Baseball America

BA 2022 ALMANAC

BASEBALL AMERICA INC. · DURHAM, N.C.

Baseball America

ESTABLISHED 1981

P.O. BOX 12877, DURHAM, NC 27709 • PHONE (919) 682-9635

PRESIDENT Tom Dondero
EDITOR IN CHIEF J.J. Cooper *@jjcoop36*
EXECUTIVE EDITOR Matt Eddy *@MattEddyBA*
CHIEF INNOVATION OFFICER Ben Badler *@benbadler*
DIRECTOR OF DIGITAL STRATEGY Mark Chiarelli *@Mark_Chiarelli*
CHIEF FINANCIAL OFFICER Dan Curvelo

EDITORIAL

SENIOR EDITOR Josh Norris *@jnorris427*
NATIONAL WRITERS Teddy Cahill *@tedcahill*
Carlos Collazo *@CarlosACollazo*
Kyle Glaser *@KyleAGlaser*
ASSOCIATE EDITOR Chris Hilburn-Trenkle *@ChrisTrenkle*
STAFF WRITER Joe Healy *@JoeHealyBA*
WEB EDITOR Kayla Lombardo *@KaylaLombardo11*
SPECIAL CONTRIBUTOR Tim Newcomb *@tdnewcomb*

PRODUCTION

CREATIVE DIRECTOR James Alworth

BUSINESS

TECHNOLOGY MANAGER Brent Lewis
MARKETING/OPERATIONS COORDINATOR Angela Lewis
CUSTOMER SERVICE Melissa Sunderman

STATISTICAL SERVICE

MAJOR LEAGUE BASEBALL ADVANCED MEDIA

Alliance
>>>> BASEBALL <<<<

BASEBALL AMERICA ENTERPRISES

CHAIRMAN & CEO Gary Green
PRESIDENT Larry Botel
GENERAL COUNSEL Matthew Pace
DIRECTOR OF MARKETING Amy Heart
INVESTOR RELATIONS Michele Balfour
DIRECTOR OF OPERATIONS Joan Disalvo
PARTNERS Stephen Alepa
Craig Amazeen
Jon Ashley
Martie Cordaro
Andrew Fox
Robert Hernreich
Glenn Isaacson
Sonny Kalsi
Peter G. Riguardi
Ian Ritchie
Brian Rothschild
Peter Ruprecht
Beryl Snyder
Tom Steiglehner
Dan Waldman
CHIEF CONTENT OFFICER Jonathan Segal

Baseball America
2022 ALMANAC

Editor
Chris Hilburn-Trenkle

Contributing Editors
Ben Badler, Teddy Cahill, Carlos Collazo, J.J. Cooper,
Matt Eddy, Joe Healy, Josh Norris

Contributing Writers
Scott Miller, Alexis Brudnicki, Bob Sutton, Mike Ashmore

Database and Application Development
Brent Lewis

Design & Production
CREATIVE DIRECTOR: James Alworth

Programming & Technical Development
Brent Lewis

Translation Assistance
Kelly Wong

Cover Photos
MAIN PHOTO: Shohei Ohtani.
PHOTO BY: Michael Owens/Getty Images

©2022 Baseball America Inc.
No portion of this book may be reprinted or reproduced without
the written consent of the publisher.
For additional copies, visit our Website at
BaseballAmerica.com or call 1-800-845-2726 to order.
US $25.95 / CAN $34.95, plus shipping and handling
per order. Expedited shipping available.
Distributed by Simon & Schuster.
ISBN-13: 978-1-7355482-5-8

Statistics provided by Major League Baseball Advanced Media
and compiled by Baseball America.

EDITOR'S NOTE: Major league statistics are based on final, unofficial 2021 averages.

» The organization statistics, which begin on page 45, include all players who participated in at least one game during the 2021 season.

» Pitchers' batting statistics are not included, nor are the pitching statistics of field players who pitched in less than two games.

» For players who played with more than one team in the same league, the player's cumulative statistics appear on the line immediately after the player's statistics with each team.

TABLE OF CONTENTS

Robbie Ray

MAJOR LEAGUES

Semblance Of Normalcy

Fans happily returned to the stands in droves following the coronavirus-shortened 2020 season.

BY SCOTT MILLER

Like the groundhog gingerly poking his head above the frosty ground each February and not seeing its shadow, baseball tentatively stepped into what it hoped would be an early spring in 2021 as players, coaches, managers and, heck, the world eagerly anticipated a return to normal following the coronavirus pandemic that ravaged 2020.

What happened next wasn't completely normal. Variants of the virus kept normalcy on edge and, for some, caused a handful of unwelcome interruptions. But baseball in 2021 did return to a full 162-game season following its abbreviated 60-game regular season a year earlier. The game did return to a regular, coast-to-coast schedule after being forced to play that abbreviated schedule in geographic pods a year earlier, with teams in the East, West and Midwest not leaving their general regions.

Some remnants from the recent past remained: The Commissioner's Office and Players' Union agreed to keep doubleheaders limited to two seven-inning games and to start extra innings of all games with a runner on second base. The rule stating that a relief pitcher entering a game must face a minimum of three batters unless the inning in which he entered ended first also stayed in place. Other remnants did not: After a universal designated hitter was used in 2020, the National League returned to its old-school, pitchers-hit ways.

Stadiums opened to limited capacities in April, and everyone pretty much in unison wished a hearty good riddance to the cardboard cutout "fans" that served as placeholders in stadium seats (along with the piped-in crowd noise, too) during the sad 2020 shortened season that was played in empty stadiums across the land. Early-season crowds of 10,000-15,000 or so gave way, according to the state-by-state, local ordinances, to full capacity crowds everywhere by June. And while some fans continued to express anxiety as the virus spiked in pockets of the country later in the summer, 50,000 fans filling Dodger Stadium was still a beautiful and welcome sight.

There were plenty of terrific sights throughout the season as baseball got its legs back under it. The Los Angeles Angels' Shohei Ohtani did things we haven't seen in MLB since Babe Ruth as a slugging DH (46 home runs) and his team's best starting pitcher (9-2, 3.18 ERA over 23 starts). Ohtani's own double duty sparked a vigorous American League Most Valuable Player debate as Toronto's young Vladimir Guerrero Jr. threatened to win

Salvador Perez tied Vladimir Guerrero Jr. for the major league lead with 48 home runs.

a Triple Crown and finished with a .311 batting average, 111 RBIs and tied with Kansas City's Salvador Perez for an MLB-leading 48 home runs.

It was a season of streaks. The St. Louis Cardinals, nearly left without a pulse in the playoff race at the end of August, won a franchise-record 17 consecutive games into September. The New York Yankees won 13 in a row in August not long after general manager Brian Cashman nearly led his team down the "seller" path at the July 31 trade deadline instead of the one marked "buyer."

But danger lurked in the shadows all season long.

In attempting to zag where the virus zigged and keep the train on the tracks, baseball encouraged each of its 30 clubs to reach an 85% vaccination rate. This included players, managers, coaches, trainers, support and traveling baseball operations personnel. And by "encouraged", it was more than verbal: Clubs that reached the 85% rate could go without wearing face masks in the dugouts and bullpens and, on road trips, could move around more freely, including going out to dinner in the city in which they were playing instead of being restricted to the hotel. By midseason, 23 of the 30 clubs reached the required threshold.

Still, it wasn't foolproof. The Yankees were one of the 23 teams with the 85% vaccination rate and yet suffered an outbreak in August following a road trip in which they played the Tampa

Bay Rays and Miami Marlins. At the time, the virus was surging in the state of Florida. Among those who were felled for a time were ace Gerrit Cole, pitcher Jordan Montgomery, catcher Gary Sanchez and first baseman Anthony Rizzo. Earlier in the year, third base coach Phil Nevin, outfielder Aaron Judge, third baseman Gio Urshela, catcher Kyle Higashioka and relievers Wandy Peralta and Jonathan Loaisiga all tested positive.

"It's a little of you don't know when and where it's spreading," Yankees manager Aaron Boone said in a statement that pretty much could be implemented league-wide.

A widespread Covid-19 outbreak in August also struck the Boston Red Sox and threatened their playoff chances. The Sox were forced to claim players from waivers, promote minor leaguers and even bring in some coaches from their farm system to replace members of manager Alex Cora's staff who were forced to quarantine.

Player-wise, there were comings and goings on and off the Covid-19 injured list all summer long throughout the league. And late in the summer, word broke that MLB would require all players participating in the Arizona Fall League to be vaccinated.

In the meantime, increasing awareness in a new era of social justice and #MeToo continued to be reflected throughout the game. The New York Mets were caught up in multiple incidents. Just one month after naming Jared Porter as their new general manager, they fired him in January following revelations that he sexually harassed a female reporter in 2016. In February, following revelations by The Athletic that he sexually harassed multiple female reporters, Mickey Callaway was sidelined as the Angels pitching coach—and, in May, MLB suspended him until at least the end of the 2022 season. That investigation spilled into the Mets organization, too, since the timeframe of some of the allegations coincided with his stint as the Mets manager. There was no break in Queens: seven months after he was named acting GM replacing Porter, Zack Scott was arrested for driving while intoxicated following a fundraiser at Mets owner Steve Cohen's home in Connecticut.

Things turned exceptionally dark and ugly for Trevor Bauer, who was the top pitcher on last winter's free agent market and the 2020 NL Cy Young winner. After signing a three-year, $102 million deal with the Dodgers, Bauer went 8-5 with a 2.59 ERA over 17 starts before being placed on administrative leave on July 2 after being accused of sexual assault by a Southern California woman during incidents in April and May. The Commissioner's Office launched an investiga-

The 2021 All-Star Game was moved to Denver due to a controversial Georgia voting rights law.

tion on July 2 and the administrative leave was extended multiple times, running out the clock on Bauer's season and, most likely, effectively ending his time with the Dodgers.

Another top free agent, outfielder Marcell Ozuna, who signed a four-year, $65 million deal to return to the Atlanta Braves, was arrested on assault charges after allegedly assaulting his wife and played his last game for the Braves on May 25. Ozuna, too, was under investigation by MLB and awaiting baseball's judgment while going through the legal process.

MLB also announced in early May that Roberto Alomar, who was in the Hall of Fame as a player and held a job in the commissioner's office, was placed on the league's ineligible list after an investigation in allegations of sexual misconduct by a baseball industry employee.

"Having reviewed all the available evidence from the now completed investigation, I have concluded that Mr. Alomar violated MLB's policies, and that termination of his consultant contract and placement on MLB's ineligible list are warranted," Manfred said. "We are grateful for the courage of the individual who came forward. MLB will continue to strive to create environments in which people feel comfortable speaking up without feat of recrimination, retaliation, or exclusion."

On the social justice trail, two enormous moments bookended the season. In April, MLB ripped the All-Star Game from Atlanta and moved

it to Denver when the state of Georgia passed a law that civil rights groups maintain is designed to restrict voting access for people of color. The move, which came just three months ahead of the All-Star Game, also included moving all of the game's festivities and the 2021 MLB draft out of Atlanta and into Denver.

"Over the last week, we have engaged in thoughtful conversations with Clubs, former and current players, the Players Association, and The Players Alliance, among others, to listen to their views," Commissioner Rob Manfred said in a statement. "I have decided that the best way to demonstrate our values as a sport is by relocating this year's All-Star Game and MLB Draft.

"Major League Baseball fundamentally supports voting rights for all Americans and opposes restrictions to the ballot box. In 2020, MLB became the first professional sports league to join the non-partisan Civic Alliance to help build a future in which everyone participates in the shaping of the United States. We proudly used our platform to encourage baseball fans and communities throughout our country to perform their civic duty and actively participate in the voting process. Fair access to voting continues to have our game's unwavering support."

Six months later, on Sept. 27, Cleveland played its final home game as … the Indians. Known by

CONTINUED ON PAGE 11

Shohei Ohtani Takes League By Storm

BY KYLE GLASER

Nez Balelo has known Shohei Ohtani as well as almost anyone since the Japanese two-way star first arrived in the United States.

Balelo, the co-head of Creative Artists Agency's baseball division, became Ohtani's agent in the winter of 2017. He guided Ohtani through a fevered recruiting process that saw nearly every team try to sign him, watched Ohtani achieve his highest highs and was up close for his lowest lows—namely, the repeated injuries that limited Ohtani each of his first three seasons in MLB.

Ohtani had Tommy John surgery in 2018, knee surgery in 2019 and suffered a forearm strain in 2020. He hit .190 and made just two, disastrous starts for the Angels last year, amplifying questions whether he should continue trying to be both a pitcher and hitter.

As those questions became more prevalent last offseason, Balelo saw a change in Ohtani.

Ohtani had always been a disciplined worker, but as he entered that winter, there was an extra layer of motivation that hadn't been there before. He shed fat, added muscle, changed his diet and sought new training methods. After an offseason split training in both Japan and the U.S., he reported to spring training bigger and stronger than he had ever been.

"He knew that he was obviously much better than what his numbers showed," Balelo said. "He was very committed to be able to say, 'I'm going to erase 2020 and watch: I'm going to come back in 2021 with a vengeance.'"

Ohtani's two-way exploits had not been seen since the days of Babe Ruth.

"And he did."

Ohtani delivered one of the greatest seasons in major league history in 2021. He performed as one of baseball's best pitchers and hitters simultaneously and, for the first time in his MLB career, maintained it over a full season.

As a hitter, Ohtani finished third in the majors with 46 home runs, fifth with a .965 OPS and eighth with 26 stolen bases. He drove in 100 runs, scored 103 runs, led MLB with eight triples and finished in the top five in walks, extra-base hits and total bases.

As a pitcher, he went 9-2, 3.18 and averaged 10.8 strikeouts per nine innings, tied for ninth among all pitchers who threw at least 130 innings. He held opponents to two runs or less in 17 of his 23 starts and limited opponents to a .205 batting average, ninth-lowest among any pitcher with 130 innings.

He became the first player in MLB history with more than 10 home runs as a hitter and 100 strikeouts as a pitcher in the same season, something not even Babe Ruth accomplished, and blew by both marks with ease. He made 14 starts on the mound during which he also led the majors in home runs.

For his singular, unprecedented season, Ohtani is the 2021 Baseball America Major League Player of the Year. ∎

LAST 10 WINNERS

2011: Matt Kemp, OF, Dodgers
2012: Mike Trout, OF, Angels
2013: Mike Trout, OF, Angels
2014: Clayton Kershaw, LHP, Dodgers
2015: Bryce Harper, OF, Nationals
2016: Mike Trout, OF, Angels
2017: Jose Altuve, 2B, Astros
2018: Mike Trout, OF, Angels
2019: Justin Verlander, RHP, Astros
2020: Freddie Freeman, 1B, Braves
Full list: BaseballAmerica.com/awards

that name since 1915, the team officially became the Guardians following a 106-year run with the only nickname almost all Clevelanders have ever known. The new name was inspired by large, landmark stone edifices that are featured on both ends of the Hope Memorial Bridge downtown that are referred to locally as "traffic guardians."

The team had stopped wearing the controversial Chief Wahoo logo on its caps and uniforms in 2018 and hinted then that there eventually would be a new nickname. At the team's final home game, stadium gift shops were briskly selling out of most "Indians" merchandise. Many fans wore T-shirts reading "Long Live the Chief" to the final home game, while one fan held a sign featuring a drawing of Chief Wahoo with a tear rolling down his face and words underneath stating simply, "The End."

New Era of Moneyball

Business as usual continued in "modern day" free agency, which is barely recognizable from the game's old winter-time feeding frenzy—and a big reason why the negotiations for a new Collective Bargaining Agreement remained contentious and the words "lockout" and "strike" continued to be whispered in the shadows leading into the winter. The current deal between the players and owners was set to expire Dec. 1.

Eventually, the top few 2021 free agents got their money: Bauer (three years, $102 million), catcher J.T. Realmuto (re-signed with the Phillies for five years and $105 million), outfielder George Springer (Toronto, five years, $150 million),

Ozuna (four years, $65 million) and second baseman D.J. LeMahieu (Yankees, six years, $90 million) all signed lucrative deals. The Springer deal was the largest in Toronto franchise history.

But in the first 70 days of the winter, just 32 free agents signed. It ranked as the most sluggish free agent market in the past decade and the players were frustrated that the game's increased emphasis on analytics and the strategy of "tanking"—or extreme rebuilding—undertaken by a handful of franchises each year (see: Baltimore Orioles, as a latest example) diluted the pool of teams bidding on free agents and threatened the game's competitive integrity.

On the other side, the owners said they took a severe financial hit during the shortened season of 2020 and, according to Manfred, took a collective $3 billion loss during the pandemic. Several owners said uncertainty over what Covid-19 would do to the 2021 season contributed to their tentativeness.

"We all lost money in the pandemic, but they're all reading from the same script," one West Coast-based agent told USA Today in January. "They say, 'I have no idea what my budget is.' Every single GM is telling me that. It's all B.S. They don't know what the budget is until they sign the player they want. They're trying to manufacture a depressed market."

The thinking of many on the players' side was that by delaying many free-agent signings, the strategy of clubs was to keep the market flooded so players signed for less than they wanted or hoped for as spring training approached.

CONTINUED ON PAGE 13

AMERICAN LEAGUE STANDINGS

East	W	L	PCT	GB	Manager	General Manager	Attendance	Avg.	Last Penn.
Tampa Bay Rays	100	62	.617	—	Kevin Cash	Erik Neander	761,072	9,377	2020
Boston Red Sox	92	70	.568	8	Alex Cora	Brian O'Halloran	1,725,323	21,300	2018
New York Yankees	92	70	.568	8	Aaron Boone	Brian Cashman	1,959,854	24,322	2009
Toronto Blue Jays	91	71	.562	9	Charlie Montoyo	Ross Atkins	805,901	10,045	1993
Baltimore Orioles	52	110	.321	48	Brandon Hyde	Mike Elias	793,229	9,921	1983
Central	**W**	**L**	**PCT**	**GB**	**Manager**	**General Manager**	**Attendance**	**Avg.**	**Last Penn.**
Chicago White Sox	93	69	.574	—	Tony La Russa	Rick Hahn	1,596,385	19,878	2005
Cleveland Indians	80	82	.494	13	Terry Francona	Mike Chernoff	1,114,368	13,881	2016
Detroit Tigers	77	85	.475	16	A.J. Hinch	Al Avila	1,102,621	13,613	2012
Kansas City Royals	74	88	.457	19	Mike Matheny	Dayton Moore	1,159,613	14,316	2015
Minnesota Twins	73	89	.451	20	Rocco Baldelli	Thad Levine	1,310,199	16,289	1991
West	**W**	**L**	**PCT**	**GB**	**Manager**	**General Manager**	**Attendance**	**Avg.**	**Last Penn.**
Houston Astros	95	67	.586	—	Dusty Baker	James Click	2,068,509	25,537	2021
Seattle Mariners	90	72	.556	5	Scott Servais	Jerry Dipoto	1,215,985	15,012	Never
Oakland Athletics	86	76	.531	9	Bob Melvin	David Forst	701,430	8,726	1990
Los Angeles Angels	77	85	.475	18	Joe Maddon	Perry Minasian	1,515,689	18,484	2002
Texas Rangers	60	102	.370	35	Chris Woodward	Chris Young	2,110,258	26,053	2011

Wild Card Game: Red Sox defeated Yankees. **Division Series:** Astros defeated White Sox 3-1 and Red Sox defeated Rays 3-1 in best-of-five series. **Championship Series:** Astros defeated Red Sox 4-2 in a best-of-seven series.

ROOKIE OF THE YEAR

Jonathan India Has Immediate Impact

BY BOBBY NIGHTENGALE

The results were immediate when Jonathan India moved to the leadoff spot for the first time on June 5. He drew a walk in his first plate appearance, hit a solo home run in his next and followed with a double.

It was the first time India hit higher than sixth in the Reds' lineup, and there was no mistaking his impact. Cincinnati vaulted into the playoff race. India leaped into the Rookie of the Year conversations. The guys hitting behind him raved about how much he helped the offense.

Jonathan India led rookies with a .376 OBP.

As the Reds' leadoff hitter, India hit .275/.383/.482 with 31 doubles, 17 home runs, 46 RBIs and 82 runs in 103 games.

Each time India was granted an opportunity this year, he ran with it. He went from a player who wasn't even on the big league spring training roster to an Opening Day starter. He spent two weeks as a backup after slumping at the end of April. He was hit by a National League-leading 23 pitches this year and, somehow, played through it all.

When the Reds were eliminated from the playoffs, manager David Bell tried to sit India for the final two games of the season. Bell said India was the player who was physically the furthest from 100% healthy. India talked his way into the lineup for the season finale, scored two runs and hit a double in a win.

It was a fitting end for an impressive rookie season. India led the Reds in games played (150) while hitting .269/.376/.459.

India is the Baseball America Rookie of the Year. To understand how he became a leader for the Reds and the league's most productive rookie, it's important to know how hard he worked when nobody kept stats.

When he arrived at the Reds' alternate site at Prasco Park in Mason, Ohio, last year, the organization wanted him to learn second base to increase his versatility. India had played shortstop in high school and third base in college, from where the Reds drafted him fifth overall out of Florida in 2018.

India was often the first player on the field with Luis Bolivar, Cincinnati's academies coordinator, for one-on-one instruction. They worked a lot on India's footwork now that he was on the opposite side of the infield.

India was one of 18 minor leaguers the Reds brought to spring training but didn't receive an official invite to big league camp. India figured he'd start the season at Triple-A Louisville. After a couple of weeks, he was the talk of camp. Scouts were impressed. Coaches loved the way he carried himself with natural leadership skills.

Reds bench coach Freddie Benavides said Bell pushed for India. Midway through camp, India was added to the big league camp roster.

India was the first Reds second baseman to make his MLB debut on Opening Day since Pete Rose in 1963.

"I just put my head down," India said, "and said, 'Screw this, I'm going to make the team. I'm going to do it.' I did. I worked really, really hard at it in spring training and at Prasco to be where I'm at. I had the motivation to make it and be on the team and help the team win this year. I definitely made it a point to do it." ∎

LAST 10 WINNERS

2012: Mike Trout, OF, Angels
2013: Jose Fernandez, RHP, Marlins
2014: Jose Abreu, 1B, White Sox
2015: Kris Bryant, 3B, Cubs
2016: Corey Seager, SS, Dodgers
2017: Aaron Judge, OF, Yankees
2018: Shohei Ohtani, RHP/DH, Angels
2019: Pete Alonso, 1B, Mets
2020: Tony Gonsolin, RHP, Dodgers
Full list: BaseballAmerica.com/awards

Adding to the players' unhappiness, financial numbers provided by the Union on the eve of spring training did not paint a brighter picture for them. The Union said the 2020 average salary would have been $3.89 million had the season been played in full and not shortened by the virus. That number was a 4.2% decrease from 2019 ($4.05 million average) and a 5.2% decrease from the record average of just under $4.1 million in 2017.

Early indications in a study of Opening Day salaries in April were that 2021 represented a fourth consecutive season in which the average player's salary decreased, falling 6.4% since the start of the 2017 season.

"We have been consistent in our position that the current trends in our game need to be addressed regarding the lack of incentive to compete and the need for the system to better reflect the value created by players throughout the service time spectrum," Union boss Tony Clark said in an email to the Associated Press in February. "While there are other forces at play, and concerns that we have in addition to the above, we look forward to discussing each of the issues I just highlighted as a way to move our industry forward."

Before 2018 and 2019, the average salary had not declined in back-to-back years since the Union started tracking it in 1967. Before the three-year decline leading into the 2021 season, the only salary decreases came in 1987, when an arbiter found clubs guilty of collusion against free agents; in 1995, following an ugly seven-and-a-half month players' strike, and in 2004.

The current trend reveals, among other things, the widening gap between top stars and other players. The average salary declined despite Gerrit Cole, Stephen Strasburg, Anthony Rendon and Christian Yelich all beginning long-term contracts guaranteeing them $215 million or more.

According to an Associated Press annual study, the median MLB salary was $1.15 million in 2021, down 18% from $1.4 million in 2019 (the last full 162-game season) and down 30% from the $1.65 million record high at the start of 2015. The current CBA went into effect at the start of the 2017 season.

As negotiations slogged forward this summer, the owners in August proposed a salary floor requiring each team to spend at least $100 million on players, according to a report in The Athletic. Tied in with that, the owners reportedly proposed to lower the luxury tax threshold to $180 million, down from the current $210 million threshold. It was the first proposal from either side to be revealed in public, and it wasn't exactly embraced by the players. One member of the Players' Association executive board likened the luxury cap threshold to a de facto salary cap, similar to the Union's stance in the past.

For the 2021 season, 12 clubs were under the $100 million team payroll: Pittsburgh ($46 million, lowest on Opening Day in a full season since Houston's $44.6 million in 2014), Cleveland ($51 million), Baltimore ($56 million), Miami ($57 million), Tampa Bay ($67 million), Detroit ($81 million), Oakland ($83 million), Seattle ($84 million), Kansas City ($89 million), Milwaukee ($94 million), Arizona ($94 million) and Texas ($98 million).

NATIONAL LEAGUE STANDINGS

East	W	L	PCT	GB	Manager	General Manager	Attendance	Avg.	Last Penn.
Atlanta Braves	88	73	.547	—	Brian Snitker	Alex Anthopoulos	2,300,247	28,858	2021
Philadelphia Phillies	82	80	.506	6.5	Joe Girardi	Sam Fuld	1,515,890	18,582	2009
New York Mets	77	85	.475	11.5	Luis Rojas	Zack Scott	1,511,926	18,414	2015
Miami Marlins	67	95	.414	21.5	Don Mattingly	Kim Ng	642,617	7,934	2003
Washington Nationals	65	97	.401	23.5	Dave Martinez	Mike Rizzo	1,465,543	18,258	2019
Central	**W**	**L**	**PCT**	**GB**	**Manager**	**General Manager**	**Attendance**	**Avg.**	**Last Penn.**
Milwaukee Brewers	95	67	.586	—	Craig Counsell	Matt Arnold	1,824,282	22,522	1982 (AL)
St. Louis Cardinals	90	72	.556	5	Mike Shildt	John Mozeliak	2,102,530	26,117	2013
Cincinnati Reds	83	79	.512	12	David Bell	Nick Krall	1,505,024	18,581	1990
Chicago Cubs	71	91	.438	24	David Ross	Jed Hoyer	1,978,934	24,431	2016
Pittsburgh Pirates	61	101	.377	34	Derek Shelton	Ben Cherington	859,498	10,611	1979
West	**W**	**L**	**PCT**	**GB**	**Manager**	**General Manager**	**Attendance**	**Avg.**	**Last Penn.**
San Francisco Giants	107	55	.660	—	Gabe Kapler	Scott Harris	1,679,484	20,734	2014
Los Angeles Dodgers	106	56	.654	1	Dave Roberts	Andrew Friedman	2,804,693	34,626	2020
San Diego Padres	79	83	.488	28	Jayce Tingler	A.J. Preller	2,191,950	27,061	1998
Colorado Rockies	74	87	.460	32.5	Bud Black	Jeff Bridich/Bill Schmidt	1,938,645	24,392	2007
Arizona Diamondbacks	52	110	.321	55	Torey Lovullo	Mike Hazen	1,043,010	12,877	2001

Wild Card Game: Dodgers defeated Cardinals. **Division Series:** Dodgers defeated Giants 3-2 and Braves defeated Brewers 3-1 in best-of-five series. **Championship Series:** Braves defeated Dodgers 4-2 in a best-of-seven series.

MAJOR LEAGUES

The game's highest payrolls were the Los Angeles Dodgers ($241 million), New York Yankees ($201 million), New York Mets ($186 million), Los Angeles Angels ($181 million), Washington ($179 million), Boston ($179 million), Houston ($176 million) and San Diego ($175 million).

As the October postseason and the Dec. 1 expiration of the CBA approached, it was clear that, like most negotiations, this one was headed toward the wire.

On-Field Ongoings

The most bruising regular season ever started on April 1 and finished on Oct. 3, and do not think for a minute that the beginning of this sentence is exaggerated hyperbole: In an era of emphasis on flamethrowers instead of control artists, pitchers hit more batters in 2021 (2,112) than ever before. San Diego reliever Austin Adams was most guilty, setting a new MLB record for the Live Ball Era (since 1920) by drilling 24 batters.

Meanwhile, as the emphasis on home runs continued, the overall batting average (.244) ranked as one of the worst in the modern era as well. The only lower averages were in the 1968 Year of the Pitcher (.237) and 1967 (.242). Both years, of course, were before the advent of the DH. And in a continuing pattern, games in 2021 averaged more strikeouts (8.68 per game) than hits (8.13). In fact, two seasons after there were more strikeouts than hits for the first time ever, there were a record 2,664 more strikeouts than hits in 2021. All of this led to the longest average game time (3 hours, 10 minutes) in history.

The season's biggest controversy erupted when MLB determined that the current emphasis on spin rate was leading to too much cheating and announced that in June there would be a crackdown on "sticky substances." The old days of pitchers using a mixture of pine tar and rosin seemed almost quaint given that some now had moved on to "spider tack", a substance most known to weightlifters for aid in carrying Atlas Stones in competitions. Beginning on June 21, umpires were instructed to physically check every pitcher in a game at least once.

Memorably, Scherzer, when he was still with Washington, and Philadelphia manager Joe Girardi got into a shouting match on the field when Girardi thought he spotted Scherzer running his hand through his hair too much and asked the umpires to check him.

"I'd have to be an absolute fool to use anything tonight when everyone's antennae are so high," Scherzer said after the dustup, which included Girardi's ejection.

Dusty Baker guided the Astros back to the World Series, where they fell in six games.

"I've seen Max a long time, since 2010," Girardi told reporters afterward. "Obviously, he's going to be a Hall of Famer. But I've never seen him wipe his head like he was doing tonight. Ever. So it was suspicious for me. He did it about four times. It was suspicious. I didn't mean to offend anyone. I just have to do what's right for our club."

Predictably, spin rates declined across the board and the percentage of plate appearances ending in strikeouts dropped from 24.2% before the crackdown to 22.7% after. The percentage of walks also dropped, from 8.9% to 8.2%, while the rate of homers increased to 3.4% from 3.1%.

Excelling under these circumstances were both the expected, the Tampa Bay Rays, and the unexpected, the San Francisco Giants. The Rays won a second consecutive AL East title for the first time in franchise history and a fourth in the past 14 years. Unquestionably, the Rays have found the key in this analytics era to continually torment their big-market AL East brethren in New York and Boston. And perhaps best of all, a year after celebrations were muted because of Covid-19, it was again OK to party with abandon.

"It was awesome," Rays second baseman Brandon Lowe said. "Confetti poppers are fun, but there's nothing that beats the burn of Champagne. It burns so good."

Out in the NL West, the Giants snapped the Dodgers' streak of eight consecutive division titles in one of the most epic races in years. To do it,

ALL-ROOKIE TEAM 2021

Pos	Player, Team	Age	AB	AVG	OBP	SLG	2B	HR	RBI	SB	Rundown
C	Tyler Stephenson, Reds	24	350	.286	.366	.431	21	10	45	0	Hit his way into prominent role; zero errors behind plate
1B	Bobby Dalbec, Red Sox	26	417	.240	.298	.494	21	25	78	2	Second among rookies in triples (five) and third in RBIs
2B	Jonathan India, Reds	24	532	.269	.376	.459	34	21	69	12	Led all qualified rookies in OBP, doubles and walks (71)
3B	Patrick Wisdom, Cubs	29	338	.231	.305	.518	13	28	61	4	Set Cubs rookie home run record in just 106 games
SS	Wander Franco, Rays	20	281	.288	.347	.463	18	7	39	2	Reached base in 43 straight games
OF	Randy Arozarena, Rays	26	529	.274	.356	.459	32	20	69	20	Finished top three among rookies in doubles, RBIs, OPS
OF	Adolis Garcia, Rangers	28	581	.243	.286	.454	26	31	90	16	Led all rookies in RBIs, second in home runs
OF	Dylan Carlson, Cardinals	22	542	.266	.343	.437	31	18	65	2	Second among rookies in walks (57), third in doubles
DH	Ryan Mountcastle, Orioles	24	534	.255	.309	.487	23	33	89	4	Led all rookies in home runs, second in RBIs

Pos	Pitcher, Team	Age	W	L	SV	ERA	IP	SO	BB	Rundown
SP	Ian Anderson, Braves	23	9	5	0	3.58	128	124	53	Tied for fourth among rookies in wins, fifth in ERA
SP	Luis Garcia, Astros	24	11	8	0	3.48	155	167	50	Led all rookies in strikeouts and innings
SP	Alek Manoah, Blue Jays	23	9	2	0	3.22	112	127	40	Posted lowest WHIP (1.05) among rookie starters
SP	Shane McClanahan, Rays	24	10	6	0	3.43	123	141	37	Led all Rays starters in wins, ERA and strikeouts
SP	Trevor Rogers, Marlins	23	7	8	0	2.64	133	157	46	Led all rookie starters in ERA and strikeouts per nine (10.6)
RP	Emmanuel Clase, Indians	23	4	5	24	1.29	70	74	16	Led all rookie relievers in ERA and saves (24)

the Giants needed to set a franchise record with 107 wins as the Dodgers (106 wins) pushed them all the way to the last day of the season. Los Angeles went 45-15 down the stretch and the Dodgers' 50-21 post-All-Star break record was the franchise's best in 68 years. July trade deadline acquisitions Scherzer and Trea Turner contributed mightily to that record. But old standbys Brandon Crawford, Buster Posey and Brandon Belt found a fountain of youth for another run in San Francisco and the Giants struck paydirt with a combination of high-producing veterans like Kevin Gausman, Anthony DeSclafani, recent discoveries like Mike Yastrzemski and Lamonte Wade Jr. and youngsters such as starter Logan Webb and closer Camilo Doval.

Milwaukee again rose to the top of the NL Central behind a pitching staff that, top to bottom, many hitters said was the best they've seen. Starter Corbin Burnes became the first Brewers pitcher ever to win an ERA title (2.43) and Brandon Woodruff (2.56) was not far behind. With weapons like Josh Hader and Devin Williams in the bullpen, the Brewers were set up for what they hoped would be a deep October run. Williams, however, broke his hand toward the conclusion of the regular season and was out the rest of the way.

Atlanta continued its dominance in the NL East by winning its fourth consecutive title. The Braves beat the odds on this one after losing star outfielder Ronald Acuna Jr. in July (anterior cruciate ligament tear), starting pitcher Mike Soroka in June (torn Achilles tendon) and outfielder Marcell Ozuna in May (arrested after a domestic disturbance at his home). General manager Alex Anthopoulos shined at midseason, adding outfielders Joc Pederson, Adam Duvall and Jorge Soler and closer Richard Rodriguez, among others. Many teams would have waved the white flag.

St. Louis won 19 of its final 20 games to cruise to the second NL wild card position, joining the Dodgers. Left out was one of the most hyped teams of the year in the preseason, the San Diego Padres, who added starters Yu Darvish, Blake Snell and Joe Musgrove in offseason trades to go with Fernando Tatis Jr., Manny Machado, Eric Hosmer, Jake Cronenworth and others. The Padres had the best record in MLB at one point in May and, when they played in Atlanta in June, the Padres had a 92% chance of making the playoffs, according to FanGraphs. A historic collapse eliminated them eight days before season's end.

In the AL, two old-time managers, Tony La Russa (77) and Dusty Baker (72), piloted the Chicago White Sox and Houston Astros to division titles that led directly to a postseason matchup between the two. The Yankees and Boston Red Sox fended off Toronto and a surprising, 90-win Seattle club for the two wild card spots.

Baseball At Its Best

When historians and fans look back at the 2021 season, in some ways it would be appropriate if they summarized it in two words: Shohei Ohtani. Four years after his debut with the Los Angeles Angels in 2018, the man finally was healthy enough to catch up to the hype. And wow, what a show it was.

Ohtani, fully back from Tommy John surgery, crushed 46 homers, knocked in 100 runs, stole 26 bases and tied for the major league lead with eight triples. On the mound, he fanned 156 hitters, finished with a 3.18 ERA and was the winning pitcher in the All-Star Game. Ohtani joins Hall of Famers Willie Mays in 1955 (51 homers) and Jim Rice in 1978 (46 homers) as the only three players in history to lead the majors in triples and hit 40 or more homers in a single season.

AMERICAN LEAGUE BEST TOOLS

A Baseball America survey of American League managers, conducted at midseason 2021, ranked players with the best tools.

Best Hitter
1. Vladimir Guerrero Jr., Blue Jays
2. Michael Brantley, Astros
3. Rafael Devers, Red Sox

Best Power
1. Shohei Ohtani, Angels
2. Vladimir Guerrero Jr., Blue Jays
3. Matt Olson, Athletics

Best Bunter
1. Cedric Mullins, Orioles
2. Cesar Hernandez, White Sox
3. Hanser Alberto, Royals

Best Strike-Zone Judgment
1. Michael Brantley, Astros
2. Vladimir Guerrero Jr., Blue Jays
3. Robbie Grossman, Tigers

Best Hit-And-Run Artist
1. David Fletcher, Angels
2. Whit Merrifield, Royals
3. Isiah Kiner-Falefa, Rangers

Best Baserunner
1. Whit Merrifield, Royals
2. Jose Ramirez, Indians
3. Cedric Mullins, Orioles

Fastest Baserunner
1. Shohei Ohtani, Angels
2. Myles Straw, Indians
3. Byron Buxton, Twins

Most Exciting Player
1. Shohei Ohtani, Angels
2. Vladimir Guerrero Jr., Blue Jays
3. Tim Anderson, White Sox

Best Pitcher
1. Lance Lynn, White Sox
2. Gerrit Cole, Yankees
3. Robbie Ray, Blue Jays

Best Fastball
1. Aroldis Chapman, Yankees
2. Raisel Iglesias, Angels
3. Gerrit Cole, Yankees

Best Curveball
1. Jose Berrios, Blue Jays
2. Nick Pivetta, Red Sox
3. Chris Bassitt, Athletics

Best Slider
1. Adam Ottavino, Red Sox
2. Gerrit Cole, Yankees
3. Carlos Rodon, White Sox

Best Changeup
1. Lucas Giolito, White Sox
2. Shohei Ohtani, Angels
3. Ryan Yarbrough, Rays

Best Control
1. Hyun-Jin Ryu, Blue Jays
2. Zack Greinke, Astros
3. Nathan Eovaldi, Red Sox

Best Pickoff Move
1. Jose Berrios, Blue Jays
2. Chris Flexen, Mariners
3. Matthew Boyd, Tigers

Best Reliever
1. Liam Hendriks, White Sox
2. Matt Barnes, Red Sox
3. Andrew Kittredge, Rays

Best Defensive Catcher
1. Christian Vazquez, Red Sox
2. Roberto Perez, Indians
3. Salvador Perez, Royals

Best Defensive 1B
1. Matt Olson, Athletics
2. Yuli Gurriel, Astros
3. Nate Lowe, Rangers

Best Defensive 2B
1. Marcus Semien, Blue Jays
2. Jose Altuve, Astros
3. DJ LeMahieu, Yankees

Best Defensive 3B
1. Matt Chapman, Athletics
2. Jose Ramirez, Indians
3. Yoan Moncada, White Sox

Best Defensive SS
1. J.P. Crawford, Mariners
2. Isiah Kiner-Falefa, Rangers
3. Andrelton Simmons, Twins

Best Infield Arm
1. Matt Chapman, Athletics
2. Carlos Correa, Astros
3. Miguel Sano, Twins

Best Defensive OF
1. Kevin Kiermaier, Rays
2. Cedric Mullins, Orioles
3. Byron Buxton, Twins

Best Outfield Arm
1. Hunter Renfroe, Red Sox
2. Joey Gallo, Rangers
3. Ramon Laureano, Athletics

Best Manager
1. Bob Melvin, Athletics
2. Dusty Baker, Astros
3. Kevin Cash, Rays

---

tough—the stress on your body—but he's doing both and playing every day as a DH and pitching every seven, every eight days," Padres righthander Yu Darvish said.

"That's a lot of stress on your body. More than two times the stress on your body."

The only negative for the Angels was inescapable and enormous: Despite Ohtani's greatness, much like that of Mike Trout in recent years, it wasn't enough to push the club anywhere near a postseason bid. Trout missed most of the season with a calf injury but, despite that, across the game, baseball lovers could only shake their heads in frustration at the way that the Angels are wasting generational talent.

Despite Ohtani's individual season unlike any other in our lifetime, Toronto's Vladimir Guerrero Jr. (.311, 48 homers, 111 RBIs) flirted with winning a Triple Crown and produced such a stellar season that in September, there was talk of his stealing the AL MVP trophy away from Ohtani. Then Guerrero's teammate Marcus Semien (.265, 45 homers, 102 RBIs, 162 games played) broke Davey Johnson's record for homers by a second baseman and nearly stole Guerrero's spotlight.

The NL MVP race turned torrid during the last two months after Fernando Tatis Jr.'s seeming vice-grip on it during the first half of the season crumbled right alongside the Padres themselves. Though Tatis finished with 42 homers, 97 RBIs and a .975 OPS, Bryce Harper (MLB-leading 1.044 OPS, 35 homers) and Juan Soto (.999 OPS, .313 batting average, 29 homers) certainly produced MVP-worthy seasons. And for those who valued statistics plus contributions to winning teams, the Giants' Brandon Crawford produced a career season individually and was perhaps the best player on the game's best team, and the Dodgers' Trea Turner did it all for the Nationals and Dodgers while winning the NL batting title (.328) and also leading the league in steals (32), hits (195) and total bases (319). Once Los Angeles acquired him, Turner quickly turned into an historical link, becoming the first Dodger to lead the league in both batting average and steals since Hall of Famer Jackie Robinson.

Philadelphia's Zack Wheeler (NL leader with 247 strikeouts and 213.1 innings pitched), the Dodgers' Max Scherzer (7-0 with an 0.78 ERA in his first nine Los Angeles starts before finishing with two clunkers) and Walker Buehler (career-best 2.47 ERA) and Milwaukee's Corbin Burnes (MLB leader in strikeouts per nine innings at 12.6 and in strikeout-to-walk ratio at 6.9) all surfaced as NL Cy Young favorites at one point or another during the season. In an example of how things

While doing so, Ohtani re-surfaced some old legends from the past, his two-way stardom reminding every day of Babe Ruth and old Negro League legends like Ted "Double-Duty" Radcliffe and Bullet Joe Rogan. He also left a trail of his fellow current players gawking.

"If you're playing only as a pitcher, the season is

have changed in the age of analytics, noticeably absent in the discussion was young Dodgers lefthander Julio Urias. All Urias did was lead the majors in wins with a 20-3 record (nobody else won 20) and post a 2.96 ERA over 32 starts. In the old days, those 20 wins would have garnered him a trophy.

As for Burnes, his control and production were remarkable, especially early: On April 20 against San Diego, he set an MLB record for most strikeouts by a starter to start a season without issuing a walk, hitting 40 to surpass the old record of 35 set by Adam Wainwright in 2013. He also set the overall record for any pitcher for most strikeouts to start a season without a walk at 58, breaking the old mark held by Kenley Jansen (51), set in 2017.

Meantime, the Yankees' Gerrit Cole's late-season fade opened up the AL Cy Young race. Cole, whose $325 million contract keeps the spotlight hot and focused on him, dominated for much of the season. Into the opening raced Toronto lefthander Robbie Ray, who pitched his Blue Jays to the season's final day before they were eliminated by the Yankees and Red Sox in the AL wild card race. Ray (13-7), long on promise and short on consistency for much of his career, was absolutely nails: He led the AL in ERA (2.84), strikeouts (248), WHIP (1.05) and quality starts (23).

Cole (16-8) battled a groin strain late and wound up third in the AL in ERA (3.23), second in WHIP (1.06) and fifth in innings pitched (181.1). On the other end of games, Chicago closer Liam Hendriks led the majors with 38 saves to aid new manager Tony La Russa's first year back managing the White Sox.

Standing in the Hall of Fame

Cooperstown, like the rest of the world, has had to adjust significantly to modern events, and so it was this year when the Hall of Fame induction ceremony returned after being canceled in 2020. However, it was a scaled back affair held on a Wednesday in early September, not the all-out celebration we are accustomed to on a Sunday in late July.

Derek Jeter, Larry Walker, Ted Simmons and the late Marvin Miller were the latest inductees—all from the Class of 2020. As for the Class of 2021, when the election results were announced in January, nobody reached the required 75% threshold required on the ballots of the Baseball Writers' Association of America voters. And because the various Veteran Committees all were put on temporary hold for a year as Hall of Fame officials waited out Covid-19, that meant that, for the first time since 1960, there would be no new

Derek Jeter was part of the Class of 2020 inducted into Cooperstown in September.

inductees for a particular year's class (it also was the first time since 2013 that the BBWAA pitched a shutout).

Because of the intentionally scaled down planning, what once was expected to be a record crowd challenging the 87,000 or so for Cal Ripken Jr. and Tony Gwynn's induction in 2007 to watch Jeter came nowhere close, but that didn't dampen enthusiasm.

Jeter got a loud ovation and old-school chants of "Der-ek Je-ter!" from those attending and, upon stepping to the podium, smiled and admitted, "I forgot how good that sounds."

In his speech, Jeter spoke of respect—for the game, for one's peers and for the fans.

"You can't be fooled," Jeter said of the fans. "You're passionate, you're loyal, knowledgeable, vocal, challenging and supporting. There's a huge responsibility that comes with wearing a Yankee uniform. You have to earn it. Every single day, I felt I was representing you and all of New York. I did it the best way I knew how."

A native of Canada, Walker said he felt he had a similar sense of responsibility—though to a different constituency.

"I share this honor with every Canadian," Walker said. "And I hope for all you Canadian kids out there that have dreams of playing in the big leagues that seeing me here today gives you another reason to go after those dreams."

Simmons was elected by the Modern Baseball

CONTINUED ON PAGE 19

ORGANIZATION OF THE YEAR

Rays player development keeps pace

BY MARC TOPKIN

The success the Rays enjoyed in 2021 started the year before with Zoom sessions and FaceTime calls and instructional and inspirational messages texted across state lines, national borders and oceans beyond.

What the Rays did in the major leagues was obviously impressive. They won an American League-high and team-record 100 games. They claimed a second straight—and fourth in 14 years—AL East title in making the playoffs for a franchise-first third straight season.

And while the Rays' season ended in the Division Series, Tampa Bay succeeded all while navigating a seemingly never-ending string of injuries and resulting roster churn that led to them using a franchise high 61 players.

But it was what the Rays did in the minor leagues that elevated the organization above the standard MLB winner. Tampa Bay's domestic affiliates posted a composite .653 winning percentage—which appears to be the highest of the past 40 years—and won three championships plus a near-miss. Rays prospects succeeded both collectively and individually, with a litany of promotions and achievements that were made all the more impressive because they followed the disruption of 2020 and the canceled minor league season.

"What immediately comes to mind: It's not the major league part of this that's most visible—though we're exceptionally proud of everything that went on there—it's the minor leagues," Rays president of baseball operations Erik Neander said.

"It's all of our staff and players, from our complexes all the way through. The people who didn't have games last year—that was

The Tampa Bay Rays won 100 games for the first time in franchise history.

tough. I can't even imagine how tough it was for many of them.

"You try to empathize, but realistically I had games in front of me. A lot of people didn't. They were at a distance. And to come out this year, and for the collective performance of our affiliates to be as strong as it was, is something that I just am incredibly grateful and appreciative and proud of all the work that went into making that possible, because of all that was endured by so many in 2020."

As a result of what they did on all levels, the Rays, for the second time in three years, were honored as the Organization of the Year.

And they feel pretty good about that.

"It's something that I personally see as a really big honor," Neander said. "Obviously, there's on-field accomplishments that we're still chasing, that ever elusive World Series championship that we hope to one day experience. But this is up there.

"Baseball America, and the incredible work they have done and continue to do in the game, for an outlet like that to recognize our organization, twice in three years—but this one in particular—it does mean a lot. And it's something that I hope our staff and our players are really proud of." ∎

LAST 10 WINNERS

2011: St. Louis Cardinals
2012: Cincinnati Reds
2013: St. Louis Cardinals
2014: Kansas City Royals
2015: Pittsburgh Pirates
2016: Chicago Cubs
2017: Los Angeles Dodgers
2018: Milwaukee Brewers
2019: Tampa Bay Rays
2020: Los Angeles Dodgers
Full list: BaseballAmerica.com/awards

CONTINUED FROM PAGE 17

Era Committee in December of 2019, and spoke eloquently of long journeys and changes.

"For those of you who are concerned that our game has changed, it has," he said. "Strikeout, walk, homer today is pretty much what you get. But our game can change back and, eventually, another George Brett will surface. He'll hit .360, he'll homer 40 times, he'll drive in 160 runs, he'll strike out 175 times, he'll walk 100 times. His on-base percentage will be .420. Our game is fluid. Hitters will begin to defeat the defensive shifts, and the pendulum will shift back. The game evolves. It's just a matter of time."

Miller was the first boss of the Players' Union and during his leadership helped usher free agency and salary arbitration into the game. He passed away in 2012 when he was 95.

Generation Next

Had the regular season lasted another two or three games, the hard-charging Blue Jays just may have caught the Yankees for the American League's second wild card spot. The Jays finished 91-71 in a stacked AL East and served notice that their young core has matured enough to become a real threat over the next few seasons. Not since they won back-to-back World Series titles in 1992 and 1993 have the Blue Jays played in the Fall Classic.

That could change as soon as 2022 given the lineage of shortstop Bo Bichette (son of former big leaguer Dante), first baseman Vladimir Guerrero Jr. (son of Hall of Famer Vladimir) and second baseman Cavan Biggio (son of Hall of Famer Craig). Toss in Lourdes Gurriel Jr., the underrated Teoscar Hernandez, Randal Grichuk and Marcus Semien and the Jays became the first team with six players to stack at least 20 homers and 80 RBIs since the 2009 Yankees. The only other teams with that many players to reach those markers are the 2003 Red Sox and the 1999 Rangers.

Of course, in recent years Tampa Bay has had a lot to say about how the AL East goes. And with sensational rookie Wander Franco, that probably will continue. The Rays recalled Franco, 20, in June and he brought immediate excitement to Tropicana Field. Not only did he bat .288 with seven homers and an .810 OPS over just 70 games, but Franco also kept fans watching nightly as he reached base in 43 consecutive games, tying Hall of Famer Frank Robinson's 43-game streak in 1956 for the longest by a player 20 or younger. Toss in outfielder Randy Arozarena, whom the Rays acquired from St. Louis and watched become the breakout star of the 2020 postseason, and

NATIONAL LEAGUE BEST TOOLS

MAJOR LEAGUES

NATIONAL LEAGUE BEST TOOLS

A Baseball America survey of National League managers, conducted at midseason 2021, ranked players with the best tools.

Best Hitter
1. Juan Soto, Nationals
2. Fernando Tatis Jr., Padres
3. Nick Castellanos, Reds

Best Power
1. Fernando Tatis Jr., Padres
2. Ronald Acuña Jr., Braves
3. Pete Alonso, Mets

Best Bunter
1. Garrett Hampson, Rockies
2. Kolten Wong, Brewers
3. Victor Robles, Nationals

Best Strike-Zone Judgment
1. Juan Soto, Nationals
2. Joey Votto, Reds
3. Freddie Freeman, Braves

Best Hit-And-Run Artist
1. Adam Frazier, Pirates
2. Yadier Molina, Cardinals
3. Luis Guillorme, Mets

Best Baserunner
1. Trea Turner, Nationals
2. Fernando Tatis Jr., Padres
3. Mookie Betts, Dodgers

Fastest Baserunner
1. Trea Turner, Nationals
2. Jorge Mateo, Padres
3. Garrett Hampson, Rockies

Most Exciting Player
1. Fernando Tatis Jr., Padres
2. Juan Soto, Nationals
3. Ronald Acuña Jr., Braves

Best Pitcher
1. Jacob deGrom, Mets
2. Zack Wheeler, Phillies
3. Brandon Woodruff, Brewers

Best Fastball
1. Jacob deGrom, Mets
2. Walker Buehler, Dodgers
3. Brandon Woodruff, Brewers

Best Curveball
1. Julio Urias, Dodgers
2. Clayton Kershaw, Dodgers
3. Charlie Morton, Braves

Best Slider
1. Jacob deGrom, Mets
2. Max Scherzer, Nationals
3. Clayton Kershaw, Dodgers

Best Changeup
1. Luis Castillo, Reds
2. Devin Williams, Brewers
3. Pablo Lopez, Marlins

Best Control
1. Kyle Hendricks, Cubs
2. Corbin Burnes, Brewers
3. Jacob deGrom, Mets

Best Pickoff Move
1. Max Fried, Braves
2. Julio Urias, Dodgers
3. Ryan Weathers, Padres

Best Reliever
1. Josh Hader, Brewers
2. Craig Kimbrel, Cubs
3. Kenley Jansen, Dodgers

Best Defensive Catcher
1. J.T. Realmuto, Phillies
2. Yadier Molina, Cardinals
3. Will Smith, Dodgers

Best Defensive 1B
1. Paul Goldschmidt, Cardinals
2. Max Muncy, Dodgers
3. Freddie Freeman, Braves

Best Defensive 2B
1. Kolten Wong, Brewers
2. Jake Cronenworth, Padres
3. Ozzie Albies, Braves

Best Defensive 3B
1. Nolan Arenado, Cardinals
2. Manny Machado, Padres
3. Justin Turner, Dodgers

Best Defensive SS
1. Francisco Lindor, Mets
2. Brandon Crawford, Giants
3. Trevor Story, Rockies

Best Infield Arm
1. Manny Machado, Padres
2. Nolan Arenado, Cardinals
3. Javier Baez, Cubs

Best Defensive OF
1. Victor Robles, Nationals
2. Jackie Bradley Jr., Brewers
3. Harrison Bader, Cardinals

Best Outfield Arm
1. Mookie Betts, Dodgers
2. Bryce Harper, Phillies
3. Cody Bellinger, Dodgers

Best Manager
1. Craig Counsell, Brewers
2. Dave Roberts, Dodgers
3. Jayce Tingler, Padres

lefthander Shane McClanahan, whose fastball velocity was the highest among rookie starters with 50 or more innings, and it is a recipe for the Rays to continue confounding their AL East rivals.

Cincinnati second baseman Jonathan India

CONTINUED ON PAGE 21

Giants catcher Buster Posey hit over .300 yet again in his final season.

The Blue Jays' Vladimir Guerrero Jr. tied for the MLB lead with 48 home runs.

FIRST TEAM

Pos.	Player, Team	AVG	OBP	SLG	AB	R	H	2B	3B	HR	RBI	BB	SO	SB	CS
C	Salvador Perez, Royals	.273	.316	.544	620	88	169	24	0	48	121	28	170	1	0
1B	Vladimir Guerrero Jr., Blue Jays	.311	.401	.601	604	123	188	29	1	48	111	86	110	4	1
2B	Trea Turner, Nationals/Dodgers	.328	.375	.536	595	107	195	34	3	28	77	41	110	32	5
3B	Jose Ramirez, Indians	.266	.355	.538	552	111	147	32	5	36	103	72	87	27	4
SS	Fernando Tatis Jr., Padres	.282	.364	.611	478	99	135	31	0	42	97	62	153	25	4
OF	Bryce Harper, Phillies	.309	.429	.615	488	101	151	42	1	35	84	100	134	13	3
OF	Aaron Judge, Yankees	.287	.373	.544	550	89	158	24	0	39	98	75	158	6	1
OF	Juan Soto, Nationals	.313	.465	.534	502	111	157	20	2	29	95	145	93	9	7
DH	Shohei Ohtani, Angels	.257	.372	.592	537	103	138	26	8	46	100	96	189	26	10

Pos.	Player, Team	W	L	ERA	G	GS	SV	IP	H	R	ER	HR	BB	SO	WHIP
SP	Walker Buehler, Dodgers	16	4	2.47	33	33	0	208	149	61	57	19	52	212	0.97
SP	Corbin Burnes, Brewers	11	5	2.43	28	28	0	167	123	47	45	7	34	234	0.94
SP	Robbie Ray, Blue Jays	13	7	2.84	32	32	0	193	150	62	61	33	52	248	1.05
SP	Max Scherzer, Nationals/Dodgers	15	4	2.46	30	30	0	179	119	53	49	23	36	236	0.86
SP	Zack Wheeler, Phillies	14	10	2.78	32	32	0	213	169	72	66	16	46	247	1.01
RP	Josh Hader, Brewers	4	2	1.23	60	0	34	59	25	8	8	3	24	102	0.84

SECOND TEAM

Pos.	Player, Team	AVG	OBP	SLG	AB	R	H	2B	3B	HR	RBI	BB	SO	SB	CS
C	Buster Posey, Giants	.304	.390	.499	395	68	120	23	0	18	56	56	87	0	0
1B	Matt Olson, Athletics	.271	.371	.540	565	101	153	35	0	39	111	88	113	4	1
2B	Marcus Semien, Blue Jays	.265	.334	.538	652	115	173	39	2	45	102	66	146	15	1
3B	Austin Riley, Braves	.303	.367	.531	590	91	179	33	1	33	107	52	168	0	1
SS	Brandon Crawford, Giants	.298	.373	.522	483	79	144	30	3	24	90	56	105	11	3
OF	Cedric Mullins, Orioles	.291	.360	.518	602	91	175	37	5	30	59	59	125	30	8
OF	Tyler O'Neill, Cardinals	.286	.352	.560	482	89	138	26	2	34	80	38	168	15	4
OF	Bryan Reynolds, Pirates	.302	.390	.522	559	93	169	35	8	24	90	75	119	5	2
DH	Nick Castellanos, Reds	.309	.362	.576	531	95	164	38	1	34	100	41	121	3	1

Pos.	Player, Team	W	L	ERA	G	GS	SV	IP	H	R	ER	HR	BB	SO	WHIP
SP	Gerrit Cole, Yankees	16	8	3.23	30	30	0	181	151	69	65	24	41	243	1.06
SP	Kevin Gausman, Giants	14	6	2.81	33	33	0	192	150	66	60	20	50	227	1.04
SP	Adam Wainwright, Cardinals	17	7	3.05	32	32	0	206	168	72	70	21	50	174	1.06
SP	Julio Urias, Dodgers	20	3	2.96	32	32	0	186	151	67	61	19	38	195	1.02
SP	Brandon Woodruff, Brewers	9	10	2.56	30	30	0	179	130	54	51	18	43	211	0.96
RP	Liam Hendriks, White Sox	8	3	2.54	69	0	38	71	45	23	20	11	7	113	0.73

EXECUTIVE OF THE YEAR

Farhan Zaidi

They led the majors and set a franchise record for wins with 107. They led the National League and set a franchise record for homers with 241. They outpaced the favored Dodgers to win their first division title since 2012.

The Giants accomplished a lot in 2021 under president of baseball operations Farhan Zaidi, who played a key role in putting this front office, group of players and coaching staff in place.

The Giants won with veteran holdovers like Buster Posey, Brandon Crawford and Brandon Belt. They won with young, emerging players like Logan Webb. They won with a rotation of Kevin Gausman, Anthony DeSclafani and Alex Wood that was built on the fly. They won role players like Darin Ruf and Wilmer Flores.

But most of all, they just won.

LAST 10 WINNERS

2011: Doug Melvin, Brewers
2012: Billy Beane, Athletics
2013: Dan Duquette, Orioles
2014: Dan Duquette, Orioles
2015: Sandy Alderson, Mets
2016: Chris Antonetti, Indians
2017: Brian Cashman, Yankees
2018: Dave Dombrowski, Red Sox
2019: Mike Rizzo, Nationals
2020: Andrew Friedman, Dodgers

Full list: BaseballAmerica.com/awards

MANAGER OF THE YEAR

Dusty Baker

Dusty Baker refused to accept the retirement so many assumed he embraced. For two years, he sat in wait for one more opportunity to complete "unfinished business."

That opportunity came after the Astros fired A.J. Hinch and Jeff Luhnow, the best manager and general manager in franchise history, in the wake of the 2019 sign-stealing investigation.

Leading the sport's most loathed team requires a remarkable touch. Baker possesses it. He has pushed the Astros deep into October in both of his seasons at the helm. In 2021, Houston narrowly lost a six-game World Series.

Even in defeat, Baker might have accomplished the impossible. He might have redeemed baseball's most loathed team.

LAST 10 WINNERS

2011: Joe Maddon, Rays
2012: Buck Showalter, Orioles
2013: Clint Hurdle, Pirates
2014: Buck Showalter, Orioles
2015: Joe Maddon, Cubs
2016: Terry Francona, Indians
2017: A.J. Hinch, Astros
2018: Bob Melvin, Athletics
2019: Craig Counsell, Brewers
2020: Brian Snitker, Braves

Full list: BaseballAmerica.com/awards

CONTINUED FROM PAGE 19

won the NL Rookie of the Year for a season of his excellent strike zone discipline at the plate and solid defense. Catcher Tyler Stephenson, India's Reds teammate, also had an encouraging rookie year in becoming that rare breed of receiver who also can hit.

From St. Louis outfielder Tyler O'Neill to Astros righthander Luis Garcia to Marlins lefthander Trevor Rogers and beyond, MLB's young talent pipeline continues to be rich and fertile. In Atlanta, Austin Riley stepped up with an enormous year just when needed after outfielder Ronald Acuna Jr. suffered a season-ending knee injury and finished with 33 homers, 107 RBIs, a .333 batting average and an .898 OPS, a total package that placed him squarely in the NL MVP debate.

As these and other highly skilled youngsters emerged, a reminder of how quickly the cycles spin

in this game was served up by the Chicago Cubs at the July trade deadline. It doesn't seem all that long ago since the Cubs were stacked, and it seems shorter still since they won their historic World Series in 2016. Yet there was Jed Hoyer, president of baseball operations, in full sell mode after the Cubs failed to win the multiple titles many predicted, faded far more quickly than anybody ever dreamed and faced hard budgetary questions.

When the dust had cleared on Chicago's North Side, the Cubs traded Kris Bryant (to the San Francisco Giants), Anthony Rizzo (Yankees) and Javier Baez (Mets) after last winter non-tendering Kyle Schwarber (who signed with the Nationals but then was traded to the Red Sox).

In place of those old standbys, the new-look Cubs toward the end of the '21 season were feeding opportunities to third baseman Patrick Wisdom, first baseman Frank Schwindel and center fielder Rafael Ortega.

"We plan to be really active in free agency," Hoyer said during a year-end exit interview. "We plan to spend money intelligently. We're scouting that market heavily."

Intelligence is something the Mets are still looking to grab onto under new owner Steve Cohen. Amid upheaval in their front office, the Mets made what many considered to be an excellent acquisition in all-star shortstop Francisco Lindor from Cleveland. But after they negotiated a $341 million deal with him, Lindor produced the worst season of his career. To make matters worse, he was an instigator of a hare-brained scheme by the players to give thumbs down gestures on the field that eventually were discovered to be the players' secret signal among themselves used for booing the fans after a severely underachieving team had become a target for boos by the spectators.

Managerial Musical Chairs

The biggest news regarding managers this season involved the returns of two men who had been suspended by MLB for the entire 2020 season for their involvement in the Astros' cheating scandal of 2017. A.J. Hinch, the Astros' manager from 2015-2019, returned to the dugout in Detroit, where Ron Gardenhire had retired. And Alex Cora, Hinch's bench coach on that 2017 World Series-winning team who then moved on to manage Boston's championship team in 2018, was rehired by the Red Sox following a year away.

Both men had positive seasons. Little was expected of the Red Sox this year and Cora helped maneuver them into the playoffs. And mired in an ongoing rebuilding stage, the Tigers under Hinch finished third in the AL Central at 77-85, their best season since 2016.

As for the biggest news involving a departure, the Cardinals took care of that in a stunning firing of Mike Shildt a week after the club's NL wild card loss to the Dodgers. Given the team's record winning streak and sensational finish, and given that Shildt had climbed the organizational ladder over 18 years, moving from scout to player development to managing in the minor leagues and then, finally, the majors, nobody saw the move. President of baseball operations John Mozeliak neglected to give details of the move, only citing a "philosophical difference in the direction that our Major League club is going."

Two other managers were fired following the 2021 season: The Mets had enough go wrong on the field and in the clubhouse that they let Luis Rojas go after two seasons. And the Padres had little choice but to let Jayce Tingler go despite his long standing relationship with A.J. Preller, presi-

San Diego native Joe Musgrove threw the first no-hitter in franchise history in April.

dent of baseball operations, after they bottomed out in what was the most humiliating season in their franchise history given the record payroll, deep talent and sky-high expectations.

Milestones & More

While baseball fans in Detroit have been starved for a winner since Justin Verlander, Max Scherzer, Torii Hunter, Rick Porcello and more left town, the one aging holdover from that era continues to hold a place in the hearts of Tigers fans. Miguel Cabrera, who is among the greatest hitters ever, crushed the 500th home run of his career on Aug. 22 in a game at Toronto.

Cabrera, 38, became just the 28th member of the 500-homer club and the first Venezuelan-born player to reach that level with his blast against lefthander Steven Matz. With two more years left on his gargantuan eight-year, $248 million deal, Cabrera, who has won four batting crowns, has a couple of other milestones in sight: He will begin the 2022 season with 2,987 hits, just 13 away from 3,000. Only six players have 500 homers and 3,000 hits.

Though no longer Cabrera's teammate, Scherzer also reached an impressive milestone with his 3,000th career strikeout on a Sunday afternoon in Dodger Stadium against the Padres. It was a still-

CONTINUED ON PAGE 24

RONALD MARTINEZ/GETTY IMAGES

Baseball's Golden Age For Young Talent

BY KYLE GLASER

Fifty years ago, the greatest All-Star Game ever played took place in Detroit. The 1971 All-Star Game featured 20 future Hall of Fame players, including Hank Aaron, Willie Mays, Reggie Jackson and Roberto Clemente.

It is not fair to put such expectations on the 2021 class of all-stars. There have been many other All-Star Games featuring otherworldly collections of talent, and none have matched 20 future Hall of Famers.

At the same time, it's not hard to imagine 50 years from now, in the year 2071, looking back at the collection of young talent that came together at Coors Field on July 13 and holding it in similar reverence.

Baseball is in a golden age of young talent, and it all came together on the same field for the first time in Denver. It was the first All-Star Game for Fernando Tatis Jr., Shohei Ohtani, Vladimir Guerrero Jr. and Juan Soto. Same for Rafael Devers, Bo Bichette, Trea Turner, Matt Olson, Alex Reyes and Corbin Burnes. All are 27 or younger.

Guerrero hit a 468-foot home run and drove in two runs to win MVP honors and lead the AL to a 5-2 win over the NL. He became the youngest player to ever win the All-Star Game MVP award. Ohtani pitched a scoreless first inning and touched 100 mph to pick up the win.

It's easy to fall into hyperbole when discussing greatness, but there is nothing hyperbolic about today's young stars.

Ohtani has redefined what is possible in MLB with his unprecedented two-way stardom. Soto owns the highest OPS by a teenager in MLB history and is the youngest player to win a batting title. Guerrero has a chance to win the Triple Crown at 22 years old, the same age as many of the players just drafted this week. Tatis' 28 home runs before the all-star break are the most ever by a shortstop

And there could have been even more talent on the field. Mike Trout, Mookie Betts, Carlos Correa and Ronald Acuña Jr. were all selected but didn't participate due to injuries. ∎

ALL-STAR GAME

Shohei Ohtani

2021 ALL-STAR GAME

JULY 13, 2021
AMERICAN LEAGUE 5, NATIONAL LEAGUE 2

American	AB	R	H	RBI	National	AB	R	H	RBI
S. Ohtani, DH	2	0	0	0	F. Tatis Jr., SS	2	0	0	0
a-J. Martinez, DH	2	0	0	0	B. Crawford, SS	1	0	0	0
d-N. Cruz, DH	1	0	0	0	T. Turner, SS	2	0	0	0
V. Guerrero Jr., 1B	3	1	1	2	M. Muncy, DH	2	0	0	0
M. Olson, 1B	2	0	0	0	e-J. Turner, DH	2	0	1	0
X. Bogaerts, SS	3	0	2	1	N. Arenado, 3B	2	0	0	0
B. Bichette, SS	1	0	0	0	M. Machado, 3B	1	1	1	0
T. Anderson, SS	0	0	0	0	E. Escobar, 3B	1	0	1	0
A. Judge, RF	2	1	0	0	F. Freeman, 1B	2	0	1	0
J. Gallo, RF	0	0	0	0	J. Cronenworth, 1B	1	0	0	0
R. Devers, 3B	2	0	1	0	N. Castellanos, RF	2	0	0	0
J. Ramirez, 3B	1	0	0	0	J. Soto, RF	0	0	0	0
J. Wendle, 3B	1	0	1	0	J. Winker, LF	1	0	0	0
M. Semien, 2B	2	0	1	1	K. Bryant, LF	2	0	0	0
b-W. Merrifield, 2B	2	0	0	0	J.T. Realmuto, C	2	1	1	1
S. Perez, C	2	0	0	0	O. Narvaez, C	2	0	0	0
M. Zunino, C	2	1	1	1	B. Reynolds, CF	2	0	0	0
T. Hernandez, LF	2	1	1	0	C. Taylor, CF	2	0	0	0
c-J. Walsh, LF	2	0	0	0	A. Frazier, 2B	2	0	1	0
C. Mullins, CF	2	1	0	0	O. Albies, 2B	2	0	1	0
A. Garcia, CF	2	0	1	0					
Totals	**36**	**5**	**9**	**5**	**Totals**	**33**	**2**	**8**	**1**

a-struck out swinging for Ohtani in the 5th. **b**-struck out swinging for Semien in the 6th. **c**-flied out to center for Hernández in the 6th. **d**-grounded to first for Martinez in the 9th. **e**-grounded to second for Muncy in the 6th
2B: Hernández (1, Rogers); Devers (1, Burnes); García (1, Kimbrel); Albies (1, Hendriks). **HR:** Zunino (1, 6th inning off Walker 0 on, 2 Out); Guerrero Jr. (1, 3rd inning off Burnes 0 on, 2 Out); Realmuto (1, 5th inning off Soto 0 on, 1 Out). **RBI:** Bogaerts (1), Semien (1), Zunino (1), Guerrero Jr. 2 (2); Realmuto (1).

Time of Game: 3:00. **Attendance:** 49,184.

American	IP	H	R	SO	National	IP	H	R	SO
S. Ohtani (w)	1.0	0	0	0	M. Scherzer	1.0	0	0	1
L. Lynn	1.0	0	0	1	C. Burnes (L)	2.0	4	2	2
K. Gibson (H)	1.0	1	0	0	G. Marquez	1.0	0	0	1
N. Eovaldi (H)	1.0	1	0	0	T. Rogers	1.0	2	2	1
G. Soto	1.0	1	1	0	T. Walker	1.0	1	1	1
C. Bassitt	1.0	1	1	1	F. Peralta	1.0	0	0	3
A. Kittredge (H)	1.0	0	0	0	M. Melancon	0.1	0	0	1
M. Barnes (H)	1.0	2	0	0	A. Reyes	0.2	1	0	1
L. Hendriks (S)	1.0	2	0	1	C. Kimbrel	0.2	1	0	0
					Z. Wheeler	0.1	0	0	1
Totals		**9**	**8**	**2**	**3**	**Totals**	**9**	**9**	**5**	**12**

CONTINUED FROM PAGE 22

new venue for Scherzer, who, along with infielder Trea Turner, was acquired by the Dodgers at the trade deadline after their big free agent signing, Trevor Bauer, was placed on MLB's administrative leave list earlier in the summer. Scherzer, 37, became only the 19th pitcher in history to record his 3,000th strikeout. Only two—Verlander and CC Sabathia—have done it during the past decade.

In April, Joe Musgrove recorded the first no-hitter in Padres' club history. The Padres were the only team in the majors never to have had a pitcher throw a no-no, and when they finally got one, it was memorable, indeed. Musgrove is a San Diego native who was a high school pitcher in the area and grew up idolizing former Padres ace Jake Peavy, among others.

In a tough season, Pete Alonso gave Mets fans reason to smile when he became the second-fastest player to 100 homers in September, reaching the milestone in his 347th game. Only Philadelphia's Ryan Howard, who only needed 325 games, did it faster.

It was a season of milestones for Cincinnati legend Joey Votto, who became just the fifth Reds player to reach the 2,000-hit plateau after he smashed his 300th career homer and collected his 1,000th RBI earlier in the season.

Votto followed Cubs Hall of Fame outfielder Billy Williams as just the second player ever to reach all three milestones in the same season, according to the Elias Sports Bureau.

The Future?

As baseball navigates a quickly changing world by working to keep its soul while changing ever so gracefully with the times, we got glimpses of what the future may look like as MLB used some of the minor leagues as an experimental laboratory. A 15-second pitch clock was implemented, for example, in the Low-A West. Reviews were very good as the crisp pace of play there resulted in a very good tempo and shorter, more manageable games. "The pitch timer was one of the more successful experiments from this season," MLB executive vice president for baseball operations Morgan Sword told Baseball America's Kyle Glaser in September. "We received very positive feedback on the timer from players, coaches, umpires, minor league operators, frankly everybody that was involved in the Low-A West league this year. We were very encouraged by how it went."

If you attended a minor league game in 2021, chances are you saw officials at work tinkering with things that may be introduced at the MLB level in the near future. The pitch clock is one of them. An automated strike zone is another. That system was introduced in the Low-A Southeast this year after first being used in the independent Atlantic League in 2019. In the Southeast, the balls and strikes were gauged by the Hawk-Eye tracking system and relayed to the home plate umpire through an earpiece.

In Triple-A, they used bigger bases for half a season. The bags went from 15 square inches to 18 square inches to see if that would help bring more stolen bases. The result? Stolen base percentages increased incrementally.

Double-A was where baseball played around with the shift. In the first half of the season, each of the four infielders were required to keep both feet in the dirt when a pitch was delivered. In the second half of the season, two infielders were required to be on each side of second base.

The shift remains a triggering topic at the MLB level. In an era when MLB looks to get more balls in play and do things to help hitters—exhibit A was the crackdown on pitchers using sticky substances—most people agree that the shift has completely changed the game.

The new Collective Bargaining Agreement was expected to deal with much of this, as well as other things. After MLB implemented a universal designated hitter during the pandemic-shortened 2020 season, things went back to normal in the NL in 2021 with pitchers batting. Again, most in the industry figure it is only a matter of time until the universal DH is adopted again, and this time for good. Expanded playoffs remain on the horizon as well, with a new CBA expected to usher in a change in the postseason format as well with more teams participating. ∎

ACTIVE LEADERS

Career leaders among players who played in a game in 2021. Batters require 3,000 plate appearances and pitchers 1,000 innings to qualify for percentage titles.

BATTERS			PITCHERS		
AVG	Miguel Cabrera	.310	ERA	Clayton Kershaw	2.49
OBP	Mike Trout	.419	SO/9	Robbie Ray	11.21
SLG	Mike Trout	.583	BB/9	Josh Tomlin	1.29
OPS	Mike Trout	1.002	HR/9	Clayton Kershaw	0.72
R	Albert Pujols	1,872	W	Justin Verlander	226
H	Albert Pujols	3,301	L	Zack Greinke	132
2B	Albert Pujols	672	SV	Craig Kimbrel	372
3B	Dexter Fowler	82	IP	Zack Greinke	3,110
HR	Albert Pujols	679	SO	Max Scherzer	3,020
RBI	Albert Pujols	2,150	BB	Jon Lester	892
BB	Albert Pujols	1,345	AVG	Clayton Kershaw	.209
SO	Justin Upton	1,948	G	Joe Smith	832
XBH	Albert Pujols	1,367	GS	Zack Greinke	488
SB	Dee Strange-Gordon	333	HR	Ervin Santana	331

ARIZONA DIAMONDBACKS
- Geraldo Perdomo...April 3
- Matt Peacock........April 6
- J.B. Bukauskas....April 20
- Stuart Fairchild......July 6
- Miguel Aguilar....July 30
- Drew Ellis.............July 30
- Tyler Gilbert........Aug. 3
- Jake McCarthy....Aug. 27
- Henry Ramos........Sept. 5
- Brandyn Sittinger.Sept. 8
- Seth Beer........Sept. 10
- Luis Frias.............Sept. 19

ATLANTA BRAVES
- Kyle Muller ....June 16
- Dylan Lee..............Oct. 1
- Spencer Strider.......Oct. 1

BALTIMORE ORIOLES
- Tyler Wells ....April 4
- Ryan McKenna....April 5
- Mac Sceroler........April 5
- Zac Lowther.......April 25
- Jay Flaa............April 27
- Isaac Mattson .... May 7
- Tyler Nevin .... May 29
- Mickey Jannis.....June 23
- Konner Wade......June 26
- Alexander Wells....June 26
- Spenser Watkins ....July 2
- Conner Greene......July 27
- Dusten Knight ...... Aug. 4
- Marcos Diplan.......Aug. 6
- Mike Baumann....Sept. 7
- Manny Barreda.....Sept. 8

BOSTON RED SOX
- Hirokazu Sawamura.April 2
- Garrett Whitlock....April 4
- Eduard Bazardo ...April 14
- Connor Wong.........June 22
- Jarren Duran........July 17
- Raynel Espinal .....Aug. 30
- Jack Lopez ....Sept. 5
- Kutter Crawford ....Sept. 5
- Connor Seabold ..Sept. 11
- Kaleb Ort ....Sept. 13

CHICAGO CUBS
- Justin Steele ....April 12
- Trevor Megill ......April 26
- Keegan Thompson. May 4
- Tommy Nance...... May 17
- P.J. Higgins .... May 19
- Cory Abbott..........June 5
- Taylor Gushue......June 30
- Manuel Rodriguez July 30
- Michael Rucker.....July 30
- Greg Deichmann....Aug. 6
- Scott Effross ....Aug. 29
- Alfonso Rivas.......Aug. 29
- Trent Giambrone Sept. 29
- Erick Castillo ..... Sept. 30
- Tyler Payne .... Oct. 3

CHICAGO WHITE SOX
- Andrew Vaughn.....April 2
- Gavin Sheets.......June 29
- Jake Burger.........July 2
- Romy Gonzalez.... Sept. 3

CINCINNATI REDS
- Jonathan India ......April 1
- Ryan Hendrix.......April 23
- Vladimir Gutiérrez May 28
- Tony Santillan.....June 13
- Alejo Lopez.......June 28
- TJ Friedl............Sept. 18
- Dauri Moreta .... Sept. 26
- Reiver Sanmartin Sept. 27
- Riley O'Brien..... Sept. 28

CLEVELAND INDIANS
- Trevor Stephan ......April 3
- Sam Hentges ......April 20
- Nick Sandlin .... May 1
- J.C. Mejia .... May 21
- Owen Miller........ May 23
- Eli Morgan .... May 28
- Ernie Clement......June 13
- Justin Garza........June 27
- Francisco Perez ....Aug. 12

COLORADO ROCKIES
- Ben Bowden..........April 2
- Jordan Sheffield ...April 2
- Alan Trejo ....April 10
- Justin Lawrence...April 29
- Lucas Gilbreath...... May 1
- Ryan Feltner .... Sept. 5
- Julian Fernandez ... Sept. 5
- Colton Welker ..... Sept. 8
- Ryan Vilade........ Sept. 18

DETROIT TIGERS
- Akil Baddoo..........April 4
- Alex Lange..........April 10
- Zack Short ....April 21
- Jason Foley ....June 6
- Matt Manning......June 17
- Jacob Robson......Aug. 12
- Drew Carlton .... Sept. 4

HOUSTON ASTROS
- Chas McCormick ....April 1
- Ronnie Dawson ...April 14
- Alex De Goti......April 16
- Peter Solomon.....April 18
- Kent Emanuel......April 24
- Tyler Ivey .... May 21
- Ralph Garza ...... May 29
- Ryan Hartman......June 30
- Jake Meyers........Aug. 1
- Jose Siri ....Sept. 3
- Seth Martinez...... Sept. 20

KANSAS CITY ROYALS
- Kyle Isbel ....April 1
- Jake Brentz..........April 3
- Daniel Lynch........ May 3
- Sebastian Rivero ...... May 8

- Jackson Kowar..........June 7
- Emmanuel Rivera...June 28
- Jon Heasley .... Sept. 17
- Dylan Coleman.... Sept. 21
- Angel Zerpa .... Sept. 30

LOS ANGELES ANGELS
- Chris Rodriguez .....April 2
- Jose Rojas............April 2
- Jack Kruger .... May 6
- Andrew Wantz......July 4
- Brandon Marsh....July 18
- Austin Warren......July 29
- Reid Detmers........Aug. 1
- Jose Marte...........Aug. 20
- Elvis Peguero ......Aug. 26
- Cooper Criswell....Aug. 27
- Janson Junk.......... Sept. 5
- Kyle Tyler .... Sept. 5
- Oliver Ortega .... Sept. 8
- Jhonathan Diaz...Sept. 17

LOS ANGELES DODGERS
- Luke Raley ....April 9
- DJ Peters.............April 23
- Edwin Uceta ....April 30
- Zach Reks ....June 21
- Jake Reed ....July 6
- Darien Núñez.........July 9
- Josiah Gray ....July 20
- Justin Bruihl ....Aug. 8
- Andre Jackson .....Aug. 16

MIAMI MARLINS
- Paul Campbell ....April 3
- Zach Pop.............April 3
- Jose Devers.........April 24
- Anthony Bender ... May 5
- Luis Madero .... May 10
- Cody Poteet .... May 12
- Luis Marte ....June 1
- Zach Thompson ...June 7
- Bryan De La Cruz ..July 30
- Brian Miller..........July 30
- Sean Guenther......Aug. 4
- Edward Cabrera ...Aug. 25
- Payton Henry....... Sept. 17
- Nick Fortes.......... Sept. 18

MILWAUKEE BREWERS
- Corey Ray.............April 24
- Mario Feliciano...... May 1
- Alec Bettinger ...... May 2
- Jake Cousins ....June 21
- Miguel Sanchez...June 22
- Aaron Ashby ....June 30

MINNESOTA TWINS
- Ben Rortvedt ......April 30
- Nick Gordon........... May 6
- Trevor Larnach....... May 8
- Bailey Ober .... May 18
- Gilberto Celestino..June 2
- Griffin Jax ....June 8
- Charlie Barnes .....July 17
- Joe Ryan.............Sept. 1
- Jovani Moran....... Sept. 12

NEW YORK METS
- Patrick Mazeika ..... May 5
- Jake Hager........... May 15
- Johneshwy Fargas May 17
- Khalil Lee............. May 17
- Tylor Megill..........June 23
- Thomas Szapucki June 30
- Akeem Bostick......July 29

NEW YORK YANKEES
- Chris Gittens ....June 5
- Trey Amburgey .....July 16
- Hoy Park ....July 16
- Luis Gil..................Aug. 3
- Brody Koerner ....Aug. 3
- Stephen Ridings...Aug. 3

OAKLAND ATHLETICS
- Ka'ai Tom ....April 1
- Luis Barrera .... May 19
- Domingo Acevedo June 21
- Jacob Wilson.......July 10

PHILADELPHIA PHILLIES
- Nick Maton ....April 19
- Bailey Falter.........April 25
- Cristopher Sanchez June 6
- Luke Williams ....June 8
- Matt Vierling ....June 19
- Damon Jones.......Aug. 10
- Hans Crouse........ Sept. 26
- Kyle Dohy ....Oct. 2

PITTSBURGH PIRATES
- Luis Oviedo............April 3
- Rodolfo Castro .....April 21
- Hunter Owen......... May 5
- Troy Stokes Jr. ...... May 9
- Max Kranick..........June 27
- Shea Spitzbarth....Aug. 2
- Roansy Contreras Sept. 29
- Oneil Cruz ....Oct. 2

ST. LOUIS CARDINALS
- Scott Hurst ....April 16
- Angel Rondon.......June 6
- Lars Nootbaar........June 22

SAN DIEGO PADRES
- Ha-Seong Kim ....April 1
- Tucupita Marcano..April 1
- Aaron Northcraft .April 24
- Ivan Castillo .... May 14
- Webster Rivas...... May 28
- Daniel Camarena June 19
- Mason Thompson June 22
- Reiss Knehr............July 9

SAN FRANCISCO GIANTS
- Camilo Doval ....April 18
- Gregory Santos ....April 22
- Jason Vosler.........April 24
- Sammy Long ....June 9
- Kervin Castro .... Sept. 7

SEATTLE MARINERS
- Taylor Trammell .....April 1
- Will Vest ....April 1
- Wyatt Mills .... May 1
- Logan Gilbert....... May 13
- Jarred Kelenic...... May 13
- Jose Godoy .... May 21
- Dillon Thomas.......June 9
- Vinny Nittoli ....June 23
- Cal Raleigh ....July 11
- Darren McCaughan July 21

TAMPA BAY RAYS
- Kevin Padlo ....April 6
- Brent Honeywell Jr.April 11
- Louis Head...........April 25
- Taylor Walls ...... May 22
- Wander Franco ....June 22
- Vidal Brujan..........July 7
- Josh Lowe.............Sept. 8
- Shane Baz...........Sept. 20

TEXAS RANGERS
- Brett de Geus........April 1
- Kohei Arihara........April 3
- Hyeon-jong Yang.April 26
- Andy Ibáñez .... May 4
- Joe Barlow...........June 24
- Curtis Terry ....July 23
- Yonny Hernandez ..Aug. 5
- Yohel Pozo...........Aug. 13
- Nick Snyder ....Aug. 21
- Jake Latz...............Aug. 25
- Ryan Dorow..........Aug. 27
- Glenn Otto............Aug. 27
- A.J. Alexy.............Aug. 30

TORONTO BLUE JAYS
- Josh Palacios ....April 9
- Ty Tice....................April 9
- Alek Manoah .... May 27
- Riley Adams ....June 8
- Tayler Saucedo ....June 17
- Nick Allgeyer ....July 2
- Kirby Snead ....July 28
- Connor Overton ...Aug. 12
- Otto Lopez...........Aug. 17
- Kevin Smith..........Aug. 18
- Bryan Baker.........Sept. 5

WASHINGTON NATIONALS
- Sam Clay...............April 7
- Cody Wilson..........April 7
- Jakson Reetz........July 10
- Gabe Klobosits......July 30
- Alberto Baldonado Sept. 2
- Jhon Romero ...... Sept. 24
- Joan Adon ....Oct. 3

CLUB BATTING

	AVG	G	AB	R	H	2B	3B	HR	RBI	BB	SO	SB	OBP	SLG
Houston	.267	162	5593	863	1496	299	14	221	834	569	1222	53	.339	.444
Toronto	.266	162	5476	846	1455	285	13	262	816	496	1218	81	.330	.466
Boston	.261	162	5495	829	1434	330	23	219	783	512	1386	40	.328	.449
Chicago	.256	162	5357	796	1373	275	22	190	757	586	1389	57	.336	.422
Kansas City	.249	162	5427	686	1349	251	29	163	647	421	1258	124	.306	.396
Los Angeles	.245	162	5437	723	1331	265	23	190	691	464	1394	79	.310	.407
Tampa Bay	.243	162	5507	857	1336	288	36	222	810	585	1542	88	.321	.429
Detroit	.242	162	5376	697	1299	236	37	179	675	490	1514	88	.308	.399
Minnesota	.241	162	5431	729	1311	271	17	228	690	525	1405	54	.314	.423
Baltimore	.239	162	5420	659	1296	266	15	195	632	451	1454	54	.304	.402
Oakland	.238	162	5395	743	1284	271	19	199	698	545	1349	88	.317	.406
Cleveland	.238	162	5332	717	1269	248	22	203	686	453	1387	109	.303	.407
New York	.237	162	5331	711	1266	213	12	222	666	621	1482	63	.322	.407
Texas	.232	162	5405	625	1254	225	24	167	598	433	1381	106	.294	.375
Seattle	.226	162	5355	697	1209	233	11	199	673	535	1492	64	.303	.385

CLUB PITCHING

	ERA	G	CG	SHO	SV	IP	H	R	ER	HR	BB	SO	AVG
Tampa Bay	3.67	162	1	13	42	1456	1264	651	593	184	436	1478	.232
Chicago	3.73	162	4	13	43	1403	1205	636	581	182	485	1588	.229
New York	3.74	162	3	13	47	1435	1243	669	596	196	492	1569	.231
Houston	3.78	162	2	8	34	1445	1231	658	607	187	549	1456	.228
Toronto	3.91	162	1	14	34	1405	1257	663	610	209	473	1468	.236
Oakland	4.02	162	3	11	39	1433	1362	687	640	191	439	1332	.247
Boston	4.26	162	0	7	49	1419	1409	749	671	176	546	1527	.258
Seattle	4.30	162	1	10	51	1440	1356	748	688	197	485	1328	.247
Detroit	4.32	162	2	7	42	1420	1370	756	681	199	571	1259	.252
Cleveland	4.34	162	0	9	39	1408	1281	727	679	216	522	1391	.240
Kansas City	4.64	162	1	7	37	1417	1375	788	731	189	591	1344	.254
Los Angeles	4.69	162	1	4	39	1422	1373	804	741	188	592	1453	.251
Texas	4.79	162	0	3	31	1424	1402	815	758	232	513	1239	.256
Minnesota	4.83	162	1	9	42	1419	1392	834	762	239	484	1317	.255
Baltimore	5.84	162	1	5	26	1402	1518	956	910	258	563	1234	.273

CLUB FIELDING

	PCT	PO	A	E	DP		PCT	PO	A	E	DP
Houston	.988	4335	1432	69	126	Cleveland	.985	4224	1400	86	138
Oakland	.987	4299	1320	72	116	Los Angeles	.985	4265	1419	88	131
Baltimore	.987	4206	1359	74	101	Toronto	.984	4216	1371	90	122
Seattle	.986	4321	1384	79	135	New York	.983	4306	1318	98	112
Tampa Bay	.986	4367	1358	80	130	Chicago	.982	4210	1210	97	112
Detroit	.986	4259	1492	83	136	Minnesota	.982	4258	1420	107	138
Texas	.986	4273	1462	83	146	Boston	.981	4257	1421	108	143
Kansas City	.985	4252	1422	84	152						

INDIVIDUAL BATTING LEADERS

	AVG	G	AB	R	H	2B	3B	HR	RBI	BB	SO	SB
Yuli Gurriel, Houston	.319	143	530	83	169	31	0	15	81	59	68	1
Michael Brantley, Houston	.311	121	469	68	146	29	3	8	47	33	53	1
Vladimir Guerrero Jr., Toronto	.311	161	604	123	188	29	1	48	111	86	110	4
Tim Anderson, Chicago	.309	123	527	94	163	29	2	17	61	22	119	18
Nicky Lopez, Kansas City	.300	151	497	78	149	21	6	2	43	49	74	22
Bo Bichette, Toronto	.298	159	640	121	191	30	1	29	102	40	137	25
Teoscar Hernandez, Toronto	.296	143	550	92	163	29	0	32	116	36	148	12
Xander Bogaerts, Boston	.295	144	529	90	156	34	1	23	79	62	113	5
Kyle Tucker, Houston	.294	140	506	83	149	37	3	30	92	53	90	14
Ty France, Seattle	.291	152	571	85	166	32	1	18	73	46	106	0

INDIVIDUAL PITCHING LEADERS

	W	L	ERA	G	GS	CG	SV	IP	H	R	ER	BB	SO
Robbie Ray, Toronto	13	7	2.84	32	32	0	0	193	150	62	61	52	248
Lance McCullers Jr., Houston	13	5	3.16	28	28	0	0	162	122	59	57	76	185
Gerrit Cole, New York	16	8	3.23	30	30	2	0	181	151	69	65	41	243
Frankie Montas, Oakland	13	9	3.37	32	32	0	0	187	164	79	70	57	207
Jose Berrios, Minnesota/Toronto	12	9	3.52	32	32	1	0	192	159	83	75	45	204
Lucas Giolito, Chicago	11	9	3.53	31	31	1	0	179	145	74	70	52	201
Chris Flexen, Seattle	14	6	3.61	31	31	0	0	180	185	74	72	40	125
Nathan Eovaldi, Boston	11	9	3.75	32	32	0	0	182	182	81	76	35	195
Dylan Cease, Chicago	13	7	3.91	32	32	1	0	166	139	77	72	68	226
Sean Manaea, Oakland	11	10	3.91	32	32	2	0	179	179	79	78	41	194

AWARD WINNERS
Selected by Baseball Writers Association of America

MOST VALUABLE PLAYER

Player	1st	2nd	3rd	Total
Shohei Ohtani, Angels	30	—	—	420
Vladimir Guerrero Jr., Blue Jays	—	29	1	269
Marcus Semien, Blue Sox	—	—	24	232
Aaron Judge, Yankees	—	—	3	171
Carlos Correa, Astros	—	—	—	163
Jose Ramirez, Indians	—	—	—	133
Salvador Perez, Royals	—	1	2	103
Matt Olson, Athletics	—	—	—	90
Cedric Mullins, Orioles	—	—	—	87
Brandon Lowe, Rays	—	—	—	34
Rafael Devers, Red Sox	—	—	—	28
Bo Bichette, Blue Jays	—	—	—	7
Xander Bogaerts, Red Sox	—	—	—	7
Jose Abreu, White Sox	—	—	—	5
Nathan Eovaldi, Red Sox	—	—	—	4
Robbie Ray, Blue Jays	—	—	—	4
Gerrit Cole, Yankees	—	—	—	4
Jose Altuve, Astros	—	—	—	3
Teoscar Hernandez, Blue Jays	—	—	—	2

CY YOUNG AWARD

Player	1st	2nd	3rd	Total
Robbie Ray, Blue Jays	29	1	—	207
Gerrit Cole, Yankees	1	29	—	123
Lance Lynn, White Sox	—	—	11	48
Nathan Eovaldi, Red Sox	—	—	8	41
Carlos Rodon, White Sox	—	—	4	34
Frankie Montas, Athletics	—	—	2	21
Lance McCullers Jr., Astros	—	—	1	14
Liam Hendriks, White Sox	—	—	3	10
Jose Berrios, Twins/Blue Jays	—	—	1	8
Chris Bassitt, Athletics	—	—	—	2
Lucas Giolito, White Sox	—	—	—	1
Raisel Iglesias, Angels	—	—	—	1

ROOKIE OF THE YEAR

Player	1st	2nd	3rd	Total
Randy Arozarena, Rays	22	4	2	124
Luis Garcia, Astros	2	15	8	63
Wander Franco, Rays	2	5	5	30
Adolis Garcia, Rangers	3	1	9	27
Emmanuel Clase, Indians	—	1	2	11
Ryan Mountcastle, Orioles	—	2	4	10
Shane McClanahan, Rays	—	—	1	3
Alek Manoah, Blue Jays	—	—	2	2

MANAGER OF THE YEAR

Player	1st	2nd	3rd	Total
Kevin Cash, Rays	19	3	5	109
Scott Servais, Mariners	5	13	7	71
Dusty Baker, Astros	2	5	8	33
Charlie Montoyo, Blue Jays	3	2	2	23
Alex Cora, Red Sox	1	3	2	16
Tony La Russa, White Sox	—	4	3	15
A.J. Hinch, Tigers	—	—	3	3

Selected by AL managers and coaches

GOLD GLOVE AWARDS
P—Dallas Keuchel, White Sox. **C**—Sean Murphy, Athletics. **1B**—Yuli Gurriel, Astros. **2B**—Marcus Semien, Blue Jays. **3B**—Matt Chapman, Athletics. **SS**—Carlos Correa, Astros. **LF**—Andrew Benintendi, Royals. **CF**—Michael A. Taylor, Royals. **RF**—Joey Gallo, Rangers/Yankees.

SILVER SLUGGER AWARDS
C—Salvador Perez, Royals. **1B**—Vladimir Guerrero Jr., Blue Jays. **2B**—Marcus Semien, Blue Jays. **3B**—Rafael Devers, Red Sox. **SS**—Xander Bogaerts, Red Sox. **OF**—Teoscar Hernandez, Blue Jays; Aaron Judge, Yankees; and Cedric Mullins, Orioles. **DH**—Shohei Ohtani, Angels.

DEPARTMENT LEADERS

BATTING

GAMES
Whit Merrifield, Kansas City	162
Marcus Semien, Toronto	162
Vladimir Guerrero Jr., Toronto	161
Salvador Perez, Kansas City	161
J.P. Crawford, Seattle	160

AT-BATS
Whit Merrifield, Kansas City	664
Marcus Semien, Toronto	652
Bo Bichette, Toronto	640
Isiah Kiner-Falefa, Texas	635
David Fletcher, Los Angeles	626

PLATE APPEARANCES
Marcus Semien, Toronto	724
Whit Merrifield, Kansas City	720
Vladimir Guerrero Jr., Toronto	698
Mitch Haniger, Seattle	691
Bo Bichette, Toronto	690

RUNS
Vladimir Guerrero Jr., Toronto	123
Bo Bichette, Toronto	121
Jose Altuve, Houston	117
Marcus Semien, Toronto	115
Jose Ramirez, Cleveland	111

HITS
Bo Bichette, Toronto	191
Vladimir Guerrero Jr., Toronto	188
Whit Merrifield, Kansas City	184
Cedric Mullins, Baltimore	175
2 others	173

TOTAL BASES
Vladimir Guerrero Jr., Toronto	363
Marcus Semien, Toronto	351
Salvador Perez, Kansas City	337
Rafael Devers, Boston	318
Shohei Ohtani, Los Angeles	318

DOUBLES
Jeimer Candelario, Detroit	42
J.D. Martinez, Boston	42
Whit Merrifield, Kansas City	42
Marcus Semien, Toronto	39
4 others	37

TRIPLES
Shohei Ohtani, Los Angeles	8
Akil Baddoo, Detroit	7
Kevin Kiermaier, Tampa Bay	7
Luis Arraez, Minnesota	6
4 others	6

EXTRA-BASE HITS
Marcus Semien, Toronto	86
Shohei Ohtani, Los Angeles	80
Vladimir Guerrero Jr., Toronto	78
Rafael Devers, Boston	76
Matt Olson, Oakland	74

HOME RUNS
Vladimir Guerrero Jr., Toronto	48
Salvador Perez, Kansas City	48
Shohei Ohtani, Los Angeles	46
Marcus Semien, Toronto	45
4 others	39

RUNS BATTED IN
Salvador Perez, Kansas City	121
Jose Abreu, Chicago	117
Teoscar Hernandez, Toronto	116
Rafael Devers, Boston	113
2 others	111

Bo Bichette

SACRIFICES
Nicky Lopez, Kansas City	12
Leury Garcia, Chicago	9
Austin Hedges, Cleveland	7
David Fletcher, Los Angeles	6
Brett Gardner, New York	5

SACRIFICE FLIES
Yuli Gurriel, Houston	12
Whit Merrifield, Kansas City	12
Matt Olson, Oakland	11
Jose Abreu, Chicago	10
3 others	9

HIT BY PITCHES
Mark Canha, Oakland	27
Ty France, Seattle	27
Jose Abreu, Chicago	22
Nick Solak, Texas	15
Bradley Zimmer, Cleveland	15

WALKS
Joey Gallo, New York	111
Robbie Grossman, Detroit	98
Shohei Ohtani, Los Angeles	96
Matt Olson, Oakland	88
Yasmani Grandal, Chicago	87

STOLEN BASES
Whit Merrifield, Kansas City	40
Cedric Mullins, Baltimore	30
Myles Straw, Cleveland	30
Jose Ramirez, Cleveland	27
Shohei Ohtani, Los Angeles	26

STOLEN BASE PERCENTAGE
Bo Bichette, Toronto	96.15
Nicky Lopez, Kansas City	95.65
Adalberto Mondesi, Toronto	93.75
Marcus Semien, Toronto	93.75
Starling Marte, Oakland	92.59

STRIKEOUTS
Joey Gallo, New York	213
Matt Chapman, Oakland	202
Adolis Garcia, Texas	194
Shohei Ohtani, Los Angeles	189
Miguel Sano, Minnesota	183

AT-BATS PER STRIKEOUT
David Fletcher, Los Angeles	10.4
Michael Brantley, Houston	8.8
Yuli Gurriel, Houston	7.8
Isiah Kiner-Falefa, Texas	7.1
Nicky Lopez, Kansas City	6.7

DOUBLE PLAYS
Jose Abreu, Chicago	28
Josh Donaldson, Minnesota	22
Giancarlo Stanton, New York	22
Miguel Cabrera, Detroit	21
Vladimir Guerrero Jr., Toronto	20

MULTI-HIT GAMES
Bo Bichette, Toronto	58
Jonathan Schoop, Detroit	53
Vladimir Guerrero Jr., Toronto	52
Aaron Judge, New York	50
Jose Altuve, Houston	49
Yuli Gurriel, Houston	49
Whit Merrifield, Kansas City	49

ON-BASE PERCENTAGE
Vladimir Guerrero Jr., Toronto	.401
Yuli Gurriel, Houston	.383
Yoan Moncada, Chicago	.375
Aaron Judge, New York	.373
Shohei Ohtani, Los Angeles	.372

ON-BASE PLUS SLUGGING
Vladimir Guerrero Jr., Toronto	1.002
Shohei Ohtani, Los Angeles	.965
Kyle Tucker, Houston	.917
Aaron Judge, New York	.916
Matt Olson, Oakland	.911

PITCHING

WINS
Gerrit Cole, New York	16
Chris Flexen, Seattle	14
Steven Matz, Toronto	14
Hyun Jin Ryu, Toronto	14
Dylan Cease, Chicago	13
Lance McCullers Jr., Houston	13
4 others	13

LOSSES
Cole Irvin, Oakland	15
Matt Harvey, Baltimore	14
Jorge Lopez, Baltimore	14
Jordan Lyles, Texas	13
Kolby Allard, Texas	12
4 others	12

GAMES
Bryan Shaw, Cleveland	81
Yusmeiro Petit, Oakland	78
Steve Cishek, Los Angeles	74
Jake Brentz, Kansas City	72
Mike Mayers, Los Angeles	72
Hansel Robles, Boston	72
Ryne Stanek, Houston	72

GAMES STARTED
Jose Berrios, Toronto	32
Dylan Cease, Chicago	32
Nathan Eovaldi, Boston	32
Cole Irvin, Oakland	32
Sean Manaea, Oakland	32
2 others	32

GAMES FINISHED
Raisel Iglesias, Los Angeles	59
Liam Hendriks, Chicago	58
Emmanuel Clase, Cleveland	51
Ryan Pressly, Houston	49
Aroldis Chapman, New York	46

Gerrit Cole

COMPLETE GAMES

Gerrit Cole, New York	2
Sean Manaea, Oakland	2
Chris Bassitt, Oakland	1
Jose Berrios, Toronto	1
Dylan Cease, Chicago	1
14 others	1

SHUTOUTS

Sean Manaea, Oakland	2
Chris Bassitt, Oakland	1
Dylan Cease, Chicago	1
Gerrit Cole, New York	1
Corey Kluber, New York	1
5 others	1

SAVES

Liam Hendriks, Chicago	38
Raisel Iglesias, Los Angeles	34
Aroldis Chapman, New York	30
Ryan Pressly, Houston	26
Matt Barnes, Boston	24
Emmanuel Clase, Cleveland	24

INNINGS PITCHED

Robbie Ray, Toronto	193.1
Jose Berrios, Toronto	192
Frankie Montas, Oakland	187
Nathan Eovaldi, Boston	182.1
Gerrit Cole, New York	181.1

HITS ALLOWED

Cole Irvin, Oakland	195
Jordan Lyles, Texas	194
Dallas Keuchel, Chicago	189
Chris Flexen, Seattle	185
Nathan Eovaldi, Boston	182

RUNS ALLOWED

Dallas Keuchel, Chicago	105
Jordan Lyles, Texas	104
Matt Harvey, Baltimore	96
Ryan Yarbrough, Tampa Bay	96
Cole Irvin, Oakland	94

HOME RUNS ALLOWED

Jordan Lyles, Texas	38
Mike Foltynewicz, Texas	35
Tarik Skubal, Detroit	35
Robbie Ray, Toronto	33
Zack Greinke, Houston	30
John Means, Baltimore	30

Liam Hendriks

WALKS ALLOWED

Lance McCullers Jr., Houston	76
Dylan Cease, Chicago	68
Nick Pivetta, Boston	65
Brad Keller, Kansas City	64
Yusei Kikuchi, Seattle	62

LOWEST WALKS PER NINE

Nathan Eovaldi, Boston	1.7
Zack Greinke, Houston	1.9
Hyun Jin Ryu, Toronto	2.0
Chris Flexen, Seattle	2.0
Gerrit Cole, New York	2.0

HIT BATTERS

Alek Manoah, Toronto	16
Jose Berrios, Toronto	15
Chris Bassitt, Oakland	11
Casey Mize, Detroit	11
Brady Singer, Kansas City	11
Framber Valdez, Houston	11

STRIKEOUTS

Robbie Ray, Toronto	248
Gerrit Cole, New York	243
Dylan Cease, Chicago	226
Frankie Montas, Oakland	207
Jose Berrios, Toronto	204

STRIKEOUTS PER NINE

Dylan Cease, Chicago	12.3
Gerrit Cole, New York	12.1
Robbie Ray, Toronto	11.5
Lance McCullers Jr., Houston	10.3
Lucas Giolito, Chicago	10.1

STRIKEOUTS PER NINE (Relievers)

Aroldis Chapman, New York	15.5
Paul Sewald, Seattle	14.5
Liam Hendriks, Chicago	14.3
Matt Barnes, Boston	13.8
Michael Kopech, Chicago	13.4

DOUBLE PLAYS

Chris Flexen, Seattle	22
Dallas Keuchel, Chicago	21
Kris Bubic, Kansas City	20
Zack Greinke, Houston	18
3 others	18

PICKOFFS

Jose Berrios, Toronto	3
Griffin Canning, Los Angeles	3
Danny Coulombe, Minnesota	3
Chris Flexen, Seattle	3
3 others	3

WILD PITCHES

Dylan Cease, Chicago	13
Lucas Giolito, Chicago	12
Jordan Montgomery, New York	12
Sam Hentges, Cleveland	11
Frankie Montas, Oakland	11
Gregory Soto, Detroit	11

WALKS PLUS HITS PER INNING

Robbie Ray, Toronto	1.04
Gerrit Cole, New York	1.06
Jose Berrios, Toronto	1.06
Lucas Giolito, Chicago	1.10
Zack Greinke, Houston	1.17

OPPONENT AVERAGE

Lance McCullers Jr., Houston	.205
Robbie Ray, Toronto	.210
Lucas Giolito, Chicago	.219
Jose Berrios, Toronto	.223
Dylan Cease, Chicago	.223
Gerrit Cole, New York	.223

WORST ERA

Dallas Keuchel, Chicago	5.82
Jordan Lyles, Texas	5.15
Tyler Anderson, Seattle	4.53
Hyun Jin Ryu, Toronto	4.37
Cole Irvin, Oakland	4.24

FIELDING

PITCHER

PCT	8 players	1.000
PO	Chris Flexen, Seattle	21
A	Dallas Keuchel, Chicago	41
DP	Chris Flexen, Seattle	22
E	Brady Singer, Kansas City	6

CATCHER

PCT	Salvador Perez, Kansas City	.998
PO	Christian Vazquez, Boston	1136
A	Salvador Perez, Kansas City	61
DP	Salvador Perez, Kansas City	12
E	Kurt Suzuki, Los Angeles	10
CS	Martin Maldonado, Houston	19
PB	3 players	10

FIRST BASE

PCT	Matt Olson, Oakland	.995
PO	Nathaniel Lowe, Texas	1164
A	Yuli Gurriel, Houston	86
DP	Nathaniel Lowe, Texas	119
E	Miguel Sano, Minnesota	13

SECOND BASE

PCT	David Fletcher, Los Angeles	.990
PO	Whit Merrifield, Kansas City	283
A	Whit Merrifield, Kansas City	382
DP	Whit Merrifield, Kansas City	103
E	2 players	12

THIRD BASE

PCT	Matt Chapman, Oakland	.987
PO	Matt Chapman, Oakland	166
A	Kyle Seager, Seattle	291
DP	Kyle Seager, Seattle	43
E	Rafael Devers, Boston	22

SHORTSTOP

PCT	Nicky Lopez, Kansas City	.987
PO	J.P. Crawford, Seattle	222
A	Isiah Kiner-Falefa, Texas	436
DP	Isiah Kiner-Falefa, Texas	98
E	Bo Bichette, Toronto	24

OUTFIELD

PCT	4 players	1.000
PO	Cedric Mullins, Baltimore	389
A	2 players	16
DP	Enrique Hernandez, Boston	4
E	Hunter Renfroe, Boston	12

CLUB BATTING

	AVG	G	AB	R	H	2B	3B	HR	RBI	BB	SO	SB	OBP	SLG
Washington	.258	162	5385	724	1388	272	20	182	686	573	1303	56	.337	.417
Cincinnati	.249	162	5423	786	1352	295	13	222	756	553	1425	36	.328	.431
San Francisco	.249	162	5462	804	1360	271	25	241	768	602	1461	66	.329	.440
Colorado	.249	161	5374	739	1338	275	34	182	709	491	1356	76	.317	.414
Los Angeles	.244	162	5445	830	1330	247	24	237	799	613	1408	65	.330	.429
Atlanta	.244	161	5363	790	1307	269	20	239	762	549	1453	59	.319	.435
St. Louis	.244	162	5351	706	1303	261	22	198	678	478	1341	89	.313	.412
San Diego	.242	162	5384	729	1305	273	21	180	695	586	1324	110	.321	.401
Philadelphia	.240	162	5366	734	1288	262	24	198	700	564	1402	77	.318	.408
New York	.239	162	5210	636	1243	228	18	176	604	495	1392	54	.315	.391
Chicago	.237	162	5306	705	1255	225	26	210	672	502	1596	86	.312	.407
Pittsburgh	.236	162	5336	609	1261	240	35	124	570	529	1328	60	.309	.364
Arizona	.236	162	5489	679	1297	308	31	144	644	537	1465	43	.309	.382
Milwaukee	.233	162	5362	738	1251	255	18	194	700	586	1465	82	.317	.396
Miami	.233	162	5348	623	1244	226	23	158	594	450	1553	106	.298	.372

CLUB PITCHING

	ERA	G	CG	SHO	SV	IP	H	R	ER	HR	BB	SO	AVG
Los Angeles	3.01	162	1	17	56	1452	1107	561	486	161	486	1599	.207
San Francisco	3.24	162	2	18	56	1455	1254	594	524	151	416	1425	.230
Milwaukee	3.50	162	2	19	44	1436	1156	623	558	168	537	1618	.218
Atlanta	3.88	161	2	18	40	1411	1237	656	608	183	516	1417	.234
New York	3.90	162	2	8	41	1379	1221	668	597	190	475	1453	.236
Miami	3.96	162	1	8	33	1415	1282	701	622	162	529	1381	.241
St. Louis	3.98	162	3	15	50	1417	1234	672	626	152	608	1225	.234
San Diego	4.10	162	2	11	43	1430	1277	708	651	205	516	1517	.237
Philadelphia	4.39	162	5	12	36	1419	1321	745	692	200	509	1480	.244
Cincinnati	4.40	162	1	8	41	1434	1330	760	702	206	617	1524	.244
Washington	4.80	162	1	8	36	1394	1364	820	743	247	548	1346	.254
Colorado	4.82	161	3	6	33	1397	1397	796	748	196	539	1269	.260
Chicago	4.87	162	1	8	40	1413	1386	839	765	235	596	1358	.255
Pittsburgh	5.08	162	0	6	25	1396	1400	833	788	213	606	1312	.260
Arizona	5.11	162	3	4	22	1417	1480	893	804	232	555	1238	.267

CLUB FIELDING

	PCT	PO	A	E	DP		PCT	PO	A	E	DP
Atlanta	.988	4232	1483	71	104	Cincinnati	.984	4303	1422	91	124
Pittsburgh	.988	4189	1378	70	139	Philadelphia	.984	4256	1439	94	142
Colorado	.987	4191	1516	73	140	Milwaukee	.984	4308	1331	94	102
San Francisco	.986	4365	1471	80	122	Washington	.983	4184	1361	96	116
San Diego	.986	4290	1399	82	139	New York	.983	4138	1312	95	121
St. Louis	.986	4251	1514	84	137	Arizona	.983	4252	1374	100	113
Chicago	.985	4238	1554	87	149	Miami	.979	4245	1443	122	146
Los Angeles	.985	4356	1303	89	94						

INDIVIDUAL BATTING LEADERS

	AVG	G	AB	R	H	2B	3B	HR	RBI	BB	SO	SB
Trea Turner, Washington/L.A.	.328	148	595	107	195	34	3	28	77	41	110	32
Juan Soto, Washington	.313	151	502	111	157	20	2	29	95	145	93	9
Bryce Harper, Philadelphia	.309	141	488	101	151	42	1	35	84	100	134	13
Nick Castellanos, Cincinnati	.309	138	531	95	164	38	1	34	100	41	121	3
Adam Frazier, Pittsburgh/S.D.	.305	155	577	83	176	36	5	5	43	48	69	10
Austin Riley, Atlanta	.303	160	590	91	179	33	1	33	107	52	168	0
Bryan Reynolds, Pittsburgh	.302	159	559	93	169	35	8	24	90	75	119	5
Freddie Freeman, Atlanta	.300	159	600	120	180	25	2	31	83	85	107	8
Brandon Crawford, San Francisco	.298	138	483	79	144	30	3	24	90	56	105	11
Paul Goldschmidt, St. Louis	.294	158	603	102	177	36	2	31	99	67	136	12

INDIVIDUAL PITCHING LEADERS

	W	L	ERA	G	GS	CG	SV	IP	H	R	ER	BB	SO
Corbin Burnes, Milwaukee	11	5	2.43	28	28	0	0	167	123	47	45	34	234
Max Scherzer, Washington/L.A.	15	4	2.46	30	30	1	0	179	119	53	49	36	236
Walker Buehler, Los Angeles	16	4	2.47	33	33	0	0	208	149	61	57	52	212
Brandon Woodruff, Milwaukee	9	10	2.56	30	30	0	0	179	130	54	51	43	211
Zack Wheeler, Philadelphia	14	10	2.78	32	32	3	0	213	169	72	66	46	247
Kevin Gausman, San Francisco	14	6	2.81	33	33	0	0	192	150	66	60	50	227
Julio Urias, Los Angeles	20	3	2.96	32	32	0	0	186	151	67	61	38	195
Marcus Stroman, New York	10	13	3.02	33	33	0	0	179	161	70	60	44	158
Max Fried, Atlanta	14	7	3.04	28	28	2	0	166	139	61	56	41	158
Adam Wainwright, St. Louis	17	7	3.05	32	32	3	0	206	168	72	70	50	174

AWARD WINNERS

Selected by Baseball Writers Association of America

MOST VALUABLE PLAYER

Player	1st	2nd	3rd	Total
Bryce Harper, Phillies	17	9	2	348
Juan Soto, Nationals	6	11	7	274
Fernando Tatis Jr., Padres	2	5	15	244
Brandon Crawford, Giants	4	2	1	213
Trea Turner, Nationals/Dodgers	1	3	3	185
Paul Goldschmidt, Cardinals	—	—	1	128
Austin Riley, Braves	—	—	—	111
Tyler O'Neill, Cardinals	—	—	1	62
Freddie Freeman, Braves	—	—	—	43
Max Muncy, Dodgers	—	—	—	38
Bryan Reynolds, Pirates	—	—	—	33
Nick Castellanos, Reds	—	—	—	24
Ozzie Albies, Braves	—	—	—	12
Max Scherzer, WSH/LAD	—	—	—	11
Corbin Burnes, Brewers	—	—	—	9
Joey Votto, Reds	—	—	—	8
Willy Adames, Brewers	—	—	—	8
Manny Machado, Padres	—	—	—	7
Zack Wheeler, Phillies	—	—	—	6
Adam Wainwright, Cardinals	—	—	—	3
LaMonte Wade Jr., Giants	—	—	—	1
Kevin Gausman, Giants	—	—	—	1
Buster Posey, Giants	—	—	—	1

CY YOUNG AWARD

Player	1st	2nd	3rd	Total
Corbin Burnes, Brewers	12	14	3	151
Zack Wheeler, Phillies	12	9	4	141
Max Scherzer, Nationals/Dodgers	6	5	13	113
Walker Buehler, Dodgers	—	2	9	70
Brandon Woodruff, Brewers	—	—	—	21
Kevin Gausman, Giants	—	—	1	7
Adam Wainwright, Cardinals	—	—	—	3
Julio Urias, Dodgers	—	—	—	3
Jacob deGrom, Mets	—	—	—	1

ROOKIE OF THE YEAR

Player	1st	2nd	3rd	Total
Jonathan India, Reds	29	1	—	148
Trevor Rogers, Marlins	1	26	3	86
Dylan Carlson, Cardinals	—	3	13	22
Patrick Wisdom, Cubs	—	—	5	5
Ian Anderson, Braves	—	—	3	3
Tyler Stephenson, Reds	—	—	2	2
Frank Schwindel, Cubs	—	—	2	2
David Bednar, Pirates	—	—	1	1

MANAGER OF THE YEAR

Player	1st	2nd	3rd	Total
Gabe Kapler, Giants	28	1	—	143
Craig Counsell, Brewers	1	22	4	75
Mike Shildt, Cardinals	1	3	11	25
Brian Snitker, Braves	—	4	9	21
Dave Roberts, Dodgers	—	—	6	6

Selected by NL managers and coaches

GOLD GLOVE AWARDS

P—Max Fried, Braves. **C**—Jacob Stallings, Pirates. **1B**—Paul Goldschmidt, Cardinals. **2B**—Tommy Edman, Cardinals. **3B**—Nolan Arenado, Cardinals. **SS**—Brandon Crawford, Giants. **LF**—Tyler O'Neill, Cardinals. **CF**—Harrison Bader, Cardinals. **RF**—Adam Duvall, Marlins/Braves.

SILVER SLUGGER AWARDS

C—Buster Posey, Giants. **1B**—Freddie Freeman, Braves. **2B**—Ozzie Albies, Braves. **3B**—Austin Riley, Braves. **SS**—Fernando Tatis Jr., Padres. **OF**—Nick Castellanos, Reds; Bryce Harper, Phillies; and Juan Soto, Nationals. **P**—Max Fried, Braves..

BATTING

GAMES
Austin Riley, Atlanta	160
Dansby Swanson, Atlanta	160
Tommy Edman, St. Louis	159
Freddie Freeman, Atlanta	159
Bryan Reynolds, Pittsburgh	159

AT-BATS
Tommy Edman, St. Louis	641
Ozzie Albies, Atlanta	629
Paul Goldschmidt, St. Louis	603
Freddie Freeman, Atlanta	600
Trea Turner, Los Angeles	595

PLATE APPEARANCES
Freddie Freeman, Atlanta	695
Tommy Edman, St. Louis	691
Ozzie Albies, Atlanta	686
Paul Goldschmidt, St. Louis	679
Austin Riley, Atlanta	662

RUNS
Freddie Freeman, Atlanta	120
Juan Soto, Washington	111
Trea Turner, Los Angeles	107
Ozzie Albies, Atlanta	103
Paul Goldschmidt, St. Louis	102

HITS
Trea Turner, Los Angeles	195
Freddie Freeman, Atlanta	180
Austin Riley, Atlanta	179
Paul Goldschmidt, St. Louis	177
Adam Frazier, San Diego	176

TOTAL BASES
Trea Turner, Los Angeles	319
Austin Riley, Atlanta	313
Paul Goldschmidt, St. Louis	310
Ozzie Albies, Atlanta	307
Nick Castellanos, Cincinnati	306

DOUBLES
Bryce Harper, Philadelphia	42
Tommy Edman, St. Louis	41
Ozzie Albies, Atlanta	40
Nick Castellanos, Cincinnati	38
2 others	36

TRIPLES
David Peralta, Arizona	8
Bryan Reynolds, Pittsburgh	8
Ozzie Albies, Atlanta	7
Jake Cronenworth, San Diego	7
Garrett Hampson, Colorado	6

EXTRA-BASE HITS
Bryce Harper, Philadelphia	78
Ozzie Albies, Atlanta	77
Nick Castellanos, Cincinnati	73
Fernando Tatis Jr., San Diego	73
Nolan Arenado, St. Louis	71

HOME RUNS
Fernando Tatis Jr., San Diego	42
Adam Duvall, Atlanta	38
Pete Alonso, New York	37
Max Muncy, Los Angeles	36
Joey Votto, Cincinnati	36

RUNS BATTED IN
Adam Duvall, Atlanta	113
Austin Riley, Atlanta	107
Ozzie Albies, Atlanta	106
Manny Machado, San Diego	106
Nolan Arenado, St. Louis	105

Freddie Freeman

SACRIFICES
Adam Wainwright, St. Louis	14
Antonio Senzatela, Colorado	12
Zach Davies, Chicago	10
Julio Urias, Los Angeles	10
3 others	9

SACRIFICE FLIES
Manny Machado, San Diego	11
Will Smith, Los Angeles	11
Dylan Carlson, St. Louis	8
Gregory Polanco, Pittsburgh	8
Austin Riley, Atlanta	8

HIT BY PITCHES
Jonathan India, Cincinnati	23
Kyle Farmer, Cincinnati	18
Will Smith, Los Angeles	18
Edmundo Sosa, St. Louis	17
Victor Robles, Washington	16

WALKS
Juan Soto, Washington	145
Bryce Harper, Philadelphia	100
Freddie Freeman, Atlanta	85
Max Muncy, Los Angeles	83
Andrew McCutchen, Philadelphia	81

STOLEN BASES
Trea Turner, Los Angeles	32
Tommy Edman, St. Louis	30
Fernando Tatis Jr., San Diego	25
Jazz Chisholm Jr., Miami	23
Starling Marte, Miami	22

STOLEN BASE PERCENTAGE
Austin Slater, San Francisco	88.24
Starling Marte, Miami	88
Trea Turner, Los Angeles	86.49
Fernando Tatis Jr., San Diego	86.21
Tommy Edman, St. Louis	85.71

STRIKEOUTS
Javier Baez, New York	184
Adam Duvall, Atlanta	174
Eugenio Suarez, Cincinnati	171
Tyler O'Neill, St. Louis	168
Austin Riley, Atlanta	168

AT-BATS PER STRIKEOUT
Kevin Newman, Pittsburgh	12.6
Adam Frazier, San Diego	8.4
Raimel Tapia, Colorado	7
Tommy Edman, St. Louis	6.7
Miguel Rojas, Miami	6.7

Juan Soto

DOUBLE PLAYS
Juan Soto, Washington	23
Josh Bell, Washington	22
Pete Alonso, New York	20
Nolan Arenado, St. Louis	20
Trea Turner, Los Angeles	18

MULTI-HIT GAMES
Trea Turner, Los Angeles	58
Freddie Freeman, Atlanta	53
Austin Riley, Atlanta	52
Nick Castellanos, Cincinnati	49
Adam Frazier, San Diego	49

ON-BASE PERCENTAGE
Juan Soto, Washington	.465
Bryce Harper, Philadelphia	.429
Freddie Freeman, Atlanta	.393
Bryan Reynolds, Pittsburgh	.390
Jonathan India, Cincinnati	.376

ON-BASE PLUS SLUGGING
Bryce Harper, Philadelphia	1.044
Juan Soto, Washington	.999
Fernando Tatis Jr., San Diego	.975
Nick Castellanos, Cincinnati	.939
Joey Votto, Cincinnati	.938

PITCHING

WINS
Julio Urias, Los Angeles	20
Adam Wainwright, St. Louis	17
Walker Buehler, Los Angeles	16
Max Scherzer, Los Angeles	15
5 others	14

LOSSES
Luis Castillo, Cincinnati	16
Patrick Corbin, Washington	16
Sandy Alcantara, Miami	15
Jake Arrieta, San Diego	14
3 others	13

GAMES
Tyler Rogers, San Francisco	80
Tim Hill, San Diego	78
Hector Neris, Philadelphia	74
Giovanny Gallegos, St. Louis	73
Blake Treinen, Los Angeles	72

GAMES STARTED
Sandy Alcantara, Miami	33
Walker Buehler, Los Angeles	33
Luis Castillo, Cincinnati	33
Kevin Gausman, San Francisco	33
Tyler Mahle, Cincinnati	33
Charlie Morton, Atlanta	33
Marcus Stroman, New York	33

GAMES FINISHED
Will Smith, Atlanta	60
Alex Reyes, St. Louis	54
Mark Melancon, San Diego	53
Kenley Jansen, Los Angeles	52
Edwin Diaz, New York	51

COMPLETE GAMES
German Marquez, Colorado	3
Adam Wainwright, St. Louis	3
Zack Wheeler, Philadelphia	3
Anthony DeSclafani, San Francisco	2
Max Fried, Atlanta	2
Joe Musgrove, San Diego	2

CARMEN MANDATO/GETTY IMAGES; G FIUME/GETTY IMAGES

SHUTOUTS

Anthony DeSclafani, San Francisco	2
Max Fried, Atlanta	2
Joe Musgrove, San Diego	2
Zack Wheeler, Philadelphia	2
10 others	1

SAVES

Mark Melancon, San Diego	39
Kenley Jansen, Los Angeles	38
Will Smith, Atlanta	37
Josh Hader, Milwaukee	34
Edwin Diaz, New York	32

INNINGS PITCHED

Zack Wheeler, Philadelphia	213.1
Walker Buehler, Los Angeles	207.2
Adam Wainwright, St. Louis	206.1
Sandy Alcantara, Miami	205.2
Kevin Gausman, San Francisco	192

HITS ALLOWED

Kyle Hendricks, Chicago	200
Patrick Corbin, Washington	192
Luis Castillo, Cincinnati	181
Antonio Senzatela, Colorado	178
Sandy Alcantara, Miami	171

RUNS ALLOWED

Patrick Corbin, Washington	114
Kyle Hendricks, Chicago	101
Zach Davies, Chicago	99
Aaron Nola, Philadelphia	95
Luis Castillo, Cincinnati	94

HOME RUNS ALLOWED

Patrick Corbin, Washington	37
Kyle Hendricks, Chicago	31
JT Brubaker, Pittsburgh	28
Yu Darvish, San Diego	28
Drew Smyly, Atlanta	27

WALKS ALLOWED

Luis Castillo, Cincinnati	75
Zach Davies, Chicago	75
Blake Snell, San Diego	69
Adrian Houser, Milwaukee	64
Tyler Mahle, Cincinnati	64
German Marquez, Colorado	64

LOWEST WALKS PER NINE

Max Scherzer, Los Angeles	1.8
Corbin Burnes, Milwaukee	1.8
Julio Urias, Los Angeles	1.8

Zack Wheeler

Zack Wheeler, Philadelphia	1.9
Aaron Nola, Philadelphia	1.9

HIT BATTERS

Austin Adams, San Diego	24
Joe Musgrove, San Diego	18
Charlie Morton, Atlanta	17
Alex Wood, San Francisco	16
Kyle Hendricks, Chicago	13

STRIKEOUTS

Zack Wheeler, Philadelphia	247
Max Scherzer, Los Angeles	236
Corbin Burnes, Milwaukee	234
Kevin Gausman, San Francisco	227
Aaron Nola, Philadelphia	223

STRIKEOUTS PER NINE

Corbin Burnes, Milwaukee	12.6
Max Scherzer, Los Angeles	11.8
Aaron Nola, Philadelphia	11.1
Yu Darvish, San Diego	10.8
Kevin Gausman, San Francisco	10.6

STRIKEOUTS PER NINE
(Relievers)

Craig Kimbrel, Chicago	15.7
Josh Hader, Milwaukee	15.7
Lucas Sims, Cincinnati	14.6
Devin Williams, Milwaukee	14.5
Tyler Chatwood, San Francisco	13.5

DOUBLE PLAYS

Luis Castillo, Cincinnati	20
Patrick Corbin, Washington	19
Antonio Senzatela, Colorado	19
Adrian Houser, Milwaukee	18
Alec Mills, Chicago	18
Logan Webb, San Francisco	18

PICKOFFS

Ryan Weathers, San Diego	9
Max Fried, Atlanta	6
Wade Miley, Cincinnati	6
Drew Smyly, Atlanta	5
3 others	4

WILD PITCHES

German Marquez, Colorado	15
Alex Reyes, St. Louis	10
Jose Alvarado, Philadelphia	9
Genesis Cabrera, St. Louis	9
6 others	9

WALKS PLUS HITS PER INNING

Max Scherzer, Los Angeles	0.86
Corbin Burnes, Milwaukee	0.94
Brandon Woodruff, Milwaukee	0.96
Walker Buehler, Los Angeles	0.97
Zack Wheeler, Philadelphia	1.01

OPPONENT AVERAGE

Max Scherzer, Los Angeles	.185
Walker Buehler, Los Angeles	.199
Brandon Woodruff, Milwaukee	.200
Corbin Burnes, Milwaukee	.201
Charlie Morton, Atlanta	.203

WORST ERA

Patrick Corbin, Washington	5.82
Kyle Hendricks, Chicago	5.28
Aaron Nola, Philadelphia	4.63
German Marquez, Colorado	4.40
Yu Darvish, San Diego	4.22

FIELDING

PITCHER

PCT	7 players	1.000
PO	Sandy Alcantara, Miami	24
A	Max Fried, Atlanta	37
DP	Luis Castillo, Cincinnati	20
E	3 players	4

CATCHER

PCT	J.T. Realmuto, Philadelphia	.999
PO	Will Smith, Los Angeles	1101
A	Willson Contreras, Chicago	57
DP	Yadier Molina, St. Louis	10
E	Willson Contreras, Chicago	7
CS	Will Smith, Los Angeles	24
PB	Jorge Alfaro, Miami	13

FIRST BASE

PCT	Paul Goldschmidt, St. Louis	.998
PO	Freddie Freeman, Atlanta	1252
A	Paul Goldschmidt, St. Louis	106
DP	Paul Goldschmidt, St. Louis	111
E	C.J. Cron, Colorado	10

SECOND BASE

PCT	Kolten Wong, Milwaukee	.995
PO	Jonathan India, Cincinnati	269
A	Ozzie Albies, Atlanta	389
DP	Jean Segura, Philadelphia	85
E	Jonathan India, Cincinnati	15

THIRD BASE

PCT	Ryan McMahon, Colorado	.979
PO	Nolan Arenado, St. Louis	125
A	Austin Riley, Atlanta	300
DP	Nolan Arenado, St. Louis	38
E	Alec Bohm, Philadelphia	15

SHORTSTOP

PCT	Kevin Newman, Pittsburgh	.993
PO	Miguel Rojas, Miami	192
A	Dansby Swanson, Atlanta	376
DP	Trevor Story, Colorado	91
E	Fernando Tatis Jr., San Diego	21

OUTFIELD

PCT	4 players	1.000
PO	Bryan Reynolds, Pittsburgh	354
A	Charlie Blackmon, Colorado	14
DP	3 players	3
E	Tyler O'Neill, St. Louis	9

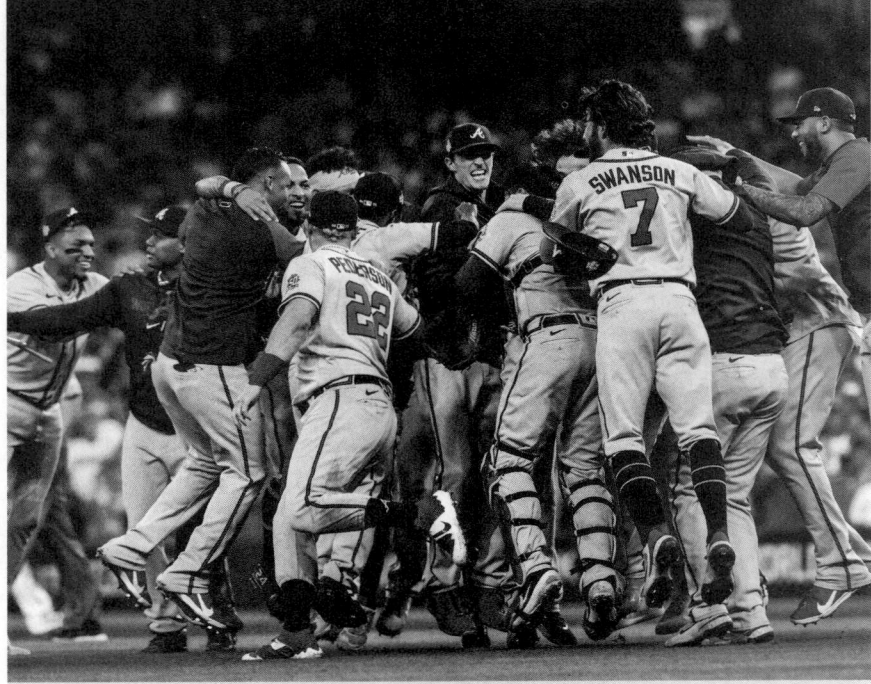

The Braves vanquished the Astros in six games for their first World Series title since 1995.

Atlanta's Improbable Run Ends With World Series Title

BY SCOTT MILLER

From April through August, check that, let's make it April through September, few people outside of the Atlanta Braves' clubhouse gave them a chance to win their first World Series since 1995.

Start with what appeared to be debilitating losses to their roster. Outfielder Ronald Acuña Jr., one of the best players on the planet, went down in a heap just before the All-Star Break while chasing a fly ball on the warning track. Acuña, 23, suffered a complete tear of the anterior cruciate ligament in his right knee, had surgery and was finished for the season.

Earlier, the Braves lost starting pitcher Mike Soroka for the season when he tore his Achilles tendon for the second time in less than a year. He was still in a walking boot at the time and, until the re-tear, the team hoped he would join

their rotation later in the summer. Add to that slugger Marcell Ozuna's arrest on domestic violence charges—he didn't play after June 1—and Atlanta, on the surface, appeared to be doomed to a lost season.

Thing is, Alex Anthopoulos, the club's president of baseball operations and general manager, and his staff didn't view it that way. Anthopoulos went on a trading spree in July during which he acquired four outfielders: Joc Pederson from the Chicago Cubs, Adam Duvall from Miami, Jorge Soler from Kansas City and Eddie Rosario from Cleveland. It was an impressive refusal to wave the white flag in light of all the bad breaks experienced by the Braves. They had staggered into the All-Star Break under .500, at 44-45. They finished July even worse, at 52-54.

It wasn't until Aug. 8 that manager Brian

The Braves clinched their fourth straight National League East title on the last day of September.

Snitker's team finally climbed over .500, to stay, at 57-56. The rebuilt outfield was beginning to jell and produce. The clubhouse was buoyed by the enormous assists from the front office.

And perhaps most importantly, nobody else in what had been predicted in the preseason to be a very strong National League East had been able to find their footing. The Mets were imploding. Philadelphia was inconsistent all season. Washington, unlike Atlanta, had waved the white flag at the trade deadline, opting to trade Max Scherzer, Trea Turner, Kyle Schwarber and others to start a rebuild. Miami was awful. In the end, the Braves took the division by 6.5 games.

The Braves clinched their fourth consecutive division title on the final day of September with a win over the Phillies. Even before knowing what October and November would bring, the link to the great Greg Maddux-Tom Glavine-John Smoltz-Chipper Jones-Bobby Cox teams was established.

"Four in a row is hard," first baseman Freddie Freeman said. "I can't imagine those 1990s teams and how they did all that."

A month or so later, this Braves team would be forever linked with Atlanta's one other World Series-winning team.

The Road To The World Series

Following the pandemic-shortened 60-game season of 2020, it was the postseason that shrank in 2021. After players and owners agreed to expand the playoffs for one year to a 16-team format in 2020, MLB returned to the familiar 10-team format in 2021. And right away there were questions regarding the format because of the sensational NL West race staged by the San Francisco Giants and Los Angeles Dodgers.

The Giants outpaced the Dodgers to end Los Angeles' streak of eight consecutive NL West championships. San Francisco finished with the best record in the majors at 107-55 and Los Angeles finished with the second best overall record at 106-56. That put the Dodgers into the precarious position of having to win the NL Wild Card Game against St. Louis, which they did, but not without stressing. Chris Taylor's bottom-of-the-ninth homer finally won it.

Immediately, critics decried the fact that the Dodgers and Giants, with those eye-popping records, were meeting in an NL Division Series instead of for the pennant in the NL Championship Series. Certainly, there seemed to be merit in seeding teams by record rather than by divisional brackets, but the playoff format—including potentially expanding beyond 10 teams—was an argument to be taken up as players and owners negotiated a new Collective Bargaining Agreement before the 2022 season.

In the meantime, the Giants and Dodgers did not disappoint, engaging in a memorable five-game series with the Dodgers finally winning in San Francisco in the last inning of Game 5, a slim 2-1 margin that was poetic in that not much separated these two teams all year, so going to the ninth inning of the 24th game between the two was perfect. Scherzer dramatically emerged to pitch the bottom of the ninth and collect the save as normal closer Kenley Jansen earned the win. But there would be repercussions.

The Dodgers faced a Braves team that shut down Milwaukee in four games in the other Division Series. The Brewers won the opener, 2-1, but Atlanta raced back to win three in a row in a series that suited historical buffs—the Braves moved to Atlanta from Milwaukee in 1966.

And though the Dodgers were favored given their powerhouse roster of Scherzer, Walker Buehler, Mookie Betts, Justin Turner, Trea Turner

and more, and given that Atlanta's 88 regular season wins were the fewest of any of the 10 teams in the postseason, the Braves stunned the Dodgers with two bottom-of-the-ninth wins in the series' first two games in Atlanta and never looked back.

Austin Riley's one-out base hit against Blake Treinen in the bottom of the ninth walked it off in Game 1, and Rosario's two-out base hit against Jansen scored Dansby Swanson to end Game 2. Though Los Angeles was able to push the series back to Atlanta by winning two of three games in Dodger Stadium, the Braves finished them off in six games after Los Angeles had to scratch Scherzer (dead arm) and start Buehler in Game 6.

In the American League, Houston's path to the World Series was not dissimilar to Atlanta's. The Astros polished off the Chicago White Sox in a tidy four games in a Division Series featuring two older (and old-school) managers in a modern game focused on youth. Dusty Baker, 72, and first-year White Sox skipper Tony La Russa, 77, had faced each other plenty over the years (particularly when Baker guided Cincinnati and La Russa St. Louis in the NL Central).

Next, Houston beat Boston in six games in the ALCS. Though the Red Sox had a relatively easy time with the Yankees in a 6-2 AL Wild Card Game waltz, took down AL East champ Tampa Bay in four games in a Division Series and then appeared World Series bound with an emphatic 12-3 Game 3 blowout to take a two-games-to-one

LAST 25 AMERICAN LEAGUE CHAMPIONS

American League postseason results since 1997, where (*) denotes wild card playoff entrant.

YEAR	CHAMPIONSHIP SERIES	ALCS MVP	DIVISION SERIES	DIVISION SERIES
2021	Houston 4, Boston 2	Yordan Alvarez, OF, Houston	Boston* 3, Tampa Bay 1	Houston 3, Chicago 1
2020	Tampa Bay 4, Houston 3	Randy Arozarena, OF, Tampa Bay	Tampa Bay 3, New York 2	Houston 3, Oakland 1
2019	Houston 4, New York 2	Jose Altuve, 2B, Houston	Houston 3, Tampa Bay* 2	New York 3, Minnesota 0
2018	Boston 4, Houston 1	Jackie Bradley Jr., OF, Boston	Boston 3, New York* 1	Houston 3, Cleveland 0
2017	Houston 4, New York 3	Justin Verlander, RHP, Houston	New York* 3, Cleveland 2	Houston 3, Boston 1
2016	Cleveland 4, Toronto 1	Andrew Miller, LHP, Cleveland	Toronto* 3, Texas 0	Cleveland 3, Boston 0
2015	Kansas City 4, Toronto 2	Alcides Escobar, SS, Kansas City	Kansas City 3, Houston* 2	Baltimore 3, Texas 2
2014	Kansas City 4, Baltimore 0	Lorenzo Cain, OF, Kansas City	Kansas City 3, Los Angeles 0	Baltimore 3, Detroit 0
2013	Boston 4, Detroit 2	Koji Uehara, RHP, Boston	Boston 3, Tampa Bay* 1	Detroit 3, Oakland 2
2012	Detroit 4, New York 0	Delmon Young, OF, Detroit	New York 3, Baltimore* 2	Detroit 3, Oakland 2
2011	Texas 4, Detroit 2	Nelson Cruz, OF, Texas	Detroit 3, New York 2	Texas 3, Tampa Bay* 1
2010	Texas 4, New York 2	Josh Hamilton, OF, Texas	Texas 3, Tampa Bay 2	New York* 3, Minnesota 0
2009	New York 4, Los Angeles 2	C.C. Sabathia, LHP, New York	New York 3, Minnesota 0	Los Angeles 3, Boston* 0
2008	Tampa Bay 4, Boston 3	Matt Garza, RHP, Tampa Bay	Boston* 3, Los Angeles 1	Tampa Bay 3, Chicago 1
2007	Boston 4, Cleveland 3	Josh Beckett, RHP, Boston	Boston 3, Los Angeles 0	Cleveland 3, New York* 1
2006	Detroit 4, Oakland 0	Placido Polanco, 2B, Detroit	Detroit* 3, New York 1	Oakland 3, Minnesota 0
2005	Chicago 4, Los Angeles 1	Paul Konerko, 1B, Chicago	Chicago 3, Boston* 0	Los Angeles 3, New York 2
2004	Boston 4, New York 3	David Ortiz, DH, Boston	Boston* 3, Anaheim 0	New York 3, Minnesota 1
2003	New York 4, Boston 3	Mariano Rivera, RHP, New York	New York 3, Minnesota 1	Boston* 3, Oakland 2
2002	Anaheim 4, Minnesota 1	Adam Kennedy, 2B, Anaheim	Anaheim* 3, New York 1	Minnesota 3, Oakland 2
2001	New York 4, Seattle 1	Andy Pettitte, LHP, New York	Seattle 3, Cleveland 2	New York 3, Oakland* 2
2000	New York 4, Seattle 2	David Justice, OF, New York	New York 3, Oakland 2	Seattle* 3, Chicago 0
1999	New York 4, Boston 1	Orlando Hernandez, RHP, New York	Boston* 3, Cleveland 2	New York 3, Texas 0
1998	New York 4, Cleveland 2	David Wells, LHP, New York	Cleveland 3, Boston* 1	New York 3, Texas 0
1997	Cleveland 4, Baltimore 2	Marquis Grissom, OF, Cleveland	Cleveland 3, New York* 2	Baltimore 3, Seattle 1

ALCS lead over Houston, Boston would score just three more runs over the next three games as the Astros reeled off three wins in a row to reach their third World Series in five years.

Brave Finish

What the 2021 World Series lacked in artistic merit it produced in pure quirkiness. And that started right away when Soler blasted the third pitch of Game 1 from Framber Valdez over the left-field fence. Jaw-dropping as it seemed to believe, it was the first top-of-the-first, leadoff homer in 117 World Series.

The Fall Classic went on to emphasize what some view as a crisis in modern pitching: Relievers worked 62% of all innings in this World Series (64.2 of 105). It wasn't until Atlanta's Max Fried threw six shutout innings in the Game 6 clincher that a starting pitcher even went as far as five innings in one of the games.

The Braves won the World Series with two "bullpen games" in Games 4 and 5, starting Tucker Davidson in only his sixth major league start in Game 5 and Dylan Lee in his first major league start in Game 4. It was a case of Snitker and pitching coach Rick Kranitz getting as creative as they needed. Atlanta's injurious season continued right into Game 1, when starter Charlie Morton's leg was fractured by a comebacker that sidelined him for the series.

That, combined with the heroics of those acquired by Anthopoulos, stretched the narrative of Atlanta's season right through to the end. Rosario was named NLCS MVP and Soler was chosen World Series MVP. It was the first time players acquired at midseason won those awards.

"This year, it was improbable," Freeman said during the celebration. "We hit every pothole, every bump you could possibly hit this year, and somehow the car still made it to the other side. It's just an incredible group."

On the other side, having lost the World Series in 2019 (to Washington) and again in 2021, the Astros moved ahead still having to answer questions regarding the legitimacy of their 2017 title having been tainted by the cheating scandal. Did the Astros feel like they had to win again to be legitimate? One huge drawback in this series was the absence of starter Lance McCullers Jr., who was sidelined with a sore arm after the ALDS.

"We obviously wanted to win," shortstop Carlos Correa said. "It didn't play out. So there's that. We're not focused on the outside noise. We're focused on the things that we can control, and that's putting in the work, showing up, showing the world how good we really are."

With Correa and one-time ace Justin Verlander (who missed all of 2021 following Tommy John surgery) headed toward free agency, their chances were running out. The Astros meekly hit .224 in the World Series with just two home runs, both from Jose Altuve. ∎

LAST 25 NATIONAL LEAGUE CHAMPIONS

National League postseason results since 1997, where (*) denotes wild card playoff entrant.

YEAR	CHAMPIONSHIP SERIES	NLCS MVP	DIVISION SERIES	DIVISION SERIES
2021	Atlanta 4, Los Angeles 2	Eddie Rosario, OF, Atlanta	Los Angeles* 3, San Francisco 2	Atlanta 3, Milwaukee 1
2020	Los Angeles 4, Atlanta 3	Corey Seager, SS, Los Angeles	Los Angeles 3, San Diego 0	Atlanta 3, Miami 0
2019	Washington 4, St. Louis 0	Howie Kendrick, 2B, Washington	Washington* 3, Los Angeles 2	St. Louis 3, Atlanta 2
2018	Los Angeles 4, Milwaukee 3	Cody Bellinger, 1B/OF, Los Angeles	Los Angeles 3, Atlanta 1	Milwaukee 3, Colorado 0*
2017	Los Angeles 4, Chicago 1	Justin Turner, 3B/Chris Taylor, CF, L.A.	Los Angeles 3, Arizona* 0	Chicago 3, Washington 2
2016	Chicago 4, Los Angeles 2	Javier Baez, 2B/Jon Lester, LHP, Chicago	Chicago 3, San Francisco* 1	Los Angeles 3, Washington 2
2015	New York 4, Chicago 0	Daniel Murphy, 2B, New York	New York 3, Los Angeles 2	Chicago* 3, St. Louis 1
2014	San Francisco 4, St. Louis 1	Madison Bumgarner, LHP, San Francisco	San Francisco 3, Washington 1	St. Louis 3, Los Angeles 1
2013	St. Louis 4, Los Angeles 2	Michael Wacha, RHP, St. Louis	St. Louis 3, Pittsburgh* 2	Los Angeles 3, Atlanta 1
2012	San Francisco 4, St. Louis 3	Marco Scutaro, 2B, San Francisco	St. Louis* 3, Washington 2	San Francisco 3, Cincinnati 2
2011	St. Louis 4, Milwaukee 2	David Freese, 3B, St. Louis	St. Louis* 3, Philadelphia 2	Milwaukee 3, Arizona 2
2010	San Francisco 4, Philadelphia 2	Cody Ross, OF, San Francisco	Philadelphia 3, Cincinnati 0	San Francisco 3, Atlanta* 1
2009	Philadelphia 4, Los Angeles 1	Ryan Howard, 1B, Philadelphia	Los Angeles 3, St. Louis 0	Philadelphia 3, Colorado* 1
2008	Philadelphia 4, Los Angeles 1	Cole Hamels, LHP, Philadelphia	Los Angeles 3, Chicago 0	Philadelphia 3, Milwaukee* 1
2007	Colorado 4, Arizona 0	Matt Holliday, OF, Colorado	Arizona 3, Chicago 0	Colorado* 3, Philadelphia 0
2006	St. Louis 4, New York 3	Jeff Suppan, RHP, St. Louis	New York 3, Los Angeles* 0	St. Louis 3, San Diego 1
2005	Houston 4, St. Louis 2	Roy Oswalt, RHP, Houston	St. Louis 3, San Diego 0	Houston* 3, Atlanta 1
2004	St. Louis 4, Houston 3	Albert Pujols, 1B, St. Louis	St. Louis 3, Los Angeles 1	Houston* 3, Atlanta 2
2003	Florida 4, Chicago 3	Ivan Rodriguez, C, Florida	Florida* 3, San Francisco 1	Chicago 3, Atlanta 2
2002	San Francisco 4, St. Louis 1	Benito Santiago, C, San Francisco	San Francisco* 3, Atlanta 2	St. Louis 3, Arizona 0
2001	Arizona 4, Atlanta 1	Craig Counsell, SS, Arizona	Atlanta 3, Houston 0	Arizona 3, St. Louis* 2
2000	New York 4, St. Louis 1	Mike Hampton, LHP, New York	St. Louis 3, Atlanta 0	New York* 3, San Francisco 1
1999	Atlanta 4, New York 2	Eddie Perez, C, Atlanta	Atlanta 3, Houston 1	New York* 3, Arizona 1
1998	San Diego 4, Atlanta 2	Sterling Hitchcock, LHP, San Diego	Atlanta 3, Chicago* 0	San Diego 3, Houston 1
1997	Florida 4, Atlanta 2	Livan Hernandez, RHP, Florida	Florida* 3, San Francisco 0	Atlanta 3, Houston 0

Year	Winner	Loser	Result
1903	Boston (AL)	Pittsburgh (NL)	5-3
1905	New York (NL)	Philadelphia (AL)	4-1
1906	Chicago (AL)	Chicago (NL)	4-2
1907	Chicago (NL)	Detroit (AL)	4-0
1908	Chicago (NL)	Detroit (AL)	4-1
1909	Pittsburgh (NL)	Detroit (AL)	4-3
1910	Philadelphia (AL)	Chicago (NL)	4-1
1911	Philadelphia (AL)	New York (NL)	4-2
1912	Boston (AL)	New York (NL)	4-3-1
1913	Philadelphia (AL)	New York (NL)	4-1
1914	Boston (NL)	Philadelphia (AL)	4-0
1915	Boston (AL)	Philadelphia (NL)	4-1
1916	Boston (AL)	Brooklyn (NL)	4-1
1917	Chicago (AL)	New York (NL)	4-2
1918	Boston (AL)	Chicago (NL)	4-2
1919	Cincinnati (NL)	Chicago (AL)	5-3
1920	Cleveland (AL)	Brooklyn (NL)	5-2
1921	New York (NL)	New York (AL)	5-3
1922	New York (NL)	New York (AL)	4-0
1923	New York (AL)	New York (NL)	4-2
1924	Washington (AL)	New York (NL)	4-3
1925	Pittsburgh (NL)	Washington (AL)	4-3
1926	St. Louis (NL)	New York (AL)	4-3
1927	New York (AL)	Pittsburgh (NL)	4-0
1928	New York (AL)	St. Louis (NL)	4-0
1929	Philadelphia (AL)	Chicago (NL)	4-1
1930	Philadelphia (AL)	St. Louis (NL)	4-2
1931	St. Louis (NL)	Philadelphia (AL)	4-3
1932	New York (AL)	Chicago (NL)	4-0
1933	New York (NL)	Washington (AL)	4-1
1934	St. Louis (NL)	Detroit (AL)	4-3
1935	Detroit (AL)	Chicago (NL)	4-2
1936	New York (AL)	New York (NL)	4-2
1937	New York (AL)	New York (NL)	4-1
1938	New York (AL)	Chicago (NL)	4-0
1939	New York (AL)	Cincinnati (NL)	4-0
1940	Cincinnati (NL)	Detroit (AL)	4-3
1941	New York (AL)	Brooklyn (NL)	4-1
1942	St. Louis (NL)	New York (AL)	4-1
1943	New York (AL)	St. Louis (NL)	4-1
1944	St. Louis (NL)	St. Louis (AL)	4-2
1945	Detroit (AL)	Chicago (NL)	4-3
1946	St. Louis (NL)	Boston (AL)	4-3
1947	New York (AL)	Brooklyn (NL)	4-3
1948	Cleveland (AL)	Boston (NL)	4-2
1949	New York (AL)	Brooklyn (NL)	4-1
1950	New York (AL)	Philadelphia (NL)	4-0
1951	New York (AL)	New York (NL)	4-2
1952	New York (AL)	Brooklyn (NL)	4-3
1953	New York (AL)	Brooklyn (NL)	4-2
1954	New York (NL)	Cleveland (AL)	4-0
1955	Brooklyn (NL)	New York (AL)	4-3
1956	New York (AL)	Brooklyn (NL)	4-3
1957	Milwaukee (NL)	New York (AL)	4-3
1958	New York (AL)	Milwaukee (NL)	4-3
1959	Los Angeles (NL)	Chicago (AL)	4-2
1960	Pittsburgh (NL)	New York (AL)	4-3
1961	New York (AL)	Cincinnati (NL)	4-1
1962	New York (AL)	San Francisco (NL)	4-3
1963	Los Angeles (NL)	New York (AL)	4-0
1964	St. Louis (NL)	New York (AL)	4-3
1965	Los Angeles (NL)	Minnesota (AL)	4-3
1966	Baltimore (AL)	Los Angeles (NL)	4-0
1967	St. Louis (NL)	Boston (AL)	4-3
1968	Detroit (AL)	St. Louis (NL)	4-3
1969	New York (NL)	Baltimore (AL)	4-1
1970	Baltimore (AL)	Cincinnati (NL)	4-1
1971	Pittsburgh (NL)	Baltimore (AL)	4-3
1972	Oakland (AL)	Cincinnati (NL)	4-3

Jorge Soler

Year	Winner	Loser	Result
1973	Oakland (AL)	New York (NL)	4-3
1974	Oakland (AL)	Los Angeles (NL)	4-1
1975	Cincinnati (NL)	Boston (AL)	4-3
1976	Cincinnati (NL)	New York (AL)	4-0
1977	New York (AL)	Los Angeles (NL)	4-2
1978	New York (AL)	Los Angeles (NL)	4-2
1979	Pittsburgh (NL)	Baltimore (AL)	4-3
1980	Philadelphia (NL)	Kansas City (AL)	4-2
1981	Los Angeles (NL)	New York (AL)	4-2
1982	St. Louis (NL)	Milwaukee (AL)	4-3
1983	Baltimore (AL)	Philadelphia (NL)	4-1
1984	Detroit (AL)	San Diego (NL)	4-1
1985	Kansas City (AL)	St. Louis (NL)	4-3
1986	New York (NL)	Boston (AL)	4-3
1987	Minnesota (AL)	St. Louis (NL)	4-3
1988	Los Angeles (NL)	Oakland (AL)	4-1
1989	Oakland (AL)	San Francisco (NL)	4-0
1990	Cincinnati (NL)	Oakland (AL)	4-0
1991	Minnesota (AL)	Atlanta (NL)	4-3
1992	Toronto (AL)	Atlanta (NL)	4-2
1993	Toronto (AL)	Philadelphia (NL)	4-2
1995	Atlanta (NL)	Cleveland (AL)	4-2
1996	New York (AL)	Atlanta (NL)	4-2
1997	Florida (NL)	Cleveland (AL)	4-3
1998	New York (AL)	San Diego (NL)	4-0
1999	New York (AL)	Atlanta (NL)	4-0
2000	New York (AL)	New York (NL)	4-1
2001	Arizona (NL)	New York (AL)	4-3
2002	Anaheim (AL)	San Francisco (NL)	4-3
2003	Florida (NL)	New York (AL)	4-2
2004	Boston (AL)	St. Louis (NL)	4-0
2005	Chicago (AL)	Houston (NL)	4-0
2006	St. Louis (NL)	Detroit (AL)	4-1
2007	Boston (AL)	Colorado (NL)	4-0
2008	Philadelphia (NL)	Tampa Bay (AL)	4-1
2009	New York (AL)	Philadelphia (NL)	4-2
2010	San Francisco (NL)	Texas (AL)	4-1
2011	St. Louis (NL)	Texas (AL)	4-3
2012	San Francisco (NL)	Detroit (AL)	4-0
2013	Boston (AL)	St. Louis (NL)	4-2
2014	San Francisco (NL)	Kansas City (AL)	4-3
2015	Kansas City (AL)	New York (NL)	4-1
2016	Chicago (NL)	Cleveland (AL)	4-3
2017	Houston (AL)	Los Angeles (NL)	4-3
2018	Boston (AL)	Los Angeles (NL)	4-1
2019	Washington (NL)	Houston (AL)	4-3
2020	Los Angeles (NL)	Tampa Bay (AL)	4-2
2021	Atlanta (NL)	Houston (AL)	4-2

WORLD SERIES BOX SCORES

GAME ONE Oct. 26, 2021

ATLANTA BRAVES 6, HOUSTON ASTROS 2

	1	2	3	4	5	6	7	8	9	R	H	E
ATLANTA	2	1	2	0	0	0	0	1	0	6	12	1
HOUSTON	0	0	0	1	0	0	0	1	0	2	8	1

ATLANTA	AB	R	H	RBI	BB	SO	LOB	AVG
Soler, DH	5	1	2	2	0	2	2	.400
Freeman, 1B	3	0	1	1	1	1	0	.333
Albies, 2B	5	1	2	0	0	0	3	.400
Riley, A, 3B	5	0	1	1	0	3	4	.200
Rosario, E, LF	5	1	2	0	0	1	1	.400
Duvall, CF-RF	4	1	1	2	1	2	1	.250
d'Arnaud, C	4	1	1	0	0	2	2	.250
Pederson, RF	4	0	1	0	0	0	0	.250
Heredia, CF	0	0	0	0	0	0	0	.000
Swanson, D, SS	3	1	1	0	1	1	2	.333
Morton, P	0	0	0	0	0	0	0	.000
Minter, P	0	0	0	0	0	0	0	.000
Jackson, L, P	0	0	0	0	0	0	0	.000
Matzek, P	0	0	0	0	0	0	0	.000
Smith, W, P	0	0	0	0	0	0	0	.000
TOTALS	**38**	**6**	**12**	**6**	**3**	**12**	**15**	**.316**

2B: Riley, A (1, Valdez, F); Rosario, E (1, Maton, P). **HR:** Soler (1, 1st inning off Valdez, F, 0 on, 0 out); Duvall (1, 3rd inning off Valdez, F, 1 on, 0 out). **TB:** Albies 2; d'Arnaud; Duvall 4; Freeman; Pederson; Riley, A 2; Rosario, E 3; Soler 5; Swanson, D. **RBI:** Duvall 2 (2); Freeman (1); Riley, A (1); Soler 2 (2).

HOUSTON	AB	R	H	RBI	BB	SO	LOB	AVG
Altuve, 2B	5	0	0	0	0	3	3	.000
Brantley, LF	5	0	3	0	0	0	1	.600
Bregman, 3B	4	0	0	0	0	2	3	.000
Alvarez, DH	3	1	1	0	1	1	1	.333
Correa, SS	3	0	0	1	1	1	0	.000
Tucker, RF	4	1	2	0	0	1	3	.500
Gurriel, 1B	4	0	2	0	0	0	1	.500
McCormick, CF	3	0	0	1	0	2	2	.000
b-Díaz, A, PH	0	0	0	0	1	0	0	.000
Maldonado, C	2	0	0	0	0	1	2	.000
a-Castro, J, PH-C	2	0	0	0	0	0	1	.000
Valdez, F, P	0	0	0	0	0	0	0	.000
García, Y, P	0	0	0	0	0	0	0	.000
Odorizzi, P	0	0	0	0	0	0	0	.000
Maton, P, P	0	0	0	0	0	0	0	.000
Stanek, P	0	0	0	0	0	0	0	.000
Raley, B, P	0	0	0	0	0	0	0	.000
TOTALS	**35**	**2**	**8**	**2**	**3**	**11**	**17**	**.229**

a-Grounded out for Maldonado in the 7th. b-Walked for McCormick in the 9th.

2B: Brantley (1, Minter); Tucker (1, Minter). **3B:** Alvarez (1, Matzek). **TB:** Alvarez 3; Brantley 4; Gurriel 2; Tucker 3. **RBI:** Correa (1); McCormick (1).

ATLANTA	IP	H	R	ER	BB	SO	HR	ERA
Morton	2.1	1	0	0	2	3	0	0.00
Minter (W, 1-0)	2.2	3	1	1	0	3	0	3.38
Jackson, L	1.2	1	0	0	0	3	0	0.00
Matzek	1.1	3	1	1	0	2	0	6.75
Smith, W	1.0	0	0	0	1	0	0	0.00
TOTALS	**9.0**	**8**	**2**	**2**	**3**	**11**	**0**	**2.00**

HOUSTON	IP	H	R	ER	BB	SO	HR	ERA
Valdez, F (L, 0-1)	2.0	8	5	5	1	2	2	22.50
García, Y	1.0	0	0	0	0	2	0	0.00
Odorizzi	2.1	1	0	0	0	5	0	0.00
Maton, P	1.0	2	0	0	1	2	0	0.00
Stanek	1.0	1	1	1	1	0	0	9.00
Raley, B	1.2	0	0	0	0	1	0	0.00
TOTALS	**9.0**	**12**	**6**	**6**	**3**	**12**	**2**	**6.00**

Valdez, F pitched to 2 batters in the 3rd. **WP:** Morton. **Pitches-strikes:** Morton 44-27; Minter 43-30; Jackson, L 20-14; Matzek 20-15; Smith, W 18-11; Valdez, F 52-30; García, Y 19-12; Odorizzi 42-26; Maton, P 22-11; Stanek 20-12; Raley, B 9-8.

GAME TWO Oct. 27, 2021

HOUSTON ASTROS 7, ATLANTA BRAVES 2

	1	2	3	4	5	6	7	8	9	R	H	E
ATLANTA	0	1	0	0	1	0	0	0	0	2	7	2
HOUSTON	1	4	0	0	0	1	1	0	X	7	9	0

ATLANTA	AB	R	H	RBI	BB	SO	LOB	AVG
Rosario, E, LF	4	0	0	0	0	1	3	.222
Freeman, 1B	4	0	1	1	0	1	1	.286
Albies, 2B	3	0	1	0	1	0	1	.375
Riley, A, 3B	4	0	1	0	0	2	1	.222
Soler, DH	4	0	1	0	0	2	3	.333
Pederson, RF	4	0	0	0	0	3	2	.125
Duvall, CF	4	0	0	0	0	0	1	.125
d'Arnaud, C	4	2	2	1	0	1	0	.375
Swanson, D, SS	3	0	1	0	1	2	1	.333
Fried, P	0	0	0	0	0	0	0	.000
Lee, P	0	0	0	0	0	0	0	.000
Chavez, J, P	0	0	0	0	0	0	0	.000
Smyly, P	0	0	0	0	0	0	0	.000
Wright, P	0	0	0	0	0	0	0	.000
TOTALS	**34**	**2**	**7**	**2**	**2**	**12**	**13**	**.264**

2B: Soler (1, Javier). **HR:** d'Arnaud (1, 2nd inning off Urquidy, 0 on, 2 out). **TB:** Albies; d'Arnaud 5; Freeman; Riley, A; Soler 2; Swanson, D. **RBI:** d'Arnaud (1); Freeman (2).

HOUSTON	AB	R	H	RBI	BB	SO	LOB	AVG
Altuve, 2B	5	2	2	1	0	1	1	.200
Brantley, LF	4	0	2	1	0	1	1	.556
Bregman, 3B	3	0	0	1	0	1	2	.000
Alvarez, DH	2	1	0	0	1	1	0	.200
Correa, SS	4	0	1	0	0	1	2	.143
Tucker, RF	3	1	1	0	1	0	2	.429
Gurriel, 1B	4	1	1	1	0	1	4	.375
Siri, CF	4	1	1	1	0	3	2	.250
Maldonado, C	4	1	1	1	0	2	2	.167
Urquidy, P	0	0	0	0	0	0	0	.000
Javier, P	0	0	0	0	0	0	0	.000
Maton, P, P	0	0	0	0	0	0	0	.000
Pressly, P	0	0	0	0	0	0	0	.000
Graveman, P	0	0	0	0	0	0	0	.000
TOTALS	**33**	**7**	**9**	**6**	**2**	**11**	**16**	**.250**

2B: Altuve (1, Fried); Brantley (2, Smyly). **HR:** Altuve (1, 7th inning off Smyly, 0 on, 0 out). **TB:** Altuve 6; Brantley 3; Correa; Gurriel; Maldonado; Siri; Tucker. **RBI:** Altuve (1); Brantley (1); Bregman (1); Gurriel (1); Maldonado (1); Siri (1).

ATLANTA	IP	H	R	ER	BB	SO	HR	ERA
Fried (L, 0-1)	5.0	7	6	6	1	6	0	10.80
Lee	0.2	0	0	0	0	1	0	0.00
Chavez, J	0.1	0	0	0	0	0	0	0.00
Smyly	1.0	2	1	1	1	1	1	9.00
Wright	1.0	0	0	0	0	3	0	0.00
TOTALS	**8.0**	**9**	**7**	**7**	**2**	**11**	**1**	**4.76**

HOUSTON	IP	H	R	ER	BB	SO	HR	ERA
Urquidy (W, 1-0)	5.0	6	2	2	0	7	1	3.60
Javier (H, 1)	1.1	1	0	0	1	2	0	0.00
Maton, P	0.2	0	0	0	0	0	0	0.00
Pressly	1.0	0	0	0	1	2	0	0.00
Graveman	1.0	0	0	0	0	1	0	0.00
TOTALS	**9.0**	**7**	**2**	**2**	**2**	**12**	**1**	**4.00**

Fried pitched to 2 batters in the 6th. **WP:** Fried; Smyly; Urquidy. **HBP:** Alvarez (by Smyly). **Pitches-strikes:** Fried 86-59; Lee 13-10; Chavez, J 3-3; Smyly 22-13; Wright 12-10; Urquidy 74-55; Javier 27-16; Maton, P 7-6; Pressly 18-13; Graveman 10-7.

GAME THREE Oct. 29, 2021

ATLANTA BRAVES 2, HOUSTON ASTROS 0

	1	2	3	4	5	6	7	8	9	R	H	E
HOUSTON	0	0	0	0	0	0	0	0	0	0	2	0
ATLANTA	0	0	1	0	0	0	0	1	X	2	6	1

HOUSTON	AB	R	H	RBI	BB	SO	LOB	AVG
Altuve, 2B	3	0	0	0	1	2	1	.154
Brantley, RF	4	0	0	0	0	1	2	.385
Bregman, 3B	2	0	1	0	1	0	0	.111
Alvarez, LF	3	0	0	0	1	1	3	.125
Correa, SS	3	0	0	0	0	0	1	.100
Tucker, CF	4	0	0	0	0	0	3	.273
Gurriel, 1B	3	0	0	0	0	1	0	.273
Maldonado, C	2	0	0	0	0	0	0	.125
b-Díaz, A, PH	1	0	1	0	0	0	0	1.000
1-Siri, PR	0	0	0	0	0	0	0	.250
Graveman, P	0	0	0	0	0	0	0	.000
Garcia, L, P	1	0	0	0	0	0	0	.000
Taylor, B, P	0	0	0	0	0	0	0	.000
a-Gonzalez, M, PH	1	0	0	0	0	1	0	.000
García, Y, P	0	0	0	0	0	0	0	.000
Raley, B, P	0	0	0	0	0	0	0	.000
Stanek, P	0	0	0	0	0	0	0	.000
c-Castro, J, PH-C	1	0	0	0	0	1	1	.000
TOTALS	28	0	2	0	3	7	11	.198

a-Struck out for Taylor, B in the 5th. **b-**Singled for Maldonado in the 8th. **c-**Struck out for Stanek in the 8th. **1-**Ran for Díaz, A in the 8th. **TB:** Bregman; Díaz, A.

ATLANTA	AB	R	H	RBI	BB	SO	LOB	AVG
Rosario, E, LF	3	1	0	1	0	1	0	.250
Freeman, 1B	4	0	1	0	0	1	1	.273
Albies, 2B	3	0	0	0	1	1	2	.273
Riley, A, 3B	4	0	1	1	0	2	1	.231
Soler, RF	2	0	0	0	2	1	0	.273
Heredia, CF	0	0	0	0	0	0	0	.000
Duvall, CF-RF	4	0	1	0	0	1	3	.167
d'Arnaud, C	4	1	2	1	0	1	5	.417
Swanson, D, SS	3	0	0	1	1	0	1	.222
Anderson, P	2	0	0	0	0	2	0	.000
Minter, P	0	0	0	0	0	0	0	.000
a-Adrianza, PH	1	0	0	0	0	0	0	.000
Jackson, L, P	0	0	0	0	0	0	0	.000
Matzek, P	0	0	0	0	0	0	0	.000
Smith, W, P	0	0	0	0	0	0	0	.000
TOTALS	30	2	6	2	5	10	14	.245

a-Grounded out for Minter in the 6th. **2B:** d'Arnaud (1, Garcia, L); Riley, A (2, Garcia, L). **HR:** d'Arnaud (2, 8th inning off Graveman, 0 on, 2 out). **TB:** d'Arnaud 6; Duvall; Freeman; Riley, A 2; Rosario, E. **RBI:** d'Arnaud (2); Riley, A (2).

HOUSTON	IP	H	R	ER	BB	SO	HR	ERA
Garcia, L (L, 0-1)	3.2	3	1	1	4	6	0	2.45
Taylor, B	0.1	1	0	0	0	1	0	0.00
García, Y	1.2	1	0	0	1	0	0	0.00
Raley, B	1.0	0	0	0	0	0	0	0.00
Stanek	0.1	0	0	0	0	1	0	6.75
Graveman	1.0	1	1	1	0	2	1	4.50
TOTALS	8.0	6	2	2	5	10	1	3.46

ATLANTA	IP	H	R	ER	BB	SO	HR	ERA
Anderson (W, 1-0)	5.0	0	0	0	3	4	0	0.00
Minter (H, 1)	1.0	0	0	0	0	2	0	2.45
Jackson, L (H, 1)	1.0	0	0	0	0	0	0	0.00
Matzek (H, 1)	1.0	1	0	0	0	1	0	3.86
Smith, W (S, 1)	1.0	1	0	0	0	0	0	0.00
TOTALS	9.0	2	0	0	3	7	0	3.12

IBB: Swanson, D (by Garcia, L). **HBP:** Correa (by Anderson); Bregman (by Minter). **Pitches-strikes:** Garcia, L 72-41; Taylor, B 8-7; García, Y 28-16; Raley, B 10-6; Stanek 4-3; Graveman 11-8; Anderson 76-39; Minter 17-12; Jackson, L 11-7; Matzek 15-10; Smith, W 14-7.

GAME FOUR Oct. 30, 2021

ATLANTA BRAVES 3, HOUSTON ASTROS 2

	1	2	3	4	5	6	7	8	9	R	H	E
HOUSTON	1	0	0	1	0	0	0	0	0	2	8	0
ATLANTA	0	0	0	0	0	1	2	0	X	3	8	1

HOUSTON	AB	R	H	RBI	BB	SO	LOB	AVG
Altuve, 2B	5	2	2	1	0	1	2	.222
Brantley, RF	4	0	1	0	1	1	2	.353
Bregman, 3B	5	0	0	0	0	2	3	.071
Alvarez, LF	3	0	0	0	2	1	0	.091
Correa, SS	4	0	1	1	0	0	2	.143
Tucker, CF	4	0	2	0	0	1	4	.333
Gurriel, 1B	2	0	0	0	2	0	1	.231
Pressly, P	0	0	0	0	0	0	0	.000
Greinke, P	2	0	1	0	0	3	0	.500
a-Gonzalez, M, PH	1	0	0	0	0	0	2	.000
Stanek, P	0	0	0	0	0	0	0	.000
Raley, B, P	0	0	0	0	0	0	0	.000
Maton, P, P	0	0	0	0	0	0	0	.000
Javier, P	0	0	0	0	0	0	0	.000
Díaz, A, 1B	1	0	0	0	0	0	0	.500
Maldonado, C	4	0	1	0	0	1	0	.167
TOTALS	35	2	8	2	5	7	19	.206

a-Flied out for Greinke in the 5th.
HR: Altuve (2, 4th inning off Wright, 0 on, 1 out). **TB:** Altuve 5; Brantley; Correa; Greinke; Maldonado; Tucker 2. **RBI:** Altuve (2); Correa (2).

ATLANTA	AB	R	H	RBI	BB	SO	LOB	AVG
Rosario, E, LF	4	1	2	0	0	1	0	.313
Freeman, 1B	3	0	1	0	1	1	1	.286
Albies, 2B	3	0	0	0	1	2	3	.214
Riley, A, 3B	4	0	2	1	0	1	2	.294
Pederson, RF	2	0	0	0	1	0	1	.100
1-Heredia, PR-CF	0	0	0	0	0	0	0	.000
d'Arnaud, C	4	0	0	0	0	3	5	.313
Duvall, CF-RF	4	0	1	0	0	1	2	.188
Swanson, D, SS	3	1	1	1	0	1	1	.250
Lee, P	0	0	0	0	0	0	0	.000
Wright, P	1	0	0	0	0	1	0	.000
Martin, P	0	0	0	0	0	0	0	.000
a-Arcia, PH	1	0	0	0	0	0	0	.000
Matzek, P	0	0	0	0	0	0	0	.000
b-Soler, PH	1	1	1	1	0	0	0	.333
Jackson, L, P	0	0	0	0	0	0	0	.000
Smith, W, P	0	0	0	0	0	0	0	.000
TOTALS	30	3	8	3	11	15	15	.250

a-Lined out for Martin in the 6th. **b-**Homered for Matzek in the 7th. **1-**Ran for Pederson in the 8th.
2B: Rosario, E (2, Raley, B). **HR:** Swanson, D (1, 7th inning off Javier, 0 on, 1 out); Soler (2, 7th inning off Javier, 0 on, 1 out). **TB:** Duvall; Freeman; Riley, A 2; Rosario, E 3; Soler 4; Swanson, D 4. **RBI:** Riley, A (3); Soler (3); Swanson, D (1).

HOUSTON	IP	H	R	ER	BB	SO	HR	ERA
Greinke	4.0	4	0	0	0	3	0	0.00
Stanek	1.0	0	0	0	0	1	0	3.86
Raley, B (H, 1)	0.1	1	1	1	1	0	0	3.00
Maton, P (H, 1)	0.2	1	0	0	1	2	0	0.00
Javier (L, 0-1)(BS, 1)	0.1	2	2	2	0	1	2	10.80
Pressly	1.2	0	0	0	1	4	0	0.00
TOTALS	8.0	8	3	3	3	11	2	3.44

ATLANTA	IP	H	R	ER	BB	SO	HR	ERA
Lee	0.1	1	1	1	2	1	0	9.00
Wright	4.2	5	1	1	3	3	1	1.59
Martin	1.0	1	0	0	0	1	0	0.00
Matzek (W, 1-0)	1.0	1	0	0	0	0	0	2.70
Jackson, L (H, 2)	1.0	0	0	0	0	1	0	0.00
Smith, W (S, 2)	1.0	0	0	0	0	1	0	0.00
TOTALS	9.0	8	2	2	5	7	1	2.83

IBB: Gurriel 2 (by Wright, by Wright); Pederson (by Maton, P). **HBP:** Pederson (by Pressly). **Pitches-strikes:** Greinke 58-37; Stanek 15-11; Raley, B 13-7; Maton, P 17-11; Javier 13-9; Pressly 33-20; Lee 15-5; Wright 75-44; Martin 9-7; Matzek 11-8; Jackson, L 17-11; Smith, W 15-10.

GAME FIVE Oct. 31, 2021
HOUSTON ASTROS 9, ATLANTA BRAVES 5

	1	2	3	4	5	6	7	8	9	R	H	E
Houston	0	2	2	0	3	0	1	1	0	9	12	0
Atlanta	4	0	1	0	0	0	0	0	0	5	8	1

HOUSTON	AB	R	H	RBI	BB	SO	LOB	AVG
Altuve, 2B	5	2	1	0	0	1	3	.217
Brantley, RF-LF	3	1	0	0	2	1	2	.300
Correa, SS	5	1	3	2	0	0	1	.263
Alvarez, LF	5	0	0	0	0	2	4	.063
Siri, CF	0	0	0	0	0	0	0	.250
Gurriel, 1B	5	2	3	1	0	1	1	.333
Tucker, CF-RF	3	2	1	0	2	0	4	.333
Bregman, 3B	4	1	1	1	1	0	3	.111
Maldonado, C	3	0	1	3	1	1	0	.200
Valdez, F, P	1	0	0	0	0	1	1	.000
Garcia, Y, P	0	0	0	0	0	0	0	.000
a-Greinke, PH	1	0	1	0	0	0	0	.667
Urquidy, P	0	0	0	0	0	0	0	.000
b-Gonzalez, M, PH	1	0	1	2	0	0	0	.333
Maton, P, P	0	0	0	0	0	0	0	.000
c-McCormick, PH	1	0	0	0	0	1	1	.000
Stanek, P	0	0	0	0	0	0	0	.000
Graveman, P	0	0	0	0	0	0	0	.000
TOTALS	38	9	12	9	6	9	20	.231

a-Singled for Garcia, Y in the 4th. b-Singled for Urquidy in the 5th. c-Struck out for Maton, P in the 7th.
2B: Bregman (1, Davidson, T); Correa (1, Chavez, J); Tucker (2, Smyly). **TB:** Altuve; Bregman 2; Correa 4; Gonzalez, M; Greinke; Gurriel 3; Maldonado; Tucker 2. **RBI:** Bregman (2); Correa 2 (4); Gonzalez, M 2 (2); Gurriel (2); Maldonado 3 (4).

ATLANTA	AB	R	H	RBI	BB	SO	LOB	AVG
Soler, RF	5	1	1	0	0	1	1	.294
Freeman, 1B	4	1	1	1	0	0	1	.278
Albies, 2B	4	1	0	0	0	2	1	.167
Riley, A, 3B	4	1	3	0	0	0	0	.381
Rosario, E, LF	2	1	0	0	2	0	2	.278
Duvall, CF	4	1	1	4	0	1	2	.200
d'Arnaud, C	4	0	2	0	0	1	1	.350
Swanson, D, SS	4	0	0	0	0	1	2	.188
Davidson, T, P	1	0	0	0	0	1	0	.000
Chavez, J, P	0	0	0	0	0	0	0	.000
Minter, P	1	0	0	0	0	0	1	.000
Martin, P	0	0	0	0	0	0	0	.000
a-Pederson, PH	1	0	0	0	0	0	1	.091
Smyly, P	0	0	0	0	0	0	0	.000
b-Adrianza, PH	1	0	0	0	0	0	0	.000
TOTALS	35	5	8	5	2	7	12	.246

a-Popped out for Martin in the 6th. b-Lined out for Smyly in the 9th.
2B: Riley, A (3, Maton, P). **HR:** Duvall (2, 1st inning off Valdez, F, 3 on, 2 out); Freeman (1, 3rd inning off Valdez, F, 0 on, 0 out). **TB:** d'Arnaud 2; Duvall 4; Freeman 4; Riley, A 4; Soler. **RBI:** Duvall 4 (6); Freeman (3).

HOUSTON	IP	H	R	ER	BB	SO	HR	ERA
Valdez, F	2.2	4	5	5	2	1	2	19.29
Garcia, Y	0.1	0	0	0	0	0	0	0.00
Urquidy (W, 2-0)	1.0	1	0	0	0	0	0	3.00
Maton, P (H, 2)	2.0	2	0	0	0	3	0	0.00
Stanek (H, 1)	1.0	0	0	0	0	1	0	2.70
Graveman	2.0	1	0	0	0	2	0	2.25
TOTALS	9.0	8	5	5	2	7	2	3.77

ATLANTA	IP	H	R	ER	BB	SO	HR	ERA
Davidson, T	2.0	2	4	2	3	1	0	9.00
Chavez, J	1.2	0	0	0	0	0	0	0.00
Minter (L, 1-1)(BS, 1)	1.0	3	3	3	2	2	0	7.71
Martin	1.1	0	0	0	0	1	0	0.00
Smyly	3.0	5	2	2	0	5	0	6.75
TOTALS	9.0	12	9	7	6	9	0	3.68

Davidson, T pitched to 2 batters in the 3rd.
IBB: Bregman (by Minter). **Pitches-strikes:** Valdez, F 47-29; Garcia, Y 12-9; Urquidy 14-10; Maton, P 29-20; Stanek 12-9; Graveman 37-23; Davidson, T 53-28; Chavez, J 24-14; Minter 24-18; Martin 16-11; Smyly 49-34.

GAME SIX Nov. 2, 2021
ATLANTA BRAVES 7, HOUSTON ASTROS 0

	1	2	3	4	5	6	7	8	9	R	H	E
Atlanta	0	0	3	0	3	0	1	0	0	7	7	1
Houston	0	0	0	0	0	0	0	0	0	0	6	0

ATLANTA	AB	R	H	RBI	BB	SO	LOB	AVG
Rosario, E, LF	4	1	0	0	1	1	0	.227
Soler, DH	3	2	1	3	1	1	0	.300
Freeman, 1B	4	1	2	2	0	1	0	.318
Riley, A, 3B	4	0	0	0	0	3	1	.320
Duvall, CF-RF	4	0	1	0	0	0	0	.208
Pederson, RF	4	0	0	0	0	1	1	.067
Heredia, CF	0	0	0	0	0	0	0	.000
Albies, 2B	3	2	2	0	1	0	0	.238
d'Arnaud, C	4	0	0	0	0	2	4	.292
Swanson, D, SS	4	1	1	2	0	0	3	.200
Fried, P	0	0	0	0	0	0	0	.000
Matzek, P	0	0	0	0	0	0	0	.000
Smith, W, P	0	0	0	0	0	0	0	.000
TOTALS	34	7	7	7	3	9	9	.239

2B: Freeman (1, Taylor, B). **HR:** Soler (3, 3rd inning off Garcia, L, 2 on, 2 out); Swanson, D (2, 5th inning off Javier, 1 on, 1 out); Freeman (2, 7th inning off Stanek, 0 on, 2 out). **TB:** Albies 2; Duvall; Freeman 6; Soler 4; Swanson, D 4. **RBI:** Freeman 2 (5); Soler 3 (6); Swanson, D 2 (3).

HOUSTON	AB	R	H	RBI	BB	SO	LOB	AVG
Altuve, 2B	4	0	1	0	0	1	1	.222
Brantley, LF-RF	4	0	2	0	0	0	2	.333
Correa, SS	4	0	1	0	0	2	4	.261
Alvarez, DH	4	0	1	0	0	0	4	.100
Gurriel, 1B	4	0	0	0	0	1	4	.273
Tucker, RF-CF	3	0	0	0	0	1	1	.286
Bregman, 3B	3	0	0	0	0	2	1	.095
Siri, CF	2	0	0	0	0	0	0	.167
a-Díaz, A, PH-LF	1	0	0	0	0	1	0	.333
Maldonado, C	2	0	1	0	0	1	0	.235
b-Gonzalez, M, PH	1	0	0	0	0	1	0	.250
Stubbs, C	0	0	0	0	0	0	0	.000
Garcia, L, P	0	0	0	0	0	0	0	.000
Raley, B, P	0	0	0	0	0	0	0	.000
Javier, P	0	0	0	0	0	0	0	.000
Taylor, B, P	0	0	0	0	0	0	0	.000
Maton, P, P	0	0	0	0	0	0	0	.000
Stanek, P	0	0	0	0	0	0	0	.000
Pressly, P	0	0	0	0	0	0	0	.000
Garcia, Y, P	0	0	0	0	0	0	0	.000
TOTALS	32	0	6	0	0	10	17	.224

a-Struck out for Siri in the 8th. b-Struck out for Maldonado in the 8th.
TB: Altuve; Alvarez; Brantley 2; Correa; Maldonado.

ATLANTA	IP	H	R	ER	BB	SO	HR	ERA
Fried (W, 1-1)	6.0	4	0	0	0	6	0	4.91
Matzek	2.0	1	0	0	0	4	0	1.69
Smith, W	1.0	1	0	0	0	0	0	0.00
TOTALS	9.0	6	0	0	0	10	0	3.06

HOUSTON	IP	H	R	ER	BB	SO	HR	ERA
Garcia, L (L, 0-2)	2.2	2	3	3	1	3	1	5.68
Raley, B	0.1	0	0	0	0	0	0	2.70
Javier	1.1	1	2	1	1	3	1	12.00
Taylor, B	0.1	1	1	1	1	0	1	13.50
Maton, P	1.1	2	0	0	0	1	0	0.00
Stanek	1.0	1	1	1	0	2	1	4.15
Pressly	1.0	0	0	0	0	0	0	7.50
Garcia, Y	1.0	0	0	0	0	0	0	0.00
TOTALS	9.0	7	7	7	3	9	3	4.33

WP: Javier.
Pitches-strikes: Fried 74-50; Matzek 28-20; Smith, W 19-12; Garcia, L 42-28; Raley, B 1-1; Javier 33-20; Taylor, B 13-5; Maton, P 20-12; Stanek 25-17; Pressly 7-5; Garcia, Y 9-7.

AMERICAN LEAGUE WILD CARD GAME

BOSTON RED SOX 6, NEW YORK YANKEES 2

NEW YORK	AVG	G	AB	R	H	2B	3B	HR	RBI	BB	SO	SB
Joey Gallo, LF	.000	1	4	0	0	0	0	0	0	0	1	0
Brett Gardner, CF	.000	1	3	0	0	0	0	0	0	0	3	0
Kyle Higashioka, C	.000	1	2	0	0	0	0	0	0	0	2	0
Aaron Judge, RF	.250	1	4	0	1	0	0	0	0	0	0	0
Rougned Odor, 3B	.000	1	2	0	0	0	0	0	0	0	1	0
Anthony Rizzo, 1B	.250	1	4	1	1	0	0	1	1	0	2	0
Gary Sanchez, C	.000	1	1	0	0	0	0	0	0	0	0	0
Giancarlo Stanton, DH	.750	1	4	1	3	0	0	1	1	0	1	0
Gleyber Torres, 2B	.000	1	4	0	0	0	0	0	0	0	1	0
Gio Urshela, 3B	.333	1	3	0	1	0	0	0	0	0	1	0
Andrew Velazquez, SS	.000	1	1	0	0	0	0	0	0	0	0	0
TOTALS	.188	1	32	2	6	0	0	2	2	0	11	0

NEW YORK	W	L	ERA	G	GS	SV	IP	H	R	ER	BB	SO
Gerrit Cole	0	1	13.50	1	1	0	2.0	4	3	3	2	3
Chad Green	0	0	0.00	1	0	0	1.2	1	0	0	1	2
Clay Holmes	0	0	0.00	1	0	0	2.0	1	0	0	1	0
Jonathan Loaisiga	0	0	18.00	1	0	0	1.0	0	2	2	3	2
Luis Severino	0	0	6.75	1	0	0	1.1	1	1	1	1	1
TOTALS	0	1	6.75	1	1	0	8.0	7	6	6	7	9

BOSTON	AVG	G	AB	R	H	2B	3B	HR	RBI	BB	SO	SB
Christian Arroyo, 2B	.000	1	3	0	0	0	0	0	0	0	1	0
Xander Bogaerts, SS	.500	1	2	2	1	0	0	1	2	2	1	0
Bobby Dalbec, 1B	.000	1	4	0	0	0	0	0	0	0	0	0
Rafael Devers, 3B	.000	1	2	1	0	0	0	0	0	2	1	0
Enrique Hernandez, CF	.333	1	3	1	1	0	0	0	0	0	1	0
Kevin Plawecki, C	.500	1	2	0	1	0	0	0	0	0	0	0
Hunter Renfroe, RF	.333	1	3	0	1	0	0	0	1	0	2	0
Kyle Schwarber, DH	.333	1	3	2	1	0	0	1	1	0	1	0
Travis Shaw, PH	.000	1	1	0	0	0	0	0	0	0	1	0
Christian Vazquez, C	.000	1	1	0	0	0	0	0	0	0	1	0
Alex Verdugo, LF	.500	1	4	0	2	1	0	0	0	3	0	0
TOTALS	.250	1	28	6	7	2	0	2	6	7	9	0

BOSTON	W	L	ERA	G	GS	SV	IP	H	R	ER	BB	SO
Ryan Brasier	0	0	0.00	1	0	0	0.2	1	0	0	0	0
Nathan Eovaldi	1	0	1.69	1	0	0	5.1	4	1	1	0	8
Tanner Houck	0	0	0.00	1	0	0	1.0	0	0	0	0	2
Hansel Robles	0	0	0.00	1	0	0	1.0	0	0	0	0	1
Garrett Whitlock	0	0	9.00	1	0	0	1.0	1	1	1	0	1
TOTALS	1	0	2.00	1	1	0	9.0	6	2	2	0	11

LOB—New York 3, Boston 5. **DP**—New York 2. **GIDP**—Plawecki, Verdugo.

SCORE BY INNING

NEW YORK	0	0	0	0	0	1	0	0	1	2
BOSTON	2	0	1	0	0	1	2	0	0	6

AMERICAN LEAGUE DIVISION SERIES

TAMPA BAY RAYS VS. BOSTON RED SOX

BOSTON	AVG	G	AB	R	H	2B	3B	HR	RBI	BB	SO	SB
Christian Arroyo, 2B	.313	4	16	1	5	1	0	0	0	0	2	0
Xander Bogaerts, SS	.333	4	18	3	6	0	0	1	2	1	3	0
Bobby Dalbec, 1B	.000	4	6	0	0	0	0	0	0	0	0	0
Rafael Devers, 3B	.333	4	18	3	6	0	0	2	6	2	5	0
Enrique Hernandez, CF	.450	4	20	4	9	3	0	2	6	0	2	0
J.D. Martinez, DH	.467	3	15	1	7	1	0	1	4	0	1	0
Kevin Plawecki, C	.000	1	2	0	0	0	0	0	0	0	0	0
Hunter Renfroe, RF	.294	4	17	2	5	1	0	0	2	2	0	
Danny Santana, DH	-	2	0	2	0	0	0	0	0	0	0	0
Kyle Schwarber, 1B	.313	4	16	4	5	0	0	1	1	2	4	1
Travis Shaw, PH	1.000	1	1	0	1	0	0	0	0	0	0	0
Christian Vazquez, C	.375	4	16	3	6	0	0	1	4	0	3	0
Alex Verdugo, LF	.316	4	19	3	6	1	0	1	3	0	2	0
TOTALS	.341	4	164	26	56	7	0	9	26	7	26	1

BOSTON	W	L	ERA	G	GS	SV	IP	H	R	ER	BB	SO
Matt Barnes	0	0	0.00	1	0	0	1.0	1	0	0	2	1
Ryan Brasier	0	0	9.00	3	0	0	2.0	3	2	2	0	4
Austin Davis	0	0	0.00	1	0	0	0.1	0	0	0	1	0
Nathan Eovaldi	0	0	3.60	1	1	0	5.0	3	2	2	1	8
Tanner Houck	1	0	3.00	2	0	0	6.0	3	2	2	0	6
Adam Ottavino	0	0	0.00	1	0	0	1.0	0	0	0	0	0
Nick Pivetta	1	0	3.12	2	0	0	8.2	7	3	3	3	11
Garrett Richards	0	0	0.00	1	0	0	0.1	0	0	0	0	0
Hansel Robles	0	0	10.80	2	0	0	1.2	4	2	2	0	3
Eduardo Rodriguez	0	1	5.40	2	2	0	6.2	5	4	4	2	7
Chris Sale	0	0	45.00	1	1	0	1.0	4	5	5	1	2
Josh Taylor	0	0	0.00	3	0	0	2.0	1	0	0	0	1
Garrett Whitlock	1	0	0.00	2	0	0	3.1	0	0	0	1	3
TOTALS	3	1	4.62	4	4	0	39.0	31	20	20	11	46

TAMPA BAY	AVG	G	AB	R	H	2B	3B	HR	RBI	BB	SO	SB
Randy Arozarena, LF	.333	4	15	4	5	1	0	1	3	4	4	2
Ji-Man Choi, 1B	.286	3	7	1	2	0	0	1	1	0	2	0
Nelson Cruz, DH	.176	4	17	2	3	0	0	1	1	1	5	0
Yandy Diaz, 3B	.200	4	15	1	3	0	0	0	2	1	2	0
Wander Franco, SS	.368	4	19	5	7	2	0	2	4	0	3	0
Kevin Kiermaier, CF	.214	4	14	2	3	3	0	0	1	2	4	0
Brandon Lowe, 2B	.000	4	18	0	0	0	0	0	0	0	9	0
Jordan Luplow, 1B	.286	4	7	2	2	1	0	1	4	1	4	0
Manuel Margot, RF	.143	3	7	1	1	0	0	0	0	1	3	0
Austin Meadows, LF	.222	3	9	1	2	1	0	1	3	0	2	0
Francisco Mejia, PH	-	1	0	0	0	0	0	0	0	1	0	0
Joey Wendle, 3B	.250	2	4	0	1	1	0	0	0	0	2	0
Mike Zunino, C	.133	4	15	1	2	1	0	0	0	0	6	0
TOTALS	.211	4	147	20	31	10	0	7	19	11	46	2

TAMPA BAY	W	L	ERA	G	GS	SV	IP	H	R	ER	BB	SO
Shane Baz	0	0	11.57	1	1	0	2.1	6	3	3	1	2
JT Chargois	0	0	0.00	4	0	0	3.1	3	0	0	1	2
Pete Fairbanks	0	0	3.38	2	0	0	2.2	1	1	1	1	2
J.P. Feyereisen	0	1	2.45	3	0	0	3.2	6	1	1	0	2
Josh Fleming	0	0	0.00	2	0	0	1.0	3	0	0	0	1
Andrew Kittredge	0	0	0.00	2	0	0	3.1	2	0	0	0	2
Shane McClanahan	1	0	7.94	2	1	0	5.2	10	5	5	1	3
Collin McHugh	0	1	7.36	2	1	0	3.2	3	3	3	1	2
Luis Patino	0	1	7.71	2	0	0	2.1	2	2	2	1	2
Drew Rasmussen	0	1	13.50	1	1	0	2.0	6	3	3	0	1
David Robertson	0	0	0.00	3	0	0	4.0	3	0	0	1	2
Michael Wacha	0	0	20.25	1	0	0	2.2	9	6	6	0	4
Matt Wisler	0	0	7.71	2	0	0	2.1	2	2	2	0	1
TOTALS	1	3	6.00	4	4	0	39.0	56	26	26	7	26

SCORE BY INNING

BOSTON	3	0	9	0	5	0	1	2	4	0	0	0	2—26
TAMPA BAY	9	0	1	0	2	3	1	4	0	0	0	0	0—20

HOUSTON ASTROS VS. CHICAGO WHITE SOX

CHICAGO	AVG	G	AB	R	H	2B	3B	HR	RBI	BB	SO	SB
Jose Abreu, 1B	.357	4	14	1	5	0	0	0	3	2	3	0
Tim Anderson, SS	.368	4	19	4	7	0	0	0	1	0	5	0
Adam Engel, RF	.000	4	7	0	0	0	0	0	0	0	1	0
Leury Garcia, RF	.200	4	15	3	3	1	0	1	4	1	7	0
Yasmani Grandal, C	.143	4	14	1	2	0	0	1	4	2	3	0
Cesar Hernandez, 2B	.286	3	7	0	2	0	0	0	0	4	3	0
Eloy Jimenez, LF	.294	4	17	0	5	0	0	0	3	0	5	0
Yoan Moncada, 3B	.250	4	16	2	4	0	0	0	0	1	3	0
Luis Robert, CF	.467	4	15	4	7	0	0	0	1	2	2	0
Gavin Sheets, 1B	.333	3	12	2	4	1	0	1	1	0	5	0
Andrew Vaughn, DH	.400	2	5	1	2	1	0	0	1	0	2	0
TOTALS	.291	4	141	18	41	3	0	3	18	12	39	0

CHICAGO	W	L	ERA	G	GS	SV	IP	H	R	ER	BB	SO
Aaron Bummer	0	1	8.10	3	0	0	3.1	5	3	3	1	7
Dylan Cease	0	0	16.20	1	1	0	1.2	2	3	3	3	2
Garrett Crochet	0	0	0.00	3	0	0	2.1	5	0	0	1	4
Lucas Giolito	0	0	8.31	1	1	0	4.1	3	4	4	5	4
Liam Hendriks	0	0	9.00	3	0	0	3.0	3	3	3	1	6
Craig Kimbrel	0	0	9.00	3	0	0	2.0	3	3	2	1	0
Michael Kopech	1	0	18.00	2	0	0	3.0	7	6	6	1	5
Reynaldo Lopez	0	0	4.50	1	0	0	2.0	1	1	1	1	2
Lance Lynn	0	1	12.27	1	1	0	3.2	6	5	5	2	4
Carlos Rodon	0	1	6.75	1	1	0	2.2	3	2	2	2	3
Jose Ruiz	0	0	0.00	1	0	0	1.1	0	0	0	1	0
Ryan Tepera	0	0	1.93	3	0	0	4.2	2	1	1	0	3
TOTALS	1	3	7.94	4	4	0	34.0	40	31	30	18	41

HOUSTON	AVG	G	AB	R	H	2B	3B	HR	RBI	BB	SO	SB
Jose Altuve, 2B	.313	4	16	9	5	2	0	1	3	4	5	1
Yordan Alvarez, LF	.273	4	11	4	3	1	0	1	3	6	6	0
Michael Brantley, LF	.368	4	19	0	7	1	0	0	4	0	5	1
Alex Bregman, 3B	.375	4	16	4	6	1	0	0	4	2	6	0
Jason Castro, PH	.000	1	1	0	0	0	0	0	0	0	1	0
Carlos Correa, SS	.385	4	13	4	5	2	0	0	4	4	2	0
Aledmys Diaz, PH	.000	1	1	0	0	0	0	0	0	0	0	0
Yuli Gurriel, 1B	.176	4	17	1	3	0	0	0	2	0	5	0
Martin Maldonado, C	.067	4	15	1	1	0	0	0	1	0	6	0
Chas McCormick, CF	.400	2	5	2	2	0	0	0	1	2	1	0
Jake Meyers, CF	.375	4	8	1	3	0	0	0	2	0	2	1
Kyle Tucker, RF	.294	4	17	5	5	1	0	2	7	0	2	2
TOTALS	.288	4	139	31	40	8	0	4	31	18	41	5

HOUSTON	W	L	ERA	G	GS	SV	IP	H	R	ER	BB	SO
Luis Garcia	0	0	16.88	1	1	0	2.2	5	5	5	3	3
Yimi Garcia	1	1	18.00	3	0	0	2.0	5	4	4	0	2
Kendall Graveman	0	0	3.00	3	0	0	3.0	3	1	1	2	1
Zack Greinke	0	0	0.00	1	0	0	1.0	2	0	0	0	1
Cristian Javier	0	0	0.00	1	0	0	2.2	0	0	0	2	6
Phil Maton	0	0	0.00	3	0	0	3.0	1	0	0	0	3
Lance McCullers Jr.	1	0	0.84	2	2	0	10.2	9	1	1	3	9
Ryan Pressly	0	0	0.00	3	0	0	3.0	3	0	0	0	4
Brooks Raley	0	0	81.00	1	0	0	0.1	5	3	3	0	0
Ryne Stanek	1	0	0.00	3	0	0	2.1	1	0	0	1	4
Framber Valdez	0	0	8.31	1	1	0	4.1	7	4	4	1	6
TOTALS	3	1	4.63	4	4	0	35.0	41	18	18	12	39

SCORE BY INNINGS

CHICAGO	2	1	5	3	3	0	0	4	0—18
HOUSTON	0	6	6	6	3	1	5	1	3—31

BOSTON	W	L	ERA	G	GS	SV	IP	H	R	ER	BB	SO
Ryan Brasier	0	0	13.50	3	0	0	1.1	4	2	2	0	1
Nathan Eovaldi	1	2	6.97	3	2	0	10.1	12	8	8	4	9
Darwinzon Hernandez	0	0	13.50	2	0	0	1.1	2	2	2	1	3
Tanner Houck	0	0	10.80	2	0	0	3.1	4	4	4	0	2
Adam Ottavino	0	0	3.00	4	0	0	3.0	3	1	1	0	3
Martin Perez	0	0	12.00	4	0	0	3.0	6	5	4	4	0
Nick Pivetta	0	0	1.80	1	1	0	5.0	2	1	1	2	3
Hansel Robles	0	1	3.38	3	0	0	2.2	3	2	1	1	1
Eduardo Rodriguez	1	0	4.50	1	1	0	6.0	5	3	3	0	7
Chris Sale	0	1	3.38	2	2	0	8.0	8	5	3	3	9
Hirokazu Sawamura	0	0	4.50	3	0	0	2.0	2	1	1	2	2
Josh Taylor	0	0	4.50	3	0	0	2.0	3	1	1	0	1
Garrett Whitlock	0	0	2.25	2	0	0	4.0	3	1	1	1	2
TOTALS	2	4	5.54	6	6	0	52.0	57	36	32	18	43

HOUSTON	AVG	G	AB	R	H	2B	3B	HR	RBI	BB	SO	SB
Jose Altuve, 2B	.125	6	24	6	3	0	0	2	4	3	3	0
Yordan Alvarez, LF	.522	6	23	7	12	3	1	1	6	2	5	0
Michael Brantley, LF	.269	6	26	3	7	1	0	0	4	0	5	0
Alex Bregman, 3B	.217	6	23	4	5	0	0	1	3	2	0	1
Jason Castro, C	.667	3	3	2	2	0	0	1	2	2	0	0
Carlos Correa, SS	.250	6	24	5	6	1	0	1	1	1	7	0
Aledmys Diaz, 1B	.000	3	2	0	0	0	0	0	0	0	2	0
Yuli Gurriel, 1B	.455	6	22	4	10	1	0	1	6	3	1	1
Martin Maldonado, C	.071	6	14	0	1	0	0	0	0	1	4	0
Chas McCormick, CF	.286	5	14	1	4	0	0	0	1	0	6	0
Jose Siri, CF	.125	3	8	1	1	0	0	0	2	0	1	0
Kyle Tucker, RF	.261	6	23	4	6	1	0	2	8	2	7	1
TOTALS	.277	6	206	36	57	7	1	9	34	18	43	2

HOUSTON	W	L	ERA	G	GS	SV	IP	H	R	ER	BB	SO
Luis Garcia	1	1	6.75	2	2	0	6.2	3	5	5	4	9
Yimi Garcia	0	0	9.00	3	0	0	3.0	3	3	3	2	4
Kendall Graveman	1	0	0.00	3	0	0	4.0	2	0	0	2	5
Zack Greinke	0	0	13.50	1	1	0	1.1	2	2	2	3	0
Cristian Javier	0	0	0.00	2	0	0	5.0	3	0	0	2	7
Phil Maton	0	0	2.45	4	0	0	3.2	1	1	1	1	3
Jake Odorizzi	0	0	9.00	1	0	0	4.0	7	4	4	0	5
Ryan Pressly	0	0	3.00	3	0	1	3.0	3	1	1	0	4
Brooks Raley	0	0	3.00	3	0	0	3.0	1	1	1	2	3
Ryne Stanek	1	0	2.08	5	0	0	4.1	2	1	1	0	2
Blake Taylor	0	0	0.00	2	0	0	2.2	2	0	0	1	4
Jose Urquidy	0	1	27.00	1	1	0	1.2	5	6	5	2	1
Framber Valdez	1	0	2.53	2	2	0	10.2	9	4	3	4	7
TOTALS	4	2	4.42	6	6	1	53.0	42	28	26	23	54

SCORE BY INNINGS

BOSTON	6	10	6	1	0	2	1	1	1—28
HOUSTON	3	1	0	6	0	8	2	5	11—36

AMERICAN LEAGUE CHAMPIONSHIP SERIES

HOUSTON ASTROS VS. BOSTON RED SOX

BOSTON	AVG	G	AB	R	H	2B	3B	HR	RBI	BB	SO	SB
Christian Arroyo, 2B	.211	6	19	3	4	0	1	1	3	0	4	0
Xander Bogaerts, SS	.192	6	26	2	5	2	0	1	2	2	10	0
Bobby Dalbec, 1B	.000	3	2	0	0	0	0	0	0	1	0	0
Rafael Devers, 3B	.292	6	24	7	7	0	0	3	6	3	2	0
Enrique Hernandez, CF	.385	6	26	4	10	1	1	3	3	0	4	0
J.D. Martinez, DH	.235	6	17	3	4	1	0	2	6	5	9	0
Kevin Plawecki, C	.000	3	3	1	0	0	0	0	0	1	0	0
Hunter Renfroe, RF	.063	6	16	2	1	1	0	0	1	4	8	1
Danny Santana, LF	.000	3	3	0	0	0	0	0	0	1	4	0
Kyle Schwarber, 1B	.120	6	25	2	3	1	0	1	4	2	7	0
Travis Shaw, 1B	.000	3	3	0	0	0	0	0	0	0	2	0
Christian Vazquez, C	.200	6	15	2	3	1	0	0	2	1	3	0
Alex Verdugo, LF	.263	6	19	2	5	1	0	0	0	5	1	1
TOTALS	.212	6	198	28	42	8	2	11	27	23	54	2

NATIONAL LEAGUE WILD CARD GAME

LOS ANGELES DODGERS 3, ST. LOUIS CARDINALS 1

ST. LOUIS	AVG	G	AB	R	H	2B	3B	HR	RBI	BB	SO	SB
Nolan Arenado, 3B	.000	1	4	0	0	0	0	0	0	0	0	0
Harrison Bader, CF	.000	1	1	0	0	0	0	0	0	1	1	0
Dylan Carlson, RF	.250	1	4	0	1	0	0	0	0	0	1	0
Paul DeJong, SS	.000	1	1	0	0	0	0	0	0	0	1	0
Tommy Edman, 2B	.600	1	5	1	3	0	0	0	0	0	1	2
Paul Goldschmidt, 1B	.333	1	3	0	1	0	0	0	0	2	1	0
Yadier Molina, C	.000	1	4	0	0	0	0	0	0	0	0	0
Tyler O'Neill, LF	.000	1	4	0	0	0	0	0	0	1	3	1
Edmundo Sosa, SS	.000	1	4	0	0	0	0	0	0	0	1	0
Adam Wainwright, P	.000	1	2	0	0	0	0	0	0	0	1	0
TOTALS	.156	1	32	1	5	0	0	0	0	4	10	3

ST. LOUIS	W	L	ERA	G	GS	SV	IP	H	R	ER	BB	SO
Giovanny Gallegos	0	0	0.00	1	0	0	1.0	1	0	0	0	2
Luis Garcia	0	0	0.00	1	0	0	1.2	1	0	0	1	0
T.J. McFarland	0	1	13.50	1	0	0	0.2	0	1	1	1	0
Alex Reyes	0	0	*.**	1	0	0	0.0	1	1	1	0	0
Adam Wainwright	0	0	1.69	1	1	0	5.1	4	1	1	2	5
TOTALS	0	1	3.12	1	1	0	8.2	7	3	3	4	7

LOS ANGELES	AVG	G	AB	R	H	2B	3B	HR	RBI	BB	SO	SB
Matt Beaty, 1B	.000	1	3	0	0	0	0	0	0	0	0	0
Cody Bellinger, CF	.500	1	2	1	1	0	0	0	0	2	1	2
Mookie Betts, RF	.500	1	4	2	2	0	0	0	0	0	0	0
Gavin Lux, PH	-	1	0	0	0	0	0	0	0	0	0	0
Billy McKinney, 1B	-	1	0	0	0	0	0	0	0	0	0	0
AJ Pollock, LF	.000	1	3	0	0	0	0	0	0	0	1	0
Albert Pujols, PH	.000	1	1	0	0	0	0	0	0	0	0	0
Luke Raley, PH	.000	1	1	0	0	0	0	0	0	0	1	0
Max Scherzer, P	-	1	0	0	0	0	0	0	0	0	0	0
Corey Seager, SS	.000	1	3	0	0	0	0	0	0	0	1	0
Will Smith, C	.000	1	3	0	0	0	0	0	0	0	1	0
Steven Souza Jr., PH	.000	1	1	0	0	0	0	0	0	0	0	0
Chris Taylor, LF	.500	1	2	1	1	0	0	1	2	0	0	0
Justin Turner, 3B	.250	1	4	1	1	0	0	1	1	0	1	0
Trea Turner, 2B	.500	1	4	0	2	0	0	0	0	0	0	0
TOTALS	.226	1	31	3	7	0	0	2	3	4	7	2

LOS ANGELES	W	L	ERA	G	GS	SV	IP	H	R	ER	BB	SO
Brusdar Graterol	0	0	0.00	1	0	0	1.0	0	0	0	0	0
Kenley Jansen	1	0	0.00	1	0	0	1.0	1	0	0	0	3
Joe Kelly	0	0	0.00	1	0	0	0.2	0	0	0	0	1
Corey Knebel	0	0	0.00	1	0	0	0.1	0	0	0	0	0
Max Scherzer	0	0	2.08	1	1	0	4.1	3	1	1	3	4
Blake Treinen	0	0	0.00	1	0	0	1.2	1	0	0	1	1
TOTALS	1	0	1.00	1	1	1	9.0	5	1	1	4	10

E—Seager. **LOB**—St. Louis 11, Los Angeles 7. **DP**—St. Louis 1. **GIDP**—T.Turner. **SAC**—Wainwright, Scherzer. **HBP**—Bader 2 (by Graterol. Scherzer). **SB**—Edman 2, O'Neill, Bellinger 2. **WP**—Kelly, Scherzer.

SCORE BY INNINGS

ST. LOUIS	1	0	0	0	0	0	0	0	0	0—1
LOS ANGELES	0	0	0	1	0	0	0	0	2—3

NATIONAL LEAGUE DIVISION SERIES

SAN FRANCISCO GIANTS VS. LOS ANGELES DODGERS

LOS ANGELES	AVG	G	AB	R	H	2B	3B	HR	RBI	BB	SO	SB
Austin Barnes, PH	.000	1	1	0	0	0	0	0	0	0	1	0
Matt Beaty, 1B	.200	4	5	0	1	0	0	0	1	0	1	0
Cody Bellinger, 1B	.267	5	15	2	4	1	0	0	3	0	7	1
Mookie Betts, RF	.450	5	20	2	9	0	0	1	4	1	2	2
Walker Buehler, P	.000	2	4	1	0	0	0	0	0	0	3	0
Gavin Lux, CF	.333	5	9	1	3	0	0	0	0	2	2	0
Billy McKinney, 1B	.000	3	1	0	0	0	0	0	0	0	1	0
AJ Pollock, LF	.273	4	11	2	3	1	0	0	2	1	5	0
Albert Pujols, 1B	.667	2	3	0	2	0	0	0	0	0	0	0
Max Scherzer, P	.000	2	1	0	0	0	0	0	0	0	1	0
Corey Seager, SS	.238	5	21	2	5	2	0	0	2	1	3	0
Will Smith, C	.333	5	18	3	6	2	0	2	3	3	2	0
Steven Souza Jr., PH	.500	3	2	0	1	0	0	0	0	1	1	0
Chris Taylor, LF	.143	4	14	3	2	1	0	0	1	2	2	0
Justin Turner, 3B	.050	5	20	1	1	0	0	0	1	4	0	0
Trea Turner, 2B	.136	5	22	1	3	2	0	0	1	0	5	0
Julio Urias, P	.333	2	3	0	1	0	0	0	0	1	0	0
TOTALS	.241	5	170	18	41	9	0	3	18	12	41	3

LOS ANGELES	W	L	ERA	G	GS	SV	IP	H	R	ER	BB	SO
Phil Bickford	0	0	0.00	3	0	0	2.1	1	0	0	0	0
Walker Buehler	0	1	3.38	2	2	0	10.2	9	4	4	3	9
Brusdar Graterol	0	0	0.00	4	0	0	3.2	3	0	0	0	3
Kenley Jansen	1	0	0.00	2	0	2	2.0	0	0	0	0	5
Joe Kelly	1	0	5.40	2	0	0	1.2	3	1	1	1	0
Corey Knebel	0	0	0.00	2	1	0	2.0	1	0	0	0	3
Max Scherzer	0	1	1.13	2	1	1	8.0	3	1	1	1	12
Blake Treinen	0	0	2.70	3	0	0	3.1	1	1	1	0	5
Julio Urias	1	0	2.00	2	1	0	9.0	6	2	2	1	10
Alex Vesia	0	0	6.75	2	0	0	1.1	2	1	1	0	2
TOTALS	3	2	2.05	5	5	1	44	29	10	10	6	49

SAN FRANCISCO	AVG	G	AB	R	H	2B	3B	HR	RBI	BB	SO	SB
Kris Bryant, CF	.471	5	17	1	8	0	0	1	2	1	3	0
Curt Casali, PH	.000	1	1	0	0	0	0	0	0	0	1	0
Brandon Crawford, SS	.250	5	20	2	5	1	0	1	2	0	4	0
Alex Dickerson, PH	.000	4	4	0	0	0	0	0	0	0	3	0
Steven Duggar, CF	.000	3	3	0	0	0	0	0	0	1	2	0
Wilmer Flores, 1B	.083	4	12	1	1	0	0	0	0	1	2	0
Kevin Gausman, P	.000	2	2	0	0	0	0	0	0	0	2	0
Tommy La Stella, 2B	.333	5	9	1	3	0	0	0	0	2	2	0
Evan Longoria, 3B	.118	5	17	2	2	0	0	1	1	0	4	0
Buster Posey, C	.300	5	20	1	6	2	0	1	2	0	6	0
Darin Ruf, LF	.091	3	11	1	1	0	0	1	2	0	5	0
Austin Slater, RF	.400	3	5	0	2	1	0	0	0	0	0	0
Donovan Solano, 2B	.000	5	8	0	0	0	0	0	0	1	3	0
LaMonte Wade Jr., LF	.100	5	10	1	1	0	0	0	0	1	4	0
Logan Webb, P	.000	2	5	0	0	0	0	0	0	0	4	0
Alex Wood, P	.000	2	0	0	0	0	0	0	0	0	0	0
Mike Yastrzemski, RF	.000	5	13	0	0	0	0	0	0	4	4	0
TOTALS	.182	5	159	10	29	4	0	5	10	6	49	0

SAN FRANCISCO	W	L	ERA	G	GS	SV	IP	H	R	ER	BB	SO
Jose Alvarez	0	0	0.00	1	0	0	0.1	0	0	0	0	0
Kervin Castro	0	0	0.00	2	0	0	1.1	0	0	0	2	0
Anthony DeSclafani	0	1	10.80	1	1	0	1.2	5	2	2	0	2
Camilo Doval	0	0	2.45	3	0	1	3.2	2	1	1	0	2
Jarlin Garcia	0	0	6.75	2	0	0	1.1	2	1	1	1	1
Kevin Gausman	0	1	6.00	2	1	0	6.0	4	4	4	3	7
Dominic Leone	0	0	16.20	2	0	0	1.2	4	3	3	2	1
Zack Littell	0	0	10.13	2	0	0	2.2	6	3	3	0	5
Jake McGee	0	0	6.75	3	0	0	2.2	2	2	2	0	1
Tyler Rogers	1	0	0.00	4	0	0	3.1	5	0	0	1	1
Logan Webb	1	0	0.61	2	2	0	14.2	9	1	1	1	17
Alex Wood	0	0	0.00	1	1	0	4.2	2	0	0	2	4
TOTALS	2	3	3.48	5	5	1	44.041	18	17	12	41

SCORE BY INNINGS

LOS ANGELES	1	3	0	2	1	5	0	5	1—18
SAN FRANCISCO	2	1	0	0	2	2	1	2	0—10

MILWAUKEE BREWERS VS. ATLANTA BRAVES

ATLANTA	AVG	G	AB	R	H	2B	3B	HR	RBI	BB	SO	SB
Ehire Adrianza, PH	.000	2	2	0	0	0	0	0	0	0	0	0
Ozzie Albies, 2B	.235	4	17	1	4	2	0	0	1	0	4	0
Ian Anderson, P	.000	1	1	0	0	0	0	0	0	0	1	0
Orlando Arcia, PH	.000	3	1	0	0	0	0	0	0	1	0	0
William Contreras, PH	.000	1	1	0	0	0	0	0	0	0	0	0
Travis d'Arnaud, C	.167	4	12	2	2	0	0	0	1	3	6	0
Adam Duvall, CF	.286	4	14	0	4	0	1	0	0	1	2	0
Freddie Freeman, 1B	.308	4	13	2	4	1	0	1	2	4	4	0
Max Fried, P	.000	1	2	0	0	0	0	0	0	0	2	0
Terrance Gore, PR	-	1	0	0	0	0	0	0	0	0	0	0
Guillermo Heredia, CF	.000	3	1	0	0	0	0	0	0	0	0	0
Charlie Morton, P	.000	2	3	0	0	0	0	0	0	0	1	0
Cristian Pache, CF	-	1	0	0	0	0	0	0	0	0	0	0
Joc Pederson, RF	.429	4	7	2	3	0	0	2	5	0	0	0
Austin Riley, 3B	.333	4	15	3	5	0	0	1	1	1	4	0
Eddie Rosario, LF	.308	4	13	0	4	0	0	0	2	1	2	0
Jorge Soler, RF	.091	3	11	1	1	1	0	0	0	2	4	0
Dansby Swanson, SS	.200	4	15	1	3	1	0	0	0	0	3	0
TOTALS	.234	4	128	12	30	5	1	4	12	13	33	0

ATLANTA	W	L	ERA	G	GS	SV	IP	H	R	ER	BB	SO
Ian Anderson	1	0	0.00	1	1	0	5.0	3	0	0	0	6
Jesse Chavez	0	0	0.00	2	0	0	1.2	1	0	0	1	2
Max Fried	1	0	0.00	1	1	0	6.0	3	0	0	0	9
Luke Jackson	0	0	0.00	4	0	0	3.1	3	0	0	2	3
Tyler Matzek	1	0	0.00	4	0	0	4.1	3	0	0	2	6
A.J. Minter	0	0	0.00	1	0	0	1.1	0	0	0	0	3
Charlie Morton	0	1	3.86	2	2	0	9.1	7	4	4	2	14
Will Smith	0	0	0.00	3	0	3	3.0	2	0	0	1	3
Huascar Ynoa	0	0	18.00	1	0	0	1.0	2	2	2	1	2
TOTALS	3	1	1.54	4	4	3	35.0	24	6	6	9	48

MILWAUKEE	AVG	G	AB	R	H	2B	3B	HR	RBI	BB	SO	SB
Willy Adames, SS	.294	4	17	0	5	1	0	0	0	0	9	0
Jackie Bradley Jr., PR	-	1	0	0	0	0	0	0	0	0	0	0
Corbin Burnes, P	.000	1	1	0	0	0	0	0	0	0	0	0
Lorenzo Cain, CF	.231	4	13	0	3	0	0	0	1	1	2	1
Eduardo Escobar, 1B	.300	4	10	0	3	1	0	0	0	0	5	0
Avisail Garcia, RF	.133	4	15	2	2	0	0	0	0	0	8	0
Eric Lauer, P	.000	1	1	0	0	0	0	0	0	0	0	0
Luke Maile, C	.000	2	2	0	0	0	0	0	0	0	1	0
Omar Narvaez, C	.375	3	8	0	3	1	0	0	1	0	0	0
Freddy Peralta, P	.000	1	1	0	0	0	0	0	0	0	1	0
Jace Peterson, RF	-	2	0	0	0	0	0	0	2	0	0	0
Manny Pina, C	.000	3	4	0	0	0	0	0	0	0	3	0
Tyrone Taylor, RF	.000	2	2	0	0	0	0	0	0	0	1	0
Rowdy Tellez, 1B	.200	4	10	2	2	0	0	2	4	0	4	0
Luis Urias, 3B	.222	3	9	1	2	0	0	0	2	0	1	0
Daniel Vogelbach, PH	.000	3	1	0	0	0	0	0	0	1	0	0
Kolten Wong, 2B	.067	4	15	0	1	0	0	0	0	1	5	0
Brandon Woodruff, P	.000	2	1	0	0	0	0	0	0	0	0	0
Christian Yelich, LF	.200	4	15	1	3	0	0	0	0	2	8	1
TOTALS	.192	4	125	6	24	3	0	2	6	9	48	2

MILWAUKEE	W	L	ERA	G	GS	SV	IP	H	R	ER	BB	SO
Aaron Ashby	0	0	6.75	2	0	0	2.2	5	2	2	2	3
Brad Boxberger	0	0	0.00	2	0	0	2.0	0	0	0	1	2
Corbin Burnes	0	0	0.00	1	1	0	6.0	2	0	0	3	6
Jake Cousins	0	0	0.00	1	0	0	1.0	1	0	0	1	1
Josh Hader	0	1	4.50	2	0	1	2.0	2	1	1	1	3
Adrian Houser	1	0	12.00	1	0	0	3.0	4	4	4	1	1
Eric Lauer	0	0	4.91	1	1	0	3.2	4	2	2	2	2
Freddy Peralta	0	0	0.00	1	1	0	4.0	3	0	0	1	5
Hunter Strickland	0	0	0.00	3	0	0	2.1	3	0	0	2	0
Brandon Woodruff	0	1	3.68	2	1	0	7.1	6	3	3	1	8
TOTALS	1	3	3.18	4	4	1	34.0	30	12	12	13	33

SCORE BY INNINGS

ATLANTA	0	0	2	2	5	1	0	2	0—12		
MILWAUKEE	0	0	0	2	2	0	2	0	0—6		

NATIONAL LEAGUE CHAMPIONSHIP SERIES
ATLANTA BRAVES VS. LOS ANGELES DODGERS

LOS ANGELES	AVG	G	AB	R	H	2B	3B	HR	RBI	BB	SO	SB
Austin Barnes, PH	.000	2	1	0	0	0	0	0	0	0	1	0
Matt Beaty, 1B	.000	4	3	0	0	0	0	0	0	0	0	0
Cody Bellinger, 1B	.412	6	17	2	7	0	0	1	4	3	3	2
Mookie Betts, RF	.174	6	23	4	4	1	0	0	1	4	3	4
Walker Buehler, P	.000	3	2	0	0	0	0	0	0	0	1	0
Andy Burns, PH	.000	2	2	0	0	0	0	0	0	0	0	0
Tony Gonsolin, P	1.000	3	1	0	1	0	0	0	0	0	0	0
Brusdar Graterol, P	.000	3	1	0	0	0	0	0	0	0	1	0
Gavin Lux, CF	.000	3	5	0	0	0	0	0	0	2	1	1
AJ Pollock, LF	.381	6	21	5	8	3	0	2	7	0	3	0
Albert Pujols, 1B	.231	6	13	2	3	0	0	0	1	5	0	
Max Scherzer, P	.000	1	2	0	0	0	0	0	0	0	0	0
Corey Seager, SS	.167	6	24	3	4	1	0	2	4	3	9	0
Will Smith, C	.217	6	23	3	5	0	0	1	1	4	5	0
Steven Souza Jr., RF	.000	6	5	0	0	0	0	0	0	0	3	0
Chris Taylor, 3B	.476	6	21	5	10	3	0	3	9	3	7	3
Justin Turner, 3B	.200	4	10	1	2	0	0	0	1	3	0	
Trea Turner, 2B	.240	6	25	2	6	0	0	1	1	7	1	
Julio Urias, P	.000	2	1	0	0	0	0	0	0	0	0	0
TOTALS	.250	6	200	27	50	8	0	9	27	22	52	11

LOS ANGELES	W	L	ERA	G	GS	SV	IP	H	R	ER	BB	SO
Phil Bickford	0	0	0.00	3	0	0	3.2	3	0	0	0	4
Justin Bruihl	0	0	0.00	3	0	0	2.0	1	0	0	0	5
Walker Buehler	0	1	7.04	2	2	0	7.2	13	8	6	6	9
Tony Gonsolin	1	0	11.25	3	0	0	4.0	5	5	5	1	4
Brusdar Graterol	0	1	2.08	3	0	0	4.1	1	1	1	0	4
Kenley Jansen	0	0	0.00	5	0	1	4.0	2	0	0	1	6
Joe Kelly	0	0	6.00	4	1	0	3.0	2	2	2	0	4
Corey Knebel	0	0	5.40	4	1	0	3.1	4	2	2	1	7
Evan Phillips	1	0	0.00	2	0	0	3.0	1	0	0	2	6
Max Scherzer	0	0	4.15	1	1	0	4.1	4	2	2	1	7
Blake Treinen	0	1	2.45	4	0	0	3.2	3	1	1	1	2
Julio Urias	0	1	10.50	2	1	0	6.0	11	7	7	2	5
Alex Vesia	0	0	0.00	5	0	0	3.0	3	0	0	3	5
TOTALS	2	4	4.50	6	1	1	52.0	53	28	26	18	68

ATLANTA	AVG	G	AB	R	H	2B	3B	HR	RBI	BB	SO	SB
Ehire Adrianza, PH	.167	6	6	1	1	0	0	0	0	2	0	
Ozzie Albies, 2B	.280	6	25	7	7	1	0	1	2	5	2	
Ian Anderson, P	.000	2	1	0	0	0	0	0	0	0	1	0
Orlando Arcia, PH	.000	2	2	0	0	0	0	0	0	0	1	0
Johan Camargo, PH	.000	4	4	0	0	0	0	0	0	0	2	0
Travis d'Arnaud, C	.211	6	19	1	4	0	0	0	3	7	0	
Adam Duvall, CF	.190	6	21	2	4	0	0	1	4	1	9	0
Freddie Freeman, 1B	.286	6	21	4	6	1	0	2	4	6	8	1
Max Fried, P	.000	2	3	0	0	0	0	0	0	0	3	0
Guillermo Heredia, CF	.000	3	2	0	0	0	0	0	0	0	2	0
Charlie Morton, P	.000	1	2	0	0	0	0	0	0	0	2	0
Cristian Pache, PR	-	1	0	0	0	0	0	0	0	0	0	0
Joc Pederson, RF	.227	6	22	2	5	0	0	1	4	1	8	0
Austin Riley, 3B	.200	6	25	3	5	2	0	1	4	2	10	0
Eddie Rosario, LF	.560	6	25	6	14	1	1	3	9	3	3	1
Drew Smyly, P	.000	1	1	0	0	0	0	0	0	0	0	0
Jorge Soler, RF	.500	2	2	0	1	1	0	0	0	0	1	0
Dansby Swanson, SS	.261	6	23	2	6	0	0	0	1	6	1	
TOTALS	.260	6	204	28	53	7	1	8	27	18	68	5

ATLANTA	W	L	ERA	G	GS	SV	IP	H	R	ER	BB	SO
Ian Anderson	0	0	3.86	2	2	0	7.0	6	3	3	4	6
Jesse Chavez	0	0	0.00	3	1	0	2.2	2	0	0	1	0
Max Fried	0	1	5.91	2	2	0	10.2	16	7	7	2	8
Luke Jackson	0	1	27.00	4	0	0	1.2	7	5	5	2	2
Dylan Lee	0	0	4.50	1	0	0	2.0	3	1	1	0	2
Chris Martin	0	0	4.50	3	0	0	2.0	3	1	1	0	1
Tyler Matzek	1	0	3.00	5	0	0	6.0	1	2	2	2	11
A.J. Minter	0	0	0.00	4	0	0	6.2	2	0	0	2	8
Charlie Morton	0	0	3.60	1	1	0	5.0	3	2	2	6	5
Will Smith	2	0	0.00	4	0	1	4.0	1	0	0	1	4
Drew Smyly	1	0	5.40	1	0	0	3.1	2	2	2	1	2
Jacob Webb	0	0	21.60	2	0	0	1.2	4	4	4	1	3
TOTALS	4	2	4.67	6	6	1	52.0	50	27	27	22	52

SCORE BY INNINGS

LOS ANGELES	4	4	1	2	4	0	4	8	0—27		
ATLANTA	4	2	2	10	2	0	0	2	6—28		

ORGANIZATION STATISTICS

Arizona Diamondbacks

SEASON IN A SENTENCE: It was always going to be tough to compete with the Dodgers, Giants and Padres in the National League West, but no one knew it would be this tough.

HIGH POINT: Behind five strong innings by Madison Bumgarner, Arizona finished April with a 7-2 win over the Rockies to improve to 14-12. That was good for only fourth place in the highly competitive NL West, but it was a promising first month.

LOW POINT: The D-backs lost a franchise-record 17 straight games in June. That losing streak began just a week after the D-backs snapped a 13-game losing skid. Arizona sat two games under .500 at 17-19 on May 11. They went 8-49 over the next two months, a stretch of futility that ranks among the worst in recent baseball history. Durig this stretch, Arizona lost an all-time record 24 straight road games.

NOTABLE ROOKIES: Pavin Smith was a fixture in the lineup while playing right field, center field and first base. The concerns about his lack of power manifested in his MLB rookie season. He hit .268/.328/.404 with 11 home runs in 145 games. Daulton Varsho matched Smith's home run total (11) in 95 games while splitting time between the uncommon combination of center field and catcher. Righthander Taylor Widener went 2-1, 4.35 in 70 innings split between the rotation and bullpen. Lefthander Tyler Gilbert, a minor league Rule 5 pick in 2020, went 2-2, 3.15 in 40 innings. Gilbert threw a no-hitter in his first MLB start on Aug. 14 and capably held down a spot in the rotation for the rest of the season, although his strikeout rate of 5.6 per nine innings will likely have to improve for him to sustain that success.

KEY TRANSACTIONS: It's a bad sign when a minor league Rule 5 pick is the most notable transaction of the year, but Tyler Gilbert quickly became one of the best minor league Rule 5 picks of all time. His 1.1 WAR ranks among the top 10 in debut seasons for Rule 5 picks in the 21st century, a list understandably dominated by major league Rule 5 picks. The most significant free agents the D-backs signed were relievers Joakim Soria and Tyler Clippard. The two tied for the team lead with six saves apiece. Soria was traded at the deadline for a pair of minor leaguers: lefthander Yaifer Perdomo and catcher JJ D'Orazio.

OPENING DAY PAYROLL: $89,077,233 (19th).

PLAYERS OF THE YEAR

MAJOR LEAGUE	MINOR LEAGUE
Ketel Marte	**Alek Thomas**
OF	OF
.318/.377/.532	(AAA/AA)
14 HR, 50 RBIs	.313/.394/.559,
143 OPS+	18 HR, 12 3B

ORGANIZATION LEADERS

Batting		*Minimum 250 AB
MAJORS		
*AVG	Ketel Marte	.318
*OPS	Ketel Marte	.909
HR	Eduardo Escobar	22
RBI	Eduardo Escobar	65
MINORS		
*AVG	Henry Ramos, Reno	.371
*OBP	Henry Ramos, Reno	.439
*SLG	Drew Ellis, Reno	.615
*OPS	Henry Ramos, Reno	1.021
R	Alek Thomas, Reno, Amarillo	86
H	Alek Thomas, Reno, Amarillo	136
TB	Alek Thomas, Reno, Amarillo	243
2B	Seth Beer, Reno	33
3B	Alek Thomas, Reno, Amarillo	12
HR	Stone Garrett, Reno, Amarillo	25
RBI	Stone Garrett, Reno, Amarillo	81
BB	Neyfy Castillo, Visalia	58
SO	Neyfy Castillo, Visalia	170
SB	Nick Dalesandro, Hillsboro	33

Pitching		#Minimum 75 IP
MAJORS		
W	2 tied	7
#ERA	Zac Gallen	4.30
SO	Zac Gallen	139
SV	2 tied	6
MINORS		
W	Luis Frias, Reno, Amarillo, Hillsboro	9
L	Matt Tabor, Reno, Amarillo, Hillsboro	11
#ERA	Ryne Nelson, Amarillo, Hillsboro	3.17
G 2 tied		43
GS 2 tied		23
SV	Miguel Aguilar, Reno	16
IP	Brandon Pfaadt, Amarillo, Hillsboro, Visalia	131.2
BB	Junior Mieses, Visalia	72
SO	Ryne Nelson, Amarillo, Hillsboro	163
#AVG	Ryne Nelson, Amarillo, Hillsboro	.206

General Manager: Mike Hazen. **Farm Director:** Josh Barfield. **Scouting Director:** Deric Ladnier.

Class	Team	League	W	L	PCT	Finish	Manager
Majors	Arizona Diamondbacks	National	52	110	.321	15th (15)	Torey Lovullo
Triple-A	Reno Aces	Triple-A West	70	54	.565	3rd (10)	Blake Lalli
Double-A	Amarillo Sod Poodles	Double-A Central	59	61	.492	7th (10)	Shawn Roof
High-A	Hillsboro Hops	High-A West	52	60	.464	4th (6)	Vince Harrison
Low-A	Visalia Rawhide	Low-A West	38	82	.317	8th (8)	Javier Colina
Rookie	ACL D-backs	Arizona Complex	21	39	.350	17th (18)	Rolando Arnedo
Rookie	DSL D-backs1	Dominican Summer	23	36	.390	t-38th (46)	Jaime Del Valle
Rookie	DSL D-backs2	Dominican Summer	27	32	.458	31st (46)	R. Ramirez/R. Ozuna
Overall 2021 Minor League Record			290	364	.443	26th (30)	

ORGANIZATION STATISTICS

ARIZONA DIAMONDBACKS
NATIONAL LEAGUE

Batting	B-T	HT	WT	DOB	AVG	vLH	vRH	G	AB	R	H	2B	3B	HR	RBI	BB	HBP	SH	SF	SO	SB	CS	SLG	OBP
Ahmed, Nick	R-R	6-2	201	3-15-90	.221	.252	.206	129	434	46	96	30	3	5	38	34	2	2	1	104	7	2	.339	.280
Beer, Seth	L-R	6-3	213	9-18-96	.444	.400	.500	5	9	4	4	1	0	1	3	1	0	0	0	3	0	0	.889	.500
Cabrera, Asdrubal	B-R	6-0	235	11-13-85	.244	.290	.221	90	283	34	69	21	0	7	40	33	2	0	3	73	1	0	.392	.324
2-team total (20 Cincinnati)					.230	.257	.215	110	309	34	71	21	0	7	42	36	3	0	4	80	1	0	.366	.313
Calhoun, Kole	L-L	5-10	205	10-14-87	.235	.122	.272	51	166	17	39	8	0	5	17	15	0	0	1	41	1	0	.373	.297
Ellis, Drew	R-R	6-3	205	12-1-95	.130	.179	.098	28	69	10	9	2	0	1	5	10	4	0	0	27	0	0	.203	.277
Escobar, Eduardo	B-R	5-10	193	1-5-89	.246	.275	.237	98	370	50	91	14	3	22	65	29	0	0	1	85	1	0	.478	.300
2-team total (48 Milwaukee)					.253	.295	.238	146	549	77	139	26	5	28	90	48	1	0	1	124	1	0	.472	.314
Fairchild, Stuart	R-R	6-0	205	3-17-96	.133	.200	.000	12	15	3	2	1	0	0	2	1	1	0	0	3	0	0	.200	.235
Hager, Jake	R-R	6-1	170	3-4-93	.111	.091	.143	9	18	1	2	0	0	0	2	4	0	0	0	11	0	0	.111	.273
2-team total (5 New York)					.115	.067	.182	14	26	2	3	0	0	0	2	4	0	0	0	14	0	0	.115	.233
Heath, Nick	L-L	6-1	190	11-27-93	.143	.000	.185	20	35	3	5	1	0	0	1	4	0	0	0	15	0	2	.171	.231
Holaday, Bryan	R-R	6-0	203	11-19-87	.194	.000	.222	13	31	2	6	2	0	0	1	1	2	0	0	15	0	0	.258	.265
Kelly, Carson	R-R	6-2	212	7-14-94	.240	.313	.198	98	304	41	73	11	1	13	46	44	6	0	5	74	0	0	.411	.343
Leyba, Domingo	B-R	5-11	205	9-11-95	.000	.000	.000	13	22	0	0	0	0	0	0	2	0	0	0	7	0	0	.000	.083
Locastro, Tim	R-R	6-1	190	7-14-92	.178	.122	.208	55	118	11	21	2	1	0	5	6	9	0	0	26	5	3	.220	.271
Marte, Ketel	B-R	6-1	210	10-12-93	.318	.387	.286	90	340	52	108	29	1	14	50	31	2	0	1	60	2	0	.532	.377
Mathisen, Wyatt	R-R	6-0	217	12-30-93	.119	.105	.130	23	42	3	5	0	0	1	8	5	3	0	1	21	0	0	.190	.255
McCarthy, Jake	L-L	6-2	215	7-30-97	.220	.190	.237	24	59	11	13	3	0	2	4	8	2	1	0	23	3	2	.373	.333
Peralta, David	L-L	6-1	210	8-14-87	.259	.267	.257	150	487	57	126	30	8	8	63	46	3	0	2	92	2	1	.402	.325
Perdomo, Geraldo	B-R	6-2	203	10-22-99	.258	.375	.217	11	31	5	8	3	1	0	1	6	0	0	0	6	0	0	.419	.378
Ramos, Henry	B-R	6-1	215	4-15-92	.200	.250	.154	18	50	5	10	2	0	1	8	4	0	0	1	12	0	0	.300	.255
Reddick, Josh	L-R	6-2	197	2-19-87	.258	.184	.294	54	151	15	39	11	0	2	21	6	0	0	1	31	0	0	.371	.285
Rojas, Josh	L-R	6-1	207	6-30-94	.264	.277	.260	139	484	69	128	32	3	11	44	58	0	1	3	137	9	4	.411	.341
Smith, Pavin	L-L	6-2	208	2-6-96	.267	.239	.277	145	498	68	133	27	4	11	49	42	4	0	1	106	1	0	.404	.328
VanMeter, Josh	L-R	5-11	194	3-10-95	.212	.326	.190	112	274	26	58	17	2	6	36	33	1	0	2	83	3	2	.354	.297
Vargas, Ildemaro	B-R	6-0	180	7-16-91	.186	.150	.217	18	43	4	8	1	1	0	4	3	0	0	0	7	0	0	.256	.239
3-team total (9 Chicago, 7 Pittsburgh)					.156	.121	.182	34	77	7	12	3	1	0	7	6	0	0	0	17	1	0	.221	.217
Varsho, Daulton	L-R	5-10	207	7-2-96	.246	.293	.228	95	284	41	70	17	2	11	38	30	0	1	0	67	6	0	.437	.318
Vogt, Stephen	L-R	6-0	216	11-1-84	.212	.357	.173	52	132	17	28	6	1	5	17	18	0	1	0	36	0	0	.386	.307
2-team total (26 Atlanta)					.195	.293	.172	78	210	24	41	6	1	7	25	26	0	1	1	56	0	0	.333	.283
Walker, Christian	R-R	6-0	208	3-28-91	.244	.240	.246	115	401	55	98	23	1	10	46	38	4	0	2	106	0	0	.382	.315
Young, Andrew	R-R	6-0	200	5-10-94	.209	.279	.146	58	91	13	19	7	0	6	15	6	6	0	1	45	0	0	.484	.298

Pitching	B-T	HT	WT	DOB	W	L	ERA	G	GS	CG	SV	IP	H	R	ER	HR	BB	SO	AVG	vLH	vRH	K/9	BB/9
Aguilar, Miguel	L-L	5-8	194	9-26-91	1	1	6.43	9	0	0	0	7	6	6	5	0	4	3	.250	.154	.364	3.86	5.14
Buchter, Ryan	L-L	6-4	230	2-13-87	0	2	6.61	18	0	0	0	16	16	13	12	5	13	16	.258	.160	.324	8.82	7.16
Bukauskas, J.B.	R-R	6-0	208	10-11-96	2	2	7.79	21	0	0	0	17	24	19	15	4	7	14	.333	.414	.279	7.27	3.63
Bumgarner, Madison	R-L	6-4	257	8-1-89	7	10	4.67	26	26	1	0	146	134	82	76	24	39	124	.242	.193	.256	7.63	2.40
Cabrera, Asdrubal	B-R	6-0	235	11-13-85	0	0	0.00	2	0	0	0	1	1	0	0	0	0	0	.250	.000	.333	0.00	0.00
Castellanos, Humberto	R-R	5-11	222	4-3-98	2	2	4.93	14	7	0	0	46	48	26	25	7	15	29	.277	.256	.299	5.72	2.96
Clarke, Taylor	R-R	6-4	217	5-13-93	1	3	4.98	43	0	0	0	43	52	28	24	4	14	39	.291	.297	.286	8.10	2.91
Clippard, Tyler	R-R	6-3	200	2-14-85	1	1	3.20	26	0	0	6	25	22	12	9	3	11	21	.232	.279	.192	7.46	3.91
Crichton, Stefan	R-R	6-3	208	2-29-92	0	4	7.33	31	0	0	4	23	33	22	19	3	12	17	.333	.400	.304	6.56	4.63
de Geus, Brett	R-R	6-2	190	11-4-97	3	2	6.56	28	0	0	0	23	31	22	17	3	12	15	.326	.436	.250	5.79	4.63
Devenski, Chris	R-R	6-3	211	11-13-90	1	0	8.59	8	0	0	1	7	11	7	7	2	5	.344	.267	.412	6.14	2.45
Duplantier, Jon	L-R	6-4	229	7-11-94	0	3	13.15	4	4	0	0	13	19	19	19	5	8	12	.322	.286	.355	8.31	5.54
Faria, Jake	R-R	6-4	230	7-30-93	0	0	5.51	23	3	0	0	33	39	21	20	5	13	32	.285	.297	.274	8.82	3.58
Frankoff, Seth	R-R	6-5	206	8-27-88	0	2	9.20	4	3	0	0	15	20	15	15	4	9	11	.333	.333	.333	6.75	5.52
Frias, Luis	R-R	6-3	245	5-23-98	0	0	2.70	3	0	0	0	3	2	1	1	0	5	3	.200	.250	.167	8.10	13.50
Gallen, Zac	R-R	6-2	189	8-3-95	4	10	4.30	23	23	1	0	121	108	61	58	19	49	139	.233	.252	.213	10.31	3.63

Name	B-T	HT	WT	DOB			ERA													AVG	vLH	vRH		
Gilbert, Tyler	L-L	6-3	223	12-22-93	2	2	3.15	9	6	1	0	40	28	17	14	4	13	25	.200	.115	.250	5.63	2.93
Ginkel, Kevin	L-R	6-4	235	3-24-94	0	1	6.35	32	0	0	0	28	30	24	20	7	14	31	.268	.317	.239	9.85	4.45
Holaday, Bryan	R-R	6-0	203	11-19-87	0	0	9.00	1	0	0	0	1	1	1	1	1	1	0	.333	.000	.500	0.00	9.00
Kelly, Merrill	R-R	6-2	202	10-14-88	7	11	4.44	27	27	0	0	158	163	82	78	21	41	130	.266	.235	.296	7.41	2.34
Lopez, Yoan	R-R	6-3	208	1-2-93	0	0	6.57	13	0	0	0	12	18	10	9	3	6	13	.333	.227	.406	9.49	4.38
Mantiply, Joe	R-L	6-4	219	3-1-91	0	3	3.40	57	0	0	0	40	45	24	15	1	17	38	.292	.261	.318	8.62	3.86
Martin, Corbin	R-R	6-2	225	12-28-95	0	3	10.69	5	3	0	0	16	23	19	19	5	14	13	.338	.258	.405	7.31	7.88
Mathisen, Wyatt	R-R	6-0	217	12-30-93	0	0	0.00	1	0	0	0	1	1	0	0	0	0	0	.250	.000	.500	0.00	0.00
Mejia, Humberto	R-R	6-4	244	3-3-97	0	3	7.25	5	5	0	0	22	32	19	18	5	9	20	.340	.364	.320	8.06	3.63
Mella, Keury	R-R	6-2	234	8-2-93	0	0	32.40	2	0	0	0	2	8	6	2	2	2	2	.615	.714	.500	10.80	10.80
Peacock, Matt	R-R	6-1	185	2-27-94	5	7	4.90	35	8	0	0	86	107	55	47	13	28	50	.304	.327	.284	5.21	2.92
Peralta, David	L-L	6-1	210	8-14-87	0	0	27.00	1	0	0	0	1	4	3	3	1	0	1	.500	.500	.500	9.00	0.00
Poppen, Sean	R-R	6-3	210	3-15-94	1	1	4.67	20	0	0	1	17	20	11	9	1	7	21	.274	.355	.214	10.90	3.63
2-team total (3 Pittsburgh)					1	1	5.32	23	0	0	1	22	31	18	13	2	9	25	.323	.400	.268	10.23	3.68
Ramirez, Noe	R-R	6-3	205	12-22-89	0	2	2.76	36	0	0	1	33	18	12	10	2	11	29	.157	.160	.154	7.99	3.03
Reddick, Josh	L-R	6-2	197	2-19-87	0	0	13.50	1	0	0	0	1	2	1	1	1	1	0	.500	.000	.667	0.00	13.50
Sittinger, Brandyn	R-R	6-1	200	6-6-94	0	1	7.71	5	0	0	0	5	5	4	4	3	2	1	.294	.200	.333	1.93	3.86
Smith, Caleb	R-L	6-0	207	7-28-91	4	9	4.83	45	13	0	0	114	93	64	61	20	63	124	.217	.250	.203	9.82	4.99
Smith, Riley	R-R	6-1	207	1-15-95	1	4	6.01	24	6	0	1	67	86	46	45	10	15	36	.308	.280	.326	4.81	2.00
Soria, Joakim	R-R	6-3	205	5-18-84	1	4	4.30	31	0	0	6	29	31	14	14	4	8	31	.270	.262	.274	9.51	2.45
Swarzak, Anthony	R-R	6-4	215	9-10-85	0	1	9.64	6	0	0	0	5	7	5	5	1	1	4	.350	.500	.286	7.71	1.93
Weaver, Luke	R-R	6-2	183	8-21-93	3	6	4.25	13	13	0	0	66	58	34	31	11	20	62	.233	.245	.224	8.50	2.74
Weems, Jordan	L-R	6-3	175	11-7-92	0	1	47.25	2	0	0	0	1	4	7	7	1	3	3	.500	.600	.333	10.25	20.25
Wendelken, J.B.	R-R	6-1	242	3-24-93	2	2	4.34	20	0	0	2	19	15	9	9	2	9	13	.221	.200	.237	6.27	4.34
Widener, Taylor	L-R	6-0	203	10-24-94	2	1	4.35	23	13	0	0	70	65	38	34	14	37	73	.241	.256	.226	9.34	4.73
Young, Alex	L-L	6-3	220	9-9-93	2	6	6.26	30	2	0	0	42	50	34	29	11	20	38	.298	.262	.318	8.21	4.32

Fielding

Catcher	PCT	G	PO	A	E	DP	PB
Holaday	.987	10	76	2	1	0	0
Kelly	.992	91	617	29	5	3	8
Varsho	.990	41	284	13	3	2	4
Vogt	.993	40	276	17	2	1	3

First Base	PCT	G	PO	A	E	DP
Beer	1.000	1	1	0	0	0
Cabrera	1.000	16	86	6	0	10
Mathisen	1.000	13	56	9	0	3
Smith	.994	54	297	31	2	25
VanMeter	1.000	1	9	0	0	0
Vogt	1.000	2	3	0	0	0
Walker	.993	107	744	66	6	64

Second Base	PCT	G	PO	A	E	DP
Ellis	1.000	4	3	5	0	2
Escobar	.992	42	53	70	1	15
Hager	1.000	5	7	9	0	2
Leyba	1.000	7	5	9	0	1
Marte	.958	20	31	37	3	12

	PCT	G	PO	A	E	DP
Rojas	.976	55	71	93	4	18
VanMeter	.976	52	65	96	4	21
Vargas	1.000	5	10	9	0	3
Young	.969	21	33	30	2	6

Third Base	PCT	G	PO	A	E	DP
Cabrera	.939	62	29	94	8	11
Ellis	1.000	17	10	17	0	2
Escobar	.946	65	31	109	8	9
Leyba	.000	1	0	0	0	0
Mathisen	.000	4	0	0	0	0
Rojas	.905	14	4	15	2	4
VanMeter	.885	25	16	38	7	5
Vargas	.929	7	2	11	1	0
Young	.000	2	0	0	1	0

Shortstop	PCT	G	PO	A	E	DP
Ahmed	.981	127	170	302	9	59
Cabrera	.000	1	0	0	0	0
Escobar	.000	1	0	0	0	0
Hager	1.000	2	1	2	0	0

	PCT	G	PO	A	E	DP
Perdomo	.976	10	14	26	1	4
Rojas	.939	42	34	74	7	13
Vargas	1.000	3	4	2	0	1

Outfield	PCT	G	PO	A	E	DP
Calhoun	.972	39	67	2	2	0
Fairchild	1.000	8	7	0	0	0
Heath	1.000	18	21	0	0	0
Locastro	1.000	42	76	1	0	0
Marte	.987	71	155	1	2	0
Mathisen	1.000	2	2	0	0	0
McCarthy	1.000	20	46	3	0	2
Peralta	.989	137	277	2	3	0
Ramos	.933	13	28	0	2	0
Reddick	.986	41	69	2	1	0
Rojas	.974	55	74	1	2	0
Smith	.990	114	192	1	2	0
VanMeter	1.000	2	2	0	0	0
Varsho	.990	54	99	2	1	0
Young	.500	1	1	0	1	0

RENO ACES

TRIPLE-A WEST

TRIPLE-A

Batting	B-T	HT	WT	DOB	AVG	vLH	vRH	G	AB	R	H	2B	3B	HR	RBI	BB	HBP	SH	SF	SO	SB	CS	SLG	OBP
Beer, Seth	L-R	6-3	213	9-18-96	.287	.278	.291	100	362	73	104	33	0	16	59	39	30	0	4	76	0	0	.511	.398
Calhoun, Kole	L-L	5-10	205	10-14-87	.500	.500	.500	2	4	3	2	0	0	2	3	0	1	0	0	0	0	0	2.000	.600
Cintron, Jancarlos	R-R	5-8	170	12-1-94	.217	.250	.211	15	46	6	10	0	0	0	2	4	0	1	0	7	2	0	.217	.280
De La Cruz, Michael	L-R	5-10	190	5-15-93	.256	.364	.219	23	43	7	11	3	0	3	6	5	0	0	0	14	0	0	.535	.333
DeLuzio, Ben	R-R	6-3	200	8-9-94	.271	.325	.252	48	155	26	42	10	5	3	18	13	1	0	1	40	6	3	.458	.329
Duzenack, Camden	R-R	5-9	170	3-8-95	.287	.256	.298	48	143	33	41	8	1	8	25	7	2	0	2	43	1	0	.524	.325
Ellis, Drew	R-R	6-3	205	12-1-95	.294	.278	.300	81	296	69	87	29	3	20	73	46	10	0	6	87	1	0	.615	.399
Fairchild, Stuart	R-R	6-0	205	3-17-96	.295	.257	.306	44	156	27	46	7	4	9	28	22	2	0	2	39	7	1	.564	.385
Garrett, Stone	R-R	6-2	195	11-22-95	.000	--	.000	2	5	0	0	0	0	0	0	1	0	0	1	0	0	0	.000	.167
Hager, Jake	R-R	6-1	170	3-4-93	.220	.316	.198	28	100	14	22	7	0	4	16	6	11	0	2	34	2	0	.410	.292
2-team total (27 Tacoma)					.220	.220	.220	55	200	30	44	14	0	10	27	22	1	0	2	59	6	0	.440	.298
Heath, Nick	L-L	6-1	190	11-27-93	.250	.289	.238	60	196	36	49	9	5	5	28	25	4	0	4	77	19	5	.423	.341
Herrera, Jose	B-R	5-10	217	2-24-97	.244	.227	.250	58	180	23	44	7	1	6	32	32	0	0	0	42	1	0	.394	.358
Holaday, Bryan	R-R	6-0	203	11-19-87	.263	.273	.260	30	95	20	25	9	0	7	30	9	0	0	4	19	1	0	.579	.315
Hummel, Cooper	B-R	5-10	198	11-28-94	.353	.351	.354	46	167	43	59	13	3	6	37	22	4	0	5	35	4	1	.575	.429
Jones, Ryder	L-R	6-2	221	6-7-94	.160	.000	.190	10	25	1	4	2	0	1	3	1	0	0	0	9	0	0	.360	.192
Leyba, Domingo	B-R	5-11	205	9-11-95	.457	.273	.542	8	35	9	16	2	1	4	14	2	0	0	0	4	0	0	.914	.486
2-team total (24 Round Rock)					.331	.324	.333	32	139	21	46	9	3	8	40	4	0	0	1	21	1	1	.612	.347
Lipka, Matt	R-R	6-1	215	4-15-92	.333	.381	.321	29	105	23	35	8	2	2	22	10	1	1	1	32	6	4	.505	.393
Lopes, Christian	R-R	6-0	211	10-1-92	.271	.431	.195	66	181	35	49	12	1	9	34	29	6	0	3	61	4	1	.497	.384
Marte, Ketel	B-R	6-1	210	10-12-93	.154	.000	.167	4	13	2	2	0	0	0	2	1	0	0	0	5	0	0	.154	.214

Name	B-T	HT	WT	DOB	AVG	vLH	vRH	G	AB	R	H	2B	3B	HR	RBI	BB	HBP	SH	SF	SO	SB	CS	SLG	OBP
Martinez, Renae	R-R	6-1	185	4-15-94	.282	.429	.250	16	39	7	11	2	1	1	8	5	1	0	0	13	1	0	.462	.378
McCarthy, Jake	L-L	6-2	215	7-30-97	.262	.278	.255	50	191	38	50	6	7	9	31	20	0	0	1	49	12	3	.508	.330
Perdomo, Geraldo	B-R	6-2	203	10-22-99	.417	.000	.500	3	12	1	5	0	0	0	3	2	0	0	0	1	0	1	.417	.500
Querecuto, Juniel	B-R	5-9	195	9-19-92	.301	.333	.293	96	362	59	109	15	7	13	79	31	0	0	3	62	9	2	.489	.354
Ramos, Henry	B-R	6-2	215	4-15-92	.371	.437	.346	75	256	62	95	16	1	12	57	29	5	0	4	48	4	5	.582	.439
Reddick, Josh	L-R	6-2	197	2-19-87	.304	.286	.308	11	46	9	14	2	0	2	8	5	0	0	1	7	0	0	.478	.365
Ritchie, Jamie	R-R	6-2	203	4-9-93	.317	.367	.304	79	284	70	90	18	1	4	43	43	7	0	2	52	0	1	.430	.417
Rojas, Josh	L-R	6-1	207	6-30-94	.300	.400	.200	3	10	4	3	0	0	3	6	3	0	0	1	4	1	1	1.200	.429
Thomas, Alek	L-L	5-11	175	4-28-00	.369	.333	.382	34	149	32	55	11	4	8	18	15	2	0	0	34	5	4	.658	.434
Thompson, Trayce	R-R	6-3	225	3-15-91	.278	.333	.250	4	18	2	5	1	0	0	2	0	0	0	0	4	0	0	.333	.350
VanMeter, Josh	L-R	5-11	194	3-10-95	.388	.421	.375	19	67	23	26	6	0	9	20	23	0	0	1	21	1	0	.881	.538
Vargas, Ildemaro	B-R	6-0	180	7-16-91	.313	.315	.313	57	249	50	78	21	0	10	39	16	0	0	3	27	3	1	.518	.351
Varsho, Daulton	L-R	5-10	207	7-2-96	.313	.409	.276	18	80	18	25	6	1	9	25	7	0	0	0	16	2	0	.750	.368
Walker, Christian	R-R	6-0	208	3-28-91	.235	.250	.231	4	17	3	4	0	0	2	4	1	0	0	0	6	0	0	.588	.278
Young, Andrew	R-R	6-0	200	5-10-94	.304	.302	.305	48	194	43	59	20	2	11	41	20	8	0	2	78	2	0	.598	.388

Pitching	B-T	HT	WT	DOB	W	L	ERA	G	GS	CG	SV	IP	H	R	ER	HR	BB	SO	AVG	vLH	vRH	K/9	BB/9
Aguilar, Miguel	L-L	5-8	194	9-26-91	4	4	5.09	43	0	0	16	41	48	28	23	7	16	45	.291	.236	.333	9.96	3.54
Arredondo, Edgar	R-R	6-3	230	5-16-97	1	3	4.55	14	9	0	0	30	30	16	15	3	13	11	.268	.327	.217	3.34	3.94
Bain, Jeff	R-R	6-4	200	3-3-96	0	1	7.88	4	2	0	0	8	11	7	7	2	1	9	.306	.273	.320	10.13	1.13
Buchter, Ryan	L-L	6-4	230	2-13-87	0	0	3.38	16	0	0	6	16	13	6	6	1	7	20	.217	.185	.242	11.25	3.94
Bukauskas, J.B.	R-R	6-0	208	10-11-96	0	2	4.26	13	0	0	1	13	9	6	6	1	4	16	.196	.174	.217	11.37	2.84
Carle, Shane	R-R	6-4	210	8-30-91	0	0	10.80	6	0	0	0	7	10	8	8	5	5	4	.370	.500	.267	5.40	6.75
2-team total (2 Tacoma)					1	0	8.31	8	0	0	0	9	11	8	8	5	5	4	.333	.500	.211	4.15	5.19
Castellanos, Humberto	R-R	5-11	222	4-3-98	6	1	4.99	12	12	1	0	58	56	32	32	14	14	59	.247	.205	.291	9.21	2.18
Castillo, Luis	R-R	6-3	212	3-10-95	2	3	6.63	17	0	0	1	19	29	17	14	3	11	14	.377	.344	.400	6.63	5.21
Clarke, Taylor	R-R	6-4	217	5-13-93	1	0	0.00	7	0	0	0	7	6	2	0	0	2	8	.250	.300	.214	10.29	2.57
Clippard, Tyler	R-R	6-3	200	2-14-85	0	0	0.00	2	0	0	0	2	1	2	0	1	0	5	.125	.200	.000	22.50	0.00
Crichton, Stefan	R-R	6-3	208	2-29-92	3	0	9.00	11	0	0	0	12	17	12	12	0	7	9	.321	.440	.214	6.75	5.25
Curtis, Keegan	R-R	6-0	175	9-30-95	1	2	7.04	9	0	0	1	8	12	8	6	1	5	5	.375	.333	.400	5.87	5.87
Donatella, Justin	R-R	6-6	236	9-16-94	0	3	8.80	5	4	0	0	15	24	16	15	5	8	13	.348	.326	.385	7.63	4.70
Duplantier, Jon	L-R	6-4	229	7-11-94	1	0	7.71	3	2	0	0	7	9	6	6	1	5	4	.310	.176	.500	5.14	6.43
Frankoff, Seth	R-R	6-5	206	8-27-88	2	0	8.14	8	3	0	0	21	26	20	19	8	14	25	.310	.383	.216	10.71	6.00
Frias, Luis	R-R	6-3	245	5-23-98	2	1	5.82	5	5	0	0	22	21	14	14	1	16	20	.256	.300	.188	8.31	6.65
Gage, Matt	R-L	6-4	240	2-11-93	2	1	5.57	36	0	0	2	32	37	22	20	7	12	40	.276	.234	.314	11.13	3.34
Gann, Cameron	R-R	6-0	203	10-8-92	2	1	8.75	20	0	0	0	24	27	24	23	6	20	23	.290	.280	.302	8.75	7.61
Garcia, Junior	L-L	5-11	220	10-1-95	1	2	3.94	29	0	0	1	32	38	18	14	4	17	31	.288	.234	.338	8.72	4.78
Gardewine, Nick	R-R	6-1	179	8-15-93	0	0	7.71	5	0	0	0	5	5	4	4	1	5	7	.263	.182	.375	13.50	9.64
Gilbert, Tyler	L-L	6-3	223	12-22-93	5	2	3.44	11	10	0	0	52	46	22	20	4	19	50	.234	.282	.206	8.60	3.27
Ginkel, Kevin	L-R	6-4	235	3-24-94	0	0	9.00	1	0	0	1	1	2	1	1	0	1	0	.500	--	.500	0.00	9.00
Green, Josh	R-R	6-3	211	8-31-95	8	4	7.34	26	15	0	0	99	149	82	81	21	30	62	.353	.351	.355	5.62	2.72
Hernandez, Kenny	L-L	6-1	197	6-24-98	0	0	11.25	1	1	0	0	4	7	5	5	1	0	4	.389	.500	.375	9.00	0.00
Holton, Tyler	L-L	6-2	200	6-13-96	0	1	7.88	8	4	0	0	16	27	14	14	1	6	22	.365	.556	.255	12.38	3.38
Lee, Zach	R-R	6-3	195	9-13-91	3	4	6.86	17	13	0	0	62	81	57	47	13	27	44	.310	.303	.319	6.42	3.94
Lemieux, Mack	L-L	6-3	205	9-6-96	1	0	2.84	4	0	0	0	6	4	3	2	0	3	5	.174	.300	.077	7.11	4.26
Liranzo, Jesus	R-R	6-2	225	3-7-95	0	0	3.06	16	0	0	2	18	15	6	6	3	3	22	.224	.208	.233	11.21	1.53
Lopez, Yoan	R-R	6-2	208	1-2-93	0	0	6.00	3	0	0	1	3	1	2	2	1	4	5	.100	.333	.000	15.00	12.00
Lucas, Josh	R-R	6-6	185	11-5-90	0	2	21.94	5	0	0	0	5	10	13	13	2	6	3	.385	.429	.333	5.06	10.13
Mantiply, Joe	R-L	6-4	219	3-1-91	0	1	1.93	5	0	0	0	5	4	2	1	1	0	10	.222	.125	.300	19.29	0.00
Martin, Corbin	R-R	6-2	225	12-28-95	2	0	5.93	6	6	0	0	27	31	21	18	7	19	30	.279	.284	.273	9.88	6.26
McCanna, Kevin	L-R	6-1	185	2-1-94	0	1	2.87	6	4	0	0	16	11	5	5	3	2	12	.220	.214	.226	6.89	1.15
Mejia, Humberto	R-R	6-4	244	3-3-97	7	5	5.53	15	15	0	0	72	83	46	44	10	27	63	.291	.300	.283	7.91	3.39
Mella, Keury	R-R	6-2	234	8-2-93	1	0	4.34	20	0	0	0	29	30	17	14	5	9	29	.256	.297	.208	9.00	2.79
Moll, Sam	L-L	5-9	190	1-3-92	0	0	5.82	21	0	0	2	22	19	17	14	3	15	30	.226	.116	.341	12.46	6.23
2-team total (12 Las Vegas)					1	1	4.58	33	0	0	2	35	31	21	18	5	20	47	.231	.114	.359	11.97	5.09
Navas, Carlos	R-R	6-0	215	8-13-92	1	0	8.51	21	2	0	0	24	34	24	23	6	14	20	.327	.361	.279	7.40	5.18
Osnowitz, Mitchell	R-R	6-5	245	7-2-91	0	0	37.13	4	0	0	0	3	8	11	11	3	6	4	.533	.429	.625	13.50	20.25
Peacock, Matt	R-R	6-1	185	2-27-94	1	1	13.50	5	0	0	1	4	7	6	6	2	3	5	.368	.125	.545	6.75	0.00
Pimentel, Chester	R-R	6-5	210	11-12-95	0	0	6.23	26	0	0	0	30	36	23	21	7	17	33	.279	.266	.292	9.79	5.04
Poppen, Sean	R-R	6-3	210	3-15-94	0	0	3.86	3	0	0	0	2	3	1	1	0	1	3	.300	.400	.400	11.57	3.86
Powers, Alex	R-R	6-4	205	2-26-92	2	2	5.29	13	0	0	0	17	14	11	10	4	5	15	.222	.200	.261	7.94	2.65
2-team total (22 El Paso)					2	2	5.40	35	3	0	0	48	47	32	29	8	21	61	.249	.225	.270	11.36	3.91
Ramirez, Noe	R-R	6-3	205	12-22-89	2	0	8.00	8	0	0	0	9	8	8	8	3	5	12	.242	.300	.154	12.00	5.00
2-team total (1 Salt Lake)					2	0	6.97	9	0	0	0	10	8	8	8	5	5	14	.216	.273	.133	12.19	4.35
Rhoades, Jeremy	R-R	6-4	250	2-12-93	1	0	8.44	18	0	0	0	21	23	21	20	9	5	27	.258	.308	.189	11.39	2.11
Sittinger, Brandyn	R-R	6-1	200	6-6-94	1	1	4.24	23	0	0	4	23	18	11	11	2	14	32	.209	.256	.170	12.34	5.40
Smith, Riley	R-R	6-1	207	1-15-95	0	0	7.94	4	4	0	0	17	22	15	15	4	4	13	.301	.333	.279	6.88	2.12
Stumpo, Mitchell	R-R	6-2	205	6-17-96	0	1	1.50	6	0	0	0	6	3	1	1	0	1	4	.167	.200	.154	6.00	1.50
Tabor, Matt	R-R	6-2	180	7-14-98	1	4	11.13	8	8	0	0	32	44	41	40	14	15	26	.336	.367	.310	7.24	4.18
Tice, Ty	R-R	5-9	185	7-4-96	0	1	12.10	11	0	0	0	10	12	13	13	3	7	11	.316	.313	.318	10.24	6.52
Tunnell, West	L-R	6-1	195	11-20-93	0	0	5.79	10	0	0	0	11	8	6	6	0	8	8	.282	.286	.273	8.68	8.68
Vernia, Justin	R-R	6-2	205	9-22-95	0	2	18.90	2	2	0	0	3	11	8	7	2	3	3	.500	.800	.412	8.10	8.10
Weaver, Luke	R-R	6-2	183	8-21-93	0	0	3.86	2	2	0	0	7	6	3	3	0	4	12	.231	.091	.333	15.43	5.14
Weems, Jordan	R-R	6-3	175	11-7-92	1	1	7.24	15	0	0	0	14	15	11	11	3	8	9	.294	.269	.320	5.93	5.27
2-team total (15 Las Vegas)					1	3	7.31	30	0	0	1	28	32	23	23	9	14	26	.294	.246	.346	8.26	4.45

	B-T	HT	WT	DOB	W	L	ERA	G	GS	CG	SV	IP	H	R	ER	HR	BB	SO	AVG	vLH	vRH	K/9	BB/9
Weiss, Ryan	R-R	6-4	210	12-10-96	4	1	5.04	21	0	0	0	30	32	19	17	2	15	38	.271	.296	.250	11.27	4.45
Widener, Taylor	L-R	6-0	203	10-24-94	0	0	3.86	1	1	0	0	5	3	2	2	1	6		.176	.200	.143	11.57	1.93
Yoshikawa, Shumpei	R-R	6-2	175	1-24-95	0	0	0.00	1	0	0	0	0	0	0	0	0	1	0	.000	.000	--	0.00	27.00
Young, Alex	L-L	6-3	220	9-9-93	1	0	4.50	2	0	0		4	5	2	2	0	0	5	.313	.444	.143	11.25	0.00

Fielding

Catcher	PCT	G	PO	A	E	DP	PB
De La Cruz	.981	7	52	0	1	0	0
Herrera	.995	45	346	20	2	2	2
Holaday	.989	21	160	13	2	1	4
Hummel	1.000	5	27	0	0	0	0
Martinez	1.000	7	58	2	0	0	1
Ritchie	.991	33	313	23	3	2	4
Varsho	.990	11	93	7	1	0	3

First Base	PCT	G	PO	A	E	DP
Beer	.990	91	685	38	7	79
Ellis	1.000	6	26	4	0	2
Garrett	1.000	1	6	0	0	0
Hager	1.000	1	8	2	0	0
Holaday	.929	2	10	3	1	1
Hummel	.900	2	9	0	1	0
Jones	1.000	1	1	0	0	0
Lopes	1.000	4	38	0	0	8
McCarthy	.975	6	37	2	1	2
Querecuto	.969	8	60	3	2	11
Ritchie	1.000	1	8	1	0	4
Vargas	1.000	2	12	0	0	0
Walker	1.000	4	24	2	0	0
Young	1.000	1	6	0	0	1

Second Base	PCT	G	PO	A	E	DP
Cintron	1.000	4	3	3	0	0
Duzenack	1.000	14	26	37	0	11

	PCT	G	PO	A	E	DP
Ellis	.960	5	10	14	1	4
Hager	1.000	2	0	2	0	0
Leyba	1.000	1	1	9	0	0
Lopes	.971	19	29	38	2	8
Querecuto	.981	24	42	64	2	18
Rojas	.000	1	0	0	0	0
VanMeter	.952	8	9	31	2	2
Vargas	.967	22	44	73	4	26
Young	.973	29	44	63	3	13

Third Base	PCT	G	PO	A	E	DP
De La Cruz	.500	1	0	3	3	0
Duzenack	1.000	5	3	5	0	0
Ellis	.969	70	48	106	5	11
Hager	.500	1	0	1	0	0
Holaday	.000	1	0	1	0	0
Hummel	.824	6	2	12	3	4
Jones	1.000	1	0	2	0	1
Lopes	.933	11	7	7	1	2
Querecuto	.970	14	12	20	1	4
VanMeter	1.000	5	6	7	0	0
Vargas	1.000	10	3	21	0	0
Young	1.000	9	3	19	0	2

Shortstop	PCT	G	PO	A	E	DP
Cintron	.975	9	16	23	1	6
Duzenack	.936	14	17	27	3	6
Hager	.980	24	25	75	2	18

	PCT	G	PO	A	E	DP
Leyba	1.000	7	6	21	0	2
Perdomo	.923	3	2	10	1	1
Querecuto	.934	45	55	114	12	23
Rojas	1.000	1	1	5	0	2
Vargas	.932	22	26	56	6	18

Outfield	PCT	G	PO	A	E	DP
Calhoun	1.000	2	4	0	0	0
DeLuzio	.978	40	87	1	2	0
Duzenack	1.000	10	12	1	0	0
Fairchild	.970	39	63	2	2	1
Heath	1.000	53	116	0	0	0
Hummel	.984	28	60	0	1	0
Jones	1.000	5	2	0	0	0
Lipka	1.000	30	62	0	0	0
Lopes	.963	10	26	0	1	0
Marte	1.000	4	9	0	0	0
McCarthy	.964	40	78	2	3	0
Querecuto	--	1	0	0	0	0
Ramos	.990	56	96	5	1	1
Reddick	1.000	11	16	0	0	0
Ritchie	1.000	16	30	0	0	0
Thomas	.988	33	78	4	1	1
Thompson	1.000	2	5	1	0	0
VanMeter	1.000	5	9	1	0	1
Varsho	.895	7	17	0	2	0
Young	1.000	7	18	0	0	0

AMARILLO SOD POODLES

DOUBLE-A

DOUBLE-A CENTRAL

Batting	B-T	HT	WT	DOB	AVG	vLH	vRH	G	AB	R	H	2B	3B	HR	RBI	BB	HBP	SH	SF	SO	SB	CS	SLG	OBP
Abreu, Osvaldo	R-R	6-0	195	6-13-94	.180	.286	.131	31	89	10	16	4	0	1	8	11	1	0	0	35	1	3	.258	.277
Alejandro Basabe, Luis	B-R	5-10	160	8-26-96	.226	.157	.249	83	283	43	64	14	2	10	32	29	1	0	1	107	7	5	.396	.299
Burt, D.J.	R-R	5-9	160	10-13-95	.200	.111	.231	11	35	3	7	1	0	0	4	4	0	0	0	12	2	1	.229	.282
2-team total (54 Wichita)					.298	.277	.307	65	215	37	64	12	1	3	20	29	0	1	2	58	21	7	.405	.378
Canzone, Dominic	L-R	6-1	190	8-16-97	.354	.483	.317	35	130	25	46	8	1	7	27	15	1	0	0	28	1	1	.592	.425
Cintron, Jancarlos	R-R	5-8	170	12-1-94	.243	.145	.278	72	263	37	64	10	0	8	32	16	2	2	1	48	10	2	.373	.291
Curpa, Jose	R-R	5-9	160	3-9-00	.273	--	.273	4	11	1	3	2	0	0	2	1	0	0	0	3	0	0	.455	.333
De La Cruz, Michael	L-R	5-10	190	5-15-93	.300	.500	.222	14	50	12	15	3	1	2	10	8	0	0	1	17	0	0	.520	.390
DeLuzio, Ben	R-R	6-3	200	8-9-94	.302	.409	.266	20	86	22	26	6	2	0	7	4	5	0	0	23	10	2	.419	.368
Diaz, Eduardo	R-R	6-2	175	7-19-97	.316	.240	.342	26	98	20	31	6	2	7	22	7	5	0	1	27	2	1	.633	.387
Duzenack, Camden	R-R	5-9	170	3-8-95	.192	.200	.190	21	78	5	15	5	0	1	8	4	1	0	0	27	3	0	.295	.241
Fletcher, Dominic	L-L	5-9	185	9-2-97	.264	.271	.261	102	402	60	106	18	5	15	56	25	7	0	6	109	3	3	.445	.314
Garrett, Stone	R-R	6-2	195	11-22-95	.280	.291	.277	103	407	65	114	19	1	25	81	20	4	0	4	118	17	5	.516	.317
Girand, Jonah	R-R	6-1	175	5-3-95	.167	.000	.214	6	18	1	3	0	0	0	0	4	0	0	0	8	0	0	.167	.318
Herrera, Jose	B-R	5-10	217	2-24-97	.278	.226	.295	36	126	22	35	4	2	5	25	19	1	0	2	39	3	1	.460	.372
Holmes, Tra	R-R	6-0	175	7-10-96	.250	.000	.375	5	12	1	3	0	0	0	1	2	0	0	0	6	1	1	.250	.357
Jones, Ryder	L-R	6-2	221	6-7-94	.301	.219	.333	61	226	31	68	18	1	10	38	15	6	0	6	51	2	1	.522	.352
Kennedy, Buddy	R-R	6-1	190	10-5-98	.278	.311	.267	66	237	46	66	6	2	17	40	39	2	0	1	73	7	2	.536	.384
Lin, Lyle	R-R	6-1	190	6-26-97	.226	.100	.286	10	31	6	7	2	0	1	6	1	1	0	0	6	0	0	.387	.273
Lipka, Matt	R-R	6-1	215	4-15-92	.071	.000	.091	4	14	0	1	0	0	0	0	2	1	0	0	6	1	0	.071	.133
Martinez, Renae	R-R	6-1	185	4-15-94	.178	.269	.147	28	101	12	18	7	0	5	12	14	1	0	0	37	1	0	.396	.284
McCarthy, Jake	L-L	6-2	215	7-30-97	.241	.314	.216	35	137	25	33	8	4	6	23	17	2	0	0	46	17	1	.489	.333
Miroglio, Dominic	R-R	6-0	205	3-10-95	.247	.241	.249	87	296	36	73	15	3	11	37	37	5	0	4	81	2	3	.429	.336
Pantoja, Alexis	L-R	5-11	186	1-18-96	.250	.400	.000	2	8	1	2	0	0	0	0	0	0	0	0	2	0	0	.250	.250
Perdomo, Geraldo	B-R	6-2	203	10-22-99	.231	.224	.233	82	286	51	66	8	5	6	32	47	7	2	2	81	8	5	.357	.351
Rei, Austin	R-R	6-0	185	10-27-93	.111	.000	.154	7	18	2	2	0	0	0	0	1	0	0	0	10	1	0	.111	.200
Reynolds, Mikey	R-R	5-9	170	8-19-90	.186	.250	.165	42	145	17	27	8	1	5	21	19	3	0	1	39	5	10	.359	.247
Rindfleisch, Jarett	R-R	6-1	225	9-4-95	.182	.235	.158	18	55	6	10	0	0	3	10	6	4	0	0	22	0	0	.345	.308
Thomas, Alek	L-L	5-11	175	4-28-00	.283	.377	.249	72	286	54	81	18	8	10	41	37	5	0	1	65	8	5	.507	.374
Yerzy, Andy	L-R	6-3	215	7-5-98	.194	.200	.193	21	72	11	14	1	1	5	13	13	0	0	0	30	0	1	.417	.326

Pitching	B-T	HT	WT	DOB	W	L	ERA	G	GS	CG	SV	IP	H	R	ER	HR	BB	SO	AVG	vLH	vRH	K/9	BB/9
Agrazal, Dario	R-R	6-2	225	12-28-94	0	0	27.00	1	0	0	0	1	4	3	3	1	0	1	.500	.333	.600	9.00	0.00
Arredondo, Edgar	R-R	6-3	230	5-16-97	4	1	3.27	14	0	0	3	22	15	8	8	4	11	31	.195	.167	.208	12.68	4.50
Bain, Jeff	R-R	6-4	200	3-3-96	3	3	4.97	24	4	0	1	54	64	33	30	6	20	51	.292	.354	.266	8.45	3.31
Brill, Matt	R-R	6-2	190	10-25-94	2	4	6.33	27	0	0	4	27	29	19	19	2	20	37	.269	.269	.268	12.33	6.67

Name	B-T	HT	WT	DOB	W	L	ERA	G	GS	CG	SV	IP	H	R	ER	HR	BB	SO	AVG	vLH	vRH	SO/9	BB/9
Castillo, Luis	R-R	6-3	212	3-10-95	1	1	2.35	12	0	0	1	15	17	5	4	1	8	21	.279	.263	.286	12.33	4.70
Curtis, Keegan	R-R	6-0	175	9-30-95	1	1	0.00	4	0	0	1	4	2	3	0	0	0	3	.154	.000	.182	7.36	0.00
Frias, Luis	R-R	6-3	245	5-23-98	5	6	5.26	16	16	1	0	79	69	52	46	16	25	91	.228	.287	.195	10.41	2.86
Gage, Matt	R-L	6-4	240	2-11-93	2	0	0.68	7	0	0	1	13	9	2	1	1	1	18	.191	.333	.103	12.15	0.68
Garcia, Junior	L-L	5-11	220	10-1-95	0	0	0.00	4	0	0	4	4	3	0	0	0	1	7	.200	.000	.231	14.54	2.08
Henry, Tommy	L-L	6-3	205	7-29-97	4	6	5.21	23	23	0	0	116	116	71	67	24	53	135	.268	.202	.287	10.50	4.12
Hernandez, Kenny	L-L	6-1	197	6-24-98	2	2	5.56	13	10	0	1	57	73	45	35	10	16	35	.312	.321	.309	5.56	2.54
Holton, Tyler	L-L	6-2	200	6-13-96	4	3	6.33	18	7	0	1	48	55	36	34	6	13	56	.282	.316	.268	10.43	2.42
Hull, Denson	B-L	6-1	220	10-21-96	0	0	5.14	4	0	0	1	7	6	4	4	1	1	5	.240	.222	.250	6.43	1.29
Jameson, Drey	R-R	6-0	165	8-17-97	3	2	4.08	8	8	0	0	46	38	22	21	6	18	68	.225	.323	.163	13.21	3.50
Jarvis, Bryce	L-R	6-2	195	12-26-97	1	2	5.66	8	8	0	0	35	32	22	22	8	17	40	.242	.132	.287	10.29	4.37
Jones, Joe	R-R	6-5	245	7-22-95	0	0	9.31	10	0	0	1	10	13	12	10	4	9	10	.295	.429	.233	9.31	8.38
Jones, Tyler	R-R	6-3	200	12-7-95	0	0	7.20	11	0	0	0	15	24	15	12	4	3	18	.364	.200	.412	10.80	1.80
Kelly, Levi	R-R	6-4	205	5-14-99	2	0	5.40	15	0	0	0	25	16	15	15	3	28	27	.195	.276	.151	9.72	10.08
Lemieux, Mack	L-L	6-3	205	9-6-96	4	2	3.43	32	0	0	2	39	36	16	15	1	25	53	.242	.106	.304	12.13	5.72
Lewis, Justin	R-R	6-7	205	8-10-95	2	1	9.53	24	0	0	0	34	37	38	36	9	19	42	.278	.140	.361	11.12	5.03
Mejia, Humberto	R-R	6-4	244	3-3-97	0	4	4.22	6	4	0	0	32	27	20	15	7	10	37	.223	.188	.247	10.41	2.81
Nelson, Ryne	R-R	6-3	184	2-1-98	3	3	3.51	14	14	1	0	77	66	31	30	13	26	104	.232	.206	.246	12.16	3.04
Osnowitz, Mitchell	R-R	6-5	245	7-2-91	0	1	2.16	8	0	0	0	8	5	2	2	2	5	10	.190	.222	.100	10.80	5.40
2-team total (15 Wichita)					1	2	4.68	23	0	0	0	33	32	18	17	4	27	36	.269	.236	.297	9.92	7.44
Pfaadt, Brandon	R-R	6-4	220	10-15-98	1	1	4.59	6	6	0	0	33	37	18	17	12	7	36	.276	.302	.264	9.72	1.89
Pimentel, Chester	R-R	6-5	210	11-12-95	2	0	1.71	14	0	0	1	21	14	4	4	0	9	27	.192	.167	.209	11.57	3.86
Rodriguez, Wesley	R-R	5-10	210	12-4-96	1	0	3.38	4	0	0	0	5	6	3	2	1	4	4	.273	.143	.333	6.75	6.75
Rogers, Blake	R-R	6-2	200	2-23-94	2	4	4.67	23	0	0	11	27	20	18	14	4	15	39	.213	.219	.210	13.00	5.00
Sittinger, Brandyn	R-R	6-1	200	6-6-94	0	1	3.94	12	0	0	1	16	11	7	7	2	3	21	.196	.125	.250	11.81	1.69
Stumpo, Mitchell	R-R	6-2	205	6-17-96	1	0	2.59	18	0	0	1	24	18	7	7	3	10	32	.202	.308	.159	11.84	3.70
Tabor, Matt	R-R	6-2	180	7-14-98	3	5	3.88	10	10	1	0	51	41	32	22	8	18	47	.214	.180	.229	8.29	3.18
Valdez, Bryan	L-L	6-3	180	11-27-94	0	0	0.00	2	0	0	0	3	3	0	0	0	2	0	.273	.250	.286	0.00	6.00
Vernia, Justin	R-R	6-2	205	9-22-95	1	0	6.17	7	0	0	0	12	14	8	8	4	1	11	.298	.471	.200	8.49	0.77
Weiss, Ryan	R-R	6-4	210	12-10-96	2	2	4.31	13	8	0	1	48	33	24	23	10	16	50	.192	.206	.183	9.38	3.00
Williams, Breckin	R-R	6-0	200	9-5-93	0	0	45.00	2	0	0	0	2	8	10	10	3	1	4	.533	.600	.500	18.00	4.50
Workman, Blake	R-R	6-3	195	10-8-97	3	6	7.84	20	0	0	0	31	39	29	27	10	8	43	.305	.268	.322	12.48	2.32
Yoshikawa, Shumpei	R-R	6-2	175	1-24-95	0	0	--	1	0	0	0	0	4	6	5	0	1	0	.800	1.000	.667	--	--

Fielding

Catcher	PCT	G	PO	A	E	DP	PB
Girand	1.000	1	7	1	0	0	1
Herrera	.994	32	318	22	2	2	3
Lin	1.000	3	36	2	0	0	0
Martinez	1.000	16	144	13	0	0	2
Miroglio	.998	59	609	37	1	4	5
Rei	1.000	1	6	1	0	1	0
Rindfleisch	1.000	1	2	0	0	0	0
Yerzy	.989	10	92	2	1	0	2

First Base	PCT	G	PO	A	E	DP
Abreu	1.000	1	5	1	0	0
Alejandro Basabe	.982	25	153	13	3	20
Canzone	1.000	7	43	5	0	6
De La Cruz	1.000	7	61	3	0	9
Garrett	1.000	1	7	2	0	0
Jones	.996	40	263	17	1	34
Martinez	1.000	3	19	0	0	3
McCarthy	1.000	5	29	0	0	2
Miroglio	.961	11	69	5	3	9
Pantoja	.000	1	0	0	0	0
Rindfleisch	1.000	16	99	11	0	13

Second Base	PCT	G	PO	A	E	DP
Abreu	.978	24	37	52	2	15
Alejandro Basabe	.889	16	26	30	7	10
Burt	.976	11	20	21	1	6
Cintron	.988	40	75	90	2	39
Curpa	.933	3	10	4	1	1
Duzenack	.983	12	29	29	1	11
Jones	1.000	2	3	2	0	0
Kennedy	.923	7	12	12	2	4
Pantoja	1.000	1	0	1	0	0
Reynolds	.973	12	17	19	1	4

Third Base	PCT	G	PO	A	E	DP
Abreu	.900	3	3	6	1	1
Alejandro Basabe	.868	31	8	51	9	8
Duzenack	1.000	9	2	18	0	1
Jones	.952	15	7	33	2	6
Kennedy	.911	55	28	105	13	11
Pantoja	1.000	1	0	2	0	0
Reynolds	1.000	11	6	15	0	3x

	PCT	G	PO	A	E	DP
Yerzy	.973	10	69	4	2	9

Shortstop	PCT	G	PO	A	E	DP
Abreu	.667	1	0	4	2	2
Cintron	.968	32	53	69	4	19
Perdomo	.957	82	98	188	13	50
Reynolds	.889	5	8	8	2	0

Outfield	PCT	G	PO	A	E	DP
Alejandro Basabe	.667	4	2	0	1	0
Canzone	1.000	27	51	3	0	0
Curpa	1.000	1	2	1	0	1
DeLuzio	1.000	18	36	1	0	0
Diaz	.980	26	46	4	1	1
Duzenack	--	2	0	0	0	0
Fletcher	.976	100	192	10	5	3
Garrett	.955	66	80	5	4	1
Holmes	1.000	5	6	0	0	0
Lipka	1.000	3	4	0	0	0
McCarthy	1.000	30	31	0	0	0
Reynolds	1.000	11	15	3	0	1
Thomas	1.000	73	138	2	0	0

HILLSBORO HOPS

HIGH CLASS A

HIGH-A WEST

Batting	B-T	HT	WT	DOB	AVG	vLH	vRH	G	AB	R	H	2B	3B	HR	RBI	BB	HBP	SH	SF	SO	SB	CS	SLG	OBP
Alexander, Blaze	R-R	6-0	160	6-11-99	.218	.292	.201	92	339	60	74	16	3	10	38	44	5	0	1	126	17	4	.372	.316
Andueza, Axel	R-R	6-0	163	10-27-98	.273	.429	.246	79	282	37	77	10	1	2	31	21	2	0	2	44	10	4	.337	.326
Barrosa, Jorge	B-L	5-9	165	2-17-01	.256	.243	.259	61	242	41	62	18	3	4	21	22	6	1	1	48	20	7	.405	.332
Brickhouse, Spencer	L-R	6-4	235	4-10-98	.206	.167	.211	64	218	27	45	10	1	9	23	30	3	0	3	102	8	3	.385	.307
Burt, D.J.	R-R	5-9	160	10-13-95	.000	.000	.000	3	9	1	0	0	0	0	1	2	0	0	0	6	1	0	.000	.182
Canzone, Dominic	R-L	6-1	190	8-16-97	.263	.185	.278	44	171	22	45	8	3	7	25	17	3	0	2	43	18	3	.468	.337
Carroll, Corbin	L-L	5-10	165	8-21-00	.435	.000	.476	7	23	9	10	1	2	2	5	6	0	0	0	7	3	1	.913	.552
Coursey, Cam	L-R	5-8	155	8-25-98	.256	.310	.249	74	242	39	62	10	5	2	29	31	2	0	5	43	14	6	.364	.339
Curpa, Jose	R-R	5-9	160	3-9-00	.125	.000	.143	4	8	0	1	0	0	0	1	2	0	0	0	2	0	1	.125	.300
Dalesandro, Nick	R-R	6-1	175	10-3-96	.261	.270	.259	74	222	35	58	10	1	1	28	34	2	0	2	73	33	7	.329	.362
Diaz, Eduardo	R-R	6-2	175	7-19-97	.227	.333	.203	56	216	39	49	7	1	14	36	14	2	0	2	63	11	4	.463	.278
English, Tristin	R-R	6-3	208	5-14-97	.242	.231	.244	83	302	40	73	15	0	10	48	28	11	0	7	87	7	4	.391	.322
Greene, Elijah	L-L	5-11	165	11-25-97	.167	--	.167	12	36	2	6	1	0	0	5	4	0	0	0	18	0	1	.194	.250

	B-T	HT	WT	DOB	AVG	vLH	vRH	G	AB	R	H	2B	3B	HR	RBI	BB	HBP	SH	SF	SO	SB	CS	OBP	SLG
Hampton, Reece	B-R	5-10	170	7-19-96	.193	.320	.164	44	135	24	26	6	4	4	17	21	1	2	1	55	16	1	.385	.304
Hernandez, Alexander	R-R	5-11	150	6-20-99	.135	.200	.125	10	37	2	5	2	0	1	6	1	0	0	0	15	1	0	.270	.158
Holmes, Tra	R-R	6-0	175	7-10-96	.245	.250	.244	29	94	15	23	2	1	1	9	9	1	0	0	49	10	3	.319	.317
Kelly, Carson	R-R	6-2	212	7-14-94	.200	--	.200	3	10	2	2	2	0	0	1	2	0	0	1	3	0	0	.400	.308
Kennedy, Buddy	R-R	6-1	190	10-5-98	.315	.444	.290	30	111	15	35	5	0	5	20	11	3	0	2	25	9	2	.495	.386
Martinez, Ricky	R-R	6-0	175	2-22-98	.147	.133	.150	31	95	10	14	2	1	2	12	4	5	0	1	46	10	1	.253	.219
Miranda, Elian	R-R	6-1	200	5-31-99	.175	.000	.206	15	40	5	7	0	1	0	5	10	0	0	0	10	1	4	.225	.340
Oriente, Danny	R-R	6-0	190	10-8-97	.324	.250	.333	10	34	4	11	1	1	0	3	4	1	0	0	8	0	1	.412	.410
Perez, Leodany	R-R	5-10	160	5-13-00	.214	.233	.212	79	238	23	51	6	1	0	22	28	4	0	1	72	24	4	.248	.306
Ruiz, Roman	R-R	5-11	175	1-3-01	.227	.100	.246	25	75	7	17	3	0	0	6	3	1	0	0	24	1	3	.267	.266
Simon, Ronny	B-R	5-9	150	4-17-00	.232	.111	.247	20	82	8	19	6	0	2	11	3	2	0	1	20	6	1	.378	.273
Valbuena, Luvin	R-R	5-9	165	5-7-99	.158	.000	.167	8	19	1	3	0	0	0	0	1	0	0	0	9	0	0	.158	.200
Vukovich, A.J.	R-R	6-5	210	7-20-01	.298	.357	.290	30	121	13	36	4	2	3	20	3	0	0	0	28	6	3	.438	.315
Yerzy, Andy	L-R	6-3	215	7-5-98	.229	.286	.223	61	205	29	47	9	0	14	39	31	8	0	2	68	5	0	.478	.350

Pitching	B-T	HT	WT	DOB	W	L	ERA	G	GS	CG	SV	IP	H	R	ER	HR	BB	SO	AVG	vLH	vRH	K/9	BB/9
Arroyo, Mailon	B-R	6-0	200	1-2-98	2	2	5.18	21	0	0	5	24	26	16	14	5	4	25	.271	.229	.295	9.25	1.48
Ay, Bobby	R-R	6-3	190	5-28-97	0	1	3.92	13	0	0	0	21	16	10	9	1	20	20	.219	.240	.208	8.71	8.71
Backhus, Kyle	L-L	6-4	185	1-31-98	0	0	5.79	2	2	0	0	9	10	6	6	0	2	9	.263	.167	.350	8.68	1.93
Cecconi, Slade	R-R	6-4	219	6-24-99	4	2	4.12	12	12	0	0	59	53	28	27	5	20	63	.240	.256	.230	9.61	3.05
Frias, Julio	L-L	6-2	160	6-1-98	0	1	4.60	11	0	0	1	16	10	10	8	1	16	17	.179	.167	.184	9.77	9.19
Frias, Luis	R-R	6-3	245	5-23-98	2	0	0.82	2	2	0	0	11	5	1	1	0	4	15	.139	.111	.167	12.27	3.27
Fuenmayor, Liu	L-L	5-11	170	2-2-99	0	0	1.56	11	0	0	4	17	15	3	3	2	2	27	.227	.138	.290	14.02	1.04
Grammes, Conor	R-R	6-1	200	7-13-97	0	2	7.46	8	7	0	0	25	35	21	21	5	12	32	.327	.289	.355	11.37	4.26
Haworth, Hunter	R-R	6-4	210	10-2-96	2	1	6.60	7	0	0	0	15	27	17	11	4	3	16	.386	.500	.278	9.60	1.80
Hernandez, Kenny	L-L	6-1	197	6-24-98	3	3	3.92	10	6	0	0	41	29	23	18	6	18	49	.196	.225	.185	10.67	3.92
Hiraldo, Yaramil	R-R	6-1	180	12-31-95	0	1	4.13	19	0	0	9	24	19	13	11	2	14	25	.213	.179	.240	9.38	5.25
Hull, Denson	B-L	6-1	220	10-21-96	0	3	6.00	19	0	0	1	21	20	16	14	6	21	21	.260	.214	.286	9.00	6.86
Jameson, Drey	R-R	6-0	165	8-17-97	2	4	3.92	13	12	1	0	64	60	31	28	9	18	77	.246	.269	.229	10.77	2.52
Jarvis, Bryce	L-R	6-2	195	12-26-97	1	2	3.62	7	7	0	0	37	30	19	15	4	13	42	.217	.203	.230	10.13	3.13
Jones, Joe	R-R	6-5	245	7-22-95	0	2	3.46	13	0	0	6	13	7	9	5	0	10	15	.152	.167	.136	10.38	6.92
Jones, Tyler	R-R	6-3	200	12-7-95	0	2	2.25	8	0	0	0	12	11	3	3	1	5	14	.256	.176	.308	10.50	3.75
Lewis, Justin	R-R	6-7	205	8-10-95	1	1	2.40	9	0	0	1	15	10	5	4	2	6	11	.192	.250	.167	6.60	3.60
Lin, Kai-Wei	R-R	5-10	175	3-19-96	0	2	4.78	29	0	0	0	43	38	26	23	4	19	43	.233	.296	.202	8.93	3.95
McMinn, Josh	R-R	6-4	205	4-29-96	1	2	12.67	9	2	0	0	16	25	24	23	2	16	20	.362	.400	.341	11.02	8.82
Nelson, Ryne	R-R	6-3	184	2-1-98	4	1	2.52	8	8	0	0	39	21	11	11	3	14	59	.153	.174	.132	13.50	3.20
Ogando, Gerald	R-R	6-2	180	7-28-00	1	0	2.19	8	0	0	0	12	11	3	3	0	3	13	.250	.300	.208	9.49	2.19
Pfaadt, Brandon	R-R	6-4	220	10-15-98	5	4	2.48	9	9	1	0	58	39	19	16	5	14	67	.186	.185	.186	10.40	2.17
Pope, Austin	R-R	6-3	210	10-26-98	1	0	2.55	8	0	0	0	18	15	7	5	0	3	18	.238	.136	.293	9.17	1.53
Rice, Jake	L-L	6-1	220	7-19-97	0	0	3.00	1	1	0	0	3	3	1	1	0	1	2	.273	.286	.250	6.00	3.00
Rodriguez, Wesley	R-R	5-10	210	12-4-96	1	4	3.45	28	0	0	0	44	46	18	17	3	22	42	.275	.291	.268	8.53	4.47
Santamaria, Jose	R-R	6-2	190	11-26-98	1	0	6.75	2	0	0	0	3	2	3	2	1	1	1	.182	.000	.400	3.38	3.38
Snyder, Nick	L-L	6-7	220	11-19-97	2	7	4.24	34	0	0	5	40	29	23	19	5	34	45	.203	.160	.226	10.04	7.59
Stout, Kyler	R-R	6-0	195	10-13-94	0	4	4.55	27	4	0	0	30	30	25	15	4	24	40	.252	.359	.200	12.13	7.28
Stumpo, Mitchell	R-R	6-2	205	6-17-96	0	0	1.08	5	0	0	0	8	3	2	1	1	1	12	.103	.077	.125	12.96	1.08
Sullivan, Collin	R-R	6-1	211	9-19-97	2	2	8.79	4	4	0	0	14	17	14	14	1	4	14	.283	.273	.296	8.79	2.51
Tabor, Matt	R-R	6-2	180	7-14-98	2	2	3.00	4	3	0	0	24	18	10	8	2	6	23	.207	.171	.239	8.63	2.25
Tineo, Marcos	R-R	6-2	205	3-14-97	2	1	3.04	4	4	0	0	24	21	10	8	3	8	21	.236	.294	.200	7.99	3.04
Vernia, Justin	R-R	6-2	205	9-22-95	4	5	6.92	18	11	0	0	68	104	59	52	8	13	56	.361	.327	.382	7.45	1.73
Walston, Blake	L-L	6-5	175	6-28-01	2	3	4.13	11	11	0	0	52	52	33	24	12	16	57	.252	.313	.223	9.80	2.75
Widener, Taylor	L-R	6-0	203	10-24-94	0	0	9.00	1	1	0	0	4	6	4	4	0	1	6	.316	.500	.294	13.50	2.25
Workman, Blake	R-R	6-3	195	10-8-97	0	2	3.74	10	0	0	2	22	21	11	9	3	5	28	.263	.162	.349	11.63	2.08
Yoshikawa, Shumpei	R-R	6-2	175	1-24-95	0	1	6.20	6	6	0	0	20	18	16	14	5	8	29	.228	.200	.245	12.84	3.54

Fielding

Catcher	PCT	G	PO	A	E	DP	PB
Andueza	.968	25	224	19	8	3	5
Dalesandro	.991	57	508	36	5	3	13
Kelly	1.000	2	20	0	0	0	1
Valbuena	1.000	7	52	5	0	0	1
Yerzy	.997	30	273	21	1	2	6
Hernandez	1.000	2	3	5	0		2
Kennedy	.923	4	2	10	1		1
Martinez	.980	16	24	24	1		7
Perez	.941	14	24	24	3		7
Ruiz	1.000	8	13	13	0		6
Simon	.923	14	9	27	3		6
Simon	.895	6	4	13	2		2

First Base	PCT	G	PO	A	E	DP
Andueza	.993	38	254	11	2	28
Brickhouse	.988	49	322	10	4	36
Canzone	1.000	4	27	1	0	1
English	.960	7	47	1	2	2
Kennedy	1.000	5	38	2	0	6
Miranda	1.000	5	32	2	0	4
Yerzy	.962	8	49	1	2	8

Second Base	PCT	G	PO	A	E	DP
Burt	1.000	1	1	2	0	1
Coursey	.969	57	93	129	7	41
Curpa	.667	2	0	2	1	0

Third Base	PCT	G	PO	A	E	DP
Coursey	1.000	3	4	4	0	1
English	.945	52	38	66	6	6
Hernandez	.941	6	6	10	1	2
Kennedy	.911	16	10	31	4	3
Martinez	1.000	2	2	1	0	0
Ruiz	1.000	6	1	13	0	1
Vukovich	.944	29	26	41	4	4

Shortstop	PCT	G	PO	A	E	DP
Alexander	.943	86	96	202	18	46
Martinez	.914	12	8	24	3	3
Ruiz	.936	11	13	31	3	7

Outfield	PCT	G	PO	A	E	DP
Barrosa	.994	60	154	2	1	1
Burt	1.000	1	2	0	0	0
Canzone	1.000	33	45	1	0	0
Carroll	.952	7	19	1	1	0
Coursey	.929	5	13	0	1	0
Curpa	1.000	2	4	0	0	0
Dalesandro	1.000	18	29	3	0	0
Diaz	.960	52	90	6	4	1
English	.962	15	24	1	1	0
Greene	.905	12	19	0	2	0
Hampton	.975	42	76	2	2	1
Holmes	.986	30	66	2	1	0
Miranda	1.000	5	5	0	0	0
Oriente	1.000	5	11	0	0	0
Perez	.980	63	96	3	2	0

LOW-A WEST

Batting	B-T	HT	WT	DOB	AVG	vLH	vRH	G	AB	R	H	2B	3B	HR	RBI	BB	HBP	SH	SF	SO	SB	CS	SLG	OBP
Barrosa, Jorge	B-L	5-9	165	2-17-01	.333	.344	.330	35	147	30	49	8	0	3	16	7	7	1	1	31	9	4	.449	.389
Berne, Mason	R-R	6-3	225	3-11-96	.210	.167	.218	29	105	11	22	5	0	3	11	12	0	0	1	37	0	0	.343	.288
Bliss, Ryan	R-R	5-9	165	12-13-99	.259	.361	.230	37	158	22	41	9	1	6	23	13	2	1	1	40	11	4	.443	.322
Castillo, Neyfy	R-R	6-3	175	3-2-01	.230	.224	.232	103	382	74	88	14	4	21	72	58	12	0	3	170	26	9	.453	.347
Chen, Sheng-Ping	L-R	5-9	165	10-27-00	.188	.164	.194	80	298	37	56	13	1	6	34	33	4	2	2	118	11	1	.299	.276
Cuevas, Dairon	B-R	6-1	155	4-5-02	.222	.273	.206	13	45	4	10	1	0	0	0	2	0	0	0	23	2	0	.244	.255
Curpa, Jose	R-R	5-9	160	3-9-00	.143	.182	.137	28	84	10	12	0	4	0	5	22	3	1	0	31	11	2	.238	.339
De Los Santos, Deyvison	R-R	6-1	185	6-21-03	.276	.344	.257	37	145	26	40	12	0	3	20	13	1	0	0	43	2	0	.421	.340
Del Castillo, Adrian	L-R	5-11	208	9-27-99	.244	.250	.242	22	78	12	19	6	2	1	14	9	3	0	1	28	0	0	.410	.341
Espinal, Jeferson	L-L	6-0	180	6-7-02	.216	.185	.222	42	153	22	33	8	0	1	13	16	0	0	1	63	7	2	.288	.288
Garcia, Manuel	R-R	5-11	170	1-28-00	.179	.250	.163	42	151	16	27	9	0	1	17	15	4	0	1	57	3	0	.258	.269
Hernandez, Alexander	R-R	5-11	150	6-20-99	.295	.250	.317	20	61	6	18	4	0	2	7	8	1	1	0	18	1	3	.459	.386
Hill Jr., Glenallen	B-R	5-9	170	9-30-00	.212	.225	.208	101	368	51	78	20	3	7	31	38	10	3	1	168	31	3	.340	.302
Lin, Lyle	R-R	6-1	200	6-26-97	.221	.167	.245	45	140	22	31	8	0	0	11	19	5	1	2	35	0	2	.279	.331
Malave, Ramses	R-R	5-11	175	9-29-00	.219	.236	.213	63	219	26	48	13	1	11	37	25	4	0	2	103	1	2	.438	.308
Miranda, Elian	R-R	6-1	200	5-18-00	.251	.224	.260	56	203	26	51	16	1	9	41	20	11	0	4	65	2	3	.473	.345
Muntz, Shane	R-R	6-4	240	2-23-99	.143	.333	.000	5	14	3	2	0	0	2	3	2	2	0	1	5	0	0	.571	.316
Oriente, Danny	R-R	6-0	190	10-8-97	.231	.222	.234	44	160	20	37	4	1	1	14	21	3	0	0	37	3	3	.288	.332
Ortiz, Channy	B-R	5-10	165	4-11-99	.256	.000	.301	25	86	12	22	1	0	0	8	10	1	1	1	28	3	1	.267	.337
Patino, Wilderd	R-R	6-1	175	7-18-01	.210	.294	.176	30	119	18	25	2	1	2	8	5	0	0	0	49	6	3	.294	.288
Roberts, Caleb	L-R	6-1	195	2-9-00	.214	.190	.220	34	112	22	24	4	2	1	15	18	4	0	2	36	3	1	.313	.338
Rubio, Luis	R-R	5-10	155	1-10-02	.000	.000	.000	6	17	0	0	0	0	0	0	2	0	1	0	7	1	1	.000	.105
Ruiz, Roman	R-R	5-11	175	1-3-01	.163	.125	.171	14	43	6	7	0	0	1	6	1	0	1	0	14	3	2	.233	.269
Santos, Oscar	R-R	5-9	175	9-24-00	.250	.500	.200	3	12	4	3	0	0	1	3	1	0	0	0	4	0	0	.500	.308
Simon, Ronny	B-R	5-9	150	4-17-00	.249	.270	.244	77	301	44	75	17	3	15	52	43	1	2	2	81	13	3	.475	.343
Tawa, Tim	R-R	6-0	196	4-7-99	.264	.057	.333	36	140	27	37	9	2	5	19	22	1	0	1	36	13	0	.464	.366
Vukovich, A.J.	R-R	6-5	210	7-20-01	.259	.250	.262	62	247	42	64	15	1	10	42	19	6	0	4	77	10	1	.449	.322
Yerzy, Andy	L-R	6-3	215	7-5-98	.220	.143	.235	12	41	6	9	3	0	2	9	9	5	0	0	10	2	0	.439	.418

Pitching	B-T	HT	WT	DOB	W	L	ERA	G	GS	CG	SV	IP	H	R	ER	HR	BB	SO	AVG	vLH	vRH	K/9	BB/9
Acosta, Enmanuel	R-R	6-2	200	6-6-99	1	3	9.82	31	0	0	1	40	57	49	44	5	37	41	.335	.359	.321	9.15	8.26
Albright, Luke	R-R	6-4	215	12-13-99	2	0	3.47	6	6	0	0	23	21	10	9	3	11	22	.247	.323	.204	8.49	4.24
Alcantara, Jose	R-R	6-2	180	8-3-99	2	1	3.51	17	0	0	1	33	33	20	13	3	11	36	.254	.240	.263	9.72	2.97
Alvarez, Jhosmer	R-R	6-1	155	6-29-01	0	0	0.00	1	0	0	0	2	2	0	0	0	2	2	.250	.000	.333	9.00	9.00
Arroyo, Mailon	B-R	6-0	200	1-2-98	1	1	0.55	12	0	0	4	16	17	4	1	1	3	17	.266	.250	.281	9.37	1.65
Ay, Bobby	R-R	6-3	190	5-28-97	2	2	6.00	13	3	0	0	24	18	20	16	3	13	32	.202	.256	.160	12.00	4.88
Backhus, Kyle	L-L	6-4	185	1-31-98	2	0	3.78	5	5	0	0	17	15	11	7	1	7	15	.231	.250	.226	8.10	3.78
Barnes, Zach	R-R	6-0	180	4-10-99	0	0	9.00	1	1	0	0	3	4	4	3	2	1	2	.308	.286	.333	6.00	3.00
Beriguete, Francis	L-L	6-3	165	8-11-99	0	0	7.82	11	0	0	0	13	10	11	11	1	15	18	.208	.200	.211	12.79	10.66
Borbolla, Rigoberto	L-L	6-2	170	8-20-01	0	2	10.54	6	3	0	0	14	18	17	16	2	16	10	.310	.273	.333	6.59	10.54
Carver, John	R-R	6-2	191	8-27-99	0	2	4.09	8	0	0	1	22	21	13	10	0	11	33	.241	.276	.224	13.50	4.50
Castillo, Bryan	R-R	6-3	185	1-18-99	0	1	15.43	7	0	0	0	5	6	8	8	0	13	2	.353	.286	.400	3.86	25.07
Del Moral, Adrian	R-R	6-1	190	2-17-99	1	10	8.90	16	13	0	1	59	88	69	58	12	23	46	.341	.357	.329	7.06	3.53
Elbis, Joe	R-R	6-1	150	9-24-02	0	1	3.86	3	3	0	0	14	13	7	6	0	3	13	.236	.259	.214	8.36	1.93
Fisher, Hugh	R-L	6-6	210	2-11-99	1	1	4.73	13	0	0	2	13	12	11	7	1	7	15	.240	.176	.273	10.13	4.73
Francis, Harrison	R-R	6-2	195	10-26-98	1	2	9.79	24	0	0	0	27	31	34	29	6	35	31	.279	.208	.345	10.46	11.81
Fuenmayor, Liu	L-L	5-11	170	2-2-99	0	2	4.81	24	0	0	1	24	24	15	13	3	14	26	.258	.241	.266	9.62	5.18
Gelabert, Michel	L-L	6-3	200	1-7-97	0	0	5.40	3	0	0	0	5	5	5	3	1	2	6	.238	.375	.154	10.80	3.60
Haworth, Hunter	R-R	6-4	210	10-2-96	0	0	4.30	9	0	0	0	15	13	9	7	2	7	13	.245	.318	.194	7.98	4.30
Hill, Jamison	R-R	6-1	180	3-28-99	0	0	0.00	2	0	0	0	7	4	1	0	0	2	6	.167	.000	.250	7.71	2.57
Hull, Denson	B-L	6-1	220	10-21-96	2	3	2.70	10	0	0	0	17	13	9	5	1	4	20	.213	.059	.273	10.80	2.16
Liebelt, Jared	R-R	6-0	169	1-20-97	0	1	15.75	5	0	0	0	4	8	8	7	1	3	5	.421	.500	.333	11.25	6.75
Martinez, Justin	R-R	6-3	180	7-30-01	1	3	6.65	7	7	0	0	23	25	20	17	1	15	24	.284	.295	.273	9.39	5.87
McMinn, Josh	R-R	6-4	205	4-29-96	0	0	0.00	3	0	0	0	3	0	0	0	0	3	5	.167	.182	.143	7.50	4.50
Mendez, Eric	R-R	6-0	175	12-3-99	1	1	3.33	19	0	0	2	24	22	13	9	2	10	36	.234	.243	.228	13.32	3.70
Mieses, Junior	R-R	6-1	168	10-15-99	2	9	7.59	22	15	0	0	81	90	81	68	10	72	89	.283	.318	.251	9.93	8.03
Norris, Liam	L-L	6-4	215	8-13-01	0	6	9.08	14	12	0	0	38	42	44	38	2	53	48	.290	.243	.306	11.47	12.66
Ogando, Gerald	R-R	6-2	180	7-28-00	1	1	3.86	14	0	0	1	19	21	12	8	3	6	18	.273	.276	.273	8.68	2.89
Olivero, Deyni	R-R	6-1	165	1-7-98	0	0	9.00	1	1	0	0	2	3	2	2	1	0	3	.333	.200	.500	13.50	0.00
Patrick, Chad	R-R	6-1	205	8-14-98	0	0	4.76	2	0	0	0	6	11	3	3	0	1	6	.423	.571	.368	9.53	1.59
Perdomo, Yaifer	L-L	5-10	160	8-9-01	0	0	7.20	2	0	0	0	5	6	4	4	1	5	8	.286	.500	.200	14.40	9.00
Pfaadt, Brandon	R-R	6-4	220	10-15-98	2	2	3.12	7	7	0	0	40	29	17	14	5	7	57	.191	.228	.151	12.72	1.56
Pope, Austin	R-R	6-3	210	10-26-98	0	10	8.71	18	15	0	1	72	99	77	70	8	36	84	.322	.310	.333	10.45	4.48
Randall, Scott	R-R	6-0	172	8-3-98	2	0	0.47	5	2	0	0	19	8	1	1	0	4	23	.127	.111	.139	10.89	1.89
Rice, Jake	L-L	6-2	220	7-19-97	2	1	3.14	4	0	0	1	14	11	7	5	1	3	19	.212	.214	.211	11.93	1.88
Sanchez, David	R-R	6-1	175	1-6-99	3	1	6.07	25	0	0	3	30	33	24	20	3	27	24	.289	.135	.368	7.28	8.19
Santamaria, Jose	R-R	6-2	190	11-26-98	1	2	5.10	20	0	0	0	30	32	21	17	2	10	26	.271	.300	.250	7.80	3.00
Short, Avery	R-L	6-1	205	3-14-01	2	5	7.38	15	14	0	0	57	76	54	47	6	23	60	.309	.281	.317	9.42	3.61
Stumpo, Mitchell	R-R	6-2	205	6-17-96	0	0	4.26	7	0	0	0	13	13	6	6	1	1	18	.255	.292	.222	12.79	0.71
Sullivan, Collin	R-R	6-1	211	9-19-97	1	0	0.00	2	1	0	0	10	2	2	0	0	0	8	.063	.077	.053	7.45	0.00
Swales, Josh	R-R	6-2	195	10-28-01	0	1	5.63	3	0	0	0	8	12	6	5	0	5	7	.353	.421	.267	7.88	5.63

Name	B-T	HT	WT	DOB	W	L	ERA	G	GS	CG	SV	IP	H	R	ER	HR	BB	SO	AVG	vLH	vRH	K/9	BB/9
Tineo, Marcos	R-R	6-0	165	3-14-97	2	4	5.51	16	2	0	0	51	60	41	31	6	18	71	.284	.349	.216	12.61	3.20
Valdez, Alex	R-R	6-2	185	12-24-99	0	1	5.63	33	0	0	1	40	45	34	25	4	19	33	.283	.270	.294	7.43	4.28
Valdez, Jhonny	R-R	6-3	187	8-10-98	1	1	6.75	17	0	0	0	23	26	24	17	3	12	18	.286	.341	.240	7.15	4.76
Walston, Blake	L-L	6-5	175	6-28-01	2	2	3.32	8	8	0	0	43	34	18	16	4	17	60	.209	.194	.213	12.46	3.53

Fielding

Catcher

	PCT	G	PO	A	E	DP	PB
Del Castillo	.961	16	140	8	6	0	6
Garcia	.963	25	206	25	9	3	9
Lin	.992	35	359	28	3	3	0
Malave	.985	27	238	24	4	1	11
Muntz	1.000	3	27	2	0	0	0
Roberts	.983	14	104	14	2	0	2
Santos	1.000	2	15	0	0	1	0
Yerzy	.982	5	47	9	1	1	3

	PCT	G	PO	A	E	DP
Cuevas	.929	4	3	10	1	1
Curpa	.950	5	9	10	1	3
Hernandez	1.000	3	3	5	0	1
Hill Jr.	.978	10	26	19	1	5
Ortiz	.947	12	27	27	3	5
Rubio	.870	6	11	9	3	1
Ruiz	1.000	3	4	11	0	0
Simon	.953	38	81	102	9	29
Tawa	1.000	4	3	11	0	0

	PCT	G	PO	A	E	DP
Chen	.935	39	48	82	9	17
Cuevas	.923	9	12	24	3	4
Curpa	.933	4	5	9	1	1
Hernandez	.800	1	2	2	1	0
Ortiz	1.000	1	3	1	0	0
Ruiz	.976	9	12	28	1	5
Simon	.949	22	38	55	5	16

First Base

	PCT	G	PO	A	E	DP
Berne	.966	24	160	10	6	9
Castillo	.976	31	229	13	6	22
De Los Santos	1.000	1	1	0	0	0
Garcia	.833	2	4	1	1	0
Hernandez	.882	3	27	3	4	2
Lin	.964	6	51	3	2	9
Malave	.976	21	158	8	4	19
Miranda	.984	31	229	23	4	21
Yerzy	.974	6	37	1	1	1

Third Base

	PCT	G	PO	A	E	DP
Curpa	1.000	3	0	6	0	1
De Los Santos	.909	35	27	73	10	5
Hernandez	.875	6	4	10	2	1
Miranda	.920	10	4	19	2	1
Ortiz	.941	8	3	13	1	0
Ruiz	1.000	1	2	1	0	0
Simon	1.000	6	3	10	0	2
Vukovich	.868	53	30	82	17	7

Outfield

	PCT	G	PO	A	E	DP
Barrosa	.973	36	70	3	2	0
Castillo	.970	61	90	6	3	1
Curpa	.900	15	18	0	2	0
Espinal	.946	38	65	5	4	1
Hernandez	1.000	5	5	0	0	1
Hill Jr.	.986	90	141	4	2	0
Miranda	1.000	3	2	1	0	0
Oriente	.931	41	54	0	4	0
Patino	.971	31	67	0	2	0
Roberts	.865	20	31	1	5	0
Ruiz	1.000	1	1	0	0	0
Tawa	.982	29	50	4	1	1

Second Base

	PCT	G	PO	A	E	DP
Chen	.968	38	60	93	5	21

Shortstop

	PCT	G	PO	A	E	DP
Bliss	.963	37	58	98	6	16

ACL D-BACKS   *ROOKIE*
ARIZONA COMPLEX LEAGUE

Batting	B-T	HT	WT	DOB	AVG	vLH	vRH	G	AB	R	H	2B	3B	HR	RBI	BB	HBP	SH	SF	SO	SB	CS	SLG	OBP
Baez, Franyel	B-R	6-3	170	3-1-03	.154	.000	.200	9	26	1	4	0	1	0	1	2	0	0	0	14	0	0	.231	.214
Batista, Juan	R-R	6-1	175	1-9-01	.304	.353	.282	23	56	9	17	3	0	2	7	6	0	1	1	19	3	3	.464	.365
Bliss, Ryan	R-R	5-9	165	12-13-99	.429	.667	.250	2	7	1	3	1	0	0	1	0	0	0	0	2	0	0	.571	.429
Cabrera, Asdrubal	B-R	6-0	235	11-13-85	.167	.000	.250	2	6	0	1	0	0	0	0	1	0	0	0	4	0	0	.167	.286
Caicuto, Luis	R-R	5-10	160	3-5-03	.200	1.000	.111	7	10	0	2	0	0	0	1	0	1	0	0	2	0	0	.200	.273
Caldera, Ricardo	R-R	6-1	175	4-6-02	.080	.000	.091	9	25	3	2	0	0	0	2	4	0	0	0	12	0	1	.080	.207
Calhoun, Kole	L-L	5-10	205	10-14-87	.250	.500	.000	2	4	2	1	0	0	1	2	1	1	0	0	1	0	0	1.000	.500
Chen, Sheng-Ping	L-R	5-9	165	10-27-00	.500	.000	.556	3	10	4	5	0	0	0	1	0	0	0	0	4	0	1	.500	.500
Conticello, Gavin	L-R	6-4	195	6-11-03	.289	.429	.263	15	45	6	13	3	0	0	3	2	4	0	0	11	2	1	.356	.373
Corniel, Juan	B-R	5-11	150	10-2-02	.245	.182	.258	52	188	23	46	9	3	0	27	12	1	0	6	51	6	3	.324	.285
Cuevas, Dairon	B-R	6-1	155	4-5-02	.161	.154	.167	14	31	7	5	1	0	0	4	3	1	0	0	9	1	0	.290	.257
Curpa, Angel	R-R	5-9	160	3-9-00	.200	.182	.222	7	20	2	4	1	0	0	2	3	0	0	0	4	5	2	.250	.304
De Los Santos, Deyvison	R-R	6-1	185	6-21-03	.329	.174	.390	25	82	19	27	4	2	5	17	13	0	0	0	24	1	1	.610	.421
Del Castillo, Adrian	L-R	5-11	208	9-27-99	.600	.500	.667	2	5	1	3	0	0	0	0	2	0	0	0	1	0	0	.600	.714
D'Orazio, J.J.	R-R	6-1	170	12-28-01	.095	.000	.125	9	21	1	2	0	0	0	1	5	0	0	0	6	0	0	.095	.296
Espinal, Jeferson	L-L	6-0	180	6-7-02	.352	.375	.345	20	71	17	25	6	1	1	10	10	2	0	0	21	9	1	.507	.446
Estrada, Deivi	B-R	5-10	155	1-17-01	.118	.000	.125	8	17	4	2	2	0	0	2	0	1	0	0	10	0	0	.235	.211
Estrada, Endy	R-R	5-11	175	4-6-02	.286	.235	.300	27	77	9	22	4	0	1	15	7	3	0	1	13	1	1	.377	.364
Fairchild, Stuart	R-R	6-0	205	3-17-96	.333	--	.333	2	6	1	2	1	0	0	0	0	0	0	0	2	0	0	.500	.333
Fernandez, Jose	R-R	6-3	165	9-22-03	.250	.182	.267	36	112	14	28	4	1	0	14	11	1	0	1	39	4	1	.304	.320
Franco, Junior	L-L	5-9	165	9-13-02	.304	.316	.300	27	79	21	24	5	3	2	10	13	1	0	1	24	10	1	.519	.404
Garcia, Manuel	R-R	5-11	170	1-28-00	.194	.250	.185	11	31	4	6	3	1	0	4	6	2	0	2	11	1	0	.355	.341
Gonnella, Dominic	L-R	5-11	205	9-16-01	.000	--	.000	2	3	0	0	0	0	0	0	1	0	0	0	1	0	0	.000	.250
Gutierrez, Sergio	B-R	6-1	195	1-18-01	.146	.167	.138	21	41	6	6	1	1	0	5	11	1	0	0	13	1	0	.293	.340
Guzman, Alvin	R-R	6-1	166	10-20-01	.208	.250	.202	42	125	28	26	6	1	0	13	18	4	1	1	50	15	3	.344	.324
Jones, Ryder	L-R	6-2	221	6-7-94	.308	.000	.333	4	13	2	4	1	0	0	0	0	0	0	0	4	0	0	.385	.286
Kelly, Carson	R-R	6-2	212	7-14-94	.000	.000	.000	1	2	0	0	0	0	0	0	1	0	0	0	2	0	0	.000	.333
Lawlar, Jordan	R-R	6-2	190	7-17-02	.400	--	.400	2	5	0	2	1	0	0	0	1	0	0	0	1	1	0	.600	.500
Marte, Ketel	B-R	6-1	210	10-12-93	.000	--	.000	1	2	0	0	0	0	0	0	1	0	0	0	1	0	0	.000	.333
Martinez, Asdrubal	R-R	5-11	170	1-4-02	.214	.000	.250	8	14	1	3	0	0	0	1	0	0	0	0	7	0	0	.214	.214
Muntz, Shane	R-R	6-4	240	2-23-99	.163	.000	.171	15	43	7	7	3	0	0	5	8	2	0	0	12	0	0	.233	.321
Ortiz, Angel	L-L	6-0	180	10-3-02	.234	.292	.218	35	111	15	26	2	0	3	20	15	0	0	3	22	5	3	.333	.318
Ortiz, Channy	B-R	5-10	165	4-11-99	.000	.000	.000	1	4	0	0	0	0	0	0	0	0	0	0	1	0	0	.000	.000
Patino, Wilderd	R-R	6-1	175	7-18-01	.250	.143	.286	8	28	2	7	1	1	0	1	1	0	0	0	9	0	2	.357	.276
Polanco, Ronny	R-R	5-11	180	8-23-03	.221	.222	.220	50	163	27	36	7	0	4	23	18	2	0	2	52	3	2	.337	.303
Roberson, Jacen	L-L	6-1	192	5-23-00	.257	.167	.276	14	35	6	9	2	0	1	5	6	0	0	0	9	0	0	.400	.366
Roberts, Caleb	L-R	6-1	195	2-9-00	.000	.000	.000	1	3	0	0	0	0	0	0	2	0	0	0	2	0	0	.000	.000
Rubio, Luis	R-R	5-10	155	1-10-02	.137	.143	.135	20	51	6	7	1	0	0	6	9	0	0	1	24	0	1	.157	.262
Sanabria, Danyer	L-L	6-1	155	3-7-02	.107	.200	.098	19	56	8	6	0	1	1	10	7	0	0	1	25	2	0	.196	.203
Santos, Oscar	R-R	5-9	175	9-24-00	.348	.200	.389	9	23	7	8	1	0	2	6	2	0	0	0	6	2	0	.652	.423
Tawa, Tim	R-R	6-0	196	4-7-99	.400	1.000	.000	2	5	1	2	0	0	1	3	2	0	0	0	2	1	0	1.000	.571

Batting	B-T	HT	WT	DOB	AVG	vLH	vRH	G	AB	R	H	2B	3B	HR	RBI	BB	HBP	SH	SF	SO	SB	CS	SLG	OBP
Valbuena, Luvin	R-R	5-9	165	5-7-99	.222	.000	.286	7	18	2	4	0	0	0	0	0	0	0	0	6	0	0	.222	.222
Walters, Jean	B-R	5-11	155	8-13-01	.342	.154	.440	21	38	5	13	0	0	0	9	8	0	0	0	10	1	1	.342	.457

Pitching	B-T	HT	WT	DOB	W	L	ERA	G	GS	CG	SV	IP	H	R	ER	HR	BB	SO	AVG	vLH	vRH	K/9	BB/9
Acosta, Enmanuel	R-R	6-2	200	6-6-99	0	0	0.00	2	0	0	0	2	0	0	0	0	2	5	.000	.000	.000	22.50	9.00
Alcantara, Jose	R-R	6-2	180	8-3-99	1	0	0.00	3	0	0	0	6	2	0	0	0	4	11	.111	.000	.167	16.50	6.00
Alvarez, Jhosmer	R-R	6-1	155	6-29-01	0	0	0.00	4	0	0	0	8	2	0	0	0	3	16	.077	.000	.111	18.00	3.38
Andujar, Hamilton	R-R	6-3	175	9-14-99	0	1	2.70	10	0	0	2	10	9	4	3	0	5	8	.237	.167	.269	7.20	4.50
Bascunan, Mauricio	R-R	6-4	170	10-3-01	0	6	5.35	11	6	0	0	37	40	27	22	2	22	29	.284	.283	.284	7.05	5.35
Beriguete, Francis	L-L	6-3	165	8-11-99	1	0	3.86	8	0	0	0	7	5	3	3	1	7	8	.217	.167	.235	10.29	9.00
Bumgarner, Madison	R-L	6-4	257	8-1-89	0	0	8.10	2	2	0	0	7	14	10	6	0	2	6	.412	1.000	.375	8.10	2.70
Calzadilla, Abraham	R-R	6-1	170	12-12-01	2	4	5.66	14	6	0	0	35	38	24	22	4	23	40	.279	.319	.258	10.29	5.91
Castillo, Bryan	R-R	6-3	185	1-18-99	3	0	1.69	6	0	0	0	11	7	2	2	1	5	15	.184	.250	.154	12.66	4.22
Clarke, Taylor	R-R	6-4	217	5-13-93	0	1	67.50	1	1	0	0	1	2	5	5	0	2	1	.500	.000	.667	13.50	27.00
Clippard, Tyler	R-R	6-3	200	2-14-85	0	0	11.57	2	0	0	0	2	4	3	3	1	0	3	.400	.429	.333	11.57	0.00
De Dios, Fredely	R-R	6-2	165	11-3-00	0	0	5.40	8	0	0	0	5	9	9	9	1	16	13	.188	.238	.148	7.80	9.60
De Jesus, Henler	L-L	6-4	170	6-15-98	1	0	6.59	11	0	0	0	14	17	11	10	2	6	14	.304	.231	.326	9.22	3.95
Diaz, Luis	R-R	6-5	230	3-9-01	2	2	5.79	19	0	0	1	23	27	21	15	1	23	27	.314	.242	.358	10.41	8.87
Duplantier, Jon	L-R	6-4	229	7-11-94	0	0	9.00	1	1	0	0	1	1	1	1	0	1	1	.400	.000	.500	9.00	9.00
Elbis, Joe	R-R	6-1	150	9-24-02	3	2	3.40	9	7	0	0	40	39	17	15	4	4	46	.260	.175	.291	10.44	0.91
Gardewine, Nick	R-R	6-1	179	8-15-93	0	0	0.00	1	0	0	0	1	0	0	0	0	1	3	.000	--	.000	27.00	9.00
Gil, Miguel	R-R	6-1	160	5-12-01	0	4	6.67	14	1	0	2	27	33	29	20	3	23	35	.292	.275	.301	11.67	7.67
Isea, Edgar	R-R	6-3	185	8-20-02	0	1	9.00	2	0	0	0	4	5	6	4	0	4	5	.278	.000	.455	11.25	9.00
Jarvis, Bryce	L-R	6-2	195	12-26-97	0	0	0.00	1	1	0	0	3	1	0	0	0	0	7	.100	.200	.000	21.00	0.00
Kelly, Merrill	R-R	6-2	202	10-14-88	0	0	4.50	1	1	0	0	4	3	2	2	0	2	7	.188	.429	.000	15.75	4.50
Marcelino, Jean	R-R	6-2	170	7-19-00	1	0	7.11	5	2	0	0	13	14	10	10	3	10	12	.286	.462	.222	8.53	7.11
Mendez, Eric	R-R	6-0	175	12-3-99	2	0	0.00	5	0	0	1	6	3	1	0	0	3	5	.143	.167	.133	7.94	4.76
Meran, Andreuris	R-R	6-1	185	8-9-99	0	0	12.06	12	0	0	0	16	22	22	21	0	16	17	.333	.542	.214	9.77	9.19
Meza, Carlos	L-L	6-1	155	2-10-01	1	4	4.97	11	7	0	0	38	43	29	21	4	18	42	.272	.333	.256	9.95	4.26
Norris, Liam	L-L	6-4	215	8-13-01	0	1	11.57	2	2	0	0	3	7	6	6	0	7	6	.214	.667	.091	11.57	13.50
Pacheco, Cristian	R-R	6-2	175	4-23-01	0	0	7.71	2	1	0	0	2	3	3	2	0	4	0	.333	.500	.286	0.00	15.43
Perez, Jheyson	R-R	6-3	175	2-2-00	0	0	0.00	1	0	0	1	2	0	0	0	0	0	0	.500	--	.500	0.00	0.00
Pimentel, Yoscar	R-R	6-2	160	11-3-01	2	2	6.18	11	7	0	0	44	47	39	30	8	24	36	.276	.228	.301	7.42	4.95
Polanco, Sarlin	R-R	6-1	190	2-23-02	0	1	18.78	6	0	0	0	8	13	16	16	0	12	7	.406	.333	.500	8.22	14.09
Ramirez, Noe	R-R	6-3	205	12-22-89	0	0	0.00	1	1	0	0	1	0	0	0	0	0	2	.000	--	.000	18.00	0.00
Rubio, Luis	R-R	5-10	155	1-10-02	0	0	0.00	1	0	0	0	0	0	0	0	0	0	0	.000	--	--	0.00	0.00
Sanchez, David	R-R	6-1	175	1-6-99	0	1	6.00	2	0	0	0	3	1	3	2	1	4	3	.091	.000	.125	9.00	12.00
Sierra, Diomede	L-L	6-2	170	9-11-01	0	4	7.36	8	6	0	0	18	24	22	15	0	13	24	.289	.269	.298	11.78	6.38
Smith, Riley	R-R	6-1	207	1-15-95	0	1	10.50	2	2	0	0	6	12	7	7	1	1	2	.414	.200	.526	10.50	1.50
Steinmetz, Jacob	R-R	6-5	220	7-19-03	0	1	6.75	1	0	0	0	1	3	1	1	0	4	0	.167	.000	.333	0.00	27.00
Swales, Josh	R-R	6-2	195	10-28-01	0	0	0.00	1	0	0	0	2	4	0	0	1	2	4	.444	.500	.400	9.00	4.50
Telleria, Carlos	R-R	6-0	150	11-7-99	0	2	10.93	18	0	0	1	14	22	22	17	2	17	20	.349	.320	.368	12.86	10.93
Valdez, Alex	R-R	6-2	185	12-24-99	0	0	4.15	2	0	0	0	4	3	2	2	0	1	7	.188	.400	.091	14.54	2.08
Valdez, Bryan	L-L	6-3	180	11-27-94	1	0	13.50	1	0	0	0	1	2	2	2	0	1	2	.333	--	.333	13.50	6.75
Walters, Jean	B-R	5-11	155	8-13-01	0	0	0.00	1	0	0	0	2	0	0	0	0	2	2	.333	.250	.500	13.50	0.00
Weaver, Luke	R-R	6-2	183	8-21-93	0	0	3.00	1	1	0	0	3	4	1	1	0	0	6	.308	.333	.300	18.00	0.00
Widener, Taylor	L-R	6-0	203	10-24-94	0	1	16.88	1	1	0	0	3	9	5	5	2	0	4	.563	.625	.500	13.50	0.00
Yoshikawa, Shumpei	R-R	6-2	175	1-24-95	0	0	18.00	1	0	0	0	1	2	2	2	0	1	1	.250	.000	.500	9.00	9.00

Fielding

C: Caicuto 7, Caldera 8, Del Castillo 2, D_Orazio 6, Garcia 10, Gutierrez 17, Kelly 1, Muntz 9, Santos 4, Valbuena 7.
1B: De Los Santos 7, Estrada 20, Gutierrez 2, Jones 1, Polanco 21, Sanabria 12.
2B: Chen 2, Corniel 19, Cuevas 7, Fernandez 14, Ortiz 1, Polanco 3, Rubio 6, Walters 11.
3B: Cabrera 2, Conticello 12, Curpa 4, De Los Santos 15, Fernandez 2, Jones 3, Polanco 20, Rubio 2, Tawa 1, Walters 3.
SS: Bliss 2, Corniel 35, Cuevas 3, Fernandez 19, Lawlar 2, Rubio 1.
OF: Baez 10, Batista 22, Calhoun 9, Curpa 2, Espinal 21, Estrada 3, Estrada 3, Fairchild 2, Franco 26, Gonnella 2, Guzman 41, Marte 1, Martinez 7, Ortiz 34, Patino 7, Roberson 14, Roberts 1, Rubio 5, Sanabria 8, Tawa 1, Walters 5.

DSL D-BACKS   ROOKIE
DOMINICAN SUMMER LEAGUE

Batting	B-T	HT	WT	DOB	AVG	vLH	vRH	G	AB	R	H	2B	3B	HR	RBI	BB	HBP	SH	SF	SO	SB	CS	SLG	OBP
Alcala, Moises	R-R	5-9	155	2-10-03	.203	.375	.176	26	59	4	12	2	1	0	10	7	2	0	1	16	0	0	.271	.304
Alvarado, Fernando	R-R	5-9	145	9-22-03	.206	.000	.304	18	34	4	7	1	0	0	7	7	2	0	0	6	5	1	.235	.372
Antigua, Ronal	R-R	6-1	180	1-27-03	.238	.400	.216	34	84	15	20	2	0	1	8	8	3	0	0	21	0	4	.298	.326
Aparicio, Juan	R-R	6-0	165	9-25-02	.198	.200	.198	45	116	18	23	6	0	0	9	21	5	1	1	23	5	4	.250	.343
Benitez, Johan	B-R	6-3	170	8-7-03	.304	.222	.319	39	112	12	34	10	0	0	9	14	3	0	0	23	4	1	.393	.395
Benua, Alexander	R-R	6-2	185	10-19-03	.156	.250	.147	48	128	18	20	5	1	0	9	15	7	0	2	35	11	1	.211	.276
Cabeza, Diosfran	B-R	5-10	155	5-13-03	.286	.316	.279	36	105	18	30	3	3	2	15	15	1	0	1	14	3	5	.429	.377
Cabral, Riquelmin	R-R	5-10	165	5-12-03	.231	.417	.208	34	108	20	25	3	0	0	6	10	6	0	0	20	9	2	.259	.331
Caldera, Ricardo	R-R	6-1	175	4-6-02	.109	.250	.070	20	55	5	6	1	0	0	4	5	7	0	3	20	1	0	.127	.257
Castillo, Kenny	R-R	6-2	170	5-13-04	.295	.211	.307	48	156	20	46	16	0	1	22	12	5	0	1	24	2	2	.417	.362
Ciprian, Alberto	R-R	5-11	165	11-5-02	.275	.231	.282	31	91	14	25	4	1	0	16	16	2	0	2	26	2	2	.352	.387
Colmenarez, Anderson	B-R	5-8	145	1-12-04	.310	.500	.296	15	29	7	9	1	0	0	1	7	1	1	0	7	2	0	.345	.459
De Jesus, Eskoly	L-L	6-2	185	9-7-03	.154	.120	.163	45	117	14	18	4	3	1	12	29	0	0	1	58	1	1	.265	.320
De La Cruz, Lewin	B-R	5-10	160	8-7-03	.169	.267	.156	42	124	14	21	4	1	1	7	19	6	1	0	42	7	5	.242	.309

	B-T	HT	WT	DOB	AVG	vLH	vRH	G	AB	R	H	2B	3B	HR	RBI	BB	HBP	SH	SF	SO	SB	CS	OBP	SLG
De Leon, Adrian	R-R	5-7	180	2-9-04	.222	.133	.246	29	72	11	16	3	0	1	5	10	4	0	2	20	1	0	.306	.341
Encarnacion, Berny	R-R	6-0	190	10-1-02	.146	.333	.117	34	89	8	13	1	0	2	11	6	0	0	1	38	1	1	.225	.198
Estrella, Cristian	L-L	6-1	175	11-12-01	.000	.000	.000	2	5	0	0	0	0	0	0	0	0	0	0	2	0	0	.000	.000
Garcia, Juan	B-R	5-10	165	5-28-03	.189	.273	.179	38	106	16	20	3	0	1	12	9	5	1	1	10	4	0	.245	.281
Gomez, Adrian	R-R	5-10	150	9-6-02	.000	--	.000	5	4	0	0	0	0	0	0	0	0	1	0	2	0	0	.000	.200
Gonzalez, Luis	R-R	6-0	170	9-20-02	.146	.231	.107	24	41	6	6	2	0	0	5	4	3	0	0	20	2	1	.195	.271
Gonzalez, Yohan	L-R	5-11	160	11-20-02	.200	.200	.200	24	55	5	11	4	0	0	6	18	1	0	1	18	0	1	.273	.400
Heredia, Jiter	R-R	5-11	170	1-29-03	.105	.150	.096	41	114	13	12	1	0	2	6	8	3	0	1	64	4	0	.167	.183
Josepha, Jakey	L-R	6-2	135	5-15-04	.116	.500	.098	19	43	3	5	0	0	0	1	6	0	1	0	14	1	2	.116	.224
Martinez, Asdrubal	R-R	5-11	170	1-4-02	1.000	1.000	--	1	1	1	1	0	0	0	0	0	0	0	0	0	1	0	1.000	1.000
Mendez, Mario	L-L	5-11	160	12-30-01	.128	.111	.133	16	39	5	5	2	0	0	6	1	1	0	1	10	0	0	.179	.167
Mendez, Teofilo	R-R	5-11	170	10-8-01	.259	.300	.250	56	158	21	41	13	0	0	13	15	8	0	1	42	4	5	.342	.352
Nava, Jonathan	R-R	5-11	165	9-15-03	.200	.000	.222	5	10	1	2	0	0	0	0	0	0	0	0	4	0	0	.200	.200
Pena, Jefferson	R-R	5-8	160	1-13-04	.204	.103	.228	47	152	14	31	5	0	0	10	11	2	0	2	38	9	7	.237	.263
Pena, Manuel	R-R	6-1	170	12-5-03	.253	.333	.241	57	194	30	49	5	2	4	30	26	1	0	1	46	17	7	.361	.342
Pernalete, Marco	R-R	6-4	175	9-12-02	.278	.250	.282	41	126	16	35	11	2	0	19	7	4	0	1	38	3	1	.444	.333
Rivas, Samuel	R-R	5-10	160	5-28-03	.200	.000	.250	5	10	1	2	0	0	0	1	2	0	1	0	2	1	1	.200	.333
Rojas, Anderdson	L-R	5-10	150	3-8-04	.209	.083	.234	47	148	20	31	3	2	1	20	13	6	0	1	33	10	4	.277	.298
Romero, Edward	R-R	5-10	150	5-11-02	.207	.111	.224	27	58	11	12	1	1	0	3	6	2	1	0	17	4	1	.259	.303
Salmeron, Daniel	L-R	6-1	170	9-4-02	.033	.000	.036	13	30	3	1	0	0	1	0	9	1	0	0	16	0	0	.033	.275
Sanchez, Carlos	L-L	5-9	150	1-29-04	--	--	--	1	0	0	0	0	0	0	0	0	0	0	0	0	0	0	.000	.000
Santos, Kevin	L-L	6-0	180	1-9-04	.113	.000	.125	25	53	9	6	1	0	1	4	12	3	0	0	21	3	0	.189	.309
Suero, Luis	R-R	6-2	165	5-25-03	.196	.214	.194	37	112	14	22	2	1	2	15	15	3	0	1	37	4	4	.286	.305
Surun, Ezequiel	R-R	6-0	150	7-7-04	.175	.143	.183	37	103	11	18	2	0	1	9	6	4	0	1	26	2	4	.223	.246
Torres, Daniel	R-R	5-9	150	1-10-02	.279	.143	.295	32	68	15	19	1	0	0	7	21	7	0	0	21	5	3	.294	.490
Vargas, Robinson	R-R	5-11	160	6-7-03	.189	.308	.164	29	74	9	14	1	0	2	9	9	1	0	1	21	2	1	.284	.282
Vasquez, Algenis	R-R	5-11	180	11-15-02	.175	.222	.167	30	57	11	10	1	1	0	2	6	3	2	0	21	2	1	.263	.238
Vasquez, Gensi	R-R	6-1	165	5-17-03	.129	.167	.105	13	31	2	4	1	0	0	3	0	0	0	0	18	1	1	.161	.206

Pitching	B-T	HT	WT	DOB	W	L	ERA	G	GS	CG	SV	IP	H	R	ER	HR	BB	SO	AVG	vLH	vRH	K/9	BB/9
Ache, Anyerbert	R-R	6-2	170	3-13-01	0	0	3.24	12	0	0	1	17	19	11	6	0	15	16	.288	.526	.191	8.64	8.10
Aguirre, Jose	R-R	6-1	170	10-11-03	1	1	8.64	11	1	0	1	17	18	18	16	1	13	10	.273	.231	.300	5.40	7.02
Almonte, Darlin	L-L	5-7	150	12-16-02	3	1	1.82	16	0	0	1	25	20	14	5	1	8	29	.225	.250	.217	10.58	2.92
Almonte, Jonathan	R-R	6-0	175	8-9-00	1	0	1.93	8	0	0	2	14	8	3	3	1	6	14	.163	.227	.111	9.00	3.86
Almonte, Lisandro	R-R	6-1	170	6-11-02	1	2	4.20	15	12	0	0	49	42	29	23	3	28	51	.240	.269	.222	9.30	5.11
Alvarez, Miguel	R-R	6-1	165	7-12-02	0	1	17.18	3	0	0	0	4	6	9	7	1	6	5	.353	.286	.400	12.27	14.73
Basabe, Eric	L-L	5-10	150	9-24-02	2	3	3.65	11	0	0	1	12	4	9	5	0	19	17	.091	.000	.121	12.41	13.86
Basora, Victor	R-R	6-3	170	2-4-02	1	1	2.50	11	0	0	0	18	11	7	5	0	16	11	.175	.154	.189	5.50	8.00
Cabrera, Jose	R-R	6-3	190	5-30-02	0	0	4.50	1	1	0	0	2	3	1	1	0	1	2	.429	.333	.500	9.00	4.50
Cerda, Junior	R-R	5-11	170	6-15-00	7	1	1.67	18	0	0	4	27	20	10	5	0	10	34	.213	.259	.194	11.33	3.33
Diaz, Yilber	R-R	6-0	190	8-19-00	2	3	5.13	19	1	0	0	26	24	21	15	1	18	17	.264	.286	.250	5.81	6.15
Encarnacion, Lorenzo	R-R	5-11	175	11-9-01	2	4	5.65	17	0	0	4	29	36	25	18	1	12	29	.310	.276	.322	9.10	3.77
Gonzalez, Miguel	R-R	6-4	220	9-6-02	0	1	12.38	7	1	0	0	8	10	13	11	1	10	3	.357	.333	.375	3.38	11.25
Jean, Daniel	L-L	6-1	185	3-24-03	0	4	4.56	13	3	0	0	24	20	15	12	1	18	29	.230	.333	.203	11.03	6.85
Jimenez, Jesus	R-R	6-2	185	10-2-02	3	5	5.63	14	8	0	1	38	37	26	24	2	19	23	.264	.226	.287	5.40	4.46
Kwidama, Jediah	R-R	6-3	185	7-30-02	0	2	4.37	13	5	0	1	23	25	17	11	3	13	18	.291	.344	.259	7.15	5.16
Marcelino, Jean	R-R	6-2	170	7-19-00	2	3	3.86	7	6	0	0	26	33	14	11	1	9	28	.314	.514	.206	9.82	3.16
Mendoza, Luis	R-R	6-1	190	1-4-02	2	1	4.15	12	1	0	0	26	23	15	12	0	17	30	.242	.268	.222	10.38	5.88
Morel, Osvaldo	R-R	6-3	195	6-17-01	0	2	5.79	15	0	0	3	23	22	20	15	1	10	25	.242	.348	.206	9.64	3.86
Nunez, Carlos	R-R	6-3	190	1-29-03	0	0	40.50	1	0	0	0	1	3	3	3	0	2	0	.000	--	.000	0.00	27.00
Nunez, Felix	R-R	6-1	160	9-22-03	0	0	9.95	9	0	0	0	6	9	8	7	2	11	7	.333	.533	.083	9.95	15.63
Osorio, Luis	R-R	6-2	170	1-31-03	3	2	5.83	15	6	0	0	42	33	30	27	6	20	51	.217	.242	.198	11.02	4.32
Otano, Peniel	R-R	6-4	190	10-7-02	2	6	3.05	14	13	0	0	56	49	29	19	2	14	67	.234	.250	.228	10.77	2.25
Parra, Nixon	R-R	6-1	170	1-7-04	2	3	9.31	12	5	0	0	19	29	22	20	0	25	14	.367	.407	.346	6.52	11.64
Reyes, Kelly	R-R	6-1	165	1-6-03	1	1	4.15	11	3	0	0	17	11	8	8	0	17	19	.208	.278	.171	9.87	8.83
Rincon, Hansel	R-R	6-1	160	8-23-02	2	3	3.42	15	11	0	0	53	59	23	20	3	3	55	.296	.368	.268	9.40	0.51
Roque, Arturo	R-R	6-1	155	12-2-00	3	4	2.65	16	10	0	0	58	52	27	17	3	16	52	.234	.190	.259	8.12	2.50
Sanchez, Jandel	L-L	6-4	185	6-20-02	0	0	9.00	8	0	0	0	9	14	12	9	0	11	9	.359	.556	.300	9.00	11.00
Santana, Sebastian	R-R	6-4	185	7-31-01	1	1	2.79	15	0	0	3	19	15	9	6	0	12	21	.214	.320	.156	9.78	5.59
Suarez, Jesus	R-R	6-2	170	10-1-02	0	2	7.36	4	0	0	0	4	4	5	3	0	6	2	.286	.000	.400	4.91	14.73
Tejeda, Luis	R-R	6-3	170	2-14-01	2	3	4.26	17	0	0	0	25	31	17	12	0	9	21	.295	.361	.261	7.46	3.20
Valdez, Jose	R-R	6-2	180	11-8-01	2	3	4.43	14	7	0	0	41	33	26	20	2	16	47	.220	.161	.261	10.40	3.54
Valdez, Vitico	R-R	6-4	175	11-6-03	1	1	4.15	9	6	0	0	22	16	14	10	0	19	18	.205	.222	.196	7.48	7.89
Vicent, Joiner	R-R	6-6	185	12-29-01	6	1	1.97	14	8	0	0	50	30	14	11	1	25	52	.172	.265	.113	9.30	4.47
Yan, Ricardo	R-R	6-4	180	11-14-02	0	4	3.71	12	4	0	0	27	21	16	11	3	20	24	.208	.243	.188	8.10	6.75
Zapata, Deyer	L-L	6-0	150	12-4-03	1	3	3.22	16	6	0	0	36	25	16	13	1	14	35	.192	.171	.202	8.67	3.47

Fielding

C: Alcala 19, Caldera 19, Castillo 43, De Leon 20, Gomez 5, Gonzalez 14, Nava 4, Rivas 2, Salmeron 8.

1B: Aparicio 17, Cabeza 20, Cabral 13, Ciprian 8, Colmenarez 1, De Jesus 3, Gonzalez 4, Mendez 24, Pernalete 5, Rivas 1, Rojas 5, Salmeron 3, Torres 27, Vasquez 11.

2B: Alvarado 16, Aparicio 13, Cabeza 10, Cabral 3, Colmenarez 8, De La Cruz 20, Garcia 33, Josepha 7, Rojas 8, Romero 6, Torres 3, Vasquez 4.

3B: Aparicio 6, Benitez 26, Cabeza 2, Cabral 12, Ciprian 6, Colmenarez 2, De La Cruz 9, Gonzalez 2, Josepha 2, Mendez 32, Pena 32.

SS: Benitez 4, Colmenarez 2, De La Cruz 13, Garcia 5, Pena 18, Rojas 27, Romero 22, Surun 34, Torres 1, Vasquez 1.

OF: Antigua 33, Benua 47, Ciprian 14, De Jesus 23, Encarnacion 33, Gonzalez 15, Heredia 39, Martinez 1, Mendez 13, Pena 46, Pernalete 34, Rojas 3, Santos 25, Suero 37, Torres 1, Vargas 24, Vasquez 1, Vasquez 16.

Atlanta Braves

SEASON IN A SENTENCE: On July 23, the Braves' record was 47-50, and they were six games out of the lead for the National League East with a 7% chance to make the playoffs. Their best player—Ronald Acuña Jr.—was out for the season with an injured knee. After a flurry of trades at the deadline, the Braves got hot, won their fourth straight NL East title with an 88-73 record and topped the Brewers, Dodgers and Astros to win the franchise's first World Series since 1995.

HIGH POINT: In Game 6 of the World Series, DH Jorge Soler worked a 3-2 count against Luis Garcia in the top of the third inning. He then fouled off two pitches before driving a cutter that found too much of the plate an estimated 446 feet out of Houston's Minute Maid Park. Soler's swing gave the Braves a 3-0 lead and proved to be the decisive blow of the World Series. It earned him MVP honors for the 2021 Fall Classic.

LOW POINT: Outfielder Ronald Acuña Jr. tore his right anterior cruciate ligament on July 10. At the time, he ranked second in baseball with 4.2 fWAR and was on pace for an eight-win season, but the injury ended his campaign while Atlanta was fighting to get over .500. His availability for 2022 Opening Day is in question, given the nature of ACL recovery times.

NOTABLE ROOKIES: William Contreras caught 49 games and threw out an above-average 37% of basestealers, but he was a below-average hitter, with a .215/.303/.399 slash line and 86 wRC+. The Braves got plenty of help from rookie arms, led by righthanders Ian Anderson (3.58 ERA, 128.1 innings) and Husacar Ynoa (4.05 ERA, 91 innings). Anderson has been dominant in the postseason for his career and threw five no-hit innings in Game 3. In eight playoff starts, Anderson has a 1.26 ERA.

KEY TRANSACTIONS: The Braves won the trade deadline, though it might not have been obvious at the time. To help replace the outfield production of the injured Acuña, the suspended Marcell Ozuna and the demoted Cristian Pache, Atlanta general manager Alex Anthopoulos acquired Adam Duvall, Jorge Soler, Eddie Rosario and Joc Pederson. All four came cheap, indicating more a willingness to add salary than to sacrifice future value. The Braves traded away Alex Jackson, Pablo Sandoval, Kasey Kalich and Bryce Ball in the deals. Atlanta also traded Bryse Wilson and Ricky Devito to the Pirates for reliever Richard Rodriguez.

OPENING DAY SALARY: $134,459,435 (13th).

PLAYERS OF THE YEAR

MAJOR LEAGUE
Austin Riley
3B
.303/.367/.531
Career-high 33 HR
33 2B, 107 RBIs

MINOR LEAGUE
Michael Harris
OF
(High-A)
.294/.362/.436,
7 HR, 27 SB

ORGANIZATION LEADERS

Batting		*Minimum 250 AB
MAJORS		
*AVG	Austin Riley	.303
*OPS	Ronald Acuna	.990
HR	Austin Riley	33
RBI	Austin Riley	107
MINORS		
*AVG	Johan Camargo, Gwinnett	.326
*OBP	Vaughn Grissom, Rome, Augusta	.418
*SLG	Travis Demeritte, FCL Braves, Gwinnett	.588
*OPS	Johan Camargo, Gwinnett	.958
R	Cade Bunnell, Augusta	78
H	Johan Camargo, Gwinnett	126
TB	Johan Camargo, Gwinnett	215
2B	2 tied	26
3B	5 tied	4
HR	Jesse Franklin V, Rome	24
RBI	2 tied	68
BB	Cade Bunnell, Augusta	91
SO	Cade Bunnell, Augusta	172
SB	Braulio Vasquez, Augusta	40

Pitching		#Minimum 75 IP
MAJORS		
W	2 tied	14
#ERA	Max Fried	3.04
SO	Charlie Morton	216
SV	Will Smith	37
MINORS		
W	Bryce Elder, Gwinnett, Mississippi, Rome	11
L	2 tied	8
#ERA	Bryce Elder, Gwinnett, Mississippi, Rome	2.75
G	Brooks Wilson, Gwinnett, Mississippi	39
GS	Bryce Elder, Gwinnett, Mississippi, Rome	25
SV	2 tied	7
IP	Bryce Elder, Gwinnett, Mississippi, Rome	137.2
BB	Bryce Elder, Gwinnett, Mississippi, Rome	57
SO	Bryce Elder, Gwinnett, Mississippi, Rome	155
#AVG	Joey Estes, Augusta	.184

2021 PERFORMANCE

General Manager: Alex Anthopoulos. **Farm Director:** Ben Sestanovich. **Scouting Director:** Dana Brown.

Class	Team	League	W	L	PCT	Finish	Manager
Majors	Atlanta Braves	National	88	73	.547	5th (15)	Brian Snitker
Triple-A	Gwinnett Stripers	Triple-A East	71	58	.550	8th (20)	Matt Tuiasosopo
Double-A	Mississippi Braves	Double-A South	67	44	.604	1st (8)	Wyatt Toregas
High-A	Rome Braves	High-A East	56	60	.483	6th (12)	Kanekoa Texeira
Low-A	Augusta GreenJackets	Low-A East	54	66	.450	9th (12)	Michael Saunders
Rookie	FCL Braves	Florida Complex	25	31	.446	13th (18)	Nestor Perez
Overall 2021 Minor League Record			273	259	.513	12th (30)	

ORGANIZATION STATISTICS

ATLANTA BRAVES
NATIONAL LEAGUE

Batting	B-T	HT	WT	DOB	AVG	vLH	vRH	G	AB	R	H	2B	3B	HR	RBI	BB	HBP	SH	SF	SO	SB	CS	SLG	OBP
Acuna Jr., Ronald	R-R	6-0	205	12-18-97	.283	.302	.278	82	297	72	84	19	1	24	52	49	9	0	5	85	17	6	.596	.394
Adrianza, Ehire	B-R	6-1	195	8-21-89	.247	.240	.250	109	182	32	45	9	2	5	28	21	2	1	3	42	0	0	.401	.327
Albies, Ozzie	B-R	5-8	165	1-7-97	.259	.323	.237	156	629	103	163	40	7	30	106	47	3	0	7	128	20	4	.488	.310
Almonte, Abraham	B-R	5-10	223	6-27-89	.216	.133	.237	64	148	20	32	12	0	5	19	26	0	0	1	38	1	1	.399	.331
Arcia, Orlando	R-R	6-0	187	8-4-94	.214	.273	.188	32	70	9	15	3	0	2	13	7	0	0	1	16	1	0	.343	.282
2-team total (4 Milwaukee)					.198	.273	.169	36	81	9	16	3	0	2	14	7	0	0	1	19	1	0	.309	.258
Camargo, Johan	B-R	6-0	195	12-13-93	.000	.000	.000	15	16	1	0	0	0	0	0	2	0	0	0	6	0	0	.000	.111
Contreras, William	R-R	6-0	180	12-24-97	.215	.188	.221	52	163	19	35	4	1	8	23	19	2	0	1	54	0	0	.399	.303
Duvall, Adam	R-R	6-1	215	9-4-88	.226	.182	.239	55	199	26	45	7	1	16	45	14	3	0	0	69	0	0	.513	.287
2-team total (91 Miami)					.228	.178	.245	146	513	67	117	17	2	38	113	35	4	0	3	174	5	0	.491	.281
d'Arnaud, Travis	R-R	6-2	210	2-10-89	.220	.256	.212	60	209	21	46	14	0	7	26	17	2	0	1	53	0	0	.388	.284
Freeman, Freddie	L-R	6-5	220	9-12-89	.300	.257	.317	159	600	120	180	25	2	31	83	85	8	0	2	107	8	3	.503	.393
Heredia, Guillermo	R-R	5-10	195	1-31-91	.220	.258	.204	120	305	46	67	26	0	5	26	32	9	0	1	81	0	0	.354	.311
Inciarte, Ender	L-L	5-11	190	10-29-90	.215	.231	.212	52	79	11	17	2	0	2	10	7	0	2	1	22	1	0	.316	.276
Jackson, Alex	R-R	6-2	215	12-25-95	.043	.000	.059	10	23	2	1	0	0	0	0	2	3	0	0	13	0	0	.043	.214
2-team total (42 Miami)					.137	.086	.156	52	131	13	18	4	0	3	12	13	7	0	0	73	0	0	.237	.252
Kazmar Jr., Sean	R-R	5-10	185	8-5-84	.000	.000	.000	3	2	0	0	0	0	0	0	0	0	0	0	0	0	0	.000	.000
Lucroy, Jonathan	R-R	6-0	200	6-13-86	.200	.000	.250	2	5	2	1	0	0	0	1	3	0	1	0	2	0	0	.200	.500
2-team total (5 Washington)					.316	.273	.375	7	19	2	6	1	0	0	3	3	0	1	0	4	0	0	.368	.409
Mathis, Jeff	R-R	6-0	205	3-31-83	.000	.000	.000	3	9	0	0	0	0	0	0	0	0	0	0	5	0	0	.000	.000
Ozuna, Marcell	R-R	6-1	225	11-12-90	.213	.188	.221	48	188	21	40	6	0	7	26	19	1	0	0	46	0	0	.356	.288
Pache, Cristian	R-R	6-2	215	11-19-98	.111	.133	.104	22	63	6	7	3	0	1	4	2	1	2	0	25	0	0	.206	.152
Pederson, Joc	L-L	6-1	220	4-21-92	.249	.256	.246	64	173	20	43	8	1	7	22	17	3	0	1	43	0	0	.428	.325
2-team total (73 Chicago)					.238	.265	.230	137	429	55	102	19	3	18	61	39	8	0	5	117	2	3	.422	.310
Riley, Austin	R-R	6-3	240	4-2-97	.303	.274	.312	160	590	91	179	33	1	33	107	52	12	0	8	168	0	1	.531	.367
Rosario, Eddie	R-L	6-1	180	9-28-91	.271	.231	.277	33	96	13	26	4	2	7	16	9	0	0	1	14	2	1	.573	.330
Sandoval, Pablo	B-R	5-10	268	8-11-86	.178	.167	.179	69	73	11	13	0	0	4	11	11	2	0	0	25	0	0	.342	.302
Smith, Kevan	R-R	6-4	230	6-28-88	.165	.118	.193	30	91	6	15	3	0	0	3	10	0	0	0	29	0	0	.198	.248
Soler, Jorge	R-R	6-4	235	2-25-92	.269	.214	.289	55	208	36	56	11	0	14	33	29	1	0	2	45	0	0	.524	.358
Swanson, Dansby	R-R	6-1	190	2-11-94	.248	.237	.252	160	588	78	146	33	2	27	88	52	5	1	7	167	9	3	.449	.311
Vogt, Stephen	L-R	6-0	216	11-1-84	.167	.154	.169	26	78	7	13	0	0	2	8	8	0	0	1	20	0	0	.244	.241
2-team total (52 Arizona)					.195	.293	.172	78	210	24	41	6	1	7	25	26	0	1	1	56	0	0	.333	.283

Pitching	B-T	HT	WT	DOB	W	L	ERA	G	GS	CG	SV	IP	H	R	ER	HR	BB	SO	AVG	vLH	vRH	K/9	BB/9
Anderson, Ian	R-R	6-3	170	5-2-98	9	5	3.58	24	24	0	0	128	105	51	51	16	53	124	.221	.205	.236	8.70	3.72
Biddle, Jesse	L-L	6-5	220	10-22-91	0	0	8.44	8	0	0	0	11	10	10	10	1	8	11	.263	.188	.318	9.28	6.75
Chavez, Jesse	R-R	6-1	175	8-21-83	3	2	2.14	30	4	0	0	34	23	9	8	0	11	36	.192	.192	.191	9.62	2.94
Davidson, Tucker	L-L	6-2	215	3-25-96	0	0	3.60	4	4	0	0	20	15	8	8	3	8	18	.205	.188	.211	8.10	3.60
Dayton, Grant	L-L	6-2	210	11-25-87	0	0	6.23	13	0	0	0	13	15	10	9	2	6	14	.283	.267	.289	9.69	4.15
Edwards Jr., Carl	R-R	6-3	170	9-3-91	0	0	81.00	1	0	0	0	0	3	3	3	1	1	1	.750	1.000	.667	27.00	27.00
Flaa, Jay	R-R	6-3	225	6-10-92	0	0	27.00	1	0	0	0	1	3	4	4	2	1	2	.429	.500	.333	13.50	6.75
Fried, Max	L-L	6-4	190	1-18-94	14	7	3.04	28	28	2	0	166	139	61	56	15	41	158	.227	.240	.223	8.58	2.23
Greene, Shane	R-R	6-4	200	11-17-88	0	1	8.47	19	0	0	0	17	22	16	16	5	9	17	.301	.333	.283	9.00	4.76
2-team total (9 Los Angeles)					0	1	7.23	28	0	0	1	24	25	19	19	6	14	24	.263	.263	.263	9.13	5.32
Jackson, Luke	R-R	6-2	210	8-24-91	2	2	1.98	71	0	0	0	64	45	15	14	6	29	70	.198	.196	.200	9.90	4.10
Jones, Nate	R-R	6-5	230	1-28-86	0	0	3.48	12	0	0	0	10	8	6	4	3	10	7	.205	.375	.161	6.10	8.71
2-team total (8 Los Angeles)					0	2	5.68	20	0	0	0	19	16	15	12	7	12	14	.219	.333	.163	6.63	5.68
Lee, Dylan	L-L	6-3	214	8-1-94	0	0	9.00	2	0	0	0	3	2	2	2	1	0	3	.333	.333	.333	13.50	0.00
Martin, Chris	R-R	6-8	225	6-2-86	2	4	3.95	46	0	0	1	43	49	20	19	4	6	33	.290	.303	.280	6.85	1.25
Matzek, Tyler	L-L	6-3	230	10-19-90	0	4	2.57	69	0	0	0	63	40	19	18	3	37	77	.182	.239	.141	11.00	5.29
Minter, A.J.	L-L	6-0	215	9-2-93	0	6	3.78	61	0	0	0	52	44	27	22	3	20	57	.226	.200	.245	9.80	3.44
Morton, Charlie	R-R	6-5	215	11-12-83	14	6	3.34	33	33	0	0	186	136	77	69	16	58	216	.203	.183	.221	10.47	2.81
Muller, Kyle	R-L	6-7	250	10-7-97	2	4	4.17	9	8	0	0	37	26	17	17	2	20	37	.202	.188	.206	9.08	4.91
Newcomb, Sean	L-L	6-5	255	6-12-93	2	0	4.73	32	0	0	1	32	28	17	17	1	27	43	.235	.244	.231	11.97	7.52

ATLANTA BRAVES

	B-T	HT	WT	DOB	W	L	ERA	G	GS	CG	SV	IP	H	R	ER	HR	BB	SO	AVG	vLH	vRH	K/9	BB/9
Rodriguez, Richard	R-R	6-4	220	3-4-90	1	2	3.12	27	0	0	0	26	23	9	9	6	5	9	.230	.233	.228	3.12	1.73
Santana, Edgar	R-R	6-2	205	10-16-91	3	0	3.59	41	0	0	0	43	37	20	17	7	12	33	.228	.172	.265	6.96	2.53
Smith, Will	R-L	6-5	255	7-10-89	3	7	3.44	71	0	0	37	68	49	27	26	11	28	87	.198	.212	.192	11.51	3.71
Smyly, Drew	L-L	6-2	188	6-13-89	11	4	4.48	29	23	0	0	127	133	69	63	27	41	117	.269	.285	.263	8.31	2.91
Strider, Spencer	R-R	6-0	195	10-28-98	1	0	3.86	2	0	0	0	2	2	1	1	1	1	2	.250	.286	.000	0.00	3.86
Tice, Ty	L-R	5-9	185	7-4-96	0	0	0.00	1	0	0	0	1	1	0	0	0	1	0	.250	--	.250	0.00	9.00
Tomlin, Josh	R-R	6-1	190	10-19-84	4	0	6.57	35	0	0	0	49	69	36	36	10	5	37	.327	.305	.341	6.75	0.91
Toussaint, Touki	R-R	6-3	215	6-20-96	3	3	4.50	11	10	0	0	50	43	28	25	11	22	48	.234	.208	.250	8.64	3.96
Webb, Jacob	R-R	6-2	210	8-15-93	5	4	4.19	34	0	0	1	34	38	22	16	4	14	33	.279	.254	.299	8.65	3.67
Wilson, Bryse	R-R	6-2	225	12-20-97	2	3	5.88	8	8	0	0	34	45	23	22	7	12	23	.328	.319	.338	6.15	3.21
2-team total (8 Pittsburgh)					3	7	5.35	16	16	0	0	74	85	45	44	15	22	46	.290	.279	.302	5.59	2.68
Wright, Kyle	R-R	6-4	215	10-2-95	0	1	9.95	2	2	0	0	6	7	7	7	2	5	6	.292	.400	.111	8.53	7.11
Ynoa, Huascar	R-R	6-2	220	5-28-98	4	6	4.05	18	17	0	0	91	76	42	41	14	25	100	.224	.211	.234	9.89	2.47

Fielding

Catcher	PCT	G	PO	A	E	DP	PB
Contreras	.995	49	411	21	2	0	7
d'Arnaud	.998	57	485	29	1	0	3
Jackson	.985	9	59	6	1	0	1
Lucroy	1.000	2	18	1	0	0	0
Mathis	1.000	3	23	1	0	0	1
Smith	.996	29	229	11	1	0	4
Vogt	1.000	23	169	11	0	1	2

First Base	PCT	G	PO	A	E	DP
Camargo	1.000	1	2	0	0	0
Freeman	.998	159	1252	101	3	95
Riley	1.000	10	40	3	0	8
Sandoval	1.000	2	3	0	0	0

Second Base	PCT	G	PO	A	E	DP
Adrianza	1.000	7	6	12	0	3
Albies	.987	156	231	389	8	75
Arcia	1.000	1	2	2	0	0
Camargo	1.000	1	0	2	0	0

Third Base	PCT	G	PO	A	E	DP
Adrianza	1.000	16	7	20	0	3
Camargo	.000	1	0	0	0	0
Riley	.965	156	89	300	14	18
Sandoval	.000	1	0	0	0	0

Shortstop	PCT	G	PO	A	E	DP
Adrianza	1.000	5	1	4	0	0
Arcia	.917	3	2	9	1	3
Swanson	.982	159	185	376	10	64

Outfield	PCT	G	PO	A	E	DP
Acuna Jr.	.986	82	134	4	2	0
Adrianza	1.000	21	28	1	0	0
Almonte	.966	44	55	1	2	0
Arcia	.966	14	28	0	1	0
Duvall	.983	68	108	5	2	0
Heredia	.985	129	202	0	3	0
Inciarte	1.000	41	58	1	0	0
Ozuna	1.000	48	92	2	0	0
Pache	.977	22	42	0	1	0
Pederson	1.000	60	79	1	0	0
Riley	--	1	0	0	0	0
Rosario	.962	29	51	0	2	0
Soler	.975	50	75	3	2	0

GWINNETT STRIPERS   TRIPLE-A
TRIPLE-A EAST

Batting	B-T	HT	WT	DOB	AVG	vLH	vRH	G	AB	R	H	2B	3B	HR	RBI	BB	HBP	SH	SF	SO	SB	CS	SLG	OBP
Almonte, Abraham	B-R	5-10	223	6-27-89	.403	.375	.421	19	62	16	25	4	0	3	19	21	0	0	0	14	3	3	.613	.554
Arcia, Orlando	R-R	6-0	187	8-4-94	.282	.309	.269	74	287	54	81	16	0	17	37	31	1	0	3	38	5	3	.516	.351
Brugman, Jaycob	L-L	6-0	195	1-18-92	.000	.000	.000	1	3	0	0	0	0	0	0	0	0	0	0	1	0	0	.000	.000
Camargo, Johan	B-R	6-0	195	12-13-93	.326	.323	.328	104	386	70	126	24	4	19	67	47	2	0	1	72	0	1	.557	.401
Casteel, Ryan	R-R	5-11	205	6-6-91	.224	.262	.198	68	156	13	35	6	0	8	28	15	2	0	1	49	0	0	.417	.299
Contreras, William	R-R	6-0	180	12-24-97	.290	.237	.308	44	155	26	45	8	0	9	29	13	3	0	0	36	0	0	.516	.357
Demeritte, Travis	R-R	6-0	180	9-30-94	.282	.326	.260	81	266	51	75	15	0	21	57	33	1	0	0	99	7	1	.575	.363
d'Arnaud, Travis	R-R	6-2	210	2-10-89	.235	.429	.100	6	17	2	4	0	0	0	1	2	0	0	0	4	0	0	.235	.316
Ervin, Phillip	R-R	5-10	207	7-15-92	.192	.190	.193	85	229	29	44	6	1	8	28	35	1	0	1	70	11	4	.332	.301
Franco, Maikel	R-R	6-1	225	8-26-92	.167	.000	.208	10	30	4	5	0	0	0	0	5	0	0	0	4	0	0	.167	.286
Goins, Ryan	L-R	5-10	180	2-13-88	.233	.204	.246	91	300	27	70	9	1	6	35	32	0	2	2	100	3	1	.330	.305
Gore, Terrance	R-R	5-7	160	6-8-91	.232	.231	.233	49	69	19	16	4	1	0	1	13	1	2	0	29	18	4	.319	.361
Heredia, Guillermo	R-L	5-10	195	1-31-91	.333	--	.333	1	3	0	1	0	0	0	0	0	0	0	0	0	0	0	.333	.333
Inciarte, Ender	L-L	5-11	190	10-29-90	.300	.300	.091	6	21	2	4	2	0	0	1	1	2	0	0	7	0	0	.286	.292
2-team total (15 Louisville)					.263	.286	.254	21	80	9	21	5	0	0	8	7	2	0	0	17	0	1	.325	.337
Jackson, Alex	R-R	6-2	215	12-25-95	.287	.359	.246	30	108	21	31	9	1	11	36	11	3	0	1	35	1	0	.694	.366
Kazmar Jr., Sean	R-R	5-10	185	8-5-84	.215	.196	.226	83	256	29	55	9	0	9	26	17	1	0	2	44	3	0	.355	.264
Kipnis, Jason	L-R	5-11	200	4-3-87	.290	.288	.291	59	193	36	56	10	2	10	32	27	6	0	2	50	1	0	.518	.390
Langeliers, Shea	R-R	6-0	205	11-18-97	.182	.250	.143	5	11	3	2	2	0	0	1	3	0	0	0	6	0	0	.364	.357
Lucroy, Jonathan	R-R	6-0	200	6-13-86	.220	.222	.218	31	91	10	20	4	0	2	16	17	3	0	3	20	0	0	.330	.351
Martinez, Carlos	R-R	5-11	195	5-2-95	.333	.250	.364	3	15	1	5	1	0	0	3	0	0	0	0	2	0	0	.400	.333
Morales, Jonathan	R-R	5-11	200	1-29-95	.145	.111	.159	49	152	9	22	5	0	2	12	3	0	1	1	29	0	0	.217	.160
Pache, Cristian	R-R	6-2	215	11-19-98	.265	.245	.273	89	321	50	85	15	0	11	44	30	1	1	0	97	9	7	.414	.330
Rosario, Eddie	L-R	6-1	180	9-28-91	.196	.364	.150	13	51	7	10	2	0	4	16	2	0	0	0	6	0	0	.471	.226
Sanchez, Yolmer	R-R	6-0	210	6-29-92	.216	.150	.258	102	310	36	67	9	3	9	35	35	7	2	1	88	6	3	.352	.309
Snider, Travis	L-L	6-0	230	2-2-88	.174	.139	.186	63	138	19	24	6	0	4	15	26	1	0	2	63	3	0	.304	.305
Tromp, Chadwick	R-R	5-8	221	3-1-95	.176	.200	.167	5	17	1	3	0	0	0	0	0	0	0	0	3	0	0	.176	.176
Unroe, Riley	R-R	5-11	180	8-3-95	.061	.154	.000	13	33	4	2	0	0	0	0	5	0	0	0	8	1	0	.061	.184
Waters, Drew	B-R	6-2	185	12-30-98	.240	.269	.226	103	404	70	97	22	1	11	37	47	7	0	1	142	28	9	.381	.329

Pitching	B-T	HT	WT	DOB	W	L	ERA	G	GS	CG	SV	IP	H	R	ER	HR	BB	SO	AVG	vLH	vRH	K/9	BB/9
Anderson, Ian	R-R	6-3	170	5-2-98	0	0	3.68	4	4	0	0	15	12	6	6	0	9	20	.218	.214	.222	12.27	5.52
Arano, Victor	R-R	6-2	228	2-7-95	1	2	2.50	32	0	0	2	36	25	11	10	3	15	45	.198	.218	.183	11.25	3.75
Biddle, Jesse	L-L	6-5	220	10-22-91	1	1	2.67	32	0	0	1	34	28	11	10	3	16	55	.224	.172	.269	14.70	4.28
Bradford, Chasen	R-R	6-1	229	8-5-89	5	0	3.42	36	0	0	0	53	52	21	20	7	12	45	.257	.298	.229	7.69	2.05
Burrows, Thomas	L-L	6-2	230	9-14-94	3	1	2.64	35	1	0	0	48	29	17	14	4	34	67	.176	.145	.194	12.65	6.42
Chavez, Jesse	R-R	6-1	175	8-21-83	1	0	2.25	13	0	0	2	12	6	5	3	1	5	27	.179	.148	.200	12.15	3.60
Davidson, Tucker	L-L	6-2	215	3-25-96	2	2	1.17	4	4	0	0	23	11	3	3	2	5	28	.141	.100	.167	10.96	1.96
De La Cruz, Jasseel	R-R	6-1	195	6-26-97	1	3	7.03	20	15	0	0	56	63	45	44	8	33	55	.278	.333	.234	8.79	5.27

Name	B-T	HT	WT	DOB	W	L	ERA	G	GS	CG	SV	IP	H	R	ER	HR	BB	SO	AVG	vLH	vRH		
Edwards Jr., Carl	R-R	6-3	170	9-3-91	0	0	0.00	1	0	0	0	1	0	0	0	0	1	3	.000	.000	.000	27.00	9.00
3-team total (7 Buffalo, 10 Charlotte)					1	0	2.65	18	0	0	3	17	9	5	5	2	4	26	.150	.148	.152	13.76	2.12
Elder, Bryce	R-R	6-2	220	5-19-99	2	3	3.21	7	7	0	0	37	18	10	9	1	20	40	.143	.170	.123	9.82	4.91
Flaa, Jay	R-R	6-3	225	6-10-92	1	2	5.82	31	0	0	1	34	31	25	22	3	30	43	.235	.233	.236	11.38	7.94
2-team total (1 Norfolk)					1	2	6.31	32	0	0	1	36	36	28	25	4	31	45	.254	.246	.260	11.36	7.82
Greene, Shane	R-R	6-4	200	11-17-88	0	0	2.08	4	0	0	0	4	4	1	1	0	2	5	.250	.143	.333	10.38	4.15
Hernandez, Daysbel	R-R	5-10	220	9-15-96	0	1	7.45	10	0	0	0	10	8	8	8	1	7	12	.235	.133	.316	11.17	6.52
Horacek, Mitch	L-L	6-5	185	12-3-91	1	2	4.60	14	0	0	0	16	12	8	8	3	8	16	.214	.120	.290	9.19	4.60
Johnstone, Connor	R-R	6-1	195	10-4-94	3	8	4.84	33	16	0	0	74	72	43	40	15	10	48	.258	.286	.238	5.81	1.21
Jones, Nate	R-R	6-5	230	1-28-86	0	0	0.00	1	0	0	0	1	0	0	0	0	0	2	.000	.000	.000	18.00	0.00
Kelley, Trevor	R-R	6-2	210	10-20-93	3	4	1.52	37	0	0	2	41	27	10	7	2	18	46	.193	.167	.207	10.02	3.92
Kingham, Nolan	R-R	6-4	210	8-18-96	0	5	10.13	7	6	0	0	29	46	33	33	9	14	20	.365	.381	.349	6.14	4.30
Lee, Dylan	L-L	6-3	214	8-1-94	5	1	1.54	35	0	0	1	47	29	11	8	4	6	54	.176	.211	.157	10.41	1.16
Lopez, Yoan	R-R	6-3	208	1-2-93	3	2	3.03	32	0	0	2	33	30	13	11	3	11	35	.250	.265	.239	9.64	3.03
Martin, Chris	R-R	6-8	225	6-2-86	0	0	7.36	4	0	0	0	4	4	3	3	0	1	4	.267	.143	.375	9.82	2.45
Minter, A.J.	L-L	6-0	215	9-2-93	0	0	0.00	7	0	0	6	7	0	0	0	0	3	10	.000	.000	.000	12.27	3.68
Muller, Kyle	R-L	6-7	250	10-7-97	5	4	3.39	17	17	0	0	80	66	37	30	9	42	93	.223	.207	.230	10.51	4.74
Newcomb, Sean	L-L	6-5	255	6-12-93	3	0	1.62	15	0	0	4	17	9	3	3	1	4	28	.153	.095	.184	15.12	2.16
Roark, Tanner	R-R	6-2	238	10-5-86	4	1	2.14	24	3	0	3	46	38	11	11	2	16	44	.226	.203	.240	8.55	3.11
Rodriguez, Jose	R-R	6-2	175	8-29-95	6	6	5.29	19	17	0	0	78	87	51	46	16	21	66	.281	.300	.265	7.58	2.41
Santana, Edgar	R-R	6-2	205	10-16-91	2	0	9.00	3	0	0	0	3	2	3	3	1	1	4	.182	.167	.200	12.00	3.00
Strider, Spencer	R-R	6-0	195	10-28-98	0	0	0.00	1	0	0	0	1	1	0	0	0	0	3	.250	.000	.333	27.00	0.00
Tice, Ty	L-R	5-9	185	7-4-96	1	0	7.36	11	0	0	0	11	13	9	9	4	5	8	.302	.278	.320	6.55	4.09
2-team total (1 Buffalo)					1	0	6.75	12	0	0	0	12	13	9	9	4	7	8	.283	.263	.296	6.00	5.25
Tomlin, Josh	R-R	6-1	190	10-19-84	0	0	9.00	1	0	0	0	3	4	3	3	1	1	2	.308	.000	.400	6.00	3.00
Toussaint, Touki	R-R	6-3	215	6-20-96	2	1	3.48	7	4	0	0	21	12	8	8	1	12	28	.174	.250	.108	12.19	5.23
Webb, Jacob	R-R	6-2	210	8-15-93	1	2	3.00	24	0	0	6	24	17	9	8	2	7	34	.193	.172	.203	12.75	2.63
Wilson, Brooks	L-R	6-2	205	3-15-96	0	0	1.50	6	0	0	1	6	2	1	1	0	2	11	.100	.000	.143	16.50	3.00
Wilson, Bryse	R-R	6-2	225	12-20-97	5	2	4.23	10	9	1	0	55	61	26	26	8	16	42	.284	.287	.281	6.83	2.60
Wright, Kyle	R-R	6-4	215	10-2-95	10	5	3.02	24	24	2	0	137	117	52	46	9	45	137	.228	.233	.224	9.00	2.96
Ynoa, Huascar	R-R	6-2	220	5-28-98	0	0	4.32	2	2	0	0	8	8	6	4	1	4	11	.250	.286	.222	11.88	4.32

Fielding

Catcher	PCT	G	PO	A	E	DP	PB
Casteel	1.000	6	59	4	0	0	1
Contreras	.993	34	257	13	2	1	5
d'Arnaud	1.000	6	39	4	0	0	0
Jackson	.986	23	203	13	3	3	1
Langeliers	.974	3	34	3	1	0	1
Lucroy	.996	24	220	16	1	0	1
Martinez	1.000	3	36	4	0	0	1
Morales	1.000	38	285	23	0	2	3
Tromp	.959	5	45	2	2	1	0

First Base	PCT	G	PO	A	E	DP
Camargo	.989	59	456	14	5	51
Casteel	.996	30	208	21	1	21
Demeritte	.923	1	11	1	1	3
Franco	1.000	8	66	2	0	8
Goins	1.000	1	6	1	0	0
Kazmar Jr.	1.000	11	67	4	0	8
Lucroy	1.000	2	11	0	0	3
Morales	.983	9	54	3	1	6
Snider	.991	19	105	5	1	11
Unroe	1.000	2	14	1	0	1

Second Base	PCT	G	PO	A	E	DP
Arcia	.667	1	1	1	1	0
Demeritte	1.000	1	1	1	0	1
Goins	.971	31	40	60	3	16
Kazmar Jr.	.978	24	29	58	2	11
Kipnis	.978	48	65	109	4	36
Morales	1.000	1	0	2	0	0
Sanchez	.993	41	55	92	1	22
Unroe	1.000	2	4	3	0	0

Third Base	PCT	G	PO	A	E	DP
Arcia	.889	3	3	5	1	1
Camargo	.924	47	19	66	7	8
Goins	1.000	16	10	35	0	2
Kazmar Jr.	.939	40	15	78	6	14
Morales	1.000	2	0	2	0	0
Sanchez	.923	32	25	47	6	3
Unroe	1.000	4	1	3	0	1

Shortstop	PCT	G	PO	A	E	DP
Arcia	.980	65	82	168	5	46
Camargo	.857	1	2	4	1	0
Goins	.968	46	48	101	5	25
Kazmar Jr.	1.000	1	0	2	0	0
Sanchez	.973	21	18	53	2	7
Unroe	1.000	2	0	1	0	0

Outfield	PCT	G	PO	A	E	DP
Almonte	.955	17	20	1	1	0
Arcia	1.000	4	6	0	0	0
Camargo	--	1	0	0	0	0
Demeritte	.991	61	109	5	1	1
Ervin	.991	73	110	5	1	2
Gore	1.000	24	36	0	0	0
Heredia	1.000	1	2	0	0	0
Inciarte	1.000	5	6	1	0	0
Kipnis	1.000	6	7	0	0	0
Pache	.962	83	147	3	6	0
Rosario	.964	11	26	1	1	0
Sanchez	1.000	6	6	2	0	1
Snider	1.000	18	27	0	0	1
Waters	.981	107	196	11	4	2

MISSISSIPPI BRAVES
DOUBLE-A SOUTH

DOUBLE-A

Batting	B-T	HT	WT	DOB	AVG	vLH	vRH	G	AB	R	H	2B	3B	HR	RBI	BB	HBP	SH	SF	SO	SB	CS	SLG	OBP
Alexander, CJ	L-R	6-5	215	7-17-96	.197	.132	.216	87	304	32	60	17	4	10	31	24	1	0	1	105	14	1	.378	.258
Calandra, Mitch	R-R	5-11	195	1-13-97	.333	.000	.500	3	3	1	1	0	0	1	0	0	0	0	0	2	0	0	.667	.333
Clementina, Hendrik	R-R	6-0	250	6-17-97	.206	.162	.221	45	141	17	29	3	0	8	21	11	0	0	2	49	0	0	.397	.260
Dean, Justin	R-R	5-6	185	12-6-96	.237	.253	.231	99	363	60	86	14	4	8	34	42	18	0	0	128	29	6	.364	.345
Delgado, Riley	R-R	5-10	175	2-22-95	.178	.125	.200	8	28	3	5	0	0	0	1	3	0	0	0	3	0	0	.179	.207
Harris, Trey	R-R	5-11	220	1-15-96	.247	.253	.245	96	364	46	90	15	0	8	50	26	12	0	2	72	4	3	.354	.317
Jenista, Greyson	L-R	6-4	210	12-7-96	.216	.147	.242	89	273	45	59	7	2	19	42	51	3	0	2	118	7	2	.465	.343
Langeliers, Shea	R-R	6-0	205	11-18-97	.258	.200	.277	92	329	56	85	13	0	22	52	36	4	0	1	97	1	0	.498	.338
Lugbauer, Drew	L-R	6-3	220	8-23-96	.223	.250	.217	86	300	50	67	15	0	18	51	42	7	0	1	131	0	1	.453	.331
Martinez, Carlos	R-R	5-11	195	5-2-95	.250	.364	.200	11	36	3	9	2	0	1	3	0	1	0	0	4	0	0	.389	.270
Miller, Jalen	R-R	6-0	190	12-19-96	.201	.191	.205	76	229	29	46	13	0	9	29	22	1	0	3	75	3	1	.376	.271
Neslony, Tyler	L-R	6-1	190	2-13-94	.164	.167	.162	19	55	6	9	2	0	1	4	7	1	0	0	21	0	1	.255	.270
2-team total (38 Birmingham)					.295	.341	.280	57	176	30	52	18	1	8	32	26	2	0	1	52	1	1	.545	.390
Pearson, Jacob	L-R	6-1	185	6-1-98	.171	.095	.200	53	152	17	26	2	2	4	19	18	0	2	2	43	3	3	.289	.256
Ramos, Jefrey	R-R	6-1	185	2-10-99	.183	.176	.185	58	197	24	36	5	3	6	23	14	2	0	4	65	3	1	.330	.240

Name	B-T	HT	WT	DOB	AVG	vLH	vRH	G	AB	R	H	2B	3B	HR	RBI	BB	HBP	SH	SF	SO	SB	CS	SLG	OBP
Rijo, Wendell	R-R	5-11	170	9-4-95	.236	.221	.240	92	322	49	76	16	0	15	37	34	6	2	1	83	8	2	.425	.320
Shewmake, Braden	L-R	6-4	190	11-19-97	.228	.206	.234	83	324	40	74	14	3	12	40	17	2	0	0	75	4	2	.401	.271
Unroe, Riley	B-R	5-11	180	8-3-95	.261	.257	.264	27	88	10	23	3	2	2	6	6	2	1	0	19	1	4	.409	.323
Waddell, Luke	L-R	5-9	180	7-13-98	.161	.286	.125	8	31	3	5	0	0	0	2	2	0	0	0	4	1	1	.161	.212

Pitching

Name	B-T	HT	WT	DOB	W	L	ERA	G	GS	CG	SV	IP	H	R	ER	HR	BB	SO	AVG	vLH	vRH	K/9	BB/9
Bacon, Troy	R-R	6-0	165	9-26-96	3	1	2.79	31	0	0	0	39	36	13	12	1	18	42	.247	.306	.202	9.78	4.19
Clouse, Corbin	B-L	6-0	230	6-26-95	0	0	1.59	8	0	0	1	11	9	4	2	1	6	17	.225	.176	.261	13.50	4.76
Deal, Hayden	L-L	6-4	210	11-4-94	3	2	3.77	23	17	0	1	88	81	40	37	5	33	72	.248	.267	.239	7.34	3.36
Diaz, Indigo	R-R	6-5	250	10-14-98	2	1	1.50	14	0	0	0	18	10	3	3	1	9	29	.161	.143	.176	14.50	4.50
Elder, Bryce	R-R	6-2	220	5-19-99	7	1	3.21	9	9	1	0	56	39	20	20	7	17	60	.198	.170	.220	9.64	2.73
Ferguson, Tyler	R-R	6-4	225	10-5-93	3	0	1.29	5	0	0	0	7	8	2	1	0	4	7	.308	.385	.231	9.00	5.14
Graham, Josh	R-R	6-1	215	10-14-93	1	0	2.33	13	0	0	1	19	16	7	5	1	6	20	.208	.310	.146	9.31	2.79
Hartman, Matt	R-R	6-3	220	2-28-96	0	1	6.35	3	0	0	0	6	4	6	4	1	8	7	.190	.333	.133	11.12	12.71
Hernandez, Daysbel	R-R	5-10	220	9-15-96	3	1	2.76	26	0	0	3	33	23	12	10	3	16	46	.200	.220	.185	12.67	4.41
Higginbotham, Jake	L-L	6-0	190	1-11-96	0	0	0.00	1	0	0	0	2	0	0	0	0	0	3	.000	.000	.000	13.50	0.00
Hoekstra, Kurt	L-R	6-2	210	6-27-93	0	0	3.18	13	0	0	0	17	10	6	6	0	17	16	.185	.200	.167	8.47	9.00
Javier, Odalvi	R-R	6-2	180	9-4-96	5	4	3.20	24	12	0	0	76	57	29	27	5	31	80	.208	.220	.199	9.47	3.67
Kingham, Nolan	R-R	6-4	210	8-18-96	6	1	2.08	12	10	0	2	65	54	15	15	3	10	43	.225	.217	.231	5.95	1.38
Latcham, Will	R-R	6-2	200	1-26-96	2	1	4.19	30	0	0	0	39	34	21	18	3	20	40	.230	.277	.193	9.31	4.66
McLaughlin, Sean	L-R	5-11	195	5-16-94	1	1	5.25	29	0	0	0	36	44	23	21	4	12	38	.293	.403	.205	9.50	3.00
Mora, Luis	R-R	6-4	210	6-17-95	0	1	2.08	6	0	0	0	9	6	3	2	0	10	6	.200	.111	.238	6.23	10.38
Nunn, Chris	L-L	6-5	200	10-5-90	0	2	4.24	14	0	0	1	17	10	8	8	2	12	26	.172	.154	.178	13.76	6.35
Puckett, A.J.	R-R	6-4	200	5-27-95	1	1	3.15	8	8	0	0	34	30	14	12	1	16	32	.240	.250	.232	8.39	4.19
Ramirez, Emmanuel	R-R	6-2	190	7-15-94	3	1	8.89	20	0	0	2	26	37	28	26	7	14	39	.319	.364	.279	13.33	4.78
Rangel, Alan	R-R	6-2	170	8-21-97	3	2	4.50	7	7	0	0	34	28	17	17	3	5	41	.220	.183	.254	10.85	1.32
Rodriguez, Jose	R-R	6-2	175	8-29-95	1	1	1.61	4	4	0	0	22	10	5	4	1	5	27	.135	.125	.143	10.88	2.01
Shuster, Jared	L-L	6-3	210	8-3-98	0	0	7.36	3	3	0	0	15	19	12	12	5	5	17	.306	.313	.304	10.43	3.07
Stallings, Mitch	L-L	6-2	180	6-30-95	0	2	21.60	3	2	0	0	5	9	12	12	1	5	7	.375	.182	.538	12.60	9.00
Strider, Spencer	R-R	6-0	195	10-28-98	3	7	4.71	14	14	0	0	63	48	34	33	6	29	94	.211	.259	.164	13.43	4.14
Tarnok, Freddy	R-R	6-3	185	11-24-98	3	2	2.60	9	9	0	0	45	35	15	13	2	15	61	.212	.231	.189	12.20	3.00
Toussaint, Touki	R-R	6-3	215	6-20-96	0	0	4.91	1	1	0	0	4	1	2	2	0	2	4	.083	.000	.125	9.82	4.91
Vodnik, Victor	R-R	6-0	200	10-9-99	1	4	5.35	11	11	0	0	34	32	20	20	5	22	41	.252	.345	.181	10.96	5.88
White, Brandon	R-R	6-2	215	12-21-94	4	2	2.33	32	0	0	0	39	30	15	10	1	18	43	.207	.254	.171	10.01	4.19
Wilson, Brooks	L-R	6-2	205	3-15-96	3	1	2.45	33	0	0	5	44	32	12	12	3	17	73	.201	.197	.205	14.93	3.48
Withrow, Matt	R-R	6-5	235	9-23-93	3	1	2.82	25	4	0	1	51	33	19	16	2	31	52	.188	.189	.186	9.18	5.47

Fielding

Catcher	PCT	G	PO	A	E	DP	PB
Clementina	.983	24	220	18	4	5	1
Langeliers	.995	79	774	73	4	9	3
Lugbauer	1.000	1	5	1	0	1	0
Martinez	.985	10	62	5	1	0	0

	PCT	G	PO	A	E	DP
Miller	.975	69	91	140	6	26
Rijo	.977	35	52	75	3	17
Unroe	1.000	8	12	15	0	7
Waddell	1.000	5	7	13	0	3

	PCT	G	PO	A	E	DP
Rijo	.949	26	32	43	4	11
Shewmake	.969	79	98	187	9	40
Unroe	.833	6	3	7	2	1
Waddell	1.000	2	2	4	0	1

First Base	PCT	G	PO	A	E	DP
Alexander	1.000	2	16	0	0	1
Jenista	.984	47	291	17	5	29
Lugbauer	.998	62	415	26	1	40
Unroe	1.000	2	18	1	0	0

Third Base	PCT	G	PO	A	E	DP
Alexander	.943	75	57	109	10	11
Delgado	1.000	4	1	7	0	2
Rijo	.966	30	39	45	3	10
Unroe	1.000	3	1	4	0	0
Waddell	1.000	1	0	1	0	0

Outfield	PCT	G	PO	A	E	DP
Dean	.985	99	197	6	3	2
Harris	.987	90	155	2	2	0
Jenista	.961	41	74	0	3	0
Neslony	1.000	16	35	0	0	0
Pearson	1.000	52	87	2	0	1
Ramos	.986	43	64	5	1	1
Unroe	--	2	0	0	0	0

Second Base	PCT	G	PO	A	E	DP
Delgado	1.000	3	8	12	0	6

Shortstop	PCT	G	PO	A	E	DP
Delgado	1.000	1	2	1	0	0

ROME BRAVES   HIGH CLASS A

HIGH-A EAST

Batting	B-T	HT	WT	DOB	AVG	vLH	vRH	G	AB	R	H	2B	3B	HR	RBI	BB	HBP	SH	SF	SO	SB	CS	SLG	OBP
Ball, Bryce	L-R	6-6	240	7-8-98	.206	.239	.194	54	170	24	35	12	1	6	31	40	0	0	4	59	0	0	.394	.350
Bermudez, Jose	B-R	6-2	160	7-9-97	.125	.000	.143	3	8	0	1	0	0	0	0	1	0	0	0	5	0	0	.125	.222
Brown, Logan	L-R	6-0	195	9-14-96	.209	.265	.193	60	230	19	48	8	0	6	32	10	2	0	2	64	0	1	.322	.246
Calandra, Mitch	R-R	5-11	195	1-13-97	.176	.167	.182	6	17	3	3	0	0	0	0	1	0	0	0	5	0	0	.176	.222
Campbell, Drew	L-L	5-11	170	11-10-97	.288	.286	.289	14	59	10	17	5	1	4	13	0	0		1	8	1	0	.610	.283
Delgado, Riley	L-R	5-10	175	2-22-95	.252	.260	.250	78	301	37	76	6	2	2	23	27	1	0	2	37	3	1	.306	.314
Estrada, Rusber	R-R	6-0	215	6-5-95	.205	.120	.245	50	156	21	32	9	0	7	19	23	5	0	1	67	0	0	.397	.324
Franklin V, Jesse	L-L	6-1	215	12-1-98	.244	.247	.244	101	360	55	88	24	2	24	61	34	8	0	4	115	19	4	.522	.320
Grissom, Vaughn	R-R	6-3	180	1-5-01	.378	.500	.364	12	37	12	14	2	0	2	10	11	2	0	2	5	3	0	.595	.519
Harris II, Michael	L-L	6-0	195	3-7-01	.294	.296	.293	101	374	55	110	26	3	7	64	35	7	0	4	76	27	4	.436	.362
Josephina, Kevin	B-R	6-0	170	10-2-96	.265	.294	.255	67	260	37	69	13	2	3	21	14	2	0	1	71	6	3	.365	.307
Langhorne, Brett	L-R	6-3	210	6-14-96	.189	.094	.220	68	212	18	40	8	0	7	23	28	2	0	3	104	11	1	.325	.286
Martinez, Carlos	R-R	5-11	195	5-2-95	.272	.429	.217	23	81	10	22	7	0	1	14	1	2	0	1	20	0	0	.395	.294
Michel, Shean	R-R	5-11	170	9-26-97	.205	.305	.159	75	258	35	53	11	4	5	28	23	0	0	4	78	12	4	.337	.267
Milligan, Cody	L-R	5-10	185	12-22-98	.230	.149	.257	96	352	60	81	13	3	1	31	47	6	1	4	97	15	11	.293	.328
Moritz, Andrew	L-R	5-11	180	12-22-96	.280	.162	.321	78	261	35	73	8	0	1	21	20	1	0	1	48	10	5	.322	.332
Philip, Beau	R-R	6-0	190	10-23-98	.187	.217	.176	97	337	43	63	15	2	6	24	38	3	0	2	137	16	4	.297	.274
Rodriguez, Cesar	B-R	5-10	160	12-26-00	.000	.000	--	1	1	0	0	0	0	0	0	0	0	0	0	0	0	0	.000	.000

	B-T	HT	WT	DOB	AVG	vLH	vRH	G	AB	R	H	2B	3B	HR	RBI	BB	HBP	SH	SF	SO	SB	CS	SLG	OBP
Saunders, Garrett	R-R	6-0	190	12-3-96	.179	.154	.188	35	95	5	17	1	1	0	6	11	1	0	0	41	1	4	.211	.271
Schwartz, Garrison	L-L	6-0	205	1-22-96	.088	.056	.096	34	91	8	8	2	0	1	4	17	5	0	0	50	4	2	.143	.265
Valdes, Javier	R-R	5-10	195	11-19-98	.250	.333	.231	5	16	6	4	1	0	0	1	2	1	0	0	3	0	0	.313	.368
Waddell, Luke	L-R	5-9	180	7-13-98	.304	.263	.320	21	69	15	21	1	0	6	13	7	1	0	1	13	1	1	.580	.372

Pitching	B-T	HT	WT	DOB	W	L	ERA	G	GS	CG	SV	IP	H	R	ER	HR	BB	SO	AVG	vLH	vRH	K/9	BB/9
Crouse, Marrick	R-R	6-3	200	5-2-97	4	1	5.91	32	0	0	1	43	49	31	28	4	23	43	.290	.325	.261	9.07	4.85
Daniels, Zach	L-R	5-11	160	4-21-97	3	2	2.11	30	0	0	4	47	35	19	11	0	23	46	.210	.194	.221	8.81	4.40
DeVito, Ricky	B-R	6-3	195	8-21-98	0	3	2.66	5	5	0	0	20	19	11	6	2	7	27	.232	.211	.250	11.95	3.10
Diaz, Indigo	R-R	6-5	250	10-14-98	4	1	1.00	18	0	0	5	27	11	4	3	0	7	54	.117	.150	.093	18.00	2.33
Dodd, Dylan	L-L	6-3	210	6-6-98	0	1	24.00	1	1	0	0	3	9	8	8	4	0	6	.500	.250	.571	18.00	0.00
Dum, Benjamin	L-R	6-0	215	9-30-96	2	1	3.97	8	0	0	0	11	10	7	5	3	2	14	.227	.143	.267	11.12	1.59
Elder, Bryce	R-R	6-2	220	5-19-99	2	1	2.60	9	9	0	0	45	38	17	13	2	20	55	.224	.282	.182	11.00	4.00
Ferguson, Tyler	R-R	6-4	225	10-5-93	3	4	2.49	17	0	0	1	25	17	13	7	2	8	26	.202	.244	.163	9.24	2.84
Gordon, Tanner	L-R	6-5	215	10-26-97	2	4	4.44	11	10	0	1	51	57	32	25	8	11	44	.282	.284	.280	7.82	1.95
Hartman, Matt	R-R	6-3	220	2-28-96	0	0	14.00	8	0	0	0	9	9	14	14	3	10	14	.265	.400	.158	14.00	10.00
Higginbotham, Jake	L-L	6-0	190	1-11-96	0	0	0.00	6	0	0	0	7	1	0	0	1	1	11	.045	.000	.091	13.50	1.23
Horacek, Mitch	L-L	6-5	185	12-3-91	1	0	2.25	4	0	0	0	4	2	1	1	0	0	7	.167	.200	.143	15.75	0.00
Huntley, Coleman	R-R	6-4	225	3-10-93	5	7	4.52	30	5	0	0	74	77	42	37	6	20	82	.270	.264	.276	10.02	2.44
Kalich, Kasey	R-R	6-3	220	4-25-98	0	2	3.26	20	0	0	5	30	33	11	11	2	17	35	.273	.224	.306	10.38	5.04
Lawson, Tanner	L-L	6-1	190	10-25-96	0	1	8.44	3	2	0	0	5	7	5	5	2	7	7	.304	.333	.294	11.81	11.81
McSteen, Jake	R-L	6-0	195	3-12-96	2	5	4.33	18	13	0	0	73	83	49	35	12	20	69	.279	.248	.296	8.55	2.48
Mora, Luis	R-R	6-4	210	6-17-95	0	0	0.00	3	0	0	0	3	0	0	0	0	4	2	.000	.000	.000	6.75	13.50
Noguera, Gabriel	L-L	6-2	175	5-31-96	1	1	7.33	24	0	0	1	27	21	24	22	4	33	34	.212	.200	.217	11.33	11.00
Puckett, A.J.	R-R	6-4	200	5-27-95	3	2	2.72	12	7	0	0	46	36	17	14	2	16	40	.212	.268	.184	7.77	3.11
Ramirez, Emmanuel	R-R	6-2	190	7-15-94	0	1	3.86	7	0	0	1	12	10	6	5	1	2	20	.233	.350	.130	15.43	1.54
Rangel, Alan	R-R	6-2	170	8-21-97	4	5	3.57	15	14	0	0	71	54	39	28	8	21	95	.205	.186	.219	12.10	2.67
Riley, Trey	L-R	6-3	205	4-21-98	5	1	3.29	26	0	0	0	38	26	16	14	5	11	32	.193	.188	.197	7.51	2.58
Santos, Lisandro	L-L	6-1	170	7-24-98	1	0	3.72	6	0	0	0	10	4	4	4	2	11	11	.133	.167	.125	10.24	10.24
Schwab, Davis	L-L	6-4	230	1-27-97	1	2	5.23	30	0	0	0	43	38	36	25	1	37	46	.233	.204	.248	9.63	7.74
Schwartz, Garrison	L-L	6-0	205	1-22-96	0	0	0.00	1	0	0	0	0	0	0	0	0	3	1	.000	—	.000	27.00	81.00
Shuster, Jared	L-L	6-3	210	8-3-98	2	0	3.70	15	14	0	0	58	47	24	24	10	15	73	.215	.172	.232	11.26	2.31
Spain, Dylan	R-R	6-6	205	6-21-98	0	0	0.00	1	0	0	0	1	0	0	0	0	1	1	.000	.000	.000	9.00	0.00
Stallings, Mitch	L-L	6-2	180	6-30-95	2	4	5.31	21	8	0	0	61	66	36	36	8	27	59	.277	.227	.301	8.70	3.98
Strider, Spencer	R-R	6-0	195	10-28-98	0	0	2.45	3	3	0	0	15	9	4	4	1	6	24	.170	.118	.194	14.73	3.68
Tarnok, Freddy	R-R	6-3	185	11-24-98	3	2	4.76	7	5	0	0	28	21	15	15	6	13	48	.204	.204	.204	15.25	4.13
Toussaint, Touki	R-R	6-3	215	6-20-96	0	0	3.00	1	1	0	0	3	1	1	1	1	1	2	.111	.143	.000	6.00	3.00
Vines, Darius	R-R	6-1	190	4-30-98	4	4	3.24	14	14	1	0	75	60	37	27	12	19	81	.214	.209	.217	9.72	2.28
Woods, William	R-R	6-3	190	12-29-98	0	1	4.66	4	4	0	0	10	10	5	5	3	4	7	.270	.214	.304	6.52	3.72
Yeager, Justin	L-R	6-5	215	1-20-98	2	3	2.50	13	0	0	3	18	12	7	5	1	10	25	.182	.214	.158	12.50	5.00
Ynoa, Huascar	R-R	6-2	220	5-28-98	0	1	27.00	1	0	0	0	1	2	3	3	0	1	2	.571	.667	.545	9.00	4.50

Fielding

Catcher	PCT	G	PO	A	E	DP	PB
Brown	.995	60	605	36	3	3	8
Calandra	1.000	2	8	0	0	0	0
Estrada	.986	43	414	17	6	2	2
Martinez	.979	13	84	11	2	0	0
Valdes	1.000	5	39	1	0	0	1

Grissom	1.000	2	6	5	0	1
Langhorne	1.000	1	3	1	0	0
Milligan	.956	92	105	219	15	45
Philip	1.000	2	3	4	0	3
Saunders	.919	9	8	26	3	5
Waddell	1.000	4	5	8	0	1

Shortstop	PCT	G	PO	A	E	DP
Delgado	.973	13	15	21	1	7
Grissom	.875	8	14	21	5	6
Philip	.935	70	84	174	18	28
Saunders	.868	19	22	37	9	5
Waddell	.903	8	10	18	3	5

First Base	PCT	G	PO	A	E	DP
Ball	.983	50	331	18	6	36
Delgado	1.000	5	31	1	0	4
Josephina	.923	4	24	0	2	2
Langhorne	.992	53	366	12	3	22
Martinez	.976	11	76	5	2	12

Third Base	PCT	G	PO	A	E	DP
Delgado	.951	37	17	60	4	7
Josephina	.872	45	24	71	14	8
Langhorne	.933	9	5	9	1	1
Philip	.922	19	13	34	4	4
Saunders	1.000	7	2	13	0	1
Waddell	.938	5	5	10	1	1

Outfield	PCT	G	PO	A	E	DP
Bermudez	1.000	2	4	0	0	0
Campbell	.913	14	19	2	2	0
Franklin V	.975	90	155	1	4	0
Harris II	.986	92	203	10	3	3
Langhorne	--	1	0	0	0	0
Michel	.992	70	111	11	1	1
Moritz	.966	62	83	3	3	1
Schwartz	1.000	27	40	0	0	0

Second Base	PCT	G	PO	A	E	DP
Delgado	1.000	10	18	26	0	8

AUGUSTA GREENJACKETS

LOW-A EAST

Batting	B-T	HT	WT	DOB	AVG	vLH	vRH	G	AB	R	H	2B	3B	HR	RBI	BB	HBP	SH	SF	SO	SB	CS	SLG	OBP
Bermudez, Jose	B-R	6-2	160	7-9-97	.200	.241	.167	23	65	7	13	3	0	0	2	2	1	1	0	24	5	2	.246	.235
Birdsong, Cody	R-R	6-2	195	1-19-97	.202	.216	.192	29	89	12	18	1	1	0	6	11	1	0	0	30	1	0	.236	.297
Blair, Connor	R-R	6-0	215	5-6-98	.081	.071	.088	19	62	4	5	0	0	0	2	13	0	0	1	19	3	2	.081	.237
Bunnell, Cade	L-R	6-0	182	5-14-97	.216	.194	.224	113	393	78	85	26	4	17	50	91	3	0	1	172	13	2	.433	.367
Calandra, Mitch	R-R	5-11	195	1-13-97	.250	--	.250	1	4	0	1	0	0	0	0	0	0	0	0	2	0	0	.250	.250
Campbell, Drew	L-L	5-11	170	11-10-97	.321	.286	.333	8	28	5	9	2	2	1	5	3	0	0	0	10	1	0	.643	.387
Carter, Willie	R-R	6-0	205	4-8-97	.273	.290	.273	101	349	46	97	12	3	8	68	45	15	0	4	109	18	5	.398	.380
Conley, Cal	B-R	5-10	185	7-17-99	.214	.167	.227	35	140	21	30	5	1	2	9	14	5	0	2	33	8	3	.307	.304
De Hoyos, Victor	R-R	5-9	170	2-23-98	.257	.343	.212	28	101	14	26	3	0	5	10	4	3	0	0	27	0	0	.436	.292
Grissom, Vaughn	R-R	6-3	180	1-5-01	.311	.281	.326	75	280	52	87	15	4	5	33	34	10	2	2	49	13	3	.446	.402

Horne, Bryson	L-R	6-3	220	3-6-99	.269	.282	.263	93	350	40	94	17	1	10	48	28	1	0	3	91	2	1	.409	.322
Malloy, Justyn-Henry	R-R	6-2	212	2-19-00	.270	.143	.309	37	122	23	33	5	0	5	21	24	0	0	1	30	4	2	.434	.388
Paolini, Stephen	L-L	6-2	195	11-23-00	.171	.184	.165	105	345	44	59	11	3	4	24	39	5	0	3	167	15	6	.255	.263
Parker, Brandon	R-R	6-1	205	5-27-99	.185	.259	.149	51	168	22	31	10	0	7	27	23	6	0	3	66	1	0	.369	.300
Robinson, Christian	L-L	6-2	211	11-23-99	.262	.217	.271	35	130	13	34	4	2	1	22	7	1	0	0	40	3	1	.346	.304
Rodriguez, Ricardo	R-R	5-11	185	12-20-97	.256	.267	.250	48	160	17	41	9	0	4	19	19	5	0	1	34	0	1	.388	.351
Shepherd, Cam	R-R	6-1	181	9-28-97	.173	.186	.167	87	272	26	47	7	1	2	25	37	3	1	3	76	6	0	.228	.276
Stephens, Landon	R-R	6-2	204	3-15-98	.239	.229	.243	105	364	57	87	17	2	21	68	55	7	0	2	151	7	6	.470	.348
Tolve, Tyler	L-R	6-2	180	7-16-00	.294	.333	.284	23	85	12	25	3	2	2	10	6	1	0	0	28	2	0	.447	.348
Valdes, Javier	R-R	5-10	195	11-19-98	.263	.400	.214	24	76	7	20	5	0	0	11	8	5	0	3	20	3	0	.329	.359
Vasquez, Braulio	R-R	6-0	210	4-13-99	.220	.145	.255	73	214	39	47	8	1	6	23	29	11	2	2	66	40	13	.350	.340
Zebrowski, Adam	R-R	6-3	230	9-28-00	.211	.300	.179	11	38	1	8	2	0	0	4	3	2	0	0	12	0	0	.263	.302

Pitching

Pitching	B-T	HT	WT	DOB	W	L	ERA	G	GS	CG	SV	IP	H	R	ER	HR	BB	SO	AVG	vLH	vRH	K/9	BB/9
Acuna, James	R-R	6-5	180	9-18-97	2	0	4.72	31	2	0	3	48	41	27	25	6	31	62	.229	.263	.202	11.71	5.85
Barger, Alec	R-R	6-2	201	3-24-98	4	4	4.50	30	6	0	1	60	51	37	30	7	31	79	.222	.252	.197	11.85	4.65
Birdsong, Cody	R-R	6-2	195	1-19-97	0	0	0.00	3	0	0	0	2	1	2	0	0	1	0	.167	.000	.333	0.00	5.40
Bryant, Chad	R-R	6-0	210	8-3-99	0	5	6.61	13	9	0	0	31	38	35	23	5	29	33	.290	.388	.188	9.48	8.33
Burgess, Brent	R-R	6-0	200	5-2-97	1	1	3.86	2	0	0	0	5	4	3	2	1	2	7	.222	.250	.214	13.50	3.86
Cusick, Ryan	R-R	6-6	235	11-12-99	0	1	2.76	6	6	0	0	16	15	7	5	1	4	34	.242	.207	.273	18.73	2.20
Dodd, Dylan	L-L	6-3	210	6-6-98	0	1	4.91	3	3	0	0	11	10	6	6	0	3	14	.250	.167	.286	11.45	2.45
Dum, Benjamin	L-R	6-0	215	9-30-96	1	1	3.68	22	0	0	3	37	36	18	15	4	11	38	.257	.328	.197	9.33	2.70
Estes, Joey	R-R	6-2	190	10-8-01	3	6	2.91	20	20	1	0	99	66	39	32	7	29	127	.184	.148	.213	11.55	2.64
Gordon, Tanner	L-R	6-5	215	10-26-97	4	4	3.43	11	11	1	0	58	43	24	22	5	10	65	.205	.143	.259	10.14	1.56
Hodgson, Alger	R-R	6-2	190	4-10-99	0	1	13.50	3	0	0	0	3	6	5	5	2	4	3	.375	.429	.333	8.10	10.80
Hoffmann, Andrew	R-R	6-5	210	2-2-00	2	2	2.73	7	7	0	0	30	21	10	9	2	8	37	.198	.220	.179	11.22	2.43
Johnson, Jared	R-R	6-2	225	3-15-01	0	6	7.11	12	12	0	0	38	42	35	30	8	28	50	.273	.260	.286	11.84	6.63
Linton, Carter	R-R	5-11	195	6-14-98	0	0	5.68	5	0	0	0	6	7	4	4	0	8	11	.292	.286	.294	15.63	11.37
McSteen, Jake	R-L	6-0	195	3-12-96	3	0	1.59	4	4	0	0	23	21	5	4	1	6	22	.253	.158	.281	8.74	2.38
Munoz, Roddery	R-R	6-3	190	4-14-00	1	2	6.67	8	6	0	0	30	33	23	22	3	11	33	.282	.353	.227	10.01	3.34
Munoz, Rolddy	R-R	6-2	183	4-14-00	4	2	6.21	14	1	0	0	29	30	26	20	3	16	40	.259	.311	.200	12.41	4.97
Owens, Tyler	R-R	5-10	185	1-9-01	0	3	7.07	6	4	0	0	14	22	20	11	2	6	17	.338	.208	.415	10.93	3.86
Pena, Miguel	L-R	6-1	190	11-26-98	5	2	5.51	26	1	0	2	51	59	34	31	7	24	51	.289	.316	.264	9.06	4.26
Rodriguez, Estarlin	R-R	6-0	180	10-24-99	1	3	7.74	23	2	0	2	43	52	41	37	3	28	30	.299	.276	.322	6.28	5.86
Rodriguez, Gabriel	L-L	6-1	193	4-9-99	0	3	8.44	27	1	0	0	32	22	36	30	4	46	59	.198	.220	.186	16.59	12.94
Rodriguez, Rainiery	R-R	6-2	170	8-28-00	2	4	7.00	10	9	0	0	45	63	36	35	7	17	37	.328	.303	.350	7.40	3.40
Salinas, Royber	R-R	6-3	205	4-10-01	2	0	0.64	3	3	0	0	14	6	1	1	0	8	18	.130	.154	.100	11.57	5.14
Santos, Lisandro	L-L	6-1	170	7-24-98	3	3	3.76	29	0	0	1	41	32	20	17	2	26	48	.218	.222	.215	10.62	5.75
Seipel, Zach	R-R	6-4	210	10-17-96	0	3	13.50	16	0	0	0	21	35	31	31	5	23	14	.389	.250	.500	6.10	10.02
Smith, Austin	R-R	6-3	198	6-22-99	0	0	4.50	6	0	0	0	8	5	4	4	1	5	10	.172	.000	.278	11.25	5.63
Spain, Dylan	R-R	6-6	205	6-21-98	1	0	0.00	7	0	0	1	12	6	0	0	0	2	15	.150	.056	.227	11.57	1.54
Strider, Spencer	R-R	6-0	195	10-28-98	0	0	0.59	4	4	0	0	15	6	1	1	0	5	32	.118	.083	.128	18.78	2.93
Thompson, Ben	R-R	6-5	220	12-21-97	3	1	7.11	30	0	0	0	51	60	45	40	13	25	61	.284	.304	.266	10.84	4.44
Van Buren, Malcolm	R-R	6-4	185	7-5-98	1	4	12.56	13	1	0	0	14	11	24	20	1	24	29	.196	.200	.194	18.21	15.07
Vasquez, Braulio	R-R	6-0	210	4-13-99	0	0	0.00	1	0	0	0	0	0	0	0	0	0	0	.000	.000	--	0.00	0.00
Vines, Darius	R-R	6-1	190	4-30-98	2	0	2.25	8	8	0	0	36	24	10	9	3	10	48	.180	.212	.149	12.00	2.50
Wells, Kenny	R-R	6-0	190	4-4-98	2	4	7.21	30	0	0	2	44	31	38	35	5	35	67	.199	.211	.188	13.81	7.21
Williams, Peyton	R-R	6-1	180	5-6-98	2	0	4.24	20	0	0	7	23	21	12	11	2	9	31	.233	.265	.214	11.96	3.47
Yeager, Justin	L-R	6-5	215	1-20-98	5	0	3.27	17	0	0	2	22	16	8	8	2	9	35	.193	.195	.190	14.32	3.68

Fielding

Catcher	PCT	G	PO	A	E	DP	PB
Calandra	.909	1	10	0	1	0	0
De Hoyos	.983	26	219	6	4	0	5
Rodriguez	.983	44	449	24	8	1	2
Tolve	.996	23	242	4	1	1	3
Valdes	.991	20	218	12	2	1	5
Zebrowski	.986	11	136	6	2	0	1

First Base	PCT	G	PO	A	E	DP
Birdsong	1.000	1	4	0	0	0
Bunnell	.978	14	82	8	2	8
Horne	.987	73	416	24	6	29
Stephens	.991	33	205	10	2	15
Vasquez	.944	4	17	0	1	2

Second Base	PCT	G	PO	A	E	DP
Bunnell	.973	34	38	72	3	16
Conley	.942	15	19	30	3	5
Grissom	.953	10	15	26	2	5
Shepherd	1.000	37	49	73	0	15
Vasquez	.986	29	31	37	1	10

Third Base	PCT	G	PO	A	E	DP
Birdsong	.848	19	9	19	5	2
Bunnell	.905	42	31	55	9	2
Grissom	.940	23	11	36	3	1
Malloy	.887	31	22	33	7	2
Stephens	.000	1	0	0	0	0
Vasquez	.833	13	8	7	3	0

Shortstop	PCT	G	PO	A	E	DP
Bunnell	.935	18	26	32	4	4
Conley	.924	20	28	33	5	9
Grissom	.943	35	41	59	6	13
Shepherd	.916	51	53	88	13	13

Outfield	PCT	G	PO	A	E	DP
Bermudez	.951	24	36	3	2	0
Birdsong	--	1	0	0	0	0
Blair	1.000	30	1	0	0	
Campbell	1.000	9	11	0	0	0
Carter	.977	83	122	7	3	0
Malloy	1.000	1	1	0	0	0
Paolini	.967	104	206	2	7	0
Parker	.986	48	70	2	1	0
Robinson	.968	35	58	2	2	0
Stephens	.955	55	82	3	4	0

FCL BRAVES   ROOKIE
FLORIDA COMPLEX LEAGUE

Batting	B-T	HT	WT	DOB	AVG	vLH	vRH	G	AB	R	H	2B	3B	HR	RBI	BB	HBP	SH	SF	SO	SB	CS	SLG	OBP
Backstrom, Mahki	L-L	6-5	220	10-10-01	.172	.074	.200	41	122	19	21	5	2	3	12	22	1	0	1	56	1	0	.320	.301
Barranca, Antonio	R-R	6-3	215	7-25-01	.176	.200	.172	23	68	13	12	2	0	1	12	12	5	0	3	32	1	0	.250	.330
Berne, Mason	R-R	6-3	225	3-11-96	.200	.250	.143	7	15	2	3	0	0	1	3	2	0	0	0	4	0	0	.400	.294
Campbell, Drew	L-L	5-11	170	11-10-97	.353	.000	.400	5	17	2	6	0	0	0	2	0	1	0	0	0	0	1	.353	.389
Celedonio, Jeremy	R-R	6-0	183	12-26-01	.000	--	.000	2	3	0	0	0	0	0	0	0	0	0	0	1	0	0	.000	.000
Collins, Tyler	L-R	5-11	180	3-6-03	.347	.125	.373	23	75	16	26	4	2	0	7	7	3	0	0	23	12	4	.453	.424
De Hoyos, Victor	R-R	5-9	170	2-23-98	.111	.000	.125	3	9	0	1	0	0	0	0	0	0	0	0	1	0	0	.111	.111
De Los Santos, Anderson	B-R	6-0	190	7-28-02	.178	.143	.184	14	45	3	8	1	0	0	3	1	3	1	0	11	1	0	.200	.245
Demeritte, Travis	R-R	6-0	180	9-30-94	1.000	1.000	--	1	1	1	1	0	0	1	1	1	1	0	0	0	1	0	4.000	1.000
Dilone, Jose	L-R	6-0	165	10-9-00	.195	.227	.185	30	87	7	17	3	0	0	4	7	3	0	1	27	3	0	.230	.276
Durbin, Caleb	R-R	5-8	175	2-22-00	.268	.111	.298	17	56	8	15	0	1	0	6	5	1	0	0	3	12	1	.304	.339
Fernando, Joseph	R-R	6-0	185	10-27-96	.200	.053	.237	32	95	7	19	2	0	0	5	4	0	1	0	16	6	1	.221	.232
Floyd, Francisco	R-R	6-1	167	5-25-02	.209	.300	.193	26	67	10	14	2	0	2	8	9	0	0	1	29	2	1	.328	.299
McGill, Liam	R-R	6-4	225	12-19-97	.229	.000	.235	12	35	4	8	4	0	1	6	4	1	0	0	15	1	0	.429	.325
Mezquita, Brandol	R-R	6-0	170	7-14-01	.308	.185	.336	43	146	18	45	8	2	3	25	19	4	0	0	50	15	4	.452	.402
Morton, Kadon	R-R	6-2	195	11-19-00	.196	.161	.205	45	148	23	29	10	3	1	17	25	4	0	0	62	14	3	.324	.328
Palma, Jose	L-L	6-0	170	6-9-99	.258	.211	.270	34	93	21	24	3	0	0	9	16	2	2	0	17	13	4	.290	.378
Paraguate, Carlos	R-R	5-10	170	2-2-01	.191	.313	.129	16	47	2	9	2	0	0	4	5	2	0	0	17	1	0	.234	.296
Pena, Gianfranco	R-R	6-2	180	1-24-00	.255	.250	.255	28	55	4	14	2	0	0	7	5	4	0	2	21	0	0	.291	.348
Pena, Kelvin	R-R	5-11	210	7-4-00	.158	.188	.146	27	57	3	9	1	0	1	3	6	3	1	0	24	1	0	.228	.273
Quintero, Geraldo	R-R	5-8	155	10-4-01	.207	.179	.215	40	121	23	25	2	3	0	6	17	2	0	1	26	12	5	.273	.312
Reyes, Charles	L-R	6-1	165	9-9-99	.293	.308	.286	12	41	8	12	3	1	1	3	2	0	0	0	11	2	0	.488	.326
Rodriguez, Cesar	B-R	5-10	160	12-26-00	.259	.400	.227	10	27	7	7	2	0	1	3	1	2	0	0	4	0	0	.444	.333
Stevens, Eliezel	L-R	6-0	185	10-8-00	.244	.231	.247	28	90	5	22	5	0	1	10	4	1	0	1	26	1	1	.333	.281
Tolve, Tyler	L-R	6-2	180	7-16-00	.000	.000	.000	1	2	0	0	0	0	0	0	0	0	0	0	1	0	0	.000	.000
Unroe, Riley	B-R	5-11	180	8-3-95	.500	1.000	.000	2	2	1	1	0	0	0	1	0	0	0	0	1	0	0	1.000	.667
Valdes, Javier	R-R	5-10	195	11-19-98	.063	.000	.071	5	16	0	1	0	0	0	1	2	0	0	1	7	0	0	.063	.158
Workinger, Ethan	R-R	6-3	185	10-19-01	.186	.167	.190	35	102	12	19	3	3	2	15	11	3	0	6	33	2	1	.333	.270
Zebrowski, Adam	R-R	6-3	230	9-28-00	.235	.250	.231	6	17	2	4	2	0	0	6	2	0	0	0	4	0	0	.353	.316

Pitching	B-T	HT	WT	DOB	W	L	ERA	G	GS	CG	SV	IP	H	R	ER	HR	BB	SO	AVG	vLH	vRH	K/9	BB/9
Alesandro, Ronaldo	R-R	6-0	170	5-7-98	3	0	2.45	15	0	0	2	22	12	7	6	0	17	37	.158	.067	.217	15.14	6.95
Anglin, Kris	L-L	5-11	175	8-9-01	0	1	2.38	5	3	0	0	11	6	3	3	1	6	15	.154	.222	.133	11.91	4.76
Asencio, Eudi	R-R	6-3	170	2-28-99	0	0	0.00	1	0	0	0	1	0	4	0	0	1	0	.000	--	.000	0.00	13.50
Bautista, Jorge	R-R	6-0	155	12-10-00	1	6	5.98	12	10	0	0	41	40	30	27	5	24	35	.256	.298	.232	7.75	5.31
Celedonio, Raulin	R-R	6-6	220	2-8-00	0	0	0.00	1	0	0	0	1	0	1	0	0	1	3	.000	.000	.000	27.00	9.00
Clouse, Corbin	B-L	6-0	230	6-26-95	1	0	1.38	5	3	0	0	13	8	5	2	0	5	16	.174	.200	.171	11.08	3.46
Corona, Reibyn	R-R	5-11	175	11-13-01	1	4	4.66	12	8	0	0	39	35	26	20	4	18	43	.240	.262	.231	10.01	4.19
Cubillan, Wilker	R-R	6-4	175	1-14-01	0	1	6.75	10	0	0	0	15	13	12	11	0	21	17	.241	.333	.222	10.43	12.89
Dayton, Grant	L-L	6-2	210	11-25-87	0	0	0.00	1	1	0	0	1	0	0	0	0	1	0	.000	.000	--	0.00	13.50
Florentino, Darling	R-R	6-0	210	5-25-01	0	2	4.74	11	5	0	1	25	14	15	13	1	25	25	.167	.048	.206	9.12	9.12
Higginbotham, Jake	L-L	6-0	190	1-11-96	1	0	0.00	2	0	0	0	2	0	0	0	0	1	2	.000	.000	--	9.00	4.50
Johnson, Jared	R-R	6-2	225	3-15-01	2	0	1.35	3	1	0	0	13	7	2	2	1	4	19	.152	.133	.161	12.83	2.70
Joseph, Elison	R-R	6-0	170	1-24-01	0	3	2.73	16	0	0	2	26	19	10	8	2	18	30	.198	.167	.212	10.25	6.15
Moreno, Cesari	R-R	6-4	214	12-21-01	0	4	12.66	12	0	0	0	11	4	17	15	0	23	17	.121	.167	.111	14.34	19.41
Munoz, Rolddy	R-R	6-2	183	4-14-00	0	0	1.50	2	1	0	0	6	1	1	1	0	1	8	.053	.000	.083	12.00	1.50
Niekro, J.J.	R-R	6-0	185	1-28-98	3	0	2.76	10	0	0	0	16	18	16	5	0	9	23	.265	.118	.314	12.67	4.96
Perez, Jordano	R-R	6-0	162	9-2-00	1	0	5.87	16	1	0	2	31	42	23	20	3	9	21	.323	.216	.366	6.16	2.64
Rodriguez, Estarlin	R-R	6-0	180	10-24-99	2	0	0.00	5	0	0	1	13	6	0	0	0	1	9	.143	.111	.167	6.23	0.69
Rodriguez, Rainiery	B-R	6-2	170	8-28-00	1	0	1.42	4	4	0	0	19	14	3	3	0	4	17	.222	.063	.277	8.05	1.89
Salinas, Royber	R-R	6-3	205	4-10-01	1	3	3.20	10	6	0	1	25	19	16	9	4	16	49	.207	.048	.254	17.41	5.68
Samuelson, Andy	L-L	6-4	185	5-20-99	2	2	10.17	12	5	0	0	26	39	34	29	5	24	29	.345	.313	.351	10.17	8.42
Shoemaker, Adam	L-L	6-6	205	8-24-02	0	1	6.75	3	2	0	0	5	3	5	4	0	7	6	.158	.000	.200	10.13	11.81
Sierra, Osiris	R-R	6-2	145	2-9-00	0	1	6.00	5	1	0	0	6	3	4	4	0	5	9	.158	.000	.176	13.50	7.50
Smith-Shawver, AJ	R-R	6-3	205	11-20-02	0	1	8.64	4	4	0	0	8	4	8	8	2	10	16	.143	.182	.118	17.28	10.80
Solano, Kevin	R-R	6-2	187	4-8-02	0	0	2.92	9	0	0	0	12	10	6	4	0	14	6	.227	.308	.194	4.38	10.22
Spain, Dylan	R-R	6-6	205	6-21-98	0	0	0.00	3	0	0	0	5	2	0	0	0	5	5	.118	.333	.071	9.00	0.00
Strickland, Samuel	R-L	6-2	218	3-26-99	2	0	8.03	9	0	0	1	12	13	11	11	3	8	13	.260	.333	.244	9.49	5.84
Vargas, Luis	R-R	5-11	196	5-2-02	0	0	0.00	3	0	0	0	4	4	1	0	0	3	4	.250	.250	.250	9.00	6.75
Vidal, Frankelvin	R-R	5-11	201	4-22-02	2	2	4.55	13	0	0	0	30	27	22	15	7	18	28	.252	.185	.275	8.49	5.46
Woods, William	R-R	6-3	190	12-29-98	0	0	0.00	1	1	0	0	1	1	0	0	0	0	1	.250	.333	.000	9.00	0.00

Fielding

C: Barranca 20, De Hoyos 3, McGill 5, Pena 19, Pena 11, Rodriguez 8, Tolve 1, Valdes 4, Zebrowski 5.
1B: Backstrom 38, Berne 7, McGill 3, Pena 6, Pena 12.
2B: De Los Santos 2, Dilone 2, Durbin 8, Fernando 7, Floyd 1, Quintero 16, Stevens 26.
3B: Dilone 25, Fernando 16, Floyd 7, Paraguate 2, Quintero 13.
SS: De Los Santos 12, Durbin 8, Floyd 17, Paraguate 13, Quintero 10, Unroe 1.
OF: Campbell 3, Collins 22, Demeritte 1, Mezquita 39, Morton 41, Palma 31, Reyes 11, Workinger 29.

Baltimore Orioles

SEASON IN A SENTENCE: The Orioles saw a breakout year from outfielder Cedric Mullins and a healthy return from designated hitter Trey Mancini following his battle with colon cancer, but the team still went 52-110 and tied for the worst record in the majors.

HIGH POINT: In an otherwise dismal year for Orioles pitchers, lefthander John Means authored one of the best pitching performances in franchise history when he no-hit the Mariners on May 5. Means struck out 12, didn't walk anyone and came within a dropped third strike of a perfect game.

LOW POINT: The Orioles lost 19 straight games from Aug. 3-24, tied for the fourth-longest losing streak in MLB in the last 50 years. The Orioles were outscored 163-55 during the skid, losing by an average of more than five runs per game. Their losses included scores of 16-2, 13-1, 12-3 and 10-0.

NOTABLE ROOKIES: The Orioles got solid rookie contributions in the starting lineup and bullpen. First baseman Ryan Mountcastle led all major league rookies with 33 home runs and finished second with 89 RBIs. Shortstop Ramon Urias took over as the starter in late June and hit .279/.361/.412 with seven home runs and 38 RBIs in 85 games. Righthander Tyler Wells, a Rule 5 draft pick from the Twins, went 2-3, 4.11 in 44 appearances and emerged as arguably the Orioles best middle reliever. The Orioles had less success with the rookies in the starting rotation. Lefthanders Keegan Akin (2-10, 6.63), Bruce Zimmermann (4-5, 5.04) and Zac Lowther (1-3, 6.67) and righthander Dean Kremer (0-7, 7.55) all struggled badly in their attempts to seize a rotation spot and were part of the reason why Orioles starters combined for a 5.99 ERA, worst in the majors by nearly half a run.

KEY TRANSACTIONS: The Orioles continued to trade major leaguers for prospects, sending righthander Alex Cobb and shortstop Jose Iglesias to the Angels before the season and trading shortstop Freddy Galvis to the Phillies at the trade deadline. First baseman Chris Davis missed the entire season with a hip injury and retired on Aug. 12 in the second-to-last year of his seven-year, $161 million contract with the Orioles.

OPENING DAY SALARY: $45,701,135 (29th).

PLAYERS OF THE YEAR

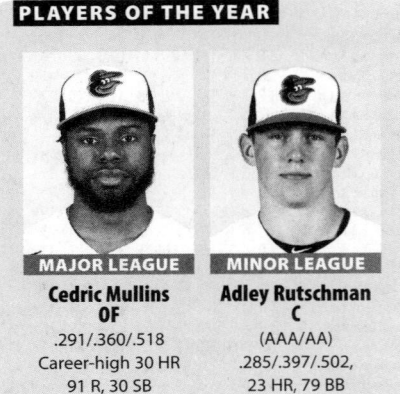

MAJOR LEAGUE	MINOR LEAGUE
Cedric Mullins	**Adley Rutschman**
OF	**C**
.291/.360/.518	(AAA/AA)
Career-high 30 HR	.285/.397/.502,
91 R, 30 SB	23 HR, 79 BB

ORGANIZATION LEADERS

Batting		*Minimum 250 AB
MAJORS		
*AVG	Cedric Mullins	.291
*OPS	Cedric Mullins	.878
HR	Ryan Mountcastle	33
RBI	Ryan Mountcastle	89
MINORS		
*AVG	J.D. Mundy, Aberdeen, Delmarva	.291
*OBP	Adley Rutschman, Norfolk, Bowie	.397
*SLG	J.D. Mundy, Aberdeen, Delmarva	.536
*OPS	J.D. Mundy, Aberdeen, Delmarva	.925
R	Adley Rutschman, Norfolk, Bowie	86
H	Adley Rutschman, Norfolk, Bowie	129
TB	Kyle Stowers, Norfolk, Bowie, Aberdeen	231
2B	Robert Neustrom, Norfolk, Bowie	31
3B	3 tied	6
HR	Kyle Stowers, Norfolk, Bowie, Aberdeen	27
RBI	Kyle Stowers, Norfolk, Bowie, Aberdeen	85
BB	Adley Rutschman, Norfolk, Bowie	79
SO	Kyle Stowers, Norfolk, Bowie, Aberdeen	171
SB	2 tied	26

PITCHING		#Minimum 75 IP
MAJORS		
W	2 tied	6
#ERA	John Means	3.62
SO	John Means	134
SV	2 tied	8
MINORS		
W	Drew Rom, Bowie, Aberdeen	11
L	2 tied	8
#ERA	Drew Rom, Bowie, Aberdeen	3.18
G	Diogenes Almengo, Norfolk, Bowie	41
GS	Grayson Rodriguez, Bowie, Aberdeen	23
SV	Diogenes Almengo, Norfolk, Bowie	16
IP	Drew Rom, Bowie, Aberdeen	107.2
BB	Kevin Smith, Norfolk, Bowie	59
SO	Grayson Rodriguez, Bowie, Aberdeen	161
#AVG	Grayson Rodriguez, Bowie, Aberdeen	.159

2021 PERFORMANCE

General Manager: Mike Elias. **Farm Director:** Matt Blood. **Scouting Director:** Brad Ciolek.

Class	Team	League	W	L	PCT	Finish	Manager
Majors	Baltimore Orioles	American	52	110	.321	15th (15)	Brandon Hyde
Triple-A	Norfolk Tides	Triple-A East	52	78	.400	t-16th (20)	Gary Kendall
Double-A	Bowie Baysox	Double-A Northeast	73	47	.608	2nd (12)	Buck Britton
High-A	Aberdeen IronBirds	High-A East	58	61	.487	5th (12)	Kyle Moore
Low-A	Delmarva Shorebirds	Low-A East	68	52	.567	t-4th (12)	Dave Anderson
Rookie	DSL Orioles1	Dominican Summer	13	39	.250	46th (46)	Elvis Morel
Rookie	DSL Orioles2	Dominican Summer	25	30	.455	32th (46)	Chris Madera
Rookie	FCL Orioles Black	Florida Complex	18	28	.391	14th (18)	Alan Mills
Rookie	FCL Orioles Orange	Florida Complex	11	34	.244	18th (18)	Kevin Bradshaw
Overall 2021 Minor League Record			318	369	.463	22nd (30)	

ORGANIZATION STATISTICS

BALTIMORE ORIOLES
AMERICAN LEAGUE

Batting	B-T	HT	WT	DOB	AVG	vLH	vRH	G	AB	R	H	2B	3B	HR	RBI	BB	HBP	SH	SF	SO	SB	CS	SLG	OBP
Ciuffo, Nick	L-R	6-0	205	3-7-95	.200	--	.200	2	5	0	1	1	0	0	0	1	0	0	0	1	0	0	.400	.333
Franco, Maikel	R-R	6-1	225	8-26-92	.210	.198	.215	104	377	31	79	22	0	11	47	20	3	0	3	67	0	0	.355	.253
Galvis, Freddy	B-R	5-10	190	11-14-89	.249	.295	.228	72	249	36	62	12	1	9	26	18	3	2	1	58	1	0	.414	.306
Gutierrez, Kelvin	R-R	6-2	215	8-28-94	.248	.326	.213	47	137	14	34	4	1	2	12	13	3	0	0	45	0	0	.336	.327
2-team total (38 Kansas City)					.232	.253	.223	85	272	23	63	8	3	3	20	19	4	0	0	76	1	1	.316	.292
Hays, Austin	R-R	6-0	205	7-5-95	.256	.308	.221	131	488	73	125	26	4	22	71	26	9	3	1	107	4	3	.461	.308
Jones, Jahmai	R-R	6-0	210	8-4-97	.149	.120	.167	26	67	5	10	3	0	0	3	4	1	0	0	26	1	0	.194	.208
Leyba, Domingo	B-R	5-11	205	9-11-95	.154	.200	.140	21	65	6	10	1	0	1	4	6	1	0	0	16	0	0	.215	.236
Mancini, Trey	R-R	6-3	230	3-18-92	.255	.288	.237	147	556	77	142	33	1	21	71	51	8	0	1	143	0	0	.432	.326
Martin, Richie	R-R	6-0	190	12-22-94	.235	.275	.207	37	98	9	23	2	0	1	8	4	1	1	1	28	0	2	.286	.269
Mateo, Jorge	R-R	6-0	182	6-23-95	.280	.271	.288	32	107	9	30	7	1	2	8	7	1	0	1	28	5	3	.421	.328
McKenna, Ryan	R-R	5-11	195	2-14-97	.183	.154	.209	90	169	20	31	6	1	2	14	24	2	2	0	74	1	0	.266	.292
Mountcastle, Ryan	R-R	6-4	230	2-18-97	.255	.266	.249	144	534	77	136	23	1	33	89	41	4	0	7	161	4	3	.487	.309
Mullins, Cedric	L-L	5-8	175	10-1-94	.291	.277	.299	159	602	91	175	37	5	30	59	59	8	1	4	125	30	8	.518	.360
Nevin, Tyler	R-R	6-4	225	5-29-97	.286	.600	.111	6	14	3	4	2	0	1	3	4	0	0	0	5	0	0	.643	.444
Ruiz, Rio	L-R	6-2	220	5-22-94	.167	.250	.154	32	90	10	15	3	0	3	6	9	1	0	0	29	2	0	.300	.250
Santander, Anthony	B-R	6-2	235	10-19-94	.241	.257	.233	110	406	54	98	24	0	18	50	23	4	1	4	101	1	1	.433	.286
Severino, Pedro	R-R	6-1	235	7-20-93	.248	.293	.220	113	379	32	94	18	0	11	46	34	1	0	5	109	0	0	.383	.308
Sisco, Chance	L-R	6-3	210	2-24-95	.154	.125	.158	23	65	4	10	2	0	0	3	6	2	0	0	18	0	0	.185	.247
Stewart, DJ	L-R	6-0	210	11-30-93	.204	.220	.201	100	270	39	55	10	0	12	33	44	4	0	0	89	0	0	.374	.324
Urias, Ramon	R-R	6-0	190	6-3-94	.279	.235	.315	85	262	33	73	14	0	7	38	28	6	0	0	76	1	2	.412	.361
Valaika, Pat	R-R	6-0	200	9-9-92	.201	.214	.192	90	259	17	52	8	0	5	25	16	2	1	3	76	1	1	.290	.250
Wilkerson, Stevie	B-R	6-2	200	1-11-92	.167	.333	.152	30	72	5	12	3	0	0	2	3	1	0	0	30	2	0	.208	.211
Wynns, Austin	R-R	6-0	190	12-10-90	.185	.256	.154	45	130	14	24	4	0	4	14	8	0	1	0	31	1	0	.308	.232

Pitching	B-T	HT	WT	DOB	W	L	ERA	G	GS	CG	SV	IP	H	R	ER	HR	BB	SO	AVG	vLH	vRH	K/9	BB/9
Abad, Fernando	L-L	6-2	235	12-17-85	0	0	5.60	16	0	0	0	18	23	12	11	1	7	10	.307	.375	.256	5.09	3.57
Akin, Keegan	L-L	5-11	235	4-1-95	2	10	6.63	24	17	0	0	95	110	70	70	17	40	82	.290	.304	.285	7.77	3.79
Anderson, Shaun	R-R	6-4	228	10-29-94	0	0	9.00	7	0	0	0	10	17	15	10	3	5	7	.347	.333	.360	6.30	4.50
2-team total (4 Minnesota)					0	0	9.16	11	0	0	0	19	30	27	19	4	10	15	.333	.417	.278	7.23	4.82
Armstrong, Shawn	R-R	6-2	225	9-11-90	0	0	8.55	20	0	0	0	20	28	20	19	5	10	22	.318	.324	.315	9.90	4.50
2-team total (11 Tampa Bay)					1	0	6.75	31	0	0	0	36	39	28	27	10	15	44	.265	.327	.228	11.00	3.75
Barreda, Manny	R-R	5-11	195	10-8-88	1	0	13.50	3	0	0	0	3	4	4	4	2	2	2	.333	.000	.571	6.75	6.75
Baumann, Mike	R-R	6-4	235	9-10-95	1	1	9.90	4	0	0	0	10	13	12	11	2	6	5	.302	.250	.333	4.50	5.40
Burdi, Zack	R-R	6-3	210	3-9-95	0	0	0.00	1	0	0	0	1	0	0	0	0	1	1	.000	.000	.000	9.00	9.00
2-team total (6 Chicago)					0	0	5.40	7	0	0	0	10	13	7	6	3	5	7	.325	.211	.429	6.30	4.50
Diplan, Marcos	R-R	6-0	200	9-18-96	2	0	4.50	23	0	0	0	30	22	16	15	6	15	24	.206	.209	.203	7.20	4.50
Ellis, Chris	L-R	6-5	205	9-22-92	0	0	2.49	6	6	0	0	25	18	7	7	3	13	16	.200	.161	.220	5.68	4.62
2-team total (1 Tampa Bay)					1	0	2.15	7	6	0	0	29	21	7	7	3	14	23	.200	.139	.232	7.06	4.30
Eshelman, Thomas	R-R	6-2	225	6-20-94	0	3	7.16	9	6	0	0	28	34	22	22	6	10	11	.298	.225	.338	3.58	3.25
Flaa, Jay	R-R	6-3	225	6-10-92	0	0	0.00	1	0	0	0	1	0	0	0	0	2	1	.000	--	.000	6.75	13.50
Fry, Paul	L-L	6-0	205	7-26-92	4	5	6.08	52	0	0	2	47	37	34	32	3	35	60	.213	.229	.202	11.41	6.65
Greene, Conner	R-R	6-4	195	4-4-95	1	3	7.71	22	1	0	0	23	30	20	20	1	12	24	.313	.308	.314	9.26	4.63
Hanhold, Eric	R-R	6-5	211	11-1-93	0	0	6.97	10	0	0	0	10	13	9	8	2	3	6	.302	.154	.367	5.23	2.61
Harvey, Hunter	R-R	6-3	210	12-9-94	0	0	4.15	9	0	0	0	9	8	4	4	1	3	6	.242	.231	.250	6.23	3.12
Harvey, Matt	R-R	6-4	220	3-27-89	6	14	6.27	28	28	0	0	128	160	96	89	19	37	95	.299	.261	.329	6.70	2.61
Jannis, Mickey	R-S	5-9	195	12-16-87	0	0	18.90	1	0	0	0	3	8	7	7	3	4	1	.471	.600	.417	2.70	10.80
Knight, Dusten	R-R	6-0	200	9-7-90	0	0	9.35	7	0	0	0	9	11	10	9	1	5	11	.289	.235	.333	11.42	5.19
Krehbiel, Joey	R-R	6-2	185	12-20-92	0	0	4.91	5	0	0	0	7	5	4	4	1	4	5	.192	.000	.250	6.14	4.91
2-team total (1 Tampa Bay)					0	0	4.32	6	0	0	0	8	5	4	4	1	5	7	.172	.000	.417	7.56	5.40
Kremer, Dean	R-R	6-2	200	1-7-96	0	7	7.55	13	13	0	0	54	63	46	45	17	25	47	.292	.261	.313	7.88	4.19
Kriske, Brooks	R-R	6-3	190	2-3-94	1	0	12.27	4	0	0	0	4	5	5	5	2	0	4	.333	.500	.273	9.82	0.00

	B-T	HT	WT	DOB	W	L	ERA	G	GS	CG	SV	IP	H	R	ER	HR	BB	SO	AVG	vLH	vRH	SO/9	BB/9
2-team total (8 New York)					2	1	14.29	12	0	0	0	11	17	19	18	7	6	11	.362	.385	.353	8.74	4.76
Lakins Sr., Travis	R-R	6-1	220	6-29-94	1	4	5.79	24	1	0	0	28	23	20	18	4	17	24	.221	.244	.203	7.71	5.46
LeBlanc, Wade	L-L	6-2	195	8-7-84	0	1	9.45	6	1	0	0	7	11	7	7	1	1	6	.355	.273	.400	8.10	1.35
Lopez, Jorge	R-R	6-3	200	2-10-93	3	14	6.07	33	25	0	0	122	142	83	82	21	56	112	.293	.294	.292	8.28	4.14
Lowther, Zac	L-L	6-2	235	4-30-96	1	3	6.67	10	6	0	0	30	36	23	22	6	13	30	.298	.440	.260	9.10	3.94
Mattson, Isaac	R-R	6-2	205	7-14-95	0	0	6.23	4	0	0	0	4	5	3	3	0	5	3	.278	.600	.154	6.23	10.38
Means, John	L-L	6-3	235	4-24-93	6	9	3.62	26	26	1	0	147	125	64	59	30	26	134	.224	.229	.223	8.22	1.60
Plutko, Adam	R-R	6-3	215	10-3-91	1	2	6.71	38	1	0	1	56	65	43	42	17	27	44	.295	.337	.270	7.03	4.31
Sceroler, Mac	R-R	6-3	215	4-9-95	0	0	14.09	5	0	0	0	8	15	15	12	6	7	11	.375	.400	.350	12.91	8.22
Scott, Tanner	R-L	6-0	235	7-22-94	5	4	5.17	62	0	0	0	54	48	34	31	6	37	70	.234	.203	.250	11.67	6.17
Sulser, Cole	R-R	6-1	190	3-12-90	5	4	2.70	60	0	0	8	63	48	20	19	5	23	73	.207	.186	.227	10.37	3.27
Tate, Dillon	R-R	6-2	195	5-1-94	0	6	4.39	62	0	0	3	68	61	35	33	7	23	49	.245	.235	.250	6.52	3.06
Valaika, Pat	R-R	6-0	200	9-9-92	0	0	0.00	2	0	0	0	1	0	0	0	0	0	0	.000	.000	.000	0.00	0.00
Valdez, Cesar	R-R	6-2	225	3-17-85	2	2	5.87	39	0	0	8	46	62	32	30	8	14	45	.320	.266	.357	8.80	2.74
Waddell, Brandon	L-L	6-3	180	6-3-94	0	0	0.00	1	0	0	0	1	0	0	0	0	0	0	.000	--	.000	0.00	9.00
2-team total (4 Minnesota)					0	1	9.00	5	0	0	0	5	10	6	5	2	4	1	.400	.500	.353	1.80	7.20
Wade, Konner	L-R	6-3	195	12-3-91	0	0	11.68	7	0	0	0	12	23	16	16	3	5	11	.390	.214	.444	8.03	3.65
Watkins, Spenser	R-R	6-2	185	8-27-92	2	7	8.07	16	10	0	0	55	74	50	49	14	19	35	.322	.296	.344	5.76	3.13
Wells, Alexander	L-L	6-1	195	2-27-97	2	3	6.75	11	8	0	0	43	53	32	32	10	16	26	.299	.294	.302	5.48	3.38
Wells, Tyler	R-R	6-8	255	8-26-94	2	3	4.11	44	0	0	4	57	40	27	26	9	12	65	.192	.167	.206	10.26	1.89
Wilkerson, Stevie	B-R	6-2	200	1-11-92	0	0	9.00	1	0	0	0	1	2	1	1	1	0	0	.400	.500	.000	0.00	9.00
Wynns, Austin	R-R	6-0	190	12-10-90	0	0	9.00	1	0	0	0	1	1	1	1	1	0	0	.250	.000	.333	0.00	9.00
Zimmermann, Bruce	L-L	6-1	215	2-9-95	4	5	5.04	14	13	0	0	64	75	37	36	14	22	56	.291	.321	.283	7.83	3.08

Fielding

Catcher	PCT	G	PO	A	E	DP	PB
Ciuffo	1.000	2	14	0	0	0	0
Severino	.995	109	797	31	4	2	10
Sisco	1.000	21	161	11	0	0	3
Wynns	.997	44	288	18	1	1	0

First Base	PCT	G	PO	A	E	DP
Franco	1.000	2	3	0	0	0
Mancini	.998	77	522	34	1	36
Mountcastle	.998	84	622	38	1	56
Nevin	.857	2	6	0	1	0
Valaika	1.000	6	28	2	0	1
Wynns	1.000	1	1	0	0	0

Second Base	PCT	G	PO	A	E	DP
Gutierrez	.000	1	0	0	0	0
Jones	.966	23	39	46	3	10
Leyba	.978	14	26	18	1	5

	PCT	G	PO	A	E	DP
Mateo	.982	18	17	39	1	6
McKenna	.000	1	0	0	0	0
Ruiz	.976	20	34	46	2	9
Urias	.954	32	50	54	5	16
Valaika	1.000	72	109	121	0	24
Wilkerson	.968	26	43	49	3	11

Third Base	PCT	G	PO	A	E	DP
Franco	.967	99	66	166	8	15
Gutierrez	.970	47	34	95	4	8
Leyba	1.000	9	5	13	0	1
Mateo	1.000	1	1	1	0	0
McKenna	.000	1	0	0	0	0
Ruiz	1.000	12	9	13	0	1
Urias	1.000	10	5	17	0	1
Valaika	1.000	2	1	2	0	1

Shortstop	PCT	G	PO	A	E	DP
Galvis	.984	72	71	173	4	18
Martin	.955	37	49	77	6	10
Mateo	.980	17	18	30	1	8
Urias	.953	48	50	91	7	16
Valaika	.980	17	18	32	1	9

Outfield	PCT	G	PO	A	E	DP
Hays	.996	148	244	9	1	2
Mateo	1.000	2	1	0	0	0
McKenna	.992	86	116	2	1	0
Mountcastle	.964	21	26	1	1	0
Mullins	.985	153	389	7	6	2
Nevin	1.000	4	9	0	0	0
Santander	.994	85	166	2	1	1
Stewart	.966	72	111	2	4	0
Valaika	1.000	3	3	0	0	0
Wilkerson	1.000	4	4	0	0	0

NORFOLK TIDES
TRIPLE-A EAST

TRIPLE-A

Batting	B-T	HT	WT	DOB	AVG	vLH	vRH	G	AB	R	H	2B	3B	HR	RBI	BB	HBP	SH	SF	SO	SB	CS	SLG	OBP
Bannon, Rylan	R-R	5-8	180	4-22-96	.176	.173	.179	84	289	43	51	11	0	15	36	47	3	0	1	71	9	1	.370	.297
Canelo, Malquin	R-R	5-10	165	9-5-94	.227	.000	.278	7	22	1	5	3	0	0	3	2	0	0	0	8	0	1	.364	.292
Ciuffo, Nick	L-R	6-0	205	3-7-95	.173	.150	.188	17	52	5	9	1	0	2	8	5	0	0	1	22	1	0	.308	.241
Cumberland, Brett	B-R	5-11	200	6-25-95	.187	.172	.195	84	267	37	50	8	0	10	23	40	28	0	0	108	1	0	.330	.352
Davis, Taylor	R-R	5-10	200	11-28-89	.289	.272	.296	12	38	6	11	3	0	0	5	5	0	0	0	5	0	0	.368	.372
2-team total (39 Indianapolis)					.248	.359	.212	51	157	22	39	6	0	2	22	22	1	0	0	21	0	0	.325	.344
Diaz, Yusniel	R-R	6-1	215	10-7-96	.157	.150	.160	54	191	19	30	4	1	4	16	14	3	0	1	69	1	2	.251	.225
Dorrian, Patrick	R-R	6-2	188	6-26-96	.125	.250	.083	4	16	0	2	0	0	0	0	0	0	0	0	8	0	0	.125	.125
Encarnacion, JC	R-R	6-3	195	1-17-98	.143	.250	.000	3	7	0	1	0	0	0	0	0	0	0	0	4	0	0	.143	.143
Escarra, J.C.	L-R	6-3	205	4-24-95	.225	.159	.265	58	182	22	41	10	1	4	21	21	5	2	4	41	4	0	.357	.316
Graffanino, AJ	R-R	6-2	170	7-16-97	.143	.000	.250	2	7	2	1	0	0	0	0	1	0	0	0	3	0	0	.143	.250
Grenier, Cadyn	R-R	5-11	188	10-31-96	.077	.000	.091	5	13	1	1	0	0	0	0	4	0	0	0	5	0	0	.077	.294
Gutierrez, Kelvin	R-R	6-2	215	8-28-94	.233	.207	.246	25	90	10	21	4	0	4	13	4	0	0	0	21	1	1	.411	.266
2-team total (9 Omaha)					.254	.326	.217	34	126	11	32	7	1	4	17	6	0	0	0	28	1	2	.421	.288
Hays, Austin	R-R	6-0	205	7-5-95	.125	.250	.000	2	8	2	1	0	0	1	1	0	0	0	0	3	0	0	.500	.125
Hudgins, Chris	R-R	6-1	190	3-2-96	.111	.000	.143	9	9	2	1	0	0	1	1	2	0	0	0	4	0	0	.444	.273
Jarrett, Zach	R-R	6-4	220	12-8-94	.221	.226	.219	91	303	39	67	12	2	10	35	40	3	1	1	109	12	8	.373	.317
Jones, Jahmai	R-R	6-0	210	8-4-97	.243	.267	.233	70	255	34	62	9	3	11	37	35	2	0	2	68	11	3	.431	.337
Leyba, Domingo	B-R	5-11	205	9-11-95	.275	.250	.289	18	69	7	19	1	0	5	20	4	0	0	1	10	0	1	.507	.311
Mantecon, Michael	R-R	5-10	180	2-2-02	.000	--	.000	1	1	0	0	0	0	0	0	0	0	0	0	1	0	0	.000	.000
Martin, Richie	R-R	6-0	190	12-24-94	.208	.275	.161	27	96	12	20	4	2	1	5	14	2	0	0	25	5	3	.323	.311
McCoy, Mason	R-R	5-11	185	3-31-95	.221	.277	.192	112	408	49	90	21	6	9	43	40	0	3	4	133	13	3	.368	.288
McKenna, Ryan	R-R	5-11	195	2-14-97	.307	.265	.328	27	101	25	31	3	1	11	23	21	0	0	0	33	7	3	.683	.423
Mejias-Brean, Seth	R-R	6-2	205	4-5-91	.211	.236	.198	50	171	21	36	6	0	5	24	17	2	0	0	42	5	1	.333	.289
Neustrom, Robert	L-L	6-2	208	11-12-96	.232	.235	.230	64	224	32	52	16	0	9	33	29	2	1	1	63	5	1	.424	.324
Nevin, Tyler	R-R	6-4	225	5-29-97	.227	.216	.233	111	401	45	91	18	0	16	52	42	5	0	5	91	1	1	.392	.305
Ripken, Ryan	L-L	6-3	215	7-26-93	.167	.174	.163	48	150	11	25	5	1	1	11	11	0	1	1	51	1	0	.233	.222

	B-T	HT	WT	DOB	AVG	OBP	SLG	G	AB	R	H	2B	3B	HR	RBI	BB	SO	SB	CS				
Roberts, Cody	R-R	6-1	195	6-16-96	.294	.313	.278	11	34	2	10	2	0	1	4	4	0	0	0	13	0	0	.441	.368
Rutschman, Adley	B-R	6-2	220	2-6-98	.312	.329	.299	43	157	25	49	9	2	5	20	24	2	0	2	33	2	2	.490	.405
Santiago, Wilbis	L-R	6-0	180	1-20-96	.250	.333	.200	7	16	1	4	0	1	0	2	0	0	0	0	1	1	0	.375	.250
Shaw, Chris	L-R	6-4	220	10-20-93	.026	.083	.000	14	39	4	1	0	0	0	1	11	0	0	0	25	0	0	.026	.240
Sisco, Chance	L-R	6-3	210	2-24-95	.205	.167	.231	12	44	7	9	3	0	1	4	7	1	0	0	17	0	0	.341	.327
2-team total (34 Syracuse)					.200	.171	.209	46	150	22	30	9	1	6	18	19	5	0	0	43	0	0	.393	.310
Stowers, Kyle	L-L	6-3	200	1-2-98	.272	.286	.261	22	81	10	22	2	0	3	11	12	0	0	0	32	1	0	.407	.366
Urias, Ramon	R-R	6-0	190	6-3-94	.258	.207	.271	24	89	14	23	6	1	4	12	9	2	1	0	25	1	1	.483	.340
Valaika, Pat	R-R	6-0	200	9-9-92	.225	.156	.271	22	80	9	18	1	0	2	7	2	0	0	0	22	0	0	.313	.244
Wilkerson, Stevie	B-R	6-2	200	1-11-92	.244	.176	.270	36	123	17	30	6	0	2	7	21	0	1	1	39	0	0	.341	.352
Wynns, Austin	R-R	6-0	190	12-10-90	.333	.375	.313	15	48	7	16	2	0	3	9	7	3	1	0	11	0	0	.563	.448
Yahn, Willy	R-R	5-11	185	11-7-95	.195	.154	.214	12	41	6	8	1	2	1	5	3	0	0	0	12	0	0	.390	.250

Pitching

	B-T	HT	WT	DOB	W	L	ERA	G	GS	CG	SV	IP	H	R	ER	HR	BB	SO	AVG	vLH	vRH	K/9	BB/9
Abad, Fernando	L-L	6-2	235	12-17-85	2	1	4.26	26	0	0	3	25	30	12	12	5	6	27	.288	.271	.304	9.59	2.13
Akin, Keegan	L-L	5-11	235	4-1-95	0	0	9.00	1	1	0	0	2	2	2	2	1	1	5	.250	.250	.250	22.50	4.50
Almengo, Diogenes	R-R	6-2	190	6-2-95	0	0	4.91	2	0	0	0	4	4	2	2	1	3	4	.267	.200	.300	9.82	7.36
Armstrong, Shawn	R-R	6-2	225	9-11-90	1	3	3.18	15	0	0	0	17	19	10	6	3	6	21	.268	.333	.200	11.12	3.18
2-team total (14 Durham)					3	4	2.90	29	0	0	2	31	29	14	10	4	8	41	.240	.259	.224	11.90	2.32
Barreda, Manny	R-R	5-11	195	10-8-88	2	3	3.79	27	2	0	1	40	47	21	17	3	12	40	.297	.319	.281	8.93	2.68
Baumann, Mike	R-R	6-4	235	9-10-95	1	1	2.00	6	6	1	0	27	18	6	6	0	13	26	.194	.222	.167	8.67	4.33
Bautista, Felix	R-R	6-5	190	6-20-95	1	3	2.45	17	0	0	5	18	11	7	5	1	9	25	.175	.080	.237	12.27	4.42
Bradish, Kyle	R-R	6-4	220	9-12-96	5	5	4.26	21	19	0	0	87	85	45	41	10	39	105	.254	.273	.233	10.90	4.05
Burdi, Zack	R-R	6-3	210	3-9-95	0	0	2.25	4	0	0	0	4	2	1	1	0	2	10	.143	.167	.125	22.50	4.50
2-team total (23 Charlotte)					0	2	6.59	27	0	0	2	29	24	24	21	9	17	45	.216	.304	.154	14.13	5.34
Carroll, Cody	R-R	6-5	230	10-15-92	2	0	5.57	22	0	0	0	21	21	14	13	5	11	23	.269	.275	.263	9.86	4.71
2-team total (3 Jacksonville)					2	0	5.63	25	0	0	0	24	26	16	15	6	12	29	.283	.271	.295	10.88	4.50
Custodio, Claudio	R-R	5-10	155	10-30-90	2	3	3.50	25	2	0	0	46	42	26	18	4	18	35	.244	.263	.229	6.80	3.50
Diplan, Marcos	R-R	6-0	200	9-18-96	3	1	4.12	17	0	0	0	20	23	10	9	1	9	26	.288	.333	.229	11.90	4.12
Eshelman, Thomas	R-R	6-2	225	6-20-94	0	4	7.80	15	3	0	0	30	42	28	26	6	3	18	.323	.317	.328	5.40	0.90
Flaa, Jay	R-R	6-3	225	6-10-92	0	0	16.20	1	0	0	0	2	5	3	3	1	1	2	.500	.400	.600	10.80	5.40
2-team total (31 Gwinnett)					1	2	6.31	32	0	0	1	36	36	28	25	4	31	45	.254	.246	.260	11.36	7.82
Fry, Paul	L-L	6-0	205	7-26-92	0	0	7.88	11	0	0	0	8	5	7	7	0	9	7	.179	.154	.200	7.88	10.13
Greene, Conner	R-R	6-4	195	4-4-95	1	3	7.39	9	3	0	0	28	38	25	23	7	17	28	.317	.344	.286	9.00	5.46
Hanhold, Eric	R-R	6-5	210	11-1-93	1	1	5.19	25	0	0	4	26	28	17	15	6	16	27	.277	.288	.265	9.35	5.54
Hartman, Ryan	L-L	6-3	234	4-21-94	2	1	4.17	10	6	0	0	37	36	19	17	2	5	30	.248	.300	.229	7.36	1.23
Harvey, Hunter	R-R	6-3	210	12-9-94	2	1	8.10	8	1	0	0	10	19	11	9	2	2	7	.396	.450	.357	6.30	1.80
Jannis, Mickey	R-R	5-9	195	12-16-87	0	5	4.98	13	5	0	1	47	45	30	26	6	25	29	.262	.321	.213	5.55	4.79
Joyner, Tyler	R-R	5-10	200	5-10-96	0	1	8.10	6	0	0	0	7	10	7	6	0	3	4	.323	.385	.278	5.40	4.05
Knight, Blaine	R-R	6-3	165	6-28-96	0	2	8.49	7	2	0	1	23	33	22	22	3	12	11	.333	.356	.313	4.24	4.63
Knight, Dusten	R-R	6-0	200	9-7-90	2	2	3.05	35	0	0	7	38	29	13	13	6	13	39	.213	.183	.246	9.16	3.05
Kremer, Dean	R-R	6-2	200	1-7-96	1	5	4.91	17	13	0	0	62	61	43	34	9	20	69	.252	.234	.267	9.96	2.89
Kriske, Brooks	R-R	6-3	190	2-3-94	0	0	0.00	1	0	0	0	1	0	0	0	0	2	2	.000	.000	.000	18.00	0.00
2-team total (24 Scranton/Wilkes-Barre)					1	1	3.68	25	0	0	2	29	15	12	12	2	14	43	.150	.114	.179	13.19	4.30
Lakins Sr., Travis	R-R	6-1	220	6-29-94	0	0	7.71	2	0	0	0	2	2	2	2	1	2	1	.222	.286	.000	3.86	7.71
Lebron, David	R-R	5-11	190	9-7-93	0	3	3.09	5	0	0	1	12	8	4	4	0	6	15	.200	.176	.217	11.57	4.50
Lowther, Zac	L-L	6-2	235	4-30-96	0	5	6.53	8	8	0	0	30	33	23	22	4	16	33	.266	.314	.247	9.79	4.75
Mattson, Isaac	R-R	6-2	205	7-14-95	0	2	6.23	18	0	0	2	17	24	13	12	3	6	24	.329	.405	.250	12.46	3.12
Means, John	L-L	6-3	235	4-24-93	0	0	6.00	1	1	0	0	3	5	2	2	0	3	4	.385	.600	.250	12.00	9.00
Peralta, Ofelky	R-R	6-5	195	4-20-97	4	2	4.91	10	9	0	0	48	46	26	26	7	25	46	.257	.250	.263	8.69	4.72
Phillips, Evan	R-R	6-2	225	9-11-94	1	1	5.04	18	0	0	3	25	21	16	14	5	14	35	.233	.283	.182	12.60	5.04
2-team total (2 Durham Bulls)					1	1	4.76	20	1	0	3	28	25	17	15	5	14	38	.240	.275	.208	12.07	4.45
Plutko, Adam	R-R	6-3	215	10-3-91	0	1	9.75	10	0	0	0	12	16	13	13	5	5	13	.314	.389	.273	9.75	3.75
Rogers, Josh	L-L	6-3	210	7-10-94	0	3	7.79	4	2	0	0	17	24	17	15	3	5	15	.324	.368	.278	7.27	1.56
2-team total (14 Rochester)					7	6	4.48	18	15	0	0	90	99	49	45	14	24	63	.274	.274	.274	6.28	2.39
Sceroler, Mac	R-R	6-3	215	4-9-95	0	0	16.62	2	2	0	0	4	8	8	8	2	2	10	.364	.294	.600	20.77	4.15
Sedlock, Cody	R-R	6-4	220	6-19-95	1	3	4.45	7	4	0	0	30	33	19	15	7	12	33	.273	.232	.308	9.79	3.56
Smith, Kevin	R-L	6-5	200	5-13-97	3	6	6.23	16	15	0	0	56	56	41	39	14	49	68	.257	.246	.261	10.86	7.83
Tate, Dillon	R-R	6-2	195	5-1-94	0	0	0.00	1	0	0	0	1	0	0	0	0	1	1	.000	.000	.000	9.00	0.00
Valdez, Cesar	R-R	6-2	225	3-17-85	0	1	1.42	9	0	0	0	13	10	3	2	0	3	12	.217	.136	.292	8.53	2.13
Vespi, Nick	L-L	6-3	215	10-10-95	2	3	6.86	16	0	0	1	20	22	17	15	6	8	25	.286	.345	.250	11.44	3.66
Waddell, Brandon	L-L	6-3	180	6-3-94	0	0	0.00	2	0	0	0	2	2	0	0	0	2	2	.250	.250	.250	7.71	0.00
2-team total (9 Memphis)					2	0	2.03	11	0	0	0	13	14	4	3	1	3	12	.280	.278	.281	8.10	2.03
Wade, Konner	L-R	6-3	199	12-3-91	4	2	2.96	20	6	1	0	73	57	28	24	11	18	50	.215	.222	.209	6.16	2.22
Watkins, Spenser	R-R	6-2	185	8-27-92	1	2	3.53	8	6	0	0	36	28	16	14	6	11	30	.212	.134	.292	7.57	2.78
Wells, Alexander	L-L	6-1	195	2-27-97	6	3	3.29	13	10	0	0	55	49	23	20	6	7	48	.232	.193	.260	7.90	1.15
Zimmermann, Bruce	L-L	6-1	215	2-9-95	1	0	2.40	4	4	0	0	15	9	4	4	2	6	15	.173	.231	.154	9.00	3.60

Fielding

Catcher

Catcher	PCT	G	PO	A	E	DP	PB
Ciuffo	.992	15	125	5	1	0	0
Cumberland	.990	55	481	30	5	4	10
Davis	1.000	2	10	0	0	1	0
Hudgins	1.000	3	26	4	0	1	0
Roberts	.987	10	71	3	1	0	5
Rutschman	1.000	29	254	19	0	4	1
Sisco	.957	6	43	1	2	0	0
Wynns	.990	12	93	9	1	1	1

First Base

First Base	PCT	G	PO	A	E	DP
Cumberland	1.000	4	29	2	0	5
Davis	1.000	1	4	0	0	1
Escarra	.994	47	322	21	2	28
Leyba	1.000	1	12	1	0	1
Nevin	.993	40	256	20	2	28
Ripken	.996	32	218	28	1	19
Rutschman	1.000	8	62	3	0	9

BALTIMORE ORIOLES

Second Base	PCT	G	PO	A	E	DP
Bannon	.992	29	44	77	1	11
Canelo	.857	3	2	4	1	0
Graffanino	1.000	2	1	1	0	0
Grenier	.875	1	5	2	1	1
Jones	.961	53	80	117	8	31
Leyba	.875	2	2	5	1	2
McCoy	.959	14	21	26	2	7
Santiago	.938	5	4	11	1	3
Urias	.939	11	19	27	3	5
Valaika	1.000	9	16	20	0	3
Wilkerson	1.000	2	1	5	0	1
Yahn	1.000	3	7	7	0	3
McCoy	1.000	7	5	6	0	3
Mejias-Brean	1.000	6	3	12	0	1
Nevin	.949	37	23	52	4	5
Urias	.909	4	1	9	1	2

Third Base	PCT	G	PO	A	E	DP
Bannon	.931	49	36	72	8	5
Canelo	.750	2	0	3	1	0
Dorrian	1.000	3	1	3	0	0
Gutierrez	.969	16	6	25	1	5
Leyba	1.000	9	4	17	0	2

Shortstop	PCT	G	PO	A	E	DP
Grenier	.947	3	8	10	1	1
Gutierrez	.857	2	2	4	1	2
Leyba	1.000	2	2	4	0	0
Martin	.979	24	36	59	2	13
McCoy	.952	80	94	202	15	41
Urias	.974	9	19	19	1	6
Valaika	1.000	8	15	22	0	8
Wilkerson	.857	2	2	4	1	0
Yahn	.000	1	0	0	0	0

Outfield	PCT	G	PO	A	E	DP
Canelo	1.000	1	1	0	0	0
Diaz	.961	47	94	5	4	1
Encarnacion	1.000	3	4	0	0	0
Gutierrez	1.000	1	3	0	0	0
Hays	.750	2	2	1	1	0
Jarrett	1.000	89	197	5	0	2
Jones	1.000	12	18	0	0	0
Leyba	1.000	1	1	0	0	0
Martin	1.000	2	2	0	0	0
McCoy	.958	8	22	1	1	1
McKenna	1.000	25	62	1	0	0
Mejias-Brean	1.000	42	79	0	0	0
Neustrom	.991	64	110	6	1	3
Nevin	.948	29	53	2	3	1
Ripken	1.000	2	6	0	0	0
Roberts	1.000	1	2	0	0	0
Shaw	.897	12	26	0	3	0
Stowers	1.000	21	36	1	0	0
Valaika	--	1	0	0	0	0
Wilkerson	1.000	26	48	1	0	0
Yahn	1.000	8	12	1	0	0

BOWIE BAYSOX   DOUBLE-A
DOUBLE-A NORTHEAST

Batting	B-T	HT	WT	DOB	AVG	vLH	vRH	G	AB	R	H	2B	3B	HR	RBI	BB	HBP	SH	SF	SO	SB	CS	SLG	OBP
Burgess, Christopher	R-R	6-0	220	5-2-97	.500	--	.500	2	4	0	2	1	0	0	0	2	0	0	0	1	0	0	.750	.667
Canelo, Malquin	R-R	5-10	165	9-5-94	.228	.154	.253	31	101	16	23	2	1	4	16	8	0	0	0	32	2	2	.386	.284
Cullen, Greg	L-R	5-10	190	11-13-96	.219	.154	.235	24	64	11	14	3	0	2	8	19	0	0	2	22	0	0	.359	.398
Daschbach, Andrew	R-R	6-3	225	10-22-97	.216	.176	.224	30	102	19	22	3	0	8	16	13	6	0	1	44	0	0	.480	.336
Diaz, Yusniel	R-R	6-1	215	10-7-96	.179	.125	.194	11	39	3	7	3	0	1	6	4	1	0	0	13	1	0	.333	.273
Dorrian, Patrick	L-R	6-2	188	6-26-96	.246	.205	.257	112	398	72	98	21	2	22	67	69	4	0	2	135	4	2	.475	.362
Encarnacion, JC	R-R	6-3	195	1-17-98	.167	.250	.000	2	6	0	1	0	0	0	0	0	0	0	0	1	0	1	.167	.167
Escarra, J.C.	R-R	6-3	205	4-24-95	.219	.219	.219	37	128	26	28	4	1	4	17	22	6	0	2	35	2	0	.359	.354
Ferguson, Jaylen	R-R	6-2	180	7-21-97	.130	.156	.128	28	100	12	15	7	1	2	12	10	2	0	3	45	5	0	.300	.235
Fontana, Shayne	L-L	6-2	195	6-21-97	.158	.143	.160	20	57	11	9	2	0	3	5	10	0	0	0	15	2	1	.351	.284
Grenier, Cadyn	R-R	5-11	188	10-31-96	.226	.200	.233	108	376	58	85	19	1	9	43	53	10	4	2	135	12	5	.354	.336
Henderson, Gunnar	R-R	6-2	210	6-29-01	.200	.000	.250	5	15	4	3	1	0	0	2	0	0	0	0	10	0	0	.267	.294
Hudgins, Chris	R-R	6-1	190	3-2-96	.198	.246	.180	60	207	29	41	11	1	8	32	22	2	1	0	84	1	0	.377	.281
Jarrett, Zach	R-R	6-4	220	12-8-94	.302	.250	.323	11	43	7	13	2	1	0	5	4	0	0	0	14	0	4	.395	.362
Lewis, Craig	L-L	5-10	190	5-22-97	.000	.000	--	1	1	0	0	0	0	0	0	0	0	0	0	0	0	0	.000	.000
Martin, Richie	R-R	6-0	190	12-22-94	.267	.333	.250	4	15	4	4	1	0	1	2	2	2	0	0	3	2	1	.533	.421
Mejias-Brean, Seth	R-R	6-2	205	4-5-91	.319	.273	.333	14	47	12	15	4	0	3	7	9	0	0	0	14	2	1	.596	.429
Neustrom, Robert	L-L	6-2	208	11-12-96	.284	.228	.302	62	229	30	65	15	3	7	50	28	2	0	2	44	7	2	.467	.364
Ortiz, Joseph	R-R	5-11	175	7-14-98	.233	.125	.250	16	60	11	14	2	0	4	9	6	1	0	0	14	1	0	.467	.313
Rizer, Johnny	L-L	6-0	192	11-7-96	.247	.254	.245	83	312	48	77	9	3	11	45	21	3	0	1	87	11	4	.401	.300
Roberts, Cody	R-R	6-1	195	6-16-96	.231	.333	.209	17	52	8	12	3	0	2	9	9	1	1	0	19	0	0	.404	.355
Rodriguez, Ramon	R-R	5-11	194	10-30-98	.176	.000	.200	6	17	0	3	1	0	0	1	1	0	0	0	7	0	0	.235	.263
Rutschman, Adley	B-R	6-2	220	2-6-98	.271	.371	.240	80	295	61	80	16	0	18	55	55	5	0	2	57	1	2	.508	.392
Santander, Anthony	R-R	6-2	235	10-19-94	.333	.200	.429	3	12	5	4	0	0	1	2	2	0	0	0	2	0	0	.583	.429
Stowers, Kyle	L-L	6-3	200	1-2-98	.283	.296	.279	66	237	38	67	15	0	17	42	34	3	0	2	84	4	1	.561	.377
Torres, Alexis	R-R	6-0	183	12-12-97	.217	.118	.250	23	69	7	15	2	1	3	13	6	0	0	0	26	0	2	.406	.280
Turchin, Doran	R-R	6-2	195	7-7-97	.186	.213	.175	49	161	22	30	7	0	8	22	19	5	1	2	67	3	2	.379	.289
Vavra, Terrin	L-R	6-1	200	5-12-97	.248	.103	.283	40	149	28	37	10	1	5	20	29	5	1	0	42	6	1	.430	.388
Watson, Zach	R-R	6-0	160	6-25-97	.246	.159	.273	49	183	25	45	8	1	12	31	8	2	1	1	57	6	3	.497	.284
Welk, Toby	R-R	6-2	205	5-2-97	.205	.203	.205	70	249	42	51	13	2	11	30	24	6	0	2	73	3	2	.406	.288
Westburg, Jordan	R-R	6-3	203	2-18-99	.232	.304	.213	30	112	15	26	6	2	4	14	14	2	0	2	32	3	0	.429	.323
Yahn, Willy	R-R	5-11	185	11-7-95	.196	.235	.176	14	51	4	10	5	0	0	4	1	0	0	0	13	0	0	.294	.212

Pitching	B-T	HT	WT	DOB	W	L	ERA	G	GS	CG	SV	IP	H	R	ER	HR	BB	SO	AVG	vLH	vRH	K/9	BB/9
Almengo, Diogenes	R-R	6-2	190	6-2-95	6	3	3.40	39	0	0	16	45	41	22	17	7	17	53	.248	.205	.283	10.60	3.40
Barreda, Manny	R-R	5-11	195	10-8-88	0	1	0.00	1	0	0	0	1	0	1	0	0	1	1	.000	--	.000	9.00	9.00
Baumann, Mike	R-R	6-4	235	9-10-95	3	2	4.89	10	10	0	0	39	29	26	21	6	18	39	.204	.231	.189	9.08	4.19
Bautista, Felix	R-R	6-5	190	6-20-95	0	1	0.68	12	0	0	4	13	2	4	1	0	11	24	.044	.000	.069	16.20	7.43
Bishop, Cameron	L-L	6-4	215	2-14-96	3	1	3.17	12	3	0	3	48	41	19	17	4	19	54	.229	.236	.224	10.06	3.54
Bradish, Kyle	R-R	6-4	220	9-12-96	1	0	0.00	3	3	0	0	14	7	0	0	0	5	26	.149	.148	.157	17.12	3.29
Brnovich, Kyle	L-R	6-2	190	10-20-97	2	1	3.86	15	11	0	0	61	54	29	26	10	15	75	.232	.216	.243	11.13	2.23
Burch, Tyler	R-R	6-2	190	9-2-97	0	0	4.35	9	0	0	0	10	8	6	5	2	5	9	.216	.250	.190	7.84	4.35
Conroy, Ryan	R-R	6-3	190	12-31-96	1	2	4.56	12	1	0	0	26	32	15	13	3	7	20	.305	.283	.322	9.47	2.45
Custodio, Claudio	R-R	5-10	155	10-30-90	1	0	6.75	3	0	0	0	4	7	3	3	1	1	4	.389	.500	.167	9.00	2.25
Erwin, Tyler	L-L	6-0	185	8-29-94	3	2	4.78	30	0	0	0	32	38	18	17	6	14	30	.304	.311	.300	8.44	3.94
Fenter, Gray	R-R	6-0	200	1-25-96	6	4	5.47	21	13	0	0	77	71	49	47	12	48	86	.243	.301	.201	10.01	5.59
Gillaspie, Logan	R-R	6-2	220	4-17-97	1	1	5.60	15	0	0	2	32	32	22	20	8		36	.288	.309	.263	11.85	2.63
Hall, D.L.	L-L	6-2	195	9-19-98	2	0	3.13	7	7	0	0	32	16	11	11	4	16	56	.145	.135	.151	15.92	4.55
Hayes, Reed	R-R	6-3	185	3-17-95	0	0	54.00	1	0	0	0	1	3	4	0	1	6	0	.600	.667	.500	0.00	13.50
Jannis, Mickey	R-R	5-9	195	12-16-87	0	2	8.07	6	6	0	0	29	42	26	26	7	13	20	.341	.353	.327	6.21	4.03

Joyner, Tyler	R-R	6-4	225	5-10-96	3	4	6.14	16	0	0	0	37	40	26	25	10	16	32	.284	.236	.314	7.85	3.93	
Klimek, Steven	L-R	6-3	205	4-4-94	5	4	4.61	36	0	0	1	53	49	35	27	8	22	70	.244	.262	.231	11.96	3.76	
Knight, Blaine	R-R	6-3	165	6-28-96	3	3	5.04	11	7	0	1	45	43	25	25	6	15	44	.259	.263	.257	8.87	3.02	
Lebron, David	R-R	5-11	190	9-7-93	6	0	3.65	22	3	0	0	62	52	30	25	15	37	91	.220	.237	.205	13.28	5.40	
Lowther, Zac	L-L	6-2	235	4-30-96	0	0	0.00	1	1	0	0	4	5	2	0	0	1	4	.278	.444	.111	9.00	2.25	
McSweeney, Morgan	R-R	6-4	210	9-21-97	1	0	1.93	8	0	0	0	9	5	2	2	1	3	13	.152	.176	.125	12.54	2.89	
Means, John	L-L	6-3	235	4-24-93	0	1	6.00	1	1	0	0	3	5	4	2	2	0	3	.333	.500	.273	9.00	0.00	
Naughton, Tim	R-R	6-3	195	11-14-95	4	2	5.36	36	0	0	4	44	39	27	26	4	39	58	.241	.109	.327	11.95	8.04	
Peralta, Ofelky	R-R	6-5	195	4-20-97	5	2	4.53	13	8	0	1	46	40	26	23	3	25	52	.234	.284	.196	10.25	4.93	
Perez, Luis	R-R	6-0	175	5-3-95	0	0	5.79	11	0	0	0	23	24	16	15	5	16	26	.264	.313	.237	10.03	6.17	
Rodriguez, Grayson	L-R	6-5	220	11-16-99	6	1	2.60	18	18	0	0	80	47	26	23	8	22	121	.165	.168	.164	13.67	2.49	
Rom, Drew	L-L	6-2	170	12-15-99	3	1	3.83	9	7	0	0	40	35	18	17	6	9	47	.230	.231	.230	10.58	2.03	
Sedlock, Cody	R-R	6-4	220	6-19-95	5	3	4.60	17	12	0	1	63	62	33	32	10	30	67	.248	.236	.255	9.62	4.31	
Smith, Kevin	R-L	6-5	200	5-13-97	0	1	1.04	6	5	0	1	26	18	4	3	1	10	37	.196	.233	.177	12.81	3.46	
Stallings, Garrett	R-R	6-2	200	8-8-97	2	3	5.54	6	3	0	0	26	27	17	16	6	8	22	.267	.264	.271	7.62	2.77	
Vespi, Nick	L-L	6-3	215	10-10-95	1	1	1.42	14	0	0	0	19	9	5	3	0	9	26	.145	.207	.091	12.32	4.26	
Wilson, Ryan	L-L	6-1	190	11-6-96	0	0	0.00	1	0	0	0	1	0	0	0	0	1	2	.000	.000	.000	18.00	9.00	
Yahn, Willy	R-R	5-11	185	11-7-95	0	0	81.00	1	0	0	0	3	3	3	1	0	0		.750	.500	1.000	0.00	0.00	
Zimmermann, Bruce	L-L	6-1	215	2-9-95	0	1	11.57	1	1	0	0	2	5	3	3	0	0	3	.417	.500	.000	11.57	0.00	

Fielding

Catcher	PCT	G	PO	A	E	DP	PB
Burgess	.955	2	19	2	1	1	1
Hudgins	.990	45	433	40	5	3	8
Roberts	1.000	17	167	13	0	0	6
Rodriguez	1.000	6	56	4	0	1	0
Rutschman	.992	53	572	37	5	5	3

First Base	PCT	G	PO	A	E	DP
Daschbach	1.000	26	192	10	0	13
Dorrian	.978	13	83	5	2	9
Escarra	.991	30	211	22	2	14
Rutschman	.994	20	141	13	1	13
Welk	.959	34	200	9	9	17

Second Base	PCT	G	PO	A	E	DP
Canelo	.984	19	27	33	1	10
Cullen	.969	21	28	35	2	5
Grenier	1.000	28	38	60	0	14
Mejias-Brean	1.000	1	2	0	0	0
Ortiz	1.000	5	8	9	0	3
Torres	1.000	16	25	23	0	7
Vavra	1.000	27	39	52	0	10

	PCT	G	PO	A	E	DP
Yahn	1.000	9	17	22	0	6

Third Base	PCT	G	PO	A	E	DP
Canelo	1.000	2	1	2	0	0
Dorrian	.938	85	45	150	13	15
Grenier	1.000	1	0	1	0	0
Henderson	1.000	1	0	1	0	0
Mejias-Brean	.917	8	5	17	2	4
Ortiz	1.000	2	0	7	0	0
Torres	.727	3	1	7	3	0
Welk	.872	14	15	19	5	3
Westburg	1.000	5	3	8	0	0
Yahn	.500	3	0	2	2	0

Shortstop	PCT	G	PO	A	E	DP
Canelo	.941	8	6	10	1	1
Grenier	.982	78	88	185	5	30
Henderson	.667	2	1	1	1	0
Martin	.889	3	3	5	1	1
Ortiz	1.000	6	6	13	0	3
Torres	.000	1	0	0	0	0
Vavra	.857	2	1	5	1	0

	PCT	G	PO	A	E	DP
Westburg	.986	21	24	47	1	12

Outfield	PCT	G	PO	A	E	DP
Canelo	1.000	1	1	0	0	0
Diaz	1.000	6	6	0	0	0
Encarnacion	1.000	2	1	0	0	0
Ferguson	.974	27	34	3	1	2
Fontana	1.000	17	30	2	0	0
Jarrett	1.000	11	16	0	0	0
Lewis	--	1	0	0	0	0
Mejias-Brean	1.000	4	3	0	0	0
Neustrom	.962	54	73	2	3	1
Rizer	.974	76	147	2	4	1
Santander	1.000	2	4	0	0	0
Stowers	.989	57	90	2	1	0
Turchin	.985	41	65	2	1	0
Vavra	1.000	9	16	0	0	0
Watson	.983	49	114	3	2	1
Welk	1.000	12	11	0	0	0
Yahn	1.000	3	2	0	0	0

ABERDEEN IRONBIRDS

HIGH CLASS A

HIGH-A EAST

Batting	B-T	HT	WT	DOB	AVG	vLH	vRH	G	AB	R	H	2B	3B	HR	RBI	BB	HBP	SH	SF	SO	SB	CS	SLG	OBP
Bannon, Rylan	R-R	5-8	180	4-22-96	.050	.000	.056	6	20	3	1	0	0	1	2	3	0	0	0	10	0	0	.200	.174
Bowens, TT	R-R	6-4	235	5-27-98	.259	.343	.221	29	112	18	29	6	0	5	9	10	1	0	0	40	1	1	.446	.325
Burgess, Christopher	R-R	6-0	220	5-2-97	.108	.063	.121	26	74	10	8	1	0	1	3	6	1	0	0	34	0	0	.162	.185
Carmona, Jean	B-R	6-1	183	10-31-99	.191	.208	.185	25	89	8	17	3	1	2	11	4	0	0	0	43	1	0	.315	.226
Cespedes, Cristopher	R-R	6-3	200	5-18-98	.263	.333	.235	29	114	12	30	9	1	3	16	8	2	0	2	38	0	0	.439	.317
Daschbach, Andrew	R-R	6-3	225	10-22-97	.268	.226	.281	75	261	41	70	16	2	8	35	29	11	0	0	100	2	0	.437	.365
Encarnacion, JC	R-R	6-3	195	1-17-98	.200	.333	.000	2	5	0	1	0	0	0	1	0	0	0	0	1	0	0	.200	.200
Fontana, Shayne	L-L	6-2	195	6-21-97	.241	.161	.264	76	278	43	67	13	6	5	32	43	4	0	2	84	4	3	.385	.349
Graffanino, AJ	L-R	6-2	170	7-16-97	.235	.227	.238	81	272	27	64	12	1	1	31	28	1	0	5	58	6	5	.298	.304
Grullon, Wilkin	R-R	6-0	220	11-28-99	.143	.500	.000	2	7	2	1	0	0	0	0	1	0	0	0	2	0	0	.143	.250
Hall, Adam	R-R	5-11	165	5-22-99	.248	.233	.253	81	294	40	73	13	2	3	27	24	16	0	3	100	26	1	.337	.335
Handley, Maverick	R-R	5-9	190	3-10-98	.201	.261	.183	60	199	24	40	10	1	5	39	27	7	0	1	71	12	2	.337	.316
Harris, Dylan	L-L	5-9	190	1-14-97	.224	.361	.181	49	152	19	34	6	1	3	17	21	0	0	2	45	5	2	.336	.314
Haskin, Hudson	R-R	6-2	200	12-31-98	.275	.529	.216	26	91	15	25	6	2	0	9	10	7	1	0	18	5	2	.385	.389
Henderson, Gunnar	L-R	6-2	210	6-29-01	.230	.194	.243	65	243	34	56	16	3	9	35	40	3	0	3	87	11	1	.432	.343
Janvrin, Mason	R-R	6-2	180	3-3-98	.118	.000	.154	6	17	2	2	1	0	0	2	1	0	0		8	1	0	.176	.211
Jones, Jahmai	R-R	6-0	210	8-4-97	.500	.500	.500	3	8	2	4	0	0	1	2	0	1	0	0	1	0	0	.875	.556
Kehe, Trevor	R-R	6-0	185	4-6-97	.179	.250	.167	21	56	7	10	2	1	1	5	7	3	0	0	29	1	1	.304	.303
Lewis, Craig	L-L	5-10	190	5-22-97	.083	.111	.067	9	24	2	2	0	0	0	4	1	0	0	0	16	0	0	.083	.241
Mantecon, Michael	R-R	5-10	180	2-2-02	.667	.000	1.000	1	3	1	2	0	0	0	0	0	0	0	0	0	0	0	.667	.667
Martinez, Andrew	R-R	5-11	180	6-17-97	.157	.120	.167	41	115	18	18	7	0	2	11	21	8	0	1	48	1	0	.270	.324
Michaels, Logan	R-R	5-11	190	8-26-98	.500	1.000	.429	2	4	1	2	1	0	0	1	1	0	0	0	1	0	0	.625	.556
Mundy, J.D.	L-R	6-0	210	5-14-98	.278	.245	.291	52	194	38	54	14	0	11	37	22	3	0	0	59	0	0	.521	.361
Ogren, Ryne	R-R	6-1	180	4-11-97	.257	.259	.256	19	70	9	18	5	0	0	10	5	1	0	2	13	0	0	.371	.308
Ortiz, Joseph	R-R	5-11	175	7-14-98	.289	.267	.295	19	76	14	22	7	2	0	8	10	2	0	1	18	3	0	.434	.382
Rizer, Johnny	L-L	6-0	192	11-7-96	.288	.200	.306	15	59	9	17	6	0	3	8	5	3	0	0	17	2	1	.542	.373
Roberts, Cody	R-R	6-1	195	6-16-96	.250	.381	.191	23	68	8	17	4	0	2	10	10	2	0	1	24	0	0	.397	.358

	B-T	HT	WT	DOB																					
Rodriguez, Ramon	R-R	5-11	194	10-30-98	.305	.364	.283	22	82	10	25	4	0	4	13	3	0	0	1	14	0	0	.500	.326
Shaw, Chris	L-R	6-4	220	10-20-93	.143	.000	.167	6	21	2	3	2	0	1	5	3	0	0	0	7	0	0	.381	.250
Sparks, Lamar	R-R	6-2	170	9-26-98	.240	.353	.186	27	104	14	25	3	4	2	12	14	1	0	0	36	3	1	.404	.336
Stowers, Kyle	L-L	6-3	200	1-2-98	.275	.290	.270	36	131	25	36	6	1	7	32	27	2	0	1	55	3	3	.496	.404
Turchin, Doran	R-R	6-2	195	7-7-97	.318	.000	.359	13	44	7	14	7	0	1	6	8	2	1	0	14	4	0	.545	.444
Vavra, Terrin	L-R	6-1	200	5-12-97	.381	.375	.385	5	21	4	8	2	1	0	1	3	0	0	0	6	0	1	.571	.458
Watson, Zach	R-R	6-0	160	6-25-97	.249	.265	.244	56	217	38	54	9	3	9	35	14	5	0	5	65	18	3	.442	.303
Welk, Toby	R-R	6-2	205	5-2-97	.265	.313	.250	36	132	21	35	5	1	2	19	20	3	0	3	33	5	1	.364	.367
Westburg, Jordan	R-R	6-3	203	2-18-99	.286	.320	.277	62	241	41	69	16	2	8	41	35	7	0	2	71	9	4	.469	.389
Yahn, Willy	R-R	5-11	185	11-7-95	.229	.286	.206	14	48	7	11	2	1	2	8	2	1	0	1	11	1	0	.438	.269

Pitching

	B-T	HT	WT	DOB	W	L	ERA	G	GS	CG	SV	IP	H	R	ER	HR	BB	SO	AVG	vLH	vRH	K/9	BB/9
Bautista, Felix	R-R	6-5	190	6-20-95	0	2	1.20	11	0	0	2	15	7	4	2	1	10	28	.137	.214	.043	16.80	6.00
Brnovich, Kyle	L-R	6-2	190	10-20-97	4	1	2.36	8	8	0	0	34	18	16	9	4	11	48	.144	.121	.164	12.58	2.88
Burch, Tyler	R-R	6-2	190	9-2-97	1	0	4.50	3	0	0	0	4	5	4	2	1	1	6	.294	.250	.308	13.50	2.25
2-team total (8 Jersey Shore)					2	0	3.00	11	0	0	4	15	12	8	5	2	3	24	.214	.300	.167	14.40	1.80
Conroy, Ryan	R-R	6-3	190	12-31-96	1	0	4.33	11	1	0	2	27	23	14	13	3	13	38	.225	.208	.241	12.67	4.33
Denoyer, Noah	B-R	6-5	225	2-17-98	0	0	2.25	5	0	0	1	12	10	3	3	1	5	10	.238	.235	.240	7.50	3.75
Farmer, Garrett	R-R	5-11	185	5-14-97	1	2	3.71	28	0	0	8	51	47	23	21	7	10	47	.246	.188	.288	8.29	1.76
Feliz, Ignacio	R-R	6-1	180	10-23-99	0	3	9.33	9	4	0	0	18	23	21	19	5	17	23	.315	.333	.297	11.29	8.35
Gillaspie, Logan	R-R	6-2	220	4-17-97	0	2	3.77	11	0	0	2	14	12	6	6	3	3	16	.226	.091	.323	10.05	1.88
Gillispie, Connor	R-R	5-11	185	11-10-97	4	8	4.97	21	12	0	2	80	70	46	44	16	29	78	.242	.300	.188	8.81	3.28
Knight, Blaine	R-R	6-3	165	6-28-96	0	1	2.41	4	4	0	0	19	14	5	5	1	1	16	.200	.257	.143	7.71	0.48
Loeprich, Conner	R-R	6-3	215	9-13-97	1	5	7.16	11	10	0	0	44	55	35	35	11	15	44	.304	.243	.342	9.00	3.07
Lowther, Zac	L-L	6-2	235	4-30-96	0	1	6.75	1	1	0	0	3	4	5	2	0	1	5	.333	.000	.364	16.88	3.38
Lucas, Easton	L-L	6-4	180	7-25-96	3	1	3.96	27	0	0	1	39	35	19	17	5	13	50	.243	.250	.240	11.64	3.03
Lyons, Jake	R-R	6-5	280	8-19-98	0	1	3.18	3	0	0	1	11	8	4	4	1	3	17	.205	.190	.222	13.50	2.38
Magee, Kevin	L-L	6-2	210	1-1-96	0	2	8.15	7	4	0	0	18	21	16	16	5	9	20	.296	.250	.326	10.19	4.58
McGinness, Clayton	R-R	6-1	180	1-13-97	3	2	3.32	28	0	0	0	38	36	20	14	6	19	40	.240	.197	.270	9.47	4.50
McLarty, Griffin	L-R	6-3	185	8-10-98	1	2	3.28	6	6	0	0	25	23	11	9	3	8	22	.247	.179	.296	8.03	2.92
McSweeney, Morgan	R-R	6-4	210	9-21-97	2	5	5.09	22	0	0	1	35	31	32	20	5	23	46	.235	.246	.225	11.72	5.86
Means, John	L-L	6-3	235	4-24-93	0	0	4.50	1	1	0	0	2	1	1	1	0	2	.143	.000		7.50	9.00
Moore, Xavier	R-R	6-2	175	1-7-99	2	9	9.00	14	0	0	0	19	15	21	19	5	14	23	.227	.190	.244	10.89	6.63
Peek, Zach	R-R	6-3	190	5-6-98	4	0	3.22	10	7	0	1	45	45	16	16	5	14	58	.250	.253	.248	11.69	2.82
Pendergast, Jonathan	R-R	6-2	200	8-25-97	0	1	9.00	12	0	0	0	16	18	17	16	4	7	18	.281	.393	.194	9.56	3.94
Perez, Luis	R-R	6-0	175	5-3-95	0	2	5.59	8	0	0	0	13	10	9	9	1	7	8	.255	.167	.303	5.14	4.50
Perkins, Shelton	R-R	5-10	215	1-28-97	0	0	3.80	17	0	0	2	21	15	10	9	5	10	24	.195	.242	.159	10.13	4.22
Prizina, Jake	L-L	6-0	190	1-24-97	3	2	3.81	21	11	0	0	78	63	38	33	7	27	69	.234	.164	.258	7.96	3.12
Rodriguez, Grayson	L-R	6-5	220	11-16-99	3	0	1.54	5	5	0	0	23	11	4	4	2	5	40	.138	.111	.159	15.43	1.93
Rom, Drew	L-L	6-2	170	12-15-99	8	3	2.79	14	13	1	0	68	60	24	21	6	17	73	.236	.218	.244	9.71	2.26
Roth, Nick	R-R	5-10	175	8-28-96	3	1	7.99	22	0	0	3	33	41	30	29	6	12	34	.297	.317	.280	9.37	3.31
Stallings, Garrett	R-R	6-2	200	8-8-97	8	3	4.39	17	16	0	0	80	84	42	39	13	12	74	.271	.298	.249	8.33	1.35
Stauffer, Adam	R-R	6-7	240	1-13-99	0	2	3.18	6	0	0	1	17	10	6	1	5	18	.169	.167	.171	9.53	2.65
Strowd, Kade	R-R	6-2	175	9-17-97	0	3	8.05	21	1	0	1	38	47	34	34	6	15	45	.309	.254	.348	10.66	3.55
Watson, Ryan	R-R	6-5	215	11-19-97	3	2	4.94	11	1	0	0	31	36	17	17	2	9	39	.293	.286	.297	11.32	2.61
Wilson, Ryan	L-L	6-1	190	11-6-96	1	2	5.49	8	3	0	0	20	12	13	12	5	12	23	.171	.100	.200	10.53	5.49
Young, Brandon	R-R	6-6	210	8-19-98	1	2	3.89	10	10	0	0	37	28	17	16	4	15	54	.207	.216	.202	13.14	3.65
Zimmermann, Bruce	L-L	6-1	215	2-9-95	0	1	3.00	1	1	0	0	3	3	2	1	0	2	.250	.500	.125	12.00	6.00

Fielding

Catcher	PCT	G	PO	A	E	DP	PB
Burgess	.988	20	149	21	2	1	4
Grullon	1.000	2	15	3	0	0	0
Handley	.992	51	470	51	4	2	3
Mantecon	1.000	1	7	0	0	0	0
Michaels	.933	2	24	4	2	0	1
Ogren	.980	10	92	8	2	0	2
Roberts	.989	18	158	19	2	1	6
Rodriguez	1.000	21	204	17	0	2	3
Yahn	1.000	1	12	0	0	0	0

First Base	PCT	G	PO	A	E	DP
Bowens	.996	29	236	14	1	18
Daschbach	.993	57	420	33	3	32
Martinez	1.000	2	10	0	0	1
Mundy	.995	26	195	8	1	16
Roberts	.917	3	10	1	1	1
Welk	.981	7	47	5	1	0
Yahn	.800	1	11	1	3	2

Second Base	PCT	G	PO	A	E	DP
Bannon	1.000	1	0	2	0	0
Carmona	1.000	2	4	7	0	3
Graffanino	.988	47	62	98	2	21
Hall	.973	47	77	104	5	22
Henderson	1.000	1	1	1	0	0
Jones	1.000	2	2	3	0	1
Martinez	.949	19	20	36	3	4
Ortiz	.938	5	6	9	1	1
Vavra	1.000	2	5	7	0	2
Yahn	1.000	1	2	5	0	0

Third Base	PCT	G	PO	A	E	DP
Bannon	1.000	3	1	6	0	0
Carmona	.902	22	10	27	4	0
Graffanino	.929	10	6	7	1	0
Henderson	.873	23	16	32	7	3
Martinez	.938	7	6	9	1	0
Ortiz	1.000	2	1	3	0	0
Rodriguez	.000	1	0	0	0	0
Welk	.871	27	17	37	8	2
Westburg	.925	20	12	25	3	2
Yahn	1.000	9	3	20	0	2

Shortstop	PCT	G	PO	A	E	DP
Carmona	1.000	1	0	1	0	0
Graffanino	1.000	17	13	41	0	7
Hall	.875	12	11	31	6	5
Henderson	.939	40	46	109	10	21
Ortiz	1.000	14	18	26	0	2
Westburg	.974	40	39	111	4	20

Outfield	PCT	G	PO	A	E	DP
Cespedes	.912	25	29	2	3	0
Daschbach	.895	12	17	0	2	0
Encarnacion	.000	1	0	0	1	0
Fontana	.976	73	112	8	3	2
Graffanino	1.000	2	3	0	0	0
Hall	1.000	3	20	1	0	0
Harris	.938	47	74	1	5	0
Haskin	1.000	26	53	1	0	1
Janvrin	1.000	5	11	0	0	0
Kehe	1.000	17	22	3	0	0
Lewis	1.000	9	9	1	0	0
Martinez	--	1	0	0	0	0
Ogren	1.000	1	1	0	0	0
Rizer	.889	10	15	1	2	0
Roberts	--	1	0	0	0	0
Shaw	.833	3	3	2	1	0
Sparks	.974	27	36	1	1	0
Stowers	.983	33	51	3	1	0
Turchin	1.000	11	20	2	0	0
Vavra	1.000	1	3	0	0	0
Watson	1.000	55	118	5	1	0
Welk	.500	1	1	0	1	0
Yahn	.800	2	4	0	1	0

DELMARVA SHOREBIRDS

LOW-A EAST

Batting	B-T	HT	WT	DOB	AVG	vLH	vRH	G	AB	R	H	2B	3B	HR	RBI	BB	HBP	SH	SF	SO	SB	CS	SLG	OBP
Alvarez, Yorkislandy	R-R	6-1	170	3-17-99	.259	.273	.255	35	116	11	30	3	0	0	12	19	1	0	0	11	2	0	.284	.368
Bowens, TT	R-R	6-4	235	5-27-98	.237	.333	.211	64	236	43	56	11	2	13	46	24	5	0	1	74	3	2	.466	.320
Burns, Collin	L-R	5-11	187	5-20-00	.279	.000	.339	19	68	14	19	2	0	0	10	8	2	0	2	15	4	2	.309	.363
Cannon, Jordan	R-R	6-3	210	11-28-96	.223	.219	.225	31	112	20	25	2	1	5	14	12	5	0	0	36	5	1	.393	.326
Carmona, Jean	B-R	6-1	183	10-31-99	.267	.314	.255	49	176	26	47	6	3	5	21	21	2	0	0	60	5	3	.420	.352
Cespedes, Cristopher	R-R	6-3	200	5-18-98	.232	.265	.220	70	259	40	60	15	0	12	51	24	2	0	1	73	5	2	.429	.301
Cook, Billy	R-R	6-1	200	1-7-99	.258	.176	.276	22	93	17	24	6	0	6	25	8	2	0	0	33	7	1	.516	.330
Cowser, Colton	L-R	6-3	195	3-20-00	.347	.692	.294	25	98	22	34	5	0	1	26	22	3	0	1	19	4	2	.429	.476
Cullen, Greg	L-R	5-10	190	11-13-96	.281	.286	.278	10	32	5	9	1	0	0	1	8	1	0	0	7	0	1	.313	.439
Deson, Mishael	B-R	6-3	155	7-7-02	.174	.250	.158	6	23	0	4	0	0	0	2	0	0	0	2	5	1	0	.174	.160
Encarnacion, JC	R-R	6-3	195	1-17-98	.154	.200	.125	4	13	1	2	0	0	1	2	0	0	0	0	8	0	0	.385	.154
Grullon, Wilkin	R-R	6-0	220	11-28-99	.087	.000	.118	11	23	2	2	0	0	1	1	5	0	0	0	10	0	0	.217	.250
Harris, Dylan	L-L	5-9	190	1-14-97	.224	.263	.212	29	85	12	19	3	0	1	15	25	5	0	2	27	2	3	.294	.419
Haskin, Hudson	R-R	6-2	200	12-31-98	.276	.241	.289	57	217	44	60	13	1	5	33	22	13	2	0	60	17	5	.415	.377
Henderson, Gunnar	L-R	6-2	210	6-29-01	.312	.195	.360	35	141	30	44	11	1	8	39	14	0	0	2	46	5	1	.574	.369
Hernaiz, Darell	R-R	6-1	170	8-3-01	.277	.270	.279	94	372	62	103	12	0	6	52	28	5	1	4	70	22	6	.358	.333
Janvrin, Mason	R-R	6-2	180	3-3-98	.203	.243	.192	82	310	68	63	9	2	10	33	47	8	0	1	105	25	0	.342	.322
Kehe, Trevor	R-R	6-0	185	4-6-97	.215	.167	.234	42	130	25	28	9	2	2	16	26	4	0	0	48	2	3	.362	.363
Lewis, Craig	L-L	5-10	190	5-22-97	.385	.400	.375	4	13	3	5	2	0	1	2	3	0	0	0	3	0	0	.769	.500
Martinez, Andrew	R-R	5-11	180	6-17-97	.193	.111	.209	37	114	19	22	6	1	6	17	26	7	0	1	39	0	0	.421	.372
Mayo, Coby	R-R	6-5	215	12-10-01	.311	.250	.322	27	106	27	33	8	1	5	26	16	3	0	0	26	5	0	.547	.416
Michaels, Logan	R-R	5-11	190	8-26-98	.232	.333	.213	15	56	9	13	0	0	0	5	3	1	0	1	11	2	0	.232	.279
Mundy, J.D.	L-R	6-0	210	5-14-98	.324	.286	.333	20	71	15	23	6	3	0	6	20	17	1	0	0	13	1	0	.577	.461
Norby, Connor	R-R	5-10	187	6-8-00	.283	.294	.280	26	99	17	28	4	1	3	17	21	3	0	3	28	5	3	.434	.413
Ogren, Ryne	R-R	6-1	180	4-11-97	.219	.296	.200	41	137	21	30	9	0	3	19	19	4	0	2	38	0	0	.350	.327
Pavolony, Connor	R-R	6-1	195	10-25-99	.164	.091	.182	18	55	10	9	3	0	1	13	18	0	0	1	17	2	0	.273	.365
Rhodes, John	R-R	6-0	200	8-15-00	.266	.400	.241	23	94	20	25	4	0	2	18	9	2	0	0	16	6	0	.372	.343
Rodriguez, Ramon	R-R	5-11	194	10-30-98	.220	.281	.186	26	91	10	20	5	0	1	15	8	2	0	1	18	0	0	.308	.294
Servideo, Anthony	L-R	5-10	175	3-11-99	.246	.182	.260	20	61	24	15	4	0	0	7	28	2	0	1	26	4	0	.311	.489
Sparks, Lamar	R-R	6-2	170	9-26-98	.256	.258	.256	45	160	20	41	5	2	4	22	22	0	0	1	43	6	4	.388	.344
Tavarez, Davis	R-R	6-2	190	1-7-99	.100	.000	.143	3	10	0	1	0	0	0	3	1	0	0	5	0	0	.300	.357
Teter, Jacob	L-L	6-6	225	2-26-99	.316	.250	.333	24	95	17	30	10	0	3	20	16	1	0	0	26	0	0	.516	.420
Trimble, Reed	B-R	6-0	180	6-6-00	.169	.167	.170	16	65	11	11	1	0	0	6	9	1	0	1	21	1	0	.185	.276
Turchin, Doran	R-R	6-2	195	7-7-97	.235	.375	.111	5	17	3	4	1	0	0	3	1	0	0	8	0	0	.294	.381
Westburg, Jordan	R-R	6-3	203	2-18-99	.366	.313	.382	20	71	18	26	5	1	3	24	12	6	0	2	24	5	1	.592	.484
Williams, Donta'	L-L	5-10	185	6-30-99	.286	.286	.286	21	77	25	22	4	1	0	9	20	1	0	1	16	5	1	.364	.434
Yahn, Willy	R-R	5-11	185	11-7-95	.250	.375	.212	22	68	17	17	2	0	1	7	7	0	0	1	12	4	0	.324	.316

Pitching	B-T	HT	WT	DOB	W	L	ERA	G	GS	CG	SV	IP	H	R	ER	HR	BB	SO	AVG	vLH	vRH	K/9	BB/9
Armbruester, Justin	R-R	6-4	235	10-21-98	0	0	2.45	7	0	0	0	7	3	2	2	1	4	13	.120	.111	.143	15.95	4.91
Baumann, Mike	R-R	6-4	235	9-10-95	0	0	0.00	2	2	0	0	5	0	0	0	0	3	6	.000	.000	.000	10.80	5.40
Bishop, Cameron	L-L	6-4	215	2-14-96	0	1	19.29	4	2	0	0	5	13	10	10	2	2	6	.500	.500	.500	11.57	3.86
Blach, Ty	R-L	6-1	215	10-20-90	0	0	1.80	10	10	0	0	15	10	3	3	0	1	14	.182	.200	.171	8.40	0.60
Conroy, Ryan	R-R	6-3	190	12-31-96	1	1	3.48	5	0	0	2	10	10	5	4	1	5	15	.244	.263	.227	13.06	4.35
Davis, Shane	R-R	6-3	180	8-26-99	4	6	5.65	21	13	0	0	73	77	54	46	11	27	76	.263	.220	.295	9.33	3.31
Del Rosario, Carlos	R-R	6-5	225	6-17-99	2	0	10.38	4	0	0	0	4	0	5	5	0	12	7	.000	.000	.000	14.54	24.92
Denoyer, Noah	B-R	6-5	225	2-17-98	5	3	2.87	15	11	0	0	60	45	21	19	6	25	71	.207	.141	.250	10.71	3.77
Elliott, Jensen	R-R	6-6	231	4-8-97	4	1	4.37	19	4	0	0	45	58	31	22	4	9	34	.304	.359	.265	6.75	1.79
Federman, Daniel	L-R	6-1	195	9-18-98	0	0	3.00	9	0	0	0	12	13	6	4	2	3	12	.265	.333	.182	9.00	2.25
Feliz, Ignacio	R-R	6-1	180	10-23-99	4	0	1.05	12	4	0	2	43	23	9	5	0	21	45	.152	.194	.119	9.42	4.40
Girard, Thomas	R-R	5-11	170	5-4-99	2	3	5.26	34	0	0	4	51	51	38	30	8	22	60	.248	.159	.314	10.52	3.86
Grady, Conor	R-R	6-2	205	10-31-98	1	0	4.97	6	0	0	0	13	9	8	7	1	9	13	.191	.167	.217	9.24	6.40
Lloyd, Daniel	R-R	6-3	232	8-8-00	1	0	6.17	9	0	0	0	12	12	8	8	1	11	16	.267	.370	.111	12.34	8.49
Lyons, Jake	R-R	6-5	280	8-19-98	4	3	3.69	19	11	0	1	68	59	31	28	6	34	85	.233	.227	.238	11.20	4.48
Martin, Kyle	R-R	6-3	215	11-25-98	2	2	5.21	18	0	0	1	19	17	15	11	2	8	20	.233	.323	.175	9.47	3.79
McLarty, Griffin	L-R	6-3	185	8-10-98	1	6	5.24	17	13	0	0	57	63	37	33	12	23	69	.283	.256	.297	10.96	3.65
Moore, Xavier	R-R	6-2	175	1-7-99	1	2	2.89	7	3	0	0	19	12	8	6	2	11	27	.182	.296	.103	13.02	5.30
Peek, Zach	R-R	6-3	190	5-6-98	2	3	4.37	13	9	0	0	45	43	25	22	2	21	64	.242	.250	.233	12.71	4.17
Pendergast, Jonathan	R-R	6-2	200	8-25-97	0	1	6.23	9	0	0	0	4	4	5	3	1	5	5	.211	.200	.222	10.38	4.15
Perez, Luis	R-R	6-0	175	5-3-95	1	2	1.54	5	1	0	0	12	8	6	2	1	8	13	.178	.235	.143	10.03	6.17
Perkins, Shelton	R-R	5-10	215	1-28-97	0	0	1.93	10	0	0	0	14	7	3	3	1	2	18	.152	.083	.227	11.57	1.29
Pham, Alex	R-R	5-11	165	10-30-99	0	2	0.00	3	0	0	0	5	3	0	0	0	5	6	.167	.000	.429	9.00	0.00
Pinto, Jean	R-R	5-11	175	1-9-01	1	1	2.51	9	7	0	0	47	29	18	13	1	13	56	.178	.127	.210	10.80	2.51
Price, Preston	L-R	6-1	198	8-18-97	1	1	11.42	8	0	0	0	9	15	11	11	2	5	10	.385	.400	.375	10.38	5.19
Prizina, Jake	L-L	6-0	190	1-24-97	2	0	0.00	2	0	0	0	5	2	0	0	0	2	5	.118	.000	.133	8.44	3.38
Ramirez, Rickey	R-R	6-0	175	10-20-96	3	1	3.21	18	0	0	4	28	22	16	10	1	12	39	.202	.234	.177	12.54	3.86
Rodriguez, Leonardo	R-R	6-7	215	11-25-97	2	2	7.68	29	0	0	3	43	60	41	37	5	31	38	.321	.358	.292	7.89	6.44
Roth, Houston	R-R	6-3	220	3-9-98	4	4	4.54	23	10	0	2	81	69	48	41	8	31	77	.223	.206	.237	8.52	3.43
Roth, Nick	R-R	5-10	175	8-28-96	1	2	4.63	6	0	0	1	12	12	6	6	0	5	12	.267	.278	.259	9.26	3.86
Stauffer, Adam	R-R	6-7	240	1-13-99	3	3	3.46	18	2	0	1	39	33	20	15	1	12	46	.219	.159	.243	10.62	2.77
Tavera, Carlos	R-R	6-1	195	10-6-98	0	0	2.25	6	3	0	0	12	4	3	3	0	12	13	.105	.190	.000	9.75	9.00

	B-T	HT	WT	DOB																
Van Loon, Peter	R-R	6-5	210	2-18-99	0	1	3.46	6	2	0	0	13	11	5	5	1	0	16	.212	.207	.217	11.08	0.00
Vasquez, Gregori	R-R	6-1	185	9-8-97	4	0	3.52	16	0	0	0	38	39	17	15	3	5	40	.257	.239	.272	9.39	1.17
Watson, Ryan	R-R	6-5	215	11-15-97	3	1	2.14	11	3	0	1	34	24	13	8	2	7	40	.190	.183	.197	10.69	1.87
Young, Brandon	R-R	6-6	210	8-19-98	3	1	3.23	13	10	0	0	47	37	23	17	4	22	60	.213	.197	.224	11.41	4.18
Zebron, Jake	R-R	6-3	180	2-4-00	0	1	8.14	16	0	0	2	21	32	22	19	3	12	15	.360	.371	.352	6.43	5.14

Fielding

Catcher	PCT	G	PO	A	E	DP	PB
Cannon	.981	24	250	10	5	1	1
Grullon	1.000	11	70	9	0	0	1
Michaels	.985	15	122	13	2	0	2
Ogren	.990	33	267	21	3	0	10
Pavolony	.989	18	158	15	2	1	5
Rodriguez	.977	26	275	19	7	1	1

First Base	PCT	G	PO	A	E	DP
Bowens	.989	56	407	26	5	27
Cook	1.000	5	36	5	0	2
Kehe	.976	15	115	7	3	9
Mundy	1.000	17	122	7	0	15
Rhodes	1.000	4	39	2	0	0
Teter	.979	21	167	17	4	12
Yahn	1.000	3	18	2	0	2

Second Base	PCT	G	PO	A	E	DP
Alvarez	.967	15	19	40	2	4
Burns	1.000	5	7	13	0	2
Carmona	.959	15	19	28	2	7
Cullen	.917	4	3	8	1	1

	PCT	G	PO	A	E	DP
Hernaiz	.963	19	25	54	3	15
Martinez	.965	17	18	37	2	2
Norby	.941	26	31	64	6	8
Servideo	.948	13	25	30	3	6
Yahn	1.000	8	13	15	0	3

Third Base	PCT	G	PO	A	E	DP
Alvarez	.927	16	12	26	3	3
Carmona	.966	11	8	20	1	1
Cullen	1.000	7	5	10	0	0
Henderson	.857	11	7	17	4	0
Hernaiz	.900	11	7	11	2	0
Kehe	.000	1	0	0	0	0
Martinez	.917	17	10	12	2	3
Mayo	.885	27	12	34	6	2
Westburg	.909	11	7	13	2	1
Yahn	1.000	11	15	17	0	2

Shortstop	PCT	G	PO	A	E	DP
Burns	.860	14	11	26	6	6
Carmona	.923	16	19	41	5	7
Henderson	.915	20	33	53	8	15

	PCT	G	PO	A	E	DP
Hernaiz	.927	61	54	148	16	22
Servideo	.909	4	11	9	2	5
Westburg	.909	8	7	13	2	4

Outfield	PCT	G	PO	A	E	DP
Cespedes	.893	48	70	5	9	2
Cook	.926	10	24	1	2	1
Cowser	.975	20	38	1	1	1
Deson	1.000	4	5	0	0	0
Encarnacion	1.000	4	6	0	0	0
Harris	.905	28	37	1	4	1
Haskin	.978	53	85	2	2	0
Janvrin	.993	80	146	6	1	0
Kehe	1.000	21	24	1	0	1
Lewis	.857	3	6	0	1	0
Rhodes	.912	16	30	1	3	0
Sparks	.960	42	68	4	3	1
Tavarez	.857	3	6	0	1	0
Trimble	.926	13	25	0	2	0
Turchin	1.000	3	8	0	0	0
Williams	.926	15	23	2	2	0

FCL ORIOLES
FLORIDA COMPLEX LEAGUE

ROOKIE

Batting

	B-T	HT	WT	DOB	AVG	vLH	vRH	G	AB	R	H	2B	3B	HR	RBI	BB	HBP	SH	SF	SO	SB	CS	SLG	OBP
Acevedo, Stiven	R-R	6-4	185	8-2-02	.254	.231	.260	39	130	21	33	3	0	3	24	11	2	0	1	34	9	0	.346	.319
Alvarez, Yorkislandy	R-R	6-1	170	3-17-99	.171	.375	.121	18	41	4	7	0	0	0	1	6	1	0	0	6	1	0	.171	.292
Bellony, Isaac	B-R	6-2	180	12-15-01	.259	.143	.287	39	108	21	28	8	0	4	11	17	0	0	0	35	2	5	.444	.360
Berroa, Jose	B-R	6-0	165	9-8-01	.277	.429	.231	36	119	22	33	5	0	1	9	13	0	0	0	32	9	5	.345	.348
Burgess, Christopher	R-R	6-0	220	5-2-97	.353	.200	.417	9	17	1	6	3	0	0	3	5	0	0	0	6	1	1	.529	.500
Burns, Collin	L-R	5-11	187	5-20-00	.429	.500	.417	5	14	4	6	2	0	0	1	1	1	0	0	1	0	1	.571	.500
Castro, Ricardo	R-R	6-0	185	12-8-99	.178	.143	.186	23	73	5	13	1	0	0	1	4	1	0	0	16	4	0	.192	.231
Cook, Billy	R-R	6-1	200	1-7-99	.286	.200	.313	7	21	3	6	2	0	0	4	1	1	0	2	8	3	0	.381	.320
Cowser, Colton	L-R	6-3	195	3-20-00	.500	.400	.529	7	22	8	11	3	0	1	8	3	0	0	0	4	3	2	.773	.560
Craig, Trendon	R-R	6-1	195	7-11-00	.294	.250	.304	24	68	12	20	5	0	1	8	8	2	0	0	17	7	3	.412	.385
Cruz, Josue	L-L	6-4	175	12-25-00	.198	.143	.211	37	116	16	23	5	2	5	20	13	1	0	2	55	3	4	.405	.280
Cullen, Greg	L-R	5-10	190	11-13-96	.417	--	.417	4	12	3	5	2	0	0	1	4	0	0	0	1	0	0	.833	.563
De Leon, Isaac	R-R	6-2	170	11-7-01	.276	.182	.293	45	145	27	40	9	1	1	23	18	3	0	0	39	5	1	.372	.367
Deson, Mishael	R-R	6-3	155	7-7-02	.369	.353	.372	32	103	19	38	2	2	3	16	9	0	1	1	23	11	2	.515	.416
Franco, Maikel	R-R	6-1	225	8-26-92	.000	.000	--	1	1	0	0	0	0	0	0	1	1	0	1	0	0	0	.000	.333
Gomez, Angel	R-R	5-11	180	6-17-01	.122	.000	.164	40	98	12	12	1	0	0	3	14	3	0	0	54	6	4	.133	.252
Gonzalez, Luis	L-L	6-4	185	11-2-02	.176	.136	.183	41	131	12	23	5	1	2	10	14	3	0	1	57	3	3	.275	.268
Grullon, Wilkin	R-R	6-0	220	11-28-99	.167	.375	.118	18	42	3	7	2	0	0	3	5	3	0	1	12	0	0	.214	.294
Hernandez, Brayan	L-R	6-0	190	11-11-01	.226	.200	.229	32	93	16	21	5	0	3	17	8	2	0	0	34	1	1	.376	.301
Herrera, Julio	L-R	6-2	180	11-20-00	.203	.100	.217	31	79	6	16	2	1	0	10	8	2	0	0	32	1	5	.253	.292
Higgins, Ryan	R-R	6-1	200	1-25-00	.250	--	.250	4	8	0	2	1	0	0	2	0	0	0	0	5	0	0	.375	.250
Infante, Kevin	R-R	6-0	180	7-14-00	.250	.125	.313	11	24	3	6	1	0	0	4	3	0	0	0	9	0	0	.292	.333
Lewis, Craig	L-L	5-10	180	5-22-97	.435	.700	.361	14	46	14	20	4	0	2	10	9	1	0	0	7	1	0	.652	.536
Mantecon, Michael	R-R	5-10	180	2-2-02	.158	.267	.131	27	76	8	12	2	0	2	7	4	2	0	0	25	2	0	.263	.220
Martin, Richie	R-R	6-0	190	12-22-94	.000	--	.000	1	2	0	0	0	0	0	0	1	1	0	0	1	2	0	.000	.667
Martinez, Roberto	B-R	6-0	145	1-16-03	.181	.300	.149	36	94	19	17	2	0	4	8	3	0	0	0	31	5	1	.202	.267
Mayo, Coby	R-R	6-5	215	12-10-01	.329	.500	.297	26	76	19	25	6	0	4	15	13	2	0	0	14	6	0	.566	.440
Norby, Connor	R-R	5-10	187	6-8-00	.182	.400	.118	7	22	3	4	2	0	0	2	1	0	0	1	7	1	0	.273	.208
Pavolony, Connor	R-R	5-11	195	10-25-99	.133	.000	.167	5	15	1	2	1	0	0	0	1	0	0	0	7	0	0	.200	.188
Placencia, Erison	R-R	6-1	180	12-31-01	.217	.000	.247	33	92	12	20	3	0	0	12	14	0	1	1	42	1	1	.250	.318
Ramirez, Moises	R-R	6-2	211	2-1-02	.314	.333	.309	34	121	14	38	8	2	5	28	4	1	0	0	26	7	3	.537	.341
Rhodes, John	R-R	6-0	200	8-15-00	.214	.000	.250	6	14	3	3	0	0	0	5	3	1	0	0	3	0	0	.214	.389
Rivera, Ricardo	L-R	5-10	176	9-29-02	.224	.111	.254	35	85	7	19	3	1	0	13	17	2	0	1	20	1	1	.282	.362
Rolle, James	L-L	6-0	240	10-28-01	.143	.357	.036	18	42	4	6	2	0	0	2	2	1	0	1	16	0	0	.190	.196
Romero, Noelberth	R-R	6-0	145	12-5-01	.229	.250	.221	40	131	22	30	8	0	3	15	13	3	1	1	28	3	2	.359	.311
Sanchez, Leonel	R-R	5-11	168	12-4-02	.073	.100	.065	18	41	5	3	0	0	0	1	4	2	0	0	27	2	0	.073	.191
Sena, Luis	R-R	5-10	140	9-16-01	.200	.455	.156	27	75	9	15	2	0	0	11	0	0	0	0	17	5	2	.227	.302
Tavarez, Davis	R-R	6-2	190	1-7-99	.344	.381	.337	37	122	19	42	10	0	2	25	11	2	1	0	20	7	5	.475	.404
Teter, Jacob	L-L	6-6	225	2-26-99	.261	.400	.222	7	23	1	6	1	1	0	2	2	0	0	0	6	0	0	.391	.320
Tolentino, Frank	R-R	6-1	180	8-5-99	.158	.100	.170	22	57	6	9	2	1	0	11	9	1	0	0	31	1	3	.228	.284
Torres, Alexis	R-R	6-0	183	12-12-97	.200	--	.200	3	5	4	1	0	0	0	0	3	0	0	0	1	0	0	.200	.500

Name	B-T	HT	WT	DOB	AVG	vLH	vRH	G	AB	R	H	2B	3B	HR	RBI	BB	HBP	SH	SF	SO	SB	CS	SLG	OBP
Trimble, Reed	B-R	6-0	180	6-6-00	.333	.500	.273	6	15	3	5	1	0	0	2	3	0	0	0	4	2	0	.400	.444
Vavra, Terrin	L-R	6-1	200	5-12-97	.500	--	.500	3	8	2	4	0	0	0	0	2	0	0	0	1	0		.500	.600
Willems, Creed	L-R	6-0	225	6-4-03	.167	.125	.188	10	24	4	4	1	0	0	1	2	2	0	0	7	0	1	.208	.286
Williams, Donta'	L-L	5-10	185	6-30-99	.333	--	.333	6	9	3	3	0	0	0	2	3	0	0	0	1	0	0	.333	.500

Pitching	B-T	HT	WT	DOB	W	L	ERA	G	GS	CG	SV	IP	H	R	ER	HR	BB	SO	AVG	vLH	vRH	K/9	BB/9
Alcantara, Darlin	R-R	6-3	180	9-20-01	2	4	6.68	14	2	0	0	32	47	28	24	3	14	28	.338	.269	.379	7.79	3.90
Angomas, Cesar	L-L	6-3	226	4-19-00	0	3	7.54	12	2	0	0	23	24	30	19	2	21	21	.264	.167	.288	8.34	8.34
Arias, Harol	R-R	6-2	180	11-7-02	1	3	8.10	12	4	0	0	27	41	26	24	5	11	19	.357	.349	.361	6.41	3.71
Armbruester, Justin	R-R	6-4	235	10-21-98	0	0	0.00	1	1	0	0	2	0	0	0	0	2	3	.167	.000	.333	13.50	9.00
Benitez, Joel	R-R	6-2	175	7-21-00	0	4	7.90	15	4	0	1	27	30	25	24	2	20	32	.288	.472	.191	10.54	6.59
Berroa, Johan	L-R	6-2	166	8-27-00	0	0	17.18	7	0	0	0	7	12	18	14	0	14	8	.364	.500	.333	9.82	17.18
Blach, Ty	R-L	6-1	215	10-20-90	1	0	0.00	6	5	0	0	7	2	1	0	0	0	9	.083	.167	.056	11.57	0.00
Carter, Carson	R-R	6-4	212	8-6-97	0	0	20.25	2	1	0	0	1	3	3	3	0	1	1	.429	.000	.750	6.75	6.75
Chace, Moises	R-R	6-0	168	6-9-03	1	3	5.64	9	5	0	0	22	25	18	14	1	12	32	.266	.222	.293	12.90	4.84
Chavez, Jesus	L-L	6-1	196	12-23-01	2	4	6.93	11	3	0	0	25	26	20	19	2	14	32	.268	.154	.310	11.68	5.11
De Los Santos, Juan	R-R	6-2	190	5-25-02	0	4	3.83	13	9	0	0	45	50	24	19	1	15	36	.289	.279	.295	7.25	3.02
Del Rosario, Carlos	R-R	6-5	225	6-17-99	2	0	2.31	9	0	0	0	12	7	5	3	0	12	15	.175	.077	.222	11.57	9.26
Elliott, Jensen	R-R	6-6	231	4-8-97	0	1	7.20	3	2	0	0	5	7	4	4	0	4	5	.333	.143	.429	9.00	7.20
Falconett, Pablo	R-R	6-2	220	10-28-00	0	0	--	1	0	0	0	0	0	0	0	0	1	0	--	--	--	--	--
Federman, Daniel	L-R	6-1	195	9-18-98	0	0	0.00	1	0	0	0	1	1	0	0	0	0	0	.250	.500	.000	0.00	0.00
Fulgencio, Orlando	R-R	5-11	168	9-6-00	1	2	13.50	16	0	0	3	18	19	32	27	0	27	17	.271	.318	.250	8.50	13.50
Gillies, Keagan	R-R	6-8	255	1-27-98	0	0	0.00	1	1	0	0	1	0	0	0	0	1	0	.000	.000	.000	9.00	0.00
Grullon, Wilkin	R-R	6-0	220	11-28-99	0	0	15.43	1	0	0	0	2	3	5	4	1	0	2	.273	.333	.200	7.71	0.00
Hammer, Dan	R-R	6-2	200	9-10-97	1	3	12.36	13	2	0	1	20	18	32	27	0	36	23	.243	.273	.231	10.53	16.47
Hayes, Reed	R-R	6-3	185	3-17-95	0	2	8.53	6	3	0	0	6	5	7	6	0	6	7	.217	.400	.167	9.95	8.53
Lacle, Adrion	L-L	6-1	175	11-6-02	2	1	5.31	14	0	0	0	20	27	20	12	3	9	19	.314	.409	.281	8.41	3.98
LaRoche, Kelvin	R-R	5-11	170	7-31-99	1	1	8.64	15	0	0	0	25	40	28	24	4	14	24	.364	.273	.424	8.64	5.04
Litscher, Dallas	R-R	6-8	215	1-10-96	0	3	4.22	6	6	0	0	11	12	11	5	2	5	16	.267	.118	.357	13.50	4.22
Lleras, Yeancarlos	R-R	6-0	150	7-22-00	1	3	6.69	16	1	0	0	35	40	34	26	1	17	34	.286	.349	.258	8.74	4.37
Lloyd, Daniel	R-R	6-3	232	8-8-00	0	0	0.00	1	0	0	0	1	0	0	0	0	0	1	.000	.000	.000	9.00	0.00
Loeprich, Conner	R-R	6-3	215	9-13-97	1	0	0.00	3	2	0	0	12	6	0	0	0	1	13	.143	.059	.200	9.75	0.75
Long, Ryan	R-R	6-6	225	10-19-99	0	2	7.71	5	4	0	0	7	9	7	6	2	1	7	.300	.125	.364	9.00	1.29
Lopez, Hector	R-R	6-1	190	10-4-01	1	1	2.39	12	2	0	0	26	20	9	7	0	14	27	.206	.200	.210	9.23	4.78
Lowther, Zac	L-L	6-2	235	4-30-96	0	0	0.00	1	0	0	0	2	1	0	0	0	0	3	.143	.000	.167	11.57	0.00
Mantecon, Michael	R-R	5-10	180	2-2-02	0	0	6.75	3	0	0	0	5	3	3	2	1	0	2	.417	.750	.250	6.75	0.00
Mendez, Alejandro	R-R	6-4	195	2-28-01	1	2	7.13	17	1	0	0	24	28	24	19	3	14	26	.280	.188	.324	9.75	5.25
Mercedes, Andry	L-L	6-3	185	12-18-00	0	0	6.00	4	0	0	0	6	4	4	4	0	5	11	.190	.500	.158	16.50	7.50
Monroy, Eduard	L-L	5-11	160	10-8-01	1	2	7.44	14	5	0	0	33	43	29	27	4	12	40	.309	.364	.292	11.02	3.31
Ortiz, Luis	L-L	6-3	195	9-17-02	1	2	5.52	7	2	0	0	15	16	10	9	6	6	17	.271	.200	.286	10.43	3.68
Padilla, Miguel	R-R	6-2	180	4-13-02	3	2	6.51	14	2	0	0	28	36	23	20	4	14	32	.300	.424	.253	10.41	4.55
Pham, Alex	R-R	5-11	165	10-10-99	1	1	8.10	5	0	0	0	7	12	7	6	0	3	7	.400	.364	.421	9.45	4.05
Pinto, Jean	R-R	5-11	175	1-9-01	1	1	1.80	5	4	0	0	20	11	5	4	2	4	28	.155	.100	.176	12.60	1.80
Portes, Edgar	R-R	6-2	165	10-2-02	2	1	6.84	14	0	0	0	25	27	22	19	1	19	25	.262	.176	.304	9.00	6.84
Price, Preston	L-R	6-1	198	8-18-97	0	0	0.00	1	0	0	0	1	1	0	0	0	0	1	.333	.000	.500	13.50	0.00
Ramirez, Rickey	R-R	6-0	168	10-20-96	1	0	8.44	5	0	0	0	5	10	6	5	0	5	6	.417	.444	.400	10.13	8.44
Rangel, Raul	R-R	6-3	150	10-9-02	2	3	3.25	12	9	0	0	36	33	17	13	4	9	45	.237	.186	.275	11.25	2.25
Rolle, James	L-L	6-0	240	10-28-01	0	0	--	1	0	0	0	0	0	0	0	0	0	1	--	--	--	--	--
Sanchez, Carlos	R-R	6-5	200	2-21-00	0	1	21.94	7	0	0	0	5	9	18	13	0	16	4	.360	.167	.421	6.75	27.00
Sanchez, Luis	R-R	6-0	167	3-4-03	0	1	13.00	8	0	0	0	9	10	13	13	1	13	7	.278	.273	.280	7.00	13.00
Vargas, Angel	R-R	6-1	173	12-1-01	1	5	5.03	15	7	0	0	34	34	26	19	4	19	29	.252	.231	.265	7.68	5.03
Zimmermann, Bruce	L-L	6-1	215	2-9-95	0	0	0.00	1	1	0	0	1	0	0	0	0	0	1	.250	.000	.333	9.00	0.00

Fielding

C: Burgess 6, Grullon 13, Hernandez 24, Herrera 22, Mantecon 5, Pavolony 5, Rivera 27, Willems 5.
1B: Alvarez 2, Bellony 19, Burgess 1, Cruz 36, De Leon 1, Grullon 1, Hernandez 3, Herrera 4, Mantecon 10, Ramirez 2, Rivera 1, Rolle 17, Sena 1, Teter 7.
2B: Alvarez 5, Cullen 3, De Leon 3, Gomez 1, Grullon 2, Infante 4, Martinez 22, Norby 7, Placencia 21, Romero 4, Sanchez 10, Sena 18, Vavra 1.
3B: Alvarez 10, De Leon 1, Franco 1, Herrera 1, Higgins 4, Infante 1, Mantecon 10, Martinez 9, Mayo 21, Placencia 7, Ramirez 32, Romero 2, Sanchez 6, Sena 3.
SS: Alvarez 2, Burns 5, De Leon 42, Martin 1, Martinez 4, Mayo 1, Placencia 4, Romero 35, Sanchez 1, Sena 4, Torres 2.
OF: Acevedo 34, Bellony 20, Berroa 1, Berroa 11, Castro 19, Cook 5, Cowser 7, Craig 20, Deson 24, Gomez 34, Gonzalez 39, Infante 4, Lewis 13, Rhodes 4, Tavarez 32, Tolentino 18, Trimble 6, Vavra 1, Williams 4.

DSL ORIOLES   ROOKIE
DOMINICAN SUMMER LEAGUE

Batting	B-T	HT	WT	DOB	AVG	vLH	vRH	G	AB	R	H	2B	3B	HR	RBI	BB	HBP	SH	SF	SO	SB	CS	SLG	OBP
Abreu, Frailyn	R-R	6-0	180	12-24-01	.206	.091	.231	26	63	13	13	3	0	1	9	20	3	0	2	26	3	0	.302	.409
Aguasvivas, Cesar	R-R	6-1	165	9-9-02	.000	.000	.000	24	50	2	0	0	0	0	3	7	0	0	2	20	0	1	.000	.119
Alvarado, Jesus	L-L	5-9	176	1-16-03	.279	.250	.286	29	86	14	24	2	0	0	9	24	3	0	0	23	6	5	.302	.451
Baez, Kenny	R-R	5-11	185	9-26-02	.231	.000	.279	23	52	8	12	3	0	0	6	10	5	1	1	12	1	2	.288	.397
Basallo, Samuel	L-R	6-3	180	8-13-04	.239	.200	.246	41	134	18	32	8	0	5	19	19	1	0	0	32	1	0	.410	.338
Beato, Lians	R-R	5-10	165	9-19-01	.250	.429	.222	21	52	5	13	3	0	1	14	14	1	0	0	12	3	2	.308	.418
Bencosme, Frederick	L-R	6-0	160	12-25-02	.310	.286	.314	44	142	18	44	6	4	2	16	11	2	2	1	18	10	3	.451	.365
Bucce, Yasmil	B-R	5-11	168	8-13-04	.236	.500	.183	26	72	9	17	2	1	0	6	11	3	0	0	17	0	0	.292	.360
Calderon, Albert	L-R	6-3	175	7-16-03	.000	.000	.000	12	27	2	0	0	0	0	0	6	2	0	0	17	1	0	.000	.229

	B-T	HT	WT	DOB	AVG	vLH	vRH	G	AB	R	H	2B	3B	HR	RBI	BB	SO	SB	CS	OBP	SLG
Castillo, Eruviel	R-R	6-1	150	12-10-03	.206	.063	.225	45	136	15	28	9	1	0	8	14	8	0	1	48	2	1	.287	.314
Celedonio, Victor	B-R	5-11	150	12-16-03	.134	.091	.141	29	82	8	11	4	0	1	4	15	7	0	0	27	3	5	.220	.317
Cortorreal, Teudis	L-L	6-1	170	12-15-03	.264	.263	.264	48	144	16	38	8	1	1	17	14	1	0	0	24	2	1	.354	.333
Cosma, Jose	B-R	6-1	184	10-1-02	.255	.500	.213	24	55	10	14	1	0	0	6	14	0	0	0	13	5	2	.273	.406
Cruz, Rolphy	B-R	5-11	164	9-21-02	.240	.125	.262	16	50	9	12	2	0	1	3	7	5	0	0	16	3	3	.340	.387
De La Cruz, Luis	L-R	6-2	190	10-15-02	.203	.222	.200	27	69	14	14	2	0	1	7	22	3	0	0	19	0	1	.275	.415
De Los Santos, Anderson	R-R	5-11	185	1-11-04	.324	.450	.297	36	111	18	36	6	2	3	17	15	1	0	0	18	3	1	.495	.409
Feliciano, Wilmer	L-R	6-3	190	4-6-04	.202	.316	.180	38	119	13	24	4	1	4	16	17	2	0	0	45	3	0	.353	.312
Gonzalez, Victor	R-R	5-10	155	10-8-02	.197	.200	.197	26	76	13	15	1	1	0	10	11	2	0	1	29	4	0	.237	.311
Hernandez, Maikol	R-R	6-3	175	10-4-03	.231	.158	.243	40	130	20	30	8	1	0	15	20	3	0	3	33	4	3	.308	.340
Isenia, J'Rudjeanon	R-R	6-1	185	12-7-01	.253	.077	.284	32	87	16	22	6	0	1	11	11	5	0	2	23	8	2	.356	.362
Jimenez, Hector	R-R	5-11	155	2-8-04	.215	.182	.222	23	65	8	14	2	0	0	9	10	0	0	0	21	3	6	.246	.354
Lara, Junior	L-L	5-11	165	1-27-04	.344	.250	.357	24	64	11	22	3	2	1	12	7	4	1	1	18	4	2	.500	.434
Martinez, Ronnie	R-R	6-0	185	11-11-02	.224	.000	.245	18	58	9	13	2	0	1	4	5	5	0	0	24	6	2	.310	.338
Mordan, Aneudis	R-R	6-1	175	6-10-04	.189	.333	.165	40	106	13	20	3	1	1	12	19	1	0	0	34	3	1	.264	.317
Nunez, Raily	L-R	6-0	160	7-1-02	.197	.286	.186	27	66	14	13	0	0	1	8	16	2	0	0	26	9	1	.242	.369
Pena, Angel	L-R	6-0	150	5-21-04	.118	.143	.114	21	51	3	6	0	0	0	3	10	0	1	0	19	3	3	.118	.262
Reyes, Anyelo	L-R	6-1	170	11-3-01	.245	.000	.300	16	49	4	12	2	0	0	2	2	0	0	0	18	1	1	.286	.275
Rodriguez, Carlos	R-R	5-11	195	10-14-03	.277	.333	.263	15	47	3	13	6	0	0	5	3	2	0	1	14	1	2	.404	.340
Rogers, Anderson	B-R	5-10	150	10-24-02	.167	.286	.146	23	48	6	8	4	0	0	4	6	0	1	0	14	0	2	.250	.259
Salazar, Grabiel	R-R	6-0	165	2-19-01	.237	.263	.233	42	135	15	32	7	0	0	17	6	0	1	0	27	9	3	.289	.268
Sandoval, Jonaiker	R-R	6-0	188	3-9-04	.229	.375	.185	24	70	6	16	4	1	0	6	4	4	0	1	21	1	1	.314	.304
Santana, Welington	R-R	6-3	182	5-20-01	.212	.385	.170	28	66	9	14	2	0	2	7	11	3	0	2	18	2	1	.333	.341
Stubbs, Dax	R-R	5-10	165	5-21-03	.079	.200	.061	17	38	7	3	0	0	0	2	11	1	0	1	24	1	1	.079	.294
Tejada, Angel	R-R	5-10	160	1-30-04	.326	.385	.316	33	92	12	30	6	2	0	14	8	4	0	0	17	3	5	.435	.404
Valdez, Damian	L-L	6-2	185	2-25-02	.206	.000	.219	15	34	5	7	2	1	0	3	4	2	0	1	15	0	1	.324	.317
Valdez, Luis	B-R	5-11	148	1-22-00	.333	.091	.370	35	84	28	28	4	1	1	12	11	3	0	2	21	13	4	.440	.420
Vicioso, Carlos	L-R	5-10	160	12-6-02	.184	.250	.173	36	87	22	16	3	2	0	8	21	1	0	0	24	11	2	.264	.349

Pitching	B-T	HT	WT	DOB	W	L	ERA	G	GS	CG	SV	IP	H	R	ER	HR	BB	SO	AVG	vLH	vRH	K/9	BB/9
Abboud, Charbel	R-R	6-6	236	10-13-02	1	1	10.80	9	0	0	0	8	1	11	10	0	17	14	.042	.000	.063	15.12	18.36
Alvarez, Cesar	R-R	6-1	175	9-11-02	3	3	2.49	12	12	0	0	47	39	17	13	0	19	63	.218	.170	.238	12.06	3.64
Beltran, Hugo	R-R	6-0	190	6-13-00	1	1	2.70	16	0	0	10	23	20	7	7	0	5	39	.222	.279	.170	15.04	1.93
Beriguete, Randy	R-R	6-4	221	11-2-02	0	5	4.93	14	14	0	0	46	51	30	25	3	16	41	.274	.212	.308	8.08	3.15
Berroa, Johan	L-L	6-2	166	8-27-00	0	1	8.71	10	0	0	0	9	17	10	0	0	18	10	.243	.333	.226	8.71	15.68
Caines, Erick	R-R	6-4	164	9-21-02	0	2	7.71	13	0	0	0	16	18	20	14	0	15	21	.265	.231	.286	11.57	8.27
Crispin, Francisco	R-R	6-6	190	12-9-02	3	2	6.19	11	0	0	1	16	18	15	11	0	11	21	.281	.280	.282	11.81	6.19
Cruz, Alexis	R-R	6-2	188	12-27-00	1	1	28.80	6	0	0	0	5	7	16	16	2	14	1	.350	.222	.455	1.80	25.20
Cruz, Deivy	L-L	5-11	154	2-13-04	2	5	5.20	13	12	0	0	45	44	31	26	2	24	63	.257	.263	.256	12.60	4.80
Duncan, Manuel	R-R	6-1	160	4-1-02	0	2	4.91	10	1	0	1	15	10	9	8	1	13	17	.192	.200	.138	10.43	7.98
Figueroa, Pedro	R-R	6-1	202	6-3-02	0	2	4.84	17	0	0	1	22	20	16	12	0	17	37	.235	.200	.250	14.91	6.85
Francisca, Elchoro	R-R	6-4	160	8-10-02	6	1	3.08	18	0	0	0	38	28	19	13	2	23	39	.211	.173	.235	9.24	5.45
Frias, Harif	R-R	6-4	163	5-19-01	1	3	6.04	17	0	0	1	22	22	21	15	1	22	23	.268	.269	.268	9.27	8.87
Gomez, Duany	R-R	6-5	186	9-30-00	0	0	0.00	3	0	0	0	3	2	1	0	0	2	3	.200	.333	.143	8.10	5.40
Gutierrez, Enmanuel	R-R	6-1	178	9-22-01	1	0	2.70	3	0	0	0	3	2	1	1	0	6	3	.200	.000	.222	8.10	16.20
Hernandez, Omar	L-L	5-8	155	1-24-04	0	2	4.82	12	12	0	0	37	41	31	20	1	33	50	.270	.179	.290	12.05	7.96
Lara, Yan	L-L	6-1	178	9-18-99	3	2	6.25	20	0	0	4	32	44	26	22	4	21	38	.317	.400	.303	10.80	5.97
Marine, Luis	R-R	6-4	210	2-12-01	1	2	3.00	12	0	0	1	15	14	8	5	0	8	11	.250	.190	.286	6.60	4.80
Morillo, Anthony	R-R	6-2	170	2-7-02	2	2	2.65	9	9	0	0	34	28	19	10	3	8	45	.215	.235	.203	11.91	2.12
Pierret, Oscar	R-R	6-2	190	3-12-01	1	1	1.52	11	0	0	0	24	16	11	4	2	13	25	.190	.214	.179	9.51	4.94
Pina, Junior	R-R	6-4	170	12-19-02	3	2	6.20	13	0	0	0	25	26	19	17	1	16	24	.257	.237	.293	8.76	5.84
Pineda, Yonatan	R-R	6-1	196	12-7-01	0	8	9.41	15	12	0	0	36	35	41	38	1	41	43	.257	.236	.272	10.65	10.16
Polanco, Elvis	L-L	5-10	165	9-16-03	1	2	6.75	13	0	0	0	33	26	28	25	1	33	35	.222	.200	.230	9.45	8.91
Ramirez, Christopher	R-R	6-4	190	7-19-01	0	2	9.64	13	0	0	1	14	24	19	15	0	16	8	.369	.423	.333	5.14	10.29
Ramirez, Jose	L-L	6-3	180	5-23-01	1	1	3.38	13	0	0	0	16	12	11	6	0	10	21	.203	.286	.178	11.81	11.25
Ramirez, Rafael	R-R	6-5	250	3-13-02	0	0	16.20	6	0	0	1	3	3	6	6	0	10	2	.231	.167	.286	5.40	27.00
Rodriguez, Eris	R-R	6-3	188	9-10-01	1	1	5.40	8	1	0	0	13	16	12	8	0	10	14	.308	.300	.313	9.45	6.75
Rogers, Anderson	B-R	5-10	150	10-24-02	0	0	0.00	1	0	0	0	1	1	0	0	0	1	0	.250	--	.250	9.00	0.00
Salas, Moises	L-L	6-2	175	10-28-02	0	1	16.88	7	1	0	0	5	4	12	10	0	13	7	.222	.000	.267	11.81	21.94
Salazar, Grabiel	R-R	6-0	165	2-19-01	0	0	0.00	1	0	0	0	1	0	0	0	0	0	1	.000	--	--	27.00	0.00
Sanchez, Brayner	R-R	6-4	189	6-2-01	1	2	3.86	14	2	0	1	30	41	22	13	0	15	20	.333	.333	.333	5.93	4.45
Sanchez, Carlos	R-R	6-5	200	2-21-00	0	1	19.29	3	0	0	0	2	1	5	5	1	6	1	.200	.000	.333	7.71	23.14
Sanchez, Luis	R-R	6-0	167	3-4-03	9	8	5.40	9	8	0	0	28	30	20	17	0	16	32	.265	.333	.221	10.16	5.08
Solano, Issac	R-R	6-6	195	10-23-01	2	3	7.16	17	17	0	0	33	29	29	26	1	25	29	.236	.298	.182	7.99	6.89
Torres, Eduardo	R-R	6-1	155	12-23-03	1	0	30.38	5	0	0	0	3	7	9	9	0	5	3	.500	.333	.625	16.88	16.88
Vasquez, Jairo	R-R	6-1	160	1-16-02	0	0	3.07	5	2	0	0	15	13	7	5	1	5	9	.265	.300	.241	5.52	3.07
Vasquez, Jordany	R-R	6-0	165	1-10-01	2	4	2.92	13	12	0	0	52	35	24	17	0	26	47	.185	.155	.198	8.08	4.47

Fielding

C: Baez 21, Basallo 27, Beato 16, Bucce 20, Mordan 21, Rodriguez 9.
1B: Abreu 4, Aguasvivas 13, Basallo 13, Beato 4, Calderon 1, Cosma 9, De La Cruz 17, Mordan 22, Reyes 2, Rodriguez 6, Rogers 9, Santana 18.
2B: Abreu 1, Bencosme 12, Celedonio 23, Cruz 11, Gonzalez 7, Nunez 15, Reyes 4, Rogers 2, Stubbs 10, Tejada 28, Valdez 7.
3B: Abreu 7, Aguasvivas 7, Bencosme 6, Calderon 8, Castillo 36, Cosma 5, De Los Santos 26, Hernandez 2, Nunez 3, Reyes 7, Rogers 7, Valdez 4.
SS: Abreu 3, Bencosme 28, Castillo 9, Celedonio 4, Cruz 5, De Los Santos 9, Gonzalez 16, Hernandez 36, Valdez 3.
OF: Alvarado 27, Cortorreal 37, De La Cruz 10, Feliciano 32, Isenia 31, Jimenez 21, Lara 24, Martinez 17, Pena 20, Salazar 45, Sandoval 17, Santana 9, Valdez 9, Valdez 15, Vicioso 34.

Boston Red Sox

SEASON IN A SENTENCE: After finishing last in the American League East in 2020, the Red Sox snapped back to become a playoff team in 2021, winning the AL Wild Card Game and the AL Division Series over the Rays before falling in six games to the Astros in the AL Championship Series.

HIGH POINT: After beating the Angels on July 5, the Red Sox were 54-32, holding a four-and-a-half-game lead over the Rays in the AL East. Their offense ranked fifth in the majors in runs scored, propelled by big years from shortstop Xander Bogaerts, third baseman Rafael Devers, center fielder Enrique Hernandez and DH J.D. Martinez.

LOW POINT: After going 55-36 in the first half, the Red Sox slowed down to go 37-34 in the second half, including a sluggish August in which they went 12-16. Starting with a July 30 series at Tampa Bay and going through the end of August, the Red Sox went 1-7 against the Rays, 1-3 against the Blue Jays and 0-3 against the Yankees, going from a one-and-a-half-game lead in the AL East entering July 30 to finishing August trailing the Rays by 10 games.

NOTABLE ROOKIES: The Red Sox plucked righthander Garrett Whitlock away from the Yankees in the Rule 5 draft. It proved to be a steal, as Whitlock emerged as one of the best relievers in the game, posting a 1.96 ERA and an 81-17 strikeout-to-walk mark in 73.1 innings. By July, righthander Tanner Houck became an important part of Boston's pitching staff, splitting time between the rotation and the bullpen with an effective fastball/slider combination. First baseman Bobby Dalbec showed big power with 25 home runs, though his free-swinging, high-whiff game ate into his production as he hit .240/.298/.494 in 133 games.

KEY TRANSACTIONS: Grabbing Whitlock away from the Yankees had the double benefit of strengthening Boston's pitching staff while taking away a potential weapon from their division rivals. A two-year contract for Hernandez was one of the best free agent signings of the offseason, as Hernandez hit .250/.337/.449 while playing good defense in center field and leading Boston's offense in the postseason. First baseman/DH Kyle Schwarber provided a jolt to the offense, hitting .291/.435/.522 in 41 games after the Nationals traded him to the Red Sox for righthander Aldo Ramirez.

OPENING DAY SALARY: $180,261,996 (3rd).

PLAYERS OF THE YEAR

MAJOR LEAGUE	MINOR LEAGUE
Rafael Devers	**Nick Yorke**
3B	**2B**
.279/.352/.538	(High-A/Low-A)
Career-high 38 HR	.325/.412/.516,
101 R, 113 RBIs	14 HR, 13 SB

ORGANIZATION LEADERS

Batting		*Minimum 250 AB
MAJORS		
*AVG	Xander Bogaerts	.295
*OPS	Rafael Devers	.890
HR	Rafael Devers	38
RBI	Rafael Devers	113
MINORS		
*AVG	Nick Yorke, Greenville, Salem	.325
*OBP	Nick Yorke, Greenville, Salem	.412
*SLG	Franchy Cordero, Worcester	.533
*OPS	Franchy Cordero, Worcester	.931
R	Nick Yorke, Greenville, Salem	76
H	Nick Yorke, Greenville, Salem	123
TB	Nick Yorke, Greenville, Salem	195
2B	2 tied	32
3B	Ceddanne Rafaela, Salem	9
HR	Tyler Dearden, Greenville	24
RBI	Tyler Dearden, Greenville	80
BB	2 tied	62
SO	Brandon Howlett, Greenville	136
SB	Ceddanne Rafaela, Salem	23

Pitching		#Minimum 75 IP
MAJORS		
W	Eduardo Rodriguez	13
#ERA	Nathan Eovaldi	3.75
SO	Nathan Eovaldi	195
SV	Matt Barnes	24
MINORS		
W	Raynel Espinal, Worcester	11
L	3 tied	9
#ERA	Brandon Walter, Greenville, Salem	2.92
G	Kaleb Ort, Worcester	42
GS	3 tied	23
SV	Kaleb Ort, Worcester	19
IP	Raynel Espinal, Worcester	117.2
BB	Stephen Gonsalves, Worcester	52
SO	Jay Groome, Portland, Greenville	134
#AVG	Brandon Walter, Greenville, Salem	.199

2021 PERFORMANCE

General Manager: Chaim Bloom. **Farm Director:** Brian Abraham. **Scouting Director:** Paul Toboni.

Class	Team	League	W	L	PCT	Finish	Manager
Majors	Boston Red Sox	American	92	70	.568	t-4th (15)	Alex Cora
Triple-A	Worcester Red Sox	Triple-A East	74	54	.578	4th (20)	Billy McMillon
Double-A	Portland Sea Dogs	Double-A Northeast	67	47	.588	4th (12)	Corey Wimberly
High-A	Greenville Drive	High-A East	67	53	.558	4th (12)	Iggy Suarez
Low-A	Salem Red Sox	Low-A East	71	49	.592	3rd (12)	Luke Montz
Rookie	DSL Red Sox Blue	Dominican Summer	38	20	.655	3rd (46)	Ozzie Chavez
Rookie	DSL Red Sox Red	Dominican Summer	31	27	.534	17th (46)	Sandy Madera
Rookie	FCL Red Sox	Florida Complex	37	20	.649	5th (18)	Jimmy Gonzalez
Overall 2021 Minor League Record			385	270	.588	3rd (30)	

ORGANIZATION STATISTICS

BOSTON RED SOX
AMERICAN LEAGUE

Batting	B-T	HT	WT	DOB	AVG	vLH	vRH	G	AB	R	H	2B	3B	HR	RBI	BB	HBP	SH	SF	SO	SB	CS	SLG	OBP
Arauz, Jonathan	B-R	6-0	195	8-3-98	.185	.208	.171	28	65	9	12	3	0	3	8	8	0	2	0	15	0	0	.369	.274
Arroyo, Christian	R-R	6-1	210	5-30-95	.262	.329	.213	57	164	22	43	12	0	6	25	8	7	1	0	44	1	0	.445	.324
Bogaerts, Xander	R-R	6-2	218	10-1-92	.295	.284	.301	144	529	90	156	34	1	23	79	62	5	0	7	113	5	1	.493	.370
Chavis, Michael	R-R	5-10	210	8-11-95	.190	.188	.191	31	79	12	15	4	1	2	6	1	1	0	1	32	1	1	.342	.207
Cordero, Franchy	L-R	6-3	226	9-2-94	.189	.188	.189	48	127	12	24	6	0	1	9	8	0	1	0	51	1	1	.260	.237
Dalbec, Bobby	R-R	6-4	227	6-29-95	.240	.278	.212	133	417	50	100	21	5	25	78	28	7	0	1	156	2	0	.494	.298
Devers, Rafael	L-R	6-0	240	10-24-96	.279	.278	.280	156	591	101	165	37	1	38	113	62	7	0	4	143	5	5	.538	.352
Duran, Jarren	L-R	6-2	212	9-5-96	.215	.185	.225	33	107	17	23	3	2	2	10	4	0	0	1	40	2	1	.336	.241
Gonzalez, Marwin	B-R	6-1	205	3-14-89	.202	.271	.174	77	242	25	49	14	0	2	20	19	8	1	1	70	3	2	.285	.281
2-team total (14 Houston)					.199	.250	.177	91	276	30	55	14	0	5	28	20	9	1	1	78	3	2	.304	.275
Hernandez, Enrique	R-R	5-11	190	8-24-91	.250	.260	.244	134	508	84	127	35	3	20	60	61	9	0	7	110	1	0	.449	.337
Iglesias, Jose	R-R	5-11	195	1-5-90	.356	.381	.342	23	59	8	21	4	1	1	7	3	2	0	0	9	0	0	.508	.406
2-team total (114 Los Angeles)					.271	.297	.260	137	483	65	131	27	2	9	48	21	6	0	1	75	5	2	.391	.309
Lopez, Jack	R-R	5-10	160	12-16-92	.154	.000	.182	7	13	2	2	0	0	0	1	0	2	0	6	0	0	.308	.214
Martinez, J.D.	R-R	6-3	230	8-21-87	.286	.279	.290	148	570	92	163	42	3	28	99	55	3	0	5	150	0	1	.518	.349
Motter, Taylor	R-R	6-1	195	9-18-89	.333	.500	.250	3	6	3	2	1	1	0	1	1	0	0	0	2	0	0	.833	.429
Munoz, Yairo	R-R	5-11	200	1-23-95	.091	.000	.200	5	11	0	1	0	0	0	0	0	0	0	0	2	0	0	.091	.091
Plawecki, Kevin	R-R	6-2	208	2-26-91	.287	.310	.267	64	157	15	45	7	0	3	15	12	3	1	0	26	0	0	.389	.349
Renfroe, Hunter	R-R	6-1	230	1-28-92	.259	.276	.250	144	521	89	135	33	0	31	96	44	1	0	6	130	1	2	.501	.315
Santana, Danny	B-R	5-11	195	11-7-90	.181	.179	.182	38	116	15	21	2	1	5	14	10	1	0	0	30	4	2	.345	.252
Schwarber, Kyle	L-R	6-0	229	3-5-93	.291	.313	.279	41	134	34	39	10	0	7	18	33	1	0	0	39	0	0	.522	.435
Shaw, Travis	L-R	6-4	230	4-16-90	.238	--	.238	28	42	6	10	3	0	3	11	5	0	1	0	17	0	0	.524	.319
Vazquez, Christian	R-R	5-9	205	8-21-90	.258	.219	.277	138	458	51	118	23	1	6	49	33	2	1	4	84	8	4	.352	.308
Verdugo, Alex	L-L	6-0	192	5-15-96	.289	.228	.321	146	544	88	157	32	2	13	63	51	4	0	5	96	6	2	.426	.351
Wong, Connor	R-R	6-1	181	5-19-96	.308	.167	.429	6	13	3	4	1	1	0	1	1	0	0	0	7	0	0	.538	.357

Pitching	B-T	HT	WT	DOB	W	L	ERA	G	GS	CG	SV	IP	H	R	ER	HR	BB	SO	AVG	vLH	vRH	K/9	BB/9
Andriese, Matt	R-R	6-2	215	8-28-89	2	3	6.03	26	0	0	1	37	55	29	25	7	11	38	.344	.367	.330	9.16	2.65
2-team total (8 Seattle)					2	3	5.21	34	0	0	1	48	65	35	28	7	13	50	.323	.342	.311	9.31	2.42
Arauz, Jonathan	B-R	6-0	195	8-3-98	0	0	9.00	1	0	0	0	1	2	1	1	0	0	0	.500	--	.500	0.00	0.00
Arroyo, Christian	R-R	6-1	210	5-30-95	0	0	0.00	1	0	0	0	1	1	2	0	1	1	0	.250	.500	.000	0.00	9.00
Barnes, Matt	R-R	6-4	208	6-17-90	6	5	3.79	60	0	0	24	55	41	25	23	8	20	84	.206	.156	.230	13.83	3.29
Bazardo, Eduard	R-R	6-0	165	9-1-95	0	0	0.00	2	0	0	0	3	1	0	0	0	2	3	.100	.000	.250	9.00	6.00
Brasier, Ryan	R-R	6-0	227	8-26-87	1	1	1.50	13	0	0	0	12	12	5	2	2	4	9	.267	.474	.115	6.75	3.00
Brennan, Brandon	R-R	6-4	207	7-26-91	0	0	0.00	1	0	0	0	3	3	0	0	0	2	1	.333	.600	.000	3.00	6.00
Brewer, Colten	R-R	6-4	222	10-29-92	0	0	36.00	1	0	0	0	1	4	4	4	0	3	1	.667	1.000	.600	9.00	27.00
Brice, Austin	R-R	6-4	238	6-19-92	0	0	6.59	13	0	0	0	14	14	10	10	2	7	12	.264	.250	.270	7.90	4.61
Crawford, Kutter	R-R	6-1	209	4-1-96	0	1	22.50	1	1	0	0	2	5	5	5	1	2	2	.556	.000	.714	9.00	9.00
Davis, Austin	L-L	6-4	235	2-3-93	1	1	4.86	19	0	0	0	17	18	10	9	2	7	17	.273	.179	.342	9.18	3.78
Eovaldi, Nathan	R-R	6-2	217	2-13-90	11	9	3.75	32	32	0	0	182	182	81	76	15	35	195	.262	.241	.263	9.63	1.73
Espinal, Raynel	R-R	6-3	215	10-6-91	0	0	9.00	1	0	0	0	2	2	2	2	0	1	0	.286	.200	.500	0.00	4.50
Feliz, Michael	R-R	6-4	250	6-28-93	0	0	3.38	4	0	0	0	5	4	2	2	1	5	.222	.125	.300	8.44	1.69
2-team total (1 Oakland)					0	0	3.18	5	0	0	0	6	5	2	2	2	5	.250	.111	.364	7.94	3.18
Gonsalves, Stephen	L-L	6-5	218	7-8-94	0	0	4.15	3	0	0	0	4	2	2	2	0	2	4	.133	.125	.143	8.31	4.15
Gonzalez, Marwin	B-R	6-1	205	3-14-89	0	0	0.00	1	0	0	0	1	0	0	0	0	0	0	.000	.000	.000	0.00	0.00
Hernandez, Darwinzon	L-L	6-2	255	12-17-96	2	2	3.38	48	0	0	0	40	29	17	15	5	31	54	.203	.204	.202	12.15	6.98
Houck, Tanner	R-R	6-5	230	6-29-96	1	5	3.52	18	13	0	1	69	57	32	27	4	21	87	.223	.231	.215	11.35	2.74
Ort, Kaleb	R-R	6-4	240	2-5-92	0	0	0.00	1	0	0	0	1	0	0	0	1	0	.500	1.000	.000	0.00	27.00
Ottavino, Adam	B-R	6-5	246	11-22-85	7	3	4.21	69	0	0	11	62	55	31	29	5	35	71	.239	.274	.219	10.31	5.08
Peacock, Brad	R-R	6-1	207	2-2-88	0	1	15.19	2	1	0	0	5	6	9	9	2	3	3	.273	.111	.385	5.06	5.06
Perez, Martin	L-L	6-0	200	4-4-91	7	8	4.74	36	22	0	0	114	136	71	60	19	36	97	.296	.253	.308	7.66	2.84
Pivetta, Nick	R-R	6-5	214	2-14-93	9	8	4.53	31	30	0	1	155	137	80	78	24	65	175	.234	.233	.235	10.16	3.77

Plawecki, Kevin R-R 6-2 208 2-26-91 0 0 0.00 1 0 0 0 1 0 0 0 0 0 0 .000 .000 .000 0.00 0.00
Richards, Garrett R-R 6-2 210 5-27-88 7 8 4.87 40 22 0 3 137 158 86 74 19 60 115 .289 .257 .309 7.57 3.95
Rios, Yacksel R-R 6-3 215 6-27-93 3 0 3.70 20 0 0 0 24 13 10 10 3 14 21 .159 .156 .160 7.77 5.18
  2-team total (3 Seattle) 3 0 4.28 23 0 0 0 27 18 13 13 3 16 23 .189 .139 .220 7.57 5.27
Robles, Hansel R-R 6-0 220 8-13-90 0 1 3.60 27 0 0 4 25 21 11 10 2 13 33 .223 .206 .233 11.88 4.68
  2-team total (45 Minnesota) 3 5 4.43 72 0 0 14 69 58 39 34 8 37 76 .228 .219 .235 9.91 4.83
Rodriguez, Eduardo L-L 6-2 231 4-7-93 13 8 4.74 32 31 0 0 158 172 87 83 19 47 185 .277 .258 .282 10.56 2.68
Sale, Chris L-L 6-6 183 3-30-89 5 1 3.16 9 9 0 0 43 45 19 15 6 12 52 .269 .154 .291 10.97 2.53
Sawamura, Hirokazu R-R 6-0 212 4-3-88 5 1 3.06 55 0 0 0 53 45 24 18 9 32 61 .227 .218 .231 10.36 5.43
Schreiber, John R-R 6-2 210 3-5-94 0 0 3.00 1 0 0 0 3 4 1 1 0 1 5 .333 .250 .375 15.00 3.00
Seabold, Connor R-R 6-2 190 1-24-96 0 0 6.00 1 1 0 0 3 2 2 1 2 0 2 .300 .500 .167 0.00 6.00
Taylor, Josh L-L 6-5 245 3-2-93 1 0 3.40 61 0 0 1 48 45 18 18 2 23 60 .246 .146 .327 11.33 4.34
Valdez, Phillips R-R 6-2 160 11-16-91 2 0 5.85 28 0 0 1 40 35 29 26 4 19 35 .238 .311 .186 7.88 4.28
Weber, Ryan R-R 6-1 175 8-12-90 0 0 17.47 1 0 0 0 6 13 11 11 4 2 7 .481 .500 .480 11.12 3.18
  2-team total (2 Seattle Mariners) 0 0 13.50 3 0 0 0 9 14 13 13 5 4 8 .389 .400 .387 8.31 4.15
Whitlock, Garrett R-R 6-5 225 6-11-96 8 4 1.96 46 0 0 2 73 64 22 16 6 17 81 .233 .293 .199 9.94 2.09
Workman, Brandon R-R 6-5 235 8-13-88 1 0 4.95 19 0 0 0 20 24 11 11 2 14 14 .304 .192 .358 6.30 6.30

Fielding

Catcher	PCT	G	PO	A	E	DP	PB
Plawecki	.995	53	382	12	2	1	3
Vazquez	.994	132	1136	58	7	6	10
Wong	1.000	5	31	1	0	0	0

First Base	PCT	G	PO	A	E	DP
Arroyo	1.000	1	2	0	0	0
Chavis	.978	8	44	1	1	9
Cordero	1.000	11	47	2	0	3
Dalbec	.988	123	828	51	11	79
Gonzalez	.978	15	83	6	2	9
Plawecki	1.000	2	1	0	0	0
Santana	1.000	14	86	3	0	16
Schwarber	.985	10	65	1	1	8
Shaw	.952	11	37	3	2	4
Vazquez	1.000	1	1	1	0	0

Second Base	PCT	G	PO	A	E	DP
Arauz	.935	12	9	20	2	4
Arroyo	1.000	51	75	96	0	25
Chavis	.986	22	25	46	1	13
Devers	1.000	2	0	1	0	0
Gonzalez	.969	37	49	77	4	27
Hernandez	.976	47	67	98	4	25
Iglesias	.978	18	17	28	1	7
Lopez	.962	6	9	16	1	6
Motter	.750	2	1	2	1	1
Munoz	1.000	3	2	3	0	0
Vazquez	1.000	2	0	1	0	0

Third Base	PCT	G	PO	A	E	DP
Arauz	1.000	2	1	2	0	0
Dalbec	.944	14	2	15	1	3
Devers	.950	151	147	269	22	37
Gonzalez	.933	6	3	11	1	1
Vazquez	.000	2	0	0	0	0

Shortstop	PCT	G	PO	A	E	DP
Arauz	.971	13	13	21	1	5
Arroyo	1.000	2	0	1	0	0
Bogaerts	.983	138	152	362	9	76
Dalbec	1.000	2	2	0	0	0
Gonzalez	.949	12	8	29	2	3
Hernandez	1.000	8	4	7	0	1
Iglesias	1.000	5	7	9	0	0

Outfield	PCT	G	PO	A	E	DP
Cordero	.959	35	44	3	2	1
Duran	1.000	29	47	1	0	1
Gonzalez	1.000	14	22	0	0	0
Hernandez	.978	93	169	8	4	4
Martinez	.985	38	63	4	1	1
Munoz	--	1	0	0	0	0
Renfroe	.957	146	253	16	12	3
Santana	1.000	20	33	1	0	0
Schwarber	1.000	15	23	1	0	2
Verdugo	.983	156	217	9	4	1

WORCESTER RED SOX
TRIPLE-A

TRIPLE-A EAST

Batting	B-T	HT	WT	DOB	AVG	vLH	vRH	G	AB	R	H	2B	3B	HR	RBI	BB	HBP	SH	SF	SO	SB	CS	SLG	OBP
Arauz, Jonathan	B-R	6-0	195	8-3-98	.245	.171	.276	68	233	32	57	8	1	6	30	30	0	0	4	45	2	0	.365	.326
Arroyo, Christian	R-R	6-1	210	5-30-95	.091	.000	.143	11	33	4	3	1	0	0	2	2	0	1	12	1	0	.121	.184
Bandy, Jett	R-R	6-4	235	3-26-90	.208	.211	.206	34	101	16	21	3	0	3	16	11	4	0	2	34	0	0	.327	.305
Casas, Triston	L-R	6-4	252	1-15-00	.242	.111	.292	9	33	6	8	3	1	1	7	8	0	0	1	8	1	0	.485	.381
Chavis, Michael	R-R	5-10	210	8-11-95	.263	.216	.293	24	95	19	25	2	0	6	17	8	2	0	2	30	1	0	.474	.327
2-team total (25 Indianapolis)					.271	.262	.275	49	192	38	52	8	0	14	37	14	9	0	2	56	2	1	.531	.346
Cordero, Franchy	L-R	6-3	226	9-2-94	.300	.267	.313	78	287	53	86	24	2	13	56	42	5	0	0	94	12	1	.533	.398
Cubillan, Ricardo	B-R	6-0	155	2-1-98	.000	--	.000	1	1	0	0	0	0	0	0	0	0	0	0	1	0	0	.000	.000
De La Guerra, Chad	L-R	5-11	195	11-24-92	.197	.238	.182	49	152	22	30	11	1	3	13	23	2	0	0	57	6	0	.342	.311
DeShields, Delino	R-R	5-9	190	8-16-92	.210	.333	.180	18	62	10	13	4	1	1	4	13	1	0	0	24	5	1	.355	.355
Downs, Jeter	R-R	5-11	195	7-27-98	.190	.177	.195	99	357	39	68	9	0	14	39	38	4	1	5	131	18	3	.333	.272
Duran, Jarren	L-R	6-2	212	9-5-96	.258	.296	.243	60	244	46	63	11	2	16	36	30	8	0	1	66	16	3	.516	.357
Fitzgerald, Ryan	L-R	6-0	185	6-17-94	.262	.364	.226	13	42	9	11	2	1	3	9	4	1	0	0	13	0	1	.571	.340
Gettys, Michael	R-R	6-1	217	10-22-95	.201	.178	.212	46	149	24	30	7	0	5	14	12	3	0	2	60	7	1	.349	.271
Gonzalez, Marwin	R-R	6-1	205	3-14-89	.333	.000	.500	2	6	1	2	0	0	1	1	0	0	0	1	0	0	.833	.429
Hernandez, Enrique	R-R	5-11	190	8-24-91	.333	--	.333	2	6	3	2	0	0	2	5	0	1	0	0	2	0	0	1.333	.429
Hernandez, Ronaldo	R-R	6-1	230	11-11-97	.333	.000	.360	7	27	1	9	3	0	0	5	1	2	0	0	7	0	0	.444	.400
Herrmann, Chris	L-R	6-0	200	11-24-87	.222	.240	.214	48	153	26	34	9	1	7	20	23	3	0	2	56	0	0	.431	.328
Lopez, Jack	R-R	5-10	160	12-16-92	.274	.258	.280	68	223	29	61	14	1	3	33	19	7	0	3	54	15	2	.386	.345
Matheny, Tate	R-R	6-0	185	2-9-94	.225	.275	.206	62	182	27	41	15	1	5	28	20	0	0	0	74	4	1	.401	.302
Meneses, Joey	R-R	6-3	220	5-6-92	.260	.270	.257	38	146	14	38	9	2	5	27	13	0	0	3	39	0	0	.452	.315
Mieses, Johan	R-R	6-2	185	7-13-95	.211	.244	.201	59	199	28	42	9	1	8	26	26	6	0	3	64	3	1	.387	.304
Motter, Taylor	R-R	6-1	195	9-18-89	.222	.333	.194	14	45	5	10	2	0	0	6	7	0	0	0	13	0	0	.267	.327
Munoz, Yairo	R-R	5-11	200	1-23-95	.308	.294	.313	88	351	45	108	16	4	8	36	17	2	1	3	53	18	5	.444	.340
Ockimey, Josh	L-R	6-1	238	10-18-95	.225	.271	.207	98	293	35	66	11	0	15	45	62	1	0	4	117	0	0	.416	.358
Pereda, Jhonny	R-R	6-1	202	4-18-96	.247	.350	.211	25	77	8	19	2	0	0	11	9	0	0	2	10	1	0	.273	.318
Puello, Cesar	R-R	6-2	220	4-1-91	.158	.214	.125	15	38	6	6	1	0	0	7	8	6	0	2	8	6	1	.184	.370
2-team total (33 Syracuse)					.224	.196	.225	48	174	16	25	5	1	1	17	13	9	0	2	30	9	1	.282	.333
Rivera, Jeremy	R-R	5-9	150	1-30-95	.270	.189	.300	45	137	23	37	7	0	2	12	15	2	2	0	28	3	0	.365	.351
Santana, Danny	B-R	5-11	195	11-7-90	.300	.600	.257	12	40	8	12	5	0	2	4	7	0	0	0	9	2	0	.575	.404
Williams, Grant	L-R	5-10	180	10-3-95	.265	.429	.222	11	34	5	9	0	1	0	4	3	0	2	0	7	2	1	.324	.324

BOSTON RED SOX

					AVG	OBP	SLG	G	AB	R	H	2B	3B	HR	RBI	BB	HBP	SH	SF	SO	SB	CS	vLH	vRH
Wilson, Marcus	R-R	6-2	198	8-15-96	.242	.317	.214	64	219	34	53	10	3	10	30	41	4	0	1	88	10	1	.452	.370
Wong, Connor	R-R	6-1	181	5-19-96	.256	.289	.247	50	199	22	51	13	0	8	26	9	0	0	0	58	7	1	.442	.288

Pitching	B-T	HT	WT	DOB	W	L	ERA	G	GS	CG	SV	IP	H	R	ER	HR	BB	SO	AVG	vLH	vRH	K/9	BB/9
Adames, Jose	R-R	6-2	165	1-17-93	2	0	6.32	16	0	0	0	16	19	15	11	2	12	19	.297	.212	.387	10.91	6.89
Andriese, Matt	R-R	6-2	215	8-28-89	0	0	0.00	3	0	0	0	4	3	0	0	0	0	1	.200	.143	.250	9.00	0.00
Barnes, Matt	R-R	6-4	208	6-17-90	0	0	0.00	1	0	0	0	1	0	0	0	0	0	1	.000	.000	.000	9.00	0.00
Bazardo, Eduard	R-R	6-0	165	9-1-95	1	1	8.74	11	0	0	3	11	16	11	11	3	5	12	.327	.391	.269	9.53	3.97
Blair, Seth	R-R	6-2	185	3-3-89	3	1	3.80	17	1	0	0	24	17	11	10	1	11	30	.202	.231	.178	11.41	4.18
Brasier, Ryan	R-R	6-0	227	8-26-87	1	0	19.29	5	0	0	0	5	9	10	10	1	3	3	.409	.455	.364	5.79	5.79
Brennan, Brandon	R-R	6-4	207	7-26-91	1	2	5.97	32	0	0	1	38	44	28	25	3	15	37	.293	.370	.221	8.84	3.58
Brewer, Colten	R-R	6-4	222	10-29-92	1	1	4.00	11	0	0	1	18	15	8	8	2	9	18	.224	.241	.211	9.00	4.50
Brice, Austin	R-R	6-4	238	6-19-92	3	0	3.27	26	2	0	2	33	25	12	12	4	14	34	.212	.250	.177	9.27	3.82
Claudio, Alex	L-L	6-3	188	1-31-92	0	0	6.17	8	2	0	1	12	15	9	8	0	3	13	.313	.211	.379	10.03	2.31
Crawford, Kutter	R-R	6-1	209	4-1-96	3	4	5.21	10	9	0	0	48	49	29	28	5	15	67	.259	.286	.235	12.48	2.79
De Jesus, Enmanuel	L-L	6-3	190	12-10-96	0	1	3.60	1	1	0	0	5	4	2	2	1	3	2	.200	.125	.250	5.40	1.80
Espinal, Raynel	R-R	6-3	215	10-6-91	11	4	3.44	23	21	0	0	118	86	50	45	12	43	115	.202	.185	.219	8.80	3.29
Feliz, Michael	R-R	6-4	250	6-28-93	1	0	0.00	2	0	0	0	2	1	0	0	0	0	4	.143	.000	.200	18.00	0.00
2-team total (13 Louisville)					2	0	1.72	15	0	0	0	16	9	3	3	0	1	19	.161	.143	.171	10.91	0.57
Feltman, Durbin	R-R	6-0	208	4-18-97	2	1	2.59	17	0	0	1	24	18	7	7	3	4	25	.200	.239	.159	9.25	1.48
Gonsalves, Stephen	L-L	6-5	218	7-8-94	5	4	4.68	22	10	0	1	73	65	41	38	13	52	103	.241	.222	.250	12.70	6.41
Gossett, Daniel	R-R	6-0	185	11-13-92	7	5	4.22	20	18	0	0	98	94	54	46	14	46	81	.249	.259	.242	7.44	4.22
Grotz, Zac	R-R	6-2	195	2-17-93	1	0	9.58	8	1	0	0	10	11	11	11	3	4	7	.378	.467	.214	6.10	3.48
Hall, Matt	L-L	6-0	200	7-23-93	2	2	7.36	28	0	0	1	37	50	34	30	4	26	37	.327	.400	.296	9.08	6.38
Hart, Kyle	L-L	6-5	200	11-23-92	6	9	4.22	23	20	1	0	107	100	58	50	19	47	90	.246	.250	.245	7.59	3.97
Hartlieb, Geoff	R-R	6-5	240	12-9-93	1	0	0.00	4	0	0	0	4	0	1	0	0	4	2	.000	.000	.000	9.00	9.82
3-team total (9 Indianapolis, 10 Syracuse)					3	2	3.76	23	0	0	0	26	21	13	11	4	17	29	.206	.146	.259	9.91	5.81
Hernandez, Darwinzon	L-L	6-2	255	12-17-96	0	0	0.00	1	0	0	0	1	0	0	0	0	1	1	.000	.000	.000	9.00	9.00
Houck, Tanner	R-R	6-5	230	6-29-96	0	2	5.14	6	6	0	0	21	19	13	12	1	7	26	.241	.250	.222	11.14	3.00
Kelly, Zack	R-R	6-3	205	3-3-95	1	0	2.89	15	0	0	1	19	13	6	6	1	5	29	.191	.133	.237	13.98	2.41
Kent, Matthew	L-L	6-0	180	9-13-92	1	0	5.40	3	2	0	0	12	9	7	7	1	4	9	.209	.125	.259	6.94	3.09
Matheny, Tate	R-R	6-0	185	2-9-94	0	0	0.00	1	0	0	0	1	1	0	0	0	0	0	.250	.500	.000	0.00	0.00
McCarthy, Kevin	R-R	6-3	210	2-22-92	1	2	7.13	28	2	0	1	35	54	31	28	5	6	35	.340	.329	.349	8.92	1.53
2-team total (7 Charlotte)					1	2	7.12	35	2	0	1	43	62	37	34	7	9	41	.330	.322	.337	8.58	1.88
Ort, Kaleb	R-R	6-4	240	2-5-92	1	3	2.98	42	0	0	19	45	40	19	15	4	20	62	.233	.319	.175	12.31	3.97
Peacock, Brad	R-R	6-1	207	2-2-88	0	3	13.50	2	0	0	0	2	4	3	3	2	2	3	.444	.667	.333	13.50	9.00
2-team total (11 Columbus)					0	4	8.00	13	10	0	0	36	43	33	32	8	16	41	.293	.300	.286	10.25	4.00
Perez, Martin	L-L	6-0	200	4-4-91	1	0	0.00	1	0	0	0	1	1	0	0	0	0	1	.250	.500	.000	9.00	0.00
Poyner, Bobby	L-L	6-0	220	12-1-92	0	0	9.69	8	0	0	0	13	22	15	14	6	2	12	.361	.563	.289	8.31	1.38
Rios, Yacksel	R-R	6-3	215	6-27-93	0	0	7.50	5	0	0	1	6	10	5	5	0	3	8	.370	.286	.462	12.00	4.50
2-team total (12 Durham)					2	0	2.75	17	0	0	3	20	18	7	6	1	5	25	.243	.231	.257	11.44	2.29
Sale, Chris	L-L	6-6	183	3-30-89	1	0	0.93	2	2	0	0	10	7	1	1	0	4	15	.194	.167	.208	13.97	3.72
Sawamura, Hirokazu	R-R	6-0	212	4-3-88	0	0	0.00	1	1	0	0	1	0	0	0	0	0	1	.000	.000	.000	9.00	0.00
Schreiber, John	R-R	6-2	210	3-5-94	3	3	2.71	33	8	0	1	66	61	23	20	3	26	65	.242	.283	.200	8.82	3.53
Seabold, Connor	R-R	6-2	190	1-24-96	4	3	3.50	11	11	0	0	54	43	24	21	6	19	52	.215	.146	.279	8.67	3.17
Simpson, Caleb	R-R	6-4	231	9-15-91	1	0	3.86	13	0	0	0	14	9	6	6	2	8	21	.180	.158	.194	13.50	5.14
Valdez, Phillips	R-R	6-2	160	11-16-91	1	0	3.94	17	0	0	1	16	13	7	7	2	14	20	.228	.222	.233	11.25	7.88
Walden, Marcus	R-R	5-10	198	9-13-88	5	3	4.01	27	3	0	0	43	46	23	19	5	19	40	.269	.240	.292	8.44	4.01
2-team total (11 Iowa)					6	4	4.87	38	3	0	0	57	70	39	31	9	23	58	.294	.255	.326	9.10	3.61
Weber, Ryan	R-R	6-1	175	8-12-90	2	2	4.63	7	6	0	0	35	35	22	18	5	10	33	.265	.271	.262	8.49	2.57
2-team total (2 Nashville)					2	3	5.02	9	8	0	0	43	48	28	24	6	11	43	.287	.318	.267	9.00	2.30
Winckowski, Josh	R-R	6-4	202	6-28-98	1	1	2.25	2	2	0	0	12	5	3	3	1	3	13	.122	.118	.125	9.75	2.25
Workman, Brandon	R-R	6-5	235	8-13-88	0	0	1.29	7	0	0	1	7	3	1	1	0	4	10	.130	.286	.063	12.86	5.14

Fielding

Catcher	PCT	G	PO	A	E	DP	PB
Bandy	.995	25	199	11	1	1	4
Hernandez	1.000	5	51	3	0	0	0
Herrmann	1.000	37	309	13	0	2	2
Pereda	.987	23	210	15	3	0	6
Wong	.995	44	399	16	2	1	6

First Base	PCT	G	PO	A	E	DP
Bandy	1.000	1	8	0	0	0
Casas	1.000	7	46	3	0	3
Chavis	.987	18	150	3	2	12
Cordero	.956	7	35	8	2	6
Gonzalez	1.000	1	4	0	0	0
Herrmann	1.000	2	4	0	0	1
Meneses	.986	10	65	6	1	5
Munoz	.970	9	59	5	2	7
Ockimey	.984	78	504	38	9	56
Santana	1.000	4	22	4	0	0

Second Base	PCT	G	PO	A	E	DP
Arauz	.983	41	60	113	3	23
Arroyo	1.000	8	10	12	0	2
Chavis	.960	6	14	10	1	2
De La Guerra	1.000	3	2	5	0	1
Downs	.971	21	44	55	3	20
Fitzgerald	1.000	4	4	9	0	2
Gonzalez	1.000	1	0	1	0	0
Lopez	.978	26	30	59	2	18
Matheny	.667	1	2	0	1	0
Motter	1.000	3	3	4	0	0
Munoz	1.000	4	6	6	0	1
Rivera	1.000	11	14	24	0	6
Santana	1.000	1	0	1	0	0
Williams	1.000	11	21	19	0	3
Wong	.667	1	2	4	3	0

Third Base	PCT	G	PO	A	E	DP
Arauz	.931	12	9	18	2	3
De La Guerra	.906	39	22	36	6	5
Fitzgerald	.889	5	6	10	2	1
Lopez	.919	16	12	22	3	3
Motter	1.000	8	3	6	0	0
Munoz	.939	54	41	98	9	13
Rivera	.667	4	1	3	2	0
Santana	1.000	1	1	2	0	0

Shortstop	PCT	G	PO	A	E	DP
Arauz	1.000	13	18	37	0	8
Downs	.965	79	83	166	9	40
Fitzgerald	1.000	2	1	5	0	1
Lopez	.982	18	23	32	1	12
Munoz	.971	11	13	20	1	4
Rivera	.958	8	11	12	1	1

Outfield	PCT	G	PO	A	E	DP
Cordero	.944	63	100	1	6	1
Cubillan	--	1	0	0	0	0
DeShields	.975	18	39	0	1	0
Duran	.991	58	111	4	1	1

Fitzgerald	1.000	1	1	0 0 0
Gettys	.949	33	69	6 4 1
Hernandez	1.000	1	2	1 0 0
Herrmann	1.000	2	1	0 0 0
Lopez	1.000	13	33	1 0 0

Matheny	1.000	61	127	2 0 0
Meneses	1.000	24	34	1 0 1
Mieses	.957	32	42	2 2 0
Motter	--	1	0	0 0 0
Munoz	.833	8	10	0 2 0

Puello	1.000	10	20	0 0 0
Rivera	.977	22	40	2 1 0
Santana	1.000	4	2	0 0 0
Wilson	.990	58	93	2 1 1

PORTLAND SEA DOGS

DOUBLE-A NORTHEAST

DOUBLE-A

Batting

Batting	B-T	HT	WT	DOB	AVG	vLH	vRH	G	AB	R	H	2B	3B	HR	RBI	BB	HBP	SH	SF	SO	SB	CS	SLG	OBP
Baldwin, Roldani	R-R	5-11	211	3-16-96	.242	.219	.248	45	149	18	36	8	1	4	18	13	5	0	1	61	1	0	.389	.321
Cannon, Cameron	R-R	5-10	205	10-16-97	.223	.190	.233	24	94	15	21	6	0	3	14	5	0	0	0	18	0	2	.383	.263
Casas, Triston	L-R	6-4	252	1-15-00	.284	.234	.299	77	275	57	78	12	2	13	52	49	3	0	2	63	6	3	.484	.395
Castellanos, Pedro	R-R	6-3	244	12-11-97	.289	.309	.284	87	325	66	94	14	3	13	44	32	8	0	3	63	2	4	.471	.364
Cottam, Kole	R-R	6-3	235	5-30-97	.282	.364	.269	25	78	11	22	5	1	4	9	3	4	0	1	33	0	0	.526	.337
Cubillan, Ricardo	B-R	6-0	155	2-1-98	.125	.000	.182	10	16	0	2	0	0	0	0	1	0	0	0	8	0	0	.125	.176
Dalton, Wil	R-R	6-0	182	8-27-97	.240	.500	.217	8	25	3	6	4	0	0	3	0	2	0	0	3	0	0	.400	.296
Fitzgerald, Ryan	L-R	6-0	185	6-17-94	.271	.222	.283	95	321	46	87	30	3	13	49	33	8	0	3	68	4	4	.505	.351
Granberg, Devlin	R-R	6-2	224	9-8-95	.286	.388	.263	69	262	48	75	16	1	10	45	11	7	0	1	54	4	1	.469	.331
Hernandez, Ronaldo	R-R	6-1	230	11-11-97	.280	.273	.281	92	336	44	94	26	1	16	53	11	9	0	2	70	0	2	.506	.319
Lopez, Jack	R-R	5-10	160	12-16-92	.421	.000	.471	5	19	5	8	3	0	1	9	2	0	0	0	4	0	0	.737	.476
Matheny, Tate	R-R	6-0	185	2-9-94	.293	.300	.292	16	58	9	17	1	1	5	11	9	0	0	0	18	5	0	.603	.388
Meneses, Joey	R-R	6-3	220	5-6-92	.303	.279	.310	50	188	31	57	22	1	10	43	12	3	0	4	35	0	1	.590	.348
Mieses, Johan	R-R	6-2	185	7-13-95	.286	.227	.306	23	84	19	24	3	0	11	22	9	2	0	0	19	0	0	.714	.368
Nishioka, Tanner	R-R	5-11	180	10-22-94	.253	.250	.254	54	150	25	38	6	0	6	19	8	7	1	3	45	1	2	.413	.315
Osinski, Michael	R-R	6-2	195	8-4-95	.100	.250	.000	4	10	0	1	0	0	0	1	0	0	0	1	4	0	0	.100	.091
Pereda, Jhonny	R-R	6-1	202	4-18-96	.246	.273	.237	39	126	14	31	12	1	0	9	22	0	0	0	17	0	0	.357	.358
Potts, Hudson	R-R	6-3	205	10-28-98	.217	.229	.215	78	281	33	61	18	0	11	47	16	4	0	6	100	0	0	.399	.264
Rangel, Oscar	L-R	5-11	184	5-27-98	.154	.000	.182	7	13	0	2	0	0	0	0	0	0	0	0	3	0	0	.154	.214
Reed, Tyreque	R-R	6-1	250	6-6-97	.239	.130	.261	44	138	20	33	9	0	3	21	18	3	0	2	54	0	0	.370	.335
Rivera, Jeremy	B-R	5-9	150	1-30-95	.150	.077	.185	26	80	11	12	2	0	0	1	11	2	0	0	24	1	0	.175	.269
Rosario, Jeisson	L-L	6-1	191	10-22-99	.232	.244	.228	98	345	48	80	15	1	3	36	50	5	2	3	113	11	7	.307	.335
Santana, Danny	B-R	5-11	195	11-7-90	.412	1.000	.375	5	17	5	7	0	0	3	6	1	0	0	0	4	2	0	.941	.444
Sogard, Nick	B-R	6-1	180	9-9-97	.263	.667	.241	18	57	8	15	0	1	0	2	5	1	0	0	11	1	0	.298	.333
Williams, Grant	L-R	5-10	180	10-3-95	.270	.268	.271	72	248	39	67	10	2	1	14	11	2	3	1	18	8	3	.339	.305

Pitching

Pitching	B-T	HT	WT	DOB	W	L	ERA	G	GS	CG	SV	IP	H	R	ER	HR	BB	SO	AVG	vLH	vRH	K/9	BB/9
Adames, Jose	R-R	6-2	165	1-17-93	0	0	2.33	19	0	0	10	19	11	5	5	1	8	27	.169	.188	.163	12.57	3.72
Barnes, Matt	R-R	6-4	208	6-17-90	1	0	18.00	1	1	0	0	1	3	2	2	0	0	2	.500	.667	.333	18.00	0.00
Bello, Brayan	R-R	6-1	170	5-17-99	2	3	4.66	15	15	0	0	64	66	34	33	5	24	87	.266	.260	.270	12.30	3.39
Blair, Seth	R-R	6-2	185	3-3-89	0	1	2.12	15	0	0	2	17	9	4	4	1	4	21	.153	.105	.175	11.12	2.12
Brasier, Ryan	R-R	6-0	227	8-26-87	0	0	0.00	3	0	0	0	3	1	0	0	0	0	4	.100	.000	.125	6.00	0.00
Crawford, Kutter	R-R	6-1	209	4-1-96	3	2	3.30	10	10	1	0	46	33	17	17	7	5	64	.200	.224	.187	12.43	0.97
De Jesus, Enmanuel	L-L	6-3	190	12-10-96	5	2	3.97	21	8	0	1	59	66	33	26	2	26	71	.281	.196	.307	10.83	3.97
Disla, Jose	R-R	6-2	165	3-11-96	0	2	13.50	9	0	0	0	9	13	13	13	3	8	6	.325	.350	.300	6.23	8.31
Feltman, Durbin	R-R	6-0	208	4-18-97	6	0	3.29	22	0	0	1	27	23	11	10	5	10	37	.228	.172	.250	12.18	3.29
German, Frank	R-R	6-2	195	9-22-97	3	9	5.12	24	18	0	2	84	99	61	48	12	30	72	.285	.277	.290	7.68	3.20
Gomez, Rio	L-L	6-0	190	10-20-94	1	1	3.43	26	0	0	0	39	37	16	15	3	12	50	.252	.188	.283	11.44	2.75
Groome, Jay	L-L	6-6	262	8-23-98	2	0	2.30	3	3	0	0	16	12	4	4	0	4	26	.211	.250	.204	14.94	2.30
Kelly, Zack	R-R	6-3	205	3-3-95	3	1	1.69	21	0	0	5	27	18	6	5	1	13	40	.196	.171	.211	13.50	4.39
Kent, Matthew	L-L	6-0	180	9-13-92	6	3	3.41	24	1	0	0	61	65	36	23	4	11	48	.278	.161	.315	7.12	1.63
Lau, Adam	R-R	6-2	210	7-5-94	1	0	4.50	7	0	0	0	8	5	4	4	2	3	10	.258	.333	.227	11.25	3.38
LoBrutto, Dominic	L-L	6-1	185	5-31-96	2	2	5.35	33	0	0	4	39	49	26	23	3	14	38	.306	.311	.304	8.84	3.26
Martinez, Joan	R-R	6-3	195	8-29-96	0	1	2.48	33	0	0	5	36	23	12	10	0	20	51	.180	.243	.154	12.63	4.95
Murphy, Chris	L-L	6-1	175	6-9-98	4	2	5.45	7	6	0	0	33	30	21	20	4	13	47	.242	.152	.275	12.82	3.55
Olson, Tyler	R-L	6-3	205	10-2-89	4	1	2.61	31	0	0	1	31	25	13	9	3	13	37	.214	.128	.256	10.74	3.77
Politi, Andrew	R-R	6-0	193	6-4-96	6	9	6.36	21	15	0	0	75	77	59	53	11	38	89	.258	.286	.244	10.68	4.56
Reyes, Denyi	R-R	6-4	255	11-2-96	4	2	4.21	20	5	0	0	58	64	30	27	10	16	63	.278	.275	.280	9.83	1.56
Sale, Chris	L-L	6-6	183	3-30-89	0	0	2.45	2	2	0	0	7	6	2	2	1	1	15	.214	.125	.333	18.41	1.23
Santos, Victor	R-R	6-1	191	7-12-00	4	2	2.58	10	8	1	0	45	43	15	13	5	6	45	.240	.192	.277	8.93	1.19
2-team total (4 Reading)					5	3	2.73	14	12	1	0	66	60	22	20	7	10	60	.236	.179	.285	8.18	1.36
Schellenger, Zach	R-R	6-5	210	1-9-96	1	0	9.53	13	0	0	0	11	10	13	12	3	14	16	.227	.333	.154	12.71	11.11
Scherff, Alex	B-R	6-3	205	2-5-98	1	0	1.35	6	0	0	0	7	5	2	1	0	2	9	.192	.375	.111	12.15	2.70
Thompson, Jake	R-R	6-1	215	9-22-94	2	0	4.13	27	0	0	0	28	28	17	13	2	18	28	.259	.200	.288	8.89	5.72
Ward, Thaddeus	R-R	6-3	192	1-16-97	0	0	5.63	2	2	0	0	8	11	5	5	0	5	11	.324	.500	.286	12.38	5.63
Winckowski, Josh	R-R	6-4	202	6-28-98	8	3	4.14	21	20	0	0	100	100	54	46	10	30	88	.253	.303	.228	7.92	2.70

Fielding

Catcher	PCT	G	PO	A	E	DP	PB
Baldwin	.992	12	116	12	1	0	7
Cottam	.988	17	156	8	2	0	0
Hernandez	.990	61	576	36	6	2	14
Pereda	.988	25	223	17	3	1	2
Rangel	1.000	5	26	0	0	0	0

First Base	PCT	G	PO	A	E	DP
Casas	.986	73	514	34	8	41
Cottam	1.000	2	10	1	0	1
Fitzgerald	1.000	2	6	0	0	0
Granberg	1.000	2	10	1	0	2
Hernandez	1.000	1	11	0	0	1
Meneses	.985	8	61	4	1	5

	PCT	G	PO	A	E	DP
Osinski	1.000	2	12	1	0	2
Pereda	.976	6	40	1	1	3
Reed	.993	19	132	10	1	14
Santana	1.000	3	9	1	0	0

Second Base	PCT	G	PO	A	E	DP
Baldwin	.931	6	10	17	2	1

	PCT	G	PO	A	E	DP
Cannon	.944	19	32	53	5	11
Cubillan	.895	7	8	9	2	5
Fitzgerald	1.000	2	0	3	0	0
Lopez	1.000	2	3	3	0	0
Nishioka	.889	24	34	38	9	13
Rivera	1.000	3	3	3	0	0
Sogard	1.000	6	9	14	0	4
Williams	.981	54	89	121	4	26

Third Base	PCT	G	PO	A	E	DP
Baldwin	.902	14	9	28	4	1
Fitzgerald	.857	9	3	15	3	2
Lopez	1.000	1	2	0	0	0
Nishioka	.946	16	13	22	2	2
Osinski	1.000	2	0	3	0	0

	PCT	G	PO	A	E	DP
Potts	.939	74	37	116	10	13
Rivera	1.000	3	3	6	0	0

Shortstop	PCT	G	PO	A	E	DP
Cannon	.857	4	1	5	1	0
Cubillan	1.000	2	0	2	0	0
Fitzgerald	.980	75	81	159	5	32
Lopez	1.000	1	3	3	0	0
Rivera	.946	12	10	25	2	4
Sogard	1.000	12	13	29	0	6
Williams	.955	20	19	44	3	7

Outfield	PCT	G	PO	A	E	DP
Baldwin	1.000	1	1	0	0	0
Castellanos	.978	82	125	7	3	2

	PCT	G	PO	A	E	DP
Dalton	.917	8	10	1	1	0
Fitzgerald	.963	15	26	0	1	0
Granberg	.989	64	86	1	1	0
Lopez	--	1	0	0	0	0
Matheny	1.000	16	29	0	0	0
Meneses	1.000	30	43	1	0	0
Mieses	1.000	14	26	0	0	0
Osinski	.000	1	0	0	1	0
Reed	.923	19	21	3	2	0
Rivera	1.000	10	21	0	0	0
Rosario	.954	101	159	6	8	1
Santana	1.000	2	2	0	0	0

GREENVILLE DRIVE HIGH CLASS A
HIGH-A EAST

Batting	B-T	HT	WT	DOB	AVG	vLH	vRH	G	AB	R	H	2B	3B	HR	RBI	BB	HBP	SH	SF	SO	SB	CS	SLG	OBP
Bandy, Luke	R-R	6-0	185	1-5-98	.104	.125	.098	19	67	5	7	1	0	1	4	7	0	0	1	41	2	0	.164	.187
Brannen, Cole	L-R	6-0	170	8-4-98	.152	.143	.154	74	224	39	34	9	3	2	21	37	0	5	2	68	7	6	.246	.270
Cannon, Cameron	R-R	5-10	205	10-16-97	.302	.290	.305	74	311	46	94	24	0	8	39	17	7	0	1	34	9	4	.457	.351
Cottam, Kole	R-R	6-3	235	5-30-97	.276	.296	.271	46	156	22	43	13	1	6	24	25	1		3	64	0	0	.487	.386
Cubillan, Ricardo	B-R	6-0	155	2-1-98	.313	.750	.167	4	16	3	5	1	0	0	3	2	0	0	0	4	0	0	.375	.389
Dalton, Wil	R-R	6-0	182	8-27-97	.182	.190	.180	60	214	30	39	11	1	7	29	23	1	1	0	67	1	2	.341	.264
Davis, Joe	R-R	6-0	230	10-31-96	.261	.304	.246	47	188	24	49	7	0	9	29	8	4	0	1	33	0	0	.441	.303
Dearden, Tyler	L-R	6-2	185	7-6-98	.261	.269	.259	97	352	73	92	20	0	24	80	55	7	0	4	114	1	0	.523	.368
D_Alessandro, Dominic	R-R	6-1	223	10-20-96	.218	.227	.215	51	179	21	39	6	1	6	22	13	5	0	2	70	0	0	.363	.286
Esplin, Tyler	L-R	6-3	230	7-6-99	.202	.075	.230	78	297	42	60	14	1	2	30	38	2	0	1	90	4	0	.276	.296
Granberg, Devlin	R-R	6-2	224	9-8-95	.326	.429	.309	27	95	21	31	7	1	7	29	12	4	0	2	16	1	0	.642	.416
Groshans, Jaxx	R-R	6-0	200	7-20-98	.262	.242	.270	34	122	13	32	6	3	4	16	9	1	0	1	28	0	0	.459	.316
Howlett, Brandon	R-R	6-1	205	9-12-99	.253	.235	.258	96	360	62	91	19	4	17	57	44	8	0	2	136	2	0	.469	.345
Koss, Christian	R-R	6-1	182	1-27-98	.271	.279	.269	104	428	65	116	18	7	15	55	31	5	0	4	100	10	4	.451	.325
MacKenzie, Jake	R-R	5-10	195	5-23-99	.265	.071	.315	25	68	14	18	4	1	0	3	8	4	1	0	18	3	1	.353	.375
Marrero, Alan	R-R	5-10	213	2-25-98	.105	.000	.122	18	57	9	6	1	0	1	6	13	1	0	0	34	0	1	.175	.282
Marrero, Christian	B-R	5-9	185	6-21-97	.287	.265	.293	57	174	32	50	14	1	1	23	25	2	1	4	38	14	3	.397	.376
Miller, Dean	R-R	6-2	235	1-30-97	.158	.167	.154	13	38	6	6	2	0	2	4	4	0	0	0	11	2	0	.368	.238
Osinski, Michael	R-R	6-2	195	8-4-95	.273	.000	.300	7	22	5	6	2	0	1	4	3	0	0	1	8	0	0	.500	.346
Reed, Tyreque	R-R	6-1	250	6-4-97	.296	.239	.316	48	179	40	53	8	1	14	50	30	4	0	2	55	4	2	.587	.405
Santana, Danny	B-R	5-11	195	11-7-90	.400	.500	.375	3	10	2	4	1	0	1	2	0	0	0	1	3	0	0	.800	.364
Scott, Stephen	L-R	5-11	207	5-23-97	.338	.394	.321	39	142	24	48	12	1	8	29	23	0	0	0	32	1	0	.606	.430
Sogard, Nick	B-R	6-1	180	9-9-97	.279	.354	.260	62	240	44	67	12	1	13	40	27	2	0	6	48	7	3	.500	.349
Yorke, Nick	R-R	6-0	200	4-2-02	.333	.333	.333	21	84	17	28	6	1	4	15	11	0	0	1	22	2	1	.571	.406

Pitching	B-T	HT	WT	DOB	W	L	ERA	G	GS	CG	SV	IP	H	R	ER	HR	BB	SO	AVG	vLH	vRH	K/9	BB/9
Bello, Brayan	R-R	6-1	170	5-17-99	5	0	2.27	6	6	0	0	32	25	10	8	3	7	45	.217	.204	.230	12.79	1.99
Bryant, Zach	R-R	6-1	210	6-5-98	3	3	3.54	37	0	0	6	48	31	25	19	6	18	65	.177	.186	.171	12.10	3.35
Cellucci, Brendan	L-L	6-4	211	6-30-98	2	3	5.30	36	0	0	0	37	36	24	22	3	28	59	.252	.315	.213	14.22	6.75
Cobb, Casey	R-R	5-10	200	6-27-96	2	0	1.35	6	0	0	0	20	14	3	3	2	3	24	.194	.158	.235	10.80	1.35
Espada, Jose	R-R	6-0	170	2-22-97	2	0	3.09	28	2	0	0	44	32	17	15	9	16	53	.199	.242	.168	10.92	3.30
Fernandez, Ryan	R-R	6-0	170	6-11-98	1	0	4.32	7	0	0	0	17	13	8	8	3	5	18	.213	.216	.208	9.72	2.70
Gambrell, Grant	L-R	6-4	225	11-21-97	1	6	7.16	8	8	0	0	33	44	29	26	8	14	38	.314	.412	.258	10.47	3.86
Gomez, Rio	L-L	6-0	190	10-20-94	0	0	4.70	3	0	0	0	8	10	4	4	1	1	10	.313	.455	.238	11.74	1.17
Groome, Jay	L-L	6-6	262	8-23-98	3	8	5.29	18	18	0	0	82	76	52	48	12	32	108	.244	.308	.211	11.90	3.53
Mosqueda, Oddanier	L-L	5-10	155	5-6-99	2	1	3.61	32	0	0	3	47	30	21	19	2	25	66	.182	.116	.229	12.55	4.75
Murphy, Chris	L-L	6-1	175	6-5-98	5	3	4.21	14	14	0	0	68	62	36	32	17	23	81	.240	.141	.278	10.67	3.03
Nail, Brendan	R-L	6-0	190	10-18-95	6	0	3.69	31	0	0	3	46	34	23	19	4	16	73	.199	.183	.207	14.18	3.11
Padron-Artiles, Yusniel	R-R	6-0	215	11-12-97	3	7	5.60	25	13	0	0	90	101	57	56	20	26	104	.277	.261	.288	10.40	2.60
Pantoja, Yorvin	L-L	5-11	175	9-22-97	4	3	4.83	37	0	0	2	50	59	34	27	6	17	73	.284	.321	.262	13.05	3.04
Santana, Yasel	R-R	6-1	180	12-14-96	1	0	1.80	7	0	0	0	10	9	3	2	1	9	5	.265	.333	.211	4.50	8.10
Scherff, Alex	B-R	6-3	205	2-5-98	2	1	2.78	17	0	0	3	23	17	8	7	1	11	37	.198	.167	.220	14.69	4.37
Scroggins, Cody	R-R	6-0	195	8-17-96	1	0	5.82	18	0	0	2	22	18	15	14	4	17	20	.228	.275	.179	8.31	7.06
Shugart, Chase	L-R	5-10	198	10-24-96	6	6	4.78	22	22	0	0	105	122	58	56	12	24	93	.292	.289	.294	7.95	2.05
Spacke, Dylan	B-R	6-0	194	3-11-98	4	2	3.07	29	4	0	0	67	63	24	23	7	22	83	.250	.296	.215	11.09	2.94
Thompson, Jake	R-R	6-1	215	9-22-94	0	0	8.10	3	0	0	0	3	8	6	3	0	3	3	.421	.667	.308	8.10	8.10
Van Belle, Brian	R-R	6-3	185	9-3-96	4	3	4.10	18	18	0	0	79	86	41	36	12	13	82	.276	.228	.313	9.34	1.48
Wallace, Jacob	R-R	6-1	190	8-13-98	3	3	5.92	39	0	0	4	49	41	33	32	5	25	76	.223	.280	.176	14.05	4.62
Walter, Brandon	L-L	6-2	200	9-8-96	4	3	3.70	12	12	0	0	58	46	35	24	6	14	86	.211	.160	.241	13.27	2.16
Wu-Yelland, Jeremy	L-L	6-2	210	6-24-99	1	1	3.00	3	3	0	0	9	6	3	3	1	6	13	.194	.000	.261	13.00	6.00

Fielding

Catcher	PCT	G	PO	A	E	DP	PB
Cottam	.995	35	365	18	2	1	3
Groshans	.996	24	259	12	1	0	5
Marrero	.974	13	100	13	3	0	1
Marrero	.977	46	524	33	13	5	6
Scott	1.000	5	57	5	0	1	1

First Base	PCT	G	PO	A	E	DP
Davis	.997	44	284	19	1	27
D_Alessandro	.986	13	69	1	1	3

Granberg	.992	15	121	7	1 6
Osinski	1.000	3	15	1	0 1
Reed	.992	40	242	12	2 26
Scott	.984	9	58	2	1 5

Second Base	PCT	G	PO	A	E	DP
Cannon	.951	50	62	94	8	22
Cubillan	1.000	1	1	1	0	0
Koss	1.000	7	13	21	0	5
MacKenzie	.980	15	21	28	1	8
Osinski	1.000	1	2	1	0	1
Santana	1.000	1	1	0	0	0
Sogard	1.000	30	41	59	0	13
Yorke	1.000	19	31	33	0	9

Third Base	PCT	G	PO	A	E	DP
Cubillan	.800	2	3	1	1	0
Groshans	.000	1	0	0	0	0
Howlett	.886	86	46	86	17	8
MacKenzie	.923	10	9	15	2	2
Osinski	1.000	1	1	2	0	0
Sogard	.906	22	16	32	5	0

Shortstop	PCT	G	PO	A	E	DP
Cannon	1.000	15	11	32	0	6
Cubillan	1.000	1	1	1	0	0
Koss	.961	97	141	230	15	49
Santana	.750	1	1	2	1	0

Sogard	1.000	6	11	19	0 6

Outfield	PCT	G	PO	A	E	DP
Bandy	.972	19	34	1	1	0
Brannen	1.000	74	147	7	0	0
Dalton	.973	59	104	6	3	1
Dearden	.958	86	106	7	5	1
D_Alessandro	1.000	15	23	1	0	0
Esplin	.980	75	135	9	3	2
Granberg	1.000	9	12	1	0	0
Miller	.944	11	16	1	1	1
Santana	--	1	0	0	0	0
Scott	.929	19	23	3	2	0

SALEM RED SOX
LOW-A EAST

LOW CLASS A

Batting	B-T	HT	WT	DOB	AVG	vLH	vRH	G	AB	R	H	2B	3B	HR	RBI	BB	HBP	SH	SF	SO	SB	CS	SLG	OBP
Arnold, Jecorrah	R-R	6-2	190	1-6-99	.143	.154	.138	33	91	12	13	2	2	3	8	8	1	0	2	42	3	1	.308	.216
Bandy, Luke	R-R	6-0	185	1-5-98	.156	.400	.111	11	32	5	5	0	0	1	4	3	1	0	0	17	1	0	.250	.250
Belen, Darel	R-R	6-4	204	5-21-00	.158	.000	.231	8	19	4	3	0	0	1	2	5	0	0	0	12	0	0	.316	.333
Bonaci, Brainer	B-R	5-10	164	7-9-02	.224	.000	.244	13	49	5	11	3	1	0	8	3	0	0	0	8	0	0	.327	.269
Dalton, Wil	R-R	6-0	182	8-27-97	.265	.231	.278	31	98	14	26	6	4	4	17	13	1	0	1	31	4	1	.449	.354
Davis, Joe	R-R	6-0	230	10-31-96	.333	.349	.329	48	189	32	63	16	0	10	49	17	1	0	4	41	0	1	.577	.384
Decker, Nick	L-L	6-0	207	10-2-99	.276	.250	.280	68	250	55	69	18	1	8	39	37	4	0	1	83	4	2	.452	.377
Diaz, Jonathan	L-R	5-11	170	7-7-99	.282	.400	.241	11	39	5	11	1	0	2	12	3	0	0	0	11	0	0	.462	.333
Erro, Alex	B-R	5-10	182	12-5-97	.242	.138	.267	90	327	50	79	16	2	2	33	41	3	1	1	75	6	4	.321	.331
Flores, Antoni	R-R	6-1	207	10-14-00	.232	.292	.220	45	151	23	35	12	0	1	22	21	4	0	3	38	2	1	.331	.335
Garcia, Jose	R-R	5-11	225	5-3-98	.000	--	.000	2	7	0	0	0	0	0	0	0	0	0	0	3	1	0	.000	.000
Groshans, Jaxx	R-R	6-0	200	7-20-98	.298	.273	.306	40	141	26	42	7	0	5	21	31	0	0	3	35	1	1	.454	.417
Hickey, Nathan	L-R	6-0	210	11-23-99	.125	--	.125	3	8	1	1	0	0	0	1	3	0	0	1	2	0	0	.125	.333
Jimenez, Gilberto	B-R	5-11	212	7-8-00	.306	.211	.330	94	373	64	114	16	6	3	56	19	8	1	7	86	13	8	.405	.346
Jordan, Blaze	R-R	6-2	220	12-19-02	.250	.125	.286	9	36	7	9	1	0	2	7	2	0	0	0	8	0	0	.444	.289
Kavadas, Niko	L-R	6-1	235	10-27-98	.286	.250	.294	7	21	6	6	2	0	1	4	8	0	0	0	7	0	0	.524	.483
Lopez, Eduardo	B-R	6-0	187	5-8-02	.206	.167	.214	9	34	5	7	1	0	0	5	8	1	0	0	15	0	0	.235	.372
Lugo, Matthew	R-R	6-1	187	5-9-01	.270	.160	.294	105	418	61	113	21	3	4	50	38	7	1	5	94	15	4	.364	.338
MacKenzie, Jake	R-R	5-10	195	5-23-99	.228	.294	.210	29	79	12	18	2	0	2	4	12	3	0	1	18	1	1	.329	.347
Maita, Angel	R-R	5-11	160	5-28-01	.245	.250	.244	42	139	26	34	3	2	0	14	15	3	1	1	28	4	0	.295	.329
Marrero, Alan	R-R	5-10	213	2-25-98	.138	.400	.083	18	58	7	8	3	0	0	5	9	2	0	2	23	0	0	.190	.254
McDonough, Tyler	B-R	5-10	180	4-2-99	.296	.368	.281	27	108	23	32	4	4	3	14	17	1	0	0	24	3	1	.491	.397
Miller, Dean	R-R	6-2	235	1-30-97	.189	.318	.157	33	111	15	21	6	1	4	17	9	2	0	1	46	0	1	.369	.260
Miller, Tyler	L-R	6-2	193	12-17-99	.359	.333	.361	9	39	9	14	2	1	2	8	4	0	0	0	11	1	1	.615	.419
Northcut, Nicholas	R-R	6-1	206	6-13-99	.261	.215	.271	96	345	68	90	32	2	17	77	46	5	1	5	91	0	0	.513	.352
Rafaela, Ceddanne	R-R	5-8	152	9-18-00	.251	.267	.248	102	394	73	99	20	9	10	53	25	7	2	4	79	23	3	.424	.305
Scott, Stephen	L-R	5-11	207	12-17-97	.259	.281	.256	61	212	49	55	17	0	8	42	39	4	0	2	46	2	1	.453	.381
Yorke, Nick	R-R	6-0	200	4-2-02	.323	.228	.346	76	294	59	95	14	4	10	47	41	7	0	4	47	11	8	.500	.413

Pitching	B-T	HT	WT	DOB	W	L	ERA	G	GS	CG	SV	IP	H	R	ER	HR	BB	SO	AVG	vLH	vRH	K/9	BB/9
Andrew, Merfy	R-R	6-1	200	11-12-96	0	0	31.50	2	0	0	0	2	6	8	7	1	3	2	.462	.500	.444	9.00	13.50
Arredondo, Jacinto	R-R	5-9	170	12-7-97	2	2	4.09	34	0	0	4	51	53	31	23	4	27	45	.265	.243	.278	7.99	4.80
Blalock, Bradley	R-R	6-2	200	12-25-00	3	6	4.27	23	23	0	0	86	96	49	41	5	36	85	.277	.236	.311	8.86	3.75
Cobb, Casey	R-R	5-10	200	6-27-96	2	0	2.18	24	1	0	3	54	38	17	13	3	13	58	.200	.209	.195	9.73	2.18
DiValerio, Jordan	R-R	6-1	200	10-9-97	9	4	5.72	31	1	0	0	72	83	50	46	8	16	72	.287	.269	.298	8.96	1.99
Drohan, Shane	L-L	6-3	195	1-7-99	7	4	3.96	23	23	0	0	89	81	44	39	3	45	86	.245	.312	.224	8.73	4.57
Fernandez, Ryan	R-R	6-0	170	6-11-98	3	1	1.50	17	0	0	2	36	33	10	6	0	9	42	.239	.190	.260	10.50	2.25
Gonzalez, Wilkelman	R-R	6-0	167	3-25-02	0	0	1.53	4	4	0	0	18	13	5	3	1	8	20	.206	.304	.150	10.19	4.08
Kwiatkowski, Robert	R-R	6-1	190	6-8-97	6	0	3.58	31	1	0	1	70	69	40	28	3	20	39	.255	.276	.243	4.99	2.56
Larez, Jose	R-R	6-4	195	1-12-97	0	1	13.50	1	0	0	0	2	4	3	3	0	2	2	.444	.500	.400	9.00	9.00
Liu, Chih-Jung	B-R	6-0	185	4-7-99	5	1	4.29	12	12	0	0	50	49	26	24	4	19	54	.257	.292	.235	9.66	3.40
Milam, Cole	R-R	6-5	240	3-13-98	0	0	5.23	14	0	0	0	21	21	12	12	1	10	14	.263	.233	.280	6.10	4.35
Montero, Alexander	R-R	6-3	180	9-21-97	4	2	5.68	20	1	0	0	38	33	26	24	3	26	50	.226	.204	.237	11.84	6.16
Nail, Brendan	R-L	6-0	190	10-18-95	0	0	0.00	1	0	0	0	1	1	0	0	0	1	1	.250	--	.250	9.00	9.00
Olds, Wyatt	R-R	6-0	183	8-5-99	0	0	2.45	5	3	0	0	11	11	3	3	0	6	20	.268	.263	.273	16.36	4.91
Perry, Aaron	R-R	5-11	175	5-7-99	2	3	2.26	13	1	0	0	23	28	17	16	2	8	33	.292	.258	.308	12.91	3.13
Ramirez, Aldo	R-R	6-0	191	5-6-01	1	1	2.03	8	8	0	0	31	27	9	7	1	8	32	.221	.255	.194	9.29	2.32
Rodriguez, Jorge	L-L	5-11	171	8-25-00	5	6	5.56	18	8	0	0	68	95	49	42	5	19	54	.326	.413	.294	7.15	2.51
Roedahl, Devon	R-R	6-2	225	11-29-96	7	5	2.52	37	0	0	11	61	48	26	17	7	12	62	.211	.170	.236	9.20	1.78
Santana, Yasel	R-R	6-1	180	12-14-96	2	2	7.62	17	0	0	1	28	43	25	24	4	15	32	.347	.238	.402	10.16	4.76
Scroggins, Cody	R-R	6-0	195	8-17-96	3	2	1.33	19	0	0	6	27	22	12	4	1	12	30	.224	.220	.228	10.00	4.00
Stock, Joey	R-R	6-5	210	9-8-97	1	0	2.08	9	0	0	0	13	12	4	3	0	6	15	.235	.100	.323	10.38	4.15
Suero, Miguel	R-R	6-1	185	1-4-97	1	2	7.76	16	0	0	0	27	43	27	23	3	10	26	.347	.304	.372	8.78	3.38
Tellier, Nate	R-R	5-9	180	6-5-98	2	0	2.51	9	0	0	0	14	7	6	4	0	20	16	.156	.250	.121	10.05	12.56
Walter, Brandon	L-L	6-2	200	9-8-96	1	1	1.45	13	2	0	0	31	21	7	5	0	6	46	.178	.206	.167	13.35	1.74
Webb, Jacob	L-R	6-5	246	3-23-99	2	0	0.90	6	0	0	0	10	5	1	1	0	6	12	.143	.133	.150	10.80	5.40

Name	B-T	HT	WT	DOB	W	L	ERA	G	GS	CG	SV	IP	H	R	ER	HR	BB	SO	AVG	vLH	vRH	K/9	BB/9
Wu-Yelland, Jeremy	L-L	6-2	210	6-24-99	1	3	4.03	20	20	0	0	67	50	33	30	4	36	77	.204	.226	.198	10.34	4.84
Zeferjahn, Ryan	R-R	6-5	209	2-28-98	1	4	6.91	12	12	0	0	42	53	41	32	2	15	41	.301	.354	.270	8.86	3.24

Fielding

Catcher	PCT	G	PO	A	E	DP	PB
Diaz	1.000	8	83	4	0	0	0
Erro	.994	57	483	49	3	5	16
Garcia	1.000	2	18	1	0	0	0
Groshans	.996	24	220	14	1	2	7
Hickey	1.000	1	12	0	0	0	2
Marrero	.985	15	126	9	2	0	2
Scott	1.000	14	107	11	0	0	3

First Base	PCT	G	PO	A	E	DP
Belen	.929	3	13	0	1	0
Davis	.990	35	291	10	3	21
Erro	1.000	7	49	3	0	5
Jordan	1.000	2	16	1	0	0
Kavadas	1.000	7	43	6	0	4
Miller	.900	1	8	1	1	0
Northcut	.990	38	295	12	3	31
Scott	.987	31	207	13	3	15

Second Base	PCT	G	PO	A	E	DP
Bonaci	.941	5	3	13	1	2
Erro	1.000	3	2	4	0	2
Flores	.964	9	13	14	1	6
Lugo	.935	6	10	19	2	2
MacKenzie	.938	20	36	39	5	11
McDonough	.972	8	15	20	1	2
Rafaela	1.000	8	8	19	0	5
Yorke	.971	66	128	178	9	39

Third Base	PCT	G	PO	A	E	DP
Erro	.943	15	13	20	2	2
Flores	.897	36	29	58	10	4
Jordan	.833	5	2	3	1	1
MacKenzie	.000	1	0	0	0	0
Miller	1.000	4	0	6	0	0
Northcut	.884	47	18	66	11	7
Rafaela	.942	20	17	32	3	2

Shortstop	PCT	G	PO	A	E	DP
Bonaci	1.000	8	12	17	0	2
Lugo	.911	93	97	239	33	42
MacKenzie	.929	6	3	10	1	1
Rafaela	.951	16	31	47	4	14

Outfield	PCT	G	PO	A	E	DP
Arnold	.982	31	53	1	1	0
Bandy	.941	11	15	1	1	1
Belen	1.000	2	4	0	0	0
Dalton	.948	36	54	1	3	0
Decker	.948	52	85	6	5	1
Jimenez	.978	90	171	7	4	0
Lopez	1.000	9	21	0	0	0
Maita	.965	42	79	3	3	1
McDonough	.952	17	40	0	2	0
Miller	.975	25	36	3	1	1
Rafaela	.992	62	122	9	1	5
Scott	1.000	9	7	2	0	0

FCL RED SOX

ROOKIE

FLORIDA COMPLEX LEAGUE

Batting	B-T	HT	WT	DOB	AVG	vLH	vRH	G	AB	R	H	2B	3B	HR	RBI	BB	HBP	SH	SF	SO	SB	CS	SLG	OBP
Belen, Darel	R-R	6-4	204	5-21-00	.208	.158	.224	25	77	11	16	6	0	0	8	15	2	0	1	34	4	2	.286	.347
Bess, Cuba	L-R	6-2	215	9-29-97	.250	.250	.250	21	52	12	13	5	2	2	13	13	3	0	1	20	1	0	.538	.420
Bonaci, Brainer	B-R	5-10	164	7-9-02	.252	.235	.257	36	139	27	35	13	1	2	17	21	2	0	0	37	12	0	.403	.358
Cubillan, Ricardo	B-R	6-0	155	2-1-98	.462	.167	.714	4	13	3	6	0	0	0	3	1	0	0	0	3	1	0	.462	.500
Decker, Nick	L-L	6-0	207	10-2-99	.154	.333	.100	5	13	1	2	0	0	0	1	4	0	0	0	4	0	0	.154	.353
Diaz, Danny	R-R	6-1	170	1-2-01	.173	.250	.145	22	75	10	13	5	0	2	12	9	1	0	2	25	1	1	.320	.264
Diaz, Jonathan	L-R	5-11	170	7-7-99	.250	.400	.182	6	16	0	4	4	0	0	8	3	0	1	0	4	0	1	.500	.368
Feliz, Albert	R-R	6-2	200	4-13-02	.180	.000	.237	20	50	4	9	5	0	0	5	10	0	0	0	22	0	1	.280	.317
Flores, Antoni	R-R	6-1	207	10-14-00	.222	.000	.286	8	27	4	6	0	0	0	2	6	0	0	0	9	0	0	.222	.364
Garcia, Jose	R-R	5-11	225	5-3-98	.264	.167	.293	19	53	9	14	4	1	1	12	9	3	0	1	17	0	0	.434	.394
Gonzalez, Bryan	R-R	6-2	220	9-18-01	.230	.317	.194	39	139	28	32	5	1	5	27	19	1	0	2	54	8	0	.388	.323
Herbert, Jacob	R-R	6-2	220	6-29-00	.400	.500	.333	3	5	2	2	1	0	0	0	0	0	0	0	0	0	0	.600	.400
Hickey, Nathan	L-R	6-0	210	11-23-99	.250	.250	.250	8	20	4	5	2	0	0	1	6	1	0	1	8	0	0	.350	.429
Jordan, Blaze	R-R	6-2	220	12-19-02	.362	.550	.286	19	69	12	25	7	1	4	19	6	0	0	1	13	0	0	.667	.408
Kavadas, Niko	L-R	6-1	235	10-27-98	.227	.600	.118	8	22	4	5	2	0	1	2	7	0	0	0	6	0	0	.455	.414
Lopez, Eduardo	R-R	6-0	187	5-8-02	.333	1.000	.200	2	6	1	2	0	0	0	3	0	0	0	0	0	0	0	.333	.333
Maita, Angel	B-R	5-11	160	5-28-01	.273	.000	.300	4	11	2	3	0	1	0	2	0	0	0	0	4	0	0	.545	.273
Marcano, Naysbel	R-R	6-0	175	5-23-02	.296	.364	.250	13	27	4	8	2	0	0	2	1	1	0	0	9	0	0	.370	.345
Mayer, Marcelo	L-R	6-3	188	12-12-02	.275	.321	.254	26	91	25	25	4	1	3	17	15	0	0	0	27	7	1	.440	.377
McDonough, Tyler	R-R	5-10	180	4-22-99	.308	1.000	.250	4	13	2	4	3	0	0	1	0	0	0	0	4	0	0	.538	.308
McElveny, Daniel	R-R	6-0	190	4-21-03	.174	.167	.176	9	23	5	4	1	0	0	1	3	4	1	0	10	0	0	.217	.367
Mejicano, Yorberto	R-R	5-11	185	11-21-00	.415	.375	.424	18	41	11	17	2	0	3	13	6	0	0	3	10	0	1	.683	.460
Meredith, Kier	L-L	5-10	200	9-12-99	.156	.250	.121	18	45	8	7	0	0	0	8	1	0	0	0	16	5	1	.156	.296
Miller, Tyler	L-R	6-2	193	12-17-99	.306	.313	.304	18	62	9	19	5	1	1	12	7	3	0	0	16	2	0	.468	.403
Montero, Juan	R-R	5-11	180	6-10-02	.179	.000	.233	16	39	6	7	3	0	1	9	11	0	0	0	13	1	1	.333	.360
Paulino, Eddinson	R-R	5-10	155	7-2-02	.336	.290	.354	36	113	25	38	16	4	0	13	15	5	0	0	21	5	2	.549	.436
Paulino, Leon	B-R	6-3	205	11-15-00	.125	.333	.000	5	8	3	1	0	0	0	0	1	0	0	0	4	0	0	.125	.222
Perez, Bramdon	L-R	6-3	180	12-9-99	.154	.000	.200	6	13	0	2	1	0	0	2	1	0	0	0	6	0	0	.231	.214
Sikes, Phillip	R-R	6-2	190	4-27-99	.392	.263	.436	24	74	18	29	8	0	3	18	8	2	0	0	24	5	1	.622	.464
Simas, Karson	R-R	6-6	175	6-2-01	.310	.269	.328	30	87	17	27	6	2	1	18	2	1	0	2	22	4	0	.460	.381
Ugueto, Miguel	R-R	6-2	185	9-3-02	.331	.267	.351	35	127	26	42	15	2	2	20	7	1	0	0	26	7	1	.528	.370
Valdez, Freddy	R-R	6-3	212	12-6-01	.229	.185	.246	31	96	18	22	6	2	0	16	18	2	0	2	27	0	0	.333	.356
Vaughan, Eduardo	R-R	5-11	179	1-12-02	.226	.174	.246	28	84	16	19	6	0	3	18	18	1	0	2	24	5	0	.405	.362
Vela, B.J.	R-R	5-9	175	10-2-99	.219	.200	.227	11	32	5	7	0	0	1	4	2	0	0	0	10	1	0	.313	.265

Pitching	B-T	HT	WT	DOB	W	L	ERA	G	GS	CG	SV	IP	H	R	ER	HR	BB	SO	AVG	vLH	vRH	K/9	BB/9
Andrew, Merfy	R-R	6-1	200	11-12-96	4	1	7.41	18	0	0	5	17	19	15	14	1	7	15	.275	.250	.286	7.94	3.71
Bastardo, Angel	R-R	6-1	175	6-18-02	1	3	6.67	10	6	0	0	30	45	29	22	1	12	33	.338	.298	.360	10.01	3.64
Bautista, Adenys	R-R	6-3	170	8-6-98	0	1	10.80	3	0	0	0	3	5	4	4	1	3	4	.333	.000	.385	10.80	8.10
Bazardo, Eduard	R-R	6-0	165	9-1-95	1	0	0.00	3	0	0	0	4	2	0	0	0	1	9	.133	.250	.091	20.25	2.25
Brewer, Colten	R-R	6-4	222	10-29-92	1	0	4.91	4	1	0	0	7	7	4	4	0	3	8	.250	.200	.278	11.05	3.68
Campbell, Maceo	R-R	6-1	215	6-17-99	1	0	2.19	11	0	0	1	12	7	3	3	0	8	16	.167	.133	.185	11.68	5.84
Cepeda, Felix	R-R	6-3	170	7-15-00	1	2	4.64	6	5	0	0	21	18	15	11	2	18	26	.214	.217	.213	10.97	7.59
Cruz, Nathanael	R-R	6-2	175	2-4-03	0	0	3.18	4	3	0	0	6	4	2	2	3	2	8	.200	.286	.154	12.71	4.76
Daniel Encarnacion, Juan	R-R	6-2	173	3-30-01	2	1	2.96	12	10	0	0	46	34	17	15	7	11	56	.201	.200	.202	11.04	2.17
De La Rosa, Luis	R-R	6-1	170	7-6-02	1	0	3.04	8	5	0	1	27	19	9	9	1	9	21	.207	.219	.200	7.09	3.04
De La Rosa, Osvaldo	R-R	6-4	240	10-28-97	0	0	6.94	8	0	0	0	12	14	13	9	5	4	8	.292	.333	.267	6.17	3.09
De Leon, Jose	R-R	6-2	215	8-7-92	0	1	9.00	2	0	0	0	2	3	2	2	1	0	4	.333	.250	.400	18.00	0.00

Pitcher	B-T	HT	WT	DOB	W	L	ERA	G	GS	CG	SV	IP	H	R	ER	HR	BB	SO	AVG	vLH	vRH	K/9	BB/9
Disla, Jose	R-R	6-2	165	3-11-96	0	0	0.00	1	0	0	0	1	1	0	0	0	1	0	.333	.000	.500	0.00	9.00
Felix, Jhonny	B-R	6-0	180	9-4-98	0	1	30.00	5	0	0	0	3	7	10	10	1	6	6	.467	.500	.444	18.00	18.00
Feliz, Albert	R-R	6-2	200	4-13-02	0	0	13.50	1	0	0	0	1	1	1	1	1	0	1	.333	--	.333	13.50	0.00
Gettys, Michael	R-R	6-1	217	10-22-95	1	0	3.60	5	0	0	0	5	5	2	2	1	4	5	.263	.400	.214	9.00	7.20
Gonzalez, Wilkelman	R-R	6-0	167	3-25-02	4	2	3.60	8	7	1	0	35	29	16	14	1	8	46	.223	.277	.193	11.83	2.06
Herbert, Jacob	R-R	6-2	220	6-29-00	0	0	0.00	1	0	0	0	1	0	0	0	0	0	1	.000	--	.000	6.75	0.00
Jackson, Gabriel	R-R	6-2	180	9-7-01	2	0	3.57	10	2	0	0	18	15	9	7	1	11	17	.217	.130	.261	8.66	5.60
Larez, Jose	R-R	6-4	195	1-12-97	5	0	2.04	9	0	0	0	18	14	6	4	2	6	24	.215	.238	.205	12.23	3.06
Liu, Chih-Jung	B-R	6-0	185	4-7-99	0	0	3.60	1	1	0	0	5	3	2	2	2	0	6	.167	.000	.188	10.80	0.00
Loubier, Blake	R-R	6-5	189	10-13-00	2	4	9.00	8	1	0	0	14	21	14	14	3	7	16	.339	.474	.279	10.29	4.50
Lucas, Bryan	R-R	6-2	160	12-13-97	1	0	2.92	7	0	0	1	12	14	8	4	2	2	15	.275	.286	.270	10.95	1.46
Milam, Cole	R-R	6-5	240	3-13-98	1	0	2.14	11	0	0	1	21	10	9	5	0	13	28	.133	.174	.115	12.00	5.57
Nunez, Henry	R-R	6-4	200	4-30-01	2	2	6.23	9	4	0	0	30	26	23	21	5	20	46	.236	.250	.232	13.65	5.93
Olds, Wyatt	R-R	6-0	183	8-5-99	0	0	0.00	1	0	0	0	1	1	0	0	0	1	1	.250	.000	.333	9.00	0.00
Perez, Bramdon	L-R	6-3	180	12-9-99	0	0	40.50	1	0	0	0	1	2	3	3	0	4	0	.667	.500	1.000	0.00	54.00
Sale, Chris	L-L	6-6	183	3-30-89	0	0	0.00	1	1	0	0	3	4	0	0	0	0	5	.308	.333	.300	15.00	0.00
Schellenger, Zach	R-R	6-5	210	1-9-96	1	0	0.00	2	0	0	0	2	0	0	0	0	1	6	.000	.000	.000	23.14	3.86
Seabold, Connor	R-R	6-2	190	1-24-96	0	0	3.18	2	2	0	0	6	3	2	2	0	3	12	.136	.125	.143	19.06	4.76
Segovia, Gregori	R-R	6-1	175	6-27-00	3	0	3.86	13	0	0	0	14	9	8	6	1	8	15	.173	.150	.188	9.64	5.14
Sena, Reidis	R-R	5-10	160	4-7-01	1	0	3.22	9	3	0	0	22	22	8	8	1	13	31	.268	.190	.295	12.49	5.24
Stock, Joey	R-R	6-5	210	9-8-97	1	0	2.70	9	0	0	1	13	8	5	4	1	3	17	.163	.077	.194	11.48	2.03
Suero, Miguel	R-R	6-1	185	1-4-97	0	0	0.00	3	0	0	0	5	3	1	0	0	0	4	.176	.000	.214	7.71	0.00
Tellier, Nate	R-R	5-9	180	6-5-98	1	1	2.00	6	0	0	1	9	3	2	2	0	5	14	.107	.125	.100	14.00	5.00
Troye, Christopher	R-R	6-4	225	2-8-99	0	0	4.50	2	0	0	0	2	2	1	1	0	0	5	.222	.250	.200	22.50	0.00
Uberstine, Tyler	R-R	6-1	200	6-1-99	1	1	1.17	5	1	0	1	8	4	3	1	0	1	8	.138	.267	.000	9.39	1.17
Webb, Jacob	L-R	6-5	246	3-23-99	0	0	0.00	2	1	0	0	2	1	1	0	0	0	8	.111	.000	.167	22.50	0.00
Zeferjahn, Ryan	R-R	6-5	209	2-28-98	0	0	3.21	4	4	0	0	14	12	6	5	2	3	18	.231	.250	.222	11.57	1.93

Fielding

C: Diaz 6, Garcia 19, Herbert 2, Hickey 4, Marcano 12, Mejicano 17, Montero 15.
1B: Belen 17, Bess 15, Diaz 14, Jordan 3, Kavadas 7, Miller 4.
2B: Bonaci 10, Cubillan 1, Flores 8, McDonough 2, McElveny 5, Paulino 12, Simas 20, Vela 6.
3B: Cubillan 3, Diaz 6, Jordan 13, Miller 13, Paulino 20, Simas 2, Vela 3.
SS: Bonaci 25, Mayer 24, Paulino 2, Simas 8.
OF: Belen 4, Decker 4, Feliz 17, Gonzalez 20, Lopez 2, Maita 4, McDonough 1, McElveny 1, Meredith 16, Paulino 4, Perez 5, Sikes 23, Simas 1, Ugueto 34, Valdez 26, Vaughan 29.

DSL RED SOX   ROOKIE
DOMINICAN SUMMER LEAGUE

Batting	B-T	HT	WT	DOB	AVG	vLH	vRH	G	AB	R	H	2B	3B	HR	RBI	BB	HBP	SH	SF	SO	SB	CS	SLG	OBP
Alvarez, Alixandri	B-R	5-9	152	2-13-02	.177	.333	.131	36	79	17	14	2	1	0	10	14	3	2	0	17	3	1	.228	.323
Asigen, Albertson	R-R	5-10	175	8-27-01	.254	.000	.283	22	67	15	17	3	2	1	12	9	0	0	1	13	1	0	.463	.338
Astacio, Frank	R-R	5-11	150	10-14-00	.317	.333	.316	31	82	18	26	7	2	1	7	15	1	0	0	21	3	1	.488	.429
Avila, Rivaldo	R-R	6-0	172	9-11-00	.186	.208	.179	33	102	13	19	2	0	1	14	15	1	0	0	41	1	1	.235	.297
Ayubi, Karim	R-R	0-0	0	12-8-03	.210	.333	.196	24	62	10	13	5	0	0	10	10	1	0	0	20	2	0	.290	.329
Barajas, Moises	R-R	6-0	149	2-14-02	.111	--	.111	5	9	2	1	0	0	0	0	0	0	1	0	7	0	1	.222	.200
Bleis, Miguel	R-R	6-3	170	3-1-04	.252	.095	.286	36	119	17	30	6	1	4	17	12	3	0	2	25	7	4	.420	.331
Camejo, Jackson	R-R	5-10	163	12-27-02	.400	--	.400	5	10	0	4	0	0	0	3	1	1	0	0	3	1	1	.400	.500
Castillo, Josue	R-R	5-9	162	10-29-03	.081	.000	.091	19	37	3	3	1	0	0	2	9	0	1	0	16	1	1	.108	.261
Castro, Allan	B-R	6-1	170	5-24-03	.232	.250	.228	46	164	24	38	8	7	3	19	21	6	0	3	43	3	2	.421	.335
Castro, Elvys	R-R	0-0	0	10-15-03	.254	.091	.292	21	59	6	15	2	1	0	6	4	1	0	0	14	3	2	.322	.313
Chacon, Juan	R-R	6-2	171	12-4-02	.311	.389	.289	47	164	45	51	5	2	1	8	26	7	0	0	26	11	7	.384	.426
Diaz, Carlos	R-R	5-10	155	12-24-02	.000	.000	.000	12	25	1	0	0	0	0	0	3	0	0	0	15	1	0	.000	.107
Diaz, Kelvin	R-R	6-0	148	3-17-03	.234	.296	.219	46	141	23	33	5	2	2	16	13	7	0	2	39	13	6	.340	.325
Flores, Renny	R-R	5-9	170	4-1-03	.167	.333	.143	14	24	2	4	1	0	0	2	3	0	0	4	0	0	.208	.259
Garcia, Jhon	R-R	6-2	168	10-10-02	.171	.167	.171	17	41	4	7	2	0	0	3	7	1	0	2	11	0	1	.220	.294
Garcia, Jhostynxon	R-R	6-0	163	12-11-02	.281	.320	.273	45	135	36	38	7	4	4	27	33	1	0	1	32	5	4	.481	.424
Garcia, Kevin	R-R	6-5	209	7-11-99	.214	.000	.231	19	42	7	9	1	0	1	6	8	3	0	2	6	1	0	.310	.364
Guerra, Sebastian	R-R	6-0	153	11-16-02	.200	.077	.231	28	65	9	13	0	0	0	6	3	3	1	1	10	4	3	.200	.264
Hernandez, Alexis	R-R	6-1	170	10-5-02	.256	.296	.244	41	117	27	30	7	1	3	18	17	2	0	1	14	6	2	.410	.358
James, Axel	L-R	5-11	153	10-5-02	.186	.100	.202	40	129	23	24	7	4	3	23	21	1	0	1	46	4	4	.372	.303
James, Lyonell	R-R	6-3	165	10-14-02	.283	.219	.298	51	173	24	49	11	1	1	33	22	6	0	2	23	5	3	.376	.379
Liendo, Ahbram	B-R	5-8	170	2-1-04	.251	.321	.237	46	167	26	42	6	4	1	21	25	1	0	2	30	11	4	.353	.349
Lira, Enderso	R-R	6-1	185	10-11-03	.246	.263	.243	41	122	16	30	7	2	0	15	32	5	0	3	18	1	1	.336	.414
Mendez, Jose	R-R	6-1	153	11-16-02	.250	.143	.273	20	40	10	10	2	0	0	3	22	0	0	1	10	0	0	.300	.508
Mota, Helison	B-R	5-11	160	9-24-03	.221	.273	.210	42	122	18	27	6	1	0	11	27	2	0	1	34	5	1	.287	.368
Ramirez, Ronny	R-R	5-11	175	11-11-03	.195	.214	.190	29	77	16	15	3	1	0	9	14	11	0	0	25	3	2	.260	.392
Ravelo, Luis	B-R	5-10	187	11-5-03	.243	.091	.270	43	144	20	35	4	2	1	13	19	2	0	3	22	0	1	.319	.333
Reinita, Yevganni	L-R	5-7	135	10-17-02	.238	.250	.237	16	42	10	10	0	0	0	2	10	1	1	0	7	1	2	.238	.396
Richetti, Claudio	R-R	6-0	175	12-19-01	.238	.286	.229	14	42	4	10	1	0	0	6	3	0	0	1	13	0	0	.310	.283
Rodriguez, Diego	B-R	6-0	150	6-20-03	.209	.278	.184	31	67	14	14	3	0	0	9	20	3	1	3	24	6	1	.254	.398
Rojas, Miguel	R-R	5-9	157	1-4-02	.209	.143	.217	26	67	10	14	4	0	1	14	9	2	0	2	15	0	0	.313	.313
Rosario, Ronald	R-R	6-0	175	1-1-03	.500	.500	.500	6	16	4	8	1	0	1	5	4	0	0	0	1	0	0	.750	.600
Saavedra, Diego	L-L	6-0	175	3-15-03	.095	.000	.111	17	21	6	2	1	0	0	3	6	3	0	1	13	1	0	.238	.355

	B-T	HT	WT	DOB	AVG	vLH	vRH	G	AB	R	H	2B	3B	HR	RBI	BB	HBP	SH	SF	SO	SB	CS	OBP	SLG
Salazar, Johnfrank	R-R	6-1	159	8-5-03	.269	.278	.267	50	167	27	45	8	1	2	22	16	6	1	1	21	5	2	.365	.353
Santana, Giancarlos	R-R	6-1	180	11-6-01	.188	.235	.170	39	64	15	12	0	1	1	9	14	1	0	0	21	7	7	.266	.342
Sierra, Armando	R-R	6-2	189	1-17-04	.284	.286	.284	53	169	24	48	10	0	2	35	21	3	0	0	41	0	2	.379	.373
Viloria, Diego	R-R	5-10	165	2-23-03	.278	.471	.218	25	72	12	20	2	2	0	8	4	5	0	0	13	2	0	.361	.358
Zapete, Alex	R-R	6-0	180	9-11-01	.314	.375	.304	52	159	37	50	10	0	2	23	30	4	0	5	30	6	0	.415	.424

Pitching	B-T	HT	WT	DOB	W	L	ERA	G	GS	CG	SV	IP	H	R	ER	HR	BB	SO	AVG	vLH	vRH	K/9	BB/9
Adames, Stiwar	L-L	6-2	180	8-8-02	4	0	2.35	11	3	0	0	23	20	6	6	0	13	13	.235	.273	.222	5.09	5.09
Astacio, Frank	R-R	5-11	150	10-14-00	0	0	18.00	1	0	0	0	1	2	2	2	0	1	0	.400	.000	.500	0.00	9.00
Blanco, Royman	R-R	6-1	170	4-17-01	2	3	4.15	19	2	0	1	39	46	23	18	1	13	36	.286	.281	.289	8.31	3.00
Burnet, Yizreel	R-R	0-0	0	1-15-04	0	0	1.59	6	5	0	0	17	9	3	3	0	8	15	.170	.160	.179	7.94	4.24
Carlos Reyes, Jean	R-R	6-2	203	12-17-03	2	1	3.06	14	14	0	0	50	39	18	17	0	22	36	.218	.189	.189	6.48	3.96
De Leon, Victor	R-R	6-3	185	1-21-97	2	0	4.50	3	0	0	0	4	1	2	2	0	11	4	.091	.125	.000	9.00	24.75
Diaz, Efren	R-R	6-0	178	2-20-02	4	0	1.30	17	0	0	2	35	29	11	5	1	12	39	.228	.156	.253	10.13	3.12
Flores, Anddy	L-L	5-10	182	4-26-04	1	1	15.00	7	0	0	0	6	3	13	10	0	16	7	.130	.000	.143	10.50	24.00
Garcia, Jogly	R-R	6-1	175	9-8-03	0	2	12.00	5	0	0	0	3	1	5	4	0	14	5	.100	.250	.000	15.00	42.00
Gregorio, Faysel	R-R	6-2	150	5-9-02	1	0	8.34	15	0	0	0	23	22	23	21	1	23	20	.256	.162	.327	7.94	9.13
Hernandez, Francis	R-R	6-2	170	9-4-01	0	5	2.92	13	13	0	0	49	39	21	16	3	11	47	.217	.232	.207	8.57	2.01
Lopez, Angel	R-R	5-11	167	11-12-03	1	1	14.14	6	2	0	0	7	7	12	11	0	9	3	.241	.286	.200	3.86	11.57
Medina, Irving	R-R	6-1	175	6-12-03	4	0	7.29	13	0	0	0	21	26	19	17	1	6	14	.295	.385	.224	6.00	2.57
Mejias, Alvaro	R-R	0-0	0	9-13-03	0	0	3.78	8	8	0	0	17	16	7	7	0	4	12	.254	.250	.257	6.48	2.16
Monegro, Yordanny	R-R	6-4	180	10-14-02	0	1	3.63	13	13	0	0	40	34	17	16	0	25	41	.239	.164	.319	9.30	5.67
Morales, Henry	L-R	6-3	185	10-4-01	6	0	2.78	15	0	0	1	23	18	14	7	0	18	22	.214	.182	.235	8.74	7.15
Ortuno, Andres	R-R	6-3	167	9-20-01	3	2	2.37	16	3	0	1	38	34	16	10	3	9	44	.234	.222	.239	10.42	2.13
Pacheco, Simon	R-R	5-11	164	6-14-02	1	3	6.67	16	2	0	0	27	36	31	20	2	15	19	.313	.311	.314	6.33	5.00
Paez, Jedixson	R-R	6-1	170	1-17-04	2	1	2.86	13	13	0	0	50	43	18	16	5	9	49	.228	.203	.245	8.76	1.61
Parra, Robinson	R-R	6-3	190	9-28-98	5	1	3.08	18	0	0	2	26	22	9	9	0	13	26	.237	.154	.296	8.89	4.44
Perales, Luis	R-R	6-1	160	4-14-03	0	0	4.50	1	1	0	0	2	1	1	1	0	1	3	.143	.000	.200	13.50	4.50
Perez, Railin	R-R	6-3	185	9-2-01	2	3	1.35	21	0	0	10	33	24	8	5	1	16	38	.198	.229	.181	10.26	4.32
Pinero, Barbaro	R-R	6-0	190	6-18-99	2	2	3.13	13	6	0	0	37	25	14	13	0	13	42	.182	.206	.162	10.13	3.13
Ramirez, Jose	R-R	6-0	142	3-28-01	5	1	2.36	13	11	0	0	50	44	19	13	0	19	46	.244	.208	.258	8.34	3.44
Reyes, Carlos	R-R	6-3	190	9-17-01	5	1	5.33	15	0	0	0	25	23	19	15	0	26	26	.237	.194	.262	9.24	9.24
Rodriguez, Yonfi	R-R	5-10	160	7-30-02	1	0	5.68	6	0	0	0	6	7	5	4	0	9	2	.318	.500	.278	2.84	12.79
Rosillo, Jesus	R-R	6-3	185	1-19-00	1	1	1.00	18	0	0	4	27	19	7	3	0	12	22	.196	.167	.209	7.33	4.00
Ruiz, Cesar	R-R	6-3	170	6-4-03	0	1	4.50	8	8	0	0	20	14	10	10	0	11	17	.200	.263	.179	7.65	4.95
Sanchez, Frailyn	R-R	6-4	192	4-23-01	5	0	3.86	18	0	0	1	30	29	18	13	2	13	22	.252	.297	.231	6.53	3.86
Santos, Starlin	L-L	6-3	180	5-13-02	3	3	3.73	13	8	0	0	51	45	23	21	3	22	42	.242	.263	.240	7.46	3.91
Soto, Cesar	R-R	6-0	170	1-20-02	2	6	7.12	15	1	0	0	30	36	31	24	3	30	21	.310	.271	.338	6.23	8.90
Talavera, Luis	R-R	6-3	175	2-6-02	3	1	1.76	15	1	0	2	31	25	11	6	0	10	25	.221	.222	.221	7.34	2.93
Valera, Michael	R-R	6-2	176	2-12-99	1	3	7.96	19	2	0	1	32	34	32	28	2	19	39	.279	.343	.253	11.08	5.40
Velez, Carlos	L-L	6-2	190	5-4-99	1	4	4.11	18	0	0	0	35	27	19	16	1	19	40	.209	.189	.217	10.29	4.89

Fielding

C: Avila 29, Diaz 8, Flores 3, Lira 32, Richetti 1, Rojas 25, Rosario 4, Viloria 25, Zapete 1.
1B: Astacio 23, Camejo 2, Castro 5, Garcia 13, Garcia 15, Guerra 7, Hernandez 13, Richetti 10, Sierra 8, Zapete 41.
2B: Alvarez 23, Castillo 19, Garcia 1, Guerra 8, Hernandez 1, Liendo 43, Reinita 15, Rodriguez 20.
3B: Alvarez 4, Astacio 8, Garcia 3, Guerra 13, James 49, Liendo 2, Mendez 4, Mota 42, Santana 1.
SS: Alvarez 8, Liendo 1, Mendez 16, Ravelo 43, Rodriguez 9, Salazar 49.
OF: Asigen 20, Ayubi 20, Barajas 4, Bleis 34, Camejo 1, Castro 38, Castro 12, Chacon 44, Diaz 48, Garcia 40, Garcia 3, Hernandez 19, James 17, Ramirez 26, Saavedra 15, Santana 35, Sierra 32.

Chicago Cubs

SEASON IN A SENTENCE: The greatest run of success in franchise history came to an end as the Cubs steered into a rebuild, trading ace Yu Darvish before the season and franchise cornerstones Anthony Rizzo, Kris Bryant and Javier Baez, among others, for prospects at the trade deadline.

HIGH POINT: Zach Davies, Andrew Chafin, Ryan Tepera and Craig Kimbrel pitched a combined no-hitter in a 4-0 win against the Dodgers on June 24. With the win, the Cubs remained tied for first place in the National League Central and appeared on track for one final playoff appearance with their core intact.

LOW POINT: The Cubs tore down at the trade deadline and summarily went on a 12-game losing streak from Aug. 5-16. They suffered losses of 10-0, 17-4 and 14-5 during the skid, the franchise's longest losing streak since 1997.

NOTABLE ROOKIES: A pair of older rookies stepped in to provide a boost during an otherwise dismal season. Third baseman Patrick Wisdom, 29, led all National League rookies with 28 home runs and emerged as one of the league's top defensive third basemen. First baseman Frank Schwindel, 29, hit .326 with 14 home runs and 43 RBIs in only 64 games and led all qualified major league rookies with a .962 OPS. Righthander Adbert Alzolay led all Cubs starters with a 4.58 ERA and 9.2 strikeouts per nine innings.

KEY TRANSACTIONS: In a signal that a rebuild was near, the Cubs traded Darvish and catcher Victor Caratini to the Padres before the season for Davies and four teenaged prospects: shortstops Reggie Preciado and Yeison Santana and outfielders Owen Caissie and Ismael Mena. Only Santana had played a professional game at the time of the trade. At the deadline, the Cubs completed their teardown by trading Rizzo to the Yankees, Bryant to the Giants and Baez to the Mets. They also traded Kimbrel and Tepera to the White Sox, Chafin to the Athletics, righthander Trevor Williams to the Mets and outfielders Joc Pederson and Jake Marisnick to the Braves and Padres, respectively. In return, the Cubs received young major leaguers Nick Madrigal and Codi Heuer from the White Sox and 10 prospects, headlined by outfielders Pete Crow-Armstrong (Baez trade) and Kevin Alcantara (Rizzo).

OPENING DAY SALARY: $149,665,500 (10th).

PLAYERS OF THE YEAR

MAJOR LEAGUE
Willson Contreras
C
.237/.340/.438
Career-high 61 R
21 HR, 57 RBI

MINOR LEAGUE
Brennen Davis
OF
(AAA/AA/High-A)
.260/.375/.494,
19 HR, 8 SB

ORGANIZATION LEADERS

Batting		*Minimum 250 AB
MAJORS		
*AVG	Rafael Ortega	.291
*OPS	Kris Bryant	.861
HR	Patrick Wisdom	28
RBI	Ian Happ	66
MINORS		
*AVG	Jared Young, Iowa, Tennessee	.290
*OBP	Nick Martini, Iowa	.387
*SLG	Nelson Velazquez, Tennessee, South Bend	.496
*OPS	Brennen Davis, Iowa, Tennessee, South Bend	.869
R	Brennen Davis, Iowa, Tennessee, South Bend	66
H	Yohendrick Pinango, South Bend, Myrtle Beach	116
TB	Nelson Velazquez, Tennessee, South Bend	191
2B	Brennen Davis, Iowa, Tennessee, South Bend	25
3B	Ezequiel Pagan, ACL Cubs, South Bend, Myrtle Beach	7
HR	Trayce Thompson, Iowa, Reno	21
RBI	Nelson Velazquez, Tennessee, South Bend	73
BB	Tyler Durna, South Bend	55
SO	Christopher Morel, Iowa, Tennessee	134
SB	Delvin Zinn, Tennessee, South Bend	44

Pitching		#Minimum 75 IP
MAJORS		
W	Kyle Hendricks	14
#ERA	Adbert Alzolay	4.58
SO	Kyle Hendricks	131
SV	Craig Kimbrel	23
MINORS		
W	2 tied	7
L	Luis Lugo, Iowa, Tennessee	10
#ERA	DJ Herz, Myrtle Beach, South Bend	3.31
G	2 tied	39
GS	Manuel Espinoza, Myrtle Beach	22
SV	2 tied	8
IP	Matt Swarmer, Iowa, Tennessee	112.2
BB	Max Bain, South Bend	56
SO	DJ Herz, Myrtle Beach, South Bend	131
#AVG	DJ Herz, Myrtle Beach, South Bend	.157

2021 PERFORMANCE

General Manager: Jed Hoyer. **Farm Director:** Bobby Basham. **Scouting Director:** Dan Kantrovitz.

Class	Team	League	W	L	PCT	Finish	Manager
Majors	Chicago Cubs	National	71	91	.438	11th (15)	David Ross
Triple-A	Iowa Cubs	Triple-A East	51	78	.395	18th (20)	Marty Pevey
Double-A	Tennessee Smokies	Double-A South	46	63	.422	7th (8)	Mark Johnson
High-A	South Bend Cubs	High-A Central	52	67	.437	11th (12)	Michael Ryan
Low-A	Myrtle Beach Pelicans	Low-A East	59	61	.492	6th (12)	Buddy Bailey
Rookie	ACL Cubs	Arizona Complex	34	26	.567	5th (18)	Lance Rymel
Rookie	DSL Cubs Blue	Dominican Summer	26	33	.441	t-33rd (46)	Jovanny Rosario
Rookie	DSL Cubs Red	Dominican Summer	28	30	.483	26th (46)	Carlos Ramirez
Overall 2021 Minor League Record			296	358	.453	25th (30)	

ORGANIZATION STATISTICS

CHICAGO CUBS
NATIONAL LEAGUE

Batting	B-T	HT	WT	DOB	AVG	vLH	vRH	G	AB	R	H	2B	3B	HR	RBI	BB	HBP	SH	SF	SO	SB	CS	SLG	OBP
Alcantara, Sergio	B-R	5-9	151	7-10-96	.205	.145	.232	89	220	30	45	6	3	5	17	30	2	1	2	74	3	0	.327	.303
Baez, Javier	R-R	6-0	190	12-1-92	.248	.301	.233	91	335	48	83	9	2	22	65	15	7	0	3	131	13	3	.484	.292
2-team total (47 New York)					.265	.291	.256	138	502	80	133	18	2	31	87	28	13	0	3	184	18	5	.494	.319
Bote, David	R-R	6-1	205	4-7-93	.199	.213	.193	97	291	32	58	10	2	8	35	27	5	1	3	73	0	1	.330	.276
Bryant, Kris	R-R	6-5	230	1-4-92	.267	.342	.243	93	326	58	87	19	2	18	51	39	8	0	1	89	4	2	.503	.358
2-team total (51 San Francisco)					.265	.284	.259	144	513	86	136	32	2	25	73	62	9	0	2	135	10	2	.481	.353
Castillo, Erick	R-R	5-11	178	2-25-93	.250	.500	.167	4	8	0	2	0	0	0	0	1	0	0	0	1	0	0	.250	.333
Chirinos, Robinson	R-R	6-1	220	6-5-84	.227	.188	.246	45	97	13	22	5	1	5	15	9	5	1	0	36	0	0	.454	.324
Contreras, Willson	R-R	6-1	225	5-13-92	.237	.284	.219	128	413	61	98	20	0	21	57	52	14	0	4	138	5	4	.438	.340
Deichman, Greg	L-R	6-2	205	5-31-95	.133	.500	.077	14	30	0	4	0	0	0	1	1	0	0	0	14	0	0	.133	.161
Duffy, Matt	R-R	6-2	190	1-15-91	.287	.270	.295	97	289	45	83	12	0	5	30	25	7	0	1	63	8	1	.381	.357
Fargas, Johneshwy	R-R	6-1	180	12-15-94	.226	.188	.267	15	31	3	7	0	1	0	2	1	0	0	0	8	1	2	.290	.250
2-team total (7 New York)					.250	.217	.276	22	52	4	13	3	2	0	5	1	0	1	0	15	1	2	.385	.264
Giambrone, Trent	R-R	5-8	175	12-20-93	.154	.400	.000	5	13	0	2	0	0	0	0	0	0	0	0	4	0	0	.154	.154
Gushue, Taylor	B-R	6-1	233	12-19-93	.000	.000	.000	2	4	0	0	0	0	0	0	0	0	0	0	3	0	0	.000	.000
Happ, Ian	B-R	6-0	205	8-12-94	.226	.213	.230	148	465	63	105	20	1	25	66	62	5	2	1	156	9	2	.434	.323
Hermosillo, Michael	R-R	6-0	205	1-17-95	.194	.286	.136	16	36	5	7	2	0	3	7	1	1	0	0	12	0	0	.500	.237
Heyward, Jason	L-L	6-5	240	8-9-89	.214	.235	.208	104	323	35	69	15	2	8	30	27	3	0	0	68	5	1	.347	.280
Higgins, P.J.	R-R	5-10	195	5-10-93	.043	.000	.050	9	23	1	1	0	0	0	0	2	0	0	0	8	0	0	.043	.120
Hoerner, Nico	R-R	6-1	200	5-13-97	.302	.244	.327	44	149	13	45	10	0	0	16	17	3	0	1	25	5	3	.369	.382
Ladendorf, Tyler	R-R	5-11	195	3-7-88	.000	.000	--	1	1	0	0	0	0	0	0	0	0	0	0	0	0	0	.000	.000
Lobaton, Jose	B-R	6-1	212	10-21-84	.000	.000	.000	6	11	1	0	0	0	0	0	2	0	0	0	5	0	0	.000	.154
Marisnick, Jake	R-R	6-4	220	3-30-91	.227	.295	.164	65	128	17	29	6	3	5	22	9	4	1	2	43	3	1	.438	.294
2-team total (34 San Diego)					.216	.259	.179	99	176	21	38	7	3	5	24	11	7	2	2	65	4	1	.375	.286
Martini, Nick	L-L	5-11	205	6-27-90	.270	.200	.281	25	37	4	10	1	0	0	4	6	0	0	2	10	0	1	.297	.356
Ortega, Rafael	L-R	5-11	180	5-15-91	.291	.128	.321	103	296	44	86	14	2	11	33	30	2	2	0	70	12	6	.463	.360
Payne, Tyler	R-R	5-11	210	10-25-92	.000	.000	.000	1	2	0	0	0	0	0	0	0	0	0	0	2	0	0	.000	.000
Pederson, Joc	L-L	6-1	220	4-21-92	.230	.271	.218	73	256	35	59	11	2	11	39	22	5	0	4	74	2	3	.418	.300
2-team total (64 Atlanta)					.238	.265	.230	137	429	55	102	19	3	18	61	39	8	0	5	117	2	3	.422	.310
Rivas, Alfonso	L-L	5-11	190	9-13-96	.318	.250	.344	18	44	7	14	1	0	1	3	4	1	0	0	16	0	0	.409	.388
Rizzo, Anthony	L-L	6-3	240	8-8-89	.248	.333	.216	92	323	41	80	16	3	14	40	36	14	0	3	59	4	2	.446	.346
Romine, Andrew	B-R	6-1	190	12-24-85	.183	.150	.200	26	60	7	11	2	0	1	5	4	0	0	0	24	0	1	.267	.234
Romine, Austin	R-R	6-1	216	11-22-88	.217	.500	.075	28	60	5	13	2	0	1	5	2	0	0	0	22	0	0	.300	.242
Schwindel, Frank	R-R	6-1	220	6-29-92	.342	.356	.337	56	222	42	76	19	1	13	40	16	1	0	0	36	2	1	.613	.389
Sogard, Eric	L-R	5-10	180	5-22-86	.249	.214	.260	78	169	16	42	6	1	1	12	9	0	0	2	30	3	1	.314	.283
Thompson, Trayce	R-R	6-3	225	3-15-91	.250	.462	.067	15	28	6	7	1	0	4	9	7	0	0	0	11	2	0	.714	.400
Vargas, Ildemaro	B-R	6-0	180	7-16-91	.143	.000	.250	9	21	3	3	2	0	0	2	3	0	0	0	7	1	0	.238	.250
3-team total (18 Arizona, 7 Pittsburgh)					.156	.121	.182	34	77	7	12	3	1	0	7	6	0	0	0	17	1	0	.221	.217
Wisdom, Patrick	R-R	6-2	220	8-27-91	.231	.223	.234	106	338	54	78	13	0	28	61	32	4	0	0	153	4	1	.518	.305
Wolters, Tony	L-R	5-10	195	6-9-92	.125	.000	.176	14	24	3	3	0	0	0	5	3	0	0	0	12	0	1	.125	.276

Pitching	B-T	HT	WT	DOB	W	L	ERA	G	GS	CG	SV	IP	H	R	ER	HR	BB	SO	AVG	vLH	vRH	K/9	BB/9
Abbott, Cory	R-R	6-1	210	9-20-95	0	0	6.75	7	1	0	0	17	20	15	13	7	11	12	.286	.333	.243	6.23	5.71
Adam, Jason	R-R	6-3	229	8-4-91	1	0	5.91	12	0	0	0	11	10	7	7	1	6	19	.244	.250	.238	16.03	5.06
Alcantara, Sergio	B-R	5-9	151	7-10-96	0	0	0.00	1	0	0	0	0	0	0	0	0	0	0	.000	--	.000	0.00	0.00
Alzolay, Adbert	R-R	6-1	208	3-1-95	5	13	4.58	29	21	0	1	126	112	66	64	25	34	128	.236	.269	.206	9.17	2.44
Arrieta, Jake	R-R	6-4	230	3-6-86	5	11	6.88	20	20	0	0	86	113	75	66	21	39	74	.315	.316	.314	7.71	4.07
2-team total (4 San Diego)					5	14	7.39	24	24	0	0	99	131	91	81	24	44	83	.320	.321	.320	7.57	4.01
Biagini, Joe	R-R	6-5	235	5-29-90	1	0	0.00	1	0	0	0	3	2	0	0	0	1	2	.200	.167	.250	6.00	3.00
Brothers, Rex	L-L	6-0	205	12-18-87	3	2	5.26	57	0	0	1	53	41	31	31	9	35	75	.212	.179	.235	12.74	5.94
Chafin, Andrew	R-L	6-2	235	6-17-90	0	2	2.06	43	0	0	0	39	21	9	9	1	12	37	.154	.164	.147	8.47	2.75
Davies, Zach	R-R	6-0	180	2-7-93	6	12	5.78	32	32	0	0	148	162	99	95	25	75	114	.281	.251	.302	6.93	4.56

Name	B-T	HT	WT	DOB	W	L	ERA	G	GS	CG	SV	IP	H	R	ER	HR	BB	SO	AVG	vLH	vRH	K/9	BB/9
Duffy, Matt	R-R	6-2	190	1-15-91	0	0	0.00	1	0	0	0	0	0	0	0	0	0	0	.000	--	.000	0.00	0.00
Effross, Scott	R-R	6-2	202	12-28-93	2	1	3.68	14	0	0	0	15	13	6	6	2	1	18	.250	.227	.267	11.05	0.61
Hendricks, Kyle	R-R	6-3	190	12-7-89	14	7	4.77	32	32	1	0	181	200	101	96	31	44	131	.278	.287	.271	6.51	2.19
Heuer, Codi	R-R	6-5	200	7-3-96	3	3	3.14	25	0	0	2	29	20	12	10	2	13	17	.206	.267	.154	5.34	4.08
Jewell, Jake	R-R	6-2	217	5-16-93	0	2	9.90	10	0	0	0	10	18	12	11	5	5	10	.391	.533	.323	9.00	4.50
Kimbrel, Craig	R-R	6-0	215	5-28-88	2	3	0.49	39	0	0	23	37	13	6	2	1	13	64	.106	.100	.113	15.71	3.19
Maples, Dillon	R-R	6-2	230	5-9-92	1	0	2.59	28	0	0	0	31	15	10	9	2	25	40	.144	.087	.190	11.49	7.18
Megill, Trevor	L-R	6-8	250	12-5-93	1	2	8.37	28	0	0	0	24	36	24	22	7	8	30	.343	.273	.393	11.41	3.04
Meisinger, Ryan	R-R	6-4	235	5-4-94	0	0	12.27	7	0	0	0	7	11	10	10	2	5	6	.355	.385	.333	7.36	6.14
Miller, Shelby	R-R	6-3	225	10-10-90	0	0	31.50	3	0	0	0	2	7	7	7	0	5	1	.583	.750	.500	4.50	22.50
2-team total (10 Pittsburgh)					0	1	9.24	13	0	0	0	13	16	13	13	3	11	8	.327	.364	.296	5.68	7.82
Mills, Alec	R-R	6-4	205	11-30-91	6	7	5.07	32	20	0	1	119	137	75	67	16	34	87	.291	.326	.263	6.58	2.57
Morgan, Adam	L-L	6-1	200	2-27-90	2	1	4.26	34	0	0	2	25	22	15	12	6	12	28	.237	.125	.405	9.95	4.26
Nance, Tommy	R-R	6-6	235	3-19-91	1	1	7.22	27	0	0	0	29	25	23	23	5	13	30	.227	.167	.286	9.42	4.08
Rizzo, Anthony	L-L	6-3	240	8-8-89	0	0	0.00	1	0	0	0	1	0	0	0	0	1	1	.000	.000	.000	13.50	13.50
Rodriguez, Manuel	R-R	5-11	210	8-6-96	3	3	6.11	20	0	0	1	18	18	18	12	3	12	16	.257	.324	.182	8.15	6.11
Romine, Andrew	B-R	6-1	190	12-24-85	0	0	9.00	1	0	0	0	1	2	1	1	1	0	1	.400	.500	.333	9.00	0.00
Rucker, Michael	R-R	6-1	195	4-27-94	0	0	6.99	20	0	0	1	28	32	25	22	5	11	30	.286	.271	.302	9.53	3.49
Ryan, Kyle	L-L	6-5	215	9-25-91	0	0	6.75	13	0	0	1	13	17	10	10	3	6	8	.315	.240	.379	5.40	4.05
Sampson, Adrian	R-R	6-2	210	10-7-91	1	2	2.80	10	5	0	0	35	30	15	11	8	8	28	.231	.226	.235	7.13	2.04
Sogard, Eric	L-R	5-10	180	5-22-86	0	0	6.23	5	0	0	0	4	7	3	3	2	0	1	.350	.286	.385	2.08	0.00
Steele, Justin	L-L	6-2	205	7-11-95	4	4	4.26	20	9	0	0	57	50	29	27	12	27	59	.233	.098	.264	9.32	4.26
Stewart, Kohl	R-R	6-3	200	10-7-94	1	1	5.27	4	3	0	0	14	17	12	8	2	6	11	.309	.323	.292	7.24	3.95
Stock, Robert	L-R	6-1	214	11-21-89	0	1	11.25	1	1	0	0	4	4	5	5	1	6	3	.267	.250	.286	6.75	13.50
2-team total (2 New York)					0	2	8.00	3	3	0	0	9	10	8	8	3	9	9	.286	.235	.333	9.00	9.00
Strop, Pedro	R-R	6-1	220	6-13-85	1	0	0.00	2	0	0	0	2	2	0	0	0	2	3	.250	.500	.167	13.50	9.00
Tepera, Ryan	R-R	6-1	195	11-3-87	0	2	2.91	43	0	0	1	43	22	14	14	3	12	50	.150	.100	.175	10.38	2.49
Thompson, Keegan	R-R	6-1	210	3-13-95	3	3	3.38	32	6	0	1	53	48	22	20	9	31	55	.233	.240	.226	9.28	5.23
Wick, Rowan	L-R	6-3	234	11-9-92	0	1	4.30	22	0	0	5	23	17	12	11	1	14	29	.205	.182	.231	11.35	5.48
Wieck, Brad	L-L	6-8	257	10-14-91	0	0	0.00	15	0	0	0	17	10	0	0	0	10	28	.136	.179	.104	14.82	5.29
Williams, Trevor	R-R	6-3	235	4-25-92	4	2	5.06	13	12	0	0	59	68	37	33	10	22	61	.286	.293	.279	9.36	3.38
2-team total (10 New York)					4	2	4.35	23	15	0	0	91	105	51	44	11	31	90	.287	.272	.302	8.90	3.07
Winkler, Dan	R-R	6-3	205	2-2-90	1	3	5.22	47	0	0	0	40	32	24	23	5	30	40	.213	.229	.200	9.08	6.81
Workman, Brandon	R-R	6-5	235	8-13-88	0	2	6.75	10	0	0	0	8	12	9	6	2	7	11	.333	.375	.300	12.38	7.88

Fielding

Catcher

Player	PCT	G	PO	A	E	DP	PB
Castillo	1.000	4	15	3	0	2	0
Chirinos	.995	27	188	7	1	2	4
Contreras	.993	116	885	57	7	6	3
Gushue	1.000	1	1	0	0	0	0
Higgins	1.000	6	54	3	0	1	1
Lobaton	1.000	5	28	1	0	0	1
Payne	1.000	1	2	0	0	0	0
Romine	.992	21	121	3	1	0	1
Wolters	1.000	8	65	3	0	1	0

First Base

Player	PCT	G	PO	A	E	DP
Bryant	.989	12	83	7	1	6
Duffy	1.000	2	3	0	0	0
Gushue	1.000	1	5	0	0	1
Higgins	1.000	1	6	0	0	0
Pederson	.000	1	0	0	0	0
Rivas	1.000	5	28	1	0	5
Rizzo	.996	92	660	94	3	68
Schwindel	.998	51	412	22	1	50
Sogard	.000	1	0	0	0	0
Wisdom	.988	13	78	4	1	7

Second Base

Player	PCT	G	PO	A	E	DP
Alcantara	.975	22	28	50	2	9
Bote	.991	61	103	130	2	40
Chirinos	.000	2	0	0	0	0
Duffy	.987	21	34	44	1	13
Giambrone	.941	4	9	7	1	4
Happ	.917	8	4	7	1	0
Hoerner	.992	30	39	84	1	16
Rizzo	.000	1	0	0	0	0
Romine	1.000	2	3	3	0	1
Sogard	.992	43	51	75	1	17
Vargas	1.000	4	3	4	0	2
Wolters	.000	2	0	0	0	0

Third Base

Player	PCT	G	PO	A	E	DP
Alcantara	.800	3	0	4	1	0
Bote	.947	24	16	38	3	6
Bryant	.964	29	15	38	2	7
Contreras	.000	1	0	0	0	0
Duffy	.973	56	33	109	4	15
Happ	.000	2	0	0	0	0
Hoerner	.000	1	0	0	0	0
Sogard	.917	10	1	10	1	0
Wisdom	.962	77	47	128	7	17

Shortstop

Player	PCT	G	PO	A	E	DP
Alcantara	.970	55	57	134	6	31
Baez	.954	88	134	240	18	51
Bryant	1.000	1	0	1	0	0
Duffy	1.000	5	2	10	0	1
Hoerner	.979	12	11	35	1	2
Romine	.967	16	19	39	2	7
Sogard	1.000	4	2	9	0	2
Vargas	.800	2	2	1	0	0

Outfield

Player	PCT	G	PO	A	E	DP
Bryant	.989	71	91	2	1	0
Contreras	--	1	0	0	0	0
Deichmann	.923	9	11	1	1	0
Duffy	1.000	3	4	0	0	0
Fargas	1.000	9	9	1	0	1
Happ	1.000	137	205	4	0	0
Hermosillo	1.000	13	22	0	0	0
Heyward	1.000	97	157	3	0	1
Hoerner	1.000	5	3	0	0	0
Marisnick	.973	49	71	0	2	0
Martini	1.000	14	9	0	0	0
Ortega	.987	99	154	0	2	0
Pederson	.989	71	92	1	1	0
Rivas	.923	9	12	0	1	0
Thompson	1.000	13	20	0	0	0
Wisdom	1.000	18	28	1	0	0
Wolters	--	1	0	0	0	0

IOWA CUBS

TRIPLE-A

TRIPLE-A EAST

Batting	B-T	HT	WT	DOB	AVG	vLH	vRH	G	AB	R	H	2B	3B	HR	RBI	BB	HBP	SH	SF	SO	SB	CS	SLG	OBP
Alcantara, Sergio	B-R	5-9	151	7-10-96	.305	.350	.290	25	82	19	25	3	0	3	9	21	0	0	0	23	3	0	.451	.447
Artis, D.J.	L-L	5-9	165	3-20-97	--	--	--	1	0	1	0	0	0	0	0	1	0	0	0	0	0	0	--	1.000
Avelino, Abiatal	R-R	6-0	210	2-14-95	.266	.277	.262	106	380	49	101	18	3	6	48	43	6	1	3	71	16	4	.376	.347
Bote, David	R-R	6-1	205	4-7-93	.125	.000	.133	5	16	1	2	1	0	0	1	3	0	0	0	4	0	0	.188	.263
Burch, Matt	L-R	5-7	175	12-13-97	.129	.000	.138	13	31	2	4	1	0	0	1	0	0	0	0	13	0	0	.161	.129
Castillo, Erick	R-R	5-11	178	2-25-93	.184	.100	.214	40	114	11	21	4	0	0	8	13	5	2	2	22	0	0	.219	.291
Contreras, Willson	R-R	6-1	225	5-13-92	.182	.000	.250	3	11	3	2	0	0	2	2	1	0	0	0	3	0	0	.727	.250
Davis, Brennen	R-R	6-4	210	11-2-99	.268	.333	.237	15	56	10	15	3	0	4	12	11	1	0	0	15	0	0	.536	.397

Player	B-T	HT	WT	DOB	AVG	vLH	vRH	G	AB	R	H	2B	3B	HR	RBI	BB	HBP	SH	SF	SO	SB	CS	SLG	OBP
Davis, Zach	B-R	5-11	175	6-29-94	.203	.250	.174	29	74	14	15	2	0	0	3	8	2	1	0	15	7	1	.230	.298
Deichmann, Greg	L-R	6-2	205	5-31-95	.227	.231	.226	34	119	14	27	8	2	3	13	11	1	0	0	38	3	2	.403	.298
Duffy, Matt	R-R	6-2	190	1-15-91	.313	.000	.333	5	16	0	5	1	0	0	1	2	0	0	1	4	0	0	.375	.368
Fargas, Johneshwy	R-R	6-1	180	12-15-94	.247	.269	.236	23	81	12	20	4	1	2	6	4	0	0	0	26	6	2	.395	.282
2-team total (8 Syracuse)					.246	.265	.238	31	114	20	28	6	1	3	9	8	0	0	0	34	14	2	.395	.295
Figuera, Edwin	R-R	5-10	160	9-2-97	.179	.231	.163	23	56	8	10	1	0	1	3	3	1	1	0	19	0	0	.250	.233
Giambrone, Trent	R-R	5-8	175	12-20-93	.174	.164	.178	72	235	27	41	8	1	3	16	31	2	1	2	79	5	3	.255	.274
Gushue, Taylor	R-B	6-1	233	12-18-93	.223	.206	.229	75	247	29	55	14	0	8	39	25	1	2	2	83	0	0	.377	.295
Hermosillo, Michael	R-R	6-0	205	1-17-95	.306	.313	.303	43	147	34	45	10	1	10	29	26	12	0	1	48	8	3	.592	.446
Heyward, Jason	L-L	6-5	240	8-9-89	.400	--	.400	2	5	1	2	0	0	1	1	1	0	0	0	1	0	0	1.000	.500
Higgins, P.J.	R-R	5-10	195	5-10-93	.333	.333	.333	11	39	7	13	2	1	1	6	8	1	0	0	11	0	0	.513	.458
Hoerner, Nico	R-R	6-1	200	5-13-97	.269	.167	.300	8	26	3	7	1	0	0	2	0	2	0	0	6	0	0	.308	.321
Huma, Josue	B-R	6-1	175	3-17-00	.167	.000	.250	3	12	1	2	0	0	0	1	0	0	0	0	5	0	0	.167	.167
Jordan, Levi	R-R	5-8	170	9-24-95	.236	.400	.186	42	127	13	30	7	1	3	17	16	3	1	2	46	1	0	.378	.331
Knight, Caleb	R-R	5-11	220	1-2-96	.231	.222	.235	17	26	6	6	2	0	2	7	9	0	1	0	5	0	0	.538	.429
Ladendorf, Tyler	R-R	5-11	195	3-7-88	.241	.129	.295	59	191	29	46	11	0	8	29	13	3	1	2	53	1	0	.424	.297
Lobaton, Jose	B-R	6-1	212	10-21-84	.179	.083	.222	15	39	5	7	3	0	2	9	10	0	0	0	15	0	0	.410	.347
Marisnick, Jake	R-R	6-4	220	3-30-91	.167	--	.167	2	6	0	1	0	0	0	0	0	0	0	0	3	0	0	.333	.167
Martini, Nick	L-L	5-11	205	6-27-90	.267	.239	.280	78	270	56	72	9	3	11	40	42	11	0	0	70	2	1	.444	.387
Matt, Peter	R-R	6-2	220	5-22-98	.000	--	.000	1	4	0	0	0	0	0	0	0	0	0	0	3	0	0	.000	.000
Maybin, Cameron	R-R	6-3	215	4-4-87	.103	.000	.129	10	39	5	4	1	0	1	3	4	0	0	0	14	1	0	.205	.186
2-team total (12 Syracuse)					.145	.125	.157	22	83	10	12	3	0	1	8	9	0	0	0	28	1	0	.217	.228
Mervis, Matt	L-R	6-4	225	4-16-98	.286	.333	.273	3	14	2	4	1	0	0	2	1	0	0	0	4	0	0	.357	.333
Miller, Ian	R-L	6-0	170	2-21-92	.261	.245	.266	106	368	38	96	14	4	3	33	37	5	0	3	75	20	1	.345	.334
Morel, Christopher	R-R	5-11	145	6-24-99	.257	.385	.182	9	35	6	9	1	0	1	2	4	0	0	0	10	2	0	.371	.333
Olson, Jacob	R-R	6-0	200	5-21-97	.174	.211	.148	16	46	2	8	3	0	1	4	1	3	0	0	13	0	0	.304	.240
Opitz, Casey	B-R	5-11	200	7-30-98	.250	.500	.000	2	4	1	1	0	0	0	0	0	0	0	0	2	0	0	.250	.625
Ortega, Rafael	L-R	5-11	180	5-15-91	.250	.188	.271	16	64	11	16	3	0	4	11	8	0	0	0	13	1	1	.484	.333
Payne, Tyler	R-R	5-11	210	10-25-92	--	--	--	1	0	0	0	0	0	0	0	0	0	0	0	0	0	0	--	--
Rivas, Alfonso	L-L	5-11	190	9-13-96	.284	.239	.298	58	197	22	56	13	0	4	32	35	5	0	0	49	0	1	.411	.405
Romine, Andrew	B-R	6-1	190	12-24-85	.290	.281	.293	61	214	28	62	7	2	1	17	20	2	7	0	42	2	4	.355	.356
Romine, Austin	R-R	6-1	216	11-22-88	.500	--	.500	2	6	2	3	1	0	0	0	0	0	0	0	1	0	0	.667	.500
Schwindel, Frank	R-R	6-1	220	6-29-92	.189	.125	.207	9	37	2	7	1	0	1	8	1	0	0	1	10	0	0	.297	.205
Serra, Bryan	L-R	5-10	173	9-7-98	.250	.000	.286	7	8	1	2	0	0	0	0	2	0	0	0	3	0	0	.250	.400
Spence, Liam	R-R	6-1	190	4-9-98	.455	.667	.375	3	11	2	5	0	0	0	3	1	0	0	1	2	1	0	.455	.462
3-team total (16 Indianapolis, 10 Nashville)					.233	.195	.253	28	120	13	28	6	0	1	10	4	2	1	0	21	3	0	.308	.270
Thompson, Trayce	R-R	6-3	225	3-15-91	.233	.179	.251	88	305	48	71	14	1	21	63	45	7	0	1	116	3	1	.492	.344
Vizcaino, Vance	L-R	6-3	215	8-1-94	.253	.280	.242	34	87	8	22	4	0	0	13	6	2	1	0	34	3	1	.299	.316
Wisdom, Patrick	R-R	6-2	220	8-27-91	.160	.182	.143	8	25	7	4	1	0	3	11	6	2	0	1	12	1	0	.560	.353
Wolters, Tony	L-R	5-10	195	6-9-92	.261	.222	.273	38	115	18	30	4	0	4	17	18	4	1	0	33	1	1	.400	.380
Young, Jared	L-R	6-2	185	7-9-95	.254	.355	.221	37	126	14	32	4	1	5	18	14	0	0	1	33	1	1	.421	.326

Pitching	B-T	HT	WT	DOB	W	L	ERA	G	GS	CG	SV	IP	H	R	ER	HR	BB	SO	AVG	vLH	vRH	K/9	BB/9
Abbott, Cory	R-R	6-1	210	9-20-95	5	6	5.91	19	19	0	0	96	97	69	63	20	53	130	.257	.318	.208	12.19	4.97
Adam, Jason	R-R	6-3	229	8-4-91	1	0	0.00	5	0	0	1	6	4	0	0	0	1	6	.174	.182	.167	8.53	1.42
Alzolay, Adbert	R-R	6-1	208	3-1-95	0	1	18.00	1	1	0	0	2	3	4	4	1	1	3	.333	.400	.250	13.50	4.50
Angel Rodriguez, Luis	L-L	6-1	190	9-10-99	0	1	36.00	1	1	0	0	2	5	8	8	3	4	0	.455	.500	.444	0.00	18.00
Biagini, Joe	R-R	6-5	235	5-29-90	3	8	5.50	22	19	0	0	92	99	57	56	14	43	85	.272	.266	.276	8.35	4.22
Chalmers, Dakota	R-R	6-3	175	10-8-96	0	0	4.50	1	0	0	0	2	2	1	1	0	1	2	.250	.250	.250	9.00	4.50
Cingrani, Tony	L-L	6-4	217	7-5-89	1	1	3.60	12	0	0	0	10	7	5	4	0	4	15	.200	.143	.238	13.50	3.60
Effross, Scott	R-R	6-2	202	12-28-93	4	2	3.64	23	2	0	2	42	28	19	17	6	10	46	.192	.230	.165	9.86	2.14
Figuera, Edwin	R-R	5-10	160	9-2-97	0	0	27.00	1	0	0	0	1	4	3	3	1	0	0	.667	1.000	.500	0.00	0.00
Gamez, Juan	R-R	5-11	247	3-7-94	1	3	9.92	15	0	0	1	16	24	19	18	1	11	11	.343	.316	.375	6.06	6.06
Hauschild, Mike	R-R	6-3	210	1-22-90	0	7	6.96	13	12	0	0	54	66	49	42	24	28	33	.299	.290	.305	5.47	4.64
Holder, Jonathan	R-R	6-2	232	6-9-93	0	0	9.00	1	0	0	0	1	1	1	1	0	1	1	.250	.000	.500	9.00	9.00
Holmes, Ben	L-L	6-1	195	9-12-91	1	0	6.52	2	2	0	0	10	7	7	7	3	8	9	.206	.200	.208	8.38	7.45
Hudson, Bryan	L-L	6-8	220	5-8-97	0	1	27.00	4	0	0	0	4	9	13	12	3	8	4	.429	.600	.375	9.00	18.00
Jewell, Jake	R-R	6-2	217	5-16-93	2	1	2.78	23	0	0	4	32	21	12	10	3	13	35	.184	.235	.143	9.74	3.62
Kellogg, Ryan	R-L	6-6	230	2-4-94	1	3	4.43	12	6	0	0	45	52	30	22	5	12	25	.287	.245	.303	5.04	2.42
Kobos, Scott	L-L	6-2	200	8-3-97	0	0	27.00	3	0	0	0	2	5	7	7	1	6	1	.417	.500	.400	3.86	23.14
Lawlor, Ryan	R-L	6-1	185	1-8-94	0	1	13.50	11	0	0	0	12	20	18	17	6	10	17	.364	.176	.447	13.50	7.94
Leeper, Ben	R-R	6-0	195	6-15-97	3	1	1.31	17	0	0	2	21	6	4	3	2	9	31	.091	.074	.103	13.50	3.92
Little, Brendon	L-L	6-2	195	8-11-96	0	1	3.44	13	0	0	2	18	22	7	7	2	7	26	.293	.208	.333	12.76	3.44
Lugo, Luis	L-L	6-5	200	3-5-94	1	6	6.75	8	8	0	0	37	40	29	28	8	25	26	.276	.268	.279	6.27	6.03
Maples, Dillon	R-R	6-2	205	5-9-92	3	1	5.40	18	1	0	0	20	14	12	12	3	18	26	.203	.219	.189	11.70	8.10
McClelland, Jackson	R-R	6-5	220	7-19-94	1	0	5.59	6	0	0	0	10	12	6	6	2	10	6	.333	.200	.429	5.59	9.31
2-team total (15 Buffalo)					2	1	5.54	21	0	0	1	26	30	17	16	5	18	17	.300	.214	.362	5.88	6.23
Megill, Trevor	L-R	6-8	250	12-5-93	0	5	5.14	12	0	0	1	14	12	8	8	2	8	20	.222	.214	.225	12.86	5.14
Meisinger, Ryan	R-R	6-4	235	5-4-94	2	4	4.25	24	0	0	3	30	24	15	14	6	16	45	.218	.217	.219	13.65	4.85
Mekkes, Dakota	R-R	6-7	275	11-6-94	0	3	4.74	27	2	0	0	38	29	22	20	3	24	35	.207	.250	.175	8.29	5.68
Miller, Shelby	R-R	6-3	225	10-10-90	0	1	0.74	3	3	0	0	10	4	4	2	1	6	15	.111	.050	.188	13.05	5.23
2-team total (10 Indianapolis)					2	1	2.96	13	4	0	0	24	14	11	8	2	9	37	.157	.125	.195	13.68	3.33
Miller, Tyson	R-R	6-4	225	7-29-95	0	0	5.06	3	1	0	0	5	5	3	3	1	2	6	.250	.111	.364	10.13	3.38
Mills, Alec	R-R	6-4	205	11-30-91	0	2	5.40	3	3	0	0	12	14	7	7	1	3	10	.292	.250	.333	7.71	2.31

	B-T	HT	WT	DOB	W	L	ERA	G	GS	CG	SV	IP	H	R	ER	HR	BB	SO	AVG	vLH	vRH	SO/9	BB/9
Morgan, Adam	L-L	6-1	200	2-27-90	0	1	2.20	15	0	0	0	16	10	5	4	1	3	21	.172	.208	.147	11.57	1.65
Nance, Tommy	R-R	6-6	235	3-19-91	1	0	2.35	10	0	0	0	15	7	4	4	1	3	18	.130	.125	.133	10.57	1.76
Reed, Sheldon	L-R	6-2	205	7-30-97	0	0	4.50	1	0	0	0	2	1	1	1	1	0	0	.143	.250	.000	0.00	0.00
Roberts, Ethan	R-R	5-10	180	7-4-97	3	2	4.50	15	0	0	0	22	19	12	11	0	8	27	.244	.163	.286	11.05	3.27
Rodriguez, Manuel	R-R	5-11	210	8-6-96	0	0	0.00	7	0	0	1	7	6	0	0	0	2	8	.231	.385	.077	9.82	2.45
Romine, Andrew	B-R	6-1	190	12-24-85	0	0	0.00	1	0	0	0	1	0	0	0	0	1	0	.000	.000	.000	0.00	18.00
Rosario, Aneuris	R-R	6-0	165	3-4-95	0	0	8.10	10	0	0	0	10	10	10	9	4	10	14	.250	.267	.240	12.60	9.00
Rucker, Michael	R-R	6-1	195	4-27-94	3	0	4.81	19	0	0	0	39	44	22	21	8	9	49	.282	.288	.278	11.21	2.06
Ryan, Kyle	L-L	6-5	215	9-25-91	2	0	2.52	19	0	0	1	25	16	7	7	2	7	24	.188	.194	.185	8.64	2.52
Sampson, Adrian	R-R	6-2	210	10-7-91	4	5	4.96	16	14	0	0	82	92	47	45	19	33	61	.289	.265	.310	6.72	3.64
Serra, Bryan	L-R	5-10	173	9-7-98	0	0	0.00	2	0	0	0	2	3	0	0	0	2	2	.375	.250	.500	10.80	10.80
Steele, Justin	L-L	6-2	205	7-11-95	2	0	1.32	9	5	0	0	27	14	6	4	1	13	29	.147	.174	.139	9.55	4.28
Stewart, Kohl	R-R	6-3	200	10-7-94	2	3	3.46	6	5	0	0	26	16	10	10	3	6	26	.174	.176	.172	9.00	2.08
Stock, Robert	L-R	6-1	214	11-21-89	0	3	4.12	9	2	0	0	20	17	10	9	4	4	25	.224	.235	.214	11.44	1.83
2-team total (4 Syracuse)					1	3	3.57	13	6	0	0	35	33	17	14	5	12	39	.244	.213	.270	9.93	3.06
Swarmer, Matt	R-R	6-5	195	9-25-93	3	8	5.22	19	15	0	1	90	87	57	52	20	28	90	.252	.270	.237	9.03	2.81
Thompson, Keegan	R-R	6-1	210	3-13-95	0	0	0.00	4	4	0	0	15	5	0	0	0	5	16	.104	.143	.074	9.82	3.07
Uelmen, Erich	R-R	6-3	195	5-19-96	0	2	10.02	12	0	0	0	21	22	26	23	7	10	24	.268	.400	.170	10.45	4.35
Valdez, Dauris	R-R	6-8	254	10-22-95	0	0	0.00	1	0	0	0	1	0	0	0	0	3	1	.000	.000	.000	9.00	27.00
Vargas, Didier	R-L	6-0	175	3-13-99	0	0	54.00	1	0	0	0	1	6	6	6	1	2	2	.667	1.000	.625	18.00	18.00
Walden, Marcus	R-R	5-10	198	9-13-88	1	1	7.36	11	0	0	0	15	24	16	12	4	4	18	.358	.290	.417	11.05	2.45
2-team total (27 Worcester)					6	4	4.87	38	3	0	0	57	70	39	31	9	23	58	.294	.255	.326	9.10	3.61
Whitney, Blake	R-R	6-3	185	5-25-96	0	1	7.11	11	1	0	0	19	19	16	15	4	16	25	.268	.281	.256	11.84	7.58
Wick, Rowan	L-R	6-3	234	11-9-92	0	0	10.38	5	0	0	0	4	6	5	5	0	3	8	.316	.571	.167	16.62	6.23
Wieck, Brad	L-L	6-8	257	10-14-91	0	0	4.70	6	0	0	0	8	5	6	4	0	8	12	.192	.231	.154	14.09	9.39
Williams, Trevor	R-R	6-3	235	4-25-92	1	0	0.00	2	2	0	0	7	2	1	0	0	1	5	.087	.143	.063	6.43	1.29
2-team total (2 Syracuse)					2	0	1.42	4	4	0	0	19	11	4	3	1	3	15	.164	.226	.111	7.11	1.42

Fielding

Catcher	PCT	G	PO	A	E	DP	P
Castillo	.991	38	317	23	3	1	4
Contreras	.955	3	19	2	1	0	1
Gushue	.989	44	348	25	4	0	5
Higgins	1.000	6	53	2	0	0	0
Knight	1.000	7	39	2	0	2	1
Lobaton	.991	10	107	1	1	0	1
Opitz	1.000	2	26	4	0	1	0
Ortega	.000	1	0	0	0	0	0
Payne	1.000	1	2	0	0	0	0
Romine	1.000	2	8	1	0	0	0
Wolters	.990	30	256	29	3	1	3

First Base	PCT	G	PO	A	E	DP
Castillo	.000	1	0	0	0	0
Gushue	1.000	8	60	4	0	5
Higgins	1.000	5	41	4	0	1
Ladendorf	.992	15	114	6	1	7
Martini	.982	26	148	19	3	16
Mervis	1.000	3	21	2	0	1
Olson	1.000	6	30	3	0	2
Rivas	.997	46	343	32	1	39
Romine	1.000	1	1	0	0	1
Schwindel	1.000	6	48	2	0	6
Wisdom	1.000	4	30	3	0	2
Wolters	1.000	2	9	1	0	0
Young	.994	22	161	8	1	15

Second Base	PCT	G	PO	A	E	DP
Alcantara	1.000	5	6	0	1	
Avelino	.950	23	30	46	4	13

	PCT	G	PO	A	E	DP
Bote	1.000	3	3	4	0	3
Burch	.778	4	1	6	2	0
Figuera	1.000	6	8	6	0	3
Giambrone	.971	62	66	133	6	31
Hoerner	.875	4	2	5	1	0
Jordan	.882	10	11	19	4	7
Ladendorf	.938	3	7	8	1	2
Morel	1.000	1	0	2	0	0
Romine	1.000	23	39	50	0	7
Spence	1.000	1	1	2	0	1
Strange-Gordon	1.000	8	12	17	0	8

Third Base	PCT	G	PO	A	E	DP
Avelino	.933	33	26	57	6	2
Bote	.750	2	3	3	2	1
Duffy	.875	5	1	6	1	0
Figuera	.818	4	1	8	2	1
Giambrone	.429	7	2	1	4	0
Huma	1.000	3	2	5	0	1
Jordan	.959	33	19	51	3	4
Knight	1.000	1	0	2	0	0
Ladendorf	.986	34	24	49	1	10
Morel	.909	4	4	6	1	1
Romine	1.000	9	4	13	0	2
Spence	1.000	2	1	4	0	0
Wisdom	1.000	3	4	1	0	0
Wolters	1.000	4	4	2	0	0
Young	.800	6	3	5	2	0

Shortstop	PCT	G	PO	A	E	DP
Alcantara	.967	23	31	57	3	10

	PCT	G	PO	A	E	DP
Avelino	.954	41	48	98	7	24
Figuera	.969	11	2	29	1	4
Giambrone	1.000	1	2	0	0	0
Hoerner	1.000	4	2	6	0	0
Jordan	.000	1	0	0	0	0
Ladendorf	.923	7	10	14	2	2
Romine	.962	31	32	68	4	17
Strange-Gordon	.952	21	23	36	3	8

Outfield	PCT	G	PO	A	E	DP
Avelino	1.000	3	2	0	0	0
Davis	.960	15	24	0	1	0
Davis	1.000	20	24	0	0	0
Deichmann	1.000	28	56	0	0	0
Fargas	1.000	20	27	1	0	1
Giambrone	1.000	2	3	0	0	0
Hermosillo	.972	35	67	2	2	1
Heyward	1.000	2	1	0	0	0
Higgins	--	1	0	0	0	0
Marisnick	1.000	2	4	0	0	0
Martini	1.000	51	78	5	0	1
Maybin	1.000	9	7	0	0	0
Miller	1.000	100	163	7	0	3
Morel	1.000	4	4	0	0	0
Olson	--	3	0	0	0	0
Ortega	1.000	17	24	1	0	0
Rivas	1.000	10	8	2	0	0
Thompson	.986	78	139	5	2	1
Vizcaino	.935	25	29	0	2	0
Wisdom	1.000	1	2	0	0	0
Young	1.000	4	3	1	0	1

TENNESSEE SMOKIES
DOUBLE-A

DOUBLE-A SOUTH

Batting	B-T	HT	WT	DOB	AVG	vLH	vRH	G	AB	R	H	2B	3B	HR	RBI	BB	HBP	SH	SF	SO	SB	CS	SLG	OBP
Amaya, Miguel	R-R	6-2	230	3-9-99	.215	.304	.179	23	79	11	17	4	0	1	13	21	5	0	1	22	2	0	.304	.406
Artis, D.J.	L-L	5-9	165	3-20-97	.171	.167	.172	26	76	15	13	4	0	3	12	11	4	0	1	25	6	0	.342	.304
Balego, Cam	R-R	5-11	205	6-12-95	.220	.286	.194	15	50	9	11	3	2	1	11	10	0	0	0	13	0	0	.420	.350
Beesley, Bradlee	R-R	5-10	180	2-21-98	.194	.143	.207	10	36	1	7	2	1	0	4	2	1	0	0	14	1	1	.389	.256
Burch, Matt	L-R	5-7	175	12-13-97	.053	.000	.059	6	19	1	1	0	0	0	1	0	0	0	0	8	0	0	.053	.100
Byrd, Grayson	L-R	6-3	205	6-16-96	.223	.190	.232	50	184	20	41	11	0	1	16	20	2	0	2	60	1	2	.299	.303
Castillo, Erick	R-R	5-11	178	2-25-93	.228	.143	.262	17	57	6	13	1	0	1	7	3	1	1		12	0	0	.298	.338
Davis, Brennen	R-R	6-4	210	11-2-99	.252	.123	.287	76	266	50	67	20	0	13	36	36	13	0	1	97	6	4	.474	.367
Davis, Zach	B-R	5-11	175	6-29-94	.261	.391	.217	27	92	12	24	3	0	2	7	11	1	0	1	31	11	3	.359	.343
Donahue, Christian	L-R	5-8	180	5-4-95	.196	.111	.216	13	46	5	9	2	0	0	1	7	2	1	0	16	3	1	.239	.327

Name	B-T	HT	WT	DOB	AVG	vLH	vRH	G	AB	R	H	2B	3B	HR	RBI	BB	HBP	SH	SF	SO	SB	CS	SLG	OBP
Figuera, Edwin	R-R	5-10	160	9-2-97	.288	.214	.316	15	52	6	15	2	0	0	4	2	3	0	0	10	0	0	.327	.351
Garcia, Reivaj	B-R	5-11	175	8-12-01	.146	.091	.162	17	48	1	7	1	0	0	3	1	0	0	0	16	0	0	.167	.163
Hill, Darius	L-L	6-1	190	8-17-97	.277	.246	.286	60	249	40	69	5	0	5	31	22	1	1	1	47	2	2	.357	.337
Jordan, Levi	R-R	5-8	170	9-24-95	.267	.306	.250	32	120	12	32	5	0	5	20	8	4	0	2	32	0	0	.433	.328
Knight, Caleb	R-R	5-11	220	1-2-96	.120	.091	.143	8	25	1	3	0	0	0	2	3	1	0	1	7	0	0	.120	.233
Maldonado, Nelson	R-R	5-10	195	8-13-96	.303	.245	.319	67	244	39	74	18	2	6	34	23	4	0	1	49	1	0	.467	.371
Morel, Christopher	R-R	5-11	145	6-24-99	.220	.278	.204	101	368	59	81	17	5	17	64	41	3	0	5	124	16	3	.432	.300
Myers, Connor	R-R	5-10	185	2-3-94	.221	.226	.220	32	113	10	25	6	1	1	8	6	6	0	1	53	8	2	.319	.294
Payne, Tyler	R-R	5-11	210	10-25-92	.231	.224	.233	59	212	26	49	14	1	4	30	17	2	0	3	66	1	0	.363	.291
Sepulveda, Carlos	L-R	5-10	170	8-27-96	.213	.245	.205	73	263	29	56	10	1	3	21	38	3	0	1	57	2	4	.293	.318
Serra, Bryan	L-R	5-10	173	9-7-98	.000	.000	.000	1	5	0	0	0	0	0	0	0	0	0	0	0	0	0	.000	.000
Slaughter, Jake	R-R	6-3	200	10-24-96	.053	.111	.000	6	19	3	1	1	0	0	2	3	0	0	0	11	0	0	.105	.250
Strumpf, Chase	R-R	6-1	170	3-8-98	.211	.226	.206	62	213	25	45	15	0	7	29	38	2	0	1	65	1	0	.380	.335
Susnara, Tim	L-R	5-11	185	4-17-96	.241	.200	.253	35	112	9	27	4	1	3	9	15	1	0	2	47	0	0	.375	.331
Vazquez, Luis	R-R	6-1	165	10-10-99	.241	.200	.250	8	29	2	7	1	0	0	1	1	0	0	0	8	0	0	.276	.267
Velazquez, Nelson	R-R	6-0	190	12-26-98	.290	.429	.262	34	124	19	36	10	1	8	27	10	3	0	0	35	5	0	.581	.358
Vizcaino, Vance	L-R	6-3	215	8-1-94	.200	.167	.205	14	45	7	9	0	0	3	6	8	1	0	0	7	1	2	.400	.333
Washer, Jake	R-R	6-0	220	2-23-96	.000	.000	.000	2	3	0	0	0	0	0	0	0	0	0	0	1	0	0	.000	.000
Weber, Andy	L-R	6-1	190	7-24-97	.214	.226	.210	41	131	17	28	12	1	0	7	13	4	0	1	52	0	0	.321	.302
Wenson, Harrison	R-R	6-3	235	4-21-95	.273	.333	.263	7	22	3	6	2	0	2	7	3	0	0	1	10	0	0	.636	.346
Wilson, D.J.	L-L	5-8	177	10-8-96	.375	--	.375	3	8	3	3	1	1	0	1	1	0	1	0	3	1	0	.750	.444
Young, Jared	L-R	6-2	185	7-9-95	.326	.227	.346	35	129	27	42	11	1	4	22	14	1	0	0	22	3	0	.519	.396
Zinn, Delvin	R-R	5-10	170	5-29-97	.159	.235	.141	27	88	5	14	2	0	0	7	2	6	1	0	20	2	6	.227	.239

Pitching	B-T	HT	WT	DOB	W	L	ERA	G	GS	CG	SV	IP	H	R	ER	HR	BB	SO	AVG	vLH	vRH	K/9	BB/9
Assad, Javier	R-R	6-1	200	7-30-97	4	8	5.32	21	20	0	0	93	111	67	55	12	32	74	.297	.275	.311	7.16	3.10
Bocchi, Matteo	R-R	6-4	205	7-19-96	0	1	9.00	2	0	0	0	7	13	8	7	2	4	4	.433	.500	.389	5.14	5.14
Burch, Matt	L-R	5-7	175	12-13-97	0	0	9.00	2	0	0	0	2	5	2	2	1	0	0	.455	.400	.500	0.00	0.00
Carraway, Burl	L-L	6-0	173	5-27-99	0	0	0.00	4	0	0	0	5	4	0	0	0	4	3	.235	.600	.083	5.79	7.71
Castillo, Erick	R-R	5-11	178	2-25-93	0	1	108.00	2	0	0	0	0	3	5	4	1	1	1	.750	.000	1.000	27.00	27.00
Chalmers, Dakota	R-R	6-3	175	10-8-96	2	5	5.37	15	14	0	0	57	47	34	34	9	35	63	.221	.169	.246	9.95	5.53
Clark, Bailey	R-R	6-4	220	12-3-94	0	0	6.75	4	0	0	0	7	7	6	5	2	8	7	.280	.200	.333	9.45	10.80
Effross, Scott	R-R	6-2	202	12-28-93	3	0	2.89	8	0	0	0	19	16	9	6	2	5	20	.232	.379	.125	9.64	2.41
Espinoza, Anderson	R-R	6-0	190	3-9-98	0	1	1.35	3	3	0	0	13	11	2	2	0	8	16	.239	.150	.308	10.80	5.40
Gamez, Juan	R-R	5-11	247	3-7-94	3	0	3.18	12	0	0	0	17	14	8	6	1	9	23	.219	.333	.150	12.18	4.76
Hudson, Bryan	L-L	6-8	220	5-8-97	6	3	3.13	31	0	0	0	55	38	25	19	2	22	51	.200	.132	.226	8.40	3.62
Hughes, Brandon	B-L	6-2	215	12-1-95	0	0	1.76	18	0	0	1	31	24	7	6	3	13	43	.214	.241	.205	12.62	3.82
Jensen, Ryan	R-R	6-0	190	11-23-97	1	0	3.00	4	4	0	0	18	14	6	6	2	7	15	.222	.167	.256	7.50	3.50
Katz, Alex	L-L	5-11	195	10-12-94	3	3	6.15	13	3	0	0	34	46	27	23	6	20	31	.338	.290	.352	8.29	5.35
Kellogg, Ryan	R-L	6-6	230	2-4-94	0	1	5.03	8	2	0	0	20	25	14	11	3	6	17	.301	.440	.241	7.78	2.75
Kelly, Garrett	R-R	6-1	210	8-2-94	0	1	5.76	22	0	0	1	25	25	20	16	5	21	29	.260	.241	.269	10.44	7.56
Kilian, Caleb	R-R	6-4	180	6-2-97	1	2	4.02	4	4	1	0	16	15	7	7	3	4	16	.250	.296	.212	9.19	2.30
King, Bryan	R-L	6-1	184	11-5-96	0	1	6.00	4	0	0	0	6	10	4	4	1	1	4	.400	.375	.412	6.00	1.50
Kobos, Scott	L-L	6-2	200	8-3-97	0	0	0.00	6	0	0	3	7	1	0	0	0	0	8	.045	.200	.000	10.29	0.00
Lawlor, Ryan	R-L	6-1	185	1-8-94	3	0	4.35	8	0	0	0	10	8	5	5	2	4	15	.211	.125	.233	13.06	3.48
Lawson, Graham	R-R	6-1	225	6-7-96	1	2	13.85	10	0	0	0	13	18	20	20	9	12	16	.321	.273	.353	11.08	8.31
Leeper, Ben	R-R	6-0	195	6-15-97	1	2	1.26	10	0	0	1	14	9	5	2	0	4	22	.167	.185	.148	13.81	2.51
Little, Brendon	L-L	6-2	195	8-11-96	0	3	3.09	13	0	0	2	23	17	8	8	2	12	27	.207	.214	.204	10.41	4.63
Lugo, Luis	L-L	6-5	200	3-5-94	5	4	3.90	17	12	0	0	58	50	27	25	7	27	74	.227	.156	.256	11.55	4.21
Mekkes, Dakota	R-R	6-7	275	11-6-94	1	0	0.00	2	0	0	0	3	4	0	0	1	1	4	.286	.167	.375	10.80	2.70
Nahas, Joe	R-R	6-1	185	11-14-99	0	4	7.98	4	3	0	0	15	23	16	13	4	7	9	.377	.519	.265	5.52	4.30
Payne, Tyler	R-R	5-11	210	10-25-92	0	0	0.00	1	0	0	0	1	0	0	0	0	0	1	.000	.000	.000	13.50	0.00
Ramos, Eury	R-R	6-3	152	10-10-97	0	2	4.50	9	0	0	0	10	11	7	5	1	5	7	.275	.077	.370	6.30	4.50
Remy, Peyton	L-R	6-2	170	8-20-96	1	3	6.43	8	8	1	0	35	42	26	25	6	11	26	.300	.306	.297	6.69	2.83
Reyes, Samuel	R-R	5-11	180	3-13-96	2	1	4.11	9	0	0	0	15	14	7	7	3	4	15	.246	.368	.184	8.80	2.35
Roberts, Ethan	R-R	5-10	180	7-4-97	1	0	1.97	24	0	0	4	32	16	9	7	2	9	45	.144	.154	.139	12.66	2.53
Rodriguez, Manuel	R-R	5-11	210	8-6-96	1	1	2.03	13	0	0	4	13	8	5	3	0	3	19	.178	.278	.111	12.83	6.75
Sanders, Cam	R-R	6-2	175	12-9-96	4	7	5.32	18	18	0	0	90	74	56	53	16	44	107	.227	.220	.232	10.74	4.42
Short, Wyatt	L-L	5-8	180	10-14-94	1	4	5.27	26	2	0	1	41	36	29	24	8	21	46	.228	.184	.242	10.10	4.61
Swarmer, Matt	R-R	6-5	195	9-25-93	0	0	3.13	5	5	0	0	23	17	9	8	2	8	30	.198	.162	.224	11.74	3.13
Ueckert, Cayne	R-R	6-3	195	5-28-96	1	1	1.61	24	0	0	7	28	11	5	5	3	12	31	.124	.167	.102	9.96	3.86
Uelmen, Erich	R-R	6-3	195	5-19-96	2	7	4.52	19	11	0	2	70	64	38	35	9	31	64	.243	.320	.199	8.27	4.00
Valdez, Dauris	R-R	6-8	254	10-22-95	0	0	16.88	7	0	0	0	5	9	10	10	0	7	5	.360	.091	.571	8.44	11.81
Washer, Jake	R-R	6-0	220	2-23-96	0	0	36.00	1	0	0	0	1	3	4	4	1	2	1	.500	.667	.333	9.00	18.00

Fielding

Catcher	PCT	G	PO	A	E	DP	PB
Amaya	1.000	12	139	15	0	2	4
Balego	1.000	3	30	0	0	0	0
Castillo	.982	13	105	7	2	1	1
Knight	.955	3	19	2	1	0	0
Payne	.992	41	358	25	3	1	2
Susnara	.990	30	271	20	3	3	5
Washer	1.000	2	9	0	0	0	0
Wenson	1.000	7	53	5	0	0	2

First Base	PCT	G	PO	A	E	DP
Amaya	1.000	2	16	0	0	1
Balego	1.000	7	50	1	0	4
Byrd	.993	37	257	12	2	37
Castillo	1.000	1	3	0	0	0
Maldonado	.977	24	157	10	4	15
Payne	1.000	9	72	5	0	13
Slaughter	1.000	3	13	1	0	2
Young	.995	29	202	11	1	16

Second Base	PCT	G	PO	A	E	DP
Byrd	.909	3	4	6	1	1
Donahue	.960	8	10	14	1	1
Figuera	1.000	1	1	1	0	1
Garcia	1.000	8	13	11	0	7
Jordan	.978	13	14	31	1	6
Morel	1.000	12	23	28	0	5
Sepulveda	.986	53	88	122	3	41
Serra	1.000	1	1	6	0	1

	PCT	G	PO	A	E	DP
Strumpf	.943	9	15	18	2	10
Zinn	.938	4	7	8	1	2

Third Base	PCT	G	PO	A	E	DP
Byrd	.900	12	5	13	2	1
Castillo	1.000	3	3	4	0	0
Figuera	.700	4	3	4	3	0
Garcia	.000	1	0	0	0	0
Jordan	.882	13	4	11	2	2
Morel	.873	19	16	32	7	3
Slaughter	1.000	4	1	6	0	0
Strumpf	.957	52	33	101	6	13
Weber	.000	1	0	0	0	0
Zinn	1.000	5	4	5	0	0

Shortstop	PCT	G	PO	A	E	DP
Donahue	1.000	2	4	7	0	0
Figuera	.909	9	10	20	3	3
Garcia	.923	9	8	16	2	3
Jordan	.917	4	5	6	1	2
Morel	.934	14	22	35	4	12
Sepulveda	1.000	13	18	32	0	4
Vazquez	1.000	8	12	31	0	12
Weber	.912	40	53	81	13	23
Zinn	.938	15	27	34	4	8

Outfield	PCT	G	PO	A	E	DP
Artis	1.000	22	23	0	0	0

	PCT	G	PO	A	E	DP
Beesley	1.000	10	13	1	0	0
Davis	.985	70	127	4	2	3
Davis	1.000	27	57	0	0	0
Donahue	1.000	3	6	0	0	0
Hill	1.000	59	85	3	0	0
Hughes	1.000	1	1	0	0	0
Morel	.992	57	126	3	1	2
Myers	.968	32	58	2	2	0
Velazquez	1.000	34	65	5	0	2
Vizcaino	1.000	11	17	0	0	0
Wilson	1.000	2	3	0	0	0
Young	.875	6	7	0	1	0
Zinn	1.000	3	4	0	0	0

SOUTH BEND CUBS

HIGH-A CENTRAL

HIGH CLASS A

Batting	B-T	HT	WT	DOB	AVG	vLH	vRH	G	AB	R	H	2B	3B	HR	RBI	BB	HBP	SH	SF	SO	SB	CS	SLG	OBP
Aliendo, Pablo	R-R	6-0	170	5-29-01	.118	.200	.083	15	51	7	6	0	0	0	3	3	0	2	1	14	0	1	.118	.164
Americaan, Edmond	L-L	6-1	170	3-26-97	.202	.147	.213	64	198	35	40	6	4	1	10	25	9	1	1	72	20	2	.288	.318
Artis, D.J.	L-L	5-9	165	3-20-97	.200	.227	.194	33	120	24	24	2	1	4	13	25	4	0	0	42	12	3	.333	.356
Balego, Cam	R-R	5-11	205	6-12-95	.188	.200	.182	5	16	1	3	0	0	0	4	4	1	0	1	3	0	0	.188	.364
Ball, Bryce	L-R	6-6	240	7-8-98	.207	.269	.182	53	184	24	38	9	1	7	21	40	1	0	0	62	0	0	.380	.351
Beesley, Bradlee	R-R	5-10	180	2-21-98	.226	.208	.229	38	133	16	30	8	1	4	21	14	2	1	0	43	12	1	.391	.307
Burch, Matt	L-R	5-7	175	12-13-97	.158	.333	.143	14	38	3	6	2	0	1	5	5	1	0	0	16	0	1	.289	.273
Byrd, Grayson	L-R	6-3	205	6-16-96	.200	.143	.208	16	55	7	11	3	0	1	7	5	1	0	0	19	0	0	.309	.279
Canario, Alexander	R-R	6-1	165	5-7-00	.224	.255	.209	42	170	19	38	6	1	9	28	10	0	0	2	46	6	5	.429	.264
Davis, Brennen	R-R	6-4	210	11-2-99	.321	.400	.304	8	28	6	9	2	0	2	5	3	1	0	0	6	2	0	.607	.406
Durna, Tyler	L-L	6-0	205	11-13-96	.232	.220	.237	97	357	46	83	17	0	5	46	55	5	1	3	74	2	2	.322	.340
Garcia, Reivaj	B-R	5-11	175	8-12-01	.179	.286	.143	9	28	3	5	2	0	0	3	1	0	0	0	7	1	0	.250	.207
Hoerner, Nico	R-R	6-1	200	5-13-97	.000	.000	--	1	1	0	0	0	0	0	0	0	0	0	0	0	0	0	.000	.000
Huma, Josue	B-R	6-1	175	3-17-00	.243	.219	.248	52	173	25	42	9	2	2	21	18	3	4	1	47	5	1	.353	.323
Knight, Caleb	R-R	5-11	220	1-2-96	.118	.000	.143	6	17	2	2	1	0	0	1	3	1	0	0	5	1	0	.176	.286
McKeon, Scott	R-R	6-0	185	10-30-97	.158	.154	.159	22	57	9	9	1	0	0	5	4	3	0	2	14	1	1	.175	.242
Nevarez, Dean	R-R	6-0	220	1-4-97	.276	.143	.318	7	29	6	8	3	0	2	9	2	0	0	0	10	0	0	.586	.323
Olson, Jacob	R-R	6-0	200	5-21-97	.183	.231	.156	22	71	8	13	7	0	0	4	6	1	0	0	17	0	1	.282	.272
Pabon, Miguel	R-R	6-0	165	8-30-00	.125	.000	.167	7	24	3	3	0	1	0	3	1	1	0	1	12	0	0	.208	.185
Pagan, Ezequiel	L-R	6-1	163	7-8-00	.000	.000	.000	2	7	0	0	0	0	0	0	0	0	0	0	5	0	0	.000	.000
Pena, Raymond	R-R	5-10	160	4-7-97	.111	--	.111	3	9	0	1	0	0	0	0	0	0	0	0	4	0	0	.111	.111
Perlaza, Yonathan	B-R	5-11	170	11-10-98	.280	.267	.285	99	357	54	100	24	1	15	64	38	3	1	5	95	6	4	.479	.350
Pinango, Yohendrick	L-L	5-11	170	5-7-02	.289	.240	.306	24	97	9	28	4	1	1	9	7	1	0	0	12	0	0	.381	.343
Reynolds, Ryan	B-R	6-2	215	7-17-97	.215	.316	.183	21	79	12	17	4	0	1	10	6	2	0	1	21	0	2	.304	.284
Roederer, Cole	L-L	6-0	180	9-24-99	.229	.188	.241	20	70	9	16	5	0	0	8	12	1	0	1	20	4	1	.300	.345
Serra, Bryan	L-R	5-10	173	9-7-98	.000	--	.000	2	3	1	0	0	0	0	0	3	0	0	0	2	0	0	.000	.500
Slaughter, Jake	R-R	6-3	200	10-24-96	.252	.400	.198	96	341	47	86	11	3	3	34	21	10	1	2	101	16	7	.328	.313
Spence, Liam	R-R	6-1	190	4-9-98	.102	.136	.074	16	49	2	5	0	0	0	5	2	0	0	0	17	0	1	.102	.185
Strumpf, Chase	R-R	6-1	170	3-8-98	.309	.286	.317	16	55	15	17	4	0	0	7	7	4	0	1	17	3	1	.382	.418
Vazquez, Luis	R-R	6-1	165	10-10-99	.282	.300	.273	23	85	14	24	1	0	2	11	12	3	0	0	27	5	1	.365	.390
Velazquez, Nelson	R-R	6-0	190	12-26-98	.261	.286	.255	69	261	37	68	13	1	12	46	20	4	1	2	97	12	2	.456	.321
Warkentin, Matt	R-L	6-6	250	1-28-97	.158	.143	.167	6	19	2	3	1	0	1	3	1	2	0	0	10	0	1	.368	.273
Washer, Jake	R-R	6-0	220	2-23-96	.164	.122	.178	46	159	13	26	5	0	2	12	13	1	1	0	55	2	0	.233	.231
Wenson, Harrison	R-R	6-3	235	4-21-95	.195	.208	.190	28	87	13	17	4	0	2	14	11	5	0	2	33	3	2	.310	.314
Wilson, D.J.	L-L	5-8	177	10-8-96	.375	.500	.333	4	8	3	3	2	0	0	3	0	0	0	1	1	0	0	.625	.545
Windham, Bryce	L-R	6-1	190	9-25-96	.273	.289	.267	52	176	26	48	9	2	3	29	24	1	1	2	28	3	1	.398	.360
Zinn, Delvin	R-R	5-10	170	5-29-97	.234	.180	.246	67	261	42	61	7	3	4	25	25	2	2	5	60	42	6	.330	.300

Pitching	B-T	HT	WT	DOB	W	L	ERA	G	GS	CG	SV	IP	H	R	ER	HR	BB	SO	AVG	vLH	vRH	K/9	BB/9
Albertos, Jose	R-R	6-1	185	11-7-98	5	0	8.24	23	1	0	0	44	62	48	40	9	29	45	.330	.277	.371	9.27	5.98
Allen, Chris	L-L	6-4	180	6-13-98	0	0	0.00	1	0	0	1	1	0	0	0	0	2	1	.200	.000	.333	6.75	13.50
Bain, Max	R-R	6-5	240	9-25-97	5	9	5.52	22	21	0	0	93	82	64	57	11	56	113	.234	.231	.236	10.94	5.42
Beesley, Bradlee	R-R	5-10	180	2-21-98	0	0	0.00	2	0	0	1	0	0	0	0	0	0	0	.000	.000	.000	0.00	0.00
Bigge, Hunter	R-R	6-1	205	6-12-98	1	2	5.66	17	0	0	1	21	19	16	13	4	17	29	.235	.229	.239	12.63	7.40
Bocchi, Matteo	R-R	6-4	205	7-19-96	2	0	3.77	18	7	0	0	57	41	24	24	6	23	70	.199	.206	.192	10.99	3.61
Carraway, Burl	L-L	6-0	173	5-27-99	3	3	6.10	29	0	0	2	31	13	26	21	3	42	51	.129	.167	.113	14.81	12.19
Casey, Derek	R-R	6-2	190	2-15-96	5	5	3.24	11	11	0	0	58	56	27	21	2	20	73	.250	.208	.288	11.26	3.09
Clarke, Chris	R-R	6-7	215	5-13-98	0	6	4.65	10	9	0	0	50	60	27	26	6	13	46	.286	.275	.296	8.23	2.32
Combs, Shane	R-R	6-2	219	1-14-97	0	0	13.50	1	0	0	0	1	1	4	1	0	2	2	.250	.000	1.000	27.00	27.00
Correa, Danis	R-R	5-11	150	8-26-99	1	2	2.45	8	0	0	0	11	9	4	3	0	6	16	.225	.118	.304	13.09	4.91
Deppermann, Bradford	R-R	6-0	195	6-15-96	2	3	5.53	17	5	0	1	41	39	29	25	4	16	40	.242	.259	.225	8.85	3.54
Espinoza, Anderson	R-R	6-0	190	3-9-98	2	5	5.06	5	5	0	0	16	9	9	9	1	11	27	.179	.263	.135	15.19	6.19
2-team total (12 Fort Wayne)					3	5	5.04	17	17	0	0	45	39	28	25	4	24	64	.235	.211	.253	12.90	4.84
Gamez, Juan	R-R	5-11	247	3-7-94	0	0	6.23	6	0	0	1	9	4	6	6	0	4	7	.143	.154	.133	7.27	4.15
Herz, DJ	R-L	6-2	175	1-4-01	1	0	2.81	3	3	0	0	16	10	6	5	1	6	26	.175	.105	.211	14.63	3.38
Horn, Bailey	L-L	6-2	210	1-15-98	0	4	4.98	7	4	0	0	22	22	13	12	4	11	24	.253	.400	.194	9.97	4.57

Player	B-T	HT	WT	DOB	W	L	ERA	G	GS	CG	SV	IP	H	R	ER	HR	BB	SO	AVG	vLH	vRH	K/9	BB/9
Hughes, Brandon	B-L	6-2	215	12-1-95	2	1	1.59	8	0	0	0	11	7	3	2	1	4	17	.171	.167	.172	13.50	3.18
Jaramillo, Gabriel	R-R	6-1	176	11-3-98	0	1	3.38	4	0	0	0	5	7	2	2	1	3	4	.333	.333	.333	6.75	5.06
Jensen, Ryan	R-R	6-0	190	11-23-97	2	7	4.50	16	16	0	0	62	42	32	31	8	24	75	.189	.237	.152	10.89	3.48
Jesson-Dalton, Tanner	R-R	6-2	195	8-25-96	2	3	7.61	26	0	0	1	37	41	32	31	3	39	44	.283	.206	.351	10.80	9.57
Kachmar, Chris	R-R	6-3	180	9-3-96	0	3	5.84	10	10	0	0	45	45	31	29	3	20	42	.262	.288	.239	8.46	4.03
Katz, Alex	L-L	5-11	195	10-12-94	0	1	9.00	6	0	0	0	11	18	11	11	0	10	12	.360	.400	.350	9.82	8.18
Kelly, Garrett	R-R	6-1	210	8-2-94	0	0	4.26	6	0	0	0	6	6	3	3	2	3	9	.240	.200	.267	12.79	4.26
King, Bryan	R-L	6-1	184	11-5-96	1	2	4.30	19	0	0	1	38	35	22	18	3	26	38	.257	.304	.233	9.08	6.21
Knight, Caleb	R-R	5-11	220	1-2-96	0	0	0.00	1	0	0	0	1	0	0	0	0	0	1	.000	--	.000	9.00	0.00
Kobos, Scott	L-L	6-2	200	8-3-97	1	0	0.71	8	0	0	1	13	6	1	1	0	7	22	.136	.214	.100	15.63	4.97
Lawson, Graham	R-R	6-1	225	6-7-96	1	1	3.33	21	0	0	1	24	22	15	9	1	18	26	.244	.342	.173	9.62	6.66
Leigh, Zachary	R-R	6-0	170	11-14-97	0	0	1.80	3	0	0	0	5	3	1	1	0	3	8	.158	.333	.000	14.40	5.40
Nahas, Joe	R-R	6-1	185	11-14-99	4	2	3.95	12	8	0	0	55	52	26	24	12	15	46	.254	.267	.243	7.57	2.47
Nevarez, Dean	R-R	6-0	220	1-4-97	0	0	0.00	1	0	0	0	1	0	0	0	0	1	0	.400	.000	.667	0.00	9.00
Nunez, Eduarniel	R-R	6-2	170	6-7-99	1	3	4.63	28	0	0	5	35	31	26	18	3	33	37	.226	.309	.145	9.51	8.49
Padilla, Nicholas	R-R	6-2	220	12-24-96	0	0	16.20	2	0	0	0	2	4	3	3	0	2	2	.500	.800	.000	10.80	10.80
Pena, Raymond	R-R	5-10	160	4-7-97	0	0	18.00	1	0	0	1	1	3	2	2	0	1	1	.500	.250	1.000	9.00	9.00
Ramos, Eury	R-R	6-3	152	10-10-97	1	1	3.73	23	0	0	6	31	17	14	13	3	13	39	.149	.140	.156	11.20	3.73
Reid, Bailey	R-R	6-2	195	7-3-98	1	1	18.00	5	0	0	1	4	5	8	8	1	5	6	.333	.500	.222	13.50	11.25
Remy, Peyton	L-R	6-2	170	8-20-96	1	2	3.70	5	5	0	0	24	20	11	10	4	10	28	.220	.186	.250	10.36	3.70
Reyes, Samuel	R-R	5-11	180	3-13-96	3	4	5.26	24	2	0	1	39	41	28	23	4	29	44	.268	.225	.305	10.02	6.64
Santana, Tyler	R-R	6-1	205	5-13-98	1	0	1.50	8	1	0	0	18	16	4	3	1	10	20	.250	.350	.205	10.00	5.00
Stambaugh, Dalton	R-L	6-0	195	2-11-97	2	0	3.99	11	1	0	1	29	22	14	13	5	13	34	.216	.133	.250	10.43	3.99
Suellentrop, Tyler	R-R	6-3	217	1-22-97	2	0	8.82	10	0	0	0	16	19	18	16	3	13	16	.284	.306	.258	8.82	7.16
Ueckert, Cayne	R-R	6-3	195	5-28-96	0	0	0.00	2	0	0	1	3	2	0	0	0	0	6	.167	.000	.333	18.00	0.00
Vizcaino, Alexander	R-R	6-2	160	5-22-97	0	1	5.27	6	5	0	0	14	8	9	8	1	9	19	.163	.200	.138	12.51	5.93
Washer, Jake	R-R	6-0	220	2-23-96	0	0	0.00	1	0	0	0	1	0	0	0	0	0	0	.000	.000	.000	0.00	0.00
Whitney, Blake	R-R	6-3	185	5-25-96	0	2	10.05	9	1	0	0	14	20	16	16	5	2	24	.313	.184	.500	15.07	1.26
Wick, Rowan	L-R	6-3	234	11-9-92	1	0	0.00	3	0	0	0	3	1	0	0	0	0	7	.100	.000	.250	21.00	0.00
Wicks, Jordan	L-L	6-3	220	9-1-99	0	0	5.14	4	4	0	0	7	7	4	4	0	3	5	.250	.125	.300	6.43	3.86

Fielding

Catcher	PCT	G	PO	A	E	DP	PB
Aliendo	.975	15	144	12	4	2	2
Balego	1.000	3	28	0	0	0	1
Knight	1.000	6	49	5	0	0	1
Nevarez	.986	6	63	6	1	1	0
Pena	.960	3	23	1	1	0	0
Washer	.988	46	463	38	6	6	6
Wenson	1.000	28	285	25	0	0	4
Windham	.976	15	150	16	4	0	0

First Base	PCT	G	PO	A	E	DP
Ball	.984	18	121	4	2	10
Byrd	.974	5	31	6	1	1
Durna	.992	82	582	41	5	37
Olson	.900	5	27	0	3	5
Reynolds	1.000	1	4	0	0	1
Slaughter	.818	2	9	0	2	0
Warkentin	1.000	6	34	3	0	1

Second Base	PCT	G	PO	A	E	DP
Burch	.943	12	13	20	2	4
Garcia	.909	5	2	8	1	2
Huma	.954	35	31	72	5	12
McKeon	1.000	4	3	5	0	1
Reynolds	.963	4	10	16	1	4
Serra	1.000	2	1	2	0	0
Slaughter	.976	12	20	21	1	8
Spence	.892	9	14	19	4	1
Strumpf	.974	9	21	17	1	4
Vazquez	1.000	2	5	1	0	1
Windham	.981	25	38	66	2	13
Zinn	.900	8	4	5	1	0

Third Base	PCT	G	PO	A	E	DP
Balego	1.000	1	0	4	0	0
Burch	.333	1	0	1	2	0
Byrd	1.000	7	2	8	0	1
Garcia	.800	5	3	5	2	2
Huma	1.000	4	1	7	0	0
Olson	1.000	1	1	0	0	0
Reynolds	.944	13	6	11	1	0
Slaughter	.899	79	44	126	19	12
Strumpf	.692	4	7	2	4	0
Windham	.846	4	2	9	2	1
Zinn	1.000	3	1	5	0	1

Shortstop	PCT	G	PO	A	E	DP
Hoerner	1.000	1	0	2	0	0
Huma	.909	14	10	30	4	6
McKeon	.930	16	19	34	4	8
Pabon	.870	7	3	17	3	2
Spence	1.000	7	5	10	0	3
Vazquez	.950	21	31	45	4	9
Zinn	.939	58	82	134	14	21

Outfield	PCT	G	PO	A	E	DP
Americaan	.958	60	112	3	5	0
Artis	.975	33	38	1	1	0
Beesley	.983	32	56	2	1	0
Canario	.978	44	83	6	2	0
Davis	1.000	5	8	0	0	0
Olson	1.000	13	25	1	0	1
Pagan	1.000	2	2	0	0	0
Perlaza	.984	72	123	1	2	0
Pinango	.950	24	37	1	2	0
Roederer	.938	18	30	0	2	0
Velazquez	.976	63	116	7	3	2
Wilson	1.000	5	6	0	0	0
Zinn	--	1	0	0	0	0

MYRTLE BEACH PELICANS — LOW CLASS A

LOW-A EAST

Batting	B-T	HT	WT	DOB	AVG	vLH	vRH	G	AB	R	H	2B	3B	HR	RBI	BB	HBP	SH	SF	SO	SB	CS	SLG	OBP
Aliendo, Pablo	R-R	6-0	170	5-29-01	.249	.290	.229	64	213	42	53	10	0	5	27	22	15	1	2	72	2	1	.366	.357
Americaan, Edmond	L-L	6-1	170	3-26-97	.244	.182	.265	23	90	18	22	4	2	3	12	7	1	0	0	31	3	1	.433	.306
Bautista, Flemin	B-R	5-10	170	3-10-00	.194	.147	.211	36	124	11	24	7	0	2	17	16	2	0	2	38	0	0	.298	.292
Byrd, Grayson	L-R	6-3	205	6-16-96	.300	.000	.500	3	10	1	3	2	0	0	0	1	0	0	1	1	0	0	.500	.364
Caissie, Owen	L-R	6-4	190	7-8-02	.233	.217	.240	22	73	15	17	4	0	1	9	16	0	0	1	28	0	0	.329	.367
Fabrizio, Miguel	L-R	5-11	178	9-26-00	.000	--	.000	2	6	0	0	0	0	0	0	0	0	0	0	3	0	0	.000	.000
Franklin, Christian	R-R	5-11	195	11-30-99	.200	.308	.173	20	65	13	13	3	0	1	5	17	5	0	0	23	1	4	.292	.402
Garcia, Reivaj	B-R	5-11	175	8-12-01	.212	.250	.190	9	33	3	7	1	0	0	3	4	0	0	0	14	1	0	.242	.297
Hearn, Ethan	L-R	5-10	200	8-31-00	.176	.148	.187	62	193	20	34	8	1	6	33	22	5	1	5	100	0	1	.321	.271
Hill, Darius	L-L	6-1	190	8-17-97	.375	.200	.455	7	32	2	12	3	0	0	5	0	0	0	0	7	1	0	.469	.375
Howard, Ed	R-R	6-2	185	1-28-02	.225	.160	.249	80	302	33	68	9	3	4	31	18	4	1	1	98	7	2	.315	.277
Huma, Josue	B-R	6-1	175	3-17-00	.198	.231	.186	32	96	12	19	3	1	1	11	14	2	3	1	19	3	1	.281	.310
Made, Kevin	R-R	5-10	160	9-10-02	.272	.237	.289	58	235	19	64	13	3	1	20	6	2	0	0	57	2	0	.366	.296
Matt, Peter	R-R	6-2	220	5-22-98	.185	.250	.158	16	54	3	10	2	0	0	4	8	0	0	0	16	2	0	.222	.290
Mervis, Matt	L-R	6-4	225	4-16-98	.204	.219	.198	69	245	38	50	11	1	9	42	36	3	0	4	66	6	0	.367	.309

	B-T	HT	WT	DOB																				
Nwogu, Jordan	R-R	6-3	230	3-10-99	.248	.190	.274	94	323	48	80	12	2	10	40	42	6	1	1	105	16	4	.390	.344
Opitz, Casey	B-R	5-11	200	7-30-98	.245	.111	.275	16	49	9	12	1	0	0	3	10	0	1	0	11	0	0	.265	.373
Pagan, Ezequiel	L-R	6-1	163	7-8-00	.245	.195	.265	39	143	19	35	6	2	1	9	10	6	0	3	26	2	1	.336	.315
Pena, Raymond	R-R	5-10	160	4-7-97	.094	.083	.100	13	32	0	3	1	0	0	1	0	0	0	0	19	0	0	.125	.094
Pertuz, Fabian	R-R	6-0	156	9-1-00	.223	.267	.201	67	224	29	50	7	0	4	21	16	4	1	0	70	3	2	.308	.287
Pinango, Yohendrick	L-L	5-11	170	5-7-02	.272	.281	.268	84	324	50	88	16	2	4	27	24	1	0	2	57	8	2	.370	.322
Reynolds, Ryan	B-R	6-2	215	7-17-97	.275	.148	.328	29	91	19	25	7	4	3	15	11	5	0	0	26	1	0	.538	.383
Santana, Yeison	R-R	5-11	170	12-7-00	.147	.125	.157	20	75	8	11	2	0	0	1	9	0	1	0	28	3	3	.173	.238
Serra, Bryan	L-R	5-10	173	9-7-98	1.000	--	1.000	1	1	1	1	0	0	0	0	0	0	0	0	0	0	0	1.000	1.000
Sierra, Jonathan	L-L	6-3	190	10-17-98	.249	.284	.234	77	273	34	68	13	1	3	43	34	4	1	1	61	1	1	.337	.340
Stevens, Felix	R-R	6-4	225	7-30-99	.133	.333	.000	5	15	1	2	1	0	0	1	0	1	0	0	5	0	0	.200	.188
Verdugo, Luis	R-R	6-0	160	10-12-00	.187	.148	.200	62	214	22	40	12	1	3	25	11	1	0	1	65	2	1	.294	.229
Warkentin, Matt	R-R	6-6	250	1-28-97	.208	.147	.263	21	72	12	15	2	1	4	16	4	0	0	0	21	0	0	.431	.305
Wetzel, Jacob	L-L	5-11	215	3-26-00	.229	.226	.230	86	288	49	66	5	3	8	45	40	8	6	0	87	7	3	.351	.339

Pitching	B-T	HT	WT	DOB	W	L	ERA	G	GS	CG	SV	IP	H	R	ER	HR	BB	SO	AVG	vLH	vRH	K/9	BB/9
Albertos, Jose	R-R	6-1	185	11-7-98	2	1	3.38	6	0	0	0	13	9	5	5	1	5	13	.200	.375	.103	8.78	3.38
Almonte, Jose	R-R	6-2	185	9-8-95	3	2	6.61	17	0	0	0	31	28	25	23	1	40	39	.235	.175	.290	11.20	11.49
Angel Rodriguez, Luis	L-L	6-1	190	9-10-99	3	0	1.74	3	0	0	0	10	5	2	2	1	5	18	.143	.267	.050	15.68	4.35
Correa, Danis	R-R	5-11	150	8-26-99	3	0	1.73	18	0	0	1	26	12	5	5	0	12	44	.133	.100	.160	15.23	4.15
Devers, Luis	R-R	6-3	178	4-24-00	0	0	6.00	2	0	0	0	3	6	3	2	0	3	5	.429	.500	.250	15.00	9.00
Espinoza, Manuel	R-R	5-11	150	11-17-00	4	9	5.11	22	22	0	0	99	113	66	56	18	26	92	.282	.283	.281	8.39	2.37
Estrada, Jeremiah	B-R	6-1	185	11-1-98	1	1	1.57	11	2	0	0	23	18	8	4	2	18	38	.214	.226	.208	14.87	2.35
Gallardo, Richard	R-R	6-1	180	9-6-01	3	9	4.53	21	21	0	0	91	92	55	46	8	32	75	.257	.276	.243	7.39	3.15
Heidenfelder, Adam	R-R	6-5	265	12-11-95	0	0	33.75	2	0	0	0	1	4	5	5	0	2	1	.571	1.000	.400	6.75	13.50
Herz, DJ	R-L	6-2	175	1-4-01	3	7	3.43	17	17	0	0	66	32	25	25	6	38	105	.152	.184	.142	14.39	5.21
Hodge, Porter	R-R	6-4	230	2-21-01	1	1	3.74	7	3	0	0	22	19	10	9	0	8	29	.232	.186	.282	12.05	3.32
Jaramillo, Gabriel	R-R	6-1	176	11-3-98	4	2	2.33	21	0	0	0	39	21	10	10	1	18	49	.162	.148	.171	11.41	4.19
Katz, Alex	L-L	5-11	195	10-12-94	0	0	0.00	1	0	0	0	2	0	0	0	0	0	1	.000	.000	.000	3.86	0.00
Kobos, Scott	L-L	6-2	200	8-3-97	2	0	0.00	8	0	0	0	11	6	0	0	0	4	19	.154	.000	.188	15.55	3.27
Krzeminski, Austin	R-R	6-2	210	9-30-96	0	0	0.00	1	0	0	0	3	1	0	0	0	2	4	.143	.000	.200	13.50	6.75
Laskey, Adam	R-L	6-3	205	3-9-98	0	2	8.44	15	9	0	0	37	46	36	35	5	33	40	.309	.282	.318	9.64	7.96
Martin, Riley	L-L	6-1	215	3-19-98	0	0	5.52	8	0	0	0	15	12	11	9	3	10	21	.222	.118	.270	12.89	6.14
Miguel Gonzalez, Jose	R-R	6-2	173	12-5-97	4	8	5.84	23	12	0	0	74	79	51	48	13	43	61	.274	.339	.229	7.42	5.23
Moreno, Jose	R-R	6-4	165	7-31-96	0	0	21.60	2	0	0	0	2	3	4	4	0	5	1	.429	.750	.000	5.40	27.00
Nahas, Joe	R-R	6-1	185	11-14-99	2	1	2.70	9	1	0	0	23	18	16	7	1	10	34	.202	.167	.215	13.11	3.86
Nevarez, Dean	R-R	6-0	220	1-4-97	0	0	13.50	1	0	0	0	1	3	1	1	0	0	0	.600	.667	.500	0.00	0.00
Nunez, Eduarniel	R-R	6-2	170	6-7-99	0	1	2.61	7	0	0	0	10	7	3	3	1	5	13	.194	.250	.167	11.32	4.35
Ocampo, Carlos	R-R	6-2	181	9-3-98	0	4	5.85	29	0	0	3	48	46	33	31	6	15	67	.250	.203	.282	12.65	2.83
Palencia, Daniel	R-R	5-11	160	2-5-00	1	0	3.67	7	7	0	0	27	17	11	11	2	18	38	.179	.089	.260	12.67	6.00
Pena, Raymond	R-R	5-10	160	4-7-97	0	0	0.00	1	0	0	0	1	1	0	0	0	1	1	.333	.500	.000	9.00	9.00
Powell, Walker	R-R	6-8	210	6-11-96	0	0	4.50	5	0	0	0	6	8	3	3	0	0	3	.320	.333	.300	4.50	0.00
Reed, Sheldon	L-R	6-2	205	7-30-97	1	0	2.00	6	0	0	0	9	13	2	2	1	6	14	.342	.381	.314	14.00	6.00
Reid, Bailey	R-R	6-2	195	7-3-98	4	5	3.69	34	0	0	7	46	40	26	19	4	27	69	.229	.212	.239	13.40	5.24
Reindl, Jake	R-R	6-1	190	1-15-97	2	1	5.97	24	0	0	1	35	39	27	23	4	21	45	.281	.250	.301	11.68	5.45
Rodriguez, Dawel	R-R	6-3	200	12-15-98	0	2	8.47	8	0	0	1	17	16	22	16	1	12	15	.239	.250	.226	7.94	6.35
Scalzo Jr., Frankie	R-R	6-3	185	11-25-99	0	0	1.13	5	0	0	0	8	6	2	1	1	1	7	.207	.154	.250	7.88	1.13
Schlaffer, Tyler	R-R	6-1	180	5-24-01	2	5	4.65	9	9	0	0	41	47	23	21	6	17	40	.296	.308	.284	8.85	3.76
Sojo, Alberto	R-R	5-11	160	9-23-00	1	0	4.34	8	0	0	1	19	20	10	9	2	3	17	.278	.241	.302	8.20	1.45
Stambaugh, Dalton	R-L	6-0	195	2-11-97	1	0	0.00	2	0	0	0	6	2	2	0	0	3	6	.095	.000	.143	8.53	4.26
Suellentrop, Tyler	R-R	6-3	217	1-22-97	1	0	0.96	10	0	0	2	19	8	7	2	1	13	29	.133	.130	.119	13.98	6.27
Thoresen, Sam	R-R	6-3	210	9-21-98	0	2	3.13	7	7	0	0	23	14	9	8	0	17	36	.173	.259	.130	14.09	6.65
Vargas, Didier	R-L	6-0	175	3-13-99	4	2	5.55	18	10	0	0	60	71	39	37	6	22	58	.290	.294	.288	8.70	3.30
Warkentin, Matt	R-L	6-6	250	1-28-97	0	0	0.00	1	0	0	0	1	0	0	0	0	0	1	.000	.000	.000	13.50	0.00
Whitney, Blake	R-R	6-3	185	5-25-96	0	0	1.38	7	0	0	0	13	6	2	2	2	3	18	.130	.105	.148	12.46	2.08
Wright, Jarod	R-R	6-3	205	12-15-96	2	3	3.59	26	0	0	3	53	37	23	21	7	19	50	.194	.225	.171	8.54	3.25

Fielding

Catcher	PCT	G	PO	A	E	DP	PB
Aliendo	.984	52	504	40	9	5	11
Hearn	.980	51	501	43	11	3	6
Opitz	.987	15	141	16	2	1	2
Pena	.975	11	73	4	2	0	2

First Base	PCT	G	PO	A	E	DP
Byrd	1.000	2	8	0	0	1
Huma	.750	1	3	0	1	0
Matt	1.000	6	34	5	0	4
Mervis	.993	59	420	38	3	25
Pena	1.000	1	4	0	0	0
Reynolds	.984	10	58	2	1	4
Sierra	.980	24	129	17	3	3
Stevens	1.000	1	4	0	0	0
Warkentin	.993	19	135	12	1	12

Second Base	PCT	G	PO	A	E	DP
Bautista	.915	36	39	68	10	14
Garcia	1.000	3	4	6	0	2
Howard	.970	21	28	37	2	4
Huma	1.000	9	11	19	0	5
Pertuz	.969	37	52	73	4	12
Santana	.961	14	22	27	2	3
Verdugo	1.000	4	4	6	0	2

Third Base	PCT	G	PO	A	E	DP
Aliendo	1.000	1	0	2	0	0
Garcia	.941	6	2	14	1	0
Huma	1.000	21	12	15	0	1
Made	.906	13	10	19	3	3
Mervis	1.000	1	1	0	0	0
Pertuz	.915	22	25	40	6	6
Reynolds	.947	10	8	10	1	0

	PCT	G	PO	A	E	DP
Verdugo	.922	51	25	70	8	3

Shortstop	PCT	G	PO	A	E	DP
Aliendo	.000	1	0	0	0	0
Garcia	.750	2	0	3	1	0
Howard	.947	58	62	118	10	21
Huma	1.000	1	1	0	0	0
Made	.951	41	58	97	8	11
Pertuz	.893	8	11	14	3	3
Santana	.955	7	3	18	1	4
Verdugo	1.000	7	5	9	0	1

Outfield	PCT	G	PO	A	E	DP
Americaan	1.000	22	54	1	0	0
Caissie	.931	14	24	3	2	0
Franklin	.972	15	35	0	1	0
Hill	1.000	6	10	0	0	0

Matt	.947	8	18	0	1	0	Pagan	.974	35	73	2	2	0	Sierra	.988	43	77	4	1	1
Mervis	.500	1	2	0	2	0	Pena	.000	1	0	0	1	0	Stevens	1.000	3	7	0	0	0
Nwogu	.978	79	125	6	3	0	Pinango	.978	63	85	6	2	1	Wetzel	.984	79	122	4	2	3

ACL CUBS   ROOKIE
ARIZONA COMPLEX LEAGUE

Batting	B-T	HT	WT	DOB	AVG	vLH	vRH	G	AB	R	H	2B	3B	HR	RBI	BB	HBP	SH	SF	SO	SB	CS	SLG	OBP
Ademan, Aramis	L-R	5-11	160	9-13-98	.304	.286	.313	9	23	4	7	2	0	0	2	3	0	0	0	3	2	0	.391	.385
Alcantara, Kevin	R-R	6-6	188	7-12-02	.337	.280	.358	25	92	27	31	3	5	4	21	13	0	1	1	28	3	0	.609	.415
Apostel, Shendrik	R-R	6-5	245	4-24-00	.186	.000	.200	18	43	8	8	2	0	1	6	10	3	0	1	23	0	0	.302	.368
Balego, Cam	R-R	5-11	205	6-12-95	.615	1.000	.500	4	13	4	8	4	0	1	3	1	0	0	0	3	0	0	1.154	.643
Bautista, Flemin	B-R	5-10	170	3-10-00	.175	.000	.206	18	40	9	7	1	0	1	7	6	0	0	2	17	0	0	.275	.271
Beesley, Bradlee	R-R	5-10	180	2-21-98	.111	.000	.125	3	9	1	1	0	0	1	3	0	1	0	0	2	0	0	.444	.200
Burch, Matt	L-R	5-7	175	12-13-97	.455	1.000	.400	5	11	3	5	2	0	0	2	3	0	0	0	1	0	0	.636	.571
Caissie, Owen	L-R	6-4	190	7-8-02	.349	.250	.383	32	109	20	38	7	1	6	20	26	1	0	0	39	1	2	.596	.478
Chavers, Parker	L-R	5-11	185	7-25-98	.059	.000	.083	5	17	2	1	1	0	0	1	1	0	0	0	3	1	0	.118	.111
Collier, Manny	R-R	5-10	170	12-19-00	1.000	1.000	--	2	1	4	1	0	0	0	1	4	1	0	0	0	2	0	1.000	1.000
Cuevas, Yovanny	R-R	6-0	170	7-28-98	.239	.250	.237	24	46	13	11	3	2	1	11	19	0	1	0	19	1	2	.457	.455
Fabrizio, Miguel	L-R	5-11	180	9-26-00	.372	.269	.402	33	113	23	42	16	1	2	28	14	0	0	0	38	2	0	.584	.441
Franklin, Christian	R-R	5-11	195	11-30-99	.455	.000	.833	4	11	4	5	0	0	0	3	3	0	0	0	2	3	0	.455	.571
Gamargo, Edgar	R-R	5-10	172	2-1-02	.400	.333	.412	9	20	4	8	1	0	0	3	6	0	0	0	3	0	0	.450	.538
Garcia, Reivaj	B-R	5-11	175	8-12-01	.314	.333	.310	11	35	5	11	1	0	1	3	2	0	1	0	10	0	0	.429	.351
Heredia, Nestor	R-R	6-1	179	11-25-00	.000	--	.000	2	4	0	0	0	0	0	0	0	0	0	0	0	0	0	.000	.000
Herrera, Rafael	R-R	5-11	170	9-18-00	.000	.000	.000	3	4	1	0	0	0	0	1	2	1	0	0	3	0	0	.000	.429
Joaquin, Widimer	R-R	6-2	180	9-8-00	.250	1.000	.143	4	8	1	2	0	0	0	3	0	0	0	0	4	0	1	.250	.455
Jordan, Levi	R-R	5-8	190	9-24-95	.300	.000	.333	3	10	1	3	0	0	0	3	1	0	0	0	1	0	0	.300	.364
Lopez, Jose O.	L-R	5-10	172	1-4-02	.119	.133	.114	22	59	8	7	2	2	1	6	9	0	1	1	28	0	1	.271	.232
Matt, Peter	R-R	6-2	220	5-22-98	.154	.100	.333	5	13	0	2	0	0	1	0	2	1	0	0	7	0	0	.154	.313
McKeon, Scott	R-R	6-0	185	10-30-97	.111	.000	.125	3	9	2	1	0	0	0	0	2	1	0	0	4	1	0	.111	.333
Mena, Ismael	L-L	6-3	185	11-30-02	.224	.171	.240	44	156	24	35	3	1	2	21	15	1	0	6	45	9	3	.295	.287
Mora, Juan	R-R	5-9	176	9-30-99	.351	.273	.365	29	74	21	26	4	2	3	23	15	3	0	1	21	7	1	.581	.473
Morel, Rafael	R-R	6-0	170	11-22-01	.203	.174	.211	39	118	18	24	4	1	3	23	14	3	1	3	38	6	1	.331	.297
Morfa, Carlos	R-R	6-2	190	12-2-00	.200	--	.200	2	5	1	1	0	0	1	0	0	0	0	0	3	0	0	.800	.200
Murray Jr., BJ	B-R	6-0	205	1-5-00	.286	.111	.368	16	56	12	16	3	1	2	8	5	0	0	0	14	2	0	.482	.344
Nevarez, Dean	R-R	6-0	220	1-4-97	.333	.500	.000	1	3	0	1	0	0	0	0	1	0	0	0	1	0	0	.333	.250
Olivo, Christian	R-R	5-11	168	10-29-03	.071	--	.071	6	14	2	1	0	0	0	2	0	1	0	0	8	0	0	.071	.133
Opitz, Casey	B-R	5-11	200	7-30-98	.333	.000	1.000	1	3	0	1	0	0	0	0	0	0	0	0	0	0	0	.333	.333
Pabon, Miguel	R-R	6-0	165	8-30-00	.364	.600	.167	5	11	2	4	1	0	0	0	0	0	0	0	3	0	0	.455	.364
Pagan, Ezequiel	L-R	6-1	163	7-8-00	.336	.125	.374	27	107	24	36	6	5	6	19	3	3	0	2	20	3	0	.654	.365
Pina, Oswaldo	R-R	5-10	170	8-9-98	.333	--	.333	2	6	1	2	0	0	0	2	0	0	0	0	0	0	0	.333	.333
Preciado, Reginald	R-R	6-4	185	5-16-03	.333	.300	.347	34	141	28	47	10	3	3	25	11	1	0	1	35	7	1	.511	.383
Quintero, Malcom	R-R	6-0	165	7-29-00	.333	.320	.338	39	99	24	33	5	0	2	11	22	1	0	1	29	2	0	.444	.455
Quintero, Ronnier	L-R	5-10	195	11-13-02	.182	1.000	.151	20	55	8	10	1	1	2	8	7	0	0	1	18	0	0	.345	.270
Romine, Austin	R-R	6-1	216	11-22-88	.250	--	.250	2	4	0	1	1	0	0	0	0	0	0	0	0	0	0	.500	.250
Santana, Yeison	R-R	5-11	170	12-7-00	.292	.364	.269	32	89	19	26	3	1	1	15	11	3	0	1	24	6	4	.382	.385
Spence, Liam	R-R	6-1	190	4-9-98	.333	--	.333	1	3	0	1	0	0	0	1	0	0	0	0	0	0	0	.333	.333
Stevens, Felix	R-R	6-4	225	7-30-99	.298	.222	.314	30	104	22	31	7	2	7	25	8	3	0	0	37	1	1	.606	.365
Triantos, James	R-R	6-1	195	1-29-03	.327	.233	.366	25	101	27	33	7	1	6	19	7	1	0	0	18	3	3	.594	.376
Vazquez, Luis	R-R	6-1	165	10-10-99	.182	.000	.200	3	11	1	2	0	0	0	1	0	0	0	0	4	0	0	.182	.250
Weber, Andy	L-R	6-1	190	7-24-97	.375	.000	.429	3	8	4	3	0	0	0	1	1	0	0	0	1	0	0	.375	.545
Windham, Bryce	L-R	6-1	190	9-25-96	.333	--	.333	3	9	2	3	0	0	0	1	1	0	0	0	1	0	0	.333	.400

Pitching	B-T	HT	WT	DOB	W	L	ERA	G	GS	CG	SV	IP	H	R	ER	HR	BB	SO	AVG	vLH	vRH	K/9	BB/9
Adam, Jason	R-R	6-3	229	8-4-91	2	0	3.00	3	1	0	0	3	4	1	1	0	1	3	.308	.000	.500	9.00	3.00
Almanzar, Elian	L-R	6-4	210	2-1-00	1	2	8.61	14	2	0	0	23	36	29	22	4	24	32	.350	.281	.380	12.52	9.39
Angel Rodriguez, Luis	L-L	6-1	190	9-10-99	1	0	1.73	9	4	0	2	26	14	5	5	2	7	39	.156	.176	.151	13.50	2.42
Baez, Rony	R-R	6-0	180	4-21-99	2	1	5.14	14	0	0	0	28	22	17	16	1	12	30	.216	.256	.190	9.64	3.86
Cabrera, Yovanny	R-R	6-2	180	3-22-01	1	2	6.70	12	10	0	0	42	34	36	31	4	21	41	.221	.237	.216	8.86	4.54
Clarke, Chris	R-R	6-7	215	5-13-98	0	0	0.00	1	1	0	0	3	3	0	0	0	0	3	.250	.250	.250	9.00	0.00
Combs, Shane	R-R	6-2	219	1-14-97	0	0	0.00	1	0	0	1	1	0	0	0	0	0	0	.000	.000	.000	0.00	0.00
Devers, Luis	R-R	6-3	178	4-24-00	2	4	3.33	12	11	0	0	51	48	24	19	3	14	54	.245	.247	.244	9.47	2.45
Feliz, Kelvin	R-R	6-1	165	9-30-00	1	1	17.05	7	0	0	0	6	11	13	12	3	11	6	.379	.438	.308	8.53	15.63
Figueroa, Wilfri	R-R	6-0	172	5-11-01	0	1	7.59	14	0	0	0	21	15	19	18	0	25	20	.214	.226	.205	8.44	10.55
Gonzalez, Angel	R-R	6-2	180	1-26-00	2	1	8.36	19	0	0	0	28	21	29	26	1	32	33	.212	.256	.183	10.61	10.29
Gray, Drew	L-L	6-2	190	5-10-03	0	1	0.00	2	2	0	0	4	3	1	0	0	1	9	.200	.000	.231	20.25	2.25
Hambley, Dominic	R-R	6-2	230	4-24-03	0	0	13.50	1	0	0	0	2	4	2	2	0	2	0	.286	.250	.333	0.00	13.50
Hernandez, Angel	L-L	6-2	180	5-6-00	2	0	3.27	15	0	0	0	22	22	20	8	0	11	26	.247	.250	.247	10.64	4.50
Hodge, Porter	R-R	6-4	230	2-21-01	1	2	7.45	7	7	0	0	29	36	31	24	5	9	35	.298	.293	.300	10.86	2.79
Holder, Jonathan	R-R	6-2	232	6-9-93	0	0	0.00	1	1	0	0	1	0	0	0	0	0	1	.200	.000	.250	9.00	0.00
Leigh, Zachary	R-R	6-0	170	11-14-97	0	0	0.00	2	0	0	0	4	1	0	0	0	0	9	.091	.200	.000	22.09	0.00
Little, Luke	L-L	6-8	220	8-30-00	0	1	4.91	5	4	0	0	11	6	8	6	1	5	19	.154	.222	.133	15.55	4.09
Machado, Joel	L-L	6-1	160	2-9-02	0	1	1.13	2	2	0	0	8	9	6	1	2	1	7	.265	.333	.250	7.88	1.13
McAvene, Michael	R-R	6-3	207	8-24-97	0	0	40.50	1	1	0	0	2	4	3	1	2	4	1	.500	.000	.667	27.00	27.00
Montano, Gregori	R-R	5-11	175	8-18-99	0	0	11.57	3	0	0	0	2	2	3	3	1	4	1	.250	.000	.286	3.86	15.43

CHICAGO CUBS

Name	B-T	HT	WT	DOB	W	L	ERA	G	GS	CG	SV	IP	H	R	ER	HR	BB	SO	AVG	vLH	vRH	K/9	BB/9
Mora, Juan	R-R	5-9	176	9-30-99	0	0	0.00	1	0	0	0	0	0	0	0	0	0	0	.000	--	.000	0.00	0.00
Oquendo, Johzan	R-R	6-2	180	1-6-01	4	3	4.57	18	5	0	2	41	34	24	21	2	21	49	.221	.236	.212	10.67	4.57
Powell, Walker	R-R	6-8	210	6-11-96	0	0	9.00	2	0	0	0	2	2	3	2	0	1	5	.200	.000	.400	22.50	4.50
Prieto, Marco	R-R	6-2	165	7-29-99	0	3	19.85	12	0	0	1	11	19	28	25	2	20	9	.373	.571	.297	7.15	15.88
Reed, Sheldon	L-R	6-2	205	7-30-97	0	0	0.00	3	0	0	0	3	1	0	0	0	1	5	.111	.000	.143	15.00	3.00
Remon, Jorge	R-R	6-2	160	2-3-01	0	1	14.21	7	0	0	0	6	6	13	10	2	13	4	.250	.143	.294	5.68	18.47
Rodriguez, Dawel	R-R	6-3	200	12-15-98	1	0	2.79	6	0	0	1	10	4	3	3	0	4	9	.138	.000	.182	8.38	3.72
Rodriguez, Robinson	R-R	6-2	190	4-12-00	1	1	2.84	6	0	0	0	6	3	7	2	0	12	9	.130	.111	.143	12.79	17.05
Rosario, Aneuris	R-R	6-0	165	3-4-95	0	0	0.00	2	1	0	0	2	0	0	0	0	0	6	.000	.000	.000	27.00	0.00
Salvador, Andricson	L-L	5-11	180	7-24-00	3	1	3.41	11	4	0	0	29	25	14	11	0	8	35	.214	.222	.212	10.86	2.48
Santana, Tyler	R-R	6-1	205	5-13-98	0	0	0.00	1	0	0	1	2	1	0	0	0	0	3	.143	.333	.000	13.50	0.00
Scalzo Jr., Frankie	R-R	6-3	185	11-25-99	0	0	0.00	1	0	0	0	1	1	0	0	0	0	1	.250	--	.250	9.00	0.00
Schlaffer, Tyler	R-R	6-1	180	5-24-01	2	1	4.40	3	3	0	0	14	16	7	7	1	5	15	.276	.438	.214	9.42	3.14
Serra, Bryan	L-R	5-10	173	9-7-98	0	0	0.00	1	0	0	0	0	1	0	0	0	0	0	.500	.500	--	0.00	0.00
Sojo, Alberto	R-R	5-11	160	9-23-00	1	0	1.80	2	0	0	0	5	3	1	1	0	2	8	.167	.200	.154	14.40	3.60
Stambaugh, Dalton	R-L	6-0	195	2-11-97	1	0	6.75	2	0	0	0	3	2	2	2	1	0	6	.200	.333	.143	20.25	0.00
Suiter, Jerrick	R-R	6-3	240	3-4-93	2	0	2.70	3	0	0	0	3	3	1	1	0	0	5	.250	.500	.200	13.50	0.00
Valdez, Dauris	R-R	6-8	254	10-22-95	1	0	10.80	3	0	0	0	3	2	4	4	0	3	5	.182	.500	.111	13.50	8.10
Watkins, Chase	L-L	6-4	215	10-4-99	2	0	1.59	5	0	0	0	11	10	2	2	0	2	20	.222	.364	.176	15.88	1.59

Fielding

C: Balego 4, Fabrizio 10, Nevarez 1, Opitz 1, Quintero 39, Quintero 13, Romine 2, Windham 3.
1B: Apostel 18, Fabrizio 18, Gamargo 4, Matt 3, Murray Jr. 6, Pabon 1, Stevens 16.
2B: Ademan 7, Bautista 5, Burch 4, Garcia 9, Heredia 1, Joaquin 1, Jordan 1, McKeon 1, Mora 18, Morel 9, Pabon 1, Pina 1, Santana 7, Spence 1, Triantos 8.
3B: Garcia 2, Joaquin 3, Jordan 1, Mora 9, Morel 24, Murray Jr. 8, Pina 1, Preciado 16, Santana 1.
SS: Ademan 2, Jordan 1, McKeon 2, Mora 1, Morel 4, Olivo 6, Pabon 3, Preciado 17, Santana 19, Triantos 7, Vazquez 3, Weber 3.
OF: Alcantara 21, Bautista 4, Beesley 2, Caissie 28, Chavers 4, Collier 1, Cuevas 22, Franklin 4, Herrera 2, Lopez 20, Matt 2, Mena 43, Morfa 1, Pagan 28, Stevens 11.

DSL CUBS ROOKIE
DOMINICAN SUMMER LEAGUE

Batting	B-T	HT	WT	DOB	AVG	vLH	vRH	G	AB	R	H	2B	3B	HR	RBI	BB	HBP	SH	SF	SO	SB	CS	SLG	OBP
Altuve, Brayan	R-R	5-11	160	1-22-03	.208	.217	.206	43	154	27	32	6	0	5	29	15	5	0	0	51	10	3	.344	.299
Alvarez, Ezequiel	B-R	5-11	150	4-10-02	.221	.273	.211	24	68	14	15	1	1	0	8	8	1	1	1	10	19	1	.265	.308
Ballesteros, Moises	L-R	5-10	195	11-8-03	.266	.348	.252	48	154	22	41	10	0	3	25	31	2	0	0	24	6	1	.390	.396
Bolivar, Wilmer	R-R	6-0	167	3-23-03	.190	.176	.193	36	105	24	20	2	1	1	10	12	1	3	0	48	11	1	.257	.280
Coran, Raino	R-R	6-4	210	5-13-02	.179	.000	.198	40	106	29	19	4	0	3	10	36	5	0	0	51	16	4	.302	.408
Cruz, Andrws	R-R	5-10	150	12-3-02	.304	.143	.331	40	148	28	45	9	1	1	25	11	3	2	2	17	14	3	.399	.360
Duarte, Samuel	R-R	5-11	175	1-20-01	.213	.154	.224	31	80	16	17	5	1	0	10	16	4	0	1	17	7	3	.300	.366
Espinoza, Leonel	R-R	6-0	165	4-7-03	.225	.262	.214	53	173	29	39	5	1	8	28	21	9	0	1	43	11	3	.405	.338
Fabian, Elias	R-R	5-11	169	3-15-01	.225	.455	.183	19	71	8	16	2	1	1	9	2	1	0	2	16	3	4	.324	.250
Ferreira, Daniel	R-R	5-10	170	10-2-03	.161	.161	.160	49	137	13	22	5	0	0	14	25	4	1	1	53	4	2	.197	.305
Granadillo, Dilan	B-R	5-9	175	5-18-01	.141	.125	.147	33	99	8	14	2	1	0	9	12	4	0	1	31	3	1	.182	.259
Guzman, Raul	L-L	5-11	145	10-18-03	.165	.207	.154	41	133	14	22	5	1	1	8	18	4	2	1	38	4	6	.241	.282
Hernandez, Cristian	R-R	6-2	175	12-13-03	.285	.258	.291	47	158	38	45	5	1	5	22	30	1	0	2	39	21	3	.424	.398
Hernandez, Frank	R-R	5-11	165	12-10-01	.287	.270	.292	53	181	29	52	6	2	1	22	20	8	0	3	26	9	6	.359	.377
Hernandez, Oferman	L-R	6-0	160	10-15-03	.155	.280	.118	36	110	10	17	5	1	0	8	19	2	0	0	39	2	2	.218	.290
Herrera, Jose	R-R	5-11	162	4-3-03	.130	.000	.145	28	69	11	9	2	0	1	10	16	8	0	2	34	1	2	.203	.347
Lubo, Geuri	R-R	6-2	185	9-24-03	.202	.083	.216	33	109	11	22	3	0	0	6	12	2	0	1	22	3	2	.229	.290
Mateo, Starlin	R-R	6-1	180	7-15-02	.190	.118	.205	36	105	16	20	3	0	3	15	15	5	0	2	29	4	7	.305	.315
Maza, Luis	L-R	5-10	150	10-10-02	.176	.000	.205	29	91	9	16	2	2	0	8	9	3	0	0	26	7	4	.242	.272
Montenegro, Fredy	R-R	5-10	160	9-12-03	.194	.182	.196	30	67	8	13	4	1	0	5	6	5	0	0	17	0	1	.284	.308
More, Cristian	L-L	5-10	170	8-11-01	.252	.296	.242	42	159	27	40	6	4	0	18	13	3	0	2	27	15	5	.340	.316
Ramirez, Pedro	B-R	5-9	165	4-1-04	.359	.423	.349	50	195	37	70	11	7	1	30	13	7	0	1	20	9	7	.503	.417
Ramos, Carlos	R-R	5-10	170	12-14-03	.243	.269	.235	40	107	20	26	2	1	0	16	17	2	1	3	14	3	5	.280	.349
Rojas, Joanfran	R-R	5-10	160	6-19-01	.301	.412	.279	33	103	31	31	6	0	0	7	10	5	0	0	10	10	3	.359	.390
Ruiz, Lizardo	R-R	5-11	165	8-20-02	.221	.314	.190	44	140	19	31	2	1	1	11	14	0	0	0	37	3	1	.271	.292
Soto, Wally	L-R	5-10	170	1-5-03	.283	.286	.282	36	106	25	30	9	1	3	20	22	6	0	1	29	5	2	.472	.430
Suriel, Anderson	L-L	6-1	175	4-11-03	.295	.280	.298	50	176	16	52	15	5	0	28	14	3	0	1	19	11	7	.438	.356
Tatis, Esmarly	B-R	5-10	165	4-11-00	.250	.250	.250	31	92	23	23	5	2	0	9	12	2	0	0	17	8	2	.348	.349
Torres, Jerry	L-R	6-1	185	10-4-02	.185	.167	.190	44	130	20	24	6	1	0	18	29	5	0	0	40	4	2	.246	.354

Pitching	B-T	HT	WT	DOB	W	L	ERA	G	GS	CG	SV	IP	H	R	ER	HR	BB	SO	AVG	vLH	vRH	K/9	BB/9
Agrazal, Gabriel	R-R	6-1	185	9-10-03	2	1	5.06	7	2	0	0	16	22	11	9	0	5	9	.355	.188	.413	5.06	2.81
Alcila, Jose	R-R	5-11	170	4-5-00	0	5	5.34	14	5	0	0	32	27	23	19	1	35	28	.231	.327	.162	7.88	9.84
Arias, Michael	R-R	6-0	155	11-15-01	4	1	3.09	16	0	0	3	23	16	11	8	2	14	22	.193	.200	.189	8.49	5.40
Carrasquel, Gregoris	R-R	6-3	178	10-13-99	3	1	4.24	13	0	0	1	17	15	10	8	1	11	19	.238	.379	.118	10.06	5.82
Crispin, Yohan	R-R	6-2	175	7-15-01	3	5	7.58	15	4	0	0	38	49	37	32	2	13	34	.301	.305	.298	8.05	3.08
De La Cruz, Enmanuel	R-R	6-2	168	4-7-02	2	1	2.14	14	11	0	0	46	27	12	11	1	11	43	.173	.188	.167	8.35	2.14
Delgado, Kenneddy	R-R	6-0	170	9-21-03	0	0	3.27	5	0	0	0	11	9	6	4	0	7	5	.231	.133	.292	4.09	5.73
Duran, Joandy	R-R	6-0	200	11-12-01	2	1	3.47	15	0	0	0	23	26	13	9	0	9	21	.277	.205	.327	8.10	3.47
Fabian, Waimer	R-R	6-2	180	4-4-01	0	0	2.51	9	0	0	1	14	6	5	4	0	6	13	.136	.095	.174	8.16	3.77
Feliz, Anderson	R-R	6-3	165	11-26-01	1	2	6.38	17	0	0	1	24	24	19	17	2	22	16	.276	.290	.268	6.00	8.25
Garcia, Carlos	L-L	6-4	190	7-12-02	1	1	1.67	15	8	0	0	43	25	15	8	1	14	47	.164	.120	.173	9.84	2.93
Gomez, Leury	R-R	6-2	160	9-16-02	0	2	6.20	12	0	0	2	20	27	18	14	2	17	20	.321	.318	.323	8.85	7.52

Name	B-T	Ht	Wt	DOB	W	L	ERA	G	GS	CG	SV	IP	H	R	ER	HR	BB	SO	AVG	vLH	vRH		
Imbriano, Zhiorman	L-L	6-0	180	1-30-03	1	0	5.82	7	4	0	0	17	22	14	11	1	4	16	.306	.300	.306	8.47	2.12
Jimenez, Joel	R-R	6-0	160	7-23-00	4	0	4.38	14	2	0	0	37	30	20	18	1	26	26	.236	.258	.229	6.32	6.32
Lebron, Scarlyn	R-R	6-3	178	1-2-02	2	2	4.21	10	1	0	0	26	18	13	12	2	25	16	.207	.179	.220	5.61	8.77
Lopez, Jose M.	R-R	6-2	170	7-21-03	3	1	1.35	11	0	0	2	20	9	4	3	0	8	18	.134	.053	.167	8.10	3.60
Marte, Luis	R-R	6-0	200	2-13-01	0	1	8.22	6	0	0	0	8	3	9	7	1	14	12	.120	.000	.176	14.09	16.43
Martinez, Adrian	R-R	6-2	190	10-24-02	0	3	12.83	10	8	0	0	13	13	23	19	0	32	12	.260	.316	.226	8.10	21.60
Martinez, Anthony	R-R	6-3	175	1-10-00	5	1	4.21	16	1	0	4	36	24	18	17	3	19	46	.188	.147	.202	11.39	4.71
Mateo, Starlin	R-R	6-1	180	7-15-02	0	1	0.00	1	0	0	0	1	0	2	0	0	1	1	.000	.000	--	9.00	9.00
Mendez, Anthony	R-R	6-1	190	8-4-02	4	1	3.28	14	3	0	0	36	31	21	13	2	13	33	.230	.200	.250	8.33	3.28
Mercedes, Edgar	R-R	6-8	190	11-1-00	0	3	27.00	5	3	0	0	3	3	12	8	0	14	3	.333	.250	.400	10.13	47.25
Morales, Gleiber	R-R	5-10	165	9-28-02	2	3	4.28	15	1	0	0	40	27	24	19	5	23	33	.184	.157	.208	7.43	5.18
Olivo, David	R-R	6-0	170	9-28-02	0	3	12.74	14	1	0	0	18	26	31	25	2	32	10	.366	.310	.405	5.09	16.30
Perez, Kenyi	R-R	6-2	165	8-9-01	0	4	7.91	13	13	0	0	39	40	37	34	2	44	46	.268	.233	.283	10.71	10.24
Pichardo, Starlyn	R-R	6-0	175	1-12-04	0	2	5.01	14	13	0	0	32	27	20	18	2	27	23	.231	.211	.241	6.40	7.52
Quintero, Welington	R-R	6-0	185	12-17-00	1	4	9.31	14	0	0	2	19	32	25	20	4	7	17	.376	.269	.424	7.91	3.26
Reyes, Luis R.	R-R	6-0	185	10-22-02	2	2	2.86	15	0	0	3	28	27	20	9	0	20	31	.248	.265	.240	9.85	6.35
Rodriguez, Samuel	L-L	6-3	178	9-2-01	1	3	2.63	14	8	0	0	48	43	22	14	0	16	41	.240	.214	.248	7.69	3.00
Rojas, Cristian	R-R	6-1	153	7-29-02	0	3	3.38	13	13	0	0	37	32	17	14	0	17	39	.237	.274	.205	9.40	4.10
Romero, Jose	R-R	5-10	185	4-20-01	3	0	2.67	18	0	0	1	30	20	10	9	1	17	42	.185	.188	.183	12.46	5.04
Roque, Oliver	R-R	6-3	180	1-10-02	1	1	0.85	16	2	0	1	32	13	9	3	0	8	26	.125	.146	.111	7.39	2.27
Sanchez, Tomy	R-R	5-8	163	2-9-03	3	1	3.25	13	0	0	0	28	22	13	10	0	12	32	.210	.209	.210	10.41	3.90
Santana, Albaro	R-R	6-0	165	10-12-01	1	1	2.89	16	0	0	1	28	14	11	9	1	12	30	.151	.148	.152	9.64	3.86
Santy, Marino	L-L	5-11	170	3-4-02	0	1	3.33	10	9	0	0	24	18	14	9	0	25	31	.194	.227	.183	11.47	9.25
Sierra, Joel	R-R	6-1	190	12-31-01	1	0	5.75	16	0	0	1	20	14	16	13	0	19	24	.197	.258	.150	10.62	8.41
Valenzuela, Luis	R-R	6-2	170	10-23-01	2	2	7.89	16	0	0	0	22	25	26	19	0	24	13	.301	.368	.281	5.40	9.97

Fielding

C: Ballesteros 41, Granadillo 31, Herrera 28, Montenegro 23, Ramos 24, Soto 16.

1B: Altuve 4, Ballesteros 25, Coran 1, Duarte 4, Granadillo 5, Hernandez 10, Hernandez 7, Herrera 14, Mateo 12, Montenegro 8, Ramos 3, Ruiz 3, Soto 11, Suriel 14, Torres 27.

2B: Alvarez 19, Cruz 6, Lubo 11, Maza 17, Montenegro 1, Ramirez 23, Ramos 14, Rojas 13, Ruiz 5, Tatis 18.

3B: Altuve 10, Cruz 21, Hernandez 3, Hernandez 1, Lubo 10, Maza 9, Montenegro 3, Ramirez 4, Ramos 1, Rojas 17, Ruiz 28, Soto 10, Tatis 9.

SS: Cruz 20, Hernandez 47, Lubo 12, Maza 2, Ramirez 24, Rojas 4, Ruiz 10, Tatis 5.

OF: Altuve 16, Alvarez 3, Bolivar 31, Coran 36, Duarte 22, Espinoza 49, Fabian 16, Ferreira 32, Guzman 39, Hernandez 37, Hernandez 16, Mateo 15, More 41, Suriel 20, Torres 12.

Chicago White Sox

SEASON IN A SENTENCE: The White Sox used a strong pitching staff and the seventh-best offense in baseball to post one of the franchise's best seasons this century. The club went 93-69 and won the American League Central for the first time since 2008 before losing in the American League Division Series to the Astros.

HIGH POINT: The White Sox clinched the division after beating the Indians 7-2 in the first game of a doubleheader on Sept. 23. Sure, Chicago went on to lose the second game of the two-game set, but that wasn't going to take away from the triumph of taking the division title after a stretch of seasons that included five straight fourth-place finishes after a 2013 season when the White Sox were the third-worst team in baseball.

LOW POINT: Any low point based on playoff performance should be taken with a grain of salt, because getting into the playoffs is an accomplishment in its own right, but the White Sox looked overmatched in their ALDS series against the Astros—where Houston outscored them 31-18. The decisive Game 4 10-1 loss was particularly hard to swallow because the team's best pitcher—lefthander Carlos Rodon—got the nod and managed just 2.2 innings after pitching the best season of his seven-year major league career.

NOTABLE ROOKIES: Power-armed relievers Michael Kopech and Garrett Crochet logged plenty of innings for the White Sox out of the bullpen. Crochet posted a 2.82 ERA while Kopech posted a 3.50 ERA and also started four games. Ryan Burr was also effective in 36.2 innings, with a 2.45 ERA and both Codi Heuer (5.12 ERA) and Jose Ruiz (3.05 ERA) were solidly in the mix as well. Yermin Mercedes was one of the hottest hitters in baseball to start the season and hit .415/.455/.659 in April with five home runs before cooling off down the stretch, while Gavin Sheets and Andrew Vaughn added 11 and 15 homers, respectively.

KEY TRANSACTIONS: The White Sox made a splashy trade deadline move in an attempt to shore up the bullpen, sending Heuer and second baseman Nick Madrigal to the Cubs in exchange for Craig Kimbrel. It was an aggressive move to trade the No. 3 prospect in the system to their inner-city rival and after being lights out for the Cubs (0.49 ERA), Kimbrel struggled in 23 innings (5.09 ERA) for the White Sox.

OPENING DAY SALARY: $125,987,500 (15th).

PLAYERS OF THE YEAR

MAJOR LEAGUE	MINOR LEAGUE
Lance Lynn **RHP**	**Romy Gonzalez** **SS**
11-6, 2.69	(AAA/AA)
AL CY Young finalist	.283/.364/.532,
176 SO in 157 IP	24 HR, 24 SB

ORGANIZATION LEADERS

Batting		*Minimum 250 AB
MAJORS		
*AVG	Luis Robert	.338
*OPS	Luis Robert	.946
HR	Jose Abreu	30
RBI	Jose Abreu	117
MINORS		
*AVG	Yolbert Sanchez, Birmingham, Winston-Salem	.308
*OBP	Matt Reynolds, Charlotte	.373
*SLG	Romy Gonzalez, Charlotte, Birmingham	.532
*OPS	Romy Gonzalez, Charlotte, Birmingham	.896
R	Jose Rodriguez, Birmingham, Winston-Salem, Kannapolis	79
H	Jose Rodriguez, Birmingham, Winston-Salem, Kannapolis	141
TB	Jose Rodriguez, Birmingham, Winston-Salem, Kannapolis	220
2B	Luis Mieses, Winston-Salem, Kannapolis	31
3B	Bryan Ramos, Kannapolis	6
HR	Mikie Mahtook, Charlotte	26
RBI	Luis Mieses, Winston-Salem, Kannapolis	74
BB	Bryan Ramos, Kannapolis	51
BB	Matt Reynolds, Charlotte	51
SO	Luis Curbelo, Winston-Salem	152
SB	Jose Rodriguez, Birmingham, Winston-Salem, Kannapolis	30
Pitching		#Minimum 75 IP
MAJORS		
W	Dylan Cease	13
W	Carlos Rodon	13
#ERA	Carlos Rodon	2.37
SO	Dylan Cease	226
SV	Liam Hendriks	38
MINORS		
W	Homer Cruz, ACL White Sox, Kannapolis	8
L	5 tied	9
#ERA	Emilio Vargas, Birmingham	2.90
G	Lane Ramsey, Charlotte, Birmingham, Winston-Salem	44
GS	Johan Dominguez, Charlotte, Birmingham, Winston-Salem	24
GS	Kade McClure, Charlotte, Birmingham	24
SV	Caleb Freeman, Birmingham, Winston-Salem	9
SV	McKinley Moore, Winston-Salem, Kannapolis	9
IP	John Parke, Charlotte, Birmingham	112.2
BB	Andrew Dalquist, Kannapolis	56
SO	Johan Dominguez, Charlotte, Birmingham, Winston-Salem	118
#AVG	Mike Wright Jr., Charlotte	.202

General Manager: Rick Hahn. **Farm Director:** Chris Getz. **Scouting Director:** Mike Shirley.

Class	Team	League	W	L	PCT	Finish	Manager
Majors	Chicago White Sox	American	93	69	.574	3rd (15)	Tony La Russa
Triple-A	Charlotte Knights	Triple-A East	47	81	.367	20th (20)	Wes Helms
Double-A	Birmingham Barons	Double-A South	62	56	.525	3rd (8)	Justin Jirschele
High-A	Winston-Salem Dash	High-A East	43	76	.361	12th (12)	Ryan Newman
Low-A	Kannapolis Cannon Ballers	Low-A East	40	79	.336	12th (12)	Guillermo Quiroz
Rookie	ACL White Sox	Arizona Complex	25	34	.424	13th (18)	Mike Gellinger
Rookie	DSL White Sox	Dominican Summer	26	33	.441	t-33rd (46)	Guillermo Reyes
Overall 2021 Minor League Record			243	359	.404	29th (30)	

ORGANIZATION STATISTICS

CHICAGO WHITE SOX
AMERICAN LEAGUE

Batting	B-T	HT	WT	DOB	AVG	vLH	vRH	G	AB	R	H	2B	3B	HR	RBI	BB	HBP	SH	SF	SO	SB	CS	SLG	OBP
Abreu, Jose	R-R	6-3	235	1-29-87	.261	.294	.251	152	566	86	148	30	2	30	117	61	22	0	10	143	1	0	.481	.351
Anderson, Tim	R-R	6-1	185	6-23-93	.309	.319	.306	123	527	94	163	29	2	17	61	22	1	0	1	119	18	7	.469	.338
Burger, Jake	R-R	6-2	230	4-10-96	.263	.091	.333	15	38	5	10	3	1	1	3	4	0	0	0	15	0	0	.474	.333
Collins, Zack	L-R	6-3	220	2-6-95	.210	.176	.222	78	195	25	41	13	0	4	26	34	1	1	0	69	1	1	.338	.330
Eaton, Adam	L-L	5-9	180	12-6-88	.201	.156	.210	58	189	33	38	8	2	5	28	20	6	4	0	55	2	0	.344	.298
2-team total (25 Los Angeles)					.201	.178	.206	83	254	38	51	10	2	6	30	22	7	4	1	71	3	0	.327	.282
Engel, Adam	R-R	6-2	215	12-9-91	.252	.200	.282	39	123	21	31	9	0	7	18	11	5	0	1	31	7	1	.496	.336
Garcia, Leury	B-R	5-8	190	3-18-91	.267	.282	.261	126	415	60	111	22	4	5	54	41	4	9	5	97	6	2	.376	.335
Gonzalez, Luis	L-L	6-1	185	9-10-95	.250	.000	.286	6	8	2	2	2	0	0	0	3	0	0	0	2	0	0	.500	.455
Gonzalez, Romy	R-R	6-1	215	9-6-96	.250	.400	.182	10	32	4	8	3	0	0	2	1	0	0	0	11	0	0	.344	.273
Goodwin, Brian	L-R	6-0	205	11-2-90	.221	.136	.250	72	235	33	52	10	1	8	29	33	1	1	1	58	1	0	.374	.319
Grandal, Yasmani	B-R	6-2	225	11-8-88	.240	.266	.233	93	279	60	67	9	0	23	62	87	3	1	5	82	0	0	.520	.420
Hamilton, Billy	R-R	6-0	160	9-9-90	.220	.229	.215	71	127	23	28	8	3	2	11	4	0	3	1	47	9	0	.378	.242
Hernandez, Cesar	B-R	5-10	195	5-23-90	.232	.212	.239	53	194	24	45	4	0	3	15	21	1	0	1	45	1	1	.299	.309
2-team total (96 Cleveland)					.232	.215	.239	149	570	84	132	21	2	21	62	59	5	0	3	135	1	1	.386	.308
Jimenez, Eloy	R-R	6-4	240	11-27-96	.249	.170	.275	55	213	23	53	10	0	10	37	16	1	0	1	57	0	0	.437	.303
Lamb, Jake	L-R	6-3	215	10-9-90	.212	.333	.194	43	113	20	24	2	0	6	13	17	1	0	0	38	0	0	.389	.321
2-team total (12 Toronto)					.194	.208	.192	55	144	25	28	4	0	7	19	22	2	0	2	51	0	0	.368	.306
Madrigal, Nick	R-R	5-8	175	3-5-97	.305	.373	.277	54	200	30	61	10	4	2	21	11	3	0	1	17	1	2	.425	.349
Mendick, Danny	R-R	5-10	195	9-28-93	.220	.219	.220	71	164	14	36	5	0	2	20	18	2	1	1	42	0	1	.287	.303
Mercedes, Yermin	R-R	5-11	245	2-14-93	.271	.338	.246	68	240	26	65	9	1	7	37	20	1	0	1	46	0	1	.404	.328
Moncada, Yoan	B-R	6-2	225	5-27-95	.263	.252	.268	144	520	74	137	33	1	14	61	84	10	0	2	157	3	2	.412	.375
Robert, Luis	R-R	6-2	220	8-3-97	.338	.397	.321	68	275	42	93	22	1	13	43	14	5	0	2	61	6	1	.567	.378
Sheets, Gavin	L-L	6-5	230	4-23-96	.250	.111	.268	54	160	23	40	8	0	11	34	16	2	0	1	40	0	0	.506	.324
Vaughn, Andrew	R-R	6-0	215	4-3-98	.235	.269	.221	127	417	56	98	22	0	15	48	41	6	0	5	101	1	1	.396	.309
Williams, Nick	L-L	6-3	215	9-8-93	.000	--	.000	4	10	2	0	0	0	0	0	1	2	0	0	4	0	0	.000	.231
Zavala, Seby	R-R	5-11	205	8-28-93	.183	.125	.203	37	93	15	17	3	0	5	15	6	1	4	0	41	0	0	.376	.240

Pitching	B-T	HT	WT	DOB	W	L	ERA	G	GS	CG	SV	IP	H	R	ER	HR	BB	SO	AVG	vLH	vRH	K/9	BB/9
Bummer, Aaron	L-L	6-3	215	9-21-93	5	5	3.22	62	0	0	2	56	42	28	22	3	29	75	.202	.151	.230	11.98	4.63
Burdi, Zack	R-R	6-3	210	3-9-95	0	0	6.00	9	0	0	0	9	13	7	6	3	4	6	.351	.222	.474	6.00	4.00
2-team total (1 Baltimore)					0	0	5.40	7	0	0	0	10	13	7	6	3	5	7	.325	.211	.429	6.30	4.50
Burr, Ryan	R-R	6-4	220	5-28-94	2	1	2.45	34	1	0	0	37	28	11	10	3	21	33	.224	.246	.206	8.10	5.15
Cease, Dylan	R-R	6-2	195	12-28-95	13	7	3.91	32	32	1	0	166	139	77	72	20	68	226	.223	.226	.220	12.28	3.69
Crochet, Garrett	L-L	6-6	230	6-21-99	3	5	2.82	54	0	0	0	54	42	22	17	2	27	65	.213	.171	.236	10.77	4.47
Foster, Matt	R-R	6-0	215	1-27-95	2	1	6.00	37	0	0	1	39	43	27	26	9	13	40	.274	.286	.264	9.23	3.00
Fry, Jace	L-L	6-1	220	7-9-93	0	1	10.80	6	0	0	0	7	10	8	8	1	6	3	.417	.429	.412	4.05	8.10
Giolito, Lucas	R-R	6-6	245	7-14-94	11	9	3.53	31	31	1	0	179	145	74	70	27	52	201	.219	.221	.217	10.13	2.62
Gonzalez, Romy	R-R	6-1	215	9-6-96	0	0	0.00	1	0	0	0	0	0	0	0	0	0	1	.000	--	.000	27.00	0.00
Hendriks, Liam	R-R	6-0	235	2-10-89	8	3	2.54	69	0	0	38	71	45	23	20	11	7	113	.174	.133	.215	14.32	0.89
Heuer, Codi	R-R	6-5	200	7-3-96	4	1	5.12	40	0	0	0	39	45	22	22	5	10	39	.296	.328	.275	9.08	2.33
Keuchel, Dallas	L-L	6-2	205	1-1-88	9	9	5.28	32	30	0	0	162	189	105	95	25	59	95	.290	.304	.286	5.28	3.28
Kimbrel, Craig	R-R	6-0	215	5-28-88	2	2	5.09	24	0	0	1	23	18	13	13	5	10	36	.217	.250	.200	14.09	3.91
Kopech, Michael	R-R	6-3	210	4-30-96	4	3	3.50	44	4	0	0	69	54	27	27	9	24	103	.210	.176	.235	13.37	3.12
Lambert, Jimmy	R-R	6-2	190	11-18-94	1	1	6.23	4	3	0	0	13	16	9	9	3	6	10	.314	.300	.323	6.92	4.15
Lopez, Reynaldo	R-R	6-1	225	1-4-94	4	4	3.43	20	9	0	0	58	42	27	22	10	13	55	.205	.219	.193	8.58	2.03
Lynn, Lance	B-R	6-5	270	5-12-87	11	6	2.69	28	28	1	0	157	123	52	47	18	45	176	.209	.227	.192	10.09	2.58
Marshall, Evan	R-R	6-2	235	4-18-90	0	2	5.60	27	0	0	0	27	28	17	17	5	9	26	.277	.205	.323	8.56	2.96
McRae, Alex	R-R	6-2	220	4-6-93	0	0	4.50	2	0	0	0	2	3	1	1	0	1	1	.333	.400	.250	4.50	4.50
Mendick, Danny	R-R	5-10	195	9-28-93	0	0	0.00	1	0	0	1	1	0	0	0	0	1	.250	.000	.333	9.00	0.00
Mercedes, Yermin	R-R	5-11	245	2-14-93	0	0	9.00	1	0	0	0	1	3	1	1	0	2	0	.600	1.000	.500	0.00	18.00
Rodon, Carlos	L-L	6-3	245	12-10-92	13	5	2.37	24	24	1	0	133	91	39	35	13	36	185	.189	.240	.175	12.55	2.44
Ruiz, Jose	R-R	6-1	245	10-21-94	1	3	3.05	59	0	0	0	65	51	26	22	8	25	63	.210	.208	.211	8.72	3.46

Stiever, Jonathan	R-R	6-2	210	5-12-97	0	0	--	1	0	0	0	0	4	3	3	0	0	0	1.000	1.000	1.000	--	--
Tepera, Ryan	R-R	6-1	195	11-3-87	0	0	2.50	22	0	0	1	18	13	5	5	1	7	24	.197	.208	.190	12.00	3.50
Wright Jr., Mike	R-R	6-6	240	1-3-90	0	1	5.50	13	0	0	0	18	17	12	11	1	11	11	.254	.250	.256	5.50	5.50

Fielding

Catcher	PCT	G	PO	A	E	DP	PB
Collins	.994	73	611	29	4	1	3
Grandal	.989	80	688	22	8	2	7
Mercedes	1.000	2	2	0	0	0	
Zavala	.997	33	296	12	1	0	8

First Base	PCT	G	PO	A	E	DP
Abreu	.995	135	980	35	5	93
Collins	1.000	1	1	0	0	0
Grandal	1.000	8	30	2	0	2
Lamb	.833	2	4	1	1	0
Mercedes	.000	1	0	1	0	0
Sheets	.983	10	58	1	1	7
Vaughn	.987	15	71	4	1	3

Second Base	PCT	G	PO	A	E	DP
Garcia	.972	36	44	59	3	13
Gonzalez	.800	1	2	2	1	1
Hernandez	.975	53	65	127	5	30
Madrigal	.973	53	76	106	5	28
Mendick	.988	28	28	52	1	12
Vaughn	1.000	1	2	1	0	1
Mendick	1.000	28	18	43	0	3

Third Base	PCT	G	PO	A	E	DP
Abreu	.000	1	0	0	0	0
Burger	1.000	8	5	9	0	0
Garcia	.952	11	6	14	1	2
Gonzalez	1.000	4	4	2	0	0
Lamb	1.000	6	2	12	0	0
Mendick	1.000	4	0	2	0	0
Moncada	.953	138	90	236	16	28
Vaughn	1.000	2	0	1	0	0

Shortstop	PCT	G	PO	A	E	DP
Anderson	.977	122	152	270	10	59
Garcia	1.000	19	18	39	0	8
Gonzalez	1.000	1	1	0	0	0
Hernandez	.000	1	0	0	0	0

Outfield	PCT	G	PO	A	E	DP
Eaton	.961	56	97	2	4	2
Engel	.988	40	82	2	1	0
Garcia	.982	86	106	2	2	0
Gonzalez	1.000	5	4	1	0	0
Gonzalez	1.000	4	1	0	0	0
Goodwin	.985	76	126	2	2	0
Hamilton	1.000	67	79	1	0	0
Jimenez	.984	37	59	1	1	0
Lamb	1.000	25	25	0	0	0
Mendick	1.000	11	9	0	0	0
Robert	.976	67	159	3	4	1
Sheets	.941	17	16	0	1	0
Vaughn	.981	113	153	3	3	0
Williams	1.000	3	5	0	0	0

CHARLOTTE KNIGHTS — TRIPLE-A
TRIPLE-A EAST

Batting	B-T	HT	WT	DOB	AVG	vLH	vRH	G	AB	R	H	2B	3B	HR	RBI	BB	HBP	SH	SF	SO	SB	CS	SLG	OBP
Adolfo, Micker	R-R	6-4	225	9-11-96	.240	.233	.243	44	150	23	36	9	1	10	23	12	1	0	0	53	3	0	.513	.301
Beckham, Tim	R-R	6-0	215	1-27-90	.279	.277	.280	45	165	32	46	11	0	11	32	14	0	0	3	44	1	0	.545	.330
Booker, Joel	R-R	6-1	190	11-1-93	.100	.000	.200	8	20	1	2	1	0	0	0	0	0	1	0	9	0	0	.150	.100
Burger, Jake	R-R	6-2	230	4-10-96	.274	.312	.258	82	310	46	85	16	2	18	54	24	4	0	2	91	0	0	.513	.332
Collins, Zack	L-R	6-3	220	2-6-95	.143	.071	.190	9	35	5	5	0	0	3	5	3	0	0	0	13	0	0	.400	.211
Cruz, Johan	R-R	6-2	188	10-8-95	.125	.000	.250	2	8	0	1	1	0	0	0	0	0	0	0	2	0	0	.250	.125
DeCarlo, Joe	R-R	5-10	210	9-13-93	.182	.304	.048	16	44	6	8	0	0	0	1	7	0	0	0	16	0	0	.182	.294
Engel, Adam	R-R	6-2	215	12-9-91	.222	.250	.206	15	54	7	12	2	0	2	5	3	2	0	1	16	5	0	.370	.283
Forbes, Ti'Quan	R-R	6-4	225	8-26-96	.237	.268	.220	50	156	15	37	4	2	11	14	2	0	2	45	2	1	.340	.305
Gonzalez, Luis	L-L	6-1	185	9-10-95	.241	.262	.232	40	137	24	33	4	0	7	20	22	2	1	1	41	9	2	.423	.352
Gonzalez, Romy	R-R	6-1	215	9-6-96	.370	.250	.405	15	54	9	20	6	0	4	14	5	0	0	1	15	3	0	.704	.417
Goodwin, Brian	L-R	6-0	205	11-2-90	.244	.219	.259	24	86	12	21	4	0	3	11	9	0	0	0	31	2	2	.395	.316
Grandal, Yasmani	B-R	6-2	225	11-8-88	.273	.375	.214	7	22	3	6	1	0	1	1	2	1	0	0	8	0	0	.455	.360
Grullon, Deivy	R-R	5-11	240	2-17-96	.200	.111	.226	11	40	4	8	2	0	2	5	2	0	0	0	17	0	0	.400	.238
3-team total (21 Durham, 11 Syracuse)					.196	.205	.192	43	143	21	28	5	0	10	25	14	1	0	1	59	0	0	.441	.270
Hamilton, Billy	R-R	6-0	160	9-9-90	.158	.000	.214	6	19	2	3	1	0	0	0	2	0	0	0	8	1	0	.211	.238
Hernandez, Marco	L-R	6-0	210	9-6-92	.266	.310	.248	97	334	35	89	18	2	5	34	10	2	1	7	60	1	2	.377	.286
Jimenez, Eloy	R-R	6-4	240	11-27-96	.263	.250	.267	10	38	3	10	2	0	1	2	2	0	0	1	14	0	0	.395	.293
Lamb, Jake	L-R	6-3	215	10-9-90	.246	.333	.217	16	61	6	15	5	0	3	8	8	0	0	0	15	0	0	.475	.333
Mahtook, Mikie	R-R	6-2	220	11-30-89	.251	.229	.261	106	367	60	92	18	1	26	62	31	7	1	4	102	8	2	.518	.318
Mendick, Danny	R-R	5-10	195	9-28-93	.271	.185	.304	25	96	16	26	4	0	3	11	7	1	0	0	20	1	1	.406	.327
Mercedes, Yermin	R-R	5-11	245	2-14-93	.275	.259	.280	59	222	32	61	7	1	11	29	11	4	0	2	39	3	0	.464	.318
Nolan, Nate	R-R	6-1	210	10-11-94	.157	.173	.149	54	153	20	24	6	0	6	14	11	1	0	2	80	0	1	.314	.216
Perez, Carlos	R-R	5-11	205	9-10-96	.077	.250	.000	4	13	2	1	1	0	0	0	2	0	0	0	1	0	0	.154	.200
Remillard, Zach	R-R	6-2	185	2-21-94	.193	.250	.169	82	269	40	52	8	0	12	23	27	7	2	1	85	10	3	.357	.283
Reynolds, Matt	R-R	6-1	200	12-3-90	.269	.275	.266	93	309	40	83	20	2	5	35	51	3	0	4	93	5	3	.395	.373
Rivera, Laz	R-R	6-1	185	9-20-94	.317	.417	.292	18	60	7	19	4	0	2	10	3	0	0	2	9	5	1	.483	.369
Robert, Luis	R-R	6-2	220	8-3-97	.276	.286	.273	8	29	4	8	1	0	1	3	5	2	0	0	9	2	0	.414	.417
Rutherford, Blake	L-R	6-3	205	5-2-97	.250	.221	.262	115	448	59	112	30	3	11	54	21	3	0	4	119	4	1	.404	.286
Sheets, Gavin	L-L	6-5	230	4-23-96	.295	.262	.309	60	227	36	67	15	0	16	46	25	0	0	2	55	1	1	.507	.362
Skoug, Evan	L-R	5-11	200	10-21-95	.143	.000	.167	3	7	1	1	1	0	0	0	0	0	0	0	2	0	0	.286	.143
Tejada, Ruben	R-R	5-11	200	10-27-89	.250	.308	.200	8	28	1	7	0	0	1	5	2	0	0	0	12	0	0	.357	.300
2-team total (72 Lehigh Valley)					.233	.284	.215	80	253	27	59	5	1	1	20	34	6	0	1	58	1	3	.273	.337
Williams, Nick	L-L	6-3	215	9-8-93	.262	.175	.302	39	126	15	33	7	1	4	13	7	3	1	1	36	4	0	.429	.314
Zavala, Seby	R-R	5-11	205	8-28-93	.168	.192	.155	43	155	19	26	5	0	8	20	20	1	0	3	75	0	1	.355	.263

Pitching	B-T	HT	WT	DOB	W	L	ERA	G	GS	CG	SV	IP	H	R	ER	HR	BB	SO	AVG	vLH	vRH	K/9	BB/9
Banks, Tanner	R-L	6-1	210	10-24-91	3	3	4.53	25	5	0	0	60	69	33	30	10	13	70	.289	.246	.305	10.56	1.96
Burdi, Zack	R-R	6-3	230	3-9-95	0	2	7.30	23	0	0	2	25	22	23	20	8	15	35	.227	.325	.158	12.77	5.47
2-team total (4 Norfolk)					0	2	6.59	27	0	0	2	29	24	24	21	9	17	45	.216	.304	.154	14.13	5.34
Burr, Ryan	R-R	6-4	220	5-28-94	1	2	4.60	15	0	0	3	16	17	11	8	3	7	14	.262	.346	.205	8.04	4.02
Carter, Will	L-R	6-3	195	1-18-93	3	3	5.02	37	2	0	1	38	40	27	21	1	24	45	.274	.365	.223	10.75	5.73
Crick, Kyle	L-R	6-4	225	11-30-92	2	0	0.87	8	0	0	0	10	4	1	1	0	3	15	.121	.200	.087	13.06	2.61
DeCarlo, Joe	R-R	5-10	210	9-13-93	0	0	0.00	1	0	0	0	1	3	6	0	1	3	0	.500	.500	.500	0.00	40.50
Dominguez, Johan	R-R	6-4	190	1-18-96	0	1	16.50	2	2	0	0	6	12	12	11	3	1	4	.400	.474	.273	6.00	1.50
Dopico, Danny	R-R	6-3	205	12-18-93	0	3	5.95	21	0	0	0	20	12	16	13	1	27	21	.179	.179	.179	9.61	12.36

Player	T	HT	WT	DOB	W	L	ERA	G	GS	CG	SV	IP	H	R	ER	HR	BB	SO	AVG	vLH	vRH	K/9	BB/9
Edwards Jr., Carl	R-R	6-3	170	9-3-91	0	0	2.00	10	0	0	0	9	4	2	2	0	3	15	.129	.143	.118	15.00	3.00
3-team total (7 Buffalo, 1 Gwinnett)					1	0	2.65	18	0	0	3	17	9	5	5	2	4	26	.150	.148	.152	13.76	2.12
Foster, Matt	R-R	6-0	215	1-27-95	0	2	4.30	14	0	0	0	15	14	7	7	2	2	23	.241	.185	.290	14.11	1.23
Fry, Jace	L-L	6-1	220	7-9-93	1	4	2.93	34	1	0	2	40	22	19	13	3	20	60	.158	.237	.129	13.50	4.50
Gomez, Ofreidy	R-R	6-3	230	7-6-95	0	1	8.20	16	0	0	0	19	20	17	17	2	13	17	.282	.300	.275	8.20	6.27
Guerrero, Tayron	R-R	6-8	225	1-9-91	1	0	6.63	18	1	0	0	19	30	16	14	2	12	25	.361	.407	.339	11.84	5.68
Johnson, Tyler	R-R	6-3	210	8-21-95	0	1	12.41	13	0	0	0	12	21	23	17	2	16	17	.362	.421	.333	12.41	11.68
Kubat, Kyle	L-L	6-1	195	12-4-92	2	3	5.33	24	5	0	0	52	59	33	31	9	16	50	.280	.274	.283	8.60	2.75
Lambert, Jimmy	R-R	6-2	190	11-18-94	3	3	4.76	19	19	0	0	64	49	38	34	11	32	82	.210	.206	.214	11.47	4.48
Lindgren, Jacob	R-L	5-11	195	3-12-93	0	0	10.13	8	0	0	0	8	5	12	9	1	15	8	.192	.250	.182	9.00	16.88
Lopez, Reynaldo	R-R	6-1	225	1-4-94	1	6	7.62	10	10	0	0	39	53	33	33	6	21	50	.327	.339	.321	11.54	4.85
Marshall, Evan	R-R	6-2	235	4-18-90	0	0	2.08	5	0	0	0	4	4	1	1	0	3	6	.286	.375	.167	12.46	6.23
McCarthy, Kevin	R-R	6-3	210	2-22-92	0	0	7.04	7	0	0	0	8	8	6	6	2	3	6	.276	.286	.267	7.04	3.52
2-team total (28 Worcester)					1	2	7.12	35	2	0	1	43	62	37	34	7	9	41	.330	.322	.337	8.58	1.88
McClure, Kade	R-R	6-7	220	2-12-96	2	3	6.81	9	9	0	0	37	46	29	28	6	15	36	.315	.370	.246	8.76	3.65
McRae, Alex	R-R	6-2	220	4-6-93	2	9	5.38	26	18	0	0	89	103	54	53	12	42	86	.290	.325	.265	8.73	4.26
Medeiros, Kodi	L-L	6-1	195	5-25-96	0	1	5.52	30	0	0	0	29	24	18	18	5	25	37	.218	.190	.235	11.35	7.67
Parke, John	L-L	6-4	220	1-3-95	2	3	3.62	11	11	0	0	55	46	25	22	7	16	38	.225	.146	.250	6.26	2.63
Paulino, Felix	R-R	6-1	185	3-24-95	1	2	13.21	5	5	0	0	16	22	23	23	5	12	17	.310	.282	.344	9.77	6.89
Ramsey, Lane	R-R	6-9	245	7-16-96	1	5	6.35	21	2	0	0	23	25	16	16	2	13	25	.275	.313	.254	9.93	5.16
Reynolds, Matt	R-R	6-1	200	12-3-90	0	0	5.40	4	0	0	0	3	6	2	2	0	1	1	.375	.167	.500	2.70	2.70
Roper, Kaleb	R-R	6-0	193	11-22-95	0	0	4.50	3	0	0	0	4	2	4	2	0	4	6	.143	.143	.143	13.50	9.00
Sadzeck, Connor	R-R	6-7	235	10-1-91	2	2	5.86	23	0	0	1	28	24	18	18	4	20	28	.238	.302	.190	9.11	6.51
2-team total (17 Nashville)					3	3	4.84	40	0	0	1	45	39	25	24	5	28	49	.235	.299	.180	9.87	5.64
Sampson, Keyvius	R-R	6-2	225	1-6-91	0	1	7.20	6	0	0	0	5	5	5	4	2	3	5	.250	.000	.313	9.00	5.40
Schryver, Hunter	L-L	6-1	205	4-3-95	1	0	4.98	40	0	0	1	43	42	26	24	7	28	48	.249	.242	.252	9.97	5.82
Severino, Anderson	L-L	5-10	190	9-17-94	0	1	0.64	13	0	0	0	14	9	1	1	0	7	20	.176	.179	.174	12.86	4.50
Sousa, Bennett	L-L	6-3	220	4-6-95	4	2	3.97	21	0	0	1	23	23	12	10	3	5	33	.258	.154	.340	13.10	1.99
Stiever, Jonathan	R-R	6-2	210	5-12-97	5	5	5.84	17	17	0	0	74	80	51	48	13	28	88	.265	.236	.286	10.70	3.41
Tago, Peter	R-R	6-3	205	7-5-92	2	0	0.00	9	0	0	0	11	3	0	0	0	4	20	.086	.154	.045	15.88	3.18
Tomshaw, Matt	R-L	6-1	210	12-17-88	0	4	7.45	11	5	0	0	39	35	34	32	16	8	36	.236	.256	.229	8.38	1.86
2-team total (3 Rochester)					0	6	7.86	14	8	0	0	53	52	48	46	23	10	46	.251	.216	.271	7.86	1.71
Turley, Nik	L-L	6-4	230	9-11-89	1	4	5.02	43	0	0	5	43	28	26	24	5	21	60	.179	.224	.159	12.56	4.40
Wright Jr., Mike	R-R	6-6	240	1-3-90	7	5	3.40	16	16	0	0	95	71	38	36	11	29	90	.202	.193	.209	8.50	2.74

Fielding

Catcher

Player	PCT	G	PO	A	E	DP	PB
Collins	1.000	9	80	8	0	2	3
DeCarlo	1.000	1	6	0	0	0	0
Grandal	1.000	5	50	4	0	0	1
Grullon	.980	10	94	2	2	1	0
Mercedes	.982	18	159	6	3	0	9
Nolan	.996	53	455	21	2	2	6
Perez	1.000	3	34	2	0	0	1
Skoug	1.000	3	17	0	0	0	0
Zavala	.995	35	337	28	2	1	7

First Base

Player	PCT	G	PO	A	E	DP
Beckham	1.000	10	79	6	0	7
DeCarlo	.977	12	78	6	2	10
Forbes	.991	32	202	15	2	15
Grandal	1.000	2	3	0	0	0
Mahtook	.941	2	16	0	1	1
Mendick	1.000	3	23	3	0	0
Mercedes	.993	19	146	3	1	7
Remillard	1.000	24	171	13	0	16
Sheets	.985	35	246	18	4	25
Zavala	1.000	3	26	0	0	2

Second Base

Player	PCT	G	PO	A	E	DP
Beckham	1.000	2	3	1	0	0
Burger	.895	5	7	10	2	2
DeCarlo	1.000	1	0	5	0	0
Forbes	1.000	4	6	5	0	2
Gonzalez	1.000	3	2	6	0	0
Hernandez	.979	86	97	177	6	43
Mendick	1.000	2	2	1	0	0
Remillard	1.000	3	4	3	0	4
Reynolds	.971	26	33	66	3	9
Rivera	.857	1	3	3	1	2
Tejada	.889	3	3	5	1	1

Third Base

Player	PCT	G	PO	A	E	DP
Beckham	1.000	12	4	24	0	1
Burger	.933	65	31	108	10	9
Cruz	1.000	2	3	1	0	0
DeCarlo	.750	3	2	1	1	0
Forbes	.960	12	10	14	1	2
Gonzalez	1.000	2	3	1	0	0
Hernandez	1.000	2	3	2	0	1
Lamb	.923	5	6	6	1	0
Mendick	1.000	3	4	6	0	1
Mercedes	.000	1	0	0	0	0
Remillard	.905	17	9	29	4	5
Rivera	.864	16	8	30	6	2

Shortstop

Player	PCT	G	PO	A	E	DP
Beckham	.919	16	17	40	5	10
Gonzalez	.914	10	11	21	3	5
Hernandez	1.000	1	1	1	0	0
Mendick	.976	12	10	31	1	5
Remillard	.990	30	29	68	1	13
Reynolds	.959	62	66	192	11	36
Tejada	1.000	5	1	9	0	0

Outfield

Player	PCT	G	PO	A	E	DP
Adolfo	.971	40	64	3	2	0
Booker	1.000	8	10	0	0	0
Engel	.966	13	28	0	1	0
Gonzalez	.978	35	44	1	1	0
Goodwin	1.000	19	36	0	0	0
Hamilton	1.000	4	5	0	0	0
Jimenez	.929	8	13	0	1	0
Lamb	1.000	10	16	0	0	0
Mahtook	.975	96	155	2	4	0
Mendick	1.000	5	4	0	0	0
Remillard	.895	15	17	0	2	0
Reynolds	--	1	0	0	0	0
Robert	1.000	5	7	0	0	0
Rutherford	.987	104	150	6	2	0
Sheets	.930	26	39	1	3	0
Williams	.977	27	41	2	1	0

BIRMINGHAM BARONS — DOUBLE-A

DOUBLE-A SOUTH

Batting

Player	B-T	HT	WT	DOB	AVG	vLH	vRH	G	AB	R	H	2B	3B	HR	RBI	BB	HBP	SH	SF	SO	SB	CS	SLG	OBP
Adolfo, Micker	R-R	6-4	225	9-11-96	.249	.255	.247	57	217	33	54	10	0	15	46	19	4	0	2	85	1	0	.525	.318
Booker, Joel	R-R	6-1	190	11-1-93	.232	.268	.221	53	177	25	41	7	0	5	15	4	3	0	2	64	15	2	.356	.258
Cespedes, Yoelqui	R-R	5-9	205	9-24-97	.298	.375	.282	27	94	14	28	3	2	1	7	3	3	0	0	27	8	4	.404	.340
Dawkins, Ian	R-R	5-11	205	7-6-95	.249	.234	.253	59	209	25	52	7	2	5	28	13	0	0	0	57	11	1	.373	.293
DeCarlo, Joe	R-R	5-10	210	9-13-93	.203	.133	.227	36	118	14	24	3	0	3	10	13	1	0	1	33	0	0	.305	.286
Dedelow, Craig	L-R	6-4	210	11-15-94	.224	.171	.239	107	366	51	82	20	1	17	56	46	4	1	3	138	3	1	.423	.315
Fernandez, Xavier	R-R	5-11	245	7-15-95	.282	.289	.280	58	195	27	55	5	0	9	29	21	2	0	3	44	1	0	.446	.353
Fisher, Jameson	L-R	6-2	210	12-18-93	.287	.250	.295	88	328	53	94	18	2	12	47	35	3	0	2	84	2	0	.463	.359

	B-T	HT	WT	DOB	AVG	vLH	vRH	G	AB	R	H	2B	3B	HR	RBI	BB	HBP	SH	SF	SO	SB	CS	SLG	OBP
Forbes, Ti'Quan	R-R	6-4	225	8-26-96	.299	.313	.296	40	147	25	44	9	1	4	17	8	5	0	0	45	4	0	.456	.356
Gonzalez, Romy	R-R	6-1	215	9-6-96	.267	.290	.261	78	303	52	81	11	0	20	47	38	3	0	0	97	21	6	.502	.355
Grandal, Yasmani	B-R	6-2	225	11-8-88	.364	1.000	.300	4	11	2	4	0	0	0	2	1	0	0	1	3	0	0	.364	.385
Granite, Zack	L-L	6-1	185	9-17-92	.226	.094	.275	51	195	33	44	7	3	5	24	32	2	1	2	49	7	4	.369	.338
Muno, JJ	L-R	6-0	190	12-21-93	.210	.172	.217	63	186	29	39	5	2	6	26	19	17	2	1	64	14	4	.355	.336
Neslony, Tyler	L-R	6-1	190	2-13-94	.355	.462	.326	38	121	24	43	16	1	7	28	19	1	0	1	31	1	0	.678	.444
2-team total (19 Mississippi)					.295	.341	.280	57	176	30	52	18	1	8	32	26	2	0	1	52	1	1	.545	.390
Perez, Carlos	R-R	5-11	205	9-10-96	.264	.239	.271	107	409	46	108	22	1	13	59	25	5	0	2	45	1	0	.418	.313
Remillard, Zach	R-R	6-2	185	2-21-94	.295	.357	.267	13	44	13	13	2	1	1	7	9	5	0	1	7	4	1	.455	.458
Rivera, Laz	R-R	6-1	185	9-20-94	.259	.227	.272	47	158	27	41	7	1	5	25	9	6	0	1	41	9	3	.411	.322
Rodriguez, Jose	R-R	5-11	175	5-13-01	.214	--	.214	4	14	2	3	1	0	0	0	0	0	0	0	2	0	1	.286	.214
Roman, Mitch	R-R	6-0	185	3-22-95	.206	.246	.191	70	218	29	45	6	1	1	18	28	2	1	1	79	15	2	.257	.301
Rusconi, Jagger	B-R	5-11	165	7-18-96	.308	.000	.320	8	26	6	8	1	0	0	4	1	0	0	6	0	0	.346	.333
Sanchez, Yolbert	R-R	5-11	176	3-3-97	.343	.348	.342	39	143	15	49	6	0	4	13	5	1	6	0	16	3	0	.469	.369
Sosa, Lenyn	R-R	6-0	180	1-25-00	.214	.286	.198	33	117	10	25	5	0	1	7	2	2	0	0	28	0	1	.282	.240
Troutwine, Gunnar	R-R	6-1	220	3-6-96	.318	.333	.313	6	22	2	7	1	0	0	1	1	0	0	0	5	0	0	.364	.348

Pitching	B-T	HT	WT	DOB	W	L	ERA	G	GS	CG	SV	IP	H	R	ER	HR	BB	SO	AVG	vLH	vRH	K/9	BB/9
Arobio, Vince	R-R	5-11	185	3-31-95	0	0	1.93	4	0	0	0	5	3	1	1	0	1	5	.176	.222	.125	9.64	1.93
Battenfield, Blake	R-R	6-3	225	8-22-94	7	8	4.75	23	20	0	0	106	128	70	56	15	21	79	.293	.297	.290	6.71	1.78
Bilous, Jason	R-R	6-2	185	8-11-97	2	7	6.51	17	17	0	0	65	71	48	47	8	30	80	.278	.220	.311	11.08	4.15
Cronin, Declan	R-R	6-4	225	9-24-97	2	0	2.16	7	0	0	0	8	7	3	2	0	3	6	.226	.286	.176	6.48	3.24
Dominguez, Johan	R-R	6-4	190	1-18-96	2	2	4.33	7	7	0	0	35	37	17	17	5	8	40	.278	.323	.235	10.19	2.04
Elliott, Jake	R-R	6-7	230	3-22-95	5	2	3.72	30	0	0	0	56	48	26	23	8	21	48	.230	.165	.269	7.76	3.40
Freeman, Caleb	R-R	6-1	195	2-23-98	0	1	2.70	14	0	0	3	17	15	5	5	2	5	22	.231	.200	.250	11.88	2.70
Glowicki, Brian	R-R	5-11	190	10-19-94	0	1	4.32	5	0	0	1	8	7	4	4	1	3	6	.233	.214	.250	6.48	3.24
Gomez, Ofreidy	R-R	6-3	230	7-6-95	5	2	3.13	15	5	0	2	32	14	11	11	1	19	42	.132	.163	.111	11.94	5.40
Hansen, Alec	R-R	6-8	260	10-10-94	1	2	6.04	22	0	0	0	22	14	25	15	0	37	43	.179	.267	.125	17.33	14.91
Kincanon, Will	L-R	6-3	215	10-27-95	0	0	0.00	4	0	0	0	4	1	0	0	0	1	4	.083	.250	.000	9.00	2.25
Kubat, Kyle	L-L	6-1	195	12-4-92	1	0	2.25	3	0	0	1	8	7	4	2	0	1	11	.226	.167	.263	12.38	1.13
Ledo, Luis	R-R	6-4	240	5-28-95	4	1	4.17	34	0	0	4	41	35	20	19	2	20	52	.229	.224	.232	11.41	4.39
Martin, Davis	L-R	6-2	200	1-4-97	1	2	3.54	6	6	0	0	20	19	8	8	2	8	20	.250	.294	.214	8.85	3.54
McClure, Kade	R-R	6-7	230	2-12-96	2	4	3.82	15	15	0	0	69	63	30	29	10	20	77	.243	.273	.221	10.14	2.63
Muckenhirn, Zach	L-L	6-0	205	2-27-95	3	1	1.77	30	0	0	1	41	30	8	8	3	19	42	.204	.192	.211	9.30	4.20
Muno, JJ	L-R	6-0	190	12-21-93	0	0	0.00	1	0	0	0	2	2	0	0	0	0	1	.286	.000	.667	4.50	0.00
Olson, J.B.	L-R	6-2	195	2-15-95	4	2	6.28	30	0	0	0	43	56	32	30	5	7	33	.313	.276	.340	6.91	1.47
Parke, John	L-L	6-4	220	1-3-95	3	4	4.66	14	12	1	0	58	57	34	30	5	21	48	.249	.232	.256	7.45	3.26
Paulino, Felix	R-R	6-1	185	3-24-95	2	1	4.05	15	0	0	1	27	21	13	12	5	7	28	.214	.256	.182	9.45	2.36
Perez, Andrew	L-L	6-2	215	7-25-97	2	1	3.50	31	0	0	1	44	40	17	17	6	12	59	.238	.241	.237	12.16	2.47
Pilkington, Konnor	L-L	6-3	240	9-12-97	4	4	3.48	14	14	0	0	62	36	24	24	9	21	71	.173	.149	.180	10.31	3.05
Ramsey, Lane	R-R	6-9	245	7-16-96	1	0	3.21	13	0	0	4	14	12	6	5	0	7	18	.222	.154	.286	11.57	4.50
Severino, Anderson	L-L	5-10	190	9-17-94	1	2	3.13	27	0	0	4	32	19	14	11	0	25	33	.178	.226	.158	9.38	7.11
Silven, Yoelvin	R-R	6-1	176	6-26-99	0	0	7.71	4	0	0	0	5	8	4	4	0	2	3	.364	.300	.417	5.79	3.86
Sousa, Bennett	L-L	6-3	220	4-6-95	0	1	3.28	20	0	0	3	25	14	11	9	4	15	38	.159	.111	.171	13.86	5.47
Tago, Peter	R-R	6-3	205	7-5-92	2	1	3.97	26	1	0	0	45	42	21	20	4	18	50	.253	.306	.211	9.93	3.57
Vargas, Emilio	R-R	6-3	220	8-12-96	7	4	2.90	21	15	0	0	84	69	36	27	9	28	99	.225	.241	.210	10.65	3.01
Varnell, Taylor	L-L	6-1	190	5-5-95	1	3	5.68	6	6	0	0	19	22	12	12	2	8	19	.293	.368	.268	9.00	3.79

Fielding

Catcher	PCT	G	PO	A	E	DP	PB
DeCarlo	.000	1	0	0	0	0	0
Fernandez	.985	26	248	18	4	2	5
Grandal	1.000	1	4	0	0	0	0
Perez	.995	88	755	69	4	4	3
Troutwine	1.000	6	60	6	0	1	0

First Base	PCT	G	PO	A	E	DP
DeCarlo	1.000	18	108	7	0	8
Fernandez	1.000	8	52	3	0	2
Fisher	.989	68	508	28	6	43
Forbes	1.000	16	88	3	0	12
Perez	.968	9	58	3	2	8
Remillard	1.000	2	19	0	0	2

Second Base	PCT	G	PO	A	E	DP
Forbes	1.000	5	8	8	0	2
Gonzalez	.951	10	16	23	2	5
Muno	1.000	16	35	41	0	8

Remillard	1.000	5	12	12	0	3
Rivera	.981	14	22	29	1	13
Roman	.969	39	45	78	4	16
Rusconi	.955	6	7	14	1	3
Sanchez	.986	19	27	41	1	7
Sosa	1.000	9	15	17	0	2

Third Base	PCT	G	PO	A	E	DP
DeCarlo	.885	15	6	17	3	2
Forbes	.930	17	11	29	3	3
Gonzalez	1.000	3	1	3	0	2
Muno	.885	29	19	50	9	5
Rivera	.944	24	12	55	4	4
Roman	.855	26	15	38	9	6
Sanchez	1.000	3	1	4	0	0
Sosa	.833	4	2	3	1	1

Shortstop	PCT	G	PO	A	E	DP
Gonzalez	.946	61	73	139	12	22

Muno	.975	10	15	24	1	7
Remillard	.950	5	8	11	1	6
Rivera	.929	4	3	10	1	2
Rodriguez	1.000	4	6	4	0	1
Roman	1.000	1	0	2	0	0
Sanchez	.956	16	22	43	3	4
Sosa	.949	20	18	38	3	3

Outfield	PCT	G	PO	A	E	DP
Adolfo	.944	39	65	3	4	0
Booker	.976	51	115	5	3	0
Cespedes	.972	26	67	3	2	0
Dawkins	.991	58	108	0	1	0
Dedelow	.982	100	156	10	3	1
Granite	.987	47	73	2	1	1
Muno	1.000	3	8	0	0	0
Neslony	.982	30	52	2	1	0
Roman	--	1	0	0	0	0
Rusconi	1.000	2	1	0	0	0

WINSTON-SALEM DASH
HIGH-A EAST

HIGH CLASS A

Batting	B-T	HT	WT	DOB	AVG	vLH	vRH	G	AB	R	H	2B	3B	HR	RBI	BB	HBP	SH	SF	SO	SB	CS	SLG	OBP
Bossard, Brandon	R-R	6-1	185	6-10-97	.197	.133	.216	26	66	7	13	3	1	0	4	11	1	1	1	31	1	0	.273	.316
Burks, Jeremiah	R-R	6-2	215	1-8-97	.224	.222	.224	20	76	4	17	1	1	1	10	5	1	0	0	27	1	2	.303	.280

CHICAGO WHITE SOX

Name	B-T	HT	WT	DOB	AVG	vLH	vRH	G	AB	R	H	2B	3B	HR	RBI	BB	HBP	SH	SF	SO	SB	CS	OBP	SLG
Bush, Bryce	R-R	6-0	200	12-14-99	.147	.250	.115	8	34	3	5	0	0	1	2	4	0	0	0	13	2	2	.235	.237
Cespedes, Yoelqui	R-R	5-9	205	9-24-97	.278	.313	.271	45	176	34	49	17	0	7	20	13	8	2	0	56	10	2	.494	.355
Cruz, Johan	R-R	6-2	188	10-8-95	.221	.217	.222	39	122	15	27	6	0	3	13	14	0	0	3	41	0	0	.344	.295
Curbelo, Luis	R-R	6-3	185	11-10-97	.223	.258	.213	109	403	59	90	27	2	22	66	34	4	0	1	152	2	1	.464	.290
Dawkins, Ian	R-R	5-11	205	7-6-95	.246	.179	.267	28	114	13	28	2	1	3	14	10	2	0	1	23	3	0	.360	.315
Destino, Alex	L-L	6-2	215	10-24-95	.231	.230	.231	105	386	66	89	15	3	21	60	50	4	0	3	131	1	0	.448	.323
Duenez, Samir	L-R	6-1	230	6-11-96	.218	.150	.230	39	133	13	29	4	0	6	18	15	1	0	0	41	1	1	.383	.302
Ellis, Duke	L-L	6-2	180	1-16-98	.200	.167	.213	73	260	30	52	8	0	4	18	23	4	1	1	77	23	4	.277	.274
Fernandez, Xavier	R-R	5-11	245	7-15-95	.214	.250	.200	4	14	3	3	0	0	1	2	1	1	0	0	4	0	0	.429	.313
Gill, AJ	R-R	6-2	220	4-15-98	.189	.200	.186	29	90	9	17	3	0	3	8	11	3	0	0	53	0	0	.322	.298
Jimenez, Eloy	R-R	6-4	240	11-27-96	.429	.500	.400	2	7	2	3	0	0	1	2	1	0	0	0	0	0	0	.857	.500
Lartigue, Henri	B-R	6-0	205	2-24-95	.118	.167	.091	7	17	2	2	1	0	0	1	7	1	0	0	5	0	0	.176	.400
Leal, Lazaro	R-R	6-2	210	1-30-97	.225	.163	.248	62	182	17	41	8	0	4	20	15	4	0	0	43	1	1	.335	.299
Mendoza, Harvin	L-L	6-2	185	2-18-99	.246	.220	.258	40	134	15	33	5	0	2	16	12	4	0	1	21	2	0	.328	.325
Mieses, Luis	L-L	6-3	180	5-31-00	.236	.224	.240	58	220	30	52	19	2	9	33	11	2	0	1	48	0	1	.464	.278
Millwee, Daniel	R-R	5-10	205	8-2-95	.182	.000	.235	8	22	5	4	0	0	1	1	4	2	0	0	12	1	0	.318	.357
Moniot, Travis	R-R	6-1	190	6-9-97	.162	.103	.179	61	173	26	28	7	0	7	23	30	3	1	1	63	9	2	.324	.295
Osik, Tyler	R-R	5-10	203	11-15-96	.165	.200	.153	24	79	9	13	4	0	1	7	10	2	0	0	23	1	0	.253	.275
Reese, E.P.	L-R	5-10	175	3-4-98	.100	.000	.111	3	10	0	1	0	0	0	0	1	0	0	0	3	0	0	.100	.182
Robert, Luis	R-R	6-2	220	8-3-97	.250	.000	.300	4	12	1	3	1	0	0	3	1	0	0	0	3	0	0	.333	.308
Rodriguez, Jose	R-R	5-11	175	5-13-01	.361	.367	.360	29	119	19	43	4	1	5	19	5	0	0	2	13	10	5	.538	.381
Rusconi, Jagger	B-R	5-11	165	7-18-96	.260	.167	.273	26	100	19	26	5	2	1	12	8	3	0	2	39	0	0	.380	.327
Sanchez, Kleyder	R-R	5-10	170	12-13-99	.167	.000	.333	6	12	2	2	1	0	0	0	0	0	0	0	7	0	0	.250	.167
Sanchez, Yolbert	R-R	5-11	176	3-3-97	.286	.286	.286	60	217	28	62	7	0	5	29	18	0	4	0	33	2	1	.387	.340
Skoug, Evan	L-R	5-11	200	10-21-95	.175	.056	.191	49	154	18	27	6	1	7	19	22	4	0	1	48	0	1	.364	.293
Sosa, Lenyn	R-R	6-0	180	1-25-00	.290	.282	.293	82	334	45	97	19	1	10	49	14	2	0	2	77	3	4	.443	.321
Tatum, Terrell	L-L	6-0	167	7-27-99	.200	--	.200	4	10	4	2	0	0	0	2	4	0	0	1	6	4	0	.200	.400
Troutwine, Gunnar	R-R	6-1	220	3-6-96	.272	.405	.229	47	147	27	40	9	0	5	18	26	3	0	1	45	0	0	.435	.390
Weaver, Caberea	R-R	6-3	180	12-1-99	.177	.200	.170	19	62	6	11	1	1	1	7	1	1	1	1	29	4	1	.274	.200

Pitching

Name	B-T	HT	WT	DOB	W	L	ERA	G	GS	CG	SV	IP	H	R	ER	HR	BB	SO	AVG	vLH	vRH	K/9	BB/9
Aiello, Vincenzo	R-R	6-2	220	8-6-94	0	0	3.00	4	0	0	1	6	3	2	2	0	5	5	.150	.154	.143	7.50	7.50
Arobio, Vince	R-R	5-11	185	3-31-95	0	0	6.48	9	0	0	0	8	5	6	6	0	10		.172	.063	.308	10.80	6.48
Biasi, Sal	R-R	5-11	205	9-30-95	0	1	6.56	19	0	0	0	23	23	19	17	6	15	22	.258	.243	.269	8.49	5.79
Bilous, Jason	R-R	6-2	185	8-11-97	1	1	2.45	3	3	0	0	15	11	6	4	0	2	26	.208	.133	.304	15.95	1.23
Bradford, Cooper	R-R	5-11	180	4-13-98	3	4	7.93	34	2	0	1	48	61	44	42	5	27	47	.308	.305	.310	8.87	5.10
Broadway, Taylor	R-R	5-11	205	4-8-97	0	0	3.00	6	1	0	0	6	4	3	2	0	1	6	.167	.083	.250	9.00	1.50
Burke, Jeremiah	R-R	6-2	195	5-16-98	1	3	3.18	10	9	0	1	34	27	16	12	2	9	28	.213	.261	.185	7.41	2.38
Butler, Hansen	R-R	5-11	180	10-30-95	0	0	11.57	3	0	0	0	5	3	3	0	4	1		.500	.250	.667	3.86	15.43
Carranza, Isaiah	R-R	6-5	180	3-2-97	1	7	6.25	15	8	0	0	45	52	35	31	5	23	37	.283	.316	.259	7.46	4.63
Cronin, Declan	R-R	6-4	225	9-24-97	3	2	5.08	28	0	0	0	39	33	23	22	4	19	37	.226	.260	.208	8.54	4.38
Cruz, Johan	R-R	6-2	188	10-8-95	0	0	0.00	1	0	0	0	1	2	0	0	0	1		.500	.333	1.000	9.00	0.00
Dominguez, Johan	R-R	6-4	190	1-18-96	3	6	4.80	15	15	0	0	66	58	36	35	8	17	74	.231	.200	.248	10.14	2.33
Folman, Kevin	R-R	6-2	215	10-23-94	0	3	8.74	11	4	0	0	23	34	25	22	5	7	26	.347	.324	.359	10.32	2.78
Freeman, Caleb	R-R	6-1	195	2-23-98	2	2	3.62	25	0	0	0	27	22	13	11	5	14	33	.218	.162	.250	10.87	4.61
Glowicki, Brian	R-R	5-11	190	10-19-94	1	1	4.55	23	0	0	0	30	29	16	15	2	8	55	.254	.349	.197	16.69	2.43
Horn, Bailey	L-L	6-2	210	1-15-98	1	1	13.09	6	4	0	0	11	12	16	16	3	11	13	.273	.250	.278	10.64	9.00
Jeans, Trey	L-L	5-10	195	1-31-96	1	1	5.94	29	0	0	0	47	48	35	31	7	25	64	.257	.254	.258	12.26	4.79
Johnson, Tyler	R-R	6-3	210	8-21-95	0	0	0.00	1	0	0	0	1	0	0	0	0	1		.000	--	.000	9.00	9.00
Leal, Lazaro	R-R	6-2	210	1-30-97	0	0	20.25	3	0	0	0	3	7	6	6	2	3	0	.467	.625	.286	0.00	10.13
Madrigal, Ty	L-L	6-0	190	3-5-97	0	1	6.60	8	0	0	0	15	17	12	11	1	12	23	.279	.148	.382	13.80	7.20
Martin, Davis	L-R	6-2	200	1-4-97	3	5	5.32	17	17	0	0	68	80	47	40	9	26	78	.297	.271	.312	10.37	3.46
Mejia, Dilmer	L-L	5-11	160	7-9-97	0	1	27.00	1	0	0	0	1	5	4	4	0	1	1	.625	.500	.750	6.75	6.75
Metzdorf, Dan	L-L	5-10	165	5-28-96	4	6	5.98	23	12	0	0	81	90	57	54	11	36	84	.287	.198	.329	9.30	3.98
Mikel, Jordan	R-R	6-5	190	3-24-99	1	1	8.53	9	0	0	0	13	20	15	12		6	17	.339	.296	.375	12.08	4.26
Milto, Pauly	R-R	6-3	245	3-6-97	0	0	7.20	3	1	0	0	5	7	4	4	0	3	5	.318	.357	.250	9.00	5.40
Moore, McKinley	R-R	6-2	225	8-24-98	1	1	4.00	18	0	0	3	18	19	8	8	2	7	24	.264	.265	.263	12.00	3.50
Navarro, Edgar	R-R	6-1	180	2-5-98	2	2	8.45	35	0	0	0	44	47	43	41	6	33	37	.275	.333	.246	7.63	6.80
Olson, J.B.	L-R	6-2	195	2-15-95	0	0	0.00	1	0	0	0	2	0	0	0	0	3		.000	.000	.000	13.50	0.00
Patel, Karan	R-R	6-0	215	1-2-97	0	2	5.28	5	4	0	0	15	17	9	9	1	6	20	.283	.250	.306	11.74	3.52
Peralta, Sammy	L-L	6-2	205	5-10-98	2	0	4.35	12	0	0	0	21	22	11	10	1	4	19	.275	.231	.296	8.27	1.74
Perez, Wilber	R-R	6-2	170	11-3-97	3	3	6.52	29	2	0	1	59	58	45	43	16	35	64	.259	.242	.271	9.71	5.31
Ramsey, Lane	R-R	6-9	245	7-16-96	1	0	1.64	10	1	0	3	11	9	3	2	0	1	13	.225	.294	.174	10.64	0.82
Roper, Kaleb	R-R	6-0	193	11-22-95	1	9	7.61	17	16	0	0	63	72	55	53	19	26	89	.283	.324	.253	12.78	3.73
Shilling, Luke	R-R	6-4	230	11-18-97	0	0	2.95	16	0	0	1	18	16	6	6	2	8	27	.235	.321	.175	13.25	3.93
Silven, Yoelvin	R-R	6-1	176	6-26-99	0	0	2.77	7	2	0	0	13	9	5	4	3	2	11	.191	.222	.172	7.62	1.38
Solesky, Chase	R-R	6-3	201	9-26-97	0	2	5.29	4	4	0	0	17	22	17	10	4	4	12	.301	.250	.333	9.00	2.12
Valles, Jesus	R-R	6-3	178	12-15-97	0	1	5.40	4	4	0	0	17	20	11	10	5	5	12	.278	.200	.333	6.48	2.70
Varnell, Taylor	L-L	6-1	190	5-5-95	4	3	2.89	13	10	0	0	56	40	19	18	6	20	61	.200	.167	.212	9.80	3.21
Williamson, Ryan	L-L	6-2	190	4-28-95	1	4	6.15	28	0	0	0	41	48	32	28	11	31	52	.294	.378	.263	11.41	6.80

Fielding

Catcher	PCT	G	PO	A	E	DP	PB
Fernandez	.975	4	38	1	1	0	1
Lartigue	1.000	7	76	3	0	0	1
Millwee	1.000	8	60	2	0	0	1
Osik	1.000	9	71	5	0	0	7
Sanchez	1.000	6	21	1	0	0	1
Skoug	.992	47	462	43	4	1	12
Troutwine	.987	43	420	23	6	4	10

First Base	PCT	G	PO	A	E	DP
Duenez	.972	22	128	11	4	13
Gill	.974	13	75	0	2	7
Leal	.977	27	161	6	4	20
Mendoza	.982	35	264	11	5	13
Moniot	.991	19	111	1	1	5
Osik	.988	13	77	2	1	9
Troutwine	1.000	2	1	0	0	1

Second Base	PCT	G	PO	A	E	DP
Bossard	1.000	17	16	28	0	6
Burks	.930	20	26	40	5	6
Cruz	1.000	9	14	21	0	6
Curbelo	1.000	2	2	8	0	2
Moniot	.917	4	6	5	1	1
Rusconi	.917	23	33	44	7	8
Sanchez	.991	34	40	66	1	14

	PCT	G	PO	A	E	DP
Sosa	.988	21	37	44	1	9

Third Base	PCT	G	PO	A	E	DP
Bossard	.846	3	2	9	2	1
Cruz	.932	25	11	44	4	5
Curbelo	.958	90	53	106	7	11
Moniot	1.000	2	2	5	0	0
Rusconi	.000	1	0	1	0	0

Shortstop	PCT	G	PO	A	E	DP
Bossard	1.000	6	5	14	0	0
Rodriguez	.943	29	34	66	6	15
Sanchez	.942	24	18	47	4	6
Sosa	.967	64	85	146	8	31

Outfield	PCT	G	PO	A	E	DP
Cespedes	1.000	24	32	0	0	0

	PCT	G	PO	A	E	DP
Cruz	.909	4	9	1	1	0
Dawkins	1.000	30	52	1	0	0
Destino	.968	82	141	10	5	2
Ellis	.989	76	171	6	2	1
Gill	.923	8	12	0	1	0
Jimenez	.667	1	2	0	1	0
Leal	.914	27	31	1	3	0
Mieses	.969	60	89	4	3	1
Moniot	1.000	41	57	3	0	1
Reese	1.000	3	5	0	0	0
Robert	1.000	4	8	0	0	0
Rusconi	1.000	5	5	1	0	0
Tatum	1.000	4	7	0	0	0
Weaver	1.000	19	36	2	0	0

KANNAPOLIS CANNON BALLERS

LOW CLASS A

LOW-A EAST

Batting	B-T	HT	WT	DOB	AVG	vLH	vRH	G	AB	R	H	2B	3B	HR	RBI	BB	HBP	SH	SF	SO	SB	CS	SLG	OBP
Abbott, Sam	L-R	6-4	225	4-9-99	.119	.167	.100	14	42	3	5	0	0	1	2	14	0	0	0	30	0	0	.190	.339
Bailey, Benyamin	R-R	6-4	215	9-18-01	.156	.136	.164	21	77	4	12	0	0	1	3	7	0	0	0	25	0	0	.195	.226
Beard, James	R-R	5-10	170	9-24-00	.192	.170	.199	73	234	30	45	5	1	5	14	37	2	0	0	107	9	2	.286	.308
Bossard, Brandon	R-R	6-1	185	6-10-97	.167	.091	.194	18	42	7	7	2	0	1	1	19	1	0	0	21	0	0	.214	.435
Burks, Jeremiah	R-R	6-2	215	1-8-97	.263	.167	.281	12	38	4	10	2	1	0	6	8	1	0	0	15	0	2	.368	.404
Comas, Anderson	L-L	6-3	185	2-10-00	.048	.000	.059	13	42	0	2	0	0	0	0	1	1	0	0	21	0	0	.048	.091
Delgado, Lency	R-R	6-3	215	6-20-99	.194	.152	.214	42	144	14	28	2	0	5	12	11	1	1	0	79	0	0	.313	.256
Garcia, Richard	R-R	6-1	185	9-20-98	.188	.091	.216	14	48	5	9	0	0	1	4	2	0	0	0	25	0	0	.250	.220
Gill, AJ	R-R	6-2	220	4-15-98	.196	.409	.138	33	102	12	20	3	0	2	10	20	4	0	0	45	0	0	.284	.349
Gladney, DJ	R-R	6-3	195	7-14-01	.191	.213	.185	71	256	20	49	11	1	7	28	31	6	0	1	124	1	0	.324	.293
Gonzalez, Ivan	R-R	5-9	190	10-28-96	.186	.125	.204	20	70	4	13	3	0	1	8	6	2	0	0	16	1	0	.271	.269
Gonzalez, Jayson	R-R	6-2	220	4-26-99	.143	.000	.171	15	49	4	7	1	0	0	4	5	2	0	0	25	0	0	.163	.250
Gonzalez, Misael	R-R	6-0	175	5-23-01	.178	.250	.167	31	90	12	16	4	0	3	10	11	3	0	1	40	1	0	.322	.286
Goosenberg, Shawn	R-R	6-1	195	12-5-99	.213	.083	.235	23	80	11	17	5	1	1	5	14	3	0	0	33	4	1	.338	.351
Hackenberg, Adam	R-R	6-1	225	9-8-99	.346	.167	.377	21	81	8	28	4	1	1	14	4	1	0	0	16	0	0	.457	.384
Krogman, Chase	L-L	5-11	180	2-27-01	.200	.286	.183	77	250	30	50	7	0	10	27	49	10	0	2	130	4	0	.348	.350
Laureano, Johnabiell	R-R	6-0	180	10-11-00	.158	.273	.111	15	38	2	6	0	0	0	2	6	2	0	0	14	0	0	.158	.304
Mendoza, Harvin	L-L	6-2	185	2-18-99	.314	.298	.319	71	261	35	82	15	2	3	36	32	1	0	3	41	0	1	.421	.387
Mieses, Luis	L-L	6-3	180	5-31-00	.305	.271	.316	52	203	31	62	12	1	6	41	13	3	0	6	33	0	0	.463	.347
Millwee, Daniel	R-R	5-10	205	8-2-95	.250	.375	.219	15	40	5	10	2	0	0	6	11	9	1	0	20	1	0	.300	.500
Osik, Tyler	R-R	5-10	203	11-15-96	.364	.250	.429	3	11	3	4	1	0	0	2	2	0	0	0	1	0	0	.455	.462
Polanco, Samil	L-R	6-0	160	2-21-00	.256	.180	.271	78	308	42	79	19	4	5	40	15	5	0	4	74	1	3	.393	.298
Ramos, Bryan	R-R	6-2	190	3-12-02	.244	.287	.231	115	431	64	105	23	6	13	57	51	18	0	4	110	13	4	.415	.345
Rodriguez, Jose	R-R	5-11	175	5-13-01	.283	.256	.293	78	336	58	95	22	4	9	32	21	2	0	1	57	20	5	.452	.328
Rusconi, Jagger	B-R	5-11	165	7-18-96	.235	.000	.333	5	17	2	4	1	0	0	1	2	1	0	0	6	0	0	.294	.350
Sanchez, Kleyder	R-R	5-10	170	12-13-99	.000	--	.000	4	11	0	0	0	0	0	0	1	0	0	0	2	0	0	.000	.083
Sanchez, Wilber	R-R	5-10	160	2-21-02	.200	.154	.206	34	115	12	23	2	1	4	13	7	2	0	2	55	11	1	.339	.254
Torres, Victor	R-R	6-0	180	7-29-00	.195	.227	.184	52	169	16	33	6	0	3	18	8	6	1	1	39	1	0	.284	.255
Weaver, Caberea	R-R	6-3	180	12-1-99	.214	.203	.217	80	290	42	62	11	2	7	30	31	6	0	1	117	25	7	.338	.302

Pitching	B-T	HT	WT	DOB	W	L	ERA	G	GS	CG	SV	IP	H	R	ER	HR	BB	SO	AVG	vLH	vRH	K/9	BB/9
Acevedo, Angel	R-R	6-1	205	9-19-98	3	6	5.52	20	14	0	0	73	87	55	45	11	30	73	.300	.302	.298	8.96	3.68
Alston, Garvin	R-L	6-4	175	3-12-97	3	3	6.75	26	0	0	0	43	48	38	32	4	28	40	.286	.188	.325	8.44	5.91
Biasi, Sal	R-R	5-11	205	9-30-95	1	1	18.00	2	0	0	0	2	2	4	4	0	2	3	.286	.500	.200	13.50	9.00
Bossard, Brandon	R-R	6-1	185	6-10-97	0	0	0.00	4	0	0	0	2	4	5	0	2	4	1	.333	.200	.400	3.86	15.43
Broadway, Taylor	R-R	5-11	205	4-8-97	0	0	1.59	5	0	0	0	6	2	1	1	1	1	7	.105	.143	.083	11.12	1.59
Burke, Jeremiah	R-R	6-2	195	5-16-98	1	1	4.22	3	0	0	0	11	13	6	5	0	4	15	.310	.375	.269	12.66	3.38
Burke, Sean	R-R	6-6	230	12-18-99	0	1	3.21	5	5	0	0	14	9	6	5	0	10	20	.191	.261	.125	12.86	6.43
Cable, Zach	R-R	6-0	215	10-22-97	0	2	4.00	9	0	0	2	9	12	8	4	1	4	14	.333	.368	.294	14.00	4.00
Carrasco, Martin	R-R	6-0	165	11-22-97	1	8	5.85	26	10	0	1	72	82	55	47	9	33	65	.288	.230	.331	8.09	4.11
Cruz, Homer	R-R	6-0	175	9-21-99	2	0	14.21	5	0	0	0	6	10	12	10	2	10	8	.357	.364	.353	11.37	14.21
Dalquist, Andrew	R-R	6-1	175	11-13-00	3	9	4.99	23	23	0	0	83	87	57	46	1	56	79	.269	.215	.307	8.57	6.07
Denlinger, Theo	R-R	6-3	240	7-10-96	0	0	2.45	14	0	0	2	15	10	6	4	1	6	26	.192	.235	.171	15.95	3.68
Ellard, Fraser	L-L	6-2	205	11-6-97	1	0	4.96	11	0	0	0	16	19	11	9	1	10	21	.275	.261	.283	11.57	5.51
Evey, Marcus	R-R	5-10	175	8-4-97	0	0	10.80	18	0	0	0	25	45	31	30	5	13	20	.402	.449	.365	7.20	4.68
Fernandez, Rigo	L-L	6-0	190	11-27-97	2	2	9.27	23	0	0	1	33	39	37	34	5	30	41	.285	.389	.248	11.18	8.18
Folman, Kevin	R-R	6-2	215	10-23-94	3	3	5.52	13	4	0	0	29	38	23	18	0	10	23	.317	.389	.258	7.06	3.07
Gosswein, Brooks	L-L	6-2	205	10-9-98	0	0	4.00	3	3	0	0	9	6	4	4	1	5	7	.200	.125	.227	7.00	5.00
Green, Haylen	L-L	5-11	185	8-12-97	0	0	0.00	2	0	0	0	2	1	0	0	0	0	1	.143	.000	.200	4.50	0.00
Hazelwood, Everhett	R-R	6-2	210	5-21-99	2	0	0.00	3	0	0	0	5	2	0	0	0	4	9	.111	.091	.200	7.20	0.00
Horn, Bailey	L-L	6-2	210	1-15-98	1	2	2.63	8	6	0	0	27	21	13	8	0	7	32	.206	.217	.203	10.54	2.30
Jeans, Trey	L-L	5-10	195	1-31-96	0	0	6.75	5	0	0	0	8	14	9	6	0	3	14	.368	.400	.357	15.75	3.38
Jenkins, Brandon	R-R	6-1	205	10-2-98	0	0	2.50	14	0	0	0	18	11	8	5	1	20	26	.175	.038	.270	13.00	10.00

Pitcher	B-T	HT	WT	DOB	W	L	ERA	G	GS	CG	SV	IP	H	R	ER	HR	BB	SO	AVG	vLH	vRH	SO/9	BB/9
Johnson, Tyler	R-R	6-3	210	8-21-95	0	0	0.00	2	0	0	0	3	2	0	0	0	2	4	.222	.500	.143	13.50	6.75
Kelley, Jared	R-R	6-3	230	10-3-01	0	5	6.86	10	10	0	0	21	21	23	16	1	22	25	.241	.286	.220	10.71	9.43
Luna Jr., Gil	L-L	5-10	173	7-29-99	0	0	0.00	4	0	0	2	6	2	0	0	0	2	7	.111	.143	.091	9.95	2.84
Madrigal, Ty	L-L	6-0	190	3-5-97	0	2	5.86	24	0	0	1	43	41	30	28	3	25	48	.250	.208	.270	10.05	5.23
Mejia, Dilmer	L-L	5-11	160	7-9-97	0	1	5.73	4	0	0	0	11	17	10	7	0	4	9	.333	.273	.350	7.36	3.27
Messer, Tyson	R-R	6-0	215	1-7-97	0	2	7.18	30	0	0	1	31	31	30	25	2	31	28	.256	.304	.227	8.04	8.90
Metzdorf, Dan	L-L	5-10	165	5-28-96	0	1	10.80	1	0	0	0	3	5	4	4	0	4	3	.385	.200	.500	8.10	10.80
Mikel, Jordan	R-R	6-5	190	3-24-99	3	2	2.63	19	0	0	1	27	21	10	8	0	17	34	.208	.211	.206	11.20	5.60
Milto, Pauly	R-R	6-3	245	3-6-97	0	0	1.23	4	0	0	1	7	2	1	1	0	3	11	.087	.167	.000	13.50	3.68
Moore, McKinley	R-R	6-6	225	8-24-98	1	1	4.37	19	0	0	6	23	18	15	11	1	14	35	.209	.200	.214	13.90	5.56
Patel, Karan	R-R	6-0	215	1-2-97	0	2	4.96	10	0	0	0	16	20	11	9	5	8	22	.313	.345	.286	12.12	4.41
Peralta, Sammy	L-L	6-2	205	5-10-98	1	1	3.89	19	0	0	2	35	32	22	15	3	12	49	.237	.178	.267	12.72	3.12
Sampson, Keyvius	R-R	6-2	225	1-6-91	0	0	4.50	2	0	0	0	2	1	1	1	0	2	2	.167	.000	.250	9.00	9.00
Silven, Yoelvin	R-R	6-1	176	6-26-99	2	4	6.68	13	3	0	0	31	41	27	23	4	10	32	.304	.354	.276	9.29	2.90
Simas, Kohl	R-R	6-1	190	12-22-99	2	0	1.50	10	0	0	1	18	9	5	3	1	4	23	.148	.179	.121	11.50	2.00
Solesky, Chase	R-R	6-3	201	9-26-97	1	5	5.08	14	14	0	0	51	56	34	29	7	20	71	.268	.247	.280	12.45	3.51
Speer, Hunter	R-R	6-0	180	5-18-95	1	2	10.43	14	0	0	0	15	14	19	17	3	23	10	.246	.217	.265	6.14	14.11
Stone, Corey	L-L	6-2	195	12-27-98	1	1	12.94	18	0	0	0	16	20	27	23	0	24	16	.317	.375	.298	9.00	13.50
Thompson, Matthew	R-R	6-3	195	8-11-00	2	8	5.90	19	19	0	0	72	83	49	47	7	38	77	.296	.317	.279	9.67	4.77
Valles, Jesus	R-R	6-3	178	12-15-97	3	4	5.12	18	8	0	0	65	85	39	37	10	9	35	.311	.316	.308	4.85	1.25
Veras, Frander	L-R	6-5	185	10-8-98	0	0	12.79	6	0	0	0	6	9	9	9	1	10	5	.321	.333	.313	7.11	14.21

Fielding

Catcher	PCT	G	PO	A	E	DP	PB
Garcia	.953	14	111	11	6	0	7
Gonzalez	.989	18	170	15	2	1	2
Hackenberg	.981	21	180	26	4	1	4
Millwee	.975	14	140	14	4	2	6
Sanchez	.968	4	29	1	1	0	1
Torres	.983	52	463	55	9	5	13

First Base	PCT	G	PO	A	E	DP
Abbott	.991	14	100	6	1	5
Gill	.983	12	55	4	1	6
Gladney	1.000	6	47	0	0	8
Gonzalez	.991	15	98	11	1	10
Mendoza	.986	71	513	38	8	43
Osik	1.000	3	20	1	0	1

Second Base	PCT	G	PO	A	E	DP
Bossard	.976	12	17	23	1	6

(Second Base)	PCT	G	PO	A	E	DP
Burks	.949	9	20	17	2	4
Delgado	.915	21	24	30	5	3
Goosenberg	.969	21	42	52	3	16
Polanco	.883	23	36	62	13	17
Ramos	.955	25	37	48	4	11
Rodriguez	1.000	3	1	6	0	3
Rusconi	1.000	1	2	4	0	0
Sanchez	.933	7	10	18	2	5

Third Base	PCT	G	PO	A	E	DP
Bossard	1.000	1	1	0	0	0
Delgado	.800	10	3	13	4	0
Gill	.889	5	1	7	1	0
Gladney	.919	45	43	59	9	4
Polanco	.875	28	11	38	7	1
Ramos	.928	34	25	52	6	7
Rodriguez	.000	1	0	0	0	0

Shortstop	PCT	G	PO	A	E	DP
Bossard	1.000	5	3	8	0	1
Polanco	.985	18	20	44	1	10
Rodriguez	.920	71	89	152	21	30
Sanchez	.991	27	40	68	1	10

Outfield	PCT	G	PO	A	E	DP
Bailey	.929	22	26	0	2	0
Beard	.952	72	135	4	7	1
Comas	.933	12	14	0	1	0
Gill	1.000	8	14	0	0	0
Gonzalez	.983	31	56	1	1	0
Krogman	.919	76	120	4	11	0
Laureano	.955	17	20	1	1	0
Mieses	.964	53	77	3	3	0
Rusconi	1.000	5	1	0	0	0
Weaver	.966	81	163	5	6	2

ACL WHITE SOX
ARIZONA COMPLEX LEAGUE

ROOKIE

Batting	B-T	HT	WT	DOB	AVG	vLH	vRH	G	AB	R	H	2B	3B	HR	RBI	BB	HBP	SH	SF	SO	SB	CS	SLG	OBP
Abbott, Sam	L-R	6-4	225	4-9-99	.171	.056	.194	35	111	11	19	5	0	4	11	13	3	0	1	58	1	0	.324	.273
Bailey, Benyamin	R-R	6-4	215	9-18-01	.216	.211	.217	40	125	20	27	2	1	3	11	24	1	0	0	46	3	1	.320	.347
Benavides, Ruben	R-R	6-1	178	8-9-01	.194	.000	.222	12	31	5	6	3	0	0	7	6	1	0	0	15	0	0	.290	.342
Betancourt, Jhoneiker	R-R	6-1	174	5-2-00	.368	.333	.385	8	19	3	7	0	0	1	1	5	1	0	0	2	1	0	.526	.520
Burks, Jeremiah	R-R	6-2	215	1-8-97	.300	.000	.333	4	10	3	3	1	0	0	2	1	2	0	1	3	0	0	.400	.429
Bush, Bryce	R-R	6-0	200	12-14-99	.000	--	--	1	2	0	0	0	0	0	0	1	0	0	0	2	0	0	.000	.333
Butler, Cameron	R-R	6-0	175	10-3-02	.083	.067	.091	18	48	4	4	2	0	0	0	11	0	0	0	27	1	2	.125	.254
Comas, Anderson	L-L	6-3	185	2-10-00	.345	.250	.360	8	29	6	10	4	0	4	9	0	0	1	0	10	0	0	.897	.345
Duenez, Samir	R-R	6-1	230	6-11-96	.182	.500	.111	3	11	0	2	0	0	0	0	3	0	0	0	6	0	0	.182	.357
Espinoza, Anthony	R-R	5-10	165	9-27-01	.243	.290	.091	31	107	15	26	3	0	0	5	8	0	0	2	31	3	2	.271	.296
Garcia, Richard	R-R	6-1	185	9-20-98	.571	.667	.500	3	7	3	4	0	0	2	4	0	0	0	0	2	0	0	1.429	.571
Glass, Logan	R-R	6-4	215	4-9-01	.159	.167	.157	45	145	23	23	7	3	3	15	10	12	0	78	2	1	.310	.269
Gonzalez, Jayson	R-R	6-0	175	4-26-99	.250	.200	.267	6	20	3	5	2	0	0	3	4	2	0	0	10	0	0	.350	.423
Gonzalez, Misael	R-R	6-0	175	5-23-01	.311	.167	.324	21	74	14	23	6	0	5	23	6	4	0	0	26	4	2	.595	.393
Goosenberg, Shawn	R-R	6-1	195	12-5-99	.273	.250	.278	6	22	8	6	3	0	1	4	1	3	0	6	0	0	.545	.385
Hackenberg, Adam	R-R	6-1	225	9-8-99	.211	.200	.214	6	19	3	4	3	0	0	2	4	1	0	0	6	0	0	.368	.375
Kath, Wes	L-R	6-3	200	8-3-02	.212	.261	.198	28	104	15	22	0	2	3	15	8	3	0	0	42	1	0	.337	.287
Laureano, Johnabiell	R-R	6-0	180	10-11-00	.255	.259	.254	41	145	20	37	1	4	3	22	13	1	0	0	44	3	1	.338	.321
Mendoza, Jefferson	R-R	6-0	220	1-10-01	.200	.207	.190	32	102	15	22	3	0	5	15	11	5	0	1	33	0	0	.392	.319
Montgomery, Colson	R-R	6-4	205	2-27-02	.287	.300	.284	26	94	16	27	3	1	2	13	4	0	0	2	22	0	1	.362	.396
Peralta, Edwin	R-R	6-3	175	5-10-01	.146	.250	.135	27	82	6	12	4	0	1	6	5	1	0	1	33	0	1	.232	.202
Reese, E.P.	L-R	5-10	175	3-4-98	.250	.500	.222	7	20	3	5	0	0	0	4	3	1	0	0	3	1	1	.250	.375
Rusconi, Jagger	B-R	5-11	165	7-18-96	.250	.000	.273	4	12	4	3	2	0	0	0	3	0	0	0	3	0	0	.417	.400
Sanchez, Wilber	R-R	5-10	160	2-21-02	.269	.500	.243	19	78	10	21	3	0	2	8	5	0	0	0	23	6	0	.385	.313
Sinatro, Danny	L-R	6-0	180	9-18-97	.000	.000	.000	2	4	0	0	0	0	0	0	1	0	0	0	1	0	0	.000	.200
Smelley, Colby	R-R	6-2	205	3-15-00	.241	.400	.208	9	29	2	7	2	0	0	5	1	0	0	0	8	0	1	.310	.267
Tatis, Elijah	R-R	5-11	155	9-27-01	.106	.111	.105	32	113	9	12	3	0	0	6	8	0	0	1	58	0	1	.133	.164
Tatum, Terrell	L-L	6-0	167	7-27-99	.265	.263	.265	22	68	15	18	8	0	1	10	21	1	0	0	28	3	0	.426	.444
Thornquist, Nick	R-R	5-8	175	9-23-97	.100	.333	.000	6	10	1	1	0	0	1	1	1	0	0	0	4	0	0	.400	.182

	B-T	HT	WT	DOB	AVG	vLH	vRH	G	AB	R	H	2B	3B	HR	RBI	BB	HBP	SH	SF	SO	SB	CS	SLG	OBP
Torres, Victor	R-R	6-0	180	7-29-00	.387	.444	.364	8	31	5	12	1	0	0	4	0	0	0	0	9	1	0	.419	.387
Veras, Wilfred	R-R	6-2	180	11-15-02	.322	.250	.339	46	152	25	49	16	2	4	26	21	4	0	1	42	3	1	.533	.416

Pitching

	B-T	HT	WT	DOB	W	L	ERA	G	GS	CG	SV	IP	H	R	ER	HR	BB	SO	AVG	vLH	vRH	K/9	BB/9
Alston, Garvin	R-L	6-4	175	3-12-97	0	0	0.00	1	0	0	0	1	0	0	0	0	0	2	.000	.000	.000	18.00	0.00
Arobio, Vince	R-R	5-11	185	3-31-95	0	0	22.50	2	0	0	0	2	5	5	5	2	3	3	.455	.571	.250	13.50	13.50
Beauchamp, Cam	L-L	6-2	221	3-13-98	1	1	5.56	7	0	0	0	11	16	8	7	1	6	10	.320	.444	.250	7.94	4.76
Bello, Erick	R-R	5-11	170	8-18-02	1	2	5.47	21	0	0	4	26	33	18	16	1	28	30	.317	.357	.290	10.25	9.57
Broadway, Taylor	R-R	5-11	205	4-8-97	1	0	0.00	1	0	0	0	1	0	0	0	0	0	2	.000	--	.000	18.00	0.00
Burke, Sean	R-R	6-6	230	12-18-99	0	0	0.00	2	2	0	0	3	1	0	0	0	1	5	.100	.000	.167	15.00	3.00
Butler, Hansen	R-R	5-11	180	10-30-95	0	0	0.00	1	0	0	0	1	0	0	0	0	0	2	.000	--	.000	27.00	0.00
Cable, Zach	R-R	6-0	215	10-22-97	0	0	3.68	6	0	0	1	7	4	5	3	0	5	11	.148	.071	.231	13.50	6.14
Cruz, Homer	R-R	6-0	175	9-21-99	6	0	2.23	17	4	0	0	44	32	15	11	2	20	55	.201	.209	.196	11.17	4.06
Denlinger, Theo	R-R	6-3	240	7-10-96	0	1	9.00	2	0	0	0	2	3	2	2	0	1	5	.375	.500	.250	22.50	4.50
Diaz, Deivi	L-L	5-10	197	6-9-99	2	2	6.32	12	0	0	1	16	17	16	11	1	18	17	.283	.263	.293	9.77	10.34
Edwards, Christian	R-R	6-3	205	3-4-00	0	0	3.00	7	0	0	0	9	6	3	3	1	5	8	.200	.154	.235	8.00	5.00
Ellard, Fraser	L-L	6-4	205	11-6-97	1	0	2.25	3	0	0	0	4	5	1	1	0	0	6	.294	.375	.222	13.50	0.00
Evey, Marcus	R-R	5-10	175	8-4-97	0	0	108.00	1	0	0	0	0	2	5	4	0	2	0	1.000	1.000	1.000	0.00	54.00
Fernandez, Rigo	L-L	6-0	190	11-27-97	0	0	0.00	4	0	0	0	8	1	0	0	0	0	12	.040	.000	.053	14.09	0.00
Gilliland, Jacob	R-R	6-2	180	1-16-00	2	5	10.50	10	7	1	0	30	53	40	35	2	16	31	.376	.444	.304	9.30	4.80
Gosswein, Brooks	L-L	6-2	205	10-9-98	0	1	1.13	3	3	0	0	8	6	1	1	0	1	8	.214	.250	.200	9.00	1.13
Green, Haylen	L-L	5-11	185	8-12-97	0	0	0.00	7	0	0	2	8	5	0	0	0	0	13	.167	.500	.143	14.63	0.00
Guzman, Ronaldo	L-L	6-0	150	8-23-02	1	5	7.62	14	8	0	0	39	38	37	33	8	48	46	.250	.294	.228	10.62	11.08
Hazelwood, Everhett	R-R	6-2	210	5-12-99	1	1	4.15	7	0	0	0	9	10	7	4	1	3	9	.278	.133	.381	9.35	3.12
Hutchinson, Bryce	R-R	6-6	245	10-21-98	0	0	4.15	5	0	0	0	4	7	3	2	1	8	5	.389	.200	.462	10.38	16.62
Jenkins, Brandon	R-R	6-1	205	10-2-98	1	1	9.82	12	0	0	0	15	21	19	16	2	16	29	.318	.393	.263	17.80	9.82
Kelley, Jared	R-R	6-3	230	10-3-01	0	2	13.50	2	2	0	0	3	3	4	4	2	4	2	.300	.400	.200	6.75	13.50
Luna Jr., Gil	L-L	5-10	173	7-29-99	0	0	0.00	6	0	0	2	9	3	0	0	0	4	17	.103	.167	.087	17.00	4.00
McDougal, Tanner	R-R	6-5	185	4-3-03	1	2	9.31	6	4	0	0	10	10	10	10	2	5	17	.278	.200	.333	15.83	4.66
Mejia, Dilmer	L-L	5-11	160	7-9-97	0	1	3.73	12	6	0	0	51	59	27	21	5	9	57	.285	.310	.275	10.13	1.60
Mena, Cristian	R-R	6-2	170	12-21-02	1	4	7.82	13	12	0	0	48	69	44	42	8	21	62	.337	.387	.283	11.54	3.91
Milto, Pauly	R-R	6-3	245	3-6-97	0	0	0.00	2	0	0	0	2	2	0	0	0	0	4	.250	--	.250	15.43	0.00
Nightengale, Drake	R-R	6-0	195	5-8-96	0	0	4.15	4	0	0	0	4	5	2	2	0	3	4	.313	.286	.333	8.31	6.23
Owen, Noah	L-R	6-4	200	10-1-00	0	1	2.00	8	3	0	0	18	12	4	4	1	3	25	.176	.120	.209	12.50	1.50
O'Neil, Conner	R-R	6-2	195	9-25-94	1	0	0.00	3	0	0	0	4	2	0	0	0	0	4	.154	.167	.143	9.00	0.00
Patel, Karan	R-R	6-0	215	1-2-97	0	0	21.60	2	0	0	0	2	4	4	4	1	2	3	.444	.500	.429	16.20	10.80
Perez, Erick	R-R	6-1	175	12-9-98	0	0	0.00	1	0	0	0	0	1	0	0	0	2	1	.500	1.000	.000	27.00	54.00
Perez, Keiter	R-R	6-4	190	4-9-01	0	1	7.36	3	0	0	0	4	1	3	3	0	7	5	.091	.000	.167	12.27	17.18
Plymell, Chase	R-R	6-4	205	5-29-98	0	0	0.00	2	0	0	0	2	0	0	0	0	1	2	.000	.000	.000	9.00	4.50
Ray, Johnny	R-R	6-2	220	10-10-98	3	0	9.75	8	1	0	0	12	12	13	13	1	8	15	.267	.250	.273	11.25	6.00
Schoenle, Garrett	L-L	6-5	185	6-21-98	0	0	2.70	10	0	0	3	10	11	3	3	0	3	11	.297	.364	.269	9.90	2.70
Simas, Kohl	R-R	6-1	190	10-24-97	0	1	3.00	3	0	0	0	3	3	1	1	0	1	2	.273	.333	.250	6.00	3.00
Sommer, Tommy	L-L	6-4	220	9-25-98	0	1	2.16	8	6	0	0	25	13	6	6	3	7	33	.149	.093	.205	11.88	2.52
Speer, Hunter	R-R	6-0	180	5-18-95	1	0	5.79	5	0	0	1	5	4	3	3	1	3	10	.222	.375	.100	19.29	5.79
Stone, Corey	L-L	6-2	195	12-27-98	0	0	0.00	5	0	0	0	6	2	0	0	0	2	7	.105	.000	.125	10.50	3.00
Suddreth, Jake	R-R	6-3	215	4-22-97	1	1	18.00	1	0	0	0	1	5	4	2	0	1	2	.500	.600	.400	18.00	9.00
Thompson, Matthew	R-R	6-3	195	8-11-00	1	0	9.00	1	1	0	0	2	3	2	2	1	0	1	.333	.500	.286	4.50	0.00
Veras, Frander	L-R	6-5	185	10-8-98	0	1	13.50	4	0	0	0	5	6	9	7	1	3	6	.300	.385	.143	11.57	5.79

Fielding

C: Benavides 8, Betancourt 5, Garcia 3, Hackenberg 6, Mendoza 26, Smelley 5, Thornquist 6, Torres 8.
1B: Abbott 28, Betancourt 3, Duenez 1, Gonzalez 4, Peralta 10, Veras 18.
2B: Burks 2, Butler 5, Espinoza 26, Goosenberg 4, Peralta 1, Rusconi 3, Sanchez 2, Tatis 18.
3B: Burks 1, Espinoza 3, Gonzalez 1, Kath 25, Laureano 1, Peralta 1, Rusconi 1, Veras 13.
SS: Espinoza 1, Goosenberg 2, Montgomery 26, Sanchez 16, Tatis 14.
OF: Bailey 33, Butler 11, Comas 7, Glass 43, Gonzalez 18, Kath 1, Laureano 38, Reese 6, Sinatro 1, Tatum 22

DSL WHITE SOX   ROOKIE
DOMINICAN SUMMER LEAGUE

Batting	B-T	HT	WT	DOB	AVG	vLH	vRH	G	AB	R	H	2B	3B	HR	RBI	BB	HBP	SH	SF	SO	SB	CS	SLG	OBP
Aguero, Alvaro	R-R	6-0	160	3-19-03	.246	.250	.245	52	175	31	43	12	3	2	17	11	4	0	2	55	22	3	.383	.302
Aguilar, Ricardo	R-R	6-0	180	12-13-02	.173	.500	.146	23	52	4	9	0	0	0	6	8	1	0	2	18	0	1	.173	.286
Bennett, Godwin	R-R	6-2	170	10-4-02	.235	.200	.238	33	85	18	20	2	3	4	15	18	2	0	1	35	9	1	.471	.377
Bernal, Alberto	R-R	6-1	215	6-13-02	.169	.500	.158	22	59	6	10	2	0	2	15	5	3	0	1	28	0	0	.305	.265
Borrero, Dario	L-L	6-5	190	11-13-03	.357	.000	.455	5	14	2	5	1	0	0	0	1	1	0	0	2	2	2	.429	.438
Gomez, Carlos	L-L	6-0	180	9-26-01	.179	.273	.161	28	67	11	12	0	0	0	5	12	2	0	1	26	5	1	.179	.317
Guariman, Manuel	R-R	6-0	196	2-9-04	.317	.250	.323	31	101	16	32	3	1	0	15	6	4	0	0	11	2	1	.366	.378
Gutierrez, Roberth	R-R	6-0	170	11-8-01	.232	.091	.250	33	99	12	23	1	3	0	10	24	1	0	0	31	7	3	.303	.387
Hernandez, Arxy	R-R	6-2	170	7-29-03	.200	.200	.200	24	70	11	14	1	1	1	6	10	3	0	1	25	4	2	.286	.321
Jimenez, Carlos	L-L	6-4	220	2-3-02	.206	.091	.220	34	102	14	21	4	1	2	15	16	1	0	0	18	4	0	.324	.319
Jimenez, Cesar	R-R	5-10	160	11-8-00	.255	.222	.259	35	94	12	24	3	0	1	10	12	1	0	2	27	8	5	.319	.339
Mercedes, Juan	R-R	6-2	160	6-4-00	.171	.300	.150	30	70	11	12	1	0	0	4	14	6	0	1	16	3	2	.186	.352
Mondesi, Randel	R-R	6-3	190	12-4-02	.229	.100	.250	25	70	8	16	3	0	1	4	10	3	0	0	26	6	1	.314	.349
Mora, Javier	R-R	5-11	170	3-23-03	.152	.000	.156	33	99	10	15	4	0	0	4	18	2	0	1	27	3	4	.192	.292
Pineda, Luis	R-R	6-1	209	3-19-02	.248	.273	.245	35	109	12	27	3	0	2	17	8	2	0	2	27	3	3	.330	.306

Quezada, Victor	R-R	6-1	185	12-27-03	.250	.500	.229	49	156	28	39	11	0	6	20	26	0	0	2	52	14	2	.436	.353
Tapia, Layant	R-R	6-1	160	1-4-02	.208	.231	.206	49	144	36	30	5	4	2	17	39	1	2	3	54	16	4	.340	.374
Vargas, Fernando	R-R	6-2	185	8-3-02	.204	.286	.191	35	108	11	22	5	0	1	7	18	3	0	0	34	5	2	.278	.333

Pitching	B-T	HT	WT	DOB	W	L	ERA	G	GS	CG	SV	IP	H	R	ER	HR	BB	SO	AVG	vLH	vRH	K/9	BB/9
Benitez, Francisco	R-R	6-2	187	9-15-00	1	3	6.08	14	0	0	0	27	25	24	18	2	19	30	.245	.212	.280	10.13	6.41
Carrion, Brian	R-R	6-2	180	1-1-99	1	2	5.40	8	5	0	0	18	17	13	11	0	13	21	.258	.308	.225	10.31	6.38
Castro, Oriel	L-L	6-0	175	5-5-01	1	3	5.45	17	4	0	0	38	42	32	23	3	28	53	.284	.205	.317	12.55	6.63
Cuevas, Guillermo	L-L	6-0	180	5-13-99	3	3	4.64	8	7	0	0	33	28	18	17	2	14	47	.228	.200	.235	12.82	3.82
Ferrer, Jorge	L-L	6-3	180	9-5-00	2	2	5.10	12	8	0	1	30	28	24	17	1	24	42	.246	.265	.238	12.60	7.20
Gil, Adrian	R-R	5-11	195	10-21-01	0	0	4.91	2	2	0	0	4	5	2	2	0	4	6	.357	.429	.286	14.73	9.82
Gonzalez, Daniel	L-L	6-3	160	11-27-01	1	4	4.71	20	1	0	2	36	37	29	19	3	26	34	.264	.267	.264	8.42	6.44
Hinestroza, Carlos	R-R	6-1	190	2-4-03	4	1	2.45	22	0	0	6	37	30	20	10	0	12	27	.233	.271	.210	6.63	2.95
Jimenez, Dionicio	R-R	6-4	190	1-7-01	0	1	6.98	12	1	0	1	19	20	15	15	1	14	18	.290	.400	.176	8.38	6.52
Mercedes, Juan	R-R	6-2	190	6-4-00	0	0	6.75	2	0	0	0	1	2	1	1	0	0	0	.333	.500	.250	0.00	0.00
Nolasco, Yohemy	R-R	6-3	160	7-12-03	0	3	5.32	13	7	0	0	24	26	16	14	1	9	19	.271	.194	.317	7.23	3.42
Rodriguez, Gabriel	R-R	5-11	172	11-20-02	1	4	4.19	16	8	0	0	43	44	24	20	3	31	44	.260	.200	.309	9.21	6.49
Talavera, Emerson	R-R	5-10	160	10-1-02	4	2	2.47	17	5	0	2	51	36	21	14	2	22	47	.197	.269	.155	8.29	3.88
Toribio, Miguel	R-R	6-1	165	12-8-01	2	2	9.55	14	0	0	1	22	30	28	23	2	16	20	.326	.410	.264	8.31	6.65
Veloz, Manuel	R-R	6-2	185	1-28-01	5	3	4.08	12	4	0	0	46	51	29	21	3	3	47	.279	.269	.284	9.13	0.58
Vera, Norge	R-R	6-4	185	6-1-00	1	0	0.00	8	7	0	0	19	9	2	0	0	5	34	.141	.238	.093	16.11	2.37

Fielding

C: Aguilar 23, Guariman 15, Pineda 29.
1B: Bernal 19, Borrero 3, Guariman 5, Gutierrez 8, Jimenez 10, Mercedes 19, Quezada 2.
2B: Jimenez 23, Mora 31, Tapia 7.
3B: Gutierrez 7, Hernandez 5, Jimenez 2, Quezada 47, Tapia 1.
SS: Hernandez 17, Jimenez 6, Mora 1, Tapia 38.
OF: Aguero 50, Bennett 29, Borrero 2, Gomez 29, Gutierrez 15, Jimenez 5, Mercedes 10, Mondesi 24, Vargas 32.

Cincinnati Reds

SEASON IN A SENTENCE: A lot of things went right for Cincinnati in 2021 as Joey Votto had his best season in years, Nick Castellanos starred and Jonathan India was a revelation, but that wasn't enough as the Reds sagged down the stretch to finish a disappointing 83-79, seven games out of the wild card race.

HIGH POINT: Wade Miley and Jeff Hoffman combined on a six-hit shutout of the Marlins on Aug. 27. With two more games against the Marlins followed by a series against the Cardinals to begin September, the Reds were on track to snag the final wild card spot in the National League. At that point, they were 71-59 and held the fourth-best record in the NL, which meant they held a one-and-a-half game lead over the Padres for the second and final wild card spot.

LOW POINT: From Aug. 28 until the end of the season, the Reds' promising season fell apart. Cincinnati went 12-20 over its final 32 games for the fourth-worst finish in the National League. Instead of returning to the playoffs, the Reds barely finished with a winning record.

NOTABLE ROOKIES: Second baseman Jonathan India proved to be one of the best players in the Reds lineup. He hit .269/.376/.459 with 21 home runs and a team-best 12 stolen bases. Catcher Tyler Stephenson proved a potent addition to the lineup as he shared the team's catching responsibilities with veteran Tucker Barnhart. Stephenson hit .286/.366/.431 with 10 home runs in 132 games. Righthander Vladimir Gutierrez went 9-6, 4.74 in 22 starts in the Reds rotation. Righthander Tony Santillan was a useful part of the Reds bullpen. He went 1-3, 2.91 with 56 strikeouts in 43 innings.

KEY TRANSACTIONS: To cut payroll, the Reds dealt righthander Raisel Iglesias to the Angels in the offseason for righthander Noe Ramirez and minor league shortstop Leonardo Rivas. Ramirez was released by the Reds at the end of spring training. Iglesias' absence was felt. He was one of the better relievers in the American League in 2021. Righthander Art Warren was a low-key offseason acquisition, but he proved to be a very useful reliever. The rookie went 3-0, 1.29 with only 11 hits and eight walks allowed in 21 innings. He struck out 34. The Reds did attempt to bolster their bullpen at the trade deadline, acquiring Mychal Givens, Luis Cessa and Justin Wilson in a pair of minor trades.

OPENING DAY PAYROLL: $118,748,164 (17th).

PLAYERS OF THE YEAR

MAJOR LEAGUE	MINOR LEAGUE
Nick Castellanos OF	**Jose Barrero** SS
.309/.362/.576	(AAA/AA)
Career-high 34 HR	.303/.380/.539,
95 R, 100 RBIs	19 HR, 16 SB

ORGANIZATION LEADERS

Batting		*Minimum 250 AB
MAJORS		
*AVG	Nick Castellanos	.309
*OPS	Jesse Winker	.949
HR	Joey Votto	36
RBI	Nick Castellanos	100
MINORS		
*AVG	Alejo Lopez, Louisville, Chattanooga	.320
*OBP	Jacob Hurtubise, Dayton	.413
*SLG	Jose Barrero, Louisville, Chattanooga	.539
*OPS	Jose Barrero, Louisville, Chattanooga	.919
R	Jacob Hurtubise, Dayton	77
H	Lorenzo Cedrola, Louisville, Chattanooga	139
TB	Lorenzo Cedrola, Louisville, Chattanooga	202
2B	Alejo Lopez, Louisville, Chattanooga	27
3B	Elly De La Cruz, ACL Reds, Daytona	9
HR	Jose Barrero, Louisville, Chattanooga	19
RBI	Jose Barrero, Louisville, Chattanooga	66
BB	Daniel Vellojin, Daytona	72
SO	Wendell Marrero, ACL Reds, Daytona	110
SO	Alex McGarry, Dayton, Daytona	110
SB	Jacob Hurtubise, Dayton	39

Pitching		#Minimum 75 IP
MAJORS		
W	Tyler Mahle	13
#ERA	Wade Miley	3.37
SO	Tyler Mahle	210
SV	Mychal Givens/Heath Hembree	8
MINORS		
W	Graham Ashcraft, Chattanooga, Dayton	11
L	3 tied	8
#ERA	Hunter Greene, Louisville, Chattanooga	3.30
G	Phillip Diehl, Louisville	58
GS	Graham Ashcraft, Chattanooga, Dayton	22
GS	Riley O'Brien, Louisville	22
SV	Vincent Timpanelli, Dayton, Daytona	14
IP	Riley O'Brien, Louisville	112.2
BB	Riley O'Brien, Louisville	55
SO	Hunter Greene, Louisville, Chattanooga	139
#AVG	Graham Ashcraft, Chattanooga, Dayton	.212

General Manager: Nick Krall. **Farm Director:** Shawn Pender. **Scouting Director:** Rob Coughlin.

Class	Team	League	W	L	PCT	Finish	Manager
Majors	Cincinnati Reds	National	83	79	.512	6th (15)	David Bell
Triple-A	Louisville Bats	Triple-A East	55	73	.430	14th (20)	Pat Kelly
Double-A	Chattanooga Lookouts	Double-A South	58	54	.518	4th (8)	Ricky Gutierrez
High-A	Dayton Dragons	High-A Central	65	55	.542	t-3rd (12)	Jose Moreno
Low-A	Daytona Tortugas	Low-A Southeast	60	60	.500	6th (10)	Gookie Dawkins
Rookie	ACL Reds	Arizona Complex	33	26	.559	6th (18)	Bryan LaHair
Rookie	DSL Reds	Dominican Summer	30	27	.526	18th (46)	Luis Terrero
Overall 2021 Minor League Record		301		295	.505 15th (30)		

ORGANIZATION STATISTICS

CINCINNATI REDS
NATIONAL LEAGUE

Batting	B-T	HT	WT	DOB	AVG	vLH	vRH	G	AB	R	H	2B	3B	HR	RBI	BB	HBP	SH	SF	SO	SB	CS	SLG	OBP
Akiyama, Shogo	L-R	6-0	190	4-16-88	.204	.240	.197	88	162	16	33	8	0	0	12	14	4	1	1	40	2	3	.253	.282
Aquino, Aristides	R-R	6-4	220	4-22-94	.190	.198	.183	84	174	25	33	6	1	10	23	27	1	0	2	75	2	2	.408	.299
Barnhart, Tucker	L-R	5-11	192	1-7-91	.247	.255	.246	116	348	41	86	21	0	7	48	29	8	0	3	100	0	0	.368	.317
Barrero, Jose	R-R	6-2	175	4-5-98	.200	.227	.179	21	50	4	10	4	1	0	3	3	3	0	0	17	1	0	.320	.286
Blandino, Alex	R-R	6-0	190	11-6-92	.200	.176	.208	43	70	9	14	4	0	0	5	8	4	0	0	28	1	0	.257	.317
Cabrera, Asdrubal	B-R	6-0	235	11-13-85	.077	.063	.100	20	26	0	2	0	0	0	2	3	1	0	1	7	0	0	.077	.194
2-team total (90 Arizona)					.230	.257	.215	110	309	34	71	21	0	7	42	36	3	0	4	80	1	0	.366	.313
Castellanos, Nick	R-R	6-4	203	3-4-92	.309	.306	.310	138	531	95	164	38	1	34	100	41	7	0	6	121	3	1	.576	.362
DeShields, Delino	R-R	5-9	190	8-16-92	.255	.182	.320	25	47	4	12	5	0	1	6	9	0	2	0	11	2	1	.426	.375
Farmer, Kyle	R-R	6-0	205	8-17-90	.263	.257	.265	147	483	60	127	22	2	16	63	22	18	1	5	97	2	3	.416	.316
Freeman, Mike	L-R	6-0	195	8-4-87	.186	.231	.174	37	59	6	11	0	0	0	3	5	1	0	0	20	1	1	.186	.262
Friedl, TJ	L-L	5-10	180	8-14-95	.290	.333	.280	14	31	9	9	1	0	1	2	4	0	0	1	2	0	0	.419	.361
Heineman, Scott	R-R	6-1	220	12-4-92	.100	.120	.000	19	30	5	3	0	0	2	3	3	1	0	0	15	0	0	.300	.206
India, Jonathan	R-R	6-0	200	12-15-96	.269	.297	.259	150	532	98	143	34	2	21	69	71	23	1	4	141	12	3	.459	.376
Lopez, Alejo	B-R	5-10	170	5-5-96	.261	.286	.222	14	23	3	6	0	0	0	0	0	0	0	0	5	0	0	.261	.261
Moustakas, Mike	L-R	6-0	225	9-11-88	.208	.086	.236	62	183	21	38	12	0	6	22	18	2	0	3	46	0	0	.372	.282
Naquin, Tyler	L-R	6-2	195	4-24-91	.270	.197	.283	127	411	52	111	24	2	19	70	35	5	0	3	106	5	3	.477	.333
Payton, Mark	L-L	5-8	180	12-7-91	.182	.500	.111	24	22	2	4	0	0	0	2	2	0	0	0	7	0	0	.182	.250
Schrock, Max	L-R	5-9	185	10-12-94	.288	.100	.304	53	125	19	36	7	2	3	14	8	0	0	1	24	1	1	.448	.328
Senzel, Nick	R-R	6-1	205	6-29-95	.252	.333	.237	36	111	18	28	4	0	1	8	12	0	0	1	16	2	5	.315	.323
Stephenson, Tyler	R-R	6-4	225	8-16-96	.286	.291	.283	132	350	56	100	21	0	10	45	41	6	0	5	75	0	0	.431	.366
Suarez, Eugenio	R-R	5-11	213	7-18-91	.198	.172	.208	145	505	71	100	23	0	31	79	56	8	0	5	171	0	1	.428	.286
Votto, Joey	L-R	6-2	220	9-10-83	.266	.215	.289	129	448	73	119	23	1	36	99	77	4	0	4	127	1	0	.563	.375
Winker, Jesse	L-L	6-3	215	8-17-93	.305	.176	.346	110	423	77	129	32	1	24	71	53	9	0	0	75	1	0	.556	.394

Pitching	B-T	HT	WT	DOB	W	L	ERA	G	GS	CG	SV	IP	H	R	ER	HR	BB	SO	AVG	vLH	vRH	K/9	BB/9
Alaniz, R.J.	R-R	6-4	220	6-14-91	0	0	3.38	3	0	0	0	3	1	1	1	1	3	3	.111	.167	.000	10.13	10.13
Antone, Tejay	R-R	6-4	230	12-5-93	2	0	2.14	23	0	0	3	34	17	8	8	3	13	42	.152	.172	.130	11.23	3.48
Bedrosian, Cam	R-R	6-1	225	10-2-91	0	0	11.12	6	0	0	0	6	10	7	7	2	6	7	.400	.375	.412	11.12	9.53
2-team total (11 Philadelphia)					0	0	6.75	17	1	0	0	16	18	12	12	4	13	15	.286	.250	.308	8.44	7.31
Blandino, Alex	R-R	6-0	190	11-6-92	0	0	9.82	4	0	0	0	4	4	5	4	1	4	1	.286	.375	.167	2.45	9.82
Brach, Brad	R-R	6-6	215	4-12-86	1	2	6.30	35	0	0	1	30	30	26	21	5	18	33	.254	.250	.257	9.90	5.40
Castillo, Luis	R-R	6-2	200	12-12-92	8	16	3.98	33	33	0	0	188	181	94	83	19	75	192	.255	.245	.264	9.21	3.60
Cessa, Luis	R-R	6-0	208	4-25-92	2	1	2.05	24	0	0	0	26	24	7	6	3	2	23	.245	.250	.240	7.86	0.68
De Leon, Jose	R-R	6-2	215	8-7-92	0	1	8.35	9	2	0	0	18	22	17	17	4	11	33	.289	.294	.286	16.20	5.40
Doolittle, Sean	L-L	6-2	204	9-26-86	3	1	4.46	45	0	0	1	38	40	21	19	6	18	41	.267	.229	.300	9.63	4.23
Feliz, Michael	R-R	6-4	250	6-28-93	0	0	16.20	9	0	0	1	7	13	12	12	2	4	9	.394	.357	.421	12.15	5.40
2-team total (7 Pittsburgh)					0	0	8.79	16	0	0	1	14	21	15	14	2	5	17	.333	.310	.353	10.67	3.14
Freeman, Mike	L-R	6-0	195	8-4-87	0	0	0.00	1	0	0	0	0	0	0	0	0	1	0	.000	—	.000	27.00	0.00
Fulmer, Carson	R-R	6-0	210	12-13-93	0	0	6.66	20	0	0	0	26	26	20	19	3	13	24	.265	.233	.291	8.42	4.56
Garcia, Edgar	R-R	6-1	205	10-4-96	0	1	16.62	5	0	0	0	4	10	10	8	2	1	4	.435	.333	.500	8.31	2.08
Garrett, Amir	R-L	6-5	239	5-3-92	0	4	6.04	63	0	0	7	48	46	34	32	9	29	61	.249	.226	.267	11.52	5.48
Givens, Mychal	R-R	6-0	230	5-13-90	1	1	4.22	23	0	0	8	21	18	11	10	2	13	20	.234	.278	.195	8.44	5.48
2-team total (31 Colorado)					4	3	3.35	54	0	0	8	51	43	22	19	7	27	54	.234	.214	.250	9.53	4.76
Goudeau, Ashton	R-R	6-6	220	7-23-92	0	0	4.00	5	0	0	0	9	8	4	4	1	9	5	.235	.222	.250	5.00	9.00
2-team total (11 Colorado)					2	1	4.19	16	1	0	0	34	24	16	16	4	17	22	.202	.232	.160	5.77	4.46
Gray, Sonny	R-R	5-10	195	11-7-89	7	9	4.19	26	26	0	0	135	115	67	63	19	50	155	.225	.208	.239	10.31	3.33
Gutierrez, Vladimir	R-R	6-1	190	9-18-95	9	6	4.74	22	22	0	0	114	115	61	60	20	46	88	.263	.255	.271	6.95	3.63
Hembree, Heath	R-R	6-4	220	1-13-89	2	7	6.38	45	0	0	8	42	32	33	30	10	19	68	.203	.295	.144	14.46	4.04
2-team total (15 New York)					3	8	5.59	60	0	0	9	58	45	39	36	12	24	83	.208	.253	.181	12.88	3.72
Hendrix, Ryan	R-R	6-3	215	12-16-94	5	1	5.97	36	0	0	0	32	33	23	21	8	16	35	.268	.212	.310	9.95	4.55
Hoffman, Jeff	R-R	6-5	235	1-8-93	3	5	4.56	31	11	0	0	73	70	41	37	12	45	79	.248	.261	.236	9.74	5.55
Lorenzen, Michael	R-R	6-3	217	1-4-92	1	2	5.59	27	0	0	4	29	26	18	18	2	14	21	.241	.226	.261	6.52	4.34

Mahle, Tyler	R-R	6-3	210	9-29-94	13	6	3.75	33	33	0	0	180	158	78	75	24	64	210	.234	.198	.270	10.50	3.20
Miley, Wade	L-L	6-2	220	11-13-86	12	7	3.37	28	28	1	0	163	166	64	61	17	50	125	.265	.218	.276	6.90	2.76
Moreta, Dauri	R-R	6-2	185	4-15-96	0	0	2.45	4	0	0	0	4	2	1	1	1	1	4	.154	.250	.000	9.82	2.45
Osich, Josh	L-L	6-2	235	9-3-88	2	0	5.02	17	0	0	1	14	15	9	8	4	5	9	.273	.296	.250	5.65	3.14
O'Brien, Riley	R-R	6-4	180	2-6-95	0	1	13.50	1	1	0	0	1	2	2	2	2	3	2	.333	.500	.250	13.50	20.25
Perez, Cionel	R-L	5-11	162	4-21-96	1	2	6.38	25	0	0	0	24	21	21	17	5	20	25	.233	.222	.241	9.38	7.50
Romano, Sal	L-R	6-5	255	10-12-93	0	0	5.23	14	0	0	0	21	20	14	12	4	9	12	.244	.194	.283	5.23	3.92
2-team total (1 Milwaukee)					0	1	6.23	15	0	0	0	22	24	18	15	5	9	12	.270	.225	.306	4.98	3.74
Sanmartin, Reiver	L-L	6-2	160	4-15-96	2	0	1.54	2	2	0	0	12	12	2	2	0	2	11	.267	.158	.346	8.49	1.54
Santillan, Tony	R-R	6-3	240	4-15-97	1	3	2.91	26	4	0	0	43	34	15	14	7	21	56	.217	.242	.198	11.63	4.36
Schrock, Max	L-R	5-9	185	10-12-94	0	0	0.00	2	0	0	0	2	0	0	0	1	0	0	.000	.000	.000	5.40	0.00
Sims, Lucas	R-R	6-2	225	5-10-94	5	3	4.40	47	0	0	7	47	34	26	23	6	18	76	.200	.214	.190	14.55	3.45
Warren, Art	R-R	6-3	230	3-23-93	3	0	1.29	26	0	0	0	21	11	3	3	1	8	34	.153	.143	.159	14.57	3.43
Wilson, Justin	L-L	6-2	205	8-18-87	0	0	2.81	21	0	0	0	16	14	5	5	1	7	14	.237	.348	.167	7.88	3.94

Fielding

Catcher	PCT	G	PO	A	E	DP	PB
Barnhart	.998	102	880	47	2	4	3
Stephenson	1.000	78	661	22	0	4	7

First Base	PCT	G	PO	A	E	DP
Barnhart	1.000	2	3	0	0	1
Blandino	1.000	17	70	7	0	8
Cabrera	.944	3	16	1	1	1
Farmer	1.000	5	17	2	0	2
Freeman	1.000	9	20	2	0	1
Heineman	1.000	2	3	1	0	1
Moustakas	1.000	11	41	4	0	2
Schrock	1.000	5	22	0	0	1
Stephenson	.993	23	128	10	1	8
Votto	.993	123	853	99	7	91

Second Base	PCT	G	PO	A	E	DP
Barrero	.875	2	5	2	1	2
Blandino	1.000	5	1	3	0	0
Farmer	1.000	9	5	12	0	3
Freeman	1.000	2	2	2	0	0
India	.976	148	269	336	15	78

	PCT	G	PO	A	E	DP
Lopez	1.000	3	2	5	0	0
Moustakas	.000	1	0	0	0	0
Schrock	1.000	8	10	13	0	4
Senzel	.875	8	6	8	2	0

Third Base	PCT	G	PO	A	E	DP
Blandino	1.000	9	2	12	0	2
Cabrera	1.000	3	0	2	0	0
Farmer	.929	10	4	9	1	1
Freeman	1.000	7	2	4	0	0
Lopez	.667	3	0	2	1	0
Moustakas	.948	44	23	68	5	3
Schrock	1.000	9	5	1	0	0
Senzel	1.000	3	2	3	0	0
Suarez	.967	104	69	193	9	21

Shortstop	PCT	G	PO	A	E	DP
Barrero	.971	9	12	22	1	11
Blandino	.000	1	0	0	0	0
Farmer	.988	121	128	270	5	53
Freeman	.950	12	5	14	1	0
Suarez	.936	34	40	77	8	17

Outfield	PCT	G	PO	A	E	DP
Akiyama	.977	61	86	0	2	0
Aquino	.966	76	84	1	3	0
Barrero	1.000	7	12	0	0	0
Blandino	1.000	3	1	0	0	0
Castellanos	.991	135	226	7	2	0
DeShields	.972	21	35	0	1	0
Farmer	--	2	0	0	0	0
Freeman	1.000	4	1	0	0	0
Friedl	.867	11	12	1	2	0
Heineman	1.000	12	11	0	0	0
Lopez	--	3	0	0	0	0
Lorenzen	1.000	2	1	0	0	0
Naquin	.980	135	188	5	4	0
Payton	.857	5	6	0	1	0
Schrock	.943	24	33	0	2	0
Senzel	.978	29	44	0	1	0
Stephenson	--	1	0	0	0	0
Winker	.987	107	152	4	2	0

LOUISVILLE BATS   TRIPLE-A

TRIPLE-A EAST

Batting	B-T	HT	WT	DOB	AVG	vLH	vRH	G	AB	R	H	2B	3B	HR	RBI	BB	HBP	SH	SF	SO	SB	CS	SLG	OBP
Akiyama, Shogo	L-R	6-0	190	4-16-88	.111	.200	.000	2	9	0	1	0	0	0	0	0	0	0	0	3	0	0	.111	.111
Aquino, Aristides	R-R	6-4	220	4-22-94	.263	.333	.231	6	19	5	5	2	0	1	5	8	0	0	0	1	0	0	.526	.481
Barrero, Jose	R-R	6-2	175	4-5-98	.306	.308	.305	45	170	31	52	10	0	13	38	20	6	1	3	44	8	3	.594	.392
Bell, Brantley	R-R	6-3	185	11-16-94	.199	.167	.212	85	236	27	47	9	2	1	17	24	2	1	1	59	8	2	.267	.278
Blandino, Alex	R-R	6-0	190	11-6-92	.102	.100	.102	18	59	5	6	3	0	0	3	14	2	0	1	16	0	0	.153	.289
Cedrola, Lorenzo	R-R	5-8	152	1-12-98	.257	.182	.292	9	35	5	9	3	0	1	1	2	2	0	0	2	2	0	.429	.333
Crook, Narciso	R-R	6-3	220	7-12-95	.245	.190	.272	86	241	35	59	16	0	11	41	36	8	0	1	77	7	3	.448	.360
Cuthbert, Cheslor	R-R	6-1	205	11-16-92	.203	.154	.229	21	74	8	15	4	0	2	11	14	0	0	0	14	1	0	.338	.330
2-team total (76 Syracuse)					.222	.191	.235	97	302	42	67	13	1	16	47	43	5	0	0	68	1	1	.430	.329
De Leon, Michael	B-R	6-1	160	1-14-97	.258	.307	.235	98	275	31	71	15	0	7	43	17	1	1	2	69	0	0	.389	.302
Delmonico, Nicky	L-R	6-3	230	7-12-92	.221	.130	.267	19	68	7	15	5	0	2	10	9	0	0	0	23	0	0	.382	.312
Freeman, Mike	L-R	6-0	195	8-4-87	.242	.140	.281	56	178	34	43	10	1	6	23	37	1	0	1	46	2	0	.410	.373
Friedl, TJ	L-L	5-10	180	8-14-95	.264	.302	.246	113	386	59	102	15	5	12	36	44	13	2	3	65	13	7	.422	.357
Gale, Rocky	R-R	6-1	185	2-22-88	.208	.270	.150	26	77	1	16	3	0	0	5	1	1	1	0	15	0	0	.247	.228
Heineman, Scott	R-R	6-1	220	12-4-92	.279	.286	.275	17	61	10	17	3	1	1	4	5	2	0	0	12	4	1	.410	.353
Hernandez, Jan	R-R	6-1	195	1-3-95	.167	.100	.196	29	66	8	11	2	0	3	8	6	2	0	0	34	0	0	.333	.257
Inciarte, Ender	L-L	5-11	190	10-29-90	.288	.273	.292	15	59	7	17	3	0	0	7	6	0	0	0	10	0	1	.339	.354
2-team total (6 Gwinnett)					.263	.286	.254	21	80	9	21	5	0	0	8	7	2	0	0	17	0	1	.325	.337
Kolozsvary, Mark	R-R	5-8	180	9-4-95	.190	.308	.156	19	58	9	11	2	1	1	2	3	6	0	0	23	0	0	.310	.299
Lee, Braxton	L-R	5-10	185	8-23-93	.233	.200	.243	51	150	15	35	7	2	0	15	19	0	1	1	40	1	2	.307	.318
Lopez, Alejo	B-R	5-10	170	5-5-96	.303	.338	.289	67	251	54	76	18	0	6	31	33	3	0	3	21	6	2	.446	.386
Morrison, Logan	L-L	6-3	245	8-25-87	.347	.200	.412	16	49	8	17	5	1	2	12	10	0	0	0	8	0	0	.612	.458
Mount, Drew	L-R	5-11	205	3-24-96	.111	.000	.143	4	9	1	0	0	0	0	1	0	0	0	0	0	0	0	.111	.200
Moustakas, Mike	L-R	6-0	225	9-11-88	.353	.167	.455	5	17	3	6	1	0	1	1	1	0	0	0	1	0	0	.588	.389
Okey, Chris	R-R	5-11	200	12-29-94	.237	.328	.181	71	169	22	40	7	1	5	23	22	2	0	1	47	0	0	.379	.330
Payton, Mark	L-L	5-8	180	12-7-91	.281	.314	.261	35	139	19	39	7	2	4	14	11	0	0	1	23	4	1	.446	.331
2-team total (40 Syracuse)					.293	.326	.278	75	290	42	85	19	3	8	33	30	2	0	3	50	6	3	.462	.360
Rey, Brian	R-R	5-11	170	2-22-98	.385	.500	.286	4	13	1	5	1	0	0	3	3	1	0	0	2	0	0	.462	.529
Robinson, Errol	R-R	5-11	170	10-1-94	.176	.294	.118	36	102	13	18	4	1	1	7	17	0	0	0	33	2	1	.265	.294
Rodriguez, Alfredo	R-R	6-0	190	6-17-94	.283	.322	.268	117	410	36	116	16	2	3	48	27	7	1	7	78	23	5	.354	.333
Schrock, Max	L-R	5-9	185	10-12-94	.289	.237	.311	38	128	14	37	4	0	6	19	7	2	0	1	25	0	0	.461	.333
Schuyler, Jay	R-R	6-1	194	4-11-97	.167	.000	.250	3	6	1	1	0	0	1	3	0	0	0	0	2	0	0	.667	.167

	B-T	HT	WT	DOB	AVG	vLH	vRH	G	AB	R	H	2B	3B	HR	RBI	BB	HBP	SH	SF	SO	SB	CS	OBP	SLG
Senzel, Nick	R-R	6-1	205	6-29-95	.286	.444	.231	10	35	5	10	3	1	0	2	2	0	0	1	2	0	0	.429	.316
Smith Jr., Dwight	L-R	6-0	210	10-26-92	.220	.186	.238	36	127	7	28	5	0	1	17	20	0	0	0	34	1	1	.283	.327
Smith, Mallex	L-R	5-10	180	5-6-93	.231	.190	.250	22	65	7	15	1	0	1	5	6	0	0	0	19	4	2	.292	.296
2-team total (7 Buffalo)					.265	.190	.290	29	83	14	22	1	1	3	11	11	0	0	0	22	7	3	.410	.351
Taylor, Beau	L-R	5-11	205	2-13-90	.232	.122	.268	75	198	21	46	8	0	4	23	28	5	1	2	56	0	0	.333	.339
Urbaez, Francisco	R-R	5-11	195	10-13-97	.231	.238	.226	14	52	6	12	4	0	0	4	3	0	0	0	8	0	0	.308	.273
Votto, Joey	L-R	6-2	220	9-10-83	.190	.375	.077	6	21	2	4	1	1	0	2	1	0	0	0	5	0	0	.333	.227
Willems, Jonathan	R-R	5-11	190	11-7-98	.111	.100	.118	19	27	4	3	1	0	0	1	2	1	1	0	12	0	0	.148	.200
Winker, Jesse	L-L	6-3	215	8-17-93	.000	.000	.000	2	5	0	0	0	0	0	0	0	0	0	0	2	0	0	.000	.000

Pitching	B-T	HT	WT	DOB	W	L	ERA	G	GS	CG	SV	IP	H	R	ER	HR	BB	SO	AVG	vLH	vRH	K/9	BB/9
Adleman, Tim	R-R	6-5	225	11-13-87	1	1	3.80	31	3	0	0	45	39	20	19	5	11	41	.228	.195	.255	8.20	2.20
Alaniz, R.J.	R-R	6-4	220	6-14-91	1	3	3.46	33	0	0	1	39	42	20	15	1	17	45	.286	.364	.239	10.38	3.92
Antone, Tejay	R-R	6-4	230	12-5-93	0	0	2.70	7	0	0	1	7	4	2	2	1	3	10	.174	.100	.231	13.50	4.05
Baker, Dylan	R-R	6-2	205	4-6-92	0	1	18.00	1	0	0	0	2	4	5	4	0	2	3	.444	.250	.600	13.50	9.00
Brach, Brad	R-R	6-6	215	4-12-86	0	0	0.00	8	0	0	0	9	5	1	0	0	1	5	.167	.000	.278	15.58	1.04
Byrne, Michael	R-R	6-3	205	4-16-97	0	0	0.00	1	0	0	0	0	0	0	0	0	1	0	.000	.000	--	0.00	27.00
Carle, Shane	R-R	6-4	210	8-30-91	0	2	3.45	19	0	0	1	16	16	8	6	1	5	15	.262	.227	.282	8.62	2.87
De Leon, Jose	R-R	6-2	215	8-7-92	1	1	4.63	12	0	0	1	12	8	7	6	1	7	19	.190	.267	.148	14.66	5.40
Demurias, Eddy	R-R	6-0	184	8-1-97	0	0	9.00	2	0	0	0	2	3	2	2	0	2	0	.375	.400	.333	0.00	4.50
Diehl, Phillip	L-L	6-2	169	7-16-94	2	3	2.47	58	0	0	3	55	39	21	15	9	12	71	.200	.197	.202	11.69	1.98
Duarte, Daniel	R-R	6-0	170	12-4-96	2	0	0.00	3	0	0	1	4	0	0	0	0	0	7	.000	.000	.000	15.75	0.00
Feliz, Michael	R-R	6-4	250	6-28-93	1	0	1.98	13	0	0	0	14	8	3	3	0	1	15	.163	.158	.167	9.88	0.66
2-team total (2 Worcester)					2	0	1.72	15	0	0	0	16	9	3	3	0	1	19	.161	.143	.171	10.91	0.57
Finnegan, Brandon	L-L	5-11	216	4-14-93	4	3	5.53	40	1	0	0	55	58	34	34	8	36	57	.274	.253	.286	9.27	5.86
Fulmer, Carson	R-R	6-0	210	12-13-93	1	5	4.61	37	2	0	1	41	40	29	21	4	25	51	.253	.197	.293	11.20	5.49
Garcia, Edgar	R-R	6-1	205	10-4-96	2	0	3.38	24	0	0	1	24	17	9	9	0	13	29	.205	.226	.192	10.88	4.88
2-team total (13 St. Paul)					4	1	3.20	37	0	0	2	45	28	16	16	1	29	49	.178	.180	.177	9.80	5.80
Goudeau, Ashton	R-R	6-6	220	7-23-92	1	3	4.65	8	5	0	0	31	30	17	16	5	13	22	.252	.227	.267	6.39	3.77
Gray, Sonny	R-R	5-10	195	11-7-89	0	0	0.00	1	1	0	0	3	1	0	0	0	3	4	.125	.000	.200	12.00	9.00
Greene, Hunter	R-R	6-5	230	8-6-99	5	8	4.13	14	14	0	0	65	59	35	30	11	25	79	.240	.267	.225	10.88	3.44
Gutierrez, Vladimir	R-R	6-1	190	9-18-95	2	0	2.65	3	3	0	0	17	9	5	5	3	7	21	.153	.136	.162	11.12	3.71
Hendrix, Ryan	R-R	6-3	215	12-16-94	1	0	8.62	16	0	0	0	16	15	17	15	4	9	15	.250	.174	.297	8.62	5.17
Hoffman, Jeff	R-R	6-5	235	1-8-93	0	0	1.76	4	4	0	0	15	11	4	3	2	4	20	.196	.056	.263	11.74	2.35
Howard, Nick	R-R	6-4	215	4-6-93	0	1	7.20	20	0	0	0	20	14	16	16	3	24	16	.206	.241	.179	7.20	10.80
Kuhnel, Joel	R-R	6-4	280	2-19-95	0	0	0.00	4	0	0	0	4	2	0	0	0	1	3	.143	.286	.000	6.75	2.25
Lee, Braxton	L-R	5-10	185	8-23-93	0	0	0.00	1	0	0	0	1	0	0	0	0	1	0	.000	.000	.000	0.00	9.00
Lee, Zach	R-R	6-3	195	9-13-91	1	0	4.26	7	3	0	0	19	16	9	9	4	6	17	.229	.313	.158	8.05	2.84
Lodolo, Nick	L-L	6-5	205	2-5-98	0	1	5.40	3	3	0	0	7	4	4	2	2	2	10	.269	.273	.267	13.50	3.60
Lopez, Diomar	R-R	5-11	165	12-15-96	1	0	1.80	9	0	0	0	15	9	4	3	1	6	15	.173	.130	.207	9.00	3.60
Lorenzen, Michael	R-R	6-3	217	1-4-92	0	0	2.08	4	0	0	1	4	2	1	1	1	1	6	.133	.250	.091	12.46	2.08
Mariot, Michael	R-R	6-0	190	10-20-88	6	5	4.02	19	18	0	0	103	96	47	46	15	31	83	.245	.242	.247	7.25	2.71
Milone, Tommy	L-L	6-0	215	2-16-87	0	2	14.40	3	3	0	0	5	9	8	8	1	3	10	.375	.500	.333	18.00	5.40
2-team total (8 Buffalo)					0	2	5.79	11	7	0	0	19	18	14	12	3	8	19	.247	.292	.224	9.16	3.86
Moreta, Dauri	R-R	6-2	185	4-15-96	2	0	0.68	24	0	0	8	26	14	4	2	2	4	21	.149	.143	.153	7.18	1.37
Osich, Josh	L-L	6-2	235	9-3-88	1	2	5.40	11	2	0	0	15	11	9	9	2	6	15	.196	.188	.200	9.00	3.60
O'Brien, Riley	R-R	6-4	180	2-6-95	7	7	4.55	23	22	0	0	113	93	59	57	16	55	121	.222	.214	.227	9.67	4.39
Perez, Cionel	R-L	5-11	162	4-21-96	1	2	3.26	31	0	0	2	30	26	13	11	1	13	41	.226	.325	.173	12.16	3.86
Perez, Hector	R-R	6-3	223	6-6-96	0	0	8.44	8	0	0	0	11	10	10	10	1	10	11	.244	.267	.231	8.44	9.28
Pidich, Matt	R-R	6-2	220	12-25-94	0	2	5.56	10	0	0	0	11	12	13	7	4	2	14	.250	.240	.261	11.12	1.59
Pucheu, Jacques	L-L	6-2	210	1-1-97	0	1	45.00	1	1	0	0	1	7	5	5	2	0	1	.700	.667	.750	9.00	0.00
Robinson, Errol	R-R	5-11	170	10-1-94	0	0	0.00	1	0	0	0	0	0	0	0	0	0	1	.000	.500	--	0.00	9.00
Sanmartin, Reiver	L-L	6-2	160	4-15-96	8	2	3.94	21	14	0	0	82	80	40	36	6	23	89	.253	.223	.266	9.73	2.51
Santillan, Tony	R-R	6-3	240	4-15-97	1	3	2.13	13	6	1	2	38	25	10	9	5	15	51	.182	.250	.136	12.08	3.55
Shipley, Braden	R-R	6-1	190	2-22-92	1	5	7.07	18	4	0	0	28	34	25	22	7	17	34	.288	.220	.338	10.93	5.46
Sims, Lucas	R-R	6-2	225	5-10-94	0	0	3.86	5	2	0	0	5	6	2	2	0	3	4	.333	.200	.500	7.71	5.79
Takahashi, Bo	R-R	6-0	225	1-23-97	3	7	4.45	18	17	0	0	89	82	47	44	14	32	89	.244	.288	.216	9.00	3.24
Warren, Art	R-R	6-3	230	3-23-93	1	2	5.06	15	0	0	2	16	18	10	9	1	5	30	.269	.348	.227	16.88	2.81

Fielding

Catcher

Catcher	PCT	G	PO	A	E	DP	PB
Gale	.996	23	217	14	1	2	0
Kolozsvary	.986	16	134	9	2	0	0
Okey	.995	46	361	23	2	4	2
Schuyler	.889	1	8	0	1	0	0
Taylor	.992	56	497	22	4	3	8

First Base

First Base	PCT	G	PO	A	E	DP
Bell	.987	49	275	24	4	30
Blandino	.959	6	43	4	2	3
Crook	.000	1	0	0	0	0
Cuthbert	1.000	4	21	0	0	1
De Leon	.988	31	159	12	2	10
Delmonico	.993	18	131	4	1	8
Freeman	1.000	4	35	3	0	3
Gale	1.000	1	2	0	0	0
Heineman	1.000	6	36	4	0	4
Morrison	1.000	14	88	7	0	11
Rodriguez	.992	19	123	7	1	12
Schrock	.944	2	16	1	1	3
Taylor	.000	1	0	0	0	0
Votto	1.000	2	14	2	0	1

Second Base

Second Base	PCT	G	PO	A	E	DP
Bell	.667	2	1	1	1	0
Blandino	.957	7	8	14	1	4
De Leon	1.000	5	3	4	0	0
Freeman	.967	7	20	9	1	6
Lopez	1.000	24	30	63	0	19
Robinson	1.000	12	15	19	0	2
Rodriguez	.988	45	65	96	2	26
Schrock	.975	20	27	50	2	10
Urbaez	.949	13	23	33	3	9
Willems	1.000	15	10	17	0	3

Third Base

Third Base	PCT	G	PO	A	E	DP
Barrero	.667	2	1	3	2	1
Bell	1.000	1	0	1	0	0
Blandino	.846	6	2	9	2	1
Cuthbert	.921	16	7	28	3	1
De Leon	.963	49	22	57	3	8
Freeman	.909	17	8	32	4	2
Lopez	.969	30	12	50	2	5
Moustakas	1.000	4	1	3	0	0
Rodriguez	1.000	11	2	13	0	1

Schrock	.800	10	3	9 3 0	

Shortstop	PCT	G	PO	A	E	DP
Barrero	.971	43	54	111	5	23
De Leon	.000	1	0	0	0	0
Freeman	.957	26	24	65	4	15
Lopez	1.000	1	2	0	0	0
Robinson	.926	20	24	39	5	9
Rodriguez	.967	44	38	108	5	17
Senzel	1.000	2	2	2	0	0

Outfield PCT G PO A E DP

Akiyama	1.000	2	4	0	0	0
Aquino	1.000	5	9	1	0	0
Bell	.974	27	36	2	1	0
Cedrola	1.000	9	28	1	0	0
Crook	.974	75	112	0	3	0
Freeman	1.000	1	1	0	0	0
Friedl	.995	117	193	3	1	1
Heineman	1.000	9	9	0	0	0
Hernandez	.966	24	25	3	1	0
Inciarte	1.000	15	35	0	0	0
Lee	.952	49	71	8	4	3

Lopez	1.000	10	16	0	0	0
Mount	1.000	3	5	0	0	0
Okey	1.000	1	1	0	0	0
Payton	1.000	34	66	1	0	0
Robinson	1.000	1	6	0	0	0
Schrock	1.000	3	6	0	0	0
Senzel	1.000	7	14	0	0	0
Smith Jr.	.978	31	41	3	1	0
Smith	.974	19	37	1	1	1
Winker	1.000	2	1	0	0	0

CHATTANOOGA LOOKOUTS
DOUBLE-A SOUTH

DOUBLE-A

CINCINNATI REDS

Batting	B-T	HT	WT	DOB	AVG	vLH	vRH	G	AB	R	H	2B	3B	HR	RBI	BB	HBP	SH	SF	SO	SB	CS	SLG	OBP
Barrero, Jose	R-R	6-2	175	4-5-98	.300	.240	.327	40	160	31	48	9	1	6	28	16	2	0	2	40	8	1	.481	.367
Bautista, Mariel	R-R	6-3	194	10-15-97	.211	.250	.200	9	19	2	4	1	0	0	3	0	0	0	0	2	0	1	.263	.211
Cedrola, Lorenzo	R-R	5-8	152	1-12-98	.320	.345	.310	106	406	68	130	16	7	9	61	17	8	2	4	50	8	8	.461	.356
Crook, Narciso	R-R	6-3	220	7-12-95	.241	.294	.216	14	54	7	13	3	0	3	13	5	2	0	0	19	1	0	.463	.328
De Leon, Michael	B-R	6-1	160	1-14-97	.316	.250	.333	5	19	1	6	1	0	1	4	2	0	0	0	2	0	0	.526	.381
Garcia, Wilson	R-R	5-11	227	1-11-94	.290	.204	.324	103	400	44	116	17	0	18	64	15	5	0	5	77	0	0	.468	.320
Hernandez, Miguel	R-R	6-0	194	4-13-99	.255	.323	.222	25	94	13	24	4	1	0	11	6	0	0	0	26	0	1	.319	.300
Hopkins, TJ	R-R	6-0	195	1-16-97	.268	.300	.254	74	257	42	69	14	7	5	33	26	4	2	3	71	3	0	.436	.341
Kolozsvary, Mark	R-R	5-8	180	9-4-95	.233	.204	.247	40	146	33	34	12	0	6	26	20	4	0	0	53	0	0	.438	.341
Lee, Braxton	L-R	5-10	185	8-23-93	.212	.182	.225	29	113	12	24	5	1	0	13	7	2	1	0	29	2	1	.274	.270
Lloyd, Matt	L-R	6-1	205	3-17-96	.235	.278	.225	32	98	13	23	3	0	7	14	12	3	0	1	36	0	1	.480	.333
Lopez, Alejo	B-R	5-10	170	5-5-96	.362	.348	.366	25	105	18	38	9	0	0	13	12	2	0	0	11	3	1	.448	.437
McAfee, Quincy	R-R	5-11	185	9-16-97	.238	.194	.256	47	122	21	29	5	1	2	16	22	9	1	2	32	5	2	.344	.387
Mount, Drew	L-R	5-11	205	3-24-96	.279	.292	.275	53	197	33	55	5	2	11	24	14	3	0	1	59	1	3	.492	.335
Rey, Brian	R-R	5-11	170	2-22-98	.255	.250	.257	68	243	31	62	7	0	3	31	21	15	1	3	49	4	6	.321	.348
Reyes, Reyny	R-R	6-2	185	3-20-99	.250	.000	.333	2	4	0	1	0	0	0	0	0	0	0	0	1	0	0	.250	.400
Rivas, Leonardo	B-R	5-10	150	10-10-97	.274	.269	.275	60	190	30	52	6	3	0	21	32	2	1	1	45	9	5	.337	.382
Robinson, Chuckie	R-R	5-11	221	12-14-94	.248	.224	.257	66	210	40	52	8	0	8	24	28	6	0	0	46	2	2	.400	.352
Robinson, Errol	R-R	5-11	170	10-1-94	.213	.208	.215	29	89	13	19	4	0	0	5	14	1	0	0	34	5	3	.258	.327
Schuyler, Jay	R-R	6-1	194	4-11-97	.182	.233	.154	40	121	9	22	6	0	1	11	11	3	0	1	49	0	0	.256	.265
Tello, Jose	R-R	6-0	170	5-21-98	.192	.250	.143	7	26	1	5	3	0	0	1	0	0	0	0	7	0	0	.308	.192
Tenerowicz, Robbie	R-R	6-1	185	1-6-95	.264	.244	.272	93	303	48	80	17	2	14	46	27	17	0	6	89	3	6	.472	.351
Urbaez, Francisco	R-R	5-11	195	10-13-97	.200	.125	.219	14	40	3	8	2	1	0	3	6	2	0	0	5	0	0	.300	.333
Willems, Jonathan	R-R	5-11	190	11-7-98	.273	.000	.333	3	11	1	3	2	0	0	0	0	0	0	0	4	0	0	.455	.273
Yanqui, Yoel	L-L	6-1	210	4-25-96	.235	.230	.237	80	272	37	64	9	3	7	35	35	11	0	2	83	4	6	.368	.323

Pitching	B-T	HT	WT	DOB	W	L	ERA	G	GS	CG	SV	IP	H	R	ER	HR	BB	SO	AVG	vLH	vRH	K/9	BB/9
Ashcraft, Graham	L-R	6-2	240	2-11-98	7	3	3.36	14	14	1	0	72	58	30	27	4	24	74	.218	.152	.261	9.21	2.99
Baker, Dylan	R-R	6-2	205	4-6-92	0	1	5.29	15	8	0	0	48	62	28	28	6	22	35	.323	.380	.283	6.61	4.15
Byrne, Michael	R-R	6-3	205	4-16-97	5	5	3.24	33	3	0	2	50	39	19	18	2	22	36	.217	.236	.206	6.84	3.96
Curlis, Connor	L-L	6-1	180	11-29-96	5	7	5.03	20	20	0	0	98	88	58	55	21	48	88	.240	.274	.228	8.05	4.39
Demurias, Eddy	R-R	6-0	184	8-1-97	3	3	2.43	30	0	0	1	41	24	13	11	2	21	42	.168	.127	.193	9.30	4.65
Diaz, Alexis	R-R	6-2	224	9-28-96	3	1	3.83	35	0	0	2	42	30	20	18	2	20	70	.194	.173	.206	14.88	4.25
Duarte, Daniel	R-R	6-0	170	12-4-96	0	1	5.84	11	0	0	6	12	14	8	8	2	5	18	.280	.389	.219	13.14	3.65
Figueroa, Miguel	R-R	6-2	165	8-9-97	0	1	5.40	29	0	0	0	40	44	25	24	7	25	60	.273	.288	.266	13.50	5.63
Ghyzel, John	R-R	6-5	200	5-18-96	1	0	8.18	12	0	0	0	11	13	14	10	2	10	18	.271	.286	.259	14.73	8.18
Greene, Hunter	R-R	6-5	230	8-6-99	0	0	1.98	7	7	0	0	41	27	9	9	2	14	60	.186	.161	.202	13.17	3.07
Howard, Nick	R-R	6-4	215	4-6-93	1	0	2.25	22	0	0	8	24	17	8	6	2	12	35	.191	.207	.183	13.13	4.50
Keys, JC	R-R	5-10	173	10-9-96	1	3	6.11	14	1	0	0	18	18	12	12	3	10	22	.254	.333	.195	11.21	5.09
Lillie, Ryan	R-R	6-0	210	5-9-96	0	0	4.35	8	0	0	0	10	13	7	5	0	7	15	.295	.190	.391	13.06	6.10
Lodolo, Nick	L-L	6-6	205	2-5-98	2	1	1.84	10	10	0	0	44	31	9	9	1	6	68	.196	.180	.204	13.91	1.84
Lopez, Diomar	R-R	5-11	165	12-15-96	0	0	2.67	18	1	0	0	30	21	10	9	4	13	27	.188	.257	.156	8.01	3.86
Moreta, Dauri	R-R	6-2	185	4-15-96	0	0	1.35	18	0	0	0	27	17	6	4	3	5	37	.179	.179	.179	12.49	1.69
Olson, Ryan	R-R	6-2	195	11-22-94	1	1	7.71	5	0	0	0	5	7	4	4	0	4	5	.318	.500	.167	5.79	7.71
Perez, Hector	R-R	6-3	223	6-6-96	0	1	5.27	25	0	0	4	27	23	16	16	0	36	38	.225	.167	.258	12.51	11.85
Pidich, Matt	R-R	6-2	220	12-25-94	2	6	7.51	23	4	0	0	38	55	33	32	3	13	42	.337	.262	.388	9.86	3.05
Pinto, Julio	R-R	6-2	223	11-18-95	2	1	2.76	29	0	0	1	33	18	12	10	3	27	36	.161	.159	.162	9.92	7.44
Pucheu, Jacques	L-L	6-2	210	1-1-97	1	0	1.69	5	2	0	0	16	9	4	3	3	4	20	.158	.056	.205	11.25	2.25
Robertson, Wes	R-R	6-2	190	3-11-96	0	2	40.50	5	0	0	0	3	7	12	12	3	7	2	.467	.444	.500	6.75	23.63
Roxby, Braxton	R-R	6-3	215	3-12-99	0	0	15.00	6	0	0	0	6	14	10	10	2	2	8	.438	.583	.350	12.00	3.00
Salazar, Eduardo	R-R	6-2	177	5-5-98	0	1	6.00	1	1	0	0	3	5	4	2	0	1	2	.333	.167	.444	6.00	3.00
Salinas, Ricky	R-R	6-2	220	3-26-96	5	7	4.76	17	17	0	0	76	82	51	40	12	32	88	.271	.276	.267	10.47	3.81
Sanmartin, Reiver	L-L	6-2	160	4-15-96	2	0	0.50	4	3	0	0	18	8	2	1	0	5	23	.133	.056	.167	11.50	2.50
Sceroler, Mac	R-R	6-3	215	4-9-95	1	0	8.42	10	7	0	0	36	48	39	34	7	11	38	.304	.290	.313	9.41	2.72
Wynne, Randy	R-R	6-1	180	3-9-93	8	4	4.94	25	14	0	1	89	105	53	49	13	11	67	.285	.319	.265	6.75	1.11

Fielding

Catcher	PCT	G	PO	A	E	DP	PB
Kolozsvary	.997	36	331	25	1	1	2
Robinson	.990	58	543	36	6	5	4
Schuyler	.989	20	164	11	2	2	0
Tello	.967	3	25	4	1	0	3

CINCINNATI REDS

First Base	PCT	G	PO	A	E	DP
Garcia	.992	36	245	12	2	17
Lloyd	1.000	9	50	3	0	3
Schuyler	1.000	6	31	3	0	2
Tello	1.000	1	7	1	0	1
Tenerowicz	1.000	6	19	3	0	2
Yanqui	.995	60	385	29	2	36

Second Base	PCT	G	PO	A	E	DP
De Leon	1.000	1	0	2	0	0
Lloyd	1.000	2	2	1	0	1
Lopez	.986	21	28	44	1	7
McAfee	1.000	20	33	43	0	12
Rey	.955	46	75	95	8	19
Rivas	.983	20	23	36	1	6
Robinson	1.000	1	2	5	0	1
Tenerowicz	.000	1	0	0	0	0
Urbaez	.958	7	8	15	1	2

	PCT	G	PO	A	E	DP
Willems	.909	3	4	6	1	0

Third Base	PCT	G	PO	A	E	DP
De Leon	.875	4	3	4	1	0
Lloyd	1.000	5	2	7	0	0
McAfee	1.000	7	1	6	0	0
Reyes	1.000	1	3	1	0	1
Rivas	.931	16	7	20	2	0
Schuyler	1.000	1	0	2	0	0
Tenerowicz	.934	85	59	124	13	14
Urbaez	1.000	4	1	6	0	2

Shortstop	PCT	G	PO	A	E	DP
Barrero	.940	37	48	77	8	12
De Leon	1.000	1	0	4	0	0
Hernandez	.931	25	33	48	6	6
McAfee	.857	8	7	11	3	1
Reyes	.000	1	0	0	0	0

Outfield	PCT	G	PO	A	E	DP
Rivas	.956	15	17	26	2	6
Robinson	.931	27	33	61	7	12
Bautista	1.000	7	6	0	0	0
Cedrola	.987	108	217	7	3	3
Crook	.950	12	19	0	1	0
Hopkins	.985	74	127	4	2	0
Lee	1.000	28	52	0	0	0
Lloyd	1.000	16	23	0	0	0
McAfee	1.000	11	10	0	0	0
Mount	.991	52	102	4	1	0
Rey	1.000	20	43	0	0	0
Rivas	1.000	8	8	0	0	0
Schuyler	.955	14	18	3	1	0
Yanqui	1.000	12	19	0	0	0

DAYTON DRAGONS — HIGH CLASS A
HIGH-A CENTRAL

Batting	B-T	HT	WT	DOB	AVG	vLH	vRH	G	AB	R	H	2B	3B	HR	RBI	BB	HBP	SH	SF	SO	SB	CS	SLG	OBP
Bautista, Mariel	R-R	6-3	194	10-15-97	.257	.348	.233	36	113	17	29	6	2	5	17	6	2	0	3	36	4	1	.478	.298
Cerda, Allan	R-R	6-3	170	11-24-99	.273	.364	.236	21	77	15	21	8	1	3	13	10	0	0	0	20	1	1	.519	.356
Cotton, Quin	R-R	5-11	200	3-31-98	.231	.225	.233	92	338	34	78	13	1	10	41	20	3	0	3	108	24	8	.364	.277
Free, James	R-R	6-2	205	4-14-98	.232	.283	.216	56	185	21	43	13	0	3	27	27	1	0	3	56	1	0	.351	.329
Hernandez, Miguel	R-R	6-0	194	4-13-99	.267	.271	.266	71	262	25	70	14	0	2	37	19	2	0	3	49	6	2	.344	.318
Hurtubise, Jacob	L-R	6-0	180	12-11-97	.283	.226	.302	102	332	77	94	12	3	0	33	58	17	2	2	73	39	10	.337	.413
Johnson, Ivan	B-R	6-0	190	10-11-98	.265	.176	.284	27	98	17	26	5	0	4	18	14	2	0	0	39	3	2	.439	.368
Martinez, Juan	R-R	6-0	219	11-8-98	.253	.265	.249	77	269	32	68	16	3	7	36	25	6	0	3	64	0	0	.413	.327
McAfee, Quincy	R-R	5-11	185	9-16-97	.222	.237	.217	42	144	28	32	13	0	4	29	22	3	0	1	32	2	1	.396	.335
McGarry, Alex	L-L	6-2	202	5-11-98	.230	.250	.224	78	270	30	62	16	0	7	29	15	4	0	0	101	6	1	.367	.280
McLain, Matt	R-R	5-11	180	8-6-99	.273	.259	.278	29	99	15	27	6	0	3	19	17	2	0	1	24	10	2	.424	.387
Nelson, Matheu	R-R	5-11	209	1-14-99	.208	.250	.200	8	24	3	5	2	1	0	3	4	1	0	0	15	0	1	.375	.345
Ozuna, Reniel	R-R	6-2	202	7-29-98	.174	.182	.172	28	86	10	15	7	0	1	8	9	1	0	2	35	0	0	.291	.255
Rey, Brian	R-R	5-11	170	2-22-98	.423	.500	.395	13	52	7	22	5	1	6	19	2	0	0	3	3	1	2	.904	.421
Reyes, Reyny	R-R	6-2	185	3-20-99	.233	.308	.213	21	60	10	14	2	0	1	3	4	0	2	1	16	0	0	.317	.277
Rogers, Jack	L-L	6-2	185	4-5-99	.188	.083	.212	18	64	10	12	1	1	3	8	3	0	0	1	32	1	0	.375	.221
Ruiz, Victor	R-R	6-1	190	10-20-99	.237	.233	.238	81	300	32	71	16	3	5	37	16	0	0	6	77	3	2	.360	.270
Siani, Michael	L-L	6-1	188	7-16-99	.216	.259	.203	97	352	60	76	13	4	6	26	50	5	0	1	103	30	10	.327	.321
Spillane, Bren	R-R	6-4	223	9-21-96	.138	.333	.087	12	29	6	4	0	0	2	6	7	0	0	0	21	3	0	.345	.306
Tello, Jose	R-R	6-0	170	5-21-98	.217	.273	.204	30	115	15	25	4	0	4	15	6	1	0	0	31	0	0	.357	.262
Urbaez, Francisco	R-R	5-11	195	10-13-97	.333	.316	.339	67	246	40	82	16	1	4	29	32	6	1	0	44	3	1	.455	.423
Willems, Jonathan	R-R	5-11	190	11-7-98	.242	.200	.257	37	99	16	24	5	0	1	11	6	2	0	1	37	6	2	.354	.296
Wolforth, Garrett	R-R	6-4	220	10-13-97	.257	.125	.296	9	35	7	9	2	2	1	5	4	0	0	0	8	0	0	.514	.333
Yang, Eric	R-R	5-11	185	3-26-98	.203	.193	.206	76	227	31	46	11	1	3	19	38	13	1	2	65	2	2	.300	.346

Pitching	B-T	HT	WT	DOB	W	L	ERA	G	GS	CG	SV	IP	H	R	ER	HR	BB	SO	AVG	vLH	vRH	K/9	BB/9
Ashcraft, Graham	L-R	6-2	240	2-11-98	4	1	2.33	8	8	0	0	39	28	12	10	0	13	55	.200	.182	.216	12.80	3.03
Bonnin, Bryce	R-R	6-2	190	10-11-98	0	2	7.36	3	3	0	0	11	7	11	9	4	8	20	.175	.167	.182	16.36	6.55
Branche, Stevie	R-R	6-4	205	5-18-97	2	0	1.29	13	0	0	1	21	8	4	3	0	11	32	.116	.129	.105	13.71	4.71
Davis, Noah	R-R	6-2	195	4-22-97	3	6	3.60	13	13	1	0	65	44	29	26	3	35	77	.193	.150	.235	10.66	4.85
Demurias, Eddy	R-R	6-0	184	8-1-97	0	0	0.00	6	0	0	2	9	3	0	0	0	6	10	.107	.000	.176	10.00	6.00
Duarte, Daniel	R-R	6-0	170	12-4-96	0	1	3.38	4	0	0	1	5	5	2	2	0	6	4	.263	.273	.250	6.75	10.13
Farr, Thomas	R-R	6-0	203	4-29-99	0	0	3.00	1	1	0	0	3	1	1	1	1	1	4	.000	.250	.000	12.00	3.00
Feliz, Michael	R-R	6-4	250	6-28-93	0	2	15.00	1	0	0	0	3	4	5	5	2	1	5	.308	.333	.000	15.00	3.00
Fisher, Andy	L-L	6-1	185	1-9-96	5	1	3.80	26	0	0	1	45	36	19	19	1	24	64	.225	.210	.235	12.80	4.80
Garbee, Tyler	R-R	6-3	210	10-8-96	0	2	11.32	9	0	0	0	10	15	13	13	3	16	14	.349	.381	.318	12.19	13.94
Garcia, Pedro	R-R	5-11	220	3-21-95	7	4	4.20	28	0	0	3	41	34	28	19	3	24	53	.231	.236	.227	11.73	5.31
Ghyzel, John	R-R	6-5	200	5-18-96	3	2	6.53	22	0	0	4	21	15	19	15	0	29	28	.205	.167	.258	12.19	12.63
Gilbert, Jake	R-R	6-7	220	11-24-96	1	4	5.83	20	0	0	2	29	30	20	19	3	18	31	.265	.304	.239	9.51	5.52
Gill, Matt	L-R	6-5	240	4-22-98	0	2	3.73	20	0	0	0	31	33	13	13	3	8	24	.268	.206	.345	6.89	2.30
Hellinger, Sam	R-R	6-1	195	9-6-94	3	2	6.39	26	0	0	1	31	29	26	22	4	25	38	.244	.262	.224	11.03	7.26
Hoffman, Jeff	R-R	6-5	235	1-8-93	0	1	12.00	1	1	0	0	3	5	4	4	3	1	5	.357	.250	.500	15.00	3.00
Karcher, Ricky	R-R	6-4	195	9-18-97	1	0	5.12	18	0	0	4	19	10	13	11	1	30	29	.152	.154	.150	13.50	13.97
Keys, JC	R-R	5-10	173	10-9-96	3	2	4.70	17	5	0	0	38	34	24	20	2	27	40	.238	.213	.265	9.39	6.34
Kravetz, Evan	L-L	6-8	240	12-19-96	0	1	7.02	6	2	0	0	17	20	15	13	0	12	22	.286	.222	.308	11.88	6.48
Lindell, Karsen	R-R	6-3	190	6-25-96	0	1	10.57	7	0	0	0	8	11	9	9	3	14	8	.333	.467	.222	9.39	16.43
Marinan, James	R-R	6-5	239	10-10-98	1	0	0.00	2	2	0	0	12	4	0	0	0	6	17	.105	.111	.100	12.75	4.50
Medrano, Miguel	R-R	6-0	165	1-4-98	0	0	12.00	4	1	0	0	9	14	14	12	2	7	14	.326	.357	.267	14.00	7.00
Peguero, Francis	R-R	6-1	185	3-11-97	1	1	4.96	28	0	0	6	33	33	19	18	3	7	36	.258	.278	.232	9.92	1.93
Proctor, James	R-R	6-5	215	7-18-98	0	1	4.41	4	4	0	0	16	13	8	8	3	12	20	.213	.167	.258	11.02	6.61
Pucheu, Jacques	L-L	6-2	210	1-1-97	4	1	3.45	20	9	0	0	60	38	24	23	5	33	62	.179	.186	.175	9.30	4.95
Richardson, Lyon	B-R	6-2	192	1-18-00	2	5	5.09	19	18	1	0	76	74	54	43	9	38	91	.248	.238	.261	10.78	4.50

Player	B-T	HT	WT	DOB			ERA					IP									SO			SLG	OBP
Roa, Christian	R-R	6-4	220	4-2-99	2	2	4.15	8	7	0	0	35	32	16	16	4	15	37	.244	.288	.208	9.61	3.89
Roxby, Braxton	R-R	6-3	215	3-12-99	2	2	2.41	25	0	0	5	34	23	12	9	1	21	53	.189	.218	.164	14.17	5.61
Salazar, Eduardo	R-R	6-2	177	5-5-98	4	5	3.49	19	19	1	0	98	81	43	38	6	32	107	.222	.193	.253	9.83	2.94
Salinas, Ricky	R-R	6-2	220	3-26-96	1	0	4.32	3	1	0	0	8	4	4	4	1	5	13	.143	.077	.200	14.04	5.40
Schneider, Johnnie	R-R	6-5	180	6-30-97	0	2	14.29	6	0	0	1	6	2	9	9	0	16	8	.111	.100	.125	12.71	25.41
Spiers, Carson	R-R	6-3	205	11-11-97	6	4	3.64	20	16	0	0	89	68	39	36	8	29	103	.215	.225	.203	10.42	2.93
Stallings, Jesse	R-R	6-2	194	10-27-94	0	0	4.50	5	0	0	0	6	8	3	3	1	4	6	.320	.400	.200	9.00	6.00
Stockton, Spencer	R-R	6-3	210	4-24-96	4	3	5.63	26	9	0	0	72	71	49	45	8	26	74	.263	.265	.260	9.25	3.25
Timpanelli, Vincent	R-R	6-2	210	10-2-98	0	0	4.35	17	0	0	5	21	8	12	10	3	13	35	.113	.176	.054	15.24	5.66
Urbaez, Francisco	R-R	5-11	195	10-13-97	0	0	0.00	1	0	0	0	1	0	0	0	0	0	1	.000	.000	.000	9.00	0.00

Fielding

Catcher	PCT	G	PO	A	E	DP	PB
Free	.996	28	261	21	1	2	3
Nelson	.964	8	76	5	3	0	1
Tello	1.000	14	122	10	0	1	4
Wolforth	.923	1	12	0	1	0	0
Yang	.990	76	764	57	8	6	4

First Base	PCT	G	PO	A	E	DP
Free	.992	16	110	9	1	9
Martinez	.971	21	123	12	4	17
McAfee	1.000	1	3	0	0	0
McGarry	.985	57	357	31	6	22
Ozuna	1.000	1	2	0	0	0
Rogers	1.000	3	21	2	0	3
Ruiz	1.000	6	38	3	0	1
Spillane	.962	4	22	3	1	3
Tello	.991	15	105	6	1	7
Wolforth	1.000	6	44	0	0	5

Second Base	PCT	G	PO	A	E	DP
Johnson	.932	14	9	32	3	8
McAfee	.947	15	17	19	2	5
Rey	1.000	8	17	23	0	2
Reyes	.962	9	11	14	1	4
Ruiz	.909	10	17	13	3	5
Urbaez	.963	49	57	101	6	20
Willems	.973	24	27	45	2	9

Third Base	PCT	G	PO	A	E	DP
Martinez	.940	47	26	68	6	7
McAfee	.909	10	6	14	2	0
Reyes	1.000	6	2	7	0	0
Ruiz	.920	53	29	75	9	6
Urbaez	.900	5	4	5	1	0
Willems	.800	5	0	4	1	0

Shortstop	PCT	G	PO	A	E	DP
Hernandez	.939	70	90	142	15	35

	PCT	G	PO	A	E	DP
Johnson	.969	9	9	22	1	3
McAfee	1.000	3	1	3	0	0
McLain	.959	27	37	57	4	13
Reyes	.917	7	6	16	2	0
Urbaez	1.000	5	4	13	0	3

Outfield	PCT	G	PO	A	E	DP
Bautista	.976	29	40	0	1	0
Cerda	.963	19	25	1	1	0
Cotton	.970	86	122	6	4	1
Hurtubise	.988	92	152	10	2	1
McAfee	1.000	14	21	1	0	0
McGarry	.750	5	3	0	1	0
Ozuna	1.000	24	50	2	0	0
Rey	1.000	5	6	0	0	0
Rogers	1.000	12	12	0	0	0
Siani	.950	75	148	5	8	1
Spillane	1.000	7	8	0	0	0
Willems	1.000	1	1	0	0	0

DAYTONA TORTUGAS
LOW-A SOUTHEAST

LOW CLASS A

Batting	B-T	HT	WT	DOB	AVG	vLH	vRH	G	AB	R	H	2B	3B	HR	RBI	BB	HBP	SH	SF	SO	SB	CS	SLG	OBP
Amador, Ranser	R-R	6-2	165	3-15-99	.244	.286	.237	27	90	15	22	3	2	1	6	5	0	0	1	35	4	0	.356	.281
Astudillo, Wilfred	B-R	5-11	209	3-14-00	.217	.167	.225	13	46	8	10	0	0	2	5	4	0	0	0	6	0	0	.348	.280
Callihan, Tyler	L-R	6-1	205	6-22-00	.299	.316	.294	23	87	14	26	6	0	2	10	8	0	0	2	13	5	1	.437	.351
Cerda, Allan	R-R	6-3	170	11-24-99	.242	.176	.261	66	227	42	55	14	4	14	42	31	14	0	4	85	1	7	.524	.362
Creal, Ashton	R-R	6-1	205	3-23-99	.197	.111	.224	25	76	13	15	5	0	0	5	8	1	1	1	35	5	0	.263	.279
De La Cruz, Elly	B-R	6-2	150	1-11-02	.269	.324	.256	50	197	22	53	12	7	5	29	10	1	0	2	65	8	5	.477	.305
Dunn, Blake	R-R	6-0	210	9-5-98	.357	.000	.385	5	14	1	5	1	0	1	5	0	0	1	0	5	0	0	.643	.357
Franco, Rafael	R-R	6-2	155	6-20-01	.034	.000	.042	11	29	5	1	0	0	0	3	11	1	1	0	12	2	1	.034	.317
Gomez, Justin	L-R	5-10	195	4-29-97	.167	.000	.200	9	24	1	4	1	0	1	2	7	0	0	0	9	0	1	.333	.355
Hendrick, Austin	L-L	6-0	195	6-15-01	.211	.244	.201	63	209	30	44	16	0	15	29	51	6	0	0	100	4	2	.388	.380
Hinds, Rece	R-R	6-4	215	9-5-00	.251	.276	.246	43	167	33	42	10	2	10	27	13	4	0	1	52	6	2	.515	.319
Ibarra, Ruben	R-R	6-5	290	4-26-99	.195	.000	.222	27	82	9	16	3	0	1	8	16	6	0	2	29	0	0	.268	.358
Johnson, Ivan	B-R	6-0	190	10-11-98	.263	.250	.268	52	186	27	49	14	2	6	23	27	3	0	0	61	8	5	.457	.366
Lantigua, Danny	B-R	6-1	165	3-7-99	.229	.288	.212	69	231	27	53	22	0	5	24	20	4	0	2	106	2	3	.390	.300
Leyton, Brandon	R-R	5-10	165	12-17-98	.248	.239	.250	80	303	47	75	22	2	6	36	17	6	0	5	60	4	2	.393	.296
Marrero, Wendell	L-L	6-2	195	11-28-00	.203	.225	.198	65	212	30	43	7	2	5	17	29	8	0	2	85	0	2	.325	.319
McGarry, Alex	L-L	6-2	200	5-11-98	.360	1.000	.304	7	25	7	9	1	1	4	7	6	0	0	1	9	0	0	.960	.469
Reyes, Reyny	R-R	6-2	185	3-20-99	.248	.292	.236	32	113	15	28	1	0	2	15	5	0	2	1	26	1	2	.310	.277
Santana, Debby	R-R	6-2	185	8-24-00	.221	.256	.210	50	163	22	36	5	0	3	18	10	3	0	0	56	1	0	.307	.278
Seminati, Leonardo	R-R	6-2	210	1-2-99	.211	.167	.222	69	227	32	48	10	1	10	36	30	2	0	1	103	6	1	.396	.308
Steiger, Gus	R-R	5-11	185	4-20-99	.213	.222	.211	68	216	27	46	6	0	1	24	31	0	2	1	64	14	6	.255	.310
Thompson, Justice	R-R	6-4	205	7-8-00	.217	.500	.180	21	69	6	15	2	0	2	9	13	0	1	0	23	1	0	.333	.341
Torres, Jose	R-R	6-0	171	9-28-99	.337	.615	.293	25	95	15	32	4	3	4	17	8	1	0	3	17	6	2	.568	.383
Trautwein, Michael	L-R	6-1	185	9-13-99	.200	.400	.160	11	30	2	6	2	0	0	2	3	1	0	0	13	2	1	.267	.294
Triana, Michel	L-R	6-3	230	11-23-99	.227	.172	.238	49	172	23	39	11	1	2	23	14	6	0	2	66	3	3	.337	.304
Vellojin, Daniel	L-R	5-11	160	3-15-00	.247	.226	.252	88	283	56	70	21	1	7	34	72	3	0	4	73	5	3	.403	.401
Wolforth, Garrett	B-R	6-4	220	10-13-97	.221	.327	.194	74	258	38	57	12	5	7	36	26	1	0	2	95	3	2	.388	.293

Pitching	B-T	HT	WT	DOB	W	L	ERA	G	GS	CG	SV	IP	H	R	ER	HR	BB	SO	AVG	vLH	vRH	K/9	BB/9
Abbott, Andrew	L-L	6-0	180	6-1-99	0	0	4.91	4	3	0	0	11	11	6	6	2	4	19	.250	.154	.290	15.55	3.27
Aguilera, Gabriel	R-R	6-0	165	8-19-00	0	2	3.28	6	4	0	0	25	19	9	9	0	14	22	.226	.239	.211	8.03	5.11
Aranguren, Frainger	R-R	6-2	190	3-17-97	6	8	4.63	26	2	0	0	70	74	39	36	4	41	57	.272	.294	.258	7.33	5.27
Benschoter, Sam	R-R	6-3	215	11-11-98	0	1	3.60	2	2	0	0	5	3	4	2	2	10	10	.167	.167	.167	18.00	3.60
Bonnin, Bryce	R-R	6-2	190	10-11-98	0	1	1.41	7	7	0	0	32	18	9	5	0	8	46	.162	.137	.183	12.38	2.25
Boyle, Joe	R-R	6-7	240	8-14-99	0	0	3.55	4	4	0	0	13	6	5	5	1	13	28	.143	.063	.192	19.89	9.24
Branche, Stevie	R-R	6-4	205	5-18-97	1	3	3.62	18	1	0	3	37	23	17	15	2	24	68	.169	.140	.190	16.39	5.79
Cachutt, Manuel	R-R	6-0	185	6-7-97	3	4	4.62	22	0	0	3	49	52	35	25	3	29	53	.267	.282	.255	9.80	5.36
Cardona, Ryan	R-R	6-1	200	5-7-00	1	1	5.00	4	3	0	0	9	10	5	5	1	5	7	.278	.235	.316	7.00	5.00
Cooper, Tanner	R-R	6-3	215	9-8-99	0	3	6.49	11	3	0	1	26	27	19	19	2	14	27	.270	.364	.224	9.23	4.78

Name	B-T	HT	WT	DOB	W	L	ERA	G	GS	CG	SV	IP	H	R	ER	HR	BB	SO	AVG	vLH	vRH	SO/9	BB/9
Farr, Thomas	R-R	6-0	203	4-29-99	0	0	0.00	2	1	0	0	6	4	0	0	0	0	8	.200	.250	.167	12.00	0.00
Franco, Jose	R-R	6-2	175	11-25-00	2	5	6.71	19	11	0	0	59	50	45	44	12	42	77	.222	.210	.229	11.75	6.41
Garbee, Tyler	R-R	6-3	210	10-8-96	2	1	2.08	6	0	0	1	13	7	4	3	1	5	10	.156	.050	.240	6.92	3.46
Garcia, Pedro	R-R	5-11	220	3-21-95	1	1	1.50	4	0	0	0	12	7	2	2	1	2	18	.167	.238	.095	13.50	1.50
Gonzalez, Alberto	R-R	6-1	180	7-26-99	2	0	3.80	13	0	0	1	21	14	9	9	3	21	29	.192	.400	.083	12.23	8.86
Gozzo, Jake	R-R	6-5	221	1-5-97	4	4	5.01	28	0	0	3	32	20	23	18	3	41	31	.192	.286	.129	8.63	11.41
Hanson, Nick	R-R	6-6	205	6-10-98	3	3	3.55	23	1	0	2	38	30	18	15	0	23	33	.213	.176	.247	7.82	5.45
Hellinger, Sam	R-R	6-1	195	9-6-94	0	1	1.62	6	0	0	2	17	7	3	3	1	3	25	.123	.105	.132	13.50	1.62
Karcher, Ricky	R-R	6-4	195	9-18-97	0	1	1.13	9	0	0	0	8	1	2	1	0	9	19	.038	.000	.059	21.38	10.13
Koch, Ian	R-R	6-4	220	8-18-97	2	0	6.75	11	0	0	0	19	14	14	14	2	27	14	.209	.292	.163	6.75	13.02
Kravetz, Evan	L-L	6-8	240	12-19-96	0	1	1.64	6	6	0	0	22	10	5	4	1	10	33	.133	.231	.113	13.50	4.09
Lockwood, Brett	L-R	6-4	220	4-15-97	1	0	4.89	29	0	0	2	53	55	34	29	6	33	55	.263	.316	.231	9.28	5.57
Manuel Abril, Juan	R-R	6-0	160	3-11-98	1	1	6.49	16	0	0	0	26	16	22	19	2	32	37	.170	.200	.156	12.65	10.94
Marinan, James	R-R	6-5	239	10-10-98	1	6	5.30	13	10	0	0	53	45	34	31	5	35	46	.227	.264	.198	7.86	5.98
Medrano, Miguel	R-R	6-0	165	1-4-98	5	2	3.64	16	9	0	1	59	49	25	24	6	33	58	.231	.250	.213	8.80	5.01
Mey, Luis	R-R	6-2	160	6-24-01	0	0	6.00	6	0	0	2	9	8	7	6	1	9	10	.229	.167	.241	10.00	9.00
Parker, Jason	R-R	5-11	197	10-27-97	4	3	4.05	19	18	0	0	80	63	41	36	7	33	91	.215	.259	.189	10.24	3.71
2-team total (1 Tampa)					4	3	4.18	20	19	0	0	84	68	44	39	9	35	96	.220	.264	.196	10.29	3.75
Proctor, James	R-R	6-5	215	7-18-98	3	0	1.60	14	12	0	0	45	31	15	8	0	22	57	.194	.159	.220	11.40	4.40
Roa, Christian	R-R	6-4	220	4-2-99	1	1	3.57	5	5	0	0	18	18	8	7	2	9	21	.261	.200	.295	10.70	4.58
Robertson, Wes	R-R	6-2	190	3-11-96	1	0	9.22	13	0	0	2	14	16	16	14	3	9	13	.296	.313	.289	8.56	5.93
Rudd, Carson	R-R	6-5	190	9-17-98	1	3	4.02	6	3	0	0	16	14	13	7	1	6	23	.237	.190	.263	13.21	3.45
Shenefield, Hayden	R-R	6-1	195	5-6-95	1	0	6.48	3	0	0	0	8	9	6	6	1	1	6	.273	.000	.346	6.48	1.08
Spiers, Carson	R-R	6-3	205	11-11-97	2	0	3.18	5	4	0	1	23	19	8	8	1	5	27	.241	.171	.295	10.72	1.99
Steiger, Gus	R-R	5-11	185	4-20-99	0	1	18.00	1	0	0	0	1	2	3	2	1	0	0	.400	.500	.333	0.00	0.00
Timpanelli, Vincent	R-R	6-2	210	10-2-98	0	1	1.82	20	0	0	9	25	7	6	5	0	17	41	.089	.080	.093	14.96	6.20
Williams, Case	R-R	6-3	210	2-16-02	2	5	5.74	12	11	0	0	47	45	35	30	7	33	34	.253	.254	.252	6.51	6.32
Wolforth, Garrett	R-R	6-4	220	10-13-97	0	0	10.80	1	0	0	0	2	3	2	2	0	1	1	.429	.500	.400	5.40	5.40
Zimmerman, Anthony	R-R	6-5	250	9-9-96	2	0	2.57	11	0	0	3	21	15	7	6	1	10	31	.200	.231	.167	13.29	4.29

Fielding

Catcher	PCT	G	PO	A	E	DP	PB
Astudillo	.986	13	126	12	2	3	2
Gomez	.986	9	63	9	1	1	2
Trautwein	1.000	8	72	5	0	0	1
Vellojin	.987	74	714	73	10	4	11
Wolforth	.995	22	195	14	1	3	5

First Base	PCT	G	PO	A	E	DP
Amador	1.000	1	4	0	0	0
Ibarra	.995	24	189	14	1	19
McGarry	1.000	3	12	0	0	0
Seminati	.996	31	245	16	1	24
Triana	.982	49	314	22	6	25
Wolforth	.983	16	115	2	2	13

Second Base	PCT	G	PO	A	E	DP
Amador	.778	2	4	3	2	0
Callihan	.956	23	39	47	4	12

	PCT	G	PO	A	E	DP
Leyton	.973	75	123	200	9	47
Reyes	.955	14	17	25	2	7
Steiger	.946	9	11	24	2	5

Third Base	PCT	G	PO	A	E	DP
De La Cruz	.916	28	19	57	7	7
Hinds	.895	33	22	46	8	3
Reyes	.929	14	17	22	3	1
Santana	.885	31	14	32	6	5
Seminati	.964	13	6	21	1	2
Steiger	1.000	8	3	10	0	1

Shortstop	PCT	G	PO	A	E	DP
Amador	1.000	1	2	2	0	1
De La Cruz	.989	20	30	58	1	14
Johnson	.936	50	63	113	12	26
Leyton	.926	6	8	17	2	2
Reyes	1.000	2	2	2	0	0

	PCT	G	PO	A	E	DP
Steiger	.941	29	40	55	6	13
Torres	.968	18	23	37	2	7

Outfield	PCT	G	PO	A	E	DP
Amador	.914	22	31	1	3	0
Cerda	.951	63	97	1	5	0
Creal	.956	22	43	0	2	0
Dunn	1.000	5	4	0	0	0
Franco	1.000	11	24	3	0	1
Hendrick	.960	61	90	6	4	2
Lantigua	.889	56	67	5	9	0
Marrero	.976	59	79	4	2	2
McGarry	1.000	2	2	0	0	0
Seminati	.946	22	33	2	2	0
Steiger	.968	22	29	1	1	1
Thompson	.964	21	26	1	1	1
Wolforth	1.000	5	4	1	0	1

ACL REDS   ROOKIE
ARIZONA COMPLEX LEAGUE

Batting	B-T	HT	WT	DOB	AVG	vLH	vRH	G	AB	R	H	2B	3B	HR	RBI	BB	HBP	SH	SF	SO	SB	CS	SLG	OBP
Alcantara, Deivid	R-R	6-2	180	6-14-03	.213	.296	.190	39	127	14	27	6	2	3	12	20	1	0	1	50	4	5	.362	.322
Allen II, Jay	R-R	6-3	190	11-22-02	.328	.250	.356	19	61	20	20	3	1	3	11	8	5	0	1	12	14	1	.557	.440
Almonte, Sebastian	R-R	6-0	185	10-22-99	.256	.308	.242	43	121	15	31	8	1	4	18	11	4	0	2	46	5	5	.438	.333
Antonia, Donovan	R-R	5-10	182	8-13-03	.155	.125	.167	33	110	11	17	4	2	1	4	14	3	0	0	52	4	1	.255	.268
Astudillo, Wilfred	B-R	5-11	209	3-14-00	.294	.269	.301	41	119	22	35	4	0	7	22	10	1	0	2	18	3	1	.504	.348
Callahan, Austin	L-R	6-3	215	6-6-01	.182	.111	.200	17	44	11	8	2	0	3	10	9	1	0	0	17	0	0	.432	.333
Castro, Fidel	L-R	6-3	175	12-26-98	.303	.182	.352	32	76	17	23	3	2	5	18	17	3	1	0	27	6	0	.592	.448
Confidan, Yerlin	L-L	6-3	170	12-16-02	.315	.311	.316	50	178	33	56	9	2	11	34	12	1	0	1	48	7	3	.573	.359
Creal, Ashton	R-R	6-1	205	3-23-99	.290	.222	.318	11	31	13	9	2	1	3	7	8	2	0	0	9	5	0	.710	.463
De La Cruz, Elly	B-R	6-2	150	1-11-02	.400	.250	.429	11	50	13	20	6	2	3	13	4	1	0	0	15	2	0	.780	.455
Dunn, Blake	R-R	6-0	210	9-5-98	.214	.250	.200	6	14	2	3	0	0	0	2	0	1	0	0	3	5	0	.214	.313
Fernandez, Ilvin	R-R	6-1	160	9-8-01	.217	.107	.253	40	115	15	25	7	0	1	12	11	1	0	0	35	5	1	.304	.291
Franco, Rafael	R-R	6-2	155	6-20-01	.220	.200	.226	32	82	19	18	5	1	1	9	17	3	0	1	23	4	3	.341	.369
Gomez, Elvis	R-R	6-0	170	5-27-99	.400	.250	.500	9	10	6	4	0	0	1	2	4	1	0	0	3	0	0	.700	.600
Guzman, Darlin	L-L	6-1	165	9-27-00	.200	.000	.222	5	5	0	1	0	0	0	0	0	0	0	0	1	0	0	.200	.200
Hinds, Rece	R-R	6-4	215	9-5-00	.294	.250	.318	11	34	6	10	3	2	2	5	4	2	0	1	13	1	1	.676	.390
Ibarra, Ruben	R-R	6-5	290	4-26-99	.400	.333	.500	4	10	3	4	1	0	1	2	2	0	0	0	3	0	0	.800	.500
Jones, Hayden	R-R	6-1	215	4-27-00	.287	.364	.111	12	29	4	6	1	0	0	4	4	1	0	0	14	1	0	.241	.324
Lloyd, Matt	L-R	6-1	205	3-17-96	.333	.333	.333	4	12	3	4	1	1	0	1	1	0	0	0	4	0	0	.667	.385
Lopez, Luis	R-R	5-11	165	11-30-99	.135	.111	.143	12	37	3	5	1	1	0	1	2	3	0	0	23	0	0	.216	.238
Marrero, Wendell	L-L	6-2	195	11-28-00	.231	.154	.256	17	52	9	12	1	2	4	11	6	2	0	0	25	0	1	.558	.333

Batting	B-T	HT	WT	DOB	AVG	vLH	vRH	G	AB	R	H	2B	3B	HR	RBI	BB	HBP	SH	SF	SO	SB	CS	SLG	OBP
McLain, Matt	R-R	5-11	180	8-6-99	.429	.000	.750	2	7	2	3	2	1	0	0	0	0	0	0	0	0	0	1.000	.429
Melo, Junior	R-R	6-2	175	5-10-97	.179	.000	.238	15	28	2	5	0	0	1	3	3	1	0	0	5	0	0	.286	.281
Miller, Jackson	L-R	6-0	195	1-3-02	.500	--	.500	3	4	1	2	0	0	0	2	2	1	0	0	0	0	0	.500	.714
Minier, Braylin	L-R	6-0	160	6-11-03	.255	.282	.245	39	145	19	37	11	0	3	26	11	1	0	2	47	0	4	.393	.308
Mount, Drew	L-R	5-11	205	3-24-96	.444	.500	.429	5	9	6	4	2	0	1	4	4	6	0	0	0	2	0	1.000	.737
Nelson, Matheu	R-R	5-11	209	1-14-99	.000	.000	.000	2	4	1	0	0	0	0	0	2	0	0	0	2	0	0		.333
Pino, Yassel	R-R	6-2	200	10-4-01	.272	.208	.289	42	114	22	31	7	1	5	23	28	0	0	0	29	7	4	.482	.415
Rogers, Jack	L-L	6-2	185	4-5-99	.364	.250	.429	4	11	4	4	1	0	0	1	1	0	0	1	3	0		.455	.417
Salcedo, Andruw	B-R	5-11	175	9-29-02	.362	.417	.343	31	94	15	34	5	0	4	11	12	5	0	0	30	0	1	.543	.459
Steiger, Gus	R-R	5-11	185	4-20-99	.240	.200	.250	8	25	4	6	3	0	0	3	0	2	0	0	4	3	0	.360	.296
Tamares, Junior	L-R	6-0	165	9-26-01	.208	.111	.231	23	48	9	10	1	1	0	1	5	1	0	0	22	3	2	.271	.296
Thompson, Justice	R-R	6-4	205	7-8-00	.316	.750	.200	7	19	4	6	2	1	0	3	3	1	0	0	5	1	1	.526	.435
Torres, Jose	R-R	6-0	171	9-28-99	.300	.000	.375	3	10	3	3	0	1	1	2	2	0	0	0	1	0	0	.800	.417
Trautwein, Michael	L-R	6-1	185	9-13-99	.000	.000	.000	3	4	0	0	0	0	0	0	1	2	0	0	0	2	0	.000	.333

Pitching	B-T	HT	WT	DOB	W	L	ERA	G	GS	CG	SV	IP	H	R	ER	HR	BB	SO	AVG	vLH	vRH	K/9	BB/9
Abbott, Andrew	L-L	6-0	180	6-1-99	0	0	0.00	2	2	0	0	2	1	0	0	0	0	3	.143	.200	.000	13.50	0.00
Abel, Kevin	R-R	6-1	195	2-19-99	0	0	9.00	3	3	0	0	4	2	4	4	1	3	6	.154	.000	.333	13.50	6.75
Aguiar, Julian	L-R	6-3	180	6-5-01	3	0	3.12	5	0	0	1	9	9	4	3	1	0	14	.243	.125	.333	14.54	0.00
Aguilera, Gabriel	R-R	6-0	165	8-19-00	0	1	1.29	5	4	0	0	21	11	4	3	1	4	35	.151	.212	.100	15.00	1.71
Benoit, Donovan	R-R	6-3	203	1-22-99	0	1	2.70	6	1	0	0	10	11	5	3	1	3	23	.275	.278	.273	20.70	2.70
Benschoter, Sam	R-R	6-3	215	3-17-98	0	0	0.00	3	0	0	1	4	1	0	0	0	2	9	.077	.000	.091	20.25	4.50
Boatman, Dennis	R-R	6-5	225	11-20-99	1	0	1.42	4	1	0	0	6	3	1	1	0	2	5	.150	.125	.167	7.11	2.84
Bonnin, Bryce	R-R	6-2	190	10-11-98	0	0	2.25	1	1	0	0	4	2	1	1	0	1	7	.143	.000	.182	15.75	2.25
Boyle, Joe	R-R	6-7	240	8-14-99	0	0	0.00	4	4	0	0	7	3	0	0	0	1	13	.130	.083	.182	16.71	1.29
Cardona, Ryan	R-R	6-1	200	5-7-00	0	0	0.00	3	1	0	1	4	2	1	0	0	0	3	.143	.167	.125	6.75	0.00
Cruz, Rynardo	R-R	6-2	165	10-24-01	1	1	3.38	7	2	0	1	21	15	19	8	1	15	30	.188	.250	.146	12.66	6.33
Duarte, Daniel	R-R	6-0	170	12-4-96	0	0	9.00	1	0	0	0	2	2	2	2	1	1	3	.250	.000	.333	13.50	4.50
Farr, Thomas	R-R	6-0	203	4-29-99	0	0	0.00	1	1	0	0	1	1	0	0	0	0	2	.000	.000	.333	18.00	0.00
Fransen, Arij	R-R	6-3	190	5-20-01	3	1	3.78	9	5	0	0	33	34	16	14	3	4	43	.266	.263	.268	11.61	0.81
Garbee, Tyler	R-R	6-3	210	10-8-96	0	0	0.00	5	0	0	4	6	2	0	0	0	0	7	.095	.111	.083	9.95	0.00
Gayman, Myles	R-R	6-4	200	2-19-98	1	1	4.11	10	0	0	0	15	20	9	7	1	2	23	.308	.400	.200	13.50	1.17
Gilbert, Jake	R-R	6-7	220	12-1-96	4	1	1.33	10	0	0	1	20	11	4	3	0	10	36	.164	.077	.220	15.93	4.43
Gonzalez, Alberto	R-R	6-1	180	7-26-99	0	3	3.00	5	0	0	0	9	4	3	3	0	10	13	.138	.188	.077	13.00	10.00
Gozzo, Jake	L-L	6-5	221	1-5-97	0	2	4.50	3	0	0	0	4	4	4	2	1	2	7	.267	.400	.200	15.75	4.50
Heatherly, Jacob	L-L	6-1	215	5-20-98	0	1	5.19	5	3	0	0	9	5	5	3	0	9	27	.286	.280	.280	9.35	3.12
Henderson, Damian	L-L	6-1	220	7-14-97	0	1	16.62	12	0	0	0	9	9	18	16	0	22	17	.250	.400	.226	17.65	22.85
Holt, Owen	R-R	6-3	225	4-22-99	2	1	7.71	4	1	0	0	7	7	6	6	1	2	11	.233	.083	.333	14.14	2.57
Johnson, Alexander	R-R	6-6	220	7-2-00	1	0	4.50	3	0	0	0	4	2	3	2	0	3	8	.143	.250	.100	18.00	6.75
Kravetz, Evan	L-L	6-8	240	12-19-96	0	0	2.50	5	5	0	0	18	20	6	5	0	2	27	.282	.176	.315	13.50	1.00
Kuhnel, Joel	R-R	6-4	280	2-19-95	0	1	2.25	4	1	0	1	4	4	1	1	0	0	8	.250	.500	.000	18.00	0.00
Lopez, Jefferson	R-R	6-1	185	2-18-01	0	0	4.66	13	0	0	0	19	19	12	10	1	9	20	.257	.280	.245	9.31	4.19
Lorenzen, Michael	R-R	6-3	217	1-4-92	0	0	0.00	1	1	0	0	1	0	0	0	0	1		.000	--	.000	18.00	0.00
Manuel Abril, Juan	R-R	6-0	160	3-11-98	2	1	4.20	8	0	0	0	15	8	9	7	1	12	18	.160	.294	.091	10.80	7.20
Maysonet, Yomil	R-R	6-1	180	1-9-00	1	2	4.28	12	8	0	0	34	30	26	16	2	25	32	.234	.222	.243	8.55	6.68
Medina, Fredy	R-R	5-10	160	9-26-97	1	1	8.40	8	0	0	0	15	18	16	14	3	12	18	.295	.440	.194	10.80	7.20
Melo, Junior	R-R	6-2	175	5-10-97	0	0	0.00	1	0	0	0	1	0	0	0	0	0		.000	--	.000	0.00	0.00
Moreno, Pedro	R-R	6-5	200	3-8-98	2	0	6.27	13	0	0	0	19	23	15	13	3	14	33	.295	.400	.229	15.91	6.75
Parks, Hunter	R-R	6-4	187	4-28-00	1	0	1.59	6	3	0	0	11	8	2	2	0	4	13	.200	.167	.227	10.32	3.18
Peralta, Jose	R-R	6-1	170	10-2-99	3	2	5.87	15	3	0	0	38	46	35	25	6	6	32	.289	.343	.250	7.51	1.41
Pinazzi, Nicolo	L-L	6-2	195	10-25-99	2	1	2.60	14	0	0	0	17	15	6	5	1	14	31	.231	.143	.273	16.10	7.27
Roa, Christian	R-R	6-4	220	4-2-99	1	0	0.00	2	1	0	0	7	1	0	0	0	2	9	.045	.091	.000	12.79	2.84
Robertson, Wes	R-R	6-2	190	3-11-96	0	0	4.26	6	0	0	0	2	6	7	4	3	0	3	4	.269	.364	.200	5.68	4.26
Rudd, Carson	R-R	6-5	190	9-17-98	0	0	40.50	1	1	0	0	1	3	3	1	3	2	.333	.000	1.000	27.00	40.50
Salazar, Martin	R-R	6-2	175	5-10-00	0	0	5.94	12	6	0	0	33	41	27	22	4	13	35	.301	.344	.267	9.45	3.51
Sandridge, Jayvien	L-L	6-3	220	2-11-99	0	3	7.00	7	0	0	0	9	6	11	7	1	8	12	.188	.333	.100	12.00	8.00
Schneider, Johnnie	R-R	6-5	180	6-30-97	2	2	8.10	12	0	0	1	13	9	16	12	1	18	23	.184	.192	.174	15.53	12.15
Stallings, Jesse	R-R	6-2	194	10-27-94	0	0	0.00	1	0	0	1	1	1	0	0	0	1		.333	--	.333	9.00	9.00
Stevenson, Jake	R-R	6-4	225	3-24-97	0	0	4.50	2	1	0	0	2	1	1	1	1	2	4	.143	.200	.000	18.00	9.00
Zimmerman, Anthony	R-R	6-5	250	9-9-96	1	2	7.20	8	0	0	0	10	15	10	8	2	2	19	.333	.250	.400	17.10	1.80

Fielding

C: Astudillo 25, Gomez 8, Jones 9, Melo 4, Miller 3, Nelson 2, Salcedo 27, Trautwein 2
1B: Almonte 12, Astudillo 10, Castro 1, Ibarra 3, Lloyd 3, Melo 10, Pino 32
2B: Almonte 14, Antonia 31, Fernandez 15, Lopez 2, Steiger 3,
3B: Almonte 14, Callahan 16, De La Cruz 7, Fernandez 3, Hinds 7, Lloyd 1, Lopez 9, Pino 11, Steiger 1,
SS: De La Cruz 3, Fernandez 21, Lopez 1, McLain 2, Minier 35, Steiger 2, Torres 3,
OF: Alcantara 30, Allen II 19, Castro 27, Confidan 43, Creal 10, Dunn 4, Franco 28, Guzman 1, Marrero 13, Mount 4, Rogers 3, Tamares 19, Thompson 7

DSL REDS   ROOKIE

DOMINICAN SUMMER LEAGUE

Batting	B-T	HT	WT	DOB	AVG	vLH	vRH	G	AB	R	H	2B	3B	HR	RBI	BB	HBP	SH	SF	SO	SB	CS	SLG	OBP
Almonte, Ariel	L-L	6-1	170	12-1-03	.278	.188	.288	48	162	35	45	9	1	5	33	26	7	0	1	52	15	6	.438	.398
Ascanio, Johnny	B-R	5-10	150	7-4-03	.333	.308	.337	42	111	32	37	5	3	0	24	19	8	1	2	22	12	7	.432	.457
Balcazar, Leonardo	R-R	0-0	0	6-17-04	.259	.375	.240	29	112	26	29	5	4	6	15	13	3	0	2	29	8	4	.536	.346

Name	B-T	HT	WT	DOB	AVG	vLH	vRH	G	AB	R	H	2B	3B	HR	RBI	BB	SO	SB	CS	OBP	SLG
Chirino, Ray-Jackson	R-R	6-1	175	12-24-02	.231	.273	.227	40	108	20	25	7	0	2	12	10	4	0	0	.352	.320
Espinoza, Iverson	R-R	5-10	155	1-6-03	.303	.214	.314	42	119	32	36	7	2	2	16	13	9	0	0	.445	.411
Garcia, Juan	R-R	5-11	185	5-3-03	.180	.182	.180	23	61	9	11	3	0	1	8	11	3	0	0	.279	.333
Inirio, Wencer	R-R	6-3	190	10-28-02	.229	.300	.222	36	118	21	27	6	0	5	17	6	7	0	1	.347	.303
Isturiz, Eddy	R-R	0-0	0	1-16-04	.236	.200	.240	21	55	11	13	4	1	0	5	6	2	0	1	.345	.328
Jorge, Carlos	R-R	0-0	0	9-22-03	.346	.444	.333	47	159	38	55	8	10	3	33	24	3	0	2	.579	.436
Leones, Luis	L-L	5-10	155	6-12-03	.189	.000	.200	24	53	10	10	2	1	1	10	4	2	0	0	.321	.271
Martinez, Cesar	B-R	6-0	173	11-18-02	.234	.417	.192	32	64	13	15	3	0	2	10	10	5	1	0	.375	.380
Omana, Diego	R-R	5-11	165	1-10-03	.371	.286	.381	25	70	13	26	3	0	1	14	8	3	0	2	.457	.446
Reyes, Luis	R-R	5-11	193	11-15-03	.261	.375	.200	8	23	1	6	0	0	0	0	1	1	0	0	.261	.320
Rijo, Brayan	R-R	0-0	0	11-24-03	.294	.313	.292	46	136	21	40	1	4	1	16	11	0	0	0	.382	.347
Serrano, Jose	R-R	6-0	180	10-14-03	.287	.250	.293	35	115	15	33	6	4	0	15	12	0	0	0	.409	.354
Torres, Esmil	R-R	6-0	150	1-18-02	.000	--	.000	3	2	2	0	0	0	0	0	3	2	0	0	.000	.714
Torres, Jesus	R-R	6-0	160	10-2-02	.286	.231	.298	25	70	15	20	1	1	0	14	4	1	0	0	.329	.333
Valdez, Malvin	R-R	6-2	178	10-14-03	.218	.136	.230	51	170	32	37	7	3	3	21	36	4	0	2	.347	.363
Ysabel, Vladimir	B-R	6-0	150	3-7-02	.235	.333	.214	8	17	4	4	1	0	0	0	2	1	0	0	.294	.350

Pitching	B-T	HT	WT	DOB	W	L	ERA	G	GS	CG	SV	IP	H	R	ER	HR	BB	SO	AVG	vLH	vRH	K/9	BB/9
Alcantara, Eddy	L-L	6-5	180	2-11-00	0	1	8.44	5	0	0	0	5	5	8	5	1	9	9	.250	.429	.154	15.19	15.19
Ascanio, Johnny	B-R	5-10	150	7-4-03	0	0	0.00	1	0	0	1	2	2	0	1	0	1		.400	--	.400	13.50	0.00
Castillo, Fraiber	L-L	6-0	160	5-15-03	1	1	4.91	12	0	0	0	18	16	20	10	0	17	11	.232	.353	.192	5.40	8.35
Castillo, Oswaldo	R-R	6-1	170	6-11-02	2	1	1.10	5	0	0	1	16	9	4	2	1	1	21	.155	.222	.125	11.57	0.55
Castro, Luis	R-R	6-4	180	3-31-02	0	2	5.11	5	1	0	0	12	10	14	7	0	14	19	.217	.182	.250	13.86	10.22
Chirinos, Elkyn	R-R	6-1	160	9-20-00	2	2	3.28	11	11	1	0	47	32	20	17	2	25	47	.198	.152	.229	9.06	4.82
Cruz, Rynardo	R-R	6-2	165	10-24-01	0	0	1.06	4	4	0	0	17	11	4	2	1	5	26	.180	.313	.133	13.76	2.65
Davila, Vladimir	R-R	5-11	158	9-10-02	1	3	5.97	12	6	0	0	38	45	28	25	4	20	29	.294	.267	.312	6.93	4.78
Galindo, Cristian	L-L	6-2	150	10-14-02	0	1	10.80	4	0	0	0	3	3	4	4	1	7	4	.250	.500	.125	10.80	18.90
Garcia, Gregory	R-R	6-1	175	12-16-02	0	0	1.00	2	2	0	0	9	3	2	1	0	1	7	.103	.000	.158	7.00	1.00
Gonzalez, Eduardo	L-L	6-1	155	7-23-03	3	0	1.99	8	2	0	1	23	15	6	5	1	16	28	.190	.310	.120	11.12	6.35
Gonzalez, Juventino	R-R	6-6	195	2-5-02	0	0	9.00	1	0	0	0	1	2	1	1	0	1	1	.400	--	.400	9.00	9.00
Gutierrez, Dualvert	R-R	6-0	185	1-25-01	3	2	3.29	13	9	0	1	52	47	22	19	3	16	76	.236	.268	.219	13.15	2.77
Lorant, Nestor	R-R	6-2	175	5-4-02	2	2	2.70	9	9	0	0	33	23	11	10	1	12	45	.198	.170	.217	12.15	3.24
Marcano, Brian	R-R	6-3	175	11-23-01	1	2	10.50	11	0	0	0	18	14	22	21	1	29	12	.215	.071	.324	6.00	14.50
Martinez, Cesar	B-R	6-0	173	11-18-02	0	0	5.40	2	0	0	0	2	3	2	1	1	1	3	.375	.333	.400	16.20	5.40
Martinez, Juan	R-R	6-1	160	12-30-02	2	4	4.03	11	9	0	0	45	46	24	20	1	23	50	.267	.241	.281	10.07	4.63
Ramirez, Marwin	R-R	6-2	175	9-10-00	6	3	4.63	15	0	0	2	33	20	14	12	2	10	35	.227	.182	.255	13.50	3.86
Rodriguez, Alejandro	R-R	6-1	160	11-14-03	0	0	6.53	15	0	0	1	21	21	16	15	2	17	10	.276	.269	.280	4.35	7.40
Rojas, Jesus	R-R	6-3	185	3-22-02	0	1	3.00	5	0	0	0	6	4	4	2	0	3	3	.190	.222	.167	4.50	4.50
Ros, Roberto	R-R	5-10	150	7-6-00	5	2	6.93	15	2	0	0	25	15	22	19	0	36	39	.179	.133	.204	14.23	13.14
Valdez, Kelvin	R-R	6-3	200	5-8-03	1	0	4.63	13	0	0	0	12	9	11	6	1	15	13	.191	.222	.172	10.03	11.57
Vargas, Videlson	R-R	6-2	175	3-23-02	0	0	16.62	9	0	0	0	9	16	21	16	2	21	8	.381	.368	.391	8.31	21.81
Yanez, Williams	R-R	6-2	175	11-7-01	0	0	0.00	2	2	0	0	6	5	0	0	1	4		.227	.273	.182	6.00	1.50
Zapata, Wilder	R-R	6-4	170	12-26-01	1	0	18.00	3	0	0	0	2	3	4	4	0	3	1	.333	.333	.333	4.50	13.50

Fielding

C: Garcia 23, Isturiz 18, Omana 23, Torres 2.
1B: Chirino 36, Espinoza 2, Inirio 20, Martinez 9, Torres 1, Torres 2.
2B: Ascanio 13, Balcazar 8, Espinoza 15, Jorge 9, Martinez 8, Serrano 16.
3B: Ascanio 6, Chirino 1, Espinoza 22, Inirio 14, Martinez 2, Reyes 8, Serrano 16.
SS: Ascanio 21, Balcazar 19, Espinoza 2, Jorge 19.
OF: Almonte 38, Leones 19, Marcano 1, Martinez 9, Rijo 46, Torres 21, Valdez 51, Ysabel 8.

Cleveland Indians

SEASON IN A SENTENCE: The Indians ran a lean operation in 2021—they ranked 30th in Opening Day payroll, and only Jose Ramirez earned as much as $5 million annually—yet still finished just two games under .500 and in second place in the American League Central.

HIGH POINT: The Indians peaked at 41-31 on June 24, but injuries that month to righthanders Shane Bieber and Aaron Civale plus outfielder Josh Naylor contributed to a 39-51 finish. Off the field, the franchise officially ditched its Indians nickname in favor of Guardians on Nov. 19.

LOW POINT: Cleveland lost reigning AL Cy Young Award winner Shane Bieber to a shoulder strain for three months following his June 13 start.

NOTABLE ROOKIES: Cleveland had the youngest team in MLB and featured three standout rookies plus a few other contributors. First baseman Bobby Bradley popped 16 home runs and ranked seventh among qualified rookies with a .237 isolated slugging. Righthander Triston McKenzie pitched to a 4.95 ERA in 120 innings, but with a strikeout rate of 10.1 per nine innings that ranked fifth among qualified rookie starters. Righthander Emmanuel Clase picked up the closer's role when James Karinchak faltered and finished with 24 saves, tops among rookies. He finished fifth in AL Rookie of the Year balloting. Other rookies of note included second baseman Owen Miller, righthander Eli Morgan and lefthander Sam Hentges.

KEY TRANSACTIONS: In January, the Indians traded franchise icon Francisco Lindor to the Mets for a four-player return headlined by shortstops Amed Rosario, the Mets' starter in 2020, and prospect Andres Gimenez. At the trade deadline, Cleveland focused on shedding the salaries of veterans like Cesar Hernandez, Jordan Luplow and Eddie Rosario. The club brought back two pitching prospects of note: righthander Peyton Battenfield from the Rays and lefthander Konnor Pilkington from the White Sox. The Indians also added Myles Straw, their potential regular center fielder next season, in a trade with the Astros.

DOWN ON THE FARM: Akron won the Double-A Northeast title in a sweep of Bowie. Shortstop Brayan Rocchio and outfielder George Valera headlined a young Akron roster. Battlefield and Pilkington combined to toss 12 innings in the playoffs, allowing three runs. The Indians' domestic affiliates finished with an overall .533 winning percentage that ranked seventh in baseball.

OPENING DAY PAYROLL: $50,220,534 (30th).

PLAYERS OF THE YEAR

MAJOR LEAGUE	MINOR LEAGUE
Jose Ramirez	**Daniel Espino**
3B	RHP
.266/.355/.538	(High-A/Low-A)
36 HR, 141 OPS+	3-8, 3.73
111 R, 103 RBIs, 27 SB	152 SO in 91.2 IP

ORGANIZATION LEADERS

Batting		*Minimum 250 AB
MAJORS		
*AVG	Amed Rosario	.282
*OPS	Jose Ramirez	.893
HR	Jose Ramirez	36
RBI	Jose Ramirez	103
MINORS		
*AVG	Jhonkensy Noel, ACL, Lake County, Lynchburg	.340
*OBP	Steven Kwan, Columbus, Akron	.407
*SLG	Jhonkensy Noel, ACL, Lake County, Lynchburg	.615
*OPS	Jhonkensy Noel, ACL, Lake County, Lynchburg	1.005
R	Brayan Rocchio, Akron, Lake County	79
H	Oscar Gonzalez, Columbus, Akron	140
TB	Oscar Gonzalez, Columbus, Akron	259
2B	Richie Palacios, Columbus	33
3B	Will Benson, Columbus, Akron	6
3B	Petey Halpin, Lynchburg	6
3B	Angel Martinez, Lynchburg	6
HR	Oscar Gonzalez, Columbus, Akron	31
RBI	Oscar Gonzalez, Columbus, Akron	83
BB	Will Benson, Columbus, Akron	74
SO	Will Benson, Columbus, Akron	146
SB	Luis Durango, ACL Indians	28

Pitching		#Minimum 75 IP
MAJORS		
W	Aaron Civale	12
#ERA	Cal Quantrill	2.89
SO	Triston McKenzie	136
SV	Emmanuel Clase	24
MINORS		
W	Juan Hillman, Columbus, Akron	10
L	Hunter Gaddis, Lake County	11
#ERA	Logan Allen, Akron, Lake County	2.26
G	Robert Broom, Columbus	45
GS	Kirk McCarty, Columbus	24
SV	Jerson Ramirez, Lake County, Lynchburg	17
IP	Kirk McCarty, Columbus	124
BB	Lenny Torres, Lynchburg	48
SO	Daniel Espino, Lake County, Lynchburg	152
#AVG	Daniel Espino, Lake County, Lynchburg	.192

2021 PERFORMANCE

General Manager: Chris Antonetti. **Farm Director:** James Harris. **Scouting Director:** Scott Barnsby.

Class	Team	League	W	L	PCT	Finish	Manager
Majors	Cleveland Indians	American	80	82	.494	9th (15)	Terry Francona
Triple-A	Columbus Clippers	Triple-A East	59	68	.465	13th (20)	Andy Tracy
Double-A	Akron RubberDucks	Double-A Northeast	73	46	.613	1st (12)	Rouglas Odor
High-A	Lake County Captains	High-A Central	65	55	.542	t-3rd (12)	Greg DiCenzo
Low-A	Lynchburg Hillcats	Low-A East	58	62	.483	7th (12)	Dennis Malave
Rookie	ACL Indians	Arizona Complex	35	23	.603	3rd (18)	Jerry Owens
Rookie	DSL Indians Red	Dominican Summer	21	38	.356	t-42nd (46)	Omir Santos/Jesus Tavarez
Rookie	DSL Indians Blue	Dominican Summer	34	25	.576	t-13th (46)	Jesus Tavarez/Omir Santos

Overall 2021 Minor League Record 345 317 .521 11th (30)

ORGANIZATION STATISTICS

CLEVELAND INDIANS
AMERICAN LEAGUE

Batting	B-T	HT	WT	DOB	AVG	vLH	vRH	G	AB	R	H	2B	3B	HR	RBI	BB	HBP	SH	SF	SO	SB	CS	SLG	OBP
Bauers, Jake	L-L	6-1	195	10-6-95	.190	.286	.174	43	100	7	19	3	0	2	6	12	0	0	0	27	0	1	.280	.277
2-team total (72 Seattle)					.209	.231	.203	115	282	27	59	7	0	4	19	30	2	0	0	78	6	1	.277	.290
Bradley, Bobby	L-R	6-1	225	5-29-96	.208	.162	.226	74	245	36	51	10	0	16	41	25	6	0	3	99	0	0	.445	.294
Chang, Yu	R-R	6-1	180	8-18-95	.228	.226	.230	89	237	32	54	14	3	9	39	11	2	0	1	69	1	0	.426	.267
Clement, Ernie	R-R	6-0	170	3-22-96	.231	.225	.235	40	121	16	28	4	0	3	9	7	2	3	0	19	0	1	.339	.285
Gamel, Ben	L-L	5-11	177	5-17-92	.071	.000	.083	11	14	1	1	1	0	0	0	3	0	0	0	6	0	0	.143	.235
Gimenez, Andres	L-R	5-11	161	9-4-98	.218	.194	.224	68	188	23	41	10	0	5	16	11	7	1	3	54	11	0	.351	.282
Hedges, Austin	R-R	6-1	223	8-18-92	.178	.179	.178	88	286	32	51	7	0	10	31	15	1	7	3	87	1	0	.308	.220
Hernandez, Cesar	B-R	5-10	195	5-23-90	.231	.217	.239	96	376	60	87	17	2	18	47	38	4	0	2	90	0	0	.431	.307
2-team total (53 Chicago)					.232	.215	.239	149	570	84	132	21	2	21	62	59	5	0	3	135	1	1	.386	.308
Johnson, Daniel	L-L	5-10	200	7-11-95	.221	.286	.214	30	77	9	17	0	0	4	5	4	0	0	0	27	1	0	.377	.259
Lavarnway, Ryan	R-R	6-3	239	8-7-87	.250	.286	.238	9	28	2	7	3	0	0	0	1	0	1	0	10	0	0	.357	.276
Luplow, Jordan	R-R	6-1	195	9-26-93	.173	.140	.208	36	98	12	17	5	0	7	20	21	2	0	0	31	0	2	.439	.331
2-team total (25 Tampa Bay)					.202	.167	.247	61	163	23	33	8	0	11	28	28	2	0	0	57	1	2	.454	.326
Mercado, Oscar	R-R	6-2	197	12-16-94	.224	.294	.178	72	214	27	48	11	1	6	19	21	2	1	0	42	7	1	.369	.300
Miller, Owen	R-R	6-0	185	11-15-96	.204	.198	.209	60	191	17	39	8	0	4	18	9	1	0	1	54	2	0	.309	.243
Naylor, Josh	L-L	5-11	250	6-22-97	.253	.193	.287	69	233	28	59	13	0	7	21	14	2	0	0	45	1	0	.399	.301
Perez, Roberto	R-R	5-11	220	12-23-88	.149	.173	.135	44	141	13	21	3	0	7	17	17	1	2	0	56	1	0	.319	.245
Ramirez, Harold	R-R	5-10	232	9-6-94	.268	.288	.258	99	339	33	91	21	1	7	41	14	5	0	3	56	3	1	.398	.305
Ramirez, Jose	B-R	5-9	190	9-17-92	.266	.289	.254	152	552	111	147	32	5	36	103	72	7	0	5	87	27	4	.538	.355
Ramos, Wilson	R-R	6-1	241	8-10-87	.226	.308	.167	9	31	3	7	0	0	2	7	3	0	0	1	7	0	0	.419	.286
2-team total (35 Detroit)					.205	.175	.216	44	151	15	31	5	0	8	20	9	0	0	1	36	0	0	.397	.248
Reyes, Franmil	R-R	6-5	265	7-7-95	.254	.260	.251	115	418	57	106	18	2	30	85	43	2	0	3	149	4	1	.522	.324
Rivera, Rene	R-R	5-10	215	7-31-83	.236	.304	.188	21	55	6	13	3	0	2	9	4	1	3	0	24	0	0	.400	.300
Rosario, Amed	R-R	6-2	190	11-20-95	.282	.313	.267	141	550	77	155	25	6	11	57	31	3	0	4	120	13	0	.409	.321
Rosario, Eddie	L-R	6-1	180	9-28-91	.254	.270	.246	78	233	47	59	12	1	7	46	17	1	2	3	47	9	2	.389	.296
Straw, Myles	R-R	5-10	178	10-17-94	.285	.267	.293	60	239	42	68	16	0	2	14	29	0	0	0	50	13	1	.377	.362
2-team total (98 Houston)					.271	.243	.285	158	564	86	153	29	1	4	48	67	2	1	4	121	30	6	.348	.349
Zimmer, Bradley	L-R	6-4	185	11-27-92	.227	.211	.233	99	299	44	68	9	1	8	35	30	15	0	4	122	15	3	.344	.325

Pitching	B-T	HT	WT	DOB	W	L	ERA	G	GS	CG	SV	IP	H	R	ER	HR	BB	SO	AVG	vLH	vRH	K/9	BB/9
Allen, Logan	R-L	6-3	200	5-23-97	2	7	6.26	14	11	0	0	50	58	39	35	12	17	37	.291	.342	.280	6.62	3.04
Bieber, Shane	R-R	6-3	200	5-31-95	7	4	3.17	16	16	0	0	97	84	36	34	11	33	134	.229	.249	.210	12.48	3.07
Civale, Aaron	R-R	6-2	215	6-12-95	12	5	3.84	21	21	0	0	124	108	56	53	23	31	99	.236	.215	.257	7.17	2.24
Clase, Emmanuel	R-R	6-2	206	3-18-98	4	5	1.29	71	0	0	24	70	51	18	10	2	16	74	.195	.179	.209	9.56	2.07
Garza, Justin	R-R	5-10	170	3-20-94	2	1	4.71	21	0	0	0	29	27	16	15	5	18	29	.250	.259	.231	9.10	5.65
Gose, Anthony	L-L	6-0	200	8-10-90	0	0	1.35	6	0	0	0	7	2	1	1	0	2	9	.091	.000	.118	12.15	2.70
Hentges, Sam	L-L	6-6	245	7-18-96	1	4	6.68	30	12	0	0	69	90	54	51	10	32	68	.318	.258	.336	8.91	4.19
Johnson, DJ	L-R	6-4	230	8-30-89	0	1	5.40	1	0	0	0	2	2	1	1	1	0	3	.286	.333	.000	16.20	0.00
2-team total (3 Tampa Bay)					0	0	2.08	4	0	0	0	4	2	1	1	1	0	5	.133	.222	.000	10.38	0.00
Karinchak, James	R-R	6-3	215	9-22-95	7	4	4.07	60	0	0	11	55	35	27	25	9	32	78	.176	.158	.200	12.69	5.20
Maton, Phil	R-R	6-2	206	3-25-93	2	0	4.57	38	1	0	0	41	36	21	21	4	20	61	.237	.239	.235	13.28	4.35
2-team total (27 Houston)					6	0	4.73	65	1	0	0	67	65	36	35	6	32	85	.256	.233	.275	11.48	4.32
McKenzie, Triston	R-R	6-5	165	8-2-97	5	9	4.95	25	24	0	0	120	84	66	66	21	58	136	.194	.203	.186	10.20	4.35
Mejia, J.C.	R-R	6-5	240	8-26-96	1	7	8.25	17	11	0	0	52	60	48	48	13	24	47	.286	.328	.227	8.08	4.13
Morgan, Eli	R-R	5-10	190	5-13-96	5	7	5.34	18	18	0	0	89	90	54	53	20	22	81	.259	.261	.257	8.16	2.22
Nelson, Kyle	L-L	6-1	175	7-8-96	0	0	9.31	10	0	0	0	10	10	10	10	0	8	8	.256	.143	.281	7.45	7.45
Parker, Blake	R-R	6-3	225	6-19-85	2	1	3.09	47	0	0	0	44	43	15	15	5	14	37	.257	.215	.311	7.63	2.89
Perez, Francisco	B-L	6-2	225	7-20-97	0	0	4.05	4	0	0	0	7	6	3	3	0	5	5	.250	.364	.154	6.75	4.05
Perez, Oliver	L-L	6-3	225	8-15-81	0	1	0.00	5	0	0	0	4	5	1	0	0	1	4	.294	.333	.273	9.82	2.45
Plesac, Zach	R-R	6-3	220	1-21-95	10	6	4.67	25	25	0	0	143	137	79	74	23	34	100	.248	.234	.260	6.31	2.14

Name	B-T	HT	WT	DOB	W	L	ERA	G	GS	CG	SV	IP	H	R	ER	HR	BB	SO	AVG	vLH	vRH	K/9	BB/9
Quantrill, Cal	L-R	6-3	195	2-10-95	8	3	2.89	40	22	0	0	150	129	55	48	16	47	121	.234	.214	.254	7.28	2.83
Sandlin, Nick	R-R	5-11	175	1-10-97	1	1	2.94	34	0	0	0	34	21	15	11	2	17	48	.176	.146	.192	12.83	4.54
Shaw, Bryan	B-R	6-1	226	11-8-87	6	7	3.49	81	0	0	2	77	69	33	30	10	38	71	.235	.225	.245	8.26	4.42
Stephan, Trevor	R-R	6-5	225	11-25-95	3	1	4.41	43	0	0	1	63	58	32	31	15	31	75	.235	.241	.230	10.66	4.41
Wittgren, Nick	R-R	6-2	216	5-29-91	2	9	5.05	60	1	0	1	62	61	38	35	13	17	61	.261	.320	.219	8.81	2.45
Young, Alex	L-L	6-3	220	9-9-93	0	0	7.84	10	0	0	0	10	15	9	9	1	7	5	.341	.350	.333	4.35	6.10

Fielding

Catcher	PCT	G	PO	A	E	DP	PB
Hedges	.997	87	720	45	2	7	2
Lavarnway	.962	8	76	0	3	0	0
Perez	.990	43	375	11	4	1	3
Ramos	1.000	9	66	4	0	1	2
Rivera	1.000	20	168	10	0	1	4

First Base	PCT	G	PO	A	E	DP
Bauers	1.000	41	244	17	0	23
Bradley	.990	68	457	47	5	54
Chang	.991	49	296	22	3	28
Miller	.986	18	135	5	2	17
Naylor	.978	15	78	11	2	6
Perez	1.000	1	1	1	0	1
Ramirez	1.000	1	3	0	0	0

Second Base	PCT	G	PO	A	E	DP

Second Base (cont.)	PCT	G	PO	A	E	DP
Chang	.955	8	6	15	1	1
Clement	.976	22	35	45	2	15
Gimenez	.991	25	44	64	1	17
Hernandez	.976	89	110	176	7	43
Miller	.982	29	40	71	2	21

Third Base	PCT	G	PO	A	E	DP
Chang	.974	21	11	26	1	9
Clement	1.000	16	14	30	0	3
Miller	.900	7	2	7	1	0
Ramirez	.955	133	105	213	15	34

Shortstop	PCT	G	PO	A	E	DP
Chang	1.000	7	11	15	0	4
Clement	.000	1	0	0	0	0
Gimenez	.965	42	52	113	6	22

	PCT	G	PO	A	E	DP
Miller	1.000	1	0	1	0	1
Rosario	.976	121	112	292	10	59

Outfield	PCT	G	PO	A	E	DP
Clement	--	2	0	0	0	0
Gamel	1.000	10	5	0	0	0
Johnson	.956	28	40	3	2	1
Luplow	1.000	36	49	2	0	2
Mercado	.992	72	125	3	1	1
Naylor	.977	51	79	5	2	0
Ramirez	.989	103	183	0	2	0
Reyes	1.000	11	14	2	0	0
Rosario	1.000	18	26	0	0	0
Rosario	.992	72	120	4	1	1
Straw	.987	60	152	1	2	0
Zimmer	.995	100	187	1	1	0

COLUMBUS CLIPPERS

TRIPLE-A EAST

TRIPLE-A

Batting	B-T	HT	WT	DOB	AVG	vLH	vRH	G	AB	R	H	2B	3B	HR	RBI	BB	HBP	SH	SF	SO	SB	CS	SLG	OBP
Arias, Gabriel	R-R	6-1	217	2-27-00	.284	.269	.289	115	436	64	124	29	3	13	55	39	5	0	3	110	5	1	.454	.348
Benson, Will	L-L	6-5	230	6-16-98	.161	.160	.162	27	93	7	15	5	1	3	9	14	0	0	0	42	0	2	.333	.271
Bradley, Bobby	L-R	6-1	225	5-29-96	.196	.261	.176	26	97	16	19	1	0	9	19	7	3	0	2	35	0	0	.485	.266
Brooks, Trenton	L-L	6-0	195	7-3-95	.253	.263	.249	79	289	42	73	23	0	8	37	31	1	2	2	67	2	0	.415	.325
Call, Alex	R-R	5-11	188	9-27-94	.229	.172	.249	66	231	34	53	8	0	10	27	33	4	0	1	38	3	3	.394	.335
Chang, Yu	L-R	6-1	180	8-18-95	.322	.250	.327	15	59	9	19	5	0	4	13	5	2	0	0	19	1	2	.610	.394
Clement, Ernie	R-R	6-0	170	3-22-96	.250	.300	.240	33	124	11	31	12	1	1	10	9	0	2	3	22	2	1	.387	.294
Collins, Gavin	R-R	5-11	205	7-17-95	.182	.333	.147	50	148	16	27	3	0	5	22	19	6	0	1	44	1	1	.304	.299
Fermin, Jose	R-R	5-11	200	3-29-99	.364	.000	.500	4	11	4	4	1	0	1	2	1	0	0	0	4	0	0	.727	.417
Gamel, Ben	L-L	5-11	177	5-17-92	.600	1.000	.500	1	5	1	3	1	0	0	0	0	0	0	0	0	1	0	.800	.600
Gimenez, Andres	R-R	5-11	161	9-4-98	.287	.224	.317	52	209	30	60	13	1	10	31	12	6	5	1	55	8	4	.502	.342
Gonzalez, Gianpaul	R-R	6-0	185	1-11-96	.000	--	.000	1	1	0	0	0	0	0	0	0	0	0	0	0	0	0	.000	.000
Gonzalez, Oscar	R-R	6-4	240	1-10-98	.269	.246	.276	72	290	39	78	12	1	18	42	11	4	0	0	76	0	1	.503	.305
Johnson, Daniel	L-L	5-10	200	7-11-95	.222	.148	.243	72	279	36	62	16	2	14	39	35	3	0	1	106	7	1	.444	.314
Jones, Nolan	L-R	6-4	195	5-7-98	.238	.259	.231	99	341	60	81	25	1	13	48	59	5	0	2	122	10	2	.431	.356
Krieger, Tyler	B-R	6-2	190	1-16-94	.169	.140	.178	60	172	16	29	6	0	3	9	12	0	2	0	57	1	2	.238	.223
Kwan, Steven	L-L	5-9	170	9-5-97	.311	.150	.349	26	103	23	32	3	1	5	13	14	1	2	0	8	2	0	.505	.398
Lavarnway, Ryan	R-R	6-3	239	8-7-87	.260	.222	.267	49	177	29	46	7	0	13	40	20	1	0	0	54	0	0	.520	.338
Lavastida, Bryan	R-R	6-0	200	11-27-98	.158	.000	.188	7	19	2	3	0	0	1	3	2	0	0	0	10	0	0	.316	.238
Lopez Alvarez, Angel	R-R	5-10	194	3-14-97	.154	.250	.111	5	13	0	2	0	0	0	2	0	0	0	0	6	0	0	.308	.154
Luplow, Jordan	L-R	6-1	195	9-26-93	.261	.167	.294	8	23	6	6	4	0	2	7	5	0	0	0	4	0	0	.696	.393
2-team total (7 Durham)					.222	.167	.259	15	45	8	10	5	0	2	9	10	0	0	0	10	0	1	.467	.364
Marabell, Connor	L-L	6-1	195	3-28-94	.291	.301	.287	99	337	41	98	23	2	8	49	18	6	0	2	65	4	4	.442	.336
Mercado, Oscar	R-R	6-2	197	12-16-94	.216	.179	.227	45	171	29	37	13	1	5	23	23	6	1	2	32	9	1	.392	.327
Miller, Owen	R-R	6-0	185	11-15-96	.297	.231	.315	48	182	25	54	12	1	7	22	21	2	0	1	52	0	0	.489	.374
Monasterio, Andruw	R-R	6-0	193	5-30-97	.279	.235	.299	33	111	23	31	12	0	1	10	18	1	0	0	37	1	0	.414	.385
Palacios, Richie	L-R	5-10	180	5-16-97	.292	.435	.256	37	113	19	33	9	1	1	12	25	4	2	1	28	10	0	.416	.434
Perez, Roberto	R-R	5-11	220	12-23-88	.125	.000	.200	8	24	3	3	0	0	0	3	6	0	0	1	7	0	0	.125	.290
Ramos, Wilson	R-R	6-1	241	8-10-87	.317	.214	.348	16	60	6	19	3	0	3	9	1	0	0	0	6	0	0	.517	.328
Reyes, Franmil	R-R	6-5	265	7-7-95	.333	.333	.333	4	12	1	4	0	0	1	2	0	0	0	0	2	0	0	.583	.333
Rivera, Mike	R-R	5-9	200	12-12-95	.230	.222	.232	23	74	4	17	3	0	0	8	4	0	0	0	18	0	0	.270	.269
Zimmer, Bradley	L-R	6-4	185	11-27-92	.267	.308	.255	18	60	9	16	3	0	1	8	10	5	0	0	26	4	2	.367	.413

Pitching	B-T	HT	WT	DOB	W	L	ERA	G	GS	CG	SV	IP	H	R	ER	HR	BB	SO	AVG	vLH	vRH	K/9	BB/9
Allen, Logan	R-L	6-3	200	5-23-97	2	3	7.95	12	11	0	0	49	61	43	43	9	29	52	.310	.333	.299	9.62	5.36
Alvarez, Manuel	R-R	6-3	226	9-17-95	0	2	16.20	8	1	0	0	7	7	15	12	0	14	8	.280	.375	.235	10.80	18.90
Bieber, Shane	R-R	6-3	200	5-31-95	0	0	3.38	1	1	0	0	3	3	1	1	0	1	3	.273	.000	.429	10.13	3.38
Broom, Robert	R-R	6-1	190	9-17-96	2	3	5.29	45	3	0	2	49	45	29	29	9	23	52	.246	.297	.218	9.49	4.20
Dowdy, Kyle	R-R	6-1	195	2-3-93	4	4	4.80	39	0	0	1	60	55	41	32	9	40	63	.241	.261	.229	9.45	6.00
Draper, Zach	L-L	6-3	200	10-18-94	0	2	8.31	4	0	0	0	4	6	4	4	1	4	4	.316	.375	.273	8.31	8.31
Fillmyer, Heath	R-R	6-1	195	5-16-94	4	7	6.18	21	16	0	0	83	85	57	57	17	37	79	.265	.272	.259	8.57	4.01
Garza, Justin	R-R	5-10	170	3-20-94	1	1	1.59	14	0	0	1	23	8	5	4	2	13	31	.110	.115	.106	12.31	5.16
Godley, Zack	R-R	6-3	250	4-21-90	1	2	6.00	6	6	0	0	24	30	19	16	5	15	18	.303	.326	.286	6.75	4.13
3-team total (6 Nashville, 9 Syracuse)					7	7	4.39	21	18	0	0	98	90	52	48	13	52	85	.251	.277	.228	7.78	4.76
Gose, Anthony	L-L	6-0	200	8-10-90	6	1	3.55	28	1	0	2	33	20	14	13	4	28	49	.172	.156	.183	13.36	7.64
Hentges, Sam	L-L	6-6	245	7-18-96	0	0	6.23	3	0	0	0	4	1	3	3	0	2	6	.071	.000	.111	12.46	4.15

CLEVELAND INDIANS

Name	B-T	HT	WT	DOB	W	L	ERA	G	GS	CG	SV	IP	H	R	ER	HR	BB	SO	AVG	vLH	vRH	SO9	BB9
Herget, Kevin	L-R	5-10	185	4-3-91	7	5	4.48	28	7	0	2	80	82	49	40	18	23	85	.260	.240	.274	9.52	2.58
Hill, Cam	R-R	6-1	200	5-24-94	1	1	8.03	24	1	0	0	25	33	22	22	3	16	18	.330	.457	.262	6.57	5.84
Hillman, Juan	L-L	6-1	195	5-15-97	0	0	11.57	1	1	0	0	2	5	3	3	0	2	2	.455	.000	.556	7.71	7.71
Johnson, DJ	L-R	6-4	230	8-30-89	1	2	3.32	21	0	0	6	22	24	10	8	3	11	35	.267	.229	.291	14.54	4.57
Karinchak, James	R-R	6-3	215	9-22-95	1	1	3.00	7	0	0	0	6	3	2	2	1	3	9	.143	.286	.071	13.50	4.50
Koch, Matt	L-R	6-3	215	11-2-90	4	2	5.83	34	4	0	0	63	62	42	41	11	29	52	.259	.239	.272	7.39	4.12
Krauth, Ben	L-L	6-0	190	3-10-94	1	0	3.00	5	1	0	0	9	7	3	3	0	5	9	.219	.083	.300	9.00	5.00
Lopez Alvarez, Angel	R-R	5-10	194	3-14-97	0	0	3.00	3	0	0	0	3	4	1	1	0	2	1	.308	.400	.250	3.00	6.00
McCarty, Kirk	L-L	5-8	185	10-12-95	9	6	5.01	24	24	0	0	124	117	73	69	25	44	104	.246	.280	.233	7.55	3.19
McKenzie, Triston	R-R	6-5	165	8-2-97	1	1	2.95	5	5	0	0	21	18	8	7	5	12	23	.228	.156	.277	9.70	5.06
Mejia, J.C.	R-R	6-5	240	8-26-96	1	3	6.75	10	6	0	0	25	24	19	19	8	16	27	.245	.286	.204	9.59	5.68
Morgan, Eli	R-R	5-10	190	5-13-96	0	1	4.03	5	5	0	0	22	20	10	10	1	11	21	.253	.308	.200	8.46	4.43
Morris, Cody	R-R	6-4	205	11-4-96	2	1	1.72	9	8	0	0	37	25	11	7	1	12	52	.191	.212	.169	12.76	2.95
Moss, Scott	L-L	6-6	225	10-6-94	1	5	7.08	9	7	0	0	20	20	16	16	2	15	29	.247	.381	.200	12.84	6.64
Mota, Juan	R-R	6-4	265	5-4-96	2	2	6.86	17	0	0	0	20	17	17	15	3	17	25	.236	.286	.205	11.44	7.78
Nelson, Kyle	L-L	6-1	175	7-8-96	0	1	6.66	25	0	0	1	26	23	22	19	1	20	30	.237	.282	.207	10.52	7.01
Ocker, Nathan	R-R	6-0	190	12-3-96	0	0	0.00	1	0	0	0	2	1	0	0	0	1	3	.143	.500	.000	13.50	4.50
Parker, Blake	R-R	6-3	225	6-19-85	0	0	0.00	12	0	0	4	11	2	0	0	0	5	15	.059	.071	.050	12.27	4.09
Peacock, Brad	R-R	6-1	207	2-2-88	0	4	7.68	11	10	0	0	34	39	30	29	6	14	38	.283	.284	.282	10.06	3.71
2-team total (2 Worcester)					0	4	8.00	13	10	0	0	36	43	33	32	8	16	41	.293	.300	.286	10.25	4.00
Perez, Francisco	B-L	6-2	215	7-20-97	1	0	3.12	19	0	0	1	26	20	9	9	2	20	36	.211	.233	.200	12.46	6.92
Scott, Adam	L-L	6-4	230	10-10-95	0	3	6.00	3	3	0	0	12	12	9	8	2	10	12	.255	.125	.282	9.00	7.52
Siri, Dalbert	R-R	6-1	200	7-19-95	2	1	7.06	15	0	0	0	22	23	17	17	5	9	23	.277	.333	.245	9.55	3.74
Stephens, Jordan	R-R	6-1	200	9-12-92	3	0	4.72	37	0	0	6	48	55	30	25	10	20	48	.304	.288	.306	9.06	3.78
Tully, Tanner	L-L	6-2	205	11-30-94	0	3	5.08	9	6	0	0	39	42	23	22	4	14	33	.273	.258	.276	7.62	3.23
Young, Alex	L-L	6-3	220	9-9-93	0	0	5.00	8	0	0	0	9	8	5	5	1	4	7	.250	.100	.318	7.00	4.00
Young, Danny	L-L	6-3	200	5-27-94	2	2	4.47	40	0	0	0	52	52	30	26	9	26	58	.256	.165	.322	9.97	4.47

Fielding

Catcher	PCT	G	PO	A	E	DP	PB
Collins	.993	49	409	30	3	2	14
Gonzalez	.000	1	0	0	0	0	0
Lavarnway	.997	39	354	20	1	0	3
Lavastida	.960	6	46	2	2	0	0
Lopez Alvarez	1.000	4	40	0	0	0	0
Perez	.982	9	53	3	1	0	0
Ramos	1.000	10	89	3	0	1	1
Rivera	1.000	23	186	7	0	1	1

First Base	PCT	G	PO	A	E	DP
Bradley	1.000	23	140	16	0	21
Brooks	.991	72	506	26	5	50
Chang	1.000	2	18	0	0	2
Jones	1.000	1	13	0	0	0
Lavarnway	1.000	1	3	0	0	0
Marabell	.987	23	135	15	2	17
Miller	1.000	8	46	3	0	7

Second Base	PCT	G	PO	A	E	DP
Arias	.971	9	18	16	1	4
Chang	1.000	4	2	7	0	2
Clement	1.000	7	8	18	0	6
Fermin	1.000	3	5	7	0	1
Gimenez	.972	17	36	33	2	13
Krieger	.976	42	48	76	3	24
Miller	.972	23	41	63	3	18
Monasterio	1.000	8	19	18	0	3
Palacios	.981	26	44	59	2	14

Third Base	PCT	G	PO	A	E	DP
Arias	.946	19	12	23	2	1
Chang	1.000	5	6	4	0	0
Clement	.875	12	8	20	4	5
Fermin	1.000	1	0	0	0	0
Jones	.960	67	56	113	7	18
Miller	.923	8	5	7	1	2
Monasterio	.941	22	18	30	3	6

Shortstop	PCT	G	PO	A	E	DP
Arias	.963	82	98	190	11	48
Chang	.957	4	9	13	1	5
Clement	.935	8	8	21	2	4
Gimenez	.980	32	30	70	2	13
Miller	.929	5	5	8	1	1
Monasterio	1.000	4	2	5	0	1

Outfield	PCT	G	PO	A	E	DP
Benson	.955	25	40	2	2	0
Call	1.000	63	133	4	0	1
Clement	.909	5	9	1	1	0
Gamel	--	1	0	0	0	0
Gonzalez	.962	56	96	5	4	1
Johnson	1.000	63	114	6	0	1
Jones	.979	25	45	2	1	0
Kwan	.963	24	51	1	2	0
Luplow	.938	7	14	1	1	0
Marabell	.988	59	78	3	1	0
Mercado	.990	43	94	1	1	0
Miller	1.000	1	2	0	0	0
Palacios	1.000	6	10	0	0	0
Zimmer	1.000	16	33	2	0	0

AKRON RUBBERDUCKS   DOUBLE-A
DOUBLE-A NORTHEAST

Batting	B-T	HT	WT	DOB	AVG	vLH	vRH	G	AB	R	H	2B	3B	HR	RBI	BB	HBP	SH	SF	SO	SB	CS	SLG	OBP
Benson, Will	L-L	6-5	230	6-16-98	.221	.217	.223	80	262	63	58	13	5	14	42	60	5	1	2	104	14	3	.469	.374
Brennan, Will	L-L	6-0	195	2-2-98	.280	.295	.274	40	150	28	42	6	0	2	20	18	5	1	3	29	2	2	.360	.369
Brooks, Trenton	L-L	6-0	195	7-3-95	.268	.333	.254	23	71	14	19	3	1	4	19	20	3	0	2	18	1	0	.507	.438
Call, Alex	R-R	5-11	188	9-27-94	.310	.400	.292	43	155	34	48	13	1	5	23	21	1	0	3	26	12	2	.503	.389
Clement, Ernie	R-R	6-0	170	3-22-96	.143	.000	.333	2	7	0	1	0	0	0	0	0	0	0	0	3	0	0	.286	.143
Engelmann, Jonathan	R-R	6-3	205	9-18-96	.222	.310	.199	58	198	30	44	9	1	7	23	22	4	0	1	66	1	2	.384	.311
Fermin, Jose	R-R	5-11	200	3-29-99	.258	.259	.257	84	295	40	76	15	2	6	39	23	10	4	3	38	4	4	.383	.329
Freeman, Ike	R-R	5-10	199	6-17-98	.189	.231	.177	41	122	19	23	4	0	1	10	13	2	3	0	43	0	1	.246	.277
Freeman, Tyler	R-R	6-0	190	5-21-99	.323	.276	.333	41	164	26	53	14	2	2	19	8	6	0	2	21	4	2	.470	.372
Gonzalez, Marcos	R-R	5-11	185	10-12-99	.224	.195	.232	61	205	26	46	11	0	7	19	12	0	1	0	75	0	2	.380	.289
Gonzalez, Oscar	R-R	6-4	240	1-10-98	.330	.375	.323	49	188	31	62	12	0	13	41	11	0	0	0	36	1	0	.601	.367
Kwan, Steven	L-L	5-9	170	9-5-97	.337	.353	.331	51	193	42	65	12	3	7	31	22	3	2	1	23	4	2	.539	.411
Lavastida, Bryan	R-R	6-0	200	11-27-98	.291	.273	.296	29	103	16	30	7	1	3	17	12	2	1	1	28	2	3	.466	.373
Lopez Alvarez, Angel	R-R	5-10	194	3-14-97	.222	--	.222	6	18	1	4	1	0	0	1	1	1	0	0	5	0	0	.278	.300
Monasterio, Andruw	R-R	5-8	185	5-30-97	.291	.365	.272	74	265	49	77	14	4	7	51	30	4	0	5	76	6	4	.453	.365
Naylor, Bo	L-R	6-0	195	2-21-00	.188	.158	.195	87	313	41	59	13	1	10	44	37	3	1	1	112	10	0	.332	.280
Nova, Victor	R-R	5-9	160	1-6-00	.241	.308	.227	23	79	10	19	3	0	0	5	10	0	1	0	25	0	1	.278	.326
Palacios, Richie	L-R	5-10	180	5-16-97	.299	.196	.323	66	244	53	73	24	3	6	36	33	4	0	2	42	10	3	.496	.389
Perez, Roberto	R-R	5-11	220	12-23-88	.357	.500	.250	6	14	1	5	2	0	0	3	1	0	0	0	3	0	0	.500	.400
Reyes, Franmil	R-R	6-5	265	7-7-95	.429	--	.429	3	7	2	3	0	0	2	3	0	0	0	0	3	0	0	1.286	.429

	B-T	HT	WT	DOB	AVG	vLH	vRH	G	AB	R	H	2B	3B	HR	RBI	BB	HBP	SH	SF	SO	SB	CS	SLG	OBP
Rivera, Mike	R-R	5-9	200	12-12-95	.163	.111	.176	26	86	11	14	3	0	3	15	10	2	0	3	25	0	0	.302	.257
Rocchio, Brayan	B-R	5-10	170	1-13-01	.293	.341	.279	44	184	34	54	13	4	6	30	13	6	0	0	41	7	4	.505	.360
Rodriguez, Eric	R-R	6-0	200	7-28-98	.182	.000	.333	5	11	2	2	0	0	1	3	1	1	0	0	5	0	0	.455	.308
Rolette, Josh	L-R	6-0	205	5-21-96	.163	.231	.149	24	80	7	13	4	0	1	10	6	0	1	1	31	0	1	.250	.218
Roller, Chris	R-R	6-0	190	10-8-96	.203	.214	.201	70	246	25	50	12	2	1	27	23	5	1	4	72	14	4	.280	.281
Schneemann, Daniel	L-R	6-1	180	1-23-97	.268	.235	.277	25	82	7	22	3	0	3	17	9	1	0	0	20	3	1	.415	.348
Scolamiero, Clark	L-L	6-0	175	1-24-96	.136	.222	.125	27	81	9	11	4	0	2	6	8	3	1	0	41	4	1	.259	.239
Valera, George	L-L	5-11	185	11-13-00	.267	.278	.265	23	86	6	23	3	0	3	22	11	0	0	3	30	1	0	.407	.340
Wade, Austen	L-L	6-1	185	2-17-96	.154	.000	.182	4	13	1	2	1	0	0	1	0	0	0	0	5	0	1	.231	.154

Pitching	B-T	HT	WT	DOB	W	L	ERA	G	GS	CG	SV	IP	H	R	ER	HR	BB	SO	AVG	vLH	vRH	K/9	BB/9
Allen, Logan	R-L	6-0	190	9-5-98	4	0	2.85	12	10	0	0	60	40	20	19	9	13	76	.186	.165	.202	11.40	1.95
Alvarez, Manuel	R-R	6-3	226	9-17-95	1	0	5.70	28	0	0	3	36	32	23	23	4	30	51	.237	.221	.254	12.63	7.43
Arias, Skylar	L-L	6-3	204	6-30-97	7	2	6.92	36	0	0	0	40	35	33	31	2	35	53	.232	.175	.273	11.83	7.81
Battenfield, Peyton	R-R	6-4	224	8-10-97	2	1	3.28	7	7	0	0	36	24	13	13	4	7	36	.183	.167	.200	9.08	1.77
Bieber, Shane	R-R	6-3	200	5-31-95	0	0	8.10	1	1	0	0	3	3	3	3	2	1	4	.231	.167	.286	10.80	2.70
Cantillo, Joey	L-L	6-4	220	12-18-99	0	2	4.50	5	1	0	0	8	8	4	4	0	10	12	.258	.400	.190	13.50	11.25
Civale, Aaron	R-R	6-2	215	6-12-95	1	0	1.29	2	2	0	0	7	4	2	1	0	3	8	.167	.158	.200	10.29	3.86
Clemmer, Dakody	R-R	6-3	220	1-19-96	3	2	3.40	35	0	0	0	50	32	28	19	2	33	62	.181	.225	.144	11.09	5.90
Curry, Xzavion	R-R	5-11	190	7-27-98	0	0	3.86	1	1	0	0	5	6	2	2	2	0	5	.300	.300	.300	9.64	0.00
Draper, Zach	L-L	6-3	200	10-18-94	0	2	6.43	7	3	0	0	21	25	18	15	5	7	18	.287	.293	.283	7.71	3.00
Enright, Nic	R-R	6-3	205	1-8-97	3	4	4.31	23	0	0	2	40	28	21	19	5	10	56	.190	.246	.141	12.71	2.27
Garza, Justin	R-R	5-10	170	3-20-94	0	0	0.00	1	0	0	0	1	0	0	0	0	2	1	.000	.000	.000	9.00	18.00
Hillman, Juan	L-L	6-1	195	5-15-97	10	4	3.77	21	20	1	0	107	110	49	45	16	32	85	.272	.280	.267	7.13	2.68
Krauth, Ben	L-L	6-0	190	3-10-94	3	2	4.66	20	0	0	2	29	23	17	15	5	13	37	.221	.300	.172	11.48	4.03
Lingos, Eli	L-L	5-11	200	5-21-96	3	1	4.95	6	6	0	0	20	22	11	11	0	9	16	.282	.333	.244	7.20	4.05
Marman, Kyle	R-R	6-3	190	3-3-97	4	0	5.85	20	0	0	1	20	20	15	13	4	13	20	.260	.297	.225	9.00	5.85
McCarthy, Shane	R-R	6-2	215	7-29-96	0	2	5.02	7	7	0	0	29	22	18	16	4	13	28	.208	.232	.180	8.79	4.08
Miednik, Jake	R-L	5-11	190	5-1-96	2	0	3.12	32	0	0	1	43	39	20	15	6	20	55	.238	.236	.239	11.42	4.15
Mikolajchak, Nick	R-R	6-2	215	11-21-97	2	5	3.18	30	0	0	8	40	34	17	14	7	9	57	.222	.276	.169	12.93	2.04
Misiaszek, Andrew	R-L	6-2	213	8-24-97	0	0	27.00	1	0	0	0	1	5	4	4	0	1	1	.625	1.000	.500	6.75	6.75
Mock, Eric	R-R	6-2	215	7-12-96	0	1	4.67	5	3	0	0	17	17	10	9	4	7	20	.246	.270	.219	10.38	3.63
Morris, Cody	R-R	6-4	205	11-4-96	0	0	1.35	5	5	0	0	20	14	3	3	1	7	29	.197	.211	.182	13.05	3.15
Mota, Juan	R-R	6-4	265	5-4-96	2	1	4.20	23	0	0	5	30	26	18	14	2	18	49	.241	.313	.183	14.70	5.40
Perez, Francisco	B-L	6-2	215	7-20-97	3	0	0.67	11	0	0	2	27	8	2	2	0	9	46	.091	.140	.044	15.33	3.00
Pilkington, Konnor	L-L	6-3	230	9-12-97	3	2	2.33	8	7	0	0	39	25	11	10	2	18	49	.187	.268	.128	11.41	4.19
Pinto, Aaron	L-R	5-10	210	7-3-96	3	1	2.30	25	0	0	5	43	31	11	11	5	13	67	.197	.300	.115	14.02	2.72
Plesac, Zach	R-R	6-3	220	1-21-95	0	1	5.79	2	2	0	0	5	5	4	3	1	2	6	.278	.182	.429	11.57	3.86
Ponticelli, Thomas	R-R	6-1	200	4-15-97	7	5	3.09	27	12	0	0	87	73	38	30	8	33	77	.229	.247	.207	7.94	3.40
Royalty, Alex	R-R	6-3	190	3-19-97	1	2	4.95	9	9	0	0	40	39	26	22	4	14	37	.258	.186	.354	8.33	3.15
Scolamiero, Clark	L-L	6-0	175	1-24-96	0	0	0.00	1	0	0	0	1	0	0	0	0	0	1	.000	.000	.000	9.00	0.00
Scott, Adam	L-L	6-4	230	10-10-95	3	2	3.49	11	11	0	0	49	39	21	19	5	18	60	.215	.184	.238	11.02	3.31
Tully, Tanner	L-L	6-2	205	11-30-94	6	3	2.68	17	12	0	1	74	81	26	22	6	18	64	.277	.252	.298	7.78	2.19
Wisely, Alec	R-R	5-9	184	8-13-97	0	1	23.14	3	0	0	1	2	6	6	6	1	2	4	.462	.750	.333	15.43	7.71

Fielding

Catcher	PCT	G	PO	A	E	DP	PB
Lavastida	.988	15	156	11	2	0	0
Lopez Alvarez	.970	4	30	2	1	1	1
Naylor	.993	73	707	54	5	4	10
Perez	1.000	6	29	4	0	0	0
Rivera	.991	23	209	7	2	1	0
Rodriguez	1.000	5	36	4	0	0	1
Rolette	1.000	2	6	0	0	0	0

First Base	PCT	G	PO	A	E	DP
Brooks	.985	19	119	11	2	13
Engelmann	.992	38	240	12	2	21
Freeman	1.000	17	101	7	0	14
Gonzalez	.986	32	194	14	3	17
Rivera	1.000	1	1	0	0	1
Rolette	.985	19	119	14	2	14
Schneemann	1.000	1	3	1	0	0

Second Base	PCT	G	PO	A	E	DP
Fermin	.990	28	44	57	1	6

	PCT	G	PO	A	E	DP
Freeman	.964	22	26	55	3	9
Freeman	1.000	7	18	18	0	5
Gonzalez	.875	2	3	4	1	0
Monastero	1.000	21	48	51	0	15
Palacios	.973	42	68	115	5	27
Rocchio	1.000	2	6	7	0	5
Schneemann	1.000	2	5	2	0	1

Third Base	PCT	G	PO	A	E	DP
Fermin	.916	40	24	52	7	7
Freeman	.333	3	1	0	2	0
Freeman	.950	7	4	15	1	5
Gonzalez	.781	17	14	11	7	4
Monastero	.955	33	16	47	3	3
Nova	.953	23	8	33	2	3

Shortstop	PCT	G	PO	A	E	DP
Clement	1.000	1	0	2	0	1
Fermin	.969	14	14	17	1	5
Freeman	.955	26	34	50	4	11

	PCT	G	PO	A	E	DP
Monastero	.912	18	23	39	6	9
Rocchio	.975	43	67	90	4	23
Schneemann	.968	22	19	41	2	6

Outfield	PCT	G	PO	A	E	DP
Benson	1.000	71	105	4	0	1
Brennan	.983	38	58	1	1	0
Brooks	1.000	2	8	0	0	0
Call	.987	37	74	1	1	0
Engelmann	1.000	7	8	0	0	0
Gonzalez	--	1	0	0	0	0
Gonzalez	.971	40	61	5	2	1
Kwan	.980	47	93	3	2	0
Palacios	.946	19	34	1	2	0
Roller	1.000	60	118	4	0	2
Scolamiero	1.000	27	48	1	0	1
Valera	1.000	22	44	3	0	1
Wade	1.000	3	5	0	0	0

LAKE COUNTY CAPTAINS

HIGH CLASS A

HIGH-A CENTRAL

Batting	B-T	HT	WT	DOB	AVG	vLH	vRH	G	AB	R	H	2B	3B	HR	RBI	BB	HBP	SH	SF	SO	SB	CS	SLG	OBP
Amditis, Michael	R-R	5-11	190	8-14-97	.192	.333	.163	34	104	15	20	7	0	4	14	14	2	1	0	28	1	0	.375	.300
Bracho, Aaron	B-R	5-11	175	4-24-01	.174	.244	.160	70	241	27	42	9	0	7	27	32	1	0	5	89	1	2	.299	.269
Bradley, Bobby	L-R	6-1	225	5-29-96	.000	.000	.000	3	7	1	0	0	0	0	0	2	0	0	0	4	0	0	.000	.222
Brennan, Will	L-L	6-0	195	2-2-98	.290	.261	.297	62	238	42	69	22	1	4	30	25	5	0	1	43	13	4	.441	.368

Player	B-T	HT	WT																					
Cairo, Christian	R-R	5-8	170	6-11-01	.268	.533	.196	21	71	16	19	5	0	3	7	12	2	1	0	21	4	1	.465	.388
Delgado, Raynel	B-R	6-2	185	4-4-00	.208	.119	.227	100	336	33	70	13	1	8	35	31	6	1	3	108	14	7	.324	.285
Donovan, Joe	R-R	5-11	180	1-20-99	.165	.091	.183	43	115	15	19	3	1	4	7	13	7	0	0	46	3	0	.313	.289
Engelmann, Jonathan	R-R	6-3	205	9-18-96	.179	.300	.158	22	67	9	12	5	0	0	7	12	1	0	2	20	3	0	.254	.305
Escobedo, Julian	L-L	5-11	190	6-10-98	.206	.294	.193	38	136	21	28	7	2	1	12	13	3	0	0	51	5	6	.309	.289
Farhat, Cody	R-R	6-1	185	9-26-96	.286	.286	.286	8	28	7	8	2	0	2	3	1	2	0	0	5	1	1	.571	.355
Gonzalez, Gianpaul	R-R	6-0	185	1-11-96	.239	.000	.289	15	46	3	11	3	0	0	5	5	0	0	0	18	1	0	.304	.314
Gonzalez, Joab	R-R	5-11	175	12-2-99	.000	--	.000	4	5	0	0	0	0	0	1	0	0	0	4	0	0	.000	.167
Holmes, Quentin	R-R	6-3	175	7-7-99	.226	.242	.223	64	199	20	45	5	2	2	19	16	1	1	2	79	17	6	.302	.284
Lavastida, Bryan	R-R	6-0	200	11-27-98	.303	.417	.284	48	165	32	50	12	0	5	31	26	3	0	4	30	14	5	.467	.399
Lopez Alvarez, Angel	R-R	5-10	194	3-14-97	.188	.250	.167	5	16	2	3	1	1	0	0	1	0	0	0	5	0	0	.375	.235
Naranjo, Joe	L-L	5-8	198	5-11-01	.235	.241	.234	109	374	44	88	13	1	6	50	44	6	0	2	115	7	1	.324	.324
Noel, Jhonkensy	R-R	6-1	180	7-15-01	.280	.192	.311	26	100	13	28	3	0	8	25	9	2	0	0	31	3	1	.550	.351
Nova, Victor	L-R	5-9	160	1-6-00	.207	.158	.217	75	241	38	50	9	3	5	32	37	3	0	2	77	10	4	.332	.318
Peralta, Wilfri	B-R	6-0	155	12-10-00	.207	.143	.227	14	29	5	6	1	0	0	7	7	3	0	0	14	3	1	.241	.410
Pries, Micah	L-R	6-4	190	2-27-98	.267	.240	.272	45	161	19	43	6	1	7	21	12	6	0	0	55	8	1	.447	.341
Ramirez, Harold	R-R	5-10	232	9-6-94	.308	.000	.333	4	13	1	4	0	0	1	1	0	0	0	0	1	0	0	.538	.308
Rocchio, Brayan	B-R	5-10	170	1-13-01	.265	.386	.239	64	257	45	68	13	1	9	33	20	9	0	2	65	14	6	.428	.337
Rodriguez, Johnathan	R-R	6-3	180	11-4-99	.215	.267	.203	24	79	9	17	4	0	2	11	9	2	0	0	22	2	1	.342	.311
Schneemann, Daniel	L-R	6-1	180	1-23-97	.235	.333	.214	26	85	9	20	3	1	3	13	6	0	0	1	24	6	0	.400	.283
Scolamiero, Clark	L-L	6-0	175	1-24-96	.190	.167	.200	8	21	6	4	1	0	2	3	6	2	0	0	7	0	0	.524	.414
Tena, Jose	L-R	5-10	160	3-20-01	.281	.295	.277	107	413	58	116	25	2	16	58	27	5	0	2	117	10	5	.467	.331
Valera, George	L-L	5-11	185	11-13-00	.256	.222	.264	63	199	45	51	2	4	16	43	55	7	0	2	58	10	5	.548	.430
Wade, Austen	L-L	6-1	185	2-17-96	.181	.160	.188	34	94	19	17	2	0	2	9	20	0	1	23	1	1	.266	.322

Pitching

Player	B-T	HT	WT	DOB	W	L	ERA	G	GS	CG	SV	IP	H	R	ER	HR	BB	SO	AVG	vLH	vRH	K/9	BB/9
Allen, Logan	R-L	6-0	190	9-5-98	5	0	1.58	9	9	0	0	51	37	13	9	3	13	67	.200	.189	.205	11.75	2.28
Burgos, Raymond	L-L	6-5	170	11-29-98	0	2	5.59	3	3	0	0	10	16	8	6	1	2	8	.372	.273	.406	7.45	1.86
Burns, Tanner	R-R	6-0	180	12-28-98	2	5	3.57	18	18	0	0	76	64	36	30	10	29	91	.229	.214	.243	10.82	3.45
Civale, Aaron	R-R	6-2	215	6-12-95	0	0	0.00	1	1	0	0	4	1	0	0	0	0	4	.067	.143	.000	8.31	0.00
Coulter, Kevin	R-R	6-5	227	8-12-96	9	4	5.10	23	13	0	0	78	86	47	44	9	26	73	.281	.283	.280	8.46	3.01
Curry, Xzavion	R-R	5-11	190	7-27-98	5	1	2.66	13	13	0	0	68	53	22	20	10	12	80	.209	.212	.205	10.64	1.60
Draper, Zach	L-L	6-3	200	10-18-94	2	2	4.47	12	4	0	2	44	45	24	22	10	11	34	.265	.292	.254	6.90	2.23
Enright, Nic	R-R	6-3	205	1-8-97	1	0	1.47	11	0	0	3	18	12	3	3	0	3	32	.179	.143	.205	15.71	1.47
Espino, Daniel	R-R	6-2	205	1-5-01	2	6	4.04	10	10	0	0	49	30	23	22	7	16	88	.177	.200	.163	16.16	2.94
Gaddis, Hunter	R-R	6-5	202	4-9-98	4	11	4.16	20	19	1	0	97	83	65	45	20	28	127	.222	.238	.207	11.74	2.59
Gallagher, Nick	R-R	6-3	200	9-9-95	1	3	4.61	36	0	0	3	55	43	31	28	7	28	70	.216	.239	.198	11.52	4.61
Gonzalez, Gianpaul	R-R	6-0	185	1-11-96	0	0	13.50	2	0	0	0	2	3	3	3	1	1	0	.333	.250	.400	0.00	4.50
Herrin, Tim	L-L	6-5	225	10-8-96	4	3	2.57	36	0	0	2	74	60	30	21	3	32	85	.219	.180	.238	10.38	3.91
Hickman, Mason	R-R	6-6	228	12-23-98	8	8	4.88	20	20	0	0	98	89	59	53	15	37	110	.237	.204	.264	10.14	3.41
Janczak, Jared	R-R	6-1	205	6-23-95	5	0	4.72	35	0	0	1	55	46	35	29	8	38	65	.227	.242	.213	10.57	6.18
Kelly, Kevin	R-R	6-2	200	11-24-97	5	5	4.66	40	0	0	7	56	56	33	29	7	8	81	.253	.273	.238	13.02	1.29
Lopez, Jonathan	L-R	6-2	175	8-13-99	0	0	0.00	1	0	0	0	1	0	0	0	0	1	1	.000	--	.000	9.00	9.00
Misiaszek, Andrew	R-L	6-2	213	8-24-97	1	0	5.91	7	0	0	0	11	11	11	7	2	6	18	.256	.294	.231	15.19	5.06
Mock, Eric	R-R	6-2	215	7-12-96	0	2	10.20	8	2	0	1	15	17	17	17	3	11	17	.298	.444	.167	10.20	6.60
Ocker, Nathan	R-R	6-0	190	12-3-96	8	0	3.03	34	1	0	3	74	65	27	25	10	23	88	.228	.165	.283	10.65	2.78
Ponticelli, Thomas	R-R	6-1	200	4-15-97	0	0	0.00	1	0	0	0	4	2	0	0	0	0	5	.154	.000	.182	11.25	0.00
Ramirez, Jerson	R-R	6-1	185	11-24-98	3	0	3.21	20	0	0	0	11	28	21	14	10	1	10	38	.208	.286	.153	12.21	3.21
Rholl, Kellen	L-L	6-3	200	5-13-96	0	1	17.50	23	0	0	2	18	33	40	35	3	34	17	.388	.259	.448	8.50	17.00
Royalty, Alex	R-R	6-3	190	3-19-97	1	0	0.00	2	2	1	0	9	5	2	0	0	5	5	.161	.000	.278	5.00	5.00
Smith, Cade	R-R	6-5	230	5-9-99	0	0	0.00	3	0	0	1	3	0	0	0	0	1	4	.000	.000	.000	12.00	3.00
Turner, Matt	L-L	6-4	180	8-4-99	0	2	3.94	4	4	0	0	16	18	14	7	4	7	12	.290	.412	.244	6.75	3.94
Wisely, Alec	R-R	5-9	184	8-13-97	1	0	5.40	7	0	0	1	12	14	8	7	2	5	11	.298	.429	.192	8.49	3.86
Zapata, Juan	R-R	6-1	198	11-19-98	0	0	0.00	1	1	0	0	6	1	0	0	0	3	3	.056	.000	.091	4.76	4.76

Fielding

Catcher	PCT	G	PO	A	E	DP	PB
Amditis	.991	34	305	19	3	2	5
Donovan	.978	42	383	26	9	2	9
Gonzalez	.992	13	124	8	1	1	2
Lavastida	.984	38	348	29	6	2	5
Lopez Alvarez	.985	5	62	2	1	0	0

First Base	PCT	G	PO	A	E	DP
Bracho	.990	12	93	4	1	8
Bradley	1.000	2	9	0	0	2
Delgado	.952	3	19	1	1	3
Engelmann	1.000	3	23	0	0	1
Naranjo	.990	97	635	37	7	54
Pries	.955	6	41	1	2	3

Second Base	PCT	G	PO	A	E	DP
Bracho	.969	30	33	62	3	16
Cairo	.967	9	14	15	1	2
Delgado	.967	44	55	93	5	18
Gonzalez	1.000	3	1	5	0	0

	PCT	G	PO	A	E	DP
Nova	1.000	1	1	2	0	1
Peralta	1.000	9	7	12	0	1
Rocchio	.970	16	21	44	2	9
Schneemann	1.000	3	7	8	0	2
Tena	.974	11	11	26	1	5

Third Base	PCT	G	PO	A	E	DP
Bracho	.885	12	8	15	3	1
Cairo	1.000	7	6	9	0	2
Delgado	.848	30	20	47	12	2
Noel	.946	17	10	25	2	5
Nova	.917	29	11	17	38	5	2
Rocchio	.966	12	8	20	1	2
Schneemann	1.000	1	0	2	0	0
Tena	.919	13	14	20	3	4

Shortstop	PCT	G	PO	A	E	DP
Cairo	1.000	2	5	1	0	0
Peralta	.800	3	1	3	1	0
Rocchio	.949	36	54	75	7	19

	PCT	G	PO	A	E	DP
Tena	.988	81	96	157	3	34

Outfield	PCT	G	PO	A	E	DP
Brennan	1.000	59	119	4	0	1
Engelmann	.935	19	29	0	2	0
Escobedo	1.000	39	61	2	0	1
Farhat	1.000	8	11	1	0	0
Holmes	.944	60	101	1	6	0
Nova	.892	28	32	1	4	0
Pries	.978	30	42	2	1	0
Ramirez	1.000	3	4	0	0	0
Rodriguez	.930	22	39	1	3	1
Schneemann	1.000	12	14	0	0	0
Scolamiero	1.000	7	14	0	0	0
Valera	.983	59	114	3	2	0
Wade	.962	33	50	1	2	1

LYNCHBURG HILLCATS

LOW-A EAST

LOW CLASS A

Batting

Batting	B-T	HT	WT	DOB	AVG	vLH	vRH	G	AB	R	H	2B	3B	HR	RBI	BB	HBP	SH	SF	SO	SB	CS	SLG	OBP
Bartlett, Will	R-R	6-3	215	2-2-01	.179	.190	.176	33	106	16	19	2	2	4	10	18	4	0	0	38	0	1	.349	.320
Burgos, Jorge	L-L	6-0	165	12-26-01	.293	.214	.308	23	92	16	27	5	3	1	9	8	0	0	0	19	2	1	.446	.350
Cairo, Christian	R-R	5-8	170	6-11-01	.210	.250	.199	58	181	36	38	6	2	3	17	37	8	1	2	63	15	2	.315	.364
Diaz, Yainer	R-R	6-0	195	9-21-98	.314	.292	.319	61	239	30	75	19	1	5	50	15	2	0	2	42	1	1	.464	.357
2-team total (12 Fayetteville)					.300	.250	.313	73	287	33	86	21	1	6	57	15	2	0	3	46	2	1	.443	.336
Escobedo, Julian	L-L	5-11	190	6-10-98	.254	.267	.250	18	67	12	17	3	0	3	12	4	2	0	0	20	4	1	.433	.315
Farhat, Cody	R-R	6-1	185	9-26-96	.255	.371	.222	46	161	29	41	6	5	6	20	14	5	2	2	47	8	3	.466	.330
Freeman, Ike	R-R	5-10	199	6-17-98	.270	.200	.281	11	37	5	10	1	0	1	5	5	1	0	0	13	1	0	.378	.372
Halpin, Petey	L-R	6-0	185	5-26-02	.294	.350	.278	54	221	34	65	14	6	1	18	21	3	1	0	50	11	9	.425	.363
Holland, Korey	R-R	5-11	170	1-1-00	.252	.225	.258	68	230	34	58	7	3	6	34	29	3	1	6	92	10	3	.387	.336
Idrogo, Cesar	B-R	5-11	170	3-26-01	.184	.333	.156	12	38	3	7	3	0	0	3	3	0	0	0	7	0	0	.263	.244
Jerez, Miguel	R-R	6-1	178	10-24-97	.177	.167	.179	50	164	24	29	8	1	7	23	21	5	1	2	63	0	0	.366	.286
Lopez, Jonathan	L-R	6-2	175	8-13-99	.286	.000	.400	6	14	1	4	1	0	0	1	2	0	0	0	5	0	0	.357	.375
Martinez, Angel	B-R	6-0	165	1-27-02	.241	.165	.262	97	377	62	91	20	6	7	46	43	1	1	2	88	13	6	.382	.319
Melendez, Andres	R-R	5-10	150	5-21-01	.247	.133	.273	73	239	41	59	16	2	8	46	44	3	0	3	80	2	1	.431	.367
Nelson, Hosea	L-L	6-0	210	11-22-96	.194	.176	.200	18	67	6	13	5	0	0	5	5	0	1	0	20	2	1	.269	.250
Noel, Jhonkensy	R-R	6-1	180	7-15-01	.393	.382	.397	38	150	36	59	10	1	11	40	7	3	0	2	27	2	1	.693	.426
Pena, Landy	B-R	6-1	180	11-6-01	.111	.200	.077	14	36	3	4	1	0	1	3	0	1	0	0	25	0	0	.222	.179
Peralta, Wilfri	R-R	6-0	155	12-10-00	.290	.375	.261	10	31	4	9	3	0	1	6	1	1	1	0	8	1	0	.484	.333
Planez, Alexfri	R-R	6-2	180	8-17-01	.264	.279	.261	103	390	61	103	19	5	16	53	13	5	1	4	121	11	3	.462	.294
Pries, Micah	L-R	6-4	190	2-27-98	.320	.160	.400	22	75	17	24	7	2	2	13	9	3	0	2	19	6	0	.547	.404
Ramirez, Micael	R-R	5-11	170	6-8-99	.225	.125	.244	30	102	16	23	3	0	0	9	14	2	0	2	13	2	0	.255	.325
Rodriguez, Eric	R-R	6-0	200	7-28-98	.129	.000	.154	12	31	3	4	1	0	0	3	0	0	0	0	10	1	1	.161	.206
Rodriguez, Gabriel	R-R	6-2	162	2-22-02	.236	.278	.226	97	373	44	88	18	1	3	34	25	3	3	2	111	3	1	.314	.288
Rodriguez, Johnathan	R-R	6-3	180	11-4-99	.314	.342	.308	59	220	29	69	13	1	5	33	16	2	0	2	54	3	1	.450	.363
Tolentino, Milan	L-R	6-0	185	11-17-01	.206	.000	.241	16	63	6	13	2	0	1	9	6	0	1	0	22	0	0	.286	.275
Valdes, Yordys	B-R	6-0	170	8-16-01	.212	.258	.200	93	312	35	66	12	2	0	22	24	3	5	5	92	16	4	.263	.270

Pitching

Pitching	B-T	HT	WT	DOB	W	L	ERA	G	GS	CG	SV	IP	H	R	ER	HR	BB	SO	AVG	vLH	vRH	K/9	BB/9
Abney, Alaska	R-R	6-1	205	5-5-00	0	0	0.82	8	0	0	1	11	4	1	1	0	4	16	.105	.150	.056	13.09	3.27
Arias-Bautista, Jaime	R-L	6-0	200	1-21-99	8	4	3.81	23	9	0	2	87	67	40	37	12	15	111	.208	.253	.192	11.44	1.55
Benton, Trey	R-R	6-4	209	6-18-98	0	2	7.41	18	0	0	1	17	12	15	14	0	29	24	.211	.261	.176	12.71	15.35
Brito, Serafino	R-R	6-0	200	4-28-97	0	1	4.12	13	0	0	1	20	19	11	9	4	5	25	.247	.150	.351	11.44	2.29
Curry, Xzavion	R-R	5-11	190	7-27-98	3	0	1.07	5	5	0	0	25	12	4	3	1	4	38	.135	.077	.180	13.50	1.42
Davenport, Aaron	R-R	6-0	185	7-25-00	0	1	3.27	4	4	0	0	11	5	4	4	0	8	15	.139	.188	.100	12.27	6.55
Dion, Will	L-L	5-10	180	4-17-00	0	0	0.00	1	0	0	0	3	0	0	0	0	2	3	.000	.000	.000	9.00	6.00
Espino, Daniel	R-R	6-2	205	1-5-01	1	2	3.38	10	10	0	0	43	34	17	16	2	23	64	.217	.214	.218	13.50	4.85
Feliz, Daritzon	L-L	6-2	175	8-19-99	4	3	7.09	29	0	0	1	53	75	45	42	10	31	59	.326	.368	.312	9.96	5.23
Forrester, Jacob	R-R	6-0	185	12-5-95	2	2	9.27	16	0	0	1	22	34	27	23	4	10	13	.347	.349	.345	5.24	4.03
Gervacio, Yeury	L-L	6-1	168	7-1-99	0	1	6.14	9	0	0	0	15	14	11	10	2	7	21	.250	.250	.250	12.89	4.30
Hart, Zach	R-R	6-4	235	5-17-97	8	2	3.35	30	1	0	0	75	55	34	28	2	45	105	.205	.188	.213	12.54	5.38
Idrogo, Cesar	B-R	5-11	170	3-26-01	0	0	18.00	1	0	0	0	1	4	5	2	1	0	0	.444	.286	1.000	0.00	0.00
Jenkins, Liam	R-R	6-8	225	4-9-97	3	0	3.98	10	1	0	0	20	18	9	9	2	14	30	.234	.259	.220	13.28	6.20
Jerez, Elvis	R-R	6-4	185	2-5-00	0	0	4.91	2	0	0	0	4	1	2	2	0	3	6	.083	.000	.143	14.73	7.36
Jerez, Miguel	R-R	6-1	178	10-24-97	0	0	0.00	1	0	0	0	1	0	0	0	0	0	0	.000	.000	.000	0.00	0.00
Jones, Jordan	R-R	6-2	195	10-2-97	3	10	4.63	20	20	0	0	89	93	52	46	5	43	82	.272	.269	.274	8.26	4.33
Labaut, Randy	L-L	6-1	202	10-1-96	3	2	3.09	22	3	0	0	44	29	18	15	5	23	58	.182	.136	.200	11.95	4.74
Lopez, Jonathan	L-R	6-2	175	8-13-99	0	0	54.00	1	0	0	0	1	2	6	6	0	3	1	.667	.500	1.000	9.00	27.00
Misiaszek, Andrew	R-L	6-2	213	8-24-97	3	2	2.32	24	0	0	1	50	45	25	13	4	20	68	.238	.095	.274	12.16	3.58
Mock, Eric	R-R	6-2	215	7-12-96	2	0	1.98	4	0	0	1	14	9	3	3	1	3	10	.184	.240	.125	6.59	1.98
Morillo, Sergio	R-R	6-3	190	9-13-99	0	2	11.30	6	0	0	0	14	18	19	18	0	13	16	.305	.143	.356	10.05	8.16
Munoz, Brauny	R-R	6-1	170	8-20-00	4	4	6.55	15	11	0	1	58	73	47	42	10	17	48	.311	.366	.275	7.49	2.65
Ramirez, Jerson	R-R	6-1	185	11-24-98	0	1	1.23	16	0	0	6	22	7	5	3	1	9	31	.095	.036	.130	12.68	3.68
Rodriguez, Eric	R-R	6-0	200	7-28-98	0	0	0.00	1	0	0	0	1	0	0	0	0	0	0	.000	---	.000	0.00	0.00
Smith, Cade	R-R	6-5	230	5-9-99	2	3	4.28	30	0	0	4	40	25	23	19	3	21	64	.177	.222	.149	14.40	4.73
Torres, Lenny	R-R	6-1	190	10-15-00	2	7	6.29	20	19	0	0	69	68	53	48	5	48	73	.256	.239	.268	9.57	6.29
Villalobos, Hugo	R-R	5-10	170	7-27-01	0	2	1.98	12	1	0	1	27	28	16	6	3	10	18	.264	.308	.239	5.93	3.29
Vinicio, Miguel	R-R	6-3	170	9-1-99	3	1	0.82	6	0	0	0	22	12	4	2	0	12	21	.158	.208	.135	8.59	4.91
Wisely, Alec	R-R	5-9	184	8-13-97	3	2	2.89	24	0	0	1	37	33	14	12	3	19	46	.232	.271	.213	11.09	4.58
Wolf, Josh	R-R	6-3	170	9-1-00	1	3	5.35	18	17	0	1	66	73	43	39	3	34	67	.283	.280	.285	9.18	4.66
Zapata, Juan	R-R	6-1	198	11-19-98	3	5	5.45	16	13	0	0	73	89	49	44	4	20	44	.302	.306	.299	5.45	2.48

Fielding

Catcher	PCT	G	PO	A	E	DP	PB
Diaz	.995	36	381	22	2	3	7
Lopez	.941	3	13	3	1	0	1
Melendez	.983	55	521	45	10	6	12
Ramirez	.986	21	193	20	3	1	4
Rodriguez	1.000	11	70	5	0	0	2

First Base	PCT	G	PO	A	E	DP
Bartlett	.995	30	175	11	1	16
Cairo	1.000	1	2	0	0	0
Diaz	1.000	2	14	1	0	1
Freeman	.981	7	49	3	1	5
Idrogo	1.000	4	24	2	0	1
Jerez	.988	48	306	26	4	25
Noel	.993	18	139	11	1	13
Peralta	.971	10	62	4	2	5

	PCT	G	PO	A	E	DP
Pries	.972	6	33	2	1	4
Ramirez	1.000	3	11	1	0	3
Rodriguez	.857	1	6	0	1	3

Second Base	PCT	G	PO	A	E	DP
Cairo	.970	34	52	78	4	22
Freeman	1.000	1	1	2	0	1
Martinez	.960	49	82	109	8	25

Pena	.926	6	9	16	2	3
Peralta	.000	1	0	0	0	0
Tolentino	.971	11	15	19	1	2
Valdes	.990	24	35	61	1	14

Third Base	PCT	G	PO	A	E	DP
Cairo	.913	22	10	32	4	2
Freeman	.000	1	0	0	0	0
Martinez	1.000	13	10	17	0	3
Noel	.917	13	11	22	3	4
Pena	1.000	5	4	5	0	0
Rodriguez	.933	55	30	67	7	7

Rodriguez	.000	1	0	0	0	0
Valdes	.933	16	5	23	2	2

Shortstop	PCT	G	PO	A	E	DP
Martinez	.920	32	46	69	10	19
Rodriguez	.906	31	35	61	10	11
Tolentino	1.000	5	9	10	0	2
Valdes	.983	54	56	120	3	26

Outfield	PCT	G	PO	A	E	DP
Burgos	.971	18	33	0	1	0
Escobedo	1.000	15	25	0	0	0

Farhat	.981	47	99	4	2	0
Halpin	1.000	46	98	5	0	2
Holland	.981	61	97	4	2	0
Idrogo	1.000	6	7	0	0	0
Nelson	.963	18	26	0	1	0
Planez	.959	97	152	12	7	2
Pries	1.000	9	12	0	0	0
Rodriguez	1.000	3	6	0	0	0
Rodriguez	.990	55	99	1	1	1
Valdes	--	1	0	0	0	0

ACL INDIANS
ROOKIE

ARIZONA COMPLEX LEAGUE

Batting	B-T	HT	WT	DOB	AVG	vLH	vRH	G	AB	R	H	2B	3B	HR	RBI	BB	HBP	SH	SF	SO	SB	CS	SLG	OBP
Amditis, Michael	R-R	5-11	190	8-14-97	.250	.000	.333	4	12	2	3	0	0	0	2	1	0	0	0	5	0	0	.250	.308
Bartlett, Will	R-R	6-3	215	2-2-01	.235	.400	.167	5	17	1	4	1	0	0	1	0	0	0	0	8	0	0	.294	.235
Brown, Jordan	R-R	6-3	185	9-9-01	.154	.211	.139	26	91	10	14	3	0	2	13	11	2	0	1	38	0	2	.253	.257
Burgos, Jorge	L-L	6-0	165	12-26-01	.353	.320	.364	31	102	25	36	11	0	0	14	18	3	0	0	26	4	1	.461	.463
Caddell, Seth	R-R	5-11	200	5-29-99	.000	--	.000	1	2	0	0	0	0	0	0	0	0	0	0	0	0	0	.000	.000
Cooper, Michael	L-R	6-5	180	7-27-99	.191	.222	.184	15	47	8	9	3	0	1	8	6	1	0	2	10	0	1	.319	.286
Devers, Jose	R-R	5-9	140	5-17-03	.212	.114	.243	43	146	24	31	3	0	3	23	20	2	0	2	49	6	3	.295	.312
Durango, Luis	L-L	5-10	135	4-8-03	.308	.275	.319	46	156	37	48	6	0	3	20	18	7	1	2	31	28	7	.404	.399
Escobedo, Julian	L-L	5-11	190	6-10-98	.300	.333	.292	8	30	5	9	1	0	2	9	4	0	0	0	8	2	1	.533	.382
Fascia, Zac	L-R	6-1	225	9-15-98	1.000	--	1.000	1	3	2	3	2	0	0	0	0	0	0	0	0	0	0	1.667	1.000
Fox, Jake	L-R	6-0	185	2-12-03	.405	.231	.483	13	42	10	17	1	0	0	6	6	0	0	1	9	7	0	.429	.469
Frias, Dayan	B-R	5-7	140	6-25-02	.322	.366	.306	42	152	32	49	12	3	4	24	27	3	0	6	38	3	2	.520	.420
Greene, Isaiah	L-L	6-1	180	8-29-01	.289	.297	.287	43	152	31	44	9	0	1	16	35	1	1	2	42	5	4	.368	.421
Kokx, Connor	R-R	6-1	200	2-24-00	.238	.182	.258	15	42	9	10	1	1	1	4	6	8	0	0	11	5	1	.381	.429
Lara, Jesus	R-R	5-8	160	6-23-02	.173	.188	.167	19	52	11	9	2	0	2	8	11	3	0	0	15	0	1	.327	.348
Luplow, Jordan	R-R	6-1	195	9-26-93	.333	--	.333	3	3	3	1	0	0	0	1	0	0	0	0	0	0	0	.333	.714
Noel, Jhonkensy	R-R	6-1	180	7-15-01	.200	.500	.154	6	15	1	3	1	0	0	1	1	1	0	0	4	0	1	.267	.294
Pastrano, Jose	B-R	5-9	145	9-12-02	.225	.217	.228	32	102	19	23	8	2	0	14	20	1	0	1	28	2	2	.343	.355
Paz, Richard	L-R	5-7	150	6-12-01	.360	.192	.429	26	89	18	32	5	1	6	25	11	6	0	4	16	0	0	.640	.445
Planchart, Victor	B-R	5-8	165	5-17-01	.276	.333	.258	28	87	18	24	9	1	3	16	14	3	0	1	16	0	0	.506	.390
Pries, Micah	L-R	6-4	190	2-27-98	.471	.800	.333	5	17	4	8	0	1	3	6	1	0	0	0	3	0	0	1.118	.500
Ramirez, Micael	R-R	5-11	170	6-8-99	.429	.389	.447	17	56	15	24	11	0	0	13	11	2	1	1	11	1	1	.625	.529
Rodriguez, Skeiling	R-R	6-0	175	2-26-01	.291	.375	.247	34	117	25	34	7	2	5	24	11	1	0	0	27	1	2	.533	.357
Romero, Sterling	L-L	5-10	145	3-2-02	.259	.200	.273	10	27	3	7	2	1	1	4	2	0	0	0	6	1	0	.519	.310
Sanquintin, Junior	B-R	6-0	172	1-8-02	.250	.220	.262	47	176	35	44	11	1	8	36	14	2	0	3	59	4	0	.460	.308
Tolentino, Milan	L-R	6-0	185	11-17-01	.301	.300	.301	32	123	27	37	4	1	6	31	10	3	0	2	40	3	1	.496	.362
Tucker, Carson	R-R	6-2	180	1-24-02	.150	.250	.125	6	20	6	3	0	0	1	3	5	0	0	4	1	1	.300	.320

Pitching	B-T	HT	WT	DOB	W	L	ERA	G	GS	CG	SV	IP	H	R	ER	HR	BB	SO	AVG	vLH	vRH	K/9	BB/9
Abney, Alaska	R-R	6-1	205	5-5-00	0	0	0.00	4	0	0	1	5	3	0	0	0	3	6	.176	.000	.375	10.80	5.40
Artiles, Reny	R-R	6-0	160	1-17-02	1	1	4.94	9	8	0	0	27	30	15	15	4	12	43	.275	.289	.266	14.16	3.95
Brito, Serafino	R-R	6-0	200	4-28-97	1	0	4.50	2	0	0	0	2	5	1	1	0	0	3	.556	.167	.500	13.50	0.00
Burgos, Raymond	L-L	6-5	170	11-29-98	0	0	3.86	3	1	0	0	2	2	1	1	0	2	2	.286	1.000	.167	7.71	7.71
Candelario, Elmson	R-R	6-4	185	11-9-00	3	2	3.77	10	8	0	0	31	27	20	13	4	15	34	.225	.273	.207	9.87	4.35
Cantillo, Joey	L-L	6-4	220	12-18-99	0	0	0.00	2	1	0	0	5	2	0	0	0	1	7	.125	.000	.182	12.60	1.80
Casetta-Stubbs, Damon	R-R	6-4	225	7-22-99	1	0	0.00	1	0	0	0	6	3	0	0	0	1	7	.143	.429	.000	17.47	3.18
Davenport, Aaron	R-R	6-0	185	7-25-00	1	0	3.18	3	2	0	0	6	3	3	2	2	2	11	.143	.429	.000	17.47	3.18
Dion, Will	L-L	5-10	180	4-17-00	0	0	0.00	4	3	0	0	9	1	1	0	0	3	18	.036	.100	.000	18.00	3.00
Figueroa, Daniel	R-R	6-0	172	9-25-00	2	2	3.81	20	0	0	1	28	34	19	12	4	15	35	.312	.517	.238	11.12	4.76
Forrester, Jacob	R-R	6-0	185	12-5-95	1	1	3.38	4	0	0	0	5	6	2	2	0	4	10	.273	.500	.188	16.88	6.75
Garcia, Luis D.	R-R	6-2	180	6-23-00	1	1	5.73	7	0	0	0	11	14	7	7	3	3	6	.298	.389	.241	4.91	2.45
Gervacio, Yeury	L-L	6-1	168	7-5-01	1	0	0.00	8	0	0	1	10	2	1	0	0	2	15	.063	.080	.13.06	1.74	
Hernandez, Allan	R-R	6-5	225	1-19-01	0	0	7.20	3	1	0	0	5	5	4	4	3	2	7	.250	.000	.294	12.60	3.60
Jerez, Elvis	R-R	6-4	185	2-5-00	2	0	2.05	20	0	0	1	22	8	6	5	1	18	44	.114	.192	.068	18.00	7.36
Jimenez, Diarlin	R-R	6-5	180	3-18-00	3	1	6.68	17	0	0	0	31	36	27	23	9	13	28	.286	.283	.288	8.13	3.77
Lopez, Euclides	R-R	5-10	170	10-13-00	1	1	11.94	19	0	0	0	17	22	26	23	0	30	17	.319	.300	.327	8.83	15.58
Mateo, Juan	R-R	5-11	190	9-9-92	4	1	5.10	22	0	0	0	30	28	25	17	2	12	27	.243	.209	.264	8.10	3.60
Mock, Eric	R-R	6-2	215	7-12-96	1	0	0.00	2	0	0	0	2	0	0	0	0	0	4	.000	.000	.000	15.43	0.00
Morris, Cody	R-R	6-4	205	11-4-96	0	0	2.08	1	1	0	0	4	2	2	1	1	1	12	.133	.000	.167	24.92	2.08
Perez, Steven	L-L	6-0	155	4-21-01	2	0	6.52	13	6	0	1	39	39	34	28	7	16	47	.257	.289	.243	10.94	3.72
Planchart, Victor	B-R	5-8	165	5-17-01	0	0	0.00	1	0	0	0	1	1	0	0	0	1	1	.000	.000	--	9.00	9.00
Reyes, Tomas	L-L	5-11	150	9-23-99	3	1	5.97	12	4	0	0	38	40	26	25	3	14	33	.267	.300	.262	7.88	3.35
Richardson, Alonzo	R-R	5-11	165	10-7-02	1	3	8.42	12	8	0	0	31	45	30	29	8	18	35	.341	.375	.321	10.16	5.23
Rodriguez, Adrian	R-R	5-11	155	8-21-00	2	2	7.71	19	0	0	0	30	38	28	26	8	17	30	.304	.354	.273	8.90	5.04
Scott, Adam	L-L	6-4	230	10-10-95	0	1	16.88	1	1	0	0	3	5	5	5	2	2	5	.385	.667	.300	16.88	6.75
Soteldo, Victor	R-R	6-1	165	8-27-01	1	0	3.21	10	0	0	0	14	15	5	5	0	4	12	.288	.286	.290	7.71	2.57
Turner, Matt	L-L	6-4	180	8-4-99	0	0	0.00	3	3	0	0	4	1	0	0	0	1	8	.077	.000	.091	18.00	2.25
Vasquez, Samuel	R-R	6-3	170	9-20-99	0	4	8.33	12	7	0	0	27	31	31	25	3	23	22	.324	.256	.365	7.33	7.67

	B-T	HT	WT	DOB	W	L	ERA	G	GS	CG	SV	IP	H	R	ER	HR	BB	SO	AVG	vLH	vRH	K/9	BB/9
Vasquez, Wardquelin	R-R	6-3	194	7-25-01	0	1	2.50	11	1	0	0	18	11	5	5	1	7	24	.172	.100	.205	12.00	3.50
Vergara, Jhon	R-R	6-3	170	4-4-00	0	0	10.80	4	2	0	0	8	12	11	10	2	4	8	.343	.333	.348	8.64	4.32
Villalobos, Hugo	R-R	5-10	170	7-27-01	2	1	6.00	6	0	0	1	9	10	6	6	1	2	9	.294	.357	.250	9.00	2.00

Fielding

C: Amditis 3, Caddell 1, Fascia 1, Paz 25, Planchart 21, Ramirez 11.
1B: Bartlett 4, Brown 1, Cooper 14, Planchart 5, Pries 2, Ramirez 6, Sanquintin 33.
2B: Devers 15, Fox 5, Frias 4, Lara 11, Pastrano 21, Tolentino 7, Tucker 1.
3B: Brown 2, Devers 19, Fox 2, Frias 13, Lara 5, Noel 5, Pastrano 3, Sanquintin 10, Tolentino 9.
SS: Devers 7, Fox 4, Frias 23, Pastrano 7, Tolentino 14, Tucker 4.
OF: Brown 18, Burgos 25, Durango 43, Escobedo 6, Greene 39, Kokx 12, Luplow 2, Pries 2, Rodriguez 32, Romero 10.

DSL INDIANS ROOKIE

DOMINICAN SUMMER LEAGUE

Batting	B-T	HT	WT	DOB	AVG	vLH	vRH	G	AB	R	H	2B	3B	HR	RBI	BB	HBP	SH	SF	SO	SB	CS	SLG	OBP
Alduey, Fran	B-R	5-7	140	1-7-04	.265	.286	.257	38	136	21	36	4	3	3	17	12	5	0	1	45	12	4	.404	.344
Andrade, Lerwin	B-R	5-7	137	3-21-04	.213	.133	.233	31	75	15	16	3	2	0	9	20	5	0	0	19	6	1	.307	.410
Aranguren, Nelson	R-R	5-11	183	8-26-03	.194	.000	.226	12	36	7	7	1	0	0	3	6	3	0	0	6	0	0	.222	.356
Benjamin, Juan	B-R	5-8	150	4-25-03	.250	.077	.291	20	68	9	17	4	1	0	12	10	1	1	1	18	1	2	.338	.350
Caminero, Junior	R-R	5-11	157	7-5-03	.295	.351	.275	43	146	26	43	8	0	9	33	20	2	0	3	28	2	0	.534	.380
Caripa, Erick	R-R	6-1	160	.1-29-03	.219	.296	.200	38	137	23	30	9	0	3	20	14	1	0	1	33	5	2	.350	.294
Cedeno, Oscar	B-R	5-7	138	8-2-03	.184	.125	.200	28	76	13	14	3	0	1	12	14	8	0	0	17	1	2	.263	.367
Cepeda, Adonis	B-R	0-0	0	1-20-04	.266	.182	.277	33	94	14	25	5	1	1	17	15	0	0	0	15	1	1	.372	.367
Collado, Maick	B-R	5-11	160	12-24-02	.227	.176	.237	37	110	24	25	5	1	1	18	27	4	0	3	23	2	1	.318	.367
Contreras, Angel	B-R	5-7	142	1-14-03	.237	.000	.265	30	76	18	18	6	1	2	11	12	15	0	1	29	1	1	.421	.433
Espinola, Christopher	L-L	5-7	165	9-19-03	.252	.333	.240	38	119	21	30	6	0	1	18	17	1	0	1	29	1	3	.328	.348
Flores, Maikol	L-R	5-9	154	11-11-02	.258	.438	.219	30	89	16	23	1	1	1	9	14	0	0	1	23	5	4	.326	.356
Genao, Angel	B-R	5-9	150	5-10-04	.265	.292	.260	46	151	36	40	4	4	1	14	39	2	0	0	29	16	0	.364	.422
Gomez, Jhoan	B-R	5-6	130	10-29-02	.240	.294	.229	31	100	12	24	1	4	2	18	16	0	0	1	14	3	1	.390	.342
Gonzalez, Esteban	L-R	5-8	150	3-19-03	.298	.368	.284	35	114	27	34	9	5	0	13	17	7	0	0	27	9	2	.465	.420
Gutierrez, Carlos	L-L	5-6	158	6-18-04	.167	.091	.194	28	84	20	14	2	1	0	8	18	4	0	0	20	6	0	.214	.340
Hernandez, Wilmer	R-R	5-11	165	9-10-02	.215	.143	.228	32	93	12	20	2	1	0	11	14	4	0	2	24	3	1	.258	.336
Hidalgo, Reyden	L-R	0-0	0	5-17-04	.272	.143	.281	34	103	17	28	1	1	0	13	9	1	1	0	8	4	2	.301	.336
Leon, David	L-R	5-11	156	5-10-02	.203	.000	.235	24	59	8	12	1	0	0	4	19	2	1	0	15	2	1	.254	.413
Lopez, Miguel	B-R	5-6	135	8-20-04	.248	.154	.260	33	109	14	27	5	1	0	14	9	9	0	1	24	3	4	.321	.352
Lopez, Robert	L-R	5-10	150	1-2-04	.167	.250	.146	32	102	13	17	5	1	2	10	17	5	0	0	32	2	1	.294	.315
Mejias, Manuel	B-R	5-7	146	6-13-04	.241	.125	.260	35	112	14	27	4	0	2	18	15	2	0	1	16	0	1	.330	.336
Mendoza, Angel	L-L	5-10	160	10-9-02	.343	.286	.367	22	70	15	24	5	3	0	7	8	3	0	1	27	5	1	.500	.427
Montilla, Jesus	B-R	5-8	130	2-29-04	.255	.353	.235	30	102	19	26	3	0	0	12	20	1	0	0	22	4	1	.284	.382
Parra, Samuel	L-L	5-10	155	5-7-03	.190	.200	.188	27	84	10	16	3	1	0	9	9	2	0	1	26	1	2	.250	.281
Pena, Ronald	R-R	0-0	0	8-14-04	.163	.278	.135	27	92	14	15	1	1	0	5	11	2	0	0	24	1	1	.196	.267
Perez, Luis	L-R	5-6	140	2-7-04	.278	.333	.269	31	79	19	22	3	1	0	13	14	2	0	1	18	4	1	.342	.396
Polanco, Richard	B-R	5-9	150	10-29-03	.125	.125	.125	35	104	9	13	0	0	0	6	16	2	0	1	34	4	1	.125	.252
Purroy, Emerson	B-R	5-9	146	2-25-04	.153	.150	.154	35	111	15	17	4	0	0	9	20	3	0	2	39	5	1	.189	.294
Rivas, Kevin	B-R	5-7	128	4-7-03	.241	.280	.222	33	79	17	19	4	1	0	14	25	1	1	1	29	2	3	.316	.425
Rivera, Yefri	B-R	5-8	142	2-12-04	.207	.080	.240	34	121	16	25	6	1	0	8	11	0	1	0	22	3	2	.273	.273
Rodriguez, Juan	L-L	6-1	145	4-8-03	.159	.111	.165	32	88	16	14	2	1	0	9	22	3	1	2	39	3	2	.205	.339
Rodriguez, Simon	L-R	5-9	135	9-23-02	.248	.185	.268	36	109	18	27	4	3	0	8	19	2	0	1	34	7	4	.339	.366
Romero, Alan	L-R	5-10	165	10-27-01	.327	.385	.308	17	52	7	17	4	0	2	8	6	0	0	1	20	0	0	.519	.390
Saduy, Lexer	L-L	5-10	148	10-14-02	.261	.286	.255	34	115	23	30	8	1	0	12	20	3	0	1	25	4	1	.348	.381
Sarita, Erickson	L-L	5-7	140	11-9-02	.231	.444	.186	18	52	10	12	2	0	1	9	10	2	0	1	12	2	1	.327	.369
Taveras, Emilio	R-R	5-10	175	9-18-02	.265	.286	.262	28	68	18	18	5	0	2	19	12	2	0	0	23	0	0	.426	.390

Pitching	B-T	HT	WT	DOB	W	L	ERA	G	GS	CG	SV	IP	H	R	ER	HR	BB	SO	AVG	vLH	vRH	K/9	BB/9
Aldeano, Austin	R-R	6-1	180	6-6-04	0	3	2.84	10	10	0	0	38	37	16	12	1	8	35	.252	.269	.242	8.29	1.89
Almanzar, Pedro	R-R	5-10	165	11-5-02	1	7	6.59	19	0	0	2	27	40	25	20	4	13	22	.345	.267	.429	7.24	4.28
Almonte, Luis	R-R	5-10	184	7-19-99	6	0	1.01	18	0	0	2	36	12	4	4	1	7	51	.102	.071	.118	12.87	1.77
Batista, Dahan	R-R	6-1	170	3-15-00	2	4	5.23	16	0	0	0	33	34	21	19	2	9	24	.286	.333	.250	6.61	2.48
Breton, Albert	R-R	6-3	165	10-7-00	3	2	2.92	16	4	0	1	37	21	15	12	1	25	32	.168	.200	.150	7.78	6.08
Brito, Abel	R-R	6-1	175	3-4-01	0	5	3.63	12	12	0	0	40	29	27	16	0	23	33	.206	.145	.244	7.49	5.22
Capellan, Bryant	R-R	6-5	217	1-3-02	0	2	24.55	5	1	0	0	4	2	10	10	0	18	4	.182	.222	.000	9.82	44.18
Castro, Alexandro	L-L	5-11	162	2-6-01	0	1	3.55	10	0	0	0	13	8	8	5	0	12	10	.190	.111	.212	7.11	8.53
Contreras, Jose	R-R	6-2	175	5-13-02	0	8	15.09	11	11	0	0	23	24	45	38	0	41	16	.276	.136	.435	6.35	16.28
Cordones, Miguel	R-R	6-6	180	9-16-99	1	2	7.50	10	0	0	0	24	33	27	20	1	15	24	.317	.276	.333	9.00	5.63
Cruz, Robert	R-R	6-3	170	4-11-00	4	0	1.35	17	0	0	0	33	26	10	5	0	10	24	.210	.260	.176	6.48	2.70
Cuevas, Jansel	R-R	6-2	221	9-2-02	0	0	54.00	3	0	0	0	1	1	8	8	0	11	1	.333	.000	.500	6.75	74.25
Diaz, Olmandi	R-R	5-10	155	5-27-02	2	1	4.12	17	0	0	1	39	43	19	18	0	7	33	.289	.276	.297	7.55	1.60
Flores, David	L-L	5-10	180	11-2-00	4	0	5.22	15	0	0	0	29	25	22	17	1	21	25	.225	.241	.220	7.67	6.44
Franco, Logan	R-R	6-3	170	10-11-99	0	0	1.23	6	0	0	0	7	7	5	1	0	5	8	.233	.267	.200	9.82	6.14
Garcia, Frederic	R-R	6-4	195	12-17-00	5	0	2.04	18	0	0	0	35	31	11	8	1	18	32	.238	.167	.260	8.15	4.58
Garcia, Luis	R-R	6-1	175	8-15-02	5	1	2.96	19	0	0	1	27	22	18	9	2	14	24	.214	.216	.212	7.90	4.61
Garcia, Victor	R-R	6-0	168	2-8-03	0	0	2.21	7	7	0	0	20	20	6	5	1	9	19	.260	.308	.235	8.41	3.98
Garcia, Yonaiker	R-R	5-11	165	12-15-00	1	1	6.98	17	0	0	0	30	31	28	23	0	28	29	.281	.241	.295	8.49	8.49
Gomez, Yorman	R-R	5-11	167	11-10-02	1	2	3.58	12	12	0	0	50	42	26	20	7	16	49	.228	.239	.221	8.76	2.86
Hidalgo, Reyden	L-R	0-0	0	5-17-04	0	0	54.00	1	0	0	0	1	6	4	4	0	0	1	.750	.714	1.000	13.50	0.00

Medina, Danny	R-R	6-3	170	11-21-02	0	1	24.00	10	0	0	0	12	7	35	32	1	35	11	.179	.118	.227	8.25	26.25
Navarro, Diego	R-R	5-11	176	12-29-02	1	2	1.69	12	11	0	0	48	30	12	9	0	8	44	.184	.182	.187	8.25	1.50
Peguero, Luis	R-R	6-1	165	11-15-99	0	1	7.94	17	0	0	0	34	35	37	30	2	26	34	.257	.233	.276	9.00	6.88
Perez, Luis	L-R	5-6	140	2-7-04	0	0	27.00	1	0	0	0	1	3	3	2	0	2	0	.500	.400	1.000	0.00	27.00
Pinto, Kenny	L-L	6-0	160	5-8-03	0	3	8.35	11	11	0	0	32	43	36	30	0	26	16	.336	.154	.357	4.45	7.24
Polanco, Bienvenido	R-R	6-1	170	10-3-01	3	1	3.09	14	6	0	0	35	30	17	12	3	10	28	.227	.235	.216	7.20	2.57
Polanco, Felix	L-L	6-2	190	6-26-00	4	2	4.09	18	2	0	0	33	29	27	15	4	15	34	.234	.240	.232	9.27	4.09
Quezada, Elian	R-R	6-1	178	7-24-01	0	4	6.03	12	12	0	0	34	35	28	23	1	20	28	.259	.349	.181	7.34	5.24
Reyes, Tomas	L-L	5-11	150	9-23-99	0	0	0.00	1	1	0	0	5	1	0	0	0	0	5	.059	.000	.111	9.00	0.00
Rodriguez, Adrian	R-R	5-11	155	8-21-00	0	0	16.20	2	0	0	0	2	5	5	3	0	0	2	.556	.500	.667	10.80	0.00
Ruviera, Jose	R-R	6-3	168	9-4-01	0	2	9.26	4	4	0	0	12	13	12	12	0	6	9	.283	.091	.458	6.94	4.63
Santos, Felipito	R-R	6-2	180	7-20-99	6	1	4.66	17	0	0	2	39	31	25	20	1	30	39	.215	.179	.258	9.08	6.98
Sosa, Christian	R-R	6-2	181	1-2-01	3	0	2.52	14	0	0	1	25	18	11	7	1	9	17	.191	.146	.226	6.12	3.24
Tovar, Javier	R-R	5-10	184	11-4-01	2	1	3.33	9	4	0	0	27	20	10	10	1	13	24	.220	.264	.158	8.00	4.33
Urena, Dielmon	R-R	6-6	166	5-15-01	0	3	9.23	11	10	0	0	26	24	29	27	2	38	25	.250	.179	.298	8.54	12.99
Vicente, Adauri	R-R	6-2	188	12-18-00	1	3	6.12	17	0	0	2	32	34	29	22	1	13	40	.268	.213	.300	11.13	3.62

Fielding

C: Aranguren 7, Hernandez 25, Leon 12, Lopez 28, Mejias 31, Romero 14, Taveras 19.

1B: Andrade 1, Aranguren 5, Caminero 10, Cedeno 13, Collado 17, Contreras 7, Gomez 2, Hernandez 9, Hidalgo 1, Leon 10, Lopez 7, Lopez 3, Mejias 2, Parra 1, Perez 9, Polanco 6, Purroy 5, Rivas 6, Rivera 1, Rodriguez 1, Romero 3, Taveras 9.

2B: Alduey 2, Andrade 13, Benjamin 7, Caminero 4, Cedeno 4, Contreras 7, Genao 5, Gomez 12, Hidalgo 13, Lopez 8, Montilla 11, Perez 5, Polanco 10, Purroy 9, Rivas 13, Rivera 11.

3B: Alduey 3, Andrade 7, Benjamin 4, Caminero 18, Cedeno 10, Collado 15, Contreras 7, Gomez 12, Hidalgo 9, Lopez 9, Montilla 7, Perez 3, Polanco 10, Purroy 5, Rivas 6, Rivera 5.

SS: Alduey 23, Andrade 1, Benjamin 2, Caminero 5, Cedeno 1, Contreras 1, Genao 34, Hidalgo 4, Lopez 6, Montilla 10, Polanco 4, Purroy 14, Rivas 5, Rivera 15.

OF: Caripa 37, Cepeda 30, Contreras 2, Espinola 37, Flores 29, Gonzalez 35, Gutierrez 28, Hidalgo 2, Mendoza 16, Parra 25, Pena 17, Perez 7, Rodriguez 30, Rodriguez 33, Saduy 33, Sarita 12.

Colorado Rockies

SEASON IN A SENTENCE: The Rockies decided to trade away star third baseman Nolan Arenado in the offseason when it became clear that he couldn't co-exist with GM Jeff Bridich, but by May, the Rockies had neither after Bridich resigned.

HIGH POINT: The Rockies were the surprise recipients of the 2021 All-Star Game after it was moved out of Georgia in response to a voting law the state passed. The Midsummer Classic gave Rockies fans a chance to see the game's best on a national stage and to honor likely-to-depart free agent shortstop Trevor Story when he competed in the Home Run Derby.

LOW POINT: After trading away Arenado in the offseason, the expectations for the 2021 season were quite low. Colorado ended up being a little better than expected over the course of the season, but a 3-11 start ensured that few noticed. Colorado went 18-34 over the first two months, and then played roughly .500 ball the rest of the season.

NOTABLE ROOKIES: Center fielder Yonathan Daza became a semi-regular in the outfield for the Rockies, although his .282/.332/.355 season offered a demonstration that he'll have to figure out a way to provide more impact at the plate if he's going to hold onto a long-term role. Left fielder Connor Joe provided an unexpected boost to the Rockies lineup in limited action. Joe hit .285/.379/.469 with eight home runs in 63 games with Colorado. Righthander Jordan Sheffield, a 2020 MLB Rule 5 pick, proved to be one of the more reliable relievers in the Rockies bullpen. He posted a 3.38 ERA in 30 appearances (29.1 innings).

KEY TRANSACTIONS: Signing first baseman C.J. Cron to a minor league deal before the season proved to be an astute pickup. Cron proved to be the Rockies' best hitter. He led the team with 28 home runs while hitting .281/.375/.530. At the trade deadline, the Rockies were surprisingly quiet. Even with Story, Righthander Jon Gray and Cron all slated to become free agents at the end of the season, Colorado largely stood pat. Righthander Mychal Givens was traded to the Reds in a minor deal, but that was the lone move even though the Rockies sat 19.5 games back and in fourth place in the NL West at the trade deadline.

OPENING DAY PAYROLL: $103,986,666 (18th).

PLAYERS OF THE YEAR

MAJOR LEAGUE

C.J. Cron
1B
.281/.375/.530
Career-high 92 RBIs
28 HR, 31 2B

MINOR LEAGUE

Zac Veen
OF
(Low-A)
.301/.399/.501,
15 HR, 36 SB

ORGANIZATION LEADERS

Batting		*Minimum 250 AB
MAJORS		
*AVG	Brendan Rodgers	.284
*OPS	C.J. Cron	.905
HR	C.J. Cron	28
RBI	C.J. Cron	92
MINORS		
*AVG	Hunter Stovall, Spokane	.316
*OBP	Isaac Collins, Spokane, Fresno	.407
*SLG	Alan Trejo, Albuquerque	.569
*OPS	Zac Veen, Fresno	.900
R	Zac Veen, Fresno	83
H	Ryan Vilade, Albuquerque	133
TB	Elehuris Montero, Albuquerque, Hartford	228
2B	Coco Montes, Hartford	37
3B	Wynton Bernard, Albuquerque	6
3B	Alan Trejo, Albuquerque	6
HR	Taylor Snyder, Albuquerque, Hartford	30
RBI	Greg Bird, Albuquerque	91
BB	Michael Toglia, Hartford, Spokane	65
SO	Michael Toglia, Hartford, Spokane	142
SB	Eddy Diaz, Spokane, Fresno	59

Pitching		#Minimum 75 IP
MAJORS		
W	German Marquez	12
#ERA	Kyle Freeland	4.33
SO	German Marquez	176
SV	Daniel Bard	20
MINORS		
W	Mitchell Kilkenny, Spokane, Fresno	12
L	Karl Kauffmann, Hartford, Spokane	12
L	Jose Mujica, Albuquerque	12
#ERA	Ryan Feltner, Albuquerque, Hartford, Spokane	2.96
G	Logan Cozart, Albuquerque	54
GS	Ryan Castellani, Albuquerque	23
GS	Frank Duncan, Albuquerque, Hartford	23
SV	Dugan Darnell, Spokane, Fresno	15
IP	Frank Duncan, Albuquerque, Hartford	122.2
BB	Ryan Castellani, Albuquerque	71
SO	Ryan Feltner, Albuquerque, Hartford, Spokane	127
#AVG	Ryan Feltner, Albuquerque, Hartford, Spokane	.233

General Manager: Bill Schmidt. **Farm Director:** Chris Forbes. **Scouting Director:** Vacant.

Class	Team	League	W	L	PCT	Finish	Manager
Majors	Colorado Rockies	National	74	87	.460	10th (15)	Bud Black
Triple-A	Albuquerque Isotopes	Triple-A West	58	72	.446	7th (10)	Warren Schaeffer
Double-A	Hartford Yard Goats	Double-A Northeast	39	79	.331	12th (12)	Chris Denorfia
High-A	Spokane Indians	High-A West	67	49	.578	2nd (6)	Scott Little
Low-A	Fresno Grizzlies	Low-A West	74	41	.643	1st (8)	Robinson Cancel
Rookie	ACL Rockies	Arizona Complex	44	15	.746	1st (18)	Jake Opitz
Rookie	DSL Colorado	Dominican Summer	39	20	.661	2nd (46)	Eugenio Jose
Rookie	DSL Rockies	Dominican Summer	37	22	.627	7th (46)	Mauricio Gonzalez
Overall 2021 Minor League Record		358		298	.546	5th (30)	

ORGANIZATION STATISTICS

COLORADO ROCKIES
NATIONAL LEAGUE

Batting	B-T	HT	WT	DOB	AVG	vLH	vRH	G	AB	R	H	2B	3B	HR	RBI	BB	HBP	SH	SF	SO	SB	CS	SLG	OBP
Adams, Matt	L-R	6-3	245	8-31-88	.167	.000	.182	22	36	3	6	1	0	0	2	4	0	0	0	9	0	0	.194	.250
Blackmon, Charlie	L-L	6-3	221	7-1-86	.270	.287	.265	150	514	76	139	25	4	13	78	54	11	0	3	91	3	0	.411	.351
Cron, C.J.	R-R	6-4	235	1-5-90	.281	.311	.269	142	470	70	132	31	1	28	92	60	13	0	4	117	1	0	.530	.375
Daza, Yonathan	R-R	6-2	207	2-28-94	.282	.296	.275	107	301	26	85	12	2	2	30	21	2	6	1	60	2	1	.355	.332
Diaz, Elias	R-R	6-1	223	11-17-90	.246	.242	.248	106	338	52	83	18	1	18	44	30	2	0	1	60	0	0	.464	.310
Fuentes, Joshua	R-R	6-2	209	2-19-93	.225	.238	.219	95	271	30	61	11	1	7	33	12	0	0	1	65	0	0	.351	.257
Hampson, Garrett	R-R	5-11	196	10-10-94	.234	.271	.217	147	453	69	106	21	6	11	33	33	3	3	2	118	17	7	.380	.289
Hilliard, Sam	L-L	6-5	236	2-21-94	.215	.255	.202	81	214	32	46	7	2	14	34	23	1	0	0	87	5	0	.463	.294
Joe, Connor	R-R	6-0	205	8-16-92	.285	.306	.277	63	179	23	51	9	0	8	35	26	3	0	3	41	0	0	.469	.379
McMahon, Ryan	L-R	6-2	219	12-14-94	.254	.229	.264	151	528	80	134	32	1	23	86	59	4	0	5	147	6	2	.449	.331
Motter, Taylor	R-R	6-1	195	9-18-89	.150	.182	.111	13	20	2	3	0	0	0	2	0	0	0	0	6	0	0	.150	.227
Nunez, Dom	L-R	6-1	212	1-17-95	.189	.158	.195	81	228	31	43	12	3	10	33	34	0	0	1	91	0	0	.399	.293
Owings, Chris	R-R	5-10	185	8-12-91	.326	.471	.231	21	43	9	14	4	3	1	5	7	0	0	0	15	2	1	.628	.420
Rodgers, Brendan	R-R	6-0	204	8-9-96	.284	.317	.273	102	387	49	110	21	3	15	51	19	7	0	2	84	0	0	.470	.328
Ruiz, Rio	L-R	6-2	220	5-22-94	.171	.250	.161	30	35	1	6	1	0	0	4	3	0	0	2	9	0	0	.200	.225
Story, Trevor	R-R	6-2	213	11-15-92	.251	.297	.234	142	526	88	132	34	5	24	75	53	11	0	5	139	20	6	.471	.329
Tapia, Raimel	L-L	6-3	175	2-4-94	.273	.292	.266	133	487	69	133	26	2	6	50	40	1	1	4	70	20	6	.372	.327
Trejo, Alan	R-R	6-2	205	5-30-96	.217	.250	.200	28	46	7	10	2	0	1	3	3	0	0	1	6	0	0	.326	.260
Vilade, Ryan	R-R	6-2	226	2-18-99	.000	.000	--	3	6	0	0	0	0	0	0	1	0	0	0	1	0	0	.000	.143
Welker, Colton	R-R	6-1	235	10-9-97	.189	.083	.240	19	37	7	7	1	0	0	2	3	0	0	0	11	0	0	.216	.250

Pitching	B-T	HT	WT	DOB	W	L	ERA	G	GS	CG	SV	IP	H	R	ER	HR	BB	SO	AVG	vLH	vRHK/9	BB/9
Almonte, Yency	R-R	6-5	223	6-4-94	1	3	7.55	48	0	0	0	48	47	42	40	9	29	47	.260	.299	.223	8.875.48
Bard, Daniel	R-R	6-4	215	6-25-85	7	8	5.21	67	0	0	20	66	69	41	38	8	36	80	.265	.319	.208	10.964.93
Bowden, Ben	L-L	6-4	249	10-21-94	3	2	6.56	39	0	0	0	36	44	30	26	6	21	42	.288	.309	.271	10.605.30
Castellani, Ryan	R-R	6-4	218	4-1-96	0	0	5.40	1	1	0	0	3	5	2	2	1	4	2	.417	.500	.375	5.4010.80
Chacin, Jhoulys	R-R	6-3	215	1-7-88	3	2	4.34	46	1	0	0	64	53	32	31	8	28	47	.222	.202	.242	6.583.92
Estevez, Carlos	R-R	6-6	277	12-28-92	3	5	4.38	64	0	0	11	62	71	32	30	8	21	60	.293	.287	.300	8.763.06
Feltner, Ryan	R-R	6-4	190	9-2-96	0	1	11.37	2	2	0	0	6	9	8	8	3	5	6	.346	.100	.500	8.537.11
Fernandez, Julian	R-R	6-6	233	12-5-95	0	0	10.80	6	0	0	0	7	9	8	8	2	4	4	.310	.389	.182	5.405.40
Freeland, Kyle	L-L	6-4	204	5-14-93	7	8	4.33	23	23	0	0	121	133	59	58	20	38	105	.284	.303	.276	7.832.83
Fuentes, Joshua	R-R	6-2	209	2-19-93	0	0	0.00	1	0	0	0	1	0	0	0	0	0	0	.250	.000	.500	0.000.00
Gilbreath, Lucas	L-L	6-1	185	3-5-96	3	2	3.38	47	1	0	1	43	33	18	16	5	23	44	.208	.228	.188	9.284.85
Givens, Mychal	R-R	6-0	230	5-13-90	3	2	2.73	31	0	0	0	30	25	11	9	5	14	34	.234	.167	.288	10.314.25
2-team total (23 Cincinnati)					4	3	3.35	54	0	0	8	51	43	22	19	7	27	54	.234	.214	.250	9.534.76
Gomber, Austin	L-L	6-5	220	11-23-93	9	9	4.53	23	23	0	0	115	102	64	58	20	41	113	.232	.223	.235	8.823.20
Gonzalez, ChiChi	R-R	6-3	210	1-15-92	3	7	6.46	24	18	0	0	102	127	74	73	18	28	56	.311	.305	.317	4.962.48
Goudeau, Ashton	R-R	6-6	220	7-23-92	2	1	4.26	11	1	0	0	25	16	12	12	3	8	17	.188	.235	.186	6.042.84
2-team total (5 Cincinnati)					2	1	4.19	16	1	0	0	34	24	16	16	4	17	22	.202	.232	.160	5.774.46
Gray, Jon	R-R	6-4	225	11-5-91	8	12	4.59	29	29	0	0	149	140	83	76	21	58	157	.245	.235	.258	9.483.50
Kinley, Tyler	R-R	6-4	220	1-31-91	3	2	4.73	70	0	0	0	70	59	37	37	12	26	68	.223	.195	.250	8.703.33
Lambert, Peter	R-R	6-2	208	4-18-97	0	0	11.12	2	2	0	0	6	12	7	7	2	2	3	.429	.563	.250	4.763.18
Lawrence, Justin	R-R	6-3	213	11-25-94	1	0	8.64	19	0	0	0	17	21	16	16	0	19	17	.333	.227	.390	9.1810.26
Marquez, German	R-R	6-1	230	2-22-95	12	11	4.40	32	32	3	0	180	165	92	88	21	64	176	.242	.245	.238	8.823.20
Rosscup, Zac	R-L	6-2	220	6-9-88	0	0	3.00	4	0	0	0	3	3	1	1	1	1	4	.300	.250	.333	12.003.00
Santos, Antonio	R-R	6-3	223	10-6-96	0	1	4.76	7	0	0	0	11	9	7	6	1	5	10	.220	.167	.241	7.943.97
Senzatela, Antonio	R-R	6-1	236	1-21-95	4	10	4.42	28	28	0	0	157	178	84	77	12	32	105	.287	.294	.281	6.031.84
Sheffield, Jordan	R-R	5-10	190	6-1-95	0	0	3.38	30	0	0	0	29	19	11	11	2	13	20	.190	.220	.166	6.143.99
Stephenson, Robert	R-R	6-3	205	2-24-93	2	1	3.13	49	0	0	1	46	42	20	16	5	18	52	.241	.241	.242	10.173.52
Tinoco, Jesus	R-R	6-4	258	4-30-95	0	0	33.75	1	0	0	0	1	5	5	5	3	1	0	.625	.500	.667	0.006.75

Fielding

Catcher	PCT	G	PO	A	E	DP	PB
Diaz	.995	98	699	48	4	5	8
Nunez	.995	77	581	28	3	2	6

First Base	PCT	G	PO	A	E	DP
Adams	1.000	7	35	7	0	3
Cron	.991	130	1040	90	10	103
Fuentes	.982	32	104	5	2	12
Joe	.982	14	100	9	2	13
Nunez	.000	1	0	0	0	0
Ruiz	1.000	1	8	1	0	1
Welker	1.000	2	15	2	0	0

Second Base	PCT	G	PO	A	E	DP
Hampson	1.000	47	54	93	0	19
McMahon	.990	52	76	132	2	28
Owings	1.000	3	10	11	0	4

	PCT	G	PO	A	E	DP
Rodgers	.988	81	127	203	4	47
Trejo	.926	10	9	16	2	4

Third Base	PCT	G	PO	A	E	DP
Fuentes	.963	60	44	113	6	13
Hampson	1.000	2	0	3	0	0
McMahon	.979	113	64	171	5	16
Motter	1.000	3	2	5	0	0
Owings	.000	1	0	0	0	0
Ruiz	1.000	5	4	9	0	0
Welker	1.000	5	2	6	0	0

Shortstop	PCT	G	PO	A	E	DP
Hampson	.900	5	3	6	1	1
Owings	1.000	1	2	2	0	1
Rodgers	.984	26	16	46	1	10
Story	.975	138	190	348	14	91

	PCT	G	PO	A	E	DP
Trejo	1.000	9	2	6	0	1

Outfield	PCT	G	PO	A	E	DP
Blackmon	.991	137	211	14	2	3
Daza	.994	91	159	3	1	0
Freeland	--	1	0	0	0	0
Fuentes	1.000	2	1	0	0	0
Hampson	1.000	91	183	1	0	1
Hilliard	1.000	74	118	2	0	0
Joe	.968	32	58	3	2	0
Motter	1.000	1	2	1	0	0
Owings	1.000	7	5	0	0	0
Ruiz	--	2	0	0	0	0
Tapia	.984	125	178	7	3	0
Vilade	1.000	2	3	0	0	0

ALBUQUERQUE ISOTOPES
TRIPLE-A

TRIPLE-A WEST

Batting	B-T	HT	WT	DOB	AVG	vLH	vRH	G	AB	R	H	2B	3B	HR	RBI	BB	HBP	SH	SF	SO	SB	CS	SLG	OBP
Adams, Matt	L-R	6-3	245	8-31-88	.000	.000	.000	2	7	0	0	0	0	0	0	0	0	0	0	3	0	0	.000	.000
Bernard, Wynton	R-R	6-2	195	9-24-90	.254	.294	.239	100	319	57	81	12	6	7	30	26	5	0	1	76	23	2	.395	.319
Bird, Greg	L-R	6-4	220	11-9-92	.267	.244	.274	112	393	63	105	21	1	27	91	58	4	0	6	106	0	1	.532	.362
Briceno, Jose	R-R	6-1	225	9-19-92	.218	.250	.205	33	101	14	22	7	0	5	15	6	1	0	3	24	1	0	.436	.261
Burcham, Scott	R-R	5-11	185	6-17-93	.234	.308	.200	52	124	14	29	5	1	1	9	7	0	0	1	45	0	1	.315	.273
Daza, Yonathan	R-R	6-2	207	2-28-94	.308	.400	.286	6	26	4	8	0	0	0	2	0	0	0	0	4	1	0	.308	.308
Edgeworth, Danny	L-R	6-3	210	7-26-95	.181	.200	.176	42	105	11	19	4	0	3	9	6	3	1	0	38	0	0	.305	.246
Fuentes, Joshua	R-R	6-2	209	2-19-93	.269	.303	.263	49	193	29	52	12	2	9	32	11	5	0	1	43	1	3	.492	.324
Garneau, Dustin	R-R	6-2	205	8-13-87	.229	.273	.208	11	35	5	8	3	0	1	6	6	1	0	0	9	0	0	.400	.357
Gomez, Jose	R-R	5-11	175	12-10-96	.202	.250	.188	29	84	13	17	2	1	2	6	6	0	0	1	30	0	1	.321	.253
Hatch, LJ	R-R	5-11	175	5-18-94	.248	.333	.222	47	105	16	26	5	2	2	14	7	1	2	1	45	0	2	.390	.298
Hilliard, Sam	L-L	6-5	236	2-21-94	.239	.176	.263	53	188	31	45	12	2	14	37	23	1	0	1	61	6	1	.548	.324
Joe, Connor	R-R	6-0	205	8-16-92	.326	.429	.296	26	92	20	30	7	0	9	25	15	1	0	2	22	1	0	.696	.418
Jones, Mylz	R-R	6-1	185	4-13-94	.000	.000	.000	9	18	0	0	0	0	0	0	0	0	0	0	7	0	0	.000	.000
Longhi, Nick	R-L	6-2	230	8-16-95	.242	.257	.235	80	219	30	53	10	0	5	26	28	4	0	1	67	0	0	.356	.337
MacIver, Willie	R-R	6-2	205	10-28-96	.000	.000	--	3	4	0	0	0	0	0	0	0	0	0	0	1	0	0	.000	.200
Montero, Elehuris	R-R	6-3	235	8-17-98	.278	.357	.250	28	108	23	30	9	1	6	17	10	3	0	0	20	0	0	.546	.355
Motter, Taylor	R-R	6-1	195	9-18-89	.332	.403	.303	68	214	54	71	16	1	24	57	49	2	0	2	50	0	2	.752	.457
Owings, Chris	R-R	5-10	185	8-12-91	.167	.400	.077	5	18	1	3	2	0	1	3	1	0	0	0	6	0	0	.444	.211
Rabago, Chris	R-R	5-11	204	4-22-93	.234	.194	.246	53	154	21	36	5	0	3	15	21	2	0	0	43	4	2	.325	.333
Rodgers, Brendan	R-R	6-0	204	8-9-96	.467	.400	.500	5	15	1	7	2	0	0	3	1	0	0	0	3	0	0	.600	.500
Ruiz, Rio	L-R	6-2	220	5-22-94	.304	.276	.313	59	224	38	68	20	1	7	28	20	2	0	3	39	3	1	.496	.361
Serven, Brian	R-R	6-0	207	5-5-95	.250	.237	.254	73	252	36	63	12	2	16	38	16	6	0	2	61	1	0	.504	.308
Snyder, Taylor	R-R	6-2	165	9-28-94	.245	.191	.260	61	216	36	53	12	1	12	31	14	1	0	0	63	9	0	.477	.294
Stamets, Eric	R-R	6-0	183	9-25-91	.157	.190	.148	34	102	16	16	4	1	3	8	13	2	1	0	23	2	0	.304	.265
Tapia, Raimel	L-L	6-3	175	2-4-94	.357	.000	.417	4	14	2	5	3	0	0	2	0	0	0	0	2	2	0	.571	.357
Tomlinson, Kelby	R-R	6-2	175	6-16-90	.167	.182	.143	9	18	1	3	1	0	0	1	2	1	0	0	3	2	0	.222	.286
Trejo, Alan	R-R	6-2	205	5-30-96	.278	.241	.291	90	334	56	93	34	6	17	72	23	1	2	3	78	2	4	.569	.324
Vilade, Ryan	R-R	6-2	226	2-18-99	.284	.308	.276	117	468	82	133	28	5	7	44	38	4	2	6	92	12	5	.410	.339
Welker, Colton	R-R	6-1	235	10-9-97	.286	.333	.280	23	84	13	24	5	1	3	18	12	1	0	1	20	0	0	.476	.378

Pitching	B-T	HT	WT	DOB	W	L	ERA	G	GS	CG	SV	IP	H	R	ER	HR	BB	SO	AVG	vLH	vRH	K/9	BB/9
Almonte, Yency	R-R	6-5	223	6-4-94	0	0	0.00	2	0	0	0	2	1	0	0	0	1	1	.167	.000	.333	4.50	4.50
Bird, Jake	R-R	6-3	200	12-4-95	5	1	3.99	29	1	0	0	38	34	17	17	3	19	36	.241	.273	.213	8.45	4.46
Bowden, Ben	L-L	6-4	249	10-21-94	1	0	0.00	12	0	0	2	12	2	0	0	0	4	17	.056	.200	.032	13.11	3.09
Castellani, Ryan	R-R	6-4	218	4-1-96	3	11	6.25	24	23	0	0	95	90	71	66	16	71	86	.256	.255	.256	8.15	6.73
Clarkin, Ian	L-L	6-2	215	2-14-95	3	5	8.77	17	9	0	0	51	66	53	50	11	34	19	.316	.268	.341	3.33	5.96
Cozart, Logan	R-R	6-2	215	1-27-93	1	2	3.68	54	0	0	7	51	47	26	21	5	25	54	.237	.288	.203	9.47	4.38
Diaz, Jairo	R-R	6-0	254	5-27-91	0	1	7.36	9	0	0	0	7	8	6	6	0	7	10	.267	.273	.263	12.27	8.59
Duncan, Frank	R-R	6-4	215	1-30-92	5	3	3.92	16	15	0	0	80	78	37	35	9	23	79	.252	.298	.214	8.85	2.58
Estevez, Carlos	R-R	6-6	277	12-28-92	0	0	0.00	1	0	0	0	1	2	0	0	0	0	3	.400	.500	.333	27.00	0.00
Feltner, Ryan	R-R	6-4	190	9-2-96	0	0	16.88	1	1	0	0	4	5	5	2	2	2	3	.364	.000	.444	6.75	6.75
Fernandez, Julian	R-R	6-6	233	12-5-95	1	0	0.64	10	0	0	0	14	10	2	1	0	4	18	.204	.227	.185	11.57	2.57
Fisk, Conor	R-R	6-2	220	4-4-92	0	0	18.00	1	0	0	0	1	4	2	2	0	0	1	.571	1.000	.250	9.00	0.00
Flores Jr., Bernardo	L-L	6-4	190	8-23-95	0	2	5.73	3	2	0	0	11	13	9	7	2	7	9	.302	.143	.333	7.36	5.73
Freeland, Kyle	L-L	6-4	204	5-14-93	1	1	1.80	2	2	0	0	10	4	2	2	2	4	4	.118	.000	.133	3.60	1.80
Gilbreath, Lucas	L-L	6-1	185	3-5-96	0	0	0.00	2	0	0	0	2	1	0	0	0	1	3	.167	.333	.000	16.20	5.40
Givens, Mychal	R-R	6-0	230	5-13-90	0	0	9.00	3	1	0	0	2	5	2	2	0	1	2	.500	.571	.333	9.00	0.00
Gold, Brandon	R-R	6-3	203	9-16-94	3	7	6.15	18	17	0	0	86	103	60	59	12	23	76	.296	.272	.320	7.92	2.40
Gomber, Austin	L-L	6-5	220	11-23-93	0	1	6.75	1	1	0	0	4	5	3	3	1	0	4	.294	--	.294	9.00	0.00
Gonzalez, Brian	R-L	6-3	230	10-25-95	0	0	2.45	8	0	0	0	7	6	2	2	0	8	14	.222	.182	.250	17.18	9.82
Gonzalez, Nelson	R-R	6-1	170	2-15-90	4	0	5.47	22	0	0	0	25	27	15	15	6	12	24	.281	.300	.268	8.76	4.38
Goudeau, Ashton	R-R	6-6	220	7-23-92	0	0	6.75	3	1	0	0	8	13	7	6	2	1	3	.361	.667	.208	3.38	1.13

Name	B-T	HT	WT	DOB	W	L	ERA	G	GS	CG	SV	IP	H	R	ER	HR	BB	SO	AVG	vLH	vRH	K/9	BB/9
Gray, Jon	R-R	6-4	225	11-5-91	0	0	4.50	1	1	0	0	4	5	2	2	1	1	6	.294	.400	.250	13.50	2.25
Griep, Nate	R-R	6-2	210	10-11-93	2	0	1.00	9	0	0	0	9	5	4	1	1	2	11	.156	.158	.154	11.00	2.00
Harvey, Joe	R-R	6-2	236	1-9-92	0	0	2.63	15	0	0	0	14	12	4	4	2	9	20	.245	.333	.179	13.17	5.93
Holder, Heath	R-R	6-6	211	8-23-92	3	3	9.91	37	0	0	0	46	61	55	51	9	36	47	.319	.316	.321	9.13	6.99
Lambert, Peter	R-R	6-2	208	4-18-97	0	0	0.00	1	1	0	0	3	2	0	0	0	1	3	.222	.000	.333	10.13	3.38
Lawrence, Justin	R-R	6-3	213	11-25-94	6	5	4.73	31	0	0	13	32	32	20	17	3	12	30	.256	.333	.177	8.35	3.34
Mujica, Jose	R-R	6-2	249	6-29-96	2	12	8.77	24	21	0	0	91	128	95	89	27	26	85	.327	.337	.320	8.38	2.56
Rodriguez, Dereck	R-R	6-0	208	6-5-92	4	6	6.72	22	19	0	0	86	112	69	64	17	30	87	.312	.298	.323	9.14	3.15
Rolison, Ryan	R-L	6-2	213	7-11-97	2	2	5.91	10	10	0	0	46	51	30	30	7	16	45	.280	.273	.283	8.87	3.15
Rosscup, Zac	R-L	6-2	220	6-9-88	1	0	2.48	30	0	0	5	29	21	9	8	1	14	41	.198	.152	.219	12.72	4.34
Rusin, Chris	L-L	6-2	200	10-22-86	0	0	10.41	30	0	0	0	32	50	38	37	14	14	23	.357	.286	.388	6.47	3.94
Santos, Antonio	R-R	6-3	223	10-6-96	0	5	7.94	34	2	0	0	45	54	41	40	10	27	32	.302	.308	.297	6.35	5.36
Scioneaux, Tate	R-R	6-0	219	12-14-92	3	2	8.07	31	0	0	1	36	45	34	32	13	15	29	.308	.333	.291	7.32	3.79
Sheffield, Jordan	R-R	5-10	190	6-1-95	0	0	0.00	1	0	0	0	1	0	0	0	0	0	0	.000	.000	.000	0.00	0.00
Smith, Chad	R-R	6-4	200	6-8-95	2	1	2.97	36	0	0	3	33	22	13	11	1	19	37	.190	.204	.177	9.99	5.13
Stephenson, Robert	R-R	6-3	205	2-24-93	0	0	18.00	1	1	0	0	1	2	2	2	0	1	1	.400	.000	.500	9.00	9.00
Tinoco, Jesus	R-R	6-4	258	4-30-95	3	2	6.00	36	2	0	0	54	65	36	36	6	27	58	.304	.383	.224	9.67	4.50
Todd, Reagan	L-L	6-3	218	8-30-95	1	0	5.40	10	0	0	0	8	11	6	5	1	8	10	.333	.308	.350	10.80	8.64
Wynkoop, Jack	L-L	6-5	200	11-2-93	2	0	2.83	12	0	0	0	29	27	9	9	2	12	22	.250	.244	.254	6.91	3.77

Fielding

Catcher	PCT	G	PO	A	E	DP	PB
Briceno	.983	15	98	19	2	2	3
Garneau	1.000	10	80	10	0	1	0
MacIver	1.000	1	15	0	0	0	0
Rabago	.988	41	311	24	4	1	3
Serven	.990	66	565	44	6	2	6

	PCT	G	PO	A	E	DP
Motter	.984	16	27	34	1	7
Owings	1.000	2	6	0	0	0
Rodgers	1.000	3	5	7	0	1
Ruiz	.991	29	40	76	1	13
Snyder	1.000	10	10	15	0	6
Stamets	.957	5	12	10	1	3
Tomlinson	1.000	5	3	13	0	1
Trejo	1.000	10	14	22	0	4

	PCT	G	PO	A	E	DP
Hatch	.886	7	12	19	4	8
Motter	.941	6	5	11	1	0
Owings	1.000	1	3	1	0	0
Rodgers	1.000	1	1	5	0	2
Snyder	1.000	3	2	15	0	2
Stamets	.964	26	28	78	4	11
Tomlinson	1.000	3	2	4	0	0
Trejo	.974	75	95	207	8	45

First Base	PCT	G	PO	A	E	DP
Adams	.938	2	13	2	1	0
Bird	.994	86	660	57	4	62
Briceno	1.000	1	1	0	0	0
Edgeworth	1.000	7	42	5	0	5
Fuentes	1.000	3	17	1	0	1
Joe	1.000	7	50	7	0	5
Longhi	1.000	12	76	8	0	11
Montero	.982	9	51	3	1	5
Motter	.000	1	0	0	0	0
Ruiz	1.000	2	13	4	0	0
Vilade	1.000	5	25	2	0	3
Welker	1.000	6	49	2	0	5

Third Base	PCT	G	PO	A	E	DP
Burcham	1.000	11	3	9	0	1
Edgeworth	.963	24	5	21	1	2
Fuentes	.957	20	7	38	2	4
Gomez	.889	7	4	12	2	3
Hatch	1.000	3	2	5	0	0
Montero	.882	19	15	30	6	4
Motter	.912	23	15	37	5	1
Ruiz	.960	21	17	31	2	5
Snyder	1.000	2	1	2	0	0
Stamets	1.000	2	1	3	0	0
Trejo	.857	2	3	3	1	1
Welker	1.000	14	7	26	0	3

Outfield	PCT	G	PO	A	E	DP
Bernard	.980	91	194	1	4	0
Burcham	--	1	0	0	0	0
Daza	1.000	6	11	0	0	0
Edgeworth	1.000	2	5	0	0	0
Fuentes	1.000	11	1	2	0	0
Hilliard	.992	51	126	5	1	2
Joe	.963	18	25	1	1	0
Jones	1.000	7	11	1	0	0
Longhi	.966	49	54	2	2	0
Motter	1.000	15	23	0	0	0
Owings	--	2	0	0	0	0
Ruiz	1.000	4	6	0	0	0
Snyder	.949	47	72	3	4	1
Tapia	1.000	4	3	0	0	0
Vilade	.979	119	184	3	4	0

Second Base	PCT	G	PO	A	E	DP
Burcham	.974	27	35	41	2	8
Fuentes	1.000	10	15	21	0	4
Gomez	.900	10	14	22	4	6
Hatch	.987	24	39	37	1	15

Shortstop	PCT	G	PO	A	E	DP
Burcham	.750	3	2	1	1	0
Gomez	.946	13	9	26	2	2

HARTFORD YARD GOATS

DOUBLE-A

DOUBLE-A NORTHEAST

Batting	B-T	HT	WT	DOB	AVG	vLH	vRH	G	AB	R	H	2B	3B	HR	RBI	BB	HBP	SH	SF	SO	SB	CS	SLG	OBP
Abreu, Willie	L-L	6-4	225	3-21-95	.232	.314	.218	70	228	19	53	14	0	7	35	14	6	1	2	71	5	3	.386	.292
Bouchard, Sean	R-R	6-3	215	5-16-96	.266	.356	.242	91	342	58	91	30	3	14	46	33	4	0	2	101	8	4	.494	.336
Czinege, Todd	R-R	6-2	204	7-28-94	.187	.265	.157	47	123	10	23	4	0	4	8	12	2	0	0	55	1	0	.317	.270
Edgeworth, Danny	L-R	6-3	210	7-26-95	.000	.000	.000	7	14	1	0	0	0	0	0	4	3	0	0	7	0	0	.000	.333
George, Max	R-R	5-10	190	4-7-96	.191	.255	.169	68	199	27	38	6	2	9	22	35	9	1	1	89	11	2	.377	.336
Golden, Casey	R-R	6-2	185	9-1-94	.236	.381	.210	39	140	17	33	10	1	6	19	12	3	0	0	70	1	0	.450	.310
Gomez, Jose	R-R	5-11	175	12-10-96	.237	.158	.265	64	219	25	54	10	0	3	17	13	1	0	0	62	7	1	.333	.292
Guevara, Javier	R-R	5-11	165	9-25-97	.167	.125	.175	19	48	4	8	1	0	3	8	11	1	0	0	24	0	0	.375	.333
Hannah, Jameson	L-L	5-9	185	8-10-97	.255	.178	.268	79	302	41	77	16	2	3	17	29	4	0	4	99	11	2	.351	.324
Hatch, LJ	R-R	5-11	185	5-18-94	.211	.286	.167	7	19	1	4	0	0	0	2	2	1	0	0	6	1	0	.211	.318
Hearn, Matt	L-R	5-9	165	2-29-96	.200	.184	.203	79	245	28	49	6	0	0	8	23	1	4	2	59	27	6	.224	.269
Herron, Jimmy	R-L	6-1	195	7-27-96	.167	.250	.125	5	12	2	2	0	0	0	1	3	0	0	0	5	1	0	.167	.333
Jones, Greg	L-R	6-2	220	10-17-94	.150	.250	.167	11	20	1	3	0	0	0	1	1	1	0	0	11	0	0	.300	.227
Jones, Mylz	R-R	6-1	185	4-13-94	.077	.000	.125	5	13	1	1	0	0	0	0	0	0	0	0	10	0	0	.077	.077
MacIver, Willie	R-R	6-2	205	10-28-96	.167	.143	.171	54	192	21	32	4	0	5	13	16	3	0	1	64	10	2	.266	.241
McLaughlin, Matt	R-R	6-1	185	2-2-96	.211	.277	.192	84	279	38	59	12	0	3	17	27	7	1	1	63	2	5	.287	.296
Melendez, Manuel	L-L	5-11	165	1-10-97	.199	.245	.189	82	266	24	53	13	0	6	25	23	3	2	1	65	5	5	.316	.270
Montero, Elehuris	R-R	6-3	235	8-17-98	.279	.288	.277	92	323	46	90	11	1	22	69	43	4	0	9	90	0	0	.523	.361
Montes, Coco	R-R	6-1	200	10-7-96	.258	.348	.240	116	431	51	111	37	3	13	60	33	6	0	4	120	3	4	.448	.316
Snyder, Taylor	R-R	6-2	165	9-20-94	.255	.261	.253	60	216	44	55	14	0	18	46	30	0	0	4	62	3	1	.569	.340
Toglia, Michael	B-L	6-5	226	8-16-98	.217	.320	.195	41	143	16	31	10	1	5	18	23	2	0	1	51	3	0	.406	.331

Pitching	B-T	HT	WT	DOB	W	L	ERA	G	GS	CG	SV	IP	H	R	ER	HR	BB	SO	AVG	vLH	vRH	K/9	BB/9
Aybar, Yoan	L-L	6-2	210	7-3-97	2	6	6.22	49	0	0	2	46	50	36	32	8	33	53	.266	.350	.227	10.29	6.41

	B-T	HT	WT	DOB	W	L	ERA	G	GS	CG	SV	IP	H	R	ER	HR	BB	SO	AVG	vLH	vRH	K/9	BB/9
Baayoun, Zak	L-L	6-1	180	5-1-98	0	1	17.55	3	0	0	0	7	15	13	13	2	4	2	.417	.250	.464	2.70	5.40
Baird, Michael	R-R	6-5	210	7-9-95	1	3	7.27	12	3	0	0	26	28	21	21	7	12	34	.269	.171	.319	11.77	4.15
Biddy, Jared	R-R	6-2	180	7-25-96	0	0	27.00	1	0	0	0	1	3	3	3	0	1	0	.750	1.000	.667	0.00	9.00
Bird, Jake	R-R	6-3	200	12-4-95	1	0	2.21	10	1	0	0	20	20	10	5	1	7	23	.250	.238	.263	10.18	3.10
Bush, Nick	L-L	6-0	195	8-23-96	0	4	5.40	7	7	0	0	35	51	24	21	4	12	30	.342	.290	.356	7.71	3.09
Clarkin, Ian	L-L	6-2	215	2-14-95	0	2	5.19	4	3	0	0	17	23	12	10	3	4	13	.319	.286	.328	6.75	2.08
Dennis, Matt	R-R	6-1	210	1-3-95	4	9	5.81	23	17	0	0	96	120	62	62	12	20	79	.308	.277	.329	7.41	1.88
Doyle, Tommy	R-R	6-6	244	5-1-96	0	1	9.64	10	0	0	0	9	17	10	14	4	3	8	.395	.353	.423	7.71	2.89
Duncan, Frank	R-R	6-4	215	1-30-92	2	3	2.76	8	8	1	0	42	43	17	13	3	6	33	.256	.254	.257	7.02	1.28
Feltner, Ryan	R-R	6-4	190	9-2-96	5	2	2.85	13	13	0	0	73	68	23	23	7	22	80	.248	.264	.240	9.91	2.72
Fernandez, Julian	R-R	6-6	233	12-5-95	2	2	3.45	30	0	0	1	29	25	14	11	4	12	24	.229	.209	.242	7.53	3.77
Gaddis, Will	R-R	6-1	185	3-12-96	2	8	5.91	37	7	0	4	67	84	50	44	12	21	50	.305	.324	.293	6.72	2.82
Gonzalez, Brian	R-L	6-3	230	10-25-95	1	2	4.74	30	1	0	0	38	41	26	20	6	20	53	.270	.146	.327	12.55	4.74
Griep, Nate	R-R	6-2	210	10-11-93	1	0	0.69	13	0	0	3	13	6	2	1	0	4	13	.133	.100	.143	9.00	2.77
Guevara, Javier	R-R	5-11	165	9-25-97	0	0	--	0	0	0	0	0	0	0	0	0	0	0	--	--	--	--	--
Harris, Nate	R-R	6-0	190	9-7-94	1	3	8.49	24	8	0	0	70	97	68	66	19	36	55	.324	.410	.278	7.07	4.63
Hill, David	R-R	6-2	195	5-27-94	2	5	5.25	16	15	0	1	74	88	50	43	16	19	64	.298	.295	.301	7.82	2.32
Jones, Greg	L-R	6-2	220	10-17-94	0	0	0.00	2	0	0	0	1	0	0	0	0	1	0	.000	.000	.000	6.75	0.00
Kaczor, Micah	R-R	6-1	205	5-21-97	1	0	0.00	1	0	0	0	5	1	0	0	0	1	3	.067	.000	.111	5.40	1.80
Kauffmann, Karl	R-R	6-2	200	8-15-97	2	11	7.35	19	18	0	0	82	123	73	67	18	41	65	.343	.362	.327	7.13	4.50
Kennedy, Nick	R-L	6-1	200	6-20-96	1	3	6.55	39	0	0	0	44	54	40	32	9	21	58	.298	.176	.372	11.86	4.30
Lambert, Peter	R-R	6-2	208	4-18-97	0	0	3.18	2	2	0	0	6	5	2	2	1	0	9	.250	.125	.333	14.29	0.00
Matson, Zach	L-L	6-3	225	10-24-95	2	2	5.73	35	0	0	0	33	28	24	21	6	15	57	.226	.229	.224	15.55	4.09
Moore, Alex	R-R	6-3	205	10-25-96	0	0	2.84	4	0	0	0	6	7	3	2	1	3	6	.292	.000	.467	8.53	4.26
Poulin, PJ	R-L	6-1	195	7-25-96	2	1	4.98	22	0	0	0	22	17	13	12	2	9	22	.218	.087	.273	9.14	3.74
Quezada, Andrew	L-R	6-1	185	6-28-97	0	1	8.10	1	1	0	0	3	3	5	3	2	4	2	.231	.500	.111	5.40	10.80
Rolison, Ryan	R-L	6-2	213	7-11-97	2	1	3.07	3	3	0	0	15	11	6	5	1	2	20	.204	.280	.138	12.27	1.23
Schilling, Garrett	R-R	6-2	185	10-25-95	1	6	5.61	11	11	1	0	51	67	33	32	8	18	49	.321	.263	.373	8.59	3.16
Scioneaux, Tate	R-R	6-0	219	12-14-92	0	0	1.02	15	0	0	0	18	12	2	2	1	1	25	.182	.214	.158	12.74	0.51
Stringer, Cole	L-L	6-0	175	8-10-96	0	0	45.00	1	0	0	0	1	2	5	5	1	2	0	.400	.500	.333	0.00	18.00
Todd, Reagan	L-L	6-3	218	8-30-95	4	2	4.36	39	0	0	6	43	39	22	21	7	15	59	.245	.286	.227	12.25	3.12
Watson, Derrik	R-R	6-2	175	8-21-94	0	1	27.00	2	0	0	0	2	3	6	6	0	6	2	.375	.500	.250	9.00	27.00

Fielding

Catcher	PCT	G	PO	A	E	DP	PB
George	.987	55	427	32	6	4	9
Guevara	.985	14	123	11	2	2	2
Jones	.980	8	43	5	1	0	0
MacIver	.986	46	395	31	6	8	4

First Base	PCT	G	PO	A	E	DP
Abreu	1.000	1	1	0	0	1
Bouchard	1.000	25	168	23	0	17
Czinege	1.000	4	26	1	0	2
McLaughlin	1.000	2	13	1	0	3
Montero	.989	40	257	13	3	25
Snyder	1.000	8	49	5	0	4
Toglia	1.000	41	306	30	0	39

Second Base	PCT	G	PO	A	E	DP
Hatch	1.000	1	4	1	0	1
McLaughlin	.968	36	51	71	4	21
Montes	.971	77	125	179	9	46
Snyder	.917	5	13	9	2	2

Third Base	PCT	G	PO	A	E	DP
Bouchard	.882	9	6	9	2	0
Edgeworth	1.000	6	3	8	0	1
Hatch	1.000	1	0	2	0	0
Jones	1.000	1	1	0	0	0
McLaughlin	.914	37	25	49	7	4
Montero	.879	42	31	63	13	6
Montes	.909	19	12	28	4	2
Snyder	.900	7	1	8	1	0

Shortstop	PCT	G	PO	A	E	DP
Gomez	.960	64	87	174	11	45
Hatch	.917	3	5	6	1	1
Montes	.921	16	19	39	5	8
Snyder	.968	35	37	83	4	19

Outfield	PCT	G	PO	A	E	DP
Abreu	.988	51	84	1	1	0
Bouchard	1.000	40	75	1	0	0
Czinege	1.000	31	32	3	0	1
Golden	.980	28	46	3	1	0
Hannah	.989	72	171	6	2	1
Hatch	1.000	1	2	0	0	0
Hearn	.986	73	141	4	2	1
Herron	1.000	4	8	0	0	0
Jones	1.000	4	7	0	0	0
Melendez	.963	79	122	7	5	2
Snyder	1.000	1	2	0	0	0

SPOKANE INDIANS
HIGH-A WEST
HIGH CLASS A

Batting	B-T	HT	WT	DOB	AVG	vLH	vRH	G	AB	R	H	2B	3B	HR	RBI	BB	HBP	SH	SF	SO	SB	CS	SLG	OBP
Bernard, Austin	B-R	5-10	195	3-14-96	.138	.000	.174	11	29	3	4	2	0	0	3	3	2	0	1	12	1	0	.207	.257
Blomgren, Jack	R-R	5-10	180	9-27-98	.284	.156	.309	86	278	61	79	13	4	3	32	45	14	5	3	74	30	7	.392	.406
Collins, Isaac	B-R	5-9	185	7-22-97	.312	.231	.328	78	311	62	97	22	4	9	48	40	8	1	4	80	20	5	.495	.399
Cope, Daniel	R-R	6-0	195	6-15-97	.278	.346	.262	41	133	19	37	3	0	4	19	23	2	1	1	32	3	3	.391	.390
Cresto, John	R-R	6-3	225	12-15-96	.172	.273	.149	19	58	6	10	1	0	2	5	4	1	0	0	27	0	0	.293	.238
Datres, Kyle	R-R	6-0	205	1-5-96	.222	.216	.224	58	189	31	42	9	1	9	40	35	7	0	5	52	14	2	.423	.356
Decolati, Niko	R-R	6-1	215	8-12-97	.264	.250	.267	100	371	67	98	14	2	11	56	40	6	2	5	98	26	5	.402	.341
Diaz, Eddy	R-R	6-0	175	2-14-00	.192	.077	.215	21	78	12	15	1	1	0	5	8	2	1	0	30	11	5	.231	.284
Doyle, Brenton	R-R	6-3	200	5-14-98	.279	.282	.279	97	390	70	109	16	2	16	47	30	3	1	0	134	21	6	.454	.336
Guevara, Javier	R-R	5-11	165	9-25-97	.198	.429	.177	30	86	10	17	4	0	1	16	14	0	3	1	37	0	1	.279	.307
Harris, Cade	L-R	6-2	195	5-27-97	.193	.083	.211	61	171	28	33	8	1	7	22	35	2	2	2	63	6	1	.374	.333
Hatch, LJ	R-R	5-11	175	5-18-94	.114	.125	.111	13	35	2	4	1	0	0	3	5	1	0	0	11	0	1	.143	.244
Lavigne, Grant	L-R	6-4	220	8-27-99	.225	.389	.194	32	111	17	25	5	1	2	18	22	1	2	1	39	2	1	.342	.362
Lewis, AJ	R-R	5-10	195	5-31-98	.179	.125	.188	21	56	10	10	2	0	1	8	12	3	2	1	20	2	2	.268	.347
MacIver, Willie	R-R	6-2	205	10-28-96	.286	.235	.299	46	168	25	48	11	1	10	30	25	6	1	1	49	10	3	.542	.395
Montano, Daniel	L-R	6-1	204	3-31-99	.284	.292	.284	44	166	24	47	7	1	0	25	20	0	2	4	47	5	5	.337	.353
Morgan, Luke	R-R	6-2	195	5-13-96	.125	.222	.097	14	40	6	5	3	0	0	2	8	1	0	0	10	2	0	.200	.286
Navarro, Cristopher	R-R	6-0	170	6-14-99	.246	.125	.283	21	69	6	17	2	0	0	3	3	1	1	0	21	1	0	.275	.303
Schunk, Aaron	R-R	6-2	205	7-24-97	.223	.239	.220	89	358	57	80	12	4	8	45	25	8	0	4	111	13	5	.346	.286

	B-T	HT	WT	DOB	AVG	vLH	vRH	G	AB	R	H	2B	3B	HR	RBI	BB	HBP	SH	SF	SO	SB	CS	SLG	OBP
Stovall, Hunter	R-R	5-8	170	9-5-96	.316	.280	.322	89	320	48	101	13	4	6	46	40	2	3	2	69	25	7	.438	.393
Toglia, Michael	B-L	6-5	226	8-16-98	.234	.218	.238	74	282	50	66	10	2	17	66	42	2	0	4	91	7	3	.465	.333
Tovar, Ezequiel	R-R	6-0	162	8-1-01	.239	.118	.256	32	134	19	32	9	0	4	18	3	2	4	0	19	3	2	.396	.266
Welker, Colton	R-R	6-1	235	10-9-97	.194	.000	.214	8	31	5	6	1	0	3	7	2	1	0	1	10	0	0	.516	.257

Pitching	B-T	HT	WT	DOB	W	L	ERA	G	GS	CG	SV	IP	H	R	ER	HR	BB	SO	AVG	vLH	vRH	K/9	BB/9
Barlow, Trysten	L-L	6-1	215	12-31-96	0	2	9.35	10	0	0	0	9	6	10	9	1	13	11	.200	.182	.211	11.42	13.50
Biddy, Jared	R-R	6-2	180	7-25-96	1	1	3.40	25	1	0	0	48	55	23	18	6	8	48	.282	.271	.291	9.06	1.51
Bush, Nick	L-L	6-0	195	8-23-96	4	2	2.58	10	7	0	1	52	40	15	15	3	9	60	.211	.279	.172	10.32	1.55
Ceja, Moises	R-R	6-0	175	8-17-95	0	2	7.43	24	0	0	0	36	53	32	30	10	10	33	.344	.403	.299	8.17	2.48
Chevalier, Luke	R-R	6-1	200	3-1-96	0	0	90.00	4	0	0	0	1	5	11	10	0	5	1	.556	.600	.500	9.00	45.00
Darnell, Dugan	L-R	6-2	205	6-26-97	4	3	2.38	36	0	0	15	42	27	13	11	3	10	63	.188	.167	.208	13.61	2.16
Davis, Noah	R-R	6-2	195	4-22-97	3	1	3.60	6	6	1	0	35	32	15	14	3	8	29	.250	.241	.265	7.46	2.06
Del Bonta-Smith, Fineas	R-R	6-0	190	2-2-97	3	4	3.35	27	0	0	1	38	28	16	14	4	12	44	.201	.186	.217	10.51	2.87
DiPiazza, Andrew	R-R	6-7	215	10-7-95	0	0	0.00	4	0	0	0	8	3	0	0	0	3	12	.111	.154	.071	13.50	3.38
Ethridge, Will	R-R	6-5	240	12-20-97	4	5	5.70	12	12	0	0	66	66	45	42	9	18	56	.260	.258	.262	7.60	2.44
Eusebio, Breiling	L-L	6-1	175	10-21-96	2	3	9.82	7	6	0	0	26	38	29	28	5	14	26	.330	.250	.367	9.12	4.91
Feltner, Ryan	R-R	6-4	190	9-2-96	3	1	2.17	7	7	0	0	37	26	9	9	1	18	45	.191	.210	.176	10.85	4.34
Fennell, Trent	R-R	6-5	205	11-26-95	1	3	4.52	31	8	0	1	68	61	41	34	8	36	82	.236	.264	.210	10.91	4.79
Gotsis, Noah	R-R	6-0	160	6-17-96	0	0	0.00	1	0	0	0	1	0	0	0	0	1	6	.500	.000	1.000	27.00	27.00
Hill, David	R-R	6-2	195	5-27-94	2	1	2.66	6	6	0	0	24	17	8	7	3	7	27	.202	.222	.179	10.27	2.66
Johnson, Boby	R-R	6-1	185	4-8-97	5	0	5.06	37	0	0	2	53	70	35	30	3	24	51	.332	.296	.363	8.61	4.05
Jones, Stephen	R-R	6-4	195	7-30-97	4	1	3.41	26	0	0	1	29	25	13	11	3	10	39	.250	.306	.167	12.10	3.10
Kauffmann, Karl	R-R	6-2	200	8-15-97	1	1	2.89	2	2	0	0	9	5	3	3	0	2	6	.167	.154	.176	5.79	1.93
Kilkenny, Mitchell	R-R	6-4	206	3-24-97	9	1	3.95	15	15	0	0	82	77	40	36	10	17	71	.245	.221	.275	7.79	1.87
Lackey, Shelby	R-R	6-3	190	7-8-97	1	1	2.79	20	0	0	6	19	16	6	6	1	8	29	.216	.179	.257	13.50	3.72
Lambert, Peter	R-R	6-2	208	4-18-97	0	0	5.87	4	4	0	0	8	8	6	5	2	6	7	.267	.200	.333	8.22	7.04
McMahon, Chris	R-R	6-2	217	2-4-99	10	3	4.17	22	20	0	0	114	119	57	53	13	32	119	.268	.284	.252	9.37	2.52
Moore, Alex	R-R	6-3	205	10-25-97	1	1	4.43	14	0	0	0	20	14	13	10	4	6	22	.203	.207	.200	9.74	2.66
Olivarez, Helcris	L-L	6-2	192	8-8-00	4	9	6.05	22	21	0	0	100	89	74	67	10	68	112	.248	.227	.258	10.11	6.14
Pint, Riley	R-R	6-5	225	11-6-97	1	0	3.38	10	0	0	0	11	7	8	4	3	10	17	.184	.190	.176	14.34	8.44
Poulin, PJ	R-L	6-1	195	7-25-96	1	0	2.35	22	0	0	4	23	11	7	6	2	6	37	.141	.111	.157	14.48	2.35
Rolison, Ryan	R-L	6-2	213	7-11-97	0	0	3.60	1	1	0	0	5	4	2	2	1	2	3	.250	.250	.250	5.40	3.60
Rosa, Raymells	R-R	6-2	180	12-6-98	0	0	15.43	2	0	0	0	2	2	4	4	0	4	1	.222	.250	.200	3.86	15.43
Sheffield, Jordan	R-R	5-10	190	6-1-95	0	0	54.00	1	0	0	0	1	3	4	4	2	1	0	.600	.667	.500	0.00	13.50
Sommers, Jake	R-R	6-2	190	5-5-97	3	2	5.59	25	0	0	0	37	42	25	23	3	19	51	.288	.310	.267	12.41	4.62
Tribucher, Will	L-L	6-3	210	9-23-96	0	0	63.00	2	0	0	0	1	8	7	7	1	3	2	.800	.667	1.000	18.00	27.00
Watson, Derrik	R-R	6-2	175	8-21-94	0	2	5.03	17	0	0	0	20	18	13	11	2	13	24	.237	.188	.273	10.98	5.95

Fielding

Catcher	PCT	G	PO	A	E	DP	PB
Bernard	.988	11	78	1	0	2	
Cope	.991	40	406	17	4	3	4
Guevara	.991	28	214	14	2	1	8
Lewis	1.000	6	47	5	0	0	
MacIver	.991	38	388	32	4	3	3

First Base	PCT	G	PO	A	E	DP
Cresto	.867	1	12	1	2	1
Datres	.992	16	112	14	1	7
Lavigne	.986	30	194	13	3	25
Schunk	1.000	2	8	2	0	0
Toglia	.991	67	493	69	5	53
Welker	1.000	1	9	0	0	0

Second Base PCT G PO A E DP

	PCT	G	PO	A	E	DP
Blomgren	.977	32	39	89	3	13
Collins	.916	21	24	52	7	13
Diaz	.972	10	13	22	1	6
Hatch	.000	1	0	0	0	0
Schunk	.968	38	55	96	5	24
Stovall	.990	23	31	64	1	14

Third Base	PCT	G	PO	A	E	DP
Datres	.811	21	8	22	7	1
Hatch	.941	6	5	11	1	0
Navarro	1.000	2	1	4	0	1
Schunk	.986	46	21	50	1	8
Stovall	.962	44	35	65	4	10
Welker	1.000	5	4	1	0	0

Shortstop PCT G PO A E DP

	PCT	G	PO	A	E	DP
Blomgren	.967	53	78	124	7	29
Diaz	.941	13	15	33	3	7
Hatch	1.000	5	6	11	0	2
Navarro	.970	19	20	44	2	9
Tovar	.957	32	47	65	5	17

Outfield	PCT	G	PO	A	E	DP
Collins	1.000	52	100	3	0	0
Cresto	1.000	9	7	0	0	0
Decolati	.963	92	155	3	6	0
Doyle	.971	83	157	13	5	2
Harris	.970	59	91	7	3	0
Hatch	1.000	1	1	0	0	0
Montano	1.000	40	71	4	0	1
Morgan	1.000	14	15	1	0	0
Stovall	.957	17	22	0	1	0

FRESNO GRIZZLIES — LOW CLASS A
LOW-A WEST

Batting	B-T	HT	WT	DOB	AVG	vLH	vRH	G	AB	R	H	2B	3B	HR	RBI	BB	HBP	SH	SF	SO	SB	CS	SLG	OBP
Aeilts, Joe	R-R	6-2	200	1-1-98	.268	.224	.286	63	205	29	55	9	1	5	33	18	3	2	3	77	6	2	.395	.332
Barnwell, Jacob	R-R	6-0	200	8-8-97	.000	--	.000	1	2	0	0	0	0	0	0	1	0	1	0	2	0	0	.000	.333
Bernabel, Warming	R-R	6-0	180	6-6-02	.205	.150	.222	21	83	9	17	6	0	1	7	7	3	0	1	14	4	1	.313	.287
Boone, Trevor	R-R	6-2	210	9-9-97	.191	.207	.185	33	110	13	21	4	2	5	18	7	2	0	1	50	1	0	.400	.250
Carreras, Julio	R-R	6-2	190	1-12-00	.254	.288	.245	94	362	61	92	19	5	7	44	24	5	8	5	102	15	4	.392	.306
Collins, Isaac	B-R	5-9	185	7-17-97	.290	.385	.265	17	62	11	18	3	1	0	6	15	2	0	0	20	1	1	.371	.443
Diaz, Eddy	R-R	6-0	175	2-14-00	.295	.320	.287	81	329	67	97	13	3	1	32	28	13	4	2	58	48	14	.362	.371
Edgeworth, Danny	L-R	6-3	210	7-26-95	.000	--	.000	1	4	0	0	0	0	0	0	0	0	0	0	3	0	0	.000	.000
Gil, Mateo	R-R	6-1	180	7-24-00	.249	.186	.268	94	366	53	91	25	1	9	56	21	4	1	4	99	8	6	.396	.294
Lavigne, Grant	L-R	6-4	220	8-27-99	.281	.255	.288	72	260	49	73	13	4	7	40	39	7	1	1	73	7	2	.442	.388
Lewis, AJ	R-R	5-10	195	5-31-98	.283	.333	.265	15	46	6	13	3	0	1	5	5	6	0	0	12	0	2	.413	.421
Martin Jr., Robby	L-R	6-3	190	8-17-99	.274	.364	.255	17	62	10	17	5	0	1	9	4	3	0	1	18	3	2	.403	.343
Montano, Daniel	L-R	6-1	204	3-31-99	.301	.400	.278	52	186	28	56	9	3	4	25	24	1	2	2	53	6	3	.446	.380
Morgan, Luke	R-R	6-2	195	5-13-96	.238	.222	.250	8	21	6	5	1	0	1	1	2	0	0	0	9	1	0	.429	.304

COLORADO ROCKIES

	B-T	HT	WT	DOB	AVG	vLH	vRH	G	AB	R	H	2B	3B	HR	RBI	BB	HBP	SH	SF	SO	SB	CS	SLG	OBP
Navarro, Cristopher	R-R	6-0	170	6-14-99	.262	.273	.259	34	107	14	28	6	0	1	9	8	1	2	0	24	3	2	.346	.319
Palma, Ronaiker	R-R	5-10	180	1-2-00	.221	.333	.180	23	68	7	15	1	0	0	6	2	1	1	1	6	1	0	.235	.250
Quijada, Bryant	R-R	5-10	167	7-2-99	.200	.200	.200	32	90	7	18	0	0	1	8	14	5	1	3	16	2	1	.233	.330
Restituyo, Bladimir	R-R	5-10	151	7-2-01	.259	.183	.283	84	290	37	75	7	3	3	24	12	2	5	5	73	31	5	.334	.288
Romo, Drew	B-R	6-1	205	8-29-01	.314	.218	.351	79	312	48	98	17	2	6	47	19	0	0	8	50	23	6	.439	.345
Simpson, Colin	L-R	5-9	228	7-23-96	.237	.115	.256	56	198	31	47	12	2	7	39	23	1	0	3	60	2	0	.424	.316
Tovar, Ezequiel	R-R	6-0	162	8-1-01	.309	.300	.311	72	298	60	92	21	3	11	54	14	5	5	4	38	21	4	.510	.346
Veen, Zac	L-R	6-4	190	12-12-01	.301	.289	.304	106	399	83	120	27	4	15	75	64	6	2	7	126	36	17	.501	.399
Yalowitz, Jack	L-L	5-11	180	10-19-96	.140	.000	.182	21	57	6	8	2	1	1	4	5	0	0	0	21	2	1	.263	.210

Pitching	B-T	HT	WT	DOB	W	L	ERA	G	GS	CG	SV	IP	H	R	ER	HR	BB	SO	AVG	vLH	vRH	K/9	BB/9
Amarista, Anderson	R-R	6-1	185	9-15-98	6	5	6.01	16	15	0	0	73	81	56	49	10	33	75	.278	.298	.263	9.20	4.05
Bido, Anderson	R-R	6-3	205	5-7-99	3	1	3.97	34	0	0	1	48	46	26	21	5	23	32	.258	.262	.256	6.04	4.34
Calvo, Blair	R-R	6-3	195	2-27-96	4	2	4.54	33	0	0	2	71	68	40	36	6	23	75	.258	.248	.265	9.46	2.90
Darnell, Dugan	L-R	6-2	205	6-26-97	0	0	0.66	8	0	0	0	14	5	1	1	0	0	17	.111	.133	.100	11.20	0.00
Del Bonta-Smith, Fineas	R-R	6-0	190	2-2-97	0	2	3.00	10	0	0	1	15	10	7	5	1	5	21	.185	.136	.219	12.60	3.00
DiPiazza, Andrew	R-R	6-7	215	10-7-95	4	0	2.51	7	6	0	0	29	22	8	8	2	17	33	.218	.297	.172	10.36	5.34
Ethridge, Will	R-R	6-5	240	12-20-97	3	1	2.56	6	6	0	0	32	22	9	9	3	2	32	.191	.191	.191	9.09	0.57
Eusebio, Breiling	L-L	6-1	175	10-21-96	5	0	3.19	11	11	0	0	59	52	24	21	10	16	64	.236	.149	.260	9.71	2.43
Goldsberry, Blake	R-R	6-4	220	5-21-97	5	1	3.06	23	2	0	1	32	27	13	11	3	9	29	.229	.241	.219	8.07	2.51
Gotsis, Noah	R-R	6-0	160	6-17-96	3	2	3.14	8	4	0	0	29	30	19	10	2	8	25	.254	.309	.206	7.85	2.51
Hernandez, Robinson	R-R	6-0	186	6-11-99	5	3	3.40	40	0	0	14	50	42	23	19	4	19	52	.247	.288	.213	9.30	3.40
Hollowell, Gavin	R-R	6-7	215	11-4-97	2	0	2.45	22	0	0	4	22	15	8	6	1	5	31	.185	.176	.191	12.68	2.05
James, Keegan	R-R	6-3	214	4-1-97	3	1	3.83	20	7	0	0	49	42	22	21	5	20	52	.231	.333	.168	9.49	3.65
Jones, Stephen	R-R	6-4	195	7-30-97	1	0	4.50	19	0	0	5	20	14	10	10	1	9	24	.206	.250	.182	10.80	4.05
Kilkenny, Mitchell	R-R	6-4	206	3-24-97	3	2	1.45	6	6	0	0	31	27	9	5	1	5	36	.225	.189	.254	10.45	1.45
Kitchen, Austin	L-L	6-0	200	2-11-97	1	4	4.97	19	8	0	0	51	66	34	28	3	14	38	.316	.288	.325	6.75	2.49
Locey, Tony	R-R	6-3	239	7-29-98	3	0	3.34	25	10	0	0	65	52	27	24	3	44	80	.227	.196	.252	11.13	6.12
Mejia, Juan	R-R	6-3	200	7-4-00	3	5	4.82	43	1	0	8	47	44	27	25	2	23	66	.242	.179	.288	12.73	4.44
Pilar, Anderson	R-R	6-2	210	3-2-98	6	0	1.61	33	1	0	1	62	47	16	11	2	17	57	.209	.211	.208	8.32	2.48
Propst, Tanner	L-L	6-0	190	6-7-98	3	1	3.54	36	0	0	2	41	36	18	16	5	13	63	.231	.268	.210	13.94	2.88
Ruff, Mike	R-R	6-2	212	3-31-98	6	2	4.34	17	17	0	0	75	68	41	36	5	35	83	.239	.273	.213	10.00	4.22
Tribucher, Will	L-L	6-3	210	9-23-96	0	0	3.68	11	0	0	0	15	11	6	6	0	8	21	.220	.105	.290	12.89	4.91
Weatherly, Sam	L-L	6-4	205	5-28-99	4	6	4.83	15	15	0	0	69	59	39	37	7	32	96	.233	.226	.235	12.52	4.17
Williams, Case	R-R	6-3	210	2-16-02	1	3	5.72	7	6	0	0	28	31	23	18	2	14	17	.272	.250	.288	5.40	4.45

Fielding

Catcher	PCT	G	PO	A	E	DP	PB
Barnwell	1.000	1	11	0	0	0	0
Palma	.993	16	127	10	1	1	0
Quijada	.993	28	238	34	2	4	0
Romo	.992	69	663	55	6	5	12
Simpson	1.000	7	76	7	0	0	2

First Base	PCT	G	PO	A	E	DP
Boone	.992	18	121	6	1	13
Edgeworth	1.000	1	9	0	0	0
Lavigne	.990	64	477	19	5	65
Navarro	.971	9	63	5	2	4
Quijada	1.000	3	19	0	0	1
Simpson	1.000	27	155	10	0	16

Second Base PCT G PO A E DP

(Second Base)	PCT	G	PO	A	E	DP
Carreras	1.000	2	5	2	0	1
Collins	.963	10	12	14	1	2
Diaz	.973	69	129	162	8	30
Gil	.985	32	59	72	2	18
Lewis	1.000	1	1	4	0	0
Navarro	1.000	2	2	2	0	1

Third Base	PCT	G	PO	A	E	DP
Bernabel	.805	17	6	27	8	1
Carreras	.971	50	36	97	4	6
Gil	.918	39	33	56	8	5
Navarro	.964	15	12	15	1	0

Shortstop	PCT	G	PO	A	E	DP
Carreras	.948	41	56	108	9	22
Diaz	.867	3	6	7	2	3

	PCT	G	PO	A	E	DP
Gil	1.000	1	0	1	0	0
Navarro	.931	9	10	17	2	4
Tovar	.961	64	80	169	10	37

Outfield	PCT	G	PO	A	E	DP
Aeilts	.981	62	105	1	2	1
Boone	.895	14	17	0	2	0
Collins	1.000	5	12	1	0	0
Lewis	.917	11	11	0	1	0
Martin Jr.	1.000	14	27	0	0	0
Montano	.986	50	63	5	1	2
Morgan	1.000	3	3	0	0	0
Restituyo	.968	81	178	5	6	0
Simpson	1.000	9	15	0	0	0
Veen	.972	95	166	8	5	0
Yalowitz	1.000	20	29	0	0	0

ACL ROCKIES

ARIZONA COMPLEX LEAGUE

ROOKIE

Batting	B-T	HT	WT	DOB	AVG	vLH	vRH	G	AB	R	H	2B	3B	HR	RBI	BB	HBP	SH	SF	SO	SB	CS	SLG	OBP
Amador, Adael	B-R	6-0	160	4-11-03	.299	.205	.333	47	164	41	49	10	1	4	24	27	2	2	5	29	10	7	.445	.394
Andrews Jr., EJ	R-R	6-1	210	9-28-00	.250	.286	.240	16	32	6	8	1	0	0	3	6	0	0	9	9	0	0	.281	.368
Bernabel, Warming	R-R	6-0	180	6-6-02	.432	.389	.446	22	74	18	32	5	0	6	31	5	2	0	5	12	5	1	.743	.453
Bernard, Austin	B-R	5-10	195	3-14-96	.179	.167	.182	11	28	5	5	1	0	0	1	8	1	0	0	11	1	0	.214	.378
Boone, Trevor	R-R	6-2	210	9-9-97	.308	.286	.316	8	26	9	8	2	1	2	7	6	0	0	0	7	3	0	.692	.438
Brito, Juan	B-R	5-11	162	9-24-01	.295	.360	.270	27	88	20	26	3	0	3	11	15	2	3	1	21	5	4	.432	.406
Cabrera, Walking	R-R	6-3	184	8-26-00	.252	.278	.243	45	139	27	35	7	2	6	24	21	1	2	1	31	11	2	.460	.352
Cordova, Jose	R-R	6-0	180	1-11-00	.405	.222	.464	19	37	3	15	3	1	0	4	2	1	0	0	8	3	1	.541	.450
Daza, Yonathan	R-R	6-2	207	2-28-94	.273	.500	.143	4	11	4	3	1	2	0	3	4	0	0	0	4	0	0	.727	.467
Fulford, Braxton	R-R	5-11	190	12-9-98	.267	.167	.333	14	30	8	8	4	0	0	3	10	3	1	0	14	2	0	.400	.488
Golden, Casey	R-R	6-2	185	9-1-94	.478	.500	.471	8	23	9	11	1	0	3	11	8	0	0	1	10	0	0	.913	.594
Goodman, Hunter	R-R	6-1	210	10-8-99	.300	.500	.239	22	60	16	18	7	0	2	12	9	4	0	1	14	1	0	.517	.419
Guerrero, Juan	R-R	6-1	160	9-10-01	.318	.226	.342	47	148	32	47	13	1	4	26	16	4	1	2	29	9	5	.500	.394
Kent, Nic	R-R	6-2	185	4-10-00	.218	.222	.216	19	55	10	12	2	0	0	6	4	3	2	0	11	3	2	.255	.306
Kokoska, Zach	L-L	6-0	200	10-20-98	.395	.435	.375	20	43	13	17	1	1	1	7	3	2	0	0	6	8	1	.535	.458
Martin Jr., Robby	L-R	6-3	190	8-17-99	.188	.000	.267	8	16	3	3	0	0	2	3	5	0	0	0	6	0	0	.563	.381
Montgomery, Benny	R-R	6-4	200	9-9-02	.340	.333	.344	14	47	7	16	0	1	0	6	5	0	0	0	9	5	1	.383	.404

Batting	B-T	HT	WT	DOB	AVG	vLH	vRH	G	AB	R	H	2B	3B	HR	RBI	BB	HBP	SH	SF	SO	SB	CS	SLG	OBP
Ordonez, Jesus	R-R	5-8	180	12-26-99	.304	.100	.361	23	46	10	14	5	1	1	12	4	3	0	1	11	0	2	.522	.389
Ortiz, Francisco	R-R	6-0	160	9-15-99	.200	.100	.218	24	65	8	13	1	2	2	16	3	1	0	1	26	0	0	.369	.243
Palma, Ronaiker	R-R	5-10	180	1-2-00	.294	.400	.250	7	17	4	5	1	0	0	7	1	1	0	0	0	0	1	.353	.368
Perez, Jean	R-R	5-10	178	7-20-02	.250	.143	.288	40	80	10	20	3	1	1	16	6	2	1	1	14	3	1	.350	.315
Rodriguez, Aiverson	R-R	6-0	170	4-1-02	.228	.375	.190	35	79	18	18	5	1	1	12	8	6	2	0	19	4	2	.354	.344
Sems, Benjamin	L-R	6-3	200	2-16-98	.265	.333	.243	21	49	7	13	2	0	0	7	11	2	0	2	12	8	2	.306	.406
Stamets, Eric	R-R	6-0	183	9-25-91	.235	.125	.333	6	17	5	4	0	0	1	1	3	1	0	0	6	0	1	.412	.381
Torrealba, Yorvis	R-R	6-0	195	7-14-97	.356	.387	.345	43	118	42	42	8	0	3	26	20	4	1	0	20	26	5	.500	.465
Ward, Braiden	L-R	5-10	160	1-18-99	.308	.000	.333	17	26	6	8	0	0	0	3	7	4	0	0	6	3	2	.308	.514
Welker, Colton	R-R	6-1	235	10-9-97	.200	.000	.333	2	5	0	1	1	0	0	1	1	0	0	0	1	0	0	.400	.333
Woodard, L.A.	B-R	5-11	165	6-3-97	.217	.500	.158	17	23	7	5	0	1	0	1	5	3	1	0	11	4	0	.304	.419
Yalowitz, Jack	L-L	5-11	180	10-19-96	.300	.400	.267	8	20	7	6	0	0	0	2	7	0	0	0	7	0	1	.300	.481
Zabowski, Cole	L-L	6-5	240	11-5-97	.289	.385	.261	39	114	21	33	9	0	4	30	18	1	0	2	35	1	1	.474	.385

Pitching	B-T	HT	WT	DOB	W	L	ERA	G	GS	CG	SV	IP	H	R	ER	HR	BB	SO	AVG	vLH	vRH	K/9	BB/9
Ahearn, Tyler	R-R	6-2	202	8-25-98	1	1	2.25	5	0	0	2	4	2	1	1	1	0	6	.143	.143		13.50	0.00
Amoroso, Luis	R-R	6-1	192	12-12-99	0	2	1.47	17	0	0	10	18	8	7	3	1	1	23	.129	.050	.167	11.29	0.49
Baayoun, Zak	L-L	6-1	180	5-1-98	6	1	3.38	10	6	1	0	45	46	19	17	2	13	50	.260	.207	.286	9.93	2.58
Baird, Michael	R-R	6-5	210	7-9-95	0	0	2.57	2	1	0	0	7	5	2	2	1	2	8	.192	.091	.267	10.29	2.57
Brown, McCade	R-R	6-6	225	5-15-00	0	0	6.75	4	3	0	0	8	10	7	6	2	3	9	.313	.273	.333	10.13	3.38
Cande, Jarrod	R-R	6-2	215	8-16-99	2	0	2.45	4	0	0	0	4	4	1	1	0	0	4	.267	.250	.286	9.82	0.00
Castillo, Brayan	R-R	6-0	145	9-11-00	3	1	5.11	8	5	0	0	25	27	17	14	0	16	28	.273	.244	.293	10.22	5.84
Chacin, Jhoulys	R-R	6-3	215	1-7-88	0	0	18.00	1	1	0	0	1	2	2	2	1	0	1	.400	.667	.000	9.00	0.00
Chevalier, Luke	R-R	6-1	200	3-1-96	0	1	8.10	4	0	0	0	3	5	4	3	0	6	4	.333	.400	.300	10.80	16.20
Condreay, Joel	L-R	6-3	185	7-5-96	0	0	4.82	10	0	0	1	9	9	5	5	0	7	12	.265	.214	.300	11.57	6.75
Diaz, Jairo	R-R	6-0	254	5-27-91	0	0	0.00	1	0	0	0	2	1	0	0	0	0	4	.143	.333	.000	18.00	0.00
Flores Jr., Bernardo	L-L	6-4	190	8-23-95	0	0	2.57	2	2	0	0	7	5	2	2	0	0	7	.200	.250	.176	9.00	0.00
Gonzalez, Chi-Chi	R-R	6-3	210	1-15-92	0	0	0.00	1	1	0	0	3	3	0	0	0	1	4	.250	.000	.429	13.50	3.38
Gotsis, Noah	R-R	6-0	160	6-17-96	2	0	2.89	4	3	0	0	19	15	6	6	1	3	22	.221	.292	.182	10.61	1.45
Green, Mason	L-L	6-1	195	2-5-99	2	0	0.00	4	0	0	0	5	4	0	0	0	1	7	.222	.000	.308	12.60	1.80
Griep, Nate	R-R	6-2	210	10-11-93	0	0	0.00	3	1	0	0	3	2	1	0	0	0	7	.167	.250	.125	21.00	0.00
Hammer, Zachary	R-R	6-2	165	7-4-00	2	0	2.70	10	0	0	0	10	5	4	3	0	8	14	.156	.385	.062	7.20	7.20
Hollowell, Gavin	R-R	6-7	215	11-4-97	1	0	0.00	2	0	0	1	2	2	0	0	0	2	2	.286	--	.286	9.00	9.00
Juarez, Victor	R-R	6-0	173	6-19-03	0	1	6.30	3	2	0	0	10	13	7	7	2	1	13	.317	.227	.421	11.70	0.90
Justice, Evan	L-L	6-4	205	7-7-98	0	0	3.00	3	0	0	0	3	2	1	1	1	2	4	.200	.500	.125	12.00	6.00
Kaczor, Micah	R-R	6-1	205	5-21-97	5	3	4.18	12	8	0	0	52	59	25	24	10	9	41	.284	.241	.299	7.14	1.57
Kafka, Cullen	R-R	6-4	210	4-16-99	0	0	0.00	4	0	0	1	5	3	0	0	0	0	5	.158	.000	.231	9.00	0.00
Kostyshock, Jacob	R-R	6-4	175	1-2-98	0	0	15.43	3	2	0	0	2	6	4	4	1	2	0	.545	.333	.800	0.00	7.71
Lorenzini, Braxton	R-R	6-4	172	4-5-95	1	0	74.25	1	0	0	0	1	6	11	11	1	11	3	.600	.750	.500	20.25	74.25
McGowan, Bryce	R-R	6-1	205	3-20-00	0	0	0.00	4	0	0	0	4	1	0	0	0	2	4	.083	.143	.000	9.00	4.50
Quezada, Andrew	L-R	6-1	185	6-28-97	3	1	3.30	8	6	0	0	30	28	12	11	3	8	33	.250	.195	.282	9.90	2.40
Ramires, Felix	L-L	6-4	175	9-26-99	3	0	2.89	18	0	0	1	19	22	7	6	0	8	26	.310	.250	.333	12.54	3.86
Ras, Tyler	B-R	6-4	205	11-9-99	0	0	0.00	5	0	0	0	4	0	0	0	0	1	10	.000	.000	.000	20.77	2.08
Rivera, Francis	R-R	6-4	160	9-14-00	0	1	4.34	17	0	0	1	19	21	12	9	0	8	29	.276	.310	.255	13.98	3.86
Rock, Joe	L-L	6-6	205	7-29-00	1	0	1.13	4	2	0	0	8	5	2	1	0	1	11	.179	.333	.136	12.38	1.13
Rolison, Ryan	R-L	6-2	213	7-11-97	0	0	7.11	2	2	0	0	6	10	7	5	0	2	9	.370	.400	.364	12.79	2.84
Sanchez, Sergio	R-R	6-0	180	1-13-01	4	2	6.38	17	0	0	1	18	16	17	13	1	9	25	.225	.214	.233	12.27	4.42
Senzatela, Antonio	R-R	6-1	236	1-21-95	0	0	0.00	1	1	0	0	4	3	0	0	0	0	3	.231	.500	.111	6.75	0.00
Shawver, Evan	R-L	6-0	175	9-11-99	0	0	0.00	4	0	0	0	4	1	0	0	0	1	1	.083	.000	.111	2.25	2.25
Sheffield, Jordan	R-R	5-10	190	6-1-95	0	0	0.00	1	1	0	0	1	1	0	0	0	1	2	.250	.000	.500	18.00	9.00
Stringer, Cole	L-L	6-1	175	8-10-96	3	1	4.40	11	9	0	0	45	51	29	22	4	16	50	.280	.256	.287	10.00	3.20
Sweeney, Nathan	R-R	6-4	185	8-21-97	1	0	8.76	14	0	0	0	12	16	12	12	1	9	9	.320	.176	.394	6.57	6.57
Taggart, Luke	R-R	6-3	228	10-10-97	1	0	0.00	2	0	0	0	3	0	0	0	0	0	6	.000	.000	.000	18.00	9.00
Tribucher, Will	L-L	6-3	210	9-23-96	0	0	0.00	8	0	0	1	8	5	0	0	0	2	12	.185	.286	.150	13.50	2.25

Fielding

C: Andrews Jr. 1, Bernard 9, Cordova 6, Fulford 12, Goodman 12, Ordonez 22, Ortiz 10, Palma 7, Zabowski 1.
1B: Boone 5, Cordova 10, Ortiz 11, Rodriguez 2, Zabowski 37.
2B: Amador 6, Brito 22, Kent 8, Perez 10, Rodriguez 11, Sems 8, Stamets 1, Woodard 7.
3B: Bernabel 18, Kent 4, Perez 26, Rodriguez 14, Sems 10, Welker 2.
SS: Amador 38, Kent 7, Perez 4, Rodriguez 8, Sems 4, Stamets 3.
OF: Andrews Jr. 13, Boone 1, Cabrera 39, Daza 3, Golden 6, Guerrero 41, Kokoska 16, Martin Jr. 8, Montgomery 12, Torrealba 42, Ward 16, Woodard 9, Yalowitz 9.

DSL ROCKIES ROOKIE

DOMINICAN SUMMER LEAGUE

Batting	B-T	HT	WT	DOB	AVG	vLH	vRH	G	AB	R	H	2B	3B	HR	RBI	BB	HBP	SH	SF	SO	SB	CS	SLG	OBP
Alcantara, Elisandro	R-R	6-0	175	10-29-02	.136	.200	.114	29	59	16	8	0	0	0	2	7	2	1	0	26	4	1	.136	.250
Betancourt, Bryant	L-R	5-11	170	10-12-03	.262	.364	.250	39	107	15	28	5	2	1	14	17	1	2	4	12	1	2	.374	.357
Bugarin, Jesus	R-R	5-10	180	12-2-01	.339	.450	.324	51	165	37	56	6	0	4	31	18	6	0	2	25	14	10	.448	.419
Carlito, Jairold	L-R	6-0	150	4-21-02	.171	.250	.162	20	41	7	7	0	0	0	4	9	1	0	0	19	0	0	.171	.333
Castillo, Juan	R-R	6-0	170	1-16-03	.255	.185	.273	34	104	13	26	2	0	1	10	5	0	1	0	26	5	1	.298	.284
Colina, Jose	B-R	5-8	155	2-25-04	.087	.200	.073	19	46	10	4	0	0	0	1	9	1	0	0	17	3	1	.087	.250
Cruz, Fadriel	L-R	5-10	170	11-12-00	.288	.387	.259	48	139	25	40	8	2	3	21	25	0	4	0	31	21	5	.439	.396
Fernandez, Yanquiel	L-L	6-2	198	1-1-03	.333	.289	.345	54	177	29	59	17	0	6	34	22	1	0	2	26	0	0	.531	.406

Batter	B-T	HT	WT	DOB	AVG	vLH	vRH	G	AB	R	H	2B	3B	HR	RBI	BB	HBP	SH	SF	SO	SB	CS	SLG	OBP
Garcia, Francisco	R-R	6-0	190	11-10-02	.267	.176	.276	57	180	33	48	12	0	6	35	15	11	0	1	54	7	2	.433	.357
Gil, Gabriel	R-R	5-10	173	3-9-01	.225	.300	.214	32	80	13	18	4	1	1	8	13	0	2	0	18	0	2	.338	.333
Gomez, Esneider	R-R	5-11	185	9-18-02	.264	.250	.267	51	163	24	43	4	0	4	22	4	8	0	0	24	2	1	.362	.314
Guerra, Jorluis	R-R	5-11	165	1-11-04	.181	.000	.194	30	72	16	13	5	0	0	4	7	3	0	0	13	2	0	.250	.280
Hernandez, Sandry	R-R	5-11	155	2-28-03	.315	.295	.321	54	184	42	58	11	1	0	10	20	7	3	0	33	24	5	.386	.403
James, Michael	L-R	5-11	170	12-4-01	.148	.118	.156	30	81	13	12	0	0	3	18	8	5	0	1	32	3	2	.259	.263
Mendez, Luis	L-R	5-11	157	10-30-02	.263	.211	.269	58	194	36	51	10	4	5	41	22	6	0	2	48	12	6	.433	.353
Mendoza, Robert	B-R	6-0	175	10-9-01	.273	.250	.280	27	66	7	18	3	0	2	15	11	2	0	0	18	1	0	.409	.392
Mota, Pedro	R-R	6-1	160	9-24-01	.245	.182	.263	37	102	19	25	8	0	2	10	13	7	3	0	32	1	3	.382	.369
Novas, Ronny	L-R	5-10	165	11-20-00	.232	.333	.221	38	95	19	22	4	1	0	10	10	0	0	2	28	8	3	.295	.299
Oferman, Justin	B-R	5-10	145	1-12-01	.203	.273	.175	27	79	8	16	4	1	0	17	11	3	2	2	19	4	1	.278	.316
Paiva, Moises	R-R	5-7	150	3-11-03	.262	.150	.297	37	84	18	22	1	1	0	6	10	3	4	0	14	6	2	.298	.361
Palma, Francisco	L-L	5-11	165	7-4-01	.118	.000	.133	7	17	3	2	1	0	0	2	4	2	0	0	3	0	0	.176	.348
Paredes, Luis	L-L	5-10	170	3-21-04	.299	.336	.297	55	177	28	53	9	2	7	24	23	3	0	2	47	7	4	.492	.385
Perez, Andy	L-R	6-3	165	6-3-04	.291	.279	.295	52	175	30	51	5	3	0	28	13	2	3	5	26	11	7	.354	.338
Perez, Jean	R-R	5-10	178	7-20-02	.400	.125	.529	8	25	3	10	1	0	1	3	1	1	1	0	8	0	2	.560	.444
Pinto, Adrian	R-R	5-6	156	9-22-02	.360	.333	.363	54	175	64	63	15	4	3	27	38	7	2	2	18	41	8	.543	.486
Rada, Oswal	R-R	6-1	200	2-17-03	.211	.100	.224	35	95	9	20	7	0	2	18	3	5	5	2	22	1	1	.347	.267
Ramos, Gerard	R-R	6-3	175	1-19-01	.272	.270	.273	50	158	21	43	12	0	9	27	11	2	1	0	45	0	0	.519	.327
Rodriguez, David	R-R	6-3	190	7-25-04	.288	.188	.316	24	73	12	21	3	0	1	9	5	1	0	2	17	0	1	.370	.333
Tena, Felix	R-R	6-0	196	9-27-03	.294	.333	.289	43	126	13	37	7	1	2	18	4	5	1	1	32	4	4	.413	.338
Terrero, Gabriel	L-R	6-3	169	12-21-03	.289	.357	.281	45	135	29	39	7	1	0	20	18	2	2	0	35	6	2	.356	.381

Pitching	B-T	HT	WT	DOB	W	L	ERA	G	GS	CG	SV	IP	H	R	ER	HR	BB	SO	AVG	vLH	vRH	K/9	BB/9
Barbosa, Gabriel	R-R	6-0	165	1-22-02	3	2	2.20	13	9	0	0	45	31	17	11	2	4	37	.188	.246	.154	7.40	0.80
Barcenas, Jose	R-R	6-0	180	9-7-02	2	1	3.71	12	4	0	0	17	15	8	7	2	12	9	.238	.200	.263	4.76	6.35
Benavides, Cristian	R-R	6-3	175	1-15-04	1	1	4.50	8	0	0	0	10	12	6	5	1	7	5	.324	.176	.450	4.50	6.30
Borges, Juan	R-R	6-2	160	1-6-98	0	1	2.66	8	5	0	0	20	19	7	6	0	4	19	.250	.188	.295	8.41	1.77
Brioso, Cristian	R-R	6-0	188	6-14-01	2	0	3.26	15	0	0	0	19	17	10	7	1	7	20	.230	.286	.196	9.31	3.26
Cabrera, Jerald	R-R	6-1	185	8-26-01	5	3	6.04	17	0	0	1	22	16	19	15	2	9	24	.193	.172	.204	9.67	3.63
Chivilli, Angel	R-R	6-2	162	7-28-02	0	3	3.49	11	8	0	0	39	37	18	15	1	8	45	.253	.204	.278	10.47	1.86
Cruz, Rony	R-R	6-1	196	3-3-04	2	0	2.31	17	0	0	3	23	13	8	6	2	12	33	.163	.118	.196	12.73	4.63
Feliciano, Janer	R-R	6-3	220	8-8-01	1	2	6.75	21	0	0	4	19	16	19	14	1	15	17	.225	.136	.265	8.20	7.23
Fernandez, Wuardo	R-R	6-1	168	12-14-00	2	0	0.82	13	12	0	0	44	28	8	4	0	15	37	.187	.176	.192	7.63	3.09
Flores, Jose	R-R	6-0	170	12-30-03	0	0	27.00	1	0	0	0	1	3	3	3	0	2	0	.000	.000	--	0.00	54.00
Galva, Claudio	R-R	6-3	176	10-13-03	3	1	1.89	12	7	0	0	38	28	13	8	1	8	40	.201	.153	.238	9.47	1.89
Garcia, Kevin	L-L	6-0	170	11-25-99	3	1	1.69	13	8	0	0	37	24	11	7	1	11	42	.185	.100	.200	10.13	2.65
George, Aneudis	R-R	6-1	172	9-27-03	2	2	3.91	13	1	0	0	23	26	14	10	2	8	18	.292	.323	.276	7.04	3.13
Gomez, Redinson	R-R	6-2	170	7-26-04	1	2	3.38	12	6	0	0	27	15	13	10	2	10	18	.158	.200	.120	6.08	3.38
Herrera, Welinton	L-L	6-0	166	4-3-04	2	0	5.16	18	0	0	1	23	17	14	13	1	11	28	.200	.263	.185	11.12	4.37
Juarez, Victor	R-R	6-0	173	6-19-03	2	0	0.68	7	6	0	0	27	11	4	2	0	6	34	.122	.069	.148	11.48	2.03
Luciano, Ismael	R-R	6-0	170	3-14-02	2	3	7.36	16	3	0	1	22	25	20	18	6	9	24	.287	.333	.255	9.82	3.68
Mena, Bryan	R-R	6-2	185	6-14-04	0	0	1.57	13	2	0	1	34	21	6	6	1	10	35	.169	.132	.186	9.17	2.62
Moron, Wilny	R-R	6-0	175	12-28-00	3	0	3.86	12	0	0	1	14	14	8	6	1	7	16	.255	.200	.286	10.29	4.50
Ochoa, Nelvis	R-R	5-10	158	5-18-00	3	1	3.79	8	1	0	0	19	20	9	8	0	3	15	.267	.273	.264	7.11	1.42
Olivares, Manuel	R-R	5-11	145	12-4-01	5	1	2.23	11	7	0	0	44	31	14	11	2	12	32	.196	.174	.205	6.50	2.44
Pacheco, Alberto	L-L	6-1	176	11-29-02	4	1	2.93	11	11	1	0	46	37	16	15	3	9	51	.222	.273	.214	9.98	1.76
Perdomo, Alan	R-R	6-4	150	8-24-01	1	4	3.78	11	6	0	0	33	33	17	14	2	6	33	.264	.265	.264	8.91	1.62
Perez, Bryan	R-R	6-2	167	9-8-03	0	1	2.78	11	9	0	0	32	27	13	10	3	10	35	.225	.217	.230	9.74	2.78
Perez, Carlos	R-R	6-3	161	7-17-01	1	0	2.13	10	1	0	2	13	7	5	3	1	4	16	.163	.125	.185	11.37	2.84
Pichardo, Rodery	R-R	6-0	150	10-24-01	0	0	18.00	1	0	0	0	1	2	2	2	1	0	1	.400	.000	.667	9.00	0.00
Pio, Enmanuel	R-R	5-11	145	4-11-00	2	2	5.19	19	0	0	1	17	21	13	10	1	11	15	.276	.240	.294	7.79	5.71
Ramirez, Felix	L-L	6-3	200	9-26-00	1	0	0.00	5	0	0	1	5	3	1	0	0	0	4	.167	.333	.133	7.71	0.00
Rebolledo, Jose	R-R	5-11	195	4-7-03	1	3	9.53	5	0	0	1	6	10	8	6	3	2	10	.435	.571	.375	15.88	3.18
Rivera, Francis	R-R	6-4	160	9-14-00	0	0	7.20	6	0	0	3	5	5	4	4		4	6	.278	.000	.385	10.80	7.20
Rudecindo, Isaac	R-R	6-2	210	1-27-01	3	0	3.72	21	0	0	9	19	20	10	8	1	15	19	.270	.214	.304	8.84	6.98
Ruiz, Wilker	L-L	6-0	150	3-11-02	4	0	1.86	14	0	0	0	19	16	5	4	0	13	20	.242	.167	.271	9.31	6.05
Sanchez, Sergio	R-R	6-0	180	1-13-01	0	0	0.00	3	0	0	0	5	1	0	0	0	2	8	.103	.000	.154	15.43	3.86
Sanchez, Stalyn	R-R	6-1	161	7-10-00	3	3	3.86	19	0	0	4	30	30	20	13	3	13	38	.246	.250	.244	11.27	3.86
Valencia, Angel	R-R	6-4	165	6-16-02	3	1	2.08	13	0	0	1	26	16	13	6	3	14	29	.172	.194	.161	10.04	4.85
Vargas, Jordy	R-R	6-3	153	11-6-03	2	0	1.30	11	9	0	0	35	18	8	5	0	16	46	.145	.121	.154	11.94	4.15
Vargas, Juan	R-R	6-0	190	10-10-00	2	2	2.73	15	3	0	0	26	27	14	8	0	12	19	.267	.216	.297	6.49	4.10
Zamora, Martin	L-L	5-11	170	11-3-01	1	0	12.27	4	0	0	0	4	8	5	5	2	2	2	.471	.200	.583	4.91	4.91

Fielding

C: Betancourt 12, Castillo 29, Gil 29, Mendoza 22, Rada 24, Rodriguez 12.
1B: Betancourt 24, Carlito 1, Fernandez 1, Garcia 1, Gomez 1, Guerra 8, Mendoza 1, Mota 9, Perez 2, Rada 11, Ramos 50, Terrero 18.
2B: Colina 11, Guerra 7, Mendez 8, Mota 10, Oferman 16, Paiva 30, Perez 7, Pinto 35, Terrero 2.
3B: Colina 4, Garcia 43, Gomez 50, Guerra 13, Mota 6, Oferman 6, Terrero 5.
SS: Mendez 45, Mota 7, Oferman 2, Perez 49, Perez 1, Pinto 12, Terrero 4.
OF: Alcantara 25, Bugarin 54, Carlito 14, Colina 1, Cruz 48, Fernandez 43, Hernandez 53, James 16, Novas 32, Palma 2, Paredes 49, Pinto 5, Tena 43.

COLORADO ROCKIES

Detroit Tigers

SEASON IN A SENTENCE: Mediocrity continued for the Tigers, who had their fifth straight losing season and missed the playoffs for the seventh year in a row, though young pitching in the organization gave a glimpse of hope for the team's future.

HIGH POINT: After a rough April, the Tigers went 69-66 the rest of the season, which isn't exactly a championship-caliber team but is a marked improvement from where they were in 2020 and 2019. Their top young pitchers showed plenty of promising signs, with righthander Casey Mize posting a 3.71 ERA in 150.1 innings and lefthander Tarik Skubal striking out 164 in 149.1 innings. Third baseman Jeimer Candelario was the bright spot on offense, hitting .271/.351/.443 in 149 games.

LOW POINT: What little hopes the Tigers had to be a playoff contender in 2021 quickly disappeared as they went 8-19 in April. Starting on April 15, the Tigers went on a stretch where they lost 18 of their next 21 games, dropping them to 9-24 and 9.5 games back in the American League Central by May 7.

NOTABLE ROOKIES: Center fielder Akil Baddoo turned into one of the most productive Rule 5 picks in recent years. Baddoo, plucked from the Twins system, hit .259/.330/.436 in 124 games as a 22-year-old, immediately stepping in as one of Detroit's best hitters. Mize, Skubal and righthander Matt Manning all had their ups and downs but showed hope for the future of the team's starting rotation. Catcher Eric Haase, a 2011 draft pick and 28-year-old rookie, didn't get on base much but hit for power with 22 home runs and a .231/.286/.459 line in 98 games.

KEY TRANSACTIONS: Getting Baddoo in the Rule 5 draft proved to be an astute decision. So was the two-year, $10 million deal they gave in the offseason to outfielder Robbie Grossman, who hit .239/.357/.415 with 23 home runs in 156 games to become one of Detroit's top hitters. The Tigers signed righthander Wily Peralta to a minor league deal before the season and he turned in a 3.07 ERA in 93.2 innings as a starter.

OPENING DAY SALARY: $80,398,600 (23rd).

PLAYERS OF THE YEAR

MAJOR LEAGUE	MINOR LEAGUE
Casey Mize	**Spencer Torkelson**
RHP	**1B/3B**
7-9, 3.71	(AAA/AA/High-A)
118 SO in 150.1 IP	.267/.383/.552,
1.14 WHIP, 114 ERA+	30 HR, 77 BB

ORGANIZATION LEADERS

Batting		*Minimum 250 AB
MAJORS		
*AVG	Harold Castros	.283
*OPS	Jeimer Candelario	.795
HR	Robbie Grossman	23
RBI	Jonathan Schoop	84
MINORS		
*AVG	Riley Greene, Toledo, Erie	.301
*OBP	Jacob Robson, Toledo, Erie	.417
*SLG	Josh Lester, Toledo, Erie	.587
*OPS	Spencer Torkelson, Toledo, Erie, West Michigan	.935
R	Riley Greene, Toledo, Erie	95
R	Ryan Kreidler, Toledo, Erie	95
H	Riley Greene, Toledo, Erie	146
TB	Riley Greene, Toledo, Erie	259
2B	Gage Workman, West Michigan, Lakeland	37
3B	Riley Greene, Toledo, Erie	8
HR	Josh Lester, Toledo, Erie	32
RBI	Aderlin Rodriguez, Toledo	94
BB	Spencer Torkelson, Toledo, Erie, West Michigan	77
SO	Ryan Kreidler, Toledo, Erie	158
SB	Eric De La Rosa, Erie, West Michigan, Lakeland	34

Pitching		#Minimum 75 IP
MAJORS		
W	Tarik Skubal	8
#ERA	Wily Peralta	3.07
SO	Tarik Skubal	164
SV	Gregory Soto	18
MINORS		
W	Ricardo Pinto, Toledo, Erie	14
L	Carlos Guzman, Lakeland	9
L	Brendan White, West Michigan	9
#ERA	Garrett Hill, Erie, West Michigan	2.74
G	Zack Hess, Erie, West Michigan	45
G	Jared Tobey, West Michigan	45
GS	Pedro Payano, Toledo, Erie	24
SV	Zack Hess, Erie, West Michigan	13
IP	Pedro Payano, Erie, Toledo	124
BB	Pedro Payano, Erie, Toledo	68
SO	Mark Leiter Jr., Erie, Toledo	145
#AVG	Austin Bergner, West Michigan, Lakeland	.211

General Manager: Al Avila. **Farm Director:** Dave Littlefield. **Scouting Director:** Scott Pleis.

Class	Team	League	W	L	PCT	Finish	Manager
Majors	Detroit Tigers	American	77	85	.475	t-10th (15)	A.J. Hinch
Triple-A	Toledo Mud Hens	Triple-A East	74	56	.569	6th (20)	Tom Prince
Double-A	Erie SeaWolves	Double-A Northeast	64	55	.538	5th (12)	Arnie Beyeler
High-A	West Michigan Whitecaps	High-A Central	58	62	.483	t-7th (12)	Brayan Pena
Low-A	Lakeland Flying Tigers	Low-A Southeast	55	63	.466	8th (10)	Andrew Graham
Rookie	DSL Tigers	Dominican Summer	23	36	.390	t-38th (46)	Ramon Zapata
Rookie	FCL Tigers East	Florida Complex	19	32	.373	15th (18)	Gary Cathcart
Rookie	FCL Tigers West	Florida Complex	18	33	.353	17th (18)	Ryan Minor

Overall 2021 Minor League Record 311 337 .480 20th (30)

ORGANIZATION STATISTICS

DETROIT TIGERS
AMERICAN LEAGUE

Batting	B-T	HT	WT	DOB	AVG	vLH	vRH	G	AB	R	H	2B	3B	HR	RBI	BB	HBP	SH	SF	SO	SB	CS	SLG	OBP
Baddoo, Akil	L-L	6-1	214	8-16-98	.259	.214	.273	124	413	60	107	20	7	13	55	45	0	0	3	122	18	4	.436	.330
Cabrera, Miguel	R-R	6-4	267	4-18-83	.256	.269	.251	130	472	48	121	16	0	15	75	40	5	0	9	118	0	0	.386	.316
Cameron, Daz	R-R	6-2	185	1-15-97	.194	.175	.206	35	103	16	20	5	0	4	13	10	2	0	0	38	6	0	.359	.278
Candelario, Jeimer	B-R	6-1	216	11-24-93	.271	.273	.270	149	557	75	151	42	3	16	67	65	4	0	0	135	0	0	.443	.351
Castro, Harold	L-R	5-10	195	11-30-93	.283	.214	.293	106	315	35	89	13	1	3	37	14	1	4	5	72	1	1	.359	.310
Castro, Willi	R-R	6-1	206	4-24-97	.220	.281	.193	125	413	56	91	15	6	9	38	23	8	3	3	109	9	4	.351	.273
Garneau, Dustin	R-R	6-2	205	8-13-87	.210	.250	.190	20	62	9	13	5	0	6	11	3	1	0	2	18	0	0	.581	.250
Goodrum, Niko	B-R	6-3	215	2-28-92	.214	.274	.185	90	290	39	62	11	2	9	33	29	4	0	2	107	14	5	.359	.292
Greiner, Grayson	R-R	6-6	238	10-11-92	.236	.208	.250	31	72	7	17	4	0	1	7	9	0	1	0	31	0	0	.333	.321
Grossman, Robbie	B-L	6-0	209	9-16-89	.239	.279	.221	156	557	88	133	23	3	23	67	98	8	2	6	155	20	5	.415	.357
Haase, Eric	R-R	5-10	210	12-18-92	.231	.283	.203	98	351	48	81	12	1	22	61	26	2	0	2	119	2	0	.459	.286
Hill, Derek	R-R	6-2	190	12-30-95	.259	.311	.218	49	139	19	36	3	3	3	14	10	1	0	0	42	6	3	.388	.313
Jones, JaCoby	R-R	6-2	211	5-10-92	.170	.150	.183	36	100	9	17	2	0	2	9	5	0	0	0	42	2	2	.250	.210
Mazara, Nomar	L-L	6-4	224	4-26-95	.212	.095	.229	50	165	12	35	5	2	3	19	15	0	0	1	45	0	0	.321	.276
Nunez, Renato	R-R	6-1	220	4-4-94	.189	.100	.209	14	53	7	10	3	0	4	7	1	1	0	0	16	0	0	.472	.218
Paredes, Isaac	R-R	5-11	213	2-18-99	.208	.286	.159	23	72	7	15	3	1	1	5	10	1	0	2	11	0	0	.319	.306
Ramos, Wilson	R-R	6-1	241	8-10-87	.200	.111	.226	35	120	12	24	5	0	6	13	6	0	0	0	29	0	0	.392	.238
	2-team total (9 Cleveland)				.205	.175	.216	44	151	15	31	5	0	8	20	9	0	0	1	36	0	0	.397	.248
Reyes, Victor	B-R	6-5	194	10-5-94	.258	.323	.229	76	209	26	54	10	4	5	22	8	0	2	1	55	5	1	.416	.284
Robson, Jacob	L-R	5-10	182	11-20-94	.000	--	.000	4	7	1	0	0	0	0	0	0	0	0	0	4	0	0	.000	.000
Rogers, Jake	R-R	6-1	201	4-18-95	.239	.256	.229	38	113	17	27	5	3	6	17	11	0	3	0	46	1	0	.496	.306
Schoop, Jonathan	R-R	6-1	247	10-16-91	.278	.333	.256	156	623	85	173	30	1	22	84	37	6	0	8	133	2	0	.435	.320
Short, Zack	R-R	5-10	180	5-29-95	.141	.134	.146	61	156	21	22	4	0	6	20	22	0	0	6	59	2	0	.282	.239

Pitching	B-T	HT	WT	DOB	W	L	ERA	G	GS	CG	SV	IP	H	R	ER	HR	BB	SO	AVG	vLH	vRH	K/9	BB/9
Alexander, Tyler	R-L	6-2	203	7-14-94	2	4	3.81	41	15	0	0	106	106	47	45	16	28	87	.255	.193	.272	7.36	2.37
Boyd, Matthew	L-L	6-3	223	2-2-91	3	8	3.89	15	15	0	0	79	77	37	34	9	23	67	.255	.270	.250	7.67	2.63
Burrows, Beau	R-R	6-2	210	9-18-96	0	0	21.60	1	0	0	0	2	2	4	4	0	2	3	.286	.000	.500	16.20	10.80
	2-team total (5 Minnesota)				0	1	13.91	6	1	0	0	11	16	18	17	5	10	8	.364	.267	.414	6.55	8.18
Carlton, Drew	R-R	6-1	215	9-8-95	0	0	4.91	4	0	0	0	4	6	2	2	1	4	1	.429	.500	.375	2.45	9.82
Castro, Harold	L-R	5-10	195	11-30-93	0	0	0.00	3	0	0	0	3	0	0	0	0	0	3	.000	.000	.000	0.00	10.13
Cisnero, Jose	R-R	6-3	258	4-11-89	4	4	3.65	67	0	0	4	62	51	34	25	6	31	62	.226	.260	.208	9.05	4.52
Del Pozo, Miguel	L-L	6-1	205	10-14-92	0	0	3.38	5	0	0	0	5	8	2	2	0	2	4	.348	.200	.462	6.75	3.38
Farmer, Buck	L-R	6-4	232	2-20-91	0	0	6.37	36	0	0	0	35	40	25	25	9	21	37	.278	.298	.268	9.42	5.35
Foley, Jason	R-R	6-4	215	11-1-95	0	0	2.61	11	0	0	0	8	8	3	3	1	5	6	.216	.077	.292	5.23	4.35
Fulmer, Michael	R-R	6-3	224	3-15-93	5	6	2.97	52	4	0	14	70	69	27	23	7	20	73	.256	.190	.309	9.43	2.58
Funkhouser, Kyle	R-R	6-3	229	3-16-94	7	4	3.42	57	2	0	1	68	58	32	26	6	38	63	.229	.248	.216	8.30	5.00
Garcia, Bryan	R-R	6-1	205	4-19-95	3	2	7.55	39	0	0	2	39	48	38	33	10	25	32	.294	.364	.247	7.32	5.72
Garcia, Rony	R-R	6-3	200	12-19-97	0	0	2.45	2	0	0	0	4	1	1	1	0	2	2	.100	.333	.000	4.91	4.91
Holland, Derek	B-L	6-2	223	10-9-86	3	2	5.07	39	1	0	0	50	58	29	28	6	20	51	.287	.257	.305	9.24	3.62
Hutchison, Drew	L-R	6-3	215	8-22-90	3	1	2.11	9	2	0	0	21	20	11	5	1	11	10	.260	.200	.298	4.22	4.64
Jimenez, Joe	R-R	6-3	277	1-17-95	6	1	5.96	52	0	0	1	45	34	33	30	6	35	57	.206	.219	.198	11.32	6.95
Krol, Ian	L-L	6-1	210	5-9-91	0	0	4.34	18	0	0	0	19	23	10	9	2	8	18	.303	.304	.302	8.68	3.86
Lange, Alex	R-R	6-3	202	10-2-95	1	3	4.04	36	0	0	1	36	37	18	16	5	16	39	.259	.239	.276	9.84	4.04
Manning, Matt	R-R	6-6	195	1-28-98	4	7	5.80	18	18	0	0	85	96	59	55	10	33	57	.279	.253	.301	6.01	3.48
Mize, Casey	R-R	6-3	212	5-1-97	7	9	3.71	30	30	1	0	150	130	64	62	24	41	118	.234	.256	.215	7.06	2.45
Norris, Daniel	L-L	6-2	207	4-25-93	1	3	5.89	38	0	0	1	37	38	25	24	4	15	40	.271	.200	.333	9.82	3.68
Peralta, Wily	R-R	6-1	255	5-8-89	4	5	3.07	19	18	0	0	94	87	41	32	12	38	58	.247	.192	.300	5.57	3.65
Ramirez, Erasmo	R-R	6-0	220	5-2-90	1	1	5.74	17	0	0	0	27	24	17	17	4	5	20	.238	.324	.188	6.75	1.69
Rogers, Jake	R-R	6-1	201	4-18-95	0	0	18.00	1	0	0	0	1	2	2	2	0	1	0	.400	.500	.000	0.00	9.00
Skubal, Tarik	R-L	6-3	240	11-20-96	8	12	4.34	31	29	0	0	149	141	76	72	35	47	164	.245	.264	.240	9.88	2.83
Soto, Gregory	L-L	6-1	234	2-11-95	6	3	3.39	62	0	0	18	64	46	30	24	7	40	76	.198	.183	.205	10.74	5.65
Teheran, Julio	R-R	6-2	205	1-27-91	1	0	1.80	1	1	0	0	5	4	1	1	1	3	3	.235	.231	.250	5.40	5.40

DETROIT TIGERS

| Turnbull, Spencer | R-R | 6-3 | 210 | 9-18-92 | 4 | 2 | 2.88 | 9 | 9 | 1 | 0 | 50 | 37 | 18 | 16 | 2 | 12 | 44 | .203 | .176 | .231 | 7.92 | 2.16 |
| Urena, Jose | R-R | 6-2 | 208 | 9-12-91 | 4 | 8 | 5.81 | 26 | 18 | 0 | 0 | 101 | 119 | 70 | 65 | 14 | 42 | 67 | .292 | .325 | .261 | 5.99 | 3.75 |

Fielding

Catcher	PCT	G	PO	A	E	DP	PB
Garneau	.987	20	142	9	2	1	3
Greiner	.990	31	201	7	2	0	3
Haase	.990	66	487	23	5	3	7
Ramos	1.000	25	171	7	0	1	2
Rogers	.997	37	289	17	1	3	3

First Base	PCT	G	PO	A	E	DP
Cabrera	.997	44	312	26	1	34
Castro	1.000	15	59	4	0	5
Goodrum	.000	1	0	0	0	0
Haase	1.000	1	2	0	0	0
Nunez	1.000	8	72	5	0	8
Schoop	.992	114	826	58	7	79

Second Base	PCT	G	PO	A	E	DP
Castro	.992	33	52	69	1	19

	PCT	G	PO	A	E	DP
Castro	.978	91	141	211	8	47
Goodrum	1.000	9	8	21	0	5
Paredes	.978	10	15	30	1	6
Schoop	.984	38	85	95	3	26
Short	.917	2	3	8	1	2

Third Base	PCT	G	PO	A	E	DP
Candelario	.976	142	91	273	9	30
Castro	.938	12	9	21	2	5
Paredes	1.000	8	10	10	0	2
Rogers	.000	1	0	0	0	0
Schoop	1.000	1	0	1	0	1
Short	1.000	3	1	3	0	0

Shortstop	PCT	G	PO	A	E	DP
Castro	1.000	43	34	83	0	12
Castro	.968	20	25	35	2	8

Goodrum	.969	66	77	175	8	37
Paredes	.938	5	3	12	1	2
Short	.982	52	56	159	4	30

Outfield	PCT	G	PO	A	E	DP
Baddoo	.988	127	252	4	3	1
Cameron	1.000	34	62	0	0	0
Castro	1.000	5	4	0	0	0
Castro	1.000	10	16	1	0	0
Goodrum	.947	15	18	0	1	0
Grossman	1.000	155	268	1	0	1
Haase	.968	22	29	1	1	0
Hill	.990	45	100	3	1	1
Jones	1.000	32	74	0	0	0
Mazara	.957	41	65	1	3	0
Reyes	.992	64	115	2	1	0
Robson	1.000	4	2	0	0	0

TOLEDO MUD HENS
TRIPLE-A
TRIPLE-A EAST

Batting	B-T	HT	WT	DOB	AVG	vLH	vRH	G	AB	R	H	2B	3B	HR	RBI	BB	HBP	SH	SF	SO	SB	CS	SLG	OBP
Baddoo, Akil	L-L	6-1	214	8-16-98	.143	.000	.167	4	14	2	2	1	0	0	2	4	0	0	0	5	1	0	.214	.333
Cameron, Daz	R-R	6-2	185	1-15-97	.296	.303	.292	39	162	33	48	11	2	6	23	15	3	0	1	39	7	3	.500	.365
Castro, Willi	B-R	6-1	206	4-24-97	.391	.500	.368	5	23	7	9	2	0	1	2	0	0	0	0	2	2	0	.609	.391
Centeno, Juan	L-R	5-9	195	11-16-89	.277	.333	.250	53	166	15	46	9	1	1	17	14	0	1	0	25	0	0	.361	.333
Clemens, Kody	L-R	6-1	170	5-15-96	.247	.264	.239	97	369	66	91	15	6	18	59	36	2	0	6	94	4	1	.466	.312
Garneau, Dustin	R-R	6-2	205	8-13-87	.176	.200	.161	17	51	8	9	1	0	4	9	7	1	0	1	20	0	0	.431	.283
Gonzalez, Yariel	R-R	6-1	190	6-1-94	.259	.233	.271	78	263	45	68	10	0	14	51	27	1	0	4	65	0	2	.456	.325
Goodrum, Niko	B-R	6-3	215	2-28-92	.185	.400	.136	14	54	7	10	0	0	0	2	7	0	0	1	16	1	0	.185	.274
Greene, Riley	L-L	6-3	200	9-28-00	.308	.318	.304	40	159	36	49	9	3	8	30	22	3	0	1	51	4	0	.553	.400
Greiner, Grayson	R-R	6-6	238	10-11-92	.202	.200	.202	33	119	9	24	6	0	1	9	13	1	0	1	49	0	0	.277	.284
Haase, Eric	R-R	5-10	210	12-18-92	.348	.222	.429	7	23	3	8	3	0	1	5	5	0	0	0	10	1	0	.609	.464
Hill, Derek	R-R	6-2	190	12-30-95	.320	.375	.301	34	125	21	40	5	3	4	15	10	2	3	1	39	4	1	.504	.377
Jones, JaCoby	R-R	6-2	211	5-10-92	.230	.242	.224	73	269	31	62	14	0	7	26	28	4	0	0	103	1	2	.361	.312
Kreidler, Ryan	R-R	6-4	208	11-12-97	.304	.306	.303	41	135	28	41	8	0	7	22	24	1	0	2	39	5	2	.519	.407
Lester, Josh	L-R	6-3	180	7-17-94	.216	.130	.246	25	88	9	19	4	0	7	13	7	0	0	0	19	0	0	.500	.274
Mazara, Nomar	L-L	6-4	224	4-26-95	.167	.000	.286	3	12	2	2	0	0	1	2	1	0	0	0	5	0	0	.417	.231
Nunez, Renato	R-R	6-1	220	4-4-94	.291	.262	.304	74	265	59	77	14	2	20	64	31	11	0	4	76	1	0	.585	.383
2-team total (21 Nashville)					.268	.245	.279	95	332	66	89	16	2	21	68	37	13	0	4	93	1	0	.518	.360
Paredes, Isaac	R-R	5-11	213	2-18-99	.265	.298	.249	72	253	39	67	10	2	11	42	56	2	0	4	47	0	0	.451	.397
Peterson, Cole	L-R	5-11	160	8-2-95	.199	.115	.235	58	171	23	34	8	4	0	13	14	2	1	3	29	7	2	.292	.263
Pinero, Daniel	R-R	6-5	210	5-2-94	.200	.222	.190	11	30	6	6	4	0	1	5	6	1	0	1	9	0	0	.433	.342
Policelli, Brady	R-R	5-10	195	6-24-95	.101	.030	.132	37	109	9	11	3	0	2	13	11	0	1	0	41	1	0	.183	.183
Proctor, Christopher	L-R	6-1	175	3-8-97	.206	.357	.100	15	34	6	7	0	0	0	3	1	0	0	0	13	0	0	.206	.229
Reyes, Victor	R-R	6-5	194	10-5-94	.385	.357	.391	20	78	13	30	7	2	1	10	10	2	0	1	17	5	2	.564	.462
Robson, Jacob	L-R	5-10	182	11-20-94	.259	.262	.259	78	239	37	62	10	3	5	28	46	3	0	0	104	15	9	.389	.385
Rodriguez, Aderlin	R-R	6-3	210	11-18-91	.290	.256	.305	116	434	67	126	26	3	29	94	42	7	0	0	127	1	1	.565	.362
Rogers, Jake	R-R	6-1	201	4-18-95	.000	--	.000	1	3	1	0	0	0	0	0	1	0	0	0	3	0	0	.000	.250
Rosa, Dylan	R-R	6-2	200	6-27-96	.240	.167	.281	19	50	8	12	5	1	0	2	1	2	0	0	19	0	0	.380	.283
Rosoff, Jon	L-R	5-9	175	11-14-94	.083	.250	.000	10	24	4	2	0	0	0	2	6	1	1	0	12	1	0	.083	.290
Short, Zack	R-R	5-10	180	5-23-95	.236	.265	.222	46	157	30	37	7	0	9	29	33	7	0	1	47	2	1	.452	.389
Stewart, Christin	L-R	6-0	220	12-10-93	.254	.220	.267	89	303	51	77	13	5	21	58	33	6	0	0	100	2	1	.538	.339
Torkelson, Spencer	R-R	6-1	220	8-26-99	.238	.279	.221	40	147	35	35	8	1	11	27	23	4	0	3	36	1	0	.531	.350

Pitching	B-T	HT	WT	DOB	W	L	ERA	G	GS	CG	SV	IP	H	R	ER	HR	BB	SO	AVG	vLH	vRH	K/9	BB/9
Bass, Brad	R-R	6-6	250	2-15-96	0	0	0.00	2	0	0	0	2	1	0	0	1	2	.143	.500	.000	9.00	4.50	
Blackwood, Nolan	R-R	6-5	185	3-16-95	5	0	4.92	37	2	0	1	60	62	40	33	5	23	51	.257	.297	.229	7.61	3.43
Boyd, Matthew	L-L	6-3	223	2-2-91	0	0	0.00	3	3	0	0	9	5	0	0	0	11	.161	.000	.217	10.61	0.00	
Burrows, Beau	R-R	6-2	210	9-18-96	1	1	6.23	9	1	0	0	17	21	12	12	4	6	17	.296	.313	.282	8.83	3.12
2-team total (13 St. Paul)					4	6	5.10	22	10	0	0	65	60	39	37	14	28	65	.236	.261	.215	8.95	3.86
Carlton, Drew	R-R	6-1	215	9-8-95	3	3	2.92	33	2	0	4	52	46	22	17	5	10	49	.232	.244	.224	8.43	1.72
De Jesus, Angel	R-R	6-4	200	2-13-97	3	4	4.21	35	2	0	5	51	32	27	24	7	32	62	.176	.150	.196	10.87	5.61
DeCaster, Ethan	R-R	6-3	190	10-27-94	0	0	7.71	4	0	0	0	5	7	4	4	0	2	5	.333	.600	.250	9.64	3.86
Del Pozo, Miguel	L-L	6-1	205	10-14-92	1	3	2.82	34	0	0	4	38	22	12	12	6	16	54	.161	.131	.184	12.68	3.76
Farmer, Buck	L-R	6-4	232	2-20-91	0	2	3.97	9	0	0	0	11	11	5	5	0	4	7	.256	.368	.167	5.56	3.18
Foley, Jason	R-R	6-4	215	11-1-95	1	1	4.41	32	0	0	2	35	34	18	17	5	19	36	.264	.375	.178	9.35	4.93
Fulmer, Michael	R-R	6-3	224	3-15-93	0	0	0.00	2	1	0	0	2	1	0	0	2	1	.167	.000	.333	9.00	9.00	
Garcia, Bryan	R-R	6-1	205	4-19-95	0	1	5.40	19	0	0	1	23	25	15	14	3	8	19	.266	.256	.273	7.33	3.09
Garcia, Rony	R-R	6-3	200	12-19-97	0	1	3.20	4	4	0	0	20	13	7	7	4	10	24	.183	.216	.147	10.98	4.58
Holland, Derek	B-L	6-2	223	10-9-86	0	0	6.75	4	1	0	0	4	5	3	3	2	3	4	.333	.625	.000	9.00	6.75

DETROIT TIGERS

Pitching	B-T	HT	WT	DOB	W	L	ERA	G	GS	CG	SV	IP	H	R	ER	HR	BB	SO	AVG	vLH	vRH	K/9	BB/9
Hutchison, Drew	L-R	6-3	215	8-22-90	8	3	3.77	19	19	0	0	88	78	42	37	8	41	89	.236	.183	.292	9.07	4.18
Jimenez, Joe	R-R	6-3	277	1-17-95	0	0	9.00	1	0	0	1	1	1	1	1	1	0	1	.250	.000	.500	9.00	0.00
Krol, Ian	L-L	6-1	210	5-9-91	2	0	2.45	20	1	0	4	26	20	8	7	4	12	31	.215	.179	.241	10.87	4.21
Ladwig, A.J.	R-R	6-5	180	12-24-92	0	0	0.00	3	0	0	0	7	3	0	0	0	0	5	.125	.182	.077	6.43	0.00
Lange, Alex	R-R	6-3	202	10-2-95	2	1	4.57	19	0	0	1	22	22	12	11	0	17	27	.265	.257	.271	11.22	7.06
Leiter Jr., Mark	R-R	6-0	210	3-13-91	8	4	3.34	17	15	0	0	89	67	38	33	10	23	110	.206	.206	.205	11.12	2.33
Manning, Matt	R-R	6-6	195	1-28-98	1	3	8.07	7	7	0	0	32	40	29	29	11	10	36	.303	.303	.303	10.02	2.78
Martinez, Henry	R-R	6-1	180	4-27-94	2	0	6.20	14	0	0	0	20	22	14	14	2	12	23	.275	.244	.308	10.18	5.31
Moreno, Gerson	R-R	6-0	218	9-10-95	0	0	6.75	2	0	0	0	3	2	2	2	0	5	5	.222	.400	.000	16.88	16.88
Navilhon, Joe	R-R	6-0	200	7-13-93	0	0	8.22	6	0	0	0	8	12	8	7	0	4	6	.375	.357	.389	7.04	4.70
Payano, Pedro	R-R	6-2	170	9-27-94	5	7	5.12	19	18	0	0	95	91	58	54	12	54	81	.253	.272	.239	7.67	5.12
Peralta, Wily	R-R	6-1	255	5-8-89	1	0	2.75	6	6	0	0	20	15	6	6	2	8	21	.211	.286	.139	9.61	3.66
Pinto, Ricardo	R-R	6-0	195	1-20-94	11	3	4.63	18	17	0	0	95	100	55	49	13	40	82	.269	.259	.277	7.74	3.78
Pinto, Wladimir	R-R	5-11	210	2-12-98	3	4	4.62	37	3	0	4	51	38	32	26	9	35	60	.207	.210	.204	10.66	6.22
Ramirez, Erasmo	R-R	6-0	220	5-2-90	1	0	3.38	5	0	0	0	8	4	3	3	0	3	10	.138	.091	.167	11.25	3.38
Rodriguez, Elvin	R-R	6-3	160	3-31-98	0	0	0.00	1	0	0	0	2	1	0	0	0	0	3	.143	.000	.200	13.50	0.00
Rodriguez, Nivaldo	R-R	6-1	214	4-16-97	2	1	4.93	13	5	0	0	35	40	25	19	6	12	19	.280	.221	.333	4.93	3.12
Rosoff, Jon	L-R	5-9	175	11-14-94	0	0	27.00	1	0	0	0	2	1	1	0	0	0	3	.667	1.000	.500	0.00	0.00
Ross Jr., Robbie	L-L	5-11	215	6-24-89	2	8	7.03	27	1	0	2	32	40	29	25	6	10	26	.299	.276	.316	7.31	2.81
Shore, Logan	R-R	6-2	215	12-28-94	7	3	3.95	16	15	0	0	73	65	32	32	6	30	64	.243	.237	.248	7.89	3.70
St. John, Locke	L-L	6-3	180	1-31-93	4	0	2.58	36	5	0	2	59	53	17	17	4	25	75	.232	.222	.239	11.38	3.79
Urena, Jose	R-R	6-2	208	9-12-91	0	0	0.00	2	2	0	0	3	0	0	0	0	1	2	.000	.000	.000	6.00	3.00
Vest, Will	R-R	6-0	180	6-6-95	1	3	4.91	23	0	0	2	26	27	14	14	3	8	25	.270	.327	.216	8.77	2.81

Fielding

Catcher	PCT	G	PO	A	E	DP	PB
Centeno	.997	51	366	27	1	1	5
Garneau	.994	17	145	9	1	0	4
Greiner	.997	31	307	30	1	2	1
Haase	1.000	4	30	1	0	0	0
Policelli	.992	28	221	16	2	2	3
Rogers	1.000	1	12	1	0	0	0
Rosoff	.986	8	65	3	1	0	0

First Base	PCT	G	PO	A	E	DP
Clemens	1.000	7	47	6	0	6
Lester	1.000	4	20	4	0	1
Nunez	.997	39	270	17	1	23
Pinero	1.000	3	15	2	0	0
Policelli	.000	1	0	0	0	0
Rodriguez	.986	45	347	17	5	40
Torkelson	.987	37	291	21	4	27

Second Base	PCT	G	PO	A	E	DP
Castro	1.000	4	6	12	0	1
Centeno	1.000	1	1	1	0	0
Clemens	.989	72	103	175	3	38
Gonzalez	1.000	17	16	42	0	8

	PCT	G	PO	A	E	DP
Goodrum	1.000	2	6	6	0	0
Jones	1.000	3	5	4	0	1
Lester	1.000	3	4	7	0	2
Paredes	.987	22	35	41	1	11
Peterson	1.000	5	3	8	0	3
Pinero	1.000	4	6	10	0	4
Short	1.000	12	13	26	0	8

Third Base	PCT	G	PO	A	E	DP
Clemens	.000	1	0	0	0	0
Gonzalez	.970	54	25	71	3	8
Kreidler	1.000	7	5	8	0	0
Lester	.947	5	5	13	1	1
Paredes	.933	32	22	61	6	7
Pinero	.875	3	3	4	1	0
Policelli	1.000	2	3	2	0	1
Rodriguez	.854	31	21	49	12	1
Short	.818	7	3	6	2	0

Shortstop	PCT	G	PO	A	E	DP
Castro	1.000	1	2	6	0	1
Gonzalez	.963	8	13	13	1	3
Goodrum	1.000	5	7	8	0	1
Kreidler	.931	35	43	79	9	15

	PCT	G	PO	A	E	DP
Paredes	.964	12	13	40	2	5
Peterson	.985	51	76	119	3	27
Short	.956	26	44	64	5	16

Outfield	PCT	G	PO	A	E	DP
Baddoo	1.000	3	1	0	0	0
Cameron	.986	37	69	3	1	0
Clemens	1.000	24	36	2	0	0
Goodrum	1.000	5	6	0	0	0
Greene	.971	41	64	4	2	0
Haase	1.000	3	3	0	0	0
Hill	1.000	33	58	0	0	0
Jones	.981	69	102	3	2	0
Lester	1.000	15	22	1	0	0
Mazara	1.000	2	3	0	0	0
Policelli	1.000	5	7	0	0	0
Proctor	.960	10	24	0	1	0
Reyes	1.000	19	31	0	0	0
Robson	.986	78	143	3	2	2
Rosa	1.000	18	24	2	0	0
Rosoff	1.000	2	4	0	0	0
Short	1.000	3	5	1	0	0
Stewart	.980	62	93	4	2	0

ERIE SEAWOLVES

DOUBLE-A

DOUBLE-A NORTHEAST

Batting	B-T	HT	WT	DOB	AVG	vLH	vRH	G	AB	R	H	2B	3B	HR	RBI	BB	HBP	SH	SF	SO	SB	CS	SLG	OBP
Bojarski, Ulrich	R-R	6-3	212	9-15-98	.429	.333	1.000	2	7	0	3	1	0	0	0	1	0	0	2	0	0	.571	.500
Cabrera, Daniel	L-L	6-3	200	9-5-98	.174	.095	.208	17	69	8	12	2	0	4	9	1	1	0	0	18	1	0	.377	.197
Carpenter, Kerry	L-R	6-2	220	9-2-97	.262	.271	.259	112	416	57	109	24	1	15	74	29	9	0	7	94	5	6	.433	.319
Centeno, Juan	L-R	5-9	195	11-16-89	.316	.333	.300	5	19	3	6	2	0	1	4	4	0	0	0	3	0	0	.579	.435
De La Rosa, Eric	R-R	6-3	186	6-3-97	.226	.259	.212	29	93	15	21	6	1	3	8	9	7	0	0	32	5	2	.409	.339
Dingler, Dillon	R-R	6-3	210	9-17-98	.202	.250	.182	50	188	24	38	3	3	4	20	9	8	0	3	62	1	0	.314	.264
Gonzalez, Yariel	B-R	6-1	190	6-1-94	.365	.368	.364	14	52	13	19	1	0	3	12	7	1	0	1	21	2	0	.558	.443
Greene, Riley	L-L	6-3	200	9-28-00	.298	.391	.261	84	326	59	97	16	5	16	54	41	4	0	2	102	12	1	.525	.381
Joyce, Corey	R-R	6-1	190	8-19-98	.171	.250	.161	11	35	1	6	0	0	1	0	1	0	0	1	5	0	0	.171	.194
Kenley, Jack	L-R	6-0	185	10-8-97	.119	.143	.114	14	42	1	5	1	0	0	1	2	0	0	0	15	0	0	.143	.159
Kreidler, Ryan	R-R	6-4	208	11-12-97	.256	.283	.246	88	347	67	89	15	0	15	36	32	5	0	4	119	10	4	.429	.325
Lester, Josh	L-R	6-3	180	7-17-94	.277	.169	.317	84	307	65	85	18	5	25	65	26	3	0	1	109	3	2	.612	.338
Lipcius, Andre	R-R	6-1	190	5-22-98	.235	.185	.253	94	341	51	80	18	2	9	46	39	1	0	4	82	4	1	.378	.312
MacLaren, Cole	R-R	5-9	193	6-10-97	.235	.111	.280	15	34	3	8	0	0	0	2	15	3	0	0	10	1	0	.235	.500
Mendoza, Carlos	L-R	5-9	165	12-14-99	.200	.333	.000	2	5	2	1	0	0	0	1	0	0	0	2	0	0	.200	.333
Myers, Dane	R-R	6-2	205	3-8-96	.278	.167	.315	27	97	8	27	5	1	3	14	4	1	1	1	27	0	1	.443	.311
Navigato, Andrew	R-R	5-11	188	5-28-98	.245	.185	.268	27	98	11	24	2	1	3	11	10	3	0	0	30	3	2	.378	.333
Peterson, Cole	L-R	5-11	160	8-2-95	.385	.400	.375	3	13	3	5	0	0	0	0	1	0	0	0	1	0	0	.385	.429
Policelli, Brady	R-R	5-10	195	6-24-95	.258	.286	.243	46	159	17	41	12	0	6	24	15	2	1	1	42	11	1	.447	.328
Proctor, Christopher	L-R	6-1	175	3-8-97	.155	.333	.075	17	58	9	9	2	0	1	5	4	0	0	2	27	0	0	.241	.203
Quiggle, Kona	L-L	6-1	200	2-1-98	.087	.000	.100	9	23	3	2	1	0	0	2	5	2	0	2	9	0	0	.130	.281

Name	B-T	HT	WT	DOB	AVG	vLH	vRH	G	AB	R	H	2B	3B	HR	RBI	BB	HBP	SH	SF	SO	SB	CS	SLG	OBP
Robson, Jacob	L-R	5-10	182	11-20-94	.424	.471	.408	18	66	17	28	9	2	2	10	14	1	1	0	21	4	1	.712	.531
Rosa, Dylan	R-R	6-2	200	6-27-96	.229	.156	.248	46	157	18	36	9	1	8	27	9	4	0	0	59	1	3	.452	.288
Rosoff, Jon	L-R	5-9	175	11-14-94	.206	.235	.196	43	136	12	28	6	0	0	4	14	0	0	1	34	3	1	.250	.278
Torkelson, Spencer	R-R	6-1	220	8-26-99	.263	.288	.252	50	175	33	46	10	0	14	36	30	3	0	4	50	1	1	.560	.373
Valente, John	R-R	5-11	190	6-23-95	.301	.338	.286	66	229	26	69	15	3	4	22	19	3	0	0	54	9	2	.445	.363
Ward, Drew	L-R	6-3	231	11-25-94	.240	.171	.269	78	275	46	66	10	1	16	54	33	4	0	4	105	1	2	.458	.326
Woodrow, Danny	L-R	5-10	155	1-26-95	.179	.167	.184	35	117	12	21	4	1	0	6	5	0	2	0	34	1	0	.231	.213

Pitching	B-T	HT	WT	DOB	W	L	ERA	G	GS	CG	SV	IP	H	R	ER	HR	BB	SO	AVG	vLH	vRH	K/9	BB/9
Bass, Brad	R-R	6-6	250	2-15-96	2	3	4.40	29	2	0	2	57	51	34	28	7	18	65	.235	.256	.220	10.20	2.83
Brieske, Beau	R-R	6-3	200	4-5-98	3	1	2.66	8	8	0	0	44	36	14	13	2	8	40	.225	.233	.218	8.18	1.64
Chentouf, Yaya	R-R	5-9	205	6-18-97	4	3	4.00	25	0	0	3	45	44	23	20	7	21	42	.267	.312	.227	8.40	4.20
Coshow, Cale	R-R	6-5	270	7-16-92	5	1	4.13	33	0	0	7	48	55	22	22	3	17	57	.288	.259	.309	10.69	3.19
De Jesus, Angel	R-R	6-4	200	2-13-97	1	0	0.00	9	1	0	1	13	6	1	0	0	5	18	.130	.000	.231	12.15	3.38
DeCaster, Ethan	R-R	6-3	190	10-27-94	1	0	0.40	15	1	0	0	22	11	3	1	0	10	23	.149	.156	.143	9.27	4.03
Fernander, Chavez	R-R	6-3	205	7-7-97	1	1	3.60	22	1	0	3	40	31	18	16	5	18	38	.212	.250	.179	8.55	4.05
Garcia, Ruben	R-R	6-4	220	8-2-96	2	2	4.83	26	0	0	0	41	38	27	22	4	29	51	.245	.265	.230	11.20	6.37
Green, Max	L-L	6-1	175	5-28-96	1	3	7.27	16	1	0	1	26	36	21	21	5	8	27	.330	.419	.295	9.35	2.77
Hess, Zack	R-R	6-6	219	2-25-97	0	0	0.00	2	0	0	0	3	2	0	0	0	1	3	.200	.000	.286	9.00	3.00
Hill, Garrett	R-R	6-0	185	1-16-96	3	1	3.20	4	4	0	0	20	15	7	7	1	10	28	.208	.200	.219	12.81	4.58
Kirby, Chance	R-R	5-11	165	7-19-95	4	2	5.51	11	7	0	0	47	42	30	29	10	20	37	.240	.267	.212	7.04	3.80
Ladwig, A.J.	R-R	6-5	180	12-24-92	6	7	4.80	21	21	0	0	101	101	56	54	23	18	82	.253	.223	.283	7.28	1.60
Leiter Jr., Mark	R-R	6-0	210	3-13-91	2	4	5.26	8	4	0	0	26	25	15	15	4	8	35	.253	.244	.259	12.27	2.81
Lescher, Billy	R-R	6-4	215	9-17-95	2	0	4.60	27	0	0	1	31	29	19	16	5	11	40	.240	.170	.294	11.49	3.16
Martinez, Henry	R-R	6-1	180	4-27-94	4	3	4.93	24	0	0	2	35	32	23	19	3	11	42	.241	.230	.250	10.90	2.86
Moreno, Gerson	R-R	6-0	218	9-10-95	5	3	4.47	35	0	0	7	46	34	24	23	9	24	68	.198	.225	.178	13.21	4.66
Navilhon, Joe	R-R	6-0	200	7-13-93	4	3	2.60	32	0	0	2	55	47	17	16	4	15	69	.226	.188	.262	11.22	2.44
Olson, Reese	R-R	6-1	160	7-31-99	2	1	4.74	5	5	0	0	25	18	13	13	1	14	21	.202	.277	.119	7.66	5.11
Payano, Pedro	R-R	6-2	170	9-27-94	3	1	3.10	6	6	0	0	29	16	10	10	2	14	36	.167	.233	.113	11.17	4.34
Pinto, Ricardo	R-R	6-0	195	1-20-94	3	1	3.18	6	6	0	0	28	23	10	10	2	7	25	.221	.175	.250	7.94	2.22
Pinto, Wladimir	R-R	5-11	170	2-12-98	0	0	0.00	1	0	0	2	1	0	0	0	0	1	1	.167	.000	.200	4.50	4.50
Richan, Paul	R-R	6-2	200	3-26-97	0	0	3.72	8	8	0	0	29	25	12	12	7	9	26	.234	.234	.233	8.07	2.79
Rodriguez, Elvin	R-R	6-3	160	3-31-98	4	6	5.83	18	18	0	0	76	69	52	49	18	29	80	.237	.281	.202	9.52	3.45
Rodriguez, Jesus	R-R	6-3	170	2-16-98	2	5	5.76	16	13	1	0	70	78	52	45	14	24	60	.275	.295	.254	7.68	3.07
Rosoff, Jon	L-R	5-9	175	11-14-94	0	0	0.00	1	0	0	0	0	0	0	0	0	0	0	.000	--	.000	0.00	0.00
Wentz, Joey	L-L	6-5	220	10-6-97	0	4	3.71	13	13	0	0	53	41	25	22	7	33	58	.209	.232	.197	9.79	5.57

Fielding

Catcher	PCT	G	PO	A	E	DP	PB
Centeno	.983	5	57	2	1	0	2
Dingler	.997	40	359	25	1	4	2
MacLaren	.993	15	132	10	1	2	1
Policelli	.976	10	76	7	2	0	2
Proctor	1.000	11	103	6	0	0	0
Rosoff	.984	39	361	12	6	3	2

First Base	PCT	G	PO	A	E	DP
Carpenter	1.000	1	6	0	0	1
Lester	.994	47	318	27	2	34
Myers	1.000	4	23	2	0	1
Torkelson	1.000	23	154	13	0	12
Ward	.997	45	274	22	1	17

Second Base	PCT	G	PO	A	E	DP
Gonzalez	1.000	3	6	6	0	2
Joyce	1.000	5	5	12	0	3
Kenley	.973	13	10	26	1	2
Lester	1.000	18	15	38	0	6
Lipcius	.987	45	65	92	2	25
Mendoza	1.000	2	2	2	0	0
Peterson	1.000	3	4	8	0	5
Policelli	.957	12	15	30	2	3
Valente	.968	21	24	36	2	7

Third Base	PCT	G	PO	A	E	DP
Gonzalez	.905	7	2	17	2	1
Lipcius	.950	49	37	78	6	8
Myers	.882	16	8	22	4	1
Policelli	1.000	1	1	3	0	0
Torkelson	.854	27	13	28	7	4
Valente	.966	12	8	20	1	0
Ward	.938	9	5	10	1	1

Shortstop	PCT	G	PO	A	E	DP
Gonzalez	.000	1	0	0	0	0
Joyce	1.000	3	2	5	0	1
Kreidler	.981	88	140	174	6	37
Navigato	.956	27	44	64	5	11
Policelli	.833	2	1	4	1	0

Outfield	PCT	G	PO	A	E	DP
Cabrera	1.000	17	29	2	0	0
Carpenter	.964	98	156	4	6	1
De La Rosa	1.000	27	60	0	0	0
Greene	.990	84	189	2	2	0
Lester	.947	11	17	1	1	0
Policelli	.957	20	43	1	2	0
Proctor	1.000	5	13	0	0	0
Quiggle	.857	6	6	0	1	0
Robson	.974	18	34	3	1	1
Rosa	.971	39	67	1	2	0
Rosoff	1.000	3	7	0	0	0
Valente	.947	7	16	2	1	1
Woodrow	.987	34	74	1	1	0

WEST MICHIGAN WHITECAPS

HIGH CLASS A

HIGH-A CENTRAL

Batting	B-T	HT	WT	DOB	AVG	vLH	vRH	G	AB	R	H	2B	3B	HR	RBI	BB	HBP	SH	SF	SO	SB	CS	SLG	OBP
Alfonzo, Eliezer	B-R	5-10	155	9-23-99	.272	.250	.280	59	213	21	58	11	0	1	26	16	0	0	3	24	1	2	.338	.319
Bojarski, Ulrich	R-R	6-3	212	9-15-98	.159	.091	.191	29	69	4	11	3	2	1	8	5	0	0	2	36	0	1	.304	.211
Cabrera, Daniel	L-L	6-3	200	9-5-98	.242	.250	.239	99	380	54	92	19	6	9	64	34	0	6	6	95	7	4	.395	.300
Cruz, Trei	B-R	6-2	204	7-5-98	.159	.214	.147	26	82	10	13	5	1	0	6	22	0	2	1	35	1	1	.244	.333
De La Rosa, Eric	R-R	6-3	186	6-3-97	.293	.271	.300	59	208	37	61	14	6	3	27	19	8	1	1	72	22	6	.462	.373
Dingler, Dillon	R-R	6-3	210	9-17-98	.287	.185	.316	32	122	25	35	6	1	8	24	13	5	0	1	36	0	0	.549	.376
Esquerra, Trevin	B-B	6-1	205	5-20-98	.080	.200	.000	8	25	4	2	0	0	0	4	1	0	0	11	0	0	.080	.233
Holton, Jake	R-R	6-0	210	3-2-98	.308	.321	.303	30	104	21	32	8	1	3	20	16	7	0	1	24	0	2	.490	.430
Johnson, Cooper	R-R	5-11	209	4-25-98	.177	.206	.169	57	164	20	29	14	0	1	14	32	2	2	2	53	0	1	.280	.315
Joyce, Corey	R-R	6-1	189	8-19-98	.184	.250	.159	28	87	11	16	3	0	1	5	15	3	0	0	27	5	0	.253	.324
Keith, Colt	L-R	6-3	211	8-14-01	.162	.188	.154	18	68	7	11	1	1	1	6	8	0	0	0	27	0	0	.250	.250
Kenley, Jack	R-R	6-0	185	10-8-97	.250	--	.250	2	4	2	1	0	0	0	1	0	0	0	0	0	0	0	.250	.400
Kerr, Jimmy	L-R	6-0	203	3-21-97	.218	.192	.227	34	101	16	22	6	1	3	18	15	0	0	1	41	1	2	.386	.316

Name	B-T	HT	WT	DOB	AVG	vLH	vRH	G	AB	R	H	2B	3B	HR	RBI	BB	HBP	SH	SF	SO	SB	CS	OBP	SLG
King, Jose	L-R	5-10	182	1-16-99	.221	.167	.238	69	226	31	50	12	1	4	29	15	3	3	4	85	4	2	.336	.274
Lipcius, Andre	R-R	6-1	190	5-22-98	.277	.333	.258	22	83	14	23	4	2	3	13	12	0	0	3	16	3	1	.482	.357
MacLaren, Cole	R-R	5-9	193	6-10-97	.176	.222	.160	14	34	4	6	2	0	0	3	3	0	1	0	8	0	0	.235	.243
Meadows, Parker	L-R	6-5	205	11-2-99	.208	.280	.187	94	355	50	74	15	2	8	44	37	6	5	5	99	9	8	.330	.290
Murr, Austin	L-L	6-2	218	1-26-99	.344	.318	.353	25	90	17	31	4	0	1	8	10	1	3	1	20	2	0	.422	.412
Myers, Dane	R-R	6-2	205	3-8-96	.333	.400	.286	4	12	3	4	1	0	1	1	3	0	0	0	1	0	0	.667	.467
Navigato, Andrew	R-R	5-11	188	5-29-97	.236	.212	.243	44	144	23	34	6	1	3	14	23	3	0	2	38	5	4	.354	.349
Packard, Bryant	L-R	6-3	200	10-6-97	.222	.195	.229	54	198	30	44	11	0	6	22	17	9	0	2	53	5	3	.369	.310
Perez, Wenceel	B-R	5-11	203	10-30-99	.245	.280	.234	90	330	51	81	13	6	3	31	31	2	5	1	64	13	1	.348	.313
Proctor, Christopher	L-R	6-1	175	3-8-97	.133	--	.133	5	15	3	2	2	0	0	0	5	0	0	0	8	0	0	.267	.350
Quiggle, Kona	L-L	6-1	200	2-1-98	.000	.000	.000	3	9	1	0	0	0	0	0	2	0	0	0	5	0	0	.000	.182
Rivera, Reynaldo	L-R	6-6	250	6-14-97	.207	.260	.192	95	323	45	67	15	0	21	60	33	7	0	6	135	0	1	.449	.290
Schultz, Austin	R-R	5-9	200	2-21-00	.278	.500	.214	4	18	1	5	0	2	0	3	0	1	0	0	5	0	0	.500	.316
Silverio, Gresuan	B-R	6-0	175	1-5-99	.211	.286	.167	9	19	3	4	1	0	0	2	3	0	0	0	8	0	0	.263	.318
Torkelson, Spencer	R-R	6-1	220	8-26-99	.312	.320	.310	31	109	21	34	11	1	5	28	24	4	0	4	28	3	2	.569	.440
Valencia, Eduardo	R-R	6-2	180	1-25-00	.800	1.000	.667	4	5	0	4	1	0	0	1	0	0	0	0	0	0	0	1.000	.800
Workman, Gage	B-R	6-3	202	10-24-99	.237	.250	.250	67	257	42	61	21	2	9	39	23	2	0	3	97	9	5	.440	.302

Pitching	B-T	HT	WT	DOB	W	L	ERA	G	GS	CG	SV	IP	H	R	ER	HR	BB	SO	AVG	vLH	vRH	K/9	BB/9
Bergner, Austin	R-R	6-5	210	5-1-97	4	0	2.90	17	10	0	0	59	50	23	19	8	25	76	.224	.230	.221	11.59	3.81
Bienlien, Michael	R-R	6-3	246	3-19-98	3	2	5.00	21	0	0	1	36	43	25	20	2	16	32	.289	.293	.287	8.00	4.00
Brieske, Beau	R-R	6-3	200	4-5-98	6	3	3.45	13	13	1	0	63	49	28	24	5	15	76	.213	.187	.236	10.91	2.15
Chentouf, Yaya	R-R	5-9	205	6-18-97	3	1	0.66	9	0	0	0	14	7	2	1	0	5	15	.156	.125	.190	9.88	3.29
De La Cruz, Isrrael	B-R	5-11	175	6-15-97	1	0	2.00	3	0	0	0	9	4	2	2	1	2	9	.133	.333	.048	9.00	2.00
De La Cruz, Sandel	R-R	6-2	225	8-6-96	1	3	5.23	29	4	0	0	53	36	34	31	7	32	65	.187	.200	.178	10.97	5.40
Fernander, Chavez	R-R	6-3	205	7-7-97	1	1	3.86	11	2	0	0	19	16	9	8	1	8	18	.232	.242	.222	8.68	3.86
Garcia, Ruben	R-R	6-4	220	8-2-96	0	0	2.35	12	0	0	0	15	8	7	4	1	5	21	.151	.143	.156	12.33	2.93
Hess, Zack	R-R	6-6	219	2-25-97	2	5	3.62	43	0	0	13	50	38	26	20	6	34	66	.212	.289	.146	11.96	6.16
Hill, Garrett	R-R	6-0	185	1-16-96	3	0	2.57	13	13	0	0	56	47	19	16	2	18	71	.223	.200	.240	11.41	2.89
Houston, Zac	R-R	6-5	260	11-30-94	1	0	1.35	5	0	0	0	7	5	1	1	0	3	13	.217	.000	.294	17.55	4.05
Javier, Xavier	R-R	6-4	225	2-9-98	0	1	10.03	19	0	0	0	23	39	27	26	4	20	17	.371	.431	.315	6.56	7.71
Kessler, Sam	R-R	6-2	192	12-16-97	0	0	3.12	16	0	0	0	17	8	7	6	0	23	21	.145	.087	.188	10.90	11.94
King, Jose	L-R	5-10	182	1-16-99	0	0	18.00	2	0	0	0	3	7	6	6	2	4	0	.467	.600	.400	0.00	12.00
Kirby, Chance	R-R	5-11	165	7-19-95	3	3	3.25	8	8	0	0	36	29	17	13	4	11	29	.213	.177	.243	7.25	2.75
Magno, Andrew	R-L	5-11	190	4-30-98	0	0	3.00	4	0	0	0	6	5	2	2	0	4	10	.220	.000	.357	15.00	6.00
Mauloni, Chris	L-R	6-2	200	6-16-98	1	3	5.48	11	0	0	0	21	25	16	13	2	11	33	.294	.294	.294	13.92	4.64
Montero, Keider	R-R	6-1	145	7-6-00	4	8	5.28	15	15	0	0	61	84	42	36	6	19	59	.321	.326	.315	8.66	2.79
Olson, Reese	R-R	6-1	160	7-31-99	1	0	0.00	2	2	0	0	11	6	0	0	0	2	14	.154	.167	.133	11.45	1.64
2-team total (14 Wisconsin)					6	4	3.71	16	16	0	0	80	64	34	33	5	37	93	.218	.163	.266	10.46	4.16
O'Loughlin, Jack	L-L	6-5	223	3-14-00	2	1	3.54	5	5	0	0	20	18	11	8	0	11	9	.250	.400	.226	3.98	4.87
Petit, RJ	R-R	6-8	300	9-23-99	0	1	20.25	2	1	0	0	3	5	6	6	1	2	4	.385	.000	.500	13.50	6.75
Reyes, Angel	R-R	6-2	205	10-17-97	2	4	3.51	40	0	0	0	59	47	29	23	5	17	54	.210	.159	.239	8.24	2.59
Rodriguez, Jesus	R-R	6-3	170	2-16-98	1	3	3.73	8	7	0	0	31	29	17	13	3	9	27	.242	.200	.283	7.76	2.59
Shepherd, Zac	R-R	6-3	185	9-14-95	6	3	4.87	28	6	0	0	78	81	47	42	9	15	61	.264	.288	.249	7.07	1.74
Tassin, Bryce	R-R	6-2	209	1-11-97	4	5	2.44	30	0	0	6	44	33	18	12	1	11	39	.210	.155	.242	7.92	2.23
Tobey, Jared	R-L	6-4	225	3-11-96	2	1	5.36	45	0	0	3	49	46	31	29	4	25	66	.250	.238	.260	12.21	4.62
White, Brendan	R-R	5-11	185	11-18-98	3	9	4.17	26	18	0	0	101	103	55	47	9	27	107	.256	.251	.259	9.50	2.40
Wolf, Adam	L-L	6-6	215	12-26-96	4	5	4.20	16	16	0	0	79	76	39	37	9	25	74	.250	.194	.266	8.39	2.84

Fielding

Catcher	PCT	G	PO	A	E	DP	PB
Alfonzo	.980	32	281	17	6	0	0
Dingler	1.000	24	240	15	0	1	4
Johnson	.992	54	487	30	4	4	6
MacLaren	.983	10	54	5	1	0	1
Proctor	1.000	3	27	1	0	0	0
Silverio	1.000	4	21	0	0	0	2
Valencia	1.000	2	3	0	0	0	0

First Base	PCT	G	PO	A	E	DP
Alfonzo	.956	8	41	2	2	10
Holton	.994	22	145	9	1	13
Kerr	.990	27	178	11	2	15
MacLaren	.000	1	0	0	0	0
Murr	.968	4	29	1	1	3
Packard	.967	3	28	1	1	1
Rivera	.980	53	373	25	8	27
Torkelson	.990	15	90	13	1	8

Second Base	PCT	G	PO	A	E	DP
Joyce	1.000	12	8	23	0	4
Keith	.889	2	4	4	1	2

	PCT	G	PO	A	E	DP
Kenley	1.000	2	1	3	0	0
King	.988	24	30	53	1	13
Lipcius	.840	9	11	10	4	3
Navigato	.965	15	19	36	2	6
Perez	.951	59	113	138	13	37

Third Base	PCT	G	PO	A	E	DP
Joyce	.800	4	2	2	1	0
Keith	.884	15	6	32	5	4
Kerr	1.000	6	3	12	0	2
King	.967	23	14	60	5	3
Lipcius	.975	13	16	23	1	0
Navigato	.937	23	14	60	5	3
Perez	.892	24	18	40	7	2
Torkelson	.953	16	15	26	2	0

Shortstop	PCT	G	PO	A	E	DP
Cruz	.926	26	18	57	6	13
Joyce	.941	12	14	18	2	5
King	.932	19	29	39	5	5
Workman	.960	65	86	179	11	32

Outfield	PCT	G	PO	A	E	DP
Bojarski	.943	29	33	0	2	0
Cabrera	.969	98	151	7	5	1
De La Rosa	.978	54	89	0	2	0
Esquerra	1.000	8	27	1	0	0
Holton	1.000	10	16	0	0	0
Kerr	1.000	3	6	0	0	0
King	1.000	3	1	0	0	0
Meadows	.994	90	171	4	1	0
Murr	.944	24	31	3	2	2
Myers	1.000	3	3	0	0	0
Navigato	1.000	6	5	2	0	0
Packard	.986	45	67	1	1	0
Proctor	1.000	1	4	1	0	0
Quiggle	1.000	3	1	1	0	0
Rivera	--	1	0	0	0	0
Schultz	1.000	4	5	0	0	0

DETROIT TIGERS

Batting	B-T	HT	WT	DOB	AVG	vLH	vRH	G	AB	R	H	2B	3B	HR	RBI	BB	HBP	SH	SF	SO	SB	CS	SLG	OBP
Alfonzo, Eliezer	B-R	5-10	155	9-23-99	.308	.353	.295	39	156	25	48	7	1	7	29	12	2	0	1	11	2	0	.500	.363
Bojarski, Ulrich	R-R	6-3	212	9-15-98	.157	.148	.160	35	121	13	19	2	0	0	5	11	1	1	0	57	3	1	.174	.233
Cameron, Daz	R-R	6-2	185	1-15-97	.000	.000	.000	3	10	1	0	0	0	0	0	4	0	0	0	4	1	0	.000	.286
Chacon, Esney	R-R	6-1	160	3-17-00	.224	.318	.200	32	107	13	24	1	0	0	14	19	0	0	1	35	4	0	.234	.339
Clemens, Kody	L-R	6-1	170	5-15-96	.182	.000	.200	3	11	0	2	0	0	0	2	0	0	0	0	4	0	0	.182	.182
Crouch, Josh	R-R	6-0	200	12-7-98	.230	.111	.261	24	87	12	20	1	1	2	16	5	0	1	4	31	0	0	.333	.260
Cruz, Trei	B-R	6-2	204	7-5-98	.162	.150	.165	33	111	23	18	6	1	2	9	33	1	0	1	31	11	2	.288	.356
De La Cruz, Jose	R-R	6-0	216	1-3-02	.127	.091	.138	39	142	15	18	3	1	1	10	10	5	0	1	74	6	1	.183	.209
De La Rosa, Eric	R-R	6-1	186	6-3-97	.276	.182	.298	16	58	9	16	2	0	2	15	9	2	0	0	20	7	1	.414	.391
Dey, Griffin	R-R	6-0	220	7-19-96	.250	.100	.318	10	32	2	8	1	0	0	4	0	1	0	9	0	0	.281	.333
Dingler, Dillon	R-R	6-3	210	9-17-98	.333	.200	.429	3	12	1	4	1	0	0	2	0	0	0	0	3	0	0	.417	.333
Garneau, Dustin	R-R	6-2	205	8-13-87	.400	.250	.500	4	10	1	4	2	1	0	2	3	0	0	1	2	0	0	.800	.500
Gonzalez, Alvaro	B-R	6-0	165	9-16-00	.200	.194	.201	64	205	28	41	7	0	2	17	30	9	0	2	61	2	3	.263	.325
Goodrum, Niko	B-R	6-3	215	2-28-92	.667	.500	1.000	1	3	1	2	2	0	0	0	0	0	0	0	1	1	1	1.333	.667
Hill, Derek	R-R	6-2	190	12-30-95	.333	.200	.385	4	18	0	6	1	0	0	2	1	0	0	0	6	0	0	.389	.368
Holton, Jake	R-R	6-0	200	3-2-98	.261	.148	.286	45	153	19	40	8	3	5	25	25	7	0	2	42	1	0	.451	.385
Irigoyen, Carlos	R-R	6-2	165	3-21-01	.207	.222	.204	37	116	9	24	2	0	0	7	11	0	2	0	34	0	0	.224	.276
Jimenez, Jeremy	R-R	6-2	180	3-3-01	.250	--	.250	1	4	1	1	0	0	0	0	0	0	0	0	1	0	0	.250	.250
Johnson, Cooper	R-R	6-1	209	4-25-98	.233	.133	.250	28	103	17	24	5	0	2	17	19	2	1	0	39	2	0	.340	.363
Joyce, Corey	R-R	6-1	190	8-19-98	.278	.200	.294	6	18	2	5	0	0	1	3	2	1	0	0	4	2	0	.444	.381
Keith, Colt	L-R	6-3	211	8-14-01	.320	.400	.299	44	147	32	47	6	3	1	21	30	2	0	2	39	4	1	.422	.436
Kerr, Jimmy	L-R	6-0	203	3-21-97	.225	.150	.246	54	182	22	41	10	1	5	31	24	3	0	4	67	3	1	.374	.319
King, Jose	L-R	5-10	182	1-16-99	.182	.125	.191	15	55	8	10	1	1	0	1	5	1	0	0	15	5	1	.236	.262
Liniak, Kingston	R-R	6-1	200	11-11-99	.193	.156	.202	107	404	48	78	14	6	10	44	42	7	1	2	121	19	6	.332	.279
MacLaren, Cole	R-R	5-9	193	6-10-97	.333	.000	.500	3	3	0	1	0	0	0	0	1	0	0	0	1	0	0	.333	.500
Malgeri, Ben	R-R	6-1	215	1-12-00	.266	.200	.278	40	158	23	42	6	3	2	21	15	5	0	0	42	6	2	.380	.348
McLaughlin, J.D.	R-R	6-3	195	12-28-00	.111	.000	.125	3	9	4	1	0	0	0	0	5	0	0	0	2	0	0	.111	.429
McMillan, Sam	R-R	5-10	193	12-14-98	.203	.278	.179	23	74	12	15	2	0	0	5	9	5	0	0	26	3	1	.230	.330
Meadows, Parker	L-R	6-5	205	11-2-99	.273	.000	.300	3	11	2	3	1	0	0	1	0	1	0	0	3	0	0	.364	.333
Mendoza, Carlos	L-R	5-9	165	12-14-99	.288	.455	.258	21	73	15	21	4	1	0	5	14	3	0	0	13	3	0	.370	.422
Meyers, Chris	L-R	6-3	210	4-27-99	.205	.143	.217	25	83	13	17	5	1	1	11	11	3	0	0	18	1	1	.325	.320
Murr, Austin	L-L	6-2	218	1-26-99	.262	.000	.314	13	42	13	11	3	0	0	4	17	2	0	0	9	2	1	.333	.492
Myers, Dane	R-R	6-2	205	3-8-96	.311	.273	.324	14	45	15	14	3	0	0	9	9	4	0	2	20	5	0	.378	.450
Navigato, Andrew	R-R	5-11	188	5-28-98	.260	.071	.305	24	73	12	19	8	0	3	16	11	2	1	3	18	6	2	.493	.360
Paredes, Isaac	R-R	5-11	213	2-18-99	.111	--	.111	3	9	4	1	0	0	1	2	3	0	0	0	3	0	0	.444	.333
Pelegrin, Carlos	R-R	6-2	180	6-21-00	.020	.000	.024	14	49	1	1	0	0	0	1	5	0	0	0	30	0	0	.041	.111
Perez, Wenceel	B-R	5-11	203	10-30-99	.293	.278	.297	23	92	16	27	5	1	1	12	12	2	0	1	21	9	1	.402	.383
Perry, Connor	L-L	5-11	185	4-22-97	.000	.000	.231	6	18	2	3	2	0	0	1	2	0	0	0	8	2	0	.278	.250
Pinero, Daniel	R-R	6-5	210	5-2-94	.286	.250	.333	4	7	0	2	0	0	0	2	3	0	0	0	2	0	0	.286	.500
Proctor, Christopher	L-R	6-1	175	3-8-97	.129	.000	.160	11	31	3	4	2	0	0	0	8	1	0	0	13	3	0	.194	.325
Quintana, Nick	R-R	5-10	180	10-13-97	.196	.214	.191	82	286	46	56	16	0	9	46	51	7	0	3	73	4	1	.346	.329
Ramos, Wilson	R-R	6-1	241	8-10-87	.000	.000	.000	1	4	0	0	0	0	0	1	0	0	0	0	0	0	0	.000	.000
Reyes, Victor	B-R	6-5	194	10-5-94	.273	1.000	.200	5	11	3	3	1	0	0	1	5	1	0	1	3	0	0	.364	.500
Rothenberg, Mike	R-R	6-3	215	10-5-98	.263	.273	.262	24	76	10	20	5	0	1	10	14	4	0	1	17	0	0	.368	.400
Schultz, Austin	R-R	5-9	200	2-21-00	.262	.167	.283	17	65	11	17	1	0	2	8	7	2	0	0	13	3	0	.369	.351
Silverio, Gresuan	B-R	6-0	175	1-5-99	.222	.182	.240	13	36	0	8	3	0	0	4	6	0	0	0	12	1	0	.306	.333
Valencia, Eduardo	R-R	6-2	180	1-25-00	.139	.200	.129	12	36	2	5	0	0	0	3	5	0	0	1	8	1	0	.139	.238
Woodrow, Danny	L-R	5-10	155	1-26-95	.154	.000	.250	3	13	1	2	0	0	0	0	1	0	0	0	4	0	0	.154	.214
Workman, Gage	B-R	6-3	202	10-24-99	.256	.121	.284	51	195	26	50	16	4	3	19	30	1	1	1	60	22	3	.426	.357

Pitching	B-T	HT	WT	DOB	W	L	ERA	G	GS	CG	SV	IP	H	R	ER	HR	BB	SO	AVG	vLH	vRH	K/9	BB/9
Arriera, Gio	R-R	6-2	236	6-7-98	1	5	5.30	9	9	0	0	37	34	27	22	3	19	38	.250	.194	.297	9.16	4.58
Beattie, Matt	R-R	6-3	225	1-5-99	0	0	10.80	12	0	0	0	12	14	15	14	3	15	14	.298	.353	.267	10.80	11.57
Bergner, Austin	R-R	6-5	210	5-1-97	2	2	4.44	10	0	0	1	24	15	12	12	3	8	34	.176	.175	.178	12.58	2.96
Bienlien, Michael	R-R	6-3	246	3-19-98	1	1	2.19	13	0	0	1	25	16	6	6	0	13	33	.182	.108	.235	12.04	4.74
Davila, Nick	R-R	6-3	202	11-21-98	6	8	3.54	27	13	0	2	94	86	46	37	6	35	99	.241	.227	.250	9.48	3.35
De La Cruz, Israel	B-R	5-11	175	6-15-97	3	2	5.86	26	0	0	4	43	48	32	28	6	21	64	.274	.296	.260	13.40	4.40
Dellinger, Jack	R-R	6-4	210	2-12-98	0	1	22.50	3	0	0	0	2	5	6	5	1	3	3	.455	.500	.400	13.50	4.50
Flores, Wilmer	R-R	6-4	225	2-20-01	4	3	3.40	11	11	0	0	53	47	25	20	1	22	72	.239	.218	.255	12.23	3.74
Gardea, Dario	R-R	6-2	210	1-29-99	0	1	3.26	9	1	0	0	19	18	7	7	2	4	23	.257	.206	.306	10.71	1.86
Guzman, Carlos	R-R	6-1	210	5-16-98	7	9	4.65	23	22	0	0	99	110	57	51	9	46	102	.282	.295	.271	9.30	4.20
Haase, Aaron	R-R	5-8	193	5-24-00	0	0	6.75	4	0	0	0	4	2	3	3	1	2	4	.143	.333	.091	9.00	4.50
Javier, Xavier	R-R	6-4	225	2-9-98	0	1	2.89	7	0	0	0	9	8	3	3	0	7	5	.229	.214	.238	4.82	6.75
Kessler, Sam	R-R	6-1	192	12-16-97	0	0	2.77	7	0	0	0	13	10	5	4	1	10	14	.213	.182	.240	9.69	6.92
King, Carson	R-R	6-2	207	12-5-99	1	3	6.34	17	1	0	0	33	38	30	23	6	15	28	.290	.340	.256	7.71	4.13
Magno, Andrew	R-L	5-11	190	4-30-98	0	1	3.68	23	0	0	1	29	14	13	12	0	30	37	.144	.167	.111	11.35	9.20
Mauloni, Chris	L-R	6-2	208	3-18-98	2	2	3.68	21	0	0	2	37	28	17	15	6	16	54	.207	.228	.192	13.25	3.93
Moore, Andrew	R-R	6-0	195	6-2-94	0	0	2.70	1	1	0	0	3	4	1	1	0	0	3	.000	.000	.000	10.80	8.10
Moreno, Williander	R-R	6-0	160	3-13-99	3	3	3.16	25	2	0	0	57	56	30	20	8	21	67	.252	.292	.222	10.58	3.32
O'Loughlin, Jack	L-L	6-5	223	3-14-00	3	0	2.19	8	8	1	0	37	32	9	9	2	10	39	.239	.290	.223	9.49	2.43

Pena, Carlos	L-L	5-11	160	9-7-98	1	0	2.93	9	6	0	0	40	31	15	13	3	9	33	.209	.265	.182	7.43	2.03
Perez, Cleiverth	L-L	6-0	211	2-5-00	0	0	4.50	2	2	0	0	6	8	3	3	1	2	6	.320	.000	.364	9.00	3.00
Petit, RJ	R-R	6-8	300	9-23-99	0	0	0.00	3	0	0	0	4	2	1	0	0	1	2	.133	.000	.250	4.50	2.25
Pinales, Erick	R-R	6-2	185	1-27-99	2	0	4.76	12	0	0	0	17	14	10	9	0	18	14	.219	.269	.184	7.41	9.53
Salazar, Joseph	R-R	6-1	175	9-24-99	1	8	8.23	18	17	0	0	62	78	61	57	12	27	68	.302	.295	.308	9.82	3.90
Sequeira, Gabriel	L-L	6-0	200	8-18-97	5	3	4.72	34	0	0	10	48	51	28	25	1	20	74	.270	.283	.264	13.97	3.78
Shore, Logan	R-R	6-2	215	12-28-94	0	0	2.84	2	2	0	0	6	5	2	2	0	1	9	.208	.333	.133	12.79	1.42
Sommerfeld, Luke	R-R	6-6	244	7-8-96	0	0	7.20	5	0	0	0	5	5	5	4	0	6	2	.250	.250	.250	3.60	10.80
Stuka, Ted	R-R	6-7	225	5-13-97	5	4	5.91	25	9	0	2	64	56	48	42	3	64	54	.230	.227	.231	7.59	9.00
Tassin, Bryce	R-R	6-2	209	1-11-97	2	0	1.46	9	0	0	3	12	8	2	2	1	4	15	.182	.150	.208	10.95	2.92
Walker, Matt	L-L	6-3	217	6-15-98	4	1	4.09	25	4	0	0	62	61	34	28	3	31	62	.253	.270	.243	9.05	4.52
Wentz, Joey	L-L	6-5	220	10-6-97	0	3	6.75	5	5	0	0	19	23	17	14	5	8	24	.311	.417	.260	11.57	3.86
Wolf, Adam	L-L	6-6	215	12-26-96	2	2	3.90	7	5	0	0	28	26	13	12	3	6	34	.250	.212	.268	11.06	1.95

Fielding

Catcher	PCT	G	PO	A	E	DP	PB
Alfonzo	.996	27	260	16	1	0	1
Crouch	.987	16	130	20	2	1	3
Dingler	1.000	1	8	0	0	0	1
Garneau	1.000	2	14	0	0	0	0
Johnson	.996	21	245	13	1	3	3
McMillan	.994	20	168	9	1	4	1
Proctor	1.000	9	72	8	0	1	1
Rothenberg	1.000	11	101	7	0	0	1
Silverio	.982	7	53	3	1	0	0
Valencia	.988	9	78	2	1	0	0

First Base	PCT	G	PO	A	E	DP
Dey	.980	7	45	4	1	6
Gonzalez	1.000	1	4	0	0	0
Holton	.997	42	271	22	1	29
Irigoyen	1.000	1	1	0	0	0
Kerr	.997	39	274	14	1	34
Meyers	1.000	25	167	8	0	9
Myers	.909	1	10	0	1	0
Rothenberg	1.000	2	15	0	0	0
Silverio	1.000	2	20	3	0	2

Second Base	PCT	G	PO	A	E	DP
Clemens	1.000	2	4	3	0	2
Gonzalez	.968	56	75	104	6	26
Irigoyen	1.000	6	4	10	0	1
Joyce	1.000	2	2	9	0	1
Keith	.956	14	18	25	2	7
King	1.000	5	6	7	0	3
Mendoza	.953	15	32	29	3	5
Navigato	1.000	2	1	0	0	0
Paredes	1.000	1	1	2	0	0
Perez	.937	21	30	59	6	13
Schultz	1.000	2	1	2	0	0

Third Base	PCT	G	PO	A	E	DP
Irigoyen	1.000	4	5	4	0	1
Keith	.903	27	27	38	7	8
King	1.000	6	4	3	0	1
Mendoza	.800	4	3	5	2	0
Myers	.786	5	2	9	3	0
Navigato	.667	2	2	0	1	0
Paredes	1.000	1	1	0	0	0
Pinero	1.000	2	3	2	0	1
Quintana	.941	72	34	109	9	15

Shortstop	PCT	G	PO	A	E	DP
Cruz	.902	32	44	57	11	10
Gonzalez	.714	1	5	0	2	0
Goodrum	1.000	1	2	1	0	0
Irigoyen	.911	26	34	58	9	9
Joyce	.889	3	4	4	1	1
King	1.000	5	6	5	0	0
Navigato	.923	4	5	7	1	3
Pinero	1.000	1	3	2	0	1
Workman	.944	47	51	100	9	24

Outfield	PCT	G	PO	A	E	DP
Bojarski	.963	34	51	1	2	0
Cameron	1.000	1	2	0	0	0
Chacon	1.000	32	64	0	0	0
De La Cruz	.965	38	51	4	2	2
De La Rosa	1.000	16	30	1	0	0
Hill	1.000	1	4	0	0	0
Holton	1.000	3	3	0	0	0
Kerr	1.000	10	10	2	0	0
Liniak	.983	106	222	9	4	3
Malgeri	.981	36	49	3	1	0
McLaughlin	1.000	3	2	1	0	0
Meadows	1.000	1	1	0	0	0
Mendoza	1.000	2	5	1	0	0
Murr	1.000	12	21	0	0	0
Myers	1.000	4	5	1	0	0
Navigato	.968	14	27	3	1	0
Pelegrin	.971	14	30	3	1	1
Perry	.933	6	14	0	1	0
Proctor	1.000	2	5	1	0	0
Reyes	1.000	4	4	0	0	0
Schultz	.944	15	17	0	1	0
Woodrow	1.000	2	4	0	0	0

FCL TIGERS   ROOKIE
FLORIDA COMPLEX LEAGUE

Batting	B-T	HT	WT	DOB	AVG	vLH	vRH	G	AB	R	H	2B	3B	HR	RBI	BB	HBP	SH	SF	SO	SB	CS	SLG	OBP
Acevedo, Yoneiry	B-R	5-10	150	12-4-00	.193	.286	.165	47	150	26	29	9	4	2	15	25	3	1	1	49	7	1	.347	.318
Benitez, Lazaro	R-R	6-0	190	10-15-99	.304	.261	.315	37	112	20	34	7	3	2	18	12	5	0	0	25	1	2	.473	.395
Bigbie, Justice	R-R	6-3	200	1-24-99	.253	.190	.269	29	99	14	25	4	1	2	18	17	1	0	1	25	0	0	.374	.364
Calderon, Cesar	R-R	6-2	170	11-1-01	.213	.300	.183	30	80	8	17	2	0	2	8	12	3	0	1	33	1	2	.313	.333
Calzadilla, Cristian	R-R	5-10	160	10-17-01	.286	.333	.268	23	56	5	16	3	1	0	9	12	2	0	2	7	0	1	.375	.417
Campos, Roberto	R-R	6-3	200	6-14-03	.228	.242	.223	39	136	20	31	5	0	8	19	17	1	0	1	41	3	0	.441	.316
Chacon, Esney	R-R	6-2	160	3-17-00	.294	.182	.325	18	51	7	15	2	2	0	6	8	2	0	0	11	1	1	.412	.410
Cruz, Jose	R-R	6-2	204	7-5-98	.167	--	.167	4	12	1	2	1	0	0	0	0	0	0	0	4	0	0	.250	.167
De La Cruz, Danuerys	R-R	5-11	160	4-27-01	.283	.400	.247	40	127	28	36	8	2	7	26	31	3	0	1	38	3	2	.543	.432
De La Cruz, Jose	R-R	6-0	216	1-3-02	.270	.368	.240	44	159	20	43	9	1	4	15	17	6	0	1	58	7	7	.415	.361
Figuereo, Adonis	L-L	6-2	206	5-5-01	.149	.000	.189	27	67	9	10	3	0	1	10	15	2	0	3	26	0	1	.239	.310
Garcia, Pedro	R-R	6-1	170	5-22-01	.175	.222	.167	22	57	5	10	2	1	0	6	7	1	0	2	22	0	0	.246	.269
Gonzalez, Alvaro	B-R	6-0	165	9-16-00	.333	--	.333	2	9	2	3	2	0	0	1	1	0	0	0	3	0	0	.556	.400
Irigoyen, Carlos	R-R	6-2	165	3-21-01	.149	.182	.139	14	47	7	7	2	0	0	5	4	2	0	0	19	0	2	.191	.245
Jimenez, Jeremy	R-R	6-2	180	3-3-01	.200	.278	.160	17	43	6	9	1	0	0	5	6	0	0	1	14	0	0	.233	.300
Joyce, Corey	R-R	6-1	190	8-19-98	.417	--	.417	4	12	4	5	2	0	3	3	0	0	0	0	2	0	0	1.333	.417
Keith, Colt	L-R	6-3	211	8-14-01	.667	.500	.714	3	9	2	6	1	1	0	5	3	0	1	0	0	0	0	1.000	.692
Leonardo, Iverson	L-L	6-0	173	8-21-01	.224	.115	.250	45	134	20	30	7	2	5	22	24	7	0	0	48	5	2	.418	.370
Malgeri, Ben	R-R	6-1	215	1-12-00	.286	--	.286	2	7	2	2	0	0	2	4	0	0	0	0	0	0	0	1.143	.286
Martinez Jr., Pedro	R-R	6-2	185	8-30-00	.168	.125	.176	36	101	12	17	9	0	1	15	8	5	0	3	31	0	1	.287	.256
McLaughlin, J.D.	R-R	6-3	195	12-28-00	.274	.172	.312	28	106	13	29	5	0	0	8	12	0	0	0	29	5	0	.321	.347
Mendoza, Carlos	L-R	5-9	165	12-14-99	.415	.545	.389	26	65	25	27	2	1	1	10	25	4	0	1	9	12	0	.523	.589
Meyers, Chris	L-R	6-3	210	4-27-99	.188	.200	.182	9	32	3	6	1	0	1	4	5	0	0	0	6	5	0	.313	.297
Mojica, Jimmy	R-R	6-0	175	5-4-00	.235	.324	.207	47	153	21	36	3	2	4	19	16	8	0	2	33	3	6	.359	.335
Murr, Austin	L-L	6-2	218	1-26-99	.333	--	.333	1	3	1	1	0	0	0	0	0	0	0	0	0	0	0	.333	.333
Olivas, Martin	R-R	6-1	170	7-25-01	.205	.118	.227	31	83	11	17	4	1	2	7	6	4	0	0	23	2	0	.349	.290
Pacheco, Izaac	L-R	6-4	225	11-18-02	.226	.233	.224	30	106	16	24	4	2	1	7	18	0	0	0	43	1	0	.330	.339
Pelegrin, Carlos	R-R	6-2	180	6-21-00	.237	.357	.198	37	114	17	27	7	0	4	16	26	3	1	0	42	2	2	.404	.392

	B-T	HT	WT	DOB	AVG	vLH	vRH	G	AB	R	H	2B	3B	HR	RBI	BB	HBP	SH	SF	SO	SB	CS	SLG	OBP
Perez, Yerjeni	R-R	6-1	165	2-6-00	.183	.214	.169	35	93	11	17	2	0	0	7	12	0	0	1	41	1	0	.204	.274
Quintana, Nick	R-R	5-10	180	10-13-97	.080	.000	.182	7	25	3	2	1	0	0	1	2	1	0	0	13	0	0	.120	.179
Rea, Yoandy	R-R	6-0	165	6-12-00	.318	.214	.346	23	66	8	21	5	0	1	8	5	2	0	0	11	0	1	.439	.384
Reina, Jose	R-R	6-2	160	2-28-01	.173	.143	.182	35	98	11	17	2	0	1	8	12	2	0	1	37	1	2	.224	.274
Reyes, Adinso	R-R	6-1	195	10-22-01	.184	.209	.175	48	163	21	30	7	0	7	18	12	8	0	1	73	1	1	.356	.272
Rothenberg, Mike	B-R	6-3	215	10-5-98	.286	.500	.250	5	14	1	4	2	0	0	4	1	0	0	0	1	0	0	.429	.333
Schultz, Austin	R-R	5-9	200	2-21-00	.333	.000	.500	4	12	1	4	1	1	0	1	1	1	0	0	2	1	0	.583	.429
Sequera, Manuel	R-R	6-1	170	9-28-02	.246	.233	.250	46	171	31	42	12	0	11	40	15	4	0	1	57	1	1	.509	.314
Tapia, Sergio	R-R	5-10	160	8-24-02	.281	.500	.231	13	32	11	9	1	0	0	4	6	2	0	1	5	1	0	.313	.415
Valencia, Eduardo	R-R	6-2	180	1-25-00	.319	.235	.338	29	91	18	29	6	0	1	14	11	7	1	1	13	1	0	.418	.427
Veliz, Frank	R-R	5-11	160	9-10-99	.228	.211	.233	49	158	22	36	6	2	2	13	18	1	0	1	48	4	3	.329	.309

Pitching

	B-T	HT	WT	DOB	W	L	ERA	G	GS	CG	SV	IP	H	R	ER	HR	BB	SO	AVG	vLH	vRH	K/9	BB/9
Anderson, Jack	R-R	6-3	197	11-23-99	0	0	7.50	5	0	0	0	6	6	5	5	3	4	3	.250	.222	.267	4.50	6.00
Appleton, Jose	R-R	6-3	170	7-2-97	1	0	4.24	18	0	0	2	23	20	14	11	4	12	27	.238	.231	.241	10.41	4.63
Baez, Joel	R-R	6-4	185	8-19-02	2	5	14.81	17	3	0	0	21	27	36	34	2	37	26	.310	.231	.344	11.32	16.11
Bastardo, Yeremi	L-L	5-9	160	1-13-02	0	2	8.66	12	0	0	0	18	18	18	17	3	10	22	.254	.300	.246	11.21	5.09
Bauza, Adolfo	R-R	6-2	160	9-27-00	1	3	8.33	13	13	0	0	36	41	42	33	6	35	45	.287	.231	.308	11.36	8.83
Beattie, Matt	R-R	6-3	225	1-5-99	0	0	9.00	1	0	0	0	2	1	2	2	0	4	3	.143	.000	.250	13.50	18.00
Brete, Jaison	R-R	6-1	160	4-27-01	0	0	0.00	1	0	0	0	1	1	0	0	0	0	2	.250	.000	.333	18.00	0.00
Cortes, Maximo	R-R	6-1	170	11-18-99	3	3	7.77	18	0	0	1	22	26	21	19	1	20	25	.306	.350	.292	10.23	8.18
Cruz, Jesus	R-R	6-4	185	10-8-00	1	0	7.00	20	0	0	0	27	23	24	21	0	25	45	.215	.324	.164	15.00	8.33
Di Monte, Daniele	R-R	6-2	187	2-16-02	1	8	9.84	17	10	0	0	32	40	43	35	8	29	33	.310	.432	.261	9.28	8.16
Diaz, Jose	R-R	6-5	200	5-12-00	1	2	6.30	13	12	0	0	40	43	29	28	3	26	45	.279	.277	.280	10.13	5.85
Fajardo, Rodolfo	L-L	6-3	244	2-17-00	1	1	3.12	15	0	0	0	35	25	13	12	4	14	35	.212	.231	.207	9.09	3.63
Fenelon, Wilmer	R-R	6-3	170	10-18-00	1	2	9.26	10	0	0	0	12	12	14	12	4	13	17	.261	.400	.194	13.11	10.03
Fenelon, Wilmer A.	R-R	6-3	175	6-12-03	4	4	5.57	16	5	0	0	32	23	22	20	4	30	27	.205	.276	.181	7.52	8.35
Flores, Wilmer	R-R	6-4	225	2-20-01	2	1	4.85	3	2	0	0	13	15	8	7	0	2	18	.288	.292	.286	12.46	1.38
Francisco, Roberto	R-R	6-3	190	3-1-99	0	1	4.97	11	0	0	2	13	19	11	7	1	9	11	.358	.368	.353	7.82	6.39
Gonzalez, Eliezer	R-R	6-1	160	12-21-00	0	0	--	1	0	0	0	0	3	3	0	3	0	--	--	--	--	--
Haase, Aaron	R-R	5-8	193	5-24-00	0	0	12.00	3	0	0	0	3	3	4	4	0	3	6	.250	.500	.000	18.00	9.00
Herrera, Martin	L-R	6-0	175	9-22-00	2	1	5.28	16	1	0	0	29	28	17	17	2	12	17	.259	.276	.253	5.28	3.72
Houston, Zac	R-R	6-5	260	11-30-94	0	0	0.00	2	2	0	0	3	1	0	0	0	0	4	.100	.000	.167	12.00	0.00
Ibarra, Edgardo	L-L	6-0	160	6-2-03	1	6	6.31	16	12	0	0	41	38	33	29	8	26	48	.245	.231	.248	10.45	5.66
Jimenez, Francisco	R-R	6-2	194	3-2-99	0	0	2.35	16	0	0	2	23	8	7	6	1	19	28	.113	.040	.152	10.96	7.43
King, Carson	R-R	6-2	207	12-5-99	1	1	4.97	6	5	0	0	25	24	15	14	3	13	14	.258	.250	.261	4.97	4.62
Nunez, Hendry	R-R	6-4	180	7-22-99	0	5	10.09	15	10	0	1	36	47	45	40	4	27	40	.329	.318	.333	10.09	6.81
Olivas, Martin	R-R	6-1	170	7-25-01	0	0	0.00	2	0	0	0	1	1	0	0	0	0	1	.250	.000	.333	9.00	0.00
O'Loughlin, Jack	L-L	6-5	223	3-14-00	0	1	2.25	1	1	0	0	4	3	1	1	0	2	4	.214	--	.214	9.00	4.50
Pena, Carlos	L-L	5-11	160	9-7-98	1	3	4.19	5	4	0	0	19	20	15	9	2	4	26	.253	.111	.271	12.10	1.86
Peraza, Jose	R-R	5-11	160	10-29-01	3	2	6.83	16	3	0	0	29	28	27	22	4	23	40	.267	.268	.266	12.41	7.14
Perez, Yerjeni	R-R	6-1	165	2-6-00	0	0	9.00	2	0	0	0	2	3	3	2	2	0	1	.300	.500	.167	4.50	0.00
Petit, RJ	R-R	6-8	300	9-23-99	0	0	0.00	1	0	0	0	1	0	0	0	0	0	2	.000	.000	.000	18.00	0.00
Pimentel, Yoldi	R-R	5-11	190	9-15-00	0	1	10.00	1	0	0	0	9	15	12	10	2	4	9	.375	.200	.433	9.00	4.00
Pina, Jose	R-R	6-3	170	5-24-01	0	0	1.59	5	0	0	0	6	3	1	1	0	5	8	.150	.333	.071	12.71	7.94
Quinones, Emmanuel	R-R	6-1	185	4-15-99	3	4	8.74	15	5	0	0	34	45	34	33	7	17	31	.319	.324	.317	8.21	4.50
Richmond, Nick	R-R	6-4	195	4-2-98	2	1	8.86	16	0	0	0	21	26	30	21	4	19	15	.302	.227	.328	6.33	8.02
Rodriguez, Erick	R-R	5-10	185	3-21-02	1	2	6.46	19	1	0	0	31	41	26	22	5	14	27	.333	.294	.348	7.92	4.11
Rodriguez, Moises	R-R	6-2	170	3-3-02	1	0	5.84	9	0	0	0	12	14	10	8	1	11	9	.269	.200	.286	6.57	8.03
Santana, Andy	R-R	6-3	190	10-27-99	0	3	4.50	19	3	0	1	34	40	21	17	2	9	30	.286	.375	.259	7.94	2.38
Shore, Logan	R-R	6-2	215	12-28-94	0	0	6.75	1	1	0	0	3	5	3	2	1	0	4	.385	.000	.455	13.50	0.00
Silva, Ricardo	L-L	6-1	165	4-14-00	2	1	5.75	12	9	0	0	41	56	34	26	5	8	37	.313	.316	.312	8.19	1.77
Sommerfeld, Luke	R-R	6-6	244	7-8-96	1	1	3.97	17	0	0	0	23	23	15	10	0	8	28	.258	.231	.270	11.12	3.18
Terrero, Richard	L-L	6-6	220	9-9-97	0	1	8.22	8	0	0	0	8	6	8	7	0	15	3	.222	.000	.250	3.52	17.61
Tortosa, Cristhian	L-L	6-4	170	10-30-98	1	0	6.67	17	0	0	0	28	29	23	21	4	26	41	.259	.263	.258	13.02	8.26

Fielding

C: Calzadilla 13, De La Cruz 21, Garcia 18, Jimenez 9, Rea 15, Rothenberg 5, Tapia 11, Valencia 19.
1B: Bigbie 24, Calderon 19, Calzadilla 1, De La Cruz 18, Jimenez 7, Martinez Jr. 21, Meyers 9, Perez 1, Rea 1, Valencia 9.
2B: Acevedo 38, Gonzalez 1, Keith 1, Mendoza 10, Olivas 4, Perez 2, Veliz 47.
3B: Acevedo 1, Calderon 9, Irigoyen 9, Keith 1, Martinez Jr. 9, Mendoza 12, Olivas 22, Perez 27, Quintana 4, Reyes 19, Veliz 1.
SS: Acevedo 8, Calderon 1, Cruz 2, Irigoyen 4, Joyce 3, Pacheco 26, Reyes 23, Sequera 40, Veliz 1.
OF: Benitez 25, Bigbie 7, Calzadilla 1, Campos 34, Chacon 19, De La Cruz 1, De La Cruz 42, Figuereo 17, Leonardo 38, Malgeri 2, McLaughlin 25, Mendoza 4, Mojica 46, Murr 1, Pelegrin 37, Perez 3, Reina 32.

DSL TIGERS   ROOKIE

DOMINICAN SUMMER LEAGUE

Batting	B-T	HT	WT	DOB	AVG	vLH	vRH	G	AB	R	H	2B	3B	HR	RBI	BB	HBP	SH	SF	SO	SB	CS	SLG	OBP
Bastidas, Abel	B-R	6-2	165	11-24-03	.188	.167	.192	54	181	24	34	4	3	2	27	35	2	0	1	46	12	5	.276	.324
Bautista, Sebastian	R-R	6-3	190	5-17-03	.138	.150	.133	29	80	10	11	4	0	1	7	12	1	0	0	36	1	1	.225	.258
Bolivar, Jesus	R-R	6-0	165	3-23-02	.244	.303	.228	45	160	21	39	10	2	3	24	10	2	0	1	39	8	3	.388	.295
Bravo, Yoan	R-R	6-1	165	10-14-01	.167	.207	.152	39	108	12	18	2	1	0	7	23	3	0	0	37	5	8	.204	.328
De Leon, Jensy	R-R	6-0	175	5-14-04	.214	.333	.191	27	56	13	12	2	0	0	5	10	3	0	0	15	3	1	.250	.362
De Los Santos, Raudy	R-R	5-11	155	3-18-03	.301	.423	.268	40	123	16	37	4	1	0	14	15	1	0	2	20	12	7	.350	.376
Fana, Nomar	B-R	5-11	175	9-28-02	.234	.208	.241	38	107	15	25	8	0	1	14	13	0	0	1	28	5	2	.336	.314

Name	B-T	HT	WT	DOB	AVG	vLH	vRH	G	AB	R	H	2B	3B	HR	RBI	BB	HBP	SH	SF	SO	SB	CS	OBP	SLG
Lopez, Abelaldo	R-R	6-1	160	9-5-02	.091	.148	.079	47	154	11	14	7	0	2	14	26	4	0	2	85	3	1	.175	.237
Perea, Randy	R-R	5-11	150	1-21-04	.169	.000	.208	22	59	9	10	1	1	0	5	7	2	0	1	33	5	3	.220	.275
Riera, Elian	L-L	5-10	150	2-23-04	.263	.200	.273	19	38	6	10	1	1	0	6	9	2	0	0	10	1	2	.342	.429
Rodriguez, Justin	R-R	5-10	155	3-11-04	.238	.174	.252	39	126	16	30	3	3	1	12	5	1	0	1	43	7	3	.333	.271
Rojas, Samuel	R-R	5-10	190	11-6-02	.219	.143	.237	26	73	9	16	3	0	0	7	6	3	0	0	14	0	0	.260	.305
Rondon, Newremberg	R-R	5-11	170	7-10-03	.303	.467	.270	33	89	15	27	9	0	0	14	8	1	0	4	23	2	0	.404	.353
Santana, Cristian	R-R	6-0	165	11-25-03	.269	.194	.286	54	171	40	46	12	2	9	27	30	15	0	0	46	12	7	.520	.421
Valero, Moises	R-R	6-2	185	3-1-02	.275	.333	.260	39	120	27	33	9	1	4	14	9	6	0	0	17	7	5	.467	.356
Viloria, Yoel	B-R	5-10	160	4-25-03	.195	.111	.219	16	41	12	8	2	1	0	5	6	2	0	0	12	1	1	.293	.327

Pitching	B-T	HT	WT	DOB	W	L	ERA	G	GS	CG	SV	IP	H	R	ER	HR	BB	SO	AVG	vLH	vRH	K/9	BB/9
Bellorin, Luis	R-R	5-11	170	7-26-00	3	2	4.15	20	0	0	3	26	24	18	12	0	13	20	.245	.235	.250	6.92	4.50
Boyer, Jorge	L-L	6-4	182	4-15-03	1	0	3.52	12	0	0	1	15	10	6	6	1	12	20	.185	.154	.195	11.74	7.04
Briceno, Ignacio	L-L	5-11	155	6-4-01	3	0	2.22	14	0	0	0	24	19	11	6	2	11	20	.202	.308	.185	7.40	4.07
Campos, Ulices	R-R	5-10	170	12-14-01	0	4	3.26	14	13	0	0	50	36	27	18	1	25	47	.208	.204	.210	8.52	4.53
Castillo, Rayner	R-R	6-3	180	6-30-04	4	2	2.88	14	14	0	0	59	52	26	19	1	15	55	.225	.227	.224	8.34	2.28
Chalas, Ronny	R-R	5-10	162	8-19-02	2	2	6.95	15	2	0	0	22	29	22	17	1	18	29	.302	.273	.311	11.86	7.36
Herrera, Juan	R-R	6-3	170	9-24-01	0	1	9.00	5	1	0	0	4	3	4	4	0	7	2	.200	.500	.154	4.50	15.75
Landaeta, Abraham	R-R	6-2	175	11-29-00	0	0	15.00	3	0	0	0	3	3	6	5	0	4	1	.273	.333	.250	3.00	12.00
Marcano, Carlos	R-R	6-2	150	7-8-03	5	6	5.25	18	1	0	1	36	39	25	21	1	10	41	.283	.357	.250	10.25	2.50
Martinez, Jose	R-R	6-2	170	8-27-02	0	0	2.79	6	0	0	1	10	5	4	3	1	4	11	.147	.222	.120	10.24	3.72
Melendez, Anderson	R-R	6-1	170	10-12-02	1	1	3.00	16	1	0	0	24	17	13	8	2	13	19	.205	.161	.231	7.13	4.88
Raciel, Alfredo	R-R	6-2	165	6-2-00	0	1	21.21	5	0	0	0	5	8	11	11	0	11	5	.364	.429	.333	9.64	21.21
Reyes, Gabriel	L-L	6-1	170	7-1-03	2	3	3.42	15	5	0	2	24	20	13	9	0	4	32	.213	.250	.205	12.17	1.52
Rivas, Jose	R-R	5-11	160	12-20-01	1	3	3.91	16	0	0	2	25	21	13	11	3	12	33	.219	.269	.200	11.72	4.26
Rodriguez, Hector	R-R	5-11	175	6-6-03	0	1	8.66	15	0	0	3	18	19	19	17	2	10	15	.271	.158	.314	7.64	5.09
Rodriguez, Jesus A.	L-L	5-11	145	10-15-03	0	5	6.25	13	10	0	0	36	42	31	25	4	21	33	.288	.156	.325	8.25	5.25
Salgado, Keni	R-R	6-2	170	11-18-03	0	1	7.53	16	0	0	1	14	16	13	12	0	13	13	.267	.353	.233	8.16	8.16
Sirit, Rolando	R-R	6-3	165	11-12-01	1	3	5.61	16	12	0	0	43	50	36	27	3	28	39	.292	.300	.288	8.10	5.82
Vallenilla, Luis	R-R	5-10	170	2-10-03	0	0	8.10	3	0	0	0	3	4	4	3	2	2	3	.267	.000	.364	8.10	5.40
Zambrano, Darwyn	R-R	6-2	175	7-27-00	0	1	7.20	9	0	0	1	10	12	10	8	1	6	12	.286	.222	.303	10.80	5.40

Fielding

C: Rojas 26, Rondon 31, Valero 8.
1B: Bravo 28, De Leon 1, Valero 29, Viloria 7.
2B: De Leon 17, De Los Santos 25, Rodriguez 15, Viloria 5.
3B: Bastidas 13, Bravo 12, De Leon 2, De Los Santos 4, Rodriguez 14, Santana 17.
SS: Bastidas 24, De Leon 1, De Los Santos 4, Santana 35.
OF: Bautista 18, Bolivar 45, Fana 37, Lopez 47, Perea 24, Riera 18.

Houston Astros

SEASON IN A SENTENCE: The Astros won 95 games and the American League West, capping a dominant five-year stretch in which the club advanced to the AL Championship Series each season, won pennants in 2017, 2019 and 2021 and won a title in the 2017 World Series.

HIGH POINT: No AL club had appeared in the League Championship Series five consecutive years since the 1971-75 Athletics. Those Oakland clubs advanced straight to the ALCS, while these Astros teams had to win a playoff round first to even reach the Championship Series.

LOW POINT: The Astros defeated tough White Sox and Red Sox teams in the playoffs. But a postseason injury to Lance McCullers Jr. proved too much to overcome. Short on pitchers, Houston lost the World Series to Atlanta in six games.

NOTABLE ROOKIES: In recent years, the Astros have lost core players to free agency, including Gerrit Cole following 2019, George Springer following 2020 and, in all likelihood, Carlos Correa this offseason. Houston has kept winning by integrating new core players into the mix, most notably Alex Bregman, Yordan Alvarez, Kyle Tucker and a slew of young pitchers headlined by Framber Valdez, Jose Urquidy and Cristian Javier. Add Luis Garcia to that list. The 24-year-old rookie righthander did not have a rotation spot assured in 2021 but quickly emerged with a 3.48 ERA over 155 innings and a 2.6 WAR total that was second only to McCullers among Astros pitchers. Garcia pitched perhaps the Astros' biggest game of the year, delivering 5.2 shutout innings against the Red Sox in the clinching Game 6 of the ALCS. The Astros paved the way for rookie center fielders Chas McCormick (107 OPS+, 2.3 WAR) and Jake Meyers (107 OPS+, 1.2 WAR) by trading Myles Straw to Cleveland at the deadline.

KEY TRANSACTIONS: The Astros focused on bulking up their bullpen at the 2021 trade deadline, adding relievers Kendall Graveman, Yimi Garcia and Phil Maton in three trades that sacrificed young position players Abraham Toro, Bryan de la Cruz and Myles Straw.

ON THE FARM: Hit hard with draft penalties incurred from the 2017 sign-stealing scandal, the Astros' farm system has fallen back from the pack, both in terms of winning percentage (.492, 18th) and impact potential (29th in organization talent rankings).

OPENING DAY PAYROLL: $194,472,041 (fourth). ■

PLAYERS OF THE YEAR

MAJOR LEAGUE	MINOR LEAGUE
Carlos Correa	**Jake Meyers**
SS	OF
.279/.366/.485	(AAA)
26 HR, 34 2B, 92 RBIs	.343/.408/.598,
7.2 WAR (third in AL)	16 HR, 10 SB

ORGANIZATION LEADERS

Batting		*Minimum 250 AB
*AVG	Yuli Gurriel	.319
*OPS	Kyle Tucker	.917
HR	Yordan Alvarez	33
RBI	Yordan Alvarez	104

MINORS

*AVG	Jake Meyers, Sugar Land	.343
*OBP	Marty Costes, Sugar Land, Corpus Christi	.419
*SLG	Jake Meyers, Sugar Land	.598
*OPS	Jake Meyers, Sugar Land	1.006
R	Shay Whitcomb, Asheville, Fayetteville	81
H	C.J. Hinojosa, Sugar Land	131
TB	Joe Perez, Corpus Christi, Asheville, Fayetteville	34
2B	C.J. Hinojosa, Sugar Land	35
3B	Justin Dirden, Asheville, Fayetteville	6
HR	Enmanuel Valdez, Corpus Christi, Asheville	26
RBI	Enmanuel Valdez, Corpus Christi, Asheville	90
BB	Michael Papierski, Sugar Land	64
SO	Matthew Barefoot, Corpus Christi, Asheville, Fayetteville	135
SO	J.J. Matijevic, Sugar Land, Corpus Christi	135
SB	Roilan Machandy, FCL Astros	30
SB	Shay Whitcomb, Asheville, Fayetteville	30

Pitching		#Minimum 75 IP

MAJORS

W	Lance McCullers	13
#ERA	Framber Valdez	3.14
SO	Lance McCullers	185
SV	Ryan Pressly	26

MINORS

W	J.P. France, Sugar Land, Corpus Christi	9
L	Tyler Brown, Corpus Christi, Asheville	8
L	Brett Daniels, Corpus Christi	8
L	Cesar Gomez, Asheville, Fayetteville	8
#ERA	Jonathan Bermudez, Sugar Land, Corpus Christi	3.24
G	Ronel Blanco, Sugar Land	42
GS	Jonathan Bermudez, Sugar Land, Corpus Christi	20
SV	Ronel Blanco, Sugar Land	22
IP	J.P. France, Sugar Land, Corpus Christi	114
BB	Jayson Schroeder, FCL Astros, Fayetteville	82
SO	J.P. France, Sugar Land, Corpus Christi	157
#AVG	Misael Tamarez, Asheville, Fayetteville	.206

2021 PERFORMANCE

General Manager: James Click. **Farm Director:** Pete Putila. **Scouting Director:** Kris Gross.

Class	Team	League	W	L	PCT	Finish	Manager
Majors	Houston Astros	American	95	67	.586	2nd (15)	Dusty Baker Jr.
Triple-A	Sugar Land Skeeters	Triple-A West	75	55	.577	2nd (10)	Mickey Storey
Double-A	Corpus Christi Hooks	Double-A Central	54	65	.454	9th (10)	Gregorio Petit
High-A	Asheville Tourists	High-A East	54	62	.466	8th (12)	Nate Shaver
Low-A	Fayetteville Woodpeckers	Low-A East	55	65	.458	8th (12)	Ray Hernandez
Rookie	DSL Astros	Dominican Summer	24	34	.414	36th (46)	Carlos Lugo
Rookie	FCL Astros	Florida Complex	28	28	.500	7th (18)	Ricardo Rivera/Wladimir Sutil
Overall 2021 Minor League Record		290		309	.484 18th (30)		

ORGANIZATION STATISTICS

HOUSTON ASTROS
AMERICAN LEAGUE

Batting	B-T	HT	WT	DOB	AVG	vLH	vRH	G	AB	R	H	2B	3B	HR	RBI	BB	HBP	SH	SF	SO	SB	CS	SLG	OBP
Altuve, Jose	R-R	5-6	166	5-6-90	.278	.278	.278	146	601	117	167	32	1	31	83	66	4	1	6	91	5	3	.489	.350
Alvarez, Yordan	L-R	6-5	225	6-27-97	.277	.283	.274	144	537	92	149	35	1	33	104	50	8	0	3	145	1	0	.531	.346
Brantley, Michael	L-L	6-2	209	5-15-87	.311	.219	.363	121	469	68	146	29	3	8	47	33	5	0	1	53	1	0	.437	.362
Bregman, Alex	R-R	6-0	192	3-30-94	.270	.300	.254	91	348	54	94	17	0	12	55	44	4	0	4	53	1	0	.422	.355
Castro, Jason	L-R	6-3	215	6-18-87	.235	.180	.263	66	149	22	35	7	0	8	21	25	3	2	0	54	0	0	.443	.356
Correa, Carlos	R-R	6-4	220	9-22-94	.279	.290	.274	148	555	104	155	34	1	26	92	75	4	0	6	116	0	0	.485	.366
Dawson, Ronnie	L-R	6-2	217	5-19-95	.200	--	.200	3	5	2	1	0	0	0	1	0	0	0	0	0	0	0	.200	.333
De Goti, Alex	R-R	6-0	192	8-19-94	.333	.400	.000	2	6	2	2	0	0	0	1	1	0	0	0	2	0	0	.333	.429
Diaz, Aledmys	R-R	6-1	195	8-1-90	.259	.265	.255	84	294	28	76	19	0	8	45	16	9	0	0	62	0	1	.405	.317
Garcia, Robel	B-R	6-0	195	3-28-93	.151	.278	.125	46	106	8	16	3	0	1	8	8	1	1	1	42	0	0	.208	.216
Gonzalez, Marwin	B-R	6-1	205	3-14-89	.176	.143	.200	14	34	5	6	0	0	3	8	1	1	0	0	8	0	0	.441	.222
2-team total (77 Boston)					.199	.250	.177	91	276	30	55	14	0	5	28	20	9	1	1	78	3	2	.304	.275
Gurriel, Yuli	R-R	6-0	215	6-9-84	.319	.326	.315	143	530	83	169	31	0	15	81	59	4	0	12	68	1	1	.462	.383
Jones, Taylor	R-R	6-7	230	12-6-93	.245	.367	.194	35	102	11	25	8	1	2	16	4	0	0	2	29	0	0	.402	.269
Maldonado, Martin	R-R	6-0	230	8-16-86	.172	.212	.154	125	373	40	64	10	1	12	36	47	5	0	1	127	0	0	.300	.272
McCormick, Chas	R-L	6-0	208	5-7-95	.257	.244	.262	108	284	47	73	12	0	14	50	25	4	0	7	104	4	2	.447	.319
Meyers, Jake	R-L	6-0	200	6-18-96	.260	.304	.233	49	146	22	38	8	0	6	28	10	4	2	1	50	3	0	.438	.323
Siri, Jose	R-R	6-2	175	7-22-95	.304	.333	.290	21	46	10	14	0	1	4	9	1	2	0	0	17	3	1	.609	.347
Straw, Myles	R-R	5-10	178	10-17-94	.262	.226	.279	98	325	44	85	13	1	2	34	38	2	1	4	71	17	5	.326	.339
2-team total (60 Cleveland)					.271	.243	.285	158	564	86	153	29	1	4	48	67	2	1	4	121	30	6	.348	.349
Stubbs, Garrett	L-R	5-10	170	5-26-93	.176	.167	.179	18	34	2	6	2	0	0	3	2	0	2	0	7	0	0	.235	.222
Toro, Abraham	B-R	6-0	206	12-20-96	.211	.304	.186	35	109	17	23	1	0	6	20	9	3	0	1	21	3	1	.385	.287
2-team total (60 Seattle)					.239	.250	.233	95	335	45	80	12	0	11	46	31	7	0	2	54	6	3	.373	.315
Tucker, Kyle	L-R	6-4	199	1-17-97	.294	.286	.299	140	506	83	149	37	3	30	92	53	1	0	5	90	14	2	.557	.359
Wilson, Jacob	R-R	5-11	219	7-29-90	.154	.000	.222	6	13	2	2	1	1	0	1	1	0	0	0	2	0	0	.385	.214
2-team total (6 Oakland)					.150	.091	.222	12	20	3	3	1	1	0	1	1	0	0	0	3	0	0	.300	.190

Pitching	B-T	HT	WT	DOB	W	L	ERA	G	GS	CG	SV	IP	H	R	ER	HR	BB	SO	AVG	vLH	vRH	K/9	BB/9
Abreu, Bryan	R-R	6-1	225	4-22-97	3	3	5.75	31	0	0	1	36	35	26	23	4	18	36	.254	.302	.224	9.00	4.50
Baez, Pedro	R-R	6-0	232	3-11-88	0	0	2.08	4	0	0	0	4	2	1	1	1	1	5	.143	.000	.250	10.38	2.08
Bielak, Brandon	L-R	6-2	208	4-2-96	3	4	4.50	28	2	0	1	50	48	29	25	5	21	46	.254	.256	.252	8.28	3.78
Emanuel, Kent	L-L	6-4	225	6-4-92	1	0	2.55	10	0	0	0	18	12	5	5	4	4	13	.190	.233	.162	6.62	2.04
Garcia, Luis	R-R	6-1	244	12-13-96	11	8	3.48	30	28	0	0	155	133	62	60	19	50	167	.232	.282	.182	9.68	2.90
Garcia, Robel	B-R	6-0	195	3-28-93	0	0	36.00	1	0	0	0	1	5	4	4	2	0	0	.625	.500	.667	0.00	0.00
Garcia, Yimi	R-R	6-2	228	8-18-90	1	2	5.48	23	0	0	0	21	18	15	13	3	5	25	.225	.273	.191	10.55	2.11
Garza Jr., Ralph	R-R	6-2	220	4-6-94	1	2	4.09	9	0	0	0	11	11	6	5	2	7	14	.262	.235	.280	11.45	5.73
2-team total (18 Minnesota)					1	4	3.56	27	0	0	1	30	24	15	12	5	14	29	.214	.195	.225	8.60	4.15
Graveman, Kendall	R-R	6-2	200	12-21-90	1	1	3.13	23	0	0	0	23	20	8	8	1	12	27	.238	.295	.175	10.57	4.70
2-team total (30 Seattle)					5	1	1.77	53	0	0	10	56	35	15	11	3	20	61	.180	.253	.117	9.80	3.21
Greinke, Zack	R-R	6-2	200	10-21-83	11	6	4.16	30	29	1	0	171	164	82	79	30	36	120	.252	.199	.285	6.32	1.89
Hartman, Ryan	L-L	6-3	234	4-21-94	0	0	3.86	1	0	0	0	2	3	1	1	1	0	2	.300	.000	.333	7.71	0.00
Ivey, Tyler	R-R	6-4	195	5-12-96	0	0	7.71	1	1	0	0	5	6	4	4	1	1	3	.316	.300	.333	5.79	1.93
James, Josh	R-R	6-3	234	3-8-93	0	0	5.40	5	0	0	0	5	4	3	3	1	2	8	.211	.182	.250	14.40	3.60
Javier, Cristian	R-R	6-1	213	3-26-97	4	1	3.55	36	9	0	2	101	67	41	40	16	53	130	.186	.230	.155	11.55	4.71
Martinez, Seth	R-R	6-2	200	8-29-94	0	0	15.00	3	0	0	0	3	5	5	5	0	3	3	.385	.333	.429	9.00	9.00
Maton, Phil	R-R	6-2	206	3-25-93	4	0	4.97	27	0	0	0	25	29	15	14	2	12	24	.284	.224	.340	8.53	4.26
2-team total (38 Cleveland)					6	0	4.73	65	1	0	0	67	65	36	35	6	32	85	.256	.233	.275	11.48	4.32
McCullers Jr., Lance	L-R	6-1	210	10-2-93	13	5	3.16	28	28	0	0	162	122	59	57	13	76	185	.205	.223	.188	10.26	4.21
Montero, Rafael	R-R	6-0	190	10-17-90	0	1	0.00	4	0	0	0	6	3	1	0	0	2	5	.158	.143	.167	7.50	3.00
2-team total (40 Seattle)					5	4	6.39	44	0	0	7	49	59	40	35	4	17	42	.296	.276	.309	7.66	3.10
Odorizzi, Jake	R-R	6-2	190	3-27-90	6	7	4.21	24	23	0	0	105	97	51	49	16	34	91	.243	.250	.238	7.82	2.92
Paredes, Enoli	R-R	5-11	171	9-28-95	0	0	6.23	12	0	0	0	9	7	10	6	0	17	15	.212	.273	.182	15.58	17.65

Name	B-T	HT	WT	DOB	W	L	ERA	G	GS	CG	SV	IP	H	R	ER	HR	BB	SO	AVG	vLH	vRH	K/9	BB/9
Pressly, Ryan	R-R	6-2	206	12-15-88	5	3	2.25	64	0	0	26	64	49	19	16	4	13	81	.208	.194	.219	11.39	1.83
Pruitt, Austin	R-R	5-10	185	8-31-89	0	1	6.75	2	0	0	0	3	3	2	2	2	0	1	.273	.500	.143	3.38	0.00
Raley, Brooks	L-L	6-3	200	6-29-88	2	3	4.78	58	0	0	2	49	43	30	26	6	16	65	.232	.195	.259	11.94	2.94
Rodriguez, Nivaldo	R-R	6-1	214	4-16-97	0	0	2.45	4	0	0	0	7	4	2	2	2	4	3	.167	.000	.308	3.68	4.91
Scrubb, Andre	R-R	6-4	270	1-13-95	1	1	5.03	18	0	0	0	20	15	11	11	5	14	21	.214	.130	.255	9.61	6.41
Smith, Joe	R-R	6-2	211	3-22-84	1	1	7.48	27	0	0	0	22	35	18	18	4	4	17	.376	.320	.397	7.06	1.66
2-team total (23 Seattle)					4	4	4.99	50	0	0	0	40	47	23	22	5	8	34	.297	.250	.314	7.71	1.82
Solomon, Peter	R-R	6-4	211	8-16-96	1	0	1.29	6	0	0	0	14	10	2	2	0	8	10	.217	.250	.167	6.43	5.14
Stanek, Ryne	R-R	6-4	226	7-26-91	3	5	3.42	72	0	0	2	68	46	32	26	8	37	83	.186	.245	.148	10.93	4.87
Taylor, Blake	L-L	6-3	220	8-17-95	4	4	3.16	51	0	0	0	43	38	19	15	6	22	41	.233	.123	.306	8.65	4.64
Urquidy, Jose	R-R	6-0	217	5-1-95	8	3	3.62	20	20	0	0	107	87	43	43	17	19	90	.218	.190	.238	7.57	1.60
Valdez, Framber	R-L	5-11	239	11-19-93	11	6	3.14	22	22	1	0	135	110	52	47	12	58	125	.220	.225	.219	8.35	3.88

Fielding

Catcher

Catcher	PCT	G	PO	A	E	DP	PB
Castro	.995	52	363	13	2	1	3
Maldonado	.993	123	1049	44	8	9	7
Stubbs	1.000	14	76	2	0	0	1

First Base

First Base	PCT	G	PO	A	E	DP
Diaz	1.000	12	87	7	0	5
Garcia	1.000	1	2	0	0	0
Gonzalez	1.000	2	21	0	0	1
Gurriel	.995	142	1057	86	6	95
Jones	1.000	14	83	7	0	7
Maldonado	1.000	1	9	0	0	2
Toro	1.000	2	15	1	0	1

Second Base

Second Base	PCT	G	PO	A	E	DP
Altuve	.985	144	199	344	8	76
De Goti	1.000	2	2	0	0	0
Diaz	.976	13	11	29	1	7
Garcia	1.000	9	10	12	0	5
Gonzalez	.833	2	3	7	2	2
Wilson	1.000	1	1	0	0	0

Third Base

Third Base	PCT	G	PO	A	E	DP
Bregman	.964	90	59	158	8	13
Diaz	.988	30	22	60	1	5
Garcia	.962	15	5	20	1	1
Gonzalez	1.000	5	2	8	0	1
Gurriel	.000	1	0	0	0	0
Toro	.963	30	15	62	3	7
Wilson	1.000	5	1	5	0	0

Shortstop

Shortstop	PCT	G	PO	A	E	DP
Correa	.981	148	183	384	11	70
Diaz	.947	9	4	14	1	0
Garcia	.974	13	10	27	1	8

Outfield

Outfield	PCT	G	PO	A	E	DP
Alvarez	.981	41	49	3	1	0
Brantley	.992	92	128	2	1	1
Diaz	1.000	16	21	0	0	0
Jones	1.000	10	6	2	0	0
McCormick	.994	106	166	2	1	1
Meyers	.988	46	84	1	1	0
Siri	1.000	18	12	2	0	0
Straw	1.000	96	234	5	0	2
Stubbs	1.000	2	1	0	0	0
Tucker	.989	137	254	6	3	2

SUGAR LAND SKEETERS   TRIPLE-A

TRIPLE-A WEST

Batting	B-T	HT	WT	DOB	AVG	vLH	vRH	G	AB	R	H	2B	3B	HR	RBI	BB	HBP	SH	SF	SO	SB	CS	SLG	OBP
Bregman, Alex	R-R	6-0	192	3-30-94	.250	.111	.296	11	36	6	9	3	0	1	5	7	1	0	0	2	0	0	.417	.386
Butera, Drew	R-R	6-1	212	8-9-83	.106	.000	.139	15	47	8	5	1	0	2	5	8	2	0	1	15	1	0	.255	.259
2-team total (49 Salt Lake)					.195	.205	.193	64	205	36	40	8	1	6	16	27	8	2	1	65	4	1	.332	.311
Castro, Jason	L-R	6-3	215	6-18-87	.200	.000	.333	3	5	0	1	0	0	0	1	4	1	0	0	2	0	0	.200	.600
Costes, Marty	R-R	5-9	200	12-18-95	.262	.375	.235	40	122	21	32	8	2	4	19	25	3	0	3	27	4	2	.459	.392
Dawson, Ronnie	L-R	6-2	217	5-19-95	.249	.216	.260	94	353	59	88	21	1	7	43	46	4	2	2	84	15	8	.374	.341
De Goti, Alex	R-R	6-0	192	8-19-94	.260		.223	104	383	54	89	22	5	5	41	46	5	1	3	108	7	0	.355	.320
De La Cruz, Bryan	R-R	6-2	175	12-16-96	.324	.256	.351	66	272	48	88	17	0	12	50	17	1	0	3	59	2	4	.518	.362
Garcia, Robel	B-R	6-0	195	3-28-93	.162	.176	.157	32	117	13	19	6	0	6	18	17	1	0	1	45	0	0	.368	.272
Gonzalez, Marwin	B-R	6-1	205	3-14-89	.286	1.000	.167	2	7	1	2	1	0	0	1	1	0	0	0	2	0	0	.429	.375
Gonzalez, Norel	L-R	6-1	240	6-26-94	.253	.231	.263	23	83	14	21	3	0	3	9	8	0	0	1	16	4	0	.398	.315
Hinojosa, C.J.	R-R	5-10	185	7-15-94	.316	.292	.325	104	414	68	131	35	0	11	67	23	1	1	4	77	4	2	.481	.351
Jones, Taylor	R-R	6-7	230	12-6-93	.331	.308	.338	48	178	36	59	15	0	10	44	31	0	0	3	43	0	1	.584	.425
Lee, AJ	R-R	6-0	180	5-26-97	.217	.125	.267	8	23	1	5	2	0	0	3	0	1	0	1	11	0	0	.304	.217
Lee, Korey	R-R	6-2	210	7-25-98	.229	.286	.214	9	35	2	8	4	0	0	4	2	0	0	1	9	0	0	.343	.263
Leon, Pedro	R-R	5-10	170	5-28-98	.131	.154	.125	17	61	11	8	2	0	0	2	14	0	0	0	23	4	2	.164	.293
Machado, Carlos	R-R	6-2	170	6-5-98	.200	.333	.000	2	5	0	1	1	0	0	0	0	0	0	0	1	0	0	.400	.200
Matijevic, J.J.	L-R	6-0	206	11-14-95	.245	.222	.252	78	282	46	69	19	3	16	48	33	1	0	1	98	4	0	.504	.325
McCormick, Chas	R-L	6-0	208	4-19-95	.500	.571	.000	2	8	3	4	1	0	0	1	1	0	0	0	2	0	0	.625	.556
Mendoza, Sean	B-S	5-8	150	6-2-00	.235	.333	.214	6	17	0	4	1	0	0	0	0	1	0	0	8	0	0	.294	.278
Meyers, Jake	R-R	6-0	200	6-18-96	.343	.321	.352	68	271	52	93	17	2	16	51	25	6	0	2	59	10	3	.598	.408
Papierski, Michael	B-R	6-3	224	2-26-96	.246	.250	.245	103	333	41	82	18	2	7	46	64	9	1	3	85	1	5	.375	.379
Pena, Jeremy	R-R	6-0	202	9-22-97	.287	.222	.305	30	122	22	35	4	2	10	19	6	5	0	0	35	5	1	.598	.346
Quintana, Lorenzo	R-R	5-10	205	3-1-89	.311	.346	.299	28	103	11	32	3	0	0	4	9	1	0	0	19	2	0	.340	.372
Rivera, Yadiel	R-R	6-3	190	5-2-92	.232	.353	.192	19	69	3	16	2	0	0	8	2	0	1	1	17	2	1	.261	.250
Salazar, Cesar	L-R	5-9	185	3-15-96	.750	1.000	.667	1	4	1	3	2	0	0	1	0	0	0	0	0	0	0	1.250	.750
Shaver, Colton	R-R	6-1	249	9-16-97	.192	.164	.205	59	182	26	35	4	0	12	28	31	7	0	0	87	0	0	.412	.332
Sierra, Miguelangel	R-R	5-11	201	12-2-97	.193	.143	.209	68	207	41	40	7	2	0	10	31	21	7	1	2	82	3	0	.391	.287
Siri, Jose	R-R	6-2	175	7-22-95	.318	.330	.313	94	362	70	115	29	4	16	72	26	5	1	3	122	24	3	.552	.369
Stubbs, Garrett	L-R	5-10	170	5-26-93	.265	.250	.271	37	113	25	30	5	0	2	15	30	1	0	2	29	4	0	.363	.418
Taylor, Chandler	L-L	6-1	210	2-7-96	.333	--	.333	1	3	1	1	0	0	0	0	0	0	0	0	2	0	0	.333	.333
Toro, Abraham	B-R	6-0	206	12-20-96	.352	.333	.364	17	54	10	19	5	1	2	11	11	3	0	0	8	2	1	.593	.485
Wielansky, Michael	R-R	6-2	175	3-18-97	.000	.000	.000	6	7	0	0	0	0	0	0	5	0	0	0	0	0	0	.000	.222
Wilson, Jacob	R-R	5-11	219	7-29-90	.173	.200	.169	20	75	4	13	0	0	1	6	6	1	0	1	19	0	0	.213	.241
2-team total (49 Las Vegas)					.255	.323	.232	69	259	43	66	17	2	15	52	32	6	0	4	62	0	0	.510	.346

Pitching	B-T	HT	WT	DOB	W	L	ERA	G	GS	CG	SV	IP	H	R	ER	HR	BB	SO	AVG	vLH	vRH	K/9	BB/9
Abreu, Bryan	R-R	6-1	225	4-22-97	0	0	1.76	15	0	0	0	15	11	3	3	0	13	24	.200	.167	.226	14.09	7.63
Baez, Pedro	R-R	6-0	232	3-11-88	1	1	5.59	9	1	0	0	10	13	6	6	1	2	7	.333	.353	.318	6.52	1.86
Bermudez, Jonathan	L-L	6-2	237	10-16-95	2	1	3.06	7	5	0	0	32	21	12	11	3	13	40	.181	.194	.176	11.13	3.62

Pitching	B-T	HT	WT	DOB	W	L	ERA	G	GS	CG	SV	IP	H	R	ER	HR	BB	SO	AVG	vLH	vRH	K/9	BB/9
Bielak, Brandon	L-R	6-2	208	4-2-96	2	0	2.08	6	3	0	0	17	16	7	4	0	4	22	.235	.289	.167	11.42	2.08
Blanco, Ronel	R-R	6-0	180	8-31-93	5	3	3.40	42	0	0	22	45	29	19	17	7	16	57	.178	.155	.190	11.40	3.20
Brown, Hunter	R-R	6-2	212	8-29-98	5	1	3.88	11	8	0	0	51	47	24	22	6	21	55	.246	.217	.269	9.71	3.71
Conine, Brett	R-R	6-3	218	10-16-96	8	4	5.66	25	18	0	1	99	105	75	62	20	43	83	.267	.226	.291	7.57	3.92
De Goti, Alex	R-R	6-0	192	8-19-94	0	0	0.00	1	0	0	0	1	1	0	0	0	0	0	.250	.000	.333	0.00	0.00
Donato, Chad	R-R	6-0	195	6-3-95	2	4	5.00	10	6	1	1	36	35	20	20	5	12	27	.254	.189	.294	6.75	3.00
Dubin, Shawn	R-R	6-1	171	9-6-95	4	3	3.44	16	8	0	1	50	35	19	19	4	19	69	.201	.190	.207	12.50	3.44
Eades, Ryan	R-R	6-2	210	12-15-91	0	1	9.00	6	0	0	0	6	7	6	6	2	4	9	.259	.364	.188	13.50	6.00
Ferrell, Riley	R-R	6-2	225	10-18-93	0	4	2.93	38	0	0	2	40	27	21	13	3	27	48	.189	.228	.163	10.80	6.08
France, J.P.	R-R	6-0	216	4-4-95	6	1	3.59	17	13	0	0	80	67	39	32	12	38	107	.220	.250	.203	11.99	4.26
Garza Jr., Ralph	R-R	6-2	220	4-6-94	2	0	1.26	10	0	0	0	14	5	2	2	2	8	17	.104	.100	.107	10.67	5.02
Greinke, Zack	R-R	6-2	200	10-21-83	0	0	0.00	1	1	0	0	2	1	0	0	0	0	3	.143	.000	.200	13.50	0.00
Hansen, Austin	R-R	6-0	204	8-25-96	0	2	7.36	9	6	0	1	26	23	21	21	7	23	27	.240	.257	.230	9.47	8.06
Hartman, Ryan	L-L	6-3	234	4-21-94	3	3	5.03	13	12	0	0	63	62	36	35	16	18	59	.255	.291	.245	8.47	2.59
Hernandez, Nick	R-R	6-1	212	12-30-94	0	0	0.00	1	0	0	0	2	0	0	0	0	3	1	.000	.000	.000	4.50	13.50
Ivey, Tyler	R-R	6-4	195	5-12-96	0	1	4.91	4	3	0	0	11	14	10	6	2	8	13	.304	.429	.250	10.64	6.55
James, Josh	R-R	6-3	234	3-8-93	1	2	3.38	20	0	0	1	19	17	8	7	0	8	27	.233	.303	.175	13.02	3.86
Kelly, Michael	R-R	6-4	185	9-6-92	3	4	2.82	35	0	0	0	45	40	16	14	4	17	53	.238	.270	.219	10.68	3.43
LaRue, Carson	R-R	6-1	175	3-6-96	2	1	4.50	5	1	0	1	16	12	9	8	2	7	16	.200	.105	.244	9.00	3.94
Martes, Francis	R-R	6-0	249	11-24-95	0	3	13.11	10	0	0	0	12	10	21	17	3	20	13	.238	.250	.231	10.03	15.43
Martinez, Seth	R-R	6-2	200	8-29-94	5	3	2.81	36	0	0	0	58	35	21	18	5	20	78	.171	.133	.192	12.17	3.12
McCullers Jr., Lance	L-R	6-1	202	10-2-93	0	0	2.25	1	1	0	0	4	2	1	1	0	0	4	.143	.250	.100	9.00	0.00
McKee, Colin	R-R	6-3	225	6-21-94	5	2	4.42	30	1	0	0	39	32	23	19	6	23	57	.222	.245	.209	13.27	5.35
Mushinski, Parker	L-L	6-0	218	11-22-95	0	0	2.84	8	1	0	0	13	14	7	4	3	3	18	.264	.222	.273	12.79	2.13
Odorizzi, Jake	R-R	6-2	190	3-27-90	0	1	4.70	2	2	0	0	8	10	4	4	1	1	11	.313	.125	.500	12.91	1.17
Olczak, Jon	R-R	6-0	180	11-14-93	2	1	4.34	11	0	0	0	19	18	10	9	2	4	19	.243	.303	.195	9.16	1.93
Paredes, Enoli	R-R	5-11	171	9-28-95	1	0	4.28	26	0	0	1	27	27	13	13	7	20	38	.255	.366	.185	12.51	6.59
Pruitt, Austin	R-R	5-10	185	8-31-89	1	0	3.68	5	2	0	0	7	7	3	3	1	1	6	.259	.273	.250	7.36	1.23
Raley, Brooks	L-L	6-3	200	6-29-88	0	0	0.00	1	0	0	0	1	1	0	0	0	0	3	.250	.000	.333	9.00	0.00
Rodriguez, Nivaldo	R-R	6-1	214	4-16-97	2	1	5.93	10	6	0	0	27	33	19	18	5	16	25	.295	.196	.364	8.23	5.27
Scheetz, Kit	L-L	5-10	185	5-18-94	2	2	3.93	38	2	0	1	55	50	25	24	6	31	44	.244	.275	.234	7.20	5.07
Scrubb, Andre	R-R	6-4	270	1-13-95	0	0	1.80	15	0	0	0	15	7	3	3	1	13	20	.137	.267	.083	12.00	7.80
Smith, Joe	R-R	6-2	211	3-22-84	1	0	0.00	2	1	0	0	2	0	0	0	0	0	3	.000	.000	.000	13.50	0.00
Solomon, Peter	R-R	6-4	211	8-16-96	8	1	4.70	21	18	0	1	98	89	55	51	16	42	112	.235	.259	.220	10.32	3.87
Taylor, Blake	L-L	6-3	220	8-17-95	0	0	6.00	3	0	0	0	3	6	2	2	1	0	3	.400	.167	.556	9.00	0.00
Torres, Jojanse	R-R	6-2	188	8-4-95	0	3	7.32	8	5	0	0	20	19	17	16	4	19	23	.257	.360	.204	10.53	8.69
Urquidy, Jose	R-R	6-0	217	5-1-95	1	0	2.00	2	2	0	0	9	5	2	2	0	0	11	.156	.105	.231	11.00	0.00
Valdez, Framber	R-L	5-11	239	11-19-93	0	1	1.29	2	2	0	0	7	9	5	1	0	2	5	.290	.000	.346	6.43	2.57
Velazquez, Hector	R-R	6-0	218	11-26-88	1	1	1.46	14	2	0	1	25	23	5	4	2	8	22	.247	.214	.275	8.03	2.92

Fielding

Catcher	PCT	G	PO	A	E	DP	PB
Butera	1.000	11	110	4	0	0	3
Castro	1.000	3	21	2	0	0	0
Lee	1.000	4	45	1	0	0	1
Papierski	.997	64	623	22	2	1	7
Quintana	.974	10	73	1	2	0	0
Salazar	1.000	1	15	0	0	0	0
Shaver	.985	16	131	4	2	0	0
Stubbs	.986	28	276	12	4	3	1

First Base	PCT	G	PO	A	E	DP
Butera	1.000	2	11	0	0	0
De Goti	1.000	1	5	0	0	2
Gonzalez	1.000	4	18	1	0	1
Jones	1.000	22	169	10	0	13
Lee	.933	2	14	0	1	2
Matijevic	1.000	27	179	16	0	14
Papierski	.985	28	190	11	3	17
Quintana	.967	13	87	1	3	12
Rivera	.923	3	12	0	1	1
Shaver	.989	29	172	11	2	17
Toro	1.000	2	13	2	0	1
Wilson	1.000	3	24	1	0	4

Second Base	PCT	G	PO	A	E	DP
De Goti	.977	36	54	75	3	11
Garcia	.974	12	17	20	1	6
Hinojosa	.992	34	52	71	1	24
Lee	1.000	6	6	7	0	0
Mendoza	1.000	4	8	7	0	3
Rivera	1.000	4	1	6	0	0
Sierra	.957	29	33	56	4	11
Stubbs	1.000	6	5	10	0	1
Toro	.933	3	6	8	1	2
Wilson	1.000	1	1	1	0	1

Third Base	PCT	G	PO	A	E	DP
Bregman	.947	10	1	17	1	4
De Goti	.971	18	13	20	1	1
Garcia	.800	8	0	8	2	0
Gonzalez	.000	1	0	0	0	0
Hinojosa	.896	32	7	36	5	3
Jones	.850	16	10	24	6	1
Leon	.818	6	4	5	2	0
Mendoza	.750	2	0	3	1	0
Pena	1.000	2	0	2	0	0
Rivera	.938	6	9	6	1	2
Shaver	.889	5	3	5	1	2
Sierra	.912	21	8	23	3	2
Toro	.957	8	4	18	1	0
Wielansky	1.000	3	1	2	0	0
Wilson	.938	7	3	12	1	1

Shortstop	PCT	G	PO	A	E	DP
De Goti	.988	45	51	109	2	30
Garcia	1.000	3	3	10	0	4
Hinojosa	.932	33	27	82	8	16
Lee	1.000	1	0	2	0	0
Leon	.957	7	9	13	1	3
Pena	.970	25	29	68	3	8
Rivera	1.000	6	6	19	0	5
Sierra	.918	14	8	37	4	6
Toro	1.000	1	1	2	0	0

Outfield	PCT	G	PO	A	E	DP
Costes	.957	35	63	3	3	2
Dawson	.973	84	143	2	4	1
De Goti	.900	8	9	0	1	0
De La Cruz	1.000	57	99	1	0	0
Garcia	1.000	2	1	0	0	0
Gonzalez	1.000	1	1	0	0	0
Gonzalez	.958	14	22	1	1	0
Jones	1.000	11	10	3	0	0
Leon	1.000	4	13	0	0	0
Machado	1.000	2	4	0	0	0
Matijevic	.966	34	55	1	2	0
McCormick	1.000	3	1	0	0	0
Meyers	1.000	61	147	4	0	2
Rivera	1.000	2	1	0	0	0
Siri	.970	84	159	2	5	0
Toro	--	1	0	0	0	0
Wilson	1.000	9	14	1	0	0

CORPUS CHRISTI HOOKS — DOUBLE-A
DOUBLE-A CENTRAL

Batting	B-T	HT	WT	DOB	AVG	vLH	vRH	G	AB	R	H	2B	3B	HR	RBI	BB	HBP	SH	SF	SO	SB	CS	SLG	OBP
Adams, Jake	R-R	6-2	250	12-23-95	.141	.259	.092	27	92	8	13	2	0	3	13	4	4	0	3	48	1	1	.261	.204

HOUSTON ASTROS

Name	B-T	HT	WT	DOB	AVG	vLH	vRH	G	AB	R	H	2B	3B	HR	RBI	BB	HBP	SH	SF	SO	SB	CS	SLG	OBP
Adolph, Ross	L-R	6-1	190	12-17-96	.245	.250	.243	65	216	33	53	9	3	10	37	24	7	0	1	77	3	3	.454	.339
Arias, Bryan	R-R	6-0	205	6-6-97	.191	.250	.148	15	47	7	9	0	0	2	6	9	1	1	0	18	1	1	.319	.333
Barefoot, Matthew	R-L	6-0	205	9-20-97	.175	.214	.158	36	137	13	24	5	0	4	16	7	2	0	0	50	4	1	.299	.226
Berryhill, Luke	R-R	6-2	227	5-28-98	.313	.500	.200	9	32	2	10	1	0	0	3	7	2	0	0	15	0	1	.344	.463
Biermann, Zach	L-L	6-3	225	6-2-97	.133	.000	.154	5	15	2	1	0	0	1	2	1	0	0	0	0	0	0	.200	.278
Castro, Jason	L-R	6-3	215	6-18-87	.250	.000	.333	1	4	1	1	0	0	0	0	0	0	0	0	0	0	0	.250	.250
Ceuta, Yorbin	B-R	6-0	165	1-14-00	.200	.333	.167	4	15	3	3	1	0	0	1	0	1	0	0	0	0	0	.267	.250
Costes, Marty	R-R	5-9	200	12-18-95	.332	.313	.340	61	208	36	69	10	0	2	30	31	9	0	2	43	7	3	.409	.436
Diaz, Aledmys	R-R	6-1	195	8-1-90	.154	.167	.143	4	13	1	2	0	0	0	0	4	0	0	0	3	0	0	.154	.353
Gonzalez, Norel	L-R	6-1	240	6-26-94	.283	.250	.298	65	233	32	66	17	0	12	40	25	5	0	0	51	1	5	.511	.365
Hensley, David	R-R	6-6	190	3-28-96	.293	.339	.274	105	396	54	116	25	3	9	51	46	2	0	1	104	11	3	.439	.369
Holderbach, Alex	R-R	6-0	205	12-26-96	.234	.188	.258	13	47	3	11	2	1	1	2	4	0	0	0	20	0	0	.383	.294
Julks, Corey	R-R	6-1	185	2-27-96	.287	.290	.286	85	338	67	97	23	2	14	36	32	1	0	1	84	15	5	.491	.349
Kessinger, Grae	R-R	6-2	204	8-25-97	.209	.286	.178	86	297	46	62	9	0	9	26	27	6	0	1	81	12	5	.330	.287
Krabbe, Tyler	R-R	6-2	220	1-13-97	.154	.200	.125	5	13	0	2	0	0	0	0	0	0	0	0	0	0	0	.154	.154
Lee, AJ	R-R	6-0	180	5-26-97	.000	.000	.000	11	23	1	0	0	0	0	0	2	0	0	0	10	0	0	.000	.080
Lee, Korey	R-R	6-2	210	7-25-98	.254	.288	.241	50	185	25	47	9	1	8	27	17	1	0	0	35	3	1	.443	.320
Leon, Pedro	R-R	5-10	170	5-28-98	.249	.304	.230	52	185	29	46	7	1	9	33	25	7	0	0	67	13	8	.443	.359
Machado, Carlos	R-R	6-2	170	6-5-98	.200	--	.200	1	5	1	1	1	0	0	0	0	0	0	0	1	0	0	.400	.200
Manea, Scott	R-R	5-11	237	12-21-95	.286	.295	.282	65	210	32	60	10	0	9	38	39	3	0	0	52	0	3	.462	.405
Matijevic, J.J.	L-R	6-0	206	11-14-95	.275	.233	.289	31	120	21	33	4	0	9	27	20	0	0	0	37	2	1	.533	.379
McKenna, Alex	R-R	6-2	204	9-6-97	.206	.234	.190	38	131	12	27	5	1	2	15	17	4	0	1	55	1	2	.305	.314
Mendoza, Sean	B-R	5-8	150	6-2-00	.214	.200	.222	5	14	2	3	1	0	0	1	0	0	0	0	4	0	0	.286	.214
Perez, Joe	R-R	6-2	198	8-12-99	.267	.216	.293	69	281	34	75	19	0	8	27	24	0	0	2	80	2	1	.420	.322
Salazar, Cesar	L-R	5-9	185	3-15-96	.243	.258	.237	32	107	12	26	5	1	8	19	9	4	0	2	24	2	1	.533	.320
Schreiber, Scott	R-R	6-3	230	10-13-95	.264	.167	.315	39	140	19	37	8	0	7	28	8	5	0	1	32	2	2	.471	.325
Shaver, Colton	R-R	6-1	249	9-18-95	.118	.000	.160	11	34	3	4	1	0	1	4	4	3	0	0	16	0	0	.235	.268
Stubbs, C.J.	R-R	6-3	207	11-12-96	.190	.130	.213	24	84	10	16	3	0	0	10	10	3	0	0	27	2	2	.226	.299
Taylor, Chandler	L-L	6-1	210	2-7-96	.148	.095	.162	62	196	24	29	3	0	8	14	33	5	0	1	100	7	3	.286	.285
Valdez, Enmanuel	L-R	5-9	191	12-28-98	.256	.179	.296	23	82	11	21	6	0	5	18	13	2	0	1	22	0	1	.512	.367
Wielansky, Michael	R-R	6-2	175	3-18-97	.156	.182	.143	12	32	7	5	0	0	0	1	7	0	0	0	10	0	1	.156	.308

Pitching	B-T	HT	WT	DOB	W	L	ERA	G	GS	CG	SV	IP	H	R	ER	HR	BB	SO	AVG	vLH	vRH	K/9	BB/9
Adams, Jake	R-R	6-2	250	12-23-95	0	0	0.00	1	0	0	0	1	0	0	0	0	0	1	.000	.000	.000	9.00	0.00
Bermudez, Jonathan	L-L	6-2	237	10-16-95	3	5	3.32	18	15	0	1	79	72	33	29	7	21	106	.238	.272	.226	12.13	2.40
Bravo, Jose	R-R	6-3	213	6-10-97	0	2	4.76	5	1	0	0	11	14	6	6	3	5	10	.292	.429	.235	7.94	3.97
Brown, Hunter	R-R	6-2	212	8-29-98	1	4	4.20	13	11	0	1	49	45	23	23	6	29	76	.245	.207	.275	13.86	5.29
Brown, Tyler	R-R	6-4	242	10-2-98	1	3	6.26	8	4	0	0	27	26	20	19	4	24	40	.252	.257	.250	13.17	7.90
Cobos, Franny	R-R	5-9	182	2-1-01	0	0	3.86	1	0	0	0	2	1	1	1	1	1	1	.125	.200	.000	3.86	3.86
Collado, Willy	R-R	6-2	168	3-30-98	1	1	6.75	4	0	0	0	7	5	6	5	2	9	6	.217	.222	.214	8.10	12.15
Conn, Devin	R-R	5-11	169	4-3-97	1	2	2.67	21	0	0	4	34	25	13	10	5	10	31	.205	.152	.237	8.29	2.67
Daniels, Brett	R-R	6-0	194	2-25-96	5	8	6.58	22	18	0	0	90	96	71	66	12	48	112	.273	.296	.260	11.16	4.78
DeJuneas, Tommy	R-R	6-1	202	10-24-95	1	1	7.53	17	0	0	0	29	27	26	24	2	27	19	.260	.244	.271	5.97	8.48
Donato, Chad	R-R	6-0	195	6-3-95	1	1	3.60	5	3	0	0	20	18	10	8	3	3	25	.228	.257	.205	11.25	1.35
Endersby, Jimmy	R-R	6-0	194	1-16-98	5	6	3.48	16	13	0	0	67	56	31	26	5	40	67	.231	.258	.215	8.96	5.35
France, J.P.	R-R	6-0	216	4-4-95	3	2	4.28	8	5	0	0	34	28	17	16	2	14	50	.222	.241	.206	13.37	3.74
Freure, R.J.	R-R	6-1	210	7-6-97	1	1	4.95	6	4	0	1	20	22	12	11	3	15	16	.282	.308	.269	7.20	6.75
Henderson, Layne	R-R	6-4	200	6-8-96	5	2	3.81	26	0	0	0	50	40	23	21	5	29	61	.217	.227	.208	11.05	5.26
Hernandez, Nick	R-R	6-1	212	12-30-94	3	1	1.67	32	1	0	6	54	28	15	10	5	28	68	.152	.123	.175	11.33	4.67
Horrell, Michael	R-R	6-3	195	12-18-96	0	1	2.25	16	0	0	1	28	22	12	7	1	13	20	.216	.289	.172	6.43	4.18
Kelly, Michael	R-R	6-4	185	9-6-92	2	0	1.69	6	0	0	0	5	4	1	1	1	1	9	.190	.200	.182	15.19	1.69
Lawson, Brandon	L-R	6-3	205	12-13-94	2	5	4.15	25	10	1	2	95	88	47	44	5	29	75	.254	.215	.278	7.08	2.74
Macuare, Angel	R-R	6-2	250	3-3-00	3	1	1.80	6	4	0	0	25	11	5	5	1	17	19	.139	.061	.196	6.84	6.12
McKee, Colin	R-R	6-3	225	6-21-94	2	0	9.45	4	0	0	0	7	12	7	7	1	4	8	.375	.467	.294	10.80	5.40
Melendez, Jaime	L-R	5-8	190	9-26-01	1	1	5.87	3	1	0	0	8	8	5	5	0	4	11	.235	.357	.150	12.91	4.70
Moclair, Mark	R-R	6-2	205	3-13-97	0	0	18.00	1	0	0	0	1	1	3	2	0	2	1	.250	--	.250	9.00	18.00
Mushinski, Parker	L-L	6-0	218	10-7-95	4	3	3.78	15	9	0	1	52	52	30	22	3	20	66	.256	.267	.252	11.35	3.44
Olczak, Jon	R-R	6-0	180	11-14-93	2	0	1.84	25	0	0	6	29	16	6	6	1	6	34	.154	.143	.159	10.43	1.84
Paredes, Enoli	R-R	5-11	171	9-28-95	0	0	0.00	4	0	0	0	5	1	0	0	1	9	.071	.000	.111	16.20	1.80
Peck, Hunter	L-L	6-2	195	5-5-97	1	0	4.32	5	0	0	0	8	9	4	4	3	4	14	.265	.333	.227	15.12	4.32
Record, Joe	R-R	6-3	232	1-12-95	5	2	3.36	19	7	0	0	62	44	24	23	5	36	53	.203	.205	.201	7.74	5.25
Riggs, Nolan	R-R	6-8	255	5-22-93	0	0	6.75	2	0	0	0	1	3	1	1	0	0	1	.429	.000	.500	6.75	0.00
Rosado, Cesar	R-R	6-1	172	6-22-96	1	6	7.04	16	9	0	1	54	64	53	42	9	29	67	.295	.351	.264	11.24	4.86
Ruppenthal, Matt	R-R	6-4	225	10-21-95	1	1	6.33	8	3	0	0	21	19	15	15	2	17	17	.244	.265	.227	7.17	7.17
Serrano, Kyle	R-R	6-3	223	7-6-95	1	0	9.00	5	0	0	1	6	6	6	6	1	11	9	.300	.500	.167	13.50	16.50
Sprinkle, Jonathan	R-R	6-6	237	7-8-98	0	1	0.87	6	0	0	0	10	7	2	1	0	3	12	.194	.267	.143	10.45	2.61
Taylor, Chandler	L-L	6-1	210	2-7-96	0	0	4.50	1	0	0	0	2	2	1	1	0	1	0	.286	.200	.500	0.00	4.50
Tejada, Felipe	R-R	6-1	190	2-27-98	3	4	4.62	27	0	0	2	37	40	20	19	5	12	46	.268	.200	.309	11.19	2.92
Urquidy, Jose	R-R	6-0	217	5-1-95	0	0	0.00	1	1	0	0	4	2	0	0	0	2	3	.182	.286	.000	7.36	4.91

Fielding

Catcher	PCT	G	PO	A	E	DP	PB
Berryhill	1.000	7	81	3	0	0	2
Castro	1.000	1	3	0	0	1	0
Holderbach	.988	10	82	3	1	0	1
Lee	.986	38	315	26	5	2	6
Manea	.990	34	355	22	4	5	0
Salazar	.984	14	114	9	2	2	0
Shaver	1.000	3	32	0	0	0	0
Stubbs	.991	19	197	15	2	3	5

First Base	PCT	G	PO	A	E	DP
Adams	.982	8	48	7	1	5

First Base	PCT	G	PO	A	E	DP
Arias	.966	4	24	4	1	5
Berryhill	1.000	1	4	2	0	0
Biermann	1.000	5	28	2	0	2
Gonzalez	.984	29	182	6	3	14
Hensley	.977	9	37	5	1	3
Holderbach	1.000	3	24	2	0	1
Lee	1.000	1	3	0	0	0
Lee	1.000	3	15	1	0	2
Manea	.989	15	82	5	1	11
Matijevic	.964	16	102	6	4	11
Perez	1.000	4	35	3	0	2
Salazar	1.000	6	56	4	0	3
Schreiber	1.000	17	118	4	0	9
Shaver	1.000	2	10	3	0	2
Stubbs	1.000	2	13	2	0	1

Second Base	PCT	G	PO	A	E	DP
Arias	1.000	4	9	5	0	1
Ceuta	1.000	2	2	1	0	0
Hensley	.966	46	79	93	6	25
Kessinger	.991	34	46	61	1	11
Lee	.958	7	10	13	1	4
Mendoza	1.000	4	6	7	0	2

	PCT	G	PO	A	E	DP
Salazar	1.000	7	9	16	0	4
Valdez	.985	13	26	39	1	5
Wielansky	1.000	9	12	17	0	3

Third Base	PCT	G	PO	A	E	DP
Adams	.929	14	10	16	2	4
Arias	.833	2	1	4	1	0
Diaz	1.000	1	1	1	0	0
Hensley	.963	17	11	15	1	3
Julks	.500	1	0	1	1	0
Kessinger	.967	14	10	19	1	2
Lee	1.000	4	4	4	0	0
Matijevic	1.000	1	1	3	0	0
Perez	.879	63	39	84	17	10
Shaver	.571	6	0	4	3	0
Stubbs	1.000	1	0	1	0	0
Valdez	1.000	1	1	3	0	0
Wielansky	1.000	3	2	3	0	0

Shortstop	PCT	G	PO	A	E	DP
Arias	1.000	2	1	5	0	2
Ceuta	1.000	1	1	2	0	0
Diaz	1.000	1	0	1	0	0

Hensley	.973	35	58	86	4	17
Kessinger	.980	42	42	102	3	21
Leon	.943	41	57	59	7	14
Mendoza	.800	1	1	3	1	0
Valdez	1.000	1	1	3	0	1

Outfield	PCT	G	PO	A	E	DP
Adolph	1.000	61	111	4	0	1
Arias	1.000	1	1	0	0	0
Barefoot	.972	34	65	5	2	2
Costes	.981	57	103	1	2	0
Diaz	.500	1	1	0	1	0
Gonzalez	.972	23	34	1	1	0
Julks	1.000	70	129	9	0	3
Lee	1.000	1	1	0	0	0
Leon	1.000	9	20	0	0	0
Machado	--	1	0	0	0	0
Matijevic	1.000	12	9	0	0	0
McKenna	.962	35	72	3	3	0
Schreiber	.968	15	27	3	1	1
Stubbs	1.000	2	3	0	0	0
Taylor	1.000	51	77	6	0	0

ASHEVILLE TOURISTS

HIGH-A EAST

HIGH CLASS A

Batting	B-T	HT	WT	DOB	AVG	vLH	vRH	G	AB	R	H	2B	3B	HR	RBI	BB	HBP	SH	SF	SO	SB	CS	SLG	OBP
Abreu, Wilyer	L-L	6-0	217	6-24-99	.268	.288	.262	82	287	52	77	15	1	16	50	38	5	0	1	99	10	11	.495	.363
Arias, Bryan	R-R	6-0	205	6-6-97	.237	.217	.250	17	59	9	14	3	0	5	13	4	1	0	0	20	1	0	.542	.297
Barber, Colin	L-L	6-0	194	12-4-00	.214	.222	.212	16	42	10	9	1	0	3	7	9	1	0	0	22	1	1	.452	.365
Barefoot, Matthew	R-L	6-0	205	9-20-97	.287	.357	.259	49	195	26	56	14	1	12	35	12	4	0	0	64	7	2	.554	.341
Berryhill, Luke	R-R	6-1	227	5-28-98	.277	.278	.276	29	94	21	26	10	0	5	19	10	5	0	1	38	1	1	.543	.373
Biermann, Zach	L-L	6-3	225	6-2-97	.200	.333	.176	6	20	2	4	1	0	1	1	5	0	0	0	7	0	0	.400	.360
Carrasco, Deury	L-R	5-9	165	9-20-99	.226	.103	.256	42	146	29	33	11	1	4	18	25	1	0	0	67	2	2	.397	.343
Ceuta, Yorbin	B-R	6-0	165	1-14-00	.000	.000	.000	1	3	1	0	0	0	0	0	0	0	0	0	0	0	0	.000	.000
Correa, J.C.	R-R	6-0	219	9-15-98	.314	.260	.333	45	185	33	58	13	0	4	25	7	0	0	1	29	3	2	.449	.337
Daniels, Zach	R-R	6-1	211	1-23-99	.219	.235	.214	40	146	24	32	8	0	3	18	23	4	0	1	64	8	3	.336	.339
Diaz, Yainer	R-R	6-0	195	9-21-98	.396	.357	.412	25	96	28	38	4	0	11	33	8	0	1	0	17	2	0	.781	.438
Dirden, Justin	L-R	6-3	209	7-16-97	.289	.235	.303	25	83	13	24	3	3	4	17	12	3	0	3	26	2	3	.542	.386
Guerrero, Luis	R-R	5-11	195	11-9-98	.234	.323	.197	32	107	17	25	3	0	4	12	12	0	0	0	34	2	1	.374	.311
Holderbach, Alex	R-R	6-0	205	12-26-96	.223	.274	.203	63	220	38	49	7	0	12	36	24	1	0	2	106	1	1	.418	.300
Hurtado, Carlos	R-R	6-0	170	5-18-01	.235	.333	.214	5	17	3	4	1	0	0	0	3	0	0	4	0	0		.294	.350
Krabbe, Tyler	R-R	6-2	220	1-13-97	.226	.333	.182	11	31	4	7	3	0	0	5	2	2	0	0	10	0	0	.323	.314
Lee, AJ	R-R	6-0	180	5-26-97	.122	.167	.107	24	74	10	9	2	0	1	4	7	3	0	1	43	3	0	.189	.224
Lee, Korey	R-R	6-2	210	7-25-98	.330	.348	.326	29	109	24	36	5	0	3	14	12	0	0	0	24	1	0	.459	.397
Machado, Carlos	R-R	6-2	170	6-5-98	.326	.200	.393	12	43	5	14	1	0	0	2	4	1	0	0	9	1	2	.349	.396
McKenna, Alex	R-R	6-2	204	9-6-97	.305	.250	.320	41	164	41	50	8	2	13	31	21	3	0	2	49	7	1	.616	.389
Nova, Freudis	R-R	6-1	178	1-12-00	.224	.225	.224	73	254	33	57	14	1	4	19	26	2	0	0	91	9	1	.335	.301
Orr, Cody	R-R	6-2	212	4-2-99	.243	.200	.259	31	111	19	27	5	0	2	9	8	1	1	1	45	8	1	.342	.298
Perez, Joe	R-R	6-2	198	8-12-99	.354	.321	.366	25	99	24	35	11	0	8	26	10	0	0	0	21	1	1	.707	.413
Rodriguez, Ramiro	L-L	5-10	145	2-2-98	.205	.214	.202	40	132	18	27	6	0	3	15	14	2	0	0	43	3	0	.318	.291
Salazar, Cesar	L-R	5-9	185	3-15-96	.238	.100	.257	23	80	10	19	4	0	3	12	9	1	0	2	22	2	0	.400	.344
Santana, Luis	R-R	5-8	198	7-20-99	.229	.093	.276	49	170	23	39	10	0	6	24	13	5	0	2	43	5	2	.394	.300
Schreiber, Scott	R-R	6-3	230	10-13-95	.319	.316	.320	41	160	37	51	7	2	10	29	15	2	0	1	41	6	3	.575	.382
Stubbs, C.J.	R-R	6-3	207	11-12-96	.229	.275	.212	67	253	40	58	15	3	12	35	23	2	0	2	104	6	4	.455	.296
Valdez, Enmanuel	L-R	5-9	191	12-28-98	.254	.231	.261	75	283	52	72	16	1	21	72	25	2	0	6	67	5	1	.541	.313
Whitcomb, Shay	R-R	6-3	202	9-28-98	.300	.215	.333	58	233	49	70	22	0	16	56	19	3	0	2	81	16	3	.601	.358

Pitching	B-T	HT	WT	DOB	W	L	ERA	G	GS	CG	SV	IP	H	R	ER	HR	BB	SO	AVG	vLH	vRH	K/9	BB/9
Alberto Rivera, Jose	R-R	6-3	193	2-14-97	0	1	7.94	5	3	0	0	11	10	12	10	2	9	17	.227	.222	.231	13.50	7.15
Arias, Bryan	R-R	6-0	205	6-6-97	0	0	7.71	2	0	0	0	2	4	2	2	0	0	0	.364	.167	.600	0.00	0.00
Bravo, Jose	R-R	6-3	213	6-10-97	2	5	5.37	14	6	0	1	57	65	36	34	14	14	72	.286	.289	.283	11.37	2.21
Brown, Tyler	R-R	6-4	242	10-2-98	3	5	7.25	15	11	0	0	63	71	52	51	14	32	68	.278	.308	.252	9.66	4.55
Carrasco, Deury	L-R	5-9	165	9-20-99	0	0	18.00	1	0	0	0	1	1	2	2	0	0	3	.250	.000	.333	0.00	27.00
Casey, Chandler	R-R	6-2	195	5-30-96	4	2	5.60	27	1	0	3	53	66	39	33	11	11	35	.299	.284	.311	5.94	1.87
Ceballos, Yeremi	L-L	6-2	165	12-21-98	2	2	8.74	19	1	0	1	23	25	35	22	5	31	31	.269	.100	.349	12.31	12.31
Cody, Danny	R-R	6-3	175	3-6-97	1	6	7.27	25	12	0	2	69	86	62	56	17	44	90	.301	.270	.325	11.68	5.71
Conn, Devin	R-R	5-11	190	4-3-97	1	1	4.91	13	0	0	1	18	13	11	10	5	7	22	.191	.233	.158	10.80	3.44
De Paula, Brayan	L-L	6-3	175	6-25-99	0	3	6.67	10	5	0	0	28	36	24	21	6	18	34	.313	.262	.342	10.80	5.72
Deason, Cody	R-R	6-4	214	12-26-96	0	0	5.14	2	0	0	0	7	9	5	4	1	4	10	.333	.333	.333	12.86	5.14
DeJuneas, Tommy	R-R	6-2	202	10-24-95	2	1	4.76	14	0	0	2	23	23	15	12	4	14	24	.256	.293	.243	9.53	5.56
Endersby, Jimmy	R-R	6-1	194	1-16-98	2	1	4.85	8	4	0	1	30	29	17	16	3	13	43	.252	.226	.274	13.04	3.94
Freure, R.J.	R-R	6-1	210	7-6-97	3	5	6.31	17	9	0	0	61	54	46	43	14	38	88	.229	.202	.254	12.91	5.58
Gaither, Ray	R-R	6-4	224	3-4-98	2	1	6.00	5	0	0	1	6	8	5	4	1	2	3	.333	.385	.273	4.50	3.00

HOUSTON ASTROS

Garcia, Freylin	R-R	6-3	170	12-6-97	0	1	2.35	9	0	0	0	15	10	5	4	1	9	18	.189	.167	.207	10.57	5.28
Gomez, Cesar	L-R	6-3	179	7-9-98	1	1	1.62	4	2	0	0	17	22	12	3	0	3	14	.306	.281	.325	7.56	1.62
Gruller, Kyle	R-R	6-3	234	5-21-98	0	0	6.06	6	4	0	0	16	9	13	11	3	17	16	.167	.148	.185	8.82	9.37
Henderson, Layne	R-R	6-4	200	6-8-96	0	0	0.00	3	0	0	0	3	1	0	0	0	0	6	.100	.000	.167	16.20	0.00
Henley, Blair	R-R	6-3	190	5-14-97	0	2	7.02	5	3	0	0	17	26	15	13	3	9	23	.356	.350	.364	12.42	4.86
Holcomb, Kevin	R-R	6-5	210	1-5-99	3	0	5.68	9	0	0	0	19	19	14	12	3	9	17	.253	.250	.256	8.05	4.26
Holderbach, Alex	R-R	6-0	205	12-26-96	0	0	4.50	2	0	0	0	2	2	1	1	0	1	2	.250	.250	.250	9.00	4.50
Horrell, Michael	R-R	6-3	195	12-18-96	0	0	2.16	15	0	0	2	25	27	16	6	1	12	27	.270	.238	.293	9.72	4.32
Jaquez, Ernesto	R-R	6-2	190	6-11-99	1	2	5.94	8	0	0	1	17	20	13	11	4	8	23	.290	.182	.389	12.42	4.32
Jimenez, Alfredi	R-R	6-1	175	10-19-99	3	4	4.80	9	7	0	0	45	52	28	24	4	10	41	.297	.304	.292	8.20	2.00
Krabbe, Tyler	R-R	6-2	220	1-13-97	0	0	3.86	3	0	0	0	2	2	1	1	0	1	2	.222	.250	.200	3.86	0.00
Macuare, Angel	R-R	6-2	250	3-3-00	0	5	9.95	8	5	0	0	25	34	30	28	6	13	32	.330	.370	.298	11.37	4.62
McDonald, Cole	L-R	6-1	220	3-11-97	0	0	0.00	1	1	0	0	1	0	0	0	2	1	0	.000	.000	--	9.00	18.00
Melendez, Jaime	L-R	5-8	190	9-26-01	2	3	4.78	11	7	0	0	32	34	19	17	2	24	41	.268	.250	.282	11.53	6.75
Moclair, Mark	R-R	6-2	205	3-13-97	1	1	5.48	22	4	0	4	43	31	29	26	4	50	55	.204	.263	.168	11.60	10.55
Pablo Lopez, Juan	L-L	6-4	216	2-17-99	6	3	6.71	16	8	0	1	56	60	48	42	9	32	65	.268	.250	.277	10.38	5.11
Procopio, Daniel	R-R	6-0	190	9-18-95	0	0	17.05	8	0	0	0	6	13	15	12	1	13	7	.419	.500	.368	9.95	18.47
Robaina, Julio	L-L	5-11	170	3-23-01	3	2	3.90	6	5	0	0	32	32	17	14	3	7	42	.246	.125	.317	11.69	1.95
Ruppenthal, Matt	R-R	6-4	225	10-21-95	4	2	5.34	15	9	0	1	61	60	37	36	7	28	71	.260	.256	.263	10.53	4.15
Serrano, Kyle	R-R	6-3	223	7-6-95	0	0	5.63	7	0	0	1	8	6	5	5	0	7	21	.200	.214	.188	23.63	7.88
Sprinkle, Jonathan	R-R	6-6	237	7-8-98	1	2	5.96	16	0	0	0	23	13	15	15	3	15	45	.167	.250	.109	17.87	5.96
Tamarez, Misael	R-R	6-1	206	1-16-00	2	1	3.48	7	7	0	0	34	30	15	13	4	10	39	.238	.250	.229	10.43	2.67
Taveras, Diosmerky	R-R	6-3	248	9-23-99	3	0	1.53	4	2	0	0	18	9	3	3	2	6	23	.145	.121	.172	11.72	3.06
Tejada, Felipe	R-R	6-1	190	2-27-98	2	0	1.23	8	0	0	0	15	9	2	2	1	6	22	.180	.350	.067	13.50	3.68
West, Derek	R-R	6-5	230	12-2-96	0	0	9.45	6	0	0	1	7	7	7	7	3	9	9	.292	.375	.250	12.15	12.15

Fielding

Catcher	PCT	G	PO	A	E	DP	PB
Berryhill	.971	12	128	5	4	0	0
Diaz	.991	12	107	5	1	0	1
Holderbach	.992	31	336	18	3	1	8
Hurtado	1.000	1	7	0	0	0	0
Krabbe	1.000	3	26	0	0	0	0
Lee	.991	20	199	13	2	1	5
Salazar	.977	11	116	9	3	0	0
Stubbs	.978	31	282	29	7	3	9

First Base	PCT	G	PO	A	E	DP
Berryhill	.967	12	55	3	2	3
Biermann	.955	3	20	1	1	2
Correa	1.000	8	56	3	0	10
Diaz	.942	8	61	4	4	1
Holderbach	.994	24	167	12	1	20
Krabbe	.971	6	32	2	1	2
Lee	1.000	2	8	1	0	1
Perez	.938	7	41	4	3	3
Salazar	.951	6	35	4	2	4
Schreiber	.994	24	149	12	1	10
Stubbs	.986	22	138	6	2	10

Second Base	PCT	G	PO	A	E	DP
Arias	.939	7	10	21	2	5
Carrasco	.946	7	15	20	2	4
Ceuta	1.000	1	0	3	0	0
Correa	.977	14	17	26	1	1
Guerrero	.800	1	2	2	1	2
Lee	1.000	2	1	7	0	0
Nova	.970	8	16	16	1	3
Orr	.923	3	7	5	1	2
Perez	1.000	1	1	1	0	0
Santana	.965	29	41	68	4	18
Valdez	.947	38	40	85	7	14
Whitcomb	1.000	10	31	16	0	7

Third Base	PCT	G	PO	A	E	DP
Arias	1.000	1	1	2	0	0
Carrasco	.960	9	6	18	1	2
Correa	.882	13	6	9	2	0
Holderbach	1.000	1	1	1	0	0
Lee	.889	3	3	5	1	1
Lee	1.000	2	2	0	0	0
Nova	.833	7	3	7	2	0
Orr	1.000	5	1	6	0	1
Perez	.963	16	8	18	1	4
Santana	.975	16	7	32	1	4
Schreiber	.667	2	0	2	1	0
Valdez	.961	29	14	35	2	3
Whitcomb	.878	20	13	30	6	1

Shortstop	PCT	G	PO	A	E	DP
Carrasco	.943	21	28	54	5	11
Correa	1.000	5	5	10	0	0
Lee	.930	16	15	25	3	7
Nova	.908	53	56	82	14	16
Orr	1.000	2	3	5	0	1
Valdez	1.000	1	3	0	0	0
Whitcomb	.953	26	35	47	4	9

Outfield	PCT	G	PO	A	E	DP
Abreu	.964	74	121	12	5	1
Arias	.875	8	6	1	1	0
Barber	1.000	15	20	1	0	0
Barefoot	.986	43	69	2	1	0
Biermann	1.000	3	1	0	0	0
Daniels	1.000	38	62	2	0	0
Dirden	1.000	23	44	5	0	0
Guerrero	.984	30	59	3	1	1
Machado	.950	12	19	0	1	0
McKenna	.987	39	69	5	1	1
Orr	.958	20	22	1	1	0
Rodriguez	.986	38	68	5	1	0
Schreiber	.950	13	19	0	1	0
Stubbs	1.000	2	1	0	0	0

FAYETTEVILLE WOODPECKERS   LOW CLASS A
LOW-A EAST

Batting	B-T	HT	WT	DOB	AVG	vLH	vRH	G	AB	R	H	2B	3B	HR	RBI	BB	HBP	SH	SF	SO	SB	CS	SLG	OBP
Alvarez, Jose	R-R	6-1	180	6-4-00	.263	.375	.245	17	57	6	15	3	0	0	7	4	0	0	1	16	2	0	.316	.306
Arias, Bryan	R-R	6-0	205	6-6-97	.200	.133	.218	19	70	13	14	2	0	3	9	9	1	0	0	22	6	2	.357	.300
Barefoot, Matthew	R-L	6-0	205	9-20-97	.344	.500	.315	16	64	14	22	4	1	4	17	7	0	0	3	21	10	1	.625	.392
Berryhill, Luke	R-R	6-1	227	5-28-98	.305	.276	.315	35	118	24	36	9	0	10	32	20	7	0	2	37	4	0	.636	.429
Brewer, Jordan	R-R	6-1	195	8-1-97	.275	.265	.277	65	251	49	69	12	2	6	41	34	8	0	3	80	21	2	.410	.375
Corona, Kenedy	R-R	5-11	184	3-21-00	.244	.262	.239	57	201	30	49	12	1	2	22	14	5	2	2	53	19	7	.343	.306
Correa, J.C.	R-R	6-0	219	9-15-98	.306	.277	.314	56	222	44	68	9	2	5	32	28	4	0	1	30	7	7	.477	.392
Daniels, Zach	R-R	6-1	211	1-23-99	.228	.250	.221	45	167	29	38	5	1	6	30	26	4	0	0	65	14	3	.377	.345
2-team total (61 Lynchburg)					.300	.250	.313	73	287	33	86	21	1	6	57	15	2	0	3	46	2	1	.443	.336
Dirden, Justin	L-R	6-3	209	7-16-97	.267	.216	.279	58	202	46	54	15	3	11	41	40	6	0	1	74	8	1	.535	.402
Giron, Adonis	R-R	5-10	190	2-22-01	.133	.000	.153	29	98	10	13	2	0	2	8	11	3	0	0	41	0	1	.214	.241
Gonzalez, Cristian	R-R	6-3	180	4-24-00	.244	.263	.240	30	123	19	30	4	1	2	14	9	1	0	1	41	1	2	.341	.299
Guerrero, Luis	R-R	5-11	195	11-9-98	.229	.000	.242	13	35	7	8	2	1	0	5	3	0	0	1	7	1	1	.343	.341
Hamilton, Quincy	L-L	5-10	190	6-12-98	.261	.400	.232	33	115	18	30	5	0	2	20	18	4	0	5	28	9	2	.357	.366
Hurtado, Carlos	R-R	6-0	170	5-18-01	.273	1.000	.200	3	11	1	3	1	0	0	2	0	0	0	0	1	0	0	.364	.273
Kato, Kobe	L-R	6-1	170	3-19-99	.242	.000	.275	31	91	15	22	3	0	2	14	24	1	0	0	16	3	3	.341	.405

	B-T	HT	WT	DOB	AVG	vLH	vRH	G	AB	R	H	2B	3B	HR	RBI	BB	HBP	SH	SF	SO	SB	CS	OBP	SLG
Loperfido, Joey	L-R	6-4	195	5-11-99	.116	.000	.129	19	69	10	8	4	0	2	6	8	8	0	2	31	1	0	.261	.276
Machado, Carlos	R-R	6-2	170	6-5-98	.250	--	.250	1	4	0	1	0	0	0	0	0	0	0	0	0	0	0	.250	.250
Martinez, Yohander	R-R	5-10	175	1-8-02	.265	.333	.250	43	132	16	35	1	0	1	21	27	4	0	2	32	4	3	.295	.400
Mascai, Victor	L-R	6-2	188	2-10-01	.174	.190	.171	41	132	20	23	5	1	7	23	31	2	0	2	56	1	0	.386	.335
Mendoza, Sean	B-R	5-8	150	6-2-00	.194	.455	.148	23	72	10	14	1	0	3	10	3	4	0	1	26	4	0	.333	.263
Orr, Cody	R-R	6-2	212	4-2-99	.150	1.000	.056	8	20	4	3	0	1	0	2	5	0	0	1	6	4	0	.250	.308
Palma, Miguel	R-S	5-10	170	1-4-02	.308	.000	.343	15	39	8	12	4	0	0	8	8	5	0	1	13	2	0	.410	.472
Paulino, Juan	L-R	5-11	192	12-10-97	.213	.222	.209	18	61	8	13	2	0	2	4	7	0	0	0	24	3	1	.344	.294
2-team total (14 Fredericksburg)					.250	.211	.260	32	96	13	24	5	0	3	10	13	0	0	0	36	10	2	.396	.339
Perez, Joe	R-R	6-2	198	8-12-99	.300	.333	.295	12	50	7	15	4	0	2	8	9	0	0	0	13	0	2	.500	.407
Perry, Nathan	L-R	6-2	207	7-7-99	.220	.333	.205	51	182	24	40	13	1	5	30	21	7	0	2	45	1	1	.385	.321
Pinto, Franklin	R-R	6-1	160	4-26-01	.286	--	.286	3	7	1	2	1	0	0	2	0	1	0	0	2	0	0	.429	.375
Ramirez, Yeuris	R-R	6-0	170	11-28-98	.257	.259	.256	43	152	24	39	7	2	3	28	16	6	0	0	54	18	5	.388	.351
Rodriguez, Nerio	R-R	6-2	228	9-21-99	.247	.233	.250	83	312	44	77	14	3	4	43	48	3	0	3	90	2	1	.349	.350
Sandle, Michael	R-R	5-10	185	9-21-98	.287	.167	.311	35	143	30	41	10	4	6	22	10	4	0	0	36	9	1	.538	.350
Stevens, Chad	R-R	6-4	215	2-3-99	.147	.100	.156	34	116	12	17	4	1	1	12	12	2	0	0	53	3	2	.224	.238
Urdaneta, Ronaldo	R-R	5-10	155	11-18-98	.229	.152	.247	52	179	33	41	6	1	5	19	24	3	0	2	60	23	2	.358	.327
Wagner, Will	L-R	6-0	185	7-29-98	.299	.250	.309	31	117	22	35	8	1	2	14	16	1	0	0	33	5	0	.436	.388
Whitcomb, Shay	R-R	6-3	202	9-28-98	.282	.270	.286	41	163	32	46	3	0	7	22	20	3	0	1	53	14	2	.429	.369
Williams, Justin	R-R	6-3	215	6-26-00	.213	.143	.226	36	127	18	27	7	0	5	16	15	3	0	0	51	4	4	.386	.310

Pitching	B-T	HT	WT	DOB	W	L	ERA	G	GS	CG	SV	IP	H	R	ER	HR	BB	SO	AVG	vLH	vRH	K/9	BB/9
Arrighetti, Spencer	R-R	6-2	186	1-2-00	2	1	2.79	4	2	0	0	10	3	3	3	1	2	16	.091	.071	.105	14.90	1.86
Baez, Pedro	R-R	6-0	232	3-11-88	0	0	0.00	2	0	0	0	2	1	0	0	0	1	1	.167	.500	.000	4.50	4.50
Barry, Shea	R-R	6-2	195	12-22-97	2	1	6.59	10	7	0	1	27	32	22	20	4	17	20	.294	.333	.255	6.59	5.60
Batista, Edinson	R-R	6-2	185	5-19-02	0	0	0.00	1	0	0	0	1	0	0	0	0	0	0	.000	.000	.000	0.00	0.00
Betances, Jose	R-R	6-0	170	10-17-99	0	4	6.75	24	0	0	3	39	29	33	29	4	37	53	.209	.263	.171	12.34	8.61
Brockhouse, Walker	R-R	6-4	197	2-22-99	0	1	3.00	10	0	0	0	15	12	8	5	3	11	18	.222	.217	.226	10.80	6.60
Brown, Aaron	R-R	6-4	220	3-19-99	1	3	5.95	5	3	0	0	20	20	15	13	4	3	28	.263	.229	.293	12.81	1.37
Calderon, Carlos	R-R	6-0	175	10-4-01	2	1	5.02	9	3	0	1	29	25	18	16	1	23	46	.225	.220	.230	14.44	7.22
De Paula, Brayan	L-L	6-3	175	6-25-99	2	0	1.78	8	4	0	0	30	13	10	6	0	16	40	.126	.120	.128	11.87	4.75
Deason, Cody	R-R	6-4	214	12-26-96	0	1	5.40	1	1	0	0	3	3	4	2	0	3	6	.231	.286	.167	16.20	8.10
DeLabio, Jacob	R-R	6-5	205	9-19-97	0	0	1.80	5	0	0	1	5	3	1	1	0	8	7	.167	.200	.125	12.60	14.40
Drennan, Whit	L-L	6-7	190	2-25-97	2	2	8.37	18	0	0	1	24	20	24	22	5	37	28	.222	.038	.297	10.65	14.07
Ford, Kasey	L-R	6-6	275	1-10-98	1	2	5.06	12	0	0	1	16	15	10	9	2	9	20	.242	.304	.205	11.25	5.06
Gaither, Ray	R-R	6-4	224	3-4-98	0	0	1.50	5	0	0	0	6	4	1	1	0	2	9	.190	.182	.200	13.50	3.00
Garcia, Elvis	R-R	6-0	165	9-24-02	1	1	1.96	6	3	0	0	23	15	7	5	1	9	19	.188	.200	.175	7.43	3.52
Garcia, Freylin	R-R	6-3	170	12-6-97	1	1	5.68	15	0	0	1	19	15	14	12	0	22	19	.221	.192	.238	9.00	10.42
Garcia, Ronny	R-R	6-3	170	12-2-99	1	1	3.24	7	0	0	1	8	11	9	3	2	8	14	.324	.467	.211	15.12	8.64
Gomez, Cesar	L-R	6-3	179	7-9-98	2	7	6.81	18	11	0	1	70	91	58	53	7	28	62	.314	.350	.288	7.97	3.60
Gruller, Kyle	R-R	6-3	234	5-21-98	0	0	2.45	3	1	0	1	11	5	3	3	0	6	18	.152	.000	.217	14.73	4.91
Hiraldo, Carlos	R-R	6-2	170	6-28-98	1	0	4.30	12	0	0	3	23	22	15	11	0	13	25	.239	.293	.196	9.78	5.09
Holcomb, Kevin	R-R	6-5	210	1-5-99	2	2	5.04	18	0	0	0	25	21	19	14	1	28	36	.223	.143	.258	12.96	10.08
James, Josh	R-R	6-3	234	3-8-93	0	0	0.00	2	2	0	0	2	2	0	0	0	2	1	.250	.333	.200	4.50	9.00
Jaquez, Ernesto	R-R	6-2	190	6-11-99	1	3	7.97	18	0	0	1	20	22	18	18	4	20	24	.278	.310	.260	10.62	8.85
Jimenez, Alfredi	R-R	6-1	175	10-19-99	1	3	4.11	12	6	0	1	50	45	26	23	5	14	55	.234	.259	.215	9.83	2.50
Kato, Kobe	L-R	6-1	170	3-19-99	0	0	13.50	1	0	0	0	1	1	1	1	0	1	0	.333	.500	.000	0.00	13.50
Kouba, Rhett	R-R	6-0	180	9-3-99	0	0	1.35	4	3	0	0	13	11	2	2	1	1	13	.220	.214	.222	8.78	0.68
Lopez, Jairo	R-R	5-11	220	11-21-00	1	1	10.13	4	2	0	0	11	17	13	12	3	5	14	.370	.524	.240	11.81	4.22
Macuare, Angel	R-R	6-2	250	3-3-00	1	1	1.15	4	2	0	1	16	8	4	2	1	5	24	.143	.211	.108	13.79	2.87
Martinez, Yohander	R-R	5-10	175	1-8-02	0	0	0.00	2	0	0	0	1	1	0	0	0	1	0	.200	.000	.250	0.00	6.75
McDermott, Chayce	L-R	6-3	197	8-22-98	0	0	3.44	6	4	0	0	18	11	8	7	3	10	33	.172	.188	.156	16.20	4.91
Mejias, Christian	R-R	6-0	160	5-19-99	1	1	7.50	4	3	0	0	12	17	11	10	1	5	21	.315	.316	.314	15.75	3.75
Melendez, Jaime	L-R	5-8	190	9-26-01	2	2	0.49	6	3	0	0	18	7	2	1	1	5	38	.111	.160	.079	18.65	2.45
Mendoza, Sean	B-R	5-8	150	6-2-00	0	0	9.00	1	0	0	0	1	1	1	1	0	1	0	.250	.000	.333	9.00	0.00
Meszaros, Janos	R-R	6-3	215	9-12-94	0	0	40.50	2	0	0	0	1	3	6	6	0	4	1	.500	.500	.500	6.75	27.00
Mezquita, Cristofer	L-L	6-0	175	6-6-00	0	0	4.76	4	0	0	0	6	4	5	3	0	4	3	.182	.400	.118	4.76	6.35
Moclair, Mark	R-R	6-2	205	3-13-97	1	0	1.69	3	2	0	0	11	5	2	2	0	9	18	.143	.200	.120	15.19	7.59
Palmer, Alex	B-R	5-10	160	5-15-98	0	0	1.80	1	0	0	0	5	2	1	1	0	0	8	.118	.333	.000	14.40	0.00
Paulino, Juan	L-R	5-11	192	12-10-97	0	0	0.00	1	0	0	0	1	0	0	0	0	0	0	.000	--		0.00	0.00
Plumlee, Peyton	R-R	6-3	201	2-10-97	2	2	3.94	9	6	0	0	30	24	17	13	5	9	34	.218	.214	.221	10.31	2.73
Procopio, Daniel	R-R	6-0	190	9-18-95	1	0	7.71	8	0	0	0	9	7	9	8	0	11	11	.200	.167	.235	10.61	10.61
Pruitt, Austin	R-R	5-10	185	8-31-89	0	2	11.57	2	2	0	0	2	5	4	3	0	1	5	.385	.200	.500	3.86	3.86
Ramirez, Yeuris	R-R	6-0	170	11-28-98	0	0	9.00	1	0	0	0	1	1	1	1	1	1	0	.250	.000	.333	0.00	9.00
Reina, Fabricio	R-R	6-3	175	2-26-00	3	4	7.65	17	5	0	0	42	33	47	36	5	50	37	.216	.239	.195	7.87	10.63
Robaina, Julio	L-L	5-11	170	3-23-01	4	1	3.63	11	4	0	0	45	39	23	18	1	18	46	.227	.288	.200	9.27	3.63
Rodriguez, Elian	R-R	6-4	205	3-10-97	1	2	5.47	9	4	0	0	26	23	18	16	4	27	28	.237	.300	.193	9.57	9.23
Salgado, Bryant	R-R	6-1	205	3-2-00	1	1	3.97	4	1	0	0	11	8	6	5	1	9	10	.195	.133	.231	7.94	7.15
Santos II, Alex	R-R	6-4	194	2-10-02	2	2	3.46	12	7	0	0	42	31	18	16	2	30	48	.205	.193	.213	10.37	6.48
Schroeder, Jayson	R-R	6-2	196	11-14-99	2	2	9.06	17	9	0	0	49	42	51	49	2	65	50	.239	.313	.172	9.25	12.02
Sprinkle, Jonathan	R-R	6-6	237	7-8-98	1	0	0.82	9	0	0	0	11	4	2	1	0	9	22	.103	.000	.129	18.00	7.36
Tamarez, Misael	R-R	6-1	206	1-16-00	4	2	3.98	12	6	0	1	43	28	21	19	3	28	64	.181	.214	.153	13.40	5.86
Taveras, Diosmerky	R-R	6-3	248	9-23-99	3	4	5.19	17	9	0	0	61	53	41	35	1	43	72	.239	.291	.206	10.68	6.38
Tokar, Heitor	R-R	6-6	256	10-25-00	3	3	4.73	11	4	0	2	40	39	24	21	3	8	37	.250	.189	.305	8.33	1.80
Urdaneta, Ronaldo	R-R	5-10	155	11-18-98	0	0	0.00	1	0	0	0	1	1	0	0	0	1	0	.333	1.000	.000	0.00	9.00

HOUSTON ASTROS

	B-T	HT	WT	DOB	W	L	ERA	G	GS	CG	SV	IP	H	R	ER	HR	BB	SO	AVG	vLH	vRH	K/9	BB/9
Vega, Luis	R-R	6-3	165	11-16-01	1	2	6.05	7	1	0	0	19	13	15	13	2	12	23	.188	.125	.243	10.71	5.59
Wagner, Will	L-R	6-0	185	7-29-98	0	0	0.00	1	0	0	0	1	0	0	0	0	0	2	.000	.000	.000	13.50	0.00

Fielding

Catcher	PCT	G	PO	A	E	DP	PB
Alvarez	.940	8	72	6	5	0	3
Berryhill	.987	16	145	9	2	1	1
Diaz	1.000	5	55	6	0	0	0
Hurtado	.947	2	16	2	1	0	0
Palma	.965	13	130	7	5	1	4
Paulino	1.000	4	33	2	0	0	4
Perry	.991	28	280	34	3	3	3
Rodriguez	.982	47	479	25	9	0	1

	PCT	G	PO	A	E	DP
Kato	.958	20	22	47	3	11
Martinez	.981	30	39	65	2	16
Mendoza	1.000	5	7	10	0	2
Ramirez	.973	8	11	25	1	5
Stevens	.880	5	9	13	3	5
Urdaneta	.913	23	35	28	6	6
Wagner	.982	14	18	36	1	7
Whitcomb	1.000	5	9	7	0	4
Williams	1.000	5	6	4	0	0

	PCT	G	PO	A	E	DP
Gonzalez	.871	23	27	47	11	8
Kato	1.000	3	2	6	0	1
Martinez	.919	10	16	18	3	2
Orr	1.000	1	0	1	0	0
Stevens	.940	20	32	47	5	10
Urdaneta	.818	3	2	7	2	1
Wagner	1.000	7	6	15	0	0
Whitcomb	.940	22	19	44	4	5
Williams	.800	1	0	4	1	1

First Base	PCT	G	PO	A	E	DP
Alvarez	1.000	6	44	0	0	0
Arias	1.000	2	14	1	0	1
Berryhill	1.000	11	89	1	0	3
Correa	.983	11	55	3	1	6
Diaz	1.000	2	13	3	0	0
Mascai	.980	33	228	20	5	17
Paulino	.985	11	61	3	1	4
Perez	.833	1	5	0	1	0
Perry	1.000	12	101	3	0	7
Ramirez	.976	16	117	6	3	11
Rodriguez	.983	8	52	7	1	7
Williams	.981	8	50	1	1	6

Third Base	PCT	G	PO	A	E	DP
Arias	.700	3	3	4	3	0
Correa	.964	9	5	22	1	1
Gonzalez	1.000	3	1	7	0	2
Guerrero	1.000	1	3	1	0	0
Kato	1.000	6	5	6	0	1
Martinez	.800	2	1	3	1	0
Mendoza	.935	15	8	21	2	2
Perez	.813	9	2	11	3	0
Ramirez	.898	17	18	26	5	0
Stevens	.909	9	3	7	1	0
Urdaneta	1.000	12	2	10	0	3
Wagner	.909	8	4	6	1	1
Whitcomb	.889	11	12	20	4	3
Williams	.977	19	14	29	1	3

Outfield	PCT	G	PO	A	E	DP
Alvarez	1.000	1	2	0	0	0
Arias	.917	9	9	2	1	0
Barefoot	.947	9	18	0	1	0
Brewer	1.000	55	96	6	0	1
Corona	1.000	57	121	4	0	0
Correa	1.000	3	2	0	0	0
Daniels	.988	39	78	4	1	1
Dirden	.958	53	86	6	4	1
Giron	.939	25	31	0	2	0
Guerrero	1.000	8	10	1	0	0
Hamilton	.980	28	48	2	1	0
Kato	--	1	0	0	0	0
Loperfido	.963	16	25	1	1	0
Mascai	.929	8	13	0	1	0
Orr	1.000	7	8	2	0	1
Pinto	1.000	1	1	0	0	0
Sandle	1.000	34	47	1	0	0
Urdaneta	.933	13	13	1	1	0

Second Base	PCT	G	PO	A	E	DP
Arias	1.000	1	2	2	0	0
Correa	1.000	4	6	4	0	0
Gonzalez	.000	1	0	0	0	0
Guerrero	1.000	5	6	9	0	1

Shortstop	PCT	G	PO	A	E	DP
Arias	.750	2	2	1	1	1
Correa	.979	30	30	63	2	13

FCL ASTROS — ROOKIE

FLORIDA COMPLEX LEAGUE

Batting	B-T	HT	WT	DOB	AVG	vLH	vRH	G	AB	R	H	2B	3B	HR	RBI	BB	HBP	SH	SF	SO	SB	CS	SLG	OBP
Alvarez, Jose	R-R	6-1	180	6-4-00	.318	.250	.357	17	44	5	14	2	1	0	6	5	1	0	1	10	3	1	.409	.392
Balogh, Ricardo	B-R	6-3	175	7-9-02	.185	.095	.202	46	135	15	25	4	1	2	13	8	1	0	0	48	2	2	.274	.234
Ceuta, Yorbin	B-R	6-0	165	1-14-00	.283	.353	.256	22	60	13	17	4	0	1	4	8	2	0	0	7	6	1	.400	.386
Cortabarria, Yimmi	R-R	6-2	175	1-10-01	.194	.200	.192	10	31	4	6	1	0	0	3	1	0	0	19	0	0	.226	.286
Cruz, Narbe	R-R	6-3	181	10-1-00	.221	.133	.239	34	86	17	19	3	0	1	7	14	6	0	2	24	2	2	.291	.361
Diaz, Aledmys	R-R	6-1	195	8-1-90	.400	--	.400	2	5	1	2	1	0	0	2	1	0	0	0	1	0	0	.600	.500
Diaz, Omar	L-L	6-1	180	9-23-01	.324	.353	.316	29	74	12	24	4	0	1	10	14	3	0	0	23	1	0	.419	.451
Giron, Adonis	R-R	5-10	190	2-22-01	.268	.400	.226	14	41	10	11	1	1	2	8	10	3	0	0	13	0	0	.488	.444
Gonzalez, Cristian	R-R	6-3	180	10-22-01	.310	.429	.286	13	42	8	13	2	0	2	13	5	0	0	0	10	3	0	.500	.383
Gonzalez, Marwin	B-R	6-1	205	3-14-89	.250	--	.250	1	4	0	1	0	0	0	0	0	0	0	0	2	0	0	.250	.250
Gonzalez, Richi	R-R	6-2	182	12-29-02	.180	.167	.158	42	131	17	21	4	0	3	12	14	5	0	0	68	3	1	.260	.267
Guerrero, Luis	R-R	5-11	195	11-9-98	.375	1.000	.286	9	8	6	3	1	0	0	3	8	0	0	0	2	2	0	.500	.688
Guilamo, Freddy	R-R	5-11	160	12-10-00	.231	.188	.245	28	65	11	15	5	0	5	15	11	1	0	2	20	2	1	.538	.342
Hurtado, Carlos	R-R	6-0	170	5-18-01	.167	.000	.200	4	6	0	1	0	0	0	0	1	0	0	0	1	0	0	.167	.167
Leon, Pedro	R-R	5-10	170	5-28-98	.222	--	.222	3	9	0	2	0	0	0	0	1	0	0	0	2	1	0	.222	.222
Liranzo, Jesus	R-R	6-1	185	12-3-01	.174	.250	.158	11	23	0	4	1	0	0	2	1	1	0	0	14	0	0	.217	.240
Lorenzo, Dauri	B-R	5-9	186	10-29-02	.248	.219	.257	41	141	15	35	6	0	1	12	14	0	0	0	35	5	1	.312	.316
Machandy, Roilan	R-R	6-2	195	2-10-01	.252	.344	.223	46	135	27	34	3	2	3	20	22	12	0	1	49	30	7	.370	.400
Mascai, Victor	L-R	6-2	188	2-10-01	.225	.286	.212	12	40	8	9	2	0	0	9	5	0	0	0	15	0	0	.425	.311
Mendoza, Jose	R-R	5-11	165	6-19-01	.000	.000	.000	7	10	1	0	0	0	0	0	2	0	0	0	3	0	0	.000	.167
Mendoza, Sean	B-R	5-8	150	6-2-00	.222	.250	.200	5	9	2	2	0	0	1	1	3	1	0	0	2	0	0	.556	.462
Monzon, Andres	R-R	5-11	152	12-5-01	.300	.250	.313	9	20	4	6	3	0	0	3	1	0	0	0	7	1	1	.450	.333
Nieves, Hector	L-R	6-3	185	7-8-03	.224	.286	.203	26	85	5	19	4	3	2	10	5	1	0	2	26	1	2	.412	.269
Palma, Miguel	R-R	5-10	170	1-4-02	.196	.200	.195	21	46	11	9	2	0	3	9	17	1	0	2	11	0	1	.435	.409
Pena, Jeremy	R-R	6-0	202	9-22-97	.348	.000	.381	7	23	3	8	1	1	0	2	2	2	0	0	6	1	0	.609	.444
Perez, Frank	R-R	6-2	180	12-24-01	.103	.000	.133	21	39	10	4	0	0	2	1	11	5	0	0	19	1	2	.103	.364
Pinto, Franklin	R-R	6-1	160	4-26-01	.250	.250	.250	7	16	4	4	0	0	0	5	4	0	0	0	2	2	0	.250	.400
Rivas, Rainier	L-L	6-3	220	6-29-01	.298	.167	.320	40	121	10	36	11	1	2	22	10	2	0	0	37	0	2	.455	.361
Santana, Luis	R-R	5-8	198	7-20-99	.000	.000	.000	2	4	1	0	0	0	0	0	0	0	0	0	0	0	0	.000	.333
Santander, Juan	R-R	6-2	180	12-9-02	.194	.200	.194	24	72	12	14	3	0	0	7	2	3	0	1	24	6	0	.236	.244
Uceta, Raider	L-L	6-0	215	1-29-01	.400	.000	.667	2	5	1	2	0	0	0	1	0	0	1	0	1	2	0	.400	.333
Whitaker, Tyler	R-R	6-4	190	8-2-02	.202	.172	.213	29	104	16	21	2	1	3	6	9	0	0	1	40	8	1	.327	.263

Pitching	B-T	HT	WT	DOB	W	L	ERA	G	GS	CG	SV	IP	H	R	ER	HR	BB	SO	AVG	vLH	vRH	K/9	BB/9
Arrighetti, Spencer	R-R	6-2	186	1-2-00	1	1	2.25	2	0	0	0	4	7	2	1	0	0	6	.368	.429	.333	13.50	0.00
Batista, Edinson	R-R	6-2	185	5-19-02	1	2	7.77	11	0	0	1	24	32	22	21	1	19	33	.314	.308	.317	12.21	7.03
Beltre, Reimy	R-R	6-3	170	12-12-00	0	0	0.00	2	0	0	0	2	0	0	0	0	0	4	.000	.000	.000	18.00	0.00

HOUSTON ASTROS

Pitching	B-T	HT	WT	DOB	W	L	ERA	G	GS	CG	SV	IP	H	R	ER	HR	BB	SO	AVG	vLH	vRH	K/9	BB/9
Bojorquez, Gerardo	R-R	6-3	195	10-23-97	0	0	0.00	1	0	0	0	1	0	0	0	0	0	3	.000	.000	.000	27.00	0.00
Brockhouse, Walker	R-R	6-4	197	2-22-99	0	0	0.00	1	0	0	0	1	0	0	0	0	0	2	.000	.000	.000	18.00	0.00
Brown, Aaron	R-R	6-4	220	3-19-99	0	0	0.00	1	1	0	0	2	1	1	0	0	1	4	.125	.000	.250	18.00	4.50
Cabral, Riley	R-R	5-11	211	1-25-97	0	0	11.57	5	0	0	0	5	6	6	6	0	6	8	.316	.286	.333	15.43	11.57
Calderon, Carlos	R-R	6-0	175	10-4-01	1	0	4.43	5	2	0	0	20	17	11	10	3	8	28	.227	.368	.179	12.39	3.54
Carrillo, Yefri	R-R	6-2	170	1-13-01	3	3	3.86	13	5	0	0	47	23	23	20	3	38	53	.144	.145	.143	10.22	7.33
Chaidez, Adrian	R-R	6-1	180	6-10-99	1	0	7.11	4	0	0	0	6	7	5	5	0	3	15	.259	.200	.294	21.32	4.26
Chavez, Jervic	L-L	6-0	175	2-8-97	1	0	4.50	3	1	0	0	8	6	5	4	0	6	11	.194	.273	.150	12.38	6.75
Deason, Cody	R-R	6-4	214	12-26-96	0	0	0.00	3	3	0	0	7	0	1	0	0	8	15	.000	.000	.000	19.29	10.29
DeLabio, Jacob	R-R	6-5	205	9-19-97	0	0	0.00	4	0	0	0	5	2	0	0	0	1	12	.118	.100	.143	21.60	1.80
Drennan, Whit	L-L	6-0	190	2-25-97	0	0	0.00	1	0	0	0	1	0	0	0	0	2	3	.000	.000	.000	27.00	0.00
Eades, Ryan	R-R	6-2	210	12-15-91	0	0	0.00	1	1	0	0	1	1	0	0	0	1	3	.250	.000	.333	27.00	9.00
Foggo, Ian	R-R	6-1	200	6-1-98	1	0	0.00	6	0	0	0	7	3	1	0	0	4	14	.125	.083	.167	18.00	5.14
Ford, Kasey	L-R	6-6	275	1-10-98	0	0	0.00	1	0	0	0	1	0	0	0	0	0	1	.000	--	.000	9.00	0.00
Gaither, Ray	R-R	6-4	224	3-4-98	0	0	5.40	2	0	0	0	2	1	1	1	0	2	3	.167	.000	.500	16.20	10.80
Garcia, Elvis	R-R	6-0	165	9-24-02	2	1	4.26	5	5	0	0	19	14	11	9	2	11	22	.206	.194	.216	10.42	5.21
Garcia, Ronny	R-R	6-3	170	12-2-99	1	0	1.38	9	0	0	2	13	10	3	2	0	5	14	.227	.100	.333	9.69	3.46
Gruller, Kyle	R-R	6-3	234	5-21-98	0	0	0.00	1	1	0	0	2	0	0	0	1	3	.000	.000	.000	13.50	4.50
Hiraldo, Carlos	R-R	6-2	170	6-28-98	0	0	0.66	5	2	0	1	14	13	8	1	0	9	6	.236	.222	.243	3.95	5.93
Hunt, Marshall	R-R	6-3	200	7-8-99	0	1	7.71	4	1	0	0	5	2	4	4	1	5	8	.133	.000	.222	15.43	9.64
Ivey, Tyler	R-R	6-4	195	5-12-96	0	0	0.00	1	1	0	0	2	1	0	0	0	1	3	.167	.000	.250	13.50	4.50
Kouba, Rhett	R-R	6-0	180	9-3-99	0	0	5.40	2	0	0	0	5	6	3	3	1	1	7	.300	.250	.333	12.60	1.80
Lopez, Jairo	R-R	5-11	220	11-0-00	0	1	2.51	5	4	0	0	14	14	7	4	0	2	14	.259	.360	.172	8.79	1.26
Martes, Francis	R-R	6-0	249	11-24-95	0	2	6.00	3	0	0	0	3	5	3	2	0	3	5	.357	.400	.333	15.00	9.00
Matthews, Zack	B-R	6-0	205	1-31-99	0	1	6.75	2	2	0	0	1	1	1	1	1	2	2	.167	.000	.250	13.50	13.50
McDermott, Chayce	L-R	6-3	197	8-22-98	0	0	0.00	1	0	0	0	3	1	0	0	0	1	7	.100	.000	.167	21.00	3.00
McDonald, Cole	L-R	6-1	220	3-11-97	0	2	2.08	3	0	0	0	9	6	5	2	0	4	18	.188	.100	.333	18.69	4.15
Miley, Deylen	R-R	6-2	210	1-25-98	1	0	2.08	5	1	0	0	13	10	4	3	0	5	24	.192	.143	.250	16.62	3.46
Molero, Jeremy	R-R	6-2	170	11-8-99	2	2	6.20	11	1	0	1	20	15	14	14	0	17	30	.205	.161	.238	13.28	7.52
Nodal, Jose	L-L	6-3	195	7-16-02	2	1	6.49	10	3	0	0	26	22	19	19	1	20	28	.224	.208	.230	9.57	6.84
Palmer, Alex	B-R	5-10	160	5-15-98	1	2	1.08	8	4	0	0	25	18	4	3	1	12	38	.200	.188	.207	13.68	4.32
Pereira, Jherson	R-R	6-2	175	1-27-97	0	0	0.00	1	0	0	0	1	0	0	0	0	1	1	.000	.000	.000	9.00	9.00
Perez, Bryan	R-R	5-11	160	4-14-00	2	1	3.95	6	1	0	0	14	17	15	6	2	9	19	.309	.355	.250	12.51	5.93
Rodriguez, Elian	R-R	6-4	205	3-10-97	1	1	3.95	5	1	0	0	14	12	7	6	0	8	21	.231	.250	.219	13.83	5.27
Salgado, Bryant	R-R	6-1	205	3-2-00	0	0	6.75	1	0	0	0	1	2	1	1	0	3	3	.333	.000	.400	20.25	20.25
Santa, Alimber	R-R	5-10	163	5-3-03	0	0	3.68	3	1	0	0	7	5	4	3	2	2	8	.185	.231	.143	9.82	2.45
Schroeder, Jayson	R-R	6-2	196	11-14-99	0	2	4.02	5	4	0	0	16	11	10	7	0	17	17	.212	.273	.167	9.77	9.77
Scrubb, Andre	R-R	6-4	270	1-13-95	0	0	0.00	1	0	0	0	1	1	0	0	0	0	1	.250	1.000	.000	9.00	0.00
Solano, Bryan	R-R	6-4	190	1-25-98	1	0	0.00	3	0	0	0	3	1	0	0	0	5	5	.111	.333	.000	15.00	15.00
Swanson, Nic	R-R	6-2	180	7-8-99	1	0	5.63	4	1	0	1	8	8	6	5	1	7	9	.250	.364	.190	10.13	7.88
Tokar, Heitor	R-R	6-6	256	10-25-00	2	1	3.86	6	0	0	0	14	9	8	6	2	6	18	.173	.063	.222	11.57	3.86
Ullola, Miguel	R-R	6-1	184	6-19-02	0	0	3.00	2	0	0	0	3	2	1	1	0	4	4	.182	.333	.125	12.00	12.00
Urquidy, Jose	R-R	6-0	217	5-1-01	0	0	0.00	1	1	0	0	3	1	0	0	0	0	6	.091	.000	.250	18.00	0.00
Vega, Luis	R-R	6-3	165	11-16-01	3	3	5.18	10	4	0	0	33	34	24	19	2	14	31	.258	.356	.207	8.45	3.82
West, Derek	R-R	6-5	230	12-2-96	0	0	0.00	2	1	0	0	3	2	0	0	0	0	6	.200	.333	.143	18.00	0.00

Fielding

C: Alvarez 12, Ceuta 1, Guilamo 22, Hurtado 4, Palma 17, Santander 14.
1B: Alvarez 4, Balogh 4, Ceuta 10, Cruz 8, Diaz 13, Guilamo 5, Liranzo 1, Mascai 11, Palma 2, Rivas 5, Santander 1.
2B: Balogh 9, Ceuta 2, Cruz 18, Lorenzo 23, Mendoza 1, Mendoza 2, Nieves 8, Santana 1.
3B: Balogh 26, Ceuta 4, Cruz 7, Diaz 1, Gonzalez 3, Gonzalez 1, Leon 1, Lorenzo 7, Mendoza 3, Mendoza 2, Nieves 3, Santana 1, Whitaker 4.
SS: Balogh 7, Ceuta 4, Diaz 1, Gonzalez 11, Leon 1, Lorenzo 11, Machandy 6, Mendoza 2, Mendoza 1, Nieves 16, Pena 5, Perez 1.
OF: Cortabarria 9, Diaz 11, Giron 10, Gonzalez 34, Guerrero 2, Leon 1, Liranzo 1, Machandy 38, Monzon 7, Nieves 1, Perez 19, Pinto 7, Rivas 22, Whitaker 24.

DSL ASTROS   ROOKIE
DOMINICAN SUMMER LEAGUE

Batting	B-T	HT	WT	DOB	AVG	vLH	vRH	G	AB	R	H	2B	3B	HR	RBI	BB	HBP	SH	SF	SO	SB	CS	SLG	OBP
Arcila, Carlos	R-R	5-11	155	1-2-04	.190	.300	.165	41	105	7	20	4	0	2	17	9	0	0	2	21	2	1	.286	.250
Caldera, Fernando	R-R	5-11	170	10-10-02	.167	.100	.190	41	78	5	13	4	0	0	10	9	1	1	0	27	1	3	.295	.261
Cooper, Everette	R-R	6-0	165	9-16-02	.163	.217	.147	46	98	12	16	2	0	0	4	9	3	0	0	34	1	2	.184	.255
De La Cruz, Denfry	R-R	6-1	190	2-20-03	.100	.250	.000	5	10	1	1	1	0	0	0	0	0	0	0	3	0	0	.200	.100
Del Rosario, Richel	R-R	6-0	191	2-27-04	.196	.130	.214	45	107	18	21	2	1	0	7	14	6	2	0	26	14	2	.234	.323
Encarnacion, Luis	R-R	5-8	150	9-25-02	.320	.275	.333	55	169	23	54	11	2	1	25	19	4	0	0	22	15	3	.426	.401
Encarnacion, Yamal	B-R	5-8	150	9-8-03	.250	.267	.246	56	152	31	38	8	2	1	17	23	1	0	0	28	12	4	.349	.352
Familia, Daniel	R-R	6-0	203	9-5-02	.206	.222	.203	28	68	12	14	3	0	4	10	10	2	0	2	27	2	3	.426	.317
Fernandez, Jesus	R-R	6-0	150	8-26-03	.241	.115	.280	48	108	12	26	3	0	0	10	15	3	0	1	27	8	3	.269	.346
Molina, Leosdany	R-R	6-0	182	1-9-00	.311	.333	.304	54	164	29	51	6	3	1	27	24	2	0	2	37	25	5	.402	.401
Morales, Christopher	R-R	6-1	170	9-30-02	.277	.316	.268	43	101	17	28	11	0	2	11	21	1	0	0	49	0	4	.446	.407
Nolasco, Brayan	R-R	5-9	178	9-24-03	.200	.143	.222	38	75	18	15	3	0	0	7	13	4	0	0	23	11	6	.240	.348
Ortiz, Ayendy	B-R	6-1	170	3-9-02	--	--	--	1	0	0	0	0	0	0	0	0	0	0	0	0	0	0	--	1.000
Payano, Josue	R-R	5-10	150	6-22-03	.200	.190	.203	43	100	11	20	2	2	0	7	2	2	1	2	38	4	5	.260	.226
Perez, Luis	R-R	5-10	193	10-24-02	.345	.158	.385	51	110	34	38	5	1	3	18	23	6	0	1	24	16	4	.491	.479
Ramirez, Tomas	R-R	6-1	172	11-21-01	.102	.231	.065	29	59	6	6	0	0	1	4	11	1	0	0	28	0	3	.153	.254

	B-T	HT	WT	DOB																							
Sanchez, Anderson	R-R	6-1	170	11-6-03	.150	.000	.194	24	40	4	6	1	0	0	3	6	1	0	0	19	4	4	.175	.277			
Toro, Ricardo	R-R	6-1	170	2-24-01	.314	.360	.302	50	121	17	38	4	0	3	25	16	5	0	2	12	2	1	.421	.410			

Pitching	B-T	HT	WT	DOB	W	L	ERA	G	GS	CG	SV	IP	H	R	ER	HR	BB	SO	AVG	vLH	vRH	K/9	BB/9
Andujar, Jose	R-R	5-10	158	2-10-02	4	5	5.28	13	7	0	0	31	25	23	18	0	27	42	.227	.217	.234	12.33	7.92
Bolivar, Jose	R-R	5-11	175	11-21-02	2	3	5.56	13	0	0	2	23	16	19	14	1	16	14	.205	.133	.250	5.56	6.35
Caldera, Fernando	R-R	5-11	170	10-10-02	0	0	0.00	1	0	0	0	2	2	0	0	0	0	1	.250	.000	.286	4.50	0.00
Chirinos, Amilcar	R-R	6-3	200	11-7-01	1	0	2.61	6	0	0	1	10	3	4	3	0	3	13	.088	.056	.125	11.32	2.61
Cooper, Everette	R-R	6-0	165	9-16-02	0	0	--	0	0	0	0	0	0	0	0	0	0	0	--	--	--	--	--
Cuevas, Hector	R-R	6-6	223	8-24-01	0	0	0.00	2	0	0	0	2	1	0	0	0	3	2	.125	.250	.000	7.71	11.57
De Pena, Freilyn	R-R	5-10	173	3-13-03	0	0	6.26	13	0	0	0	27	27	26	19	0	26	26	.257	.351	.206	8.56	8.56
Encarnacion, Yamal	B-R	5-8	150	9-8-03	0	1	9.00	1	0	0	0	1	2	1	1	0	1	0	.500	--	.500	0.00	9.00
Eusebio, Marcos	R-R	6-1	180	9-5-00	2	2	4.55	16	1	0	2	30	20	19	15	3	29	31	.189	.231	.164	9.40	8.80
Familia, Daniel	R-R	6-0	203	9-5-02	0	0	0.00	1	0	0	0	0	0	0	0	0	0	0	.000	.000	--	0.00	0.00
Fernandez, Jesus	R-R	6-0	150	8-26-03	1	0	4.15	2	0	0	0	4	5	3	2	0	1	1	.263	.200	.286	2.08	2.08
Figuereo, Johan	R-R	6-0	172	6-27-00	2	3	4.17	12	7	0	0	37	33	27	17	2	25	32	.237	.226	.244	7.85	6.14
Geraldo, Jorge	R-R	6-6	197	12-7-01	1	1	1.98	8	0	0	1	14	7	3	3	0	10	19	.159	.133	.172	12.51	6.59
Guzman, Danyuri	R-R	6-0	154	2-11-03	0	0	0.00	1	1	0	0	1	1	0	0	0	0	2	.250	.333	.000	18.00	0.00
Leon, Ricardo	L-L	6-4	165	3-26-01	0	5	7.36	13	9	0	0	37	35	40	30	0	28	50	.240	.158	.269	12.27	6.87
Martich, Eurys	R-R	6-3	206	8-20-02	0	3	14.35	14	7	0	0	26	20	44	42	1	52	43	.211	.241	.197	14.70	17.77
Mercedes, Abel	R-R	6-1	185	6-29-02	0	2	7.91	10	0	0	0	19	22	19	17	0	22	21	.293	.324	.263	9.78	10.24
Perez, Chanderson	R-R	6-0	195	9-22-01	0	0	2.57	6	0	0	0	7	8	3	2	0	10	8	.286	.200	.333	10.29	12.86
Ramirez, Johangel	R-R	6-2	193	9-10-01	4	1	2.45	14	9	0	0	48	34	18	13	4	27	38	.205	.197	.210	7.17	5.10
Rosario, Darwin	R-R	6-3	180	6-15-00	1	0	12.46	4	0	0	0	4	4	8	6	1	7	8	.267	.500	.182	16.62	14.54
Santa, Alimber	R-R	5-10	163	5-3-03	0	2	3.29	6	3	0	1	14	14	7	5	0	6	14	.275	.333	.250	9.22	3.95
Soto, Juan	R-R	6-2	209	4-30-03	3	3	5.45	13	5	0	1	35	26	23	21	0	37	44	.200	.194	.206	11.42	9.61
Subero, Danny	R-R	6-4	194	11-2-01	1	1	4.60	17	2	0	3	29	16	18	15	2	25	30	.155	.146	.161	9.20	7.67
Toro, Ricardo	R-R	6-1	170	2-24-01	0	0	5.79	2	0	0	0	5	7	4	3	2	4	0	.304	.333	.286	0.00	7.71
Torres, Normar	R-R	6-0	184	10-28-02	0	0	9.00	2	0	0	0	3	5	4	3	0	1	2	.357	.400	.333	6.00	3.00
Ullola, Miguel	R-R	6-1	184	6-19-02	1	1	4.22	8	5	0	0	21	10	11	10	1	17	34	.139	.192	.109	14.34	7.17
Villega, Elvin	R-R	6-2	173	7-13-02	1	1	1.76	8	2	0	1	15	10	5	3	0	12	19	.196	.125	.229	11.15	7.04

Fielding

C: Arcila 17, Caldera 34, Encarnacion 12, Toro 26,
1B: Arcila 10, Caldera 4, De La Cruz 3, Del Rosario 7, Encarnacion 33, Fernandez 1, Payano 2, Toro 22,
2B: Del Rosario 3, Encarnacion 6, Encarnacion 21, Fernandez 31, Molina 1, Ortiz 1, Payano 10, Perez 1,
3B: Del Rosario 24, Encarnacion 22, Familia 2, Fernandez 11, Molina 7, Morales 1, Payano 18
SS: Encarnacion 17, Molina 47, Payano 6,
OF: Cooper 44, Del Rosario 23, Encarnacion 1, Encarnacion 2, Familia 19, Fernandez 1, Molina 1, Morales 30, Nolasco 36, Payano 3, Perez 48, Ramirez 21, Sanchez 22,

Kansas City Royals

SEASON IN A SENTENCE: A season that began with faint aspirations of contending for the AL Central quickly dissipated after the Royals went 18-37 in May and June, though the club played .521 ball in the second half and avoided 90 losses.

HIGH POINT: Salvador Perez tied the Blue Jays' Vladimir Guerrero Jr. for the MLB lead with 48 home runs. The 31-year-old also established an MLB record for home runs in a season by a primary catcher, besting the 45 Johnny Bench hit in 1970. Perez's 337 total bases were third most ever by a catcher, while his MLB-leading 121 RBIs were 13th most ever by a catcher.

LOW POINT: The Royals entered May seven games over .500 but then lost 11 straight from May 2 to 13 to fall to 16-20. They never reached .500 again. Most troubling was the club's 4.97 ERA from starting pitchers, the organization's perceived strength heading into 2021. A trio of top 2018 draft picks fared particularly poorly. Brady Singer ran up a 4.91 ERA in 128 innings, while rookies Daniel Lynch (5.89 ERA in 68 IP) and Jackson Kowar (11.27 ERA in 30 IP) were worse.

NOTABLE ROOKIES: While Lynch and Kowar scuffled as rookies, 24-year-old righthander Carlos Hernandez was a revelation. He opened the year in the bullpen but moved to the rotation on July 18 and went 5-2, 3.23 with 44 strikeouts and 26 walks in 64 innings after making the switch.

KEY TRANSACTIONS: The Royals made few transactions of note. They dealt pending free agents Jorge Soler and Danny Duffy at the trade deadline, as much for salary relief as future value. Soler would go on to win the World Series MVP award for the Braves.

ON THE FARM: Most of the Royals' positive developments happened on the farm. Quad Cities won High-A Central to help boost the Royals' organizational winning percentage for domestic affiliates to .510, which ranked 14th among 30 clubs. More significantly, the Royals' system climbed to No. 3 in the organizational talent rankings, buoyed by five of the top 80 qualified hitters in the minors, per wRC+. Minor league home run champ MJ Melendez ranked sixth, followed by Nick Pratto (ninth), Vinnie Pasquantino (15th), Minor League Player of the Year Bobby Witt Jr. (44th) and Michael Massey (80th). Melendez, Pratto and Witt were first-team Minor League All-Stars, with Melendez and Pratto authoring the two largest turnarounds from 2019 to 2021.

OPENING DAY PAYROLL: $86,565,788 (23rd).

PLAYERS OF THE YEAR

MAJOR LEAGUE	MINOR LEAGUE
Salvador Perez	**Bobby Witt Jr.**
C	SS
.273/.316/.544	(AAA/AA)
MLB-leading 48 HR	.290/.361/.575,
and 121 RBIs	33 HR, 29 SB

ORGANIZATION LEADERS

Batting		*Minimum 250 AB
MAJORS		
*AVG	Nicky Lopez	.300
*OPS	Salvador Perez	.859
HR	Salvador Perez	48
RBI	Salvador Perez	121
MINORS		
*AVG	Edward Olivares, Omaha	.313
*OBP	Edward Olivares, Omaha	.397
*SLG	MJ Melendez, NW Arkansas, Omaha	.625
*OPS	MJ Melendez, NW Arkansas, Omaha	1.011
R	Bobby Witt Jr., NW Arkansas, Omaha	99
H	Bobby Witt Jr., NW Arkansas, Omaha	144
TB	Bobby Witt Jr., NW Arkansas, Omaha	286
2B	Vinnie Pasquantino, NW Arkansas, Quad Cities	37
3B	Maikel Garcia, Quad Cities, Columbia	7
3B	Nick Pratto, NW Arkansas, Omaha	7
3B	Tyler Tolbert, ACL Royals Blue, Columbia, Quad Cities	7
HR	MJ Melendez, NW Arkansas, Omaha	41
RBI	MJ Melendez, NW Arkansas, Omaha	103
BB	Nick Pratto, Omaha, NW Arkansas	83
SO	Nick Pratto, Omaha, NW Arkansas	157
SB	Tyler Tolbert, ACL Royals Blue, Columbia, Quad Cities	55

Pitching		#Minimum 75 IP
MAJORS		
W	Brad Keller/Mike Minor	8
#ERA	Carlos Hernandez	3.68
SO	Mike Minor	149
SV	Scott Barlow	16
MINORS		
W	Mitch Ellis, Columbia, Quad Cities/Jackson Kowar, Omaha	9
L	Adrian Alcantara, Columbia	9
L	Marcelo Martinez, Omaha, NW Arkansas	9
#ERA	Drew Parrish, NW Arkansas, Quad Cities	2.83
G	Grant Gavin, Omaha	48
G	Collin Snider, Omaha, NW Arkansas	48
GS	Marcelo Martinez, Omaha, NW Arkansas	24
SV	Josh Dye, Omaha, NW Arkansas	9
IP	Marcelo Martinez, Omaha, NW Arkansas	112.2
BB	Stephen Woods Jr., NW Arkansas	45
SO	Anthony Veneziano, Quad Cities	127
#AVG	Drew Parrish, NW Arkansas, Quad Cities	.198

2021 PERFORMANCE

General Manager: J.J. Picollo. **Farm Director:** Vacant. **Scouting Director:** Danny Ontiveros.

Class	Team	League	W	L	PCT	Finish	Manager
Majors	Kansas City Royals	American	74	88	.457	12th (15)	Mike Matheny
Triple-A	Omaha Storm Chasers	Triple-A East	73	56	.566	7th (20)	Brian Poldberg
Double-A	N.W. Arkansas Naturals	Double-A Central	64	55	.538	t-2nd (10)	Scott Thorman
High-A	Quad Cities River Bandits	High-A Central	77	41	.653	1st (12)	Chris Widger
Low-A	Columbia Fireflies	Low-A East	48	71	.403	10th (12)	Brooks Conrad
Rookie	ACL Royals Gold	Arizona Complex	20	33	.377	15th (18)	Andre David
Rookie	ACL Royals Blue	Arizona Complex	20	34	.370	16th (18)	Omar Ramirez
Rookie	DSL Royals White	Dominican Summer	20	32	.385	40th (46)	Sergio De Luna
Rookie	DSL Royals Blue	Dominican Summer	32	20	.615	8th (46)	Ramon Martinez
Overall 2021 Minor League Record		354		342	.509 13th (30)		

ORGANIZATION STATISTICS

KANSAS CITY ROYALS
AMERICAN LEAGUE

Batting	B-T	HT	WT	DOB	AVG	vLH	vRH	G	AB	R	H	2B	3B	HR	RBI	BB	HBP	SH	SF	SO	SB	CS	SLG	OBP
Alberto, Hanser	R-R	5-11	215	10-17-92	.270	.286	.254	103	241	25	65	20	3	2	24	4	4	4	2	26	3	1	.402	.291
Benintendi, Andrew	L-L	5-9	180	7-6-94	.276	.303	.264	134	493	63	136	27	2	17	73	36	2	1	6	97	8	9	.442	.324
Dozier, Hunter	R-R	6-4	220	8-22-91	.216	.204	.220	144	487	55	105	27	6	16	54	43	7	0	6	154	5	4	.394	.285
Dyson, Jarrod	L-R	5-9	165	8-15-84	.221	.200	.227	77	122	13	27	2	6	0	10	6	0	3	1	28	8	3	.311	.256
2-team total (25 Toronto)					.207	.179	.215	102	135	17	28	7	2	0	10	10	0	3	1	33	10	5	.289	.260
Gallagher, Cam	R-R	6-3	230	12-6-92	.250	.229	.260	48	112	9	28	6	0	1	7	8	0	2	1	20	0	0	.330	.298
Gutierrez, Kelvin	R-R	6-2	215	8-28-94	.215	.156	.233	38	135	9	29	4	2	1	8	4	1	0	0	31	0	1	.296	.254
2-team total (47 Baltimore)					.232	.253	.223	85	272	23	63	8	3	3	20	19	4	0	0	76	0	1	.316	.292
Isbel, Kyle	L-R	5-11	190	3-3-97	.276	.333	.266	28	76	16	21	5	2	1	7	7	0	0	0	23	2	0	.434	.337
Lopez, Nicky	L-R	5-11	180	3-13-95	.300	.288	.304	151	497	78	149	21	6	2	43	49	4	12	3	74	22	1	.378	.365
McBroom, Ryan	R-L	6-3	220	4-9-92	.250	.250	.250	7	8	1	2	0	0	0	1	0	0	0	0	6	0	0	.250	.333
Merrifield, Whit	R-R	6-1	195	1-24-89	.277	.276	.277	162	664	97	184	42	3	10	74	40	4	0	12	103	40	4	.395	.317
Mondesi, Adalberto	B-R	6-1	200	7-27-95	.230	.256	.218	35	126	19	29	8	1	6	17	6	1	3	0	43	15	1	.452	.271
Olivares, Edward	R-R	6-2	190	3-6-96	.238	.205	.263	39	101	14	24	2	0	5	12	5	3	1	1	19	2	2	.406	.291
O'Hearn, Ryan	L-L	6-3	220	7-26-93	.225	.161	.234	84	236	23	53	5	1	9	29	13	2	0	3	71	0	0	.369	.268
Perez, Salvador	R-R	6-3	255	5-10-90	.273	.302	.261	161	620	88	169	24	0	48	121	28	13	0	4	170	1	2	.544	.316
Rivera, Emmanuel	R-R	6-2	225	6-29-96	.256	.259	.254	29	90	13	23	4	0	1	5	8	0	0	0	21	2	0	.333	.316
Rivero, Sebastian	R-R	6-1	210	11-16-98	.175	.167	.176	17	40	1	7	2	0	0	3	3	1	0	0	15	0	0	.225	.250
Santana, Carlos	B-R	5-11	215	4-8-86	.214	.283	.184	158	565	66	121	15	0	19	69	86	3	0	5	102	2	0	.342	.319
Soler, Jorge	R-R	6-4	235	2-25-92	.192	.230	.176	94	308	38	59	16	0	13	37	38	5	0	3	97	0	0	.370	.288
Taylor, Michael A.	R-R	6-4	215	3-26-91	.244	.295	.224	142	483	58	118	16	1	12	54	33	5	2	5	144	14	7	.356	.297

Pitching	B-T	HT	WT	DOB	W	L	ERA	G	GS	CG	SV	IP	H	R	ER	HR	BB	SO	AVG	vLH	vRH	K/9	BB/9
Alberto, Hanser	R-R	5-11	215	10-17-92	0	0	0.00	1	0	0	0	0	0	0	0	0	0	0	.000	.000	--	0.00	0.00
Barlow, Scott	R-R	6-3	210	12-18-92	5	3	2.42	71	0	0	16	74	61	20	20	4	28	91	.223	.235	.214	11.02	3.39
Blewett, Scott	R-R	6-6	245	4-10-96	0	0	1.80	3	0	0	0	5	3	1	1	0	5	4	.188	.111	.286	7.20	9.00
Bolanos, Ronald	R-R	6-2	230	8-23-96	0	0	1.42	3	0	0	0	6	4	1	1	0	2	10	.174	.333	.071	14.21	2.84
Brentz, Jake	L-L	6-1	205	9-14-94	5	2	3.66	72	0	0	2	64	45	32	26	7	37	76	.197	.116	.231	10.69	5.20
Bubic, Kris	L-L	6-3	225	8-19-97	6	7	4.43	29	20	0	0	130	121	67	64	22	59	114	.248	.238	.251	7.89	4.08
Coleman, Dylan	R-R	6-5	230	9-16-96	0	0	1.42	5	0	0	0	6	5	1	1	0	1	7	.208	.375	.125	9.95	1.42
Davis, Wade	R-R	6-5	225	9-7-85	0	3	6.75	40	0	0	2	43	44	33	32	8	19	38	.270	.257	.280	8.02	4.01
Duffy, Danny	L-L	6-3	205	12-21-88	4	3	2.51	13	12	0	0	61	52	19	17	6	22	65	.226	.217	.228	9.59	3.25
Hahn, Jesse	R-R	6-5	205	7-30-89	0	0	13.50	5	0	0	1	3	5	5	5	2	4	3	.357	.333	.500	8.10	10.80
Heasley, Jon	R-R	6-3	225	1-27-97	1	1	4.91	3	3	0	0	15	15	8	8	3	6	14	.278	.200	.375	3.68	1.84
Hernandez, Carlos	R-R	6-4	245	3-11-97	6	2	3.68	24	11	0	0	86	69	36	35	7	41	74	.223	.184	.254	7.77	4.31
Holland, Greg	R-R	5-10	210	11-20-85	3	5	4.85	57	0	0	8	56	49	32	30	9	26	53	.229	.205	.246	8.57	4.20
Junis, Jakob	R-R	6-3	220	9-16-92	2	4	5.26	16	6	0	0	39	43	24	23	7	12	41	.279	.294	.261	9.38	2.75
Keller, Brad	R-R	6-5	255	7-29-95	8	12	5.39	26	26	0	0	134	158	89	80	18	64	120	.297	.301	.293	8.08	4.31
Kowar, Jackson	R-R	6-5	200	10-4-96	0	6	11.27	9	6	0	0	30	43	38	38	7	20	29	.336	.333	.338	8.60	5.93
Lovelady, Richard	L-L	6-0	185	7-7-95	2	0	3.48	20	0	0	1	21	16	9	8	3	6	23	.211	.156	.250	10.02	2.61
Lynch, Daniel	L-L	6-6	200	11-17-96	4	6	5.69	15	15	0	0	68	80	46	43	9	31	55	.295	.161	.313	7.28	4.10
Minor, Mike	R-L	6-4	210	12-26-87	8	12	5.05	28	28	0	0	159	156	92	89	26	41	149	.252	.253	.252	8.45	2.33
Newberry, Jake	R-R	6-2	200	11-20-94	0	0	16.62	4	0	0	0	4	10	8	8	2	3	5	.476	.556	.417	10.38	6.23
Payamps, Joel	R-R	6-2	225	4-7-94	1	1	4.43	15	1	0	0	20	23	12	10	3	3	16	.277	.235	.306	7.08	1.33
2-team total (22 Toronto)					1	3	3.40	37	1	0	0	50	44	22	19	6	14	38	.232	.176	.262	6.79	2.50
Santana, Ervin	R-R	6-2	175	12-12-82	2	2	4.68	38	2	0	0	65	65	35	34	9	22	52	.259	.275	.248	7.16	3.03
Singer, Brady	R-R	6-5	215	8-4-96	5	10	4.91	27	27	1	0	128	146	81	70	14	53	131	.281	.268	.296	9.19	3.72
Speier, Gabe	L-L	5-11	200	4-12-95	0	0	1.17	7	0	0	0	8	10	3	1	0	0	5	.313	.154	.421	5.87	0.00
Staumont, Josh	R-R	6-3	200	12-21-93	4	3	2.88	64	0	0	5	66	43	24	21	6	27	72	.183	.211	.164	9.87	3.70
Swarzak, Anthony	R-R	6-4	215	9-10-85	0	0	9.39	7	0	0	0	8	13	8	8	3	0	5	.382	.538	.286	5.87	0.00
Tapia, Domingo	R-R	6-3	263	8-4-91	4	1	2.84	32	0	0	0	32	21	10	10	1	14	25	.191	.161	.203	7.11	3.98

					2-team total (2 Seattle)	4	1	2.67	34	0	0	0	34	25	10	10	1	15	26	.208	.194	.214	6.95	4.01
Zerpa, Angel	L-L	6-0	220	9-27-99		0	1	0.00	1	1	0	0	5	3	2	0	0	1	4	.176	.000	.231	7.20	1.80
Zimmer, Kyle	R-R	6-3	225	9-13-91		4	1	4.83	52	2	0	2	54	46	32	29	7	30	46	.243	.179	.288	7.67	5.00
Zuber, Tyler	R-R	5-11	195	6-16-95		0	3	6.26	31	0	0	0	27	26	20	19	6	17	25	.250	.308	.192	8.23	5.60

Fielding

Catcher	PCT	G	PO	A	E	DP	PB
Gallagher	.983	46	281	13	5	0	1
Perez	.998	124	975	61	2	12	1
Rivero	1.000	17	95	8	0	0	2

First Base	PCT	G	PO	A	E	DP
Dozier	1.000	19	99	8	0	10
Gutierrez	1.000	1	1	0	0	0
O'Hearn	.973	20	102	5	3	11
Rivera	1.000	1	7	0	0	0
Santana	.993	136	1001	50	7	117

Second Base	PCT	G	PO	A	E	DP
Alberto	.952	31	25	35	3	10
Lopez	1.000	4	9	11	0	3
Merrifield	.988	149	283	382	8	103

Third Base	PCT	G	PO	A	E	DP
Alberto	.955	49	32	53	4	8
Dozier	.956	57	33	75	5	11
Gutierrez	.909	37	27	63	9	11
Mondesi	.964	20	14	40	2	6
Rivera	.934	28	23	48	5	3

Shortstop	PCT	G	PO	A	E	DP
Alberto	1.000	17	15	39	0	7

	PCT	G	PO	A	E	DP
Lopez	.987	148	156	371	7	77
Mondesi	1.000	11	10	22	0	4

Outfield	PCT	G	PO	A	E	DP
Benintendi	.987	129	225	6	3	1
Dozier	.985	74	122	6	2	0
Dyson	.990	71	95	3	1	0
Isbel	1.000	27	46	1	0	0
Merrifield	1.000	20	28	1	0	0
Olivares	.957	37	42	2	2	0
O'Hearn	1.000	26	35	1	0	0
Soler	.985	46	66	0	1	0
Taylor	.992	139	351	11	3	3

OMAHA STORM CHASERS
TRIPLE-A EAST

TRIPLE-A

Batting	B-T	HT	WT	DOB	AVG	vLH	vRH	G	AB	R	H	2B	3B	HR	RBI	BB	HBP	SH	SF	SO	SB	CS	SLG	OBP
Blanco, Dairon	R-R	6-0	170	4-26-93	.252	.270	.245	38	131	21	33	6	0	5	15	11	4	2	0	31	9	5	.412	.329
Cancel, Gabriel	R-R	6-0	205	12-8-96	.238	.175	.262	57	206	35	49	12	1	14	35	20	0	0	1	68	12	2	.510	.304
Castellano, Angelo	R-R	6-0	165	1-13-95	.226	.258	.215	80	252	29	57	7	0	8	32	20	4	3	4	63	8	2	.349	.289
Dini, Nick	R-R	5-8	190	7-27-93	.303	.385	.270	26	89	10	27	5	0	4	16	5	3	0	1	18	1	0	.494	.357
Dozier, Hunter	R-R	6-4	220	8-22-91	.167	.000	.188	4	18	1	3	2	0	0	3	0	0	0	0	5	0	0	.278	.167
Escobar, Alcides	R-R	6-1	205	12-16-86	.274	.294	.267	35	124	23	34	7	0	5	16	6	1	1	1	29	2	0	.452	.311
Esposito, Nate	R-R	5-11	180	6-25-93	.200	.333	.158	15	25	2	5	1	0	1	2	2	2	0	0	12	0	1	.360	.310
Fermin, Freddy	R-R	5-10	200	5-16-95	.231	.167	.286	4	13	4	3	1	0	0	2	2	0	1	0	6	0	0	.308	.333
Fox, Lucius	B-R	6-1	185	7-2-97	.242	.241	.242	57	215	41	52	14	0	4	21	33	2	1	1	61	19	2	.363	.347
Gallagher, Cam	R-R	6-3	230	12-6-92	.222	.500	.200	7	27	4	6	0	0	1	3	5	0	0	4	0	0	0	.333	.344
Govern, Jimmy	R-R	5-11	190	12-11-96	.269	.000	.318	7	26	1	7	2	0	1	3	1	0	0	0	3	1	0	.462	.296
Gutierrez, Kelvin	R-R	6-2	215	8-28-94	.306	.571	.136	9	36	1	11	3	1	0	4	2	0	0	0	7	0	1	.444	.342
				2-team total (25 Norfolk)	.254	.326	.217	34	126	11	32	7	1	4	17	6	0	0	0	28	1	2	.421	.288
Isbel, Kyle	L-R	5-11	190	3-3-97	.269	.258	.273	105	394	62	106	18	3	15	55	45	10	0	2	91	22	5	.444	.357
Jones, Travis	R-R	6-4	210	9-29-95	.200	.071	.230	35	75	14	15	1	0	2	5	14	3	0	0	27	1	1	.293	.348
Martin, Rudy	L-L	5-7	155	1-31-96	.223	.105	.240	46	148	23	33	4	1	6	20	24	1	2	1	60	11	0	.385	.333
McBroom, Ryan	R-L	6-3	220	4-9-92	.261	.236	.269	115	433	78	113	14	2	32	88	47	5	0	4	109	3	1	.524	.337
Mejia, Erick	B-R	5-11	195	11-9-94	.246	.288	.232	55	203	22	50	10	1	7	30	22	0	1	2	41	1	2	.409	.317
Melendez, MJ	L-R	6-1	190	11-29-98	.293	.257	.304	44	150	37	44	4	3	13	38	32	0	0	2	39	1	2	.620	.413
Merrell, Kevin	L-R	6-1	180	12-14-95	.258	.308	.222	13	31	5	8	1	0	0	3	4	1	1	1	9	2	0	.290	.351
Miller, Anderson	L-L	6-3	215	5-6-94	.215	.250	.200	69	219	35	47	6	0	12	35	24	5	1	2	67	9	2	.406	.304
Mondesi, Adalberto	B-R	6-1	200	7-27-95	.204	.154	.222	14	49	8	10	1	0	2	2	2	0	0	0	13	5	1	.347	.235
Mondesi, Paul	R-R	6-0	240	7-7-98	.333	.500	.250	4	12	2	4	0	0	0	0	0	0	0	1	0	0	0	.333	.333
Olivares, Edward	R-R	6-2	190	3-6-96	.313	.339	.304	66	256	54	80	12	3	15	36	29	7	0	0	46	12	4	.559	.397
O'Hearn, Ryan	L-L	6-3	220	7-26-93	.375	.238	.431	19	72	22	27	4	0	12	25	9	1	0	0	15	3	0	.931	.451
Pratto, Nick	L-L	6-1	215	10-6-98	.259	.286	.251	63	224	54	58	15	3	21	55	37	4	0	5	77	5	0	.634	.367
Rivera, Emmanuel	R-R	6-2	225	6-29-96	.286	.328	.271	63	255	48	73	17	2	19	57	22	3	0	2	58	3	0	.592	.348
Rivero, Sebastian	R-R	6-1	210	11-16-98	.260	.263	.259	42	150	18	39	7	1	3	26	10	3	0	0	45	2	1	.380	.319
Starling, Bubba	R-R	6-4	220	8-3-92	.258	.206	.286	27	97	18	25	6	1	7	17	7	0	0	1	25	1	0	.557	.305
Viloria, Meibrys	L-R	5-11	225	2-15-97	.233	.154	.267	54	172	19	40	9	1	5	18	32	5	2	1	68	2	2	.384	.367
Witt Jr., Bobby	R-R	6-1	200	6-14-00	.285	.321	.274	62	253	55	72	24	0	17	46	26	2	1	3	64	15	3	.581	.352

Pitching	B-T	HT	WT	DOB	W	L	ERA	G	GS	CG	SV	IP	H	R	ER	HR	BB	SO	AVG	vLH	vRH	K/9	BB/9
Adams, Chance	R-R	6-1	215	8-10-94	0	0	27.00	1	0	0	0	1	1	2	2	1	2	0	.333	.000	1.000	0.00	27.00
Barker, Brandon	R-R	6-3	210	8-20-92	2	3	7.79	15	11	0	0	52	76	47	45	13	18	46	.342	.352	.333	7.96	3.12
Blewett, Scott	R-R	6-6	245	4-10-96	6	3	6.39	23	10	0	0	69	80	54	49	19	31	64	.285	.289	.281	8.35	4.04
Bolanos, Ronald	R-R	6-2	230	8-23-96	0	3	6.34	10	10	0	0	38	39	28	27	10	27	34	.271	.238	.296	7.98	6.34
Butler, Eddie	R-R	6-2	180	3-13-91	7	3	6.01	27	13	0	0	79	97	56	53	14	33	55	.302	.306	.299	6.24	3.74
Coleman, Dylan	R-R	6-5	230	9-16-96	4	0	3.55	27	0	0	3	33	19	16	13	2	17	56	.167	.176	.159	15.27	4.64
Cox, Austin	L-L	6-4	235	3-28-97	0	0	18.00	2	1	0	0	5	9	10	10	3	5	4	.375	.286	.412	7.20	9.00
Cuas, Jose	R-R	6-3	195	6-28-94	1	0	0.00	3	0	0	0	5	2	0	0	0	1	4	.125	.167	.100	7.20	1.80
Dye, Josh	L-L	6-5	180	9-14-96	0	0	3.60	2	0	0	0	5	4	2	2	1	1	5	.222	.167	.250	9.00	1.80
Esposito, Nate	R-R	5-11	180	6-25-93	0	0	0.00	3	0	0	0	3	2	0	0	0	0	1	.222	.167	.333	3.38	0.00
Gavin, Grant	R-R	6-2	185	7-10-95	1	3	4.36	48	0	0	4	74	59	40	36	11	35	92	.219	.161	.267	11.14	4.24
Griffin, Foster	R-L	6-5	205	7-27-95	0	0	3.60	6	6	0	0	25	29	12	10	1	10	19	.290	.444	.233	6.84	3.60
Hahn, Jesse	R-R	6-5	205	7-30-89	0	0	5.40	1	1	0	0	2	1	1	1	0	1	2	.167	.000	.333	10.80	5.40
Hernandez, Carlos	R-R	6-4	245	3-11-97	2	1	4.44	6	6	0	0	26	28	15	13	6	6	26	.272	.315	.224	8.89	2.05
Junis, Jakob	R-R	6-3	220	9-16-92	0	2	5.60	6	6	0	0	18	22	14	11	4	8	18	.297	.393	.217	9.17	4.08
Kalish, Jake	B-L	6-2	210	7-9-91	3	6	6.94	30	15	0	0	96	110	75	74	31	35	106	.286	.267	.297	9.94	3.28
Kowar, Jackson	R-R	6-5	200	10-4-96	9	4	3.46	17	16	0	0	81	66	31	31	7	34	115	.220	.203	.236	12.83	3.79
Lovelady, Richard	L-L	6-0	185	7-7-95	0	0	1.08	7	0	0	0	8	5	1	1	0	4	9	.179	.000	.313	9.72	4.32

	B-T	HT	WT	DOB	W	L	ERA	G	GS	CG	SV	IP	H	R	ER	HR	BB	SO	AVG	vLH	vRH	K/9	BB/9
Lynch, Daniel	L-L	6-6	200	11-17-96	4	3	5.84	12	11	0	0	57	74	39	37	10	18	62	.318	.397	.285	9.79	2.84
Marquez, Emilio	L-L	5-8	170	4-28-98	0	0	0.00	1	0	0	0	1	0	0	0	0	0	0	.000	.000	.000	0.00	0.00
Martinez, Marcelo	L-L	6-2	190	8-10-96	5	7	5.12	18	17	0	0	84	90	52	48	19	27	84	.268	.267	.268	8.96	2.88
Newberry, Jake	R-R	6-2	200	11-20-94	3	5	5.07	44	0	0	2	60	69	36	34	6	21	75	.292	.330	.263	11.19	3.13
Nunez, Andres	R-R	6-4	240	9-20-95	0	0	6.35	17	1	0	0	23	23	17	16	3	10	27	.267	.364	.167	10.72	3.97
Payamps, Joel	R-R	6-2	225	4-7-94	1	0	4.50	8	0	0	2	8	10	5	4	0	4	14	.286	.300	.267	15.75	4.50
2-team total (4 Buffalo)					2	1	5.25	12	0	0	2	12	17	8	7	2	4	15	.327	.357	.292	11.25	3.00
Ramirez, Ruben	R-R	6-0	190	11-14-98	0	0	24.00	3	0	0	0	3	5	8	8	0	5	5	.385	.800	.125	15.00	15.00
Sanabria, Carlos	R-R	6-3	200	1-24-97	0	5	5.27	18	0	0	0	27	25	19	16	1	18	29	.245	.279	.220	9.55	5.93
Shawaryn, Mike	R-R	6-2	240	9-17-94	1	0	4.63	9	0	0	0	12	6	7	6	0	16	16	.154	.188	.130	12.34	12.34
Singer, Brady	R-R	6-5	215	8-4-96	0	2	13.50	2	2	0	0	5	8	7	7	1	1	2	.400	.333	.455	3.86	1.93
Snider, Collin	R-R	6-4	195	10-10-95	3	2	6.30	21	0	0	0	30	39	23	21	7	12	23	.312	.358	.278	6.90	3.60
Sotillet, Andres	R-R	6-1	215	3-2-97	2	0	6.75	13	1	0	0	15	21	15	11	0	16	18	.328	.355	.303	11.05	9.82
Speier, Gabe	L-L	5-11	200	4-12-95	3	0	2.98	45	0	0	5	45	45	15	15	5	9	57	.253	.207	.302	11.32	1.79
Swarzak, Anthony	R-R	6-4	215	9-10-85	1	0	2.89	9	0	0	4	9	7	3	3	2	0	14	.212	.167	.267	13.50	0.00
Tapia, Domingo	R-R	6-3	263	8-4-91	1	0	4.50	18	0	0	2	22	20	12	11	4	15	22	.238	.189	.277	9.00	6.14
Vines, Jace	R-R	6-3	215	9-4-94	6	4	4.10	44	1	0	2	68	58	32	31	2	35	67	.234	.229	.237	8.87	4.63
Zerpa, Angel	L-L	6-0	220	9-27-99	0	2	13.50	2	1	0	0	1	2	3	3	1	1	1	.333	.500	.250	6.75	6.75
Zimmer, Kyle	R-R	6-3	225	9-13-91	1	1	3.00	8	0	0	0	9	7	3	3	0	4	11	.219	.154	.263	11.00	4.00
Zuber, Tyler	R-R	5-11	195	6-16-95	1	3	2.83	28	0	0	8	29	15	10	9	3	16	43	.152	.150	.153	13.50	5.02

Fielding

Catcher	PCT	G	PO	A	E	DP	PB
Dini	1.000	23	203	7	0	0	2
Esposito	1.000	10	49	5	0	1	0
Fermin	.935	4	39	4	3	1	1
Gallagher	.982	6	50	4	1	1	0
Melendez	.990	29	274	13	3	2	4
Mondesi	1.000	1	2	0	0	0	0
Rivero	.994	36	334	24	2	2	2
Viloria	.997	30	283	18	1	2	1

First Base	PCT	G	PO	A	E	DP
Gutierrez	1.000	4	25	4	0	2
Jones	1.000	11	55	5	0	4
McBroom	.995	47	337	34	2	44
O'Hearn	1.000	8	66	8	0	6
Pratto	.998	52	375	28	1	43
Rivera	.973	9	65	7	2	5
Viloria	1.000	5	26	2	0	5

Second Base	PCT	G	PO	A	E	DP
Cancel	.972	37	61	77	4	29
Castellano	.995	46	60	125	1	26
Escobar	.931	8	8	19	2	5
Fox	.975	33	46	70	3	19
Govern	.833	2	2	3	1	1
Mejia	.920	8	8	15	2	3
Merrell	1.000	2	2	6	0	0

Third Base	PCT	G	PO	A	E	DP
Cancel	.964	15	6	21	1	4
Castellano	.962	17	9	16	1	2
Dozier	1.000	2	3	5	0	1
Escobar	1.000	2	1	3	0	0
Govern	1.000	5	4	6	0	1
Gutierrez	1.000	3	2	7	0	4
Jones	.897	19	13	22	4	4
Mejia	.919	15	9	25	3	5
Melendez	.920	9	9	14	2	1
Rivera	.968	45	30	91	4	11
Witt Jr.	1.000	10	8	7	0	1

Shortstop	PCT	G	PO	A	E	DP
Castellano	.930	18	16	37	4	13
Escobar	.989	24	26	62	1	13
Fox	.937	16	22	37	4	7
Mejia	.977	11	17	25	1	8
Merrell	.963	11	7	19	1	3
Mondesi	.943	13	10	23	2	7
Witt Jr.	.975	52	52	106	4	25

Outfield	PCT	G	PO	A	E	DP
Blanco	1.000	38	71	1	0	0
Cancel	--	1	0	0	0	0
Castellano	1.000	1	0	1	0	0
Dozier	1.000	2	2	0	0	0
Fox	1.000	8	18	2	0	0
Isbel	.990	100	187	6	2	2
Jones	1.000	4	3	0	0	0
Martin	.965	45	77	6	3	1
McBroom	.944	18	16	1	1	0
Mejia	.966	26	54	2	2	1
Miller	.965	64	103	6	4	2
Olivares	.963	62	102	2	4	0
O'Hearn	1.000	8	11	0	0	0
Pratto	1.000	3	8	1	0	0
Starling	.976	27	39	1	1	0

NORTHWEST ARKANSAS NATURALS

DOUBLE-A

DOUBLE-A CENTRAL

Batting	B-T	HT	WT	DOB	AVG	vLH	vRH	G	AB	R	H	2B	3B	HR	RBI	BB	HBP	SH	SF	SO	SB	CS	SLG	OBP
Bewley, Brhet	R-R	5-11	182	1-30-97	.230	.196	.242	56	204	29	47	9	0	6	34	15	2	0	4	55	1	4	.363	.284
Blanco, Dairon	R-R	6-0	170	4-26-93	.289	.289	.288	79	291	62	84	11	5	9	38	25	8	4	1	64	32	9	.454	.360
Carrasco, Dennicher	R-R	5-11	195	10-12-95	.212	.239	.200	43	151	17	32	7	0	5	20	14	0	0	0	65	0	1	.358	.279
Castellano, Angelo	R-R	6-0	165	1-13-95	.267	.385	.219	14	45	10	12	1	0	1	4	4	0	0	0	13	0	0	.356	.327
Cropley, Tyler	R-R	5-11	185	12-10-95	.194	.167	.204	26	67	8	13	2	0	2	6	8	5	0	0	15	0	0	.313	.325
Dennis, Austin	R-R	5-11	170	6-6-97	.179	.125	.194	18	39	3	7	0	0	1	5	5	1	0	1	14	2	1	.256	.283
Dungan, Clay	L-R	6-1	190	6-2-96	.288	.284	.290	108	444	74	128	17	4	9	56	40	9	3	3	73	28	11	.405	.357
Fermin, Freddy	R-R	5-10	200	5-16-95	.279	.254	.287	73	269	45	75	13	1	10	45	29	4	0	1	50	1	1	.446	.356
Govern, Jimmy	R-R	5-11	190	12-11-96	.215	.346	.186	44	144	19	31	8	0	6	23	11	3	2	3	34	2	1	.396	.281
Guzman, Jeison	B-R	6-2	205	10-8-98	.216	.154	.232	32	125	17	27	8	0	2	15	6	2	3	0	41	2	3	.328	.263
Hicklen, Brewer	R-R	6-2	208	2-9-96	.243	.202	.255	107	362	70	88	15	3	16	57	52	6	2	2	132	40	4	.434	.346
Jones, Travis	R-R	6-4	210	9-29-95	.225	.296	.204	37	120	20	27	4	2	3	14	24	2	0	0	38	4	1	.367	.363
Martin, Rudy	L-L	5-7	155	1-31-96	.318	.313	.320	43	129	31	41	7	0	5	31	28	3	5	0	38	10	4	.488	.450
Matias, Seuly	R-R	6-3	225	9-4-98	.193	.375	.149	23	83	14	16	4	0	7	14	8	2	0	0	35	2	0	.494	.280
Melendez, MJ	L-R	6-1	190	11-29-98	.285	.311	.274	79	298	58	85	18	0	28	65	43	1	0	5	76	2	4	.628	.372
Merrell, Kevin	L-R	6-1	180	12-14-95	.185	.212	.174	41	119	15	22	5	0	3	9	13	1	2	0	39	5	0	.303	.271
Mondesi, Adalberto	B-R	6-1	200	7-27-95	.214	.000	.250	5	14	1	3	0	0	1	3	1	0	0	0	4	0	0	.429	.267
Pasquantino, Vinnie	L-L	6-4	245	10-10-97	.310	.368	.287	55	200	35	62	17	0	11	42	31	3	0	3	26	2	0	.560	.405
Perkins, Blake	B-R	5-11	181	9-10-96	.202	.298	.171	72	238	33	48	8	1	7	30	40	1	1	0	81	9	2	.332	.319
Pratto, Nick	L-L	6-1	215	10-6-98	.271	.226	.289	61	221	44	60	13	4	15	43	46	5	0	3	80	7	5	.570	.404
Rivera, Emmanuel	R-R	6-2	225	6-29-96	.267	.000	.308	4	15	1	4	0	0	0	1	2	0	0	1	6	0	0	.267	.333
Stupienski, Gavin	L-R	6-1	220	3-12-94	.000	.000	--	1	1	0	0	0	0	0	0	0	0	0	0	0	0	0	.000	.000
Viloria, Meibrys	L-R	5-11	225	2-15-97	.257	.250	.259	31	109	18	28	5	0	3	13	18	2	0	1	32	1	1	.385	.369
Witt Jr., Bobby	R-R	6-1	200	6-14-00	.295	.381	.265	61	244	44	72	11	4	16	51	25	6	0	4	67	14	8	.570	.369

Pitching

Pitching	B-T	HT	WT	DOB	W	L	ERA	G	GS	CG	SV	IP	H	R	ER	HR	BB	SO	AVG	vLH	vRH	K/9	BB/9
Adams, Derrick	L-L	6-3	215	3-8-97	2	3	8.40	22	3	0	0	50	72	52	47	10	34	47	.326	.333	.322	8.40	6.08
Bewley, Brhet	R-R	5-11	182	1-30-97	0	0	45.00	1	0	0	0	1	5	5	5	2	0	0	.625	.750	.500	0.00	0.00
Bolanos, Ronald	R-R	6-2	230	8-23-96	0	0	7.11	3	3	0	0	6	7	6	5	2	8	7	.280	.182	.357	9.95	11.37
Bowlan, Jonathan	R-R	6-6	240	12-1-96	2	0	1.59	4	4	0	0	17	13	3	3	0	3	25	.206	.222	.194	13.24	1.59
Capps, Holden	R-L	6-2	180	3-24-95	3	2	7.48	12	0	0	0	22	41	20	18	2	9	19	.406	.485	.368	7.89	3.74
Coleman, Dylan	R-R	6-5	230	9-16-96	1	1	2.92	18	0	0	4	25	19	8	8	2	5	37	.211	.289	.154	13.50	1.82
Cox, Austin	L-L	6-4	235	3-28-97	4	1	3.00	15	15	1	0	63	54	23	21	8	25	56	.232	.254	.223	8.00	3.57
Cuas, Jose	R-R	6-3	195	6-28-94	3	1	1.95	22	0	0	3	32	31	11	7	1	7	32	.252	.265	.243	8.91	1.95
Davila, Garrett	L-L	6-2	180	1-17-97	0	0	6.91	7	0	0	0	14	13	12	11	2	8	12	.245	.118	.306	7.53	5.02
Del Rosario, Yefri	R-R	6-2	180	9-23-99	2	4	5.99	26	11	0	0	71	79	51	47	12	35	78	.280	.356	.238	9.93	4.46
Dye, Josh	L-L	6-5	180	9-14-96	4	2	2.52	38	0	0	9	61	53	19	17	5	18	68	.231	.200	.247	10.09	2.67
Eldred, C.J.	R-R	6-2	220	5-6-95	2	0	4.35	4	1	0	0	10	10	6	5	1	4	12	.256	.250	.261	10.45	3.48
Garcia, Robert	R-L	6-4	225	6-14-96	4	3	5.63	33	0	0	1	48	49	31	30	7	23	60	.259	.227	.276	11.25	4.31
Gray, Peyton	R-R	6-3	200	6-2-95	1	2	6.28	8	0	0	0	14	16	12	10	3	8	22	.271	.200	.308	13.81	5.02
Griffin, Foster	R-L	6-3	225	7-27-95	0	2	3.55	3	3	0	0	13	12	5	5	0	2	13	.255	.188	.290	9.24	1.42
Heasley, Jon	R-R	6-3	225	1-27-97	7	3	3.33	22	21	1	0	105	95	42	39	18	34	120	.244	.245	.243	10.25	2.91
Marsh, Alec	R-R	6-2	220	5-14-98	1	3	4.97	6	6	0	0	25	20	14	14	4	13	42	.217	.237	.204	14.92	4.62
Martinez, Marcelo	L-L	6-2	190	8-10-96	1	2	5.08	7	7	0	0	28	21	16	16	7	11	33	.206	.345	.151	10.48	3.49
Nunez, Andres	R-R	6-4	240	9-20-95	6	3	2.94	30	0	0	4	52	46	21	17	5	15	58	.234	.242	.229	10.04	2.60
Parrish, Drew	L-L	5-11	200	12-8-97	5	4	3.36	18	17	1	0	83	65	34	31	8	25	95	.215	.204	.220	10.30	2.71
Sanabria, Carlos	R-R	6-3	200	1-24-97	3	0	2.61	20	0	0	2	31	14	10	9	4	18	30	.132	.105	.147	8.71	5.23
Snider, Collin	R-R	6-4	195	10-10-95	2	1	2.97	27	0	0	3	36	32	12	12	1	14	41	.241	.275	.226	10.16	3.47
Sotillet, Andres	R-R	6-1	215	3-2-97	1	2	4.94	21	0	0	0	31	29	18	17	4	13	32	.240	.250	.234	9.29	3.77
Tillo, Daniel	L-L	6-5	215	6-13-96	0	3	4.63	17	2	0	0	23	21	12	12	1	15	22	.244	.250	.241	8.49	5.79
Watson, Nolan	R-R	6-2	195	1-25-97	5	3	5.80	25	6	0	0	68	86	46	44	12	31	41	.315	.349	.299	5.40	4.08
Woods Jr., Stephen	R-R	6-2	195	6-10-95	5	7	7.42	22	7	0	1	47	59	44	39	5	45	48	.307	.270	.326	9.13	8.56
Zerpa, Angel	L-L	6-0	220	9-27-99	0	3	5.96	13	13	0	0	45	51	30	30	7	19	54	.287	.309	.276	10.72	3.77

Fielding

Catcher	PCT	G	PO	A	E	DP	PB
Cropley	1.000	21	152	9	0	1	0
Fermin	.990	32	286	16	3	3	3
Melendez	.982	52	499	35	10	2	3
Viloria	1.000	21	172	17	0	1	1

First Base	PCT	G	PO	A	E	DP
Carrasco	1.000	3	19	3	0	3
Jones	1.000	2	11	0	0	0
Merrell	1.000	2	6	0	0	1
Pasquantino	.991	54	400	31	4	42
Pratto	.998	61	438	36	1	33

Second Base	PCT	G	PO	A	E	DP
Bewley	.970	23	46	51	3	17
Dennis	.963	7	13	13	1	6
Dungan	.992	71	92	162	2	30
Govern	1.000	4	8	10	0	3

Third Base	PCT	G	PO	A	E	DP
Bewley	.811	23	13	30	10	2
Carrasco	.885	32	21	48	9	3
Castellano	1.000	6	4	6	0	0
Dennis	1.000	2	0	1	0	0
Dungan	1.000	2	0	2	0	0
Govern	.973	40	20	90	3	8
Jones	1.000	5	7	6	0	0
Merrell	.778	6	2	5	2	1
Rivera	1.000	4	0	5	0	2
Witt Jr.	1.000	8	4	10	0	1

Shortstop	PCT	G	PO	A	E	DP
Castellano	.944	6	8	9	1	2
Dennis	1.000	1	0	4	0	1
Dungan	.963	35	37	92	5	15
Merrell	.988	19	36	46	1	13
Guzman	.961	27	33	66	4	12
Merrell	.938	4	5	10	1	2
Mondesi	1.000	4	2	7	0	0
Witt Jr.	.975	50	49	107	4	20

Outfield	PCT	G	PO	A	E	DP
Bewley	.923	6	12	0	1	0
Blanco	.994	79	151	6	1	1
Castellano	1.000	4	2	0	0	0
Dennis	1.000	5	4	0	0	0
Guzman	1.000	5	7	0	0	0
Hicklen	.984	103	171	10	3	1
Jones	.971	23	33	1	1	0
Martin	.959	43	67	4	3	0
Matias	.930	21	37	3	3	0
Merrell	1.000	10	18	0	0	0
Perkins	.986	72	139	3	2	1
Stupienski	--	1	0	0	0	0

QUAD CITIES RIVER BANDITS

HIGH CLASS A

HIGH-A CENTRAL

Batting	B-T	HT	WT	DOB	AVG	vLH	vRH	G	AB	R	H	2B	3B	HR	RBI	BB	HBP	SH	SF	SO	SB	CS	SLG	OBP
Bates, Parker	L-R	6-1	205	11-16-97	.243	.091	.308	11	37	3	9	2	0	0	5	6	0	0	0	8	1	0	.297	.349
Bradley, Tucker	L-L	6-0	206	5-6-98	.280	.298	.276	86	307	53	86	18	5	6	42	42	3	6	2	77	9	1	.430	.370
Cole, Eric	B-R	5-11	170	1-17-97	.240	.211	.247	100	366	71	88	14	3	12	61	53	3	2	10	72	9	3	.393	.333
Eaton, Nathan	R-R	5-11	185	12-22-96	.243	.245	.243	70	259	44	63	13	1	6	37	35	5	5	0	71	23	3	.371	.344
Emodi, Michael	R-R	6-4	225	4-18-96	.143	.000	.200	5	21	0	3	0	0	0	0	1	0	0	0	10	0	0	.143	.182
Emshoff, Kale	R-R	6-2	228	5-2-98	.222	.273	.188	8	27	1	6	2	0	0	2	6	0	0	0	13	0	0	.296	.364
Garcia, Maikel	R-R	6-0	145	3-3-00	.281	.415	.238	53	217	38	61	8	4	3	24	24	0	1	1	40	11	3	.396	.351
Gentry, Tyler	R-R	6-2	210	2-1-99	.259	.308	.248	44	147	29	38	10	0	6	28	29	6	1	3	55	4	0	.449	.395
Govern, Jimmy	R-R	5-11	190	12-11-96	.313	.320	.311	41	147	23	46	13	0	4	27	8	4	1	0	24	3	0	.483	.365
Guzman, Jeison	R-R	6-2	205	10-8-98	.289	.217	.303	34	142	25	41	11	1	4	22	12	3	1	2	35	9	3	.465	.352
Hancock, William	L-R	6-2	200	10-31-96	.192	.216	.188	69	229	30	44	11	1	5	35	28	5	2	4	98	0	0	.314	.289
Hughes, Gage	B-R	6-1	170	8-15-99	.188	.333	.154	6	16	2	3	2	0	0	1	0	0	0	0	7	0	0	.313	.235
Jaquez, Rubendy	B-R	5-11	174	2-13-99	.377	.308	.400	19	53	15	20	5	0	0	7	6	0	3	1	9	7	2	.472	.433
Loftin, Nick	L-R	6-1	180	9-25-98	.289	.351	.273	90	356	67	103	22	5	10	57	42	7	3	2	60	11	2	.463	.373
Massey, Michael	L-R	6-0	190	3-22-98	.289	.225	.305	99	388	76	112	27	2	21	87	33	8	3	7	68	12	2	.531	.351
Matias, Seuly	R-R	6-3	225	9-4-98	.213	.148	.228	36	141	26	30	5	3	10	28	12	6	0	0	58	3	0	.504	.302
Means, Jake	R-R	6-2	215	4-14-96	.227	.193	.237	69	247	32	56	13	2	10	34	39	3	0	1	78	3	0	.417	.338
Mondesi, Paul	R-R	6-0	240	7-7-98	.333	.500	.286	2	9	0	3	0	0	0	0	0	0	0	0	0	0	0	.333	.333
Pasquantino, Vinnie	L-L	6-4	245	10-10-97	.301	.277	.295	61	237	44	69	20	3	13	42	33	4	0	2	38	4	0	.565	.384
Porter, Logan	R-R	6-0	200	7-12-95	.241	.319	.213	77	257	53	62	10	1	14	45	45	7	0	1	81	1	0	.451	.368
Rave, John	L-L	6-0	185	12-30-97	.252	.283	.246	77	278	49	70	8	3	14	51	38	5	1	0	93	13	0	.453	.352
Stupienski, Gavin	L-R	6-1	220	3-12-94	.264	.308	.258	37	110	24	29	7	1	5	19	20	1	1	2	26	0	0	.482	.376

	B-T	HT	WT	DOB	AVG	vLH	vRH	G	AB	R	H	2B	3B	HR	RBI	BB	HBP	SH	SF	SO	SB	CS	SLG	OBP
Tolbert, Tyler	R-R	6-0	160	1-27-98	.188	.286	.111	6	16	4	3	1	0	1	4	3	0	0	0	6	4	0	.438	.316

Pitching	B-T	HT	WT	DOB	W	L	ERA	G	GS	CG	SV	IP	H	R	ER	HR	BB	SO	AVG	vLH	vRH	K/9	BB/9
Biasi, Dante	L-L	6-0	205	12-4-97	5	2	3.77	24	6	0	2	72	53	35	30	9	33	84	.203	.212	.198	10.55	4.14
Block, A.J.	L-L	6-5	218	4-16-98	4	5	3.81	19	16	0	0	85	67	39	36	7	33	98	.215	.156	.242	10.38	3.49
Capps, Holden	R-L	6-2	180	3-24-95	1	0	2.25	5	0	0	0	8	8	2	2	0	4	10	.276	.000	.364	11.25	4.50
Chamberlain, Christian	L-L	5-10	173	7-20-99	1	0	4.91	2	0	0	0	4	3	2	2	0	1	6	.214	.000	.300	14.73	2.45
Cosby, Christian	R-R	6-5	215	12-21-96	4	3	4.50	20	10	0	0	72	66	40	36	12	17	81	.238	.234	.242	10.13	2.13
Davila, Garrett	L-L	6-2	180	1-17-97	6	2	2.45	27	0	0	4	51	37	18	14	2	20	42	.202	.131	.238	7.36	3.51
Dipoto, Jonah	R-R	6-1	225	9-3-96	1	0	3.19	22	0	0	8	31	18	12	11	1	23	39	.159	.204	.125	11.32	6.68
Eldred, C.J.	R-R	6-2	220	5-6-95	0	0	8.82	5	1	0	0	16	26	17	16	5	6	17	.366	.333	.395	9.37	3.31
Ellis, Mitch	B-R	6-3	200	8-22-95	8	2	5.36	28	1	0	2	49	55	33	29	5	21	56	.284	.303	.267	10.36	3.88
Gambrell, Grant	L-R	6-4	225	11-21-97	2	1	4.37	5	5	0	0	23	16	12	11	5	7	18	.190	.238	.143	7.15	2.78
Gray, Peyton	R-R	6-3	200	6-2-95	2	1	1.26	15	0	0	6	29	16	6	4	2	15	47	.163	.163	.163	14.76	4.71
Haake, Zach	R-R	6-4	186	10-8-96	4	1	3.74	11	10	0	0	46	35	20	19	9	22	47	.208	.211	.205	9.26	4.34
Kalich, Kasey	R-R	6-3	220	4-25-98	2	2	4.12	14	0	0	0	20	23	10	9	2	6	23	.280	.306	.261	10.53	2.75
Klein, Will	R-R	6-5	230	11-28-99	7	1	3.20	36	0	0	4	70	43	28	25	4	44	121	.173	.188	.163	15.48	5.63
Lacy, Asa	L-L	6-4	215	6-2-99	2	5	5.19	14	14	0	0	52	41	31	30	5	41	79	.222	.284	.180	13.67	7.10
Lukas, Adam	R-R	6-4	230	7-31-98	1	1	3.38	6	0	0	2	8	5	3	3	0	5	9	.179	.083	.250	10.13	5.63
Marquez, Emilio	L-L	5-8	170	4-28-98	1	0	10.13	4	2	0	0	13	20	15	15	7	4	14	.345	.273	.362	9.45	2.70
Monke, Caden	L-L	6-3	170	9-2-99	0	0	1.42	5	0	0	0	6	4	1	1	0	1	5	.200	.375	.083	7.11	1.42
Morel, Yohanse	R-R	6-0	170	8-23-00	4	2	6.66	30	2	0	2	50	54	44	37	8	32	45	.278	.289	.268	8.10	5.76
Murdock, Noah	R-R	6-8	205	8-20-98	2	1	3.18	7	6	0	0	23	15	9	8	0	11	19	.181	.173	.194	7.54	4.37
Neuweiler, Charlie	R-R	6-1	205	2-8-99	2	3	4.81	13	12	0	0	58	64	37	31	7	23	50	.278	.330	.234	7.76	3.57
Parrish, Drew	L-L	5-11	200	12-8-97	1	0	0.00	4	1	0	1	16	5	0	0	0	3	23	.096	.067	.108	13.21	1.72
Paulino, Anderson	R-R	6-2	200	9-12-98	1	1	4.91	3	1	0	0	7	9	7	4	1	3	7	.300	.333	.278	8.59	3.68
Phillips, Zack	L-L	6-0	170	7-11-98	0	1	2.21	10	0	0	1	20	18	6	5	1	9	14	.228	.214	.235	6.20	3.98
Ramirez, Ruben	R-R	6-0	190	11-14-98	0	0	9.82	4	0	0	0	7	10	8	8	2	5	8	.333	.273	.368	9.82	6.14
Ratliff, Tad	R-R	6-2	240	4-3-96	0	0	9.82	3	0	0	0	4	4	4	4	1	2	7	.267	.200	.400	17.18	4.91
Smith, Patrick	L-L	6-2	215	10-14-96	1	1	3.57	10	0	0	0	18	14	7	7	3	10	20	.222	.222	.222	10.19	5.09
Stupienski, Gavin	L-R	6-1	220	3-12-94	0	1	27.00	2	0	0	0	1	5	5	4	1	2	0	.625	.250	1.000	0.00	13.50
Veneziano, Anthony	L-L	6-5	205	9-1-97	6	4	3.75	22	22	0	0	94	76	46	39	11	37	127	.222	.186	.237	12.20	3.56
Watson, Nolan	R-R	6-2	195	1-25-97	1	0	11.05	3	1	0	0	7	15	10	9	0	3	5	.429	.353	.500	6.14	3.68
Webb, Nathan	R-R	6-2	215	8-20-97	4	1	4.41	17	0	0	1	33	26	17	16	2	9	46	.215	.286	.167	12.67	2.48
Zerpa, Angel	L-L	6-0	220	9-27-99	4	0	2.59	8	8	0	0	42	32	12	12	2	8	53	.205	.211	.202	11.45	1.73

Fielding

Catcher	PCT	G	PO	A	E	DP	PB
Emodi	1.000	5	66	1	0	2	0
Emshoff	1.000	5	49	2	0	0	0
Hancock	.987	67	639	49	9	3	11
Porter	.992	44	448	19	4	3	6
Stupienski	1.000	2	12	0	0	0	0

First Base	PCT	G	PO	A	E	DP
Means	.994	23	151	10	1	18
Pasquantino	.995	52	374	25	2	22
Porter	.994	23	155	5	1	21
Stupienski	.995	25	179	9	1	11

Second Base	PCT	G	PO	A	E	DP
Eaton	1.000	2	0	4	0	0
Govern	1.000	7	4	11	0	3
Guzman	.917	2	2	9	1	2
Hughes	1.000	4	3	6	0	0

Jaquez	1.000	8	8	18	0	4
Loftin	.943	21	22	44	4	9
Massey	.989	81	108	173	3	32
Tolbert	1.000	1	2	2	0	1

Third Base	PCT	G	PO	A	E	DP
Eaton	.900	41	30	69	11	10
Govern	.870	25	9	31	6	3
Guzman	1.000	5	3	10	0	1
Hughes	1.000	1	0	3	0	0
Jaquez	.833	5	1	4	1	0
Loftin	.923	11	6	18	2	4
Means	.917	37	17	60	7	10
Porter	.000	1	0	0	0	0

Shortstop	PCT	G	PO	A	E	DP
Eaton	1.000	4	0	4	0	0
Garcia	.954	48	54	112	8	20

	PCT	G	PO	A	E	DP
Guzman	.910	20	31	40	7	11
Hughes	1.000	1	0	1	0	0
Jaquez	1.000	1	0	1	0	0
Loftin	.949	47	62	86	8	22
Means	.500	1	0	1	1	0
Tolbert	.923	3	7	5	1	1

Outfield	PCT	G	PO	A	E	DP
Bates	1.000	11	19	0	0	0
Bradley	.993	88	129	9	1	1
Cole	.994	94	154	6	1	1
Eaton	.974	20	34	4	1	1
Gentry	.986	43	72	1	1	0
Guzman	1.000	5	4	0	0	0
Matias	.904	29	45	2	5	0
Means	1.000	1	1	0	0	0
Rave	.982	75	159	1	3	0
Tolbert	1.000	1	1	0	0	0

COLUMBIA FIREFLIES   LOW CLASS A
LOW-A EAST

Batting	B-T	HT	WT	DOB	AVG	vLH	vRH	G	AB	R	H	2B	3B	HR	RBI	BB	HBP	SH	SF	SO	SB	CS	SLG	OBP
Bradley, Tucker	L-L	6-0	206	5-6-98	.348	.250	.368	8	23	2	8	1	0	0	3	4	3	0	0	3	3	1	.391	.500
Carlos Negret, Juan	R-R	6-1	190	6-19-99	.170	.200	.160	100	358	56	61	13	0	23	76	56	11	0	5	155	3	2	.399	.298
Collins, Darryl	L-R	6-2	185	9-16-01	.246	.203	.258	86	317	45	78	8	3	5	54	52	10	2	2	55	15	5	.338	.367
Dennis, Austin	R-R	5-11	170	6-6-97	.400	--	.400	2	5	1	2	0	0	1	1	1	0	0	0	0	1	0	1.000	.500
Dixon, Burle	L-L	6-5	185	10-15-98	.237	.217	.243	56	186	34	44	9	2	4	20	27	5	1	2	75	17	5	.371	.345
Emshoff, Kale	R-R	6-2	228	5-2-98	.273	.282	.270	55	198	29	54	7	1	10	43	30	5	0	1	74	0	0	.505	.380
Familia, Felix	R-R	6-2	205	10-13-98	.265	.228	.277	66	234	17	62	7	0	1	25	21	7	0	1	55	0	0	.308	.342
Garcia, Maikel	R-R	6-0	145	3-3-00	.303	.262	.314	51	195	40	59	13	3	1	26	38	0	0	4	33	24	3	.415	.409
Garza, Saul	R-R	6-3	227	4-9-98	.281	.298	.274	43	153	26	43	14	0	3	21	18	7	0	0	60	2	1	.431	.382
Gonzalez, Herard	B-R	5-11	167	5-16-01	.235	.215	.241	90	311	63	73	16	3	7	44	62	6	3	5	125	13	5	.373	.367
Hernandez, Diego	L-L	6-0	150	11-21-00	.274	.215	.294	74	266	47	73	9	2	1	19	32	3	6	3	66	34	10	.335	.355
Hernandez, Omar	R-R	5-11	170	12-10-01	.174	.233	.155	69	241	21	42	11	2	3	20	17	2	2	2	68	3	0	.274	.233
Hughes, Gage	B-R	6-1	170	8-15-99	.213	.204	.216	58	188	26	40	8	1	4	18	16	5	4	3	42	7	1	.330	.288
Jaquez, Rubendy	B-R	5-11	174	2-13-99	.200	.292	.167	56	180	28	36	8	2	0	10	17	2	0	2	41	13	5	.267	.274
Marquez, Jose	B-R	6-0	195	10-7-97	.164	.133	.174	19	61	7	10	1	0	2	6	5	2	1	0	23	3	2	.279	.250

	B-T	HT	WT	DOB	AVG	vLH	vRH	G	AB	R	H	2B	3B	HR	RBI	BB	HBP	SH	SF	SO	SB	CS	SLG	OBP
McConnell, Brady	R-R	6-3	195	5-24-98	.196	.091	.224	30	107	12	21	6	1	3	17	14	0	1	0	49	3	0	.355	.289
Means, Jake	R-R	6-2	215	4-14-96	.208	.273	.189	28	96	23	20	6	0	6	18	20	2	0	0	32	2	1	.458	.356
Ramirez, Jean	L-L	5-10	190	10-25-00	.194	.150	.213	24	67	7	13	3	1	1	5	16	3	3	0	30	3	5	.313	.372
Schmidt, Matthew	R-R	6-2	210	1-15-97	.135	.294	.091	49	155	22	21	5	0	3	16	25	2	2	0	87	0	1	.226	.264
Shrum, Dillan	R-L	6-0	200	3-4-98	.194	.167	.211	9	31	3	6	0	0	1	2	3	1	0	0	13	0	0	.290	.286
Tolbert, Tyler	R-R	6-0	160	1-27-98	.219	.247	.209	80	283	56	62	10	7	5	32	51	8	3	2	95	49	2	.357	.352
Tresh, Luca	R-R	6-0	193	1-11-00	.143	.250	.111	10	35	0	5	1	0	0	5	4	0	0	0	11	0	0	.171	.231
Valdez, Enrique	L-R	6-0	185	5-15-01	.185	.045	.229	26	92	12	17	5	0	2	9	6	2	0	1	38	1	1	.304	.248
Wilson, Peyton	B-R	5-9	180	11-1-99	.231	.222	.233	11	39	6	9	3	1	0	1	4	2	0	1	10	5	0	.359	.326

Pitching

	B-T	HT	WT	DOB	W	L	ERA	G	GS	CG	SV	IP	H	R	ER	HR	BB	SO	AVG	vLH	vRH	K/9	BB/9
Alcantara, Adrian	R-R	6-1	178	8-29-99	5	9	5.33	24	20	0	0	96	102	67	57	18	30	98	.266	.251	.279	9.16	2.80
Aquino, Ismael	R-R	6-2	170	9-2-98	0	2	2.57	11	0	0	2	14	8	7	4	2	12	13	.154	.136	.167	8.36	7.71
Arias, Wander	R-R	6-4	230	11-3-99	0	3	7.36	6	4	0	0	22	32	20	18	3	16	17	.364	.333	.395	6.95	6.55
Avila, Luinder	R-R	6-3	195	8-21-01	2	4	4.10	6	6	0	0	26	27	16	12	0	6	24	.260	.268	.254	8.20	2.05
Block, A.J.	L-L	6-5	218	4-16-98	1	0	0.56	4	2	0	0	16	6	1	1	1	3	26	.107	.000	.136	14.63	1.69
Bloye, Taylor	R-R	6-2	194	2-28-95	1	2	8.59	8	0	0	0	15	17	16	14	1	14	13	.279	.208	.324	7.98	8.59
Capellan, Delvin	R-R	6-1	167	12-6-98	1	2	3.48	9	6	0	0	34	30	13	13	3	16	34	.244	.259	.232	9.09	4.28
Cosby, Christian	R-R	6-5	215	12-21-96	1	1	2.45	5	0	0	0	15	12	4	4	2	6	23	.235	.250	.229	14.11	3.68
De Avila, Luis	L-L	5-11	160	5-29-01	5	4	5.16	24	0	0	0	52	69	38	30	4	19	59	.315	.309	.318	10.15	3.27
Eldred, C.J.	R-R	6-2	220	5-6-95	0	0	6.75	2	2	0	0	8	7	6	6	2	5	4	.259	.154	.357	4.50	5.63
Ellis, Mitch	B-R	6-3	200	8-22-95	1	0	0.00	2	0	0	0	5	3	1	0	0	0	6	.167	.333	.083	10.13	0.00
Franklin, A.J.	L-L	6-1	180	4-18-96	0	0	2.45	10	0	0	1	15	8	4	4	1	16	15	.178	.375	.069	9.20	9.82
Garcia, Heribert	R-R	6-0	220	10-2-99	0	4	8.75	7	3	0	0	24	36	26	23	6	7	27	.346	.302	.377	10.27	2.66
Gray, Peyton	R-R	6-3	200	6-2-95	0	0	0.00	1	0	0	1	2	1	0	0	0	0	2	.143	.000	.167	9.00	0.00
Griffin, Foster	R-L	6-3	225	7-27-95	0	0	0.00	2	2	0	0	8	2	0	0	0	1	10	.077	.091	.067	10.80	1.08
Guerrero, Tyson	L-L	6-1	188	2-16-99	0	1	9.00	3	3	0	0	7	10	7	7	2	4	6	.323	.556	.227	7.71	5.14
Halligan, Patrick	R-R	6-6	230	10-4-99	0	1	6.75	5	0	0	1	9	13	9	7	2	5	12	.342	.400	.304	11.57	4.82
Hernandez, Ben	R-R	6-2	205	7-1-01	1	2	4.31	9	9	0	0	31	32	15	15	2	17	31	.271	.286	.261	8.90	4.88
Jaquez, Rubendy	B-R	5-11	174	2-13-99	0	0	0.00	1	0	0	0	0	0	0	0	0	1	0	.000	--	.000	27.00	27.00
Kaufman, Rylan	L-L	6-4	225	6-23-99	2	5	5.95	23	20	0	0	82	77	57	54	10	37	94	.248	.275	.234	10.36	4.08
Marquez, Emilio	L-L	5-8	170	4-28-98	6	1	1.86	20	5	0	1	63	38	15	13	4	16	87	.170	.141	.183	12.43	2.29
McMillon, John	L-R	6-3	230	1-27-98	0	0	7.36	4	0	0	0	4	1	3	3	1	4	7	.083	.000	.167	17.18	9.82
Monke, Caden	L-L	6-3	170	9-2-99	0	0	0.00	2	0	0	0	3	1	3	0	1	5	5	.100	.250	.000	16.88	10.13
Noriega, Cruz	R-R	6-1	175	10-1-97	5	3	3.97	17	11	0	1	70	69	36	31	7	13	76	.255	.244	.263	9.73	1.66
Paulino, Anderson	R-R	6-2	200	9-12-98	6	6	4.54	21	11	0	0	79	91	52	40	9	21	79	.278	.282	.275	8.96	2.38
Pennington, Walter	L-L	6-2	205	4-14-98	3	3	3.18	23	0	0	4	40	36	15	14	2	14	37	.240	.190	.272	8.39	3.18
Peralta, Dario	R-R	6-1	190	10-12-00	0	0	6.92	10	0	0	1	13	15	14	10	2	9	8	.273	.261	.281	5.54	6.23
Phillips, Zack	L-L	6-0	170	7-11-98	0	3	1.95	15	0	0	2	28	22	8	6	2	4	37	.218	.216	.219	12.04	1.30
Rollings, Kipp	R-R	6-2	188	9-13-96	1	0	4.50	7	0	0	0	16	21	9	8	1	3	22	.313	.269	.341	12.38	1.69
Simonelli, Anthony	R-R	6-2	200	12-23-98	0	1	1.80	4	1	0	0	10	5	2	2	0	3	15	.143	.000	.217	13.50	2.70
Smith, Patrick	L-L	6-2	215	10-14-96	2	4	3.75	22	0	0	1	36	27	18	15	3	24	39	.209	.217	.205	9.75	6.00
Stil, Matt	R-R	6-3	190	7-5-00	2	2	4.64	17	14	0	0	52	46	29	27	8	33	55	.242	.186	.275	9.46	5.68
Wallace, Chase	R-R	6-2	195	11-13-98	3	4	5.28	25	0	0	1	46	52	33	27	3	24	41	.280	.321	.248	8.02	4.70
Wang, Chih-Ting	L-L	6-1	240	1-24-99	0	1	1.84	7	0	0	0	15	11	3	3	0	7	18	.204	.250	.184	11.05	4.30
Webb, Nathan	R-R	6-2	215	8-20-97	0	2	3.38	18	0	0	4	27	14	10	10	3	12	43	.154	.184	.132	14.51	4.05
Willis, Marlin	L-L	6-4	190	6-5-98	0	1	5.70	23	0	0	1	36	28	27	23	1	38	57	.209	.205	.211	14.12	9.41

Fielding

Catcher	PCT	G	PO	A	E	DP	PB
Emshoff	.995	33	362	20	2	2	3
Familia	1.000	21	179	16	0	0	5
Garza	.929	2	24	2	2	1	0
Hernandez	.989	58	505	47	6	5	6
Tresh	1.000	7	67	0	0	0	6

First Base	PCT	G	PO	A	E	DP
Familia	.989	44	337	24	4	29
Garza	.994	22	167	13	1	10
Schmidt	.989	49	342	22	4	27
Shrum	.979	6	42	5	1	9

Second Base	PCT	G	PO	A	E	DP
Dennis	1.000	1	1	0	0	0
Gonzalez	.941	62	101	140	15	29
Jaquez	.973	8	14	22	1	7

	PCT	G	PO	A	E	DP
Marquez	.980	12	16	34	1	4
Tolbert	.991	28	41	69	1	9
Wilson	.955	11	13	29	2	8

Third Base	PCT	G	PO	A	E	DP
Dennis	1.000	1	0	1	0	1
Gonzalez	1.000	1	2	0	0	0
Hughes	.894	53	34	84	14	6
Jaquez	.971	25	19	48	2	6
Marquez	.875	6	3	4	1	0
McConnell	1.000	3	0	4	0	0
Means	.933	26	19	51	5	6
Valdez	.923	6	3	9	1	3

Shortstop	PCT	G	PO	A	E	DP
Garcia	.981	41	45	107	3	16
Gonzalez	.956	23	26	60	4	6

	PCT	G	PO	A	E	DP
Hughes	1.000	4	9	7	0	0
Jaquez	.937	20	34	40	5	9
McConnell	.778	3	4	3	2	1
Tolbert	.914	13	16	37	5	5
Valdez	.941	20	24	40	4	11

Outfield	PCT	G	PO	A	E	DP
Bradley	.909	8	7	3	1	0
Carlos Negret	.969	81	116	7	4	0
Collins	1.000	75	109	1	0	0
Dixon	.956	56	86	1	4	0
Hernandez	.978	72	131	3	3	0
McConnell	1.000	9	10	0	0	0
Ramirez	.977	23	40	2	1	0
Tolbert	.983	39	57	2	1	0

ACL ROYALS

ARIZONA COMPLEX LEAGUE

ROOKIE

Batting	B-T	HT	WT	DOB	AVG	vLH	vRH	G	AB	R	H	2B	3B	HR	RBI	BB	HBP	SH	SF	SO	SB	CS	SLG	OBP
Bates, Parker	L-R	6-1	205	11-16-97	.321	.308	.333	10	28	2	9	5	1	0	2	3	2	0	1	6	3	3	.571	.412
Bewley, Brhet	R-R	5-11	182	1-30-97	.278	.400	.231	6	18	3	5	2	0	1	5	3	0	0	0	3	0	0	.611	.381
Camarillo, Gary	R-R	6-1	157	7-5-01	.000	.000	.000	1	3	0	0	0	0	0	0	0	0	0	0	3	0	0	.000	.000
Cancel, Gabriel	R-R	6-0	205	12-8-96	.333	.500	.313	6	18	3	6	1	0	0	2	0	0	0	0	9	2	0	.389	.333

Name	B-T	HT	WT	DOB	AVG	vLH	vRH	G	AB	R	H	2B	3B	HR	RBI	BB	HBP	SH	SF	SO	SB	CS	OBP	SLG
Candelario, Wilmin	B-R	5-11	195	9-11-01	.154	.040	.181	38	130	20	20	2	3	3	13	8	1	1	2	73	9	1	.285	.206
Cepero, Ryan	R-R	6-1	180	2-11-03	.088	.000	.130	13	34	3	3	0	0	1	2	4	2	1	0	20	1	0	.176	.225
Collins, Darnel	L-L	6-1	185	7-12-04	.228	.219	.232	38	127	18	29	4	2	0	20	11	1	0	1	30	2	0	.291	.293
De Los Santos, Jaswel	L-R	6-1	180	1-28-02	.267	.270	.266	42	146	20	39	5	2	6	22	19	1	3	0	53	4	4	.452	.355
Dennis, Austin	R-R	5-11	170	6-6-97	.400	.200	.467	7	20	8	8	1	0	0	7	4	2	1	0	3	2	1	.450	.538
Dixon, Burle	L-L	6-5	185	10-15-98	.250	1.000	.000	1	4	0	1	0	0	0	0	0	0	0	0	3	0	0	.500	.250
Dooney, Dayton	B-R	6-0	190	8-21-99	.250	.353	.185	15	44	4	11	5	0	1	5	7	0	0	0	14	0	0	.432	.353
Duarte, German	R-R	6-0	190	10-30-02	.200	.500	.154	5	15	1	3	2	0	0	3	2	1	0	1	5	0	0	.333	.316
Eaton, Nathan	R-R	5-11	185	12-22-96	.231	.200	.250	5	13	3	3	1	0	0	2	4	1	0	0	4	0	0	.308	.444
Florentino, Omar	B-R	5-9	170	10-26-01	.220	.233	.216	40	132	18	29	7	0	2	9	23	3	0	0	48	5	5	.318	.348
Fox, Lucius	B-R	6-1	185	7-2-97	.286	.000	.333	5	14	3	4	1	0	1	3	4	0	0	0	6	0	0	.571	.444
Garza, Saul	R-R	6-3	227	4-9-98	.385	.750	.222	5	13	2	5	2	0	0	0	3	0	0	0	2	1	0	.538	.500
Grullon, Francis	B-R	5-10	185	10-13-00	.234	.350	.203	33	94	19	22	2	2	2	12	18	4	2	0	27	7	0	.362	.379
Guzman, Diego	R-R	6-1	170	9-12-03	.224	.143	.250	31	85	12	19	4	0	1	8	12	2	1	0	40	3	2	.306	.333
Hernandez, Diego	L-L	6-0	150	11-21-00	.067	.000	.083	5	15	1	1	0	0	0	1	2	0	0	0	5	1	1	.067	.176
Hollie, David	R-R	6-2	217	10-25-99	.179	.000	.226	33	78	13	14	3	0	3	12	14	4	0	0	51	4	2	.333	.333
Hovey, Jordan	L-R	6-1	190	8-1-97	.154	.091	.171	21	52	10	8	2	0	1	7	10	3	0	0	20	4	0	.250	.323
Jackson, Kevon	R-R	5-9	189	6-14-00	.242	.222	.246	28	66	11	16	4	0	2	11	16	4	0	0	35	5	2	.394	.342
Jensen, Carter	L-R	6-1	210	7-3-03	.281	.278	.282	19	57	9	16	2	1	1	7	10	0	0	0	24	0	0	.404	.388
Leyton, Roger	R-R	6-1	180	2-3-03	.209	.069	.259	36	110	24	23	10	1	3	15	19	3	0	1	40	5	1	.400	.338
Maican, Diego	R-R	6-3	220	10-24-00	.220	.152	.242	43	132	25	29	3	0	1	13	19	5	0	0	44	6	0	.265	.340
Marinez, Neyfi	L-R	6-1	190	9-7-00	.216	.100	.244	19	51	5	11	2	0	0	4	4	1	0	1	24	0	1	.255	.281
Marquez, Jose	B-R	6-0	195	10-7-97	.241	.200	.250	9	29	7	7	0	0	2	5	6	0	0	0	9	1	0	.448	.371
Martinez, Edgar	R-R	5-10	180	2-14-01	.189	.172	.194	37	122	21	23	7	2	2	11	20	3	0	0	51	10	3	.328	.317
Matias, Seuly	R-R	6-3	225	9-4-98	.364	.000	.444	5	11	4	4	1	0	1	5	4	1	0	1	5	0	0	.727	.529
McNair, Brennon	R-R	6-1	175	9-15-02	.323	.273	.350	10	31	7	10	1	0	2	8	3	3	2	0	9	4	2	.548	.432
Medina, Yesi	R-R	5-10	185	4-18-00	.125	.000	.167	10	24	1	3	0	0	0	2	2	0	0	0	15	0	0	.125	.192
Mondesi, Paul	R-R	6-0	240	7-7-98	.241	.000	.259	10	29	5	7	2	0	1	3	0	0	1	0	7	1	0	.414	.241
Moreno, Oliver	R-R	6-1	210	6-28-01	.111	.000	.130	24	63	8	7	1	0	1	6	10	0	0	1	31	2	0	.175	.230
Nivar, Kevin	R-R	5-10	170	9-28-00	.176	.000	.188	8	17	2	3	0	0	0	1	4	0	0	0	6	1	0	.176	.364
Pena, Erick	L-R	6-3	205	2-20-03	.161	.088	.184	40	137	14	22	10	1	3	15	15	3	0	1	57	4	4	.314	.256
Pire, Enmanuel	R-R	5-10	175	5-18-01	.253	.188	.269	28	83	16	21	3	0	1	10	14	2	0	0	21	0	1	.325	.374
Quintana, Guillermo	R-R	6-1	180	3-16-01	.298	.263	.308	33	84	16	25	7	0	2	13	21	3	0	0	16	1	0	.452	.454
Ramirez, Jean	L-L	5-10	190	10-25-00	.235	.333	.226	12	34	8	8	2	1	0	4	5	1	1	1	10	6	0	.353	.341
Reyes, Kevin	B-R	5-10	160	5-5-02	.243	.143	.267	16	37	6	9	2	0	0	6	7	0	0	0	16	3	0	.297	.364
Rivera, Joshua	R-R	5-11	185	1-30-99	.288	.286	.289	22	52	7	15	3	1	3	18	5	1	0	1	21	1	1	.558	.356
Rodriguez, Omar	R-R	6-1	230	4-9-00	.118	.000	.129	12	34	5	4	2	0	0	4	2	3	0	1	16	0	0	.176	.225
Seijas, Rothaikeg	R-R	5-11	170	7-22-02	.243	.125	.276	38	111	24	27	4	1	3	21	20	3	0	2	38	8	4	.378	.368
Shrum, Dillan	R-L	6-0	200	3-4-98	.300	.500	.250	8	20	4	6	0	0	2	8	1	2	0	0	8	1	0	.600	.391
Tolbert, Tyler	R-R	6-0	160	7-1-98	.455	.667	.375	3	11	5	5	0	0	0	0	1	0	0	0	4	2	0	.455	.500
Town, River	L-R	5-11	181	7-8-99	.220	.071	.267	21	59	9	13	4	0	0	5	8	5	0	0	13	6	0	.288	.361
Tresh, Luca	R-R	6-0	193	1-11-00	.389	.333	.444	6	18	2	7	3	0	1	3	1	0	0	0	4	0	0	.722	.421
Valdez, Enrique	L-R	6-0	185	5-15-01	.288	.235	.302	28	80	15	23	2	4	3	16	12	5	1	1	30	7	3	.525	.408
Williams, Cam	B-R	6-2	195	2-7-98	.298	.462	.250	20	57	10	17	6	1	1	7	6	2	0	1	22	2	1	.491	.397
Wilson, Peyton	B-R	5-9	180	11-1-99	.200	.111	.231	12	35	7	7	3	1	1	7	6	3	0	1	11	2	2	.429	.356

Pitching	B-T	HT	WT	DOB	W	L	ERA	G	GS	CG	SV	IP	H	R	ER	HR	BB	SO	AVG	vLH	vRH	K/9	BB/9
Adams, Chance	R-R	6-1	215	8-10-94	0	0	6.35	5	3	0	0	6	7	5	4	3	1	9	.292	.455	.154	14.29	1.59
Aldrich, Jack	L-L	5-11	204	6-12-99	2	3	3.60	9	3	0	0	15	15	9	6	1	2	14	.250	.313	.227	8.40	1.20
Aquino, Ismael	R-R	6-2	170	9-2-98	0	0	16.20	3	1	0	0	3	7	6	6	0	2	3	.412	.500	.400	8.10	5.40
Arias, Wander	R-R	6-4	230	11-3-99	2	2	5.82	9	2	0	0	34	36	23	22	6	10	38	.271	.294	.256	10.06	2.65
Avila, Luinder	R-R	6-3	195	8-21-01	1	2	5.12	8	4	0	0	32	22	19	18	3	11	27	.198	.182	.205	7.67	3.13
Barroso, Luis	R-R	6-3	165	9-7-98	0	0	27.00	1	0	0	0	3	3	3	1	1	0		.500	1.000	.400	0.00	9.00
Beethe, Harrison	R-R	6-5	220	4-3-98	0	1	10.80	1	0	0	0	3	7	4	4	1	0	6	.438	.125	.750	16.20	0.00
Blewett, Scott	R-R	6-6	245	4-10-96	0	0	2.25	2	2	0	0	4	4	1	1	0	2		.250	.200	.273	4.50	0.00
Bloye, Taylor	R-R	6-2	194	2-28-95	1	1	4.71	5	1	0	0	21	23	11	11	3	8	22	.280	.459	.133	9.43	3.43
Bolanos, Ronald	R-R	6-2	230	8-23-96	0	1	23.14	2	2	0	0	2	5	6	6	1	2	3	.455	.333	.500	11.57	7.71
Cabrera, Daury	R-R	6-4	230	10-23-00	2	5	8.14	15	6	0	0	45	52	47	41	6	26	31	.287	.266	.299	6.15	5.16
Capellan, Delvin	R-R	6-1	167	12-6-98	0	2	9.82	3	3	0	0	4	4	5	4	2	1	5	.375	.500	.333	12.27	2.45
Capps, Holden	R-L	6-2	180	3-24-95	0	0	4.70	5	3	0	0	6	5	4	2	2	7		.214	.333	.158	8.22	2.35
Cerantola, Eric	R-R	6-5	225	5-2-00	0	0	1.93	4	2	0	0	5	1	1	1	0	7	9	.067	.000	.111	17.36	13.50
Connolly, Shane	L-L	6-2	175	2-19-98	0	1	7.20	10	2	0	1	25	19	12	3	9	21		.347	.318	.360	12.60	5.40
Cuas, Jose	R-R	6-3	195	6-28-94	1	0	0.00	2	0	0	0	4	0	0	0	1	8		.000	.000	.000	16.62	0.00
De Avila, Luis	L-L	5-11	160	5-29-01	3	0	3.38	3	0	0	0	5	4	2	2	0	5	5	.182	.300	.083	8.44	8.44
Diaz, Andres	R-R	6-1	155	7-6-01	4	1	3.77	15	1	0	1	29	32	18	12	3	5	25	.274	.286	.268	7.85	1.57
Eldred, C.J.	R-R	6-2	220	5-6-95	3	1	4.74	5	1	0	0	19	20	14	10	3	2	27	.260	.207	.292	12.79	0.95
Franklin, A.J.	L-L	6-1	180	8-18-96	0	1	3.65	9	0	0	1	12	16	11	5	0	6	21	.302	.316	.294	15.32	4.38
Garcia, Heribert	R-R	6-0	220	10-2-99	2	1	2.62	8	4	0	0	34	28	11	10	3	6	40	.217	.116	.267	10.49	1.57
Griffin, Foster	R-L	6-3	225	7-27-95	0	1	10.50	4	0	0	0	6	7	7	7	0	5	9	.280	.143	.313	13.50	7.50
Guerrero, Tyson	L-L	6-1	188	2-16-99	1	0	1.80	6	4	0	0	10	8	2	2	0	4	14	.242	.143	.269	12.60	3.60
Haake, Zach	R-R	6-4	186	10-8-96	0	0	1.13	4	4	0	0	8	5	2	1	0	1	11	.185	.308	.071	12.38	1.13
Halligan, Colton	R-R	6-6	230	10-4-99	0	0	2.57	5	1	0	0	7	11	3	2	0	3	7	.344	.462	.263	9.00	3.86
Harm, Parker	L-L	6-2	195	2-2-97	1	1	6.16	10	1	0	1	19	23	15	13	2	6	26	.295	.211	.322	12.32	2.84
Henry, Isaiah	R-R	6-3	212	3-22-99	0	0	0.00	5	4	0	0	5	2	0	0	0	2	10	.111	.286	.000	16.88	3.38
Hernandez, Ben	R-R	6-2	205	7-1-01	0	0	4.50	3	3	0	0	4	5	2	2	0	0	2	.313	.455	.000	4.50	0.00

Jin, Woo-Young	R-R	6-2	210	2-5-01	3	3	5.46	18	1	0	3	31	39	21	19	5	9	49	.310	.407	.236	14.07	2.59
Junis, Jakob	R-R	6-3	220	9-16-92	0	0	5.06	3	3	0	0	5	9	3	3	1	0	8	.375	.182	.538	13.50	0.00
Maduro, Cal	R-R	6-0	165	10-25-01	1	4	4.76	21	0	0	1	34	43	25	18	2	3	35	.295	.208	.337	9.26	0.79
Marsili, Matt	R-R	5-11	205	10-19-96	2	2	4.82	17	0	0	1	28	22	17	15	3	22	42	.222	.200	.234	13.50	7.07
McMillon, John	L-R	6-3	230	1-27-98	0	1	7.43	9	1	0	0	13	15	12	11	3	9	25	.273	.188	.308	16.88	6.08
Monke, Caden	L-L	6-3	170	9-2-99	0	0	1.93	4	0	0	0	5	2	1	1	0	3	7	.118	.000	.125	13.50	5.79
Moreno, Oliver	R-R	6-1	210	6-28-01	0	0	0.00	1	0	0	0	1	0	0	0	0	0	0	.000	--	.000	0.00	0.00
Neuweiler, Charlie	R-R	6-1	205	2-8-99	0	0	0.00	2	2	0	0	5	3	0	0	0	6	6	.176	.167	.182	11.57	0.00
Noriega, Cruz	R-R	6-1	175	10-1-97	0	1	6.00	2	2	0	0	3	3	2	2	0	1	5	.250	.167	.333	15.00	3.00
Ovalle, Luilly	R-R	6-3	170	10-13-00	1	2	8.03	6	2	0	1	12	13	12	11	2	17	8	.277	.313	.258	5.84	12.41
Palacios, Leo	L-L	6-4	215	2-10-00	0	0	0.00	2	0	0	0	2	1	0	0	1	1	5	.143	1.000	.000	22.50	4.50
Pennington, Walter	L-L	6-2	205	4-14-98	0	0	4.91	2	0	0	0	4	2	2	2	1	1	3	.154	.333	.100	7.36	2.45
Peralta, Dario	R-R	6-1	190	10-12-00	1	3	3.45	10	1	0	0	16	16	11	6	2	6	17	.258	.182	.300	9.77	3.45
Ramirez, Ruben	R-R	6-0	190	11-14-98	0	1	12.60	4	0	0	2	5	10	7	7	2	1	7	.417	.700	.214	12.60	1.80
Ratliff, Tad	R-R	6-2	240	4-3-96	0	0	0.00	4	4	0	0	6	2	0	0	0	4	6	.105	.167	.077	6.00	0.00
Reynoso, Jeffry	R-R	6-2	185	10-1-01	0	2	12.27	6	3	0	0	7	9	10	10	2	7	5	.321	.300	.333	6.14	8.59
Rollings, Kipp	R-R	6-2	188	9-15-96	1	1	5.40	8	3	0	2	15	15	10	9	3	4	20	.254	.263	.250	12.00	2.40
Russell, Ashe	R-R	6-4	201	8-28-96	0	0	6.75	4	0	0	0	4	2	7	3	1	8	6	.143	.333	.091	13.50	18.00
Simonelli, Anthony	R-R	6-2	200	12-23-98	1	0	0.93	6	1	0	0	10	7	4	1	1	1	9	.194	.200	.192	8.38	0.93
Solano, Adrian	R-R	6-1	180	10-17-99	2	1	7.23	6	2	0	0	19	32	19	15	3	11	14	.390	.360	.404	6.75	5.30
Stil, Matt	R-R	6-3	190	7-5-00	0	1	9.00	3	2	0	0	5	7	5	5	0	5	4	.350	.500	.200	7.20	9.00
Tillo, Daniel	L-L	6-5	215	6-13-96	0	0	1.59	3	3	0	0	6	3	1	1	0	5	5	.167	.143	.182	7.94	7.94
Valenzuela, Oscar	R-R	5-11	171	3-2-01	2	3	6.95	14	0	0	3	34	42	31	26	5	12	33	.294	.370	.247	8.82	3.21
Valerio, Samuel	R-R	6-4	230	10-8-01	3	0	5.06	4	0	0	0	11	15	6	6	1	5	6	.333	.400	.300	5.06	4.22
Villar, Luis	L-L	5-10	195	11-8-00	1	6	6.03	12	1	0	0	31	38	34	21	7	18	42	.290	.257	.302	12.06	5.17
Wang, Chih-Ting	L-L	6-1	240	1-24-99	0	2	2.64	10	3	0	2	31	18	9	9	0	13	42	.164	.292	.128	12.33	3.82
Willis, Marlin	L-L	6-4	190	6-5-98	0	0	9.64	3	0	0	0	5	9	6	5	0	1	5	.429	.500	.412	9.64	1.93

Fielding

C: Duarte 5, Garza 2, Jensen 11, Medina 10, Mondesi 6, Pire 27, Quintana 29, Rodriguez 11, Tresh 4.
1B: Collins 34, Hovey 6, Maican 43, Mondesi 4, Quintana 3, Shrum 7.
2B: Bewley 3, Cancel 3, Dennis 1, Dooney 6, Florentino 29, Grullon 29, Hovey 2, Marquez 4, Martinez 1, Nivar 3, Reyes 8, Rivera 7, Tolbert 2, Valdez 4, Wilson 10.
3B: Bewley 3, Cancel 2, Dennis 5, Eaton 4, Guzman 25, Martinez 22, Nivar 3, Rivera 11, Valdez 14, Williams 14.
SS: Candelario 32, Cepero 13, Florentino 8, Fox 4, Guzman 7, Martinez 13, McNair 9, Reyes 8, Valdez 10.
OF: Bates 10, De Los Santos 42, Dixon 1, Hernandez 5, Hollie 29, Hovey 3, Jackson 23, Leyton 34, Marinez 14, Martinez 2, Matias 5, Moreno 24, Pena 37, Ramirez 10, Seijas 3, Tolbert 1, Town 21.

DSL ROYALS   ROOKIE
DOMINICAN SUMMER LEAGUE

Batting	B-T	HT	WT	DOB	AVG	vLH	vRH	G	AB	R	H	2B	3B	HR	RBI	BB	HBP	SH	SF	SO	SB	CS	SLG	OBP
Advincola, Yeudi	R-R	6-1	170	10-9-01	.283	.200	.307	38	113	19	32	7	0	0	16	10	2	0	0	30	9	1	.345	.352
Borges, Meiver	R-R	5-10	165	10-12-02	.243	.313	.224	26	74	9	18	2	0	0	7	8	0	1	1	18	1	0	.270	.313
Bravo, Osman	R-R	5-11	170	6-16-04	.140	.091	.156	18	43	2	6	0	0	0	4	5	3	0	0	10	0	0	.140	.275
Calderon, Junior	R-R	6-0	175	12-9-01	.268	.259	.270	48	138	27	37	10	0	2	30	26	2	0	7	19	6	6	.384	.376
Castillo, Marino	L-R	5-11	150	10-13-02	.210	.080	.245	39	119	25	25	3	1	0	10	17	3	1	0	25	19	5	.252	.324
Celado, Jorge	R-R	6-0	163	1-14-03	.236	.136	.269	35	89	10	21	1	1	2	13	5	1	0	1	27	1	0	.337	.281
Cespedes, Steven	L-R	5-9	170	10-23-03	.139	.200	.129	28	72	7	10	5	0	0	2	7	1	0	0	23	0	1	.208	.225
Chacon, Jose	R-R	6-0	165	11-29-02	.222	.231	.220	43	126	22	28	6	1	2	8	22	4	2	1	33	5	4	.333	.353
Cruz, Reymond	R-R	6-1	165	4-14-01	.236	.250	.231	30	55	12	13	1	1	0	6	10	0	0	0	19	9	3	.291	.354
De Cuba, Ethan	B-R	6-0	145	4-14-03	.211	.222	.208	33	90	17	19	2	0	0	10	19	2	1	1	25	1	6	.233	.357
Echenique, Luis	L-L	5-11	175	11-25-02	.239	.300	.232	39	92	19	22	3	2	0	9	12	3	1	2	12	12	3	.315	.339
Fernandez, Yosmi	B-R	5-11	165	4-15-04	.093	.308	.063	40	108	7	10	1	1	0	7	16	2	0	1	47	7	3	.120	.220
Freites, Jose	R-R	6-1	180	11-25-01	.194	.278	.163	27	67	10	13	2	0	0	8	14	3	0	0	24	3	0	.224	.357
Garcia, Eduardo	L-R	6-1	183	9-10-01	.261	.150	.283	43	119	19	31	11	0	3	23	17	3	0	0	32	2	0	.429	.367
Lucas, Aldrin	R-R	5-10	165	2-7-03	.194	.348	.147	38	98	14	19	1	0	1	9	12	4	2	3	21	2	2	.235	.299
Marin, Junior	R-R	6-2	220	3-15-04	.380	.278	.405	32	92	17	35	8	0	7	32	16	1	0	2	19	5	2	.696	.468
Melendez, Mario	R-R	5-10	180	4-4-03	.317	.450	.291	42	123	23	39	6	0	2	23	18	2	0	1	32	1	0	.415	.410
Meli, Densi	R-R	6-0	170	1-24-01	.218	.200	.222	27	55	8	12	3	0	0	8	4	6	0	1	23	7	3	.273	.333
Mendez, Jairo	L-L	6-0	155	10-6-02	.239	.250	.237	37	117	24	28	3	4	3	13	17	2	0	2	39	7	4	.410	.341
Morales, Jorge	R-R	6-0	170	12-2-02	.208	.150	.221	40	106	13	22	3	1	0	12	17	3	2	0	30	1	0	.255	.328
Nuel, Omar	R-R	6-1	170	5-12-03	.273	.214	.280	38	121	26	33	4	1	3	18	12	1	0	0	39	3	2	.397	.343
Parra, Angel	L-L	6-0	156	1-26-04	.202	.200	.202	39	109	15	22	3	0	1	9	14	3	1	0	29	11	5	.257	.310
Perdomo, Jhonny	R-R	5-10	168	6-9-02	.256	.222	.262	40	121	17	31	8	1	1	16	11	5	4	0	25	13	2	.364	.357
Ramirez, Sebastian	L-L	6-2	180	10-1-03	.173	.286	.162	39	75	17	13	2	1	1	7	19	6	0	0	31	9	3	.267	.380
Rodriguez, Lizandro	B-R	5-11	165	11-16-02	.309	.158	.346	34	97	27	30	5	1	6	23	21	3	0	0	18	14	4	.567	.446
Salon, Dionmy	R-R	6-2	190	11-18-01	.211	.250	.200	25	57	7	12	3	0	1	7	12	2	0	0	13	2	2	.316	.366
Santana, Angel	R-R	5-10	160	4-27-03	.255	.357	.220	23	55	4	14	0	1	0	1	2	2	0	0	15	3	0	.291	.305
Silva, Gabriel	R-R	5-10	195	12-10-03	.194	.188	.195	36	93	19	18	4	0	4	18	22	4	0	0	27	1	2	.366	.370
Ulloa, Francisco	R-R	5-11	170	10-13-03	.152	.154	.151	29	66	11	10	1	0	0	8	7	5	1	0	27	1	3	.167	.282
Vargas, Yeison	R-R	0-0	0	9-10-03	.237	.222	.242	32	93	15	22	4	0	0	9	13	3	0	1	23	4	5	.280	.345
Vazquez, Daniel	R-R	6-0	150	12-15-03	.186	.125	.198	32	102	17	19	3	1	1	10	14	0	0	2	31	4	0	.265	.280

Pitching	B-T	HT	WT	DOB	W	L	ERA	G	GS	CG	SV	IP	H	R	ER	HR	BB	SO	AVG	vLH	vRH	K/9	BB/9
Arronde, Felix	R-R	6-3	185	4-25-03	2	4	5.25	11	2	0	0	24	26	27	14	1	14	24	.271	.235	.290	9.00	5.25

Name	B-T	Ht	Wt	DOB	W	L	ERA	G	GS	CG	SV	IP	H	R	ER	HR	BB	SO	AVG	vLH	vRH		
Betemit Jr., Wilson	R-R	6-1	170	7-27-03	2	2	5.61	12	1	0	0	26	30	19	16	2	10	16	.286	.237	.313	5.61	3.51
Breton, Fraicy	L-L	6-3	196	6-10-01	1	3	2.11	11	10	0	0	43	33	13	10	2	10	44	.209	.211	.208	9.28	2.11
Cabrera, Daury	R-R	6-4	230	10-23-00	0	1	1.50	2	2	0	0	6	5	2	1	0	2	4	.208	.600	.105	6.00	3.00
Castillo, Emilio	L-L	5-10	150	10-18-02	3	0	2.91	11	0	0	0	22	17	9	7	0	14	30	.221	.200	.224	12.46	5.82
Catano, Jose	L-L	6-3	180	6-10-01	0	0	1.27	12	12	0	0	43	19	7	6	0	15	57	.135	.105	.139	12.02	3.16
Colon, Jose	R-R	6-2	182	2-12-01	3	1	4.39	12	3	0	1	27	20	16	13	1	16	20	.211	.105	.281	6.75	5.40
Cordero, Pedro	R-R	6-3	170	11-29-01	2	0	4.86	7	3	0	0	17	15	12	9	0	7	9	.238	.263	.227	4.86	3.78
Cruz, Julio	R-R	6-0	190	7-26-00	3	2	3.96	13	0	0	2	25	21	12	11	0	8	26	.231	.227	.234	9.36	2.88
Cuevas, Frandy	L-L	5-11	180	1-19-02	2	2	11.44	14	1	0	1	20	22	30	25	0	24	21	.278	.200	.297	9.61	10.98
De Jesus, Dary	L-L	6-1	165	2-21-03	2	0	6.57	7	0	0	0	12	10	9	9	0	10	20	.222	.222	.222	14.59	7.30
Espinoza, Weskendry	R-R	6-1	185	3-18-02	1	3	4.38	12	10	0	0	39	41	28	19	2	11	28	.270	.254	.280	6.46	2.54
Gomez, Jhonny	R-R	5-11	180	8-27-02	0	1	3.05	12	0	0	4	21	21	8	7	2	6	20	.269	.250	.289	8.71	2.61
Gonzalez, Adrian	R-R	6-2	170	9-30-00	2	3	1.91	12	0	0	0	28	21	10	6	1	6	20	.216	.278	.180	6.35	1.91
Gonzalez, Willians	R-R	6-0	190	12-6-00	2	0	3.71	10	6	0	0	27	25	13	11	2	9	25	.240	.333	.197	8.44	3.04
Hernandez, Miguel	R-R	6-0	174	10-26-01	1	0	3.95	8	0	0	3	14	16	6	6	1	3	8	.271	.409	.189	5.27	1.98
Leal, Jemir	R-R	6-2	155	4-7-03	0	3	5.01	12	5	0	2	23	30	19	13	3	13	14	.319	.326	.313	5.40	5.01
Lorenzo, Ricardito	L-L	6-3	200	8-3-03	0	0	9.00	1	0	0	0	1	2	3	1	0	0	2	.333	--	.333	18.00	0.00
Martinez, Juan	R-R	5-11	170	4-6-01	4	1	1.83	11	2	0	1	20	17	8	4	1	16	23	.246	.412	.192	10.53	7.32
Martinez, Luis	L-L	6-1	180	9-17-03	0	4	9.61	11	3	0	0	20	17	35	21	2	26	23	.227	.154	.242	10.53	11.90
Mendez, Eslahiber	R-R	5-11	160	12-9-03	0	2	9.95	4	0	0	0	6	5	10	7	0	9	8	.217	.250	.200	11.37	12.79
Michel, Ismael	R-R	6-3	175	2-14-02	1	0	3.78	9	2	0	0	17	9	9	7	1	8	23	.150	.045	.211	12.42	4.32
Novas, Elvis	R-R	6-0	180	9-2-02	2	0	3.91	11	0	0	1	23	29	12	10	1	7	27	.319	.296	.328	10.57	2.74
Nunez, Jan	L-L	6-2	180	11-18-02	0	1	16.88	7	0	0	0	8	12	16	15	0	14	10	.364	.400	.357	11.25	15.75
Paulino, Christian	L-L	6-1	166	10-2-01	0	3	8.26	13	4	0	0	28	24	27	26	2	25	27	.240	.400	.222	8.58	7.94
Pena, Victor	L-L	5-11	165	12-21-02	0	1	3.74	10	6	0	0	22	21	12	9	0	13	24	.256	.294	.246	9.97	5.40
Polanco, Luis	R-R	6-3	219	8-10-00	1	0	5.79	11	0	0	0	19	20	13	12	2	6	23	.278	.281	.275	11.09	2.89
Rayo, Oscar	L-L	6-1	180	1-13-02	1	0	3.92	9	3	0	0	21	18	9	9	1	3	25	.234	.083	.262	10.89	1.31
Reynoso, Jeffry	R-R	6-2	185	10-1-01	0	0	4.50	3	1	0	0	4	2	2	2	1	2	3	.133	.000	.154	6.75	4.50
Rodriguez, Edwin	R-R	6-2	170	8-24-03	2	2	5.79	13	0	0	1	23	25	19	15	0	14	33	.281	.207	.317	12.73	5.40
Rosado, Jarold	R-R	6-3	215	7-13-02	0	1	2.70	4	4	0	0	10	9	6	3	0	6	5	.237	.167	.250	4.50	5.40
Rosario, Axel	R-R	6-5	192	5-22-00	7	1	2.74	12	0	0	3	23	15	9	7	0	12	44	.172	.190	.156	17.22	4.70
Santana, Angel	R-R	5-10	160	4-27-03	0	1	27.00	1	0	0	0	1	3	4	3	0	1	1	.500	.500	.500	9.00	9.00
Santana, Osiris	R-R	5-11	165	10-11-01	2	5	3.35	12	12	0	0	46	38	19	17	1	4	39	.218	.094	.291	7.69	0.79
Sosa, Yenfri	L-L	6-0	170	12-29-03	2	1	2.03	6	0	0	0	13	10	4	3	0	2	9	.204	.222	.200	6.08	1.35
Veliz, Mauricio	R-R	6-2	170	7-17-02	1	3	6.35	12	11	0	0	34	39	26	24	4	11	28	.279	.233	.299	7.41	2.91
Vicente, Jheremy	R-R	6-1	170	10-1-03	3	1	5.40	12	1	0	0	25	24	19	15	0	18	28	.247	.250	.246	10.08	6.48

Fielding

C: Borges 23, Bravo 8, Cespedes 15, Lucas 11, Melendez 10, Salon 22, Silva 26.
1B: Calderon 34, Celado 12, Freites 12, Garcia 29, Lucas 24, Melendez 4.
2B: Celado 5, Chacon 13, Fernandez 14, Perdomo 38, Rodriguez 21, Vargas 24.
3B: Calderon 13, Celado 19, Chacon 30, Garcia 2, Meli 9, Morales 38, Rodriguez 8.
SS: Advincola 33, Chacon 3, Fernandez 29, Meli 16, Rodriguez 1, Vargas 4, Vazquez 30.
OF: Castillo 35, Cruz 25, De Cuba 35, Echenique 33, Freites 9, Marin 27, Mendez 37, Nuel 38, Parra 37, Ramirez 34, Santana 22, Ulloa 28.

Los Angeles Angels

SEASON IN A SENTENCE: Despite a historic, two-way season from Shohei Ohtani, the Angels continued to struggle in the American League West, finishing in fourth place for the fourth straight year with a 77-85 record. The Angels have had a losing season in six consecutive years and been to the playoffs just once in Mike Trout's career.

HIGH POINT: There wasn't a singular moment in the season more impressive or that will be remembered more fondly than the totality of Ohtani's 2021 season. He hit 46 home runs and led the league with eight triples, while posting a .257/.372/.592 slash line and 152 wRC+. At the same time, Ohtani made 23 starts and posted a 3.18 ERA over 130.1 innings. He was a 9-win player according to Baseball-Reference when combining his value as a hitter and pitcher—easily the best in baseball.

LOW POINT: Is it too obvious to say that losing Mike Trout for the season after straining his calf on May 17 was the low point? While the Angels desperately needed to find pitching, it's still possible that a full season of Trout—who was excellent when on the field, hitting .333/.466/.624 with a 190 wRC+ in 36 games—could have helped Los Angeles push for the playoffs.

NOTABLE ROOKIES: The Angels didn't get more than a single win above replacement from any rookie this season. Brandon Marsh was the most notable, though his .254/.317/.356 line was below major league average over 70 games and his strikeout rate (35%) is concerning. Top prospect Jo Adell and Jack Mayfield both struggled to get on base at a decent clip, while the Angels got innings from 17 different rookie pitchers—the best of whom was Austin Warren, who posted a 1.77 ERA in 20.1 innings out of the bullpen.

KEY TRANSACTIONS: The Albert Pujols era in Anaheim came to an end this year when the team released the future Hall of Famer in May. In total, Pujols played 1,181 games for the Angels over 10 seasons, hitting .256/.311/.447 with 222 home runs and a 108 OPS+. The Angels traded Jahmai Jones to the Orioles in February for Alex Cobb, who started 18 games and posted a 3.76 ERA over 93.1 innings.

OPENING DAY SALARY: $177,353,000 (4th).

PLAYERS OF THE YEAR

MAJOR LEAGUE	MINOR LEAGUE
Shohei Ohtani **DH/RHP**	**Reid Detmers** **LHP**
.257/.372/.592	(AAA/AA)
Career-high 46 HR	3-4, 3.19,
9-2, 3.18, 10.8 SO/9	108 SO, 19 BB in 62 IP

ORGANIZATION LEADERS

Batting		*Minimum 250 AB
MAJORS		
*AVG	Jared Walsh	.277
*OPS	Shohei Ohtani	1.167
HR	Shohei Ohtani	46
RBI	Shohei Ohtani	100
MINORS		
*AVG	Michael Stefanic, Salt Lake, Rocket City	.336
*OBP	Braxton Martinez, Tri-City, Inland Empire	.439
*SLG	Jo Adell, Salt Lake	.592
*OPS	Braxton Martinez, Tri-City, Inland Empire	1.027
R	Brendon Davis, Salt Lake, Rocket City, Tri-City	91
H	Michael Stefanic, Salt Lake, Rocket City	165
TB	Brendon Davis, Salt Lake, Rocket City, Tri-City	271
2B	David MacKinnon, Rocket City	30
3B	Livan Soto, Rocket City, Tri-City	8
HR	Brendon Davis, Salt Lake, Rocket City, Tri-City	30
RBI	Jake Gatewood, Salt Lake	84
BB	Matt Thaiss, Salt Lake	60
SO	Jake Gatewood, Salt Lake	170
SB	Jeremy Arocho, Salt Lake, Tri-City, Inland Empire	31
SB	D'Shawn Knowles, Inland Empire	31

Pitching		#Minimum 75 IP
MAJORS		
W	Shohei Ohtani	9
#ERA	Shohei Ohtani	3.18
SO	Shohei Ohtani	156
SV	Raisel Iglesias	34
MINORS		
W	Cristopher Molina, Rocket City, Tri-City	10
L	Thomas Pannone, Salt Lake	11
#ERA	Cristopher Molina, Rocket City, Tri-City	3.38
G	Tim Peterson, Salt Lake	43
GS	Ryan Smith, Salt Lake, Rocket City, Tri-City, Inland Empire	23
SV	Emilker Guzman, Inland Empire	12
IP	Ryan Smith, Salt Lake, Rocket City, Tri-City, Inland Empire	129.1
BB	Hector Yan, Tri-City	58
SO	Davis Daniel, Salt Lake, Rocket City, Tri-City	154
#AVG	Robinson Pina, Rocket City, Tri-City, Inland Empire	.209

General Manager: Perry Minasian. **Farm Director:** Andrew Ball. **Scouting Director:** Matt Swanson.

Class	Team	League	W	L	PCT	Finish	Manager
Majors	Los Angeles Angels	American	77	85	.475	t-10th (15)	Joe Maddon
Triple-A	Salt Lake Bees	Triple-A West	55	74	.426	9th (10)	Lou Marson
Double-A	Rocket City Trash Pandas	Double-A South	54	56	.491	6th (8)	Jay Bell
High-A	Tri-City Dust Devils	High-A West	43	68	.387	6th (6)	Jack Santora/Andy Schatzley
Low-A	Inland Empire 66ers	Low-A West	56	61	.479	5th (8)	Jack Howell
Rookie	ACL Angels	Arizona Complex	30	28	.517	10th (18)	Dave Stapleton
Rookie	DSL Angels	Dominican Summer	32	26	.552	16th (46)	Hector De La Cruz
Overall 2021 Minor League Record		270		313	.463	21st (30)	

ORGANIZATION STATISTICS

LOS ANGELES ANGELS
AMERICAN LEAGUE

Batting	B-T	HT	WT	DOB	AVG	vLH	vRH	G	AB	R	H	2B	3B	HR	RBI	BB	HBP	SH	SF	SO	SB	CS	SLG	OBP
Adell, Jo	R-R	6-3	215	4-8-99	.246	.250	.244	35	130	17	32	5	2	4	26	8	1	1	0	32	2	1	.408	.295
Bemboom, Anthony	L-R	6-2	200	1-18-90	.222	.500	.174	8	27	2	6	0	0	0	2	1	0	0	0	10	0	0	.222	.250
Butera, Drew	R-R	6-1	212	8-9-83	.094	.167	.077	12	32	1	3	1	0	0	5	0	0	3	1	16	0	0	.125	.091
Eaton, Adam	L-L	5-9	180	12-6-88	.200	.231	.192	25	65	5	13	2	0	1	2	2	1	0	1	16	1	0	.277	.232
2-team total (58 Chicago)					.201	.178	.206	83	254	38	51	10	2	6	30	22	7	4	1	71	3	0	.327	.282
Fletcher, David	R-R	5-9	185	5-31-94	.262	.316	.238	157	626	74	164	27	3	2	47	31	1	6	1	60	15	3	.324	.297
Fowler, Dexter	B-R	6-5	205	3-22-86	.250	.400	.200	7	20	3	5	0	0	0	1	1	0	0	6	1	0	.250	.286
Gosselin, Phil	R-R	6-1	188	10-3-88	.261	.275	.251	104	345	40	90	14	0	7	47	24	3	0	1	81	4	2	.362	.314
Iglesias, Jose	R-R	5-11	195	1-5-90	.259	.283	.249	114	424	57	110	23	1	8	41	18	4	0	1	66	5	2	.375	.295
2-team total (23 Boston)					.271	.297	.260	137	483	65	131	27	2	9	48	21	6	0	1	75	5	2	.391	.309
Jay, Jon	L-L	5-9	200	3-15-85	.357	.250	.400	5	14	2	5	0	0	0	1	0	0	0	0	2	0	0	.357	.357
Kruger, Jack	R-R	6-1	195	10-26-94	--	--	--	1	0	0	0	0	0	0	0	0	0	0	0	0	0	0	--	--
Lagares, Juan	R-R	6-2	219	3-17-89	.236	.252	.227	112	309	39	73	20	2	6	38	12	1	4	1	76	1	2	.372	.266
Marsh, Brandon	L-R	6-4	215	12-18-97	.254	.260	.252	70	236	27	60	12	3	2	19	20	2	1	1	91	6	1	.356	.317
Mayfield, Jack	R-R	5-11	190	9-30-90	.224	.236	.219	75	232	28	52	14	0	10	36	16	3	3	1	58	5	0	.414	.282
2-team total (11 Seattle)					.218	.223	.215	86	266	30	58	15	0	10	39	17	3	3	1	68	5	0	.387	.272
Ohtani, Shohei	L-R	6-4	210	7-5-94	.257	.263	.254	155	537	103	138	26	8	46	100	96	4	0	2	189	26	10	.592	.372
Pujols, Albert	R-R	6-3	235	1-16-80	.198	.259	.169	24	86	9	17	0	0	5	12	3	3	0	0	13	1	0	.372	.250
Rendon, Anthony	R-R	6-1	200	6-6-90	.240	.194	.260	58	217	24	52	13	0	6	34	29	1	0	2	41	0	0	.382	.329
Rengifo, Luis	B-R	5-10	195	2-26-97	.201	.212	.197	54	174	22	35	1	0	6	18	9	2	3	2	38	1	0	.310	.246
Rojas, Jose	L-R	6-0	200	2-24-93	.208	.237	.200	61	168	26	35	14	0	6	15	15	1	0	0	50	2	1	.399	.277
Schebler, Scott	L-R	6-1	228	10-6-90	.147	.000	.208	14	34	3	5	3	0	0	0	0	0	0	0	17	0	0	.235	.147
Stassi, Max	R-R	5-10	200	3-15-91	.241	.194	.256	87	282	45	68	11	1	13	35	28	8	0	1	101	0	0	.426	.326
Suzuki, Kurt	R-R	5-11	210	10-4-83	.224	.242	.208	72	219	17	49	8	0	6	16	12	11	2	3	44	0	0	.342	.294
Thaiss, Matt	L-R	6-0	215	5-6-95	.143	.500	.000	3	7	1	1	0	0	0	0	1	0	0	1	1	0	0	.143	.250
Trout, Mike	R-R	6-2	235	8-7-91	.333	.265	.361	36	117	23	39	8	1	8	18	27	2	0	0	41	2	0	.624	.466
Upton, Justin	R-R	6-1	215	8-25-87	.211	.225	.205	89	318	47	67	12	0	17	41	39	1	0	3	107	4	1	.409	.296
Walsh, Jared	L-L	6-0	210	7-30-93	.277	.170	.333	144	530	70	147	34	1	29	98	48	4	0	3	152	2	1	.509	.340
Ward, Taylor	R-R	6-1	200	12-14-93	.250	.303	.225	65	208	33	52	15	0	8	33	20	6	2	1	55	1	1	.438	.332
Wong, Kean	L-R	5-9	189	4-17-95	.167	.167	.167	32	60	3	10	2	1	0	2	0	4	0	0	17	0	0	.233	.194

Pitching	B-T	HT	WT	DOB	W	L	ERA	G	GS	CG	SV	IP	H	R	ER	HR	BB	SO	AVG	vLH	vRH	K/9	BB/9
Barria, Jaime	R-R	6-1	210	7-18-96	2	4	4.61	13	11	0	0	57	70	29	29	8	19	35	.307	.313	.303	5.56	3.02
Bemboom, Anthony	L-R	6-2	200	1-18-90	0	0	18.00	1	0	0	0	1	3	2	2	1	0	0	.429	.500	.333	0.00	0.00
Bundy, Dylan	B-R	6-1	225	11-15-92	2	9	6.06	23	19	0	0	91	89	64	61	20	34	84	.253	.238	.263	8.34	3.38
Canning, Griffin	R-R	6-2	180	5-11-96	5	4	5.60	14	13	0	0	63	65	41	39	14	28	62	.264	.252	.273	8.90	4.02
Cishek, Steve	R-R	6-6	215	6-18-86	0	2	3.42	74	0	0	0	68	61	32	26	2	41	64	.238	.209	.253	8.43	5.40
Claudio, Alex	L-L	6-3	188	1-31-92	1	2	5.51	41	0	0	1	33	37	22	20	6	15	30	.278	.275	.281	8.27	4.13
Cobb, Alex	R-R	6-3	205	10-7-87	8	3	3.76	18	18	0	0	93	85	46	39	5	33	98	.240	.228	.251	9.45	3.18
Criswell, Cooper	R-R	6-6	200	7-24-96	0	1	20.25	1	1	0	0	1	6	3	3	0	0	0	.600	.500	.667	0.00	0.00
Detmers, Reid	L-L	6-2	210	7-8-99	1	3	7.40	5	5	0	0	21	26	17	17	5	11	19	.295	.318	.288	8.27	4.79
Diaz, Jhonathan	L-L	6-0	170	7-10-96	1	0	4.15	3	2	0	0	13	11	6	6	1	7	9	.220	.059	.303	6.23	4.85
Eaton, Adam	L-L	5-9	180	12-6-88	0	0	0.00	1	0	0	0	2	0	0	0	0	0	0	.400	.333	.500	0.00	0.00
Guerra, Junior	R-R	6-0	235	1-16-85	5	2	6.06	41	1	0	0	65	67	45	44	6	46	61	.262	.304	.238	8.40	6.34
Heaney, Andrew	L-L	6-2	200	6-5-91	6	7	5.27	18	18	0	0	94	92	56	55	16	31	113	.252	.270	.245	10.82	2.97
2-team total (12 New York)					8	9	5.83	30	23	0	0	130	130	85	84	29	41	150	.256	.260	.255	10.41	2.85
Herget, Jimmy	R-R	6-3	170	9-9-93	2	2	4.30	14	0	0	0	15	15	7	7	0	4	18	.283	.250	.297	11.05	2.45
2-team total (4 Texas)					2	3	5.30	18	0	0	0	19	20	12	11	1	4	20	.286	.211	.314	9.64	1.93
Hoyt, James	R-R	6-6	230	9-30-86	0	0	6.75	9	0	0	0	9	9	7	7	3	8	11	.324	.200	.370	12.38	7.88
Iglesias, Raisel	R-R	6-2	190	1-4-90	7	5	2.57	65	0	0	34	70	53	25	20	11	12	103	.207	.223	.194	13.24	1.54
Junk, Janson	R-R	6-1	177	1-15-96	0	1	3.86	4	4	0	0	16	20	11	7	5	2	10	.294	.333	.250	5.51	1.10
Marte, Jose	R-R	6-3	180	6-14-96	0	1	9.00	4	0	0	0	4	4	5	4	1	3	5	.267	.429	.125	11.25	6.75

Pitching	B-T	HT	WT	DOB	W	L	ERA	G	GS	CG	SHO	SV	IP	H	R	ER	HR	BB	SO	AVG	vLH	vRH		
Mayers, Mike	R-R	6-2	220	12-6-91	5	5	3.84	72	2	0	2	75	71	32	32	11	26	90	.250	.250	.250	10.80	3.12
Naughton, Packy	R-L	6-2	195	4-16-96	0	4	6.35	7	5	0	0	23	27	18	16	3	14	12	.290	.296	.288	4.76	5.56
Ohtani, Shohei	L-R	6-4	210	7-5-94	9	2	3.18	23	23	0	0	130	98	48	46	15	44	156	.207	.235	.178	10.77	3.04
Ortega, Oliver	R-R	6-0	165	10-2-96	1	0	4.82	8	0	0	0	9	12	5	5	1	2	4	.333	.429	.273	3.86	1.93
Peguero, Elvis	R-R	6-5	208	3-20-97	0	1	27.00	3	0	0	0	2	7	7	7	0	3	0	.538	.400	.625	0.00	11.57
Pena, Felix	R-R	6-2	220	2-25-90	0	0	37.80	2	0	0	0	2	7	7	7	0	4	2	.583	.750	.500	10.80	21.60
Petricka, Jake	R-R	6-4	218	6-5-88	0	1	15.00	7	0	0	0	6	6	10	10	1	7	8	.261	.333	.182	12.00	10.50
Quijada, Jose	L-L	5-11	215	11-9-95	0	2	4.56	26	0	0	0	26	20	14	13	2	15	30	.213	.263	.179	13.32	5.26
Quintana, Jose	R-L	6-1	220	1-24-89	0	3	6.75	24	10	0	0	53	66	45	40	9	29	73	.297	.180	.342	12.32	4.89
Ramirez, Noe	R-R	6-3	205	12-22-89	0	0	5.40	2	0	0	0	3	5	2	2	1	1	0	.357	.571	.143	0.00	2.70
Ramos, AJ	R-R	5-10	200	9-20-86	0	0	0.00	4	0	0	0	5	0	0	0	0	2	3	.000	.000	.000	5.79	3.86
Rodriguez, Chris	R-R	6-2	185	7-20-98	2	1	3.64	15	2	0	0	30	28	14	12	0	15	29	.243	.213	.265	8.80	4.55
Rowen, Ben	R-R	6-4	200	11-15-88	0	0	5.56	8	0	0	0	11	12	8	7	3	2	8	.273	.333	.217	6.35	1.59
Sandoval, Patrick	L-L	6-3	190	10-18-96	3	6	3.62	17	14	0	1	87	69	38	35	11	36	94	.215	.151	.241	9.72	3.72
Selman, Sam	R-L	6-2	198	11-14-90	0	1	6.35	18	0	0	0	17	16	13	12	1	8	11	.258	.235	.267	5.82	4.24
Slegers, Aaron	R-R	6-10	260	9-4-92	2	2	6.97	29	0	0	0	31	43	24	24	6	15	25	.326	.395	.298	7.26	4.35
Strickland, Hunter	R-R	6-3	225	9-24-88	0	0	9.95	9	0	0	0	6	11	9	7	3	4	4	.379	.364	.389	5.68	5.68
2-team total (13 Tampa Bay)					0	0	4.03	22	0	0	0	22	25	13	10	4	10	20	.281	.313	.263	8.06	4.03
Suarez, Jose	L-L	5-10	225	1-3-98	8	8	3.75	23	14	1	0	98	85	45	41	11	36	85	.230	.315	.202	7.78	3.29
Tyler, Kyle	R-R	6-0	185	12-20-97	0	0	2.92	5	0	0	0	12	8	4	4	1	6	6	.190	.067	.259	4.38	4.38
Wantz, Andrew	R-R	6-4	235	10-13-95	1	0	4.94	21	0	0	0	27	23	17	15	5	11	38	.219	.282	.182	12.51	3.62
Warren, Austin	R-R	6-0	170	2-5-96	3	0	1.77	16	0	0	1	20	16	5	4	0	5	20	.205	.143	.228	8.85	2.21
Watson, Tony	L-L	6-3	224	5-30-85	3	3	4.64	36	0	0	0	33	25	18	17	3	14	25	.207	.213	.203	6.82	3.82

Fielding

Catcher	PCT	G	PO	A	E	DP	PB
Bemboom	.973	7	71	1	2	0	0
Butera	1.000	12	99	2	0	0	3
Kruger	1.000	1	1	0	0	0	0
Stassi	.994	86	697	25	4	1	8
Suzuki	.984	69	597	33	10	5	7
Ward	1.000	1	2	0	0	0	0

First Base	PCT	G	PO	A	E	DP
Eaton	1.000	1	1	0	0	0
Gosselin	1.000	23	135	12	0	13
Pujols	.986	20	137	8	2	13
Rojas	.833	2	5	0	1	0
Thaiss	1.000	2	17	1	0	0
Walsh	.995	128	897	73	5	96

Second Base	PCT	G	PO	A	E	DP
Fletcher	.990	142	261	354	6	86
Gosselin	.923	4	4	8	1	2
Rengifo	.941	4	7	9	1	2
Rojas	.975	14	20	19	1	8
Wong	1.000	10	15	20	0	6

Third Base	PCT	G	PO	A	E	DP
Gosselin	.955	32	25	38	3	7
Mayfield	.955	66	36	114	7	15
Pujols	.000	1	0	0	0	0
Rendon	.993	57	31	114	1	12
Rengifo	.828	12	2	22	5	4
Rojas	.974	12	6	31	1	2
Wong	1.000	6	2	1	0	1

Shortstop	PCT	G	PO	A	E	DP
Fletcher	.971	20	15	51	2	7
Iglesias	.958	114	115	250	16	44
Mayfield	.971	12	10	23	1	9
Rengifo	.981	26	30	74	2	16

Outfield	PCT	G	PO	A	E	DP
Adell	1.000	44	82	2	0	1
Bemboom	1.000	1	1	0	0	0
Canning	--	1	0	0	0	0
Eaton	1.000	25	31	1	0	0
Fowler	1.000	7	7	0	0	0
Gosselin	1.000	40	69	0	0	0
Jay	1.000	5	8	0	0	0
Lagares	1.000	122	167	5	0	0
Marsh	.994	70	154	1	1	0
Ohtani	--	7	0	0	0	0
Rengifo	.960	15	24	0	1	0
Rojas	1.000	34	44	2	0	0
Schebler	1.000	11	21	0	0	0
Trout	1.000	36	53	0	0	0
Upton	.984	88	121	3	2	1
Walsh	.957	18	22	0	1	0
Ward	.984	81	124	2	2	0
Wong	1.000	8	13	0	0	0

SALT LAKE BEES   TRIPLE-A
TRIPLE-A WEST

Batting	B-T	HT	WT	DOB	AVG	vLH	vRH	G	AB	R	H	2B	3B	HR	RBI	BB	HBP	SH	SF	SO	SB	CS	SLG	OBP
Adell, Jo	R-R	6-3	215	4-8-99	.289	.323	.280	73	311	57	90	17	4	23	69	22	4	0	2	99	8	2	.592	.342
Arcia, Francisco	L-R	5-11	200	9-14-89	.357	.286	.381	10	28	4	10	1	0	0	2	2	0	0	0	9	2	0	.393	.400
Arocho, Jeremy	B-R	5-10	165	10-6-98	.000	--	.000	1	3	0	0	0	0	0	0	1	0	0	0	2	0	0	.000	.250
Aviles Jr., Luis	R-R	6-1	170	3-16-95	.000	--	.000	1	0	0	0	0	0	0	0	0	0	0	0	0	0	0	.000	.000
Bemboom, Anthony	L-R	6-2	200	1-18-90	.255	.143	.284	40	137	22	35	6	2	7	30	23	2	0	3	33	2	0	.482	.364
2-team total (25 Oklahoma City)					.232	.200	.244	65	211	35	49	8	3	8	37	38	3	0	4	55	2	0	.412	.352
Butera, Drew	R-R	6-1	212	8-9-83	.222	.273	.208	49	158	28	35	7	1	4	11	19	6	2	0	50	3	1	.354	.328
2-team total (15 Sugar Land)					.195	.205	.193	64	205	36	40	8	1	6	16	27	8	2	1	65	4	1	.332	.311
Cecchini, Gavin	R-R	6-2	200	12-22-93	.288	.278	.291	49	177	15	51	16	0	0	17	8	0	0	1	29	4	0	.379	.317
Davis, Brendon	R-R	6-4	185	7-28-97	.333	.320	.337	31	117	25	39	8	2	8	25	10	5	0	0	28	3	1	.641	.409
Gatewood, Jake	R-R	6-5	190	9-25-95	.227	.242	.223	116	450	60	102	22	2	28	84	29	6	0	2	170	6	2	.471	.281
Griffin, Spencer	R-R	6-1	170	10-24-96	.000	.000	.000	2	3	0	0	0	0	0	0	0	0	0	0	1	0	0	.000	.000
Hunter Jr., Torii	R-R	6-2	180	6-7-95	.125	.000	.154	5	16	3	2	0	0	1	2	2	0	0	0	7	0	0	.313	.222
Jay, Jon	L-L	5-11	200	3-15-85	.362	.500	.327	18	69	16	25	4	0	1	5	2	1	0	1	9	2	0	.464	.384
Lund, Brennon	L-R	5-9	185	11-27-94	.224	.125	.252	79	286	34	64	16	2	11	38	17	5	0	2	86	3	2	.409	.277
Marsh, Brandon	L-R	6-4	215	12-18-97	.255	.267	.253	24	94	26	24	5	3	3	8	16	0	0	0	29	2	0	.468	.364
Matthews, Gabe	L-R	6-2	219	11-24-97	.107	.167	.091	16	56	3	6	2	0	0	5	6	1	0	0	19	0	0	.143	.206
Mayfield, Jack	R-R	5-11	190	9-30-90	.329	.313	.333	15	70	14	23	2	3	5	11	5	1	0	0	8	1	1	.657	.382
2-team total (1 Tacoma)					.342	.316	.351	16	76	16	26	2	3	5	12	5	1	0	0	9	1	1	.645	.390
Mulrine, Anthony	R-R	6-1	205	3-30-98	.118	.000	.143	5	17	1	2	0	0	0	3	0	0	0	0	7	0	0	.118	.250
Palmeiro, Preston	L-R	5-11	180	1-22-95	.243	.283	.229	109	399	53	97	18	2	14	48	32	1	0	2	94	5	3	.404	.300
Pompey, Dalton	B-R	6-2	200	12-11-92	.367	.500	.346	10	30	5	11	3	0	0	2	4	1	0	0	9	1	2	.467	.457
Rengifo, Luis	B-R	5-10	195	2-26-97	.329	.385	.315	53	207	46	68	16	4	8	32	17	3	0	1	32	13	5	.560	.386
Rojas, Jose	L-R	6-0	200	2-24-93	.259	.230	.271	55	216	32	56	11	1	8	34	23	0	0	2	38	4	1	.431	.328
Schebler, Scott	L-R	6-1	228	10-6-90	.216	.218	.215	69	255	31	55	14	0	11	40	17	12	0	1	86	3	1	.400	.295

Player	B-T	HT	WT	DOB	AVG	vLH	vRH	G	AB	R	H	2B	3B	HR	RBI	BB	HBP	SH	SF	SO	SB	CS	SLG	OBP
Stassi, Max	R-R	5-10	200	3-15-91	.308	.000	.333	4	13	1	4	2	0	0	2	2	0	0		5	0	0	.462	.400
Stefanic, Michael	R-R	5-10	180	2-24-96	.334	.303	.343	104	404	67	135	21	0	16	54	45	7	0	2	62	6	3	.505	.408
Thaiss, Matt	L-R	6-0	215	5-6-95	.280	.265	.285	101	379	71	106	23	4	17	69	60	6	0	4	92	2	1	.496	.383
Torres, Franklin	R-R	6-0	175	10-27-96	.220	.000	.250	13	41	3	9	2	0	0	5	1	0	0		11	0	0	.268	.238
Upton, Justin	R-R	6-1	215	8-25-87	.143	--	.143	2	7	1	1	0	0	1	1	0	0	0		4	0	0	.571	.250
Walding, Mitch	L-R	6-3	190	9-10-92	.238	.333	.218	33	122	20	29	8	0	6	25	15	1	0	0	65	1	1	.451	.326
Wallach, Chad	R-R	6-2	246	11-4-91	.223	.233	.220	39	148	30	33	7	0	8	22	20	2	0	1	45	0	0	.432	.322
2-team total (1 Oklahoma City)					.219	.219	.218	40	151	31	33	7	0	8	22	21	2	0	1	46	0	0	.424	.320
Ward, Taylor	R-R	6-1	200	12-14-93	.429	.364	.447	13	49	15	21	9	0	4	10	9	1	0	0	12	2	0	.857	.525
Wenson, Harrison	R-R	6-3	235	4-21-95	.286	1.000	.167	4	14	2	4	0	0	1	3	1	0	1	1	6	1	0	.500	.313
Wong, Kean	L-R	5-9	189	4-17-95	.339	.317	.345	46	189	31	64	10	2	4	22	14	0	0	0	32	10	3	.476	.384

Pitching	B-T	HT	WT	DOB	W	L	ERA	G	GS	CG	SV	IP	H	R	ER	HR	BB	SO	AVG	vLH	vRH	K/9	BB/9
Ahearn, Taylor	R-R	6-1	190	11-25-94	0	2	10.29	2	2	0	0	7	14	9	8	1	5	7	.400	.318	.538	9.00	6.43
Barria, Jaime	R-R	6-1	210	7-18-96	3	2	4.41	10	10	1	0	49	54	30	24	10	8	34	.270	.286	.253	6.24	1.47
Biegalski, Boomer	R-R	6-2	177	7-13-94	0	1	12.00	1	0	0	0	3	5	4	4	1	3	1	.357	.143	.571	3.00	9.00
Buchanan, Jake	R-R	6-0	232	9-24-89	3	4	7.12	16	6	0	0	43	62	36	34	8	14	39	.333	.333	.333	8.16	2.93
Canning, Griffin	R-R	6-2	180	5-11-96	0	0	27.00	1	1	0	0	2	3	6	6	1	5	4	.333	.500	.000	18.00	22.50
Criswell, Cooper	R-R	6-6	200	7-24-96	3	5	6.51	9	9	0	0	47	57	35	34	8	12	43	.302	.371	.214	8.23	2.30
Daniel, Davis	R-R	6-1	190	6-11-97	0	2	10.29	5	4	0	0	21	37	25	24	7	6	24	.381	.408	.354	10.29	2.57
Danish, Tyler	R-R	6-0	200	9-12-94	4	3	4.33	29	3	0	0	60	68	34	29	9	15	67	.281	.359	.208	9.99	2.24
Dashwood, Jack	L-L	6-6	240	11-17-97	1	2	8.03	6	5	0	1	25	43	25	22	7	6	21	.381	.410	.365	7.66	2.19
Detmers, Reid	L-L	6-2	210	7-8-99	1	0	1.13	2	2	0	0	8	7	1	1	0	1	11	.233	.182	.263	12.38	1.13
Diaz, Jhonathan	L-L	6-0	170	9-13-96	0	3	4.11	3	3	0	0	15	15	7	7	0	8	14	.250	.273	.237	8.22	4.70
Faria, Jake	R-R	6-4	230	7-30-93	3	2	5.65	7	7	0	0	37	41	23	23	7	15	46	.281	.290	.273	11.29	3.68
Herget, Jimmy	R-R	6-3	170	9-9-93	0	1	13.50	4	0	0	0	5	7	7	7	1	3	5	.350	.308	.429	9.64	5.79
2-team total (27 Round Rock)					2	3	3.83	31	0	0	3	42	35	21	18	6	15	53	.215	.202	.228	11.27	3.19
Higgins, Connor	R-L	6-5	240	7-21-96	0	1	12.00	8	0	0	0	6	6	8	8	1	14	5	.273	.100	.417	7.50	21.00
Hoyt, James	R-R	6-6	230	9-30-86	1	2	9.42	33	0	0	3	35	51	41	37	10	20	36	.336	.397	.278	9.17	5.09
Johnson, Brian	L-L	6-3	250	12-7-90	3	4	5.72	14	10	0	0	61	62	41	39	8	23	47	.261	.168	.328	6.90	3.38
Marte, Jose	R-R	6-3	180	6-14-96	1	2	8.59	7	0	0	0	7	10	9	7	0	5	7	.323	.385	.278	8.59	6.14
Naughton, Packy	R-L	6-2	195	4-16-96	2	2	4.76	13	9	0	0	57	69	30	30	7	13	53	.299	.278	.312	8.42	2.06
Ortega, Oliver	R-R	6-0	165	10-2-96	0	0	3.75	9	0	0	0	12	11	6	5	2	5	15	.224	.160	.304	11.25	3.75
Pannone, Thomas	L-L	6-1	205	4-28-94	5	11	7.07	24	21	0	0	118	160	103	93	24	40	82	.322	.337	.314	6.24	3.04
Peguero, Elvis	R-R	6-5	208	3-20-97	0	0	6.75	6	0	0	0	8	9	6	6	0	2	7	.281	.400	.176	7.88	2.25
Pena, Felix	R-R	6-2	220	2-25-90	5	4	8.03	31	7	0	0	68	82	64	61	14	27	59	.293	.295	.287	7.77	3.56
Peters, Dillon	L-L	5-11	190	8-31-92	2	2	4.35	8	8	0	0	41	47	21	20	12	13	48	.285	.313	.274	10.45	2.83
Peterson, Tim	R-R	6-1	215	2-22-91	3	1	4.63	43	0	0	9	47	47	27	24	8	16	47	.257	.272	.242	9.06	3.09
Petricka, Jake	R-R	6-4	218	6-5-88	6	2	4.25	23	0	0	1	36	41	17	17	5	12	34	.287	.234	.329	8.50	3.00
Quijada, Jose	L-L	5-11	215	11-9-95	3	1	1.53	22	0	0	1	29	17	8	5	2	11	37	.163	.200	.145	11.35	3.38
Ramirez, Noe	R-R	6-3	205	12-22-89	0	0	0.00	1	0	0	0	1	0	0	0	0	0	2	.000	.000	.000	13.50	0.00
2-team total (8 Reno)					2	0	6.97	9	0	0	0	10	8	8	3	5	14		.216	.273	.133	12.19	4.35
Ramos, AJ	R-R	5-10	200	9-20-86	0	2	5.26	42	0	0	2	53	55	35	31	9	26	76	.257	.240	.272	12.91	4.42
Reed, Jake	R-R	6-2	195	9-29-92	0	0	8.44	8	0	0	1	11	13	10	10	1	6	17	.302	.455	.143	14.34	5.06
2-team total (9 Oklahoma City)					0	0	5.57	17	0	0	1	21	25	13	13	2	7	28	.301	.452	.212	12.00	3.00
Rodriguez, Chris	R-R	6-2	185	7-20-98	0	1	5.87	3	2	0	0	8	7	5	5	1	6	5	.250	.462	.067	5.87	7.04
Rogalla, Keith	R-R	6-3	205	9-15-95	0	0	0.00	2	0	0	0	2	0	0	0	0	0	0	.000	.000	.000	0.00	0.00
Rowen, Ben	R-R	6-4	200	11-15-88	1	2	6.82	21	0	0	0	30	34	24	23	3	8	18	.293	.352	.242	5.34	2.37
Ryan, Zac	R-R	6-1	201	5-28-94	1	3	6.97	23	0	0	1	31	37	31	24	6	23	39	.291	.254	.328	11.32	6.68
Slegers, Aaron	R-R	6-10	260	9-4-92	0	1	6.43	16	5	0	0	28	43	25	20	9	10	12	.347	.355	.339	3.86	3.21
Smith, Ryan	L-L	5-11	185	8-13-97	0	1	8.46	5	5	0	0	22	28	24	21	6	11	21	.292	.289	.293	8.46	4.43
Suarez, Jose	L-L	5-10	225	1-3-98	0	0	1.50	2	2	0	0	6	4	1	1	0	1	4	.308	.333	.294	6.00	1.50
Tyler, Kyle	R-R	6-0	185	12-27-96	1	2	5.14	5	2	0	0	14	20	8	8	1	3	19	.333	.314	.360	12.21	1.93
Wantz, Andrew	R-R	6-4	235	10-13-95	1	0	1.78	12	5	0	0	30	22	9	6	2	6	30	.200	.275	.136	8.90	1.78
Warren, Austin	R-R	6-0	170	2-5-96	2	3	6.19	22	1	0	1	36	42	26	25	5	18	45	.292	.304	.280	11.15	4.46

Fielding

Catcher	PCT	G	PO	A	E	DP	PB
Arcia	.979	6	43	4	1	0	1
Bemboom	.989	20	176	6	2	1	4
Butera	.995	26	201	8	1	0	1
Mulrine	1.000	4	43	3	0	1	0
Stassi	1.000	2	12	1	0	0	0
Thaiss	.986	54	457	23	7	0	5
Torres	1.000	2	9	0	0	0	0
Wallach	.993	15	128	9	1	1	3
Wenson	1.000	4	44	0	0	0	1

First Base	PCT	G	PO	A	E	DP
Arcia	.875	3	14	0	2	1
Bemboom	.933	2	12	2	1	0
Butera	.981	20	145	13	3	12
Gatewood	.971	4	32	2	1	3
Jay	1.000	3	11	0	0	4
Matthews	.987	16	139	10	2	15
Palmeiro	.998	61	428	26	1	42
Rojas	.968	7	58	3	2	9
Stefanic	1.000	2	14	4	0	2
Thaiss	.985	17	126	7	2	18
Torres	1.000	2	10	0	0	0
Wallach	1.000	1	8	0	0	1

Second Base	PCT	G	PO	A	E	DP
Cecchini	1.000	6	3	12	0	1
Mayfield	1.000	1	2	4	0	3
Palmeiro	.917	9	15	18	3	5
Rengifo	.981	15	24	38	1	7
Rojas	.909	5	9	11	2	3
Stefanic	.973	72	112	173	8	46
Torres	1.000	1	2	2	0	1
Wong	.975	25	55	60	3	21

Third Base	PCT	G	PO	A	E	DP
Cecchini	1.000	7	4	6	0	1
Davis	1.000	3	1	3	0	0
Gatewood	.946	35	19	68	5	10
Palmeiro	1.000	4	2	5	0	1
Rojas	.953	26	15	46	3	4
Stefanic	.982	20	15	39	1	7
Thaiss	.333	3	1	0	2	0
Walding	.892	25	16	50	8	4
Wong	.962	12	6	19	1	1

Shortstop	PCT	G	PO	A	E	DP
Arocho	1.000	1	1	1	0	0
Cecchini	.967	31	25	63	3	11
Davis	.978	20	30	57	2	17
Gatewood	.951	27	28	69	5	16
Mayfield	.981	14	15	38	1	8
Rengifo	.946	37	47	93	8	22
Stefanic	1.000	5	5	14	0	3

Outfield	PCT	G	PO	A	E	DP
Adell	.979	70	135	5	3	1
Aviles Jr.	1.000	1	1	0	0	0
Bemboom	1.000	1	2	0	0	0
Cecchini	1.000	3	4	0	0	0
Davis	1.000	8	16	0	0	0
Gatewood	.984	57	123	0	2	0
Griffin	1.000	2	1	0	0	0
Hunter Jr.	1.000	2	4	0	0	0
Jay	1.000	15	35	0	0	0
Lund	.976	72	119	2	3	0
Marsh	.967	14	27	2	1	0
Palmeiro	.984	36	56	4	1	1
Pompey	1.000	10	13	0	0	0
Rojas	.962	13	25	0	1	0
Schebler	.962	63	125	0	5	0
Stefanic	.667	4	2	0	1	0
Torres	1.000	5	12	0	0	0
Upton	.833	2	5	0	1	0
Ward	.958	13	23	0	1	0
Wong	1.000	10	14	1	0	0

ROCKET CITY TRASH PANDAS

DOUBLE-A

DOUBLE-A SOUTH

Batting	B-T	HT	WT	DOB	AVG	vLH	vRH	G	AB	R	H	2B	3B	HR	RBI	BB	HBP	SH	SF	SO	SB	CS	SLG	OBP
Aviles Jr., Luis	R-R	6-1	170	3-16-95	.236	.232	.237	66	267	45	63	15	1	15	46	18	3	0	5	73	12	2	.468	.287
Cabbiness, Cade	L-R	6-4	232	2-16-98	.154	.500	.091	4	13	1	2	0	0	0	2	1	0	0	9	1	0	.154	.313
Cecchini, Gavin	R-R	6-2	200	12-22-93	.228	.240	.222	42	167	16	38	3	0	5	19	9	0	3	33	3	1	.335	.263
Cruz, Michael	L-R	5-11	210	1-13-96	.218	.233	.215	64	179	27	39	5	0	9	29	20	11	0	1	60	0	0	.397	.332
Davis, Brendon	R-R	6-4	185	7-28-97	.268	.125	.292	30	112	25	30	4	1	8	18	18	0	0	1	34	4	0	.536	.366
Didder, Ray-Patrick	R-R	6-0	170	10-1-94	.240	.181	.264	96	329	53	79	21	5	5	39	37	9	0	3	84	16	8	.380	.331
Greene, Elijah	L-L	5-11	165	11-25-97	.000	--	.000	4	6	1	0	0	0	0	0	0	0	0	0	3	0	0	.000	.143
Griffin, Spencer	R-R	6-1	170	10-24-96	.071	.000	.091	6	14	2	1	0	0	1	2	3	0	0	0	10	0	0	.286	.235
Guzman, Jose	B-R	5-11	162	9-15-00	.167	.000	.200	10	12	4	2	1	0	0	2	1	0	0	4	1	0	.250	.333
Herrera, Carlos	L-R	6-0	145	9-23-96	.200	.143	.208	17	55	4	11	2	0	2	3	3	2	0	0	11	4	0	.345	.267
Hunter Jr., Torii	R-R	6-2	180	6-7-95	.239	.205	.250	91	293	37	70	14	1	7	24	31	3	2	1	109	12	5	.365	.317
Isabel, Ibandel	R-R	6-4	225	6-20-95	.196	.215	.188	62	219	28	43	7	1	13	28	24	4	0	0	96	0	0	.416	.287
Jones, Matt	R-R	6-0	195	4-14-92	.169	.105	.200	18	59	7	10	3	0	4	9	4	0	0	1	21	0	0	.424	.219
MacKinnon, David	R-R	6-2	200	12-15-94	.285	.313	.277	99	365	53	104	30	0	13	65	52	6	0	3	83	2	2	.474	.380
Martinez, Orlando	L-L	6-0	185	2-17-98	.258	.242	.262	102	400	58	103	23	2	16	54	30	3	0	2	119	5	3	.445	.313
Matthews, Carson	R-R	5-10	180	1-27-00	.273	.000	.300	3	11	0	3	0	0	0	0	0	0	0	0	2	0	1	.273	.273
Molfetta, Christian	R-R	5-10	190	10-17-96	.161	.143	.167	13	31	0	5	1	1	0	3	5	1	0	0	14	0	1	.258	.297
Mulrine, Anthony	R-R	6-1	205	3-30-98	.217	.167	.234	55	166	16	36	7	0	4	17	16	11	0	1	42	0	1	.331	.325
Nay, Mitch	R-R	6-3	200	9-20-93	.237	.231	.239	106	367	61	87	20	0	23	54	59	3	0	1	113	1	1	.480	.347
Pompey, Dalton	B-R	6-2	200	12-11-92	.247	.240	.250	27	97	20	24	2	1	5	10	11	1	0	0	20	1	0	.443	.330
Soto, Livan	L-R	6-0	160	6-20-00	.225	.111	.258	12	40	3	9	1	0	0	4	3	1	0	0	11	0	0	.250	.295
Stefanic, Michael	R-R	5-10	180	2-24-96	.345	.370	.333	21	87	11	30	5	0	1	9	7	2	0	0	15	0	2	.437	.406
Wilson, Izzy	L-R	6-3	185	3-6-98	.247	.250	.246	83	296	51	73	8	0	21	53	36	1	0	2	102	25	7	.486	.328

Pitching	B-T	HT	WT	DOB	W	L	ERA	G	GS	CG	SV	IP	H	R	ER	HR	BB	SO	AVG	vLH	vRH	K/9	BB/9
Almeida, Adrian	L-L	6-0	160	2-25-95	3	0	4.70	24	0	0	0	31	20	17	16	2	34	41	.187	.200	.181	12.03	9.98
Bates, Nathan	R-R	6-6	205	3-1-94	4	0	3.83	28	0	0	1	42	34	20	18	7	19	39	.224	.279	.187	8.29	4.04
Biegalski, Boomer	R-R	6-2	177	7-13-94	3	5	4.38	16	3	0	0	49	46	26	24	11	15	59	.243	.211	.265	10.76	2.74
Brady, Denny	R-R	6-1	200	1-18-97	0	1	7.04	5	5	0	0	15	22	14	12	2	9	23	.333	.385	.300	13.50	5.28
Clark, Ryan	R-R	6-5	220	12-9-93	0	1	8.85	12	0	0	0	20	31	21	20	4	10	17	.340	.331	.333	7.52	4.43
Criswell, Cooper	R-R	6-6	200	7-24-96	6	4	3.71	12	12	1	0	70	68	33	29	9	8	85	.245	.237	.252	10.88	1.02
Daniel, Davis	R-R	6-1	190	6-11-97	1	3	2.68	9	9	0	0	47	39	15	14	4	8	66	.222	.176	.255	12.64	1.53
Danish, Tyler	R-R	6-0	200	9-12-94	1	0	0.90	3	0	0	1	10	4	1	1	0	1	12	.118	.091	.130	10.80	0.90
Detmers, Reid	L-L	6-2	210	7-8-99	2	4	3.50	12	12	0	0	54	45	24	21	10	18	97	.223	.227	.222	16.17	3.00
Diaz, Jhonathan	L-L	6-0	170	9-13-96	5	3	3.98	13	9	1	0	61	50	27	27	5	12	78	.223	.167	.244	11.51	1.77
Dietz, Matthias	R-R	6-5	220	9-20-95	1	1	4.20	9	0	0	0	15	13	8	7	2	7	15	.236	.150	.286	9.00	4.20
Harding, Houston	L-L	6-1	230	5-28-98	0	0	5.40	2	0	0	0	5	7	3	3	1	0	3	.318	.429	.267	5.40	0.00
Hernandez, Aaron	R-R	6-1	170	12-2-96	3	4	7.11	11	10	1	0	44	52	44	35	7	31	58	.278	.250	.301	11.77	6.29
Herrin, Travis	R-R	6-2	220	4-29-95	0	0	6.75	1	1	0	0	4	7	4	3	1	3	3	.368	.375	.364	6.75	6.75
Higgins, Connor	R-L	6-5	240	7-21-96	1	2	3.55	30	0	0	8	38	41	17	15	3	19	43	.283	.265	.292	10.18	4.50
Ingram, Kolton	L-L	5-9	170	10-21-96	0	0	1.26	12	0	0	4	14	9	2	2	0	6	17	.184	.188	.182	10.67	3.77
Junk, Janson	R-R	6-1	177	1-15-96	2	2	5.27	5	5	0	0	27	32	21	16	5	7	29	.281	.205	.329	9.55	2.30
Kerry, Brett	R-R	6-0	213	4-12-97	0	0	0.00	1	1	0	0	5	2	0	0	1	2	5	.133	.000	.182	3.60	1.80
Lee, Jake	R-R	6-4	215	6-30-95	1	3	5.31	5	5	0	0	20	23	17	12	2	8	23	.288	.161	.360	10.18	3.54
Leftwich, Luke	R-R	6-3	205	6-9-94	1	1	5.96	17	0	0	0	23	23	15	15	0	16	32	.264	.172	.310	12.71	6.35
Linginfelter, Zach	L-R	6-5	220	4-10-97	0	1	2.70	6	0	0	0	7	3	2	2	1	6	6	.136	.000	.214	8.10	8.10
Lovegrove, Kieran	R-R	6-4	200	7-28-94	2	1	7.20	25	0	0	0	40	39	32	32	10	41	49	.253	.259	.250	11.03	9.23
Marte, Jose	R-R	6-3	180	6-14-96	0	0	0.00	3	0	0	0	3	1	0	0	0	2	5	.100	.333	.000	15.00	6.00
Molina, Cristopher	R-R	6-3	170	6-10-97	6	1	3.51	8	6	0	0	41	28	17	16	4	14	40	.193	.209	.179	8.78	3.07
Molnar, Kyle	R-R	6-3	211	11-14-96	0	2	13.21	11	0	0	1	16	30	27	23	3	11	16	.400	.375	.419	9.19	6.32
Naughton, Packy	R-L	6-2	195	4-16-96	0	0	6.75	1	1	0	0	4	7	7	3	2	1	2	.333	.000	.389	4.50	2.25
Ortega, Oliver	R-R	6-0	165	10-2-96	2	3	6.16	25	0	0	5	31	33	28	21	3	13	46	.266	.233	.284	13.50	3.82
Peguero, Elvis	R-R	6-3	205	9-22-96	1	1	8.44	4	0	0	0	5	7	5	5	2	1	8	.304	.500	.200	13.50	1.69
Pina, Robinson	R-R	6-4	180	11-26-98	0	3	9.39	4	4	0	0	15	19	16	16	7	9	22	.297	.261	.317	12.91	5.28
Rodriguez, Chris	R-R	6-2	185	7-20-98	0	0	4.26	5	5	0	0	13	15	9	6	1	5	17	.283	.227	.323	12.08	3.55
Rodriguez, Hansel	R-R	6-2	170	2-27-97	0	0	7.71	1	0	0	0	2	2	3	2	0	2	1	.222	.000	.400	3.86	7.71
Rogalla, Keith	R-R	6-3	205	9-15-95	2	3	3.83	29	0	0	3	42	44	19	18	2	14	44	.270	.344	.225	9.35	2.97
Silseth, Chase	R-R	6-0	217	5-18-00	0	2	13.50	2	2	0	0	3	6	6	5	1	0	3	.353	.286	.400	8.10	0.00
Smith, Ryan	L-L	5-11	185	8-13-97	2	2	4.28	6	6	0	0	34	42	18	16	5	8	36	.307	.241	.324	9.62	2.14
Swanda, John	R-R	6-1	185	3-18-99	0	1	10.57	2	2	0	0	8	12	9	9	1	2	2	.375	.385	.368	2.35	2.35
Tyler, Kyle	R-R	6-0	185	12-27-96	5	2	3.38	15	12	1	1	72	64	31	27	8	22	73	.233	.240	.227	9.13	2.5

Fielding

Catcher	PCT	G	PO	A	E	DP	PB
Cruz	.985	50	425	35	7	1	5
Jones	.993	14	133	9	1	1	2
Molfetta	1.000	2	6	0	0	0	0
Mulrine	.997	55	546	38	2	4	9

First Base	PCT	G	PO	A	E	DP
Isabel	.986	9	62	6	1	5
Jones	1.000	1	1	0	0	0
MacKinnon	.995	86	602	35	3	39
Nay	.990	18	91	9	1	10

Second Base	PCT	G	PO	A	E	DP
Aviles Jr.	.986	22	29	42	1	9
Cecchini	.968	19	24	37	2	5
Davis	1.000	9	7	24	0	4
Didder	.989	27	33	54	1	9
Guzman	1.000	1	1	2	0	1
Herrera	.960	12	18	30	2	5

	PCT	G	PO	A	E	DP
MacKinnon	.889	1	3	5	1	0
Matthews	.933	3	7	7	1	3
Soto	.857	2	4	2	1	1
Stefanic	.985	15	23	41	1	9

Third Base	PCT	G	PO	A	E	DP
Aviles Jr.	.946	15	13	22	2	4
Cecchini	.000	1	0	0	1	0
Davis	.895	9	5	12	2	0
Didder	.500	1	0	1	1	0
Guzman	1.000	3	0	1	0	0
Nay	.923	80	56	100	13	9
Stefanic	1.000	4	4	4	0	1

Shortstop	PCT	G	PO	A	E	DP
Aviles Jr.	.912	16	13	39	5	4
Cecchini	.971	22	26	41	2	5
Davis	1.000	7	2	16	0	4
Didder	.925	49	53	96	12	17

Outfield	PCT	G	PO	A	E	DP
Guzman	1.000	2	4	3	0	1
Herrera	.800	3	2	6	2	2
Soto	1.000	10	7	29	0	5
Stefanic	1.000	1	2	2	0	0

Outfield	PCT	G	PO	A	E	DP
Aviles Jr.	1.000	11	21	0	0	0
Cabbiness	.875	4	7	0	1	0
Cruz	1.000	1	0	1	0	0
Davis	1.000	3	5	1	0	0
Didder	1.000	19	40	0	0	0
Greene	1.000	2	2	0	0	0
Griffin	.889	5	8	0	1	0
Hunter Jr.	.972	91	138	2	4	1
Martinez	.970	100	157	5	5	0
Pompey	1.000	22	39	2	0	0
Stefanic	1.000	1	1	0	0	0
Wilson	.939	80	134	4	9	0

TRI-CITY DUST DEVILS

HIGH CLASS A

HIGH-A WEST

Batting	B-T	HT	WT	DOB	AVG	vLH	vRH	G	AB	R	H	2B	3B	HR	RBI	BB	HBP	SH	SF	SO	SB	CS	SLG	OBP
Adams, Jordyn	R-R	6-2	180	10-18-99	.217	.167	.227	71	277	37	60	7	2	5	27	28	1	0	1	116	18	4	.310	.290
Arocho, Jeremy	B-R	5-10	165	10-6-98	.351	.000	.382	19	74	10	26	1	0	0	9	11	0	0	0	19	8	1	.365	.435
Davis, Brendon	R-R	6-4	185	7-28-97	.280	.300	.276	63	254	41	71	17	3	14	40	19	5	0	4	75	9	3	.535	.337
De La Cruz, Julio	R-R	5-11	182	8-3-00	.068	.000	.075	15	44	4	3	1	0	0	1	5	0	0	1	28	1	0	.091	.160
Del Valle, Francisco	L-L	6-1	187	8-18-98	.217	.173	.225	94	327	41	71	15	1	11	46	45	7	0	4	102	3	2	.370	.321
Diaz, Pedro	R-R	6-3	210	1-9-99	.129	.250	.111	11	31	3	4	0	0	0	1	0	0	0	0	23	0	0	.129	.129
Greene, Ty	L-R	6-0	185	5-4-97	.194	.000	.226	15	36	6	7	0	0	0	1	6	0	1	0	13	0	0	.194	.310
Griffin, Spencer	R-R	6-1	170	10-24-96	.211	.125	.229	42	133	14	28	3	3	2	14	7	2	0	0	64	8	0	.323	.261
Herrera, Carlos	R-R	6-0	145	9-23-96	.273	.119	.300	70	275	33	75	23	2	5	34	10	3	1	2	71	14	2	.425	.303
Humphreys, Zach	R-R	5-10	195	10-9-97	.226	.273	.200	10	31	2	7	2	0	0	3	1	0	0	1	6	1	0	.290	.314
Kasser, Kyle	L-R	5-10	180	10-12-95	.251	.192	.264	80	279	33	70	15	0	1	24	28	1	3	3	46	6	2	.315	.318
Maitan, Kevin	B-R	6-2	190	2-12-00	.207	.071	.224	32	121	9	25	3	0	1	12	6	2	1	0	33	0	0	.256	.254
Martinez, Braxton	R-R	6-3	220	3-3-94	.308	--	.308	7	26	4	8	1	0	3	5	3	0	0	1	10	0	0	.692	.367
Mazur, Griffin	R-R	5-11	180	4-8-97	.296	.333	.292	17	54	8	16	3	0	1	10	9	0	0	2	18	0	0	.407	.385
Morgan, Gareth	R-R	6-4	265	4-12-96	.181	.267	.158	38	144	17	26	4	0	4	15	9	0	0	0	71	3	0	.292	.229
Palmeiro, Preston	L-R	5-11	180	1-22-95	.000	--	.000	1	2	0	0	0	0	0	0	2	0	0	0	1	0	0	.000	.500
Paris, Kyren	R-R	6-0	165	11-11-01	.231	.600	.191	13	52	6	12	2	1	1	6	2	1	0	0	20	4	0	.365	.273
Peabody, Mike	L-R	6-4	200	10-1-98	.000	--	.000	2	5	0	0	0	0	0	0	0	0	0	0	2	0	0	.000	.000
Pina, Keinner	R-R	5-10	175	2-2-97	.197	.231	.192	37	117	14	23	5	0	1	14	10	1	1	3	33	0	0	.265	.260
Reina, Carlos	B-R	6-0	175	12-11-98	.133	--	.133	4	15	1	2	0	0	0	1	0	0	0	0	7	0	0	.133	.188
Rivas, Steven	L-L	6-1	208	6-28-99	.145	.200	.137	27	83	8	12	2	0	3	6	6	1	0	1	32	2	0	.277	.209
Rivera, William	R-R	6-3	184	4-21-00	.059	.000	.077	5	17	0	1	0	0	0	1	0	0	0	1	7	0	0	.059	.056
Rondon, Adrian	R-R	6-1	190	7-7-98	.237	.147	.251	68	249	24	59	11	1	4	38	21	0	0	2	82	0	0	.337	.294
Selma, Quentin	L-R	6-3	205	6-8-98	.143	.000	.167	5	14	0	2	0	0	0	0	3	1	0	0	8	0	0	.143	.333
Soto, Livan	R-R	6-0	160	6-22-00	.217	.217	.217	91	360	49	78	14	8	7	36	39	2	0	5	99	14	5	.358	.293
Torres, Franklin	R-R	6-0	175	10-27-96	.251	.211	.262	54	187	14	47	12	0	3	17	18	1	1	0	54	0	0	.364	.320
Verrier, Jose	R-R	6-1	180	12-2-97	.148	.083	.158	29	88	8	13	6	0	1	4	14	4	1	0	40	0	1	.250	.292
Watson Jr., Kevin	L-R	6-1	190	5-25-99	.267	.333	.250	5	15	0	4	0	1	0	4	0	0	0	0	6	0	1	.400	.421
Wenson, Harrison	R-R	6-0	235	4-21-95	.125	.000	.150	15	48	6	6	2	0	3	6	6	1	0	0	24	4	1	.354	.236
White, Brandon	R-R	5-11	160	8-28-97	.125	.235	.103	45	104	9	13	1	1	0	7	13	2	1	0	37	3	3	.154	.235
Williams-Nelson, Drevian	R-R	5-7	175	1-10-00	.178	.300	.159	26	73	9	13	2	0	1	4	5	3	0	0	31	2	1	.247	.259
Yovan, Kenyon	R-R	6-2	221	12-28-97	.231	.077	.250	33	117	17	27	6	0	5	13	11	4	0	0	58	2	0	.410	.318

Pitching	B-T	HT	WT	DOB	W	L	ERA	G	GS	CG	SV	IP	H	R	ER	HR	BB	SO	AVG	vLH	vRH	K/9	BB/9
Ahearn, Taylor	R-R	6-1	190	11-25-94	0	4	7.16	12	6	0	0	33	51	32	26	5	13	29	.340	.373	.313	7.99	3.58
Albanese Jr., Glenn	R-R	6-6	240	10-22-98	0	1	2.35	6	6	0	0	15	17	5	4	0	4	15	.274	.167	.342	8.80	2.35
Alvarado, Luis	R-R	6-4	210	1-5-97	3	2	5.49	23	2	0	1	39	38	25	24	4	22	45	.253	.262	.247	10.30	5.03
Armstrong, Ivan	R-R	6-5	247	7-27-00	0	1	6.16	10	0	0	1	19	27	14	13	0	8	17	.342	.458	.291	8.05	3.79
Bachman, Sam	R-R	6-1	235	9-30-99	0	2	3.77	5	5	0	0	14	13	7	6	1	4	15	.245	.333	.211	9.42	2.51
Burns, Nathan	R-R	6-1	193	6-1-99	0	0	0.00	1	0	0	1	2	0	0	0	0	1	2	.000	.000	.000	9.00	4.50
Bush, Ky	L-L	6-6	240	11-12-99	0	2	4.50	5	5	0	0	12	14	7	6	0	5	20	.292	.471	.194	15.00	3.75
Chaney, Chase	R-R	6-1	180	12-16-99	0	0	4.50	1	0	0	0	4	6	3	2	1	1	4	.375	.750	.250	9.00	2.25
Costeiu, Ryan	R-R	6-0	200	11-28-00	0	0	0.00	2	0	0	0	3	1	0	0	0	0	6	.111	.000	.200	18.00	0.00
Daniel, Davis	R-R	6-1	190	6-11-97	3	2	2.31	9	9	0	0	47	26	12	12	4	20	64	.163	.208	.125	12.34	3.86
Dashwood, Jack	L-L	6-6	240	11-17-97	3	1	5.01	5	1	0	0	20	33	15	16	13	3	6	18	.350	.406	.324	6.94	2.31
Dietz, Matthias	R-R	6-5	220	9-20-95	1	1	1.08	4	0	0	0	8	5	2	1	0	3	13	.179	.071	.286	14.04	3.24
Donovan, Dakota	R-R	6-6	230	7-25-97	1	1	4.02	12	0	0	2	16	18	10	7	1	6	21	.273	.190	.311	12.06	3.45
Duensing, Cole	L-R	6-4	175	5-16-99	0	0	6.30	17	0	0	0	30	29	23	21	3	18	30	.246	.212	.273	9.90	5.40
Dufault, Brandon	R-R	6-5	195	10-19-98	0	1	13.50	2	0	0	0	2	3	3	3	1	1	4	.333	.000	.375	18.00	4.50
Erla, Mason	R-R	6-4	200	8-19-97	0	1	3.86	1	1	0	0	2	2	1	1	0	0	2	.200	.333	.143	7.71	0.00
Hernandez, Aaron	R-R	6-1	170	12-2-96	1	2	1.93	5	5	0	0	19	11	4	4	0	13	20	.175	.269	.108	9.64	6.27

Pitching	B-T	HT	WT	DOB	W	L	ERA	G	GS	CG	SV	IP	H	R	ER	HR	BB	SO	AVG	vLH	vRH	SO/9	BB/9
Ingram, Kolton	L-L	5-9	170	10-21-96	1	0	5.23	16	0	0	2	21	15	12	12	2	13	31	.205	.167	.218	13.50	5.66
Julio, Erick	R-R	6-1	175	9-22-96	0	4	6.10	27	1	0	1	41	45	35	28	2	33	46	.274	.282	.269	10.02	7.19
Kasser, Kyle	L-R	5-10	180	10-12-95	0	0	0.00	1	0	0	0	1	0	0	0	0	0	2	.000	.000	.000	18.00	0.00
Killam, Brent	L-L	5-11	180	3-26-98	0	2	4.24	5	5	0	0	17	11	8	8	2	11	21	.200	.211	.194	11.12	5.82
King, Dylan	R-R	6-3	190	12-5-96	2	4	7.55	12	5	0	1	39	43	36	33	10	14	64	.265	.276	.256	14.64	3.20
Kristofak, Zac	R-R	5-9	185	12-8-97	1	2	6.14	38	0	0	3	44	53	33	30	3	20	46	.301	.292	.308	9.41	4.09
Linginfelter, Zach	L-R	6-5	220	4-10-97	2	6	4.26	21	13	0	1	63	59	40	30	8	41	73	.239	.250	.232	10.37	5.83
McMillan, Matthew	L-R	6-5	220	11-24-99	0	0	1.50	1	1	0	0	6	4	1	1	0	0	5	.200	.167	.214	7.50	0.00
Molina, Cristopher	R-R	6-3	170	6-10-97	4	2	3.27	19	2	0	2	52	50	25	19	2	20	59	.253	.301	.210	10.15	3.44
Molnar, Kyle	R-R	6-3	211	11-14-96	2	1	3.28	14	0	0	1	25	27	13	9	0	10	27	.278	.268	.286	9.85	3.65
Murphy, Luke	R-R	6-5	190	11-5-99	0	1	3.00	7	0	0	2	9	7	3	3	0	1	15	.206	.000	.269	15.00	1.00
Pina, Robinson	R-R	6-4	180	11-26-98	2	7	4.40	13	13	0	0	57	38	29	28	4	41	85	.191	.242	.165	13.34	6.44
Ramirez, Luis	R-R	5-11	175	9-14-97	4	1	6.92	29	0	0	1	39	43	31	30	10	21	39	.283	.284	.282	9.00	4.85
Seminaris, Adam	R-L	6-0	185	10-19-98	2	0	2.84	4	4	0	0	19	15	6	6	0	7	18	.217	.316	.180	8.53	3.32
Smith, Jake	R-R	6-4	190	10-4-99	1	1	5.56	5	3	0	0	11	15	7	7	4	3	13	.313	.400	.273	10.32	2.38
Smith, Ryan	L-L	5-11	185	8-13-97	3	3	3.74	8	8	0	0	46	32	21	19	7	7	52	.194	.188	.195	10.25	1.38
Smith, Tyler	R-R	6-0	200	10-19-98	1	1	5.45	24	0	0	0	33	32	27	20	5	23	38	.248	.286	.219	10.36	6.27
Sykes, Chad	R-R	5-11	180	2-11-96	2	3	5.24	35	0	0	2	45	33	26	26	7	28	47	.204	.174	.226	9.47	5.64
Torres, Eric	L-L	6-0	195	9-22-99	0	1	5.40	8	0	0	0	8	7	5	5	1	4	13	.219	.500	.125	14.04	4.32
Veliz, Greg	L-R	6-2	200	4-10-97	1	1	5.11	8	0	0	0	12	10	9	7	3	6	18	.213	.200	.222	13.14	4.38
Walsh, Joey	L-L	6-1	224	10-5-97	0	0	4.91	1	0	0	0	4	2	2	2	1	1	6	.154	.500	.091	14.73	2.45
Yan, Hector	L-L	5-11	180	4-26-99	3	7	5.25	20	16	1	0	82	69	57	48	15	58	94	.225	.230	.224	10.28	6.34

Fielding

Catcher	PCT	G	PO	A	E	DP	PB
Greene	.982	12	104	6	2	0	1
Humphreys	1.000	7	65	6	0	0	0
Mazur	.989	17	168	13	2	3	3
Pina	.989	35	340	35	4	1	3
Reina	.974	4	35	2	1	1	2
Torres	.978	30	316	35	8	3	6
Wenson	.992	12	113	19	1	3	3

First Base	PCT	G	PO	A	E	DP
De La Cruz	.958	7	45	1	2	3
Greene	.800	2	4	0	1	1
Kasser	.993	44	264	23	2	23
Maitan	.964	3	26	1	1	1
Martinez	1.000	5	33	1	0	2
Morgan	1.000	1	1	0	0	0
Rondon	.992	18	114	10	1	7
Selma	1.000	4	24	1	0	2
Torres	.970	18	119	12	4	12
Yovan	.977	18	118	11	3	10

Second Base	PCT	G	PO	A	E	DP
Arocho	.952	12	24	36	3	8

	PCT	G	PO	A	E	DP
Davis	.966	8	10	18	1	3
De La Cruz	1.000	2	1	4	0	1
Herrera	.960	45	61	107	7	14
Kasser	.966	12	25	31	2	8
Maitan	.882	4	3	12	2	2
Paris	.900	2	4	5	1	1
Rondon	.978	12	26	19	1	6
Soto	.984	14	30	30	1	9
Williams-Nelson	.667	3	2	4	3	0

Third Base	PCT	G	PO	A	E	DP
Davis	.927	41	43	59	8	8
Herrera	.815	11	4	18	5	1
Kasser	.833	4	5	5	2	0
Maitan	.927	19	10	28	3	5
Rondon	.917	29	17	38	5	8
Yovan	.867	8	3	10	2	2

Shortstop	PCT	G	PO	A	E	DP
Arocho	.833	3	1	14	3	1
Davis	.949	10	15	22	2	5
Herrera	.942	14	10	39	3	6
Paris	.914	9	14	18	3	3

	PCT	G	PO	A	E	DP
Rondon	1.000	6	7	13	0	2
Soto	.945	69	69	136	12	24

Outfield	PCT	G	PO	A	E	DP
Adams	.931	62	106	2	8	0
Arocho	1.000	4	7	0	0	0
Davis	1.000	3	2	0	0	0
Del Valle	.966	83	138	2	5	0
Diaz	.857	4	6	0	1	0
Greene	--	1	0	0	0	0
Griffin	.984	39	63	0	1	0
Kasser	.964	19	24	3	1	0
Morgan	.982	30	53	3	1	1
Palmeiro	1.000	1	1	0	0	0
Peabody	1.000	2	5	0	0	0
Rivas	.949	25	33	4	2	2
Rivera	.800	5	4	0	1	0
Verrier	1.000	18	25	1	0	0
Watson Jr.	1.000	5	8	0	0	0
White	1.000	39	62	0	0	0
Williams-Nelson	.897	17	26	0	3	0

INLAND EMPIRE 66ERS
LOW-A WEST
LOW CLASS A

Batting	B-T	HT	WT	DOB	AVG	vLH	vRH	G	AB	R	H	2B	3B	HR	RBI	BB	HBP	SH	SF	SO	SB	CS	SLG	OBP
Arocho, Jeremy	B-R	5-10	165	10-6-98	.294	.333	.284	63	228	49	67	5	3	1	21	42	2	0	1	50	23	3	.355	.407
Bonilla, Jose	R-R	6-0	185	4-2-02	.189	.226	.173	28	106	9	20	3	0	1	9	6	2	0	2	46	1	0	.245	.241
Brown, Spencer	L-R	5-10	185	7-14-99	.163	.154	.166	52	190	20	31	7	3	5	15	9	3	0	0	90	4	0	.311	.213
Cabbiness, Cade	L-R	6-4	232	2-16-98	.186	.154	.190	28	97	13	18	3	2	5	15	12	1	0	1	53	0	0	.412	.279
Campero, Gustavo	B-R	5-6	182	9-20-97	.245	.235	.248	41	139	17	34	4	0	4	16	12	3	2	1	40	8	4	.360	.316
De La Cruz, Julio	R-R	5-11	182	8-3-00	.184	.158	.190	32	103	13	19	1	3	1	13	14	1	1	0	42	6	1	.282	.288
Emmerson, Myles	R-R	5-11	185	5-15-98	.247	.267	.241	23	73	11	18	5	0	1	8	15	3	0	0	23	0	2	.356	.396
Gill, Starlin	R-R	5-10	150	3-16-00	.156	.167	.154	16	64	9	10	2	1	0	6	1	0	0	0	20	0	0	.219	.169
Greene, Elijah	L-L	5-11	165	11-25-97	.277	.208	.300	62	213	36	59	13	4	1	22	44	1	4	1	61	8	5	.390	.402
Greene, Ty	L-R	6-0	185	5-4-97	.429	--	.429	2	7	3	3	1	1	0	1	0	1	0	0	3	0	0	.857	.556
Guzman, Jose	B-R	5-11	162	9-15-00	.260	.292	.251	89	323	63	84	20	4	5	40	37	5	2	2	93	18	7	.393	.343
Jackson, Jeremiah	R-R	6-0	165	3-26-00	.263	.241	.268	45	167	29	44	14	3	8	46	24	1	0	4	65	11	3	.527	.352
Knowles, D'Shawn	B-R	6-0	165	1-16-01	.227	.222	.228	84	361	61	82	21	5	5	48	25	2	4	1	114	31	1	.355	.280
Martinez, Braxton	R-R	6-3		3-3-94	.333	.337	.335	79	282	50	94	27	3	12	59	56	5	0	5	52	1	2	.578	.444
Matthews, Carson	R-R	5-10	180	1-27-00	.253	.143	.272	23	95	15	24	6	0	1	11	8	1	0	0	32	6	2	.347	.317
Matthews, Gabe	L-R	6-2	219	11-24-97	.269	.308	.263	25	93	16	25	6	1	4	19	17	5	0	0	29	2	0	.484	.409
Mora Jr., Darimen	B-R	5-11	160	7-16-02	.000	--	.000	2	8	1	0	0	0	0	0	0	0	0	0	3	0	0	.000	.000
Moreno, Darwin	R-R	6-2	175	1-26-02	.000	.000	.000	1	4	0	0	0	0	0	0	0	0	0	0	4	0	0	.000	.000
Paris, Kyren	R-R	6-0	165	11-11-01	.274	.333	.261	29	106	29	29	5	6	2	18	27	3	0	0	41	16	4	.491	.434
Pina, Keinner	R-R	5-10	175	2-12-97	.215	.231	.209	29	93	9	20	4	0	0	7	13	3	0	2	27	0	0	.258	.324
Quero, Edgar	B-R	5-11	170	4-6-03	.206	.500	.167	10	34	2	7	2	0	1	6	5	1	0	2	16	1	0	.353	.310
Ramirez, Alexander	R-R	6-2	180	8-29-02	.083	.000	.102	19	72	4	6	0	1	0	4	7	2	0	0	34	1	1	.111	.185
Reina, Carlos	B-R	6-0	175	12-11-98	.192	.105	.212	30	104	13	20	4	0	1	7	12	3	0	1	35	0	0	.260	.292

	B-T	HT	WT	DOB	AVG	vLH	vRH	G	AB	R	H	2B	3B	HR	RBI	BB	HBP	SH	SF	SO	SB	CS	SLG	OBP
Reyes, Jose	L-R	6-2	180	9-22-00	.212	.217	.211	90	325	35	69	13	4	6	45	25	2	0	4	117	1	2	.332	.270
Rivera, William	R-R	6-3	184	4-21-00	.286	.400	.250	6	21	6	6	0	0	0	2	5	0	0	0	4	2	0	.286	.423
Scires, Caleb	L-L	6-0	195	9-1-98	.240	.132	.266	52	196	34	47	12	1	7	27	16	7	0	0	80	6	1	.418	.320
Teodosio, Bryce	R-L	6-2	220	6-18-99	.279	.200	.293	17	68	9	19	8	0	1	8	5	0	0	0	28	4	3	.441	.329
Vera, Arol	B-R	6-2	170	9-12-02	.280	.231	.290	19	82	10	23	0	0	0	5	6	2	0	0	20	9	2	.280	.344
Wallace, Paxton	R-R	5-11	215	1-6-99	.280	.143	.294	23	75	9	21	1	1	4	16	14	1	0	0	17	1	1	.480	.400
Watson Jr., Kevin	L-R	6-1	190	5-25-99	.292	.500	.273	6	24	4	7	1	2	1	4	5	0	0	0	9	1	0	.625	.414
Yon, Edwin	R-R	6-5	180	7-24-98	.240	.207	.246	54	200	38	48	8	4	14	44	20	3	0	1	104	0	1	.530	.317

Pitching	B-T	HT	WT	DOB	W	L	ERA	G	GS	CG	SV	IP	H	R	ER	HR	BB	SO	AVG	vLH	vRH	K/9	BB/9
Ahearn, Taylor	R-R	6-1	190	11-25-94	0	1	3.38	3	0	0	0	5	5	2	2	1	3	8	.238	.125	.308	13.50	5.06
Alcantara, Jhosua	R-R	6-6	200	9-30-97	0	0	3.62	20	0	0	0	27	22	12	11	2	15	15	.222	.256	.200	4.94	4.94
Blake, Andrew	R-R	6-5	227	3-24-98	0	0	0.00	1	1	0	0	5	4	1	0	0	0	8	.211	.200	.214	14.40	0.00
Burns, Nathan	R-R	6-1	193	6-1-99	0	0	0.00	6	0	0	0	10	5	0	0	0	4	14	.135	.000	.176	12.19	3.48
Caceres, Kelvin	R-R	6-1	180	1-26-00	0	4	9.16	9	2	0	0	19	18	24	19	0	27	23	.247	.286	.222	11.09	13.02
Campero, Gustavo	B-R	5-6	182	9-20-97	0	0	27.00	1	0	0	0	1	1	3	3	0	3	0	.333	.500	.000	0.00	27.00
Chaney, Chase	R-R	6-1	180	12-16-99	2	1	3.65	10	0	0	0	25	31	12	10	1	7	36	.304	.375	.258	13.14	2.55
Costeiu, Ryan	R-R	6-0	200	11-28-00	1	0	4.30	9	0	0	2	15	14	10	7	3	6	25	.250	.313	.225	15.34	3.68
Courtney, Justin	R-R	6-5	225	7-24-96	3	1	5.63	22	0	0	2	40	49	26	25	6	10	46	.302	.250	.340	10.35	2.25
Crow, Coleman	R-R	6-0	175	12-30-00	4	3	4.19	13	10	0	0	62	68	39	29	7	29	62	.273	.312	.250	8.95	4.19
Dashwood, Jack	L-L	6-6	240	11-17-97	3	1	3.43	15	4	0	3	58	50	24	22	5	8	69	.227	.254	.217	10.77	1.25
Donovan, Dakota	R-R	6-6	230	7-25-97	4	2	1.70	23	0	0	5	42	33	17	8	2	12	53	.210	.254	.174	11.27	2.55
Dufault, Brandon	R-R	6-5	195	10-19-98	0	0	3.52	9	0	0	1	15	12	9	6	2	9	20	.211	.190	.222	11.74	5.28
Goff, Julio	R-R	5-10	200	1-11-00	5	7	3.67	23	10	0	1	96	87	58	39	8	38	87	.239	.245	.235	8.18	3.57
Guzman, Emilker	R-R	5-10	160	2-10-99	3	5	2.26	35	0	0	12	52	43	26	13	3	15	53	.219	.239	.208	9.23	2.61
Ingram, Kolton	L-L	5-9	170	10-21-96	0	1	3.09	8	0	0	4	12	9	5	4	1	6	19	.209	.267	.179	14.66	4.63
Jones, Nick	L-L	6-6	209	1-22-99	0	0	13.50	3	0	0	0	3	5	5	5	1	3	4	.333	.500	.222	10.80	8.10
Kelso, Shane	R-R	6-3	220	8-26-97	0	1	20.25	4	0	0	0	4	8	9	9	1	4	9	.421	.500	.400	20.25	9.00
Kerry, Brett	R-R	6-0	213	4-12-99	0	0	1.93	4	4	0	0	9	6	2	2	0	4	17	.182	.091	.227	16.39	3.86
Killam, Brent	L-L	5-11	180	3-26-98	1	2	2.63	5	5	0	0	24	14	8	7	2	9	41	.171	.273	.133	15.38	3.38
Kochanowicz, Jack	L-R	6-6	220	12-22-00	4	2	6.91	20	18	0	0	83	102	72	64	12	35	73	.297	.292	.300	7.88	3.78
Lawson, Garrett	L-L	6-3	200	7-2-98	2	4	7.99	30	0	0	1	42	47	45	37	3	30	48	.281	.279	.282	10.37	6.48
Martinez, Alex	R-R	5-10	170	9-15-02	0	0	9.00	1	0	0	0	2	2	2	2	0	3	0	.286	.250	.333	0.00	13.50
Mondak, Nick	L-L	6-4	200	6-2-98	2	0	0.00	2	0	0	0	10	5	0	0	0	0	12	.147	.000	.208	10.80	0.00
Olthoff, Braden	R-R	6-4	228	3-12-99	0	1	10.57	2	2	0	0	8	13	9	9	1	2	10	.371	.286	.429	11.74	2.35
Peters, Andrew	R-R	6-2	191	11-25-98	2	4	9.26	10	2	0	0	12	13	14	12	1	9	20	.283	.308	.273	15.43	6.94
Pina, Robinson	R-R	6-4	180	11-26-98	0	1	1.19	4	4	0	0	23	15	3	3	2	6	33	.185	.200	.179	13.10	2.38
Rivera, Erik	L-L	6-2	200	4-2-01	0	0	0.00	1	1	0	0	3	1	0	0	0	1	6	.091	.000	.100	16.20	2.70
Rivera, Jerryell	L-L	6-3	180	4-19-99	1	2	8.03	10	0	0	0	12	20	14	11	2	8	13	.385	.417	.375	9.49	5.84
Salvador, Jose	L-L	6-2	170	9-21-99	6	5	5.91	20	17	0	0	96	100	66	63	10	47	115	.272	.313	.260	10.78	4.41
Seigler, Blake	R-R	6-3	205	2-16-98	0	0	20.25	1	0	0	0	1	1	3	3	0	5	2	.200	1.000	.000	13.50	33.75
Seminaris, Adam	R-L	6-0	185	10-19-98	4	5	5.46	16	14	0	0	64	73	47	39	9	19	94	.275	.264	.278	13.15	2.66
Smith, Ryan	L-L	5-11	185	8-13-97	2	1	1.63	5	4	0	0	28	14	5	5	2	7	44	.147	.094	.175	14.31	2.28
Swanda, John	R-R	6-2	185	3-18-99	7	5	4.14	20	15	0	0	104	104	61	48	13	33	92	.250	.268	.238	7.94	2.85
Van Scoyoc, Connor	R-R	6-6	210	11-26-99	0	2	7.99	7	4	0	0	24	37	21	21	1	14	30	.366	.367	.365	11.41	5.32

Fielding

Catcher	PCT	G	PO	A	E	DP	PB
Campero	.976	30	296	32	8	4	9
Emmerson	.980	23	221	22	5	2	2
Greene	1.000	2	21	2	0	0	0
Pina	.997	29	305	31	1	0	5
Quero	1.000	9	100	9	0	3	2
Reina	.992	26	225	18	2	1	3

First Base	PCT	G	PO	A	E	DP
Arocho	1.000	2	3	0	0	0
Brown	.965	32	235	13	9	18
Gill	1.000	10	62	4	0	2
Martinez	.994	58	453	25	3	38
Matthews	1.000	17	152	9	0	5
Wallace	1.000	2	10	1	0	3

Second Base	PCT	G	PO	A	E	DP
Arocho	.974	24	44	68	3	11
De La Cruz	.924	25	39	46	7	10
Guzman	.977	34	41	86	3	14

	PCT	G	PO	A	E	DP
Jackson	.927	9	18	20	3	7
Matthews	.953	12	28	21	2	5
Mora Jr.	1.000	1	3	3	0	3
Paris	.932	11	21	20	3	5
Vera	1.000	7	15	14	0	2

Third Base	PCT	G	PO	A	E	DP
Arocho	.840	34	23	66	17	1
Bonilla	.845	28	12	37	9	4
De La Cruz	.714	7	1	4	2	0
Gill	.923	6	3	9	1	0
Guzman	.929	7	3	10	1	0
Martinez	.870	11	6	14	3	1
Matthews	.933	10	9	19	2	6
Mora Jr.	.500	1	0	1	1	0
Wallace	.979	19	8	39	1	0

Shortstop	PCT	G	PO	A	E	DP
Arocho	1.000	1	3	5	0	1
Guzman	.951	49	47	126	9	13

	PCT	G	PO	A	E	DP
Jackson	.900	31	42	57	11	9
Knowles	.900	8	12	15	3	2
Matthews	1.000	1	1	1	0	0
Paris	.894	17	24	52	9	12
Vera	.961	12	13	36	2	4

Outfield	PCT	G	PO	A	E	DP
Arocho	1.000	8	14	0	0	0
Cabbiness	.955	26	41	1	2	0
Greene	.970	62	93	5	3	2
Knowles	.960	68	143	2	6	0
Moreno	1.000	1	1	0	0	0
Ramirez	.964	19	26	1	1	1
Reyes	.966	77	105	7	4	1
Rivera	.875	6	7	0	1	0
Scires	.940	45	77	2	5	0
Teodosio	.964	17	27	0	1	0
Watson Jr.	1.000	6	6	0	0	0
Yon	.918	28	43	2	4	0

ACL ANGELS　　ROOKIE

ARIZONA COMPLEX LEAGUE

Batting	B-T	HT	WT	DOB	AVG	vLH	vRH	G	AB	R	H	2B	3B	HR	RBI	BB	HBP	SH	SF	SO	SB	CS	SLG	OBP
Blakely, Werner	L-R	6-3	185	2-21-02	.182	.158	.186	44	148	22	27	6	0	3	19	33	3	0	2	69	15	2	.284	.339
Bonilla, Jose	R-R	6-0	185	4-2-02	.227	.158	.244	30	97	15	22	5	0	2	14	5	3	0	2	26	4	0	.340	.280
Calabrese, David	L-R	5-11	160	9-26-02	.201	.077	.229	42	144	25	29	8	2	1	17	20	1	0	0	54	5	1	.306	.303

Name	B-T	HT	WT	DOB	AVG	vLH	vRH	G	AB	R	H	2B	3B	HR	RBI	BB	HBP	SH	SF	SO	SB	CS	OBP	SLG
De La Cruz, Julio	R-R	5-11	182	8-3-00	.150	.000	.200	9	20	1	3	0	0	0	3	2	0	0	0	10	0	0	.150	.227
Deveaux, Trent	R-R	6-0	160	5-4-00	.299	.313	.294	22	67	11	20	1	2	0	8	7	0	0	2	16	2	0	.373	.355
Diaz, Pedro	R-R	6-3	210	1-9-99	.146	.125	.150	14	48	3	7	3	1	0	5	2	2	0	0	22	0	0	.250	.212
Gill, Starlin	R-R	5-10	150	3-16-00	.250	.250	.250	26	76	18	19	1	0	0	6	12	4	1	0	15	4	3	.263	.380
Holmes, William	R-R	6-2	185	12-22-00	.150	--	.150	7	20	1	3	0	0	0	1	1	0	0	0	11	0	0	.150	.190
Jackson, Jeremiah	R-R	6-0	165	3-26-00	.381	.200	.438	6	21	5	8	1	0	2	4	1	0	0	0	7	2	0	.714	.409
Jimenez, Jorge	R-R	5-9	150	6-9-02	.180	.091	.205	21	50	9	9	1	0	0	4	10	1	1	1	10	4	0	.200	.323
Lovelace, Kyle	R-R	5-10	170	8-3-98	.368	.286	.417	7	19	2	7	1	0	0	3	3	1	0	0	7	1	0	.421	.478
Maitan, Kevin	B-R	6-2	190	2-12-00	.273	.250	.286	5	11	1	3	0	0	0	1	1	0	0	0	3	0	0	.273	.333
Marcano, Marlon	R-R	5-11	211	9-14-99	.000	--	.000	2	3	0	0	0	0	0	1	0	0	0	1	1	0	0	.000	.000
Marsh, Brandon	L-R	6-4	215	12-18-97	.500	.000	.538	4	14	6	7	1	1	1	7	4	0	0	0	3	0	0	.929	.611
Mora Jr., Darimen	B-R	5-11	160	7-16-02	.190	.125	.206	18	42	10	8	0	0	1	7	8	1	0	0	11	4	1	.262	.333
Moreno, Darwin	R-R	6-2	175	1-26-02	.206	.000	.241	25	68	10	14	3	0	0	7	8	4	0	0	34	2	3	.250	.325
Paris, Kyren	R-R	6-0	165	11-11-01	.357	.000	.385	5	14	3	5	0	0	1	1	1	0	0	0	3	2	0	.571	.400
Placencia, Adrian	B-R	5-11	155	6-2-03	.175	.235	.167	43	143	29	25	3	3	5	19	28	4	0	0	49	4	2	.343	.326
Podaras, Straton	R-R	6-1	210	12-9-97	.375	.333	.385	17	48	9	18	5	1	1	13	7	7	0	0	11	1	0	.583	.516
Quero, Edgar	B-R	5-11	170	4-6-03	.253	.143	.263	29	87	21	22	8	1	4	24	23	6	0	0	28	1	1	.506	.440
Ramirez, Alexander	R-R	6-2	180	8-29-02	.276	.200	.286	35	127	30	35	7	4	5	27	22	4	0	1	50	3	3	.512	.396
Reina, Carlos	B-R	6-0	175	12-11-98	.100	--	.100	3	10	0	1	0	0	0	0	0	0	0	0	3	0	0	.100	.100
Rivera, William	R-R	6-3	184	4-21-00	.189	.400	.156	14	37	2	7	0	0	0	3	2	2	0	0	10	1	0	.189	.268
Rodriguez, Gabriel	R-R	6-1	154	9-29-02	.286	.333	.275	21	63	6	18	5	0	1	10	3	2	0	1	15	0	0	.413	.333
Santana, Natanael	R-R	6-1	190	7-27-01	.239	.308	.226	48	163	30	39	8	2	2	14	11	7	0	1	70	13	2	.350	.313
Selma, Quentin	L-R	6-3	205	6-8-98	.275	.250	.278	12	40	8	11	3	0	1	7	6	0	0	0	11	1	0	.425	.370
Teodosio, Bryce	R-L	6-3	220	6-18-99	.240	.500	.217	8	25	5	6	0	1	2	7	8	0	0	0	8	1	0	.560	.424
Vera, Arol	B-R	6-2	170	9-12-02	.317	.176	.336	38	145	24	46	16	3	0	17	12	5	0	2	39	2	2	.469	.384
Walding, Mitch	L-R	6-3	190	9-10-92	.500	--	.500	4	8	3	4	2	1	0	3	0	0	0	0	3	1	0	1.000	.636
Ward, Taylor	R-R	6-1	200	12-14-93	.143	.000	.167	3	7	0	1	0	0	0	1	0	0	0	0	4	0	0	.286	.250
Watson Jr., Kevin	L-R	6-1	190	5-25-99	.348	.100	.417	24	46	12	16	2	1	0	10	20	2	2	0	11	6	0	.435	.543

Pitching	B-T	HT	WT	DOB	W	L	ERA	G	GS	CG	SV	IP	H	R	ER	HR	BB	SO	AVG	vLH	vRH	K/9	BB/9
Albright, Mason	L-L	6-0	190	11-26-02	1	0	0.00	3	2	0	0	8	3	0	0	0	2	8	.107	.000	.125	9.00	2.25
Aleman, Jose	R-R	6-1	165	2-1-03	1	1	6.56	15	1	0	0	23	27	21	17	2	14	22	.287	.324	.263	8.49	5.40
Aquino, Ewdy	R-R	5-9	170	2-24-00	0	1	27.00	1	0	0	0	1	2	2	2	0	2	1	.500	.667	.000	13.50	0.00
Aquino, Stiward	R-R	6-6	170	6-20-99	0	0	5.40	5	0	0	0	5	3	3	3	0	2	10	.167	.143	.182	18.00	3.60
Buchanan, Jake	R-R	6-0	232	9-24-89	0	0	3.00	2	2	0	0	3	2	1	1	0	0	3	.200	.333	.000	9.00	0.00
Burns, Nathan	R-R	6-1	193	6-1-99	1	0	0.00	3	0	0	0	4	1	0	0	0	1	9	.071	.200	.000	20.25	2.25
Caceres, Kelvin	R-R	6-1	180	1-26-00	0	2	4.30	7	6	0	0	29	24	16	14	2	21	42	.218	.255	.190	12.89	6.44
Carlos Lucas, Jean	R-R	6-3	185	12-2-00	2	0	2.91	15	0	0	1	22	20	8	7	1	11	21	.270	.314	.231	8.72	4.57
Chaney, Chase	R-R	6-1	180	12-16-99	1	2	6.39	4	3	0	0	13	23	17	9	4	14	16	.365	.400	.342	9.95	2.84
Charle, Sandi	R-R	6-5	180	9-5-02	1	4	7.94	10	2	0	0	28	34	31	25	4	19	28	.283	.245	.310	8.89	6.04
De La Rosa, Manuel	R-R	6-2	210	4-17-02	0	0	9.00	1	0	0	0	1	0	1	1	0	2	2	.000	.000	.000	18.00	18.00
Diaz, Danifer	R-R	6-0	165	7-26-01	0	0	24.00	1	0	0	0	3	7	9	8	3	5	5	.412	.571	.300	15.00	15.00
Duran, Emmanuel	R-R	6-2	182	10-9-00	3	3	4.75	18	1	0	0	36	29	27	19	1	18	48	.209	.192	.218	12.00	4.50
Erla, Mason	R-R	6-4	200	8-19-97	1	0	0.00	2	1	0	0	5	2	0	0	0	0	9	.125	1.000	.067	16.20	0.00
Garcia, Leonard	L-L	6-2	165	8-11-03	3	0	4.24	12	5	0	0	40	45	28	19	5	18	48	.268	.327	.244	10.71	4.02
Goebel, Harrison	R-R	6-6	245	9-25-96	0	1	--	1	0	0	0	0	2	3	3	1	2	0	1.000	1.000	--	--	--
Grech, Zach	R-R	6-0	182	6-5-98	0	0	4.50	4	0	0	0	4	5	2	2	0	3	2	.333	.200	.400	4.50	6.75
Guanare, Fernando	R-R	6-1	140	6-21-03	0	0	0.00	1	1	0	0	4	1	0	0	0	0	4	.071	.000	.143	9.00	0.00
Harding, Houston	L-L	6-1	230	5-28-98	0	0	3.60	2	0	0	0	5	5	2	2	0	1	5	.250	.333	.214	9.00	1.80
Hernandez, Gabriel	R-R	6-1	160	1-22-02	1	2	4.50	19	0	0	8	22	22	13	11	1	10	24	.244	.219	.259	9.82	4.09
Herrin, Travis	R-R	6-2	220	4-29-95	0	0	0.00	2	1	0	0	2	0	0	0	0	0	3	.000	.000	.000	13.50	0.00
Hidalgo, Alejandro	R-R	6-1	160	5-20-03	3	2	4.67	7	6	0	0	27	26	18	14	6	9	31	.241	.182	.267	10.33	3.00
Holmes, William	R-R	6-2	185	12-22-00	0	0	--	1	0	0	0	0	0	1	1	0	2	0	--	--	--	--	--
Jones, Nick	L-L	6-6	209	1-22-99	1	0	3.27	7	0	0	0	11	10	6	4	0	3	15	.227	.455	.152	12.27	2.45
Killam, Brent	L-L	5-11	180	3-26-98	0	0	0.00	1	1	0	0	1	3	0	0	0	0	2	.600	.000	.750	18.00	0.00
King, Dylan	R-R	6-3	190	11-5-99	0	0	0.00	2	2	0	0	3	0	0	0	0	0	3	.000	.000	.000	9.00	0.00
Marceaux, Landon	R-R	6-0	179	10-8-99	1	0	14.73	2	2	0	0	4	7	6	6	0	0	6	.389	.400	.385	14.73	0.00
Martinez, Alex	R-R	5-10	170	9-15-02	3	1	0.83	16	0	0	0	22	16	4	2	0	10	33	.203	.313	.128	13.71	4.15
McMillan, Matthew	L-R	6-5	220	11-24-99	1	0	1.80	6	4	0	0	15	16	6	3	1	11	21	.283	.333	.222	6.60	0.60
Mondak, Nick	L-L	6-4	200	6-2-98	1	1	3.97	5	3	0	0	11	11	6	5	1	3	14	.268	.222	.281	11.12	2.38
Natera, Jose	R-R	6-1	180	11-30-99	0	0	3.38	6	1	0	0	8	6	5	3	0	2	6	.207	.222	.182	6.75	2.25
Nunan, Daniel	L-L	6-6	215	5-25-00	1	1	4.50	7	1	0	0	14	9	10	7	2	11	21	.184	.167	.194	13.50	7.07
Nunez, Luis	R-R	6-2	175	9-19-01	0	0	2.51	10	0	0	0	14	5	4	4	0	11	16	.104	.167	.083	10.05	6.91
Olthoff, Braden	R-R	6-4	228	3-12-99	0	1	2.00	3	3	0	0	9	7	6	2	0	2	16	.194	.077	.261	16.00	2.00
Reinoso, Dayan	R-R	6-1	210	8-27-98	0	0	0.00	2	0	0	0	2	1	1	0	0	1	2	.143	.000	.200	9.00	4.50
Rosario, Yordi	R-R	6-2	185	1-30-99	0	0	9.00	1	0	0	0	1	2	1	1	0	0	1	.500	.000	.667	9.00	0.00
Rowen, Ben	R-R	6-4	200	11-15-88	0	0	0.00	2	1	0	0	2	0	0	0	0	0	2	.000	.000	.000	7.71	0.00
Sanchez, Edwin	R-R	6-0	160	11-3-00	2	1	2.39	7	3	0	0	26	23	9	7	1	7	22	.237	.209	.259	7.52	2.39
Santa Maria, Tulio	R-R	6-1	170	6-6-00	0	0	0.00	2	0	0	0	1	0	0	0	0	1	0	.000	.000	.000	9.00	9.00
Seigler, Blake	R-R	6-3	205	2-16-98	0	0	0.00	2	0	0	0	3	0	0	0	0	1	4	.000	.000	.000	10.80	2.70
Silseth, Chase	R-R	6-0	217	5-18-00	0	0	4.50	1	0	0	0	2	1	1	0	1	1	4	.143	.000	.250	18.00	4.50
Tapia, Gabriel	R-R	6-1	160	5-20-02	0	1	43.20	7	2	0	0	3	8	18	16	0	9	5	.421	.375	.455	13.50	24.30
Tejada, Cristofer	R-R	6-1	175	6-1-01	0	0	9.00	3	0	0	0	3	3	3	3	1	2	6	.231	.286	.167	18.00	6.00
Van Scoyoc, Connor	R-R	6-6	210	11-26-99	0	1	4.50	5	4	0	0	18	16	10	9	1	10	21	.235	.286	.213	10.50	5.00
Walsh, Joey	L-L	6-1	224	10-5-97	1	0	3.38	7	0	0	2	16	13	7	6	0	4	13	.217	.200	.222	7.31	2.25

Fielding

C: Lovelace 6, Marcano 2, Podaras 6, Quero 22, Reina 3, Rodriguez 19, Watson Jr. 4.
1B: De La Cruz 3, Diaz 12, Gill 20, Jimenez 10, Podaras 7, Selma 8, Walding 1.
2B: Blakely 14, Jimenez 11, Mora Jr. 9, Paris 1, Placencia 27, Vera 6.
3B: Blakely 14, Bonilla 29, De La Cruz 5, Gill 3, Maitan 3, Mora Jr. 7, Selma 5, Walding 2.
SS: Blakely 14, Jackson 5, Paris 3, Placencia 14, Vera 28.
OF: Calabrese 41, Deveaux 19, Diaz 1, Holmes 1, Marsh 3, Moreno 26, Ramirez 29, Rivera 14, Santana 47, Teodosio 8, Ward 3.

DSL ANGELS   ROOKIE
DOMINICAN SUMMER LEAGUE

Batting	B-T	HT	WT	DOB	AVG	vLH	vRH	G	AB	R	H	2B	3B	HR	RBI	BB	HBP	SH	SF	SO	SB	CS	SLG	OBP
Alfonso, Edgar	B-R	5-9	175	3-27-04	.231	.115	.256	49	147	27	34	6	2	1	15	20	1	3	1	39	17	7	.320	.325
Betancourt, Eiver	L-R	5-11	185	10-2-03	.231	.000	.250	11	26	5	6	1	0	0	1	4	2	0	0	8	1	0	.269	.375
Chirinos, Jorge	R-R	6-0	170	5-11-03	.217	.154	.234	22	60	10	13	6	0	1	10	6	4	0	0	28	1	1	.367	.329
Falcon, Isaias	R-R	5-10	165	10-26-00	.252	.154	.276	46	131	27	33	9	0	3	18	15	3	1	0	50	25	5	.389	.342
Garcia, Cristian	B-R	6-1	168	7-26-04	.232	.143	.250	45	125	14	29	10	1	1	21	25	3	0	2	24	8	7	.352	.368
Guzman, Denzer	R-R	6-1	180	2-8-04	.213	.167	.222	44	141	21	30	10	1	3	27	20	1	0	2	24	11	7	.362	.311
Hidalgo, Edwin	R-R	0-0	0	8-12-03	.220	.179	.233	36	118	12	26	10	0	2	19	5	9	0	2	31	2	1	.356	.299
Lopez, Kleiver	R-R	0-0	0	7-14-04	.211	.259	.198	42	123	21	26	6	0	0	6	16	3	1	1	26	9	5	.260	.315
Macias, Johan	B-R	5-9	150	1-6-03	.221	.455	.182	37	77	15	17	3	2	0	9	10	6	6	0	13	5	3	.312	.355
Manon, Junior	L-R	5-10	165	2-6-03	.095	.111	.091	21	42	5	4	2	0	0	5	10	2	1	2	16	1	0	.143	.286
Mota, Juan	L-R	6-2	160	10-23-03	.179	.167	.183	26	78	8	14	3	1	0	4	4	0	0	0	22	2	0	.244	.220
Munroe, Kristin	R-R	6-1	175	8-6-04	.207	.188	.211	32	92	14	19	2	2	0	9	15	4	0	0	44	8	5	.272	.342
Ortega, Jesus	R-R	6-0	170	1-18-01	.260	.200	.275	52	150	32	39	5	1	2	24	11	7	5	1	44	14	5	.347	.337
Perez, Diego	L-R	6-3	170	7-7-03	.184	.167	.192	18	38	6	7	0	0	2	13	7	5	0	0	20	7	1	.342	.380
Ruiz, Jorge	L-L	5-10	164	6-30-04	.270	.318	.263	53	174	32	47	9	2	1	15	22	11	2	3	25	19	6	.362	.381
Scull, Anthony	L-L	6-0	165	1-26-04	.115	.000	.143	10	26	6	3	0	1	0	7	3	2	0	2	11	3	0	.192	.242
Villahermosa, Yeremi	B-R	5-9	150	10-16-02	.158	.077	.182	32	57	16	9	0	1	0	5	19	4	2	0	12	11	2	.193	.400

Pitching	B-T	HT	WT	DOB	W	L	ERA	G	GS	CG	SV	IP	H	R	ER	HR	BB	SO	AVG	vLH	vRH	K/9	BB/9
Cedano, Milleran	L-L	6-0	165	3-23-03	2	4	3.02	16	6	0	0	42	30	18	14	2	26	39	.199	.207	.197	8.42	5.62
Cordero, Daniel	R-R	6-2	170	4-23-03	4	1	2.61	17	0	0	1	31	24	10	9	2	17	40	.220	.161	.244	11.61	4.94
De La Rosa, Manuel	R-R	6-2	210	4-17-02	0	1	1.48	10	2	0	4	24	17	5	4	0	15	16	.202	.226	.189	5.92	5.55
Diaz, Wrayan	L-L	6-2	150	9-2-02	0	1	13.50	6	0	0	0	7	4	13	11	1	14	12	.160	.125	.176	14.73	17.18
Francia, Darlin	R-R	6-5	200	11-29-03	2	0	1.29	5	2	0	0	14	11	5	2	0	7	9	.200	.286	.171	5.79	4.50
Gomez, Yendy	R-R	6-2	170	12-19-03	1	4	6.59	12	8	0	0	41	51	42	30	5	18	29	.302	.317	.294	6.37	3.95
Guanare, Fernando	R-R	6-1	140	6-21-03	4	1	1.96	9	9	1	0	46	40	13	10	0	1	49	.231	.189	.250	9.59	0.20
Hernandez, Bryan	R-R	6-1	145	5-25-04	1	2	1.96	13	0	0	0	23	12	9	5	2	18	21	.152	.042	.200	8.22	7.04
Key, Keythel	R-R	6-3	180	10-10-03	0	0	1.64	4	3	0	0	11	6	2	2	0	3	7	.154	.000	.200	5.73	2.45
Marcheco, Jorge	R-R	6-1	185	8-6-02	0	0	0.00	3	3	0	0	9	0	0	0	0	0	0	.000	.000	.000	0.00	0.00
Mendez, Haminton	R-R	6-1	177	6-5-04	0	2	6.00	9	3	0	0	15	16	11	10	0	13	8	.276	.167	.304	4.80	7.80
Pena, Adrian	R-R	6-4	180	11-11-02	3	1	1.94	10	8	0	0	42	24	15	9	1	14	36	.160	.122	.174	7.78	3.02
Perez, Diego	L-R	6-3	170	7-7-03	0	0	9.00	5	0	0	0	4	4	5	4	1	4	0	.267	.500	.111	0.00	9.00
Reyes, Yokelvin	L-L	6-1	195	3-29-04	3	1	3.10	12	1	0	1	20	17	8	7	0	17	26	.239	.400	.196	11.51	7.52
Segura, Dawry	R-R	6-2	140	8-5-03	1	0	2.97	8	5	0	0	30	29	10	10	3	3	24	.250	.185	.270	7.12	0.89
Sifontes, Enderjer	R-R	6-0	135	11-19-02	0	1	5.87	3	3	0	0	8	11	6	5	0	2	7	.324	.500	.300	8.22	2.35
Torres, Julio	L-L	6-0	165	5-30-03	0	3	9.17	12	4	0	0	18	17	21	18	2	22	18	.270	.154	.300	9.17	11.21
Valdespina, Edinson	R-R	6-6	190	5-31-04	0	0	9.00	5	1	0	0	4	4	4	4	0	9	5	.286	.333	.250	11.25	20.25
Valerio, Welmy	R-R	5-11	155	3-16-02	4	1	5.92	14	0	0	1	24	29	19	16	1	4	21	.287	.256	.306	7.77	1.48
Viloria, Luis	L-L	5-10	150	9-24-03	6	3	2.97	15	0	0	2	30	23	14	10	1	11	41	.209	.130	.230	12.16	3.26

Fielding

C: Betancourt 7, Chirinos 16, Hidalgo 14, Villahermosa 30.
1B: Betancourt 3, Garcia 44, Hidalgo 5, Manon 7, Munroe 1.
2B: Alfonso 29, Lopez 30, Macias 6, Manon 1.
3B: Garcia 1, Lopez 11, Macias 17, Manon 5, Mota 17, Munroe 18.
SS: Alfonso 19, Guzman 37, Macias 2.
OF: Falcon 46, Macias 11, Manon 4, Ortega 50, Perez 16, Ruiz 51, Scull 8.

Los Angeles Dodgers

SEASON IN A SENTENCE: The Dodgers overcame myriad injuries and Trevor Bauer's suspension following sexual assault allegations to win 106 games, but their World Series title defense ended with a loss to the Braves in the National League Championship Series.

HIGH POINT: The Dodgers and Giants engaged in a thrilling division title race, with the Giants finishing one game ahead of the Dodgers at 107-55. The longtime rivals met in the NLDS for their first-ever postseason matchup and went back and forth in a tense, five-game series. In the decisive Game 5 at Oracle Park, Cody Bellinger hit the go-ahead RBI single in the top of the ninth inning and Max Scherzer came out of the bullpen to close out the Giants for the save, keeping the Dodgers' title dreams alive and ending their rivals' season on their home field.

LOW POINT: The Dodgers signed Bauer to a three-year, $102 million deal before the season despite his history of troubling interactions with women on social media. In late June, a 27-year-old San Diego woman filed a domestic violence restraining order against Bauer alleging sexual assault, including that he choked her until she was unconscious and punched her repeatedly in the face. Both the Pasadena (Calif.) Police Department and Major League Baseball opened investigations into the case and Bauer did not pitch for the Dodgers the rest of the season.

NOTABLE ROOKIES: Righthander Phil Bickford was selected off waivers from the Brewers in May and became one of the Dodgers top middle relievers. He went 4-2, 2.50 in 56 appearances and made six scoreless appearances in the postseason. Righthander Mitch White posted a 3.66 ERA in 21 appearances (four starts) and Zach McKinstry appeared in 60 games while playing four positions.

KEY TRANSACTIONS: Hit hard by injuries in their starting rotation and infield, the Dodgers went aggressive at the trade deadline and acquired Scherzer and shortstop Trea Turner from the Nationals for four prospects in arguably the biggest deal of the year. Scherzer went 7-0, 1.98 in 11 starts with the Dodgers and Turner hit .338/.385/.565 in 52 games to cement the NL batting title. The Dodgers also signed first baseman Albert Pujols in May after the Angels released him, and the 41-year-old veteran became a clubhouse leader while serving as an effective platoon hitter against lefties.

OPENING DAY SALARY: $235,412,876 (1st).

PLAYERS OF THE YEAR

MAJOR LEAGUE	MINOR LEAGUE
Walker Buehler RHP	**Miguel Vargas** 3B
16-4, 2.47	(AA/High-A)
Career-high 33 GS	.319/.380/.526,
212 SO in 207.2 IP	23 HR, 27 2B

ORGANIZATION LEADERS

Batting		*Minimum 250 AB
MAJORS		
*AVG	Corey Seager	.306
*OPS	Corey Seager	.915
HR	Max Muncy	36
RBI	Max Muncy	94
MINORS		
*AVG	Justin Yurchak, Tulsa, Great Lakes	.365
*OBP	Justin Yurchak, Tulsa, Great Lakes	.443
*SLG	Matt Davidson, Oklahoma City	.629
*OPS	Matt Davidson, Oklahoma City	.995
R	Miguel Vargas, Tulsa, Great Lakes	98
H	Miguel Vargas, Tulsa, Great Lakes	154
TB	Miguel Vargas, Tulsa, Great Lakes	254
2B	Sam McWilliams, Great Lakes, R. Cucamonga	33
3B	James Outman, Tulsa, Great Lakes	9
HR	Andy Pages, Great Lakes	31
RBI	Andy Pages, Great Lakes	88
BB	Andy Pages, Great Lakes	77
SO	Leonel Valera, Great Lakes	148
SB	James Outman, Tulsa, Great Lakes	23

Pitching		#Minimum 75 IP
MAJORS		
W	Julio Urias	20
#ERA	Walker Buehler	2.47
SO	Walker Buehler	212
SV	Kenley Jansen	38
MINORS		
W	Austin Bibens-Dirkx, Oklahoma City	10
L	Ryan Pepiot, Oklahoma City, Tulsa	9
#ERA	Hyun-il Choi, Great Lakes, R. Cucamonga	3.55
G	James Pazos, Oklahoma City	48
GS	Clayton Beeter, Tulsa, Great Lakes	27
SV	Kevin Quackenbush, Oklahoma City	23
IP	Yefry Ramirez, Oklahoma City	113
BB	Yefry Ramirez, Oklahoma City	51
SO	Gavin Stone, Great Lakes, R. Cucamonga	138
#AVG	Andre Jackson, Oklahoma City, Tulsa, R. Cucamonga	.214

General Manager: Andrew Friedman. **Farm Director:** Will Rhymes. **Scouting Director:** Billy Gasparino.

Class	Team	League	W	L	PCT	Finish	Manager
Majors	Los Angeles Dodgers	National	106	56	.654	2nd (15)	Dave Roberts
Triple-A	Oklahoma City Dodgers	Triple-A West	67	62	.519	t-4th (10)	Travis Barbary
Double-A	Tulsa Drillers	Double-A Central	63	57	.525	5th (10)	Scott Hennessey
High-A	Great Lakes Loons	High-A Central	63	57	.525	5th (12)	J. Shoemaker/A. Chubb
Low-A	R. Cucamonga Quakes	Low-A West	67	53	.558	3rd (8)	A. Chubb/J. Shoemaker
Rookie	ACL Dodgers	Arizona Complex	32	27	.542	7th (18)	Danny Dorn/Tony Cappucilli
Rookie	DSL Dodgers Shoemaker	Dominican Summer	29	28	.509	21st (46)	Cordell Hipolito
Rookie	DSL Dodgers Bautista	Dominican Summer	32	25	.561	15th (46)	Jair Fernandez

Overall 2021 Minor League Record 353 309 .533 8th (30)

ORGANIZATION STATISTICS

LOS ANGELES DODGERS
NATIONAL LEAGUE

Batting	B-T	HT	WT	DOB	AVG	vLH	vRH	G	AB	R	H	2B	3B	HR	RBI	BB	HBP	SH	SF	SO	SB	CS	SLG	OBP
Barnes, Austin	R-R	5-10	187	12-28-89	.215	.212	.216	77	200	28	43	8	0	6	23	20	4	1	0	56	1	0	.345	.299
Beaty, Matt	L-R	6-0	215	4-28-93	.270	.350	.261	120	204	35	55	4	1	7	40	20	10	0	0	44	2	2	.402	.363
Bellinger, Cody	L-L	6-4	203	7-13-95	.165	.116	.183	95	315	39	52	9	2	10	36	31	1	0	3	94	3	1	.302	.240
Betts, Mookie	R-R	5-9	180	10-7-92	.264	.266	.263	122	466	93	123	29	3	23	58	68	11	0	5	86	10	5	.487	.367
Burns, Andy	R-R	6-2	205	8-7-90	.273	.222	.500	9	11	2	3	1	0	0	3	1	0	0	1	0	0	0	.364	.467
Lux, Gavin	L-R	6-2	190	11-23-97	.242	.188	.260	102	335	49	81	12	4	7	46	41	3	0	2	83	4	1	.364	.328
McKinney, Billy	L-L	6-1	205	8-23-94	.146	.294	.108	37	82	8	12	2	1	1	7	14	1	0	1	24	0	0	.232	.276
3-team total (40 Milwaukee, 39 New York)					.192	.220	.184	116	265	32	51	11	3	9	27	32	1	0	2	79	2	0	.358	.280
McKinstry, Zach	L-R	6-0	180	4-29-95	.215	.224	.211	60	158	19	34	9	0	7	29	10	1	1	2	50	1	1	.405	.263
Muncy, Max	L-R	6-0	215	8-25-90	.249	.276	.240	144	497	95	124	26	2	36	94	83	11	0	1	120	2	1	.527	.368
Neuse, Sheldon	R-R	6-0	232	12-10-94	.169	.073	.333	33	65	6	11	1	0	3	4	1	0	0	0	26	1	1	.323	.182
Peters, DJ	R-R	6-6	225	12-12-95	.192	.143	.400	18	26	5	5	2	0	1	4	8	0	0	0	14	0	0	.385	.382
Pollock, AJ	R-R	6-1	210	12-5-87	.297	.288	.301	117	384	53	114	27	1	21	69	30	6	0	2	80	9	1	.536	.355
Pujols, Albert	R-R	6-3	235	1-16-80	.254	.303	.188	85	189	20	48	3	0	12	38	11	2	0	2	32	1	0	.460	.299
Raley, Luke	L-R	6-4	235	9-19-94	.182	.000	.240	33	66	5	12	1	0	2	4	2	4	0	0	25	0	0	.288	.250
Reks, Zach	L-R	6-2	190	11-12-93	.000	.000	.000	6	10	2	0	0	0	0	0	0	0	0	0	7	0	0	.000	.000
Rios, Edwin	L-R	6-3	220	4-21-94	.078	.000	.103	25	51	4	4	0	0	1	1	7	2	0	0	18	0	0	.137	.217
Ruiz, Keibert	B-R	6-0	225	7-20-98	.143	.000	.167	6	7	1	1	0	0	1	1	0	0	0	0	5	0	0	.571	.143
2-team total (23 Washington)					.273	.357	.233	29	88	10	24	3	0	3	15	6	2	0	0	9	0	0	.409	.333
Seager, Corey	L-R	6-4	215	4-27-94	.306	.330	.294	95	353	54	108	22	3	16	57	48	5	0	3	66	1	1	.521	.394
Smith, Will	R-R	5-10	195	3-28-95	.258	.231	.270	130	414	71	107	19	2	25	76	58	18	0	11	101	3	0	.495	.365
Souza Jr., Steven	R-R	6-4	225	4-24-89	.152	.222	.067	17	33	2	5	1	1	1	3	2	1	0	0	14	0	0	.333	.222
Taylor, Chris	R-R	6-1	196	8-29-90	.254	.296	.237	148	507	92	129	25	4	20	73	63	8	1	3	167	13	1	.438	.344
Tsutsugo, Yoshi	L-R	6-1	225	11-26-91	.120	.000	.167	12	25	2	3	0	0	0	2	6	0	0	0	12	0	0	.120	.290
2-team total (43 Pittsburgh)					.243	.273	.227	55	152	22	37	8	1	8	27	21	1	0	1	45	0	1	.467	.337
Turner, Justin	R-R	5-11	202	11-23-84	.278	.258	.286	151	533	87	148	22	0	27	87	61	12	0	6	98	3	0	.471	.361
Turner, Trea	R-R	6-2	185	6-30-93	.338	.365	.329	52	207	41	70	17	0	10	28	15	2	0	2	33	11	2	.565	.385
2-team total (96 Washington)					.328	.392	.305	148	595	107	195	34	3	28	77	41	6	0	4	110	32	5	.536	.375

Pitching	B-T	HT	WT	DOB	W	L	ERA	G	GS	CG	SV	IP	H	R	ER	HR	BB	SO	AVG	vLH	vRH	K/9	BB/9
Alexander, Scott	L-L	6-2	195	7-10-89	0	2	2.93	18	0	0	0	15	15	6	5	2	4	8	.242	.179	.348	4.70	2.35
Bauer, Trevor	R-R	6-1	205	1-17-91	8	5	2.59	17	17	1	0	108	71	36	31	19	37	137	.182	.220	.146	11.45	3.09
Bickford, Phil	R-R	6-4	200	7-10-95	4	2	2.50	56	0	0	1	50	34	16	14	6	18	59	.190	.196	.188	10.55	3.22
2-team total (1 Milwaukee)					4	2	2.81	57	0	0	1	51	36	18	16	7	19	59	.197	.222	.186	10.34	3.33
Bruihl, Justin	L-L	6-2	215	6-26-97	0	1	2.89	21	2	0	0	19	13	7	6	1	7	11	.203	.150	.292	5.30	3.38
Buehler, Walker	R-R	6-2	185	7-28-94	16	4	2.47	33	33	0	0	208	149	61	57	19	52	212	.199	.201	.198	9.19	2.25
Burns, Andy	R-R	6-2	205	8-7-90	0	0	18.00	1	0	0	0	1	3	2	2	1	0	1	.500	.667	.333	9.00	0.00
Cleavinger, Garrett	R-L	6-1	220	4-23-94	2	4	3.00	22	1	0	0	18	20	11	6	4	12	21	.290	.243	.344	10.50	6.00
Feliz, Neftali	R-R	6-3	235	5-2-88	0	0	0.00	3	0	0	0	3	1	0	0	0	1	1	.100	.000	.167	3.00	3.00
2-team total (2 Philadelphia)					0	1	9.00	5	0	0	0	4	5	4	4	1	1	3	.294	.333	.250	6.75	2.25
Gonsolin, Tony	R-R	6-3	205	5-14-94	4	1	3.23	15	13	0	0	56	41	20	20	8	34	65	.202	.213	.185	10.51	5.50
Gonzalez, Victor	L-L	6-0	180	11-16-95	3	1	3.57	44	1	0	1	35	32	14	14	3	19	33	.244	.200	.295	8.41	4.84
Graterol, Brusdar	R-R	6-1	265	8-26-98	3	0	4.59	34	1	0	0	33	34	18	17	2	13	27	.260	.286	.244	7.29	3.51
Gray, Josiah	R-R	6-1	190	12-21-97	0	0	6.75	2	1	0	0	8	7	6	6	4	5	13	.233	.167	.278	14.63	5.63
2-team total (12 Washington)					2	2	5.48	14	13	0	0	71	63	44	43	19	33	76	.238	.221	.252	9.68	4.20
Greene, Conner	R-R	6-4	195	4-4-95	0	0	0.00	2	0	0	0	2	2	0	0	0	2	2	.250	.333	.000	9.00	0.00
Greene, Shane	R-R	6-4	200	11-17-88	0	0	4.05	9	0	0	1	7	3	3	3	1	5	7	.136	.091	.182	9.45	6.75
2-team total (19 Atlanta)					0	1	7.23	28	0	0	1	24	25	19	19	6	14	24	.263	.263	.263	9.13	5.32
Jackson, Andre	R-R	6-3	210	5-1-96	0	1	2.31	3	0	0	1	12	10	3	3	1	6	10	.238	.261	.211	7.71	4.63
Jansen, Kenley	B-R	6-5	265	9-30-87	4	4	2.22	69	0	0	38	69	36	21	17	4	36	86	.153	.169	.136	11.22	4.70

Name	B-T	HT	WT	DOB	W	L	ERA	G	GS	CG	SV	IP	H	R	ER	HR	BB	SO	AVG	vLH	vRH	K/9	BB/9
Jones, Nate	R-R	6-5	230	1-28-86	0	0	8.31	8	0	0	0	9	8	9	8	4	2	7	.235	.313	.167	7.27	2.08
2-team total (12 Atlanta)					0	2	5.68	20	0	0	0	19	16	15	12	7	12	14	.219	.333	.163	6.63	5.68
Kelly, Joe	R-R	6-1	174	6-9-88	2	0	2.86	48	0	0	2	44	28	16	14	3	15	50	.174	.183	.167	10.23	3.07
Kershaw, Clayton	L-L	6-4	225	3-19-88	10	8	3.55	22	22	0	0	122	103	51	48	15	21	144	.224	.178	.242	10.65	1.55
Kickham, Mike	L-L	6-4	220	12-12-88	0	0	13.50	1	0	0	0	2	5	3	3	1	1	2	.500	.500	.500	9.00	4.50
Knebel, Corey	R-R	6-3	224	11-26-91	4	0	2.45	27	4	0	3	26	16	8	7	2	9	30	.176	.140	.208	10.52	3.16
May, Dustin	R-R	6-6	180	9-6-97	1	1	2.74	5	5	0	0	23	16	8	7	4	6	35	.186	.159	.214	13.70	2.35
Nelson, Jimmy	R-R	6-6	250	6-5-89	1	2	1.86	28	1	0	0	29	14	8	6	0	13	44	.143	.174	.115	13.66	4.03
Nunez, Darien	L-L	6-2	205	3-19-93	0	1	8.22	6	1	0	0	8	8	8	7	3	4	8	.276	.400	.143	9.39	4.70
Phillips, Evan	R-R	6-2	215	9-11-94	1	1	3.48	7	0	0	0	10	8	5	4	0	5	9	.200	.143	.263	7.84	4.35
Price, David	L-L	6-5	215	8-26-85	5	2	4.03	39	11	0	1	74	79	35	33	8	26	58	.272	.276	.270	7.09	3.18
Quackenbush, Kevin	R-R	6-4	235	11-28-88	0	0	27.00	1	0	0	0	3	1	1	0	0	1	0	.750	--	.750	27.00	0.00
Ramirez, Yefry	R-R	6-2	215	11-28-93	0	0	0.00	1	0	0	0	2	0	0	0	0	1	2	.000	.000	.000	9.00	4.50
Reed, Jake	R-R	6-2	195	9-29-92	0	0	3.38	6	1	0	0	5	5	3	2	1	2	5	.238	.000	.278	8.44	3.38
2-team total (4 New York)					0	1	3.60	10	1	0	0	10	10	6	4	1	2	10	.250	.143	.273	9.00	1.80
Santana, Dennis	R-R	6-2	190	4-12-96	0	0	6.00	16	0	0	0	15	18	11	10	0	11	8	.300	.353	.279	4.80	6.60
Scherzer, Max	R-R	6-3	208	7-27-84	7	0	1.98	11	11	0	0	68	48	17	15	5	8	89	.189	.231	.142	11.72	1.05
2-team total (19 Washington)					15	4	2.46	30	30	1	0	179	119	53	49	23	36	236	.185	.192	.177	11.84	1.81
Sherfy, Jimmie	R-R	6-0	175	12-27-91	1	1	4.15	4	0	0	0	4	3	3	2	1	0	3	.188	.250	.167	6.23	0.00
2-team total (10 San Francisco)					2	1	4.20	14	0	0	0	15	12	8	7	3	4	12	.218	.174	.250	7.20	2.40
Treinen, Blake	R-R	6-5	225	6-30-88	6	5	1.99	72	0	0	7	72	46	20	16	5	25	85	.179	.140	.207	10.58	3.11
Turner, Justin	R-R	5-11	202	11-23-84	0	0	0.00	1	0	0	0	1	2	0	0	0	0	0	.400	.000	1.000	0.00	0.00
Uceta, Edwin	R-R	6-0	155	1-9-98	0	3	6.64	14	1	0	0	20	19	18	15	3	12	25	.253	.304	.172	11.07	5.31
Urias, Julio	L-L	6-0	225	8-12-96	20	3	2.96	32	32	0	0	186	151	67	61	19	38	195	.219	.210	.222	9.45	1.84
Vasquez, Andrew	L-L	6-6	228	9-14-93	0	0	0.00	2	0	0	0	2	1	1	0	0	3	0	.167	.333	.000	16.20	0.00
Vesia, Alex	L-L	6-1	209	4-11-96	3	1	2.25	41	0	0	1	40	17	17	10	6	22	54	.126	.123	.129	12.15	4.95
White, Mitch	R-R	6-3	210	12-28-94	1	3	3.66	21	4	0	0	47	38	28	19	6	17	49	.215	.230	.200	9.45	3.28

Fielding

Catcher	PCT	G	PO	A	E	DP	PB
Barnes	.989	52	515	15	6	3	3
Ruiz	1.000	2	3	0	0	0	0
Smith	.995	117	1101	43	6	1	9

First Base	PCT	G	PO	A	E	DP
Beaty	1.000	21	110	8	0	11
Bellinger	.923	4	23	1	2	3
Burns	1.000	2	5	0	0	0
McKinney	1.000	1	6	1	0	1
Muncy	.998	122	771	47	2	48
Pujols	.997	56	257	30	1	22
Rios	1.000	10	50	6	0	3
Smith	1.000	1	0	0	0	0
Tsutsugo	1.000	1	2	0	0	0

Second Base	PCT	G	PO	A	E	DP
Barnes	.833	7	2	3	1	1
Betts	1.000	7	6	9	0	3
Burns	1.000	3	0	1	0	0
Lux	.988	27	31	48	1	7
McKinstry	.902	20	17	29	5	7
Muncy	.991	39	50	61	1	15
Neuse	.923	13	6	18	2	4
Taylor	.964	46	60	73	5	17
Turner	.973	49	70	110	5	20

Third Base	PCT	G	PO	A	E	DP
Beaty	.800	5	1	3	1	0
Burns	1.000	2	1	1	0	0
Lux	.500	1	0	2	2	0
McKinstry	1.000	12	5	16	0	1
Muncy	1.000	7	3	4	0	0
Neuse	1.000	8	2	8	0	0
Rios	.917	6	2	9	1	0
Smith	.000	1	0	0	1	0
Taylor	.842	11	6	10	3	0
Turner	.961	143	82	211	12	18

Shortstop	PCT	G	PO	A	E	DP
Lux	.966	59	67	129	7	18
Seager	.975	92	104	202	8	22
Taylor	.973	23	26	46	2	8
Turner	1.000	3	2	2	0	0

Outfield	PCT	G	PO	A	E	DP
Beaty	.919	48	33	1	3	0
Bellinger	.989	94	172	1	2	0
Betts	.985	128	201	1	3	1
Lux	1.000	18	17	1	0	1
McKinney	1.000	23	38	1	0	0
McKinstry	1.000	37	31	3	0	0
Neuse	1.000	5	5	0	0	0
Peters	1.000	15	26	0	0	0
Pollock	1.000	111	177	4	0	1
Raley	1.000	29	23	0	0	0
Reks	1.000	5	7	0	0	0
Rios	--	2	0	0	0	0
Souza Jr.	1.000	13	9	0	0	0
Taylor	.986	99	146	0	2	0
Tsutsugo	1.000	8	15	0	0	0

OKLAHOMA CITY DODGERS   TRIPLE-A
TRIPLE-A WEST

Batting	B-T	HT	WT	DOB	AVG	vLH	vRH	G	AB	R	H	2B	3B	HR	RBI	BB	HBP	SH	SF	SO	SB	CS	SLG	OBP
Asuaje, Carlos	L-R	5-8	160	11-2-91	.249	.255	.248	83	261	44	65	13	3	2	26	33	4	0	2	38	7	2	.345	.340
Avans, Drew	L-L	5-10	195	6-13-96	.275	.259	.279	90	233	51	64	15	4	5	32	43	1	1	1	59	19	2	.438	.388
Beaty, Matt	L-R	6-0	215	4-28-93	.357	.429	.333	9	28	5	10	3	0	0	4	2	5	0	0	8	0	0	.464	.486
Bellinger, Cody	L-L	6-4	203	7-13-95	.200	.400	.133	5	20	3	4	0	0	2	3	1	0	0	0	4	0	0	.500	.238
Bemboom, Anthony	L-R	6-2	200	1-18-90	.189	.259	.149	25	74	13	14	2	1	1	7	15	1	0	1	22	0	0	.284	.330
2-team total (40 Salt Lake)					.232	.200	.244	65	211	35	49	8	3	8	37	38	3	0	4	55	2	0	.412	.352
Berman, Stevie	R-R	6-2	225	11-28-94	.111	.000	.143	2	9	0	1	1	0	0	2	1	0	0	0	3	0	0	.222	.200
Betancourt, Kenneth	R-R	5-8	160	2-5-00	.091	.500	.000	6	11	0	1	0	0	0	1	0	0	0	0	5	0	0	.182	.091
Blankenhorn, Travis	L-R	6-2	235	8-3-96	.000	--	.000	3	3	0	0	0	0	0	0	0	0	0	0	2	0	0	.000	.000
2-team total (4 Tacoma)					.217	.500	.190	7	23	1	5	0	0	1	4	0	0	0	0	7	0	0	.348	.217
Burns, Andy	R-R	6-2	205	8-7-90	.232	.235	.230	54	177	36	41	12	1	6	24	36	1	0	2	52	10	2	.412	.361
Daniel, Clayton	R-R	5-7	170	5-10-95	.222	.500	.105	12	27	2	6	1	0	0	3	3	0	0	0	8	0	1	.259	.300
Davidson, Matt	R-R	6-3	230	3-26-91	.294	.256	.308	84	313	60	92	21	0	28	81	33	5	0	5	90	0	0	.629	.365
De Jongh, Aldrich	L-R	5-9	160	9-1-98	.242	.429	.250	13	31	3	9	5	0	0	5	2	0	0	0	9	0	0	.452	.333
Estevez, Omar	R-R	5-10	185	2-25-98	.199	.219	.192	106	361	47	72	12	0	9	48	40	3	0	5	106	0	1	.307	.281
Federowicz, Tim	R-R	5-10	215	8-5-87	.200	.250	.185	25	70	10	14	3	0	3	9	9	0	0	0	17	0	0	.371	.291
Liput, Deacon	L-R	5-10	185	6-27-96	.176	.200	.167	10	34	8	6	0	0	1	6	3	0	0	0	17	0	0	.441	.222
Lux, Gavin	L-R	6-2	190	11-23-97	.279	.273	.283	17	68	18	19	4	0	1	10	6	0	0	0	15	0	0	.382	.338
Marte, Hamlet	R-R	5-10	180	2-3-94	.189	.160	.198	38	111	12	21	5	1	3	15	8	1	0	0	50	0	0	.333	.250
McKinney, Billy	L-L	6-1	205	8-23-94	.267	.000	.364	4	15	1	4	3	0	0	0	0	0	0	0	6	0	0	.467	.267

LOS ANGELES DODGERS

Name	B-T	HT	WT	DOB	AVG	vLH	vRH	G	AB	R	H	2B	3B	HR	RBI	BB	HBP	SH	SF	SO	SB	CS	SLG	OBP
McKinstry, Zach	L-R	6-0	180	4-29-95	.272	.262	.276	40	147	35	40	8	3	7	21	20	3	0	1	26	4	2	.510	.368
Neuse, Sheldon	R-R	6-0	232	12-10-94	.293	.393	.253	78	314	57	92	13	3	13	56	29	2	0	4	84	6	0	.478	.352
Noriega, Andres	R-R	6-1	190	1-3-01	.000	--	.000	1	1	0	0	0	0	0	0	0	0	0	0	1	0	0	.000	.000
Peters, DJ	R-R	6-6	225	12-12-95	.233	.279	.219	50	180	24	42	9	2	4	19	20	3	0	1	58	1	1	.372	.319
Raley, Luke	L-R	6-4	235	9-19-94	.294	.305	.291	72	272	60	80	14	2	19	69	27	18	0	1	74	8	3	.570	.393
Ravelo, Rangel	R-R	6-1	235	4-24-92	.407	.375	.418	26	91	20	37	8	0	8	27	17	3	0	2	11	0	0	.758	.504
Reks, Zach	L-R	6-2	190	11-12-93	.280	.269	.284	87	321	69	90	24	1	19	67	46	8	0	2	108	0	1	.539	.382
Ruiz, Keibert	B-R	6-0	225	7-20-98	.311	.291	.318	52	206	39	64	18	0	16	45	23	1	0	1	27	0	0	.631	.381
Santana, Cristian	R-R	6-2	175	2-24-97	.311	.375	.288	91	331	40	103	20	0	8	51	11	1	0	4	68	0	2	.444	.331
Soto, Elliot	R-R	5-9	160	8-21-89	.230	.191	.244	54	174	23	40	9	0	0	15	19	3	1	1	41	3	1	.282	.315
Souza Jr., Steven	R-R	6-4	225	4-24-89	.274	.326	.259	56	186	39	51	14	1	12	35	34	4	0	1	61	4	0	.554	.396
Tsutsugo, Yoshi	L-R	6-1	225	11-26-91	.257	.371	.221	43	148	28	38	7	0	10	32	26	1	0	5	32	0	0	.507	.361
Wallach, Chad	R-R	6-2	246	11-4-91	.000	.000	.000	1	3	1	0	0	0	0	0	0	0	0	0	1	0	0	.000	.250
2-team total (39 Salt Lake)					.219	.219	.218	40	151	31	33	7	0	8	22	21	2	0	1	46	0	0	.424	.320
Wolters, Tony	L-R	5-10	195	6-9-92	.215	.059	.240	26	93	10	20	6	1	2	13	8	5	0	1	20	0	1	.366	.308
Zabala, Juan	R-R	5-10	170	7-3-99	.500	--	.500	2	4	0	2	0	0	0	1	0	0	0	0	1	0	0	.500	.500

Pitching	B-T	HT	WT	DOB	W	L	ERA	G	GS	CG	SV	IP	H	R	ER	HR	BB	SO	AVG	vLH	vRH	K/9	BB/9
Alexander, Scott	L-L	6-2	195	7-10-89	0	0	1.93	5	0	0	0	5	3	1	1	0	0	5	.188	.143	.222	9.64	0.00
Bibens-Dirkx, Austin	R-R	6-1	210	4-29-85	10	6	5.13	25	17	0	0	109	133	71	62	14	26	87	.296	.292	.298	7.21	2.15
Bickford, Phil	R-R	6-4	200	7-10-95	1	0	5.40	5	0	0	0	5	5	3	3	0	0	12	.238	.182	.300	21.60	0.00
Bruihl, Justin	L-L	6-2	215	6-26-97	3	0	3.57	18	1	0	0	23	22	11	9	2	7	30	.259	.148	.310	11.91	2.78
Cleavinger, Garrett	R-L	6-1	220	4-23-94	1	0	1.54	11	0	0	0	12	9	3	2	0	5	25	.220	.091	.267	19.29	3.86
Cuello, Edward	R-R	6-0	170	10-20-98	1	0	9.18	14	1	0	0	17	22	17	17	6	7	12	.310	.290	.325	6.48	3.78
Feliz, Neftali	R-R	6-3	235	5-2-88	2	1	4.39	20	1	0	0	27	24	14	13	5	10	42	.242	.259	.236	14.18	3.38
Gonsolin, Tony	R-R	6-3	205	5-14-94	0	0	3.48	3	3	0	0	10	6	4	4	2	3	9	.162	.077	.208	7.84	2.61
Gonzalez, Victor	L-L	6-0	180	11-16-95	2	0	3.72	12	0	0	0	10	10	4	4	1	2	15	.256	.133	.333	13.97	1.86
Graterol, Brusdar	R-R	6-1	265	8-26-98	2	2	6.48	17	0	0	1	17	12	12	12	1	5	20	.194	.240	.162	10.80	2.70
Gray, Josiah	R-R	6-1	190	12-21-97	1	1	2.87	4	3	0	0	16	8	5	5	3	2	22	.145	.174	.125	12.64	1.15
Jackson, Andre	R-R	6-3	210	5-1-96	2	3	5.13	6	5	0	0	26	26	16	15	6	9	23	.250	.208	.263	7.86	3.08
Jewell, Jake	R-R	6-2	217	5-16-93	0	0	0.00	2	0	0	0	2	3	0	0	0	1	5	.300	--	.300	19.29	3.86
2-team total (8 Sacramento)					0	0	4.97	10	0	0	0	13	14	7	7	1	6	15	.286	.375	.242	10.66	4.26
Jones, Nate	R-R	6-5	230	1-28-86	0	0	12.00	3	0	0	0	3	5	4	4	1	1	6	.357	.222	.600	18.00	3.00
Kasowski, Marshall	L-R	6-2	215	3-10-95	0	0	5.14	7	0	0	0	7	9	4	4	0	7	9	.333	.429	.300	11.57	9.00
Kershaw, Clayton	L-L	6-4	225	3-19-88	0	0	6.00	1	1	0	0	3	4	2	2	1	0	3	.308	.100	.364	9.00	0.00
Kickham, Mike	L-L	6-4	220	12-12-88	0	3	6.51	20	9	0	0	47	58	34	34	10	24	43	.301	.321	.293	8.23	4.60
Knebel, Corey	R-R	6-3	224	11-26-91	0	0	1.59	6	1	0	0	6	4	1	1	0	1	11	.190	.000	.250	17.47	1.59
Martinson, Jordan	L-L	6-0	210	3-7-97	0	1	6.39	11	0	0	0	13	11	9	9	1	11	11	.234	.222	.241	7.82	7.82
Meisinger, Ryan	R-R	6-3	235	5-4-94	1	0	0.84	10	0	0	0	11	11	2	1	2	4	17	.256	.308	.233	14.34	3.38
Moseley, Ryan	R-R	6-3	190	10-6-94	2	5	7.55	40	1	0	0	48	63	44	40	7	31	39	.313	.309	.316	7.36	5.85
Nunez, Darien	L-L	6-2	205	3-19-93	7	0	2.42	31	1	0	0	52	30	15	14	4	20	80	.168	.226	.143	13.85	3.46
Nuno, Vidal	L-L	5-11	210	7-26-87	6	2	6.58	18	7	0	0	53	65	42	39	10	11	43	.297	.295	.297	7.26	1.86
Pazos, James	R-L	6-2	252	5-5-91	1	6	3.72	48	1	0	0	46	48	23	19	7	24	62	.265	.378	.228	12.13	4.70
Pepiot, Ryan	R-R	6-3	215	8-21-97	2	5	7.13	11	9	0	0	42	54	41	33	12	21	46	.305	.333	.294	9.94	4.54
Quackenbush, Kevin	R-R	6-4	235	11-28-88	1	7	1.65	45	0	0	0	44	35	13	8	1	22	48	.217	.194	.232	9.89	4.53
Ramirez, Yefry	R-R	6-2	215	11-28-93	6	4	5.02	25	22	0	0	113	113	73	63	14	51	115	.257	.255	.258	9.16	4.06
2-team total (8 Salt Lake)					0	0	5.57	17	0	0	0	21	25	13	13	2	7	28	.301	.452	.212	12.00	3.00
Reed, Jake	R-R	6-2	195	9-29-92	0	0	2.61	9	0	0	0	10	12	3	3	1	1	11	.300	.444	.258	9.58	0.87
Salow, Logan	L-L	6-1	185	9-27-94	3	0	3.73	38	0	0	0	41	32	20	17	2	33	47	.212	.298	.173	10.32	7.24
Santana, Dennis	R-R	6-2	190	4-12-96	0	0	10.13	3	3	0	0	5	9	6	6	2	4	6	.375	.333	.417	10.13	6.75
2-team total (4 Round Rock)					0	0	5.79	7	3	0	0	9	9	6	6	2	5	15	.250	.267	.238	14.46	4.82
Schwaab, Andrew	R-R	6-1	205	2-8-93	1	1	4.78	24	0	0	0	26	24	15	14	6	14	31	.238	.219	.246	10.59	4.78
Sierra, Yaisel	R-R	6-1	170	6-5-91	0	1	13.78	23	0	0	0	16	36	26	25	6	12	18	.429	.406	.442	9.92	6.61
Solbach, Markus	R-R	6-5	205	8-26-91	0	6	8.12	17	9	0	0	48	67	46	43	3	18	40	.327	.338	.320	7.55	3.40
Tropeano, Nick	R-R	6-4	205	8-27-90	1	0	4.91	9	5	0	0	26	29	19	14	4	12	28	.279	.263	.288	9.82	4.21
2-team total (3 Sacramento)					2	0	4.33	12	8	0	0	35	38	23	17	5	17	41	.270	.278	.264	10.44	4.33
Uceta, Edwin	R-R	6-0	155	1-9-98	2	3	4.71	10	3	0	0	29	27	16	15	4	13	38	.243	.212	.256	11.93	4.08
Vasquez, Andrew	L-L	6-6	220	9-14-93	0	0	3.00	6	0	0	0	6	6	2	2	0	2	11	.250	.300	.214	16.50	3.00
Vesia, Alex	L-L	6-1	209	4-11-96	0	0	1.00	9	0	0	2	9	3	1	1	0	3	19	.107	.091	.118	19.00	3.00
Wahl, Bobby	R-R	6-3	216	3-21-92	0	0	12.96	11	0	0	0	8	15	13	12	3	9	8	.395	.375	.400	8.64	9.72
Watson, Cyrillo	R-R	6-1	195	8-10-97	0	0	24.55	5	0	0	0	4	10	10	10	3	3	6	.500	.400	.600	14.73	7.36
White, Mitch	R-R	6-3	210	12-28-94	1	0	1.69	10	7	0	0	32	28	9	6	1	12	39	.228	.163	.263	10.97	3.38
Wilkerson, Aaron	R-R	6-2	230	5-24-89	8	5	3.86	23	19	0	0	112	98	50	48	12	24	125	.235	.252	.227	10.04	1.93

Fielding

Catcher	PCT	G	PO	A	E	DP	PB
Bemboom	1.000	21	203	8	0	2	1
Berman	1.000	2	21	0	0	0	0
Federowicz	.982	16	162	5	3	2	2
Marte	.990	32	283	9	3	2	4
Ruiz	.989	44	417	18	5	2	3
Wallach	1.000	1	8	0	0	0	0
Wolters	.985	20	190	11	3	1	1
Zabala	1.000	2	9	0	0	0	0

First Base	PCT	G	PO	A	E	DP
Beaty	.935	3	27	2	2	1
Bellinger	1.000	1	7	2	0	0
Burns	1.000	2	9	3	0	0
Davidson	.993	59	374	24	3	35
Federowicz	1.000	2	6	0	0	1
Liput	.857	1	5	1	1	0
Marte	1.000	2	9	0	0	1
Neuse	1.000	4	20	2	0	3
Raley	1.000	2	16	0	0	1
Ravelo	.993	21	133	10	1	7
Santana	.969	20	121	2	4	9
Souza Jr.	1.000	2	7	0	0	1
Tsutsugo	1.000	19	132	10	0	14

Second Base	PCT	G	PO	A	E	DP
Asuaje	.966	53	68	103	6	26
Betancourt	1.000	3	6	1	0	0
Burns	.974	11	18	19	1	4
Daniel	1.000	2	2	3	0	1

BaseballAmerica.com

Estevez	.957	23	39	28	3	8
Liput	.000	1	0	0	0	0
Lux	1.000	8	13	19	0	2
McKinstry	.982	12	20	36	1	5
Neuse	.978	30	59	72	3	30

Third Base	PCT	G	PO	A	E	DP
Betancourt	.800	1	2	2	1	0
Burns	.889	29	15	41	7	5
Daniel	1.000	2	2	0	0	0
Davidson	1.000	13	6	20	0	1
Liput	.941	8	4	12	1	1
Lux	.833	4	0	5	1	0
McKinstry	.909	4	2	8	1	2
Neuse	.974	20	11	27	1	5

Santana	.926	62	27	85	9	8

Shortstop	PCT	G	PO	A	E	DP
Asuaje	.982	19	15	41	1	4
Estevez	.981	37	32	74	2	13
McKinstry	.945	15	15	37	3	6
Neuse	.952	17	24	35	3	12
Soto	.964	52	59	100	6	23

Outfield	PCT	G	PO	A	E	DP
Avans	.981	85	151	3	3	2
Beaty	1.000	4	4	0	0	0
Bellinger	.875	4	7	0	1	0
Burns	.950	10	19	0	1	0
Daniel	1.000	6	5	0	0	0

De Jongh	1.000	9	11	0	0	0
Estevez	.986	34	66	2	1	0
Lux	1.000	2	7	1	0	1
McKinney	1.000	4	3	0	0	0
McKinstry	.933	7	13	1	1	0
Neuse	1.000	6	9	1	0	1
Peters	.967	48	86	3	3	1
Raley	.993	68	138	4	1	0
Ravelo	1.000	2	5	1	0	0
Reks	.993	82	137	3	1	1
Souza Jr.	.973	46	67	4	2	1
Tsutsugo	.971	22	33	0	1	0

TULSA DRILLERS

DOUBLE-A CENTRAL

DOUBLE-A

Batting	B-T	HT	WT	DOB	AVG	vLH	vRH	G	AB	R	H	2B	3B	HR	RBI	BB	HBP	SH	SF	SO	SB	CS	SLG	OBP
Amaya, Jacob	R-R	6-0	180	9-3-98	.216	.176	.229	113	417	60	90	15	1	12	47	52	2	0	5	103	5	0	.343	.303
Berman, Stevie	R-R	6-2	225	11-28-94	.165	.154	.169	36	115	10	19	5	0	1	9	19	5	1	0	18	0	0	.235	.309
2-team total (6 Wichita)					.179	.156	.186	42	134	11	24	6	0	2	14	19	5	1	1	25	0	0	.269	.302
Betancourt, Kenneth	R-R	5-8	160	2-5-00	.385	.000	.556	5	13	1	5	2	0	0	1	0	0	0	0	4	1	0	.538	.385
Busch, Michael	L-R	6-1	210	11-9-97	.267	.198	.288	107	409	84	109	27	1	20	67	70	12	0	4	129	2	3	.484	.386
Casey, Donovan	R-R	6-2	190	2-23-96	.296	.309	.291	73	301	51	89	15	1	11	36	26	6	0	1	102	15	4	.462	.362
Cuadrado, Romer	R-R	6-4	185	9-12-97	.227	.259	.212	81	278	30	63	3	0	10	32	28	1	0	2	117	0	1	.345	.298
Daniel, Clayton	R-R	5-7	170	5-10-95	.232	.195	.248	48	142	21	33	4	0	2	16	14	0	0	0	27	1	0	.303	.301
Feduccia, Hunter	L-R	6-2	215	6-5-97	.254	.355	.225	86	284	44	72	9	1	10	45	39	1	0	3	62	0	0	.398	.343
Hoese, Kody	R-R	6-4	200	7-13-97	.188	.293	.152	59	229	26	43	7	0	2	17	15	2	0	3	55	2	2	.245	.241
Kendall, Jeren	L-R	5-11	190	2-4-96	.209	.222	.206	57	201	24	42	7	2	10	33	25	5	0	0	92	15	8	.413	.312
Mann, Devin	R-R	6-3	180	2-11-97	.244	.265	.236	110	369	51	90	27	1	14	62	49	15	0	7	100	6	4	.436	.350
Marte, Hamlet	R-R	5-10	180	2-3-94	.300	.375	.250	7	20	4	6	0	0	0	5	4	0	0	1	6	1	0	.300	.400
Noda, Ryan	L-L	6-3	217	3-30-96	.250	.213	.262	113	384	73	96	15	1	29	78	74	12	0	5	127	3	1	.521	.383
Noriega, Andres	R-R	6-1	190	1-3-01	.250	.286	.231	7	20	1	5	2	0	0	2	0	1	0	1	8	0	0	.350	.273
Outman, James	L-R	6-3	215	5-14-97	.289	.317	.280	39	166	40	48	9	1	9	24	18	3	0	0	51	2	2	.518	.369
Rincon, Carlos	R-R	6-3	190	10-14-97	.263	.259	.264	63	232	33	61	12	0	12	48	25	5	0	3	72	0	0	.470	.343
Vargas, Miguel	R-R	6-3	205	11-17-99	.321	.337	.314	83	327	67	105	16	1	16	60	36	2	0	5	57	7	1	.523	.386
Yanel Diaz, Luis	R-R	5-11	170	9-9-99	.000	.000	.000	1	3	0	0	0	0	0	0	0	0	0	0	1	0	0	.000	.000
Yurchak, Justin	L-R	6-1	204	9-17-96	.383	.207	.438	30	115	21	44	8	0	2	27	13	1	0	4	22	0	0	.504	.436
Zabala, Juan	R-R	5-10	170	7-3-99	.267	.167	.292	11	30	3	8	1	0	1	4	4	0	0	0	9	0	1	.400	.353

Pitching	B-T	HT	WT	DOB	W	L	ERA	G	GS	CG	SV	IP	H	R	ER	HR	BB	SO	AVG	vLH	vRH	K/9	BB/9
Beeter, Clayton	R-R	6-2	220	10-9-98	0	2	4.20	5	5	0	0	15	10	8	7	2	7	23	.189	.250	.152	13.80	4.20
Brickhouse, Bryan	R-R	6-0	195	6-6-92	1	3	3.45	19	10	0	0	60	51	27	23	6	16	51	.226	.202	.244	7.65	2.40
Bruihl, Justin	L-L	6-2	215	6-26-97	1	0	1.20	8	0	0	0	15	7	2	2	1	3	20	.140	.100	.167	12.00	1.80
Carrillo, Gerardo	R-R	5-10	170	9-13-98	3	2	4.25	15	14	0	0	59	49	31	28	9	29	70	.221	.210	.231	10.62	4.40
Cuello, Edward	R-R	6-0	170	10-20-98	0	0	6.35	6	1	0	0	11	13	11	8	2	6	6	.277	.250	.296	4.76	4.76
Drury, Austin	L-L	5-11	190	8-13-97	3	1	4.53	20	3	0	0	44	41	22	22	6	14	49	.243	.313	.200	10.10	2.89
Gamboa, Max	R-R	6-5	190	11-22-95	1	1	1.69	3	0	0	0	5	2	2	1	1	5	8	.118	.091	.167	13.50	8.44
Gibbens, Cameron	L-R	6-8	194	7-4-95	0	1	7.88	13	0	0	0	16	20	14	14	3	18	25	.299	.320	.286	14.06	10.13
Grove, Michael	R-R	6-3	200	12-18-96	1	4	7.86	21	19	0	0	71	85	62	62	19	42	88	.290	.268	.307	11.15	5.32
Hagenman, Justin	R-R	6-3	205	10-7-96	7	4	3.45	38	2	0	6	63	54	25	24	6	18	77	.230	.225	.233	11.06	2.59
Jackson, Andre	R-R	6-3	210	5-1-96	3	2	3.27	15	13	0	0	63	46	24	23	12	20	75	.201	.194	.206	10.66	2.84
Jimenez, Andres	B-R	6-0	170	7-23-99	0	2	20.52	6	0	0	0	8	16	19	19	6	8	9	.400	.571	.308	9.72	8.64
Knack, Landon	L-R	6-2	220	7-15-97	2	1	4.37	6	6	0	0	23	19	11	11	6	3	27	.221	.171	.267	10.72	1.19
Martinez, Jose	R-R	6-0	194	4-23-99	1	4	7.44	9	7	0	0	33	58	39	27	7	12	22	.372	.493	.276	6.06	3.31
Martinson, Jordan	L-L	6-0	210	3-7-97	1	4	9.55	18	1	0	0	27	32	35	29	7	16	27	.276	.234	.304	8.89	5.27
Miller, Bobby	L-R	6-5	220	4-5-99	0	0	4.82	3	3	0	0	9	10	5	5	1	2	14	.256	.235	.273	13.50	1.93
Nunez, Darien	L-L	6-2	205	3-19-93	0	0	0.00	1	0	0	0	1	2	0	0	0	0	3	.400	1.000	.250	27.00	0.00
Ochsenbein, Aaron	R-R	6-3	225	2-29-96	3	2	3.32	38	1	0	8	57	46	30	21	15	22	69	.215	.207	.220	10.89	3.47
Pepiot, Ryan	R-R	6-3	215	8-21-97	3	4	2.87	15	13	0	0	60	30	19	19	7	26	81	.149	.143	.153	12.22	3.92
Plunkett, Zack	R-R	6-2	225	2-16-96	2	1	6.92	7	0	0	0	13	15	11	10	3	7	11	.283	.300	.273	7.62	4.85
Robertson, Nick	R-R	6-6	265	7-16-98	2	4	3.53	39	1	0	4	59	55	28	23	5	17	63	.248	.300	.212	9.66	2.61
Rooney, John	R-L	6-5	215	1-28-97	2	4	2.08	8	5	0	0	29	25	13	13	3	21	42	.231	.225	.235	13.19	6.59
Schwaab, Andrew	R-R	6-1	205	2-8-93	5	0	2.79	20	0	0	0	39	28	16	12	2	15	47	.196	.222	.175	10.94	3.49
Serrano, Elio	R-R	5-11	160	8-2-98	0	0	0.00	1	0	0	0	2	3	0	0	0	2	3	.333	.333	.333	11.57	7.71
Solbach, Markus	R-R	6-5	205	8-26-91	0	0	4.91	1	0	0	0	4	3	2	2	1	3	5	.214	.200	.222	7.36	0.00
Speer, Hunter	R-R	6-0	180	5-18-95	0	0	6.00	6	0	0	0	6	7	4	4	0	10	8	.269	.400	.188	12.00	15.00
Varland, Gus	L-R	6-1	205	11-6-96	1	4	5.71	16	14	0	0	35	33	23	22	7	18	22	.252	.298	.216	5.71	4.67
Warzek, Bryan	L-L	6-0	205	1-17-97	3	2	5.67	31	0	0	0	46	49	34	29	12	42	54	.275	.270	.279	10.57	8.22
Washington, Mark	R-R	6-7	205	3-24-96	1	2	1.00	31	1	0	3	63	45	16	14	0	27	81	.202	.200	.209	3.96	3.86
Watson, Cyrillo	R-R	6-1	195	8-10-97	4	2	4.62	30	1	0	1	39	33	24	20	5	28	41	.224	.210	.235	9.46	6.46
Willeman, Zach	R-R	6-2	219	3-27-96	3	2	3.78	33	0	0	3	48	42	25	20	3	23	59	.232	.286	.192	11.14	4.34
Zuniga, Guillermo	R-R	6-5	230	10-10-98	7	2	3.06	25	0	0	2	35	25	16	12	5	13	49	.194	.230	.162	12.48	3.31

LOS ANGELES DODGERS

LOS ANGELES DODGERS

Fielding

Catcher	PCT	G	PO	A	E	DP	PB
Berman	.995	35	363	17	2	3	4
Feduccia	.999	70	636	39	1	3	8
Marte	.986	7	68	4	1	0	1
Noriega	.983	6	55	2	1	0	0
Zabala	.981	11	101	5	2	0	0

First Base	PCT	G	PO	A	E	DP
Busch	.986	11	60	10	1	2
Mann	.987	34	218	12	3	13
Noda	.997	47	286	20	1	21
Vargas	.985	9	62	4	1	5
Yurchak	.983	24	163	8	3	15

Second Base	PCT	G	PO	A	E	DP
Betancourt	1.000	1	1	3	0	0
Busch	.978	88	111	194	7	35
Daniel	1.000	9	13	19	0	6
Mann	.962	13	10	15	1	2
Vargas	.982	15	24	30	1	7

Third Base	PCT	G	PO	A	E	DP
Daniel	1.000	7	6	7	0	1
Hoese	.931	53	42	66	8	5
Mann	1.000	12	6	14	0	2
Vargas	.924	53	30	79	9	5

Shortstop	PCT	G	PO	A	E	DP
Amaya	.950	112	151	228	20	43
Betancourt	1.000	3	3	1	0	1
Daniel	.957	9	8	14	1	2
Hoese	.000	1	0	0	0	0
Yanel Diaz	1.000	1	0	4	0	0

Outfield	PCT	G	PO	A	E	DP
Casey	.975	76	150	3	4	0
Cuadrado	.952	69	115	5	6	1
Daniel	1.000	2	2	0	0	0
Kendall	.992	56	124	6	1	1
Mann	.988	46	84	1	1	0
Noda	.937	46	74	0	5	0
Outman	1.000	39	93	1	0	0
Rincon	.972	39	65	5	2	1
Yurchak	1.000	3	6	1	0	0

GREAT LAKES LOONS

HIGH CLASS A

HIGH-A CENTRAL

Batting	B-T	HT	WT	DOB	AVG	vLH	vRH	G	AB	R	H	2B	3B	HR	RBI	BB	HBP	SH	SF	SO	SB	CS	SLG	OBP
Barbary, Chase	R-R	6-2	180	4-7-97	.000	.000	.000	3	8	0	0	0	0	0	0	1	0	0	0	6	0	0	.000	.111
Betancourt, Kenneth	R-R	5-8	160	2-5-00	.220	.125	.238	18	50	8	11	0	0	0	1	3	0	0	0	15	1	1	.220	.264
Ching, Zac	R-R	5-9	180	5-29-97	.240	.213	.245	89	308	42	74	13	3	13	52	24	8	1	2	129	9	4	.429	.310
Chirinos, Yhostin	R-R	5-10	165	9-29-00	.000	.000	.000	6	13	0	0	0	0	0	0	1	0	0	0	9	0	0	.000	.071
Deluca, Jonny	R-R	5-11	196	7-10-98	.232	.324	.205	44	164	27	38	6	2	7	21	15	3	0	0	35	7	0	.421	.308
Heyer, Luke	R-R	6-0	205	9-26-96	.045	.200	.000	8	22	1	1	1	0	0	1	1	0	0	1	11	0	0	.091	.083
January, Ryan	L-R	6-4	200	5-27-97	.191	.200	.190	65	188	37	36	11	0	11	31	35	15	0	1	79	1	0	.426	.360
Leonard, Eddys	R-R	6-0	160	11-10-00	.299	.194	.328	41	164	30	49	10	2	8	24	17	3	0	0	42	3	1	.530	.375
Lewis, Brandon	R-R	6-2	222	10-23-98	.262	.277	.257	55	214	33	56	7	1	20	51	14	5	0	1	70	2	0	.584	.321
Liput, Deacon	L-R	5-10	185	6-27-96	.225	.224	.225	89	320	41	72	9	3	12	36	22	4	2	2	107	13	4	.384	.282
McWilliams, Sam	R-R	6-0	178	5-26-98	.143	.000	.200	5	14	0	2	1	0	0	0	0	0	0	0	5	1	0	.214	.143
Outman, James	L-R	6-3	215	5-14-97	.250	.250	.250	65	248	50	62	12	8	9	30	45	10	0	1	88	21	2	.472	.385
Pages, Andy	R-R	6-1	212	12-8-00	.265	.229	.273	120	438	96	116	25	1	31	88	77	19	0	4	132	6	3	.539	.394
Taylor, Carson	B-R	6-2	205	6-2-99	.278	.323	.265	79	291	52	81	16	1	9	54	45	1	0	5	63	1	0	.433	.371
Valera, Leonel	R-R	6-2	200	7-9-99	.224	.234	.221	95	362	51	81	15	7	16	58	34	9	0	2	148	16	4	.436	.305
Vargas, Miguel	R-R	6-3	205	11-17-99	.314	.381	.304	37	156	31	49	11	1	7	16	9	5	0	2	32	4	0	.532	.366
Vivas, Jorbit	L-R	5-10	171	3-9-01	.318	.360	.300	23	85	12	27	6	0	1	14	13	3	0	1	33	3	1	.424	.422
Vranesh, Joe	R-R	6-2	200	1-23-98	.229	.293	.213	86	297	45	68	17	3	9	37	36	6	0	1	121	17	3	.397	.324
Ward, Ryan	L-R	5-11	200	2-23-98	.278	.210	.293	109	439	91	122	21	3	27	84	47	5	0	3	118	8	6	.524	.352
Yurchak, Justin	L-R	6-1	204	9-17-96	.356	.371	.353	62	225	42	80	10	1	5	31	38	2	0	4	47	2	1	.476	.446
Zabala, Juan	R-R	5-10	170	7-3-99	.097	.000	.115	9	31	3	3	1	0	1	4	3	0	0	1	10	0	0	.226	.171

Pitching	B-T	HT	WT	DOB	W	L	ERA	G	GS	CG	SV	IP	H	R	ER	HR	BB	SO	AVG	vLH	vRH	K/9	BB/9
Acosta, Aldry	R-R	6-4	226	9-7-99	1	1	7.00	12	0	0	0	18	19	15	14	2	9	22	.279	.333	.229	11.00	4.50
Alejo, Carlos	R-R	6-1	165	8-23-99	0	0	9.00	1	0	0	0	1	4	4	1	0	0	1	.500	1.000	.333	9.00	0.00
Beeter, Clayton	R-R	6-2	220	10-9-98	0	4	3.13	23	22	0	0	37	28	16	13	3	15	55	.212	.232	.190	13.26	3.62
Belge, Jeff	L-L	6-5	225	12-4-97	2	2	5.61	31	0	0	5	43	39	33	27	4	34	63	.235	.224	.241	13.08	7.06
Betancourt, Kenneth	R-R	5-8	160	2-5-00	0	0	0.00	1	0	0	0	1	0	0	0	0	0	0	.000	.000	.000	0.00	0.00
Boyer, Logan	R-R	6-3	215	1-24-98	0	5	5.58	28	24	0	0	40	43	29	25	6	21	42	.261	.250	.274	9.37	4.69
Cantleberry, Jacob	L-L	6-1	180	8-8-97	1	1	5.48	17	1	0	1	21	25	13	13	3	8	31	.291	.235	.327	13.08	3.38
Choi, Hyun-il	R-R	6-2	200	5-27-00	0	3	4.17	9	9	0	0	41	38	19	19	4	11	31	.248	.264	.235	6.80	2.41
Cooper, Morgan	R-R	6-5	210	9-12-94	0	1	6.43	9	0	0	0	14	8	10	10	2	12	12	.170	.174	.167	7.71	7.71
Cuello, Edward	R-R	6-0	170	10-20-98	0	0	6.43	3	0	0	0	7	4	5	5	2	2	4	.182	.091	.273	5.14	2.57
De La Paz, Franklin	L-L	6-2	190	3-29-99	2	2	2.66	13	0	0	0	20	17	8	6	0	7	27	.224	.259	.204	11.95	3.10
Drury, Austin	L-L	5-11	190	8-13-97	3	1	3.00	11	0	0	0	24	21	9	8	3	9	22	.231	.290	.200	8.25	3.38
Duran, Carlos	R-R	6-7	230	7-30-01	0	1	8.59	2	2	0	0	7	10	8	7	0	6	6	.323	.364	.222	7.36	7.36
Fink, Braidyn	L-L	6-1	216	3-7-98	2	4	5.31	31	0	0	1	41	43	26	24	5	21	41	.276	.230	.305	9.07	4.65
Gamboa, Alec	B-L	6-1	205	1-17-97	4	5	4.21	22	11	0	0	77	71	37	36	9	30	71	.241	.214	.252	8.30	3.51
Gibbens, Cameron	L-R	6-8	194	7-4-95	3	0	1.33	15	0	0	2	20	9	3	3	1	10	35	.136	.107	.158	15.49	4.43
Hernandez, Jose	L-L	6-3	170	12-31-97	1	2	3.60	10	2	0	0	15	10	6	6	2	9	20	.182	.111	.216	12.00	5.40
Heyer, Luke	R-R	6-0	205	9-26-96	0	0	9.00	1	0	0	0	1	2	1	1	0	0	0	.333	.667	.000	0.00	0.00
Hobbs, Michael	R-R	6-3	220	7-10-99	1	1	4.91	7	0	0	1	7	4	5	4	2	6	12	.154	.267	.000	14.73	7.36
Jimenez, Melvin	B-R	6-0	170	7-23-99	2	2	4.35	30	0	0	3	39	33	24	19	7	18	46	.220	.257	.188	10.53	4.12
Knack, Landon	R-R	6-2	200	7-15-97	5	0	2.50	10	5	0	0	40	31	11	11	2	5	55	.235	.138	.278	12.48	1.13
Knowles, Antonio	R-R	6-1	180	1-15-00	0	0	4.50	2	0	0	0	2	2	1	1	0	1	5	.222	.500	.143	22.50	4.50
Liput, Deacon	L-R	5-10	185	6-27-96	0	0	54.00	1	0	0	0	4	2	2	0	0	0		.800	1.000	.500	0.00	0.00
Little, Jack	L-R	6-4	190	11-30-97	3	1	6.75	24	0	0	2	31	35	25	23	5	11	31	.278	.306	.250	9.10	3.23
Lockhart, Lael	B-L	6-3	220	12-31-97	2	1	3.55	9	0	0	0	13	10	5	5	1	7	23	.222	.250	.200	16.34	4.97
Malisheski, Kevin	R-R	6-3	200	9-7-97	4	0	5.79	22	0	0	1	28	24	20	18	2	20	41	.231	.240	.222	13.18	6.43
Martinez, Jose	R-R	6-0	194	4-23-99	5	1	4.19	15	8	0	0	62	76	37	29	2	14	47	.297	.303	.290	6.79	2.02
Miller, Bobby	L-R	6-5	220	4-5-99	2	2	1.91	14	11	0	0	47	30	16	10	1	11	56	.178	.139	.211	10.72	2.11
Mokma, Mike	R-R	6-7	235	5-6-98	5	4	4.14	27	0	0	1	46	42	26	21	6	13	47	.235	.265	.208	9.26	2.56
Morillo, Juan	R-R	6-1	150	3-19-99	0	0	0.00	1	1	0	0	2	2	0	0	0	0	4	.286	.000	.400	21.60	0.00
Ortiz, Robinson	L-L	6-0	180	1-4-00	2	1	0.77	4	2	0	0	12	6	1	1	0	13	12	.150	.150	.150	9.26	10.03

	B-T	HT	WT	DOB	W	L	ERA	G	GS	CG	SV	IP	H	R	ER	HR	BB	SO	AVG	vLH	vRH	K/9	BB/9
Percival, Cole	R-R	6-5	220	2-26-99	5	3	3.34	26	2	0	1	73	55	29	27	6	41	68	.204	.190	.215	8.42	5.08
Plunkett, Zack	R-R	6-2	225	2-16-96	0	2	4.24	24	0	0	1	34	31	21	16	6	18	43	.240	.200	.275	11.38	4.76
Rodulfo, Jose	R-R	6-0	165	8-20-00	0	1	6.75	10	0	0	0	16	19	15	12	4	8	8	.311	.323	.300	4.50	4.50
Shaps, Andrew	L-L	6-1	185	12-5-95	0	1	0.98	22	0	0	0	18	8	5	2	0	15	17	.133	.042	.194	8.35	7.36
Sheehan, Emmet	R-R	6-5	215	11-15-99	0	0	16.20	1	1	0	0	2	0	3	3	0	3	4	.000	.000	.000	21.60	16.20
Smith, Julian	R-L	6-4	190	6-6-97	0	0	4.80	9	0	0	0	15	14	8	8	0	6	12	.255	.250	.256	7.20	3.60
Speer, Hunter	R-R	6-0	180	5-18-95	0	0	0.00	2	0	0	0	2	0	0	0	0	0	2	.000	.000	.000	9.00	0.00
Stone, Gavin	R-R	6-1	175	10-15-98	1	0	3.86	5	5	0	0	21	18	9	9	2	5	37	.234	.200	.281	15.86	2.14
Vargas, Jesus	R-R	6-2	175	8-18-98	8	5	4.40	24	14	0	0	102	102	58	50	18	14	88	.256	.221	.289	7.74	1.23
Watson, Cyrillo	R-R	6-1	195	8-10-97	0	0	6.75	2	0	0	0	3	5	3	2	0	5	2	.385	.200	.500	6.75	16.88
Widell, Ryley	L-L	6-3	180	6-1-97	0	0	8.71	6	0	0	0	10	8	10	10	0	11	10	.242	.300	.217	8.71	9.58

Fielding

Catcher	PCT	G	PO	A	E	DP	PB
Barbary	1.000	3	14	1	0	0	0
January	.988	62	523	30	7	6	4
Taylor	.988	56	532	31	7	8	8
Zabala	1.000	9	75	4	0	0	0

Catcher	PCT	G	PO	A	E	DP	PB
Ching	.944	53	61	106	10	19	
Chirinos	1.000	2	0	3	0	0	
Leonard	1.000	11	14	16	0	4	
Liput	.983	42	60	118	3	18	
McWilliams	1.000	2	0	4	0	0	
Vargas	1.000	2	1	3	0	0	
Vivas	1.000	9	7	16	0	3	

Shortstop	PCT	G	PO	A	E	DP
Betancourt	.500	1	0	1	1	0
Ching	.958	24	27	65	4	9
Leonard	.933	6	6	8	1	2
Valera	.936	93	108	197	21	37

First Base	PCT	G	PO	A	E	DP
Betancourt	1.000	1	6	0	0	1
Ching	.963	8	49	3	2	3
Heyer	1.000	8	58	4	0	4
Lewis	.983	24	149	21	3	14
Liput	.995	25	179	13	1	16
Vargas	1.000	1	6	0	0	0
Ward	1.000	2	4	0	0	0
Yurchak	.996	60	466	35	2	32

Third Base	PCT	G	PO	A	E	DP
Betancourt	.750	6	2	4	2	0
Ching	.933	6	6	8	1	1
Chirinos	.778	4	1	6	2	1
Heyer	.000	1	0	0	0	0
Leonard	.889	15	7	17	3	1
Lewis	.982	27	23	32	1	2
Liput	.880	26	14	30	6	2
Vargas	.952	31	31	49	4	6
Vivas	.949	14	12	25	2	4

Outfield	PCT	G	PO	A	E	DP
Betancourt	1.000	2	3	0	0	0
Deluca	.989	44	91	2	1	1
Leonard	1.000	11	25	0	0	0
Liput	--	1	0	0	0	0
McWilliams	1.000	1	4	1	0	1
Outman	1.000	64	119	7	0	0
Pages	.950	110	180	9	10	3
Shaps	1.000	18	30	2	0	1
Vranesh	.978	52	82	6	2	1
Ward	.955	69	103	2	5	0

Second Base	PCT	G	PO	A	E	DP
Betancourt	1.000	7	11	21	0	3

RANCHO CUCAMONGA QUAKES
LOW-A WEST

Batting	B-T	HT	WT	DOB	AVG	vLH	vRH	G	AB	R	H	2B	3B	HR	RBI	BB	HBP	SH	SF	SO	SB	CS	SLG	OBP
Alcantara, Ismael	R-R	6-1	165	9-25-98	.307	.309	.307	61	205	44	63	8	7	12	36	20	3	2	0	66	7	3	.590	.377
Betancourt, Kenneth	R-R	5-8	160	2-5-00	.196	.200	.195	17	51	7	10	3	0	0	5	2	0	1	2	10	0	1	.255	.218
Cartaya, Diego	R-R	6-3	219	9-7-01	.298	.313	.293	31	114	31	34	6	0	10	31	18	4	0	1	37	0	0	.614	.409
Chalo, Wladimir	R-R	5-8	197	4-21-00	.197	.273	.164	52	183	19	36	10	0	5	17	13	7	0	3	59	0	0	.333	.272
De Jesus, Alex	R-R	6-2	170	3-22-02	.268	.253	.273	97	351	67	94	25	1	12	73	69	0	0	2	128	1	0	.447	.386
De Jongh, Aldrich	L-R	5-9	160	9-1-98	.248	.172	.267	46	149	20	37	7	4	5	22	12	0	0	1	59	4	0	.450	.302
Deluca, Jonny	R-R	5-11	196	7-10-98	.287	.265	.297	57	223	48	64	17	3	15	43	31	1	0	0	48	13	2	.592	.376
Fernandez, Yeiner	R-R	5-9	170	9-19-02	.516	.667	.480	7	31	4	16	1	0	1	10	2	1	0	0	3	0	0	.645	.559
Hernandez, Marco	R-R	6-2	170	6-22-98	.205	.161	.219	37	127	28	26	6	0	3	22	21	6	0	0	32	0	0	.323	.344
Lao, Sauryn	R-R	6-2	182	8-14-99	.244	.281	.232	94	356	65	87	21	4	11	46	37	9	0	1	119	5	1	.419	.330
Leonard, Eddys	R-R	6-0	160	11-10-00	.295	.337	.274	66	261	59	77	19	2	14	57	34	12	0	1	74	6	2	.544	.399
Lewis, Brandon	R-R	6-2	222	10-23-98	.278	.157	.331	44	169	36	47	14	1	10	35	26	3	0	2	63	0	1	.550	.380
Mateo, Edwin	B-L	5-9	160	11-18-98	.274	.265	.277	94	329	68	90	18	6	4	40	35	13	0	2	86	22	3	.401	.364
McKenzie, Luke	L-R	6-2	210	7-16-98	.057	.125	.037	12	35	2	2	1	0	0	3	4	0	0	0	16	0	0	.086	.154
McWilliams, Sam	R-R	6-0	178	5-26-98	.304	.250	.327	87	355	82	108	32	2	14	70	44	5	0	5	117	12	5	.524	.384
Pollock, AJ	R-R	6-1	210	12-5-87	.222	.286	.000	4	9	2	2	0	0	1	1	0	0	0	1	0	0	.556	.300
Ramos, Jose	R-R	6-1	200	1-1-01	.313	.241	.340	47	195	30	61	18	3	8	44	16	6	0	3	57	1	4	.559	.377
Vargas, Imanol	L-R	6-3	185	6-29-98	.246	.226	.252	72	264	42	65	11	4	17	55	36	2	0	2	95	2	1	.511	.339
Vivas, Jorbit	L-R	5-10	171	3-9-01	.311	.213	.350	83	328	73	102	20	4	13	73	27	17	0	3	42	5	3	.515	.389
Vogel, Jake	R-R	5-11	165	10-12-01	.233	.255	.221	76	323	54	75	14	6	3	27	33	12	0	2	111	12	4	.338	.323
Wulff, Brandon	R-R	6-1	225	12-19-96	.159	.111	.192	18	44	8	7	3	0	1	5	10	2	0	1	16	1	0	.295	.333
Yanel Diaz, Luis	R-R	5-11	170	9-9-99	.241	.242	.241	30	112	21	27	3	4	6	20	7	2	0	0	53	2	1	.500	.298

Pitching	B-T	HT	WT	DOB	W	L	ERA	G	GS	CG	SV	IP	H	R	ER	HR	BB	SO	AVG	vLH	vRH	K/9	BB/9
Acosta, Aldry	R-R	6-4	226	9-7-99	4	3	3.15	23	0	0	3	34	37	22	12	0	12	43	.268	.338	.200	11.27	3.15
Alcantara, Ismael	R-R	6-1	165	9-25-98	0	0	3.86	3	0	0	0	2	1	1	1	0	2		.125	.250	.000	7.71	0.00
Alejo, Carlos	R-R	6-1	185	8-23-99	2	3	6.03	32	0	0	8	34	32	26	23	2	22	43	.241	.340	.175	11.27	5.77
Alexander, Scott	L-L	6-2	195	7-10-89	0	0	0.00	1	0	0	0	1	0	0	0	0	0	0	.000	--	.000	0.00	0.00
Cabrera, Jeisson	R-R	6-2	170	9-5-98	1	0	4.50	2	0	0	0	2	3	1	1	0	2	6	.333	.250	.400	27.00	9.00
Cantleberry, Jacob	L-L	6-1	180	8-8-97	4	0	1.98	7	0	0	1	14	7	3	3	0	5	27	.149	.158	.143	17.78	3.29
Casparius, Ben	R-R	6-0	208	2-11-99	0	0	3.00	2	0	0	0	3	4	2	1	0	3	4	.333	.333	.333	12.00	9.00
Choi, Hyun-il	R-R	6-2	200	5-27-00	8	3	3.17	15	2	0	0	65	47	25	23	8	7	75	.197	.197	.198	10.33	0.96
Contreras, Nelfri	B-L	6-0	175	12-25-98	3	1	3.80	31	0	0	2	47	50	32	20	7	25	47	.263	.200	.286	8.94	4.75
Cruz, Daniel	R-R	6-3	185	10-5-97	3	2	4.89	30	0	0	2	39	27	23	21	3	16	61	.190	.179	.200	14.20	3.72
De Jongh, Aldrich	L-R	5-9	160	9-1-98	0	0	0.00	1	0	0	0	1	1	0	0	0	0	0	.333	.000	1.000	0.00	0.00
De La Paz, Franklin	L-L	6-2	190	3-29-99	2	0	2.45	13	1	0	0	18	16	7	5	1	8	25	.219	.160	.250	12.27	3.93
De Los Santos, Carlos	R-R	6-2	170	11-18-00	1	1	5.70	33	0	0	3	43	42	29	27	2	28	55	.253	.236	.266	11.60	5.91
De Paula, Reinaldo	R-R	5-11	177	10-20-98	3	1	4.96	11	0	0	1	16	17	12	9	0	6	19	.258	.308	.225	10.47	3.31
Duran, Carlos	R-R	6-7	230	7-30-01	2	4	5.25	20	18	0	0	74	81	50	43	9	24	109	.266	.286	.250	13.32	2.93

Fisher, Braydon	R-R	6-4	180	7-26-00	5	3	6.56	23	2	0	1	70	89	59	51	8	26	83	.308	.304	.311	10.67	3.34
Gibbens, Cameron	L-R	6-8	194	7-4-95	1	1	0.87	7	0	0	1	10	6	1	1	0	4	23	.167	.167	.167	20.03	3.48
Gonsolin, Tony	R-R	6-3	205	5-14-94	0	0	3.86	1	1	0	0	2	3	1	1	0	1	1	.333	.500	.200	3.86	3.86
Gonzalez, Victor	L-L	6-0	180	11-16-95	0	1	20.25	2	1	0	0	1	2	3	3	1	1	3	.333	.000	.400	20.25	6.75
Harris, Ben	L-L	6-1	195	2-22-00	0	0	6.75	4	0	0	0	4	6	3	3	1	3	7	.333	.333	.333	15.75	6.75
Henriquez, Edgardo	R-R	6-4	200	6-24-02	0	0	18.00	1	1	0	0	2	3	4	4	0	2	3	.375	.500	.333	13.50	9.00
Hernandez, Jose	L-L	6-3	170	12-31-97	2	0	4.75	22	3	0	1	30	32	17	16	1	13	41	.274	.189	.313	12.16	3.86
Hurt, Kyle	R-R	6-3	215	5-30-98	1	2	5.51	8	1	0	1	16	12	11	10	1	10	28	.200	.233	.167	15.43	5.51
Jackson, Andre	R-R	6-3	210	5-1-96	0	0	1.59	1	1	0	0	6	4	1	1	1	1	5	.182	.154	.222	7.94	1.59
Kelly, Joe	R-R	6-1	174	6-9-88	0	0	0.00	2	1	0	0	1	0	0	0	0	2	2	.000	.000	.000	13.50	13.50
Leasure, Jordan	R-R	6-2	195	8-15-98	1	0	4.76	4	0	0	0	6	5	4	3	2	3	6	.227	.364	.091	9.53	4.76
Lewis, Jimmy	R-R	6-6	200	11-2-00	0	3	6.79	23	18	0	0	50	65	52	38	10	29	37	.305	.308	.303	6.62	5.19
Lin, Huei-Sheng	R-R	6-2	198	10-9-98	1	1	5.50	11	4	0	1	36	39	28	22	4	12	34	.264	.313	.222	8.50	3.00
Martinez, Michael	R-R	6-1	185	7-11-99	2	2	6.87	12	0	0	0	18	19	14	14	3	10	24	.264	.231	.283	11.78	4.91
Nastrini, Nick	R-R	6-3	215	2-18-00	0	0	2.08	6	6	0	0	13	6	6	3	2	7	30	.130	.143	.120	20.77	4.85
Peto, Robbie	R-R	6-4	225	7-10-98	1	4	5.22	20	18	0	0	71	75	46	41	12	29	72	.263	.229	.287	9.17	3.69
Ramirez, Adolfo	R-R	6-0	165	6-1-99	1	2	6.91	11	1	0	2	29	40	23	22	5	9	29	.323	.392	.274	9.10	2.83
Robles, Benony	L-L	6-4	185	10-1-00	0	1	3.00	1	1	0	0	3	4	1	1	1	2	0	.286	1.000	.231	0.00	6.00
Rosario, Jerming	R-R	6-1	175	5-8-02	0	2	39.27	3	2	0	0	4	13	18	16	1	4	6	.520	.364	.643	14.73	9.82
Santana, Martin	R-R	6-4	165	1-30-01	0	0	8.59	7	0	0	0	7	11	7	7	0	7	10	.344	.417	.300	12.27	8.59
Scoggins, Adam	L-L	6-3	220	1-21-98	0	0	9.82	2	0	0	0	4	6	4	4	2	1	6	.353	1.000	.313	14.73	2.45
Serrano, Elio	R-R	5-11	160	8-2-98	1	0	10.80	9	0	0	0	10	18	12	12	4	3	11	.383	.444	.300	9.90	2.70
Sheehan, Emmet	R-R	6-5	215	11-15-99	3	0	4.15	5	0	0	0	13	10	6	6	2	5	27	.204	.200	.200	18.69	3.46
Smith, Julian	R-L	6-4	190	6-6-97	6	5	7.16	23	0	0	0	44	58	39	35	5	20	54	.312	.279	.328	11.05	4.09
Stone, Gavin	R-R	6-1	175	10-15-98	1	2	3.73	18	17	0	0	70	69	35	29	5	20	101	.253	.196	.292	12.99	2.57
Sublette, Ryan	R-R	6-2	190	10-1-98	1	1	3.72	6	0	0	0	10	9	5	4	1	1	12	.237	.176	.286	11.17	0.93
Valdez, Joan	R-R	6-4	175	3-10-99	2	2	4.03	17	0	0	0	29	22	14	13	5	9	38	.212	.267	.169	11.79	2.79
White, Mitch	R-R	6-3	210	12-28-94	2	0	1.54	2	2	0	0	12	7	2	2	1	1	14	.175	.167	.179	10.80	0.77
Williams, Kendall	R-R	6-6	205	8-24-00	3	3	4.53	23	19	0	1	93	106	62	47	14	22	87	.277	.251	.300	8.39	2.12

Fielding

Catcher	PCT	G	PO	A	E	DP	PB
Cartaya	.997	31	309	24	1	2	11
Chalo	.978	52	496	37	12	4	14
Fernandez	.984	5	56	5	1	0	3
Hernandez	.993	35	427	16	3	3	10

First Base	PCT	G	PO	A	E	DP
Alcantara	1.000	3	5	1	0	1
Lao	.983	59	431	32	8	31
Lewis	.968	9	54	6	2	1
McKenzie	1.000	2	4	1	0	0
Vargas	.986	56	389	26	6	23
Wulff	1.000	4	7	1	0	1

Second Base	PCT	G	PO	A	E	DP
Alcantara	1.000	5	4	4	0	0
Betancourt	.882	6	7	8	2	1
Lao	1.000	1	0	1	0	0
Leonard	.984	16	22	39	1	9

	PCT	G	PO	A	E	DP
McWilliams	.967	61	70	132	7	16
Vivas	.978	38	44	87	3	15
Yanel Diaz	.857	5	2	4	1	0

Third Base	PCT	G	PO	A	E	DP
Alcantara	.000	1	0	0	0	0
Betancourt	.000	1	0	0	0	0
De Jesus	.000	1	0	0	0	0
Lao	.840	35	20	43	12	5
Leonard	.903	9	8	20	3	4
Lewis	.952	32	19	60	4	7
Vargas	.000	1	0	0	0	0
Vivas	.938	34	15	60	5	4
Yanel Diaz	.962	18	17	34	2	0

Shortstop	PCT	G	PO	A	E	DP
Betancourt	.875	10	11	24	5	3
De Jesus	.904	75	79	156	25	22
Lao	.000	1	0	0	0	0

	PCT	G	PO	A	E	DP
Leonard	.922	32	33	73	9	13
Vivas	1.000	2	1	0	0	0
Yanel Diaz	.864	9	4	15	3	0

Outfield	PCT	G	PO	A	E	DP
Alcantara	.950	45	71	5	4	1
Betancourt	--	1	0	0	0	0
De Jongh	.912	39	49	3	5	0
Deluca	.977	57	81	4	2	2
Mateo	.976	91	162	2	4	0
McKenzie	.909	8	9	1	1	0
McWilliams	1.000	22	29	1	0	0
Pollock	1.000	3	2	0	0	0
Ramos	.922	44	65	6	6	2
Vargas	1.000	2	1	0	0	0
Vivas	--	1	0	0	0	0
Vogel	.952	71	96	3	5	0
Wulff	1.000	12	9	2	0	0
Yanel Diaz	--	1	0	0	0	0

ACL DODGERS   ROOKIE
ARIZONA COMPLEX LEAGUE

Batting	B-T	HT	WT	DOB	AVG	vLH	vRH	G	AB	R	H	2B	3B	HR	RBI	BB	HBP	SH	SF	SO	SB	CS	SLG	OBP
Allison, Chet	R-R	6-2	215	4-30-99	.143	.200	.120	16	35	9	5	1	0	1	2	5	4	0	0	16	0	0	.257	.318
Bolivar, Roimer	R-R	6-0	175	12-10-99	.224	.143	.247	30	98	19	22	8	0	4	17	9	8	0	1	36	2	0	.429	.336
Burns, Andy	R-R	6-2	205	8-7-90	.333	.000	.375	4	9	4	3	0	0	1	2	5	0	0	1	1	1	0	.667	.571
Carrion, Julio	R-R	6-2	185	12-29-98	.253	.258	.252	53	174	33	44	9	1	3	25	27	10	0	2	45	2	0	.368	.380
Chirinos, Yhostin	R-R	5-10	165	9-29-00	.224	.357	.182	24	58	10	13	4	0	0	10	15	0	1	0	24	1	0	.293	.378
Fernandez, Yeiner	R-R	5-9	170	9-19-02	.319	.261	.331	35	141	24	45	11	1	2	15	10	5	0	1	27	1	3	.454	.382
Garcia, Jose	B-R	5-10	190	10-4-01	.265	.308	.255	20	68	13	18	3	1	2	14	6	0	0	2	23	2	0	.426	.324
Garcia, Yunior	R-R	6-0	198	7-29-01	.300	.286	.303	31	110	20	33	5	1	4	16	10	3	0	1	29	2	0	.473	.371
Gauthier, Austin	R-R	6-0	188	5-7-99	.255	.286	.250	30	98	22	25	3	2	0	17	23	0	0	3	38	5	1	.327	.387
Hoese, Kody	R-R	6-4	200	7-13-97	.258	.250	.261	10	31	2	8	1	0	0	3	2	0	0	1	4	0	0	.290	.294
Keith, Damon	R-R	6-3	195	5-28-00	.333	.231	.357	23	69	13	23	6	3	1	13	13	3	0	1	24	2	0	.551	.453
Kendall, Jeren	L-R	5-11	190	2-4-96	.077	.000	.125	4	13	1	1	0	0	0	2	2	0	0	0	6	1	0	.077	.200
Martinez, Hector	R-R	6-0	135	8-22-00	.240	.333	.214	44	125	20	30	4	1	0	12	15	2	1	0	30	2	1	.288	.331
McKenzie, Luke	L-R	6-2	210	7-16-98	.298	.308	.294	17	47	12	14	4	2	0	2	8	1	0	0	18	3	3	.468	.411
Quiroz, Nelson	B-R	5-8	194	11-5-01	.272	.294	.267	30	92	17	25	11	0	0	14	16	2	0	1	12	0	0	.391	.387
Ramos, Jose	R-R	6-1	200	1-1-01	.383	.417	.375	15	60	13	23	6	0	3	15	7	1	0	0	14	1	0	.633	.456
Restituyo, Harold	R-R	6-2	185	9-1-00	.300	.222	.311	21	70	9	21	5	0	2	8	6	1	0	1	18	0	1	.457	.359
Rodriguez, Frank	R-R	5-11	197	9-28-01	.242	.286	.229	32	91	14	22	3	1	1	12	10	3	0	2	19	0	0	.330	.330
Rodriguez, Luis	R-R	6-2	175	9-16-02	.216	.189	.222	54	199	40	43	4	1	8	28	27	7	0	3	73	1	1	.367	.354
Santiago, Carlos	B-R	5-11	145	7-24-01	.168	.161	.169	44	167	19	28	4	2	5	25	15	1	0	3	60	1	0	.305	.237

	B-T	HT	WT	DOB	AVG	vLH	vRH	G	AB	R	H	2B	3B	HR	RBI	BB	HBP	SH	SF	SO	SB	CS	SLG	OBP
Seager, Corey	L-R	6-4	215	4-27-94	.500	--	.500	1	2	0	1	0	0	0	0	1	0	0	0	0	0	0	.500	.667
Soto, Elliot	R-R	5-9	160	8-21-89	.500	.333	.600	3	8	1	4	0	1	0	1	1	0	0	0	3	0	0	.750	.556
Tomsjansen, Rushenten	R-R	6-0	150	5-14-01	.125	.000	.143	13	24	2	3	1	0	0	3	0	2	0	1	8	0	0	.167	.185
Vogel, Jake	R-R	5-11	165	10-12-01	.000	--	.000	1	2	0	0	0	0	0	0	0	1	0	0	1	0	0	.000	.333
Yan, Luis	B-R	6-3	180	1-1-99	.190	.167	.200	8	21	2	4	0	0	0	0	2	0	0	0	11	0	0	.190	.261
Yanel Diaz, Luis	R-R	5-11	170	9-9-99	.289	.318	.278	22	76	9	22	5	1	4	20	6	2	0		37	4	3	.539	.357

Pitching	B-T	HT	WT	DOB	W	L	ERA	G	GS	CG	SV	IP	H	R	ER	HR	BB	SO	AVG	vLH	vRH	K/9	BB/9
Acevedo, Axel	R-R	6-2	170	9-23-00	3	1	7.62	12	0	0	0	13	15	13	11	4	11	16	.278	.389	.222	11.08	7.62
Alvarez, Yadier	R-R	6-3	175	3-7-96	0	0	7.36	3	1	0	0	4	3	3	3	0	1	7	.231	.333	.143	17.18	2.45
Andujar, Horacio	R-R	6-2	161	1-14-99	2	1	4.15	16	0	0	1	22	33	14	10	1	4	24	.347	.325	.364	9.97	1.66
Baro, Heisell	R-R	6-1	185	2-20-02	0	3	5.79	14	10	0	0	37	39	26	24	7	26	41	.269	.238	.308	9.88	6.27
Bautista, Kelvin	L-L	5-11	155	7-7-99	1	1	1.82	19	0	0	1	25	17	6	5	0	12	32	.198	.158	.209	11.68	4.38
Becerra, Octavio	L-L	6-3	209	2-3-01	1	1	1.77	14	2	0	1	20	3	14	4	0	15	42	.044	.038	.048	18.59	6.64
Bruns, Maddux	L-L	6-2	205	6-20-02	0	2	16.20	4	4	0	0	5	8	9	9	2	7	5	.364	.556	.231	9.00	12.60
Casparius, Ben	R-R	6-0	208	2-11-99	0	0	3.00	3	1	0	0	3	4	1	1	0	0	6	.308	.400	.250	18.00	0.00
Castillo, Yamil	R-R	6-1	200	8-18-99	0	0	3.27	8	0	0	0	11	14	5	4	0	4	14	.311	.364	.261	11.45	3.27
Cheng, Hao-Chun	R-R	6-3	205	9-17-97	0	1	5.40	7	0	0	0	8	8	5	5	0	1	8	.242	.333	.167	8.64	1.08
De Paula, Reinaldo	R-R	5-11	177	10-20-98	0	0	1.50	6	0	0	0	6	4	1	1	0	2	7	.190	.111	.250	10.50	3.00
Edwards, Jonathan	R-R	6-6	185	1-26-00	0	0	0.00	6	0	0	0	5	2	0	0	0	4	7	.125	.250	.000	11.81	6.75
Emmett, Gabe	R-R	6-5	175	5-22-01	0	0	7.36	3	0	0	0	4	2	3	3	2	4	4	.167	.250	.125	9.82	9.82
Feliz, Frankelyn	R-R	6-1	170	12-24-01	1	0	6.92	11	0	0	0	13	17	13	10	1	10	12	.304	.350	.278	8.31	6.92
Galindo, Harold	R-R	6-2	175	1-22-01	5	1	5.32	17	0	0	0	22	13	13	13	0	19	19	.176	.257	.103	7.77	7.77
Garcia, Jose	B-R	6-1	190	10-4-01	0	0	0.00	1	0	0	0	0	0	0	0	0	0	0	.000	.000	--	0.00	0.00
Gutierrez, Osvanni	R-R	6-1	170	5-24-01	2	0	3.41	13	4	0	1	37	35	15	14	2	9	37	.261	.327	.220	9.00	2.19
Gutierrez, Roque	R-R	5-9	177	9-7-02	0	0	12.46	4	0	0	0	4	6	6	6	1	2	4	.300	.385	.143	8.31	4.15
Harris, Ben	L-L	6-1	195	2-22-00	0	0	6.75	2	0	0	0	1	1	1	1	0	3	2	.200	1.000	.000	13.50	20.25
Henriquez, Edgardo	R-R	6-4	200	6-24-02	2	3	4.13	12	8	0	0	33	20	15	15	3	22	47	.179	.224	.143	12.95	6.06
Heubeck, Peter	R-R	6-3	170	7-22-02	0	0	0.00	2	1	0	0	4	1	0	0	0	2	9	.077	.000	.167	20.25	4.50
Hobbs, Michael	R-R	6-3	220	7-10-99	0	0	9.00	1	0	0	0	1	2	1	1	0	1	1	.400	.000	.500	9.00	9.00
Hurt, Kyle	R-R	6-3	215	5-30-98	1	0	5.79	4	3	0	0	5	6	3	3	1	0	8	.300	.444	.182	15.43	0.00
Kasowski, Marshall	L-R	6-3	215	3-10-95	1	0	3.38	6	3	0	0	5	6	2	2	0	2	8	.286	.200	.364	13.50	3.38
Knowles, Antonio	R-R	6-1	180	1-15-00	0	0	0.00	2	0	0	0	2	1	0	0	0	0	6	.143	.333	.000	27.00	0.00
Kopp, Ronan	L-L	6-7	250	7-29-02	0	0	0.00	3	0	0	0	2	0	0	0	0	1	5	.250	.000	.286	22.50	4.50
Leasure, Jordan	R-R	6-2	195	8-15-98	0	0	5.79	4	0	0	0	5	3	3	3	1	0	7	.176	.273	.000	13.50	0.00
Lin, Huei-Sheng	R-R	6-2	198	10-9-98	0	1	7.11	3	0	0	0	6	10	5	5	0	0	10	.357	.417	.313	14.21	0.00
Lockhart, Lael	B-L	6-3	220	12-31-97	0	0	9.00	1	0	0	0	1	2	1	1	0	0	2	.500	--	.500	18.00	0.00
Martinez, Francisco	L-L	6-1	180	5-4-01	0	1	81.00	1	0	0	0	0	1	3	3	0	2	0	.500	--	.500	0.00	54.00
Martinez, Michael	R-R	6-1	185	7-11-99	0	1	8.31	4	0	0	0	4	3	6	4	0	4	6	.188	.167	.200	12.46	8.31
Nastrini, Nick	R-R	6-3	215	2-18-00	0	0	0.00	1	1	0	0	1	0	0	0	0	0	2	.333	.500	.000	18.00	0.00
Paez, Isaul	R-R	6-2	180	8-15-99	1	2	4.85	11	0	0	0	13	15	7	7	1	1	19	.289	.235	.315	13.15	0.69
Robles, Benony	L-L	6-4	185	10-1-00	1	2	3.35	13	8	0	1	46	31	20	17	3	15	61	.189	.186	.190	12.02	2.96
Rodulfo, Jose	R-R	6-0	165	8-20-00	1	0	0.00	2	0	0	0	2	2	0	0	0	1	2	.250	.000	.333	9.00	4.50
Rosario, Jerming	R-R	6-1	175	5-8-02	0	4	4.17	11	5	0	0	37	32	22	17	5	13	48	.229	.237	.222	11.78	3.19
Santana, Martin	R-R	6-4	165	1-30-01	5	1	2.04	12	0	0	0	18	10	5	4	1	2	25	.140	.304	.081	12.74	1.02
Scoggins, Adam	L-L	6-3	220	1-21-98	0	1	5.79	5	0	0	0	5	7	4	3	0	4	10	.333	.444	.250	19.29	7.71
Sheehan, Emmet	R-R	6-5	215	11-15-99	0	0	0.00	1	1	0	0	1	0	0	0	0	0	3	.000	.000	.000	27.00	0.00
Suarez, Christian	L-L	5-11	160	11-25-00	2	0	3.12	15	0	0	1	17	20	13	6	1	5	20	.274	.200	.313	10.38	2.60
Sublette, Ryan	R-R	6-2	190	10-1-98	0	0	0.00	1	0	0	0	1	0	0	0	0	0	2	.000	--	.000	18.00	0.00
Uceta, Edwin	R-R	6-0	155	1-9-98	0	0	0.00	1	1	0	0	1	0	0	0	0	0	2	.000	--	.000	18.00	0.00
Zambrano, Jhan	R-R	6-3	165	12-21-01	2	1	2.15	12	5	0	0	38	29	11	9	2	12	27	.213	.192	.226	6.45	2.87

Fielding

C: Fernandez 19, Garcia 10, Quiroz 22, Rodriguez 15.
1B: Carrion 33, Garcia 9, Rodriguez 18, Yan 8.
2B: Chirinos 15, Gauthier 15, Martinez 34, Santiago 1, Yanel Diaz 2.
3B: Burns 3, Carrion 23, Chirinos 2, Gauthier 1, Hoese 7, Martinez 9, Rodriguez 1, Yanel Diaz 20.
SS: Chirinos 10, Gauthier 7, Martinez 1, Santiago 44, Seager 1, Soto 1, Yanel Diaz 1.
OF: Allison 13, Bolivar 21, Garcia 22, Keith 22, Kendall 22, McKenzie 16, Ramos 16, Restituyo 21, Rodriguez 57, Tomsjansen 7, Vogel 1, Yanel Diaz 1.

DSL DODGERS   ROOKIE
DOMINICAN SUMMER LEAGUE

Batting	B-T	HT	WT	DOB	AVG	vLH	vRH	G	AB	R	H	2B	3B	HR	RBI	BB	HBP	SH	SF	SO	SB	CS	SLG	OBP
Alonso, Juan	R-R	0-0	0	11-3-03	.239	.050	.278	32	117	19	28	6	0	1	14	13	3	0	0	32	6	6	.316	.331
Armas, Javier	L-R	5-10	155	8-27-03	.262	.130	.293	42	122	26	32	10	1	1	17	22	3	2	3	31	11	4	.385	.380
Avila, Carlos	R-R	0-0	0	12-4-03	.206	.143	.224	21	63	7	13	1	0	1	5	6	2	0	0	16	2	1	.254	.296
Campos, Elio	R-R	5-9	157	1-2-04	.266	.333	.245	39	128	21	34	1	1	0	15	14	3	1	1	19	11	6	.289	.349
Caraballo, Roger	R-L	6-1	185	8-14-01	.262	.318	.242	53	168	35	44	10	2	7	31	19	9	0	4	39	2	0	.470	.360
De La Rosa, Bladimir	R-R	6-1	175	10-15-01	.194	.235	.183	48	160	25	31	8	1	8	27	20	3	0	1	59	4	3	.406	.293
Diaz, Juan	B-R	6-2	190	2-20-02	.256	.269	.254	50	160	26	41	9	0	4	29	32	7	0	0	38	2	2	.388	.402
Diaz, Victor	R-R	5-9	215	5-2-02	.000	--	--	1	3	1	0	0	0	0	0	0	0	0	1	0	2	0	0	.000	.000
Diaz, Victor	R-R	5-10	175	11-25-01	.364	.200	.500	4	11	3	4	1	0	1	1	2	0	0	0	4	0	0	.727	.462
Diaz, Wilman	R-R	6-2	182	11-15-03	.235	.278	.224	24	85	13	20	5	1	0	9	9	0	0	0	26	8	4	.353	.309
Doncon, Rayne	R-R	6-2	176	9-22-03	.283	.286	.282	31	99	20	28	4	2	3	15	16	2	0	2	28	7	1	.455	.387
Dotel, Rafael	R-R	6-1	165	9-17-02	.194	.071	.229	25	62	8	12	4	1	1	12	4	2	0	0	20	1	0	.339	.265

	B-T	HT	WT	DOB	AVG	vLH	vRH	G	AB	R	H	2B	3B	HR	RBI	BB	SO	SB	CS	HBP	SO	SB	CS	OBP	SLG
Droz, Miguel	R-R	6-0	170	10-2-01	.212	.130	.232	39	118	19	25	5	1	2	17	21	3	0	1	31	9	4	.322	.343
Enrique, Julio	R-R	6-1	184	2-21-00	.310	.273	.321	45	145	39	45	10	2	2	21	23	8	1	1	43	23	7	.448	.429
Espinosa, Andy	R-R	5-11	195	1-25-03	.277	.345	.259	48	141	31	39	10	1	7	30	29	7	1	0	52	3	4	.511	.424
Figueroa, Derlin	L-R	6-0	163	9-7-03	.164	.214	.151	49	134	14	22	3	2	0	14	27	2	0	4	40	2	4	.216	.305
Galiz, Jesus	R-R	6-0	183	12-19-03	.218	.269	.200	31	101	14	22	5	1	0	12	7	3	0	1	17	2	0	.287	.286
Garcia, Darol	R-R	5-11	178	9-12-02	.219	.238	.212	48	155	30	34	8	0	1	12	25	2	0	0	52	19	4	.290	.335
Guerra, Luis	R-R	6-1	180	10-4-03	.279	.190	.296	40	129	17	36	6	0	0	20	14	1	0	1	29	5	1	.326	.352
Hernandez, Jose	R-R	6-1	145	4-30-03	.242	.333	.220	46	124	21	30	5	1	0	16	31	5	0	2	29	6	6	.298	.407
Lasso, Roger	B-R	6-0	180	2-27-04	.244	.280	.235	42	127	20	31	13	3	1	21	21	1	0	3	28	1	0	.417	.349
Liranzo, Thayron	B-R	6-3	195	7-5-03	.250	.222	.260	21	68	11	17	4	0	1	9	14	2	0	0	20	3	1	.353	.393
Lopez, Goalber	R-R	5-10	145	10-20-02	.200	.125	.213	24	55	13	11	2	1	0	6	11	2	0	2	18	5	0	.273	.343
Meza, Jose	R-R	6-1	160	4-22-03	.258	.313	.244	52	163	28	42	7	3	3	20	23	10	1	3	48	8	6	.393	.377
Morales, Luis	R-R	5-9	162	12-6-00	.222	.235	.218	43	135	25	30	5	2	5	24	21	1	0	1	48	12	0	.400	.323
Nahr, Cliyano	R-R	6-1	170	11-7-01	.139	.056	.164	34	79	15	11	2	0	1	10	26	10	0	0	32	10	1	.203	.409
Puerta, Jorge	R-R	5-11	178	12-5-01	.299	.409	.274	39	107	33	32	6	0	5	23	24	4	0	1	16	4	0	.495	.441
Rojas, Carlos	R-R	6-0	165	7-25-02	.243	.346	.212	41	111	21	27	2	0	1	17	22	6	1	3	15	4	1	.288	.387
Segura, Yohensy	R-R	6-0	170	4-2-03	.167	.333	.111	4	12	0	2	0	0	0	0	0	0	0	0	4	0	0	.167	.167
Sosa, Victor	L-L	6-1	165	1-7-03	.277	.250	.283	45	148	29	41	6	1	2	19	28	0	0	2	23	4	1	.372	.388
Valencia, Geremias	R-R	6-3	200	10-5-01	.212	.050	.253	38	99	13	21	5	0	3	10	14	5	1	1	30	2	1	.354	.336
Valladares, Jefferson	R-R	6-0	190	5-30-02	.298	.333	.293	22	47	6	14	2	1	0	5	8	5	0	1	10	4	3	.383	.443

Pitching	B-T	HT	WT	DOB	W	L	ERA	G	GS	CG	SV	IP	H	R	ER	HR	BB	SO	AVG	vLH	vRH	K/9	BB/9
Abad, Dailoui	R-R	6-0	168	5-2-02	1	2	3.26	19	6	0	0	30	30	12	11	1	10	13	.273	.275	.271	3.86	2.97
Bastardo, Miguel	R-R	6-3	166	1-14-03	2	1	1.98	9	0	0	1	14	6	5	3	1	4	23	.128	.154	.118	15.15	2.63
Benua, Alvaro	R-R	6-4	198	1-11-03	0	0	0.00	3	0	0	3	2	0	0	0	0	1	2	.167	.000	.250	6.00	3.00
Bernardo, Smeily	R-R	6-2	180	10-22-01	0	3	6.75	13	0	0	1	19	17	16	14	2	13	20	.250	.308	.214	9.64	6.27
Bucan, Jesus	L-L	5-11	160	2-3-01	1	0	3.27	9	0	0	0	11	12	5	4	0	8	8	.286	.308	.276	6.55	6.55
Cabrera, Felix	L-L	6-3	170	4-8-02	0	0	7.17	16	4	0	0	21	25	21	17	2	20	18	.284	.273	.288	7.59	8.44
Capriata, Franniel	R-R	6-2	190	8-30-02	3	2	1.71	17	1	0	2	26	13	8	5	3	9	20	.148	.139	.154	6.84	3.08
Castillo, Yhonkervix	L-L	6-1	158	9-28-02	1	2	2.18	15	0	0	3	21	18	8	5	0	5	17	.247	.316	.222	7.40	2.18
Castro, Fran	R-R	6-0	175	7-9-00	0	0	3.95	17	0	0	0	27	33	20	12	3	11	30	.292	.395	.240	9.88	3.62
De Jesus, Antonio	R-R	6-1	205	2-25-03	0	1	8.64	12	1	0	0	8	7	11	8	0	22	10	.233	.000	.304	10.80	23.76
Diaz, Brian	R-R	6-1	179	6-5-03	0	0	5.40	18	0	0	0	20	23	15	12	3	18	23	.277	.281	.275	10.35	8.10
Dominguez, Eduardo	L-L	6-3	186	4-17-01	3	0	4.85	16	0	0	2	26	26	22	14	2	14	18	.268	.217	.284	6.23	4.85
Gonzalez, Jorge	R-R	6-5	203	8-30-02	1	2	7.45	16	7	0	1	19	20	23	16	2	15	20	.253	.250	.255	9.31	6.98
Grateron, Jose	R-R	6-0	155	5-21-02	3	4	2.67	17	0	0	1	27	20	17	8	3	14	23	.211	.205	.214	7.67	4.67
Gutierrez, Roque	R-R	5-9	177	9-7-02	0	2	3.27	8	0	0	3	11	10	6	4	0	5	6	.263	.105	.421	4.91	4.09
Herrera, Jean	R-R	6-0	178	11-14-00	3	0	2.84	14	1	0	3	19	14	9	6	1	3	25	.203	.192	.209	11.84	1.42
Ibarra, Joel	R-R	6-0	176	7-10-02	2	1	5.16	18	0	0	3	23	20	17	13	1	15	31	.247	.300	.216	12.31	5.96
Idrogo, Juan	R-R	6-2	175	9-5-02	0	1	7.94	5	0	0	0	6	5	6	5	1	8	5	.217	.600	.111	7.94	12.71
Jimenez, Jhonny	R-R	6-5	180	11-9-03	1	5	6.52	14	7	0	0	29	34	21	21	3	18	11	.306	.358	.259	3.41	5.59
Joseph, Luis	R-R	6-4	176	4-22-03	2	3	3.79	11	9	0	0	36	38	20	15	1	5	28	.266	.290	.259	7.07	1.26
Lopez, Goalber	R-R	5-10	145	10-20-02	0	0	0.00	2	0	0	0	1	0	0	0	0	0	0	.000	.000	--	0.00	0.00
Lucumi, Francisco	R-R	6-2	170	6-14-02	3	0	4.20	18	0	0	0	30	32	16	14	5	9	30	.276	.263	.282	9.00	2.70
Luna, Jesus	R-R	6-6	165	11-6-00	3	1	0.71	18	0	0	1	25	13	6	2	1	14	22	.153	.083	.204	7.82	4.97
Martines, Denverick	L-L	6-0	170	5-31-01	1	1	4.67	15	0	0	0	17	17	13	9	1	9	16	.250	.222	.254	8.31	4.67
Martinez, Carlos	R-R	6-3	190	11-9-01	2	0	3.04	15	3	0	0	27	19	13	9	0	20	30	.196	.241	.176	10.13	6.75
Martinez, Felix	L-L	6-1	170	10-20-01	0	0	8.31	4	0	0	0	4	1	4	4	0	6	6	.071	.000	.083	12.46	12.46
Martinez, Maximo	R-R	6-2	185	6-21-04	1	2	4.76	12	12	0	0	28	27	19	15	2	16	21	.260	.175	.313	6.67	5.08
Matos, Alberluis	L-L	6-0	175	9-30-01	4	2	1.32	16	0	0	5	27	15	6	4	1	9	28	.174	.143	.181	9.22	2.96
Medrano, Lesther	R-R	6-2	185	3-5-03	1	1	2.88	13	9	0	0	41	39	20	13	1	11	36	.252	.183	.295	7.97	2.43
Moya, Abel	R-R	6-1	172	6-6-01	4	2	1.95	17	0	0	1	32	28	12	7	1	7	30	.224	.175	.265	8.35	1.95
Omosako, Kinn	R-R	6-4	210	6-24-04	0	2	7.47	12	4	0	1	16	16	16	13	2	13	9	.271	.286	.263	5.17	7.47
Pinales, Darlin	R-R	6-4	240	8-28-02	1	2	5.28	12	8	0	0	29	25	19	17	1	20	24	.231	.324	.183	7.45	6.21
Portes, Denis	R-R	6-1	170	3-9-02	1	0	23.63	4	0	0	0	3	2	7	7	1	8	2	.222	.167	.333	10.13	27.00
Ramirez, Kelvin	R-R	6-4	187	6-10-01	2	1	6.48	6	2	0	0	8	6	7	6	1	8	13	.207	.000	.300	14.04	8.64
Rodriguez, Jose	B-R	6-6	200	7-18-01	2	0	5.40	15	0	0	1	18	20	16	11	2	8	18	.270	.212	.310	8.84	3.93
Romero, Christian	R-R	6-3	195	12-11-02	1	1	3.72	10	5	0	0	29	22	14	12	1	9	32	.212	.283	.155	9.93	2.79
Santana, Waylin	R-R	6-1	155	3-13-03	1	2	7.23	10	9	0	0	24	28	20	19	2	13	24	.308	.256	.354	9.13	4.94
Santillan, Pedro	R-R	6-4	200	7-7-01	4	1	3.58	20	0	0	3	28	27	17	11	3	12	25	.255	.182	.288	8.13	3.90
Soto, Missael	R-R	0-0		9-21-03	0	2	11.37	13	13	0	0	19	21	29	24	1	19	12	.269	.278	.262	5.68	9.00
Tiburcio, David	R-R	6-2	195	12-29-01	2	3	3.94	15	0	0	0	30	22	16	13	0	10	27	.196	.170	.215	8.19	3.03
Tua, Rafael	R-R	5-10	145	10-26-01	3	3	3.73	13	5	0	0	41	34	17	17	6	11	46	.224	.156	.252	10.10	2.41
Valdez, Luis	L-L	6-2	158	7-18-03	0	0	1.50	3	3	0	0	6	3	1	1	0	1	9	.150	.000	.158	13.50	1.50
Vilchez, Michael	R-R	6-3	180	6-3-04	1	1	3.10	12	5	0	0	20	23	13	7	0	8	10	.291	.241	.320	4.43	3.54

Fielding

C: Avila 19, Diaz 1, Galiz 15, Liranzo 12, Lopez 19, Puerta 22, Rojas 38, Valladares 12.
1B: Caraballo 1, Diaz 16, Diaz 3, Dotel 1, Hernandez 19, Liranzo 6, Lopez 6, Puerta 16, Rojas 11, Sosa 20, Valencia 30, Valladares 6.
2B: Armas 16, Campos 27, De La Rosa 16, Doncon 6, Dotel 4, Droz 1, Espinosa 7, Figueroa 13, Garcia 14, Guerra 16, Hernandez 12, Lopez 1.
3B: Armas 21, Campos 2, De La Rosa 16, Droz 14, Espinosa 26, Figueroa 7, Garcia 9, Guerra 15, Hernandez 17, Lopez 1.
SS: Armas 6, Campos 7, De La Rosa 2, Diaz 14, Doncon 18, Droz 23, Figueroa 31, Garcia 25, Guerra 1, Hernandez 5.
OF: Alonso 27, Campos 3, Caraballo 49, De La Rosa 13, Diaz 33, Dotel 12, Enrique 44, Garcia 1, Guerra 6, Lasso 21, Meza 57, Morales 43, Nahr 34, Puerta 1, Segura 4, Sosa 24, Valencia 7, Valladares 1.

Miami Marlins

SEASON IN A SENTENCE: The Marlins showed hints of promise throughout the season but ultimately settled for fourth place in the National League East, 21.5 games behind the eventual World Series-champion Braves.

HIGH POINT: On Sept. 8, ace righty Sandy Alcantara tossed the best game of his season when he whiffed 14 in a one-run complete game victory over the Mets. His effort that day earned him a game score of 88, the best of the season by any Marlins pitcher.

LOW POINT: The Nationals battered the Marlins on July 19 by a score of 18-1 in a game in which starter Ross Detwiler allowed four home runs in the first inning. The game finished with catcher Sandy Leon on the mound allowing one of Juan Soto's two home runs on the day.

NOTABLE ROOKIES: Lefty starter Trevor Rogers, who debuted in 2020 but still met the rookie threshold for 2021, continued his star turn. Rogers finished 7-8, 2.64 with 157 strikeouts in 133 innings. He was joined by Jazz Chisholm, who showed plenty of flashes of brilliance and star power both at the plate and in the field. Chisholm slammed 18 home runs and stole 23 bases as part of a 2.5 bWAR season. The Marlins also got contributions from outfielder Jesus Sanchez, first baseman Lewin Diaz—trade pieces from the Rays and Twins, respectively—and catcher Nick Fortes, as well as reclamation project Zach Thompson, who pitched 75 innings and worked to a 3-7, 3.25 mark. Reliever Anthony Bender also gave the club 1.2 bWAR in relief after being signed in the offseason as a minor league free agent. Bender was one of 13 Marlins to make their big league debut in 2021. The list also included righthander Zach Pop, infielders Jose Devers and Luis Marte and outfielder Brian Miller.

KEY TRANSACTIONS: The Marlins were sellers at the deadline, choosing to aim themselves for the future rather than make a long-odds run at a wild card spot. Instead, they turned Starling Marte into former Oakland top prospect Jesus Luzardo, spun Adam Duvall to Atlanta for catcher Alex Jackson, received Bryan De La Cruz and Austin Pruitt from Houston for reliever Yimi Garcia and got catcher Payton Henry from Milwaukee for reliever John Curtiss. Those trades each brought controllable big league pieces to a team looking toward the future with a farm system stocked with an enviable supply of pitching.

OPENING DAY PAYROLL: $49,425,000 (27th).

PLAYERS OF THE YEAR

MAJOR LEAGUE	MINOR LEAGUE
Trevor Rogers	**Eury Perez**
LHP	**RHP**
7-8, 2.64	(High-A/Low-A)
NL ROY finalist	3-5, 1.96,
157 SO in 133 IP	108 SO in 78 IP

ORGANIZATION LEADERS

Batting		*Minimum 250 AB
MAJORS		
*AVG	Miguel Rojas	.265
*OPS	Jesus Aguilar	.788
HR	Jesus Aguilar	22
HR	Adam Duvall	22
RBI	Jesus Aguilar	93
MINORS		
*AVG	Troy Johnston, Beloit, Jupiter	.300
*OBP	Troy Johnston, Beloit, Jupiter	.399
*SLG	Griffin Conine, Pensacola, Beloit	.530
*OPS	Troy Johnston, Beloit, Jupiter	.867
R	Connor Scott, Beloit	80
H	Troy Johnston, Beloit, Jupiter	132
TB	Griffin Conine, Pensacola, Beloit	209
2B	Kameron Misner, Pensacola, Beloit	29
3B	Ricky Aracena, Beloit	11
3B	Victor Mesa Jr., Jupiter	11
HR	Griffin Conine, Pensacola, Beloit	36
RBI	Troy Johnston, Beloit, Jupiter	85
BB	Peyton Burdick, Jacksonville, Pensacola	79
SO	Griffin Conine, Pensacola, Beloit	185
SB	Brian Miller, Jacksonville	36
Pitching		#Minimum 75 IP
MAJORS		
W	Sandy Alcantara	9
#ERA	Trevor Rogers	2.64
SO	Sandy Alcantara	201
SV	Dylan Floro	15
SV	Yimi Garcia	15
MINORS		
W	6 tied	7
L	Zach McCambley, Pensacola, Beloit	10
#ERA	Max Meyer, Jacksonville, Pensacola	2.27
G	Colton Hock, Jacksonville, Pensacola	44
GS	Bryan Hoeing, Beloit	22
GS	Max Meyer, Jacksonville, Pensacola	22
SV	Colton Hock, Jacksonville, Pensacola	19
IP	Bryan Hoeing, Beloit	121
BB	M.D. Johnson, Beloit, Jupiter	63
SO	Kyle Nicolas, Pensacola, Beloit	136
#AVG	Eury Perez, Beloit, Jupiter	.158

General Manager: Kim Ng. **Farm Director:** Gary Denbo. **Scouting Director:** D.J. Svihlik.

Class	Team	League	W	L	PCT	Finish	Manager
Majors	Miami Marlins	National	67	95	.414	12th (15)	Don Mattingly
Triple-A	Jacksonville Jumbo Shrimp	Triple-A East	75	55	.577	5th (20)	Al Pedrique
Double-A	Pensacola Blue Wahoos	Double-A South	57	54	.514	5th (8)	Kevin Randel
High-A	Beloit Snappers	High-A Central	55	65	.458	9th (12)	Mike Jacobs
Low-A	Jupiter Hammerheads	Low-A Southeast	61	56	.521	5th (10)	Jorge Hernandez
Rookie	DSL Marlins	Dominican Summer	23	34	.404	37th (46)	Rigoberto Silverio
Rookie	FCL Marlins	Florida Complex	27	28	.491	8th (18)	Luis Dorante
Overall 2021 Minor League Record		298		292	.505 16th (30)		

ORGANIZATION STATISTICS

MIAMI MARLINS
NATIONAL LEAGUE

Batting	B-T	HT	WT	DOB	AVG	vLH	vRH	G	AB	R	H	2B	3B	HR	RBI	BB	HBP	SH	SF	SO	SB	CS	SLG	OBP
Aguilar, Jesus	R-R	6-3	277	6-30-90	.261	.259	.261	131	449	49	117	23	0	22	93	46	3	0	7	93	0	0	.459	.329
Alfaro, Jorge	R-R	6-3	230	6-11-93	.244	.259	.238	92	295	22	72	15	1	4	30	11	5	0	0	99	8	1	.342	.283
Alvarez, Eddy	B-R	5-9	185	1-30-90	.188	.100	.227	24	64	8	12	4	1	1	6	4	6	0	0	18	1	0	.328	.297
Anderson, Brian	R-R	6-3	208	5-19-93	.249	.158	.278	67	233	24	58	9	0	7	28	26	5	0	0	65	5	0	.378	.337
Berti, Jon	R-R	5-10	190	1-22-90	.210	.161	.240	85	233	35	49	10	1	4	19	32	3	1	2	61	8	4	.313	.311
Brinson, Lewis	R-R	6-5	212	5-8-94	.226	.256	.212	89	274	24	62	14	0	9	33	13	1	1	1	72	1	1	.376	.263
Chisholm Jr., Jazz	L-R	5-11	184	2-1-98	.248	.237	.252	124	464	70	115	20	4	18	53	34	4	2	3	145	23	8	.425	.303
Cooper, Garrett	R-R	6-5	235	12-25-90	.284	.344	.258	71	215	30	61	10	1	9	33	30	4	0	1	68	1	1	.465	.380
De La Cruz, Bryan	R-R	6-2	175	12-16-96	.296	.347	.280	58	199	17	59	7	2	5	19	18	1	0	1	53	1	1	.427	.356
Devers, Jose	L-R	6-0	174	12-7-99	.244	.167	.257	21	41	7	10	3	0	0	5	3	1	0	1	11	0	0	.317	.304
Diaz, Isan	L-R	5-11	201	5-27-96	.193	.169	.205	89	238	25	46	9	0	4	17	34	1	1	3	73	1	1	.282	.293
Diaz, Lewin	L-L	6-4	217	11-19-96	.205	.179	.217	40	122	16	25	4	1	8	13	6	0	0	0	33	0	0	.451	.242
Dickerson, Corey	L-R	6-1	200	5-22-89	.263	.268	.262	63	205	27	54	12	3	2	14	16	3	0	1	45	2	4	.380	.324
Duvall, Adam	R-R	6-1	215	9-4-88	.229	.176	.249	91	314	41	72	10	1	22	68	21	1	0	3	105	5	0	.478	.277
2-team total (55 Atlanta)					.228	.178	.245	146	513	67	117	17	2	38	113	35	4	0	3	174	5	0	.491	.281
Fortes, Nick	R-R	5-11	198	11-11-96	.290	.250	.316	14	31	6	9	0	0	4	7	3	0	0	0	8	1	0	.677	.353
Harrison, Monte	R-R	6-3	225	8-10-95	.200	.143	.333	9	10	0	2	1	0	0	0	0	0	1	0	3	0	1	.300	.200
Henry, Payton	R-R	6-2	215	6-24-97	.267	.333	.222	5	15	0	4	1	0	0	1	0	0	0	0	5	0	0	.333	.313
Jackson, Alex	R-R	6-2	215	12-25-95	.157	.103	.177	42	108	11	17	4	0	3	12	11	4	0	0	60	0	0	.278	.260
2-team total (10 Atlanta)					.137	.086	.156	52	131	13	18	4	0	3	12	13	7	0	0	73	0	0	.237	.252
Leon, Sandy	B-R	5-10	235	3-13-89	.183	.228	.166	83	202	15	37	5	0	4	14	12	3	1	2	65	0	0	.267	.237
Marrero, Deven	R-R	6-0	190	8-25-90	.188	.000	.273	10	16	4	3	0	0	1	1	3	0	0	0	6	1	0	.375	.316
Marte, Luis	R-R	6-1	188	12-15-93	.167	.000	.250	4	6	2	1	0	0	0	0	1	0	0	0	2	0	0	.167	.286
Marte, Starling	R-R	6-1	195	10-9-88	.305	.258	.323	64	233	52	71	11	1	7	25	32	8	1	1	57	22	3	.451	.405
Miller, Brian	L-R	6-1	196	8-20-95	.273	.500	.143	5	11	1	3	0	0	0	0	0	0	0	0	3	0	0	.273	.273
Panik, Joe	L-R	6-1	205	10-30-90	.172	.088	.205	53	122	8	21	3	0	1	7	9	2	1	0	20	2	0	.221	.241
Rojas, Miguel	R-R	6-0	188	2-24-89	.265	.317	.244	132	495	66	131	30	3	9	48	37	5	1	1	74	13	3	.392	.322
Sanchez, Jesus	L-R	6-3	222	10-7-97	.251	.257	.248	64	227	27	57	8	2	14	36	20	3	0	1	78	0	1	.489	.319
Sierra, Magneuris	L-L	5-11	178	4-7-96	.230	.245	.225	123	209	27	48	6	1	0	5	15	0	1	0	50	11	0	.268	.281
Wallach, Chad	R-R	6-2	246	11-4-91	.200	.190	.205	23	60	2	12	2	1	0	6	3	1	0	2	32	0	0	.267	.242

Pitching	B-T	HT	WT	DOB	W	L	ERA	G	GS	CG	SV	IP	H	R	ER	HR	BB	SO	AVG	vLH	vRH	K/9	BB/9
Alcantara, Sandy	R-R	6-5	200	9-7-95	9	15	3.19	33	33	1	0	206	171	85	73	21	50	201	.223	.229	.215	8.80	2.19
Bass, Anthony	R-R	6-2	200	11-1-87	3	9	3.82	70	1	0	0	61	55	33	26	11	24	58	.241	.300	.195	8.51	3.52
Bellatti, Andrew	R-R	6-1	190	8-5-91	0	0	13.50	3	0	0	0	3	6	5	5	0	2	4	.353	.300	.429	10.80	5.40
Bender, Anthony	R-R	6-4	205	2-3-95	3	2	2.79	60	1	0	3	61	45	22	19	5	20	71	.207	.247	.180	10.42	2.93
Bleier, Richard	L-L	6-3	215	4-16-87	3	2	2.95	68	0	0	0	58	51	20	19	4	6	44	.241	.211	.262	6.83	0.93
Cabrera, Edward	R-R	6-5	217	4-13-98	0	3	5.81	7	7	0	0	26	24	20	17	6	19	28	.247	.259	.233	9.57	6.49
Campbell, Paul	L-R	6-0	210	7-26-95	2	3	6.41	16	1	0	0	27	32	24	19	5	10	26	.288	.286	.290	8.78	3.38
Castano, Daniel	L-L	6-3	231	9-17-94	0	2	4.87	5	4	0	0	20	22	12	11	3	8	13	.268	.250	.274	5.75	3.54
Cimber, Adam	R-R	6-3	195	8-15-90	1	2	2.88	33	0	0	0	34	30	14	11	0	11	21	.242	.196	.269	5.50	2.88
Curtiss, John	R-R	6-5	220	4-5-93	3	1	2.48	35	2	0	0	40	34	13	11	4	9	40	.227	.234	.221	9.00	2.03
2-team total (6 Milwaukee)					3	1	3.45	41	2	0	0	44	42	21	17	6	12	44	.244	.260	.232	8.93	2.44
Detwiler, Ross	R-L	6-5	210	3-6-86	2	1	4.96	46	5	0	0	45	41	26	25	8	15	56	.234	.273	.211	11.12	2.98
2-team total (7 San Diego)					3	1	4.64	53	5	0	0	52	44	28	27	10	20	62	.222	.237	.213	10.66	3.44
Floro, Dylan	L-R	6-2	203	12-27-90	6	6	2.81	68	0	0	15	64	53	25	20	2	25	62	.217	.236	.201	8.72	3.52
Garcia, Yimi	R-R	6-2	228	8-18-90	3	7	3.47	39	0	0	15	36	31	18	14	5	13	35	.233	.241	.227	8.67	3.22
Garrett, Braxton	R-L	6-2	202	8-5-97	1	2	5.03	8	7	0	0	34	42	20	19	3	20	32	.318	.394	.293	8.47	5.29
Guenther, Sean	L-L	5-11	194	12-29-95	0	1	9.30	14	0	0	0	20	31	22	21	1	10	15	.348	.447	.275	6.64	4.43
Guilmet, Preston	R-R	6-2	200	7-27-87	0	0	4.50	2	0	0	0	2	2	1	1	1	0	1	.286	.333	.250	4.50	0.00
Guzman, Jorge	R-R	6-1	246	1-28-96	0	0	32.40	2	0	0	0	2	4	6	6	0	6	3	.444	.000	.500	16.20	32.40
Hernandez, Elieser	R-R	6-0	214	5-3-95	1	3	4.18	11	11	0	0	52	54	26	24	13	14	53	.265	.282	.245	9.23	2.44

Hess, David	R-R	6-1	215	7-10-93	2	2	8.00	14	1	0	0	18	24	18	16	7	10	16	.324	.368	.278	8.00	5.00
Holloway, Jordan	R-R	6-6	230	6-13-96	2	3	4.00	13	4	0	0	36	23	19	16	3	26	36	.177	.193	.164	9.00	6.50
Leon, Sandy	B-R	5-10	235	3-13-89	0	0	7.50	6	0	0	0	6	7	5	5	3	1	2	.280	.214	.364	3.00	1.50
Lopez, Pablo	L-R	6-4	225	3-7-96	5	5	3.07	20	20	0	0	103	89	37	35	11	26	115	.233	.245	.221	10.08	2.28
Luzardo, Jesus	L-L	6-0	218	9-30-97	4	5	6.44	12	12	0	0	57	60	41	41	9	32	58	.269	.235	.279	9.10	5.02
Madero, Luis	R-R	6-1	195	4-15-97	0	0	9.00	6	0	0	0	12	13	12	12	3	8	4	.277	.423	.095	3.00	6.00
Mitchell, Bryan	L-R	6-2	215	4-19-91	0	0	4.50	2	0	0	0	4	5	2	2	2	0	4	.313	.000	.455	9.00	4.50
Morimando, Shawn	L-L	6-0	206	11-20-92	0	0	9.58	4	0	0	0	10	18	11	11	2	5	9	.375	.500	.357	7.84	4.35
Neidert, Nick	R-R	6-1	202	11-20-96	1	2	4.54	8	7	0	0	36	31	18	18	4	23	21	.246	.300	.197	5.30	5.80
Okert, Steven	L-L	6-2	202	7-9-91	3	1	2.75	34	0	0	0	36	22	12	11	5	15	40	.183	.140	.214	10.00	3.75
Pop, Zach	R-R	6-4	220	9-20-96	1	0	4.12	50	0	0	0	55	54	29	25	3	24	51	.254	.220	.275	8.40	3.95
Poteet, Cody	R-R	6-1	190	7-30-94	2	3	4.99	7	7	0	0	31	25	17	17	7	16	32	.216	.197	.236	9.39	4.70
Pruitt, Austin	R-R	5-10	185	8-31-89	0	0	1.93	4	0	0	0	5	4	1	1	0	0	4	.235	.333	.182	7.71	0.00
Rogers, Trevor	L-L	6-5	217	11-13-97	7	8	2.64	25	25	0	0	133	107	46	39	6	46	157	.218	.259	.206	10.62	3.11
Thompson, Zach	R-R	6-7	230	10-23-93	3	7	3.24	26	14	0	0	75	63	35	27	6	28	66	.227	.262	.196	7.92	3.36
Williams, Taylor	B-R	5-11	185	7-21-91	0	0	7.11	6	0	0	0	6	9	6	5	1	5	3	.346	.313	.400	4.26	7.11
2-team total (5 San Diego)					0	0	4.63	11	0	0	0	12	12	7	6	1	8	9	.273	.217	.333	6.94	6.17

Fielding

Catcher	PCT	G	PO	A	E	DP	PB
Alfaro	.996	61	467	19	2	1	13
Fortes	.982	7	50	5	1	1	4
Henry	1.000	5	43	1	0	1	0
Jackson	.992	34	248	11	2	1	2
Leon	.994	60	444	20	3	3	4
Wallach	.988	19	161	3	2	1	4

First Base	PCT	G	PO	A	E	DP
Aguilar	.991	113	824	83	8	94
Alfaro	1.000	3	17	1	0	0
Cooper	1.000	19	115	7	0	12
Diaz	1.000	32	204	34	0	24
Marrero	.000	1	0	0	0	0
Panik	.978	6	42	2	1	3

Second Base	PCT	G	PO	A	E	DP
Alvarez	1.000	4	8	11	0	4
Berti	.987	27	32	44	1	12
Chisholm Jr.	.959	91	120	209	14	57

	PCT	G	PO	A	E	DP
Devers	1.000	13	5	18	0	1
Diaz	.982	35	44	66	2	13
Marrero	1.000	1	2	1	0	0
Marte	1.000	1	1	5	0	1
Panik	1.000	17	26	28	0	9

Third Base	PCT	G	PO	A	E	DP
Aguilar	1.000	2	0	2	0	0
Alvarez	.909	17	8	32	4	1
Anderson	.970	65	37	124	5	17
Berti	.927	46	22	79	8	5
Diaz	.934	37	17	68	6	8
Leon	.000	1	0	0	0	0
Marrero	1.000	3	1	3	0	0
Marte	1.000	1	0	1	0	0
Panik	.882	11	4	11	2	1

Shortstop	PCT	G	PO	A	E	DP
Anderson	1.000	1	2	3	0	0
Berti	1.000	2	3	0	0	0

	PCT	G	PO	A	E	DP
Chisholm Jr.	.925	37	46	77	10	20
Devers	.900	5	5	4	1	2
Marrero	1.000	4	2	6	0	1
Marte	1.000	1	0	1	0	0
Rojas	.977	128	192	282	11	80

Outfield	PCT	G	PO	A	E	DP
Alfaro	.913	21	20	1	2	0
Berti	1.000	12	11	0	0	0
Brinson	.980	88	139	5	3	1
Cooper	.984	41	61	1	1	0
De La Cruz	.975	63	113	3	3	1
Dickerson	.988	52	83	2	1	1
Duvall	.988	90	152	7	2	1
Harrison	1.000	7	7	1	0	0
Jackson	--	1	0	0	0	0
Marte	.986	63	133	6	2	3
Miller	1.000	5	2	1	0	0
Sanchez	.961	62	120	3	5	0
Sierra	.982	78	109	3	2	1

JACKSONVILLE JUMBO SHRIMP
TRIPLE-A

TRIPLE-A EAST

Batting	B-T	HT	WT	DOB	AVG	vLH	vRH	G	AB	R	H	2B	3B	HR	RBI	BB	HBP	SH	SF	SO	SB	CS	SLG	OBP
Alfaro, Jorge	R-R	6-3	230	6-11-93	.250	.500	.000	5	16	3	4	0	0	2	5	0	0	0	1	0	0	.625	.250
Alvarez, Eddy	B-R	5-9	185	1-30-90	.288	.303	.282	31	111	23	32	5	0	4	16	18	8	1	0	27	2	5	.441	.423
Anderson, Brian	R-R	6-3	208	5-19-93	.077	.333	.000	5	13	2	1	0	0	0	1	0	1	0	1	6	0	0	.077	.133
Arcaya, Luis	R-R	6-1	170	2-26-99	.000	--	.000	2	5	0	0	0	0	0	0	0	0	0	0	2	0	0	.000	.000
Bird, Corey	L-L	6-1	185	8-11-95	.239	.164	.260	94	280	47	67	18	2	6	24	37	2	0	0	67	15	2	.382	.332
Bradshaw, Davis	L-R	6-3	175	4-25-98	.154	.333	.100	7	13	1	2	0	0	0	0	1	0	0	0	3	0	0	.154	.214
Brigman, Bryson	R-R	5-11	180	6-19-95	.282	.264	.288	104	376	54	106	19	5	5	33	46	3	4	4	68	10	5	.399	.361
Brinson, Lewis	R-R	6-2	212	5-8-94	.283	.333	.265	12	46	3	13	1	1	1	3	2	0	0	0	11	2	0	.413	.313
Burdick, Peyton	R-R	6-0	205	2-26-97	.143	.111	.158	8	28	5	4	3	0	0	1	3	0	0	0	11	0	0	.250	.226
Chavez, Santiago	R-R	5-11	211	8-5-95	.186	.083	.219	33	97	14	18	4	0	2	6	6	5	2	0	38	1	0	.289	.269
Chinea, Chris	R-R	5-11	220	5-3-94	.150	.000	.231	8	20	2	3	1	0	1	1	1	0	0	6	0	0	.350	.227
Chisholm Jr., Jazz	L-R	5-11	184	2-1-98	.444	1.000	.375	3	9	3	4	1	0	1	4	1	0	0	0	2	1	2	.889	.500
Cooper, Garrett	R-R	6-5	235	12-25-90	.400	--	.400	2	5	1	2	0	0	0	0	1	0	0	1	0	0	0	.400	.500
Cribbs Jr., Galli	L-R	6-0	190	10-8-92	.071	.000	.091	10	14	0	1	0	0	0	0	0	3	0	0	8	0	1	.071	.235
Devers, Jose	L-R	6-0	174	12-7-99	.231	.400	.172	12	39	4	9	1	1	0	3	1	0	1	0	5	0	0	.308	.250
Diaz, Isan	L-R	5-11	201	5-27-96	.243	.280	.231	29	103	16	25	8	1	5	15	11	2	0	0	30	0	2	.485	.328
Diaz, Lewin	L-L	6-4	217	11-19-96	.248	.237	.252	74	278	52	69	15	0	20	51	26	7	0	1	60	2	0	.518	.327
Dunand, Joe	R-R	6-2	205	9-20-95	.201	.226	.190	64	204	20	41	9	1	8	32	17	5	1	2	70	0	0	.373	.276
Fortes, Nick	R-R	5-11	198	11-11-96	.237	.286	.220	38	135	16	32	7	0	4	21	10	7	0	0	18	0	0	.378	.322
Fowler, Dustin	L-L	6-0	195	12-29-94	.295	.357	.273	28	105	13	31	2	1	6	24	2	1	0	2	33	0	0	.505	.309
2-team total (13 Indianapolis)					.289	.300	.284	41	142	21	41	4	2	9	30	11	2	0	2	49	2	0	.535	.344
Hairston, Devin	R-R	5-8	175	4-7-96	.175	.067	.240	14	40	3	7	0	1	1	4	5	0	1	1	12	0	0	.300	.261
Harrison, Monte	R-R	6-3	225	8-10-95	.242	.218	.251	74	269	47	65	8	1	15	52	31	6	0	2	121	24	3	.446	.331
Henry, Payton	R-R	6-2	215	6-24-97	.188	.222	.176	22	69	7	13	2	0	4	8	10	1	0	0	26	0	1	.391	.300
2-team total (19 Nashville)					.223	.200	.230	41	130	14	29	5	0	5	17	14	5	0	2	43	0	1	.377	.318
Justus, Connor	R-R	6-0	190	11-2-94	.201	.146	.222	45	149	9	30	4	1	0	7	10	3	2	1	45	0	2	.242	.264
Kone, Zack	R-R	6-3	202	11-5-96	.333	1.000	.000	2	3	0	1	0	0	0	0	0	1	0	0	0	0	0	.333	.500
Marrero, Deven	R-R	6-1	190	8-25-90	.215	.204	.220	59	181	23	39	7	0	5	21	21	1	3	1	60	0	1	.337	.299
Marte, Luis	R-R	6-1	188	12-15-93	.202	.158	.215	27	84	7	17	2	0	3	11	2	0	0	2	20	3	1	.333	.216
Marte, Starling	R-R	6-1	195	10-9-88	.000	.000	.000	2	6	0	0	0	0	0	0	0	0	0	0	1	0	0	.000	.000
Miller, Brian	L-R	6-1	196	8-20-95	.268	.224	.284	113	396	53	106	16	3	2	34	34	2	7	4	88	36	8	.338	.326

Name	B-T	HT	WT	DOB																				
Mitchell, Tevin	R-R	6-1	170	5-2-97	.111	.111	.111	9	18	5	2	0	1	1	1	2	3	0	0	11	0	1	.389	.304
Navarreto, Brian	R-R	6-0	237	12-29-94	.214	.241	.203	33	98	15	21	3	1	5	17	12	1	0	2	34	0	0	.418	.301
Osborne, J.D.	R-R	6-1	215	7-13-95	.216	.111	.250	13	37	2	8	2	0	0	2	1	1	0	0	10	0	0	.270	.256
Pompey, Tristan	B-R	6-4	200	3-23-97	.194	.227	.178	25	67	9	13	3	1	0	6	13	0	0	1	25	0	0	.269	.321
Quintana, Lorenzo	R-R	5-10	205	3-1-89	.294	.263	.306	64	204	28	60	14	3	9	34	14	6	0	2	45	0	0	.525	.354
Rojas, Miguel	R-R	6-0	188	2-24-89	.500	.000	.571	2	8	1	4	1	0	0	1	0	0	0	0	1	0	0	.625	.500
Sanchez, Jesus	L-R	6-3	222	10-7-97	.348	.349	.347	37	141	23	49	5	4	10	31	12	2	0	0	29	1	0	.652	.406
Twine, Justin	R-R	5-11	205	10-7-95	.229	.212	.236	71	231	35	53	10	4	5	26	6	6	0	4	97	12	1	.372	.263
Wallach, Chad	R-R	6-2	246	11-4-91	.204	.160	.218	31	103	11	21	2	0	7	17	23	4	0	0	35	0	0	.427	.369
Zehner, Zack	R-R	6-4	215	8-8-92	.259	.298	.239	60	170	19	44	9	1	4	19	20	0	0	2	55	3	0	.394	.333
2-team total (12 Scranton/Wilkes-Barre)					.239	.308	.207	72	205	23	49	11	2	4	23	30	0	0	2	70	6	0	.371	.333

Pitching

	B-T	HT	WT	DOB	W	L	ERA	G	GS	CG	SV	IP	H	R	ER	HR	BB	SO	AVG	vLH	vRH	K/9	BB/9
Alexander, Jason	R-R	6-3	200	3-1-93	1	1	1.84	5	4	0	0	15	12	5	3	1	3	18	.222	.241	.200	11.05	1.84
Bellatti, Andrew	R-R	6-1	190	8-5-91	1	2	1.52	26	0	0	11	30	15	7	5	2	10	38	.149	.160	.137	11.53	3.03
Bugg, Parker	R-R	6-6	210	10-26-94	6	2	4.46	32	4	0	0	67	49	41	33	10	45	85	.201	.193	.208	11.48	6.08
Cabrera, Edward	R-R	6-5	217	4-13-98	1	3	3.68	6	6	0	0	29	22	13	12	4	19	48	.206	.243	.186	14.73	5.83
Campbell, Paul	L-R	6-0	210	7-26-95	0	0	0.84	3	3	0	0	11	3	1	1	1	6	9	.086	.000	.107	7.59	5.06
Carroll, Cody	R-R	6-5	230	10-15-92	0	0	6.00	3	0	0	0	3	5	2	2	1	1	6	.357	.250	.500	18.00	3.00
2-team total (22 Norfolk)					2	0	5.63	25	0	0	0	24	26	16	15	6	12	29	.283	.271	.295	10.88	4.50
Castano, Daniel	L-L	6-3	231	9-17-94	7	2	3.91	14	14	1	0	78	69	35	34	16	16	54	.235	.220	.243	6.20	1.84
Eibner, Brett	R-R	6-4	215	12-2-88	1	2	3.46	11	0	0	3	13	13	7	5	0	6	14	.250	.250	.250	9.69	4.15
Eveld, Tommy	R-R	6-5	214	12-30-93	5	3	3.63	36	0	0	6	45	38	20	18	8	16	54	.230	.241	.221	10.88	3.22
Fishman, Jake	L-L	6-3	195	2-8-95	5	1	3.67	34	2	0	1	56	44	26	23	7	17	51	.213	.200	.222	8.15	2.72
Garrett, Braxton	R-L	6-2	202	8-5-97	5	4	3.89	18	18	0	0	86	73	41	37	10	32	86	.231	.244	.227	9.04	3.36
Guenther, Sean	L-L	5-11	194	12-29-95	3	1	4.76	15	1	0	1	23	21	15	12	2	4	28	.247	.242	.250	11.12	1.59
Guerrero, Alberto	R-R	6-3	192	12-13-97	1	1	4.70	11	0	0	0	15	15	10	8	3	7	14	.283	.357	.256	8.22	4.11
Guillen, Alexander	R-R	6-2	206	11-23-95	1	1	5.84	13	1	0	1	25	30	16	16	4	10	21	.294	.277	.309	7.66	3.65
Guilmet, Preston	R-R	6-2	200	7-27-87	5	2	3.78	32	0	0	6	52	37	24	22	8	13	67	.194	.196	.191	11.52	2.24
Guzman, Jorge	R-R	6-1	246	1-28-96	0	1	3.52	9	0	0	4	15	14	8	6	1	9	20	.230	.192	.257	11.74	5.28
Hernandez, Elieser	R-R	6-0	214	5-3-95	0	1	2.95	5	5	0	0	21	11	8	7	3	3	32	.149	.276	.067	13.50	1.27
Hock, Colton	R-R	6-4	220	3-15-96	2	1	5.56	8	0	0	0	11	16	8	7	1	2	9	.333	.154	.400	7.15	1.59
Holloway, Jordan	R-R	6-6	230	6-13-96	0	5	4.88	8	6	0	0	31	29	20	17	5	14	29	.248	.266	.226	8.33	4.02
Leban, Zack	R-R	6-3	245	5-30-96	0	1	4.50	4	0	0	0	8	7	4	4	1	7	8	.250	.300	.222	9.00	7.88
Leibrandt, Brandon	L-L	6-4	190	12-13-92	2	6	5.18	14	11	1	0	57	61	34	33	12	19	53	.279	.284	.275	8.32	2.98
Lopez, Pablo	L-R	6-4	225	3-7-96	0	0	0.00	2	2	0	0	5	1	0	0	0	0	5	.067	.091	.000	9.00	0.00
Madero, Luis	R-R	6-1	195	4-15-97	7	3	2.84	17	7	0	0	57	46	28	18	4	24	58	.215	.253	.183	9.16	3.79
McKenna, Brian	R-R	6-0	202	11-19-92	0	0	20.25	1	0	0	0	3	3	3	3	2	1	1	.429	.500	.400	6.75	6.75
Melotakis, Mason	R-L	6-2	220	6-28-91	3	1	5.59	22	0	0	2	29	37	21	18	9	16	23	.311	.245	.357	7.14	4.97
Mesa Jr., Jose	R-R	6-4	215	8-13-93	0	0	10.13	5	0	0	0	8	15	9	9	3	4	7	.395	.389	.400	7.88	4.50
Meyer, Max	L-R	6-0	196	3-12-99	0	1	0.90	2	2	0	0	10	6	5	1	1	2	17	.167	.188	.150	15.30	1.80
Mitchell, Bryan	L-R	6-2	215	4-19-91	1	0	2.76	11	3	0	0	29	20	9	9	3	13	37	.192	.132	.227	11.35	3.99
2-team total (20 Lehigh Valley)					4	1	4.37	31	3	0	1	58	52	29	28	5	29	57	.248	.264	.236	8.90	4.53
Morimando, Shawn	L-L	6-0	206	11-20-92	3	4	4.32	18	16	0	0	90	90	45	43	17	31	86	.259	.255	.261	8.63	3.11
Neidert, Nick	R-R	6-1	202	11-20-96	6	4	3.67	14	13	1	0	69	71	41	28	8	21	52	.264	.308	.211	6.82	2.75
Okert, Steven	L-L	6-2	202	7-9-91	2	0	1.80	15	0	0	4	20	13	4	4	1	4	29	.188	.179	.195	13.05	1.80
Poteet, Cody	R-R	6-1	190	7-30-94	1	0	3.38	2	2	0	0	8	6	3	3	1	3	12	.207	.182	.222	13.50	3.38
Pruitt, Austin	R-R	5-10	185	8-31-89	1	0	4.50	8	0	0	0	8	9	9	5	1	3	11	.237	.235	.238	9.90	2.70
Smith, Josh A.	R-R	6-2	210	8-7-87	2	0	2.76	8	6	0	0	33	24	10	10	1	13	30	.197	.213	.180	8.27	3.58
Stout, Eric	L-L	6-3	205	3-27-93	0	2	10.19	7	4	0	0	18	19	22	20	6	18	21	.268	.176	.296	10.70	9.17
Thompson, Zach	R-R	6-7	230	10-23-93	0	0	6.60	8	0	0	0	15	22	11	11	4	2	21	.338	.385	.269	12.60	1.20
Walters, Jake	R-R	6-0	190	3-11-96	0	0	0.00	2	0	0	0	7	3	1	0	0	7	7	.130	.077	.200	9.00	9.00
Zastryzny, Rob	R-L	6-3	205	3-26-92	3	0	3.68	24	0	0	2	29	29	12	12	7	15	41	.248	.261	.239	12.58	4.60

Fielding

Catcher	PCT	G	PO	A	E	DP	PB
Alfaro	1.000	3	19	3	0	0	2
Chavez	.996	28	215	17	1	1	4
Fortes	.988	27	250	6	3	0	4
Henry	.986	16	139	5	2	0	1
Navarreto	.997	31	294	20	1	5	2
Osborne	1.000	2	2	0	0	0	0
Quintana	1.000	10	79	6	0	1	0
Wallach	1.000	24	221	16	0	0	6

First Base	PCT	G	PO	A	E	DP
Arcaya	1.000	1	10	1	0	0
Chavez	1.000	3	20	2	0	1
Chinea	.941	2	16	0	1	1
Cooper	1.000	1	9	0	0	0
Diaz	.996	63	455	41	2	39
Dunand	1.000	8	59	2	0	4
Marrero	1.000	19	97	4	0	10
Marte	.933	3	13	1	1	2

	PCT	G	PO	A	E	DP
Osborne	.945	7	49	3	3	4
Quintana	.979	34	228	6	5	19

Second Base	PCT	G	PO	A	E	DP
Alvarez	.983	15	22	37	1	11
Brigman	1.000	31	29	62	0	9
Chisholm Jr.	.714	3	2	3	2	1
Cribbs Jr.	1.000	3	2	10	0	1
Devers	1.000	3	1	5	0	1
Diaz	.857	8	9	9	3	3
Hairston	1.000	11	14	19	0	6
Justus	1.000	8	4	17	0	3
Marrero	1.000	2	2	0	0	0
Marte	1.000	10	6	10	0	3
Twine	.952	48	66	92	8	21

Third Base	PCT	G	PO	A	E	DP
Alvarez	.893	10	7	18	3	0
Anderson	1.000	4	2	5	0	0
Brigman	1.000	3	1	7	0	1

	PCT	G	PO	A	E	DP
Diaz	.980	20	16	33	1	6
Dunand	.945	41	22	81	6	10
Justus	.963	14	3	23	1	2
Marrero	.953	24	15	46	3	3
Marte	.938	4	6	9	1	0
Quintana	.500	1	1	1	2	0
Twine	.872	19	8	26	5	2

Shortstop	PCT	G	PO	A	E	DP
Alvarez	1.000	4	4	8	0	1
Brigman	.969	63	80	142	7	28
Cribbs Jr.	.889	5	6	2	1	0
Devers	.957	8	8	14	1	5
Dunand	.979	15	20	27	1	5
Hairston	1.000	3	2	12	0	1
Justus	.961	27	28	46	3	7
Kone	1.000	2	2	0	0	0
Marrero	1.000	8	6	10	0	1
Marte	.966	9	12	16	1	2
Rojas	1.000	2	2	5	0	1

Outfield	PCT	G	PO	A	E	DP
Arcaya	--	1	0	0	0	0
Bird	.979	83	138	1	3	0
Bradshaw	1.000	5	4	0	0	0
Brinson	1.000	9	19	0	0	0
Burdick	.833	7	5	0	1	0
Cooper	1.000	1	1	1	0	0
Diaz	1.000	4	8	0	0	0
Fowler	1.000	25	54	3	0	0
Harrison	.994	64	150	7	1	1
Marrero	1.000	4	5	0	0	0
Marte	1.000	3	5	0	0	0
Marte	1.000	1	1	0	0	0
Miller	.986	112	198	6	3	1
Mitchell	1.000	7	2	0	0	0
Pompey	1.000	22	33	0	0	0
Sanchez	.985	32	60	6	1	1
Twine	.750	1	3	0	1	0
Zehner	.987	53	73	1	1	0

PENSACOLA BLUE WAHOOS
DOUBLE-A SOUTH

DOUBLE-A

MIAMI MARLINS

Batting	B-T	HT	WT	DOB	AVG	vLH	vRH	G	AB	R	H	2B	3B	HR	RBI	BB	HBP	SH	SF	SO	SB	CS	SLG	OBP
Alonso, Lazaro	L-R	6-3	220	12-17-94	.217	.136	.240	63	198	22	43	9	0	5	20	40	1	0	0	85	1	0	.338	.351
Bleday, JJ	L-L	6-3	205	11-10-97	.212	.256	.199	110	397	52	84	22	3	12	54	64	3	0	4	101	5	3	.373	.323
Burdick, Peyton	R-R	6-0	205	2-26-97	.231	.225	.232	106	373	71	86	17	2	23	52	76	11	0	0	135	9	5	.472	.376
Chavez, Santiago	R-R	5-11	211	8-5-95	.134	.000	.141	22	67	4	9	1	0	0	6	6	0	2	0	21	0	0	.149	.205
Chinea, Chris	R-R	5-11	220	5-3-94	.263	.200	.280	38	137	11	36	6	0	4	16	11	4	0	1	28	0	2	.394	.333
Conine, Griffin	L-R	6-1	213	7-11-97	.176	.211	.171	42	159	18	28	4	0	13	25	12	2	0	0	82	0	1	.447	.243
Cribbs Jr., Galli	L-R	6-0	190	10-8-92	.201	.083	.223	46	154	14	31	8	1	1	12	6	3	4	2	58	4	1	.286	.242
Encarnacion, Jerar	R-R	6-5	239	10-22-97	.222	.200	.229	63	230	24	51	12	1	9	28	24	5	0	1	99	5	5	.400	.308
Fortes, Nick	R-R	5-11	198	11-11-96	.251	.319	.230	57	195	21	49	10	1	3	23	22	5	0	3	36	5	2	.359	.338
Hairston, Devin	R-R	5-8	175	4-7-96	.200	.175	.208	50	165	18	33	8	0	3	18	11	0	2	1	57	4	0	.303	.249
Hampton, Lorenzo	R-R	6-5	225	8-8-97	.154	.000	.186	16	52	7	8	1	0	1	5	9	2	0	0	21	0	1	.231	.302
Hollins, Bubba	R-R	6-1	200	12-6-95	.177	.154	.184	20	62	3	11	4	0	1	7	6	1	0	1	16	1	0	.290	.257
Justus, Connor	R-R	6-0	190	11-2-94	.203	.087	.227	43	133	19	27	7	0	2	19	20	2	0	1	42	2	1	.301	.314
Kone, Zack	R-R	5-11	202	11-5-96	.229	.250	.226	13	35	3	8	1	0	0	2	2	0	1	0	12	0	0	.257	.270
Lovullo, Nick	R-R	6-0	175	12-1-93	.302	.300	.303	16	53	5	16	4	1	1	9	6	0	0	0	13	1	2	.472	.373
Mahan, Riley	L-R	6-3	220	12-31-95	.204	.209	.203	81	275	26	56	13	1	6	24	23	3	0	3	105	1	3	.324	.270
Misner, Kameron	L-L	6-4	218	1-8-98	.309	.375	.298	14	55	12	17	7	0	1	3	7	0	0	0	17	2	2	.491	.387
Mitchell, Tevin	R-R	6-1	170	5-2-97	.143	--	.143	2	7	0	1	0	0	0	1	0	0	1	0	0	0	0	.286	.250
Navarreto, Brian	R-R	6-0	237	12-29-94	.176	.091	.189	22	85	8	15	3	0	4	5	1	1	0	0	12	0	0	.353	.195
Nunez, Jhon	B-R	5-9	165	12-5-94	.204	.200	.205	16	49	3	10	2	0	2	7	3	4	1	0	12	0	1	.367	.304
Orr, J.D.	L-L	5-11	185	9-11-96	.347	.400	.339	22	72	9	25	5	1	0	3	4	1	0	0	16	5	2	.444	.390
Osborne, J.D.	R-R	6-1	215	7-13-95	.250	.294	.229	17	52	9	13	1	0	3	11	9	3	0	0	22	0	1	.442	.391
Pompey, Tristan	B-R	6-4	200	3-23-97	.196	.167	.205	31	97	8	19	1	1	1	10	16	0	0	1	41	1	1	.258	.310
Rivera, Marcos	R-R	6-1	160	5-13-97	.000	.000	.000	4	14	1	0	0	0	0	2	0	0	8	0	0	0	.000	.125
Sims, Demetrius	R-R	6-2	200	7-14-95	.196	.083	.219	81	276	31	54	10	0	4	18	31	6	1	1	113	17	4	.275	.290
Twine, Justin	R-R	5-11	205	10-7-95	.000	.000	.000	2	6	0	0	0	0	0	0	1	0	0	1	0	0	.000	.000
Victor Mesa, Victor	R-R	5-11	188	7-20-96	.093	.036	.128	21	75	8	7	1	0	0	4	1	1	0	0	19	0	1	.107	.231

Pitching	B-T	HT	WT	DOB	W	L	ERA	G	GS	CG	SV	IP	H	R	ER	HR	BB	SO	AVG	vLH	vRH	K/9	BB/9
Alexander, Jason	R-R	6-3	200	3-1-93	0	1	0.00	1	1	0	0	3	4	1	0	0	0	2	.333	.400	.286	6.00	0.00
Andrews, Tanner	R-R	6-3	220	11-15-95	0	0	11.12	4	0	0	0	6	5	7	7	3	1	9	.227	.286	.200	14.29	1.59
Bellatti, Andrew	R-R	6-1	190	8-5-91	0	0	0.00	4	0	0	0	3	1	1	0	0	2	4	1.000	.500	.000	10.80	5.40
Bice, Dylan	L-R	6-4	220	8-17-97	5	3	3.13	36	0	0	2	55	40	20	19	7	23	49	.203	.218	.191	8.07	3.79
Cabrera, Edward	R-R	6-5	217	4-13-98	2	1	2.77	5	5	0	0	26	19	10	8	3	6	33	.211	.286	.164	11.42	2.08
Carroll, Cody	R-R	6-5	230	10-15-92	0	0	1.29	4	0	0	0	7	4	1	1	0	1	14	.160	.231	.083	18.00	1.29
Carter, C.J.	R-R	6-0	165	5-27-97	0	1	27.00	1	0	0	0	1	3	3	3	1	1	3	.500	.600	.000	27.00	9.00
Eder, Jake	L-L	6-4	215	10-9-98	3	5	1.77	15	15	0	0	71	43	19	14	3	27	99	.169	.095	.194	12.49	3.41
Evans, Justin	R-R	6-0	185	9-9-96	0	1	7.71	4	0	0	0	5	5	7	4	1	6	6	.278	.300	.250	11.57	11.57
Guenther, Sean	L-L	5-11	194	12-29-95	1	0	1.02	11	0	0	0	18	11	3	2	1	3	26	.180	.185	.176	13.25	1.53
Guerrero, Alberto	R-R	6-3	192	12-13-97	2	1	2.28	18	0	0	0	28	19	8	7	2	6	31	.198	.244	.157	10.08	1.95
Guillen, Alexander	R-R	6-2	206	11-23-95	1	1	1.57	15	0	0	1	23	18	4	4	2	6	14	.212	.184	.234	5.48	2.35
Hernandez, Elieser	R-R	6-0	214	5-3-95	0	0	0.00	1	1	0	0	3	1	0	0	0	3	.110	.500	.000	10.13	0.00
Hock, Colton	R-R	6-4	220	3-5-96	1	2	2.95	36	0	0	19	40	31	16	13	4	13	46	.214	.212	.215	10.44	2.95
Leban, Zack	R-R	6-3	245	5-30-96	1	1	3.49	28	0	0	1	39	36	16	15	4	9	39	.245	.171	.312	9.08	2.09
Leibrandt, Brandon	L-R	6-4	190	12-13-92	2	3	6.61	7	7	0	0	31	39	27	23	4	14	21	.320	.167	.384	6.03	4.02
Lindgren, Jeff	R-R	6-1	200	9-17-96	8	8	3.82	20	19	0	0	106	103	49	45	17	31	85	.252	.278	.227	7.22	2.63
Maldonado, Anthony	R-R	6-4	200	2-6-98	0	1	3.38	5	0	0	3	5	4	2	2	0	1	8	.211	.200	.214	13.50	1.69
McCambley, Zach	L-R	6-2	220	5-4-99	1	6	5.18	9	9	0	0	40	41	28	23	11	20	47	.270	.289	.246	10.58	4.50
McInvale, Andrew	R-R	6-2	195	11-3-96	3	2	5.70	21	0	0	0	24	21	16	15	5	16	36	.231	.238	.224	13.69	6.08
McKenna, Brian	R-R	6-0	202	11-19-92	3	0	4.11	11	0	0	1	15	9	7	7	2	3	22	.170	.250	.121	12.91	1.76
Mesa Jr., Jose	R-R	6-4	215	8-13-93	2	0	6.00	11	3	0	0	21	18	17	14	5	9	19	.214	.040	.288	8.14	3.86
Meyer, Max	L-R	6-0	196	3-12-99	6	3	2.41	20	20	0	0	101	84	35	27	7	40	113	.226	.216	.234	10.07	3.56
Mitzel, Tyler	R-R	6-4	210	5-10-96	0	2	2.70	6	0	0	0	7	5	5	2	1	2	8	.185	.214	.154	10.80	2.70
Nardi, Andrew	L-L	6-3	201	8-18-98	1	1	2.60	11	0	0	0	17	10	7	5	2	9	19	.164	.240	.111	9.87	4.67
Nicolas, Kyle	R-R	6-4	223	2-22-99	3	2	2.52	8	8	0	0	39	23	11	11	3	25	50	.167	.209	.127	11.44	5.72
Pobereyko, Matt	R-R	6-3	220	12-24-91	1	0	1.17	12	0	0	0	15	9	4	2	2	6	21	.173	.100	.261	12.33	3.52
Roberson, Josh	R-R	6-3	175	5-12-96	1	1	8.10	20	0	0	1	27	30	25	24	5	19	39	.280	.234	.317	13.16	6.41
Rose, Jackson	R-R	6-2	185	4-25-96	0	1	4.15	3	0	0	0	4	4	3	2	1	1	3	.250	.571	.000	6.23	2.08
Stevens, Tyler	R-R	6-1	215	4-4-96	3	0	3.41	23	0	0	1	32	27	14	12	8	15	37	.223	.261	.214	10.52	4.26
Stewart, Will	L-L	6-1	180	7-14-97	5	8	4.33	20	20	0	0	100	96	54	48	9	38	85	.257	.256	.258	7.68	3.43
Velez, Antonio	L-L	6-1	195	3-31-97	2	0	0.50	3	3	0	0	18	12	2	1	0	2	18	.190	.333	.146	9.00	1.00
Wolf, Zach	R-R	5-8	175	11-15-97	1	2	5.57	13	0	0	0	21	21	14	13	4	5	23	.256	.281	.240	9.86	2.14
Yan, Jefry	L-L	6-3	170	8-17-96	0	0	1.93	10	0	0	0	14	8	6	3	0	11	19	.167	.176	.161	12.21	7.07

MIAMI MARLINS

Fielding

Catcher	PCT	G	PO	A	E	DP	PB
Chavez	.977	17	151	16	4	0	0
Chinea	.978	12	89	2	2	1	2
Fortes	.988	48	466	33	6	6	4
Navarreto	.983	21	226	10	4	4	2
Nunez	.986	15	126	11	2	0	1
Osborne	.909	1	9	1	1	0	0

First Base	PCT	G	PO	A	E	DP
Alonso	.980	51	319	28	7	44
Chavez	1.000	1	2	0	0	0
Chinea	.985	19	124	10	2	11
Encarnacion	.986	16	131	10	2	14
Hollins	1.000	3	24	3	0	1
Mahan	1.000	12	104	10	0	6
Osborne	.977	12	80	6	2	15

Second Base	PCT	G	PO	A	E	DP
Cribbs Jr.	1.000	3	5	4	0	2

	PCT	G	PO	A	E	DP
Hairston	.989	19	29	58	1	19
Justus	1.000	10	16	18	0	3
Kone	.900	6	12	15	3	7
Lovullo	.909	6	10	20	3	5
Mahan	.966	43	71	101	6	27
Rivera	.857	1	2	4	1	2
Sims	.968	22	38	53	3	8
Twine	1.000	2	3	5	0	2

Third Base	PCT	G	PO	A	E	DP
Chavez	1.000	6	7	13	0	2
Hairston	.667	5	0	8	4	2
Hollins	.912	17	15	16	3	2
Justus	.918	27	16	40	5	6
Kone	1.000	6	2	4	0	1
Lovullo	.917	9	8	14	2	1
Mahan	.897	20	15	20	4	2
Rivera	1.000	3	2	4	0	1
Sims	.915	24	11	43	5	2

Shortstop	PCT	G	PO	A	E	DP
Cribbs Jr.	.960	43	65	103	7	23
Hairston	.947	26	30	59	5	18
Justus	1.000	6	6	8	0	3
Lovullo	.750	1	1	2	1	0
Sims	.938	35	44	78	8	22

Outfield	PCT	G	PO	A	E	DP
Bleday	.989	89	166	11	2	3
Burdick	.982	90	159	4	3	1
Conine	.985	34	61	5	1	0
Encarnacion	.958	39	66	2	3	0
Hampton	1.000	12	17	2	0	0
Misner	1.000	12	22	0	0	0
Mitchell	1.000	2	4	0	0	0
Orr	.960	19	24	0	1	0
Pompey	.920	18	23	0	2	0
Victor Mesa	.976	20	38	2	1	0

BELOIT SNAPPERS HIGH CLASS A

HIGH-A CENTRAL

Batting	B-T	HT	WT	DOB	AVG	vLH	vRH	G	AB	R	H	2B	3B	HR	RBI	BB	HBP	SH	SF	SO	SB	CS	SLG	OBP
Aracena, Ricky	B-R	5-8	160	10-2-97	.228	.169	.244	110	378	61	86	11	11	3	36	44	3	3	4	116	28	12	.339	.310
Banfield, Will	R-R	6-1	207	11-18-99	.180	.245	.164	67	266	30	48	14	1	6	42	25	4	0	3	95	1	0	.308	.258
Cody, Javeon	R-R	6-3	205	7-29-99	.333	--	.333	3	3	1	1	0	0	0	0	0	1	0	0	0	0	0	.333	.500
Conine, Griffin	L-R	6-1	213	7-11-97	.247	.203	.261	66	235	45	58	7	2	23	59	46	6	0	1	103	3	0	.587	.382
Enright, Kole	B-R	6-1	175	1-21-98	.239	.421	.167	18	67	5	16	3	0	1	5	3	1	0	0	21	0	0	.328	.282
Hairston, Devin	R-R	5-8	175	4-7-96	.167	.071	.192	21	66	10	11	4	0	2	3	10	0	0	2	23	1	0	.318	.276
Hollins, Bubba	R-R	6-1	200	12-6-95	.301	.316	.297	29	93	10	28	11	0	3	23	17	7	0	2	22	1	0	.516	.437
Hostetler, Bennett	R-R	6-0	195	9-23-97	.265	.286	.259	10	34	10	9	2	0	2	8	2	3	0	0	12	3	0	.500	.359
Johnston, Troy	L-L	6-0	210	6-22-97	.289	.232	.305	96	357	54	103	22	1	14	72	57	5	0	1	91	6	1	.473	.393
Jones, Thomas	R-R	6-4	195	12-9-97	.213	.221	.211	103	375	58	80	13	5	8	38	47	18	1	4	132	23	7	.339	.327
Kone, Zack	R-R	6-3	202	11-5-96	.190	.000	.250	5	21	1	4	0	0	0	5	1	0	0	0	6	1	0	.190	.227
Marinez, Ynmanol	R-R	6-0	190	4-12-01	.234	.239	.233	79	290	35	68	13	5	4	24	12	6	0	2	90	2	2	.355	.277
Martinez, David	R-R	5-10	195	10-16-96	.190	.091	.212	18	63	9	12	1	0	2	5	11	2	0	1	30	0	0	.302	.325
Mercado, Jan	R-R	6-0	200	8-28-99	.195	.200	.194	21	77	5	15	1	1	2	7	4	3	0	0	38	0	0	.312	.262
Misner, Kameron	L-L	6-4	218	1-8-98	.244	.250	.242	88	340	58	83	22	3	11	56	50	7	0	3	119	24	2	.424	.350
Mitchell, Tevin	R-R	6-1	170	5-2-97	.167	.067	.200	25	60	8	10	4	0	2	9	4	3	0	0	27	0	1	.333	.254
Orr, J.D.	L-L	5-11	185	9-11-96	.206	.182	.217	9	34	8	7	2	0	0	6	0	0	0	0	3	6	1	.265	.325
Owings, Zachary	L-R	6-1	195	12-17-98	.201	.200	.318	8	32	2	9	5	0	5	0	1	0	1	4	1	0	.438	.294
Ready, Nic	R-R	6-3	239	2-13-97	.169	.175	.167	76	267	41	45	15	0	8	32	26	4	0	3	105	1	1	.315	.250
Rivera, Marcos	R-R	6-1	160	5-13-97	.207	.205	.208	52	188	20	39	9	0	9	34	12	0	0	2	81	1	0	.399	.252
Santos, Angeudis	R-R	6-1	168	9-19-01	.200	.000	.286	3	10	0	2	0	0	0	1	0	0	0	0	4	0	0	.200	.200
Scott, Connor	L-L	6-3	187	10-8-99	.276	.378	.249	96	395	80	109	25	6	10	46	31	4	0	2	92	14	6	.446	.333
Skelton, Dustin	R-R	6-0	202	7-31-97	.182	.170	.186	51	192	26	35	6	0	8	19	17	3	0	0	76	0	0	.339	.259
Victor Mesa, Victor	R-R	5-11	188	7-20-96	.306	.213	.333	51	206	31	63	12	1	4	25	16	1	1	1	37	11	1	.432	.357

Pitching	B-T	HT	WT	DOB	W	L	ERA	G	GS	CG	SV	IP	H	R	ER	HR	BB	SO	AVG	vLH	vRH	K/9	BB/9
Bice, Dylan	L-R	6-4	220	8-17-97	0	0	0.00	5	1	0	0	5	1	0	0	0	0	6	.071	.000	.250	11.57	5.79
Brabrand, Evan	R-R	6-3	205	11-23-95	1	2	6.53	11	0	0	0	21	29	18	15	4	10	15	.322	.348	.295	6.53	4.35
Brito, Raul	R-R	6-1	180	5-23-97	2	1	7.23	11	0	0	0	19	22	17	15	4	17	18	.289	.412	.190	8.68	8.20
Carter, C.J.	R-R	6-0	165	5-27-97	1	1	4.32	8	0	0	0	8	6	5	4	2	6	14	.200	.100	.250	15.12	6.48
Cha, Erik	L-L	6-2	190	6-19-97	0	0	7.71	3	0	0	0	2	3	2	2	0	6	2	.300	.000	.375	7.71	23.14
Curtiss, John	R-R	6-5	220	4-5-93	0	0	0.00	1	1	0	0	1	0	0	0	0	0	2	.000	.000	.000	18.00	0.00
Evans, Justin	R-R	6-0	185	9-9-96	2	2	7.52	20	0	0	2	26	32	27	22	6	13	30	.291	.255	.327	10.25	4.44
Fulton, Dax	L-L	6-7	225	10-16-01	0	1	5.49	5	5	0	0	20	21	13	12	3	8	18	.276	.238	.291	8.24	3.66
Guerrero, Alberto	R-R	6-3	192	12-13-97	1	2	6.37	7	6	0	0	30	29	23	21	3	11	35	.254	.305	.200	10.62	3.34
Hoeing, Bryan	R-R	6-6	225	10-19-96	7	6	4.83	22	22	0	0	121	130	72	65	13	24	96	.267	.276	.258	7.14	1.79
Johnson, M.D.	R-R	6-5	190	7-7-97	3	4	2.58	11	11	0	0	59	37	18	17	7	26	59	.182	.188	.178	8.95	3.94
King, Zach	L-L	6-6	228	4-30-98	3	2	5.88	16	16	0	0	78	91	57	51	14	33	79	.287	.253	.299	9.12	3.81
Leban, Zack	R-R	6-3	245	5-30-96	0	0	0.00	4	0	0	2	4	1	0	0	0	0	6	.083	.000	.125	13.50	0.00
Maldonado, Anthony	R-R	6-4	200	2-6-98	1	3	4.26	13	0	0	0	19	21	11	9	1	4	20	.273	.368	.179	9.47	1.89
McCambley, Zach	L-R	6-2	220	5-4-99	2	4	3.79	11	11	0	0	57	52	27	24	10	6	73	.234	.262	.200	11.53	0.95
Mincey, Cody	R-R	5-11	175	4-23-92	2	1	1.35	12	0	0	1	33	22	9	5	1	7	38	.182	.214	.154	10.26	1.89
Mitzel, Tyler	R-R	6-4	210	5-10-96	2	7	4.34	32	0	0	9	37	35	22	18	3	19	44	.259	.186	.338	10.61	4.58
Nardi, Andrew	L-L	6-3	201	8-18-98	2	1	4.66	10	0	0	0	19	21	13	10	4	4	27	.273	.276	.271	12.57	1.86
Nicolas, Kyle	R-R	6-4	223	2-22-99	3	2	5.28	13	13	0	0	60	57	36	35	13	24	86	.246	.229	.263	12.97	3.62
Perez, Eury	R-R	6-8	200	4-15-03	1	2	2.86	5	5	0	0	22	11	10	7	5	5	26	.145	.156	.136	10.64	2.05
Puckett, Brady	R-R	6-8	220	7-31-95	6	2	6.46	26	0	0	1	47	58	39	34	9	27	39	.301	.363	.245	7.42	5.13
Reed, Remey	R-R	6-5	230	5-5-95	1	1	3.60	15	0	0	0	30	28	12	12	1	9	34	.252	.304	.215	10.20	2.70
Roberson, Josh	R-R	6-3	175	5-12-96	2	0	3.48	5	0	0	0	10	8	4	4	1	4	14	.205	.400	.083	12.19	3.48
Rose, Jackson	R-R	6-2	185	4-25-96	2	2	2.91	23	0	0	0	56	46	21	18	10	14	70	.217	.194	.235	11.32	2.26

Name	B-T	HT	WT	DOB	W	L	ERA	G	GS	CG	SV	IP	H	R	ER	HR	BB	SO	AVG	vLH	vRH	K/9	BB/9
Simpson, Josh	L-L	6-2	190	8-19-97	0	2	5.61	18	4	0	0	43	37	29	27	6	19	58	.226	.204	.236	12.05	3.95
Soriano, George	R-R	6-2	170	3-24-99	4	1	3.74	11	11	0	0	55	58	24	23	5	19	67	.267	.313	.231	10.90	3.09
Steele, Joey	R-R	6-2	195	11-15-95	0	1	9.00	9	0	0	0	13	17	13	13	3	5	13	.304	.355	.240	9.00	3.46
Sterner, Justin	R-R	6-1	215	8-29-96	0	0	7.36	5	0	0	0	7	6	7	6	3	6	10	.214	.250	.188	12.27	7.36
Tavarez, Eddy	R-R	6-6	245	5-16-95	0	0	54.00	1	0	0	0	1	2	4	4	0	1	1	.500	.667	.000	13.50	13.50
Velez, Antonio	L-L	6-1	195	3-31-97	5	2	3.00	20	11	0	0	81	62	32	27	10	9	75	.205	.179	.217	8.33	1.00
Villalobos, Eli	R-R	6-4	195	6-26-97	1	3	4.07	17	0	0	2	24	20	11	11	3	9	42	.211	.268	.167	15.53	3.33
Walters, Jake	R-R	6-0	190	3-11-96	2	3	4.06	15	5	0	1	51	43	26	23	2	22	54	.226	.264	.179	9.53	3.88
Wolf, Zach	R-R	5-8	175	11-15-97	0	0	9.00	1	0	0	0	2	4	2	2	0	1	2	.444	.167	1.000	9.00	4.50

Fielding

Catcher	PCT	G	PO	A	E	DP	PB
Banfield	.994	58	597	49	4	4	3
Martinez	1.000	9	102	2	0	0	0
Mercado	.994	17	165	11	1	1	2
Skelton	.982	36	311	23	6	2	6

First Base	PCT	G	PO	A	E	DP
Hollins	1.000	6	45	3	0	1
Johnston	.988	94	681	48	9	41
Owings	1.000	8	55	0	0	4
Ready	1.000	13	106	10	0	8

Second Base	PCT	G	PO	A	E	DP
Aracena	.955	109	155	251	19	43
Enright	.963	8	12	14	1	2

	PCT	G	PO	A	E	DP
Hairston	1.000	1	1	2	0	1
Hollins	.750	1	1	2	1	1
Marinez	1.000	2	2	4	0	0

Third Base	PCT	G	PO	A	E	DP
Enright	1.000	2	1	3	0	1
Hollins	.966	20	22	35	2	3
Hostetler	1.000	9	7	16	0	2
Kone	.857	2	1	5	1	0
Marinez	1.000	4	0	6	0	0
Ready	.955	56	48	102	7	3
Rivera	.932	27	13	55	5	4
Santos	.857	3	0	6	1	1

Shortstop	PCT	G	PO	A	E	DP

	PCT	G	PO	A	E	DP
Enright	1.000	2	2	0	0	0
Hairston	.972	20	27	43	2	8
Kone	.889	3	4	4	1	0
Marinez	.919	73	82	145	20	27
Rivera	.949	26	23	52	4	8

Outfield	PCT	G	PO	A	E	DP
Cody	1.000	1	3	0	0	0
Conine	.965	55	105	5	4	1
Jones	.970	83	126	3	4	1
Misner	.968	81	146	5	5	1
Mitchell	.957	15	21	1	1	0
Orr	.900	9	9	0	1	0
Scott	.973	80	136	9	4	1
Victor Mesa	.977	47	125	2	3	0

MIAMI MARLINS

JUPITER HAMMERHEADS   *LOW CLASS A*
LOW-A SOUTHEAST

Batting	B-T	HT	WT	DOB	AVG	vLH	vRH	G	AB	R	H	2B	3B	HR	RBI	BB	HBP	SH	SF	SO	SB	CS	SLG	OBP
Allen, Tanner	L-R	5-11	190	6-5-98	.189	.083	.202	30	111	16	21	1	2	2	10	9	2	0	2	21	1	3	.288	.258
Alonso, Lazaro	L-R	6-3	220	12-17-94	.000	--	.000	1	1	0	0	0	0	0	1	0	0	1	0	0	0	.000	.000
Alvarez, Eddy	B-R	5-9	185	1-30-90	.600	.800	.500	4	15	5	9	0	0	2	8	3	1	0	0	2	2	0	1.000	.684
Arcaya, Luis	R-R	6-1	170	2-26-99	.000	.000	.000	5	15	1	0	0	0	0	0	1	0	0	0	9	0	0	.000	.063
Barstad, Cameron	L-R	6-1	195	11-29-00	.191	.148	.200	47	162	16	31	7	1	4	14	22	2	0	0	74	1	0	.321	.296
Bradshaw, Davis	L-R	6-3	175	4-25-98	.299	.273	.304	59	201	27	60	7	4	1	32	15	9	1	2	31	8	8	.388	.370
Burgos, Diowill	L-R	6-1	207	1-29-01	.185	.179	.187	54	178	20	33	10	1	2	16	33	1	0	1	75	1	0	.287	.315
Caballero, Jorge	R-R	6-1	170	1-10-00	.000	.000	.000	5	10	0	0	0	0	0	1	4	0	0	0	4	0	0	.000	.286
Chiu, Marcus	R-R	6-2	208	1-13-97	.234	.171	.248	58	192	28	45	11	2	6	28	18	12	0	0	66	0	1	.406	.338
Cody, Javeon	R-R	6-3	205	7-29-99	.240	.313	.216	36	129	20	31	5	2	0	16	23	0	0	0	51	7	3	.310	.355
Combs, Casey	R-R	6-2	205	7-29-96	.000	.000	.000	2	3	0	0	0	0	0	0	1	0	0	0	0	0	0	.000	.250
Cumana, Arquimedes	R-R	6-3	175	4-28-00	.077	.000	.083	4	13	1	1	0	0	0	2	3	0	0	1	10	0	0	.077	.235
Dunand, Joe	R-R	6-2	205	9-20-95	.143	.500	.083	5	14	0	2	0	0	0	0	1	0	0	0	7	0	0	.143	.200
Easley, Ashton	R-R	6-0	200	8-7-97	.111	.167	.095	9	27	2	3	0	0	1	4	3	2	0	0	11	0	0	.222	.250
Encarnacion, Jerar	R-R	6-5	239	10-22-97	.200	--	.200	2	5	1	1	0	0	0	1	1	0	0	0	3	0	0	.200	.333
Fish, Keegan	B-R	5-11	190	9-19-99	.295	.273	.303	13	44	5	13	1	0	0	2	4	1	1	0	15	0	0	.318	.367
Hampton, Lorenzo	R-R	6-5	225	8-8-97	.000	.000	.000	5	8	0	0	0	0	0	0	2	0	0	0	5	0	0	.000	.200
Harrison, Monte	R-R	6-3	225	8-10-95	.250	.000	.308	6	16	3	4	2	0	0	0	1	2	0	0	6	2	0	.375	.368
Hostetler, Bennett	R-R	6-1	195	9-23-97	.337	.188	.364	27	104	17	35	6	0	3	25	4	2	1	3	32	0	0	.481	.369
Johnson, Osiris	R-R	6-1	198	10-18-00	.196	.250	.184	65	255	36	50	8	1	3	29	23	3	0	2	80	6	1	.271	.269
Johnston, Troy	L-L	6-0	210	6-22-97	.349	.267	.368	24	83	12	29	5	0	1	13	11	1	0	1	12	0	0	.446	.427
Kone, Zack	R-R	6-3	202	11-5-96	.224	.333	.197	23	76	8	17	3	0	0	14	1	0	0	0	16	0	0	.342	.234
Marinez, Ynmanol	R-R	6-0	190	4-12-01	.000	.000	.000	2	9	1	0	0	0	0	0	0	0	0	0	6	0	0	.000	.000
McIntosh, Paul	R-R	6-1	220	11-20-97	.253	.200	.267	23	75	14	19	6	2	6	20	15	3	0	1	20	0	0	.627	.394
Mercado, Jan	R-R	6-0	200	8-28-99	.220	.121	.244	47	164	23	36	3	1	4	21	18	7	0	0	71	2	0	.323	.323
Mesa Jr., Victor	L-L	6-0	175	9-8-01	.266	.218	.277	111	428	66	114	21	11	5	71	33	3	0	10	102	12	5	.402	.316
Mitchell, Tevin	R-R	6-1	170	5-2-97	.000	.000	.000	1	3	0	0	0	0	0	0	0	0	0	0	1	0	0	.000	.000
Morissette, Cody	L-R	6-0	175	1-16-00	.204	.063	.223	34	137	22	28	8	1	0	10	20	1	0	1	38	0	2	.299	.308
Navarreto, Brian	R-R	6-0	237	12-29-94	.556	--	.556	3	9	2	5	2	0	0	4	2	0	0	0	2	0	0	.778	.636
Nunez, Nasim	B-R	5-9	158	8-18-00	.243	.179	.260	52	189	33	46	2	1	0	10	35	2	1	1	46	33	10	.265	.366
Orr, J.D.	L-L	5-11	185	9-11-96	.282	.333	.274	41	131	25	37	7	2	0	8	21	0	2	0	30	12	6	.366	.382
Owings, Zachary	L-R	6-1	195	12-17-97	.125	--	.125	2	8	1	1	0	0	0	0	0	0	0	0	2	0	0	.125	.125
Polanco, Federico	L-R	5-10	155	3-20-01	.236	.368	.215	78	284	35	67	13	3	2	25	20	7	2	1	70	5	4	.324	.301
Praytor, Sam	R-R	5-10	205	4-4-99	.220	.250	.213	20	59	5	13	6	0	0	3	12	3	0	1	20	0	0	.322	.373
Ready, Nic	R-R	6-3	239	2-13-97	.167	.000	.182	3	12	1	2	0	0	1	2	1	0	0	0	3	0	0	.417	.231
Rosario, Dalvy	R-R	6-0	185	7-22-00	.224	.246	.218	60	241	29	54	12	2	3	30	33	5	3	3	75	17	2	.308	.309
Rowan, Thomas	R-R	6-1	200	11-8-95	.098	.000	.128	23	61	5	6	1	0	1	5	10	5	0	0	22	0	0	.164	.276
Salas, Jose	B-R	6-2	191	4-26-03	.250	.214	.255	27	108	12	27	4	0	1	8	11	3	0	1	28	6	0	.315	.333
Santos, Angeudis	B-R	6-1	168	9-19-01	.163	.154	.165	34	98	19	16	3	1	1	4	23	1	0	2	24	0	1	.204	.304

Pitching	B-T	HT	WT	DOB	W	L	ERA	G	GS	CG	SV	IP	H	R	ER	HR	BB	SO	AVG	vLH	vRH	K/9	BB/9
Bergin, Jesse	R-R	6-4	205	10-8-99	0	2	16.88	4	4	0	0	8	20	19	15	1	5	6	.465	.526	.417	6.75	5.63
Bierman, Gabe	R-R	6-2	200	9-3-99	1	0	3.93	5	4	0	1	18	15	8	8	2	8	23	.217	.229	.206	11.29	3.93
Bordner, Sam	R-R	6-5	228	10-16-96	3	0	1.35	11	0	0	0	20	11	4	3	0	10	30	.159	.238	.125	13.50	4.50

Player	B-T	HT	WT	DOB	W	L	ERA	G	GS	CG	SV	IP	H	R	ER	HR	BB	SO	AVG	vLH	vRH	K/9	BB/9
Brabrand, Evan	R-R	6-3	205	11-23-95	2	2	8.87	13	0	0	0	23	34	26	23	6	12	21	.351	.351	.350	8.10	4.63
Brito, Raul	R-R	6-1	180	5-23-97	0	2	4.74	13	0	0	1	19	18	15	10	1	11	26	.250	.269	.239	12.32	5.21
Cabrera, Edward	R-R	6-5	217	4-13-98	0	0	0.00	2	2	0	0	6	4	0	0	0	0	11	.182	.125	.214	16.50	0.00
Carroll, Cody	R-R	6-5	230	10-15-92	0	0	3.38	2	0	0	0	3	3	1	1	0	0	1	.273	.333	.200	8.00	0.00
Carter, C.J.	R-R	6-0	165	5-27-97	1	0	1.69	3	0	0	0	5	3	1	1	1	3	7	.176	.200	.167	11.81	5.06
Cruz, Troy	R-R	5-8	158	12-28-93	4	1	2.49	12	0	0	0	22	16	8	6	0	6	17	.208	.111	.293	7.06	2.49
Evans, Justin	R-R	6-0	185	9-9-96	1	3	3.86	10	0	0	3	14	13	6	6	1	5	17	.250	.176	.286	10.93	3.21
Eveld, Tommy	R-R	6-5	214	12-30-93	0	0	0.00	2	0	0	0	4	4	0	0	0	1	5	.286	.375	.167	11.25	2.25
Fitterer, Evan	R-R	6-3	192	6-26-00	0	1	4.56	7	6	0	0	26	30	14	13	1	6	27	.286	.179	.348	9.47	2.10
Fulton, Dax	L-L	6-7	225	10-16-01	2	4	4.30	15	14	0	0	59	50	35	28	3	30	66	.229	.119	.256	10.13	4.60
Galindez, Geremy	R-R	6-1	200	4-29-98	0	1	10.50	3	0	0	0	6	10	8	7	1	4	2	.357	.167	.409	3.00	6.00
Givin, Matt	R-R	6-3	180	6-17-99	4	6	3.80	19	14	0	0	90	89	47	38	8	37	74	.256	.293	.234	7.40	3.70
Holloway, Jordan	R-R	6-6	230	6-13-96	0	0	13.50	2	2	0	0	2	7	3	3	0	1	2	.538	.500	.571	9.00	4.50
Jimenez, Yeuris	R-R	6-3	218	3-23-01	0	0	0.00	1	0	0	0	1	0	0	0	0	0	1	.000	.000	.000	9.00	0.00
Johnson, M.D.	R-R	6-5	190	7-7-97	3	4	3.19	10	7	0	0	42	22	18	15	3	37	48	.153	.159	.150	10.20	7.87
Jones Jr., Holt	R-R	6-8	235	5-8-99	0	1	13.50	3	0	0	0	5	7	7	7	0	3	4	.350	.300	.400	7.71	5.79
Jozwiak, Chandler	L-L	6-0	185	2-15-98	0	0	5.79	7	0	0	3	9	13	7	6	0	3	14	.317	.273	.333	13.50	2.89
Lara, Yeremin	R-R	6-1	160	11-6-98	5	0	2.48	13	3	0	0	40	31	15	11	1	16	44	.214	.227	.208	9.90	3.60
Maldonado, Anthony	R-R	6-4	200	2-6-98	0	1	9.00	1	0	0	0	2	3	2	2	1	2	1	.375	.333	.400	4.50	9.00
Martinez, Robinson	R-R	6-0	190	3-20-98	2	2	3.86	19	0	0	4	30	25	19	13	1	10	35	.229	.256	.214	10.38	2.97
Mendez, Josan	R-R	6-2	180	7-10-00	3	0	2.05	13	0	0	0	22	19	5	5	2	6	23	.238	.243	.233	9.41	2.45
Mokma, Chris	R-R	6-4	210	2-11-01	2	7	6.60	20	20	0	0	93	122	75	68	17	28	78	.314	.291	.329	7.58	2.72
Nardi, Andrew	L-L	6-3	201	8-18-98	1	1	3.45	8	0	0	2	16	14	6	6	0	3	23	.241	.222	.250	13.21	1.72
Palacios, Luis	L-L	6-2	160	7-1-00	5	6	3.88	12	10	2	1	65	48	29	28	10	16	66	.199	.333	.163	9.14	2.22
Perdue, Hunter	R-R	6-3	210	3-4-99	0	2	4.05	6	3	0	0	20	17	10	9	0	12	24	.230	.212	.244	10.80	5.40
Perez, Eury	R-R	6-8	200	4-15-03	2	3	1.61	15	15	0	0	56	32	14	10	2	21	82	.163	.159	.165	13.18	3.38
Pettitte, Jared	L-L	6-3	218	5-28-98	0	1	6.75	4	0	0	0	5	5	4	4	1	4	8	.238	.400	.188	13.50	6.75
Pop, Zach	R-R	6-4	220	9-20-96	0	0	3.86	2	1	0	0	2	3	1	1	0	0	3	.333	.400	.250	11.57	0.00
Reynolds, Sean	L-R	6-8	240	4-19-98	2	1	3.09	19	0	0	2	32	26	14	11	0	23	37	.215	.178	.237	10.41	6.47
Roberson, Josh	R-R	6-3	175	5-12-96	0	0	6.00	4	2	0	0	6	3	4	4	0	4	8	.158	.000	.250	12.00	6.00
Rodriguez, Eliezer	L-L	6-1	160	2-17-99	0	0	3.00	3	0	0	0	3	4	1	1	0	4	1	.333	.667	.222	3.00	12.00
Rogers, Trevor	L-L	6-5	217	11-13-97	1	0	0.00	2	2	0	0	8	4	0	0	0	3	12	.138	.125	.154	12.96	3.24
Rose, Jackson	R-R	6-2	185	4-25-96	0	1	1.29	3	0	0	0	7	6	5	1	0	2	16	.207	.100	.263	20.57	2.57
Sanchez, Edgar	R-R	6-1	190	8-2-00	0	0	31.50	3	0	0	0	2	4	9	7	0	8	4	.364	.250	.429	18.00	36.00
Sanchez, Jesus E.	R-R	6-0	188	4-8-99	7	3	4.68	23	1	0	0	65	53	37	34	6	27	84	.217	.235	.208	11.57	3.72
Soriano, George	R-R	6-2	170	3-24-99	3	0	2.91	7	7	0	0	34	26	14	11	3	18	47	.205	.178	.220	12.44	4.76
Steele, Joey	R-R	6-2	195	11-15-95	3	1	1.89	20	0	0	5	33	20	8	7	2	9	61	.164	.146	.173	16.47	2.43
Sterner, Justin	R-R	6-1	215	8-29-96	2	1	1.38	7	0	0	3	13	3	2	2	0	5	20	.073	.067	.077	13.85	3.46
Suriel, Edison	L-L	5-10	185	10-24-98	1	1	8.22	6	0	0	0	8	8	8	7	0	12	8	.267	.250	.269	9.39	14.09
Tavarez, Eddy	R-R	6-6	245	5-16-95	0	0	1.32	9	0	0	0	8	3	2	1	1	11	18	.182	.250	.143	11.85	7.24
Villalobos, Eli	R-R	6-4	195	6-26-97	1	0	3.10	15	0	0	2	20	19	9	7	2	7	30	.238	.120	.291	13.28	3.10
Yan, Jefry	L-L	6-3	170	8-17-96	0	1	3.18	11	0	0	0	17	16	10	6	2	14	32	.232	.222	.233	16.94	7.41

Fielding

Catcher

Catcher	PCT	G	PO	A	E	DP	PB
Barstad	.975	31	283	31	8	4	5
Combs	1.000	2	17	0	0	0	0
Fish	.986	13	129	11	2	1	1
McIntosh	.978	9	84	3	2	0	1
Mercado	.994	44	453	36	3	2	7
Navarreto	.962	3	23	2	1	0	0
Praytor	.988	19	155	12	2	1	1
Rowan	1.000	2	8	1	0	0	0

First Base

First Base	PCT	G	PO	A	E	DP
Alonso	1.000	1	4	0	0	0
Arcaya	.931	5	26	1	2	3
Chiu	.990	58	373	25	4	35
Cumana	.968	4	30	0	1	1
Encarnacion	.875	1	7	0	1	1
Johnston	.993	16	130	6	1	11
Kone	1.000	7	39	2	0	3
McIntosh	1.000	1	7	0	0	1
Owings	1.000	2	14	1	0	0
Reynolds	.984	8	55	6	1	6
Rowan	.964	17	104	4	4	6

Second Base

Second Base	PCT	G	PO	A	E	DP
Alvarez	1.000	3	11	5	0	2
Johnson	.848	23	42	36	14	9
Morissette	.946	16	19	34	3	10
Polanco	.964	50	97	90	7	28
Rosario	.920	13	17	29	4	10
Santos	.960	17	19	29	2	7

Third Base

Third Base	PCT	G	PO	A	E	DP
Dunand	1.000	1	0	1	0	0
Hostetler	.932	21	12	29	3	6
Johnson	.667	5	2	2	2	0
Kone	.976	16	11	29	1	1
Marinez	1.000	1	1	3	0	0
Morissette	.971	14	6	27	1	2
Polanco	.938	18	7	23	2	1
Ready	1.000	3	0	7	0	0
Rosario	.936	34	23	65	6	6
Santos	.750	8	5	10	5	2

Shortstop

Shortstop	PCT	G	PO	A	E	DP
Dunand	1.000	1	1	0	0	0
Hostetler	.882	4	8	7	2	2
Morissette	.889	2	3	5	1	1
Nunez	.960	48	63	107	7	21
Rosario	.938	35	27	63	6	4
Salas	.869	25	26	47	11	14
Santos	.842	7	7	9	3	1

Outfield

Outfield	PCT	G	PO	A	E	DP
Allen	1.000	23	27	1	0	0
Bradshaw	.969	47	62	1	2	0
Burgos	.931	48	60	7	5	2
Caballero	.875	5	7	0	1	0
Cody	.964	36	52	1	2	0
Easley	1.000	9	11	0	0	0
Encarnacion	1.000	1	1	0	0	0
Hampton	1.000	5	2	0	0	0
Harrison	1.000	3	4	0	0	0
Johnson	1.000	27	54	3	0	1
Johnson	.889	8	8	0	1	0
McIntosh	1.000	3	7	0	0	0
Mesa Jr.	.973	106	212	7	6	2
Mitchell	--	1	0	0	0	0
Orr	.943	40	63	3	4	1
Rosario	.963	8	24	2	1	0

FCL MARLINS — ROOKIE

FLORIDA COMPLEX LEAGUE

Batting	B-T	HT	WT	DOB	AVG	vLH	vRH	G	AB	R	H	2B	3B	HR	RBI	BB	HBP	SH	SF	SO	SB	CS	SLG	OBP
Allen, Tanner	L-R	5-11	190	6-5-98	.111	--	.111	3	9	0	1	0	0	0	0	2	0	0	0	1	0	0	.111	.273
Alonso, Lazaro	L-R	6-3	220	12-17-94	.375	.000	.429	2	8	3	3	1	0	1	1	1	0	0	0	1	0	0	.875	.444
Alvarez, Eddy	B-R	5-9	185	1-30-90	.000	--	.000	1	2	0	0	0	0	0	0	0	0	0	0	0	0	0	.000	.000

Name	B-T	HT	WT	DOB	AVG	vLH	vRH	G	AB	R	H	2B	3B	HR	RBI	BB	HBP	SH	SF	SO	SB	CS	SLG	OBP
Arcaya, Luis	R-R	6-1	170	2-26-99	.077	.000	.083	6	13	1	1	0	0	1	3	1	0	0	0	6	0	0	.308	.143
Arroyo, Carlos	R-R	5-9	170	7-11-01	.167	.000	.200	8	18	4	3	0	0	0	3	3	1	0	0	2	1	0	.167	.318
Burgos, Diowill	L-R	6-1	207	1-29-01	.204	.083	.222	30	93	14	19	8	2	2	12	18	1	0	0	27	0	0	.398	.339
Caballero, Jorge	R-R	6-1	170	1-10-00	.348	.143	.385	15	46	12	16	2	1	2	13	8	1	0	0	15	0	0	.565	.455
Campos, Brhayan	R-R	6-1	185	9-17-98	.143	.000	.167	12	28	1	4	1	0	0	3	5	2	0	0	9	0	1	.179	.314
Castillo, Kyler	R-R	5-11	185	10-29-97	.317	.083	.375	18	60	7	19	5	0	0	6	8	0	0	0	8	1	4	.400	.397
Chiu, Marcus	R-R	6-2	208	1-13-97	.250	.500	.167	3	8	1	2	2	0	0	1	1	1	0	0	1	0	0	.500	.400
Cody, Javeon	R-R	6-3	205	7-29-99	.220	.429	.176	12	41	9	9	0	1	0	3	8	2	0	0	13	8	2	.268	.373
Combs, Casey	R-R	6-2	205	7-29-96	--	--	--	1	0	0	0	0	0	0	0	0	0	0	0	0	0	0	--	--
Cumana, Arquimedes	R-R	6-3	175	4-28-00	.170	.000	.216	25	47	6	8	2	0	1	7	10	3	0	1	24	0	1	.277	.344
Estrada, Jose	R-R	5-10	175	5-5-00	.274	.250	.278	22	62	8	17	8	0	0	9	6	0	0	0	10	0	0	.403	.338
Fish, Keegan	R-R	5-11	190	9-19-99	.500	.500	.500	8	20	7	10	2	0	0	3	4	3	0	1	4	1	0	.600	.607
Hollins, Bubba	R-R	6-1	200	12-6-95	.000	--	.000	1	2	0	0	0	0	0	0	0	0	0	0	0	0	0	.000	.000
Johnson, Osiris	R-R	6-1	198	10-18-00	.281	.300	.279	27	96	21	27	9	1	8	26	11	1	0	0	24	2	0	.646	.361
Kessler, Coltyn	L-R	6-2	220	4-22-99	.150	.143	.152	17	40	4	6	0	0	0	3	9	2	0	0	12	0	1	.150	.333
Leon, Ene	R-R	5-10	170	11-3-01	.333	--	.333	2	3	0	1	0	0	0	0	0	0	0	0	0	0	0	.333	.333
Lewis, Ian	B-R	5-10	177	3-4-03	.302	.450	.279	43	149	24	45	10	5	3	27	11	1	0	0	24	9	4	.497	.354
Mack, Joe	L-R	6-1	210	12-27-02	.132	.231	.100	19	53	9	7	1	0	1	2	20	1	0	1	22	0	1	.208	.373
McCants, Jordan	L-R	6-1	165	5-21-02	.224	.364	.200	23	76	10	17	5	0	0	4	6	1	1	2	22	1	2	.237	.286
McIntosh, Paul	R-R	6-1	220	11-20-97	.000	--	.000	1	1	0	0	0	0	0	0	0	0	0	0	0	0	0	.000	.500
Osorio, Jhonaiker	L-R	6-0	160	9-2-00	.067	.200	.000	10	15	1	1	0	0	0	1	0	0	0	0	4	0	0	.067	.067
Paulino, Jandel	R-R	6-1	193	11-3-00	.360	.250	.381	11	25	6	9	1	0	2	7	0	0	0	0	9	0	0	.640	.360
Pena, Yelinson	R-R	5-11	175	9-16-00	.455	.667	.375	10	11	4	5	1	0	1	4	3	1	0	0	1	1	0	.818	.600
Praytor, Sam	R-R	5-10	205	4-4-99	.286	.500	.200	3	7	1	2	1	0	0	1	0	1	0	0	1	0	0	.429	.375
Ready, Nic	R-R	6-3	239	2-13-97	.417	.000	.455	3	12	2	5	3	0	0	2	0	0	0	0	1	1	0	.667	.417
Rodriguez, Cristhian	L-R	6-1	160	12-23-01	.218	.118	.230	46	156	20	34	12	2	0	18	15	2	0	0	59	3	1	.321	.295
Roman, Richard	R-R	6-1	210	12-22-01	.125	.214	.100	23	64	3	8	2	0	1	3	5	1	0	0	33	0	1	.203	.200
Salas, Jose	B-R	6-2	191	4-26-03	.370	.500	.346	28	92	14	34	10	0	1	11	11	4	0	0	23	8	5	.511	.458
Sanchez, Yoelvis	L-L	6-2	163	4-27-02	.151	.182	.147	32	86	20	13	1	2	1	10	17	3	1	0	46	10	2	.279	.311
Santos, Angeudis	B-R	6-1	160	9-19-01	.255	.250	.257	14	47	9	12	2	1	0	5	7	0	0	0	16	5	1	.340	.352
Sosa, Maicol	R-R	6-2	185	2-9-99	.191	.000	.236	24	68	9	13	2	0	0	9	12	2	0	1	28	0	1	.221	.325
Torres, Chris	B-R	5-11	170	2-6-98	.200	.000	.250	4	10	2	2	0	1	0	1	0	0	0	0	4	0	0	.400	.273
Watson, Kahlil	L-R	5-9	178	4-16-03	.394	.000	.419	9	33	13	13	3	2	0	5	8	1	0	0	7	4	1	.606	.524
Williamson, Noah	R-R	6-4	220	8-23-00	.147	.053	.179	23	75	8	11	4	0	0	7	3	5	1	0	40	1	1	.200	.229
Zubia, Zach	R-R	6-4	230	11-4-97	.167	.167	.167	24	72	4	12	2	0	0	7	11	1	0	1	32	0	0	.194	.282

Pitching	B-T	HT	WT	DOB	W	L	ERA	G	GS	CG	SV	IP	H	R	ER	HR	BB	SO	AVG	vLH	vRH	K/9	BB/9
Alegre, Delvis	R-R	6-2	180	2-2-01	5	1	3.56	11	4	0	0	43	42	22	17	4	12	43	.247	.221	.269	9.00	2.51
Alexander, Jason	R-R	6-3	200	3-1-93	0	0	0.00	1	1	0	0	2	0	0	0	0	0	2	.000	.000		9.00	0.00
Almanzar, Stiven	R-R	5-10	155	12-24-01	0	1	9.82	3	0	0	0	7	10	8	8	3	8	7	.345	.462	.250	8.59	9.82
Bargallo, Sandro	L-L	6-1	180	12-29-01	1	3	8.13	12	7	0	0	28	27	27	25	3	31	34	.245	.317	.203	11.06	10.08
Bergin, Jesse	R-R	6-4	205	10-8-99	1	0	0.90	3	2	0	0	10	7	2	1	0	0	13	.189	.133	.227	11.70	0.00
Bierman, Gabe	R-R	6-2	200	9-3-99	0	0	5.59	3	3	0	0	10	11	6	6	2	3	8	.324	.111	.563	7.45	2.79
Carroll, Cody	R-R	6-5	230	10-15-92	0	0	0.00	1	0	0	0	1	0	0	0	0	1	0	.000	.000	.000	0.00	13.50
Carter, C.J.	R-R	6-0	165	5-27-97	0	0	9.82	3	0	0	0	4	5	4	4	0	2	7	.294	.250	.333	17.18	4.91
Doble, Mario	R-R	6-4	178	11-1-00	1	0	6.62	6	4	0	0	18	22	14	13	2	9	21	.297	.256	.343	10.70	4.58
Eckberg, Tyler	R-R	6-4	220	9-4-97	1	1	6.75	5	0	0	0	8	12	6	6	0	0	12	.353	.417	.318	13.50	0.00
Encarnacion, Breidy	R-R	6-3	185	11-9-00	2	2	8.18	9	1	0	0	22	25	21	20	4	18	21	.294	.375	.245	8.59	7.36
Fall, Justin	L-L	6-6	240	6-11-99	0	1	5.14	5	0	0	0	7	7	4	4	0	3	9	.259	.167	.286	11.57	3.86
Fitterer, Evan	R-R	6-3	192	6-26-00	0	1	1.93	2	2	0	0	5	2	1	1	0	4	6	.125	.200	.091	11.57	7.71
Galindez, Geremy	R-R	6-1	200	4-29-98	0	3	4.70	9	0	0	0	15	16	10	8	2	5	12	.267	.269	.265	7.04	2.93
Gonzalez, Luis	L-L	6-2	200	2-21-00	2	1	5.65	10	0	0	0	14	16	9	9	1	8	19	.281	.438	.220	11.93	5.02
Guillen, Alexander	R-R	6-2	206	11-23-95	0	0	18.00	1	0	0	0	1	2	2	2	0	1	2	.400	--	.400	18.00	9.00
Jimenez, Yeuris	R-R	6-3	218	3-23-01	2	3	3.60	14	1	0	0	25	22	13	10	2	8	25	.232	.290	.203	9.00	2.88
Jones Jr., Holt	R-R	6-8	235	5-8-99	0	0	2.08	2	0	0	0	4	5	1	1	0	1	7	.278	.222	.333	14.54	2.08
Leon, Maycold	L-L	6-1	160	4-29-02	0	0	0.00	2	0	0	0	4	0	0	0	0	0	4	.000	.000	9.82	0.00	
Maldonado, Anthony	R-R	6-4	200	2-6-98	0	1	3.00	2	2	0	0	3	3	1	1	0	0	5	.250	.400	.143	15.00	0.00
Melotakis, Mason	R-L	6-2	220	6-28-91	0	0	0.00	1	0	0	0	1	0	0	0	0	0	2	.000	--	.000	18.00	0.00
Mendez, Josan	R-R	6-2	180	7-10-00	2	0	0.00	5	0	0	1	9	3	1	0	0	0	8	.097	.083	.105	7.71	0.00
Montesino, Kendry	R-R	6-4	180	2-1-03	0	2	8.44	4	0	0	0	11	7	11	10	1	16	9	.194	.000	.233	7.59	13.50
Monteverde, Pat	R-L	6-2	190	9-24-97	0	0	3.07	7	1	0	2	15	14	6	5	1	4	16	.246	.261	.235	9.82	2.45
Perdue, Hunter	R-R	6-3	210	3-4-99	0	1	0.00	2	2	0	0	5	3	2	0	0	2	7	.158	.100	.222	12.60	3.60
Pettitte, Jared	L-L	6-3	195	5-28-98	0	0	0.00	4	0	0	0	7	4	0	0	0	5	15	.167	.273	.077	19.29	6.43
Quinonez, Yoilan	R-R	6-4	200	8-11-99	0	1	3.97	9	0	0	0	11	13	7	5	1	2	13	.271	.286	.259	10.32	1.59
Rivera, Yaqui	R-R	6-2	150	7-19-03	0	1	1.64	3	3	0	0	11	11	2	2	2	4	10	.262	.214	.286	8.18	3.27
Roberson, Josh	R-R	6-3	175	5-12-96	0	0	0.00	1	1	0	0	2	3	0	0	0	0	3	.333	.250	.400	13.50	0.00
Rodriguez, Eliezer	L-L	6-1	160	2-17-99	0	0	3.07	12	0	0	4	15	5	5	5	0	8	13	.111	.083	.121	7.98	4.91
Sanchez, Edgar	R-R	6-1	190	8-2-00	1	1	4.12	9	1	0	0	20	18	13	9	1	8	23	.225	.303	.170	10.53	3.66
Schrand, Jake	R-R	6-2	180	8-8-99	2	0	3.00	6	4	0	2	12	10	4	4	2	2	10	.190	.167	.200	15.00	3.00
Simpson, Josh	L-L	6-2	190	8-19-97	0	0	11.57	1	1	0	0	2	3	3	3	0	0	4	.300	--	.600	15.43	0.00
Smith, Josh A.	R-R	6-2	210	8-7-87	0	0	0.00	1	1	0	0	2	1	0	0	0	0	3	.143	.000	.167	13.50	0.00
Suriel, Edison	L-L	5-10	185	10-24-98	1	0	5.40	10	0	0	0	17	19	13	10	0	4	23	.284	.250	.294	12.42	2.16
Tineo, Dameivi	L-L	6-3	170	8-1-03	0	1	4.35	4	4	0	0	13	15	7	5	1	0	12	.289	.250	.303	10.45	0.00
Vizcaino, Luis	R-R	6-4	199	7-9-01	4	2	2.92	12	8	0	0	49	35	23	16	4	24	51	.198	.192	.202	9.30	4.38
Wurster, Caleb	L-L	5-11	182	9-21-98	2	1	2.38	8	0	0	1	11	9	5	3	0	4	16	.220	.182	.233	12.71	3.18

Zastryzny, Rob   R-L 6-3 205 3-26-92 0 0 0.00 1 1 0 0 1 0 0 0 0 0 3 .000 .000 .000 27.00 0.00

Fielding
C: Arcaya 2, Campos 4, Combs 1, Cumana 7, Estrada 21, Fish 6, Kessler 7, Leon 1, Mack 11, McIntosh 1, Osorio 9, Praytor 3.
1B: Alonso 2, Arcaya 2, Burgos 11, Campos 2, Chiu 3, Cumana 14, Kessler 2, Rodriguez 3, Zubia 23.
2B: Alvarez 1, Arroyo 8, Lewis 32, McCants 5, Rodriguez 5, Salas 6, Santos 7.
3B: Cumana 4, Hollins 1, Kessler 5, Lewis 5, Pena 8, Ready 3, Rodriguez 33, Salas 3, Santos 5.
SS: Lewis 3, McCants 14, Pena 1, Rodriguez 10, Salas 20, Santos 3, Torres 4, Watson 8.
OF: Allen 3, Burgos 11, Caballero 9, Castillo 19, Cody 11, Johnson 20, Paulino 10, Roman 21, Sanchez 29, Sosa 21, Williamson 23.

DSL MARLINS   ROOKIE
DOMINICAN SUMMER LEAGUE

Batting	B-T	HT	WT	DOB	AVG	vLH	vRH	G	AB	R	H	2B	3B	HR	RBI	BB	HBP	SH	SF	SO	SB	CS	SLG	OBP
Adderley, Steven	R-R	6-0	160	12-5-02	.160	.111	.188	9	25	2	4	1	0	0	2	3	0	0	0	16	4	1	.200	.250
Arthur, Andre	R-R	6-4	185	6-9-03	.187	.120	.207	36	107	25	20	6	1	1	14	20	12	0	0	34	7	1	.290	.374
Cappe, Yiddi	R-R	6-3	175	9-17-02	.270	.121	.301	54	189	31	51	17	1	2	27	19	1	0	7	35	9	8	.402	.329
Chourio, Reiner	L-R	5-10	155	12-12-03	.185	.100	.205	24	54	12	10	2	0	1	10	20	2	0	1	25	1	1	.278	.416
Colina, Oscar	R-R	6-0	150	1-28-04	.231	.000	.273	6	13	3	3	1	0	0	3	4	0	0	6	4	0	.308	.412
Duran, Edward	R-R	5-10	170	5-29-04	.340	.286	.349	20	50	12	17	5	0	0	6	7	3	0	0	6	3	1	.440	.450
Flores, Gabriel	R-R	5-10	175	9-15-01	.188	1.000	.133	13	32	5	6	1	0	1	5	11	0	0	1	11	0	0	.313	.386
Guerrero, Kevin	R-R	6-3	165	4-17-04	.260	.333	.243	39	131	24	34	3	1	0	11	23	2	1	2	38	13	3	.298	.373
Hernandez, Jesus	R-R	5-11	150	2-20-04	.263	.227	.271	39	118	17	31	3	0	0	9	19	1	0	1	20	10	4	.288	.367
Hernandez, Ronald	B-R	6-1	155	10-23-03	.209	.148	.224	43	134	30	28	5	3	3	26	31	3	0	2	32	3	1	.358	.365
Hidalgo, Renny	R-R	5-9	165	9-5-02	.239	.188	.247	38	113	21	27	6	6	0	26	16	5	0	1	31	7	1	.398	.356
Melenciano, Jhonny	L-R	6-0	155	12-13-01	.267	.308	.258	45	150	18	40	6	3	0	24	11	1	0	4	30	9	3	.347	.313
Pena, Yelinson	R-R	5-11	175	9-16-00	.163	.000	.171	16	43	4	7	0	1	1	5	7	1	0	1	15	1	0	.279	.288
Rodriguez, Miguel	R-R	6-0	160	11-8-02	.157	.111	.169	30	89	12	14	3	0	0	10	15	2	0	1	28	4	3	.191	.290
Ruiz, Germain	R-R	6-3	165	12-25-02	.261	.222	.269	36	111	25	29	4	2	0	14	19	10	0	0	40	10	5	.333	.414
Sanoja, Javier	R-R	5-9	150	9-3-02	.233	.256	.227	55	219	43	51	11	1	3	26	18	6	0	1	11	11	5	.333	.307
Vegas, Derek	R-R	6-2	175	12-22-01	.226	.212	.231	40	137	21	31	7	0	0	17	10	9	0	1	29	1	0	.277	.318

Pitching	B-T	HT	WT	DOB	W	L	ERA	G	GS	CG	SV	IP	H	R	ER	HR	BB	SO	AVG	vLH	vRH	K/9	BB/9
Almanzar, Stiven	R-R	5-10	155	12-24-01	2	1	2.45	8	5	0	0	26	16	7	7	2	14	26	.184	.152	.204	9.12	4.91
Araba, Oscar	R-R	6-4	195	9-19-02	0	0	6.00	3	0	0	0	3	3	2	2	0	5	3	.273	.000	.375	9.00	15.00
Baldiris, Luis	L-L	5-11	150	5-7-04	1	1	6.06	14	0	0	0	16	16	12	11	0	14	31	.250	.100	.278	17.08	7.71
Burguillos, Yoelvis	R-R	6-2	150	9-7-02	2	3	5.13	12	8	0	0	26	13	20	15	1	24	25	.144	.172	.131	8.54	8.20
De La Rosa, Wander	B-R	6-0	160	10-22-01	2	3	2.54	15	0	0	0	28	28	14	8	1	7	21	.257	.220	.288	6.67	2.22
Dilonex, Wilmer	R-R	6-6	200	12-28-01	0	0	36.00	3	0	0	0	1	4	8	4	1	5	0	.500	.667	.400	0.00	45.00
Duarte, Franyer	R-R	6-0	160	2-2-04	1	2	3.33	10	4	0	0	27	16	12	10	1	10	25	.170	.167	.172	8.33	3.33
Hernandez, Gerardo	R-R	0-0	0	10-16-03	3	0	5.40	14	0	0	0	17	15	10	10	1	12	10	.242	.217	.256	5.40	6.48
Leon, Jesus	L-L	6-3	160	5-5-04	2	0	6.55	16	0	0	0	22	19	17	16	2	9	18	.229	.143	.246	7.36	3.68
Leon, Maycold	L-L	6-1	160	4-29-02	1	0	0.00	8	0	0	1	9	4	1	0	0	5	10	.148	.000	.222	10.38	5.19
Lopez, Luis	R-R	6-3	185	10-8-01	0	0	2.95	12	4	0	0	40	37	14	13	3	3	33	.250	.265	.242	7.49	0.68
Medina, Manuel	L-L	5-10	140	3-25-02	2	3	1.25	14	0	0	1	22	20	13	3	0	5	35	.235	.500	.215	14.54	2.08
Montero, Euri	R-R	6-4	170	3-28-02	2	0	4.63	12	3	0	0	35	37	22	18	2	13	29	.264	.211	.301	7.46	3.34
Montesino, Kendry	R-R	6-4	180	2-1-03	0	4	9.53	8	8	0	0	17	23	19	18	2	23	13	.333	.484	.211	6.88	12.18
Perez, Ivan	L-L	6-6	200	8-30-01	0	0	27.00	6	0	0	0	3	10	11	10	0	7	2	.500	.667	.429	5.40	18.90
Polanco, Natanael	R-R	6-1	170	4-24-03	0	3	8.53	13	4	0	0	19	25	23	18	1	15	16	.329	.176	.373	7.58	7.11
Ramirez, Alan	L-L	5-10	205	7-20-99	1	1	6.88	16	0	0	0	17	12	14	13	1	15	26	.190	.000	.226	13.76	7.94
Reyes, Jean	R-R	5-11	165	8-16-02	0	1	7.94	11	0	0	1	11	9	15	10	0	13	17	.243	.222	.263	13.50	10.32
Reynoso, Juan	R-R	6-0	165	4-4-04	0	1	4.80	7	1	0	0	15	15	9	8	1	9	17	.254	.348	.194	10.20	5.40
Rivera, Yaqui	R-R	6-2	150	7-9-03	0	1	4.50	9	9	0	0	28	23	16	14	0	14	35	.223	.154	.294	11.25	4.50
Rojas, Jose	R-R	6-0	160	4-19-03	0	4	4.32	13	0	0	2	17	15	13	8	1	9	24	.234	.250	.231	12.96	4.86
Serrano, Jhoniel	R-R	0-0	0	10-17-03	2	5	4.94	11	9	0	0	27	21	17	15	1	16	32	.202	.200	.203	10.54	5.27
Tineo, Dameivi	L-L	6-3	170	8-1-03	0	0	1.29	2	2	0	0	7	2	1	1	0	3	6	.100	.200	.067	7.71	3.86
Valencia, Williams	R-R	6-0	167	7-21-00	2	1	2.95	12	0	0	2	18	14	7	6	1	12	16	.219	.259	.189	7.85	5.89

Fielding
C: Duran 13, Flores 10, Hernandez 27, Vegas 13.
1B: Duran 5, Pena 13, Rodriguez 17, Vegas 25.
2B: Chourio 22, Hernandez 29, Sanoja 11.
3B: Hernandez 1, Pena 2, Rodriguez 13, Sanoja 43.
SS: Cappe 50, Hernandez 12.
OF: Adderley 7, Arthur 24, Colina 6, Guerrero 37, Hidalgo 39, Melenciano 38, Ruiz 31, Sanoja 3.

Milwaukee Brewers

SEASON IN A SENTENCE: Behind a strong pitching staff that ranked third in the majors in runs allowed, the Brewers won the National League Central to reach the playoffs for the fourth straight season, though it ended quickly in the NL Division Series against the Braves.

HIGH POINT: From June 22 to July 3, the Brewers won 11 straight games. When the winning streak started, the Brewers were tied with the Cubs for first place in the NL Central. By the time it ended—including a three-game sweep of the Cubs—Milwaukee held an eight-game lead in the division and did not relinquish first place the rest of the season. Brandon Woodruff, Corbin Burnes and Freddy Peralta, all of whom came up through the Brewers farm system, anchored one of the best starting rotations in baseball, while Josh Hader and Devin Williams formed one of the most potent high-leverage bullpen duos in the game.

LOW POINT: The Dodgers bludgeoned the Brewers, 16-4, on May 2, the start of a six-game losing streak for Milwaukee. That stretch, which included a four-game sweep in Philadelphia, dropped the Brewers to 17-16 and second place in the NL Central. Christian Yelich, the NL MVP in 2018 and runner-up in 2019, has seen his performance decline precipitously since then, while Jackie Bradley Jr. struggled mightily in the first year of his two-year contract.

NOTABLE ROOKIES: The lack of upper-level prospects in the minor league system entering the season was evident, with few rookies making an impact at the big league level in 2021. Outfielder Tyrone Taylor, a 27-year-old rookie, proved to be a useful player, hitting .247/.321/.457 in 99 games while playing all three outfield spots with good defense.

KEY TRANSACTIONS: On May 21, the Brewers traded righthanders J.P. Feyereisen and Drew Rasmussen to the Rays for shortstop Willy Adames and righthander Trevor Richards. While Rasmussen emerged as a productive arm for the Rays, Adames became the best hitter on the Brewers, batting .285/.366/.521 over 99 games with Milwaukee. He formed a strong middle infield partnership with Kolten Wong, who signed a two-year contract with the Brewers before the season and hit .272/.335/.447 in 116 games.

OPENING DAY SALARY: $87,569,366 (21st).

PLAYERS OF THE YEAR

MAJOR LEAGUE	MINOR LEAGUE
Corbin Burnes RHP	**Joey Wiemer** OF
11-5, 2.43	(High-A/Low-A)
NL Cy Young finalist	.295/.403/.556,
234 SO in 167 IP	27 HR, 30 SB

ORGANIZATION LEADERS

Batting		*Minimum 250 AB
MAJORS		
*AVG	Willy Adames	.285
*OPS	Willy Adames	.886
HR	Avisail Garcia	29
RBI	Avisail Garcia	86
MINORS		
*AVG	Freddy Zamora, Carolina, Wisconsin	.300
*OBP	Ashton McGee, Carolina, Wisconsin	.423
*SLG	Joey Wiemer, Carolina, Wisconsin	.556
*OPS	Joey Wiemer, Carolina, Wisconsin	.958
R	Felix Valerio, Carolina, Wisconsin	90
H	Felix Valerio, Carolina, Wisconsin	124
TB	Joey Wiemer, Carolina, Wisconsin	220
2B	Felix Valerio, Carolina, Wisconsin	37
3B	David Hamilton, Biloxi, Wisconsin	11
HR	Joey Wiemer, Wisconsin, Carolina	27
RBI	Joe Gray Jr., Carolina, Wisconsin	90
BB	Hayden Cantrelle, Biloxi, Wisconsin	82
SO	Zach Green, Nashville	148
SB	David Hamilton, Biloxi, Wisconsin	52

Pitching		#Minimum 75 IP
MAJORS		
W	Brent Suter	12
#ERA	Corbin Burnes	2.43
SO	Corbin Burnes	234
SV	Josh Hader	34
MINORS		
W	Justin Bullock, Biloxi, Wisconsin, Carolina	8
W	Brandon Knarr, Wisconsin, Carolina	8
L	Jesus Castillo, Nashville, Biloxi	9
#ERA	Ethan Small, ACL Brewers Gold, Biloxi, Nashville	1.98
G	Luke Barker, Nashville	53
GS	Victor Castaneda, Nashville, Wisconsin	22
GS	Noah Zavolas, Biloxi	22
SV	Luke Barker, Nashville	13
SV	Cam Robinson, Biloxi, Wisconsin, Carolina	13
IP	Noah Zavolas, Biloxi	120.2
BB	Michele Vassalotti, Carolina	60
SO	Victor Castaneda, Nashville, Wisconsin	131
#AVG	Evan Reifert, Wisconsin, Carolina	.168

2021 PERFORMANCE

General Manager: David Stearns. **Farm Director:** Tom Flanagan. **Scouting Director:** Tod Johnson.

Class	Team	League	W	L	PCT	Finish	Manager
Majors	Milwaukee Brewers	National	95	67	.586	3rd (15)	Craig Counsell
Triple-A	Nashville Sounds	Triple-A East	70	58	.547	9th (20)	Rick Sweet
Double-A	Biloxi Shuckers	Double-A South	45	69	.395	8th (8)	Mike Guerrero
High-A	Wisconsin Timber Rattlers	High-A Central	59	60	.496	6th (12)	Matt Erickson
Low-A	Carolina Mudcats	Low-A East	68	52	.567	t-4th (12)	Joe Ayrault
Rookie	ACL Brewers Blue	Arizona Complex	21	33	.389	14th (18)	Rafael Neda
Rookie	ACL Brewers Gold	Arizona Complex	27	24	.529	8th (18)	David Tufo
Rookie	DSL Brewers2	Dominican Summer	29	30	.492	t-24th (46)	Fidel Pena
Rookie	DSL Brewers1	Dominican Summer	31	28	.525	t-19th (46)	Victor Estevez
Overall 2021 Minor League Record			350	354	.497	17th (30)	

ORGANIZATION STATISTICS

MILWAUKEE BREWERS
NATIONAL LEAGUE

Batting	B-T	HT	WT	DOB	AVG	vLH	vRH	G	AB	R	H	2B	3B	HR	RBI	BB	HBP	SH	SF	SO	SB	CS	SLG	OBP
Adames, Willy	R-R	6-0	210	9-2-95	.285	.263	.293	99	365	61	104	26	2	20	58	47	0	0	1	105	4	2	.521	.366
Arcia, Orlando	R-R	6-0	187	8-4-94	.091	--	.091	4	11	0	1	0	0	0	1	0	0	0	0	3	0	0	.091	.091
2-team total (32 Atlanta)					.198	.273	.169	36	81	9	16	3	0	2	14	7	0	0	1	19	1	0	.309	.258
Bradley Jr., Jackie	L-R	5-10	196	4-19-90	.163	.169	.161	134	387	39	63	14	3	6	29	28	10	0	3	132	7	1	.261	.236
Cain, Lorenzo	R-R	6-2	214	4-13-86	.257	.206	.275	78	257	40	66	13	0	8	36	26	2	0	1	48	13	2	.401	.329
Escobar, Eduardo	B-R	5-10	193	1-5-89	.268	.328	.240	48	179	27	48	12	2	6	25	19	1	0	0	39	0	0	.458	.342
2-team total (98 Arizona)					.253	.295	.238	146	549	77	139	26	5	28	90	48	1	0	1	124	1	0	.472	.314
Feliciano, Mario	R-R	6-1	200	11-20-98	--	--	--	1	0	1	0	0	0	0	0	1	0	0	0	0	0	0	--	1.000
Fisher, Derek	L-R	6-3	215	8-21-93	.250	.000	.286	4	8	1	2	0	1	0	1	0	0	0	0	1	0	0	.500	.250
Garcia, Avisail	R-R	6-4	250	6-12-91	.262	.279	.258	135	461	68	121	18	0	29	86	38	11	0	5	121	8	4	.490	.330
Hiura, Keston	R-R	6-0	202	8-2-96	.168	.130	.185	61	173	16	29	9	1	4	19	14	7	2	1	77	3	0	.301	.256
Lopes, Tim	R-R	5-11	180	6-24-94	.100	.000	.143	7	10	1	1	0	0	0	0	1	0	0	0	4	0	1	.100	.182
Maile, Luke	R-R	6-3	225	2-6-91	.300	.750	.231	15	30	6	9	4	0	0	3	3	1	0	0	7	0	0	.433	.382
McKinney, Billy	L-L	6-1	205	8-23-94	.207	.227	.200	40	92	9	19	3	1	3	6	7	0	0	1	24	1	0	.359	.260
3-team total (37 Los Angeles, 39 New York)					.192	.220	.184	116	265	32	51	11	3	9	27	32	1	0	2	79	2	0	.358	.280
Narvaez, Omar	L-R	5-11	220	2-10-92	.266	.152	.289	123	391	54	104	20	0	11	49	41	7	0	6	84	0	0	.402	.342
Nottingham, Jacob	R-R	6-2	220	4-3-95	.214	.375	.000	5	14	2	3	1	0	2	4	0	0	0	0	8	0	0	.714	.214
Peterson, Jace	L-R	6-0	215	5-9-90	.247	.271	.242	94	259	36	64	11	1	6	31	38	3	0	2	68	10	1	.367	.348
Pina, Manny	R-R	6-0	202	6-5-87	.189	.221	.165	75	180	27	34	6	0	13	33	22	5	0	1	38	0	0	.439	.293
Ray, Corey	L-L	6-0	196	9-22-94	.000	--	.000	1	2	1	0	0	0	0	0	1	0	0	0	1	0	0	.000	.333
Reyes, Pablo	R-R	5-8	175	9-5-93	.256	.270	.244	53	78	12	20	5	0	1	3	9	0	0	0	15	4	0	.359	.333
Robertson, Daniel	R-R	5-11	210	3-22-94	.164	.158	.167	50	73	10	12	2	0	2	4	12	3	1	1	28	0	0	.274	.303
Shaw, Travis	L-R	6-4	230	4-16-90	.191	.154	.201	56	178	14	34	8	0	6	28	19	3	1	1	51	0	0	.337	.279
Taylor, Tyrone	R-R	6-0	194	1-22-94	.247	.298	.220	93	243	33	60	9	3	12	43	20	7	0	1	59	6	1	.457	.321
Tellez, Rowdy	L-L	6-4	255	3-16-95	.272	.278	.270	56	158	22	43	10	1	7	28	14	1	0	1	32	0	0	.481	.333
Urias, Luis	R-R	5-9	186	6-3-97	.249	.243	.251	150	490	77	122	25	1	23	75	63	10	1	3	116	5	1	.445	.345
Vogelbach, Daniel	L-R	6-0	270	12-17-92	.219	.097	.239	93	215	30	47	8	0	9	24	43	0	0	0	57	0	0	.381	.349
Wong, Kolten	L-R	5-7	185	10-10-90	.272	.297	.261	116	445	70	121	32	2	14	50	31	13	0	3	83	12	5	.447	.335
Yelich, Christian	L-R	6-3	195	12-5-91	.248	.187	.271	117	399	70	99	19	2	9	51	70	3	0	3	113	9	3	.373	.362

Pitching	B-T	HT	WT	DOB	W	L	ERA	G	GS	CG	SV	IP	H	R	ER	HR	BB	SO	AVG	vLH	vRH	K/9	BB/9
Anderson, Brett	L-L	6-4	230	2-1-88	4	9	4.22	24	24	0	0	96	102	52	45	11	28	58	.276	.303	.270	5.44	2.63
Ashby, Aaron	R-L	6-2	181	5-24-98	3	2	4.55	13	4	0	1	32	25	20	16	4	12	39	.210	.375	.184	11.08	3.41
Axford, John	R-R	6-5	234	4-1-83	0	0	54.00	1	0	0	0	2	2	2	2	0	1	0	.667	1.000	.500	0.00	27.00
Bettinger, Alec	R-R	6-2	210	7-13-95	0	1	13.50	4	1	0	0	10	18	15	15	3	3	5	.391	.350	.423	4.50	2.70
Bickford, Phil	R-R	6-4	200	7-10-95	0	0	18.00	1	0	0	0	1	2	2	2	1	1	0	.500	.667	.000	0.00	9.00
2-team total (56 Los Angeles)					4	2	2.81	57	0	0	1	51	36	18	16	7	19	59	.197	.222	.186	10.34	3.33
Boxberger, Brad	R-R	5-10	211	5-27-88	5	4	3.34	71	0	0	4	65	44	26	24	8	25	83	.192	.139	.240	11.55	3.48
Burnes, Corbin	R-R	6-3	225	10-22-94	11	5	2.43	28	28	0	0	167	123	47	45	7	34	234	.201	.220	.179	12.61	1.83
Cousins, Jake	R-R	6-4	185	7-14-94	1	0	2.70	30	0	0	0	30	16	9	9	3	19	44	.158	.146	.167	13.20	5.70
Curtiss, John	R-R	6-5	220	4-5-93	0	0	12.46	6	0	0	0	4	8	8	6	2	3	4	.364	.444	.308	8.31	6.23
2-team total (35 Miami)					3	1	3.45	41	2	0	0	44	42	21	17	6	12	44	.244	.260	.232	8.93	2.44
Feyereisen, J.P.	R-R	6-2	215	2-7-93	0	2	3.26	21	0	0	0	19	10	9	7	2	11	20	.154	.172	.139	9.31	5.12
Godley, Zack	R-R	6-3	250	4-21-90	0	1	16.20	2	1	0	0	3	4	7	6	2	5	5	.286	1.000	.313	5.10	13.50
Gustave, Jandel	R-R	6-3	220	10-12-92	1	2	3.44	14	0	0	0	18	15	10	7	2	5	13	.224	.200	.238	6.38	2.45
Hader, Josh	L-L	6-3	180	4-7-94	4	2	1.23	60	0	0	34	59	25	8	8	3	24	102	.127	.133	.125	15.65	3.68
Hardy, Blaine	L-L	6-2	218	3-14-87	0	1	18.00	1	0	0	0	1	3	3	2	1	1	1	.600	.500	.667	9.00	9.00
Houser, Adrian	R-R	6-3	222	2-2-93	10	6	3.22	28	26	1	0	142	118	61	51	12	64	105	.228	.273	.192	6.64	4.05
Lauer, Eric	R-L	6-3	228	6-3-95	7	5	3.19	24	20	0	0	119	94	46	42	16	41	117	.215	.228	.211	8.87	3.11
Lindblom, Josh	R-R	6-4	240	6-15-87	0	0	9.72	8	0	0	0	17	23	18	18	5	10	17	.324	.280	.348	9.18	5.40

Name	B-T	HT	WT	DOB	W	L	ERA	G	GS	CG	SV	IP	H	R	ER	HR	BB	SO	AVG	vLH	vRH	SO/9	BB/9
Maile, Luke	R-R	6-3	225	2-6-91	0	0	9.00	1	0	0	0	1	2	1	1	1	0	0	.400	.667	.000	0.00	0.00
Milner, Hoby	L-L	6-3	175	1-13-91	0	0	5.40	19	0	0	0	22	30	15	13	8	3	30	.323	.250	.361	12.46	1.25
Norris, Daniel	L-L	6-2	207	4-25-93	1	0	6.64	18	0	0	0	20	17	16	15	5	15	18	.227	.222	.228	7.97	6.64
Peralta, Freddy	R-R	5-11	199	6-4-96	10	5	2.81	28	27	1	0	144	84	47	45	14	56	195	.165	.157	.174	12.16	3.49
Perdomo, Angel	L-L	6-8	265	5-7-94	1	0	6.35	19	0	0	0	17	12	12	12	4	16	28	.200	.087	.270	14.82	8.47
Peterson, Jace	L-R	6-0	215	5-9-90	0	0	9.00	2	0	0	0	2	4	2	2	0	1	2	.400	.333	.500	9.00	4.50
Rasmussen, Drew	R-R	6-1	211	7-27-95	0	1	4.24	15	0	0	1	17	13	11	8	2	12	25	.200	.150	.222	13.24	6.35
Rea, Colin	R-R	6-5	235	7-1-90	0	0	7.50	1	0	0	0	6	7	5	5	2	0	5	.304	.444	.214	7.50	0.00
Richards, Trevor	R-R	6-2	195	5-15-93	3	0	3.20	15	0	0	0	20	15	7	7	3	9	25	.208	.132	.294	11.44	4.12
Robertson, Daniel	R-R	5-11	210	3-22-94	0	0	0.00	1	0	0	0	1	1	0	0	0	0	0	.250	.000	.333	0.00	0.00
Romano, Sal	L-R	6-5	255	10-12-93	0	1	27.00	1	0	0	0	1	4	4	3	1	0	0	.571	.500	.667	0.00	0.00
2-team total (14 Cincinnati)					0	1	6.23	15	0	0	0	22	24	18	15	5	9	12	.270	.225	.306	4.98	3.74
Sanchez, Miguel	R-R	6-3	205	12-31-93	2	1	4.15	28	0	0	0	26	27	14	12	4	14	23	.267	.265	.269	7.96	4.85
Strickland, Hunter	R-R	6-3	225	9-24-88	3	2	1.73	35	0	0	0	36	21	8	7	4	12	38	.165	.205	.145	9.41	2.97
Suter, Brent	L-L	6-4	213	8-29-89	12	5	3.07	61	1	0	1	73	72	34	25	9	24	69	.252	.215	.269	8.47	2.95
Topa, Justin	R-R	6-4	200	3-7-91	0	0	29.70	4	0	0	0	3	12	11	11	2	1	1	.545	.857	.400	2.70	2.70
Weber, Ryan	R-R	6-1	175	8-12-90	0	0	0.00	1	0	0	0	1	1	0	0	0	0	0	.333	.000	.500	0.00	0.00
Weigel, Patrick	R-R	6-6	240	7-8-94	0	0	4.50	3	0	0	0	4	4	2	2	1	4	9	.250	.143	.333	20.25	9.00
Williams, Devin	R-R	6-2	200	9-21-94	8	2	2.50	58	0	0	3	54	36	17	15	5	28	87	.186	.190	.181	14.50	4.67
Woodruff, Brandon	L-R	6-4	243	2-10-93	9	10	2.56	30	30	0	0	179	130	54	51	18	43	211	.200	.182	.219	10.59	2.16
Yardley, Eric	R-R	6-0	170	8-18-90	0	0	6.75	17	0	0	0	19	24	15	14	3	10	5	.324	.500	.240	2.41	4.82
Zimmermann, Jordan	R-R	6-2	225	5-23-86	0	0	7.94	2	0	0	0	6	8	5	5	1	2	0	.348	.300	.385	0.00	3.18

Fielding

Catcher	PCT	G	PO	A	E	DP	PB
Maile	1.000	12	82	5	0	0	0
Narvaez	.994	111	1005	52	6	2	5
Nottingham	1.000	3	22	2	0	0	2
Pina	.994	65	511	27	3	1	3

First Base	PCT	G	PO	A	E	DP
Escobar	1.000	18	79	7	0	7
Hiura	.991	49	304	19	3	25
McKinney	1.000	9	28	0	0	3
Peterson	.965	26	79	4	3	9
Robertson	1.000	3	3	2	0	0
Shaw	1.000	20	34	6	0	2
Tellez	.988	46	313	17	4	31
Vogelbach	.997	59	330	16	1	20

Second Base	PCT	G	PO	A	E	DP
Hiura	1.000	7	1	10	0	1
Lopes	1.000	3	3	5	0	0
Narvaez	.000	1	0	0	0	0
Peterson	.991	35	52	60	1	17
Reyes	1.000	2	1	3	0	0
Robertson	.957	9	8	14	1	4
Urias	.984	25	27	33	1	5
Wong	.995	113	164	229	2	51

Third Base	PCT	G	PO	A	E	DP
Arcia	1.000	1	1	5	0	1
Escobar	.945	34	9	43	3	8
Peterson	.938	11	6	9	1	2
Reyes	.966	28	5	23	1	2
Robertson	.952	24	7	13	1	2
Shaw	.952	48	23	76	5	4
Urias	.940	68	40	100	9	8

Shortstop	PCT	G	PO	A	E	DP
Adames	.968	96	110	226	11	40
Arcia	1.000	2	0	2	0	0
Peterson	.000	1	0	0	0	0
Reyes	1.000	2	3	4	0	1
Robertson	1.000	8	8	12	0	1
Urias	.935	68	61	139	14	23

Outfield	PCT	G	PO	A	E	DP
Bradley Jr.	1.000	120	215	3	0	2
Cain	.994	70	154	2	1	1
Fisher	1.000	3	2	0	0	0
Garcia	.972	122	204	4	6	0
Hiura	1.000	1	1	0	0	0
McKinney	1.000	20	29	1	0	0
Peterson	1.000	28	31	0	0	0
Ray	1.000	1	2	0	0	0
Reyes	1.000	1	1	0	0	0
Taylor	1.000	82	113	0	0	0
Yelich	.994	108	170	5	1	0

NASHVILLE SOUNDS

TRIPLE-A

TRIPLE-A EAST

Batting	B-T	HT	WT	DOB	AVG	vLH	vRH	G	AB	R	H	2B	3B	HR	RBI	BB	HBP	SH	SF	SO	SB	CS	SLG	OBP
Broxton, Keon	R-R	6-3	200	5-7-90	.111	.000	.133	15	36	4	4	0	0	0	1	5	1	0	0	22	2	1	.111	.238
2-team total (73 St. Paul)					.175	.197	.168	88	257	42	45	6	0	9	27	35	4	0	3	135	12	2	.304	.281
Cain, Lorenzo	R-R	6-2	214	4-13-86	.241	.429	.182	9	29	1	7	1	0	0	2	0	0	0	0	8	1	0	.276	.290
Castro, Luis	R-R	6-1	187	9-19-95	.333	.000	.400	2	6	1	2	1	0	1	3	1	1	0	0	3	0	0	1.000	.500
Coca, Yeison	B-R	5-10	155	5-22-99	.296	.286	.300	13	27	6	8	1	0	0	2	1	0	0	0	7	0	1	.333	.321
Cozens, Dylan	L-L	6-6	245	5-31-94	.177	.069	.240	31	79	17	14	4	1	2	7	19	1	1	0	43	4	1	.329	.343
Dahl, David	L-R	6-2	197	4-1-94	.327	.130	.379	31	110	18	36	12	1	3	15	8	1	0	1	17	0	0	.536	.375
Diaz, Brent	R-R	6-1	205	3-22-96	.250	1.000	.000	2	4	0	1	0	0	0	1	0	0	0	0	1	0	0	.250	.250
Feliciano, Mario	R-R	6-1	200	11-20-98	.210	.219	.205	32	105	12	22	2	0	3	19	4	2	0	3	26	1	0	.314	.246
Fisher, Derek	L-R	6-3	215	8-21-93	.205	.111	.233	25	78	11	16	5	0	1	8	7	0	0	0	23	0	0	.308	.271
Forsythe, Logan	R-R	6-1	205	1-14-87	.250	.286	.231	17	20	4	5	3	0	0	8	1	0	0	7	0	0	.400	.483
Fry, David	R-R	6-2	215	11-20-95	.288	.286	.289	19	52	8	15	4	1	1	5	7	1	0	0	17	0	0	.462	.383
Green, Zach	R-R	6-2	224	3-7-94	.214	.209	.216	101	327	39	70	18	0	15	64	40	7	0	4	148	0	1	.407	.310
Hager, Jake	R-R	6-1	170	3-4-93	.211	.211	.212	18	71	13	15	7	0	2	9	8	0	0	1	15	1	0	.394	.288
2-team total (9 Syracuse)					.279	.250	.288	27	108	19	30	9	0	5	18	10	0	0	1	20	1	0	.500	.336
Henry, Payton	R-R	6-2	215	6-24-97	.262	.167	.286	19	61	7	16	3	0	1	9	4	4	0	2	17	0	0	.361	.338
2-team total (22 Jacksonville)					.223	.200	.230	41	130	14	29	5	0	5	17	14	5	0	2	43	0	1	.377	.318
Hiura, Keston	R-R	6-0	202	8-2-96	.236	.388	.203	51	172	22	44	12	0	8	24	29	4	0	1	69	2	1	.465	.374
Hummel, Cooper	B-R	5-10	198	11-28-94	.254	.265	.250	46	126	27	32	8	3	6	15	41	0	0	1	26	0	0	.508	.435
Kelley, Christian	R-R	5-10	190	9-23-93	.268	.438	.211	49	127	12	34	7	0	1	22	20	1	0	1	37	0	1	.346	.369
Kramer, Kevin	R-R	6-0	195	10-3-93	.245	.364	.214	23	53	8	13	4	0	0	5	11	1	0	1	14	0	0	.321	.379
2-team total (51 Indianapolis)					.207	.176	.220	74	232	27	48	9	2	3	26	35	10	0	3	72	0	1	.302	.332
Lipka, Matt	R-R	6-1	215	4-15-92	.285	.238	.302	70	242	46	69	10	1	9	32	18	5	1	1	65	24	3	.446	.346
Longo, Mitch	L-R	6-0	195	1-12-95	.182	.200	.178	20	55	10	10	1	1	1	4	4	0	0	0	21	4	0	.291	.237
Lopes, Tim	R-R	5-11	180	6-24-94	.226	.211	.232	93	327	52	74	16	4	11	39	34	5	0	4	92	9	3	.401	.305
Lujano, Jesus	L-L	5-10	160	2-18-99	.143	.000	.250	6	7	2	1	0	0	0	0	3	1	0	0	3	1	0	.143	.250
Maile, Luke	R-R	6-3	225	2-6-91	.225	.222	.226	46	129	17	29	9	0	1	15	22	3	1	0	50	2	0	.318	.351

Name	B-T	HT	WT	DOB	AVG	vLH	vRH	G	AB	R	H	2B	3B	HR	RBI	BB	HBP	SH	SF	SO	SB	CS	SLG	OBP
Nunez, Renato	R-R	6-1	220	4-4-94	.179	.192	.171	21	67	7	12	2	0	1	4	6	2	0	0	17	0	0	.254	.267
2-team total (74 Toledo)					.268	.245	.279	95	332	66	89	16	2	21	68	37	13	0	4	93	1	0	.518	.360
Perez, Hernan	R-R	6-1	213	3-26-91	.357	.333	.367	23	84	8	30	6	0	3	18	6	0	0	1	16	4	1	.536	.396
Peterson, Dustin	R-R	6-2	210	9-10-94	.271	.258	.278	77	291	42	79	15	0	9	56	30	5	0	3	44	0	1	.416	.347
Peterson, Jace	L-R	6-0	215	5-9-90	.236	.154	.262	17	55	12	13	4	0	5	19	9	0	0	0	19	1	0	.582	.344
Ray, Corey	L-L	6-0	196	9-22-94	.274	.308	.255	39	146	18	40	11	2	6	19	10	1	0	0	45	2	0	.500	.325
Reyes, Pablo	R-R	5-8	175	9-5-93	.226	.207	.231	34	133	26	30	7	0	4	20	15	1	0	4	24	1	3	.368	.301
Robertson, Daniel	R-R	5-11	210	3-22-94	.115	.150	.103	28	78	6	9	3	0	0	3	10	0	0	0	25	0	0	.154	.216
Shaw, Travis	L-R	6-4	230	4-16-90	.273	.300	.261	11	33	6	9	1	0	2	8	7	1	0	0	8	0	0	.485	.415
Spanberger, Chad	L-R	6-3	235	11-1-95	.125	.250	.000	4	8	1	1	0	0	1	2	0	0	0	0	5	0	0	.500	.125
Stokes Jr., Troy	R-R	5-9	205	2-2-96	.199	.212	.194	69	136	18	27	5	2	2	9	16	3	0	0	38	5	2	.309	.297
2-team total (29 Indianapolis)					.188	.164	.197	98	207	29	39	7	3	4	14	27	5	0	0	56	9	2	.309	.297
Strange-Gordon, Dee	L-R	5-11	166	4-22-88	.333	.286	.357	10	42	10	14	2	1	1	2	3	0	0	0	5	2	1	.500	.378
3-team total (16 Indianapolis Indians, 28 Iowa Cubs)					.248	.228	.258	54	230	36	57	11	1	5	21	11	2	1	0	35	6	1	.370	.288
Taylor, Tyrone	R-R	6-0	194	1-22-94	.500	.571	.429	9	28	10	14	4	0	3	10	5	0	0	2	4	0	0	.964	.543
Tellez, Rowdy	L-L	6-4	255	3-16-95	.333	--	.333	2	6	2	2	0	0	1	3	2	0	0	0	1	0	0	.833	.500
2-team total (13 Buffalo)					.302	.250	.317	15	53	10	16	4	0	5	14	8	2	0	0	12	0	0	.660	.413
Turang, Brice	R-R	6-0	173	11-21-99	.245	.225	.252	44	143	19	35	7	0	1	14	32	0	0	1	35	9	2	.315	.381
Vogelbach, Daniel	L-R	6-0	270	12-17-92	.313	.375	.300	18	48	8	15	0	0	3	8	16	0	0	1	13	0	0	.500	.477
Westbrook, Jamie	R-R	5-9	193	6-18-95	.287	.349	.266	70	251	45	72	15	1	11	47	21	7	0	4	42	2	0	.486	.353
Wilson, Weston	R-R	6-3	215	9-19-94	.267	.245	.274	70	217	34	58	11	1	16	35	28	1	0	0	57	8	2	.548	.354
Yelich, Christian	L-R	6-3	195	12-5-91	.000	.000	.000	3	5	0	0	0	0	0	0	2	0	0	0	2	0	0	.000	.286

Pitching	B-T	HT	WT	DOB	W	L	ERA	G	GS	CG	SV	IP	H	R	ER	HR	BB	SO	AVG	vLH	vRH	K/9	BB/9
Alvarez, R.J.	R-R	6-1	230	6-8-91	0	3	4.08	38	0	0	0	35	34	19	16	3	18	44	.246	.317	.187	11.21	4.58
Andrews, Clayton	L-L	5-6	160	1-4-97	1	1	4.82	7	0	0	0	9	6	7	5	1	6	11	.171	.375	.111	10.61	5.79
Ashby, Aaron	R-L	6-2	181	5-24-98	5	4	4.41	21	12	0	0	63	55	35	31	4	32	100	.227	.183	.246	14.21	4.55
Barker, Luke	R-R	6-3	230	3-11-92	7	5	2.35	53	0	0	13	61	39	24	16	9	10	77	.178	.163	.190	11.30	1.47
Bettinger, Alec	R-R	6-2	210	7-13-95	3	7	4.75	21	18	0	0	97	104	56	51	15	26	98	.272	.268	.275	9.12	2.42
Brown, Zack	R-R	6-1	199	12-15-94	1	0	0.00	3	0	0	0	5	2	0	0	0	4	4	.154	.143	.167	7.71	7.71
Castaneda, Victor	R-R	6-1	185	8-27-98	1	1	2.25	3	2	0	0	12	9	3	3	0	8	17	.205	.286	.130	12.75	6.00
Castillo, Jesus	R-R	6-3	205	8-27-95	0	0	6.75	7	1	0	0	11	8	9	8	1	8	11	.195	.286	.100	9.28	6.75
Cousins, Jake	R-R	6-4	185	7-14-94	1	0	1.86	9	1	0	1	10	6	3	2	1	2	16	.171	.294	.056	14.90	1.86
Derby, Bubba	L-R	5-11	185	2-24-94	3	0	4.70	13	0	0	0	23	20	12	12	3	9	24	.230	.286	.192	9.39	3.52
File, Dylan	R-R	6-1	205	6-4-96	2	4	5.27	9	9	0	0	43	53	26	25	7	12	36	.314	.326	.301	7.59	2.53
Francis, Bowden	R-R	6-5	225	4-22-96	4	2	3.49	7	7	0	0	39	26	17	15	4	12	39	.197	.185	.209	9.08	2.79
2-team total (14 Buffalo)					10	6	3.95	21	20	0	0	112	82	55	49	19	43	110	.205	.228	.185	8.87	3.47
Godley, Zack	R-R	6-3	250	4-21-90	3	2	2.40	6	5	0	0	30	21	9	8	4	12	34	.198	.158	.221	10.20	3.60
3-team total (6 Columbus, 9 Syracuse)					7	7	4.39	21	18	0	0	98	90	52	48	13	52	85	.251	.277	.228	7.78	4.76
Gustave, Jandel	R-R	6-3	220	10-12-92	0	1	1.50	6	0	0	0	6	3	1	1	0	0	8	.150	.222	.091	12.00	0.00
2-team total (15 Indianapolis Indians)					1	1	3.00	21	0	0	5	21	15	7	7	0	5	26	.197	.200	.196	11.14	2.14
Hardy, Blaine	L-L	6-2	218	3-14-87	6	6	2.63	30	8	0	0	68	57	25	20	10	29	62	.228	.216	.235	8.17	3.82
Jankins, Thomas	R-R	6-2	220	7-2-95	2	6	6.11	25	15	0	0	84	94	61	57	13	31	62	.287	.277	.293	6.64	3.32
Kramer, Kevin	L-R	6-0	195	10-3-93	0	0	9.00	1	0	0	0	1	1	1	1	0	1	0	.200	.000	.333	0.00	0.00
Lauer, Eric	R-L	6-3	228	6-3-95	0	0	0.00	1	1	0	0	5	1	0	0	0	2	12	.067	.000	.083	21.60	3.60
LeBlanc, Wade	L-L	6-2	195	8-7-84	1	1	3.78	4	4	0	0	17	12	7	7	1	7	14	.197	.222	.186	7.56	3.78
Lindblom, Josh	R-R	6-4	240	6-15-87	5	4	3.10	22	20	0	0	105	102	38	36	10	26	117	.250	.267	.233	10.06	2.24
Lobstein, Kyle	L-L	6-3	220	8-12-89	1	0	4.94	23	0	0	0	24	30	15	13	3	9	20	.294	.178	.386	7.61	3.42
2-team total (16 Rochester)					3	0	3.40	39	0	0	1	45	45	19	17	3	17	45	.256	.176	.334	9.00	3.40
Milner, Hoby	L-L	6-3	175	1-13-91	1	1	1.69	30	0	0	5	32	19	6	6	2	2	48	.168	.170	.167	13.50	0.56
Otero, Andy	L-L	5-9	165	6-3-92	0	2	9.15	7	5	0	0	21	30	27	21	4	9	23	.330	.371	.304	10.02	3.92
Perdomo, Angel	L-L	6-8	265	5-7-94	1	0	1.29	14	1	0	0	14	8	3	2	1	4	25	.170	.333	.094	16.07	2.57
Rea, Colin	R-R	6-5	235	7-1-90	4	2	2.27	7	7	0	0	36	33	9	9	2	4	35	.241	.268	.212	8.83	1.01
Sadzeck, Connor	R-R	6-7	235	10-1-91	1	1	3.18	17	0	0	0	17	15	7	6	1	8	21	.231	.294	.161	11.12	4.24
2-team total (23 Charlotte)					3	3	4.84	40	0	0	1	45	39	25	24	5	28	49	.235	.299	.180	9.87	5.64
Sanchez, Miguel	R-R	6-3	205	12-31-93	2	0	3.60	19	0	0	5	25	22	15	10	3	9	24	.229	.229	.230	8.64	3.24
Small, Ethan	L-L	6-4	215	2-14-97	2	0	2.06	9	9	0	0	35	27	9	8	3	21	24	.216	.300	.176	6.17	5.40
Sobotka, Chad	R-R	6-7	225	7-10-93	2	1	4.85	43	0	0	0	39	32	24	21	2	23	29	.230	.164	.292	6.69	5.31
Strzelecki, Peter	R-R	6-2	195	10-24-94	0	0	3.60	4	0	0	0	5	4	2	2	1	1	6	.235	.400	.000	10.80	1.80
Topa, Justin	R-R	6-4	200	3-7-91	1	0	3.00	10	0	0	0	9	7	3	3	0	2	9	.206	.150	.286	9.00	2.00
Torres-Costa, Quintin	L-L	5-11	190	9-11-94	3	1	6.81	35	0	0	0	36	32	31	27	2	38	50	.239	.211	.250	12.62	9.59
Wahl, Bobby	R-R	6-3	216	3-21-92	1	0	7.27	11	0	0	1	7	7	7	7	1	7	14	.226	.400	.143	14.54	7.27
Weber, Ryan	R-R	6-1	175	8-12-90	1	1	6.75	2	2	0	0	8	13	6	6	1	1	10	.371	.444	.294	11.25	1.13
2-team total (7 Worcester)					2	3	5.02	9	8	0	0	43	48	28	24	6	11	43	.287	.318	.267	9.00	2.30
Weigel, Patrick	R-R	6-6	240	7-8-94	2	1	7.27	36	1	0	2	43	47	40	35	6	38	48	.275	.253	.293	9.97	7.89
Wilson, Weston	R-R	6-3	215	9-11-94	0	0	0.00	1	0	0	0	1	3	0	0	0	0	0	.600	1.000	.000	0.00	0.00
Yardley, Eric	R-R	6-0	170	8-18-90	4	1	3.22	39	0	0	0	36	37	14	13	2	9	30	.257	.306	.220	7.43	2.23

Fielding

Catcher	PCT	G	PO	A	E	DP	PB
Diaz	1.000	1	13	0	0	0	0
Feliciano	.985	30	258	8	4	0	0
Fry	.971	5	34	0	1	0	0
Henry	1.000	18	155	11	0	0	0
Hummel	.971	4	31	2	1	0	0
Kelley	.995	42	349	18	2	2	1
Maile	.995	41	377	22	2	2	3

First Base	PCT	G	PO	A	E	DP
Castro	1.000	2	8	1	0	0
Fry	.962	3	22	3	1	0
Green	.987	33	210	13	3	16
Hiura	.979	24	173	12	4	17
Hummel	1.000	5	29	0	0	4
Lipka	1.000	2	14	1	0	2
Maile	.500	2	0	1	1	0
Nunez	.993	19	134	12	1	15

	PCT	G	PO	A	E	DP
Perez	1.000	3	20	2	0	0
Peterson	.987	17	69	5	1	8
Peterson	1.000	3	15	1	0	3
Tellez	1.000	2	12	0	0	1
Vogelbach	.990	16	95	9	1	11
Wilson	1.000	22	157	17	0	13

Second Base	PCT	G	PO	A	E	DP
Coca	.000	1	0	0	0	0
Forsythe	1.000	6	3	6	0	1
Hiura	.964	23	34	72	4	12
Kramer	1.000	2	0	2	0	1
Lopes	.965	23	28	54	3	10
Perez	1.000	6	2	11	0	2
Peterson	1.000	7	8	12	0	3
Reyes	.946	12	23	30	3	4
Robertson	1.000	4	2	12	0	4
Strange-Gordon	1.000	3	7	12	0	2
Westbrook	.982	41	68	96	3	28
Wilson	.871	10	8	19	4	3

Third Base	PCT	G	PO	A	E	DP
Coca	.000	3	0	0	0	0
Forsythe	1.000	2	1	3	0	0
Fry	.952	10	8	12	1	1
Green	.929	63	32	85	9	10

	PCT	G	PO	A	E	DP
Kramer	1.000	4	1	5	0	0
Lopes	.941	25	13	35	3	0
Nunez	1.000	1	1	2	0	0
Perez	.000	1	0	0	0	0
Peterson	1.000	3	1	6	0	1
Reyes	1.000	6	3	14	0	2
Robertson	.889	8	4	4	1	0
Shaw	.941	9	4	12	1	0
Westbrook	.840	12	5	16	4	4
Wilson	1.000	7	1	14	0	2

Shortstop	PCT	G	PO	A	E	DP
Coca	.944	5	7	10	1	5
Forsythe	1.000	2	1	2	0	0
Hager	.927	17	13	38	4	4
Kramer	.956	14	11	32	2	8
Lopes	1.000	10	15	22	0	9
Perez	1.000	9	9	16	0	5
Reyes	.871	10	7	20	4	1
Robertson	.978	14	15	29	1	6
Strange-Gordon	.900	7	4	14	2	2
Turang	.982	44	62	105	3	22
Westbrook	1.000	1	2	1	0	0
Wilson	.932	13	15	26	3	5

Outfield	PCT	G	PO	A	E	DP

	PCT	G	PO	A	E	DP
Broxton	.923	16	12	0	1	0
Cain	1.000	9	15	0	0	0
Cozens	.975	27	39	0	1	0
Dahl	1.000	28	39	2	0	0
Fisher	.947	24	35	1	2	0
Fry	--	2	0	0	0	0
Hager	1.000	2	1	0	0	0
Hummel	1.000	25	33	1	0	0
Lipka	.975	67	112	6	3	1
Longo	1.000	17	29	1	0	0
Lopes	.967	41	57	1	2	0
Lujano	.500	2	1	0	1	0
Perez	1.000	11	12	0	0	0
Peterson	.978	64	86	3	2	0
Peterson	1.000	1	1	0	0	0
Ray	.989	38	87	4	1	1
Reyes	1.000	5	7	0	0	0
Spanberger	1.000	4	2	0	0	0
Stokes Jr.	.982	51	55	0	1	0
Taylor	1.000	9	19	0	0	0
Westbrook	.842	16	15	1	3	0
Wilson	1.000	12	10	0	0	0
Yelich	1.000	3	4	0	0	0

BILOXI SHUCKERS
DOUBLE-A SOUTH

DOUBLE-A

Batting	B-T	HT	WT	DOB	AVG	vLH	vRH	G	AB	R	H	2B	3B	HR	RBI	BB	HBP	SH	SF	SO	SB	CS	SLG	OBP
Aguilar, Ryan	L-L	6-2	168	9-11-94	.146	.146	.145	74	213	41	31	4	0	6	21	37	5	3	0	90	9	1	.249	.286
Cabrera, Jhonnys	R-R	5-11	150	6-5-02	.000	--	.000	1	1	0	0	0	0	0	0	0	0	0	0	1	0	0	.000	.000
Cantrelle, Hayden	B-R	5-11	175	11-25-98	.143	.083	.174	13	35	9	5	0	2	0	2	5	3	0	0	12	1	1	.257	.302
Castillo, Daniel	R-R	5-11	150	1-25-01	.143	.000	.250	4	7	0	1	0	0	0	0	1	0	0	0	3	0	0	.143	.250
Castro, Luis	R-R	6-1	187	9-19-95	.212	.188	.219	63	231	30	49	11	1	8	25	24	7	0	0	89	3	0	.372	.305
Coca, Yeison	B-R	5-10	155	5-22-99	.211	.250	.182	5	19	4	4	3	0	0	1	0	0	0	0	5	1	0	.368	.250
Devanney, Cam	R-R	6-1	195	4-13-97	.175	.162	.179	87	291	23	51	10	0	5	30	31	8	0	4	94	1	2	.261	.269
Diaz, Brent	R-R	6-1	205	3-22-96	.208	.188	.212	58	178	21	37	7	0	5	24	15	11	1	1	68	2	2	.331	.307
Dillard, Thomas	B-R	6-0	230	8-28-97	.256	.346	.219	27	90	9	23	3	0	2	8	18	1	0	0	34	1	0	.356	.385
Friis, Tyler	B-R	5-9	180	2-12-96	.267	.345	.237	34	105	15	28	4	2	0	8	11	0	1	2	20	8	3	.343	.331
Fry, David	R-R	6-2	215	11-20-95	.248	.274	.240	75	262	39	65	15	2	11	41	31	6	0	0	71	1	1	.447	.341
Garcia, Gabriel	R-R	6-3	212	12-16-97	.217	.269	.202	32	115	13	25	8	0	4	12	9	2	0	0	44	0	2	.391	.286
Hamilton, David	L-R	5-10	175	9-29-97	.248	.258	.245	33	133	16	33	5	4	3	12	15	0	1	1	32	11	3	.414	.322
Henry, Payton	R-R	6-2	215	6-24-97	.315	.296	.321	30	111	11	35	5	1	1	16	12	2	0	0	32	0	0	.405	.392
Holt, Gabe	L-R	5-11	175	1-7-98	.316	.500	.281	15	38	3	12	2	0	0	4	6	0	1	0	5	0	0	.368	.409
Howell, Korry	R-R	6-3	180	9-1-98	.235	.222	.239	28	98	18	23	5	1	4	16	15	0	0	1	44	4	3	.429	.318
Longo, Mitch	L-R	6-0	195	1-12-95	.308	.313	.307	75	263	47	81	15	4	11	36	23	4	1	2	56	18	2	.521	.370
Lujano, Jesus	L-L	5-10	160	2-18-99	.304	.300	.306	17	46	2	14	4	0	0	3	2	0	0	0	11	0	1	.391	.333
Lutz, Tristen	R-R	6-2	210	8-22-98	.217	.311	.184	64	240	25	52	12	1	7	31	20	6	0	2	86	2	5	.363	.291
Mitchell, Garrett	L-R	6-3	215	9-4-98	.186	.167	.192	35	129	16	24	1	0	3	10	18	1	0	0	41	5	1	.264	.291
Palma, Alexander	R-R	6-0	201	10-18-95	.250	.302	.231	85	320	33	80	14	0	13	55	19	1	0	6	61	0	2	.416	.289
Rios, Kekai	R-R	5-11	196	6-6-97	.105	.000	.118	6	19	0	2	1	0	0	2	0	0	0	6	1	0	.158	.190
Spanberger, Chad	L-R	6-3	235	11-1-95	.204	.127	.222	86	294	38	60	15	1	12	41	31	5	0	2	111	2	0	.384	.289
Turang, Brice	L-R	6-0	173	11-21-99	.264	.290	.256	73	288	40	76	14	3	5	39	28	1	1	2	48	11	7	.385	.329
Westbrook, Jamie	R-R	5-9	193	6-18-95	.261	.429	.218	19	69	12	18	1	1	1	7	9	2	0	2	12	1	0	.348	.354

Pitching	B-T	HT	WT	DOB	W	L	ERA	G	GS	CG	SV	IP	H	R	ER	HR	BB	SO	AVG	vLH	vRH	K/9	BB/9
Beckman, Cody	R-L	6-2	205	11-1-94	0	3	6.36	30	2	0	0	47	50	36	33	6	30	53	.272	.291	.257	10.22	5.79
Bennett, Nick	L-L	6-4	210	9-1-97	1	4	4.66	10	6	0	0	46	37	29	24	10	24	43	.223	.196	.235	8.35	4.66
Brown, Zack	R-R	6-1	199	12-15-94	0	0	4.50	14	1	0	0	20	20	13	10	4	14	23	.267	.269	.265	10.35	6.30
Bullock, Justin	R-R	6-2	195	5-12-99	2	5	6.55	8	8	0	0	34	41	30	25	8	12	30	.293	.328	.260	7.86	3.15
Castillo, Jesus	R-R	6-1	205	8-27-95	5	9	4.74	19	18	0	0	95	113	55	50	18	13	60	.297	.305	.291	5.68	1.23
Contreras, Luis	R-R	6-1	175	4-29-96	1	1	5.19	3	3	0	0	9	9	7	5	2	3	19	.250	.250	.250	19.73	3.12
Cousins, Jake	R-R	6-4	185	7-14-94	0	1	3.00	8	0	0	3	9	6	3	3	1	3	14	.182	.154	.200	14.00	3.00
Crawford, Leo	L-L	6-0	180	2-2-97	2	5	4.92	25	9	0	1	64	60	37	35	10	26	66	.242	.232	.247	9.28	3.66
Derby, Bubba	L-R	5-11	185	2-24-94	1	2	9.72	12	3	0	0	25	34	27	27	6	11	25	.318	.245	.379	9.00	3.96
Erceg, Lucas	L-R	6-3	196	5-1-95	2	6	5.29	22	13	0	0	48	38	35	28	5	35	45	.218	.200	.232	8.50	6.61
Floyd, Taylor	R-R	6-1	185	12-8-97	1	0	0.00	7	0	0	0	2	7	4	0	0	2	12	.160	.375	.059	14.73	2.45
Francis, Bowden	R-R	6-5	215	4-22-96	3	1	3.86	4	4	0	0	21	18	9	9	5	5	26	.222	.128	.310	11.14	2.14
Hall, Brooks	R-R	6-5	235	6-26-90	0	0	9.82	2	2	0	0	4	5	4	4	1	2	6	.333	.375	.286	14.73	4.91
Hardy, Matt	L-R	6-0	160	7-15-95	1	3	3.83	27	1	0	0	42	35	21	18	8	19	52	.230	.228	.232	11.06	4.04
Hintzen, J.T.	R-R	6-0	185	6-1-96	5	3	3.88	36	1	0	3	58	50	31	25	11	18	79	.230	.290	.212	12.26	2.79
Hitt, Robbie	R-R	6-2	185	6-21-96	4	1	2.98	36	0	0	0	42	33	18	14	4	20	47	.208	.254	.177	9.99	4.25
Kirby, Nathan	L-L	6-2	200	11-23-93	0	1	1.93	17	0	0	0	19	12	8	4	1	13	19	.182	.043	.256	9.16	6.27

Pitcher	B-T	HT	WT	DOB	W	L	ERA	G	GS	CG	SV	IP	H	R	ER	HR	BB	SO	AVG	vLH	vRH	K/9	BB/9
Luna, Carlos	R-R	6-1	175	9-25-96	1	3	3.07	6	6	0	0	29	27	10	10	4	4	26	.241	.273	.211	7.98	1.23
Otero, Andy	L-L	5-9	165	6-3-92	5	0	2.10	16	7	0	0	51	33	13	12	5	8	65	.181	.221	.158	11.40	1.40
Robinson, Cam	R-R	5-11	187	9-6-99	0	0	0.00	1	0	0	0	1	1	0	0	0	0	2	.250	.000	.333	18.00	0.00
Small, Ethan	L-L	6-4	215	2-14-97	2	2	1.96	8	8	0	0	41	26	10	9	1	21	67	.184	.132	.204	14.59	4.57
Strzelecki, Peter	R-R	6-2	195	10-24-94	0	2	3.45	36	0	0	1	47	42	19	18	5	17	65	.237	.300	.196	12.45	3.26
Topa, Justin	R-R	6-4	200	3-7-91	0	0	2.25	4	0	0	0	4	2	1	1	0	2	2	.154	.000	.286	4.50	4.50
Vennaro, Zach	R-R	6-6	220	6-3-96	1	3	7.61	37	0	0	2	37	47	35	31	8	23	50	.311	.318	.306	12.27	5.65
Wahl, Bobby	R-R	6-3	216	3-21-92	0	0	21.60	2	0	0	0	2	3	4	4	2	2	4	.375	.250	.500	21.60	10.80
Webb, Braden	R-R	6-3	200	4-25-95	4	7	4.59	41	0	0	3	49	40	29	25	7	30	67	.223	.189	.248	12.31	5.51
Zavolas, Noah	R-R	6-1	190	5-11-96	5	7	4.40	22	22	0	0	121	113	61	59	18	31	121	.248	.218	.272	9.02	2.31

Fielding

Catcher	PCT	G	PO	A	E	DP	PB
Diaz	.994	57	491	19	3	4	4
Dillard	1.000	2	19	0	0	0	0
Fry	.992	28	246	12	2	2	6
Henry	.997	27	272	25	1	3	3
Rios	1.000	6	70	4	0	1	0

First Base	PCT	G	PO	A	E	DP
Aguilar	.995	28	183	15	1	12
Castro	.987	41	278	24	4	28
Dillard	1.000	13	89	6	0	13
Erceg	1.000	3	15	1	0	1
Fry	.955	7	40	2	2	4
Garcia	1.000	3	20	3	0	0
Spanberger	.995	25	180	19	1	17

Second Base	PCT	G	PO	A	E	DP
Cantrelle	.976	10	15	26	1	7
Castillo	.667	3	2	0	1	0
Castro	1.000		0	3	0	0

	PCT	G	PO	A	E	DP
Coca	.944	5	7	10	1	3
Devanney	.989	48	66	116	2	28
Friis	.990	32	42	61	1	11
Fry	1.000	5	11	12	0	4
Hamilton	.818	3	2	7	2	1
Holt	1.000	6	3	9	0	2
Howell	.941	5	6	10	1	1
Westbrook	1.000	5	5	4	0	1

Third Base	PCT	G	PO	A	E	DP
Cantrelle	1.000	1	1	3	0	0
Castro	1.000	2	1	2	0	0
Devanney	.942	32	14	51	4	2
Erceg	1.000	4	2	2	0	1
Fry	.956	34	18	47	3	5
Garcia	.854	27	11	30	7	1
Holt	.818	7	2	7	2	0
Howell	1.000	7	3	13	0	1
Westbrook	1.000	7	4	17	0	1

Shortstop	PCT	G	PO	A	E	DP
Devanney	1.000	9	12	12	0	6
Friis	1.000	1	0	1	0	0
Hamilton	.972	30	41	63	3	21
Howell	.950	4	7	12	1	2
Turang	.952	71	96	164	13	29

Outfield	PCT	G	PO	A	E	DP
Aguilar	.965	47	80	3	3	1
Castro	1.000	21	35	0	0	0
Fry	1.000	4	7	0	0	0
Garcia	1.000	3	4	0	0	0
Howell	1.000	13	22	0	0	0
Longo	.968	74	116	4	4	0
Lujano	1.000	14	21	0	0	0
Lutz	.962	60	96	4	4	1
Mitchell	.987	33	77	0	1	0
Palma	.978	33	40	4	1	1
Spanberger	.968	53	87	4	3	0
Westbrook	1.000	5	5	0	0	0

WISCONSIN TIMBER RATTLERS — HIGH CLASS A

HIGH-A CENTRAL

Batting	B-T	HT	WT	DOB	AVG	vLH	vRH	G	AB	R	H	2B	3B	HR	RBI	BB	HBP	SH	SF	SO	SB	CS	SLG	OBP
Cantrelle, Hayden	B-R	5-11	175	11-25-98	.175	.235	.159	77	252	44	44	12	1	7	32	77	7	1	4	90	28	8	.313	.376
Castillo, LG	R-R	6-2	215	7-18-99	.280	.311	.266	69	243	35	68	13	0	9	39	11	2	1	0	86	7	2	.444	.316
Coca, Yeison	B-R	5-10	155	5-22-99	.204	.179	.211	50	167	21	34	6	0	2	18	16	2	0	0	60	6	4	.275	.281
Dillard, Thomas	B-R	6-0	230	8-28-97	.245	.229	.250	78	282	44	69	12	2	16	67	49	4	0	5	112	4	2	.472	.359
Frelick, Sal	L-R	5-9	175	4-19-00	.167	.250	.136	15	60	7	10	1	1	1	5	10	1	0	0	13	3	0	.267	.296
Garcia, Gabriel	R-R	6-3	212	12-16-97	.217	.250	.203	28	92	15	20	6	0	2	17	12	1	0	3	41	2	1	.348	.306
Gray Jr., Joe	R-R	6-1	195	3-12-00	.219	.224	.217	59	215	32	47	7	2	8	37	20	9	0	4	70	11	3	.381	.306
Hall, Alex	B-R	5-8	161	6-8-99	.250	.667	.136	8	28	4	7	2	0	1	6	2	1	0	0	8	0	1	.429	.323
Hamilton, David	L-R	5-10	175	9-29-97	.263	.194	.284	68	270	50	71	14	7	5	31	35	2	1	1	58	41	6	.422	.351
Howell, Korry	R-R	6-3	180	9-1-98	.248	.230	.254	69	258	65	64	12	4	12	36	34	12	0	1	88	20	3	.465	.361
Kahle, Nick	R-R	5-10	210	2-28-98	.186	.096	.212	69	231	23	43	11	0	4	26	26	5	0	3	81	2	0	.286	.279
Lujano, Jesus	L-L	5-10	160	2-18-99	.252	.321	.232	36	123	19	31	6	0	3	18	15	5	0	0	42	4	1	.374	.352
McClanahan, Chad	L-R	6-5	200	12-22-97	.205	.182	.211	77	254	40	52	14	0	8	40	37	2	0	3	117	1	3	.354	.307
McGee, Ashton	L-R	6-1	215	11-19-98	.224	.091	.263	15	49	12	11	3	0	1	2	11	0	0	0	15	1	0	.347	.367
Mitchell, Garrett	L-R	6-3	215	9-4-98	.359	.294	.373	29	92	33	33	5	2	5	20	28	0	0	0	30	12	1	.620	.508
Pinero, Antonio	R-R	6-1	152	3-15-99	.222	.222	.222	30	99	13	22	3	0	1	9	11	0	0	1	34	2	0	.283	.297
Rios, Kekai	R-R	5-11	196	6-6-97	.270	.206	.295	42	122	16	33	8	0	3	16	16	2	1	3	36	0	0	.410	.357
Rodriguez, Carlos	L-L	5-10	150	12-7-00	.267	.198	.288	94	345	43	92	17	4	1	38	35	1	1	0	75	15	6	.348	.336
Valerio, Felix	R-R	5-7	165	12-26-00	.229	.206	.238	29	118	19	27	13	0	5	16	15	1	0	0	22	4	1	.466	.321
Ward, Je'Von	L-R	6-5	190	10-25-99	.234	.266	.225	75	282	39	73	17	2	5	49	23	1	0	5	85	9	5	.387	.312
Warren, Zavier	B-R	6-0	190	1-8-99	.267	.278	.263	36	135	21	36	7	1	3	18	18	2	0	2	32	5	0	.400	.357
Wiemer, Joey	R-R	6-5	215	2-11-99	.336	.270	.363	34	128	33	43	7	0	14	33	18	4	0	2	36	8	2	.719	.428
Zamora, Freddy	R-R	6-1	190	11-1-98	.342	.217	.393	22	79	12	27	9	0	1	9	12	0	0	0	19	1	0	.494	.435

Pitching	B-T	HT	WT	DOB	W	L	ERA	G	GS	CG	SV	IP	H	R	ER	HR	BB	SO	AVG	vLH	vRH	K/9	BB/9
Adames, Freisis	R-R	6-3	175	11-18-96	5	2	5.57	26	9	0	0	82	82	51	51	17	42	75	.259	.236	.283	8.20	4.59
Bennett, Nick	L-L	6-4	210	9-1-97	3	4	4.31	12	11	0	0	56	59	32	27	7	19	72	.263	.329	.234	11.50	3.04
Bullock, Justin	R-R	6-2	195	5-12-99	5	2	3.65	8	8	1	0	44	34	21	18	5	9	43	.206	.253	.167	8.73	1.83
Castaneda, Victor	R-R	6-1	185	8-27-98	5	7	5.20	20	20	1	0	97	90	58	56	18	37	114	.243	.252	.237	10.58	3.43
Chirino, Harold	R-R	6-2	173	1-12-98	6	5	3.88	35	0	0	7	51	51	30	22	9	23	75	.254	.208	.295	13.24	4.06
File, Dylan	R-R	6-1	205	6-4-96	0	1	7.20	2	2	0	0	5	7	4	4	1	6	6	.333	.300	.364	10.80	7.20
Floyd, Taylor	R-R	6-1	185	12-8-97	4	2	3.33	33	0	0	8	49	34	18	18	4	22	72	.193	.238	.156	13.32	4.07
Garcia, Gabriel	R-R	6-3	212	12-16-97	0	0	0.00	1	0	0	0	1	0	0	0	0	0	0	.000	--	.000	0.00	0.00
Hasler, Kent	R-R	5-10	195	10-15-95	1	1	3.86	6	0	0	0	9	10	6	4		3	16	.256	.250	.259	15.43	3.86
Jarvis, Justin	R-R	6-1	195	2-20-00	1	7	5.40	17	17	0	0	63	63	42	38	9	35	62	.254	.274	.234	8.81	4.97
Kahle, Nick	R-R	5-10	210	2-28-98	0	0	0.00	1	0	0	0	0	0	0	0	0	0	0	.000	.000	--	0.00	0.00
Kelly, Antoine	L-L	6-6	205	12-5-99	0	1	54.00	1	1	0	0	1	3	8	8	0	3	3	.500	.667	.333	20.25	20.25
Knarr, Brandon	R-L	5-10	215	6-2-98	1	1	6.04	5	5	0	0	22	21	18	15	4	14	25	.233	.355	.169	10.07	5.64

Name	B-T	HT	WT	DOB	W	L	ERA	G	GS	CG	SV	IP	H	R	ER	HR	BB	SO	AVG	vLH	vRH	K/9	BB/9
LaRossa, John	L-R	6-1	205	2-24-95	1	1	12.72	24	0	0	0	35	47	49	49	12	29	41	.311	.411	.218	10.64	7.53
Luna, Carlos	R-R	6-1	175	9-25-96	3	1	1.79	9	5	0	2	40	22	9	8	5	6	48	.155	.130	.178	10.71	1.34
Matulovich, Joey	R-R	6-3	195	7-6-97	1	2	6.55	8	7	0	0	34	42	25	25	9	14	39	.290	.338	.231	10.22	3.67
McClanahan, Chad	L-R	6-5	200	12-22-97	0	0	13.50	2	0	0	0	2	6	3	3	2	1	0	.500	.500	.500	0.00	4.50
Mort, Zach	R-R	6-1	205	5-22-97	1	4	7.13	16	13	0	0	64	88	53	51	18	22	56	.322	.400	.257	7.83	3.08
Olson, Reese	R-R	6-1	160	7-31-99	5	4	4.30	14	14	0	0	69	58	34	33	5	35	79	.228	.162	.280	10.30	4.57
2-team total (2 West Michigan)					6	4	3.71	16	16	0	0	80	64	34	33	5	37	93	.218	.163	.266	10.46	4.16
Patterson, Nathan	R-R	6-1	180	2-5-96	0	1	13.50	5	0	0	0	5	9	8	7	1	7	3	.409	.455	.364	5.79	13.50
Reifert, Evan	R-R	6-4	190	5-14-99	1	3	2.29	32	0	0	6	51	31	18	13	4	32	87	.169	.159	.175	15.35	5.65
Rios, Kekai	R-R	5-11	196	6-6-97	0	0	0.00	1	0	0	0	1	1	0	0	0	0	0	.250	.333	.000	0.00	0.00
Robinson, Cam	R-R	5-11	187	9-6-99	2	1	4.60	12	0	0	1	16	18	9	8	0	11	21	.281	.258	.303	12.06	6.32
Sabouri, Arman	R-L	5-10	200	6-28-98	0	3	7.81	22	0	0	0	28	42	26	24	2	13	43	.347	.423	.290	13.99	4.23
Schanuel, Brady	R-R	6-3	180	2-21-97	6	0	5.37	37	0	0	0	57	49	41	34	6	40	76	.226	.185	.256	12.00	6.32
Shook, TJ	R-R	6-3	226	5-29-98	1	1	7.20	5	5	0	0	20	22	16	16	3	14	25	.278	.289	.268	11.25	6.30
Sierra, Cristian	R-R	6-3	180	4-1-98	2	3	4.30	32	2	0	1	61	46	30	29	6	41	68	.212	.225	.200	10.09	6.08
Walters, Nash	R-R	6-5	210	5-18-97	5	3	4.33	43	0	0	2	60	61	37	29	7	29	82	.261	.282	.244	12.23	4.33

Fielding

Catcher	PCT	G	PO	A	E	DP	PB
Dillard	.984	7	61	0	1	0	2
Hall	1.000	8	89	4	0	0	0
Kahle	.996	69	722	38	3	4	3
Rios	.992	42	355	35	3	3	3
Warren	1.000	3	33	1	0	0	0
Coca	1.000	13	19	22	0	6	
Hamilton	.968	10	12	18	1	5	
Pinero	.833	3	4	6	2	2	
Valerio	.985	27	30	34	1	4	
Hamilton	.934	57	66	133	14	20	
Howell	.889	9	10	14	3	3	
Pinero	.951	18	20	38	3	9	
Zamora	.947	21	20	34	3	4	

First Base	PCT	G	PO	A	E	DP
Dillard	.980	60	381	20	8	28
Garcia	1.000	9	46	6	0	2
McClanahan	.988	29	153	12	2	9
McGee	1.000	15	91	2	0	5
Warren	1.000	10	49	3	0	4

Second Base	PCT	G	PO	A	E	DP
Cantrelle	.967	67	86	150	8	28

Third Base	PCT	G	PO	A	E	DP
Coca	.902	28	17	29	5	0
Garcia	.889	19	15	17	4	1
Howell	.889	9	8	8	2	1
McClanahan	.929	35	36	56	7	4
Pinero	.889	9	6	2	1	0
Warren	.980	21	15	34	1	2

Shortstop	PCT	G	PO	A	E	DP
Cantrelle	.947	7	10	8	1	4
Coca	.885	8	8	15	3	4

Outfield	PCT	G	PO	A	E	DP
Castillo	.983	38	55	3	1	0
Frelick	1.000	13	26	1	0	0
Gray Jr.	.983	51	111	3	2	0
Howell	.959	51	112	4	5	1
Lujano	.982	33	52	2	1	0
McClanahan	.957	12	20	2	1	1
Mitchell	1.000	15	34	1	0	1
Rodriguez	.977	91	162	8	4	1
Ward	.940	33	62	1	0	0
Wiemer	1.000	26	42	0	0	0

CAROLINA MUDCATS
LOW CLASS A
LOW-A EAST

Batting	B-T	HT	WT	DOB	AVG	vLH	vRH	G	AB	R	H	2B	3B	HR	RBI	BB	HBP	SH	SF	SO	SB	CS	SLG	OBP
Bello, Micah	R-R	5-11	165	7-21-00	.241	.182	.249	47	191	24	46	14	0	4	24	11	2	0	2	64	1	1	.377	.286
Binelas, Alex	L-R	6-3	225	5-26-00	.314	.500	.288	29	118	29	37	11	0	9	27	12	1	0	1	33	0	0	.636	.379
Black, Tyler	L-R	6-2	190	7-26-00	.222	.200	.225	23	81	11	18	4	0	0	6	20	2	0	0	29	3	2	.272	.388
Campbell, Noah	B-R	6-0	208	6-6-99	.270	.370	.254	100	341	71	92	21	2	5	53	58	10	0	3	94	20	3	.387	.388
Castillo, Daniel	R-R	5-11	150	1-25-01	.153	.286	.111	19	59	12	9	1	0	1	14	9	3	0	1	28	5	0	.220	.292
Cipion, Arbert	R-R	6-2	186	5-9-00	.095	.154	.085	29	95	13	9	0	0	0	10	17	2	0	2	57	9	1	.095	.241
Clarke, Wes	R-R	6-2	236	10-13-99	.206	.308	.182	21	68	13	14	3	0	4	19	21	4	0	2	21	0	1	.426	.411
Frelick, Sal	L-R	5-9	175	4-19-00	.437	.375	.444	16	71	17	31	6	1	1	12	9	0	0	1	10	6	2	.592	.494
Garcia, Eduardo	R-R	6-2	160	7-10-02	.333	--	.333	10	33	8	11	4	0	0	7	6	2	0	1	13	1	0	.455	.452
Gray Jr., Joe	R-R	6-1	195	3-12-00	.231	.289	.231	79	266	52	55	15	7	12	53	33	6	0	2	61	12	0	.632	.407
Hall, Alex	B-R	5-8	161	6-8-99	.233	.167	.245	44	163	21	38	9	4	2	26	17	1	0	3	56	2	2	.374	.304
Holt, Gabe	L-R	5-11	175	1-7-98	.279	.255	.283	82	323	70	90	14	1	1	36	62	7	0	3	47	17	2	.337	.403
Martinez, Ernesto	L-L	6-6	229	6-20-99	.274	.235	.280	79	266	52	73	15	5	11	48	32	10	0	3	84	30	4	.492	.370
McGee, Ashton	L-R	6-2	215	11-19-98	.301	.250	.309	71	239	52	72	20	1	10	54	54	3	0	1	92	0	1	.519	.434
Miller, Darrien	L-R	6-0	175	3-10-01	.263	.233	.269	52	160	37	42	4	0	7	31	33	10	1	0	45	4	0	.419	.419
Murray, Ethan	R-R	6-0	200	5-13-00	.232	.273	.228	28	112	19	26	3	2	3	14	17	2	0	1	29	3	1	.375	.341
Nnebe, Andre	R-R	6-3	230	11-14-97	.205	.146	.218	69	220	32	45	12	1	6	39	28	1	0	3	103	14	0	.350	.294
Perez, Hedbert	L-L	5-10	160	4-4-03	.169	.000	.180	16	65	5	11	2	0	1	7	1	2	0	0	25	0	0	.246	.206
Raabe, Zack	R-R	5-10	180	8-18-99	.255	.250	.255	17	55	12	14	0	0	0	6	11	1	0	1	17	0	1	.255	.382
Sibrian, Jose	R-R	5-11	175	10-24-98	.333	.300	.375	5	18	5	6	3	2	0	0	1	0	0	0	5	0	0	.444	.333
Valerio, Felix	R-R	5-7	165	12-26-00	.314	.310	.315	85	309	71	97	24	3	6	63	54	11	0	3	49	27	8	.469	.430
Warren, Zavier	B-R	6-0	190	1-8-99	.251	.171	.269	53	191	34	48	8	2	10	30	33	5	0	1	49	1	0	.471	.374
Wiemer, Joey	R-R	6-5	215	2-11-99	.276	.395	.257	75	268	53	74	11	2	13	44	45	6	0	1	69	22	4	.478	.391
Wilson, Mike	L-R	6-0	200	3-29-98	.188	.000	.210	25	69	13	13	3	1	1	3	11	4	0	0	39	0	1	.391	.325
Zamora, Freddy	R-R	6-1	190	11-1-98	.287	.359	.275	70	268	58	77	13	1	5	40	45	5	0	3	57	9	5	.399	.396

Pitching	B-T	HT	WT	DOB	W	L	ERA	G	GS	CG	SV	IP	H	R	ER	HR	BB	SO	AVG	vLH	vRH	K/9	BB/9
Baker, Robbie	R-R	6-1	185	1-31-95	2	0	4.01	11	0	0	0	25	21	11	11	1	10	27	.226	.227	.224	9.85	3.65
Begue, Brock	R-L	6-3	210	4-19-99	1	1	7.18	20	4	0	1	36	42	42	29	5	32	40	.284	.351	.261	9.91	7.93
Belzer, Nick	R-R	6-2	185	8-1-95	6	4	3.55	12	12	1	0	63	58	31	25	5	19	45	.253	.239	.262	6.39	2.70
Bullock, Justin	R-R	6-2	195	5-12-99	1	1	1.42	4	4	0	0	19	9	3	3	0	5	27	.141	.130	.146	12.79	2.37
Campbell, Noah	B-R	6-0	208	6-6-99	0	0	8.10	4	0	0	0	3	3	3	3	1	0	2	.231	.333	.143	5.40	0.00
Cornielle, Alexander	R-R	6-2	180	8-22-01	0	1	10.13	2	2	0	0	8	15	9	9	2	2	10	.405	.409	.400	11.25	2.25
Cruz, Jhoan	R-R	5-9	147	5-31-00	6	6	6.42	20	15	0	1	81	114	60	58	16	23	79	.331	.323	.336	8.74	2.55
Figueroa, Jefferson	R-R	6-0	180	8-22-00	0	1	4.74	5	5	0	0	19	15	11	10	2	12	21	.208	.289	.118	9.95	5.68

Player	B-T	HT	WT	DOB	W	L	ERA	G	GS	CG	SV	IP	H	R	ER	HR	BB	SO	AVG	vLH	vRH	K/9	BB/9
Geraldo, Juan	R-R	6-0	175	8-6-01	3	2	5.69	27	0	0	2	49	55	34	31	4	22	54	.284	.286	.282	9.92	4.04
Gillis, Jackson	R-L	6-3	235	11-27-97	0	0	9.24	9	0	0	0	13	13	17	13	3	13	11	.255	.273	.250	7.82	9.24
Guerrero, Miguel	R-R	6-5	180	7-15-00	6	4	5.75	31	4	1	1	56	66	46	36	6	29	59	.289	.270	.299	9.43	4.63
Hasler, Kent	R-R	5-10	195	10-15-95	3	2	2.86	24	0	0	2	35	26	18	11	3	20	64	.197	.184	.202	16.62	5.19
Kelly, Antoine	L-L	6-6	205	12-5-99	0	1	6.88	7	7	0	0	17	13	13	13	0	16	24	.213	.100	.268	12.71	8.47
Knarr, Brandon	R-L	5-10	215	6-2-98	7	2	3.84	16	13	0	0	75	61	35	32	8	35	103	.223	.294	.206	12.36	4.20
Lemons, Caden	R-R	6-6	175	12-2-98	0	3	9.53	4	3	0	0	11	14	12	12	2	15	14	.318	.182	.364	11.12	11.91
Long, Peyton	R-R	6-4	210	10-28-97	2	0	8.39	22	0	0	1	34	42	33	32	7	14	30	.294	.327	.273	7.86	3.67
Matulovich, Joey	R-R	6-3	195	7-6-97	2	0	1.80	16	2	0	1	40	25	9	8	4	21	56	.179	.306	.135	12.60	4.73
McCarville, Keegan	R-R	6-1	210	2-3-98	1	1	8.35	11	0	0	0	18	28	19	17	3	4	20	.350	.333	.362	9.82	1.96
McGee, Ashton	L-R	6-1	215	11-19-98	0	0	9.00	4	0	0	0	4	7	4	4	0	1	0	.412	.375	.444	0.00	2.25
Meeker, James	R-R	6-4	215	3-22-95	1	2	0.50	12	0	0	5	18	12	4	1	0	5	22	.185	.182	.188	11.00	2.50
Miller, Justin	R-R	6-4	183	5-17-98	1	1	16.50	9	0	0	0	12	19	24	22	2	11	10	.339	.250	.389	7.50	8.25
Montero, Junior	R-R	6-3	175	9-20-98	1	0	1.93	5	0	0	0	14	14	3	3	1	10	10	.264	.222	.308	6.43	6.43
Mort, Zach	R-R	6-1	205	5-22-97	4	1	4.41	6	6	0	0	33	28	16	16	3	10	45	.233	.183	.283	12.40	2.76
Munsch, Jason	L-L	6-2	230	5-12-99	1	1	6.39	5	1	0	0	13	9	9	9	2	6	13	.196	.111	.216	9.24	4.26
Murphy, Brendan	L-L	6-4	200	1-2-99	5	6	5.74	20	14	1	0	74	75	49	47	6	44	73	.266	.245	.271	8.92	5.38
Peden, Nate	R-R	6-4	170	10-16-98	2	0	5.23	17	0	0	0	41	54	26	24	4	14	39	.331	.266	.367	8.49	3.05
Reifert, Evan	R-R	6-4	190	5-14-99	2	0	1.00	5	0	0	2	9	5	1	1	0	4	16	.161	.167	.160	16.00	4.00
Robinson, Cam	R-R	5-11	187	9-6-99	1	1	2.45	26	0	0	12	33	30	14	9	1	19	39	.236	.242	.234	10.64	5.18
Rodriguez, Brailin	R-R	6-2	185	8-10-02	0	1	5.06	3	2	0	0	11	9	6	6	2	9	9	.231	.333	.185	7.59	7.59
Shook, TJ	R-R	6-3	226	5-29-98	4	1	3.86	6	6	0	0	28	21	12	12	3	11	36	.214	.179	.229	11.57	3.54
Tripp, Christian	R-R	6-7	220	3-13-97	0	1	4.97	10	3	0	0	25	24	19	14	1	20	33	.245	.235	.250	11.72	7.11
Uribe, Abner	R-R	6-2	200	6-20-00	1	0	4.01	17	4	0	3	34	24	19	15	2	25	52	.195	.195	.195	13.90	6.68
Vassalotti, Michele	R-R	6-2	180	8-2-00	5	8	7.24	22	13	0	0	68	59	61	55	5	60	82	.237	.271	.216	10.80	7.90

Fielding

Catcher	PCT	G	PO	A	E	DP	PB
Campbell	.000	1	0	0	0	0	0
Clarke	.980	9	90	8	2	1	2
Hall	.971	43	402	37	13	3	4
Miller	.981	50	480	34	10	4	3
Sibrian	.980	5	46	3	1	0	0
Warren	.978	17	162	18	4	3	7

First Base	PCT	G	PO	A	E	DP
Binelas	1.000	5	29	1	0	4
Campbell	.975	17	75	3	2	3
Clarke	.980	8	47	1	1	8
Martinez	.985	67	367	28	6	35
McGee	1.000	25	153	5	0	7
Miller	1.000	1	1	0	0	1
Warren	1.000	9	72	6	0	7

Second Base	PCT	G	PO	A	E	DP
Black	.917	15	20	24	4	6
Campbell	1.000	3	6	5	0	2

	PCT	G	PO	A	E	DP
Holt	.982	48	66	94	3	22
Murray	1.000	9	15	21	0	6
Raabe	1.000	8	15	19	0	4
Valerio	.959	40	59	58	5	12

Third Base	PCT	G	PO	A	E	DP
Binelas	.880	20	10	12	3	1
Campbell	.871	17	7	20	4	1
Castillo	.950	5	3	16	1	2
Garcia	.000	1	0	0	0	0
Holt	.941	19	7	25	2	1
McGee	.939	30	20	26	3	9
Murray	.875	7	4	10	2	2
Raabe	1.000	3	0	4	0	0
Valerio	.912	17	9	22	3	1
Warren	.931	13	7	20	2	1

Shortstop	PCT	G	PO	A	E	DP
Campbell	1.000	7	2	5	0	2
Castillo	.886	14	18	21	5	6

	PCT	G	PO	A	E	DP
Garcia	.979	10	22	24	1	8
Murray	.933	12	15	27	3	4
Raabe	1.000	2	5	5	0	2
Valerio	.950	18	21	36	3	8
Zamora	.954	63	102	145	12	24

Outfield	PCT	G	PO	A	E	DP
Bello	.989	49	84	4	1	1
Campbell	.987	58	72	6	1	3
Cipion	.976	27	40	0	1	0
Frelick	.972	14	33	2	1	1
Gray Jr.	.953	48	95	6	5	1
Martinez	1.000	4	4	0	0	0
Nnebe	.961	64	96	3	4	1
Perez	1.000	17	44	1	0	1
Raabe	--	1	0	0	0	0
Wiemer	.988	78	153	12	2	2
Wilson	1.000	23	41	3	0	1

ACL BREWERS ROOKIE
ARIZONA COMPLEX LEAGUE

Batting	B-T	HT	WT	DOB	AVG	vLH	vRH	G	AB	R	H	2B	3B	HR	RBI	BB	HBP	SH	SF	SO	SB	CS	SLG	OBP
Bautista, Erys	B-R	6-1	220	11-9-01	.263	.125	.307	32	99	12	26	7	1	4	25	4	2	0	1	44	1	1	.475	.302
Bello, Micah	R-R	5-11	165	7-21-00	.217	1.000	.182	6	23	3	5	0	0	0	2	0	0	0	10	2	0	.217	.280
Binelas, Alex	L-R	6-3	225	5-26-00	.286	.200	.313	7	21	4	6	0	0	0	2	5	1	0	0	6	1	1	.286	.444
Black, Tyler	L-R	6-2	190	7-26-00	.500	.000	.600	3	6	4	3	0	0	1	2	6	0	0	2	2	0	1.000	.750
Broxton, Keon	R-R	6-3	200	5-7-90	.111	.000	.125	3	9	3	1	0	0	0	2	1	0	0	6	0	0	.111	.333
Caballero, Jose	R-R	5-10	140	3-26-03	.206	.217	.203	36	97	14	20	9	1	1	13	9	2	1	3	22	7	4	.351	.279
Cabrera, Jhonnys	R-R	5-11	150	6-5-02	.147	.091	.174	15	34	2	5	2	0	0	3	2	1	0	0	14	0	0	.206	.216
Castillo, Daniel	R-R	5-11	150	1-25-01	.333	.385	.320	25	63	10	21	2	1	1	6	7	1	0	2	19	4	0	.444	.397
Chirinos, Jesus	R-R	6-0	165	7-27-01	.296	.333	.287	45	142	30	42	8	1	5	29	30	0	0	0	43	0	0	.472	.419
Cipion, Arbert	R-R	6-2	186	5-9-00	.156	.034	.194	42	122	19	19	6	2	4	14	15	1	0	0	47	8	5	.336	.254
Clarke, Wes	R-R	6-2	236	10-13-99	.250	.500	.167	3	8	1	2	0	0	1	2	0	0	0	0	6	0	0	.625	.250
David, Jhonny	R-R	6-3	195	7-5-01	.111	.250	.094	17	36	5	4	3	0	0	1	4	0	0	0	20	0	0	.194	.200
Diaz, Blayberg	R-R	5-11	190	1-31-03	.283	.231	.299	35	113	15	32	3	0	4	14	8	5	0	1	22	2	0	.416	.354
Doston, Terence	L-R	5-10	160	9-20-02	.272	.294	.268	41	114	27	31	3	0	1	8	23	8	1	0	26	9	4	.325	.428
Ernesto, Larry	B-R	6-2	175	9-12-00	.200	.318	.155	28	80	6	16	5	0	0	3	9	0	0	0	31	3	2	.263	.281
Feliciano, Mario	R-R	6-1	200	11-20-98	.360	.500	.348	7	25	7	9	3	1	0	4	1	3	0	0	6	0	0	.560	.448
Fernandez, Eduarqui	R-R	6-2	176	11-20-01	.208	.160	.219	40	130	25	27	1	1	6	19	21	2	0	0	58	11	4	.369	.327
Ferrer, Alberis	R-R	6-1	150	12-17-00	.308	.250	.320	40	117	20	36	5	4	6	24	13	1	0	1	37	9	3	.573	.379
Frelick, Sal	L-R	5-9	175	4-19-00	.467	.667	.417	4	15	4	7	1	1	0	4	2	0	0	0	2	3	0	.667	.529
Frias, Juan	R-R	6-0	175	11-7-00	.000	.000	.000	5	5	2	0	0	0	0	0	2	0	0	0	2	0	0	.000	.286
Garcia, Eduardo	R-R	6-2	160	7-10-02	.252	.286	.246	36	135	27	34	12	3	4	27	10	5	0	0	42	2	3	.474	.327
Garcia, Jesus	R-R	5-7	163	10-2-02	.205	.200	.205	16	44	9	9	1	0	1	5	2	3	0	0	12	0	0	.295	.286
Garcia, Nader	L-R	5-9	160	5-14-02	.150	.077	.185	21	40	5	6	1	0	1	6	6	0	0	0	14	0	0	.250	.261

Batter	B-T	HT	WT	DOB	AVG	vLH	vRH	G	AB	R	H	2B	3B	HR	RBI	BB	SO	SB	CS				OBP	SLG
Jaraba, Branlyn	R-R	6-2	196	3-20-02	.231	.250	.225	16	52	5	12	2	0	1	10	3	2	0	0	22	1	0	.327	.298
Leones, Oswel	L-R	6-0	165	10-6-00	.310	.444	.286	38	116	20	36	6	2	0	21	16	0	0	0	22	1	1	.397	.394
Low, Quinton	L-R	6-6	215	9-5-02	.364	.333	.385	9	22	3	8	0	0	0	3	4	0	0	0	6	0	1	.364	.462
Medina, Luis	L-L	6-2	168	2-24-03	.228	.172	.242	40	149	18	34	4	3	1	12	5	1	0	2	45	1	4	.315	.255
Mendez, Hendry	L-L	6-2	175	11-7-03	.333	.235	.370	19	63	6	21	4	2	0	10	10	0	1	0	10	3	1	.460	.425
Mercado, Reidy	B-R	5-11	153	1-6-01	.248	.308	.233	38	129	24	32	3	3	1	5	13	2	0	0	39	12	2	.341	.326
Murray, Ethan	R-R	6-0	200	5-13-00	.227	.000	.313	8	22	1	5	1	0	0	3	3	0	0	0	2	0	0	.273	.320
Nicasia, Kaylan	B-R	6-2	176	4-10-02	.190	.200	.189	16	42	6	8	0	0	0	3	8	0	0	0	18	1	1	.190	.320
Parra, Jesus	R-R	6-2	184	8-30-02	.200	.160	.213	35	105	9	21	5	0	2	15	4	5	0	1	35	0	0	.305	.261
Pastran, Beyker	R-R	5-10	162	4-1-03	.227	.185	.238	41	128	19	29	5	1	0	10	8	1	0	1	29	5	3	.281	.275
Perez, Hedbert	L-L	5-10	160	4-4-03	.333	.214	.349	32	120	19	40	11	0	6	21	8	4	0	0	34	2	0	.575	.394
Peters, Tristan	L-R	6-0	180	2-29-00	.239	.143	.281	13	46	9	11	0	2	1	6	8	0	0	1	14	6	1	.391	.345
Pinero, Antonio	R-R	6-1	152	3-15-99	.458	1.000	.381	8	24	7	11	2	0	0	4	3	0	0	0	5	4	0	.542	.519
Quero, Jefferson	R-R	5-10	165	10-8-02	.309	.286	.315	23	68	15	21	5	1	2	8	12	3	0	0	10	4	3	.500	.434
Raabe, Zack	R-R	5-10	180	8-18-99	.107	.000	.120	11	28	3	3	0	0	0	1	6	0	0	1	10	0	0	.107	.257
Roa, Carlos	R-R	5-11	165	9-4-01	.154	.150	.155	36	104	10	16	5	0	3	14	9	3	0	1	34	0	2	.288	.239
Sibrian, Jose	R-R	5-11	175	10-24-98	.209	.143	.222	26	86	11	18	3	0	0	5	4	3	0	0	17	0	0	.244	.269
Silva, Luis	R-R	6-0	178	7-6-01	.180	.222	.173	31	61	7	11	4	0	0	8	6	0	1	1	23	1	0	.246	.271
Smith, Drew	R-R	5-10	190	9-2-98	.294	.375	.269	12	34	8	10	2	0	0	5	4	3	0	1	4	2	1	.353	.405
Valdez, Alwinson	R-R	6-3	175	4-1-01	.265	.167	.292	29	83	8	22	4	0	0	9	5	2	0	1	35	8	2	.313	.319
Vargas, Jheremy	R-R	5-10	160	5-10-03	.230	.265	.218	44	135	22	31	2	3	2	20	29	5	0	5	42	8	4	.333	.374

Pitching

Pitcher	B-T	HT	WT	DOB	W	L	ERA	G	GS	CG	SV	IP	H	R	ER	HR	BB	SO	AVG	vLH	vRH	K/9	BB/9
Beasley, Wade	R-R	6-3	210	12-14-99	0	0	--	1	0	0	0	0	0	0	0	0	0	1	0	--	--	--	--
Bender, Kelvin	L-L	5-11	165	3-11-00	1	1	0.66	9	0	0	1	14	4	1	1	0	9	20	.095	.000	.148	13.17	5.93
Brown, Zack	R-R	6-1	199	12-15-94	0	0	3.86	2	0	0	2	2	1	1	1	1	1	1	.286	.000	.500	3.86	3.86
Cabrera, Jhonnys	R-R	5-11	150	6-5-02	0	0	0.00	2	0	0	0	1	0	0	0	0	1	0	.000	.000	.000	13.50	0.00
Carrasco, Ramon	R-R	6-0	167	8-9-02	2	1	6.00	13	0	0	2	33	29	24	22	1	27	21	.250	.317	.213	5.73	7.36
Carvajal, Breiner	R-R	6-3	170	10-22-01	0	1	10.13	7	1	0	0	8	6	11	9	0	13	12	.200	.000	.286	13.50	14.63
Castaneda, Oscar	R-R	5-11	205	5-9-01	4	1	7.86	16	1	0	1	26	33	25	23	3	16	33	.306	.289	.317	11.28	5.47
Chavez, Jose	R-R	6-2	150	1-9-03	0	1	10.34	11	3	0	0	16	24	18	18	2	14	26	.353	.417	.318	14.94	8.04
Chourio, Wilkerman	R-R	6-1	170	10-20-00	2	2	4.63	9	0	0	1	12	11	7	6	1	10	11	.244	.154	.281	8.49	7.71
Cornielle, Alexander	R-R	6-2	180	8-22-01	4	2	4.64	9	4	0	0	33	26	18	17	2	16	50	.211	.186	.234	13.64	4.36
Dario, Samuel	R-R	6-3	175	12-23-02	2	5	7.15	12	10	0	0	34	39	31	27	6	26	33	.291	.364	.221	8.74	6.88
De La Cruz, Leoni	L-L	6-0	175	5-22-98	0	0	0.84	4	0	0	1	11	6	1	1	0	2	10	.162	.333	.107	8.44	1.69
Elizondo, Santiago	R-R	5-9	154	10-25-99	2	0	6.75	11	2	0	0	16	26	14	12	3	6	24	.347	.353	.341	13.50	3.38
Figueroa, Jefferson	R-R	6-0	180	8-22-00	0	0	0.90	4	2	0	0	10	3	1	1	1	2	14	.094	.000	.120	12.60	1.80
File, Dylan	R-R	6-1	205	6-4-96	0	0	3.38	2	2	0	0	3	5	1	1	0	0	3	.385	.000	.455	10.13	0.00
Garabitos, Pablo	L-L	6-1	170	7-30-00	2	0	2.40	10	0	0	3	15	13	4	4	0	2	19	.245	.182	.262	11.40	1.20
Garcia, Andy	R-R	6-0	160	1-16-02	1	4	7.03	10	8	0	0	32	37	34	25	3	25	36	.291	.309	.278	10.13	7.03
Garcia, Nader	L-R	5-9	160	5-14-02	0	0	21.60	2	0	0	0	2	4	4	4	1	1	0	.500	--	.500	0.00	5.40
Garcia, Rafael	R-R	6-1	158	4-28-01	2	4	6.16	12	10	0	0	50	49	39	34	9	29	52	.261	.175	.304	9.42	5.26
Herrera, Yujanyer	R-R	6-3	175	8-17-03	3	3	9.00	11	4	0	0	35	50	40	35	7	28	37	.331	.328	.334	9.51	7.20
Jimenez, Edwin	R-R	6-3	175	12-12-01	0	4	5.25	7	4	0	1	24	28	15	14	3	5	27	.283	.267	.290	10.13	1.88
Jordan, Brannon	R-R	6-2	190	7-20-94	1	0	4.26	4	2	0	0	6	3	3	3	1	3	10	.143	.222	.083	14.21	4.26
Kelly, Antoine	L-L	6-6	205	12-5-99	0	0	0.00	1	0	0	0	1	0	0	0	0	0	0	.000	.000	.000	0.00	0.00
Maldonado, Fraudy	L-L	6-0	155	3-21-03	2	1	3.79	17	0	0	7	19	12	11	8	0	23	28	.188	.143	.200	13.26	10.89
McCarville, Keegan	R-R	6-1	210	2-3-98	0	1	5.40	4	0	0	0	5	8	3	3	0	1	6	.320	.333	.318	10.80	1.80
Miller, Justin	R-R	6-4	183	5-17-98	1	3	7.20	10	0	0	1	15	14	12	12	1	9	15	.241	.269	.219	9.00	5.40
Montero, Junior	R-R	6-3	175	9-20-98	0	0	2.11	12	0	0	3	21	17	6	5	1	10	31	.215	.154	.245	13.08	4.22
Moore, Ryne	R-R	6-4	210	11-27-98	0	0	0.73	6	2	0	1	12	4	1	1	0	4	8	.100	.143	.077	5.84	2.92
Morales, Karlos	L-L	6-2	178	8-10-99	2	2	5.34	19	0	0	1	29	34	32	17	1	15	42	.272	.333	.257	13.19	4.71
Morelo, Fray	R-R	6-2	178	5-23-02	1	0	3.86	6	0	0	0	9	8	4	4	0	10	10	.242	.313	.176	9.64	9.64
Olguin, Fernando	R-R	5-9	155	3-4-01	4	1	2.87	10	3	0	0	31	26	11	10	4	8	30	.230	.263	.213	8.62	2.30
Peden, Nate	R-R	6-0	178	10-16-98	0	1	5.40	4	0	0	0	7	10	5	4	0	1	14	.323	.333	.316	18.90	1.35
Pena, Jeison	R-R	6-1	165	9-14-02	0	1	5.14	11	2	0	1	28	30	23	16	1	18	35	.283	.313	.270	11.25	5.79
Perez, Mario	R-R	5-11	148	4-18-02	0	2	5.36	11	6	1	0	40	47	28	24	5	24	34	.307	.161	.392	7.59	5.36
Puello, Israel	R-R	6-3	200	10-10-00	1	4	4.94	10	10	0	0	27	24	18	15	2	9	37	.238	.227	.246	12.18	2.96
Ramey, Brandon	R-R	6-3	170	8-31-00	0	3	11.12	5	4	0	0	6	9	7	7	0	5	8	.360	.250	.412	12.71	7.94
Robinson, Edrian	R-R	6-5	170	3-1-02	3	1	8.31	15	0	0	0	22	21	24	20	2	23	23	.247	.286	.228	9.55	9.55
Rodriguez, Brailin	R-R	6-2	185	8-10-02	2	2	4.60	9	7	0	0	31	32	18	16	1	19	35	.269	.298	.250	10.05	5.46
Rodriguez, Yerlin	R-R	6-2	172	3-22-02	1	9	6.75	11	9	0	1	37	37	30	28	3	34	53	.262	.264	.261	12.78	8.20
Segura, Miguel	R-R	6-1	160	2-15-02	1	0	1.86	5	3	0	0	19	7	4	4	1	14	22	.113	.000	.167	10.24	6.52
Shook, TJ	R-R	6-3	226	5-29-98	0	0	1.93	2	2	0	0	5	1	1	1	1	3	10	.067	.000	.111	19.29	5.79
Silva, Luis	R-R	6-0	178	7-6-01	0	0	22.50	2	0	0	0	2	7	5	5	0	1	1	.538	.800	.375	4.50	4.50
Silverio, Phili	R-R	6-2	190	7-27-01	0	2	5.59	13	0	0	0	19	16	17	12	0	20	30	.219	.222	.217	13.97	9.31
Small, Ethan	L-L	6-4	215	2-14-97	0	0	0.00	1	1	0	0	1	2	0	0	0	0	1	.400	.333	.500	9.00	0.00
Tietz, Trevor	R-R	6-3	205	7-14-00	0	0	0.00	3	0	0	0	4	1	0	0	0	1	6	.071	.000	.100	10.38	2.08
Topa, Justin	R-R	6-4	200	3-7-91	0	0	0.00	2	0	0	0	2	1	0	0	0	0	5	.143	.000	.167	22.50	0.00
Tripp, Christian	R-R	6-7	220	3-13-97	1	0	0.00	5	0	0	2	11	3	1	0	0	3	15	.083	.083	.083	12.66	2.53
Vire, Caden	L-L	6-6		9-9-03	0	0	3.38	3	1	0	0	3	1	3	1	1	4	2	.100	.000	.143	6.75	13.50
Zhao, Jolon	R-R	5-10	180	8-29-01	2	1	1.04	6	0	0	0	9	6	2	1	0	2	13	.194	.273	.150	13.50	2.08

Fielding

C: Cabrera 14, Diaz 27, Feliciano 5, Garcia 16, Garcia 16, Quero 14, Sibrian 24.
1B: Bautista 25, Castillo 2, Chirinos 44, Clarke 3, Diaz 2, Frias 2, Jaraba 6, Low 7, Parra 10, Silva 22, Vargas 3.

2B: Black 3, Caballero 14, Castillo 13, Ferrer 3, Murray 2, Nicasia 5, Parra 2, Pastran 20, Raabe 9, Roa 27, Smith 11, Vargas 7.
3B: Binelas 6, Castillo 8, Ferrer 21, Jaraba 10, Nicasia 1, Parra 23, Pastran 16, Roa 7, Silva 9, Vargas 17.
SS: Caballero 22, Castillo 3, Ferrer 10, Garcia 35, Murray 5, Nicasia 10, Pastran 2, Pinero 7, Roa 1, Silva 1, Vargas 17.
OF: Bautista 5, Bello 6, Broxton 1, Cipion 36, David 11, Doston 39, Ernesto 16, Fernandez 37, Frelick 4, Frias 1, Leones 26, Medina 36, Mendez 13, Mercado 34, Perez 29, Peters 12, Valdez 23.

DSL BREWERS   ROOKIE
DOMINICAN SUMMER LEAGUE

Batting	B-T	HT	WT	DOB	AVG	vLH	vRH	G	AB	R	H	2B	3B	HR	RBI	BB	HBP	SH	SF	SO	SB	CS	SLG	OBP
Alvis, Deivid	R-R	6-2	170	10-19-01	.155	.211	.135	26	71	6	11	4	1	1	16	4	5	0	3	27	0	2	.282	.241
Areinamo, Jadher	R-R	5-10	160	11-28-03	.276	.522	.233	44	152	32	42	7	2	0	10	17	5	0	1	22	5	4	.349	.366
Barrios, Gregory	B-R	6-0	180	4-8-04	.208	.294	.190	30	101	19	21	4	0	0	6	14	0	0	1	14	9	1	.248	.302
Bautista, Angel	R-R	5-8	160	4-10-02	.207	.286	.182	22	58	7	12	1	0	0	2	5	0	0	1	14	1	0	.224	.266
Briceno, Miguel	R-R	5-9	155	7-6-03	.237	.195	.250	52	177	31	42	10	3	2	22	17	1	0	1	18	10	3	.362	.306
Burciaga, Sebastian	R-R	5-7	158	9-7-01	.088	.100	.086	27	68	12	6	2	1	1	4	8	2	0	0	17	3	0	.191	.205
Castillo, Luis	L-L	5-11	175	10-11-03	.252	.103	.291	43	139	14	35	7	0	0	13	15	1	0	1	24	3	1	.302	.327
Chourio, Jackson	R-R	6-1	165	3-11-04	.296	.379	.277	45	159	31	47	7	1	5	25	23	3	0	4	28	8	3	.447	.386
Ciprian, Alberto	R-R	5-11	160	11-5-02	.378	.000	.412	12	37	6	14	5	0	0	8	5	1	0	0	8	2	0	.514	.465
Colina, Eduarh	R-R	5-11	160	6-6-03	.278	.129	.313	50	162	28	45	8	0	3	29	16	7	0	5	38	2	1	.383	.358
Curbata, Isaac	R-R	5-11	165	2-24-02	.174	.000	.190	10	23	0	4	1	0	0	2	1	1	0	0	10	0	0	.217	.240
Feliz, Enmanuel	R-R	6-0	157	12-11-02	.154	.333	.139	16	39	7	6	1	0	0	2	7	0	0	0	14	2	2	.179	.283
Ferreira, Mendy	R-R	6-0	165	1-27-03	.195	.200	.194	38	82	14	16	5	0	0	10	24	1	0	1	34	16	3	.256	.380
Garcia, Duncan	R-R	6-1	170	10-31-03	.224	.296	.204	39	125	25	28	5	0	3	12	18	3	0	0	44	15	5	.336	.336
Garcia, Mauro	B-R	5-9	150	10-14-02	.273	.500	.250	8	22	3	6	0	0	0	2	2	0	0	0	3	0	0	.273	.333
Gonzalez, Jose	R-R	5-10	165	10-2-02	.276	.214	.291	42	145	30	40	10	2	1	24	14	3	0	1	30	9	1	.393	.350
Herrera, Yesbel	R-R	5-11	155	5-29-03	.232	.190	.246	30	82	14	19	5	0	2	11	6	3	0	0	27	4	1	.366	.308
Larez, Diego	R-R	6-1	165	12-9-02	.228	.138	.255	43	123	27	28	1	5	3	19	15	11	0	0	29	4	3	.390	.362
Leon, Henry	R-R	5-9	175	1-30-02	.160	.250	.143	10	25	2	4	0	0	0	3	4	1	0	1	7	0	0	.160	.290
Lora, Darlin	R-R	5-10	175	7-23-03	.222	.300	.205	20	54	7	12	3	0	1	9	4	1	0	1	13	2	0	.333	.283
Martinez, Eric	R-R	6-0	175	4-6-04	.230	.267	.217	24	61	10	14	1	0	0	4	12	4	0	0	11	3	1	.246	.390
Martinez, Rafael	B-R	5-11	170	9-20-01	.257	.111	.308	24	70	13	18	3	0	2	14	13	2	0	0	24	8	2	.386	.388
Mendez, Hendry	L-L	6-2	175	11-7-03	.296	.222	.311	21	54	10	16	5	1	1	9	7	2	0	1	2	0	0	.481	.391
Nino, Bryan	R-R	6-0	169	4-22-02	.226	.353	.178	22	62	7	14	3	0	0	4	10	0	0	0	23	1	1	.274	.333
Ollarve, Jason	L-R	5-10	160	5-20-04	.227	.154	.245	20	66	9	15	4	0	0	9	3	6	0	0	12	2	0	.288	.320
Ordonez, Edgardo	R-R	5-11	155	9-24-03	.298	.133	.333	27	84	13	25	10	1	0	15	14	5	0	0	20	3	1	.440	.427
Oropeza, Brayan	R-R	6-1	175	11-18-03	.216	.333	.206	12	37	5	8	0	0	0	5	4	1	0	0	12	1	0	.216	.310
Perez, Alexander	R-R	5-9	160	3-12-03	.214	.235	.211	44	140	23	30	7	0	1	20	21	3	0	3	36	7	0	.286	.323
Perez, Yeison	L-L	5-10	165	1-13-04	.244	.080	.275	43	156	15	38	9	1	1	27	9	2	0	0	41	1	0	.333	.293
Reyes, Erick	R-R	5-10	145	4-17-04	.082	.063	.088	27	73	6	6	2	0	0	4	10	0	0	0	31	1	2	.110	.193
Riera, Pedro	R-R	6-1	160	11-11-03	.170	.000	.200	31	88	16	15	4	0	0	12	22	3	0	2	40	1	1	.216	.348
Rodriguez, Arnys	B-R	5-11	173	8-12-03	.160	.000	.183	33	94	14	15	2	0	1	8	17	0	0	0	24	1	2	.213	.288
Rojas, Richard	R-R	5-10	155	1-19-04	.132	.000	.147	26	76	5	10	0	0	0	5	12	2	0	0	24	1	2	.132	.267
Ruiz, Manuel	R-R	6-0	170	3-1-02	.250	1.000	.182	6	12	0	3	0	0	0	3	4	0	0	0	3	0	0	.250	.438
Serrano, Ney	R-R	6-0	150	5-8-04	.255	.267	.252	43	149	26	38	11	0	1	17	19	5	0	0	39	11	6	.349	.358
Valderrama, Felipe	R-R	6-0	170	7-24-03	.255	.227	.262	34	106	16	27	5	0	0	13	12	7	0	0	31	1	0	.302	.368
Watter, Luis	R-R	5-8	150	11-10-03	.211	.294	.192	34	95	16	20	2	1	1	9	16	3	0	0	28	12	2	.284	.342
Winterdaal, Egduard	R-R	5-10	155	9-30-03	.143	.133	.148	17	42	6	6	1	0	0	4	5	3	1	1	16	1	0	.167	.275
Zalm, Jamal	B-R	5-10	155	9-21-02	.274	.222	.289	38	117	27	32	9	1	1	15	13	5	0	0	26	15	1	.393	.370

Pitching	B-T	HT	WT	DOB	W	L	ERA	G	GS	CG	SV	IP	H	R	ER	HR	BB	SO	AVG	vLH	vRH	K/9	BB/9
Albir, Jared	R-R	6-2	161	8-27-02	0	3	4.50	12	12	0	0	46	42	30	23	1	34	32	.266	.324	.222	6.26	6.65
Alcantara, Erovis	R-R	6-4	175	11-1-00	1	0	4.50	2	0	0	0	2	1	3	1	1	2	5	.143	.000	.200	22.50	9.00
Aquino, Patricio	R-R	6-0	175	5-1-03	1	2	2.66	11	11	0	0	44	35	17	13	0	27	54	.224	.250	.212	11.05	5.52
Baez, Gregory	R-R	6-3	180	12-29-01	2	1	5.13	17	0	0	1	26	23	20	15	1	19	23	.237	.150	.298	7.86	6.49
Bautista, Angel	R-R	5-8	160	4-10-02	0	0	0.00	2	0	0	0	2	0	0	0	0	1	0	.000	.000	.000	0.00	4.50
Briceno, Kevin	R-R	6-1	160	10-15-02	2	0	3.12	12	2	0	2	26	19	11	9	0	7	26	.202	.182	.205	9.00	2.42
Caldera, Albert	L-L	6-1	170	11-30-01	2	3	5.93	10	0	0	0	14	10	10	9	0	17	12	.204	.000	.233	7.90	11.20
Calzadilla, Gerson	R-R	5-11	155	4-5-03	2	3	2.80	13	8	0	1	45	41	21	14	1	15	35	.244	.222	.260	7.00	3.00
Camacho, Rafael	R-R	5-0	165	8-8-02	4	4	2.20	16	3	0	1	45	36	16	11	1	11	42	.220	.328	.150	8.40	2.20
Castillo, Jairo	R-R	6-4	170	11-14-03	0	0	11.57	3	0	0	0	2	0	4	3	0	8	3	.000	.000	.000	11.57	30.86
Castillo, Junior	L-L	5-10	160	1-28-03	1	3	3.05	13	7	0	0	41	28	17	14	1	21	36	.194	.034	.235	7.84	4.57
Ciprian, Braudin	R-R	6-2	220	3-20-01	1	2	5.11	9	0	0	0	12	8	12	7	0	11	13	.174	.313	.100	9.49	8.03
Cruz, Jonathan	R-R	6-2	165	5-9-02	3	2	6.20	17	0	0	3	25	16	20	17	1	26	35	.176	.139	.200	12.77	9.49
Cruz, Stiven	R-R	6-2	165	11-11-03	3	3	1.17	12	11	0	0	53	31	13	8	0	23	73	.168	.204	.154	12.47	3.93
Cuevas, Nelson	R-R	6-2	145	4-25-01	1	3	2.81	18	0	0	4	26	22	15	8	0	15	29	.234	.227	.236	10.17	5.26
De La Cruz, Leoni	L-L	6-0	175	5-22-98	3	0	1.45	11	0	0	2	19	14	8	3	1	8	29	.197	.125	.206	13.98	3.86
Encarnacion, Stanley	R-R	6-1	185	11-22-01	4	1	3.89	18	0	0	2	37	38	21	16	1	17	38	.260	.258	.261	9.24	4.14
Feliz, Enmanuel	R-R	6-0	157	12-11-02	0	0	9.00	1	0	0	0	1	2	1	1	0	0	1	1.000	1.000	1.000	0.00	0.00
Garrido, Henry	R-R	5-10	160	2-25-02	0	1	9.82	5	5	0	0	11	11	15	12	0	14	7	.262	.294	.240	5.73	11.45
Geraldo, Dencer	R-R	6-1	160	3-5-03	0	1	11.88	7	0	0	0	8	8	11	11	1	10	12	.242	.333	.222	12.96	10.80
Gonzalez, Arielbi	R-R	5-10	180	11-16-02	3	2	2.08	11	10	0	0	43	36	14	10	0	18	38	.234	.286	.218	7.89	3.74
Guzman, Delson	R-R	5-11	160	9-10-02	0	1	9.64	2	2	0	0	5	7	6	5	0	3	5	.333	.583	.000	9.64	5.79
Herrera, Yesbel	R-R	5-11	155	5-29-03	0	1	27.00	1	0	0	0	1	6	3	2	0	3	0	.000	--	.000	0.00	40.50
Jimenez, Edwin	R-R	6-3	175	12-12-01	1	1	1.72	5	4	0	0	16	10	5	3	0	7	21	.182	.176	.184	12.06	4.02

Name	B-T	Ht	Wt	DOB	W	L	ERA	G	GS	CG	SV	IP	H	R	ER	HR	BB	SO	AVG	vLH	vRH		
Mejia, Domingo	R-R	6-3	175	8-31-01	4	2	1.98	11	11	0	0	50	38	15	11	0	13	67	.203	.269	.167	12.06	2.34
Mendoza, Raul	R-R	5-11	168	12-9-00	2	2	2.84	11	0	0	0	19	13	7	6	2	7	22	.194	.083	.218	10.42	3.32
Morelo, Fray	R-R	6-2	178	5-23-02	0	2	4.00	7	2	0	1	18	15	9	8	0	11	22	.224	.455	.179	11.00	5.50
Mota, Henrison	R-R	6-3	193	7-4-03	6	1	3.20	17	0	0	2	25	14	12	9	2	16	34	.165	.219	.132	12.08	5.68
Ozuna, Erik	R-R	6-7	200	5-10-02	1	1	30.00	10	0	0	0	6	7	20	20	3	23	3	.318	.222	.385	4.50	34.50
Perdomo, Michael	R-R	6-0	170	11-22-01	1	3	3.00	18	0	0	1	36	28	19	12	2	8	47	.217	.244	.202	11.75	2.00
Perez, Anthony	R-R	6-3	190	10-28-01	1	2	6.85	13	7	0	0	22	14	18	17	0	25	25	.179	.000	.215	10.07	10.07
Reyes, Rosmel	R-R	5-11	155	2-18-03	3	0	5.50	11	0	0	0	18	14	12	11	1	18	27	.209	.222	.204	13.50	9.00
Rivero, Jesus	R-R	6-1	175	5-14-03	1	1	2.22	10	6	0	0	28	15	8	7	2	21	38	.156	.118	.165	12.07	6.67
Rodriguez, Waldin	R-R	6-3	176	1-5-02	1	2	7.58	15	0	0	1	19	19	21	16	3	20	25	.253	.273	.245	11.84	9.47
Sanchez, Dikember	R-R	5-11	160	2-20-04	3	3	4.54	15	4	0	1	40	34	26	20	0	29	35	.238	.219	.243	7.94	6.58
Segura, Miguel	R-R	6-1	160	2-15-02	1	0	1.50	6	4	0	0	18	6	3	3	0	7	25	.107	.077	.116	12.50	3.50
Vallecillo, Alexander	R-R	6-2	150	7-1-02	2	0	1.80	9	9	0	0	40	25	9	8	3	13	36	.176	.161	.186	8.10	2.93
Vasquez, Hamlet	R-R	6-3	175	9-9-02	0	2	7.15	10	0	0	0	11	13	10	9	0	8	17	.283	.429	.256	13.50	6.35

Fielding

C: Leon 5, Lora 15, Martinez 17, Ollarve 17, Ordonez 15, Oropeza 10, Ruiz 4, Valderrama 29, Winterdaal 15.

1B: Alvis 13, Bautista 18, Briceno 1, Curbata 7, Feliz 10, Herrera 11, Leon 4, Lora 4, Martinez 3, Nino 7, Ollarve 3, Ordonez 11, Perez 11, Reyes 1, Riera 1, Rodriguez 24, Ruiz 1.

2B: Areinamo 8, Barrios 1, Bautista 1, Briceno 13, Burciaga 17, Chourio 6, Garcia 5, Perez 4, Reyes 12, Riera 6, Rodriguez 10, Rojas 9, Serrano 7, Watter 10, Zalm 18.

3B: Areinamo 11, Bautista 1, Briceno 14, Burciaga 9, Ciprian 11, Garcia 1, Perez 22, Reyes 8, Riera 17, Rodriguez 1, Rojas 12, Serrano 4, Watter 3, Zalm 10.

SS: Areinamo 21, Barrios 28, Briceno 24, Perez 12, Reyes 1, Riera 7, Rojas 3, Serrano 25, Zalm 2.

OF: Alvis 10, Castillo 29, Chourio 32, Colina 46, Curbata 3, Feliz 6, Ferreira 36, Garcia 37, Gonzalez 41, Herrera 19, Larez 38, Martinez 16, Mendez 15, Nino 8, Perez 24, Watter 20.

Minnesota Twins

SEASON IN A SENTENCE: After winning the American League Central in back-to-back years, the Twins took a massive step back in 2021, posting a 73-89 record and finishing last in the division for the first time since 2016.

HIGH POINT: The Twins started the season well for about a week, sitting in first place of the division for three days in early April and watching Byron Buxton perform like one of the best players in baseball in the 61 games he was healthy. Buxton hit a career-high 19 home runs and managed a 169 wRC+ while playing some of the best center field defense in baseball.

LOW POINT: After starting 5-2, the Twins proceeded to lose five straight games and never again reached the .500 mark on the season. That led to the team eventually trading Nelson Cruz—who had been a stalwart in Minnesota's lineup for two and a half years—and Jose Berrios in late July.

NOTABLE ROOKIES: The Twins finished with a league average offense despite injuries to Buxton and top prospect Alex Kirilloff, but needed more help on the pitching side. Bailey Ober posted a 4.19 ERA over 20 starts and 92.1 innings and Joe Ryan pitched better than his results would indicate in five starts after he was acquired from the Rays. Jorge Alcala was just OK out of the bullpen (3.92 ERA, 59.2 innings). Ryan Jeffers wasn't quite the hitter he flashed in 2020, but still hit 14 homers and received well behind the plate. Trevor Larnach hit well early (.811 OPS in first 37 games) before major league pitchers figured him out (.559 OPS in last 42 games).

KEY TRANSACTIONS: Minnesota made two big moves for the future at the deadline by shipping Nelson Cruz to the Rays for righthanders Joe Ryan and Drew Strotman and sending Jose Berrios to the Blue Jays for infielder/outfielder Austin Martin—who immediately became the organization's top prospect—and righthander Simeon Woods Richardson. The Twins' preseason signing of shortstop Andrelton Simmons did upgrade the team's infield defense (Simmons was +15 defensive runs saved at the position) but he had a career-worst year at the plate with a .223/.283/.274 slash line and 56 wRC+.

OPENING DAY SALARY: $121,003,834 (16th).

PLAYERS OF THE YEAR

MAJOR LEAGUE	MINOR LEAGUE
Jorge Polanco **2B**	**Jose Miranda** **3B**
.269/.323/.503	(AAA/AA)
Career-high 33 HR	.344/.401/.572,
97 R, 98 RBIs, 11 SB	30 HR, 94 RBIs

ORGANIZATION LEADERS

Batting		*Minimum 250 AB
MAJORS		
*AVG	Luis Arraez	.294
*OPS	Nelson Cruz	.907
HR	Jorge Polanco	33
RBI	Jorge Polanco	98
MINORS		
*AVG	Jose Miranda, St. Paul, Wichita	.344
*OBP	Edouard Julien, Cedar Rapids, Fort Myers	.434
*SLG	Jose Miranda, St. Paul, Wichita	.572
*OPS	Jose Miranda, St. Paul, Wichita	.973
R	Jose Miranda, St. Paul, Wichita	97
H	Jose Miranda, St. Paul, Wichita	184
TB	Jose Miranda, St. Paul, Wichita	306
2B	Jose Miranda, St. Paul, Wichita	32
3B	Wander Javier, Cedar Rapids	10
HR	Jose Miranda, St. Paul, Wichita	30
RBI	Jose Miranda, St. Paul, Wichita	94
BB	Edouard Julien, Cedar Rapids, Fort Myers	110
SO	Trey Cabbage, Wichita, Cedar Rapids	160
SB	Aaron Whitefield, Wichita	36

Pitching		#Minimum 75 IP
MAJORS		
W	Michael Pineda	9
#ERA	Jose Berrios	3.48
SO	Jose Berrios	126
SV	Alex Colome	17
MINORS		
W	Louie Varland, Cedar Rapids, Fort Myers	10
L	Sawyer Gipson-Long, Cedar Rapids, Fort Myers	8
L	Austin Schulfer, Wichita	8
#ERA	Louie Varland, Cedar Rapids, Fort Myers	2.10
G	Yennier Cano, St. Paul, Wichita	42
GS	Austin Schulfer, Wichita	24
SV	Melvi Acosta, Wichita, Cedar Rapids	9
SV	Denny Bentley, Cedar Rapids, Fort Myers	9
SV	Zach Featherstone, Cedar Rapids	9
IP	Austin Schulfer, Wichita	110
BB	Bryan Sammons, St. Paul, Wichita	61
BB	Chris Vallimont, Wichita, Fort Myers	61
SO	Louie Varland, Cedar Rapids, Fort Myers	142
#AVG	Cole Sands, Wichita	.203

2021 PERFORMANCE

General Manager: Derek Falvey. **Farm Director:** Alex Hassan. **Scouting Director:** Sean Johnson.

Class	Team	League	W	L	PCT	Finish	Manager
Majors	Minnesota Twins	American	73	89	.451	13th (15)	Rocco Baldelli
Triple-A	St. Paul Saints	Triple-A East	67	63	.515	10th (20)	Toby Gardenhire
Double-A	Wichita Wind Surge	Double-A Central	69	51	.575	1st (10)	Ramon Borrego
High-A	Cedar Rapids Kernels	High-A Central	67	53	.558	2nd (12)	Brian Dinkelman
Low-A	Fort Myers Mighty Mussels	Low-A Southeast	60	54	.526	3rd (10)	Brian Meyer
Rookie	DSL Twins	Dominican Summer	21	38	.356	t-42nd (46)	Seth Feldman
Rookie	FCL Twins	Florida Complex	21	38	.356	16th (18)	Takashi Miyoshi
Overall 2021 Minor League Record			305	297	.507	14th (30)	

ORGANIZATION STATISTICS

MINNESOTA TWINS
AMERICAN LEAGUE

Batting	B-T	HT	WT	DOB	AVG	vLH	vRH	G	AB	R	H	2B	3B	HR	RBI	BB	HBP	SH	SF	SO	SB	CS	SLG	OBP
Arraez, Luis	L-R	5-10	175	4-9-97	.294	.253	.307	121	428	58	126	17	6	2	42	43	2	0	6	48	2	2	.376	.357
Astudillo, Willians	R-R	5-9	225	10-14-91	.236	.241	.232	72	208	17	49	8	0	7	21	3	4	0	1	12	0	0	.375	.259
Blankenhorn, Travis	L-R	6-2	235	8-3-96	--	--	--	1	0	1	0	0	0	0	0	0	0	0	0	0	0	0	--	--
Buxton, Byron	R-R	6-2	190	12-18-93	.306	.325	.297	61	235	50	72	23	0	19	32	13	6	0	0	62	9	1	.647	.358
Cave, Jake	L-L	6-0	200	12-4-92	.189	.122	.211	76	164	14	31	6	1	3	13	10	3	1	0	62	1	1	.293	.249
Celestino, Gilberto	R-L	6-0	170	2-13-99	.136	.111	.174	23	59	7	8	3	0	2	3	3	0	0	0	14	0	0	.288	.177
Cruz, Nelson	R-R	6-2	230	7-1-80	.294	.362	.257	85	296	44	87	13	1	19	50	35	5	0	7	63	3	0	.537	.370
2-team total (55 Tampa Bay)					.265	.316	.240	140	513	79	136	21	1	32	86	51	7	0	9	126	3	0	.497	.334
Donaldson, Josh	R-R	6-1	210	12-8-85	.247	.257	.243	135	457	73	113	26	0	26	72	74	4	0	8	114	0	0	.475	.352
Garlick, Kyle	R-R	6-1	210	1-26-92	.232	.271	.175	36	99	17	23	8	0	5	10	6	1	0	1	32	1	0	.465	.280
Garver, Mitch	R-R	6-1	220	1-15-91	.256	.215	.289	68	207	29	53	15	0	13	34	31	3	0	2	71	1	1	.517	.358
Gordon, Nick	L-R	6-0	160	10-24-95	.240	.244	.239	73	200	19	48	9	1	4	23	12	3	0	1	55	10	1	.355	.292
Jeffers, Ryan	R-R	6-4	235	6-3-97	.199	.225	.185	85	267	28	53	10	1	14	35	22	4	0	0	108	0	1	.401	.270
Kepler, Max	L-L	6-4	225	2-10-93	.211	.157	.232	121	426	61	90	21	4	19	54	54	6	0	4	96	10	0	.413	.306
Kirilloff, Alex	L-L	6-2	195	11-9-97	.251	.279	.238	59	215	23	54	11	1	8	34	14	1	0	1	52	1	1	.423	.299
Larnach, Trevor	L-R	6-4	223	2-26-97	.223	.183	.242	79	260	29	58	12	0	7	28	31	8	0	2	104	1	0	.350	.322
Lin, Tzu-Wei	L-R	5-9	180	2-15-94	--	--	--	1	0	0	0	0	0	0	0	0	0	0	0	0	0	0	--	--
Polanco, Jorge	B-R	5-11	208	7-5-93	.269	.273	.267	152	588	97	158	35	2	33	98	45	5	0	6	118	11	6	.503	.323
Refsnyder, Rob	R-R	6-0	205	3-26-91	.245	.304	.205	51	139	21	34	7	0	2	12	17	0	0	1	40	1	0	.338	.325
Riddle, JT	L-R	6-1	190	10-12-91	.333	1.000	.200	4	6	1	2	0	0	0	0	0	0	0	0	0	0	0	.333	.333
Rooker, Brent	R-R	6-3	225	11-1-94	.201	.212	.195	58	189	25	38	10	0	9	16	15	9	0	0	70	0	0	.397	.291
Rortvedt, Ben	L-R	5-10	205	9-25-97	.169	.111	.183	39	89	8	15	1	0	3	7	6	1	2	0	29	0	0	.281	.229
Sano, Miguel	R-R	6-4	272	5-11-93	.223	.238	.216	135	470	68	105	24	0	30	75	59	2	0	1	183	2	1	.466	.312
Simmons, Andrelton	R-R	6-2	195	9-4-89	.223	.245	.211	131	412	37	92	12	0	3	31	32	3	3	1	62	1	0	.274	.283

Pitching	B-T	HT	WT	DOB	W	L	ERA	G	GS	CG	SV	IP	H	R	ER	HR	BB	SO	AVG	vLH	vRH	K/9	BB/9
Albers, Andrew	R-L	6-1	200	10-6-85	1	2	7.58	5	3	0	0	19	24	16	16	9	9	12	.304	.261	.321	5.68	4.26
Alcala, Jorge	R-R	6-3	205	7-28-95	3	6	3.92	59	0	0	1	60	45	29	26	10	13	61	.214	.214	.214	9.20	1.96
Anderson, Shaun	R-R	6-4	228	10-29-94	0	0	9.35	4	0	0	0	9	13	12	9	1	6	8	.317	.583	.207	8.31	5.19
2-team total (7 Baltimore)					0	0	9.16	11	0	0	0	19	30	27	19	4	10	15	.333	.417	.278	7.23	4.82
Astudillo, Willians	R-R	5-9	225	10-14-91	0	0	2.25	4	0	0	0	4	1	1	1	1	2	0	.071	.000	.111	0.00	4.50
Barnes, Charlie	L-L	6-2	190	10-1-95	0	3	5.92	9	8	0	0	38	46	27	25	4	16	20	.303	.258	.314	4.74	3.79
Barraclough, Kyle	R-R	6-3	229	5-23-90	2	0	5.54	10	0	0	0	13	12	8	8	4	8	18	.245	.286	.229	12.46	5.54
Berrios, Jose	R-R	6-0	205	5-27-94	7	5	3.48	20	20	1	0	122	95	53	47	14	32	126	.213	.260	.170	9.32	2.37
2-team total (12 Toronto)					12	9	3.52	32	32	1	0	192	159	83	75	22	45	204	.223	.254	.193	9.56	2.11
Burrows, Beau	R-R	6-2	210	9-18-96	0	1	12.54	5	1	0	0	9	14	14	13	5	8	5	.378	.333	.400	4.82	7.71
2-team total (1 Detroit)					0	1	13.91	6	1	0	0	11	16	18	17	5	10	8	.364	.267	.414	6.55	8.18
Colome, Alex	R-R	6-1	225	12-31-88	4	4	4.15	67	0	0	17	65	68	41	30	8	23	58	.264	.302	.237	8.03	3.18
Coulombe, Danny	L-L	5-10	190	10-26-89	3	2	3.67	29	1	0	0	34	35	17	14	5	7	33	.267	.250	.276	8.65	1.83
Dobnak, Randy	R-R	6-1	230	1-17-95	1	7	7.64	14	6	0	1	51	66	44	43	11	12	27	.310	.327	.296	4.80	2.13
Duffey, Tyler	R-R	6-3	220	12-27-90	3	3	3.18	64	0	0	3	62	48	25	22	4	28	61	.216	.253	.197	8.81	4.04
Farrell, Luke	L-R	6-6	200	6-7-91	1	1	4.74	20	1	0	0	25	28	13	13	4	13	25	.280	.265	.289	9.12	4.74
Gant, John	R-R	6-4	200	8-6-92	1	5	5.61	14	7	0	0	34	31	24	21	4	15	36	.242	.271	.225	9.62	4.01
Garcia, Edgar	R-R	6-1	205	10-4-96	0	0	10.45	6	0	0	0	10	9	12	12	3	7	8	.225	.267	.200	6.97	6.10
Garza Jr., Ralph	R-R	6-2	220	4-6-94	0	2	3.26	18	0	0	1	19	13	9	7	3	7	15	.186	.167	.196	6.98	3.26
2-team total (9 Houston)					1	4	3.56	27	0	0	1	30	24	15	12	5	14	29	.214	.195	.225	8.60	4.15
Gibaut, Ian	R-R	6-3	250	11-19-93	0	0	2.70	3	0	0	0	7	7	2	2	2	2	4	.280	.429	.091	5.40	2.70
Happ, J.A.	L-L	6-5	205	10-19-82	5	6	6.77	19	19	0	0	98	125	76	74	21	31	77	.306	.301	.307	7.05	2.84
Jax, Griffin	R-R	6-2	195	11-22-94	4	5	6.37	18	14	0	0	82	82	62	58	23	29	65	.256	.254	.258	7.13	3.18
Law, Derek	R-R	6-3	225	9-14-90	0	0	4.20	9	0	0	0	15	16	7	7	2	8	14	.276	.348	.229	8.40	4.80
Maeda, Kenta	R-R	6-1	185	4-11-88	6	5	4.66	21	21	0	0	106	106	60	55	16	32	113	.258	.258	.257	9.56	2.71
Minaya, Juan	R-R	6-4	210	9-18-90	2	1	2.48	29	0	0	0	40	27	12	11	4	20	43	.189	.250	.158	9.68	4.50
Moran, Jovani	L-L	6-1	167	4-24-97	0	0	7.88	5	0	0	0	8	9	7	7	0	7	10	.290	.250	.304	11.25	7.88

	B-T	HT	WT	DOB	W	L	ERA	G	GS	CG	SV	IP	H	R	ER	HR	BB	SO	AVG	vLH	vRH	K/9	BB/9
Ober, Bailey	R-R	6-9	260	7-12-95	3	3	4.19	20	20	0	0	92	92	45	43	20	19	96	.258	.288	.235	9.36	1.85
Pineda, Michael	R-R	6-7	280	1-18-89	9	8	3.62	22	21	0	0	109	114	49	44	17	21	88	.265	.290	.246	7.24	1.73
Robles, Hansel	R-R	6-0	220	8-13-90	3	4	4.91	45	0	0	10	44	37	28	24	6	24	43	.231	.225	.236	8.80	4.91
2-team total (27 Boston)					3	5	4.43	72	0	0	14	69	58	39	34	8	37	76	.228	.219	.235	9.91	4.83
Rogers, Taylor	L-L	6-3	190	12-17-90	2	4	3.35	40	0	0	9	40	38	18	15	4	8	59	.247	.170	.287	13.17	1.79
Ryan, Joe	R-R	6-2	205	6-5-96	2	1	4.05	5	5	0	0	27	16	12	12	4	5	30	.168	.149	.188	10.13	1.69
Shoemaker, Matt	R-R	6-2	225	9-27-86	3	8	8.06	16	11	0	0	60	73	56	54	15	27	40	.297	.331	.264	5.97	4.03
Smeltzer, Devin	R-L	6-3	195	9-7-95	0	0	0.00	1	0	0	0	5	1	1	0	0	1	3	.077	.143	.000	5.79	1.93
Stashak, Cody	R-R	6-2	180	6-4-94	0	0	6.89	15	0	0	0	16	16	12	12	2	10	26	.258	.400	.162	14.94	5.74
Thielbar, Caleb	R-L	6-0	205	1-31-87	7	0	3.23	59	0	0	0	64	55	24	23	8	20	77	.232	.217	.240	10.83	2.81
Thorpe, Lewis	R-L	6-1	218	11-23-95	0	2	4.70	5	4	0	0	15	14	11	8	2	7	6	.237	.273	.229	3.52	4.11
Vincent, Nick	R-R	5-10	185	7-12-86	1	0	0.71	7	0	0	0	13	6	1	1	1	5	9	.146	.067	.192	6.39	3.55
Waddell, Brandon	L-L	6-3	180	6-3-94	0	1	11.25	4	0	0	0	4	10	6	5	2	3	1	.455	.500	.429	2.25	6.75
2-team total (1 Baltimore)					0	1	9.00	5	0	0	0	5	10	6	5	2	4	1	.400	.500	.353	1.80	7.20

Fielding

Catcher	PCT	G	PO	A	E	DP	PB
Astudillo	1.000	10	33	2	0	1	1
Garver	.998	59	426	12	1	2	4
Jeffers	.994	84	626	30	4	2	6
Rortvedt	.989	39	244	14	3	2	2

First Base	PCT	G	PO	A	E	DP
Astudillo	1.000	27	179	8	0	19
Garver	.857	4	5	1	1	1
Kirilloff	1.000	29	181	15	0	10
Sano	.986	118	878	43	13	94

Second Base	PCT	G	PO	A	E	DP
Arraez	.987	48	68	85	2	26
Astudillo	.833	4	3	2	1	2
Blankenhorn	.000	1	0	0	1	0
Gordon	.977	17	20	23	1	8
Polanco	.974	120	164	294	12	70

Third Base	PCT	G	PO	A	E	DP
Arraez	.957	55	40	95	6	11
Astudillo	.969	29	20	43	2	7
Donaldson	.952	92	71	187	13	19
Gordon	.667	2	0	2	1	0
Sano	.750	9	3	6	3	1

Shortstop	PCT	G	PO	A	E	DP
Gordon	1.000	14	14	23	0	4
Polanco	.948	39	24	67	5	11
Riddle	1.000	3	0	6	0	1
Simmons	.976	131	167	322	12	67

Outfield	PCT	G	PO	A	E	DP
Arraez	1.000	27	36	3	0	1
Astudillo	1.000	1	1	0	0	0
Buxton	.994	60	179	0	1	0
Cave	.980	77	96	4	2	1
Celestino	.958	25	44	2	2	1
Garlick	1.000	35	54	2	0	1
Gordon	1.000	46	72	1	0	0
Kepler	1.000	119	215	5	0	1
Kirilloff	.981	40	51	2	1	1
Larnach	.979	80	134	4	3	1
Lin	--	1	0	0	0	0
Refsnyder	.988	51	81	2	1	1
Rooker	.987	46	72	2	1	0

ST. PAUL SAINTS

TRIPLE-A EAST

TRIPLE-A

Batting	B-T	HT	WT	DOB	AVG	vLH	vRH	G	AB	R	H	2B	3B	HR	RBI	BB	HBP	SH	SF	SO	SB	CS	SLG	OBP
Arraez, Luis	L-R	5-10	175	4-9-97	.250	.000	.400	2	8	2	2	0	0	0	2	1	0	0	0	0	0	0	.250	.333
Astudillo, Willians	R-R	5-9	225	10-14-91	.281	.321	.262	22	89	13	25	3	0	2	8	3	2	0	0	4	3	0	.382	.319
Banuelos, David	R-R	6-0	205	10-1-96	.211	.280	.185	30	90	13	19	5	2	3	14	5	0	0	1	34	0	0	.411	.250
Blankenhorn, Travis	L-R	6-2	235	8-3-96	.182	1.000	.100	3	11	1	2	1	0	0	1	2	0	0	0	6	0	0	.273	.308
2-team total (48 Syracuse)					.250	.179	.271	51	172	23	43	11	0	9	31	31	2	0	1	59	3	2	.471	.369
Boyd, BJ	L-R	5-11	230	7-16-93	.209	.087	.250	26	91	17	19	3	1	1	11	7	2	0	0	26	3	0	.297	.280
Broxton, Keon	R-R	6-3	200	5-7-90	.186	.217	.174	73	221	38	41	6	0	9	26	30	3	0	3	113	10	1	.335	.288
2-team total (15 Nashville)					.175	.197	.168	88	257	42	45	6	0	9	27	35	4	0	3	135	12	2	.304	.281
Buxton, Byron	R-R	6-2	190	12-18-93	.409	.667	.313	7	22	6	9	2	1	3	9	2	0	0	2	3	0	0	1.000	.423
Cave, Jake	L-L	6-0	200	12-4-92	.367	.556	.286	8	30	6	11	1	0	1	5	5	1	0	0	10	0	1	.500	.472
Celestino, Gilberto	R-L	6-0	170	2-13-99	.290	.333	.275	49	183	27	53	13	0	5	24	24	4	0	0	43	4	0	.443	.384
Contreras, Mark	L-R	6-0	195	1-24-95	.248	.174	.272	95	343	62	85	26	2	18	63	34	13	0	4	117	12	5	.493	.335
Descalso, Daniel	L-R	5-10	190	10-19-86	.093	.100	.092	24	75	9	7	2	0	2	4	14	1	0	0	31	0	0	.200	.244
Encarnacion, Yeltsin	L-R	5-11	170	6-28-98	.200	.000	.240	11	30	1	6	1	0	0	2	2	0	0	0	14	0	0	.233	.250
Garlick, Kyle	R-R	6-1	210	1-26-92	.286	.000	.400	2	7	0	2	0	0	0	1	1	0	0	0	1	0	0	.286	.375
Garver, Mitch	R-R	6-1	220	1-15-91	.231	.500	.150	7	26	4	6	0	0	0	2	3	1	0	0	8	0	0	.231	.333
Gordon, Nick	L-R	6-0	160	10-24-95	.282	.125	.302	18	71	11	20	0	1	3	9	6	0	0	0	12	7	2	.437	.338
Hamilton, Caleb	R-R	6-0	185	2-5-95	.103	.000	.143	11	29	1	3	0	0	1	3	2	0	0	0	14	0	0	.207	.161
Jeffers, Ryan	R-R	6-4	235	6-3-97	.217	.200	.219	24	83	13	18	4	0	5	16	16	1	0	3	26	0	0	.446	.340
Johnson, Sherman	L-R	5-10	190	7-15-90	.215	.231	.213	64	195	30	42	8	2	5	30	40	4	0	0	63	2	1	.354	.360
Kepler, Max	L-L	6-4	225	2-10-93	.091	--	.091	3	11	0	1	0	0	0	0	0	0	0	0	1	0	0	.091	.091
Kerrigan, Jimmy	R-R	6-1	215	3-16-94	.263	.312	.245	107	354	59	93	16	2	19	56	34	6	0	4	135	10	2	.480	.334
Kirilloff, Alex	L-L	6-2	195	11-9-97	.500	--	.250	2	6	2	3	0	0	2	3	0	0	0	0	2	0	0	1.500	.500
Larnach, Trevor	L-R	6-4	223	2-26-97	.176	.063	.229	14	51	13	9	1	0	3	7	6	5	0	0	21	0	0	.373	.323
Lin, Tzu-Wei	L-R	5-9	180	2-15-94	.269	.250	.273	7	26	8	7	1	0	0	4	4	0	0	0	8	3	0	.308	.367
Maggi, Drew	R-R	6-0	192	5-16-89	.252	.271	.243	95	318	59	80	13	2	16	50	40	11	0	1	114	12	5	.456	.354
Miranda, Jose	R-R	6-2	210	6-29-98	.343	.358	.338	80	341	61	117	24	0	17	56	25	6	0	1	49	0	2	.563	.397
Ozoria, Daniel	B-R	5-9	135	8-24-00	.000	--	.000	3	3	0	0	0	0	0	0	0	0	0	0	1	0	0	.000	.000
Pena, Roberto	R-R	6-0	250	6-9-92	.202	.240	.186	27	84	5	17	4	0	2	11	7	1	0	1	12	0	0	.321	.269
Refsnyder, Rob	R-R	6-0	205	3-26-91	.318	.286	.333	18	66	13	21	5	0	5	14	12	1	0	1	13	0	0	.621	.425
Riddle, JT	L-R	6-1	190	10-12-91	.202	.153	.216	91	317	42	64	13	2	7	40	23	7	0	3	62	3	3	.322	.269
Rooker, Brent	R-R	6-3	225	11-1-94	.245	.167	.267	62	220	40	54	8	1	20	49	38	6	0	3	80	1	2	.564	.367
Rortvedt, Ben	L-R	5-10	205	9-25-97	.254	.250	.256	34	122	18	31	6	0	5	22	10	3	0	1	35	0	0	.426	.324
Schmidt, Kyle	R-R	6-0	205	7-13-97	.000	.000	--	1	1	0	0	0	0	0	0	0	0	0	0	0	0	0	.000	.000
Stankiewicz, Drew	B-R	5-10	160	6-18-93	.253	.125	.289	45	146	23	37	12	1	2	12	19	1	0	1	38	1	0	.390	.333
Telis, Tomas	R-R	5-8	220	6-19-91	.296	.288	.298	101	423	51	125	22	1	12	50	26	3	1	0	58	5	1	.418	.340
Tomscha, Damek	R-R	6-2	200	8-27-91	.241	.226	.247	82	274	38	66	14	1	10	38	21	6	0	0	74	0	1	.409	.309
Wiel, Zander	R-R	6-3	220	1-11-93	.250	1.000	.143	2	8	0	2	0	0	0	0	0	0	0	0	3	0	0	.250	.250

	B-T	HT	WT	DOB	W	L	ERA	G	GS	CG	SV	IP	H	R	ER	HR	BB	SO	AVG	vLH	vRH	K/9	BB/9
Yake, Ernie	L-R 5-11 165 11-20-97 .000 -- .000 1 1 0 0 0 0 0 0 0 0 0 0 0 0 0 .000 .000																						

Pitching

Pitching	B-T	HT	WT	DOB	W	L	ERA	G	GS	CG	SV	IP	H	R	ER	HR	BB	SO	AVG	vLH	vRH	K/9	BB/9
Albers, Andrew	R-L	6-1	200	10-6-85	8	4	3.88	18	17	0	0	102	120	54	44	15	11	88	.285	.261	.296	7.76	0.97
Anderson, Shaun	R-R	6-4	228	10-29-94	1	0	0.00	5	0	0	0	6	2	0	0	0	3	5	.105	.111	.100	7.50	4.50
Barnes, Charlie	L-L	6-2	190	10-1-95	6	4	3.79	16	16	0	0	76	73	35	32	7	24	62	.251	.259	.248	7.34	2.84
Barraclough, Kyle	R-R	6-3	229	5-23-90	4	1	2.49	21	0	0	0	25	15	7	7	4	10	38	.172	.241	.138	13.50	3.55
2-team total (11 Scranton/Wilkes-Barre)					8	1	2.75	32	0	0	0	39	20	12	12	6	21	62	.153	.184	.134	14.19	4.81
Burrows, Beau	R-R	6-2	210	9-18-96	3	5	4.69	13	9	0	0	48	39	27	25	10	22	48	.213	.241	.188	9.00	4.13
2-team total (9 Toledo)					4	6	5.10	22	10	0	0	65	60	39	37	14	28	65	.236	.261	.215	8.95	3.86
Cano, Yennier	R-R	6-4	185	3-9-94	2	3	3.86	30	1	0	0	4	51	45	23	22	4	29	58	.238	.277	.208	10.17	5.08
Coulombe, Danny	L-L	5-10	190	10-26-89	1	1	1.77	14	0	0	2	20	16	6	4	1	3	27	.211	.200	.216	11.95	1.33
Dobnak, Randy	R-R	6-1	230	1-17-95	0	1	3.00	4	4	0	0	18	15	6	6	0	10	13	.234	.216	.259	6.50	5.00
Duran, Jhoan	R-R	6-5	230	1-8-98	0	3	5.06	5	4	0	0	16	16	9	9	1	13	22	.258	.207	.303	12.38	7.31
Farrell, Luke	L-R	6-6	200	6-7-91	0	1	4.00	7	0	0	0	9	5	4	4	0	6	16	.167	.100	.200	16.00	6.00
Garcia, Edgar	R-R	6-1	205	10-4-96	2	1	3.00	13	0	0	1	21	11	7	7	1	16	20	.149	.133	.159	8.57	6.86
2-team total (24 Louisville)					4	1	3.20	37	0	0	2	45	28	16	16	1	29	49	.178	.180	.177	9.80	5.80
Garcia, Jason	R-R	6-0	185	11-21-92	0	0	4.60	5	4	0	0	16	15	8	8	1	6	12	.259	.259	.258	6.89	3.45
Garza Jr., Ralph	R-R	6-2	220	4-6-94	0	0	7.36	3	0	0	1	4	3	3	3	1	2	5	.214	.000	.300	12.27	4.91
Gibaut, Ian	R-R	6-3	250	11-19-93	1	4	6.80	32	1	0	0	45	54	34	34	5	21	54	.293	.284	.300	10.80	4.20
Hackimer, Tom	R-R	5-11	195	6-28-94	0	0	16.20	6	0	0	0	1	5	6	9	9	0	15	7	.300	.400	.200	12.60	27.00
2-team total (15 Syracuse)					0	0	5.95	21	0	0	5	12	13	13	2	29	27	.174	.132	.226	12.36	13.27
Hamilton, Ian	R-R	6-1	200	6-16-95	4	3	4.12	38	3	0	4	59	46	31	27	5	39	86	.217	.194	.235	13.12	5.95
Harvey, Joe	R-R	6-2	236	1-9-92	0	1	18.00	4	0	0	0	3	6	6	6	2	6	4	.429	.400	.444	12.00	18.00
Jax, Griffin	R-R	6-2	195	11-22-94	4	1	3.76	8	8	0	0	41	37	17	17	2	16	36	.242	.235	.247	7.97	3.54
Law, Derek	R-R	6-3	225	9-14-90	1	1	2.54	18	3	0	4	28	25	8	8	1	12	28	.238	.204	.268	8.89	3.81
Leyer, Robinson	R-R	6-2	185	3-13-93	1	4	6.95	35	1	0	0	45	42	37	35	11	32	51	.240	.305	.183	10.13	6.35
Maeda, Kenta	R-R	6-1	185	4-11-88	0	0	2.25	1	1	0	0	4	1	1	1	1	1	5	.077	.250	.000	11.25	2.25
Mason, Ryan	R-R	6-6	215	10-4-94	1	0	3.38	13	0	0	1	19	14	8	7	1	10	25	.197	.172	.214	12.05	4.82
Minaya, Juan	R-R	6-4	210	9-18-90	2	3	3.41	17	0	0	0	29	29	14	11	3	15	37	.254	.250	.258	11.48	4.66
Moran, Jovani	L-L	6-1	167	4-24-97	2	1	3.03	15	0	0	1	30	14	11	10	3	18	45	.140	.182	.119	13.65	5.46
Mullenbach, Matt	R-R	6-4	195	10-6-96	0	0	0.00	0	0	0	0	2	2	0	0	0	1	0	.250	.250	.250	0.00	4.50
Nittoli, Vinny	R-R	6-1	210	11-11-90	0	1	2.45	7	0	0	1	7	3	2	2	1	3	10	.125	.100	.143	12.27	3.68
Nunn, Chris	L-L	6-5	200	10-5-90	1	1	3.66	16	0	0	0	20	11	10	8	1	15	19	.162	.222	.122	8.69	6.86
Ober, Bailey	R-R	6-9	260	7-12-95	1	0	2.81	4	4	0	0	16	13	5	5	0	5	21	.217	.222	.208	11.81	2.81
Pineda, Michael	R-R	6-7	280	1-18-89	0	1	9.00	1	1	0	0	4	4	5	4	0	3	1	.267	.300	.200	2.25	6.75
Ryan, Joe	R-R	6-2	205	6-5-96	0	0	2.00	2	2	0	0	9	5	2	2	1	2	17	.161	.188	.133	17.00	2.00
2-team total (12 Durham)					4	3	3.41	14	13	0	0	66	40	27	25	9	12	92	.173	.214	.141	12.55	1.64
Sammons, Bryan	L-L	6-4	235	4-27-95	1	3	6.61	13	9	0	0	49	57	38	36	11	32	33	.291	.200	.331	6.06	5.88
Shepherd, Chandler	R-R	6-1	215	8-25-92	9	6	5.33	26	17	0	0	105	132	67	62	18	30	68	.311	.307	.316	5.85	2.58
Shoemaker, Matt	R-R	6-2	225	9-27-86	1	0	1.80	4	3	0	0	20	12	4	4	1	8	17	.182	.172	.189	7.65	3.60
Sparkman, Glenn	R-R	6-2	215	5-11-92	0	0	3.00	2	0	0	0	3	2	1	1	0	6	.182	.000	.333	18.00	0.00
Stankiewicz, Drew	B-R	5-10	160	6-18-93	0	0	18.00	1	0	0	0	1	4	3	2	1	0	1	.500	.750	.250	9.00	0.00
Stashak, Cody	R-R	6-2	180	6-4-94	0	0	0.00	2	2	0	0	2	2	0	0	0	0	3	.222	.200	.250	11.57	0.00
Strotman, Drew	R-R	6-3	195	9-3-96	3	3	7.33	12	12	0	0	54	65	44	44	9	30	42	.298	.274	.317	7.00	5.00
2-team total (13 Durham)					10	5	5.29	25	24	0	0	112	115	69	66	12	63	104	.267	.247	.283	8.33	5.05
Thorpe, Lewis	R-L	6-1	218	11-23-95	6	2	4.76	6	2	0	0	17	12	9	9	1	7	12	.190	.176	.196	6.35	3.71
Vasquez, Andrew	L-L	6-6	228	9-14-93	4	0	3.61	33	0	0	0	42	21	21	17	5	22	68	.143	.069	.191	14.46	4.68
Vincent, Nick	R-R	5-10	185	7-12-86	3	1	4.55	24	0	0	6	32	28	20	16	8	7	38	.228	.213	.242	10.80	1.99
Whalen, Rob	R-R	6-2	220	1-31-94	0	4	8.59	10	4	0	2	22	26	22	21	3	14	17	.292	.318	.267	6.95	5.73
Winder, Josh	R-R	6-5	210	10-11-96	1	0	4.67	4	4	0	0	17	14	9	9	4	3	15	.219	.067	.353	7.79	1.56

Fielding

Catcher	PCT	G	PO	A	E	DP	PB
Astudillo	.984	7	56	5	1	1	1
Banuelos	.979	29	225	9	5	3	4
Garver	1.000	5	28	4	0	0	1
Hamilton	1.000	6	45	2	0	0	2
Jeffers	.993	13	141	5	1	0	4
Pena	.982	14	101	9	2	0	1
Rortvedt	.996	29	275	7	1	0	5
Telis	.997	36	321	18	1	3	0

First Base	PCT	G	PO	A	E	DP
Astudillo	1.000	4	29	0	0	1
Blankenhorn	.889	1	7	1	1	1
Hamilton	1.000	2	18	2	0	0
Jeffers	1.000	1	1	0	0	0
Johnson	1.000	24	176	18	0	16
Miranda	.983	14	112	4	2	7
Pena	.988	10	75	4	1	9
Rooker	1.000	1	2	0	0	0
Telis	.989	44	336	26	4	26
Tomscha	.993	35	244	26	2	25
Wiel	.938	2	14	1	1	0

Second Base	PCT	G	PO	A	E	DP
Arraez	1.000	1	2	2	0	1
Blankenhorn	1.000	2	4	6	0	1
Broxton	1.000	1	0	1	0	0
Descalso	.935	9	9	20	2	5
Encarnacion	.971	9	11	22	1	6
Gordon	1.000	1	3	1	0	0
Johnson	.987	16	30	45	1	11
Lin	.923	4	3	9	1	1
Maggi	.972	25	38	65	3	15
Miranda	.944	20	24	44	4	10
Ozoria	.000	2	0	0	0	0
Riddle	1.000	16	20	39	0	8
Stankiewicz	.979	32	44	99	3	15
Telis	1.000	2	3	3	0	0
Yake	1.000	1	1	1	0	1

Third Base	PCT	G	PO	A	E	DP
Astudillo	.944	5	3	14	1	1
Descalso	1.000	15	5	33	0	3
Gordon	.667	1	1	1	1	0
Johnson	.938	15	11	34	3	1

	PCT	G	PO	A	E	DP
Lin	1.000	1	0	2	0	0
Maggi	1.000	14	4	26	0	2
Miranda	.948	39	23	69	5	9
Ozoria	.000	1	0	0	0	0
Riddle	.909	6	1	9	1	1
Stankiewicz	1.000	2	1	1	0	0
Telis	.667	1	0	2	1	0
Tomscha	.982	41	32	80	2	7

Shortstop	PCT	G	PO	A	E	DP
Encarnacion	1.000	1	0	3	0	1
Gordon	.921	11	12	23	3	6
Lin	1.000	2	3	3	0	0
Maggi	.973	50	48	96	4	18
Riddle	.967	61	66	142	7	29
Stankiewicz	.970	11	10	22	1	4

Outfield	PCT	G	PO	A	E	DP
Arraez	1.000	1	1	0	0	0
Boyd	1.000	17	31	1	0	0
Broxton	.993	67	134	2	1	1
Buxton	1.000	6	8	1	0	0

MINNESOTA TWINS

	PCT	G	PO	A	E	DP
Cave	1.000	5	7	2	0	0
Celestino	.961	43	71	2	3	1
Contreras	1.000	87	140	5	0	1
Garlick	1.000	1	1	0	0	0
Gordon	1.000	3	5	0	0	0
Johnson	--	2	0	0	0	0
Kepler	1.000	2	4	0	0	0
Kerrigan	.991	97	210	9	2	6
Kirilloff	1.000	1	1	0	0	0
Larnach	1.000	8	20	0	0	0
Maggi	1.000	5	7	1	0	0
Miranda	1.000	3	5	0	0	0
Refsnyder	1.000	12	15	3	0	1
Riddle	1.000	9	8	1	0	0
Rooker	.987	51	74	1	1	0

WICHITA WIND SURGE

DOUBLE-A

DOUBLE-A CENTRAL

Batting	B-T	HT	WT	DOB	AVG	vLH	vRH	G	AB	R	H	2B	3B	HR	RBI	BB	HBP	SH	SF	SO	SB	CS	SLG	OBP
Banuelos, David	R-R	6-0	205	10-1-96	.185	.182	.186	15	54	7	10	2	0	0	4	3	1	0	1	19	0	0	.222	.237
Bechtold, Andrew	R-R	6-1	185	4-18-96	.239	.275	.223	99	351	55	84	23	0	18	48	45	2	0	2	131	1	1	.459	.328
Berman, Stevie	R-R	6-2	225	11-28-94	.263	.167	.308	6	19	1	5	1	0	1	5	0	0	0	1	7	0	0	.474	.250
2-team total (36 Tulsa)					.179	.156	.186	42	134	11	24	6	0	2	14	19	5	1	1	25	0	0	.269	.302
Boyd, BJ	L-R	5-11	230	7-16-93	.319	.365	.301	66	260	50	83	13	1	15	62	21	3	0	3	49	8	0	.550	.373
Burt, D.J.	R-R	5-9	160	10-13-95	.317	.304	.323	54	180	34	57	11	1	3	20	25	0	1	2	46	19	6	.439	.396
2-team total (11 Amarillo)					.298	.277	.307	65	215	37	64	12	1	3	20	29	0	1	2	58	21	7	.405	.378
Cabbage, Trey	L-R	6-3	204	5-3-97	.262	.194	.286	68	244	40	64	10	1	18	49	31	2	0	1	110	2	0	.533	.349
Cabrera, Leobaldo	R-R	6-1	170	1-21-98	.235	.250	.226	52	170	37	40	7	1	11	33	26	0	1	1	65	5	1	.482	.335
Celestino, Gilberto	R-L	6-0	170	2-13-99	.250	.269	.241	21	84	10	21	5	0	2	7	11	1	0	0	24	0	1	.381	.344
Contreras, Mark	R-R	6-1	195	1-24-95	.269	.188	.294	19	67	10	18	4	1	2	11	9	0	0	2	23	3	0	.448	.355
De La Trinidad, Ernie	L-L	5-9	165	1-3-96	.266	.235	.276	80	289	39	77	12	2	9	39	21	14	0	2	81	4	2	.415	.344
Encarnacion, Yeltsin	L-R	5-11	170	6-28-98	.125	.105	.138	14	48	5	6	1	0	0	7	6	0	0	1	16	2	1	.146	.218
Garland, Nick	R-R	6-0	200	11-3-95	.200	.250	.167	4	10	1	2	0	0	1	1	0	0	0	0	5	0	0	.500	.200
Hamilton, Caleb	R-R	6-0	185	2-5-95	.192	.183	.196	67	203	24	39	8	1	8	28	41	1	0	3	79	4	1	.360	.327
Johnson, Sherman	L-R	5-10	190	7-15-90	.107	.200	.087	11	28	6	3	2	0	0	3	6	2	0	0	7	1	0	.179	.306
Kerrigan, Jimmy	R-R	6-1	215	3-16-94	.125	.200	.000	2	8	0	1	0	1	0	0	0	0	0	0	3	0	0	.375	.125
Martin, Austin	R-R	6-0	185	3-23-99	.254	.297	.237	37	134	24	34	8	0	3	19	23	10	0	1	30	5	1	.381	.399
Miranda, Jose	R-R	6-2	210	6-29-98	.345	.455	.302	47	194	36	67	8	0	13	38	17	5	0	2	25	4	2	.588	.408
Mooney, Peter	R-R	5-6	155	8-19-90	.163	.267	.131	36	129	11	21	0	1	2	12	14	0	0	0	31	1	1	.225	.245
Morales, Roy	R-R	6-2	195	6-25-95	.306	.371	.280	87	333	43	102	14	1	1	33	35	5	0	2	47	5	4	.363	.379
Palacios, Jermaine	R-R	6-0	145	7-19-96	.259	.276	.252	110	410	69	106	17	0	19	54	46	7	1	4	109	18	8	.439	.340
Santiago, Wilbis	L-R	6-0	180	1-20-96	.218	.188	.231	18	55	6	12	3	0	1	6	2	0	0	1	6	0	0	.327	.246
Snyder, Gabe	L-L	6-5	235	3-4-95	.000	.000	.000	4	12	0	0	0	0	0	0	0	0	0	0	6	0	0	.000	.000
Steer, Spencer	R-R	5-11	185	12-7-97	.241	.219	.250	65	249	45	60	11	2	14	42	20	5	0	6	73	4	0	.470	.304
Tomscha, Damek	R-R	6-2	200	8-27-91	.250	.000	.333	5	16	4	4	1	0	0	3	2	1	0	0	6	1	0	.313	.368
Whitefield, Aaron	R-R	6-4	210	9-2-96	.257	.250	.259	111	397	62	102	12	4	6	58	42	3	1	7	112	36	12	.353	.327
Williams, Chris	R-R	6-1	225	11-23-96	.225	.281	.193	28	89	17	20	5	1	3	15	13	1	0	3	33	0	0	.404	.321

Pitching	B-T	HT	WT	DOB	W	L	ERA	G	GS	CG	SV	IP	H	R	ER	HR	BB	SO	AVG	vLH	vRH	K/9	BB/9
Acosta, Melvi	R-R	6-1	215	6-2-95	0	0	0.00	1	0	0	0	3	1	1	0	0	1	2	.100	.200	.000	6.00	3.00
Balazovic, Jordan	R-R	6-5	215	9-17-98	5	4	3.62	20	20	0	0	97	98	48	39	9	38	102	.255	.272	.236	9.46	3.53
Beck, Tyler	R-R	6-1	190	11-16-95	1	2	4.21	5	2	0	0	26	22	13	12	6	14	27	.234	.240	.227	9.47	4.91
Cano, Yennier	R-R	6-4	185	3-9-94	3	1	1.47	12	0	0	1	18	17	7	3	1	5	28	.227	.242	.214	13.75	2.45
Chalmers, Dakota	R-R	6-3	175	10-8-96	0	0	9.49	5	2	0	0	12	10	15	13	5	15	13	.217	.273	.167	9.49	10.95
Cheshire, Jonathan	L-R	6-1	185	11-15-94	0	0	4.50	2	0	0	0	2	4	1	1	0	3	2	.500	.333	.600	9.00	13.50
Faucher, Calvin	R-R	6-1	190	9-22-95	1	1	7.04	19	0	0	1	31	39	29	24	6	24	42	.310	.286	.329	12.33	7.04
Funderburk, Kody	L-L	6-4	230	11-27-96	3	0	1.25	7	0	0	3	22	13	7	3	1	7	23	.169	.176	.163	9.55	2.91
Garcia, Jason	R-R	6-0	185	11-21-92	1	2	5.08	12	5	0	0	28	35	19	16	4	19	31	.310	.345	.276	9.85	6.04
Gilmartin, Sean	L-L	6-2	205	5-8-90	1	0	12.27	3	0	0	0	4	5	5	5	0	4	5	.294	.333	.273	12.27	9.82
Gore, Jordan	B-R	6-0	180	8-3-94	3	1	1.61	20	0	0	6	28	15	5	5	1	11	30	.156	.068	.231	9.64	3.54
Gross, Ben	R-R	6-1	210	10-5-96	0	2	6.75	4	1	0	0	13	20	11	10	1	9	16	.377	.276	.500	10.80	6.08
Hackimer, Tom	R-R	5-11	195	6-28-94	2	0	0.00	4	0	0	0	7	5	0	0	1	1	11	.200	.273	.143	13.50	1.23
Koch, Brandon	R-R	6-1	205	12-25-93	1	0	4.73	9	0	0	1	13	13	9	7	2	6	14	.260	.227	.286	9.45	4.05
Kuzia, Joe	R-R	6-5	190	10-3-93	0	0	9.00	6	0	0	0	5	5	5	5	1	6	6	.263	.444	.100	10.80	9.00
2-team total (3 Frisco)					1	1	18.00	9	0	0	0	7	11	14	14	1	11	6	.367	.600	.133	7.71	14.14
Lau, Adam	R-R	6-2	210	7-5-94	3	0	5.08	22	2	0	1	34	28	19	19	6	15	31	.219	.220	.218	8.29	4.01
Lujan, Hector	R-R	6-3	220	8-23-94	3	2	3.62	18	0	0	0	32	25	13	13	8	9	33	.208	.176	.232	9.19	2.51
Manoah Jr., Erik	R-R	6-2	190	12-22-95	1	1	4.61	11	0	0	1	14	9	7	7	2	8	18	.180	.174	.185	11.85	5.27
Mason, Ryan	R-R	6-6	215	10-4-94	3	2	2.29	25	0	0	6	35	31	14	9	3	18	38	.230	.242	.219	9.68	4.58
Milbrath, Jordan	R-R	6-6	215	8-1-91	0	0	10.00	6	0	0	0	9	8	11	10	0	14	12	.242	.313	.176	12.00	14.00
Mitchell, Josh	R-L	6-2	220	9-8-94	1	1	4.05	4	0	0	1	7	6	5	3	1	1	4	.231	.364	.133	5.40	1.35
Morales, Roy	R-R	6-2	195	6-25-95	0	0	0.00	1	0	0	0	1	0	0	0	0	0	0	.500	.000	1.000	0.00	0.00
Moran, Jovani	L-L	6-1	167	4-24-97	2	1	1.91	20	0	0	2	38	14	8	3	14	64		.112	.154	.082	15.29	3.35
Neff, Zach	L-L	6-1	195	3-14-96	8	3	4.78	31	0	0	3	53	41	30	28	9	19	54	.208	.186	.225	9.23	3.25
Nunn, Chris	R-R	6-2	190	10-5-90	0	0	4.91	5	0	0	1	7	6	4	4	1	7	10	.222	.000	.333	12.27	8.59
Osnowitz, Mitchell	R-R	6-5	245	7-2-91	1	1	5.55	15	0	0	0	24	27	16	15	2	22	26	.297	.267	.326	9.62	8.14
2-team total (8 Amarillo)					1	2	4.68	23	0	0	0	33	32	18	17	4	27	36	.269	.236	.297	9.92	7.44
Phillips, Alex	R-R	6-4	220	12-16-94	2	4	5.44	30	0	0	1	50	51	31	30	9	13	23	.258	.250	.264	9.60	2.36
Rozek, Aaron	L-L	6-2	225	8-20-95	1	0	0.00	1	0	0	0	3	2	0	0	0		2	.200	.000	.286	6.00	0.00
Salinas, Jhonleider	R-R	6-7	215	9-25-95	0	0	7.36	13	0	0	1	18	18	15	15	6	21	15	.261	.179	.317	7.36	10.31
Sammons, Bryan	L-L	6-4	235	4-27-95	3	4	6.44	14	12	0	0	59	51	43	42	13	29	67	.236	.216	.246	10.28	4.45
Sands, Cole	R-R	6-3	215	7-17-97	4	2	2.46	19	18	0	0	80	59	27	22	6	35	96	.203	.243	.167	10.76	3.92
Schulfer, Austin	R-R	6-2	175	12-22-95	6	8	4.34	24	24	0	0	110	109	61	53	7	49	105	.260	.256	.262	8.59	4.01
Sisk, Evan	L-L	6-2	209	4-23-97	1	1	4.87	13	0	0	0	20	22	14	11	2	15	23	.265	.237	.289	10.18	6.64

	B-T	HT	WT	DOB	W	L	ERA	G	GS	CG	SV	IP	H	R	ER	HR	BB	SO	AVG	vLH	vRH	K/9	BB/9
2-team total (16 Springfield)					3	1	4.24	29	0	0	1	40	41	26	19	4	27	51	.255	.288	.232	11.38	6.02
Vallimont, Chris	R-R	6-5	220	3-18-97	5	7	6.03	21	21	0	0	91	91	64	61	15	61	130	.258	.284	.232	12.86	6.03
Whalen, Rob	R-R	6-2	220	1-31-94	0	0	9.00	1	0	0	0	2	2	2	2	1	1	2	.286	.333	.250	9.00	4.50
Winder, Josh	R-R	6-5	210	10-11-96	3	0	1.98	10	10	0	0	55	41	12	12	5	10	65	.208	.172	.236	10.70	1.65
Woods Richardson, Simeon	R-R	6-3	210	9-27-00	1	1	6.75	4	3	0	0	8	6	6	6	0	8	10	.207	.188	.231	11.25	9.00

Fielding

Catcher	PCT	G	PO	A	E	DP	PB
Banuelos	.995	15	172	16	1	0	0
Bechtold	1.000	1	10	1	0	0	0
Berman	.985	6	64	3	1	0	1
Hamilton	.990	39	377	17	4	2	4
Morales	.988	42	397	26	5	3	5
Williams	.991	22	214	16	2	1	2

First Base	PCT	G	PO	A	E	DP
Bechtold	.988	27	155	11	2	15
Cabbage	.973	9	66	6	2	5
Hamilton	.975	22	141	12	4	13
Miranda	1.000	14	98	4	0	8
Morales	.993	43	263	21	2	26
Palacios	.964	5	24	3	1	2
Santiago	1.000	2	3	0	0	0
Snyder	.947	3	18	0	1	0
Tomscha	1.000	2	8	0	0	1
Williams	1.000	4	28	0	0	3

Second Base PCT G PO A E DP

	PCT	G	PO	A	E	DP
Bechtold	1.000	1	2	3	0	1
Burt	.976	43	59	105	4	18
Encarnacion	.929	6	7	19	2	5
Johnson	1.000	2	1	7	0	1
Miranda	1.000	14	19	24	0	9
Mooney	.980	28	41	56	2	12
Palacios	1.000	5	9	9	0	1
Santiago	.947	10	13	23	2	6
Steer	.970	18	24	40	2	6

Third Base	PCT	G	PO	A	E	DP
Bechtold	.962	64	38	87	5	7
Burt	.800	1	0	4	1	1
Johnson	1.000	2	1	1	0	0
Miranda	.927	15	12	26	3	1
Palacios	1.000	5	2	8	0	0
Steer	.962	36	26	49	3	5
Tomscha	1.000	1	2	2	0	1

Shortstop	PCT	G	PO	A	E	DP
Encarnacion	.000	1	0	0	0	0

	PCT	G	PO	A	E	DP
Martin	.887	16	27	20	6	9
Miranda	.875	2	4	3	1	1
Mooney	.500	2	1	0	1	0
Palacios	.962	93	134	195	13	40
Steer	.931	8	11	16	2	5

Outfield	PCT	G	PO	A	E	DP
Boyd	.979	50	92	3	2	2
Burt	1.000	8	12	1	0	0
Cabbage	.983	31	54	4	1	1
Cabrera	.967	51	84	3	3	1
Celestino	1.000	19	39	0	0	0
Contreras	1.000	15	23	2	0	1
De La Trinidad	.962	61	93	8	4	2
Encarnacion	1.000	1	1	0	0	0
Hamilton	.667	4	2	0	1	0
Kerrigan	1.000	2	2	1	0	1
Martin	1.000	20	41	3	0	1
Whitefield	.983	111	219	9	4	0

MINNESOTA TWINS

CEDAR RAPIDS KERNELS

HIGH-A CENTRAL

HIGH CLASS A

Batting	B-T	HT	WT	DOB	AVG	vLH	vRH	G	AB	R	H	2B	3B	HR	RBI	BB	HBP	SH	SF	SO	SB	CS	SLG	OBP
Cabbage, Trey	L-R	6-3	204	5-3-97	.266	.190	.297	40	143	21	38	10	1	9	33	16	1	0	1	50	4	0	.538	.342
Cabrera, Leobaldo	R-R	6-1	170	1-21-98	.194	.375	.143	14	36	8	7	1	0	2	6	13	0	0	0	17	0	0	.389	.408
Camargo, Jair	R-R	5-10	150	7-1-99	.236	.211	.245	71	263	32	62	7	1	13	36	12	4	0	1	106	3	1	.418	.279
Encarnacion, Yeltsin	L-R	5-11	170	6-28-98	.106	.077	.118	16	47	2	5	0	0	0	4	3	0	0	1	18	0	0	.106	.157
Gray, Seth	L-R	6-3	205	5-30-98	.212	.213	.212	113	429	61	91	13	3	11	53	17	0	0	2	142	5	1	.333	.321
Hall, Allante	R-R	6-0	175	4-9-99	.000	--	.000	2	1	0	0	0	0	0	0	1	0	0	0	0	0	0	.000	.000
Helman, Michael	R-R	6-1	195	5-23-96	.246	.236	.250	111	398	71	98	21	4	19	57	51	3	0	1	87	21	5	.462	.336
Isola, Alex	R-R	6-1	215	7-22-98	.243	.198	.257	98	362	47	88	15	0	17	52	53	2	0	1	89	1	0	.425	.342
Javier, Wander	R-R	6-1	165	12-29-98	.225	.253	.216	96	378	48	85	15	10	12	53	25	5	0	3	141	1	3	.413	.280
Julien, Edouard	L-R	6-2	195	4-30-99	.247	.230	.253	65	247	52	61	16	0	15	48	60	2	0	1	90	13	3	.494	.397
Keirsey, DaShawn	L-L	6-2	195	5-13-97	.199	.235	.187	45	141	17	28	4	4	7	24	18	3	0	3	50	10	3	.433	.297
Maciel, Gabriel	B-R	5-10	170	1-10-99	.238	.164	.264	73	235	26	56	7	2	2	21	25	1	1	3	50	17	3	.311	.311
Morales, Jefferson	R-R	5-8	170	5-13-99	.301	.381	.278	25	93	11	28	5	0	5	22	5	2	0	0	20	0	1	.516	.350
Ozoria, Daniel	B-R	5-9	135	8-24-00	.252	.200	.263	49	119	18	30	6	0	1	11	5	1	0	0	37	8	4	.328	.288
Prato, Anthony	R-R	5-10	186	5-11-98	.289	.200	.333	14	45	8	13	3	0	0	1	8	2	0	0	13	0	1	.356	.418
Sabato, Aaron	R-R	6-2	230	6-4-99	.253	.350	.218	22	75	21	19	3	0	8	15	19	1	0	2	32	0	0	.613	.402
Schmidt, Kyle	R-R	6-0	205	7-13-97	.185	.278	.149	22	65	6	12	1	0	0	1	9	2	0	0	24	0	1	.200	.303
Severino, Yunior	B-R	6-1	189	10-3-99	.321	.241	.343	35	134	19	43	12	1	3	17	20	2	0	1	50	1	0	.493	.414
Smith, Max	L-R	6-1	210	3-10-97	.244	.219	.250	54	172	29	42	9	1	6	20	33	1	0	1	74	3	0	.413	.367
Snyder, Gabe	L-L	6-5	235	3-4-95	.230	.161	.253	35	126	26	29	8	2	6	14	24	2	0	0	37	3	0	.468	.362
Steer, Spencer	R-R	5-11	185	12-7-97	.274	.444	.227	45	168	37	46	7	1	10	24	35	4	0	1	32	4	4	.506	.409
Wallner, Matt	L-R	6-5	220	12-12-97	.264	.230	.277	66	258	39	68	14	2	15	47	28	7	0	1	98	0	1	.508	.350
Williams, Chris	R-R	6-1	225	11-23-96	.100	.182	.077	17	50	4	5	3	0	0	2	13	0	0	0	27	1	0	.160	.286

Pitching	B-T	HT	WT	DOB	W	L	ERA	G	GS	CG	SV	IP	H	R	ER	HR	BB	SO	AVG	vLH	vRH	K/9	BB/9
Acosta, Melvi	R-R	6-1	215	6-2-95	3	1	3.86	37	0	0	9	58	54	31	25	2	17	67	.236	.275	.205	10.34	2.62
Beck, Tyler	R-R	6-1	190	11-16-95	2	2	2.47	14	11	0	0	58	42	18	16	2	16	64	.194	.234	.156	9.87	2.47
Bentley, Denny	L-L	6-2	195	5-28-98	1	0	1.93	8	0	0	0	14	18	3	3	0	6	19	.316	.400	.286	12.21	3.86
Cabezas, Andrew	R-R	5-10	175	12-5-96	4	1	3.57	23	8	0	0	71	55	30	28	8	26	82	.209	.198	.219	10.44	3.31
Canterino, Matt	R-R	6-2	222	12-14-97	1	0	0.86	5	5	0	0	21	10	3	2	1	4	43	.135	.135	.135	18.43	1.71
Cheshire, Jonathan	L-R	6-1	185	11-15-94	3	3	4.41	13	0	0	0	16	14	10	8	1	7	14	.226	.227	.225	7.71	3.86
Cruz, Steven	R-R	6-7	225	6-15-99	0	0	8.10	2	0	0	0	3	2	4	3	0	4	4	.182	.000	.286	10.80	8.10
Encarnacion, Yeltsin	L-R	5-11	170	6-28-98	0	0	13.50	2	0	0	0	1	3	2	2	1	0	1	.429	.500	.500	6.75	0.00
Enlow, Blayne	R-R	6-3	170	3-21-99	1	1	1.84	3	3	0	0	15	13	4	3	1	6	23	.250	.238	.258	14.11	3.68
Featherstone, Zach	L-L	6-2	215	12-18-95	3	4	2.13	40	0	0	9	55	28	22	13	4	42	93	.149	.125	.161	15.22	6.87
Funderburk, Kody	L-L	6-4	230	11-27-96	3	3	3.18	11	10	0	1	45	33	19	16	1	21	59	.199	.240	.181	11.71	4.17
German, Osiris	R-R	6-1	170	11-2-98	2	2	4.55	20	0	0	1	28	29	16	14	1	11	41	.257	.170	.318	13.34	3.58
Gipson-Long, Sawyer	R-R	6-4	225	12-12-97	3	3	4.55	6	6	0	0	30	28	16	15	4	9	39	.250	.211	.270	11.83	2.73
Gore, Jordan	B-R	6-0	180	8-3-94	5	1	2.95	19	0	0	1	40	21	13	13	2	17	58	.156	.213	.108	13.16	3.86
Griffith, Owen	R-R	6-1	195	2-6-98	4	3	6.35	19	1	0	0	28	33	22	20	2	13	38	.280	.258	.258	12.07	4.13
Gross, Ben	R-R	6-1	210	10-5-96	5	2	3.62	17	16	0	0	82	79	42	33	9	23	106	.243	.245	.241	11.63	2.52
Koch, Brandon	R-R	6-1	205	12-25-93	0	0	0.00	1	0	0	0	1	0	0	0	1	0	2	.000	.000	.000	18.00	9.00

Name	B-T	HT	WT	DOB	W	L	ERA	G	GS	CG	SV	IP	H	R	ER	HR	BB	SO	AVG	vLH	vRH	K/9	BB/9
Laweryson, Cody	L-R	6-4	205	1-1-99	2	5	4.91	15	14	0	0	59	59	36	32	6	19	73	.255	.202	.292	11.20	2.91
Legumina, Casey	R-R	6-2	195	6-19-97	0	0	5.79	1	1	0	0	5	6	3	3	0	2	7	.300	.000	.333	13.50	3.86
Manoah Jr., Erik	R-R	6-2	190	12-22-95	1	2	1.86	12	0	0	1	19	14	7	4	1	4	27	.200	.128	.290	12.57	1.86
Molina, Derek	L-R	6-3	206	7-27-97	7	1	4.65	32	0	0	1	62	51	37	32	5	26	81	.223	.242	.210	11.76	3.77
Mooney, Sean	R-R	6-1	200	1-11-98	0	1	6.23	3	3	0	0	13	8	9	9	1	6	19	.167	.167	.167	13.15	4.15
Olsen, Jon	R-R	6-2	190	5-13-97	1	4	4.03	16	13	0	0	67	53	30	30	6	31	57	.217	.230	.203	7.66	4.16
Ozoria, Daniel	B-R	5-9	135	8-24-00	0	0	22.50	3	0	0	0	2	3	5	5	0	3	1	.333	.286	.500	4.50	13.50
Palm, Tyler	R-R	6-9	226	12-10-94	3	4	5.05	27	0	0	0	46	43	35	26	4	25	49	.244	.263	.229	9.52	4.86
Rijo, Luis	R-R	6-1	200	9-6-98	0	0	9.95	4	2	0	0	6	10	7	7	0	6	7	.385	.357	.417	9.95	8.53
Rozek, Aaron	L-L	6-2	225	8-20-95	1	1	4.03	5	4	0	0	22	17	11	10	4	5	28	.202	.300	.172	11.28	2.01
Shreve, Ryan	R-R	6-6	215	6-23-98	4	3	3.63	22	1	0	2	35	21	17	14	1	16	49	.167	.185	.153	12.72	4.15
Smith, Max	L-R	6-1	210	3-10-97	0	0	6.75	2	0	0	0	1	2	1	1	0	2	1	.400	.500	.000	6.75	13.50
Snyder, Gabe	L-L	6-5	235	3-4-95	0	0	--	1	0	0	0	0	3	5	5	0	2	0	1.000	1.000	1.000	--	--
Suniaga, Carlos	R-R	6-2	187	5-26-97	0	0	7.88	5	0	0	0	1	8	8	7	7	2	6	3	.267	.111	.333	3.38	6.75
Varland, Louie	L-R	6-1	205	12-9-97	2	2	2.10	10	10	0	0	56	41	14	13	4	14	66	.202	.198	.206	10.67	2.26
Watson, Tyler	R-L	6-6	240	5-22-97	2	4	4.78	23	12	0	1	70	62	43	37	8	35	59	.238	.194	.255	7.62	4.52
Williams, Breckin	R-R	6-0	200	9-5-93	2	0	2.51	12	0	0	0	14	10	5	4	1	5	23	.189	.292	.103	14.44	3.14

Fielding

Catcher	PCT	G	PO	A	E	DP	PB
Camargo	.982	43	445	43	9	0	11
Hall	1.000	1	1	0	0	0	0
Isola	.978	45	470	11	11	2	3
Morales	.964	9	98	9	4	0	1
Schmidt	.989	18	173	4	2	1	2
Williams	.992	11	118	7	1	0	0

First Base	PCT	G	PO	A	E	DP
Cabbage	.980	7	46	4	1	2
Camargo	.989	12	82	4	1	4
Isola	.987	29	216	13	3	10
Julien	.992	17	114	6	1	11
Sabato	.993	20	146	5	1	5
Schmidt	1.000	2	15	0	0	1
Snyder	.982	33	245	24	5	16
Williams	1.000	2	15	0	0	1

Second Base	PCT	G	PO	A	E	DP
Encarnacion	.960	11	17	31	2	6
Helman	.974	16	8	29	1	1
Julien	.960	26	44	51	4	9
Ozoria	.905	18	21	36	6	5
Prato	1.000	5	5	12	0	3
Severino	.913	24	21	42	6	6
Steer	.962	28	37	65	4	14

Third Base	PCT	G	PO	A	E	DP
Gray	.933	104	52	183	17	13
Julien	.875	7	3	11	2	0
Ozoria	1.000	2	0	1	0	0
Severino	.833	4	1	4	1	0
Steer	1.000	5	2	3	0	0

Shortstop	PCT	G	PO	A	E	DP
Encarnacion	.000	1	0	0	0	0

	PCT	G	PO	A	E	DP
Helman	.750	4	2	4	2	0
Javier	.940	86	92	191	18	27
Ozoria	.985	20	22	42	1	5
Prato	1.000	5	8	10	0	0
Steer	.969	7	14	17	1	2

Outfield	PCT	G	PO	A	E	DP
Cabbage	.941	29	30	2	2	0
Cabrera	1.000	15	18	3	0	0
Helman	.989	95	172	14	2	1
Julien	.923	12	11	1	1	0
Keirsey	1.000	43	85	2	0	1
Maciel	.991	72	113	0	1	0
Morales	.909	9	10	0	1	0
Ozoria	.500	2	1	0	1	0
Prato	1.000	4	4	0	0	0
Smith	.980	45	45	3	1	0
Wallner	.918	57	74	4	7	0

FORT MYERS MIGHTY MUSSELS

LOW CLASS A

LOW-A SOUTHEAST

Batting	B-T	HT	WT	DOB	AVG	vLH	vRH	G	AB	R	H	2B	3B	HR	RBI	BB	HBP	SH	SF	SO	SB	CS	SLG	OBP
Anderson, Nick	R-R	5-11	200	3-16-97	.165	.235	.145	33	79	13	13	2	1	0	10	29	4	1	1	29	7	2	.215	.407
Cabrera, Leobaldo	R-R	6-1	170	1-21-98	.077	.000	.091	5	13	1	1	0	0	0	1	0	0	0	0	6	1	0	.154	.143
Cavaco, Keoni	R-R	6-2	195	6-2-01	.233	.273	.224	60	236	27	55	6	2	2	24	18	4	0	2	89	5	2	.301	.296
Encarnacion-Strand, Christian	R-R	6-0	224	12-1-99	.391	.500	.380	22	87	17	34	2	2	4	18	5	0	0	0	26	2	0	.598	.424
Fedko, Kyler	R-R	6-2	210	9-21-99	.235	.188	.250	23	68	11	16	2	0	0	8	11	1	0	1	19	2	0	.265	.346
Feliz, Jesus	R-R	6-0	185	6-7-00	.222	.267	.213	45	171	19	38	6	0	7	19	8	8	0	0	49	3	0	.380	.289
Garland, Nick	R-R	6-1	200	11-3-95	.053	.000	.067	13	19	1	1	0	0	0	2	7	0	0	0	13	1	0	.053	.308
Hall, Allante	R-R	6-0	175	4-9-99	.125	.000	.143	2	8	0	1	0	0	0	0	0	0	0	0	4	0	0	.125	.125
Holland, Will	R-R	5-10	181	4-18-98	.214	.308	.197	76	252	40	54	15	1	10	27	33	13	1	0	99	19	5	.401	.336
Joe Garry Jr., Willie	L-L	6-2	187	5-29-00	.197	.178	.201	95	294	44	58	7	6	4	31	38	5	0	2	112	24	6	.303	.298
Julien, Edouard	L-R	6-2	195	4-30-99	.299	.276	.305	47	147	41	44	12	1	3	24	50	6	0	1	54	21	2	.456	.490
Mack, Charles	L-R	6-0	190	11-12-99	.229	.324	.211	73	231	37	53	7	2	7	30	52	0	0	1	75	2	0	.368	.370
McKinnon, Kole	R-R	6-0	195	7-19-97	.189	.000	.226	14	37	4	7	1	0	0	2	5	0	0	0	15	2	0	.216	.286
Morales, Jeferson	R-R	5-8	170	5-13-99	.237	.271	.229	71	236	43	56	19	0	7	31	42	12	0	2	52	12	2	.407	.377
Ozoria, Daniel	B-R	5-9	135	8-24-00	.125	.000	.143	5	8	1	1	0	0	0	0	0	0	0	0	4	2	0	.125	.125
Perez, Mikey	R-R	6-0	185	8-24-99	.500	.500	.500	9	26	4	13	5	0	0	6	4	0	0	0	4	2	0	.692	.567
Prato, Anthony	R-R	5-10	186	5-11-98	.253	.333	.231	28	83	12	21	3	0	0	7	18	2	0	0	19	6	1	.289	.398
Rucker, Jake	R-R	6-2	195	9-14-99	.265	.250	.267	22	68	10	18	2	1	0	10	10	4	0	3	16	2	1	.324	.376
Sabato, Aaron	R-R	6-2	230	6-4-99	.189	.240	.178	85	286	48	54	15	0	11	42	73	7	0	1	117	1	0	.357	.365
Santana, Ruben	B-R	5-9	160	11-30-97	.208	.222	.204	47	130	15	27	3	0	1	17	17	0	1	3	33	5	1	.254	.293
Schmidt, Kyle	R-R	6-2	205	7-13-97	.302	.444	.265	25	86	17	26	6	1	1	12	17	1	0	0	20	0	0	.430	.423
Severino, Yunior	B-R	6-1	189	10-3-99	.245	.286	.237	63	229	30	56	17	1	5	53	32	5	0	2	75	2	0	.393	.347
Smith, Max	L-R	6-1	210	3-10-97	.107	.000	.125	7	28	4	3	0	0	1	6	1	2	0	1	13	1	0	.214	.188
Snyder, Gabe	L-L	6-5	235	3-4-95	.000	--	.000	1	2	0	0	0	0	0	0	1	0	0	0	0	0	0	.000	.333
Soularie, Alerick	R-R	6-0	175	7-5-99	.219	.278	.207	58	105	21	23	3	1	2	12	19	1	0	0	31	9	1	.324	.344
Urbina, Misael	R-R	6-0	175	4-26-02	.191	.200	.189	101	367	50	70	12	4	5	52	54	7	1	10	82	16	6	.286	.299
Valdez, Wander	R-R	6-2	200	11-22-99	.158	.571	.065	15	38	6	6	0	0	1	5	6	0	0	0	16	0	0	.237	.273
Washington, Justin	R-R	6-4	190	5-6-00	.191	.111	.168	57	164	20	26	5	1	1	15	22	3	0	1	63	22	4	.220	.268
Winkel, Patrick	L-R	6-1	200	1-27-00	.243	.308	.228	21	70	7	17	5	0	1	11	13	1	0	0	22	0	0	.357	.369

Pitching	B-T	HT	WT	DOB	W	L	ERA	G	GS	CG	SV	IP	H	R	ER	HR	BB	SO	AVG	vLH	vRH	K/9	BB/9
Bellair, Cole	R-R	6-1	230	4-8-97	0	0	9.00	1	0	0	0	1	1	2	1	0	3	1	.333	.000	1.000	9.00	27.00
Bentley, Denny	L-L	6-2	195	5-28-98	4	3	3.05	28	1	0	9	44	32	19	15	0	27	68	.200	.234	.186	13.80	5.48

	B-T	HT	WT	DOB	W	L	ERA	G	GS	CG	SV	IP	H	R	ER	HR	BB	SO	AVG	vLH	vRH	SO/9	BB/9
Breek, Donny	R-R	6-2	205	11-8-99	0	0	27.00	4	0	0	0	4	6	11	11	0	12	2	.375	.667	.308	4.91	29.45
Campbell, Logan	R-R	6-2	205	7-22-99	2	0	3.75	7	0	0	0	12	12	9	5	0	5	13	.250	.267	.242	9.75	3.75
Canterino, Matt	R-R	6-2	222	12-14-97	0	0	0.00	1	1	0	0	2	0	0	0	0	0	2	.000	.000	.000	9.00	0.00
Cruz, Steven	R-R	6-7	225	6-15-99	4	2	4.05	26	2	0	1	47	33	31	21	3	30	76	.190	.212	.176	14.66	5.79
Dobnak, Randy	R-R	6-1	230	1-17-95	0	0	0.00	1	1	0	0	3	0	0	0	0	0	5	.000	.000	.000	15.00	0.00
Escobar, Anthony	R-R	5-11	170	8-25-00	1	0	0.00	2	0	0	0	4	3	2	0	0	1	5	.176	.167	.182	11.25	2.25
Festa, David	R-R	6-6	185	3-8-00	0	0	10.80	2	0	0	0	3	2	5	4	0	4	4	.167	.000	.333	10.80	10.80
Garland, Nick	R-R	6-1	200	11-3-95	0	0	0.00	1	0	0	0	0	0	0	0	0	0	0	—	—	—	27.00	0.00
German, Osiris	R-R	6-1	170	11-2-98	0	0	2.27	18	0	0	3	32	18	11	8	2	13	49	.162	.156	.165	13.93	3.69
Gipson-Long, Sawyer	R-R	6-4	225	12-12-97	5	5	4.54	14	13	0	0	67	71	40	34	6	18	95	.257	.308	.218	12.70	2.41
Grace, Regi	L-R	6-2	215	12-10-99	1	0	2.76	8	8	0	0	29	20	9	9	3	11	32	.190	.244	.156	9.82	3.38
Hanner, Bradley	R-R	6-4	210	2-10-99	2	1	7.13	26	1	0	2	42	45	34	33	0	34	49	.278	.317	.253	10.58	7.34
Headrick, Brent	L-L	6-6	235	12-17-97	3	5	3.82	15	14	0	0	61	64	32	26	5	33	86	.264	.224	.280	12.62	4.84
Hicks, Jackson	R-R	6-1	225	2-15-98	0	0	--	1	1	0	0	0	1	1	1	0	1	0	1.000	1.000	--	--	--
Labas, A.J.	R-R	6-3	223	12-8-98	1	2	11.00	6	1	0	1	9	21	11	11	2	2	12	.447	.500	.400	12.00	2.00
Leach, Landon	R-R	6-4	220	7-12-99	1	3	6.91	9	6	0	0	29	25	29	22	1	23	27	.234	.171	.273	8.48	7.22
Legumina, Casey	R-R	6-2	195	6-19-97	4	2	3.02	14	8	0	0	45	31	15	15	4	14	56	.191	.148	.218	11.28	2.82
Manoah Jr., Erik	R-R	6-2	190	12-22-95	0	1	1.00	6	0	0	2	9	4	2	1	0	2	15	.125	.091	.143	15.00	2.00
McKinnon, Kole	R-R	6-0	195	7-19-97	0	0	0.00	1	0	0	0	1	2	0	0	0	1	0	.400	1.000	.250	9.00	0.00
McMahon, Hunter	R-R	6-3	185	4-9-98	1	1	3.00	4	2	0	0	18	16	6	6	0	4	20	.229	.259	.209	10.00	2.00
Milacki, Bobby	R-R	6-2	210	11-6-96	0	2	3.86	11	8	0	0	42	45	23	18	4	7	42	.266	.238	.283	9.00	1.50
Mooney, Sean	R-R	6-1	200	1-11-98	0	1	1.24	10	9	0	0	29	14	8	4	1	17	52	.140	.158	.129	16.14	5.28
Mullenbach, Matt	R-R	6-4	195	10-6-96	1	0	4.70	7	1	0	1	15	23	9	8	0	5	19	.359	.250	.396	11.15	2.93
Ozoria, Daniel	B-R	5-9	135	8-24-00	0	0	0.00	1	0	0	0	3	1	0	0	0	1	6	.111	.500	.000	9.00	3.38
Pichardo, Juan	L-L	6-1	175	6-25-98	3	5	6.45	28	0	0	4	45	43	44	32	3	32	53	.250	.167	.277	10.68	6.45
Pineda, Ramon	R-R	6-3	200	2-3-98	2	1	6.00	5	0	0	0	6	6	5	4	1	4	4	.261	.375	.200	6.00	6.00
Povich, Cade	L-L	6-3	185	4-12-00	0	0	1.13	3	2	0	0	8	6	2	1	0	2	16	.194	.111	.227	18.00	2.25
Puentes, Zaquiel	R-R	6-1	160	12-30-00	2	2	1.25	14	0	0	1	22	21	9	3	1	20	23	.236	.333	.179	9.55	8.31
Rodriguez, Miguel	R-R	6-2	180	2-25-99	3	5	4.50	15	10	0	0	52	54	31	26	4	26	58	.261	.235	.273	10.04	4.50
Rodriguez, Orlando	R-R	6-2	195	12-16-95	1	1	4.15	4	2	0	0	17	21	10	8	2	7	23	.292	.229	.351	11.94	3.63
Rozek, Aaron	L-L	6-2	225	8-20-95	0	1	1.80	8	3	0	0	25	19	6	5	2	0	31	.207	.136	.229	11.16	0.00
Sharpe, Zarion	R-L	6-5	207	9-30-98	1	2	3.62	22	6	0	0	60	62	31	24	1	26	57	.262	.196	.282	8.60	3.92
Shreve, Ryan	R-R	6-6	215	6-23-98	0	1	3.21	6	0	0	1	14	10	6	5	1	7	21	.185	.174	.194	13.50	4.50
Stankiewicz, John	R-R	6-4	230	9-8-98	1	0	2.70	7	4	0	0	23	18	7	7	0	8	24	.212	.275	.156	9.26	3.09
Suniaga, Carlos	R-R	6-2	187	5-26-97	2	3	3.98	18	0	0	0	32	31	19	14	3	8	32	.244	.229	.253	9.09	2.27
Swain, Matthew	R-R	6-7	225	8-20-97	6	2	4.60	35	1	0	5	61	44	35	31	9	31	70	.194	.174	.206	10.38	4.60
Vallimont, Chris	R-R	6-5	220	3-18-97	0	0	0.00	1	1	0	0	3	2	0	0	0	6	6	.182	.167	.200	18.00	0.00
Varland, Louie	L-R	6-1	205	12-9-97	4	2	2.09	10	8	0	0	47	41	14	11	2	16	76	.228	.219	.234	14.45	3.04
Wilson, John	L-L	6-0	195	7-17-97	0	1	19.29	3	0	0	0	2	3	5	5	0	3	2	.300	.000	.375	7.71	11.57

Fielding

Catcher	PCT	G	PO	A	E	DP	PB
Garland	1.000	5	24	3	0	0	0
Mack	.986	56	602	44	9	5	17
McKinnon	1.000	9	81	3	0	0	0
Morales	.962	21	191	13	8	0	5
Schmidt	.987	20	219	16	3	0	5
Winkel	.990	9	89	11	1	0	4

First Base	PCT	G	PO	A	E	DP
Anderson	1.000	2	12	0	0	2
Encarnacion-Strand	.992	17	115	6	1	6
Feliz	.987	10	74	1	1	6
Garland	1.000	3	7	0	0	1
Julien	1.000	4	12	3	0	0
Sabato	.986	77	500	51	8	36
Snyder	1.000	1	6	1	0	0
Valdez	.875	1	7	0	1	2
Winkel	1.000	3	21	1	0	1

Second Base	PCT	G	PO	A	E	DP
Feliz	1.000	2	2	5	0	1
Holland	.952	5	11	9	1	1
Julien	.915	13	18	25	4	5
Ozoria	.000	1	0	0	0	0
Perez	1.000	5	6	9	0	1
Prato	1.000	15	22	20	0	3
Rucker	1.000	5	6	6	0	0
Santana	.958	38	47	68	5	16
Severino	.914	20	20	44	6	9
Soularie	.926	18	27	36	5	3
Valdez	1.000	1	0	2	0	0

Third Base	PCT	G	PO	A	E	DP
Encarnacion-Strand	1.000	4	3	7	0	2
Feliz	.974	25	8	30	1	2
Holland	.828	14	10	14	5	2
Julien	.909	16	7	13	2	2
Ozoria	1.000	2	1	2	0	0
Rucker	.906	16	9	20	3	0
Severino	.882	36	19	48	9	3
Valdez	.733	6	1	10	4	0

Shortstop	PCT	G	PO	A	E	DP
Cavaco	.864	55	49	104	24	11
Feliz	.750	3	2	4	2	0
Holland	.923	45	53	102	13	19
Ozoria	.000	1	0	0	0	0
Perez	1.000	3	1	6	0	0
Prato	.905	7	5	14	2	0
Santana	.952	7	10	10	1	5

Outfield	PCT	G	PO	A	E	DP
Anderson	1.000	25	28	1	0	0
Cabrera	1.000	5	6	0	0	0
Fedko	.969	18	29	2	1	0
Garland	--	1	0	0	0	0
Holland	.962	13	24	1	1	0
Joe Garry Jr.	.925	94	127	8	11	1
Julien	1.000	6	7	0	0	0
Mack	1.000	1	2	0	1	0
Morales	.965	35	53	2	2	0
Prato	.923	6	11	1	1	0
Smith	1.000	6	11	0	0	0
Soularie	.923	9	12	0	1	0
Urbina	.967	93	144	3	5	1
Washington	.962	57	97	3	4	1

FCL TWINS   ROOKIE
FLORIDA COMPLEX LEAGUE

Batting	B-T	HT	WT	DOB	AVG	vLH	vRH	G	AB	R	H	2B	3B	HR	RBI	BB	HBP	SH	SF	SO	SB	CS	SLG	OBP
Aguiar, Carlos	L-L	6-2	175	8-12-03	.216	.071	.241	29	97	11	21	1	1	8	20	9	0	0	1	40	2	1	.495	.280
Angel Vallejo, Miguel	R-R	6-1	190	8-21-01	.143	.333	.111	10	21	3	3	3	0	0	2	3	0	0	0	8	0	0	.286	.250
Baez, Luis	R-R	5-11	170	11-23-00	.298	.389	.273	28	84	14	25	3	3	0	4	8	4	0	0	22	3	3	.405	.385
Cardenas, Noah	R-R	6-1	190	9-10-99	.300	.000	.353	13	20	3	6	1	0	1	4	3	1	0	1	3	0	0	.500	.400
Castro, Wilfri	R-R	5-11	165	3-21-01	.259	.250	.259	29	58	8	15	2	2	3	18	9	2	0	0	20	0	1	.517	.377
Cavaco, Keoni	R-R	6-2	195	6-2-01	.222	--	.222	3	9	2	2	1	0	0	0	0	0	0	0	1	0	0	.333	.300
Cespedes, Rubel	L-R	6-2	180	8-29-00	.157	.267	.143	39	127	13	20	3	2	3	15	13	2	0	1	42	3	1	.283	.245

Name	B-T	HT	WT	DOB	AVG	vLH	vRH	G	AB	R	H	2B	3B	HR	RBI	BB	HBP	SH	SF	SO	SB	CS	OBP	SLG
Duran, Gregory	L-R	6-2	201	10-8-02	.267	.167	.292	13	30	3	8	1	1	0	2	5	1	0	0	13	1	0	.367	.389
Feliz, Jesus	R-R	6-0	185	6-7-00	.364	.000	.381	6	22	7	8	2	0	2	3	1	0	0	0	6	0	0	.727	.391
Garland, Nick	R-R	6-1	200	11-3-95	1.000	--	1.000	1	1	0	1	0	0	0	0	0	0	0	0	0	0	0	1.000	1.000
Gomez, Luis	L-R	5-11	160	10-22-00	.243	.250	.242	30	70	8	17	5	0	0	3	20	2	0	0	21	1	1	.314	.424
Hall, Allante	R-R	6-0	175	4-9-99	.125	.000	.143	6	8	0	1	0	0	0	1	1	0	0	1	2	0	0	.125	.200
Jimenez, Argenis	R-R	5-11	160	4-21-03	.136	.000	.143	28	81	5	11	2	2	1	5	7	1	0	0	28	3	1	.247	.213
Keirsey, DaShawn	L-L	6-2	195	5-13-97	.364	.333	.375	3	11	4	4	0	0	0	0	0	1	0	0	1	1	0	.364	.417
McKinnon, Kole	R-R	6-0	195	7-19-97	.400	--	.400	3	5	0	2	1	0	0	0	2	0	0	0	1	1	0	.600	.571
Miller, Noah	B-R	6-0	185	11-12-02	.238	.545	.192	22	84	11	20	3	1	2	14	9	1	1	1	26	1	1	.369	.316
Nigro, Frank	R-R	6-4	200	8-1-97	.120	.200	.100	16	25	1	3	0	0	0	3	3	1	1	0	12	0	0	.120	.241
Olivar, Ricardo	R-R	5-10	176	8-10-01	.204	.167	.209	34	49	5	10	2	1	1	5	8	2	0	0	17	3	0	.347	.339
Pena, Alexander	R-R	6-2	175	4-12-02	.321	.600	.284	26	84	11	27	6	0	0	10	7	1	0	0	25	3	1	.393	.380
Perez, Mikey	R-R	6-0	185	8-24-99	.750	.000	1.000	1	4	2	3	0	0	1	2	1	0	0	0	1	0	1	1.500	.800
Prato, Anthony	R-R	5-10	186	5-11-98	.222	.000	.235	5	18	4	4	0	0	0	2	3	2	0	0	5	1	0	.222	.391
Ramirez, Breilin	R-R	6-1	170	9-6-02	.056	.000	.071	14	36	4	2	1	0	0	2	1	0	0	0	26	0	0	.083	.227
Roberto, Nelson	R-R	6-2	170	10-27-00	.158	.200	.154	24	57	10	9	1	0	2	5	5	1	0	0	25	2	2	.281	.238
Rodriguez, Emmanuel	L-L	5-10	165	2-28-03	.214	.000	.231	37	126	31	27	5	2	10	23	23	3	0	1	56	9	4	.524	.346
Rodriguez, Endy	L-R	5-9	148	6-10-03	.229	.125	.250	23	48	11	11	2	2	1	4	15	1	0	1	21	1	1	.417	.415
Rosario, Kala'i	R-R	6-1	205	7-2-02	.277	.200	.288	51	188	32	52	10	4	5	40	19	0	0	1	66	4	0	.452	.341
Smith, LaRon	R-R	6-2	200	9-16-00	.171	.500	.141	28	70	10	12	2	1	5	12	13	3	0	0	26	1	1	.443	.326
Snyder, Gabe	L-L	6-5	235	3-4-95	.235	--	.235	6	17	2	4	1	0	0	2	2	0	0	1	5	0	0	.294	.300
Sosa, Malfrin	R-R	6-1	198	9-13-02	.218	.500	.170	18	55	6	12	4	0	2	11	4	1	0	0	22	1	0	.400	.283
Soto, Yonardy	R-L	5-11	180	1-31-03	.228	.000	.241	31	92	9	21	4	0	1	7	15	1	0	0	32	3	1	.304	.343
Soularie, Alerick	R-R	6-0	175	7-5-99	.350	1.000	.316	6	20	3	7	1	0	1	3	4	1	0	0	6	0	0	.550	.480
Tatum, Dillon	R-R	6-1	220	5-24-00	.000	--	.000	5	7	2	0	0	0	0	0	0	0	0	0	4	0	0	.000	.300
Valdez, Wander	R-R	6-2	200	11-22-99	.246	.235	.248	40	122	25	30	8	0	3	11	17	5	0	1	45	4	0	.385	.359
Vasquez, Amilcar	B-R	5-8	170	12-26-01	.167	.500	.000	6	6	3	1	1	0	0	1	2	2	0	0	3	0	0	.333	.500
Wallner, Matt	L-R	6-5	220	12-12-97	.333	--	.333	2	6	2	2	0	0	0	0	0	0	0	0	0	0	0	.333	.333
Wiel, Zander	R-R	6-3	220	1-11-93	.120	1.000	.083	9	25	4	3	2	0	1	4	2	3	0	1	8	0	0	.320	.258
Yake, Ernie	L-R	5-11	165	11-20-97	.238	.200	.250	7	21	4	5	2	0	0	3	5	0	0	0	4	3	0	.333	.385

Pitching	B-T	HT	WT	DOB	W	L	ERA	G	GS	CG	SV	IP	H	R	ER	HR	BB	SO	AVG	vLH	vRH	K/9	BB/9
Adams, Travis	R-R	6-1	197	1-19-00	0	1	20.25	1	1	0	0	1	2	3	3	0	2	3	.333	.000	.400	20.25	13.50
Aria, Develson	L-L	6-0	155	3-20-01	3	2	3.16	13	6	0	0	26	14	10	9	0	23	39	.161	.172	.155	13.68	8.06
Barrington, Malik	R-R	6-2	236	10-8-97	1	1	3.46	5	0	0	2	13	11	5	5	0	4	22	.224	.188	.242	15.23	2.77
Bellair, Cole	R-R	6-1	230	4-8-97	0	2	6.43	10	0	0	1	21	27	24	15	4	7	34	.290	.256	.315	14.57	3.00
Breek, Donny	R-R	6-2	205	11-8-99	0	1	21.60	3	2	0	0	2	0	9	4	0	7	1	.000	--	.000	5.40	37.80
Campbell, Logan	R-R	6-2	205	7-22-99	0	0	2.25	3	0	0	0	4	3	1	1	0	1	3	.214	.125	.333	6.75	2.25
Carr, Jordan	B-L	6-2	210	7-17-97	0	0	3.00	5	0	0	0	9	9	4	3	1	1	11	.243	.100	.296	11.00	1.00
Feliz, Rafael	R-R	6-0	160	11-20-00	0	4	10.32	13	2	0	0	23	35	28	26	4	13	22	.340	.394	.314	8.74	5.16
Festa, David	R-R	6-6	185	3-8-00	1	0	0.00	2	0	0	0	5	1	0	0	0	0	8	.063	.000	.111	14.40	0.00
German, Giovahniey	R-R	6-2	165	10-8-00	2	4	5.59	12	11	0	0	39	33	27	24	3	32	43	.226	.238	.221	10.01	7.45
Gilmartin, Sean	L-L	6-2	205	5-8-90	0	0	16.62	3	1	0	0	4	7	8	8	1	2	8	.455	.667	.421	16.62	4.15
Goree, Zach	L-L	6-0	180	7-9-98	0	0	20.25	2	0	0	1	5	4	3	3	0	4	4	.500	.500	.500	27.00	20.25
Grace, Regi	L-R	6-2	215	12-10-99	0	0	0.00	1	0	0	0	2	0	0	0	0	0	3	.000	.000	.000	13.50	0.00
Headrick, Brent	L-L	6-0	235	12-17-97	0	0	0.00	1	1	0	0	2	1	1	0	0	2	2	.167	.333	.000	10.80	10.80
Hicks, Jackson	R-R	6-1	225	2-15-98	0	2	7.07	5	1	0	0	14	16	15	11	0	2	16	.271	.273	.270	10.29	1.29
Koch, Brandon	R-R	6-1	205	12-25-93	0	0	6.00	2	0	0	0	3	3	2	2	1	0	2	.231	.000	.375	6.00	0.00
Labas, A.J.	R-R	6-3	223	12-8-98	1	0	4.50	1	0	0	0	2	3	1	1	0	0	2	.375	.667	.200	9.00	0.00
Lavallee, Johnathan	R-R	6-4	240	8-11-99	0	0	4.50	1	0	0	0	2	2	1	1	0	0	3	.222	.500	.143	13.50	0.00
Leach, Landon	R-R	6-4	220	7-12-99	0	0	2.57	3	3	0	0	7	8	2	2	0	3	6	.276	.125	.333	7.71	3.86
MacLeod, Christian	R-R	6-3	227	4-12-00	0	0	0.00	1	0	0	0	2	1	0	0	0	2	5	.167	.000	.200	27.00	10.80
McMahon, Hunter	R-R	6-3	185	4-9-98	0	0	0.00	1	1	0	0	2	1	0	0	0	0	4	.143	.333	.000	18.00	0.00
Mendez, Juan	R-R	6-4	240	10-18-98	2	3	3.58	12	5	0	1	28	21	13	11	2	14	37	.196	.119	.246	12.04	4.55
Moreno, Danny	R-R	6-0	180	10-19-96	1	2	7.54	15	0	0	0	23	23	22	19	0	18	21	.256	.241	.262	8.34	7.15
Moreno, Erasmo	R-R	6-1	170	6-22-02	0	2	5.20	12	6	0	0	36	31	23	21	3	21	33	.220	.239	.239	8.17	5.20
Mullenbach, Matt	R-R	6-4	195	10-6-96	1	1	3.44	9	0	0	0	18	20	10	7	0	8	18	.274	.190	.308	8.84	3.93
Nowlin, Jaylen	L-L	6-2	185	1-29-01	0	1	81.00	1	0	0	0	2	4	3	0	2	1	.667	--	.667	27.00	54.00
Ohl, Pierson	R-R	6-1	180	9-19-00	0	0	16.20	1	0	0	0	2	5	3	3	1	0	1	.500	1.000	.286	5.40	0.00
Paredes, Mike	R-R	5-11	185	7-27-00	0	0	2.25	2	1	0	0	4	1	1	1	0	1	6	.077	.000	.111	13.50	2.25
Perez, Elpidio	L-L	6-3	248	11-11-98	0	1	7.77	11	2	0	0	22	25	20	19	4	18	24	.281	.263	.286	9.82	7.36
Perez, Samuel	L-L	5-11	175	11-29-99	4	2	1.45	13	1	0	0	37	29	9	6	1	5	39	.210	.281	.189	9.40	1.21
Petty, Chase	R-R	6-1	190	4-4-03	0	1	5.40	2	1	0	0	5	6	3	3	0	1	6	.300	.000	.333	10.80	1.80
Pineda, Ramon	R-R	6-3	200	2-3-98	0	3	4.35	13	0	0	2	21	22	12	10	2	2	17	.272	.233	.294	7.40	0.87
Povich, Cade	L-L	6-3	185	4-10-00	0	0	0.00	1	1	0	0	1	0	0	0	0	0	3	.143	--	.143	13.50	0.00
Reyes, Wilker	L-L	6-0	170	2-25-02	1	3	5.14	11	6	0	0	42	47	25	24	2	17	37	.292	.294	.291	7.93	3.64
Rimmel, Niklas	R-R	6-3	200	7-5-99	0	0	3.86	3	3	0	0	7	6	4	3	0	1	7	.222	.167	.267	9.00	1.29
Rodriguez, Orlando	R-R	6-2	195	12-16-95	0	1	27.00	1	0	0	0	2	4	4	1	2	0	0	.333	.500	.250	0.00	13.50
Rozek, Aaron	L-L	6-2	225	8-20-95	1	0	0.00	1	0	0	0	8	8	0	0	0	2	13	.182	.000	.190	19.50	3.00
Shreve, Ryan	R-R	6-6	215	6-23-98	1	0	9.00	1	0	0	0	1	2	1	1	0	0	2	.400	.000	.500	27.00	0.00
Stankiewicz, John	R-R	6-4	230	9-8-98	0	0	4.50	1	1	0	0	2	2	1	1	0	1	6	.222	.000	.500	27.00	4.50
Thorpe, Lewis	R-L	6-1	218	11-23-95	0	1	3.18	2	2	0	0	6	5	2	2	0	1	8	.150	.000	.214	11.12	1.59
Velez, Ricardo	R-R	6-1	180	8-21-98	0	5	5.40	5	0	0	0	7	8	6	4	2	5	8	.286	.182	.353	10.80	6.75
Wilson, John	L-L	6-0	195	7-17-97	0	1	3.86	14	0	0	2	23	32	17	10	1	4	16	.327	.435	.293	6.17	1.54

Fielding
C: Cardenas 13, Castro 26, Hall 5, McKinnon 3, Nigro 14, Olivar 33, Smith 5, Tatum 5, Vasquez 6.
1B: Castro 2, Cespedes 7, Duran 11, Garland 1, Hall 1, Nigro 1, Pena 15, Ramirez 1, Smith 16, Snyder 2, Valdez 14, Wiel 6.
2B: Cespedes 17, Gomez 13, Rodriguez 13, Soto 18, Soularie 4, Yake 2.
3B: Cespedes 19, Feliz 2, Gomez 1, Pena 6, Perez 1, Ramirez 7, Smith 2, Soto 1, Valdez 25, Yake 4.
SS: Cavaco 3, Feliz 3, Gomez 17, Miller 22, Prato 4, Rodriguez 10, Soto 10, Yake 1.
OF: Aguiar 22, Angel Vallejo 8, Baez 26, Jimenez 28, Keirsey 3, Pena 1, Roberto 21, Rodriguez 33, Rosario 38, Sosa 15, Wallner 2.

DSL TWINS

ROOKIE

DOMINICAN SUMMER LEAGUE

Batting	B-T	HT	WT	DOB	AVG	vLH	vRH	G	AB	R	H	2B	3B	HR	RBI	BB	HBP	SH	SF	SO	SB	CS	SLG	OBP
Centeno, Andres	R-R	6-1	183	10-23-03	.176	.214	.165	38	119	13	21	4	2	2	15	12	3	0	0	45	2	2	.294	.269
Contreras, Deiner	R-R	6-0	198	4-14-04	.071	.125	.050	11	28	2	2	0	0	0	2	3	4	0	0	13	0	0	.071	.257
Cruz, Rafael	R-R	6-1	166	11-13-03	.218	.257	.208	46	165	19	36	7	1	2	11	12	1	0	1	47	3	0	.309	.274
De Andrade, Danny	R-R	5-11	173	4-10-04	.264	.370	.227	50	178	16	47	13	1	0	16	15	6	0	1	27	6	2	.348	.340
De La Cruz, Jefferson	L-L	6-1	176	11-26-03	.235	.190	.245	36	119	16	28	5	0	1	9	5	8	0	1	36	3	1	.303	.308
Del Valle, Junior	R-R	5-11	173	3-23-04	.179	.083	.205	37	112	14	20	1	3	1	12	10	1	0	1	31	4	1	.268	.250
Gervis, Denyerbe	B-R	5-8	139	9-5-03	.193	.045	.246	32	83	8	16	1	1	0	10	14	1	0	3	28	9	3	.229	.307
Madrigal, Reynaldo	R-R	6-1	174	9-23-03	.172	.200	.165	34	99	15	17	4	1	1	6	10	4	0	0	44	11	1	.263	.274
Marino, Junior	R-R	5-11	165	8-19-04	.290	.154	.321	26	69	10	20	5	1	0	5	8	1	0	0	17	2	0	.391	.372
Marrero, Kevin	R-R	6-0	175	1-24-02	.208	.148	.228	38	106	12	22	3	1	0	6	13	9	0	0	35	8	2	.255	.344
Martinez, Santo	L-R	5-9	152	1-31-04	.207	.231	.200	39	111	14	23	4	1	1	9	20	1	0	1	40	2	1	.288	.331
Michel, Fredy	B-R	5-10	154	7-10-04	.175	.188	.171	43	137	24	24	5	4	0	17	18	10	0	1	62	18	7	.270	.313
Moreno, Javier	R-R	5-10	187	12-29-03	.125	.000	.150	15	48	3	6	1	0	0	1	4	0	0	0	25	0	0	.146	.192
Perez, Ismael	L-L	5-11	175	12-16-03	.220	.129	.250	41	127	11	28	3	3	1	12	14	6	0	0	32	7	3	.315	.327
Rivero, Giovanny	B-R	5-10	173	10-19-03	.213	.389	.158	28	75	11	16	5	0	0	8	10	0	0	1	24	2	0	.280	.302
Rodriguez, Luis	B-R	5-10	169	9-15-03	.145	.238	.125	43	117	16	17	3	1	3	16	18	8	0	0	42	2	0	.265	.301

Pitching	B-T	HT	WT	DOB	W	L	ERA	G	GS	CG	SV	IP	H	R	ER	HR	BB	SO	AVG	vLH	vRH	K/9	BB/9
Andrade, Hector	R-R	6-2	175	7-3-04	1	0	19.13	8	0	0	0	8	15	21	17	0	13	8	.395	.313	.455	9.00	14.63
Boadas, Miguelangel	R-R	6-1	181	12-7-02	0	0	3.63	12	3	0	0	35	26	15	14	0	8	34	.205	.216	.200	8.83	2.08
Bonilla, Julio	R-R	6-3	180	11-15-00	0	2	7.50	14	0	0	0	24	16	25	20	0	16	24	.168	.250	.141	9.00	6.00
Brito, Jose	R-R	6-1	168	9-19-99	0	2	8.31	10	0	0	2	9	5	9	8	1	10	8	.179	.000	.263	8.31	10.38
Chaviel, Edgardo	L-L	6-0	209	2-17-04	0	2	5.17	10	5	0	0	16	12	14	9	2	8	11	.197	.200	.196	6.32	4.60
Cleto, Tomas	R-R	6-2	206	10-9-00	1	3	2.55	12	12	0	0	42	30	19	12	2	16	39	.199	.196	.200	8.29	3.40
Duran, Roger	R-R	6-1	185	8-25-04	1	3	11.03	15	1	0	1	24	38	37	29	1	26	16	.352	.378	.338	6.08	9.89
Gutierrez, Carlos	R-R	6-3	180	1-16-00	2	4	4.05	14	4	0	0	47	30	27	21	0	19	53	.175	.129	.202	10.22	3.66
Huizi, Eiker	R-R	6-0	155	9-24-00	2	0	2.79	12	0	0	0	19	16	8	6	1	8	17	.229	.143	.265	7.91	3.72
Jimenez, Cristian	R-R	6-2	180	5-16-04	0	1	4.30	9	1	0	1	15	18	17	7	1	7	17	.277	.267	.280	10.43	4.30
Landaeta, Yon	R-R	6-1	170	3-16-00	1	3	3.86	12	4	0	1	28	20	16	12	0	25	43	.215	.118	.271	13.82	8.04
Maldonado, Cleiber	L-L	6-0	200	11-20-03	1	1	3.26	10	1	0	0	19	18	11	7	0	7	31	.247	.067	.293	14.43	3.26
Marino, Junior	R-R	5-11	165	8-19-04	0	0	19.64	3	0	0	0	4	9	8	8	0	2	4	.450	.333	.471	9.82	4.91
Marrero, Kevin	R-R	6-0	175	1-24-02	0	0	0.00	3	0	0	0	5	6	3	0	0	1	2	.300	.000	.353	3.86	1.93
Nunez, Juan	R-R	5-11	190	12-7-00	2	4	2.14	11	10	0	0	46	32	17	11	1	15	62	.194	.216	.184	12.04	2.91
Olivares, Jose	R-R	6-1	199	1-18-03	3	2	5.40	10	5	0	0	15	18	11	9	1	10	15	.300	.269	.324	9.00	6.00
Paredes, Oscar	R-R	6-0	176	10-2-03	2	3	5.68	11	0	0	0	25	26	16	16	0	10	22	.265	.355	.224	7.82	3.55
Polanco, Lenny	L-L	6-4	180	1-2-02	0	0	0.00	1	0	0	1	1	0	0	0	0	2	2	.000	.000	18.00	18.00
Rojas, Juan	L-L	6-0	165	1-31-04	0	2	1.80	13	9	0	1	40	25	19	8	0	14	49	.170	.273	.152	11.03	3.15
Soriano, Eduardo	R-R	6-1	190	10-4-02	3	3	4.85	10	1	0	0	13	8	10	7	1	8	11	.178	.214	.161	7.62	5.54
Tovar, Jesus	R-R	6-1	175	12-8-03	2	3	4.43	12	3	0	0	20	12	14	10	0	25	20	.179	.208	.163	8.85	11.07

Fielding
C: Contreras 10, Marino 18, Moreno 13, Rivero 24.
1B: Cruz 22, Marrero 6, Martinez 22, Rodriguez 13.
2B: Gervis 30, Martinez 9, Michel 14, Rodriguez 9.
3B: Cruz 24, De Andrade 13, Gervis 2, Rodriguez 22.
SS: De Andrade 38, Martinez 1, Michel 22, Rodriguez 1.
OF: Centeno 28, De La Cruz 26, Del Valle 32, Madrigal 28, Marino 1, Marrero 27, Martinez 6, Michel 8, Perez 32.

New York Mets

SEASON IN A SENTENCE: A season that began with World Series aspirations heralded by new owner Steve Cohen and blockbuster trade acquisition Francisco Lindor ended with the Mets squarely out of the postseason and in third place in the National League East, 11.5 games behind the division-winning Braves, who won just 88 games.

HIGH POINT: A beat-up Mets team improbably built a lead in the NL East in May and June—17 total games versus the D-backs, Marlins, Orioles and Rockies helped—as the Braves and Phillies stumbled through the first half. New York peaked at 11 games over .500 on June 16 and led the division by as many as 5.5 games on June 26.

LOW POINT: The second half was a complete disaster for the Mets. New York drafted Vanderbilt ace Kumar Rocker 10th overall but failed to sign him after his physical turned up something the club didn't like. On the field, the Mets went 29-45 after the all-star break and made history by becoming the first team to spend so many days in first place (103) and finish with a losing record.

NOTABLE ROOKIE: The 2021 Mets weren't an old team, but they weren't exactly a young team either. Only one rookie made a meaningful contribution, and that rookie entered the season ranked as the organization's No. 28 prospect. Six-foot-seven righthander Tylor Megill showed enhanced velocity and a deeper repertoire at Double-A and Triple-A, where he put up a 3.35 ERA and 1.09 WHIP with 59 strikeouts in 40.1 innings, to earn a June 23 callup. The 26-year-old Megill averaged near 95 mph in the big leagues and missed enough bats to profile as at least a back-end starter.

KEY TRANSACTIONS: Shortstop Francisco Lindor slumped through much of the first half and spent time sidelined with an oblique injury, but his outstanding glove and acquisition cost—Amed Rosario and Andres Gimenez were key pieces sent to Cleveland—made his January acquisition worthwhile. At the trade deadline, the Mets traded 2020 first-rounder Pete Crow-Armstrong, a potentially elite defensive center fielder, to the Cubs for pending free agent Javier Baez.

ON THE FARM: Mets domestic affiliates went 237-282 (.457) to rank 21st among all 30 organizations. A lack of upper-level depth was apparent. Only the Florida Complex League club and Low-A St. Lucie finished with winning records. Triple-A Syracuse, Double-A Binghamton and High-A Brooklyn finished deep in the second division.

OPENING DAY PAYROLL: $167,415,024 (8th).

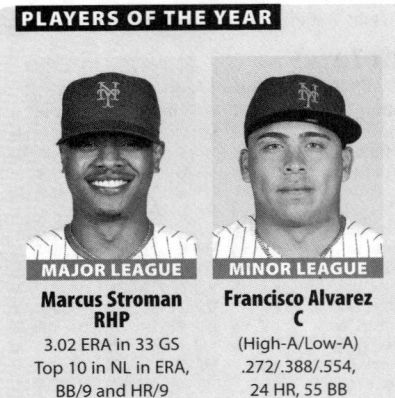

PLAYERS OF THE YEAR

MAJOR LEAGUE	MINOR LEAGUE
Marcus Stroman RHP	**Francisco Alvarez** C
3.02 ERA in 33 GS	(High-A/Low-A)
Top 10 in NL in ERA,	.272/.388/.554,
BB/9 and HR/9	24 HR, 55 BB

ORGANIZATION LEADERS

Batting		*Minimum 250 AB
MAJORS		
*AVG	Brandon Nimmo	.292
*OPS	Pete Alonso	.862
HR	Pete Alonso	37
RBI	Pete Alonso	94
MINORS		
*AVG	Brett Baty, Binghamton, Brooklyn	.292
*OBP	Khalil Lee, Syracuse	.451
*SLG	Mark Vientos, Syracuse, Binghamton	.581
*OPS	Khalil Lee, Syracuse	.951
R	Jaylen Palmer, Brooklyn, St. Lucie	79
H	Ronny Mauricio, Binghamton, Brooklyn	105
TB	Ronny Mauricio, Binghamton, Brooklyn	190
2B	Carlos Cortes, Binghamton	26
3B	Jaylen Palmer, Brooklyn, St. Lucie	6
HR	Mark Vientos, Syracuse, Binghamton	25
RBI	Francisco Alvarez, Brooklyn, St. Lucie	70
BB	Khalil Lee, Syracuse	71
SO	Jaylen Palmer, Brooklyn, St. Lucie	146
SB	Jaylen Palmer, Brooklyn, St. Lucie	30

Pitching		#Minimum 75 IP
MAJORS		
W	Marcus Stroman	10
#ERA	Jacob deGrom	1.08
SO	Marcus Stroman	158
SV	Edwin Diaz	32
MINORS		
W	Jerad Eickhoff, Syracuse	9
W	Adam Oller, Syracuse, Binghamton	9
W	Josh Walker, Syracuse, Binghamton, Brooklyn	9
L	Alec Kisena, Binghamton, Brooklyn	11
#ERA	Adam Oller, Syracuse, Binghamton	3.45
G	Bradley Roney, Syracuse, Binghamton	36
GS	Adam Oller, Syracuse, Binghamton	23
SV	Reyson Santos, Brooklyn, St. Lucie	9
IP	Adam Oller, Syracuse, Binghamton	120
BB	Jesus Reyes, Syracuse	60
SO	Adam Oller, Syracuse, Binghamton	138
#AVG	Josh Walker, Syracuse, Binghamton, Brooklyn	.211

General Manager: Zack Scott. **Farm Director:** Jeremy Barnes. **Scouting Director:** Marc Tramuta.

Class	Team	League	W	L	PCT	Finish	Manager
Majors	New York Mets	National	77	85	.475	9th (15)	Luis Rojas
Triple-A	Syracuse Mets	Triple-A East	50	75	.400	t-16th (20)	Chad Kreuter
Double-A	Binghamton Rumble Ponies	Double-A Northeast	47	60	.439	9th (12)	Lorenzo Bundy
High-A	Brooklyn Cyclones	High-A East	48	70	.407	10th (12)	Ed Blankmeyer
Low-A	St. Lucie Mets	Low-A Southeast	60	55	.522	4th (10)	Reid Brignac
Rookie	DSL Mets2	Dominican Summer	27	29	.482	27th (46)	Yucary De La Cruz
Rookie	DSL Mets1	Dominican Summer	25	33	.431	35th (46)	Manny Martinez
Rookie	FCL Mets	Florida Complex	32	22	.593	6th (18)	C. Newell/R. Robinson
Overall 2021 Minor League Record			289	344	.457	24th (30)	

ORGANIZATION STATISTICS

NEW YORK METS
NATIONAL LEAGUE

Batting	B-T	HT	WT	DOB	AVG	vLH	vRH	G	AB	R	H	2B	3B	HR	RBI	BB	HBP	SH	SF	SO	SB	CS	SLG	OBP
Almora Jr., Albert	R-R	6-2	190	4-16-94	.115	.143	.097	47	52	3	6	3	0	0	0	2	0	0	0	17	0	0	.173	.148
Alonso, Pete	R-R	6-3	245	12-7-94	.262	.237	.273	152	561	81	147	27	3	37	94	60	12	0	4	127	3	0	.519	.344
Baez, Javier	R-R	6-0	190	12-1-92	.299	.278	.310	47	167	32	50	9	0	9	22	13	6	0	0	53	5	2	.515	.371
2-team total (91 Chicago)					.265	.291	.256	138	502	80	133	18	2	31	87	28	13	0	3	184	18	5	.444	.319
Blankenhorn, Travis	L-R	6-2	235	8-3-96	.174	.000	.190	23	23	3	4	2	0	1	4	1	0	0	0	8	0	0	.391	.208
Conforto, Michael	R-L	6-1	215	3-1-93	.232	.205	.243	125	406	52	94	20	0	14	55	59	12	0	2	104	1	0	.384	.344
Davis, J.D.	R-R	6-3	218	4-27-93	.285	.241	.304	73	179	18	51	12	0	5	23	24	6	0	2	68	1	0	.436	.384
Drury, Brandon	R-R	6-2	230	8-21-92	.274	.278	.271	51	84	7	23	5	0	4	14	3	1	0	0	22	0	0	.476	.307
Fargas, Johneshwy	R-R	6-1	180	12-15-94	.286	.286	.286	7	21	1	6	3	1	0	3	0	0	1	0	7	0	0	.524	.286
2-team total (15 Chicago)					.250	.217	.276	22	52	4	13	3	2	0	5	1	0	1	0	15	1	2	.385	.264
Guillorme, Luis	L-R	5-10	190	9-27-94	.265	.265	.265	69	132	13	35	3	0	1	5	23	0	1	0	23	0	2	.311	.374
Hager, Jake	R-R	6-1	170	3-4-93	.125	.000	.250	5	8	1	1	0	0	0	0	0	0	0	0	3	0	0	.125	.125
2-team total (9 Arizona)					.115	.067	.182	14	26	2	3	0	0	0	2	4	0	0	0	14	0	0	.115	.233
Lee, Khalil	L-L	5-10	170	6-26-98	.056	.000	.071	11	18	2	1	1	0	0	1	0	0	0	0	13	0	0	.111	.056
Lindor, Francisco	B-R	5-11	190	11-14-93	.230	.240	.225	125	452	73	104	16	3	20	63	58	5	6	3	96	10	4	.412	.322
Maybin, Cameron	R-R	6-3	215	4-4-87	.036	.000	.045	9	28	2	1	0	0	0	0	3	2	0	0	12	1	0	.036	.182
Mazeika, Patrick	L-R	6-3	210	10-14-93	.190	.200	.185	37	79	6	15	3	0	1	6	4	3	0	1	18	0	0	.266	.253
McCann, James	R-R	6-3	220	6-13-90	.232	.257	.221	121	375	29	87	12	1	10	46	32	2	0	3	115	1	2	.349	.294
McKinney, Billy	L-L	6-1	205	8-23-94	.220	.150	.239	39	91	15	20	6	1	5	14	11	0	0	0	31	1	0	.473	.304
3-team total (37 Los Angeles, 40 Milwaukee)					.192	.220	.184	116	265	32	51	11	3	9	27	32	1	0	2	79	2	0	.358	.280
McNeil, Jeff	L-R	6-1	195	4-8-92	.251	.253	.251	120	386	48	97	19	1	7	35	29	10	0	1	58	3	0	.360	.319
Nido, Tomas	R-R	6-0	211	4-12-94	.222	.200	.230	58	153	16	34	5	1	3	13	5	3	0	0	44	1	0	.327	.261
Nimmo, Brandon	L-R	6-3	206	3-27-93	.292	.306	.286	92	325	51	95	17	3	8	28	54	5	2	0	79	5	4	.437	.401
Peraza, Jose	R-R	6-0	210	4-30-94	.204	.175	.228	64	142	21	29	7	0	6	20	9	3	0	0	26	1	0	.380	.266
Pillar, Kevin	R-R	6-0	200	1-4-89	.231	.240	.225	124	325	40	75	11	2	15	47	11	10	0	1	81	4	3	.415	.277
Sisco, Chance	L-R	6-3	210	2-24-95	.111	.000	.250	5	9	1	1	1	0	0	1	1	0	0	0	3	0	0	.222	.200
Smith, Dominic	L-L	6-0	239	6-15-95	.244	.312	.218	145	446	43	109	20	0	11	58	32	9	0	6	112	2	1	.363	.304
Tovar, Wilfredo	R-R	5-7	180	8-11-91	.182	.000	.200	6	11	0	2	0	0	0	1	0	0	0	0	4	0	0	.182	.250
Villar, Jonathan	B-R	6-0	233	5-2-91	.249	.281	.234	142	454	63	113	18	2	18	42	46	3	2	0	132	14	7	.416	.322
Williams, Mason	L-R	6-1	195	8-21-91	.212	.143	.231	17	33	3	7	1	0	1	1	4	0	0	0	9	0	1	.333	.297

Pitching	B-T	HT	WT	DOB	W	L	ERA	G	GS	CG	SV	IP	H	R	ER	HR	BB	SO	AVG	vLH	vRH	K/9	BB/9
Almora Jr., Albert	R-R	6-2	190	4-16-94	0	0	27.00	1	0	0	0	1	3	3	3	1	1	0	.250	.000	.333	0.00	9.00
Banda, Anthony	L-L	6-2	230	8-10-93	1	0	7.36	5	0	0	0	7	14	8	6	2	1	7	.400	.333	.435	8.59	1.23
2-team total (25 Pittsburgh)					2	2	4.28	30	0	0	0	34	39	18	16	6	13	32	.287	.224	.322	8.55	3.48
Barnes, Jacob	R-R	6-2	231	4-14-90	1	1	6.27	19	0	0	2	19	19	13	13	6	5	18	.260	.226	.286	8.68	2.41
Betances, Dellin	R-R	6-8	265	3-23-88	0	0	9.00	1	0	0	0	1	0	1	1	0	1	1	.000	.000	.000	9.00	9.00
Bostick, Akeem	R-R	6-6	250	5-4-95	0	0	0.00	1	0	0	0	1	0	0	0	0	1	0	.000	.000	.000	0.00	9.00
Carrasco, Carlos	R-R	6-4	224	3-21-87	1	5	6.04	12	12	0	0	54	59	39	36	12	18	50	.272	.245	.296	8.39	3.02
Castro, Miguel	R-R	6-7	205	12-24-94	3	4	3.45	69	2	0	0	70	48	30	27	7	43	77	.189	.198	.180	9.85	5.50
deGrom, Jacob	L-R	6-4	180	6-19-88	7	2	1.08	15	15	1	0	92	40	14	11	6	11	146	.129	.128	.130	14.28	1.08
Diaz, Edwin	R-R	6-3	165	3-22-94	5	6	3.45	63	0	0	32	63	43	27	24	3	23	89	.195	.165	.223	12.78	3.30
Diaz, Yennsy	R-R	6-1	210	11-15-96	0	2	5.40	20	0	0	0	25	25	16	15	5	12	21	.255	.267	.245	7.56	4.32
Drury, Brandon	R-R	6-2	230	8-21-92	0	0	27.00	1	0	0	0	1	3	2	2	1	1	0	.600	.667	.500	0.00	13.50
Eickhoff, Jerad	R-R	6-4	246	7-2-90	0	2	8.69	5	4	0	0	20	30	24	19	9	10	13	.333	.432	.239	5.95	4.58
Familia, Jeurys	R-R	6-3	240	10-10-89	9	4	3.94	65	0	0	1	59	57	31	26	10	27	72	.248	.270	.231	10.92	4.10
Gsellman, Robert	R-R	6-4	200	7-18-93	0	1	3.77	17	1	0	0	29	27	14	12	3	7	17	.248	.261	.238	5.34	2.20
Guillorme, Luis	L-R	5-10	190	9-27-94	0	0	18.00	1	0	0	0	1	3	2	2	0	1	0	.500	.000	.600	0.00	9.00
Hand, Brad	L-L	6-3	224	3-20-90	1	0	2.70	16	0	0	0	13	12	7	4	1	5	14	.250	.250	.250	9.45	3.38
2-team total (41 Washington)					6	5	3.38	57	0	0	21	56	43	29	21	6	23	56	.214	.230	.207	9.00	3.70
Hartlieb, Geoff	R-R	6-5	240	12-9-93	0	0	14.54	3	0	0	0	4	7	7	7	0	6	5	.350	.300	.400	10.38	12.46
2-team total (4 Pittsburgh)					0	0	11.00	7	0	0	0	9	10	11	11	0	11	9	.278	.250	.300	9.00	11.00

NEW YORK METS

Pitcher	B-T	HT	WT	DOB	W	L	ERA	G	GS	CG	SV	IP	H	R	ER	HR	BB	SO	AVG	vLH	vRH	SO/9	BB/9
Hembree, Heath	R-R	6-4	220	1-13-89	0	0	3.45	15	0	0	1	16	13	6	6	2	5	15	.220	.111	.268	8.62	2.87
2-team total (45 Cincinnati)					2	7	5.59	60	0	0	9	58	45	39	36	12	24	83	.207	.253	.181	12.88	3.72
Hildenberger, Trevor	R-R	6-2	205	12-15-90	0	0	15.43	2	0	0	0	2	3	4	4	1	3	4	.300	.000	.333	15.43	11.57
Hill, Rich	L-L	6-5	221	3-11-80	1	4	3.84	13	12	0	0	63	62	29	27	7	19	59	.257	.200	.278	8.38	2.70
Hunter, Tommy	R-R	6-3	250	7-3-86	0	0	0.00	4	1	0	0	8	4	0	0	3	6		.148	.167	.133	6.75	3.38
Loup, Aaron	L-L	5-11	210	12-19-87	6	0	0.95	65	2	0	0	57	37	9	6	1	16	57	.192	.167	.211	9.05	2.54
Lucchesi, Joey	L-L	6-5	225	6-6-93	1	4	4.46	11	8	0	0	38	34	20	19	4	11	41	.245	.276	.236	9.63	2.58
Lugo, Seth	R-R	6-4	225	11-17-89	4	3	3.50	46	0	0	1	46	41	18	18	6	19	55	.237	.237	.237	10.68	3.69
May, Trevor	R-R	6-5	240	9-23-89	7	3	3.59	68	0	0	4	63	55	29	25	10	24	83	.227	.240	.217	11.92	3.45
Megill, Tylor	R-R	6-7	230	7-28-95	4	6	4.52	18	18	1	0	90	88	46	45	19	27	99	.255	.315	.200	9.94	2.71
Nogosek, Stephen	R-R	6-2	205	1-11-95	0	1	6.00	1	0	0	0	3	3	2	2	2	0	5	.250	.143	.400	15.00	0.00
Oswalt, Corey	R-R	6-5	250	9-3-93	1	1	3.48	3	1	0	0	10	12	4	4	1	2	10	.300	.400	.240	8.71	1.74
Peterson, David	L-L	6-6	240	9-3-95	2	6	5.54	15	15	0	0	67	64	44	41	11	29	69	.255	.281	.246	9.32	3.92
Pillar, Kevin	R-R	6-0	200	1-4-89	0	0	0.00	1	0	0	0	0	0	0	0	0	0	0	.000	—	.000	0.00	0.00
Reed, Jake	R-R	6-2	195	9-29-92	0	1	3.86	4	0	0	0	5	5	3	2	0	5	3	.263	.250	.267	9.64	0.00
2-team total (6 Los Angeles)					0	1	3.60	10	1	0	0	10	10	6	4	1	2	10	.250	.143	.273	9.00	1.80
Reid-Foley, Sean	R-R	6-3	230	8-30-95	2	1	5.23	12	0	0	0	21	22	15	12	3	9	26	.265	.243	.283	11.32	3.92
Smith, Drew	R-R	6-2	190	9-24-93	3	1	2.40	31	1	0	0	41	28	13	11	7	16	41	.192	.145	.226	8.93	3.48
Stock, Robert	L-R	6-1	214	11-21-89	0	1	5.40	2	2	0	0	5	6	3	3	2	3	6	.300	.222	.364	10.80	5.40
2-team total (1 Chicago)					0	2	8.00	3	3	0	0	9	10	8	8	3	9	9	.286	.235	.333	9.00	9.00
Stroman, Marcus	R-S	5-7	180	5-1-91	10	13	3.02	33	33	0	0	179	161	70	60	17	44	158	.242	.239	.245	7.94	2.21
Syndergaard, Noah	L-R	6-6	242	8-29-92	0	1	9.00	2	2	0	0	2	3	2	2	1	0	2	.375	.333	.400	9.00	0.00
Szapucki, Thomas	R-L	6-2	181	6-12-96	0	1	14.73	1	0	0	0	4	7	6	6	2	3	4	.412	.500	.400	9.82	7.36
Tarpley, Stephen	R-L	6-0	202	2-17-93	0	0	—	1	0	0	0	0	1	2	2	0	2	0	1.000	1.000	—	—	—
Tropeano, Nick	R-R	6-4	205	8-27-90	0	0	4.50	1	0	0	0	2	4	1	1	1	1	0	.400	.333	.500	0.00	4.50
2-team total (4 San Francisco)					1	0	2.25	5	0	0	0	8	8	3	2	1	3	2	.267	.235	.308	2.25	3.38
Walker, Taijuan	R-R	6-4	235	8-13-92	7	11	4.47	30	29	0	0	159	133	84	79	26	55	146	.225	.192	.250	8.26	3.11
Williams, Trevor	R-R	6-3	235	4-25-92	0	0	3.06	10	3	0	0	32	37	14	11	1	9	29	.289	.235	.350	8.07	2.51
2-team total (13 Chicago)					4	2	4.35	23	15	0	0	91	105	51	44	11	31	90	.287	.272	.302	8.90	3.07
Yamamoto, Jordan	R-R	6-0	185	5-11-96	1	1	4.05	2	1	0	0	7	10	6	3	0	2	3	.345	.300	.368	4.05	2.70

Fielding

Catcher	PCT	G	PO	A	E	DP	PB
Mazeika	.989	24	166	11	2	1	2
McCann	.993	107	877	33	6	2	8
Nido	.989	52	415	23	5	5	2
Sisco	1.000	4	12	1	0	0	

First Base	PCT	G	PO	A	E	DP
Alonso	.993	148	978	98	8	98
Drury	1.000	3	9	0	0	0
Mazeika	1.000	1	5	0	0	0
McCann	1.000	6	37	5	0	4
Smith	.981	15	45	7	1	5

Second Base	PCT	G	PO	A	E	DP
Baez	.968	35	58	64	4	18
Blankenhorn	.778	5	4	3	2	2
Drury	1.000	2	2	2	0	0
Guillorme	1.000	18	20	35	0	11
McNeil	.976	79	96	148	6	36
Peraza	1.000	36	47	59	0	12
Tovar	1.000	4	1	7	0	0
Villar	.964	9	11	16	1	4

Third Base	PCT	G	PO	A	E	DP
Davis	.960	50	36	60	4	6
Drury	.938	7	4	11	1	2
Guillorme	.927	27	9	29	3	2
McNeil	1.000	2	2	0	0	0
Nido	.000	1	0	0	0	0
Peraza	.917	9	2	19	2	1
Villar	.933	97	60	134	14	17

Shortstop	PCT	G	PO	A	E	DP
Baez	.953	12	18	23	2	2
Guillorme	.897	11	9	17	3	2
Lindor	.978	124	160	275	10	58
Peraza	.000	1	0	0	0	0
Villar	1.000	26	28	61	0	13

Outfield	PCT	G	PO	A	E	DP
Almora Jr.	.976	36	40	0	1	0
Blankenhorn	1.000	2	2	0	0	0
Conforto	.975	117	192	7	5	2
Drury	1.000	12	12	0	0	0
Fargas	1.000	7	14	0	0	0
Hager	1.000	3	1	1	0	0
Lee	1.000	11	9	0	0	0
Maybin	1.000	13	13	0	0	0
McKinney	.976	35	41	0	1	0
McNeil	.960	28	47	1	2	0
Nimmo	.995	94	203	2	1	1
Peraza	—	1	0	0	0	0
Pillar	1.000	131	162	5	0	0
Smith	.994	114	159	2	1	0
Williams	1.000	16	25	0	0	0

SYRACUSE METS — TRIPLE-A
TRIPLE-A EAST

Batting	B-T	HT	WT	DOB	AVG	vLH	vRH	G	AB	R	H	2B	3B	HR	RBI	BB	HBP	SH	SF	SO	SB	CS	SLG	OBP
Almora Jr., Albert	R-R	6-2	190	4-16-94	.270	.213	.295	41	152	24	41	6	0	6	18	13	2	0	2	18	2	5	.428	.331
Blankenhorn, Travis	L-R	6-2	235	8-3-96	.255	.158	.285	48	161	22	41	10	0	9	30	29	2	0	1	53	3	2	.484	.373
2-team total (3 St. Paul)					.250	.179	.271	51	172	23	43	11	0	9	31	31	2	0	1	59	3	2	.471	.369
Bohanek, Cody	R-R	6-1	195	7-2-95	.191	.179	.197	34	89	10	17	4	1	1	6	17	6	1	2	32	6	2	.292	.351
Brodey, Quinn	L-L	6-1	195	12-1-95	.189	.143	.208	23	74	12	14	1	1	4	12	11	1	1	2	28	6	1	.392	.295
Calixte, Orlando	R-R	6-0	183	2-3-92	.235	.220	.239	64	196	27	46	10	0	2	24	20	0	1	3	45	13	4	.316	.301
Cervenka, Martin	R-R	6-4	225	8-3-92	.183	.140	.202	72	186	20	34	7	1	7	19	25	1	0	2	54	1	0	.344	.280
Colina, Jose	B-R	6-2	250	3-26-98	.250	—	.250	3	4	1	1	0	0	1	0	3	0	0	1	0	0	0	1.000	.571
Conforto, Michael	L-R	6-1	215	3-1-93	.182	.000	.200	3	11	2	2	1	0	0	0	0	0	0	0	3	0	0	.273	.182
Conti, Nick	R-S	5-9	160	2-14-97	.125	.000	.200	4	8	0	1	0	0	0	0	1	2	0	1	2	0	0	.125	.273
Cuthbert, Cheslor	R-R	6-1	205	11-16-92	.228	.206	.236	76	228	34	52	9	1	14	36	29	5	0	0	54	0	1	.461	.328
2-team total (21 Louisville)					.222	.191	.235	97	302	42	67	13	1	16	47	43	5	0	0	68	1	1	.430	.329
Davis, J.D.	R-R	6-3	218	4-27-93	.316	.333	.300	14	38	8	12	4	0	4	7	10	1	0	0	14	0	0	.737	.469
Drury, Brandon	R-R	6-2	230	8-21-92	.257	.262	.255	56	214	28	55	14	0	9	32	19	1	0	2	49	0	0	.449	.318
Elizalde, Sebastian	L-R	6-0	195	11-20-91	.186	.211	.176	22	70	9	13	2	0	1	6	9	0	0	0	10	6	1	.257	.278
Fargas, Johneshwy	R-R	6-1	180	12-15-94	.242	.250	.240	8	33	8	8	2	0	1	3	4	0	0	0	8	8	3	.394	.324
2-team total (23 Iowa)					.246	.265	.238	31	114	20	28	6	1	3	9	13	0	0	0	34	14	2	.395	.295
Ferguson, Drew	R-R	5-11	188	8-3-92	.186	.190	.182	36	97	11	18	2	0	1	7	18	0	0	0	39	8	2	.237	.313
Grullon, Deivy	R-R	5-11	240	2-17-96	.146	.125	.152	11	41	3	6	2	0	2	8	1	0	0	0	16	0	0	.341	.167

	B-T	HT	WT	DOB	AVG	vLH	vRH	G	AB	R	H	2B	3B	HR	RBI	BB	HBP	SH	SF	SO	SB	CS	OBP	SLG
3-team total (11 Charlotte, 21 Durham)					.196	.205	.192	43	143	21	28	5	0	10	25	14	1	0	1	59	0	0	.441	.270
Guillorme, Luis	L-R	5-10	190	9-27-94	.304	.500	.263	9	23	4	7	0	0	0	1	3	1	0	1	2	0	0	.304	.393
Hager, Jake	R-R	6-1	170	3-4-93	.405	.333	.429	9	37	6	15	2	0	3	9	2	0	0	5	0	0	.703	.436
2-team total (18 Nashville)					.278	.250	.288	27	108	19	30	9	0	5	18	10	0	0	1	20	1	0	.500	.336
Jackson, Drew	R-R	6-2	200	7-28-93	.251	.278	.240	85	243	38	61	11	2	9	37	53	7	4	2	78	24	3	.424	.397
Lagrange, Wagner	R-R	5-11	187	9-6-95	.321	.200	.389	12	28	5	9	2	0	0	5	2	0	0	1	6	0	0	.393	.355
Lee, Khalil	L-L	5-10	170	6-26-98	.274	.316	.259	102	292	67	80	20	2	14	37	71	24	0	1	115	8	10	.500	.451
Loyo, Juan	R-R	5-11	180	3-16-99	1.000	--	1.000	1	1	0	1	0	0	0	0	0	0	0	0	0	0	0	1.000	1.000
Martinez, Jose	R-R	6-6	215	7-25-88	.263	.385	.200	12	38	6	10	2	0	3	6	4	0	0	0	8	0	0	.553	.333
Maxwell, Bruce	L-R	6-1	250	12-20-90	.174	.000	.267	9	23	4	4	1	0	1	6	7	0	0	1	9	0	0	.348	.355
Maybin, Cameron	R-R	6-3	215	4-4-87	.182	.167	.200	12	44	5	8	2	0	0	5	5	0	0	0	14	0	0	.227	.265
2-team total (10 Iowa)					.145	.125	.157	22	83	10	12	3	0	1	8	9	0	0	0	28	1	0	.217	.228
Mazeika, Patrick	L-R	6-3	210	10-14-93	.280	.196	.315	44	157	22	44	9	0	7	33	17	3	0	3	19	0	0	.471	.356
McNeil, Jeff	R-R	6-1	195	4-8-92	.400	.000	.429	4	15	4	6	2	0	1	2	1	0	0	0	4	0	0	.733	.438
Meyer, Nick	R-R	6-1	200	2-18-97	.286	.200	.313	11	42	2	12	3	0	0	6	5	0	1	0	7	1	2	.357	.362
Nido, Tomas	R-R	6-0	211	4-12-94	.364	--	.364	3	11	2	4	0	0	0	2	0	0	0	0	0	0	0	.364	.364
Nimmo, Brandon	R-R	6-3	206	3-27-93	.172	.100	.211	9	29	5	5	1	0	0	0	5	2	0	0	3	0	0	.207	.333
Payton, Mark	L-L	5-8	180	12-7-91	.305	.341	.291	40	151	23	46	12	1	4	19	19	2	0	2	27	2	2	.477	.385
2-team total (35 Louisville)					.293	.326	.278	75	290	42	85	19	3	8	33	30	2	0	3	50	6	3	.462	.360
Peraza, Jose	R-R	6-0	210	4-30-94	.270	.200	.296	10	37	5	10	2	0	0	4	2	0	0	0	2	1	0	.324	.308
Puello, Cesar	R-R	6-2	220	4-1-91	.241	.188	.277	33	79	10	19	4	0	1	10	5	3	0	0	22	3	0	.329	.310
2-team total (15 Worcester)					.214	.196	.225	48	117	16	25	5	0	1	17	13	9	0	2	30	9	1	.282	.333
Reddick, Josh	L-R	6-2	197	2-19-87	.182	.077	.250	11	33	4	6	1	0	1	4	4	1	0	0	13	0	0	.303	.289
Rizzie, Dan	R-R	6-2	200	11-26-93	.000	.000	.000	2	4	1	0	0	0	0	0	1	0	0	0	1	0	0	.000	.200
Rodriguez, David	R-R	6-1	215	2-25-96	.261	.320	.227	23	69	5	18	2	0	2	5	6	0	0	0	17	1	0	.377	.320
Sisco, Chance	L-R	6-3	210	2-24-95	.198	.176	.202	34	106	15	21	6	1	5	14	12	4	0	0	26	0	0	.415	.303
2-team total (12 Norfolk)					.200	.171	.209	46	150	22	30	9	1	6	18	19	5	0	0	43	0	0	.393	.310
Struble, LT	L-R	5-9	182	7-3-96	.500	.500	--	2	2	0	1	0	0	0	0	0	1	0	0	0	0	0	.500	.667
Thompson, David	R-R	6-2	210	8-28-93	.228	.224	.230	67	219	29	50	10	2	13	39	22	11	0	0	68	10	1	.470	.329
Tovar, Wilfredo	R-R	5-7	180	8-11-91	.276	.333	.252	100	355	52	98	16	0	7	51	45	3	0	4	46	13	4	.380	.359
Vientos, Mark	R-R	6-4	185	12-11-99	.278	.273	.280	11	36	9	10	2	0	3	4	7	0	0	0	13	0	1	.583	.395
Villar, Jonathan	B-R	6-0	233	5-2-91	.000	--	.000	2	6	1	0	0	0	0	0	1	0	0	0	6	0	0	.000	.143
Williams, Mason	L-R	6-1	195	8-21-91	.281	.306	.273	70	210	31	59	13	0	5	29	17	2	1	3	51	7	0	.414	.336
Winaker, Matt	L-L	6-1	195	11-29-95	.125	.000	.167	5	8	2	1	1	0	0	0	4	0	0	0	2	0	0	.250	.462

Pitching	B-T	HT	WT	DOB	W	L	ERA	G	GS	CG	SV	IP	H	R	ER	HR	BB	SO	AVG	vLH	vRH	K/9	BB/9
Banda, Anthony	L-L	6-2	230	8-10-93	1	0	5.23	9	0	0	0	10	9	7	6	2	2	10	.225	.313	.167	8.71	1.74
Betances, Dellin	R-R	6-8	265	3-23-88	0	0	20.25	2	0	0	0	1	2	3	3	0	2	2	.400	.500	.333	13.50	13.50
Bostick, Akeem	R-R	6-5	250	5-4-95	1	4	5.08	16	8	0	1	51	52	31	29	9	30	37	.267	.216	.308	6.49	5.26
Campos, Yeizo	R-R	5-11	175	4-29-96	1	1	3.14	12	0	0	0	14	10	5	5	1	5	11	.196	.208	.185	6.91	3.14
Carrasco, Carlos	R-R	6-4	224	3-21-87	0	1	9.64	2	2	0	0	5	5	5	5	3	3	7	.263	.500	.154	13.50	5.79
Cobb, Trey	R-R	6-1	190	6-24-94	1	3	8.70	24	1	0	0	40	59	39	39	13	19	31	.343	.329	.354	6.92	4.24
De La Cruz, Oscar	R-R	6-6	250	3-4-95	1	1	18.90	4	0	0	0	7	15	14	14	0	7	7	.417	.389	.444	9.45	9.45
Diaz, Yennsy	R-R	6-1	210	11-15-96	0	3	6.75	15	0	0	1	17	14	16	13	5	9	19	.209	.273	.147	9.87	4.67
Dillon, Justin	R-R	6-3	225	9-5-93	0	0	0.00	3	0	0	0	4	0	0	0	0	2	7	.000	.000	.000	14.54	4.15
Eickhoff, Jerad	R-R	6-4	246	7-2-90	9	2	4.86	16	16	0	0	80	80	47	43	17	20	79	.261	.252	.267	8.92	2.26
Elizalde, Sebastian	L-R	6-0	195	11-20-91	0	0	0.00	1	0	0	0	1	0	0	0	0	0	0	.000	.000	.000	0.00	0.00
Familia, Jeurys	R-R	6-3	240	10-10-89	0	0	0.00	1	1	0	0	1	0	0	0	0	0	0	.000	.000	.000	0.00	0.00
Godley, Zack	R-R	6-3	250	4-21-90	3	3	4.87	9	7	0	0	44	39	24	24	4	29	33	.253	.306	.188	6.70	5.89
3-team total (6 Columbus, 6 Nashville)					7	7	4.39	21	18	0	0	98	90	52	48	13	52	85	.251	.277	.228	7.78	4.76
Gsellman, Robert	R-R	6-4	200	7-18-93	1	1	5.79	4	0	0	0	5	6	3	3	0	2	5	.300	.400	.200	5.79	3.86
Hackimer, Tom	R-R	5-11	195	6-28-94	0	0	2.45	15	0	0	4	15	6	4	4	2	14	20	.122	.036	.238	12.27	8.59
2-team total (6 St. Paul)					0	0	5.95	21	0	0	5	20	12	13	13	2	29	27	.174	.132	.226	12.36	13.27
Hartlieb, Geoff	R-R	6-5	240	12-9-93	1	1	6.23	10	0	0	0	13	16	10	9	3	9	14	.276	.222	.323	9.69	6.23
3-team total (9 Indianapolis, 4 Worcester)					3	2	3.76	23	0	0	0	26	21	13	11	4	17	29	.206	.146	.259	9.91	5.81
Hejka, Josh	R-R	6-1	175	3-20-97	0	0	10.13	3	0	0	0	3	7	3	3	1	1	1	.467	.556	.333	3.38	3.38
Hildenberger, Trevor	R-R	6-2	205	12-15-90	0	1	6.75	2	0	0	0	3	2	3	2	0	4	6	.182	.333	.000	20.25	13.50
Jackson, Drew	R-R	6-2	200	7-28-93	0	0	18.00	2	0	0	0	3	6	6	6	3	2	0	.462	.250	.556	0.00	6.00
Kilome, Franklyn	R-R	6-6	175	6-25-95	3	3	3.91	21	5	1	1	46	34	20	20	5	29	40	.207	.203	.212	7.83	5.67
Lugo, Seth	R-R	6-4	225	11-17-89	0	0	2.70	3	0	0	0	3	4	3	1	0	4	5	.267	.250	.273	13.50	10.80
Maxwell, Bruce	L-R	6-1	250	12-20-90	0	0	0.00	1	0	0	0	1	0	0	0	0	0	1	.500	.000	1.000	0.00	0.00
McWilliams, Sam	R-R	6-7	230	3-4-95	0	1	10.80	7	0	0	0	8	10	11	10	3	8	10	.294	.438	.167	10.80	8.64
Megill, Tylor	R-R	6-7	230	7-28-95	0	0	3.77	3	3	0	0	14	11	6	6	2	5	19	.204	.200	.207	10.63	3.14
Mitchell, Andrew	L-L	6-2	200	10-23-94	0	0	9.00	5	0	0	0	10	13	10	10	3	6	9	.333	.300	.345	8.10	5.40
Nogosek, Stephen	R-R	6-2	205	1-11-95	1	5	5.14	27	0	0	6	35	35	23	20	2	16	52	.254	.246	.260	13.37	4.11
Oller, Adam	R-R	6-4	225	10-17-94	4	1	2.45	8	8	0	0	44	27	12	12	1	18	43	.179	.203	.153	8.80	3.68
Orze, Eric	R-R	6-4	195	8-21-97	1	0	2.19	10	0	0	0	12	7	3	3	1	7	16	.171	.176	.167	11.68	5.11
Oswalt, Corey	R-R	6-5	250	9-3-93	1	1	4.15	6	2	0	0	13	12	6	6	4	3	15	.240	.304	.185	10.38	2.08
Ramirez, Roel	R-R	6-0	235	5-26-95	0	2	8.31	12	0	0	2	13	18	15	12	3	11	16	.321	.286	.343	11.08	7.62
2-team total (20 Memphis)					0	3	5.57	32	0	0	3	42	44	32	26	5	19	48	.273	.315	.239	10.29	4.07
Reed, Jake	R-R	6-2	195	9-29-92	0	1	4.50	8	0	0	0	8	7	5	4	1	2	8	.233	.375	.071	9.00	2.25
2-team total (1 Durham)					0	1	3.86	9	0	0	0	9	8	5	4	1	2	8	.235	.412	.059	7.71	1.93
Reid-Foley, Sean	R-R	6-3	230	8-30-95	0	2	2.38	10	0	0	0	11	5	3	3	1	6	15	.132	.176	.095	15.09	3.93
Renteria, Marcel	R-R	5-11	185	9-27-94	4	0	9.00	14	0	0	0	19	16	21	19	2	14	28	.211	.314	.122	13.26	6.63
Reyes, Jesus	R-R	6-2	180	2-21-93	4	9	5.34	25	19	0	0	118	128	74	70	18	60	105	.284	.284	.283	8.01	4.58

Name	B-T	HT	WT	DOB	W	L	ERA	G	GS	CG	SV	IP	H	R	ER	HR	BB	SO	AVG	vLH	vRH	SO/9	BB/9
Roney, Bradley	R-R	6-1	193	9-1-92	2	4	6.08	33	0	0	6	40	30	30	27	3	31	56	.205	.152	.250	12.60	6.98
Sanabia, Alex	R-R	6-2	210	9-8-88	0	2	4.76	10	5	0	1	28	38	17	15	6	7	11	.330	.321	.339	3.49	2.22
Schugel, A.J.	R-R	6-0	195	6-27-89	1	1	5.56	16	0	0	0	23	29	15	14	3	13	21	.302	.341	.269	8.34	5.16
Smith, Drew	R-R	6-2	190	9-24-93	0	0	0.00	1	0	0	1	2	2	0	0	0	1	0	.286	.200	.500	0.00	4.50
Stock, Robert	L-R	6-1	214	11-21-89	1	0	2.87	4	4	0	0	16	16	7	5	1	8	14	.271	.185	.344	8.04	4.60
2-team total (9 Iowa)					1	3	3.57	13	6	0	0	35	33	17	14	5	12	39	.244	.213	.270	9.93	3.06
Syndergaard, Noah	L-R	6-6	242	8-29-92	0	0	0.00	2	2	0	0	2	1	0	0	0	2	3	.143	--	.143	9.00	0.00
Szapucki, Thomas	R-L	6-2	181	6-12-96	0	4	4.10	10	9	0	0	42	42	28	19	5	28	41	.263	.293	.252	8.86	6.05
Tarpley, Stephen	R-L	6-0	202	2-17-93	1	2	15.58	9	0	0	0	9	20	17	15	3	6	10	.465	.533	.429	10.38	6.23
Tropeano, Nick	R-R	6-4	205	8-27-90	1	0	1.64	5	1	0	0	11	6	2	2	0	7	10	.167	.167	.167	8.18	5.73
Vizcaino, Arodys	R-R	6-0	245	11-13-90	0	0	2.35	7	0	0	0	8	5	2	2	2	2	14	.185	.267	.083	16.43	2.35
Walker, Josh	L-L	6-6	225	12-1-94	1	3	5.19	9	9	0	0	50	43	31	29	5	18	33	.232	.143	.271	5.90	3.22
Williams, Trevor	R-R	6-3	235	4-25-92	1	0	2.25	2	2	0	0	12	9	3	3	1	2	10	.205	.250	.150	7.50	1.50
2-team total (2 Iowa)					2	0	1.42	4	4	0	0	19	11	4	3	1	3	15	.164	.226	.111	7.11	1.42
Windle, Tom	L-L	6-4	215	3-10-92	1	4	5.48	22	0	0	0	23	14	16	14	2	21	14	.187	.190	.185	5.48	8.22
Worley, Vance	R-R	6-2	240	9-25-87	4	6	5.23	16	15	0	0	86	108	55	50	17	32	39	.303	.302	.305	4.08	3.35
Yamamoto, Jordan	R-R	6-0	185	5-11-96	0	3	5.96	7	6	0	0	23	27	15	15	7	7	20	.293	.385	.226	7.94	2.78
Zamora, Daniel	L-L	6-3	195	4-15-93	0	2	20.25	4	1	0	0	7	10	16	15	3	10	7	.357	.250	.400	9.45	13.50

Fielding

Catcher	PCT	G	PO	A	E	DP	PB
Cervenka	.985	58	378	29	6	3	5
Colina	1.000	2	15	1	0	0	0
Grullon	.966	7	52	5	2	1	0
Maxwell	1.000	5	38	1	0	0	0
Mazeika	.981	22	189	13	4	3	1
Meyer	.974	9	68	6	2	2	1
Nido	.955	3	20	1	1	0	0
Rizzie	1.000	1	7	0	0	1	0
Rodriguez	.991	14	109	5	1	2	1
Sisco	.976	17	117	5	3	1	1

First Base	PCT	G	PO	A	E	DP
Blankenhorn	1.000	5	33	2	0	1
Bohanek	1.000	2	7	0	0	1
Cuthbert	.993	45	252	13	2	38
Davis	.909	3	16	4	2	1
Drury	1.000	17	100	9	0	12
Elizalde	1.000	8	49	1	0	8
Jackson	.857	2	6	0	1	0
Maxwell	.909	2	9	1	1	2
Mazeika	1.000	14	77	3	0	8
Meyer	.929	2	13	0	1	1
Rodriguez	1.000	2	16	2	0	2
Thompson	.994	43	286	22	2	27
Winaker	1.000	2	7	0	0	1

Second Base	PCT	G	PO	A	E	DP
Blankenhorn	.988	29	28	54	1	11
Bohanek	1.000	1	2	3	0	0
Calixte	.964	26	39	42	3	12
Conti	1.000	4	7	6	0	3
Cuthbert	.957	5	10	12	1	2
Drury	1.000	10	13	19	0	4
Guillorme	1.000	3	7	6	0	3
Hager	1.000	4	9	5	0	1
Jackson	.981	32	49	57	2	20
McNeil	1.000	4	6	6	0	3
Peraza	1.000	4	3	13	0	0
Tovar	.983	29	48	67	2	23
Williams	1.000	2	1	1	0	0

Third Base	PCT	G	PO	A	E	DP
Bohanek	1.000	3	3	6	0	0
Calixte	.907	38	23	45	7	6
Cuthbert	.942	24	19	30	3	5
Davis	1.000	10	4	10	0	3
Drury	.959	23	14	33	2	8
Guillorme	.750	3	2	1	1	0
Jackson	.920	10	7	16	2	2
Meyer	1.000	1	1	0	0	0
Peraza	1.000	2	4	5	0	1
Thompson	.918	19	9	36	4	5
Tovar	1.000	4	1	2	0	0
Vientos	1.000	9	4	18	0	0
Villar	1.000	2	0	3	0	0

Shortstop	PCT	G	PO	A	E	DP
Bohanek	.980	28	32	65	2	18
Calixte	1.000	4	2	3	0	0
Guillorme	1.000	3	3	10	0	1
Hager	1.000	4	6	6	0	1
Jackson	.948	27	30	61	5	17
Tovar	.966	72	105	177	10	42

Outfield	PCT	G	PO	A	E	DP
Almora Jr.	.982	40	106	2	2	0
Blankenhorn	1.000	17	28	0	0	0
Brodey	1.000	21	33	4	0	0
Conforto	1.000	3	5	0	0	0
Drury	1.000	3	5	0	0	0
Elizalde	1.000	12	22	0	0	0
Fargas	1.000	8	21	1	0	0
Ferguson	.985	37	62	2	1	0
Hager	1.000	2	1	0	0	0
Jackson	.967	21	26	3	1	0
Lagrange	1.000	6	4	0	0	0
Lee	.979	98	177	7	4	1
Martinez	1.000	10	19	2	0	1
Maybin	.917	8	10	1	1	0
Nimmo	1.000	9	14	0	0	0
Payton	.988	38	80	2	1	2
Peraza	1.000	4	8	0	0	0
Puello	1.000	28	36	2	0	0
Reddick	1.000	9	14	1	0	0
Struble	1.000	2	1	0	0	0
Vientos	1.000	1	1	0	0	0
Williams	.960	60	93	4	4	3
Winaker	--	1	0	0	0	0

BINGHAMTON RUMBLE PONIES

DOUBLE-A

DOUBLE-A NORTHEAST

Batting	B-T	HT	WT	DOB	AVG	vLH	vRH	G	AB	R	H	2B	3B	HR	RBI	BB	HBP	SH	SF	SO	SB	CS	SLG	OBP
Baty, Brett	L-R	6-3	210	11-13-99	.272	.289	.265	40	151	16	41	8	0	5	22	22	1	0	2	45	2	0	.424	.364
Beracierta, Raul	R-R	6-1	215	5-24-99	.200	.000	.286	3	10	0	2	0	0	0	1	0	0	0	0	2	0	0	.200	.273
Brodey, Quinn	L-L	6-1	195	12-1-95	.172	.135	.185	40	145	17	25	6	1	0	9	10	2	0	2	61	8	2	.228	.233
Carpio, Luis	R-R	5-11	190	7-11-97	.249	.264	.243	87	305	38	76	20	0	7	32	33	2	0	1	89	6	5	.384	.326
Conti, Nick	R-R	5-9	160	2-14-97	.250	.222	.267	19	48	6	12	3	0	1	5	8	0	0	0	17	0	0	.375	.357
Cortes, Carlos	L-B	5-7	197	6-30-97	.257	.198	.282	79	304	50	78	26	1	14	57	35	2	0	5	85	1	2	.487	.332
Duplantis, Antoine	L-L	5-11	180	9-5-96	.143	.091	.176	7	28	3	4	1	0	1	2	1	1	0	0	7	1	1	.286	.200
Elizalde, Sebastian	L-R	6-0	195	11-20-91	.286	.300	.280	9	35	2	10	3	0	0	6	0	0	0	1	5	1	0	.371	.390
Fargas, Johneshwy	R-R	6-1	180	12-15-94	.214	.000	.300	5	14	4	3	0	0	0	2	3	1	0	0	4	3	0	.214	.389
Fermin, Edgardo	R-R	6-0	171	5-28-98	.200	.231	.191	18	60	4	12	3	0	1	4	1	0	0	0	22	0	0	.300	.213
Gaddis, Nic	R-R	5-11	171	10-12-96	.000	.000	.000	1	2	0	0	0	0	0	0	1	0	0	0	1	0	0	.000	.333
Lagrange, Wagner	R-R	5-11	187	9-6-95	.262	.239	.270	67	256	23	67	11	1	8	33	14	5	0	3	54	2	3	.406	.309
Lindsay, Desmond	R-R	6-0	200	1-15-97	.155	.105	.179	18	58	8	9	3	0	2	4	8	1	0	0	33	0	0	.310	.269
Mangum, Jake	B-L	6-1	179	3-8-96	.294	.289	.296	75	303	56	89	21	4	7	41	16	8	0	3	58	14	6	.459	.342
Mauricio, Ronny	B-R	6-3	166	4-4-01	.323	.273	.350	8	31	3	10	1	0	1	1	2	0	0	0	11	2	0	.452	.364
Mena, Jose	R-R	6-0	208	12-22-96	.273	.500	.143	3	11	1	3	1	0	0	2	0	0	0	0	5	0	0	.364	.385
Meyer, Nick	R-R	6-1	200	2-18-97	.243	.265	.234	51	177	27	43	4	0	3	12	19	6	4	3	39	5	2	.316	.332
Ortega, Jake	L-R	5-10	175	7-31-96	.200	.000	.250	5	10	2	2	0	0	0	0	2	0	0	0	2	0	0	.200	.333
Rincon, Carlos	R-R	6-3	190	10-14-97	.268	.270	.268	38	149	22	40	8	1	10	29	11	0	0	0	44	3	0	.537	.319
Rizzie, Dan	R-R	6-2	200	11-26-93	.130	.000	.200	8	23	0	3	1	0	0	3	6	0	0	1	9	0	0	.174	.300

Name	B-T	HT	WT	DOB	AVG	vLH	vRH	G	AB	R	H	2B	3B	HR	RBI	BB	HBP	SH	SF	SO	SB	CS	SLG	OBP
Rodriguez, David	R-R	6-1	215	2-25-96	.232	.167	.262	32	95	12	22	5	0	4	10	15	2	0	0	28	0	0	.411	.348
Rodriguez, Manny	R-R	5-10	166	7-4-96	.210	.134	.242	70	224	30	47	9	0	6	26	15	6	2	2	87	2	3	.330	.275
Romero, Yoel	R-R	6-3	196	4-10-98	.253	.292	.238	67	229	26	58	14	0	4	33	21	2	3	2	72	0	0	.367	.319
Senger, Hayden	R-R	6-1	210	4-3-97	.254	.208	.271	50	181	23	46	13	1	3	10	16	7	0	1	62	0	0	.387	.337
Toffey, Will	L-R	6-1	205	12-31-94	.178	.091	.203	34	101	18	18	3	0	6	15	17	4	0	1	47	6	0	.386	.317
Vasquez, Jeremy	L-L	6-1	205	7-17-96	.171	.192	.165	32	105	11	18	4	0	1	11	15	0	0	1	33	0	0	.238	.273
Vientos, Mark	R-R	6-4	185	12-11-99	.281	.200	.314	72	274	43	77	16	0	22	59	26	3	0	3	87	0	1	.580	.346
Winaker, Matt	L-L	6-1	195	11-29-95	.260	.219	.268	59	181	25	47	8	2	2	14	29	9	0	0	47	1	1	.359	.388

Pitching	B-T	HT	WT	DOB	W	L	ERA	G	GS	CG	SV	IP	H	R	ER	HR	BB	SO	AVG	vLH	vRH	K/9	BB/9
Beggs, Dustin	R-R	6-3	180	6-14-93	4	3	4.13	10	8	0	0	48	46	23	22	6	14	28	.254	.313	.222	5.25	2.63
Bostick, Akeem	R-R	6-6	250	5-4-95	0	0	1.29	2	0	0	1	7	4	1	1	0	1	9	.167	.083	.250	11.57	1.29
Butto, Jose	R-R	6-1	202	3-19-98	3	2	3.12	8	8	0	0	40	33	15	14	6	9	50	.219	.180	.238	11.16	2.01
Campos, Yeizo	R-R	5-11	175	4-29-96	1	1	3.89	19	2	0	0	44	44	22	19	6	16	39	.259	.303	.223	7.98	3.27
Cavallaro, Joe	R-R	6-4	190	7-19-95	0	0	0.00	2	0	0	0	4	4	0	0	0	1	4	.143	.333	.000	9.00	2.25
Cobb, Trey	R-R	6-1	190	6-24-94	0	0	4.50	3	0	0	0	4	6	2	2	0	3	3	.353	.429	.300	6.75	6.75
De La Cruz, Oscar	R-R	6-6	250	3-4-95	1	5	7.24	16	13	0	0	60	77	50	48	7	25	60	.316	.394	.267	9.05	3.77
Dibrell, Tony	R-R	6-3	190	11-8-95	2	1	4.45	7	5	0	0	28	25	16	14	6	12	25	.240	.150	.297	7.94	3.81
Dillon, Justin	R-R	6-3	225	9-5-93	0	0	1.35	5	0	0	0	7	5	1	1	0	3	8	.192	.000	.278	10.80	4.05
Edwards, Andrew	L-L	6-2	216	5-12-97	1	0	0.96	6	0	0	0	9	5	2	1	0	4	11	.161	.100	.190	10.61	3.86
Gilliam, Ryley	R-R	5-10	170	8-11-96	2	4	9.88	20	0	0	1	27	31	33	30	4	13	25	.277	.264	.288	8.23	4.28
Goggin, Dan	R-R	6-2	206	6-9-97	0	1	9.87	8	0	0	0	17	28	20	19	4	10	13	.368	.395	.342	6.75	5.19
Gordon, Cole	L-R	6-5	226	10-2-95	4	3	3.69	20	13	1	1	83	49	37	34	12	35	85	.170	.189	.158	9.22	3.80
Grey, Connor	R-R	6-0	180	5-6-94	1	4	4.55	7	5	0	0	32	31	18	16	3	6	37	.263	.220	.286	10.52	1.71
Hackimer, Tom	R-R	5-11	195	6-28-94	0	1	5.14	9	0	0	1	14	10	8	8	1	5	16	.200	.250	.167	10.29	3.21
Hall, Dylan	R-R	6-5	210	9-7-97	0	2	13.50	2	2	0	0	7	14	12	11	2	4	8	.412	.429	.385	9.82	4.91
Hejka, Josh	R-R	6-1	175	3-20-97	0	0	3.72	6	0	0	0	5	5	4	4	0	1	6	.147	.091	.174	5.59	0.93
Holderman, Colin	R-R	6-7	240	10-8-95	0	2	3.26	11	2	0	4	19	13	7	7	2	6	20	.191	.219	.167	9.31	2.79
Kisena, Alec	L-R	6-5	268	10-12-95	0	2	7.50	2	1	0	0	6	9	6	5	1	4	8	.333	.286	.350	12.00	6.00
Lasko, Justin	R-R	6-4	208	3-16-97	1	4	8.14	5	5	0	0	21	34	20	19	2	10	13	.366	.429	.328	5.57	4.29
Loyo, Juan	R-R	5-11	180	3-16-99	0	1	0.00	1	0	0	0	1	1	1	0	0	1	0	.333	.000	.500	0.00	9.00
McIlraith, Thomas	R-R	6-4	220	2-17-94	1	2	6.23	14	0	0	0	22	24	17	15	1	15	30	.273	.342	.220	12.46	6.23
Megill, Tylor	R-R	6-7	230	7-28-95	2	1	3.12	5	5	0	0	26	21	9	9	1	7	42	.221	.182	.275	14.54	2.42
Metoyer, Brian	R-R	6-3	173	11-13-96	0	0	3.00	2	0	0	0	3	2	1	1	0	3	6	.182	.400	.000	18.00	9.00
Miller, Troy	R-R	6-4	210	2-13-97	1	1	5.23	2	2	0	0	10	11	7	6	2	2	11	.289	.467	.174	9.58	1.74
2-team total (4 New Hampshire)					2	3	6.53	6	5	0	0	30	35	23	22	6	9	27	.287	.286	.288	8.01	2.67
Mitchell, Andrew	L-L	6-1	200	10-23-94	3	1	2.15	17	0	0	2	29	23	7	7	1	7	34	.217	.262	.188	10.43	2.15
Montes de Oca, Bryce	R-R	6-7	265	4-23-96	0	0	0.00	2	0	0	0	2	1	0	0	0	1	5	.167	.500	.000	27.00	0.00
Oller, Adam	R-R	6-4	225	10-17-94	5	3	4.03	15	15	0	0	76	66	39	34	8	29	95	.230	.200	.255	11.25	3.43
Orze, Eric	R-R	6-4	195	8-21-97	2	0	2.60	11	0	0	4	17	12	5	5	2	1	25	.190	.211	.182	12.98	0.52
Parra, Franklin	L-L	6-1	202	9-13-99	0	0	3.00	2	0	0	0	3	3	2	1	1	2	2	.250	.000	.429	6.00	6.00
Ragan, Mitch	R-R	6-0	216	4-1-97	2	1	5.54	8	0	0	0	13	12	8	8	1	6	14	.250	.231	.257	9.69	4.15
Rennie, Luc	R-R	6-2	215	4-26-94	1	6	9.54	13	11	0	0	50	72	55	53	14	17	48	.330	.287	.373	8.64	3.06
Renteria, Marcel	R-R	5-11	185	9-27-94	0	0	0.00	3	0	0	0	7	2	0	0	0	3	10	.091	.083	.100	12.86	3.86
Rizzie, Dan	R-R	6-2	200	11-26-93	0	0	0.00	1	0	0	0	1	1	0	0	0	0	0	.250	.250	--	0.00	0.00
Robinson, Jared	R-R	6-0	190	11-20-94	1	4	3.78	29	0	0	5	48	45	25	20	11	20	72	.239	.288	.204	13.59	3.78
Roney, Bradley	R-R	6-1	193	9-1-92	0	0	0.00	3	0	0	0	4	2	0	0	0	1	10	.154	.111	.250	22.50	2.25
Sanabia, Alex	R-R	6-2	210	9-8-88	1	1	3.00	2	2	0	0	9	6	3	3	1	4	6	.188	.250	.150	5.00	4.00
Shaw, Joe	R-R	6-5	225	12-20-93	0	0	0.00	4	0	0	1	5	3	0	0	0	2	4	.167	.000	.333	7.71	3.86
Taveras, Willy	R-R	5-11	163	1-20-98	0	0	0.00	2	0	0	0	3	2	0	0	0	2	2	.182	.000	.222	6.00	6.00
Tewes, Sam	R-R	6-5	200	2-6-95	0	1	3.00	1	1	0	0	3	2	5	1	0	3	3	.167	.333	.111	9.00	9.00
Walker, Josh	L-L	6-6	225	12-1-94	5	1	2.64	8	7	0	0	44	32	17	13	3	7	42	.196	.220	.186	8.53	1.42
Wilson, Tommy	R-R	6-4	220	5-26-96	1	0	2.35	10	0	0	1	15	10	6	4	1	5	18	.182	.261	.125	10.57	2.93
Winans, Allan	R-R	6-2	165	8-10-95	1	1	1.65	14	0	0	3	27	12	5	5	3	8	29	.129	.156	.115	9.55	2.63
Zanghi, Joe	R-R	6-3	240	12-1-94	1	1	8.69	15	0	0	0	20	26	20	19	5	9	26	.317	.432	.222	11.90	4.12

Fielding

Catcher	PCT	G	PO	A	E	DP	PB
Loyo	1.000	1	7	0	0	0	0
Mena	1.000	3	26	2	0	0	0
Meyer	.979	44	389	32	9	2	9
Ortega	1.000	2	11	1	0	0	0
Rizzie	1.000	5	38	4	0	0	0
Rodriguez	.992	11	119	8	1	0	1
Senger	.989	44	402	35	5	4	8

First Base	PCT	G	PO	A	E	DP
Brodey	1.000	8	50	3	0	1
Fermin	.900	1	9	0	1	0
Gaddis	1.000	1	3	0	0	0
Meyer	1.000	2	14	0	0	3
Rizzie	1.000	2	14	1	0	1
Rodriguez	1.000	6	38	2	0	2
Romero	1.000	3	15	4	0	1
Senger	1.000	1	5	0	0	0

	PCT	G	PO	A	E	DP
Toffey	1.000	12	64	7	0	3
Vasquez	.983	26	160	9	3	12
Vientos	.972	11	65	5	2	8
Winaker	.997	42	289	27	1	20

Second Base	PCT	G	PO	A	E	DP
Carpio	.990	55	75	126	2	22
Conti	.932	16	23	32	4	9
Fermin	1.000	8	10	10	0	1
Rodriguez	.800	3	6	2	2	0
Romero	.927	31	49	53	8	5

Third Base	PCT	G	PO	A	E	DP
Baty	.862	24	14	36	8	2
Carpio	1.000	10	1	12	0	0
Conti	.000	1	0	0	0	0
Fermin	.000	1	0	0	0	0
Romero	.961	23	15	34	2	0

	PCT	G	PO	A	E	DP
Toffey	1.000	14	9	18	0	0
Vientos	.868	41	20	46	10	2

Shortstop	PCT	G	PO	A	E	DP
Carpio	.919	24	25	54	7	7
Fermin	.833	7	5	10	3	1
Mauricio	.933	8	8	20	2	3
Rodriguez	.940	64	85	136	14	35
Romero	.941	5	5	11	1	3

Outfield	PCT	G	PO	A	E	DP
Baty	1.000	15	29	1	0	0
Beracierta	1.000	2	4	0	0	0
Brodey	1.000	32	64	4	0	1
Cortes	.993	64	135	6	1	1
Duplantis	1.000	7	16	0	0	0
Elizalde	1.000	8	11	0	0	0
Fargas	1.000	4	7	0	0	0

Fermin	1.000	1	1	0	0	0		Mangum	1.000	70	172	1	0	0		Toffey	1.000	3	4	0	0	0
Lagrange	.973	55	105	2	3	1		Rincon	1.000	28	37	2	0	0		Vientos	1.000	12	24	0	0	0
Lindsay	1.000	7	17	0	0	0		Romero	.900	3	9	0	1	0		Winaker	1.000	13	23	0	0	0

BROOKLYN CYCLONES

HIGH CLASS A

HIGH-A EAST

Batting	B-T	HT	WT	DOB	AVG	vLH	vRH	G	AB	R	H	2B	3B	HR	RBI	BB	HBP	SH	SF	SO	SB	CS	SLG	OBP
Alvarez, Francisco	R-R	5-10	233	11-19-01	.247	.324	.221	84	279	55	69	13	1	22	58	40	8	0	6	82	6	3	.538	.351
Ashford, Zach	L-R	5-10	175	2-9-97	.236	.238	.235	72	225	23	53	10	2	1	21	23	7	1	0	49	5	3	.311	.325
Baty, Brett	L-R	6-3	210	11-13-99	.309	.269	.326	51	181	27	56	14	1	7	34	24	3	0	1	53	4	3	.514	.397
Beracierta, Raul	R-R	6-1	215	5-24-99	.143	.500	.000	4	14	1	2	0	0	0	3	1	0	0	1	4	0	0	.143	.188
Bohanek, Cody	R-R	6-1	195	7-2-95	.195	.143	.215	64	205	35	40	12	1	9	22	32	12	1	2	75	10	3	.395	.335
Campos, Oscar	R-R	5-10	170	12-8-96	.174	.000	.200	8	23	2	4	1	0	1	4	0	0	0	1	6	0	0	.348	.167
Duplantis, Antoine	L-L	5-11	180	9-5-96	.253	.297	.237	98	396	62	100	18	4	5	34	36	2	1	1	87	8	6	.356	.317
Fermin, Edgardo	R-R	6-0	171	5-28-98	.232	.125	.275	16	56	12	13	2	0	2	8	10	0	0	0	18	2	0	.375	.348
Fryman, Branden	R-R	6-2	176	3-16-98	.158	.667	.063	5	19	0	3	1	0	0	1	0	0	0	0	2	0	0	.211	.158
Gaddis, Nic	R-R	5-11	171	10-12-96	.188	.238	.163	22	64	10	12	5	0	4	14	14	3	1	1	20	1	1	.453	.354
Genord, Joe	R-R	6-1	227	8-17-96	.203	.203	.203	59	207	20	42	8	1	7	20	15	3	0	2	64	2	0	.353	.264
Gonzalez, Luis	R-R	6-0	175	7-28-94	.269	.234	.279	60	201	30	54	8	1	6	26	13	0	1	1	52	3	1	.408	.312
Hernandez, Adrian	R-R	5-9	210	2-8-01	.133	.192	.111	30	98	3	13	0	0	1	3	4	0	0	0	42	0	2	.163	.167
Kleszcz, Cole	R-R	6-0	206	6-16-97	.111	.000	.188	8	27	4	3	0	0	0	1	1	0	0	1	14	0	0	.111	.138
Mangum, Jake	B-L	6-1	179	3-8-96	.206	.182	.217	9	34	7	7	1	0	2	6	3	1	0	0	15	0	1	.412	.289
Martinez, Jose	R-R	6-6	215	7-25-88	.182	.167	.200	4	11	1	2	0	0	0	1	3	0	0	0	3	0	0	.182	.357
Mauricio, Ronny	B-R	6-3	166	4-4-01	.242	.274	.231	100	392	55	95	14	5	19	63	24	3	0	1	101	9	7	.449	.290
McNeil, Jeff	L-R	6-1	195	4-8-92	.000	--	.000	1	2	0	0	0	0	0	0	0	0	0	0	0	0	0	.000	.000
Mena, Jose	R-R	6-0	208	12-22-96	.167	.233	.130	28	84	6	14	3	0	1	6	5	0	0	0	23	0	0	.238	.213
Molina, Gerson	R-R	6-3	186	3-13-96	.125	.133	.122	21	56	4	7	2	0	1	2	5	0	0	0	22	1	0	.214	.197
Murphy, Tanner	R-R	6-4	199	5-1-98	.180	.111	.209	23	61	4	11	3	1	0	6	8	1	0	0	26	3	0	.262	.286
Ota, Scott	L-L	5-11	195	8-16-97	.273	--	.273	3	11	1	3	0	0	0	1	2	0	0	0	3	0	0	.273	.385
Palmer, Jaylen	R-R	6-4	208	7-31-00	.189	.200	.186	39	143	28	27	5	2	4	15	25	1	0	0	65	7	1	.336	.314
Peroza, Jose	R-R	6-1	221	6-15-00	.218	.265	.202	38	133	20	29	7	0	5	17	13	2	0	2	44	1	0	.383	.293
Reyes, Wilmer	R-R	6-0	161	12-22-97	.400	.500	.379	9	35	5	14	1	0	2	9	4	0	0	1	7	0	0	.600	.450
Ritter, Luke	R-R	5-11	187	2-15-97	.232	.260	.220	73	250	31	58	9	0	14	44	25	5	0	3	94	3	1	.436	.311
Senger, Hayden	R-R	6-1	210	4-3-97	.302	.182	.344	11	43	16	13	5	1	2	4	3	1	0	0	16	0	0	.605	.362
Struble, LT	L-R	5-9	182	7-3-96	.207	.143	.227	25	58	9	12	1	1	0	5	13	1	2	0	27	2	1	.259	.361
Suozzi, Joe	R-R	6-3	215	2-28-98	.175	.190	.167	23	57	7	10	3	2	1	6	5	2	0	0	27	1	0	.351	.266
Tiberi, Blake	L-R	6-0	205	2-16-95	.182	.214	.175	23	77	9	14	5	0	2	4	13	1	0	0	38	1	0	.325	.308
Titus, Jimmy	R-R	6-1	195	1-25-98	.000	.000	.000	4	9	0	0	0	0	0	0	0	0	0	0	5	0	0	.000	.000
Uriarte, Juan	R-R	6-0	182	9-17-97	.188	.083	.212	20	64	7	12	1	1	0	4	3	3	0	0	20	0	0	.234	.257
Vasquez, Jeremy	L-L	6-1	195	7-17-96	.273	.244	.282	51	165	25	45	15	0	7	30	27	1	1	4	35	1	2	.491	.371
Walters, Anthony	R-R	6-1	185	12-17-97	.161	.158	.162	18	56	5	9	5	0	0	5	8	1	0	0	24	0	0	.250	.277
Winaker, Matt	L-L	6-1	195	11-29-95	.292	.333	.278	7	24	8	7	1	0	0	2	8	1	0	0	5	0	0	.333	.485

Pitching	B-T	HT	WT	DOB	W	L	ERA	G	GS	CG	SV	IP	H	R	ER	HR	BB	SO	AVG	vLH	vRH	K/9	BB/9
Bryant, Garrison	L-R	6-3	202	12-3-98	0	0	18.00	1	1	0	0	3	7	6	6	1	2	2	.438	.500	.417	6.00	6.00
Butto, Jose	R-R	6-1	202	3-19-98	1	4	4.32	12	12	1	0	58	51	31	28	11	15	60	.232	.250	.224	9.26	2.31
Carrasco, Carlos	R-R	6-4	224	3-21-87	0	0	0.00	1	1	0	0	2	1	0	0	0	0	2	.143	.000	.200	9.00	0.00
Cavallaro, Joe	R-R	6-4	190	7-19-95	0	0	4.05	6	0	0	1	7	6	3	3	0	4	9	.250	.300	.214	12.15	5.40
Chacin, Jose	R-R	6-4	192	3-25-97	3	1	3.57	4	4	0	0	23	15	9	9	2	7	24	.183	.077	.232	9.53	2.78
Clenney, Nolan	L-R	6-2	200	6-16-96	0	0	3.68	4	0	0	0	7	7	3	3	0	1	8	.259	.000	.350	9.82	1.23
Edwards, Andrew	L-L	6-2	216	5-12-97	0	3	2.22	18	0	0	1	24	18	6	6	1	15	31	.202	.172	.217	11.47	5.55
Ginn, J.T.	R-R	6-2	200	5-20-99	3	4	3.38	10	10	0	0	53	49	22	20	0	12	46	.240	.291	.208	7.76	2.03
Goggin, Dan	R-R	6-2	206	6-9-97	0	0	0.00	2	0	0	0	3	2	0	0	0	1	5	.182	.250	.143	15.00	3.00
Grey, Connor	R-R	6-0	180	5-6-94	1	1	3.22	4	4	0	0	22	14	11	8	2	10	25	.182	.190	.179	10.07	4.03
Griffin, David	R-R	6-5	205	1-9-00	3	1	4.18	7	7	0	0	32	35	20	15	4	13	30	.267	.273	.263	8.35	3.62
Hall, Dylan	R-R	6-5	210	9-7-97	0	0	1.69	4	0	0	0	5	5	1	1	0	1	6	.238	.375	.154	10.13	1.69
Hejka, Josh	R-R	6-1	175	3-20-97	2	1	3.28	24	0	0	1	49	58	30	18	1	11	40	.296	.262	.311	7.30	2.01
Kisena, Alec	L-R	6-5	268	10-12-95	2	9	4.74	18	16	0	0	80	75	45	42	8	34	102	.246	.235	.251	11.52	3.84
Lasko, Justin	R-R	6-4	208	3-16-97	4	5	2.81	11	11	0	0	64	52	20	20	6	13	64	.226	.156	.271	9.00	1.83
MacDonald, Nick	R-R	6-1	175	6-11-98	0	0	5.06	6	0	0	0	11	13	7	6	1	2	14	.289	.357	.258	11.81	1.69
Metoyer, Brian	R-R	6-3	173	11-13-96	3	2	2.18	21	0	0	1	33	14	10	8	1	16	46	.130	.163	.108	12.55	4.36
Montas, Luis	R-R	6-2	203	9-16-00	0	1	11.57	5	0	0	0	7	11	9	9	0	2	7	.379	.364	.389	9.00	2.57
Montes de Oca, Bryce	R-R	6-7	265	4-23-96	1	3	4.73	26	0	0	6	32	22	20	17	1	27	42	.188	.220	.171	11.69	7.52
Morris, Colby	R-R	6-3	190	5-17-97	2	1	4.11	27	1	0	1	50	43	24	23	4	20	57	.230	.298	.200	10.19	3.58
Opp, Cam	L-R	5-10	185	11-4-95	1	9	7.69	13	12	0	0	50	67	49	43	5	20	51	.306	.273	.314	9.12	3.58
Orze, Eric	R-R	6-4	195	8-21-97	1	2	4.05	13	0	0	1	20	19	10	9	2	6	26	.244	.250	.241	11.70	2.70
Otanez, Michel	R-R	6-4	218	7-3-97	3	1	5.13	35	0	0	1	40	30	24	23	3	41	58	.204	.122	.245	12.94	9.15
O'Neil, Conner	R-R	6-2	195	9-25-94	1	1	7.71	17	0	0	0	26	33	24	22	6	13	26	.308	.308	.309	9.12	4.56
Parsons, Hunter	R-R	6-2	215	6-24-97	2	0	2.61	12	0	0	2	39	29	24	15	2	24	48	.206	.224	.196	10.98	5.49
Ragan, Mitch	R-R	6-0	216	4-1-97	3	2	1.33	18	0	0	2	27	19	12	4	1	11	28	.202	.135	.246	9.33	3.67
Rennie, Luc	R-R	6-2	215	4-26-94	3	0	6.75	7	7	0	0	28	30	21	21	4	15	33	.273	.256	.292	10.61	4.82
Rojas, Jose	R-R	5-11	200	5-5-99	0	4	7.23	6	6	0	0	24	34	23	19	6	13	15	.330	.290	.347	5.70	4.94
Ruibal, Evy	R-R	6-4	232	9-29-95	2	1	4.91	19	0	0	2	22	20	14	12	3	18	26	.241	.188	.275	10.64	7.36
Santos, Reyson	R-R	6-0	218	1-22-99	1	0	10.80	3	0	0	0	3	4	4	4	0	3	4	.286	.333	.273	10.80	8.10

	B-T	HT	WT	DOB															AVG	OBP	SLG	ERA	
Syndergaard, Noah	L-R	6-6	242	8-29-92	0	0	9.00	1	1	0	0	1	1	1	1	1	0	1	.250	.000	.500	9.00	0.00
Taveras, Willy	R-R	5-11	163	1-20-98	2	0	1.77	12	0	0	3	20	14	4	4	1	4	24	.189	.167	.205	10.62	1.77
Vilera, Jaison	R-R	6-0	188	6-19-97	3	8	7.24	20	20	0	0	87	107	77	70	22	29	72	.294	.252	.319	7.45	3.00
Walker, Josh	L-L	6-6	225	12-1-94	3	0	2.57	4	4	0	0	21	14	6	6	1	4	23	.189	.111	.214	9.86	1.71
Winans, Allan	R-R	6-2	165	8-10-95	1	2	1.83	12	0	0	0	20	11	5	4	0	7	16	.167	.150	.174	7.32	3.20

Fielding

Catcher	PCT	G	PO	A	E	DP	PB
Alvarez	.983	49	428	28	8	4	13
Campos	1.000	8	75	5	0	0	0
Gaddis	1.000	12	105	5	0	0	2
Mena	.983	26	217	13	4	0	4
Senger	.991	9	98	7	1	0	0
Uriarte	.988	20	152	15	2	0	1

First Base	PCT	G	PO	A	E	DP
Bohanek	.980	12	95	5	2	11
Genord	.992	51	367	25	3	35
Martinez	1.000	1	3	0	0	0
Reyes	.980	8	48	2	1	3
Ritter	.990	13	98	1	1	8
Suozzi	.000	1	0	0	0	0
Vasquez	.992	35	250	7	2	21
Winaker	1.000	2	18	0	0	2

Second Base	PCT	G	PO	A	E	DP
Bohanek	1.000	3	8	6	0	2
Fermin	1.000	4	6	9	0	1
Gonzalez	.988	42	72	90	2	19
McNeil	1.000	1	1	1	0	0

	PCT	G	PO	A	E	DP
Peroza	1.000	4	2	11	0	4
Reyes	1.000	1	1	2	0	1
Ritter	.986	55	89	118	3	29
Struble	.857	2	1	5	1	1
Tiberi	.778	1	2	5	2	1
Titus	1.000	2	1	0	0	0
Walters	.946	11	13	22	2	9

Third Base	PCT	G	PO	A	E	DP
Baty	.941	41	23	89	7	8
Bohanek	.938	23	20	41	4	5
Fermin	.958	7	7	16	1	2
Gaddis	1.000	2	0	2	0	0
Gonzalez	.833	6	3	7	2	2
Palmer	1.000	4	0	3	0	0
Peroza	.875	32	16	40	8	5
Tiberi	.875	7	8	13	3	0

Shortstop	PCT	G	PO	A	E	DP
Bohanek	.907	10	15	24	4	2
Fermin	1.000	3	2	3	0	0
Fryman	1.000	5	4	17	0	2
Gonzalez	.971	9	10	23	1	5

	PCT	G	PO	A	E	DP
Mauricio	.944	87	103	237	20	42
Reyes	.857	1	0	6	1	1
Walters	.857	4	4	8	2	1

Outfield	PCT	G	PO	A	E	DP
Ashford	.976	69	76	4	2	1
Baty	.800	3	4	0	1	0
Beracierta	1.000	4	10	0	0	0
Bohanek	1.000	13	21	1	0	0
Duplantis	.994	100	173	6	1	2
Hernandez	.957	27	44	0	2	0
Kleszcz	1.000	8	5	0	0	0
Mangum	.923	8	12	0	1	0
Martinez	1.000	3	5	0	0	0
Molina	1.000	21	32	1	0	0
Murphy	1.000	23	43	1	0	0
Ota	1.000	3	3	0	0	0
Palmer	1.000	37	68	0	0	0
Struble	1.000	18	24	0	0	0
Suozzi	.970	18	31	1	1	0
Tiberi	1.000	12	20	0	0	0
Vasquez	.900	8	9	0	1	0
Winaker	1.000	6	3	1	0	0

ST. LUCIE METS
LOW-A SOUTHEAST

LOW CLASS A

Batting	B-T	HT	WT	DOB	AVG	vLH	vRH	G	AB	R	H	2B	3B	HR	RBI	BB	HBP	SH	SF	SO	SB	CS	SLG	OBP
Adon, Ranfy	R-R	6-3	195	8-2-97	.193	.000	.225	26	83	14	16	2	0	1	9	16	3	1	1	33	12	5	.253	.340
Alvarez, Francisco	R-R	5-10	233	11-19-01	.417	.500	.409	15	48	12	20	5	0	2	12	15	3	0	1	7	2	2	.646	.567
Ashford, Zach	L-R	5-10	175	2-9-97	.340	.571	.302	14	50	6	17	3	0	0	6	5	5	0	0	12	1	0	.400	.459
Berbesi, Cesar	L-R	6-0	160	4-13-00	.170	.222	.158	18	47	8	8	3	1	0	4	17	0	0	0	23	2	2	.277	.391
Brodey, Quinn	L-L	6-1	195	12-1-95	.158	--	.158	6	19	3	3	1	0	1	1	3	1	0	0	5	0	0	.368	.304
Colina, Jose	B-R	6-2	250	3-26-98	.198	.167	.204	38	111	18	22	5	1	2	15	20	3	0	1	45	1	0	.315	.333
Conti, Nick	R-R	5-9	160	2-14-97	.000	--	.000	4	9	1	0	0	0	0	0	3	0	0	0	3	0	0	.000	.250
Crow-Armstrong, Pete	L-L	6-0	184	3-25-02	.417	.333	.429	6	24	6	10	2	0	0	4	7	1	0	0	6	2	3	.500	.563
De Los Santos, Omar	R-R	6-1	172	8-8-99	.241	.100	.252	38	133	14	32	8	2	0	17	7	3	0	1	50	12	1	.331	.292
Dyer, Matt	R-R	6-4	185	7-14-98	.194	.241	.179	36	124	20	24	7	2	7	20	23	3	0	2	47	6	1	.452	.329
Fargas, Johneshwy	R-R	6-1	180	12-15-94	.231	.333	.200	4	13	3	3	0	0	3	6	1	1	0	0	4	0	0	.923	.333
Fermin, Edgardo	R-R	6-0	171	5-28-98	.222	.400	.154	5	18	4	4	0	0	1	2	5	1	0	0	8	1	0	.389	.417
Fryman, Brandon	R-R	6-2	176	3-16-98	.229	.289	.218	69	249	34	57	11	0	3	26	21	4	0	2	47	14	4	.309	.297
Gaddis, Nic	R-R	5-11	171	10-12-96	.250	.111	.268	25	80	17	20	4	1	3	18	22	3	0	2	22	1	0	.438	.421
Gonzalez, Luis	R-R	6-0	175	7-28-94	.250	.250	.250	3	12	1	3	1	0	0	2	0	0	0	0	3	0	0	.333	.250
Guerrera, Justin	R-R	5-9	185	1-11-00	.212	.267	.196	19	66	12	14	2	1	3	5	8	1	0	1	22	2	0	.409	.303
Jordan, Rowdey	B-R	5-10	190	1-27-99	.229	.214	.232	30	109	15	25	4	0	1	13	18	0	1	2	28	2	3	.294	.333
Kendall, Kevin	L-R	5-10	175	6-25-99	.327	.280	.341	31	113	22	37	7	2	1	11	5	4	0	1	24	8	2	.451	.421
Kleszcz, Cole	R-R	6-0	206	6-16-97	.167	.308	.138	28	78	20	13	2	2	2	15	24	4	0	0	29	2	1	.321	.387
Loyo, Juan	R-R	5-11	180	3-24-99	.000	--	.000	1	2	1	0	0	0	0	0	1	1	0	0	2	0	0	.000	.500
Martinez, Jose	R-R	6-6	215	7-25-88	.143	.000	.250	3	7	1	1	0	0	0	0	1	0	0	0	1	0	0	.143	.250
McIlwain, Brandon	R-R	6-1	205	5-31-98	.255	.196	.271	74	239	36	61	11	1	7	40	36	7	0	5	89	8	3	.397	.362
Murphy, Tanner	R-R	6-4	199	5-19-00	.183	.273	.167	21	71	14	13	3	0	3	13	10	3	0	1	33	4	1	.352	.306
Newton, Shervyen	B-R	6-4	209	4-24-99	.190	.118	.202	30	116	17	22	6	0	2	24	20	2	1	3	58	1	1	.293	.312
O'Neill, Matt	R-R	6-0	205	8-20-97	.187	.148	.196	52	139	19	26	3	0	3	12	48	3	0	2	74	1	0	.273	.401
Palmer, Jaylen	R-R	6-4	208	7-31-00	.276	.227	.287	66	246	51	68	13	4	2	24	39	3	0	3	81	23	5	.386	.378
Peroza, Jose	R-R	6-0	221	6-15-00	.274	.324	.266	64	226	46	62	15	1	7	47	41	9	0	1	67	5	0	.442	.404
Ramirez, Alex	R-R	6-3	170	1-13-03	.258	.091	.296	76	302	41	78	15	4	5	35	23	8	0	1	104	16	7	.384	.326
Romero, Yoel	R-R	6-3	196	4-10-98	.000	.000	.000	2	5	1	0	0	0	0	1	2	1	0	1	2	0	0	.000	.333
Saunders, Warren	R-R	6-3	205	12-17-98	.249	.211	.257	93	337	51	84	8	2	3	44	29	8	0	4	75	1	2	.312	.320
Schwartz, JT	L-R	6-4	215	12-17-99	.195	.056	.234	25	82	9	16	5	0	0	8	13	3	0	2	12	2	0	.256	.320
Struble, LT	L-R	5-9	182	7-3-96	.286	.333	.278	7	21	1	6	0	0	0	3	4	0	1	0	7	4	1	.286	.400
Suozzi, Joe	R-R	6-3	215	2-28-98	.292	.318	.286	30	113	21	33	4	0	2	17	10	5	0	1	33	13	0	.381	.372
Thompson, David	R-R	6-2	211	8-28-93	.500	.333	.600	3	8	2	4	2	0	1	3	0	0	0	1	1	0	1	1.125	.500
Titus, Jimmy	R-R	6-1	195	1-25-98	.233	.143	.243	38	129	22	30	3	1	1	17	18	4	0	1	28	0	1	.295	.342
Uriarte, Juan	R-R	6-0	182	9-17-97	.180	.286	.167	19	61	8	11	3	1	0	2	1	3	0	0	13	0	0	.262	.231
Vasquez, Jeremy	L-L	6-4	215	7-17-96	.211	.000	.286	5	19	2	4	2	0	0	3	1	0	0	1	3	0	0	.316	.200
Walters, Anthony	R-R	6-1	185	12-17-97	.151	.143	.152	17	53	9	8	3	0	0	3	12	2	0	0	17	3	0	.208	.328
Wold, Jack-Thomas	L-L	5-10	220	9-16-99	.279	.429	.250	25	86	12	24	4	2	2	13	5	0	0	1	17	0	0	.442	.315

NEW YORK METS

Pitching	B-T	HT	WT	DOB	W	L	ERA	G	GS	CG	SV	IP	H	R	ER	HR	BB	SO	AVG	vLH	vRH	K/9	BB/9
Beck, Jace	R-R	6-9	200	6-14-00	0	0	27.00	1	0	0	0	1	3	3	3	0	2	1	.600	.333	1.000	9.00	18.00
Betances, Dellin	R-R	6-8	265	3-23-88	0	1	19.29	5	0	0	0	2	5	5	5	0	3	4	.417	.625	.000	15.43	11.57
Bryant, Garrison	L-R	6-3	202	12-3-98	1	1	2.57	2	2	0	0	7	6	2	2	1	1	7	.222	.294	.100	9.00	1.29
Cavallaro, Joe	R-R	6-4	190	7-19-95	0	0	21.60	1	0	0	0	2	1	4	4	0	4	1	.167	.000	.200	5.40	21.60
Chacin, Jose	R-R	6-4	192	3-25-97	3	2	3.86	5	5	0	0	28	24	13	12	4	8	25	.226	.200	.255	8.04	2.57
Clenney, Nolan	L-R	6-2	200	6-16-96	1	1	3.98	13	0	0	1	20	18	11	9	2	6	29	.243	.250	.239	12.84	2.66
Cleveland, Matt	R-R	6-3	187	3-18-98	0	0	0.00	5	0	0	0	7	2	0	0	0	5	9	.087	.200	.000	11.05	6.14
Colina, Robert	R-R	5-11	175	4-24-01	3	1	3.18	6	5	1	0	28	27	14	10	4	12	27	.248	.224	.267	8.58	3.81
Colon, Jeffrey	R-R	6-1	170	11-9-99	1	0	6.27	14	0	0	0	19	28	14	13	5	11	17	.359	.286	.419	8.20	5.30
deGrom, Jacob	L-R	6-4	180	6-19-88	0	0	0.00	1	1	0	0	3	0	0	0	0	0	8	.000	.000	.000	24.00	0.00
Dillon, Justin	R-R	6-3	225	9-5-93	0	0	9.00	2	0	0	0	2	1	2	2	1	1	1	.143	.000	.167	4.50	4.50
Dominguez, Christofer	L-L	6-2	222	1-3-00	0	1	13.50	1	0	0	0	2	3	3	3	0	2	2	.333	.333	.333	9.00	9.00
Faith, Austin	R-R	6-6	215	5-13-98	3	5	7.56	25	5	0	0	42	34	38	35	4	33	55	.219	.234	.209	11.88	7.13
Ginn, J.T.	R-R	6-2	200	5-20-99	2	1	2.56	8	8	0	0	39	26	12	11	3	10	35	.195	.222	.177	8.15	2.33
Goggin, Dan	R-R	6-2	206	6-9-97	0	0	0.00	1	0	0	0	2	0	0	0	0	0	2	.000	.000	.000	9.00	0.00
Gonzalez, Brailin	L-L	6-2	180	9-23-99	1	2	6.97	18	0	0	0	21	23	21	16	3	20	32	.250	.182	.271	13.94	8.71
Gonzalez, Saul	R-R	6-7	235	12-28-99	0	1	8.71	4	2	0	0	10	18	10	10	1	3	10	.360	.400	.320	8.71	2.61
Griffin, David	R-R	6-0	205	7-16-96	2	1	3.05	7	7	0	0	38	24	13	13	2	18	48	.178	.117	.227	11.27	4.23
Gsellman, Robert	R-R	6-4	200	7-18-93	0	0	21.60	2	2	0	0	2	4	4	4	0	1	2	.500	1.000	.200	10.80	5.40
Hall, Dylan	R-R	6-5	210	9-7-97	0	0	3.00	2	1	0	0	6	4	2	2	0	4	7	.190	.100	.273	10.50	6.00
Hardy, Brendan	R-R	6-4	170	12-15-99	0	0	13.83	11	0	0	0	14	13	21	21	2	21	17	.255	.333	.167	11.20	13.83
Hartwig, Grant	R-R	6-5	235	12-18-97	0	0	1.93	4	0	0	3	5	3	2	1	0	1	3	.176	.286	.100	5.79	1.93
Holderman, Colin	R-R	6-7	240	10-8-95	0	0	3.86	4	0	0	1	5	3	2	2	0	2	5	.176	.250	.154	13.50	3.86
Juarez, Daniel	L-L	5-11	155	9-28-00	1	0	0.00	1	0	0	0	2	0	0	0	0	1	2	.000	.000	.000	7.71	3.86
Kubichek, Kolby	R-R	6-0	180	11-28-99	0	3	8.15	6	2	0	0	18	22	20	16	2	11	10	.297	.314	.282	5.09	5.60
Lasko, Justin	R-R	6-4	208	3-16-97	2	0	1.96	4	2	0	0	23	15	5	5	2	4	25	.185	.293	.075	9.78	1.57
Lugo, Seth	R-R	6-4	225	11-17-89	0	0	0.00	1	1	0	0	1	0	0	0	0	0	0	.000	--	.000	0.00	0.00
McCall, Liam	R-R	6-4	180	2-19-99	3	1	4.01	22	0	0	1	34	26	16	15	6	22	34	.215	.093	.313	9.09	5.88
McLoughlin, Trey	R-R	6-2	210	6-11-99	0	2	6.41	6	1	0	0	20	20	14	14	7	7	18	.267	.235	.293	8.24	3.20
Montas, Luis	R-R	6-2	203	9-16-00	5	0	0.90	19	0	0	7	30	24	4	3	2	7	29	.220	.237	.211	8.70	2.10
Moreno, Luis	R-R	6-2	170	5-29-99	6	4	5.42	21	12	1	1	73	70	51	44	9	56	64	.261	.271	.253	7.89	6.90
Morris, Colby	R-R	6-3	190	5-17-97	0	0	1.80	4	0	0	1	5	3	2	1	1	0	8	.176	.077	.500	14.40	0.00
Nightengale, Drake	R-R	6-0	195	5-8-94	3	4	4.07	25	0	0	2	42	38	26	19	6	23	44	.252	.250	.253	9.43	4.93
Nogosek, Stephen	R-R	6-2	205	1-11-95	0	0	3.00	3	2	0	0	3	4	1	1	0	1	3	.333	.333	.333	3.00	3.00
Opp, Cam	L-L	5-10	185	11-4-95	2	0	0.79	3	2	0	0	11	10	2	1	0	6	9	.238	.294	.200	7.15	4.76
Oswalt, Corey	R-R	6-5	250	9-3-93	0	0	0.00	3	3	0	0	4	2	0	0	0	1	2	.133	.143	.125	4.50	2.25
Parra, Franklin	L-L	6-1	202	9-13-99	3	4	6.00	18	8	0	0	57	61	51	38	3	53	48	.280	.263	.286	7.58	8.37
Parsons, Hunter	R-R	6-2	215	6-24-97	2	0	1.80	4	0	0	0	10	8	2	2	0	3	18	.216	.300	.118	16.20	2.70
Reid-Foley, Sean	R-R	6-3	230	8-30-95	0	0	0.00	2	1	0	0	2	0	0	0	0	3	2	.000	.000	.000	7.71	11.57
Rincones, Ronny	R-R	5-10	160	10-31-01	0	0	9.00	1	0	0	0	2	1	1	1	0	1	2	.500	.500	.500	18.00	9.00
Rodriguez, Luis	L-L	6-3	190	12-3-02	0	1	7.71	3	2	0	0	7	10	6	6	1	2	5	.345	.200	.421	6.43	2.57
Rojas, Oscar	R-R	5-11	200	5-5-99	6	3	3.66	15	14	3	0	84	71	36	34	7	25	81	.234	.246	.226	8.71	2.69
Sanchez, Franklin	R-R	6-6	183	9-12-00	0	0	0.00	3	0	0	1	3	1	1	0	0	5	4	.111	.000	.200	12.00	15.00
Santos, Junior	R-R	6-7	244	8-16-01	6	6	4.59	21	16	2	0	96	108	60	49	8	38	79	.287	.286	.288	7.41	3.56
Santos, Reyson	R-R	6-0	218	1-22-99	3	2	5.09	27	0	0	9	35	26	21	20	5	22	44	.208	.217	.203	11.21	5.60
Suarez, Joander	R-R	6-3	223	2-27-00	0	3	7.66	6	6	0	0	25	28	23	21	3	16	26	.280	.339	.205	9.49	5.84
Syndergaard, Noah	L-R	6-6	242	8-29-92	0	0	0.00	2	2	0	0	5	1	0	0	0	1	6	.059	.000	.077	10.80	1.80
Tavarez, Sammy	R-R	6-7	225	10-20-98	0	2	5.81	24	0	0	1	31	22	22	20	1	34	52	.198	.220	.186	15.10	9.87
Taveras, Willy	R-R	5-11	163	1-20-98	1	3	3.33	18	0	0	0	24	22	9	9	2	2	34	.247	.213	.286	12.58	0.74
Yamamoto, Jordan	R-R	6-0	185	5-11-96	0	0	1.00	3	3	0	0	9	4	1	1	0	1	8	.129	.182	.100	8.00	1.00

Fielding

Catcher	PCT	G	PO	A	E	DP	PB
Alvarez	.966	10	108	6	4	1	1
Colina	.961	17	106	16	5	4	3
Dyer	.973	9	65	8	2	1	0
Gaddis	.994	18	153	9	1	0	0
Loyo	1.000	1	9	0	0	0	0
O'Neill	.994	50	419	45	3	1	6
Uriarte	1.000	19	148	15	0	2	1

First Base	PCT	G	PO	A	E	DP
Brodey	.958	4	22	1	1	3
Colina	1.000	15	83	5	0	15
Dyer	1.000	10	67	3	0	7
Peroza	1.000	6	43	1	0	2
Saunders	.979	55	351	30	8	41
Schwartz	.977	24	156	12	4	9
Vasquez	.969	4	30	1	1	5
Wold	1.000	2	14	0	0	4

Second Base	PCT	G	PO	A	E	DP
Berbesi	.864	8	10	9	3	2
Conti	1.000	3	4	3	0	1
Fermin	1.000	1	0	2	0	0
Fryman	.990	21	44	52	1	16
Gonzalez	1.000	1	1	1	0	1
Guerrera	.870	11	17	23	6	5
Kendall	.938	4	9	6	1	3
Newton	1.000	5	9	12	0	5
Palmer	.967	11	22	36	2	12
Peroza	.980	25	38	58	2	20
Romero	1.000	1	0	2	0	0
Saunders	1.000	1	2	3	0	1
Struble	.900	3	3	6	1	1
Titus	.967	16	33	26	2	9
Walters	.970	7	17	15	1	8

Third Base	PCT	G	PO	A	E	DP
Berbesi	.917	5	3	8	1	1
Dyer	.941	9	3	13	1	1
Gaddis	1.000	5	0	7	0	0
Guerrera	.786	5	4	7	3	0
Palmer	.904	27	15	32	5	4
Peroza	.867	28	17	35	8	8
Romero	1.000	1	0	2	0	0
Saunders	.905	26	15	42	6	5
Thompson	.800	3	1	3	1	0
Titus	.895	7	6	11	2	1
Walters	1.000	2	1	3	0	0

Shortstop	PCT	G	PO	A	E	DP
Berbesi	1.000	5	2	15	0	3
Conti	1.000	1	1	4	0	0
Fermin	.667	2	1	1	1	0
Fryman	.972	45	71	134	6	22
Gonzalez	1.000	2	2	6	0	1
Kendall	.969	26	36	59	3	14
Newton	.953	22	28	54	4	17
Titus	1.000	6	10	7	0	2
Walters	.958	9	7	16	1	6

Outfield	PCT	G	PO	A	E	DP
Adon	.971	24	32	1	1	0
Ashford	1.000	13	21	1	0	0
Crow-Armstrong	.933	5	12	2	1	1
De Los Santos	.950	37	53	4	3	0
Dyer	1.000	2	5	0	0	0
Fargas	1.000	4	8	0	0	0
Fermin	1.000	1	3	0	0	0
Jordan	.984	25	58	2	1	0

Kleszcz	.962	25	47	4	2	2		Palmer	1.000	19	38	0	0	0		Suozzi		.977	25	42	0	1	0
Martinez	1.000	3	1	0	0	0		Ramirez	.969	73	155	2	5	0									
McIlwain	.978	64	86	4	2	0		Saunders	--	1	0	0	0	0									
Murphy	1.000	20	28	2	0	0		Struble	1.000	4	4	0	0	0		Wold		.968	16	30	0	1	0

FCL METS   ROOKIE
FLORIDA COMPLEX LEAGUE

Batting	B-T	HT	WT	DOB	AVG	vLH	vRH	G	AB	R	H	2B	3B	HR	RBI	BB	HBP	SH	SF	SO	SB	CS	SLG	OBP
Aybar, Ronis	L-R	6-0	180	1-13-00	.265	.154	.282	32	98	16	26	7	1	4	18	6	1	0	0	38	6	0	.480	.314
Beracierta, Raul	R-R	6-1	215	5-24-99	.281	.227	.292	39	128	20	36	16	1	5	23	13	2	0	0	38	5	1	.539	.357
Berbesi, Cesar	L-R	6-0	160	4-13-00	.382	.333	.387	11	34	11	13	3	1	1	6	10	1	0	1	9	5	1	.618	.522
Brodey, Quinn	L-L	6-1	195	12-1-95	.000	--	.000	1	4	0	0	0	0	0	0	0	0	0	0	4	0	0	.000	.000
Consuegra, Stanley	R-R	6-2	167	9-24-00	.270	.235	.281	20	74	10	20	9	1	2	10	4	3	0	2	21	3	3	.500	.325
De Los Santos, Omar	R-R	6-1	172	8-8-99	.429	.200	.478	7	28	6	12	0	1	3	8	1	0	0	0	3	2	0	.821	.448
Dominguez, Carlos	R-R	6-1	190	10-11-99	.262	.296	.254	46	145	27	38	7	1	10	28	9	10	0	0	57	7	3	.531	.348
Fargas, Johneshwy	R-R	6-1	180	12-15-94	.200	--	.200	2	5	1	1	0	0	0	1	1	0	0	0	2	0	0	.200	.333
Fermin, Edgardo	R-R	6-0	171	5-28-98	.300	1.000	.125	4	10	5	3	1	0	0	1	4	1	0	0	4	0	0	.400	.533
Guerrera, Justin	R-R	5-9	185	1-11-00	.410	.000	.500	11	39	8	16	3	0	2	10	5	1	0	1	11	1	0	.641	.478
Guerrero, Gregory	R-R	6-0	186	1-20-99	.220	.313	.202	35	100	13	22	6	0	3	9	9	0	0	0	31	0	2	.370	.284
Loyo, Juan	R-R	5-11	180	3-16-99	.324	.000	.353	16	37	4	12	1	0	0	4	4	2	0	0	13	0	1	.351	.419
Lugo, William	R-R	6-3	215	1-2-02	.218	.182	.228	46	156	28	34	6	0	6	22	23	3	0	1	52	5	1	.372	.328
Martinez, Yeral	L-R	6-3	220	10-30-02	.116	.300	.094	33	95	11	11	5	0	2	9	17	0	0	1	58	1	0	.232	.248
McIntosh, Blaine	L-L	6-4	180	6-9-01	.121	.250	.080	17	33	5	4	1	1	0	4	9	0	0	0	19	1	0	.212	.310
Murphy, Tanner	R-R	6-4	199	5-1-98	.273	.000	.300	4	11	4	3	2	0	0	1	2	0	0	0	3	2	0	.455	.385
Ortega, Jake	L-R	5-10	175	7-31-96	.269	.154	.308	19	52	8	14	4	0	0	2	6	2	0	0	10	3	0	.346	.367
Osborn, Drake	R-R	5-10	190	7-22-98	.178	.250	.162	16	45	9	8	2	0	0	3	7	1	0	1	18	0	0	.222	.296
Perozo, Vincent	L-R	6-0	170	3-6-03	.173	.182	.171	18	52	7	9	2	0	1	6	10	4	0	0	21	0	2	.269	.348
Reyes, Wilmer	R-R	6-0	161	12-22-97	.261	.250	.267	7	23	2	6	1	0	0	1	2	1	0	0	3	0	1	.304	.346
Rivera, Jose	R-R	5-9	190	9-7-99	.182	.000	.250	4	11	0	2	2	0	0	0	0	1	0	0	2	1	0	.364	.250
Rodriguez, Manny	R-R	5-10	166	7-4-96	.000	.000	.000	3	10	0	0	0	0	0	0	0	0	0	0	8	0	0	.000	.000
Rudick, Matt	L-L	5-9	170	7-2-98	.303	.333	.295	21	76	17	23	2	3	1	12	12	1	0	0	11	6	0	.447	.404
Salazar, Eduardo	R-R	6-3	167	12-15-00	.308	.125	.355	25	78	11	24	7	0	1	11	5	6	0	1	15	2	0	.436	.389
Suarez, Albert	L-R	5-11	150	11-30-99	.167	.111	.176	25	60	4	10	1	0	0	6	3	1	1	0	18	1	1	.267	.219
Tilien, Junior	R-R	6-1	168	9-9-02	.165	.267	.148	32	103	11	17	7	0	0	7	6	2	0	1	24	0	0	.233	.223
Titus, Jimmy	R-R	6-1	195	1-25-98	.125	.000	.200	2	8	2	1	1	0	0	1	2	0	0	0	2	0	0	.250	.300
Villalobos, Fernando	L-R	6-0	195	6-24-02	.132	.000	.185	14	38	3	5	1	0	3	3	3	1	0	0	13	0	0	.237	.214
Young, Wyatt	L-R	5-7	160	12-5-99	.370	.227	.414	26	92	15	34	8	1	0	13	9	0	0	0	21	4	2	.478	.426

Pitching	B-T	HT	WT	DOB	W	L	ERA	G	GS	CG	SV	IP	H	R	ER	HR	BB	SO	AVG	vLH	vRH	K/9	BB/9
Abad, Yeremi	R-R	6-1	165	1-25-02	0	0	11.57	2	0	0	0	2	5	3	3	0	3	2	.417	.286	.600	7.71	11.57
Acuna, Jose	R-R	6-2	175	10-20-02	1	0	3.86	4	3	0	0	7	3	3	3	2	3	7	.130	.091	.167	9.00	3.86
Alfonseca, Angel	L-L	5-10	171	1-10-01	0	0	4.35	8	1	0	0	10	6	6	5	1	9	13	.182	.000	.222	11.32	7.84
Alfonseca, Miguel	R-R	6-0	190	2-13-00	2	2	5.52	14	7	0	1	31	38	21	19	2	14	39	.297	.322	.275	11.32	4.06
Askew, Keyshawn	L-L	6-4	190	1-5-00	2	0	1.00	4	1	0	0	9	3	1	1	1	4	14	.103	.143	.091	14.00	4.00
Beck, Jace	R-R	6-9	200	6-14-00	1	4	6.65	10	6	0	0	22	18	17	16	1	19	31	.222	.200	.239	12.88	7.89
Bryant, Garrison	L-R	6-3	202	12-3-98	0	0	1.04	4	3	0	0	9	6	2	1	0	1	9	.194	.133	.250	9.35	1.04
Cavallaro, Joe	R-R	6-4	190	7-19-95	0	0	0.00	2	1	0	0	2	0	0	0	0	2	5	.000	.000	.000	19.29	7.71
Chacin, Jose	R-R	6-4	192	3-25-97	1	0	0.90	5	2	0	0	10	2	1	1	1	2	9	.063	.071	.056	8.10	1.80
Cleveland, Matt	R-R	6-3	187	3-18-98	0	1	7.71	3	0	0	0	2	5	5	2	1	2	2	.385	.375	.400	7.71	7.71
Colina, Robert	R-R	5-11	175	4-24-01	2	1	2.70	6	3	0	1	23	21	8	7	1	6	32	.231	.278	.200	12.34	2.31
Colon, Jeffrey	R-R	6-1	170	11-9-99	2	1	1.45	9	1	0	1	19	14	4	3	0	3	27	.209	.194	.226	13.02	1.45
Courtney, Justin	R-R	6-5	225	7-24-96	0	0	0.00	2	0	0	0	3	0	0	0	0	1	1	.000	.000	.000	3.00	3.00
Davidson, Kody	R-R	5-9	170	11-10-98	0	0	0.00	2	0	0	0	2	2	0	0	0	3	3	.286	.333	.250	16.20	16.20
Dominguez, Christofer	L-L	6-2	222	1-3-00	3	2	4.09	15	0	0	2	22	24	10	10	1	10	24	.282	.261	.290	9.82	4.09
Dominguez, Robert	R-R	6-5	195	11-30-01	1	1	8.25	10	1	0	1	12	15	12	11	1	9	10	.300	.467	.229	7.50	6.75
Encarnacion, Yeily	R-R	6-3	195	2-10-00	0	0	9.00	6	1	0	0	12	13	13	12	1	12	11	.271	.263	.276	8.25	9.00
Garcia, Benito	R-R	6-0	165	3-10-00	1	0	6.28	9	0	0	2	14	22	10	10	3	3	8	.361	.333	.387	5.02	1.88
Gomez, Kevin	R-R	6-1	184	1-31-01	2	0	6.23	15	0	0	3	17	31	19	12	3	10	19	.397	.371	.419	9.87	5.19
Gonzalez, Brailin	L-L	6-2	180	9-23-99	1	0	0.90	7	0	0	1	10	4	3	1	0	4	14	.143	.083	.130	12.60	3.60
Gonzalez, Saul	R-R	6-7	235	12-28-99	2	0	3.68	8	5	0	0	29	23	14	12	1	9	31	.207	.245	.177	9.51	2.76
Hall, Dylan	R-R	6-5	210	9-7-97	0	0	0.00	2	0	0	0	3	2	0	0	0	4	4	.222	.250	.200	13.50	13.50
Hamel, Dominic	R-R	6-2	206	3-2-99	0	0	0.00	2	2	0	0	3	0	0	0	0	7	0	.000	.000	.000	21.00	0.00
Hardy, Brendan	R-R	6-4	170	12-15-99	3	1	10.80	13	1	0	1	12	11	15	14	0	17	14	.262	.318	.200	10.80	13.11
Hartwig, Grant	R-R	6-5	235	12-18-97	0	1	3.86	4	3	0	0	7	7	5	3	1	3	9	.259	.400	.083	11.57	3.86
Juarez, Daniel	L-L	5-11	155	9-23-00	2	1	2.76	16	1	0	1	29	11	11	9	2	18	44	.113	.167	.096	13.50	5.52
Kubichek, Kolby	R-R	6-0	180	11-28-99	0	0	0.00	1	1	0	0	1	1	0	0	0	0	2	.250	.500	.000	18.00	0.00
Lavender, Nathan	L-L	6-2	210	1-20-00	0	0	1.35	4	0	0	0	3	7	3	1	0	2	12	.130	.000	.167	16.20	2.70
McLoughlin, Trey	R-R	6-2	210	6-11-99	0	0	0.00	1	0	0	0	1	0	0	0	0	0	1	.000	.000	.000	9.00	0.00
Nogosek, Stephen	R-R	6-2	205	11-11-95	0	0	0.00	1	1	0	0	1	0	0	0	0	0	2	.000	.000	.000	18.00	0.00
Parra, Franklin	L-L	6-1	202	9-13-99	0	0	0.00	1	0	0	0	2	1	1	0	0	2	3	.111	.143	.000	11.57	7.71
Rincones, Ronny	R-R	5-10	160	10-31-01	1	0	4.50	4	0	0	1	8	7	4	4	1	3	9	.241	.250	.231	10.13	3.38
Rodriguez, Luis	R-R	6-2	190	12-3-00	0	1	1.69	4	2	0	0	5	2	4	1	0	3	6	.125	.100	.185	5.06	5.06
Sanchez, Franklin	R-R	6-6	183	9-12-00	2	3	7.30	14	1	0	0	25	20	23	20	0	16	31	.222	.257	.200	11.31	5.84
Scott, Christian	R-R	6-4	215	6-15-99	0	0	3.00	3	0	0	0	3	3	1	1	0	1	1	.300	.500	.000	3.00	3.00

Player	B-T	HT	WT	DOB	AVG	vLH	vRH	G	AB	R	H	2B	3B	HR	RBI	BB	HBP	SH	SF	SO	SB	CS	SLG	OBP
Seymour, Carson	R-R	6-6	260	12-16-98	0	0	2.08	4	0	0	0	4	3	3	1	0	6	4	.214	.000	.333	8.31	12.46
Vasil, Mike	L-R	6-5	225	3-19-00	0	0	1.29	3	3	0	0	7	3	1	1	0	0	10	.125	.214	.000	12.86	0.00
Vasquez, Christopher	R-R	6-0	160	3-17-01	3	1	7.15	16	2	0	1	23	28	19	18	4	16	25	.301	.395	.236	9.93	6.35
Yamamoto, Jordan	R-R	6-0	185	5-11-96	0	0	0.00	1	1	0	0	1	1	0	0	0	0	1	.250	.250	--	9.00	0.00
Yera, Ariel	R-R	6-3	215	1-20-97	1	0	0.00	8	0	0	0	9	5	0	0	0	7	3	.156	.143	.167	2.89	6.75
Zorrilla, Jose	B-L	6-1	180	10-2-98	0	0	3.00	3	1	0	0	3	2	1	1	0	3	2	.182	.250	.143	6.00	9.00
Zwack, Nick	L-L	6-3	230	8-1-98	1	0	0.00	5	0	0	0	7	6	1	0	0	2	13	.261	.125	.333	16.71	2.57

Fielding

C: Loyo 15, Ortega 12, Osborn 14, Perozo 6, Rivera 3, Villalobos 12.
1B: Beracierta 20, Brodey 1, Guerrero 12, Lugo 2, Martinez 14, Perozo 5, Reyes 1, Salazar 3.
2B: Berbesi 1, De Los Santos 1, Fermin 1, Guerrera 2, Guerrero 5, Ortega 3, Reyes 1, Rivera 1, Suarez 13, Tilien 15, Young 19.
3B: Berbesi 5, Fermin 1, Guerrera 1, Guerrero 16, Reyes 2, Suarez 6, Tilien 11, Titus 2, Young 3.
SS: Berbesi 5, Fermin 1, Guerrera 5, Guerrero 2, Lugo 31, Reyes 2, Rodriguez 2, Suarez 3, Tilien 5, Young 4.
OF: Aybar 24, Beracierta 14, Consuegra 19, De Los Santos 5, Dominguez 42, Fargas 2, Guerrera 1, Martinez 15, McIntosh 11, Murphy 3, Rudick 20, Salazar 16, Suarez 1.

DSL METS   ROOKIE
DOMINICAN SUMMER LEAGUE

Batting	B-T	HT	WT	DOB	AVG	vLH	vRH	G	AB	R	H	2B	3B	HR	RBI	BB	HBP	SH	SF	SO	SB	CS	SLG	OBP
Almonte, Jostyn	R-R	5-11	193	5-10-03	.164	.077	.183	25	73	12	12	3	0	0	7	5	3	0	0	21	4	2	.205	.247
Aular, Jose	R-R	5-11	175	1-2-04	.200	.286	.125	7	15	0	3	1	0	0	1	3	0	1	4	0	0	0	.267	.350
Camacaro, Samuel	R-R	0-0	0	11-23-03	.187	.200	.183	33	91	10	17	1	0	0	8	12	1	0	1	22	5	0	.220	.286
Campos, Dyron	R-R	5-10	155	12-26-00	.233	.111	.259	37	103	18	24	4	0	2	18	11	2	0	2	22	2	4	.330	.314
Castillo, Lewis	R-R	6-0	163	6-23-03	.264	.231	.270	30	87	10	23	3	1	0	9	7	2	0	0	15	4	2	.322	.333
Castillo, Luis	L-R	6-1	180	11-13-01	.165	.250	.138	41	85	7	14	4	2	0	7	13	5	0	1	30	4	0	.259	.308
Castro, Sebastian	L-R	6-3	185	8-27-04	.163	.222	.146	43	123	12	20	2	2	1	14	22	2	0	1	50	3	4	.236	.297
Cuevas, Yohairo	L-L	6-3	172	9-16-03	.155	.200	.141	41	103	15	16	6	0	0	8	23	5	0	2	41	5	0	.214	.331
De Leon, Francis	R-R	0-0	0	10-4-03	.214	.333	.188	35	84	14	18	4	0	3	10	18	7	0	0	39	6	3	.369	.394
De Los Santos, Jefrey	L-R	6-0	154	5-30-03	.248	.462	.198	42	137	26	34	1	5	2	14	18	2	0	0	40	6	3	.372	.344
Flores, Joel	R-R	6-1	175	4-28-03	.208	.192	.213	36	106	15	22	4	1	2	15	11	3	0	2	34	1	4	.321	.295
Gomez, Tommy	R-R	5-10	188	4-21-04	.154	.500	.000	5	13	1	2	0	0	0	2	2	1	0	0	7	1	0	.154	.313
Gonzalez, Jhoandry	R-R	6-2	165	1-29-02	.147	.000	.167	14	34	7	5	1	0	0	2	15	0	0	0	15	2	1	.176	.408
Guance, Manuel	R-R	5-10	150	11-6-03	.175	.176	.174	17	40	4	7	2	1	0	3	10	0	0	1	16	1	1	.275	.340
Guerrero, Angel	L-R	6-1	185	11-17-03	.188	.000	.200	6	16	0	3	0	0	0	0	1	2	0	0	5	1	0	.188	.316
Hendrick, Robert	R-R	6-2	190	4-22-03	.120	.133	.117	31	75	10	9	3	0	1	5	8	12	0	0	35	1	1	.200	.305
Ibarguen, Mike	R-R	0-0	0	3-25-04	.192	.333	.150	13	26	4	5	3	0	0	5	4	3	0	1	9	1	1	.308	.353
Lander, Adrian	R-R	5-9	145	3-13-03	.174	.048	.229	28	69	6	12	2	0	0	3	6	0	0	0	15	0	1	.203	.240
Lara, Wilfredo	R-R	5-10	180	4-28-04	.208	.360	.155	31	96	14	20	6	1	2	13	10	4	0	0	26	3	2	.354	.309
Leal, Gregory	R-R	6-0	171	2-14-03	.082	.000	.098	28	49	6	4	1	0	1	4	10	3	0	2	18	0	0	.163	.266
Lechuga, Isaac	B-R	5-10	145	9-10-02	.167	.077	.207	19	42	3	7	2	0	0	3	10	0	0	1	19	5	2	.214	.321
Leon, Alejandro	L-R	5-10	167	9-19-01	.000	.000	.000	2	5	0	0	0	0	0	1	0	1	0	0	1	0	0	.000	.167
Linares, Franklin	R-R	6-0	165	11-5-00	.217	.091	.255	47	143	21	31	2	3	0	9	15	5	0	1	42	19	6	.273	.311
Machado, Fabian	R-R	6-2	180	4-25-03	.280	.200	.299	38	107	16	30	10	0	1	15	15	4	0	2	25	3	2	.402	.383
Marcano, Jose	R-R	6-0	160	5-6-04	.316	.000	.364	16	38	6	12	3	0	0	6	4	2	0	0	7	4	1	.395	.409
Marquez, Gustavo	R-R	0-0	0	10-4-03	.176	.095	.200	34	91	11	16	3	0	0	5	3	5	0	1	42	2	3	.209	.240
Marte, Frederick	B-R	6-1	160	2-20-04	.183	.150	.196	29	71	7	13	4	0	0	9	18	1	0	2	27	2	0	.239	.348
Mata, Yohenny	R-R	6-2	175	6-3-04	.211	.235	.200	22	57	5	12	2	0	0	0	3	0	0	0	13	3	0	.246	.237
Mejia, Gerald	B-R	6-0	156	6-14-03	.238	.217	.244	33	101	15	24	2	2	3	15	12	0	0	2	45	6	2	.386	.313
Melendez, Jose	R-R	0-0	0	10-3-03	.233	.190	.246	36	90	6	21	3	0	0	8	9	2	0	1	24	1	3	.267	.314
Minaya, Boris	L-L	6-1	168	12-8-02	.128	.143	.120	17	39	3	5	3	0	0	2	7	3	0	0	10	1	0	.205	.306
Monegro, Isnael	R-R	6-0	150	10-1-02	.163	.143	.167	20	49	4	8	3	0	0	2	4	2	0	0	13	6	1	.224	.255
Mosquera, Diego	R-R	0-0	0	3-14-04	.326	.294	.333	32	92	21	30	3	2	0	7	14	3	0	0	15	3	3	.402	.431
Perez, Yoandy	L-R	6-0	155	4-17-04	.184	.077	.240	16	38	2	7	1	1	0	3	0	0	1	1	13	1	1	.263	.238
Rodriguez, Hector	R-R	0-0	0	3-11-04	.301	.310	.298	42	123	17	37	8	2	3	15	13	3	0	2	17	6	8	.472	.376
Sanchez, Roberto	L-L	6-1	162	3-7-03	.194	.250	.179	16	36	5	7	0	0	1	0	10	1	0	0	12	2	1	.194	.383
Santana, Eric	B-R	6-0	180	11-2-02	.172	.375	.104	24	64	8	11	2	1	2	7	14	0	0	1	29	1	1	.328	.316
Santana, Luis	L-R	6-2	160	8-1-02	.250	.000	.333	2	4	1	1	0	0	0	1	1	2	0	0	1	0	0	.750	.571
Serrano, Enyer	L-R	5-11	165	5-14-04	.143	.333	.067	20	42	7	6	1	1	0	1	6	1	0	0	18	1	0	.214	.265
Silvestre, Jensy	B-R	6-0	170	11-9-03	.128	.222	.100	20	39	4	5	1	1	0	1	7	0	0	0	15	2	0	.205	.261
Valdez, Enrique	R-R	6-0	180	9-1-01	.109	.077	.121	20	46	9	5	2	1	0	4	14	2	0	1	23	1	2	.217	.333
Villavicencio, Kevin	R-R	5-10	172	11-24-03	.303	.417	.267	45	152	25	46	12	1	1	17	15	2	0	0	17	14	3	.414	.373
Yustiz, Ruben	R-R	6-2	175	1-2-04	.148	.100	.157	31	61	8	9	3	0	1	11	11	1	0	0	27	1	0	.246	.288

Pitching	B-T	HT	WT	DOB	W	L	ERA	G	GS	CG	SV	IP	H	R	ER	HR	BB	SO	AVG	vLH	vRH	K/9	BB/9
Alvarez, Luis	R-R	6-5	185	5-5-03	0	0	0.00	1	0	0	0	1	0	0	0	0	0	1	.000	--	.000	9.00	0.00
Atencio, Javier	L-L	6-0	160	11-26-01	1	3	2.44	15	14	0	0	48	28	16	13	1	19	76	.171	.186	.165	14.25	3.56
Baptist, Ricardo	R-R	6-0	192	10-16-02	2	1	7.71	15	2	0	0	12	4	11	10	0	22	14	.105	.182	.074	10.80	16.97
Calderon, Jean	R-R	6-0	220	11-15-00	0	2	9.58	10	0	0	3	11	11	11	9	0	20	8	.206	.000	.111	17.42	7.84
Camilo, Luis	L-L	5-9	178	7-22-02	1	0	9.95	6	0	0	6	3	3	1	0	7	11	3	.136	.000	.167	4.26	15.63
Cepeda, Yoerison	R-R	6-4	190	10-14-01	0	1	7.71	6	0	0	1	7	5	6	1	5	5	.200	.143	.222	6.43	6.43
Contreras, Kelvin	L-L	6-0	152	5-12-01	0	3	9.82	11	1	0	0	11	17	18	12	0	20	9	.340	.500	.289	7.36	16.36
De La Cruz, Felipe	L-L	6-0	180	5-26-01	0	4	3.13	14	12	0	0	46	38	22	16	1	16	46	.218	.323	.196	9.00	3.13
De Leon, Jorge	R-R	6-5	180	11-24-02	0	3	1.85	13	12	0	0	39	25	16	8	0	16	49	.177	.161	.188	11.31	3.69
Diaz, Joel	R-R	0-0	0	2-26-04	0	2	0.54	15	15	0	0	50	29	9	3	0	9	63	.164	.120	.181	11.26	1.61

Name	B-T	Ht	Wt	DOB	W	L	ERA	G	GS	CG	SV	IP	H	R	ER	HR	BB	SO	AVG	vL	vR		
Garcia, Saul	R-R	6-2	180	6-11-03	1	1	7.50	5	0	0	0	6	4	7	5	0	4	11	.182	.222	.154	16.50	6.00
Gomez, Raimon	R-R	6-2	175	9-6-01	1	1	2.19	9	2	0	0	12	10	6	3	1	6	14	.213	.222	.207	10.22	4.38
Lora, Yeudi	R-R	6-2	170	8-25-03	2	3	8.35	15	0	0	0	18	21	19	17	1	17	17	.292	.143	.353	8.35	8.35
Martinez, Aaron	R-R	6-1	185	11-10-03	0	1	2.45	8	8	0	0	18	15	7	5	0	12	11	.221	.111	.293	5.40	5.89
Mejia, Leandro	R-R	6-7	221	4-27-01	2	1	5.40	10	0	0	0	12	5	8	7	0	17	10	.135	.167	.120	7.71	13.11
Mejia, Nicolandy	R-R	6-1	175	7-2-01	1	4	7.22	23	0	0	1	29	36	34	23	2	22	27	.313	.314	.313	8.48	6.91
Mercedes, Daniel	L-L	6-2	175	1-17-02	1	0	9.58	9	0	0	0	10	7	12	11	1	16	11	.194	.000	.212	9.58	13.94
Nunez, Ellian	R-R	6-2	167	12-8-03	0	0	10.13	2	0	0	0	3	3	3	3	0	2	1	.333	.667	.167	3.38	6.75
Nunez, Rikelvis	R-R	6-5	195	5-6-02	2	1	6.19	14	0	0	1	16	15	11	11	0	13	25	.246	.192	.286	14.06	7.31
Orellana, Douglas	R-R	6-1	196	5-1-02	2	2	8.05	17	0	0	0	19	22	22	17	2	20	14	.293	.263	.304	6.63	9.47
Ovalles, Layonel	R-R	6-3	175	6-16-03	0	2	2.83	12	6	0	1	35	16	14	11	0	8	34	.132	.100	.148	8.74	2.06
Pacheco, Juan	R-R	6-1	178	9-19-02	5	3	5.68	21	0	0	2	25	23	20	16	4	18	31	.242	.289	.211	11.01	6.39
Palacios, Jonaiker	R-R	6-0	170	5-7-03	4	4	5.01	22	1	0	3	32	37	25	18	2	16	38	.289	.324	.277	10.58	4.45
Peguero, Jeremy	L-L	6-2	175	5-3-02	3	3	5.54	19	8	0	0	39	41	27	24	2	26	48	.270	.265	.271	11.08	6.00
Pena, Herlyn	R-R	6-2	168	9-24-03	2	1	4.86	19	4	0	1	37	36	24	20	2	11	39	.257	.238	.273	9.49	2.68
Ramirez, Jawilme	R-R	6-2	170	11-28-01	5	5	2.14	14	13	0	0	55	22	14	13	2	20	56	.119	.098	.127	9.22	3.29
Ramos, Lenerd	R-R	6-2	190	9-23-03	1	2	6.35	19	3	0	2	28	26	28	20	1	16	28	.228	.208	.233	8.89	5.08
Reyes, Brawny	R-R	6-3	165	3-7-03	0	1	43.88	4	1	0	0	3	6	14	13	0	10	2	.400	.500	.333	6.75	33.75
Ribon, Kevin	R-R	6-0	157	9-20-02	3	1	1.20	17	8	0	0	53	39	15	7	0	13	40	.205	.192	.210	6.84	2.22
Rodriguez, Jorge	R-R	6-3	180	12-18-01	0	0	0.00	2	0	0	0	3	1	0	0	0	3	2	.100	.000	.125	6.00	9.00
Rodriguez, Luis	R-R	6-4	175	2-27-03	3	1	2.49	16	1	0	3	25	15	7	7	0	13	34	.179	.290	.113	12.08	4.62
Rodriguez, Marcos	L-L	6-3	176	10-28-02	2	1	7.62	21	0	0	0	28	31	28	24	1	23	36	.279	.185	.310	11.44	7.31
Santana, Angel	R-R	6-1	150	2-27-03	2	1	3.96	15	1	0	0	25	20	11	11	0	9	19	.220	.152	.259	6.84	3.24
Sierra, Brian	R-R	6-3	188	1-5-04	3	3	6.91	21	1	0	2	29	31	27	22	0	14	28	.261	.381	.195	8.79	4.40
Veliz, Juan	L-L	6-1	200	6-12-04	3	0	1.08	10	1	0	0	17	10	2	2	0	8	15	.172	.400	.125	8.10	4.32

Fielding

C: Aular 7, Flores 7, Gomez 5, Lander 13, Leal 27, Leon 2, Marcano 14, Melendez 33, Yustiz 31.

1B: Castillo 27, Castillo 25, Hendrick 21, Lander 11, Marte 12, Melendez 3, Monegro 7, Perez 9, Valdez 10.

2B: Camacaro 4, Castillo 2, Castillo 1, De Los Santos 19, Guance 16, Lechuga 10, Marte 9, Mata 1, Monegro 3, Mosquera 4, Perez 4, Rodriguez 25, Silvestre 11, Villavicencio 14.

3B: Camacaro 19, Castillo 1, Castillo 9, De Los Santos 4, Lander 3, Lara 29, Lechuga 1, Linares 8, Marte 4, Mata 17, Monegro 6, Perez 1, Rodriguez 13, Silvestre 1, Villavicencio 3.

SS: Camacaro 8, Castillo 5, De Los Santos 18, Guance 1, Lara 1, Linares 28, Marte 3, Mosquera 28, Villavicencio 27.

OF: Almonte 20, Campos 37, Castro 40, Cuevas 39, De Leon 28, Flores 26, Gonzalez 12, Guerrero 2, Hendrick 8, Ibarguen 11, Machado 33, Marquez 32, Mejia 29, Minaya 13, Rodriguez 2, Sanchez 12, Santana 5, Santana 1, Serrano 20.

New York Yankees

SEASON IN A SENTENCE: The Yankees overcame injuries and a boom-or-bust offense and a torrent of injuries to win 92 games, but fell to the rival Red Sox in the Wild Card Game.

HIGH POINT: With their playoff hopes hanging in the balance, the Yankees ripped off a streak of 13 straight wins in the middle of August that rejuvenated morale and helped boost them up the standings in the three-way wild card maelstrom with Boston and Toronto. The team needed every one of those wins, because the hot streak was immediately followed by a stretch of overall poor play. The Yankees finished tied with Boston in the regular season and just one game better than Toronto.

LOW POINT: Ace righthander Gerrit Cole spit the bit in the team's Wild Card Game loss to the rival Red Sox, who threw salt in the wound by closing the game with righty Garrett Whitlock, whom Boston popped in the Rule 5 draft after the Yankees left him unprotected as he finished his rehab from Tommy John surgery.

NOTABLE ROOKIES: The most significant of the Yankees rookies was Luis Gil, the team's top pitching prospect. He made his big league debut in August and showed excellent stuff, albeit with wandering control and command. He made six starts with the club and whiffed 38 in 29.1 innings. The team also sprinkled in appearances from players like Stephen Ridings, Chris Gittens, Clarke Schmidt, Deivi Garcia, Estevan Florial, Trey Amburgey and the since-traded Hoy Park.

KEY TRANSACTIONS: The Yankees made a slew of moves at the deadline, the centerpiece of which was landing slugger Joey Gallo from the Rangers for a package of four prospects. Beyond Gallo, the team also imported first baseman Anthony Rizzo from the Cubs, lefty Andrew Heaney from the Angels and relievers Joely Rodriguez and Clay Holmes from the Rangers and Pirates, respectively. Heaney was a near-immediate bust, while the other four—especially the mercurial Gallo—experienced ups and downs. Before the season, the Yankees used a four-prospect package to add righthander Jameson Taillon from the Pirates. Holmes and his nasty sinker and Rodriguez's excellent changeup added different elements to a bullpen that had been taxed throughout the year by an array of injuries to starters Luis Severino, Taillon and Corey Kluber, while Gallo and Rizzo gave the team's predominantly righthanded lineup a couple of hard-hitting doses of power from the left side.

OPENING DAY PAYROLL: $191,205,631 (2nd).

PLAYERS OF THE YEAR

MAJOR LEAGUE	MINOR LEAGUE
Aaron Judge	**Anthony Volpe**
OF	SS
.287/.373/.544	(High-A/Low-A)
39 HR, 98 RBIs	.294/.423/.604,
89 R, 149 OPS+	27 HR, 33 SB

ORGANIZATION LEADERS

Batting   *Minimum 250 AB

MAJORS

*AVG	Aaron Judge	.287
*OPS	Aaron Judge	.916
HR	Aaron Judge	39
RBI	Aaron Judge	98

MINORS

*AVG	Brandon Lockridge, Somerset, Hudson Valley	.298
*OBP	Anthony Volpe, Hudson Valley, Tampa	.423
*SLG	Anthony Volpe, Hudson Valley, Tampa	.604
*OPS	Anthony Volpe, Hudson Valley, Tampa	1.027
R	Anthony Volpe, Hudson Valley, Tampa	113
H	O. Peraza, Somerset, Scranton/W-B, Somerset, Hudson Valley	138
TB	O. Cabrera, Somerset, Scranton/W-B, Somerset	249
TB	Anthony Volpe, Hudson Valley, Tampa	249
2B	Anthony Volpe, Hudson Valley, Tampa	35
3B	Michael Beltre, Somerset	8
HR	Dermis Garcia, Somerset	31
RBI	O. Cabrera, Somerset, Scranton/W-B, Somerset	89
BB	Anthony Volpe, Hudson Valley, Tampa	78
SO	Dermis Garcia, Somerset	168
SB	O. Peraza, Somerset, Scranton/W-B, Somerset, Hudson Valley	38

Pitching   #Minimum 75 IP

MAJORS

W	Gerrit Cole	16
#ERA	Nestor Cortes	2.90
SO	Gerrit Cole	243
SV	Aroldis Chapman	30

MINORS

W	H. Wesneski, Scranton/W-B, Somerset, Hudson Valley	11
L	3 tied	7
#ERA	Randy Vasquez, Somerset, Hudson Valley, Tampa	2.52
G	Ron Marinaccio, Somerset, Scranton/W-B, Somerset	40
G	Greg Weissert, Somerset, Scranton/W-B, Somerset	40
GS	H. Wesneski, Scranton/W-B, Somerset, Hudson Valley	24
SV	Derek Craft, Hudson Valley, Tampa	11
SV	Luis Garcia, Scranton/W-B	11
IP	H. Wesneski, Scranton/W-B, Somerset, Hudson Valley	130.1
BB	Deivi Garcia, Scranton/W-B	68
SO	Ken Waldichuk, Somerset, Hudson Valley	163
#AVG	Matt Krook, Somerset, Scranton/W-B, Somerset	.175

2021 PERFORMANCE

General Manager: Brian Cashman. **Farm Director:** Kevin Reese. **Scouting Director:** Damon Oppenheimer.

Class	Team	League	W	L	PCT	Finish	Manager
Majors	New York Yankees	American	92	70	.568	t-4th (15)	Aaron Boone
Triple-A	Scranton/W.B. RailRiders	Triple-A East	75	52	.591	3rd (20)	Doug Davis
Double-A	Somerset Patriots	Double-A Northeast	72	47	.605	3rd (12)	Julio Mosquera
High-A	Hudson Valley Renegades	High-A East	71	49	.592	3rd (12)	Dan Fiorito
Low-A	Tampa Tarpons	Low-A Southeast	73	43	.629	1st (10)	David Adams
Rookie	DSL Yankees2	Dominican Summer	30	29	.508	22nd (46)	Victor Rey
Rookie	DSL Yankees1	Dominican Summer	31	28	.525	t-19th (46)	Rainiero Coa
Rookie	FCL Yankees	Florida Complex	36	16	.692	2nd (18)	Tyson Blaser/Julio Borbon
Overall 2021 Minor League Record			388	264	.595	2nd (30)	

ORGANIZATION STATISTICS

NEW YORK YANKEES
AMERICAN LEAGUE

Batting	B-T	HT	WT	DOB	AVG	vLH	vRH	G	AB	R	H	2B	3B	HR	RBI	BB	HBP	SH	SF	SO	SB	CS	SLG	OBP
Allen, Greg	B-R	6-0	185	3-15-93	.270	.500	.185	15	37	9	10	4	1	0	2	5	5	0	1	13	5	0	.432	.417
Amburgey, Trey	R-R	6-2	210	10-24-94	.000	.000	--	2	4	0	0	0	0	0	0	0	0	0	0	2	0	0	.000	.000
Andujar, Miguel	R-R	6-0	211	3-2-95	.253	.222	.275	45	154	19	39	2	0	6	12	7	0	0	1	28	0	1	.383	.284
Brantly, Rob	L-R	6-0	191	7-14-89	.150	.000	.176	6	20	0	3	1	0	0	0	1	0	0	0	4	0	0	.200	.190
Bruce, Jay	L-L	6-3	230	4-3-87	.118	.167	.091	10	34	3	4	1	0	1	3	5	0	0	0	13	0	0	.235	.231
Davis, Jonathan	R-R	5-8	190	5-12-92	.059	.000	.200	12	17	4	1	0	0	0	0	1	0	0	0	5	0	0	.059	.111
2-team total (52 Toronto)					.126	.103	.146	64	87	20	11	1	0	1	4	12	3	0	1	26	4	1	.172	.252
Florial, Estevan	L-R	6-1	195	11-25-97	.300	.000	.400	11	20	3	6	2	0	1	2	5	0	0	0	6	1	0	.550	.440
Ford, Mike	L-R	6-0	225	7-4-92	.133	.100	.140	22	60	6	8	0	0	3	5	11	1	0	0	23	0	0	.283	.278
Frazier, Clint	R-R	5-11	212	9-6-94	.186	.188	.184	66	183	20	34	9	0	5	15	32	3	0	0	65	2	0	.317	.317
Gallo, Joey	L-R	6-5	250	11-19-93	.160	.115	.181	58	188	33	30	7	0	13	22	37	2	0	1	88	0	0	.404	.303
2-team total (95 Texas)					.199	.200	.198	153	498	90	99	13	1	38	77	111	6	0	1	213	6	0	.458	.351
Gardner, Brett	L-L	5-11	195	8-24-83	.222	.253	.212	140	387	47	86	16	4	10	39	60	3	5	6	100	4	0	.362	.327
Gittens, Chris	R-R	6-4	250	2-4-94	.111	.188	.050	16	36	1	4	0	0	1	5	7	0	0	1	13	0	0	.194	.250
Hicks, Aaron	B-R	6-1	205	10-2-89	.194	.242	.173	32	108	13	21	3	0	4	14	14	2	0	2	30	0	0	.333	.294
Higashioka, Kyle	R-R	6-1	202	4-20-90	.181	.234	.155	67	193	20	35	10	0	10	29	17	0	0	1	59	0	0	.389	.246
Judge, Aaron	R-R	6-7	282	4-26-92	.287	.298	.283	148	550	89	158	24	0	39	98	75	3	0	5	158	6	1	.544	.373
LaMarre, Ryan	R-L	6-1	215	11-21-88	.190	.214	.143	9	21	3	4	0	0	2	4	0	0	0	0	6	1	0	.476	.292
LeMahieu, DJ	R-R	6-4	220	7-13-88	.268	.266	.269	150	597	84	160	24	1	10	57	73	4	0	5	94	4	2	.362	.349
Locastro, Tim	R-R	6-1	190	7-14-92	.190	.500	.000	9	21	4	4	2	0	1	2	1	0	0	1	7	0	0	.429	.217
Odor, Rougned	L-R	5-11	200	2-3-94	.202	.227	.191	102	322	42	65	12	0	15	39	27	11	1	0	100	0	1	.379	.286
Park, Hoy	L-R	6-1	175	4-7-96	.000	--	.000	1	1	0	0	0	0	0	0	0	0	0	0	0	0	0	.000	.000
Rizzo, Anthony	L-L	6-3	240	8-8-89	.249	.313	.211	49	173	32	43	7	0	8	21	16	9	0	2	28	2	0	.428	.340
Sanchez, Gary	R-R	6-2	230	12-2-92	.204	.230	.193	117	383	54	78	13	1	23	54	52	5	0	0	121	0	0	.423	.307
Stanton, Giancarlo	R-R	6-6	245	11-8-89	.273	.271	.273	139	510	64	139	19	0	35	97	63	3	0	3	157	0	0	.516	.354
Tauchman, Mike	L-L	6-2	220	12-3-90	.214	.429	.000	11	14	1	3	1	0	0	0	1	0	1	0	6	2	0	.286	.267
Torres, Gleyber	R-R	6-1	205	12-13-96	.259	.293	.245	127	459	50	119	22	0	9	51	50	1	2	4	104	14	6	.366	.331
Urshela, Gio	R-R	6-0	215	10-11-91	.267	.293	.254	116	420	42	112	18	2	14	49	20	1	0	1	109	1	0	.419	.301
Velazquez, Andrew	B-R	5-9	170	7-14-94	.224	.208	.233	28	67	11	15	4	1	1	6	1	0	0	0	23	4	1	.358	.235
Voit, Luke	R-R	6-3	255	2-13-91	.239	.259	.227	68	213	26	51	7	1	11	35	21	7	0	0	74	0	0	.437	.328
Wade, Tyler	L-R	6-1	188	11-23-94	.268	.325	.241	103	127	31	34	5	1	0	5	16	1	0	0	37	17	6	.323	.354

Pitching	B-T	HT	WT	DOB	W	L	ERA	G	GS	CG	SV	IP	H	R	ER	HR	BB	SO	AVG	vLH	vRH	K/9	BB/9
Abreu, Albert	R-R	6-2	190	9-26-95	2	0	5.15	28	0	0	1	37	27	21	21	8	19	35	.206	.208	.205	8.59	4.66
Britton, Zack	L-L	6-1	200	12-22-87	0	1	5.89	22	0	0	1	18	17	14	12	2	14	16	.262	.176	.292	7.85	6.87
Cessa, Luis	R-R	6-0	208	4-25-92	3	1	2.82	29	0	0	0	38	31	17	12	2	17	31	.218	.161	.256	7.28	3.99
Chapman, Aroldis	L-L	6-4	218	2-28-88	6	4	3.36	61	0	0	30	56	36	23	21	9	38	97	.182	.116	.200	15.50	6.07
Cole, Gerrit	R-R	6-4	220	9-8-90	16	8	3.23	30	30	2	0	181	151	69	65	24	41	243	.223	.216	.229	12.06	2.03
Cortes, Nestor	R-L	5-11	210	12-10-94	2	3	2.90	22	14	0	0	93	75	32	30	14	25	103	.217	.228	.214	9.97	2.42
Garcia, Deivi	R-R	5-9	163	5-19-99	0	2	6.48	2	2	0	0	8	8	7	6	1	4	7	.250	.353	.133	7.56	4.32
German, Domingo	R-R	6-2	181	8-4-92	4	5	4.58	22	18	0	0	98	89	52	50	17	27	98	.234	.214	.251	8.97	2.47
Gil, Luis	R-R	6-2	185	6-3-98	1	1	3.07	6	6	0	0	29	20	11	10	4	19	38	.183	.167	.194	11.66	5.83
Green, Chad	L-R	6-3	215	5-24-91	10	7	3.12	67	0	0	6	84	57	32	29	14	17	99	.193	.200	.188	10.65	1.83
Heaney, Andrew	L-L	6-2	200	6-5-91	2	2	7.32	12	5	0	0	36	38	29	29	13	10	37	.268	.222	.278	9.34	2.52
2-team total (18 Los Angeles)					8	9	5.83	30	23	0	0	130	130	85	84	29	41	150	.256	.260	.255	10.41	2.85
Holmes, Clay	R-R	6-5	245	3-27-93	5	2	1.61	25	0	0	0	28	18	8	5	2	4	34	.180	.200	.179	10.93	1.29
King, Michael	R-R	6-3	210	5-25-95	2	4	3.55	22	6	0	0	63	57	29	25	6	24	62	.236	.256	.225	8.81	3.41
Kluber, Corey	R-R	6-4	215	4-10-86	5	3	3.83	16	16	1	0	80	74	37	34	8	33	82	.247	.218	.267	9.23	3.71
Koerner, Brody	R-R	6-2	220	10-17-93	0	0	3.00	2	0	0	0	3	2	1	1	0	2	1	.200	.333	.143	3.00	6.00
Kriske, Brooks	R-R	6-3	190	2-3-94	1	1	15.26	8	0	0	0	8	12	14	13	5	6	7	.375	.333	.391	8.22	7.04
2-team total (4 Baltimore)					2	1	14.29	12	0	0	0	11	17	19	18	7	6	11	.362	.385	.353	8.74	4.76
Loaisiga, Jonathan	R-R	5-11	165	11-2-94	9	4	2.17	57	0	0	5	71	56	19	17	3	16	69	.215	.238	.200	8.79	2.04

Luetge, Lucas	L-L	6-4	205	3-24-87	4	2	2.74	57	1	0	1	72	67	30	22	6	15	78	.238	.196	.259	9.71	1.87
Montgomery, Jordan	L-L	6-6	228	12-27-92	6	7	3.83	30	30	0	0	157	150	73	67	19	51	162	.250	.227	.256	9.27	2.92
Nelson, Nick	R-R	6-1	205	12-5-95	0	2	8.79	11	2	0	0	14	15	16	14	0	16	22	.263	.259	.267	13.81	10.05
O'Day, Darren	R-R	6-4	220	10-22-82	0	0	3.38	12	0	0	0	11	9	4	4	2	4	11	.220	.083	.276	9.28	3.38
Peralta, Wandy	L-L	6-0	217	7-27-91	3	3	2.95	46	1	0	3	43	38	19	14	5	18	35	.235	.203	.252	7.38	3.80
Ridings, Stephen	R-R	6-8	220	8-14-95	0	0	1.80	5	0	0	0	5	4	2	1	0	2	7	.235	.000	.444	12.60	3.60
Rodriguez, Joely	L-L	6-1	200	11-14-91	1	0	2.84	21	0	0	0	19	21	8	6	1	6	17	.304	.240	.341	8.05	2.84
2-team total (31 Texas)					2	3	4.66	52	0	0	1	46	53	27	24	4	18	47	.294	.203	.339	9.13	3.50
Romano, Sal	L-R	6-5	255	10-12-93	0	1	5.40	4	0	0	0	3	7	2	2	0	2	5	.412	.200	.500	13.50	5.40
Schmidt, Clarke	R-R	6-1	209	2-20-96	0	0	5.68	2	1	0	0	6	11	8	4	1	5	6	.355	.500	.200	8.53	7.11
Severino, Luis	R-R	6-2	218	2-20-94	1	0	0.00	4	0	0	0	6	2	0	0	1	8	.100	.333	.059	12.00	1.50
Taillon, Jameson	R-R	6-5	230	11-18-91	8	6	4.30	29	29	0	0	144	130	73	69	24	44	140	.238	.225	.247	8.73	2.74
Wilson, Justin	L-L	6-2	205	8-18-87	1	1	7.50	21	0	0	0	18	18	17	15	5	9	15	.250	.318	.220	7.50	4.50
Wojciechowski, Asher	R-R	6-4	235	12-21-88	0	0	4.50	1	1	0	0	4	3	2	2	1	3	4	.200	.143	.250	9.00	6.75

Fielding

Catcher	PCT	G	PO	A	E	DP	PB
Brantly	1.000	5	37	3	0	0	0
Higashioka	.995	66	609	18	3	1	6
Sanchez	.994	110	932	54	6	1	8

First Base	PCT	G	PO	A	E	DP
Andujar	1.000	2	21	0	0	2
Brantly	1.000	1	4	0	0	1
Bruce	1.000	10	55	2	0	5
Ford	1.000	21	130	9	0	19
Gittens	1.000	13	79	4	0	4
LeMahieu	.997	55	286	13	1	21
Rizzo	.991	47	308	24	3	30
Voit	.983	42	277	15	5	21

Second Base	PCT	G	PO	A	E	DP
LeMahieu	.993	83	117	156	2	48

	PCT	G	PO	A	E	DP
Odor	.962	74	89	140	9	29
Torres	.986	19	33	39	1	11
Wade	.950	19	21	17	2	7

Third Base	PCT	G	PO	A	E	DP
Andujar	1.000	4	0	4	0	1
LeMahieu	.930	39	18	62	6	6
Odor	.940	33	12	51	4	8
Urshela	.959	96	56	175	10	26
Wade	.939	27	9	22	2	3

Shortstop	PCT	G	PO	A	E	DP
Torres	.952	108	121	236	18	37
Urshela	.970	28	23	42	2	6
Velazquez	.963	28	25	54	3	5
Wade	1.000	31	15	31	0	3

Outfield	PCT	G	PO	A	E	DP
Allen	1.000	17	28	0	0	0
Amburgey	1.000	2	6	0	0	0
Andujar	.985	37	62	3	1	0
Davis	1.000	10	17	1	0	0
Florial	1.000	11	16	0	0	0
Frazier	.988	70	82	1	1	0
Gallo	.972	60	98	5	3	0
Gardner	.996	140	253	3	1	1
Hicks	.983	32	56	1	1	1
Judge	.988	137	246	10	3	2
LaMarre	.889	9	8	0	1	0
Locastro	1.000	9	13	0	0	0
Park	1.000	1	2	0	0	0
Stanton	.980	26	50	0	1	0
Tauchman	1.000	9	12	0	0	0
Wade	1.000	25	22	1	0	0

SCRANTON/WILKES-BARRE RAILRIDERS   TRIPLE-A

TRIPLE-A EAST

Batting	B-T	HT	WT	DOB	AVG	vLH	vRH	G	AB	R	H	2B	3B	HR	RBI	BB	HBP	SH	SF	SO	SB	CS	SLG	OBP
Allen, Greg	B-R	6-0	185	3-15-93	.326	.317	.329	73	215	49	70	13	1	5	28	26	19	3	0	45	26	2	.465	.442
Alvarez, Armando	R-R	6-1	195	7-14-94	.236	.257	.227	106	360	46	85	25	0	10	52	37	0	0	5	70	2	1	.389	.303
Amburgey, Trey	R-R	6-2	210	10-24-94	.276	.356	.235	71	257	36	71	23	2	8	52	25	1	0	5	81	1	0	.475	.337
Andujar, Miguel	R-R	6-0	211	3-2-95	.333	.417	.310	16	54	13	18	1	0	5	13	7	0	0	2	6	0	0	.630	.397
Brantly, Rob	L-R	6-0	191	7-14-89	.289	.231	.307	68	228	35	66	9	1	9	43	20	14	0	2	41	1	0	.456	.379
Brito, Socrates	L-L	6-2	205	9-6-92	.251	.311	.227	107	375	57	94	16	2	9	53	32	6	0	6	95	23	3	.376	.315
Burt, Max	R-R	6-2	185	8-28-96	.187	.269	.160	36	107	16	20	8	0	1	10	11	0	1	1	33	2	0	.290	.261
Cabrera, Oswaldo	B-R	5-10	145	3-1-99	.500	.250	.538	9	30	11	15	2	1	5	11	5	1	0	0	9	1	0	1.133	.583
Chirinos, Robinson	R-R	6-1	220	6-5-84	.278	.389	.167	13	36	6	10	1	0	3	6	9	0	0	0	16	0	0	.556	.422
Cuevas, Frederick	L-L	5-11	185	10-27-97	.167	.200	.158	8	24	4	4	1	0	1	2	1	0	1	0	4	1	0	.333	.200
Davis, Jonathan	R-R	5-8	190	5-12-92	.193	.063	.244	17	57	13	11	2	1	2	8	9	5	0	1	20	4	2	.368	.347
2-team total (3 Buffalo)					.194	.053	.250	20	67	16	13	2	1	2	9	12	6	0	1	23	5	2	.343	.360
Deglan, Kellin	L-R	6-2	205	5-3-92	.233	.667	.185	12	30	3	7	1	0	1	3	2	0	0	0	10	0	0	.367	.281
2-team total (27 Buffalo Bisons)					.211	.273	.204	39	109	13	23	4	0	4	16	14	4	0	1	40	1	0	.358	.320
Dietrich, Derek	L-R	6-2	205	7-18-89	.215	.222	.213	36	107	19	23	4	0	5	22	27	9	0	0	46	0	0	.393	.413
2-team total (43 Rochester)					.163	.164	.163	79	239	32	39	7	0	8	35	40	23	0	0	97	0	0	.293	.338
Florial, Estevan	L-R	6-1	195	11-25-97	.218	.211	.221	78	312	65	68	17	1	13	41	42	3	3	2	112	13	7	.404	.315
Ford, Mike	L-R	6-0	225	7-4-92	.083	.000	.167	7	24	3	2	0	0	1	3	1	0	1	0	8	0	0	.083	.207
3-team total (40 Durham, 29 Rochester)					.213	.152	.238	76	268	35	57	10	1	14	44	35	3	0	1	81	1	0	.414	.309
Gittens, Chris	R-R	6-4	250	2-4-94	.301	.447	.232	45	146	37	44	8	0	14	44	36	1	0	1	46	0	0	.644	.440
Holder, Kyle	L-R	6-1	204	5-25-94	.216	.234	.210	78	250	23	54	10	1	3	23	24	5	6	2	67	2	2	.276	.295
Illig, Chase	B-R	6-0	210	9-14-96	1.000	--	1.000	1	1	0	1	0	0	0	0	0	0	0	0	0	0	0	1.000	1.000
LaMarre, Ryan	R-L	6-1	215	11-21-88	.277	.254	.289	60	206	27	57	13	2	6	34	27	7	0	0	62	14	6	.447	.379
Lopez, Jason	R-R	5-10	160	3-16-98	.300	.333	.286	3	10	1	3	1	0	1	3	2	0	0	0	5	0	0	.700	.417
McDowell, Max	R-R	6-1	208	1-12-94	.227	.240	.218	45	128	26	29	6	0	1	10	20	12	1	0	35	3	1	.297	.381
Milone, Thomas	L-L	5-11	190	1-26-95	.285	.214	.316	40	137	19	39	8	1	4	13	11	2	0	0	41	5	2	.445	.347
Park, Hoy	L-R	6-1	175	4-7-96	.327	.324	.330	48	171	44	56	9	1	10	29	46	3	2	1	46	8	4	.567	.475
2-team total (8 Indianapolis)					.306	.239	.326	56	193	46	59	9	1	10	32	53	4	2	2	53	9	4	.518	.460
Peraza, Oswald	R-R	6-0	165	6-15-00	.286	.200	.304	8	28	5	8	0	0	1	2	2	0	0	1	5	2	1	.393	.323
Perez, Cristian	R-R	5-10	170	10-26-98	.220	.167	.244	47	132	20	29	5	0	1	13	14	2	1	0	23	5	0	.280	.304
Pita, Matt	R-R	5-10	175	4-21-97	.228	.250	.216	27	79	12	18	2	0	7	15	6	3	0	0	24	2	4	.519	.307
Sands, Donny	R-R	6-2	190	5-16-96	.272	.390	.226	42	147	20	40	6	0	8	29	16	0	0	2	32	0	1	.476	.339
Torres, Gleyber	R-R	6-1	205	12-13-96	.167	.500	.000	2	6	0	1	0	0	0	1	0	0	1	0	1	0	0	.167	.286
Velazquez, Andrew	R-R	5-9	170	7-14-94	.273	.278	.270	77	264	40	72	20	3	7	46	37	1	2	2	87	29	3	.451	.362
Voit, Luke	R-R	6-3	255	2-13-91	.344	.143	.400	9	32	8	11	3	0	4	9	3	1	0	0	8	0	0	.813	.417
Wagner, Brandon	L-R	6-0	210	8-24-95	.158	.125	.168	57	133	18	21	3	0	4	16	27	2	1	1	67	1	1	.263	.307
Zehner, Zack	R-R	6-4	215	8-8-92	.143	.375	.074	12	35	4	5	2	1	0	4	10	0	0	0	15	3	0	.257	.333

Pitching	B-T	HT	WT	DOB	W	L	ERA	G	GS	CG	SV	IP	H	R	ER	HR	BB	SO	AVG	vLH	vRH	K/9	BB/9
2-team total (60 Jacksonville)																			.239	.308	.207	72	205 23 49 11 2 4 23 30 0 0 2 70 6 0 .371 .333
Abreu, Albert	R-R	6-2	190	9-26-95	1	0	3.78	10	0	0	2	17	10	7	7	0	11	31	.169	.095	.211	16.74	5.94
Barraclough, Kyle	R-R	6-3	229	5-23-90	4	0	3.21	11	0	0	0	14	5	5	5	2	11	24	.114	.100	.125	15.43	7.07
2-team total (21 St. Paul)					8	1	2.75	32	0	0	0	39	20	12	12	6	21	62	.153	.184	.134	14.19	4.81
Boyle, Sean	R-R	6-1	205	10-29-96	2	0	1.07	6	4	1	0	25	15	3	3	1	4	25	.170	.200	.146	8.88	1.42
Bristo, Braden	R-R	6-0	180	11-1-94	5	3	4.86	38	1	0	0	50	40	28	27	7	30	61	.221	.237	.210	10.98	5.40
Britton, Zack	L-L	6-1	200	12-22-87	0	0	27.00	2	1	0	0	1	3	4	4	1	2	1	.500	.500	.500	6.75	13.50
Cortes, Nestor	R-L	5-11	210	12-10-94	1	1	1.20	5	1	0	1	15	8	2	2	1	1	18	.160	.071	.194	10.80	0.60
Gadea, Kevin	R-R	6-5	240	12-6-94	0	0	0.00	2	0	0	0	5	1	1	0	0	1	5	.063	.143	.000	9.00	1.80
Garcia, Deivi	R-R	5-9	163	5-19-99	3	7	6.85	24	22	0	0	91	102	73	69	21	68	97	.285	.339	.237	9.63	6.75
Garcia, Luis	R-R	6-2	240	1-30-87	1	2	3.63	18	0	0	11	17	16	8	7	2	3	19	.246	.320	.200	9.87	1.56
German, Domingo	R-R	6-2	181	8-4-92	1	0	2.25	2	0	0	0	4	4	1	1	0	2	7	.267	.273	.250	15.75	4.50
Gil, Luis	R-R	6-2	185	6-3-98	4	0	4.81	13	10	0	1	49	35	26	26	7	32	67	.202	.198	.207	12.39	5.92
Goody, Nick	R-R	5-11	200	7-6-91	4	3	4.28	28	0	0	1	34	24	18	16	7	11	46	.198	.182	.208	12.30	2.94
2-team total (11 Rochester)					4	6	4.53	39	0	0	1	48	37	28	24	8	18	59	.211	.177	.230	11.14	3.40
Green, Nick	R-R	6-1	175	3-25-95	3	2	3.95	25	7	0	0	55	47	29	24	3	35	53	.234	.169	.286	8.73	5.76
Keller, Brian	R-R	6-3	210	6-21-94	2	2	2.77	26	11	0	0	55	43	21	17	3	46	65	.214	.198	.225	10.57	7.48
King, Michael	R-R	6-3	210	5-25-95	0	1	4.76	3	1	0	1	6	5	3	3	1	0	11	.227	.273	.182	17.47	0.00
Kluber, Corey	R-R	6-4	215	4-10-86	1	0	9.00	1	0	0	0	3	2	3	3	1	2	4	.182	.000	.222	12.00	6.00
Koerner, Brody	R-R	6-2	220	10-17-93	3	4	3.39	26	15	0	0	77	75	30	29	8	23	64	.258	.214	.294	7.48	2.69
Kriske, Brooks	R-R	6-2	190	2-3-94	1	1	3.81	24	0	0	1	28	15	12	12	2	14	41	.155	.116	.185	13.02	4.45
2-team total (1 Norfolk)					1	1	3.68	25	0	0	1	29	15	12	12	2	14	43	.150	.114	.179	13.19	4.30
Krook, Matt	L-L	6-4	225	10-21-94	6	5	3.17	17	14	0	0	77	51	33	27	4	49	88	.185	.154	.197	10.33	5.75
Lane, Trevor	L-L	5-11	185	4-24-94	4	0	1.99	17	0	0	1	23	20	6	5	1	5	28	.241	.167	.283	11.12	1.99
Maciejewski, Josh	R-L	6-3	175	8-14-95	0	2	6.50	4	4	0	0	18	24	14	13	3	10	11	.316	.333	.309	5.50	5.00
Marinaccio, Ron	R-R	6-2	205	7-1-95	1	0	2.36	18	0	0	2	27	18	8	7	2	8	41	.186	.226	.136	13.84	2.70
McClain, Reggie	R-R	6-2	180	11-16-92	5	2	1.79	36	1	0	0	55	37	12	11	1	26	57	.193	.228	.168	9.27	4.23
Montgomery, Mike	L-L	6-5	220	7-1-89	1	2	7.56	4	4	0	0	17	19	15	14	2	9	16	.288	.211	.319	8.64	4.86
Nelson, Nick	R-R	6-1	205	12-5-95	3	4	3.81	29	5	0	1	52	50	31	22	6	29	62	.250	.244	.254	10.73	5.02
Otto, Glenn	R-R	6-3	240	3-11-96	1	0	4.35	2	2	0	0	10	14	5	5	0	3	12	.311	.333	.300	10.45	2.61
O'Day, Darren	R-R	6-4	220	10-22-82	0	0	0.00	3	0	0	0	3	2	0	0	0	0	6	.182	.200	.167	18.00	0.00
Ridings, Stephen	R-R	6-8	220	8-14-95	1	0	2.70	8	0	0	1	10	8	6	3	2	2	12	.211	.167	.231	10.80	1.80
Romano, Sal	L-R	6-5	255	10-12-93	1	1	3.56	25	0	0	2	30	36	18	12	1	5	25	.298	.386	.247	7.42	1.48
Russ, Addison	R-R	6-1	200	10-29-94	0	0	8.74	8	0	0	0	11	12	11	11	2	14	13	.279	.313	.259	10.32	11.12
Schmidt, Clarke	R-R	6-1	209	2-20-96	0	1	2.10	6	5	0	0	26	25	14	6	4	8	32	.245	.208	.278	11.22	2.81
Sears, JP	R-L	5-11	180	2-19-96	7	0	2.87	10	10	0	0	53	41	19	17	5	11	65	.215	.254	.197	10.97	1.86
Semple, Shawn	R-R	6-1	220	10-9-95	0	1	16.20	3	2	0	0	5	8	10	9	0	7	1	.364	.455	.273	1.80	12.60
Taillon, Jameson	R-R	6-5	230	11-18-91	0	0	6.00	1	1	0	0	3	4	2	2	0	2	2	.308	.250	.333	6.00	6.00
Wagner, Brandon	L-R	6-0	210	8-24-95	0	1	0.00	2	0	0	0	2	1	0	0	0	2	2	.250	.333	.200	9.00	9.00
Warren, Adam	R-R	6-1	224	8-25-87	4	4	3.59	38	1	0	2	58	55	26	23	5	29	60	.252	.239	.262	9.36	4.53
Weissert, Greg	R-R	6-2	215	2-4-95	3	1	1.96	28	0	0	2	37	20	11	8	2	22	40	.156	.207	.114	9.82	5.40
Wesneski, Hayden	R-R	6-3	210	12-5-97	2	1	3.27	3	2	0	0	11	10	4	4	0	5	12	.244	.286	.222	9.82	4.09
Wilson, Justin	L-L	6-2	205	8-18-87	0	0	0.00	3	0	0	0	3	0	0	0	0	2	2	.000	.000	.000	6.00	6.00
Wojciechowski, Asher	R-R	6-4	235	12-21-88	0	1	5.68	4	3	0	1	13	14	8	8	1	5	17	.298	.368	.250	12.08	3.55

Fielding

Catcher	PCT	G	PO	A	E	DP	PB
Brantly	.975	43	373	23	10	4	5
Chirinos	.990	11	99	5	1	0	0
Deglan	1.000	7	38	5	0	0	0
Illig	1.000	1	5	0	0	0	0
Lopez	.971	3	31	2	1	0	1
McDowell	.995	39	346	20	2	5	3
Sands	.995	37	361	10	2	3	1

First Base	PCT	G	PO	A	E	DP
Alvarez	.985	20	116	12	2	12
Andujar	1.000	3	15	0	0	1
Brantly	.977	20	116	9	3	9
Burt	1.000	1	6	1	0	0
Deglan	.000	1	0	0	0	0
Dietrich	.979	11	43	3	1	4
Ford	.975	6	35	4	1	8
Gittens	.988	38	234	16	3	18
LaMarre	1.000	2	2	0	0	0
Sands	.000	1	0	0	0	0
Voit	.944	6	32	2	2	4
Wagner	.992	45	244	17	2	32

Second Base	PCT	G	PO	A	E	DP
Alvarez	1.000	6	5	11	0	1
Burt	.966	14	23	34	2	7

Cabrera	1.000	7	10	16	0	6
Dietrich	.970	17	26	39	2	7
Holder	.989	28	39	47	1	14
Park	.987	23	25	49	1	12
Perez	.962	12	18	33	2	7
Pita	1.000	9	13	18	0	3
Velazquez	.982	24	49	58	2	19
Wagner	1.000	3	1	0	0	0

Third Base	PCT	G	PO	A	E	DP
Alvarez	.925	81	45	116	13	13
Andujar	1.000	1	0	1	0	0
Burt	.973	18	19	17	1	3
Cabrera	.667	1	2	2	1	0
Dietrich	1.000	9	5	12	0	4
Holder	.889	8	4	12	2	2
Perez	1.000	14	3	23	0	4
Sands	.000	1	0	0	0	0
Velazquez	.952	10	7	13	1	0
Wagner	1.000	6	0	4	0	0

Shortstop	PCT	G	PO	A	E	DP
Burt	1.000	6	1	8	0	1
Cabrera	1.000	1	0	1	0	0
Holder	.944	44	44	75	7	20
Park	.973	20	26	46	2	11

Peraza	.964	7	4	23	1	3
Perez	.986	18	26	42	1	8
Torres	1.000	2	0	3	0	0
Velazquez	.968	42	47	75	4	19

Outfield	PCT	G	PO	A	E	DP
Allen	.980	64	92	4	2	1
Amburgey	.987	47	74	3	1	0
Andujar	1.000	11	8	1	0	0
Brito	.992	84	124	2	1	0
Cuevas	.938	7	14	1	1	0
Davis	.970	16	29	3	1	0
Florial	.972	73	135	4	4	2
Holder	1.000	1	1	0	0	0
LaMarre	.991	49	105	5	1	2
Milone	.983	38	56	1	1	0
Park	1.000	6	9	0	0	0
Pita	1.000	11	16	0	0	0
Velazquez	1.000	4	2	0	0	0
Wagner	1.000	1	3	0	0	0
Zehner	1.000	9	9	0	0	0

SOMERSET PATRIOTS

DOUBLE-A

DOUBLE-A NORTHEAST

NEW YORK YANKEES

Batting	B-T	HT	WT	DOB	AVG	vLH	vRH	G	AB	R	H	2B	3B	HR	RBI	BB	HBP	SH	SF	SO	SB	CS	SLG	OBP
Alexander, Evan	L-L	6-2	175	2-26-98	.235	.333	.214	4	17	2	4	1	0	1	1	2	0	0	0	5	0	0	.471	.316
Bastidas, Jesus	R-R	5-10	145	9-14-98	.278	.303	.263	29	90	22	25	6	0	5	16	14	4	0	2	25	3	2	.511	.391
Bell, Chad	L-R	6-3	210	3-4-97	.178	.128	.206	30	107	13	19	1	0	5	9	10	0	0	0	41	1	0	.327	.248
Beltre, Michael	L-R	6-3	220	7-3-95	.256	.250	.259	109	398	72	102	21	8	16	54	50	4	0	1	110	37	5	.470	.344
Breaux, Josh	R-R	6-1	220	10-7-97	.240	.300	.214	26	100	14	24	8	0	6	17	4	1	0	1	26	1	0	.500	.274
Burt, Max	R-R	6-2	185	8-28-96	.241	.162	.264	49	162	24	39	8	0	5	19	14	2	0	0	41	4	0	.383	.309
Cabrera, Oswaldo	B-R	5-10	145	3-1-99	.256	.227	.269	109	437	61	112	29	1	24	78	36	0	2	3	118	20	5	.492	.311
Castillo, Diego	R-R	5-11	185	10-28-97	.277	.300	.268	58	224	44	62	18	0	11	32	21	3	0	1	34	8	3	.504	.345
2-team total (28 Altoona)					.278	.310	.267	86	334	55	93	21	0	16	48	31	3	1	1	43	9	5	.485	.344
Cuevas, Frederick	L-L	5-11	185	10-27-97	.148	.143	.150	8	27	4	4	0	0	1	1	4	0	0	0	10	1	0	.259	.258
Dunn, Oliver	L-R	5-10	185	9-2-97	.182	.233	.159	35	99	18	18	4	0	4	17	17	0	1	1	40	5	1	.343	.299
Florial, Estevan	L-R	6-1	195	11-25-97	.229	.250	.217	9	35	5	8	2	0	4	6	4	0	0	0	9	0	1	.629	.308
Frazier, Clint	R-R	5-11	212	9-6-94	.333	1.000	.200	2	6	0	2	0	0	0	0	1	0	0	0	1	0	0	.333	.429
Garcia, Dermis	R-R	6-3	200	1-7-98	.210	.200	.214	109	385	58	81	11	1	31	67	52	3	0	3	168	10	2	.486	.307
Gasper, Mickey	B-R	5-10	205	10-11-95	.343	.300	.360	10	35	10	12	2	2	1	7	2	2	0	1	6	2	0	.600	.400
Gilliam, Isiah	B-R	6-3	220	7-23-96	.235	.228	.238	100	328	40	77	22	1	11	41	47	4	0	4	116	26	10	.409	.334
Gittens, Chris	R-R	6-4	250	2-4-94	.375	.333	.400	2	8	3	3	0	0	1	3	1	0	0	0	2	0	0	.750	.444
Illig, Chase	B-R	6-0	210	9-14-96	.087	.000	.167	11	23	0	2	1	0	0	3	6	0	0	0	11	0	0	.130	.276
Lockridge, Brandon	R-R	6-1	185	3-14-97	.328	.352	.317	43	174	33	57	10	0	10	24	13	3	0	1	58	13	1	.557	.382
Lopez, Jason	R-R	5-10	160	3-16-98	.196	.128	.224	49	163	17	32	4	1	4	18	25	0	0	5	58	7	0	.307	.303
McDowell, Max	R-R	6-1	208	1-12-94	.133	.167	.111	5	15	5	2	2	0	0	2	4	2	0	0	8	0	0	.267	.381
Milone, Thomas	L-L	5-11	190	1-26-95	.276	.233	.298	56	174	27	48	9	2	6	25	34	1	0	2	54	10	7	.454	.393
Palensky, Aaron	R-R	5-11	190	9-22-98	.216	.118	.260	37	111	11	24	8	2	2	14	21	4	0	0	38	0	3	.378	.360
Park, Hoy	L-R	6-1	175	4-7-96	.194	.182	.200	10	31	4	6	1	0	1	3	6	0	1	1	3	0	1	.323	.316
Peraza, Oswald	R-R	6-0	165	6-15-00	.294	.244	.314	79	326	51	96	16	2	12	40	23	4	0	0	82	20	8	.466	.348
Perez, Cristian	R-R	5-10	170	10-26-98	.214	.167	.227	9	28	4	6	1	0	0	0	2	1	0	0	6	3	0	.250	.290
Pita, Matt	R-R	5-10	175	4-21-97	.225	.370	.173	33	102	18	23	11	0	1	12	7	4	0	1	32	10	1	.363	.298
Sanchez, Gary	R-R	6-2	230	12-2-92	.000	.000	.000	1	2	0	0	0	0	0	0	1	0	0	0	0	0	0	.000	.333
Sands, Donny	R-R	6-2	190	5-16-96	.257	.248	.260	52	194	27	49	10	0	10	27	16	3	0	2	25	2	0	.459	.316
Torrealba, Eduardo	R-R	5-8	140	3-26-99	.182	.000	.250	3	11	0	2	0	0	0	0	0	0	0	0	2	0	0	.182	.182
Torres, Gleyber	R-R	6-1	205	12-13-96	.500	.500	--	1	2	1	1	0	0	1	1	2	0	0	0	0	0	0	2.000	.750
Urshela, Gio	R-R	6-0	215	10-11-91	.500	.500	.500	2	8	3	4	1	0	0	0	1	0	0	0	1	0	0	.625	.556
Voit, Luke	R-R	6-3	255	2-13-91	.438	.286	.556	5	16	4	7	1	0	2	6	1	0	0	0	5	0	0	.875	.471
Wagner, Brandon	L-R	6-0	210	8-24-95	.227	.500	.167	6	22	1	5	0	0	0	2	2	0	0	0	8	0	0	.227	.292
Zehner, Zack	R-R	6-4	215	8-8-92	.300	.286	.308	7	20	4	6	1	0	0	1	1	0	0	0	7	0	1	.350	.462

Pitching	B-T	HT	WT	DOB	W	L	ERA	G	GS	CG	SV	IP	H	R	ER	HR	BB	SO	AVG	vLH	vRH	K/9	BB/9
Anderson, Reid	R-R	6-0	200	9-6-95	1	0	3.95	8	0	0	0	14	9	7	6	2	7	21	.180	.083	.211	13.83	4.61
Boyle, Sean	R-R	6-1	205	10-29-96	2	0	1.32	4	0	0	0	14	13	5	2	0	3	17	.255	.160	.346	11.20	1.98
Brito, Jhony	R-R	6-2	160	2-17-98	3	3	5.01	8	8	0	0	47	50	28	26	8	9	45	.269	.310	.232	8.68	1.74
Britton, Zack	L-L	6-1	200	12-22-87	0	0	6.00	3	2	0	0	3	2	2	2	1	1	4	.167	.000	.222	12.00	3.00
Curtis, Keegan	R-R	6-0	175	9-30-95	1	1	3.94	12	0	0	2	16	14	9	7	0	7	27	.241	.158	.282	15.19	3.94
Ernst, Nick	R-R	6-3	195	8-27-96	0	2	3.31	11	0	0	3	16	6	7	6	1	7	25	.105	.167	.061	13.78	3.86
Espinal, Carlos	R-R	5-11	175	10-21-96	1	1	6.75	8	0	0	0	16	18	13	12	3	11	20	.286	.261	.300	11.25	6.19
Gadea, Kevin	R-R	6-5	240	12-6-94	2	1	2.97	26	0	0	1	36	28	14	12	2	22	53	.214	.141	.284	13.13	5.45
Gil, Luis	R-R	6-2	185	6-3-98	1	1	2.64	7	7	0	0	31	24	11	9	2	13	50	.207	.289	.167	14.67	3.82
Gomez, Michael	R-R	6-3	210	8-15-96	4	2	3.12	31	0	0	2	49	38	24	17	4	14	50	.203	.195	.209	9.18	2.57
Green, Nick	R-R	6-1	175	3-25-95	1	2	3.31	6	1	0	0	16	12	6	6	2	10	12	.200	.148	.242	6.61	5.51
Greene, Zach	R-R	6-1	215	8-29-96	2	5	3.66	25	0	0	2	39	33	19	16	4	13	58	.226	.304	.156	13.27	2.97
Junk, Janson	R-R	6-1	177	1-15-96	4	1	1.78	14	12	0	1	66	43	13	13	6	20	68	.185	.186	.185	9.32	2.74
Kluber, Corey	R-R	6-4	215	4-10-86	0	0	12.60	2	2	0	0	5	7	7	7	0	5	5	.350	.500	.200	9.00	9.00
Krook, Matt	L-L	6-4	225	10-21-94	1	1	2.15	7	7	0	0	29	15	9	7	1	11	44	.147	.094	.171	13.50	3.38
Loseke, Barrett	R-R	6-0	170	11-12-96	1	1	4.33	14	0	0	2	27	23	13	13	6	13	33	.228	.204	.250	11.00	4.33
Marinaccio, Ron	R-R	6-2	205	7-1-95	1	1	1.82	22	0	0	3	40	17	8	8	2	19	64	.129	.132	.127	14.52	4.31
Medina, Luis	R-R	6-1	175	5-3-99	4	3	3.67	15	14	0	0	74	65	35	30	7	41	83	.239	.259	.218	10.14	5.01
Otto, Glenn	R-R	6-3	240	3-11-96	6	3	3.17	11	10	0	0	65	46	23	23	6	14	103	.197	.185	.206	14.19	1.93
Peguero, Elvis	R-R	6-5	208	3-20-97	1	0	1.50	6	0	0	0	12	6	4	2	1	5	17	.140	.118	.154	12.75	3.75
Peralta, Wandy	L-L	6-0	217	7-27-91	1	0	0.00	3	1	0	0	3	1	0	0	0	1	5	.091	.000	.125	13.50	2.70
Ridings, Stephen	R-R	6-8	220	8-14-95	4	0	0.47	14	0	0	2	19	8	2	1	0	2	30	.123	.034	.194	14.21	0.95
Russ, Addison	R-R	6-1	200	10-29-94	3	2	1.91	27	0	0	4	33	23	8	7	3	13	42	.198	.160	.227	11.45	3.55
Schmidt, Clarke	R-R	6-1	209	2-20-96	0	1	4.26	2	2	0	0	6	5	3	3	2	2	5	.208	.250	.188	7.11	2.84
Sears, JP	R-L	5-11	180	2-19-96	3	2	4.09	15	8	0	1	51	45	24	23	6	18	71	.242	.250	.237	12.61	3.20
Semple, Shawn	R-R	6-1	220	10-9-95	6	3	3.76	15	10	0	0	65	52	31	27	7	21	74	.214	.157	.255	10.30	2.92
Severino, Luis	R-R	6-2	218	2-20-94	0	0	2.84	2	2	0	0	6	2	2	2	1	1	9	.095	.200	.000	12.79	1.42
Valdez, Jefry	R-R	6-1	165	8-20-95	4	1	3.86	16	0	0	1	30	24	15	13	3	10	26	.212	.167	.246	7.71	2.97
Vasquez, Randy	R-R	6-0	165	11-3-98	2	1	4.22	4	4	0	0	21	23	15	10	2	7	19	.258	.240	.282	8.02	2.95
Waldichuk, Ken	L-L	6-4	220	1-8-98	4	3	4.20	16	14	0	0	79	64	44	37	13	38	108	.218	.183	.234	12.25	4.31
Weissert, Greg	R-R	6-2	215	2-4-95	1	2	0.71	12	0	0	4	13	9	2	1	0	3	20	.191	.154	.206	14.21	3.55
Wesneski, Hayden	R-R	6-3	210	12-5-97	8	4	4.01	15	15	2	0	83	76	40	37	11	22	92	.241	.228	.255	9.98	2.39

Fielding

Catcher	PCT	G	PO	A	E	DP	PB
Breaux	1.000	20	213	5	0	0	1
Gasper	.970	8	94	2	3	0	1
Illig	1.000	7	50	1	0	0	0
Lopez	.998	43	440	44	1	4	4
McDowell	.983	4	54	3	1	0	0
Sanchez	1.000	1	3	0	0	0	0
Sands	.993	39	435	23	3	0	3

First Base	PCT	G	PO	A	E	DP
Bell	.983	8	54	5	1	3
Burt	.992	19	116	6	1	11
Garcia	.977	87	530	67	14	49
Gittens	1.000	1	4	0	0	0
Illig	1.000	1	1	0	0	0
Voit	1.000	4	24	2	0	2
Wagner	1.000	4	30	2	0	2

Second Base	PCT	G	PO	A	E	DP
Bastidas	.978	22	30	57	2	10
Bell	.933	4	5	9	1	2
Cabrera	.988	43	68	93	2	25

	PCT	G	PO	A	E	DP	PB
Castillo	.975	23	28	50	2	11	
Dunn	.976	16	24	16	1	3	
Park	.818	4	4	5	2	1	
Perez	1.000	2	4	4	0	0	
Pita	1.000	7	10	11	0	2	
Torrealba	1.000	2	4	5	0	0	

Third Base	PCT	G	PO	A	E	DP
Bastidas	.923	6	3	9	1	2
Bell	.871	18	10	17	4	0
Burt	.962	22	10	41	2	4
Cabrera	.939	35	17	60	5	3
Castillo	.792	14	2	17	5	4
Dunn	.895	11	3	14	2	1
Garcia	1.000	5	3	3	0	0
Park	.667	2	0	2	1	0
Perez	1.000	6	5	10	0	2
Urshela	1.000	2	0	1	0	0
Wagner	1.000	1	1	1	0	0

Shortstop	PCT	G	PO	A	E	DP
Burt	1.000	7	3	12	0	1

	PCT	G	PO	A	E	DP
Cabrera	.965	24	26	56	3	6
Castillo	.956	14	12	31	2	4
Dunn	1.000	2	2	6	0	1
Park	1.000	4	5	8	0	2
Peraza	.972	69	84	122	6	30
Torrealba	.667	1	0	2	1	0
Torres	1.000	1	0	2	0	0

Outfield	PCT	G	PO	A	E	DP
Alexander	1.000	4	7	0	0	0
Beltre	.989	104	171	6	2	1
Cuevas	1.000	7	15	0	0	0
Dunn	1.000	3	5	0	0	0
Florial	.923	7	12	0	1	0
Frazier	1.000	1	1	0	0	0
Gilliam	.964	83	129	4	5	0
Lockridge	1.000	42	73	1	0	1
Milone	1.000	53	92	4	0	0
Palensky	.957	27	43	1	2	0
Pita	.957	24	22	0	1	0
Zehner	.941	7	15	1	1	0

HUDSON VALLEY RENEGADES
HIGH-A EAST

HIGH CLASS A

Batting	B-T	HT	WT	DOB	AVG	vLH	vRH	G	AB	R	H	2B	3B	HR	RBI	BB	HBP	SH	SF	SO	SB	CS	SLG	OBP
Alexander, Evan	L-L	6-2	175	2-26-98	.192	.000	.217	12	26	3	5	1	0	1	4	5	0	0	0	15	0	0	.346	.323
Bell, Chad	L-R	6-3	210	3-4-97	.255	.300	.237	39	137	17	35	4	2	10	28	20	1	0	1	53	1	0	.533	.352
Breaux, Josh	R-R	6-1	220	10-7-97	.252	.232	.260	64	250	34	63	12	0	17	46	22	0	0	4	73	0	0	.504	.308
Chaparro, Andres	R-R	6-1	200	5-4-99	.264	.417	.248	36	129	19	34	4	3	8	22	24	2	0	0	34	1	1	.527	.387
Chirinos, Roberto	R-R	5-11	172	9-8-00	.286	.143	.333	7	28	3	8	3	0	1	4	0	1	0	0	7	0	0	.500	.310
Cuevas, Frederick	L-L	5-11	185	10-27-97	.222	.250	.215	49	153	26	34	11	0	3	17	24	0	1	2	36	8	2	.353	.324
DeMarco, Pat	R-R	5-9	192	3-10-98	.220	.219	.220	42	150	23	33	11	1	7	14	3	2	0	0	41	2	0	.447	.245
Dunham, Elijah	L-L	6-0	213	5-29-98	.257	.313	.244	64	241	40	62	19	0	9	32	22	3	0	2	62	17	1	.448	.325
Dunn, Oliver	L-R	5-10	185	9-2-97	.209	.138	.235	37	110	21	23	3	4	3	8	26	1	0	0	37	5	0	.391	.365
Duran, Ezequiel	R-R	5-11	185	5-22-99	.290	.316	.282	67	259	42	75	15	6	12	48	28	8	0	2	71	12	7	.533	.374
2-team total (38 Hickory)					.267	.262	.268	105	416	67	111	22	6	19	79	40	10	0	5	130	19	9	.486	.342
Gasper, Mickey	B-R	5-10	205	10-11-95	.318	.333	.316	7	22	6	7	1	0	1	2	2	2	0	0	6	0	0	.500	.423
Guerrero, Alex	L-R	6-0	185	3-10-00	.375	1.000	.286	3	8	1	3	1	0	0	2	2	0	0	1	4	0	0	.500	.455
Illig, Chase	B-R	6-0	210	9-14-96	.000	.000	.000	2	7	0	0	0	0	0	0	0	0	0	1	3	0	0	.000	.000
Lockridge, Brandon	R-R	6-1	185	3-14-97	.256	.310	.240	32	125	18	32	6	2	3	22	9	1	0	1	27	5	1	.408	.309
MacDonald, Kyle	L-R	6-3	240	6-17-96	.266	.263	.267	64	139	18	37	9	1	4	25	9	4	0	1	40	7	1	.432	.327
Narvaez, Carlos	R-R	6-0	190	11-26-98	.304	.333	.300	16	56	12	17	1	0	2	13	5	2	0	2	18	1	0	.429	.369
Nelson, James	R-R	6-2	180	10-18-97	.246	.232	.250	77	276	33	68	13	0	6	40	25	6	0	3	90	16	7	.359	.319
Olivares, Pablo	R-R	6-0	160	1-27-98	.244	.227	.248	58	193	24	47	16	0	2	20	25	5	0	2	42	7	3	.358	.342
Pasteur, Isaiah	R-R	6-2	182	6-19-96	.159	.172	.155	43	126	19	20	6	1	1	11	18	1	0	1	64	6	3	.246	.267
Peraza, Oswald	R-R	6-0	165	6-15-00	.306	.368	.293	28	111	20	34	10	0	5	16	12	3	0	1	24	16	1	.532	.386
Pereira, Everson	R-R	6-0	191	4-10-01	.259	.333	.250	27	108	27	28	3	0	14	32	15	2	0	2	38	5	2	.676	.354
Perez, Cristian	R-R	5-10	170	10-26-98	.200	.000	.222	3	10	2	2	1	0	0	1	0	0	0	1	0	0	0	.300	.273
Sanford, Jake	L-R	6-2	215	10-24-97	.278	.227	.294	49	187	22	52	6	4	9	30	13	5	0	0	61	2	1	.497	.341
Santos, Luis	R-R	5-8	160	1-4-00	.175	.000	.186	20	63	9	11	1	0	1	6	9	0	0	0	11	0	0	.238	.278
Seigler, Anthony	B-B	6-0	200	6-20-99	.219	.136	.252	41	151	24	33	12	1	4	24	23	1	0	1	46	1	2	.391	.324
Sensley, Steven	L-L	6-1	220	9-6-95	.278	.000	.357	5	18	2	5	2	0	1	6	1	0	0	0	8	0	0	.556	.316
Smith, Josh H.	L-R	5-10	172	8-7-97	.320	.342	.308	28	103	29	33	12	3	3	9	16	5	1	0	27	12	3	.583	.435
2-team total (9 Hickory)					.313	.333	.304	37	147	39	46	15	3	4	16	18	8	1	0	36	14	3	.537	.416
Torrealba, Eduardo	R-R	5-8	140	3-26-99	.304	.227	.316	49	158	24	48	4	1	3	13	13	4	1	0	24	8	2	.399	.371
Torres, Saul	R-R	6-2	190	2-19-99	.235	.263	.224	27	68	11	16	1	0	1	10	9	0	0	2	28	0	0	.294	.316
Volpe, Anthony	R-R	5-11	180	4-28-01	.286	.222	.304	55	213	57	61	17	1	15	37	27	12	0	4	58	12	4	.587	.391
Wagaman, Eric	R-R	6-4	210	8-14-97	.222	.208	.225	47	162	20	36	6	2	3	16	6	2	0	2	50	0	1	.340	.330
Wells, Austin	L-R	6-2	220	7-12-99	.274	.167	.289	38	146	21	40	6	1	7	22	20	4	0	0	55	5	0	.473	.376

Pitching	B-T	HT	WT	DOB	W	L	ERA	G	GS	CG	SV	IP	H	R	ER	HR	BB	SO	AVG	vLH	vRH	K/9	BB/9
Aguilar, Clay	L-L	6-1	210	3-26-99	0	0	0.00	1	1	0	0	6	3	0	0	0	0	5	.150	.250	.125	7.50	0.00
Alvarez, Nelson	R-R	6-4	220	6-11-98	3	2	8.55	30	0	0	1	40	43	43	38	9	32	41	.270	.333	.235	9.23	7.20
Anderson, Reid	R-R	6-0	200	9-6-95	1	2	3.98	7	7	0	0	32	25	16	14	3	14	32	.227	.268	.203	9.09	3.98
Barclay, Edgar	L-L	5-10	200	5-25-98	1	3	5.65	11	4	0	0	29	29	21	18	6	8	39	.254	.207	.271	12.24	2.51
Boyle, Sean	R-R	6-1	205	10-29-96	1	1	3.38	6	2	0	1	19	11	8	7	2	6	22	.169	.152	.188	10.61	2.89
Brito, Jhony	R-R	6-2	160	2-17-98	4	4	2.57	14	14	1	0	70	59	31	20	2	12	73	.219	.269	.188	9.39	1.54
Correa, Nelvin	R-R	6-1	170	1-25-97	0	2	6.48	10	0	0	0	17	22	13	12	3	10	14	.324	.368	.306	7.56	5.40
Craft, Derek	R-R	6-8	220	7-11-96	1	3	3.82	27	0	0	10	35	28	21	15	6	17	47	.211	.250	.188	11.97	4.33
Ernst, Nick	R-R	6-3	195	8-27-96	4	0	5.09	24	0	0	3	41	31	26	23	3	26	71	.205	.203	.207	15.71	5.75
Espinal, Carlos	R-R	5-11	175	10-21-96	1	1	6.48	12	0	0	2	17	13	13	12	3	9	25	.203	.148	.243	13.50	4.86
Greene, Zach	R-R	6-1	215	8-29-96	2	2	2.21	9	0	0	1	20	6	7	5	2	8	33	.092	.154	.051	14.61	3.54

Name	B-T	HT	WT	DOB	W	L	ERA	G	GS	CG	SV	IP	H	R	ER	HR	BB	SO	AVG	vLH	vRH	SO/9	BB/9
Holloway, Trevor	R-R	6-2	200	6-22-97	1	1	4.05	18	0	0	2	33	25	16	15	3	16	35	.207	.214	.203	9.45	4.32
Loseke, Barrett	R-R	6-0	170	11-12-96	3	1	3.03	15	1	0	0	39	26	13	13	3	18	58	.187	.250	.154	13.50	4.19
MacDonald, Kyle	L-R	6-3	240	6-17-96	0	0	13.50	1	0	0	0	1	1	1	1	1	1	1	.333	.000	.500	13.50	13.50
Maciejewski, Josh	R-L	6-3	175	8-14-95	9	4	4.10	18	13	0	0	83	69	41	38	13	24	94	.220	.218	.220	10.15	2.59
Medina, Luis	R-R	6-1	175	5-3-99	2	1	2.76	7	7	0	0	33	18	10	10	4	19	50	.162	.204	.129	13.78	5.23
Minnick, Matt	R-L	6-2	210	3-11-96	5	2	4.40	30	0	0	0	45	38	26	22	9	25	66	.221	.292	.194	13.20	5.00
Munoz, Anderson	R-R	5-8	158	8-4-98	2	1	4.41	8	8	0	0	33	23	18	16	5	12	48	.192	.257	.165	13.22	3.31
Myatt, Tanner	R-R	6-7	220	5-21-98	1	0	7.71	9	0	0	1	12	6	11	10	0	14	15	.150	.182	.138	11.57	10.80
Orozco, Jio	R-R	6-1	210	8-15-97	0	0	13.50	1	1	0	0	2	3	3	3	0	1	2	.300	.500	.250	9.00	4.50
Peguero, Elvis	R-R	6-5	208	3-20-97	3	1	2.51	15	0	0	2	32	22	10	9	2	11	40	.186	.308	.127	11.13	3.06
Perez, Freicer	R-R	6-8	240	3-14-96	0	1	6.19	13	0	0	0	16	13	11	11	2	13	11	.217	.222	.214	6.19	7.31
Ruegger, Charlie	R-R	6-6	218	7-14-97	6	4	6.80	33	0	0	1	48	61	42	36	4	22	53	.299	.353	.272	10.01	4.15
Sauer, Matt	R-R	6-4	195	1-21-99	3	2	5.20	8	8	0	0	45	35	33	26	7	15	51	.205	.204	.205	10.20	3.00
Semple, Shawn	R-R	6-1	220	10-19-95	4	1	2.48	6	6	0	0	36	22	11	10	6	9	49	.172	.143	.190	12.14	2.23
Severino, Luis	R-R	6-2	218	2-20-94	0	0	5.40	1	1	0	0	2	1	1	1	0	1	3	.167	.000	.333	16.20	5.40
Spence, Mitch	R-R	6-1	185	5-6-98	7	6	3.94	23	20	0	0	105	99	52	46	10	37	118	.249	.223	.266	10.11	3.17
Valdez, Jairo	R-R	6-1	165	8-20-95	0	0	4.91	6	1	0	1	11	12	7	6	1	6	10	.286	.188	.346	8.18	4.91
Vasquez, Randy	R-R	6-0	165	11-3-98	3	0	1.75	6	6	0	0	36	33	8	7	0	8	53	.241	.333	.181	13.25	2.00
Vizcaino, Alexander	R-R	6-2	160	5-22-97	0	1	9.00	4	2	0	0	4	5	5	4	0	7	3	.313	.500	.125	6.75	15.75
Waldichuk, Ken	L-L	6-4	220	1-8-98	2	0	0.00	7	7	0	0	31	12	0	0	0	13	55	.120	.267	.057	16.14	3.82
Way, Beck	R-R	6-4	200	8-6-99	1	2	7.71	4	4	0	0	16	18	14	14	3	9	29	.281	.391	.220	15.98	4.96
Wesneski, Hayden	R-R	6-3	210	12-5-97	1	1	1.49	7	7	0	0	36	24	8	6	2	9	47	.194	.254	.123	11.64	2.23
Wilson, Justin	R-R	6-0	180	9-9-96	0	0	4.76	10	0	0	3	11	8	6	6	1	7	15	.211	.000	.276	11.91	5.56

Fielding

Catcher	PCT	G	PO	A	E	DP	PB
Breaux	.991	38	432	24	4	0	7
Gasper	1.000	5	53	3	0	1	1
Guerrero	1.000	1	12	2	0	0	0
Illig	.920	2	20	3	2	0	1
Narvaez	.977	12	119	10	3	0	2
Seigler	.986	23	202	15	3	0	5
Torres	.980	26	220	19	5	1	4
Wells	1.000	23	243	16	0	0	6

First Base	PCT	G	PO	A	E	DP
Bell	.994	21	169	8	1	18
Chaparro	.992	17	125	3	1	7
Dunham	1.000	3	6	1	0	1
MacDonald	.990	39	266	22	3	15
Sensley	1.000	2	9	0	0	0
Wagaman	.984	42	279	37	5	19

Second Base	PCT	G	PO	A	E	DP
Bell	.938	5	7	8	1	2
Chirinos	1.000	4	7	9	0	3

Second Base (cont.)	PCT	G	PO	A	E	DP
Dunn	.988	22	31	52	1	12
Duran	.982	42	58	107	3	22
MacDonald	1.000	1	1	0	0	0
Perez	1.000	1	1	1	0	0
Santos	.939	18	28	34	4	5
Torrealba	.977	30	35	51	2	9
Volpe	.667	1	2	2	2	0

Third Base	PCT	G	PO	A	E	DP
Bell	.931	13	6	21	2	2
Chaparro	.917	18	8	36	4	0
Dunn	.960	10	6	18	1	3
MacDonald	.000	1	0	0	1	0
Nelson	.875	74	40	114	22	10
Perez	1.000	2	2	4	0	0
Santos	.000	1	0	0	0	0
Torrealba	.909	5	2	8	1	0

Shortstop	PCT	G	PO	A	E	DP
Chirinos	.909	3	4	6	1	0
Dunn	.875	3	1	6	1	0
Duran	.978	16	21	23	1	5
Peraza	.966	25	24	60	3	6
Smith	.989	23	20	66	1	12
Torrealba	.941	7	6	10	1	1
Volpe	.971	45	57	108	5	21

Outfield	PCT	G	PO	A	E	DP
Alexander	1.000	12	13	0	0	0
Cuevas	.969	50	60	3	2	0
DeMarco	.967	43	55	3	2	0
Dunham	.988	58	82	2	1	0
Dunn	--	1	0	0	0	0
Lockridge	1.000	30	49	1	0	0
MacDonald	1.000	2	2	0	0	0
Olivares	.979	57	90	3	2	1
Pasteur	.961	45	47	2	2	1
Pereira	.970	22	31	1	1	0
Sanford	.976	50	81	1	2	0
Seigler	--	1	0	0	0	0
Sensley	1.000	3	0	1	0	0
Torrealba	1.000	9	11	0	0	0

TAMPA TARPONS
LOW-A SOUTHEAST
LOW CLASS A

Batting	B-T	HT	WT	DOB	AVG	vLH	vRH	G	AB	R	H	2B	3B	HR	RBI	BB	HBP	SH	SF	SO	SB	CS	SLG	OBP
Alexander, Evan	L-L	6-2	175	2-26-98	.225	.222	.226	41	111	26	25	6	1	2	8	23	4	0	0	38	12	3	.351	.377
Bastidas, Jesus	R-R	5-10	145	9-14-98	.218	.263	.206	38	87	20	19	0	0	4	18	12	4	0	0	28	5	1	.356	.340
Battle, Kyle	R-R	6-1	190	12-4-97	.222	.000	.333	3	9	1	2	0	0	0	3	1	0	0	0	2	1	0	.222	.300
Bell, Chad	L-R	6-3	210	3-4-97	.279	.167	.313	29	104	24	29	5	2	6	19	17	0	0	0	32	1	0	.538	.380
Bowman, Cooper	R-R	6-0	205	1-25-00	.237	.320	.206	27	93	17	22	8	1	3	22	11	6	0	2	26	11	1	.441	.348
Burt, Max	R-R	6-2	185	8-28-96	.423	.400	.429	6	26	5	11	3	0	1	6	1	0	0	0	6	0	0	.654	.444
Chaparro, Andres	R-R	6-1	200	5-4-99	.270	.255	.273	65	230	52	62	17	0	7	51	36	7	0	5	59	3	3	.435	.378
Chirinos, Roberto	R-R	5-11	172	9-8-00	.250	.174	.271	33	108	15	27	4	0	4	16	11	3	0	1	33	2	2	.398	.333
Cowles, Benjamin	R-R	6-1	180	2-15-00	.237	.000	.277	32	97	12	23	7	0	4	23	12	4	0	1	42	1	1	.433	.342
De Leon, Juan	R-R	6-2	185	9-13-97	.185	.087	.200	56	168	33	31	9	1	9	32	27	6	0	2	73	3	1	.411	.315
DeMarco, Pat	R-R	5-9	192	3-10-98	.274	.188	.294	48	168	42	46	11	0	7	32	31	1	0	1	50	3	2	.464	.388
Diaz, Pedro	R-R	6-2	202	11-6-97	.233	.333	.213	25	73	12	17	1	1	1	11	10	2	0	0	34	1	0	.315	.341
Dominguez, Jasson	B-R	5-10	190	2-7-03	.258	.170	.288	49	186	26	48	9	1	5	18	21	5	0	2	67	7	3	.398	.346
Dunham, Elijah	L-L	6-0	213	5-29-98	.276	.222	.296	29	98	32	27	6	2	4	25	25	4	0	0	23	11	4	.500	.441
Frazier, Clint	R-R	5-11	212	9-6-94	.500	.500	.500	1	4	1	2	1	0	0	0	0	0	0	0	2	0	0	.750	.500
Garcia, Anthony	B-R	6-5	204	9-5-00	.291	.100	.333	16	55	16	16	2	0	6	16	13	0	0	0	25	5	0	.655	.426
Gomez, Antonio	R-R	6-2	210	11-13-01	.197	.250	.184	17	61	10	12	2	0	2	7	10	0	0	0	18	1	0	.328	.310
Green, Ryder	R-R	6-0	200	5-5-00	.231	.243	.227	43	156	27	36	9	0	6	22	13	7	0	1	62	11	1	.404	.316
Hardman, Tyler	R-R	6-3	200	1-27-99	.238	.316	.220	30	101	18	24	5	0	4	17	9	2	0	2	45	4	1	.406	.307
Hauver, Trevor	L-R	6-0	205	11-20-98	.288	.311	.283	66	229	48	66	17	2	9	49	64	3	0	3	78	2	0	.498	.445
Henson, Spencer	R-R	6-2	235	11-3-97	.400	.250	.500	5	10	5	4	0	0	2	7	3	2	0	0	3	0	0	1.500	.600
Narvaez, Carlos	R-R	6-0	190	11-26-98	.239	.294	.228	60	205	41	49	8	0	7	30	43	3	0	3	76	2	0	.380	.374
Pereira, Everson	R-R	6-0	191	4-10-01	.361	.435	.327	19	72	17	26	5	1	5	22	10	1	0	0	21	4	1	.667	.446
Rice, Ben	L-R	6-2	205	2-22-99	.210	.100	.231	20	62	8	13	2	0	3	12	12	3	0	1	18	1	0	.387	.359

	B-T	HT	WT	DOB	AVG	vLH	vRH	G	AB	R	H	2B	3B	HR	RBI	BB	HBP	SH	SF	SO	SB	CS	SLG	OBP
Sanchez, Aldenis	R-R	6-1	165	9-26-98	.413	.385	.418	23	80	18	33	8	0	2	14	11	3	0	0	15	13	6	.588	.500
Sanford, Jake	L-R	6-2	215	10-24-97	.291	.313	.284	52	203	34	59	7	1	7	31	22	4	0	1	55	2	1	.438	.370
Santos, Luis	R-R	5-8	160	1-4-00	.226	.143	.250	13	31	11	7	0	0	1	9	15	3	0	1	10	6	0	.323	.500
Santos, Madison	L-R	5-10	165	9-6-99	.209	.077	.241	22	67	16	14	4	0	1	9	17	0	0	1	20	9	4	.313	.365
Smith, Josh H.	L-R	5-10	172	8-7-97	.333	.417	.296	11	39	15	13	0	0	6	15	7	4	0	0	6	5	0	.795	.480
Sweeney, Trey	L-R	6-4	200	4-24-00	.245	.182	.261	29	110	26	27	4	4	6	13	18	1	0	0	29	3	1	.518	.357
Torrealba, Eduardo	R-R	5-8	140	3-26-99	.310	.231	.345	13	42	9	13	0	0	1	12	5	2	0	2	2	1	0	.381	.392
Vallejo, Dionys	R-R	6-2	159	5-25-00	.105	.000	.111	7	19	1	2	0	0	0	1	5	0	0	0	12	0	0	.105	.292
Volpe, Anthony	R-R	5-11	180	4-28-01	.302	.462	.263	54	199	56	60	18	5	12	49	51	6	0	1	43	21	5	.623	.455
Wagaman, Eric	R-R	6-4	210	8-14-97	.216	.176	.224	31	102	11	22	8	1	3	18	12	0	0	3	29	1	0	.402	.291
Wells, Austin	L-R	6-2	220	7-12-99	.258	.277	.254	65	236	61	61	17	4	9	54	51	7	0	5	62	11	0	.479	.398

Pitching	B-T	HT	WT	DOB	W	L	ERA	G	GS	CG	SV	IP	H	R	ER	HR	BB	SO	AVG	vLH	vRH	K/9	BB/9
Abeyta, Blane	R-R	6-3	185	9-4-98	5	3	5.24	14	7	0	0	46	35	30	27	3	32	59	.211	.243	.188	11.46	6.22
Aguilar, Clay	L-L	6-1	210	3-26-99	1	2	2.15	21	4	0	0	46	27	15	11	3	11	66	.164	.146	.171	12.91	2.15
Anderson, Ryan	L-L	6-6	205	9-9-98	0	3	10.03	12	6	0	0	23	29	28	26	1	29	26	.309	.143	.356	10.03	11.19
Barclay, Edgar	L-L	5-10	200	5-25-98	3	1	2.22	18	2	0	0	49	24	14	12	1	17	73	.145	.103	.157	13.50	3.14
Boyle, Sean	R-R	6-1	205	10-29-96	3	2	2.22	11	4	0	0	28	25	16	7	1	9	34	.234	.311	.177	10.80	2.86
Calderon, Yorlin	R-R	6-3	155	8-17-01	0	0	9.00	1	0	0	0	4	4	5	4	2	2	0	.250	.167	.300	0.00	4.50
Carela, Juan	R-R	6-3	186	12-15-01	0	2	11.51	6	6	0	0	20	32	27	26	3	18	22	.368	.429	.327	9.74	7.97
Castano, Blas	R-R	5-10	162	9-8-98	6	1	4.23	8	7	0	0	38	44	20	18	2	8	43	.288	.361	.239	10.10	1.88
Castro, Yon	R-R	6-0	203	5-23-99	0	0	0.00	1	1	0	0	3	0	0	0	0	4	4	.000	.000	.000	12.00	12.00
Coleman, Carson	R-R	6-2	190	4-7-98	2	3	6.11	31	0	0	5	35	35	26	24	2	26	49	.257	.302	.229	12.48	6.62
Correa, Nelvin	R-R	6-1	170	1-25-97	5	0	1.06	21	0	0	5	42	25	7	5	2	17	48	.169	.206	.138	10.20	3.61
Cortijo, Harold	R-R	6-2	180	9-29-98	0	0	6.10	6	1	0	0	10	9	7	7	0	12	11	.243	.176	.300	9.58	10.45
Craft, Derek	R-R	6-8	220	7-11-96	1	0	3.12	6	0	0	0	9	6	3	3	2	1	10	.182	.231	.150	10.38	1.04
Diaz, Pedro	R-R	6-2	202	11-6-97	1	0	10.80	2	0	0	0	2	2	3	2	1	1	0	.250	.000	.400	0.00	5.40
Diaz, Wellington	R-R	6-4	190	4-25-97	4	3	5.17	27	0	0	2	38	29	23	22	5	27	53	.209	.241	.185	12.44	6.34
Giacone, Michael	L-L	6-0	175	10-23-96	8	0	3.71	20	0	0	1	44	33	20	18	1	20	60	.208	.243	.197	12.37	4.12
Gomez, Carlos	R-R	6-1	175	6-14-98	1	1	5.12	8	0	0	0	19	18	13	11	1	15	24	.240	.257	.225	11.17	6.98
Gomez, Yoendrys	R-R	6-3	175	10-15-99	0	0	3.42	9	9	0	0	24	14	10	9	3	9	29	.163	.122	.200	11.03	3.42
Holloway, Trevor	R-R	6-2	200	6-22-97	7	1	2.78	17	0	0	3	36	24	13	11	0	13	49	.185	.216	.165	12.36	3.28
Keizer, Ben	L-L	6-2	215	8-28-97	2	3	12.94	9	0	0	0	16	20	26	23	3	22	13	.308	.200	.356	7.31	12.38
Kohn, Zach	R-R	6-4	190	9-30-97	1	0	4.73	9	0	0	1	13	9	8	7	0	14	16	.200	.263	.154	10.80	9.45
Lessar, Jarod	R-R	6-4	225	6-22-97	0	0	0.00	1	0	0	0	2	0	1	0	0	6	1	.000	.000	--	4.50	27.00
McNeely, Shaine	L-R	6-4	210	5-10-98	0	0	0.00	1	0	0	0	2	1	0	0	0	2	2	.167	.333	.000	10.80	0.00
Milam, Kevin	R-R	6-0	200	2-13-98	0	0	7.30	8	0	0	1	12	15	13	10	1	7	17	.288	.300	.281	12.41	5.11
Montas, Kenlly	R-R	6-0	187	5-31-96	0	0	9.53	6	0	0	1	11	12	13	12	2	11	9	.273	.412	.185	7.15	8.74
Munoz, Anderson	R-R	5-8	158	8-4-98	4	0	2.50	8	1	0	0	18	13	5	5	1	7	26	.197	.133	.250	13.00	3.50
Munoz, Jhonatan	R-R	5-10	200	8-10-99	7	3	4.37	23	9	0	0	60	54	36	29	9	39	75	.237	.268	.214	11.31	5.88
Myatt, Tanner	R-R	6-7	220	5-21-98	0	0	1.35	6	0	0	0	7	4	1	1	0	2	10	.174	.273	.083	13.50	2.70
Neely, Jack	R-R	6-8	225	6-5-00	0	0	0.00	2	0	0	0	2	0	0	0	0	0	5	.000	.000	.000	22.50	0.00
Paciorek, Nick	R-R	6-2	195	6-1-98	0	0	4.91	4	0	0	0	7	3	4	4	0	6	12	.120	.143	.091	14.73	7.36
Panacual, Josue	R-R	5-10	158	1-13-02	0	1	6.75	1	1	0	0	4	3	3	3	0	1	4	.214	.250	.200	9.00	2.25
Parker, Jason	R-R	5-11	197	10-27-97	0	0	6.75	1	1	0	0	4	5	3	3	2	2	5	.313	.500	.286	11.25	4.50
2-team total (19 Daytona)					4	3	4.18	20	19	0	0	84	68	44	39	9	35	96	.220	.264	.196	10.29	3.75
Pellerin, Connor	R-R	6-4	210	7-22-99	0	0	7.71	4	0	0	0	5	2	4	4	1	12	8	.125	.333	.000	15.43	23.14
Rodriguez, Nicio	R-R	6-3	175	9-3-99	2	2	5.06	9	8	0	0	37	37	22	21	5	17	43	.264	.224	.293	10.37	4.10
Santana, Enrique	R-R	5-11	190	9-23-97	1	1	4.37	16	0	0	1	23	25	11	11	2	14	20	.284	.209	.356	7.94	5.56
Sauer, Matt	R-R	6-4	195	1-21-99	2	4	4.34	15	13	0	0	66	58	38	32	6	32	76	.227	.250	.213	10.31	4.34
Schmidt, Clarke	R-R	6-1	209	2-20-96	0	0	3.00	1	1	0	0	3	1	1	1	0	2	4	.111	.250	.000	12.00	6.00
Severino, Luis	R-R	6-2	218	2-20-94	0	0	3.38	1	1	0	0	3	2	1	1	0	1	3	.200	.500	.000	10.13	3.38
Vasquez, Randy	R-R	6-0	165	11-3-98	3	3	2.34	13	11	0	0	50	35	24	13	2	23	58	.189	.134	.233	10.44	4.14
Vega, Alfred	R-R	6-1	169	1-19-01	0	1	2.25	1	1	0	0	4	2	1	1	1	3	6	.143	.000	.222	13.50	6.75
Watson, Danny	R-R	6-7	235	10-6-00	0	0	16.88	3	0	0	0	3	3	5	5	0	4	2	.273	.333	.250	6.75	13.50
Way, Beck	R-R	6-2	205	8-6-99	3	1	2.68	15	14	0	0	47	23	15	14	2	29	54	.144	.171	.122	10.34	5.55
Yulie, Tyrone	R-R	6-4	180	8-4-01	1	1	8.89	9	8	0	0	28	28	29	28	5	26	37	.255	.315	.196	11.75	8.26

Fielding

Catcher	PCT	G	PO	A	E	DP	PB
Gomez	.980	15	135	15	3	1	4
Narvaez	.979	40	418	40	10	6	1
Rice	.994	15	147	14	1	2	2
Wells	.990	47	462	25	5	2	10

First Base	PCT	G	PO	A	E	DP
Bell	.991	17	102	6	1	10
Chaparro	.976	18	108	13	3	13
Diaz	.992	21	112	13	1	9
Garcia	.954	13	77	6	4	6
Hardman	.975	17	104	12	3	11
Henson	1.000	4	25	4	0	1
Wagaman	.991	29	208	10	2	12

Second Base	PCT	G	PO	A	E	DP
Bastidas	1.000	11	14	23	0	6
Bell	1.000	2	5	3	0	0
Bowman	.973	24	42	68	3	14
Burt	1.000	2	2	3	0	0
Chirinos	1.000	4	2	6	0	2
Cowles	.944	11	14	20	2	5
Hauver	.960	56	83	110	8	23
Santos	1.000	6	12	10	0	3
Smith	1.000	1	1	2	0	1
Torrealba	1.000	2	4	4	0	1
Vallejo	1.000	1	2	2	0	0
Volpe	1.000	1	0	2	0	0

Third Base	PCT	G	PO	A	E	DP
Bastidas	.833	8	4	6	2	0
Bell	.941	10	3	13	1	0
Burt	.667	2	0	4	2	0
Chaparro	.912	46	35	69	10	9
Chirinos	1.000	13	13	19	0	3
Cowles	.958	10	14	9	1	3
Hardman	1.000	8	7	14	0	1
Hauver	1.000	1	0	2	0	0
Santos	1.000	5	0	8	0	0
Torrealba	.955	8	9	12	1	2
Vallejo	.813	7	4	9	3	0
Volpe	1.000	3	5	4	0	1

Shortstop	PCT	G	PO	A	E	DP
Bastidas	.931	19	6	21	2	1
Burt	1.000	3	3	4	0	0
Chirinos	.926	16	18	32	4	5

							Outfield	PCT	G	PO	A	E	DP							
Cowles	.941	11	18	14	2	7								Dunham	.958	29	45	1	2	0
Santos	1.000	2	2	3	0	0	Alexander	1.000	38	44	1	0	0	Green	1.000	40	53	4	0	0
Smith	1.000	7	5	10	0	0	Battle	1.000	3	5	0	0	0	Pereira	1.000	15	20	0	0	0
Sweeney	.927	25	20	56	6	11	De Leon	.958	54	64	5	3	0	Sanchez	.926	21	25	0	2	0
Torrealba	.800	3	2	2	1	0	DeMarco	.988	47	79	2	1	0	Sanford	.963	50	74	5	3	1
Volpe	.951	40	32	84	6	13	Dominguez	.964	38	53	1	2	0	Santos	1.000	22	33	2	0	1

FCL YANKEES   ROOKIE
FLORIDA COMPLEX LEAGUE

Batting	B-T	HT	WT	DOB	AVG	vLH	vRH	G	AB	R	H	2B	3B	HR	RBI	BB	HBP	SH	SF	SO	SB	CS	SLG	OBP
Alcantara, Kevin	R-R	6-6	188	7-12-02	.370	.167	.429	9	27	5	10	1	0	1	3	4	0	0	0	8	2	0	.519	.452
Battle, Kyle	R-R	6-1	190	12-4-97	.302	.214	.333	20	53	16	16	4	0	3	15	13	3	0	2	11	5	0	.547	.451
Bowman, Cooper	R-R	6-0	205	1-25-00	.444	.333	.500	3	9	3	4	1	0	1	1	0	0	0	0	4	2	0	.889	.444
Cabrera, Marcos	R-R	6-3	189	10-10-01	.217	.147	.242	42	129	36	28	3	0	8	23	29	7	0	1	38	12	4	.426	.386
Chirinos, Roberto	R-R	5-11	172	9-8-00	.240	.143	.278	10	25	4	6	1	1	1	3	5	0	0	0	7	4	0	.480	.367
Colmenares, Jose	R-R	5-11	173	4-3-02	.250	.250	.250	11	28	7	7	0	1	1	2	6	0	0	0	7	2	0	.429	.382
Cowles, Benjamin	R-R	6-1	180	2-15-00	.429	.333	.500	3	7	2	3	0	1	0	2	1	0	0	0	1	0	1	.714	.500
Crisp, Juan	R-R	6-1	170	5-23-00	.273	.000	.500	12	11	4	3	1	0	0	1	2	1	0	0	4	0	0	.364	.429
Dominguez, Jasson	R-R	5-10	190	2-7-03	.200	.143	.231	7	20	5	4	0	0	0	1	6	1	0	0	6	2	0	.200	.407
Garcia, Anthony	B-R	6-5	204	9-5-00	.318	.211	.362	23	66	19	21	1	0	8	21	18	0	0	1	25	10	1	.697	.459
Gasper, Mickey	B-R	5-10	205	10-11-95	.222	.333	.167	4	9	2	2	0	0	0	2	3	0	0	1	2	0	0	.222	.385
Gomez, Antonio	R-R	6-2	210	11-13-01	.305	.226	.344	29	95	18	29	8	1	2	16	16	2	0	0	31	4	0	.474	.416
Gomez, Nelson	R-R	6-1	220	10-8-97	.243	.278	.231	25	70	11	17	7	0	3	20	7	4	0	1	22	2	0	.471	.341
Green, Ryder	R-R	6-0	200	5-5-00	.286	.000	.444	7	14	5	4	2	0	0	0	11	1	0	0	5	2	0	.429	.615
Guerrero, Alex	L-R	6-0	185	3-10-00	.407	.333	.439	26	59	14	24	8	1	3	19	8	1	0	1	17	1	1	.729	.478
Hardman, Tyler	R-R	6-3	204	1-27-99	.333	1.000	.000	3	6	2	2	2	0	0	2	1	0	0	1	0	0	0	.667	.375
Knowles, D'Vaughn	R-R	5-10	161	1-16-01	.130	.125	.133	10	23	3	3	0	1	0	2	2	1	0	0	10	1	0	.217	.231
Marte, Miguel	R-R	5-11	165	5-26-01	.270	.143	.300	10	37	4	10	1	0	0	3	1	0	0	1	11	1	0	.297	.282
Martinez, Jose	R-R	6-0	198	1-28-99	.213	.190	.225	28	61	16	13	0	1	4	17	15	0	0	2	28	0	1	.443	.359
Mazza, John	R-R	5-11	195	2-15-95	.000	.000	.000	5	5	0	0	0	0	0	0	0	0	0	0	1	0	0	.000	.000
Pereira, Everson	R-R	6-0	191	4-10-01	.375	.500	.250	3	8	3	3	2	0	1	3	3	0	0	0	6	0	0	1.000	.545
Pries, Jake	R-R	6-4	226	10-11-96	.259	.267	.256	24	54	9	14	3	0	2	12	13	2	0	0	12	1	0	.426	.420
Ramirez, Agustin	R-R	6-0	210	9-10-01	.220	.143	.243	32	91	19	20	10	0	4	15	15	0	0	3	33	0	1	.462	.321
Rice, Ben	L-R	6-2	205	2-22-99	.000	.000	.000	2	4	0	0	0	0	0	1	1	0	0	1	3	0	0	.000	.167
Richardson, Grant	L-L	6-2	210	7-13-99	.269	.250	.275	27	93	24	25	8	3	3	18	14	2	0	0	28	10	1	.516	.374
Rojas, Angel	R-R	6-0	160	11-26-00	.230	.250	.220	28	74	16	17	3	1	2	9	7	0	0	0	31	6	2	.378	.296
Rosario, Hemmanuel	R-R	6-2	200	8-21-00	.233	.250	.231	13	30	5	7	1	0	1	8	2	0	0	0	12	0	0	.367	.281
Rosario, Stanley	R-R	6-2	195	12-1-00	.216	.250	.207	19	37	6	8	0	2	3	10	8	1	0	0	13	0	0	.568	.370
Salinas, Raimfer	R-R	6-0	175	12-31-00	.250	.205	.265	45	152	33	38	8	3	6	28	13	8	0	3	46	10	3	.461	.335
Sanchez, Aldenis	R-R	6-1	165	9-26-98	.000	.000	.000	3	7	0	0	0	0	0	0	0	0	0	0	2	0	0	.000	.000
2-team total (2 FCL Rays)					.133	.000	.154	5	15	2	2	1	0	0	1	2	0	0	0	4	1	0	.200	.235
Santos, Luis	R-R	5-8	160	1-4-00	.286	.500	.250	7	14	4	4	0	0	0	2	0	1	0	2	0	0	0	.286	.294
Santos, Madison	L-R	5-10	165	9-6-99	.386	.286	.433	15	44	15	17	5	3	3	19	11	1	0	1	15	9	0	.841	.509
Sensley, Steven	L-L	6-1	220	9-6-95	.083	.000	.125	4	12	0	1	1	0	0	1	0	0	0	0	5	0	0	.167	.083
Smith, Sincere	R-R	5-11	170	3-13-00	.222	.222	.222	19	45	6	10	1	0	0	3	5	1	0	0	16	2	2	.244	.314
Sweeney, Trey	L-R	6-4	200	4-24-00	.600	.500	.667	3	5	4	3	0	0	1	1	4	0	0	0	1	1	0	1.200	.778
Vallejo, Dionys	R-R	6-2	159	5-25-00	.160	.143	.167	19	25	9	4	1	0	1	3	12	0	0	0	8	3	0	.320	.432
Vargas, Alexander	B-R	5-11	148	10-29-01	.273	.229	.287	42	150	37	41	7	1	3	26	20	2	0	2	40	17	8	.393	.362

Pitching	B-T	HT	WT	DOB	W	L	ERA	G	GS	CG	SV	IP	H	R	ER	HR	BB	SO	AVG	vLH	vRH	K/9	BB/9
Abeyta, Blane	R-R	6-3	185	9-4-98	0	0	6.00	3	3	0	0	9	8	7	6	1	3	12	.216	.300	.185	12.00	3.00
Anderson, Ryan	L-L	6-6	205	9-9-98	1	0	9.95	4	1	0	0	6	10	8	7	0	4	6	.370	.222	.444	8.53	5.68
Barrios, Wilser	R-R	6-2	160	3-21-98	2	0	1.17	7	0	0	2	15	12	2	2	1	2	14	.214	.083	.250	8.22	1.17
Calderon, Yorlin	R-R	6-3	155	8-17-01	2	2	11.02	6	1	0	0	16	25	25	20	4	5	18	.352	.385	.333	9.92	2.76
Carela, Juan	R-R	6-3	186	12-15-01	2	0	1.64	6	5	0	0	22	14	8	4	0	5	27	.182	.105	.207	11.05	2.05
Castano, Blas	R-R	5-10	162	9-8-98	0	1	3.86	2	1	0	0	7	4	3	3	0	2	12	.174	.250	.133	15.43	2.57
Castro, Yon	R-R	6-0	203	5-23-99	1	1	2.66	10	4	0	1	24	20	9	7	1	7	31	.217	.304	.188	11.79	2.66
Cortijo, Harold	R-R	6-2	180	9-29-98	0	0	13.50	2	1	0	0	2	4	3	3	1	2	3	.222	.333	.167	13.50	9.00
Dees, Bailey	R-R	6-8	250	2-5-99	0	0	7.71	3	1	0	0	2	4	5	2	2	1	5	.333	.667	.222	19.29	3.86
Diaz, Yoljeldriz	R-R	5-11	165	7-14-01	2	0	9.64	8	0	0	1	9	5	11	10	0	9	13	.147	.182	.130	12.54	8.68
Gabonia, Ocean	R-R	6-1	175	7-31-01	0	0	1.93	5	2	0	0	9	3	3	2	0	7	9	.097	.125	.087	8.68	6.75
Gomez, Carlos	R-R	6-1	175	6-14-98	1	0	0.00	4	0	0	0	9	1	0	0	0	4	17	.036	.000	.048	17.00	4.00
Keizer, Ben	L-L	6-3	215	8-28-97	3	1	1.50	4	0	0	0	12	8	2	2	0	4	12	.195	.000	.229	9.00	3.00
Kohn, Zach	R-R	6-4	190	9-30-97	1	1	15.00	3	1	0	0	3	4	5	5	1	6	4	.286	.000	.400	12.00	18.00
Larrondo, Denny	R-R	6-2	180	5-31-02	5	1	4.56	11	3	0	0	26	19	16	13	2	16	38	.204	.192	.209	13.32	5.61
Lessar, Jarod	R-R	6-4	225	6-22-97	1	0	3.09	8	0	0	2	12	16	5	4	0	1	11	.333	.250	.361	8.49	0.77
Martinez, Nolan	R-R	6-2	165	6-30-98	0	0	6.75	3	2	0	0	4	4	3	1	0	6	3	.353	.600	.250	13.50	13.50
Mazza, John	R-R	5-11	195	2-15-95	0	0	0.00	1	0	0	0	1	0	0	0	0	0	0	.000	.000	.000	0.00	0.00
Milam, Kevin	R-R	6-0	200	2-13-98	3	1	8.74	10	0	0	0	11	17	13	11	1	5	18	.340	.231	.378	14.29	3.97
Montas, Kenlly	R-R	6-0	187	5-31-96	0	1	5.40	9	0	0	0	15	15	15	9	3	13	17	.254	.188	.279	10.20	7.80
Paciorek, Nick	R-R	6-4	190		0	0	0.00	1	0	0	0	3	0	0	0	0	1	0	.000	.000	.000	0.00	9.00
Panacual, Josue	R-R	5-10	158	1-13-02	4	2	6.26	11	4	0	0	27	24	25	19	2	16	33	.229	.308	.182	10.87	5.27
Paredes, Edward	R-R	5-11	170	1-7-99	0	0	2.13	8	0	0	0	13	11	6	3	1	6	12	.234	.167	.257	8.53	4.26
Pellerin, Connor	R-R	6-4	210	7-22-99	0	1	10.13	2	2	0	0	3	4	3	3	0	2	2	.400	.000	.500	6.75	6.75

	B-T	HT	WT	DOB	W	L	ERA	G	GS	CG	SV	IP	H	R	ER	HR	BB	SO	AVG	vLH	vRH	K/9	BB/9
Perez, Freicer	R-R	6-8	240	3-14-96	0	2	9.53	4	3	0	0	6	4	6	6	0	7	11	.190	.333	.133	17.47	11.12
Perez, Starling	R-R	6-3	182	9-2-00	0	1	5.54	12	1	0	1	26	28	20	16	3	20	24	.277	.167	.324	8.31	6.92
Pestana, Leonardo	R-R	6-4	198	7-30-98	1	0	5.79	2	0	0	0	5	2	3	3	1	1	8	.125	.250	.083	15.43	1.93
Rodriguez, Nicio	R-R	6-3	175	9-3-99	0	0	9.64	2	1	0	0	5	5	5	5	0	3	7	.294	.500	.231	13.50	5.79
Rodriguez, Osiel	R-R	6-2	210	11-22-01	0	0	4.15	6	0	0	0	9	9	6	4	1	2	11	.265	.000	.360	11.42	2.08
Ruiz, Yarison	R-R	6-4	216	3-26-00	1	1	2.08	5	4	0	0	17	8	6	4	0	18	29	.138	.000	.186	15.06	9.35
Sanchez, Brandom	L-L	6-2	207	2-17-00	1	0	15.43	7	0	0	0	7	10	12	12	0	10	3	.345	.000	.357	3.86	12.86
Schmidt, Clarke	R-R	6-1	209	2-20-96	0	0	0.00	1	1	0	0	3	1	0	0	0	0	5	.111	.000	.143	15.00	0.00
Selvidge, Brock	R-L	6-3	205	8-28-02	0	0	2.45	3	2	0	0	4	2	2	1	0	1	4	.154	.000	.250	9.82	2.45
Sumoza, Christian	R-R	5-10	164	11-18-00	2	1	7.11	13	0	0	1	19	23	18	15	2	8	25	.299	.474	.241	11.84	3.79
Vega, Alfred	R-R	6-1	169	1-19-01	1	0	1.64	11	6	0	0	33	17	9	6	2	17	40	.153	.154	.153	10.91	4.64
Velasquez, Luis	R-R	5-10	155	7-1-01	1	0	5.00	7	0	0	0	9	8	7	5	0	11	7	.235	.182	.261	7.00	11.00
Vizcaino, Alexander	R-R	6-2	160	5-22-97	0	0	4.50	2	1	0	0	2	1	1	1	0	3	4	.167	--	.167	18.00	13.50
Yulie, Tyrone	R-R	6-4	180	8-4-01	1	0	0.00	3	2	0	0	10	2	0	0	0	5	13	.063	.167	.038	11.32	4.35
Zurak, Kyle	R-R	6-1	208	11-28-94	0	0	0.00	1	0	0	0	1	0	0	0	0	0	0	.000	.000	.000	0.00	0.00

Fielding

C: Crisp 10, Gasper 3, Gomez 23, Guerrero 9, Mazza 1, Ramirez 20, Rice 1, Rosario 8.
1B: Crisp 1, Garcia 14, Gomez 17, Guerrero 9, Hardman 3, Martinez 20, Pries 1, Ramirez 1, Sensley 2.
2B: Bowman 3, Chirinos 6, Colmenares 11, Cowles 1, Marte 8, Rojas 9, Santos 3, Smith 16, Vallejo 6.
3B: Cabrera 41, Chirinos 1, Cowles 2, Gomez 6, Martinez 2, Santos 2, Vallejo 12.
SS: Chirinos 3, Marte 3, Rojas 17, Santos 3, Smith 2, Sweeney 3, Vargas 35.
OF: Alcantara 6, Battle 21, Dominguez 6, Garcia 5, Green 5, Knowles 10, Pereira 3, Pries 22, Richardson 27, Rosario 20, Salinas 46, Sanchez 3, Santos 18.

DSL YANKEES — ROOKIE

DOMINICAN SUMMER LEAGUE

Batting	B-T	HT	WT	DOB	AVG	vLH	vRH	G	AB	R	H	2B	3B	HR	RBI	BB	HBP	SH	SF	SO	SB	CS	SLG	OBP
Altagracia, Ramiro	R-R	5-11	180	1-18-04	.198	.214	.194	38	131	21	26	3	1	1	13	25	2	0	1	68	5	2	.260	.333
Arias, Daury	L-L	5-10	172	8-7-01	.287	.267	.291	49	181	41	52	10	1	8	49	38	2	0	0	30	9	2	.486	.416
Bersing, Gabriel	R-R	6-1	195	10-17-02	.324	.571	.259	24	68	9	22	3	1	2	8	8	3	0	1	19	4	2	.485	.413
Bonifacio, Mauro	R-R	6-7	226	8-31-01	.247	.381	.200	24	81	15	20	4	0	7	16	5	2	0	2	37	1	0	.556	.300
Castellano, Enger	R-R	6-0	190	12-2-02	.226	.217	.228	40	137	18	31	7	0	2	23	21	1	0	2	49	5	4	.321	.329
Castillo, Darwin	R-R	5-10	153	2-26-03	.195	.100	.209	31	77	15	15	1	0	0	6	8	2	0	1	18	6	2	.208	.284
Duran, Edinson	R-R	5-7	180	7-22-02	.233	.438	.189	32	90	15	21	4	1	4	19	9	5	0	1	24	2	3	.433	.333
Escanio, Brenny	B-R	5-9	145	12-16-02	.250	.268	.244	50	172	43	43	13	1	6	27	38	6	0	1	54	20	7	.442	.401
Espino, Kelvin	L-R	6-1	193	12-8-01	.115	.000	.125	8	26	2	3	1	0	0	5	7	0	0	1	11	0	0	.154	.294
Familia, Christopher	L-L	5-11	170	6-10-00	.266	.161	.289	48	173	30	46	16	0	2	28	22	7	0	1	39	9	4	.393	.369
Fleitas, Osmany	R-R	5-9	133	1-7-02	.397	.417	.391	29	58	18	23	5	2	0	6	13	0	0	0	12	10	1	.552	.507
Garcia, Alex	B-R	5-10	155	12-8-01	.208	.250	.200	35	77	21	16	1	2	1	12	18	1	0	0	28	7	4	.312	.365
Garcia, Nicolas	R-R	5-11	200	6-15-01	.259	.300	.250	19	58	11	15	5	0	2	13	8	0	0	0	25	1	0	.448	.348
Gonzalez, Josue	R-R	5-9	170	10-30-03	.217	.125	.237	18	46	9	10	2	1	1	8	11	0	0	0	11	1	1	.370	.403
Herrera, Carlos	R-R	5-10	165	9-1-02	.143	--	.143	5	14	2	2	0	0	0	1	2	0	0	0	4	0	1	.143	.250
Imbert, Jhon	R-R	6-1	172	9-1-03	.267	.000	.333	5	15	2	4	1	1	0	3	1	0	0	0	10	1	0	.467	.313
Marte, Miguel	R-R	5-11	165	5-26-01	.158	.250	.133	9	19	2	3	0	1	0	4	3	1	0	1	3	1	2	.263	.292
Martinez, Omar	L-R	5-11	192	7-5-01	.250	.200	.260	49	148	31	37	9	0	6	27	35	6	0	3	47	1	3	.432	.406
Medina, Nelson	R-R	6-2	175	9-14-00	.241	.276	.228	43	108	29	26	8	1	1	13	29	2	0	3	28	13	2	.361	.401
Mejia, Alan	R-R	6-0	165	7-20-01	.288	.333	.283	47	156	29	45	9	2	8	28	26	1	0	1	43	15	7	.526	.391
Mendez, Joel	R-R	6-1	180	1-28-03	.220	.250	.213	49	173	43	38	9	1	7	26	38	3	0	0	84	7	2	.405	.369
Montero, Fidel	R-R	6-0	178	12-19-03	.193	.292	.177	52	171	39	33	7	3	4	14	44	10	0	0	90	19	4	.339	.387
Montero, Hans	R-R	5-11	160	12-25-03	.200	.179	.205	51	190	31	38	5	1	1	22	33	8	0	2	74	15	4	.253	.339
Montero, Willy	R-R	6-4	202	8-4-04	.191	.167	.195	16	47	8	9	1	0	0	8	7	3	0	4	18	0	4	.213	.311
Negueis, Felix	R-R	6-0	200	12-29-00	.299	.387	.282	53	194	41	58	17	0	4	34	33	6	0	1	61	16	5	.448	.415
Palencia, Manuel	R-R	6-0	175	9-5-02	.302	.400	.281	33	116	21	35	8	0	0	17	11	3	0	1	15	5	2	.371	.374
Perez, Dayro	R-R	6-2	180	1-31-02	.266	.415	.231	57	214	54	57	12	3	6	28	37	13	0	1	83	35	9	.435	.404
Rodriguez, Jesus	R-R	5-10	182	4-23-02	.294	.370	.273	39	126	28	37	15	0	0	22	22	1	0	2	24	8	3	.413	.397
Rojas, Ronny	B-R	6-1	180	8-23-01	.224	.212	.228	50	147	31	33	6	2	8	28	39	5	0	1	57	4	0	.456	.401
Rosa, Juan	R-R	6-0	189	11-18-02	.194	.200	.194	14	36	7	7	3	0	2	6	8	1	0	0	19	2	3	.444	.356
Serna, Jared	R-R	5-8	168	6-1-02	.238	.318	.225	50	151	34	36	9	2	3	16	34	8	0	0	27	24	4	.384	.404
Silverio, Oscar	L-R	5-9	170	10-25-01	.238	.154	.260	27	63	12	15	3	0	3	19	10	1	0	0	21	2	1	.429	.351
Torres, Miguel	R-R	6-0	170	3-3-00	.198	.235	.189	38	91	16	18	2	0	5	28	18	4	0	1	19	3	1	.385	.351
Valenzuela, Anthony	R-R	5-11	180	6-16-01	.100	.000	.111	7	10	5	1	1	0	0	1	5	3	0	0	5	0	1	.200	.500
Vargas, Sergio	R-R	6-1	170	6-16-02	.167	--	.167	2	6	1	1	0	0	0	0	1	0	0	0	3	0	0	.167	.286
Verdecia, Carlos	B-R	5-11	170	3-16-02	.189	.125	.203	34	95	19	18	5	1	1	12	10	5	2	1	20	5	2	.263	.342

Pitching	B-T	HT	WT	DOB	W	L	ERA	G	GS	CG	SV	IP	H	R	ER	HR	BB	SO	AVG	vLH	vRH	K/9	BB/9
Abrego, Gerardo	R-R	6-3	190	4-16-01	3	2	2.68	12	10	0	0	47	32	23	14	2	22	56	.193	.227	.180	10.72	4.21
Alfaro, Ricardo	R-R	6-5	175	11-27-01	0	0	0.00	2	0	0	1	0	0	0	0	0	2	1	.000	--	.000	27.00	54.00
Aparicio, Kevin	R-R	6-3	180	1-6-03	5	0	4.50	15	0	0	4	16	15	9	8	0	7	25	.238	.280	.211	14.06	3.94
Arejula, Luis	R-R	6-1	170	2-20-02	2	4	4.30	12	10	0	1	44	38	23	21	3	13	60	.229	.277	.210	12.27	2.66
Arias, Brian	R-R	6-0	177	11-18-03	0	1	6.19	8	6	0	0	16	13	14	11	1	13	19	.213	.150	.244	10.69	7.31
Barrios, Wilser	R-R	6-2	160	3-21-98	1	1	0.00	2	0	0	0	4	3	2	0	1	5	20	.200	.000	.250	10.38	2.08
Beltran, Lester	L-L	6-0	190	1-28-00	1	1	4.80	12	0	0	0	15	17	11	8	3	5	13	.250	.000	.315	7.80	3.00
Bersing, Gabriel	R-R	6-1	195	10-17-02	0	0	135.00	1	0	0	0	0	4	5	5	0	2	0	.800	.667	1.000	0.00	54.00
Borges, Ernesto	R-R	6-2	188	5-17-01	1	1	6.87	11	0	0	1	18	16	16	14	4	12	16	.258	.400	.190	7.85	5.89
Calderon, Daniel	L-L	6-1	170	10-13-97	0	0	3.38	11	0	0	1	19	17	8	7	1	17	23	.246	.214	.255	11.09	8.20

Name	B-T	Ht	Wt	DOB	W	L	ERA	G	GS	CG	SV	IP	H	R	ER	HR	BB	SO	AVG	vLH	vRH	BB/9	SO/9
Calderon, Yorlin	R-R	6-3	155	8-17-01	0	0	7.20	3	2	0	0	10	14	10	8	2	1	17	.318	.538	.226	15.30	0.90
Castillo, Ruben	R-R	6-1	160	6-18-01	1	1	2.12	17	1	0	3	30	15	10	7	0	6	32	.147	.152	.145	9.71	1.82
Cordero, Diego	R-R	5-11	216	10-21-99	1	3	5.20	13	0	0	0	28	38	25	16	3	11	27	.330	.289	.357	8.78	3.58
Corniel, Franklin	R-R	6-2	165	10-8-01	1	3	6.90	13	9	0	0	44	47	48	34	0	30	51	.273	.203	.315	10.35	6.09
Espana, Juan	R-R	5-9	145	2-19-02	1	1	9.24	10	0	0	0	13	18	24	13	1	12	8	.305	.235	.333	5.68	8.53
Facundo, Allen	L-L	6-0	171	9-3-02	0	3	4.25	14	11	0	0	49	34	29	23	0	27	84	.195	.121	.213	15.53	4.99
Fleitas, Osmany	R-R	5-9	133	1-7-02	0	0	0.00	1	0	0	0	1	0	0	0	0	0	0	.000	--	.000	0.00	0.00
Garcia, Donys	R-R	6-2	175	2-18-01	2	3	3.57	12	6	0	1	35	19	15	14	2	25	41	.161	.087	.208	10.44	6.37
Gomez, Alejandro	R-R	6-4	180	8-3-02	2	0	5.06	10	0	0	1	21	26	13	12	3	11	22	.289	.353	.250	9.28	4.64
Guerrero, Daniel	R-R	6-4	204	1-26-04	0	3	7.63	6	5	0	0	15	17	17	13	1	8	14	.274	.261	.282	8.22	4.70
Guzman, Jose	R-R	5-11	185	12-26-01	1	0	0.00	3	0	0	1	9	1	0	0	0	4	10	.036	.000	.048	10.00	4.00
Henriquez, Nolberto	R-R	6-4	170	10-16-99	6	1	4.69	14	8	0	0	56	53	35	29	6	26	57	.251	.233	.261	9.22	4.20
Hernandez, Franyer	R-R	5-11	204	2-1-01	1	3	3.16	16	0	0	0	31	29	15	11	0	13	28	.250	.214	.270	8.04	3.73
Lalane, Henry	L-L	6-7	211	5-18-04	1	3	3.70	12	12	0	0	41	42	29	17	2	25	39	.264	.333	.250	8.49	5.44
Martinez, Omar	L-R	5-11	192	7-5-01	0	0	0.00	1	0	0	0	2	1	0	0	0	0	3	.167	.000	.250	16.20	0.00
Mendoza, Jordarlin	R-R	6-0	175	11-14-03	0	0	0.00	1	0	0	0	2	2	0	0	0	1	3	.286	.000	.400	13.50	4.50
Oropeza, Riordan	R-R	6-3	181	1-12-02	3	4	6.00	13	0	0	0	21	25	21	14	3	12	26	.305	.214	.352	11.14	5.14
Peguero, Geremias	L-L	6-1	198	2-7-00	0	0	3.60	3	2	0	0	5	2	2	2	0	8	9	.118	.000	.133	16.20	14.40
Pena, Jan	R-R	6-4	180	6-15-00	6	0	2.89	13	0	0	1	53	40	18	17	0	19	61	.207	.231	.195	10.36	3.23
Perrone, Sebastian	R-R	5-11	180	4-8-00	4	0	1.55	13	0	0	0	29	17	7	5	0	11	38	.167	.216	.138	11.79	3.41
Pichardo, Yordi	R-R	6-3	180	7-12-02	2	1	9.60	12	0	0	0	15	14	17	16	2	13	17	.233	.136	.289	10.20	7.80
Polimir, Edwar	L-L	5-11	145	11-5-00	1	0	0.00	1	0	0	0	1	0	0	0	0	0	1	.000	.000	.000	6.75	0.00
Pozo, Miguel	L-L	5-11	155	9-9-01	3	1	2.58	12	5	0	0	38	27	18	11	1	20	48	.194	.261	.181	11.27	4.70
Rodriguez, Pedro	L-L	5-10	145	8-11-02	3	0	9.00	16	0	0	1	20	26	24	20	2	13	30	.302	.235	.319	13.50	5.85
Rosario, Carlos	R-R	6-2	170	6-26-00	2	3	6.65	13	10	0	0	47	55	46	35	1	24	55	.279	.257	.293	10.46	4.56
Ruiz, Yarison	R-R	6-4	216	3-26-00	0	1	4.97	4	4	0	0	13	13	9	7	1	10	20	.265	.190	.321	14.21	7.11
Salas, Daniel	R-R	6-3	189	2-16-03	1	3	8.25	12	0	0	1	12	18	21	11	3	11	11	.333	.263	.371	8.25	8.25
Santana, Geralmi	R-R	6-3	173	12-7-00	2	0	3.75	12	5	0	0	36	29	21	15	1	16	39	.203	.163	.223	9.75	4.00
Serna, Luis	R-R	5-11	144	7-20-04	1	5	2.25	12	11	0	0	40	25	16	10	0	17	46	.176	.188	.170	10.35	3.83
Urbano, Luis	L-L	6-2	163	10-1-02	0	1	8.04	11	0	0	0	16	19	19	14	0	20	14	.311	.286	.319	8.04	11.49
Vargas, Miguel	L-L	5-10	180	2-22-01	5	3	3.67	13	1	0	1	49	51	26	20	3	18	55	.270	.333	.256	10.10	3.31

Fielding

C: Bersing 1, Duran 12, Garcia 3, Gonzalez 13, Herrera 2, Martinez 26, Palencia 33, Rodriguez 29, Silverio 11, Torres 12.

1B: Bersing 22, Castellano 1, Duran 20, Garcia 1, Garcia 14, Herrera 2, Martinez 19, Rodriguez 8, Rojas 1, Silverio 15, Torres 23, Vargas 2.

2B: Castellano 1, Castillo 12, Escanio 35, Fleitas 12, Garcia 15, Imbert 1, Marte 2, Rojas 3, Serna 34, Verdecia 13.

3B: Castellano 37, Fleitas 7, Garcia 2, Imbert 4, Marte 7, Rojas 48, Serna 16, Verdecia 13.

SS: Castillo 15, Escanio 13, Montero 40, Perez 46, Serna 1, Verdecia 5.

OF: Altagracia 29, Arias 38, Bersing 1, Bonifacio 18, Espino 7, Familia 38, Fleitas 8, Garcia 10, Medina 41, Mejia 43, Mendez 38, Montero 40, Montero 12, Negueis 42, Rosa 13, Serna 1, Valenzuela 7.

Oakland Athletics

SEASON IN A SENTENCE: Oakland again looked the part of an American League playoff contender until fishtailing through the second half, finishing 86-76 and nine games back in the AL West, inviting skepticism that the team's competitive window is beginning to close.

HIGH POINT: While not quite the famed 20-game winning streak of the 'Moneyball' era in 2002, Oakland ripped off a 13-game win streak in late April to erase an 0-6 start. The A's outscored their opponents by 45 runs during the stretch. Matt Olson's play also deserves credit—Oakland's all-star first baseman hit a career-best 39 homers, tied for the sixth most in baseball.

LOW POINT: August was rough from start to finish. Oakland lost outfielder Ramon Laureano to a PED suspension on Aug. 6 and ace right-hander Chris Bassitt suffered a devastating head injury on a comebacker on Aug. 17. The following week, Oakland lost six consecutive games to three playoff contenders—the Giants, Mariners and Yankees. Three of those games were blown saves and Oakland was tied entering the ninth inning in a 7-6 loss to the Yankees. The A's fell out of one of the top two wild card spots during that stretch and never played their way back in.

NOTABLE ROOKIES: Once a touted draft prospect, a series of arm injuries wiped out three seasons of development for righthander James Kaprielian from 2016-2018. The righty finally carved out a regular role in the big leagues in his age-27 season, though, posting a 4.07 ERA over 119.1 innings and looking the part of a future rotation piece.

KEY TRANSACTIONS: The A's most notably acquired former all-star center fielder Starling Marte at the deadline in exchange for lefthander Jesus Luzardo, one of their prized young arms. Marte was tremendous, accumulating 2.0 WAR in just 56 games with Oakland while hitting .312 and stealing 25 bases. Oakland's quiet acquisition of lefthander Cole Irvin in January 2021 also proved prescient—he made 32 starts, pitching to a 4.24 ERA.

OPENING DAY PAYROLL: $74,615,000 (24th).

PLAYERS OF THE YEAR

MAJOR LEAGUE

Matt Olson
1B
.271/.371/.540
Career-high 39 HR
101 R, 111 RBIs

MINOR LEAGUE

Nick Allen
SS
(AAA/AA)
.288/.346/.403,
17 2B, 12 SB

ORGANIZATION LEADERS

Batting		*Minimum 250 AB
MAJORS		
*AVG	Tony Kemp	.279
*OPS	Matt Olson	.911
HR	Matt Olson	39
RBI	Matt Olson	111
MINORS		
*AVG	Austin Allen, Las Vegas	.317
*OBP	Jonah Bride, Midland	.407
*SLG	Austin Allen, Las Vegas	.584
*OPS	Austin Allen, Las Vegas	.935
R	Max Schuemann, Las Vegas, Midland, Lansing	83
H	Max Schuemann, Las Vegas, Midland, Lansing	121
TB	Carlos Perez, Las Vegas	215
2B	Max Schuemann, Las Vegas, Midland, Lansing	25
3B	Devin Foyle, Midland	7
HR	Carlos Perez, Las Vegas	31
RBI	Carlos Perez, Las Vegas	89
BB	Logan Davidson, Midland	62
SO	Logan Davidson, Midland	155
SB	Max Schuemann, Las Vegas, Midland, Lansing	52
Pitching		#Minimum 75 IP
MAJORS		
W	Frankie Montas	13
#ERA	Chris Bassitt	3.15
SO	Frankie Montas	207
SV	Lou Trivino	22
MINORS		
W	Colin Peluse, Midland, Lansing	9
L	Reid Birlingmair, Lansing	10
#ERA	Jack Cushing, Midland, Lansing, Stockton	3.22
G	Aaron Brown, Las Vegas, Midland	51
G	James Naile, Las Vegas	51
GS	Brady Feigl, Las Vegas, Midland	25
SV	Aaron Brown, Las Vegas, Midland	12
SV	Charles Hall, Lansing	12
IP	Brady Feigl, Las Vegas, Midland	122.1
BB	Pedro Santos, Stockton	62
SO	Brady Feigl, Las Vegas, Midland	123
#AVG	Charles Hall, Lansing	.191

2021 PERFORMANCE

General Manager: David Forst. **Farm Director:** Ed Sprague. **Scouting Director:** Eric Kubota.

Class	Team	League	W	L	PCT	Finish	Manager
Majors	Oakland Athletics	American	86	76	.531	8th (15)	Bob Melvin
Triple-A	Las Vegas Aviators	Triple-A West	65	61	.516	6th (10)	Fran Riordan
Double-A	Midland RockHounds	Double-A Central	59	60	.496	6th (10)	Bobby Crosby
High-A	Lansing Lugnuts	High-A Central	58	62	.483	t-7th (12)	Scott Steinmann
Low-A	Stockton Ports	Low-A West	42	75	.359	7th (8)	Rico Brogna
Rookie	ACL Athletics	Arizona Complex	16	43	.271	18th (18)	Adam Rosales
Rookie	DSL Athletics	Dominican Summer	20	36	.357	41st (46)	Carlos Casimiro/Luis Baez
Overall 2021 Minor League Record			260	337	.436	27th (30)	

ORGANIZATION STATISTICS

OAKLAND ATHLETICS
AMERICAN LEAGUE

Batting	B-T	HT	WT	DOB	AVG	vLH	vRH	G	AB	R	H	2B	3B	HR	RBI	BB	HBP	SH	SF	SO	SB	CS	SLG	OBP
Allen, Austin	L-R	6-2	219	1-16-94	.250	.000	.400	4	8	2	2	0	0	1	1	0	0	0	0	3	0	0	.625	.250
Andrus, Elvis	R-R	6-0	210	8-26-88	.243	.190	.269	146	497	60	121	25	2	3	37	31	6	3	4	81	12	2	.320	.294
Barrera, Luis	L-L	6-0	195	11-15-95	.250	.000	.286	6	8	1	2	0	0	0	0	0	0	0	0	2	0	0	.250	.250
Bolt, Skye	B-R	6-2	180	1-15-94	.089	.048	.114	32	56	5	5	1	0	1	4	1	0	2	0	14	2	0	.161	.105
Brown, Seth	L-L	6-1	223	7-13-92	.214	.136	.220	111	281	43	60	13	1	20	48	23	1	0	2	89	4	1	.480	.274
Canha, Mark	R-R	6-2	209	2-15-89	.231	.221	.237	141	519	93	120	22	4	17	61	77	27	0	2	128	12	2	.387	.358
Chapman, Matt	R-R	6-0	215	4-28-93	.210	.228	.201	151	529	75	111	15	3	27	72	80	4	0	9	202	3	2	.403	.314
Davis, Khris	R-R	5-11	205	12-21-87	.255	.250	.261	20	51	3	13	4	0	1	5	2	0	0	0	15	0	0	.392	.283
2-team total (22 Texas)					.206	.208	.204	42	102	11	21	5	1	3	10	10	0	0	2	31	0	0	.363	.272
Garcia, Aramis	R-R	6-1	228	1-12-93	.205	.238	.194	32	88	8	18	1	0	3	7	1	3	2	0	28	0	0	.318	.239
Gomes, Yan	R-R	6-2	212	7-19-87	.221	.259	.192	40	131	19	29	4	0	5	17	6	2	0	1	31	0	0	.366	.264
Harrison, Josh	R-R	5-8	190	7-8-87	.254	.279	.239	48	185	19	47	10	0	2	22	6	6	0	2	25	4	3	.341	.296
Kemp, Tony	L-R	5-6	160	10-31-91	.279	.240	.290	131	330	54	92	16	3	8	37	52	6	4	5	51	8	2	.418	.382
Kozma, Pete	R-R	6-0	190	4-11-88	.091	.000	.125	3	11	0	1	0	0	0	0	0	1	0	0	4	0	0	.091	.167
Laureano, Ramon	R-R	5-11	203	7-15-94	.246	.304	.217	88	341	43	84	21	2	14	39	27	9	0	1	98	12	5	.443	.317
Lowrie, Jed	B-R	6-0	180	4-17-84	.245	.259	.237	139	457	55	112	28	0	14	69	49	2	0	4	108	0	0	.398	.318
Machin, Vimael	L-R	5-11	185	9-25-93	.125	.222	.087	15	32	1	4	0	0	0	1	3	0	2	0	10	0	0	.125	.200
Marte, Starling	R-R	6-1	195	10-9-88	.316	.286	.333	56	234	37	74	16	2	5	30	11	5	0	1	42	25	2	.466	.359
Moreland, Mitch	L-L	6-3	245	9-6-85	.227	.154	.242	81	229	28	52	11	1	10	30	18	2	0	3	58	0	0	.415	.286
Murphy, Sean	R-R	6-3	228	10-4-94	.216	.194	.227	119	393	47	85	23	0	17	59	40	12	0	3	114	0	0	.405	.306
Olson, Matt	L-R	6-5	225	3-29-94	.271	.270	.271	156	565	101	153	35	0	39	111	88	9	0	11	113	4	1	.540	.371
Pinder, Chad	R-R	6-2	210	3-29-92	.243	.291	.198	75	214	30	52	16	1	6	27	16	2	0	1	62	1	0	.411	.300
Piscotty, Stephen	R-R	6-4	211	1-14-91	.220	.256	.181	72	173	14	38	8	0	5	16	13	2	0	0	48	1	0	.353	.282
Schwindel, Frank	R-R	6-1	220	6-29-92	.150	.167	.125	8	20	2	3	1	0	1	3	0	0	0	0	5	0	0	.350	.150
Tom, Ka'ai	L-R	5-9	185	5-29-94	.063	.333	.000	9	16	1	1	0	0	0	1	0	0	0	0	6	0	0	.063	.063
Wilson, Jacob	R-R	5-11	219	7-29-90	.143	.143	—	6	7	1	1	0	0	0	0	0	0	0	0	1	0	0	.143	.143
2-team total (6 Houston)					.150	.091	.222	12	20	3	3	1	1	0	1	1	0	0	0	3	0	0	.300	.190

Pitching	B-T	HT	WT	DOB	W	L	ERA	G	GS	CG	SV	IP	H	R	ER	HR	BB	SO	AVG	vLH	vRH	K/9	BB/9
Acevedo, Domingo	R-R	6-7	240	3-6-94	0	0	3.27	10	0	0	0	11	9	4	4	3	4	9	.225	.200	.240	7.36	3.27
Bassitt, Chris	R-R	6-5	217	2-22-89	12	4	3.15	27	27	1	0	157	127	55	55	15	39	159	.218	.196	.238	9.10	2.23
Bedrosian, Cam	R-R	6-1	225	10-2-91	0	0	2.00	9	0	0	0	9	9	2	2	2	4	8	.265	.273	.261	8.00	4.00
Blackburn, Paul	R-R	6-1	196	12-4-93	1	4	5.87	9	9	0	0	38	52	26	25	8	10	26	.319	.333	.309	6.10	2.35
Chafin, Andrew	L-L	6-2	235	6-17-90	2	2	1.53	28	0	0	5	29	24	5	5	3	7	27	.226	.182	.247	8.28	2.15
Diekman, Jake	R-L	6-4	195	1-21-87	3	3	3.86	67	0	0	7	61	47	29	26	10	34	83	.211	.229	.200	12.31	5.04
Feliz, Michael	R-R	6-4	250	6-28-93	0	0	0.00	1	0	0	0	0	1	0	0	0	1	0	.500	.000	1.000	0.00	27.00
2-team total (4 Boston)					0	0	3.18	5	0	0	0	6	5	2	2	2	2	5	.250	.111	.364	7.94	3.18
Fiers, Mike	R-R	6-2	211	6-15-85	0	2	7.71	2	2	0	0	9	15	8	8	4	4	5	.366	.455	.333	4.82	3.86
Guduan, Reymin	L-L	6-4	205	3-16-92	0	0	6.28	11	0	0	0	14	19	11	10	1	5	5	.345	.118	.447	3.14	3.14
Guerra, Deolis	R-R	6-5	245	4-17-89	4	1	4.11	53	0	0	0	66	53	34	30	8	20	62	.218	.217	.219	8.50	2.74
Irvin, Cole	L-L	6-4	217	1-31-94	10	15	4.24	32	32	0	0	178	195	94	84	23	42	125	.275	.289	.270	6.31	2.12
Jefferies, Daulton	L-R	6-0	182	8-2-95	1	0	3.60	5	1	0	0	15	11	6	6	1	4	8	.208	.231	.185	4.80	2.40
Kaprielian, James	R-R	6-3	225	3-2-94	8	5	4.07	24	21	0	0	119	105	55	54	19	41	123	.233	.266	.201	9.28	3.09
Kolarek, Adam	L-L	6-3	215	1-14-89	0	0	8.00	12	0	0	0	9	16	8	8	2	5	4	.341	.211	.440	4.00	5.00
Luzardo, Jesus	L-L	6-0	218	9-30-97	2	4	6.87	13	6	0	0	38	46	32	29	11	16	40	.297	.275	.304	9.47	3.79
Manaea, Sean	R-L	6-5	245	2-1-92	11	10	3.91	32	32	2	0	179	179	79	78	25	41	194	.255	.204	.271	9.74	2.06
Moll, Sam	L-L	5-9	190	1-3-92	0	0	3.48	8	0	0	0	10	8	4	4	1	5	8	.216	.333	.136	6.97	4.35
Montas, Frankie	R-R	6-2	255	3-21-93	13	9	3.37	32	32	0	0	187	164	79	70	20	57	207	.232	.225	.238	9.96	2.74
Moreland, Mitch	L-L	6-3	245	9-6-85	0	0	0.00	1	0	0	0	1	1	0	0	0	0	1	.250	.000	.500	9.00	0.00
Petit, Yusmeiro	R-R	6-1	252	11-22-84	8	3	3.92	78	0	0	2	78	69	35	34	12	12	37	.233	.219	.242	4.27	1.38
Puk, A.J.	L-L	6-7	248	4-25-95	0	3	6.08	12	0	0	0	13	18	9	9	1	6	16	.310	.267	.326	10.80	4.05
Romo, Sergio	R-R	5-11	185	3-4-83	1	1	4.67	66	0	0	3	62	56	33	32	9	21	60	.238	.235	.240	8.76	3.06
Smith, Burch	R-R	6-4	225	4-12-90	1	1	5.40	31	0	0	0	43	49	27	26	5	11	28	.280	.316	.263	5.82	2.28

Player	L-R	HT	WT	DOB	W	L	ERA	G	GS	CG	SV	IP	H	R	ER	HR	BB	SO	AVG	vLH	vRH	K/9	BB/9
Tom, Ka'ai	L-R	5-9	185	5-29-94	0	0	0.00	1	0	0	0	1	1	0	0	0	0	0	.250	.333	.000	0.00	0.00
Trivino, Lou	R-R	6-5	235	10-1-91	7	8	3.18	71	0	0	22	74	58	32	26	5	34	67	.216	.282	.171	8.19	4.15
Weems, Jordan	L-R	6-3	175	11-7-92	0	0	6.23	5	0	0	0	4	2	3	3	1	3	4	.133	.000	.200	8.31	6.23
Wendelken, J.B.	R-R	6-1	242	3-24-93	2	1	4.32	26	0	0	25	29	15	12	2	13	26	.279	.357	.226	9.36	4.68

Fielding

Catcher	PCT	G	PO	A	E	DP	PB
Allen	.955	2	18	3	1	0	0
Garcia	.991	30	217	9	2	0	4
Gomes	.992	31	236	7	2	0	1
Murphy	.993	112	873	42	6	6	1

First Base	PCT	G	PO	A	E	DP
Brown	.967	6	27	2	1	4
Canha	1.000	2	2	0	0	0
Moreland	1.000	7	49	4	0	5
Olson	.995	152	1156	73	6	98
Schwindel	1.000	1	1	0	0	1

Second Base	PCT	G	PO	A	E	DP
Harrison	1.000	32	37	54	0	12
Kemp	.980	89	103	148	5	34
Lowrie	.986	71	80	125	3	18
Machin	1.000	3	5	6	0	1

	PCT	G	PO	A	E	DP
Pinder	1.000	7	7	10	0	4
Wilson	1.000	3	1	4	0	1

Third Base	PCT	G	PO	A	E	DP
Chapman	.987	150	166	274	6	40
Harrison	1.000	12	7	16	0	1
Lowrie	1.000	1	2	0	0	0
Machin	.500	3	0	1	1	1
Pinder	.938	6	3	12	1	0
Wilson	.000	1	0	0	0	0

Shortstop	PCT	G	PO	A	E	DP
Andrus	.971	143	161	337	15	61
Chapman	1.000	3	0	1	0	0
Harrison	.857	8	2	16	3	2
Kemp	1.000	1	0	2	0	0
Kozma	1.000	3	1	14	0	1
Machin	.944	8	3	14	1	3

	PCT	G	PO	A	E	DP
Pinder	1.000	8	8	9	0	5

Outfield	PCT	G	PO	A	E	DP
Barrera	1.000	5	4	0	0	0
Bolt	1.000	25	48	0	0	0
Brown	.988	98	163	3	2	1
Canha	.988	156	243	3	3	0
Davis	1.000	1	1	0	0	0
Harrison	1.000	3	3	0	0	0
Kemp	1.000	49	69	1	0	0
Laureano	.990	83	199	7	2	1
Marte	.993	56	147	2	1	0
Pinder	.989	56	87	0	1	0
Piscotty	1.000	67	103	0	0	0
Tom	1.000	5	8	0	0	0
Wilson	1.000	1	3	0	0	0

LAS VEGAS AVIATORS
TRIPLE-A WEST
TRIPLE-A

Batting	B-T	HT	WT	DOB	AVG	vLH	vRH	G	AB	R	H	2B	3B	HR	RBI	BB	HBP	SH	SF	SO	SB	CS	SLG	OBP
Allen, Austin	L-R	6-2	219	1-16-94	.317	.347	.306	72	281	50	89	15	0	20	53	13	3	0	2	55	0	0	.584	.351
Allen, Nick	R-R	5-8	166	10-8-98	.243	.286	.231	39	136	17	33	8	0	0	10	11	1	2	1	30	4	1	.301	.302
Barrera, Luis	L-L	6-0	195	11-15-95	.276	.297	.268	96	341	53	94	16	6	4	37	39	1	1	4	67	10	2	.393	.348
Bechina, Marty	R-R	6-0	200	10-31-96	.189	.190	.189	56	164	19	31	9	0	9	28	5	4	0	5	72	3	1	.409	.225
Beck, Austin	R-R	6-1	200	11-21-98	.150	.000	.176	8	20	4	3	0	0	3	6	2	0	0		13	0	0	.600	.227
Bolt, Skye	B-R	6-2	180	1-15-94	.387	.391	.385	51	163	41	63	12	2	9	29	32	3	0	1	43	5	0	.650	.492
Brown, Seth	L-L	6-1	223	7-13-92	.286	.000	.400	3	14	3	4	1	1	0	1	0	0	0	0	5	0	0	.500	.286
Davis, Khris	R-R	5-11	205	12-21-87	.333	.375	.327	16	63	16	21	3	2	10	25	4	1	0	0	13	0	0	.921	.382
2-team total (1 Round Rock)					.313	.375	.305	17	67	16	21	3	2	10	25	4	1	0	0	15	0	0	.866	.361
Deichmann, Greg	L-R	6-2	205	5-31-95	.300	.186	.344	60	210	48	63	14	3	4	35	50	0	0	1	60	7	1	.452	.433
Diaz, Edwin	R-R	6-2	223	8-25-95	.111	.056	.139	18	54	5	6	0	0	2	4	7	0	0	0	26	0	0	.222	.213
Garcia, Aramis	R-R	6-1	228	1-12-93	.268	.333	.250	30	112	15	30	8	0	2	15	9	1	0	2	27	0	0	.393	.323
Gelof, Zack	R-R	6-3	205	10-19-99	.583	1.000	.500	3	12	3	7	1	0	0	6	1	0	0	0	2	0	0	.667	.615
Kozma, Pete	R-R	6-0	190	4-11-88	.244	.220	.254	113	454	62	111	24	3	4	40	37	5	2	2	97	6	1	.337	.307
Machin, Vimael	L-R	5-11	185	9-25-93	.295	.217	.320	89	336	65	99	17	6	11	58	49	5	0	3	72	2	1	.479	.389
McDonald, Mickey	L-R	6-2	215	6-2-95	.333	.436	.307	56	192	44	64	11	3	1	22	26	1		3	42	10	0	.438	.423
Mondou, Nate	L-R	5-10	205	3-24-95	.282	.333	.266	85	308	53	87	20	1	8	49	40	7	0	6	55	0	2	.432	.371
Pena, Francisco	R-R	6-2	230	10-12-89	.250	.225	.259	105	392	68	98	13	0	23	81	37	9	0	9	92	1	0	.459	.322
Peralta, Elvis	L-R	5-9	160	12-7-96	.000	--	.000	2	1	0	0	0	0	0	0	0	0	0	0	1	0	0	.000	.000
Perez, Carlos	R-R	6-0	210	10-27-90	.269	.232	.281	97	376	61	101	19	1	3	89	34	6	0	2	63	0	0	.572	.337
Pinder, Chad	R-R	6-2	210	3-29-92	.286	.500	.200	7	28	6	8	2	0	2	10	2	0	0	1	8	0	0	.571	.323
Reed, Buddy	B-R	6-4	218	4-27-95	.247	.292	.233	43	97	20	24	5	1	1	13	15	1	1	0	41	3	2	.351	.354
Schuemann, Max	R-R	6-1	186	6-11-97	.231	.143	.263	8	26	2	6	1	1	0	1	5	0	0		7	1	0	.346	.355
Schwindel, Frank	R-R	6-2	220	6-29-92	.317	.294	.326	45	189	42	60	11	0	16	41	13	2	0	3	35	0	0	.630	.362
Theroux, Collin	R-R	6-2	220	3-10-94	.238	.000	.294	7	21	4	5	1	0	1	3	5	0	0	0	11	0	0	.429	.385
Thomas, Cody	L-R	6-4	211	10-8-94	.289	.388	.281	59	218	46	63	20	4	18	52	25	1	0	1	78	0	0	.665	.363
Uhl, Cooper	R-R	5-10	185	10-19-97	.000	--	.000	2	2	0	0	0	0	0	0	0	0	0	0	1	0	0	.000	.333
White, Mikey	R-R	6-1	200	9-3-93	.133	.167	.111	11	30	8	4	0	1	0	4	6	1	0	0	11	1	0	.200	.297
Wilson, Jacob	R-R	5-11	219	7-29-90	.288	.345	.264	49	184	39	53	17	2	14	46	26	5	0	3	43	0	0	.630	.385
2-team total (20 Sugar Land)					.255	.323	.232	69	259	43	66	17	2	15	52	32	6	0	4	62	0	0	.510	.346

Pitching	B-T	HT	WT	DOB	W	L	ERA	G	GS	CG	SV	IP	H	R	ER	HR	BB	SO	AVG	vLH	vRH	K/9	BB/9
Acevedo, Domingo	R-R	6-7	240	3-6-94	2	0	2.48	30	0	0	9	33	22	12	9	3	6	53	.186	.191	.180	14.60	1.65
Anderson, Tanner	R-R	6-2	203	5-27-93	3	0	3.60	12	0	0	0	15	14	6	6	3	12	3	.259	.333	.167	1.80	7.20
Angulo, Argenis	R-R	6-2	225	2-26-94	3	1	7.33	13	2	0	0	43	55	35	35	11	28	47	.313	.294	.384	9.84	5.86
Bailey, Homer	R-R	6-4	223	5-3-86	2	7	6.88	13	13	0	0	52	67	41	40	7	21	56	.312	.339	.283	9.63	3.61
Bedrosian, Cam	R-R	6-1	225	10-2-91	0	0	0.00	4	0	0	1	5	2	0	0	1	5		.118	.182	.000	9.00	1.80
Blackburn, Paul	R-R	6-1	196	12-4-93	4	7	4.97	17	16	0	0	89	114	59	49	8	27	80	.311	.300	.323	8.12	2.74
Blackham, Matt	R-R	5-10	150	1-7-93	0	2	8.03	22	1	0	0	25	27	22	22	7	21	37	.278	.217	.378	13.50	7.66
Bracewell, Ben	R-R	6-0	200	9-19-90	5	3	4.07	49	0	0	6	60	75	35	27	10	20	56	.305	.274	.331	8.45	3.02
Brown, Aaron	L-L	6-2	223	6-20-92	2	1	2.49	20	0	0	3	25	17	11	7	0	15	20	.191	.162	.212	7.11	5.33
Dunshee, Parker	R-R	6-0	215	2-12-95	1	5	6.65	10	9	0	0	43	48	36	32	7	17	38	.273	.294	.243	7.89	3.53
Erwin, Zack	L-L	6-5	195	1-24-94	3	0	3.32	15	0	0	0	19	17	9	7	1	9	23	.230	.152	.293	10.89	4.26
Feigl, Brady	R-R	6-4	235	11-27-95	1	2	8.55	5	5	0	0	20	23	19	19	5	12	17	.295	.370	.188	7.65	5.40
Fiers, Mike	R-R	6-2	211	6-15-85	0	1	9.00	1	1	0	0	5	9	7	5	1	1	2	.360	.400	.300	3.60	1.80
Friedrichs, Kyle	R-R	6-1	195	1-22-92	1	1	4.81	8	5	0	0	39	41	21	21	4	6	28	.273	.254	.291	6.41	1.37
Guduan, Reymin	L-L	6-4	205	3-16-92	4	3	5.06	30	0	0	0	32	39	20	18	2	14	34	.300	.354	.246	9.56	3.94

Name	B-T	HT	WT	DOB	W	L	ERA	G	GS	CG	SV	IP	H	R	ER	HR	BB	SO	AVG	vLH	vRH	K/9	BB/9
Holmes, Grant	L-R	6-0	226	3-22-96	1	2	8.01	36	7	0	0	66	99	62	59	11	40	71	.341	.323	.363	9.63	5.43
Howard, Brian	R-R	6-9	213	4-25-95	7	4	5.86	24	21	0	0	111	126	78	72	22	40	96	.284	.297	.269	7.81	3.25
Jackson, Zach	R-R	6-4	230	12-25-94	1	1	5.40	11	0	0	1	12	11	7	7	1	6	13	.256	.308	.176	10.03	4.63
Jefferies, Daulton	R-R	6-0	182	8-2-95	5	1	4.91	15	15	0	0	77	90	44	42	13	11	68	.288	.297	.280	7.95	1.29
Kaprielian, James	R-R	6-3	225	3-2-94	0	1	3.86	1	1	0	0	5	8	2	2	0	1	5	.400	.462	.286	9.64	1.93
Kolarek, Adam	L-L	6-3	215	1-14-89	1	0	6.75	37	0	0	0	39	48	33	29	5	20	27	.300	.222	.380	6.28	4.66
Luzardo, Jesus	L-L	6-0	218	9-30-97	2	2	6.52	8	8	0	0	29	33	24	21	3	15	26	.289	.186	.352	8.07	4.66
Milburn, Matt	R-R	6-3	210	7-29-93	1	2	11.95	10	5	0	0	20	38	28	27	11	5	11	.396	.404	.385	4.87	2.21
Moll, Sam	L-L	5-9	190	1-3-92	1	1	2.63	12	0	0	2	14	12	4	4	2	5	17	.240	.111	.391	11.20	3.29
2-team total (21 Reno)					1	1	4.58	33	0	0	2	35	31	21	18	5	20	47	.231	.114	.359	11.97	5.09
Mondou, Nate	L-R	5-10	205	3-24-95	0	0	0.00	2	0	0	0	2	2	0	0	0	0	2	.250	.250	.250	9.00	0.00
Naile, James	R-R	6-4	185	2-8-93	8	0	4.04	51	0	0	0	62	77	30	28	7	15	51	.306	.339	.273	7.36	2.17
Puk, A.J.	L-L	6-7	248	4-25-95	2	5	6.10	29	4	0	1	49	61	40	33	12	19	58	.303	.212	.331	10.73	3.51
Romero, Miguel	R-R	6-0	202	4-23-94	3	6	6.27	28	13	0	2	75	86	56	52	15	34	54	.284	.280	.288	6.51	4.10
Schlitter, Brian	R-R	6-3	238	12-21-85	1	1	9.00	5	0	0	0	7	11	7	7	1	3	8	.344	.375	.250	10.29	3.86
2-team total (36 Tacoma)					2	0	4.72	41	5	0	2	48	56	26	25	6	19	37	.284	.259	.318	6.99	3.59
Smith, Burch	R-R	6-4	225	4-12-90	0	0	10.13	4	0	0	0	5	9	6	6	3	4	7	.360	.467	.200	11.81	6.75
Weems, Jordan	L-R	6-3	175	11-7-92	0	1	7.36	15	0	0	1	15	17	12	12	6	6	17	.293	.226	.370	10.43	3.68
2-team total (15 Reno)					1	3	7.31	30	0	0	1	28	32	23	23	9	14	26	.294	.246	.346	8.26	4.45
Wendelken, J.B.	R-R	6-1	242	3-24-93	0	0	3.60	4	0	0	0	5	2	2	2	1	2	5	.125	.111	.143	9.00	3.60
Zambrano, Jesus	R-R	5-10	204	8-23-96	1	1	9.37	11	0	0	0	16	21	19	17	6	9	11	.309	.262	.385	6.06	4.96

Fielding

Catcher	PCT	G	PO	A	E	DP	PB
Allen	.998	46	388	21	1	1	1
Garcia	.985	23	180	13	3	0	2
Pena	.987	27	202	21	3	1	5
Perez	.996	31	244	24	1	1	4
Theroux	1.000	7	58	3	0	1	2

First Base	PCT	G	PO	A	E	DP
Allen	.857	1	6	0	1	0
Machin	1.000	2	1	0	0	0
Pena	.994	56	442	22	3	47
Perez	.988	30	226	17	3	23
Schwindel	.995	42	358	17	2	39
White	1.000	1	12	0	0	0

Second Base	PCT	G	PO	A	E	DP
Allen	1.000	14	21	46	0	8
Bechina	1.000	2	2	5	0	1
Diaz	1.000	3	1	6	0	1
Kozma	.970	19	24	40	2	7

	PCT	G	PO	A	E	DP
Machin	.971	26	31	69	3	16
Mondou	.974	63	83	179	7	37
Schuemann	1.000	3	5	8	0	2
White	1.000	7	8	20	0	6
Wilson	1.000	2	2	5	0	2

Third Base	PCT	G	PO	A	E	DP
Bechina	.885	10	9	14	3	1
Diaz	.955	8	6	15	1	2
Gelof	.800	3	1	3	1	1
Machin	.961	58	46	77	5	7
McDonald	.966	12	5	23	1	4
Mondou	.842	12	5	11	3	0
White	1.000	3	0	3	0	0
Wilson	.976	34	23	58	2	6

Shortstop	PCT	G	PO	A	E	DP
Allen	.942	22	43	54	6	14
Diaz	1.000	7	8	15	0	2
Kozma	.962	90	133	248	15	56

	PCT	G	PO	A	E	DP
Machin	.952	4	4	16	1	6
Mondou	1.000	2	3	3	0	0
Pinder	.923	3	4	8	1	1

Outfield	PCT	G	PO	A	E	DP
Barrera	.942	98	155	7	10	0
Bechina	.983	40	55	4	1	0
Beck	1.000	7	4	0	0	0
Bolt	1.000	49	102	2	0	1
Brown	1.000	2	5	0	0	0
Deichmann	.971	57	96	6	3	1
McDonald	.988	48	81	4	1	0
Mondou	1.000	1	1	0	0	0
Perez	.967	20	27	2	1	0
Pinder	1.000	3	2	0	0	0
Reed	.957	41	64	3	3	0
Schuemann	1.000	5	7	0	0	0
Thomas	.979	56	92	3	2	2
Wilson	1.000	13	18	1	0	0

MIDLAND ROCKHOUNDS

DOUBLE-A

DOUBLE-A CENTRAL

Batting	B-T	HT	WT	DOB	AVG	vLH	vRH	G	AB	R	H	2B	3B	HR	RBI	BB	HBP	SH	SF	SO	SB	CS	SLG	OBP
Allen, Nick	R-R	5-8	166	10-8-98	.319	.440	.279	50	204	31	65	9	2	6	31	18	2	2	3	46	8	6	.471	.374
Bechina, Marty	R-R	6-0	200	10-31-96	.227	.150	.247	26	97	16	22	7	1	0	10	8	2	1	1	31	1	0	.320	.296
Bride, Jonah	R-R	5-10	200	12-27-95	.265	.339	.244	78	264	45	70	11	2	9	49	57	9	0	4	57	2	0	.424	.407
Calabuig, Chase	L-L	5-11	185	12-10-95	.214	.158	.231	92	323	42	69	11	0	5	34	43	2	0	3	62	2	1	.294	.307
Cross, Matt	R-R	6-1	205	7-28-98	.111	.500	.000	3	9	1	1	0	0	0	1	0	0	0	0	1	0	0	.111	.111
Davidson, Logan	B-R	6-3	185	12-26-97	.212	.119	.239	119	448	53	95	22	1	7	48	62	1	1	3	155	4	3	.313	.307
Diaz, Edwin	R-R	6-2	223	8-25-95	.243	.429	.198	41	144	19	35	7	0	7	17	14	2	0	0	56	1	0	.438	.319
Eierman, Jeremy	R-R	6-0	205	9-10-96	.247	.289	.236	60	223	34	55	13	1	10	30	21	9	1	1	92	9	4	.448	.335
Foyle, Devin	L-L	6-3	190	11-18-96	.257	.190	.276	99	362	62	93	14	7	12	61	42	7	0	3	91	8	5	.434	.343
McCann, Kyle	R-R	6-2	217	12-10-97	.166	.156	.168	93	320	40	53	11	0	8	39	47	6	0	2	139	1	0	.275	.283
McDonald, Mickey	L-R	6-2	175	6-2-95	.273	.259	.276	50	172	25	47	6	1	1	16	25	4	1	0	47	8	0	.337	.378
Paulino, Jhoan	R-R	6-1	176	6-11-01	.375	.500	.333	3	8	0	3	0	0	0	1	0	0	0	0	4	0	0	.375	.444
Peralta, Elvis	L-R	5-9	160	12-7-96	.182	.000	.235	9	22	3	4	1	0	0	0	1	0	0	0	4	0	0	.227	.217
Ramirez, Tyler	L-L	5-9	185	2-21-95	.263	.182	.293	23	80	10	21	8	0	0	16	15	2	0	1	16	1	1	.363	.388
Santos, Jhonny	R-R	6-0	160	10-2-96	.242	.242	.242	86	322	46	78	16	0	13	59	34	0	1	1	84	1	2	.413	.314
Schuemann, Max	R-R	6-1	186	6-11-97	.320	.346	.311	57	219	38	70	13	1	2	21	23	7	0	2	46	17	3	.416	.398
Schwarz, JJ	R-R	6-2	225	3-28-96	.240	.364	.197	72	254	30	61	11	1	6	36	37	0	0	1	69	0	0	.362	.336
Suddleson, Jake	R-R	6-3	205	12-30-97	.250	.273	.243	67	236	39	59	6	1	7	23	26	10	0	1	56	1	0	.373	.348
Theroux, Collin	R-R	6-2	220	3-10-94	.123	.068	.142	50	171	18	21	3	0	4	18	15	5	0	0	82	0	0	.211	.215
Vargas, Yerdel	R-R	6-0	170	2-17-00	.128	.143	.121	15	47	4	6	1	0	0	0	0	0	0	0	20	1	0	.149	.128
White, Mikey	R-R	6-1	200	9-3-93	.194	.000	.200	9	31	1	6	0	0	0	1	6	3	1	0	15	0	0	.290	.278

Pitching	B-T	HT	WT	DOB	W	L	ERA	G	GS	CG	SV	IP	H	R	ER	HR	BB	SO	AVG	vLH	vRH	K/9	BB/9
Briggs, Austin	R-L	6-1	205	10-11-95	3	2	6.38	41	0	0	2	55	57	42	39	7	28	41	.282	.200	.313	6.71	4.58
Brown, Aaron	L-L	6-2	223	6-20-92	1	3	3.58	28	0	0	9	38	35	19	15	3	18	36	.257	.225	.271	8.60	4.30
Cohen, Chase	L-R	6-1	183	4-26-97	1	1	3.00	16	0	0	0	27	24	9	9	1	14	33	.245	.244	.246	11.00	4.67
Conley, Bryce	R-R	6-3	200	8-22-94	5	5	4.39	29	14	0	0	94	80	48	46	6	44	88	.235	.219	.244	8.40	4.20
Cushing, Jack	R-R	6-3	195	12-3-96	0	5	4.68	5	5	0	0	25	35	15	13	1	7	20	.327	.323	.329	7.20	2.52

	B-T	HT	WT	DOB	W	L	ERA	G	GS	CG	SV	IP	H	R	ER	HR	BB	SO	AVG	vLH	vRH	K/9	BB/9
Damron, Ty	L-L	6-2	200	7-28-94	2	7	5.94	22	20	0	0	89	115	65	59	11	29	84	.315	.360	.301	8.46	2.92
DuRapau, Montana	R-R	5-10	190	3-27-92	4	1	3.98	37	0	0	9	54	44	24	24	4	16	40	.227	.180	.248	6.63	2.65
Erwin, Zack	L-L	6-5	195	1-24-94	3	4	4.30	34	0	0	3	44	47	23	21	3	14	44	.278	.333	.258	9.00	2.86
Feigl, Brady	R-R	6-4	235	11-27-95	7	7	3.96	20	20	0	0	102	94	50	45	13	34	106	.242	.245	.240	9.32	2.99
Friedrichs, Kyle	R-R	6-1	195	1-22-92	4	3	4.36	15	13	0	0	66	65	36	32	8	19	45	.254	.278	.241	6.14	2.59
Graves, Brett	R-R	6-1	170	1-30-93	1	2	7.11	21	0	0	1	25	21	22	20	0	24	29	.223	.143	.271	10.30	8.53
Highberger, Nick	R-R	5-11	200	11-4-93	0	1	6.41	32	1	0	1	39	46	31	28	6	25	34	.303	.340	.284	7.78	5.72
Jackson, Zach	R-R	6-4	230	12-25-94	1	1	0.55	14	0	0	5	16	7	3	1	0	4	34	.127	.154	.103	18.73	3.86
Koenig, Jared	R-L	6-5	235	1-24-94	7	5	3.26	24	21	0	0	121	108	56	44	14	43	100	.240	.203	.255	7.42	3.19
Marinez, Eric	B-R	6-1	160	9-12-95	0	1	4.64	21	0	0	1	21	19	13	11	2	20	20	.244	.273	.222	8.44	8.44
McIntyre, Aiden	R-R	6-5	220	8-27-95	1	2	3.94	21	1	0	0	30	33	15	13	3	12	36	.287	.346	.270	10.92	3.64
Milburn, Matt	R-R	6-3	210	7-29-93	4	4	4.46	14	10	0	0	71	82	40	35	10	6	44	.289	.236	.313	5.60	0.76
Peluse, Colin	R-R	6-3	230	6-11-98	2	0	1.80	3	3	0	0	15	9	3	3	1	4	17	.176	.071	.216	10.20	2.40
Reininger, Zac	B-R	6-3	190	1-29-93	1	4	4.63	5	5	0	0	23	27	13	12	1	2	23	.290	.323	.274	8.87	0.77
Ruiz, Norge	R-R	5-10	180	3-15-94	2	0	2.08	3	0	0	0	4	3	1	1	0	1	3	.231	.667	.100	6.23	2.08
Sawyer, Dalton	L-L	6-5	210	11-22-93	1	0	4.82	7	0	0	0	9	7	5	5	1	8	11	.206	.222	.200	10.61	7.71
Theroux, Collin	R-R	6-2	220	3-10-94	0	0	0.00	1	0	0	1	0	0	0	0	0	1	0	.000	.000	.000	9.00	9.00
Weisenburger, Jack	R-R	6-3	220	10-8-97	4	0	4.58	28	0	0	1	37	37	20	19	5	32	48	.255	.319	.224	11.57	7.71
Zambrano, Jesus	R-R	5-10	204	8-23-96	5	2	4.10	21	0	0	1	37	29	19	17	3	18	41	.218	.244	.205	9.88	4.34

Fielding

Catcher	PCT	G	PO	A	E	DP	PB
Cross	1.000	1	13	1	0	0	0
McCann	.998	56	454	41	1	0	6
Schwarz	.995	25	188	18	1	1	0
Theroux	.980	42	312	34	7	2	7

First Base	PCT	G	PO	A	E	DP
Bride	.998	45	395	13	1	35
Calabuig	.994	23	163	7	1	15
Cross	1.000	1	3	0	0	0
Davidson	1.000	1	12	0	0	2
McCann	.982	24	202	11	4	22
Schwarz	.994	23	170	10	1	22
White	.973	6	33	3	1	7

Second Base	PCT	G	PO	A	E	DP
Allen	1.000	22	43	72	0	16
Bechina	.938	11	19	26	3	7
Bride	.952	9	15	25	2	8
Davidson	.963	5	8	18	1	7
Diaz	1.000	1	2	1	0	0
Eierman	.981	15	23	29	1	10
Paulino	1.000	1	2	2	0	1
Peralta	1.000	6	14	7	0	4
Schuemann	.974	42	78	106	5	33
Vargas	.964	12	22	32	2	10
White	1.000	1	3	3	0	1

Third Base	PCT	G	PO	A	E	DP
Bride	1.000	16	11	29	0	6
Davidson	.982	40	30	81	2	8
Diaz	.943	25	14	36	3	5
Eierman	.960	35	19	77	4	10
McDonald	1.000	4	3	5	1	0
Paulino	.714	2	0	5	2	0
White	1.000	1	1	2	0	1

Shortstop	PCT	G	PO	A	E	DP
Allen	.946	26	32	55	5	14
Davidson	.956	71	98	204	14	39
Diaz	.932	14	15	40	4	9
Eierman	1.000	6	9	20	0	4
Schuemann	.900	3	3	6	1	1

Outfield	PCT	G	PO	A	E	DP
Bechina	1.000	14	25	0	0	0
Calabuig	1.000	63	97	6	0	0
Foyle	.973	83	138	6	4	1
McDonald	1.000	44	86	3	0	0
Peralta	--	2	0	0	0	0
Ramirez	1.000	18	24	3	0	1
Santos	.988	76	161	6	2	1
Schuemann	1.000	13	32	4	0	0
Suddleson	.985	53	129	5	2	0
Vargas	--	1	0	0	0	0

LANSING LUGNUTS   HIGH CLASS A
HIGH-A CENTRAL

Batting	B-T	HT	WT	DOB	AVG	vLH	vRH	G	AB	R	H	2B	3B	HR	RBI	BB	HBP	SH	SF	SO	SB	CS	SLG	OBP
Armenteros, Lazaro	R-R	6-0	182	5-22-99	.195	.265	.179	56	174	20	34	5	0	4	16	13	4	2	0	80	13	4	.293	.267
Beck, Austin	R-R	6-1	200	11-21-98	.202	.206	.200	69	248	20	50	12	2	7	33	15	3	0	3	91	3	1	.351	.253
Brito, Marcos	B-R	6-0	165	3-6-00	.094	.083	.096	19	64	5	6	1	0	0	5	4	0	1	0	39	3	0	.109	.147
Butler, Jonny	R-L	6-1	200	2-12-99	.203	.067	.234	25	79	9	16	2	1	1	9	9	0	0	2	22	1	0	.291	.278
Butler, Lawrence	L-R	6-3	210	7-10-00	.340	.300	.367	14	50	14	17	4	0	2	8	4	0	0	0	15	3	1	.540	.389
Diaz, Jordan	R-R	5-10	175	8-13-00	.288	.265	.294	90	333	46	96	24	1	13	56	25	2	0	5	58	2	3	.483	.337
Greer, Jalen	R-R	6-3	185	7-19-01	.000	.000	.000	3	1	0	0	0	0	0	0	0	0	0	0	3	0	0	.000	.091
Gridley, Ryan	R-R	5-8	180	5-4-95	.231	.083	.269	32	117	14	27	7	0	0	10	11	5	0	0	17	6	0	.291	.323
Guldberg, Michael	R-R	6-0	171	6-22-99	.259	.161	.280	48	174	29	45	9	2	5	18	17	7	6	1	36	11	1	.420	.347
Harris, Brett	R-R	6-3	208	6-24-98	.222	.300	.197	25	81	14	18	3	0	3	11	8	4	1	0	20	3	1	.370	.323
Lee, DJ	L-R	6-2	185	7-15-96	.148	.000	.174	14	27	5	4	1	0	0	1	1	1	1	0	10	2	0	.185	.351
Madden, Lester	R-R	6-2	190	1-19-99	.199	.122	.221	64	221	22	44	13	1	3	27	10	4	1	1	75	0	3	.308	.246
McColl, Patrick	L-R	6-6	215	6-22-97	.180	.139	.190	64	183	33	33	6	2	6	24	29	5	2	4	64	10	2	.333	.303
McDonald, Jared	R-R	6-0	180	12-5-96	.222	.238	.216	51	176	16	39	10	0	4	16	9	6	0	4	70	1	0	.347	.277
Millas, Drew	B-R	6-2	205	1-15-98	.255	.158	.275	59	220	34	56	12	1	3	28	41	2	0	3	39	10	2	.359	.372
Pantoja, Enrry	R-R	5-11	215	9-27-96	.188	.500	.143	7	16	1	3	0	0	0	1	1	0	0	0	5	0	0	.188	.235
Peralta, Elvis	L-R	5-9	160	12-7-96	.216	.250	.208	67	213	32	46	12	0	0	19	23	4	2	1	73	17	2	.300	.303
Schuemann, Max	R-R	6-1	186	6-11-97	.224	.387	.194	54	201	43	45	11	1	5	20	25	14	1	2	50	34	2	.363	.347
Selman, Shane	R-L	5-11	198	8-30-96	.260	.234	.265	78	258	36	67	14	2	12	36	39	3	1	1	79	5	3	.469	.362
Simoneit, William	R-R	6-3	235	10-14-96	.273	.257	.278	90	322	40	88	20	1	10	53	38	6	0	1	85	7	1	.435	.360
Suddleson, Jake	R-R	6-3	205	12-30-97	.284	.294	.282	24	95	15	27	9	1	4	19	7	3	0	2	24	1	0	.526	.346
Swift, Drew	R-R	6-0	165	2-15-99	.174	.182	.171	32	92	18	16	5	0	1	5	21	2	2	1	34	12	1	.261	.336
Uhl, Cooper	R-R	5-10	185	10-19-97	.115	.167	.100	10	26	2	3	0	0	0	3	3	1	0	0	12	0	0	.115	.233
Vance, Cobie	R-R	5-8	185	8-24-97	.252	.250	.253	108	373	54	94	20	3	3	31	52	11	2	4	74	11	0	.346	.353
Vargas, Yerdel	R-R	6-0	170	2-17-00	.214	.290	.186	35	117	7	25	6	2	1	14	5	1	1	0	34	2	0	.325	.252

Pitching	B-T	HT	WT	DOB	W	L	ERA	G	GS	CG	SV	IP	H	R	ER	HR	BB	SO	AVG	vLH	vRH	K/9	BB/9
Acton, Garrett	L-R	6-2	215	6-15-98	1	0	3.63	14	0	0	2	17	10	7	7	3	4	34	.161	.250	.067	17.65	2.08
Basso, Brady	R-L	6-2	213	10-8-97	2	2	4.71	7	4	0	0	21	21	12	11	2	7	26	.247	.258	.241	11.14	3.00
Berrios, Osvaldo	R-R	6-2	200	11-29-99	2	1	5.86	6	5	0	0	28	35	18	18	4	10	20	.318	.370	.268	6.51	3.25
Birlingmair, Reid	L-R	5-10	210	11-13-96	4	10	4.54	21	21	0	0	103	88	56	52	13	52	84	.233	.249	.212	7.34	4.54

Pitcher	B-T	HT	WT	DOB	W	L	ERA	G	GS	CG	SV	IP	H	R	ER	HR	BB	SO	AVG	vLH	vRH	SO/9	BB/9
Cerny, Charlie	L-R	6-5	230	9-23-96	0	2	12.83	20	1	0	0	27	44	39	38	3	30	20	.379	.373	.390	6.75	10.13
Criswell, Jeff	R-R	6-4	225	3-10-99	0	0	4.50	5	5	0	0	12	9	6	6	1	4	12	.200	.219	.154	9.00	3.00
Cushing, Jack	R-R	6-3	195	12-3-96	6	1	2.74	8	7	1	0	46	41	14	14	3	10	48	.236	.224	.254	9.39	1.96
Danielak, Michael	R-R	6-4	215	3-16-94	1	1	5.12	14	0	0	0	19	25	16	11	4	5	20	.316	.310	.324	9.31	2.33
Emanuels, Stevie	R-R	6-5	210	1-30-99	1	3	6.26	7	6	0	0	27	27	20	19	6	13	25	.260	.214	.313	8.23	4.28
Gridley, Ryan	R-R	5-8	180	5-4-95	0	0	0.00	2	0	0	0	3	0	0	0	0	0	1	.000	.000	.000	3.38	0.00
Guasch, Richard	R-R	6-4	205	4-10-98	1	4	4.67	13	9	0	0	54	54	38	28	7	29	68	.255	.282	.221	11.33	4.83
Hall, Charles	R-R	5-10	170	9-6-94	6	3	2.11	43	0	0	12	64	42	21	15	3	21	79	.191	.202	.178	11.11	2.95
Juan, Jorge	R-R	6-8	200	3-6-99	0	2	11.12	2	2	0	0	6	7	7	7	2	6	9	.280	.357	.182	14.29	9.53
Kelly, Rafael	R-R	6-2	190	6-9-97	0	1	2.82	5	4	0	0	22	23	13	7	2	7	19	.267	.256	.279	7.66	2.82
Leal, David	L-L	6-5	250	4-22-97	1	4	4.43	11	10	0	0	43	48	21	21	7	7	49	.281	.303	.267	10.34	1.48
McIntyre, Aiden	R-R	6-5	220	8-27-95	1	0	1.27	17	0	0	2	21	14	5	3	2	5	31	.182	.182	.182	13.08	2.11
Mora, Jose	R-R	6-3	200	10-1-97	1	2	11.09	15	0	0	0	19	26	26	23	5	15	24	.313	.392	.188	11.57	7.23
Nightengale, Bryce	R-R	6-5	215	8-16-96	2	1	4.44	14	2	0	0	26	24	17	13	1	21	38	.233	.263	.196	12.99	7.18
Owen, Jack	L-L	6-2	204	5-26-98	0	1	4.50	7	4	0	0	20	26	13	10	3	4	21	.295	.267	.310	9.45	1.80
Peluse, Colin	R-R	6-3	230	6-11-98	7	3	3.66	18	15	0	0	86	82	42	35	10	22	92	.251	.194	.326	9.63	2.30
Pineda, Leudeny	R-R	6-1	205	1-29-96	2	1	5.45	26	1	0	1	40	37	29	24	4	24	42	.248	.238	.261	9.53	5.45
Rafuse, Zach	R-R	6-0	185	12-3-96	1	1	1.00	6	0	0	0	9	7	2	1	0	2	10	.200	.278	.118	10.00	2.00
Romero, Sam	R-R	6-2	180	1-1-97	0	0	9.82	4	0	0	0	4	9	5	4	0	4	2	.450	.500	.417	4.91	9.82
Ruiz, Norge	R-R	5-10	180	3-15-94	0	0	11.12	4	0	0	0	6	9	7	7	0	2	7	.360	.267	.500	11.12	3.18
Sawyer, Dalton	L-L	6-5	210	11-22-93	2	2	4.03	33	0	0	3	38	28	24	17	6	20	62	.203	.194	.211	14.68	4.74
Selman, Shane	R-L	5-11	198	8-30-96	0	0	0.00	1	0	0	0	1	0	0	0	0	0	0	.000	.000	--	0.00	0.00
Shuman, Seth	R-R	6-1	195	12-1-97	2	3	2.25	13	11	0	0	56	44	16	14	4	15	62	.216	.200	.238	9.96	2.41
Simoneit, William	R-R	6-4	235	10-14-96	0	0	9.00	5	0	0	0	6	11	8	6	2	1	1	.379	.450	.222	1.50	1.50
Tomioka, Shohei	R-R	6-0	190	2-29-96	4	7	4.65	25	9	0	0	72	71	47	37	6	25	78	.252	.247	.258	9.80	3.14
Uhl, Cooper	R-R	5-10	185	10-19-97	0	0	18.90	4	0	0	0	3	11	7	7	2	1	1	.550	.556	.545	2.70	2.70
Virbitsky, Kyle	R-R	6-7	235	10-8-98	1	2	3.38	7	3	0	0	16	21	7	6	1	4	22	.328	.333	.321	12.38	2.25
Weisenburger, Jack	R-R	6-3	220	10-8-97	0	1	1.76	13	0	0	4	15	9	3	3	0	4	26	.170	.185	.154	15.26	2.35
Whittlesey, Brock	R-R	6-3	210	2-27-97	5	2	4.47	32	1	0	5	46	45	26	23	4	11	52	.246	.238	.256	10.10	2.14
Withers, Brandon	R-R	6-0	200	7-4-94	3	2	4.39	35	0	0	0	55	58	36	27	4	22	72	.264	.307	.217	11.71	3.58

Fielding

Catcher	PCT	G	PO	A	E	DP	PB
McDonald	.986	34	319	28	5	4	10
Millas	.983	50	476	39	9	0	11
Simoneit	.988	33	321	18	4	0	4
Uhl	1.000	7	46	4	0	1	0

First Base	PCT	G	PO	A	E	DP
Butler	1.000	6	36	7	0	3
Diaz	.968	23	138	11	5	11
McColl	.992	52	343	21	3	19
Simoneit	.997	48	347	32	1	30

Second Base	PCT	G	PO	A	E	DP
Brito	.909	4	5	5	1	2
Gridley	.988	20	31	53	1	12
Harris	1.000	3	3	11	0	1
Peralta	.970	33	40	58	3	6
Schuemann	1.000	2	1	9	0	1
Swift	1.000	2	4	3	0	1

	PCT	G	PO	A	E	DP
Vance	.981	30	35	68	2	15
Vargas	.955	33	39	66	5	10

Third Base	PCT	G	PO	A	E	DP
Diaz	.875	52	27	57	12	8
Greer	1.000	2	1	0	0	0
Gridley	1.000	3	4	7	0	0
Harris	.976	20	14	27	1	3
Peralta	.000	1	0	0	0	0
Vance	.911	52	37	65	10	4

Shortstop	PCT	G	PO	A	E	DP
Brito	.921	15	31	27	5	4
Harris	.923	4	6	6	1	0
Peralta	.938	9	11	19	2	4
Schuemann	.944	51	58	110	10	17
Swift	.990	29	32	66	1	15
Vance	.969	16	34	28	2	6
Vargas	1.000	1	1	1	0	0

Outfield	PCT	G	PO	A	E	DP
Armenteros	.975	45	79	0	2	0
Beck	.989	61	90	1	1	0
Butler	.977	26	41	1	1	0
Butler	.923	7	12	0	1	0
Diaz	1.000	4	3	0	0	0
Greer	.500	1	1	0	1	0
Guldberg	1.000	43	75	4	0	0
Lee	1.000	12	16	1	0	0
Madden	.970	54	61	3	2	0
McColl	.947	10	18	0	1	0
McDonald	1.000	1	1	0	0	0
Pantoja	.778	6	6	1	2	1
Peralta	.902	24	37	0	4	0
Selman	.960	65	93	3	4	0
Suddleson	.973	23	36	0	1	0
Vance	1.000	17	24	3	0	1

STOCKTON PORTS

LOW CLASS A

LOW-A WEST

Batting	B-T	HT	WT	DOB	AVG	vLH	vRH	G	AB	R	H	2B	3B	HR	RBI	BB	HBP	SH	SF	SO	SB	CS	SLG	OBP
Armenteros, Lazaro	R-R	6-0	182	5-22-99	.431	.571	.392	15	65	9	28	6	0	2	10	5	0	0	0	26	8	4	.615	.471
Bautista, Danny	R-R	6-2	185	9-20-00	.208	.232	.201	72	245	38	51	15	3	2	23	33	5	5	2	68	6	2	.318	.312
Bell, George	R-R	6-2	170	1-3-00	.135	.154	.128	15	52	3	7	2	0	0	1	5	2	0	0	23	0	0	.173	.237
Bonilla, Jose	R-R	6-3	180	2-20-01	.250	.500	.214	5	16	2	4	0	0	0	2	4	0	0	0	9	0	0	.250	.400
Brito, Marcos	B-R	6-0	165	3-6-00	.262	.167	.300	14	42	8	11	1	0	0	2	10	0	0	0	19	2	2	.286	.404
Brown, Seth	L-L	6-1	223	7-13-92	.400	--	.400	1	5	2	2	0	0	1	1	0	0	0	0	3	0	0	1.000	.400
Brueser, Nick	R-L	6-3	212	9-29-98	.113	.083	.120	16	62	5	7	0	0	1	4	5	1	0	0	28	0	0	.161	.191
Buelvas, Brayan	R-R	5-11	155	6-8-02	.219	.217	.220	88	347	54	76	11	4	16	50	37	7	0	1	95	17	7	.412	.306
Butler, Lawrence	L-R	6-3	210	7-10-00	.263	.253	.266	88	335	62	88	20	4	17	67	55	1	0	5	131	26	4	.499	.364
Campos, Alexander	R-R	6-0	178	2-20-00	.177	.000	.208	23	62	10	11	3	0	2	7	16	2	0	0	17	0	1	.323	.363
Cross, Matt	R-R	6-1	205	7-28-98	.250	.500	.250	13	34	4	10	4	0	1	8	3	1	0	0	13	0	0	.500	.368
Gelof, Zack	R-R	6-3	205	10-19-99	.298	.250	.308	32	124	26	37	8	1	7	22	19	1	0	1	36	11	2	.548	.393
Jones, Gavin	R-R	6-2	210	7-19-98	.192	.171	.200	37	120	14	23	4	1	1	11	16	3	1	0	47	1	1	.267	.302
Perez, Junior	R-R	6-1	165	7-4-01	.207	.239	.198	95	329	54	68	16	5	8	34	51	3	1	2	145	24	7	.359	.317
Piscotty, Stephen	R-R	6-4	211	1-14-91	.000	--	.000	1	4	0	0	0	0	0	0	0	0	0	0	2	0	0	.000	.000
Puason, Robert	B-R	6-3	165	9-11-02	.215	.275	.197	91	302	43	65	12	1	3	27	24	5	4	2	139	3	1	.291	.282
Ricciardi, Mariano	L-R	5-7	170	6-29-98	.143	.000	.167	4	14	0	2	1	0	0	0	0	0	0	0	6	1	1	.214	.200
Richards, Kevin	R-R	6-2	160	1-8-00	.244	.286	.230	58	221	26	54	10	1	3	25	20	0	0	0	63	3	6	.339	.316
Rivas, Jose	R-R	5-11	220	8-5-98	.230	.173	.248	60	213	25	49	9	0	5	31	17	12	0	1	65	0	0	.343	.321
Rodriguez, CJ	R-R	5-10	200	7-7-00	.160	.000	.194	22	81	5	13	2	0	1	4	4	0	0	1	13	0	0	.222	.198

Name	B-T	HT	WT	DOB	AVG	vLH	vRH	G	AB	R	H	2B	3B	HR	RBI	BB	HBP	SH	SF	SO	SB	CS	SLG	OBP
Romero, Jorge	R-R	6-2	185	5-30-00	.278	.500	.214	5	18	2	5	0	0	0	3	0	1	0	0	6	1	0	.278	.316
Schofield-Sam, T.J.	L-R	6-1	185	6-20-01	.246	.247	.245	105	391	51	96	20	5	9	62	35	13	0	7	105	6	4	.391	.323
Soderstrom, Tyler	L-R	6-2	200	11-24-01	.306	.375	.283	57	222	39	68	20	1	12	49	27	4	0	1	61	2	1	.568	.390
Uhl, Cooper	R-R	5-10	185	10-19-97	.160	.250	.118	20	50	6	8	2	0	1	4	11	0	0	0	16	0	0	.260	.311
Valenzuela, Sahid	B-R	5-9	165	9-16-97	.216	.270	.204	60	199	32	43	9	2	1	16	23	8	1	0	51	4	0	.296	.322
Winkler, Jack	R-R	6-2	185	11-4-98	.148	.077	.167	15	61	8	9	3	0	0	2	5	2	0	0	14	2	2	.197	.235
Wright, Joshwan	R-R	5-8	170	11-9-00	.243	.264	.237	84	317	45	77	17	1	5	46	29	7	3	2	64	5	2	.350	.318

Pitching	B-T	HT	WT	DOB	W	L	ERA	G	GS	CG	SV	IP	H	R	ER	HR	BB	SO	AVG	vLH	vRH	K/9	BB/9
Acton, Garrett	L-R	6-2	215	6-15-98	2	0	3.72	20	0	0	0	36	31	15	15	6	14	53	.233	.190	.253	13.13	3.47
Baram, Edward	R-R	6-3	205	6-2-97	3	3	6.98	29	0	0	3	58	69	55	45	8	30	64	.296	.286	.303	9.93	4.66
Berrios, Osvaldo	R-R	6-2	200	11-29-99	3	6	5.97	16	11	0	0	75	90	56	50	12	20	70	.299	.320	.283	8.36	2.39
Breault, Hunter	R-R	6-2	228	6-12-99	1	1	2.57	8	0	0	0	14	15	8	4	0	3	9	.283	.238	.313	5.79	1.93
Carrasco, Luis	R-R	6-1	180	12-19-01	0	0	4.38	7	0	0	0	12	14	8	6	1	4	11	.286	.238	.321	8.03	2.92
Cohn, Aaron	R-R	6-0	195	10-30-98	0	2	6.75	8	0	0	0	9	10	9	7	0	7	6	.263	.350	.167	5.79	6.75
Coletti, Vince	R-R	6-2	210	11-3-96	1	1	0.00	3	0	0	0	2	2	1	0	0	0	4	.222	.500	.143	15.43	0.00
Cota, Clark	R-R	6-2	230	10-6-96	0	1	10.13	2	0	0	0	3	2	3	3	1	3	4	.200	.333	.143	13.50	10.13
Cross, Matt	R-R	6-1	205	7-28-98	0	0	6.00	3	0	0	0	3	4	2	2	1	0	0	.308	.400	.250	0.00	0.00
Cushing, Jack	R-R	6-3	195	12-3-96	1	1	2.88	8	7	0	0	41	37	19	13	5	10	43	.243	.281	.221	9.52	2.21
DeMers, Joe	R-R	6-1	240	11-9-96	1	2	6.30	10	1	0	0	20	32	17	14	8	8	13	.364	.390	.340	5.85	3.60
Dicochea, Jose	R-R	6-3	180	3-21-01	2	2	11.05	6	5	0	0	15	19	18	18	4	8	23	.306	.333	.293	14.11	4.91
Florentino, Luis	R-R	6-2	190	3-13-00	1	1	7.53	5	0	0	0	14	21	14	12	3	6	9	.362	.391	.343	5.65	3.77
Garcia, Gerald	L-L	6-2	200	12-21-01	0	0	2.51	3	3	0	0	14	11	6	4	1	6	16	.212	.375	.139	10.05	3.77
Gonzalez, James	L-L	6-2	230	9-15-00	0	0	3.38	2	0	0	1	8	10	7	3	1	2	5	.303	.250	.310	5.63	2.25
Granado, Diego	R-R	6-1	200	1-13-97	2	2	6.46	30	6	0	2	70	84	55	50	15	24	74	.297	.333	.275	9.56	3.10
Guante, Wander	R-R	6-1	180	6-15-00	0	0	3.00	3	0	0	0	6	7	2	2	1	1	8	.280	.364	.214	12.00	1.50
Holman, Grant	R-R	6-6	250	5-31-00	0	1	4.20	6	4	0	0	15	15	8	7	3	4	15	.263	.364	.200	9.00	2.40
Infante, Angello	R-R	6-1	180	4-16-99	3	3	6.20	10	6	0	0	45	67	40	31	8	8	30	.351	.376	.330	6.00	1.60
Johnson, Colton	L-L	6-4	222	7-28-98	0	1	5.40	3	0	0	0	3	2	2	2	0	0	7	.167	.000	.182	18.90	0.00
Juan, Jorge	R-R	6-2	200	3-6-99	1	1	3.86	6	4	0	0	21	15	10	9	2	7	31	.203	.214	.188	13.29	3.00
Judkins, Grant	L-R	6-3	200	8-6-97	0	6	6.29	14	11	0	0	49	55	40	34	11	21	63	.284	.237	.314	11.65	3.88
Kubo, Trayson	R-R	6-0	180	9-26-97	2	2	6.52	9	1	0	0	19	30	23	14	1	13	18	.345	.289	.388	8.38	6.05
Lage, Jesus	B-R	6-1	155	12-1-97	0	0	0.00	1	0	0	0	2	1	0	0	0	1	2	.167	.500	.000	9.00	4.50
Leal, David	L-L	6-5	250	4-22-97	1	1	3.71	7	4	0	0	27	25	12	11	4	1	29	.245	.250	.244	9.79	0.34
Martinez, Daniel	L-R	5-11	190	7-28-98	3	5	9.00	18	5	0	0	54	83	57	54	13	28	54	.352	.372	.338	9.00	4.67
Mora, Jose	R-R	6-3	200	10-1-97	3	2	3.04	18	0	0	5	24	19	11	8	2	11	37	.194	.114	.241	12.49	3.71
Morban, Jose	R-R	6-2	162	12-24-97	0	3	6.57	5	3	0	0	12	14	10	9	4	13	11	.280	.389	.219	8.03	9.49
Nambiar, Kumar	L-L	5-11	188	4-17-98	1	6	6.09	15	12	0	0	65	77	51	44	13	22	66	.287	.345	.272	9.14	3.05
Palencia, Daniel	R-R	5-11	160	2-5-00	0	2	6.91	6	6	0	0	14	17	12	11	3	6	14	.309	.217	.375	8.79	3.77
Romero, Sam	R-R	6-2	180	1-1-97	1	0	10.87	16	0	0	0	27	44	35	33	7	20	32	.358	.318	.380	10.54	6.59
Sanchez, Yehizon	R-R	6-2	170	11-16-00	0	0	2.25	1	1	0	0	4	3	1	1	0	4	2	.231	.167	.286	4.50	9.00
Santos, Pedro	R-R	6-4	205	1-7-00	3	7	6.32	21	12	0	0	68	64	55	48	4	62	87	.243	.239	.247	11.46	8.17
Tovar, Oscar	R-R	6-2	200	3-19-98	3	3	3.52	28	0	0	5	38	41	20	15	1	15	38	.272	.286	.261	8.92	3.52
Uhl, Cooper	R-R	5-10	185	10-19-97	0	0	63.00	1	0	0	0	1	7	7	7	2	0	0	.700	.800	.600	0.00	0.00
Vazquez, Robin	R-R	6-2	187	4-15-98	0	0	4.26	6	0	0	0	13	14	8	6	1	7	14	.275	.316	.250	9.95	4.97
Walkinshaw, Jake	R-R	6-3	200	7-7-96	5	4	4.85	16	14	0	0	72	82	43	39	6	25	63	.291	.248	.320	7.84	3.11
Whittlesey, Brock	R-R	6-3	210	2-27-97	0	0	0.00	9	0	0	2	10	6	0	0	0	0	10	.171	.267	.100	8.71	0.00
Woolfolk, Dallas	R-R	6-2	225	10-30-96	1	3	6.68	23	1	0	1	34	38	30	25	5	31	29	.286	.203	.362	7.75	8.29
Wright, Joshwan	R-R	5-8	170	11-9-00	0	0	18.00	1	0	0	0	1	2	2	2	1	0	0	.400	1.000	.250	0.00	0.00

Fielding

Catcher	PCT	G	PO	A	E	DP	PB
Cross	.973	10	64	8	2	1	0
Rivas	.976	43	374	31	10	5	3
Rodriguez	.989	20	150	26	2	0	6
Soderstrom	.985	38	346	40	6	3	15
Uhl	1.000	18	121	10	0	2	1

First Base	PCT	G	PO	A	E	DP
Brueser	.992	14	112	7	1	15
Butler	.988	47	321	19	4	32
Cross	1.000	3	16	1	0	0
Jones	1.000	14	120	3	0	10
Rivas	1.000	1	1	0	0	0
Schofield-Sam	.992	38	241	14	2	25
Soderstrom	.983	9	55	3	1	5

Second Base	PCT	G	PO	A	E	DP
Brito	.957	7	5	17	1	0
Campos	.947	13	14	22	2	5
Jones	1.000	3	2	6	0	1
Ricciardi	.941	4	9	7	1	1
Valenzuela	.967	39	62	83	5	17
Winkler	1.000	5	13	18	0	5
Wright	.962	53	93	108	8	31

Third Base	PCT	G	PO	A	E	DP
Campos	1.000	1	1	0	0	1
Gelof	.877	30	19	38	8	4
Jones	.962	18	7	18	1	1
Schofield-Sam	.954	54	34	70	5	9
Valenzuela	1.000	4	2	2	0	1
Wright	.979	20	14	33	1	3

Shortstop	PCT	G	PO	A	E	DP
Brito	.909	4	8	12	2	3
Campos	.861	8	12	19	5	2
Puason	.919	91	120	209	29	49
Valenzuela	.906	12	5	24	3	6
Winkler	.978	9	21	24	1	6

Outfield	PCT	G	PO	A	E	DP
Armenteros	1.000	4	5	0	0	0
Bautista	.961	60	117	7	5	1
Bell	1.000	15	28	1	0	0
Bonilla	1.000	5	9	2	0	0
Brown	1.000	1	4	1	0	1
Buelvas	.969	87	151	4	5	2
Butler	.973	39	67	5	2	0
Perez	.972	95	200	9	6	3
Piscotty	1.000	1	3	0	0	0
Richards	.974	47	70	4	2	2
Romero	1.000	5	8	0	0	0

ACL ATHLETICS ROOKIE
ARIZONA COMPLEX LEAGUE

Batting	B-T	HT	WT	DOB	AVG	vLH	vRH	G	AB	R	H	2B	3B	HR	RBI	BB	HBP	SH	SF	SO	SB	CS	SLG	OBP
Alvarez, Wilson	R-R	5-10	155	5-19-98	.222	.375	.170	30	63	9	14	3	0	0	9	13	1	0	3	17	2	2	.270	.350
Amaya, Carlos	R-R	5-10	165	12-28-01	.294	--	.294	7	17	1	5	2	0	0	1	0	0	0	6	0	0	.412	.333
Basilia, Givaine	R-R	6-1	160	6-22-00	.080	.000	.103	28	50	9	4	0	0	0	2	6	0	1	0	23	2	1	.080	.179

Name	B-T	HT	WT	DOB	AVG	vLH	vRH	G	AB	R	H	2B	3B	HR	RBI	BB	HBP	SH	SF	SO	SB	CS	OBP	SLG
Bautista, Danny	R-R	6-2	185	9-20-00	.200	--	.200	3	5	2	1	0	0	0	0	3	0	0	0	1	1	0	.200	.500
Bell, George	R-R	6-2	170	1-3-00	.266	.222	.273	24	64	10	17	1	0	2	10	4	1	0	0	26	1	0	.375	.319
Bonilla, Jose	R-R	6-3	180	2-20-01	.175	.167	.178	28	63	9	11	1	0	2	5	11	1	0	1	37	0	0	.286	.303
Brito, Marcos	B-R	6-0	165	3-6-00	.296	.400	.273	11	27	8	8	1	2	1	8	5	0	0	0	13	3	0	.593	.406
Brueser, Nick	R-L	6-3	212	9-29-98	.304	.000	.318	8	23	0	7	1	0	0	3	2	1	0	0	11	0	0	.348	.385
Butler, Jonny	L-R	6-1	200	2-12-99	.300	.000	.333	4	10	2	3	0	0	1	3	2	0	0	1		0	0	.600	.417
Campos, Alexander	R-R	6-0	178	2-20-00	.250	.000	.313	7	20	3	5	0	1	0	3	1	1	0	0	3	0	0	.350	.318
Clarke, Denzel	R-R	6-5	220	5-1-00	.316	--	.316	7	19	2	6	2	0	1	1	3	0	0		6	1	2	.429	.409
Cross, Matt	R-R	6-1	205	7-28-98	.235	.333	.214	6	17	0	4	1	0	0	0	1	0	0		4	0	0	.294	.278
Cruz, Cristopher	R-R	6-0	180	3-28-02	.067	.000	.077	22	45	6	3	1	1	0	3	6	4	0	1	23	0	0	.133	.232
Davila, Geykler	R-R	5-11	180	10-19-00	.000	.000	.000	4	3	1	0	0	0	0	0	0	2	1	0	2	0	0	.000	.500
Davis, Khris	R-R	5-11	205	12-21-87	.091	.000	.125	4	11	3	1	0	0	0	1	3	1	0	0	4	0	0	.091	.333
Diaz, Edwin	R-R	6-2	223	8-25-95	.273	.000	.300	4	11	1	3	0	0	0	0	1	1	0	0	3	0	0	.273	.385
Diaz, Jasmed	L-L	6-0	175	4-16-03	.000	.000	.000	1	3	0	0	0	0	0	0	0	0	0	0	1	0	0	.000	.000
Escorche, Jose	R-R	5-10	145	4-29-02	.232	.125	.264	34	69	5	16	1	0	1	6	11	0	1	0	18	2	0	.290	.338
Franco, Carlos	R-R	5-10	150	2-17-03	.269	.222	.294	9	26	1	7	1	0	0	1	1	0	0	0	2	0	0	.308	.296
Gelof, Zack	R-R	6-3	205	10-19-99	1.000	--	1.000	1	2	1	2	0	0	0	2	0	1	0	0	0	0	2	1.000	1.000
Gordon, Jorge	R-R	5-10	175	10-28-97	.385	.400	.381	19	52	6	20	4	0	1	11	1	2	0	0	11	0	1	.519	.418
Greer, Jalen	R-R	6-3	185	7-19-01	.259	.316	.247	36	108	12	28	3	1	1	5	19	4	0	0	43	4	1	.333	.389
Harris, Brett	R-R	6-3	208	6-24-98	.667	.500	1.000	2	3	2	2	0	0	0	3	2	0	0	0	0	0	0	.667	.800
Jones, Gavin	R-R	6-2	210	7-19-98	.286	.333	.273	7	14	2	4	0	1	0	2	3	0	0	1	3	0	1	.429	.389
Lee, DJ	L-R	6-2	185	7-15-96	.344	.200	.370	16	32	6	11	3	0	1	4	10	2	0	0	11	2	0	.531	.523
Lopez, Hansen	R-R	5-9	170	7-3-00	.136	.111	.143	21	44	4	6	0	1	0	3	4	1	0	1	28	1	0	.182	.220
Mackey, Davonn	R-R	6-2	170	10-10-00	.244	.143	.263	21	45	7	11	1	0	0	1	10	1	0	0	22	0	0	.267	.393
Marinez, Luis	R-R	6-1	155	10-11-01	.100	.000	.167	6	10	1	1	0	0	0	1	3	0	0	0	6	0	0	.100	.308
Martinez, Ramon	R-R	6-0	170	11-17-01	.143	.000	.167	26	56	10	8	2	0	0	4	19	0	0	0	31	0	2	.179	.360
McGuire, Shane	L-R	6-0	195	4-12-99	.280	.250	.283	19	50	7	14	3	0	0	9	7	1	0	3	11	1	0	.340	.361
Mujica, Jose	R-R	6-0	164	3-28-01	.241	.261	.236	34	112	13	27	9	0	2	19	5	0	0	0	20	0	0	.375	.274
Muncy, Max	R-R	6-1	180	8-25-02	.129	.333	.107	11	31	3	4	0	0	0	4	3	0	0	0	12	1	0	.129	.206
Paulino, Jhoan	R-R	6-1	176	6-11-01	.244	.286	.235	27	82	15	20	3	1	4	15	5	3	0	0	23	0	0	.451	.311
Pineda, Pedro	R-R	6-1	170	9-6-03	.258	.000	.302	23	62	15	16	2	2	1	8	13	2	0	0	28	3	3	.403	.403
Reed, Buddy	B-R	6-4	218	4-27-95	.400	.000	.500	2	5	1	2	1	0	0	1	2	0	0	0	2	0	0	.600	.571
Ricciardi, Mariano	L-R	5-7	170	6-29-98	.222	--	.222	7	18	2	4	2	0	0	1	2	1	0	0	2	0	0	.333	.333
Rodriguez, CJ	R-R	5-10	200	7-7-00	.000	--	.000	1	3	0	0	0	0	0	0	0	0	0	0	2	0	0	.000	.000
Romero, Jorge	R-R	6-2	185	5-30-00	.176	.182	.175	23	51	7	9	2	0	0	7	6	4	0	1	21	0	1	.216	.306
Salom, Dereck	R-R	5-10	135	2-22-01	.270	.429	.233	17	37	3	10	4	0	0	4	7	1	0	0	12	2	0	.378	.386
Sanchez, Saul	B-R	5-11	160	1-5-01	.184	.167	.189	22	49	8	9	0	0	0	0	10	0	0	0	18	2	0	.184	.322
Swift, Drew	R-R	6-0	165	2-15-99	.000	--	.000	2	4	2	0	0	0	0	0	1	1	0	0	2	0	0	.000	.333
Uhl, Cooper	R-R	5-10	185	10-19-97	.000	.000	.000	3	4	0	0	0	0	0	0	0	0	0	0	1	0	0	.000	.000
White, Mikey	R-R	6-1	200	9-3-93	.182	.500	.111	4	11	1	2	0	0	0	2	1	1	0	0	3	0	0	.182	.308
Winkler, Jack	R-R	6-2	185	11-4-98	.286	.000	.296	9	28	2	8	2	1	0	3	2	0	0	1	6	2	0	.429	.323

Pitching	B-T	HT	WT	DOB	W	L	ERA	G	GS	CG	SV	IP	H	R	ER	HR	BB	SO	AVG	vLH	vRH	K/9	BB/9
Alvarez, Wilson	R-R	5-10	155	5-19-98	0	0	8.10	3	0	0	1	3	5	3	3	0	0	2	.385	.500	.333	5.40	0.00
Anderson, Luke	R-R	6-2	205	8-5-98	0	0	0.00	2	0	0	0	3	1	0	0	0	0	3	.100	.250	.000	9.00	0.00
Bailey, Homer	R-R	6-4	223	5-3-86	0	1	14.73	2	2	0	0	4	9	7	6	0	2	6	.500	.500	.500	14.73	4.91
Basilia, Givaine	R-R	6-1	160	6-22-00	0	1	0.00	4	0	0	0	2	1	1	0	0	0	0	.200	.000	.333	0.00	0.00
Baum, Tyler	R-R	6-2	195	1-14-98	0	3	12.08	8	6	0	0	13	12	19	17	1	20	11	.267	.176	.321	7.82	14.21
Beers, Blake	R-R	6-4	215	7-15-98	0	0	9.00	1	1	0	0	1	2	1	1	0	1	4	.400	.000	.667	9.00	9.00
Bell, George	R-R	6-2	170	1-3-00	0	0	5.40	2	0	0	0	2	6	4	1	1	2	1	.545	.750	.429	5.40	10.80
Breault, Hunter	R-R	6-2	228	6-12-99	1	1	13.50	2	0	0	0	3	5	4	4	0	1	2	.417	.400	.429	6.75	3.38
Cantillo, Marshall	R-R	6-1	183	3-28-01	0	3	11.32	11	0	0	0	10	16	15	13	1	13	7	.364	.348	.381	6.10	11.32
Carrasco, Luis	R-R	6-1	180	12-19-01	1	1	3.94	10	6	0	0	32	37	17	14	2	6	33	.285	.298	.274	9.28	1.69
Cedano, Alexis	R-R	6-0	180	11-12-97	1	3	4.84	19	0	0	1	22	22	14	12	1	8	20	.262	.244	.279	8.06	3.22
Cerny, Charlie	L-R	6-5	230	9-23-96	0	0	4.50	4	1	0	0	6	5	4	3	0	2	7	.217	.125	.267	10.50	3.00
Cohn, Aaron	R-R	6-0	195	10-30-98	1	0	6.23	5	1	0	0	9	11	7	6	1	1	13	.306	.385	.261	13.50	1.04
Coletti, Vince	R-R	6-2	210	11-3-96	0	1	0.00	4	0	0	0	4	5	3	0	0	2	7	.263	.143	.333	14.54	4.15
DeMers, Joe	R-R	6-1	240	11-4-96	0	1	9.53	4	1	0	0	6	8	6	6	1	3	8	.333	.333	.333	12.71	4.76
Dunshee, Parker	R-R	6-0	215	2-12-95	0	0	4.50	1	1	0	0	2	2	1	1	0	0	3	.250	.000	.400	13.50	0.00
Emanuels, Stevie	R-R	6-5	210	1-30-99	0	0	0.00	1	1	0	0	1	1	0	0	0	1	0	.250	.500		0.00	9.00
Florentino, Luis	R-R	6-2	190	3-13-00	1	1	6.66	11	1	0	0	24	27	20	18	4	14	29	.276	.289	.267	10.73	5.18
Garcia, Gerald	L-R	6-2	200	10-21-01	0	2	4.79	8	5	0	0	21	27	17	11	0	5	28	.307	.167	.343	12.19	2.18
Garza, Roberto	R-R	6-2	175	6-22-02	2	3	6.75	9	3	0	0	20	17	19	15	3	12	24	.230	.238	.226	10.80	5.40
Gonzalez, James	L-L	6-2	230	9-15-00	1	0	1.80	8	4	0	0	20	15	4	4	0	4	22	.205	.000	.227	9.90	1.80
Guante, Wander	R-R	6-1	180	6-15-00	1	1	5.85	9	3	0	0	29	19	14	13	2	9	27	.253	.289	.216	12.15	4.05
Holiday, Aaron	R-R	6-3	205	5-28-00	2	0	0.00	3	0	0	0	6	3	0	0	0	2	8	.158	.000	.250	12.71	3.18
Infante, Angello	R-R	6-1	180	4-16-99	0	0	0.00	5	1	0	0	15	5	1	0	0	0	15	.102	.074	.136	9.20	0.00
Jones, Gavin	R-R	6-2	210	7-19-98	0	0	0.00	1	0	0	0	1	1	0	0	0	0	1	.250	.333	.000	9.00	0.00
Kubo, Trayson	R-R	6-0	180	9-26-97	0	2	0.00	2	1	0	0	2	2	0	0	0	1	2	.222	.250	.200	9.00	4.50
Lage, Jesus	B-R	6-1	155	12-1-97	0	1	9.19	13	0	0	0	16	22	18	16	1	11	16	.328	.478	.250	9.19	6.32
Lopez, Hansen	R-R	5-9	170	7-3-00	0	0	0.00	2	0	0	0	1	1	0	0	0	0	1	.400	1.000	.250	9.00	4.50
Martinez, Daniel	L-R	5-11	190	7-28-98	0	1	4.50	2	0	0	0	4	5	2	2	0	2	7	.313	.500	.250	15.75	4.50
Martinez, Luis	R-R	6-2	170	3-30-01	0	1	43.20	1	1	0	0	2	10	9	8	1	1	1	.667	.571	.750	5.40	5.40
Miller, Mason	R-R	6-5	200	8-24-98	0	1	1.50	3	2	0	0	6	4	1	1	0	3	9	.190	.333	.133	13.50	4.50
Morban, Jose	R-R	6-2	162	12-24-97	0	2	4.42	7	1	0	0	18	19	11	9	2	4	30	.266	.200	.302	14.73	1.96
Nightengale, Bryce	R-R	6-5	215	8-16-96	0	0	0.00	1	0	0	0	1	1	0	0	0	0	2	.250	--	.250	18.00	0.00

	B-T	HT	WT	DOB	W	L	ERA	G	GS	CG	SV	IP	H	R	ER	HR	BB	SO	AVG	vLH	vRH	K/9	BB/9
Rivera, Eduardo	L-L	6-7	237	6-13-03	0	0	0.00	1	1	0	0	1	0	0	0	0	0	1	.000	.000	.000	9.00	0.00
Ruiz, Norge	R-R	5-10	180	3-15-94	0	0	0.00	1	0	0	0	2	0	0	0	0	0	0	.667	--	.667	0.00	0.00
Sanchez, Yehizon	R-R	6-2	170	11-16-00	1	4	8.59	8	2	0	0	22	28	24	21	3	14	28	.315	.265	.345	11.45	5.73
Silverio, Jesus	R-R	6-2	180	7-15-02	0	1	3.48	4	3	0	0	10	11	8	4	0	8	7	.268	.167	.310	6.10	6.97
Szynski, Skylar	L-R	6-2	195	7-14-97	1	2	16.20	18	0	0	0	18	26	37	33	2	26	16	.333	.393	.300	7.85	12.76
Uhl, Cooper	R-R	5-10	185	10-19-97	0	0	67.50	1	0	0	0	1	5	5	5	0	1	0	.714	.500	.800	0.00	13.50
Vazquez, Robin	R-R	6-2	187	4-15-98	2	2	4.56	13	4	0	1	26	26	14	13	0	18	21	.263	.302	.232	7.36	6.31
Woolfolk, Dallas	R-R	6-2	225	10-30-96	0	0	15.43	2	0	0	0	2	2	5	4	0	2	5	.200	.333	.143	19.29	7.71

Fielding

C: Amaya 5, Cross 3, Davila 2, Franco 6, Gordon 11, Lopez 13, Marinez 4, McGuire 10, Mujica 14, Rodriguez 1, Uhl 2.
1B: Bonilla 7, Brueser 7, Cross 1, Cruz 6, Franco 1, Gordon 4, Lopez 6, Marinez 1, McGuire 5, Mujica 14, Paulino 9, White 1.
2B: Alvarez 20, Basilia 11, Brito 4, Campos 2, Diaz 1, Escorche 11, Greer 5, Jones 2, Paulino 1, Ricciardi 6, Salom 6, Sanchez 1, Swift 2, White 1.
3B: Alvarez 3, Campos 1, Cruz 1, Diaz 1, Escorche 8, Gelof 1, Greer 6, Harris 2, Jones 3, Paulino 12, Salom 3, Sanchez 9, White 1, Winkler 5,.
SS: Alvarez 2, Brito 7, Campos 3, Diaz 2, Escorche 14, Greer 20, Muncy 11, Salom 5, Winkler 4.
OF: Alvarez 1, Basilia 16, Bautista 2, Bell 24, Bonilla 18, Butler 4, Clarke 6, Diaz 1, Escorche 1, Greer 6, Lee 15, Mackey 23, Martinez 28, Pineda 24, Reed 2, Romero 17, Sanchez 13.

DSL ATHLETICS

ROOKIE

DOMINICAN SUMMER LEAGUE

OAKLAND ATHLETICS

Batting	B-T	HT	WT	DOB	AVG	vLH	vRH	G	AB	R	H	2B	3B	HR	RBI	BB	HBP	SH	SF	SO	SB	CS	SLG	OBP
Amaya, Carlos	R-R	5-10	165	12-28-01	.457	.600	.439	15	46	11	21	4	1	0	12	9	1	0	1	6	2	2	.587	.544
Arevalo, Angel	R-R	5-11	160	10-2-03	.297	.250	.303	27	74	16	22	5	4	0	15	18	2	0	2	19	1	3	.473	.438
Avila, Albert	L-L	6-2	160	9-26-00	.182	.000	.214	14	33	4	6	1	0	0	5	10	1	0	1	15	3	1	.212	.378
Baldallo, Dayker	L-R	5-10	135	11-29-03	.197	.444	.154	23	61	15	12	1	0	0	5	21	2	1	1	20	1	1	.213	.412
Beltran, Nelson	R-R	5-10	160	12-28-01	.263	.333	.250	44	114	19	30	6	2	0	17	14	7	0	1	41	13	1	.351	.375
Freitez, Luis	R-R	6-0	180	5-17-03	.225	.235	.222	32	89	13	20	3	1	2	15	8	3	1	0	26	2	1	.348	.310
Fuentes, Erubiel	R-R	5-8	160	1-15-03	.170	.176	.169	32	94	16	16	3	0	0	11	19	5	1	1	55	5	3	.202	.336
Gainza, Jayson	R-R	5-8	160	11-11-02	.121	.222	.102	22	58	4	7	0	0	0	4	6	0	0	0	14	0	0	.121	.203
Gallardo, Moises	R-R	6-0	160	4-23-03	.135	.000	.147	17	37	5	5	2	0	0	6	7	1	0	1	22	0	0	.189	.283
Garcia, Kelvin	R-R	6-3	194	10-14-00	.100	.000	.105	9	20	2	2	1	0	1	5	2	0	0	0	12	0	0	.300	.182
Garrett, Ray	R-R	5-10	155	3-23-04	.243	.000	.279	25	70	11	17	3	3	0	8	12	2	0	0	25	2	2	.371	.369
Gomez, Mario	L-R	5-10	185	12-30-02	.308	.154	.338	26	78	12	24	6	0	0	14	13	0	0	0	20	1	1	.385	.407
Hipolito, Cesar	R-R	5-9	160	6-3-02	.167	.200	.158	11	24	4	4	0	0	0	2	4	1	0	0	8	2	0	.167	.310
Lelis, Matheus	R-R	5-9	160	6-12-02	.145	.250	.128	25	55	7	8	0	0	0	4	10	1	0	0	14	1	0	.145	.288
Machado, Anderson	R-R	6-1	170	10-10-03	.217	.167	.225	29	83	17	18	4	0	0	10	12	1	0	0	20	2	1	.265	.323
Martinez, Beyker	B-R	6-1	165	3-21-04	.234	.455	.197	30	77	14	18	3	1	0	3	14	2	0	0	20	5	3	.299	.366
Montero, Adriel	B-R	6-2	170	5-11-02	.217	.125	.232	38	115	17	25	5	2	0	15	20	0	0	1	24	6	1	.296	.331
Ortiz, German	B-R	0-0	0	8-2-04	.256	.000	.286	13	39	7	10	1	1	0	3	7	1	0	0	13	1	2	.333	.383
Pariguan, Javier	R-R	5-10	160	2-5-04	.245	.300	.231	23	49	8	12	0	2	0	5	12	5	0	2	19	0	0	.327	.426
Pastrano, Jose	B-R	5-9	145	11-25-00	.220	.429	.186	24	50	9	11	2	1	0	5	6	2	1	0	14	2	2	.300	.328
Pineda, Pedro	R-R	6-1	170	9-6-03	.200	.500	.182	10	35	4	7	1	1	0	1	5	0	0	0	13	3	2	.286	.300
Santana, Juan	L-L	6-2	180	7-17-01	.264	.125	.289	38	106	15	28	2	2	1	16	23	2	0	1	32	2	2	.349	.402
Santana, Ronny	B-R	6-1	155	12-30-01	.105	.167	.077	9	19	3	2	1	0	0	1	4	0	0	0	8	0	0	.158	.261
Vallejo, Otoniel	R-L	6-2	180	7-16-01	.207	.190	.211	39	111	18	23	4	3	0	10	16	3	3	3	31	9	2	.297	.316

Pitching	B-T	HT	WT	DOB	W	L	ERA	G	GS	CG	SV	IP	H	R	ER	HR	BB	SO	AVG	vLH	vRH	K/9	BB/9
Breindembach, Marco	R-R	6-0	160	11-7-02	0	1	10.91	13	0	0	1	16	27	21	19	0	14	16	.386	.423	.364	9.19	8.04
De Jesus, Dairon	R-R	6-3	180	3-27-04	1	0	1.48	7	4	0	0	24	16	5	4	0	11	24	.190	.152	.216	8.88	4.07
De La Rosa, Franck	R-R	6-8	200	6-9-00	1	4	6.75	9	4	0	0	19	22	18	14	0	14	19	.289	.325	.250	9.16	6.75
De Paula, Willy	R-R	6-2	180	4-1-02	0	4	7.11	10	6	0	0	25	27	21	20	0	21	20	.284	.290	.281	7.11	7.46
Gimenez, Dheygler	R-R	6-2	170	12-3-01	3	2	6.03	11	4	0	0	31	28	23	21	1	9	27	.237	.238	.237	7.76	2.59
Gonzalez, Adriel	R-R	6-2	145	4-28-02	0	5	3.98	10	7	0	1	41	47	27	18	2	14	43	.285	.323	.262	9.52	3.10
Gonzalez, Dangiover	R-R	6-0	149	2-26-02	1	4	5.70	10	4	0	0	24	23	22	15	0	20	12	.261	.222	.266	4.56	7.61
Gonzalez, Jose	R-R	6-0	160	1-5-02	0	2	5.06	11	4	0	0	27	30	21	15	1	12	28	.283	.281	.284	9.45	4.05
Hernandez, Moises	R-R	0-0	0	2-20-04	0	1	30.38	7	4	0	0	5	4	18	18	0	20	5	.190	.500	.067	8.44	33.75
Mijares, Jeremy	L-L	6-0	170	10-19-02	1	0	0.59	8	1	0	1	15	12	3	1	0	3	15	.222	.167	.229	8.80	1.76
Montero, Darlyn	B-R	6-2	170	5-11-02	0	0	0.00	3	0	0	0	3	3	2	0	0	1	3	.273	.000	.429	10.13	3.38
Perdigon, Jesus	R-R	6-2	195	3-21-03	0	2	34.71	10	4	0	0	7	13	29	27	0	24	8	.406	.429	.400	10.29	30.86
Restituyo, Brayan	L-L	5-11	160	1-17-02	2	4	6.48	11	5	0	0	33	34	31	24	0	21	43	.272	.571	.234	11.61	5.67
Ribeiro, Sulivan	L-L	6-4	220	12-16-03	0	2	12.79	6	3	0	0	6	6	12	9	0	16	5	.286	.000	.333	7.11	22.74
Rodriguez, Franyelson	R-R	6-1	160	5-20-02	2	1	4.21	13	0	0	0	26	27	15	12	1	6	14	.273	.316	.246	4.91	2.10
Rodriguez, Roger	R-R	6-1	145	9-11-01	4	0	1.45	10	3	0	0	37	28	8	6	1	8	33	.207	.162	.254	7.96	1.93
Rojas, Gimy	R-R	6-1	145	10-31-03	2	1	11.66	11	0	0	0	15	26	22	19	1	8	8	.382	.375	.385	4.91	4.91
Sarmiento, Carlos	L-L	5-11	145	8-19-03	1	1	3.94	10	2	0	0	32	31	18	14	2	14	23	.252	.333	.248	6.47	3.94
Silverio, Jesus	R-R	6-2	180	7-15-02	0	0	2.57	2	1	0	0	7	4	2	2	0	2	8	.174	.125	.200	10.29	2.57
Torrealba, Pedro	R-R	6-0	180	6-4-03	2	1	5.59	13	0	0	0	19	17	12	12	2	13	18	.224	.263	.184	8.38	6.05
Vallejo, Otoniel	R-L	6-2	180	7-16-01	0	0	0.00	2	0	0	0	1	1	0	0	0	0	1	.333	.500	.000	9.00	0.00

Fielding

C: Amaya 6, Gainza 17, Lelis 25, Pariguan 23.
1B: Amaya 10, Beltran 14, Gainza 4, Garcia 1, Gomez 14, Lelis 1, Montero 17, Santana 1.
2B: Arevalo 2, Baldallo 5, Fuentes 7, Garrett 20, Hipolito 11, Machado 2, Pastrano 17, Santana 1.
3B: Arevalo 7, Beltran 2, Fuentes 11, Machado 22, Montero 11, Ortiz 4, Pastrano 2, Santana 2.
SS: Arevalo 13, Baldallo 18, Fuentes 14, Garrett 3, Machado 5, Ortiz 6, Santana 1.
OF: Avila 13, Beltran 22, Freitez 30, Gallardo 13, Martinez 30, Montero 6, Pastrano 1, Pineda 7, Santana 25, Santana 1, Vallejo 37.

Philadelphia Phillies

SEASON IN A SENTENCE: Thanks in large part to the excellence of outfielder Bryce Harper and righthander Zack Wheeler, the Phillies finished above .500 for the first time since the 2011 season, but it was still not enough to break their playoff drought, as they were eliminated from postseason contention on the last day of September.

HIGH POINT: Buoyed by the confidence of dealing for righthanders Kyle Gibson and Ian Kennedy, the Phillies started the month of August with eight consecutive wins to move into a two-game lead in the National League East. The run included a four-game sweep of the Nationals and a three-game sweep of the Mets.

LOW POINT: The Phillies met the Braves for a three-game set beginning Sept. 28 with a chance to take sole possession of first place with a series sweep. Instead, the Phillies got swept themselves, managing just six runs across three games as they were eliminated from postseason contention. In the final game of the series Gibson was knocked out of the contest in the fifth inning after giving up five runs (four earned).

NOTABLE ROOKIES: After helping Team USA earn a spot in the Olympics, utilityman Luke Williams quickly found his way to the major leagues. He provided a big boost for the club in the month of June before cooling off down the stretch and finishing the season with a .245/.315/.316 slash line. Middle infielder Nick Maton provided solid depth and was mostly used as a pinch hitter, slashing .256/.323/.385 in 117 at-bats. Outfielder Matt Vierling impressed the organization with his play during 2020 fall instructional league and had an encouraging big league debut, with a 126 OPS+ in 71 at-bats. Righthander Connor Brogdon proved to be a reliable weapon out of the bullpen, appearing in 56 games and posting a 3.43 ERA.

KEY TRANSACTIONS: The Phillies made a big splash at the end of July by trading former top prospect Spencer Howard and two minor league pitchers to the Rangers for Gibson, Kennedy and righthander Hans Crouse, who slots in as the team's No. 7 prospect. Gibson struggled over 11 starts, but Kennedy helped stabilize the bullpen. Crouse made his big league debut in September and should take on a bigger role next season. The Phillies also acquired shortstop Freddy Galvis from the Orioles for righthander Tyler Burch. Galvis appeared in 32 games and hit .224 while providing steady defense.

OPENING DAY PAYROLL: $174,009,000 (5th).

PLAYERS OF THE YEAR

MAJOR LEAGUE	MINOR LEAGUE
Bryce Harper	**Bryson Stott**
OF	SS
.309/.429/.615	(AAA/AA/High-A)
MLB-best 1.044 OPS	.299/.390/.486,
35 HR, 100 BB, 13 SB	16 HR, 10 SB

ORGANIZATION LEADERS

Batting   *Minimum 250 AB

MAJORS

*AVG	Bryce Harper	.309
*OPS	Bryce Harper	1.044
HR	Bryce Harper	35
RBI	Bryce Harper	84

MINORS

*AVG	Bryson Stott, Lehigh Valley, Reading, Jersey Shore	.299
*OBP	Bryson Stott, Lehigh Valley, Reading, Jersey Shore	.390
*SLG	Jorge Bonifacio, Lehigh Valley, Reading	.506
*OPS	Bryson Stott, Lehigh Valley, Reading, Jersey Shore	.876
R	Bryson Stott, Lehigh Valley IronPigs	71
H	Bryson Stott, Lehigh Valley IronPigs	125
TB	Bryson Stott, Lehigh Valley IronPigs	203
2B	Darick Hall, Lehigh Valley	27
3B	Mickey Moniak, Lehigh Valley	8
HR	Jhailyn Ortiz, Reading, Jersey Shore	23
RBI	Mickey Moniak, Lehigh Valley	65
BB	Baron Radcliff, Clearwater, Phillies	71
SO	McCarthy Tatum, Reading, Jersey Shore	126
SB	Johan Rojas, Jersey Shore, Clearwater, Phillies	34

Pitching   #Minimum 75 IP

MAJORS

W	Zack Wheeler	14
#ERA	Ranger Suarez	1.36
SO	Zack Wheeler	247
SV	Hector Neris	12

MINORS

W	Austin Ross, Lehigh Valley, Reading	8
W	Victor Vargas, Lehigh Valley, Jersey Shore, Clearwater	8
L	Francisco Morales, Lehigh Valley, Reading	14
#ERA	Adam Leverett, Lehigh Valley, Reading, Jersey Shore	3.48
G	Mike Adams, Lehigh Valley, Jersey Shore	44
G	Jeffrey Singer, Lehigh Valley	44
GS	Francisco Morales, Lehigh Valley, Reading	22
SV	Brian Marconi, Lehigh Valley, Reading, Jersey Shore	15
IP	Jack Perkins, Lehigh Valley, Reading, Jersey Shore	100.2
BB	Francisco Morales, Lehigh Valley, Reading	67
SO	Francisco Morales, Lehigh Valley, Reading	117
#AVG	Josh Hendrickson, Lehigh Valley, Reading, Jersey Shore	.220

2021 PERFORMANCE

General Manager: Dave Dombrowski. **Farm Director:** Preston Mattingly. **Scouting Director:** Brian Barber.

Class	Team	League	W	L	PCT	Finish	Manager
Majors	Philadelphia Phillies	National	82	80	.506	7th (15)	Joe Girardi
Triple-A	Lehigh Valley IronPigs	Triple-A East	53	75	.414	15th (20)	Gary Jones
Double-A	Reading Fightin Phils	Double-A Northeast	48	65	.425	10th (12)	Shawn Williams
High-A	Jersey Shore BlueClaws	High-A East	56	62	.475	7th (12)	Chris Adamson
Low-A	Clearwater Threshers	Low-A Southeast	52	64	.448	9th (10)	Milver Reyes/Marty Malloy
Rookie	DSL Phillies White	Dominican Summer	36	20	.643	4th (46)	Orlando Munoz
Rookie	DSL Phillies Red	Dominican Summer	33	24	.579	12th (46)	Waner Santana
Rookie	FCL Phillies	Florida Complex	26	14	.650	4th (18)	Roly de Armas
Overall 2021 Minor League Record		304		324	.484 19th (30)		

ORGANIZATION STATISTICS

PHILADELPHIA PHILLIES
NATIONAL LEAGUE

Batting	B-T	HT	WT	DOB	AVG	vLH	vRH	G	AB	R	H	2B	3B	HR	RBI	BB	HBP	SH	SF	SO	SB	CS	SLG	OBP
Bohm, Alec	R-R	6-5	218	8-3-96	.247	.289	.228	115	380	46	94	15	0	7	47	31	2	0	4	111	4	0	.342	.305
Bonifacio, Jorge	R-R	6-1	220	6-4-93	.091	.125	.000	7	11	0	1	0	0	0	2	1	0	0	0	6	0	0	.091	.167
Galvis, Freddy	B-R	5-10	190	11-14-89	.224	.206	.233	32	107	17	24	3	0	5	14	9	2	0	2	19	0	0	.393	.292
Gregorius, Didi	L-R	6-3	205	2-18-90	.209	.157	.226	103	368	35	77	16	2	13	54	25	8	0	7	67	3	0	.370	.270
Harper, Bryce	L-R	6-3	210	10-16-92	.309	.257	.333	141	488	101	151	42	1	35	84	100	5	2	4	134	13	3	.615	.429
Haseley, Adam	L-L	6-1	190	4-12-96	.190	.167	.200	9	21	2	4	1	0	0	0	0	0	0	0	4	0	0	.238	.190
Herrera, Odubel	L-R	5-11	205	12-29-91	.260	.252	.264	124	450	59	117	27	2	13	51	29	6	1	5	77	6	1	.416	.310
Hoskins, Rhys	R-R	6-4	245	3-17-93	.247	.250	.245	107	389	64	96	29	0	27	71	47	5	0	2	108	3	2	.530	.334
Jankowski, Travis	L-R	6-2	190	6-15-91	.252	.300	.243	76	131	24	33	6	2	1	10	22	1	2	0	29	5	0	.351	.364
Joyce, Matt	L-R	6-2	194	8-3-84	.091	.091	.091	43	55	6	5	1	0	2	7	12	1	0	1	16	0	0	.218	.261
Kingery, Scott	R-R	5-10	180	4-29-94	.053	.071	.000	15	19	1	1	0	0	0	0	0	0	0	0	12	0	0	.053	.053
Knapp, Andrew	B-R	6-1	189	11-9-91	.152	.125	.165	62	145	13	22	3	0	2	11	10	2	1	1	61	0	0	.214	.215
Marchan, Rafael	B-R	5-9	170	2-25-99	.231	.304	.172	20	52	7	12	1	1	1	4	4	0	0	0	10	0	0	.346	.286
Maton, Nick	L-R	6-2	178	2-18-97	.256	.325	.221	52	117	16	30	7	1	2	14	10	2	1	1	39	2	0	.385	.323
McCutchen, Andrew	R-R	5-11	195	10-10-86	.222	.293	.186	144	482	78	107	24	1	27	80	81	4	0	7	132	6	1	.444	.334
Miller, Brad	L-R	6-2	195	10-18-89	.227	.169	.244	140	331	53	75	9	3	20	49	45	1	0	0	112	3	0	.453	.321
Moniak, Mickey	L-R	6-2	195	5-13-98	.091	.000	.120	21	33	3	3	0	0	1	3	3	0	1	0	16	0	0	.182	.167
Quinn, Roman	B-R	5-10	175	5-14-93	.173	.115	.231	28	52	8	9	2	2	0	2	6	4	0	0	19	4	3	.288	.306
Realmuto, J.T.	R-R	6-1	212	3-18-91	.263	.241	.271	134	476	64	125	25	4	17	73	48	11	0	2	129	13	3	.439	.343
Segura, Jean	R-R	5-10	220	3-17-90	.290	.313	.279	131	514	76	149	27	3	14	58	39	9	1	4	78	9	3	.436	.348
Torreyes, Ronald	R-R	5-8	155	9-2-92	.242	.284	.218	111	318	30	77	10	1	7	41	19	1	5	1	41	2	1	.346	.286
Vierling, Matt	R-R	6-3	205	9-16-96	.324	.341	.300	34	71	11	23	3	1	2	6	4	1	0	1	20	2	0	.479	.364
Williams, Luke	R-R	6-1	186	8-9-96	.245	.288	.179	58	98	8	24	4	0	1	6	10	0	0	0	23	2	2	.316	.315

Pitching	B-T	HT	WT	DOB	W	L	ERA	G	GS	CG	SV	IP	H	R	ER	HR	BB	SO	AVG	vLH	vRH	K/9	BB/9
Alvarado, Jose	L-L	6-2	245	5-21-95	7	1	4.20	64	0	0	5	56	42	30	26	5	47	68	.213	.123	.266	10.99	7.60
Anderson, Chase	R-R	6-1	210	11-30-87	2	4	6.75	14	9	0	0	48	51	36	36	10	20	35	.268	.174	.357	6.56	3.75
Bedrosian, Cam	R-R	6-1	225	10-2-91	0	0	4.35	11	1	0	0	10	8	5	5	2	7	8	.211	.188	.227	6.97	6.10
2-team total (6 Cincinnati)				0	0	6.75	17	1	0	0	16	18	12	12	4	13	15	.286	.250	.308	8.44	7.31
Bradley, Archie	R-R	6-4	215	8-10-92	7	3	3.71	53	0	0	2	51	51	24	21	5	22	40	.258	.227	.282	7.06	3.88
Brogdon, Connor	R-R	6-5	205	1-29-95	5	1	3.43	56	1	0	1	58	47	27	22	6	18	50	.221	.218	.223	7.80	2.81
Coonrod, Sam	R-R	6-1	225	9-22-92	2	2	4.04	42	2	0	2	42	41	21	19	5	15	48	.247	.247	.247	10.20	3.19
Crouse, Hans	L-R	6-4	180	9-15-98	0	2	5.14	2	2	0	0	7	4	4	4	2	7	2	.167	.200	.111	2.57	9.00
De Los Santos, Enyel	R-R	6-3	235	12-25-95	1	1	6.75	26	0	0	0	28	34	28	21	7	14	42	.288	.296	.281	13.50	4.50
2-team total (7 Pittsburgh)				2	1	6.37	33	0	0	0	35	43	32	25	8	18	48	.291	.284	.296	12.23	4.58
Dohy, Kyle	L-L	6-2	202	9-17-96	0	0	0.00	1	0	0	0	1	1	0	0	0	1	1	.250	.000	.500	9.00	9.00
Dominguez, Seranthony	R-R	6-1	225	11-25-94	0	0	0.00	1	0	0	0	1	0	0	0	0	0	1	.000	.000	.000	9.00	0.00
Eflin, Zach	R-R	6-6	220	4-8-94	4	7	4.17	18	18	0	0	106	116	52	49	15	16	99	.276	.264	.286	8.43	1.36
Falter, Bailey	R-L	6-4	175	4-24-97	2	1	5.61	22	1	0	0	34	34	21	21	5	6	34	.262	.288	.244	9.09	1.60
Feliz, Neftali	R-R	6-3	235	5-2-88	0	1	36.00	2	0	0	0	1	4	4	4	1	1	2	.571	.600	.500	18.00	9.00
2-team total (3 Los Angeles)				0	1	9.00	5	0	0	0	4	5	4	4	1	3	.294	.333	.250	6.75	2.25
Gibson, Kyle	R-R	6-6	215	10-23-87	4	6	5.09	12	11	0	0	69	66	40	39	8	23	61	.250	.282	.198	7.96	3.00
Hale, David	R-R	6-2	210	9-27-87	0	2	6.41	17	1	0	0	27	30	20	19	5	9	21	.283	.167	.359	7.09	3.04
Hammer, JD	R-R	6-3	202	7-12-94	1	1	4.95	20	0	0	0	20	21	11	11	3	11	22	.259	.244	.275	9.90	4.95
Howard, Spencer	R-R	6-3	210	7-28-96	0	2	5.72	11	7	0	0	28	25	19	18	2	17	31	.236	.184	.281	9.85	5.40
Jones, Damon	L-L	6-5	233	9-30-94	0	0	0.00	1	0	0	0	1	0	0	0	0	2	0	.500	--	.500	0.00	54.00
Kennedy, Ian	R-R	6-0	210	12-19-84	3	1	4.13	23	0	0	10	24	18	11	11	7	10	27	.202	.237	.176	10.13	3.75
Kintzler, Brandon	R-R	5-10	200	8-1-84	2	1	6.37	29	1	0	0	30	45	23	21	7	8	22	.344	.283	.385	6.67	2.43
Knapp, Andrew	B-R	6-1	189	11-9-91	0	0	0.00	1	0	0	0	0	0	0	0	0	0	0	.000	--	.000	0.00	0.00
Llovera, Mauricio	R-R	5-11	224	4-11-96	1	0	9.45	6	0	0	0	7	10	7	7	5	4	7	.333	.462	.235	9.45	5.40
Maton, Nick	L-R	6-2	178	2-18-97	0	0	0.00	1	0	0	0	0	0	0	0	0	1	0	.000	--	.000	27.00	0.00
Medina, Adonis	R-R	6-1	187	12-18-96	0	0	3.52	4	1	0	0	8	9	3	3	0	4	6	.310	.462	.188	7.04	4.70

Name	B-T	HT	WT	DOB	W	L	ERA	G	GS			IP	H	R	ER	HR	BB	SO	AVG				
Moore, Matt	L-L	6-3	210	6-18-89	2	4	6.29	24	13	0	0	73	78	54	51	15	38	63	.274	.289	.267	7.77	4.68
Neris, Hector	R-R	6-2	227	6-14-89	4	7	3.63	74	0	0	12	74	55	34	30	12	32	98	.202	.223	.185	11.87	3.87
Nola, Aaron	R-R	6-2	200	6-4-93	9	9	4.63	32	32	1	0	181	165	95	93	26	39	223	.237	.221	.254	11.11	1.94
Paulino, David	R-R	6-6	240	2-6-94	0	0	9.00	1	0	0	0	2	3	2	2	1	0	0	.333	.400	.250	0.00	0.00
Romero, JoJo	L-L	5-11	200	9-9-96	0	0	7.00	1	0	0	0	9	12	8	7	4	4	8	.308	.250	.368	8.00	4.00
Rosso, Ramon	R-R	6-4	240	6-9-96	0	0	5.63	7	0	0	0	8	10	6	5	2	3	7	.313	.385	.263	7.88	3.38
Sanchez, Cristopher	L-L	6-1	165	12-12-96	1	0	4.97	7	1	0	0	13	16	8	7	1	7	13	.320	.300	.333	9.24	4.97
Suarez, Ranger	L-L	6-1	217	8-26-95	8	5	1.36	39	12	1	4	106	73	20	16	4	33	107	.194	.109	.225	9.08	2.80
Torreyes, Ronald	R-R	5-8	155	9-2-92	0	0	13.50	2	0	0	0	3	6	4	4	2	0	1	.429	.500	.400	3.38	0.00
Velasquez, Vince	R-R	6-3	212	6-7-92	3	6	5.95	21	17	0	0	82	76	55	54	17	45	85	.244	.297	.208	9.37	4.96
2-team total (4 San Diego)					3		9 6.30	25		21	0	0	94	91	68	66	23	49	101	.251	.297	.221	9.64	4.67
Wheeler, Zack	L-R	6-4	195	5-30-90	14	10	2.78	32	32	3	0	213	169	72	66	16	46	247	.215	.213	.218	10.42	1.94

Fielding

Catcher	PCT	G	PO	A	E	DP	PB
Knapp	.997	47	340	16	1	1	4
Marchan	.991	17	107	6	1	0	1
Realmuto	.999	118	1057	30	1	5	6

First Base	PCT	G	PO	A	E	DP
Bohm	.963	7	24	2	1	2
Galvis	1.000	1	2	0	0	1
Harper	.000	1	0	0	0	0
Hoskins	.995	103	735	79	4	81
Knapp	1.000	6	4	0	0	0
Marchan	.000	1	0	0	0	0
Miller	.992	58	325	36	3	35
Realmuto	.984	16	54	6	1	5
Vierling	1.000	9	45	2	0	6
Williams	1.000	6	5	1	0	1

Second Base	PCT	G	PO	A	E	DP
Galvis	1.000	2	3	3	0	0
Kingery	.800	4	1	3	1	1

	PCT	G	PO	A	E	DP	PB
Knapp	1.000	1	0	1	0	1	
Maton	1.000	21	19	40	0	6	
Miller	1.000	13	14	19	0	7	
Segura	.981	128	224	335	11	85	
Torreyes	.957	11	8	14	1	6	
Williams	1.000	8	10	11	0	3	

Third Base	PCT	G	PO	A	E	DP
Bohm	.936	103	67	154	15	17
Galvis	.956	19	10	33	2	8
Kingery	1.000	1	0	1	0	0
Miller	1.000	8	4	10	0	0
Torreyes	1.000	50	33	69	0	9
Williams	.900	8	4	5	1	0

Shortstop	PCT	G	PO	A	E	DP
Galvis	.944	10	17	17	2	4
Gregorius	.953	101	131	236	18	49
Maton	.933	20	18	38	4	12
Segura	.000	1	0	0	0	0

	PCT	G	PO	A	E	DP
Torreyes	.978	44	48	86	3	19
Williams	1.000	5	4	9	0	1

Outfield	PCT	G	PO	A	E	DP
Bonifacio	1.000	5	5	0	0	0
Harper	.996	139	214	10	1	1
Haseley	1.000	10	15	0	0	0
Herrera	.986	128	214	5	3	2
Jankowski	1.000	59	69	0	0	0
Joyce	1.000	18	21	0	0	0
Kingery	1.000	7	4	1	0	1
McCutchen	.980	135	189	4	4	0
Miller	.909	20	20	0	2	0
Moniak	1.000	17	15	0	0	0
Quinn	1.000	27	35	2	0	1
Torreyes	1.000	1	1	0	0	0
Vierling	1.000	21	13	0	0	0
Williams	.952	25	20	0	1	0

LEHIGH VALLEY IRONPIGS
TRIPLE-A
TRIPLE-A EAST

Batting	B-T	HT	WT	DOB	AVG	vLH	vRH	G	AB	R	H	2B	3B	HR	RBI	BB	HBP	SH	SF	SO	SB	CS	SLG	OBP
Bohm, Alec	R-R	6-5	218	8-3-96	.271	.389	.220	15	59	8	16	5	0	1	6	7	1	0	1	15	3	1	.407	.353
Bonifacio, Jorge	R-R	6-1	220	6-4-93	.261	.239	.271	44	153	28	40	13	2	5	19	28	1	0	1	41	4	2	.471	.377
Brito, Daniel	L-R	6-1	170	1-23-98	.286	.143	.333	8	28	6	8	1	1	2	8	4	0	0	0	7	0	1	.607	.375
Cabral, Edgar	R-R	5-11	210	9-12-95	.221	.188	.229	29	86	11	19	5	1	0	11	14	1	0	1	32	0	0	.302	.333
Chatham, C.J.	R-R	6-4	185	12-22-94	.271	.286	.267	50	155	20	42	6	1	3	23	13	6	0	2	27	0	1	.381	.347
Conley, Jack	R-R	6-1	190	1-16-97	.111	.333	.067	7	18	3	2	2	0	0	3	0	0	0	0	10	0	0	.222	.238
Cordell, Ryan	R-R	6-4	200	3-31-92	.198	.205	.196	57	197	31	39	6	0	12	28	24	3	0	2	87	8	1	.411	.292
Duran, Rodolfo	R-R	5-9	181	2-19-98	.267	.500	.182	4	15	3	4	1	0	1	3	1	0	0	0	4	0	0	.533	.313
Elmore, Jake	R-R	5-10	180	6-15-87	.225	.375	.188	15	40	7	9	2	0	0	9	10	1	0	0	6	1	1	.275	.392
Fassnacht, Nate	R-R	5-11	180	1-5-98	.667	--	.667	2	3	2	2	0	0	0	1	0	1	0	0	1	0	0	.667	.750
Francisco, Freddy	R-R	5-11	180	2-7-01	1.000	.500	--	2	2	0	1	0	0	0	0	0	0	0	0	1	0	0	.500	.667
Friscia, Vito	R-R	6-3	225	12-19-96	.333	--	.333	1	3	1	1	0	0	0	1	0	0	0	0	1	0	0	.667	.500
Galvis, Freddy	B-R	5-10	190	11-14-89	.222	.200	.250	5	18	1	4	0	0	1	2	1	0	0	0	4	0	0	.389	.300
Gamboa, Arquimedes	B-R	6-0	190	9-23-97	.234	.269	.221	36	94	16	22	3	1	2	9	16	1	0	0	24	4	1	.351	.351
Gozzo, Sal	B-R	6-0	196	3-29-98	.149	.130	.156	39	87	9	13	1	0	0	6	9	1	1	0	27	0	0	.161	.237
Gregorius, Didi	L-R	6-3	205	2-18-90	.474	.000	.563	7	19	4	9	2	0	1	4	4	0	0	0	1	0	0	.737	.565
Guthrie, Dalton	R-R	5-11	160	12-23-95	.292	.325	.278	37	130	17	38	13	0	2	13	5	2	2	0	31	2	1	.438	.328
Hall, Darick	L-R	6-4	232	7-25-95	.230	.239	.227	120	400	46	92	27	0	14	60	55	12	0	3	100	0	2	.403	.338
Haseley, Adam	L-L	6-1	190	4-12-96	.224	.286	.207	41	156	18	35	2	0	3	14	12	1	0	1	33	7	2	.295	.282
Heineman, Tyler	B-R	5-10	199	6-19-91	.274	.375	.239	20	62	5	17	2	0	0	6	9	0	3	0	12	0	1	.306	.366
2-team total (21 Memphis)					.264		.370	.235	41	129	13	34	6	0	0	11	16	1	3	2	29	0	3	.310	.345
Herrera, Odubel	L-R	5-11	205	12-29-91	.500	.600	.333	2	8	2	4	0	0	1	2	2	0	0	0	1	1	0	.875	.600
Iser, Herbert	L-R	6-3	210	12-14-97	.000	--	.000	1	1	0	0	0	0	0	0	0	0	0	0	0	0	0	.000	.000
Jankowski, Travis	L-R	6-2	190	6-15-91	.304	.308	.302	19	56	16	17	4	0	0	6	15	0	1	0	9	4	3	.375	.451
Joyce, Matt	L-R	6-2	194	8-3-84	.333	--	.333	2	9	1	3	1	0	1	3	1	0	0	0	1	0	0	.778	.400
Kingery, Scott	R-R	5-10	180	4-29-94	.181	.083	.200	23	72	11	13	4	2	0	5	13	1	0	2	27	3	0	.292	.307
Knapp, Andrew	B-R	6-1	189	11-9-91	.125	--	.125	3	8	1	1	0	0	0	0	4	0	0	0	4	0	0	.125	.417
Listi, Austin	R-R	6-0	214	11-5-93	.221	.273	.205	56	190	16	42	7	0	1	20	19	3	0	2	46	0	0	.274	.299
Marchan, Rafael	B-R	5-9	170	2-25-99	.203	.179	.212	67	237	28	48	7	0	0	19	23	4	0	1	45	1	0	.232	.283
Maton, Nick	L-R	6-2	178	2-18-97	.199	.184	.204	63	206	29	41	11	2	5	27	38	4	2	2	60	3	2	.345	.332
Moniak, Mickey	L-R	6-2	195	5-13-98	.238	.224	.243	99	365	42	87	15	8	15	65	31	4	1	8	101	5	2	.447	.299
Moore, Logan	L-R	6-3	220	8-22-90	.164	.125	.170	22	55	8	9	0	0	1	5	12	1	2	1	18	0	0	.218	.319
Muzziotti, Simon	L-L	6-1	175	12-27-98	.200	.333	.182	8	25	2	5	0	0	0	2	0	0	2	0	4	2	0	.200	.333
O'Hoppe, Logan	R-R	6-2	3-9-00	1.000	.500	.158	16	21	2	4	1	0	1	3	2	0	0	0	4	0	0	.381	.261
Quinn, Roman	B-R	5-10	175	5-14-93	.333	.500	.250	2	6	0	2	0	0	0	1	1	0	1	0	2	0	0	.333	.429
Randolph, Cornelius	L-R	5-11	205	6-2-97	.234	.250	.230	48	145	26	34	7	0	5	20	19	0	0	0	50	5	0	.386	.323

Player	B-T	HT	WT	DOB	AVG	OBP	SLG	G	AB	R	H	2B	3B	HR	RBI	BB	HBP	SH	SF	SO	SB	CS	vLH	vRH
Rivera, T.J.	R-R	6-1	203	10-27-88	.314	.318	.313	31	86	13	27	5	0	4	24	5	4	0	4	16	1	0	.512	.364
2-team total (57 Indianapolis)					.269	.338	.246	88	279	35	75	17	0	9	48	18	5	2	7	58	1	1	.427	.317
Segura, Jean	R-R	5-10	220	3-17-90	.750	.667	1.000	2	4	2	3	1	0	0	0	1	0	0	0	0	0	0	1.000	.800
Stephen, Josh	L-L	6-0	185	9-22-97	.000	.000	.000	3	8	1	0	0	0	0	0	0	2	0	0	0	2	0	0	.000	.200
Stott, Bryson	L-R	6-3	200	10-6-97	.303	.400	.286	10	33	4	10	0	0	1	3	8	0	0	0	8	1	0	.394	.439
Tejada, Ruben	R-R	5-11	200	10-27-89	.231	.278	.216	72	225	26	52	5	1	0	15	32	6	0	1	46	1	3	.262	.341
2-team total (8 Charlotte Knights)					.233	.284	.215	80	253	27	59	5	1	1	20	34	6	0	1	58	1	3	.273	.337
Tilson, Charlie	L-L	6-1	190	12-2-92	.296	.255	.309	59	203	42	60	13	3	1	27	17	5	4	2	47	13	2	.404	.361
Torreyes, Ronald	R-R	5-8	155	9-2-92	.276	.182	.333	9	29	3	8	4	0	0	4	6	1	0	0	6	0	0	.414	.417
Vierling, Matt	R-R	6-3	205	9-16-96	.248	.321	.220	55	206	25	51	6	1	5	31	24	3	0	3	46	5	1	.359	.331
Williams, Corbin	R-R	6-2	170	1-19-98	.000	.000	.000	2	1	0	0	0	0	0	0	0	0	0	0	1	0	0	.000	.000
Williams, Luke	R-R	6-1	186	8-9-96	.270	.310	.258	32	126	21	34	5	2	0	15	12	1	0	4	29	7	3	.341	.329

Pitching	B-T	HT	WT	DOB	W	L	ERA	G	GS	CG	SV	IP	H	R	ER	HR	BB	SO	AVG	vLH	vRH	K/9	BB/9
Adams, Mike	R-R	5-11	175	9-7-94	1	1	3.65	30	0	0	0	37	35	15	15	1	19	29	.257	.260	.256	7.05	4.62
Alexander, Tyler	L-L	6-1	180	9-22-91	2	2	4.44	9	4	0	0	26	26	13	13	4	12	21	.250	.240	.253	7.18	4.10
Alvarado, Jose	L-L	6-2	245	5-21-95	0	0	0.00	1	1	0	0	1	0	0	0	0	1	1	.000	.000	.000	9.00	9.00
Anderson, Chase	R-R	6-1	210	11-30-87	1	2	5.71	5	5	0	0	17	21	11	11	2	5	14	.300	.200	.375	7.27	2.60
Appel, Mark	R-R	6-5	220	7-15-91	3	5	6.17	15	9	0	0	47	38	33	32	8	34	36	.226	.200	.247	6.94	6.56
Bedrosian, Cam	R-R	6-1	225	10-2-91	2	2	2.25	16	0	0	2	20	18	7	5	1	7	20	.240	.286	.213	9.00	3.15
Bradley, Archie	R-R	6-4	215	8-10-92	0	0	4.50	2	0	0	0	2	2	1	1	0	1	1	.250	.000	.667	4.50	4.50
Brogdon, Connor	R-R	6-6	205	1-29-95	0	0	0.00	1	1	0	0	1	0	0	0	0	0	2	.000	.000	.000	18.00	9.00
Conley, Jack	R-R	6-1	190	1-16-97	0	0	9.00	1	0	0	0	1	1	1	1	0	2	1	.250	.000	.333	9.00	18.00
Coonrod, Sam	R-R	6-2	225	9-22-92	0	0	1.69	5	0	0	0	5	2	1	1	1	2	4	.118	.333	.000	6.75	3.38
Crouse, Hans	L-R	6-4	180	9-15-98	0	0	6.23	1	1	0	0	4	5	3	3	1	3	6	.294	.375	.222	12.46	6.23
De Los Santos, Enyel	R-R	6-3	235	12-25-95	0	1	2.70	10	0	0	0	13	3	4	4	1	5	24	.073	.125	.040	16.20	3.38
Dohy, Kyle	L-L	6-2	202	9-17-96	0	0	8.44	6	0	0	0	5	4	5	5	1	12	9	.200	.167	.214	15.19	20.25
Dominguez, Seranthony	R-R	6-1	225	11-25-94	0	1	7.30	12	0	0	0	12	13	13	10	1	8	16	.250	.375	.143	11.68	5.84
Eastman, Colton	R-R	6-3	185	8-22-96	1	1	3.00	4	4	1	0	21	18	7	7	1	7	14	.237	.175	.306	6.00	3.00
Evanko, Ethan	L-L	6-4	185	6-7-95	3	1	4.24	10	1	0	0	23	21	12	11	3	8	17	.247	.240	.250	6.56	3.09
Falter, Bailey	R-L	6-4	175	4-24-97	2	1	1.76	8	6	0	0	31	23	6	6	3	8	44	.205	.212	.203	12.91	2.35
Feliz, Neftali	R-R	6-3	235	5-2-88	2	1	1.26	15	0	0	4	14	8	4	2	1	6	23	.160	.125	.192	14.44	3.77
Garcia, Julian	L-R	6-3	206	5-13-95	0	4	8.07	14	3	0	0	36	37	37	32	8	30	33	.259	.361	.183	8.33	7.57
Glogoski, Kyle	R-R	6-2	183	1-6-99	0	0	54.00	1	1	0	0	1	2	6	6	1	3	3	.400	.667	.000	27.00	27.00
Guerrieri, Taylor	R-R	6-3	225	12-1-92	0	0	6.48	7	0	0	0	8	11	7	6	2	3	10	.333	.308	.350	10.80	3.24
Hammer, JD	R-R	6-3	202	7-12-94	2	0	3.80	20	0	0	1	24	20	11	10	3	13	36	.225	.143	.298	13.69	4.94
Hendrickson, Josh	L-L	6-4	215	9-18-97	1	0	6.23	1	0	0	0	4	1	3	3	0	6	3	.071	.000	.143	6.23	12.46
Hernandez, Jakob	L-L	6-4	260	5-19-96	3	2	4.86	27	0	0	2	33	32	21	18	2	16	36	.252	.238	.259	9.72	4.32
Howard, Spencer	R-R	6-3	210	7-28-96	1	0	1.25	6	4	0	0	22	13	3	3	1	9	28	.171	.139	.200	11.63	3.74
Jones, Daman	L-L	6-5	233	9-30-94	1	5	5.44	34	0	0	1	41	39	27	25	3	36	57	.248	.192	.276	12.41	7.84
Kaminsky, Rob	R-L	6-0	195	9-2-94	0	0	0.00	1	0	0	0	1	0	0	0	0	1	2	.000	.000	.000	18.00	9.00
Kintzler, Brandon	R-R	5-10	200		0	0	0.00	2	0	0	0	2	0	0	0	0	1	0	.000	.000	.000	0.00	4.50
Lackney, Nick	L-L	6-4	210	6-5-97	0	0	18.00	1	0	0	0	1	3	2	2	0	2	0	.600	.000	.750	0.00	18.00
Lail, Brady	R-R	6-2	200	8-9-93	1	0	6.08	31	1	0	0	40	38	28	27	9	25	43	.257	.254	.258	9.68	5.63
Leverett, Adam	L-R	6-4	190	9-19-98	1	0	4.00	2	2	0	0	9	8	4	4	2	3	8	.250	.250	.250	8.00	3.00
Listi, Austin	R-R	6-0	214	11-5-93	0	0	0.00	1	0	0	0	1	0	0	0	0	0	0	.000	.000	.000	0.00	0.00
Llovera, Mauricio	R-R	5-11	224	4-17-96	2	2	3.46	32	4	0	0	52	41	21	20	5	24	48	.212	.205	.219	8.31	4.15
Marconi, Brian	R-L	6-3	175	5-9-97	0	0	15.75	4	0	0	0	4	9	7	7	0	6	2	.474	.375	.545	4.50	13.50
McAllister, Zach	R-R	6-6	240	12-8-87	1	1	5.19	9	0	0	0	9	12	6	5	2	6	8	.300	.308	.320	8.31	6.23
Medina, Adonis	R-R	6-1	187	12-18-96	4	5	5.05	17	17	0	0	68	71	48	38	10	26	55	.264	.301	.237	7.32	3.46
Mitchell, Bryan	L-R	6-2	215	4-19-91	3	1	6.04	20	0	0	1	28	32	20	19	2	16	20	.302	.367	.246	6.35	5.08
2-team total (11 Jacksonville)					4	1	4.37	31	3	0	1	58	52	29	28	5	29	57	.248	.264	.236	8.90	4.53
Moore, Matt	L-L	6-3	210	6-18-89	0	2	4.66	5	5	0	0	19	20	10	10	5	11	22	.267	.318	.245	10.24	5.12
Morales, Francisco	R-R	6-4	185	10-27-99	0	1	0.00	2	2	0	0	9	6	4	0	0	7	7	.188	.278	.071	7.27	7.27
Ogle, Braeden	L-L	6-2	215	7-30-97	1	3	9.95	20	0	0	0	19	30	23	21	5	14	18	.380	.304	.411	8.53	6.63
2-team total (24 Indianapolis)					3	5	5.68	44	0	0	1	51	49	36	32	7	37	60	.259	.246	.267	10.66	6.57
Parkinson, David	R-L	6-2	210	12-14-95	1	11	7.93	20	18	0	0	78	109	73	69	16	28	68	.323	.326	.323	7.81	3.22
Paulino, David	R-R	6-6	240	2-6-94	4	4	4.06	30	7	0	2	75	67	36	34	7	34	79	.238	.254	.225	9.44	4.06
Perkins, Jack	R-R	6-2	200	8-6-97	0	3	5.40	6	6	0	0	25	33	17	15	3	7	21	.320	.298	.339	7.56	2.52
Ross, Austin	R-R	6-1	185	8-16-94	1	0	1.04	7	1	0	0	9	3	2	1	0	6	12	.100	.067	.133	12.46	6.23
Rosso, Ramon	R-R	6-4	240	6-9-96	0	2	4.60	21	3	0	0	29	28	23	15	2	19	28	.259	.333	.200	8.59	5.83
Sanchez, Cristopher	L-L	6-1	165	12-12-96	5	6	4.68	19	17	0	0	73	58	39	38	4	48	89	.211	.139	.240	10.97	5.92
Singer, Jeffrey	L-L	6-0		9-13-93	3	3	4.75	44	0	0	3	53	51	30	28	2	26	67	.254	.231	.265	11.38	4.42
Vargas, Victor	R-R	6-1	175	9-3-00	1	0	0.00	1	1	0	0	5	2	0	0	0	2	3	.118	.125	.111	5.40	3.60
Velasquez, Vince	R-R	6-3	212	6-7-92	0	0	2.70	2	2	0	0	7	2	2	1	3	12		.095	.125	.077	16.20	4.05
Warren, Zach	L-L	6-5	205	6-9-96	0	0	60.75	2	0	0	0	1	8	9	9	0	3	2	.667	1.000	.556	13.50	20.25
Zarbnisky, Braden	L-R	6-2	191	12-26-96	1	1	7.24	8	0	0	0	14	12	13	11	4	5	11	.226	.304	.167	7.24	3.29

Fielding

Catcher	PCT	G	PO	A	E	DP	PB
Cabral	.992	25	234	8	2	1	2
Conley	.978	5	43	2	1	0	0
Duran	1.000	4	38	0	0	0	0
Francisco	1.000	1	1	0	0	0	1
Friscia	1.000	1	10	0	0	0	0
Heineman	.979	15	129	9	3	0	1
Knapp	1.000	3	29	2	0	0	0
Marchan	.992	58	460	42	4	2	3
Moore	.985	18	126	8	2	1	2
O'Hoppe	.977	5	41	1	1	0	0

First Base	PCT	G	PO	A	E	DP
Bohm	.969	3	31	0	1	5
Hall	.998	114	768	56	2	70
Listi	1.000	10	47	1	0	3
Rivera	1.000	2	17	0	0	3
Vierling	1.000	6	45	2	0	2

	PCT	G	PO	A	E	DP
Williams	1.000	1	9	0	0	0

Second Base

	PCT	G	PO	A	E	DP
Brito	1.000	5	7	10	0	0
Chatham	1.000	21	33	46	0	12
Elmore	1.000	11	13	19	0	8
Fassnacht	1.000	1	1	2	0	1
Galvis	1.000	1	1	3	0	1
Gamboa	.941	14	23	25	3	6
Gozzo	.937	26	31	43	5	6
Guthrie	.971	10	16	18	1	6
Kingery	.979	10	17	29	1	6
Maton	.967	15	23	36	2	11
Rivera	1.000	9	12	22	0	4
Segura	1.000	2	3	1	0	1
Tejada	1.000	14	10	28	0	3
Torreyes	1.000	1	0	1	0	0
Williams	1.000	14	21	30	0	6

Third Base

	PCT	G	PO	A	E	DP
Bohm	.966	12	8	20	1	4
Brito	1.000	1	0	3	0	1
Galvis	1.000	2	2	7	0	1
Gozzo	1.000	4	1	3	0	0
Guthrie	.957	9	6	16	1	4

	PCT	G	PO	A	E	DP
Kingery	1.000	3	0	2	0	0
Listi	.940	46	19	59	5	3
Maton	1.000	13	5	15	0	2
Rivera	.906	13	9	20	3	1
Tejada	.983	27	10	47	1	3
Torreyes	1.000	1	1	2	0	0
Vierling	.938	11	1	29	2	2
Williams	1.000	9	5	12	0	1

Shortstop

	PCT	G	PO	A	E	DP
Brito	1.000	2	2	3	0	0
Chatham	.972	26	24	46	2	9
Elmore	1.000	1	0	1	0	0
Galvis	1.000	2	0	2	0	0
Gamboa	.959	14	13	34	2	6
Gozzo	1.000	1	1	1	0	1
Gregorius	.958	7	7	16	1	2
Guthrie	.951	16	19	39	3	9
Kingery	.900	4	2	7	1	0
Maton	1.000	38	39	73	0	19
Stott	1.000	10	9	16	0	4
Tejada	.977	19	20	22	1	5
Torreyes	1.000	3	5	7	0	3
Williams	1.000	4	4	5	0	3

Outfield

	PCT	G	PO	A	E	DP
Bonifacio	.967	33	56	3	2	1
Cordell	.975	41	77	1	2	0
Elmore	1.000	3	9	0	0	0
Gamboa	1.000	6	5	0	0	0
Guthrie	1.000	7	6	0	0	0
Haseley	1.000	38	75	0	0	0
Herrera	1.000	2	7	1	0	0
Jankowski	1.000	17	11	3	0	0
Joyce	.600	2	3	0	2	0
Kingery	1.000	5	13	0	0	0
Listi	1.000	5	8	0	0	0
Maton	1.000	2	1	0	0	0
Moniak	.989	94	175	4	2	0
Muzziotti	1.000	8	17	0	0	0
Quinn	1.000	2	4	1	0	0
Randolph	.951	42	77	1	4	0
Stephen	1.000	2	3	0	0	0
Tilson	.991	51	104	1	1	0
Torreyes	1.000	3	2	0	0	0
Vierling	1.000	40	78	2	0	0
Williams	1.000	1	1	0	0	0
Williams	1.000	11	22	2	0	0

READING FIGHTIN PHILS — DOUBLE-A

DOUBLE-A NORTHEAST

Batting	B-T	HT	WT	DOB	AVG	vLH	vRH	G	AB	R	H	2B	3B	HR	RBI	BB	HBP	SH	SF	SO	SB	CS	SLG	OBP
Bonifacio, Jorge	R-R	6-1	220	6-4-93	.251	.300	.237	49	171	31	43	13	0	12	41	24	1	0	2	41	1	0	.538	.343
Brito, Daniel	L-R	6-1	170	1-23-98	.296	.259	.307	63	247	37	73	14	4	6	22	23	3	2	0	46	3	3	.457	.363
Cedeno, Jose	L-L	6-2	168	3-19-01	--	--	--	1	0	0	0	0	0	0	0	0	1	0	0	0	0	0	--	1.000
Conley, Jack	R-R	6-1	190	1-16-97	.155	.097	.173	44	142	20	22	5	1	4	12	16	1	2	0	46	1	0	.289	.245
Cornelius, Chris	R-R	6-0	186	9-4-97	.220	.241	.210	26	91	11	20	5	1	5	3	0	1	0	23	0	1	.308	.245
Cumana, Grenny	R-R	5-5	145	11-10-95	.259	.289	.248	42	147	18	38	5	0	2	18	12	3	0	0	16	0	0	.333	.327
Duran, Rodolfo	R-R	5-9	181	2-19-98	.193	.238	.183	31	114	10	22	7	0	5	10	5	0	0	0	24	0	0	.386	.227
Fitch, Colby	L-R	5-11	215	7-27-95	.176	.194	.169	39	102	14	18	6	2	2	5	28	2	0	0	42	5	0	.333	.364
Gamboa, Arquimedes	B-R	6-0	190	9-23-97	.230	.222	.233	68	230	33	53	12	0	8	26	40	0	0	1	69	6	0	.387	.343
Gonzalez, Oscar	R-R	6-0	184	11-21-00	.294	.500	.182	6	17	1	5	0	0	0	1	0	0	0	0	8	0	0	.294	.333
Gozzo, Sal	B-R	6-0	196	3-29-98	.119	.071	.143	17	42	7	5	1	0	0	1	4	0	0	0	17	0	0	.143	.196
Guthrie, Dalton	R-R	5-11	160	12-23-95	.242	.270	.234	47	165	17	40	4	2	4	15	15	3	1	0	41	3	2	.364	.317
Hearn, Hunter	R-R	6-2	205	10-30-96	.162	.143	.174	12	37	3	6	1	0	0	0	6	0	0	0	9	1	0	.189	.279
Joyce, Matt	L-R	6-2	194	8-3-84	.250	.333	.222	5	12	1	3	0	0	1	3	3	1	0	1	4	0	0	.500	.412
Kroon, Matt	R-R	6-1	195	12-5-96	.301	.308	.298	45	163	19	49	6	3	5	22	13	3	1	1	45	6	4	.466	.361
Landon, Logan	R-R	6-2	180	2-17-93	.198	.235	.188	26	81	4	16	4	0	1	9	3	1	0	1	24	1	0	.284	.233
Marchan, Rafael	B-R	5-9	170	2-25-99	.200	--	.200	1	5	1	1	1	0	0	0	0	0	0	0	1	0	0	.400	.200
Matera, Nick	R-R	6-2	215	8-29-96	.208	.316	.170	21	72	12	15	2	0	5	9	11	0	0	0	23	0	0	.444	.313
Miller, Luke	R-R	6-2	192	7-17-96	.213	.309	.182	88	277	35	59	15	0	13	39	21	6	0	3	97	0	0	.408	.280
Muzziotti, Simon	L-L	6-1	175	12-27-98	.313	--	.313	4	16	1	5	2	0	0	1	0	1	0	2	0	0	0	.438	.353
Ortiz, Jhailyn	R-R	6-3	215	11-18-98	.208	.143	.245	21	77	7	16	1	0	4	6	9	2	0	0	27	0	0	.377	.307
O'Hoppe, Logan	R-R	6-2	185	2-9-00	.296	.222	.311	13	54	6	16	1	0	3	7	1	2	0	0	9	0	0	.481	.333
Stassi, Brock	L-L	6-1	190	8-7-89	.169	.167	.169	25	71	8	12	0	0	2	8	20	0	1	0	10	0	0	.254	.348
Stephen, Josh	L-L	6-0	185	9-22-97	.208	.121	.231	97	317	34	66	15	2	8	44	42	5	0	3	87	5	3	.344	.305
Stokes, Madison	R-R	6-2	200	4-25-96	.240	.259	.233	94	342	41	82	21	2	11	40	31	3	0	3	104	2	2	.406	.306
Stott, Bryson	L-R	6-3	200	10-6-97	.301	.271	.313	80	312	49	94	22	2	10	36	35	0	4	2	78	6	2	.481	.368
Tatum, McCarthy	R-R	6-2	210	5-15-96	.181	.152	.190	59	193	20	35	8	1	7	19	15	7	0	3	74	3	2	.342	.261
Vierling, Matt	R-R	6-3	205	9-16-96	.345	.333	.349	24	87	16	30	6	1	6	16	12	1	0	2	18	5	1	.644	.422
Williams, Corbin	R-R	6-2	170	1-19-98	.000	.000	.000	1	2	0	0	0	0	0	0	1	0	0	0	2	1	0	.000	.333

Pitching	B-T	HT	WT	DOB	W	L	ERA	G	GS	CG	SV	IP	H	R	ER	HR	BB	SO	AVG	vLH	vRH	K/9	BB/9
Appel, Mark	R-R	6-5	220	7-15-91	0	1	5.84	8	6	0	0	25	28	16	16	4	15	24	.292	.306	.283	8.76	5.47
Armenta, Erubiel	L-L	6-3	189	3-11-00	1	0	0.00	1	0	0	0	2	1	0	0	0	1	2	.143	.000	.200	9.00	4.50
Brown, Andrew	R-R	6-1	180	10-24-97	0	0	12.38	5	0	0	0	8	17	16	11	4	4	8	.395	.500	.263	9.00	4.50
Brown, Blake	R-R	6-1	195	8-18-98	0	0	0.00	1	0	0	0	1	0	0	0	0	2	1	.000	.000	.000	9.00	18.00
Carr, Tyler	R-R	5-10	175	5-1-96	1	0	5.61	33	0	0	0	51	57	34	32	8	22	44	.291	.313	.274	7.71	3.86
Cesar, Joel	R-R	5-11	191	1-26-96	0	1	10.29	6	0	0	0	7	7	8	8	2	8	7	.250	.250	.250	9.00	10.29
Crouse, Hans	L-R	6-4	180	9-15-98	2	2	2.73	6	6	0	0	30	24	9	9	3	12	38	.222	.255	.189	11.53	3.64
Dohy, Kyle	L-L	6-2	202	9-17-96	4	0	2.17	26	0	0	2	37	17	9	9	2	16	56	.135	.229	.099	13.50	3.86
Dominguez, Seranthony	R-R	6-1	225	11-25-94	1	0	14.40	4	0	0	0	5	8	8	8	4	3	3	.333	.200	.429	5.40	5.40
Eastman, Colton	R-R	6-3	185	8-22-96	0	3	3.55	11	7	0	0	33	24	15	13	4	16	34	.198	.200	.197	9.27	4.36
Eflin, Zach	R-R	6-6	220	4-8-94	0	0	0.00	1	1	0	0	2	1	0	0	0	2	3	.125	.333	.000	11.57	0.00
Evanko, Ethan	L-L	6-4	195	1-6-99	0	0	0.00	2	0	0	0	2	1	0	0	0	1	2	.143	.167	.000	9.00	4.50
Garcia, Julian	L-R	6-3	206	5-13-95	0	4	10.69	6	4	0	0	16	32	24	19	5	4	17	.405	.432	.371	9.56	2.25
Glogoski, Kyle	R-R	6-2	183	1-6-99	0	2	8.03	5	3	0	0	12	17	13	11	5	13	15	.327	.238	.387	10.95	9.49

Name	B-T	HT	WT	DOB	W	L	ERA	G	GS	CG	SV	IP	H	R	ER	HR	BB	SO	AVG	vLH	vRH		
Hendrickson, Josh	L-L	6-4	215	9-18-97	4	3	3.64	14	11	0	0	72	63	29	29	12	21	63	.240	.256	.234	7.91	2.64
Hennigan, Jonathan	L-L	6-4	193	8-27-94	0	3	7.04	32	0	0	0	38	45	33	30	3	27	41	.287	.192	.333	9.63	6.34
Hernandez, Jakob	L-L	6-4	260	5-19-96	1	1	4.50	15	0	0	4	20	18	11	10	3	5	33	.237	.156	.295	14.85	2.25
Lackney, Nick	L-L	6-4	210	6-5-97	3	1	3.74	19	0	0	0	34	25	16	14	4	24	27	.214	.233	.203	7.22	6.42
Lehman, Taylor	L-L	6-8	240	12-30-95	1	0	3.52	5	3	0	0	15	14	7	6	0	11	20	.241	.263	.231	11.74	6.46
Leverett, Adam	L-R	6-4	190	9-19-98	2	5	5.50	8	8	0	0	36	38	24	22	6	13	36	.273	.234	.293	9.00	3.25
Lindow, Ethan	R-L	6-3	180	10-15-98	0	2	6.11	6	5	0	0	18	19	12	12	5	11	23	.268	.226	.300	11.72	5.60
Marconi, Brian	R-L	6-3	175	5-9-97	1	2	2.27	34	0	0	15	44	31	12	11	5	21	56	.200	.180	.210	11.54	4.33
McArthur, James	R-R	6-7	230	12-11-96	2	6	4.48	19	15	0	0	74	74	41	37	9	23	78	.258	.223	.287	9.44	2.78
Mezquita, Jhordany	L-L	6-1	185	1-30-98	0	0	3.00	1	1	0	0	3	4	1	1	0	2	4	.333	.250	.500	12.00	6.00
Morales, Francisco	R-R	6-4	185	10-27-99	4	13	6.94	22	20	0	0	83	76	72	64	11	60	110	.240	.242	.238	11.93	6.51
Parkinson, David	R-L	6-2	210	12-14-95	0	0	0.00	1	0	0	1	3	0	0	0	0	0	5	.000	.000	.000	15.00	0.00
Paulino, David	R-R	6-6	240	2-6-94	1	0	1.50	1	1	0	0	6	3	2	1	1	2	5	.150	.200	.100	7.50	3.00
Perkins, Jack	R-R	6-4	200	8-6-97	3	2	4.25	12	11	0	0	59	62	29	28	10	20	52	.268	.222	.293	7.89	3.03
Phillips, Tyler	R-R	6-5	225	10-27-97	0	0	6.35	4	4	0	0	11	12	9	8	2	3	11	.267	.263	.269	8.74	2.38
Potter, Mark	R-R	6-6	284	11-12-97	0	1	14.73	4	0	0	0	4	6	7	6	1	6	6	.375	.455	.200	14.73	14.73
Reyes, Carlo	R-R	6-0	212	7-4-98	1	1	2.53	8	0	0	0	11	14	9	3	3	4	9	.292	.294	.290	7.59	3.38
Ross, Austin	R-R	6-1	185	8-16-94	7	2	5.58	27	0	0	0	40	34	26	25	6	27	49	.230	.258	.209	10.93	6.02
Santos, Victor	R-R	6-1	191	7-12-00	1	1	3.05	4	4	0	0	21	17	7	7	2	4	15	.227	.154	.306	6.53	1.74
2-team total (10 Portland)					5	3	2.73	14	12	1	0	66	60	22	20	7	10	60	.236	.179	.285	8.18	1.36
Skirrow, Noah	R-R	6-3	215	7-21-98	1	3	5.70	7	3	0	0	24	29	17	15	5	9	18	.284	.250	.303	6.85	3.42
Sullivan, Billy	R-R	6-2	195	4-16-99	1	1	3.00	15	0	0	2	18	12	8	6	0	10	27	.190	.125	.231	13.50	5.00
Warren, Zach	L-L	6-5	205	6-9-96	1	2	2.64	37	0	0	3	44	28	17	13	5	34	70	.177	.250	.142	14.21	6.90
Zabala, Aneurys	R-R	6-3	259	12-21-96	1	2	7.52	19	0	0	0	26	28	24	22	5	11	43	.269	.209	.311	14.70	3.76
Zarbnisky, Braden	L-R	6-2	191	12-26-96	4	1	3.26	19	0	0	5	30	21	12	11	6	5	33	.189	.167	.206	9.79	1.48

Fielding

Catcher	PCT	G	PO	A	E	DP	PB
Conley	.990	40	366	28	4	3	4
Duran	.993	28	254	24	2	2	4
Fitch	.982	18	153	15	3	1	5
Gonzalez	1.000	1	11	1	0	0	0
Marchan	1.000	1	8	0	0	0	0
Matera	.988	16	162	7	2	1	1
O'Hoppe	1.000	11	121	6	0	0	0

First Base	PCT	G	PO	A	E	DP
Kroon	1.000	6	44	4	0	3
Miller	.972	57	313	32	10	33
Stassi	.987	22	142	9	2	14
Stokes	.992	35	238	21	2	22
Tatum	1.000	5	26	1	0	1

Second Base	PCT	G	PO	A	E	DP
Brito	.973	58	86	129	6	32
Cornelius	.978	25	32	55	2	14
Gamboa	1.000	5	4	9	0	4
Gozzo	.929	4	4	9	1	3
Guthrie	.950	8	8	11	1	2
Stokes	.978	12	22	23	1	6
Stott	.950	4	8	11	1	3

Third Base	PCT	G	PO	A	E	DP
Brito	.900	3	6	3	1	0
Gamboa	.950	9	5	14	1	1
Gozzo	.875	8	5	9	2	1
Guthrie	1.000	15	10	17	0	3
Kroon	.857	5	1	5	1	1
Miller	1.000	2	1	2	0	1
Stokes	.946	25	17	36	3	5
Stott	1.000	5	4	15	0	3
Tatum	.960	47	29	68	4	6

Shortstop	PCT	G	PO	A	E	DP
Brito	1.000	2	1	5	0	1
Gamboa	.962	27	51	75	5	13
Gozzo	1.000	1	2	2	0	1
Guthrie	.933	12	18	24	3	8
Stokes	.875	3	4	3	1	1
Stott	.979	71	91	147	5	25

Outfield	PCT	G	PO	A	E	DP
Bonifacio	.988	45	76	3	1	0
Cumana	.984	35	59	2	1	0
Fitch	1.000	4	7	0	0	0
Gamboa	1.000	23	49	1	0	0
Guthrie	1.000	13	25	2	0	2
Hearn	1.000	12	15	1	0	0
Joyce	.909	4	10	0	1	0
Kroon	.963	35	49	3	2	0
Landon	1.000	24	38	1	0	0
Miller	1.000	1	1	0	0	0
Muzziotti	1.000	4	5	0	0	0
Ortiz	.962	20	49	1	2	0
Stassi	1.000	2	6	0	0	0
Stephen	.985	82	128	2	2	0
Stokes	1.000	23	39	5	0	0
Tatum	1.000	4	5	0	0	0
Vierling	1.000	25	40	4	0	1
Williams	1.000	1	1	0	0	0

JERSEY SHORE BLUECLAWS   HIGH CLASS A

HIGH-A EAST

Batting	B-T	HT	WT	DOB	AVG	vLH	vRH	G	AB	R	H	2B	3B	HR	RBI	BB	HBP	SH	SF	SO	SB	CS	SLG	OBP
Cornelius, Chris	R-R	6-0	186	9-4-97	.263	.000	.303	13	38	3	10	0	1	0	4	2	2	0	2	14	0	0	.316	.318
De La Cruz, Carlos	R-R	6-8	210	10-6-99	.242	.154	.265	17	62	10	15	4	0	3	14	5	0	0	1	23	0	0	.452	.294
Fassnacht, Nate	R-R	5-11	180	1-5-98	.207	.250	.198	69	227	41	47	10	3	6	28	44	1	0	0	110	7	4	.357	.338
Francisco, Freddy	R-R	5-11	180	2-7-01	.500	--	.500	1	4	0	2	0	0	0	0	0	0	0	0	1	0	0	.500	.500
Friscia, Vito	R-R	5-9	225	12-19-96	.265	.305	.253	76	257	32	68	14	2	7	40	45	5	0	5	88	3	0	.416	.378
Garcia, Luis	B-R	5-11	170	10-1-00	.224	.333	.218	16	58	6	13	2	0	2	8	10	0	1	1	19	4	0	.362	.333
Gonzalez, Oscar	R-R	6-0	184	11-21-00	.000	.000	.000	1	4	0	0	0	0	0	1	1	0	0	0	1	0	0	.000	.200
Gozzo, Jake	R-R	6-0	196	3-29-98	.154	.200	.143	7	26	1	4	0	0	0	3	1	0	0	0	5	0	0	.154	.185
Greenwalt, Keaton	R-R	6-3	175	11-23-97	.172	.103	.185	62	186	12	32	4	0	2	11	22	3	0	0	65	9	1	.226	.270
Guzman, Jonathan	R-R	6-0	156	8-17-99	.185	.143	.193	105	379	42	70	9	5	6	25	29	1	5	3	108	17	5	.282	.243
Haseley, Adam	L-L	6-1	190	4-12-96	.281	.667	.192	8	32	7	9	1	0	1	4	5	0	0	1	5	0	0	.406	.368
Hearn, Hunter	R-R	6-2	205	10-30-96	.106	.143	.096	30	94	7	10	4	0	2	7	9	2	0	2	43	1	1	.213	.196
Iser, Herbert	L-R	6-3	210	12-14-97	.177	.152	.181	68	232	18	41	11	2	5	31	13	3	0	5	80	0	0	.306	.225
Kroon, Matt	R-R	6-1	195	12-5-96	.235	.000	.308	4	17	2	4	2	0	0	0	1	0	0	0	5	0	0	.353	.278
Markwardt, Hunter	L-L	6-1	185	8-22-97	.236	.226	.238	55	195	33	46	3	4	3	19	18	4	6	1	66	17	1	.338	.312
Martin, Casey	R-R	5-11	175	4-7-99	.136	.273	.102	29	110	15	15	4	0	1	7	13	1	1	1	52	2	4	.200	.232
Matera, Nick	R-R	6-2	215	8-29-96	.196	.200	.194	13	46	8	9	1	0	2	7	5	1	0	0	19	0	0	.348	.288
Muzziotti, Simon	L-L	6-1	175	12-27-98	.412	--	.412	4	17	7	7	1	0	0	3	2	0	0	0	2	0	0	.471	.474
Ortiz, Jhailyn	R-R	6-3	215	11-18-98	.262	.250	.265	74	263	52	69	11	0	19	48	29	10	0	6	86	4	1	.521	.358
O'Hoppe, Logan	R-R	6-2	185	2-9-00	.270	.352	.254	85	318	43	86	17	2	13	48	30	4	0	6	63	6	3	.459	.335
Pelletier, Ben	R-R	6-2	190	8-22-98	.200	.000	.219	12	35	5	7	0	1	2	6	3	2	0	0	14	0	0	.429	.300

Name	B-T	HT	WT	DOB	AVG	vLH	vRH	G	AB	R	H	2B	3B	HR	RBI	BB	HBP	SH	SF	SO	SB	CS	SLG	OBP
Pichardo, Kervin	R-R	6-0	180	10-15-01	.000	.000	--	1	2	0	0	0	0	0	0	1	0	0	0	2	0	0	.000	.333
Rojas, Johan	R-R	6-1	165	8-14-00	.344	.500	.333	17	64	16	22	3	1	3	11	7	2	0	1	8	8	3	.563	.419
Rott, Rudy	L-R	6-0	212	9-7-96	.221	.200	.224	23	77	4	17	5	1	0	12	9	2	0	0	19	3	1	.312	.318
Stewart, D.J.	R-R	6-2	205	2-2-99	.245	.227	.249	77	290	34	71	10	3	11	42	24	4	0	4	66	5	1	.414	.307
Stobbe, Cole	R-R	6-2	194	8-30-97	.122	.240	.102	56	172	20	21	5	0	5	16	19	7	1	3	89	6	1	.238	.234
Stott, Bryson	L-R	6-3	200	10-6-97	.288	.286	.288	22	73	18	21	4	0	5	10	22	0	0	0	22	3	2	.548	.453
Tatum, McCarthy	R-R	6-6	210	5-15-96	.201	.250	.194	43	159	15	32	5	0	4	15	17	5	0	2	52	1	0	.308	.295
Torres, Nicolas	R-R	5-10	155	9-23-99	.388	.429	.382	27	103	18	40	4	1	0	14	7	1	2	1	18	5	0	.447	.429
Tortolero, Jose	R-R	5-11	154	12-31-99	.203	.308	.190	40	118	16	24	2	0	2	10	13	2	3	2	33	4	1	.271	.289
Williams, Corbin	R-R	6-2	170	1-19-98	.171	.222	.161	34	105	13	18	2	0	1	3	9	2	3	0	45	18	1	.219	.250

Pitching

Name	B-T	HT	WT	DOB	W	L	ERA	G	GS	CG	SV	IP	H	R	ER	HR	BB	SO	AVG	vLH	vRH	K/9	BB/9
Adams, Mike	R-R	5-11	175	9-7-94	1	1	7.59	14	0	0	0	11	14	10	9	0	9	13	.298	.263	.321	10.97	7.59
Anderson, Aidan	R-R	6-1	195	6-21-97	2	1	4.91	27	0	0	5	48	39	29	26	14	23	43	.223	.275	.189	8.12	4.34
Armenta, Erubiel	L-L	6-3	189	3-11-00	0	0	3.14	11	0	0	2	14	11	6	5	1	11	30	.204	.385	.146	18.84	6.91
Brown, Andrew	R-R	6-1	180	10-24-97	3	2	2.60	19	0	0	0	35	23	12	10	2	20	46	.183	.172	.191	11.94	5.19
Brown, Ben	R-R	6-6	210	9-9-99	0	0	7.50	4	2	0	0	12	12	10	10	2	7	14	.261	.188	.300	10.50	5.25
Brown, Blake	R-R	6-1	195	8-18-98	2	1	3.15	33	0	0	8	40	22	16	14	2	34	58	.158	.143	.171	13.05	7.65
Burch, Tyler	R-R	6-2	190	9-2-97	1	0	2.45	8	0	0	4	11	7	4	3	1	2	18	.179	.313	.087	14.73	1.64
2-team total (3 Aberdeen)					2	0	3.00	11	0	0	4	15	12	8	5	2	3	24	.214	.300	.167	14.40	1.80
De La Cruz, Jonas	R-R	6-3	175	1-1-98	1	1	8.69	11	0	0	0	20	26	19	19	6	18	19	.321	.414	.269	8.69	8.24
Dominguez, Seranthony	R-R	6-1	225	11-25-94	0	0	0.00	3	3	0	0	3	1	0	0	0	1	4	.111	.167	.000	12.00	3.00
Francisco, Carlos A	R-R	6-4	220	7-2-99	2	0	6.14	11	0	0	0	15	13	10	10	2	8	17	.224	.400	.132	10.43	4.91
Garcia, Julian	L-R	6-3	206	5-13-95	1	1	6.75	1	1	0	0	4	5	3	3	0	2	3	.313	1.000	.267	6.75	4.50
Gowdy, Kevin	R-R	6-4	170	11-16-97	4	5	4.43	14	12	0	0	61	68	34	30	5	15	63	.280	.328	.234	9.30	2.21
2-team total (6 Hickory)				6	6	4.20	20	16	0	0	90	98	48	42	9	25	89	.275	.324	.231	8.90	2.50		
Hendrickson, Josh	L-L	6-4	215	9-18-97	0	1	2.75	6	3	0	0	20	12	6	6	3	5	27	.174	.200	.163	12.36	2.29
Hughes, Jonathan	R-R	6-2	196	1-8-97	4	8	5.92	23	13	0	1	73	90	54	48	5	37	57	.307	.319	.297	7.03	4.56
Lackney, Nick	R-R	6-4	210	6-5-97	1	0	0.90	6	0	0	1	10	7	1	1	0	8	12	.179	.222	.143	10.80	7.20
Leverett, Adam	L-R	6-4	190	9-19-98	1	1	1.56	11	7	0	0	40	22	7	7	0	15	46	.159	.143	.176	10.26	3.35
Lindow, Ethan	R-L	6-3	180	10-15-98	3	6	3.21	12	10	1	0	67	65	25	24	11	11	59	.260	.310	.235	7.89	1.47
Lopez, Victor	R-R	6-4	192	9-2-99	0	0	2.92	6	0	0	0	12	8	4	4	1	6	8	.186	.071	.241	5.84	4.38
Marconi, Brian	R-L	6-3	175	5-9-97	0	0	0.00	3	0	0	0	6	2	0	0	0	4	9	.118	.000	.200	14.29	6.35
McArthur, James	R-R	6-7	230	12-11-96	0	0	0.00	1	0	0	1	4	1	0	0	0	1	5	.077	.000	.100	11.25	2.25
McGarry, Griff	R-R	6-2	190	6-8-99	1	0	2.70	3	3	0	0	13	7	4	4	0	7	21	.152	.000	.179	14.18	4.73
McKay, Tyler	R-R	6-6	180	8-18-97	2	4	4.76	13	9	0	0	45	42	32	24	3	22	31	.253	.200	.283	6.15	4.37
Mezquita, Jhordany	L-L	6-1	185	1-30-98	4	8	6.09	21	16	0	0	75	75	51	51	8	46	79	.262	.296	.249	9.44	5.50
Miller, Erik	L-L	6-5	240	2-13-98	0	0	0.00	1	1	0	0	3	3	0	0	0	3	4	.231	.000	.300	10.80	8.10
Perkins, Jack	R-R	6-4	200	8-6-97	0	1	5.51	5	3	0	0	16	17	10	10	2	3	16	.262	.333	.211	8.82	1.65
Phillips, Tyler	R-R	6-5	225	10-27-97	0	0	0.00	1	1	0	0	3	2	0	0	0	1	1	.200	.000	.250	3.00	3.00
Pipkin, Dominic	R-R	6-4	160	11-5-99	4	3	4.97	16	12	0	0	58	58	34	32	6	27	64	.264	.283	.248	9.93	4.19
Potter, Mark	R-R	6-4	284	11-12-97	2	2	8.13	28	0	0	3	34	45	35	31	10	18	48	.313	.304	.318	12.58	4.72
Reyes, Carlo	R-R	6-0	212	7-4-98	5	2	3.00	19	3	0	0	39	27	16	13	4	15	60	.188	.132	.220	13.85	3.46
Santos, Victor	R-R	6-1	191	7-12-00	2	1	1.33	9	1	0	1	20	17	7	3	2	5	25	.221	.175	.270	11.07	2.21
Silva, Manuel	L-L	6-2	145	12-9-98	1	0	3.24	19	2	0	3	42	32	19	15	5	21	39	.209	.068	.266	8.42	4.54
Skirrow, Noah	R-R	6-3	215	7-21-98	0	2	3.73	9	6	0	0	31	26	14	13	2	16	40	.224	.214	.230	11.49	4.60
Sullivan, Billy	R-R	6-2	195	4-16-99	0	0	1.59	5	0	0	0	6	1	1	1	1	3	8	.059	.000	.077	12.71	4.76
Sutera, Tom	L-R	6-5	190	5-29-97	4	3	5.89	16	2	0	0	37	47	26	24	5	11	23	.313	.232	.362	5.65	2.70
Vargas, Victor	R-R	6-1	175	9-3-00	3	4	10.47	8	8	0	0	33	48	39	38	7	17	31	.350	.321	.369	8.54	4.68
Wilson, Riley	L-L	6-0	180	8-2-96	0	1	15.63	5	0	0	0	6	13	12	11	1	5	9	.394	.364	.409	12.79	7.11
Woodward, J.P.	L-L	6-6	215	11-13-98	0	0	4.00	13	0	0	1	18	23	18	8	3	9	17	.299	.222	.322	8.50	4.50
Yanez, Gabriel	L-L	6-3	168	7-22-99	1	0	3.38	6	0	0	1	5	3	5	3	0	4	6	.200	.000	.273	10.13	4.50
Zabala, Aneurys	R-R	6-3	259	12-21-96	2	3	5.51	14	0	0	3	16	14	12	10	3	6	20	.237	.238	.237	11.02	3.31
Zarbnisky, Braden	L-R	6-2	191	12-26-96	1	1	1.69	3	0	0	5	6	1	1	1	3	7	.286	.500	.200	11.81	5.06	

Fielding

Catcher	PCT	G	PO	A	E	DP	PB
Francisco	1.000	1	8	0	0	0	0
Friscia	.967	4	28	1	1	0	2
Gonzalez	1.000	1	3	1	0	0	0
Iser	.993	43	379	29	3	1	12
Matera	.991	11	110	2	1	0	1
O'Hoppe	.992	60	587	35	5	2	8

First Base	PCT	G	PO	A	E	DP
Fassnacht	1.000	1	7	0	0	0
Friscia	.992	34	233	9	2	25
Iser	1.000	12	72	3	0	14
Rott	1.000	18	125	9	0	14
Stewart	.983	49	328	18	6	36
Stobbe	1.000	3	26	1	0	0
Tatum	1.000	4	28	1	0	4

Second Base	PCT	G	PO	A	E	DP
Cornelius	1.000	3	5	9	0	3
Fassnacht	.966	14	21	36	2	10
Garcia	.952	4	12	8	1	3
Gozzo	1.000	1	2	3	0	0
Guzman	.987	37	58	95	2	16
Martin	.933	10	23	19	3	9
Stobbe	.980	13	20	30	1	8
Stott	1.000	6	7	19	0	4
Torres	1.000	8	8	16	0	5
Tortolero	.954	25	44	60	5	11

Third Base	PCT	G	PO	A	E	DP
Cornelius	.929	9	3	10	1	1
Fassnacht	.940	37	13	50	4	1
Gozzo	.875	5	2	5	1	1
Guzman	.944	4	5	12	1	0
Pichardo	1.000	1	1	4	0	0
Stewart	.942	26	23	42	4	8
Tatum	.965	27	11	44	2	2
Torres	1.000	4	1	9	0	0
Tortolero	.810	11	8	9	4	0

Shortstop	PCT	G	PO	A	E	DP
Cornelius	1.000	1	2	2	0	1
Fassnacht	1.000	1	4	2	0	1
Garcia	.974	11	10	27	1	4
Gozzo	1.000	1	2	5	0	0
Guzman	.986	62	81	134	3	38
Martin	.953	19	30	52	4	12
Stott	.962	16	19	31	2	5
Torres	.920	5	13	10	2	4
Tortolero	.818	4	5	2	2	

Outfield	PCT	G	PO	A	E	DP
De La Cruz	.957	14	22	0	1	0
Fassnacht	.970	15	30	2	1	0
Greenwalt	.976	56	78	3	2	1
Haseley	1.000	7	23	0	0	0
Hearn	1.000	25	33	2	0	0

Kroon	.889	4	6	2	1	0	Pelletier	1.000	10	10	0	0	0	Torres	1.000	11	36	0	0	0
Markwardt	.969	54	92	2	3	0	Rojas	1.000	17	45	1	0	0							
Muzziotti	1.000	3	7	0	0	0	Stobbe	.984	40	62	1	1	0							
Ortiz	.958	70	112	3	5	2	Tatum	1.000	11	22	0	0	0	Williams	.972	34	66	4	2	1

CLEARWATER THRESHERS
LOW-A SOUTHEAST

LOW CLASS A

Batting	B-T	HT	WT	DOB	AVG	vLH	vRH	G	AB	R	H	2B	3B	HR	RBI	BB	HBP	SH	SF	SO	SB	CS	SLG	OBP
Aparicio, Juan	R-R	5-11	175	5-26-01	.213	.292	.200	54	169	25	36	3	1	6	21	21	5	0	2	43	0	0	.349	.315
Baylor, Jamari	R-R	5-11	190	8-25-00	.214	.455	.156	15	56	5	12	1	0	0	5	1	2	0	0	27	1	0	.232	.254
Burke, Chris	L-R	5-11	180	8-16-01	.217	.188	.233	14	46	7	10	4	0	0	4	5	0	0	0	16	2	1	.304	.294
Carr, Jared	L-R	6-1	180	5-24-99	.277	.313	.271	32	101	18	28	4	1	4	17	17	3	0	2	32	7	3	.455	.390
Cerny, Logan	R-R	6-1	185	9-28-99	.133	.000	.200	5	15	1	2	0	0	0	0	2	0	0	0	4	0	1	.133	.235
De Freitas, Arturo	R-R	6-0	170	5-28-01	.176	.500	.156	13	34	2	6	0	0	0	2	1	3	0	0	9	0	0	.176	.263
De La Cruz, Carlos	R-R	6-8	210	10-6-99	.148	.214	.139	37	122	10	18	5	0	2	11	13	4	0	0	56	2	0	.238	.252
Dipre, Guarner	R-R	6-0	160	10-26-00	.067	.000	.069	9	30	4	2	0	0	0	1	3	0	0	0	12	0	0	.067	.152
Edwards, Mitchell	B-R	5-11	200	8-1-99	.250	.000	.286	3	8	0	2	0	0	0	1	2	0	0	0	3	0	0	.250	.455
Flores, Wilfredo	L-R	5-10	170	5-14-00	.417	--	.417	5	12	1	5	1	0	0	1	0	0	0	0	3	0	1	.500	.417
Francisco, Freddy	R-R	5-11	180	2-7-01	.143	.000	.167	4	14	1	2	2	0	0	2	1	0	0	0	4	0	0	.286	.200
Garcia, Luis	B-R	5-11	170	10-1-00	.246	.298	.238	87	333	57	82	16	5	11	42	54	4	2	2	93	11	6	.423	.356
Garcia, Yhoswar	R-R	6-0	150	9-13-01	.229	.375	.210	18	70	7	16	1	1	0	8	6	1	0	0	23	11	2	.271	.299
Gutierrez, Abrahan	R-R	6-0	214	10-31-99	.288	.269	.291	50	177	30	51	10	0	5	32	37	4	0	1	31	0	0	.429	.420
2-team total (22 Bradenton)					.290	.354	.274	72	245	46	71	18	2	5	36	53	7	0	1	44	0	0	.441	.428
Iser, Herbert	R-R	6-3	210	12-14-97	.000	--	.000	1	3	0	0	0	0	0	0	0	0	0	0	1	0	0	.000	.000
Joyce, Matt	L-R	6-2	194	8-3-84	.313	.500	.286	7	16	2	5	1	0	0	3	5	0	0	1	2	0	0	.375	.455
Lee Sang, Marcus	L-L	6-0	200	1-2-01	.212	.000	.233	11	33	0	7	1	0	0	5	4	0	0	0	11	0	0	.242	.297
Made, Edgar	B-R	5-10	145	12-15-99	.136	.059	.151	38	103	12	14	4	0	1	9	15	1	0	3	31	3	0	.204	.246
Markwardt, Hunter	L-L	6-1	185	8-22-97	.313	.333	.308	5	16	2	5	1	0	0	2	3	1	0	0	5	2	1	.375	.450
Martin, Casey	R-R	5-11	175	4-7-99	.223	.222	.224	69	264	33	59	17	0	6	35	28	8	0	1	68	15	3	.356	.316
Matera, Nick	R-R	6-2	215	8-29-96	.263	.250	.267	5	19	5	5	2	0	1	4	0	1	0	0	4	0	0	.526	.300
Minyety, Freylin	R-R	5-10	185	10-22-99	.286	.105	.338	28	84	17	24	1	0	3	13	14	6	0	0	23	3	2	.405	.423
Muzziotti, Simon	L-L	6-1	175	12-27-98	.300	.500	.250	3	10	1	3	0	1	0	1	1	0	0	0	2	0	1	.500	.364
Ortega, Junior	R-R	5-11	175	9-30-99	.000	--	.000	4	10	0	0	0	0	0	0	1	0	0	0	8	0	0	.000	.083
Pelletier, Ben	R-R	6-2	190	8-22-98	.190	.111	.207	31	105	12	20	6	0	3	10	7	0	0	0	41	0	1	.333	.241
Pichardo, Kervin	R-R	6-0	180	10-15-01	.146	.000	.176	19	41	9	6	2	0	1	8	19	0	0	0	18	2	1	.268	.417
Radcliff, Baron	L-R	6-4	228	2-9-99	.189	.200	.187	86	254	50	48	8	0	11	39	70	3	0	3	112	3	3	.350	.367
Reyes, Felix	R-R	6-4	195	3-26-01	.206	.182	.209	30	97	12	20	4	1	1	7	7	5	0	0	27	6	2	.299	.294
Rojas, Johan	R-R	6-1	165	8-14-00	.240	.213	.244	78	313	51	75	15	3	7	38	26	5	4	3	69	25	6	.374	.305
Rumfield, T.J.	L-R	6-5	225	5-17-00	.250	.100	.273	27	76	13	19	1	0	0	7	21	3	0	1	11	0	0	.263	.426
Sanchez, Jadiel	B-R	6-2	185	5-10-01	.297	.214	.317	21	74	13	22	3	1	2	6	8	1	0	0	14	0	2	.446	.373
Simmons, Logan	R-R	6-2	180	4-11-00	.226	.056	.252	41	137	20	31	10	2	6	15	13	6	0	0	38	4	2	.460	.321
Stewart, D.J.	R-R	6-2	205	2-2-99	.353	.467	.321	17	68	9	24	3	0	3	21	6	1	0	0	13	1	1	.529	.413
Torres, Nicolas	R-R	5-10	155	9-23-99	.239	.360	.224	69	226	32	54	8	2	4	27	35	0	1	0	69	10	4	.345	.341
Tortolero, Jose	R-R	5-11	154	12-31-99	.243	.000	.273	13	37	1	9	1	0	0	4	6	2	1	0	8	0	0	.270	.378
Viloria, Uziel	B-R	5-9	155	10-6-01	.071	.250	.042	10	28	3	2	0	0	0	0	6	1	0	0	13	0	0	.071	.257
Williams, Corbin	R-R	6-2	170	1-19-98	.214	.000	.333	5	14	2	3	1	0	0	1	0	1	0	0	7	0	1	.286	.267
Wilson, Ethan	L-L	6-1	210	11-7-99	.215	.188	.220	30	107	15	23	4	2	3	17	10	0	0	2	25	2	2	.374	.282
Wingrove, Rixon	L-R	6-5	260	5-23-00	.206	.065	.232	79	287	29	59	13	1	11	37	25	7	0	2	98	1	0	.373	.283
Yonamine, Micah	R-R	6-4	210	10-10-00	.211	.286	.194	16	38	6	8	1	0	0	5	18	0	2	0	6	0	0	.237	.464

Pitching	B-T	HT	WT	DOB	W	L	ERA	G	GS	CG	SV	IP	H	R	ER	HR	BB	SO	AVG	vLH	vRH	K/9	BB/9
Abel, Mick	R-R	6-5	190	8-18-01	1	3	4.43	14	14	0	0	45	27	23	22	5	27	66	.174	.101	.233	13.30	5.44
Adams, Tyler	L-L	6-1	203	3-17-98	1	3	7.48	19	0	0	0	22	19	21	18	1	33	29	.229	.231	.228	12.05	13.71
Aldegheri, Samuel	L-L	6-1	180	9-19-01	0	1	2.92	5	2	0	0	12	9	4	4	0	7	18	.200	.167	.205	13.14	5.11
Anderson, Aidan	R-R	6-1	195	6-21-97	1	0	1.69	4	0	0	0	5	2	1	1	0	1	2	.118	.286	.000	3.38	1.69
Antonac, Yoan	R-R	6-9	183	7-27-00	0	1	19.29	3	0	0	0	2	5	6	5	0	4	2	.417	.250	.500	7.71	15.43
Aponte, Leonel	R-R	6-4	144	7-2-99	1	2	5.96	14	0	0	0	23	24	17	15	2	13	23	.261	.259	.262	9.13	5.16
Armenta, Erubiel	L-L	6-3	189	3-11-01	2	0	0.00	4	0	0	1	7	3	0	0	0	4	17	.125	.500	.091	22.95	5.40
Ash, Konnor	R-R	5-11	191	3-17-99	3	0	3.48	6	1	0	0	10	7	4	4	1	7	8	.206	.125	.231	6.97	6.10
Baker, Andrew	R-R	6-3	190	3-24-00	1	2	11.70	7	1	0	0	10	4	14	13	1	17	16	.118	.125	.115	14.40	15.30
Bell, Brendan	R-R	5-11	175	3-11-00	1	5	5.50	18	0	0	0	18	21	14	11	1	18	20	.280	.250	.298	10.00	9.00
Burch, Tyler	R-R	6-2	190	9-2-97	3	3	4.91	15	0	0	3	18	17	12	10	4	6	31	.239	.212	.263	15.22	2.95
Castaneda, Dylan	R-R	6-2	190	7-16-01	2	4	9.92	11	3	0	0	33	38	40	36	9	28	36	.288	.346	.250	9.92	7.71
Castillo, Starlyn	R-R	6-0	210	2-24-02	0	2	4.35	6	3	0	0	21	17	10	10	1	10	20	.218	.289	.150	8.71	4.35
Cotto, Gabriel	L-L	6-5	175	5-15-00	2	3	4.11	8	6	0	0	35	31	18	16	4	18	38	.238	.077	.256	9.77	4.63
Francisco, Carlos A	R-R	6-4	220	7-2-99	1	0	2.84	14	0	0	3	13	8	6	4	2	7	18	.178	.192	.158	12.79	4.97
Garbrick, Alex	R-R	6-1	210	6-4-98	0	1	9.49	4	1	0	0	12	16	14	13	1	9	13	.333	.400	.316	9.49	6.57
Garrido, Maikel	L-L	6-4	175	1-24-00	2	0	5.48	14	0	0	0	23	30	18	14	3	20	29	.303	.217	.329	11.35	7.83
Gherbaz, Wilson	R-R	6-2	145	9-30-00	0	0	9.00	1	0	0	0	1	1	1	1	0	2	1	.250	1.000	.000	9.00	18.00
Hernandez, Cristian	R-R	6-3	180	9-23-00	2	7	3.69	18	15	0	0	71	62	31	29	11	29	86	.235	.170	.278	10.95	3.69
Hsu, Chi-Ling	R-R	6-2	202	8-9-99	1	1	3.38	2	0	0	0	5	6	2	2	0	0	2	.286	.500	.263	3.38	0.00
Jacobsak, Sam	R-R	6-5	200	6-11-98	1	0	4.91	2	0	0	0	4	3	2	2	0	4	9	.300	.200	.400	7.36	17.18
Jefferson, DJ	R-R	6-5	185	1-9-01	0	1	14.73	1	0	0	0	4	5	6	6	3	2	3	.313	.667	.100	7.36	4.91
Kuznetsov, Anton	R-L	6-1	185	5-26-98	0	0	2.79	5	0	0	0	10	11	3	3	1	4	8	.289	.167	.346	7.45	3.72

Name	B-T	HT	WT	DOB	W	L	ERA	G	GS	CG	SV	IP	H	R	ER	HR	BB	SO	AVG	vLH	vRH	H/9	BB/9
Lackney, Nick	L-L	6-4	210	6-5-97	0	0	0.00	6	0	0	0	7	6	0	0	0	3	5	.240	.167	.263	6.43	3.86
Lin, Hsin-Chieh	R-R	6-2	198	3-18-99	0	3	7.20	8	4	0	0	20	21	20	16	3	19	28	.269	.240	.283	12.60	8.55
Lopez, Victor	R-R	6-4	192	9-2-99	0	1	3.72	6	0	0	1	10	11	5	4	0	3	15	.275	.385	.222	13.97	2.79
Lozano, Fernando	R-R	6-2	186	1-11-00	3	2	2.60	17	6	0	0	52	36	22	15	6	21	51	.188	.213	.171	8.83	3.63
Made, Alejandro	R-R	6-4	190	12-29-97	1	2	11.25	10	0	0	0	12	14	22	15	2	17	10	.269	.321	.208	7.50	12.75
Made, Edgar	B-R	5-10	145	12-15-99	0	0	0.00	1	0	0	0	0	0	0	0	0	2	0	.000	.000	--	0.00	54.00
Marcano, Rafael	L-L	6-1	170	4-20-00	1	3	3.76	17	8	0	0	53	53	26	22	4	27	67	.259	.250	.261	11.45	4.61
Martinez, Jordi	L-L	6-2	185	7-18-00	3	0	2.53	10	6	0	0	32	25	10	9	2	11	34	.212	.237	.200	9.56	3.09
Mayer, Gunner	R-R	6-6	190	7-27-00	0	7	10.03	11	7	0	0	23	31	32	26	5	22	33	.320	.357	.304	12.73	8.49
McCollum, Tommy	R-R	6-5	260	6-8-99	0	0	6.39	9	0	0	1	13	9	9	9	1	16	15	.196	.125	.211	10.66	11.37
McGarry, Griff	R-R	6-2	190	6-8-99	0	0	3.27	5	1	0	1	11	6	4	4	0	7	22	.154	.077	.192	18.00	5.73
McGowan, Christian	R-R	6-3	205	3-7-00	0	0	0.00	3	0	0	0	4	2	0	0	0	1	5	.154	1.000	.083	11.25	2.25
McKenney, Alex	R-R	6-3	245	5-11-99	2	1	1.56	9	1	0	0	17	10	7	3	0	10	17	.172	.214	.159	8.83	5.19
Miller, Erik	L-L	6-5	240	2-13-98	0	0	3.18	2	2	0	0	6	4	5	2	0	5	10	.190	.000	.286	15.88	7.94
Osterberg, Matt	L-L	6-2	200	4-21-99	2	1	1.83	7	3	0	1	20	13	5	4	1	8	21	.194	.200	.193	9.61	3.66
Reyes, Carlo	R-R	6-0	212	7-4-98	1	0	0.00	8	0	0	1	10	5	0	0	0	4	13	.147	.133	.158	11.32	3.48
Ruffcorn, Jason	R-R	6-2	215	7-21-98	0	0	5.84	12	0	0	3	12	12	8	8	1	7	13	.240	.267	.229	9.49	5.11
Russell, Matt	R-R	6-2	190	3-28-99	2	2	3.06	9	1	0	0	18	17	7	6	1	4	22	.243	.444	.173	11.21	2.04
Sanchez, Rodolfo	R-R	5-10	165	1-12-00	1	3	4.67	18	8	0	0	54	40	31	28	6	27	73	.198	.163	.221	12.17	4.50
Segovia, Eduar	R-R	6-0	180	1-10-01	3	5	5.58	17	10	0	1	50	40	36	31	8	31	67	.215	.192	.230	12.06	5.58
Soriano, Christopher	L-L	6-1	160	9-17-01	0	0	8.38	4	2	0	0	10	12	9	9	2	6	6	.308	.286	.313	5.59	5.59
Van Scoyoc, Spencer	L-L	6-4	200	10-4-97	0	0	4.26	3	3	0	0	6	3	3	3	0	7	11	.143	--	.143	15.63	9.95
Vargas, Victor	R-R	6-1	175	9-3-00	4	1	3.62	13	6	0	2	50	49	27	20	4	12	54	.254	.253	.255	9.79	2.17
Velasquez, Vince	R-R	6-3	212	6-7-92	1	0	2.57	4	2	0	0	7	4	2	2	1	1	12	.160	.375	.059	15.43	1.29
Wetherbee, Jared	R-R	5-10	203	8-14-98	1	0	1.08	8	0	0	3	8	1	1	1	0	4	6	.038	.250	.000	16.20	4.32
Woodward, J.P.	L-L	6-6	215	11-13-98	1	0	2.08	14	0	0	0	17	10	5	4	1	6	18	.169	.136	.189	9.35	3.12
Wynne, Cam	R-R	6-6	220	1-11-99	0	0	6.75	7	0	0	1	9	12	15	7	1	9	10	.293	.429	.222	9.64	8.68
Yanez, Gabriel	L-L	6-3	168	7-22-99	5	0	2.14	22	0	0	1	34	33	12	8	5	14	46	.252	.182	.276	12.30	3.74

Fielding

Catcher	PCT	G	PO	A	E	DP	PB
Aparicio	.983	40	362	38	7	2	1
Burke	.986	14	127	9	2	0	1
De Freitas	.983	13	106	12	2	0	2
Edwards	1.000	1	14	0	0	0	0
Francisco	1.000	1	9	0	0	0	0
Gutierrez	.994	39	423	41	3	3	4
Iser	1.000	1	7	0	0	0	1
Matera	1.000	5	49	5	0	0	4
Yonamine	1.000	6	45	1	0	0	0

First Base	PCT	G	PO	A	E	DP
Aparicio	1.000	6	30	1	0	2
Made	1.000	2	8	0	0	3
Pichardo	1.000	3	13	1	0	0
Reyes	1.000	4	18	1	0	0
Rumfield	.993	19	130	4	1	11
Stewart	1.000	10	56	4	0	7
Torres	1.000	1	3	0	0	0
Wingrove	.981	69	450	25	9	39
Yonamine	.980	8	45	3	1	1

Second Base	PCT	G	PO	A	E	DP
Baylor	1.000	8	20	21	0	4
Dipre	1.000	2	3	4	0	2

	PCT	G	PO	A	E	DP
Flores	1.000	1	2	3	0	0
Garcia	.948	30	53	56	6	9
Made	.920	12	22	24	4	11
Martin	.991	25	52	58	1	15
Minyety	.870	7	10	10	3	4
Simmons	1.000	12	9	20	0	2
Torres	.957	15	19	26	2	3
Tortolero	.857	3	4	2	1	1
Viloria	1.000	4	10	4	0	3

Third Base	PCT	G	PO	A	E	DP
Dipre	.700	6	3	4	3	0
Flores	.667	2	1	1	1	0
Made	.737	15	3	11	5	1
Minyety	.839	19	7	19	5	1
Pichardo	.958	16	6	40	2	5
Simmons	.852	22	13	33	8	1
Stewart	1.000	7	6	9	0	1
Torres	.865	23	15	17	5	1
Tortolero	1.000	9	7	9	0	0
Viloria	1.000	6	1	10	0	1

Shortstop	PCT	G	PO	A	E	DP
Baylor	.913	7	8	13	2	1
Dipre	.857	1	3	3	1	0

	PCT	G	PO	A	E	DP
Garcia	.919	57	57	114	15	26
Martin	.942	43	53	94	9	16
Simmons	.833	6	6	9	3	2
Torres	.933	5	7	7	1	3

Outfield	PCT	G	PO	A	E	DP
Carr	1.000	30	49	2	0	0
Cerny	1.000	5	6	0	0	0
De La Cruz	.984	34	61	0	1	0
Flores	1.000	1	1	0	0	0
Garcia	.962	18	23	2	1	1
Joyce	1.000	5	6	1	0	1
Lee Sang	1.000	7	14	0	0	0
Made	1.000	2	1	0	0	0
Markwardt	1.000	5	4	0	0	0
Muzziotti	1.000	3	8	0	0	0
Ortega	1.000	4	3	0	0	0
Pelletier	.949	23	35	2	2	0
Radcliff	.973	62	69	3	2	0
Reyes	.929	19	24	2	2	0
Rojas	.978	77	173	5	4	2
Sanchez	1.000	22	40	1	0	0
Torres	1.000	27	37	1	0	0
Williams	.750	3	3	0	1	0
Wilson	1.000	22	26	0	0	0

FCL PHILLIES
FLORIDA COMPLEX LEAGUE

ROOKIE

Batting	B-T	HT	WT	DOB	AVG	vLH	vRH	G	AB	R	H	2B	3B	HR	RBI	BB	HBP	SH	SF	SO	SB	CS	SLG	OBP
Azuaje, Alexeis	R-R	5-10	155	4-24-02	.400	.400	.400	19	45	17	18	6	0	5	16	4	6	1	0	5	4	0	.867	.509
Barboza, Edward	R-R	5-11	175	4-2-01	.292	.000	.333	9	24	4	7	3	2	0	1	3	0	0	1	7	2	0	.583	.370
Baylor, Jamari	R-R	5-11	190	8-25-00	.303	.077	.342	25	89	24	27	8	1	5	16	18	3	0	0	33	11	5	.584	.436
Burke, Chris	L-R	5-11	180	8-16-01	.357	.500	.346	13	28	3	10	1	0	0	1	3	0	0		5	4	1	.393	.419
Cedeno, Jose	L-L	6-2	168	3-19-01	.100	.000	.115	14	30	7	3	2	0	0	3	6	1	0	1	13	2	0	.167	.263
Cerny, Logan	R-R	6-1	185	9-8-99	.250	.400	.200	8	20	6	5	1	1	0	2	6	0	0	0	8	6	1	.400	.423
Chatham, C.J.	R-R	6-4	185	12-22-94	.286	.000	.333	2	7	1	2	0	0	0	1	0	0	0	0	0	0	0	.286	.250
Cornelius, Chris	R-R	6-0	186	9-4-97	.400	.000	.500	2	5	2	2	0	0	0	1	0	0	0	0	0	0	0	.400	.400
Cumana, Grenny	R-R	5-5	145	11-10-95	.000	.000	.000	4	9	0	0	0	0	0	1	1	1	0	0	0	1	0	.000	.182
De Freitas, Arturo	R-R	5-10	190	5-28-01	.250	.000	.333	8	20	5	5	0	0	0	3	1	0	0		3	1	0	.400	.318
De La Cruz, Carlos	R-R	6-8	210	10-6-99	.200	.000	.222	9	20	3	4	0	0	0	1	8	2	0	0	8	3	0	.200	.467
Dipre, Guarner	R-R	6-0	160	10-26-00	.132	.000	.147	23	38	8	5	0	1	0	8	1	0	1	0	17	0	2	.184	.292
Edwards, Mitchell	B-R	5-11	200	8-1-99	.344	.000	.370	11	32	5	11	3	0	0	4	2	0	0	1	7	0	0	.438	.371
Fitch, Colby	L-R	5-11	215	7-27-95	.167	--	.167	2	6	0	1	0	0	0	1	0	0	0		3	1	0	.167	.286
Flores, Wilfredo	L-R	5-10	170	5-14-00	.222	.000	.261	12	27	6	6	0	0	2	6	2	1	0	0	5	1	0	.444	.300

	B-T	HT	WT	DOB	AVG	vLH	vRH	G	AB	R	H	2B	3B	HR	RBI	BB	HBP	SH	SF	SO	SB	CS	SLG	OBP
Francisco, Freddy	R-R	5-11	180	2-7-01	.103	.000	.125	17	29	2	3	2	0	0	1	4	1	0	1	10	0	1	.172	.229
Gonzalez, Oscar	R-R	6-0	184	11-21-00	.194	.333	.179	20	31	6	6	1	0	0	4	5	1	0	0	8	0	0	.226	.324
Goodheart, Matt	L-R	6-1	185	12-10-98	.381	.000	.444	8	21	5	8	1	0	0	2	2	1	0	0	4	1	1	.429	.458
Guthrie, Dalton	R-R	5-11	160	12-23-95	.143	--	.143	3	7	2	1	0	0	1	2	1	0	0	0	1	0	0	.571	.250
Haseley, Adam	L-L	6-1	190	4-12-96	.222	.000	.235	7	18	5	4	1	0	1	3	7	0	0	0	4	0	0	.444	.440
Herrera, Juan	R-R	6-3	165	12-14-99	.357	.000	.385	9	14	3	5	1	0	0	5	3	0	0	0	6	1	0	.429	.471
Jerez, Albert	R-R	6-2	165	5-18-01	.143	.333	.091	15	28	6	4	1	0	0	8	5	2	0	0	9	3	0	.179	.314
Kroon, Matt	R-R	6-1	195	12-5-96	.154	--	.154	4	13	1	2	1	0	0	1	2	1	0	0	2	1	1	.231	.313
Lee Sang, Marcus	L-L	6-0	200	1-2-01	.273	.222	.286	26	88	18	24	6	1	5	17	7	1	0	0	25	11	3	.534	.333
Made, Edgar	B-R	5-10	145	12-15-99	.182	.400	.143	17	33	10	6	1	0	1	5	12	1	0	1	8	3	1	.303	.404
Markwardt, Hunter	L-L	6-1	185	8-22-97	.364	--	.364	5	11	5	4	0	0	1	2	0	2	0	1	3	1	0	.636	.429
Matera, Nick	R-R	6-2	215	8-29-96	.667	.000	1.000	1	3	2	2	0	0	1	1	1	0	0	0	0	0	0	1.667	.750
Mejia, Adony	R-R	5-11	170	6-9-01	.200	.000	.250	4	5	2	1	0	0	0	1	0	2	0	0	0	0	0	.200	.429
Muzziotti, Simon	L-L	6-1	175	12-27-98	.333	--	.333	1	3	1	1	1	0	0	0	0	0	0	0	0	0	0	.667	.333
Nava, Andrick	B-R	5-11	175	10-6-01	.333	.000	.400	3	6	2	1	0	0	0	0	0	0	0	0	4	0	0	.500	.333
Ortega, Junior	R-R	5-11	175	9-30-99	.233	.500	.205	20	43	10	10	1	1	1	7	5	5	0	1	12	3	0	.372	.370
Pelletier, Ben	R-R	6-2	190	8-22-98	.529	--	.529	7	17	5	9	4	0	1	6	4	1	0	1	3	0	0	.941	.609
Pichardo, Kervin	R-R	6-0	180	10-15-01	.400	.500	.385	15	30	11	12	4	2	1	8	4	0	0	1	10	0	0	.767	.571
Pineda, Leandro	L-L	6-1	165	6-4-02	.130	.077	.143	33	69	14	9	3	0	1	9	20	2	0	2	23	3	1	.217	.333
Quirion, Anthony	R-R	6-2	205	10-29-97	.313	.000	.385	11	16	5	5	0	1	2	5	3	1	0	0	3	1	0	.813	.450
Radcliff, Baron	L-R	6-4	228	2-9-99	.667	--	.667	1	3	2	2	0	0	2	0	3	1	0	0	0	0	0	2.667	.750
Randolph, Cornelius	L-R	5-11	205	6-2-97	.308	.000	.333	5	13	3	4	1	0	0	3	4	0	0	1	5	1	0	.385	.444
Reyes, Felix	R-R	6-4	195	3-26-01	.294	.333	.286	7	17	4	5	1	0	2	9	1	2	0	0	2	0	1	.706	.400
Rojas, Johan	R-R	6-1	165	8-14-00	.750	--	.750	1	4	2	3	0	0	1	3	0	0	0	0	0	1	0	1.500	.750
Sanchez, Jadiel	B-R	6-2	185	5-10-01	.217	.167	.235	7	23	2	5	0	0	0	4	3	0	0	1	5	1	0	.217	.296
Simmons, Logan	R-R	6-2	180	4-11-00	.200	.000	.286	5	10	1	2	1	0	0	1	3	1	0	0	3	3	0	.300	.429
Stassi, Brock	L-L	6-1	190	8-7-89	.333	.000	.500	1	3	1	1	0	0	0	0	0	0	0	0	0	0	0	.333	.333
Tonkel, Gavin	R-R	6-2	180	11-6-02	.261	.000	.286	11	23	5	6	1	0	0	2	4	3	0	1	8	2	1	.304	.419
Valdez, Wilson	R-R	6-2	168	10-25-99	.227	.000	.263	31	44	5	10	1	2	0	4	3	0	0	1	8	0	3	.341	.327
Valerio, Christian	R-R	6-1	155	2-27-00	.000	.000	.000	6	10	1	0	0	0	0	0	2	0	0	0	4	0	0	.000	.167
Viars, Jordan	L-L	6-4	215	7-18-03	.255	.429	.225	22	47	13	12	1	0	3	18	11	3	0	3	12	2	0	.468	.406
Viloria, Uziel	B-R	5-9	155	10-6-01	.205	.400	.138	22	39	6	8	2	0	0	7	10	0	0	0	13	3	1	.256	.367
Wingrove, Rixon	L-R	6-5	260	5-23-00	.158	.000	.200	7	19	3	3	0	0	0	2	5	1	0	0	6	1	0	.158	.360
Yonamine, Micah	R-R	6-4	210	10-10-00	.200	--	.200	5	10	2	2	0	0	2	0	3	2	1	0	0	1	0	.400	.385
Yu Lee, Hao	R-R	5-10	190	2-3-03	.364	.333	.368	9	22	9	8	2	2	1	5	3	0	0	0	5	0	0	.773	.440

Pitching	B-T	HT	WT	DOB	W	L	ERA	G	GS	CG	SV	IP	H	R	ER	HR	BB	SO	AVG	vLH	vRH	K/9	BB/9
Adams, Tyler	L-L	6-1	203	3-17-98	0	1	4.35	5	0	0	0	10	10	8	5	0	4	15	.256	.143	.281	13.06	3.48
Aldegheri, Samuel	L-L	6-1	180	9-19-01	1	0	2.08	3	1	0	0	9	8	3	2	0	3	14	.235	.167	.250	14.54	3.12
Antonac, Yoan	R-R	6-9	183	7-27-00	0	0	5.40	12	0	0	0	17	18	13	10	1	7	16	.273	.222	.292	8.64	3.78
Aponte, Leonel	R-R	6-4	144	7-2-99	0	0	0.00	4	0	0	1	3	2	0	0	0	2	1	.200	--	.200	3.38	6.75
Ash, Konnor	R-R	5-11	191	3-17-99	0	0	4.50	3	1	0	1	4	4	3	2	1	1	6	.235	.143	.300	13.50	2.25
Baker, Andrew	R-R	6-3	190	3-24-00	0	0	0.00	3	0	0	0	2	1	0	0	0	0	4	.143	.000	.167	18.00	0.00
Bell, Brendan	R-R	5-11	175	3-11-00	2	0	3.55	4	1	0	1	13	8	5	5	3	4	12	.167	.091	.189	8.53	2.84
Betancourt, Carlos	R-R	6-1	160	3-27-01	0	0	6.00	3	0	0	0	3	2	2	2	0	2	3	.222	1.000	.125	9.00	6.00
Binns, Malik	R-R	6-7	240	1-5-99	0	0	0.00	2	2	0	0	3	1	0	0	0	1	1	.111	.500	.000	3.00	3.00
Brown, Ben	R-R	6-6	210	9-9-99	1	0	2.25	3	0	0	0	4	2	1	1	0	1	3	.143	.000	.200	6.75	2.25
Castaneda, Dylan	R-R	6-2	190	7-16-01	1	0	5.06	3	1	0	0	11	11	7	6	1	4	14	.250	.100	.294	11.81	3.38
Collins, Ty	L-R	6-3	165	8-29-01	1	0	10.80	4	0	0	0	3	3	5	4	1	8	5	.231	.200	.250	13.50	21.60
Cotto, Gabriel	L-L	6-5	175	5-15-00	2	0	0.00	4	1	0	0	11	8	0	0	0	12	18	.205	.500	.171	14.29	9.53
De La Cruz, Jonas	R-R	6-3	175	1-1-98	0	1	10.50	4	1	0	0	6	11	9	7	1	3	11	.355	.286	.375	16.50	4.50
Fowler, Jordan	L-L	6-3	180	3-9-99	1	0	3.38	7	1	0	0	8	8	3	3	1	1	4	.242	.500	.207	4.50	1.13
Francisco, Carlos A	R-R	6-4	220	7-2-99	0	0	18.00	1	0	0	0	1	3	2	2	0	0	0	.750	.667	1.000	0.00	0.00
Garbrick, Alex	R-R	6-1	210	6-4-98	0	0	7.20	3	0	0	0	5	5	4	4	1	6	7	.238	.200	.250	12.60	10.80
Garcia, Julian	L-R	6-3	206	5-13-95	0	0	0.00	1	0	0	0	2	1	0	0	0	0	6	.143	.000	.200	27.00	0.00
Garnett, Tristan	L-L	6-6	240	3-29-98	1	3	6.57	7	0	0	0	12	21	9	9	2	6	14	.382	.222	.413	10.22	4.38
Garrido, Maikel	L-L	6-4	175	1-24-00	0	0	3.86	2	0	0	0	2	1	2	1	0	4	5	.091	.000	.100	19.29	15.43
Gessner, Josh	R-R	6-1	205	6-25-00	0	0	4.66	4	3	0	0	10	8	7	5	0	5	18	.216	.286	.200	16.76	4.66
Gherbaz, Wilson	R-R	6-2	145	9-30-00	4	1	5.93	8	0	0	0	14	9	10	9	2	14	6	.209	.455	.125	3.95	9.22
Glogoski, Kyle	R-R	6-2	183	1-6-99	0	0	3.60	4	0	0	0	5	7	2	2	1	3	4	.333	.250	.353	7.20	5.40
Hernandez, Cristian	R-R	6-3	180	9-23-00	0	0	1.80	2	2	0	0	5	2	1	1	0	1	8	.118	.333	.071	14.40	1.80
Hsu, Chi-Ling	R-R	6-2	202	8-9-99	0	1	4.85	7	0	3	0	13	17	8	7	0	2	12	.304	.200	.326	8.31	1.38
Jacobsak, Sam	R-R	6-5	200	6-11-98	0	0	0.00	4	0	0	0	8	7	1	0	0	2	8	.226	.500	.160	9.00	2.25
Jefferson, DJ	R-R	6-5	185	1-9-01	0	1	13.50	7	2	0	0	12	18	18	18	2	9	16	.353	.333	.357	12.00	6.75
Kuznetsov, Anton	R-L	6-1	185	5-26-98	0	0	0.00	1	0	0	0	2	0	0	0	0	2	1	.000	--	.000	3.86	7.71
Lin, Hsin-Chieh	R-R	6-2	198	4-30-99	1	0	9.00	1	0	0	0	4	6	4	4	3	0	2	.333	.000	.353	4.50	0.00
Lopez, Victor	R-R	6-4	192	9-2-99	0	0	0.00	5	0	0	1	6	3	0	0	0	4	4	.150	.400	.067	6.35	0.00
Lozano, Fernando	R-R	6-2	186	1-11-00	0	1	2.25	3	1	0	1	4	2	1	1	1	1	4	.143	.167	.167	9.00	2.25
Marcano, Rafael	L-L	6-1	170	4-20-00	2	0	2.08	3	0	0	0	4	2	1	1	1	0	5	.133	.000	.154	10.38	0.00
Mayer, Gunner	R-R	6-6	190	7-27-00	0	0	0.00	1	1	0	0	3	0	0	0	0	0	5	.000	.000	.000	15.00	0.00
McAllister, Zach	R-R	6-6	240	12-8-87	0	0	0.00	2	2	0	0	2	2	0	0	0	0	2	.222	.200	.250	9.00	0.00
McGowan, Christian	R-R	6-3	205	3-7-00	0	0	0.00	1	0	0	0	1	0	0	0	0	0	3	.000	.000	.000	27.00	0.00
McKay, Ty	R-R	6-6	180	8-18-97	0	3	3.00	3	3	0	1	3	3	1	1	0	2	2	.273	.600	.000	6.00	6.00
McKenna, Jake	R-L	6-6	215	4-24-02	0	0	15.00	6	1	0	1	6	7	10	10	0	13	12	.280	.000	.304	18.00	19.50
Miller, Erik	L-L	6-5	240	2-13-98	0	0	0.00	2	2	0	0	4	1	0	0	0	3	2	.083	1.000	.000	4.91	7.36

Name	B-T	HT	WT	DOB	W	L	ERA	G	GS	CG	SV	IP	H	R	ER	HR	BB	SO	AVG	vLH	vRH	K/9	BB/9
Osterberg, Matt	L-L	6-2	200	4-21-99	0	0	0.00	1	0	0	0	1	0	0	0	0	1	3	.000	.000	.000	27.00	9.00
Ottenbreit, Micah	R-R	6-4	190	5-7-03	1	0	4.50	5	0	0	0	6	6	3	3	0	3	4	.273	.250	.278	6.00	4.50
Painter, Andrew	R-R	6-7	215	4-10-03	0	0	0.00	4	4	0	0	6	4	0	0	0	0	12	.190	.286	.143	18.00	0.00
Pena Jr., Jose	R-R	6-3	200	7-8-03	1	0	13.50	4	0	0	0	3	3	4	4	0	3	5	.273	.333	.250	16.88	10.13
Phelan, Corey	L-L	6-2	180	7-3-02	1	0	0.93	5	0	0	0	10	7	1	1	0	4	6	.219	.000	.241	5.59	3.72
Rosario, Dalvin	R-R	6-1	167	6-15-00	0	1	3.00	2	0	0	0	3	3	1	1	0	2	1	.273	.000	.333	3.00	6.00
Sanchez, Rodolfo	R-R	5-10	165	1-12-00	0	0	0.00	2	0	0	0	3	3	0	0	0	1	4	.273	.000	.300	12.00	3.00
Skirrow, Noah	R-R	6-3	215	7-21-98	0	0	0.00	2	1	0	0	3	1	0	0	0	2	6	.125	.500	.000	6.00	6.00
Smith, Jaylen	L-L	5-11	170	11-5-99	1	0	4.30	13	0	0	4	15	8	8	7	2	12	12	.151	.000	.174	7.36	7.36
Soriano, Christopher	L-L	6-1	160	9-17-01	1	1	9.00	5	0	0	0	7	7	9	7	0	10	7	.250	.333	.240	9.00	12.86
Sutera, Tom	L-R	6-5	190	5-29-97	0	2	9.00	3	2	0	0	6	11	8	6	2	1	7	.355	.400	.346	10.50	1.50
Tae Lee, Ji	R-R	6-2	240	1-12-01	1	0	22.50	3	0	0	0	2	5	5	5	0	6	1	.333	.000	.400	4.50	27.00
Ulloa, Jose	R-R	6-2	200	5-6-99	1	2	7.11	6	1	0	0	6	10	7	5	2	4	3	.333	.222	.381	4.26	5.68
Van Scoyoc, Spencer	L-L	6-4	200	10-4-97	0	0	0.00	4	4	0	0	6	1	0	0	0	4	9	.056	.000	.059	13.50	6.00
Wetherbee, Jared	R-R	5-10	203	8-14-98	0	0	0.00	2	0	0	0	3	2	2	0	0	2	4	.167	.000	.200	12.00	6.00
Wilson, Riley	L-L	6-0	180	8-2-96	0	0	0.00	3	0	0	0	3	1	0	0	0	0	6	.100	.000	.143	13.50	0.00
Woodward, J.P.	L-L	6-6	215	11-13-98	1	0	0.00	1	0	0	0	1	0	0	0	0	0	1	.000	.000	.000	9.00	0.00
Yanez, Gabriel	L-L	6-3	168	7-22-99	0	0	0.00	1	0	0	0	1	0	0	0	0	0	1	.000	.000	.000	9.00	0.00

Fielding

C: Barboza 4, Burke 8, De Freitas 6, Edwards 6, Fitch 2, Francisco 16, Gonzalez 10, Matera 1, Mejia 4, Nava 3, Quirion 11, Yonamine 5.
1B: Barboza 3, De Freitas 2, Gonzalez 10, Goodheart 6, Herrera 6, Jerez 6, Kroon 1, Made 8, Reyes 5, Viars 8, Wingrove 6.
2B: Azuaje 5, Baylor 8, Chatham 1, Cornelius 1, Cumana 2, Dipre 6, Flores 5, Guthrie 1, Jerez 1, Pichardo 2, Valdez 6, Viloria 15, Yu Lee 8.
3B: Azuaje 4, Dipre 5, Flores 3, Herrera 2, Jerez 6, Made 6, Pichardo 13, Simmons 2, Valdez 13, Valerio 2, Viloria 6.
SS: Azuaje 9, Baylor 16, Chatham 1, Cornelius 1, Dipre 11, Guthrie 2, Jerez 2, Simmons 3, Valdez 10, Valerio 4, Viloria 1.
OF: Cedeno 13, Cerny 8, Cumana 2, De La Cruz 8, Flores 1, Haseley 7, Kroon 3, Lee Sang 25, Markwardt 5, Muzziotti 1, Ortega 17, Pelletier 7, Pineda 31, Radcliff 1, Randolph 4, Reyes 2, Rojas 1, Sanchez 7, Stassi 1, Tonkel 10, Viars 12.

DSL PHILLIES   ROOKIE
DOMINICAN SUMMER LEAGUE

Batting	B-T	HT	WT	DOB	AVG	vLH	vRH	G	AB	R	H	2B	3B	HR	RBI	BB	HBP	SH	SF	SO	SB	CS	SLG	OBP
Alderete, Alfredo	R-R	5-9	150	2-16-04	.244	.333	.238	19	45	9	11	2	1	0	6	6	1	0	0	6	5	3	.333	.346
Avila, Kliubert	R-R	5-10	170	5-19-03	.317	.250	.329	33	82	11	26	6	3	1	17	17	1	0	1	19	3	1	.500	.436
Barria, Erick	R-R	5-11	155	1-31-03	.216	.000	.242	17	37	7	8	2	0	0	2	9	1	1	1	12	2	1	.270	.375
Brito, Erick	R-R	5-10	134	5-25-02	.327	.367	.317	54	153	29	50	4	1	0	21	40	4	2	3	28	20	6	.366	.470
Cabrera, Deivi	R-R	0-0	0	1-26-04	.220	.091	.256	23	50	10	11	0	1	1	8	12	4	0	0	6	3	1	.320	.409
Colmenarez, Jose	R-R	5-9	160	11-24-02	.190	.000	.276	21	42	7	8	1	0	0	8	5	3	0	0	11	3	2	.214	.320
Corona, Jeury	R-R	5-11	140	9-7-01	.333	.300	.338	32	81	13	27	6	1	0	13	12	2	1	0	11	16	3	.432	.432
Escobar, Derek	B-R	5-11	170	1-28-02	.178	.333	.164	37	73	15	13	0	0	3	15	10	1	0	0	17	10	3	.178	.388
Flores, Yemal	R-R	5-11	206	11-22-03	.171	.136	.179	37	117	18	20	9	1	2	14	21	2	0	0	50	7	1	.316	.307
Garcia, Jorge	L-R	5-11	145	2-6-04	.308	.111	.412	9	26	8	3	3	0	0	4	6	0	0	0	5	2	0	.423	.438
Gil, Reiberth	R-R	6-0	165	4-9-02	.000	.000	.000	10	18	3	0	0	0	0	1	6	0	1	0	4	2	2	.000	.240
Gonzalez, Diego	R-R	5-11	160	6-7-03	.274	.200	.286	43	146	20	40	7	1	1	18	12	2	0	3	22	3	7	.356	.331
Graterol, Enyer	B-R	5-10	160	1-18-03	.120	.333	.053	13	25	3	3	0	1	0	0	3	0	1	0	9	0	0	.200	.214
Guevara, Jhorjan	R-R	6-2	160	5-19-02	.224	.158	.235	44	134	12	30	5	0	1	15	15	3	0	1	37	10	9	.284	.314
Heredia, Raylin	R-R	0-0	0	11-10-03	.500	--	.500	2	4	0	2	0	0	0	1	0	0	0	0	1	0	0	.500	.500
Hernandez, Fernando	R-R	5-11	165	3-30-03	.274	.444	.239	37	106	18	29	6	0	0	9	15	5	0	0	30	11	4	.330	.389
Heureaux, Julio	B-R	5-10	168	12-18-01	.219	.429	.193	21	64	6	14	3	1	0	4	5	0	0	1	15	1	1	.297	.271
Leanez, Jose	R-R	6-0	145	1-13-03	.306	.296	.308	52	144	30	44	6	2	0	10	16	6	1	0	30	11	10	.375	.398
Martinez, Jarol	R-R	6-2	150	7-19-03	.138	.083	.147	37	87	12	12	4	0	0	8	19	0	0	1	39	2	4	.184	.290
Mejia, Adony	R-R	5-10	170	6-9-01	.316	.333	.314	23	57	11	18	6	0	0	9	7	4	0	2	15	3	2	.421	.414
Mendez, Jorge	R-R	5-10	160	8-1-03	.219	.083	.250	29	64	7	14	3	0	0	6	9	6	0	0	6	3	1	.266	.367
Muller, Arquedion	R-R	5-10	170	6-19-04	.176	.222	.160	16	34	4	6	2	0	0	3	9	1	0	0	17	1	4	.235	.364
Perez, Rickardo	L-R	5-10	172	12-4-03	.256	.154	.269	43	121	15	31	3	0	0	9	22	1	0	2	15	3	1	.281	.370
Pertuz, Jackie	L-R	6-0	188	11-1-02	.262	.118	.284	44	126	14	33	7	0	0	20	12	5	0	0	22	2	2	.317	.350
Ramos, Yoangel	R-R	6-2	165	1-21-04	.183	.185	.183	44	131	18	24	2	1	1	9	8	5	0	1	39	7	2	.237	.255
Rodriguez, Albert	R-R	6-2	170	12-11-02	.238	.056	.277	35	101	11	24	9	1	0	19	14	4	0	1	26	11	2	.347	.350
Rodriguez, Solardo	R-R	5-11	170	11-24-03	.231	.278	.225	47	156	25	36	9	3	2	23	11	1	0	3	17	8	3	.365	.293
Rondon, Carlos	B-R	5-10	155	4-18-02	.267	.167	.286	30	75	17	20	5	0	0	11	8	1	0	0	14	6	2	.333	.345
Rondon, Leonardo	R-R	5-8	160	3-10-04	.208	.067	.246	30	72	14	15	0	2	0	6	7	2	3	1	11	6	2	.264	.293
Rosario, Ricardo	R-R	6-1	160	2-8-03	.235	.318	.221	49	162	28	38	6	3	1	24	18	5	0	6	31	12	3	.327	.319
Rosario, Yemil	R-R	5-10	150	4-12-04	.125	.111	.127	30	80	13	10	3	0	0	7	13	1	1	1	31	5	2	.163	.253
Sevilla, Jehisbert	R-R	5-11	149	3-21-03	.261	.214	.273	44	138	27	36	10	2	0	22	14	5	0	2	31	3	3	.362	.346
Silva, Brahian	R-R	5-11	170	12-30-00	.098	.100	.097	22	41	1	4	1	0	0	3	11	0	0	0	9	1	1	.122	.288
Soto, Marco	B-R	5-11	145	3-8-04	.174	.143	.177	23	69	14	12	2	0	0	2	8	4	2	0	16	4	0	.203	.296
Tirado, Gabriel	L-R	5-10	144	9-6-02	.245	.400	.229	21	53	8	13	2	0	0	4	10	2	0	1	17	7	3	.283	.379
Torres, Santiago	R-R	6-1	160	9-20-02	.203	.182	.207	46	143	14	29	5	1	1	13	10	2	3	1	37	5	6	.273	.263
Vasquez, Randy	R-R	6-0	170	12-16-02	.240	.188	.248	40	121	13	29	4	1	0	14	17	0	2	1	38	5	2	.289	.331
Vina, Javier	R-R	5-11	180	3-25-02	.143	.286	.119	20	49	5	7	2	0	0	3	5	4	1	0	23	3	1	.184	.276

Pitching	B-T	HT	WT	DOB	W	L	ERA	G	GS	CG	SV	IP	H	R	ER	HR	BB	SO	AVG	vLH	vRH	K/9	BB/9
Alcala, Saul	R-R	6-1	158	11-7-00	6	2	3.90	15	1	0	1	32	24	17	14	1	17	32	.209	.200	.213	8.91	4.73
Angulo, Joalbert	L-L	6-5	165	10-30-01	2	1	6.10	15	0	0	0	21	22	20	14	1	14	23	.262	.190	.286	10.02	6.10
Astudillo, Hermes	R-R	5-11	160	3-2-02	3	0	0.00	5	0	0	1	8	4	0	0	0	2	7	.160	.286	.111	7.88	2.25
Cabrera, Jean	R-R	6-0	145	10-20-01	3	2	1.54	13	13	0	0	53	34	13	9	1	10	61	.185	.254	.152	10.42	1.71

Castellano, Eiberson	R-R	6-3	160	5-9-01	2	1	1.09	16	1	0	3	33	17	7	4	1	16	36	.148	.162	.141	9.82	4.36
Estanista, Jaydenn	R-R	6-3	180	10-3-01	1	1	3.23	10	6	0	1	31	19	12	11	1	19	33	.188	.161	.200	9.68	5.58
Fuenmayor, Javier	R-R	6-2	170	1-20-03	3	4	3.47	15	9	0	1	49	48	26	19	1	15	37	.247	.214	.266	6.75	2.74
Garibaldi, Alexis	L-L	6-4	195	3-19-04	0	2	13.50	6	0	0	0	4	6	7	6	0	9	4	.353	.000	.375	9.00	20.25
Gomez, Luis	R-R	6-1	174	5-14-01	1	1	0.00	9	0	0	5	10	5	1	0	0	2	14	.139	.167	.125	12.19	1.74
Ibarra, Neyker	L-L	5-11	165	3-30-02	0	0	2.70	3	0	0	0	3	1	1	1	0	3	2	.111	.000	.125	5.40	8.10
Jimenez, Estibenzon	R-R	6-1	172	1-25-02	6	0	1.59	16	3	0	2	45	24	13	8	2	13	41	.154	.093	.186	8.14	2.58
Linares, Diego	R-R	6-2	180	9-29-02	2	2	4.34	11	0	0	0	19	17	9	9	1	8	17	.239	.278	.223	8.20	3.86
Loyo, Jared	L-L	6-4	175	1-14-03	1	2	6.75	12	0	0	0	13	17	19	10	0	14	9	.304	.556	.255	6.08	9.45
Medina, Oswald	R-R	6-0	145	12-2-01	2	2	2.16	14	14	0	0	58	48	20	14	4	6	65	.226	.194	.241	10.03	0.93
Mejia, Daniel	R-R	6-5	164	4-19-02	2	0	3.94	11	0	0	1	16	13	11	7	0	9	9	.210	.417	.160	5.06	5.06
Melendez, Juan	R-R	6-3	170	7-19-04	1	2	21.94	7	1	0	0	5	8	15	13	0	15	5	.348	.333	.357	8.44	25.31
Mijares, Douglas	R-R	6-3	165	4-27-00	8	2	2.58	17	0	0	1	38	28	16	11	3	16	38	.209	.167	.228	8.92	3.76
Millan, Carlos	R-R	6-2	160	7-19-03	1	0	5.06	9	1	0	0	16	16	9	9	0	8	17	.258	.375	.217	9.56	4.50
Ortega, Fernando	R-R	6-4	160	10-10-01	0	0	4.60	10	0	0	0	16	15	10	8	0	11	13	.246	.294	.227	7.47	6.32
Paz, Ender	R-R	6-1	170	3-26-04	0	0	3.38	9	0	0	0	11	9	5	4	0	16	13	.243	.250	.241	10.97	13.50
Petit, Jonathan	R-R	6-2	174	4-19-01	4	2	2.27	12	8	0	0	44	36	11	11	1	5	41	.226	.250	.217	8.45	1.03
Pulido, Danyony	R-R	6-1	165	10-19-02	3	2	5.46	14	0	0	1	28	18	21	17	0	25	31	.180	.240	.160	9.96	8.04
Querales, Jesus	R-R	6-0	175	2-18-03	2	2	1.38	19	0	0	8	26	25	8	4	0	5	31	.258	.265	.254	10.73	1.73
Ramirez, Ronny	L-L	5-10	160	11-3-02	1	2	6.23	11	0	0	0	13	13	12	9	1	10	12	.250	.167	.261	8.31	6.92
Reyes, Pedro	R-R	6-3	175	11-26-02	2	2	2.93	13	10	0	0	46	36	22	15	2	15	32	.213	.196	.221	6.26	2.93
Rivas, Jonathan	R-R	5-11	160	9-1-01	1	1	4.26	7	0	0	2	13	8	8	6	1	6	9	.170	.154	.176	6.39	4.26
Sanchez, Sergio	L-L	6-1	160	12-16-00	2	1	3.38	17	1	0	4	24	21	10	9	1	8	21	.233	.158	.254	7.88	3.00
Urias, Manuel	R-R	6-6	200	3-8-01	2	2	1.82	14	14	0	0	54	43	14	11	1	6	63	.211	.214	.209	10.44	0.99
Valdez, Joel	L-L	6-4	171	4-28-00	1	1	1.63	15	15	0	0	55	43	12	10	0	16	54	.218	.172	.226	8.78	2.60
Velasquez, Giussepe	R-R	6-1	170	4-30-03	1	2	2.75	14	14	0	0	52	50	25	16	3	19	56	.249	.246	.250	9.63	3.27
Ventura, Ezequiel	R-R	6-1	151	6-20-02	3	1	3.45	16	2	0	2	31	23	12	12	0	18	34	.207	.233	.198	9.77	5.17
Zuniga, Edgar	R-R	6-2	185	9-15-02	3	2	3.47	13	0	0	1	23	28	15	9	1	7	13	.311	.231	.344	5.01	2.70

Fielding

C: Avila 21, Colmenarez 20, Corona 1, Mejia 15, Mendez 24, Perez 35, Pertuz 30, Silva 10, Vina 3.

1B: Avila 10, Brito 17, Corona 7, Escobar 3, Heureaux 3, Martinez 16, Mejia 13, Mendez 4, Muller 6, Perez 5, Pertuz 1, Ramos 15, Rodriguez 13, Rondon 4, Rosario 5, Silva 2, Vina 3.

2B: Alderete 11, Barria 3, Brito 2, Cabrera 10, Escobar 1, Gonzalez 4, Graterol 11, Hernandez 9, Heureaux 13, Rondon 13, Rondon 19, Rosario 2, Sevilla 16, Soto 22, Vasquez 4.

3B: Alderete 3, Brito 21, Cabrera 2, Gonzalez 3, Hernandez 21, Martinez 12, Muller 3, Ramos 17, Rondon 5, Rondon 3, Rosario 7, Sevilla 7, Vasquez 23.

SS: Alderete 3, Barria 15, Brito 11, Cabrera 13, Gonzalez 36, Hernandez 8, Martinez 1, Ramos 4, Rondon 6, Rosario 13, Sevilla 20, Soto 2.

OF: Brito 10, Corona 25, Escobar 30, Flores 31, Garcia 8, Gil 7, Guevara 44, Heredia 2, Leanez 53, Rodriguez 35, Rodriguez 20, Rosario 50, Tirado 20, Torres 46.

Pittsburgh Pirates

SEASON IN A SENTENCE: Pittsburgh is in the doldrums of a rebuild, going 61-101 to finish last in the NL Central and 34 games out of first place.

HIGH POINT: OF Bryan Reynolds represented a rare bright spot. The 26-year-old outfielder was among the top players in the National League, finishing tied for fifth in fWAR (5.5) and wRC+ (142), while posting the best walk rate, strikeout rate, on-base percentage and slugging percentage of his career. Reynolds earned his first all-star appearance and is joined by third baseman Ke'Bryan Hayes as two building blocks for the Pirates to build around.

LOW POINT: Pittsburgh was just one game below .500 after April, but May and June were disastrous. The Pirates went 17-37 during a stretch punctuated by a 10-game losing streak in early June, their longest of the season.

NOTABLE ROOKIES: Righthander David Bednar quickly assumed high-leverage responsibilities, displaying a penchant for limiting hard contact by mixing his 97 mph fastball, curveball and splitter to great success. He struck out 32.5% of all hitters he faced and held them to a .189 expected batting average. Pittsburgh acquired Bednar, who grew up in nearby Mars, Pa., from the Padres in last winter's Joe Musgrove trade. He looks the part of a late-inning reliever for years to come. Hayes went on the injured list multiple times with a left wrist injury, and struggled in 96 games after an outstanding 2020 debut.

KEY TRANSACTIONS: Ben Cherington's month of July may end up being one of the fulcrum points of Pittsburgh's rebuild. He drafted catcher Henry Davis No. 1 overall and signed him to a deal $2 million below slot. The savings allowed the Pirates to draft and sign three premium high schoolers, walking away with four of the 32 best prospects in the 2021 draft class. Cherington then made a series of trades at the deadline, including dealing all-star second baseman Adam Frazier, that netted Pittsburgh nine more prospects to add to its system.

OPENING DAY PAYROLL: $35,905,000 (30th).

PLAYERS OF THE YEAR

MAJOR LEAGUE	MINOR LEAGUE
Bryan Reynolds	**Matt Fraizer**
OF	OF
.302/.390/.522	(AA/High-A)
Career-high 24 HR	.306/.388/.552,
MLB-leading 8 3B	23 HR, 15 SB

ORGANIZATION LEADERS

Batting		*Minimum 250 AB
MAJORS		
*AVG	Bryan Reynolds	.302
*OPS	Bryan Reynolds	.912
HR	Bryan Reynolds	24
RBI	Bryan Reynolds	90
MINORS		
*AVG	Oneil Cruz, Indianapolis, Altoona	.310
*OBP	Matt Fraizer, Altoona, Greensboro	.388
*SLG	Oneil Cruz, Indianapolis, Altoona	.594
*OPS	Oneil Cruz, Indianapolis, Altoona	.970
R	Matt Fraizer, Altoona, Greensboro	84
H	Matt Fraizer, Altoona, Greensboro	133
TB	Matt Fraizer, Altoona, Greensboro	240
2B	Mason Martin, Indianapolis, Altoona	29
2B	Jared Triolo, Greensboro	29
3B	Sergio Campana, Bradenton, FCL Pirates Gold	7
HR	Mason Martin, Indianapolis, Altoona	25
RBI	Mason Martin, Indianapolis, Altoona	81
BB	Hudson Head, Bradenton	68
SO	Mason Martin, Indianapolis, Altoona	171
SB	Lolo Sanchez, Greensboro	30

Pitching		#Minimum 75 IP
MAJORS		
W	Chris Stratton	7
#ERA	Chris Stratton	3.63
SO	JT Brubaker	129
SV	Chris Stratton	8
MINORS		
W	Bear Bellomy, Indianapolis, Greensboro	9
W	Steven Jennings, Altoona, Greensboro, Bradenton	9
L	Travis MacGregor, Altoona/ Beau Sulser, Indianapolis	9
#ERA	Adrian Florencio, Bradenton	2.46
G	Shea Spitzbarth, Indianapolis	42
GS	Beau Sulser, Indianapolis	24
SV	Enmanuel Mejia, Greensboro, Bradenton	9
SV	Cristofer Melendez, Altoona, Greensboro	9
SV	Austin Roberts, Indianapolis, Greensboro	9
IP	James Marvel, Indianapolis	131.2
BB	James Marvel, Indianapolis	54
SO	Adrian Florencio, Bradenton	117
#AVG	Logan Hofmann, Bradenton	.196

2021 PERFORMANCE

General Manager: Ben Cherington. **Farm Director:** John Baker. **Scouting Director:** Joe Delli Carri.

Class	Team	League	W	L	PCT	Finish	Manager
Majors	Pittsburgh Pirates	National	61	101	.377	14th (15)	Derek Shelton
Triple-A	Indianapolis Indians	Triple-A East	61	67	.477	t-11th (20)	Brian Esposito
Double-A	Altoona Curve	Double-A Northeast	58	59	.496	7th (12)	Miguel Perez
High-A	Greensboro Grasshoppers	High-A East	74	46	.617	2nd (12)	Kieran Mattison
Low-A	Bradenton Marauders	Low-A Southeast	71	48	.597	2nd (10)	Jonathan Johnston
Rookie	DSL Pirates Black	Dominican Summer	34	22	.607	9th (46)	Jose Mendez
Rookie	DSL Pirates Gold	Dominican Summer	19	37	.339	45th (46)	Jose Mosquera
Rookie	FCL Pirates Gold	Florida Complex	30	14	.682	3rd (18)	Gera Alvarez
Rookie	FCL Pirates Black	Florida Complex	19	23	.452	12th (18)	M. Lopez/S. Morales
Overall 2021 Minor League Record			366	316	.537	6th (30)	

ORGANIZATION STATISTICS

PITTSBURGH PIRATES
NATIONAL LEAGUE

Batting	B-T	HT	WT	DOB	AVG	vLH	vRH	G	AB	R	H	2B	3B	HR	RBI	BB	HBP	SH	SF	SO	SB	CS	SLG	OBP
Alford, Anthony	R-R	6-1	215	7-20-94	.233	.156	.273	49	133	14	31	6	1	5	11	12	3	0	0	58	5	6	.406	.311
Castro, Rodolfo	B-R	6-0	205	5-21-99	.198	.276	.158	31	86	9	17	2	0	5	8	6	1	0	0	27	0	0	.395	.258
Chavis, Michael	R-R	5-10	210	8-11-95	.357	.421	.304	12	42	4	15	3	0	1	5	0	0	0	0	10	0	1	.500	.357
Craig, Will	R-R	6-3	235	11-16-94	.217	.235	.209	18	60	5	13	2	0	1	3	5	0	0	0	22	0	0	.300	.277
Cruz, Oneil	L-R	6-7	210	10-4-98	.333	.000	.600	2	9	2	3	0	0	1	3	0	0	0	0	4	0	0	.667	.333
Davis, Taylor	R-R	5-10	200	11-28-89	.400	.400	--	2	5	0	2	0	0	0	0	1	0	0	0	0	0	0	.400	.500
Difo, Wilmer	B-R	5-11	200	4-2-92	.269	.234	.284	116	219	25	59	7	3	4	24	20	0	0	1	54	1	0	.384	.329
Evans, Phillip	R-R	5-10	210	9-10-92	.206	.242	.191	76	214	23	44	5	0	5	16	28	5	0	0	53	1	0	.299	.312
Fowler, Dustin	L-L	6-0	195	12-29-94	.171	.143	.176	18	41	3	7	1	0	0	2	3	1	0	1	20	1	0	.195	.239
Frazier, Todd	R-R	6-3	215	2-12-86	.086	.125	.074	13	35	3	3	1	0	0	4	3	2	0	0	6	0	0	.114	.200
Gamel, Ben	L-L	5-11	177	5-17-92	.255	.242	.260	111	326	42	83	17	3	8	26	48	3	2	4	99	3	6	.399	.352
Gonzalez, Erik	R-R	6-3	205	8-31-91	.232	.294	.204	71	220	17	51	7	1	2	21	8	0	0	1	40	2	2	.300	.258
Hayes, Ke'Bryan	R-R	5-10	205	1-28-97	.257	.279	.247	96	362	49	93	20	2	6	38	31	1	0	2	87	9	1	.373	.316
Moran, Colin	L-R	6-4	225	10-1-92	.258	.171	.288	99	318	29	82	12	0	10	50	36	2	0	3	87	1	0	.390	.334
Newman, Kevin	R-R	6-0	185	8-4-93	.226	.221	.229	148	517	50	117	22	3	5	39	27	1	6	3	41	6	1	.309	.265
Nogowski, John	R-L	6-0	245	1-5-93	.261	.275	.254	33	111	12	29	7	0	1	14	11	0	0	1	22	0	1	.351	.325
2-team total (19 St. Louis)					.233	.262	.218	52	129	14	30	7	0	1	14	12	1	0	1	22	0	1	.310	.301
Oliva, Jared	R-R	6-2	205	11-27-95	.175	.267	.120	20	40	4	7	2	0	0	2	3	0	0	0	10	2	0	.225	.233
Owen, Hunter	R-R	5-11	200	9-22-93	.000	--	.000	3	4	0	0	0	0	0	0	0	0	1	0	3	0	0	.000	.200
Park, Hoy	L-R	6-1	175	4-7-96	.197	.292	.175	44	127	16	25	5	2	3	14	18	1	1	1	38	1	1	.339	.299
Perez, Michael	L-R	5-10	195	8-7-92	.143	.154	.141	70	210	19	30	8	1	7	21	19	2	0	0	68	0	1	.290	.221
Reynolds, Bryan	B-R	6-3	210	1-27-95	.302	.325	.293	159	559	93	169	35	8	24	90	75	8	0	4	119	5	2	.522	.390
Stallings, Jacob	R-R	6-5	225	12-22-89	.246	.200	.272	112	374	38	92	20	1	8	53	49	2	0	2	85	0	0	.369	.335
Stokes Jr., Troy	R-R	5-9	205	2-2-96	.111	.000	.143	8	18	2	2	1	0	0	2	1	1	0	0	5	1	0	.167	.200
Tom, Ka'ai	L-R	5-9	185	5-29-94	.152	.190	.141	39	92	9	14	2	1	2	11	17	5	0	3	30	1	0	.261	.308
Tsutsugo, Yoshi	L-R	6-1	225	11-26-91	.268	.313	.241	43	127	20	34	8	1	8	25	15	1	0	1	33	0	1	.535	.347
2-team total (12 Los Angeles)					.243	.273	.227	55	152	22	37	8	1	8	27	21	1	0	1	45	0	1	.467	.337
Tucker, Cole	B-R	6-3	205	7-3-96	.222	.161	.244	43	117	15	26	4	2	2	12	13	0	0	1	33	2	2	.342	.298
Vargas, Ildemaro	B-R	6-0	180	7-16-91	.077	.250	.000	7	13	0	1	0	0	0	1	0	0	0	0	3	0	0	.077	.077
3-team total (18 Arizona, 9 Chicago)					.156	.121	.182	34	77	7	12	3	1	0	7	6	0	0	0	17	1	0	.221	.217

Pitching	B-T	HT	WT	DOB	W	L	ERA	G	GS	CG	SV	IP	H	R	ER	HR	BB	SO	AVG	vLH	vRH	K/9	BB/9
Anderson, Tanner	R-R	6-2	203	5-27-93	0	0	3.60	1	0	0	0	5	5	2	2	0	0	1	.263	.200	.333	1.80	0.00
Anderson, Tyler	L-L	6-2	220	12-30-89	5	8	4.35	18	18	0	0	103	99	52	50	16	25	86	.251	.206	.268	7.49	2.19
Banda, Anthony	L-L	6-2	230	8-10-93	1	2	3.42	25	0	0	0	26	25	10	10	4	12	25	.248	.189	.281	8.54	4.10
2-team total (5 New York)					2	2	4.28	30	0	0	0	34	39	18	16	6	13	32	.287	.224	.322	8.55	3.48
Bednar, David	L-R	6-1	245	10-10-94	3	1	2.23	61	0	0	3	61	40	15	15	5	19	77	.185	.178	.190	11.42	2.82
Brault, Steven	L-L	6-0	195	4-29-92	0	3	5.86	7	7	0	0	28	33	18	18	3	12	19	.292	.133	.316	6.18	3.90
Brubaker, JT	R-R	6-3	180	11-17-93	5	13	5.36	24	24	0	0	124	123	75	74	28	38	129	.254	.269	.239	9.34	2.75
Cahill, Trevor	R-R	6-4	223	3-1-88	1	5	6.57	9	8	0	0	37	42	29	27	4	14	32	.286	.349	.238	7.78	3.41
Contreras, Roansy	R-R	6-0	175	11-7-99	0	0	0.00	1	1	0	0	3	3	0	0	0	1	4	.273	.250	.286	12.00	3.00
Crick, Kyle	L-R	6-4	225	11-30-92	1	1	4.44	27	0	0	0	24	14	14	12	0	19	21	.175	.147	.196	7.77	7.03
Crowe, Wil	R-R	6-2	235	9-9-94	4	8	5.48	26	25	0	0	117	126	75	71	25	57	111	.276	.239	.304	8.56	4.40
Davis, Austin	L-L	6-4	235	2-3-93	0	0	5.59	10	0	0	0	10	6	7	6	2	5	11	.167	.105	.235	10.24	4.66
De Jong, Chase	L-R	6-4	230	12-29-93	1	4	5.77	9	9	0	0	44	49	28	28	11	19	39	.280	.300	.253	8.04	3.92
De Los Santos, Enyel	R-R	6-3	235	12-25-95	1	0	4.91	7	0	0	0	7	9	4	4	1	4	6	.300	.231	.353	7.36	4.91
2-team total (26 Philadelphia)					2	1	6.37	33	0	0	0	35	43	32	25	8	18	48	.291	.284	.296	12.23	4.58
Difo, Wilmer	B-R	5-11	200	4-2-92	0	0	36.00	2	0	0	0	2	9	8	8	1	3	1	.643	.750	.600	4.50	13.50
Evans, Phillip	R-R	5-10	210	9-10-92	0	0	0.00	1	0	0	0	1	0	0	0	0	0	0	.000	--	.000	0.00	0.00
Feliz, Michael	R-R	6-4	250	6-28-93	0	0	2.35	7	0	0	0	8	8	3	2	0	1	8	.267	.267	.267	9.39	1.17

Name	B-T	HT	WT	DOB	W	L	ERA	G	GS	CG	SV	IP	H	R	ER	HR	BB	SO	AVG	vLH	vRH	SO/9	BB/9
2-team total (9 Cincinnati)					0	0	8.79	16	0	0	1	14	21	15	14	2	5	17	.333	.310	.353	10.67	3.14
Hartlieb, Geoff	R-R	6-5	240	12-9-93	0	0	7.71	4	0	0	0	5	3	4	4	0	5	4	.188	.167	.200	7.71	9.64
2-team total (3 New York)					0	0	11.00	7	0	0	0	9	10	11	11	0	11	9	.278	.250	.300	9.00	11.00
Holmes, Clay	R-R	6-5	245	3-27-93	3	2	4.93	44	0	0	0	42	35	24	23	3	25	44	.220	.295	.173	9.43	5.36
Howard, Sam	R-L	6-4	195	3-5-93	3	4	5.60	54	1	0	0	45	34	29	28	7	32	60	.211	.158	.259	12.00	6.40
Keller, Kyle	R-R	6-4	205	4-28-93	1	1	6.48	32	0	0	0	33	30	27	24	9	22	36	.234	.255	.219	9.72	5.94
Keller, Mitch	R-R	6-2	220	4-4-96	5	11	6.17	23	23	0	0	101	131	69	69	10	49	92	.322	.345	.300	8.23	4.38
Kranick, Max	R-R	6-3	210	7-21-97	2	3	6.28	9	9	0	0	39	47	28	27	4	19	32	.301	.333	.269	7.45	4.42
Kuhl, Chad	R-R	6-3	205	9-10-92	5	7	4.82	28	14	0	0	80	73	50	43	13	42	75	.252	.257	.247	8.40	4.71
Mears, Nick	R-R	6-2	200	10-7-96	1	0	5.01	30	0	0	0	23	25	14	13	5	13	23	.269	.282	.259	8.87	5.01
Miller, Shelby	R-R	6-3	225	10-10-90	0	1	5.06	10	0	0	0	11	9	6	6	3	6	7	.243	.278	.211	5.91	5.06
2-team total (3 Chicago)					0	1	9.24	13	0	0	0	13	16	13	13	3	11	8	.327	.364	.296	5.68	7.82
Nogowski, John	R-L	6-0	245	1-5-93	0	0	15.00	3	0	0	0	3	8	5	5	0	0	0	.500	.200	.636	0.00	0.00
Overton, Connor	L-R	6-0	190	7-24-93	0	1	8.31	5	3	0	0	9	10	8	8	2	3	11	.294	.389	.188	11.42	3.12
Oviedo, Luis	R-R	6-4	235	5-15-99	1	2	8.80	22	1	0	0	30	33	32	29	4	26	31	.282	.302	.266	9.40	7.89
Peters, Dillon	L-L	5-11	190	8-31-92	1	2	3.71	6	6	0	0	27	26	12	11	2	10	23	.245	.200	.266	7.76	3.38
Ponce, Cody	R-R	6-6	255	4-25-94	0	6	7.04	15	2	0	0	38	56	34	30	8	11	36	.344	.338	.347	8.45	2.58
Poppen, Sean	R-R	6-3	210	3-15-94	0	0	7.71	3	0	0	0	5	11	7	4	1	2	4	.478	.556	.429	7.71	3.86
2-team total (20 Arizona)					1	1	5.32	23	0	0	0	1	22	31	18	13	2	9	25	.323	.400	.268	10.23	3.68
Shreve, Chasen	L-L	6-4	180	7-12-90	3	3	3.20	57	0	0	0	56	43	20	20	7	28	45	.212	.200	.221	7.19	4.47
Spitzbarth, Shea	R-R	6-1	215	10-4-94	0	0	3.60	5	0	0	0	5	4	2	2	1	2	1	.211	.250	.182	1.80	3.60
Stratton, Chris	R-R	6-2	205	8-22-90	7	1	3.63	68	0	0	0	8	79	70	34	32	9	33	86	.233	.260	.213	9.76	3.74
Underwood Jr., Duane	R-R	6-2	210	7-20-94	2	3	4.33	43	0	0	0	73	77	40	35	9	27	65	.270	.296	.250	8.05	3.34
Wilson, Bryse	R-R	6-2	225	12-20-97	1	4	4.91	8	8	0	0	40	40	22	22	8	10	23	.256	.247	.268	5.13	2.23
2-team total (8 Atlanta)					3	7	5.35	16	16	0	0	74	85	45	44	15	22	46	.290	.279	.302	5.59	2.68
Yajure, Miguel	R-R	6-1	220	5-1-98	0	2	8.40	4	3	0	0	15	17	14	14	6	7	11	.283	.353	.192	6.60	4.20

Fielding

Catcher	PCT	G	PO	A	E	DP	PB
Davis	1.000	2	11	0	0	0	0
Perez	.994	58	457	20	3	4	2
Stallings	.995	104	868	49	5	2	0

First Base	PCT	G	PO	A	E	DP
Chavis	1.000	1	7	1	0	0
Craig	.991	18	101	9	1	10
Evans	.984	20	107	15	2	18
Frazier	1.000	4	35	0	0	3
Gamel	1.000	4	11	0	0	3
Gonzalez	1.000	13	61	8	0	1
Moran	.992	84	564	42	5	62
Nogowski	1.000	29	178	13	0	26
Perez	.000	1	0	0	0	0
Stallings	1.000	1	3	0	0	0
Tsutsugo	1.000	15	79	7	0	8
Tucker	1.000	1	2	0	0	1

Second Base	PCT	G	PO	A	E	DP
Castro	.951	20	36	41	4	12
Chavis	1.000	7	10	9	0	4

	PCT	G	PO	A	E	DP
Difo	.972	28	29	40	2	11
Frazier	.986	94	144	213	5	47
Newman	1.000	15	17	22	0	7
Park	.982	16	24	30	1	9
Tucker	1.000	9	17	21	0	6

Third Base	PCT	G	PO	A	E	DP
Castro	1.000	5	2	7	0	1
Chavis	1.000	4	3	6	0	1
Difo	.935	18	8	21	2	3
Evans	.967	14	5	24	1	4
Frazier	1.000	3	4	5	0	1
Gonzalez	.969	38	20	73	3	5
Hayes	.988	95	73	173	3	28
Moran	.000	1	0	0	0	0
Park	1.000	9	5	11	0	2
Vargas	1.000	3	0	3	0	0

Shortstop	PCT	G	PO	A	E	DP
Cruz	1.000	2	1	4	0	1
Difo	1.000	4	3	6	0	2
Gonzalez	.962	17	19	31	2	5
Newman	.993	132	164	286	3	62

	PCT	G	PO	A	E	DP
Park	1.000	8	5	13	0	4
Tucker	.942	17	22	27	3	5

Outfield	PCT	G	PO	A	E	DP
Alford	.985	39	63	1	1	0
Chavis	1.000	1	2	0	0	0
Difo	.900	12	18	0	2	0
Evans	.920	31	44	2	4	0
Fowler	1.000	13	26	0	0	0
Frazier	1.000	7	4	0	0	0
Gamel	1.000	101	184	3	0	0
Nogowski	--	1	0	0	0	0
Oliva	1.000	19	25	0	0	0
Owen	--	1	0	0	0	0
Park	1.000	9	12	0	0	0
Polanco	.980	92	191	2	4	0
Reynolds	.994	154	354	4	2	1
Stokes Jr.	1.000	4	12	0	0	0
Tom	1.000	31	55	1	0	0
Tsutsugo	.970	22	31	1	1	0
Tucker	1.000	14	12	0	0	0
Vargas	1.000	2	1	0	0	0

INDIANAPOLIS INDIANS

TRIPLE-A

TRIPLE-A EAST

Batting	B-T	HT	WT	DOB	AVG	vLH	vRH	G	AB	R	H	2B	3B	HR	RBI	BB	HBP	SH	SF	SO	SB	CS	SLG	OBP
Alford, Anthony	R-R	6-1	215	7-20-94	.307	.356	.292	56	189	37	58	12	0	14	41	33	4	0	0	78	9	4	.593	.420
Bethancourt, Christian	R-R	6-3	205	9-2-91	.281	.333	.263	92	331	46	93	18	1	14	60	28	2	0	2	73	4	1	.468	.339
Busby, Dylan	R-R	6-2	196	11-28-95	.077	.000	.083	4	13	0	1	0	0	0	1	0	0	0	0	4	0	0	.077	.077
Castillo, Diego	R-R	5-11	185	10-28-97	.278	.313	.263	18	54	18	15	3	0	3	13	1	0	2	13	0	0	.500	.414
Castro, Rodolfo	B-R	6-0	205	5-21-99	.286	.385	.227	8	35	7	10	4	0	3	8	3	0	0	11	0	0	.657	.342
Chavis, Michael	R-R	5-10	210	8-11-95	.278	.333	.260	25	97	19	27	6	0	8	20	6	7	0	0	26	1	1	.588	.364
2-team total (24 Worcester)					.271	.262	.275	49	192	38	52	8	0	14	37	14	9	0	2	56	2	1	.531	.346
Craig, Will	R-R	6-3	235	11-16-94	.287	.257	.299	33	122	23	35	8	0	8	23	14	2	0	1	28	0	0	.549	.367
Cruz, Oneil	L-R	6-7	210	10-4-98	.524	.636	.400	6	21	11	11	1	0	5	7	8	0	0	0	5	1	0	1.286	.655
Davis, Taylor	R-R	5-10	200	11-28-89	.235	.393	.187	39	119	16	28	3	0	2	17	17	1	0	0	16	0	0	.311	.336
2-team total (12 Norfolk)					.248	.359	.212	51	157	22	39	6	0	2	24	21	1	0	0	21	0	0	.325	.344
Delay, Jason	R-R	5-11	200	3-7-95	.265	.444	.200	13	34	6	9	2	0	2	4	4	0	0	0	10	0	0	.500	.342
Difo, Wilmer	B-R	5-11	200	4-2-92	.244	.235	.250	12	41	6	10	2	0	2	4	0	0	1	0	10	0	0	.293	.304
Evans, Phillip	R-R	5-10	210	9-10-92	.253	.260	.256	38	127	18	32	10	0	0	10	15	1	0	1	25	0	0	.331	.333
Fowler, Dustin	L-L	6-0	195	12-29-94	.270	.167	.320	13	37	8	10	2	1	3	6	9	1	0	0	16	2	0	.622	.426
2-team total (28 Jacksonville)					.289	.300	.284	41	142	21	41	4	2	9	30	11	2	0	2	49	2	0	.535	.344
Gonzalez, Erik	R-R	6-3	205	8-31-91	.140	.000	.174	16	43	6	2	1	0	4	4	2	0	1	10	0	0	.233	.240
Hayes, Ke'Bryan	R-R	5-10	205	1-28-97	.250	.143	.294	7	24	6	6	2	0	2	3	2	0	0	0	7	0	0	.583	.308
Hudson, Joe	R-R	6-0	210	5-21-91	.188	.229	.176	47	154	11	29	7	0	3	18	18	0	0	3	45	0	0	.292	.269

Name	B-T	HT	WT	DOB	AVG	OBP	SLG	G	AB	R	H	2B	3B	HR	RBI	BB	HBP	SH	SF	SO	SB	CS	vLH	vRH
Kaiser, Connor	R-R	6-4	195	11-20-96	.111	.333	.000	5	9	1	1	1	0	0	0	2	0	0	0	4	0	0	.222	.273
Kramer, Kevin	L-R	6-0	195	10-3-93	.196	.140	.221	51	179	19	35	5	2	3	22	24	9	0	2	58	0	1	.296	.318
2-team total (23 Nashville)					.207	.176	.220	74	232	27	48	9	2	3	26	35	10	0	3	72	0	1	.302	.332
Macias, Fabricio	R-R	6-0	188	3-11-98	.245	.222	.253	38	102	13	25	2	0	2	9	4	4	1	0	27	2	1	.324	.300
Madris, Bligh	L-R	6-0	208	2-29-96	.272	.247	.282	104	334	43	91	25	1	9	55	40	4	1	6	70	2	4	.434	.352
Marcano, Tucupita	L-R	6-0	170	9-16-99	.230	.255	.219	48	183	29	42	4	1	1	12	26	0	1	0	33	8	1	.279	.325
Martin, Mason	L-R	6-0	220	6-2-99	.240	.333	.211	8	25	4	6	0	0	3	6	1	1	0	0	10	0	1	.600	.296
Mitchell, Cal	L-L	6-0	205	3-8-99	.250	.000	.333	7	20	1	5	1	0	0	1	0	1	0	0	4	0	0	.300	.286
Moran, Colin	L-R	6-0	225	10-1-92	.200	.300	.133	9	25	4	5	2	0	2	11	3	0	0	1	7	0	0	.520	.276
Nogowski, John	R-L	6-0	245	1-5-93	.259	.333	.244	20	54	5	14	2	0	1	10	13	1	0	1	10	3	0	.352	.406
2-team total (36 Memphis)					.214	.167	.224	56	182	21	39	6	0	4	24	28	6	0	1	41	6	0	.313	.336
Oliva, Jared	R-R	6-2	205	11-27-95	.249	.196	.263	64	225	27	56	12	4	2	23	19	5	0	0	67	10	3	.364	.321
Owen, Hunter	R-R	5-11	200	9-22-93	.235	.337	.198	97	328	55	77	11	0	20	53	29	6	0	3	124	2	2	.451	.306
2-team total (48 Scranton/Wilkes-Barre)					.306	.299	.310	56	193	46	59	9	1	10	32	53	4	2	2	53	9	4	.518	.460
Paul, Ethan	L-R	5-10	180	8-27-96	.205	.077	.238	49	127	12	26	3	0	1	14	20	2	1	0	52	3	0	.252	.322
Rivera, T.J.	R-R	6-1	203	10-27-88	.249	.348	.218	57	193	22	48	12	0	5	24	13	1	2	3	42	0	1	.389	.295
2-team total (31 Lehigh Valley)					.269	.338	.246	88	279	35	75	17	0	9	48	18	5	2	7	58	1	1	.427	.317
Sharpe, Chris	R-R	6-1	195	6-6-96	.196	.175	.203	108	317	45	62	25	0	5	29	41	9	2	2	111	6	3	.322	.304
Smith-Njigba, Canaan	L-R	6-0	240	4-30-99	.095	.333	.056	7	21	1	2	0	0	0	2	2	0	0	0	9	0	0	.095	.174
Stokes Jr., Troy	R-R	5-9	205	2-2-96	.169	.091	.204	29	71	11	12	2	1	2	5	11	2	0	0	18	4	0	.310	.298
2-team total (69 Nashville)					.188	.164	.197	98	207	29	39	7	3	4	14	27	5	0	0	56	9	2	.309	.297
Strange-Gordon, Dee	L-R	5-11	166	4-22-88	.221	.250	.205	16	68	13	15	3	0	3	9	4	0	0	0	19	1	0	.397	.264
3-team total (28 Iowa, 10 Nashville)					.248	.228	.258	54	230	36	57	11	1	5	21	11	2	1	0	35	6	1	.370	.288
Susac, Andrew	R-R	6-1	220	3-22-90	.222	.100	.269	11	36	5	8	2	0	2	3	4	0	0	0	12	0	0	.444	.300
Swaggerty, Travis	L-L	5-11	200	8-19-97	.220	.222	.219	12	41	6	9	0	0	3	7	6	1	0	0	8	3	0	.439	.333
Tom, Ka'ai	L-R	5-9	185	5-29-94	.190	.231	.178	23	58	6	11	1	0	2	7	5	4	0	0	19	0	0	.310	.299
Tucker, Cole	B-R	6-3	205	7-3-96	.223	.273	.210	61	220	33	49	11	2	6	20	41	2	0	0	58	9	3	.373	.350
Wilson, Eli	R-R	6-2	190	7-6-98	.333	--	.333	1	3	0	1	0	0	1	0	0	1	0	0	0	1	0	.667	.500

Pitching	B-T	HT	WT	DOB	W	L	ERA	G	GS	CG	SV	IP	H	R	ER	HR	BB	SO	AVG	vLH	vRH	K/9	BB/9
Alldred, Cam	L-L	6-3	205	7-25-96	0	0	0.71	5	0	0	1	13	12	2	1	2	7	10	.261	.067	.355	7.11	4.97
Anderson, Tanner	R-R	6-2	203	5-27-93	2	4	4.17	17	4	0	0	37	36	20	17	2	14	25	.259	.211	.309	6.14	3.44
Bashlor, Tyler	R-R	6-0	195	4-16-93	1	2	2.39	37	0	0	6	38	30	14	10	5	19	45	.214	.175	.247	10.75	4.54
Bellomy, Bear	R-R	6-4	205	11-29-96	0	0	0.00	1	0	0	0	1	1	0	0	0	0	0	.250	--	.250	0.00	0.00
Bethancourt, Christian	R-R	6-3	205	9-2-91	0	0	0.00	2	0	0	0	2	1	0	0	0	1	1	.167	.250	.000	4.50	4.50
Bido, Osvaldo	R-R	6-3	175	10-18-95	0	0	8.22	2	2	0	0	8	11	10	7	2	4	7	.333	.615	.150	8.22	4.70
Brault, Steven	L-L	6-0	195	4-29-92	0	1	1.64	3	3	0	0	11	6	2	2	2	1	9	.162	.077	.208	7.36	0.82
Contreras, Roansy	R-R	6-0	175	11-7-99	0	0	2.45	1	1	0	0	4	4	1	1	0	1	6	.267	.429	.125	14.73	2.45
Crowe, Wil	R-R	6-2	235	9-9-94	0	0	0.00	1	0	0	0	1	0	0	0	0	0	0	.000	.000	.000	0.00	0.00
Davis, Austin	L-L	6-4	235	2-3-93	0	1	2.57	11	0	0	0	14	6	5	4	0	5	18	.136	.150	.125	11.57	3.21
Davis, Taylor	R-R	5-10	200	11-28-89	0	0	27.00	1	0	0	0	1	4	3	3	0	0	1	.571	.667	.500	0.00	0.00
De Jong, Chase	L-R	6-4	230	12-29-93	2	0	3.60	4	4	0	0	20	16	8	8	3	8	26	.216	.189	.243	12.60	3.60
De Los Santos, Yerry	R-R	6-2	215	12-12-97	0	0	0.00	4	0	0	0	6	2	0	0	0	1	6	.105	.250	.000	9.00	1.50
Eckelman, Matt	R-R	6-3	281	10-6-93	3	5	4.91	36	0	0	0	66	81	43	36	12	14	54	.303	.322	.288	7.36	1.91
Ford, Grant	R-R	6-1	175	3-11-98	0	0	54.00	2	0	0	0	1	6	8	8	2	4	2	.600	.500	.667	13.50	27.00
Gustave, Jandel	R-R	6-3	220	10-12-92	1	1	3.60	15	0	0	5	15	12	6	6	0	5	18	.214	.190	.229	10.80	3.00
2-team total (6 Nashville)					1	1	3.00	21	0	0	5	21	15	7	7	0	5	26	.197	.200	.196	11.14	2.14
Hartlieb, Geoff	R-R	6-5	240	12-9-93	1	1	1.86	9	0	0	0	10	5	2	2	1	4	13	.147	.067	.211	12.10	3.72
3-team total (10 Syracuse, 4 Worcester)					3	2	3.76	23	0	0	0	26	21	13	11	4	17	29	.206	.146	.259	9.91	5.81
Howard, Sam	R-L	6-4	195	3-5-93	0	0	0.00	4	1	0	0	5	2	0	0	0	2	6	.125	.250	.000	11.57	3.86
Jacques, Joe	L-L	6-4	210	3-11-95	3	1	4.31	37	0	0	1	48	48	25	23	5	20	53	.261	.232	.278	9.94	3.75
Keller, Kyle	R-R	6-5	205	4-28-93	2	0	1.96	13	1	0	0	18	13	4	4	2	3	31	.200	.188	.212	15.22	1.47
Keller, Mitch	R-R	6-2	220	4-4-96	1	1	3.21	8	6	0	0	28	27	18	10	2	13	39	.241	.278	.207	12.54	4.18
Kranick, Max	R-R	6-3	210	7-21-97	4	4	4.14	12	12	0	0	54	53	30	25	6	16	45	.252	.316	.200	7.45	2.65
Kuhl, Chad	R-R	6-3	205	9-10-92	0	0	1.42	2	2	0	0	6	2	1	1	0	3	9	.095	.125	.077	12.79	4.26
Manasa, Alex	L-R	6-4	195	1-6-98	0	0	13.50	1	0	0	0	3	4	4	4	0	3	3	.333	.250	.375	10.13	10.13
Marvel, James	R-R	6-4	215	9-17-93	7	7	5.26	25	22	0	0	132	145	87	77	21	54	98	.285	.252	.316	6.70	3.69
Mears, Nick	R-R	6-2	200	10-7-96	2	2	5.30	17	0	0	1	19	16	12	11	2	9	25	.229	.286	.190	12.05	4.34
Mella, Keury	R-R	6-2	234	8-2-93	2	0	7.11	16	0	0	3	19	17	16	15	1	12	23	.239	.267	.220	10.89	5.68
Miller, Shelby	R-R	6-3	225	10-10-90	2	1	3.86	10	1	0	0	14	10	7	6	1	3	22	.189	.179	.204	14.14	1.93
2-team total (3 Iowa)					2	1	2.96	13	4	0	0	24	14	11	8	2	9	37	.157	.125	.195	13.68	3.33
Mlodzinski, Carmen	R-R	6-2	232	2-19-99	0	1	4.50	1	0	0	0	2	3	2	1	0	2	2	.333	.500	.286	9.00	9.00
Ogle, Braeden	L-L	6-2	215	7-30-97	2	3	3.13	24	0	0	1	32	19	13	11	2	23	42	.173	.217	.141	11.94	6.54
2-team total (20 Lehigh Valley)					3	5	5.68	44	0	0	1	51	49	36	32	7	37	60	.259	.246	.267	10.66	6.57
Overton, Connor	L-R	6-0	190	7-24-93	0	0	0.00	1	0	0	0	1	0	0	0	0	1	2	.000	--	.000	18.00	9.00
2-team total (21 Buffalo)					2	1	1.99	22	7	0	0	59	52	14	13	3	11	52	.241	.263	.223	7.98	1.69
Oviedo, Luis	R-R	6-4	235	5-15-99	0	2	8.00	4	3	0	0	9	11	8	8	1	6	11	.297	.350	.235	11.00	6.00
O'Reilly, John	R-R	6-5	225	10-4-95	0	2	6.68	16	3	0	1	32	46	24	24	3	7	13	.341	.375	.316	3.62	1.95
Peters, Dillon	L-L	5-11	190	8-31-92	1	0	1.50	5	2	0	0	12	4	2	2	0	6	16	.100	.138	.111	11.25	4.50
Ponce, Cody	R-R	6-6	255	4-25-94	1	4	4.71	15	8	0	0	57	55	30	30	8	18	59	.253	.276	.235	9.26	2.83
Poppen, Sean	R-R	6-3	210	3-15-94	1	0	4.50	2	0	0	0	4	3	2	2	1	1	4	.214	.167	.250	9.00	2.25
2-team total (19 Durham)					3	3	1.95	21	0	0	2	32	26	9	7	2	12	34	.228	.275	.203	9.46	3.34
Roberts, Austin	R-R	6-2	219	7-27-98	0	0	0.00	1	0	0	0	1	0	0	0	0	3	1	.000	.000	.000	27.00	0.00
Shreve, Chasen	L-L	6-4	180	7-12-90	0	0	0.00	2	1	0	0	2	1	0	0	0	0	3	.143	.200	.000	13.50	0.00

	B-T	HT	WT	DOB	W	L	ERA	G	GS	CG	SV	IP	H	R	ER	HR	BB	SO	AVG	vLH	vRH	K/9	BB/9
Spitzbarth, Shea	R-R	6-1	215	10-4-94	3	3	2.12	42	0	0	2	47	35	15	11	4	21	41	.210	.158	.253	7.91	4.05
Stratton, Hunter	R-R	6-4	225	11-17-96	0	2	3.42	18	0	0	0	24	21	11	9	2	12	26	.233	.250	.217	9.89	4.56
Sulser, Beau	R-R	6-2	195	5-5-94	7	9	5.65	26	24	0	0	123	150	87	77	21	53	102	.299	.308	.290	7.48	3.89
Vieaux, Cam	L-L	6-3	200	12-5-93	2	2	7.67	8	8	0	0	29	38	28	25	6	21	28	.322	.375	.302	8.59	6.44
Weiman, Blake	R-L	6-3	210	11-5-95	5	0	4.76	35	0	0	0	45	37	25	24	11	12	45	.218	.156	.255	8.93	2.38
Wright, Steven	R-R	6-2	215	8-30-84	4	7	6.68	18	12	0	1	63	74	51	47	5	44	70	.294	.268	.320	9.95	6.25
Yajure, Miguel	R-R	6-1	220	5-1-98	2	3	3.09	9	9	0	0	44	33	17	15	6	13	40	.209	.233	.188	8.24	2.68

Fielding

Catcher	PCT	G	PO	A	E	DP	PB
Bethancourt	.996	28	224	14	1	3	3
Davis	.994	37	296	27	2	5	5
Delay	.989	11	86	8	1	0	1
Hudson	.995	47	410	26	2	3	8
Susac	.990	9	96	2	1	0	1
Wilson	.917	1	11	0	1	0	0

First Base	PCT	G	PO	A	E	DP
Bethancourt	.986	28	199	10	3	18
Chavis	.983	7	53	5	1	7
Craig	.997	32	266	23	1	23
Evans	.984	15	116	8	2	11
Gonzalez	1.000	3	17	1	0	2
Martin	1.000	5	33	0	0	2
Moran	1.000	8	43	5	0	8
Nogowski	.986	17	122	19	2	13
Owen	1.000	9	58	4	0	9
Rivera	1.000	13	89	10	0	15
Susac	1.000	1	6	0	0	0

Second Base	PCT	G	PO	A	E	DP
Castillo	.952	6	9	11	1	6
Castro	1.000	1	1	1	0	0
Chavis	.953	10	16	25	2	7
Difo	1.000	6	5	15	0	2
Evans	1.000	1	1	2	0	0
Gonzalez	1.000	2	0	2	0	0
Kaiser	1.000	4	7	2	0	1
Kramer	1.000	9	11	17	0	3
Marcano	.981	34	63	88	3	21
Park	1.000	2	1	2	0	0
Paul	.943	28	39	60	6	16
Rivera	.981	27	36	65	2	11
Strange-Gordon	.971	5	15	19	1	5
Tucker	1.000	4	3	7	0	1

Third Base	PCT	G	PO	A	E	DP
Busby	1.000	4	1	6	0	1
Castillo	1.000	2	1	2	0	0
Castro	1.000	4	2	6	0	2
Chavis	1.000	3	1	5	0	1
Craig	.000	1	0	0	0	0
Difo	.952	6	3	17	1	0
Evans	1.000	11	2	16	0	2
Gonzalez	.857	5	5	7	2	3
Hayes	1.000	4	6	10	0	1
Kramer	1.000	16	13	23	0	2
Marcano	.750	4	2	4	2	1
Owen	.953	73	47	117	8	21
Paul	.833	5	3	2	1	0
Rivera	1.000	4	1	5	0	0

Shortstop	PCT	G	PO	A	E	DP
Castillo	.897	9	6	20	3	2
Castro	.909	3	3	7	1	1
Cruz	.906	5	10	19	3	4
Gonzalez	.962	5	5	20	1	4
Kaiser	.000	1	0	0	0	0
Kramer	.987	23	29	49	1	12
Marcano	1.000	1	1	0	0	1
Park	1.000	5	4	18	0	2
Paul	.942	12	18	31	3	11
Rivera	1.000	8	11	24	0	6
Strange-Gordon	1.000	11	9	27	0	6
Tucker	.962	48	65	137	8	26

Outfield	PCT	G	PO	A	E	DP
Alford	.956	50	84	2	4	0
Bethancourt	.941	12	16	0	1	0
Chavis	1.000	1	3	0	0	0
Evans	1.000	5	9	0	0	0
Fowler	1.000	11	16	1	0	1
Kramer	1.000	1	3	0	0	0
Macias	1.000	23	29	1	0	0
Madris	.984	82	120	4	2	0
Marcano	1.000	8	20	0	0	0
Mitchell	1.000	5	6	0	0	0
Oliva	.992	60	119	5	1	0
Owen	1.000	14	12	0	0	0
Park	1.000	1	1	0	0	0
Sharpe	.988	97	166	5	2	1
Smith-Njigba	.857	5	6	0	1	0
Stokes Jr.	.972	21	35	0	1	0
Swaggerty	.958	9	22	1	1	1
Tom	.966	15	28	0	1	0
Tucker	.917	10	11	0	1	0

ALTOONA CURVE

DOUBLE-A NORTHEAST

DOUBLE-A

Batting	B-T	HT	WT	DOB	AVG	vLH	vRH	G	AB	R	H	2B	3B	HR	RBI	BB	HBP	SH	SF	SO	SB	CS	SLG	OBP
Amaral, Daniel	R-R	6-0	190	3-7-97	.218	.236	.209	68	220	32	48	12	0	7	22	24	3	0	1	62	9	4	.368	.302
Bae, Ji-hwan	L-R	6-1	185	7-26-99	.278	.243	.289	83	320	63	89	12	5	7	31	38	4	0	3	83	20	8	.413	.359
Bins, Carter	R-R	6-0	205	10-7-98	.200	.467	.100	16	55	4	11	2	0	0	6	10	1	0	0	19	0	0	.236	.333
Bissonette, Josh	R-R	6-0	185	11-1-96	.229	.230	.229	71	231	28	53	10	0	1	21	24	1	1	2	51	1	1	.286	.302
Busby, Dylan	R-R	6-2	196	11-28-95	.182	.000	.200	3	11	3	2	0	0	1	2	1	0	0	0	3	0	0	.455	.250
Castillo, Diego	R-R	5-11	185	10-28-97	.282	.333	.265	28	110	11	31	3	0	5	16	10	0	1	0	9	1	2	.445	.342
2-team total (58 Somerset)					.278	.310	.267	86	334	55	93	21	0	16	48	31	3	1	1	43	9	5	.485	.344
Castro, Rodolfo	B-R	6-0	205	5-21-99	.242	.200	.255	72	285	43	69	14	1	12	47	19	4	0	4	72	7	4	.425	.295
Citta, Brendt	R-R	6-2	180	7-12-96	.294	.257	.304	47	160	16	47	9	2	2	23	10	3	0	0	36	0	1	.413	.347
Cruz, Oneil	L-R	6-7	210	10-4-98	.292	.328	.281	62	250	51	73	15	5	12	40	20	1	0	1	64	18	3	.536	.346
Davis, Jonah	L-R	5-10	181	7-2-97	.211	.179	.219	60	190	29	40	7	3	8	19	26	5	0	0	95	4	6	.405	.321
Delay, Jason	R-R	5-11	200	3-7-95	.117	.000	.143	17	60	1	7	2	0	0	3	0	0	0	0	23	0	0	.150	.117
Finol, Claudio	R-R	5-11	171	4-13-00	.000	--	.000	2	2	1	0	0	0	0	0	0	0	0	0	2	0	0	.000	.000
Fraizer, Matt	L-R	6-3	217	1-12-98	.288	.267	.294	37	132	20	38	12	3	3	18	13	2	0	2	34	1	2	.492	.356
Hernandez, Raul	R-R	6-0	182	12-20-95	.229	.250	.222	10	35	4	8	1	0	0	4	1	0	0	0	9	0	0	.343	.250
Jimenez, Joe	R-R	5-10	185	2-22-98	.167	--	.167	2	6	1	1	0	0	1	1	2	0	0	0	1	0	0	.667	.375
Kaiser, Connor	R-R	6-4	195	11-20-96	.195	.154	.209	48	149	25	29	7	0	4	14	17	1	0	1	42	0	0	.322	.280
Koch, Grant	R-R	6-0	195	2-5-97	.130	.167	.125	16	54	4	7	2	0	1	4	2	0	0	0	18	0	0	.222	.161
Madris, Bligh	L-R	6-0	208	2-29-96	.192	.000	.250	10	26	2	5	0	0	0	1	7	0	0	0	6	0	0	.192	.364
Martin, Mason	L-R	6-0	220	6-2-99	.242	.227	.246	112	414	62	100	29	2	22	75	38	12	0	7	161	0	2	.481	.318
Mitchell, Cal	L-L	6-0	205	3-8-99	.280	.211	.301	108	382	43	107	19	1	12	61	24	7	0	5	71	6	7	.429	.330
Murray, Chase	L-R	6-0	188	6-3-98	.320	.600	.250	9	25	1	8	1	0	0	0	1	0	0	0	6	0	0	.360	.346
Pabst, Arden	R-R	6-1	205	3-14-95	.194	.254	.170	61	206	21	40	7	0	7	28	7	0	1	0	73	0	0	.330	.220
Paul, Ethan	R-R	5-10	180	8-27-96	.217	.250	.211	8	23	2	5	1	0	0	1	4	0	0	0	7	0	0	.261	.333
Smith-Njigba, Canaan	L-R	6-0	240	4-30-99	.274	.255	.279	66	219	35	60	11	0	6	40	45	1	0	1	66	13	1	.406	.398
Stafford, Deon	R-R	5-11	211	3-17-96	.161	.333	.053	14	31	5	5	1	0	2	3	2	0	0	0	11	0	0	.387	.212
Suwinski, Jack	L-L	6-2	215	7-29-98	.252	.206	.265	45	151	21	38	9	0	4	21	25	2	1	3	51	4	2	.391	.359
Valdez, Jesus	R-R	6-0	175	12-29-97	.171	.083	.207	13	41	3	7	0	0	1	1	1	0	0	0	13	0	0	.244	.190

Pitching	B-T	HT	WT	DOB	W	L	ERA	G	GS	CG	SV	IP	H	R	ER	HR	BB	SO	AVG	vLH	vRH	K/9	BB/9
Alldred, Cam	L-L	6-3	205	7-25-96	4	0	2.53	28	0	0	1	53	33	17	15	5	23	49	.176	.143	.198	8.27	3.88
Bido, Osvaldo	R-R	6-3	175	10-18-95	4	8	5.09	21	19	0	0	94	95	61	53	13	33	91	.257	.268	.249	8.74	3.17

	B-T	HT	WT	DOB	W	L	ERA	G	GS	CG	SV	IP	H	R	ER	HR	BB	SO	AVG	vLH	vRH	K/9	BB/9
Case, Brad	R-R	6-6	242	9-13-96	2	3	5.24	28	2	0	0	67	80	41	39	13	21	57	.295	.298	.293	7.66	2.82
Contreras, Roansy	R-R	6-0	175	11-7-99	3	2	2.65	12	12	0	0	54	37	21	16	5	12	76	.185	.245	.132	12.59	1.99
Cruz, Omar	L-L	6-0	200	1-26-99	3	4	3.44	14	14	0	0	71	70	32	27	6	22	60	.260	.313	.238	7.64	2.80
De Los Santos, Yerry	R-R	6-2	215	12-12-97	3	2	2.04	12	0	0	2	18	11	6	4	2	6	19	.177	.231	.139	9.68	3.06
Gardner, Will	R-R	6-2	200	5-8-96	2	5	7.71	33	0	0	0	42	38	39	36	7	29	43	.239	.209	.261	9.21	6.21
Jennings, Steven	R-R	6-2	175	11-13-98	3	0	6.67	13	0	0	0	30	40	23	22	4	11	20	.313	.304	.319	6.07	3.34
Kirby, Nathan	L-L	6-2	200	11-23-93	1	0	6.52	17	0	0	1	19	19	18	14	1	15	37	.247	.267	.234	17.22	6.98
Kranick, Max	R-R	6-3	210	7-21-97	1	0	4.02	3	3	0	0	16	14	7	7	2	3	16	.233	.208	.250	9.19	1.15
MacGregor, Travis	R-R	6-3	180	10-15-97	4	9	6.25	22	21	0	0	91	92	69	63	13	41	88	.264	.239	.285	8.74	4.07
Manasa, Alex	L-R	6-4	195	1-6-98	0	0	15.75	2	0	0	0	4	15	10	7	2	0	1	.556	.571	.538	2.25	0.00
McGough, Trey	L-L	6-3	195	3-29-98	6	5	3.41	18	18	1	0	95	89	39	36	7	21	77	.247	.228	.256	7.29	1.99
Melendez, Cristofer	R-R	6-3	226	9-16-97	3	3	4.41	28	0	0	7	33	21	21	16	2	18	39	.179	.176	.182	10.74	4.96
Murray, Shea	R-R	6-6	215	11-5-93	4	3	4.12	37	0	0	4	44	41	25	20	3	38	51	.255	.228	.269	10.51	7.83
Nunez, Oddy	L-L	6-8	230	12-20-96	2	1	8.32	28	0	0	1	44	48	43	41	5	37	51	.271	.229	.299	10.35	7.51
O'Reilly, John	R-R	6-5	225	10-4-95	3	3	5.09	22	0	0	3	35	47	24	20	1	8	22	.331	.297	.322	5.60	2.04
Pabst, Arden	R-R	6-1	205	3-14-95	0	0	0.00	1	0	0	0	0	0	0	0	0	0	0	.000	.000	--	0.00	0.00
Passantino, Jeffrey	R-R	5-10	225	9-24-95	1	8	4.62	18	15	0	1	76	77	41	39	12	20	74	.256	.237	.271	8.76	2.37
Stratton, Hunter	R-R	6-4	225	11-17-96	2	0	1.42	20	0	0	7	25	16	4	4	1	13	44	.182	.108	.235	15.63	4.62
Toribio, Noe	R-R	6-2	194	8-25-99	2	2	4.32	14	8	0	0	50	46	29	24	5	13	40	.238	.250	.228	7.20	2.34
Vieaux, Cam	L-L	6-3	200	12-5-93	5	1	3.68	17	5	0	0	44	35	21	18	5	16	44	.211	.258	.183	9.00	3.27

Fielding

Catcher	PCT	G	PO	A	E	DP	PB
Bins	.985	15	128	7	2	1	0
Delay	.991	17	109	4	1	0	2
Hernandez	.979	9	85	8	2	1	1
Jimenez	1.000	2	17	0	0	0	0
Koch	1.000	14	134	5	0	0	1
Pabst	.995	61	522	25	3	2	2
Stafford	1.000	1	15	3	0	1	0

First Base	PCT	G	PO	A	E	DP
Busby	.800	1	4	0	1	0
Citta	1.000	8	69	2	0	7
Martin	.990	108	767	64	8	65

Second Base	PCT	G	PO	A	E	DP
Amaral	1.000	2	0	3	0	0
Bae	.940	65	97	124	14	29

Bissonette	.983	12	20	37	1	8
Castillo	.957	9	9	13	1	2
Castro	.957	24	43	69	5	15
Kaiser	1.000	1	2	1	0	0
Paul	1.000	8	10	27	0	5

Third Base	PCT	G	PO	A	E	DP
Bissonette	.939	46	24	83	7	13
Busby	.750	1	1	2	1	0
Castillo	1.000	7	5	16	0	1
Castro	.915	44	32	75	10	11
Finol	1.000	2	1	0	0	0
Kaiser	.867	7	5	8	2	2
Valdez	.818	12	6	12	4	1

Shortstop	PCT	G	PO	A	E	DP
Bissonette	.933	13	9	19	2	4

Castillo	.947	12	10	26	2	2
Castro	.867	4	6	7	2	4
Cruz	.931	54	63	112	13	17
Kaiser	.985	41	45	88	2	18

Outfield	PCT	G	PO	A	E	DP
Amaral	.975	56	114	4	3	1
Bae	.900	9	15	3	2	2
Citta	.667	2	2	0	1	0
Davis	.979	57	138	2	3	1
Fraizer	1.000	32	67	2	0	1
Madris	1.000	11	11	0	0	0
Mitchell	.984	97	186	3	3	1
Murray	1.000	5	1	0	0	0
Smith-Njigba	.991	61	106	2	1	1
Stafford	1.000	3	2	0	0	0
Suwinski	.976	37	76	4	2	0

GREENSBORO GRASSHOPPERS

HIGH CLASS A

HIGH-A EAST

Batting	B-T	HT	WT	DOB	AVG	vLH	vRH	G	AB	R	H	2B	3B	HR	RBI	BB	HBP	SH	SF	SO	SB	CS	SLG	OBP
Acuna, Francisco	R-R	5-6	150	1-12-00	.160	.111	.178	31	100	13	16	5	0	2	9	14	3	0	0	30	6	1	.270	.282
Alvarez, Andres	R-R	5-10	175	3-29-97	.288	.229	.308	39	139	29	40	9	0	6	20	17	1	0	1	38	10	2	.482	.367
Davis, Henry	R-R	6-2	210	9-21-99	.263	.250	.267	6	19	6	5	0	1	2	3	4	0	0	1	8	1	0	.684	.375
Davis, Jonah	L-R	5-10	181	7-2-97	.196	.194	.197	32	107	17	21	5	0	7	19	19	6	0	0	58	2	3	.439	.348
Fajardo, Yoyner	L-R	6-0	179	4-6-99	.246	.167	.293	19	65	10	16	3	0	0	4	8	2	0	0	13	6	5	.292	.347
Finol, Claudio	R-R	5-11	171	4-13-00	.067	.000	.100	5	15	2	1	0	0	0	1	3	0	0	0	6	0	0	.067	.222
Fraizer, Matt	L-R	6-3	217	1-12-98	.314	.321	.311	75	303	64	95	14	3	20	50	43	2	0	1	74	14	6	.578	.401
Gonzales, Nick	R-R	5-10	195	5-27-99	.302	.354	.285	80	324	53	98	23	4	18	54	40	4	0	1	101	7	2	.565	.385
Gorski, Matt	R-R	6-4	198	12-22-97	.223	.165	.243	95	358	62	80	18	0	17	56	34	4	0	5	125	18	1	.416	.294
Herman, Jack	R-R	5-9	190	9-30-99	.115	.222	.059	15	52	3	6	3	0	0	1	2	0	0	0	26	1	1	.173	.148
Jarvis, Mike	R-R	5-10	180	5-12-98	.267	.333	.222	5	15	1	4	0	1	0	0	1	2	0	0	4	3	0	.400	.389
Koch, Grant	R-R	6-0	195	2-5-97	.192	.148	.211	54	182	34	35	8	0	9	32	22	3	1	3	51	0	1	.385	.296
Macias, Fabricio	R-R	6-0	188	3-11-98	.316	.265	.336	44	171	27	54	9	2	6	38	10	3	0	0	41	5	3	.497	.364
Matthiessen, Will	R-R	6-7	220	1-9-98	.245	.269	.238	77	277	51	68	14	0	13	65	30	1	0	2	107	1	3	.437	.319
Murray, Chase	L-R	6-0	188	6-3-98	.264	.188	.297	14	53	10	14	1	0	3	8	1	0	0	16	4	0	.453	.278
Peguero, Liover	R-R	6-1	200	12-31-00	.270	.295	.260	90	374	67	101	19	2	14	45	33	3	4	3	105	28	6	.444	.332
Sabol, Blake	L-R	6-4	215	1-7-98	.296	.200	.325	52	199	39	59	12	3	11	33	27	1	0	2	72	6	0	.553	.380
Sanchez, Lolo	R-R	5-11	168	4-23-99	.264	.240	.272	104	364	79	96	18	0	17	58	55	11	2	5	72	30	9	.453	.372
Shackelford, Aaron	L-R	5-10	205	10-16-96	.210	.208	.211	97	372	51	78	15	2	22	69	36	8	0	5	133	3	0	.438	.290
Shockley, Dylan	R-R	5-11	195	4-10-97	.113	.105	.116	20	62	7	7	3	0	1	6	6	3	0	1	21	0	1	.210	.222
Triolo, Jared	R-R	6-3	212	2-8-98	.304	.304	.304	108	421	74	128	29	0	15	78	42	4	0	4	94	25	6	.480	.369
Valdez, Jesus	R-R	6-0	175	12-29-97	.250	.182	.273	13	44	9	11	1	0	4	7	4	1	0	0	13	3	0	.545	.327
Wilkie, Kyle	R-R	5-10	205	10-20-97	.118	.111	.120	10	34	3	4	0	0	0	3	0	0	0	0	12	0	0	.118	.189
Wilson, Eli	R-R	6-2	190	7-6-98	.203	.222	.195	16	59	12	12	3	2	1	8	5	3	0	0	21	0	0	.373	.299

Pitching	B-T	HT	WT	DOB	W	L	ERA	G	GS	CG	SV	IP	H	R	ER	HR	BB	SO	AVG	vLH	vRH	K/9	BB/9
Alvarez, Andres	R-R	5-10	175	3-29-97	0	0	18.90	3	0	0	0	3	7	9	7	2	2	1	.438	.125	.750	2.70	5.40
Ashcraft, Braxton	L-R	6-5	195	10-5-99	1	1	5.35	10	10	0	0	39	35	23	23	8	12	41	.246	.154	.325	9.54	2.79
Bellomy, Bear	R-R	6-4	205	3-29-98	9	2	4.57	34	0	0	2	67	59	36	34	13	17	85	.230	.225	.233	11.42	2.28
Burrows, Michael	R-R	6-2	183	11-8-99	2	2	2.20	13	13	0	0	49	24	15	12	3	20	66	.143	.164	.126	12.12	3.67
Carey, Jack	R-R	6-0	205	9-20-99	0	0	6.23	3	0	0	0	4	5	3	3	0	2	4	.294	.667	.091	8.31	4.15

Name	B-T	HT	WT	DOB	W	L	ERA	G	GS	CG	SV	IP	H	R	ER	HR	BB	SO	AVG	vLH	vRH	H/9	BB/9
Cruz, Omar	L-L	6-0	200	1-26-99	3	3	3.45	7	7	0	0	29	17	13	11	4	14	38	.168	.100	.185	11.93	4.40
Florez, Santiago	R-R	6-5	222	5-9-00	3	3	7.53	11	9	0	0	43	57	37	36	9	21	36	.329	.296	.359	7.53	4.40
Flowers, J.C.	R-R	6-3	190	5-19-98	5	2	4.23	15	11	0	1	62	64	36	29	6	22	69	.266	.233	.290	10.07	3.21
Ford, Grant	R-R	6-1	175	3-11-98	8	4	6.04	25	10	0	0	76	77	52	51	17	40	91	.258	.237	.275	10.78	4.74
Garcia, Oliver	R-R	6-3	213	1-8-98	4	2	4.42	36	0	0	8	53	46	30	26	10	32	52	.231	.204	.255	8.83	5.43
Gonzalez, Domingo	R-R	6-0	185	9-27-99	2	2	6.46	8	6	0	0	39	48	28	28	12	17	35	.306	.323	.293	8.08	3.92
Jennings, Steven	R-R	6-2	175	11-13-98	4	1	4.50	10	1	0	0	28	28	14	14	3	5	20	.262	.174	.328	6.43	1.61
Junker, Cameron	R-R	6-5	220	9-3-97	0	0	9.00	3	0	0	0	4	5	4	4	1	1	7	.294	.250	.333	15.75	2.25
Kobos, Will	R-R	6-2	180	8-3-97	6	2	2.16	27	0	0	5	42	19	13	10	4	23	68	.129	.108	.153	14.69	4.97
Leonard, Garrett	R-R	6-3	190	9-25-96	3	2	5.81	29	0	0	1	62	49	42	40	15	49	71	.220	.208	.230	10.31	7.11
Linarez, Valentin	R-R	6-5	226	2-14-00	0	2	5.00	2	2	0	0	9	8	5	5	3	2	7	.235	.333	.182	7.00	2.00
Manasa, Alex	L-R	6-4	195	1-6-98	1	1	5.55	20	0	0	1	49	54	34	30	11	8	46	.278	.306	.257	8.51	1.48
Matthiessen, Will	R-R	6-7	220	1-9-98	1	0	45.00	1	0	0	0	1	4	6	5	1	1	0	.571	.333	.750	0.00	9.00
McGough, Trey	L-L	6-3	195	3-29-98	0	0	2.00	6	1	0	0	18	12	4	4	1	4	13	.197	.250	.152	6.50	2.00
Mejia, Enmanuel	R-R	5-11	185	12-22-98	1	1	1.10	11	0	0	1	16	11	7	2	2	10	18	.193	.235	.175	9.92	5.51
Melendez, Cristofer	R-R	6-3	226	9-16-97	0	0	2.00	6	0	0	2	9	6	2	2	1	2	13	.188	.176	.200	13.00	2.00
Miliano, Michell	R-R	6-3	185	12-22-99	2	2	6.30	16	0	0	0	20	20	18	14	1	26	23	.267	.267	.267	10.35	11.70
Mlodzinski, Carmen	R-R	6-2	232	2-19-99	2	3	3.93	14	14	0	0	50	45	26	22	7	20	64	.237	.211	.260	11.44	3.58
Priester, Quinn	R-R	6-3	210	9-16-00	7	4	3.04	20	20	0	0	98	82	40	33	8	39	98	.225	.238	.212	9.03	3.59
Roberts, Austin	R-R	6-0	219	7-27-98	4	3	4.55	39	0	0	9	65	64	39	33	15	25	99	.252	.264	.243	13.64	3.44
Selby, Colin	R-R	6-1	218	10-24-97	3	1	4.37	31	0	0	6	60	39	29	29	7	35	67	.183	.247	.137	10.15	5.28
Shockley, Dylan	R-R	5-11	195	4-10-97	0	0	0.00	1	0	0	0	1	2	0	0	0	0	2	.400	--	.400	18.00	0.00
Thomas, Tahnaj	R-R	6-4	190	6-16-99	3	3	5.19	16	16	0	0	61	61	40	35	13	35	62	.256	.266	.250	9.20	5.19
Umana, Sergio	R-R	6-0	175	5-21-00	0	0	31.50	2	0	0	0	2	6	7	7	4	1	1	.500	.500	.500	4.50	4.50

Fielding

Catcher	PCT	G	PO	A	E	DP	PB
Davis	1.000	4	32	2	0	0	2
Koch	.985	51	493	38	8	2	8
Sabol	.997	25	285	11	1	1	2
Shockley	.995	20	191	10	1	0	4
Wilkie	.983	8	53	4	1	0	0
Wilson	1.000	14	123	15	0	0	4

First Base	PCT	G	PO	A	E	DP
Gorski	1.000	3	28	0	0	0
Matthiessen	.988	57	386	26	5	37
Shackelford	.996	55	422	21	2	33
Valdez	.940	7	41	6	3	2

Second Base	PCT	G	PO	A	E	DP
Acuna	.955	10	15	27	2	7
Alvarez	.976	11	14	26	1	7
Fajardo	1.000	1	0	1	0	0

	PCT	G	PO	A	E	DP
Finol	1.000	2	2	4	0	1
Gonzales	.981	73	95	161	5	34
Shackelford	.969	27	32	61	3	12

Third Base	PCT	G	PO	A	E	DP
Acuna	1.000	2	0	2	0	0
Alvarez	.966	14	11	17	1	2
Fajardo	.000	1	0	0	0	0
Finol	.500	1	0	1	1	0
Shackelford	1.000	1	1	0	0	0
Triolo	.961	102	81	163	10	19
Valdez	.750	2	1	2	1	0

Shortstop	PCT	G	PO	A	E	DP
Acuna	.921	19	19	39	5	7
Alvarez	1.000	12	11	19	0	6
Finol	1.000	2	1	6	0	2
Gonzales	1.000	1	0	1	0	0

	PCT	G	PO	A	E	DP
Jarvis	.000	1	0	0	0	0
Peguero	.934	86	115	210	23	34
Triolo	1.000	5	6	10	0	1

Outfield	PCT	G	PO	A	E	DP
Davis	.969	32	60	2	2	1
Fajardo	.889	12	15	1	2	0
Fraizer	.979	68	137	3	3	0
Gorski	.989	89	177	9	2	2
Herman	.944	11	17	0	1	0
Jarvis	1.000	4	9	0	0	0
Macias	.984	30	60	0	1	0
Matthiessen	1.000	11	12	1	0	0
Murray	1.000	12	16	2	0	0
Sabol	.958	10	23	0	1	0
Sanchez	.993	86	130	4	1	0

BRADENTON MARAUDERS   LOW CLASS A
LOW-A SOUTHEAST

Batting	B-T	HT	WT	DOB	AVG	vLH	vRH	G	AB	R	H	2B	3B	HR	RBI	BB	HBP	SH	SF	SO	SB	CS	SLG	OBP
Acuna, Francisco	R-R	5-6	150	1-12-00	.208	.211	.207	39	101	22	21	7	0	1	9	20	9	0	1	27	0	1	.307	.382
Bowen, Jase	R-R	6-0	190	9-2-00	.220	.288	.203	103	354	51	78	12	2	14	60	32	15	0	4	111	16	1	.384	.309
Campana, Sergio	R-R	6-1	160	3-29-02	.169	.138	.176	51	160	27	27	5	3	0	9	24	2	0	2	67	13	1	.238	.282
Dixon, Jasiah	R-R	6-0	180	8-31-01	.175	.222	.170	27	97	14	17	2	0	0	4	13	4	1	0	34	13	0	.196	.298
Escotto, Maikol	R-R	5-11	180	6-4-02	.234	.339	.211	89	320	61	75	13	1	7	38	54	6	0	1	116	22	5	.347	.354
Fajardo, Yoyner	L-R	6-0	179	4-6-99	.309	.000	.313	31	68	9	21	4	2	1	12	8	2	0	0	15	8	0	.471	.397
Finol, Claudio	R-R	5-11	171	4-13-00	.176	.000	.200	6	17	2	3	0	0	0	1	2	1	0	0	2	1	1	.176	.300
Glenn, Jackson	R-R	5-9	205	10-24-97	.337	.450	.309	28	101	22	34	12	1	0	14	22	0	0	1	21	1	1	.475	.452
Goforth, Ethan	R-R	5-10	190	6-25-97	.286	1.000	.167	4	7	1	2	0	0	0	1	1	0	0	0	3	3	0	.286	.375
Gutierrez, Abrahan	R-R	6-0	214	10-31-99	.294	.455	.217	22	68	16	20	8	2	0	8	16	3	0	0	13	0	0	.471	.448
2-team total (50 Clearwater)					.290	.354	.274	72	245	46	71	18	2	5	36	53	7	0	1	44	0	0	.441	.428
Head, Hudson	L-L	6-1	180	4-8-01	.213	.097	.243	101	348	67	74	16	1	15	50	68	15	0	3	137	3	1	.394	.362
Herman, Jack	R-R	5-9	190	9-30-99	.253	.214	.263	54	217	39	55	11	1	13	49	23	1	0	2	70	2	1	.493	.325
Lopez, Dariel	R-R	6-1	183	2-7-02	.258	.333	.240	98	361	52	93	17	1	10	64	41	8	0	6	103	1	2	.393	.341
Marcos, Norkis	R-R	6-0	170	5-26-01	.193	.333	.168	40	119	18	23	4	1	0	14	21	1	0	2	50	7	3	.244	.315
Matthiessen, Will	R-R	6-7	220	1-9-98	.256	.429	.219	12	39	6	10	3	1	2	11	12	0	0	0	21	0	0	.538	.431
Mojica, Alexander	R-R	6-1	195	8-2-02	.209	.148	.223	87	287	38	60	11	0	9	43	41	6	0	3	90	1	0	.341	.322
Ordonez, Ernny	R-R	6-1	210	1-17-99	.252	.255	.251	75	258	37	65	14	3	7	45	24	3	0	2	64	1	0	.411	.321
Rivero, Daniel	R-R	6-0	191	1-22-01	.241	.190	.253	40	108	17	26	3	2	1	14	25	0	0	1	20	1	2	.333	.381
Rodriguez, Endy	B-R	6-0	170	5-26-00	.294	.319	.289	98	377	73	111	25	6	15	73	50	4	0	3	77	2	0	.512	.380
Sabol, Blake	L-R	6-4	215	1-7-98	.370	.250	.381	14	46	11	17	2	0	2	12	12	1	0	0	12	2	0	.543	.508
Shockley, Dylan	R-R	5-11	195	4-10-97	.308	.000	.333	8	26	7	8	2	0	0	6	5	2	0	0	9	0	0	.385	.455
Siani, Sammy	L-L	5-10	195	12-14-00	.215	.237	.210	62	200	48	43	7	2	8	35	52	2	0	4	63	9	2	.390	.376
Snider, Jack	L-R	6-1	190	5-19-98	.462	--	.462	7	13	7	6	1	0	0	0	5	0	0	0	2	0	0	.538	.611
Wilkie, Kyle	R-R	5-10	205	10-20-97	.271	.500	.225	17	48	7	13	4	0	1	6	5	0	0	0	10	0	0	.417	.340
Wilson, Eli	R-R	6-2	190	7-6-98	.328	.316	.330	39	116	23	38	8	0	3	22	31	4	0	1	38	0	0	.474	.480

PITTSBURGH PIRATES

Pitching

Pitching	B-T	HT	WT	DOB	W	L	ERA	G	GS	CG	SV	IP	H	R	ER	HR	BB	SO	AVG	vLH	vRH	K/9	BB/9
Acuna, Francisco	R-R	5-6	150	1-12-00	0	0	0.00	1	0	0	0	1	2	3	0	0	2	1	.400	.000	.500	9.00	18.00
Aquino, Alex	R-R	6-2	165	7-6-96	0	0	0.00	4	0	0	2	5	0	0	0	0	0	8	.000	.000	.000	14.40	3.60
Brahms, Parker	R-R	6-3	209	12-2-97	1	2	9.24	18	0	0	0	25	29	28	26	4	29	36	.293	.333	.275	12.79	10.30
Brault, Steven	L-L	6-0	195	4-29-92	0	0	0.00	1	1	0	0	2	1	0	0	0	2	3	.167	.000	.250	16.20	10.80
Campos, Carlos	R-R	6-1	169	5-10-01	2	2	4.84	13	1	0	0	22	25	15	12	6	10	25	.272	.273	.271	10.07	4.03
Charle, Cristian	R-R	6-1	208	6-2-00	0	2	6.55	5	0	0	0	11	14	11	8	1	3	10	.298	.353	.267	8.18	2.45
Chen, Po-Yu	L-R	6-2	187	10-2-01	1	1	5.63	4	4	0	0	16	15	12	10	2	12	15	.246	.333	.209	8.44	6.75
Concepcion, Xavier	R-R	6-2	175	1-22-98	0	0	7.36	3	0	0	1	4	4	5	3	0	4	2	.286	.286	.286	4.91	9.82
Davis, Austin	L-L	6-4	235	2-3-93	0	0	3.00	2	0	0	0	3	2	1	1	0	1	6	.200	.000	.400	18.00	3.00
Dombkowski, Nick	R-L	6-2	195	8-9-98	1	0	3.86	11	0	0	2	19	13	8	8	3	6	23	.178	.167	.182	11.09	2.89
Fellows, Drake	L-R	6-5	216	3-6-98	1	0	9.82	2	0	0	0	4	5	4	4	1	6	4	.313	.500	.250	9.82	14.73
Florencio, Adrian	R-R	6-6	205	10-11-98	6	4	2.46	20	19	0	0	95	70	35	26	5	30	117	.198	.232	.175	11.08	2.84
Florez, Santiago	R-R	6-5	222	5-9-00	5	2	1.37	10	9	2	1	53	31	10	8	0	14	71	.165	.077	.247	12.13	2.39
Flowers, J.C.	R-R	6-3	190	5-19-98	0	1	2.12	6	2	0	0	17	11	4	4	1	3	23	.183	.160	.200	12.18	1.59
Garcia, Nick	L-R	6-4	215	4-20-99	5	4	4.22	21	13	0	1	75	66	48	35	9	35	83	.232	.242	.226	10.00	4.22
Gonzalez, Domingo	R-R	6-0	185	9-27-99	3	3	3.72	12	8	0	0	48	38	27	20	8	20	69	.215	.235	.202	12.85	3.72
Hofmann, Logan	L-R	5-10	190	11-18-99	6	4	3.59	22	13	0	0	83	59	40	33	12	33	103	.196	.136	.230	11.21	3.59
Jennings, Steven	R-R	6-2	175	11-13-98	2	0	2.76	6	0	0	0	16	14	5	5	1	5	19	.222	.208	.231	10.47	2.76
Jones, Jared	L-R	6-1	180	8-6-01	3	6	4.64	18	15	0	0	66	63	44	34	6	34	103	.245	.179	.291	14.05	4.64
Junker, Cameron	R-R	6-5	220	9-3-97	2	0	3.00	14	0	0	1	30	14	12	10	2	20	47	.143	.136	.148	14.10	6.00
Maldonado, Jose	R-R	6-2	198	1-17-99	0	0	1.59	3	2	0	0	6	1	1	1	0	4	11	.056	.000	.100	17.47	6.35
Malone, Brennan	R-R	6-4	205	9-8-00	0	0	0.00	3	0	0	0	4	4	4	0	0	5	2	.286	.200	.333	4.91	12.27
Marcos, Norkis	R-R	6-0	170	5-26-01	0	0	--	1	0	0	0	2	5	5	0	3	0	1	1.000	--	1.000	--	--
Mateo, Oliver	R-R	6-2	170	11-7-97	5	2	4.78	33	0	0	7	38	17	21	20	2	40	82	.135	.173	.108	19.59	9.56
Meis, Justin	R-R	6-2	160	11-23-99	1	1	2.04	10	0	0	0	18	14	9	4	2	9	27	.203	.083	.267	13.75	4.58
Mejia, Enmanuel	R-R	5-11	185	12-22-98	4	1	0.00	21	0	0	8	26	15	4	0	0	17	35	.161	.152	.167	11.96	5.81
Montout, Wandi	R-R	6-2	190	3-21-97	6	0	4.66	24	0	0	1	39	29	22	20	1	30	52	.204	.288	.156	12.10	6.98
Ortiz, Estalin	L-L	6-4	213	11-20-98	0	0	67.50	2	0	0	0	1	5	10	10	2	5	2	.556	.000	.625	13.50	33.75
Ortiz, Luis	R-R	6-2	163	1-27-99	5	3	3.09	22	19	0	0	87	82	46	30	5	28	113	.241	.276	.218	11.65	2.89
Rodriguez, Endy	B-R	6-0	170	5-26-00	0	0	0.00	1	0	0	0	1	1	0	0	0	0	0	.333	.500	.000	0.00	0.00
Roman, Brayan	L-L	5-9	180	9-30-98	3	2	6.33	11	0	0	1	21	27	15	15	3	14	21	.325	.222	.375	8.86	5.91
Roth, Alex	R-R	6-5	220	12-9-97	1	0	4.13	17	1	0	0	24	21	12	11	6	18	29	.231	.273	.207	10.88	6.75
Samaniego, Tyler	R-L	6-4	205	12-30-99	1	0	1.29	5	0	0	0	7	4	2	1	1	2	15	.154	.222	.118	19.29	2.57
Soriano, Jose	R-R	6-3	220	10-20-98	0	0	14.73	2	2	0	0	4	6	7	6	0	3	6	.353	.429	.300	14.73	7.36
Troutman, Ryan	R-R	6-1	205	12-25-96	2	1	9.00	16	0	0	0	23	24	25	23	2	31	22	.270	.270	.269	8.61	12.13
Umana, Sergio	R-R	6-0	175	5-21-00	0	4	6.21	23	0	0	0	42	59	35	29	5	5	27	.322	.333	.314	5.79	1.07
Wilkie, Kyle	R-R	5-10	205	10-20-97	0	0	7.36	3	0	0	0	4	3	3	1	3	2	.286	.222	.400	4.91	7.36
Yajure, Miguel	R-R	6-1	220	5-1-98	1	0	6.75	2	2	0	0	4	6	5	3	1	1	5	.333	.500	.286	11.25	2.25
Yean, Eddy	R-R	6-1	180	6-25-01	5	2	5.27	22	8	0	1	67	56	45	39	8	39	69	.224	.245	.207	9.32	5.27

Fielding

Catcher

Catcher	PCT	G	PO	A	E	DP	PB
Goforth	1.000	2	7	2	0	0	0
Gutierrez	.974	13	110	3	3	1	0
Rodriguez	.990	54	553	40	6	1	8
Sabol	1.000	3	25	3	0	0	0
Shockley	1.000	8	81	11	0	1	0
Wilkie	.989	16	166	10	2	3	0
Wilson	.995	33	339	24	2	3	2

First Base

First Base	PCT	G	PO	A	E	DP
Finol	1.000	1	7	0	0	0
Goforth	.917	2	11	0	1	2
Marcos	.968	11	58	2	2	9
Matthiessen	.986	10	68	2	1	5
Mojica	.993	21	137	8	1	11
Ordonez	.977	66	439	23	11	38
Rodriguez	.988	18	80	4	1	7
Wilkie	1.000	1	1	0	0	0

Second Base

Second Base	PCT	G	PO	A	E	DP
Acuna	.947	21	29	42	4	7
Bowen	.948	41	54	93	8	26
Escotto	.957	10	13	9	1	3
Fajardo	1.000	22	25	30	0	7
Finol	1.000	2	2	1	0	0
Glenn	.971	24	25	43	2	7
Lopez	.912	9	18	13	3	5
Marcos	.962	8	14	11	1	5

Third Base

Third Base	PCT	G	PO	A	E	DP
Acuna	.939	14	14	17	2	2
Bowen	1.000	4	2	2	0	1
Fajardo	1.000	2	3	0	0	0
Finol	1.000	3	2	4	0	1
Glenn	1.000	3	0	3	0	0
Lopez	.867	45	20	58	12	4
Marcos	.929	9	9	17	2	5
Mojica	.907	48	27	80	11	10
Ordonez	1.000	2	0	1	0	0

Shortstop

Shortstop	PCT	G	PO	A	E	DP
Acuna	.727	3	2	6	3	2
Escotto	.907	77	82	153	24	37
Lopez	.839	35	34	60	18	8
Marcos	.897	13	9	17	3	3

Outfield

Outfield	PCT	G	PO	A	E	DP
Bowen	.988	57	81	1	1	0
Campana	.950	50	73	3	4	0
Dixon	.941	27	30	2	2	0
Fajardo	1.000	1	5	1	0	1
Head	.973	92	140	3	4	1
Herman	.967	46	55	3	2	0
Rivero	.970	37	59	5	2	1
Rodriguez	.500	4	1	0	1	0
Sabol	1.000	4	6	0	0	0
Siani	.976	61	80	2	2	1
Snider	1.000	5	4	0	0	0

FCL PIRATES
FLORIDA COMPLEX LEAGUE

ROOKIE

Batting	B-T	HT	WT	DOB	AVG	vLH	vRH	G	AB	R	H	2B	3B	HR	RBI	BB	HBP	SH	SF	SO	SB	CS	SLG	OBP
Bae, Ji-hwan	L-R	6-1	185	7-26-99	.429	.500	.400	2	7	3	3	0	0	1	2	0	0	0	0	0	0	0	.857	.429
Baez, Darwin	R-R	6-0	186	11-6-00	.231	.000	.279	24	52	11	12	0	1	1	7	7	1	1	1	15	1	1	.327	.328
Basabe, Angel	L-L	6-0	153	12-12-00	.214	.444	.194	38	117	18	25	5	3	0	16	11	7	2	2	28	5	0	.308	.314
Bastardo, Franrielis	R-R	6-2	196	7-19-02	.215	.143	.226	36	107	11	23	6	0	3	16	8	3	0	0	33	0	0	.355	.288
Bishop, Braylon	L-L	6-2	193	4-23-03	.192	.000	.238	8	26	3	5	0	0	0	2	2	0	0	0	8	3	0	.192	.250
Brown, Lane	L-R	5-10	195	3-12-98	.174	.500	.147	17	45	5	7	0	1	0	5	5	0	0	3	11	1	0	.200	.226
Busby, Dylan	R-R	6-2	196	11-28-95	.250	.000	.286	3	8	3	2	0	0	1	2	1	0	0	0	6	0	0	.625	.333
Campana, Sergio	R-R	6-1	160	3-29-02	.272	.333	.246	30	92	20	25	3	4	1	18	14	4	1	0	30	7	3	.424	.391

	B-T	HT	WT	DOB	AVG	vLH	vRH	G	AB	R	H	2B	3B	HR	RBI	BB	HBP	SH	SF	SO	SB	CS	OBP	SLG
Canache, Carlos	R-R	6-1	170	11-4-00	.241	.000	.278	30	83	18	20	7	2	0	7	15	1	0	0	24	10	0	.373	.364
Chandler, Bubba	B-R	6-3	200	9-14-02	.167	.143	.174	11	30	3	5	1	0	1	2	5	2	0	0	16	0	0	.300	.324
Cheng, Tsung-Che	L-R	5-7	154	7-26-01	.311	.370	.295	38	122	32	38	8	1	4	31	30	2	1	2	14	16	6	.492	.449
Davis, Henry	R-R	6-2	210	9-21-99	.429	.500	.400	2	7	1	3	2	0	1	4	0	0	0	0	2	0	0	1.143	.429
Dixon, Brenden	R-R	6-1	205	11-20-00	.313	.375	.292	12	32	6	10	1	1	2	6	10	1	0	0	12	2	0	.594	.488
Dixon, Jasiah	R-R	6-0	180	8-31-01	.244	.200	.263	27	82	22	20	2	0	1	9	19	4	0	0	26	4	2	.305	.410
Finol, Claudio	R-R	5-11	171	4-13-00	.276	.176	.317	21	58	7	16	6	1	1	10	5	2	0	1	16	1	0	.466	.348
Fowler, Dustin	L-L	6-0	195	12-29-94	.200	.000	.214	5	15	2	3	0	1	1	2	1	1	0	0	6	0	0	.533	.294
Glenn, Jackson	R-R	5-9	205	10-24-97	.400	--	.400	2	5	1	2	2	0	0	1	1	0	0	0	1	0	0	.800	.500
Goforth, Ethan	R-R	5-10	190	6-25-97	.000	.000	.000	2	2	1	0	0	0	0	0	1	1	0	0	0	0	0	.000	.500
Graham, A.J.	R-R	6-3	180	10-2-02	.100	.000	.125	4	10	2	1	0	0	0	1	1	1	0	0	4	1	0	.100	.250
Hendrie, Wyatt	R-R	5-11	200	2-8-99	.237	.000	.273	15	38	6	9	2	1	1	6	7	0	0	1	8	0	0	.421	.348
Herman, Jack	R-R	5-9	190	9-30-99	.360	.167	.421	8	25	7	9	3	0	2	9	4	0	0	0	7	0	0	.720	.448
Hernandez, Luis	R-R	5-9	150	9-6-00	.184	.000	.209	29	76	12	14	3	0	0	13	6	6	0	3	29	0	0	.224	.286
Jarvis, Mike	R-R	5-10	180	5-12-98	.357	.500	.313	13	42	16	15	3	2	2	8	3	4	0	0	4	8	0	.667	.449
Jerez, Juan	R-R	6-0	160	11-28-01	.296	.286	.298	43	152	26	45	9	2	6	28	24	2	1	2	46	10	4	.500	.394
Jimenez, Joe	R-R	5-10	185	2-22-98	.000	--	.000	6	5	0	0	0	0	0	0	1	0	0	0	2	0	0	.000	.000
Maguire, Solomon	L-R	5-11	168	3-4-03	.146	.111	.154	17	48	6	7	1	0	2	6	10	0	0	1	15	0	1	.292	.288
Marcos, Norkis	R-R	6-0	170	5-26-01	.194	.240	.181	37	108	22	21	4	1	0	8	24	4	0	0	38	8	4	.250	.360
Montero, Eliazer	R-R	5-10	157	9-15-00	.197	.154	.208	26	61	15	12	3	0	1	8	10	1	1	1	20	4	1	.295	.315
Nadal, Deivis	B-R	5-11	150	2-8-02	.165	.190	.159	36	109	12	18	0	0	0	3	7	7	2	1	31	7	4	.165	.258
Nolasco, Rodolfo	R-R	6-1	175	9-23-01	.284	.182	.317	42	134	27	38	8	2	8	32	26	3	0	1	43	0	0	.552	.409
Nova, Fleury	R-R	5-11	160	1-17-01	.176	.222	.160	19	34	4	6	0	1	0	4	2	0	1	0	12	0	0	.235	.222
Planchart, Geovanny	R-R	6-0	176	9-17-01	.321	.458	.267	26	84	12	27	7	1	1	15	12	0	0	2	23	1	0	.464	.398
Polanco, Gustavo	R-R	6-0	190	6-13-97	.230	.091	.260	21	61	6	14	1	1	0	14	4	2	1	0	8	1	0	.279	.299
Polanco, Jhan	B-R	5-11	175	11-4-00	.188	.667	.138	13	32	7	6	3	0	1	9	19	2	0	0	10	0	0	.375	.509
Quintero, Francisco	R-R	5-10	167	9-19-00	.289	.222	.306	22	45	7	13	3	0	1	4	8	1	0	0	18	1	2	.422	.407
Rivero, Daniel	R-R	6-0	191	1-22-01	.270	.333	.240	11	37	5	10	0	1	0	9	2	1	0	2	7	1	0	.324	.310
Romero, Randy	R-R	5-11	155	8-10-99	.252	.273	.243	40	151	30	38	5	4	0	15	11	2	4	2	24	15	2	.338	.307
Romero, Rayber	B-R	5-10	155	5-28-02	.270	.278	.269	39	111	31	30	1	1	1	13	31	6	3	2	22	7	1	.324	.447
Shockley, Dylan	R-R	5-11	195	4-10-97	.222	.250	.200	8	18	8	4	1	0	1	6	7	1	0	1	6	0	0	.444	.444
Stafford, Deon	R-R	5-11	211	3-17-96	.364	.200	.412	6	22	6	8	3	0	2	5	3	1	0	0	5	0	0	.773	.462
Tejeda, Luis	R-R	5-11	170	8-26-02	.196	.158	.204	37	112	16	22	7	0	2	19	15	1	0	3	33	2	1	.313	.290
Walker, Deion	R-R	6-4	180	8-20-01	.200	.500	.176	33	80	18	16	1	2	1	8	15	2	0	0	23	9	2	.300	.340
White Jr., Lonnie	R-R	6-3	212	12-31-02	.258	.000	.308	9	31	6	8	2	0	2	5	2	0	0	0	14	0	0	.516	.303
Wood, Cory	L-R	5-9	180	6-26-97	.091	.000	.143	4	11	1	1	0	0	0	1	0	0	0	0	1	0	0	.091	.167
Wright, Jake	L-L	5-9	195	9-5-97	.154	.000	.200	7	13	3	2	0	0	0	1	6	1	0	0	6	0	0	.154	.450

Pitching	B-T	HT	WT	DOB	W	L	ERA	G	GS	CG	SV	IP	H	R	ER	HR	BB	SO	AVG	vLH	vRH	K/9	BB/9
Bidois, Brandan	R-R	6-2	158	6-21-01	0	0	4.50	3	0	0	0	6	8	3	3	0	4	6	.320	.500	.200	9.00	6.00
Brahms, Parker	R-R	6-3	209	12-2-97	1	0	13.50	2	0	0	0	3	4	4	4	0	2	2	.400	.333	.429	6.75	6.75
Campos, Carlos	R-R	6-1	169	5-10-01	2	0	1.93	5	0	0	0	14	9	3	3	0	4	20	.188	.077	.229	12.86	2.57
Carey, Jack	R-R	6-0	205	9-20-99	1	0	0.00	1	0	0	0	1	0	0	0	0	1	0	--	.000	.000	9.00	0.00
Charle, Cristian	R-R	6-1	208	6-2-00	4	2	2.56	11	0	0	2	32	25	10	9	1	5	37	.208	.174	.230	10.52	1.42
Chen, Po-Yu	L-R	6-2	187	10-2-01	2	0	0.69	6	6	0	0	26	18	3	2	0	0	29	.191	.200	.186	10.04	0.00
Cruz, Cristopher	R-R	6-2	170	1-6-03	1	5	6.44	10	8	0	0	29	27	28	21	2	25	23	.241	.324	.205	7.06	7.67
De Dios, Arlinthon	R-R	6-2	183	1-24-00	2	2	3.96	13	1	0	1	36	28	17	16	1	14	36	.212	.204	.218	8.92	3.47
Del Rosario, Joelvis	R-R	5-11	170	4-16-01	4	2	3.26	12	7	0	1	39	32	15	14	3	10	52	.224	.255	.207	12.10	2.33
Disla, Kelvin	R-R	6-0	170	7-5-01	0	1	13.15	11	0	0	0	13	19	19	19	3	16	13	.339	.200	.390	9.00	11.08
Dotel, Bladimir	R-R	6-3	178	9-25-02	2	0	3.34	11	5	0	0	30	20	18	11	2	18	34	.185	.200	.179	10.31	5.46
Ercolani, Alessandro	R-R	6-2	185	4-20-04	2	3	5.40	10	0	0	0	18	20	13	11	1	8	20	.278	.296	.267	9.82	3.93
Fellows, Drake	L-R	6-5	216	3-6-98	0	0	0.00	3	2	0	0	8	5	0	0	0	4	5	.172	.250	.160	5.63	4.50
Garcia, Darvin	R-R	6-3	170	4-25-99	4	2	2.73	14	0	0	2	33	22	12	10	3	9	44	.188	.200	.183	12.00	2.45
Garcia, Mario	R-R	6-1	183	12-27-98	2	1	3.86	6	0	0	1	9	7	4	4	0	3	6	.212	.091	.273	5.79	2.89
Harbin, Ryan	R-R	6-4	195	8-6-01	0	1	7.53	5	5	0	0	14	19	13	12	1	9	17	.322	.269	.364	10.67	5.65
Jimenez, Carlos	R-R	6-2	140	7-14-02	3	2	3.15	10	8	0	0	34	25	21	12	2	15	44	.190	.200	.198	11.53	3.93
Linarez, Valentin	R-R	6-5	226	2-14-00	1	2	2.63	8	8	0	0	24	16	9	7	0	11	38	.188	.250	.158	14.25	4.13
Maldonado, Andy	R-R	6-4	196	7-21-02	2	0	2.45	9	6	1	0	29	21	10	8	1	22	44	.194	.220	.179	13.50	6.75
Malone, Brennan	R-R	6-4	205	9-8-00	0	0	5.23	6	5	0	0	7	6	6	5	1	5	8	.194	.235	.158	12.19	4.35
Marcos, Norkis	R-R	6-0	170	5-26-01	0	0	0.00	1	0	0	0	1	1	0	0	0	2	2	.250	.000	.500	18.00	18.00
Mendez, Adrian	L-L	6-1	160	3-7-02	1	2	8.00	12	0	0	0	18	25	20	16	1	15	17	.342	.444	.309	8.50	7.50
Mendoza, Dante	R-R	6-5	186	12-16-98	1	0	7.36	3	2	0	0	4	5	3	3	1	2	6	.313	.200	.364	14.73	4.91
Montero, Johan	R-R	6-3	187	8-26-99	2	0	7.31	11	0	0	1	16	19	13	13	1	10	14	.284	.292	.279	7.88	5.63
Ortiz, Estalin	L-L	6-4	213	11-20-98	1	0	6.00	2	0	0	0	3	3	3	2	0	3	4	.214	.000	.300	12.00	9.00
Peralta, Luis	L-L	5-11	170	1-6-01	0	3	3.41	9	7	0	0	29	20	15	11	1	18	36	.200	.200	.200	11.17	5.59
Ramos, Jorge	R-R	6-0	150	6-5-02	2	1	2.25	10	0	0	1	20	17	13	5	1	11	20	.227	.200	.200	9.00	4.95
Ramos, Wilkin	R-R	6-5	165	10-31-00	2	1	3.69	12	5	0	1	39	45	22	16	3	17	36	.292	.245	.314	8.31	3.92
Reyes, Yoelvis	L-R	6-2	192	12-10-99	1	2	6.55	16	0	0	1	22	25	19	16	2	15	27	.287	.364	.262	11.05	6.14
Rodriguez, Sebastian	R-R	6-0	168	10-17-01	1	1	4.71	6	4	0	0	21	26	12	11	2	6	16	.310	.351	.277	6.86	2.57
Romero, Wander	R-R	6-3	184	7-25-99	0	2	14.40	9	0	0	0	10	13	23	16	2	12	8	.302	.111	.353	7.20	10.80
Sosa, Listher	R-R	6-4	208	9-6-01	3	1	4.31	11	2	0	0	31	30	16	15	3	5	33	.254	.205	.278	9.48	1.44
Suero, Angel	R-R	6-4	202	8-27-99	0	0	9.00	3	0	0	0	3	7	9	3	1	3	3	.438	.667	.385	3.00	9.00
Sweeney, Jake	R-L	6-7	240	6-14-00	2	2	4.26	9	4	0	0	25	12	15	12	0	21	36	.140	.067	.155	12.79	7.46
Thibo, Yunior	R-R	6-4	185	6-24-98	0	1	7.80	15	0	0	2	15	17	17	13	2	9	12	.279	.263	.286	7.20	5.40
Troutman, Ryan	R-R	6-1	205	12-25-96	0	0	5.06	3	0	0	0	5	5	3	3	0	4	8	.278	.500	.214	13.50	6.75

Fielding

C: Baez 12, Davis 2, Finol 2, Goforth 2, Hendrie 12, Hernandez 19, Jimenez 5, Planchart 25, Polanco 6, Polanco 9, Shockley 6, Stafford 6.
1B: Baez 13, Bastardo 30, Canache 3, Finol 13, Hernandez 10, Marcos 18, Polanco 13, Quintero 1, Shockley 1.
2B: Bae 2, Cheng 14, Dixon 8, Dixon 1, Finol 1, Glenn 1, Jarvis 6, Jerez 4, Marcos 2, Montero 11, Nadal 5, Quintero 6, Romero 34, Tejeda 1, Wood 3.
3B: Busby 3, Cheng 12, Finol 5, Glenn 1, Jerez 27, Marcos 17, Montero 11, Nadal 2, Quintero 13, Romero 1, Tejeda 2.
SS: Chandler 3, Cheng 12, Dixon 1, Graham 4, Jarvis 5, Montero 1, Nadal 28, Quintero 2, Romero 5, Tejeda 35, Wood 1.
OF: Basabe 34, Bastardo 1, Bishop 8, Brown 16, Campana 29, Canache 31, Dixon 24, Fowler 5, Herman 4, Jarvis 1, Maguire 19, Montero 1, Nolasco 20, Nova 15, Rivero 10, Romero 39, Walker 33, White Jr. 9, Wright 3.

DSL PIRATES   ROOKIE
DOMINICAN SUMMER LEAGUE

Batting	B-T	HT	WT	DOB	AVG	vLH	vRH	G	AB	R	H	2B	3B	HR	RBI	BB	HBP	SH	SF	SO	SB	CS	SLG	OBP
Alfonzo, Omar	L-R	6-1	180	8-3-03	.232	.143	.256	39	99	21	23	2	1	2	10	32	2	0	0	30	0	0	.333	.429
Armas, Gustavo	R-R	6-2	175	12-12-03	.231	.100	.252	51	147	26	34	3	1	0	12	34	3	1	4	52	7	5	.265	.378
Carrasco, Eudys	R-R	6-1	180	10-4-01	.176	.167	.177	35	74	7	13	4	0	0	6	7	3	0	0	35	0	0	.230	.274
Castillo, Jesus	R-B	5-9	144	7-12-03	.245	.235	.248	49	147	24	36	2	1	0	12	17	5	0	1	30	15	5	.272	.341
Custodio, Jauri	R-R	5-10	162	9-21-01	.304	.167	.320	19	56	11	17	4	1	1	5	7	0	0	0	10	5	3	.464	.381
De La Cruz, Rodolfo	L-L	6-0	160	11-24-03	.161	.000	.187	43	124	14	20	4	2	2	15	27	2	0	0	54	3	7	.274	.320
De Paula, Robert	R-R	5-11	193	3-23-03	.188	.000	.222	15	32	4	6	1	0	0	5	5	4	0	0	13	0	1	.219	.366
Diaz, Kelvin	R-R	6-0	143	10-3-02	.154	.083	.175	25	52	10	8	4	0	1	9	10	5	0	2	22	3	0	.288	.333
Dipre, Isaias	R-R	5-11	159	6-7-03	.245	.167	.268	21	53	11	13	4	0	0	5	9	1	0	2	15	5	2	.321	.354
Escalante, Rafael	R-R	5-11	160	9-13-01	.275	.130	.324	41	91	15	25	5	0	0	14	15	5	0	0	18	4	1	.330	.405
Escalona, Eybert	R-R	6-0	180	10-27-02	.294	.000	.323	16	34	2	10	4	1	0	6	6	2	0	0	10	0	0	.471	.429
Escudero, Samuel	R-R	0-0	0	2-27-04	.151	.500	.108	36	73	5	11	2	0	0	2	10	1	0	1	11	1	1	.178	.259
Espinal, Ewry	L-R	6-0	185	12-18-02	.155	.167	.151	45	116	23	18	5	3	1	13	30	4	0	0	60	2	0	.276	.347
Figuereo, Pedro	B-R	5-10	150	3-28-03	.135	.000	.156	34	74	10	10	1	1	0	9	12	0	0	3	42	0	1	.176	.247
Gavilan, Osvaldo	L-L	5-11	150	10-10-01	.220	.286	.206	37	82	14	18	4	1	2	15	14	1	0	2	16	5	4	.366	.333
Lebron, Rubel	R-R	5-10	154	9-13-03	.214	.250	.208	23	56	7	12	1	1	0	7	7	0	0	0	17	4	1	.268	.302
Machado, Juan	L-R	5-11	145	6-4-03	.235	.200	.244	30	51	7	12	2	1	0	8	13	2	0	1	19	3	0	.314	.403
Montalban, Heiron	R-R	6-1	170	8-28-02	.231	.000	.281	18	39	5	9	3	0	1	6	7	1	0	1	14	3	2	.385	.354
Pena, Jhonson	R-R	6-0	155	8-3-02	.321	.429	.304	34	53	14	17	2	0	0	4	10	4	2	0	10	7	1	.358	.463
Polanco, Shalin	L-L	5-11	168	2-6-04	.204	.212	.202	47	157	16	32	6	3	3	22	18	0	0	1	44	6	2	.338	.284
Ramirez, Delfin	R-R	6-0	160	9-26-02	.191	.200	.190	42	89	14	17	2	0	0	8	12	3	1	1	35	4	2	.213	.305
Rivas, Javier	R-R	6-3	165	9-1-02	.133	.071	.153	51	173	19	23	5	1	0	10	11	7	0	1	56	6	4	.173	.214
Rodriguez, Eddy	R-R	6-0	181	11-5-03	.253	.231	.256	36	91	20	23	5	1	3	23	14	2	0	2	16	2	1	.429	.358
Sanchez, Ronny	R-R	5-11	191	7-22-02	.327	.360	.318	38	113	14	37	7	3	0	19	5	7	0	0	24	4	2	.442	.392
Sosa, Miguel	R-R	5-11	181	12-4-03	.239	.750	.175	32	71	9	17	2	0	1	9	12	3	1	1	18	0	1	.310	.368
Terrero, Enmanuel	L-L	5-11	160	9-14-02	.237	.300	.220	49	139	29	33	6	1	1	11	33	2	0	0	24	6	4	.317	.391
Toledo, Jeral	B-R	6-0	135	1-22-03	.236	.280	.228	52	148	33	35	9	0	1	21	35	6	0	3	24	9	6	.318	.396
Urbina, Fabian	L-R	5-8	175	10-25-01	.266	.368	.233	28	79	10	21	3	0	0	6	8	2	0	0	11	0	1	.304	.348
Valdez, Dioris	R-R	6-1	180	11-16-02	.258	.091	.279	40	97	11	25	4	0	1	8	20	2	0	1	25	0	1	.330	.392
Valdez, Esmerlyn	R-R	6-2	181	1-27-04	.248	.238	.250	45	129	20	32	8	0	5	21	16	6	1	1	39	3	1	.426	.355
Vizcaya, Ruben	R-R	5-10	155	7-20-01	.221	.261	.210	42	104	18	23	6	3	0	16	21	2	3	2	32	4	1	.337	.357
Zapata, Wesley	B-R	5-10	152	3-2-04	.186	.231	.179	39	97	12	18	1	0	0	8	22	1	0	0	21	3	4	.196	.342
Zorrilla, John	R-R	6-1	173	5-23-04	.000	--	.000	11	3	0	0	0	0	0	0	1	0	0	0	1	1	0	.000	.500

Pitching	B-T	HT	WT	DOB	W	L	ERA	G	GS	CG	SV	IP	H	R	ER	HR	BB	SO	AVG	vLH	vRH	K/9	BB/9
Brito, Luis	L-L	6-1	164	11-25-01	5	0	8.27	16	0	0	1	21	27	23	19	3	19	22	.297	.290	.300	9.58	8.27
Carrasco, Eudys	R-R	6-1	180	10-4-01	0	0	27.00	1	0	0	0	1	3	3	3	1	2	1	.500	.500	.500	9.00	18.00
Chiquillo, Diego	L-L	5-11	185	12-9-02	6	0	5.92	13	1	0	0	24	15	17	16	1	31	29	.179	.000	.217	10.73	11.47
Clode, Jesus	R-R	6-2	180	8-28-01	5	3	5.51	17	0	0	1	33	31	21	20	3	16	25	.254	.222	.273	6.89	4.41
De La Paz, Yoldin	L-L	6-0	165	5-10-02	1	2	2.03	11	0	0	0	40	25	13	9	1	15	40	.180	.258	.157	9.00	3.38
Diaz, Darlin	R-R	6-0	177	11-30-03	5	0	4.81	13	1	0	2	24	19	13	13	0	16	18	.209	.158	.245	6.66	5.92
Diaz, Miguel	R-R	6-0	160	8-19-01	4	0	2.30	16	0	0	4	27	16	11	7	0	12	29	.158	.125	.174	9.55	3.95
Dominguez, Argenys	R-R	6-3	170	5-10-01	0	0	16.20	6	0	0	0	5	11	11	9	0	6	3	.423	.286	.583	5.40	10.80
Farington, Luis	R-R	5-11	187	5-27-03	3	1	5.18	15	0	0	1	24	23	16	14	1	17	29	.237	.355	.182	10.73	6.29
Figuereo, Pedro	B-R	5-10	150	3-28-03	1	0	0.00	1	0	0	0	1	0	0	0	0	3	0	.000	--	.000	0.00	40.50
Fuentes, Juan	R-R	6-3	165	9-30-01	0	0	5.40	11	1	0	1	18	13	13	11	1	16	13	.197	.103	.270	6.38	7.85
Garces, Jose	R-R	6-2	149	6-9-04	0	2	5.16	12	9	0	1	30	28	24	17	0	15	32	.241	.262	.230	9.71	4.55
Garcia, Roelmy	R-R	6-2	172	4-12-03	0	3	4.74	12	10	0	0	25	15	18	13	2	32	39	.174	.108	.224	14.23	11.68
Gonzalez, Luis C	L-L	6-0	160	11-19-01	4	3	1.63	19	0	0	3	28	24	11	5	2	11	23	.233	.222	.235	7.48	3.58
Guzman, Lewys	R-R	6-1	180	2-9-02	2	1	6.64	13	1	0	0	20	16	17	15	3	18	24	.213	.158	.232	10.62	7.97
Hernandez, Kevison	R-R	6-5	188	7-20-02	1	3	2.78	10	9	0	0	23	18	9	7	0	15	27	.212	.219	.208	10.72	5.96
Hernandez, Luigi	R-R	6-0	185	9-21-03	0	6	7.18	12	11	0	0	31	31	31	25	3	14	37	.246	.279	.229	10.63	4.02
Joseph, Luis	R-R	6-1	180	6-15-02	2	2	4.40	10	0	0	0	14	8	9	7	1	13	13	.163	.071	.200	8.16	8.16
Kelly, Antwone	R-R	5-10	183	9-1-03	1	2	4.14	12	12	0	0	37	36	19	17	2	14	39	.259	.294	.239	9.49	3.41
Martinez, Wilbur	R-R	6-2	162	8-3-01	1	0	1.59	4	0	0	1	6	3	1	1	0	4	1	.158	.250	.133	1.59	6.35
Mendez, Greiber	R-R	6-0	150	4-3-04	0	1	27.00	1	0	0	0	3	5	1	0	0	3	5	.600	.500	1.000	27.00	0.00
Mendez, Rafael	R-R	6-3	170	8-14-02	0	4	3.38	22	0	0	2	29	29	19	11	3	17	12	.254	.326	.206	3.68	5.22
Olantilo, Francis	R-R	6-0	170	10-21-02	1	0	7.11	9	0	0	0	13	10	10	10	2	17	8	.217	.133	.258	5.68	12.08
Osoria, Yojeiry	L-L	6-1	188	1-24-03	0	4	6.12	10	10	0	0	25	22	21	17	1	16	20	.227	.267	.209	7.20	5.76
Quintanilla, Keneth	R-R	6-0	154	11-1-03	1	0	0.90	10	0	0	4	10	7	3	1	0	7	12	.194	.267	.143	10.80	6.30
Ress, Patricio	R-R	6-2	165	6-26-03	3	1	1.91	14	1	0	0	33	24	15	7	1	17	25	.194	.216	.178	6.82	4.64
Rodriguez, Sebastian	R-R	6-0	168	10-17-00	0	1	0.00	3	3	0	0	10	4	2	0	0	2	4	.118	.000	.200	3.60	1.80

Romero, Eliecer	R-R	6-0	185	9-8-01	1	3	2.31	15	2	0	4	35	31	16	9	1	16	33	.228	.211	.244	8.49	4.11
Salazar, Jonathan	R-R	6-3	180	12-22-03	1	0	6.23	15	0	0	1	22	22	21	15	1	26	13	.259	.214	.281	5.40	10.80
Santos, Juan	R-R	6-3	178	10-18-02	1	1	7.04	5	0	0	0	8	7	6	6	0	5	7	.241	.143	.333	8.22	5.87
Santos, Reyson	R-R	6-3	180	9-7-01	0	2	12.06	13	0	0	2	16	17	23	21	0	30	11	.283	.400	.225	6.32	17.23
Sierra, Andres	R-R	6-1	189	10-25-03	1	0	3.60	4	0	0	0	5	8	6	2	0	6	2	.381	.400	.375	3.60	10.80
Silvera, Andres	R-R	6-0	188	7-20-04	0	4	2.97	13	11	0	0	36	37	21	12	0	10	29	.257	.250	.261	7.18	2.48
Tejada, Joaquin	R-R	5-11	160	7-16-03	1	1	3.80	8	7	0	0	24	23	11	10	2	13	25	.245	.211	.268	9.51	4.94
2-team total (2 DSL Mariners)					1	1	4.40	10	8	0	0	29	24	17	14	2	17	33	.216	.190	.232	10.36	5.34
Toussaint, Weslyn	R-R	6-2	183	12-7-02	0	3	5.73	16	0	0	1	22	18	19	14	1	14	25	.209	.200	.214	10.23	5.73
Uribe, Isaias	L-L	6-3	172	8-13-02	0	1	2.76	11	11	0	0	33	25	15	10	0	17	25	.208	.056	.235	6.89	4.68
Valdez, Wilkin	R-R	6-5	210	7-14-01	2	4	4.88	12	2	0	0	24	21	26	13	0	22	24	.236	.171	.278	9.00	8.25
Zapata, Eduardo	R-R	6-2	160	8-27-03	1	1	8.04	10	0	0	0	16	18	14	14	2	12	15	.290	.346	.250	8.62	6.89

Fielding

C: Alfonzo 37, Escalante 18, Escalona 11, Escudero 35, Montalban 1, Sosa 27, Urbina 7.
1B: Alfonzo 1, Carrasco 28, De Paula 7, Escalante 11, Escalona 3, Gavilan 11, Rodriguez 13, Sanchez 36, Urbina 2, Valdez 18.
2B: Castillo 26, Diaz 11, Dipre 11, Escalante 3, Figuereo 15, Lebron 1, Machado 8, Pena 5, Ramirez 34, Toledo 12, Urbina 3, Zapata 5.
3B: Carrasco 5, Castillo 13, Diaz 13, Dipre 1, Escalante 8, Figuereo 18, Pena 26, Ramirez 6, Rivas 4, Sanchez 1, Toledo 4, Urbina 16, Zapata 19, Zorrilla 2.
SS: Castillo 14, Figuereo 4, Rivas 46, Toledo 42, Zapata 17, Zorrilla 5.
OF: Armas 50, Custodio 12, De La Cruz 44, De Paula 5, Espinal 32, Gavilan 19, Machado 18, Montalban 8, Polanco 42, Rodriguez 11, Sosa 1, Terrero 47, Valdez 15, Valdez 33, Vizcaya 39.

St. Louis Cardinals

SEASON IN A SENTENCE: The Cardinals entered the All-Star Break two games under. 500 at 44-46, but exploded for 46 wins in the second half, capped off by a 17-game winning streak, to earn a spot in the National League Wild Card Game before falling to the Dodgers on a walkoff home run.

HIGH POINT: The Cardinals woke up on Sept. 11 with a 71-69 record, 15 games behind the division-leading Brewers, before stringing together 17 consecutive wins to set a franchise record. The win streak included three-game sweeps against the Mets and Padres and four-game sweeps against the Brewers and Cubs.

LOW POINT: The Cardinals had an abysmal month of June, losing 17 of 27 games to fall from half a game back in the division to eight games back. The month included a six-game losing streak, a series loss against the last-place Pirates and three shutout losses.

NOTABLE ROOKIES: After an up-and-down campaign during the shortened 2020 season, outfielder Dylan Carlson solidified himself as a permanent fixture in the Cardinals lineup, hitting .266/.343/.437 with 18 home runs and a 117 OPS+ while playing impressive defensive in right and center field. Carlson finished fourth among all NL outfielders with eight outfield assists and was named an NL Rookie of the Year finalist. Fellow outfielder Lars Nootbaar impressed the organization with his play at the Triple-A level and spent the second half of the season in the majors, where he mostly filled in as a pinch hitter. Nootbaar posted a .739 OPS, hit five home runs and showed an encouraging approach at the plate while splitting time between left and right field. Righthander Johan Oviedo bounced between the big league rotation and Triple-A, making 13 starts and posting an 0-5, 4.91 mark. Oviedo showed off a plus fastball, but struggled with his control and walked 5.3 batters per nine innings.

KEY TRANSACTIONS: With a record hovering around .500, the Cardinals weren't aggressive at the trade deadline. They made one significant move, acquiring lefthander Jon Lester from the Nationals for outfielder Lane Thomas to bolster their rotation. Lester was solid in 12 starts, posting a 4-1, 4.36 mark while helping patch up a struggling rotation. Thomas, meanwhile, quickly earned a starting spot with the Nationals, posting a 133 OPS+ with seven home runs in 45 games.

OPENING DAY SALARY: $135,047,200 (12th).

PLAYERS OF THE YEAR

MAJOR LEAGUE	MINOR LEAGUE
Tyler O'Neill	**Jordan Walker**
OF	3B
.286/.352/.560	(High-A/Low-A)
Career-high 34 HR	.317/.388/.548,
89 R, 80 RBIs, 15 SB	14 HR, 14 SB

ORGANIZATION LEADERS

Batting		*Minimum 250 AB
MAJORS		
*AVG	Paul Goldschmidt	.294
*OPS	Tyler O'Neill	.912
HR	Nolan Arenado	34
HR	Tyler O'Neill	34
RBI	Nolan Arenado	105
MINORS		
*AVG	Jordan Walker, Peoria, Palm Beach	.317
*OBP	Nick Plummer, Memphis, Springfield	.415
*SLG	Juan Yepez, Memphis, Springfield	.586
*OPS	Juan Yepez, Memphis, Springfield	.969
R	Masyn Winn, Peoria, Palm Beach	76
H	Nolan Gorman, Memphis, Springfield	134
TB	Nolan Gorman, Memphis, Springfield	231
2B	Juan Yepez, Memphis, Springfield	29
3B	Nick Plummer, Memphis, Springfield	6
HR	Juan Yepez, Memphis, Springfield	27
RBI	Juan Yepez, Memphis, Springfield	77
BB	Nick Plummer, Memphis, Springfield	73
SO	Francisco Hernandez, Peoria, Palm Beach	145
SB	Masyn Winn, Peoria, Palm Beach	32

Pitching		#Minimum 75 IP
MAJORS		
W	Adam Wainwright	17
#ERA	Giovanny Gallegos	3.02
SO	Adam Wainwright	174
SV	Alex Reyes	29
MINORS		
W	Matthew Liberatore, Memphis	9
L	Dalton Roach, Springfield	10
L	Domingo Robles, Springfield	10
L	Zack Thompson, Memphis	10
#ERA	Wilfredo Pereira, Peoria	3.33
G	Connor Jones, Memphis	47
GS	Connor Lunn, Peoria	23
SV	Freddy Pacheco, Memphis, Springfield, Peoria	11
IP	Matthew Liberatore, Memphis	124.2
BB	Levi Prater, Palm Beach	68
SO	Matthew Liberatore, Memphis	123
#AVG	Wilfredo Pereira, Peoria	.211

2021 PERFORMANCE

General Manager: John Mozeliak. **Farm Director:** Gary LaRocque. **Scouting Director:** Randy Flores.

Class	Team	League	W	L	PCT	Finish	Manager
Majors	St. Louis Cardinals	National	90	72	.556	4th (15)	Mike Shildt
Triple-A	Memphis Redbirds	Triple-A East	61	67	.477	t-11th (20)	Ben Johnson
Double-A	Springfield Cardinals	Double-A Central	45	75	.375	10th (10)	Jose Leger
High-A	Peoria Chiefs	High-A Central	45	75	.375	12th (12)	J. Leon/C. Swauger
Low-A	Palm Beach Cardinals	Low-A Southeast	37	80	.316	10th (10)	C. Swauger/J. Leon
Rookie	DSL Cardinals Red	Dominican Summer	27	30	.474	29th (46)	Estuar Ruiz
Rookie	DSL Cardinals Blue	Dominican Summer	21	38	.356	t-42nd (46)	Fray Peniche
Rookie	FCL Cardinals	Florida Complex	24	29	.453	11th (18)	J. Lopez/R. Espinoza
Overall 2021 Minor League Record			260	394	.398	30th (30)	

ORGANIZATION STATISTICS

ST. LOUIS CARDINALS
NATIONAL LEAGUE

Batting	B-T	HT	WT	DOB	AVG	vLH	vRH	G	AB	R	H	2B	3B	HR	RBI	BB	HBP	SH	SF	SO	SB	CS	SLG	OBP
Arenado, Nolan	R-R	6-2	215	4-16-91	.255	.295	.245	157	593	81	151	34	3	34	105	50	3	0	7	96	2	0	.494	.312
Bader, Harrison	R-R	6-0	210	6-3-94	.267	.243	.273	103	367	45	98	21	1	16	50	27	5	0	2	85	9	4	.460	.324
Carlson, Dylan	B-L	6-2	205	10-23-98	.266	.341	.243	149	542	79	144	31	4	18	65	57	11	1	8	152	2	1	.437	.343
Carpenter, Matt	L-R	6-4	210	11-26-85	.169	.056	.180	130	207	18	35	11	1	3	21	35	6	0	1	77	2	0	.275	.305
Dean, Austin	R-R	6-0	215	10-14-93	.233	.222	.250	22	30	5	7	2	0	1	7	6	0	0	2	11	0	0	.400	.342
DeJong, Paul	R-R	6-0	205	8-2-93	.197	.163	.207	113	356	44	70	10	1	19	45	35	9	0	2	103	4	1	.390	.284
Edman, Tommy	B-R	5-10	180	5-9-95	.262	.267	.261	159	641	91	168	41	3	11	56	38	6	2	4	95	30	5	.387	.308
Goldschmidt, Paul	R-R	6-3	220	9-10-87	.294	.350	.279	158	603	102	177	36	2	31	99	67	4	0	5	136	12	0	.514	.365
Hurst, Scott	L-R	5-10	175	3-25-96	.000	.000	.000	7	5	0	0	0	0	0	0	0	0	0	0	1	0	0	.000	.000
Knizner, Andrew	R-R	6-1	225	2-3-95	.174	.089	.207	63	161	18	28	7	0	1	9	20	4	0	0	39	0	0	.236	.281
Molina, Yadier	R-R	5-11	225	7-13-82	.252	.278	.247	121	440	45	111	19	0	11	66	24	5	0	3	79	3	0	.370	.297
Moroff, Max	B-R	5-10	190	5-13-93	.063	.000	.077	6	16	0	1	0	0	0	1	0	0	0	0	10	0	0	.063	.063
Nogowski, John	R-L	6-0	245	1-5-93	.056	.000	.063	19	18	2	1	0	0	0	0	1	1	0	0	2	0	0	.056	.150
2-team total (33 Pittsburgh)					.233	.262	.218	52	129	14	30	7	0	1	14	12	1	0	1	22	0	1	.310	.301
Nootbaar, Lars	L-R	6-3	210	9-8-97	.239	.273	.230	58	109	15	26	3	1	5	15	13	0	1	1	28	2	1	.422	.317
O_Neill, Tyler	R-R	5-11	200	6-22-95	.286	.289	.286	138	482	89	138	26	2	34	80	38	13	0	4	168	15	4	.560	.352
Rondon, Jose	R-R	6-1	215	3-3-94	.263	.393	.192	63	80	13	21	3	0	3	9	8	0	0	2	17	2	0	.413	.322
Sanchez, Ali	R-R	6-1	200	1-20-97	.500	1.000	.333	2	4	0	2	2	0	0	0	0	0	0	0	0	0	0	1.000	.500
Sosa, Edmundo	R-R	6-0	210	3-6-96	.271	.217	.288	113	288	39	78	8	4	6	27	17	17	1	2	63	4	4	.389	.346
Thomas, Lane	R-R	6-0	185	8-23-95	.104	.267	.030	32	48	2	5	1	0	0	1	10	0	0	0	17	2	1	.125	.259
2-team total (45 Washington)					.235	.381	.178	77	226	35	53	15	2	7	28	37	0	0	1	63	6	3	.412	.341
Williams, Justin	L-R	6-1	235	8-20-95	.160	.133	.163	51	119	10	19	0	0	4	11	17	1	0	0	46	0	1	.261	.270

Pitching	B-T	HT	WT	DOB	W	L	ERA	G	GS	CG	SV	IP	H	R	ER	HR	BB	SO	AVG	vLH	vRH	K/9	BB/9
Cabrera, Genesis	L-L	6-2	180	10-10-96	4	5	3.73	71	0	0	0	70	52	31	29	3	36	77	.209	.261	.178	9.90	4.63
Carpenter, Matt	L-R	6-4	210	11-26-85	0	0	0.00	1	0	0	0	1	2	0	0	0	0	0	.400	.500	.333	0.00	0.00
Dickson, Brandon	R-R	6-5	190	11-3-84	0	0	13.50	2	0	0	0	2	5	3	3	1	0	1	.500	.000	.714	4.50	0.00
Elledge, Seth	R-R	6-3	240	5-20-96	0	0	4.63	11	0	0	0	12	13	6	6	1	7	11	.302	.273	.333	8.49	5.40
Fernandez, Junior	R-R	6-3	215	3-2-97	1	0	5.66	18	0	0	0	21	25	13	13	2	15	15	.305	.378	.244	6.53	6.53
Flaherty, Jack	R-R	6-4	225	10-15-95	9	2	3.22	17	15	0	0	78	57	35	28	12	26	85	.199	.195	.204	9.77	2.99
Flores Jr., Bernardo	L-L	6-4	190	8-23-95	0	0	--	1	0	0	0	1	1	1	0	2	0	1.000	1.000	--	--	--
Gallegos, Giovanny	R-R	6-2	215	8-14-91	6	5	3.02	73	0	0	14	80	51	28	27	6	20	95	.183	.176	.190	10.64	2.24
Gant, John	R-R	6-4	200	8-6-92	4	6	3.42	25	14	0	0	76	64	32	29	6	56	56	.229	.205	.248	6.60	6.60
Garcia, Luis	R-R	6-2	240	1-30-87	1	1	3.24	34	0	0	2	33	25	12	12	2	8	34	.202	.289	.152	9.18	2.16
Happ, J.A.	L-L	6-5	205	10-19-82	5	2	4.00	11	11	0	0	54	52	24	24	9	17	45	.251	.186	.277	7.50	2.83
Helsley, Ryan	R-R	6-2	230	7-18-94	6	4	4.56	51	0	0	1	47	40	24	24	4	27	47	.227	.250	.214	8.94	5.13
Hicks, Jordan	R-R	6-2	220	9-6-96	0	0	5.40	10	0	0	0	10	5	6	6	0	10	10	.147	.182	.130	9.00	9.00
Hudson, Dakota	R-R	6-5	215	9-15-94	1	0	2.08	2	1	0	0	9	7	2	2	1	1	6	.219	.231	.211	6.23	1.04
Hyun Kim, Kwang	L-L	6-2	195	7-22-88	7	7	3.46	27	21	0	1	107	98	46	41	12	39	80	.242	.156	.267	6.75	3.29
LeBlanc, Wade	L-L	6-2	195	8-7-84	0	1	3.61	12	8	0	0	42	45	17	17	7	16	23	.269	.291	.259	4.89	3.40
Lester, Jon	L-L	6-4	249	1-7-84	4	1	4.36	12	12	0	0	66	68	34	32	11	26	40	.270	.275	.269	5.45	3.55
2-team total (16 Washington)					7	6	4.71	28	28	0	0	141	159	84	74	25	55	91	.285	.246	.295	5.79	3.50
Martinez, Carlos	R-R	6-0	200	9-21-91	4	9	6.23	16	16	0	0	82	77	58	57	8	36	57	.246	.261	.226	6.23	3.94
McFarland, T.J.	L-L	6-3	200	6-8-89	4	1	2.56	38	0	0	0	39	32	11	11	3	9	21	.237	.167	.276	4.89	2.09
Mikolas, Miles	R-R	6-4	230	8-23-88	2	3	4.23	9	9	0	0	45	43	24	21	6	11	31	.253	.273	.232	6.25	2.22
Miller, Andrew	L-L	6-7	200	5-21-85	0	0	4.75	40	0	0	0	36	41	19	19	5	16	40	.293	.182	.392	10.00	4.00
Miller, Justin	R-R	6-3	225	6-13-87	1	0	4.50	18	0	0	1	16	15	8	8	2	5	9	.254	.217	.278	5.06	2.81
2-team total (5 Washington)					1	0	6.16	23	0	0	1	19	20	13	13	5	6	13	.258	.250	.295	6.16	2.84
Oviedo, Johan	R-R	6-5	245	3-2-98	0	5	4.91	14	13	0	0	62	61	39	34	8	37	51	.251	.272	.229	7.36	5.34
Ponce de Leon, Daniel	R-R	6-3	200	1-16-92	1	1	6.21	24	2	0	2	33	32	24	23	5	22	24	.252	.267	.239	6.48	5.94
Ramirez, Roel	R-R	6-0	235	5-26-95	0	0	81.00	1	0	0	0	0	1	3	3	0	2	0	.500	.000	1.000	0.00	54.00

	B-T	HT	WT	DOB	W	L	ERA	G	GS	CG	SV	IP	H	R	ER	HR	BB	SO	AVG	vLH	vRH	K/9	BB/9
Reyes, Alex	R-R	6-4	220	8-29-94	10	8	3.24	69	0	0	29	72	46	32	26	9	52	95	.176	.155	.195	11.82	6.47
Rondon, Angel	R-R	6-1	205	12-1-97	0	0	0.00	2	0	0	0	2	1	0	0	0	1	1	.167	.200	.000	4.50	4.50
Waddell, Brandon	L-L	6-3	180	6-3-94	0	0	4.15	4	0	0	0	4	4	2	2	0	5	6	.235	.333	.125	12.46	10.38
Wainwright, Adam	R-R	6-7	230	8-30-81	17	7	3.05	32	32	3	0	206	168	72	70	21	50	174	.220	.229	.209	7.59	2.18
Webb, Tyler	L-L	6-5	240	7-20-90	0	0	13.22	22	0	0	0	16	22	26	24	1	19	14	.310	.286	.333	7.71	10.47
Whitley, Kodi	R-R	6-3	220	2-21-95	0	0	2.49	25	0	0	0	25	15	8	7	1	12	27	.172	.200	.154	9.59	4.26
Woodford, Jake	R-R	6-4	215	10-28-96	3	4	3.99	26	8	0	0	68	66	32	30	7	25	50	.261	.317	.208	6.65	3.33

Fielding

Catcher	PCT	G	PO	A	E	DP	PB
Knizner	.992	57	368	21	3	4	1
Molina	.997	118	869	49	3	10	6
Sanchez	1.000	2	7	0	0	0	

First Base	PCT	G	PO	A	E	DP
Carpenter	.988	14	72	12	1	9
Goldschmidt	.998	153	1144	106	2	111
Knizner	1.000	1	1	0	0	0
Molina	1.000	1	1	0	0	0
Nogowski	1.000	3	6	0	0	0
Rondon	.000	1	0	0	0	0

Second Base	PCT	G	PO	A	E	DP
Carpenter	.974	34	50	61	3	15

	PCT	G	PO	A	E	DP
Edman	.990	130	195	308	5	64
Moroff	1.000	4	6	7	0	3
Rondon	1.000	2	1	1	0	0
Sosa	.987	25	38	39	1	13
Thomas	1.000	1	1	0	0	0

Third Base	PCT	G	PO	A	E	DP
Arenado	.974	155	125	287	11	38
Carpenter	1.000	6	2	5	0	0
Moroff	.667	1	0	2	1	0
Rondon	.933	7	6	8	1	2
Sosa	1.000	9	7	7	0	0

Shortstop	PCT	G	PO	A	E	DP
DeJong	.980	107	129	256	8	51

	PCT	G	PO	A	E	DP
Edman	1.000	4	9	9	0	3
Sosa	.961	71	79	169	10	30

Outfield	PCT	G	PO	A	E	DP
Bader	.990	103	289	4	3	1
Carlson	.987	156	297	8	4	3
Dean	1.000	9	13	0	0	0
Edman	.970	41	63	1	2	0
Hurst	1.000	6	1	0	0	0
Nootbaar	.967	35	55	3	2	1
O_Neill	.962	131	221	7	9	1
Rondon	1.000	9	11	0	0	0
Sosa	--	1	0	0	0	0
Thomas	.962	19	25	0	1	0
Williams	.970	43	60	4	2	1

MEMPHIS REDBIRDS · TRIPLE-A
TRIPLE-A EAST

Batting	B-T	HT	WT	DOB	AVG	vLH	vRH	G	AB	R	H	2B	3B	HR	RBI	BB	HBP	SH	SF	SO	SB	CS	SLG	OBP
Antonini, Aaron	L-R	6-0	200	7-27-98	.000	.000	.000	4	9	1	0	0	0	0	0	0	1	0	0	5	0	0	.000	.100
Ascanio, Rayder	R-R	5-11	155	3-17-96	.225	.151	.256	74	182	22	41	5	0	8	18	18	0	4	0	39	2	1	.385	.295
Bader, Harrison	R-R	6-0	210	6-3-94	.500	.500	--	1	2	1	1	1	0	0	1	0	0	0	1	0	0	1.000	.667
Baker, Luken	R-R	6-4	280	3-10-97	.333	.000	1.000	2	6	1	2	1	0	0	2	0	1	0	0	2	0	0	.500	.429
Burleson, Alec	L-L	6-2	212	11-25-98	.234	.238	.232	45	154	19	36	7	0	4	22	17	0	0	0	27	0	1	.357	.310
Capel, Conner	L-L	6-1	185	5-19-97	.261	.220	.273	114	357	55	93	17	4	14	51	43	3	0	4	79	6	4	.448	.342
Coulter, Clint	R-R	6-3	225	7-30-93	.234	.229	.237	57	128	19	30	5	0	8	20	12	1	0	1	46	0	0	.461	.303
Dean, Austin	R-R	6-1	215	10-14-93	.213	.313	.161	14	47	6	10	6	0	1	8	7	2	0	0	19	0	1	.404	.339
DeJong, Paul	R-R	6-0	205	8-2-93	.100	.000	.125	4	10	1	1	1	0	0	0	0	0	0	0	2	0	0	.200	.100
Donovan, Brendan	L-R	6-1	195	1-16-97	.288	.375	.253	33	111	23	32	5	0	6	25	25	4	0	1	23	4	2	.495	.389
Gorman, Nolan	L-R	6-1	210	5-10-00	.274	.217	.295	76	303	45	83	14	1	14	48	20	2	0	3	63	3	1	.465	.320
Heineman, Tyler	B-R	5-10	199	6-19-91	.254	.364	.232	21	67	8	17	4	0	0	5	7	1	0	2	17	0	2	.313	.325
2-team total (20 Lehigh Valley)					.264	.370	.235	41	129	13	34	6	0	0	11	16	1	3	2	29	0	3	.310	.345
Herrera, Ivan	R-R	5-11	220	6-1-00	.000	.000	.000	1	4	0	0	0	0	0	0	0	0	0	0	0	0	0	.000	.000
Hurst, Scott	L-R	5-10	175	3-25-96	.203	.254	.187	70	266	39	54	12	1	4	18	33	1	3	2	94	5	4	.301	.291
Lopez, Irving	L-R	5-9	175	6-30-95	.229	.083	.254	37	83	4	19	6	1	0	7	6	1	0	0	17	0	0	.325	.289
Mendoza, Evan	R-R	6-2	205	6-28-96	.242	.259	.238	116	396	51	96	14	1	1	27	36	3	3	7	105	15	6	.290	.305
Moroff, Max	B-R	6-0	190	5-13-93	.538	.250	.591	7	26	11	14	3	0	4	9	6	2	0	0	3	1	0	1.115	.647
Nogowski, John	R-L	6-0	245	1-5-93	.195	.095	.215	36	128	16	25	4	0	3	14	15	5	0	0	31	3	0	.297	.304
2-team total (20 Indianapolis)					.214	.167	.224	56	182	21	39	6	0	4	24	28	6	0	1	41	6	0	.313	.336
Nootbaar, Lars	L-R	6-3	210	9-8-97	.308	.211	.327	35	117	21	36	2	1	6	19	17	2	0	0	25	1	3	.496	.404
Ortega, Dennis	R-R	6-3	230	6-11-97	.231	.250	.226	57	160	19	37	7	0	2	13	15	1	1	0	49	0	0	.313	.301
Plummer, Nick	L-L	5-10	200	7-31-96	.267	.300	.244	27	75	19	20	3	2	2	8	20	6	0	0	18	4	1	.440	.455
Robertson, Kramer	R-R	5-10	166	9-20-94	.253	.167	.284	118	391	66	99	22	4	11	62	62	9	1	3	81	11	1	.414	.366
Rondon, Jose	R-R	6-1	215	3-3-94	.235	.294	.221	21	85	14	20	5	0	6	19	8	0	0	0	22	0	0	.482	.301
Sanchez, Ali	R-R	6-1	200	1-20-97	.275	.315	.264	70	251	24	69	10	0	4	22	18	0	0	1	47	0	2	.363	.322
Szczur, Matt	R-R	6-0	200	7-20-89	.186	.056	.214	30	102	8	19	3	1	5	11	7	0	1	1	29	0	0	.382	.236
Thomas, Lane	R-R	6-0	185	8-23-95	.265	.346	.251	30	113	18	30	5	2	4	20	12	1	0	1	35	3	2	.451	.339
2-team total (3 Rochester)					.278	.370	.253	33	126	20	35	6	2	5	23	12	1	0	1	37	3	2	.476	.343
Toerner, Justin	L-L	5-11	185	8-11-96	.250	.000	.318	11	28	3	7	1	1	1	5	3	1	1	0	9	0	0	.464	.344
Williams, Justin	L-R	6-1	235	8-20-95	.274	.227	.290	23	84	10	23	4	0	6	19	3	1	0	0	23	1	0	.560	.307
Yepez, Juan	R-R	6-1	200	2-19-98	.289	.260	.302	94	304	56	88	25	0	22	63	42	6	0	4	69	1	3	.589	.382

Pitching	B-T	HT	WT	DOB	W	L	ERA	G	GS	CG	SV	IP	H	R	ER	HR	BB	SO	AVG	vLH	vRH	K/9	BB/9
Ascanio, Rayder	R-R	5-11	155	3-17-96	0	0	0.00	1	0	0	0	1	0	0	0	0	1	0	.000	.000	.000	0.00	9.00
Black, Grant	R-R	6-5	225	7-21-94	0	0	3.91	14	2	0	1	23	22	10	10	2	9	23	.250	.182	.318	9.00	3.52
Bosiokovic, Jacob	R-R	6-5	240	12-21-93	1	0	2.16	7	0	0	3	8	7	3	2	0	1	12	.219	.273	.190	12.96	1.08
Cruz, Jesus	R-R	6-1	230	4-15-95	0	3	3.06	37	0	0	3	35	29	14	12	1	26	38	.223	.245	.210	9.68	6.62
Dickson, Brandon	R-R	6-5	190	11-3-84	1	0	8.74	12	0	0	0	11	20	13	11	4	7	7	.392	.556	.303	5.56	3.18
Elledge, Seth	R-R	6-3	240	5-20-96	2	2	6.56	30	0	0	2	36	44	28	26	3	22	46	.299	.283	.310	11.61	5.55
FaGalde, Alex	R-R	6-2	225	4-29-94	1	0	4.76	8	0	0	0	11	8	7	6	2	13	9	.211	.182	.250	7.15	10.32
Fernandez, Junior	R-R	6-3	215	3-2-97	1	2	6.28	13	0	0	1	14	18	11	10	3	5	22	.305	.267	.345	13.81	3.14
Flaherty, Jack	R-R	6-4	225	10-15-95	0	0	3.60	2	2	0	0	5	5	2	2	0	1	8	.250	.429	.154	14.40	1.80
Flores Jr., Bernardo	L-L	6-4	190	8-23-95	2	2	5.74	8	5	0	0	31	40	24	20	6	18	26	.315	.283	.333	7.47	5.17
Hicks, Jordan	R-R	6-2	220	9-6-96	0	0	15.00	3	3	0	0	3	5	5	5	2	3	3	.417	1.000	.300	9.00	9.00
Hudson, Dakota	R-R	6-5	215	9-15-94	0	0	1.80	1	1	0	0	5	2	2	1	0	3	2	.125	.111	.143	3.60	5.40

Pitcher	B-T	HT	WT	DOB	W	L	ERA	G	GS	CG	SV	IP	H	R	ER	HR	BB	SO	AVG	vLH	vRH	SO/9	BB/9
Hyun Kim, Kwang	L-L	6-2	195	7-22-88	0	0	9.00	1	1	0	0	2	2	2	2	2	0	2	.250	1.000	.143	9.00	0.00
Jones, Connor	R-R	6-3	220	10-10-94	5	6	5.91	47	0	0	5	56	74	40	37	3	31	50	.329	.376	.295	7.99	4.95
Kruczynski, Evan	L-L	6-4	205	3-31-95	2	0	6.38	18	0	0	0	18	14	13	13	6	14	22	.215	.105	.261	10.80	6.87
Liberatore, Matthew	L-L	6-4	200	11-6-99	9	9	4.04	22	18	0	0	125	123	66	56	19	33	123	.257	.243	.262	8.88	2.38
McFarland, T.J.	L-L	6-3	200	6-8-89	1	0	2.57	4	0	0	1	7	6	3	2	0	2	8	.214	.167	.250	10.29	2.57
2-team total (18 Rochester)					2	2	4.65	22	0	0	2	31	29	17	16	3	7	34	.240	.143	.323	9.87	2.03
Mikolas, Miles	R-R	6-4	230	8-23-88	1	1	2.33	5	5	0	0	19	17	5	5	2	3	13	.243	.333	.147	6.05	1.40
Miller, Andrew	L-L	6-7	200	5-21-85	0	0	3.00	3	1	0	0	3	1	1	1	1	2	5	.100	.000	.143	15.00	6.00
Miller, Justin	R-R	6-3	225	6-13-87	0	0	9.00	2	1	0	0	2	3	2	2	1	0	4	.333	1.000	.143	18.00	0.00
2-team total (13 RochesteR)					1	0	1.47	15	1	0	5	18	12	4	3	1	4	33	.185	.200	.171	16.20	1.96
Oviedo, Johan	R-R	6-5	245	3-2-98	1	6	6.13	12	11	0	0	54	55	38	37	7	29	59	.262	.313	.216	9.77	4.80
Pacheco, Freddy	R-R	5-11	203	4-17-98	0	0	0.00	2	0	0	0	3	1	0	0	1	5		.100	.000	.143	15.00	3.00
Pallante, Andre	R-R	6-0	203	9-18-98	0	0	3.60	2	1	0	0	5	7	2	2	0	4	4	.304	.200	.333	7.20	7.20
Parsons, Thomas	R-R	6-4	220	9-1-95	2	6	5.86	24	9	0	1	74	84	48	48	19	24	70	.292	.300	.285	8.55	2.93
Ponce de Leon, Daniel	R-R	6-3	200	1-16-92	0	0	0.00	5	5	0	0	9	3	0	0	0	8	9	.107	.222	.053	9.00	8.00
Quezada, Johan	R-R	6-9	255	8-25-94	0	0	0.00	3	0	0	0	3	1	0	0	0	2	2	.091	.250	.000	5.40	5.40
Ramirez, Roel	R-R	6-0	235	5-26-95	0	1	4.34	20	0	0	1	29	26	17	14	2	8	32	.248	.327	.170	9.93	2.48
2-team total (12 Syracuse)					0	3	5.57	32	0	0	3	42	44	32	26	5	19	48	.273	.315	.239	10.29	4.07
Rondon, Angel	R-R	6-1	205	12-1-97	6	4	4.58	19	13	0	0	77	85	46	39	15	22	68	.275	.223	.329	7.98	2.58
Santos, Ramon	R-R	6-3	230	9-20-94	1	1	12.46	5	0	0	0	4	7	6	6	0	4	6	.368	.375	.364	12.46	8.31
Thomas, Connor	L-L	5-11	173	5-29-98	6	4	3.10	22	14	2	1	102	108	51	35	11	30	92	.269	.250	.276	8.14	2.66
Thompson, Zack	L-L	6-2	215	10-28-97	2	10	7.06	22	19	0	2	93	114	76	73	18	57	82	.302	.286	.307	7.94	5.52
Waddell, Brandon	L-L	6-3	180	6-3-94	2	0	2.45	9	0	0	0	11	12	4	3	1	3	10	.286	.286	.286	8.18	2.45
2-team total (2 Norfolk)					2	0	2.03	11	0	0	0	13	14	4	3	1	3	12	.280	.278	.281	8.10	2.03
Walsh, Jake	R-R	6-1	192	7-20-95	0	1	9.00	4	0	0	0	4	4	2	4	1	3	9	.143	.500	.083	20.25	6.75
Warner, Austin	L-L	5-11	185	6-27-94	7	3	3.34	41	5	0	2	73	57	33	27	8	22	75	.213	.228	.206	9.29	2.72
Webb, Tyler	L-L	6-5	240	7-20-90	0	2	5.82	18	0	0	0	22	17	15	14	5	14	32	.207	.222	.200	13.29	5.82
Whitley, Kodi	R-R	6-3	220	2-21-95	3	0	1.69	12	0	0	3	16	11	4	3	1	7	21	.193	.316	.132	11.81	3.94
Williams, Garrett	L-L	6-1	200	9-15-94	1	1	6.61	26	0	0	0	33	23	28	24	2	35	37	.198	.143	.222	10.19	9.64
Woodford, Jake	R-R	6-4	215	10-28-96	2	3	4.50	7	7	0	0	34	41	21	17	4	12	25	.299	.234	.356	6.62	3.18
Zeuch, T.J.	R-R	6-7	245	8-1-95	2	0	4.93	9	5	0	1	38	36	22	21	6	15	35	.248	.302	.207	8.22	3.52
2-team total (12 Buffalo)					4	3	4.39	21	14	0	1	96	101	56	47	14	28	77	.266	.290	.246	7.19	2.62

Fielding

Catcher	PCT	G	PO	A	E	DP	PB
Antonini	1.000	2	10	0	0	0	0
Coulter	1.000	4	30	1	0	0	1
Heineman	1.000	16	162	9	0	2	0
Herrera	1.000	1	11	1	0	1	0
Ortega	.990	45	381	14	4	2	5
Sanchez	.989	64	531	32	6	5	3

First Base	PCT	G	PO	A	E	DP
Ascanio	.990	16	94	10	1	10
Baker	1.000	2	16	1	0	1
Donovan	.993	17	129	5	1	14
Mendoza	1.000	14	69	7	0	6
Nogowski	.991	31	202	18	2	18
Sanchez	1.000	1	3	0	0	1
Yepez	.985	60	415	38	7	47

Second Base	PCT	G	PO	A	E	DP
Ascanio	1.000	2	2	6	0	0
Donovan	1.000	2	3	5	0	1
Gorman	.989	61	109	162	3	43
Lopez	.927	12	20	18	3	7
Mendoza	1.000	5	6	11	0	3
Moroff	1.000	3	5	9	0	3
Robertson	.995	50	94	93	1	29

Third Base	PCT	G	PO	A	E	DP
Ascanio	.972	30	20	49	2	7
Donovan	.900	12	2	16	2	1
Gorman	.957	9	5	17	1	2
Lopez	.953	18	9	32	2	4
Mendoza	1.000	2	0	5	0	2
Moroff	.800	4	0	4	1	0
Robertson	.906	43	19	77	10	5
Rondon	.964	12	11	16	1	3
Yepez	.889	11	5	19	3	4

Shortstop	PCT	G	PO	A	E	DP
Ascanio	.963	9	5	21	1	5
DeJong	1.000	4	1	6	0	0
Donovan	.933	2	6	8	1	2
Mendoza	.972	92	145	277	12	58
Robertson	.955	19	17	46	3	7
Rondon	.969	9	10	21	1	3

Outfield	PCT	G	PO	A	E	DP
Ascanio	1.000	5	8	1	0	0
Bader	1.000	1	2	0	0	0
Burleson	.982	39	53	2	1	1
Capel	.984	107	174	11	3	3
Coulter	1.000	25	27	3	0	1
Dean	1.000	8	8	1	0	0
Donovan	1.000	2	3	0	0	0
Hurst	1.000	65	132	5	0	2
Lopez	--	1	0	0	0	0
Mendoza	1.000	2	4	0	0	0
Nogowski	1.000	5	7	0	0	0
Nootbaar	1.000	35	61	2	0	0
Plummer	.974	25	36	1	1	0
Szczur	.984	28	59	1	1	1
Thomas	.980	25	45	4	1	0
Toerner	1.000	12	25	1	0	1
Williams	1.000	20	40	1	0	1
Yepez	.933	11	14	0	1	0

SPRINGFIELD CARDINALS

DOUBLE-A

DOUBLE-A CENTRAL

Batting	B-T	HT	WT	DOB	AVG	vLH	vRH	G	AB	R	H	2B	3B	HR	RBI	BB	HBP	SH	SF	SO	SB	CS	SLG	OBP
Antonini, Aaron	L-R	6-0	200	7-27-98	.189	.091	.214	35	106	12	20	3	0	4	13	18	7	0	0	36	0	0	.330	.344
Baker, Luken	R-R	6-4	280	3-10-97	.248	.294	.233	91	347	51	86	20	0	26	68	38	2	0	4	103	0	0	.530	.322
Burleson, Alec	L-L	6-2	212	11-25-98	.288	.254	.299	63	260	34	75	10	0	14	44	19	0	0	3	59	2	0	.488	.333
Capel, Conner	L-L	6-1	185	5-19-97	.167	--	.167	3	12	0	2	0	0	0	0	0	0	0	0	2	0	0	.167	.167
Castillo, Moises	R-R	5-11	170	7-04-94	.132	.211	.088	19	53	5	7	0	0	0	1	6	2	0	0	16	0	0	.132	.246
Cedeno, Leandro	R-R	6-2	195	8-22-98	.257	.208	.280	19	74	8	19	4	0	3	16	4	2	0	1	13	1	0	.432	.309
Diaz, Imeldo	R-R	6-0	175	11-2-97	.254	.294	.238	16	59	4	15	0	0	0	3	0	0	0	1	14	0	2	.254	.250
Donovan, Brendan	L-R	6-1	195	1-16-97	.319	.205	.355	50	185	35	59	10	1	4	28	25	6	0	3	39	8	5	.449	.411
Dunn, Nick	L-R	5-10	185	1-29-97	.259	.228	.269	95	324	40	84	14	0	6	36	36	6	0	5	52	4	2	.358	.340
Gorman, Nolan	L-R	6-1	210	5-10-00	.288	.167	.319	43	177	26	51	6	0	11	27	18	0	0	0	52	4	0	.508	.354
Herrera, Ivan	R-R	5-11	220	6-1-00	.231	.237	.229	98	363	50	84	13	0	17	63	60	7	0	7	96	2	3	.408	.346
Koperniak, Matt	L-R	6-0	200	2-8-98	.271	.206	.293	33	133	19	36	7	0	3	15	9	2	0	0	20	1	2	.391	.326
Lopez, Irving	L-R	5-9	175	6-30-95	.235	.270	.223	43	149	19	35	4	2	3	19	9	5	3	2	40	2	0	.349	.297
Nunez, Malcom	R-R	5-11	205	3-9-01	.257	.283	.246	54	202	28	52	5	0	6	19	21	1	0	0	44	2	1	.371	.330

Name	B-T	HT	WT	DOB	AVG	vLH	vRH	G	AB	R	H	2B	3B	HR	RBI	BB	HBP	SH	SF	SO	SB	CS	SLG	OBP
Perez, Delvin	R-R	6-3	175	11-24-98	.265	.301	.253	98	389	62	103	9	4	4	23	28	5	0	1	98	24	8	.339	.322
Pinder, Chase	R-R	5-11	185	3-16-96	.226	.200	.237	18	53	10	12	1	0	2	4	9	1	0	0	13	0	0	.358	.349
Plummer, Nick	L-L	5-10	200	7-31-96	.283	.288	.282	90	311	52	88	17	4	13	46	53	11	0	1	108	9	8	.489	.404
Raposo, Nick	R-R	5-10	200	6-3-98	.267	.341	.227	42	116	19	31	4	2	1	12	17	2	1	1	27	1	0	.362	.368
Redmond, Chandler	L-R	6-1	231	1-9-97	.303	.212	.337	32	122	13	37	9	0	5	25	11	0	0	0	50	0	1	.500	.361
Rodriguez, Julio E.	R-R	6-0	245	6-11-97	.196	.125	.217	29	107	10	21	2	0	3	10	7	1	0	0	23	1	0	.299	.252
Toerner, Justin	L-L	5-11	185	8-11-96	.210	.219	.206	71	243	36	51	11	0	7	27	37	8	1	0	82	3	2	.342	.333
Vinsky, David	R-L	6-0	198	7-9-98	.210	.169	.225	73	210	33	44	6	2	3	21	33	4	1	4	80	3	2	.300	.323
Yepez, Juan	R-R	6-1	200	2-19-98	.270	.462	.220	19	63	11	17	4	0	5	14	9	3	0	0	13	0	0	.571	.387

Pitching	B-T	HT	WT	DOB	W	L	ERA	G	GS	CG	SV	IP	H	R	ER	HR	BB	SO	AVG	vLH	vRH	K/9	BB/9
Black, Grant	R-R	6-5	225	7-21-94	1	3	5.70	16	4	0	1	36	39	26	23	3	26	39	.277	.351	.226	9.66	6.44
Bosiokovic, Jacob	R-R	6-5	240	12-21-93	6	3	4.28	31	0	0	4	48	35	29	23	4	28	70	.194	.226	.178	13.03	5.21
Brettell, Michael	R-R	6-3	195	7-13-97	1	5	7.97	23	6	0	0	70	96	65	62	15	27	57	.331	.308	.347	7.33	3.47
Dayton, Patrick	L-L	6-0	170	7-20-95	0	1	18.80	13	0	0	0	19	39	41	39	7	16	13	.443	.381	.463	6.27	7.71
Diaz, Imeldo	R-R	6-0	175	11-2-97	0	0	0.00	1	0	0	0	2	0	0	0	0	0	0	.667	.000	1.000	0.00	0.00
Escobar, Edgar	R-R	6-1	220	1-20-97	1	3	5.88	25	0	0	4	41	34	32	27	12	15	53	.219	.208	.225	11.54	3.27
FaGalde, Alex	R-R	6-2	225	4-29-94	0	0	1.59	7	0	0	0	11	11	8	2	2	8	11	.244	.304	.182	8.74	6.35
Flaherty, Jack	R-R	6-4	225	10-15-95	0	0	6.75	1	1	0	0	4	3	3	3	1	0	3	.214	.333	.000	6.75	0.00
Gonzalez, Edgar	R-R	6-1	200	12-22-96	0	0	0.00	1	0	0	0	1	1	0	0	0	1	0	.333	1.000	.000	9.00	0.00
Hudson, Dakota	R-R	6-5	215	9-15-94	1	0	0.77	3	3	0	0	12	8	3	1	0	5	7	.205	.300	.105	5.40	3.86
Justo, Salvador	R-R	6-5	210	10-14-94	0	1	6.48	22	0	0	1	25	21	22	18	5	22	22	.226	.229	.224	7.92	7.92
Leahy, Kyle	R-R	6-5	200	6-4-97	0	8	8.20	25	10	0	0	87	130	86	79	17	44	63	.352	.308	.373	6.54	4.57
Marnon, Kevin	R-R	6-3	245	3-16-94	0	1	18.90	7	0	0	0	10	23	21	21	5	10	12	.451	.360	.538	10.80	9.00
McGovern, Kevin	L-L	6-2	190	5-22-89	1	5	6.33	15	14	0	0	70	80	55	49	18	31	75	.288	.253	.305	9.69	4.00
Mikolas, Miles	R-R	6-4	230	8-23-88	1	0	6.97	2	2	0	0	10	15	8	8	3	3	7	.375	.364	.389	6.10	2.61
Pacheco, Freddy	R-R	5-11	203	4-17-98	1	0	1.83	15	0	0	3	20	7	4	4	1	8	33	.106	.103	.108	15.10	3.66
Pallante, Andre	R-R	6-0	203	9-18-98	4	7	3.82	21	21	0	0	94	102	53	40	8	42	82	.273	.267	.277	7.82	4.01
Patterson, Jacob	R-L	6-2	200	10-30-95	0	0	14.14	11	0	0	0	14	15	25	22	3	23	6	.263	.188	.293	3.86	14.79
Pike, Tyler	L-L	6-0	180	1-26-94	4	4	4.85	15	10	1	0	69	80	45	37	5	16	68	.291	.245	.316	8.91	2.10
Ponce de Leon, Daniel	R-R	6-3	200	1-16-92	1	0	16.20	1	0	0	0	2	2	3	3	1	1	1	.286	.200	.500	5.40	5.40
Quezada, Johan	R-R	6-9	255	8-25-94	0	1	10.80	8	0	0	0	12	20	16	14	3	6	14	.364	.370	.357	10.80	4.63
Raposo, Nick	R-R	5-10	200	6-3-98	0	0	0.00	1	0	0	0	1	0	0	0	1	0	0	.000	--	.000	6.75	6.75
Roach, Dalton	R-R	6-2	210	4-8-96	7	10	5.65	24	19	0	0	115	135	76	72	27	45	119	.291	.347	.250	9.34	3.53
Roberts, Griffin	R-R	6-3	210	6-13-96	0	1	40.50	2	0	0	0	1	2	6	6	1	6	2	.400	.500	.333	13.50	40.50
Robles, Domingo	L-L	6-2	170	4-29-98	3	10	6.09	23	21	1	1	92	115	74	62	18	24	78	.303	.339	.286	7.66	2.36
Santos, Ramon	R-R	6-3	230	9-20-94	5	4	2.79	29	0	0	2	61	35	25	19	7	39	96	.164	.197	.145	14.09	5.72
Seijas, Alvaro	R-R	6-1	195	10-10-98	1	2	8.78	6	4	0	0	13	14	15	13	1	21	8	.275	.263	.281	5.40	14.18
Sisk, Evan	L-L	6-2	209	4-23-97	2	0	3.60	16	0	0	1	20	19	12	8	2	12	28	.244	.357	.180	12.60	5.40
2-team total (13 Wichita)					3	1	4.24	29	0	0	1	40	41	26	19	4	27	51	.255	.288	.232	11.38	6.02
Thomas, Connor	R-L	5-11	173	5-29-98	0	2	4.87	4	4	0	0	20	26	13	11	5	3	24	.321	.417	.281	10.62	1.33
Thompson, Cory	R-R	5-11	180	9-23-94	1	1	3.44	9	0	0	0	18	18	10	7	1	9	12	.257	.333	.189	5.89	4.42
Walsh, Jake	R-R	6-2	192	7-20-95	2	1	1.50	13	0	0	0	18	11	3	3	0	5	25	.169	.091	.209	12.50	2.50
Whitley, Kodi	R-R	6-3	220	2-21-95	1	2	13.50	6	1	0	0	5	5	8	7	1	3	8	.278	.200	.308	15.43	5.79
Williams, Garrett	L-L	6-1	200	9-15-94	1	0	3.32	11	0	0	0	19	18	7	7	2	8	25	.265	.310	.231	11.84	3.79

Fielding

Catcher	PCT	G	PO	A	E	DP	PB
Antonini	.987	16	143	12	2	2	3
Herrera	.987	71	636	53	9	3	7
Raposo	.971	22	156	14	5	1	2
Rodriguez	.971	16	119	14	4	2	2

First Base	PCT	G	PO	A	E	DP
Baker	.991	84	617	36	6	66
Burleson	1.000	1	8	0	0	1
Cedeno	1.000	5	23	2	0	1
Diaz	1.000	1	4	0	0	0
Donovan	1.000	7	45	1	0	8
Redmond	.966	18	129	13	5	22
Rodriguez	.970	4	32	0	1	3
Yepez	1.000	7	40	3	0	3

Second Base	PCT	G	PO	A	E	DP
Castillo	.944	5	6	11	1	1
Diaz	1.000	2	1	3	0	1

	PCT	G	PO	A	E	DP
Donovan	.944	3	8	9	1	2
Dunn	.966	86	117	193	11	53
Gorman	.947	16	23	48	4	13
Lopez	.980	13	22	26	1	4

Third Base	PCT	G	PO	A	E	DP
Castillo	.875	7	4	3	1	0
Diaz	.842	7	3	13	3	0
Donovan	.958	18	14	32	2	4
Dunn	1.000	3	1	5	0	0
Gorman	.933	23	19	37	4	6
Lopez	.906	15	6	23	3	1
Nunez	.902	48	29	81	12	11
Redmond	1.000	1	0	1	0	0
Yepez	1.000	4	1	11	0	2

Shortstop	PCT	G	PO	A	E	DP
Castillo	.958	8	12	11	1	1
Diaz	.960	7	9	15	1	3

	PCT	G	PO	A	E	DP
Donovan	1.000	9	7	23	0	5
Lopez	.912	9	11	20	3	5
Perez	.956	97	138	251	18	59

Outfield	PCT	G	PO	A	E	DP
Burleson	.983	55	112	2	2	0
Capel	.889	3	7	1	1	0
Cedeno	.972	15	33	2	1	0
Donovan	1.000	15	24	0	0	0
Koperniak	1.000	32	68	1	0	1
Lopez	1.000	7	13	1	0	0
Pinder	1.000	18	42	1	0	0
Plummer	.965	83	135	4	5	1
Redmond	.667	4	2	0	1	0
Toerner	1.000	71	154	4	0	0
Vinsky	.946	69	98	7	6	2
Yepez	1.000	5	6	0	0	0

PEORIA CHIEFS   HIGH CLASS A
HIGH-A CENTRAL

Batting	B-T	HT	WT	DOB	AVG	vLH	vRH	G	AB	R	H	2B	3B	HR	RBI	BB	HBP	SH	SF	SO	SB	CS	SLG	OBP
Antonini, Aaron	L-R	6-0	200	7-27-98	.160	.188	.153	24	75	9	12	3	0	2	9	12	8	0	1	26	0	0	.280	.333
Buchberger, Jacob	R-R	6-2	215	10-1-97	.163	.130	.175	21	80	7	13	5	2	0	5	5	0	0	0	22	2	0	.275	.212
Burleson, Alec	L-L	6-2	212	11-25-98	.286	.111	.333	11	42	8	12	1	0	4	10	6	0	0	1	15	1	0	.595	.367
Castillo, Moises	R-R	6-1	170	7-14-99	.236	.218	.241	69	246	27	58	11	1	6	33	19	9	0	0	72	5	3	.362	.314

Batting	B-T	HT	WT	DOB	AVG	vLH	vRH	G	AB	R	H	2B	3B	HR	RBI	BB	HBP	SH	SF	SO	SB	CS	SLG	OBP
Cedeno, Leandro	R-R	6-2	195	8-22-98	.261	.290	.252	77	287	37	75	18	1	9	44	18	6	0	0	101	0	2	.425	.318
Chamberlain, Matt	L-R	6-0	200	10-31-98	.207	.136	.228	83	256	34	53	6	1	7	28	43	5	1	2	106	8	7	.320	.330
Diaz, Imeldo	R-R	6-0	175	11-2-97	.221	.200	.226	23	77	7	17	2	0	1	2	3	2	0	0	19	1	0	.286	.268
Donovan, Brendan	L-R	6-1	195	1-16-97	.295	.318	.288	25	95	15	28	6	0	2	13	10	4	0	0	15	7	1	.421	.385
Francisco, Thomas	L-R	6-0	211	6-26-99	.211	.200	.214	10	38	5	8	1	0	1	4	2	1	0	0	5	1	1	.316	.268
Hernandez, Francisco	R-R	5-11	190	10-8-99	.186	.175	.190	91	311	29	58	11	3	3	21	31	3	0	1	141	8	6	.270	.266
Jew, Tommy	R-R	6-1	185	10-26-97	.143	.000	.170	21	63	6	9	4	1	0	5	8	3	0	0	26	3	1	.238	.270
Koperniak, Matt	L-R	6-0	200	2-8-98	.429	.667	.364	4	14	0	6	3	0	0	3	2	2	0	0	3	0	0	.643	.556
Longa, Cristhian	R-R	5-11	180	4-28-00	.273	.259	.278	30	99	11	27	6	0	1	7	4	3	0	0	26	0	0	.364	.321
Lott, Todd	R-R	6-4	235	8-22-97	.243	.303	.226	39	148	19	36	7	1	7	17	9	3	0	2	58	4	4	.446	.296
Nunez, Malcom	R-R	5-11	205	3-9-01	.285	.333	.267	35	137	18	39	10	2	3	20	11	3	0	0	27	5	2	.453	.351
Pages, Pedro	R-R	6-1	234	9-17-98	.249	.304	.230	80	301	28	75	12	1	9	39	34	7	0	2	82	1	2	.385	.337
Redmond, Chandler	L-R	6-1	231	1-9-97	.234	.200	.244	63	222	33	52	11	0	13	34	35	5	0	1	88	3	1	.459	.350
Reichenborn, Tyler	R-R	5-11	180	7-23-98	.207	.254	.191	81	276	30	57	19	2	6	29	30	7	0	2	86	6	6	.355	.298
Richardson, Zade	R-R	6-1	200	5-10-00	.180	.189	.177	73	245	40	44	7	1	12	37	38	13	0	0	94	2	1	.363	.321
Torres, Jhon	R-R	6-4	199	3-29-00	.238	.204	.249	97	383	47	91	25	3	6	32	27	9	0	1	98	3	4	.366	.302
Walker, Jordan	R-R	6-5	220	5-22-02	.292	.365	.270	55	226	39	66	14	3	8	27	15	3	0	0	66	13	2	.487	.344
Whalen, Brady	B-R	6-1	180	1-15-98	.255	.234	.262	49	192	28	49	7	0	9	27	15	3	0	1	44	1	1	.432	.318
Winn, Masyn	R-R	5-11	180	3-21-02	.209	.222	.205	36	148	26	31	4	2	2	10	6	0	0	0	40	16	3	.304	.240

Pitching	B-T	HT	WT	DOB	W	L	ERA	G	GS	CG	SV	IP	H	R	ER	HR	BB	SO	AVG	vLH	vRH	K/9	BB/9
Aker, Cole	R-R	6-2	205	9-18-96	3	1	7.62	20	0	0	0	28	27	25	24	3	28	23	.250	.233	.271	7.31	8.89
Bedell, Ian	R-R	6-2	198	9-5-99	0	1	10.13	1	2	0	0	3	7	4	3	0	2	4	.500	.375	.667	13.50	6.75
Blanco, Fabian	L-L	6-0	205	12-22-97	2	6	8.72	37	0	0	0	42	67	55	41	9	25	58	.347	.365	.336	12.33	5.31
Brettell, Michael	R-R	6-3	195	7-13-97	1	0	2.84	4	0	0	0	13	13	5	4	0	5	13	.289	.348	.227	9.24	3.55
Cordero, Diego	L-L	6-3	175	9-8-97	0	2	3.60	10	0	0	0	15	9	7	6	3	8	9	.191	.200	.185	5.40	4.80
Dalatri, Gianluca	R-R	6-6	250	4-4-98	1	0	11.57	4	0	0	0	5	10	6	6	2	4	2	.435	.545	.333	11.57	3.86
Gragg, Logan	R-R	6-5	200	8-8-98	2	7	4.45	25	20	0	0	99	108	58	49	15	27	80	.273	.278	.265	7.27	2.45
Heredia, Nathanael	L-L	6-3	190	9-10-00	1	2	7.71	14	3	0	0	19	17	19	16	1	31	21	.243	.429	.119	10.13	14.95
Kealey, Sean	L-L	6-7	225	10-15-97	1	1	4.76	15	0	0	1	23	30	13	12	1	14	29	.313	.235	.355	11.51	5.56
Lardner, Mac	R-L	6-4	195	12-29-97	0	6	5.91	21	14	0	1	67	74	46	44	10	22	73	.273	.305	.253	9.81	2.96
Lunn, Connor	R-R	6-3	215	7-8-98	6	8	3.96	24	23	0	0	120	117	61	53	12	20	121	.254	.268	.234	9.05	1.50
Marnon, Kevin	R-L	6-7	245	3-16-99	0	0	4.15	4	0	0	1	4	4	2	2	1	5	2	.250	.400	.182	10.38	2.08
Mikolas, Miles	R-R	6-4	230	8-23-88	1	0	3.86	1	1	0	0	7	6	3	3	0	0	8	.231	.429	.000	10.29	0.00
Oxnevad, Ian	R-L	6-4	205	10-3-96	0	0	0.00	2	0	0	1	4	4	0	0	0	3	4	.286	.250	.300	9.82	7.36
Pacheco, Freddy	R-R	5-11	203	4-17-98	0	0	5.17	24	0	0	8	31	20	18	18	5	20	57	.182	.212	.136	16.37	5.74
Pereira, Wilfredo	R-R	5-11	197	4-26-99	3	8	3.33	29	13	0	1	97	76	44	36	9	40	115	.211	.180	.252	10.63	3.70
Ralston, Jack	R-R	6-6	231	8-13-97	2	5	3.49	28	11	0	2	67	41	28	26	4	36	101	.171	.181	.154	13.57	4.84
Redmond, Chandler	L-R	6-1	231	1-9-97	0	0	0.00	1	0	0	0	1	0	0	0	0	0	0	.000	.000	.000	0.00	0.00
Schlesener, Jacob	L-L	6-3	175	10-8-96	5	5	7.64	39	0	0	0	53	55	48	45	4	66	71	.272	.244	.292	12.06	11.21
Schmid, Colin	L-L	6-1	195	8-13-97	0	1	3.00	4	2	0	0	9	13	3	3	0	3	10	.333	.286	.360	10.00	3.00
Schwendel, Paul	R-R	6-5	220	8-9-89	2	1	3.98	17	0	0	4	20	13	9	9	2	16	39	.178	.184	.167	17.26	7.08
Sisk, Evan	L-L	6-2	209	4-23-97	0	0	2.84	10	0	0	3	13	13	11	4	0	8	18	.250	.278	.235	12.79	5.68
Solano, Enmanuel	R-R	6-1	160	9-23-98	5	1	4.42	32	0	0	1	57	52	36	28	10	26	53	.239	.285	.179	8.37	4.11
Taveras, Leonardo	R-R	6-5	190	9-7-98	1	6	6.22	41	0	0	3	46	34	34	32	5	54	64	.207	.263	.130	12.43	10.49
Thompson, Cory	R-R	5-11	180	9-23-94	2	0	3.70	17	0	0	2	24	24	10	10	1	10	37	.255	.240	.273	13.68	3.70
Troglic-Iverson, Nick	R-R	6-1	175	10-3-97	6	5	5.10	21	11	0	0	67	92	41	38	9	24	50	.333	.327	.342	6.72	3.22
Winn, Masyn	R-R	5-11	180	3-21-02	0	0	0.00	1	0	0	0	1	0	0	0	0	0	1	.000	.000	.000	9.00	0.00
YaSenka, Michael	R-R	6-1	195	5-26-98	1	9	6.11	24	21	0	0	96	92	75	65	17	57	103	.246	.259	.228	9.69	5.36

Fielding

Catcher	PCT	G	PO	A	E	DP	PB
Antonini	.992	14	119	10	1	3	1
Longa	1.000	3	30	2	0	0	1
Pages	.982	63	606	47	12	2	4
Richardson	.971	41	408	24	13	2	10

First Base	PCT	G	PO	A	E	DP
Antonini	1.000	1	1	0	0	0
Buchberger	1.000	1	11	1	0	2
Cedeno	1.000	23	144	14	0	17
Francisco	1.000	10	56	4	0	5
Lott	.965	22	150	14	6	17
Pages	1.000	4	1	0	2	
Redmond	.991	16	108	4	1	8
Whalen	.987	46	272	23	4	17

Second Base	PCT	G	PO	A	E	DP

Buchberger	1.000	16	22	31	0	8
Castillo	.925	13	17	20	3	1
Diaz	.949	10	13	24	2	2
Donovan	.951	22	30	47	4	11
Hernandez	.988	52	62	105	2	24
Redmond	.967	10	12	17	1	3

Third Base	PCT	G	PO	A	E	DP
Buchberger	.600	4	2	1	2	0
Diaz	1.000	7	1	10	0	0
Donovan	1.000	1	0	2	0	0
Hernandez	.957	7	10	12	1	0
Nunez	.945	34	26	43	4	6
Redmond	.905	15	6	13	2	3
Walker	.876	54	51	62	16	5

Shortstop	PCT	G	PO	A	E	DP

Castillo	.936	56	100	104	14	21
Diaz	1.000	2	2	2	0	0
Hernandez	.962	33	69	59	5	12
Winn	.949	31	41	70	6	18

Outfield	PCT	G	PO	A	E	DP
Burleson	1.000	10	13	0	0	0
Cedeno	.963	45	74	4	3	0
Chamberlain	1.000	80	178	8	0	1
Diaz	1.000	3	1	0	0	0
Donovan	1.000	1	2	0	0	0
Jew	1.000	20	34	0	0	0
Koperniak	1.000	4	6	1	0	1
Lott	.885	10	23	0	3	0
Redmond	.968	20	7	3	1	0
Reichenborn	.958	79	151	7	7	1
Torres	.972	94	163	9	5	2

PALM BEACH CARDINALS
LOW-A SOUTHEAST

LOW CLASS A

Batting	B-T	HT	WT	DOB	AVG	vLH	vRH	G	AB	R	H	2B	3B	HR	RBI	BB	HBP	SH	SF	SO	SB	CS	SLG	OBP
Antico, Mike	L-R	5-10	200	2-16-98	.266	.154	.291	39	143	21	38	8	3	6	19	13	3	0	0	33	8	1	.490	.340
Bader, Harrison	R-R	6-0	210	6-3-94	.333	--	.333	3	9	1	3	1	0	0	1	1	0	0	1	1	0	0	.444	.364

Buchberger, Jacob	R-R	6-2	215	10-1-97	.308	.368	.298	72	266	36	82	14	3	3	34	34	4	0	2	57	5	2	.417	.392
Cabell, Elijah	R-R	6-2	225	6-30-99	.246	.333	.217	19	61	6	15	2	1	3	8	7	3	0	0	29	0	0	.459	.352
Chambers, Mack	B-R	6-0	180	8-10-99	.203	.150	.214	34	118	15	24	5	1	0	11	15	1	0	2	26	1	2	.263	.294
Cruz, Adanson	R-R	6-2	175	10-6-00	.200	.200	.200	7	25	4	5	3	0	0	2	3	1	0	0	13	0	1	.320	.310
Dean, Austin	R-R	6-0	215	10-14-93	.400	.000	.444	4	10	3	4	0	0	1	2	2	0	0	0	3	0	0	.700	.500
Del Villar, Darlyn	R-R	6-0	176	11-8-00	.183	.200	.180	27	71	7	13	3	0	0	7	12	1	0	0	31	1	1	.225	.310
Francisco, Thomas	L-R	6-0	211	6-26-99	.333	.333	.333	23	81	11	27	7	0	2	11	8	4	0	1	16	1	0	.494	.415
Fuller, Terry	L-R	6-4	210	12-5-98	.110	.063	.118	42	109	14	12	5	1	0	8	32	2	0	1	49	2	0	.174	.319
Heredia, Roblin	L-R	6-0	200	7-22-02	.209	.111	.224	19	67	10	14	5	0	0	7	5	2	0	0	28	0	0	.284	.284
Hernandez, Francisco	R-R	5-11	190	10-8-99	.000	.000	.000	3	9	0	0	0	0	0	1	1	0	0	1	4	0	0	.000	.091
Holgate, Ryan	L-L	6-2	193	6-8-00	.193	.130	.209	30	114	15	22	2	0	3	14	13	1	0	1	46	0	0	.289	.279
Jew, Tommy	R-R	6-1	185	10-26-97	.213	.179	.219	54	188	31	40	5	2	5	30	27	3	0	1	78	11	4	.340	.320
Jones, L.J.	R-R	6-0	225	6-27-99	.243	.286	.236	86	329	43	80	17	2	7	38	23	6	0	2	73	1	1	.371	.303
Koperniak, Matt	L-R	6-0	200	2-8-98	.322	.207	.344	58	183	28	59	15	0	4	23	30	12	0	3	32	3	1	.470	.443
Lott, Todd	R-R	6-4	235	8-22-97	.263	.206	.276	52	186	29	49	19	2	6	31	24	9	0	2	62	0	0	.484	.371
Machado, Jonatan	L-L	5-9	155	1-21-99	.000	.000	.000	1	2	0	0	0	0	0	0	0	0	0	0	0	0	0	.000	.000
McKeithan, Aaron	R-R	6-1	220	12-13-99	.154	.154	.154	22	65	9	10	2	0	0	4	6	4	0	1	17	0	0	.185	.263
Mendlinger, Noah	L-R	5-9	180	8-9-00	.275	.182	.310	29	80	12	22	5	1	0	5	18	2	0	0	14	0	2	.363	.420
Mendoza, Ramon	R-R	5-11	174	8-31-00	.077	.000	.095	12	26	2	1	0	0	1	0	1	0	0	6	0	0	0	.115	.226
Rodriguez, Edgardo	R-R	6-0	207	11-29-00	.213	.300	.196	17	61	2	13	1	0	0	5	1	0	0	1	18	0	0	.230	.222
Rodriguez, Luis	R-R	6-0	175	2-26-00	.154	.000	.167	9	26	1	4	2	0	0	1	3	0	0	0	11	0	0	.231	.241
Romeri, Patrick	R-R	6-3	195	6-29-01	.236	.283	.226	79	276	36	65	17	0	7	30	42	4	0	0	95	3	4	.373	.345
Soto, Carlos	L-R	6-1	225	4-27-99	.227	.344	.211	75	264	33	60	15	2	8	42	52	3	0	3	73	0	1	.390	.357
Soto, Franklin	R-R	5-11	168	9-23-99	.208	.190	.211	81	274	27	57	10	0	4	29	24	5	1	3	87	3	3	.288	.281
Stauss, Wade	L-R	6-2	225	4-4-99	.143	.000	.162	15	42	2	6	2	0	1	4	6	2	0	1	26	0	0	.262	.275
Tovalin, Osvaldo	L-R	6-2	225	10-31-99	.269	.235	.275	32	108	16	29	6	1	2	16	4	3	0	0	27	0	1	.398	.313
Walker, Jordan	R-R	6-5	220	5-22-02	.374	.600	.333	27	99	24	37	11	1	6	21	18	3	0	2	21	1	0	.687	.475
Whalen, Brady	B-R	6-4	180	1-15-98	.275	.167	.294	11	40	4	11	1	0	0	4	4	1	0	0	9	0	0	.300	.356
Williams, Donivan	R-R	6-0	190	7-25-99	.220	.143	.233	46	141	19	31	4	0	1	12	24	1	0	1	51	4	1	.270	.335
Williams, Justin	L-R	6-1	235	8-20-95	.143	--	.143	2	7	0	1	0	0	0	0	0	0	0	0	1	0	1	.143	.143
Winn, Masyn	R-R	5-11	180	3-21-02	.262	.371	.243	61	237	50	62	15	3	3	34	40	3	0	4	60	16	2	.388	.370
Zapata, Jose	R-R	5-11	195	2-14-01	.188	.143	.200	10	32	4	6	1	0	1	4	2	0	0	0	13	0	0	.313	.235

Pitching

Pitching	B-T	HT	WT	DOB	W	L	ERA	G	GS	CG	SV	IP	H	R	ER	HR	BB	SO	AVG	vLH	vRH	K/9	BB/9
Beller, John	L-L	5-11	175	3-6-99	0	7	4.59	21	19	0	1	80	78	54	41	6	44	98	.244	.254	.241	10.98	4.93
Cuenca, Angel	R-R	6-1	160	7-10-01	1	1	7.04	4	0	0	0	8	9	12	6	0	7	10	.257	.462	.136	11.74	8.22
Dalatri, Gianluca	R-R	6-6	250	4-4-98	0	3	5.60	13	1	0	1	18	16	13	11	1	7	24	.242	.174	.279	12.23	3.57
Davila, Jose	R-R	6-3	177	11-9-02	0	1	10.80	4	0	0	0	8	12	10	10	0	10	5	.375	.600	.273	5.40	10.80
Del Villar, Darlyn	R-R	6-0	176	11-8-00	0	0	9.00	1	0	0	0	1	1	1	1	0	1	1	.333	--	.333	9.00	9.00
Garcia, Roy	R-R	6-0	190	8-28-00	0	0	7.71	6	0	0	0	7	9	10	6	0	4	6	.300	.200	.400	7.71	5.14
Graceffo, Gordon	R-R	6-4	210	3-17-00	1	0	1.73	11	1	0	1	26	28	9	5	1	9	37	.267	.324	.239	12.81	3.12
Granillo, Andre	R-R	6-4	245	5-12-00	2	3	1.50	14	0	0	2	18	10	12	3	1	9	23	.159	.091	.195	11.50	4.50
Guay, Will	R-R	6-3	216	5-30-97	3	2	5.53	16	0	0	0	28	25	17	17	3	27	33	.240	.217	.259	10.73	8.78
Heredia, Nathanael	L-L	6-3	190	9-10-00	1	1	4.82	16	1	0	0	37	30	21	20	0	28	49	.224	.240	.220	11.81	6.75
Hudson, Dakota	R-R	6-5	215	9-15-94	0	0	0.00	1	1	0	0	2	2	0	0	0	0	1	.250	.250	.250	4.50	0.00
Jimenez, Ludwin	R-R	6-2	165	8-9-01	0	9	6.17	23	18	0	0	77	89	61	53	8	51	89	.287	.241	.312	10.36	5.94
Justo, Francisco	R-R	6-4	217	10-12-98	2	0	4.85	15	0	0	1	26	24	20	14	2	24	23	.242	.355	.191	7.96	8.31
Kealey, Sean	L-L	6-7	225	10-15-97	2	3	3.68	12	0	0	0	15	15	11	6	0	6	25	.259	.250	.262	15.34	3.68
Loutos, Ryan	R-R	6-5	215	1-29-99	1	2	5.56	12	1	0	0	23	28	15	14	0	6	26	.292	.343	.262	10.32	2.38
Love, Austin	R-R	6-3	232	1-26-00	0	0	0.00	2	0	0	0	3	1	0	0	0	1	4	.111	.333	.000	12.00	3.00
Manzo, Edgar	R-R	5-11	181	10-24-00	6	5	4.91	25	6	0	1	66	62	40	36	5	30	65	.249	.219	.271	8.86	4.09
Marnon, Kevin	R-L	6-7	245	3-16-94	0	2	4.66	10	0	0	2	10	6	5	5	1	4	14	.182	.167	.185	13.03	3.72
Marrero, Andrew	R-R	5-10	196	5-8-00	0	2	10.13	10	0	0	0	13	16	20	15	1	14	22	.286	.304	.273	14.85	9.45
McGreevy, Michael	R-R	6-4	215	7-8-00	0	0	9.00	5	5	0	0	6	10	6	6	1	1	4	.357	.455	.294	6.00	1.50
Mendoza, Ramon	R-R	5-11	174	8-31-00	0	0	0.00	1	0	0	0	2	0	0	0	0	1	1	.000	--	.000	4.50	4.50
Moreno, Jose	R-R	6-1	197	8-20-00	1	5	5.53	23	16	0	0	81	83	56	50	5	56	102	.263	.254	.269	11.29	6.20
Nunez, Edwin	R-R	6-3	185	11-5-01	3	5	10.90	32	2	0	0	54	64	72	65	7	56	59	.303	.298	.308	9.89	9.39
Ortiz, Luis	R-R	6-3	170	7-23-00	2	4	6.68	33	0	0	1	61	71	54	45	4	47	75	.284	.337	.248	11.13	6.97
Paniagua, Inohan	R-R	6-1	148	2-6-00	4	1	3.88	16	5	0	2	46	37	24	20	3	19	62	.219	.207	.230	12.04	3.69
Portillo, Reinys	R-R	6-2	165	1-14-01	1	1	8.53	4	0	0	0	6	6	7	6	1	10	8	.231	.167	.250	11.37	14.21
Prater, Levi	B-L	6-0	184	6-20-99	1	9	6.72	24	16	0	0	68	63	60	51	13	68	104	.248	.200	.266	13.70	8.96
Richard, Yordy	R-R	6-1	195	8-27-02	1	2	8.59	9	0	0	0	15	23	17	14	2	11	16	.365	.387	.344	9.82	6.75
Rodriguez, Dionys	L-R	6-0	188	9-3-00	4	5	3.36	22	12	0	0	70	52	28	26	5	22	88	.201	.185	.185	11.37	2.84
Rodriguez, Gustavo J.	R-R	6-3	160	1-8-01	0	5	7.36	16	10	0	0	40	51	40	33	3	27	41	.309	.259	.333	9.15	6.02
Rodriguez, Luis	R-R	6-0	175	2-26-00	0	0	0.00	1	0	0	0	0	0	0	0	0	0	0	.000	--	.000	0.00	0.00
Santos, Ramon	R-R	6-3	230	9-20-94	1	0	2.84	6	0	0	1	6	6	2	2	0	1	6	.261	.267	.250	8.53	1.42
Solano, Enmanuel	R-R	6-1	160	9-23-98	0	1	7.04	4	0	0	0	8	8	7	6	2	3	5	.286	.368	.111	5.87	3.52
Soto, Hector	R-R	6-1	175	3-2-99	0	1	3.38	5	0	0	1	5	7	4	2	1	1	7	.292	.444	.200	11.81	1.69
Tena, Luis	R-R	5-11	172	10-21-99	0	1	7.66	22	0	0	0	25	36	24	21	2	18	30	.330	.262	.373	10.95	6.57
Trogrlic-Iverson, Nick	R-R	6-1	175	10-3-97	0	1	2.25	3	3	0	0	16	11	6	4	1	5	11	.208	.250	.118	6.19	2.81

Fielding

Catcher	PCT	G	PO	A	E	DP	PB
Heredia	1.000	13	127	9	0	1	2
McKeithan	1.000	20	176	11	0	2	1
Rodriguez	.993	13	132	9	1	0	2
Rodriguez	1.000	8	86	9	0	0	1
Soto	.995	57	522	48	3	2	5
Stauss	.987	8	71	6	1	0	2
Zapata	.958	5	42	4	2	1	0

First Base	PCT	G	PO	A	E	DP
Buchberger	1.000	25	141	6	0	20
Francisco	.984	19	109	17	2	9
Jones	.992	21	118	10	1	13
Lott	.969	36	205	17	7	19
Soto	1.000	9	55	5	0	5
Whalen	.983	9	55	4	1	5

Second Base	PCT	G	PO	A	E	DP
Buchberger	1.000	1	0	2	0	0
Hernandez	1.000	1	1	1	0	0
Mendlinger	.960	21	33	39	3	10
Mendoza	1.000	6	6	7	0	3
Soto	.911	61	101	113	21	27
Williams	.968	35	63	59	4	19

Third Base	PCT	G	PO	A	E	DP
Buchberger	.875	34	24	53	11	5
Del Villar	.667	10	2	4	3	0
Hernandez	1.000	2	3	4	0	1
Mendlinger	.941	9	7	9	1	2
Mendoza	.833	6	4	6	2	0
Rodriguez	.000	1	0	0	0	0
Tovalin	.881	31	19	40	8	5
Walker	.875	22	22	20	6	4
Williams	1.000	10	7	12	0	0

Shortstop	PCT	G	PO	A	E	DP
Chambers	.886	34	43	58	13	11
Del Villar	.818	15	14	13	6	5
Soto	.857	21	15	39	9	8
Williams	1.000	2	0	3	0	0
Winn	.920	55	71	136	18	27

Outfield	PCT	G	PO	A	E	DP
Antico	.983	35	55	2	1	0
Bader	1.000	2	5	0	0	0
Buchberger	1.000	8	6	0	0	0
Cabell	.923	17	24	0	2	0
Cruz	1.000	7	16	2	0	0
Dean	1.000	2	4	0	0	0
Fuller	.967	36	55	4	2	0
Holgate	.979	28	47	0	1	0
Jew	1.000	51	100	6	0	2
Jones	.987	49	68	7	1	3
Koperniak	.966	56	107	5	4	2
Machado	1.000	1	2	0	0	0
Romeri	.975	74	113	6	3	1
Williams	1.000	1	2	0	0	0

FCL CARDINALS   ROOKIE
FLORIDA COMPLEX LEAGUE

Batting	B-T	HT	WT	DOB	AVG	vLH	vRH	G	AB	R	H	2B	3B	HR	RBI	BB	HBP	SH	SF	SO	SB	CS	SLG	OBP
Baez, Joshua	R-R	6-4	220	6-28-03	.158	.267	.131	23	76	18	12	3	1	2	8	14	3	0	2	28	5	0	.303	.305
Burns, Jake	L-R	6-0	199	2-17-03	.205	.190	.209	35	112	14	23	5	0	2	13	18	1	0	2	36	2	1	.304	.316
Cruz, Adanson	R-R	6-2	175	10-6-00	.272	.333	.250	34	103	15	28	3	1	2	15	19	2	0	0	43	3	0	.379	.395
De Los Santos, Joerlin	R-R	5-11	175	9-16-00	.220	.100	.245	22	59	12	13	2	0	0	6	15	3	0	0	14	6	3	.254	.403
Del Villar, Darlyn	R-R	6-0	176	11-8-00	.235	.200	.250	10	34	2	8	3	0	1	4	5	0	0	0	14	1	0	.412	.333
Fletcher, Tre	R-R	6-2	200	4-30-01	.222	.000	.250	7	27	3	6	2	0	1	2	2	0	0	0	11	0	0	.407	.276
Garcia, Joyser	R-R	5-10	165	10-14-99	.250	.000	.429	5	12	0	3	1	0	0	3	0	0	0	0	2	0	0	.333	.250
Heredia, Roblin	L-R	6-0	200	7-22-02	.167	.067	.202	38	114	9	19	5	0	0	10	23	1	0	1	45	3	0	.211	.309
Hernandez, Brandon	L-R	6-0	190	8-21-01	.180	.136	.194	29	89	11	16	4	1	0	10	8	1	0	2	33	3	2	.247	.250
Inoa, Albert	R-R	5-11	170	12-4-01	.137	.000	.161	27	73	9	10	0	0	0	3	16	0	0	0	33	3	2	.137	.292
Mendoza, Ramon	R-R	5-11	174	8-31-00	.271	.238	.286	24	70	15	19	5	1	0	6	11	2	0	1	16	1	1	.371	.381
Montano, Luis	L-R	6-2	170	4-10-00	.275	.321	.261	35	120	21	33	10	2	4	17	12	0	0	0	37	2	0	.492	.341
Moquete, Darlin	R-R	5-11	175	9-19-99	.329	.286	.339	24	73	12	24	4	0	0	10	9	2	0	0	20	1	1	.384	.417
Mora, Sander	R-R	5-9	155	2-23-01	.159	.045	.200	27	82	18	13	2	1	2	9	12	3	0	0	27	1	0	.280	.289
Orecchia, Jesus	R-R	6-1	175	4-22-01	.229	.111	.256	23	48	7	11	2	0	1	9	8	0	0	2	12	0	0	.333	.328
Otamendi, Hansel	R-R	5-9	180	2-15-02	.296	.300	.295	28	98	15	29	4	2	1	15	9	1	0	0	22	7	3	.408	.361
Pinder, Chase	R-R	5-11	185	3-16-96	.182	.250	.143	5	11	3	2	1	0	1	1	4	2	0	0	0	0	0	.545	.471
Rivas, Jeremy	R-R	6-0	172	3-4-03	.271	.250	.277	48	177	22	48	7	1	0	16	15	6	0	2	32	6	5	.322	.345
Rodriguez, Edgardo	R-R	6-0	207	11-29-00	.282	.273	.286	13	39	3	11	0	0	2	8	3	1	0	2	9	1	0	.436	.333
Rodriguez, Julio E.	R-R	6-0	245	6-11-97	.286	.333	.273	7	14	2	4	0	0	0	2	5	2	0	1	3	0	0	.286	.500
Rodriguez, Luis	R-R	6-1	175	2-26-00	.347	.000	.370	22	49	7	17	2	0	0	11	8	0	0	0	18	0	1	.388	.439
Vargas, Smith	R-R	5-10	160	8-30-01	.088	.000	.103	18	34	9	3	2	0	0	4	0	0	0	0	17	2	1	.206	.184
Velasquez, Diego	R-R	5-10	175	3-25-02	.143	.000	.167	5	14	1	2	0	0	0	1	0	1	0	0	3	1	0	.143	.200
Whalen, Brady	B-R	6-4	180	1-15-98	.160	.125	.176	7	25	2	4	1	0	0	5	3	0	0	2	2	1	1	.200	.233
Williams, Justin	L-R	6-1	235	8-20-95	.143	.000	.167	4	14	1	2	1	0	0	3	0	1	0	0	3	0	0	.214	.200
Zapata, Jose	R-R	5-11	195	2-14-01	.250	.375	.200	10	28	4	7	3	0	0	4	2	0	0	0	11	0	0	.357	.300

Pitching	B-T	HT	WT	DOB	W	L	ERA	G	GS	CG	SV	IP	H	R	ER	HR	BB	SO	AVG	vLH	vRH	K/9	BB/9
Baird, Ben	R-R	6-3	190	1-7-98	1	1	4.38	14	0	0	0	12	18	10	6	1	4	12	.327	.300	.343	8.76	2.92
Baker, Trent	R-R	6-3	240	12-28-98	0	0	5.87	8	0	0	0	8	9	5	5	2	2	10	.281	.333	.214	11.74	2.35
Cordero, Diego	L-L	6-3	175	9-8-97	0	0	1.80	6	0	0	0	10	5	2	2	0	7	9	.161	.147	.160	8.10	6.30
Cornwell, Alex	L-L	6-2	200	5-9-99	1	0	2.25	8	0	0	0	8	6	2	2	1	2	5	.207	.000	.273	5.63	2.25
Davila, Jose	R-R	6-3	177	11-9-02	1	3	3.77	11	9	1	0	45	33	28	19	1	24	49	.281	.244	.159	9.73	4.76
Garcia, Roy	R-R	6-0	190	8-28-00	3	0	1.42	10	0	0	0	19	11	5	3	1	3	23	.159	.192	.140	10.89	1.42
Gerard, Chris	R-L	5-10	175	11-23-99	0	1	4.70	7	0	0	0	8	6	5	4	1	2	10	.200	.200	.200	11.74	2.35
Giulianelli, Ettore	R-R	6-3	190	3-30-03	0	2	4.30	14	1	0	0	15	13	8	7	0	11	22	.245	.269	.222	13.50	6.75
Hart, Thomas	R-R	6-2	155	12-5-00	2	1	15.88	10	3	0	0	11	18	20	20	3	16	7	.360	.318	.393	5.56	12.71
Heinecke, Hayes	L-L	6-0	210	6-28-99	0	1	6.75	3	0	0	0	3	5	4	2	0	2	3	.417	.500	.400	10.13	6.75
Hence, Tink	R-R	6-1	175	8-6-02	0	1	9.00	8	1	0	1	8	11	10	8	1	3	14	.306	.385	.261	15.75	3.38
Love, Austin	R-R	6-3	232	1-26-99	0	0	1.80	5	5	0	0	5	2	1	1	0	1	9	.118	.000	.182	16.20	0.00
McGreevy, Michael	R-R	6-4	215	7-8-00	0	2	10.80	2	2	0	0	2	4	2	2	0	1	3	.444	.500	.400	16.20	5.40
Mills, Zane	R-R	6-4	220	7-4-00	0	0	1.17	7	0	0	0	8	4	1	1	0	1	9	.154	.091	.200	10.57	0.00
Miranda, William	R-R	6-1	170	2-14-01	0	0	15.88	6	0	0	0	6	9	10	10	2	11	8	.346	.400	.313	12.71	17.47
Peralta, Juan	R-R	6-2	175	8-9-02	1	0	1.08	8	0	0	0	8	5	2	1	1	2	16	.167	.000	.227	10.80	2.16
Pope, Bryan	R-R	6-2	195	1-27-99	0	0	1.04	7	0	0	0	9	11	4	1	1	1	9	.306	.313	.300	9.35	1.04
Portillo, Reinys	R-R	6-2	165	1-14-01	1	6	7.51	12	9	0	1	38	36	37	32	5	27	40	.259	.271	.250	9.39	6.34
Quezada, Johan	R-R	6-9	255	8-25-94	1	0	3.00	7	2	0	0	9	7	3	3	0	1	12	.219	.200	.235	12.00	1.00
Richard, Yordy	R-R	6-1	195	8-27-02	3	6	4.27	12	11	0	0	46	51	28	22	6	9	48	.271	.213	.299	9.32	1.75
Rodriguez, Gustavo J.	R-R	6-3	160	1-8-01	1	1	6.75	5	1	0	0	8	12	6	6	1	3	11	.353	.462	.286	12.38	3.38
Rodriguez, Luis	R-R	6-0	175	2-26-00	0	0	0.00	1	0	0	1	1	0	0	0	0	0	1	.333	--	.333	13.50	0.00
Ruiz, Alfredo	L-L	6-0	200	3-12-00	1	0	1.04	8	0	0	1	9	8	4	1	0	2	12	.267	.250	.273	12.46	2.08
Saldana, Enrique	R-R	5-11	155	6-26-99	1	1	3.72	11	5	0	0	29	23	14	12	1	10	29	.223	.234	.214	9.00	3.10
Sanchez, Omar	R-L	5-10	185	4-23-02	3	0	1.50	17	0	0	7	24	11	4	4	0	15	30	.138	.130	.140	11.25	5.63

Name	B-T	HT	WT	DOB	W	L	ERA	G	GS	CG	SV	IP	H	R	ER	HR	BB	SO	AVG	SLG	OBP

| | | | | | | | | | | | | | | | | | | | | | |

Schmid, Colin | L-L | 6-1 | 195 | 8-13-97 | 1 | 0 | 2.37 | 8 | 3 | 0 | 0 | 19 | 18 | 8 | 5 | 1 | 2 | 17 | .243 | .263 | .236 | 8.05 | 0.95
Soto, Hector | R-R | 6-1 | 175 | 3-2-99 | 0 | 0 | 2.70 | 5 | 0 | 0 | 0 | 7 | 6 | 2 | 2 | 2 | 2 | 11 | .250 | .333 | .200 | 14.85 | 2.70
Statler, Tyler | R-R | 6-6 | 230 | 7-1-01 | 1 | 1 | 8.46 | 14 | 0 | 0 | 1 | 22 | 26 | 25 | 21 | 3 | 20 | 24 | .274 | .317 | .241 | 9.67 | 8.06
Tena, Luis | R-R | 5-11 | 172 | 10-21-99 | 0 | 0 | 0.00 | 2 | 0 | 0 | 0 | 2 | 0 | 0 | 0 | 0 | 0 | 3 | .000 | .000 | .000 | 13.50 | 0.00
Villanueva, Victor | R-R | 6-1 | 170 | 3-26-01 | 2 | 2 | 5.75 | 16 | 0 | 0 | 0 | 20 | 27 | 16 | 13 | 6 | 8 | 15 | .310 | .278 | .333 | 6.64 | 3.54
Willis, Alec | R-R | 6-5 | 220 | 3-30-03 | 0 | 0 | 0.00 | 1 | 1 | 0 | 0 | 1 | 0 | 0 | 0 | 0 | 0 | 1 | .000 | .000 | -- | 9.00 | 0.00

Fielding

C: Burns 19, Garcia 1, Heredia 21, Orecchia 4, Rodriguez 7, Rodriguez 5, Rodriguez 2, Velasquez 4, Zapata 4.
1B: Garcia 3, Heredia 10, Orecchia 19, Rodriguez 18, Velasquez 1, Whalen 7, Zapata 4.
2B: Del Villar 2, Hernandez 11, Inoa 25, Mendoza 13, Montano 1, Mora 3, Rivas 1.
3B: Del Villar 7, Hernandez 17, Mendoza 10, Mora 20, Rodriguez 2.
SS: Del Villar 1, Hernandez 1, Mendoza 3, Mora 4, Rivas 48.
OF: Baez 21, Cruz 31, De Los Santos 18, Fletcher 6, Montano 27, Moquete 20, Otamendi 25, Pinder 5, Vargas 14, Williams 4.

DSL CARDINALS   ROOKIE
DOMINICAN SUMMER LEAGUE

Batting	B-T	HT	WT	DOB	AVG	vLH	vRH	G	AB	R	H	2B	3B	HR	RBI	BB	HBP	SH	SF	SO	SB	CS	SLG	OBP
Avendano, Christian	R-R	6-0	168	9-4-03	.231	.154	.246	24	78	7	18	3	0	0	8	3	7	0	1	11	1	1	.269	.315
Bernal, Leonardo	B-R	6-0	200	2-13-04	.209	.214	.208	44	158	23	33	9	1	5	29	17	3	0	0	28	3	1	.373	.298
Bolivar, Javier	R-R	6-2	170	12-19-02	.200	.286	.174	20	60	5	12	0	1	0	2	13	2	0	0	18	1	0	.233	.360
Cabrera, Romtres	R-R	6-0	182	9-13-03	.244	.321	.227	52	160	37	39	7	5	5	30	26	11	0	1	70	11	8	.444	.384
Carbonara, Santiago	R-R	6-0	187	9-23-02	.209	.400	.184	13	43	8	9	2	1	0	5	7	0	0	0	7	0	0	.302	.320
Carmona, Carlos	R-R	6-2	190	7-1-04	.210	.111	.226	37	124	20	26	7	1	0	11	13	5	0	2	39	6	2	.282	.306
Cordoba, Jose	R-R	5-11	165	1-3-03	.225	.240	.222	43	142	24	32	3	2	3	19	10	7	0	1	35	5	4	.338	.306
De La Rosa, Samil	R-R	5-8	175	9-24-03	.288	.333	.277	37	125	23	36	8	3	1	21	14	9	0	1	28	2	2	.424	.396
Diaz, Fernando	L-R	6-4	185	1-12-02	.220	.036	.257	49	168	22	37	8	1	3	24	13	6	0	2	55	0	1	.333	.296
Encarnacion, Anyelo	R-R	6-0	164	1-2-04	.205	.261	.192	37	122	18	25	3	3	1	11	22	0	0	0	48	4	3	.303	.326
Encarnacion, Bryan	B-R	6-1	140	4-20-03	.141	.000	.175	28	78	10	11	1	1	0	7	9	2	0	2	46	1	0	.179	.242
Espinoza, Lizandro	R-R	5-7	158	11-20-02	.291	.294	.290	46	117	27	34	7	2	0	8	17	4	2	1	21	10	6	.385	.396
Grant, Adari	R-R	5-11	163	1-2-04	.220	.154	.232	43	164	27	36	9	1	1	10	21	5	0	0	53	7	3	.305	.326
Guerrero, Justin	R-R	6-1	195	5-20-03	.092	.200	.073	22	65	2	6	0	0	0	3	9	0	0	0	21	0	0	.092	.203
Guerrero, Yancel	R-R	6-1	169	4-16-04	.263	.091	.290	29	80	13	21	2	2	0	4	7	6	0	0	31	2	1	.338	.366
Guzman, Raul	R-R	6-0	180	9-14-02	.190	.222	.184	43	105	19	20	3	1	2	9	31	7	0	0	50	4	1	.295	.406
Hernandez, Maikel	B-R	6-0	163	2-20-03	.222	.200	.226	22	63	7	14	4	0	1	4	5	4	0	1	23	0	0	.333	.315
Justo, Maycol	B-R	5-10	141	2-2-03	.331	.267	.346	47	166	38	55	5	2	1	14	21	7	0	2	25	6	5	.404	.423
Linarez, Carlos	R-R	6-0	170	10-24-01	.305	.286	.308	22	59	4	18	1	1	1	11	9	0	0	6	0	0	.407	.397
Loaiza, Alejandro	R-R	5-11	163	12-23-03	.149	.385	.093	25	67	6	10	2	0	1	5	6	3	0	0	36	0	2	.224	.250
Lopez, Robelyn	R-R	6-4	190	10-10-03	.158	.077	.175	28	76	9	12	2	1	0	8	12	1	0	0	38	1	0	.211	.281
Perez, Marcelo	R-R	6-2	181	1-7-04	.144	.120	.151	37	111	19	16	4	0	0	3	24	2	0	0	34	0	0	.180	.307
Pino, Luis	R-R	5-11	155	4-9-04	.247	.125	.281	42	146	18	36	7	0	6	19	17	10	0	1	52	1	2	.418	.362
Ramos, Jeremy	R-R	6-3	173	4-4-03	.310	.158	.340	37	116	25	36	10	2	2	25	12	3	0	0	39	13	2	.483	.389
Reynoso, Elias	R-R	5-10	158	11-25-03	.155	.143	.157	40	129	30	20	6	1	0	7	36	2	0	1	47	9	1	.217	.345
Reynoso, Francis	R-R	6-5	206	12-26-02	.195	.158	.202	36	113	10	22	5	0	3	20	15	3	0	0	49	0	3	.319	.305
Rodriguez, Jose	R-R	6-3	200	8-4-02	.258	.333	.244	28	93	8	24	8	2	1	19	6	1	0	1	38	0	0	.419	.307
Rombley, Keshawn	L-R	6-0	171	8-11-03	.191	.138	.206	43	136	22	26	4	2	3	16	17	1	0	3	58	2	2	.316	.280
Sanchez, Juan	R-R	5-11	170	10-15-01	.160	.000	.190	10	25	1	4	1	0	1	4	2	3	0	0	9	0	0	.320	.300
Suarez, Jose	R-R	6-2	200	8-9-04	.295	.357	.284	31	88	10	26	3	1	1	9	17	1	0	1	31	0	1	.386	.411
Taveras, Felix	L-R	6-1	186	3-8-03	.301	.176	.319	39	133	23	40	9	3	6	30	13	2	0	1	37	7	2	.549	.369
Vargas, Miguel	L-L	6-0	176	3-14-04	.229	.214	.232	27	83	10	19	1	0	1	12	10	0	0	0	25	2	0	.277	.312
Velasquez, Diego	R-R	5-10	175	3-25-02	.111	.000	.154	15	36	6	4	0	0	2	3	7	3	0	0	10	2	1	.278	.304

Pitching	B-T	HT	WT	DOB	W	L	ERA	G	GS	CG	SV	IP	H	R	ER	HR	BB	SO	AVG	vLH	vRH	K/9	BB/9
Almonte, Marlyn	R-R	6-2	174	11-9-02	1	0	6.38	17	0	0	0	18	23	16	13	2	14	7	.315	.185	.391	3.44	6.87
Arias, Benjamin	R-R	6-5	195	11-5-01	3	3	1.94	12	12	0	0	51	39	18	11	2	14	61	.204	.148	.231	10.76	2.47
Bautista, Roberto	R-R	6-3	168	11-23-02	0	2	10.13	6	2	0	0	5	7	8	6	0	5	3	.304	.167	.353	5.06	8.44
Beltre, Alexander	R-L	6-1	169	11-5-02	3	3	7.85	24	2	0	0	39	46	42	34	6	28	44	.282	.273	.284	10.15	6.46
Calderon, Augusto	R-R	6-0	190	10-6-00	3	1	2.25	20	0	0	5	28	16	9	7	2	11	34	.165	.088	.206	10.93	3.54
Cervantes, Alejandro	R-R	6-2	189	5-15-01	3	3	4.50	20	0	0	3	32	30	19	16	1	13	33	.246	.212	.258	9.28	3.66
Clemente, Randel	R-R	6-3	173	11-17-01	1	5	4.86	17	5	0	0	33	30	34	18	3	29	35	.234	.184	.256	9.45	7.83
Contreras, Esteban	R-R	6-1	187	4-16-03	1	1	6.57	10	0	0	3	12	12	9	9	1	9	17	.261	.250	.267	12.41	6.57
Cuello, Antoni	R-R	6-5	186	11-7-02	0	1	6.75	9	2	0	0	11	13	9	8	0	7	8	.317	.429	.259	6.75	5.91
Curvelo, Uriel	R-R	6-3	182	9-30-02	0	0	11.32	13	0	0	1	10	17	13	13	0	13	12	.370	.400	.355	10.45	11.32
De La Cruz, Carlos	R-R	5-11	167	11-14-02	1	0	5.06	6	0	0	0	5	4	4	3	0	8	2	.222	.333	.167	3.38	13.50
Dominguez, Yonael	R-R	6-2	175	10-24-01	3	2	5.22	12	12	0	0	50	71	35	29	3	6	50	.332	.393	.307	9.00	1.08
Fabian, Samuel	R-R	6-4	177	5-21-03	1	1	9.68	14	2	0	0	18	26	23	19	1	21	10	.363	.373	.359	5.06	10.70
Gomez, Henry	R-R	6-1	163	10-17-01	1	8	5.33	12	12	0	0	49	62	33	29	1	14	36	.310	.360	.293	6.61	2.57
Guerrero, Diorys	L-L	6-1	170	2-1-01	3	2	2.56	10	9	0	0	46	39	16	13	1	9	54	.231	.174	.240	10.64	1.77
Guzman, Frankely	R-R	6-3	147	6-18-03	1	0	11.51	16	0	0	0	20	39	28	26	3	18	15	.394	.364	.409	6.64	7.97
Herrera, Victor	R-R	6-2	175	2-16-02	2	6	11.74	16	2	0	0	23	38	44	30	2	25	21	.388	.405	.377	8.22	9.78
Lopez, Bruno	R-R	6-4	220	4-18-02	5	1	2.38	16	0	0	0	23	20	10	6	0	8	22	.230	.258	.214	8.74	3.18
Lopez, Oliver	R-R	6-2	165	4-1-02	1	1	5.21	17	0	0	1	19	12	13	11	1	20	21	.179	.100	.213	9.95	9.47
Lugo, Americo	R-R	6-1	192	8-27-00	2	0	4.13	18	0	0	2	24	21	13	11	1	9	22	.236	.182	.268	8.25	3.38
Luna, Angel	R-R	6-0	195	5-5-01	0	1	1.50	6	0	0	0	6	4	1	1	0	0	3	.182	.000	.235	4.50	0.00
Marte, Fraimin	R-R	6-3	170	7-21-01	0	1	7.17	15	1	0	2	21	17	19	17	0	21	15	.221	.226	.217	6.33	8.86

Martinez, Engels	R-R	5-11	165	5-13-02	0	4	3.51	16	8	0	0	41	40	24	16	0	16	31	.260	.318	.236	6.80	3.51
Martinez, Miguel	R-R	6-0	143	1-26-03	2	1	6.00	20	0	0	2	24	23	18	16	0	15	28	.253	.147	.316	10.50	5.63
Miranda, William	R-R	6-1	170	2-14-01	0	0	54.00	1	0	0	0	0	2	2	2	0	0	1	.667	--	.667	27.00	0.00
Oliver, Ronny	R-R	6-2	155	1-1-04	1	3	6.40	13	9	0	0	32	33	25	23	2	27	36	.268	.310	.247	10.02	7.52
Ortega, Wilmer	R-R	6-1	169	4-4-01	0	3	4.85	11	11	0	0	39	35	27	21	2	26	39	.238	.268	.220	9.00	6.00
Peralta, Juan	R-R	6-2	175	8-9-02	1	0	0.98	13	0	0	3	18	13	2	2	0	3	17	.194	.190	.196	8.35	1.47
Pimentel, Eduar	R-R	6-2	170	2-23-01	1	1	4.15	13	0	0	0	22	19	14	10	0	14	17	.241	.269	.226	7.06	5.82
Ramirez, Brayan	R-R	6-4	200	9-29-01	0	5	7.01	11	10	0	0	35	40	31	27	2	21	29	.296	.278	.303	7.53	5.45
Rincon, Hancel	R-R	6-2	160	4-28-02	0	2	1.84	11	11	0	0	49	33	14	10	1	19	55	.188	.185	.189	10.10	3.49
Saladin, Darlin	R-R	5-11	150	12-28-02	6	1	4.03	20	0	0	1	38	33	22	17	0	15	31	.224	.231	.221	7.34	3.55
Salas, Juan	R-R	6-0	189	2-14-03	0	2	2.89	12	5	0	0	19	14	7	6	1	3	17	.203	.200	.205	8.20	1.45
Severino, Juan	R-R	6-0	165	6-6-04	2	2	6.11	16	1	0	0	18	25	19	12	1	17	17	.321	.500	.220	8.66	8.66
Yanez, Omar	R-R	6-2	190	12-7-02	0	2	3.93	17	0	0	3	18	16	14	8	1	15	14	.235	.179	.275	6.87	7.36

Fielding

C: Bernal 33, Guerrero 19, Hernandez 22, Linarez 17, Loaiza 19, Sanchez 4, Velasquez 6.
1B: Carbonara 12, Diaz 47, Guerrero 1, Guzman 13, Reynoso 35, Sanchez 4, Velasquez 9.
2B: De La Rosa 10, Encarnacion 26, Encarnacion 6, Espinoza 30, Grant 31, Perez 20, Reynoso 1.
3B: Bolivar 15, De La Rosa 20, Encarnacion 9, Encarnacion 14, Espinoza 10, Guerrero 27, Guzman 30.
SS: Encarnacion 1, Encarnacion 1, Espinoza 3, Grant 12, Justo 47, Perez 18, Reynoso 40.
OF: Avendano 25, Cabrera 43, Carmona 35, Cordoba 40, Lopez 25, Pino 36, Ramos 37, Rodriguez 12, Rombley 35, Suarez 23, Taveras 30, Vargas 24.

San Diego Padres

SEASON IN A SENTENCE: The Padres entered the year expecting to contend for the World Series after a flurry of offseason activity, but injuries to the starting rotation and clubhouse discord led to a 79-83 season and the firing of manager Jayce Tingler.

HIGH POINT: Righthander Joe Musgrove, a San Diego-area native in his first season with his hometown team, threw the first no-hitter in Padres history in a 3-0 win over the Rangers on April 9. Musgrove struck out 10, didn't walk anyone and came within a hit batter of a perfect game, helping the Padres shed the ignominy of being the only franchise without a no-hitter.

LOW POINT: The Padres went 4-18 in their last 22 games to go from holding the first National League wild card spot to finishing 11 games back of the playoffs. The frustration boiled over on Sept. 18 in St. Louis when shortstop Fernando Tatis Jr. and third baseman Manny Machado had to be separated in the dugout following a heated dugout exchange in full view of the cameras.

NOTABLE ROOKIES: The Padres got few positive contributions from their rookie performers, one of the many reasons they fell short of expectations. Lefthander Ryan Weathers went 4-7, 5.32 and lost his spot as the team's fifth starter and righthander Reiss Knehr, a midseason callup, went 1-2, 4.97 with as many walks as strikeouts (20). Shortstop Ha-Seong Kim, who signed a four-year, $28 million contract out of South Korea before the season, hit .202/.270/.352. Utilityman Tucupita Marcano made the Opening Day roster but hit .182/.280/.205 before being sent back down to Triple-A and was traded to the Pirates in July.

KEY TRANSACTIONS: The Padres went for it in 2021, acquiring pitchers Yu Darvish, Blake Snell and Musgrove in offseason trades and all-star second baseman Adam Frazier at the trade deadline. They also signed Kim, utilityman Jurickson Profar and closer Mark Melancon to contracts totaling $51 million before the season. Their biggest signing before the season was a 14-year, $340 million extension for Tatis, making him the third-highest paid player in the game at the time.

OPENING DAY SALARY: $171,686,600 (6th).

PLAYERS OF THE YEAR

MAJOR LEAGUE	MINOR LEAGUE
Fernando Tatis Jr. SS/OF	**Robert Hassell** OF
.282/.364/.611	(High-A/Low-A)
NL-leading 42 HR	.302/.393/.470,
99 R, 97 RBIs, 25 SB	11 HR, 34 SB

ORGANIZATION LEADERS

Batting		*Minimum 250 AB
MAJORS		
*AVG	Fernando Tatis	.282
*OPS	Fernando Tatis	.975
HR	Fernando Tatis	42
RBI	Manny Machado	106
MINORS		
*AVG	Euribiel Angeles, Fort Wayne, Lake Elsinore	.329
*OBP	Robert Hassell III, Fort Wayne, Lake Elsinore	.393
*SLG	Brian O'Grady, El Paso	.547
*OPS	Brian O'Grady, El Paso	.913
R	Robert Hassell III, Fort Wayne, Lake Elsinore	87
H	Euribiel Angeles, Fort Wayne, Lake Elsinore	143
TB	Jose Azocar, El Paso, San Antonio	215
2B	Robert Hassell III, Fort Wayne, Lake Elsinore	33
3B	Jose Azocar, El Paso, San Antonio	14
HR	Patrick Kivlehan, El Paso	21
HR	Agustin Ruiz, San Antonio, Fort Wayne	21
RBI	Robert Hassell III, Fort Wayne, Lake Elsinore	76
RBI	Agustin Ruiz, San Antonio, Fort Wayne	76
BB	Robert Hassell III, Fort Wayne, Lake Elsinore	66
SO	Agustin Ruiz, San Antonio, Fort Wayne	135
SB	Reinaldo Ilarraza, Fort Wayne	38

Pitching		#Minimum 75 IP
MAJORS		
W	Joe Musgrove	11
#ERA	Craig Stammen	3.06
SO	Joe Musgrove	203
SV	Mark Melancon	39
MINORS		
W	Adrian Martinez, El Paso, San Antonio	8
L	Caleb Boushley, El Paso, San Antonio	11
L	Noel Vela, Fort Wayne, Lake Elsinore	11
#ERA	Moises Lugo, San Antonio, Fort Wayne	3.19
G	Jose Quezada, El Paso, San Antonio	46
GS	Caleb Boushley, El Paso, San Antonio	23
SV	Jose Quezada, El Paso, San Antonio	18
IP	Adrian Martinez, El Paso, San Antonio	125
BB	Gabe Morales, Fort Wayne, Lake Elsinore	50
SO	Adrian Martinez, El Paso, San Antonio	122
#AVG	Moises Lugo, San Antonio, Fort Wayne	.194

2021 PERFORMANCE

General Manager: A.J. Preller. **Farm Director:** Sam Geaney. **Scouting Director:** Mark Conner.

Class	Team	League	W	L	PCT	Finish	Manager
Majors	San Diego Padres	National	79	83	.488	8th (15)	Jayce Tingler
Triple-A	El Paso Chihuahuas	Triple-A West	51	79	.392	10th (10)	Edwin Rodriguez
Double-A	San Antonio Missions	Double-A Central	57	63	.475	8th (10)	Phillip Wellman
High-A	Fort Wayne TinCaps	High-A Central	54	66	.450	10th (12)	Anthony Contreras
Low-A	Lake Elsinore Storm	Low-A West	55	65	.458	6th (8)	Mike McCoy
Rookie	ACL Padres	Arizona Complex	26	32	.448	12th (18)	Miguel Del Castillo
Rookie	DSL Padres	Dominican Summer	37	21	.638	5th (46)	M. Del Castillo/L. Mendez
Overall 2021 Minor League Record			280	326	.462	23rd (30)	

ORGANIZATION STATISTICS

SAN DIEGO PADRES
NATIONAL LEAGUE

Batting	B-T	HT	WT	DOB	AVG	vLH	vRH	G	AB	R	H	2B	3B	HR	RBI	BB	HBP	SH	SF	SO	SB	CS	SLG	OBP
Andreoli, John	R-R	6-1	218	6-9-90	.167	.000	.250	7	6	2	1	1	0	0	0	1	0	0	0	3	0	0	.333	.286
Campusano, Luis	R-R	5-11	232	9-29-98	.088	.000	.097	11	34	0	3	0	0	0	1	4	0	0	0	11	0	0	.088	.184
Caratini, Victor	B-R	6-1	215	8-17-93	.227	.271	.214	116	313	33	71	9	0	7	39	35	4	0	4	82	2	0	.323	.309
Castillo, Ivan	B-R	5-9	179	5-30-95	.333	.500	.000	3	3	0	1	0	0	0	0	1	1	0	0	0	0	0	.333	.500
Cronenworth, Jake	L-R	6-0	187	1-21-94	.266	.270	.265	152	567	94	151	33	7	21	71	55	10	3	3	90	4	3	.460	.340
Frazier, Adam	L-R	5-10	185	12-14-91	.267	.228	.284	57	191	25	51	8	1	1	11	13	4	3	0	23	5	1	.335	.327
Grisham, Trent	L-L	5-11	224	11-1-96	.242	.261	.236	132	462	61	112	28	3	15	62	54	6	1	4	119	13	5	.413	.327
Hosmer, Eric	L-L	6-4	226	10-24-89	.269	.262	.272	151	509	53	137	28	0	12	65	48	5	1	2	99	5	4	.395	.337
Kim, Ha-Seong	R-R	5-9	168	10-17-95	.202	.222	.194	117	267	27	54	12	2	8	34	22	4	2	3	71	6	1	.352	.270
Kivlehan, Patrick	R-R	6-2	215	12-22-89	.250	.250	--	5	4	3	1	0	0	0	2	2	1	0	1	3	0	0	.250	.500
Machado, Manny	R-R	6-3	218	7-6-92	.278	.246	.288	153	564	92	157	31	2	28	106	63	2	0	11	102	12	3	.489	.347
Marcano, Tucupita	L-R	6-0	170	9-16-99	.182	.222	.171	25	44	7	8	1	0	0	3	6	0	0	0	9	1	0	.205	.280
Marisnick, Jake	R-R	6-4	220	3-30-91	.188	.150	.214	34	48	4	9	1	0	0	2	2	3	1	0	22	1	0	.208	.264
2-team total (65 Chicago)					.216	.259	.179	99	176	21	38	7	3	5	24	11	7	2	2	65	4	1	.375	.286
Mateo, Jorge	R-R	6-0	182	6-23-95	.207	.217	.203	57	87	10	18	4	0	2	6	2	2	3	1	27	5	0	.322	.250
Myers, Wil	R-R	6-3	207	12-10-90	.256	.271	.250	146	442	56	113	24	2	17	63	54	0	0	4	141	8	5	.434	.334
Nola, Austin	R-R	6-0	197	12-28-89	.272	.348	.221	56	173	15	47	12	0	2	29	14	5	0	2	19	0	1	.376	.340
O'Grady, Brian	L-R	6-2	215	5-17-92	.157	.000	.174	32	51	8	8	3	0	2	9	8	0	1	1	17	0	0	.333	.267
Pham, Tommy	R-R	6-1	223	3-8-88	.229	.202	.239	155	475	74	109	24	2	15	49	78	4	0	4	128	14	6	.383	.340
Profar, Jurickson	B-R	6-0	184	2-20-93	.227	.154	.247	137	353	47	80	17	2	4	33	49	6	1	2	65	10	5	.320	.329
Rivas, Webster	R-R	6-1	219	8-8-90	.221	.273	.196	24	68	8	15	2	0	2	4	8	0	1	0	16	0	0	.338	.303
Tatis Jr., Fernando	R-R	6-3	217	1-2-99	.282	.284	.282	130	478	99	135	31	0	42	97	62	2	0	4	153	25	4	.611	.364

Pitching	B-T	HT	WT	DOB	W	L	ERA	G	GS	CG	SV	IP	H	R	ER	HR	BB	SO	AVG	vLH	vRH	K/9	BB/9
Adams, Austin	R-R	6-3	220	5-5-91	3	2	4.10	65	0	0	0	53	28	28	24	1	35	76	.159	.197	.133	12.99	5.98
Altavilla, Dan	R-R	5-11	226	9-8-92	0	0	6.75	2	0	0	0	1	1	1	1	1	0	2	.200	.333	.000	13.50	0.00
Anderson, Shaun	R-R	6-4	228	10-29-94	0	0	5.79	5	0	0	0	5	6	3	3	0	2	4	.316	.286	.333	7.71	3.86
Arrieta, Jake	R-R	6-4	230	3-6-86	0	3	10.95	4	4	0	0	12	18	16	15	3	5	9	.353	.350	.355	6.57	3.65
2-team total (20 Chicago)					5	14	7.39	24	24	0	0	99	131	91	81	24	44	83	.320	.319	.320	7.57	4.01
Avila, Pedro	R-R	5-11	210	1-14-97	0	1	2.25	1	1	0	0	4	4	2	1	1	3	5	.235	.333	.182	11.25	6.75
Camarena, Daniel	L-L	6-0	210	11-9-92	0	0	9.64	6	0	0	0	9	16	12	10	2	3	7	.364	.333	.379	6.75	2.89
Crismatt, Nabil	R-R	6-1	220	12-25-94	3	1	3.76	45	0	0	0	81	87	40	34	10	24	71	.274	.295	.258	7.86	2.66
Cronenworth, Jake	L-R	6-0	187	1-21-94	0	0	0.00	1	0	0	0	1	1	0	0	0	0	1	.500	1.000	.000	13.50	0.00
Darvish, Yu	R-R	6-5	219	8-16-86	8	11	4.22	30	30	0	0	166	138	81	78	28	44	199	.222	.221	.221	10.77	2.38
Detwiler, Ross	R-L	6-5	210	3-6-86	1	0	2.57	7	0	0	0	7	3	2	2	2	5	6	.130	.000	.231	7.71	6.43
2-team total (46 Miami)					3	1	4.64	53	5	0	0	52	44	28	27	10	20	62	.222	.237	.213	10.66	3.44
Diaz, Miguel	R-R	6-0	224	11-28-94	3	1	3.64	25	2	0	1	42	31	19	17	8	19	46	.204	.172	.227	9.86	4.07
Guerra, Javy	L-R	6-0	185	9-25-95	0	0	4.91	4	0	0	0	4	4	2	2	0	2	3	.333	.200	.200	7.36	4.91
Hill, Tim	R-L	6-4	200	2-10-90	6	6	3.62	78	0	0	1	60	51	34	24	9	23	56	.230	.210	.252	8.45	3.47
Hudson, Daniel	R-R	6-3	215	3-9-87	1	2	5.21	23	0	0	0	19	17	13	11	4	9	27	.236	.286	.205	12.79	4.26
2-team total (31 Washington)					5	3	3.31	54	0	0	0	52	40	22	19	8	16	75	.226	.256	.179	13.06	2.79
Johnson, Pierce	R-R	6-2	202	5-10-91	3	4	3.22	63	2	0	0	59	47	21	21	6	27	77	.220	.230	.211	11.81	4.14
Kela, Keone	R-R	6-1	220	4-16-93	2	2	5.06	12	0	0	0	11	11	8	6	3	3	13	.244	.179	.353	10.97	2.53
Knehr, Reiss	L-R	6-2	205	11-3-96	1	2	4.97	12	5	0	0	29	23	16	16	2	20	20	.221	.182	.250	6.21	6.21
Lamet, Dinelson	R-R	6-3	228	7-18-92	2	4	4.40	22	9	0	0	47	48	24	23	6	22	57	.262	.315	.213	10.91	4.21
Melancon, Mark	R-R	6-1	215	3-28-85	4	3	2.23	64	0	0	39	65	54	21	16	4	25	59	.228	.150	.285	8.21	3.48
Morejon, Adrian	L-L	5-11	224	2-27-99	0	0	3.86	2	2	0	0	5	5	2	2	2	2	3	.278	.000	.313	5.79	3.86
Musgrove, Joe	R-R	6-5	230	12-4-92	11	9	3.18	32	31	2	0	181	142	68	64	22	54	203	.213	.231	.194	10.08	2.68
Northcraft, Aaron	R-R	6-3	229	5-28-90	1	0	2.25	5	0	0	0	8	5	2	2	1	8	5	.192	.154	.231	5.63	9.00
Norwood, James	R-R	6-2	215	12-24-93	0	0	0.00	5	0	0	0	5	6	0	0	0	3	3	.300	.333	.286	5.40	5.40
Paddack, Chris	R-R	6-5	217	1-8-96	7	7	5.07	23	22	0	0	108	115	67	61	15	22	99	.269	.214	.325	8.22	1.83

SAN DIEGO PADRES

Pitching	B-T	HT	WT	DOB	W	L	ERA	G	GS	CG	SV	IP	H	R	ER	HR	BB	SO	AVG	vLH	vRH	K/9	BB/9
Pagan, Emilio	L-R	6-2	208	5-7-91	4	3	4.83	67	0	0	0	63	56	35	34	16	18	69	.231	.210	.248	9.81	2.56
Pomeranz, Drew	R-L	6-5	246	11-22-88	1	0	1.75	27	0	0	0	26	19	6	5	2	10	30	.211	.156	.241	10.52	3.51
Ramirez, Nick	L-L	6-4	232	8-1-89	1	1	5.75	13	0	0	0	20	23	15	13	2	7	14	.277	.258	.288	6.20	3.10
Snell, Blake	L-L	6-4	225	12-4-92	7	6	4.20	27	27	0	0	129	101	61	60	16	69	170	.214	.144	.235	11.89	4.83
Stammen, Craig	R-R	6-2	228	3-9-84	6	3	3.06	67	4	0	1	88	79	31	30	13	13	83	.235	.224	.244	8.46	1.32
Strahm, Matt	R-L	6-2	190	11-12-91	0	1	8.10	6	1	0	0	7	15	6	6	0	1	4	.441	.467	.421	5.40	1.35
Thompson, Mason	R-R	6-7	223	2-20-98	0	0	3.00	4	0	0	0	3	4	1	1	0	1	2	.333	.250	.375	6.00	3.00
2-team total (27 Washington)					1	3	4.01	31	0	0	0	25	32	15	11	4	15	23	.311	.222	.358	8.39	5.47
Velasquez, Vince	R-R	6-3	212	6-7-92	0	3	8.53	4	4	0	0	13	15	13	12	6	4	16	.294	.294	.294	11.37	2.84
2-team total (21 Philadelphia)					3	9	6.30	25	21	0	0	94	91	68	66	23	49	101	.251	.297	.221	9.64	4.67
Weathers, Ryan	R-L	6-1	230	12-17-99	4	7	5.32	30	18	0	1	95	101	57	56	20	30	72	.279	.291	.273	6.85	2.85
Williams, Taylor	B-R	5-11	185	7-21-91	0	0	1.69	5	0	0	0	5	3	1	1	0	3	6	.167	.000	.273	10.13	5.06
2-team total (6 Miami)					0	0	4.63	11	0	0	0	12	12	7	6	1	8	9	.273	.217	.333	6.94	6.17

Fielding

Catcher	PCT	G	PO	A	E	DP	PB
Campusano	1.000	9	85	1	0	0	1
Caratini	.998	101	851	34	2	3	6
Nola	.998	48	428	14	1	3	4
Rivas	1.000	24	152	9	0	1	0

First Base	PCT	G	PO	A	E	DP
Caratini	1.000	5	6	0	0	0
Cronenworth	.994	24	153	9	1	17
Hosmer	.993	131	909	92	7	97
Nola	1.000	1	6	0	0	1
O'Grady	1.000	1	2	0	0	0
Profar	.991	20	108	5	1	11

Second Base	PCT	G	PO	A	E	DP
Castillo	.000	1	0	0	0	0
Cronenworth	.986	94	142	213	5	60

	PCT	G	PO	A	E	DP
Frazier	1.000	46	68	99	0	30
Kim	1.000	21	23	45	0	8
Marcano	1.000	8	5	14	0	3
Nola	1.000	4	2	1	0	1
Profar	.935	10	10	19	2	3

Third Base	PCT	G	PO	A	E	DP
Caratini	.000	2	0	0	0	0
Castillo	1.000	1	0	1	0	1
Kim	.982	23	13	41	1	5
Machado	.965	144	94	261	13	34
Marcano	.000	1	0	0	0	0
Mateo	1.000	8	2	4	0	0

Shortstop	PCT	G	PO	A	E	DP
Cronenworth	.977	41	46	81	3	20
Kim	.970	35	37	91	4	25

	PCT	G	PO	A	E	DP
Mateo	.000	1	0	0	0	0
Tatis Jr.	.940	102	113	217	21	45

Outfield	PCT	G	PO	A	E	DP
Andreoli	1.000	7	2	0	0	0
Frazier	1.000	5	6	0	0	0
Grisham	.986	127	274	2	4	1
Kivlehan	1.000	2	3	0	0	0
Marcano	.750	8	3	0	1	0
Marisnick	1.000	25	31	0	0	0
Mateo	1.000	22	28	0	0	0
Musgrove	1.000	1	0	0	0	0
Myers	1.000	131	194	2	0	1
O'Grady	1.000	16	21	1	0	0
Pham	.991	125	214	2	2	1
Profar	.976	85	120	4	3	2
Tatis Jr.	.981	27	49	2	1	2

EL PASO CHIHUAHUAS
TRIPLE-A WEST
TRIPLE-A

Batting	B-T	HT	WT	DOB	AVG	vLH	vRH	G	AB	R	H	2B	3B	HR	RBI	BB	HBP	SH	SF	SO	SB	CS	SLG	OBP
Andreoli, John	R-R	6-1	218	6-9-90	.201	.214	.198	45	139	23	28	6	3	4	19	30	1	0	1	62	6	3	.374	.345
Azocar, Jose	R-R	5-11	181	5-11-96	.289	.242	.299	49	190	26	55	14	8	0	27	6	1	0	4	45	17	3	.447	.308
Batten, Matt	R-R	5-11	180	6-22-95	.300	.247	.313	117	417	70	125	14	3	6	39	48	0	2	119	27	5	.391	.370		
Campusano, Luis	R-R	5-11	232	9-29-98	.295	.264	.301	81	292	47	86	21	3	15	45	27	6	0	1	66	1	0	.541	.365
Cantu, Michael	R-R	6-3	225	8-28-95	.186	.250	.174	58	145	15	27	2	0	3	20	18	0	0	1	56	0	0	.262	.274
Castillo, Ivan	B-R	5-9	179	5-30-95	.287	.254	.294	113	404	47	116	15	4	3	45	26	0	0	5	76	12	5	.366	.326
Florimon, Pedro	B-R	6-2	185	12-10-86	.228	.322	.207	102	329	52	75	17	3	10	43	47	1	0	3	117	12	1	.389	.324
Grisham, Trent	L-L	5-11	224	11-1-96	.200	--	.200	2	5	0	1	1	0	0	1	2	0	0	0	0	1	0	.400	.429
Katoh, Gosuke	L-R	6-1	197	10-8-94	.306	.361	.291	114	350	62	107	27	4	8	42	46	2	2	2	84	8	4	.474	.388
Kivlehan, Patrick	R-R	6-2	215	12-22-89	.261	.352	.237	91	333	49	87	19	0	21	70	26	2	0	3	100	4	3	.508	.316
Kohlwey, Taylor	L-L	6-3	200	7-20-94	.319	.295	.324	97	342	47	109	18	4	7	56	37	0	0	4	84	9	3	.456	.381
Malone, Tyler	L-R	5-11	190	11-4-97	.286	.500	.200	7	7	0	2	1	0	0	1	1	0	0	0	2	0	0	.429	.375
Marcano, Tucupita	L-R	6-0	170	9-16-99	.273	.200	.299	45	172	31	47	7	2	6	27	27	0	0	3	26	4	4	.442	.366
Mathis, Zack	L-R	5-8	188	10-11-98	.250	.500	.000	3	8	0	2	0	0	0	1	0	0	0	0	1	1	1	.250	.250
Melean, Kelvin	R-R	6-0	195	9-5-98	.000	--	.000	1	1	0	0	0	0	0	0	0	0	0	0	0	0	0	.000	.000
Nola, Austin	R-R	6-0	197	12-28-89	.303	.600	.250	11	33	3	10	1	0	1	4	5	1	0	0	7	0	0	.424	.410
O'Grady, Brian	L-R	6-2	215	5-17-92	.281	.317	.270	74	285	44	80	21	5	15	46	36	4	0	3	85	10	3	.547	.366
Podorsky, Robbie	R-R	5-8	170	1-27-95	.250	.429	.197	33	92	13	23	3	2	1	5	8	0	0	2	22	10	1	.391	.304
Profar, Jurickson	B-R	6-0	184	2-20-93	.100	--	.100	3	10	1	1	0	0	0	0	4	0	0	1	0	0	0	.100	.357
Rivas, Webster	R-R	6-1	219	8-8-90	.252	.172	.269	52	163	19	41	8	0	5	15	22	0	0	1	39	0	0	.393	.339
Rodriguez, Yorman	R-R	5-10	160	7-23-97	.323	.250	.333	32	99	11	32	4	0	6	12	2	3	0	0	20	0	2	.545	.356
Ruta, Ben	L-R	6-3	195	6-8-94	.200	.205	.198	37	125	21	25	11	0	4	19	21	0	1	1	32	4	4	.384	.313
Tanielu, Nick	R-R	5-11	214	9-4-92	.233	.217	.236	88	318	48	74	14	1	14	42	28	4	0	5	70	2	0	.415	.299

Pitching	B-T	HT	WT	DOB	W	L	ERA	G	GS	CG	SV	IP	H	R	ER	HR	BB	SO	AVG	vLH	vRH	K/9	BB/9
Anderson, Shaun	R-R	6-4	228	10-29-94	1	0	4.40	11	0	0	1	14	13	7	7	2	6	18	.236	.211	.250	11.30	3.77
2-team total (2 Round Rock)					1	0	3.63	13	0	0	1	17	13	7	7	2	7	22	.203	.167	.225	11.42	3.63
Avila, Pedro	R-R	5-11	210	1-14-97	1	0	3.22	13	1	0	0	22	18	9	8	1	15	24	.222	.320	.179	9.67	6.04
Batten, Matt	R-R	5-11	180	6-22-95	0	0	16.43	5	0	0	0	8	17	14	14	5	1	2	.459	.333	.520	2.35	1.17
Beimel, Joe	L-L	6-3	205	4-19-77	0	1	6.14	14	1	0	1	15	16	10	10	5	5	9	.296	.353	.270	5.52	3.07
Boushley, Caleb	R-R	6-3	190	10-1-93	3	8	5.85	16	15	1	0	80	98	58	52	21	21	73	.293	.311	.336	8.21	2.36
Camarena, Daniel	L-L	6-0	210	11-9-92	6	7	4.75	22	19	0	1	83	83	51	44	11	31	62	.256	.186	.282	6.70	3.35
Crismatt, Nabil	R-R	6-1	220	12-25-94	0	0	0.00	3	0	0	0	4	3	0	0	0	1	6	.214	.000	.375	14.73	2.45
Diaz, Miguel	R-R	6-0	224	11-28-94	0	4	7.47	14	2	0	0	16	22	13	13	4	14	21	.333	.294	.347	12.06	8.04
Florimon, Pedro	B-R	6-2	185	12-10-86	0	0	0.00	1	0	0	0	1	1	0	0	0	0	0	.250	.500	.000	9.00	0.00
Fox, Mason	R-R	6-2	170	1-7-97	0	0	11.57	2	0	0	0	2	3	3	3	1	1	3	.375	.000	.429	11.57	3.86
Gore, MacKenzie	L-L	6-2	197	2-24-99	0	2	5.85	6	6	0	0	20	24	17	13	3	12	18	.289	.333	.277	8.10	5.40
Guerrero, Jordan	R-R	6-5	296	8-1-96	4	0	4.02	27	0	0	1	40	43	21	18	8	18	40	.274	.222	.301	8.93	4.02

Pitching	B-T	HT	WT	DOB	W	L	ERA	G	GS	CG	SV	IP	H	R	ER	HR	BB	SO	AVG	vLH	vRH	SO/9	BB/9
Johnson, Chase	R-R	6-3	220	1-9-92	1	1	10.80	19	1	0	0	30	47	39	36	3	24	21	.367	.359	.371	6.30	7.20
Keel, Jerry	L-L	6-6	240	9-26-93	2	4	7.24	15	11	0	0	55	78	49	44	16	25	42	.336	.333	.337	6.91	4.12
Kennedy, Brett	R-R	6-0	200	8-4-94	1	6	10.35	13	10	0	0	40	64	48	46	7	22	36	.356	.348	.360	8.10	4.95
Knehr, Reiss	L-R	6-2	205	11-3-96	0	2	2.66	8	5	0	1	20	15	6	6	3	9	20	.211	.125	.255	8.85	3.98
Kuzia, Nick	R-R	6-4	190	2-7-96	0	1	3.00	4	0	0	0	6	5	3	2	0	4	11	.217	.250	.182	16.50	6.00
Leasher, Aaron	L-L	6-3	208	4-28-96	0	1	9.00	4	3	0	0	12	19	13	12	2	5	10	.365	.438	.333	7.50	3.75
Markel, Parker	R-R	6-5	240	9-15-90	3	2	4.42	41	0	0	2	57	38	29	28	7	45	91	.185	.153	.203	14.37	7.11
Martinez, Adrian	R-R	6-2	215	12-10-96	1	2	5.28	9	9	0	0	44	50	28	26	6	17	39	.291	.345	.265	7.92	3.45
McGrath, Kyle	L-L	6-2	185	7-31-92	2	3	8.06	26	5	0	0	41	60	38	37	7	19	26	.341	.375	.328	5.66	4.14
McWilliams, Sam	R-R	6-7	230	9-4-95	2	3	10.07	18	1	0	2	22	20	25	25	1	27	25	.260	.216	.300	10.07	10.88
Miller, Evan	R-L	6-2	197	5-23-95	4	4	5.33	41	4	0	0	78	93	50	46	6	27	85	.297	.353	.264	9.85	3.13
Northcraft, Aaron	R-R	6-3	229	5-28-90	0	2	8.10	13	0	0	1	13	21	17	12	1	6	11	.350	.389	.333	7.43	4.05
Norwood, James	R-R	6-2	215	12-24-93	3	4	4.43	43	0	0	4	45	40	22	22	3	21	71	.240	.232	.243	14.31	4.23
Powers, Alex	R-R	6-4	205	2-26-92	0	2	5.46	22	3	0	0	31	33	21	19	4	16	46	.262	.245	.273	13.21	4.60
2-team total (13 Reno)					2	2	5.40	35	3	0	0	48	47	32	29	8	21	61	.249	.225	.270	11.36	3.91
Quezada, Jose	R-R	5-9	165	9-7-95	0	1	6.10	11	0	0	0	10	8	7	7	1	10	13	.205	.333	.148	11.32	8.71
Ramirez, Nick	L-L	6-4	232	8-1-89	2	2	4.50	35	2	0	1	48	46	26	24	5	18	53	.242	.220	.250	9.94	3.38
Reeves, James	R-L	6-3	220	6-7-93	0	0	15.83	9	0	0	0	10	14	17	17	4	7	14	.333	.333	.333	13.03	6.52
Routzahn, Ethan	R-R	6-4	225	3-19-98	0	0	0.00	2	0	0	0	1	0	0	0	0	1	0	.000	.000	--	0.00	13.50
Scholtens, Jesse	R-R	6-4	230	4-6-94	3	10	5.05	21	20	1	0	102	104	58	57	15	34	103	.267	.269	.266	9.12	3.01
Strahm, Matt	R-L	6-2	190	11-12-91	0	0	0.00	3	0	0	0	4	2	2	0	0	0	7	.143	.000	.182	17.18	0.00
Thompson, Mason	R-R	6-7	223	2-20-98	3	2	5.74	23	0	0	7	27	25	18	17	4	8	24	.245	.233	.250	8.10	2.70
Weathers, Ryan	R-L	6-1	230	12-17-99	1	0	3.60	2	2	0	0	10	13	4	4	2	2	11	.317	.250	.324	9.90	1.80
Westphal, Luke	L-L	6-3	230	6-14-89	2	5	5.84	18	10	1	0	49	50	36	32	8	28	58	.258	.262	.256	10.58	5.11
Williams, Taylor	B-R	5-11	185	7-21-91	2	0	6.75	9	0	0	0	13	12	10	10	5	8	16	.245	.250	.241	10.80	5.40
Wilson, Steven	R-R	6-3	221	8-24-94	4	0	3.43	28	0	0	0	39	22	18	15	7	14	63	.157	.197	.122	14.42	3.20

Fielding

Catcher	PCT	G	PO	A	E	DP	PB
Campusano	.985	62	503	30	8	2	7
Cantu	.988	38	306	14	4	2	1
Nola	1.000	3	9	2	0	0	0
Rivas	.994	32	304	18	2	4	6
Rodriguez	.980	5	48	0	1	0	1

First Base	PCT	G	PO	A	E	DP
Campusano	.955	3	20	1	1	1
Cantu	1.000	7	28	1	0	3
Florimon	1.000	4	23	1	0	2
Katoh	.996	41	246	12	1	17
Kivlehan	.993	17	130	6	1	11
Kohlwey	.992	18	124	6	1	10
Mathis	1.000	1	1	0	0	0
Nola	.968	4	28	2	1	2
Profar	1.000	1	2	0	0	0
Rivas	1.000	10	46	8	0	6
Rodriguez	1.000	13	90	1	0	8
Tanielu	1.000	36	227	16	0	15

Second Base	PCT	G	PO	A	E	DP
Batten	.954	18	24	38	3	12
Castillo	.977	60	107	143	6	34
Florimon	.963	8	11	15	1	2
Katoh	1.000	43	62	89	0	19
Marcano	1.000	11	16	25	0	3
Profar	1.000	1	0	1	0	0
Rodriguez	1.000	4	5	6	0	1

Third Base	PCT	G	PO	A	E	DP
Batten	.962	34	15	61	3	6
Castillo	.973	36	16	55	2	5
Florimon	.941	17	9	23	2	2
Katoh	1.000	2	1	7	0	0
Mathis	1.000	1	0	3	0	0
Melean	1.000	1	1	0	0	0
Tanielu	.981	50	29	72	2	9

Shortstop	PCT	G	PO	A	E	DP
Batten	.989	44	67	114	2	13

	PCT	G	PO	A	E	DP
Castillo	.964	16	24	30	2	2
Florimon	.953	67	61	164	11	27
Marcano	.975	11	11	28	1	8

Outfield	PCT	G	PO	A	E	DP
Andreoli	.970	38	64	0	2	0
Azocar	.957	47	83	7	4	0
Batten	.971	18	32	1	1	0
Florimon	--	1	0	0	0	0
Grisham	1.000	2	7	0	0	0
Katoh	1.000	23	25	1	0	0
Kivlehan	1.000	55	76	3	0	0
Kohlwey	.966	77	111	3	4	1
Malone	--	2	0	0	0	0
Marcano	.974	23	36	1	1	1
O'Grady	1.000	70	142	3	0	1
Podorsky	.981	28	52	0	1	0
Profar	1.000	2	2	0	0	0
Rodriguez	1.000	4	2	0	0	0
Ruta	.970	37	62	3	2	1

SAN ANTONIO MISSIONS

DOUBLE-A

DOUBLE-A CENTRAL

Batting	B-T	HT	WT	DOB	AVG	vLH	vRH	G	AB	R	H	2B	3B	HR	RBI	BB	HBP	SH	SF	SO	SB	CS	SLG	OBP
Abrams, CJ	L-R	6-2	185	10-3-00	.296	.378	.272	42	162	26	48	14	0	2	23	15	3	1	2	36	13	2	.420	.363
Alarcon, Kelvin	B-R	6-1	155	3-6-99	.273	--	.273	4	11	0	3	2	0	0	1	1	0	0	3	0	0	.455	.333
Azocar, Jose	R-R	5-11	181	5-11-96	.276	.271	.277	79	301	46	83	8	6	9	43	35	5	1	1	71	15	11	.432	.360
Basabe, Olivier	R-R	5-11	190	7-15-97	.195	.159	.205	68	215	34	42	6	1	4	17	21	2	1	1	48	3	3	.288	.272
Batten, Matt	R-R	5-11	180	6-22-95	.174	.000	.190	6	23	2	4	1	0	0	2	5	0	0	0	7	1	1	.217	.321
Cordoba, Allen	R-R	6-1	175	12-6-95	.299	.349	.282	74	251	34	75	20	1	5	38	29	12	0	4	42	6	6	.446	.392
Curry, Michael	R-R	6-1	212	7-4-97	.230	.262	.219	75	252	28	58	10	0	8	34	36	2	0	1	83	3	1	.365	.330
Fernandez, Juan	R-R	5-11	205	3-7-99	.226	.203	.232	72	257	27	58	9	2	8	28	28	5	1	1	60	3	2	.370	.313
Givin, Chris	R-R	6-2	185	3-21-97	.160	.190	.150	31	81	9	13	4	0	1	10	9	1	1	0	26	2	0	.247	.253
Kohlwey, Taylor	L-L	6-3	200	7-20-94	.269	.429	.226	18	67	12	18	5	0	1	13	14	1	0	2	14	2	3	.388	.393
Melean, Kelvin	R-R	6-0	195	9-5-98	.170	.077	.193	43	135	11	23	3	0	1	10	13	1	2	1	24	2	0	.215	.247
Ona, Jorge	R-R	6-0	235	12-31-96	.375	.000	.429	2	8	1	3	1	0	0	2	0	0	0	0	2	0	0	.500	.375
Overstreet, Kyle	R-R	5-11	205	9-4-93	.241	.289	.228	103	361	36	87	15	0	4	46	54	2	0	6	88	2	2	.316	.338
Podorsky, Robbie	R-R	5-8	170	1-27-95	.370	.400	.364	7	27	8	10	1	2	0	5	4	0	0	0	2	2	3	.556	.452
Rodriguez, Yorman	R-R	5-10	160	7-23-97	.245	.214	.257	14	49	7	12	2	0	1	2	4	0	0	0	7	0	0	.347	.302
Rosario, Eguy	R-R	5-9	150	8-25-99	.281	.357	.253	114	420	65	118	31	3	12	61	49	6	0	5	109	30	14	.455	.360
Ruiz, Agustin	L-R	6-2	215	9-23-99	.194	.292	.173	35	134	19	26	3	0	6	20	7	3	0	1	42	0	0	.351	.248
Ruiz, Esteury	R-R	6-0	169	2-15-99	.240	.324	.228	84	309	52	77	16	2	10	42	28	9	5	2	73	36	7	.411	.328
Ruta, Ben	L-R	6-3	195	6-8-94	.159	.162	.157	39	145	13	23	4	0	2	15	12	1	0	3	37	3	0	.228	.224
Seagle, Chandler	R-R	6-0	190	5-23-96	.190	.136	.211	53	158	24	30	9	0	1	14	7	8	6	2	45	0	1	.266	.257
Skender, Ethan	R-R	5-11	185	12-22-96	.271	.222	.284	22	85	7	23	4	1	1	11	5	2	0	0	22	0	2	.376	.326

	B-T	HT	WT	DOB	AVG	vLH	vRH	G	AB	R	H	2B	3B	HR	RBI	BB	HBP	SH	SF	SO	SB	CS	SLG	OBP
Suwinski, Jack	L-L	6-2	215	7-29-98	.269	.232	.281	66	216	47	58	8	4	15	37	45	3	1	2	74	7	6	.551	.398
Williams-Sutton, Dwanya	R-R	6-2	225	7-10-97	.193	.152	.210	45	114	22	22	3	0	4	14	23	9	1	2	45	5	4	.325	.365
Zunica, Brad	L-R	6-6	254	10-21-95	.167	.071	.200	17	54	5	9	4	0	0	4	6	2	0	0	25	0	1	.241	.274

Pitching	B-T	HT	WT	DOB	W	L	ERA	G	GS	CG	SV	IP	H	R	ER	HR	BB	SO	AVG	vLH	vRH	K/9	BB/9
Avila, Pedro	R-R	5-11	210	1-14-97	1	4	4.64	23	10	0	2	52	47	29	27	4	21	58	.240	.257	.230	9.97	3.61
Basabe, Olivier	R-R	5-11	190	7-15-97	0	0	10.80	3	0	0	0	3	5	4	4	0	1	2	.333	.286	.375	5.40	2.70
Beimel, Joe	L-L	6-3	205	4-19-77	1	1	2.21	17	0	0	1	20	10	8	5	1	6	16	.145	.125	.156	7.08	2.66
Belen, Carlos	R-R	6-1	250	2-28-96	5	3	4.36	39	1	0	2	54	64	34	26	2	16	40	.296	.288	.300	6.71	2.68
Boushley, Caleb	R-R	6-3	190	10-11-93	2	3	3.79	8	8	0	0	36	42	16	15	5	9	36	.288	.309	.269	9.08	2.27
Cosgrove, Tom	L-L	6-2	190	6-14-96	1	0	2.36	22	0	0	1	27	19	8	7	2	7	32	.192	.186	.196	10.80	2.36
Elliott, Ethan	L-L	6-3	180	4-28-97	0	1	3.55	3	3	0	0	13	16	7	5	1	6	16	.308	.333	.297	11.37	4.26
Fox, Mason	R-R	6-2	170	1-7-97	3	3	10.92	22	1	0	0	30	47	38	36	7	24	42	.351	.455	.300	12.74	7.28
Gore, MacKenzie	L-L	6-2	197	2-24-99	0	0	3.00	2	2	0	0	9	6	3	3	0	8	16	.182	.167	.185	16.00	8.00
Guerra, Javy	L-R	6-0	185	9-25-95	0	0	0.00	1	0	0	0	1	0	0	0	0	0	0	.000	.000	.000	0.00	0.00
Henry, Henry	R-R	6-4	215	12-17-98	3	0	3.90	38	0	0	0	67	57	31	29	3	31	59	.226	.261	.207	7.93	4.16
Hernandez, Osvaldo	L-L	6-0	181	5-15-98	4	8	5.11	22	22	0	0	100	120	64	57	20	26	88	.286	.287	.286	7.89	2.33
Humphreys, Jordan	R-R	6-2	223	6-11-96	2	0	6.95	10	5	0	0	22	29	19	17	4	14	21	.326	.342	.314	8.59	5.73
Keel, Jerry	L-L	6-6	240	9-26-93	2	4	5.05	10	6	0	0	41	49	25	23	4	14	33	.292	.364	.274	7.24	3.07
Kennedy, Brett	R-R	6-0	200	8-4-94	0	1	2.25	1	1	0	0	4	4	1	1	1	2	4	.267	.000	.444	9.00	4.50
Knehr, Reiss	L-R	6-2	205	11-3-96	6	1	3.90	11	11	0	0	55	41	24	24	4	22	46	.209	.202	.215	7.48	3.58
Komar, Brandon	R-R	6-0	195	5-8-99	2	3	5.01	19	4	0	0	50	49	32	28	6	27	53	.251	.229	.264	9.48	4.83
Kopps, Kevin	R-R	6-0	200	3-2-97	0	0	0.00	2	0	0	2	2	0	0	0	0	1	2	.000	.000	.000	9.00	4.50
Kuzia, Nick	R-R	6-4	190	2-7-96	4	7	3.47	37	0	0	7	47	30	22	18	5	23	60	.185	.271	.136	11.57	4.44
Lawson, Reggie	R-R	6-4	205	8-2-97	0	2	9.45	4	4	0	0	7	7	10	7	2	6	9	.241	.188	.308	12.15	8.10
Leasher, Aaron	L-L	6-3	208	4-28-96	4	4	2.56	12	12	0	0	53	42	20	15	4	21	52	.219	.233	.212	8.89	3.59
Lugo, Moises	R-R	6-1	185	1-20-99	0	1	1.80	6	3	0	0	15	11	4	3	1	8	22	.200	.308	.167	13.20	4.80
Martinez, Adrian	R-R	6-2	215	12-10-96	7	3	2.34	17	13	0	0	81	64	22	21	4	24	83	.215	.202	.223	9.26	2.68
McWilliams, Sam	R-R	6-7	230	9-4-95	2	1	4.91	11	1	0	0	18	14	11	10	4	14	21	.219	.120	.282	10.31	6.87
Melean, Kelvin	R-R	6-0	195	9-5-98	0	0	0.00	1	0	0	0	1	0	0	0	0	0	0	.000	.000	.000	0.00	0.00
Quezada, Jose	R-R	5-9	165	9-7-95	0	2	4.46	35	0	0	18	40	38	23	20	4	13	53	.244	.230	.253	11.83	2.90
Reeves, James	R-L	6-3	220	6-7-93	3	0	3.27	31	0	0	0	41	23	19	15	4	27	61	.162	.157	.165	13.28	5.88
Rheault, Dylan	R-R	6-9	245	3-21-92	1	1	6.75	23	0	0	0	33	43	27	25	3	28	25	.326	.383	.294	6.75	7.56
Schlichtholz, Fred	R-L	6-3	215	9-18-95	0	1	5.93	23	1	0	0	30	32	20	20	3	16	25	.278	.233	.306	7.42	4.75
Viza, Tyler	R-R	6-3	170	10-21-94	1	3	4.71	5	5	0	0	29	40	20	15	5	8	21	.328	.378	.306	6.59	2.51
Waldron, Matt	R-R	6-2	185	9-26-96	0	4	6.61	7	7	1	0	31	35	23	23	2	16	31	.282	.184	.347	8.90	4.60
Williams, Sam	L-L	6-3	195	6-26-96	3	2	4.43	18	0	0	0	22	16	11	11	3	10	22	.200	.107	.250	8.87	4.03

Fielding

Catcher	PCT	G	PO	A	E	DP	PB
Fernandez	.989	69	609	42	7	3	9
Overstreet	1.000	1	3	0	0	0	2
Seagle	.984	53	440	50	8	2	2

First Base	PCT	G	PO	A	E	DP
Basabe	.967	7	28	1	1	2
Cordoba	.992	17	111	10	1	9
Curry	1.000	3	13	1	0	1
Givin	.964	6	26	1	1	5
Kohlwey	.985	16	125	7	2	11
Overstreet	.994	68	501	33	3	46
Rodriguez	1.000	5	45	4	0	5
Ruta	1.000	1	3	1	0	0
Zunica	1.000	5	22	6	0	4

Second Base	PCT	G	PO	A	E	DP
Abrams	1.000	6	6	10	0	2

	PCT	G	PO	A	E	DP
Basabe	.962	16	19	32	2	5
Batten	1.000	2	3	9	0	1
Givin	.975	10	16	23	1	6
Melean	.979	33	56	84	3	17
Rosario	.953	38	61	102	8	20
Skender	.986	21	35	33	1	7

Third Base	PCT	G	PO	A	E	DP
Alarcon	1.000	2	0	1	0	0
Basabe	.941	43	29	66	6	6
Batten	1.000	3	2	7	0	0
Cordoba	.943	55	36	97	8	9
Givin	1.000	1	0	3	0	0
Melean	1.000	2	2	2	0	0
Overstreet	.955	9	9	12	1	1
Rosario	.875	7	4	10	2	0

Shortstop	PCT	G	PO	A	E	DP

	PCT	G	PO	A	E	DP
Abrams	.968	33	48	74	4	17
Batten	1.000	1	2	3	0	0
Givin	.955	15	24	18	2	9
Melean	.962	8	11	14	1	2
Rosario	.937	69	89	150	16	31

Outfield	PCT	G	PO	A	E	DP
Azocar	.969	75	155	3	5	1
Basabe	--	3	0	0	0	0
Curry	1.000	34	59	4	0	2
Kohlwey	1.000	2	2	0	0	0
Ona	1.000	2	4	1	0	1
Podorsky	1.000	5	8	0	0	0
Ruiz	1.000	35	60	0	0	0
Ruiz	.994	78	172	1	1	1
Ruta	1.000	31	66	3	0	0
Suwinski	.975	63	110	7	3	3
Williams-Sutton	1.000	41	38	3	0	0

FORT WAYNE TINCAPS

HIGH CLASS A

HIGH-A CENTRAL

Batting	B-T	HT	WT	DOB	AVG	vLH	vRH	G	AB	R	H	2B	3B	HR	RBI	BB	HBP	SH	SF	SO	SB	CS	SLG	OBP
Alarcon, Kelvin	B-R	6-1	155	3-6-99	.189	.150	.198	33	111	9	21	2	2	0	8	17	0	0	0	35	0	0	.243	.297
Almanzar, Luis	R-R	6-0	205	11-1-99	.223	.167	.234	76	260	26	58	16	2	3	31	24	0	0	0	84	1	1	.335	.289
Angeles, Euribiel	R-R	5-11	175	5-11-02	.264	.429	.224	18	72	12	19	4	0	1	8	8	4	2	0	16	1	1	.361	.369
Arias, Andelson	R-R	6-1	170	6-14-00	.000	--	.000	1	3	0	0	0	0	0	0	0	0	0	0	2	0	0	.000	.000
Basabe, Olivier	R-R	5-11	190	7-15-97	.273	--	.273	4	11	1	3	1	0	0	2	0	1	0	3	0	0	.364	.385
Curran, Seamus	L-R	6-6	245	9-6-97	.204	.167	.208	33	113	14	23	8	0	3	18	25	1	0	0	45	1	1	.354	.353
Curry, Michael	R-R	6-1	212	7-4-97	.250	.500	.214	4	16	3	4	2	0	0	2	0	0	0	7	0	0	.375	.294
Duarte, Victor	R-R	5-11	170	2-23-01	.250	1.000	.200	4	16	3	4	0	0	1	3	1	0	0	6	0	0	.438	.294
Givin, Chris	R-R	6-2	185	3-21-97	.202	.138	.213	55	203	22	41	5	0	3	16	25	2	2	2	48	0	0	.271	.293
Harris, Jawuan	R-R	5-9	190	11-3-96	.142	.143	.142	44	134	22	19	7	0	1	6	25	3	3	0	69	16	2	.216	.290
Hassell III, Robert	L-L	6-2	195	8-15-01	.205	.200	.206	18	78	10	16	2	1	4	11	9	0	0	25	3	0	.410	.287
Homza, Jonny	R-R	6-0	185	6-13-99	.218	.257	.213	85	312	52	68	17	3	6	43	42	11	0	3	116	8	5	.349	.329
Ilarraza, Reinaldo	B-R	5-10	150	1-12-99	.232	.278	.224	101	349	53	81	10	6	1	29	50	3	7	5	124	38	8	.304	.329

Name	B-T	HT	WT	DOB	AVG	vLH	vRH	G	AB	R	H	2B	3B	HR	RBI	BB	HBP	SH	SF	SO	SB	CS	OBP	SLG
Kerner, Adam	R-R	5-10	185	7-31-98	.173	.208	.167	52	156	17	27	10	1	1	19	21	3	3	0	58	1	2	.269	.283
Little, Grant	R-R	6-1	185	7-8-97	.262	.152	.282	65	214	40	56	12	0	1	24	34	11	1	2	54	19	9	.332	.387
Lopez, Justin	B-R	6-2	195	5-9-00	.243	.231	.245	104	383	47	93	23	1	10	68	42	0	3	6	127	2	2	.386	.313
Malone, Tyler	L-R	5-11	190	11-4-97	.183	.500	.148	20	60	8	11	6	0	1	4	14	0	0	0	25	0	1	.333	.338
Mathis, Zack	L-R	5-8	188	10-11-98	.265	.125	.295	35	136	17	36	9	0	3	19	12	7	0	0	37	1	0	.397	.355
Melean, Kelvin	R-R	6-0	195	9-5-98	.272	.357	.254	42	158	23	43	10	2	2	23	12	6	0	1	30	4	3	.399	.345
Ornelas, Tirso	L-R	6-3	200	3-11-00	.248	.210	.255	107	383	57	95	31	1	7	55	52	6	0	4	98	3	1	.389	.344
Reyes, Ripken	B-R	5-10	180	4-1-97	.280	.167	.316	19	50	11	14	0	0	0	2	6	11	3	0	17	3	0	.280	.463
Rodriguez, Yorman	R-R	5-10	160	7-23-97	.289	.294	.288	22	90	12	26	3	1	2	13	5	1	0	0	18	3	0	.411	.333
Ruiz, Agustin	L-R	6-2	215	9-23-99	.253	.162	.266	72	281	51	71	15	0	15	56	36	4	0	3	93	3	3	.466	.343
Skender, Ethan	R-R	5-11	185	12-22-96	.258	.355	.240	60	198	37	51	13	2	2	25	25	10	2	3	60	6	3	.374	.364
Solarte, Angel	R-R	5-11	155	3-29-01	.321	.000	.360	8	28	4	9	2	0	0	0	3	0	0	0	9	0	0	.393	.387
Valenzuela, Brandon	B-R	6-0	170	10-2-00	.245	.300	.231	15	49	4	12	1	0	1	7	15	0	1	0	20	1	0	.327	.415
Williams-Sutton, Dwanya	R-R	6-2	225	7-10-97	.265	.000	.295	17	49	10	13	3	1	2	7	14	3	0	0	18	4	0	.490	.455

Pitching	B-T	HT	WT	DOB	W	L	ERA	G	GS	CG	SV	IP	H	R	ER	HR	BB	SO	AVG	vLH	vRH	K/9	BB/9
Alarcon, Kelvin	B-R	6-1	155	3-6-99	0	0	0.00	2	0	0	0	2	0	0	0	0	0	0	.000	.000	.000	0.00	0.00
Basabe, Olivier	R-R	5-11	190	7-15-97	0	0	0.00	2	0	0	0	1	0	0	0	0	0	1	.000	.000	.000	13.50	0.00
Bencomo, Edwuin	R-R	6-2	165	4-14-99	7	4	3.97	31	2	0	0	66	53	30	29	5	18	78	.221	.227	.215	10.69	2.47
Boyd, Luke	R-R	6-2	180	11-21-97	2	1	2.79	9	0	0	0	10	7	5	3	0	2	15	.200	.190	.214	13.97	1.86
Denz, Danny	L-L	5-9	198	5-20-98	0	2	3.26	13	12	0	0	50	39	19	18	3	24	47	.220	.205	.226	8.52	4.35
Elliott, Ethan	L-L	6-3	180	4-28-97	2	1	2.95	12	12	0	0	58	43	20	19	13	13	71	.204	.147	.235	11.02	2.02
Espinoza, Anderson	R-R	6-0	190	3-9-98	0	1	5.02	12	12	0	0	29	29	19	16	3	13	37	.264	.192	.328	11.62	4.08
2-team total (5 South Bend)					1	3	5.04	17	17	0	0	45	39	28	25	4	24	64	.235	.211	.253	12.90	4.84
Feole, Mason	L-L	6-1	194	8-28-98	1	1	9.00	21	0	0	0	16	14	17	16	3	20	21	.230	.200	.244	11.81	11.25
Geraldo, Jose	R-R	6-3	200	1-30-99	1	1	2.79	9	0	0	0	10	10	5	3	1	3	10	.270	.389	.158	9.31	2.79
Gore, MacKenzie	L-L	6-2	197	2-24-99	0	1	5.40	1	1	0	0	5	3	3	3	0	4	5	.176	.333	.143	9.00	7.20
Guarate, Carlos	R-R	6-2	178	3-30-01	1	6	7.30	10	9	0	0	41	55	38	33	5	14	24	.324	.413	.244	5.31	3.10
Keating, Sam	R-R	6-3	190	8-31-98	3	5	8.10	44	0	0	1	53	59	56	48	4	29	42	.285	.379	.217	7.09	4.89
Komar, Brandon	R-R	6-0	195	5-8-99	2	2	3.60	12	1	0	1	30	22	16	12	1	13	32	.196	.155	.241	9.60	3.90
Kopps, Kevin	R-R	6-0	200	3-2-97	1	0	0.00	8	0	0	3	8	2	0	0	0	4	10	.080	.100	.067	11.25	4.50
Lehmann, Connor	R-R	6-7	210	8-15-96	3	5	8.47	10	10	0	0	39	50	40	37	7	22	21	.313	.222	.386	4.81	5.03
Loewen, Carter	R-R	6-4	240	9-28-98	1	1	4.84	21	0	0	0	22	20	13	12	0	11	31	.238	.195	.279	12.49	4.43
Lugo, Moises	R-R	6-1	185	1-20-99	4	3	3.46	17	16	0	0	75	52	30	29	9	32	93	.193	.227	.163	11.11	3.82
Martinez, Edgar	R-R	5-10	155	2-26-01	0	1	7.36	3	3	0	0	7	12	6	6	1	6	6	.353	.381	.308	7.36	7.36
Miliano, Michell	R-R	6-3	185	12-22-99	0	0	6.23	4	0	0	0	4	2	3	3	0	4	7	.125	.167	.100	14.54	8.31
Minjarez, Felix	R-R	6-3	205	9-13-96	3	5	4.19	42	3	0	0	73	69	37	34	7	37	90	.255	.234	.272	11.10	4.56
Morales, Gabe	L-L	6-3	175	4-14-99	1	0	5.40	6	0	0	0	17	12	10	10	0	14	27	.194	.040	.297	14.58	7.56
Mosser, Gabe	R-R	6-4	185	6-8-96	4	8	4.39	21	14	0	0	80	80	42	39	7	23	72	.261	.301	.219	8.10	2.59
Perez, Ramon	L-L	6-1	225	7-2-99	3	0	5.30	27	0	0	3	36	26	21	21	3	28	43	.205	.250	.189	10.85	7.07
Sabrowski, Erik	R-L	6-4	235	10-31-97	2	0	1.86	8	3	0	0	29	18	6	6	1	12	41	.182	.163	.196	12.72	3.72
Schlichtholz, Fred	R-L	6-3	215	9-18-95	3	1	5.65	11	1	0	0	14	17	10	9	0	8	14	.309	.250	.326	8.79	5.02
Skender, Ethan	R-R	5-11	185	12-22-96	0	0	0.00	1	0	0	0	1	1	0	0	0	1	2	.250	.000	.333	18.00	9.00
Smith, Austin	R-R	6-4	250	7-9-96	3	5	5.10	43	0	0	0	60	65	37	34	6	24	64	.271	.282	.260	9.60	3.60
Sung, Wen-Hua	R-R	6-1	198	9-2-96	1	1	2.52	23	0	0	4	25	19	12	7	1	15	46	.196	.130	.255	16.56	5.40
Tyler, Cody	L-L	6-0	190	10-26-94	0	0	10.65	19	0	0	0	24	40	28	28	9	7	20	.374	.313	.400	7.61	2.66
Vela, Noel	L-L	6-1	165	12-21-98	0	3	3.78	8	8	0	0	33	31	15	14	2	16	44	.244	.278	.231	11.88	4.32
Waldron, Matt	R-R	6-2	185	9-26-96	3	4	3.24	13	13	0	0	72	69	37	26	6	19	72	.256	.244	.267	8.96	2.36
Walter, Chase	R-R	6-7	260	7-26-98	0	1	3.18	9	0	0	0	11	2	4	4	0	12	22	.057	.125	.000	17.47	9.53
Williams, Sam	L-L	6-3	195	6-26-96	3	3	4.72	26	0	0	1	34	36	20	18	4	12	40	.265	.256	.269	10.49	3.15

Fielding

Catcher	PCT	G	PO	A	E	DP	PB
Duarte	1.000	4	44	1	0	0	0
Homza	.987	44	416	29	6	2	2
Kerner	.994	51	461	33	3	2	12
Malone	.985	9	65	2	1	0	3
Mathis	1.000	2	27	1	0	0	0
Valenzuela	.966	14	134	6	5	0	4

First Base	PCT	G	PO	A	E	DP
Alarcon	.955	5	19	2	1	2
Almanzar	.983	49	328	14	6	32
Basabe	1.000	3	20	4	0	0
Curran	.987	27	212	18	3	11
Givin	.989	12	87	5	1	7
Homza	.969	3	29	2	1	1
Malone	1.000	1	6	0	0	0
Mathis	1.000	7	43	5	0	7
Rodriguez	1.000	17	125	8	0	12
Valenzuela	1.000	1	8	1	0	0

Second Base	PCT	G	PO	A	E	DP
Angeles	1.000	1	0	3	0	0
Givin	.987	18	27	49	1	8
Ilarraza	.940	38	47	63	7	12
Lopez	.966	24	28	56	3	11
Melean	1.000	10	9	26	0	5
Reyes	.987	18	25	51	1	12
Skender	.973	18	26	47	2	8

Third Base	PCT	G	PO	A	E	DP
Alarcon	.886	13	8	23	4	3
Angeles	1.000	1	1	20	0	2
Basabe	.000	1	0	0	0	0
Givin	1.000	5	2	7	0	0
Homza	.818	8	4	5	2	0
Lopez	1.000	5	4	10	0	2
Mathis	.937	27	13	46	4	4
Melean	.846	17	5	17	4	1
Skender	.932	42	21	61	6	5

Shortstop	PCT	G	PO	A	E	DP
Angeles	1.000	8	11	21	0	5
Givin	1.000	22	26	39	0	9
Homza	1.000	1	3	2	0	0
Lopez	.979	74	78	159	5	28
Melean	.934	16	26	31	4	7

Outfield	PCT	G	PO	A	E	DP
Almanzar	1.000	10	18	1	0	0
Curry	1.000	2	2	0	0	0
Harris	.972	42	103	3	3	0
Hassell III	.967	16	29	0	1	0
Homza	1.000	2	2	0	0	0
Ilarraza	.974	64	149	2	4	1
Little	.971	66	96	5	3	0
Malone	1.000	6	4	0	0	0
Ornelas	.973	85	143	2	4	0
Ruiz	.980	66	95	3	2	0
Solarte	1.000	8	11	0	0	0

Williams-Sutton .947 13 18 0 1 0

LAKE ELSINORE STORM

LOW CLASS A

LOW-A WEST

Batting	B-T	HT	WT	DOB	AVG	vLH	vRH	G	AB	R	H	2B	3B	HR	RBI	BB	HBP	SH	SF	SO	SB	CS	SLG	OBP
Acosta, Matthew	L-L	5-11	185	4-1-98	.264	.317	.249	81	292	60	77	18	4	6	33	47	4	4	1	69	9	1	.414	.372
Alarcon, Kelvin	B-R	6-1	155	3-6-99	.233	.333	.208	12	30	7	7	0	0	0	6	3	0	1	0	13	1	0	.233	.303
Angeles, Euribiel	R-R	5-11	175	5-11-02	.343	.307	.354	87	362	65	124	22	6	3	56	32	4	2	5	61	18	6	.461	.397
Aquino, Charlis	R-R	6-2	165	11-18-01	.216	.400	.188	12	37	4	8	1	0	0	1	3	1	0	0	11	1	0	.243	.293
Barley, Jordy	R-R	6-0	175	12-3-99	.240	.206	.253	61	242	43	58	8	2	8	28	31	4	0	2	82	33	6	.388	.333
Bender, Colton	R-R	5-9	195	1-13-99	.260	.300	.254	20	77	14	20	3	0	1	13	7	1	0	1	29	1	1	.338	.326
Cummings, Cole	L-R	6-2	205	6-20-98	.349	.300	.364	12	43	13	15	2	1	3	16	8	2	0	0	11	0	0	.651	.472
Dale, Jarryd	R-R	6-1	176	9-11-00	.269	.224	.283	102	402	66	108	23	2	6	60	32	6	3	3	109	31	8	.381	.330
Dunn, Lucas	R-R	6-0	205	4-30-99	.236	.409	.202	34	127	25	30	6	4	2	18	17	2	1	1	44	1	4	.394	.333
Ferguson, Max	L-R	6-1	180	8-23-99	.170	.071	.212	12	47	15	8	2	1	0	4	9	2	0	0	20	5	0	.255	.328
Guilbe, Sean	R-R	6-1	190	12-13-99	.194	.214	.190	74	222	38	43	9	4	1	21	28	11	3	2	91	10	1	.284	.312
Hassell III, Robert	L-L	6-2	195	8-15-01	.323	.384	.301	92	365	77	118	31	3	7	65	57	3	0	4	74	31	6	.482	.415
Heredia, Cristian	R-R	6-3	175	4-12-01	.083	.143	.069	10	36	0	3	0	0	0	2	1	0	0	0	20	0	0	.083	.108
Jones, Pierce	R-R	6-1	185	6-15-01	.188	.222	.174	10	32	4	6	1	0	1	8	3	0	0	0	15	2	1	.313	.257
Luis, Carlos	L-R	6-2	160	9-4-99	.243	.226	.248	40	148	19	36	9	1	1	19	13	0	0	0	33	0	1	.338	.304
Malone, Tyler	L-R	5-11	190	11-4-97	.056	.333	.000	5	18	0	1	1	0	0	3	2	0	0	0	7	0	0	.111	.150
Mathis, Zack	L-R	5-8	188	10-11-98	.228	.290	.205	34	114	22	26	6	0	2	6	14	4	0	0	25	0	1	.333	.333
Mears, Joshua	R-R	6-3	230	2-21-01	.244	.246	.243	71	242	45	59	10	4	17	48	36	12	0	1	114	10	5	.529	.368
Nunez, Anthony	B-R	6-1	190	7-10-01	.105	.000	.133	6	19	2	2	0	0	0	2	5	0	0	0	8	1	1	.105	.292
Quintero, Alison	R-R	5-11	175	4-24-00	.160	.217	.145	30	106	9	17	3	0	1	14	7	2	2	1	32	1	0	.217	.224
Reyes, Ripken	B-R	5-10	180	4-1-97	.364	.000	.444	9	22	6	8	3	1	0	6	7	2	1	0	5	1	1	.591	.548
Solarte, Angel	R-R	5-11	155	3-29-01	.306	.255	.321	67	248	36	76	17	1	2	37	13	6	0	4	57	11	3	.407	.351
Stronach, Jack	L-R	6-3	195	4-29-97	.224	.128	.249	65	232	31	52	15	0	5	25	28	6	0	1	65	6	2	.353	.322
Torres, Bryan	R-R	5-9	165	12-11-99	.181	.125	.198	31	105	18	19	2	1	1	13	14	1	3	2	26	3	2	.267	.279
Valenzuela, Brandon	B-R	6-0	170	10-2-00	.307	.321	.302	82	329	50	101	21	3	6	62	44	2	0	3	80	3	2	.444	.389
Vizcarra, Gilberto	R-R	5-10	180	3-1-99	.293	.262	.303	71	246	32	72	14	3	5	40	14	4	1	5	37	0	0	.435	.335

Pitching	B-T	HT	WT	DOB	W	L	ERA	G	GS	CG	SV	IP	H	R	ER	HR	BB	SO	AVG	vLH	vRH	K/9	BB/9
Alarcon, Kelvin	B-R	6-1	155	3-6-99	1	0	0.00	3	0	0	0	2	2	0	0	0	1	1	.250	.500	.167	3.86	3.86
Arias, Luarbert	R-R	6-2	176	12-12-00	1	1	3.96	15	0	0	0	25	16	12	11	6	15	44	.184	.235	.151	15.84	5.40
Collett, Keegan	R-R	6-3	215	7-27-98	0	2	6.92	23	0	0	1	26	21	22	20	4	25	49	.219	.214	.222	16.96	8.65
Dana, Cullen	R-L	6-4	240	8-7-97	2	0	0.87	7	0	0	0	10	8	1	1	0	1	12	.211	.200	.214	10.45	0.87
Galindo, Ruben	R-R	6-1	175	1-24-01	5	4	4.57	20	8	0	0	65	72	41	33	5	27	62	.289	.279	.297	8.58	3.74
Garcia, Jeferson	R-R	6-0	165	2-4-00	0	0	36.00	2	0	0	0	1	3	5	4	0	1	0	.500	1.000	.400	0.00	9.00
Garcia, Jose	L-L	5-11	169	2-19-98	2	2	5.51	27	0	0	2	47	48	39	29	5	29	30	.267	.130	.313	5.70	5.51
Gasser, Robert	L-L	6-1	190	5-31-99	0	0	1.29	5	5	0	0	14	11	4	2	1	2	13	.224	.167	.233	8.36	1.29
Geraldo, Jose	R-R	6-3	200	1-30-99	2	1	2.42	14	0	0	1	22	17	10	6	2	9	24	.200	.207	.196	9.67	3.63
Guarate, Carlos	R-R	6-2	178	3-30-01	2	2	4.94	13	8	0	0	58	60	35	32	7	10	53	.260	.235	.278	8.18	1.54
Iriarte, Jairo	R-R	6-2	160	12-15-01	0	4	27.00	4	3	0	0	9	25	27	27	5	6	9	.490	.444	.542	9.00	6.00
Jacob, Alek	L-R	6-3	190	6-16-98	2	0	0.00	12	0	0	2	19	12	1	0	0	2	26	.188	.259	.135	12.54	0.96
Lamet, Dinelson	R-R	6-3	228	7-18-92	0	0	2.25	3	0	0	0	4	2	1	1	1	1	6	.143	.000	.250	13.50	2.25
Lehmann, Connor	R-R	6-7	210	8-15-96	0	2	6.45	9	3	0	0	22	28	17	16	4	10	31	.311	.340	.279	12.49	4.03
Lopez, Frank	R-R	6-1	170	4-23-01	0	0	23.63	2	0	0	0	3	6	8	7	2	6	2	.500	.500	.500	6.75	20.25
Lugo, Jesus	R-R	5-11	170	1-27-98	0	3	4.40	15	14	0	0	45	45	25	22	8	16	54	.253	.261	.248	10.80	3.20
Mathis, Zack	L-R	5-8	188	10-11-98	0	0	13.50	1	0	0	0	2	6	3	3	0	0	1	.545	.250	.714	0.00	0.00
Matos, Dwayne	R-R	6-2	154	11-7-00	1	4	5.12	20	15	0	0	77	95	57	44	9	20	55	.305	.252	.351	6.40	2.33
Mayberry, Seth	R-R	6-3	200	6-22-00	0	1	7.50	9	0	0	0	12	15	12	10	0	6	14	.313	.278	.333	10.50	4.50
Miliano, Michell	R-R	6-3	185	12-22-99	2	2	3.16	18	0	0	0	26	15	11	9	3	21	52	.167	.200	.145	18.23	7.36
Minjarez, Felix	R-R	6-3	205	9-13-96	1	0	0.00	2	0	0	0	7	1	0	0	0	4	6	.045	.000	.059	8.10	0.00
Morales, Gabe	L-L	6-3	195	4-14-99	3	3	4.12	22	5	0	1	59	48	31	27	7	36	82	.218	.190	.228	12.51	5.49
Mundo, Alan	R-R	6-2	170	5-27-00	0	0	12.00	2	0	0	0	3	4	4	4	1	4	2	.364	.400	.333	6.00	12.00
Och, Ryan	R-L	6-0	195	7-18-98	1	0	2.70	7	0	0	1	10	4	3	3	1	6	13	.121	.200	.107	11.70	5.40
Ochoa, Duilio	R-R	6-0	180	8-2-98	2	0	4.31	22	0	0	1	31	31	17	15	2	16	40	.252	.268	.239	11.49	4.60
Perez, Ramon	L-L	6-1	225	7-2-99	3	2	3.28	15	0	0	1	25	26	17	9	2	19	32	.250	.267	.243	11.68	6.93
Quijada, Hazahel	L-L	6-2	185	9-18-97	0	1	3.32	16	0	0	1	22	23	11	8	0	15	28	.274	.100	.328	11.63	6.23
Rascon, Bodi	L-L	6-5	205	2-3-01	2	2	3.38	6	5	0	0	21	16	9	8	2	6	14	.203	.000	.225	5.91	2.53
Reynolds, Jason	R-R	6-3	200	9-25-98	6	1	2.75	33	0	0	4	56	42	24	17	5	23	57	.198	.213	.187	9.22	3.72
Rondon, Miguel	B-R	5-11	150	1-26-01	3	4	10.22	24	0	0	0	47	58	56	53	14	41	65	.309	.256	.349	12.54	7.91
Routzahn, Ethan	R-R	6-4	225	3-19-98	3	0	2.87	11	0	0	0	16	15	6	5	2	4	29	.246	.238	.250	16.66	2.30
Sanchez, Fernando	L-L	6-0	198	9-13-00	0	0	6.75	1	1	0	0	3	0	2	2	0	4	2	.000	--	.000	6.75	13.50
Thomas, Levi	R-R	5-11	185	6-29-98	3	6	5.55	22	17	0	0	84	85	57	52	9	37	90	.265	.286	.250	9.60	3.95
Thwaits, Nick	R-R	6-2	195	6-27-99	2	10	7.03	22	18	0	0	87	104	76	68	9	35	87	.292	.311	.276	9.00	3.62
Vela, Noel	L-L	6-1	165	12-21-98	1	8	3.98	13	13	0	0	54	42	36	24	5	30	63	.202	.135	.216	10.44	4.97
Walter, Chase	R-R	6-7	260	7-26-98	1	0	2.28	23	0	0	2	28	20	16	7	3	15	52	.187	.192	.182	16.92	4.88
Wolf, Jackson	L-L	6-7	200	4-22-99	0	0	3.75	5	5	0	0	12	12	5	5	1	6	19	.267	.286	.263	14.25	4.50

Fielding

Catcher	PCT	G	PO	A	E	DP	PB								
Bender	1.000	10	98	7	0	0	0	Malone	1.000	1	10	0	0	0	0
								Quintero	.995	20	185	11	1	3	8

Valenzuela .973 49 474 57 15 4 9
Vizcarra .986 49 452 52 7 6 7

SAN DIEGO PADRES

BaseballAmerica.com   Baseball America 2022 Almanac · 289

First Base	PCT	G	PO	A	E	DP
Acosta	.987	18	138	13	2	10
Alarcon	1.000	4	23	2	0	4
Cummings	.961	7	45	4	2	1
Dale	.979	7	44	3	1	1
Guilbe	.990	16	91	5	1	9
Luis	.989	27	163	20	2	16
Mathis	1.000	1	6	0	0	1
Nunez	1.000	3	22	5	0	2
Quintero	1.000	1	7	1	0	1
Stronach	.985	24	184	12	3	19
Valenzuela	.988	19	149	9	2	11

Second Base	PCT	G	PO	A	E	DP
Alarcon	.875	2	2	5	1	1
Angeles	.967	28	52	67	4	20
Aquino	.920	8	8	15	2	2
Barley	.957	15	26	41	3	8
Dale	.966	33	52	63	4	19
Ferguson	1.000	3	7	9	0	2

	PCT	G	PO	A	E	DP
Guilbe	.958	7	8	15	1	4
Mathis	1.000	4	5	4	0	2
Reyes	1.000	6	12	11	0	2
Torres	.959	24	31	39	3	8

Third Base	PCT	G	PO	A	E	DP
Alarcon	.800	4	3	5	2	0
Angeles	.865	14	9	23	5	2
Cummings	1.000	4	0	4	0	0
Dale	.911	20	11	40	5	4
Dunn	.891	22	6	43	6	2
Guilbe	.850	28	11	40	9	6
Luis	.900	5	1	8	1	1
Mathis	.836	27	11	35	9	4
Nunez	.800	2	0	4	1	0
Reyes	1.000	1	0	2	0	0
Torres	1.000	2	1	2	0	0

Shortstop	PCT	G	PO	A	E	DP
Alarcon	.000	1	0	0	0	0

	PCT	G	PO	A	E	DP
Angeles	.987	41	61	92	2	15
Aquino	1.000	3	0	9	0	1
Barley	.849	43	57	95	27	21
Dale	.934	29	33	66	7	8
Torres	.917	6	7	15	2	4

Outfield	PCT	G	PO	A	E	DP
Acosta	.944	59	82	3	5	1
Dale	1.000	11	20	0	0	0
Dunn	.929	10	10	3	1	0
Ferguson	.923	9	24	0	2	0
Guilbe	.950	15	19	0	1	0
Hassell III	.962	86	176	2	7	0
Heredia	1.000	6	3	0	0	0
Jones	.900	9	9	0	1	0
Malone	1.000	1	1	0	0	0
Mears	.960	58	89	8	4	3
Solarte	.990	67	94	5	1	1
Stronach	.974	38	71	4	2	1

ACL PADRES ROOKIE
ARIZONA COMPLEX LEAGUE

Batting	B-T	HT	WT	DOB	AVG	vLH	vRH	G	AB	R	H	2B	3B	HR	RBI	BB	HBP	SH	SF	SO	SB	CS	SLG	OBP
Alvarez-Lopez, Jared	R-R	6-2	200	1-18-01	.179	.208	.170	36	112	15	20	6	0	0	9	7	5	1	0	22	0	0	.232	.258
Andreoli, John	R-R	6-1	218	6-9-90	.333	.500	.250	5	12	4	4	0	0	2	6	4	1	0	1	6	0	1	.833	.500
Antunez, Neifi	R-R	5-10	160	4-21-02	.177	.000	.212	22	62	4	11	0	0	0	3	8	3	0	0	29	3	3	.177	.301
Aquino, Charlis	R-R	6-2	165	11-18-01	.221	.316	.197	31	95	18	21	6	1	1	10	18	3	0	1	30	1	5	.337	.359
Bender, Colton	R-S	5-9	195	1-13-99	.200	.000	.333	4	10	2	2	0	0	0	0	1	0	0	1	0	0	0	.200	.273
Castanon, Marcos	R-R	6-0	195	3-23-99	.137	.333	.056	18	51	4	7	4	0	2	12	2	2	0	1	16	0	0	.333	.196
Cedeno, Newirlian	R-R	5-11	175	3-16-02	.241	.056	.333	18	54	8	13	8	1	2	7	9	1	0	1	20	2	0	.537	.354
Cummings, Cole	L-R	6-2	205	6-20-98	.283	.286	.282	24	60	9	17	5	1	2	15	11	2	0	3	15	1	2	.500	.395
Diaz, Josttin	B-R	6-0	170	5-18-02	.109	.091	.114	21	46	2	5	1	1	0	2	4	0	1	0	16	0	1	.174	.180
Duarte, Victor	R-R	5-11	170	2-23-01	.176	.667	.071	12	34	3	6	1	0	0	3	4	0	0	0	10	0	0	.265	.263
Dunn, Lucas	R-R	6-0	205	4-30-99	.364	.200	.412	8	22	8	8	1	1	0	6	5	3	0	0	5	0	2	.500	.533
Echavarria, Vladimir	R-R	5-11	160	4-12-00	.154	.000	.182	9	26	4	4	0	0	1	2	3	2	0	0	10	1	1	.269	.290
Fabian, Albert	L-L	6-0	215	12-21-01	.217	.600	.111	7	23	4	5	1	0	0	2	3	0	0	0	10	1	1	.261	.308
Farmer, Justin	R-R	6-1	190	12-19-98	.302	.400	.273	16	43	6	13	3	0	3	11	9	0	0	1	12	0	1	.581	.415
Ferguson, Max	L-R	6-1	180	8-23-99	.239	.227	.245	25	71	14	17	4	1	0	9	22	0	0	1	22	10	1	.324	.415
Fermin, Rafael	R-R	6-0	170	12-25-01	.240	.200	.250	14	25	6	6	0	0	0	5	1	0	0	0	5	1	1	.240	.387
Heredia, Cristian	R-R	6-3	175	4-12-01	.219	.190	.231	23	73	14	16	5	1	1	8	10	3	0	0	18	2	1	.356	.337
Hernandez, Alejandro	R-R	5-11	175	10-19-99	.333	1.000	.000	1	3	2	1	0	0	0	1	1	0	0	0	0	0	0	.333	.500
Jones, Pierce	R-R	6-1	185	6-15-01	.302	.400	.271	25	63	17	19	3	1	3	11	16	2	0	2	26	6	2	.524	.446
Lomack, Taylor	R-R	5-11	185	8-22-99	.250	.167	.500	5	8	1	2	0	0	0	0	2	0	0	1	1	1	0	.250	.400
Luis, Carlos	L-R	6-2	160	9-4-99	.167	.000	.333	2	6	1	1	0	0	0	1	0	0	0	1	1	0	0	.167	.143
Merrill, Jackson	L-R	6-3	195	4-19-03	.280	.243	.300	31	107	19	30	7	2	0	10	10	0	2	1	27	5	1	.383	.339
Nunez, Anthony	B-R	6-1	190	7-10-01	.245	.100	.279	20	53	10	13	5	0	2	14	15	0	0	1	21	2	1	.453	.406
Ona, Jorge	R-R	6-0	235	12-31-96	.111	.000	.143	3	9	2	1	0	0	1	1	2	0	0	0	4	0	0	.222	.333
Paez, Luis	L-R	5-10	165	9-3-00	.200	.200	.200	11	25	3	5	0	0	0	3	6	1	0	1	3	2	0	.200	.364
Paula, Willmert	L-R	6-1	165	9-30-01	.217	.000	.281	32	83	13	18	5	2	2	13	15	0	0	1	44	1	1	.398	.333
Polanco, Matias	L-R	5-11	175	9-18-00	.258	.500	.200	12	31	5	8	1	0	1	3	3	0	0	0	6	0	0	.387	.324
Ramirez, Alex	R-R	5-9	170	1-16-02	.500	--	.500	2	4	1	2	0	1	0	1	2	0	0	0	1	0	0	1.500	.500
Reyes, Ripken	B-R	5-10	180	4-1-97	.083	.000	.100	5	12	2	1	0	0	0	0	1	0	0	0	4	0	0	.083	.154
Rojas, Edwin	R-R	6-2	170	11-12-01	.212	.167	.222	44	132	19	28	6	0	0	10	21	2	0	2	39	4	5	.258	.325
Ryan, River	R-R	6-2	195	8-17-98	.308	.313	.304	12	39	5	12	2	0	1	2	3	0	0	1	13	4	1	.436	.349
Salinas, Ruben	R-L	6-0	154	1-13-03	.333	.000	.500	2	3	0	1	0	0	0	2	0	1	0	1	1	2	0	.333	.400
Suarez, Michael	L-L	6-2	200	5-21-00	.196	.154	.212	14	46	3	9	2	1	0	6	0	0	0	0	16	0	0	.304	.196
Torres, Bryan	R-S	5-9	165	12-11-99	.357	.333	.364	5	14	3	5	0	0	0	2	6	0	0	1	0	1	2	.357	.524
Tovar, Wilfredo	R-R	6-0	174	11-13-01	.000	--	.000	3	7	0	0	0	0	0	0	0	0	0	0	2	0	0	.000	.000
Vilar, Anthony	L-R	5-10	186	4-1-99	.217	.167	.235	8	23	3	5	2	1	0	1	5	0	0	1	4	0	0	.391	.345
Wood, James	L-R	6-7	240	9-17-02	.372	.323	.400	26	86	18	32	5	0	3	22	13	2	0	0	32	10	0	.535	.465

Pitching	B-T	HT	WT	DOB	W	L	ERA	G	GS	CG	SV	IP	H	R	ER	HR	BB	SO	AVG	vLH	vRH	K/9	BB/9
Arias, Luarbert	R-R	6-2	176	12-12-00	0	0	3.52	6	0	0	0	7.2	8	3	3	0	6	13	.192	.333	.150	15.26	7.04
Baker, Blake	R-R	6-3	195	1-10-99	0	0	8.64	5	0	0	0	8.1	8	10	8	2	8	10	.242	.214	.263	10.80	8.64
Bergert, Ryan	R-R	6-1	205	3-8-00	1	0	0.00	7	3	0	1	11	3	2	0	0	0	14	.081	.059	.100	11.45	0.00
Boyd, Luke	R-R	6-2	180	11-21-00	0	0	0.00	2	0	0	0	2.1	1	0	0	0	2	5	.143	.200	.000	19.29	7.71
Castillo, Wilton	R-R	6-7	190	2-12-00	2	2	5.40	15	5	0	0	36.2	38	23	22	6	12	49	.264	.200	.303	12.03	2.95
Chacon, Javier	L-L	5-11	190	12-24-02	0	1	--	1	1	0	0	3	6	6	1	3	0		1.000	--	1.000	--	--
Dana, Cullen	R-L	6-5	240	8-7-97	0	0	0.00	2	0	0	0	2	0	0	0	0	0	2	.000	.000	.000	9.00	0.00
Denz, Danny	L-L	5-9	198	5-20-98	0	0	15.43	2	0	0	0	2.1	2	4	4	0	3	2	.222	.333	.167	7.71	11.57
Echavarria, Vladimir	R-R	5-11	160	4-12-00	0	0	10.13	4	0	0	0	2.2	3	4	3	1	2	4	.333	.600	.143	13.50	6.75
Fox, Mason	R-R	6-2	170	1-7-97	0	0	0.00	1	0	0	0	1.1	1	0	0	0	0	3	.200	.500	.000	20.25	0.00
Gasser, Robert	L-L	6-1	190	5-31-99	0	0	0.00	1	1	0	0	1	0	0	0	0	0	1	.000	.000	.000	9.00	0.00

Pitching	B-T	HT	WT	DOB	W	L	ERA	G	GS	CG	SV	IP	H	R	ER	HR	BB	SO	AVG	vLH	vRH	K/9	BB/9
Gonzalez, Jesus	L-L	5-10	160	6-12-01	1	0	4.91	2	0	0	0	4	2	2	2	0	2	3	.182	.000	.286	7.36	4.91
Gore, MacKenzie	L-L	6-2	197	2-24-99	1	0	1.65	3	3	0	0	16	13	3	3	0	4	22	.220	.167	.234	12.12	2.20
Guerra, Javy	L-R	6-0	185	9-25-95	0	0	0.00	2	1	0	0	2	0	0	0	0	0	2	.000	.000	.000	9.00	0.00
Hawkins, Garrett	R-R	6-5	230	2-10-00	3	1	2.35	7	0	0	0	15	15	6	4	1	2	27	.254	.350	.205	15.85	1.17
Heiss, Brenden	R-R	6-0	200	9-15-97	0	1	0.00	5	0	0	1	5	3	3	0	0	0	7	.176	.200	.143	5.79	13.50
Iriarte, Jairo	R-R	6-2	160	12-15-01	0	1	4.71	8	3	0	0	21	18	12	11	1	7	25	.237	.226	.244	10.71	3.00
Jacob, Alek	L-R	6-3	190	6-16-98	0	0	0.00	1	0	0	0	1	2	0	0	0	0	3	.400	.000	.667	27.00	0.00
Kennedy, Brett	R-R	6-0	200	8-4-94	0	1	5.59	3	3	0	0	10	12	6	6	1	2	14	.316	.308	.320	13.03	1.86
Kopps, Kevin	R-R	6-0	200	3-2-97	0	0	1.93	4	0	0	0	5	3	1	1	0	1	10	.176	.200	.167	19.29	1.93
Landinez, Yerry	B-R	6-1	170	1-20-01	1	1	5.40	8	0	0	1	8	9	5	5	1	3	12	.281	.300	.273	12.96	3.24
Lange, Justin	R-R	6-4	220	9-11-01	0	3	6.95	9	9	0	0	22	18	17	17	1	15	29	.217	.267	.189	11.86	6.14
Lizarraga, Victor	R-R	6-3	180	11-30-03	0	4	5.10	11	11	0	0	30	25	17	17	5	15	35	.223	.244	.209	10.50	4.50
Lopez, Frank	R-R	6-1	170	4-23-01	0	1	10.50	5	0	0	0	6	8	7	7	0	5	6	.348	.250	.400	9.00	7.50
Luis Reyes, Jose	R-R	6-3	190	8-20-02	1	3	3.68	12	0	0	0	22	17	14	9	1	13	25	.210	.231	.200	10.23	5.32
Mayberry, Seth	R-R	6-3	200	6-22-00	2	0	0.00	3	0	0	0	4	1	0	0	0	0	5	.083	.000	.111	12.27	0.00
Medina, Brayan	R-R	6-1	180	10-6-02	0	1	18.00	3	2	0	0	5	11	11	10	3	3	7	.423	.417	.429	12.60	5.40
Miller, Ben	L-L	6-4	225	9-29-99	1	1	8.00	8	0	0	1	9	8	8	8	0	6	8	.229	.000	.296	8.00	6.00
Mundo, Alan	R-R	6-2	170	5-27-00	1	2	5.94	14	0	0	3	17	17	14	11	0	14	24	.246	.207	.275	12.96	7.56
Och, Ryan	R-L	6-1	195	7-19-98	0	1	3.00	3	0	0	0	3	3	1	1	0	1	6	.300	.500	.167	18.00	3.00
Parra, Reinier	R-R	6-0	155	5-31-01	0	3	12.39	12	3	0	1	20	30	31	28	3	21	20	.370	.400	.353	8.85	9.30
Paulina, Joshua	R-R	6-6	220	2-9-02	1	1	5.18	12	1	0	1	33	28	26	19	5	18	45	.226	.241	.214	12.27	4.91
Quijada, Hazahel	L-L	6-2	185	9-18-97	1	0	0.00	2	0	0	0	3	1	0	0	0	2	5	.125	.000	.143	16.88	6.75
Rascon, Bodi	L-L	6-5	205	2-3-01	1	1	5.06	5	1	0	1	11	12	7	6	0	4	16	.279	.111	.324	13.50	3.38
Robinson, Kobe	R-R	6-2	160	3-3-01	0	0	6.00	3	0	0	1	3	6	2	2	0	2	3	.429	.571	.286	9.00	6.00
Rondon, Miguel	R-R	5-11	150	1-26-01	0	0	0.90	8	0	0	1	10	6	2	1	0	5	12	.176	.125	.192	10.80	4.50
Routzahn, Ethan	R-R	6-4	225	3-19-98	0	0	0.00	1	0	0	0	0	0	0	0	0	0	0	.000	.000	.000	16.20	0.00
Saba, Elvis	R-R	5-11	180	5-11-00	1	0	3.60	4	1	0	0	10	7	4	4	0	2	11	.194	.364	.120	9.90	1.80
Smith, Adam	R-R	6-2	180	5-9-00	1	3	6.28	7	4	0	0	14	16	11	10	3	3	15	.286	.240	.323	9.42	1.88
Sparling, Matt	R-L	5-11	200	2-24-98	0	0	0.00	7	0	0	1	9	5	0	0	0	4	11	.161	.182	.150	10.61	3.86
Sweeting, Evan	R-R	6-1	185	10-4-01	0	0	0.00	1	0	0	0	1	0	0	0	0	0	0	.000	.000	.000	40.50	13.50
Vega, Alexuan	L-L	6-2	160	6-22-99	1	1	6.89	15	0	0	0	16	20	17	12	2	17	18	.313	.188	.354	10.34	9.77
Wilson, Steven	R-R	6-3	221	8-24-94	0	0	0.00	2	0	0	0	3	1	0	0	0	0	8	.111	.000	.167	27.00	0.00
Wingenter, Trey	R-R	6-7	237	4-15-94	1	0	0.00	3	1	0	0	3	1	0	0	0	1	6	.100	.250	.000	18.00	3.00
Wolf, Jackson	L-L	6-7	200	4-22-99	0	0	0.00	2	2	0	0	3	1	2	0	0	1	5	.083	.250	.000	15.00	3.00

Fielding

C: Alvarez-Lopez 27, Bender 4, Duarte 9, Hernandez 1, Polanco 12, Tovar 1, Vilar 7.
1B: Alvarez-Lopez 6, Castanon 6, Cummings 13, Diaz 1, Dunn 1, Fabian 5, Ferguson 1, Luis 2, Nunez 16, Rojas 1, Suarez 13.
2B: Antunez 18, Aquino 9, Castanon 7, Cedeno 4, Ferguson 13, Paez 10, Reyes 4.
3B: Castanon 3, Cedeno 10, Cummings 11, Diaz 18, Dunn 2, Echavarria 8, Ferguson 7, Nunez 3, Torres 1.
SS: Antunez 3, Aquino 18, Cedeno 1, Diaz 1, Ferguson 3, Merrill 27, Torres 4.
OF: Andreoli 4, Aquino 1, Dunn 4, Fabian 2, Farmer 16, Fermin 13, Heredia 18, Jones 25, Ona 2, Paez 1, Paula 32, Rojas 41, Salinas 2, Suarez 1, Wood 22.

DSL PADRES
ROOKIE

DOMINICAN SUMMER LEAGUE

Batting	B-T	HT	WT	DOB	AVG	vLH	vRH	G	AB	R	H	2B	3B	HR	RBI	BB	HBP	SH	SF	SO	SB	CS	SLG	OBP
Acosta, Victor	B-R	5-11	170	6-10-04	.285	.270	.289	56	186	45	53	12	5	5	31	38	12	1	3	45	26	7	.484	.431
Beltre, Eddy	R-R	5-11	165	4-16-04	.295	.308	.291	32	112	35	33	8	0	3	22	19	6	0	0	23	24	4	.446	.423
Cordero, Jose	R-R	6-1	165	5-24-03	.237	.267	.229	49	135	21	32	6	0	3	25	25	6	0	1	59	8	2	.348	.377
Hernandez, Alejandro	R-R	5-11	175	10-19-99	.286	.000	.333	4	7	2	2	0	0	0	1	4	0	0	0	0	0	0	.286	.545
Linares, Oswaldo	R-R	5-11	150	4-28-03	.207	.357	.179	33	92	19	19	1	0	1	12	34	3	2	1	23	4	2	.250	.431
Montesino, Daniel	L-L	6-0	180	2-12-04	.316	.333	.311	56	190	37	60	13	4	4	48	43	5	0	5	53	8	4	.489	.444
Perez, Adrian	R-R	5-9	165	10-3-02	.312	.389	.293	29	93	19	29	5	1	3	20	15	3	0	2	31	3	1	.484	.416
Perez, Jake	R-R	6-0	165	7-5-00	.348	.391	.337	40	112	29	39	7	2	2	21	25	5	0	0	36	9	10	.500	.486
Ramos, Ignacio	R-R	6-2	175	1-18-03	.171	.100	.194	15	41	2	7	1	0	0	5	4	0	0	1	11	0	0	.195	.239
Rodriguez, Carlos	B-R	5-10	155	5-12-03	.200	.148	.214	43	125	25	25	7	1	4	18	37	5	0	2	42	3	2	.368	.396
Sanabria, Jose	R-R	5-10	150	10-30-02	.212	.238	.203	53	170	38	36	8	0	1	19	25	9	1	7	45	9	7	.276	.332
Sanchez, Hugo	L-R	6-0	180	11-6-02	.195	.154	.206	49	133	33	26	3	4	0	19	45	2	0	0	52	10	4	.278	.406
Vallejo, Samuel	R-R	6-0	160	6-17-03	.145	.111	.152	22	55	11	8	2	0	1	5	14	1	0	0	26	2	1	.236	.329
Vergara, Carlos	R-R	6-3	170	1-7-02	.056	.000	.077	12	18	4	1	0	0	0	1	0	0	0	0	11	0	0	.056	.105
Villalobos, Heber	R-R	5-11	180	9-24-03	.128	.000	.167	21	39	3	5	1	0	0	3	6	3	1	1	14	2	0	.154	.286
Zavala, Samuel	L-L	6-1	175	7-15-04	.297	.286	.301	55	195	44	58	16	6	3	40	32	4	0	4	36	11	7	.487	.400

Pitching	B-T	HT	WT	DOB	W	L	ERA	G	GS	CG	SV	IP	H	R	ER	HR	BB	SO	AVG	vLH	vRH	K/9	BB/9
Acosta, Luis	R-R	6-1	175	2-5-01	3	2	6.35	20	0	0	2	28	36	25	20	3	15	36	.300	.316	.300	11.44	4.76
Asencio, Joel	R-R	6-7	185	3-26-03	2	1	8.84	17	0	0	2	18	25	23	18	1	23	24	.333	.400	.309	11.78	11.29
Baez, Henry	R-R	6-3	175	10-12-02	0	2	4.25	12	10	0	0	36	36	27	17	0	13	37	.257	.303	.243	9.25	3.25
Castro, Manuel	R-R	5-8	180	5-11-02	2	1	1.04	9	0	0	0	17	17	6	2	0	5	25	.262	.167	.317	12.98	2.60
De Los Santos, Adrian	R-R	6-3	190	8-16-00	2	1	3.72	11	7	0	0	36	34	19	15	1	16	26	.243	.326	.206	6.44	3.47
Gutierrez, Luis	L-L	6-0	175	7-31-03	1	2	6.60	11	2	0	0	15	16	15	11	0	15	18	.286	.000	.364	10.80	9.00
Lezan, Walki	R-R	6-0	165	4-24-02	4	0	3.10	19	0	0	2	20	19	11	7	1	13	15	.244	.154	.288	6.64	5.75
Lopez, Greiber	R-R	6-1	175	2-23-00	2	2	7.16	17	0	0	5	16	18	14	13	2	14	21	.290	.368	.256	11.57	7.71
Lugo, Alejandro	R-R	6-0	165	8-20-02	3	3	3.86	17	0	0	2	21	15	10	9	2	13	27	.197	.200	.196	11.57	5.57
Luna, Adrian	R-R	6-0	160	7-27-01	4	0	3.19	14	3	0	1	31	28	17	11	2	11	26	.252	.100	.338	7.55	3.19
Medina, Brayan	R-R	6-1	180	10-6-02	0	2	3.77	11	10	0	0	29	22	15	12	1	21	42	.202	.206	.200	13.19	6.59

Player	B-T	Ht	Wt	DOB	W	L	ERA	G	GS	CG	SV	IP	H	R	ER	HR	BB	SO	AVG	vLH	vRH		
Mendez, Miguel	R-R	6-2	165	7-1-02	1	2	4.91	12	11	0	0	40	33	27	22	1	21	40	.214	.155	.250	8.93	4.69
Moreno, Yariel	R-R	6-5	190	6-28-04	1	1	5.24	11	7	0	0	34	32	22	20	4	12	32	.242	.174	.279	8.39	3.15
Peralta, Axcel	L-L	6-4	190	10-24-01	1	0	7.50	15	0	0	0	18	20	15	15	0	17	29	.274	.133	.310	14.50	8.50
Perez, Jake	R-R	6-0	165	7-5-00	0	0	0.00	1	0	0	0	0	0	1	0	0	2	0	.000	.000	.000	0.00	54.00
Rodriguez, Bradgley	R-R	6-1	160	11-16-03	2	0	6.20	10	3	0	0	25	20	18	17	3	16	27	.225	.156	.263	9.85	5.84
Rosario, Jonney	R-R	5-10	185	7-28-04	2	1	9.62	13	0	0	0	24	28	28	26	5	17	32	.275	.333	.262	11.84	6.29
Rosario, Rodrigo	R-R	6-4	170	12-10-98	1	0	36.00	3	0	0	0	1	3	5	4	0	5	0	.600	.000	.750	0.00	45.00
Saba, Elvis	R-R	5-11	180	5-11-00	0	1	3.31	4	4	0	0	16	11	7	6	1	1	20	.190	.261	.143	11.02	0.55
Vergara, Carlos	R-R	6-3	170	1-7-02	0	0	18.00	2	0	0	0	1	4	3	2	0	0	0	.500	.500	.500	0.00	0.00
Zenizo, Javier	R-R	5-8	160	1-13-03	6	1	3.48	12	1	0	0	34	32	18	13	2	6	32	.252	.220	.267	8.55	1.60

Fielding

C: Linares 17, Rodriguez 31, Villalobos 19.
1B: Hernandez 3, Montesino 32, Peralta 4, Perez 13, Perez 6, Ramos 7, Rodriguez 2, Villalobos 2.
2B: Acosta 7, Hernandez 1, Perez 2, Perez 10, Sanabria 43.
3B: Perez 9, Perez 7, Ramos 1, Sanchez 46.
SS: Acosta 46, Perez 8, Sanabria 9, Sanchez 1.
OF: Beltre 33, Cordero 48, Montesino 22, Perez 15, Vallejo 16, Vergara 8, Zavala 52.

San Francisco Giants

SEASON IN A SENTENCE: A series of shrewd pickups and improvement on the roster—plus the return of Buster Posey for one last hurrah—led the Giants to the best record in the game but couldn't keep them from an early playoff exit.

HIGH POINT: It took until their 107th win on the final day of the season, but the Giants emerged victorious in their quest for the National League West crown. The win, an 11-4 romp over the Padres, was fueled on both sides of the ball by righthander Logan Webb. On the mound, he spun seven solid innings with eight strikeouts and no walks. At the plate, he cracked a three-run home run as part of a five-run inning that busted the game open and set the wheels in motion for he and his teammates to uncork some Champagne.

LOW POINT: In the regular season, the Giants used every bullet in the chamber to hold off the rival Dodgers for the game's best record and the division title. A few days later, the tables turned as the Dodgers topped the Giants and sent them home for the winter. The finale saw the Giants stymied by a reverse-engineered Los Angeles pitching staff which led with reliever Corey Knebel and closed with all-world starter Max Scherzer. The deciding run scored in the ninth inning, when reliever Camilo Doval allowed a decisive single to Cody Bellinger.

NOTABLE ROOKIES: The Giants weren't particularly rookie-laden, but the team did get contributions on the pitching staff from reclamation project Sammy Long, as well as fireballing relievers Gregory Santos and Camilo Doval. The latter impressed enough to settle into a late-inning role in the playoffs. Fellow pitchers Caleb Baragar, Conner Menez and Kervin Castro also got innings.

KEY TRANSACTIONS: The Giants' biggest move at the deadline was the addition of third baseman Kris Bryant from the Cubs in exchange for righthander Caleb Kilian and powerful outfielder Alexander Canario. Bryant produced a .788 OPS after the move to San Francisco, then went 8-for-17 with a home run in his team's loss to the rival Dodgers in the NL Division Series. Preseason addition Kevin Gausman, who signed a one-year deal, paid off handsomely. Gausman went 14-6, 2.81 and whiffed 227 hitters on his way to an all-star berth. The Giants added Anthony DeSclafani on a one-year pact as well, then watched as he posted an MLB-best two shutouts and 3.9 wins above replacement, as measured by Baseball-Reference.

OPENING DAY PAYROLL: $127,889,003 (14th).

PLAYERS OF THE YEAR

MAJOR LEAGUE	MINOR LEAGUE
Kevin Gausman RHP	**Jairo Pomares** OF
14-6, 2.81	(High-A/Low-A)
Career-high 227 SO	.334/.378/.629,
1.04 WHIP, 192 IP	20 HR, 1.007 OPS

ORGANIZATION LEADERS

Batting		*Minimum 250 AB
MAJORS		
*AVG	Buster Posey	.304
*OPS	Brandon Belt	.975
HR	Brandon Belt	29
RBI	Brandon Crawford	90
MINORS		
*AVG	Ismael Munguia, Eugene	.336
*OBP	Braden Bishop, Sacramento, Tacoma	.388
*SLG	Jairo Pomares, Eugene, San Jose	.629
*OPS	Jairo Pomares, Eugene, San Jose	1.007
R	Luis Matos, San Jose	84
H	Luis Matos, San Jose	141
TB	Luis Matos, San Jose	223
2B	Luis Matos, San Jose	35
3B	Franklin Labour, Eugene	6
HR	Jairo Pomares, Eugene, San Jose	20
HR	David Villar, Richmond	20
RBI	Luis Matos, San Jose	86
BB	Franklin Labour, Eugene	65
SO	Tyler Fitzgerald, Eugene	139
SB	Simon Whiteman, Richmond, Eugene	34

Pitching		#Minimum 75 IP
MAJORS		
W	Kevin Gausman	14
#ERA	Tyler Rogers	2.22
SO	Kevin Gausman	227
SV	Jake McGee	31
MINORS		
W	Travis Perry, Eugene	10
L	Matt Frisbee, Sacramento, Richmond	10
#ERA	Caleb Kilian, Tennessee, Richmond, Eugene	2.13
G	Silvino Bracho, Sacramento	49
GS	Prelander Berroa, San Jose	24
GS	Sean Hjelle, Sacramento, Richmond	24
GS	Carson Ragsdale, San Jose	24
SV	Chris Wright, Eugene, San Jose	21
IP	Sean Hjelle, Sacramento, Richmond	119
BB	Seth Corry, Eugene	63
SO	Carson Ragsdale, San Jose	167
#AVG	Ryan Murphy, Eugene, San Jose	.189

2021 PERFORMANCE

General Manager: Farhan Zaidi. **Farm Director:** Kyle Haines. **Scouting Director:** Michael Holmes.

Class	Team	League	W	L	PCT	Finish	Manager
Majors	San Francisco Giants	National	107	55	.660	1st (15)	Gabe Kapler
Triple-A	Sacramento River Cats	Triple-A West	56	71	.441	8th (10)	Dave Brundage
Double-A	Richmond Flying Squirrels	Double-A Northeast	57	56	.504	6th (12)	Jose Alguacil
High-A	Eugene Emeralds	High-A West	69	50	.580	1st (6)	Dennis Pelfrey
Low-A	San Jose Giants	Low-A West	76	44	.633	2nd (8)	Lenn Sakata
Rookie	ACL Giants Orange	Arizona Complex	35	24	.593	4th (18)	C.Valderrama/L.Burkhart
Rookie	ACL Giants Black	Arizona Complex	28	31	.475	11th (18)	L.Burkhart/C.Valderrama
Rookie	DSL Giants Orange	Dominican Summer	27	27	.500	23rd (46)	Jose Montilla
Rookie	DSL Giants Black	Dominican Summer	24	28	.462	30th (46)	Juan Ciriaco
Overall 2021 Minor League Record			372	331	.529	9th (30)	

ORGANIZATION STATISTICS

SAN FRANCISCO GIANTS
NATIONAL LEAGUE

Batting	B-T	HT	WT	DOB	AVG	vLH	vRH	G	AB	R	H	2B	3B	HR	RBI	BB	HBP	SH	SF	SO	SB	CS	SLG	OBP
Bart, Joey	R-R	6-2	238	12-15-96	.333	.667	.000	2	6	1	2	0	0	0	1	0	0	0	0	2	0	0	.333	.333
Belt, Brandon	L-L	6-3	231	4-20-88	.274	.246	.280	97	325	65	89	14	2	29	59	48	7	0	1	103	3	2	.597	.378
Bolt, Skye	B-R	6-2	180	1-15-94	.000	--	.000	2	1	0	0	0	0	0	0	0	0	0	0	1	0	0	.000	.000
Bryant, Kris	R-R	6-5	230	1-4-92	.262	.200	.288	51	187	28	49	13	0	7	22	23	1	0	1	46	6	0	.444	.344
2-team total (93 Chicago)					.265	.284	.259	144	513	86	136	32	2	25	73	62	9	0	2	135	10	2	.481	.353
Casali, Curt	R-R	6-2	220	11-9-88	.210	.102	.245	77	200	20	42	11	1	5	26	26	4	1	0	66	0	0	.350	.313
Crawford, Brandon	L-R	6-1	223	1-21-87	.298	.244	.319	138	483	79	144	30	3	24	90	56	5	0	5	105	11	3	.522	.373
Davis, Jaylin	R-R	5-11	205	7-1-94	.111	.000	.333	5	9	1	1	1	0	0	0	0	0	0	0	1	0	0	.222	.111
Dickerson, Alex	L-L	6-2	226	5-26-90	.233	.286	.229	111	283	37	66	10	2	13	38	23	6	0	0	76	1	0	.420	.304
Dubon, Mauricio	R-R	6-0	173	7-19-94	.240	.250	.234	74	175	20	42	9	0	5	22	9	1	0	2	41	2	1	.377	.278
Duggar, Steven	L-R	6-1	187	11-4-93	.257	.233	.262	107	268	45	69	14	5	8	35	27	2	0	0	88	7	0	.437	.330
Estrada, Thairo	R-R	5-10	185	2-22-96	.273	.236	.303	52	121	19	33	4	0	7	22	9	2	0	0	23	1	0	.479	.333
Flores, Wilmer	R-R	6-2	213	8-6-91	.262	.288	.248	139	389	57	102	16	1	18	53	41	3	0	3	56	1	0	.447	.335
La Stella, Tommy	L-R	5-11	180	1-31-89	.250	.240	.251	76	220	26	55	11	1	7	27	18	1	0	1	26	0	0	.405	.308
Longoria, Evan	R-R	6-1	213	10-7-85	.261	.318	.241	81	253	45	66	17	0	13	46	35	1	0	2	68	1	1	.482	.351
Posey, Buster	R-R	6-1	213	3-27-87	.304	.368	.280	113	395	68	120	23	0	18	56	56	1	0	2	87	0	0	.499	.390
Ruf, Darin	R-R	6-2	232	7-28-86	.271	.283	.262	117	262	41	71	13	2	16	43	46	3	0	1	87	2	0	.519	.385
Slater, Austin	R-R	6-1	204	12-13-92	.241	.284	.171	129	274	39	66	12	1	12	32	28	4	0	0	84	15	2	.423	.320
Solano, Donovan	R-R	5-8	210	12-17-87	.280	.301	.268	101	307	35	86	17	0	7	31	25	7	1	4	58	2	0	.404	.344
Tauchman, Mike	L-L	6-2	220	12-3-90	.178	.115	.190	64	152	21	27	4	0	4	15	22	1	0	0	52	1	3	.283	.286
Tromp, Chadwick	R-R	5-8	221	3-21-95	.222	.200	.231	9	18	1	4	0	0	1	2	0	0	0	0	4	0	0	.389	.222
Vosler, Jason	L-R	6-1	220	9-6-93	.178	.250	.169	41	73	12	13	4	0	3	9	7	1	0	1	21	2	0	.356	.256
Wade Jr., LaMonte	L-L	6-1	205	1-1-94	.253	.135	.268	109	336	52	85	17	3	18	56	33	5	4	3	89	6	1	.482	.326
Yastrzemski, Mike	L-L	5-10	178	8-23-90	.224	.170	.242	139	468	75	105	28	3	25	71	51	9	1	3	131	4	0	.457	.311

Pitching	B-T	HT	WT	DOB	W	L	ERA	G	GS	CG	SV	IP	H	R	ER	HR	BB	SO	AVG	vLH	vRH	K/9	BB/9
Alvarez, Jose	L-L	5-11	195	5-6-89	5	2	2.37	67	1	0	0	65	53	23	17	2	19	42	.217	.220	.214	5.85	2.64
Baragar, Caleb	R-L	6-3	215	4-9-94	2	1	1.57	25	0	0	2	23	19	7	4	1	12	16	.235	.323	.180	6.26	4.70
Beede, Tyler	R-R	6-2	216	5-23-93	0	0	27.00	1	0	0	0	1	2	3	3	0	0	2	.400	1.000	.250	18.00	0.00
Brebbia, John	L-R	6-1	200	5-30-90	1	0	5.89	18	0	0	0	18	25	13	12	4	4	22	.316	.235	.378	10.80	1.96
Castro, Kervin	R-R	6-0	185	2-7-99	1	1	0.00	10	0	0	0	13	13	1	0	0	4	13	.260	.292	.231	8.78	2.70
Chatwood, Tyler	R-R	5-11	200	12-16-89	1	0	6.75	2	0	0	0	4	6	5	3	1	1	6	.333	.286	.500	13.50	2.25
Cueto, Johnny	R-R	5-11	229	2-15-86	7	7	4.08	22	21	0	0	115	127	57	52	15	30	98	.285	.274	.299	7.69	2.35
DeSclafani, Anthony	R-R	6-2	195	4-18-90	13	7	3.17	31	31	2	0	168	141	61	59	19	42	152	.225	.248	.204	8.16	2.25
Doval, Camilo	R-R	6-2	185	7-4-97	5	1	3.00	29	0	0	3	27	19	10	9	4	9	37	.192	.220	.172	12.33	3.00
Garcia, Jarlin	L-L	6-3	215	1-18-93	6	3	2.62	58	0	0	1	69	48	26	20	9	18	68	.196	.173	.213	8.91	2.36
Gausman, Kevin	L-R	6-2	190	1-6-91	14	6	2.81	33	33	0	0	192	150	66	60	20	50	227	.210	.214	.206	10.64	2.34
Jackson, Jay	R-R	6-1	195	10-27-87	2	1	3.74	23	1	0	0	22	15	9	9	3	12	28	.197	.167	.217	11.63	4.98
Kazmir, Scott	L-L	6-0	185	1-24-84	0	1	6.35	5	4	0	0	11	15	9	8	3	6	10	.313	.400	.273	7.94	4.76
Leone, Dominic	R-R	5-10	215	10-26-91	4	5	1.51	57	4	0	2	54	37	15	9	2	22	50	.195	.154	.223	8.39	3.69
Littell, Zack	R-R	6-4	220	10-5-95	4	0	2.92	63	2	0	2	62	46	24	20	7	24	63	.207	.250	.183	9.19	3.50
Long, Sammy	L-L	6-1	185	7-8-95	2	1	5.53	12	5	0	0	41	37	27	25	5	15	38	.237	.164	.284	8.41	3.32
McGee, Jake	L-L	6-4	229	8-6-86	3	2	2.72	62	0	0	31	60	44	25	18	7	10	58	.196	.197	.196	8.75	1.51
Menez, Conner	L-L	6-2	206	5-29-95	1	0	3.86	8	1	0	0	14	16	10	6	2	3	15	.276	.211	.308	9.64	1.93
Moronta, Reyes	R-R	5-10	265	1-6-93	0	0	2.25	4	0	0	0	4	1	1	1	1	0	2	.077	.000	.125	4.50	0.00
Peralta, Wandy	L-L	6-0	217	7-27-91	2	1	5.40	10	0	0	2	8	11	5	5	1	3	8	.333	.500	.261	8.64	3.24
Quintana, Jose	R-L	6-1	220	1-24-89	0	0	4.66	5	0	0	0	10	8	5	5	3	6	12	.216	.056	.368	11.17	5.59
Rogers, Tyler	R-R	6-3	181	12-17-90	7	1	2.22	80	0	0	13	81	74	23	20	5	13	55	.243	.177	.299	6.11	1.44
Ruf, Darin	R-R	6-2	232	7-28-86	0	0	18.00	1	0	0	0	1	3	2	2	0	0	0	.600	.500	1.000	0.00	0.00
Sanchez, Aaron	R-R	6-4	210	7-1-92	1	1	3.06	7	7	0	0	35	32	12	12	2	15	26	.234	.217	.247	6.62	3.82

Name	B-T	HT	WT	DOB	W	L	ERA	G	GS	CG	SV	IP	H	R	ER	HR	BB	SO	AVG	vLH	vRH	K/9	BB/9
Santos, Gregory	R-R	6-2	190	8-28-99	0	2	22.50	3	0	0	0	2	5	6	5	3	2	3	.455	.333	.500	13.50	9.00
Selman, Sam	R-L	6-2	198	11-14-90	0	0	4.50	7	0	0	0	8	4	4	4	2	4	8	.143	.267	.000	9.00	4.50
Sherfy, Jimmie	R-R	6-0	175	12-27-91	1	0	4.22	10	0	0	0	11	9	5	5	2	4	9	.231	.158	.300	7.59	3.38
2-team total (4 Los Angeles)					2	1	4.20	14	0	0	0	15	12	8	7	3	4	12	.218	.174	.250	7.20	2.40
Slater, Austin	R-R	6-1	204	12-13-92	0	0	0.00	1	0	0	0	0	0	0	0	0	1	0	.000	.000	--	0.00	27.00
Tauchman, Mike	L-L	6-2	220	12-3-90	0	0	9.00	1	0	0	0	1	3	1	1	0	0	0	.500	.333	.667	0.00	0.00
Tropeano, Nick	R-R	6-4	205	8-27-90	1	0	1.50	4	0	0	0	6	4	2	1	0	2	2	.200	.182	.222	3.00	3.00
2-team total (1 New York)					1	0	2.25	5	0	0	0	8	8	3	2	1	3	2	.267	.235	.308	2.25	3.38
Watson, Tony	L-L	6-3	224	5-30-85	4	1	2.96	26	0	0	0	24	15	8	8	1	4	19	.174	.171	.176	7.03	1.48
Webb, Logan	R-R	6-1	220	11-18-96	11	3	3.03	27	26	0	0	148	128	53	50	9	36	158	.234	.260	.210	9.59	2.18
Wisler, Matt	R-R	6-3	215	9-12-92	1	2	6.05	21	0	0	0	19	19	13	13	4	6	26	.253	.185	.292	12.10	2.79
Wood, Alex	R-L	6-4	215	1-12-91	10	4	3.83	26	26	0	0	139	125	63	59	14	39	152	.236	.258	.230	9.87	2.53

Fielding

Catcher	PCT	G	PO	A	E	DP	PB
Bart	1.000	1	8	0	0	0	0
Casali	.992	64	502	18	4	2	4
Posey	.997	106	884	31	3	3	2
Tromp	1.000	8	51	1	0	0	0

First Base	PCT	G	PO	A	E	DP
Belt	.996	93	681	56	3	60
Casali	1.000	3	2	0	0	0
Flores	.988	34	154	14	2	17
Ruf	.997	44	272	28	1	23
Vosler	1.000	3	13	1	0	1
Wade Jr.	.977	31	155	16	4	12

Second Base	PCT	G	PO	A	E	DP
Dubon	.976	20	16	25	1	6
Estrada	.977	16	18	24	1	4

	PCT	G	PO	A	E	DP	PB
Flores	.985	30	28	38	1	9	
La Stella	.995	54	76	105	1	28	
Solano	.978	91	121	184	7	37	
Vosler	1.000	3	0	3	0	0	

Third Base	PCT	G	PO	A	E	DP
Bryant	.929	26	14	38	4	6
Dubon	.917	12	2	9	1	1
Estrada	1.000	4	1	4	0	0
Flores	.941	58	23	89	7	6
La Stella	1.000	5	1	5	0	0
Longoria	.974	78	47	139	5	11
Vosler	.906	19	9	20	3	2

Shortstop	PCT	G	PO	A	E	DP
Crawford	.983	135	168	340	9	68
Dubon	.952	21	20	59	4	10

	PCT	G	PO	A	E	DP
Estrada	.962	19	14	37	2	8
Solano	1.000	2	1	2	0	0

Outfield	PCT	G	PO	A	E	DP
Bolt	1.000	1	2	0	0	0
Bryant	.978	35	42	2	1	1
Davis	1.000	3	4	1	0	1
Dickerson	.982	82	107	2	2	0
Dubon	1.000	27	36	1	0	0
Duggar	.988	98	165	2	2	0
Estrada	1.000	5	6	0	0	0
Ruf	1.000	38	46	3	0	1
Slater	1.000	138	143	3	0	1
Tauchman	.986	62	69	1	1	0
Vosler	1.000	3	1	0	0	0
Wade Jr.	.991	96	108	2	1	0
Yastrzemski	.996	149	259	3	1	1

SACRAMENTO RIVER CATS

TRIPLE-A

TRIPLE-A WEST

Batting	B-T	HT	WT	DOB	AVG	vLH	vRH	G	AB	R	H	2B	3B	HR	RBI	BB	HBP	SH	SF	SO	SB	CS	SLG	OBP
Alcantara, Arismendy	B-R	5-10	170	10-29-91	.280	.254	.292	71	232	43	65	10	5	17	52	21	0	0	2	82	2	0	.586	.337
Bart, Joey	R-R	6-2	238	12-15-96	.294	.237	.311	67	252	37	74	15	0	10	46	21	5	0	1	82	0	0	.472	.358
Belt, Brandon	L-L	6-3	231	4-20-88	.250	.000	.333	5	12	2	3	0	0	0	1	2	0	0	1	3	0	0	.250	.333
Bishop, Braden	R-R	6-1	178	8-22-93	.326	.337	.321	75	288	58	94	18	5	12	43	25	5	0	2	56	9	3	.549	.388
2-team total (4 Tacoma)					.318	.333	.310	79	305	61	97	19	5	12	45	27	6	0	2	60	10	3	.531	.382
Bour, Justin	L-R	6-4	270	5-28-88	.213	.087	.247	33	108	18	23	5	0	6	17	20	2	0	0	30	0	1	.426	.346
Davis, Jaylin	R-R	5-11	205	7-1-94	.230	.306	.196	43	161	34	37	7	2	11	34	17	5	0	3	59	3	1	.503	.317
Dickerson, Alex	L-L	6-2	226	5-26-90	.289	.286	.290	11	38	8	11	3	0	2	4	5	2	0	0	8	0	0	.526	.400
Dubon, Mauricio	R-R	6-0	173	7-19-94	.332	.355	.322	63	247	41	82	13	2	8	31	29	5	0	2	38	9	3	.498	.410
Duggar, Steven	L-R	6-1	187	11-4-93	.279	.357	.255	15	61	13	17	2	1	1	9	9	0	0	2	13	0	0	.393	.371
Estrada, Thairo	R-R	5-10	185	2-22-96	.333	.370	.323	50	210	37	70	14	1	9	40	20	3	0	0	35	6	4	.538	.399
Freeman, Ronnie	R-R	6-1	190	1-8-91	.188	.222	.179	20	48	9	9	1	0	4	9	7	0	0	0	15	0	0	.458	.291
Genoves, Ricardo	R-R	6-2	190	5-14-99	.455	.500	.429	6	22	4	10	3	0	3	0	1	0	0	0	6	1	0	.727	.478
Johnson, Bryce	B-R	6-1	195	10-27-95	.286	.234	.301	100	353	65	101	15	5	9	44	48	4	1	1	108	30	4	.433	.377
Krizan, Jason	L-R	6-0	185	6-28-89	.316	.290	.322	110	431	67	136	26	1	16	73	39	1	1	8	70	1	0	.492	.367
La Stella, Tommy	L-R	5-11	180	1-31-89	.200	.000	.333	12	30	8	6	2	0	0	2	7	0	0	0	5	0	0	.267	.351
Longoria, Evan	R-R	6-1	213	10-7-85	.385	.250	.444	4	13	1	5	0	0	1	4	1	0	0	0	2	0	0	.615	.429
Maris, Peter	L-R	5-10	175	9-16-93	.289	.216	.309	75	173	23	50	8	1	9	29	16	0	0	3	51	2	1	.503	.344
Martorano, Brandon	R-R	6-2	198	1-6-98	1.000	--	1.000	1	1	1	1	0	0	0	1	0	0	0	0	0	0	0	1.000	1.000
Mathisen, Wyatt	R-R	6-0	217	12-30-93	.263	.333	.231	24	76	16	20	5	0	5	12	11	2	0	0	23	0	0	.526	.371
2-team total (32 Tacoma)					.191	.250	.172	56	178	29	34	8	0	7	24	31	8	0	1	53	0	0	.354	.335
McCarthy, Joe	L-L	6-3	220	2-23-94	.305	.283	.312	74	275	48	84	18	1	15	55	32	5	0	3	61	4	1	.542	.384
Nogowski, John	R-L	6-0	245	1-5-93	.185	.250	.133	8	27	3	5	1	0	2	5	2	2	0	0	2	0	0	.444	.290
Pena, Fabian	R-R	5-11	205	10-18-96	.179	.111	.200	12	39	4	7	2	0	2	7	1	0	0	0	12	0	0	.385	.200
Ramos, Heliot	R-R	6-1	188	9-7-99	.272	.373	.234	54	213	30	58	11	2	4	30	15	1	0	0	65	8	2	.399	.323
Robinson, Drew	L-R	6-1	200	4-20-92	.115	.095	.120	38	96	13	11	3	0	3	8	14	0	0	1	61	1	0	.240	.225
Ruf, Darin	R-R	6-2	232	7-28-86	.250	.000	.400	2	8	1	2	1	0	0	2	0	0	0	0	5	0	0	.375	.250
Solano, Donovan	R-R	5-8	210	12-17-87	.375	--	.375	5	16	3	6	1	0	0	2	0	0	2	0	1	5	0	0	.438	.421
Tauchman, Mike	L-L	6-2	220	12-3-90	.266	.143	.300	42	128	25	34	9	2	3	19	20	3	0	3	36	2	1	.438	.370
Toffey, Will	L-R	6-2	205	12-31-94	.270	.250	.278	31	74	15	20	2	0	2	9	13	4	3	0	39	1	0	.378	.407
Tolman, Mitchell	L-R	5-10	195	6-8-94	.263	.218	.278	63	213	33	56	12	3	9	33	18	8	2	2	57	3	2	.474	.340
Tom, Ka'ai	L-R	5-9	185	5-29-94	.130	.286	.063	6	23	2	3	0	1	0	3	0	1	0	0	11	0	0	.217	.167
Tromp, Chadwick	R-R	5-8	221	3-21-95	.224	.220	.225	55	192	23	43	12	0	6	24	10	1	0	1	47	0	0	.380	.265
Vosler, Jason	L-R	6-1	220	9-6-93	.295	.339	.282	72	261	51	77	14	1	15	51	36	6	0	6	45	0	0	.529	.385
Wade Jr., LaMonte	L-L	6-1	205	1-1-94	.244	.143	.263	14	45	12	11	2	0	3	8	14	0	0	0	13	0	1	.489	.424

Pitching	B-T	HT	WT	DOB	W	L	ERA	G	GS	CG	SV	IP	H	R	ER	HR	BB	SO	AVG	vLH	vRH	K/9	BB/9
Alvarez, Daniel	R-R	6-2	190	6-28-96	3	1	7.00	11	0	0	0	18	17	14	14	4	10	18	.236	.296	.200	9.00	5.00
Banda, Anthony	L-L	6-2	230	8-10-93	3	2	6.86	10	5	0	0	39	52	38	30	7	18	42	.315	.362	.297	9.61	4.12

Name	B-T	Ht	Wt	DOB	W	L	ERA	G	GS	CG	SV	IP	H	R	ER	HR	BB	SO	AVG	vLH	vRH		
Baragar, Caleb	R-L	6-3	215	4-9-94	3	3	8.46	22	1	0	0	22	28	23	21	7	21	25	.304	.368	.259	10.07	8.46
Bautista, Gerson	R-R	6-3	195	5-31-95	1	3	9.00	9	0	0	0	11	10	12	11	2	15	10	.238	.280	.176	8.18	12.27
Beede, Tyler	R-R	6-2	216	5-23-93	0	6	6.66	16	16	0	0	49	50	42	36	7	45	50	.265	.271	.258	9.25	8.32
Bracho, Silvino	R-R	5-10	190	7-17-92	1	3	4.14	49	0	0	8	50	59	25	23	10	19	65	.292	.295	.289	11.70	3.42
Brebbia, John	L-R	6-1	200	5-30-90	3	0	2.93	17	2	0	0	15	9	5	5	2	5	27	.167	.231	.107	15.85	2.93
Castro, Kervin	R-R	6-0	185	2-7-99	6	1	2.86	30	0	0	1	44	31	14	14	3	22	60	.197	.269	.127	12.27	4.50
Chatwood, Tyler	R-R	5-11	200	12-16-89	0	0	0.00	4	0	0	1	6	2	0	0	0	3	6	.125	.000	.250	9.53	4.76
Cueto, Johnny	R-R	5-11	229	2-15-86	0	0	5.40	1	1	0	0	2	4	1	1	0	1	1	.444	.667	.333	5.40	5.40
Cyr, Tyler	R-R	6-1	205	5-5-93	3	0	4.91	32	2	0	0	37	23	21	20	4	21	49	.174	.152	.197	12.03	5.15
Dahlberg, Jake	L-L	6-0	205	12-1-93	1	0	0.00	2	1	0	0	9	2	0	0	0	0	10	.069	--	.069	10.00	0.00
Doval, Camilo	R-R	6-2	185	7-4-97	3	0	4.99	28	0	0	1	31	28	18	17	3	24	44	.241	.231	.250	12.91	7.04
Frisbee, Matt	R-R	6-5	215	11-18-96	1	6	7.64	11	9	0	0	53	77	50	45	16	18	46	.329	.264	.387	7.81	3.06
Garabito, Gerson	R-R	6-0	160	8-19-95	0	3	4.71	11	6	0	1	42	42	22	22	7	27	36	.269	.262	.278	7.71	5.79
Gonzalez, Luis	L-L	6-0	170	1-17-92	0	1	7.36	20	0	0	0	26	33	24	21	6	10	33	.300	.327	.279	11.53	3.51
Gott, Trevor	R-R	5-10	182	8-26-92	1	3	4.10	43	1	0	3	42	37	22	19	4	16	53	.243	.246	.241	11.45	3.46
Gudino, Norwith	R-R	6-2	200	11-22-95	4	1	5.66	15	5	0	0	35	34	24	22	8	13	47	.246	.269	.225	12.09	3.34
Herrera, Jasier	R-R	6-5	190	1-1-98	0	0	13.50	1	0	0	0	2	2	3	3	1	4	2	.250	.333	.200	9.00	18.00
Hildenberger, Trevor	R-R	6-2	205	12-15-90	2	1	4.70	20	2	0	0	23	18	13	12	1	13	23	.217	.167	.268	9.00	5.09
Hjelle, Sean	R-R	6-11	228	5-7-97	2	6	5.74	10	10	0	0	53	67	45	34	6	29	35	.307	.347	.274	5.91	4.89
Jackson, Jay	R-R	6-1	195	10-27-87	1	0	1.29	10	0	0	0	14	5	2	2	1	1	24	.106	.130	.083	15.43	0.64
Jewell, Jake	R-R	6-2	217	5-16-93	0	0	6.10	8	0	0	0	10	11	7	7	1	5	10	.282	.375	.217	8.71	4.35
2-team total (2 Oklahoma City)					0	0	4.97	10	0	0	0	13	14	7	7	1	6	15	.286	.375	.242	10.66	4.26
Kazmir, Scott	L-L	6-0	185	1-24-84	3	3	4.61	13	12	0	0	53	45	28	27	6	18	48	.234	.238	.231	8.20	3.08
Krizan, Jason	L-R	6-0	185	6-28-89	0	1	0.00	2	0	0	0	1	1	1	0	0	0	0	.200	.500	.000	9.00	0.00
Leone, Dominic	R-R	5-10	215	10-26-91	0	1	1.00	7	1	0	2	9	6	1	1	0	3	16	.194	.154	.222	16.00	3.00
Littell, Zack	R-R	6-4	220	10-5-95	0	0	9.00	2	0	0	0	2	4	2	2	1	2	1	.444	.400	.500	4.50	9.00
Long, Sammy	L-L	6-1	185	7-8-95	1	0	2.05	11	3	0	0	26	16	6	6	2	9	31	.172	.205	.148	10.59	3.08
Marte, Yunior	R-R	6-2	180	2-2-95	0	3	3.49	43	1	0	4	57	60	30	22	4	23	62	.264	.252	.274	9.85	3.65
Menez, Conner	L-L	6-2	206	5-29-95	2	3	6.75	26	5	0	1	43	56	36	32	7	29	45	.322	.344	.310	9.49	6.12
Moronta, Reyes	R-R	5-10	265	1-6-93	0	2	11.00	24	2	0	0	18	22	23	22	3	26	19	.319	.243	.406	9.50	13.00
Morris, Akeel	R-R	6-1	205	11-14-92	1	3	10.23	5	4	0	0	22	31	26	25	6	13	21	.337	.297	.364	8.59	5.32
Ondrusek, Logan	R-R	6-8	230	2-13-85	1	3	4.78	9	8	0	0	43	46	26	23	6	13	41	.269	.227	.302	8.52	2.70
Pfeifer, Phil	L-L	6-0	200	7-15-92	0	3	11.25	5	0	0	0	12	23	22	15	2	11	13	.397	.375	.412	9.75	8.25
Russell, John	R-R	6-3	195	10-17-95	0	0	6.75	2	0	0	0	3	2	2	2	0	3	3	.222	.500	.143	10.13	10.13
Sanchez, Aaron	R-R	6-4	210	7-1-92	1	1	7.79	6	6	0	0	17	24	16	15	4	10	11	.333	.257	.405	5.71	5.19
Santos, Gregory	R-R	6-2	190	8-28-99	1	5	5.17	14	0	0	0	16	16	9	9	1	9	15	.262	.348	.211	8.62	5.17
Selman, Sam	R-L	6-2	198	11-14-90	1	0	4.03	17	2	0	1	22	13	10	10	0	19	24	.169	.250	.098	9.67	7.66
Sherfy, Jimmie	R-R	6-0	175	12-27-91	0	0	0.00	6	0	0	0	8	3	0	0	1	11	.111	.154	.071	12.91	1.17	
Shoemaker, Matt	R-R	6-2	225	9-27-86	4	3	4.83	9	8	0	0	50	52	29	27	7	9	54	.271	.277	.266	9.66	1.61
Tona, Jesus	R-R	5-10	170	3-30-96	0	0	27.00	1	0	0	0	1	2	3	3	1	2	0	.400	.333	.500	9.00	18.00
Tropeano, Nick	R-R	6-4	205	8-27-90	1	2	2.79	3	3	0	0	10	9	4	3	1	5	13	.243	.313	.190	12.10	4.66
2-team total (9 Oklahoma City)					2	0	4.33	12	8	0	0	35	38	23	17	5	17	41	.270	.278	.264	10.44	4.33
Webb, Logan	R-R	6-1	220	11-18-96	0	0	4.50	1	1	0	0	2	1	1	1	0	1	5	.167	.000	.500	4.50	4.50
Weber, Ty	R-R	6-4	220	3-19-98	0	0	5.63	3	0	0	0	8	8	5	5	3	1	5	.258	.308	.222	5.63	1.13
Williams, Ronnie	R-R	6-0	170	1-6-96	0	0	4.02	5	4	0	0	16	10	9	7	2	8	8	.189	.105	.235	4.60	4.60
Wolff, Sam	R-R	6-0	205	4-14-91	1	1	4.03	24	2	0	0	22	23	10	10	2	8	29	.256	.261	.250	11.69	3.22
Yamaguchi, Shun	R-R	6-2	225	7-11-87	0	3	6.17	5	4	0	0	23	19	18	16	3	14	25	.216	.191	.244	9.64	5.40

Fielding

Catcher	PCT	G	PO	A	E	DP	PB
Bart	.991	63	584	45	6	2	6
Freeman	1.000	20	127	5	0	1	0
Genoves	1.000	6	59	7	0	1	2
Pena	1.000	7	56	4	0	0	3
Tromp	.998	43	393	12	1	3	3

First Base	PCT	G	PO	A	E	DP
Belt	1.000	5	23	3	0	2
Bour	1.000	23	160	2	0	16
Davis	1.000	1	5	0	0	0
Krizan	.990	42	282	19	3	21
La Stella	1.000	1	3	0	0	0
Mathisen	.967	4	24	5	1	5
McCarthy	.991	34	218	14	2	23
Nogowski	1.000	6	31	3	0	2
Ruf	1.000	1	2	0	0	0
Toffey	1.000	3	16	2	0	2
Vosler	.994	23	160	10	1	24
Wade Jr.	.000	1	0	0	0	0

Second Base	PCT	G	PO	A	E	DP
Alcantara	.925	15	7	30	3	5
Dubon	1.000	3	2	11	0	4
Estrada	.973	16	25	46	2	12

	PCT	G	PO	A	E	DP
Krizan	.980	36	34	62	2	14
La Stella	.923	6	1	11	1	1
Maris	.972	42	52	54	3	9
Solano	1.000	4	5	8	0	3
Toffey	1.000	4	1	6	0	0
Tolman	.948	17	21	34	3	9
Vosler	.977	12	12	30	1	6

Third Base	PCT	G	PO	A	E	DP
Alcantara	.800	9	5	11	4	3
Dubon	1.000	1	0	1	0	0
Estrada	.889	2	3	5	1	1
Krizan	.915	22	11	32	4	5
La Stella	1.000	2	0	1	0	0
Longoria	.917	4	1	10	1	2
Maris	.800	9	3	5	2	0
Mathisen	.974	18	11	26	1	2
Toffey	.971	14	14	20	1	1
Tolman	.946	29	23	47	4	6
Tromp	.000	1	0	0	0	0
Vosler	.974	31	10	65	2	5

Shortstop	PCT	G	PO	A	E	DP
Alcantara	.969	32	40	55	3	18
Dubon	.967	51	81	124	7	38

	PCT	G	PO	A	E	DP
Estrada	.896	30	30	56	10	12
Maris	1.000	3	2	4	0	1
Tolman	.939	15	16	30	3	4

Outfield	PCT	G	PO	A	E	DP
Alcantara	.920	9	23	0	2	0
Bishop	.992	69	126	2	1	1
Davis	.975	37	75	3	2	1
Dickerson	.800	6	8	0	2	0
Dubon	1.000	7	12	1	0	1
Duggar	1.000	11	24	1	0	0
Estrada	1.000	1	3	0	0	0
Johnson	.978	82	175	1	4	0
Krizan	1.000	11	11	1	0	0
McCarthy	.981	38	52	1	1	0
Nogowski	1.000	2	3	0	0	0
Ramos	.964	50	102	4	4	1
Robinson	1.000	28	40	0	0	0
Ruf	--	1	0	0	0	0
Tauchman	1.000	31	49	2	0	1
Toffey	1.000	8	19	1	0	1
Tom	1.000	6	5	0	0	0
Vosler	1.000	5	6	0	0	0
Wade Jr.	1.000	13	19	1	0	0

RICHMOND FLYING SQUIRRELS
DOUBLE-A NORTHEAST

DOUBLE-A

Batting	B-T	HT	WT	DOB	AVG	vLH	vRH	G	AB	R	H	2B	3B	HR	RBI	BB	HBP	SH	SF	SO	SB	CS	SLG	OBP
Alexander Basabe, Luis	B-R	6-0	180	8-26-96	.206	.087	.267	22	68	12	14	3	0	2	9	15	0	0	0	26	5	0	.338	.349
Angulo, Andres	R-R	5-10	181	9-5-97	.209	.212	.207	53	163	27	34	6	0	4	18	21	2	0	0	50	2	1	.319	.306
Fabian, Sandro	R-R	6-1	180	3-6-98	.264	.271	.261	89	296	37	78	13	1	15	55	11	4	0	2	57	0	0	.466	.297
Fernandez, Vince	L-R	6-3	210	7-25-95	.229	.180	.241	81	249	48	57	10	4	14	43	29	11	0	4	98	2	0	.470	.331
Freeman, Ronnie	R-R	6-1	190	1-8-91	.200	.077	.250	14	45	6	9	2	1	1	4	3	0	0	0	11	0	0	.356	.250
Heyward, Jacob	R-R	6-1	215	8-1-95	.208	.292	.168	74	202	35	42	12	0	12	24	34	9	0	1	71	2	3	.446	.346
Howard, Ryan	R-R	6-2	195	7-25-94	.207	.273	.167	24	58	7	12	4	0	2	6	5	0	0	0	23	0	0	.379	.270
Maris, Peter	L-R	5-10	175	9-16-93	.143	.333	.000	2	7	0	1	0	0	1	0	1	0	0	0	1	0	0	.429	.143
Martorano, Brandon	R-R	6-2	198	1-6-98	.176	.207	.167	38	119	14	21	4	0	6	20	21	2	0	2	44	2	0	.361	.306
Matheny, Shane	L-R	6-1	205	6-5-96	.207	.192	.213	58	174	26	36	10	1	4	16	33	1	1	2	67	3	1	.345	.333
Maxwell, Bruce	L-R	6-1	250	12-20-90	.235	.200	.241	9	34	3	8	1	0	1	6	3	0	0	1	13	0	0	.353	.289
Mottice, Kyle	L-R	5-11	185	1-18-96	.255	.378	.192	36	110	11	28	5	1	0	11	12	2	4	0	19	6	2	.318	.339
Quinn, Heath	R-R	6-3	220	6-7-95	.213	.308	.176	12	47	5	10	1	0	2	5	1	0	0	1	21	0	0	.362	.224
Ramos, Heliot	R-R	6-1	188	9-7-99	.237	.273	.224	62	236	36	56	14	1	10	26	27	3	0	0	73	7	2	.432	.323
Rincones, Diego	R-R	6-0	175	6-14-99	.290	.250	.304	51	186	31	54	8	1	10	33	16	9	0	1	37	1	0	.505	.373
Sugilio, Andy	L-R	6-2	170	10-26-96	.250	.161	.273	57	152	18	38	5	0	1	13	11	2	1	1	41	5	3	.303	.307
Tolman, Mitchell	L-R	5-10	195	6-8-94	.253	.267	.250	24	83	15	21	4	1	1	9	10	4	0	2	22	1	1	.361	.354
Torres, Bryan	L-R	5-11	165	7-2-97	.280	.423	.245	43	132	18	37	7	1	0	9	7	2	0	3	31	6	3	.348	.319
Tostado, Frankie	L-L	6-2	205	3-31-98	.249	.292	.233	100	366	46	91	18	3	14	63	28	1	0	3	92	1	0	.429	.302
Villar, David	R-R	6-1	215	1-27-97	.275	.255	.283	106	385	70	106	29	0	20	58	46	15	0	0	112	5	1	.506	.374
Whiteman, Simon	R-R	5-10	165	1-28-97	.236	.262	.228	71	267	35	63	18	1	3	23	36	5	1	0	88	17	2	.345	.338
Wilson, Will	R-R	6-0	184	7-21-98	.189	.211	.180	51	196	20	37	8	0	5	22	22	3	0	0	81	1	0	.306	.281

Pitching	B-T	HT	WT	DOB	W	L	ERA	G	GS	CG	SV	IP	H	R	ER	HR	BB	SO	AVG	vLH	vRH	K/9	BB/9
Amaya, Luis	L-L	5-11	160	8-26-98	2	0	5.57	33	3	0	0	53	51	38	33	9	33	70	.249	.227	.265	11.81	5.57
Beck, Tristan	R-R	6-4	165	6-24-96	2	2	5.89	4	4	0	0	18	20	13	12	4	7	17	.274	.161	.357	8.35	3.44
Blair, Aaron	R-R	6-5	220	5-26-92	0	3	4.46	9	9	0	0	34	30	22	17	4	20	23	.240	.234	.246	6.03	5.24
Dabovich, R.J.	R-R	6-3	208	1-11-99	1	1	3.66	20	0	0	6	20	13	9	8	1	7	34	.178	.188	.171	15.56	3.20
Frisbee, Matt	R-R	6-5	215	11-18-96	5	4	3.77	11	11	0	0	60	47	28	25	11	10	65	.213	.227	.202	9.80	1.51
Garabito, Gerson	R-R	6-0	160	8-19-95	3	3	4.30	14	6	0	0	44	47	23	21	3	15	44	.280	.253	.309	9.00	3.07
Gudino, Norwith	R-R	6-2	200	11-22-95	1	1	1.44	17	0	0	5	25	13	5	4	1	10	39	.149	.059	.208	14.04	3.60
Hjelle, Sean	R-R	6-11	228	5-7-97	3	2	3.15	14	14	0	0	66	60	32	23	8	19	69	.241	.233	.248	9.46	2.60
Kilian, Caleb	R-R	6-4	180	6-2-97	3	2	2.43	11	11	2	0	63	51	19	17	2	8	64	.221	.185	.245	9.14	1.14
Long, Sammy	L-L	6-1	185	7-8-95	0	1	3.00	4	4	0	0	15	12	6	5	0	4	22	.214	.056	.289	13.20	2.40
Marciano, Joey	L-L	6-5	250	1-11-95	3	4	3.09	39	0	0	4	47	38	22	16	4	16	59	.220	.216	.222	11.38	3.09
Marshall, Mac	R-L	6-1	187	1-27-96	0	3	10.13	12	0	0	0	16	22	19	18	1	18	22	.324	.233	.395	12.38	10.13
Marte, Jose	R-R	6-3	180	6-14-96	2	0	3.57	19	0	0	1	23	21	11	9	0	15	36	.247	.267	.236	14.29	5.96
Morris, Akeel	R-R	6-1	205	11-24-92	6	0	3.67	10	10	0	0	54	49	23	22	8	11	65	.239	.198	.272	10.83	1.83
Pfeifer, Phil	L-L	6-0	200	7-15-92	2	2	5.01	9	4	0	0	23	24	14	13	4	13	28	.273	.269	.274	10.80	5.01
Plassmeyer, Michael	L-L	6-2	197	11-5-96	3	9	5.08	16	16	0	0	80	90	51	45	11	16	91	.284	.278	.286	10.28	1.81
Rubio, Frank	R-R	5-11	185	4-23-95	4	3	3.56	37	0	0	4	43	41	23	17	4	7	34	.248	.280	.280	7.12	1.47
Ruotolo, Patrick	R-R	5-10	250	1-16-95	3	1	2.68	39	0	0	11	37	20	13	11	5	5	50	.155	.191	.134	12.16	1.22
Seelinger, Matt	R-R	6-3	190	4-19-95	3	1	3.07	36	0	0	0	41	31	15	14	6	31	64	.211	.242	.185	14.05	6.80
Toplikar, Trenton	R-R	6-4	215	5-21-96	2	8	4.90	22	18	0	0	94	108	58	51	14	36	86	.285	.292	.279	8.26	3.46
Vizcaino, Raffi	R-R	6-0	237	12-2-95	3	2	5.40	34	2	0	3	40	39	24	24	4	25	45	.255	.294	.224	10.13	5.63
Walker, Ryan	R-R	6-2	200	11-26-95	0	0	0.96	8	0	0	0	9	7	1	1	0	0	10	.206	.278	.125	9.64	0.00
Williams, Ronnie	R-R	6-0	170	1-6-96	6	4	2.45	24	1	0	1	62	43	27	17	5	28	61	.193	.263	.137	8.81	4.04

Fielding

Catcher	PCT	G	PO	A	E	DP	PB
Angulo	.979	43	388	30	9	2	5
Freeman	1.000	13	121	8	0	0	0
Martorano	.992	37	346	31	3	3	4
Maxwell	1.000	8	82	5	0	0	0
Torres	.994	21	162	15	1	3	5

First Base	PCT	G	PO	A	E	DP
Angulo	1.000	4	32	2	0	0
Howard	1.000	4	26	1	0	1
Matheny	1.000	1	3	0	0	0
Tostado	.987	93	618	44	9	49
Villar	1.000	13	85	5	0	6

Second Base	PCT	G	PO	A	E	DP
Howard	.941	6	5	11	1	3
Maris	1.000	1	2	0	0	0

	PCT	G	PO	A	E	DP	PB
Matheny	.981	13	25	28	1	6
Mottice	.962	34	39	62	4	14
Tolman	1.000	12	15	29	0	2
Torres	.943	18	15	35	3	7
Whiteman	.965	35	48	63	4	14

Third Base	PCT	G	PO	A	E	DP
Howard	1.000	2	1	0	0	0
Matheny	.929	8	4	9	1	1
Tolman	1.000	7	6	9	0	3
Torres	.750	4	3	3	2	0
Villar	.916	92	64	144	19	12
Wilson	.600	3	0	3	2	0

Shortstop	PCT	G	PO	A	E	DP
Howard	.636	3	3	4	4	1
Maris	1.000	1	0	1	0	0

	PCT	G	PO	A	E	DP
Matheny	.970	34	36	61	3	13
Mottice	1.000	1	2	1	0	1
Tolman	1.000	5	9	19	0	4
Whiteman	.960	52	29	43	3	10
Wilson	.948	48	62	83	8	11

Outfield	PCT	G	PO	A	E	DP
Alexander Basabe	.979	23	45	2	1	0
Fabian	.965	69	104	6	4	0
Fernandez	.992	63	127	2	1	0
Heyward	.965	51	81	2	3	0
Quinn	.952	7	20	0	1	0
Ramos	1.000	58	106	3	0	0
Rincones	.980	34	49	1	1	0
Sugilio	.971	45	63	3	2	1
Whiteman	.971	14	33	0	1	0

EUGENE EMERALDS
HIGH-A WEST

HIGH CLASS A

Batting	B-T	HT	WT	DOB	AVG	vLH	vRH	G	AB	R	H	2B	3B	HR	RBI	BB	HBP	SH	SF	SO	SB	CS	SLG	OBP

SAN FRANCISCO GIANTS

Name	B-T	HT	WT	DOB	AVG	vLH	vRH	G	AB	R	H	2B	3B	HR	RBI	BB	HP	SH	SF	SO	SB	CS	SLG	OBP
Adkins, Kwan	L-L	6-2	195	10-2-96	.244	.500	.138	18	41	11	10	3	0	1	2	6	1	0	0	16	5	1	.390	.354
Aldrete, Carter	R-R	6-2	205	10-12-97	.240	.214	.248	81	262	36	63	13	0	9	44	22	1	2	1	90	8	3	.393	.301
Auerbach, Brett	R-R	5-9	185	8-27-98	.256	.234	.263	53	199	40	51	8	1	15	39	18	5	1	0	60	18	2	.533	.333
Bailey, Patrick	B-R	6-1	210	5-29-99	.185	.095	.202	33	135	13	25	9	0	2	15	18	2	0	0	43	6	0	.296	.290
Bishop, Hunter	L-R	6-5	210	6-25-98	.167	.333	.111	3	12	1	2	1	0	0	1	2	1	0	0	4	0	0	.250	.333
Dempsey, Nolan	R-R	6-0	175	9-9-96	.149	.750	.093	17	47	6	7	2	0	1	7	3	2	0	0	19	0	1	.255	.231
Emery, Robert	R-R	6-0	210	10-22-96	.333	.636	.279	23	72	10	24	3	0	2	11	8	4	0	0	16	0	0	.458	.429
Fitzgerald, Tyler	R-R	6-3	205	9-15-97	.262	.239	.267	103	382	71	100	28	2	19	65	38	9	2	1	139	12	4	.495	.342
Flores, Tyler	L-L	6-2	185	1-24-96	.214	.154	.221	38	117	16	25	8	0	4	16	13	5	0	1	39	0	1	.385	.316
Genoves, Ricardo	R-R	6-2	190	5-14-99	.217	.085	.253	65	217	33	47	11	0	7	26	22	3	0	3	73	0	0	.364	.294
Gonzalez, Jacob	R-R	6-3	190	6-26-98	.174	.091	.185	27	92	10	16	4	0	1	9	8	2	0	1	21	1	0	.250	.252
Labour, Franklin	R-R	6-1	190	5-11-98	.223	.224	.223	100	318	60	71	16	6	13	58	65	5	0	4	123	13	8	.434	.360
Luciano, Marco	R-R	6-2	178	9-10-01	.217	.154	.233	36	129	16	28	3	2	1	14	10	3	0	3	54	1	0	.295	.283
Martorano, Brandon	R-R	6-2	198	1-6-98	.333	.438	.305	25	75	17	25	5	3	2	8	16	3	0	1	27	4	0	.560	.463
Munguia, Ismael	L-L	5-10	158	10-19-98	.336	.349	.333	81	333	57	112	22	3	9	53	13	5	2	4	27	15	5	.502	.366
Pena, Fabian	R-R	5-11	205	10-18-96	.333	--	.333	1	3	0	1	0	0	0	0	0	0	0	0	1	0	0	.333	.333
Pomares, Jairo	L-R	6-1	185	8-4-00	.262	.250	.266	26	103	13	27	5	1	6	15	1	0	0	0	33	1	0	.505	.269
Quinn, Heath	R-R	6-3	220	6-7-95	.265	.222	.273	35	117	21	31	5	0	8	22	8	4	0	0	40	0	1	.513	.333
Rincones, Diego	R-R	6-0	175	6-14-99	.300	.143	.348	25	90	15	27	6	0	5	15	10	3	0	1	19	0	0	.533	.385
Roby, Sean	R-R	6-2	215	7-8-98	.241	.239	.242	97	373	64	90	24	1	19	58	43	4	0	1	132	3	0	.464	.325
Smith, Armani	R-R	6-4	215	7-19-98	.279	.286	.277	69	258	43	72	14	2	8	45	25	4	0	1	84	4	1	.442	.351
Whiteman, Simon	R-R	5-10	165	1-28-97	.268	.364	.254	28	82	12	22	3	1	1	8	19	2	3	1	32	17	2	.366	.413
Williams, Javeyan	L-L	5-9	160	6-27-97	.145	.200	.140	22	62	9	9	1	0	1	9	5	2	0	1	24	5	1	.210	.229
Wilson, Will	R-R	6-0	184	7-21-98	.251	.306	.239	49	195	37	49	14	2	10	26	24	3	0	2	56	1	7	.497	.339
Wyatt, Logan	L-R	6-4	230	11-15-97	.238	.200	.245	70	227	36	54	8	1	1	24	58	3	0	1	52	2	3	.295	.398

Pitching	B-T	HT	WT	DOB	W	L	ERA	G	GS	CG	SV	IP	H	R	ER	HR	BB	SO	AVG	vLH	vRH	K/9	BB/9
Avila, Nick	R-R	6-4	195	7-25-97	5	7	6.51	25	7	0	0	76	95	59	55	12	27	78	.307	.313	.303	9.24	3.20
Bates, Solomon	R-R	6-2	210	3-16-97	2	2	4.76	32	2	0	0	51	53	30	27	4	26	62	.266	.358	.203	10.94	4.59
Corry, Seth	L-L	6-2	195	11-3-98	3	3	5.99	19	19	0	0	68	53	50	45	4	63	100	.226	.221	.228	13.30	8.38
Dabovich, R.J.	R-R	6-3	208	1-11-99	0	0	1.42	11	0	0	4	13	2	2	2	2	6	28	.050	.056	.045	19.89	4.26
Dahlberg, Jake	L-L	6-0	205	12-1-93	2	5	6.60	10	10	0	0	46	60	37	34	8	9	61	.308	.362	.278	11.85	1.75
Herrera, Jasier	R-R	6-5	190	1-1-98	1	2	3.99	24	1	0	0	56	63	30	25	5	15	57	.283	.255	.304	9.11	2.40
Kilian, Caleb	R-R	6-4	180	6-2-97	3	0	1.25	4	4	0	0	22	9	3	3	0	1	32	.122	.048	.151	13.29	0.42
Marte, Jose	R-R	6-3	180	6-14-96	0	0	0.00	5	0	0	3	6	3	0	0	0	0	14	.130	.167	.118	19.89	0.00
Morreale, Nick	R-R	6-5	220	7-27-97	2	0	6.27	9	3	0	0	19	18	14	13	1	11	24	.247	.238	.250	11.57	5.30
Murphy, Ryan	R-R	6-1	190	10-8-99	2	2	1.44	6	0	0	0	31	13	11	5	1	8	48	.124	.083	.158	13.79	2.30
Nurse, Conner	R-R	6-6	210	7-31-99	6	7	4.86	23	20	1	0	113	112	66	61	21	51	114	.258	.271	.248	9.08	4.06
Perry, Travis	R-R	6-4	190	3-8-97	10	1	2.88	29	2	0	0	59	38	25	19	4	26	71	.185	.204	.170	10.77	3.94
Phillips, Aaron	R-R	6-5	225	10-16-94	4	7	7.06	16	16	0	0	73	102	65	57	9	31	48	.338	.338	.337	5.94	3.84
Rashi, Taylor	R-R	6-4	220	1-15-96	6	3	4.44	32	2	0	2	47	27	25	23	7	22	68	.164	.211	.128	13.11	4.24
Reich, Austin	R-R	6-3	210	4-15-97	2	1	1.56	18	0	0	1	35	16	6	6	1	5	51	.137	.145	.132	13.24	1.30
Rivera, Blake	R-R	6-4	225	1-9-98	1	2	6.43	5	4	0	0	14	21	12	10	2	5	17	.350	.429	.281	10.93	3.21
Russell, John	R-R	6-3	195	10-17-95	6	0	4.01	27	1	0	1	49	38	26	22	7	23	63	.209	.205	.212	11.49	4.20
Schimpf, Tyler	R-R	6-4	210	8-7-95	1	2	4.95	31	0	0	4	44	30	29	24	7	22	69	.183	.139	.217	14.22	4.53
Teng, Kai-Wei	R-R	6-4	260	12-1-98	5	6	4.33	21	21	1	0	96	76	50	46	11	53	142	.218	.228	.211	13.36	4.99
Timmins, John	R-R	6-6	215	1-20-94	2	0	3.27	10	0	0	0	11	9	4	4	1	10	14	.220	.067	.308	11.45	8.18
Tona, Jesus	R-R	5-10	170	3-30-96	0	0	0.00	1	0	0	0	1	1	0	0	0	0	2	.250	1.000	.000	18.00	0.00
Tucker, Bryce	B-L	6-3	205	12-10-96	0	0	8.88	21	1	0	1	25	30	28	25	1	27	28	.303	.235	.338	9.95	9.59
Walker, Ryan	R-R	6-2	200	11-26-95	1	0	4.28	31	0	0	0	40	39	21	19	4	10	56	.250	.288	.227	12.60	2.25
Weber, Ty	R-R	6-4	220	3-19-98	1	0	0.00	2	0	0	0	2	0	0	0	0	3	2	.000	.000	.000	9.00	13.50
Wright, Chris	L-L	6-1	205	10-14-98	4	0	0.97	31	0	0	17	37	15	5	4	2	18	62	.122	.132	.118	15.08	4.38

Fielding

Catcher	PCT	G	PO	A	E	DP	PB
Auerbach	.993	12	130	7	1	0	0
Bailey	.994	25	283	27	2	1	5
Emery	.970	14	125	6	4	0	6
Genoves	.991	53	542	36	5	4	10
Martorano	.992	19	215	19	2	2	3
Pena	1.000	1	13	3	0	1	0

First Base	PCT	G	PO	A	E	DP
Aldrete	1.000	1	12	0	0	1
Bailey	.970	4	30	2	1	1
Emery	1.000	3	16	1	0	0
Flores	1.000	14	98	5	0	7
Genoves	.952	4	20	0	1	3
Gonzalez	1.000	6	38	2	0	4
Roby	.995	32	200	8	1	11
Wyatt	.984	58	401	21	7	37

Second Base	PCT	G	PO	A	E	DP
Aldrete	.978	29	34	57	2	4
Auerbach	.981	27	42	62	2	15
Dempsey	.960	7	5	19	1	2
Fitzgerald	1.000	46	64	110	0	19
Whiteman	.984	17	22	41	1	10
Wilson	.909	4	12	8	2	4

Third Base	PCT	G	PO	A	E	DP
Aldrete	.951	35	14	44	3	5
Auerbach	1.000	4	3	4	0	0
Emery	.000	1	0	0	0	0
Fitzgerald	.792	14	11	8	5	1
Gonzalez	.739	11	4	13	6	0
Roby	.967	54	31	85	4	7
Whiteman	.941	7	5	11	1	0

Shortstop	PCT	G	PO	A	E	DP
Aldrete	.944	3	4	13	1	3
Dempsey	.926	9	9	16	2	2
Fitzgerald	.947	32	35	55	5	10
Luciano	.915	29	30	45	7	9
Whiteman	1.000	5	2	6	0	1
Wilson	.964	42	45	90	5	18

Outfield	PCT	G	PO	A	E	DP
Adkins	.955	14	20	1	1	0
Aldrete	1.000	7	1	0	0	0
Auerbach	.917	6	11	0	1	0
Bishop	1.000	2	3	0	0	0
Flores	.941	19	31	1	2	0
Gonzalez	1.000	5	7	2	0	0
Labour	.967	93	137	10	5	2
Munguia	.988	82	159	2	2	1
Pomares	1.000	22	27	2	0	0
Quinn	.959	26	45	2	2	1
Rincones	1.000	21	20	0	0	0
Smith	.959	51	69	2	3	1
Williams	.950	22	36	2	2	1
Wyatt	1.000	5	8	0	0	0

SAN JOSE GIANTS

LOW-A WEST

Batting	B-T	HT	WT	DOB	AVG	vLH	vRH	G	AB	R	H	2B	3B	HR	RBI	BB	HBP	SH	SF	SO	SB	CS	SLG	OBP
Arteaga, Aeverson	R-R	6-1	170	3-16-03	.000	--	.000	1	3	0	0	0	0	0	0	0	0	0	0	1	0	0	.000	.000
Auerbach, Brett	R-R	5-9	185	8-27-98	.342	.375	.333	34	117	23	40	11	2	2	17	22	3	0	3	29	12	5	.521	.448
Bailey, Patrick	B-R	6-1	210	5-29-99	.322	.321	.322	47	177	45	57	16	0	7	24	28	1	0	1	47	1	1	.531	.415
Bishop, Hunter	L-R	6-5	210	6-25-98	.000	.000	.000	2	8	1	0	0	0	0	0	1	0	0	0	7	0	0	.000	.111
Bone, Rodolfo	R-R	5-11	170	3-22-00	.238	.200	.245	27	63	7	15	3	1	2	7	3	3	2	2	15	1	1	.413	.296
Canario, Alexander	R-R	6-1	165	5-7-00	.235	.282	.226	65	238	43	56	14	3	9	29	33	0	0	3	79	15	3	.433	.325
Emery, Robert	R-R	6-0	210	10-22-96	.294	.333	.286	5	17	2	5	1	0	2	2	2	0	0	0	2	0	1	.706	.368
Flores, Ronaldo	R-R	6-0	175	5-17-02	.000	--	.000	1	3	0	0	0	0	0	0	0	0	0	0	1	0	0	.000	.000
Flores, Tyler	L-L	6-2	185	1-24-96	.294	1.000	.250	5	17	3	5	1	0	0	0	2	0	0	0	3	0	0	.353	.368
Frechette, Garrett	L-L	6-3	200	12-31-00	.219	.267	.212	31	114	12	25	3	1	1	12	7	1	0	1	39	1	0	.289	.268
Freed, Harrison	R-R	5-11	205	5-13-98	.233	.171	.246	70	236	27	55	8	0	8	38	20	11	0	0	78	2	1	.369	.322
Gaskins, Najee	R-R	6-0	185	9-7-97	.281	.111	.313	15	57	8	16	3	0	1	6	2	2	1	0	14	1	0	.386	.328
Genoves, Ricardo	R-R	6-2	190	5-14-99	.338	.333	.339	38	136	30	46	11	0	6	24	22	3	0	0	29	0	0	.551	.441
Glowenke, Jimmy	R-R	5-10	200	6-5-99	.256	.154	.278	97	360	61	92	25	2	13	51	49	15	0	1	100	3	0	.444	.367
Layer, Abdiel	B-R	6-2	170	8-9-98	.212	.231	.207	84	307	46	65	11	3	13	46	22	3	2	1	123	7	1	.394	.270
Luciano, Marco	R-R	6-2	178	9-10-01	.278	.204	.295	70	266	52	74	14	3	18	50	38	3	0	1	68	5	5	.556	.373
Matos, Luis	R-R	5-11	160	1-28-02	.313	.260	.323	109	451	84	141	35	1	15	86	28	7	0	5	61	21	5	.494	.358
McCray, Grant	L-R	6-2	170	12-7-00	.250	.333	.231	24	80	8	20	2	2	2	12	6	0	1	1	30	4	1	.400	.299
Mora, Edison	R-R	6-2	165	8-13-00	.242	.267	.232	30	99	19	24	2	2	1	11	13	3	1	0	31	0	1	.333	.348
Pena, Fabian	R-R	5-11	205	10-18-96	.209	.214	.208	27	91	10	19	5	0	4	13	4	1	0	0	29	1	0	.396	.250
Pomares, Jairo	L-R	6-1	185	8-4-00	.372	.296	.384	51	199	45	74	22	0	14	44	15	7	0	3	54	0	0	.693	.429
Rodriguez, Yorlis	R-R	6-0	187	7-20-99	.250	.429	.224	27	112	21	28	7	0	4	10	6	4	0	0	21	0	1	.420	.311
Santos, Ghordy	B-R	6-1	177	9-2-99	.317	.267	.326	24	101	17	32	5	1	1	19	9	1	0	0	27	5	1	.416	.378
Schmitt, Casey	R-R	6-2	215	3-1-99	.247	.304	.234	64	251	36	62	14	1	8	29	22	5	0	2	44	2	2	.406	.318
Smith, Armani	R-R	6-4	215	7-19-98	.339	.769	.217	15	59	12	20	3	1	4	14	2	1	0	1	11	2	0	.627	.365
Toribio, Luis	L-R	6-1	185	9-28-00	.229	.095	.248	94	340	59	78	20	1	7	39	63	2	1	2	113	2	1	.356	.351
Williams, Carter	L-R	6-3	210	1-14-98	.262	.320	.255	54	225	29	59	14	4	7	37	13	1	2	2	49	6	3	.453	.303
Wright, Max	L-R	6-3	215	1-8-98	.143	.000	.167	3	7	0	1	0	0	0	0	2	0	0	0	4	0	0	.143	.125
Wyatt, Tyler	R-R	5-11	185	12-9-96	.214	.333	.167	13	42	6	9	3	0	0	6	2	0	0	0	9	0	0	.500	.340

Pitching	B-T	HT	WT	DOB	W	L	ERA	G	GS	CG	SV	IP	H	R	ER	HR	BB	SO	AVG	vLH	vRH	K/9	BB/9
Adames, Abel	R-R	6-5	190	12-8-95	3	0	3.86	17	0	0	0	30	29	15	13	2	17	37	.252	.238	.260	10.98	5.04
Armstrong, Ivan	R-R	6-5	247	7-27-00	4	1	1.88	20	0	0	2	38	24	10	8	0	14	43	.180	.188	.172	10.10	3.29
Beck, Tristan	R-R	6-4	165	6-24-96	2	0	4.91	2	0	0	0	7	9	5	4	1	1	5	.290	.400	.238	6.14	1.23
Bednar, Will	R-R	6-2	229	6-13-00	0	1	1.80	2	2	0	0	5	6	2	1	0	3	.273	.444	.154	5.40	0.00
Berroa, Prelander	R-R	5-11	170	4-18-00	5	6	3.56	24	24	0	0	99	79	52	39	13	53	135	.220	.270	.179	12.31	4.83
Castillo, Wilkelma	R-R	6-0	170	1-6-00	3	0	3.69	28	0	0	1	39	25	18	16	5	18	46	.181	.214	.159	10.62	4.15
Crawford, Brooks	R-R	6-4	215	8-19-96	6	1	1.96	32	0	0	4	46	38	12	10	2	7	57	.221	.228	.215	11.15	1.37
Crump, Justin	R-R	6-3	215	12-1-95	4	3	5.94	23	0	0	1	33	32	30	22	2	25	38	.258	.327	.203	10.26	6.75
Harrison, Kyle	R-L	6-2	200	8-12-01	4	3	3.19	23	23	0	0	99	86	43	35	3	52	157	.232	.302	.207	14.32	4.74
Helvey, Clay	R-R	6-2	195	2-14-97	3	5	3.06	39	0	0	10	53	38	22	18	4	20	83	.240	.226	.179	14.09	3.40
Jensen, Wil	R-R	6-4	180	9-2-97	7	3	3.59	23	19	0	0	103	96	46	41	12	25	109	.242	.251	.235	9.56	2.19
King, Haydn	L-L	6-2	205	11-14-98	2	2	5.31	22	1	0	0	39	38	24	23	6	21	35	.255	.293	.241	8.08	4.85
Labrador, Jorge	R-R	6-1	180	3-9-99	2	0	7.36	15	0	0	0	18	14	16	15	3	20	22	.212	.120	.268	10.80	9.82
Long, Sammy	L-L	6-1	185	7-8-95	0	0	0.00	1	0	0	0	1	1	0	0	0	0	2	.250	.000	.333	18.00	0.00
McDonald, Trevor	R-R	6-2	180	2-26-01	1	1	10.13	1	1	0	0	3	4	7	3	1	3	2	.333	.200	.429	6.75	10.13
Moreno, Luis	R-R	6-2	174	8-3-98	1	1	8.74	6	0	0	0	11	11	13	11	1	12	10	.268	.250	.294	7.94	9.53
Murphy, Ryan	R-R	6-1	190	10-8-99	4	2	2.96	15	15	0	0	76	59	33	25	11	18	116	.215	.176	.252	13.74	2.13
Pagan, Kanoa	R-R	6-2	190	9-29-98	0	0	9.82	2	0	0	0	4	3	4	4	1	4	4	.214	.286	.143	9.82	9.82
Ragsdale, Carson	R-R	6-8	225	5-25-98	8	6	4.43	24	24	0	0	114	107	61	56	13	45	167	.245	.234	.253	13.22	3.56
Reich, Clay	R-R	6-3	210	4-15-97	3	0	1.73	16	0	0	1	26	17	5	5	2	9	47	.200	.176	.216	16.27	3.12
Rodriguez, Randy	R-R	6-0	166	9-5-99	3	1	3.74	32	0	0	2	62	44	12	12	0	23	101	.193	.217	.176	14.66	3.34
Roupp, Landen	R-R	6-2	205	9-10-98	0	0	0.00	1	0	0	0	2	1	0	0	0	0	2	.143	.250	.000	9.00	0.00
Sanchez, Aaron	R-R	6-4	210	7-1-92	0	1	6.23	1	1	0	0	4	4	3	3	1	3	3	.222	.000	.400	4.15	0.00
Sanchez, Juan	L-L	6-2	165	11-12-00	4	2	4.97	31	0	0	1	51	49	37	28	3	13	66	.249	.309	.225	11.72	2.31
Swiney, Nick	R-L	6-3	185	2-12-99	7	7	0.74	7	7	0	0	24	16	4	2	0	12	42	.178	.231	.169	15.53	4.44
Tona, Jesus	R-R	5-10	170	3-30-96	1	0	3.65	10	0	0	2	12	14	6	5	0	2	11	.280	.250	.300	8.03	1.46
Waites, Cole	R-R	6-3	180	6-10-98	1	0	2.25	10	0	0	2	10	1	1	1	0	4	24	.031	.000	.042	20.90	3.48
Weber, Ty	R-R	6-4	220	3-19-98	3	4	4.50	27	3	0	0	54	63	33	27	7	8	56	.286	.283	.289	9.33	1.33
Wright, Chris	L-L	6-1	205	10-14-98	0	0	1.13	6	0	0	4	8	4	1	1	0	3	17	.143	.111	.158	19.13	3.38

Fielding

Catcher	PCT	G	PO	A	E	DP	PB
Auerbach	.986	14	132	13	2	0	2
Bailey	.986	39	429	58	7	2	7
Bone	1.000	27	194	18	0	0	2
Emery	1.000	2	28	1	0	0	0
Flores	1.000	1	15	0	0	0	1
Genoves	.993	32	404	24	3	2	14
Pena	.986	20	184	22	3	0	5
Wright	1.000	1	6	1	0	0	0

First Base	PCT	G	PO	A	E	DP
Emery	1.000	3	22	0	0	4
Flores	.714	1	5	0	2	0
Frechette	.973	29	171	10	5	19
Genoves	1.000	2	12	1	0	0
Layer	.989	30	175	9	2	10
Mora	1.000	7	32	1	0	4
Toribio	.977	47	328	12	8	26
Wyatt	.953	9	58	3	3	4

Second Base	PCT	G	PO	A	E	DP
Auerbach	.978	13	20	24	1	4
Glowenke	.976	96	160	206	9	46
Layer	1.000	5	7	12	0	2
Mora	1.000	2	2	1	0	0
Rodriguez	1.000	1	1	3	0	0
Santos	.938	3	8	7	1	2
Wyatt	.000	1	0	0	0	0

Third Base	PCT	G	PO	A	E	DP
Auerbach	1.000	3	0	2	0	1
Layer	.000	2	0	0	0	0
Mora	.909	11	7	13	2	1
Rodriguez	.864	26	10	28	6	0
Schmitt	.972	50	27	76	3	6
Toribio	.854	29	8	33	7	4
Wyatt	1.000	2	1	6	0	0

Shortstop	PCT	G	PO	A	E	DP
Arteaga	1.000	1	0	1	0	0
Glowenke	1.000	1	0	1	0	0
Layer	.934	46	64	106	12	18
Luciano	.929	60	80	115	15	26
Santos	.864	14	8	30	6	3

Outfield	PCT	G	PO	A	E	DP
Auerbach	1.000	3	7	0	0	0
Bishop	1.000	1	1	0	0	0
Canario	.980	56	92	4	2	0
Flores	1.000	4	5	0	0	0
Freed	.956	67	84	3	4	1
Gaskins	1.000	17	25	0	0	0
Layer	1.000	1	2	0	0	0
Matos	.968	104	177	4	6	1
McCray	.963	24	51	1	2	1
Mora	1.000	11	18	0	0	0
Pomares	.915	29	41	2	4	0
Smith	.952	14	20	0	1	0
Williams	.966	43	57	0	2	0
Wyatt	1.000	1	3	0	0	0

ACL GIANTS — ROOKIE

ARIZONA COMPLEX LEAGUE

Batting	B-T	HT	WT	DOB	AVG	vLH	vRH	G	AB	R	H	2B	3B	HR	RBI	BB	HBP	SH	SF	SO	SB	CS	SLG	OBP
Adkins, Kwan	L-L	6-2	195	10-2-96	.299	.438	.255	26	67	17	20	2	1	5	18	10	3	0	1	28	4	2	.582	.407
Alexander Basabe, Luis	B-R	6-0	180	8-26-96	.370	.300	.412	11	27	5	10	3	0	1	3	6	1	0	0	11	0	0	.593	.500
Arteaga, Aeverson	R-R	6-1	170	3-16-03	.294	.383	.267	56	197	42	58	12	1	9	43	23	2	0	4	69	8	0	.503	.367
Bailey, Patrick	B-R	6-1	210	5-29-99	.400	--	.400	2	5	3	2	0	0	0	0	2	0	0	1	0	0	0	.400	.571
Bell, George	R-R	6-4	215	5-8-98	.220	.167	.234	49	141	19	31	6	1	4	20	17	4	1	0	58	4	2	.362	.321
Bericoto, Victor	R-R	6-1	155	12-3-01	.333	.333	.333	7	18	5	6	1	0	2	7	1	0	0	0	6	0	0	.722	.368
Bishop, Hunter	L-R	6-5	210	6-25-98	.160	.143	.167	11	25	5	4	1	0	0	3	5	1	0	1	11	1	1	.200	.313
Brown, Vaun	R-R	6-1	190	6-23-98	.354	.333	.362	25	79	24	28	7	4	2	14	7	12	0	0	29	8	1	.620	.480
Caraballo, Andrew	R-R	6-0	175	4-29-00	.111	.091	.120	13	36	7	4	1	0	0	4	4	1	0	0	9	1	0	.139	.220
Dempsey, Nolan	R-R	6-0	175	9-9-96	.167		.250	4	12	2	2	0	0	0	3	0	0	0		3	1	0	.167	.333
Dues, Damon	L-R	6-0	180	6-21-98	.256	.368	.220	28	78	15	20	3	1	0	11	14	4	0	2	22	2	3	.321	.388
Dupere, Jared	L-R	5-11	200	1-23-99	.263	.269	.261	29	95	21	25	6	1	2	15	12	0	0	0	36	5	0	.411	.346
Flores, Ronaldo	R-R	6-0	175	5-17-02	.280	.273	.282	38	118	13	33	7	1	0	12	5	3	0	2	28	0	0	.356	.322
Forner, Tyler	R-L	5-11	195	10-18-01	.211	.192	.222	36	71	5	15	3	1	0	9	9	1	1	3	28	0	1	.282	.298
Frechette, Garrett	L-L	6-3	200	12-31-00	.331	.167	.376	50	169	20	56	13	1	1	28	13	4	0	2	52	2	0	.438	.388
Gaskins, Najee	R-R	6-0	185	9-7-97	.241	.182	.255	19	58	6	14	1	1	2	4	4	0	0	1	20	2	2	.397	.286
Gonzalez, Cesar	R-R	5-11	206	5-8-01	.258	.154	.286	20	62	5	16	5	1	1	9	2	0	0	1	22	0	0	.419	.277
Gonzalez, Jacob	R-R	6-3	190	6-26-98	.301	.381	.270	48	153	27	46	9	0	7	36	11	7	0	7	33	1	0	.497	.360
Guzman, Angel	R-R	6-0	155	5-17-00	.200	.000	.333	3	5	0	1	0	0	0	1	2	1	0	0	1	0	0	.200	.500
Hilson, P.J.	R-R	5-11	175	8-25-00	.196	.174	.202	43	112	26	22	7	1	0	8	18	7	0	1	49	7	2	.277	.341
Juliana, Richgelon	R-R	6-0	170	5-30-00	.229	.182	.250	16	35	6	8	1	0	0	2	7	0	0	0	15	0	0	.257	.357
McCray, Grant	L-R	6-2	170	12-7-00	.309	.333	.294	21	55	16	17	3	1	1	6	9	0	0	1	20	3	1	.455	.400
McIntyre, Donovan	L-L	6-2	165	12-10-02	.203	.077	.235	18	64	15	13	2	1	1	4	10	2	0	0	30	5	1	.313	.329
Medina, Omar	B-R	5-11	170	12-20-99	.200	.200	.200	14	30	4	6	0	0	0	3	3	2	0	0	11	0	0	.200	.314
Mora, Edison	R-R	6-2	165	8-13-00	.273	.276	.272	33	110	25	30	4	2	2	19	12	6	0	1	23	8	0	.400	.372
Murr III, Irvin	R-R	6-4	220	3-12-03	.109	.200	.065	16	46	3	5	0	0	1	3	3	1	0	0	22	0	1	.174	.180
Pena, Jean	R-R	6-1	175	12-22-00	.182	.067	.225	42	110	13	20	6	0	3	14	26	3	0	0	56	1	2	.318	.353
Peralta, Jose	B-R	5-11	160	7-4-01	.217	.167	.235	9	23	2	5	0	0	0	3	4	0	0	0	11	1	0	.217	.333
Rodriguez, Anthony	R-R	6-2	165	9-20-02	.224	.225	.224	53	165	26	37	7	1	4	23	29	4	0	1	62	5	0	.352	.352
Rodriguez, Yorlis	R-R	6-0	187	7-20-99	.316	.286	.328	25	79	11	25	4	1	2	11	7	1	0	1	16	1	1	.468	.375
Rosario, Dilan	R-R	6-0	175	6-16-01	.209	.233	.200	53	158	21	33	5	3	2	17	19	0	0	1	59	1	3	.316	.292
Santana, Rayner	R-R	6-2	180	8-15-02	.237	.167	.260	30	97	9	23	5	0	4	14	6	4	0	1	46	0	1	.412	.306
Santos, Ghordy	B-R	6-1	177	9-2-99	.357	.429	.333	10	28	8	10	1	2	2	8	4	0	0	0	4	1	1	.750	.438
Sivira, Anyesber	R-R	5-9	155	1-9-00	.158	.000	.188	9	19	0	3	1	0	0	2	2	0	0	4	1	0		.211	.238
Suarez, Alexander	R-R	6-2	160	12-20-01	.311	.321	.307	55	193	43	60	15	2	6	25	10	11	0	0	72	16	4	.503	.379
Sugastey, Adrian	R-R	6-1	170	10-23-02	.358	.353	.360	43	148	23	53	6	0	2	25	12	1	0	2	26	1	0	.439	.405
Torrealba, Yeiver	R-R	5-11	145	10-26-01	.256	.346	.217	32	86	17	22	3	2	0	11	18	4	1	0	30	7	1	.337	.407
Velasquez, Diego	B-R	6-1	150	10-1-03	.213	.282	.190	46	160	19	34	3	0	0	10	13	3	3	1	25	2	1	.231	.282
Williams, Javeyan	L-L	5-9	160	6-27-97	.264	.235	.273	30	72	17	19	1	0	2	6	17	2	1	0	25	10	1	.361	.418
Wright, Max	L-R	6-3	215	1-8-98	.267	.375	.227	19	60	11	16	7	0	1	9	4	3	0	1	18	1	0	.433	.338
Wyatt, Logan	L-R	6-4	230	11-15-97	.242	.091	.318	10	33	7	8	2	0	1	4	2	0	0	0	10	0	0	.394	.286
Wyatt, Tyler	R-R	5-11	185	12-9-96	.308	.333	.300	5	13	2	4	1	0	1	1	1	1	0	0	1	1	0	.615	.400

Pitching	B-T	HT	WT	DOB	W	L	ERA	G	GS	CG	SV	IP	H	R	ER	HR	BB	SO	AVG	vLH	vRH	K/9	BB/9
Acosta, Cristian	R-R	6-0	170	9-19-99	3	2	7.17	14	0	0	0	21	17	18	17	4	11	31	.210	.182	.220	13.08	4.64
Adames, Abel	R-R	6-5	190	12-8-95	0	0	0.00	1	0	0	0	1	0	0	0	0	2	0	.000	.000	.000	18.00	0.00
Beck, Tristan	R-R	6-4	165	6-24-96	0	3	7.71	6	6	0	0	12	17	11	10	0	6	17	.333	.316	.344	13.11	4.63
Bednar, Will	R-R	6-2	229	6-13-00	0	0	0.00	2	2	0	0	2	0	0	0	0	1	3	.000	.000	.000	13.50	4.50
Bonilla, Jason	R-R	6-0	165	8-30-98	1	2	5.57	17	0	0	0	21	15	17	13	0	15	39	.208	.143	.235	16.71	6.43
Brown, Marvin	L-L	6-1	177	5-21-01	2	0	3.38	8	0	0	0	13	12	6	5	0	8	20	.240	.231	.243	13.50	5.40
Civada, Odue	R-R	6-1	165	4-5-02	1	4	7.86	10	4	0	0	26	36	24	23	5	10	40	.321	.378	.284	13.67	3.42
Cruz, Jose	R-R	6-1	178	5-18-00	3	1	4.44	19	0	0	5	24	24	16	12	0	9	42	.258	.182	.300	15.53	3.33
De La Cruz, Lisander	R-R	6-2	185	8-16-01	2	1	6.07	15	4	0	0	30	37	26	20	2	20	37	.296	.324	.286	11.22	6.07
Dula, Hunter	L-R	6-1	195	3-8-99	0	1	1.80	10	0	0	1	10	6	2	2	0	4	17	.171	.222	.154	15.30	3.60
Garcia, Jorge	R-R	6-0	185	5-10-02	2	2	5.04	6	4	0	0	25	22	14	14	5	6	31	.242	.132	.321	11.16	2.16
Gates, Evan	R-R	6-0	210	1-13-98	1	1	4.50	9	0	0	0	10	12	6	5	3	2	14	.300	.190	.421	12.60	1.80
Gomez, Jesus	L-L	6-2	180	4-1-01	1	3	4.24	12	1	0	1	23	20	11	11	2	11	34	.244	.333	.219	13.11	4.24
Gonzalez, Marco	L-L	6-1	180	12-8-97	1	0	3.09	8	0	0	0	12	7	5	4	1	7	12	.171	.200	.167	9.26	5.40
Halstead, Ryan	L-R	6-5	220	5-13-92	0	0	0.00	3	0	0	0	3	1	0	0	0	1	5	.100	.000	.125	15.00	3.00

Name	B-T	HT	WT	DOB	W	L	ERA	G	GS	CG	SV	IP	H	R	ER	HR	BB	SO	AVG	vLH	vRH	K/9	BB/9
Kemlage, Joe	B-L	6-1	220	1-19-99	1	0	1.42	5	0	0	0	6	5	4	1	0	0	9	.179	.222	.158	12.79	0.00
Labrador, Jorge	R-R	6-1	180	3-9-99	1	0	5.94	14	0	0	2	17	15	11	11	0	12	35	.231	.143	.273	18.90	6.48
Lonsway, Seth	L-L	6-3	195	10-7-98	0	0	7.20	4	4	0	0	5	5	4	4	1	0	10	.250	.000	.385	18.00	0.00
Lumbert, Evan	L-R	6-0	175	5-10-96	2	2	1.59	15	0	0	2	23	18	10	4	2	11	25	.234	.239		9.93	4.37
Martinez, Rafael	R-R	6-0	160	4-18-00	2	6	7.88	13	9	0	0	48	64	47	42	8	28	55	.309	.300	.315	10.31	5.25
McDonald, Trevor	R-R	6-2	180	2-26-01	2	3	3.86	15	13	0	0	68	67	35	29	3	31	69	.266	.238	.286	9.18	4.12
Medina, Nomar	L-L	6-0	190	11-23-02	2	1	2.57	14	3	0	1	35	34	12	10	1	12	37	.258	.440	.215	9.51	3.09
Mercedes, Manuel	R-R	6-3	162	9-21-02	3	3	5.11	14	13	0	0	56	61	38	32	5	25	62	.277	.325	.252	9.91	3.99
Mikulski, Matt	L-L	6-4	205	5-8-99	0	0	1.80	4	4	0	0	5	4	2	1	0	3	5	.235	.000	.286	9.00	5.40
Moreno, Luis	R-R	6-2	174	8-3-98	4	1	2.66	14	4	0	0	41	26	14	12	4	11	51	.183	.275	.132	11.29	2.43
Morreale, Nick	R-R	6-5	220	7-27-97	0	0	1.46	7	7	0	0	12	10	2	2	0	4	20	.213	.182	.240	14.59	2.92
Mullings, Jose	R-R	6-3	170	12-22-99	3	2	3.58	9	1	0	1	28	31	19	11	3	12	27	.272	.295	.257	8.78	3.90
Myrick, Tyler	R-R	6-0	205	6-25-98	1	1	6.43	8	0	0	1	7	11	8	5	1	1	16	.333	.385	.300	20.57	1.29
Olsen, Mat	R-R	5-11	185	7-8-00	0	0	0.00	3	0	0	0	3	0	0	0	0	0	5	.000	.000	.000	15.00	0.00
Pagan, Kanoa	R-R	6-2	190	9-29-98	0	1	1.93	5	3	0	0	5	4	5	1	1	4	2	.235	.429	.100	3.86	7.71
Paulino, Freddery	R-R	6-2	181	9-12-00	4	1	4.97	6	6	0	0	29	33	19	16	3	10	29	.277	.167	.315	9.00	3.10
Ramirez, Yoniel	R-R	6-0	180	5-27-01	0	3	7.82	15	1	0	0	25	31	23	22	1	13	19	.316	.275	.345	6.75	4.62
Rivera, Blake	R-R	6-4	225	1-9-98	3	0	2.61	5	0	0	0	10	8	3	3	1	3	14	.211	.211	.211	12.19	2.61
Roupp, Landen	R-R	6-2	205	9-10-98	0	0	3.00	4	0	0	0	6	5	2	2	0	1	12	.227	.000	.313	18.00	1.50
Silva, Eric	R-R	6-1	185	10-3-02	0	1	36.00	2	0	0	1	4	4	4	0	0	3	2	.571	1.000	.500	18.00	27.00
Sinacola, Nick	L-R	6-1	190	10-29-99	0	0	0.00	5	0	0	0	6	2	0	0	0	0	11	.091	.091	.091	15.63	0.00
Standlee, Brett	R-R	6-4	223	9-14-98	0	1	0.00	9	0	0	6	9	5	1	1	0	2	9	.156	.167	.150	9.00	2.00
Suarez, Willian	R-R	6-3	175	3-21-98	4	1	4.40	15	0	0	2	29	26	18	14	3	19	39	.245	.216	.261	12.24	5.97
Swiney, Nick	R-L	6-3	185	2-12-99	0	0	1.13	5	5	0	0	8	7	1	1	0	6	16	.233	.167	.250	18.00	6.75
Tona, Jesus	R-R	5-10	170	3-30-96	1	0	0.00	7	0	0	0	8	5	1	0	0	1	10	.167	.071	.250	11.74	1.17
Vargas, Sonny	L-L	6-2	180	11-8-00	5	5	5.33	16	10	0	2	54	45	36	32	6	18	69	.226	.227	.226	11.50	3.00
Villers, Ian	R-R	6-6	245	9-1-00	1	0	2.08	9	0	0	0	8	4	2	2	1	0	12	.242	.154	.300	12.46	0.00
Vinicio, Esmerlin	L-L	6-2	141	1-31-03	3	3	2.64	14	11	0	0	58	49	22	17	2	29	70	.240	.239	.241	10.86	4.50
Waites, Cole	R-R	6-3	180	6-10-98	1	0	0.00	3	0	0	0	3	0	1	0	0	2	7	.000	.000	.000	21.00	6.00

Fielding

C: Flores 26, Gonzalez 20, Guzman 2, Medina 2, Santana 9, Sugastey 40, Wright 18.
1B: Caraballo 4, Dues 2, Flores 10, Frechette 43, Gonzalez 36, Medina 2, Mora 4, Pena 12, Santana 1, Wyatt 5, Wyatt 2.
2B: Caraballo 6, Dempsey 1, Dues 18, Mora 9, Pena 1, Peralta 8, Rodriguez 1, Rodriguez 5, Rosario 31, Santos 5, Sivira 4, Torrealba 24, Velasquez 11.
3B: Arteaga 1, Gonzalez 1, Mora 4, Murr III 7, Pena 30, Rodriguez 51, Rodriguez 21, Rosario 3, Sivira 2, Torrealba 1.
SS: Arteaga 54, Dempsey 2, Dues 1, Rodriguez 1, Rosario 21, Santos 2, Sivira 1, Velasquez 35.
OF: Adkins 25, Alexander Basabe 8, Bell 41, Bericoto 4, Bishop 11, Brown 26, Dues 2, Dupere 31, Forner 31, Frechette 4, Gaskins 17, Gonzalez 2, Hilson 41, Juliana 11, McCray 9, McIntyre 18, Mora 17, Suarez 54, Williams 28, Wyatt 2.

DSL GIANTS   ROOKIE

DOMINICAN SUMMER LEAGUE

Batting	B-T	HT	WT	DOB	AVG	vLH	vRH	G	AB	R	H	2B	3B	HR	RBI	BB	HBP	SH	SF	SO	SB	CS	SLG	OBP
Anza, Rajean	R-R	5-11	160	5-18-03	.196	.333	.180	20	56	6	11	4	0	0	8	10	0	0	3	12	3	0	.268	.304
Arrieta, Randy	R-R	5-11	150	11-1-03	.207	.333	.192	22	58	13	12	2	0	0	1	11	3	0	0	27	6	2	.241	.361
Astudillo, Jose	R-R	5-10	150	2-27-04	.208	.167	.213	21	53	8	11	3	0	0	6	5	1	0	1	5	3	0	.264	.283
Bautista, Saul	B-R	6-0	145	4-20-04	.194	.188	.196	38	108	14	21	5	0	1	10	11	0	0	0	49	5	1	.269	.269
Camacho, Jhosward	B-R	5-10	146	7-9-04	.265	.238	.269	43	151	22	40	6	1	1	22	11	0	0	3	30	10	2	.338	.309
Cardozo, Gustavo	R-R	6-1	160	10-9-03	.300	.389	.286	42	130	18	39	10	1	0	11	15	1	0	0	16	8	3	.392	.377
Cassiani, Estanlin	L-L	5-11	155	12-30-02	.290	.500	.268	19	62	14	18	4	2	0	4	3	3	2	0	8	10	1	.419	.353
Castillo, Javier	R-R	6-1	170	11-14-03	.255	.000	.286	17	47	5	12	4	0	0	7	4	1	0	1	11	1	0	.340	.321
Ferrer, Brayan	B-R	6-0	170	12-26-03	.231	.333	.217	25	78	9	18	6	0	0	8	6	2	0	2	18	0	0	.308	.295
Francisco, Javier	R-R	6-2	162	11-11-02	.188	.222	.184	32	85	11	16	3	2	2	15	13	6	0	2	18	1	0	.341	.330
Gonzalez, Diego	B-R	5-11	155	9-22-03	.270	.167	.290	17	37	5	10	4	0	0	8	1	0	0	0	5	1	1	.378	.289
Guzman, Brian	R-R	6-1	192	5-13-04	.205	.167	.212	14	39	6	8	0	0	0	3	6	1	0	0	18	1	0	.205	.326
Ladera, Oswaldo	R-R	6-2	170	2-14-03	.167	.167	.167	31	84	8	14	2	1	1	5	6	1	0	1	28	1	3	.250	.228
Laya, Derwin	R-R	6-3	187	9-15-03	.262	.300	.255	40	130	27	34	10	0	3	20	18	5	0	0	26	1	2	.408	.373
Lemos, Yeison	R-R	6-0	165	9-6-02	.225	.143	.238	44	151	32	34	8	2	5	29	14	4	0	1	49	5	0	.404	.306
Lespe, Wueslly	L-R	6-0	165	4-23-03	.244	.500	.222	31	78	16	19	1	2	2	14	18	2	0	3	29	5	2	.385	.386
Maduro, Jediael	L-L	6-1	188	12-26-03	.250	.400	.230	29	84	14	21	3	0	1	17	20	2	0	1	16	2	1	.321	.402
Montero, Eduardo	L-R	5-10	150	10-26-03	.205	.000	.235	15	39	5	8	3	0	0	8	7	0	0	0	7	0	0	.282	.326
Peralta, Ramon	R-R	5-11	165	10-2-03	.216	.207	.217	49	167	33	36	10	0	4	17	29	5	0	2	48	10	3	.347	.345
Perez, Onil	R-R	6-1	187	9-10-02	.291	.167	.308	36	103	24	30	5	0	2	15	30	0	0	1	15	6	4	.398	.448
Pierre, Mauricio	R-R	6-3	180	11-23-03	.256	.278	.252	40	133	25	34	7	1	5	23	14	2	0	0	44	6	5	.436	.336
Polo, Angel	R-R	5-11	184	11-18-03	.182	.000	.200	4	11	2	2	0	0	0	1	2	0	0	0	4	0	0	.182	.308
Quintas, Cesar	R-R	6-1	175	3-25-03	.309	.333	.304	27	81	21	25	6	0	2	13	10	9	0	2	16	2	0	.457	.431
Ramos, Jose	R-R	5-11	143	10-25-02	.245	.286	.242	30	98	18	24	3	4	3	15	11	1	0	0	24	6	3	.449	.327
Rayo, Elian	R-R	6-0	202	3-4-03	.243	.300	.232	38	115	19	28	6	1	2	19	17	2	0	0	27	1	1	.365	.387
Reyes, Samuel	R-R	6-0	170	1-27-03	.305	.263	.313	43	131	29	40	9	5	1	18	18	13	0	2	20	8	3	.473	.433
Rodriguez, Samuel	B-R	5-11	161	10-22-03	.236	.067	.282	44	140	29	33	7	0	1	15	21	2	0	1	33	11	4	.307	.341
Rosario, Brandy	R-R	6-0	145	3-24-04	.148	.000	.176	22	61	8	9	3	0	1	4	4	5	0	0	33	0	0	.246	.257
Sandoval, Julian	L-L	6-2	175	2-4-04	.222	.111	.245	38	117	13	26	6	0	4	17	11	6	0	3	37	4	3	.376	.311
Tremaria, Freddy	R-R	5-11	165	4-28-03	.169	.083	.189	23	65	11	11	5	0	0	8	10	1	0	1	22	0	0	.246	.286
Urena, Juanel	R-R	5-10	165	3-2-04	.198	.143	.203	28	86	17	17	2	0	0	9	22	1	0	1	31	9	3	.221	.364
Verbel, Diego	R-R	6-0	162	7-24-02	.148	.200	.143	23	54	9	8	2	1	0	6	10	1	0	1	25	0	0	.222	.288

SAN FRANCISCO GIANTS

Villadiego, Fabio	R-R	5-11	140	3-13-04	.200	.200	.200	34	85	21	17	2	0	0	9	13	5	0	1	21	4	1	.224	.337
Villegas, Diego	L-L	6-0	170	3-23-04	.202	.143	.207	37	99	16	20	3	1	0	11	23	2	0	0	21	2	2	.253	.363

Pitching	B-T	HT	WT	DOB	W	L	ERA	G	GS	CG	SV	IP	H	R	ER	HR	BB	SO	AVG	vLH	vRH	K/9	BB/9
Azor, Anderson	R-R	6-0	162	10-9-03	2	1	6.41	15	0	0	0	20	29	22	14	2	7	14	.312	.393	.277	6.41	3.20
Caraballo, Jan	R-R	6-6	181	10-20-03	3	2	6.30	15	0	0	3	20	23	18	14	1	13	15	.288	.526	.213	6.75	5.85
Castillo, Leandro	R-R	6-1	160	7-1-02	2	2	3.92	15	0	0	3	21	14	10	9	1	13	19	.203	.167	.216	8.27	5.66
Castillo, Luis	L-L	5-11	170	8-24-02	0	2	8.10	15	1	0	1	17	15	18	15	1	11	16	.227	.333	.204	8.64	5.94
Chires, Samir	R-R	6-0	160	9-17-03	2	0	3.33	13	3	0	0	27	37	14	10	1	6	12	.336	.351	.329	4.00	2.00
Duarte, Pavel	L-L	6-1	164	10-29-03	0	0	4.66	10	0	0	0	19	17	14	10	2	6	19	.224	.222	.224	8.84	2.79
Espinoza, Daniel	L-L	6-0	168	11-25-03	0	0	15.19	9	0	0	0	5	6	10	9	1	17	4	.273	.500	.250	6.75	28.69
Estrada, Ricardo	L-L	6-0	170	6-25-02	1	5	3.05	10	10	0	0	38	30	21	13	1	23	38	.216	.286	.203	8.92	5.40
Flores, Junior	R-R	6-1	170	2-13-02	2	1	3.50	16	0	0	3	18	10	9	7	1	17	25	.154	.100	.178	12.50	8.50
Franco, Marlon	R-R	6-2	165	9-18-02	2	1	5.52	12	0	0	0	15	15	13	9	3	7	17	.259	.313	.238	10.43	4.30
Gonzalez, Jose	R-R	6-1	180	6-15-02	3	2	5.60	14	0	0	1	18	17	13	11	1	16	21	.254	.200	.277	10.70	8.15
Gonzalez, Victor	R-R	6-1	170	4-4-02	0	0	10.32	12	0	0	0	11	13	15	13	0	16	12	.283	.214	.313	9.53	12.71
Grullon, Johnny	L-L	6-0	170	7-4-02	2	2	4.75	8	8	0	0	30	26	19	16	4	10	27	.234	.133	.250	8.01	2.97
Jimenez, Rolfi	R-R	6-0	150	10-8-02	4	1	2.35	11	11	0	0	46	46	21	12	3	17	37	.260	.308	.240	7.24	3.33
Lopez, Carlos	L-L	6-0	165	8-31-02	1	2	3.66	14	0	0	1	20	11	9	8	0	12	27	.175	.231	.160	12.36	5.49
Malave, German	R-R	6-1	187	10-23-00	1	2	3.46	9	7	0	0	26	24	21	10	0	16	23	.238	.208	.247	7.96	5.54
Maldonado, Gerelmi	R-R	6-2	170	12-21-03	2	1	5.22	13	6	0	0	29	25	19	17	0	17	30	.227	.289	.185	9.20	5.22
Manzano, Mikell	R-R	6-0	140	11-30-02	3	4	3.54	12	11	0	0	48	50	30	19	3	5	70	.249	.265	.241	13.03	0.93
Martinez, Jorge	R-R	6-0	161	11-6-01	0	4	4.50	7	7	0	0	26	27	20	13	0	11	27	.270	.355	.232	9.35	3.81
Monegro, Roberto	R-R	5-10	145	11-15-01	2	2	4.19	14	0	0	1	19	18	10	9	3	3	22	.240	.385	.163	10.24	1.40
Mora, Miguel	R-R	6-2	187	11-4-01	2	2	3.09	10	10	0	0	44	28	20	15	3	16	47	.181	.197	.170	9.69	3.30
Moreno, Angel	R-R	6-2	170	2-22-01	1	0	5.57	14	1	0	2	21	19	13	13	0	17	12	.250	.259	.245	5.14	7.29
Morillo, Juan	R-R	5-10	145	11-1-02	1	2	11.08	14	0	0	0	13	14	16	16	4	17	17	.286	.273	.289	11.77	11.77
Mota, Ismael	R-R	6-2	165	8-4-01	1	2	5.71	9	1	0	0	17	18	13	11	3	3	17	.281	.333	.256	8.83	1.56
Nunez, David	R-R	5-11	165	12-13-01	0	0	3.00	2	0	0	1	3	3	1	1	0	2	3	.250	1.000	.182	9.00	6.00
Ochoa, Yonathan	R-R	6-3	175	10-18-02	1	3	4.45	8	8	0	0	32	27	18	16	1	7	27	.223	.302	.179	7.52	1.95
Palencia, Brayan	R-R	5-11	142	1-14-03	3	1	1.96	15	0	0	2	18	13	5	4	0	4	23	.197	.278	.167	11.29	1.96
Perez, Argenis	L-L	5-10	140	4-30-03	1	3	2.19	11	1	0	0	25	19	8	6	2	10	24	.211	.150	.229	8.76	3.65
Perez, Jose T	R-R	6-2	180	8-9-03	0	0	2.70	4	0	0	0	3	4	2	1	0	1	3	.286	.000	.444	8.10	2.70
Rojas, Jose	R-R	6-1	145	1-2-04	2	0	3.69	9	7	0	0	32	22	13	13	1	15	23	.193	.200	.190	6.54	4.26
Rondon, Daniel	R-R	6-0	190	3-16-03	0	3	6.87	5	4	0	0	18	19	18	14	1	10	18	.268	.316	.250	8.84	4.91
Salas, Ken	R-R	6-2	180	7-30-01	0	2	6.48	11	0	0	0	8	10	10	6	0	8	11	.278	.286	.273	11.88	8.64
Sanchez, Angel	R-R	6-1	164	12-20-02	1	1	6.35	10	0	0	0	11	13	8	8	0	9	13	.283	.294	.276	10.32	7.15
Tortolero, Erasmo	R-R	6-1	188	8-5-02	0	0	1.17	6	0	0	0	8	6	1	1	0	3	3	.214	.250	.188	3.52	3.52
Valenzuela, Cristofer	R-R	6-1	170	10-7-01	1	4	9.93	11	10	0	0	29	38	40	32	2	25	21	.319	.333	.311	6.52	7.76
Vasquez, Fernando	R-R	5-11	180	12-2-01	4	1	5.59	16	0	0	1	19	21	15	12	2	6	16	.276	.296	.265	7.45	2.79
Yepez, Luis	R-R	5-11	165	5-7-02	1	0	7.58	12	0	0	0	19	24	17	16	3	12	17	.316	.333	.306	8.05	5.68

Fielding

C: Anza 19, Castillo 6, Ferrer 13, Gonzalez 15, Montero 14, Perez 25, Polo 1, Tremaria 23.
1B: Anza 1, Astudillo 7, Camacho 28, Castillo 8, Francisco 30, Lespe 11, Maduro 16, Verbel 13.
2B: Astudillo 7, Camacho 9, Cardozo 41, Lespe 7, Ramos 7, Rodriguez 29, Rosario 14.
3B: Astudillo 2, Camacho 2, Francisco 2, Laya 40, Lespe 7, Ramos 12, Rayo 34, Rodriguez 6, Rosario 1, Verbel 3.
SS: Cardozo 1, Lemos 41, Lespe 1, Peralta 47, Ramos 10, Rodriguez 7.
OF: Arrieta 20, Bautista 36, Cassiani 17, Guzman 6, Ladera 29, Maduro 10, Pierre 36, Quintas 22, Reyes 36, Sandoval 28, Urena 27, Verbel 6, Villadiego 31, Villegas 35.

Seattle Mariners

SEASON IN A SENTENCE: Expected to struggle through another rebuilding year, the Mariners instead remained in playoff contention until the final day of the regular season and finished 90-72, their best record in 18 years.

HIGH POINT: The Mariners entered Sept. 20 in third place in the AL West behind the A's and Astros, but promptly swept Oakland in a four-game series on the road to pull into second place.

LOW POINT: In February, a video emerged of Mariners president and CEO Kevin Mather making derogatory remarks about the organization's players in a speech to the Bellevue, Wash. Rotary Club. Mather criticized the English speaking skills of former pitcher Hisashi Iwakuma and current top prospect Julio Rodriguez, called franchise third baseman Kyle Seager "overpaid" and admitted the organization manipulated the service time of outfield prospect Jarred Kelenic. Mather's comments drew swift condemnation from Mariners ownership, Major League Baseball and the MLB Players Association, and he resigned shortly after.

NOTABLE ROOKIES: Righthander Logan Gilbert received his first big league callup in May and stayed in the Mariners rotation the rest of the year, going 6-5, 4.64 with 128 strikeouts in 119.2 innings. Kelenic debuted in May and struggled initially, resulting in a demotion back to Triple-A in June. He returned to the majors for good after the All-Star Break and improved each month, capped by hitting seven of his 14 home runs after Sept. 1. Catcher Cal Raleigh debuted in July and appeared in 47 of the Mariners' final 72 games.

KEY TRANSACTIONS: The Mariners had one of the more productive under-the-radar signings of the offseason when they signed former Mets righthander Chris Flexen to a two-year deal out of the Korea Baseball Organization. Flexen went 14-6, 3.61 in 31 starts, all of which led the team. During the season, the Mariners simultaneously made moves aimed both for the short term and long term at the trade deadline, sending closer Kendall Graveman to the Astros for infielder Abraham Toro and reliever Joe Smith, acquiring pitcher Tyler Anderson from the Pirates for two prospects and acquiring closer Diego Castillo from the Rays for prospect third baseman Austin Shenton and reliever J.T. Chargois. The trade of Graveman angered the team's players, with many using the word "betrayed" to describe seeing him sent to a division rival in the middle of a playoff race.

OPENING DAY SALARY: $64,553,500 (25th).

PLAYERS OF THE YEAR

MAJOR LEAGUE
Ty France
1B/2B
.291/.368/.445
Career-high 18 HR
32 2B, 85 R

MINOR LEAGUE
Julio Rodriguez
OF
(AA/High-A)
.347/.441/.560,
13 HR, 21 SB

ORGANIZATION LEADERS

Batting		*Minimum 250 AB
MAJORS		
*AVG	Ty France	.291
*OPS	Ty France	.812
HR	Mitch Haniger	39
RBI	Kyle Seager	101
MINORS		
*AVG	Julio Rodriguez, Arkansas, Everett	.347
*OBP	Julio Rodriguez, Arkansas, Everett	.441
*SLG	Jose Marmolejos, Tacoma	.672
*OPS	Jose Marmolejos, Tacoma	1.111
R	Noelvi Marte, Everett, Modesto	91
H	Jack Larsen, Arkansas, Everett	121
H	Noelvi Marte, Everett, Modesto	121
H	Jantzen Witte, Tacoma	121
TB	Cade Marlowe, Tacoma, Everett, Modesto	239
2B	Zach DeLoach, Arkansas, Everett	33
3B	Cade Marlowe, Tacoma, Everett, Modesto	10
HR	Cade Marlowe, Tacoma, Everett, Modesto	26
HR	Jose Marmolejos, Tacoma	26
RBI	Cade Marlowe, Tacoma, Everett, Modesto	107
BB	Jack Larsen, Arkansas, Everett	73
SO	Dariel Gomez, Everett, Modesto	151
SB	Victor Labrada, Everett, Modesto	32

Pitching		#Minimum 75 IP
MAJORS		
W	Chris Flexen	14
#ERA	Chris Flexen	3.61
SO	Yusei Kikuchi	163
SV	Drew Steckenrider	14
MINORS		
W	Logan Verrett, Tacoma	11
L	Josias De Los Santos, Modesto	8
#ERA	Matt Brash, Arkansas, Everett	2.31
G	Justin Grimm, Tacoma	45
GS	Darren McCaughan, Tacoma, Arkansas	21
SV	Darin Gillies, Tacoma, Arkansas	10
IP	Darren McCaughan, Tacoma, Arkansas	121
BB	Josias De Los Santos, Modesto	70
SO	Brandon Williamson, Arkansas, Everett	153
#AVG	Matt Brash, Arkansas, Everett	.180

2021 PERFORMANCE

General Manager: Jerry Dipoto. **Farm Director:** Andy McKay. **Scouting Director:** Scott Hunter.

Class	Team	League	W	L	PCT	Finish	Manager
Majors	Seattle Mariners	American	90	72	.556	7th (15)	Scott Servais
Triple-A	Tacoma Rainiers	Triple-A West	78	52	.600	1st (10)	Kristopher Negron
Double-A	Arkansas Travelers	Double-A Central	64	56	.533	4th (10)	Collin Cowgill
High-A	Everett AquaSox	High-A West	61	56	.521	3rd (6)	Louis Boyd
Low-A	Modesto Nuts	Low-A West	64	51	.557	4th (8)	Eric Farris
Rookie	ACL Mariners	Arizona Complex	40	18	.690	2nd (18)	Austin Knight
Rookie	DSL Mariners	Dominican Summer	35	24	.593	10th (46)	Luis Caballero
Overall 2021 Minor League Record			342	257	.571	4th (30)	

ORGANIZATION STATISTICS

SEATTLE MARINERS
AMERICAN LEAGUE

Batting	B-T	HT	WT	DOB	AVG	vLH	vRH	G	AB	R	H	2B	3B	HR	RBI	BB	HBP	SH	SF	SO	SB	CS	SLG	OBP
Bauers, Jake	L-L	6-1	195	10-6-95	.220	.216	.221	72	182	20	40	4	0	2	13	18	2	0	0	51	6	0	.275	.297
2-team total (43 Cleveland)					.209	.231	.203	115	282	27	59	7	0	4	19	30	2	0	0	78	6	1	.277	.290
Bishop, Braden	R-R	6-1	178	8-22-93	.250	.500	.000	8	4	1	1	0	0	0	0	0	0	1	0	2	0	0	.250	.250
Campbell, Eric	R-R	6-3	215	4-9-87	.273	.000	.375	4	11	1	3	0	0	0	1	0	0	0	0	1	0	0	.273	.333
Crawford, J.P.	L-R	6-2	199	1-11-95	.273	.274	.272	160	619	89	169	37	0	9	54	58	5	1	4	114	3	6	.376	.338
Fraley, Jake	L-L	6-0	195	5-25-95	.210	.169	.231	78	214	27	45	7	0	9	36	46	2	1	2	71	10	2	.369	.352
France, Ty	R-R	5-11	217	7-13-94	.291	.311	.280	152	571	85	166	32	1	18	73	46	27	0	6	106	0	0	.445	.368
Godoy, Jose	L-R	5-11	200	10-13-94	.162	.000	.182	16	37	2	6	1	0	0	3	3	0	0	0	14	0	0	.189	.225
Haggerty, Sam	B-R	5-11	175	5-26-94	.186	.107	.224	35	86	15	16	3	0	2	5	6	1	1	0	28	5	1	.291	.247
Haniger, Mitch	R-R	6-2	213	12-23-90	.253	.286	.237	157	620	110	157	23	2	39	100	54	9	0	8	169	1	0	.485	.318
Kelenic, Jarred	L-L	6-1	190	7-16-99	.181	.168	.189	93	337	41	61	13	1	14	43	36	3	0	1	106	6	4	.350	.265
Lewis, Kyle	R-R	6-4	205	7-13-95	.246	.242	.247	36	130	15	32	4	0	5	11	16	1	0	0	37	2	0	.392	.333
Long Jr., Shed	L-R	5-8	184	8-22-95	.198	.163	.226	34	111	13	22	4	1	4	17	9	0	1	0	39	1	0	.360	.258
Marmolejos, Jose	L-L	6-2	239	1-2-93	.160	.111	.165	41	106	11	17	4	0	4	12	15	0	0	1	39	0	0	.311	.262
Mayfield, Jack	R-R	5-11	190	9-30-90	.176	.182	.167	11	34	2	6	1	0	1	3	1	0	0	0	10	0	0	.206	.200
2-team total (75 Los Angeles)					.218	.223	.215	86	266	30	58	15	0	10	39	17	3	3	1	68	5	0	.387	.272
Moore, Dylan	R-R	6-0	185	8-2-92	.181	.206	.163	126	332	42	60	11	2	12	43	40	4	0	1	111	21	5	.334	.276
Murphy, Tom	R-R	6-1	218	4-3-91	.202	.232	.170	97	277	35	56	8	0	11	34	40	2	0	3	99	0	0	.350	.304
Nottingham, Jacob	R-R	6-2	220	4-3-95	.115	.083	.143	10	26	3	3	0	0	1	2	2	2	0	1	12	0	0	.231	.226
Padlo, Kevin	R-R	6-2	210	7-15-96	.000	--	.000	1	1	0	0	0	0	0	0	0	0	0	0	0	0	0	.000	.000
2-team total (9 Tampa Bay)					.077	.100	.000	10	13	1	1	1	0	0	0	2	0	0	0	9	0	0	.154	.200
Raleigh, Cal	B-R	6-3	215	11-26-96	.180	.219	.168	47	139	6	25	12	0	2	13	7	1	0	1	52	0	0	.309	.223
Seager, Kyle	L-R	6-0	216	11-3-87	.212	.219	.208	159	603	73	128	29	1	35	101	59	4	0	4	161	3	1	.438	.285
Thomas, Dillon	L-L	6-1	215	12-10-92	.111	.250	.000	4	9	1	1	0	0	0	2	0	0	0	0	7	0	0	.111	.111
Toro, Abraham	B-R	6-0	206	12-20-96	.252	.235	.262	60	226	28	57	11	0	5	26	22	4	0	1	33	3	2	.367	.328
2-team total (35 Houston)					.239	.250	.233	95	335	45	80	12	0	11	46	31	7	0	2	54	6	3	.373	.315
Torrens, Luis	R-R	6-0	208	5-2-96	.243	.275	.221	108	346	39	84	16	2	15	47	28	1	0	3	99	0	0	.431	.299
Trammell, Taylor	L-L	6-2	213	9-13-97	.160	.098	.190	51	156	23	25	7	0	8	18	17	3	2	0	75	2	3	.359	.256
Walton, Donovan	L-R	5-10	175	5-25-94	.206	.188	.213	24	63	6	13	2	1	2	7	4	0	2	0	15	1	0	.365	.254
White, Evan	R-L	6-3	220	4-26-96	.144	.067	.179	30	97	8	14	3	0	2	9	6	1	0	0	31	0	0	.237	.202

Pitching	B-T	HT	WT	DOB	W	L	ERA	G	GS	CG	SV	IP	H	R	ER	HR	BB	SO	AVG	vLH	vRH	K/9	BB/9
Anderson, Tyler	L-L	6-2	220	12-30-89	2	3	4.81	13	13	0	0	64	71	35	34	11	13	48	.280	.382	.251	6.79	1.84
Andriese, Matt	R-R	6-2	215	8-28-89	0	0	2.45	8	0	0	0	11	10	6	3	0	2	12	.244	.263	.227	9.82	1.64
2-team total (26 Boston)					2	3	5.21	34	0	0	1	48	65	35	28	7	13	50	.323	.342	.311	9.31	2.42
Castillo, Diego	R-R	6-3	250	1-18-94	3	1	2.86	24	0	0	2	22	14	9	7	4	7	26	.184	.222	.163	10.64	2.86
2-team total (37 Tampa Bay)					5	5	2.78	61	0	0	16	58	40	23	18	9	17	75	.194	.203	.190	11.57	2.62
Chargois, JT	B-R	6-3	200	12-3-90	1	0	3.00	31	0	0	0	30	23	11	10	2	6	29	.217	.184	.235	8.70	1.80
2-team total (25 Tampa Bay)					6	1	2.52	56	0	0	0	54	38	16	15	5	20	53	.202	.147	.233	8.89	3.35
Doolittle, Sean	L-L	6-2	204	9-26-86	0	0	4.76	11	0	0	0	11	10	6	6	1	5	12	.227	.200	.250	9.53	3.97
Dugger, Robert	R-R	6-0	198	7-3-95	0	2	7.36	12	4	0	0	26	34	24	21	4	12	19	.324	.293	.344	6.66	4.21
Dunn, Justin	R-R	6-2	185	9-22-95	1	3	3.75	11	11	0	0	50	37	21	21	6	29	49	.201	.200	.202	8.76	5.19
Fletcher, Aaron	L-L	6-0	220	2-25-96	0	0	12.27	4	0	0	0	4	7	5	5	1	1	2	.368	.500	.308	4.91	2.45
Flexen, Chris	R-R	6-3	250	7-1-94	14	6	3.61	31	31	0	0	180	185	74	72	19	40	125	.268	.235	.296	6.26	2.00
Gilbert, Logan	R-R	6-6	225	5-5-97	6	5	4.68	24	24	0	0	119	112	63	62	21	28	128	.241	.239	.243	9.65	2.11
Gonzales, Marco	L-L	6-1	197	2-16-92	10	6	3.96	25	25	1	0	143	125	64	63	29	42	108	.234	.210	.242	6.78	2.64
Graveman, Kendall	R-R	6-2	200	12-21-90	4	0	0.82	30	0	0	10	33	15	7	3	2	8	34	.136	.213	.079	9.27	2.18
2-team total (23 Houston)					5	1	1.77	53	0	0	10	56	35	15	11	3	20	61	.180	.253	.117	9.80	3.21
Kikuchi, Yusei	L-L	6-0	200	6-17-91	7	9	4.41	29	29	0	0	157	145	82	77	27	62	163	.243	.147	.271	9.34	3.55
Lail, Brady	R-R	6-2	200	8-9-93	0	0	13.50	2	0	0	0	2	4	3	3	1	0	1	.400	.500	.333	4.50	0.00
Margevicius, Nick	L-L	6-5	220	6-18-96	0	2	8.25	5	3	0	0	12	13	16	11	2	7	12	.250	.125	.306	9.00	5.25
Mayfield, Jack	R-R	5-11	190	9-30-90	0	0	0.00	1	0	0	0	0	0	0	0	0	0	0	.000	--	.000	0.00	0.00

Name	B-T	HT	WT	DOB	W	L	ERA	G	GS	CG	SV	IP	H	R	ER	HR	BB	SO	AVG	vLH	vRH	SO/9	BB/9
McCaughan, Darren	R-R	6-1	200	3-18-96	0	0	8.00	2	1	0	0	9	8	8	8	3	4	2	.250	.375	.125	2.00	4.00
Middleton, Keynan	R-R	6-3	215	9-12-93	1	2	4.94	32	1	0	4	31	30	20	17	2	19	24	.252	.231	.263	6.97	5.52
Mills, Wyatt	R-R	6-4	190	1-25-95	0	0	9.95	11	0	0	0	13	19	14	14	1	7	11	.352	.500	.300	7.82	4.97
Misiewicz, Anthony	R-L	6-1	200	11-1-94	5	5	4.61	66	0	0	0	55	61	30	28	7	15	53	.280	.261	.294	8.73	2.47
Montero, Rafael	R-R	6-0	190	10-17-90	5	3	7.27	40	0	0	7	43	56	39	35	4	15	37	.311	.290	.324	7.68	3.12
2-team total (4 Houston)					5	4	6.39	44	0	0	7	49	59	40	35	4	17	42	.296	.276	.309	7.66	3.10
Munoz, Andres	R-R	6-2	243	1-16-99	0	0	0.00	1	0	0	0	1	0	0	0	0	2	1	.000	--	.000	13.50	27.00
Newsome, Ljay	R-R	5-11	210	11-8-96	1	1	7.98	7	1	0	0	15	20	14	13	5	3	16	.317	.389	.289	9.82	1.84
Nittoli, Vinny	R-R	6-1	210	11-11-90	0	0	18.00	1	0	0	0	1	1	2	2	1	2	1	.250	--	.250	9.00	18.00
Paxton, James	L-L	6-4	227	11-6-88	0	0	6.75	1	1	0	0	1	0	1	0	1	2	0	.000	.000	.000	13.50	6.75
Ramirez, Yohan	R-R	6-4	190	5-6-95	1	3	3.90	25	0	0	2	28	18	14	12	6	12	35	.188	.235	.161	11.39	3.90
Rios, Yacksel	R-R	6-3	215	6-27-93	0	0	9.00	3	0	0	0	3	5	3	3	0	2	2	.385	.000	.556	6.00	6.00
2-team total (20 Boston)					3	0	4.28	23	0	0	0	27	18	13	13	3	16	23	.189	.139	.220	7.57	5.27
Sadler, Casey	R-R	6-3	205	7-13-90	0	1	0.67	42	0	0	0	40	19	4	3	1	10	37	.143	.116	.156	8.26	2.23
Santiago, Hector	R-L	6-0	215	12-16-87	1	1	3.42	13	1	0	0	26	27	10	10	2	11	30	.257	.290	.243	10.25	3.76
Sewald, Paul	R-R	6-3	207	5-26-90	10	3	3.06	62	0	0	11	65	42	24	22	10	24	104	.176	.165	.183	14.47	3.34
Sheffield, Justus	L-L	5-10	195	5-13-96	7	8	6.83	21	15	0	0	80	105	69	61	14	43	63	.316	.266	.332	7.06	4.82
Smith, Joe	R-R	6-2	211	3-22-84	3	3	2.00	23	0	0	0	18	12	5	4	1	4	17	.185	.133	.200	8.50	2.00
2-team total (27 Houston)					4	4	4.99	50	0	0	0	40	47	23	22	5	8	34	.297	.250	.314	7.71	1.82
Steckenrider, Drew	R-R	6-4	217	1-10-91	5	2	2.00	67	0	0	14	68	52	16	15	5	17	58	.214	.178	.243	7.71	2.26
Swanson, Erik	R-R	6-3	220	9-4-93	0	3	3.31	33	2	0	1	35	28	18	13	5	10	35	.212	.234	.191	8.92	2.55
Tapia, Domingo	R-R	6-3	263	8-4-91	0	0	0.00	2	0	0	0	2	4	0	0	0	1	1	.400	.400	.400	4.50	4.50
2-team total (32 Kansas City)					4	1	2.67	34	0	0	0	34	25	10	10	1	15	26	.208	.194	.214	6.95	4.01
Vest, Will	R-R	6-0	180	6-6-95	1	0	6.17	32	0	0	0	35	38	25	24	2	18	27	.288	.279	.296	6.94	4.63
Weber, Ryan	R-R	6-1	175	8-12-90	0	0	6.00	2	0	0	0	3	1	2	2	1	2	1	.111	.333	.000	3.00	6.00
2-team total (1 Boston)					0	0	13.50	3	0	0	0	9	14	13	13	5	4	8	.389	.400	.387	8.31	4.15
Zamora, Daniel	L-L	6-3	195	4-15-93	2	0	6.23	4	0	0	0	4	5	4	3	1	1	3	.294	.333	.273	6.23	2.08

Fielding

Catcher	PCT	G	PO	A	E	DP	PB
Godoy	.981	14	97	4	2	0	0
Murphy	.990	88	664	24	7	2	6
Raleigh	.997	43	303	8	1	0	5
Torrens	.997	35	278	12	1	0	1

First Base	PCT	G	PO	A	E	DP
Bauers	1.000	13	83	5	0	6
Campbell	1.000	1	8	0	0	3
France	.999	106	740	73	1	78
Marmolejos	.980	14	92	4	2	9
Nottingham	1.000	4	26	3	0	2
Torrens	.971	5	31	2	1	3
White	.992	30	227	17	2	28

Second Base	PCT	G	PO	A	E	DP
France	.972	21	32	38	2	16
Haggerty	1.000	4	3	4	0	1
Long Jr.	1.000	10	11	25	0	5
Mayfield	1.000	9	9	16	0	3
Moore	.987	66	92	137	3	36
Toro	.975	58	76	123	5	27
Walton	.981	14	22	29	1	9

Third Base	PCT	G	PO	A	E	DP
Campbell	1.000	2	0	1	0	0
France	.857	5	2	4	1	0
Mayfield	1.000	2	2	4	0	0
Moore	1.000	10	5	15	0	0
Seager	.965	149	99	291	14	43
Toro	1.000	2	0	2	0	0
Torrens	1.000	2	0	1	0	0
Walton	.667	2	0	2	1	1

Shortstop	PCT	G	PO	A	E	DP
Crawford	.981	160	222	388	12	89
Moore	1.000	4	1	2	0	1
Walton	1.000	2	0	5	0	0

Outfield	PCT	G	PO	A	E	DP
Bauers	1.000	44	66	3	0	0
Bishop	1.000	8	3	0	0	0
Fraley	.984	73	120	1	2	1
Haggerty	1.000	29	53	2	0	0
Haniger	.989	123	270	3	3	0
Kelenic	.983	94	230	2	4	1
Lewis	.989	34	86	0	1	0
Long Jr.	1.000	25	36	1	0	0
Marmolejos	1.000	13	17	1	0	1
Moore	.989	57	92	2	1	1
Thomas	1.000	4	9	1	0	0
Trammell	1.000	51	118	2	0	0
Walton	.857	5	6	0	1	0

TACOMA RAINIERS — TRIPLE-A
TRIPLE-A WEST

Batting	B-T	HT	WT	DOB	AVG	vLH	vRH	G	AB	R	H	2B	3B	HR	RBI	BB	HBP	SH	SF	SO	SB	CS	SLG	OBP
Arias, Amador	R-R	5-11	143	8-25-00	.000	.000	.000	1	3	0	0	0	0	0	1	0	0	0	1	2	0	0	.000	.000
Bishop, Braden	R-L	6-1	178	8-22-93	.176	.250	.154	4	17	3	3	1	0	0	2	2	1	0	0	4	1	0	.235	.300
2-team total (75 Sacramento)					.318	.333	.310	79	305	61	97	19	5	12	45	27	6	0	2	60	10	3	.531	.382
Blankenhorn, Travis	L-R	6-2	235	8-3-96	.250	.500	.222	4	20	1	5	0	0	1	4	0	0	0	0	5	0	0	.400	.250
2-team total (3 Oklahoma City)					.217		.190	7	23	1	5	0	0	1	4	0	0	0	0	7	0	0	.348	.217
Campbell, Eric	R-R	6-3	215	4-9-87	.260	.500	.167	13	50	8	13	5	0	1	6	4	1	0	0	17	1	0	.420	.327
Filia, Eric	L-R	6-0	189	7-6-92	.262	.302	.245	44	149	27	39	9	0	3	15	30	2	0	2	25	4	0	.383	.388
Fraley, Jake	L-L	6-0	195	5-25-95	.325	.375	.313	13	40	8	13	1	0	3	7	9	1	0	1	15	3	1	.575	.451
Godoy, Jose	L-R	5-11	200	10-13-94	.285	.183	.324	73	298	44	85	15	1	7	56	19	3	1	4	57	1	0	.413	.330
Hager, Jake	R-R	6-1	170	3-4-93	.220	.136	.244	27	100	16	22	7	0	6	11	11	1	0	0	25	4	0	.470	.304
2-team total (28 Reno)					.220	.220	.220	55	200	30	44	14	0	10	27	22	1	0	2	59	6	0	.440	.298
Hanson, Alen	B-R	6-0	170	10-22-92	.275	.235	.288	40	138	25	38	6	6	2	15	14	1	2	1	27	5	1	.449	.344
Kelenic, Jarred	L-L	6-1	190	7-16-99	.320	.258	.340	30	125	29	40	9	1	9	28	15	1	0	2	22	6	1	.624	.392
Kelly, Ty	B-R	6-0	180	7-20-88	.227	.278	.211	24	75	14	17	2	0	2	10	13	0	1	0	15	0	0	.333	.337
Liberato, Luis	L-L	6-1	175	12-18-96	.279	.303	.270	87	298	52	83	13	5	8	37	31	0	0	8	79	3	0	.436	.338
Long Jr., Shed	L-R	5-8	184	8-22-95	.323	.429	.292	7	31	8	10	3	0	1	2	2	0	0	0	5	0	0	.516	.417
Marlowe, Cade	L-R	6-1	210	6-24-97	.667	--	.667	1	3	0	2	1	0	0	1	1	0	0	0	1	1	0	1.000	.750
Marmolejos, José	L-L	6-2	239	1-2-93	.338	.365	.329	83	293	66	99	16	2	26	75	54	2	0	4	69	0	0	.672	.439
Masters, David	R-R	6-1	185	4-23-93	.083	--	.083	4	12	2	1	0	0	1	1	3	0	0	0	4	0	0	.333	.267
Mathisen, Wyatt	R-R	6-0	217	12-30-93	.137	.150	.134	32	102	13	14	3	0	2	12	20	6	0	1	30	0	0	.225	.310
2-team total (24 Sacramento)					.191	.250	.172	56	178	29	34	8	0	7	24	31	8	0	1	53	0	0	.354	.335
Mayfield, Jack	R-R	5-11	190	9-30-90	.500	.333	.667	1	6	2	3	0	0	0	1	0	0	0	0	1	0	0	.500	.500
2-team total (15 Salt Lake)					.342	.316	.351	16	76	16	26	2	3	5	12	5	1	0	0	9	1	1	.645	.390

	B-T	HT	WT	DOB	AVG	OBP	SLG	G	AB	R	H	2B	3B	HR	RBI	BB	HP	SH	SF	SO	SB	CS	vLH	vRH
Moore, Dylan	R-R	6-0	185	8-2-92	.455	.500	.444	3	11	3	5	3	0	1	1	1	0	0	0	2	1	0	1.000	.500
Nottingham, Jacob	R-R	6-2	220	4-3-95	--	--	--	1	0	0	0	0	0	0	0	0	0	0	0	0	0	0	--	--
O'Keefe, Brian	R-R	6-1	210	7-15-93	.253	.346	.224	56	217	34	55	7	0	13	30	31	0	0	0	72	1	1	.465	.347
Padlo, Kevin	R-R	6-2	210	7-15-96	.298	.333	.286	26	104	22	31	3	2	8	21	16	0	0	1	21	1	1	.596	.388
Raleigh, Cal	B-R	6-3	215	11-26-96	.324	.383	.302	44	176	34	57	21	1	9	36	14	4	0	5	25	3	2	.608	.377
Reinheimer, Jack	R-R	6-1	185	7-19-92	.242	.250	.239	91	327	46	79	13	2	4	34	31	4	0	4	84	18	3	.330	.311
Rodriguez, Brett	R-R	6-0	200	5-6-98	.143	--	.143	2	7	1	1	0	0	0	0	0	0	0	0	4	1	0	.143	.143
Rosa, Joseph	B-R	5-10	165	3-6-97	.231	.500	.111	5	13	1	3	0	0	1	4	4	0	0	0	5	0	0	.462	.412
Sheaffer, David	R-R	6-2	170	5-9-95	.125	.400	.000	4	16	1	2	1	0	0	0	0	0	0	0	4	0	0	.188	.125
Taylor, Kennie	R-R	5-11	170	10-20-96	.200	.273	.167	13	35	2	7	1	0	1	9	3	1	0	0	14	0	1	.314	.282
Thomas, Dillon	L-L	6-1	215	12-10-92	.269	.239	.277	94	335	68	90	19	1	13	47	41	18	0	1	117	12	1	.448	.377
Torrens, Luis	R-R	6-0	208	5-2-96	.219	.154	.233	19	73	12	16	4	0	6	19	10	1	0	1	22	0	0	.521	.318
Trammell, Taylor	L-L	6-2	213	9-13-97	.263	.351	.230	71	274	43	72	15	1	12	49	40	5	0	4	74	8	2	.456	.362
Travis, Sam	R-R	6-0	220	8-27-93	.256	.200	.275	71	277	38	71	19	0	11	41	22	1	0	1	88	2	3	.444	.312
Walton, Donovan	L-R	5-10	175	5-25-94	.304	.280	.313	69	283	50	86	20	1	13	60	35	11	0	5	88	1	3	.519	.395
White, Evan	R-L	6-3	220	4-26-96	.333	--	.333	4	12	2	4	0	0	2	5	1	0	0	0	2	1	0	.833	.385
Wilson, Marcus	R-R	6-2	198	8-15-96	.235	.207	.239	39	144	25	34	8	0	4	22	27	0	0	1	58	5	2	.375	.355
Witte, Jantzen	R-R	6-2	195	1-4-90	.299	.276	.307	104	405	63	121	19	1	19	70	41	3	1	4	80	3	2	.491	.364

Pitching	B-T	HT	WT	DOB	W	L	ERA	G	GS	CG	SV	IP	H	R	ER	HR	BB	SO	AVG	vLH	vRH	K/9	BB/9
Carle, Shane	R-R	6-4	210	8-30-91	1	0	0.00	2	0	0	0	2	1	0	0	0	0	0	.167	.500	.000	0.00	0.00
2-team total (6 Reno)					1	0	8.31	8	0	0	0	9	11	8	8	5	5	4	.333	.500	.211	4.15	5.19
Dugger, Robert	R-R	6-0	198	7-3-95	4	5	6.10	15	14	0	0	69	74	48	47	12	24	64	.271	.307	.233	8.31	3.12
Dull, Ryan	R-R	5-9	185	10-2-89	2	2	6.06	28	1	0	0	36	33	26	24	7	15	43	.244	.289	.186	10.85	3.79
Dunn, Justin	R-R	6-2	185	9-22-95	0	0	--	1	0	0	0	0	0	0	0	0	0	1	0	--	--	--	--
Duron, Nick	R-R	6-4	190	1-30-96	2	1	7.24	15	0	0	0	14	15	11	11	4	12	15	.288	.217	.345	9.88	7.90
Festa, Matthew	R-R	6-1	195	3-11-93	4	1	2.95	19	0	0	1	21	17	7	7	4	3	31	.215	.300	.128	13.08	1.27
Fisher, Nate	L-L	6-1	205	5-28-96	0	0	7.71	1	1	0	0	2	2	2	2	0	2	1	.250	.000	.286	3.86	7.71
Fletcher, Aaron	L-L	6-0	220	2-25-96	4	0	3.47	39	0	0	2	49	53	20	19	6	14	45	.277	.193	.343	8.21	2.55
Gilbert, Logan	R-R	6-6	225	5-5-97	1	0	1.80	1	1	0	0	5	4	1	1	0	0	5	.222	.250	.200	9.00	0.00
Gillies, Darin	R-R	6-4	220	11-6-92	3	0	3.74	18	1	0	0	22	17	9	9	3	9	22	.213	.244	.179	9.14	3.74
Gomez, Moises	R-R	6-1	215	2-8-97	0	2	5.94	13	1	0	0	17	22	13	11	2	4	18	.319	.333	.303	9.72	2.16
Graveman, Kendall	R-R	6-2	200	12-21-90	0	0	9.00	1	0	0	0	1	1	1	1	0	1	2	.250	1.000	.000	18.00	9.00
Grimm, Justin	R-R	6-3	210	8-16-88	3	1	4.37	45	1	0	5	47	43	25	23	11	21	72	.232	.255	.209	13.69	3.99
Guerrieri, Taylor	R-R	6-3	225	12-1-92	3	1	4.61	22	0	0	0	27	30	14	14	2	12	28	.273	.275	.271	9.32	3.95
Herb, Tyler	R-R	6-3	200	4-28-92	1	0	10.80	1	0	0	0	5	10	6	6	1	2	2	.435	.778	.214	3.60	0.00
Huff, David	B-L	6-1	210	8-22-84	2	3	5.25	14	9	0	0	48	61	30	28	13	9	35	.302	.250	.322	6.56	1.69
Hunter, Leon	R-R	6-3	253	3-17-97	0	0	18.00	1	0	0	0	2	3	4	4	2	1	1	.333	1.000	.000	4.50	4.50
Jerez, Williams	L-L	6-4	210	5-16-92	0	3	11.32	19	1	0	1	21	31	27	26	7	12	13	.333	.317	.346	10.02	5.23
Johnson, Evan	R-R	5-11	190	1-17-97	0	0	36.00	1	0	0	0	1	3	4	4	0	0	1	.600	.750	.000	9.00	0.00
Kerr, Ray	L-L	6-3	185	9-10-94	0	0	4.09	12	1	0	2	11	8	5	5	0	6	17	.205	.214	.200	13.91	4.91
Kuhn, Travis	R-R	5-10	195	10-2-94	0	0	0.00	1	0	0	0	1	0	0	0	0	0	2	.000	.000	.000	18.00	0.00
Lail, Brady	R-R	6-2	200	8-9-93	0	1	1.50	4	1	0	1	6	3	2	1	0	2	7	.143	.154	.125	10.50	3.00
Martin, Reeves	L-R	5-8	180	12-25-96	0	2	8.10	5	1	0	0	7	8	6	6	0	5	4	.308	.333	.273	5.40	6.75
Martinez, Bernie	R-R	6-0	195	12-24-96	0	0	7.94	2	0	0	0	6	8	5	5	1	1	5	.333	.333	.333	7.94	1.59
McCaughan, Darren	R-R	6-1	200	3-18-96	5	4	4.53	20	20	0	0	115	111	61	58	20	17	99	.251	.260	.240	7.73	1.33
McKinney, Ian	L-L	5-11	185	11-18-94	4	4	6.04	11	10	0	0	54	54	36	36	10	28	48	.260	.219	.278	8.05	4.70
Middleton, Keynan	R-R	6-3	215	9-12-93	1	0	2.35	7	1	0	0	8	7	3	2	1	2	13	.233	.333	.133	15.26	2.35
Mills, Wyatt	R-R	6-4	190	1-25-95	4	2	3.14	23	1	0	0	29	19	12	10	2	7	51	.179	.135	.222	16.01	2.20
Morgan, Reid	R-R	6-0	187	3-24-97	0	0	0.00	1	0	0	0	2	0	0	0	0	0	4	.000	.000	.000	18.00	0.00
Munoz, Andres	R-R	6-2	243	1-16-99	0	0	6.75	3	1	0	0	3	1	2	2	0	1	4	.111	.000	.250	13.50	3.38
Murfee, Penn	R-R	6-2	195	5-2-94	2	1	4.44	16	4	0	0	26	22	13	13	2	15	35	.227	.208	.245	11.96	5.13
Nittoli, Vinny	R-R	6-1	210	11-11-90	3	3	5.61	23	6	0	0	34	36	22	21	7	7	41	.275	.305	.250	10.96	1.87
Onyshko, Ben	R-L	6-2	205	10-18-96	0	0	7.71	6	1	0	0	9	10	9	8	3	9	20	.263	.200	.304	19.29	8.68
Pall, Bryan	R-R	6-2	215	10-28-95	0	1	13.50	5	2	0	0	9	13	13	13	4	9	11	.361	.400	.313	11.42	9.35
Pounders, Brooks	R-R	6-5	265	9-26-90	0	1	27.00	3	0	0	0	1	3	4	4	2	3	1	.429	.500	.000	6.75	20.25
Ramirez, Yohan	R-R	6-4	190	5-6-95	0	0	4.15	15	0	0	0	17	12	8	8	2	13	24	.200	.206	.192	12.46	6.75
Roberts, Max	L-L	6-6	190	7-23-97	1	0	3.27	7	0	0	0	11	18	5	4	1	7	10	.333	.467	.306	8.18	5.73
Sadler, Casey	R-R	6-3	205	7-13-90	0	0	0.00	3	0	0	0	3	0	0	0	0	0	4	.000	.000	.000	13.50	0.00
Santiago, Hector	R-L	6-0	215	12-16-87	1	0	4.50	3	3	0	0	14	10	7	7	5	5	22	.196	.211	.188	14.14	3.21
Schlitter, Brian	R-R	6-3	238	12-21-85	1	0	3.98	36	5	0	2	41	45	19	18	5	16	29	.273	.227	.325	6.42	3.54
2-team total (5 Las Vegas)					2	0	4.72	41	5	0	2	48	56	26	25	6	19	37	.284	.299	.318	6.99	3.59
Schultz, Jaime	R-R	5-10	205	6-20-91	2	2	15.00	5	1	0	0	6	7	11	10	2	11	8	.304	.353	.167	12.00	16.50
Sewald, Paul	R-R	6-3	207	5-26-90	0	0	0.00	2	1	0	0	2	1	0	0	0	0	2	.200	.286	.125	20.77	0.00
Sheffield, Justus	L-L	5-10	195	5-13-96	0	1	8.64	5	2	0	0	8	8	9	8	1	7	14	.258	.286	.235	15.12	7.56
Swanson, Erik	R-R	6-3	220	9-4-93	0	0	4.50	2	0	0	0	2	2	1	1	0	1	2	.250	.400	.000	4.50	0.00
Tapia, Domingo	R-R	6-3	263	8-4-91	0	0	1.42	5	0	0	0	6	2	3	1	0	2	6	.095	.154	.000	8.53	2.84
Verrett, Logan	R-R	6-2	190	6-19-90	11	4	4.74	19	19	0	0	114	123	64	60	23	16	88	.272	.294	.249	6.95	1.26
Villarreal, Fred	R-R	5-11	187	4-7-98	0	0	9.45	3	0	0	0	7	11	7	7	1	3	2	.393	.400	.385	2.70	4.05
Weber, Ryan	R-R	6-1	175	8-12-90	4	2	3.58	10	10	0	0	60	54	26	24	9	2	59	.235	.272	.190	8.80	0.30
Weiss, Zack	R-R	6-2	195	4-3-92	3	4	4.31	30	1	0	1	40	34	29	19	5	24	56	.225	.217	.232	12.71	5.45
Willrodt, Matthew	R-R	6-4	220	10-19-97	1	0	0.00	1	0	0	0	2	0	0	0	0	1	5	.000	.000	.000	5.40	10.80
Winslow, Robert	R-R	6-5	215	8-19-97	0	0	0.00	1	0	0	0	4	1	0	0	0	0	3	.077	.200	.000	6.75	0.00
Witte, Jantzen	R-R	6-2	195	1-4-90	0	0	8.22	7	0	0	0	8	11	7	7	2	0	4	.333	.294	.375	4.70	0.00
Wojciechowski, Asher	R-R	6-4	235	12-21-88	0	1	5.82	5	5	0	0	17	21	11	11	2	6	27	.296	.262	.345	14.29	3.18

Yacabonis, Jimmy R-R 6-3 225 3-21-92 4 0 2.17 30 1 0 6 37 28 9 9 3 10 37 .204 .211 .197 8.92 2.41
Zamora, Daniel L-L 6-3 195 4-15-93 3 0 4.14 28 1 0 1 37 39 24 17 5 16 47 .271 .291 .258 11.43 3.89

Fielding

Catcher	PCT	G	PO	A	E	DP	PB
Godoy	.989	48	443	22	5	1	4
O'Keefe	.985	40	361	22	6	1	5
Raleigh	.997	34	324	16	1	4	5
Sheaffer	1.000	2	21	0	0	0	0
Torrens	1.000	9	72	5	0	0	2

First Base	PCT	G	PO	A	E	DP
Campbell	1.000	1	9	2	0	0
Filia	1.000	7	36	4	0	2
Godoy	1.000	2	4	0	0	0
Marmolejos	.991	45	317	31	3	31
Mathisen	1.000	1	9	1	0	1
Raleigh	1.000	2	5	1	0	0
Torrens	.983	8	51	6	1	3
Travis	.988	55	388	40	5	29
White	1.000	1	1	0	0	1
Witte	1.000	16	128	6	0	12

Second Base	PCT	G	PO	A	E	DP
Blankenhorn	1.000	2	7	3	0	0
Hager	1.000	4	8	7	0	2
Hanson	.985	37	31	100	2	18
Kelly	1.000	13	17	30	0	9
Long Jr.	.944	6	8	9	1	1

	PCT	G	PO	A	E	DP
Masters	1.000	2	1	3	0	1
Mayfield	1.000	1	1	0	0	1
Moore	1.000	2	2	7	0	1
Reinheimer	.955	24	32	53	4	10
Rosa	.917	3	1	10	1	1
Travis	1.000	1	5	1	0	0
Walton	.972	20	28	42	2	10
Witte	1.000	22	29	43	0	11

Third Base	PCT	G	PO	A	E	DP
Campbell	.000	2	0	0	0	0
Hanson	1.000	2	2	1	0	0
Kelly	1.000	9	4	13	0	0
Mathisen	.987	31	17	60	1	5
Padlo	.956	25	9	34	2	4
Reinheimer	1.000	11	6	16	0	1
Rodriguez	1.000	1	1	0	0	0
Rosa	1.000	1	0	2	0	1
Travis	.000	2	0	0	0	0
Witte	.936	54	29	88	8	3

Shortstop	PCT	G	PO	A	E	DP
Hager	.988	23	31	54	1	18
Hanson	1.000	1	1	2	0	1
Kelly	1.000	1	0	4	0	0

	PCT	G	PO	A	E	DP
Masters	1.000	2	2	0	0	0
Reinheimer	.964	59	67	118	7	26
Rosa	1.000	1	0	1	0	0
Walton	.950	46	54	117	9	15

Outfield	PCT	G	PO	A	E	DP
Bishop	1.000	4	12	0	0	0
Blankenhorn	.857	1	5	1	1	0
Filia	.975	25	36	3	1	0
Fraley	1.000	8	9	0	0	0
Hanson	--	1	0	0	0	0
Kelenic	1.000	28	55	1	0	0
Kelly	1.000	2	4	0	0	0
Liberato	.995	85	179	3	1	1
Marlowe	--	1	0	0	0	0
Marmolejos	.982	35	55	0	1	0
Rodriguez	1.000	2	4	0	0	0
Taylor	1.000	11	21	0	0	0
Thomas	.980	85	190	4	4	1
Trammell	.959	67	135	5	6	1
Travis	1.000	1	3	0	0	0
Walton	1.000	3	3	0	0	0
Wilson	1.000	39	69	0	0	0
Witte	1.000	9	12	0	0	0

SEATTLE MARINERS

ARKANSAS TRAVELERS   DOUBLE-A
DOUBLE-A CENTRAL

Batting	B-T	HT	WT	DOB	AVG	vLH	vRH	G	AB	R	H	2B	3B	HR	RBI	BB	HBP	SH	SF	SO	SB	CS	SLG	OBP
Anchia, Jake	R-R	6-1	210	3-5-97	.177	.095	.200	27	96	12	17	3	0	3	12	7	2	0	2	33	0	0	.302	.243
Bins, Carter	R-R	6-0	205	10-7-98	.063	.111	.043	11	32	9	2	0	0	1	4	10	1	0	0	13	2	0	.156	.302
Caballero, Jose	R-R	5-10	185	8-30-96	.200	.200	.200	8	20	3	4	1	0	1	3	7	0	0	1	4	2	1	.400	.393
Cowan, Jordan	L-R	6-0	160	4-13-95	.258	.273	.252	83	295	45	76	14	3	4	24	47	4	2	0	69	18	5	.366	.367
DeLoach, Zach	L-R	6-1	205	8-18-98	.227	.267	.214	49	185	28	42	10	2	5	22	28	3	0	0	58	1	2	.384	.338
Frick, Patrick	R-R	6-2	200	2-14-97	.241	.250	.235	42	137	21	33	3	0	2	15	16	3	0	0	26	1	0	.307	.333
Honeyman, Bobby	L-R	6-1	185	5-25-96	.240	.159	.270	85	304	33	73	16	0	4	30	35	5	0	1	60	3	1	.332	.328
Kopach, Connor	R-R	6-0	170	8-4-94	.150	.208	.121	47	147	24	22	3	0	4	9	22	3	1	0	78	8	1	.252	.273
Larsen, Jack	L-L	6-1	195	1-13-95	.277	.408	.226	45	173	33	48	6	1	11	32	28	1	0	2	46	2	2	.514	.377
Lien, Connor	R-R	6-3	225	3-15-94	.150	.146	.151	45	147	26	22	3	1	5	15	25	5	0	1	84	2	4	.286	.292
Masters, David	R-R	6-1	185	4-23-93	.225	.162	.257	33	111	11	25	4	0	6	15	11	2	1	0	39	2	2	.423	.306
McGovern, Keegan	L-R	6-3	200	9-13-95	.189	.222	.178	42	143	25	27	3	1	4	11	26	4	0	0	68	5	0	.308	.329
Morgan, Josh	R-R	5-11	185	11-16-95	.246	.295	.221	64	232	29	57	9	0	9	36	33	8	0	2	56	1	3	.401	.356
O'Keefe, Brian	R-R	6-1	210	7-15-93	.286	.347	.264	49	189	24	54	7	1	11	40	17	2	0	0	59	3	1	.508	.351
Polcovich, Kaden	B-R	5-10	185	2-21-99	.133	.216	.099	36	128	13	17	4	0	2	14	16	3	0	2	41	4	1	.211	.242
Rizzo, Joe	L-R	5-10	194	3-31-98	.253	.255	.252	105	380	49	96	18	1	12	60	42	4	0	4	104	4	4	.400	.330
Rodriguez, Julio	R-R	6-3	180	12-29-00	.362	.351	.365	46	174	35	63	11	0	7	26	29	3	0	0	37	16	4	.546	.461
Scheiner, Jake	R-R	6-1	200	8-13-95	.253	.299	.234	105	395	74	100	20	3	18	60	47	9	0	4	133	2	4	.456	.343
Sheaffer, David	R-R	6-2	170	5-9-95	.278	.259	.289	24	72	11	20	3	0	2	12	11	1	0	2	17	0	0	.403	.372
Shenton, Austin	L-R	6-0	205	1-22-98	.326	.462	.267	10	43	6	14	5	0	1	8	4	1	0	0	10	0	0	.512	.396
Thompson-Williams, Dom	L-L	6-0	190	4-21-95	.184	.150	.200	58	190	15	35	9	0	5	28	17	1	0	1	71	4	3	.311	.254
Wrenn, Stephen	R-R	6-0	202	10-7-94	.244	.263	.235	91	308	39	75	12	4	7	39	33	9	0	4	108	23	5	.377	.331

Pitching	B-T	HT	WT	DOB	W	L	ERA	G	GS	CG	SV	IP	H	R	ER	HR	BB	SO	AVG	vLH	vRH	K/9	BB/9
Anderson, Jack	R-R	6-3	210	1-10-94	3	0	5.75	36	0	0	1	52	52	36	33	4	30	32	.272	.293	.259	5.57	5.23
Arias, Dayeison	R-R	6-1	160	1-7-97	2	0	2.70	16	0	0	3	20	16	6	6	2	12	33	.211	.273	.163	14.85	5.40
Brash, Matt	R-R	6-1	170	5-12-98	3	2	2.13	10	10	1	0	55	32	15	13	3	23	80	.162	.141	.175	13.09	3.76
Driver, Tyler	R-R	6-2	185	2-4-01	1	0	1.50	1	1	0	0	6	6	1	1	0	1	7	.250	.400	.211	10.50	1.50
Duron, Nick	R-R	6-4	190	1-30-96	1	1	3.18	23	0	0	4	28	16	12	10	2	12	28	.163	.143	.175	8.89	3.81
Ellingson, David	R-R	6-2	200	1-23-95	1	0	9.00	16	0	0	0	18	31	18	18	3	6	14	.388	.353	.413	7.00	3.00
Fisher, Nate	L-L	6-1	205	5-28-96	1	0	3.09	7	0	0	0	12	5	4	4	2	2	13	.128	.083	.148	10.03	1.54
Gillies, Darin	R-R	6-4	220	11-6-92	2	0	1.93	22	0	0	10	23	14	6	5	2	12	30	.175	.250	.135	11.57	4.63
Gomez, Moises	R-R	6-1	215	2-8-97	2	1	1.23	23	0	0	0	29	22	7	4	2	7	25	.216	.213	.218	7.67	2.15
Haberer, Jake	R-R	6-2	225	2-9-95	1	3	6.12	26	0	0	0	32	34	29	22	5	25	26	.266	.286	.253	7.24	6.96
Hancock, Emerson	R-R	6-4	213	5-31-99	1	1	3.29	3	3	0	0	14	10	6	5	0	4	13	.196	.150	.226	8.56	2.63
Herb, Tyler	R-R	6-3	200	4-28-92	3	6	4.16	17	15	1	0	84	91	39	39	12	15	85	.276	.320	.250	9.07	1.60
Hernandez, Joseph	R-R	5-11	150	9-26-98	0	1	13.50	1	1	0	0	4	7	6	6	2	5	4	.350	.500	.333	9.00	2.25
Hill, Adam	R-R	6-6	225	3-24-97	4	4	6.34	14	14	0	0	61	67	43	43	14	30	66	.275	.269	.279	9.74	4.43
Hunter, Leon	R-R	6-3	253	3-17-97	1	0	1.93	2	0	0	0	5	2	1	1	0	2	6	.133	.200	.100	11.57	3.86
Inman, Ryne	R-R	6-5	215	5-13-96	0	0	6.17	11	0	0	0	12	10	11	8	3	13	22	.233	.176	.269	16.97	10.03
Kerr, Ray	L-L	6-3	185	9-10-94	2	1	2.83	24	0	0	3	29	18	11	9	2	10	43	.176	.143	.208	13.50	3.14

EVERETT AQUASOX

HIGH CLASS A

HIGH-A WEST

Batting	B-T	HT	WT	DOB	AVG	vLH	vRH	G	AB	R	H	2B	3B	HR	RBI	BB	HBP	SH	SF	SO	SB	CS	SLG	OBP
Anchia, Jake	R-R	6-1	210	3-5-97	.239	.256	.234	48	184	35	44	11	1	12	40	15	4	0	3	52	0	0	.505	.306
Bins, Carter	R-R	6-0	205	10-7-98	.284	.207	.303	40	148	42	42	10	0	7	31	32	4	0	1	54	1	3	.493	.422
Caballero, Jose	R-R	5-10	185	8-30-96	.294	--	.294	4	17	7	5	2	0	0	3	3	1	0	0	4	8	1	.412	.429
DeLoach, Zach	L-R	6-1	205	8-18-98	.313	.327	.310	58	249	56	78	23	2	9	37	32	4	0	0	63	6	3	.530	.400
Frick, Patrick	R-R	6-2	200	2-14-97	.310	.347	.300	63	229	56	71	19	1	7	42	42	10	0	3	64	5	1	.493	.433
Gomez, Dariel	L-R	6-4	190	7-15-96	.263	.333	.255	51	186	32	49	16	3	12	34	24	3	0	2	79	0	0	.575	.353
Grosse, Cody	L-R	5-8	165	12-30-96	.218	.200	.222	72	220	36	48	7	1	3	23	39	3	0	4	67	12	2	.300	.338
Hoover, Connor	L-R	5-10	185	7-18-96	.231	.269	.225	102	363	77	84	26	4	19	47	66	3	1	2	116	19	4	.482	.353
Keenan, Tyler	L-R	6-4	250	2-27-99	.196	.114	.212	64	224	28	44	18	0	6	44	32	6	0	8	100	0	0	.357	.304
Labrada, Victor	L-L	5-9	165	1-16-00	.246	.231	.249	49	203	35	50	7	3	6	27	19	2	0	2	63	10	6	.399	.314
Larsen, Jack	L-L	6-1	195	1-13-95	.308	.271	.317	64	237	47	73	25	2	8	52	45	4	0	1	67	11	5	.532	.425
Lavey, Anthony	R-R	6-1	205	9-23-97	.213	.167	.221	35	122	14	26	3	1	6	20	10	0	0	1	50	2	0	.402	.271
Lepre, Anthony	R-R	5-10	195	5-29-97	.167	--	.167	6	18	1	3	0	1	0	2	0	0	0	0	10	0	0	.278	.250
Marlowe, Cade	L-R	6-1	210	6-24-97	.259	.304	.250	71	286	52	74	18	5	20	77	36	2	0	1	91	12	7	.566	.345
Marte, Noelvi	R-R	6-1	181	10-16-01	.290	.286	.292	8	31	4	9	4	0	0	2	2	0	0	0	11	1	0	.419	.333
Perez, Miguel	R-R	6-2	170	8-21-00	.136	.000	.167	7	22	4	3	1	0	1	3	4	0	0	0	13	2	0	.318	.269
Polcovich, Kaden	B-R	5-10	185	2-21-99	.271	.194	.287	58	214	55	58	12	4	10	47	47	8	0	3	64	16	3	.505	.415
Rodriguez, Alberto	L-L	5-11	180	10-6-00	.208	.250	.200	7	24	5	5	1	0	0	2	2	2	0	0	7	2	0	.250	.321
Rodriguez, Julio	R-R	6-3	180	12-29-00	.325	.211	.347	28	117	29	38	8	2	6	21	14	3	0	0	29	5	1	.581	.410
Rosa, Joseph	B-R	5-10	165	3-6-97	.254	.288	.247	85	295	50	75	20	3	8	39	34	6	0	2	81	22	4	.424	.341
Sabino, Liam	R-R	6-0	205	5-1-96	.120	.111	.122	18	50	4	6	2	0	0	4	10	0	0	0	26	1	0	.160	.267
Scheffler, Matt	R-R	6-2	190	2-6-98	.257	.000	.290	21	70	11	18	4	1	4	12	5	3	0	1	23	1	1	.486	.329
Sheaffer, David	R-R	6-2	170	5-9-95	.238	.100	.257	20	80	9	19	6	1	0	12	3	0	0	2	21	1	0	.338	.259
Shenton, Austin	L-R	6-0	205	1-22-98	.295	.279	.298	57	224	55	66	24	3	11	53	41	7	0	1	62	1	0	.576	.418
Taylor, Kennie	R-R	5-11	170	10-20-96	.287	.444	.273	31	108	17	31	5	1	2	18	8	3	0	1	33	2	1	.407	.350
Thomas, Andy	L-R	6-2	210	6-17-98	.289	.667	.219	11	38	4	11	2	0	1	4	3	1	0	1	11	0	0	.421	.349

Pitching	B-T	HT	WT	DOB	W	L	ERA	G	GS	CG	SV	IP	H	R	ER	HR	BB	SO	AVG	vLH	vRH	K/9	BB/9
Alcantara, Raul	L-L	6-0	167	1-22-01	0	0	27.00	1	0	0	0	1	3	3	3	0	2	1	.500	1.000	.250	9.00	18.00
Alford, Peyton	L-L	6-0	190	8-15-97	2	1	9.26	7	0	0	0	12	18	13	12	6	4	18	.360	.250	.433	13.89	3.09
Arias, Dayeison	R-R	6-1	160	1-7-97	1	0	2.63	16	1	0	1	24	15	8	7	4	8	36	.170	.162	.176	13.50	3.00

Pitcher	B-T	HT	WT	DOB	W	L	ERA	G	GS	CG	SV	IP	H	R	ER	HR	BB	SO	AVG	vLH	vRH	K/9	BB/9
Bayless, Jarod	R-R	6-4	225	12-29-96	0	0	4.18	20	0	0	3	24	17	11	11	3	7	33	.198	.188	.204	12.55	2.66
Brash, Matt	R-R	6-1	170	5-12-98	3	2	2.55	10	9	0	1	42	31	16	12	3	25	62	.204	.138	.245	13.18	5.31
Campbell, Isaiah	R-R	6-4	230	8-15-97	3	1	2.33	5	0	0	0	19	13	7	5	2	6	20	.194	.222	.184	9.31	2.79
Dilone, Julio	L-R	6-1	196	3-23-00	0	0	3.38	3	0	0	0	3	2	1	1	1	1	3	.200	--	.200	10.13	3.38
Dollard, Taylor	R-R	6-3	195	2-17-99	6	2	6.15	12	11	0	0	67	78	48	46	12	14	74	.283	.297	.276	9.89	1.87
Driver, Tyler	R-R	6-2	185	2-4-01	3	4	6.75	11	3	0	0	27	28	24	20	3	16	26	.277	.219	.304	8.78	5.40
Ellingson, David	R-R	6-2	200	1-23-95	2	0	1.21	20	0	0	1	30	27	7	4	1	5	36	.237	.205	.257	10.92	1.52
Elliott, Tim	R-R	6-1	200	10-11-97	5	4	6.78	19	10	0	1	82	93	69	62	20	42	90	.277	.287	.272	9.84	4.59
Festa, Matthew	R-R	6-1	195	3-11-93	0	0	0.00	2	0	0	0	2	1	0	0	0	0	3	.143	.500	.000	13.50	0.00
Fisher, Nate	L-L	6-1	205	5-28-96	1	0	2.40	8	1	0	2	15	11	6	4	0	2	20	.200	.308	.103	12.00	1.20
Hancock, Emerson	R-R	6-4	213	5-31-99	2	0	2.32	9	9	0	0	31	19	11	8	1	13	30	.178	.075	.239	8.71	3.77
Hill, Adam	R-R	6-6	225	3-24-97	1	3	3.60	5	5	0	0	30	24	16	12	5	10	36	.207	.244	.187	10.80	3.00
Hill, Kyle	R-R	5-11	200	5-12-97	1	2	3.94	26	0	0	4	32	23	17	14	0	21	36	.204	.243	.184	10.13	5.91
Hoffman, Nolan	R-R	6-4	190	8-9-97	0	1	5.32	13	1	0	1	22	22	13	13	2	5	24	.256	.280	.246	9.82	2.05
Hoover, Connor	L-R	5-10	185	7-18-96	0	0	18.00	2	0	0	0	2	8	4	4	3	0	1	.615	.600	.625	4.50	0.00
Januario, Igor	L-R	6-7	260	1-20-98	0	3	7.79	29	0	0	0	32	41	41	28	1	25	28	.306	.381	.272	7.79	6.96
Johnson, Evan	R-R	5-11	190	1-17-97	2	0	2.70	18	1	0	1	27	19	8	8	3	16	42	.200	.189	.207	14.18	5.40
Joyce, Jimmy	R-R	6-2	210	1-13-99	0	0	3.63	4	4	0	0	17	17	9	7	2	6	25	.246	.304	.217	12.98	3.12
Kirby, George	R-R	6-4	215	2-4-98	4	2	2.38	9	9	0	0	42	33	15	11	1	8	52	.214	.208	.217	11.23	1.73
Kolek, Stephen	R-R	6-3	210	4-18-97	3	3	5.93	21	9	0	0	55	55	38	36	7	20	66	.251	.320	.215	10.87	3.29
Kuhn, Travis	R-R	5-10	195	5-20-98	1	0	5.06	3	0	0	0	5	9	3	3	2	1	8	.346	.571	.263	13.50	1.69
Lavey, Justin	R-R	6-1	205	9-23-97	0	0	0.00	1	0	0	0	1	1	0	0	0	0	0	.250	--	.250	0.00	0.00
Laws, Holden	L-L	6-2	166	12-8-99	1	0	9.00	1	0	0	0	2	3	2	2	1	0	2	.300	--	.300	9.00	0.00
Limoncelli, Michael	L-R	6-2	185	5-30-00	0	2	10.80	2	1	0	0	3	5	5	4	0	4	1	.357	.333	.375	2.70	10.80
Martinez, Bernie	R-R	6-0	195	12-24-96	4	2	6.70	25	3	0	0	48	54	39	36	13	21	44	.286	.269	.295	8.19	3.91
McGuigan, Brendan	R-R	6-2	210	10-9-95	2	3	6.53	16	0	0	1	21	21	16	15	4	8	30	.263	.250	.271	13.06	3.48
Morgan, Reid	R-R	6-0	187	3-24-97	2	0	3.68	3	2	0	0	15	16	6	6	2	3	17	.271	.278	.268	10.43	1.84
Onyshko, Ben	R-L	6-2	205	10-18-96	0	5	5.54	25	0	0	2	37	38	27	23	5	16	55	.262	.255	.265	13.26	3.86
Pall, Bryan	R-R	6-1	215	10-28-95	1	1	6.00	16	1	0	1	15	17	10	10	1	7	23	.288	.261	.306	13.80	4.20
Phillips, Connor	R-R	6-2	190	5-4-01	0	1	2.25	1	1	0	0	4	2	3	1	1	2	7	.133	.000	.167	15.75	4.50
Sadler, Casey	R-R	6-3	205	7-13-90	0	0	0.00	1	0	0	0	1	0	0	0	0	0	1	.000	.000	.000	18.00	0.00
Salvatore, Mike	R-R	6-0	186	12-27-96	0	0	0.00	1	0	0	0	1	0	0	0	0	0	1	.000	.000	.000	9.00	0.00
Stoudt, Levi	R-R	6-1	195	12-4-97	6	1	3.52	12	12	0	0	64	47	28	25	6	29	67	.204	.163	.227	9.42	4.08
Then, Juan	R-R	6-1	175	2-7-00	2	5	6.46	14	14	0	0	54	68	42	39	12	19	59	.300	.313	.292	9.77	3.15
Townsend, Blake	L-L	6-4	220	4-5-01	0	1	16.20	1	0	0	0	2	2	3	3	0	2	4	.333	--	.333	21.60	10.80
Van Gurp, Franklin	R-R	6-1	225	10-26-95	0	3	6.33	14	1	0	0	27	27	20	19	6	9	33	.262	.233	.283	11.00	3.00
Villarreal, Fred	R-R	5-11	187	4-7-98	1	3	3.71	29	3	0	0	51	55	26	21	5	13	50	.275	.311	.254	8.82	2.29
Williamson, Brandon	R-L	6-6	210	4-2-98	2	1	3.19	6	6	0	0	31	21	11	11	4	10	59	.189	.200	.184	17.13	2.90
Willrodt, Matthew	R-R	6-4	220	10-19-97	0	0	0.00	1	0	0	0	3	2	0	0	0	1	9	.182	.000	.250	27.00	3.00

Fielding

Catcher	PCT	G	PO	A	E	DP	PB
Anchia	.990	39	394	16	4	3	9
Bins	.988	35	384	30	5	2	12
Lepre	.981	6	47	4	1	1	2
Scheffler	.978	16	163	11	4	0	6
Sheaffer	.979	12	125	12	3	0	1
Thomas	.991	11	98	11	1	0	5

First Base	PCT	G	PO	A	E	DP
Anchia	.931	3	25	2	2	3
Gomez	.993	41	269	21	2	21
Hoover	.990	39	280	11	3	22
Keenan	.985	17	124	4	2	7
Larsen	1.000	3	17	2	0	1
Salvatore	1.000	1	7	1	0	2
Sheaffer	.973	5	32	4	1	3
Shenton	.987	12	70	4	1	4

Second Base	PCT	G	PO	A	E	DP
Frick	1.000	2	2	6	0	1
Grosse	.987	24	30	44	1	10
Hoover	1.000	2	2	4	0	0
Lavey	1.000	12	19	21	0	3
Polcovich	1.000	24	37	65	0	9
Rosa	.972	46	59	81	4	14
Sabino	.941	13	16	32	3	3
Shenton	.833	3	3	2	1	2

Third Base	PCT	G	PO	A	E	DP
Frick	1.000	4	1	6	0	0
Hoover	.934	27	17	40	4	3
Keenan	.963	30	13	39	2	4
Lavey	.921	17	12	23	3	1
Polcovich	1.000	4	3	2	0	0
Rosa	1.000	3	0	1	0	0
Sabino	.667	1	0	2	1	0
Shenton	.959	41	24	70	4	5

Shortstop	PCT	G	PO	A	E	DP
Caballero	.889	3	3	5	1	0
Frick	.935	53	63	124	13	26
Hoover	.976	23	26	54	2	5
Lavey	1.000	5	3	5	0	1
Marte	.967	7	11	18	1	1
Polcovich	.952	14	22	37	3	10
Rosa	.933	17	13	29	3	5
Salvatore	1.000	1	1	2	0	0

Outfield	PCT	G	PO	A	E	DP
DeLoach	.962	54	70	6	3	1
Grosse	1.000	47	75	4	0	0
Hoover	.938	10	14	1	1	0
Labrada	.989	48	89	2	1	0
Larsen	.969	53	92	2	3	1
Marlowe	.968	65	120	1	4	0
Perez	1.000	7	10	2	0	2
Polcovich	.909	9	19	1	2	0
Rodriguez	.909	6	10	0	1	0
Rodriguez	.977	21	43	0	1	0
Rosa	.778	8	7	0	2	0
Taylor	.952	30	58	1	3	1

MODESTO NUTS   LOW CLASS A
LOW-A WEST

Batting	B-T	HT	WT	DOB	AVG	vLH	vRH	G	AB	R	H	2B	3B	HR	RBI	BB	HBP	SH	SF	SO	SB	CS	SLG	OBP
Arias, Amador	R-R	5-11	143	8-25-00	.207	.143	.227	8	29	5	6	1	1	1	2	3	0	0	0	11	0	0	.414	.281
Batista, Freuddy	R-R	6-0	182	12-12-99	.429	.500	.421	5	21	6	9	2	0	1	1	2	0	0	0	6	1	0	.667	.478
Bednar, Randy	R-L	5-11	200	11-30-98	.400	--	.400	6	20	4	8	1	1	0	3	2	0	0	0	5	0	0	.550	.455
Davis, Colin	R-R	6-1	190	2-8-99	.315	.429	.298	29	108	28	34	8	0	2	22	18	1	0	3	17	7	1	.444	.408
Duvall, Ty	L-R	5-11	200	7-11-97	.230	.219	.232	60	213	34	49	10	1	2	26	38	8	0	0	71	0	1	.315	.367
Gomez, Dariel	L-R	6-4	190	7-15-96	.269	.182	.291	46	167	28	45	12	1	3	26	29	4	0	1	72	0	1	.407	.388
Gonzalez, Junior	R-R	5-11	186	5-10-00	.000	--	.000	1	4	0	0	0	0	0	0	0	0	0	0	2	0	0	.000	.000
Izturis Jr., Cesar	B-R	5-11	145	11-11-99	.260	.188	.278	89	334	44	87	23	0	3	39	21	3	1	3	78	5	4	.356	.307

Name	B-T	HT	WT	DOB	AVG	vLH	vRH	G	AB	R	H	2B	3B	HR	RBI	BB	HBP	SH	SF	SO	SB	CS	SLG	OBP
Jones, Eric	R-R	6-0	193	3-20-96	.353	.421	.342	32	133	17	47	11	0	1	24	6	3	0	1	25	1	0	.459	.392
Labrada, Victor	L-L	5-9	165	1-16-00	.294	.227	.312	50	201	44	59	16	3	1	28	34	6	0	2	60	22	9	.418	.407
Lavey, Justin	R-R	6-1	205	9-23-97	.262	.278	.259	49	183	24	48	8	2	2	23	21	4	0	3	63	8	0	.361	.346
Lepre, Anthony	R-R	5-10	195	5-29-97	.091	.000	.111	3	11	3	1	0	0	0	1	4	0	0	0	5	0	0	.091	.333
Marlowe, Cade	L-R	6-1	210	6-24-97	.301	.206	.333	34	133	35	40	6	5	6	29	24	1	0	2	40	11	2	.556	.406
Marte, Noelvi	R-R	6-1	181	10-16-01	.271	.244	.278	99	413	87	112	24	2	17	69	58	6	0	1	106	23	7	.462	.368
Packard, Spencer	L-R	6-1	205	10-12-97	.250	.222	.252	29	120	20	30	4	1	3	18	13	5	0	0	19	1	0	.375	.348
Parker, James	R-R	6-1	200	3-26-00	.327	.308	.328	35	150	31	49	16	2	3	29	13	2	0	3	36	3	2	.520	.381
Perez, Milkar	R-R	5-11	173	10-16-01	.296	1.000	.269	6	27	6	8	2	0	0	0	4	1	0	0	4	0	1	.370	.406
Perez, Robert	R-R	6-1	170	6-26-00	.282	.315	.274	98	401	62	113	21	2	15	77	34	17	0	5	114	0	0	.456	.359
Querecuto, Juan	R-R	6-2	175	9-21-00	.250	.333	.205	20	68	7	17	1	0	1	5	8	3	0	0	22	2	2	.309	.354
Rodriguez, Alberto	L-L	5-11	180	10-6-00	.295	.297	.294	93	370	75	109	30	5	10	63	51	5	0	5	95	13	7	.484	.383
Rodriguez, Brett	R-R	6-0	200	5-6-98	.231	.250	.226	84	277	42	64	14	3	3	36	41	10	1	4	125	25	7	.336	.346
Rosier, Corey	L-R	5-10	184	9-7-99	.390	.368	.394	31	118	31	46	8	3	3	23	18	1	0	4	20	13	3	.585	.461
Sabino, Liam	R-R	6-0	205	5-1-96	.240	.667	.182	7	25	4	6	3	0	0	2	3	1	0	0	5	1	0	.360	.345
Scheffler, Matt	R-R	6-2	190	2-6-98	.241	.200	.255	40	141	19	34	7	2	3	26	24	3	0	1	41	1	1	.383	.361
Taylor, Kennie	R-R	5-11	170	10-20-96	.308	.357	.289	15	52	9	16	4	0	1	12	7	1	0	1	16	1	0	.442	.393
Thomas, Andy	L-R	6-2	210	6-17-98	.182	.000	.200	11	33	7	6	2	0	0	5	11	0	0	1	6	0	0	.242	.378
Tingelstad, Trent	L-R	5-10	215	6-14-98	.260	.200	.271	76	285	50	74	19	1	6	53	58	2	0	4	87	1	0	.396	.384

Pitching	B-T	HT	WT	DOB	W	L	ERA	G	GS	CG	SV	IP	H	R	ER	HR	BB	SO	AVG	vLH	vRH	K/9	BB/9
Alford, Peyton	L-L	6-0	190	8-15-97	0	0	3.60	2	0	0	1	5	3	2	2	0	2	3	.176	.200	.167	5.40	3.60
Alvarado, Elvis	R-R	6-4	183	2-23-99	0	2	6.60	31	1	0	0	45	60	43	33	3	32	33	.323	.212	.383	6.60	6.40
Benitez, Jorge	L-L	6-2	155	6-1-99	1	2	5.70	27	0	0	0	36	37	31	23	2	27	51	.257	.333	.237	12.63	6.69
Burgos, Juan	R-R	6-0	155	12-22-99	0	0	0.00	1	0	0	0	1	2	1	0	0	1	1	.333	.333	.333	6.75	6.75
Carlson, Sam	R-R	6-4	195	12-3-98	6	4	4.77	19	19	0	0	100	107	69	53	7	44	112	.268	.250	.281	10.08	3.96
Casetta-Stubbs, Damon	R-R	6-4	225	7-22-99	3	3	6.42	9	9	0	0	41	33	35	29	6	27	58	.219	.234	.207	12.84	5.98
Curvelo, Luis	R-R	6-1	170	10-21-00	5	1	3.58	37	0	0	6	55	49	31	22	4	18	80	.229	.256	.213	13.01	2.93
De Los Santos, Josias	R-R	6-2	174	7-29-99	4	8	5.27	20	20	0	0	96	100	68	56	7	70	89	.271	.250	.285	8.37	6.59
Dollard, Taylor	R-R	6-3	195	2-17-99	3	2	3.35	7	7	0	0	38	40	15	14	2	10	59	.265	.250	.274	14.10	2.39
Fleming, William	R-R	6-6	220	3-6-99	3	0	2.84	7	2	0	0	19	14	7	6	2	3	22	.203	.172	.225	10.42	1.42
Hoffman, Nolan	R-R	6-4	190	8-9-97	1	1	2.17	24	1	0	5	29	18	8	7	0	9	31	.173	.250	.125	9.62	2.79
Hunter, Leon	R-R	6-3	253	3-17-97	6	1	3.00	24	1	0	1	54	46	30	18	6	21	68	.218	.180	.246	11.33	3.50
Jones, Eric	R-R	6-0	193	3-20-96	0	1	27.00	1	0	0	0	1	2	1	0	2	1	0	.500	1.000	.000	0.00	54.00
Kingsbury, Jimmy	R-R	6-1	187	2-13-99	2	1	2.20	8	7	0	0	33	16	8	8	2	11	39	.138	.191	.101	10.74	3.03
Kolek, Stephen	R-R	6-3	210	4-18-97	1	0	6.00	2	0	0	0	3	3	2	2	0	2	2	.300	.250	.333	6.00	6.00
Kuhn, Travis	R-R	5-10	195	5-20-98	2	1	3.86	21	0	0	5	28	20	13	12	4	16	36	.196	.182	.207	11.57	5.14
Macko, Adam	L-L	6-0	170	12-30-00	2	2	4.59	9	9	0	0	33	29	19	17	1	21	56	.223	.150	.236	15.12	5.67
Mercedes, Juan	R-R	6-2	190	4-3-00	7	4	5.54	34	0	0	0	63	67	47	39	9	17	88	.263	.208	.299	12.51	2.42
Miller, Bryce	R-R	6-2	180	8-23-98	0	0	4.82	5	3	0	0	9	15	7	5	0	2	15	.357	.444	.292	14.46	1.93
Moore, Andrew	L-R	6-5	205	8-11-99	0	1	6.87	13	0	0	0	18	17	15	14	2	17	16	.246	.313	.226	7.85	8.35
Nunez, Kelvin	R-R	6-1	170	12-10-99	4	3	6.09	25	6	0	1	55	66	42	37	8	22	50	.292	.165	.378	8.23	3.62
Perez, Brayan	L-L	6-0	170	9-5-00	1	4	3.34	31	6	0	1	67	75	37	25	2	18	81	.270	.233	.280	10.83	2.41
Phillips, Connor	R-R	6-2	190	5-4-01	7	3	4.75	16	16	0	0	72	62	42	38	1	44	104	.229	.243	.220	13.00	5.50
Roberts, Max	L-L	6-6	190	7-23-97	0	0	4.30	11	5	0	0	23	16	14	11	2	14	29	.200	.250	.188	11.35	5.48
Tomczak, Anthony	R-R	6-2	200	10-17-00	0	0	9.00	1	0	0	0	1	1	1	1	0	2	2	.333	.500	.000	18.00	18.00
Willrodt, Matthew	R-R	6-4	220	10-19-97	4	3	6.02	35	1	0	4	49	55	36	33	4	28	46	.285	.300	.274	8.39	5.11
Winslow, Robert	R-R	6-5	215	8-19-97	2	4	6.28	27	2	0	2	43	41	39	30	4	32	59	.246	.221	.263	12.35	6.70

Fielding

Catcher	PCT	G	PO	A	E	DP	PB
Batista	.946	5	60	10	4	0	3
Duvall	.982	56	564	31	11	2	13
Gonzalez	.917	1	10	1	1	1	0
Jones	.958	2	23	0	1	0	1
Lepre	1.000	2	20	2	0	0	1
Scheffler	.977	39	441	33	11	3	14
Thomas	.992	11	107	13	1	2	1

First Base	PCT	G	PO	A	E	DP
Gomez	.974	32	209	19	6	19
Jones	.979	18	132	10	3	3
Perez	.975	66	471	31	13	41
Sabino	1.000	1	6	0	0	0

Second Base	PCT	G	PO	A	E	DP
Arias	.963	5	10	16	1	4
Izturis Jr.	.960	59	82	134	9	27
Lavey	.974	40	60	89	4	24
Parker	1.000	2	2	8	0	0
Querecuto	.667	1	2	0	1	0
Rodriguez	.895	12	12	22	4	3
Sabino	1.000	1	1	2	0	0

Third Base	PCT	G	PO	A	E	DP
Arias	1.000	3	5	3	0	0
Izturis Jr.	.854	21	15	26	7	4
Jones	.833	2	1	4	1	1
Lavey	.667	5	3	5	4	1
Parker	.895	21	10	41	6	3
Perez	.692	6	3	6	4	0
Perez	.750	7	2	7	3	0
Querecuto	.914	15	12	20	3	0
Rodriguez	.916	36	34	53	8	7
Sabino	.800	5	1	3	1	0

Shortstop	PCT	G	PO	A	E	DP
Izturis Jr.	1.000	8	12	16	0	2
Marte	.920	92	109	225	29	46
Parker	.930	13	12	28	3	3
Querecuto	.846	4	5	6	2	1

Outfield	PCT	G	PO	A	E	DP
Bednar	1.000	5	8	0	0	0
Davis	.982	26	53	1	1	0
Jones	1.000	3	4	0	0	0
Labrada	.951	46	77	1	4	0
Marlowe	.897	28	33	2	4	0
Packard	1.000	20	28	1	0	0
Perez	1.000	5	1	1	0	0
Rodriguez	.953	82	150	12	8	3
Rodriguez	.983	35	56	2	1	0
Rosier	.982	26	53	1	1	0
Taylor	.900	12	17	1	2	0
Tingelstad	.977	62	81	3	2	0

ACL MARINERS — ROOKIE
ARIZONA COMPLEX LEAGUE

Batting	B-T	HT	WT	DOB	AVG	vLH	vRH	G	AB	R	H	2B	3B	HR	RBI	BB	HBP	SH	SF	SO	SB	CS	SLG	OBP
Arias, Amador	R-R	5-11	143	8-25-00	.189	.120	.209	40	111	20	21	8	0	4	22	21	5	0	0	52	14	2	.369	.343

Batting	B-T	HT	WT	DOB	AVG	vLH	vRH	G	AB	R	H	2B	3B	HR	RBI	BB	HBP	SH	SF	SO	SB	CS	SLG	OBP
Arroyo, Edwin	B-B	6-0	175	8-25-03	.211	.316	.173	21	71	16	15	2	0	2	10	10	4	0	1	26	4	1	.324	.337
Barr, Cole	R-R	5-11	195	5-23-98	.292	.333	.277	27	65	10	19	3	0	0	11	18	9	0	0	26	2	1	.338	.500
Batista, Freuddy	R-R	6-0	182	12-12-99	.196	.059	.225	33	97	19	19	5	1	7	23	18	2	0	3	25	3	3	.485	.325
Bednar, Randy	R-L	5-11	200	11-30-98	.241	.273	.234	22	58	14	14	3	2	2	14	17	4	0	2	16	2	2	.466	.432
Bueno, Asdrubal	R-R	5-11	170	11-25-01	.193	.235	.182	34	83	16	16	3	0	2	11	11	8	0	1	37	4	1	.301	.340
Bumpass, AJ	L-R	6-3	195	5-30-96	.235	.158	.258	31	81	15	19	3	1	5	11	10	1	0	0	32	3	1	.481	.326
Caballero, Jose	R-R	5-10	185	8-30-96	.280	.400	.250	8	25	6	7	2	0	2	9	3	0	0	1	8	1	0	.600	.345
Chevalier, Luis	B-R	5-11	160	1-18-02	.221	.310	.198	47	140	28	31	4	1	3	21	25	2	0	1	35	2	0	.329	.345
Clase, Jonatan	L-R	5-8	150	5-23-02	.245	.400	.205	14	49	12	12	1	0	2	10	6	1	0	1	15	16	0	.388	.333
Davis, Colin	R-R	6-1	190	2-8-99	.286	--	.286	2	7	0	2	0	0	0	1	0	0	0	0	1	1	0	.286	.286
Ford, Harry	R-R	5-10	200	2-21-03	.291	.200	.311	19	55	12	16	7	0	3	10	9	1	0	0	14	3	0	.582	.400
Gonzalez, Junior	R-R	5-11	186	5-10-00	.220	.250	.216	25	59	8	13	3	1	2	14	11	1	0	2	21	0	0	.407	.342
Guerrero, Arturo	R-R	6-3	165	9-21-00	.267	.172	.294	43	131	27	35	6	5	2	19	11	9	0	1	47	9	3	.435	.362
Jones, Eric	R-R	6-0	193	3-20-96	.353	.667	.286	5	17	6	6	1	1	0	5	2	1	0	0	5	0	0	.529	.450
Lepre, Anthony	R-R	5-10	195	5-29-97	.220	.667	.159	22	50	5	11	3	0	1	6	6	0	0	0	20	0	0	.340	.304
Omosako, Gunn	R-R	6-4	190	5-12-01	.173	.143	.176	33	81	18	14	3	1	4	15	9	13	0	1	31	1	0	.383	.346
Packard, Spencer	L-R	6-1	205	10-12-97	.500	--	.500	2	4	3	2	0	0	0	1	3	0	0	1	1	0	0	.500	.714
Parker, James	R-R	6-1	200	3-26-00	.500	--	.500	1	2	1	1	0	0	0	1	0	0	0	0	0	0	0	2.000	.500
Perez, Miguel	R-R	6-2	170	8-21-00	.187	.143	.196	46	123	24	23	9	3	2	13	27	1	0	0	63	7	2	.358	.338
Perez, Milkar	R-R	5-11	173	10-16-01	.310	.286	.315	45	145	33	45	10	0	0	23	39	3	0	1	38	1	1	.379	.463
Ramirez, Ben	L-R	6-3	200	12-2-98	.277	.286	.274	28	94	11	26	6	2	2	11	7	3	1	0	21	0	1	.447	.346
Rosier, Corey	L-R	5-10	184	9-7-99	.000	--	.000	1	3	0	0	0	0	0	0	0	0	0	0	2	0	0	.000	.000
Sabino, Liam	B-R	6-0	205	5-1-96	.222	--	.222	3	9	1	2	0	0	0	0	2	0	0	0	3	3	1	.222	.364
Thomas, Andy	L-R	6-2	210	6-17-98	.500	.000	1.000	1	2	1	1	0	0	0	0	1	0	0	0	0	0	0	.500	.667
Welch, Charlie	R-R	6-0	205	2-8-00	.348	.364	.343	20	46	9	16	2	0	3	13	10	1	0	1	15	1	1	.587	.466

Pitching	B-T	HT	WT	DOB	W	L	ERA	G	GS	CG	SV	IP	H	R	ER	HR	BB	SO	AVG	vLH	vRH	K/9	BB/9
Alcantara, Raul	L-L	6-0	167	1-22-01	8	1	3.11	12	6	0	0	46	39	20	16	3	21	59	.224	.222	.225	11.46	4.08
Alford, Peyton	L-L	6-0	190	8-15-97	1	0	0.00	3	0	0	1	3	1	0	0	1	6	.083	.000	.125	16.20	2.70
Baez, Luis	R-R	6-3	165	2-6-01	2	2	5.08	12	4	0	0	28	22	24	16	2	31	41	.214	.333	.141	13.02	9.85
Burgos, Juan	R-R	6-0	155	12-22-99	0	0	4.80	13	0	0	6	15	10	12	8	0	10	18	.179	.167	.188	10.80	6.00
Castillo, Diego	R-R	6-3	250	1-18-94	0	0	0.00	1	0	0	0	1	0	0	0	0	0	2	.000	.000	.000	18.00	0.00
Chang, Danny	L-L	6-3	176	2-11-00	2	0	7.84	10	4	0	0	21	23	19	18	3	19	27	.288	.400	.250	11.76	8.27
Dilone, Julio	L-R	6-1	196	3-23-00	1	0	3.45	12	0	0	4	16	14	6	6	0	5	19	.226	.292	.184	10.91	2.87
Driver, Tyler	R-R	6-2	185	2-4-01	2	0	5.79	6	1	0	1	19	21	15	12	2	9	18	.280	.321	.255	8.68	4.34
Festa, Matthew	R-R	6-1	195	3-11-93	0	0	0.00	2	1	0	0	2	0	0	0	0	1	5	.000	.000	.000	22.50	4.50
Fisher, Nate	L-L	6-1	205	5-28-96	1	0	2.16	5	0	0	0	8	7	2	2	1	5	13	.233	.167	.250	14.04	5.40
Fleming, William	R-R	6-6	220	3-6-99	1	1	6.00	2	0	0	0	3	2	3	2	0	1	5	.000	.200	.143	15.00	3.00
Garabitos, Natanael	R-R	6-0	185	8-4-00	3	2	5.31	12	7	0	0	41	33	28	24	3	28	57	.228	.190	.190	12.61	6.20
Gonzalez, Junior	R-R	5-11	186	5-10-00	0	0	0.00	1	0	0	0	1	0	0	0	0	1	1	.000	.000	.000	9.00	9.00
Hernandez, Joseph	R-R	5-11	150	6-15-00	4	0	4.35	10	4	0	0	31	25	18	15	2	18	49	.221	.209	.229	14.23	5.23
Jefferson, Chris	L-R	6-2	200	1-24-97	2	0	1.54	6	0	0	2	12	7	2	2	1	5	17	.167	.111	.208	13.11	3.86
Jones, Eric	R-R	6-0	193	3-20-96	1	0	0.00	1	0	0	0	1	0	1	0	0	2	1	.000	.000	--	9.00	18.00
Joyce, Jimmy	R-R	6-2	210	1-13-99	0	0	1.80	2	2	0	0	5	4	1	1	0	1	6	.211	.250	.200	10.80	1.80
Laws, Holden	L-L	6-2	166	12-8-99	2	1	4.05	7	4	0	0	20	18	10	9	3	11	25	.237	.200	.261	11.25	4.95
Limoncelli, Michael	L-R	6-2	185	5-30-00	1	3	3.33	10	8	0	0	24	17	11	9	1	25	33	.193	.243	.157	12.21	9.25
Medina, Abdiel	R-R	5-11	155	1-20-02	3	1	3.76	10	3	1	1	38	35	16	16	2	7	37	.250	.208	.276	8.69	1.64
Moore, Andrew	L-R	6-5	205	8-11-99	0	0	9.00	1	0	0	0	1	1	1	1	0	1	0	.333	--	.333	0.00	9.00
Morales, Michael	R-R	6-2	205	8-13-02	0	0	18.00	1	1	0	0	1	2	2	2	0	1	1	.500	--	.500	9.00	9.00
Morillo, David	R-R	6-2	168	9-26-01	3	1	2.12	19	0	0	4	34	25	13	8	1	10	41	.197	.191	.200	10.85	2.65
Munoz, Andres	R-R	6-2	243	1-16-99	0	0	0.00	1	0	0	1	3	0	0	0	0	0	3	.000	.000	.000	27.00	0.00
Perez, Wilton	R-R	6-3	171	3-7-02	0	1	27.00	1	1	0	0	1	2	2	2	0	1	1	.333	.000	1.000	13.50	13.50
Tatiz, Yeury	R-R	6-3	175	11-22-00	2	4	3.92	11	6	0	0	39	35	23	17	4	22	45	.236	.231	.240	10.38	5.08
Tomczak, Anthony	R-R	6-2	200	10-17-00	0	0	3.68	2	1	0	0	7	3	3	3	0	4	13	.125	.143	.100	15.95	4.91
Townsend, Blake	L-L	6-4	200	4-5-01	0	0	2.63	4	3	0	0	14	9	6	4	1	5	22	.184	.091	.211	14.49	3.29
Van Gurp, Franklin	R-R	6-1	225	10-26-95	1	0	0.00	2	0	0	1	3	1	0	0	0	8	.100	.000	.111	24.00	0.00

Fielding

C: Batista 18, Ford 13, Gonzalez 19, Lepre 15, Thomas 1, Welch 11.
1B: Barr 3, Batista 12, Bueno 26, Jones 5, Lepre 2, Ramirez 15, Sabino 1, Welch 2.
2B: Arias 13, Arroyo 2, Barr 7, Bueno 5, Caballero 1, Chevalier 27, Ramirez 6, Sabino 2.
3B: Barr 10, Bueno 2, Perez 45.
SS: Arias 25, Arroyo 20, Caballero 3, Chevalier 11, Parker 1, Ramirez 2.
OF: Barr 2, Bednar 21, Bumpass 30, Chevalier 7, Clase 14, Davis 2, Guerrero 37, Omosako 21, Packard 2, Perez 47, Ramirez 5, Rosier 1.

DSL MARINERS — ROOKIE
DOMINICAN SUMMER LEAGUE

Batting	B-T	HT	WT	DOB	AVG	vLH	vRH	G	AB	R	H	2B	3B	HR	RBI	BB	HBP	SH	SF	SO	SB	CS	SLG	OBP
Aguilar, Starlin	L-R	5-11	170	1-26-04	.246	.379	.221	53	183	38	45	13	1	2	21	29	5	0	3	41	0	2	.361	.359
Bolivar, Luis	R-R	6-1	160	2-9-04	.000	--	.000	1	2	0	0	0	0	0	0	1	0	0	0	1	0	0	.000	.333
Caguana, Jose	R-R	5-10	175	4-5-02	.275	.222	.290	29	80	12	22	5	0	2	15	15	2	0	1	35	2	1	.413	.398
Cova, Ricardo	R-R	5-9	145	5-24-04	.247	.067	.290	32	77	8	19	2	0	1	9	9	4	1	1	13	4	2	.312	.352
Cruz, Juan	R-R	5-11	140	4-30-04	.255	.250	.256	32	51	19	13	6	1	1	8	9	5	1	0	21	6	2	.471	.415
Feliz, George	R-R	5-11	160	9-21-02	.277	.207	.292	46	173	32	48	7	4	5	25	21	2	0	0	46	8	1	.451	.362
Gonzalez, Gabriel	R-R	5-10	165	1-4-04	.287	.262	.295	54	188	39	54	15	4	7	36	21	7	0	5	35	9	3	.521	.371

	B-T	HT	WT	DOB	AVG	vLH	vRH	G	AB	R	H	2B	3B	HR	RBI	BB	SO	SB	CS	SO			SLG	OBP
Guilarte, German	R-R	5-10	167	3-6-03	.195	.300	.161	21	41	7	8	3	2	0	3	10	6	0	0	21	1	1	.366	.421
Jimenez, Carlos	L-L	5-10	170	2-14-03	.200	.182	.204	42	120	21	24	2	2	5	21	24	4	0	4	36	8	1	.375	.342
Mendez, Bryant	R-R	5-11	165	9-15-03	.185	.231	.171	24	54	10	10	2	0	1	4	6	2	0	0	21	5	0	.278	.290
Moncada, Gabe	L-L	6-2	175	12-17-01	.358	.368	.355	54	159	29	57	16	2	4	30	37	9	0	1	46	2	5	.560	.500
Rodriguez, Edryn	R-R	5-9	150	4-23-03	.309	.385	.291	44	136	28	42	14	1	4	28	24	4	0	2	35	5	6	.515	.422
Rojas, Yoander	B-R	5-11	175	9-9-02	.169	.250	.148	27	77	11	13	3	0	0	8	17	3	0	0	26	0	0	.208	.340
Sanchez, Axel	R-R	6-0	170	12-10-02	.261	.229	.270	52	161	33	42	7	0	1	29	20	6	1	2	46	15	4	.323	.360
Sosa, Andy	R-R	6-2	175	2-13-03	.167	.154	.170	28	66	11	11	2	0	0	5	7	1	0	1	21	4	2	.197	.253
Suisbel, Luis	B-R	6-1	190	5-23-03	.188	.208	.183	43	128	10	24	6	0	2	15	17	13	0	2	47	3	1	.281	.338

Pitching	B-T	HT	WT	DOB	W	L	ERA	G	GS	CG	SV	IP	H	R	ER	HR	BB	SO	AVG	vLH	vRH	K/9	BB/9
Aquino, Jose	L-L	6-3	175	6-27-02	1	3	3.74	12	9	0	0	43	35	22	18	2	23	65	.222	.238	.219	13.50	4.78
Brito, Lisander	R-R	6-3	175	7-9-02	2	0	4.88	9	6	0	1	24	17	15	13	5	21	22	.195	.154	.213	8.25	7.88
Cardozo, Kristian	R-R	6-2	175	11-10-02	3	4	3.62	12	11	0	0	50	42	30	20	3	19	40	.225	.278	.191	7.25	3.44
Da Costa Lemos, Pedro	R-R	6-0	179	5-22-03	0	0	0.00	1	1	0	0	3	1	1	0	0	1	4	.100	.333	.000	13.50	3.38
Diaz, Brayan	R-R	6-1	190	1-5-01	1	0	5.06	13	0	0	1	16	15	17	9	0	15	17	.246	.111	.302	9.56	8.44
Diaz, Gleiner	R-R	6-0	170	9-20-03	2	0	2.74	17	0	0	2	23	14	8	7	0	19	27	.182	.238	.161	10.57	7.43
Geraldo, Jose	R-R	5-10	185	12-3-99	3	4	1.29	19	0	0	8	28	15	8	4	1	13	43	.161	.103	.188	13.82	4.18
Jimenez, Yoryi	R-R	5-11	175	10-28-03	0	0	0.00	2	0	0	0	3	1	0	0	0	1	4	.111	.500	.000	13.50	3.38
Marcano, Emmanuel	R-R	6-0	170	12-4-02	4	1	3.28	16	2	0	2	36	31	15	13	4	10	41	.235	.243	.232	10.35	2.52
Melenge, Harold	L-L	5-10	170	1-15-02	2	0	3.77	7	0	0	1	14	12	9	6	1	6	15	.235	.500	.200	9.42	3.77
Munoz, Jean	R-R	6-1	155	9-17-02	1	6	5.23	12	11	0	0	43	38	31	25	3	25	46	.235	.246	.229	9.63	5.23
Ovando, Anyelo	R-R	6-5	222	12-25-00	4	2	3.93	11	0	0	0	18	10	9	8	1	17	22	.167	.231	.149	10.80	8.35
Pediet, Fausto	R-R	5-11	175	12-4-00	3	0	0.75	6	0	0	1	12	10	2	1	0	1	10	.217	.200	.226	7.50	0.75
Quintana, Adrian	R-R	6-0	175	11-20-02	5	1	1.97	12	11	0	0	59	32	16	13	3	9	64	.150	.171	.140	9.71	1.37
Sanchez, Steven	R-R	6-0	160	8-19-03	1	0	4.91	11	0	0	1	18	26	12	10	0	6	17	.351	.350	.352	8.35	2.95
Sosa, Gabriel	R-R	6-2	182	4-17-01	1	1	5.98	16	5	0	1	41	37	30	27	3	16	48	.234	.188	.255	10.62	3.54
Talavera, Roiber	R-R	6-0	160	3-31-04	2	2	6.89	9	2	0	0	16	19	16	12	2	9	15	.292	.391	.238	8.62	5.17
Tejada, Joaquin	R-R	5-11	160	7-16-03	0	0	7.20	2	1	0	0	5	1	6	4	0	4	8	.059	.000	.077	14.40	7.20
2-team total (8 DSL Pirates Black)					1	1	4.40	10	8	0	0	29	24	17	14	2	17	33	.216	.190	.232	10.36	5.34

Fielding

C: Caguana 23, Guilarte 19, Rojas 24.
1B: Mendez 1, Moncada 42, Sanchez 8, Sosa 4, Suisbel 10.
2B: Cova 10, Mendez 14, Rodriguez 39.
3B: Aguilar 37, Cova 6, Mendez 4, Sanchez 1, Suisbel 17.
SS: Mendez 7, Rodriguez 3, Sanchez 42, Suisbel 16.
OF: Bolivar 1, Cova 19, Cruz 27, Feliz 38, Gonzalez 47, Jimenez 42, Moncada 8, Sosa 18.

Tampa Bay Rays

SEASON IN A SENTENCE: The Rays fell short of the ultimate prize with an early playoff exit, but otherwise the season was nearly perfect with Tampa Bay finishing with the best record in the American League and winning almost everywhere in the minors thanks to a stacked farm system.

HIGH POINT: A 12-2 win over the Yankees on the second to last day of the season ensured the Rays their first 100-win season in team history, in addition to putting an exclamation point on the organization's third straight AL East title. The 2008 Rays previously held the team record with a 97-65 season.

LOW POINT: The Rays' attempt to return to the World Series for a third time and their quest for their first title ended in early October thanks to back-to-back one-run losses to the Red Sox in the American League Division Series.

NOTABLE ROOKIES: Outfielder Randy Arozarena and shortstop Wander Franco were both among the best rookies in the American League. Arozarena hit 20 home runs and stole 20 bases in a .274/.356/.459 season. Franco hit .288/.347/.463 in 70 games. shortstop Taylor Walls showed excellent defense but a light bat in 54 games with the Rays. Lefthander Shane McClanahan led the team in wins in a 10-6, 3.43 season. Patino made 15 starts and threw 77 innings for the Rays, going 5-3, 4.31. Relievers J.P. Feyereisen, Dietrich Enns and Louis Head all provided utility in the bullpen.

KEY TRANSACTIONS: Before the season, Tampa Bay traded its ace lefthander Blake Snell to the Padres in a deal that brought back four players. Two of the players in the trade, catcher Francisco Mejia and righthander Luis Patino, played significant roles for the Rays big league club in 2021. The Rays stunned much of baseball by trading starting shortstop Willy Adames and righthander Trevor Richards to the Brewers for righthanders Feyereisen and Drew Rasmussen in late May. The deal was surprising both in its timing (two months before the trade deadline) and the fact that Adames is still years away from free agency. Adames was excellent for the Brewers after the trade, but the move cleared a path for Franco to become the Rays shortstop and Rasmussen eventually stepped into the Rays rotation. At the trade deadline, the Rays acquired DH Nelson Cruz and minor league righthander Calvin Faucher for minor league righthanders Joe Ryan and Drew Strotman.

OPENING DAY PAYROLL: $60,388,600 (26th).

PLAYERS OF THE YEAR

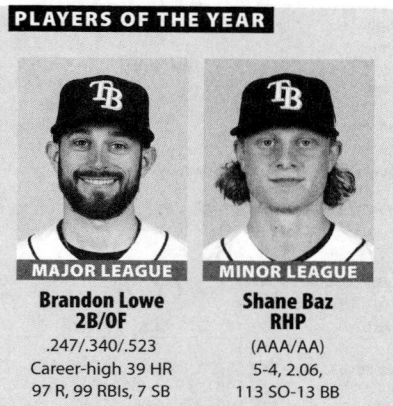

MAJOR LEAGUE	MINOR LEAGUE
Brandon Lowe	**Shane Baz**
2B/OF	**RHP**
.247/.340/.523	(AAA/AA)
Career-high 39 HR	5-4, 2.06,
97 R, 99 RBIs, 7 SB	113 SO-13 BB

ORGANIZATION LEADERS

Batting		*Minimum 250 AB
MAJORS		
*AVG	Wander Franco	.288
*OPS	Brandon Lowe	.863
HR	Brandon Lowe	39
RBI	Austin Meadows	106
MINORS		
*AVG	Jonathan Aranda, Montgomery, Bowling Green	.330
*OBP	Jonathan Aranda, Montgomery, Bowling Green	.418
*SLG	Jonathan Aranda, Montgomery, Bowling Green	.543
*OPS	Jonathan Aranda, Montgomery, Bowling Green	.962
R	Diego Infante, Bowling Green, Charleston	84
H	Curtis Mead, Durham, Bowling Green, Charleston	132
TB	Curtis Mead, Durham, Bowling Green, Charleston	219
2B	Curtis Mead, Durham, Bowling Green, Charleston	38
3B	Osleivis Basabe, Bowling Green, Charleston	6
3B	Wander Franco, Durham	6
HR	Dalton Kelly, Durham	27
RBI	Diego Infante, Bowling Green, Charleston	83
BB	Jonathan Embry, Charleston	64
SO	Niko Hulsizer, Montgomery, Bowling Green	148
SB	Vidal Brujan, Durham	44

Pitching		#Minimum 75 IP
MAJORS		
W	Josh Fleming	10
W	Shane McClanahan	10
#ERA	Tyler Glasnow	2.66
SO	Shane McClanahan	141
SV	Diego Castillo	14
MINORS		
W	Taj Bradley, Bowling Green, Charleston	12
L	Joel Peguero, Durham, Montgomery	8
#ERA	Taj Bradley, Bowling Green, Charleston	1.83
G	Brian Moran, Durham	53
GS	Taj Bradley, Bowling Green, Charleston	22
GS	Tobias Myers, Durham, Montgomery	22
SV	Colby White, Durham, Montgomery, Bowling Green, Charleston	11
IP	Tobias Myers, Durham, Montgomery	117.2
BB	Jose Lopez, Bowling Green, Charleston	39
SO	Tobias Myers, Durham, Montgomery	146
#AVG	Shane Baz, Durham, Montgomery	.181

2021 PERFORMANCE

General Manager: Erik Neander. **Farm Director:** Jeff McLerran. **Scouting Director:** RJ Harrison.

Class	Team	League	W	L	PCT	Finish	Manager
Majors	Tampa Bay Rays	American	100	62	.617	1st (15)	Kevin Cash
Triple-A	Durham Bulls	Triple-A East	86	44	.662	1st (20)	Brady Williams
Double-A	Montgomery Biscuits	Double-A South	62	55	.530	2nd (8)	Morgan Ensberg
High-A	Bowling Green Hot Rods	High-A East	82	36	.695	1st (12)	Jeff Smith
Low-A	Charleston RiverDogs	Low-A East	82	38	.683	1st (12)	Blake Butera
Rookie	DSL Rays2	Dominican Summer	28	31	.475	28th (46)	Julio Zorrilla
Rookie	DSL Rays1	Dominican Summer	29	30	.492	t-24th (46)	Esteban Gonzalez
Rookie	FCL Rays	Florida Complex	42	15	.737	1st (18)	Rafael Valenzuela
Overall 2021 Minor League Record			411	249	.623	1st (30)	

ORGANIZATION STATISTICS

TAMPA BAY RAYS
AMERICAN LEAGUE

Batting	B-T	HT	WT	DOB	AVG	vLH	vRH	G	AB	R	H	2B	3B	HR	RBI	BB	HBP	SH	SF	SO	SB	CS	SLG	OBP
Adames, Willy	R-R	6-0	210	9-2-95	.197	.180	.207	41	132	16	26	6	1	5	15	10	0	0	0	51	1	2	.371	.254
Arozarena, Randy	R-R	5-11	185	2-28-95	.274	.302	.257	141	529	94	145	32	3	20	69	56	14	0	5	170	20	10	.459	.356
Brosseau, Mike	R-R	5-10	205	3-15-94	.187	.234	.107	57	150	21	28	9	0	5	18	15	2	0	2	53	2	0	.347	.266
Brujan, Vidal	B-R	5-10	180	2-9-98	.077	.059	.111	10	26	3	2	0	0	0	2	0	0	0	0	8	1	0	.077	.077
Choi, Ji-Man	L-R	6-1	260	5-19-91	.229	.186	.245	83	258	36	59	14	0	11	45	45	2	0	0	87	0	0	.411	.348
Cruz, Nelson	R-R	6-2	230	7-1-80	.226	.242	.219	55	217	35	49	8	0	13	36	16	2	0	2	63	0	0	.442	.283
2-team total (85 Minnesota)					.265	.316	.240	140	513	79	136	21	1	32	86	51	7	0	9	126	3	0	.497	.334
Diaz, Yandy	R-R	6-2	215	8-8-91	.256	.288	.234	134	465	62	119	20	1	13	64	69	3	0	4	85	1	1	.387	.353
Franco, Wander	B-R	5-10	189	3-1-01	.288	.357	.251	70	281	53	81	18	5	7	39	24	2	0	1	37	2	1	.463	.347
Kiermaier, Kevin	L-R	6-1	210	4-22-90	.259	.268	.254	122	348	54	90	19	7	4	37	33	5	0	4	99	5	5	.388	.328
Lowe, Brandon	L-R	5-10	185	7-6-94	.247	.198	.270	149	535	97	132	31	0	39	99	68	9	0	3	167	7	1	.523	.340
Lowe, Josh	L-R	6-4	205	2-2-98	1.000	--	1.000	2	1	0	1	0	0	0	0	1	0	0	0	0	1	0	1.000	1.000
Luplow, Jordan	R-R	6-1	195	9-26-93	.246	.200	.320	25	65	11	16	3	0	4	8	7	0	0	0	26	1	0	.477	.319
2-team total (36 Cleveland)					.202	.167	.247	61	163	23	33	8	0	11	28	28	2	0	0	57	1	2	.454	.329
Margot, Manuel	R-R	5-11	180	9-28-94	.254	.273	.239	125	421	55	107	18	3	10	57	37	1	1	4	70	13	8	.382	.313
Meadows, Austin	L-L	6-3	225	5-3-95	.234	.198	.251	142	518	79	121	29	3	27	106	59	6	0	8	122	4	3	.458	.315
Mejia, Francisco	B-R	5-8	188	10-27-95	.260	.276	.248	84	250	31	65	15	3	6	35	17	7	1	2	49	0	0	.416	.322
Odom, Joseph	R-R	6-2	215	1-9-92	.000	.000	.000	2	2	0	0	0	0	0	0	0	0	0	0	1	0	0	.000	.000
Padlo, Kevin	R-R	6-2	210	7-15-96	.083	.100	.000	9	12	1	1	1	0	0	0	2	0	0	0	8	0	0	.167	.214
2-team total (1 Seattle)					.077	.100	.000	10	13	1	1	1	0	0	0	2	0	0	0	9	0	0	.154	.200
Phillips, Brett	L-R	6-0	195	5-30-94	.206	.110	.244	118	253	50	52	9	4	13	44	33	2	2	2	113	14	3	.427	.300
Smith, Kevan	R-R	6-4	230	6-28-88	.250	.000	.333	3	4	2	1	0	0	0	0	0	0	0	0	2	0	0	.250	.250
Tsutsugo, Yoshi	L-R	6-1	225	11-26-91	.167	.182	.164	26	78	5	13	4	0	0	5	8	0	1	0	27	0	0	.218	.244
Walls, Taylor	B-R	5-10	185	7-10-96	.211	.230	.198	54	152	15	32	10	0	1	15	23	0	1	0	49	4	2	.296	.314
Wendle, Joey	L-R	6-1	195	4-26-90	.265	.202	.287	136	460	73	122	31	4	11	54	28	10	0	3	113	8	6	.422	.319
Zunino, Mike	R-R	6-2	235	3-25-91	.216	.342	.151	109	333	64	72	11	2	33	62	34	7	0	1	132	0	0	.559	.301

Pitching	B-T	HT	WT	DOB	W	L	ERA	G	GS	CG	SV	IP	H	R	ER	HR	BB	SO	AVG	vLH	vRH	K/9	BB/9
Anderson, Nick	R-R	6-4	205	7-5-90	0	1	4.50	6	0	0	1	6	4	3	3	2	2	1	.190	.143	.214	1.50	3.00
Archer, Chris	R-R	6-2	195	9-26-88	1	1	4.66	6	5	0	0	19	18	11	10	3	8	21	.240	.179	.277	9.78	3.72
Armstrong, Shawn	R-R	6-2	225	9-11-90	1	0	4.50	11	0	0	0	16	11	8	8	5	5	22	.186	.333	.105	12.38	2.81
2-team total (20 Baltimore)					1	0	6.75	31	0	0	0	36	39	28	27	10	15	44	.265	.327	.228	11.00	3.75
Baz, Shane	R-R	6-2	190	6-17-99	2	0	2.03	3	3	0	0	13	6	3	3	3	3	18	.130	.250	.067	12.15	2.03
Castillo, Diego	R-R	6-3	250	1-18-94	2	4	2.72	37	0	0	14	36	26	14	11	5	10	49	.200	.190	.205	12.14	2.48
2-team total (24 Seattle)					5	5	2.78	61	0	0	16	58	40	23	18	9	17	75	.194	.203	.190	11.57	2.62
Chargois, JT	B-R	6-3	200	12-3-90	5	1	1.90	25	0	0	0	24	15	5	5	3	14	24	.183	.100	.231	9.13	5.32
2-team total (31 Seattle)					6	1	2.52	56	0	0	0	54	38	16	15	5	20	53	.202	.147	.233	8.89	3.35
Conley, Adam	L-L	6-3	209	5-24-90	0	0	2.29	17	0	0	0	20	14	5	5	2	6	16	.212	.136	.250	7.32	2.75
Ellis, Chris	L-R	6-5	205	9-22-92	1	0	0.00	1	0	0	0	4	3	0	0	1	7	.200	.000	.300	15.75	2.25
2-team total (6 Baltimore)					1	0	2.15	7	6	0	0	29	21	7	7	3	14	32	.209	.139	.232	7.06	4.30
Enns, Dietrich	L-L	6-1	210	5-16-91	2	0	2.82	9	0	0	2	22	17	8	7	1	6	25	.207	.200	.209	10.07	2.42
Fairbanks, Pete	R-R	6-6	225	12-16-93	3	6	3.59	47	0	0	5	43	40	21	17	2	21	56	.241	.343	.167	11.81	4.43
Feyereisen, J.P.	R-R	6-2	215	2-7-93	4	2	2.45	34	0	0	3	37	26	14	10	3	22	33	.197	.269	.150	8.10	5.40
Fleming, Josh	L-L	6-2	220	5-18-96	10	8	5.09	26	11	0	1	104	110	60	59	11	31	65	.268	.277	.265	5.61	2.67
Glasnow, Tyler	L-R	6-8	225	8-23-93	5	2	2.66	14	14	0	0	88	55	26	26	10	27	123	.176	.139	.205	12.58	2.76
Head, Louis	R-R	6-1	180	4-23-90	2	0	2.31	27	2	0	0	35	21	10	9	2	9	32	.175	.146	.194	8.23	2.31
Hess, David	R-R	6-1	215	7-10-93	0	0	27.00	1	0	0	0	2	8	6	6	3	1	2	.571	.500	.667	9.00	4.50
Hill, Rich	L-L	6-5	221	3-11-80	6	4	3.87	19	19	0	0	95	75	41	41	14	36	91	.220	.176	.232	8.59	3.40
Honeywell Jr., Brent	R-R	6-2	195	3-31-95	0	0	8.31	3	2	0	0	4	5	4	4	2	3	4	.278	.429	.182	8.31	6.23
Johnson, DJ	R-R	6-2	230	8-30-89	0	0	0.00	3	0	0	0	3	0	0	0	0	0	2	.000	.000	.000	6.75	0.00
2-team total (1 Cleveland)					0	0	2.08	4	0	0	0	4	2	1	1	0	5	.133	.222	.000	10.38	0.10
Kittredge, Andrew	R-R	6-1	230	3-17-90	9	3	1.88	57	4	0	8	72	55	21	15	7	15	77	.210	.200	.214	9.67	1.88

Name	B-T	HT	WT	DOB	W	L	ERA	G	GS	CG	SV	IP	H	R	ER	HR	BB	SO	AVG	vLH	vRH	SO/9	BB/9
Krehbiel, Joey	R-R	6-2	185	12-20-92	0	0	0.00	1	0	0	0	1	0	0	0	0	1	2	.000	.000	.000	18.00	9.00
2-team total (5 Baltimore)					0	0	4.32	6	0	0	0	8	5	4	4	1	5	7	.172	.000	.227	7.56	5.40
Luplow, Jordan	R-R	6-1	195	9-26-93	0	0	9.00	1	0	0	0	1	2	1	1	1	0	0	.400	.000	.500	0.00	0.00
Mazza, Chris	R-R	6-4	190	10-17-89	0	0	4.61	14	0	0	1	27	26	14	14	3	7	21	.257	.205	.290	6.91	2.30
McClanahan, Shane	L-L	6-1	200	4-28-97	10	6	3.43	25	25	0	0	123	120	49	47	14	37	141	.252	.293	.242	10.29	2.70
McHugh, Collin	R-R	6-2	191	6-19-87	6	1	1.55	37	7	0	1	64	48	15	11	3	12	74	.207	.163	.230	10.41	1.69
Mejia, Francisco	B-R	5-8	188	10-27-95	0	0	27.00	2	0	0	0	2	6	6	6	1	0	0	.500	.400	.571	0.00	0.00
Patino, Luis	R-R	6-1	192	10-26-99	5	3	4.31	19	15	0	0	77	69	40	37	12	29	74	.232	.274	.240	8.61	3.38
Phillips, Brett	L-R	6-0	195	5-30-94	0	0	9.00	1	0	0	0	1	2	1	1	0	2	0	.400	.000	.500	0.00	18.00
Phillips, Evan	R-R	6-2	215	9-11-94	0	0	3.00	1	0	0	1	3	3	1	1	1	1	2	.250	.000	.333	6.00	3.00
Poppen, Sean	R-R	6-3	210	3-15-94	0	0	0.00	1	0	0	0	1	0	0	0	0	1	0	.000	.000	.000	13.50	0.00
Rasmussen, Drew	R-R	6-1	211	7-27-95	4	0	2.44	20	10	0	0	59	44	16	16	3	13	48	.205	.214	.198	7.32	1.98
Reed, Cody	L-L	6-5	230	4-15-93	0	1	3.72	12	0	0	0	10	8	5	4	1	6	7	.235	.125	.269	6.52	5.59
Richards, Trevor	R-R	5-5	195	5-15-93	0	0	4.50	6	0	0	1	12	9	6	6	2	3	16	.205	.133	.241	12.00	2.25
2-team total (32 Toronto)					4	2	3.63	38	0	0	1	45	25	19	18	9	13	53	.160	.161	.160	10.68	2.62
Robertson, David	R-R	5-11	195	4-9-85	0	0	4.50	12	1	0	0	12	11	7	6	2	4	16	.239	.250	.231	12.00	3.00
Roe, Chaz	R-R	6-5	190	10-9-86	0	0	27.00	1	0	0	0	1	1	2	2	0	1	2	.333	1.000	.000	27.00	13.50
Sherriff, Ryan	L-L	6-1	190	5-25-90	0	1	5.52	16	0	0	1	15	14	11	9	0	9	16	.241	.214	.267	9.82	5.52
Springs, Jeffrey	L-L	6-3	218	9-20-92	5	1	3.43	43	0	0	2	45	35	21	17	9	14	63	.216	.263	.190	12.69	2.82
Strickland, Hunter	R-R	6-3	225	9-24-88	0	0	1.69	13	0	0	0	16	14	4	3	1	6	16	.233	.286	.205	9.00	3.38
2-team total (9 Los Angeles)					0	0	4.03	22	0	0	0	22	25	13	10	4	10	20	.281	.313	.263	8.06	4.03
Thompson, Ryan	R-R	6-5	210	6-26-92	3	2	2.38	36	0	0	0	34	26	11	9	3	9	37	.211	.200	.214	9.79	2.38
Wacha, Michael	R-R	6-6	215	7-1-91	3	5	5.05	29	23	0	0	125	132	73	70	23	31	121	.270	.243	.287	8.74	2.24
Wisler, Matt	R-R	6-3	215	9-12-92	2	3	2.15	27	0	0	1	29	22	11	7	2	5	36	.210	.286	.159	11.05	1.53
Yarbrough, Ryan	R-L	6-5	205	12-31-91	9	7	5.11	30	21	1	0	155	163	96	88	25	27	117	.267	.235	.275	6.79	1.57

Fielding

Catcher	PCT	G	PO	A	E	DP	PB
Mejia	.993	76	554	33	4	1	4
Odom	1.000	1	2	0	0	0	0
Smith	1.000	2	13	0	0	0	0
Zunino	.995	105	909	37	5	2	10

First Base	PCT	G	PO	A	E	DP
Brosseau	.974	10	35	3	1	3
Choi	.996	73	500	23	2	46
Cruz	1.000	1	7	0	0	0
Diaz	.996	81	510	31	2	51
Lowe	1.000	1	0	0	0	0
Luplow	1.000	17	90	6	0	8
Mejia	1.000	2	10	1	0	1
Padlo	1.000	3	3	1	0	1
Tsutsugo	1.000	15	80	4	0	9

Second Base	PCT	G	PO	A	E	DP
Brosseau	1.000	27	20	42	0	14
Brujan	.941	4	9	7	1	2
Diaz	.000	1	0	0	0	0
Franco	1.000	1	2	4	0	0
Lowe	.976	133	187	270	11	78
Luplow	.000	1	0	0	0	0
Walls	1.000	3	5	5	0	3
Wendle	1.000	16	16	28	0	3

Third Base	PCT	G	PO	A	E	DP
Brosseau	.974	23	11	27	1	2
Diaz	.983	58	35	84	2	12
Franco	.810	8	5	12	4	1
Luplow	.000	1	0	0	0	0
Padlo	.929	6	4	9	1	2
Walls	.000	1	0	0	0	0
Wendle	.959	107	81	176	11	22

Shortstop	PCT	G	PO	A	E	DP
Adames	.974	40	43	106	4	23
Franco	.977	63	69	141	5	28
Walls	.968	49	35	116	5	20
Wendle	1.000	25	23	60	0	7

Outfield	PCT	G	PO	A	E	DP
Arozarena	.995	135	207	5	1	1
Brosseau	1.000	2	3	0	0	0
Brujan	1.000	4	5	0	0	0
Kiermaier	.996	116	229	1	1	0
Lowe	.944	16	17	0	1	0
Lowe	1.000	2	4	0	0	0
Luplow	1.000	3	1	0	0	0
Margot	.985	134	266	4	4	2
Meadows	.981	79	101	5	2	0
Phillips	.982	117	213	3	4	1

DURHAM BULLS

TRIPLE-A

TRIPLE-A EAST

Batting	B-T	HT	WT	DOB	AVG	vLH	vRH	G	AB	R	H	2B	3B	HR	RBI	BB	HBP	SH	SF	SO	SB	CS	SLG	OBP
Boldt, Ryan	L-R	6-2	210	11-22-94	.260	.228	.276	85	300	38	78	21	2	11	42	33	3	0	2	98	12	1	.453	.337
Brosseau, Mike	R-R	5-10	205	3-15-94	.218	.197	.232	51	170	25	37	2	1	8	21	23	9	0	0	50	2	0	.382	.342
Brujan, Vidal	B-R	5-10	180	2-9-98	.262	.215	.287	103	389	77	102	31	1	12	56	49	1	1	1	68	44	8	.440	.345
Choi, Ji-Man	L-R	6-1	260	5-19-91	.261	.300	.231	6	23	4	6	2	0	0	2	3	0	0	1	7	0	0	.348	.333
Ford, Mike	L-R	6-0	225	7-4-92	.243	.196	.266	40	140	22	34	5	1	11	31	21	1	0	0	41	1	0	.529	.346
3-team total (29 Rochester, 7 Scranton/Wilkes-Barre)					.213	.152	.238	76	268	35	57	10	1	14	44	35	3	0	1	81	1	0	.414	.309
Franco, Wander	B-R	5-10	189	3-1-01	.313	.304	.318	40	163	31	51	11	6	7	35	14	2	0	1	21	5	4	.583	.372
Freitas, David	R-R	6-2	250	3-18-89	.245	.238	.250	16	53	13	13	1	0	3	8	11	0	0	2	11	1	0	.434	.364
Gray, Tristan	L-R	6-3	215	3-22-96	.246	.202	.268	75	248	36	61	13	4	8	33	23	2	0	2	81	1	1	.427	.313
Grullon, Deivy	R-R	5-11	240	2-17-96	.226	.259	.200	21	62	14	14	5	1	4	10	6	1	0	1	26	0	0	.532	.347
3-team total (11 Charlotte, 11 Syracuse)					.196	.205	.192	43	143	21	28	5	0	10	25	14	1	0	1	59	0	0	.441	.270
Haley, Jim	R-R	6-1	195	2-23-95	.000	.000	--	1	4	0	0	0	0	0	0	0	0	0	0	0	0	0	.000	.000
Kelly, Dalton	L-L	6-3	200	8-4-94	.244	.239	.247	110	377	69	92	20	0	27	74	60	5	0	6	129	17	3	.512	.350
Lowe, Josh	L-R	6-4	205	2-2-98	.291	.270	.303	111	402	76	117	28	2	22	78	61	1	0	6	123	26	0	.535	.381
Lukes, Nathan	L-R	5-11	185	7-12-98	.303	.245	.337	85	294	50	89	31	1	4	44	21	4	2	5	41	2	2	.456	.352
Luplow, Jordan	R-R	6-1	195	9-26-93	.182	.160	.200	7	22	2	4	1	0	0	2	5	0	0	0	6	0	0	.227	.333
2-team total (8 Columbus)					.222	.167	.259	15	45	8	10	5	0	2	9	10	0	0	0	10	0	1	.467	.364
Margot, Manuel	R-R	5-11	180	9-28-94	.286	.167	.375	3	14	1	4	0	0	0	5	1	0	0	0	4	1	1	.286	.333
Mastrobuoni, Miles	L-R	5-11	185	10-31-95	.292	.192	.339	51	161	25	47	10	3	0	14	24	0	0	0	48	2	4	.391	.384
Mathisen, Wyatt	R-R	6-0	217	12-30-93	.288	.320	.265	18	59	12	17	5	0	3	9	3	2	0	0	19	0	0	.525	.344
McKay, Brendan	L-L	6-2	220	12-18-95	.091	.125	.071	6	22	1	2	0	0	0	1	3	0	0	0	8	0	0	.091	.200
Mead, Curtis	R-R	6-2	171	10-26-00	.429	.500	.375	4	14	3	6	2	0	1	2	0	0	0	0	3	0	0	.786	.429
Odom, Joseph	R-R	6-2	215	1-9-92	.217	.143	.250	29	92	12	20	4	0	3	15	9	3	0	1	42	0	0	.359	.305
Padlo, Kevin	R-R	6-2	210	7-15-96	.194	.143	.219	69	253	40	49	11	0	12	37	25	2	0	2	93	5	2	.379	.270
Pinto, Rene	R-R	5-10	195	11-2-96	.299	.321	.283	52	201	25	60	11	0	12	35	7	2	0	1	58	2	1	.532	.327

	B-T	HT	WT	DOB	AVG	vLH	vRH	G	AB	R	H	2B	3B	HR	RBI	BB	HBP	SH	SF	SO	SB	CS	SLG	OBP
Quiroz, Esteban	L-R	5-6	199	2-17-92	.268	.235	.283	68	213	49	57	19	0	12	48	43	5	0	1	56	1	0	.526	.401
Roach, Joey	L-R	6-0	205	8-27-93	.100	.250	.000	5	10	1	1	0	0	1	1	1	1	0	0	5	0	0	.400	.250
Sullivan, Brett	L-R	6-1	195	2-22-94	.223	.216	.226	90	309	48	69	20	0	9	35	31	4	1	0	54	7	4	.375	.302
Trevino, Luis	R-R	5-11	200	5-23-96	.000	.000	--	1	2	0	0	0	0	0	0	0	1	0	0	0	0	0	.000	.333
Walls, Taylor	B-R	5-10	185	7-10-96	.247	.315	.218	52	178	41	44	9	1	8	29	40	2	0	2	58	10	5	.444	.387
Whitley, Garrett	R-R	6-1	195	3-13-97	.172	.212	.150	31	93	16	16	4	1	2	11	9	4	0	2	36	3	0	.301	.269
Williams, Alika	R-R	6-2	180	3-12-99	.222	.000	.286	4	9	1	2	0	0	1	3	0	1	0	2	0	0	0	.556	.250

Pitching	B-T	HT	WT	DOB	W	L	ERA	G	GS	CG	SV	IP	H	R	ER	HR	BB	SO	AVG	vLH	vRH	K/9	BB/9
Allie, Stetson	R-R	6-2	244	3-13-91	0	0	6.75	6	1	0	0	5	1	5	4	0	10	6	.067	.167	.000	10.13	16.88
Anderson, Nick	R-R	6-4	205	7-5-90	0	0	5.06	11	0	0	0	11	12	7	6	2	1	12	.286	.368	.217	10.13	0.84
Archer, Chris	R-R	6-2	195	9-26-88	0	1	3.86	5	5	0	0	14	9	9	6	3	3	16	.176	.136	.207	10.29	1.93
Armstrong, Shawn	R-R	6-2	225	9-11-90	2	1	2.57	14	0	0	2	14	10	4	4	1	2	20	.200	.111	.250	12.86	1.29
2-team total (15 Norfolk)					3	4	2.90	29	0	0	2	31	29	14	10	4	8	41	.240	.259	.224	11.90	2.32
Baz, Shane	R-R	6-2	190	6-17-99	3	0	1.76	10	10	0	0	46	28	10	9	6	11	64	.174	.155	.189	12.52	2.15
Brigden, Trevor	L-R	6-3	210	9-20-95	0	1	48.60	2	1	0	0	2	8	9	9	2	2	2	.615	.600	.625	10.80	10.80
Conley, Adam	L-L	6-3	209	5-24-90	2	1	4.35	27	0	0	3	31	18	15	15	4	18	34	.170	.239	.117	9.87	5.23
De Horta, Adrian	R-R	6-3	185	3-13-95	0	2	7.77	8	5	0	0	22	26	20	19	8	12	19	.299	.231	.354	7.77	4.91
Ellis, Chris	L-R	6-5	205	9-22-92	1	5	6.32	15	13	0	0	57	61	43	40	14	28	58	.272	.284	.266	9.16	4.42
Enns, Dietrich	L-L	6-1	210	5-16-91	8	2	2.64	19	11	0	0	72	46	22	21	8	18	90	.178	.164	.182	11.30	2.26
Fairbanks, Pete	R-R	6-6	225	12-16-93	0	0	4.50	2	0	0	0	2	1	1	1	0	2	.143	.500	.000	9.00	0.00
Faucher, Calvin	R-R	6-1	190	9-22-95	0	0	1.77	11	3	0	0	20	14	4	4	1	7	26	.194	.296	.133	11.51	3.10
Feyereisen, J.P.	R-R	6-2	215	2-7-93	0	0	5.79	5	0	0	0	5	4	3	3	1	1	3	.222	.125	.300	5.79	1.93
Fleming, Josh	L-L	6-2	220	5-18-96	1	0	0.90	7	0	0	1	10	7	1	1	0	1	12	.194	.300	.154	10.80	0.90
Head, Louis	R-R	6-1	180	4-23-90	0	0	2.20	26	0	0	5	29	20	7	7	2	10	37	.194	.214	.187	11.63	3.14
Hess, David	R-R	6-1	215	7-10-93	6	3	3.57	20	2	0	0	45	40	21	18	11	10	51	.229	.268	.202	10.13	1.99
Hogan, Miller	R-R	6-2	200	7-18-96	1	0	27.00	1	0	0	0	1	3	3	3	2	0	2	.500	1.000	.250	18.00	0.00
Honeywell Jr., Brent	R-R	6-2	195	3-31-95	5	4	3.97	31	13	0	2	82	74	40	36	13	24	67	.241	.226	.251	7.38	2.64
Krehbiel, Joey	R-R	6-2	185	12-20-92	3	2	4.19	44	0	0	4	43	38	24	20	8	9	52	.236	.275	.223	10.88	1.88
Mazza, Chris	R-R	6-4	190	10-17-89	4	1	3.16	26	3	0	0	37	26	14	13	3	13	47	.191	.174	.200	11.43	3.16
McGee, Easton	R-R	6-6	205	12-26-97	0	0	0.00	1	1	0	0	5	3	0	0	0	3	.200	.143	.250	5.40	0.00
Moats, Dalton	L-L	6-3	210	5-24-95	0	0	6.75	2	0	0	0	1	3	1	1	0	1	3	.429	.333	.500	20.25	6.75
Moran, Brian	L-L	6-4	225	9-30-88	1	0	2.16	53	0	0	1	50	29	15	12	1	14	65	.169	.151	.182	11.70	2.52
Myers, Tobias	R-R	6-0	193	8-5-98	3	4	4.50	12	12	0	0	58	52	31	29	11	18	65	.234	.242	.228	10.09	2.79
Ogando, Cristofer	R-R	6-3	195	10-23-93	0	0	5.40	1	0	0	0	2	2	1	1	2	2	.286	.500	.000	10.80	10.80
Patino, Luis	R-R	6-1	192	10-26-99	1	3	3.07	7	7	0	0	29	23	10	10	2	11	41	.213	.342	.143	12.58	3.38
Peguero, Joel	R-R	5-11	160	5-5-97	0	0	0.00	2	0	0	0	2	0	0	0	0	1	4	.000	.000	.000	15.43	3.86
Phillips, Evan	R-R	6-2	215	9-11-94	0	0	2.70	2	1	0	0	3	4	1	1	0	0	3	.286	.000	.333	8.10	0.00
2-team total (18 Norfolk)					1	1	4.76	20	1	0	0	28	25	17	15	5	14	38	.240	.275	.208	12.07	4.45
Poppen, Sean	R-R	6-3	210	3-15-94	2	3	1.59	19	0	0	2	28	23	7	5	1	11	30	.230	.294	.197	9.53	3.49
2-team total (2 Indianapolis)					3	3	1.95	21	0	0	2	32	26	9	7	2	12	34	.228	.275	.203	9.46	3.34
Rasmussen, Drew	R-R	6-1	211	7-27-95	2	0	0.00	8	1	0	1	11	5	0	0	0	2	23	.132	.067	.136	18.26	1.59
Reed, Cody	L-L	6-5	230	4-15-93	0	0	0.00	6	0	0	0	6	3	0	0	0	1	9	.143	.000	.200	12.79	1.42
Reed, Jake	R-R	6-2	195	9-29-92	0	0	0.00	1	0	0	0	1	1	0	0	0	0	0	.250	1.000	.000	0.00	0.00
2-team total (8 Syracuse)					0	1	3.86	9	0	0	0	8	5	4	1	2	8	.235	.412	.059	7.71	1.93
Richards, Trevor	R-R	6-2	195	5-15-93	1	0	0.00	7	0	0	0	7	3	0	0	0	1	12	.120	.200	.067	14.73	1.23
Rios, Yacksel	R-R	6-3	215	6-27-93	2	0	0.66	12	0	0	0	14	8	2	1	1	2	17	.170	.200	.136	11.20	1.32
2-team total (5 Worcester)					2	0	2.75	17	0	0	3	20	18	7	6	1	5	25	.243	.231	.257	11.44	2.29
Robertson, David	R-R	5-11	195	4-9-85	0	0	0.00	6	0	0	0	6	4	1	0	0	1	12	.200	.333	.091	18.00	1.50
Roe, Chaz	R-R	6-5	190	10-9-86	0	0	7.11	7	0	0	0	6	6	5	5	0	3	7	.250	.100	.357	9.95	4.26
Romero, Tommy	R-R	6-2	225	7-8-97	2	3	3.18	12	12	0	0	62	39	22	22	7	21	70	.178	.196	.165	10.11	3.03
Rosenberg, Kenny	L-L	6-1	195	7-9-95	4	0	2.35	14	0	0	1	31	26	8	8	4	11	43	.239	.242	.237	12.62	3.23
Ryan, Joe	R-R	6-2	205	6-5-96	4	3	3.63	12	11	0	0	57	35	25	23	8	10	75	.175	.218	.142	11.84	1.58
2-team total (2 St. Paul)					4	3	3.41	14	13	0	0	66	40	27	25	9	12	92	.173	.214	.141	12.55	1.64
Sanders, Phoenix	R-R	5-10	205	6-5-95	5	2	3.38	50	0	0	2	64	47	27	24	8	11	80	.203	.183	.213	11.25	1.55
Seymour, Ian	L-L	6-0	210	12-13-98	1	0	0.00	2	2	0	0	10	4	1	0	0	4	9	.121	.125	.120	8.10	3.60
Sherriff, Ryan	L-L	6-1	190	5-25-90	5	4	2.81	32	2	0	1	26	18	9	8	1	14	28	.198	.146	.236	9.82	4.91
Slegers, Aaron	R-R	6-10	260	9-4-92	0	0	6.75	2	2	0	0	8	9	6	6	2	0	6	.281	.250	.300	6.75	0.00
Strotman, Drew	R-R	6-3	195	9-3-96	7	2	3.39	13	12	0	0	58	50	25	22	3	33	62	.235	.222	.246	9.57	5.09
2-team total (12 St. Paul)					10	5	5.29	25	24	0	0	112	115	69	66	12	63	104	.267	.247	.283	8.33	5.05
Thompson, Ryan	R-R	6-5	210	6-26-92	1	0	0.00	4	0	0	0	3	3	0	0	0	3	7	.273	1.000	.000	16.20	8.10
White, Colby	R-R	6-0	190	7-4-98	1	0	1.86	9	0	0	2	10	6	2	2	0	4	14	.176	.273	.130	13.03	3.72
Wisler, Matt	R-R	6-3	215	9-12-92	0	0	0.00	1	0	0	0	1	1	0	0	0	3	.250	.000	1.000	27.00	0.00
Zabaleta, Ezequiel	R-R	6-0	175	8-20-95	0	0	4.50	4	0	0	0	6	5	3	3	2	2	5	.227	.167	.250	7.50	3.00
Zombro, Tyler	R-R	5-10	215	9-2-94	1	1	3.18	9	0	0	0	11	15	4	4	1	1	9	.306	.320	.292	7.15	0.79

Fielding

Catcher	PCT	G	PO	A	E	DP	PB
Freitas	1.000	5	39	4	0	0	0
Grullon	1.000	10	82	2	0	0	0
Odom	.992	21	231	4	2	1	1
Pinto	.990	34	365	16	4	0	2
Roach	1.000	2	6	1	0	0	0
Sullivan	.994	66	616	28	4	4	6

First Base	PCT	G	PO	A	E	DP
Brosseau	.955	7	40	2	2	4
Choi	1.000	5	38	2	0	4
Ford	.993	19	131	9	1	13
Freitas	1.000	1	3	0	0	0
Gray	1.000	8	48	4	0	1
Kelly	.998	77	477	58	1	53
Luplow	1.000	5	26	2	0	2
Mathisen	1.000	12	74	3	0	5
Padlo	.974	5	36	1	1	5
Roach	1.000	1	4	0	0	0

Second Base	PCT	G	PO	A	E	DP
Brosseau	1.000	8	15	14	0	5
Brujan	.990	29	40	56	1	13
Franco	1.000	3	4	3	0	2

Gray	.846	2	5	6	2	1
Mastrobuoni	.973	11	19	17	1	8
Padlo	.981	17	22	29	1	5
Quiroz	.979	58	88	95	4	34
Walls	.974	10	18	19	1	3

Third Base	PCT	G	PO	A	E	DP
Brosseau	.943	28	18	32	3	1
Brujan	.846	6	2	9	2	0
Ford	1.000	6	4	5	0	1
Franco	.944	7	3	14	1	1
Gray	.979	23	11	36	1	1
Mastrobuoni	.953	15	15	26	2	4
Mathisen	1.000	1	0	1	0	0

Mead	1.000	4	1	7	0	1
Padlo	.966	45	34	80	4	12
Walls	.933	6	1	13	1	0

Shortstop	PCT	G	PO	A	E	DP
Brosseau	.938	5	6	9	1	1
Brujan	.917	16	17	38	5	11
Franco	.973	31	37	71	3	10
Gray	.975	38	32	86	3	20
Haley	1.000	1	1	2	0	0
Mastrobuoni	.929	3	4	9	1	1
Quiroz	1.000	3	2	4	0	1
Walls	.976	36	47	77	3	22
Williams	1.000	4	2	6	0	2

Outfield	PCT	G	PO	A	E	DP
Boldt	.984	74	124	2	2	0
Brosseau	1.000	1	3	0	0	0
Brujan	.975	53	71	6	2	0
Kelly	1.000	26	40	0	0	0
Lowe	.988	104	162	6	2	2
Lukes	1.000	82	122	3	0	0
Luplow	1.000	1	1	0	0	0
Margot	1.000	3	4	0	0	0
Mastrobuoni	1.000	20	36	1	0	0
Sullivan	.889	14	24	0	3	0
Whitley	1.000	31	57	0	0	0

MONTGOMERY BISCUITS
DOUBLE-A
DOUBLE-A SOUTH

Batting	B-T	HT	WT	DOB	AVG	vLH	vRH	G	AB	R	H	2B	3B	HR	RBI	BB	HBP	SH	SF	SO	SB	CS	SLG	OBP
Aranda, Jonathan	L-R	5-10	173	5-23-98	.325	.348	.320	79	274	53	89	19	5	10	58	33	10	0	5	63	4	2	.540	.410
Betts, Chris	L-R	6-2	215	3-10-97	.117	.000	.132	23	60	4	7	1	0	2	10	10	1	0	0	28	0	0	.233	.254
Cardenas, Ruben	R-R	6-2	185	10-10-97	.262	.265	.261	75	290	43	76	9	3	15	47	12	3	0	4	84	3	3	.469	.294
Edwards, Xavier	B-R	5-10	175	8-9-99	.302	.328	.296	79	291	40	88	13	3	0	27	36	1	5	4	42	19	11	.368	.377
Gomez, Moises	R-R	5-11	200	8-27-98	.171	.134	.183	76	269	34	46	13	0	8	23	27	4	0	1	115	5	3	.309	.256
Haley, Jim	R-R	6-1	195	2-23-95	.205	.247	.191	94	336	51	69	17	2	14	39	24	10	0	3	118	18	5	.393	.276
Hollis, Connor	R-R	5-10	170	11-18-94	.375	.500	.346	10	32	3	12	5	2	0	2	4	0	0	0	10	0	1	.656	.444
Hulsizer, Niko	R-R	6-2	225	2-1-97	.243	.121	.271	51	173	31	42	10	1	8	35	20	2	0	1	78	2	0	.451	.327
Hunt, Blake	R-R	6-3	215	11-10-98	.125	.167	.114	17	56	5	7	2	0	0	6	0	1	0	0	25	0	0	.161	.210
Johnson, Kaleo	R-R	6-3	220	8-26-96	.125	.148	.108	20	64	4	8	2	0	1	7	1	0	0	0	33	0	0	.156	.222
Jones, Greg	B-R	6-2	175	3-7-98	.185	.167	.188	16	54	8	10	1	1	1	2	4	2	0	0	21	7	0	.296	.267
Mastrobuoni, Miles	L-R	5-11	185	10-31-95	.299	.300	.298	55	221	34	66	14	2	5	31	27	0	0	1	48	6	3	.448	.373
Ostberg, Erik	L-R	5-10	225	10-12-95	.190	.000	.222	6	21	0	4	0	1	0	4	0	0	0	0	7	0	0	.286	.190
Palomaki, Jake	B-R	5-10	175	7-17-95	.198	.213	.192	75	217	27	43	4	3	0	19	37	4	6	2	50	14	9	.244	.323
Paulson, Dillon	L-L	6-3	200	6-10-97	.340	.438	.297	15	53	5	18	3	0	0	13	4	0	0	2	13	0	1	.396	.373
Pinto, Rene	R-R	5-10	195	11-2-96	.242	.188	.267	41	153	25	37	9	0	8	25	15	3	0	0	56	2	1	.458	.322
Proctor, Ford	L-R	6-1	195	12-4-96	.244	.154	.267	97	308	54	75	12	3	12	47	63	7	0	3	100	4	4	.419	.381
Roach, Joey	L-R	6-0	205	8-27-93	.228	.125	.254	26	79	7	18	2	0	3	14	7	1	0	0	19	0	1	.367	.299
Shenton, Austin	L-R	6-0	205	1-22-98	.271	.364	.243	13	48	5	13	3	0	2	9	2	0	0	1	15	0	0	.458	.294
Smith, Michael	L-L	5-11	165	5-30-97	.179	.133	.192	21	67	9	12	1	1	0	7	5	1	0	2	30	1	0	.224	.240
Stevenson, Cal	L-L	5-10	175	9-12-96	.254	.268	.251	92	295	51	75	15	1	9	41	56	1	6	7	78	17	5	.403	.368
Whalen, Seaver	R-R	6-2	185	2-5-95	.214	.300	.173	60	187	20	40	12	1	6	30	8	17	1	4	43	5	3	.385	.301
Whitley, Garrett	R-R	6-1	195	3-13-97	.255	.263	.254	57	200	44	51	14	2	11	24	30	7	1	1	67	9	4	.510	.370

Pitching	B-T	HT	WT	DOB	W	L	ERA	G	GS	CG	SV	IP	H	R	ER	HR	BB	SO	AVG	vLH	vRH	K/9	BB/9
Battenfield, Peyton	R-R	6-4	224	8-10-97	3	0	2.72	7	6	0	0	36	24	13	11	5	7	46	.179	.150	.203	11.39	1.73
Baz, Shane	R-R	6-2	190	6-17-99	2	4	2.48	7	7	0	0	33	22	9	9	3	2	49	.190	.173	.203	13.50	0.55
Brink, Jordan	L-R	6-0	200	3-18-93	4	1	4.42	32	1	0	1	57	52	29	28	5	20	61	.243	.230	.252	9.63	3.16
Carrera, Faustino	L-L	5-10	165	3-9-99	2	2	3.21	16	6	0	0	48	38	19	17	4	14	32	.216	.227	.209	6.04	2.64
De Horta, Adrian	R-R	6-3	185	3-13-95	2	4	4.36	17	5	0	0	33	36	16	16	5	18	44	.202	.208	.197	12.00	4.91
Dodson, Tanner	B-R	6-1	160	5-9-97	1	2	4.86	13	0	0	2	17	17	12	9	2	9	17	.258	.231	.275	9.18	4.86
Faucher, Calvin	R-R	6-1	190	9-22-95	0	0	0.00	2	0	0	1	5	2	0	0	0	0	4	.125	.000	.222	7.71	0.00
Gau, Christopher	L-R	6-2	205	2-3-91	2	0	2.31	7	0	0	0	12	8	3	3	2	5	21	.182	.133	.207	16.20	3.86
Haley, Jim	R-R	6-1	195	2-23-95	0	0	3.38	2	0	0	0	3	4	1	1	0	0	6	.364	.000	.571	0.00	0.00
Hogan, Miller	R-R	6-2	200	7-18-96	0	1	3.18	4	4	0	0	17	18	9	6	2	0	19	.257	.321	.214	10.06	0.00
Labosky, Jack	R-R	6-3	235	7-19-96	2	4	4.20	28	11	0	0	79	71	44	37	15	16	76	.238	.208	.258	8.62	1.82
Lopez, Jacob	L-L	6-4	220	3-11-98	0	0	3.60	1	1	0	0	5	3	2	2	0	1	8	.158	.111	.200	14.40	1.80
McGee, Easton	R-R	6-6	205	12-26-97	6	2	4.07	19	18	0	0	80	77	40	36	10	13	73	.251	.270	.238	8.25	1.47
McKay, Brendan	L-L	6-2	220	12-18-95	0	2	12.86	3	3	0	0	7	10	10	10	5	4	8	.323	.273	.350	10.29	5.14
Moats, Dalton	L-L	6-3	210	5-24-91	0	0	5.46	18	0	0	0	28	35	17	17	4	8	29	.309	.329	.302	9.32	2.57
Muller, Chris	R-R	6-5	210	4-22-96	1	1	4.32	17	0	0	7	17	15	9	8	3	12	25	.234	.385	.132	13.50	6.48
Murray, Jayden	R-R	6-1	190	4-11-97	1	2	2.82	8	8	0	0	38	21	13	12	6	7	43	.157	.172	.145	10.10	1.64
Myers, Tobias	R-R	6-0	193	8-5-98	5	3	3.32	13	10	0	0	60	49	23	22	8	10	81	.222	.208	.233	12.22	1.51
Ogando, Cristofer	R-R	6-3	195	10-23-93	5	2	3.68	21	3	0	0	37	25	18	15	4	15	52	.188	.220	.162	12.76	3.68
Peguero, Joel	R-R	5-11	160	5-5-97	4	8	4.50	37	0	0	3	54	53	32	27	2	22	48	.257	.329	.213	8.00	3.67
Pelaez, Ivan	R-R	6-1	155	2-1-94	8	5	5.43	37	0	0	10	55	63	41	33	8	12	50	.285	.256	.301	8.23	1.98
Plassmeyer, Michael	L-L	6-2	197	11-5-96	2	1	3.64	7	3	0	0	30	28	13	12	4	7	33	.241	.171	.272	10.01	2.12
Romero, Tommy	R-R	6-2	225	7-8-97	1	0	1.88	11	9	0	0	48	36	13	10	3	10	75	.202	.179	.220	14.06	1.88
Rosenberg, Kenny	L-L	6-1	195	7-9-95	0	1	3.60	2	2	0	0	5	3	4	2	1	4	6	.176	.200	.167	10.80	7.20
Rosenblum-Larson, Simon	R-R	6-3	202	2-11-97	0	0	7.00	7	0	0	0	9	5	8	7	0	6	6	.156	.273	.095	15.00	6.00
Sampen, Caleb	R-R	6-2	185	7-23-96	0	1	8.66	5	4	0	0	18	21	18	17	3	10	11	.288	.273	.300	5.60	5.09
Shaffer, Brian	R-R	6-5	200	8-12-96	1	1	5.63	12	0	0	0	24	24	15	15	5	4	14	.267	.324	.226	5.25	1.50
Sterner, Justin	R-R	6-1	215	8-29-96	1	1	3.54	14	0	0	3	28	23	11	11	4	7	32	.222	.197	.229	10.29	2.25
Strong, Alan	R-R	6-3	200	10-22-96	0	1	9.82	3	0	0	0	4	6	4	4	0	3	4	.333	.250	.400	9.82	7.36
Valverde, Alex	R-R	6-2	185	9-26-96	2	5	4.88	30	10	0	3	72	69	44	39	6	29	92	.246	.270	.230	11.50	3.63
Whalen, Seaver	R-R	6-2	185	2-5-95	0	0	9.00	1	0	0	0	1	1	1	1	0	2	0	.000	.000	.000	0.00	18.00

	B-T	HT	WT	DOB	W	L	ERA	G	GS	CG	SV	IP	H	R	ER	HR	BB	SO	AVG	vLH	vRH	K/9	BB/9
White, Colby	R-R	6-0	190	7-4-98	0	0	1.38	8	0	0	2	13	4	3	2	0	3	19	.095	.063	.115	13.15	2.08
Witt, Nathan	R-R	6-4	210	4-19-96	0	1	8.44	7	2	0	0	11	8	12	10	2	8	7	.195	.250	.160	5.91	6.75
York, Mikey	R-R	6-2	190	2-24-96	2	0	3.92	14	1	0	0	21	18	10	9	4	8	20	.234	.143	.310	8.71	3.48

Fielding

Catcher	PCT	G	PO	A	E	DP	PB
Betts	.991	16	102	6	1	1	4
Hunt	.994	17	152	4	1	1	0
Ostberg	.714	1	5	0	2	0	0
Pinto	.982	28	260	11	5	2	2
Proctor	.989	58	584	23	7	5	16
Roach	1.000	3	17	0	0	0	0

First Base	PCT	G	PO	A	E	DP
Aranda	.997	48	308	21	1	31
Haley	.968	17	115	7	4	8
Johnson	.978	6	43	2	1	5
Paulson	.989	12	83	7	1	9
Pinto	.984	7	54	6	1	4
Roach	1.000	3	9	0	0	2
Shenton	1.000	1	6	0	0	1
Whalen	.992	32	215	20	2	17

Second Base	PCT	G	PO	A	E	DP
Aranda	.968	17	18	42	2	10
Edwards	.988	55	60	107	2	24
Haley	1.000	10	9	28	0	5
Hollis	.972	9	11	24	1	5
Mastrobuoni	1.000	5	11	12	0	4
Palomaki	.964	23	32	49	3	12
Proctor	.938	4	4	11	1	2

Third Base	PCT	G	PO	A	E	DP
Aranda	.889	10	4	12	2	1
Edwards	.966	22	14	42	2	5
Haley	.942	33	22	43	4	4
Hollis	1.000	1	3	0	0	0
Johnson	.875	3	2	5	1	0
Mastrobuoni	1.000	4	7	4	0	0
Palomaki	.939	15	7	24	2	2
Proctor	.947	6	3	15	1	1
Shenton	1.000	11	4	15	0	3

	PCT	G	PO	A	E	DP
Whalen	.910	21	25	36	6	2

Shortstop	PCT	G	PO	A	E	DP
Aranda	1.000	1	3	1	0	0
Haley	.922	26	23	60	7	9
Jones	.961	15	16	33	2	7
Mastrobuoni	.955	23	31	53	4	14
Palomaki	.957	29	28	62	4	12
Proctor	.967	28	32	55	3	12

Outfield	PCT	G	PO	A	E	DP
Cardenas	1.000	68	108	6	0	0
Gomez	.976	69	119	5	3	2
Haley	1.000	12	23	1	0	0
Hulsizer	.982	33	54	0	1	0
Mastrobuoni	.975	18	37	2	1	0
Smith	.974	20	37	0	1	0
Stevenson	1.000	91	157	6	0	3
Whitley	1.000	51	90	1	0	0

BOWLING GREEN HOT RODS

HIGH CLASS A

HIGH-A EAST

Batting	B-T	HT	WT	DOB	AVG	vLH	vRH	G	AB	R	H	2B	3B	HR	RBI	BB	HBP	SH	SF	SO	SB	CS	SLG	OBP
Alexander, Hill	R-R	6-2	200	6-13-96	.325	.309	.333	53	166	37	54	9	0	14	41	19	2	2	3	59	7	2	.633	.395
Alvarez, Roberto	R-R	5-11	151	7-28-99	.333	.333	.333	26	78	13	26	4	0	1	16	14	4	0	0	14	1	0	.423	.458
Aranda, Jonathan	L-R	5-10	173	5-23-98	.351	.333	.355	21	74	20	26	3	0	4	7	9	5	0	1	13	1	0	.554	.449
Basabe, Osleivis	R-R	6-1	188	9-13-00	.250	.300	.167	4	16	2	4	0	0	1	1	2	0	0	0	6	0	0	.438	.333
Cardenas, Ruben	R-R	6-2	185	10-10-97	.368	.320	.380	30	117	26	43	4	0	10	31	12	1	0	2	31	3	1	.658	.424
Driscoll, Logan	L-R	6-1	195	11-3-97	.241	.182	.262	24	87	13	21	7	0	2	10	8	0	0	2	25	0	0	.391	.299
Edwards, Evan	L-L	6-0	200	6-21-97	.226	.157	.249	94	332	55	75	11	1	22	58	56	6	0	2	137	6	1	.464	.346
Gigliotti, Michael	L-L	6-0	180	2-14-96	.203	.077	.235	21	64	15	13	3	0	3	10	9	1	0	0	24	4	1	.391	.311
Gregorio, Osmy	R-R	6-2	175	5-27-98	.162	.086	.189	38	130	14	21	7	0	1	13	8	0	2	1	36	1	1	.238	.209
Hollis, Connor	R-R	5-10	170	11-18-94	.277	.375	.240	63	231	45	64	16	1	5	26	22	5	0	2	45	12	1	.420	.350
Hulsizer, Niko	R-R	6-2	225	2-1-97	.248	.235	.252	44	153	36	38	10	0	13	41	25	2	0	0	70	7	0	.569	.361
Hunt, Blake	R-R	6-3	215	11-10-98	.225	.194	.236	59	227	41	51	15	2	9	41	26	2	0	2	79	1	0	.427	.307
Infante, Diego	R-R	6-2	178	10-22-99	.500	.156	.455	5	16	2	4	0	0	0	3	1	0	0	0	4	0	0	.600	.524
Jones, Greg	B-R	6-2	175	3-7-98	.291	.323	.277	56	220	48	64	7	3	13	38	29	7	0	1	75	27	2	.527	.389
Martinez, Pedro	B-R	5-11	165	1-28-01	.216	.250	.203	89	348	50	75	12	3	6	39	31	5	2	0	121	21	18	.319	.289
McGowan, Jacson	R-R	6-3	212	6-18-97	.241	.242	.241	67	220	42	53	5	1	17	46	33	0	0	4	97	1	0	.505	.340
Mead, Curtis	R-R	6-2	171	10-26-00	.282	.298	.275	53	206	38	58	15	1	7	32	19	4	0	4	38	2	2	.466	.348
Murray, Tanner	R-R	6-2	190	9-3-99	.154	.222	.000	3	13	1	2	1	0	0	0	0	0	0	0	3	0	0	.231	.154
Ostberg, Erik	L-R	5-10	225	10-12-95	.266	.162	.290	59	192	31	51	5	1	12	33	21	2	0	1	57	0	2	.490	.343
Qsar, Jordan	L-R	6-3	195	12-2-95	.257	.180	.283	98	343	65	88	19	4	23	69	55	1	1	3	132	15	5	.536	.366
Trevino, Luis	R-R	5-11	200	5-23-96	.295	.269	.302	35	112	18	33	13	0	1	14	12	2	0	0	20	1	1	.438	.373
Turner, Gionti	R-R	6-2	178	8-17-00	.167	.200	.143	5	12	6	2	1	0	0	1	3	0	0	0	2	0	1	.250	.333
Williams, Alika	R-R	6-2	180	3-12-99	.279	.316	.262	14	61	12	17	3	0	3	9	2	0	0	0	11	1	1	.475	.302
Wisely, Brett	L-R	5-10	180	5-8-99	.321	.389	.289	31	112	28	36	6	0	8	30	30	0	0	2	29	3	1	.589	.418
Witherspoon, Grant	L-L	6-3	200	9-27-96	.269	.211	.289	99	386	65	104	20	2	22	70	38	0	0	5	109	13	6	.503	.331

Pitching	B-T	HT	WT	DOB	W	L	ERA	G	GS	CG	SV	IP	H	R	ER	HR	BB	SO	AVG	vLH	vRH	K/9	BB/9
Battenfield, Peyton	R-R	6-4	224	8-10-97	2	0	1.45	7	6	0	0	31	18	7	5	2	5	49	.162	.156	.167	14.23	1.45
Bradley, Taj	R-R	6-2	190	3-20-01	3	0	1.96	8	8	0	0	37	28	11	8	4	11	42	.207	.169	.259	10.31	2.70
Brigden, Trevor	L-R	6-3	210	9-20-95	2	0	2.97	23	1	0	1	36	24	15	12	6	7	42	.180	.169	.191	10.40	1.73
Costanzo, Michael	L-L	6-1	190	11-14-95	2	1	4.78	30	0	0	2	49	42	34	26	10	26	51	.223	.216	.230	9.37	4.78
Cumbie, Trey	L-L	6-2	200	7-12-96	1	2	5.23	11	1	0	1	21	19	13	12	4	8	27	.226	.226	.226	11.76	3.48
Dodson, Tanner	B-R	6-1	160	5-9-97	4	0	2.50	24	1	0	2	40	38	14	11	2	14	47	.250	.296	.197	10.66	3.18
Doxakis, John	R-L	6-4	215	8-20-98	6	1	4.56	16	14	0	0	73	67	41	37	6	16	72	.240	.231	.246	8.88	1.97
Felipe, Angel	R-R	6-5	190	8-30-97	1	0	4.38	15	0	0	1	25	20	17	12	3	16	33	.217	.204	.233	12.04	5.84
Garcia, Carlos	R-R	6-3	185	11-20-98	8	2	4.23	26	6	0	0	66	54	36	31	9	27	63	.219	.238	.200	8.59	3.68
Gau, Christopher	L-R	6-2	205	2-3-97	2	2	3.41	27	0	0	6	37	33	16	14	4	8	59	.228	.197	.253	14.35	1.95
Gregorio, Osmy	R-R	6-2	175	5-27-98	0	0	0.00	1	0	0	0	1	0	0	0	0	0	0	.000	.000	--	0.00	0.00
Hogan, Miller	R-R	6-2	200	7-18-96	4	2	3.62	24	4	0	2	55	40	25	22	9	9	57	.202	.231	.183	9.38	1.48
LaSorsa, Joe	L-L	6-2	215	4-29-98	1	1	4.71	12	6	0	0	36	34	22	19	8	14	29	.245	.231	.253	7.18	3.47
Lopez, Jacob	L-L	6-4	220	3-11-98	3	1	2.30	14	10	0	2	55	40	15	14	6	17	88	.201	.250	.165	14.49	2.80
Lopez, Jose	L-L	6-1	200	2-15-99	3	1	9.72	5	0	0	0	8	11	9	9	2	5	6	.324	.290	.348	6.48	5.40
McKendry, Evan	R-R	6-3	200	2-6-98	4	3	3.73	21	10	0	3	63	51	30	26	7	12	60	.222	.230	.213	8.62	1.72
Mercado, Michael	R-R	6-4	160	4-15-99	2	5	5.35	22	18	0	0	71	68	47	42	16	23	81	.250	.235	.261	10.32	2.93
Moss, Addison	R-R	6-1	190	9-10-97	0	0	6.00	2	0	0	0	3	3	3	2	1	2	2	.231	.286	.167	6.00	3.00
Muller, Chris	R-R	6-5	210	4-22-96	0	1	7.20	4	0	0	0	5	5	4	4	1	1	7	.211	.125	.273	12.60	1.80

Name	B-T	HT	WT	DOB	W	L	ERA	G	GS	CG	SV	IP	H	R	ER	HR	BB	SO	AVG	vLH	vRH	K/9	BB/9
Murray, Jayden	R-R	6-1	190	4-11-97	7	1	1.72	12	12	0	0	58	30	18	11	5	10	53	.149	.161	.138	8.27	1.56
Ogando, Cristofer	R-R	6-3	195	10-23-93	0	1	8.31	9	0	0	0	13	15	13	12	4	7	20	.273	.222	.297	13.85	4.85
Seymour, Ian	L-L	6-0	210	12-13-98	1	0	1.80	2	2	0	0	10	6	2	2	1	2	19	.167	.176	.158	17.10	1.80
Sterner, Justin	R-R	6-1	215	8-29-96	1	2	3.00	6	0	0	0	9	9	5	3	0	3	16	.237	.217	.267	16.00	3.00
Strong, Alan	R-R	6-3	200	10-22-96	6	2	6.71	27	6	0	4	51	73	41	38	6	13	57	.333	.333	.333	10.06	2.29
Trageton, Zack	R-R	6-1	225	9-2-98	5	2	4.08	28	12	0	2	88	84	46	40	11	22	84	.250	.228	.273	8.56	2.24
White, Colby	R-R	6-0	190	7-4-98	2	2	2.31	15	1	0	3	23	8	6	6	3	7	35	.105	.135	.077	13.50	2.70
Witt, Nathan	R-R	6-4	210	4-19-96	1	0	7.45	8	0	0	0	10	10	9	8	2	6	9	.256	.348	.125	8.38	5.59
York, Mikey	R-R	6-2	190	2-24-96	0	0	6.17	9	0	0	1	12	8	9	8	3	2	20	.190	.118	.240	15.43	1.54
Zabaleta, Ezequiel	R-R	6-0	175	8-20-95	6	4	4.11	29	0	0	3	50	51	26	23	7	18	59	.258	.307	.218	10.55	3.22

Fielding

Catcher	PCT	G	PO	A	E	DP	PB
Alvarez	.988	23	222	18	3	2	1
Driscoll	.981	16	146	9	3	1	2
Hunt	.993	50	503	31	4	2	2
Ostberg	1.000	18	138	10	0	0	3
Trevino	.994	19	175	3	1	4	3
McGowan	.000	1	0	0	0	0	
Turner	.667	2	1	1	1	0	
Williams	.889	3	1	7	1	2	
Wisely	1.000	22	35	43	0	12	
Hollis	1.000	4	2	8	0	0	
Jones	.926	50	70	106	14	21	
Martinez	.944	49	65	104	10	25	
Murray	.750	1	0	3	1	0	
Williams	.906	11	8	21	3	1	

First Base	PCT	G	PO	A	E	DP
Edwards	.986	85	609	37	9	34
McGowan	.993	21	134	9	1	17
Mead	1.000	3	17	0	0	2
Ostberg	.941	6	46	2	3	7
Trevino	.975	5	38	1	1	2
Witherspoon	1.000	2	12	2	0	1

Second Base	PCT	G	PO	A	E	DP
Aranda	.917	15	11	33	4	2
Basabe	1.000	2	2	0	1	0
Gregorio	.954	21	26	57	4	17
Hollis	.983	31	43	71	2	11
Martinez	.988	27	23	60	1	6

Third Base	PCT	G	PO	A	E	DP
Alvarez	.000	1	0	0	0	0
Aranda	.846	5	2	9	2	1
Gregorio	.966	9	9	19	1	0
Hollis	1.000	6	6	9	0	0
Martinez	.929	14	9	17	2	2
McGowan	.848	37	14	42	10	4
Mead	.980	43	34	62	2	4
Murray	1.000	2	3	2	0	0
Turner	.875	2	2	5	1	2
Wisely	1.000	6	4	3	0	0

Shortstop	PCT	G	PO	A	E	DP
Aranda	1.000	1	0	1	0	0
Basabe	1.000	3	4	5	0	0
Gregorio	.909	3	3	7	1	1

Outfield	PCT	G	PO	A	E	DP
Alexander	.971	49	61	6	2	1
Cardenas	1.000	29	62	1	0	1
Driscoll	1.000	8	21	0	0	0
Gigliotti	1.000	19	46	0	0	0
Gregorio	.800	4	4	0	1	0
Hollis	1.000	13	17	2	0	0
Hulsizer	.934	39	55	2	4	1
Infante	1.000	5	11	0	0	0
McGowan	--	1	0	0	0	0
Qsar	.995	95	182	4	1	1
Turner	1.000	1	2	0	0	0
Witherspoon	.984	98	177	2	3	1

CHARLESTON RIVERDOGS
LOW-A EAST

LOW CLASS A

Batting	B-T	HT	WT	DOB	AVG	vLH	vRH	G	AB	R	H	2B	3B	HR	RBI	BB	HBP	SH	SF	SO	SB	CS	SLG	OBP
Alexander, Hill	R-R	6-2	200	6-13-96	.213	.182	.220	22	61	10	13	2	1	4	15	12	3	0	0	23	1	0	.475	.368
Basabe, Osleivis	R-R	6-1	188	9-13-00	.284	.186	.311	66	278	51	79	16	2	5	35	26	2	1	2	39	18	4	.385	.347
Berglund, Michael	L-R	6-2	175	7-18-97	.196	.267	.180	50	158	23	31	6	0	1	26	27	7	0	6	61	2	0	.253	.328
Brundage, Beau	L-R	6-3	170	4-29-97	.340	.130	.381	38	141	35	48	12	3	8	32	22	4	0	1	50	3	1	.638	.440
Driscoll, Logan	L-R	6-1	195	11-3-97	.324	.241	.354	30	111	36	36	9	1	4	15	12	4	0	1	37	2	0	.532	.406
Dyer, Matt	R-R	6-4	185	7-14-98	.336	.391	.321	27	107	25	36	7	3	5	13	6	2	0	0	35	4	2	.598	.383
Embry, Jonathan	L-R	5-11	180	11-26-96	.253	.169	.277	82	265	60	67	17	3	8	39	64	3	0	4	68	9	0	.430	.399
Hernandez, Heriberto	R-R	6-1	195	12-16-99	.252	.231	.257	73	250	54	64	15	0	12	44	49	9	0	8	90	7	4	.453	.381
Hiott, Garrett	L-R	5-11	175	7-7-97	.268	.212	.284	42	149	32	40	5	3	6	28	25	3	1	2	52	11	2	.463	.380
Infante, Diego	R-R	6-2	178	10-22-99	.296	.250	.309	101	371	83	110	20	5	16	80	56	6	0	5	114	20	8	.507	.393
Leon, Luis	B-R	6-0	175	9-10-98	.218	.107	.246	42	142	19	31	7	0	2	15	18	2	0	1	40	0	0	.310	.313
Lopez, Johan	R-R	5-10	167	7-28-00	.240	.148	.269	84	262	56	63	13	1	10	40	44	12	2	5	89	17	1	.412	.368
Marte, Jelfry	B-R	5-10	130	3-27-01	.140	.200	.132	13	43	9	6	1	0	1	3	5	1	1	1	13	1	2	.233	.240
Mead, Curtis	R-R	6-2	171	10-26-00	.356	.351	.357	47	191	36	68	21	1	7	35	15	3	0	2	30	9	2	.586	.408
Merino, Patrick	R-R	6-2	220	8-13-98	.189	.200	.185	23	74	11	14	1	1	4	20	11	3	0	0	36	0	0	.392	.318
Murray, Tanner	R-R	6-2	190	9-3-99	.339	.346	.337	27	109	23	37	12	1	2	21	9	4	0	1	20	2	2	.523	.407
Ovalles, Alexander	L-L	6-0	184	10-6-00	.248	.319	.226	89	315	45	78	13	2	8	46	43	6	2	4	68	5	4	.378	.345
Ramirez, Abiezel	B-R	5-11	160	1-26-00	.260	.145	.295	68	231	38	60	10	3	9	54	32	1	5	3	102	17	3	.446	.348
Schnell, Nick	L-R	6-3	180	3-27-00	.174	.189	.170	52	190	35	33	4	0	8	29	31	4	0	2	73	13	2	.321	.300
Trevino, Luis	R-R	5-11	200	5-23-96	.154	.000	.200	4	13	1	2	0	0	0	1	1	1	0	0	4	3	0	.154	.267
Troike, Ben	R-R	5-10	170	2-5-98	.348	.000	.364	7	23	3	8	1	0	0	2	4	2	0	0	3	2	0	.391	.483
Williams, Alika	R-R	6-2	180	3-12-99	.266	.149	.295	55	237	37	63	13	1	1	34	17	3	1	5	43	5	5	.342	.317
Wisely, Brett	L-R	5-10	180	5-8-99	.292	.240	.304	69	274	50	80	13	1	11	44	28	1	1	2	69	28	7	.467	.357

Pitching	B-T	HT	WT	DOB	W	L	ERA	G	GS	CG	SV	IP	H	R	ER	HR	BB	SO	AVG	vLH	vRH	K/9	BB/9
Alexander, Hill	R-R	6-2	200	6-13-96	0	0	0.00	1	0	0	0	1	0	0	0	0	0	0	.000	.000	.000	0.00	0.00
Bradley, Taj	R-R	6-2	190	3-20-01	9	3	1.76	15	14	1	0	67	37	17	13	4	20	81	.165	.219	.125	10.94	2.70
Brecht, Ben	L-L	6-7	215	1-7-98	5	3	3.23	19	16	0	0	75	58	32	27	9	14	70	.206	.241	.191	8.36	1.67
Brigden, Trevor	L-R	6-3	210	9-20-95	1	1	3.27	6	0	0	2	11	6	5	4	0	4	25	.154	.176	.136	20.45	3.27
Catalina, Neraldo	R-R	6-6	202	6-21-00	2	2	8.69	24	3	0	0	29	28	29	28	2	31	36	.246	.250	.242	11.17	9.62
Costanzo, Michael	L-L	6-1	190	11-14-95	0	0	0.00	1	0	0	0	3	1	0	0	0	1	4	.111	.200	.000	13.50	3.38
Cumbie, Trey	L-L	6-2	200	7-12-96	4	1	3.49	16	1	0	1	28	17	11	11	1	20	45	.173	.276	.130	14.29	6.35
Dacosta, Franklin	L-L	5-11	162	2-24-99	3	1	3.05	9	5	0	0	41	32	17	14	3	11	51	.219	.174	.240	11.10	2.40
Doxakis, John	R-L	6-4	215	8-20-98	3	1	2.43	7	7	0	0	30	16	8	8	1	3	42	.154	.167	.149	12.74	0.91
Felipe, Angel	R-R	6-5	190	8-30-97	2	0	1.42	21	0	0	7	38	31	8	6	1	17	45	.223	.281	.173	10.66	4.03
Figueroa, Hector	R-R	6-3	190	11-30-94	6	2	5.89	24	0	0	4	44	41	37	29	7	24	51	.237	.225	.245	10.35	4.87
Gaston, Sandy	R-R	6-3	200	12-16-01	2	1	3.86	7	7	0	0	30	22	16	13	2	22	38	.206	.179	.235	11.27	6.53

Player	B-T	HT	WT	DOB																				
Gross, Andrew	R-R	6-4	195	9-19-96	6	1	1.66	33	1	0	2	60	47	17	11	2	6	59	.214	.286	.169	8.90	0.91
Hiott, Garrett	L-R	5-11	175	7-7-97	0	0	36.00	1	0	0	0	1	5	4	4	2	0	1	.625	.500	.750	9.00	0.00
Jimenez, Antonio	L-L	5-11	145	5-6-01	1	1	4.70	4	2	0	0	15	13	9	8	2	7	20	.228	.273	.200	11.74	4.11
Johnson, Seth	R-R	6-1	200	9-19-98	6	6	2.88	23	16	0	0	94	86	43	30	7	33	115	.243	.194	.284	11.05	3.17
LaSorsa, Joe	L-L	6-5	215	4-29-98	0	2	2.41	19	0	0	4	34	23	11	9	2	5	40	.192	.079	.244	10.69	1.34
Leatherman, Ian	R-R	5-11	165	2-26-99	0	0	1.29	5	0	0	0	7	2	1	1	0	3	8	.095	.111	.083	10.29	3.86
Lopez, Jose	L-L	6-1	200	2-15-99	3	6	4.48	22	10	0	3	66	53	34	33	5	34	77	.217	.266	.194	10.45	4.61
Lugo, Audry	R-R	5-11	160	10-29-98	3	2	5.73	22	1	0	0	38	38	29	24	3	23	41	.259	.234	.277	9.80	5.50
Moncada, Luis	L-L	6-1	150	2-28-98	8	1	2.79	18	10	0	1	68	47	26	21	3	28	66	.197	.213	.190	8.78	3.72
Moore, Steffon	L-L	6-3	185	6-25-97	3	1	6.59	20	0	0	0	29	26	26	21	0	31	48	.241	.194	.260	15.07	9.73
Moss, Addison	R-R	6-1	190	9-10-97	2	0	10.24	7	0	0	0	10	16	11	11	1	6	13	.364	.500	.286	12.10	5.59
Munoz, Victor	R-R	6-3	160	12-25-00	0	0	2.79	3	3	0	0	10	8	3	3	1	1	9	.235	.188	.278	8.38	0.93
Peguero, Matthew	R-R	6-2	200	1-12-00	1	1	4.30	9	2	0	0	23	21	11	11	5	8	26	.244	.176	.343	10.17	3.13
Rivera, Juan	R-R	6-3	220	6-4-98	1	0	0.00	5	1	0	0	7	2	2	0	0	6	10	.087	.077	.100	12.86	7.71
Rojas, Nomar	R-R	6-4	168	3-30-01	3	1	3.33	12	0	0	0	24	17	11	9	1	15	21	.202	.229	.184	7.77	5.55
Seymour, Ian	L-L	6-0	210	12-13-98	2	0	2.55	10	9	0	0	35	16	11	10	3	13	59	.136	.139	.134	15.03	3.31
Stinson, Graeme	L-L	6-5	250	8-6-97	1	0	5.44	23	2	0	1	45	44	39	27	6	22	35	.254	.183	.292	7.05	4.43
Theriot, Brayden	R-R	6-2	195	12-19-96	2	0	0.64	10	0	0	3	14	9	1	1	0	0	26	.176	.200	.161	16.71	0.00
White, Colby	R-R	6-0	190	7-4-98	1	1	0.00	11	0	0	4	16	8	3	0	1	1	36	.138	.238	.081	19.84	0.55
Wilcox, Cole	R-R	6-5	232	7-14-99	1	0	2.03	10	10	0	0	44	33	16	10	1	5	52	.200	.174	.219	10.56	1.02
Yancey, Stephen	L-R	6-1	190	11-8-95	1	0	4.05	7	0	0	0	13	9	6	6	2	9	19	.196	.077	.242	12.83	6.08

Fielding

Catcher	PCT	G	PO	A	E	DP	PB
Berglund	.988	40	396	30	5	1	7
Driscoll	.995	17	203	7	1	1	3
Dyer	.979	9	85	9	2	2	0
Embry	.989	26	247	16	3	1	4
Leon	.992	33	345	31	3	4	8

First Base	PCT	G	PO	A	E	DP
Dyer	.980	6	49	1	1	5
Embry	.988	51	384	22	5	38
Mead	.990	15	95	6	1	8
Ovalles	.980	48	318	18	7	32
Trevino	1.000	3	20	0	0	1
Wisely	.971	6	31	2	1	4

Second Base	PCT	G	PO	A	E	DP
Basabe	.976	21	37	45	2	13
Embry	1.000	1	0	1	0	0
Lopez	.964	23	43	64	4	18
Marte	.923	10	14	22	3	8
Murray	.900	5	5	13	2	1
Ramirez	.956	19	35	52	4	13
Troike	1.000	1	1	2	0	0
Williams	.947	8	12	24	2	7
Wisely	.963	35	59	70	5	16

Third Base	PCT	G	PO	A	E	DP
Basabe	.929	6	6	7	1	0
Dyer	1.000	3	2	6	0	0
Lopez	.890	35	22	51	9	4
Mead	.938	25	20	40	4	2
Murray	1.000	9	6	10	0	3
Ramirez	.787	26	10	27	10	4
Troike	.750	5	2	4	2	0
Wisely	.957	18	12	32	2	4

Shortstop	PCT	G	PO	A	E	DP
Basabe	.922	39	38	92	11	21
Lopez	.957	22	23	65	4	14
Marte	.818	3	6	3	2	1
Murray	.962	6	9	16	1	4
Ramirez	.955	7	7	14	1	1
Williams	.967	44	52	123	6	25

Outfield	PCT	G	PO	A	E	DP
Alexander	1.000	18	19	0	0	0
Brundage	1.000	36	50	1	0	0
Driscoll	1.000	6	9	0	0	0
Dyer	1.000	9	10	4	0	1
Hernandez	.958	66	87	4	4	0
Hiott	.984	40	60	3	1	0
Infante	.977	91	119	7	3	0
Merino	.889	20	23	1	3	0
Ovalles	.959	43	65	5	3	2
Schnell	.986	45	68	1	1	1

FCL RAYS   ROOKIE
FLORIDA COMPLEX LEAGUE

Batting	B-T	HT	WT	DOB	AVG	vLH	vRH	G	AB	R	H	2B	3B	HR	RBI	BB	HBP	SH	SF	SO	SB	CS	SLG	OBP
Allen, Logan	R-R	5-10	180	8-13-98	.200	.333	.185	10	30	10	6	0	0	0	5	6	0	0	0	5	4	0	.200	.333
Alvarez, Roberto	R-R	5-11	151	7-28-99	.143	.000	.158	6	21	4	3	0	0	0	0	4	0	0	0	7	0	0	.143	.280
Auer, Mason	R-R	6-1	210	3-1-01	.265	.333	.250	11	34	7	9	2	0	0	3	6	1	0	0	7	10	1	.324	.390
Baker, Dru	R-R	5-11	205	3-22-00	.289	.250	.297	12	45	8	13	2	2	0	10	3	1	0	0	9	6	0	.422	.347
Betts, Chris	L-R	6-2	215	3-10-97	.286	.000	.308	4	14	3	4	3	0	0	4	3	0	0	1	6	0	0	.500	.389
Brosseau, Mike	R-R	5-10	205	3-15-94	.750	.667	1.000	1	4	1	3	2	0	0	1	0	0	0	0	0	0	0	1.250	.750
Brundage, Beau	L-R	6-3	170	4-29-97	.182	.000	.211	8	22	6	4	0	1	1	3	4	2	0	0	12	1	0	.409	.357
Candelario, Stir	R-R	6-0	185	9-3-00	.125	.250	.083	15	48	3	6	0	1	0	1	8	0	0	0	19	0	0	.167	.250
Castellanos, Daiwer	L-R	5-11	155	8-16-00	.235	.333	.213	29	98	18	23	3	1	1	9	15	2	1	0	28	7	3	.316	.348
Castillo, Estanli	R-R	6-3	195	10-7-01	.259	.000	.326	18	54	13	14	5	0	0	9	14	0	0	1	13	1	1	.352	.406
Chevez, Freddvil	R-R	6-4	200	3-13-00	.292	.400	.270	32	120	23	35	7	0	3	19	11	3	1	4	28	0	0	.425	.355
Choi, Ji-Man	L-R	6-1	260	5-19-91	.000	.000	.000	2	5	0	0	0	0	0	0	1	2	0	0	3	0	0	.000	.286
Dimon, Dawson	R-R	6-1	185	5-17-99	.333	.000	.429	9	9	2	3	0	0	0	2	5	0	0	0	4	0	0	.333	.571
Driscoll, Logan	L-R	6-1	195	11-3-97	.444	--	.444	3	9	3	4	2	0	0	3	4	0	0	0	2	0	1	.667	.615
Edwards, K.V.	R-R	6-1	175	3-5-98	.278	.500	.250	6	18	6	5	0	0	0	2	7	6	1	0	7	0	0	.611	.480
Fernandez, Mario	R-R	5-11	172	9-28-00	.220	.333	.188	30	82	16	18	7	0	3	14	7	6	0	0	21	0	0	.415	.326
Figuereo, Alberto	B-R	5-8	145	4-24-00	.161	.250	.148	12	31	1	5	0	0	0	3	3	1	1	0	10	2	1	.161	.257
Freitas, David	R-R	6-2	250	3-18-89	.077	.000	.091	4	13	2	1	0	0	0	0	2	1	0	0	3	0	0	.077	.250
Galarraga, Angel	L-R	6-1	178	8-1-02	.182	--	.182	4	11	2	2	0	0	0	1	2	0	0	0	3	0	0	.182	.308
Gigliotti, Michael	L-L	6-1	180	2-14-96	.333	--	.333	6	15	5	5	3	1	1	6	7	3	0	1	4	2	0	.867	.577
Huffins, Zach	R-R	6-1	185	6-16-99	.263	.429	.226	14	38	10	10	4	1	2	9	4	1	0	0	15	3	0	.579	.349
Johnson, Christian	R-R	5-11	180	6-4-01	.170	.250	.143	18	47	5	8	2	2	0	6	1	2	0	2	11	0	1	.298	.212
Kinney, Cooper	L-R	6-3	200	1-27-03	.286	.167	.310	11	35	9	10	1	1	0	5	10	2	0	0	9	2	0	.371	.468
Leon, Luis	B-R	6-0	175	9-10-98	.286	--	.286	2	7	0	2	1	0	0	1	0	0	0	1	0	0	0	.429	.286
Luplow, Jordan	R-R	6-1	195	9-26-93	.800	1.000	.750	1	5	2	4	1	0	0	3	0	0	0	0	0	0	0	1.600	.800
Manzardo, Kyle	L-R	6-1	205	7-18-00	.349	.400	.333	13	43	10	15	5	0	2	8	4	3	0	0	6	0	0	.605	.440
Manzueta, Oneill	R-R	6-0	190	2-7-01	.278	.200	.295	18	54	10	15	2	0	0	9	1	0	1	0	15	1	0	.315	.385
Marte, Jelfry	B-R	5-10	130	3-27-01	.189	.214	.183	26	74	14	14	0	2	0	7	16	4	1	1	22	5	4	.243	.358

TAMPA BAY RAYS

Batter	B-T	HT	WT	DOB	AVG	vLH	vRH	G	AB	R	H	2B	3B	HR	RBI	BB	HBP	SH	SF	SO	SB	CS	SLG	OBP
Merino, Patrick	R-R	6-2	220	8-13-98	.257	.167	.304	13	35	13	9	1	0	4	13	10	5	0	1	13	3	2	.629	.471
Meza, Julio	R-R	6-0	165	5-4-99	.222	.200	.231	8	18	4	4	1	0	0	4	5	0	0	1	8	1	0	.278	.375
Murray, Tanner	R-R	6-2	190	9-3-99	.364	.500	.355	9	33	7	12	6	1	2	12	4	2	0	0	3	2	0	.788	.462
Phillips, Brett	L-R	6-0	195	5-30-94	.250	--	.250	1	4	1	1	0	0	1	1	0	0	0	0	2	0	0	1.000	.250
Pie, Alejandro	R-R	6-4	175	1-31-02	.238	.238	.238	32	122	16	29	4	0	0	9	8	3	0	1	47	10	4	.270	.299
Pierre, Yonathan	R-R	6-1	170	6-4-99	.150	.250	.083	8	20	4	3	0	0	0	5	5	1	0	1	9	2	0	.150	.333
Piper, Kenny	R-R	5-10	190	7-12-98	.533	.500	.545	6	15	4	8	2	0	1	2	2	2	0	1	3	2	0	.867	.600
Quiroz, Esteban	L-R	5-6	199	2-17-92	.417	.000	.500	4	12	7	5	1	1	2	9	3	3	0	0	4	2	0	1.167	.611
Sanchez, Aldenis	R-R	6-1	165	9-26-98	.250	.000	.286	2	8	2	2	1	0	0	1	2	0	0	0	2	1	0	.375	.400
2-team total (3 FCL Yankees)					.133	.000	.154	5	15	2	2	1	0	0	1	2	0	0	0	4	1	0	.200	.235
Sasaki, Shane	R-R	6-0	165	7-1-00	.290	.308	.286	33	124	33	36	4	2	2	16	18	1	0	1	37	22	2	.403	.382
Seymour, Bobby	L-R	6-4	250	10-7-98	.333	.333	.333	8	30	5	10	3	0	2	10	2	0	0	1	13	1	0	.633	.364
Smith, Michael	L-L	5-11	165	5-30-97	.111	.000	.125	3	9	3	1	1	0	0	0	3	0	0	0	2	0	0	.222	.333
Soria, Nate	R-R	5-10	175	11-24-95	.222	.429	.150	15	27	8	6	2	0	0	3	7	2	0	1	6	3	0	.296	.405
Spikes, Ryan	R-R	5-9	185	3-13-03	.250	.111	.290	11	40	9	10	3	0	1	5	6	1	0	0	13	4	1	.400	.362
Troike, Ben	R-R	5-10	170	2-5-98	.278	.333	.259	15	36	8	10	1	0	0	8	7	1	0	2	10	4	0	.306	.391
Turner, Gionti	R-R	6-2	178	8-17-00	.272	.111	.317	29	81	12	22	4	0	1	8	11	3	2	1	16	4	3	.358	.375
Vasquez, Willy	R-R	6-0	191	9-6-01	.288	.324	.277	40	146	26	42	6	3	2	31	20	4	0	3	27	14	6	.411	.382
Williams, Carson	R-R	6-2	180	6-25-03	.282	.000	.333	11	39	8	11	4	1	0	8	6	2	0	0	13	2	2	.436	.404

Pitching

Pitching	B-T	HT	WT	DOB	W	L	ERA	G	GS	CG	SV	IP	H	R	ER	HR	BB	SO	AVG	vLH	vRH	K/9	BB/9
Allie, Stetson	R-R	6-2	244	3-13-91	0	0	9.82	4	0	0	0	4	5	4	4	0	4	5	.294	.200	.333	12.27	9.82
Anderson, Nick	R-R	6-4	205	7-5-90	0	0	0.00	2	1	0	0	2	1	0	0	0	0	4	.143	--	.143	18.00	0.00
Angel, Conor	R-R	6-5	190	9-30-99	0	0	0.00	1	0	0	0	1	0	0	0	0	1	1	.000	.000	--	0.00	9.00
Archer, Chris	R-R	6-2	195	9-26-88	0	0	0.00	1	1	0	0	1	1	0	0	0	1	1	.200	.000	.250	6.75	6.75
Ayala Jr., Alex	R-L	6-1	195	11-26-01	0	0	0.00	4	0	0	0	6	1	0	0	0	3	10	.059	.000	.077	15.88	4.76
Carvajal, Linse	R-R	6-2	170	12-5-98	0	0	11.05	6	0	0	0	7	13	9	9	3	5	7	.394	.500	.316	8.59	6.14
Cortorreal, Aneudy	R-R	6-3	200	12-13-99	1	0	1.29	10	0	0	1	21	13	6	3	0	13	27	.200	.159	.159	11.57	5.57
Cuevas, Jonny	R-R	6-3	200	11-20-00	0	0	7.71	2	0	0	0	2	3	2	2	0	1	3	.273	.000	.375	11.57	3.86
Dacosta, Franklin	L-L	5-11	162	2-27-00	1	0	0.57	4	1	0	1	16	11	1	1	0	3	22	.196	.174	.212	12.64	1.72
Dryer, Conor	L-R	6-3	205	8-18-98	1	0	2.00	7	0	0	0	9	7	2	2	1	0	10	.206	.231	.190	10.00	0.00
Feyereisen, J.P.	R-R	6-2	215	2-7-93	0	0	0.00	1	0	0	1	1	0	0	0	0	0	0	.000	.000	.000	9.00	0.00
Fields, Kamron	R-R	6-2	200	9-24-98	0	0	10.80	3	0	0	1	3	3	4	4	0	4	1	.250	.333	.167	2.70	10.80
Galue, Over	R-R	6-2	188	7-31-01	5	3	4.13	14	3	0	1	28	29	19	13	2	18	34	.259	.195	.296	10.80	5.72
Gaston, Sandy	R-R	6-3	200	12-16-01	1	0	3.20	7	3	0	0	20	7	8	7	1	33	32	.115	.100	.122	14.64	5.95
Goss, JJ	R-R	6-3	185	12-25-00	1	0	6.10	4	3	0	0	10	15	7	7	0	0	12	.341	.391	.286	10.45	0.00
Guzman, Cristian	R-R	5-11	153	5-8-02	2	0	0.00	5	2	0	0	10	6	0	0	0	7	16	.188	.067	.294	14.40	6.30
Hakanson, Jeff	R-R	6-0	185	8-4-98	2	0	2.84	4	0	0	0	6	2	3	2	1	1	11	.087	.000	.182	15.63	1.42
Hunley, Sean	R-R	6-4	220	7-5-99	1	0	2.35	6	0	0	1	8	6	2	2	0	0	12	.214	.182	.235	14.09	0.00
Jimenez, Antonio	L-L	5-11	145	5-6-01	2	0	1.65	8	5	0	1	33	23	6	6	1	7	44	.197	.100	.230	12.12	1.93
Leatherman, Ian	R-R	5-11	165	2-26-99	0	0	0.00	3	0	0	0	4	1	0	0	0	1	9	.077	.000	.143	20.25	2.25
Leon, Maicor	L-L	5-9	165	3-6-01	1	1	2.96	17	0	0	1	24	14	16	8	3	18	25	.159	.143	.162	9.25	6.66
Leonard, Cameron	R-R	6-4	205	7-26-99	2	0	1.64	9	0	0	0	11	14	2	2	0	1	10	.333	.600	.185	8.18	0.82
Mazza, Chris	R-R	6-2	190	10-17-89	0	0	0.00	1	1	0	0	1	0	0	0	0	1	1	.000	.000	.000	9.00	0.00
McKay, Brendan	L-L	6-2	220	12-18-95	0	0	1.59	4	4	0	0	6	5	2	1	1	1	5	.217	.286	.188	7.94	1.59
Melo, Fernando	L-L	6-6	200	12-31-99	0	0	8.64	7	0	0	0	8	4	11	8	0	13	11	.133	.000	.167	11.88	14.04
Molina, Anthony	R-R	6-2	170	1-12-02	2	1	2.61	12	3	0	2	31	29	10	9	2	8	36	.252	.306	.212	10.45	2.32
Montgomery, Mason	L-L	6-2	195	6-17-00	1	0	0.84	5	4	0	0	11	4	1	1	1	0	20	.114	.231	.045	16.88	0.84
Moss, Addison	R-R	6-1	190	9-10-97	0	0	0.00	2	0	0	0	3	1	0	0	0	3	7	.100	.000	.500	21.00	9.00
Mullen, Sean	R-R	6-1	205	9-18-99	0	0	0.00	4	0	0	2	6	3	0	0	0	0	7	.143	.000	.250	9.95	1.42
Munoz, Victor	R-R	6-3	160	12-25-00	1	1	1.95	10	7	0	0	32	32	10	7	0	6	38	.252	.333	.203	10.58	1.67
Peguero, Matthew	R-R	6-2	200	1-12-00	3	1	4.28	8	5	0	0	27	22	16	13	5	14	35	.220	.270	.190	11.52	4.61
Peoples, Ben	L-R	6-1	175	5-1-01	2	1	2.84	9	4	0	0	19	16	7	6	0	13	29	.225	.348	.167	13.74	6.16
Reed, Cody	L-L	6-5	230	4-15-93	0	0	0.00	1	0	0	0	1	0	0	0	0	1	3	.000	.000	.000	27.00	9.00
Rivera, Juan	R-R	6-3	220	6-4-98	3	0	3.93	12	0	0	1	18	15	8	8	0	9	29	.224	.185	.250	14.24	4.42
Rojas, Nomar	R-R	6-4	168	3-30-01	1	2	4.22	4	0	0	1	11	11	6	5	1	4	8	.250	.250	.250	6.75	3.38
Rosenberg, Kenny	L-L	6-1	195	7-9-95	0	0	4.50	2	2	0	0	6	5	3	3	1	1	10	.217	.250	.211	15.00	1.50
Rosenblum-Larson, Simon	R-R	6-3	202	2-11-97	1	0	16.50	6	0	0	0	6	8	12	11	2	9	11	.320	.385	.250	16.50	13.50
Sampen, Caleb	R-R	6-2	185	7-23-96	0	1	6.00	2	2	0	0	3	5	5	2	0	0	2	.313	.222	.429	6.00	0.00
Stinson, Graeme	L-L	6-5	250	8-6-97	1	0	6.75	2	0	0	0	4	5	3	3	1	2	4	.294	.000	.500	9.00	4.50
Theriot, Brayden	R-R	6-2	195	12-19-96	0	0	0.00	4	0	0	0	2	1	0	0	0	1	6	.143	.000	.250	27.00	4.50
Thompson, Ryan	R-R	6-5	210	6-26-92	0	0	0.00	1	0	0	0	1	0	0	0	0	0	2	.000	.000	.000	18.00	0.00
Vernon, Austin	R-R	6-8	265	2-8-99	2	0	0.79	5	2	0	0	11	4	1	1	0	4	17	.105	.125	.091	13.50	3.18
Whitten, Kyle	R-R	6-3	190	9-22-98	1	1	1.50	6	0	0	0	6	5	6	1	0	2	7	.239	.300	.067	10.50	3.00
Wicklander, Patrick	R-L	6-1	205	12-31-99	2	0	0.00	5	0	0	1	11	8	0	0	0	3	22	.195	.167	.217	17.47	2.38
Wisler, Matt	R-R	6-3	215	9-12-92	1	0	0.00	1	0	0	1	3	0	0	0	0	0	3	.000	.000	.000	27.00	0.00
Witt, Nathan	R-R	6-4	210	4-19-96	0	3	11.37	5	2	0	0	6	8	8	8	1	3	9	.370	.455	.313	12.79	4.26
Workman, Logan	R-R	6-2	215	12-6-98	1	0	0.87	5	0	0	2	10	6	1	1	0	5	14	.171	.176	.167	12.19	4.35

Fielding

C: Alvarez 4, Betts 3, Dimon 6, Driscoll 2, Fernandez 30, Freitas 3, Galarraga 4, Leon 1, Meza 5, Piper 5, Soria 14.
1B: Candelario 12, Chevez 28, Choi 1, Luplow 1, Manzardo 10, Seymour 5, Troike 1.
2B: Brosseau 1, Edwards 1, Figuereo 6, Kinney 8, Marte 9, Murray 2, Quiroz 2, Sasaki 1, Spikes 5, Troike 5, Turner 22.
3B: Edwards 1, Figueroa 5, Kinney 3, Marte 3, Murray 2, Pie 23, Spikes 5, Troike 4, Turner 2, Vasquez 11.
SS: Castellanos 1, Figuereo 1, Marte 11, Murray 4, Pie 6, Troike 4, Turner 1, Vasquez 27, Williams 11.
OF: Allen 10, Auer 11, Baker 12, Brundage 7, Castellanos 30, Castillo 15, Chevez 2, Edwards 3, Gigliotti 6, Huffins 12, Johnson 17, Manzueta 15, Merino

8, Pie 1, Pierre 6, Sanchez 2, Sasaki 31, Smith 3, Turner 1, Vasquez 1.

DSL RAYS — ROOKIE

DOMINICAN SUMMER LEAGUE

Batting	B-T	HT	WT	DOB	AVG	vLH	vRH	G	AB	R	H	2B	3B	HR	RBI	BB	HBP	SH	SF	SO	SB	CS	SLG	OBP
Albert Lantigua	L-R	5-9	160	10-9-99	.000	--	.000	1	1	0	0	0	0	0	0	0	0	0	0	1	0	0	.000	.000
Aponte, Cesar	R-R	6-3	160	7-16-02	.318	.412	.296	49	176	28	56	12	2	0	26	13	7	0	1	37	13	8	.409	.386
Arias, Gabriel	R-R	5-11	169	10-13-03	.250	.000	.298	26	56	7	14	6	0	0	7	8	3	0	0	27	4	2	.357	.373
Ariza, Luis	R-R	5-11	155	5-8-04	.255	.208	.264	45	153	25	39	10	1	3	24	15	3	0	2	47	4	4	.392	.329
Barete, Cristopher	L-L	5-9	155	12-10-01	.309	.250	.319	41	110	20	34	10	3	2	13	19	1	0	0	27	9	3	.509	.415
Barragan, Edwin	R-R	5-7	158	7-2-03	.299	.364	.281	44	147	23	44	4	0	2	15	16	6	0	4	15	18	9	.367	.382
Cerda, Christian	R-R	6-0	190	12-27-02	.218	.320	.194	42	133	18	29	9	2	1	18	25	6	0	0	25	5	3	.338	.366
Colmenarez, Carlos	L-R	5-10	170	11-15-03	.247	.250	.247	26	97	7	24	2	1	0	12	8	4	0	4	30	7	6	.289	.319
Croisier, Angel	R-R	5-11	162	1-4-03	.250	.500	.222	7	20	1	5	0	0	0	4	2	0	0	0	5	1	0	.250	.318
De La Cruz, Willmer	B-R	5-8	168	4-6-03	.261	.195	.282	51	165	37	43	9	2	2	19	41	3	0	1	51	21	11	.376	.414
Del Rosario, Daury	R-R	6-0	175	2-14-02	.179	.111	.191	26	56	11	10	3	0	3	8	10	8	0	1	14	2	0	.393	.373
Diaz, Jhon	L-L	5-11	160	10-1-02	.176	.148	.182	45	159	26	28	5	2	1	13	29	0	0	3	58	5	3	.252	.298
Feliz, Alexis	L-R	5-10	155	9-26-02	.275	.083	.316	29	69	11	19	4	1	0	7	7	1	3	2	15	5	4	.362	.342
Feliz, Luis	B-R	5-10	155	5-8-02	.203	.286	.182	26	69	8	14	5	1	0	3	10	1	0	0	26	8	3	.304	.313
Galarraga, Angel	L-R	6-1	178	8-1-02	.159	.111	.171	18	44	11	7	0	0	1	3	16	1	0	1	12	2	1	.227	.387
Jimenez, Arison	R-R	5-10	153	11-5-02	.185	.037	.227	40	124	16	23	3	2	1	16	24	4	0	1	40	8	4	.266	.333
Leon, Yonathan	R-R	6-0	153	10-18-02	.203	.222	.196	43	148	22	30	2	0	0	8	15	2	0	3	40	19	6	.216	.280
Martinez, Raudelis	L-R	6-0	180	5-30-02	.173	.000	.210	38	127	14	22	4	0	2	16	18	2	0	2	25	3	3	.252	.282
Millan, Santiago	R-R	6-2	174	5-27-03	.263	.256	.265	51	175	28	46	3	0	3	28	22	5	0	3	40	10	5	.331	.356
Peguero, Odalys	B-R	5-9	172	1-25-03	.273	.257	.277	50	172	37	47	4	3	1	17	36	4	0	3	39	21	6	.349	.405
Pena, Jose	R-R	6-0	185	12-24-02	.159	.103	.172	47	157	29	25	2	0	4	11	29	6	0	1	54	16	2	.248	.311
Perez, Jorge	R-R	5-8	162	10-11-02	.214	.133	.236	28	70	8	15	3	0	0	6	13	4	0	1	19	0	0	.257	.364
Perez, Jose	R-R	5-9	170	3-12-04	.206	.167	.218	33	102	14	21	4	2	1	15	18	2	0	1	27	2	5	.314	.333
Petiyan, Elias	B-R	5-11	160	12-3-01	.315	.571	.277	26	54	10	17	3	0	1	16	10	2	2	2	10	5	4	.426	.426
Piron, Jhonny	R-R	6-1	165	2-6-04	.232	.275	.219	52	168	34	39	12	1	3	17	29	7	0	1	44	17	6	.369	.366
Quevedo, Jesus	R-R	0-0	0	9-12-03	.169	.333	.151	23	59	10	10	4	0	0	8	11	2	2	1	16	2	2	.237	.315
Rangel, Roylems	R-R	5-8	163	10-17-02	.198	.118	.213	34	111	11	22	4	1	0	7	11	1	0	1	21	2	2	.252	.274
Rodriguez, Nathanael	R-R	6-0	155	12-6-03	.157	.087	.173	38	127	13	20	4	0	0	19	14	2	0	1	29	2	3	.189	.250
Rodriguez, Rhoniel	B-R	5-9	154	9-16-02	.188	.381	.133	34	96	15	18	2	2	0	17	7	4	0	1	26	5	1	.250	.269
Salguera, Felix	R-R	6-0	171	3-1-02	.292	.310	.286	37	113	15	33	6	1	2	14	14	1	0	1	21	7	3	.416	.372
Tapia, German	R-R	6-2	170	9-19-03	.214	.214	.214	49	168	22	36	8	0	0	14	26	3	0	2	52	2	7	.262	.327
Valera, Victor	B-R	5-9	146	10-15-02	.180	.278	.140	23	61	12	11	0	0	1	5	6	0	0	0	13	3	0	.230	.254
Velasquez, Wuilman	L-R	5-8	148	2-7-03	.192	.059	.232	28	73	12	14	2	0	0	3	11	0	0	1	23	5	1	.219	.294

Pitching	B-T	HT	WT	DOB	W	L	ERA	G	GS	CG	SV	IP	H	R	ER	HR	BB	SO	AVG	vLH	vRH	K/9	BB/9
Acosta, Luis	R-R	5-11	185	2-8-02	3	1	5.74	14	0	0	3	27	29	20	17	2	8	21	.284	.320	.273	7.09	2.70
Afanador, Emilio	R-R	6-1	202	2-10-03	0	2	9.00	7	1	0	1	8	12	9	8	0	8	6	.353	.364	.348	6.75	9.00
Alberto, Alexander	R-R	6-8	190	11-2-01	1	2	4.21	14	2	0	0	26	25	17	12	0	19	21	.250	.241	.254	7.36	6.66
Almonte, Adrian	L-L	6-4	199	3-4-03	1	3	8.50	13	1	0	0	18	23	25	17	1	17	18	.307	.143	.370	9.00	8.50
Andujar, Gustavo	R-R	5-11	164	4-6-00	4	3	3.38	16	0	0	1	35	24	19	13	1	14	28	.214	.200	.226	7.27	3.63
Andujar, Jordy	R-R	6-3	186	2-25-03	1	0	1.35	12	0	0	1	20	9	4	3	0	17	24	.138	.152	.125	10.80	7.65
Arredondo, Baltazar	L-L	6-1	175	1-22-04	0	3	6.05	12	4	0	1	19	23	16	13	1	16	18	.291	.316	.283	8.38	7.45
Barrios, Orlando	R-R	6-6	180	8-27-01	3	3	4.25	13	10	0	0	49	44	27	23	3	13	37	.244	.232	.255	6.84	2.40
Calmes, Nigel	R-R	6-1	175	9-21-99	2	2	1.00	15	0	0	1	27	15	8	3	1	7	31	.158	.175	.145	10.33	2.33
Castillo, Franklin	L-L	5-11	154	11-3-01	0	2	1.23	10	1	0	0	15	9	4	2	1	2	14	.176	.111	.190	8.59	1.23
Contreras, Elvis	L-L	5-11	145	2-13-00	4	2	1.17	13	6	0	0	54	38	17	7	1	13	61	.196	.186	.200	10.23	2.18
Costume, Fernando	R-R	6-2	165	5-14-03	0	0	8.18	9	3	0	0	11	5	13	10	0	23	12	.143	.250	.087	9.82	18.82
Cruz, Samuel	R-R	6-3	160	1-9-02	4	0	3.96	12	5	0	0	39	26	19	17	2	33	30	.195	.196	.195	6.98	7.68
Curet, Yoniel	R-R	6-2	190	11-3-02	2	4	3.71	14	8	0	0	51	37	25	21	0	27	63	.210	.191	.230	11.12	4.76
De Jesus, Cesar	L-L	6-1	140	9-28-03	1	0	2.70	7	1	0	1	13	8	4	4	0	11	17	.178	.100	.200	11.48	7.43
De La Rosa, Manuel	L-L	6-0	155	4-20-03	2	4	3.38	14	9	0	0	51	37	25	19	1	27	73	.207	.318	.191	12.97	4.80
Dishmey, Christopher	R-R	6-2	200	11-10-02	1	1	4.26	8	3	0	0	13	11	8	6	1	4	4	.250	.250	.250	2.84	2.84
Dominguez, Justino	R-R	5-11	178	9-26-01	2	1	4.91	7	4	0	0	11	3	7	6	0	11	13	.094	.125	.083	10.64	9.00
Feliz, Alexis	L-R	5-10	155	9-26-02	0	0	0.00	1	0	0	0	0	0	0	0	0	0	1	.000	.000	--	27.00	0.00
Fransua, Victor	R-R	6-1	180	8-13-00	3	0	2.10	13	0	0	4	26	15	7	6	0	16	26	.181	.190	.179	9.12	5.61
Geronimo, Darwin	R-R	6-2	187	3-24-00	0	0	2.25	11	0	0	2	20	15	7	5	0	16	10	.221	.238	.213	4.50	7.20
Gonzalez, Jose	R-R	6-3	175	4-1-02	2	0	7.15	8	0	0	0	11	11	9	9	2	7	11	.262	.150	.364	8.74	5.56
Guaiquirian, Angel	R-R	6-3	174	3-21-03	0	2	4.56	15	4	0	0	26	33	17	13	1	7	15	.303	.292	.311	5.26	2.45
Javier, Sebastian	R-R	6-1	185	12-26-03	1	3	18.69	4	3	0	0	4	7	10	9	0	8	2	.350	.500	.286	4.15	16.62
Jimenez, Humberto	R-R	6-2	174	9-29-01	0	1	3.20	12	5	0	1	20	21	10	7	0	18	17	.273	.317	.222	7.78	8.24
Kimura, Igor	R-R	6-1	207	4-14-99	2	0	5.09	10	1	0	2	18	15	12	10	0	7	12	.217	.241	.200	6.11	3.57
Manuela, Egory	L-L	6-1	180	9-9-03	0	0	3.38	7	5	0	0	11	8	5	4	0	17	17	.216	.333	.194	14.34	14.34
Mateo, Israel	R-R	5-11	135	11-22-01	1	6	6.08	15	7	0	1	37	32	29	25	1	27	33	.239	.277	.213	8.03	6.57
Mejia, Samuel	R-R	6-1	160	6-17-02	3	1	2.63	12	6	0	0	51	43	22	15	2	15	44	.223	.237	.216	7.71	2.63
Nunez, Cristhian	R-R	6-3	185	12-15-00	1	2	4.13	14	0	0	0	24	19	14	11	1	20	30	.238	.200	.260	11.25	7.50
Pichardo, Alexis	R-R	6-1	180	8-20-02	1	1	2.00	5	0	0	0	9	4	5	2	0	9	9	.148	.182	.125	9.00	9.00
Rodriguez, Andy	R-R	6-1	182	7-28-02	0	1	3.07	10	0	0	3	15	15	7	5	1	4	13	.263	.250	.276	7.98	2.45
Rodriguez, Juan	R-R	6-1	180	8-22-01	1	1	5.82	13	6	0	0	34	29	25	22	1	31	32	.240	.304	.200	8.47	8.21
Ruiz, Raynalf	R-R	6-3	175	4-27-01	1	0	3.86	12	0	0	3	16	14	12	7	0	12	15	.230	.261	.211	8.27	6.61

TAMPA BAY RAYS

					W	L	ERA	G	GS	CG	SV	IP	H	R	ER	HR	BB	SO	AVG				
Severino, Kikito	L-L	5-11	145	8-26-01	4	5	3.74	15	10	0	0	53	57	37	22	1	28	59	.270	.200	.298	10.02	4.75
Tavarez, Andri	L-L	6-1	165	5-23-03	3	2	2.96	13	7	0	0	52	44	22	17	2	17	57	.227	.174	.234	9.93	2.96
Uzcategui, Raimund	R-R	6-0	165	11-21-00	0	1	5.23	13	0	0	1	21	20	16	12	4	13	11	.263	.313	.227	4.79	5.66
Vilchez, Juan	R-R	6-2	179	1-9-03	0	0	0.00	1	1	0	0	1	0	0	0	0	0	0	.000	.000	.000	0.00	0.00
William, Junior	R-R	6-4	187	3-6-00	3	0	1.50	16	1	0	4	30	16	9	5	1	9	27	.152	.135	.162	8.10	2.70
Zamudio, Edwin	L-R	6-2	195	9-17-02	0	1	2.25	4	4	0	0	8	6	2	2	0	2	4	.207	.231	.188	4.50	2.25

Fielding

C: Cerda 29, Galarraga 9, Martinez 23, Perez 17, Rangel 28, Salguera 24.
1B: Aponte 26, Arias 7, Ariza 15, Croisier 3, Del Rosario 23, Martinez 13, Perez 8, Rodriguez 23, Salguera 15.
2B: Arias 11, Ariza 13, Barragan 15, De La Cruz 16, Feliz 10, Leon 6, Peguero 18, Perez 11, Petiyan 1, Quevedo 17, Rodriguez 2, Valera 13.
3B: Aponte 19, Arias 6, Ariza 11, Barragan 17, Croisier 4, Feliz 16, Leon 12, Peguero 2, Perez 8, Rodriguez 27, Rodriguez 8, Valera 1.
SS: Aponte 4, Barragan 9, Colmenarez 16, De La Cruz 24, Leon 20, Peguero 30, Pena 1, Perez 8, Quevedo 5, Rodriguez 9.
OF: Barete 39, Colmenarez 1, Del Rosario 3, Diaz 46, Feliz 24, Jimenez 32, Millan 50, Pena 38, Petiyan 25, Piron 51, Tapia 45, Velasquez 27.

Texas Rangers

SEASON IN A SENTENCE: The Rangers spun their wheels all season before breaking it down and dealing their stars for prospects to buttress their farm system, which also got a boost by adding the country's top pitching prospect, Vanderbilt righty Jack Leiter, in the first round of the draft.

HIGH POINT: After a year without fans due to the pandemic, the Rangers finally got to welcome their supporters to their brand-new Globe Life Field. The park had hosted some of the playoffs and the World Series in 2020, but the Rangers themselves had never played there in front of their own fans. So on April 5, after three games on the road in Kansas City, the Rangers welcomed 38,238 well-wishers through the turnstiles. Although the game ended in a loss to Toronto, the day was a moment when the Rangers could signal what they hope will be the beginning of a new era.

LOW POINT: On May 19, Texas was no-hit by the Yankees and former Rangers righthander Corey Kluber. As if being no-hit weren't enough, Kluber's gem was the second time in less than two months that they'd been held hitless.

NOTABLE ROOKIES: Adolis Garcia was one of the best rookies in the sport in 2021. The Cuban outfielder hit 26 doubles, 31 home runs and drove in 90 runs while accumulating 3.9 wins above replacement, as measured by Baseball-Reference. Righthander Kohei Arihara did not fare well in his first season after coming over from Japan. He worked to a 6.64 ERA, pitched just 40.2 innings and dealt with injuries as well. Including Arihara, the 2021 Rangers gave 13 players their first taste of the big leagues. Cuban utilityman Andy Ibañez was the most successful of those rookies, accruing 1.8 bWAR over 76 games.

KEY TRANSACTIONS: At the deadline, the Rangers made big moves. Chief among them was the deal that sent Joey Gallo to the Yankees for a package of prospects including infielders Ezequiel Duran, Trevor Hauver and Josh Smith and righthander Glenn Otto, who made his big league debut late in the season. Texas also spun righthanders Kyle Gibson and Ian Kennedy to Philadelphia for young, controllable starter Spencer Howard as well as minor league righties Kevin Gowdy and Josh Gessner. Beyond the Gallo deal, the Yankees and Rangers also hooked up earlier in the season when New York, in need of an infielder and a lefty bat, acquired Rougned Odor for minor leaguers Josh Stowers and Antonio Cabello.

OPENING DAY PAYROLL: $84,868,750 (22nd).

PLAYERS OF THE YEAR

MAJOR LEAGUE	MINOR LEAGUE
Adolis Garcia OF	**Cole Winn** RHP
.243/.286/.454	(AAA/AA)
Led all rookies with 90 RBIs	4-3, 2.41, 107 SO, 0.86 WHIP

ORGANIZATION LEADERS

Batting		*Minimum 250 AB
MAJORS		
*AVG	Andy Ibanez	.277
*OPS	Joey Gallo	.869
HR	Adolis Garcia	31
RBI	Adolis Garcia	90
MINORS		
*AVG	Yohel Pozo, Round Rock	.337
*OBP	Jayce Easley, Down East	.403
*SLG	Yohel Pozo, Round Rock	.622
*OPS	Josh Jung, Round Rock	.990
R	Dustin Harris, Hickory, Down East	86
H	Dustin Harris, Hickory, Down East	132
TB	Blaine Crim, Frisco, Hickory	224
2B	Ryan Dorow, Round Rock, Frisco	27
3B	Bubba Thompson, Frisco	9
HR	Blaine Crim, Frisco, Hickory	29
RBI	Dustin Harris, Hickory, Down East	85
BB	Jayce Easley, Down East	78
SO	Pedro Gonzalez, Hickory	136
SB	Jayce Easley, Down East	70

Pitching		#Minimum 75 IP
MAJORS		
W	Jordan Lyles	10
#ERA	Kyle Gibson	2.87
SO	Jordan Lyles	146
SV	Ian Kennedy	16
MINORS		
W	Jacob Lemoine, Round Rock	7
W	Collin Wiles, Round Rock	7
L	Nick Krauth, Down East	9
#ERA	Cole Winn, Round Rock, Frisco	2.41
G	Jacob Lemoine, Round Rock	45
GS	Cole Winn, Round Rock, Frisco	21
SV	Buck Farmer, Round Rock, Toledo	8
SV	Cole Uvila, Round Rock, Frisco	8
IP	Nick Krauth, Down East	102.2
BB	Gavin Collyer, Down East	48
SO	Cody Bradford, Frisco, Hickory	128
#AVG	Cole Winn, Round Rock, Frisco	.146

General Manager: Jon Daniels. **Farm Director:** Paul Kruger. **Scouting Director:** Kip Fagg.

Class	Team	League	W	L	PCT	Finish	Manager
Majors	Texas Rangers	American	60	102	.370	14th (15)	Chris Woodward
Triple-A	Round Rock Express	Triple-A West	67	62	.519	t-4th (10)	Kenny Holmberg
Double-A	Frisco RoughRiders	Double-A Central	64	55	.538	t-2nd (10)	Jared Goedert
High-A	Hickory Crawdads	High-A East	46	68	.404	11th (12)	Josh Johnson
Low-A	Down East Wood Ducks	Low-A East	72	48	.600	2nd (12)	Carlos Cardoza
Rookie	ACL Rangers	Arizona Complex	31	28	.525	9th (18)	Jay Sullenger
Rookie	DSL Rangers1	Dominican Summer	36	21	.632	6th (46)	Carlos Maldonado
Rookie	DSL Rangers2	Dominican Summer	34	24	.586	11th (46)	Alexis Infante
Overall 2021 Minor League Record			350	306	.534	7th (30)	

ORGANIZATION STATISTICS

TEXAS RANGERS
AMERICAN LEAGUE

Batting	B-T	HT	WT	DOB	AVG	vLH	vRH	G	AB	R	H	2B	3B	HR	RBI	BB	HBP	SH	SF	SO	SB	CS	SLG	OBP
Calhoun, Willie	L-R	5-8	200	11-4-94	.250	.236	.254	75	260	26	65	10	3	6	25	21	2	0	1	34	0	2	.381	.310
Culberson, Charlie	R-R	6-1	200	4-10-89	.243	.346	.123	90	247	23	60	15	2	5	22	17	2	4	1	64	7	1	.381	.296
Dahl, David	L-R	6-2	197	4-1-94	.210	.102	.253	63	205	19	43	11	0	4	18	10	1	1	3	59	2	1	.322	.247
Davis, Khris	R-R	5-11	205	12-21-87	.157	.160	.154	22	51	8	8	1	1	2	5	8	0	0	2	16	0	0	.333	.262
2-team total (20 Oakland)					.206	.208	.204	42	102	11	21	5	1	3	10	10	0	0	2	31	0	0	.363	.272
Dorow, Ryan	R-R	6-0	195	8-21-95	.000	.000	.000	3	6	0	0	0	0	0	0	1	0	0	0	3	0	0	.000	.143
Gallo, Joey	L-R	6-5	250	11-19-93	.223	.244	.209	95	310	57	69	6	1	25	55	74	4	0	0	125	6	0	.490	.379
2-team total (58 New York)					.199	.200	.198	153	498	90	99	13	1	38	77	111	6	0	1	213	6	0	.458	.351
Garcia, Adolis	R-R	6-1	205	3-2-93	.243	.232	.249	149	581	77	141	26	2	31	90	32	5	0	4	194	16	5	.454	.286
Guzman, Ronald	L-L	6-5	235	10-20-94	.063	.000	.071	7	16	1	1	0	0	1	1	1	0	0	0	6	0	0	.250	.118
Heim, Jonah	B-R	6-4	220	6-27-95	.196	.253	.174	82	265	22	52	13	0	10	32	15	1	1	3	58	3	1	.358	.239
Hernandez, Yonny	B-R	5-9	140	5-4-98	.217	.182	.232	43	143	15	31	5	0	0	6	17	4	1	1	32	11	2	.252	.315
Hicks, John	R-R	6-2	230	8-31-89	.258	.167	.316	10	31	6	8	1	0	4	7	0	0	0	0	8	0	0	.677	.258
Holt, Brock	L-R	5-10	180	6-11-88	.209	.171	.216	76	235	21	49	13	1	2	23	23	1	0	1	49	5	1	.298	.281
Ibanez, Andy	R-R	5-11	205	4-3-93	.277	.344	.238	76	253	31	70	15	2	7	25	15	2	1	1	35	0	4	.435	.321
Kiner-Falefa, Isiah	R-R	5-11	190	3-23-95	.271	.233	.289	158	635	74	172	25	3	8	53	28	11	1	2	90	20	5	.357	.312
Lowe, Nathaniel	L-R	6-4	220	7-7-95	.264	.277	.257	157	557	75	147	24	3	18	72	80	2	0	3	162	8	0	.415	.357
Martin, Jason	L-R	5-9	185	9-5-95	.208	.108	.243	58	144	14	30	3	0	6	17	8	0	1	1	41	3	1	.354	.248
Peters, DJ	R-R	6-6	225	12-12-96	.198	.150	.219	52	197	24	39	7	1	12	34	4	2	0	3	68	2	0	.426	.218
Pozo, Yohel	R-R	6-0	201	6-14-97	.284	.360	.245	21	74	8	21	4	0	1	9	3	0	0	0	10	0	0	.378	.312
Solak, Nick	R-R	5-11	185	1-11-95	.242	.266	.232	127	458	57	111	18	2	11	49	34	15	2	2	107	7	5	.362	.314
Taveras, Leody	B-R	6-2	195	9-8-98	.161	.182	.151	49	174	14	28	6	2	3	9	9	1	1	0	60	10	1	.270	.207
Tejeda, Anderson	B-R	6-0	200	5-1-98	.063	.000	.071	5	16	1	1	0	0	0	1	0	0	1	0	10	1	0	.063	.118
Terry, Curtis	R-R	6-2	258	10-6-96	.089	.059	.107	13	45	3	4	2	0	0	1	2	1	0	0	15	0	0	.133	.146
Trevino, Jose	R-R	5-11	210	11-28-92	.239	.189	.262	89	285	23	68	14	0	5	30	12	0	2	3	57	1	1	.340	.267
White, Eli	R-R	6-3	195	6-26-94	.177	.133	.203	64	198	26	35	6	1	6	15	18	4	0	0	66	4	3	.308	.259

Pitching	B-T	HT	WT	DOB	W	L	ERA	G	GS	CG	SV	IP	H	R	ER	HR	BB	SO	AVG	vLH	vRH	K/9	BB/9
Alexy, A.J.	R-R	6-4	195	4-21-98	3	1	4.70	5	4	0	0	23	13	12	12	4	17	17	.167	.114	.209	6.65	6.65
Allard, Kolby	L-L	6-1	195	8-13-97	3	12	5.41	32	17	0	0	125	128	80	75	29	31	104	.258	.246	.262	7.51	2.24
Anderson, Drew	R-R	6-3	205	3-22-94	1	1	3.27	9	1	0	0	22	20	8	8	1	6	9	.238	.216	.255	3.68	2.45
Arihara, Kohei	R-R	6-2	210	8-11-92	2	4	6.64	10	10	0	0	41	45	31	30	11	13	24	.281	.250	.304	5.31	2.88
Barlow, Joe	R-R	6-2	210	9-28-95	0	2	1.55	31	0	0	11	29	12	9	5	2	12	27	.124	.143	.109	8.38	3.72
Benjamin, Wes	R-L	6-2	210	7-26-93	0	2	8.74	13	2	0	0	23	29	23	22	6	17	19	.309	.414	.262	7.54	6.75
Bush, Matt	R-R	5-9	180	2-8-86	0	0	6.75	4	0	0	0	4	4	3	3	1	5	2	.250	.000	.364	11.25	2.25
Cody, Kyle	R-R	6-7	225	8-9-94	0	2	7.94	7	0	0	0	11	16	11	10	3	2	14	.327	.263	.367	11.12	1.59
Cotton, Jharel	R-R	5-11	200	1-19-92	2	0	3.52	23	0	0	0	31	28	12	12	2	15	30	.237	.208	.257	8.80	4.40
Culberson, Charlie	R-R	6-1	200	4-10-89	0	0	0.00	2	0	0	0	2	2	0	0	0	0	0	.286	.000	.500	0.00	0.00
de Geus, Brett	R-R	6-2	190	11-4-97	0	0	8.44	19	0	0	0	27	31	25	25	3	13	26	.292	.316	.279	8.78	4.39
Dunning, Dane	R-R	6-4	225	12-20-94	5	10	4.51	27	25	0	0	118	126	61	59	13	43	114	.275	.279	.271	8.72	3.29
Evans, Demarcus	R-R	6-5	265	10-22-96	0	2	5.13	25	0	0	0	26	24	16	15	4	16	33	.238	.333	.177	11.28	5.47
Foltynewicz, Mike	R-R	6-4	195	10-7-91	2	12	5.44	28	24	0	0	139	139	86	84	35	36	97	.260	.271	.250	6.28	2.33
Gibson, Kyle	R-R	6-6	215	10-23-87	6	3	2.87	19	19	0	0	113	92	38	36	9	41	94	.224	.240	.210	7.49	3.27
Hearn, Taylor	L-L	6-6	230	8-30-94	6	6	4.66	42	11	0	0	104	96	58	54	17	42	92	.247	.198	.267	7.94	3.62
Herget, Jimmy	R-R	6-3	170	9-9-93	0	1	9.00	4	0	0	0	4	5	5	4	1	2	0	.294	.000	.357	4.50	0.00
2-team total (14 Los Angeles)					2	3	5.30	18	0	0	0	19	20	12	11	1	4	20	.286	.211	.314	9.64	1.93
Holt, Brock	L-R	5-10	180	6-11-88	0	0	0.00	1	0	0	0	1	1	0	0	0	0	0	.333	.000	.500	0.00	0.00
Howard, Spencer	R-R	6-3	210	7-28-96	0	3	9.70	8	8	0	0	21	28	26	23	5	10	21	.308	.326	.346	8.86	4.22
Kennedy, Ian	R-R	6-0	210	12-19-84	0	0	2.51	32	0	0	16	32	27	9	9	5	7	35	.227	.226	.227	9.74	1.95
King, John	L-L	6-2	215	9-14-94	7	5	3.52	27	0	0	0	46	41	24	18	3	12	40	.233	.140	.277	7.83	2.35
Latz, Jake	R-L	6-2	185	4-8-96	0	1	5.79	1	1	0	0	5	5	3	3	0	4	.263	.000	.294	7.71	0.00

	B-T	HT	WT	DOB	W	L	ERA	G	GS	CG	SV	IP	H	R	ER	HR	BB	SO	AVG	vLH	vRH	K/9	BB/9
Lyles, Jordan	R-R	6-5	230	10-19-90	10	13	5.15	32	30	0	0	180	194	104	103	38	56	146	.278	.260	.291	7.30	2.80
Martin, Brett	L-L	6-4	200	4-28-95	4	4	3.18	66	0	0	0	62	67	31	22	5	14	42	.272	.255	.283	6.06	2.02
Otto, Glenn	R-R	6-3	240	3-11-96	0	3	9.26	6	6	0	0	23	32	24	24	2	8	28	.320	.452	.261	10.80	3.09
Patton, Spencer	R-R	6-1	200	2-20-88	2	3	3.83	42	0	0	2	42	36	20	18	4	15	48	.229	.318	.165	10.20	3.19
Rodriguez, Joely	L-L	6-1	200	11-14-91	1	3	5.93	31	0	0	1	27	32	19	18	3	12	30	.288	.176	.338	9.88	3.95
2-team total (21 New York)					2	3	4.66	52	0	0	1	46	53	27	24	4	18	47	.294	.203	.339	9.13	3.50
Santana, Dennis	R-R	6-2	190	4-12-96	2	4	3.63	39	0	0	0	40	30	20	16	4	21	38	.214	.200	.227	8.62	4.76
Sborz, Josh	R-R	6-2	215	12-17-93	4	3	3.97	63	0	0	1	59	52	29	26	7	32	69	.234	.271	.212	10.53	4.88
Snyder, Nick	R-R	6-4	190	10-10-95	0	0	4.91	4	0	0	0	4	3	2	2	0	3	1	.250	.000	.429	2.45	7.36
Wood, Hunter	R-R	6-1	175	8-12-93	0	0	3.60	5	0	0	0	5	2	2	2	1	2	5	.125	.200	.091	9.00	3.60
Yang, Hyeon-Jong	L-L	6-0	200	3-1-88	0	3	5.60	12	4	0	0	35	42	24	22	9	16	25	.296	.293	.297	6.37	4.08

Fielding

Catcher	PCT	G	PO	A	E	DP	PB
Heim	.995	78	557	25	3	3	3
Hicks	1.000	8	45	4	0	0	0
Pozo	1.000	2	15	0	0	0	0
Trevino	.991	88	644	27	6	3	4

First Base	PCT	G	PO	A	E	DP
Culberson	1.000	4	22	4	0	1
Guzman	1.000	4	21	3	0	1
Ibanez	1.000	12	82	4	0	8
Lowe	.991	148	1164	54	11	119
Terry	1.000	1	4	2	0	1

Second Base	PCT	G	PO	A	E	DP
Culberson	1.000	4	8	4	0	1
Hernandez	.976	9	16	25	1	10

Ibanez	.983	31	44	74	2	13
Solak	.989	121	169	270	5	63
Tejeda	.000	1	0	0	0	0
White	1.000	3	7	8	0	3

Third Base	PCT	G	PO	A	E	DP
Culberson	.966	68	51	121	6	12
Dorow	1.000	3	1	3	0	0
Hernandez	.988	29	22	62	1	9
Holt	.978	69	43	134	4	10
Ibanez	.963	11	5	21	1	1
Lowe	1.000	1	0	1	0	0
Tejeda	1.000	5	4	6	0	2

Shortstop	PCT	G	PO	A	E	DP
Culberson	.800	3	2	6	2	1

Hernandez	1.000	6	6	14	0	2
Kiner-Falefa	.972	156	214	436	19	98

Outfield	PCT	G	PO	A	E	DP
Calhoun	1.000	41	51	1	0	1
Culberson	1.000	7	13	1	0	0
Dahl	1.000	44	69	2	0	1
Davis	1.000	2	3	0	0	0
Gallo	.979	83	181	9	4	3
Garcia	.988	139	325	16	4	3
Guzman	--	2	0	0	0	0
Ibanez	1.000	1	3	0	0	0
Martin	.988	47	85	0	1	0
Peters	1.000	52	103	3	0	2
Taveras	.977	48	128	1	3	1
White	.983	63	114	3	2	0

ROUND ROCK EXPRESS   TRIPLE-A

TRIPLE-A WEST

Batting	B-T	HT	WT	DOB	AVG	vLH	vRH	G	AB	R	H	2B	3B	HR	RBI	BB	HBP	SH	SF	SO	SB	CS	SLG	OBP
Apostel, Sherten	R-R	6-4	235	3-11-99	.205	.182	.209	22	78	10	16	3	0	1	6	7	2	0	1	32	0	0	.282	.284
Biggers, Jax	L-R	5-11	175	4-7-97	.000	--	.000	5	13	0	0	0	0	0	0	0	0	0	0	3	0	0	.000	.000
Calhoun, Willie	L-R	5-8	200	11-4-94	.000	--	.000	2	6	1	0	0	0	0	0	1	0	0	0	1	0	0	.000	.143
Chester, Carl	R-R	6-0	200	12-12-95	.186	.220	.176	99	338	43	63	11	4	7	35	20	2	0	2	126	6	7	.305	.235
Dahl, David	L-R	6-2	197	4-1-94	.182	.000	.333	3	11	1	2	1	1	0	2	0	0	0	0	3	0	0	.455	.182
Davis, Khris	R-R	5-11	205	12-21-87	.000	--	.000	1	4	0	0	0	0	0	0	0	0	0	0	0	0	0	.000	.000
2-team total (16 Las Vegas)					.313	.375	.305	17	67	16	21	3	2	10	25	4	1	0	0	15	0	0	.866	.361
DeShields, Delino	R-R	5-9	190	8-16-92	.263	.172	.291	66	247	46	65	9	1	5	18	50	3	4	1	62	16	2	.368	.392
Dorow, Ryan	R-R	6-0	195	8-21-95	.229	.231	.229	78	279	48	64	18	2	10	32	33	3	0	3	92	3	2	.416	.314
Felix, Jose A.	R-R	5-11	190	7-23-02	.300	.000	.375	4	10	3	3	0	0	0	1	0	0	0	0	4	0	0	.300	.300
Hernandez, Elier	R-R	6-3	197	11-21-94	.231	.306	.213	92	329	42	76	14	0	16	55	21	6	0	2	107	3	1	.419	.288
Hernandez, Yonny	B-R	5-9	140	5-4-98	.250	.216	.258	61	192	42	48	7	2	1	13	51	7	1	0	44	21	10	.323	.424
Hicks, John	R-R	6-2	230	8-31-89	.290	.309	.285	64	248	41	72	18	0	13	44	16	2	0	2	79	7	1	.520	.336
Holt, Brock	L-R	5-10	180	6-11-88	.286	1.000	.167	2	7	1	2	0	0	0	0	1	0	0	0	0	0	0	.286	.375
Hoover, Jake	R-R	6-0	180	7-11-97	.222	.667	.000	3	9	0	2	0	0	0	0	0	0	0	0	4	0	0	.222	.222
Huff, Sam	R-R	6-5	240	1-14-98	.273	.200	.294	7	22	4	6	1	0	3	7	2	0	0	1	9	0	0	.727	.320
Ibanez, Andy	R-R	5-11	205	4-3-93	.342	.471	.288	30	114	21	39	11	1	7	27	12	2	0	1	18	1	0	.640	.411
Jung, Josh	R-R	6-2	214	2-12-98	.348	.185	.389	35	135	29	47	14	0	9	21	18	3	0	0	34	0	0	.652	.436
Kruger, Jack	R-R	6-1	195	10-26-94	.267	.267	.267	46	161	19	43	7	1	3	16	11	0	0	0	34	1	1	.379	.314
Leblanc, Charles	R-R	6-3	195	6-3-96	.229	.282	.215	96	332	49	76	16	4	17	57	40	1	0	1	131	5	3	.455	.313
Leyba, Domingo	B-R	5-11	205	9-11-95	.288	.348	.272	24	104	12	30	7	2	4	26	2	0	0	1	17	1	1	.510	.299
2-team total (8 Reno)					.331	.324	.333	32	139	21	46	9	3	8	40	4	0	0	1	21	1	1	.612	.347
Loehr, Trace	L-R	5-10	185	5-23-95	.261	.222	.267	37	119	10	31	8	2	0	9	9	1	0	1	33	1	0	.361	.315
Martin, Jason	L-R	5-9	185	9-5-95	.248	.250	.247	39	129	27	32	4	2	10	27	28	2	1	1	34	2	3	.543	.388
Pozo, Yohel	R-R	6-0	201	6-14-97	.337	.278	.356	77	315	46	106	17	2	23	74	7	1	0	1	42	0	0	.622	.352
Solak, Nick	R-R	5-11	185	1-11-95	.353	.250	.370	22	85	15	30	6	0	1	6	7	1	0	0	16	0	1	.459	.409
Taveras, Leody	B-R	6-2	195	9-8-98	.245	.241	.247	87	322	57	79	19	2	17	55	49	2	2	6	95	13	5	.475	.343
Tejeda, Anderson	B-R	6-0	200	5-1-98	.152	.065	.191	28	99	13	15	1	1	3	12	11	0	1	0	47	8	2	.273	.236
Terry, Curtis	R-R	6-2	258	10-6-96	.275	.232	.290	99	364	58	100	24	2	22	75	29	14	0	3	94	3	1	.533	.349
Walker, Steele	L-L	5-11	209	7-30-96	.223	.156	.237	48	184	22	41	8	0	5	21	16	1	0	1	46	2	3	.348	.287
Wendzel, Davis	R-R	6-1	206	5-23-97	.214	.200	.217	8	28	5	6	4	0	1	2	2	3	0	0	8	0	0	.464	.333
White, Eli	R-R	6-3	195	6-26-94	.343	.409	.311	20	67	19	23	2	1	3	11	12	1	0	0	20	3	1	.537	.450

Pitching	B-T	HT	WT	DOB	W	L	ERA	G	GS	CG	SV	IP	H	R	ER	HR	BB	SO	AVG	vLH	vRH	K/9	BB/9
Alexy, A.J.	R-R	6-4	195	4-21-98	0	0	1.84	3	3	0	0	15	9	3	3	2	6	19	.176	.211	.156	11.66	3.68
Anderson, Chase	R-R	6-1	210	11-30-87	0	1	4.20	5	3	0	0	15	14	9	7	5	8	14	.241	.200	.273	8.40	4.80
Anderson, Drew	R-R	6-3	205	3-22-94	4	5	3.06	15	12	0	0	71	55	26	24	8	29	86	.212	.202	.221	10.95	3.69
Anderson, Justin	L-R	6-3	230	9-28-92	0	1	3.27	11	0	0	0	11	7	4	4	1	5	19	.175	.176	.174	15.55	4.09
Anderson, Shaun	R-R	6-4	228	10-29-94	0	0	0.00	2	0	0	0	3	0	0	0	0	1	4	.000	.000	.000	12.00	3.00
2-team total (11 El Paso)					1	0	3.63	13	0	0	1	17	13	7	7	2	7	22	.203	.167	.225	11.42	3.63
Arihara, Kohei	R-R	6-2	210	8-11-92	0	1	11.17	3	3	0	0	10	11	14	12	3	5	6	.282	.500	.095	5.59	4.66

Player	B-T	HT	WT	DOB	W	L	ERA	G	GS	CG	SV	IP	H	R	ER	HR	BB	SO	AVG	vLH	vRH		
Bahr, Jason	R-R	6-5	195	2-15-95	2	1	9.00	21	5	0	0	33	37	34	33	8	30	38	.282	.169	.375	10.36	8.18
Barlow, Joe	R-R	6-2	210	9-28-95	0	1	2.57	17	0	0	7	21	8	6	6	1	8	29	.114	.185	.070	12.43	3.43
Bass, Blake	R-R	6-7	265	6-3-93	0	1	7.36	7	0	0	1	7	9	9	6	1	10	7	.300	.231	.353	8.59	12.27
Benjamin, Wes	R-L	6-2	210	7-26-93	2	5	8.29	15	10	0	0	47	72	50	43	6	25	42	.344	.328	.352	8.10	4.82
Burke, Brock	L-L	6-4	210	8-4-96	1	5	5.68	21	20	0	0	78	76	53	49	13	31	97	.253	.255	.252	11.24	3.59
Bush, Matt	R-R	5-9	180	2-8-86	0	0	0.00	4	0	0	0	3	2	0	0	0	4	3	.200	.167	.250	9.00	12.00
Cotton, Jharel	R-R	5-11	200	1-19-92	4	0	3.00	24	2	0	0	42	32	19	14	3	17	57	.205	.175	.226	12.21	3.64
Engler, Scott	R-R	6-4	220	12-12-96	2	0	4.01	25	0	0	3	34	30	18	15	4	18	32	.240	.192	.274	8.55	4.81
Evans, Demarcus	R-R	6-5	265	10-22-96	2	0	3.74	18	0	0	0	22	12	10	9	2	12	31	.156	.125	.170	12.88	4.98
Farmer, Buck	L-R	6-4	232	2-20-91	2	1	3.60	15	0	0	8	15	11	8	6	1	6	15	.208	.227	.194	9.00	3.60
Felix, Jose A.	R-R	5-11	190	7-23-02	0	0	0.00	1	0	0	0	0	0	0	0	0	0	0	.000	--	.000	0.00	0.00
Gatto, Joe	R-R	6-3	220	6-14-95	4	2	4.35	24	0	0	0	41	33	21	20	5	15	44	.223	.167	.261	9.58	3.27
Gaviglio, Sam	R-R	6-1	215	5-22-90	2	1	5.13	5	5	0	0	26	33	16	15	3	4	24	.300	.304	.297	8.20	1.37
Grant-Parks, Blake	R-R	6-1	190	7-15-93	0	0	0.00	1	0	0	0	0	0	0	0	0	0	0	.000	--	.000	0.00	0.00
Herget, Jimmy	R-R	6-3	170	9-9-93	2	2	2.63	27	0	0	3	38	28	14	11	5	12	48	.196	.183	.208	11.47	2.87
2-team total (4 Salt Lake)					2	3	3.83	31	0	0	3	42	35	21	18	6	15	53	.215	.202	.228	11.27	3.19
Howard, Spencer	R-R	6-3	210	7-28-96	0	1	4.50	1	1	0	0	2	3	1	1	0	0	3	.333	.250	.400	13.50	0.00
Jones, James	L-L	6-2	205	9-24-88	2	2	5.14	21	0	0	0	21	21	13	12	4	10	24	.269	.286	.256	10.29	4.29
King, John	L-L	6-2	215	9-14-94	0	0	0.00	2	0	0	0	2	1	0	0	0	1	2	.143	.000	.200	9.00	4.50
Kubiak, David	R-R	6-7	228	8-3-89	2	1	3.90	6	5	0	0	30	31	13	13	5	5	28	.274	.177	.250	8.40	1.50
Latz, Jake	R-L	6-2	185	4-8-96	1	1	3.55	7	6	0	0	33	31	20	13	5	16	35	.242	.265	.228	9.55	4.36
LeBlanc, Wade	L-L	6-2	195	8-7-84	2	0	2.50	3	3	0	0	18	12	5	5	3	3	19	.185	.227	.163	9.50	1.50
Lemoine, Jacob	R-R	6-5	220	11-28-93	7	4	2.86	45	1	0	3	57	41	24	18	5	29	43	.203	.237	.174	6.83	4.61
Mendez, Sal	R-L	6-4	185	2-25-95	0	1	9.64	4	0	0	0	5	7	6	5	0	3	5	.333	.000	.467	9.64	5.79
Miller, Tyson	R-R	6-4	225	7-29-95	5	3	3.05	20	9	0	0	56	44	24	19	6	23	59	.215	.258	.181	9.48	3.70
Ortiz, Luis	R-R	6-3	230	9-22-95	2	2	4.60	28	4	0	0	43	44	23	22	7	17	44	.265	.297	.239	9.21	3.56
Otto, Glenn	R-R	6-3	240	3-11-96	2	1	2.70	4	4	0	0	20	13	6	6	0	7	19	.188	.194	.184	8.55	3.15
Palumbo, Joe	L-L	6-0	195	10-26-94	1	2	13.50	6	2	0	0	7	12	11	10	4	10	7	.387	.571	.333	9.45	13.50
Patton, Spencer	R-R	6-1	200	2-20-88	2	0	0.00	11	0	0	4	12	6	0	0	0	6	12	.154	.286	.080	9.00	4.50
Phillips, Tyler	R-R	6-5	225	10-27-97	0	3	9.90	4	4	0	0	10	15	12	11	2	12	11	.341	.462	.290	9.90	10.80
Rodriguez, Yerry	R-R	6-2	198	10-15-97	3	3	8.01	13	4	0	0	30	37	28	27	5	12	37	.298	.339	.265	10.98	3.56
Ryan, Ryder	R-R	6-2	205	5-11-95	2	7	5.60	38	0	0	4	45	48	33	28	7	19	55	.264	.303	.236	11.00	3.80
Santana, Dennis	R-R	6-2	190	4-12-96	0	0	0.00	4	0	0	0	4	0	0	0	0	1	9	.000	.000	.000	20.25	2.25
2-team total (3 Oklahoma City)					0	0	5.79	7	3	0	0	9	9	6	6	2	5	15	.250	.267	.238	14.46	4.82
Snyder, Nick	R-R	6-4	190	10-10-95	1	0	6.23	5	0	0	0	4	3	3	3	1	1	5	.188	.400	.091	10.38	2.08
Thomas, Tyler	R-L	6-1	175	12-22-95	0	0	3.60	2	0	0	0	5	5	2	2	2	1	2	.278	.000	.385	1.80	3.60
Uvila, Cole	R-R	6-3	206	1-30-94	0	0	8.74	16	0	0	0	23	34	24	22	3	16	18	.354	.317	.382	7.15	6.35
Villines, Stephen	R-R	6-1	185	7-15-95	0	0	2.70	2	1	0	0	3	2	1	1	1	0	6	.167	.333	.111	0.00	2.70
Vincent, Nick	R-R	5-10	185	7-12-86	0	0	4.11	15	0	0	0	15	18	10	7	1	7	22	.273	.320	.244	12.91	4.11
Wiles, Collin	R-R	6-4	222	5-30-94	7	2	4.19	23	11	0	0	86	87	41	40	12	20	82	.264	.294	.237	8.58	2.09
Winn, Cole	R-R	6-2	190	11-25-99	1	0	3.38	2	2	0	0	8	5	3	3	1	5	10	.167	.111	.190	11.25	5.63
Wood, Hunter	R-R	6-1	175	8-12-93	0	0	3.38	2	0	0	1	3	1	1	1	0	1	5	.111	.333	.000	16.88	3.38
Yang, Hyeon-Jong	L-L	6-0	200	3-1-88	0	3	5.60	10	9	0	0	45	52	32	28	10	10	42	.287	.413	.220	8.40	2.00

Fielding

Catcher	PCT	G	PO	A	E	DP	PB
Felix	.000	1	0	0	0	0	0
Hicks	.987	38	368	19	5	3	10
Kruger	.990	41	365	24	4	4	5
Pozo	.989	51	495	23	6	3	5

First Base	PCT	G	PO	A	E	DP
Apostel	1.000	2	18	0	0	0
Hernandez	.991	17	102	3	1	9
Hicks	1.000	8	67	4	0	8
Huff	.957	4	22	0	1	2
Ibanez	1.000	3	21	2	0	1
Kruger	1.000	1	9	1	0	1
Leblanc	.993	21	127	9	1	20
Pozo	.962	4	24	1	1	1
Terry	.984	73	477	26	8	48
White	1.000	1	8	0	0	0

Second Base	PCT	G	PO	A	E	DP
Biggers	1.000	4	15	12	0	7
DeShields	.941	7	5	11	1	2
Dorow	.955	5	11	10	1	3
Hernandez	1.000	10	26	14	0	4
Hoover	.933	3	5	9	1	3
Ibanez	1.000	12	18	36	0	9
Leblanc	1.000	21	39	50	0	6
Leyba	1.000	19	37	43	0	16
Loehr	.970	27	36	61	3	16
Solak	.981	15	21	31	1	8
Tejeda	1.000	3	3	4	0	2
Wendzel	1.000	1	4	1	0	1
White	.929	7	10	16	2	3

Third Base	PCT	G	PO	A	E	DP
Apostel	.879	16	6	23	4	3
Dorow	.966	16	5	23	1	3
Hernandez	1.000	2	2	2	0	0
Hernandez	1.000	17	9	30	0	3
Hicks	.857	3	1	5	1	1
Holt	.000	1	0	0	0	0
Ibanez	.862	13	12	13	4	2
Jung	.980	24	10	40	1	5
Leblanc	.971	34	12	56	2	5
Leyba	.000	1	0	0	1	0
Loehr	1.000	2	0	2	0	0
Pozo	1.000	1	1	1	0	0
Tejeda	1.000	1	0	1	0	0
Wendzel	.833	3	1	4	1	0
White	.000	2	0	0	1	0

Shortstop	PCT	G	PO	A	E	DP
Dorow	.971	58	61	137	6	30
Hernandez	.927	34	32	82	9	15
Leblanc	.875	6	7	14	3	1
Leyba	1.000	3	5	6	0	4
Loehr	.941	6	4	12	1	3
Tejeda	.909	23	26	54	8	9
Wendzel	1.000	2	4	3	0	1

Outfield	PCT	G	PO	A	E	DP
Calhoun	--	1	0	0	0	0
Chester	.983	93	170	4	3	1
Dahl	1.000	1	1	0	0	0
DeShields	.980	53	99	1	2	0
Hernandez	.979	69	141	2	3	1
Hicks	1.000	2	4	0	0	0
Ibanez	1.000	1	2	0	0	0
Leblanc	.955	11	21	0	1	0
Martin	.969	35	61	2	2	0
Taveras	.979	81	180	7	4	1
Walker	.966	49	82	4	3	1
Wendzel	1.000	1	4	0	0	0
White	1.000	7	16	2	0	0

FRISCO ROUGHRIDERS
DOUBLE-A CENTRAL

DOUBLE-A

Batting	B-T	HT	WT	DOB	AVG	vLH	vRH	G	AB	R	H	2B	3B	HR	RBI	BB	HBP	SH	SF	SO	SB	CS	SLG	OBP

Player	B-T	HT	WT	DOB	AVG	vLH	vRH	G	AB	R	H	2B	3B	HR	RBI	BB	HBP	SH	SF	SO	SB	CS	SLG	OBP
Aparicio, Miguel	L-L	6-0	195	3-17-99	.179	.222	.167	15	39	4	7	1	1	0	2	1	0	0	1	12	0	0	.256	.195
Apostel, Sherten	R-R	6-4	235	3-11-99	.236	.216	.247	42	148	20	35	9	0	6	20	17	1	0	1	52	0	0	.419	.317
Arias, Diosbel	R-R	6-2	190	7-21-96	.266	.315	.247	102	379	43	101	17	0	5	40	36	0	0	4	72	3	1	.351	.327
Barreto, Derwin	B-R	5-9	160	9-1-00	.091	.286	.000	6	22	1	2	0	0	0	0	0	0	0	0	8	0	0	.091	.091
Biggers, Jax	L-R	5-11	175	4-7-97	.224	.173	.242	91	290	26	65	12	2	4	31	25	2	6	4	54	14	3	.321	.287
Crim, Blaine	R-R	5-11	200	6-17-97	.288	.262	.299	35	139	24	40	6	0	9	19	7	2	0	0	35	0	0	.525	.331
Dahl, David	L-R	6-2	197	4-1-94	.522	.400	.615	6	23	7	12	0	0	1	7	2	0	0	0	3	1	0	.652	.560
Dorow, Ryan	R-R	6-0	195	8-21-95	.333	.208	.379	24	90	13	30	9	0	2	15	9	0	0	0	20	0	0	.600	.394
Foscue, Justin	R-R	6-0	205	3-2-99	.247	.333	.193	26	93	14	23	7	0	2	13	8	2	0	1	29	0	1	.387	.317
Hernandez, Elier	R-R	6-3	197	11-21-94	.228	.313	.195	16	57	7	13	1	0	0	7	6	1	0	0	15	2	1	.246	.313
Holt, Brock	L-R	5-10	180	6-11-88	.000	.000	.000	2	6	0	0	0	0	0	0	1	1	0	0	0	0	0	.000	.250
Hoover, Jake	R-R	6-0	180	7-11-97	.087	.100	.077	16	46	3	4	2	0	0	5	4	1	0	0	17	0	0	.130	.176
Huff, Sam	R-R	6-5	240	1-14-98	.237	.196	.256	46	173	24	41	5	0	10	23	16	2	0	0	77	0	0	.439	.309
Jung, Josh	R-R	6-2	214	2-12-98	.308	.347	.292	43	169	25	52	8	1	10	40	13	3	0	1	42	2	2	.544	.366
Loehr, Trace	L-R	5-10	185	5-23-95	.205	.125	.250	13	44	4	9	1	0	0	4	0	1	0	0	15	1	0	.227	.222
Martinez, J.P.	L-L	5-9	174	3-21-96	.242	.338	.210	81	285	45	69	13	4	5	28	42	8	6	0	112	20	0	.368	.355
Novoa, Melvin	R-R	5-11	215	6-17-96	.310	.393	.268	28	84	11	26	8	0	5	15	15	0	0	0	28	1	0	.583	.414
Pena, Yenci	R-R	6-2	193	7-13-00	.222	.286	.000	4	9	3	2	1	0	0	0	0	1	0	0	2	0	0	.333	.300
Procyshen, Jordan	L-R	5-10	185	3-11-93	.197	.135	.221	45	132	21	26	4	0	5	20	20	6	1	2	42	1	0	.341	.325
Quiroz, Isaias	R-R	5-10	234	10-22-96	.231	.500	.182	5	13	1	3	0	0	0	1	1	0	0	0	7	0	1	.231	.286
Smith, Josh H.	L-R	5-10	172	8-7-97	.294	.280	.299	30	102	12	30	5	0	3	10	18	6	0	1	20	7	2	.431	.425
Stowers, Josh	R-R	6-0	200	2-25-97	.220	.234	.212	89	305	62	67	11	2	20	57	38	4	0	4	106	21	4	.466	.311
Tejeda, Anderson	B-R	6-0	200	5-1-98	.200	.228	.186	47	175	19	35	8	0	9	20	15	1	0	0	82	2	1	.400	.267
Thompson, Bubba	R-R	6-2	197	6-9-98	.275	.298	.264	104	429	73	118	23	9	16	52	29	4	6	2	121	25	8	.483	.325
Trevino, Jose	R-R	5-11	210	11-28-92	.286	.333	.267	6	21	5	6	2	0	1	4	2	0	0	0	4	0	0	.524	.348
Walker, Steele	L-L	5-11	209	7-30-96	.255	.316	.236	63	239	39	61	10	2	10	40	22	3	0	2	45	8	2	.439	.323
Wendzel, Davis	R-R	6-1	206	5-23-97	.239	.250	.234	45	159	23	38	6	0	6	23	21	6	0	1	43	1	2	.390	.348
Whatley, Matt	R-R	5-9	200	1-7-96	.203	.171	.217	75	227	27	46	6	0	4	14	35	3	2	1	80	7	8	.282	.316

Pitching

Pitching	B-T	HT	WT	DOB	W	L	ERA	G	GS	CG	SV	IP	H	R	ER	HR	BB	SO	AVG	vLH	vRH	K/9	BB/9
Advocate, Josh	R-R	6-0	195	1-18-94	0	0	5.68	6	0	0	0	6	6	4	1	10	10		.231	.167	.250	14.21	14.21
Alexy, A.J.	R-R	6-4	195	4-21-98	1	1	1.61	13	7	0	0	50	30	9	9	4	21	57	.174	.127	.208	10.19	3.75
Anderson, Grant	R-R	6-0	180	6-21-97	2	1	6.91	20	0	0	0	27	32	22	21	5	15	26	.288	.311	.273	8.56	4.94
Arihara, Kohei	R-R	6-2	210	8-11-92	0	0	0.00	1	1	0	0	2	1	0	0	0	0	2	.143	.000	.333	9.00	0.00
Bass, Blake	R-R	6-7	265	6-3-93	4	0	2.40	23	0	0	1	30	19	9	8	3	21	27	.186	.209	.169	8.10	6.30
Bradford, Cody	L-L	6-4	197	2-22-98	2	0	3.89	7	7	0	0	35	41	18	15	1	4	41	.293	.324	.282	10.64	1.04
Bremer, Noah	R-R	6-5	206	5-13-96	5	4	4.48	22	7	0	4	68	65	36	34	8	25	65	.255	.255	.255	8.56	3.29
Brennan, Tim	R-R	6-4	212	12-18-96	0	3	3.75	7	6	0	0	24	24	10	10	1	10	13	.267	.361	.204	4.88	3.75
Bueno, Hever	R-R	6-2	179	11-23-94	4	4	4.28	32	0	0	2	48	47	24	23	3	23	55	.246	.221	.263	10.24	4.28
Crouse, Hans	L-R	6-4	180	9-15-98	3	2	3.35	13	13	0	0	51	27	20	19	5	19	54	.157	.133	.175	9.53	3.35
Engler, Scott	R-R	6-4	220	12-12-96	1	0	3.20	12	0	0	3	20	15	8	7	2	6	32	.211	.200	.220	14.64	2.75
Gatto, Joe	R-R	6-3	220	6-14-95	1	1	0.98	11	0	0	0	18	13	4	2	1	4	25	.203	.219	.188	12.27	1.96
Henriquez, Ronny	R-R	5-10	155	6-20-00	4	4	5.04	16	11	0	0	70	65	42	39	15	17	78	.242	.242	.241	10.08	2.20
Kent, Zak	R-R	6-3	208	2-24-98	0	4	5.34	6	6	1	0	29	34	17	17	9	9	39	.298	.333	.278	12.24	2.83
Kuzia, Joe	R-R	6-5	190	10-3-93	1	1	40.50	3	0	0	0	2	6	9	9	0	6	0	.545	.833	.200	0.00	27.00
2-team total (6 Wichita)					1	1	18.00	9	0	0	0	7	11	14	14	1	11	6	.367	.600	.133	7.71	14.14
Latz, Jake	R-L	6-2	185	4-8-96	1	1	4.69	15	13	0	0	63	55	40	33	9	28	84	.233	.261	.216	11.94	3.98
Lee, Chase	R-R	6-0	170	8-13-98	0	1	3.71	13	0	0	0	17	11	7	7	2	3	27	.180	.250	.135	14.29	1.59
Mejia, Juan	L-L	5-11	160	1-9-99	0	0	0.00	1	0	0	0	1	0	0	0	0	2	2	.000	.000	.000	18.00	18.00
Mendez, Sal	L-R	6-4	185	2-25-95	6	3	4.50	24	2	0	0	60	47	31	30	6	26	58	.219	.193	.235	8.70	3.90
Ozuna, Fernery	R-R	5-8	170	11-9-95	5	3	5.32	32	0	0	3	46	42	33	27	11	17	51	.247	.292	.214	10.05	3.35
Phillips, Tyler	R-R	6-5	225	10-27-97	1	2	4.70	6	5	0	0	15	12	8	8	4	7	18	.207	.190	.216	10.57	4.11
Procyshen, Jordan	L-R	5-10	185	3-11-93	2	1	2.79	7	0	0	0	10	11	6	3	2	4	1	.306	.267	.333	0.93	3.72
Quiroz, Isaias	R-R	5-10	234	10-22-96	0	0	27.00	1	0	0	0	2	3	3	3	1	1	0	.600	.500	1.000	0.00	9.00
Ragans, Cole	L-L	6-4	190	12-12-97	3	1	5.70	9	7	0	0	36	39	27	23	8	20	33	.275	.350	.245	8.17	4.95
Robert, Daniel	L-R	6-4	210	8-30-94	0	1	2.08	12	0	0	1	17	11	5	4	2	3	31	.175	.200	.158	16.10	1.56
Rodriguez, Yerry	R-R	6-2	198	10-15-97	1	1	2.63	14	14	0	0	51	38	16	15	3	21	63	.205	.244	.178	11.05	3.68
Snyder, Nick	R-R	6-4	190	10-10-95	0	1	1.65	13	0	0	1	16	12	4	3	1	1	25	.200	.217	.189	13.78	0.55
Speas, Alex	R-R	6-3	225	3-4-98	1	2	11.25	12	0	0	0	12	10	15	15	2	21	23	.222	.235	.214	17.25	15.75
Thomas, Tyler	R-L	6-1	175	12-24-95	3	2	4.17	26	0	0	1	41	39	19	19	5	17	51	.250	.254	.247	11.20	3.73
Tiedemann, Tai	R-R	6-6	195	5-31-96	1	2	3.05	11	1	0	0	21	21	13	7	2	12	10	.259	.244	.275	4.35	5.23
Uvila, Cole	R-R	6-3	206	1-30-94	2	2	2.90	23	0	0	8	31	24	10	10	1	14	42	.212	.238	.197	12.19	4.06
Villines, Stephen	R-R	6-1	185	7-15-95	5	4	3.38	24	0	0	3	40	39	23	15	3	10	43	.255	.333	.219	9.68	2.25
Winn, Cole	R-R	6-2	190	11-25-99	3	3	2.31	19	19	0	0	78	38	21	20	6	26	97	.144	.147	.142	11.19	3.00

Fielding

Catcher	PCT	G	PO	A	E	DP	PB
Novoa	1.000	16	131	11	0	1	2
Procyshen	.993	32	269	29	2	2	4
Quiroz	.953	5	41	0	2	0	0
Trevino	.950	3	18	1	1	0	0
Whatley	.997	74	727	64	2	3	7

First Base	PCT	G	PO	A	E	DP
Apostel	.975	15	113	6	3	10

Second Base	PCT	G	PO	A	E	DP
Arias	.984	16	27	35	1	10

Outfield	PCT	G	PO	A	E	DP
Arias	.994	50	314	21	2	28
Biggers	1.000	3	6	0	0	0
Crim	.984	10	60	2	1	2
Hernandez	1.000	3	20	1	0	4
Huff	.992	34	242	8	2	21
Procyshen	.976	11	80	3	2	7

Shortstop	PCT	G	PO	A	E	DP
Biggers	.982	59	90	125	4	21
Dorow	1.000	3	3	7	0	2
Foscue	.967	24	37	52	3	11
Hoover	1.000	3	1	4	0	0
Loehr	1.000	13	25	32	0	9
Pena	1.000	1	2	1	0	1
Tejeda	1.000	1	0	5	0	0
Wendzel	1.000	4	9	11	0	1

Third Base	PCT	G	PO	A	E	DP
Apostel	.902	20	15	22	4	1
Arias	.972	32	23	47	2	4
Biggers	1.000	1	0	1	0	1
Dorow	.929	7	5	8	1	0
Holt	.000	1	0	0	0	0
Hoover	.960	12	11	13	1	0
Jung	1.000	32	12	53	0	4
Pena	.857	4	1	5	1	0
Wendzel	.977	18	15	27	1	5

Shortstop	PCT	G	PO	A	E	DP
Arias	1.000	4	2	13	0	1
Barreto	.960	6	10	14	1	4
Biggers	.889	3	2	6	1	2
Dorow	.980	13	19	29	1	9
Smith	.960	30	35	61	4	11
Tejeda	.920	46	64	108	15	16
Wendzel	.932	19	25	44	5	11

Outfield	PCT	G	PO	A	E	DP
Aparicio	1.000	14	18	1	0	1
Biggers	.935	26	24	5	2	1
Crim	.889	7	8	0	1	0
Dahl	1.000	4	8	0	0	0
Hernandez	1.000	9	13	0	0	0
Hoover	1.000	2	6	2	0	0
Martinez	1.000	78	116	4	0	0
Stowers	.988	85	155	4	2	2
Thompson	.969	94	188	0	6	0
Walker	.989	51	88	4	1	2

HICKORY CRAWDADS

HIGH CLASS A

HIGH-A EAST

Batting	B-T	HT	WT	DOB	AVG	vLH	vRH	G	AB	R	H	2B	3B	HR	RBI	BB	HBP	SH	SF	SO	SB	CS	SLG	OBP
Acosta, Jose	B-R	5-10	170	3-20-00	.250	.350	.207	37	132	21	33	4	1	4	20	4	3	2	1	44	5	4	.386	.286
Anderson, Ryan	R-R	6-1	205	8-30-95	.118	.000	.130	15	51	6	6	1	0	1	3	3	1	0	0	17	1	1	.196	.182
Aparicio, Miguel	L-L	6-0	195	3-17-99	.274	.357	.257	48	164	28	45	8	2	12	35	18	7	1	2	41	1	1	.567	.366
Barreto, Derwin	B-R	5-9	160	9-1-00	.150	.235	.087	19	40	6	6	0	0	0	1	7	1	0	0	16	0	0	.150	.292
Chavez, Frainyer	B-R	5-10	170	5-24-99	.244	.313	.220	97	315	48	77	13	1	1	38	46	6	2	3	79	10	6	.302	.349
Crim, Blaine	R-R	5-11	200	6-17-97	.300	.296	.302	73	270	48	81	10	0	20	61	21	11	0	2	64	1	1	.559	.372
Duran, Ezequiel	R-R	5-11	185	5-22-99	.229	.196	.243	38	157	25	36	7	0	7	31	12	2	0	3	59	7	2	.408	.287
2-team total (67 Hudson Valley)					.267	.262	.268	105	416	67	111	22	6	19	79	40	10	0	5	130	19	9	.486	.342
Enright, Kole	B-R	6-1	175	1-21-98	.178	.167	.182	28	90	8	16	3	0	1	6	12	3	0	0	34	0	1	.244	.295
Foscue, Justin	R-R	6-0	205	3-2-99	.296	.346	.283	33	125	34	37	11	1	14	35	16	8	0	1	39	1	1	.736	.407
Garcia, Andretty	B-R	5-11	201	2-6-00	.256	.267	.251	83	301	36	77	13	0	5	40	18	2	0	4	78	0	0	.349	.298
Gonzalez, Pedro	R-R	6-5	190	10-27-97	.185	.120	.207	90	297	28	55	16	0	6	26	28	4	0	5	136	6	1	.300	.260
Guenther, Jake	L-L	6-4	230	5-16-97	.256	.295	.243	94	308	55	79	12	0	9	43	32	10	2	6	72	3	4	.383	.340
Gutierrez, Jember	R-R	5-11	160	9-8-99	.083	.250	.000	3	12	0	1	0	0	0	0	0	0	0	0	5	0	0	.083	.083
Hair, Trey	L-R	5-10	185	4-21-95	.291	.268	.301	66	234	45	68	13	0	13	48	24	11	1	2	68	4	3	.513	.380
Harris, Dustin	L-R	6-2	185	7-8-99	.372	.341	.386	37	145	32	54	10	0	10	32	13	1	0	1	25	5	1	.648	.425
Hauver, Trevor	L-R	6-0	205	11-20-98	.246	.176	.273	33	122	20	30	4	0	6	21	20	1	0	0	47	0	0	.426	.357
Irizarry, Kenen	L-R	6-0	150	5-6-00	.167	.231	.138	17	42	4	7	1	0	0	4	2	0	0	1	11	0	0	.190	.200
Kapers, Scott	R-R	5-11	198	11-27-96	.212	.300	.190	21	52	6	11	1	0	2	10	10	4	0	2	17	0	1	.346	.368
Ornelas, Jonathan	R-R	6-0	196	5-26-00	.261	.260	.261	94	376	71	98	18	4	8	38	21	6	2	0	87	9	5	.394	.310
Piotto, Konner	L-R	5-10	195	1-1-98	.240	.143	.278	10	25	1	6	1	0	0	5	3	0	0	0	7	0	0	.280	.321
Quiroz, Isaias	R-R	5-10	234	10-22-96	.179	.172	.182	39	106	15	19	3	0	4	12	13	2	0	1	54	0	1	.321	.279
Seise, Chris	R-R	6-2	196	1-6-99	.225	.333	.206	10	40	6	9	0	1	2	4	4	0	0	0	15	0	0	.425	.295
Smith, Brady	R-R	6-1	210	11-18-98	.200	.000	.250	5	10	2	2	0	0	0	1	0	0	0	0	5	0	0	.200	.273
Smith, Josh H.	L-R	5-10	172	8-7-97	.295	.286	.297	9	44	10	13	3	0	1	7	2	3	0	0	9	2	0	.432	.367
2-team total (28 Hudson Valley)					.313	.333	.304	37	147	39	46	15	3	4	16	18	8	1	0	36	14	3	.537	.416
Strahm, Kellen	R-R	6-1	215	4-25-97	.281	.306	.273	50	192	40	54	10	2	6	26	32	2	1	1	60	5	0	.448	.388
Walker, Jared	L-R	6-2	198	2-4-96	.173	.162	.177	45	133	20	23	3	1	5	25	10	4	0	0	70	5	0	.323	.299

Pitching	B-T	HT	WT	DOB	W	L	ERA	G	GS	CG	SV	IP	H	R	ER	HR	BB	SO	AVG	vLH	vRH	K/9	BB/9
Anderson, Ben	R-R	6-4	200	5-2-98	2	0	4.06	9	4	0	0	31	32	15	14	4	8	31	.260	.255	.265	9.00	2.32
Anderson, Grant	R-R	6-0	180	6-21-97	0	3	4.61	15	0	0	3	27	22	14	14	3	14	35	.216	.313	.171	11.52	4.61
Anderson, Ryan	R-R	6-1	205	8-30-95	0	0	0.00	1	0	0	0	2	0	0	0	1	0	0	.000	.000	.000	0.00	4.50
Bradford, Cody	L-L	6-4	197	2-22-98	4	4	4.23	13	13	0	0	62	55	36	29	9	17	87	.230	.277	.213	12.70	2.48
Casanova, Jean	R-R	6-3	181	3-4-97	2	3	7.50	27	0	0	5	36	47	33	30	6	25	53	.320	.352	.301	13.25	6.25
Chandler, Sean	R-R	6-5	203	1-24-97	3	3	4.91	29	0	0	1	44	30	30	24	11	20	65	.190	.127	.223	13.30	4.09
Corbett, Joe	R-R	6-5	230	10-12-96	0	3	6.35	15	0	0	1	23	29	18	16	4	12	26	.312	.244	.365	10.32	4.76
Gowdy, Kevin	R-R	6-4	170	11-16-97	2	1	3.72	6	4	0	0	29	30	14	12	4	10	26	.265	.314	.226	8.07	3.10
2-team total (14 Jersey Shore)					6	6	4.20	20	16	0	0	90	98	48	42	9	25	89	.275	.324	.231	8.90	2.50
Hair, Trey	L-R	5-10	185	4-21-95	0	1	20.25	4	0	0	0	4	12	11	9	3	0	1	.480	.462	.500	2.25	0.00
Henriquez, Ronny	R-R	5-10	155	6-20-00	1	3	3.75	5	5	0	0	24	13	11	10	2	8	27	.153	.286	.088	10.13	3.00
Kapers, Scott	R-R	5-11	198	11-27-96	0	1	9.00	1	0	0	0	1	1	2	1	0	2	0	.250	.000	.500	0.00	18.00
Kent, Zak	R-R	6-3	208	2-24-98	6	2	2.83	14	9	0	0	66	46	20	19	5	15	78	.206	.195	.213	11.64	2.24
Kuzia, Joe	R-R	6-5	190	10-3-93	0	0	0.00	2	0	0	0	4	3	1	0	0	2	4	.200	.000	.250	9.00	4.50
Laio, Nic	R-R	6-5	205	7-28-97	0	1	7.80	14	1	0	1	30	34	30	26	9	10	40	.276	.289	.271	12.00	3.00
Linarez, Jesus	R-R	6-4	216	1-10-97	3	4	4.70	16	3	0	0	38	36	28	20	3	13	31	.245	.140	.311	7.28	3.05
Marsden, Justin	R-R	6-4	175	1-27-97	1	6	7.71	23	0	0	1	33	38	31	28	5	22	45	.295	.250	.321	12.40	6.06
McKillican, Adam	R-R	6-5	225	1-9-98	0	1	7.00	5	0	0	0	9	16	10	7	0	3	6	.364	.250	.429	6.00	3.00
Mejia, Juan	L-L	5-11	160	1-9-99	1	2	2.92	5	0	0	0	12	9	4	4	0	4	10	.196	.188	.200	7.30	2.92
Mraz, Spencer	R-R	6-10	245	5-5-98	0	0	7.45	8	1	0	0	10	13	11	8	2	5	13	.283	.200	.381	12.10	4.66
Nordlin, Seth	R-R	6-4	213	9-4-97	3	5	5.20	20	11	0	2	83	80	49	48	11	32	87	.252	.205	.281	9.43	3.47
Polley, Triston	L-L	6-0	190	12-20-96	2	1	8.16	9	0	0	0	14	14	13	13	1	12	20	.250	.389	.184	12.56	7.53
Quiroz, Isaias	R-R	5-10	234	10-22-96	0	0	0.00	1	0	0	0	1	0	0	0	0	1	0	.000		.500	0.00	9.00
Ragans, Cole	L-L	6-4	190	12-12-97	1	2	3.25	10	10	0	0	44	34	16	16	4	14	54	.217	.250	.200	10.96	2.84
Robert, Daniel	L-R	6-4	210	8-30-94	0	0	4.15	3	0	0	1	4	3	2	2	1	1	9	.188	.167	.200	18.69	2.08
Slaten, Justin	R-R	6-4	222	9-15-97	4	8	6.01	20	19	0	0	88	83	60	55	17	31	110	.283	.292	.276	12.02	3.39
Smith, Josh	L-L	6-2	205	2-5-97	1	1	3.32	14	0	0	0	22	26	16	8	4	8	20	.302	.333	.283	8.31	3.32
Snyder, Nick	R-R	6-4	190	10-10-95	0	0	2.19	10	0	0	3	12	8	3	3	2	3	17	.195	.167	.207	12.41	2.19
Starr, Nick	R-R	6-3	225	12-3-96	1	3	5.94	24	0	0	0	33	36	29	22	11	14	52	.263	.327	.224	14.04	3.78
Thomas, Tyler	R-L	6-1	175	12-22-95	0	1	2.08	5	0	0	0	13	9	5	3	0	3	19	.180	.200	.167	13.15	2.08

	B-T	HT	WT	DOB	W	L	ERA	G	GS	CG	SV	IP	H	R	ER	HR	BB	SO	AVG	vLH	vRH	K/9	BB/9
Tiedemann, Tai	R-R	6-6	195	5-31-96	4	0	4.50	15	1	0	0	36	45	19	18	3	6	27	.310	.357	.291	6.75	1.50
Weems, Avery	R-L	6-2	205	6-6-97	4	6	5.06	20	19	0	0	85	77	54	48	16	27	124	.237	.145	.269	13.08	2.85
Wolfram, Grant	L-L	6-6	235	12-12-96	2	3	4.21	17	14	0	0	66	63	38	31	11	34	99	.242	.154	.280	13.43	4.61
Yoder, Nick	R-R	6-6	190	3-3-99	0	1	13.50	4	0	0	0	4	4	6	6	1	6	2	.250	.125	.375	4.50	13.50

Fielding

Catcher

	PCT	G	PO	A	E	DP	PB
Garcia	.991	73	721	54	7	4	8
Kapers	1.000	14	154	11	0	1	1
Piotto	.960	6	43	5	2	1	1
Quiroz	.983	30	280	8	5	0	1
Smith	.947	3	18	0	1	0	0
Chavez	.987	50	63	88	2		23
Duran	.944	4	7	10	1		4
Enright	.667	1	0	2	1		0
Foscue	1.000	29	35	57	0		9
Hair	1.000	3	0	5	0		0
Hauver	.955	12	16	26	2		5
Ornelas	1.000	2	0	7	0		0

First Base

	PCT	G	PO	A	E	DP
Crim	.989	53	340	14	4	26
Guenther	.993	20	135	7	1	9
Gutierrez	1.000	1	11	0	0	0
Hair	.987	13	72	4	1	1
Harris	.977	24	156	12	4	15
Irizarry	.952	4	20	0	1	2
Kapers	1.000	1	10	0	0	0
Quiroz	.778	1	7	0	2	0
Walker	1.000	6	28	6	0	0

Second Base

	PCT	G	PO	A	E	DP
Acosta	1.000	15	27	24	0	3
Barreto	1.000	7	5	11	0	2

Third Base

	PCT	G	PO	A	E	DP
Acosta	.938	17	7	23	2	0
Barreto	1.000	9	5	13	0	1
Chavez	.961	29	16	57	3	4
Crim	.750	5	1	2	1	0
Duran	1.000	3	0	2	0	0
Gutierrez	1.000	2	2	3	0	1
Hair	.932	26	20	35	4	2
Harris	.913	11	7	14	2	0
Irizarry	.955	11	8	13	1	2
Ornelas	1.000	7	4	8	0	0
Walker	.778	7	2	5	2	1

Shortstop

	PCT	G	PO	A	E	DP
Acosta	.867	4	3	10	2	1
Chavez	.957	14	18	26	2	3
Duran	.911	25	33	69	10	12
Ornelas	.964	60	66	124	7	20
Seise	.906	9	10	19	3	3
Smith	.974	9	15	23	1	1

Outfield

	PCT	G	PO	A	E	DP
Anderson	.929	15	13	0	1	0
Aparicio	1.000	38	55	2	0	0
Chavez	--	3	0	0	0	0
Enright	.927	26	35	3	3	0
Gonzalez	.968	89	149	4	5	0
Guenther	.980	67	93	3	2	1
Hair	--	1	0	0	0	0
Hauver	.938	18	15	0	1	0
Irizarry	--	1	0	0	0	0
Ornelas	.981	27	52	1	1	0
Strahm	1.000	47	81	3	0	0
Walker	.920	30	42	4	4	0

DOWN EAST WOOD DUCKS   LOW CLASS A

LOW-A EAST

Batting

	B-T	HT	WT	DOB	AVG	vLH	vRH	G	AB	R	H	2B	3B	HR	RBI	BB	HBP	SH	SF	SO	SB	CS	SLG	OBP
Acosta, Jose	B-R	5-10	170	3-20-00	.257	.462	.227	37	101	20	26	9	0	1	7	12	5	0	0	31	9	3	.376	.364
Acuna, Luisangel	R-R	5-10	181	3-12-02	.266	.156	.297	111	413	77	110	15	3	12	74	49	4	0	7	110	44	11	.404	.345
Aponte, Angel	R-R	6-0	170	2-3-00	.247	.250	.246	48	162	27	40	5	1	3	24	15	9	0	2	42	17	3	.346	.340
Cabello, Antonio	R-R	5-10	160	11-1-00	.156	.098	.180	44	141	15	22	4	1	3	15	12	0	0	3	57	3	0	.262	.218
Carter, Evan	L-R	6-4	190	8-29-02	.236	.257	.225	32	106	22	25	8	1	2	12	34	5	0	1	28	12	4	.387	.438
Easley, Jayce	B-R	5-8	151	8-2-99	.244	.282	.232	98	311	74	76	11	3	1	28	78	6	4	2	83	70	10	.309	.403
Florentino, Randy	L-R	5-11	182	7-5-00	.148	.152	.147	52	149	19	22	5	0	3	12	20	1	1	3	54	2	2	.242	.249
Freeman, Cody	R-R	5-10	180	1-5-01	.247	.226	.253	71	243	36	60	11	2	6	35	32	10	1	1	47	11	1	.383	.357
Harris, Dustin	L-R	6-2	185	7-8-99	.301	.282	.309	73	259	54	78	11	3	10	53	34	7	0	6	48	20	1	.483	.389
Inoa, Cristian	R-R	5-10	165	7-4-99	.292	.271	.298	88	322	46	94	22	1	11	58	28	5	3	5	51	9	3	.469	.353
Mateo, Daniel	R-R	6-1	165	7-3-01	.272	.185	.294	36	136	28	37	7	0	2	20	9	0	1	4	41	11	4	.368	.315
Moss, Keithron	B-R	5-11	188	8-20-01	.171	.170	.172	61	187	27	32	8	4	5	22	48	0		2	96	14	3	.337	.296
Osuna, Alejandro	L-L	6-0	185	10-10-02	.224	.160	.233	66	201	36	45	14	0	6	36	34	5	2	1	74	17	5	.383	.349
Pena, Yenci	R-R	6-0	193	7-13-00	.262	.000	.302	20	61	15	16	5	0	2	13	7	1	0	2	19	2	0	.443	.338
Piotto, Konner	L-R	5-10	195	1-1-98	.071	--	.071	5	14	0	1	0	0	0	1	3	1	0	0	1	0	0	.071	.278
Ricumstrict, Obie	R-R	6-2	175	7-20-98	.163	.111	.183	33	98	13	16	5	0	3	15	9	3	2	1	43	6	0	.306	.252
Rodriguez, Jose	L-R	6-0	185	10-5-01	.200	.000	.281	15	45	2	9	3	0	0	1	8	0	0	0	19	1	0	.267	.321
Rodriguez, Keyber	R-R	5-10	178	10-24-00	.271	.345	.248	103	369	55	100	19	4	5	63	37	7	1	8	90	10	5	.385	.342
Saggese, Thomas	R-R	5-11	175	4-10-02	.256	.267	.254	73	242	44	62	14	3	10	37	42	3	0	1	85	11	3	.463	.372
Smith, Brady	R-R	6-1	210	11-18-98	.184	.000	.217	20	38	5	7	1	0	0	4	9	1	0	1	15	1	0	.211	.347
Smith, Marcus	L-L	5-11	185	9-11-00	.273	.667	.125	3	11	1	3	0	1	0	2	1	0	0	0	5	1	0	.455	.333
Valentin, Xavier	L-R	5-9	180	8-22-00	.224	.172	.237	43	143	12	32	10	2	2	24	12	3	0	1	59	12	3	.364	.296
Zavala, Aaron	L-R	6-0	193	6-23-00	.302	.333	.293	15	53	13	16	4	0	1	7	10	3	0	1	13	7	0	.434	.433

Pitching

	B-T	HT	WT	DOB	W	L	ERA	G	GS	CG	SV	IP	H	R	ER	HR	BB	SO	AVG	vLH	vRH	K/9	BB/9
Acker, Dane	R-R	6-2	189	4-1-99	0	1	2.84	2	2	0	0	6	4	2	2	0	1	11	.160	.125	.176	15.63	1.42
Anderson, Ben	R-R	6-4	200	5-2-98	1	1	3.24	11	0	0	0	25	21	10	9	3	11	31	.223	.154	.273	11.16	3.96
Brewer, Michael	R-R	6-5	215	8-8-00	1	1	4.30	8	0	0	0	15	8	7	7	1	7	19	.160	.043	.259	11.66	4.30
Church, Marc	R-R	6-3	189	3-30-01	3	1	4.28	19	0	0	3	27	22	13	13	4	8	49	.210	.205	.212	16.13	2.63
Cole, Mason	R-R	6-6	200	12-4-97	2	0	4.01	15	0	0	1	25	17	13	11	4	18	27	.195	.160	.210	9.85	6.57
Collyer, Gavin	R-R	6-1	165	5-12-01	3	1	3.33	21	16	0	0	73	63	31	27	6	48	84	.236	.198	.261	10.36	5.92
Corbett, Joe	R-R	6-5	230	10-14-96	1	1	2.38	10	0	0	5	11	6	3	3	0	5	18	.146	.143	.148	14.29	3.97
Dotson, Destin	L-L	6-7	231	11-17-99	3	0	4.34	16	0	0	0	29	23	20	14	2	14	38	.207	.152	.246	11.79	4.34
Englert, Mason	B-R	6-4	206	11-1-99	6	3	4.35	19	19	1	0	81	73	48	39	4	26	90	.242	.182	.282	10.04	2.90
Filpo, Eris	R-R	6-3	170	5-3-98	2	3	6.82	14	1	0	1	33	49	34	25	5	10	37	.331	.358	.316	10.09	2.73
Gomez, Orceli	R-R	6-5	175	11-23-00	0	2	3.86	3	3	0	0	9	10	4	4	1	1	8	.278	.300	.269	7.71	0.96
Inoa, Cristian	R-R	5-10	165	7-4-99	0	0	0.00	2	0	0	0	2	3	0	0	0	0	0	.333	.250	.400	0.00	0.00
Javier, Joshua	L-L	6-3	195	12-16-98	1	0	3.68	17	0	0	0	22	19	15	9	2	27	38	.224	.259	.207	15.55	11.05
Krauth, Nick	R-R	6-3	170	9-6-99	5	9	4.30	20	20	1	0	103	103	56	49	11	28	99	.258	.255	.260	6.93	2.45
Laio, Nic	R-R	6-5	205	7-28-97	3	2	2.73	10	0	0	0	26	23	8	8	5	6	39	.235	.256	.220	13.33	2.05
Linarez, Jesus	R-R	6-4	216	1-10-97	2	1	2.38	13	2	0	1	23	15	8	6	2	9	22	.190	.130	.214	8.74	3.57
Lockhart, Nick	R-R	6-6	204	2-12-01	1	1	8.49	13	2	0	0	30	32	29	28	7	19	25	.276	.279	.274	8.49	5.76
Manon, Eudrys	R-R	6-1	160	1-16-98	3	0	2.78	16	0	0	6	23	9	8	7	0	15	36	.122	.156	.095	14.29	5.96

Name	B-T	HT	WT	DOB	W	L	ERA	G	GS														AVG	vLH	vRH
Matthews, John	R-R	6-1	190	1-21-98	5	4	6.78	24	11	0	0	68	80	54	51	9	28	80	.289	.294	.286	10.64	3.72
McDowell, Theo	L-R	6-4	175	12-2-98	1	0	7.63	9	0	0	1	15	17	13	13	3	13	27	.279	.231	.314	15.85	7.63
Mendoza, Abdiel	R-R	5-10	160	9-19-98	1	3	4.95	10	7	0	0	36	41	23	20	3	16	40	.293	.380	.244	9.91	3.96
Mraz, Spencer	R-R	6-10	245	5-5-98	4	4	4.55	22	0	0	7	32	27	16	16	2	16	44	.229	.275	.205	12.51	4.55
Ortega, Teodoro	R-R	6-0	145	3-12-00	3	1	2.91	17	1	0	1	34	28	18	11	2	15	34	.219	.283	.183	9.00	3.97
Roby, Tekoah	R-R	6-1	185	9-18-01	2	2	2.45	6	6	0	0	22	14	6	6	1	7	35	.177	.172	.180	14.32	2.86
Sechler, Connor	R-R	6-3	180	4-7-99	4	2	5.40	15	0	0	0	28	22	20	17	3	23	36	.216	.311	.140	11.44	7.31
Serrano, Florencio	R-R	6-1	205	2-23-00	3	0	1.27	9	5	0	0	28	21	5	4	2	8	29	.206	.211	.203	9.21	2.54
Smith, Josh	L-L	6-5	205	2-5-97	0	0	0.82	13	0	0	2	22	17	6	2	1	7	29	.205	.250	.197	11.86	2.86
Sparks, Wyatt	R-R	6-2	195	9-27-99	1	1	4.12	10	10	0	0	44	39	23	20	5	12	34	.235	.219	.245	7.01	2.47
Starr, Nick	R-R	6-3	225	12-3-96	3	0	0.00	5	0	0	0	5	1	0	0	0	2	8	.059	.000	.091	13.50	3.38
Stephan, Josh	R-R	6-3	185	11-1-01	0	1	8.25	3	3	0	0	12	15	11	11	4	4	19	.294	.182	.379	14.25	3.00
Tejada, Leury	R-R	6-1	160	12-24-99	2	2	4.66	20	2	0	3	39	44	25	20	5	17	42	.278	.203	.323	9.78	3.96
Thompson, Tyree	R-R	6-4	165	6-12-97	1	0	2.70	7	2	0	0	20	16	8	6	2	15	19	.211	.192	.220	8.55	6.75
White, Owen	R-R	6-3	199	8-9-99	3	1	3.24	8	8	0	0	33	25	12	12	2	12	54	.205	.140	.250	14.58	3.24
Yoder, Nick	R-R	6-6	190	3-3-99	2	0	8.02	10	0	0	0	21	32	21	19	6	12	19	.344	.333	.352	8.02	5.06

Fielding

Catcher	PCT	G	PO	A	E	DP	PB
Florentino	.987	45	434	34	6	3	0
Freeman	.989	35	344	21	4	2	1
Piotto	1.000	5	39	2	0	0	0
Smith	1.000	14	95	6	0	1	0
Valentin	.994	29	294	21	2	4	7

First Base	PCT	G	PO	A	E	DP
Acosta	.981	11	49	3	1	5
Florentino	.929	6	23	3	2	3
Freeman	1.000	4	6	1	0	0
Harris	1.000	50	333	24	0	30
Inoa	.989	51	337	17	4	31
Pena	1.000	4	19	2	0	1
Rodriguez	.960	4	22	2	1	3
Smith	1.000	3	10	0	0	1

Second Base	PCT	G	PO	A	E	DP
Acosta	1.000	8	14	11	0	0

Acuna	.971	36	59	77	4	12
Inoa	.969	10	12	19	1	6
Moss	.925	48	62	122	15	25
Saggese	.986	22	30	41	1	9

Third Base	PCT	G	PO	A	E	DP
Acosta	.958	8	10	13	1	4
Easley	1.000	1	1	0	0	0
Freeman	1.000	24	22	37	0	6
Harris	.903	13	7	21	3	0
Inoa	.912	15	5	26	3	3
Moss	1.000	1	0	1	0	0
Pena	.833	9	4	11	3	0
Rodriguez	.951	29	16	42	3	5
Saggese	.867	24	14	38	8	5

Shortstop	PCT	G	PO	A	E	DP
Acosta	.850	7	8	9	3	3
Acuna	.957	42	59	98	7	22

Rodriguez	.936	63	84	120	14	22
Saggese	.953	11	14	27	2	5

Outfield	PCT	G	PO	A	E	DP
Aponte	1.000	49	68	4	0	0
Cabello	.967	43	59	0	2	0
Carter	.980	30	48	0	1	0
Easley	.995	101	184	11	1	3
Mateo	.953	38	60	1	3	0
Moss	.500	1	1	0	1	0
Osuna	.970	63	93	3	3	1
Pena	.933	4	13	1	1	1
Ricumstrict	.980	33	50	0	1	0
Rodriguez	.800	8	8	0	2	0
Rodriguez	.750	5	3	0	1	0
Smith	1.000	3	2	0	0	0
Zavala	.882	11	13	2	2	0

ACL RANGERS   ROOKIE
ARIZONA COMPLEX LEAGUE

Batting	B-T	HT	WT	DOB	AVG	vLH	vRH	G	AB	R	H	2B	3B	HR	RBI	BB	HBP	SH	SF	SO	SB	CS	SLG	OBP
Acosta, Maximo	R-R	6-1	187	10-29-02	.246	.250	.245	17	61	11	15	2	2	1	5	3	1	0	3	15	7	2	.393	.279
Amaro, Fernando	R-R	5-10	180	11-1-01	.226	.000	.292	16	31	3	7	2	0	0	2	3	2	0	0	9	0	2	.290	.333
Aponte, Angel	R-R	6-0	170	2-3-00	.474	.500	.471	5	19	4	9	5	0	0	3	0	0	0	0	5	1	0	.737	.474
Apostel, Sherten	R-R	6-4	235	3-11-99	.417	--	.417	4	12	6	5	1	0	3	8	3	1	0	0	5	0	0	1.250	.563
Bannister, Zion	R-R	6-3	189	9-9-01	.227	.091	.255	37	128	19	29	6	0	2	15	17	0	0	0	51	2	5	.320	.317
Barreto, Derwin	B-R	5-9	160	9-1-00	.324	.000	.333	13	37	12	12	0	2	1	7	11	1	0	0	11	4	0	.514	.490
Blackmon, JoJo	L-L	6-0	183	3-31-03	.236	.182	.250	18	55	10	13	1	2	0	6	12	0	0	0	29	8	1	.327	.373
Bryan, Hunter	R-R	6-0	195	4-22-01	.231	.000	.250	8	13	5	3	0	0	1	3	7	2	0	0	8	1	1	.462	.545
Cabello, Antonio	R-R	5-10	160	11-1-00	.307	.409	.264	24	75	11	23	8	1	1	13	15	0	0	0	26	2	2	.480	.422
Calhoun, Willie	L-R	5-8	200	11-4-94	.353	.000	.400	5	17	4	6	2	0	0	3	3	0	0	0	3	0	0	.647	.450
Cauley, Cameron	R-R	5-10	170	2-6-03	.255	.125	.282	24	94	20	24	4	4	0	17	8	0	0	1	31	10	1	.383	.311
Del Orbe, Alisson	R-R	6-3	185	9-6-01	.233	.105	.262	41	103	11	24	8	3	0	9	10	1	0	1	34	4	2	.369	.304
Felix, Jose A.	R-R	5-11	190	7-23-02	.000	--	.000	1	1	0	0	0	0	0	0	0	0	0	1	0	0	0	.000	.000
Foscue, Justin	R-R	6-0	205	3-2-99	.273	.333	.250	3	11	4	3	1	0	1	3	1	1	0	0	4	1	0	.636	.385
Freeman, Cody	R-R	5-10	180	1-5-01	.214	--	.214	4	14	2	3	1	0	0	1	1	0	0	1	1	0	0	.286	.250
Galan, Yosy	R-R	6-4	200	4-25-01	.254	.216	.264	51	177	34	45	5	7	10	44	18	6	0	2	80	16	1	.531	.340
Gutierrez, Jember	R-R	5-11	160	9-8-99	.318	.250	.340	28	66	10	21	1	1	1	10	5	1	0	2	14	1	2	.485	.365
Hicks, Liam	L-R	5-11	185	6-2-99	.125	.200	.105	10	24	6	3	0	0	0	2	7	1	0	0	4	0	0	.125	.344
Huff, Sam	R-R	6-5	240	1-14-98	.276	.667	.174	8	29	6	8	2	0	3	6	3	1	0	0	11	0	0	.655	.364
Irizarry, Kenen	L-R	6-0	150	5-6-00	.228	.200	.237	44	123	17	28	9	0	1	20	18	0	0	4	25	3	2	.325	.317
Lascarro, Ronier	L-L	5-10	155	1-31-01	.200	.238	.186	31	80	14	16	3	0	1	9	15	0	1	0	32	4	2	.275	.326
Mateo, Daniel	R-R	6-1	165	7-3-01	.327	.187	.347	15	55	12	18	3	3	1	9	6	1	0	1	9	8	4	.545	.397
Mitchell, Tucker	R-R	6-1	210	2-10-01	.200	.150	.233	14	50	4	10	2	1	1	5	5	2	0	0	13	1	0	.340	.298
Moller, Ian	R-R	6-0	190	10-26-02	.220	.429	.186	15	50	11	11	4	0	3	9	4	0	0	0	20	0	2	.480	.381
Moreno, Jesus	R-R	5-11	170	4-16-01	.174	.105	.200	29	69	10	12	1	1	1	8	13	5	0	1	27	2	2	.261	.341
Moss, Keithron	B-R	5-11	188	8-20-01	.259	.300	.235	37	85	7	22	7	1	0	7	3	2	0	0	10	7	0	.296	.375
Narvaez, Effrener	R-R	5-11	155	7-25-02	.353	.286	.375	35	116	18	41	7	2	2	24	14	4	0	4	30	0	2	.500	.428
Paniagua, Junior	R-R	5-10	160	10-8-01	.201	.200	.202	46	134	21	27	6	0	5	21	17	1	0	1	51	4	5	.358	.294
Pena, Yenci	R-R	6-2	193	7-13-00	.286	.667	.250	11	35	6	10	1	1	1	6	3	0	0	0	10	1	1	.457	.342
Ricumstrict, Obie	R-R	6-2	175	7-20-98	.214	.000	.273	4	14	3	3	1	0	0	1	1	0	0	0	5	0	0	.286	.267
Smith, Marcus	L-L	5-11	185	9-11-00	.188	.250	.167	11	32	4	6	1	1	1	6	4	2	0	0	18	0	0	.375	.316
Tejeda, Anderson	B-R	6-0	200	5-1-98	.429	.500	.417	4	14	5	6	3	0	0	1	1	0	0	0	3	1	0	.643	.467
Valentin, Xavier	L-R	5-9	180	8-22-00	.083	.000	.125	7	24	1	2	0	0	0	3	1	0	0	1	9	2	0	.083	.115

TEXAS RANGERS

Batting	B-T	HT	WT	DOB	AVG	vLH	vRH	G	AB	R	H	2B	3B	HR	RBI	BB	HBP	SH	SF	SO	SB	CS	SLG	OBP
Wendzel, Davis	R-R	6-1	206	5-23-97	.250	.500	.179	10	36	12	9	0	1	1	7	5	1	0	1	10	0	0	.389	.349
Zavala, Aaron	L-R	6-0	193	6-23-00	.273	.167	.313	7	22	5	6	1	0	0	2	3	1	0	0	7	2	0	.318	.385

Pitching	B-T	HT	WT	DOB	W	L	ERA	G	GS	CG	SV	IP	H	R	ER	HR	BB	SO	AVG	vLH	vRH	K/9	BB/9
Anderson, Justin	L-R	6-3	230	9-28-92	0	0	0.00	2	1	0	0	2	0	0	0	0	0	6	.000	.000	.000	27.00	0.00
Bratt, Mitch	L-L	6-1	190	7-3-03	0	0	0.00	4	0	0	0	6	4	2	0	0	0	13	.174	.286	.125	19.50	0.00
Brennan, Tim	R-R	6-4	212	12-18-96	0	0	0.00	1	1	0	0	2	0	0	0	0	0	2	.000	.000	.000	9.00	0.00
Brewer, Michael	R-R	6-5	215	8-8-00	1	0	2.87	10	0	0	0	16	14	6	5	1	10	24	.241	.320	.182	13.79	5.74
Cole, Mason	R-R	6-6	200	12-4-97	1	0	3.00	3	0	0	0	3	0	1	1	0	3	7	.000	.000	.000	21.00	9.00
Corniell, Jose	R-R	6-3	165	6-22-03	1	3	6.98	13	9	0	0	39	44	38	30	7	14	44	.282	.372	.192	10.24	3.26
Curry, Aidan	R-R	6-5	185	7-5-02	0	1	13.79	11	1	0	0	16	23	24	24	1	14	23	.343	.278	.419	13.21	8.04
Dotson, Destin	L-L	6-7	231	11-17-99	0	0	9.39	4	0	0	0	8	9	8	8	1	5	10	.310	.400	.263	11.74	5.87
Elliott, Evan	R-R	6-3	210	1-10-01	2	0	0.00	3	0	0	0	3	0	0	0	0	3	7	.000	.000	.000	21.00	9.00
Filpo, Eris	R-R	6-3	170	5-3-98	0	0	4.05	2	0	0	0	7	3	3	3	1	1	10	.130	.231	.000	13.50	1.35
Gessner, Josh	R-R	6-1	205	6-25-00	2	3	3.95	7	5	0	0	27	16	13	12	0	17	46	.168	.222	.120	15.15	5.60
Hoopii-Tuionetoa, Anthony	R-R	6-2	190	8-11-00	2	3	5.16	18	0	0	4	23	19	16	13	2	11	38	.213	.206	.218	15.09	4.37
Kindreich, Larson	L-L	6-4	210	6-21-99	0	0	1.13	6	0	0	1	8	5	1	1	0	3	18	.172	.400	.125	20.25	3.38
Lee, Chase	R-R	6-0	170	8-13-98	0	0	0.00	1	0	0	0	1	1	0	0	0	0	3	.250	.000	.333	27.00	0.00
Lockhart, Nick	R-R	6-6	204	2-12-01	1	1	4.26	5	4	0	0	19	17	10	9	1	2	27	.250	.200	.279	12.79	0.95
MacLean, Dylan	R-L	6-4	190	7-12-02	0	2	5.82	7	6	0	0	17	14	15	11	1	19	17	.226	.333	.191	9.00	10.06
Manon, Eudrys	R-R	6-1	160	1-16-98	1	0	3.38	4	0	0	0	5	4	2	2	1	3	6	.222	.273	.143	10.13	5.06
McCarty, D.J.	R-R	6-2	145	9-9-02	0	3	7.76	16	2	0	0	27	36	31	23	5	27	36	.321	.318	.324	12.15	9.11
McDowell, Theo	L-R	6-4	175	12-2-98	2	0	6.39	9	0	0	2	13	10	9	9	3	12	23	.227	.304	.143	16.34	8.53
McKillican, Adam	R-R	6-5	225	1-9-98	1	0	9.00	1	0	0	0	2	3	2	2	0	0	3	.429	.333	.500	13.50	0.00
Mejia, Juan	L-L	5-11	160	1-9-99	1	0	1.08	5	0	0	1	8	4	2	1	0	1	14	.133	.000	.174	15.12	1.08
Mendoza, Damian	L-R	6-1	175	1-25-01	2	3	7.30	14	9	0	1	41	53	37	33	4	16	43	.312	.224	.383	9.52	3.54
Moreno, Jesus	R-R	5-11	170	4-16-01	0	0	63.00	1	0	0	0	1	6	7	7	2	1	0	.750	.750	.750	0.00	9.00
Pacheco, Sergio	R-R	6-1	170	8-17-99	1	0	7.36	5	0	0	0	7	9	6	6	0	3	13	.290	.182	.350	15.95	3.68
Polley, Triston	L-L	6-0	190	12-20-96	0	0	0.00	2	2	0	0	2	0	0	0	0	2	6	.000	.000	.000	23.14	7.71
Richardson, Glen	R-R	6-1	210	7-30-98	0	1	11.57	4	0	0	0	5	7	6	6	0	3	12	.304	.333	.286	23.14	5.79
Robert, Daniel	L-R	6-4	210	8-30-94	0	0	9.00	1	0	0	0	1	2	1	1	0	1	2	.400	.333	.500	18.00	9.00
Rodriguez, Adrian	R-R	6-5	192	5-18-01	1	1	7.78	14	0	0	1	20	16	19	17	2	28	35	.222	.138	.279	16.02	12.81
Santos, Winston	R-R	6-0	160	4-15-02	2	2	3.10	10	5	0	0	29	18	12	10	1	9	32	.176	.176	.176	9.93	2.79
Schiltz, Luke	R-R	6-5	200	7-2-00	0	0	7.71	11	0	0	0	16	16	14	14	1	19	19	.246	.304	.214	10.47	10.47
Sechler, Connor	R-R	6-3	180	4-7-99	0	0	0.00	3	0	0	0	6	1	0	0	0	1	14	.056	.000	.083	22.24	1.59
Speas, Alex	R-R	6-3	225	3-4-98	1	1	10.80	3	1	0	0	3	2	5	4	0	5	7	.167	.000	.250	18.90	13.50
Stephan, Josh	R-R	6-3	185	11-1-01	2	1	3.86	7	6	0	0	28	20	15	12	3	12	31	.204	.211	.200	9.96	3.86
Tejada, Leury	R-R	6-1	160	12-24-99	0	0	3.00	2	2	0	0	3	2	1	1	1	0	5	.182	.250	.143	15.00	0.00
Teodo, Emiliano	R-R	6-1	165	2-14-01	4	2	3.38	19	0	0	0	29	24	12	11	0	18	48	.214	.157	.262	14.73	5.52
Webb, Bradford	R-R	6-3	200	4-20-98	1	0	3.12	6	0	0	0	9	4	3	3	0	0	13	.265	.125	.389	13.50	0.00
White, Owen	R-R	6-3	199	8-9-99	1	0	0.00	1	0	0	0	2	1	0	0	0	0	2	.167	.000	.200	9.00	0.00
Wynyard, Kai	R-R	6-0	176	6-22-02	1	2	5.40	15	5	0	1	28	28	19	17	1	31	40	.255	.278	.232	12.71	9.85
Yoder, Nick	R-R	6-6	190	3-3-99	0	0	0.00	1	0	0	0	2	0	0	0	0	2	4	.000	.000	.000	15.43	7.71

Fielding

C: Amaro 4, Cabello 6, Hicks 1, Mitchell 5, Moller 12, Moreno 12, Narvaez 22, Valentin 3.
1B: Amaro 5, Bryan 1, Gutierrez 3, Hicks 6, Huff 6, Irizarry 18, Mitchell 7, Moreno 9, Narvaez 7, Paniagua 2, Pena 4.
2B: Acosta 1, Barreto 7, Bryan 5, Cauley 6, Del Orbe 2, Foscue 3, Freeman 2, Gutierrez 9, Irizarry 9, Moss 6, Paniagua 9, Wendzel 2.
3B: Apostel 3, Barreto 2, Cauley 1, Del Orbe 23, Gutierrez 11, Irizarry 7, Moreno 2, Paniagua 13, Pena 8, Wendzel 1.
SS: Acosta 13, Barreto 5, Cauley 17, Del Orbe 4, Freeman 1, Paniagua 23, Tejeda 3, Wendzel 4.
OF: Amaro 4, Aponte 4, Bannister 36, Blackmon 19, Cabello 17, Calhoun 3, Felix 1, Galan 44, Gutierrez 3, Irizarry 4, Lascarro 30, Mateo 15, Ricumstrict 3, Smith 7, Zavala 5.

DSL RANGERS   ROOKIE
DOMINICAN SUMMER LEAGUE

Batting	B-T	HT	WT	DOB	AVG	vLH	vRH	G	AB	R	H	2B	3B	HR	RBI	BB	HBP	SH	SF	SO	SB	CS	SLG	OBP
Almonte, Frandy	B-R	5-8	150	10-16-03	.280	.379	.259	50	168	39	47	9	2	1	20	44	4	0	0	31	35	1	.375	.440
Barroso, Beycker	R-R	5-10	160	1-24-03	.330	.333	.330	35	115	20	38	5	3	0	14	14	4	1	5	6	5	4	.426	.406
Basabe, Edgar	R-R	6-0	155	4-27-04	.196	.167	.200	35	97	16	19	1	2	1	14	20	2	0	2	38	16	1	.278	.339
Beato, Andy	R-R	0-0	0	11-27-03	.176	.500	.156	15	34	8	6	3	0	0	9	8	2	0	0	12	1	1	.265	.364
Cueva, Danyer	L-R	6-1	160	5-27-04	.282	.259	.286	49	202	48	57	11	3	1	25	22	8	0	0	48	9	4	.381	.375
Diaz, Juan	R-R	6-2	180	1-9-04	.225	.188	.233	31	89	18	20	5	2	1	10	9	2	0	1	14	2	1	.360	.307
Figuereo, Gleider	L-R	6-0	165	6-27-04	.231	.103	.260	48	156	23	36	6	4	2	28	28	3	1	2	31	3	2	.359	.354
Gomez, Israyber	R-R	6-1	185	9-10-01	.255	.222	.263	18	47	5	12	1	0	0	2	5	0	0	1	4	1	1	.277	.321
Gonzalez, Robert	R-R	6-0	175	6-19-01	.247	.182	.258	52	154	40	38	6	0	2	16	40	9	1	1	27	23	2	.325	.426
Laya, Francisco	R-R	6-0	160	10-9-03	.150	.125	.155	36	100	14	15	4	0	0	7	16	2	2	1	22	8	3	.190	.277
Linares, Brandon	R-R	6-0	165	8-14-00	.230	.231	.230	46	161	22	37	7	2	4	29	22	11	0	1	47	9	5	.373	.359
Lora, Bayron	R-R	6-5	242	9-29-02	.218	.208	.220	47	147	34	32	9	0	6	22	48	1	0	0	73	10	2	.401	.413
Lozano, Elian	R-R	5-11	175	1-2-03	.176	.333	.000	9	17	2	3	0	0	0	0	5	1	0	0	6	1	0	.176	.391
Marcano, Rafael	R-R	5-11	165	2-26-02	.167	.000	.208	13	30	7	5	0	0	2	5	8	4	0	1	10	0	0	.167	.395
Marlin, Gedionne	R-R	0-0	0	2-5-04	.223	.200	.228	34	121	20	27	4	1	1	17	19	6	0	5	30	5	2	.298	.344
Mejia, John	R-R	5-10	163	1-12-01	.257	.375	.222	29	70	15	18	6	1	0	11	25	1	0	0	22	5	1	.371	.458
Mesa, Andres	R-R	5-11	170	10-16-02	.231	.375	.204	55	199	30	46	11	1	5	25	24	3	0	2	57	13	6	.372	.320
Morrobel, Yeison	L-L	6-2	170	12-8-03	.270	.290	.266	51	185	33	50	11	6	1	30	30	10	1	3	25	8	4	.411	.395

Name	B-T	HT	WT	DOB	AVG	vLH	vRH	G	AB	R	H	2B	3B	HR	RBI	BB	HBP	SH	SF	SO	SB	CS	OBP	SLG
Noguera, Abel	R-R	6-1	185	2-22-02	.234	.333	.215	36	111	16	26	7	1	2	18	12	4	0	0	24	0	0	.369	.331
Ogando, Jansel	B-R	5-8	160	11-21-01	.154	.167	.143	5	13	0	2	0	0	0	2	1	1	0	1	3	0	0	.154	.250
Ortega, Cesar	L-R	5-11	180	10-16-00	.263	.346	.248	52	171	30	45	8	4	1	26	24	10	0	1	20	16	4	.374	.383
Ortiz, Abimelec	L-L	6-0	205	2-22-02	.233	.000	.280	40	129	33	30	10	1	11	33	33	9	0	1	31	5	1	.581	.419
Padua, Ismael	R-R	6-1	180	9-11-02	.289	.333	.280	39	142	27	41	6	0	4	33	16	8	0	2	31	5	1	.415	.387
Pavon, Keiderson	R-R	5-7	140	12-11-03	.249	.261	.247	49	181	28	45	5	0	0	21	20	4	3	2	18	20	5	.276	.333
Pinero, Hector	B-R	5-11	155	1-12-03	.200	.200	.200	22	55	9	11	2	2	0	6	10	1	0	0	21	0	0	.309	.333
Pinto, Julio	R-R	5-10	165	6-5-04	.187	.100	.202	37	134	15	25	5	0	0	9	10	0	1	1	20	5	1	.224	.241
Reyes, Rony	R-R	6-3	175	1-22-03	.148	.000	.173	22	61	5	9	2	1	0	9	6	0	0	1	25	4	1	.213	.221
Romero, Josue	R-R	5-9	190	9-19-02	.239	.333	.218	22	67	6	16	3	0	1	8	10	2	0	0	15	1	0	.328	.354
Salazar, Marlon	R-R	5-10	160	4-3-03	.313	.333	.310	12	32	4	10	5	0	0	5	3	2	1	1	5	2	0	.469	.395
Tejeda, Justin	R-R	6-1	195	1-23-01	.056	.000	.067	6	18	5	1	0	0	0	0	5	1	0	0	8	1	0	.056	.292
Tineo, Jefferson	B-R	5-10	145	10-10-03	.208	.120	.227	45	144	25	30	6	2	1	13	27	0	1	3	48	13	3	.299	.328
Villarroel, Miguel	R-R	6-0	165	12-23-01	.302	.267	.309	50	182	28	55	8	2	2	30	18	4	0	1	21	6	2	.401	.376
Zambrano, Luis	R-R	6-1	165	10-30-01	.161	.100	.174	24	56	2	9	2	1	0	4	12	1	0	0	16	1	4	.232	.319

Pitching	B-T	HT	WT	DOB	W	L	ERA	G	GS	CG	SV	IP	H	R	ER	HR	BB	SO	AVG	vLH	vRH	K/9	BB/9
Agreda, Ismael	R-R	6-0	150	10-8-03	2	1	8.10	15	0	0	0	13	13	17	12	0	21	12	.283	.278	.286	8.10	14.18
Angulo, Gerson	R-R	6-1	180	7-26-02	1	0	1.15	9	1	0	1	16	13	4	2	0	12	17	.236	.250	.222	9.77	6.89
Ayola, Julio	R-R	6-3	173	4-8-02	2	1	4.53	13	8	0	1	44	39	25	22	1	16	34	.235	.157	.270	7.01	3.30
Calderon, Leandro	R-R	6-1	200	6-17-02	0	2	5.02	13	0	0	6	14	8	8	8	2	13	24	.160	.143	.167	15.07	8.16
Castellanos, Isaac	L-L	6-0	0	12-4-03	3	2	3.80	14	2	0	0	24	15	10	10	1	28	26	.203	.333	.191	9.89	10.65
Castillo, Wilson	R-R	6-4	210	6-13-01	0	2	9.00	4	1	0	0	11	19	12	11	0	3	11	.380	.444	.344	9.00	2.45
Cesar, Remy	R-R	5-11	182	7-11-03	0	1	21.27	14	2	0	0	11	14	26	26	0	23	7	.318	.333	.308	5.73	18.82
Cordero, Wilfredo	R-R	6-2	190	9-30-02	1	0	20.48	14	0	0	0	10	6	22	22	0	28	9	.194	.308	.111	8.38	26.07
De La Cruz, Yangely	R-R	6-3	175	9-14-99	0	0	6.00	2	0	0	0	3	2	2	2	0	2	1	.250	.333	.200	3.00	6.00
Duenas, Sebastian	L-L	6-0	155	5-29-02	0	3	6.00	9	0	0	0	12	10	8	8	1	12	11	.244	.167	.276	8.25	9.00
Duran, Jhonny	R-R	6-1	150	5-20-01	4	0	4.78	12	1	0	1	26	29	17	14	0	7	14	.287	.400	.239	4.78	2.39
Estrada, Jose	R-R	6-1	155	3-31-01	0	0	1.74	8	0	0	0	10	5	2	2	0	11	14	.152	.182	.136	12.19	6.10
Felix, Jose V.	R-R	6-0	160	4-8-02	0	3	5.58	11	11	0	0	31	30	25	19	3	22	22	.246	.200	.278	6.46	6.46
Ferreira, Elian	R-R	6-1	175	4-12-00	7	2	2.73	16	2	0	0	33	29	13	10	1	13	34	.238	.196	.268	9.27	3.55
Florentino, Dianye	R-R	6-4	200	1-7-00	1	1	4.43	22	0	0	2	20	16	16	10	0	18	16	.208	.167	.226	7.08	7.97
Flores, Eiroon	R-R	5-11	175	9-8-01	2	2	1.66	5	3	0	0	22	18	5	4	0	6	22	.234	.143	.268	9.14	2.49
Gonzalez, Jose	R-R	6-3	200	8-5-01	3	1	2.35	12	11	0	0	46	29	15	12	0	26	40	.182	.197	.169	7.83	5.09
Guzman, Stanley	R-R	6-3	170	12-28-99	1	1	2.70	3	0	0	0	3	2	2	1	0	3	2	.167	.200	.143	5.40	8.10
Hernandez, Nyan	L-R	6-2	198	7-11-01	2	0	3.24	11	0	0	2	17	12	7	6	1	8	17	.200	.150	.225	9.18	4.32
Leal, Elis	R-R	6-1	170	1-3-02	1	2	5.48	16	0	0	1	23	24	17	14	0	8	14	.264	.167	.327	5.48	3.13
Magdaleno, Bryan	L-L	6-2	202	2-22-01	0	2	2.95	10	9	0	0	37	32	18	12	1	24	35	.230	.160	.246	8.59	5.89
Medina, Rafmar	R-R	6-5	190	9-9-99	0	1	3.50	15	1	0	2	18	12	9	7	1	13	22	.188	.148	.216	11.00	6.50
Mena, Peniel	R-R	6-1	160	11-28-00	5	0	0.00	15	1	0	2	31	23	7	0	0	5	23	.204	.176	.226	6.68	1.45
Mendoza, Brayan	L-L	6-0	155	1-19-04	1	1	4.50	12	12	0	0	42	34	25	21	3	18	37	.217	.212	.218	7.93	3.86
Moreno, Raymher	R-R	6-4	195	6-20-01	2	1	5.47	12	0	0	0	26	30	17	16	4	6	16	.280	.405	.200	5.47	2.05
Mota, Alberto	R-R	5-11	170	2-17-03	2	0	3.00	14	0	0	3	18	9	6	6	0	9	37	.141	.211	.111	18.50	4.50
Munoz, Wilkerman	R-R	6-3	185	11-27-02	0	2	6.41	9	7	0	1	27	27	19	19	3	9	24	.262	.268	.258	8.10	3.04
Oviedo, Ivan	R-R	6-2	175	10-14-02	2	2	3.03	12	11	0	0	62	53	24	21	5	16	72	.226	.289	.195	10.40	2.31
Palma, Wilker	R-R	6-1	170	5-8-02	3	1	4.19	15	0	0	2	19	10	12	9	2	10	30	.152	.211	.128	13.97	4.66
Parra, Deretd	R-R	6-3	160	6-18-00	2	0	2.29	16	6	0	1	39	23	16	10	2	24	33	.182	.207	.155	7.55	5.49
Paulino, Luis	L-L	5-10	135	5-2-98	4	1	1.03	19	0	0	5	26	10	4	3	0	10	28	.112	.056	.127	9.57	3.42
Ramirez, Bladimir	R-R	6-2	190	5-20-02	0	0	6.00	3	0	0	0	3	1	3	2	0	2	3	.091	.200	.000	9.00	6.00
Ramon, Jhon	L-L	5-10	180	1-10-02	0	0	15.95	9	0	0	0	7	10	13	13	2	14	10	.313	.333	.308	12.27	17.18
Rodriguez, Josue	L-L	5-11	175	7-30-02	1	0	1.02	13	0	0	0	18	10	3	2	0	8	19	.164	.222	.154	9.68	4.08
Rosado, Eury	R-R	6-0	160	11-23-00	3	2	2.00	12	11	0	1	54	36	21	12	3	16	55	.187	.133	.227	9.17	2.67
Sanchez, Yosber	R-R	6-1	170	5-22-01	2	1	2.08	12	0	0	1	13	10	7	3	0	13	19	.200	.100	.225	13.15	9.00
Santos, Winston	R-R	6-0	160	4-15-02	0	0	4.50	1	1	0	0	4	6	4	2	0	0	4	.333	.333	.333	9.00	0.00
Simeon, Victor	R-R	6-2	160	12-4-00	0	3	2.37	13	6	0	0	30	22	11	8	1	14	33	.198	.300	.160	9.79	4.15
Torres, Gabriel	L-L	5-11	165	3-14-01	4	1	2.36	12	6	0	0	42	28	12	11	4	9	40	.188	.125	.200	8.57	1.93
Valdez, Jesus	R-R	6-2	175	5-3-01	1	1	0.00	9	0	0	0	12	7	3	0	0	3	12	.179	.250	.130	9.26	2.31
Vargas, Aron	R-R	6-1	180	1-21-00	2	1	5.56	15	2	0	0	23	16	14	14	2	22	22	.200	.217	.193	8.74	8.74
Viola, Jose	R-R	6-0	175	4-25-01	4	1	4.50	16	0	0	0	26	16	13	13	3	19	20	.170	.240	.145	6.92	6.58

Fielding

C: Barroso 30, Beato 6, Gomez 15, Lozano 1, Marcano 13, Mejia 2, Noguera 35, Romero 22, Salazar 8.
1B: Barroso 1, Gomez 1, Lozano 1, Marlin 2, Mejia 10, Noguera 1, Ortega 17, Ortiz 40, Padua 2, Pinero 4, Salazar 2, Villarroel 42, Zambrano 1.
2B: Almonte 2, Marlin 28, Mejia 1, Mesa 19, Ogando 2, Pavon 12, Pinero 2, Pinto 28, Tineo 23, Zambrano 5.
3B: Almonte 2, Figuereo 45, Marlin 1, Mejia 2, Mesa 5, Ogando 3, Pavon 31, Pinero 10, Pinto 3, Villarroel 9, Zambrano 14.
SS: Cueva 49, Marlin 1, Mesa 30, Pavon 7, Pinero 1, Pinto 6, Tineo 21, Zambrano 1.
OF: Almonte 45, Basabe 35, Diaz 24, Gonzalez 55, Laya 39, Linares 48, Lora 35, Morrobel 50, Ortega 16, Padua 13, Pinero 5, Reyes 21, Tejeda 3, Zambrano 2.

Toronto Blue Jays

SEASON IN A SENTENCE: A young, homegrown nucleus in the Blue Jays lineup led by first baseman Vladimir Guerrero Jr. powered an offense that ranked third in the majors in runs scored to a 91-win season, a formidable year but one good enough for just fourth place in a stacked AL East.

HIGH POINT: The Blue Jays saved their best stretch of the season for last, starting September with eight straight wins (including a three-game sweep against Oakland and a four-game sweep at the Yankees), going 22-9 to finish the year. Guerrero Jr. led the AL in both on-base percentage and slugging by hitting .311/.401/.601 in 161 games as a 22-year-old, and his 48 home runs tied for the AL lead. Shortstop Bo Bichette led the AL in hits while second baseman Marcus Semien led the league in extra-base hits and was one of the most productive all-around players in the league.

LOW POINT: Starting May 19, the Blue Jays lost six straight games to the Red Sox and Rays, costly losses within their division as they ended up finishing just one game behind the Red Sox and Yankees for a wild card spot. Through the end of July, the Blue Jays outscored their opponents 523-420, but they couldn't capitalize in the win column, with a 53-48 record at the time that was eight games back of the Rays and 7.5 behind the Red Sox.

NOTABLE ROOKIES: Righthander Alek Manoah looked electric in spring training and carried it over into the regular season once the Blue Jays brought him up at the end of May. He developed into one of the best starting pitchers in the AL. Santiago Espinal proved a reliable third baseman with a high-contact game, hitting .311/.376/.405 in 246 plate apperances.

KEY TRANSACTIONS: The Blue Jays started their offseason by re-signing lefthander Robbie Ray to a one-year, $8 million deal. Ray rebounded from a 6.62 ERA in 2020 to become one of the best pitchers in baseball in 2021. Steven Matz joined the Blue Jays in an offseason trade for righthanders Josh Winckowski, Sean Reid-Foley and Yennsy Diaz and performed as a solid mid-rotation starter. The Blue Jays further bolstered their starting rotation at the trade deadline by acquiring righthander Jose Berrios. The deal sent two of their top prospects, infielder/outfielder Austin Martin and righthander Simeon Woods Richardson, to the Twins. Their splashiest offseason move was the six-year, $150 million signing of outfielder George Springer, but injuries limited him to 78 games.

OPENING DAY SALARY: $137,133,333 (11th).

PLAYERS OF THE YEAR

MAJOR LEAGUE	MINOR LEAGUE
Vladimir Guerrero Jr.	**Orelvis Martinez**
1B	**SS/3B**
.311/.401/.601	(High-A/Low-A)
MLB-leading 48 HR	.261/.345/.549,
123 R, 169 OPS+	28 HR, 26 2B

ORGANIZATION LEADERS

Batting		*Minimum 250 AB
MAJORS		
*AVG	Vladimir Guerrero Jr.	.311
*OPS	Vladimir Guerrero Jr.	1.002
HR	Vladimir Guerrero Jr.	48
RBI	Teoscar Hernandez	116
MINORS		
*AVG	Vinny Capra, Buffalo, New Hampshire	.316
*OBP	Tyler White, Buffalo	.424
*SLG	Kevin Smith, Buffalo	.561
*OPS	Kevin Smith, Buffalo	.931
R	Otto Lopez, Buffalo, New Hampshire	88
H	Otto Lopez, Buffalo, New Hampshire	142
TB	Orelvis Martinez, Vancouver, Dunedin	217
2B	Otto Lopez, Buffalo, New Hampshire	32
3B	Steward Berroa, New Hampshire, Dunedin	5
3B	Sebastian Espino, Vancouver, Dunedin	5
3B	Forrest Wall, Buffalo	5
HR	Orelvis Martinez, Vancouver, Dunedin	28
RBI	Orelvis Martinez, Vancouver, Dunedin	87
BB	PK Morris, Vancouver, Dunedin	81
SO	Logan Warmoth, Buffalo	137
SB	Steward Berroa, New Hampshire, Dunedin	58

Pitching		#Minimum 75 IP
MAJORS		
W	Steven Matz	14
W	Hyun Jin Ryu	14
#ERA	Robbie Ray	2.84
SO	Robbie Ray	248
SV	Jordan Romano	23
MINORS		
W	Zach Logue, Buffalo, New Hampshire	12
L	4 tied	7
#ERA	Zach Logue, Buffalo, New Hampshire	3.67
G	Hobie Harris, Buffalo	42
GS	Zach Logue, Buffalo, New Hampshire	24
SV	Bryan Baker, Buffalo	11
IP	Zach Logue, Buffalo, New Hampshire	125
BB	Luis Quinones, New Hampshire, Vancouver	65
SO	Zach Logue, Buffalo, New Hampshire	144
#AVG	Luis Quinones, New Hampshire, Vancouver	.189

General Manager: Ross Atkins. **Farm Director:** Gil Kim. **Scouting Director:** Shane Farrell.

Class	Team	League	W	L	PCT	Finish	Manager
Majors	Toronto Blue Jays	American	91	71	.562	6th (15)	Charlie Montoyo
Triple-A	Buffalo Bisons	Triple-A East	79	47	.627	2nd (20)	Casey Candaele
Double-A	New Hampshire Fisher Cats	Double-A Northeast	52	55	.486	8th (12)	Cesar Martin
High-A	Vancouver Canadians	High-A West	55	64	.462	5th (6)	Donnie Murphy
Low-A	Dunedin Blue Jays	Low-A Southeast	57	63	.475	7th (10)	Luis Hurtado
Rookie	DSL Blue Jays	Dominican Summer	38	19	.667	1st (46)	Dane Fujinaka
Rookie	FCL Blue Jays	Florida Complex	25	29	.463	10th (18)	Brent Lavallee
Overall 2021 Minor League Record			306	277	.525	10th (30)	

ORGANIZATION STATISTICS

TORONTO BLUE JAYS
AMERICAN LEAGUE

Batting	B-T	HT	WT	DOB	AVG	vLH	vRH	G	AB	R	H	2B	3B	HR	RBI	BB	HBP	SH	SF	SO	SB	CS	SLG	OBP
Adams, Riley	R-R	6-4	246	6-26-96	.107	.167	.000	12	28	2	3	2	0	0	0	2	0	0	0	12	0	0	.179	.167
Bichette, Bo	R-R	6-0	185	3-5-98	.298	.340	.286	159	640	121	191	30	1	29	102	40	6	0	4	137	25	1	.484	.343
Biggio, Cavan	L-R	6-2	200	4-11-95	.224	.200	.232	79	250	27	56	10	1	7	27	37	1	1	4	78	3	1	.356	.322
Davis, Jonathan	R-R	5-8	190	5-12-92	.143	.148	.140	52	70	16	10	1	0	1	4	11	3	0	1	21	4	1	.200	.282
2-team total (12 New York)					.126	.103	.146	64	87	20	11	1	0	1	4	12	3	0	1	26	4	1	.172	.252
Dickerson, Corey	L-R	6-1	200	5-22-89	.282	.000	.296	46	131	16	37	6	2	4	15	9	0	0	0	23	4	1	.450	.329
Dyson, Jarrod	L-R	5-9	165	8-15-84	.077	.000	.100	25	13	4	1	0	0	0	0	4	0	0	0	5	2	2	.077	.294
2-team total (77 Kansas City)					.207	.179	.215	102	135	17	28	7	2	0	10	10	0	3	1	33	10	5	.289	.260
Espinal, Santiago	R-R	5-10	181	11-13-94	.311	.348	.285	92	222	32	69	13	1	2	17	22	1	1	0	30	6	1	.405	.376
Grichuk, Randal	R-R	6-2	216	8-13-91	.241	.246	.239	149	511	59	123	25	1	22	81	27	3	0	4	114	0	3	.423	.281
Guerrero Jr., Vladimir	R-R	6-2	250	3-16-99	.311	.295	.317	161	604	123	188	29	1	48	111	86	6	0	2	110	4	1	.601	.401
Gurriel Jr., Lourdes	R-R	6-4	215	10-10-93	.276	.269	.279	141	500	62	138	28	2	21	84	32	2	1	6	102	1	3	.466	.319
Hernandez, Teoscar	R-R	6-2	205	10-15-92	.296	.372	.273	143	550	92	163	29	0	32	116	36	7	0	2	148	12	4	.524	.346
Hoying, Jared	L-R	6-3	205	5-18-89	.000	.000	.000	2	3	0	0	0	0	0	0	0	0	0	0	1	0	0	.000	.000
Jansen, Danny	R-R	6-2	225	4-15-95	.223	.150	.258	70	184	32	41	13	0	11	28	17	3	1	0	44	0	0	.473	.299
Kirk, Alejandro	R-R	5-8	265	11-6-98	.242	.314	.211	60	165	19	40	8	0	8	24	19	3	0	2	22	0	0	.436	.328
Lamb, Jake	L-R	6-3	215	10-9-90	.129	.000	.182	12	31	5	4	2	0	1	6	5	1	0	2	13	0	0	.290	.256
2-team total (43 Chicago)					.194	.208	.192	55	144	25	28	4	0	7	19	22	2	0	2	51	0	0	.368	.306
Lopez, Otto	R-R	5-10	160	10-1-98	.000	--	.000	1	1	0	0	0	0	0	0	0	0	0	0	1	0	0	.000	.000
McGuire, Reese	L-R	6-0	215	3-2-95	.253	.175	.272	78	198	22	50	15	0	1	10	15	2	1	1	44	0	0	.343	.310
Palacios, Josh	L-R	6-1	198	7-30-95	.200	.400	.167	13	35	7	7	0	0	0	4	3	2	1	1	11	0	0	.200	.293
Panik, Joe	L-R	6-1	205	10-30-90	.246	.133	.263	42	114	9	28	6	0	2	11	8	0	0	1	14	0	0	.351	.293
Semien, Marcus	R-R	6-0	195	9-17-90	.265	.243	.274	162	652	115	173	39	2	45	102	66	3	0	3	146	15	1	.538	.334
Smith, Kevin	R-R	6-0	190	7-4-96	.094	.158	.000	18	32	2	3	0	0	1	1	3	1	0	0	11	0	0	.188	.194
Springer, George	R-R	6-3	221	9-19-89	.264	.282	.258	78	299	59	79	19	1	22	50	37	4	0	1	79	4	1	.555	.352
Tellez, Rowdy	L-L	6-4	255	3-16-95	.209	.273	.197	50	139	12	29	4	1	4	8	9	2	0	0	33	0	0	.338	.272
Valera, Breyvic	B-R	5-11	190	1-8-92	.253	.304	.234	39	87	10	22	6	0	1	15	8	0	1	1	12	1	0	.356	.313

Pitching	B-T	HT	WT	DOB	W	L	ERA	G	GS	CG	SV	IP	H	R	ER	HR	BB	SO	AVG	vLH	vRH	K/9	BB/9
Allgeyer, Nick	L-L	6-3	210	2-3-96	0	0	0.00	1	0	0	0	1	0	0	0	0	0	0	.000	.000	.000	0.00	0.00
Baker, Bryan	R-R	6-6	245	12-2-94	0	0	0.00	1	0	0	0	1	0	0	0	0	1	0	.250	--	.250	9.00	0.00
Barnes, Jacob	R-R	6-2	231	4-14-90	0	1	6.30	10	0	0	0	10	12	7	7	1	6	15	.286	.250	.308	13.50	5.40
Beasley, Jeremy	R-R	6-3	235	11-20-95	0	1	7.71	8	0	0	0	9	7	9	8	3	9	13	.200	.250	.158	12.54	8.68
Bergen, Travis	L-L	6-1	223	10-8-93	2	0	1.69	10	1	0	0	11	5	2	2	1	8	6	.139	.182	.120	5.06	6.75
Berrios, Jose	R-R	6-0	205	5-27-94	5	4	3.58	12	12	0	0	70	64	30	28	8	13	78	.238	.244	.232	9.98	1.66
2-team total (20 Minnesota)					12	9	3.52	32	32	1	0	192	159	83	75	22	45	204	.223	.254	.193	9.56	2.11
Borucki, Ryan	L-L	6-4	215	3-31-94	3	1	4.94	24	0	0	0	24	18	14	13	5	11	21	.214	.132	.283	7.99	4.18
Castro, Anthony	R-R	6-2	182	4-13-95	1	2	4.74	25	0	0	1	25	23	15	13	4	8	32	.237	.201	.254	11.68	2.92
Chatwood, Tyler	R-R	5-11	200	12-16-89	1	2	5.46	30	0	0	1	28	20	17	17	1	20	32	.196	.226	.183	10.29	6.43
Cimber, Adam	R-R	6-3	195	8-15-90	2	2	1.69	37	0	0	1	37	31	10	7	2	5	30	.226	.171	.250	7.23	1.21
Cole, A.J.	R-R	6-5	240	1-5-92	0	0	1.13	6	0	0	0	8	5	1	1	1	1	7	.207	.250	.176	7.88	1.13
Dolis, Rafael	R-R	6-4	235	1-10-88	2	5	5.63	39	0	0	3	32	29	21	20	2	27	39	.232	.213	.244	10.97	7.59
Edwards Jr., Carl	R-R	6-3	170	9-3-91	0	0	6.75	6	0	0	0	5	8	4	4	2	2	5	.348	.375	.333	8.44	3.38
Hand, Brad	L-L	6-3	224	3-20-90	0	2	7.27	11	0	0	0	9	13	10	7	3	3	5	.351	.200	.407	5.19	3.12
Hatch, Thomas	R-R	6-1	205	9-29-94	0	1	6.75	3	2	0	0	9	11	7	7	2	6	8	.289	.438	.182	7.71	5.79
Jin Ryu, Hyun	R-L	6-3	255	3-25-87	14	10	4.37	31	31	1	0	169	170	85	82	24	37	143	.258	.255	.259	7.62	1.97
Kay, Anthony	L-L	6-0	225	3-21-95	1	2	5.61	11	5	0	0	34	38	22	21	7	18	39	.281	.341	.255	10.43	4.81
Manoah, Alek	R-R	6-6	260	1-9-98	9	2	3.22	20	20	0	0	112	77	44	40	12	40	127	.208	.156	.228	10.24	3.22
Matz, Steven	R-L	6-2	201	5-29-91	14	7	3.82	29	29	0	0	151	158	70	64	18	43	144	.265	.276	.261	8.60	2.57
Mayza, Tim	L-L	6-3	220	1-15-92	5	2	3.40	61	0	0	1	53	40	21	20	5	12	57	.206	.181	.221	9.68	2.04
Merryweather, Julian	R-R	6-4	215	10-14-91	0	1	4.85	13	1	0	2	13	13	7	7	4	4	12	.265	.294	.250	8.31	2.77
Milone, Tommy	L-L	6-0	215	2-16-87	1	0	6.43	6	1	0	1	14	20	10	10	3	3	17	.323	.250	.348	10.93	1.93

Name	B-T	HT	WT	DOB	W	L	ERA	G	GS	CG	SV	IP	H	R	ER	HR	BB	SO	AVG	vLH	vRH		
Murphy, Patrick	R-R	6-5	235	6-10-95	0	1	4.82	8	0	0	0	9	12	6	5	1	4	6	.316	.214	.375	5.79	3.86
Overton, Connor	L-R	6-0	190	7-24-93	0	0	0.00	4	0	0	0	7	4	0	0	0	2	4	.182	.125	.214	5.40	2.70
Payamps, Joel	R-R	6-2	225	4-7-94	0	2	2.70	22	0	0	0	30	21	10	9	3	11	22	.196	.118	.233	6.60	3.30
2-team total (15 Kansas City)					1	3	3.40	37	1	0	0	50	44	22	19	6	14	38	.232	.176	.262	6.79	2.50
Pearson, Nate	R-R	6-6	250	8-20-96	1	1	4.20	12	1	0	0	15	14	8	7	2	12	20	.237	.273	.216	12.00	7.20
Phelps, David	R-R	6-2	198	10-9-86	0	0	0.87	11	1	0	0	10	8	2	1	0	4	15	.216	.154	.250	13.06	3.48
Ray, Robbie	L-L	6-2	215	10-1-91	13	7	2.84	32	32	0	0	193	150	62	61	33	52	248	.210	.187	.216	11.54	2.42
2-team total (6 Tampa Bay)					4	2	3.63	38	0	0	1	45	25	19	18	9	13	53	.160	.161	.160	10.68	2.62
Roark, Tanner	R-R	6-2	238	10-5-86	0	1	6.43	3	1	0	0	7	7	7	5	3	2	5	.241	.250	.231	6.43	2.57
Romano, Jordan	R-R	6-5	225	4-21-93	7	1	2.14	62	0	0	23	63	41	17	15	7	25	85	.181	.140	.211	12.14	3.57
Saucedo, Tayler	L-L	6-5	185	6-18-93	0	0	4.56	29	0	0	0	26	22	14	13	1	10	19	.229	.139	.283	6.66	3.51
Snead, Kirby	L-L	6-1	218	10-7-94	0	1	2.35	7	0	0	0	8	7	3	2	0	2	7	.259	.200	.294	8.22	2.35
Soria, Joakim	R-R	6-3	205	5-18-84	0	1	7.88	10	0	0	0	8	8	7	7	2	4	9	.267	.556	.143	10.13	4.50
Stripling, Ross	R-R	6-3	220	11-23-89	5	7	4.80	24	19	0	0	101	99	55	54	23	30	94	.251	.218	.270	8.35	2.66
Thornton, Trent	R-R	6-0	195	9-30-93	1	3	4.78	37	3	0	0	49	54	33	26	12	16	52	.278	.241	.294	9.55	2.94
Tice, Ty	L-R	5-9	185	7-4-96	0	0	5.14	4	0	0	0	7	9	4	4	1	4	6	.310	.444	.250	7.71	5.14
Zeuch, T.J.	R-R	6-7	245	8-1-95	0	2	6.60	5	3	0	0	15	21	16	11	6	9	8	.323	.400	.289	4.80	5.40

Fielding

Catcher	PCT	G	PO	A	E	DP	PB
Adams	.986	11	67	6	1	0	0
Jansen	.996	69	522	17	2	3	0
Kirk	.995	44	353	17	2	1	2
McGuire	1.000	73	547	16	0	2	4

First Base	PCT	G	PO	A	E	DP
Biggio	1.000	7	25	0	0	4
Guerrero Jr.	.993	133	1026	46	8	90
Gurriel Jr.	1.000	11	64	4	0	5
Lamb	1.000	1	8	0	0	0
Panik	1.000	3	15	0	0	0
Smith	1.000	1	2	0	0	1
Tellez	.984	19	122	4	2	9

Second Base	PCT	G	PO	A	E	DP
Biggio	1.000	7	6	3	0	3
Panik	1.000	10	13	26	0	4
Semien	.985	147	202	317	8	86
Valera	1.000	10	9	4	0	0

Third Base	PCT	G	PO	A	E	DP
Biggio	.935	52	23	106	9	12
Espinal	.980	81	33	159	4	16
Guerrero Jr.	.000	1	0	0	0	0
Lamb	.955	10	4	17	1	3
Panik	.900	21	10	35	5	4
Smith	.950	14	4	15	1	3
Valera	1.000	21	11	26	0	3

Shortstop	PCT	G	PO	A	E	DP
Bichette	.957	148	169	364	24	73
Semien	.984	21	16	46	1	5

Outfield	PCT	G	PO	A	E	DP
Biggio	1.000	16	27	1	0	0
Davis	1.000	48	48	1	0	0
Dickerson	.981	40	51	0	1	0
Dyson	1.000	21	15	1	0	0
Grichuk	1.000	167	252	1	0	0
Gurriel Jr.	.978	119	169	12	4	2
Hernandez	.982	170	260	7	5	1
Hoying	--	1	0	0	0	0
Palacios	1.000	14	14	1	0	0
Smith	--	1	0	0	0	0
Springer	.978	44	88	1	2	0

BUFFALO BISONS   TRIPLE-A

TRIPLE-A EAST

Batting	B-T	HT	WT	DOB	AVG	vLH	vRH	G	AB	R	H	2B	3B	HR	RBI	BB	HBP	SH	SF	SO	SB	CS	SLG	OBP
Adams, Riley	R-R	6-4	246	6-26-96	.239	.182	.262	35	117	20	28	6	1	7	17	16	9	0	1	46	0	0	.487	.371
2-team total (1 Rochester)					.233	.171	.259	36	120	20	28	6	1	7	17	18	9	0	1	46	0	0	.475	.372
Biggio, Cavan	L-R	6-2	200	4-11-95	.182	.059	.217	22	77	15	14	2	0	3	11	11	1	0	1	26	0	0	.325	.289
Capra, Vinny	R-R	5-8	175	7-7-96	.000	.000	.000	5	8	0	0	0	0	0	0	1	1	1	0	3	0	0	.000	.200
Colon, Christian	R-R	5-10	215	5-14-89	.258	.322	.236	100	357	56	92	16	0	15	60	40	10	1	5	49	4	7	.429	.345
Davis, Jonathan	R-R	5-8	190	5-12-92	.200	.000	.286	3	10	3	2	0	0	0	1	3	1	0		3	0	0	.200	.429
2-team total (17 Scranton/Wilkes-Barre)					.194	.053	.250	20	67	16	13	2	1	2	9	12	6	0	1	23	5	2	.343	.360
Deglan, Kellin	R-R	6-2	205	5-3-92	.203	.125	.211	27	79	10	16	3	0	3	13	12	4	0	1	30	1	0	.354	.333
2-team total (12 Scranton/Wilkes-Barre)					.211	.273	.204	39	109	13	23	4	0	4	16	14	4	0	1	40	1	0	.358	.320
Dickerson, Corey	L-R	6-1	200	5-22-89	.267	.333	.250	4	15	1	4	0	0	0	1	0	1	0	0	3	0	0	.333	.313
Espinal, Santiago	R-R	5-10	181	11-13-94	.308	--	.308	4	13	1	4	1	0	1	2	0	0	0	0	4	0	0	.615	.308
Graterol, Juan	R-R	6-1	225	2-14-89	.293	.381	.264	50	167	17	49	5	0	2	21	11	6	0	2	20	0	0	.359	.355
Herrera, Dilson	R-R	5-10	210	3-3-94	.213	.245	.200	53	174	24	37	5	1	10	27	18	2	0	2	62	0	1	.425	.291
Hoying, Jared	L-R	6-3	205	5-18-89	.333	.250	.348	7	27	7	9	4	0	3	7	1	0	0	0	10	0	0	.815	.357
Jansen, Danny	R-R	6-2	225	4-15-95	.238	.333	.200	7	21	5	5	0	0	1	4	4	0	0	1	3	0	0	.381	.346
Kirk, Alejandro	R-R	5-8	265	11-6-98	.347	.118	.469	14	49	7	17	3	0	2	13	5	0	0	2	9	0	0	.531	.393
Knight, Nash	B-R	6-0	205	9-20-92	.184	.240	.167	71	212	38	39	9	0	7	26	36	4	0	1	76	1	0	.325	.312
Large, Cullen	B-R	6-1	175	1-22-96	.256	.205	.269	115	403	54	103	22	3	8	44	50	5	0	5	102	3	5	.385	.341
Lopez, Otto	R-R	5-10	160	10-1-98	.289	.306	.285	43	173	36	50	8	3	2	25	13	4	1	3	26	15	1	.405	.347
Morales, Anthony	B-R	6-0	175	11-13-98	.333	.000	.375	9	3	1	3	0	0	0	0	2	0	0	0	3	0	0	.333	.400
Moreno, Gabriel	R-R	5-11	160	2-14-00	.111	.000	.125	3	9	0	1	0	0	0	0	1	0	0	0	2	0	0	.111	.200
Palacios, Josh	L-R	6-1	198	7-30-95	.241	.375	.184	16	54	7	13	2	0	2	5	4	0	0	5	16	1	2	.278	.349
Polanco, Gregory	L-L	6-5	240	9-14-91	.374	.300	.383	24	91	15	34	7	0	9	24	8	2	0	0	19	5	0	.747	.436
Pruitt, Reggie	R-R	6-0	180	5-7-97	.273	.500	.222	5	11	3	3	0	0	1	2	3	0	0	0	5	1	0	.545	.429
Smith, Kevin	R-R	6-0	190	7-4-96	.285	.241	.297	94	355	65	101	27	4	21	69	46	4	2	3	97	18	3	.561	.370
Smith, Mallex	L-R	5-10	180	5-6-93	.389	--	.389	7	18	7	7	0	1	0	6	5	0	0	0	3	3	1	.833	.522
2-team total (22 Louisville)					.265	.190	.290	29	83	14	22	1	1	3	11	11	0	0	0	22	7	3	.410	.351
Springer, George	R-R	6-3	221	9-19-89	.176	.167	.182	5	17	2	3	1	0	0	1	0	1	0	0	3	0	0	.235	.222
Tellez, Rowdy	L-L	6-4	255	3-16-95	.298	.250	.314	13	47	8	14	4	0	4	11	6	2	0	0	12	0	0	.638	.400
2-team total (2 Nashville)					.302	.250	.317	15	53	10	16	4	0	5	14	8	2	0	0	12	0	0	.660	.413
Urena, Richard	B-R	6-0	195	2-26-96	.272	.250	.277	92	324	41	88	25	1	9	49	16	4	2	4	81	2	2	.438	.310
Valera, Breyvic	B-R	5-11	190	1-8-92	.313	.293	.321	41	150	29	47	11	1	3	28	24	2	0	4	19	7	4	.460	.406
Vicuna, Kevin	R-R	6-0	140	1-14-98	.200	.250	.182	6	15	3	3	0	0	0	3	1	0	1	0	3	1	0	.200	.250

Player	B-T	HT	WT	DOB	AVG	vLH	vRH	G	AB	R	H	2B	3B	HR	RBI	BB	HBP	SH	SF	SO	SB	CS	SLG	OBP
Vigil, Rodrigo	R-R	6-0	165	1-3-93	.278	.313	.263	19	54	4	15	1	0	0	5	3	2	0	1	14	0	0	.296	.333
Wall, Forrest	L-R	6-1	195	11-20-95	.266	.180	.288	78	297	46	79	15	5	1	20	30	6	1	2	87	35	4	.360	.343
Warmoth, Logan	R-R	6-0	195	9-6-95	.228	.282	.212	107	342	61	78	15	1	9	41	56	10	2	3	137	17	5	.357	.350
White, Tyler	R-R	5-11	238	10-29-90	.292	.293	.292	105	353	54	103	26	0	13	65	80	5	0	5	73	2	2	.476	.424

Pitching

Player	B-T	HT	WT	DOB	W	L	ERA	G	GS	CG	SV	IP	H	R	ER	HR	BB	SO	AVG	vLH	vRH	K/9	BB/9
Allgeyer, Nick	L-L	6-3	210	2-3-96	5	5	5.34	22	17	0	0	89	95	58	53	15	52	80	.274	.344	.249	8.06	5.24
Axford, John	R-R	6-5	234	4-1-83	1	0	0.84	9	0	0	2	11	2	1	1	0	3	14	.061	.000	.100	11.81	2.53
Baker, Bryan	R-R	6-6	245	12-2-94	6	1	1.31	39	0	0	11	41	18	9	6	1	17	48	.125	.118	.132	10.45	3.70
Barnes, Jacob	R-R	6-2	231	4-14-90	1	0	0.63	14	0	0	2	14	7	1	1	0	4	10	.146	.167	.133	6.28	2.51
Beasley, Jeremy	R-R	6-3	235	11-20-95	3	0	2.89	17	2	0	0	19	13	7	6	0	15	26	.197	.280	.146	12.54	7.23
Bergen, Travis	L-L	6-1	223	10-8-93	2	0	3.18	25	0	0	0	23	18	8	8	2	15	30	.222	.231	.218	11.91	5.96
Borucki, Ryan	L-L	6-4	215	3-31-94	0	0	2.89	9	0	0	0	9	5	3	3	0	8	12	.161	.000	.192	11.57	7.71
Castro, Anthony	R-R	6-2	182	4-13-95	0	1	1.80	10	0	0	0	10	6	2	2	1	0	15	.167	.182	.160	13.50	0.00
Chatwood, Tyler	R-R	5-11	200	12-16-89	1	0	1.93	5	0	0	0	5	6	1	1	0	8	1	.353	.333	.375	1.93	15.43
Cole, A.J.	R-R	6-5	240	1-5-92	1	0	0.00	10	0	0	0	8	0	0	0	0	12	11	.211	.154	.240	10.80	0.00
Dolis, Rafael	R-R	6-4	235	1-10-88	1	2	1.59	11	0	0	0	11	11	4	2	0	7	14	.250	.200	.276	11.12	5.56
Dykstra, James	L-R	6-3	207	11-22-90	0	0	0.00	3	0	0	0	3	1	0	0	0	4	4	.125	.000	.200	13.50	13.50
Edwards Jr., Carl	R-R	6-3	170	9-3-91	1	0	3.86	7	0	0	0	7	5	3	3	2	2	8	.192	.167	.214	10.29	0.00
3-team total (10 Charlotte, 1 Gwinnett)					1	0	2.65	18	0	0	3	17	9	5	5	2	4	26	.150	.148	.152	13.76	2.12
Francis, Bowden	R-R	6-5	225	4-22-96	6	2	4.19	14	13	0	0	73	56	38	34	15	31	71	.209	.252	.174	8.75	3.82
2-team total (7 Nashville)					10	6	3.95	21	20	0	0	112	82	55	49	19	43	110	.205	.228	.185	8.87	3.47
Harris, Hobie	R-R	6-3	200	6-23-93	5	2	3.92	42	0	0	8	44	30	21	19	8	21	51	.190	.107	.235	10.51	4.33
Harris, Jon	R-R	6-4	175	10-16-93	0	1	13.50	2	0	0	0	3	6	5	5	0	2	1	.429	.429	.429	2.70	5.40
Hatch, Thomas	R-R	6-1	205	9-29-94	2	6	4.04	15	14	0	0	65	58	33	29	10	19	70	.238	.211	.259	9.74	2.64
Jimenez, Dany	R-R	6-1	182	12-23-93	3	3	2.22	39	1	0	3	45	29	13	11	5	25	73	.180	.222	.159	14.71	5.04
Johnston, Kyle	R-R	6-0	190	7-17-96	1	0	1.04	14	3	0	0	17	10	2	2	1	3	14	.169	.182	.162	7.27	1.56
Kay, Anthony	L-L	6-0	225	3-21-95	0	4	8.89	8	8	0	0	26	31	30	26	5	13	29	.287	.318	.266	9.91	4.44
Lawrence, Casey	R-R	6-2	170	10-28-87	7	2	4.85	21	10	0	0	65	65	36	35	10	13	62	.260	.313	.217	8.58	1.80
Logue, Zach	L-L	6-0	165	4-23-96	9	3	3.32	18	17	0	0	89	79	39	33	9	20	93	.236	.215	.242	9.37	2.01
Manoah, Alek	R-R	6-6	260	1-9-98	3	0	0.50	3	3	0	0	18	7	1	1	1	3	27	.119	.154	.091	13.50	1.50
Mayza, Tim	L-L	6-3	220	1-15-92	0	0	9.00	1	0	0	0	1	1	1	1	0	0	2	.250	.000	.500	0.00	0.00
McClelland, Jackson	R-R	6-5	220	7-19-94	1	1	5.51	15	0	0	1	16	18	11	10	3	8	11	.281	.222	.324	6.06	4.41
2-team total (6 Iowa)					2	1	5.54	21	0	0	1	26	30	17	16	5	18	17	.300	.214	.362	5.88	6.23
Merryweather, Julian	R-R	6-4	215	10-14-91	1	0	9.00	4	0	0	3	5	3	3	3	0	1	5	.357	.400	.333	15.00	3.00
Milone, Tommy	L-L	6-0	215	2-16-87	0	2	2.63	8	4	0	0	14	9	6	4	2	5	9	.184	.222	.161	5.93	3.29
2-team total (3 Louisville)					0	2	5.79	11	7	0	0	19	18	14	12	3	8	19	.247	.292	.224	9.16	3.86
Murphy, Patrick	R-R	6-5	235	6-10-95	1	1	0.00	10	0	0	0	15	8	1	0	0	8	17	.160	.000	.276	10.43	4.91
2-team total (3 Rochester)					1	1	0.54	13	0	0	0	17	10	2	1	0	9	20	.172	.037	.290	10.80	4.86
Overton, Connor	L-R	6-0	190	7-24-93	2	1	2.03	21	7	0	0	58	52	14	13	3	10	50	.244	.263	.229	7.80	1.56
2-team total (1 Indianapolis)					2	1	1.99	22	7	0	0	59	52	14	13	3	11	52	.241	.263	.223	7.98	1.69
Payamps, Joel	R-R	6-2	225	4-7-94	1	1	6.75	4	0	0	0	4	7	3	3	2	0	1	.412	.500	.333	2.25	0.00
2-team total (8 Omaha)					2	1	5.25	12	0	0	2	12	17	8	7	2	4	15	.327	.357	.292	11.25	3.00
Pearson, Nate	R-R	6-6	250	8-20-96	1	3	4.40	12	6	0	0	31	21	15	15	4	13	44	.189	.200	.180	12.91	3.82
Rees, Jackson	R-R	6-4	210	7-30-94	0	0	3.38	3	0	0	0	3	2	2	1	0	4	2	.250	.000	.333	6.75	13.50
Reyes, Marcus	L-L	5-11	180	3-10-95	0	0	27.00	1	0	0	0	1	3	3	3	2	0	1	.500	1.000	.400	9.00	0.00
Saucedo, Tayler	L-L	6-5	185	6-18-93	2	1	1.96	12	0	0	0	18	15	4	4	0	2	25	.231	.276	.194	12.27	0.98
Snead, Kirby	L-L	6-1	218	10-7-94	2	0	1.58	36	1	0	4	40	21	12	7	1	16	57	.151	.130	.165	12.83	3.60
Spraker, Graham	R-R	6-3	200	3-19-95	0	0	0.00	1	0	0	0	2	2	0	0	0	0	3	.250	.250	.250	13.50	0.00
Stadler, Fitz	R-R	6-9	245	4-2-97	0	0	7.62	13	0	0	1	13	12	11	11	3	9	17	.250	.389	.167	11.77	6.23
Stripling, Ross	R-R	6-3	220	11-23-89	0	0	0.00	1	1	0	0	1	0	0	0	0	1	1	.200	.000	.333	6.75	6.75
Taylor, Curtis	R-R	6-5	230	7-25-95	0	0	4.19	19	0	0	0	19	21	12	9	1	8	16	.276	.286	.271	7.45	3.72
Thornton, Trent	R-R	6-0	195	9-30-93	1	0	0.00	10	0	0	3	10	8	2	0	0	2	8	.211	.267	.174	6.97	1.74
Tice, Ty	L-R	5-9	185	7-4-96	0	0	0.00	1	0	0	0	1	0	0	0	0	2	0	.000	.000	.000	0.00	18.00
2-team total (11 Gwinnett)					1	0	6.75	12	0	0	0	12	13	9	9	4	7	8	.283	.263	.296	6.00	5.25
Waguespack, Jacob	R-R	6-6	235	11-5-93	7	2	2.86	24	10	0	1	69	63	22	22	3	21	74	.237	.252	.226	9.61	2.73
Zeuch, T.J.	R-R	6-7	245	8-1-95	2	3	4.03	12	9	0	0	58	65	34	26	8	13	42	.278	.283	.273	6.52	2.02
2-team total (9 Memphis)					4	3	4.39	21	14	0	1	96	101	56	47	14	28	77	.266	.290	.246	7.19	2.62

Fielding

Catcher

Catcher	PCT	G	PO	A	E	DP	PB
Adams	.992	25	250	14	2	1	3
Deglan	.992	26	227	10	2	0	2
Graterol	.998	46	413	24	1	3	1
Jansen	1.000	5	38	3	0	1	0
Kirk	.986	10	65	5	1	1	2
Morales	.955	3	20	1	1	0	1
Moreno	1.000	2	13	0	0	6	0
Vigil	.993	19	147	5	1	0	2
Urena	.000	1	0	0	0	0	
White	.994	86	574	45	4	53	

First Base

First Base	PCT	G	PO	A	E	DP
Knight	1.000	22	173	11	0	14
Large	1.000	6	40	4	0	3
Smith	1.000	1	3	0	0	1
Tellez	.990	11	92	10	1	8

Second Base

Second Base	PCT	G	PO	A	E	DP
Colon	.980	11	22	28	1	4
Herrera	.969	36	57	70	4	13
Knight	1.000	7	12	14	0	4
Large	.988	25	37	44	1	12
Lopez	.983	15	26	33	1	5
Urena	.992	31	46	79	1	22
Valera	1.000	4	10	6	0	4

Third Base

Third Base	PCT	G	PO	A	E	DP
Biggio	1.000	9	5	11	0	0
Capra	1.000	1	0	1	0	0
Colon	.944	30	25	59	5	7
Espinal	1.000	3	4	8	0	1
Herrera	.909	7	2	8	1	0
Knight	.958	29	16	52	3	4
Large	1.000	17	12	26	0	3
Smith	.979	17	6	41	1	5
Urena	.909	13	4	16	2	0
Valera	1.000	9	7	12	0	1
Vicuna	1.000	1	1	0	0	0
White	.000	1	1	0	0	0

Shortstop

Shortstop	PCT	G	PO	A	E	DP
Colon	.921	16	19	39	5	9
Lopez	.931	10	8	19	2	3
Smith	.968	66	89	181	9	33

Urena	.970	25	29	35	2	4
Valera	.933	6	6	8	1	2
Vicuna	.857	4	6	6	2	1

Outfield	PCT	G	PO	A	E	DP
Biggio	1.000	7	10	0	0	0
Capra	1.000	4	4	0	0	0
Colon	.962	33	49	2	2	0
Davis	1.000	3	8	0	0	0

Dickerson	1.000	2	2	0	0	0
Hoying	1.000	7	17	3	0	1
Large	.974	58	69	5	2	1
Lopez	1.000	16	29	2	0	0
Palacios	.967	14	29	0	1	0
Polanco	1.000	20	35	1	0	0
Pruitt	1.000	5	13	0	0	0
Smith	1.000	5	12	0	0	0

Smith	.889	6	8	0	1	0
Springer	1.000	4	9	0	0	0
Urena	1.000	7	8	2	0	2
Valera	.972	20	34	1	1	1
Wall	.993	75	145	6	1	1
Warmoth	.990	110	188	5	2	0

NEW HAMPSHIRE FISHER CATS

DOUBLE-A NORTHEAST

Batting	B-T	HT	WT	DOB	AVG	vLH	vRH	G	AB	R	H	2B	3B	HR	RBI	BB	HBP	SH	SF	SO	SB	CS	SLG	OBP
Bec, Chris	R-R	5-11	190	12-30-95	.181	.157	.191	49	166	20	30	2	0	2	14	19	1	0	0	47	11	3	.229	.269
Berroa, Steward	B-R	5-10	178	6-5-99	.300	.333	.286	3	10	2	3	1	0	0	3	0	0	0	1	2	3	0	.400	.273
Capra, Vinny	R-R	5-8	175	7-7-96	.327	.508	.262	72	248	39	81	17	4	10	58	25	5	1	2	74	4	1	.548	.396
Cardona, Hugo	R-R	5-11	145	9-5-99	.333	.000	.375	3	9	0	3	1	0	0	1	0	0	0	0	5	1	0	.444	.333
Ferrer, Jose	R-R	5-11	175	3-1-99	.000	.000	.000	1	3	0	0	0	0	0	0	0	0	0	0	0	0	0	.000	.000
Gold, Ryan	L-R	5-11	215	10-10-97	.167	.105	.191	21	66	4	11	2	0	2	7	7	1	0	0	20	0	0	.288	.257
Groshans, Jordan	R-R	6-3	205	11-10-99	.291	.290	.292	75	278	46	81	23	0	7	40	34	1	0	3	61	0	0	.450	.367
Horwitz, Spencer	L-R	6-0	190	11-14-97	.375	.200	.455	4	16	3	6	2	0	2	4	0	0	0	0	2	0	0	.875	.375
Kirwer, Tanner	R-R	6-0	180	3-15-96	.208	.250	.195	47	159	31	33	5	0	5	16	24	4	0	1	51	18	3	.333	.324
Lantigua, Rafael	R-R	5-8	153	4-28-98	.000	.000	.000	3	11	2	0	0	0	0	1	0	0	0	5	0	0	.000	.083
Lopez, Otto	R-R	5-10	160	10-1-98	.331	.367	.321	70	278	52	92	24	1	3	39	28	5	0	3	62	7	3	.457	.398
Lundquist, Brock	L-R	5-11	190	1-23-96	.172	.267	.154	30	93	12	16	1	0	2	18	15	3	0	3	45	0	0	.247	.298
Martin, Austin	R-R	6-0	185	3-23-99	.281	.256	.288	56	196	43	55	10	2	2	16	37	14	0	3	53	9	3	.383	.424
Morales, Anthony	B-R	6-0	175	11-13-98	.333	.000	.500	3	3	1	1	0	0	0	0	0	0	0	1	0	0	.333	.333
Moreno, Gabriel	R-R	5-11	160	2-14-00	.373	.526	.346	32	126	29	47	9	1	8	45	14	3	0	2	22	1	2	.651	.441
Orimoloye, Demi	R-R	6-4	225	1-6-97	.237	.266	.225	75	283	32	67	17	1	6	20	11	1	0	0	94	12	2	.367	.268
Podkul, Nick	R-R	6-1	200	4-11-97	.204	.226	.195	57	181	26	37	9	1	7	29	23	4	0	1	51	4	1	.381	.306
Pruitt, Reggie	R-R	6-0	180	5-7-97	.164	.136	.172	68	189	31	31	7	1	2	18	18	5	1	0	87	12	6	.243	.255
Talley, LJ	L-R	6-2	203	5-7-97	.247	.250	.245	80	296	43	73	16	1	8	51	34	1	0	4	66	3	0	.389	.322
Taylor, Samad	R-R	5-10	160	7-11-98	.294	.203	.321	87	320	69	94	17	1	16	52	42	8	0	4	110	30	8	.503	.385
Vicuna, Kevin	R-R	6-0	140	1-14-98	.247	.276	.236	76	275	26	68	14	0	2	35	15	11	1	4	68	11	3	.320	.308
Vigil, Rodrigo	R-R	6-0	165	1-3-93	.271	.333	.256	15	48	7	13	2	0	0	2	1	3	0	0	11	0	1	.313	.327
Young, Chavez	B-R	6-0	195	7-8-97	.265	.244	.274	78	279	41	74	15	2	7	52	35	4	0	5	81	20	3	.409	.350

Pitching	B-T	HT	WT	DOB	W	L	ERA	G	GS	CG	SV	IP	H	R	ER	HR	BB	SO	AVG	vLH	vRH	K/9	BB/9
Barbato, Johnny	R-R	6-1	231	7-11-92	3	4	4.35	17	13	0	0	70	72	46	34	5	25	67	.264	.315	.228	8.57	3.20
Bash, Andrew	R-R	6-0	190	8-1-96	1	0	0.00	1	0	0	0	5	3	0	0	0	1	4	.188	.375	.000	7.20	1.80
Beasley, Jeremy	R-R	6-3	235	11-26-95	1	1	7.71	3	2	0	0	5	3	4	4	1	2	8	.188	.182	.200	15.43	3.86
Capra, Vinny	R-R	5-8	175	7-7-96	0	0	0.00	1	0	0	0	0	0	0	0	0	0	0	.000	--	.000	0.00	0.00
Caracci, Parker	R-R	6-0	205	9-13-96	1	0	0.84	6	0	0	1	11	5	1	1	0	5	5	.143	.133	.150	4.22	4.22
Castillo, Maximo	R-R	6-2	256	5-4-99	11	4	4.85	21	20	0	0	102	106	60	55	12	35	89	.265	.264	.266	7.85	3.09
Dykstra, James	L-R	6-3	207	11-22-90	0	1	3.18	5	0	0	0	6	4	3	2	0	2	10	.182	.000	.364	15.88	3.18
Eisert, Brandon	L-L	6-2	205	1-18-98	1	0	2.63	10	0	0	1	14	13	4	4	0	2	17	.250	.381	.161	11.20	1.32
Ellenbest, Mike	R-R	6-4	220	8-20-94	1	4	5.50	25	3	0	1	36	34	26	22	5	13	43	.250	.362	.167	10.75	3.25
Finfrock, Cre	B-R	5-11	185	6-26-96	0	1	23.63	4	1	0	0	3	3	7	7	1	5	4	.273	.250	.286	13.50	16.88
Fraze, Nick	R-R	6-3	180	10-24-97	1	1	4.58	5	3	0	0	20	25	11	10	2	6	14	.316	.361	.279	6.41	2.75
Gaston, Willy	R-R	6-5	190	5-19-96	0	1	10.50	5	0	0	0	6	8	7	7	2	3	3	.320	.400	.300	6.00	4.50
Harris, Jon	R-R	6-4	175	10-16-93	1	3	2.93	28	0	0	2	40	29	13	13	7	12	34	.199	.211	.191	7.65	2.70
Hernandez, Adrian	R-R	5-10	168	1-22-00	0	0	2.30	10	1	0	4	16	5	4	4	2	6	27	.096	.043	.138	15.51	3.45
Hovis, Reilly	R-R	6-3	195	10-27-93	2	4	6.53	12	11	0	0	51	66	42	37	16	17	37	.311	.338	.295	6.53	3.00
Jimenez, Emerson	L-R	6-1	160	12-16-94	1	3	9.47	18	0	0	1	19	22	22	20	0	17	16	.286	.267	.298	7.58	8.05
Johnston, Kyle	R-R	6-0	190	7-17-96	1	1	1.74	21	6	0	3	52	41	10	10	2	26	41	.222	.192	.241	7.14	4.53
Law, Connor	R-R	6-4	220	4-27-94	0	2	6.75	23	0	0	0	25	30	21	19	6	22	22	.294	.216	.338	7.82	7.82
Lawrence, Casey	R-R	6-2	210	11-7-87	1	1	3.00	4	4	0	0	21	14	7	7	2	4	18	.194	.200	.191	7.71	1.71
Logue, Zach	L-L	6-0	165	4-23-96	3	1	4.54	7	7	0	0	36	33	18	18	6	7	51	.246	.244	.247	12.87	1.77
Luciano, Elvis	R-R	6-3	210	2-15-00	1	1	3.16	12	12	0	0	37	35	16	13	4	18	34	.254	.180	.312	8.27	4.38
McAffer, Will	R-R	6-2	205	5-30-97	1	0	8.18	9	0	0	0	11	13	11	10	1	8	9	.289	.313	.276	7.36	6.55
McInvale, Andrew	R-R	6-2	195	11-3-96	2	2	2.18	13	0	0	0	21	12	8	5	1	13	28	.164	.129	.190	12.19	5.66
Miller, Troy	R-R	6-4	210	2-13-97	1	2	7.20	4	3	0	0	20	24	16	16	4	7	16	.286	.206	.340	7.20	3.15
2-team total (2 Binghamton)					2	3	6.53	6	5	0	0	30	35	23	22	6	9	27	.287	.286	.288	8.01	2.67
Quinones, Luis	R-R	6-0	205	7-2-97	2	4	5.20	8	8	0	0	36	25	22	21	4	26	51	.188	.208	.175	12.63	6.44
Rackoski, Sean	R-R	6-7	225	5-12-95	1	2	4.65	25	0	0	3	31	37	19	16	2	6	21	.294	.388	.234	6.10	1.74
Reyes, Marcus	L-L	5-11	180	3-10-95	2	0	2.48	19	0	0	2	29	21	11	8	3	13	30	.198	.313	.149	9.31	4.03
Rodning, Brody	R-L	6-1	185	1-14-96	3	4	5.58	32	0	0	2	40	51	31	25	2	18	43	.307	.281	.324	9.60	4.02
Ryan, Sam	R-R	6-3	205	9-22-98	0	1	9.53	4	0	0	0	6	7	6	6	2	4	6	.333	.444	.250	6.35	6.35
Spraker, Graham	R-R	6-3	205	3-19-95	2	1	2.74	30	0	0	2	43	29	14	13	5	23	62	.190	.217	.172	13.08	4.85
Stadler, Fitz	R-R	6-9	245	4-2-97	2	1	4.79	26	1	0	1	36	26	24	19	4	26	52	.194	.135	.113	13.12	6.56
Taylor, Curtis	R-R	6-6	230	7-25-95	2	1	7.63	11	1	0	0	15	15	19	13	4	9	25	.242	.156	.333	14.67	5.28
Valdez, Julian	R-R	6-2	192	12-13-98	1	0	0.00	1	0	0	0	3	2	0	0	0	3	2	.182	.125	.333	5.40	8.10
Woods Richardson, Simeon	R-R	6-3	210	9-27-00	2	4	5.76	11	11	0	0	45	42	33	29	5	26	67	.246	.222	.267	13.30	5.16

Fielding

Catcher	PCT	G	PO	A	E	DP	PB
Bec	.996	49	422	29	2	2	7
Capra	1.000	1	1	0	0	0	0
Ferrer	1.000	1	4	1	0	0	0
Gold	.994	20	164	9	1	0	4
Morales	1.000	1	13	0	0	0	0
Moreno	1.000	27	276	22	0	3	0
Vigil	.989	13	83	6	1	1	0

First Base	PCT	G	PO	A	E	DP
Groshans	1.000	1	5	0	0	1
Horwitz	1.000	2	12	1	0	1
Podkul	.990	49	352	36	4	38
Talley	.992	37	241	16	2	24
Vicuna	.970	18	118	12	4	13
Vigil	1.000	2	9	1	0	0

Second Base	PCT	G	PO	A	E	DP
Cardona	1.000	2	2	6	0	1

	PCT	G	PO	A	E	DP	PB
Lantigua	1.000	2	3	9	0	3	
Lopez	.947	43	61	83	8	19	
Podkul	1.000	1	4	3	0	2	
Talley	.977	11	19	24	1	9	
Taylor	.983	34	56	61	2	13	
Vicuna	.972	18	30	39	2	10	

Third Base	PCT	G	PO	A	E	DP
Capra	.917	42	25	63	8	9
Groshans	.863	21	12	32	7	2
Lantigua	.000	1	0	0	0	0
Moreno	1.000	1	0	1	0	0
Talley	.871	16	9	18	4	0
Taylor	.909	14	5	15	2	1
Vicuna	.933	18	13	29	3	2

Shortstop	PCT	G	PO	A	E	DP
Capra	.944	14	21	30	3	4
Groshans	.960	43	43	78	5	19

	PCT	G	PO	A	E	DP
Lopez	1.000	1	0	2	0	0
Martin	.902	27	31	61	10	12
Taylor	1.000	5	8	12	0	6
Vicuna	.978	26	39	51	2	15

Outfield	PCT	G	PO	A	E	DP
Berroa	1.000	3	5	0	0	0
Capra	1.000	10	12	2	0	1
Cardona	1.000	1	2	0	0	0
Kirwer	1.000	37	60	2	0	0
Lopez	1.000	23	62	3	0	0
Lundquist	1.000	15	20	2	0	1
Martin	1.000	26	46	4	0	3
Orimoloye	1.000	63	101	4	0	1
Pruitt	.969	63	88	6	3	1
Taylor	.955	30	40	2	2	0
Young	.978	74	163	11	4	2

VANCOUVER CANADIANS
HIGH-A WEST   **HIGH CLASS A**

Batting	B-T	HT	WT	DOB	AVG	vLH	vRH	G	AB	R	H	2B	3B	HR	RBI	BB	HBP	SH	SF	SO	SB	CS	SLG	OBP
Aiello, John	R-R	6-2	215	2-14-97	.226	.333	.200	9	31	3	7	4	0	1	5	1	2	0	0	9	1	0	.452	.294
Ammons, Justin	L-R	5-10	180	3-16-98	.143	.000	.167	5	14	2	2	1	0	0	1	3	0	1	0	6	1	0	.214	.294
Barger, Addison	L-R	6-0	175	11-12-99	.158	.000	.250	5	19	1	3	1	0	0	2	0	0	0	0	6	0	0	.211	.158
Brito, Ronny	R-R	6-0	165	3-22-99	.166	.087	.180	41	145	21	24	6	0	7	22	15	0	0	4	72	0	1	.352	.238
Clarke, Philip	L-R	5-11	190	3-24-98	.248	.224	.252	87	327	49	81	18	1	6	48	35	14	1	1	60	1	1	.364	.345
Cook, Zac	L-R	6-1	195	4-29-98	.269	.393	.242	48	160	32	43	16	1	8	29	16	11	0	2	60	3	1	.531	.370
De Los Santos, Luis	R-R	6-1	160	6-9-98	.253	.241	.255	91	376	50	95	25	2	12	65	16	10	0	5	93	4	5	.426	.297
Eden, Cameron	R-R	6-1	181	3-31-98	.274	.206	.290	48	179	41	49	9	1	4	31	26	8	1	4	50	30	2	.402	.382
Espino, Sebastian	R-R	6-2	176	5-29-00	.295	.298	.294	61	227	38	67	15	5	8	47	23	2	2	5	71	2	4	.511	.358
Gold, Ryan	L-R	5-11	215	10-10-97	.243	.214	.249	63	235	31	57	23	3	4	36	32	7	0	1	80	0	0	.417	.349
Guerra, Andres	R-R	5-11	175	6-3-97	.247	.222	.250	25	85	11	21	5	0	1	12	7	1	0	2	33	1	0	.341	.305
Horwitz, Spencer	L-R	6-0	190	11-14-97	.290	.393	.271	105	389	65	113	28	1	10	62	70	5	0	5	66	4	5	.445	.401
Kirwer, Tanner	R-R	6-0	180	3-15-96	.285	.348	.272	36	137	36	39	6	1	6	17	27	5	1	0	33	25	2	.474	.420
Lantigua, Rafael	R-R	5-8	153	4-28-98	.280	.333	.268	80	300	65	84	22	1	11	43	42	4	0	1	76	26	6	.470	.375
Martinez, Orelvis	R-R	6-1	188	11-19-01	.214	.080	.253	27	112	17	24	4	0	9	19	10	1	0	1	28	0	1	.491	.282
Morales, Anthony	B-R	6-0	175	11-13-98	.133	.000	.182	4	15	2	2	0	0	0	1	0	0	0	0	5	0	0	.133	.188
Morris, PK	L-L	6-1	195	11-30-98	.053	.000	.077	5	19	1	1	0	0	0	0	1	0	0	0	10	0	0	.053	.100
Morris, Tanner	L-R	6-2	190	9-13-97	.285	.224	.297	103	397	55	113	19	3	7	57	58	7	2	5	90	4	1	.401	.381
Neal, DJ	R-R	6-3	220	1-11-97	.206	.200	.207	47	155	16	32	5	1	0	13	17	1	0	1	43	8	4	.252	.287
Ray, Harrison	R-R	6-0	200	1-11-98	.067	.000	.083	4	15	0	1	0	0	0	0	0	0	0	0	6	0	0	.067	.067
Rivera, Eric	R-R	6-0	185	9-19-97	.241	.200	.249	78	261	36	63	7	0	0	17	35	3	2	1	48	13	6	.268	.337
Robertson, Will	L-L	6-2	215	12-26-97	.235	.216	.239	56	221	35	52	16	1	5	26	17	8	0	2	75	2	2	.385	.310
Schneider, Davis	R-R	5-10	190	1-26-99	.231	.409	.200	45	147	26	34	7	1	9	22	26	2	1	3	59	0	1	.476	.348
Schwecke, Trevor	R-R	6-1	185	12-18-97	.205	.100	.235	13	44	4	9	2	0	0	6	8	1	0	0	14	1	3	.250	.340
Talley, LJ	L-R	6-2	203	5-7-97	.304	.500	.263	7	23	0	7	1	0	0	3	2	1	0	0	3	0	1	.348	.360

Pitching	B-T	HT	WT	DOB	W	L	ERA	G	GS	CG	SV	IP	H	R	ER	HR	BB	SO	AVG	vLH	vRH	K/9	BB/9
Bash, Andrew	R-R	6-0	190	8-1-96	3	5	5.16	9	2	0	1	23	17	14	13	4	9	20	.210	.256	.158	7.94	3.57
Bouchey, Brayden	L-R	6-5	225	9-20-95	0	0	10.80	3	0	0	0	2	1	2	2	1	3	2	.167	.000	.333	10.80	16.20
Caracci, Parker	R-R	6-0	205	9-13-96	3	2	2.64	32	0	0	8	44	32	17	13	2	22	40	.213	.208	.219	8.12	4.47
Concepcion, Jol	R-R	6-5	195	9-17-98	0	0	1.93	8	0	0	1	9	5	2	2	0	11	8	.167	.111	.190	7.71	10.61
Danner, Hagen	R-R	6-2	210	9-30-98	2	1	2.02	25	0	0	3	36	21	11	8	2	12	42	.171	.140	.197	10.60	3.03
Eisert, Brandon	L-L	6-2	205	1-18-98	5	1	4.05	20	0	0	0	47	51	22	21	5	16	60	.279	.291	.273	11.57	3.09
Estrada, Lazaro	R-R	5-10	180	4-24-99	0	0	0.00	2	0	0	0	4	1	0	0	0	1	5	.091	.000	.143	11.25	2.25
Fraze, Nick	R-R	6-3	180	10-24-97	3	2	2.14	11	9	0	0	42	27	12	10	5	10	46	.180	.140	.204	9.86	2.14
Gaston, Willy	R-R	6-5	190	5-19-96	1	3	6.91	22	1	0	0	43	55	36	33	2	34	28	.316	.301	.333	5.86	7.12
Gillingham, Luke	L-L	6-3	200	3-4-94	0	1	0.00	1	0	0	0	1	1	2	0	0	2	4	.167	.000	.250	27.00	13.50
Hernandez, Adrian	R-R	5-10	168	1-22-00	3	1	1.88	12	0	0	0	29	12	6	6	2	8	44	.125	.091	.154	13.81	2.51
Hernandez, Roither	R-R	6-4	185	3-5-98	0	1	5.53	22	0	0	0	28	34	20	17	3	14	32	.291	.276	.305	10.41	4.55
Johnson, Cobi	R-R	6-4	225	11-6-95	1	2	6.42	28	0	0	2	41	40	34	29	2	33	50	.260	.232	.282	11.07	7.30
Juenger, Hayden	R-R	6-0	180	8-9-00	2	0	2.70	10	0	0	0	20	11	6	6	4	4	17	.162	.219	.111	7.71	1.80
Kloffenstein, Adam	R-R	6-5	243	8-25-00	7	7	6.22	23	23	0	0	101	96	76	70	10	61	107	.243	.272	.219	9.50	5.42
Law, Connor	R-R	6-4	220	4-27-94	1	0	3.75	9	0	0	0	12	9	5	5	0	7	15	.200	.174	.227	11.25	5.25
Maese, Justin	R-R	6-3	190	10-24-96	3	4	4.75	33	0	0	4	53	49	31	28	4	30	63	.241	.311	.186	10.70	5.09
McAffer, Will	R-R	6-2	205	5-30-97	2	3	7.91	21	0	0	3	33	29	32	29	5	38	51	.240	.225	.247	13.91	10.36
McInvale, Andrew	R-R	6-2	195	11-3-96	0	0	4.50	2	0	0	0	4	3	2	2	1	1	6	.188	.286	.111	13.50	2.25
Melean, Alejandro	R-R	6-0	175	11-11-00	1	1	4.74	4	4	0	0	19	27	13	10	2	6	17	.329	.188	.420	8.05	2.84
Mellen, Sean	L-L	6-5	215	2-20-98	0	1	7.52	10	0	0	0	20	25	17	17	1	11	18	.309	.214	.358	7.97	4.87
Miller, Troy	R-R	6-4	210	2-13-97	2	0	1.84	3	3	0	0	15	7	3	3	1	8	17	.140	.143	.139	10.43	4.91
Nolan, Alex	R-R	6-4	225	3-21-96	1	6	7.35	17	6	0	0	49	71	43	40	11	18	32	.338	.304	.370	5.88	3.31

				W	L	ERA	G	GS	CG	SV	IP	H	R	ER	HR	BB	SO	AVG	vLH	vRH	K/9	BB/9
Ponce, Gabriel	R-R	6-2	205	4-29-99	2	2	2.65	13	0	0	1	17	15	8	5	0	12	25	.234	.219	.250	13.24	6.35
Quinones, Luis	R-R	6-0	205	7-2-97	2	3	3.00	9	9	0	0	39	26	17	13	2	39	64	.190	.172	.203	14.77	9.00
Rapp, Brian	R-R	6-0	197	8-10-95	0	4	8.68	7	5	0	0	19	24	23	18	5	17	11	.304	.306	.302	5.30	8.20
Reyes, Marcus	L-L	5-11	180	3-10-95	1	0	3.68	12	0	0	1	29	23	14	12	1	7	28	.219	.265	.197	8.59	2.15
Robberse, Sem	R-R	6-1	160	10-12-01	0	3	5.23	7	7	0	0	31	39	29	18	3	18	29	.305	.340	.280	8.42	5.23
Ruwe, Thomas	R-R	6-9	225	9-9-95	0	0	2.53	9	0	0	1	11	5	3	3	0	6	17	.147	.125	.167	14.34	5.06
Ryan, Sam	R-R	6-3	205	9-22-98	0	2	5.23	9	2	0	0	21	21	18	12	1	12	20	.259	.405	.136	8.71	5.23
Schneider, Davis	R-R	5-10	190	1-26-99	0	1	--	1	0	0	0	0	1	2	1	1	0	0	1.000	1.000	--	--	--
Schultz, Paxton	L-R	6-3	205	1-5-98	5	7	5.28	22	21	0	0	102	108	69	60	11	45	114	.276	.297	.255	10.03	3.96
Van Eyk, CJ	R-R	6-1	198	9-15-98	4	6	5.83	19	19	0	0	80	71	58	52	9	39	100	.234	.247	.222	11.20	4.37
Watson, Troy	R-R	6-2	180	6-11-97	0	0	0.00	1	1	0	0	3	1	0	0	0	2	3	.091	.000	.167	9.00	6.00
Wymer, Sean	R-R	6-1	205	3-19-97	1	3	10.17	7	7	0	0	26	40	30	29	5	13	23	.357	.333	.371	8.06	4.56

Fielding

Catcher	PCT	G	PO	A	E	DP	PB
Clarke	.991	73	682	59	7	7	13
Gold	.997	27	267	30	1	2	5
Guerra	.991	21	206	14	2	2	7
Morales	1.000	1	14	0	0	0	0

	PCT	G	PO	A	E	DP
Lantigua	.983	28	40	73	2	15
Morris	.994	43	78	87	1	18
Ray	1.000	2	2	6	0	0
Schneider	.986	18	31	41	1	10
Schwecke	1.000	4	6	12	0	1
Talley	1.000	1	0	3	0	0

Shortstop	PCT	G	PO	A	E	DP
Barger	.900	5	5	13	2	0
Brito	.923	3	5	7	1	1
De Los Santos	.967	69	92	175	9	25
Lantigua	.966	7	8	20	1	5
Martinez	.885	19	31	38	9	8
Morris	.948	17	11	44	3	11

First Base	PCT	G	PO	A	E	DP
Aiello	.968	3	30	0	1	1
Brito	.857	1	6	0	1	0
Clarke	.983	7	48	10	1	7
Gold	.987	20	142	8	2	12
Horwitz	.994	83	603	45	4	50
Morris	.935	5	43	0	3	0
Schwecke	1.000	1	5	1	0	0

Third Base	PCT	G	PO	A	E	DP
Aiello	.700	5	3	4	3	0
Brito	.847	22	10	40	9	3
De Los Santos	.900	4	1	8	1	1
Eden	.500	1	0	1	1	0
Espino	.909	18	8	22	3	0
Lantigua	.893	16	9	16	3	1
Martinez	1.000	6	3	5	0	1
Morris	.929	39	28	51	6	2
Schneider	.867	5	7	6	2	0
Schwecke	1.000	5	4	11	0	1
Talley	1.000	3	2	3	0	0

Outfield	PCT	G	PO	A	E	DP
Ammons	.929	5	13	0	1	0
Cook	.988	45	74	5	1	2
Eden	1.000	47	92	1	0	0
Espino	.927	33	49	2	4	1
Horwitz	1.000	5	4	0	0	0
Kirwer	.956	38	63	2	3	0
Lantigua	.939	22	29	2	2	0
Neal	.969	46	63	0	2	0
Rivera	.979	79	131	11	3	3
Robertson	.981	55	98	3	2	0

Second Base	PCT	G	PO	A	E	DP
Brito	.956	9	21	22	2	5
Cook	1.000	2	4	10	0	2
De Los Santos	.939	14	27	35	4	7
Horwitz	1.000	1	2	1	0	0

DUNEDIN BLUE JAYS — LOW CLASS A
LOW-A SOUTHEAST

Batting	B-T	HT	WT	DOB	AVG	vLH	vRH	G	AB	R	H	2B	3B	HR	RBI	BB	HBP	SH	SF	SO	SB	CS	SLG	OBP
Ammons, Justin	L-R	5-10	180	3-16-98	.167	.077	.186	23	72	10	12	1	0	1	8	17	0	0	0	23	6	1	.222	.326
Astudillo, Willfrann	R-R	5-10	165	8-5-01	.250	.000	.286	4	8	1	2	0	0	0	0	1	0	0	0	0	0	0	.250	.333
Barger, Addison	L-R	6-0	175	11-12-99	.249	.210	.259	91	325	53	81	21	2	18	80	36	8	0	5	123	7	0	.492	.334
Berroa, Steward	B-R	5-10	178	6-5-99	.245	.302	.228	82	278	60	68	12	5	7	37	50	1	3	1	76	55	9	.399	.361
Britton, Zach	L-R	6-1	200	9-9-98	.225	.267	.216	79	267	50	60	18	0	7	35	48	16	0	2	102	5	1	.371	.372
Brown, Dasan	R-R	6-0	185	9-25-01	.212	.279	.194	51	198	33	42	8	1	4	16	20	8	0	0	74	22	6	.323	.310
Cardona, Hugo	R-R	5-11	145	9-5-99	.250	.150	.274	32	104	14	26	6	1	2	14	11	3	1	0	45	15	2	.385	.339
Cook, Zac	L-R	6-1	195	4-29-98	.237	.192	.250	34	118	29	28	9	1	4	18	15	14	0	0	40	12	4	.432	.388
D'Orazio, J.J.	R-R	6-1	170	12-28-01	.146	.111	.156	12	41	4	6	0	0	1	6	3	0	0	1	13	0	0	.220	.200
Espino, Sebastian	R-R	6-2	176	5-29-00	.286	.500	.250	4	14	1	4	1	0	0	1	0	1	0	0	6	1	1	.357	.333
Ferrer, Jose	R-R	5-11	175	3-1-99	.130	.000	.161	25	69	3	9	3	0	0	7	5	2	0	2	29	0	0	.174	.205
Hiraldo, Miguel	R-R	5-11	170	9-5-00	.249	.320	.232	105	390	66	97	26	4	7	52	51	5	0	7	111	29	5	.390	.338
Jimenez, Leo	R-R	5-11	160	5-17-01	.315	.351	.305	54	168	35	53	8	0	1	19	51	21	0	2	35	4	1	.381	.517
Martinez, Gabriel	R-R	6-0	170	7-24-02	.333	.750	.125	3	12	1	4	1	0	0	1	1	0	0	0	4	0	1	.417	.385
Martinez, Orelvis	R-R	6-1	188	11-19-01	.279	.235	.289	71	283	49	79	22	2	19	68	33	8	0	1	85	4	1	.572	.369
Mesia, Victor	R-R	5-9	175	1-18-03	.129	.000	.154	8	31	3	4	1	0	0	2	1	0	0	0	8	0	0	.161	.156
Morales, Anthony	B-R	6-0	175	11-13-98	.222	.286	.207	12	36	0	8	2	0	0	4	3	0	0	0	19	1	2	.278	.282
Morris, PK	L-L	6-1	195	11-30-98	.251	.234	.255	100	323	58	81	21	2	9	57	81	7	0	4	116	5	0	.412	.407
Mueller, MacKenzie	R-L	6-3	225	12-16-97	.215	.260	.201	95	317	44	68	12	4	5	38	42	8	0	2	125	15	4	.325	.320
Nunez, Rainer	R-R	6-3	180	12-4-00	.263	.125	.364	6	19	4	5	0	0	1	3	3	1	0	0	4	0	0	.421	.391
Palacios, Josh	L-R	6-1	198	7-30-95	1.000	--	1.000	1	2	0	2	0	0	0	0	0	0	0	0	0	1	0	1.000	1.000
Ray, Harrison	R-R	6-0	200	1-11-98	.202	.268	.186	80	277	44	56	11	1	9	33	41	9	1	2	114	26	7	.347	.322
Rivas, Jose	R-R	5-9	165	9-5-00	.189	.083	.220	18	53	6	10	0	0	0	5	6	1	0	0	14	2	2	.189	.283
Rivera, Eric	R-R	6-0	185	9-19-97	.474	.600	.429	6	19	7	9	1	0	0	1	0	1	0	2	5	0	0	.526	.600
Santiago, Glenn	R-R	6-0	165	12-14-00	.125	.000	.167	3	8	2	1	0	0	0	0	1	0	0	0	3	1	0	.125	.222
Sloniger, Ryan	L-R	5-11	200	3-20-97	.130	.095	.146	22	69	15	9	3	0	2	8	16	2	0	0	27	1	0	.261	.310
Solarte, Jhon	B-R	6-0	165	12-9-00	.162	.111	.179	35	111	20	18	3	0	3	18	16	5	1	1	52	7	2	.270	.293
Sosa, Andres	R-R	5-11	210	11-7-97	.188	.000	.231	5	16	0	3	0	0	0	3	1	1	0	1	7	0	0	.188	.263
Sotolongo, Adriel	R-R	6-3	208	4-22-98	.182	.000	.200	3	11	0	2	1	0	0	2	0	0	0	0	5	0	0	.273	.182
Spain, Garrett	L-R	5-11	178	9-21-00	.169	.083	.191	17	59	4	10	0	0	0	5	2	0	0	1	14	0	2	.169	.194
Tirotta, Riley	R-R	6-3	195	8-21-98	.305	.273	.315	30	95	16	29	3	1	1	13	19	3	0	2	25	4	2	.389	.429

Pitching	B-T	HT	WT	DOB	W	L	ERA	G	GS	CG	SV	IP	H	R	ER	HR	BB	SO	AVG	vLH	vRH	K/9	BB/9
Alvarado, Wilgenis	L-L	6-1	160	5-18-00	1	3	8.84	8	0	0	0	19	28	21	19	4	17	15	.354	.385	.348	6.98	7.91
Bash, Andrew	R-R	6-0	190	8-1-96	4	1	6.75	6	2	0	0	28	39	22	21	2	11	26	.333	.387	.314	8.36	3.54
Burnette, Jimmy	L-L	6-2	205	10-19-98	1	0	2.19	7	0	0	0	12	6	4	3	0	7	17	.146	.143	.148	12.41	5.11

Player	B-T	Ht	Wt	DOB	W	L	ERA	G	GS	CG	SV	IP	H	R	ER	HR	BB	SO	AVG	OBP	SLG		
Caballero, Elixon	R-R	5-9	160	7-9-00	3	2	5.60	25	0	0	0	27	22	19	17	3	25	27	.220	.237	.210	8.89	8.23
Casimiri, Jiorgeny	R-R	6-1	160	7-12-01	1	2	10.70	13	0	0	0	18	24	25	21	7	13	17	.329	.333	.327	8.66	6.62
Cole, A.J.	R-R	6-5	240	1-5-92	0	0	0.00	1	1	0	0	1	0	0	0	0	0	0	.000	.000	.000	0.00	0.00
Concepcion, Jol	R-R	6-5	195	9-17-98	1	6	5.63	17	8	0	1	54	51	37	34	7	43	42	.246	.200	.263	6.96	7.12
Cooke, Connor	R-R	6-1	203	11-2-99	1	0	0.00	3	0	0	0	3	2	0	0	0	0	6	.200	.200	.200	18.00	0.00
De Paula, Juan	R-R	6-3	165	9-22-97	1	4	4.75	22	0	0	1	47	37	30	25	5	29	42	.210	.304	.167	7.99	5.51
Dominguez, Michael	R-R	5-10	175	8-17-00	1	0	3.34	7	6	0	0	30	26	11	11	2	12	31	.234	.226	.241	9.40	3.64
Dykstra, James	L-R	6-3	207	11-22-90	0	0	0.00	1	0	0	0	1	1	0	0	0	0	2	.250	.000	.500	18.00	0.00
Edwards Jr., Carl	R-R	6-3	170	9-3-91	0	1	0.00	1	0	0	0	1	1	1	0	0	0	2	.200	.500	.200	18.00	0.00
Eisert, Brandon	L-L	6-2	205	1-18-98	0	0	0.00	2	0	0	0	3	2	1	0	0	1	5	.167	.000	.286	15.00	3.00
Estrada, Lazaro	R-R	5-10	180	4-24-99	0	0	3.31	5	2	0	0	16	17	8	6	2	7	23	.250	.333	.184	12.67	3.86
Finfrock, Cre	B-R	5-11	185	6-26-96	0	0	0.00	1	0	0	0	1	1	0	0	0	1	3	.250	--	.250	27.00	9.00
Frasso, Nick	R-R	6-5	200	10-18-98	0	0	0.00	3	2	0	0	5	3	1	0	0	2	8	.158	.000	.250	14.40	3.60
Garcia, Winder	R-R	5-10	165	10-11-01	0	1	6.75	3	3	0	0	11	9	8	8	3	8	10	.231	.308	.192	8.44	6.75
Gaston, Willy	R-R	6-5	190	5-19-96	2	0	1.69	4	0	0	0	11	10	6	2	1	5	13	.233	.313	.185	10.97	4.22
Gregory, Hunter	R-R	6-3	215	11-16-98	0	1	13.50	6	0	0	1	6	9	9	9	2	3	6	.333	.438	.182	9.00	4.50
Hernandez, Adrian	R-R	5-10	168	1-22-00	0	1	4.50	9	1	0	3	18	13	13	9	1	15	37	.194	.333	.100	18.50	7.50
Hernandez, Roither	R-R	6-4	185	3-5-98	2	1	3.05	13	0	0	3	21	18	9	7	2	6	31	.237	.238	.236	13.50	2.61
Herrera, Jefferson	R-R	6-4	190	6-2-99	2	3	5.31	21	1	0	0	39	35	27	23	7	25	27	.235	.309	.191	6.23	5.77
Kelly, Justin	R-R	6-1	195	12-2-98	0	1	6.33	11	1	0	0	21	18	17	15	3	11	19	.231	.241	.224	8.02	4.64
Laws, Colton	R-R	6-7	230	11-20-95	0	0	9.00	1	0	0	0	1	2	1	1	0	0	0	.500	.500	.500	0.00	0.00
Medrano, Eliezer	R-R	6-2	180	8-17-98	0	0	5.40	2	0	0	0	2	4	3	1	0	1	0	.444	.250	.600	0.00	5.40
Melean, Alejandro	R-R	6-0	175	10-11-00	3	5	5.29	19	10	0	1	63	69	46	37	10	30	75	.268	.235	.284	10.71	4.29
Mellen, Sean	L-L	6-5	215	2-20-98	1	1	3.51	12	3	0	1	26	23	10	10	4	10	40	.237	.292	.219	14.03	3.51
Merryweather, Julian	R-R	6-4	215	10-14-91	0	0	0.00	1	1	0	0	1	1	0	0	0	1	1	.500	--	.500	9.00	9.00
Monsion, Rafael	L-L	6-3	185	8-16-99	1	0	2.42	13	1	0	0	22	22	6	6	3	8	21	.256	.250	.258	8.46	3.22
Murphy, Patrick	R-R	6-5	235	6-10-95	0	0	5.40	3	0	0	0	3	6	3	2	0	1	5	.375	.600	.273	13.50	2.70
Nolan, Alex	R-R	6-4	225	3-21-96	2	0	4.09	4	0	0	0	11	12	6	5	0	4	7	.286	.467	.185	5.73	3.27
Ohashi, Rafael	R-R	6-1	185	10-8-02	1	2	5.96	10	7	0	0	26	22	22	17	1	24	35	.227	.244	.214	12.27	8.42
Palmer, Trent	R-R	6-1	230	4-2-99	4	2	3.00	16	16	2	0	63	33	24	21	0	42	83	.153	.179	.142	11.86	6.00
Paulino, Naswell	L-L	5-11	160	4-17-00	7	4	3.82	23	23	0	0	97	75	50	41	8	57	109	.208	.235	.197	10.15	5.31
Perdomo, Yaifer	L-L	5-10	160	8-16-01	0	0	15.00	1	1	0	0	3	4	5	5	2	3	5	.308	.000	.444	15.00	9.00
Perez, Nathanael	R-R	6-1	160	6-5-98	4	3	5.61	17	16	0	0	61	64	40	38	15	27	73	.262	.276	.255	10.77	3.98
Ponce, Gabriel	R-R	6-2	205	4-29-99	1	2	5.77	22	0	0	7	34	29	22	22	5	20	50	.230	.340	.158	13.11	5.24
Rivas, Jose	R-R	5-9	165	9-5-00	0	1	27.00	1	0	0	0	1	2	1	1	0	0	0	.500	1.000	.000	0.00	0.00
Robberse, Sem	R-R	6-1	160	10-12-01	5	4	3.90	14	12	0	0	58	46	28	25	4	20	61	.214	.246	.200	9.52	3.12
Rosario, Tony	R-R	6-4	192	12-14-97	0	1	--	1	0	0	0	0	1	3	3	0	2	0	1.000	1.000	--	--
Rutkowski, Harry	R-L	6-2	230	4-23-99	3	1	2.42	12	0	0	1	22	15	7	6	2	10	24	.190	.107	.235	9.67	4.03
Ruwe, Thomas	R-R	6-9	225	9-9-95	0	0	5.03	18	0	0	2	20	17	12	11	3	15	32	.218	.192	.231	14.64	6.86
Santos, Dahian	R-R	5-11	160	2-26-03	0	2	12.60	2	2	0	0	5	8	7	7	1	4	5	.400	.625	.250	9.00	7.20
Schneider, Davis	R-R	5-10	190	1-26-99	0	0	18.00	1	0	0	0	1	3	2	2	1	1	1	.500	.667	.333	9.00	9.00
Spain, Garrett	L-R	5-11	178	9-21-00	0	1	9.00	1	0	0	0	1	2	2	1	0	0	0	.400	.333	.500	0.00	9.00
Svanson, Matt	R-R	6-5	235	1-31-99	1	1	2.30	11	0	0	5	16	8	5	4	0	8	23	.143	.217	.091	13.21	4.60
Townsend, Grant	R-R	6-0	190	8-9-97	0	1	18.90	2	0	0	0	3	5	7	7	1	6	1	.333	.500	.222	2.70	16.20
Urbaez, Geison	R-R	6-1	180	7-5-00	3	0	8.00	10	0	0	0	18	20	16	16	0	23	16	.290	.214	.309	8.00	11.50
Valdez, Julian	R-R	6-2	192	12-13-98	1	5	5.44	31	0	0	4	48	56	43	29	7	27	44	.286	.302	.278	8.25	5.06
Wallace, Trenton	L-L	6-1	200	3-31-99	0	1	4.32	5	0	0	0	8	4	4	4	0	9	11	.148	.222	.111	11.88	9.72
Zulueta, Yosver	R-R	6-1	190	1-23-98	0	0	--	1	1	0	0	0	0	0	0	0	0	0	.000	--	.000	--	--

Fielding

Catcher	PCT	G	PO	A	E	DP	PB
Astudillo	1.000	4	25	0	0	0	0
Britton	.995	44	408	24	2	0	7
D'Orazio	.991	12	102	9	1	1	2
Ferrer	.995	25	180	15	1	1	6
Mesia	.990	8	93	6	1	2	4
Morales	.987	10	71	6	1	1	1
Sloniger	.991	21	197	21	2	0	7
Sosa	.983	5	50	8	1	0	0

First Base	PCT	G	PO	A	E	DP
Barger	.985	10	65	2	1	8
Espino	1.000	1	7	0	0	1
Morris	.992	88	601	35	5	54
Mueller	.943	10	62	4	4	2
Nunez	1.000	6	30	2	0	7
Ray	.952	7	36	4	2	2

Second Base	PCT	G	PO	A	E	DP
Barger	.971	24	29	38	2	7
Berroa	.000	1	0	0	0	0

	PCT	G	PO	A	E	DP
Cardona	.905	10	21	17	4	6
Cook	.967	9	15	14	1	4
Hiraldo	.944	51	79	90	10	35
Jimenez	.977	12	16	26	1	7
Ray	.889	3	3	5	1	1
Rivas	.962	15	21	30	2	4
Schneider	1.000	1	1	1	0	0

Third Base	PCT	G	PO	A	E	DP
Barger	.875	13	6	22	4	3
Cardona	.923	6	5	7	1	1
Espino	1.000	2	2	4	0	0
Hiraldo	.843	37	18	57	14	7
Martinez	.813	12	6	20	6	3
Ray	.864	26	18	39	9	1
Schneider	1.000	1	0	2	0	1
Tirotta	.931	25	18	36	4	3

Shortstop	PCT	G	PO	A	E	DP
Barger	.905	27	25	51	8	8
Cardona	1.000	14	17	18	0	7

	PCT	G	PO	A	E	DP
Jimenez	.964	37	41	65	4	12
Martinez	.931	46	58	90	11	19
Rivas	1.000	1	2	4	0	2

Outfield	PCT	G	PO	A	E	DP
Ammons	1.000	21	43	1	0	0
Berroa	.981	79	142	9	3	2
Britton	1.000	8	3	0	0	0
Brown	.990	49	103	1	1	1
Cook	.980	25	43	5	1	0
Espino	1.000	1	3	0	0	0
Martinez	1.000	3	4	0	0	0
Mueller	.965	82	134	5	5	1
Palacios	--	2	0	0	0	0
Ray	.949	37	55	1	3	0
Rivera	1.000	6	13	1	0	0
Santiago	1.000	3	6	0	0	0
Solarte	.985	35	63	1	1	0
Sotolongo	1.000	2	3	0	0	0
Spain	1.000	17	28	2	0	1

FCL BLUE JAYS

FLORIDA COMPLEX LEAGUE

ROOKIE

Batting	B-T	HT	WT	DOB	AVG	vLH	vRH	G	AB	R	H	2B	3B	HR	RBI	BB	HBP	SH	SF	SO	SB	CS	SLG	OBP
Ammons, Justin	L-R	5-10	180	3-16-98	.308	.250	.333	15	26	9	8	3	0	0	3	5	1	0	0	8	3	0	.423	.438
Astudillo, Willfrann	R-R	5-10	165	8-5-01	.130	.400	.056	21	23	4	3	0	0	1	4	7	0	0	2	3	2	0	.261	.313
Brazoban, Amell	R-R	6-2	170	10-9-01	.317	.421	.293	38	101	24	32	11	3	2	20	14	2	0	1	28	8	5	.545	.407
Brito, Peniel	R-R	6-1	210	12-20-02	.200	.214	.197	30	75	12	15	6	0	0	9	22	2	0	0	28	0	1	.280	.394
Callez, Leonel	R-R	5-11	165	1-25-01	.333	--	.333	10	15	3	5	1	0	0	4	2	0	0	0	1	0	0	.400	.412
Cardona, Hugo	R-R	5-11	145	9-5-99	.167	.250	.125	6	12	3	2	0	1	0	4	3	1	0	0	2	1	3	.333	.375
De Castro, Rikelbin	R-R	6-0	150	1-23-03	.238	.268	.224	39	126	19	30	8	3	2	23	24	4	0	2	40	3	5	.397	.372
De La Rosa, Marcos	B-R	5-11	160	1-28-02	.197	.154	.207	29	71	13	14	2	1	0	7	10	3	0	0	26	11	6	.254	.321
Del Rosario, Angel	R-R	6-0	160	1-11-03	.241	.208	.250	41	116	29	28	2	0	1	10	15	6	0	1	28	27	2	.284	.355
Deschamps, Nicolas	L-R	5-11	180	8-25-02	.333	.000	.500	3	3	0	1	0	0	0	0	1	0	0	0	2	0	0	.333	.500
D'Orazio, J.J.	R-R	6-1	170	12-28-01	.370	.500	.324	15	46	10	17	1	1	1	9	3	0	0	1	15	0	0	.500	.400
Gonzalez, Juan	R-R	5-10	195	2-20-01	.176	.000	.200	16	34	3	6	1	1	0	6	4	2	0	2	7	0	1	.265	.286
Guzman, Darlin	L-L	6-1	165	9-27-00	.216	.000	.234	19	51	8	11	4	0	2	7	6	0	0	0	21	0	0	.412	.298
Jimenez, Leo	R-R	5-11	160	5-17-01	.385	.429	.333	5	13	6	5	2	0	0	2	3	4	0	0	1	1	0	.538	.600
Lundquist, Brock	L-R	5-11	190	1-23-96	.375	.000	.474	7	24	4	9	1	0	3	8	1	0	0	0	8	0	0	.792	.400
Machado, Estiven	B-R	5-10	170	10-4-02	1.000	1.000	--	1	1	0	1	0	0	0	0	0	0	0	0	0	0	0	1.000	1.000
Martinez, Gabriel	R-R	6-0	170	7-24-02	.330	.250	.350	31	100	16	33	8	0	0	14	21	2	0	2	18	7	2	.410	.448
Masson, J.C.	L-R	6-3	193	8-22-02	.283	.333	.270	15	46	10	13	4	0	2	12	8	0	0	1	25	2	1	.500	.382
Mesia, Victor	R-R	5-9	175	1-18-03	.288	.235	.310	21	59	15	17	5	0	2	14	6	3	0	2	12	0	0	.475	.371
Montero, Adrian	R-R	5-9	150	8-23-01	.350	.000	.412	12	20	2	7	0	1	0	5	2	1	0	1	3	0	0	.450	.417
Moreno, Gabriel	R-R	5-11	160	2-14-00	.750	--	.750	2	4	1	3	1	0	0	0	0	0	0	0	1	0	0	1.000	.750
Nunez, Rainer	R-R	6-3	180	12-4-00	.274	.333	.258	36	124	25	34	11	0	5	31	20	0	0	2	22	0	0	.484	.370
Palacios, Josh	L-R	6-1	198	7-30-95	.500	--	.500	2	4	2	2	1	0	0	2	4	0	0	0	0	1	0	.750	.750
Palmegiani, Damiano	R-R	6-1	195	1-24-00	.333	.500	.276	17	39	11	13	2	0	2	9	7	2	0	0	9	1	0	.538	.458
Perez, Yhon	R-R	5-9	150	5-5-00	.263	.250	.267	19	38	7	10	0	0	3	9	2	0	1	7	0	0	.263	.429
Pizarro, Juan	L-L	5-11	150	1-18-02	.111	.250	.000	2	9	1	1	0	0	0	1	1	0	0	0	3	0	0	.111	.200
Rivas, Jose	R-R	5-9	165	9-5-00	.321	.333	.317	23	53	21	17	3	2	0	10	20	5	0	0	10	4	0	.453	.538
Robertson, Will	L-L	6-2	215	12-26-97	.308	.500	.000	4	13	6	4	0	1	1	5	4	1	0	0	1	1	0	.692	.500
Rudd, Jaden	L-L	6-0	185	8-16-02	.218	.250	.209	20	55	11	12	4	0	1	8	11	4	0	0	14	5	1	.345	.386
Sanchez, Emmanuel	R-R	6-0	170	5-30-01	.255	.286	.247	33	102	11	26	4	0	0	11	4	1	0	0	23	2	3	.294	.290
Santiago, Glenn	R-R	6-0	165	12-14-00	.254	.176	.278	25	71	18	18	3	0	2	19	11	2	0	5	9	3	1	.380	.348
Schwecke, Trevor	R-R	6-1	185	12-18-97	.250	.000	.375	5	12	5	3	1	0	0	3	5	2	0	0	5	2	0	.333	.526
Smith, Mallex	L-R	5-10	180	5-6-93	.200	.000	.214	6	15	6	3	1	0	0	3	7	1	0	0	4	1	0	.267	.478
Solarte, Jhon	B-R	6-0	165	12-9-00	.196	.087	.232	34	92	22	18	4	0	1	14	20	3	0	2	35	11	1	.272	.350
Sosa, Andres	R-R	5-11	210	11-7-97	.333	.250	.400	9	9	1	3	1	0	0	1	0	2	0	0	3	0	0	.444	.455
Sotolongo, Adriel	R-R	6-3	208	4-22-98	.386	.217	.450	27	83	22	32	4	0	7	28	12	1	0	1	21	1	1	.687	.464
Spain, Garrett	L-R	5-11	178	9-21-00	.333	.000	.444	6	12	1	4	1	0	0	0	1	0	0	2	0	0	0	.417	.385

Pitching	B-T	HT	WT	DOB	W	L	ERA	G	GS	CG	SV	IP	H	R	ER	HR	BB	SO	AVG	vLH	vRH	K/9	BB/9
Alvarado, Wilgenis	L-L	6-1	160	5-18-00	3	3	8.04	9	0	0	0	16	15	18	14	0	14	14	.238	.462	.180	8.04	8.04
Axford, John	R-R	6-5	234	4-1-83	0	0	0.00	1	1	0	0	1	1	0	0	0	0	1	.250	.000	.500	9.00	0.00
Ayala, Cesar	R-R	6-2	180	2-17-03	1	3	9.35	11	6	0	2	26	37	30	27	8	20	30	.343	.393	.325	10.38	6.92
Bernal, Jonatan	R-R	6-1	194	6-29-02	0	3	4.43	12	9	0	0	43	56	32	21	6	12	35	.315	.326	.311	7.38	2.53
Burnette, Jimmy	L-L	6-2	205	10-19-98	0	1	15.43	3	0	0	0	2	5	4	4	0	2	2	.417	1.000	.364	7.71	7.71
Casimiri, Jiorgeny	R-R	6-1	160	7-12-01	2	1	1.35	11	0	0	0	13	9	3	2	1	8	19	.184	.125	.212	12.83	5.40
Castro, Edgar	R-R	6-1	165	2-7-02	1	2	6.38	15	1	0	0	24	23	18	17	4	14	25	.264	.143	.303	9.38	5.25
Civit, Marc	L-L	6-0	150	6-23-02	3	1	8.64	12	0	0	0	17	16	19	16	2	19	17	.254	.100	.283	9.18	10.26
Cole, A.J.	R-R	6-5	240	1-5-92	0	0	9.00	1	1	0	0	1	1	1	1	0	1	1	.333	1.000	.000	9.00	9.00
Cooke, Connor	R-R	6-1	203	11-2-99	0	0	4.50	2	0	0	0	2	2	1	1	1	1	2	.286	--	.286	9.00	4.50
Dominguez, Michael	R-R	5-10	175	8-17-00	0	2	5.00	4	0	0	0	9	13	5	5	2	2	13	.333	.313	.348	13.00	2.00
Dykstra, James	L-R	6-3	207	11-22-90	1	0	18.00	2	1	0	0	2	5	4	4	1	0	2	.455	.750	.286	9.00	0.00
Edwards Jr., Carl	R-R	6-3	170	9-3-91	0	0	0.00	1	1	0	0	1	0	0	0	0	0	2	.000	--	.000	18.00	0.00
Garcia, Winder	R-R	5-10	165	10-11-01	0	0	9.00	2	0	0	0	3	5	3	3	1	0	1	.385	.200	.500	0.00	3.00
Hiciano, Jeury	R-R	5-11	160	2-22-00	0	0	6.75	8	0	0	2	8	14	10	6	1	5	9	.389	.333	.400	10.13	5.63
Jimenez, Emerson	L-R	6-1	160	12-16-94	0	0	3.00	2	0	0	0	3	2	1	1	0	1	4	.222	.500	.000	12.00	3.00
Lara, Yunior	R-R	6-1	150	1-28-01	0	0	17.18	4	0	0	0	4	7	7	7	0	5	5	.412	.000	.500	12.27	12.27
Laws, Colton	R-R	6-7	230	11-20-95	0	0	0.00	5	4	0	0	5	2	0	0	0	5	7	.118	.222	.000	9.00	9.00
Lebron, Jackxarel	R-R	6-3	175	9-8-00	0	0	36.00	2	0	0	0	1	4	4	4	1	5	2	.333	1.000	.000	18.00	45.00
Martinez, Soenni	L-L	6-0	180	5-26-01	1	0	2.21	15	1	0	1	20	14	5	5	0	10	25	.189	.077	.213	11.07	4.43
Medrano, Elieser	R-R	6-2	180	8-17-98	1	2	9.26	11	0	0	0	12	10	13	12	0	13	9	.238	.222	.242	6.94	10.03
Mejia, Brayan	R-R	6-2	165	6-11-00	1	0	7.36	13	0	0	0	15	10	12	12	0	16	9	.200	.357	.139	5.52	9.82
Merryweather, Julian	R-R	6-4	215	10-14-91	0	0	0.00	1	1	0	0	1	0	0	0	0	0	1	.000	--	.000	9.00	0.00
Meza, Bejardi	R-R	5-11	145	11-16-00	1	2	4.50	10	1	0	0	22	22	13	11	4	14	20	.272	.190	.300	8.18	5.73
Murray, Joey	L-R	6-2	195	9-23-96	0	1	27.00	1	0	0	0	1	2	2	1	2	1	3	.333	--	.333	13.50	27.00
Ohashi, Rafael	R-R	6-1	185	10-8-02	1	2	4.09	5	0	0	0	11	5	6	5	1	7	15	.135	.059	.200	12.27	5.73
Pardinho, Eric	R-R	5-10	155	1-5-01	0	0	0.00	2	0	0	0	3	1	0	0	0	4	4	.111	.000	.143	12.00	0.00
Perdomo, Yaifer	L-L	5-10	160	8-16-01	2	0	2.45	8	7	0	0	33	19	11	9	1	14	59	.162	.222	.152	16.09	3.82
Perez, Kelvin	R-R	6-3	175	9-9-00	4	1	6.00	15	0	0	0	21	18	15	14	4	9	17	.225	.318	.190	7.29	3.86
Rojas, Kendry	L-L	6-2	190	11-26-02	0	0	2.28	8	4	0	0	24	14	6	6	1	5	39	.171	.143	.176	14.83	1.90
Rosario, Tony	R-R	6-4	192	12-14-97	0	0	2.45	4	1	0	1	4	0	1	1	0	10	5	.000	.000	.000	12.27	24.55
Santos, Dahian	R-R	5-11	165	2-26-03	1	2	4.58	10	7	0	0	35	30	20	18	5	12	53	.224	.208	.233	13.50	3.06
Urbaez, Geison	R-R	6-1	180	7-5-00	0	2	5.40	7	3	0	0	22	21	13	13	2	6	22	.253	.080	.328	9.14	2.49
Vargas, Stephen	R-R	5-10	168	2-12-02	0	0	7.11	13	0	0	0	13	10	11	10	2	15	11	.213	.400	.162	7.82	10.66
Villasmil, Guillermo	R-R	5-10	160	9-13-02	2	1	7.36	11	0	0	0	15	18	14	12	2	9	11	.300	.294	.302	6.75	5.52

Fielding

C: Astudillo 19, Callez 9, Deschamps 2, D'Orazio 15, Gonzalez 16, Mesia 21, Moreno 2, Sosa 8.
1B: Brito 14, Nunez 28, Sanchez 12, Santiago 3, Schwecke 1, Sotolongo 6.
2B: De Castro 6, De La Rosa 7, Del Rosario 20, Machado 1, Montero 9, Perez 9, Rivas 18, Santiago 1, Schwecke 1.
3B: Brito 13, Cardona 1, Del Rosario 8, Palmegiani 16, Perez 1, Rivas 1, Sanchez 19, Santiago 7, Schwecke 3, Sotolongo 1.
SS: Cardona 3, De Castro 33, Del Rosario 13, Jimenez 3, Sanchez 2, Santiago 6.
OF: Ammons 13, Astudillo 1, Brazoban 35, Cardona 3, De La Rosa 23, Del Rosario 1, Guzman 14, Lundquist 6, Martinez 28, Palacios 2, Perez 10, Pizarro 2, Rivas 3, Robertson 3, Rudd 20, Santiago 8, Smith 5, Solarte 35, Sotolongo 9, Spain 5.

DSL BLUE JAYS   ROOKIE
DOMINICAN SUMMER LEAGUE

Batting	B-T	HT	WT	DOB	AVG	vLH	vRH	G	AB	R	H	2B	3B	HR	RBI	BB	HBP	SH	SF	SO	SB	CS	SLG	OBP
Aponte, Yhoangel	R-R	5-11	190	2-12-04	.240	.158	.255	38	129	25	31	9	3	0	18	25	8	0	1	44	5	4	.357	.393
Arias, Victor	L-L	5-11	150	8-24-03	.248	.231	.250	35	109	18	27	4	0	2	13	24	1	0	0	32	5	3	.339	.388
Arnaez, Jean	R-R	5-10	160	8-22-02	.254	.250	.255	24	59	10	15	0	1	0	10	10	2	0	2	10	2	0	.288	.370
Beltre, Manuel	R-R	5-9	155	6-9-04	.225	.200	.230	53	182	39	41	10	3	2	29	42	10	0	4	33	10	4	.346	.391
Bullon, Luis	L-R	5-9	165	12-14-01	.143	.333	.111	9	21	4	3	0	0	0	3	5	0	0	0	3	0	0	.143	.308
David, Gary	R-R	6-0	170	11-23-01	.190	.000	.211	9	21	3	4	0	0	1	5	4	0	0	0	7	0	0	.333	.320
Fajardo, Francisco	B-R	5-10	163	5-26-00	.365	.308	.376	51	167	42	61	7	4	1	15	19	5	3	0	12	30	7	.473	.445
Feliz, Cristian	L-L	6-4	190	9-7-02	.291	.280	.294	44	151	29	44	7	0	4	30	18	8	0	1	49	2	1	.417	.393
Garcia, Endri	R-R	6-0	163	11-9-02	.315	.227	.333	45	124	31	39	10	0	2	23	15	8	0	1	29	4	5	.444	.419
Garcia, Luis	R-R	5-9	160	9-1-03	.307	.174	.333	36	137	26	42	10	0	0	15	13	2	0	0	20	12	3	.380	.375
Gimenez, Martin	R-R	5-11	155	2-15-04	.225	.174	.235	39	142	15	32	4	0	0	13	13	3	0	0	50	6	1	.254	.304
Hernandez, Jommer	R-R	5-11	181	10-20-00	.179	.000	.206	15	39	4	7	2	0	0	3	6	1	0	1	9	1	0	.231	.298
Munoz, Yeuni	R-R	6-1	190	10-4-03	.260	.222	.265	44	150	26	39	14	1	1	30	24	3	0	5	55	4	4	.387	.363
Oliva, Daniel	R-R	6-0	180	9-14-01	.103	.000	.143	12	29	7	3	1	0	0	3	9	2	0	0	14	2	1	.138	.350
Peguero, Jonathan	L-R	5-11	165	7-23-04	.266	.273	.265	33	94	15	25	4	0	2	14	16	2	0	0	19	3	2	.372	.384
Perez, Wilder	R-R	5-9	185	1-8-02	.143	.125	.154	10	21	2	3	0	0	0	0	2	0	0	0	6	0	0	.143	.217
Robertis, Robert	L-L	5-11	188	11-29-02	.266	.412	.243	39	128	19	34	5	1	1	19	12	2	0	2	24	7	3	.344	.333
Veracierto, Francisco	R-R	5-11	160	1-29-02	.190	.250	.176	9	21	2	4	0	0	0	2	1	0	1	0	6	0	1	.190	.346
Yege, Leafar	B-R	5-9	160	7-15-02	.233	.000	.278	23	43	8	10	0	0	0	4	9	1	0	0	10	0	2	.233	.377

Pitching	B-T	HT	WT	DOB	W	L	ERA	G	GS	CG	SV	IP	H	R	ER	HR	BB	SO	AVG	vLH	vRH	K/9	BB/9
Acosta, Pedro	R-R	6-2	155	12-21-01	4	2	5.09	12	0	0	2	18	16	11	10	0	12	19	.235	.192	.262	9.68	6.11
Alcalde, Eliander	R-R	5-9	171	8-9-03	3	4	2.93	14	13	0	0	61	43	23	20	2	32	60	.205	.110	.255	8.80	4.70
Caruci, Sergio	R-R	6-2	155	10-12-02	0	0	2.84	16	10	0	0	51	38	17	16	4	15	61	.203	.242	.167	10.84	2.66
Castro, Cristopher	L-L	6-1	150	8-17-02	0	1	0.87	4	4	0	0	10	3	1	1	1	9	16	.086	.000	.107	13.94	7.84
Cruz, Darwin	R-R	6-0	190	9-11-01	3	1	2.22	13	12	0	0	53	50	21	13	3	15	46	.249	.234	.255	7.86	2.56
De Jesus, Robin	R-R	6-0	160	9-28-02	2	2	8.78	12	0	0	0	13	12	13	13	2	18	15	.235	.500	.171	10.13	12.15
Hiciano, Jeury	R-R	5-11	160	2-22-00	0	0	1.42	5	0	0	0	6	5	4	1	0	4	5	.192	.167	.214	7.11	5.68
Jimenez, Brahiam	L-L	6-0	165	12-10-01	2	0	2.40	9	0	0	1	15	13	7	4	0	6	18	.232	.267	.220	10.80	3.60
Leon, Keiner	R-R	5-11	190	10-29-03	7	1	2.60	19	0	0	1	35	31	11	10	4	11	39	.244	.231	.253	10.13	2.86
Lopez, Jean	R-R	6-0	170	10-18-02	4	1	5.00	16	0	0	3	36	38	26	20	3	17	31	.262	.254	.268	7.75	4.25
Medina, Frank	R-R	5-11	164	10-28-00	1	1	6.23	13	0	0	2	13	15	10	9	2	13	19	.300	.273	.308	13.15	9.00
Mercedes, Francis	R-R	5-11	200	3-5-00	2	1	3.86	17	0	0	1	23	18	12	10	1	11	22	.220	.294	.167	8.49	4.24
Munoz, Pedro	L-L	5-9	150	7-29-04	0	0	8.22	8	0	0	0	8	8	7	7	2	11	8	.267	.333	.250	9.39	12.91
Obeso, Neiyerbe	R-R	6-1	174	1-9-04	4	0	5.79	10	0	0	1	14	13	12	9	1	19	6	.265	.238	.286	3.86	12.21
Ochoa, Gabriel	R-R	5-11	173	8-16-02	0	0	5.02	14	1	0	0	14	10	12	8	0	22	16	.204	.130	.269	10.05	13.81
Perez, Nathanael	R-R	5-10	159	4-2-01	2	0	4.12	12	2	0	1	20	15	11	9	2	9	10	.214	.111	.279	4.58	4.12
Rojas, Yondrei	R-R	5-10	180	11-22-02	0	1	2.95	16	0	0	7	21	25	11	7	0	9	27	.298	.259	.316	11.39	3.80
Santana, Angel	R-R	6-2	155	5-17-02	1	2	4.91	13	5	0	1	22	19	14	12	0	17	14	.241	.240	.241	5.73	6.95
Simon, Johan	L-L	6-1	166	7-1-01	3	1	3.74	7	5	0	0	22	17	11	9	1	7	25	.221	.133	.242	10.38	2.91
Villasmil, Guillermo	R-R	5-10	160	9-13-02	0	1	4.15	6	5	0	0	17	11	8	8	1	7	12	.183	.217	.162	6.23	3.63

Fielding

C: Arnaez 1, Bullon 9, David 8, Hernandez 15, Peguero 31, Perez 6, Yege 1.
1B: Arnaez 15, Fajardo 13, Feliz 24, Perez 4, Veracierto 6.
2B: Arnaez 1, Beltre 8, Fajardo 35, Garcia 11, Veracierto 1, Yege 7.
3B: Arnaez 4, Fajardo 2, Garcia 18, Gimenez 31, Veracierto 1, Yege 7.
SS: Arnaez 2, Beltre 44, Garcia 5, Gimenez 7, Veracierto 1.
OF: Aponte 29, Arias 32, Feliz 8, Garcia 40, Munoz 41, Oliva 8, Robertis 28, Yege 3.

Washington Nationals

SEASON IN A SENTENCE: The Nationals got off to a sluggish start for the third season in a row, this time ultimately resulting in a sell-off of assets at the trade deadline and a last-place finish in the National League East with a 65-97 record.

HIGH POINT: After poor showings in April and May, the Nationals went 19-9 in June, their best month since August 2019, pushing their record to 40-38 and climbing to within two games of the division lead at month's end. The stretch included a four-game winning streak and two five-game winning streaks.

LOW POINT: After the heady days of June led to a July swoon that ended with an 8-18 record for the month, the Nationals traded franchise cornerstones Max Scherzer and Trea Turner to the Dodgers on July 30, signaling the end of an era for a club two years removed from a World Series title and coming off of a solid decade of competing for division titles.

NOTABLE ROOKIES: Midseason trades provided a solid handful of promising rookie performances over the second half of the season. Righthander Josiah Gray, who came over as part of the return for Scherzer and Turner, jumped into the rotation as soon as he arrived in Washington and started 12 games. He had some ups and downs but finished the season strong, setting himself up to be a key cog in 2022. The top prospect in that same trade, catcher Keibert Ruiz, played well in a smaller sample, hitting .284/.348/.395. Righthander Mason Thompson, who arrived in the deadline deal that sent Daniel Hudson to the Padres, had a 4.15 ERA in 27 games as a reliever.

KEY TRANSACTIONS: On July 29 and 30, the Nationals traded a total of eight veterans in return for 12 players, many of whom either became immediate contributors on the big league club or top prospects in the minor league system. The biggest deal sent Scherzer and Turner to Los Angeles in return for Ruiz, Gray, righthander Gerardo Carrillo and outfielder Donovan Casey, all four of whom either ended the season in the big leagues or are knocking on the doorstep heading into 2022. Outfielder Lane Thomas quickly became a mainstay after arriving from the Cardinals in a deal for Jon Lester.

OPENING DAY SALARY: $161,907,528 (9th).

PLAYERS OF THE YEAR

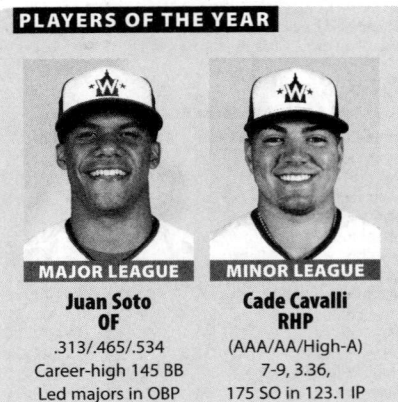

MAJOR LEAGUE	MINOR LEAGUE
Juan Soto	**Cade Cavalli**
OF	RHP
.313/.465/.534	(AAA/AA/High-A)
Career-high 145 BB	7-9, 3.36,
Led majors in OBP	175 SO in 123.1 IP

ORGANIZATION LEADERS

Batting		*Minimum 250 AB
MAJORS		
*AVG	Trea Turner	.322
*OPS	Juan Soto	.999
HR	Juan Soto	29
RBI	Juan Soto	95
MINORS		
*AVG	Jake Noll, Rochester	.300
*OBP	Daniel Palka, Rochester	.364
*SLG	Jake Noll, Rochester	.494
*OPS	Jake Noll, Rochester	.840
R	Armond Upshaw, Harrisburg, Wilmington	63
H	Jake Noll, Rochester	131
TB	Jake Noll, Rochester	216
2B	Jake Noll, Rochester	28
2B	Jacob Rhinesmith, Harrisburg, Wilmington	28
3B	Armond Upshaw, Harrisburg, Wilmington	7
HR	Daniel Palka, Rochester	18
RBI	Jake Noll, Rochester	69
BB	Daniel Palka, Rochester	61
SO	Drew Mendoza, Harrisburg, Wilmington	125
SB	Armond Upshaw, Harrisburg, Wilmington	29

Pitching		#Minimum 75 IP
MAJORS		
W	Patrick Corbin	9
#ERA	Max Scherzer	2.76
SO	Max Scherzer	147
SV	Brad Hand	21
MINORS		
W	Alex Troop, Harrisburg, Wilmington	8
L	Mitchell Parker, Wilmington, Fredericksburg	12
L	Karlo Seijas, Fredericksburg	12
#ERA	Alex Troop, Harrisburg, Wilmington	3.35
G	Jhon Romero, Rochester, Harrisburg	38
GS	Cade Cavalli, Rochester, Harrisburg, Wilmington	24
GS	Luis Reyes, Rochester, Harrisburg	24
SV	Frankie Bartow, Harrisburg	10
IP	Luis Reyes, Rochester, Harrisburg	126.2
BB	Ben Braymer, Rochester	60
BB	Cade Cavalli, Rochester, Harrisburg, Wilmington	60
SO	Cade Cavalli, Rochester, Harrisburg, Wilmington	175
#AVG	Cade Cavalli, Rochester, Harrisburg, Wilmington	.213

2021 PERFORMANCE

General Manager: Mike Rizzo. **Farm Director:** Mark Harris. **Scouting Director:** Kris Kline.

Class	Team	League	W	L	PCT	Finish	Manager
Majors	Washington Nationals	National	65	97	.401	13th (15)	Dave Martinez
Triple-A	Rochester Red Wings	Triple-A East	49	77	.389	19th (20)	Matthew LeCroy
Double-A	Harrisburg Senators	Double-A Northeast	42	76	.356	11th (12)	Tripp Keister
High-A	Wilmington Blue Rocks	High-A East	52	64	.448	9th (12)	Tommy Shields
Low-A	Fredericksburg Nationals	Low-A East	44	76	.367	11th (12)	Mario Lisson
Rookie	DSL Nationals	Dominican Summer	34	25	.576	t-13th (46)	Sandy Martinez
Rookie	FCL Nationals	Florida Complex	26	30	.464	9th (18)	Jake Lowery
Overall 2021 Minor League Record			247	348	.415	28th (30)	

ORGANIZATION STATISTICS

WASHINGTON NATIONALS
NATIONAL LEAGUE

Batting	B-T	HT	WT	DOB	AVG	vLH	vRH	G	AB	R	H	2B	3B	HR	RBI	BB	HBP	SH	SF	SO	SB	CS	SLG	OBP
Adams, Riley	R-R	6-4	246	6-26-96	.268	.222	.295	35	71	11	19	6	1	2	10	13	6	0	0	28	0	0	.465	.422
Arteaga, Humberto	R-R	6-1	160	1-23-94	.000	.000	.000	1	3	0	0	0	0	0	1	0	0	0	1	0	0	0	.000	.000
Avila, Alex	L-R	5-11	228	1-29-87	.191	.067	.216	34	89	5	17	9	1	1	9	19	2	1	0	37	0	0	.348	.345
Barrera, Tres	R-R	6-0	206	9-15-94	.264	.455	.203	30	91	8	24	3	1	2	10	12	4	0	0	22	0	0	.385	.374
Bell, Josh	B-R	6-4	255	8-14-92	.261	.245	.268	144	498	75	130	24	1	27	88	65	2	0	3	101	0	0	.476	.347
Castro, Starlin	R-R	6-2	218	3-24-90	.283	.349	.259	87	315	25	89	20	0	3	38	26	0	0	4	62	0	1	.375	.333
Escobar, Alcides	R-R	6-1	205	12-16-86	.288	.280	.292	75	319	53	92	21	2	4	28	17	9	2	2	56	3	0	.404	.340
Garcia, Luis	L-R	6-2	224	5-16-00	.242	.297	.221	70	236	29	57	18	2	6	22	11	0	0	0	43	0	2	.411	.275
Gomes, Yan	R-R	6-2	212	7-19-87	.271	.365	.232	63	218	30	59	11	1	9	35	13	4	0	0	47	0	0	.454	.323
Harrison, Josh	R-R	5-8	190	7-8-87	.294	.308	.289	90	320	39	94	23	2	6	38	25	12	0	1	50	5	2	.434	.366
Hernandez, Yadiel	L-R	5-10	188	10-9-87	.273	.300	.261	112	264	33	72	8	1	9	32	22	1	0	2	59	3	0	.413	.329
Kieboom, Carter	R-R	6-2	215	9-3-97	.207	.178	.222	62	217	26	45	6	0	6	20	25	5	0	2	62	0	0	.318	.301
Lucroy, Jonathan	R-R	6-0	200	6-13-86	.357	.300	.500	5	14	0	5	1	0	0	2	0	0	0	0	2	0	0	.429	.357
2-team total (2 Atlanta)					.316	.273	.375	7	19	2	6	1	0	0	3	3	0	1	0	4	0	0	.368	.409
Mercer, Jordy	R-R	6-3	210	8-27-86	.254	.304	.222	46	118	13	30	7	0	2	9	9	0	0	0	34	0	0	.364	.307
Parra, Gerardo	L-L	5-11	210	5-6-87	.237	.158	.256	53	97	13	23	5	0	2	10	6	2	1	1	30	1	1	.351	.292
Perez, Hernan	R-R	6-1	213	3-26-91	.053	.083	.000	10	19	1	1	0	0	0	0	2	0	0	0	10	0	0	.053	.143
Reetz, Jakson	R-R	6-0	205	1-3-96	.500	--	.500	2	2	1	1	0	0	0	0	0	0	0	0	0	0	0	1.000	.500
Rivera, Rene	R-R	5-10	215	7-31-83	.214	.200	.222	4	14	2	3	0	0	0	0	0	1	0	0	5	0	0	.214	.267
Robles, Victor	R-R	6-0	205	5-19-97	.203	.176	.214	107	315	37	64	21	1	2	19	33	16	4	1	85	8	6	.295	.310
Ruiz, Keibert	B-R	6-0	225	7-20-98	.284	.370	.241	23	81	9	23	3	0	2	14	6	2	0	0	4	0	0	.395	.348
2-team total (6 Los Angeles)					.273	.357	.233	29	88	10	24	3	0	3	15	6	2	0	0	9	0	0	.409	.333
Sanchez, Adrian	R-R	6-0	208	8-16-90	.257	.125	.296	16	35	5	9	2	0	0	1	3	0	0	0	4	0	0	.314	.316
Schwarber, Kyle	L-R	6-0	229	3-5-93	.253	.240	.258	72	265	42	67	9	0	25	53	31	5	0	2	88	1	1	.570	.340
Soto, Juan	L-L	6-2	224	10-25-98	.313	.280	.333	151	502	111	157	20	2	29	95	145	2	0	5	93	9	7	.534	.465
Stevenson, Andrew	L-L	6-0	192	6-1-94	.229	.214	.232	109	192	22	44	6	0	5	23	13	5	2	1	61	1	1	.339	.294
Thomas, Lane	R-R	6-0	185	8-23-95	.270	.417	.215	45	178	33	48	14	2	7	27	27	0	0	1	46	4	2	.489	.364
2-team total (32 St. Louis)					.235	.381	.178	77	226	35	53	15	2	7	28	37	0	0	1	63	6	3	.412	.341
Turner, Trea	R-R	6-2	185	6-30-93	.322	.406	.293	96	388	66	125	17	3	18	49	26	4	0	2	77	21	3	.521	.369
2-team total (52 Los Angeles)					.328	.392	.305	148	595	107	195	34	3	28	77	41	6	0	4	110	32	5	.536	.375
Wilson, Cody	R-R	6-2	200	7-4-96	.000	--	.000	1	0	0	0	0	0	0	0	0	0	0	0	0	0	0	.000	.000
Zimmerman, Ryan	R-R	6-3	215	9-28-84	.243	.291	.207	110	255	27	62	16	0	14	46	16	0	0	2	77	0	0	.471	.286

Pitching	B-T	HT	WT	DOB	W	L	ERA	G	GS	CG	SV	IP	H	R	ER	HR	BB	SO	AVG	vLH	vRH	K/9	BB/9
Adon, Joan	R-R	6-2	242	8-12-98	0	0	3.38	1	1	0	0	5	6	2	2	1	3	9	.300	.500	.167	15.19	5.06
Avilan, Luis	L-L	6-2	220	7-19-89	0	1	12.60	4	0	0	0	5	7	7	7	1	3	4	.333	.333	.333	7.20	5.40
Baldonado, Alberto	L-L	6-4	250	2-1-93	0	1	8.44	14	0	0	0	11	10	10	10	3	7	12	.244	.273	.211	10.13	5.91
Clay, Sam	L-L	6-3	227	6-21-93	0	5	5.60	58	0	0	0	45	55	32	28	4	22	34	.296	.250	.333	6.80	4.40
Corbin, Patrick	L-L	6-4	220	7-19-89	9	16	5.82	31	31	0	0	172	192	114	111	37	60	143	.286	.228	.302	7.50	3.15
Espino, Paolo	R-R	5-10	215	1-10-87	5	5	4.27	35	19	0	1	110	108	53	52	19	25	92	.256	.280	.230	7.55	2.05
Fedde, Erick	R-R	6-4	200	2-25-93	7	9	5.47	29	27	0	0	133	144	90	81	23	48	128	.275	.290	.258	8.64	3.24
Finnegan, Kyle	R-R	6-2	220	9-4-91	5	9	3.55	68	0	0	11	66	64	39	26	9	34	68	.251	.207	.288	9.27	4.64
Gray, Josiah	R-R	6-1	190	12-21-97	2	2	5.31	12	12	0	0	63	56	38	37	15	28	63	.238	.227	.248	9.05	4.02
2-team total (2 Los Angeles)					2	2	5.48	14	13	0	0	71	63	44	43	19	33	76	.238	.221	.252	9.68	4.20
Guerra, Javy	R-R	6-1	215	10-31-85	0	1	16.50	6	0	0	0	6	12	13	11	3	3	4	.429	.667	.250	6.00	4.50
Hand, Brad	L-L	6-3	224	3-20-90	5	5	3.59	41	0	0	21	43	31	22	17	5	18	42	.203	.216	.198	8.86	3.80
2-team total (16 New York)					6	5	3.38	57	0	0	21	56	43	29	21	6	23	56	.214	.230	.207	9.00	3.70
Harper, Ryne	R-R	6-3	217	3-27-89	0	2	4.04	34	0	0	0	36	28	16	16	6	14	31	.214	.258	.174	7.82	3.53
Harris, Will	R-R	6-4	236	8-28-84	0	1	9.00	8	0	0	0	6	7	6	6	1	5	9	.100	.353	13.50	4.50	
Hudson, Daniel	R-R	6-3	215	3-9-87	4	1	2.20	31	0	0	0	33	23	9	8	4	7	48	.195	.240	.162	13.22	1.93
2-team total (23 San Diego)					5	3	3.31	54	0	0	0	52	40	22	19	8	16	75	.211	.256	.179	13.06	2.79
Klobosits, Gabe	L-R	6-7	270	5-16-95	0	1	5.56	11	0	0	0	11	13	8	7	0	5	5	.283	.222	.368	3.97	3.97

Name	B-T	HT	WT	DOB	W	L	ERA	G	GS	CG	SV	IP	H	R	ER	HR	BB	SO	AVG	vLH	vRH	K/9	BB/9
Lester, Jon	L-L	6-4	249	1-7-84	3	5	5.02	16	16	0	0	75	91	50	42	14	29	51	.297	.224	.318	6.09	3.46
2-team total (12 St. Louis)					7	6	4.71	28	28	0	0	141	159	84	74	25	55	91	.285	.246	.295	5.79	3.50
Lobstein, Kyle	L-L	6-3	220	8-12-89	0	0	20.25	3	0	0	0	1	3	3	3	1	1	1	.429	.000	.600	6.75	6.75
Machado, Andres	R-R	6-0	220	4-22-93	1	2	3.53	40	0	0	0	36	30	17	14	4	15	30	.226	.200	.247	7.57	3.79
McGowin, Kyle	R-R	6-3	202	11-27-91	0	0	4.20	27	0	0	0	30	21	14	14	5	14	35	.188	.222	.155	10.50	4.20
Miller, Justin	R-R	6-3	225	6-13-87	0	0	15.00	5	0	0	0	3	5	5	5	3	1	4	.385	.400	.375	12.00	3.00
2-team total (18 St. Louis)					1	0	6.16	23	0	0	1	19	20	13	13	5	6	13	.278	.250	.295	6.16	2.84
Murphy, Patrick	R-R	6-5	235	6-10-95	0	2	5.30	17	0	0	0	19	19	12	11	2	6	23	.250	.243	.256	11.09	2.89
Nolin, Sean	L-L	6-4	250	12-26-89	0	2	4.39	10	5	0	0	27	32	13	13	4	13	20	.302	.297	.304	6.75	4.39
Perez, Hernan	R-R	6-1	213	3-26-91	0	0	0.00	2	0	0	0	2	1	0	0	0	0	2	.143	.250	.000	9.00	0.00
Rainey, Tanner	R-R	6-2	247	12-25-92	1	3	7.39	38	0	0	3	32	29	27	26	6	25	42	.238	.212	.257	11.94	7.11
Rodriguez, Jefry	R-R	6-6	232	7-26-93	0	0	5.92	14	1	0	0	24	25	16	16	6	17	20	.266	.250	.280	7.40	6.29
Rogers, Josh	L-L	6-3	210	7-10-94	2	2	3.28	6	6	0	0	36	32	13	13	7	14	22	.241	.143	.286	5.55	3.53
Romero, Jhon	R-R	5-10	195	1-17-95	0	0	4.50	5	0	0	0	4	5	2	2	0	4	5	.313	.333	.300	6.75	0.00
Ross, Joe	R-R	6-4	223	5-21-93	5	9	4.17	20	19	0	0	108	98	57	50	17	34	109	.237	.254	.222	9.08	2.83
Scherzer, Max	R-R	6-3	208	7-27-84	8	4	2.76	19	19	1	0	111	71	36	34	18	28	147	.182	.164	.198	11.92	2.27
2-team total (11 Los Angeles)					15	4	2.46	30	30	1	0	179	119	53	49	23	36	236	.185	.192	.177	11.84	1.81
Strasburg, Stephen	R-R	6-5	240	7-20-88	1	2	4.57	5	5	0	0	22	16	12	11	4	14	21	.200	.294	.130	8.72	5.82
Suero, Wander	R-R	6-4	216	9-15-91	2	3	6.33	45	0	0	0	43	45	35	30	11	15	44	.266	.273	.261	9.28	3.16
Thompson, Mason	R-R	6-7	223	2-20-98	1	3	4.15	27	0	0	0	22	28	14	10	4	14	21	.308	.219	.356	8.72	5.82
2-team total (4 San Diego)					1	3	4.01	31	0	0	0	25	32	15	11	4	15	23	.311	.222	.358	8.39	5.47
Voth, Austin	R-R	6-2	211	6-26-92	4	1	5.34	49	1	0	0	57	57	35	34	10	28	59	.266	.267	.265	9.26	4.40

Fielding

Catcher	PCT	G	PO	A	E	DP	PB
Adams	1.000	23	159	13	0	0	0
Avila	.996	27	235	9	1	3	0
Barrera	.992	29	222	12	2	2	2
Gomes	.989	61	494	37	6	3	2
Lucroy	1.000	4	34	0	0	0	1
Reetz	1.000	1	4	0	0	0	0
Rivera	.925	4	32	5	3	0	0
Ruiz	.995	21	178	13	1	1	0

First Base	PCT	G	PO	A	E	DP
Bell	.994	119	819	73	5	71
Mercer	1.000	2	2	0	0	0
Perez	1.000	2	3	1	0	0
Zimmerman	1.000	54	338	15	0	30

Second Base	PCT	G	PO	A	E	DP
Avila	1.000	1	1	1	0	0

(Second Base)	PCT	G	PO	A	E	DP
Escobar	1.000	18	28	43	0	10
Garcia	.962	59	88	115	8	23
Harrison	.980	70	110	141	5	36
Mercer	.941	21	22	42	4	10
Perez	1.000	3	2	1	0	0
Sanchez	1.000	9	14	29	0	5
Thomas	1.000	1	0	1	0	0

Third Base	PCT	G	PO	A	E	DP
Castro	.946	85	52	157	12	17
Harrison	.913	11	7	14	2	1
Kieboom	.958	60	39	98	6	7
Mercer	.926	14	7	18	2	1
Sanchez	1.000	2	1	3	0	0

Shortstop	PCT	G	PO	A	E	DP
Arteaga	1.000	1	2	0	0	0
Castro	1.000	1	0	1	0	0
Escobar	.969	61	97	121	7	23
Garcia	.920	8	10	13	2	3
Mercer	1.000	6	2	3	0	0
Turner	.968	95	105	223	11	40

Outfield	PCT	G	PO	A	E	DP
Bell	1.000	10	8	0	0	0
Harrison	.913	20	21	0	2	0
Hernandez	.992	61	117	1	1	1
Mercer	--	1	0	0	0	0
Parra	.957	30	44	0	2	0
Perez	1.000	2	3	0	0	0
Robles	1.000	104	215	5	0	1
Sanchez	--	1	0	0	0	0
Schwarber	.977	72	127	3	3	1
Soto	.980	144	295	5	6	1
Stevenson	.979	66	94	1	2	0
Thomas	.978	45	81	6	2	1

ROCHESTER RED WINGS — TRIPLE-A
TRIPLE-A EAST

Batting	B-T	HT	WT	DOB	AVG	vLH	vRH	G	AB	R	H	2B	3B	HR	RBI	BB	HBP	SH	SF	SO	SB	CS	SLG	OBP
Adams, Riley	R-R	6-4	246	6-26-96	.000	.000	.000	1	3	0	0	0	0	0	0	2	0	0	0	0	0	0	.000	.400
2-team total (35 Buffalo)					.233	.171	.259	36	120	20	28	6	1	7	18	9	0	1	46	0	0	.475	.372
Arteaga, Humberto	R-R	6-1	160	1-23-94	.172	.192	.166	63	209	15	36	4	1	2	11	8	1	1	0	56	2	0	.230	.206
Banks, Nick	L-L	6-0	215	11-18-94	.189	.286	.154	32	106	10	20	4	0	3	10	12	0	0	0	35	0	0	.311	.271
Barrera, Tres	R-R	6-0	206	9-15-94	.201	.262	.181	54	169	14	34	5	0	3	18	24	2	1	4	43	0	0	.284	.302
Bautista, Rafael	R-R	6-2	194	3-8-93	.238	.270	.227	78	235	24	56	10	0	5	24	12	6	1	1	47	3	1	.345	.291
Casey, Donovan	R-R	6-2	190	2-23-96	.179	.250	.153	38	134	15	24	9	0	2	9	9	3	0	1	57	5	0	.291	.245
Castillo, Ali	R-R	5-9	180	6-19-89	.211	.227	.205	61	161	15	34	3	2	0	11	8	2	0	2	28	2	0	.255	.254
Castillo, Welington	R-R	5-10	215	4-24-87	.143	.250	.063	11	28	4	4	1	0	0	1	9	0	0	0	10	0	0	.179	.351
Dietrich, Derek	L-R	6-2	205	7-18-89	.121	.107	.125	43	132	13	16	3	0	3	13	13	14	0	0	51	0	0	.212	.270
2-team total (36 Scranton/Wilkes-Barre)					.163	.164	.163	79	239	32	39	7	0	8	35	40	23	0	0	97	0	0	.293	.338
Dunlap, Alex	R-R	6-2	215	10-6-94	.173	.182	.170	24	75	7	13	2	1	2	8	7	1	1	0	26	1	0	.307	.253
Flores, Jeckson	R-R	5-11	145	10-28-93	.235	.212	.242	55	153	19	36	13	0	1	14	27	0	1	1	30	0	1	.340	.348
Flores, Ramon	L-L	5-10	190	3-26-92	.143	.143	.143	9	21	4	3	0	0	0	5	0	0	0	0	4	0	0	.143	.308
Ford, Mike	L-R	6-0	225	7-4-92	.202	.143	.217	29	104	10	21	5	0	3	12	11	1	0	0	32	0	0	.337	.284
3-team total (40 Durham, 7 Scranton/Wilkes-Barre)					.213	.152	.238	76	268	35	57	10	1	14	44	35	3	0	1	81	1	0	.414	.309
Garcia, Luis	R-R	6-2	224	5-16-00	.303	.326	.293	37	142	26	43	3	0	13	25	15	1	0	1	26	1	1	.599	.371
Hernandez, Yadiel	L-R	5-10	188	10-9-87	.288	.385	.261	15	59	9	17	2	0	5	12	5	0	0	0	11	0	1	.576	.344
Joseph, Corban	L-R	6-0	185	10-28-88	.429	.500	.421	6	21	2	9	3	1	1	5	2	0	0	1	3	0	0	.810	.458
Keller, Alec	L-R	6-2	200	5-13-92	.311	.375	.303	27	74	16	23	3	0	2	8	10	1	0	1	9	2	0	.432	.395
Kieboom, Carter	R-R	6-2	215	9-3-97	.236	.273	.221	44	148	26	35	7	0	5	23	26	7	0	0	31	1	1	.385	.376
Lara, Gilbert	R-R	6-4	198	10-30-97	.130	.000	.167	7	23	1	3	0	0	0	1	0	0	0	0	11	0	0	.261	.130
Noll, Jake	R-R	6-2	215	3-8-94	.300	.322	.291	118	437	60	131	28	3	17	69	29	4	0	4	74	4	1	.494	.346
Palka, Daniel	L-L	6-2	230	10-28-91	.256	.222	.267	106	356	61	91	19	2	18	58	61	1	0	2	90	5	0	.472	.364
Parra, Gerardo	L-L	5-11	210	5-6-87	.222	.111	.259	21	72	10	16	3	1	1	12	19	0	0	1	17	1	2	.333	.393
Perez, Wilmer	R-R	5-10	186	4-16-98	.000	.000	.000	4	4	0	0	0	0	0	0	1	0	0	0	3	0	0	.000	.200
Read, Raudy	R-R	6-0	220	10-29-93	.288	.259	.302	22	80	13	23	5	0	6	15	3	2	0	1	26	0	0	.575	.326
Reetz, Jakson	R-R	6-0	205	1-3-96	.184	.222	.172	13	38	4	7	2	0	2	8	3	0	1	0	15	0	0	.395	.289

Player	B-T	HT	WT	DOB	AVG	vLH	vRH	G	AB	R	H	2B	3B	HR	RBI	BB	HP	SH	SF	SO	SB	CS	OBP	SLG
Robles, Victor	R-R	6-0	205	5-19-97	.301	.280	.310	23	83	14	25	8	1	4	8	7	2	1	0	26	6	1	.566	.370
Ruiz, Keibert	B-R	6-0	225	7-20-98	.308	.391	.273	20	78	11	24	6	0	5	14	7	0	0	0	6	0	0	.577	.365
Sanchez, Adrian	R-R	6-0	208	8-16-90	.314	.347	.300	45	159	21	50	9	0	4	20	11	1	3	0	28	5	2	.447	.363
Snyder, Brandon	R-R	6-2	215	11-23-86	.207	.217	.203	65	203	35	42	7	0	12	32	26	8	0	1	71	0	0	.419	.319
Stevenson, Andrew	L-L	6-0	192	6-1-94	.436	.300	.467	15	55	11	24	4	0	2	8	3	0	0	0	11	2	0	.618	.466
Swihart, Blake	B-R	6-0	185	4-3-92	.198	.211	.194	70	177	26	35	6	2	5	17	26	0	0	1	51	2	3	.339	.299
Thomas, Lane	R-R	6-0	185	8-23-95	.385	1.000	.333	3	13	2	5	1	0	1	3	0	0	0	0	2	0	0	.692	.385
2-team total (30 Memphis)					.278	.370	.253	33	126	20	35	6	2	5	23	12	1	0	1	37	3	2	.476	.343
Tocci, Carlos	R-R	6-2	180	8-23-95	.172	.091	.189	32	64	5	11	3	0	1	4	10	0	0	0	16	0	0	.266	.284
Tomas, Yasmany	R-R	6-2	260	11-14-90	.185	.217	.172	26	81	14	15	6	0	3	12	13	0	0	2	28	0	1	.370	.292
Wilson, Cody	R-R	6-2	200	7-4-96	.127	.069	.151	33	102	10	13	2	1	0	7	12	1	2	0	38	7	2	.167	.226

Pitching	B-T	HT	WT	DOB	W	L	ERA	G	GS	CG	SV	IP	H	R	ER	HR	BB	SO	AVG	vLH	vRH	K/9	BB/9
Adon, Joan	R-R	6-2	242	8-12-98	0	0	0.00	1	1	0	0	4	2	0	0	0	3	7	.143	.000	.182	15.75	6.75
Armenteros, Rogelio	R-R	6-1	244	6-30-94	0	5	6.08	10	9	0	0	40	44	29	27	9	25	42	.282	.300	.271	9.45	5.63
Bacus, Dakota	R-R	6-2	212	4-2-91	4	3	3.38	36	0	0	4	51	47	24	19	5	20	49	.245	.266	.230	8.70	3.55
Baez, Joan	R-R	6-3	190	12-26-94	2	1	9.82	7	0	0	0	15	17	16	16	3	9	13	.293	.280	.303	7.98	5.52
Baldonado, Alberto	L-L	6-4	250	2-1-93	3	1	3.31	28	0	0	0	33	28	13	12	1	9	36	.228	.250	.213	9.92	2.48
Barrett, Aaron	R-R	6-3	230	1-2-88	3	2	2.22	23	0	0	2	24	18	7	6	0	15	24	.214	.273	.150	8.88	5.55
Bonnell, Bryan	L-R	6-5	240	9-28-93	1	3	4.29	36	4	0	5	65	65	35	31	5	19	59	.259	.236	.277	8.17	2.63
Braymer, Ben	L-L	6-2	212	4-28-94	7	8	5.78	25	21	0	0	100	93	65	64	19	60	79	.250	.277	.236	7.13	5.42
Castillo, Ali	R-R	5-9	180	6-19-89	0	0	6.75	3	0	0	0	4	6	3	3	1	4	1	.333	.250	.400	2.25	9.00
Cavalli, Cade	R-R	6-4	230	8-14-98	1	5	7.30	6	6	0	0	25	33	21	20	2	13	24	.317	.300	.327	8.76	4.74
Clay, Sam	L-L	6-3	227	6-21-93	0	0	1.42	6	0	0	1	6	2	1	1	0	2	7	.100	.125	.083	9.95	2.84
Eppler, Tyler	R-R	6-5	230	1-5-93	2	9	7.75	19	15	0	0	72	94	64	62	19	30	48	.319	.309	.327	6.00	3.75
Fuentes, Steven	R-R	6-2	241	5-4-97	0	5	19.96	7	5	0	0	15	37	35	34	4	14	9	.457	.488	.425	5.28	8.22
Goody, Nick	R-R	5-11	200	7-6-91	3	5	5.14	11	0	0	0	14	13	10	8	1	7	13	.241	.167	.278	8.36	4.50
2-team total (28 Scranton/Wilkes-Barre)					4	6	4.53	39	0	0	1	48	37	28	24	8	18	59	.211	.177	.230	11.14	3.40
Guerra, Javy	R-R	6-1	215	10-31-85	0	0	2.45	3	0	0	0	4	4	1	1	0	2	1	.286	.500	.125	2.45	4.91
Harper, Ryne	R-R	6-3	217	3-27-89	1	1	3.66	13	0	0	0	20	16	12	8	2	8	23	.219	.212	.225	10.53	3.66
Klobosits, Gabe	L-R	6-7	270	5-16-95	1	2	2.45	16	0	0	3	18	15	7	5	0	6	20	.211	.219	.205	9.82	2.95
Lee, Andrew	L-R	6-5	225	12-2-93	0	1	12.79	6	0	0	0	6	10	9	9	1	6	9	.370	.556	.278	12.79	8.53
Lobstein, Kyle	L-L	6-3	220	8-12-89	2	0	1.69	16	0	0	0	21	15	4	4	0	8	25	.203	.172	.222	10.55	3.38
2-team total (23 Nashville)					3	0	3.40	39	0	0	1	45	45	19	17	3	17	45	.256	.176	.314	9.00	3.40
Machado, Andres	R-R	6-0	220	4-22-93	0	0	3.68	11	0	0	0	15	17	6	6	1	4	19	.283	.233	.333	11.66	2.45
McFarland, T.J.	L-L	6-3	200	6-8-89	1	2	5.25	18	0	0	1	24	23	14	14	3	5	26	.247	.136	.347	9.75	1.88
2-team total (4 Memphis)					2	2	4.65	22	0	0	2	31	29	17	16	3	7	34	.240	.143	.323	9.87	2.03
McGowin, Kyle	R-R	6-3	202	11-27-91	1	0	0.93	9	0	0	0	10	3	2	1	0	3	10	.094	.100	.083	9.31	2.79
McMahan, Pearson	L-R	6-2	190	7-1-96	0	0	13.50	1	0	0	0	2	3	3	3	1	3	0	.500	—	.500	0.00	13.50
Miller, Justin	R-R	6-3	225	6-13-87	1	0	0.55	13	0	0	5	16	9	2	1	0	4	29	.161	.143	.179	15.98	2.20
2-team total (2 Memphis)					1	0	1.47	15	1	0	5	18	12	4	3	1	4	33	.185	.200	.171	16.20	1.96
Moreno, Diego	R-R	6-1	235	7-21-87	0	1	2.37	20	0	0	0	30	23	8	8	4	11	26	.215	.255	.173	7.71	3.26
Murphy, Patrick	R-R	6-5	235	6-10-95	0	0	4.50	3	0	0	0	2	2	1	1	0	1	3	.250	.167	.500	13.50	4.50
2-team total (10 Buffalo)					1	1	0.54	13	0	0	0	17	10	2	1	0	9	20	.172	.037	.290	10.80	4.86
Nolin, Sean	L-L	6-4	250	12-26-89	3	3	3.80	11	9	0	0	47	46	20	20	7	15	52	.253	.341	.225	9.89	2.85
Pena, Ronald	R-R	6-4	195	9-1-94	0	1	5.12	31	0	0	1	39	38	23	22	4	17	32	.250	.311	.192	7.45	3.96
Rainey, Tanner	R-R	6-2	247	12-25-92	1	0	2.35	8	1	0	0	8	3	2	2	1	5	15	.115	.133	.091	17.61	5.87
Reyes, Luis	R-R	6-2	175	9-26-94	0	5	6.05	9	9	0	0	42	45	30	28	4	27	28	.278	.291	.263	6.05	5.83
Rodriguez, Jefry	R-R	6-6	232	7-26-93	2	1	4.86	12	11	0	0	46	41	29	25	4	24	46	.240	.264	.214	8.94	4.66
Rogers, Josh	L-L	6-3	210	7-10-94	7	3	3.70	14	13	0	0	73	75	32	30	8	21	49	.261	.233	.274	6.04	2.59
2-team total (4 Norfolk)					7	6	4.48	18	15	0	0	90	99	49	45	14	24	63	.274	.274	.274	6.28	2.39
Romero, Jhon	R-R	5-10	195	1-17-95	0	0	1.23	5	0	0	0	7	5	1	1	1	1	11	.192	.222	.176	13.50	1.23
Romero, Seth	L-L	6-3	225	4-19-96	0	0	2.25	1	1	0	0	4	4	1	1	0	2	5	.267	.250	.273	11.25	4.50
Sanchez, Mario	R-R	6-1	166	10-31-94	0	0	6.48	2	0	0	0	8	10	6	6	0	2	8	.294	.294	.294	8.64	2.16
Sharp, Sterling	R-R	6-3	182	5-30-95	4	4	4.97	16	14	0	0	71	73	47	39	9	39	47	.265	.262	.269	5.99	4.97
Snyder, Brandon	R-R	6-2	215	11-23-86	0	0	18.69	4	0	0	0	4	12	9	9	4	2	2	.480	.375	.529	4.15	4.15
Strasburg, Stephen	R-R	6-5	240	7-20-88	0	0	0.00	1	1	0	0	4	2	0	0	0	2	6	.143	.000	.200	12.46	4.15
Suero, Wander	R-R	6-4	216	9-15-91	2	1	6.39	12	1	0	0	13	12	9	9	0	3	16	.255	.292	.217	11.37	2.13
Teel, Carson	L-L	6-0	160	12-17-95	0	1	4.82	5	0	0	0	9	5	5	5	2	3	8	.152	.125	.176	7.71	2.89
Tetreault, Jackson	R-R	6-5	189	6-3-96	0	1	3.27	2	1	1	0	11	10	4	4	1	3	12	.244	.125	.412	9.82	2.45
Tomshaw, Matt	R-L	6-1	210	12-17-88	0	2	9.00	3	3	0	0	14	17	14	14	7	2	10	.288	.161	.429	6.43	1.29
2-team total (11 Charlotte)					0	6	7.86	14	8	0	0	53	52	48	46	23	10	46	.251	.216	.271	7.86	1.71
Voth, Austin	R-R	6-2	211	6-26-92	0	0	0.00	2	2	0	0	3	2	0	0	0	1	4	.167	.111	.333	12.00	3.00
Wells, Nick	L-L	6-5	185	2-21-96	0	3	6.47	22	0	0	0	32	34	23	23	3	23	29	.276	.213	.316	8.16	6.47

Fielding

Catcher	PCT	G	PO	A	E	DP	PB
Adams	1.000	1	8	1	0	0	0
Barrera	.987	54	430	29	6	7	1
Castillo	.977	10	81	5	2	1	1
Dunlap	.988	22	147	23	2	1	3
Perez	1.000	1	8	0	0	0	0
Read	1.000	1	9	1	0	0	0
Reetz	1.000	13	86	10	0	1	2
Ruiz	1.000	19	139	7	0	0	0
Snyder	1.000	2	8	1	0	0	0
Swihart	1.000	14	82	4	0	1	0

First Base	PCT	G	PO	A	E	DP
Castillo	1.000	1	1	0	0	0
Castillo	1.000	1	2	0	0	0
Dietrich	.978	12	78	10	2	10
Ford	.994	21	148	7	1	20
Joseph	1.000	3	24	0	0	0
Noll	.993	36	271	17	2	26
Palka	1.000	8	49	2	0	8
Read	.977	13	85	1	2	7
Snyder	.990	20	182	8	2	10
Swihart	.962	5	23	2	1	4
Tomas	.984	17	121	6	2	6

Second Base	PCT	G	PO	A	E	DP
Arteaga	1.000	14	23	49	0	12

	PCT	G	PO	A	E	DP
Castillo	.991	35	41	68	1	14
Dietrich	1.000	9	18	27	0	6
Flores	1.000	3	3	0	0	0
Garcia	.950	9	16	22	2	5
Joseph	1.000	3	7	10	0	3
Noll	.960	54	83	108	8	27
Sanchez	.959	17	25	46	3	8
Snyder	.882	4	5	10	2	1

Third Base	PCT	G	PO	A	E	DP
Arteaga	1.000	10	6	16	0	2
Castillo	.977	22	15	27	1	4
Dietrich	1.000	16	6	19	0	1
Flores	.000	1	0	0	0	0
Kieboom	.973	40	27	82	3	8
Lara	.941	7	6	10	1	3

Noll	1.000	7	1	7	0	0
Sanchez	.962	12	6	19	1	2
Snyder	.971	28	22	45	2	10
Tomas	.000	1	0	0	0	0

Shortstop	PCT	G	PO	A	E	DP
Arteaga	.979	39	42	101	3	17
Flores	.989	49	66	122	2	33
Garcia	.889	28	28	60	11	8
Lara	1.000	1	1	1	0	1
Sanchez	.938	17	20	41	4	7

Outfield	PCT	G	PO	A	E	DP
Banks	1.000	30	44	4	0	1
Bautista	.966	67	110	2	4	1
Casey	1.000	39	66	2	0	0

Dietrich	1.000	3	4	0	0	0
Flores	1.000	7	8	1	0	0
Hernandez	1.000	12	21	0	0	0
Keller	1.000	23	34	1	0	0
Noll	.969	23	31	0	1	0
Palka	1.000	64	98	1	0	0
Parra	.893	19	24	1	3	0
Robles	1.000	22	56	0	0	0
Sanchez	1.000	2	5	0	0	0
Stevenson	.964	13	27	0	1	0
Swihart	.982	31	50	6	1	2
Thomas	1.000	3	12	0	0	0
Tocci	.978	26	43	1	1	0
Tomas	1.000	3	6	1	0	1
Wilson	.987	32	75	2	1	0

HARRISBURG SENATORS — DOUBLE-A

DOUBLE-A NORTHEAST

Batting	B-T	HT	WT	DOB	AVG	vLH	vRH	G	AB	R	H	2B	3B	HR	RBI	BB	HBP	SH	SF	SO	SB	CS	SLG	OBP
Alu, Jake	L-R	5-10	175	4-6-97	.264	.333	.234	56	197	26	52	12	1	5	23	13	2	0	1	43	5	3	.411	.315
Arteaga, Humberto	R-R	6-1	160	1-23-94	.229	.333	.207	9	35	3	8	2	0	1	2	2	0	0	0	11	0	1	.371	.270
Banks, Nick	L-L	6-0	215	11-18-94	.245	.333	.211	67	229	23	56	11	0	5	30	20	2	1	1	74	0	3	.358	.310
Berrios, Allan	R-R	6-0	190	8-9-97	.240	.167	.308	8	25	5	6	2	0	0	1	2	2	1	0	6	0	0	.320	.345
Canning, Gage	L-R	5-10	175	4-23-97	.253	.267	.248	43	158	20	40	10	0	0	8	13	2	0	0	44	1	2	.316	.318
Casey, Donovan	R-R	6-2	190	2-23-96	.347	.429	.333	12	49	6	17	2	1	3	10	1	0	0	1	9	2	1	.612	.353
Castillo, Ali	R-R	5-9	180	6-19-89	.204	.263	.171	16	54	3	11	0	0	0	4	3	1	2	0	4	2	1	.204	.259
Cluff, Jackson	R-R	6-0	185	12-3-96	.190	.171	.200	35	126	14	24	5	0	2	9	9	7	0	2	39	3	2	.278	.278
Corredor, Aldrem	L-L	6-0	202	10-27-95	.257	.240	.264	92	323	31	83	19	1	9	52	33	2	0	2	79	1	0	.406	.328
Daily, Cole	L-R	5-11	170	11-28-96	.214	.000	.290	22	42	7	9	1	1	0	0	5	0	1	0	11	0	1	.286	.298
Duarte, Osvaldo	R-R	5-9	177	1-18-96	.189	.290	.148	77	217	26	41	10	3	1	7	16	4	2	1	85	6	3	.276	.256
Dunlap, Alex	R-R	6-2	215	10-6-94	.189	.188	.190	24	74	4	14	4	0	1	8	4	2	0	0	23	0	1	.284	.250
Flores, Jecksson	R-R	5-11	145	10-28-93	.226	.200	.234	21	62	9	14	2	1	0	1	6	4	0	0	8	1	0	.290	.333
Flores, Ramon	L-L	5-10	190	3-26-92	.132	.143	.129	16	38	4	5	0	0	0	2	7	0	0	1	13	0	0	.132	.261
Freeman, Cole	R-R	5-9	175	9-27-94	.267	.321	.247	99	397	57	106	14	0	5	39	22	14	4	3	47	15	5	.340	.326
Geraldo, Manuel	B-R	6-1	170	9-23-96	.067	.000	.094	14	45	1	3	0	1	0	3	1	0	0	0	17	0	0	.111	.087
Harrison, K.J.	R-R	6-0	208	8-11-96	.243	.181	.272	90	300	40	73	20	0	14	40	28	3	0	2	100	0	0	.450	.312
Joseph, Corban	R-R	6-0	185	10-28-88	.247	.269	.238	26	89	11	22	3	0	1	8	11	0	0	0	10	0	0	.315	.330
Lara, Gilbert	R-R	6-4	198	10-30-97	.252	.207	.269	63	218	18	55	17	0	4	32	9	3	0	0	59	1	2	.385	.291
Lindsly, Brady	L-R	6-1	221	3-3-98	.258	.133	.298	20	62	7	16	2	0	0	5	7	0	0	0	15	0	0	.290	.333
Marinconz, Kyle	L-R	5-10	185	5-24-96	.150	.200	.133	13	40	4	6	2	0	0	2	2	2	0	0	11	1	0	.200	.227
Mendoza, Drew	L-R	6-5	225	10-10-97	.160	.250	.140	34	106	12	17	6	0	4	11	15	2	0	1	45	1	0	.330	.274
Mercer, Jordy	R-R	6-3	210	8-27-86	.333	--	.333	3	9	1	3	0	0	0	0	2	0	0	3	0	0	.333	.455
Meregildo, Omar	R-R	6-1	185	8-18-97	.167	.167	.167	5	18	0	3	1	0	0	0	0	0	0	0	5	0	1	.222	.167
Perez, Wilmer	R-R	5-10	186	4-16-98	1.000	--	1.000	1	3	1	3	1	0	0	2	0	0	0	1	0	0	1.333	.750
Reetz, Jakson	R-R	6-0	205	1-3-96	.190	.191	.190	64	221	31	42	13	0	4	18	24	10	0	0	69	1	1	.303	.298
Rhinesmith, Jacob	L-L	6-2	195	5-23-96	.238	.304	.213	25	84	10	20	7	1	3	14	10	1	0	1	19	0	1	.452	.323
Robles, Victor	R-R	6-0	205	5-19-97	.500	--	.500	1	2	1	1	0	0	0	0	0	0	0	0	0	0	.500	.750
Sagdal, Ian	L-R	6-2	191	1-6-93	.227	.250	.221	35	110	13	25	2	0	4	15	11	1	2	0	34	0	0	.355	.303
Tocci, Carlos	R-R	6-2	180	8-23-95	.232	.278	.211	18	56	3	13	1	0	0	2	2	0	0	0	10	0	0	.250	.259
Upshaw, Armond	B-L	6-0	190	6-20-96	.186	.182	.188	17	59	11	11	2	2	1	6	8	2	0	0	25	5	2	.339	.304
Wilson, Cody	R-R	6-2	200	7-4-96	.115	.091	.122	17	52	2	6	1	1	0	1	6	0	0	0	14	0	2	.173	.207
Wiseman, Rhett	L-R	6-0	200	6-22-94	.217	.242	.210	85	286	27	62	17	1	9	30	17	7	4	1	109	2	1	.378	.277

Pitching	B-T	HT	WT	DOB	W	L	ERA	G	GS	CG	SV	IP	H	R	ER	HR	BB	SO	AVG	vLH	vRH	K/9	BB/9
Adon, Joan	R-R	6-2	242	8-12-98	1	2	6.43	3	3	0	0	14	15	10	10	1	5	24	.263	.222	.300	15.43	3.21
Baldonado, Alberto	L-L	6-4	250	2-1-93	3	0	1.13	6	0	0	0	8	4	1	1	0	1	11	.143	.214	.071	12.38	0.00
Barrett, Aaron	R-R	6-3	230	1-2-88	1	1	1.04	6	0	0	0	9	8	4	1	0	1	15	.235	.294	.176	15.58	1.04
Bartow, Frankie	R-R	6-3	180	2-26-97	0	5	5.40	29	0	0	10	32	33	24	19	3	13	31	.260	.291	.239	8.81	3.69
Carrillo, Gerardo	R-R	5-10	170	9-13-98	0	5	5.59	8	8	0	0	37	40	28	23	5	21	38	.270	.309	.238	9.24	5.11
Cate, Tim	L-L	6-0	185	9-30-97	2	10	5.31	21	21	0	0	97	113	64	57	12	37	81	.288	.275	.295	7.54	3.44
Cavalli, Cade	R-R	6-4	230	8-14-98	3	3	2.79	11	11	0	0	58	39	19	18	2	35	80	.188	.234	.150	12.41	5.43
Cronin, Matt	L-L	6-2	195	9-20-97	0	1	5.56	10	0	0	0	11	9	9	7	2	10	18	.220	.278	.174	14.29	7.94
Dobzanski, Bryan	R-R	6-5	240	8-31-95	1	1	3.47	33	0	0	1	47	34	20	18	4	23	46	.200	.206	.196	8.87	4.44
Duarte, Osvaldo	R-R	5-9	177	1-18-96	0	0	0.00	1	0	0	0	1	0	0	0	0	0	0	.500	.000	1.000	0.00	0.00
Fuentes, Steven	R-R	6-2	241	5-4-97	0	1	6.97	2	2	0	0	10	13	8	8	4	2	11	.295	.313	.286	9.58	1.74
German, Jhonatan	R-R	6-4	238	1-24-95	0	0	3.75	10	0	0	0	12	9	5	5	2	10	9	.209	.176	.231	6.75	7.50
Guerra, Javy	R-R	6-1	215	10-31-85	0	0	0.00	1	0	0	0	1	0	0	0	0	0	1	.000	.000	.000	9.00	0.00
Karp, Andrew	R-R	6-1	204	9-30-95	0	0	9.00	1	0	0	0	1	2	1	1	0	0	0	.400	.000	.500	0.00	0.00
Klobosits, Gabe	L-R	6-7	270	5-16-95	2	1	0.90	15	0	0	3	20	13	3	2	1	8	26	.183	.118	.243	11.70	3.60
Lee, Andrew	L-R	6-5	225	12-2-95	3	5	4.62	20	8	0	1	60	51	34	31	9	25	65	.225	.214	.230	9.73	3.73
McMahan, Pearson	L-R	6-2	190	7-1-96	3	3	3.91	31	1	0	0	46	33	27	20	2	27	37	.201	.177	.224	7.24	5.28
Moreno, Diego	R-R	6-1	235	7-21-87	0	1	2.84	4	0	0	0	6	8	4	2	1	3	8	.308	.286	.333	11.37	4.26
Navas, Carlos	R-R	6-0	215	8-13-92	0	1	4.95	15	0	0	2	20	17	11	11	8	4	27	.227	.174	.250	12.15	1.80

	B-T	HT	WT	DOB	W	L	ERA	G	GS	CG	SV	IP	H	R	ER	HR	BB	SO	AVG	vLH	vRH	K/9	BB/9
Peguero, Francys	R-R	6-2	170	10-4-95	1	0	4.50	2	0	0	0	2	3	1	1	0	0	2	.333	.000	.500	9.00	0.00
Pena, Malvin	R-R	6-2	180	6-24-97	0	1	9.72	5	0	0	0	8	10	9	9	2	4	6	.313	.375	.250	6.48	4.32
Reyes, Luis	R-R	6-2	175	9-26-94	7	6	4.76	16	15	0	0	85	80	46	45	15	32	81	.252	.275	.229	8.58	3.39
Romero, Jhon	R-R	5-10	195	1-17-95	2	4	2.83	33	0	0	2	48	45	17	15	5	10	58	.243	.260	.231	10.95	1.89
Romero, Seth	L-L	6-3	225	4-19-96	0	2	5.31	6	6	0	0	20	21	13	12	2	9	34	.253	.250	.254	5.05	3.98
Sanchez, Mario	R-R	6-1	166	10-31-94	4	8	3.98	22	18	0	0	106	94	48	47	16	21	107	.234	.277	.198	9.06	1.78
Schaller, Reid	R-R	6-3	210	4-2-97	1	1	4.94	17	0	0	0	24	20	13	13	1	14	25	.235	.286	.211	9.51	5.32
Schlabach, Ike	R-L	6-5	185	12-27-96	0	0	0.00	1	0	0	0	2	0	0	0	0	2	0	.000	.000	.000	9.00	
Sharp, Sterling	R-R	6-3	182	5-30-95	0	2	1.84	3	3	0	0	15	11	10	3	3	6	12	.193	.225	.118	7.36	3.68
Tapani, Ryan	R-R	6-0	180	6-28-94	0	3	4.18	24	1	0	0	47	37	24	22	9	19	50	.215	.246	.194	9.51	3.61
Teel, Carson	L-L	6-0	160	12-17-95	2	6	4.35	28	11	0	2	81	86	49	39	15	22	69	.273	.302	.256	7.70	2.45
Tetreault, Jackson	R-R	6-5	189	6-3-96	5	3	3.74	10	10	0	0	55	56	25	23	8	19	43	.259	.272	.252	6.99	3.09
Troop, Alex	L-L	6-5	210	7-19-96	0	0	0.00	4	0	0	0	11	2	0	0	0	0	15	.059	.000	.095	12.66	0.00
Wells, Nick	L-L	6-5	185	2-21-96	0	0	2.12	10	0	0	0	17	18	5	4	0	5	20	.290	.375	.200	10.59	2.65

Fielding

Catcher	PCT	G	PO	A	E	DP	PB
Berrios	1.000	7	60	4	0	1	1
Dunlap	.994	22	159	11	1	0	2
Harrison	.985	7	61	4	1	1	2
Lindsly	.983	20	162	9	3	2	3
Perez	1.000	1	1	0	0	0	0
Reetz	.995	63	603	34	3	3	8

First Base	PCT	G	PO	A	E	DP
Alu	.750	1	3	0	1	0
Corredor	.985	56	357	37	6	34
Harrison	.997	47	320	22	1	23
Marinconz	.000	1	0	0	0	0
Mendoza	.972	19	126	13	4	13
Mercer	1.000	1	3	0	0	0
Sagdal	1.000	1	1	0	0	1

Second Base	PCT	G	PO	A	E	DP
Alu	1.000	14	23	22	0	12
Arteaga	1.000	6	13	21	0	8
Castillo	.000	1	0	0	0	0
Cluff	1.000	12	24	30	0	10
Daily	1.000	9	5	12	0	3

	PCT	G	PO	A	E	DP
Duarte	.969	50	83	104	6	20
Freeman	1.000	4	7	4	0	1
Geraldo	.818	7	4	14	4	2
Joseph	.984	19	26	34	1	5
Marinconz	.971	10	12	21	1	6
Mercer	1.000	2	1	0	0	0

Third Base	PCT	G	PO	A	E	DP
Alu	.927	33	27	49	6	6
Castillo	.974	15	15	22	1	1
Daily	.923	6	2	10	1	1
Duarte	.895	6	9	8	2	0
Freeman	.909	3	2	8	1	3
Geraldo	.857	7	1	5	1	0
Lara	.952	7	7	13	1	1
Marinconz	1.000	3	1	2	0	0
Mendoza	.968	13	12	18	1	1
Mercer	1.000	2	0	1	0	0
Meregildo	.917	5	6	5	1	0
Sagdal	.914	31	26	38	6	8

Shortstop	PCT	G	PO	A	E	DP
Arteaga	.923	3	3	9	1	0

	PCT	G	PO	A	E	DP
Castillo	.000	1	0	0	0	0
Cluff	.935	23	36	51	6	14
Daily	.750	2	1	2	1	0
Duarte	.917	14	25	30	5	8
Flores	1.000	21	21	44	0	6
Geraldo	1.000	1	0	1	0	0
Lara	.943	56	66	132	12	28

Outfield	PCT	G	PO	A	E	DP
Banks	.975	64	115	4	3	1
Canning	.975	41	76	3	2	0
Casey	1.000	12	30	2	0	0
Corredor	1.000	22	37	0	0	0
Duarte	1.000	1	2	0	0	0
Flores	.952	12	20	0	1	0
Freeman	.994	85	151	6	1	1
Rhinesmith	1.000	15	27	0	0	0
Tocci	.939	15	31	0	2	0
Upshaw	.944	16	33	1	2	2
Wilson	1.000	17	43	1	0	1
Wiseman	.981	64	96	7	2	2

WILMINGTON BLUE ROCKS   HIGH CLASS A
HIGH-A EAST

Batting	B-T	HT	WT	DOB	AVG	vLH	vRH	G	AB	R	H	2B	3B	HR	RBI	BB	HBP	SH	SF	SO	SB	CS	SLG	OBP
Agustin, Telmito	L-L	5-10	160	10-9-96	.000	--	.000	1	3	0	0	0	0	0	0	0	0	0	0	0	0	0	.000	.000
Alu, Jake	L-R	5-10	175	4-6-97	.303	.238	.315	39	145	22	44	10	1	5	19	8	4	0	0	32	8	0	.490	.357
Antuna, Yasel	B-R	6-0	195	10-26-99	.227	.197	.233	106	405	55	92	26	1	12	65	46	2	0	3	100	4	4	.385	.307
Arruda, J.T.	B-R	5-10	180	10-20-97	.186	.200	.183	49	167	14	31	8	1	2	12	16	0	0	1	49	5	2	.281	.255
Canning, Gage	L-R	5-10	175	4-23-97	.266	.158	.284	36	128	16	34	8	0	5	16	9	4	2	1	38	1	3	.445	.331
Connell, Justin	R-R	6-1	185	3-11-99	.293	.310	.290	98	372	52	109	11	5	6	38	33	5	4	3	72	21	13	.398	.356
Corredor, Aldrem	L-L	6-0	202	10-27-95	.000	.000	.000	4	8	1	0	0	0	0	0	0	1	0	0	4	0	0	.000	.111
Daily, Cole	L-R	5-11	170	11-28-96	.136	.000	.150	8	22	3	3	0	0	0	2	5	0	0	0	6	0	0	.136	.296
Dunn, Jack	R-R	6-2	185	9-5-96	.276	.303	.271	65	203	39	56	5	2	2	19	24	3	0	1	36	11	2	.350	.359
Geraldo, Manuel	B-R	6-1	170	9-23-96	.286	--	.286	2	7	1	2	0	0	0	0	0	0	0	0	2	0	0	.286	.286
Keller, Alec	L-R	6-2	200	5-13-92	.500	--	.500	2	8	2	4	0	0	0	1	0	0	0	0	0	0	0	.500	.556
Lara, Gilbert	R-R	6-4	198	10-30-97	.220	.174	.229	39	132	10	29	5	1	1	10	7	1	1	2	41	0	1	.295	.261
Lindsly, Brady	R-R	6-1	221	3-3-98	.209	.000	.237	21	67	10	14	2	1	2	8	13	0	0	1	23	1	0	.358	.333
Marinconz, Kyle	L-R	5-10	185	5-24-96	.226	.250	.222	29	106	12	24	2	0	2	11	12	3	0	1	19	4	4	.302	.320
Martina, Junior	R-R	6-0	190	12-12-97	.231	.000	.261	7	26	3	6	2	0	0	2	1	0	0	1	5	0	0	.308	.250
Mendez, Ricardo	L-L	5-10	185	1-24-00	.284	.238	.296	25	102	19	29	11	1	2	18	6	0	1	1	29	2	3	.471	.321
Mendoza, Drew	L-R	6-5	225	10-10-97	.225	.279	.214	70	253	38	57	7	0	5	30	32	10	0	2	80	5	2	.332	.333
Meregildo, Omar	R-R	6-1	185	8-19-97	.234	.228	.236	84	290	45	68	11	0	16	48	36	8	0	2	109	2	1	.438	.333
Millas, Drew	B-R	6-2	205	1-15-98	.284	.125	.314	27	102	15	29	4	0	0	20	13	2	0	1	14	5	1	.324	.373
Perez, Wilmer	R-R	5-10	186	4-16-98	.206	.286	.185	15	34	1	7	1	0	0	3	2	1	0	1	10	0	0	.235	.263
Pineda, Israel	R-R	5-11	190	4-3-00	.208	.200	.210	77	293	35	61	11	0	14	48	18	3	0	1	83	0	0	.389	.260
Pratt, Andrew	R-R	6-3	225	7-24-96	.205	.231	.198	34	112	13	23	5	1	7	24	12	3	0	1	57	0	0	.455	.297
Rhinesmith, Jacob	L-L	6-2	195	5-23-96	.253	.352	.232	30	348	48	76	21	0	6	39	40	3	0	2	59	9	0	.383	.345
Strohschein, Kevin	R-R	6-1	215	7-25-97	.135	.083	.150	15	52	5	7	2	1	0	5	5	0	0	0	16	0	0	.212	.211
Upshaw, Armond	B-L	6-0	190	6-20-96	.257	.306	.247	83	296	52	76	14	5	9	43	31	9	3	2	98	24	10	.429	.343
Wilson, Cody	R-R	6-2	200	7-4-96	.130	.000	.150	7	23	3	3	0	0	0	1	4	0	0	0	9	3	0	.130	.259
Witt, Paul	R-R	5-11	170	10-29-97	.132	.000	.163	17	53	2	7	2	0	0	2	2	0	0	0	10	1	0	.170	.132
Ydens, Jeremy	R-R	6-2	200	7-3-97	.240	.143	.267	38	129	22	31	2	0	5	13	4	8	0	0	33	3	0	.372	.305

Pitching	B-T	HT	WT	DOB	W	L	ERA	G	GS	CG	SV	IP	H	R	ER	HR	BB	SO	AVG	vLH	vRH	K/9	BB/9
Adon, Joan	R-R	6-2	242	8-12-98	6	4	4.97	17	17	1	0	87	77	51	48	7	32	91	.235	.236	.234	9.41	3.31

Name	B-T	HT	WT	DOB	W	L	ERA	G	GS	CG	SV	IP	H	R	ER	HR	BB	SO	AVG	vLH	vRH		
Alastre, Tomas	R-R	6-4	240	6-11-98	0	0	13.50	5	0	0	0	8	11	12	12	2	7	8	.344	.357	.333	9.00	7.88
Bocko, Jordan	R-R	5-11	195	1-10-97	1	2	7.89	17	1	0	0	30	44	29	26	8	11	32	.341	.355	.328	9.71	3.34
Brzykcy, Zach	R-R	6-2	225	7-12-99	6	4	5.20	28	1	0	2	62	55	37	36	8	25	86	.236	.311	.189	12.42	3.61
Cavalli, Cade	R-R	6-4	230	8-14-98	3	1	1.77	7	7	0	0	41	24	9	8	1	12	71	.171	.238	.143	15.71	2.66
Chu, Gilberto	L-L	5-11	195	11-19-97	0	0	3.86	2	0	0	0	5	8	6	2	1	3	5	.364	.556	.231	9.64	5.79
Cronin, Matt	L-L	6-2	195	9-20-97	2	0	1.23	10	0	0	4	15	8	2	2	0	5	28	.163	.154	.167	17.18	3.07
Driskill, Tanner	R-R	6-1	185	1-18-96	0	1	9.42	10	0	0	0	14	23	16	15	2	6	10	.348	.333	.359	6.28	3.77
Dunn, Jack	R-R	6-2	185	9-5-96	0	0	0.00	2	0	0	0	2	2	0	0	0	0	0	.250	.333	.200	0.00	0.00
Dyson, Tyler	R-R	6-4	220	12-24-97	1	2	2.77	7	3	0	0	26	14	8	8	2	15	26	.167	.227	.145	9.00	5.19
Fedde, Erick	R-R	6-4	200	2-25-93	0	1	3.60	1	1	0	0	5	5	2	2	0	1	3	.263	.000	.313	5.40	1.80
Fuentes, Steven	R-R	6-2	241	5-4-97	0	0	5.00	2	2	0	0	9	12	6	5	1	1	9	.324	.250	.345	9.00	1.00
German, Jhonatan	R-R	6-4	238	1-24-95	0	0	5.63	7	0	0	0	8	10	8	5	2	5	6	.294	.353	.235	6.75	5.63
Guasch, Richard	R-R	6-4	205	4-10-98	0	1	3.15	6	5	0	0	20	14	12	7	3	17	24	.192	.294	.103	10.80	7.65
Guerra, Javy	R-R	6-1	215	10-31-85	0	0	9.00	1	0	0	0	2	2	2	2	0	1	4	.250	.000	.500	18.00	4.50
Henry, Cole	R-R	6-4	215	7-15-99	3	3	1.88	9	8	0	0	43	23	10	9	3	11	63	.158	.145	.165	13.19	2.30
Hernandez, Alfonso	L-L	5-11	198	8-3-99	4	4	3.97	17	10	0	0	70	68	37	31	14	21	85	.250	.181	.287	10.88	2.69
Hinton, Kyle	R-R	6-0	200	2-12-97	0	2	8.47	13	0	0	0	17	28	19	16	3	14	22	.368	.406	.341	11.65	7.41
Karp, Andrew	R-R	6-1	204	9-30-95	1	1	3.25	23	1	0	0	53	46	29	19	5	25	64	.230	.202	.250	10.94	4.27
Lee, Evan	L-L	6-4	200	6-18-97	4	3	4.32	21	20	0	0	77	69	39	37	6	32	104	.239	.301	.214	12.16	3.74
Martina, Junior	R-R	6-0	190	12-12-97	0	0	0.00	1	0	0	0	1	1	0	0	0	0	0	.333	.000	.500	0.00	0.00
Moore, Davis	R-R	6-4	210	3-4-98	2	2	4.64	15	0	0	0	21	24	15	11	2	10	29	.279	.270	.286	12.23	4.22
Nolin, Sean	L-L	6-4	250	12-26-89	0	0	0.00	1	0	0	0	1	0	0	0	0	0	2	.000	.000	.000	18.00	0.00
Parker, Mitchell	L-L	6-4	225	9-27-99	1	5	5.89	11	11	0	0	44	56	34	29	4	17	59	.303	.283	.309	11.98	3.45
Peguero, Francys	R-R	6-2	170	10-4-95	2	4	3.61	26	3	0	1	52	47	23	21	9	18	50	.237	.253	.227	8.60	3.10
Pena, Malvin	R-R	6-2	180	6-24-97	1	3	4.70	22	0	0	2	38	34	22	20	4	22	29	.231	.259	.215	6.81	5.17
Peterson, Todd	R-R	6-5	230	1-22-98	1	1	4.15	18	3	0	3	30	28	19	14	4	12	32	.237	.208	.257	9.49	3.56
Powell, Holden	R-R	6-0	190	9-9-99	0	0	9.00	1	0	0	0	1	1	1	1	0	2	0	.333	.000	.500	0.00	18.00
Rutledge, Jackson	R-R	6-8	245	4-1-99	0	3	12.66	4	4	0	0	11	17	16	15	0	9	10	.370	.500	.300	8.44	7.59
Schaller, Reid	R-R	6-3	210	4-2-97	1	3	3.05	16	0	0	4	21	18	10	7	3	10	23	.237	.250	.232	10.02	4.35
Schlabach, Ike	R-L	6-5	185	12-27-96	0	0	3.51	13	0	0	0	26	29	11	10	2	6	30	.282	.333	.254	10.52	2.10
Shuman, Seth	R-R	6-1	195	12-1-97	0	5	6.03	8	8	0	0	34	42	25	23	8	10	31	.296	.266	.321	8.13	2.62
Stainbrook, Troy	L-L	6-7	250	10-31-96	0	0	0.00	3	0	0	0	5	3	0	0	1	7		.158	.000	.214	11.81	1.69
Tetreault, Jackson	R-R	6-5	189	6-3-96	0	2	5.14	3	3	0	0	14	14	8	8	3	4	12	.255	.412	.184	7.71	2.57
Troop, Alex	L-L	6-5	210	7-19-96	8	5	3.84	24	8	0	0	73	77	39	31	9	15	85	.268	.323	.242	10.53	1.86
Vann, Christian	L-L	6-2	195	6-25-96	3	1	12.27	13	0	0	0	15	20	22	20	2	19	16	.328	.474	.262	9.82	11.66
Willingham, Amos	R-R	6-4	217	8-21-98	1	0	14.54	6	0	0	0	13	26	21	21	6	6	14	.413	.429	.400	9.69	4.15
Witt, Paul	R-R	5-11	170	10-29-97	0	0	9.00	1	0	0	0	2	1	2	2	1	1	1	.143	.500	.000	4.50	4.50
Yankosky, Tyler	L-R	6-6	225	5-28-98	1	1	8.22	5	0	0	0	8	10	8	7	2	4	5	.333	.300	.350	5.87	4.70

Fielding

Catcher	PCT	G	PO	A	E	DP	PB
Lindsly	.980	18	188	8	4	0	3
Millas	.991	20	202	11	2	1	4
Perez	.991	14	108	7	1	0	1
Pineda	.990	58	553	65	6	3	9
Pratt	1.000	14	104	8	0	1	2

	PCT	G	PO	A	E	DP
Daily	1.000	2	2	7	0	2
Dunn	1.000	15	30	43	0	13
Marinconz	1.000	27	46	52	0	14
Witt	.941	12	16	16	2	5

	PCT	G	PO	A	E	DP
Antuna	.894	96	115	190	36	40
Arruda	.000	1	0	0	0	0
Dunn	.975	11	11	28	1	4
Lara	1.000	8	17	16	0	3

First Base	PCT	G	PO	A	E	DP
Corredor	1.000	2	6	1	0	0
Dunn	.982	8	53	1	1	5
Lara	1.000	2	6	0	0	0
Mendoza	.975	61	434	28	12	49
Meregildo	.990	43	274	16	3	21
Strohschein	.944	3	15	2	1	4

Third Base	PCT	G	PO	A	E	DP
Alu	.889	11	3	13	2	1
Arruda	1.000	2	1	2	0	0
Daily	.917	5	2	9	1	0
Dunn	.926	27	16	34	4	5
Geraldo	.800	2	1	3	1	0
Lara	.953	29	18	43	3	0
Martina	1.000	7	8	19	0	7
Mendoza	1.000	3	0	5	0	1
Meregildo	.909	35	12	58	7	8
Witt	1.000	3	2	1	0	0

Outfield	PCT	G	PO	A	E	DP
Canning	1.000	34	41	3	0	1
Connell	.972	98	165	8	5	1
Corredor	1.000	2	2	0	0	0
Dunn	--	2	0	0	0	0
Keller	.833	2	5	0	1	0
Mendez	.950	25	36	2	2	2
Rhinesmith	.981	66	104	0	2	0
Strohschein	1.000	6	12	1	0	0
Upshaw	.969	83	185	3	6	2
Wilson	1.000	7	14	2	0	0
Witt	.667	1	2	0	1	0
Ydens	.967	36	57	2	2	0

Second Base	PCT	G	PO	A	E	DP
Alu	.988	19	35	47	1	8
Arruda	.987	43	70	85	2	27

Shortstop	PCT	G	PO	A	E	DP

FREDERICKSBURG NATIONALS

LOW CLASS A

LOW-A EAST

Batting	B-T	HT	WT	DOB	AVG	vLH	vRH	G	AB	R	H	2B	3B	HR	RBI	BB	HBP	SH	SF	SO	SB	CS	SLG	OBP
Agustin, Telmito	L-L	5-10	160	10-9-96	.220	.400	.194	11	41	5	9	2	0	0	3	5	1	0	0	12	4	0	.268	.319
Arruda, J.T.	B-R	5-10	180	10-20-97	.235	.250	.231	41	136	15	32	5	2	1	9	29	1	0	0	32	9	0	.324	.373
Baker, Darren	L-R	6-0	180	2-11-99	.318	.230	.328	18	66	3	21	3	1	0	5	4	0	3	1	9	2	2	.394	.352
Barley, Jordy	R-R	6-0	175	12-3-99	.205	.095	.228	33	122	17	25	6	0	2	10	17	2	0	0	43	12	5	.303	.312
Berrios, Allan	R-R	6-0	190	8-9-97	.186	.154	.196	18	59	8	11	2	0	0	6	6	2	1	0	24	0	1	.220	.284
Boissiere, Branden	L-L	6-1	205	3-23-00	.200	.250	.195	25	85	9	17	5	0	1	12	10	2	0	0	25	1	0	.294	.299
Boone, Jake	R-R	6-0	185	3-23-99	.229	.269	.222	63	170	22	39	4	3	0	23	18	7	2	3	55	9	2	.288	.323
Cluff, Jackson	L-R	6-0	185	12-3-96	.278	.000	.313	5	18	2	5	1	0	0	0	2	2	0	0	3	1	0	.333	.409
Cornell, Zach	L-L	6-2	225	12-18-97	.175	.000	.204	18	57	11	10	4	0	0	4	9	3	0	0	13	2	1	.246	.319
Coutts, Jackson	L-R	6-3	230	9-1-98	.138	.139	.138	19	65	4	10	2	0	1	8	6	1	0	1	22	0	0	.231	.233
Daily, Cole	L-R	5-11	170	11-28-96	.200	.133	.229	14	50	9	10	1	0	0	5	9	0	0	0	12	2	1	.220	.322
De La Rosa, Jeremy	L-L	5-11	160	1-16-02	.209	.200	.211	87	326	34	68	12	4	5	22	30	2	0	0	122	7	8	.316	.279

Name	B-T	HT	WT	DOB	AVG	vLH	vRH	G	AB	R	H	2B	3B	HR	RBI	BB	HBP	SH	SF	SO	SB	CS	OBP	SLG
Diaz, Geraldi	L-R	6-0	206	7-8-00	.217	.053	.245	40	129	21	28	7	0	2	16	20	9	0	0	32	3	0	.318	.361
Diaz, Gio	R-R	5-11	180	2-9-99	.125	.000	.154	7	16	1	2	0	0	0	1	6	0	0	0	4	1	0	.125	.364
Dieterich, Landon	R-R	6-5	225	5-5-98	.188	.000	.214	15	48	7	9	1	0	1	2	4	0	0	0	27	1	0	.271	.250
Emiliani, Leandro	L-L	6-1	180	3-22-00	.155	.222	.149	32	103	12	16	1	0	5	16	15	2	0	0	39	0	0	.311	.275
Fein, Jaden	R-R	6-3	205	8-15-00	.151	.200	.147	22	73	7	11	3	0	1	4	5	3	0	1	28	1	1	.233	.232
Fernandez, Braian	R-L	6-1	170	4-15-99	.220	.333	.197	46	141	14	31	6	1	0	17	16	1	1	1	47	1	2	.277	.302
Flores, Jeckson	R-R	5-11	145	10-28-93	.304	.500	.286	6	23	3	7	2	0	0	5	0	1	0	0	2	2	0	.391	.333
Martina, Junior	R-R	6-0	190	12-12-97	.269	.241	.275	80	301	35	81	13	0	3	36	18	5	0	0	82	4	3	.342	.321
Mendez, Ricardo	L-L	5-10	185	1-24-00	.289	.353	.270	60	225	32	65	16	3	3	34	22	2	3	3	65	9	3	.427	.353
Paulino, Juan	L-R	5-11	192	12-10-97	.314	.000	.324	14	35	5	11	3	0	1	6	6	0	0	0	12	7	1	.486	.415
2-team total (18 Fayetteville)					.250	.211	.260	32	96	13	24	5	0	3	10	13	0	0	0	36	10	2	.396	.339
Pena, Viandel	B-R	5-8	148	11-22-00	.214	.211	.214	78	295	46	63	11	2	4	26	34	0	1	1	88	10	4	.305	.294
Randa, Jake	L-L	6-1	195	12-14-98	.220	.250	.213	86	305	37	67	23	2	2	40	30	2	0	6	89	3	0	.328	.289
Read, Raudy	R-R	6-0	220	10-29-93	.273	.000	.333	4	11	2	3	0	0	1	4	5	1	0	0	2	0	0	.545	.529
Sanchez, Jose	R-R	5-11	195	1-10-97	.232	.257	.227	73	233	43	54	16	1	3	31	41	5	1	0	61	1	1	.348	.358
Strohschein, Kevin	R-R	6-1	215	7-25-97	.255	.190	.269	62	235	33	60	9	1	11	34	13	1	0	0	49	0	4	.443	.297
Vega, Onix	R-R	5-10	200	9-7-98	.233	.313	.214	71	240	22	56	12	0	3	35	34	10	1	4	47	5	0	.321	.347
Williams, Steven	L-R	6-3	216	2-18-99	.160	.250	.143	7	25	3	4	0	0	0	3	3	1	0	0	7	0	0	.160	.276
Witt, Paul	R-R	5-11	170	10-29-97	.145	.200	.125	18	55	6	8	2	0	0	5	7	1	0	2	10	0	0	.182	.246
Ydens, Jeremy	R-R	6-2	200	7-3-97	.227	.222	.228	30	110	15	25	3	1	5	12	5	0	0	1	30	4	0	.409	.259
Young, Jacob	R-R	6-0	180	7-27-99	.208	.143	.213	26	101	16	21	6	0	0	5	10	1	1	1	17	13	0	.267	.283

Pitching

Name	B-T	HT	WT	DOB	W	L	ERA	G	GS	CG	SV	IP	H	R	ER	HR	BB	SO	AVG	vLH	vRH	K/9	BB/9
Alastre, Tomas	R-R	6-4	240	6-11-98	2	3	6.53	26	0	0	1	40	38	32	29	3	31	44	.247	.319	.215	9.90	6.98
Alvarez, Andrew	L-L	6-3	215	6-13-99	0	0	0.00	0	0	0	0	6	3	0	0	2	0	6	.143	.000	.214	9.00	3.00
Barrett, Aaron	R-R	6-3	230	1-2-88	0	0	3.60	4	0	0	0	5	2	3	2	0	2	11	.111	.000	.167	19.80	3.60
Bocko, Jordan	R-R	5-11	195	1-10-98	0	1	2.08	6	0	0	0	13	9	9	3	2	6	12	.176	.353	.088	8.31	4.15
Chu, Gilberto	L-L	5-11	195	11-19-97	3	0	2.79	19	4	0	1	48	32	19	15	4	15	39	.190	.344	.154	7.26	2.79
Collins, Brendan	R-R	6-4	215	9-10-99	0	2	9.53	5	0	0	0	6	10	6	6	0	6	8	.370	.333	.417	12.71	9.53
Cuevas, Michael	R-R	6-2	165	6-29-99	1	8	4.48	20	17	0	1	88	85	55	44	8	28	80	.244	.299	.209	8.15	2.85
Diaz, Gio	R-R	5-11	180	2-9-99	0	0	18.00	1	0	0	0	1	4	2	2	0	0	0	.571	.500	.600	0.00	0.00
Driskill, Tanner	R-R	6-1	185	1-18-96	0	1	4.70	13	0	0	2	23	25	13	12	2	4	18	.281	.290	.276	7.04	1.57
Gonzalez, Pedro	R-R	6-2	225	7-16-00	0	5	11.17	6	3	0	0	10	14	19	12	2	8	10	.326	.368	.292	9.31	7.45
Hernandez, Alfonso	L-L	5-11	198	8-3-99	2	1	2.81	8	5	0	0	32	27	12	10	3	12	34	.221	.250	.217	9.56	3.38
Kirian, Michael	R-L	6-6	260	2-1-99	1	1	1.50	3	0	0	1	6	5	1	1	0	4	4	.238	.286	.214	6.00	0.00
Knowles, Lucas	L-L	6-2	185	3-14-98	3	1	4.06	14	3	0	1	31	32	14	14	2	15	38	.269	.200	.287	11.03	4.35
Lara, Andry	R-R	6-4	180	1-6-03	0	1	5.19	2	2	0	0	9	6	5	5	2	8	5	.200	.286	.125	5.19	8.31
Merrill, Matt	R-R	6-4	202	6-11-98	2	2	4.66	18	7	0	0	46	43	27	24	2	22	71	.242	.260	.229	13.79	4.27
Moore, Davis	R-R	6-4	210	3-4-98	1	3	3.58	18	0	0	2	28	19	19	11	1	15	41	.188	.182	.191	13.34	4.88
Parker, Mitchell	L-L	6-4	225	9-27-99	3	7	4.08	12	10	0	0	57	47	33	26	8	21	85	.215	.111	.241	13.34	3.30
Pena, Bryan	L-L	6-1	210	1-10-00	1	3	6.50	30	4	0	0	73	75	59	53	13	47	70	.267	.255	.270	8.59	5.77
Pena, Malvin	R-R	6-2	180	6-24-97	0	1	7.50	3	0	0	0	6	9	5	5	2	5	4	.240	.111	.313	6.00	7.50
Quintanilla, Cole	R-R	6-5	225	5-31-97	0	2	4.50	5	0	0	2	6	4	3	3	0	4	7	.238	.417	.000	10.50	6.00
Romero, Carlos	R-R	6-6	179	7-15-99	3	3	4.96	17	8	0	0	45	53	33	25	7	21	38	.282	.271	.288	7.54	4.17
Romero, Seth	L-L	6-3	225	4-19-96	0	0	2.79	3	3	0	0	10	15	5	3	0	2	14	.349	.214	.414	13.03	1.86
Rutledge, Jackson	R-R	6-8	245	4-1-99	1	2	5.32	7	7	0	0	22	20	16	13	1	9	26	.235	.265	.216	10.64	3.68
Saenz, Dustin	L-L	5-11	190	6-2-99	1	0	4.76	5	1	0	0	11	14	7	6	0	4	12	.298	.400	.250	9.53	3.18
Schoff, Tyler	R-R	6-4	220	12-6-98	1	0	3.00	5	0	0	0	9	10	6	3	1	5	10	.263	.350	.167	10.00	5.00
Seijas, Karlo	R-R	6-1	215	9-6-00	3	12	6.84	22	22	0	0	97	119	85	74	16	29	82	.301	.311	.294	7.58	2.68
Stainbrook, Troy	L-L	6-7	250	10-31-96	2	1	6.33	28	0	0	2	43	47	34	30	3	18	52	.281	.290	.290	10.97	3.80
Strom, Leif	R-R	6-6	240	5-17-97	1	4	9.50	27	2	0	1	42	59	58	44	7	37	40	.321	.333	.315	8.64	7.99
Theophile, Rodney	R-R	6-5	230	9-16-99	4	11	5.56	22	22	0	0	89	96	73	55	9	47	84	.270	.288	.258	8.49	4.75
Turner, Trey	R-R	6-1	195	6-5-96	1	1	5.40	13	0	0	0	18	16	14	11	3	18	21	.232	.316	.200	10.31	8.84
Urena, Edward	R-R	6-3	185	3-21-99	1	1	6.26	18	0	0	0	27	35	21	19	2	12	29	.304	.383	.250	9.55	3.95
Vann, Christian	L-L	6-2	195	6-25-96	0	1	39.00	3	0	0	0	3	5	14	13	0	9	3	.417	.333	.500	9.00	27.00
Willingham, Amos	R-R	6-4	217	8-21-98	3	0	2.28	23	0	0	2	47	36	15	12	4	19	42	.206	.241	.188	7.99	3.61
Yankosky, Tyler	L-R	6-6	225	5-28-98	2	0	3.13	17	0	0	1	23	22	15	8	1	11	15	.229	.250	.219	5.87	4.30

Fielding

Catcher

Catcher	PCT	G	PO	A	E	DP	PB
Berrios	.990	12	95	8	1	1	5
Diaz	.973	38	317	40	10	4	7
Paulino	.988	9	65	14	1	0	1
Read	1.000	2	14	0	0	0	0
Vega	.989	59	474	53	6	3	15
Williams	1.000	5	46	2	0	0	2
Sanchez	1.000	7	46	1	0	2	
Strohschein	.962	41	283	24	12	22	
Vega	1.000	1	4	1	0	0	

First Base

First Base	PCT	G	PO	A	E	DP
Berrios	.974	5	32	6	1	5
Boissiere	.964	17	122	12	5	10
Coutts	.965	17	100	9	4	8
Daily	.978	12	84	6	2	13
Emiliani	.979	19	129	12	3	17
Paulino	.882	3	15	0	2	1
Read	.938	2	15	0	1	0

Second Base

Second Base	PCT	G	PO	A	E	DP
Arruda	.975	10	25	14	1	6
Baker	.984	17	26	37	1	8
Barley	1.000	5	7	11	0	4
Boone	.953	19	27	34	3	6
Daily	1.000	2	3	4	0	0
Diaz	1.000	1	2	2	0	0
Martina	.917	3	6	5	1	1
Pena	.954	59	114	92	10	30
Sanchez	.958	11	24	22	2	5

Third Base

Third Base	PCT	G	PO	A	E	DP
Arruda	.920	11	10	13	2	0
Boone	.750	5	1	2	1	0
Diaz	.647	6	3	8	6	0
Martina	.933	61	48	133	13	7
Pena	.958	9	7	16	1	2
Sanchez	.901	35	19	45	7	7
Witt	.667	1	0	2	1	0

Shortstop

Shortstop	PCT	G	PO	A	E	DP
Arruda	.920	19	18	28	4	7
Barley	.859	27	33	52	14	13
Boone	.973	37	49	94	4	26
Cluff	.875	4	5	9	2	3
Flores	1.000	5	8	9	0	3
Pena	.882	8	11	19	4	3
Sanchez	.875	13	11	24	5	3

Witt	.956	16	26	39	3	6

Outfield	PCT	G	PO	A	E	DP
Agustin	1.000	8	16	0	0	0
Cornell	.909	16	20	0	2	0

De La Rosa	.960	85	187	4	8	2
Dieterich	1.000	15	21	1	0	1
Fein	.921	21	35	0	3	0
Fernandez	.989	45	86	1	1	0

Mendez	.978	53	86	5	2	1
Randa	.975	73	110	9	3	2
Ydens	.985	33	64	3	1	1
Young	1.000	26	56	2	0	2

FCL NATIONALS ROOKIE
FLORIDA COMPLEX LEAGUE

Batting	B-T	HT	WT	DOB	AVG	vLH	vRH	G	AB	R	H	2B	3B	HR	RBI	BB	HBP	SH	SF	SO	SB	CS	SLG	OBP
Acosta, Jeisel	R-R	6-0	170	9-4-01	.195	.222	.188	15	41	2	8	0	0	0	3	3	3	1	0	7	0	0	.195	.298
Amparo, Yeuri	R-R	6-2	170	9-25-01	.253	.417	.182	32	79	10	20	2	0	1	10	7	1	0	1	17	4	1	.316	.318
Arias, Andry	L-L	6-3	180	6-19-00	.259	.214	.270	42	143	19	37	10	0	5	20	17	4	0	2	40	2	3	.434	.349
Avila, Alex	L-R	5-11	228	1-29-87	.000	--	.000	1	3	0	0	0	0	0	0	0	0	0	0	1	0	0	.000	.000
Baker, Darren	L-R	6-0	180	2-11-99	.400	.000	.462	4	15	2	6	1	0	0	1	2	0	0	0	2	0	0	.467	.471
Cluff, Jackson	L-R	6-0	185	12-3-96	.333	.500	.273	5	15	2	5	0	0	0	1	1	1	0	0	5	3	0	.333	.412
Cornell, Zach	L-L	6-2	225	12-18-97	.276	.000	.320	9	29	5	8	3	1	0	2	2	2	0	0	4	0	0	.448	.364
Coutts, Jackson	L-R	6-3	230	9-1-98	.411	.474	.389	21	73	17	30	9	0	1	14	13	2	0	1	9	1	1	.575	.506
Cruz, RobertAnthony	L-R	6-1	190	9-16-98	.130	.000	.188	7	23	1	3	1	0	0	1	1	0	0	0	7	0	0	.174	.167
De La Cruz, ChristopherL	L-L	5-11	145	3-29-01	.180	.000	.229	29	61	14	11	0	1	1	10	21	2	0	2	13	3	0	.262	.395
Diaz, Gio	R-R	5-11	180	2-9-99	.222	.000	.250	5	9	3	2	1	0	0	0	3	1	0	3	1	0	.333	.462
Dieterich, Landon	R-R	6-5	225	5-5-98	.230	.182	.240	26	61	1	14	4	1	1	7	5	4	0	0	23	0	1	.377	.329
Doolittle, Mason	R-R	6-4	210	7-10-98	.250	.000	.400	2	8	1	2	2	0	0	2	0	0	0	0	0	0	0	.500	.250
Emiliani, Leandro	L-L	6-1	180	3-22-00	.194	.200	.194	12	36	1	7	2	0	0	3	4	0	0	1	8	0	0	.250	.268
Frizzell, Will	L-R	6-5	225	2-21-99	.313	.429	.280	9	32	4	10	3	0	1	6	1	1	0	0	6	0	0	.500	.353
Geraldo, Angel	R-R	6-1	160	6-14-01	.190	.182	.194	32	100	10	19	4	0	0	11	6	2	0	2	22	0	0	.230	.245
Gomez, Raymi	B-R	6-0	150	10-28-99	.257	.375	.222	12	35	6	9	0	1	1	6	4	1	0	0	12	1	1	.400	.350
Gonzales, Jarrett	R-R	5-11	185	3-27-98	.000	--	.000	1	1	0	0	0	0	0	0	0	0	0	0	1	0	0	.000	.000
Halter, Gunner	R-R	6-3	180	3-18-98	.240	.000	.300	9	25	6	6	1	1	0	1	1	0	0	0	6	0	0	.400	.269
House, Brady	R-R	6-4	215	6-4-03	.322	.333	.320	16	59	14	19	3	0	4	12	7	0	0	0	13	0	0	.576	.394
Hurtado, Jorge	R-R	6-1	165	10-15-00	.164	.000	.213	20	61	11	10	3	2	3	11	8	2	0	0	20	3	0	.426	.282
Infante, Sammy	R-R	6-1	185	6-22-01	.215	.167	.223	37	121	19	26	5	2	3	15	17	4	0	1	43	3	4	.364	.329
Keller, Alec	L-R	6-2	200	5-13-92	.182	--	.182	4	11	1	2	1	0	0	2	1	0	0	0	5	1	0	.273	.250
Klein, Brian	L-R	5-11	190	6-1-98	.275	.100	.317	25	51	13	14	4	0	2	11	9	4	0	1	9	0	0	.471	.415
Lile, Daylen	L-R	6-0	195	11-30-02	.219	.250	.212	19	64	16	14	2	0	0	10	15	0	0	1	20	2	1	.250	.363
Marte, Daniel	R-R	6-0	165	1-14-02	.204	.226	.198	45	137	22	28	4	1	3	20	24	10	1	0	59	10	5	.314	.363
Matos, Wilfrido	R-R	5-11	160	9-28-00	.143	.000	.150	11	21	4	3	0	0	0	1	9	2	0	0	9	5	1	.143	.438
Murzi, Ivan	R-R	6-0	165	5-28-01	.176	.200	.172	16	34	7	6	0	0	1	2	13	2	0	0	16	1	0	.265	.429
Quintana, Roismar	R-R	6-1	175	2-6-03	.308	.333	.300	7	13	3	4	2	0	1	5	6	1	0	0	5	0	0	.692	.550
Read, Raudy	R-R	6-0	220	10-29-93	.250	--	.250	2	4	2	1	2	0	0	2	1	0	0	0	0	0	0	1.000	.400
Rivero, Yoander	R-R	5-9	155	11-22-01	.270	.222	.282	32	89	17	24	2	1	3	22	19	2	3	0	17	8	2	.416	.409
Sagdal, Ian	L-R	6-3	190	1-6-93	.154	--	.154	5	13	0	2	1	0	0	1	1	0	0	0	3	0	0	.231	.214
Sullivan, Jake	R-R	5-10	187	7-24-97	.333	.500	.308	6	15	4	5	2	0	0	2	4	0	0	0	3	0	0	.467	.474
Tomlin, Quade	L-R	6-1	185	2-11-02	.100	.000	.125	22	60	13	6	4	0	0	4	7	3	0	0	22	0	0	.167	.250
Torres, Ray	B-R	5-11	190	4-9-00	.194	.182	.200	12	36	6	7	0	1	0	4	3	1	0	1	12	0	0	.250	.268
Turbi, Frailin	R-R	6-0	165	10-19-00	.069	.000	.091	9	29	1	2	0	0	0	2	2	1	0	0	8	0	0	.069	.156
White, T.J.	B-R	6-2	210	7-23-03	.283	.167	.317	15	53	11	15	2	0	4	5	3	1	0	0	14	1	0	.547	.356
Williams, Steven	L-R	6-3	216	2-18-99	.429	.000	.600	5	14	5	6	0	0	2	5	4	0	0	0	0	0	0	.857	.556

Pitching	B-T	HT	WT	DOB	W	L	ERA	G	GS	CG	SV	IP	H	R	ER	HR	BB	SO	AVG	vLH	vRH	K/9	BB/9
Alvarez, Andrew	L-L	6-3	215	6-13-99	1	0	3.00	2	0	0	0	3	2	1	1	0	2	6	.182	.000	.333	18.00	6.00
Armenteros, Rogelio	R-R	6-1	244	6-30-94	0	0	0.00	1	0	0	0	1	0	0	0	0	1	1	.000	.000	--	9.00	9.00
Baez, Joan	R-R	6-3	190	12-26-94	0	1	6.00	2	1	0	0	3	4	2	2	0	0	3	.308	.333	.286	9.00	0.00
Beasley, Dylan	R-R	6-3	201	12-2-97	0	0	0.00	2	1	0	0	2	3	0	0	0	0	5	.333	.333	.333	22.50	0.00
Brinley, Ryan	L-R	6-1	200	4-9-93	0	0	0.00	1	1	0	0	1	2	0	0	0	0	0	.667	.667	--	0.00	0.00
Caceres, Bryan	R-R	6-1	170	2-19-00	3	1	3.98	11	6	0	0	41	30	24	18	1	23	38	.205	.230	.188	8.41	5.09
Castro, Andres	R-R	6-2	185	10-15-00	0	0	9.95	5	0	0	0	6	13	7	7	2	7	3	.419	.571	.294	4.26	9.95
Collins, Brendan	R-R	6-4	215	9-10-99	0	0	0.00	2	0	0	1	3	1	0	0	0	0	5	.100	.000	.333	15.00	0.00
Cronin, Matt	L-L	6-2	195	9-20-97	2	0	2.25	3	0	0	0	4	3	1	1	0	1	4	.214	.000	.500	9.00	2.25
Davis, Marc	R-R	6-3	195	11-11-99	0	0	3.72	5	1	0	0	10	9	4	4	0	9	12	.237	.167	.300	11.17	8.38
De La Rosa, Manuel	R-R	6-3	182	6-8-99	0	1	3.38	8	0	0	1	8	8	4	3	1	7	11	.258	.333	.188	12.38	7.88
Dyson, Tyler	R-R	6-4	220	12-24-97	0	1	3.18	3	3	0	0	6	4	2	2	0	5	4	.190	.091	.300	6.35	7.94
Ferrer, Jose A.	L-L	5-11	180	3-3-00	0	4	2.78	17	0	0	2	36	31	18	11	1	9	47	.226	.217	.231	11.86	2.27
Fuentes, Steven	R-R	6-2	241	5-4-97	0	0	0.00	1	1	0	0	3	2	0	0	0	0	7	.182	.250	.143	21.00	0.00
Glavine, Peyton	R-L	5-11	180	3-23-99	1	0	3.00	7	0	0	0	9	4	4	3	0	3	12	.129	.063	.200	12.00	3.00
Gomez, Miguel	R-R	6-3	170	9-9-00	1	3	6.85	12	4	0	0	22	28	19	17	4	6	23	.315	.316	.314	9.27	2.42
Gomez, Niomar	R-R	6-3	173	9-9-98	0	0	4.50	4	0	0	0	6	6	3	3	0	1	6	.261	.417	.091	9.00	1.50
Gonzalez, Pedro	R-R	6-2	225	7-16-00	2	5	5.40	14	3	0	1	33	35	23	20	2	20	33	.263	.254	.270	8.91	5.40
Greenhill, Cody	R-R	6-4	216	9-20-97	0	0	0.00	3	0	0	0	4	6	1	0	1	6	.316	.200	.357	12.46	2.08
Guerra, Javy	R-R	6-1	215	10-31-85	0	0	0.00	2	1	0	2	1	0	0	0	0	0	0	.143	.000	.500	0.00	0.00
Henry, Cole	R-R	6-4	215	7-15-99	0	2	6.75	2	2	0	0	4	5	3	3	0	1	7	.278	.333	.250	15.75	2.25
Hiraldo, Bernardo	R-R	6-2	160	5-20-00	2	4	4.46	12	6	0	1	42	49	31	21	3	9	44	.290	.306	.278	9.35	1.91
Kirian, Michael	R-L	6-6	260	2-1-99	1	0	5.40	4	1	0	0	7	7	4	4	0	2	4	.259	.200	.294	5.40	2.70
Knowles, Lucas	L-L	6-2	185	3-14-98	1	0	5.40	3	0	0	0	5	7	4	3	1	0	4	.304	.333	.294	7.20	1.80
Lara, Andry	R-R	6-4	180	1-6-03	3	2	4.54	9	7	0	0	40	35	21	20	5	13	47	.230	.207	.245	10.66	2.95

	B-T	HT	WT	DOB	W	L	ERA	G	GS	CG	SV	IP	H	R	ER	HR	BB	SO	AVG	vLH	vRH	K/9	BB/9
Marquez, Franklin	L-L	6-0	165	12-6-02	3	0	4.02	10	0	0	0	16	15	7	7	3	4	18	.242	.235	.244	10.34	2.30
Mercedes, Jose	R-R	6-5	178	6-2-00	0	2	11.20	11	1	0	1	14	14	19	17	1	16	12	.259	.200	.310	7.90	10.54
Otanez, Johan	R-R	6-1	168	2-19-02	2	1	5.89	11	3	0	0	18	16	17	12	0	21	23	.232	.207	.250	11.29	10.31
Peterson, Todd	R-R	6-5	230	1-22-98	1	0	1.80	2	0	0	0	5	3	1	1	0	1	4	.158	.000	.250	7.20	1.80
Powell, Holden	R-R	6-0	190	9-9-99	0	0	7.36	3	1	0	0	4	4	3	3	1	1	7	.267	.143	.375	17.18	2.45
Quintanilla, Cole	R-R	6-5	225	5-13-99	0	0	0.00	1	0	0	0	1	1	0	0	0	0	1	.250	.000	.333	9.00	0.00
Ramirez, Aldo	R-R	6-0	191	5-6-01	1	1	8.22	4	2	0	0	8	9	8	7	0	4	3	.300	.333	.250	3.52	4.70
Ribalta, Orlando	R-R	6-7	245	3-5-98	1	1	4.24	11	0	0	2	17	14	9	8	1	7	17	.222	.179	.257	9.00	3.71
Rodriguez, Kevin	R-R	6-1	145	8-13-00	1	2	5.40	13	0	0	1	20	18	14	12	3	9	18	.250	.231	.261	8.10	4.05
Romero, Seth	L-L	6-3	225	4-19-96	0	0	10.80	1	1	0	0	2	3	2	2	0	2	2	.500	--	.500	10.80	10.80
Rutledge, Jackson	R-R	6-8	245	4-1-99	0	1	7.36	2	2	0	0	4	3	3	3	1	2	5	.214	.000	.300	12.27	4.91
Saenz, Dustin	L-L	5-11	190	6-2-99	0	0	4.50	1	1	0	0	2	2	1	1	0	0	4	.250	.000	.333	18.00	0.00
Schlabach, Ike	R-L	6-5	185	12-27-96	0	0	0.00	3	0	0	0	2	1	0	0	0	1	3	.143	.000	.200	11.57	3.86
Schoff, Tyler	R-R	6-4	220	12-6-98	0	0	0.00	2	0	0	0	2	1	0	0	0	1	0	.125	.167	.000	3.86	0.00
Sinclair, Jack	R-R	6-4	170	5-3-99	0	0	5.06	6	2	0	0	11	13	9	6	1	4	8	.302	.278	.320	6.75	3.38
Tetreault, Jackson	R-R	6-5	189	6-3-96	0	1	1.93	2	2	0	0	5	2	1	1	0	2	5	.125	.000	.222	9.64	3.86
Urena, Edward	R-R	6-3	185	3-21-99	0	0	0.00	1	0	0	0	3	1	0	0	0	0	4	.100	.000	.200	12.00	0.00
Vann, Christian	L-L	6-2	195	6-25-96	0	0	0.00	6	0	0	1	7	2	0	0	0	0	11	.091	.125	.071	14.14	0.00

Fielding
C: Acosta 14, Avila 1, Gonzales 1, Murzi 16, Sullivan 6, Torres 11, Turbi 9, Williams 5.
1B: Coutts 20, Dieterich 22, Doolittle 2, Emiliani 10, Frizzell 9, Read 2, Tomlin 1.
2B: Baker 4, Diaz 1, Infante 20, Klein 14, Matos 7, Rivero 7, Tomlin 14.
3B: Cruz 7, Diaz 4, Geraldo 28, Klein 11, Rivero 8, Sagdal 4, Tomlin 7.
SS: Cluff 4, Cruz 1, Geraldo 6, Halter 1, House 16, Infante 15, Matos 5, Rivero 18.
OF: Amparo 27, Arias 30, Cornell 8, De La Cruz 27, Gomez 11, Halter 8, Hurtado 15, Keller 4, Marte 39, Quintana 7, White 15.

DSL NATIONALS ROOKIE
DOMINICAN SUMMER LEAGUE

Batting	B-T	HT	WT	DOB	AVG	vLH	vRH	G	AB	R	H	2B	3B	HR	RBI	BB	HBP	SH	SF	SO	SB	CS	SLG	OBP
Batista, Cristian	L-L	6-1	170	5-2-04	.197	.235	.185	29	71	11	14	2	0	0	6	16	4	0	1	25	2	0	.225	.370
Bustamante, Keiner	L-R	6-1	160	1-14-02	.132	.071	.148	28	68	5	9	1	0	0	3	13	2	1	1	28	1	0	.147	.286
Castro, Sebastian	R-R	6-1	168	12-25-02	.171	.111	.188	20	41	10	7	1	0	0	4	14	2	3	1	19	1	2	.195	.397
Colmenares, Jose	R-R	5-10	165	8-23-02	.235	.269	.226	44	132	19	31	9	1	1	22	15	4	1	4	19	1	1	.341	.323
Contreras, Jhoan	R-R	6-1	185	12-26-03	.244	.185	.261	39	119	23	29	5	1	0	12	16	0		2	27	4	1	.303	.338
Cruz, Armando	R-R	5-10	160	1-16-04	.232	.278	.220	48	177	22	41	8	1	1	17	16	0	2	2	27	11	4	.305	.292
De La Cruz, Edward	R-R	5-11	165	8-27-02	.200	.222	.192	17	35	3	7	1	0	0	2	5	1	0	0	10	1	1	.229	.317
Diaz, Winder	B-R	6-3	170	9-5-02	.207	.238	.202	44	135	19	28	4	2	0	12	28	6	1	2	34	6	3	.267	.363
Estrada, Jean	R-R	5-11	147	2-13-04	.113	.000	.132	22	62	7	7	2	0	0	6	4	4	0	1	24	1	1	.145	.211
Fernandez, Jenier	R-R	6-1	175	10-16-03	.245	.313	.233	36	102	11	25	2	0	0	7	2	2	0	1	28	4	2	.265	.271
Garcia, Juan	R-R	6-0	170	2-17-03	.221	.257	.211	54	163	30	36	8	2	1	12	28	10	0	1	48	10	3	.313	.366
Luis, Andy	L-R	6-0	150	1-14-03	.122	.150	.113	35	82	16	10	1	2	1	5	10	6	0	0	40	3	3	.220	.265
Martinez, Dawry	B-R	5-10	160	10-2-02	.130	.133	.129	34	77	5	10	1	1	0	4	10	2	0	1	27	6	1	.169	.244
Ramirez, Enmanuel	R-R	6-1	170	11-5-03	.168	.121	.184	42	131	16	22	5	0	2	15	11	1	0	1	34	4	2	.252	.236
Santana, Eliesel	R-R	6-2	185	10-2-02	.270	.370	.242	41	122	19	33	9	0	0	17	17	5	1	3	26	6	1	.344	.374
Tejeda, Erick	R-R	6-4	162	12-26-01	.298	.462	.255	42	124	16	37	6	0	3	24	21	6	1	2	25	3	1	.419	.418

Pitching	B-T	HT	WT	DOB	W	L	ERA	G	GS	CG	SV	IP	H	R	ER	HR	BB	SO	AVG	vLH	vRH	K/9	BB/9
Abreu, Juan	R-R	6-2	190	6-12-00	1	1	1.06	11	0	0	0	17	5	2	2	0	10	31	.093	.111	.083	16.41	5.29
Agostini, Gabriel	L-L	6-0	160	7-24-04	5	2	1.11	15	4	0	0	32	23	8	4	0	6	42	.198	.190	.200	11.69	1.67
Atencio, Jose	R-R	5-11	165	9-18-01	5	4	1.58	11	8	0	0	51	40	11	9	1	4	61	.213	.141	.256	10.69	0.70
Carmona, Josue	L-L	6-3	185	9-3-00	0	0	0.00	3	0	0	0	6	1	0	0		2	5	.056	.000	.067	7.94	3.18
Cedeno, Jose	R-R	6-3	170	10-5-01	5	0	1.24	12	10	0	0	58	32	9	8	2	11	73	.160	.095	.198	11.33	1.71
Diaz, Juan	L-L	6-0	175	6-19-98	2	2	3.60	6	0	0	1	10	9	8	4	0	7	12	.231	.250	.222	10.80	6.30
Diaz, Moises	R-R	6-0	195	4-27-01	0	2	2.12	15	0	0	4	17	9	6	4	0	5	13	.155	.250	.088	6.88	2.65
Francisco, Michael	R-R	6-1	163	5-13-01	3	0	2.00	17	0	0	2	18	13	6	4	2	5	22	.203	.174	.220	11.00	2.50
Lara, Randy	R-R	6-2	190	10-30-01	3	3	3.29	10	7	0	0	38	30	20	14	3	10	38	.214	.234	.204	8.92	2.35
Leon, Jefrem	R-R	6-1	155	9-9-02	0	0	1.46	12	3	0	0	25	13	5	4	0	10	27	.157	.156	.157	9.85	3.65
Marcano, Eliel	R-R	6-1	170	7-9-02	2	1	4.70	7	2	0	0	23	28	12	12	2	2	20	.304	.167	.353	7.83	0.78
Montero, Ronni	R-R	6-3	190	11-2-01	1	2	3.38	12	1	0	2	19	15	10	7	0	12	20	.205	.217	.200	9.64	5.79
Moron, Raynel	R-R	6-3	190	3-17-01	2	3	4.30	10	9	0	0	44	52	23	21	0	9	45	.302	.396	.266	9.20	1.84
Ogando, Adrian	R-R	6-2	190	11-20-03	0	1	10.80	5	0	0	0	7	11	10	8	1	3	8	.379	.545	.278	10.80	4.05
Olivero, Sebastian	R-R	6-2	180	1-28-02	0	1	5.40	7	0	0	1	8	13	7	5	3	10	9	.394	.500	.348	9.72	10.80
Perez, Doimil	R-R	6-3	170	11-3-02	1	2	4.67	10	6	0	0	27	25	17	14	3	4	30	.250	.246	.246	10.00	1.33
Polanco, Bryan	R-R	6-2	190	9-12-01	1	0	7.04	5	0	0	0	8	10	6	6	2		11	.300	.455	.211	12.91	2.35
Ramirez, Jorge	L-L	5-10	160	7-12-97	1	1	5.54	6	2	0	0	13	11	9	8	1	3	15	.224	.200	.231	10.38	2.08
Rivas, Gustavo	R-R	6-2	165	11-21-03	1	1	4.86	9	4	0	0	17	17	14	9	1	8	20	.266	.381	.209	6.48	4.32
Zapata, Genderson	R-R	6-3	170	6-26-04	0	0	2.45	5	3	0	0	15	8	4	4	0	3	6	.167	.133	.182	3.68	1.84

Fielding
C: Bustamante 25, Colmenares 31, De La Cruz 11.
1B: Bustamante 1, Castro 1, Colmenares 1, Contreras 17, Diaz 12, Tejeda 33.
2B: Castro 17, Diaz 20, Luis 24, Martinez 1.
3B: Castro 2, Diaz 3, Garcia 51, Tejeda 5.
SS: Cruz 47, Diaz 9, Luis 4.
OF: Batista 20, Estrada 21, Fernandez 34, Martinez 28, Ramirez 42, Santana 40, Tejeda 2.

MINOR
LEAGUES

The Dawn Of A New Era For The Minor Leagues

BY J.J. COOPER

For decades to come, 2021 will be remembered as the beginning of a brand new era of the minor leagues.

The independence (if co-dependence) that had long been a feature of Minor League Baseball was erased with the expiration of the existing Professional Baseball Agreement on Sept. 30, 2020, when Major League Baseball replaced the Professional Baseball Agreement with new Player Development Licenses (PDLs).

Those PDLs eliminated the middleman. Before, MLB dealt with MiLB. Under the new system, MLB contracted directly with MiLB teams, meaning that the relationship eliminated Minor League Baseball as a governing entity.

While Major League Baseball has many demarcation moments in its history, including 1903 (World Series era), 1947 (de-segregation), 1961 (expansion era) and 1969 (league championships mark the expansion of playoffs), Minor League Baseball has rarely had such clear and defined moments of change, in part because the minor leagues have been spread around the country often in more of a loose confederation of independent entities. But in the minors, 1962 will always stand out as the dividing line between the old system with Class B, C and D leagues and the new, streamlined version that saw the leagues reorganized into Triple-A, Double-A, Class A and eventually short-season leagues.

The 1990 PBA between the National Association (as MiLB was then known) and MLB stands as another watershed moment, as it brought the guarantee of Professional Development Contracts for four full-season affiliates for every MLB team as well as increased facility standards that led to new stadiums and massive growth in attendance and franchise values for MiLB teams.

But the complete reorganization of the governance of MiLB is more significant than either of those previous moments. Going forward, MLB has taken over control of the operations of these minor leagues. In doing so, it eliminated short-season baseball, reducing the affiliated minor leagues to four ticket-buying full-season levels (Low-A, High-A, Double-A and Triple-A). Below that, there also are the Dominican Summer, Florida and Arizona Complex leagues.

Wichita suited up for the 2021 season in a new league—the Double-A Central circuit.

MLB is now responsible for marketing and operating MiLB. It is likely that the league names will be rebranded going forward, but for 2021, the traditional league names were replaced by generic placeholders like Triple-A West, Low-A East and Double-A South.

Under the old system, MiLB teams signed Player Development Contracts with MLB teams on (mostly) two-year terms. Every two years, there was an affiliation shuffle when MiLB teams and MLB clubs could decide to find a new partner. A number of MLB teams were frustrated by the musical chairs arrangement that left the unluckiest teams stuck in less-than-ideal affiliation agreements. In multiple cases, MLB teams purchased MiLB teams to avoid being stuck with the worst options.

Beginning in 2021, the remaining 120 MiLB teams signed 10-year Professional Development Licenses with MLB clubs. As long as they meet the facility standards and other PDL provisions, these 120 teams have 10-year agreements with their MLB affiliates.

The facility standards have been significantly increased under the new PDL system, although many of those provisions will not be put into place for several years. Under the new system, teams will be required to meet increased lighting standards, expanded clubhouses and training room facilities as well as dining areas for teams, and have covered batting tunnels and locker rooms for female staff.

The new system also led to a dramatic change in how schedules are constructed. Beginning in 2021, MiLB teams across the board adopted a six-games-on, one-day-off schedule that saw teams play all week against the same opponent. All but the Triple-A West opted to have their off day on Monday while the Triple-A West league opted to have Wednesday as its weekly off day.

The six-days-on, one-day-off schedule was instituted for 2021 to reduce travel during the pandemic. With teams playing fewer but longer series, Triple-A teams were on commercial flights less often. Teams at lower levels spent less time on buses.

The reduced travel also provided financial savings to minor league teams. Cutting one round-trip flight can save a Triple-A team $10,000 or more. The savings on bus travel are a little less consistent, but the reduced travel was expected to save all teams money in 2021.

One MiLB general manager said the six-game schedule would nearly halve the miles his team traveled in 2021.

The new schedule was billed as a one-year experiment, but when schedules were announced for 2022, the six-on and one-off schedule was continued.

Just a few years ago, minor leaguers were guaranteed only one off day a month. Under the new Professional Development License system, players and staff are guaranteed one off day every 15 days. Under the current six-days-on, one-day-off schedule, they receive four off days every 28 days.

League Supervisors Hired

Under the new system, Minor League Baseball's offices in St. Petersburg, Fla. were eliminated. The elimination of league offices meant that league presidents were also eliminated in the reorganization of the minors. In their place, MLB hired five regional supervisors to handle coordinating the many daily details for all 11 affiliated full-season leagues.

The five regional supervisors came from a variety of backgrounds, including a former league president, a former farm director, two former minor league general managers and a former minor league player.

The regional supervisors are responsible for handling the day-to-day issues that arise among teams and leagues throughout the season and offseason.

Previously, many of these responsibilities had been handled by league presidents and league offices, but those were eliminated in the switch of governance of the minors from Minor League Baseball to MLB.

Ronnie Richardson was hired to be the supervisor for Triple-A East and Double-A South. Augusto "Cookie" Rojas became responsible for Double-A Central and High-A Central. Kim Parker is the supervisor for Triple-A West, Low-A West and High-A West. Eric Krupa became responsible for Low-A Southeast and High-A Mid-Atlantic, and Ronnie Glenn supervised Double-A Northeast and Low-A East.

Rosters Expand

As part of the new changes, rosters were also expanded across the minors. For Double-A and Triple-A, teams were limited to 28 active players. For High-A and Low-A the limits were 30 active players. That's a significant increase from the 25 players that were allowed for all full-season levels before. For the short-season and Rookie-level leagues, 35-player active rosters were long the norm, but teams had been limited to 25 players on an active roster for all four full-season levels before 2021.

The newly expanded rosters provided MLB teams some of the roster flexibility they had been requesting. An expanded 28-player roster allowed teams to add another arm or two that can mean the difference between using a position player and another actual pitcher in a bullpen game. It also

NAME GAME

A lot changed in the minor leagues in 2020, even though zero games were played. This chart collects everything that was different in 2021 compared with 2019.

RELOCATIONS
- **Angels:** Double-A Mobile BayBears become Double-A Rocket City Trash Pandas, based in Madison, Ala.
- **Nationals:** High-A Potomac Nationals become Low-A Fredericksburg Nationals. Both are in Virginia.
- **Red Sox:** Triple-A Pawtucket Red Sox become Triple-A Worcester Red Sox and move from R.I. to Mass.
- **Twins:** Triple-A New Orleans become Double-A Wichita. Affiliation switches from Marlins to Twins.

NEW NICKNAMES
- **Fort Myers Mighty Mussels:** formerly Miracle.
- **Jersey Shore BlueClaws:** formerly Lakewood.
- **Kannapolis Cannon Ballers:** formerly Intimidators.

INDEPENDENTS TURNED AFFILIATED
- **Triple-A St. Paul Saints (Twins)**
- **Double-A Somerset Patriots (Yankees)**
- **Triple-A Sugar Land (Astros)**

LOST FULL-SEASON AFFILIATIONS
- **Double-A:** Jackson and Trenton.
- **High-A:** Charlotte, Florida, Frederick and Lancaster.
- **Low-A:** Burlington, Clinton, Hagerstown, Kane County, Lexington and West Virginia.

allowed teams to more comfortably carry an extra position player to provide a fill-in when a player was slightly injured.

At the two Class A levels, the 30-player limit allowed teams to avoid the roster shenanigans that have long been an aspect of those levels. To get players rest and/or to get others playing time, teams often in the past have had paper moves where players (pitchers especially) were optioned to a lower level for a few days, even if they never left the team and remained part of the travel party.

Teams will not be required to carry as many active players as the roster rules allow.

Plenty Of Rules Changes

The 2021 season also brought with it a wide variety of rules changes. At the Triple-A level, the size of bases was increased from 15-by-15 inches to 18-by-18 inches. By doing so, MLB hoped the slightly shorter distance between bases would lead to a higher success rate on stolen base attempts and more infield hits on grounders and bunts. The larger bags can also decrease the number of collisions/spiking incidents at first base. The rule was in place for the first half of the season in Triple-A East and the second half of the season in Triple-A West.

At the Double-A level, teams had to have at least four players on the infield during play, which is defined as having both feet "completely in front of the outer boundary of the infield dirt."

In High-A, pitchers were required to disengage the rubber completely before throwing to any base. At Low-A, pitchers were limited to two step-offs or pickoff attempts per plate appearance. If a pitcher tried a third pickoff in a plate appearance, the move was considered a balk unless the runner was successfully picked off.

In the Low-A Southeast teams used a computerized automatic ball-strike system. In the Low-A West, teams added timers to enforce time between pitches with a 15-second clock.

Of all the changes, the stricter pitch clock in Low-A West proved to have the most significant impact. The 15-second timer was introduced into Low-A West on June 8, five weeks into the season, and led to a decrease of 21 minutes in the average time of a nine-inning game. The introduction of the pitch clock also corresponded with an increase in batting average, runs and home runs and a decrease in walks and strikeouts.

"The pitch timer was one of the more successful experiments from this season," MLB executive vice president for baseball operations Morgan Sword said. "We received very positive feedback on the timer from players, coaches, umpires, minor league operators, frankly everybody that was involved in

ORGANIZATION STANDINGS

Cumulative domestic farm club records for major league organizations, with winning percentages going back five years. Beginning in 2021, most organizations have five affiliates.

	2021 W	L	PCT	2019	2018	2017	2016
1. Rays	411	249	.623	.573	.591	.536	.529
2. Yankees	388	264	.595	.518	.500	.602	.595
3. Red Sox	385	270	.588	.459	.476	.497	.526
4. Mariners	342	257	.571	.487	.469	.487	.581
5. Rockies	358	298	.546	.472	.482	.496	.477
6. Pirates	366	316	.537	.529	.499	.499	.490
7. Rangers	350	306	.534	.559	.466	.467	.491
8. Dodgers	353	309	.533	.562	.552	.546	.527
9. Giants	372	331	.529	.516	.457	.446	.483
10. Blue Jays	306	277	.525	.496	.523	.505	.507
11. Indians	345	317	.521	.509	.529	.493	.550
12. Braves	273	259	.513	.464	.471	.471	.468
13. Royals	354	342	.509	.495	.492	.466	.452
14. Twins	305	297	.507	.539	.511	.581	.540
15. Reds	301	295	.505	.449	.453	.456	.502
16. Marlins	298	292	.505	.506	.465	.483	.454
17. Brewers	350	354	.497	.493	.502	.504	.443
18. Astros	290	309	.484	.527	.576	.521	.513
19. Phillies	304	324	.484	.494	.549	.528	.595
20. Tigers	311	337	.480	.468	.505	.502	.474
21. Angels	270	313	.463	.411	.430	.492	.451
22. Orioles	318	369	.463	.526	.471	.482	.455
23. Padres	280	326	.462	.534	.502	.505	.463
24. Mets	289	344	.457	.493	.472	.456	.480
25. Cubs	296	358	.453	.476	.459	.504	.539
26. D-backs	290	364	.443	.557	.541	.515	.507
27. Athletics	260	337	.436	.477	.515	.494	.488
28. Nationals	247	348	.415	.488	.481	.456	.508
29. White Sox	243	359	.404	.490	.515	.438	.427
30. Cardinals	260	394	.398	.448	.534	.546	.520

POSTSEASON RESULTS

League	Champion	Runner-Up
Triple-A East*	Durham (TB)	Buffalo (TOR)
Triple-A West*	Tacoma (SEA)	Sugar Land (HOU)
Double-A Northeast	Akron (CLE)	Bowie (BAL)
Double-A South	Mississippi (ATL)	Montgomery (TB)
Double-A Central	NW Arkansas (KC)	Wichita (MIN)
High-A Central	Quad Cities (KC)	Cedar Rapids (MIN)
High-A East	Bowling Green (TB)	Greensboro (PIT)
High-A West	Eugene (SF)	Spokane (COL)
Low-A West	San Jose (SF)	Fresno (COL)
Low-A East	Charleston (TB)	Down East (TEX)
Low-A Southeast	Bradenton (PIT)	Tampa (NYY)
Arizona Complex*	ACL Rockies (COL)	ACL Mariners (SEA)
Florida Complex*	FCL Rays (TB)	FCL Yankees (NYY)

* No playoffs; based on winning percentage

the Low-A West league this year. We were very encouraged by how it went."

There were two fundamental differences that made the Low-A West pitch clock more effective at reducing average game times. The first, simply, is there was less time on the clock. The pitch clock rose to 17 seconds with runners on base in Low-A West, compared to 20 seconds at higher levels.

CONTINUED ON PAGE 359

CREDIT

Bobby Witt Jr. Excels At Advanced Levels

BY CARLOS COLLAZO

PLAYER OF THE YEAR

When Royals director of hitting performance Alec Zumwalt first saw Bobby Witt Jr. in person, what stood out to him immediately was his personality.

Whether Witt was in the lineup or slotted in at DH or taking a day off, he was always smiling. There was an easygoing, exciting presence to Witt that was infectious to everyone watching him and playing with him.

But when Zumwalt got more hands-on with Kansas City's 2019 first-round pick, he quickly realized the immense talent of the high school shortstop from Colleyville, Texas.

"The kid's skill set is amazing," Zumwalt said. "I have told a lot of people this, but right from the start the thing that stood out to me was how he could simplify what was so hard for most people—and most hitters.

"His cognitive ability to simplify his thoughts and simplify his mechanics and simplify his approach, it's just so, so unique."

Witt's first pro season was limited to 37 games in the Rookie-level Arizona League in 2019, but after losing the 2020 minor league season to the pandemic, he wasted no time getting back on track.

After standing out in big league spring training, Witt was assigned to Double-A Northwest Arkansas, where he hit .295/.369/.570 with 16 home runs, 11 doubles and 14 stolen bases in 61 games. In mid July, after having recently turned 21, Witt was promoted to Triple-A Omaha. He performed equally well there, hitting .285/.352/.581 with 17 home runs, 24 doubles and 15 stolen bases.

In 123 total games, Witt batted .290/.361/.575 with 33 homers, 35 doubles and 29 stolen bases. He swiped his 30th base on Sept. 30, only to see the game canceled by rain. Thus he fell one steal shy of a 30-30 season.

Among players 21 or younger who played in the upper minors this season, Witt's offensive production as measured by OPS (.936)

stood out. D-backs outfielder Alek Thomas (.953) surpassed Witt, but other notable prospects stood a pace behind, including the Mets' Mark Vientos (.933), the Dodgers' Miguel Vargas (.906) and the Tigers' duo of Spencer Torkelson (.935) and Riley Greene (.921).

For his excellence at a young age and advanced level, Witt is the Baseball America Minor League Player of the Year.

"He is a complete player," Omaha manager Brian Poldberg said. "He can hit for power. He can hit for average. He can steal bases. He can play shortstop. Most of the young guys who we get now think the game owes them. And he plays it like he owes the game."

"He has an easiness on the field, but he works extremely hard behind the scenes," Northwest Arkansas manager Scott Thorman said. "He's done everything we've asked of him. He's hit for power. He's played defense. I mean, he's a true five-tool threat."

As Thorman mentioned, the game does appear to come just a little bit easier to Witt than other players. When asked about an area where he struggled or found difficulties this year, after skipping Class A entirely, Witt struggled to immediately come up with an answer. But he did eventually find one. "I guess sometimes on the road, after games, it's kind of tough to find a spot to eat," Witt said with a chuckle.

"That's about it." ■

Bobby Witt Jr.

CONTINUED FROM PAGE 357

Batters were also required to be in the box ready to hit with eight seconds remaining on the clock, compared to seven seconds at higher levels.

The second, and more significant, difference was how the pitch clock was enforced. Pitchers at Double-A and Triple-A can step off the mound and have the pitch clock reset with no penalty. In the Low-A West, stepping off the mound counted as one of the pitcher's pickoff attempts. He could step off twice and have the clock reset, but the third time he'd be called for a balk.

"We removed a lot of the quote-unquote loopholes that existed in the Triple-A and Double-A pitch clock," Sword said. "I think that's why we saw such a better result in Low-A West compared to some other levels."

The other rules changes generally were less impactful. The larger bases did result in higher stolen base success rates. Runners were successful on 76% of stolen base attempts at the Triple-A levels this season. The success rates ranged between 69-72% each season from 2015-19.

At Double-A, the limits on shifts did little to change how many balls got through the infield. After compiling data throughout the year, however, MLB found no significant difference in batted-ball outcomes by limiting shifts.

The batting average on balls in play at all Double-A leagues was .309 in 2018 and .305 in 2019. In 2021, with shift restrictions in place, the batting average on balls in play was .307.

The step-off rule led to an increase in the number of stolen base attempts and stolen base success rates. From 2015-19, teams averaged 2.4 stolen base attempts per game in High-A. In 2021, they averaged just under 2.85 attempts per game. The success rate on stolen bases rose from nearly 68% from 2015-19 to just under 76% this season. While there were concerns about stolen bases becoming too easy or too prevalent with the rule change, the result was less than one additional stolen base attempt every other game.

The Low-A limit on pickoff attempts also led to an increase in stolen bases. Teams averaged 2.4 stolen base attempts per game in Low-A in 2018-19. With the new limit in place, they averaged nearly 3.2 steal attempts per game this season. The success rate rose from 68% to 77%.

The test with "robo-umps" was messier. One problem that quickly arose was young pitchers at the lowest levels of the minors lacked the control to consistently throw strikes, and umpires were unable to adjust the zone to help speed games along as they normally would. With the increase

In Low-A Southeast, umpires relied on the automated balls and strikes system.

in walks lengthening game times, MLB adjusted the strike zone beginning July 26. It eliminated three-and-a-half inches off the top of the zone, widened it by two inches on each side of the plate and changed where pitches were registered from the front of the plate to the middle of the plate.

The changes correlated with slight increases in batting average and slugging percentage and a reduction in walks and strikeouts. League batters hit .234/.346/.367 with a 12.9% walk rate and 26.8% strikeout rate through July 25. They hit .238/.339/.376 with an 11.4% walk rate and 26% strikeout rate after July 26, when the zone was altered.

MiLB Players Find Their Voice

The end of the 2021 season brought with it a sign of the increased power minor league players have thanks to the power of social media, advocacy groups and the willingness of some players to speak out. MLB announced that it would cover the housing costs of some minor league players beginning in 2022. The exact details were not yet finalized, but MLB's decision to cover housing costs continued a string of small, but growing successes by a concerted campaign from groups like Advocates for Minor Leaguers and More Than Baseball.

During the 2021 season, publicity those groups brought to bear on poor housing situations and inadequate food for team meals led to teams quickly rectifying issues. The year before, negative publicity led the Oakland A's to back away from a plan to not pay their minor league players a stipend

MINOR LEAGUES

MIKE JANES/FOUR SEAM IMAGES

Royals prospect M.J. Melendez led the minor leagues with 41 home runs after a disappointing 2019 season.

during the canceled 2020 minor league season. The addition of paid-for housing will eliminate one of the biggest issues minor league players have during the season. Because of the nature of player movement, the current system where they are responsible for finding their own housing often leaves players stuck with leases (and not-always approved sublets) in cities in which they are no longer playing.

"For most minor leaguers in the past, nearly 100% of our paychecks have gone straight to paying for housing during the season, leaving no room to pocket any money and making it nearly impossible to invest in yourself off the field or provide for your family," Pirates minor league catcher Joe Hudson said. "With housing being paid for (or being provided a stipend) players will now be able to actually make some money during the season and more comfortably provide for themselves and their families. This is an enormous win for MiLBers."

Home Runs Surge Through Minors

The home run surge that swept through Triple-A in 2019 was apparently contagious. In 2021, it spread to the other three levels of the full-season minor leagues.

But the records Triple-A teams set in 2019 had

a clear explanation—the baseball changed. There is no easy answer for why teams were all of a sudden hitting the ball out of the park at much higher rates in the lower levels of the minors.

When Major League Baseball decided to bring the MLB ball to Triple-A in 2019, it sparked a record-breaking season for home runs around the minors. Balls flew out of Triple-A parks at record rates while the other levels of the minors, which used the standard minor league ball, kept hitting home runs at rates consistent with what had been seen in previous years.

In 2021, the balls kept clearing the walls, but in ways that may have been somewhat unexpected. In 2021, the home run surge was focused on every level other than Triple-A.

In 2021, the home run rate at Triple-A dropped off a little from its previous high. Double-A, High-A and Low-A all saw significant power spikes even though the type of ball they used remained unchanged.

At the Triple-A level, home runs dropped from 1.37 per game to 1.24 per game. That's still dramatically higher than the 0.71 to 0.87 home runs per game range the level saw from 2016 to 2018, but it's still 90% of the home run rate in 2019.

But at every other level of the full-season minors, teams hit home runs at rates that seem astonishing when compared to 2019.

■ At Double-A, the home run rate was up 47%, from 0.75 per game in 2019 to 1.10 this year.

■ At Low-A, the home run rate was up 33%, from 0.62 per game in 2019 to 0.82 this year

■ At High-A, the home run jump was a massive 65%, from 0.64 per game in 2019 to 1.06 in 2021

Those levels are using the same standard minor league ball they have used for years.

There are likely a variety of factors at play. Thanks to the reorganization of the minors, multiple leagues shifted levels. The High-A Florida State and California leagues became the Low-A Southeast and West leagues. The short-season Northwest League morphed into the High-A West, while the Low-A Midwest League became High-A Central. The Low-A South Atlantic League and High-A Carolina League were reshuffled to form the new Low-A East and High-A East leagues. So in many cases, the ballparks and environments within which teams play have changed. The 2021 minor league season also didn't start until May, which meant that the power-sapping cold of April did not play a factor in this year's season. And rules changes, most notably automated balls and strikes in Low-A Southeast, led to some alterations in the environment as well. But none of that explains the entirety of the jump in home runs. The teams in the Double-A leagues

K.L. Wombacher Rewards Fan Loyalty

BY J.J. COOPER

Everywhere around the country, MiLB teams received an unexpected status check in 2020. With no season and uncertainty over what the reorganized minors would look like in 2021, minor league teams had to reach out to their long-time supporters and ask them for help.

When the Hillsboro Hops reached out to their sponsors and informed them that they wouldn't have a 2020 season, not one of the sponsors asked for their money back. Instead every one of them just pushed their sponsorships to 2021.

Maybe even more impressively, 94% of the Hops season-ticket holders rolled their money over into 2021 season tickets.

Such a vote of confidence was beyond the front office's wildest dreams.

"That was a wake-up call for us. That was incredible," Hillsboro president K.L. Wombacher said. "We had hoped for 85%. That was one of those moments where you realize how much community support you have."

But such support is not all that surprising. The Hops have been an integral part of the Hillsboro community since they moved there in 2013. Facing capacity restrictions for the first couple of months of the season, Hillsboro drew 1,871 fans per game in 2021. In every other season since they arrived, Hillsboro has averaged more than 3,000 fans per game.

This year, the Hops had a lot more of a good thing. After having no baseball in 2020,

the Hops, along with the rest of what was previously known as the Northwest League, jumped from 38-game home schedules to 60 home games as the league went from being a short-season league to a High-A league. When Vancouver faced an inability to cross the U.S.-Canada border because of coronavirus restrictions, the Hops opened up their stadium, which meant that all of a sudden Hillsboro had 120 home games.

The Canadians brought some staff to Hillsboro to operate Vancouver's "home games" but the food and beverage staff for Hillsboro worked both Vancouver and Hillsboro's games.

For the Hops' consistent success in providing an excellent operation and showing adaptability, Wombacher is Baseball America's 2021 Minor League Executive of the Year. ∎

MINOR LEAGUES

---

largely played in the same parks they did in 2019, and home runs in those leagues increased at similar rates. It's fair to suggest that the emphasis on hitting for more power, and accepting a rise in strikeout rate to go with it, likely also played a role.

The strikeout rate at all four levels was higher than it was in 2019, with the jump ranging from 4.4% in Triple-A up to 16.3% in High-A. At all but the Low-A level—where robo umps led to a massive increase in walk rate in Low-A Southeast—the walk rate increases were right in line with the strikeout rate increases.

As far as run scoring, the power increases in the lower levels meant that for the first time in years, run scoring was relatively equivalent across all four levels. Runs per game at Triple-A dipped from 5.52

in 2019 to 5.11 in 2021. Double-A runs per game increased from 4.10 to 4.72. High-A jumped from 4.15 to 5.06. And Low-A skyrocketed from 4.28 to 5.27.

Across the full-season minors as a whole, the average hitter hit .247/.334/.406. The average game saw 5.04 runs per team per game, with 3.84 walks and 9.62 strikeouts.

Attendance Was Down, As Expected

In any other year, the attendance trends in 2021 would be greeted with concern and dismay.

For the 120 full-season minor league teams, attendance was down nearly 1,000 fans per game

Chris Widger Flexes Managing Chops

BY BILL MITCHELL

MANAGER OF THE YEAR

In only his second season of managing in the affiliated minor leagues, former big leaguer Chris Widger led his Quad Cities River Bandits to the High-A Central league championship. For the outstanding season, Widger is Baseball America's Minor League Manager of the Year. The Royals affiliate finished with a regular season record of 77-41.

Coming off a 2020 season in which no games were played due to the Covid-19 pandemic, Widger and the River Bandits had to navigate through plenty of obstacles both on and off the field to get to the league championship. It helped that the 10-year major league veteran had already built a solid foundation with many of the players that he took to Quad Cities for the start of the 2021 regular season thanks to his previous managing assignment with the Royals.

"Widge had built a strong relationship with the core group of this team back in Burlington (N.C.) during the 2019 season," said Alec Zumwalt, Kansas City's director of hitting performance/player development. "His players love playing for him and in turn he creates a winning environment in the clubhouse that plays out on the field."

The 2019 season in the Rookie-level Appalachian League was Widger's first managing job in the Royals system. He led that team to the league championship round before losing to Johnson City in the finals, two games to one.

One of the many challenges that Widger had to tackle over the course of the 2021 season was the turnover of players resulting from assorted injuries and promotions to the Double-A level. One of the key losses was when first baseman Vinnie Pasquantino was promoted to Northwest Arkansas in mid July.

"He was not only our best player overall," Widger said about Pasquantino, "but he was the guy that the players turned to when they had a problem or needed to be picked up."

It wasn't just how his players performed on the field, but also how they handled themselves off the field that made a difference with this team. Widger credits the Royals front office for bringing not just good players into the organization but quality individuals. ∎

---

per team. The 120 full-season minor league clubs averaged 4,201 fans per game per team in 2019 and 3,234 fans per game per team in 2021 (a 23% drop).

But this was not any other year. This was the year that the minors returned to action after losing the entirety of the 2020 season to the coronavirus pandemic. The season was shortened to 120 games for both Class A levels and Double-A and 130 games for the Triple-A level. Some teams dealt with capacity restrictions early in the season. Others faced reluctance from some fans (especially groups) to attend games all year because of the ongoing pandemic. And all teams faced a shortened selling season because of the delays in getting a 2021 minor league schedule announced.

Those complicating factors didn't affect all teams equally, but it did affect everyone in some manner. Only three minor league teams drew more fans per game in 2021 than they did in 2019, and one of those three was a team that stopped selling tickets for three out of every six home games.

In talking to a number of people around the minors, the overall sense at the end of the 2021 season is one of relief much more than panic. While there were sporadic game cancellations because of players and staff testing positive for Covid-19, those cancellations were not widespread. While teams had hurdles when it came to selling tickets, fans did return to the ballpark.

And with almost all ticket and advertising make-goods from the canceled 2020 season now off the books and the 2022 schedules being announced, teams can head into next season with the expecta-

TRIPLE-A

Pos	Player, Team (Organization)	Age	AVG	OBP	SLG	AB	H	2B	3B	HR	RBI	BB	SO	SB
C	Keibert Ruiz, Okla. City/Rochester (Dodgers/Nats)	22	.310	.377	.616	284	88	24	0	21	59	30	33	0
1B	Juan Yepez, Memphis (Cardinals)	23	.281	.374	.575	292	82	23	0	21	60	40	69	3
2B	Michael Stefanic, Salt Lake (Angels)	25	.342	.417	.520	383	131	20	0	16	54	44	60	6
3B	Drew Ellis, Reno (D-backs)	25	.296	.402	.615	291	86	29	2	20	73	46	84	1
SS	Jose Barrero, Louisville (Reds)	23	.306	.392	.594	170	52	10	0	13	38	20	44	8
OF	Khalil Lee, Syracuse (Mets)	23	.271	.449	.496	280	76	20	2	13	36	69	110	8
OF	Josh Lowe, Durham (Rays)	23	.291	.380	.538	385	112	28	2	21	75	58	118	26
OF	Jake Meyers, Sugar Land (Astros)	25	.343	.408	.598	271	93	17	2	16	51	25	59	10
DH	Jose Marmolejos, Tacoma (Mariners)	28	.350	.450	.690	274	96	14	2	25	74	51	63	0

Pos	Pitcher, Team (Organization)	Age	W	L	ERA	G	GS	IP	H	BB	SO	HR	SO/9	WHIP
SP	Jackson Kowar, Omaha (Royals)	24	9	4	3.46	17	16	81	66	34	115	7	12.8	1.24
SP	Kyle Muller, Gwinnett (Braves)	23	5	4	3.40	16	16	77	62	39	85	9	10.0	1.32
SP	Tommy Romero, Durham (Rays)	23	6	2	3.45	11	11	57	36	20	64	7	10.0	0.98
SP	Joe Ryan, Durham/St. Paul (Rays/Twins)	25	4	3	3.41	14	13	66	40	12	92	9	12.6	0.79
SP	Kyle Wright, Gwinnett (Braves)	25	9	5	3.18	23	23	130	112	44	129	9	8.9	1.20
RP	Tony Santillan, Louisville (Reds)	24	1	3	2.13	13	6	38	25	15	51	5	12.1	1.05

DOUBLE-A

Pos	Player, Team (Organization)	Age	AVG	OBP	SLG	AB	H	2B	3B	HR	RBI	BB	SO	SB
C	MJ Melendez, Northwest Arkansas (Royals)	22	.285	.372	.628	298	85	18	0	28	65	43	76	2
1B	Nick Pratto, Northwest Arkansas (Royals)	22	.271	.404	.570	221	60	13	4	15	43	46	80	7
2B	Jonathan Aranda, Montgomery (Rays)	23	.325	.410	.540	274	89	19	5	10	58	33	63	4
3B	Miguel Vargas, Tulsa (Dodgers)	21	.321	.386	.523	327	105	16	1	16	60	36	57	7
SS	Bobby Witt Jr., Northwest Arkansas (Royals)	21	.295	.369	.570	244	72	11	4	16	51	25	67	14
OF	Peyton Burdick, Pensacola (Marlins)	24	.231	.376	.472	373	86	17	2	23	52	76	136	9
OF	Riley Greene, Erie (Tigers)	20	.298	.381	.525	326	97	16	5	16	54	41	102	12
OF	Julio Rodriguez, Arkansas (Mariners)	20	.362	.461	.546	174	63	11	0	7	26	29	37	16
DH	Jose Miranda, Wichita (Twins)	23	.345	.408	.588	194	67	8	0	13	37	16	25	4

Pos	Pitcher, Team (Organization)	Age	W	L	ERA	G	GS	IP	H	BB	SO	HR	SO/9	WHIP
SP	Jake Eder, Pensacola (Marlins)	22	3	5	1.77	15	15	71	43	27	99	3	12.5	0.98
SP	Max Meyer, Pensacola (Marlins)	22	6	3	2.41	20	20	101	84	40	113	7	10.1	1.23
SP	Grayson Rodriguez, Bowie (Orioles)	21	6	1	2.60	18	18	80	47	22	121	8	13.7	0.87
SP	Josh Winder, Wichita (Twins)	24	3	0	1.98	10	10	55	41	10	65	5	10.7	0.93
SP	Cole Winn, Frisco (Rangers)	21	3	3	2.31	19	19	78	38	26	97	6	11.2	0.82
RP	Jovani Moran, Wichita (Twins)	24	2	1	1.91	20	0	38	14	14	64	3	15.3	0.74

HIGH-A

Pos	Player, Team (Organization)	Age	AVG	OBP	SLG	AB	H	2B	3B	HR	RBI	BB	SO	SB
C	Francisco Alvarez, Brooklyn (Mets)	19	.247	.351	.538	279	69	13	1	22	58	40	82	6
1B	Vinnie Pasquantino, Quad Cities (Royals)	23	.291	.384	.565	237	69	20	3	13	42	33	38	4
2B	Nick Gonzales, Greensboro (Pirates)	22	.302	.385	.565	324	98	23	4	18	54	40	101	7
3B	Austin Shenton, Everett (Mariners)	23	.295	.418	.576	224	66	24	3	11	53	41	62	1
SS	Anthony Volpe, Hudson Valley (Yankees)	20	.286	.391	.587	213	61	17	1	15	37	27	58	12
OF	Matt Fraizer, Greensboro (Pirates)	23	.314	.401	.578	303	95	14	3	20	50	43	74	14
OF	Andy Pages, Great Lakes (Dodgers)	20	.265	.394	.539	438	116	25	1	31	88	77	132	6
OF	George Valera, Lake County (Indians)	20	.256	.430	.548	199	51	2	3	16	43	55	58	10
DH	Griffin Conine, Beloit (Marlins)	23	.247	.382	.587	235	58	7	2	23	59	46	103	3

Pos	Pitcher, Team (Organization)	Age	W	L	ERA	G	GS	IP	H	BB	SO	HR	SO/9	WHIP
SP	Logan T. Allen, Lake County (Indians)	22	5	0	1.58	9	9	51	37	13	67	3	11.7	0.97
SP	Xzavion Curry, Lake County (Indians)	22	5	1	2.66	13	13	68	53	12	80	10	10.6	0.96
SP	Zak Kent, Hickory (Rangers)	23	6	2	2.83	14	9	60	46	15	78	5	11.6	1.01
SP	Louie Varland, Cedar Rapids (Twins)	23	6	2	2.10	10	10	56	41	14	66	4	10.7	0.99
SP	Ken Waldichuk, Hudson Valley (Yankees)	23	2	0	0.00	7	7	31	12	13	55	0	16.1	0.82
RP	Chris Wright, Eugene (Giants)	22	4	0	0.97	31	0	37	15	18	62	2	15.1	0.89

tion of the first "normal" offseason since 2019.

The reduction of the minor leagues to 120 full-season clubs means that the mark for what was considered an excellent attendance season in the past is now obsolete. MLB's takeover of the minors eliminated 40 teams from the affiliated minors. It also means that the Mexican League, which MiLB was affiliated with and counted in its attendance marks, no longer counts in the attendance figures.

That means that it is likely that the 43.26 million fans MiLB drew in attendance in 2008 will stand as the all-time record for the foreseeable future. MiLB drew 42.4 million in 2014 and 42.5 million in 2015, but MiLB has failed to top 42

MINOR LEAGUES

LOW-A

Pos	Player, Team (Organization)	Age	AVG	OBP	SLG	AB	H	2B	3B	HR	RBI	BB	SO	SB
C	Endy Rodriguez, Bradenton (Pirates)	21	.294	.380	.512	377	111	25	6	15	73	50	77	2
1B	Curtis Mead, Charleston (Rays)	20	.356	.408	.586	191	68	21	1	7	35	15	30	9
2B	Nick Yorke, Salem (Red Sox)	19	.323	.413	.500	294	95	14	4	10	47	41	47	11
3B	Orelvis Martinez, Dunedin (Blue Jays)	19	.279	.369	.572	283	79	22	2	19	68	33	85	4
SS	Anthony Volpe, Tampa (Yankees)	20	.302	.455	.623	199	69	18	5	12	49	51	43	21
OF	Joe Gray Jr., Carolina (Brewers)	21	.289	.407	.632	190	55	15	7	12	53	33	61	12
OF	Robert Hassell, Lake Elsinore (Padres)	19	.323	.415	.482	365	118	31	3	7	65	57	74	31
OF	Zac Veen, Fresno (Rockies)	19	.301	.399	.501	399	120	27	4	15	75	64	126	36
DH	Jairo Pomares, San Jose (Giants)	20	.372	.429	.693	199	74	22	0	14	44	15	54	0

Pos	Pitcher, Team (Organization)	Age	W	L	ERA	G	GS	IP	H	BB	SO	HR	SO/9	WHIP
SP	Taj Bradley, Charleston (Rays)	20	9	3	1.76	15	14	67	37	20	81	4	10.9	0.86
SP	Joey Estes, Augusta (Braves)	19	3	6	2.91	20	20	99	66	29	127	7	11.5	0.96
SP	Kyle Harrison, San Jose (Giants)	19	4	3	3.19	20	20	99	86	52	157	3	14.3	1.40
SP	Ryan Murphy, San Jose (Giants)	21	4	2	2.96	15	15	76	59	18	116	11	13.7	1.01
SP	Eury Perez, Jupiter (Marlins)	18	2	3	1.61	15	15	56	32	21	82	2	13.2	0.95
RP	Randy Rodriguez, San Jose (Giants)	21	6	3	1.74	32	0	62	44	23	101	0	14.7	1.08

ARIZONA & FLORIDA COMPLEX LEAGUES

Pos	Player, Team (Organization)	Age	AVG	OBP	SLG	AB	H	2B	3B	HR	RBI	BB	SO	SB
C	Andruw Salcedo, ACL Reds	18	.362	.459	.543	94	34	5	0	4	11	12	30	0
1B	Anthony Garcia, FCL Yankees	20	.318	.459	.697	66	21	1	0	8	21	18	25	10
2B	James Triantos, ACL Cubs	18	.327	.376	.594	101	33	7	1	6	19	7	18	3
3B	Blaze Jordan, FCL Red Sox	18	.362	.408	.667	69	25	7	1	4	19	6	13	1
SS	Jose Salas, FCL Marlins	18	.370	.458	.511	92	34	10	0	1	11	11	23	8
OF	Kevin Alcantara, ACL Cubs	18	.345	.423	.588	119	41	4	5	5	24	17	36	5
OF	Owen Caissie, ACL Cubs	18	.349	.478	.596	109	38	7	1	6	20	26	39	1
OF	James Wood, ACL Padres	18	.372	.465	.535	86	32	5	0	3	22	13	32	10
DH	Coby Mayo, FCL Orioles	19	.329	.440	.566	76	25	6	0	4	15	13	14	6

Pos	Pitcher, Team (Organization)	Age	W	L	ERA	G	GS	IP	H	BB	SO	HR	SO/9	WHIP
SP	Gabriel Aguilera, ACL Reds	20	0	1	1.29	5	4	21	11	4	35	1	15.0	0.71
SP	Po-Yu Chen, FCL Pirates	19	2	0	0.69	6	6	26	18	0	29	0	10.0	0.69
SP	Antonio Jimenez, FCL Rays	20	2	0	1.65	8	5	33	23	7	44	1	12.1	0.92
SP	Yaifer Perdomo, FCL Blue Jays	19	2	0	2.45	8	7	33	19	14	59	1	16.1	1.00
SP	Kendry Rojas, FCL Blue Jays	18	0	0	2.28	8	4	24	14	5	39	1	14.8	0.80

DOMINICAN SUMMER LEAGUE

Pos	Player, Team (Organization)	Age	AVG	OBP	SLG	AB	H	2B	3B	HR	RBI	BB	SO	SB
C	Onil Perez, DSL Giants	18	.313	.477	.422	83	26	3	0	2	13	27	10	6
1B	Daniel Montesino, DSL Padres	17	.322	.468	.513	152	49	12	4	3	41	40	41	8
2B	Adrian Pinto, DSL Rockies	18	.371	.486	.545	143	53	11	4	2	23	28	16	37
3B	Cristian Santana, DSL Tigers	17	.276	.418	.507	152	42	12	1	7	22	26	41	9
SS	Victor Acosta, DSL Padres	17	.292	.434	.506	154	45	8	5	5	30	30	37	23
OF	Yanquiel Fernandez, DSL Rockies	18	.340	.423	.547	150	51	16	0	5	32	22	24	0
OF	Gabriel Gonzalez, DSL Mariners	17	.306	.392	.556	160	49	14	4	6	32	20	30	8
OF	Samuel Zavala, DSL Padres	16	.304	.399	.503	161	49	14	6	2	35	25	32	11
DH	Carlos Jorge, DSL Reds	17	.361	.442	.586	133	48	7	7	3	31	18	26	22

Pos	Pitcher, Team (Organization)	Age	W	L	ERA	G	GS	IP	H	BB	SO	HR	SO/9	WHIP
SP	Gabriel Agostini, FCL Nationals	16	4	2	0.65	13	4	28	18	6	34	0	11.1	0.87
SP	Joel Diaz, FCL Mets	17	0	1	0.42	13	13	43	24	9	54	0	11.2	0.76
SP	Fernando Guanare, ACL Angels	18	4	1	1.96	9	9	46	40	1	49	0	9.6	0.89
SP	Victor Juarez, ACL Rockies	18	2	0	0.68	7	6	27	11	6	34	0	11.5	0.64
SP	Adrian Quintana, FCL Mariners	18	3	1	1.88	10	9	48	24	9	50	2	9.4	0.69

million since. In 2019, the final year of the old format, MiLB drew 41.5 million fans, for an average of 4,044 fans per game per team.

This year, that number dipped to 22.1 million fans in attendance. Comparing like to like, the 120 full-season MiLB teams in 2019 drew 33.3 million fans, but that was in a season with 1,114 additional home dates because of the longer year.

With some coronavirus cancellations this year, the overall percentage of lost dates for all causes rose, but not dramatically. In 2018, 5.4% of scheduled dates were lost. In 2019, teams lost 5.2% of scheduled dates. In 2021, that number rose to 5.9%.

The 11-million drop in fans is precipitous, but it's impossible to treat this season as close to normal. And the drop in attendance was actually significantly less as a percentage than the drop at the MLB level.

Royals catcher MJ Melendez topped the minor leagues with 41 home runs.

Nationals righthander Cade Cavalli led the minor leagues with 175 strikeouts.

FIRST TEAM

Pos	Player, Organization (Peak Level)	Age	AVG	OBP	SLG	AB	R	H	HR	RBI	BB	SO
C	M.J. Melendez, Royals (Triple-A)	22	.288	.386	.625	448	95	129	41	103	75	115
1B	Nick Pratto, Royals (Triple-A)	22	.265	.385	.602	445	98	118	36	98	83	157
2B	Jose Miranda, Twins (Triple-A)	23	.344	.401	.572	535	97	184	30	94	42	74
3B	Miguel Vargas, Dodgers (Double-A)	21	.318	.380	.525	484	98	154	23	75	45	89
SS	Bobby Witt Jr., Royals (Triple-A)	21	.290	.361	.575	497	99	144	33	97	51	131
OF	Riley Greene, Tigers (Triple-A)	20	.301	.387	.534	485	95	146	24	84	63	153
OF	Andy Pages, Dodgers (High-A)	20	.265	.394	.539	438	96	116	31	88	77	132
OF	Julio Rodriguez, Mariners (Double-A)	20	.347	.441	.560	291	64	101	13	47	43	66
DH	Anthony Volpe, Yankees (High-A)	20	.294	.423	.604	412	113	121	27	86	78	101

Pos	Pitcher, Organization (Peak Level)	Age	W	L	ERA	G	GS	IP	BB	SO	HR	AVG
SP	Taj Bradley, Rays (High-A)	20	12	3	1.83	23	22	103	31	123	8	.181
SP	Matt Brash, Mariners (Double-A)	22	6	4	2.31	20	19	97	48	142	6	.180
SP	Cade Cavalli, Nationals (Triple-A)	22	7	9	3.36	24	24	123	60	175	5	.213
SP	Max Meyer, Marlins (Double-A)	22	6	4	2.27	22	22	111	42	130	8	.221
SP	Grayson Rodriguez, Orioles (Double-A)	21	9	1	2.36	23	23	103	27	161	10	.159
RP	Chris Wright, Giants (High-A)	22	4	0	1.00	37	0	45	21	79	2	.126

SECOND TEAM

Pos	Player, Organization (Peak Level)	Age	AVG	OBP	SLG	AB	R	H	HR	RBI	BB	SO
C	Adley Rutschman, Orioles (Triple-A)	23	.285	.397	.502	452	86	129	23	75	79	90
1B	Spencer Torkelson, Tigers (Triple-A)	21	.267	.383	.552	431	89	115	30	91	77	114
2B	Nick Yorke, Red Sox (High-A)	19	.325	.412	.516	378	76	123	14	62	52	69
3B	Jordan Walker, Cardinals (High-A)	19	.317	.388	.548	325	63	103	14	48	33	87
SS	Jose Barrero, Reds (Triple-A)	23	.303	.380	.539	330	62	100	19	66	36	84
OF	Josh Lowe, Rays (Triple-A)	23	.291	.381	.535	402	76	117	22	78	61	123
OF	Jake Meyers, Astros (Triple-A)	25	.343	.408	.598	271	52	93	16	51	25	59
OF	Joey Wiemer, Brewers (High-A)	22	.295	.403	.556	396	86	117	27	77	63	105
DH	Vinnie Pasquantino, Royals (Double-A)	23	.300	.394	.563	437	79	131	24	84	64	64

Pos	Pitcher, Organization (Peak Level)	Age	W	L	ERA	G	GS	IP	BB	SO	HR	AVG
SP	Logan T. Allen, Indians (Double-A)	22	9	0	2.26	21	19	111	26	143	12	.193
SP	Shane Baz, Rays (Triple-A)	22	5	4	2.06	17	17	79	12	113	9	.181
SP	Ryne Nelson, D-backs (Double-A)	23	7	4	3.17	22	22	116	40	163	16	.206
SP	Eury Perez, Marlins (High-A)	18	3	5	1.96	20	20	78	26	108	7	.158
SP	Tommy Romero, Rays (Triple-A)	23	8	2	2.61	23	21	110	31	145	10	.189
RP	Dauri Moreta, Reds (Triple-A)	25	6	0	1.02	42	0	53	9	58	5	.164

Durham Bulls Rule The Minor Leagues

BY BOB SUTTON

The Durham Bulls were stacked with talent and perhaps even overflooded with prospects when the 2021 season finally began.

They had the game's top prospect in shortstop Wander Franco and a lineup that might have been the envy of teams in the major leagues.

Then, it got better for the Bulls.

They started playing.

"It has been an unbelievable year from start to finish," manager Brady Williams said. "Not knowing if we were going to start the season. Coming into a season where you weren't sure if you were going to have fans. Then we had fans. Then a Fourth of July sellout, which was awesome. This is how it was in '19, a packed house."

Wander Franco

Meanwhile, this edition of the Bulls was cramming the record books.

With that, they're the Minor League Team of the Year—the first Triple-A team to land that honor since 2006.

Williams had a chore managing all this talent for the top affiliate of the Rays, who finished with the best record in the American League. That meant a steady stream of player transitions between Durham and Tampa Bay.

Durham's 86-44 record matches the third-most wins in the franchise's Triple-A history while playing 14 fewer games. The .661 winning percentage is tops for the Bulls franchise.

The Bulls produced the best record in Triple-A, winning whatever team honors that were to be awarded. They took a first-place spot in Triple-A East in mid June and never relinquished it.

Five players received first-time promotions to the major leagues from the Bulls. Two others were with the Durham club in what amounted to an extended spring training when they received their first calls to the big leagues.

"If they were in a different organization or a different spot, they would be up there a lot longer," Williams said. "It's hard to crack that (Rays) lineup."

There was more than one player transaction per day involving Durham.

In all, 74 players appeared in games for the Bulls—46 pitchers and 28 position players.

Williams, who was in his second season with the Bulls after leading them to the 2019 International League playoffs, had veteran pitching coach Rick Knapp at his side.

"There was a moment in the season we weren't quite sure who was on the team and who was available to pitch," Williams said.

At one point, the Bulls lost two members of the starting rotation to the U.S. Olympic team when Joe Ryan and Shane Baz headed to Japan. When the Olympians came home, Ryan was a member of the Minnesota Twins.

By the time the season ended, Baz was pitching in the American League playoffs.

Franco, of course, made a splash with the Rays once his stay of about 6.5 weeks with the Bulls came to a close.

If not for Franco, other Bulls might have been viewed as headliners in any other season.

"I think anybody that's with Wander is going to get overlooked," Williams said.

"He's the No. 1 prospect in baseball for all the right reasons. There's a lot of other good players on this team that deserve attention just like Wander." ∎

LAST 10 WINNERS

2010: Northwest Arkansas/Texas League (Royals)
2011: Mobile BayBears/Southern League (Diamondbacks)
2012: Springfield Cardinals/Texas League (Cardinals)
2013: Daytona Cubs/Florida State League (Cubs)
2014: Portland Sea Dogs/Eastern League (Red Sox)
2015: Biloxi Shuckers/Southern League (Brewers)
2016: Rome Braves/South Atlantic League (Braves)
2017: Midland RockHounds/Texas League (Athletics)
2018: Bowling Green Hot Rods/Midwest League (Rays)
2019: Amarillo/Texas League (Padres)

Full list: BaseballAmerica.com/awards

MINOR LEAGUES

BY EMILY WALDON

When Brennen Davis arrived in Denver to represent the Cubs in the 2021 Futures Game, he made up his mind to keep things simple.

It's nothing out of the ordinary, just the way the 21-year-old outfielder has always been wired. After navigating limited play at the alternate training site in 2020, Davis is just happy to be back with the opportunity to do what he loves.

Adapting to the atmosphere of Denver, Davis knew the air will treat you differently out west than at his regular-season assignment of Knoxville, Tenn., home of the Double-A Tennessee Smokies.

Davis' introduction at the plate for the National League roster wasn't seamless, ending in a swinging strikeout.

He was late and he knew it.

Prior to his next at-bat, Davis returned to the basics and knew he needed to just slow down.

Facing Twins righthander Josh Winder in the fourth inning, Davis wasn't familiar with Winder's profile, but he had returned the pace of the game to what he wanted.

That adjustment translated to him vaulting a 95 mph fastball 428 feet to straightaway center field.

Just like always, Davis was keeping it simple.

Fast forward to the sixth inning. Orioles righthander Marcos Diplan had faced one batter the previous inning, giving Davis a preview of what he would be facing.

"When he came back out, I kind of had an idea of what he had," Davis said.

This time it was an 83 mph offspeed offering that Davis rocketed 410 feet.

Following the game, as the newly crowned Futures Game MVP slid into a seat, still donning his Cubs cap and uniform, the events of the day were still setting in and Davis didn't deny that.

"I can't put it into words, because I feel like (the Futures Game) still happening and I haven't been able to come down from what just happened and running around the bases. I don't know," he said. "You should ask me tomorrow."

The man giving him the MVP trophy? Hall of famer Ken Griffey Jr.

"Yeah, I mean being around Ken Griffey (in the clubhouse) and all the players, I really enjoyed being around all those guys," Davis added. "These are the guys that I hope to play against, and play with later on in my career. It's just awesome to be around those caliber of guys." ∎

FUTURES GAME BOX SCORE

NATIONAL LEAGUE 8, AMERICAN LEAGUE 3
JULY 11 IN DENVER

AL	AB	R	H	RBI	NL	AB	R	H	RBI
Witt Jr., SS	2	0	0	0	Thomas, LF	2	0	0	0
Martin, SS	1	0	1	1	Waters, LF	1	0	1	0
Kelenic, LF	1	0	0	0	Barrero, SS	1	2	1	1
a-Dominguez, CF	3	0	0	0	Luciano, SS	1	0	0	0
Rodriguez, RF	3	0	0	0	Gorman, 3B	2	1	1	1
Rutschman, C	1	0	0	0	Baty, 3B	2	0	0	0
Naylor, B, C	1	0	0	0	Campusano, C	1	0	0	1
Pratto, 1B	1	0	0	0	MacIver, C	2	0	0	0
Soderstrom, 1B	1	0	0	0	Harris, M, CF	2	0	0	0
Cespedes, DH	2	0	0	0	Ramos, CF	1	0	0	0
c-Leon, PH	1	0	0	0	Davis, B, RF	3	2	2	2
Greene, CF-LF	3	1	2	0	Vilade, DH	2	0	0	0
Torkelson, 3B	2	1	1	0	a-Alvarez, PH-DH	1	1	1	1
Edwards, 2B	1	0	0	0	Stott, 2B	2	1	0	0
b-Downs, Jet., 2B	2	1	1	2	Busch, 2B	1	0	1	0
					Toglia, 1B	3	1	1	2
Totals	**25**	**3**	**5**	**3**	**Totals**	**27**	**8**	**8**	**8**

							R	H	E
AMERICAN LEAGUE	000	000	3				3	5	1
NATIONAL LEAGUE	104	102	X				8	8	0

AL: 2B: Downs, Jet (1, Small). **TB:** Downs, Jet 2; Greene 2; Martin; Torkelson. **RBI:** Downs, Jet 2 (2); Martin (1). **Runners left in scoring position, 2 out:** Dominguez; Torkelson. **Team RISP:** 2-for-4. **Team LOB:** 6. **CS:** Rodríguez (1, 3rd base by Rodríguez, M/MacIver). **E:** Ragans (1, fielding).

NL: 2B: Gorman (1, Bello). **HR:** Barrero (1, 1st inning off Winn, 0 on, 1 out); Toglia (1, 3rd inning off Ragans, 1 on, 0 out); Davis 2 (2, 4th inning off Winder, 0 on, 0 out, 6th inning off Diplán, M, 0 on, 0 out); Álvarez (1, 6th inning off Diplán, M, 0 on, 0 out). **TB:** Barrero 4; Busch; Davis 8; Gorman 2; Toglia 4; Waters; Álvarez 4. **RBI:** Barrero (1); Campusano (1); Davis 2 (2); Gorman (1); Toglia (1); Álvarez (1). **Runners left in scoring position, 2 out:** Luciano; MacIver 2. **SF:** Campusano. **Team RISP:** 0-for-3. **Team LOB:** 5.

AL	IP	H	R	ER	BB	SO	NL	IP	H	R	ER	BB	SO
Winn (L)	1	1	1	1	0	1	Liberatore (W)	1	0	0	0	0	1
Baz	1	0	0	0	0	2	Meyer	0.1	0	0	0	1	0
Ragans	0.1	1	3	2	1	1	Jackson	1	1	0	0	0	0
Bello	0.2	1	1	1	0	0	Lodolo	1	0	0	0	0	1
Winder	0.1	1	1	1	1	0	Priester	0.2	0	0	0	1	1
Yan	0.2	0	0	0	1	0	Cavalli	1	0	0	0	2	2
Detmers	0.2	0	0	0	0	2	Rodriguez, M	1	0	0	0	1	1
Diplan, M	0.1	2	2	2	0	1	Eder	0.1	1	1	1	0	1
Medina	1	2	0	0	1	2	Small	0.2	3	2	2	0	2
Totals	**6**	**8**	**8**	**7**	**3**	**10**	**Totals**	**7**	**5**	**3**	**3**	**5**	**9**

WP: Bello; Winder; Medina. **Pitches-strikes:** Winn 20-13; Baz 10-8; Ragans 15-7; Bello 11-7; Winder 12-9; Yan 15-7; Detmers 10-7; Diplán, M 17-12; Medina 28-17; Liberatore 12-6; Meyer 7-2; Jackson 14-8; Lodolo 13-8; Priester 13-6; Cavalli 29-15; Rodríguez, M 14-9; Eder 7-4; Small 14-10. **T:** 2:41

Full-season teams only

DEPARTMENT LEADERS

FULL-SEASON TEAM LEADERS

WINS
Durham Bulls (Triple-A East)	86
Bowling Green Hot Rods (High-A East)	82
Charleston Riverdogs (Low-A East)	82
Buffalo Bisons (Triple-A East)	79
Tacoma Rainiers (Triple-A West)	78

LONGEST WINNING STREAK
Memphis (Triple-A East)	15
Nashville Sounds (Triple-A East)	15
Portland Sea Dogs (Double-A Northeast)	14
Buffalo Bisons (Triple-A East)	12
Frisco RoughRiders (Double-A Central)	11
Fresno Grizzlies (Low-A West)	11
Bowling Green Hot Rods (High-A East)	11
Durham Bulls (Triple-A East)	11

LOSSES
Visalia Rawhide (Low-A West)	82
Charlotte Knights (Triple-A East)	81
Palm Beach Cardinals (Low-A Southeast)	80
El Paso Chihuahuas (Triple-A West)	79
Hartford Yard Goats (Double-A Northeast)	79
Kannapolis Cannon Ballers (Low-A East)	79

LONGEST LOSING STREAK
Palm Beach Cardinals (Low-A Southeast)	18
Hickory Crawdads (High-A East)	16
Kannapolis Cannon Ballers (Low-A East)	15
Fredericksburg Nationals (Low-A East)	15
Syracuse Mets (Triple-A East)	15

BATTING AVERAGE
Reno Aces (Triple-A West)	.294
Sacramento River Cats (Triple-A West)	.279
Las Vegas Aviators (Triple-A West)	.277
Modesto Nuts (Low-A West)	.277
Tacoma Rainiers (Triple-A West)	.273

RUNS
Reno Aces (Triple-A West)	872
Rancho Cucamonga Quakes (Low-A West)	810
Las Vegas Aviators (Triple-A West)	794
Carolina Mudcats (Low-A East)	770
Everett Aquasox (High-A West)	766
Tampa Tarpons (Low-A Southeast)	766

HOME RUNS
Omaha Storm Chasers (Triple-A East)	231
Reno Aces (Triple-A West)	198
Bowling Green Hot Rods (High-A East)	197
Las Vegas Aviators (Triple-A West)	193
Toldeo Mud Hens (Triple-A East)	190

STOLEN BASES
Down East Wood Ducks (Low-A East)	290
Hillsboro Hops (High-A West)	231
Dunedin Blue Jays (Low-A Southeast)	227
Fresno Grizzlies (Low-A West)	221
Fayetteville Woodpeckers (Low-A East)	205

EARNED RUN AVERAGE
Somerset Patriots (Double-A Northeast)	3.38
Durham Bulls (Triple-A East)	3.40
Charleston Riverdogs (Low-A East)	3.45
Buffalo Bisons (Triple-A East)	3.46
Pensacola Blue Wahoos (Double-A South)	3.51

STRIKEOUTS
San Jose Giants (Low-A West)	1,439
Durham Bulls (Triple-A East)	1,326
Greenville Drive (High-A East)	1,315
Eugene Emeralds (High-A West)	1,311
Rancho Cucamonga Quakes (Low-A West)	1,310

INDIVIDUAL BATTING

BATTING AVERAGE*
Minimum 324 PA
Justin Yurchak (Great Lakes, Tulsa)	.365
Julio Rodriguez (Everett, Arkansas)	.347
Jose Miranda (St. Paul, Wichita)	.343
Jose Marmolejos (Tacoma)	.338
Yohel Pozo (Round Rock)	.337

RUNS
Anthony Volpe (Hudson Valley, Tampa)	113
Bobby Witt Jr. (NW Arkansas, Omaha)	99
Nick Pratto (Omaha, NW Arkansas)	98
Miguel Vargas (Tulsa, Great Lakes)	98
Jose Miranda (St. Paul, Wichita)	97

HITS
Jose Miranda (St. Paul, Wichita)	184
Michael Stefanic (Salt Lake, Rocket City)	165
Miguel Vargas (Tulsa, Great Lakes)	154
Riley Greene (Toledo, Erie)	146
Bobby Witt Jr. (NW Arkansas, Omaha)	144

TOP HITTING STREAKS
Yairo Muñoz (Worcester)	35
Spencer Horwitz (New Hampshire, Vancouver)	28
Cal Raleigh (Tacoma)	23
Miguel Vargas (Tulsa, Great Lakes)	23
Tanner Morris (Vancouver)	22
Yariel Gonzalez (Toledo, Erie)	22
Euribiel Angeles (Fort Wayne, Lake Elsinore)	22

MOST HITS (ONE GAME)
J.C. Correa (Asheville, Fayetteville)	6
Jorbit Vivas (Great Lakes, R. Cucamonga)	6
Izzy Wilson (Rocket City)	6
92 others	5

TOTAL BASES
Jose Miranda (St. Paul, Wichita)	306
Bobby Witt Jr. (NW Arkansas, Omaha)	286
MJ Melendez (NW Arkansas, Omaha)	280
Brendon Davis (Salt Lake, Rocket City, Tri-City)	271
Nick Pratto (Omaha, NW Arkansas)	268

EXTRA-BASE HITS
Bobby Witt Jr. (NW Arkansas, Omaha)	72
Nick Pratto (Omaha, NW Arkansas)	71
Anthony Volpe (Hudson Valley, Tampa)	68
MJ Melendez (NW Arkansas, Omaha)	66
Brendon Davis (Salt Lake, Rocket City, Tri-City)	65

DOUBLES
Curtis Mead (Charleston, Bowling Green, Durham)	38
Coco Montes (Hartford)	37
Vinnie Pasquantino (NW Arkansas, Quad Cities)	37
Felix Valerio (Wisconsin, Carolina)	37
Gage Workman (West Michigan, Lakeland)	37

TRIPLES
Jose Azocar (El Paso, San Antonio)	14
Alek Thomas (Reno, Amarillo)	12
Ricky Aracena (Beloit)	11
David Hamilton (Biloxi, Wisconsin)	11
Jake McCarthy (Reno, Amarillo)	11
Victor Mesa Jr (Jupiter)	11

HOME RUNS
MJ Melendez (NW Arkansas, Omaha)	41
Griffin Conine (Pensacola, Beloit)	36
Nick Pratto (Omaha, NW Arkansas)	36
Bobby Witt Jr. (NW Arkansas, Omaha)	33
Josh Lester (Toledo, Erie)	32
Ryan McBroom (Omaha)	32

RUNS BATTED IN
Cade Marlowe (Tacoma, Everett, Modesto)	107
MJ Melendez (NW Arkansas, Omaha)	103
Nick Pratto (Omaha, NW Arkansas)	98
Bobby Witt Jr. (NW Arkansas, Omaha)	97
Jose Miranda (St. Paul, Wichita)	94
Aderlin Rodriguez (Toledo)	94

MOST RBIs(ONE GAME)
Alexander Ovalles (Charleston)	10
Billy Cook (FCL Orioles Orange, Delmarva)	9
Noelvi Marte (Everett, Modesto)	9
Orelvis Martinez (Vancouver, Dunedin)	9
Ashton McGee (Wisconsin, Carolina)	9
Luke Raley (Oklahoma City)	9
Chad Spanberger (Nashville, Biloxi)	9
Edwin Yon (Inland Empire)	9

WALKS
Edouard Julien (Cedar Rapids, Fort Myers)	110
Aaron Sabato (Cedar Rapids, Fort Myers)	92
Cade Bunnell (Augusta)	91
Trevor Hauver (Hickory, Tampa)	84
Nick Pratto (Omaha, NW Arkansas)	83

INTENTIONAL WALKS
Jhonkensy Noel (Lake County, Lynchburg, ACL)	6
Jose Marmolejos (Tacoma)	5
Christin Stewart (Toledo)	5
Nelson Velazquez (Tennessee, South Bend)	5
Joey Wiemer (Wisconsin, Carolina)	5

Jose Miranda

STRIKEOUTS
Griffin Conine (Pensacola, Beloit)	185
Cade Bunnell (Augusta)	172
Mason Martin (Indianapolis, Altoona)	171
Kyle Stowers (Norfolk, Bowie, Aberdeen)	171
Neyfy Castillo (Visalia)	170
Jake Gatewood (Salt Lake)	170

STOLEN BASES
Jayce Easley (Down East)	70
Eddy Diaz (Spokane, Fresno)	59
Steward Berroa (New Hampshire, Dunedin)	58
Tyler Tolbert (Quad Cities, Columbia, Royals Blue)	55
David Hamilton (Biloxi, Wisconsin)	52
Max Schuemann (Las Vegas, Midland, Lansing)	52

CAUGHT STEALING
Eddy Diaz (Spokane, Fresno)	19
Pedro Martinez (Bowling Green)	18
Zac Veen (Fresno)	17
Victor Labrada (Everett, Modesto)	15
Jose Azocar (El Paso, San Antonio)	14
Dairon Blanco (Omaha, NW Arkansas)	14
Eguy Rosario (San Antonio)	14

ON-BASE PERCENTAGE*
Minimum 324 PA
Khalil Lee (Syracuse)	.451
Justin Yurchak (Great Lakes, Tulsa)	.443
Julio Rodriguez (Everett, Arkansas)	.441
Braxton Martinez (Tri-City, Inland Empire)	.439
Jose Marmolejos (Tacoma)	.439

SLUGGING PERCENTAGE*
Minimum 324 PA
Jose Marmolejos (Tacoma)	.672
Matt Davidson (Oklahoma City)	.629
Jairo Pomares (San Jose, Eugene)	.629
MJ Melendez (NW Arkansas, Omaha)	.628
Yohel Pozo (Round Rock)	.622

ON-BASE PLUS SLUGGING (OPS)*
Minimum 324 PA
Jose Marmolejos (Tacoma)	1.111
Anthony Volpe (Tampa, Hudson Valley)	1.027
Braxton Martinez (Tri-City, Inland Empire)	1.027
Drew Ellis (Reno)	1.014
MJ Melendez (NW Arkansas, Omaha)	1.011

HIT BY PITCH
Seth Beer (Reno)	30
Brett Cumberland (Norfolk)	28
Zac Cook (Vancouver, Dunedin)	25
Leo Jimenez (FCL Blue Jays, Dunedin)	25
Khalil Lee (Syracuse)	24
Austin Martin (New Hampshire, Wichita)	24

SACRIFICE BUNTS
Yolbert Sanchez (Birmingham, Winston-Salem)	10
Ezequiel Tovar (Spokane, Fresno)	9
Julio Carreras (Fresno)	8
Josue Huma (Iowa, South Bend, Myrtle Beach)	7
Reinaldo Ilarraza (Fort Wayne)	7
Rudy Martin (Omaha, NW Arkansas)	7
Brian Miller (Jacksonville)	7
Andrew Romine (Iowa)	7

SACRIFICE FLIES
Spencer Torkelson (Toledo, Erie, West Michigan)	11
Eric Cole (Quad Cities)	10
Victor Mesa Jr. (Jupiter)	10
Misael Urbina (Fort Myers)	10
Elehuris Montero (Albuquerque, Hartford)	9
Francisco Pena (Las Vegas)	9

MINOR LEAGUES

GROUNDED INTO DOUBLE PLAY

Diosbel Arias (Frisco)	21
Pete Kozma (Las Vegas)	20
Wilfredo Tovar (Syracuse)	20
Carlos Perez (Charlotte, Birmingham)	19
Christian Colon (Buffalo)	18

BATTING AVERAGE BY POSITION

CATCHERS

Yohel Pozo (Round Rock)	.337
Yainer Diaz (Asheville, Lynchburg, Fayetteville)	.324
Jamie Ritchie (Reno)	.317
Austin Allen (Las Vegas)	.317
Drew Romo (Fresno)	.314

FIRST BASEMEN

Justin Yurchak (Tulsa, Great Lakes)	.365
Jose Marmolejos (Tacoma)	.338
Braxton Martinez (Tri-City, Inland Empire)	.331
Jonathan Aranda (Montgomery, Bowling Green)	.330
Dustin Harris (Hickory, Down East)	.327

SECOND BASEMEN

Michael Stefanic (Salt Lake, Rocket City)	.336
Nick Yorke (Greenville, Salem)	.325
Alejo Lopez (Louisville, Chattanooga)	.320
C.J. Hinojosa (Sugar Land)	.316
Otto Lopez (Buffalo, New Hampshire)	.315

THIRD BASEMEN

Jose Miranda (St. Paul, Wichita)	.344
Jhonkensy Noel (Lake County, Lynchburg, ACL Indians)	.340
Josh Jung (Round Rock, Frisco)	.326
Curtis Mead (Charleston, Bowling Green, Durham)	.321
Miguel Vargas (Tulsa, Great Lakes)	.319

SHORTSTOPS

Mauricio Dubon (Sacramento)	.332
Euribiel Angeles (Fort Wayne, Lake Elsinore)	.329
Leo Jimenez (Dunedin, FCL Blue Jays)	.320
Vaughn Grissom (Rome, Augusta)	.319
Oneil Cruz (Indianapolis, Altoona)	.310

OUTFIELDERS

Henry Ramos (Reno)	.371
Julio Rodriguez (Arkansas, Everett)	.347
Jake Meyers (Sugar Land)	.343
Ismael Munguia (Eugene)	.336
Jairo Pomares (Eugene, San Jose)	.334

INDIVIDUAL PITCHING

EARNED RUN AVERAGE*
Minimum 96 IP

Taj Bradley (Charleston, Bowling Green)	1.83
Louie Varland (Fort Myers, Cedar Rapids)	2.10
Jayden Murray (Bowling Green, Montgomery)	2.16
Logan T. Allen (Lake County, Akron)	2.26
Max Meyer (Jacksonville, Pensacola)	2.41

WORST ERA*

Thomas Pannone (Salt Lake)	7.07
Karlo Seijas (Fredericksburg)	6.84
Adam Kloffenstein (Vancouver)	6.22
Helcris Olivarez (Spokane)	6.05
Jose Salvador (Inland Empire)	5.91

WINS

Ricardo Pinto (Toledo, Erie)	14
Bowden Francis (Buffalo, Nashville, Biloxi)	13
Taj Bradley (Charleston, Bowling Green)	12
Mitchell Kilkenny (Spokane, Fresno)	12
Zach Logue (Buffalo, New Hampshire)	12

LOSSES

Francisco Morales (Lehigh Valley, Reading)	14
Karl Kauffmann (Hartford, Spokane)	12
Jose Mujica (Albuquerque)	12
Mitchell Parker (Wilmington, Fredericksburg)	12
Karlo Seijas (Fredericksburg)	12

GAMES

Phillip Diehl (Louisville)	58
Logan Cozart (Albuquerque)	54
Luke Barker (Nashville)	53
Brian Moran (Durham)	53
Aaron Brown (Midland, Las Vegas)	51
James Naile (Las Vegas)	51

GAMES STARTED

Clayton Beeter (Tulsa, Great Lakes)	27
Bryce Elder (Gwinnett, Mississippi, Rome)	25
Brady Feigl (Las Vegas, Midland)	25
Prelander Berroa (San Jose)	24
Logan Boyer (Great Lakes)	24
16 others	24

COMPLETE GAMES

Caleb Kilian (Tennessee, Richmond, Eugene)	3
Oscar Rojas (Brooklyn, St. Lucie)	3
Noah Davis (Dayton, Spokane)	2
Santiago Florez (Greensboro, Bradenton)	2
Luis Palacios (Jupiter)	2
Trent Palmer (Dunedin)	2
Junior Santos (St. Lucie)	2
Connor Thomas (Memphis, Springfield)	2
Hayden Wesneski (H.V., Somerset, Scranton/WB)	2
Kyle Wright (Gwinnett)	2

SHUTOUTS

Trent Palmer (Dunedin)	2
Oscar Rojas (Brooklyn, St. Lucie)	2
Kyle Wright (Gwinnett)	2
34 others	1

GAMES FINISHED

Kevin Quackenbush (Oklahoma City)	42
Luke Barker (Nashville)	38
Ronel Blanco (Sugar Land)	38
Clay Helvey (San Jose)	35
Kaleb Ort (Worcester)	35

HOLDS

Moises Gomez (Tacoma, Arkansas)	14
Logan Cozart (Albuquerque)	12
Julian Fernandez (Albuquerque, Hartford)	12
PJ Poulin (Hartford, Spokane)	12
Chad Smith (Albuquerque)	12
Gabe Speier (Omaha)	12

SAVES

Kevin Quackenbush (Oklahoma City)	23
Ronel Blanco (Sugar Land)	22
Chris Wright (Eugene, San Jose)	21
Colton Hock (Jacksonville, Pensacola)	19
Kaleb Ort (Worcester)	19

INNINGS PITCHED

Bryce Elder (Gwinnett, Mississippi, Rome)	137.2
Kyle Wright (Gwinnett)	137.0
Bowden Francis (Buffalo, Nashville, Biloxi)	132.2
James Marvel (Indianapolis)	131.2
Brandon Pfaadt (Amarillo, Hillsboro, Visalia)	131.2

WALKS

Jayson Schroeder (FCL Astros, Fayetteville)	82
Junior Mieses (Visalia)	72
Ryan Castellani (Albuquerque)	71
Josias De Los Santos (Modesto)	70
Deivi Garcia (Scranton/W-B)	68
Helcris Olivarez (Spokane)	68
Pedro Payano (Toledo, Erie)	68
Levi Prater (Palm Beach)	68

STRIKEOUTS

Cade Cavalli (Rochester, Harrisburg, Wilmington)	175
Carson Ragsdale (San Jose)	167
Ryan Murphy (Eugene, San Jose)	164
Ryne Nelson (Amarillo, Hillsboro)	163
Ken Waldichuk (Somerset, Hudson Valley)	163

HITS ALLOWED

Thomas Pannone (Salt Lake)	160
Beau Sulser (Indianapolis)	150
Josh Green (Reno)	149
James Marvel (Indianapolis)	145
Caleb Boushley (El Paso, San Antonio)	140

HOME RUNS ALLOWED

Jake Kalish (Omaha)	31
Matt Frisbee (Sacramento, Richmond)	27
Jose Mujica (Albuquerque)	27
Dalton Roach (Springfield)	27
Caleb Boushley (El Paso, San Antonio)	26
Marcelo Martinez (Omaha, NW Arkansas)	26

STRIKEOUTS PER NINE (STARTERS)*
Minimum 96 IP

Grayson Rodriguez (Aberdeen, Bowie)	14.07
Ryan Murphy (San Jose, Eugene)	13.75
Ken Waldichuk (Somerset, Hudson Valley)	13.34
Carson Ragsdale (San Jose)	13.22
Cade Cavalli (Wilm., Harrisburg, Rochester)	12.77

STRIKEOUTS PER NINE (RELIEVERS)*
Minimum 48 IP

Freddy Pacheco (Peoria, Springfield, Memphis)	15.83
Adrian Hernandez (Dunedin, Vancouver, N.H.)	15.59
Will Klein (Quad Cities)	15.48
Evan Reifert (Carolina, Wisconsin)	15.45
Stevie Branche (Daytona, Dayton)	15.43

OPPONENT AVERAGE (STARTERS)*
Minimum 96 IP

Jayden Murray (Bowling Green, Montgomery)	.152
Grayson Rodriguez (Aberdeen, Bowie)	.159
M.D. Johnson (Jupiter, Beloit)	.170
Matt Krook (Somerset, Scranton/WB)	.175
Peyton Battenfield (B.G., Montgomery, Akron)	.176

OPPONENT AVERAGE (RELIEVERS)*
Minimum 48 IP

Colby White (Charleston, B.G., Mont., Durham)	.124
Jovani Moran (Wichita, St. Paul)	.124
Adrian Hernandez (Dunedin, Vancouver, N.H.)	.140
Nick Hernandez (Corpus Christi, Sugar Land)	.147
Stevie Branche (Daytona, Dayton)	.151

MOST STRIKEOUTS (ONE GAME)

Reid Detmers (Salt Lake, Rocket City)	16
Cade Cavalli (Rochester, Harrisburg, Wilmington)	15
Cody Bradford (Frisco, Hickory)	14
Cooper Criswell (Salt Lake, Rocket City)	14
Reid Detmers (Salt Lake, Rocket City)	14
Joey Estes (Augusta)	14
Mark Leiter Jr. (Erie, Toledo)	14
Glenn Otto (Round Rock, Scranton/WB, Somerset)	14
Hayden Wesneski (H.V., Somerset, Scranton/WB)	14

WILD PITCHES

Danny Medina (DSL Indians Blue)	38
Edwin Nunez (Palm Beach)	34
Jonathan Sprinkle (Corpus, Asheville, Fayetteville)	29
Oliver Mateo (Bradenton)	22
Jacob Schlesener (Peoria)	22

BALKS

Luis Ortiz (Palm Beach)	11
Freylin Garcia (Asheville, Fayetteville)	8
Rynardo Cruz (ACL Reds, DSL Reds)	6
Marlin Willis (ACL Royals Blue, ACL Royals Gold, Columbia)	5
8 players	4

HIT BATTERS

Edwin Nunez (Palm Beach)	17
Tom Hackimer (Syracuse, St. Paul, Bing., Wich.)	16
Sam McWilliams (Syracuse, El Paso, San Antonio)	16
Sam Keating (Fort Wayne)	15
Jose Betances (Fayetteville)	14
Tyler Palm (Cedar Rapids)	14
Kellen Rholl (Lake County)	14
Enmanuel Solano (Peoria, Palm Beach)	14
Kenny Wells (Augusta)	14

GROUNDBALL DOUBLE PLAYS

Jacob Lemoine (Round Rock)	13
Blair Calvo (Fresno)	12
Jose Garcia (Lake Elsinore)	12
Austin Briggs (Midland)	11
Tanner Anderson (Las Vegas, Indianapolis)	10
Yaya Chentouf (Erie, West Michigan)	10
Angel Felipe (Charleston, Bowling Green)	10
James Naile (Las Vegas)	10

INDIVIDUAL FIELDING

ERRORS

Yasel Antuña (Wilmington)	36
Matthew Lugo (Salem)	33
Noelvi Marte (Everett, Modesto)	29
Robert Puason (Stockton)	29
Jordy Barley (Lake Elsinore, Fredericksburg)	27

MINOR LEAGUES

BY MARK CHIARELLI

Triple-A East brimmed with prospect talent that will shape MLB for the next decade. The 20-team behemoth of a league preserved the old 14-team International League while bringing aboard six other franchises, four from what was the Pacific Coast League.

By season's end, four of the game's five best prospects—Adley Rutschman, Bobby Witt Jr., Spencer Torkelson and Riley Greene—reached Triple-A East and qualified for our prospect ranking. So, too, did shortstop Wander Franco, who opened the year as baseball's No. 1 prospect at Durham before climbing to Tampa Bay in late June.

Durham was the class of the league, going 86-44, including a 9-1 finish that secured their place as Triple-A champions. The Bulls served as an exemplary feeder system to the Rays, the American League's top team. Franco marveled in his 40-game stretch in Durham. League managers voted him Triple-A East's best batting prospect and the hitter with the best strike-zone judgment in the league. To underscore that point, he reached base in 43 straight games as a 20-year-old MLB rookie.

In addition to Franco, Durham righthander Shane Baz emerged as the league's most dominant pitching prospect. He had a 1.76 ERA in 10 starts with Durham before joining Tampa Bay's rotation in August. Outfielder Josh Lowe tied for fifth among all league hitters with 22 homers and also received a callup to Tampa Bay late in the year. ∎

TOP 10 PROSPECTS

Wander Franco

1. Wander Franco, SS, Durham (Rays)
2. Adley Rutschman, C, Norfolk (Orioles)
3. Bobby Witt Jr., SS, Omaha (Royals)
4. Riley Greene, OF, Toledo (Tigers)
5. Spencer Torkelson, 1B, Toledo (Tigers)
6. Shane Baz, RHP, Durham (Rays)
7. Vidal Brujan, 2B/OF, Durham (Rays)
8. Jose Barrero, SS, Louisville (Reds)
9. Jarren Duran, OF, Worcester (Red Sox)
10. Matthew Liberatore, LHP, Memphis (Cardinals)

ALL-STAR TEAM

C: Tomas Telis, St. Paul.
1B: Juan Yepez, Memphis.
2B: Jake Noll, Rochester.
3B: Aderlin Rodriguez, Toledo.
SS: Kevin Smith, Buffalo.
OF: Josh Lowe, Durham.
OF: Vidal Brujan, Durham.
OF: Khalil Lee, Syracuse.
DH: Ryan McBroom, Omaha.
RHP: Jackson Kowar, Omaha.
LHP: Matthew Liberatore, Memphis.
RP: Luke Barker, Nashville.

MVP: Aderlin Rodriguez, 3B, Toledo.
Pitcher of the Year: Jackson Kowar, RHP, Omaha.
Top MLB Prospect: Bobby Witt Jr., SS, Omaha.
Managers of the Year: Brady Williams, Durham; and Casey Candaele, Buffalo.

OVERALL STANDINGS

Midwest Division	W	L	PCT	GB	Manager	Attendance	Avg	Last Penn
Toledo Mud Hens (Tigers)	74	56	.569	—	Tom Prince	300,063	2,308	*2006
Omaha Storm Chasers (Royals)	73	56	.566	0.5	Brian Poldberg	245,170	1,901	**2014
St. Paul Saints (Twins)	67	63	.515	7	Toby Gardenhire	393,394	3,026	Never
Indianapolis Indians (Pirates)	61	67	.477	12	Brian Esposito	353,729	2,764	*2000
Columbus Clippers (Indians)	59	68	.465	13.5	Andy Tracy	393,879	3,101	*2019
Louisville Bats (Reds)	55	73	.430	18	Pat Kelly	269,338	2,104	*2001
Iowa Cubs (Cubs)	51	78	.395	22.5	Marty Pevey	314,749	2,44	Never

Northeast Division	W	L	PCT	GB	Manager	Attendance	Avg	Last Penn
Buffalo Bisons (Blue Jays)	79	47	.627	—	Casey Candaele	200,752	1,593	*2004
Scranton/Wilkes-Barre RailRiders (Yankees)	75	52	.591	4.5	Doug Davis	236,559	1,863	*2016
Worcester Red Sox (Red Sox)	74	54	.578	6	Billy McMillon	362,559	2,832	Never
Lehigh Valley IronPigs (Phillies)	53	75	.414	27	Gary Jones	356,355	2,784	*1995
Syracuse Mets (Mets)	50	75	.400	28.5	Chad Kreuter	215,336	1,723	*1976
Rochester Red Wings (Nationals)	49	77	.389	30	Matt LeCroy	219,941	1,746	*1997

Southeast Division	W	L	PCT	GB	Manager	Attendance	Avg	Last Penn
Durham Bulls (Rays)	86	44	.662	—	Brady Williams	320,873	2,468	2021
Jacksonville Jumbo Shrimp (Marlins)	75	55	.577	11	Al Pedrique	242,667	1,867	Never
Gwinnett Stripers (Braves)	71	58	.550	14.5	Matt Tuiasosopo	162,494	1,260	*2007
Nashville Sounds (Brewers)	70	58	.547	15	Rick Sweet	436,868	3,413	**2005
Memphis Redbirds (Cardinals)	61	67	.477	24	Ben Johnson	183,217	1,431	**2018
Norfolk Tides (Orioles)	52	78	.400	34	Gary Kendall	262,496	2,019	*1999
Charlotte Knights (White Sox)	47	81	.367	38	Wes Helms	345,305	2,698	*1985

No playoffs: Durham finished with the best record and went 9-1 during the 10-game Triple-A "final stretch."

* Refers to Triple-A International League prior to 2021. ** Refers to Triple-A Pacific Coast League prior to 2021.

CLUB BATTING

	AVG	G	AB	R	H	2B	3B	HR	RBI	BB	SO	SB	OBP	SLG
Buffalo	.262	126	4048	640	1061	219	21	136	598	505	1044	117	.353	.427
Omaha	.260	129	4350	746	1129	213	23	231	708	493	1163	150	.341	.478
Toledo	.257	130	4329	710	1111	213	38	190	677	534	1258	66	.345	.455
Durham	.255	130	4277	732	1092	262	23	183	683	532	1185	142	.343	.456
Scranton/W-B	.255	127	4121	680	1052	218	18	146	635	537	1160	148	.352	.423
Columbus	.253	127	4264	605	1079	254	16	159	574	452	1151	71	.333	.432
St. Paul	.251	130	4378	686	1098	204	20	178	642	462	1229	76	.332	.429
Charlotte	.247	128	4242	585	1049	216	15	173	548	362	1244	65	.311	.428
Louisville	.246	128	4212	531	1036	201	21	98	500	465	993	65	.329	.373
Gwinnett	.245	129	4211	614	1030	191	15	164	580	471	1197	99	.325	.414
Syracuse	.244	126	3992	582	976	199	12	142	543	529	1031	124	.343	.407
Memphis	.244	128	4150	587	1014	191	21	137	544	448	1080	60	.324	.400
Worcester	.244	128	4164	600	1015	211	23	147	569	447	1234	140	.331	.411
Iowa	.243	129	4284	588	1042	192	21	120	557	516	1199	92	.335	.382
Jacksonville	.243	130	4222	577	1026	182	33	136	535	406	1204	112	.319	.398
Nashville	.241	128	4174	618	1006	221	19	136	580	524	1233	85	.332	.401
Lehigh Valley	.236	128	4118	564	971	188	25	88	520	513	1071	81	.328	.358
Indianapolis	.235	128	4209	600	991	208	14	139	557	499	1193	71	.325	.391
Rochester	.233	127	4088	534	952	186	15	133	501	444	1048	49	.316	.383
Norfolk	.220	130	4122	527	908	171	23	141	492	498	1228	82	.312	.376

CLUB PITCHING

	ERA	G	CG	SHO	SV	IP	H	R	ER	HR	BB	SO	AVG
Durham	3.40	130	0	14	29	1126	873	469	426	143	362	1326	.212
Buffalo	3.46	126	0	9	36	1075	900	471	413	118	406	1148	.225
Gwinnett	3.72	129	3	9	31	1112	950	504	460	124	439	1191	.230
Scranton/W-B	3.79	127	1	9	30	1089	920	528	458	108	545	1241	.229
Jacksonville	3.94	130	3	9	36	1129	998	578	494	168	436	1202	.235
Nashville	4.07	128	0	12	17	1112	1019	571	503	121	439	1202	.242
Louisville	4.14	128	1	9	26	1115	982	575	513	146	457	1219	.234
Toledo	4.27	130	0	8	33	1125	1028	591	534	138	486	1144	.241
Worcester	4.39	128	1	8	36	1100	1042	600	536	135	471	1161	.248
Indianapolis	4.55	128	0	5	22	1119	1100	643	566	143	466	1104	.256
St. Paul	4.55	130	0	8	28	1142	1062	627	578	144	522	1180	.244
Norfolk	4.77	130	2	6	27	1102	1108	656	584	168	611	1099	.260
Memphis	4.79	128	2	4	28	1101	1130	666	586	158	491	1096	.265
Lehigh Valley	5.03	128	1	5	23	1083	1036	668	605	128	579	1113	.251
Rochester	5.05	127	1	6	22	1071	1073	647	601	136	483	982	.260
Iowa	5.16	129	0	7	19	1118	1067	706	641	203	524	1173	.249
Columbus	5.22	127	0	10	26	1099	1059	692	637	177	563	1160	.252
Omaha	5.26	129	0	3	32	1128	1173	710	659	187	496	1226	.267
Charlotte	5.33	128	0	6	19	1094	1062	718	648	165	530	1237	.251
Syracuse	5.35	126	1	7	27	1054	1056	686	626	167	541	972	.261

CLUB FIELDING

	PCT	PO	A	E	DP		PCT	PO	A	E	DP
Buffalo	.984	3224	1049	69	88	Indianapolis	.980	3358	1179	92	120
Lehigh Valley	.984	3248	1049	72	89	Norfolk	.980	3306	1097	90	107
Durham	.983	3378	1012	74	96	Louisville	.980	3344	1093	91	99
Gwinnett	.983	3336	1161	80	120	Jacksonville	.979	3306	1056	96	86
St. Paul	.981	3427	1186	87	98	Iowa Cubs	.979	3356	1133	97	108
Omaha	.981	3385	1156	86	120	Scranton/W-B	.979	3267	1024	94	105
Memphis	.981	3302	1176	85	113	Nashville	.977	3336	1096	103	96
Toledo	.981	3375	1152	86	104	Worcester	.977	3300	1031	101	98
Columbus	.981	3297	1038	83	106	Syracuse	.977	3161	1056	99	125
Rochester	.980	3214	1147	87	105	Charlotte	.977	3282	1126	106	89

INDIVIDUAL BATTING

Batter, Club	AVG	G	AB	R	H	2B	3B	HR	RBI	BB	SO	SB
Jose Miranda, St. Paul	.343	80	341	61	117	24	0	17	56	25	49	0
Johan Camargo, Gwinnett	.326	104	386	70	126	24	4	19	67	47	72	0
Yairo Munoz, Worcester	.308	88	351	45	108	16	4	8	36	17	53	18
Jake Noll, Rochester	.300	118	437	60	131	28	5	17	69	29	74	4
Tomas Telis, St. Paul	.296	101	423	51	125	12	2	12	56	28	58	5
Tyler White, Buffalo	.292	105	353	54	103	26	0	13	65	80	73	2
Josh Lowe, Durham	.291	111	402	76	117	28	2	22	78	61	123	26
Connor Marabell, Columbus	.291	99	337	41	98	23	2	8	49	18	65	4
Aderlin Rodriguez, Toledo	.290	116	434	67	126	26	3	29	94	42	127	1
Juan Yepez, Memphis	.289	92	304	56	88	25	0	22	63	42	69	1

INDIVIDUAL PITCHING

Pitcher, Club	W	L	ERA	G	GS	CG	SV	IP	H	R	ER	BB	SO
Kyle Wright, Gwinnett	10	5	3.02	24	24	2	0	137	117	52	46	45	137
Josh Lindblom, Nashville	5	4	3.10	22	20	0	0	105	102	38	36	26	117
Raynel Espinal, Worcester	11	4	3.44	23	21	0	0	118	86	50	45	43	115
Bowden Francis, Buffalo	10	6	3.95	21	20	0	0	112	82	55	49	43	110
Matthew Liberatore, Memphis	9	9	4.04	22	18	0	0	125	123	66	56	33	123
Kyle Hart, Worcester	6	9	4.22	23	20	1	0	107	100	58	50	47	90
Riley O'Brien, Louisville	7	7	4.55	23	22	0	0	113	93	59	57	55	121
Kirk McCarty, Columbus	9	6	5.01	24	24	0	0	124	117	73	69	44	104
James Marvel, Indianapolis	7	7	5.26	25	22	0	0	132	145	87	77	54	98
Drew Strotman, St. Paul	10	5	5.29	25	24	0	0	112	115	69	66	63	104

DEPARTMENT LEADERS

BATTING

OBP	Khalil Lee, Syracuse	.451
SLG	Juan Yepez, Memphis	.589
OPS	Juan Yepez, Memphis	.971
R	Ryan McBroom, Omaha	78
H	Jake Noll, Rochester	131
TB	Aderlin Rodriguez, Toledo	245
XBH	Aderlin Rodriguez, Toledo	58
2B	Vidal Brujan, Durham	31
2B	Nathan Lukes, Nashville	31
3B	Mickey Moniak, Lehigh Valley	8
HR	Ryan McBroom, Omaha	32
RBI	Aderlin Rodriguez, Toledo	94
SAC	Mickey Moniak, Lehigh Valley	8
BB	Tyler White, Buffalo	80
HBP	Brett Cumberland, Norfolk	28
SO	Zach Green, Nashville	148
SB	Vidal Brujan, Durham	44
CS	Khalil Lee, Syracuse	10
AB/SO	Wilfredo Tovar, Syracuse	7.72

FIELDING

C PCT	Brett Sullivan, Durham	.994
PO	Brett Sullivan, Durham	616
A	Rafael Marchan, Lehigh Valley	42
DP	Tres Barrera, Rochester	7
E	Rob Brantly, Scranton/Wilkes-Barre	10
CS	Brett Sullivan, Durham	19
SB	Tres Barrera, Rochester	55
PB	Gavin Collins, Columbus	14
1B PCT	Darick Hall, Lehigh Valley	.998
PO	Josh Ockimey, Worcester	504
A	Lewin Diaz, Jacksonville	41
DP	Dalton Kelly, Durham	53
E	3 players	5
2B PCT	Marco Hernandez, Charlotte	.979
PO	Nolan Gorman, Memphis, 109	
A	Marco Hernandez, Charlotte	177
DP	Nolan Gorman, Memphis	43
DP	Marco Hernandez, Charlotte	43
E	3 players	8
3B PCT	Armando Alvarez, Scranton/WB	.925
PO	Nolan Jones, Columbus	56
A	Hunter Owen, Indianapolis	117
DP	Hunter Owen, Indianapolis	21
E	Armando Alvarez, Scranton/WB	13
SS PCT	Evan Mendoza, Memphis	.972
PO	Evan Mendoza, Memphis	145
A	Evan Mendoza, Memphis	277
DP	Evan Mendoza, Memphis	58
E	Mason McCoy, Norfolk	15
OF PCT	3 players	1.000
PO	Jimmy Kerrigan, St. Paul	210
A	2 players	11
DP	Jimmy Kerrigan, St. Paul	6
E	Franchy Cordero, Worcester	3
E	Cristian Pache, Gwinnett	3

PITCHING

G	Phillip Diehl, Louisville	58
GS	Kirk McCarty, Columbus	24
GS	Drew Strotman, St. Paul	24
GS	Beau Sulser, Indianapolis	24
GS	Kyle Wright, Gwinnett	24
GF	Luke Barker, Nashville	38
SV	Kaleb Ort, Worcester	19
W	Raynel Espinal, Worcester	11
W	Ricardo Pinto, Toledo	11
L	David Parkinson, Lehigh Valley	11
IP	Kyle Wright, Gwinnett	137
H	Beau Sulser, Indianapolis	150
R	2 players	87
ER	James Marvel, Indianapolis	77
ER	Beau Sulser, Indianapolis	77
HB	Robert Broom, Columbus	14
BB	Deivi Garcia, Scranton/Wilkes-Barre	68
SO	Kyle Wright, Gwinnett	137
SO/9	Josh Lindblom, Nashville	10.06
SO/9 (RP)	Ilan Hamilton, St. Paul	13.12
BB/9	Andrew Albers, St. Paul	0.97
WP	Kyle Muller, Gwinnett	15
BK	Jasseel De La Cruz, Gwinnett	5
HRA	Jake Kalish, Omaha	31
BAA	Raynel Espinal, Worcester	.202

MINOR LEAGUES

BY KYLE GLASER

Triple-A West got a significant makeover as part of MLB's restructuring of the minor leagues. Formerly known as the Pacific Coast League, the league dropped from 16 teams to 10.

Iowa, Memphis, Nashville and Omaha—all members of the league since 1998—moved to the more geographically convenient Triple-A East. San Antonio dropped down to Double-A, as did New Orleans when it relocated to Wichita. Fresno, which had been in the PCL since 1998, dropped to Low-A and was replaced by Sugar Land, a former independent team that moved to affiliated status.

The reduction in teams meant a reduction in players, and thus a reduction of talent relative to previous seasons. Standouts such as Tacoma outfielder Jarred Kelenic, Oklahoma City catcher Keibert Ruiz and Salt Lake outfielder Jo Adell ensured the league still had headliners, but the talent dropped off considerably beyond the top tier of prospects.

Combined with the increased occurrence of injuries in the major leagues, rosters were in a constant state of flux throughout Triple-A West. Most teams used more than 70 different players over the course of the season as they shuttled back and forth from the majors.

Amidst that backdrop of change, Tacoma's dominance was a constant. The Rainiers went a league-best 78-52 and were declared league champion. No postseason was played under MLB's restructuring.

Tacoma got early-season boosts from Kelenic and catcher Cal Raleigh before each got called up to Seattle.

But Tacoma's most impactful player was first baseman/left fielder Jose Marmolejos. He hit .338 with 26 home runs and 75 RBIs and led the minors with a 1.111 OPS for the Rainiers. He led the league in batting average, on-base percentage (.439) and slugging percentage (.672) and finished

TOP 10 PROSPECTS

Keibert Ruiz

1. Jarred Kelenic, OF, Tacoma (Mariners)
2. Keibert Ruiz, C, Oklahoma City (Dodgers)
3. Jo Adell, OF, Salt Lake (Angels)
4. Josh Jung, 3B, Round Rock (Rangers)
5. Alek Thomas, OF, Reno (D-backs)
6. Luis Campusano, C, El Paso (Padres)
7. Joey Bart, C, Sacramento (Giants)
8. Jake Meyers, OF, Sugar Land (Astros)
9. Cal Raleigh, C, Tacoma (Mariners)
10. Bryan de la Cruz, OF, Sugar Land (Astros)

fifth in the league in home runs. With Marmolejos leading the way, the Rainiers finished tied for third in scoring despite playing in one of the league's few pitcher-friendly home parks.

Marmolejos was named MVP and Tacoma manager Kristopher Negron was named manager of the year.

Sugar Land righthander Peter Solomon was named the league's pitcher of the year after going 8-1, 4.70 and finishing third in the league with 112 strikeouts. Led by Solomon and outfielders Jake Meyers and Bryan de la Cruz, Sugar Land went 75-55 and won the East Division title in its first year in the league. Meyers and de la Cruz played well in MLB after being called up. ◼

OVERALL STANDINGS

East Division	W	L	PCT	GB	Manager	Attendance	Average	Last Penn
Sugar Land Skeeters (Astros)	75	55	.577	—	Mickey Storey	211,560	1,627	Never
Oklahoma City Dodgers (Dodgers)	67	62	.519	7.5	Travis Barbary	305,290	2,367	1965
Round Rock Express (Rangers)	67	62	.519	7.5	Kenny Holmberg	305,742	2,370	Never
Albuquerque Isotopes (Rockies)	58	72	.446	17	Warren Schaeffer	329,295	2,533	*1994
El Paso Chihuahuas (Padres)	51	79	.392	24	Eric Junge	403,657	3,105	*2016

West Division	W	L	PCT	GB	Manager	Attendance	Average	Last Penn
Tacoma Rainiers (Mariners)	78	52	.600	—	Kristopher Negron	245,706	1,890	*2010
Reno Aces (D-backs)	70	54	.565	5	Blake Lalli	233,961	1,887	*2012
Las Vegas Aviators (Athletics)	65	61	.516	11	Fran Riordan	428,369	3,400	*1998
Sacramento River Cats (Giants)	56	71	.441	20.5	Dave Brundage	259,640	2,044	*2019
Salt Lake Bees (Angels)	55	74	.426	22.5	Lou Marson	300,535	2,330	*1979

No playoffs: Tacoma finished with the league's best record.

* Refers to Triple-A Pacific Coast League prior to 2021.

CLUB BATTING

	AVG	G	AB	R	H	2B	3B	HR	RBI	BB	SO	SB	OBP	SLG
Reno	.294	124	4370	872	1284	284	50	198	816	502	1086	94	.373	.518
Sacramento	.279	127	4455	753	1241	236	34	186	713	477	1202	89	.354	.472
Las Vegas	.277	126	4424	794	1227	248	37	193	758	494	1070	53	.355	.481
Tacoma	.273	130	4472	763	1221	244	24	189	732	548	1114	85	.357	.465
Salt Lake	.269	129	4472	716	1201	250	32	189	676	426	1183	84	.339	.466
El Paso	.266	130	4377	636	1166	226	42	130	587	475	1178	128	.339	.426
Sugar Land	.266	130	4353	698	1157	258	24	153	653	516	1201	98	.350	.442
Oklahoma City	.260	129	4428	763	1150	253	23	181	729	519	1188	62	.344	.450
Albuquerque	.258	130	4325	693	1115	257	34	184	645	421	1125	68	.328	.461
Round Rock	.257	129	4356	685	1118	230	30	181	652	455	1239	96	.333	.448

CLUB PITCHING

	ERA	G	CG	SHO	SV	IP	H	R	ER	HR	BB	SO	AVG
Sugar Land	4.13	130	1	3	34	1126	985	589	517	161	527	1277	.231
Round Rock	4.62	129	0	5	34	1118	1052	650	574	153	483	1212	.246
Tacoma	4.96	130	0	7	24	1147	1152	681	632	193	392	1222	.258
Oklahoma City	5.01	129	0	4	34	1136	1189	704	632	157	465	1267	.266
Sacramento	5.33	127	0	2	34	1116	1133	742	661	161	577	1212	.262
Las Vegas	5.78	126	0	1	26	1113	1321	787	715	188	445	1046	.293
El Paso	5.86	130	3	4	23	1113	1220	787	725	178	522	1173	.277
Albuquerque	5.98	130	0	0	31	1110	1228	786	737	185	514	1052	.281
Salt Lake	6.00	129	1	5	20	1122	1334	827	748	196	420	1081	.292
Reno	6.29	124	1	3	39	1085	1266	820	759	212	488	1044	.289

CLUB FIELDING

	PCT	PO	A	E	DP		PCT	PO	A	E	DP
Tacoma	.982	3441	1085	81	85	Reno	.977	3256	1102	102	112
El Paso	.982	3339	1137	81	88	Sacramento	.977	3350	1047	103	108
Albuquerque	.979	3330	1219	97	107	Oklahoma City	.976	3407	1015	107	95
Las Vegas	.979	3339	1219	99	115	Salt Lake	.976	3365	1127	111	115
Sugar Land	.977	3379	990	102	97	Round Rock	.975	3352	1033	112	100

INDIVIDUAL BATTING

Batter, Club	AVG	G	AB	R	H	2B	3B	HR	RBI	BB	SO	SB
Jose Marmolejos, Tacoma	.338	83	293	66	99	16	2	26	75	54	69	0
Michael Stefanic, Salt Lake	.334	104	404	67	135	21	0	16	54	45	62	6
Taylor Kohlwey, El Paso	.319	97	342	47	109	18	4	7	56	37	84	9
Jose Siri, Sugar Land	.318	94	362	70	115	29	4	16	72	26	122	24
C.J. Hinojosa, Sugar Land	.316	104	414	68	131	35	0	11	67	23	77	4
Jason Krizan, Sacramento	.316	110	431	67	136	26	1	16	73	39	70	1
Gosuke Katoh, El Paso	.306	114	350	62	107	27	4	8	42	46	84	8
Juniel Querecuto, Reno	.301	96	362	59	109	15	7	13	79	31	62	9
Matt Batten, El Paso	.300	117	417	70	125	14	3	6	39	48	119	27
Jantzen Witte, Tacoma	.299	104	405	63	121	19	1	19	70	41	80	3

INDIVIDUAL PITCHING

Pitcher, Club	W	L	ERA	G	GS	CG	SV	IP	H	R	ER	BB	SO
Aaron Wilkerson, Oklahoma City	8	5	3.86	23	19	0	0	112	98	50	48	24	125
Darren McCaughan, Tacoma	5	4	4.53	20	20	0	0	115	111	61	58	17	99
Logan Verrett, Tacoma	11	4	4.74	19	19	0	0	114	123	64	60	16	88
Yefry Ramirez, Oklahoma City	6	4	5.02	25	22	0	0	113	113	73	63	51	115
Austin Bibens-Dirkx, Oklahoma City	10	6	5.13	25	17	0	0	109	133	71	62	26	97
Brian Howard, Las Vegas	7	4	5.86	24	21	0	0	111	126	78	72	40	96
Thomas Pannone, Salt Lake	5	11	7.07	24	21	0	0	118	160	103	93	40	82

ALL-STAR TEAM

C: Carlos Perez, Las Vegas. **1B:** Greg Bird, Albuquerque. **2B:** Michael Stefanic, Salt Lake.
3B: Drew Ellis, Reno. **SS:** C.J. Hinojosa, Sugar Land. **OF:** Jo Adell, Salt Lake. **OF:** Jake Meyers, Sugar Land.
OF: Jose Siri, Sugar Land. **DH:** Jose Marmolejos, Tacoma. **RHP:** Peter Solomon, Sugar Land.
LHP: Daniel Camarena, El Paso. **RP:** Ronel Blanco, Sugar Land.
MVP: Jose Marmolejos, 1B/OF, Tacoma. **Pitcher of the Year:** Peter Solomon, RHP, Sugar Land.
Top MLB Prospect: Jo Adell, OF, Salt Lake. **Manager of the Year:** Kristopher Negron, Tacoma.

DEPARTMENT LEADERS

BATTING

OBP	Jose Marmolejos, Tacoma	.439
SLG	Jose Marmolejos, Tacoma	.672
OPS	Jose Marmolejos, Tacoma	1.111
R	Ryan Vilade, Albuquerque	82
H	Jason Krizan, Sacramento	136
TB	Carlos Perez, Las Vegas	215
XBH	Alan Trejo, Albuquerque	57
2B	C.J. Hinojosa, Sugar Land	35
3B	Jose Azocar, El Paso	8
HR	Carlos Perez, Las Vegas	31
RBI	Greg Bird, Albuquerque	91
SAC	Francisco Pena, Las Vegas	9
BB	Michael Papierski, Sugar Land	64
HBP	Seth Beer, Reno	30
SO	Jake Gatewood, Salt Lake	170
SB	Bryce Johnson, Sacramento	30
CS	Yonny Hernandez, Round Rock	10
AB/SO	Donovan Walton, Tacoma	7.86

FIELDING

C	PCT	Brian Serven, Albuquerque	.990
	PO	Michael Papierski, Sugar Land	623
	A	Joey Bart, Sacramento	45
	DP	Cal Raleigh, Tacoma	4
	DP	Webster Rivas, El Paso	4
	DP	Jack Kruger, Round Rock	4
	E	Luis Campusano, El Paso	8
	CS	Brian Serven, Albuquerque	23
	SB	Luis Campusano, El Paso	47
	PB	John Hicks, Round Rock	10
1B	PCT	Seth Beer, Reno	.990
	PO	Seth Beer, Reno	685
	A	Greg Bird, Albuquerque	57
	DP	Seth Beer, Reno	79
	E	Curtis Terry, Round Rock	8
2B	PCT	Michael Stefanic, Salt Lake	.973
	PO	Michael Stefanic, Salt Lake	112
	A	Nate Mondou, Las Vegas	179
	DP	Michael Stefanic, Salt Lake	46
	E	Michael Stefanic, Salt Lake	8
3B	PCT	Drew Ellis, Reno	.969
	PO	Drew Ellis, Reno	48
	A	Drew Ellis, Reno	106
	DP	Drew Ellis, Reno	11
	E	Cristian Santana, Oklahoma City	9
SS	PCT	Pete Kozma, Las Vegas	.962
	PO	Pete Kozma, Las Vegas	133
	A	Pete Kozma, Las Vegas	248
	DP	Pete Kozma, Las Vegas	56
	E	Pete Kozma, Las Vegas	15
OF	PCT	Carl Chester, Round Rock	.983
	PO	Wynton Bernard, Albuquerque	194
	A	Jose Azocar, El Paso	7
	A	Luis Barrera, Las Vegas	7
	A	Leody Taveras, Round Rock	7
	DP	5 players	2
	E	Luis Barrera, Las Vegas	10

PITCHING

G	Logan Cozart, Albuquerque	54
GS	Ryan Castellani, Albuquerque	23
GF	Kevin Quackenbush, Oklahoma City	42
SV	Kevin Quackenbush, Oklahoma City	23
W	Logan Verrett, Tacoma	11
L	Jose Mujica, Albuquerque	12
IP	Thomas Pannone, Salt Lake	118.1
H	Thomas Pannone, Salt Lake	160
R	Thomas Pannone, Salt Lake	103
ER	Thomas Pannone, Salt Lake	93
HB	Brett Conine, Sugar Land	14
BB	Ryan Castellani, Albuquerque	71
SO	Aaron Wilkerson, Oklahoma City	125
SO/9	Aaron Wilkerson, Oklahoma City	10.04
SO/9 (RP)	Parker Markel, El Paso	14.37
BB/9	Logan Verrett, Tacoma	1.26
WP	Justin Grimm, Tacoma	12
BK	Justin Grimm, Tacoma	3
BK	Zack Weiss, Tacoma	3
HRA	Jose Mujica, Albuquerque	27
BAA	Aaron Wilkerson, Oklahoma City	.235

MINOR LEAGUES

MINOR LEAGUES

BY J.J. COOPER

Like most of the minor leagues, Double-A Central was affected by the reorganization of the minor leagues. What was long known was the Texas League. It added two teams in the process, both of them coming from Triple-A. San Antonio and Wichita joined the league, the latter after relocating from New Orleans. Wichita had been scheduled to debut in 2020 in Triple-A, but had to wait until 2021 because of the coronavirus pandemic.

Three of the top 10 prospects in all of baseball spent significant time in the league. Shortstop Bobby Witt Jr. opened the season with Northwest Arkansas and shortstop C.J. Abrams began the year with Amarillo. Outfielder Julio Rodriguez joined Arkansas for the second half of the season.

Witt and Rodriguez were in good company. They played for two of the more talented teams in the minors. In the first half of the season, Northwest Arkansas stood out thanks to Witt, first baseman Nick Pratto and catcher MJ Melendez.

After the Royals prospects moved to Triple-A, the Mariners' affiliate in Arkansas became the team to watch thanks to the promotions of Rodriguez, righthanders Matt Brash and George Kirby and lefthander Brandon Williamson.

Northwest Arkansas managed to win the Double-A Central championship even after losing so many stars to in-season promotions. The Naturals managed to keep on winning in the second half thanks to first baseman Vinnie Pasquantino, righthanders Jon Heasley and Drew Parrish and lefthander Austin Cox.

In the playoffs, the Naturals swept Wichita. Freddy Fermin singled in Jeison Guzman and Meibrys Viloria in the seventh inning of Game 1 to give Northwest Arkansas a 7-5 win. In Game 2, Yefri Del Rosario and three relievers combined to hold Wichita to one run in a 5-1 victory. And in

TOP 10 PROSPECTS

Bobby Witt Jr.

1. Bobby Witt Jr., SS, Northwest Arkansas (Royals)
2. Julio Rodriguez, OF, Arkansas (Mariners)
3. C.J. Abrams, SS, San Antonio (Padres)
5. M.J. Melendez, C, Northwest Arkansas (Royals)
6. Alek Thomas, OF, Amarillo (D-backs)
6. Matt Brash, RHP, Arkansas (Mariners)
7. Josh Jung, 3B, Frisco (Rangers)
8. Nolan Gorman, 3B/2B, Springfield (Cardinals)
9. Cole Winn, RHP, Frisco (Rangers)
10. Miguel Vargas, 3B/2B, Tulsa (Dodgers)

Game 3, a Brewer Hicklen grand slam provided all the runs the Naturals needed in a 6-2 win.

Wichita also had a roster to remember thanks to third baseman Jose Miranda, shortstop/center fielder Austin Martin and a loaded rotation that included righthanders Josh Winder, Jordan Balazovic, Cole Sands, Simeon Woods Richardson and Josh Winder.

League MVP Melendez hit 28 home runs—one off Ryan Noda's league lead—in just 79 games.

The league as a whole was filled with impressive prospects. It was also a year for impressive performances. Four different players—Nolan Gorman, Nick Plummer, Pratto and Witt—had a game with three home runs. ■

OVERALL STANDINGS

North Division	W	L	PCT	GB	Manager	Attendance	Average	Last Penn.
Wichita Wind Surge (Twins)	69	51	.575	—	Ramon Borrego	241,230	4,021	Never
Northwest Arkansas Naturals (Royals)	64	55	.538	4.5	Scott Thorman	150,473	2,487	2021
Arkansas Travelers (Mariners)	64	56	.533	5	Collin Cowgill	215,050	3,597	*2009
Tulsa Drillers (Dodgers)	63	57	.525	6	Scott Hennessey	300,270	4,955	*2018
Springfield Cardinals (Cardinals)	45	75	.375	24	Jose Leger	172,134	2,885	*2012

South Division	W	L	PCT	GB	Manager	Attendance	Average	Last Penn.
Frisco RoughRiders (Rangers)	64	55	.538	—	Jared Goedert	275,169	4,683	*2004
Midland RockHounds (Athletics)	59	60	.496	5	Bobby Crosby	186,134	3,117	*2017
Amarillo Sod Poodles (D-backs)	59	61	.492	5.5	Shawn Roof	316,288	5,286	*2019
San Antonio Missions (Padres)	57	63	.475	7.5	Phillip Wellman	184,167	3,055	*2013
Corpus Christi Hooks (Astros)	54	65	.454	10	Gregorio Petit	206,847	3,524	*2006

Finals: Northwest Arkansas defeated Wichita 3-0.   * Refers to Double-A Texas League prior to 2021

CLUB BATTING

	AVG	G	AB	R	H	2B	3B	HR	RBI	BB	SO	SB	OBP	SLG
Wichita	.257	120	4033	636	1038	178	18	150	597	459	1142	123	.339	.422
NW Arkansas	.257	119	3932	668	1012	181	25	166	619	488	1076	164	.347	.443
Amarillo	.254	120	4000	624	1016	191	40	160	588	406	1172	117	.330	.442
Springfield	.254	120	4058	577	1029	159	15	140	534	467	1087	67	.339	.404
Tulsa Drillers	.254	120	4055	644	1028	184	10	161	613	511	1160	62	.344	.423
Corpus Christi	.247	119	3932	551	970	187	13	140	524	451	1178	89	.335	.408
Frisco	.247	119	3898	536	961	175	21	136	511	405	1143	116	.324	.407
San Antonio	.241	120	3835	535	923	183	22	95	493	450	985	135	.330	.374
Arkansas	.236	120	3901	565	922	164	17	124	515	511	1214	103	.334	.382
Midland	.236	119	3956	557	934	170	18	98	515	492	1173	65	.329	.362

CLUB PITCHING

	ERA	G	CG	SHO	SV	IP	H	R	ER	HR	BB	SO	AVG
Frisco	3.98	119	1	9	30	1038	877	515	459	126	423	1183	.228
Arkansas	4.13	120	4	12	32	1036	936	527	475	124	433	1156	.240
Corpus Christi	4.22	119	1	8	28	1035	914	552	485	103	515	1163	.237
Wichita	4.35	120	0	8	28	1059	950	577	512	136	531	1210	.238
Midland	4.40	119	0	4	34	1047	1024	572	512	103	426	977	.259
San Antonio	4.43	120	1	10	31	1035	1000	575	510	108	449	1049	.252
Tulsa	4.48	120	4	0	27	1057	954	598	526	173	490	1211	.237
Northwest Arkansas	4.56	119	3	8	27	1024	1013	563	519	133	442	1104	.257
Amarillo	4.93	120	3	6	35	1043	1004	640	571	186	424	1214	.252
Springfield	5.97	120	2	2	17	1039	1161	794	689	178	507	1063	.282

CLUB FIELDING

	PCT	PO	A	E	DP		PCT	PO	A	E	DP
Midland	.982	3140	1173	81	112	Tulsa Drillers	.976	3172	884	98	68
Arkansas	.981	3107	949	77	82	Corpus Christi	.976	3105	941	99	91
Frisco	.979	3114	997	87	86	Amarillo	.976	3128	1013	103	118
NW Arkansas	.979	3072	1063	90	90	Wichita	.975	3176	961	104	87
San Antonio	.977	3105	1023	99	90	Springfield	.969	3117	1071	132	113

INDIVIDUAL BATTING

Batter, Club	AVG	G	AB	R	H	2B	3B	HR	RBI	BB	SO	SB
Miguel Vargas, Tulsa	.321	83	327	67	105	16	1	16	60	36	57	7
Roy Morales, Wichita	.306	87	333	43	102	14	1	1	33	8	45	5
Donovan Casey, Tulsa	.296	73	301	51	89	15	1	11	36	26	102	15
David Hensley, Corpus Christi	.293	105	396	54	116	25	3	9	51	46	104	11
Dairon Blanco, Northwest Arkansas	.289	79	291	62	84	11	5	9	38	25	64	32
Clay Dungan, Northwest Arkansas	.288	108	444	74	128	17	4	9	56	40	73	28
Corey Julks, Corpus Christi	.287	85	338	67	97	23	2	14	36	32	84	15
MJ Melendez, Northwest Arkansas	.285	79	298	58	85	18	0	28	65	43	76	2
Alek Thomas, Amarillo	.283	72	286	54	81	18	8	10	41	37	65	8
Nick Plummer, Springfield	.283	90	311	52	88	17	4	13	46	53	108	9

INDIVIDUAL PITCHING

Pitcher, Club	W	L	ERA	G	GS	CG	SV	IP	H	R	ER	BB	SO
Jared Koenig, Midland	7	5	3.26	24	21	0	0	121	108	56	44	43	100
Jon Heasley, Northwest Arkansas	7	3	3.33	22	21	1	0	105	95	42	39	34	120
Jordan Balazovic, Wichita	5	4	3.62	20	20	0	0	97	98	48	39	38	102
Brady Feigl, Midland	7	7	3.96	20	20	0	0	102	94	50	45	34	106
Austin Schulfer, Wichita	6	8	4.34	24	24	0	0	110	109	61	53	49	105
Osvaldo Hernandez, San Antonio	4	8	5.11	22	22	0	0	100	120	64	57	26	88
Tommy Henry, Amarillo	4	6	5.21	23	23	0	0	116	116	71	67	53	135
Dalton Roach, Springfield	7	10	5.65	24	19	0	0	115	135	76	72	45	119

ALL-STAR TEAM

C: MJ Melendez, NW Arkansas. **1B:** Nick Pratto, NW Arkansas. **2B:** Michael Busch, Tulsa.
3B: Miguel Vargas, Tulsa. **SS:** Bobby Witt Jr., NW Arkansas. **OF:** Stone Garrett, Amarillo.
OF: Julio Rodriguez, Arkansas. **OF:** Bubba Thompson, Frisco. **DH:** Ryan Noda, Tulsa.
RHP: Cole Winn, Frisco. **LHP:** Jared Koenig, Midland. **RP:** Darin Gillies, Arkansas.

MVP: MJ Melendez, C, NW Arkansas. **Pitcher of the Year:** Cole Winn, RHP, Frisco.
Top MLB Prospect: Bobby Witt Jr., NW Arkansas. **Manager of the Year:** Ramon Borrego, Wichita.

DEPARTMENT LEADERS

BATTING

OBP	Jonah Bride, Midland	.407
SLG	MJ Melendez, Northwest Arkansas	.628
OPS	MJ Melendez, Northwest Arkansas	.999
R	Michael Busch, Tulsa	84
H	Clay Dungan, Northwest Arkansas	128
TB	Stone Garrett, Amarillo	210
XBH	Michael Busch, Tulsa	48
XBH	Bubba Thompson, Frisco	48
2B	Eguy Rosario, San Antonio	31
3B	Bubba Thompson, Frisco	9
HR	Ryan Noda, Tulsa	29
RBI	Stone Garrett, Amarillo	81
SAC	Ivan Herrera, Springfield	7
SAC	Devin Mann, Tulsa	7
SAC	Aaron Whitefield, Wichita	7
BB	Ryan Noda, Tulsa	74
HBP	Devin Mann, Tulsa	15
SO	Logan Davidson, Midland	155
SB	Brewer Hicklen, Northwest Arkansas	40
CS	Eguy Rosario, San Antonio	14
AB/SO	Roy Morales, Wichita	7.09

FIELDING

C PCT	Hunter Feduccia, Tulsa	.999
PO	Matt Whatley, Frisco	727
A	Matt Whatley, Frisco	64
DP	Scott Manea, Corpus Christi	5
E	MJ Melendez, Northwest Arkansas	10
CS	Matt Whatley, Frisco	29
SB	Matt Whatley, Frisco	74
PB	Juan Fernandez, San Antonio	9
1B PCT	Luken Baker, Springfield	.991
PO	Luken Baker, Springfield	617
A	Nick Pratto, NW Arkansas	36
A	Luken Baker, Springfield	36
DP	Luken Baker, Springfield	66
E	Luken Baker, Springfield	6
2B PCT	Michael Busch, Tulsa	.978
PO	Nick Dunn, Springfield	117
A	Michael Busch, Tulsa	194
DP	Nick Dunn, Springfield	53
E	Nick Dunn, Springfield	11
3B PCT	Andrew Bechtold, Wichita	.962
PO	Kody Hoese, Tulsa	42
A	Buddy Kennedy, Amarillo	105
DP	2 players	11
E	Joe Perez, Corpus Christi	17
SS PCT	Jermaine Palacios, Wichita	.962
PO	Jacob Amaya, Tulsa	151
A	Delvin Perez, Springfield	251
DP	Delvin Perez, Springfield	59
E	Jacob Amaya, Tulsa	20
OF PCT	Stephen Wrenn, Arkansas	.994
PO	Aaron Whitefield, Wichita	219
A	Dominic Fletcher, Amarillo	10
A	Brewer Hicklen, Northwest Arkansas	10
DP	3 players	3
E	Bubba Thompson, Frisco	6
E	David Vinsky, Springfield	6
E	Romer Cuadrado, Tulsa	6

PITCHING

G	Austin Briggs, Midland	41
G	Michael Stryffeler, Arkansas	41
GS	Austin Schulfer, Wichita	24
GF	Jose Quezada, San Antonio	31
SV	Jose Quezada, San Antonio	18
W	Zach Neff, Wichita	8
L	Dalton Roach, Springfield	10
L	Domingo Robles, Springfield	10
IP	Jared Koenig, Midland	121.1
H	Dalton Roach, Springfield	135
R	Kyle Leahy, Springfield	86
ER	Kyle Leahy, Springfield	79
HB	Gerardo Carrillo, Tulsa	16
BB	Chris Vallimont, Wichita	61
SO	Tommy Henry, Amarillo	135
SO/9	Chris Vallimont, Wichita	12.86
SO/9 (RP)	Ramon Santos, Springfield	14.09
BB/9	Osvaldo Hernandez, San Antonio	2.33
WP	Michael Brettell, Springfield	14
BK	Brett Daniels, Corpus Christi	4
HRA	Dalton Roach, Springfield	27
BAA	Jared Koenig, Midland	.240

MINOR LEAGUES

BY MIKE ASHMORE

Eleven teams in Double-A Northeast were holdovers from the Eastern League. The exception was Somerset, which the Yankees plucked from the independent Atlantic League to supplant Trenton.

The league featured some of the premier prospects in baseball in 2021. Bowie and Erie were of particular interest because each featured a recent No. 1 overall pick who paid with another top 10 overall prospect in baseball.

Catcher Adley Rutschman, the top pick in 2019, formed a battery with top pitching prospect in baseball Grayson Rodriguez for much of the year in Bowie. Top 2020 pick Spencer Torkelson, a slugging first baseman, drew plenty of interest in Erie batting alongside outfielder Riley Greene.

Even past the top names, the Double-A Northeast featured extraordinary depth. Sixteen players on the end-of-season Top 100 Prospects qualified for the list. That group included a trio of players who spent the majority of their seasons on a must-watch New Hampshire team: shortstop/outfielder Austin Martin, catcher Gabriel Moreno and shortstop Jordan Groshans.

The Blue Jays traded Martin, whom they drafted fifth overall out of Vanderbilt in 2020, to the Twins at the trade deadline to acquire righthander Jose Berrios.

Akron finished with a .613 wining percentage, tops in the league. The Indians affiliate went on to win the Double-A Northeast title by sweeping Bowie three games to none in the championship series. Akron entered the eighth inning of Game 3 trailing 5-0 but pulled off an impressive comeback that culminated in a walk-off hit from catcher Bo Naylor, Cleveland's first-round pick in 2018.

Somerset, in its first year in affiliated baseball, finished with the top record in the Northeast

Division and featured league MVP Oswaldo Cabrera. The 22-year-old infielder batted .258/.311/.492 with hit 24 home runs while starting at least 20 games at second base, third base and shortstop. Cabrera's exit velocity spiked in a season in which he hit a personal best 29 home runs between Double-A and Triple-A.

Rodriguez was the league's pitcher of the year and finished the season ranked as the No. 7 prospect in baseball. He joined the league on June 2 but still led Double-A Northeast with 121 strikeouts. Among starters with at least 100 innings, Rodriguez led all minor leaguers with a 40.5% strikeout rate and tied for first with a 0.83 WHIP. ∎

TOP 10 PROSPECTS

Adley Rutschman

1. Adley Rutschman, C, Bowie (Orioles)
2. Spencer Torkelson, 1B/3B, Erie (Tigers)
3. Riley Greene, OF, Erie (Tigers)
4. Grayson Rodriguez, RHP, Bowie (Orioles)
5. Gabriel Moreno, C, New Hampshire (Blue Jays)
6. Cade Cavalli, RHP, Harrisburg (Nationals)
7. Oneil Cruz, SS, Altoona (Pirates)
8. Brayan Rocchio, SS, Akron (Indians)
9. Triston Casas, 1B, Portland (Red Sox)
10. Austin Martin, SS/OF, New Hampshire (Blue Jays)

OVERALL STANDINGS

Northeast Division	W	L	PCT	GB	Manager	Attendance	Average	Last Penn.
Somerset Patriots (Yankees)	72	47	.605	—	Julio Mosquera	205,246	3,474	Never
Portland Sea Dogs (Red Sox)	67	47	.588	2.5	Corey Wimberly	210,211	3,651	*2006
New Hampshire Fisher Cats (Blue Jays)	52	55	.486	14	Cesar Martin	183,730	3,295	*2018
Binghamton Rumble Ponies (Mets)	47	60	.439	19	Lorenzo Bundy	107,803	2,095	*1994
Reading Fightin Phils (Phillies)	48	65	.425	21	Shawn Williams	226,667	4,118	*2001
Hartford Yard Goats (Rockies)	39	79	.331	32.5	Chris Denorfia	287,752	4,971	Never

Southwest Division	W	L	PCT	GB	Manager	Attendance	Average	Last Penn.
Akron RubberDucks (Indians)	73	46	.613	—	Rouglas Odor	208,162	3,525	2021
Bowie Baysox (Orioles)	73	47	.608	0.5	Buck Britton	128,467	2,161	Never
Erie SeaWolves (Tigers)	64	55	.538	9	Arnie Beyeler	145,445	2,395	Never
Richmond Flying Squirrels (Giants)	57	56	.504	13	Jose Alguacil	275,169	4,611	*2014
Altoona Curve (Pirates)	58	59	.496	14	Miguel Perez	213,686	3,796	*2017
Harrisburg Senators (Nationals)	42	76	.356	30.5	Tripp Keister	167,810	2,664	*1999

Finals: Akron defeated Bowie 3-0

* Refers to Double-A Eastern League prior to 2021

CLUB BATTING

	AVG	G	AB	R	H	2B	3B	HR	RBI	BB	SO	SB	OBP	SLG
Portland	.262	114	3695	575	968	222	19	130	528	333	910	46	.333	.438
New Hampshire	.259	107	3533	559	916	194	15	91	520	383	1019	116	.341	.400
Akron	.254	119	3922	628	998	220	30	116	577	440	1046	100	.338	.415
Erie	.253	119	3884	584	981	192	27	152	546	378	1159	79	.327	.433
Somerset	.248	119	3880	600	962	209	20	175	546	448	1150	186	.331	.447
Altoona	.244	117	3820	535	932	186	22	119	504	371	1102	86	.316	.398
Binghamton	.244	107	3555	477	866	193	11	108	439	359	1085	57	.321	.395
Richmond	.236	113	3652	525	862	183	17	127	480	398	1124	66	.322	.400
Bowie	.235	120	3891	628	916	196	21	170	583	507	1226	78	.332	.428
Reading	.232	113	3666	457	852	176	21	121	423	400	1032	49	.313	.391
Hartford	.228	118	3808	475	869	198	13	122	433	390	1203	99	.308	.383
Harrisburg	.227	118	3820	432	869	192	14	76	388	312	1047	48	.297	.345

CLUB PITCHING

	ERA	G	CG	SHO	SV	IP	H	R	ER	HR	BB	SO	AVG
Somerset	3.38	119	2	17	28	1025	801	443	385	106	385	1300	.212
Akron	3.78	119	1	13	31	1031	876	494	433	116	420	1190	.229
Richmond	3.94	113	2	8	31	967	877	496	423	109	354	1098	.240
Harrisburg	4.16	118	0	4	21	1011	926	532	467	133	387	1050	.241
Portland	4.16	114	2	5	34	959	935	516	443	98	342	1100	.252
Erie	4.27	119	1	7	29	1014	906	528	481	143	383	1072	.237
Bowie	4.28	120	0	13	34	1040	931	552	495	152	462	1258	.237
New Hampshire	4.62	107	0	5	23	909	855	537	467	110	410	955	.246
Binghamton	4.65	107	1	6	24	926	862	534	479	117	333	1001	.244
Altoona	4.66	117	1	5	27	1005	964	591	520	114	399	999	.249
Reading	4.81	113	0	5	33	966	907	577	516	144	470	1088	.247
Hartford	5.47	118	2	3	19	996	1151	675	605	165	374	992	.288

CLUB FIELDING

	PCT	PO	A	E	DP		PCT	PO	A	E	DP
Bowie	.980	3121	985	84	80	Harrisburg	.975	3032	964	101	87
Erie	.980	3044	902	82	77	New Hampshire	.975	2728	864	93	86
Somerset	.979	3074	921	86	72	Portland	.974	2876	942	102	77
Akron	.979	3093	947	88	91	Binghamton	.973	2779	845	99	59
Reading	.977	2898	923	89	81	Richmond	.973	2900	885	104	66
Hartford	.976	2987	1006	99	102	Altoona	.971	3014	937	119	83

INDIVIDUAL BATTING

Batter, Club	AVG	G	AB	R	H	2B	3B	HR	RBI	BB	SO	SB
Otto Lopez, New Hampshire	.331	70	278	52	92	24	1	3	39	28	62	7
Bryson Stott, Reading	.301	80	312	49	94	22	2	10	36	35	78	6
Riley Greene, Erie	.298	84	326	59	97	16	5	16	54	41	102	12
Oswald Peraza, Somerset	.294	79	326	51	96	16	2	12	40	23	82	20
Samad Taylor, New Hampshire	.294	87	320	69	94	17	1	16	52	42	110	30
Jake Mangum, Binghamton	.294	75	303	56	89	21	4	7	41	16	58	14
Pedro Castellanos, Portland	.289	87	325	66	94	14	3	13	44	32	63	2
Triston Casas, Portland	.284	77	275	57	78	12	2	13	52	49	63	6
Cal Mitchell, Altoona	.280	108	382	43	107	19	1	12	61	24	71	6
Ronaldo Hernandez, Portland	.280	92	336	44	94	26	1	16	53	11	70	0

INDIVIDUAL PITCHING

Pitcher, Club	W	L	ERA	G	GS	CG	SV	IP	H	R	ER	BB	SO
Juan Hillman, Akron	10	4	3.77	21	20	1	0	107	110	49	45	32	85
Mario Sanchez, Harrisburg	4	8	3.98	22	18	0	0	106	94	48	47	21	107
Josh Winckowski, Portland	8	3	4.14	21	20	0	0	100	100	54	46	30	88
A.J. Ladwig, Erie	6	7	4.80	21	21	0	0	101	101	56	54	18	82
Maximo Castillo, New Hampshire	11	4	4.85	21	20	0	0	102	106	60	55	35	89
Tim Cate, Harrisburg	2	10	5.31	21	21	0	0	97	113	64	57	37	81
Matt Dennis, Hartford	4	9	5.81	23	17	0	0	96	120	62	62	20	79

ALL-STAR TEAM

C: Adley Rutschman, Bowie. **1B:** Mason Martin, Altoona. **2B:** Oswaldo Cabrera, Somerset.
3B: Mark Vientos, Binghamton. **SS:** Oneil Cruz, Altoona. **OF:** Michael Beltre, Somerset.
OF: Riley Greene, Erie. **OF:** Jake Mangum, Binghamton. **DH:** Josh Lester, Erie.
RHP: Grayson Rodriguez, Bowie. **LHP:** Juan Hillman, Akron. **RP:** Brian Marconi, Reading.

MVP: Oswaldo Cabrera, 2B, Somerset. **Pitcher of the Year:** Grayson Rodriguez, RHP, Bowie.
Top MLB Prospect: Adley Rutschman, C, Bowie. **Manager of the Year:** Rouglas Odor, Akron.

DEPARTMENT LEADERS

BATTING

OBP	Triston Casas, Portland	.395
SLG	Josh Lester, Erie	.612
OPS	Josh Lester, Erie	.951
R	Michael Beltre, Somerset	72
R	Patrick Dorrian, Bowie	72
H	Oswaldo Cabrera, Somerset	112
TB	Oswaldo Cabrera, Somerset	215
XBH	Oswaldo Cabrera, Somerset	54
2B	Coco Montes, Hartford	37
3B	Michael Beltre, Somerset	8
HR	Dermis Garcia, Somerset	31
RBI	Oswaldo Cabrera, Somerset	78
SAC	Elehuris Montero, Hartford	9
BB	Patrick Dorrian, Bowie	69
HBP	David Villar, Richmond	15
SO	Dermis Garcia, Somerset	168
SB	Michael Beltre, Somerset	37
CS	Isiah Gilliam, Somerset	10
AB/SO	Cole Freeman, Harrisburg	8.45

FIELDING

C PCT	Jakson Reetz, Harrisburg	.995
PO	Bo Naylor, Akron	707
A	Bo Naylor, Akron	54
DP	Willie MacIver, Hartford	8
E	Andres Angulo, Richmond	9
E	Nick Meyer, Binghamton	9
CS	Willie MacIver, Hartford	22
SB	Max George, Hartford	48
PB	Ronaldo Hernandez, Portland	14
1B PCT	Mason Martin, Altoona	.990
PO	Mason Martin, Altoona	767
A	Dermis Garcia, Somerset	67
DP	Mason Martin, Altoona	65
E	Dermis Garcia, Somerset	14
2B PCT	Coco Montes, Hartford	.971
PO	Coco Montes, Hartford	125
A	Coco Montes, Hartford	179
DP	Coco Montes, Hartford	46
E	Ji-hwan Bae, Altoona	14
3B PCT	Patrick Dorrian, Bowie	.938
PO	David Villar, Richmond	64
A	Patrick Dorrian, Bowie	150
DP	Patrick Dorrian, Bowie	15
E	David Villar, Richmond	19
SS PCT	Ryan Kreidler, Erie	.981
PO	Ryan Kreidler, Erie	140
A	Cadyn Grenier, Bowie	185
DP	Jose Gomez, Hartford	45
E	Manny Rodriguez, Binghamton	14
OF PCT	Cole Freeman, Harrisburg	.994
PO	Riley Greene, Erie	189
A	Chavez Young, New Hampshire	11
DP	Austin Martin, New Hampshire	3
E	Jeisson Rosario, Portland	8

PITCHING

G	Yoan Aybar, Hartford	49
GS	Tim Cate, Harrisburg	21
GS	A.J. Ladwig, Erie	21
GS	Travis MacGregor, Altoona	21
GF	Yoan Aybar, Hartford	28
SV	Diogenes Almengo, Bowie	16
W	Maximo Castillo, New Hampshire	11
L	Francisco Morales, Reading	13
IP	Juan Hillman, Akron	107.1
H	Karl Kauffmann, Hartford	123
R	Karl Kauffmann, Hartford	73
ER	Karl Kauffmann, Hartford	67
HB	Skylar Arias, Akron	12
HB	Juan Hillman, Akron	12
BB	Francisco Morales, Reading	60
SO	Grayson Rodriguez, Bowie	121
SO/9	Mario Sanchez, Harrisburg	9.06
SO/9 (RP)	Zach Warren, Reading	14.21
BB/9	A.J. Ladwig, Erie	1.6
WP	Francisco Morales, Reading	12
BK	9 players	2
HRA	A.J. Ladwig, Erie	23
BAA	Mario Sanchez, Harrisburg	.234

MINOR LEAGUES

BY MATT EDDY

The Southern League dropped two franchises and became Double-A South but was otherwise the same hot, humid, pitcher-friendly league it has always been. No affiliated league saw fewer runs scored per game in 2021.

Dropped from the league were Jacksonville, which moved to Triple-A, and Jackson, which lost its affiliation. Mobile relocated to Rocket City in Madison, Ala., where the park played small and featured three home runs per game. Just two Double-A parks saw a higher rate of home runs hit per game.

The prospect depth in Double-A South was below average, even for an eight-team league, though a number of pitchers stood out to scouts. In particular the crop of lefthanders was strong, led by Chattanooga's Nick Lodolo, Rocket City's Reid Detmers and Pensacola's Jake Eder.

All three southpaws ended the season on the sidelines. Lodolo moved to Triple-A in August but made just three starts before going down with a shoulder injury. Detmers was called up to Anaheim in August but missed September with Covid and returned to make two late appearances. Eder went down with an elbow injury that required Tommy John surgery in September.

Mississippi catcher Shea Langeliers and Chattanooga shortstop Jose Barrero were the top position prospects in the league. Both have the type of up-the-middle upside to become above-average MLB regulars.

Double-A South was rich in first-round talent, including Top 10 Prospects Langeliers, Lodolo, Detmers and righthanders Hunter Greene of Chattanooga and Max Meyer of Pensacola. Other first-rounders who played in the league long enough to qualify for the Top 10 were Pensacola outfielder JJ Bleday, Mississippi shortstop Braden Shewmake and lefthander Ethan Small, shortstop Brice Turang and outfielder Garrett Mitchell, all three of Biloxi.

Montgomery's Jonathan Aranda, a 23-year-old

TOP 10 PROSPECTS

Shea Langeliers

1. Shea Langeliers, C, Mississippi (Braves)
2. Jose Barrero, SS, Chattanooga (Reds)
3. Nick Lodolo, LHP, Chattanooga (Reds)
4. Reid Detmers, LHP, Rocket City (Angels)
5. Hunter Greene, RHP, Chattanooga (Reds)
6. Brennen Davis, OF, Tennessee (Cubs)
7. Jake Eder, LHP, Pensacola (Marlins)
8. Max Meyer, RHP, Pensacola (Marlins)
9. Peyton Burdick, OF, Pensacola (Marlins)
10. Jonathan Aranda, 1B/2B, Montgomery (Rays)

lefthanded hitter from Mexico, took league MVP honors. He topped Double-A South with a .325 average, .410 on-base percentage and .540 slugging percentage while starting at least 10 games at first base, second base and third base.

Meyer, the third pick in the 2020 draft out of Minnesota, was the league's pitcher of the year. He won the Double-A South ERA title (2.41) and paced a dominant Pensacola pitching staff.

South Division rivals Mississippi and Montgomery met in the Double-A South finals. The Braves prevailed in a five-game series, with outfielder Greyson Jenista delivering the go-ahead home run in the clinching game, a 2-1 Mississippi victory. The M-Braves' victory also deprived the Rays organization of a clean sweep of minor league championships. Tampa Bay affiliates won at Triple-A, High-A, Low-A and Rookie ball. ∎

OVERALL STANDINGS

North Division	W	L	PCT	GB	Manager(s)	Attendance	Average	Last Penn
Birmingham Barons (White Sox)	62	56	.525	—	Justin Jirschele	231,365	1,961	*2013
Chattanooga Lookouts (Reds)	58	54	.518	1	Ricky Gutierrez	131,322	1,173	*2017
Rocket City Trash Pandas (Angels)	54	56	.491	4	Jay Bell	274,858	2,499	Never
Tennessee Smokies (Cubs)	46	63	.422	11.5	Mark Johnson	245,821	2,255	*2004

South Division	W	L	PCT	GB	Manager(s)	Attendance	Average	Last Penn
Mississippi Braves (Braves)	67	44	.604	—	Dan Meyer	118,776	1,070	2021
Montgomery Biscuits (Rays)	62	55	.530	8	Morgan Ensberg	137,709	1,177	*2007
Pensacola Blue Wahoos (Marlins)	57	54	.514	10	Kevin Randel	235,948	2,126	*2017
Biloxi Shuckers (Brewers)	45	69	.395	23.5	Mike Guerrero	114,276	1,002	Never

Finals: Mississippi defeated Montgomery 3-2

* Refers to Double-A Southern League prior to 2021

CLUB BATTING

	AVG	G	AB	R	H	2B	3B	HR	RBI	BB	SO	SB	OBP	SLG
Chattanooga	.265	112	3699	551	981	168	29	101	500	348	919	58	.341	.408
Birmingham	.258	118	3818	557	984	177	18	134	516	350	1050	120	.330	.419
Montgomery	.242	117	3748	557	906	181	31	114	508	437	1138	116	.330	.398
Rocket City	.240	110	3585	523	862	172	13	152	487	391	1068	87	.324	.423
Tennessee	.236	109	3529	473	832	187	18	91	439	399	1048	73	.324	.376
Biloxi	.230	114	3698	476	852	166	23	104	446	387	1098	84	.312	.372
Mississippi	.222	111	3539	491	786	142	20	143	445	353	1094	78	.302	.395
Pensacola	.212	111	3473	407	737	158	12	99	374	424	1173	63	.307	.350

CLUB PITCHING

	ERA	G	CG	SHO	SV	IP	H	R	ER	HR	BB	SO	AVG
Pensacola	3.51	111	0	6	29	964	802	442	376	117	371	1051	.226
Mississippi	3.58	111	1	12	25	953	785	417	379	74	413	1083	.224
Birmingham	4.05	118	1	9	25	995	897	504	448	106	388	1077	.239
Montgomery	4.11	117	0	4	32	1001	877	516	457	125	296	1114	.232
Chattanooga	4.37	112	1	8	26	959	897	516	466	109	420	1074	.244
Biloxi	4.46	114	0	7	22	972	899	545	482	150	388	1088	.244
Tennessee	4.55	109	2	5	25	931	863	537	470	131	431	989	.246
Rocket City	4.74	110	4	6	24	932	920	558	491	126	382	1112	.255

CLUB FIELDING

	PCT	PO	A	E	DP		PCT	PO	A	E	DP
Mississippi	.982	2859	896	69	87	Birmingham	.976	2984	998	99	80
Chattanooga	.977	2876	880	87	72	Tennessee	.974	2792	914	97	102
Montgomery	.977	3002	939	92	84	Rocket City	.973	2796	842	101	60
Biloxi	.977	2916	933	90	84	Pensacola	.970	2891	940	119	103

INDIVIDUAL BATTING

Batter, Club	AVG	G	AB	R	H	2B	3B	HR	RBI	BB	SO	SB
Jonathan Aranda, Montgomery	.325	79	274	53	89	19	5	10	58	33	63	4
Lorenzo Cedrola, Chattanooga	.320	106	406	68	130	16	7	9	61	17	50	8
Xavier Edwards, Montgomery	.302	79	291	40	88	13	3	0	27	36	42	19
Wilson Garcia, Chattanooga	.290	103	400	44	116	17	0	18	64	15	77	0
Jameson Fisher, Birmingham	.287	88	328	53	94	18	2	12	47	35	84	2
David MacKinnon, Rocket City	.285	99	365	53	104	30	0	13	65	52	83	2
Romy Gonzalez, Birmingham	.267	78	303	52	81	11	0	20	47	38	97	21
Carlos Perez, Birmingham	.264	107	409	46	108	22	1	13	59	25	45	1
Robbie Tenerowicz, Chattanooga	.264	93	303	48	80	17	2	14	46	27	89	3
Shea Langeliers, Mississippi	.258	92	329	56	85	13	0	22	52	36	97	1
Orlando Martinez, Rocket City	.258	102	400	58	103	23	2	16	54	30	119	5

INDIVIDUAL PITCHING

Pitcher, Club	W	L	ERA	G	GS	CG	SV	IP	H	R	ER	BB	SO
Max Meyer, Pensacola	6	3	2.41	20	20	0	0	101	84	35	27	40	113
Jeff Lindgren, Pensacola	6	8	3.82	20	19	0	0	106	101	49	45	31	85
Will Stewart, Pensacola	5	8	4.33	20	20	0	0	100	96	54	48	38	85
Noah Zavolas, Biloxi	5	7	4.40	22	22	0	0	121	113	61	59	31	121
Blake Battenfield, Birmingham	7	8	4.75	23	20	0	0	106	128	70	56	21	79
Connor Curlis, Chattanooga	5	7	5.03	20	20	0	0	98	88	58	55	48	88

ALL-STAR TEAM

C: Shea Langeliers, Mississippi. **1B:** Jonathan Aranda, Montgomery. **2B:** Xavier Edwards, Montgomery.
3B: Mitch Nay, Rocket City. **SS:** Romy Gonzalez, Birmingham. **OF:** Peyton Burdick, Pensacola.
OF: Lorenzo Cedrola, Chattanooga. **OF:** Brennen Davis, Tennessee. **DH:** Wilson Garcia, Chattanooga.
RHP: Max Meyer, Pensacola. **LHP:** Jake Eder, Pensacola. **RP:** Colton Hock, Pensacola.

MVP: Jonathan Aranda, 1B, Montgomery.
Pitcher of the Year: Max Meyer, RHP, Pensacola.
Top MLB Prospect: Shea Langeliers, C, Mississippi.
Manager of the Year: Dan Meyer, Mississippi.

DEPARTMENT LEADERS

BATTING

OBP	Jonathan Aranda, Montgomery	.410
SLG	Jonathan Aranda, Montgomery	.540
OPS	Jonathan Aranda, Montgomery	.950
R	Peyton Burdick, Pensacola	71
H	Lorenzo Cedrola, Chattanooga	130
TB	Lorenzo Cedrola, Chattanooga	187
TB	Wilson Garcia, Chattanooga	187
XBH	David MacKinnon, Rocket City	43
XBH	Mitch Nay, Rocket City	43
2B	David MacKinnon, Rocket City	30
2B	Lorenzo Cedrola, Chattanooga	7
3B	TJ Hopkins, Chattanooga	7
HR	Peyton Burdick, Pensacola	23
HR	Mitch Nay, Rocket City	23
RBI	David MacKinnon, Rocket City	65
SAC	Cal Stevenson, Montgomery	7
BB	Peyton Burdick, Pensacola	76
HBP	Justin Dean, Mississippi	18
SO	Craig Dedelow, Birmingham	138
SB	Justin Dean, Mississippi	29
CS	Xavier Edwards, Montgomery	11
AB/SO	Carlos Perez, Birmingham	9.09

FIELDING

C	PCT	Anthony Mulrine, Rocket City	.997
	PO	Shea Langeliers, Mississippi	774
	A	Shea Langeliers, Mississippi	73
	DP	Shea Langeliers, Mississippi	9
	E	Ford Proctor, Montgomery	7
	E	Michael Cruz, Rocket City	7
	CS	Shea Langeliers, Mississippi	30
	SB	2 players	46
	PB	Ford Proctor, Montgomery	16
1B	PCT	David MacKinnon, Rocket City	.995
	PO	David MacKinnon, Rocket City	602
	A	David MacKinnon, Rocket City	35
	DP	Lazaro Alonso, Pensacola	44
	E	Lazaro Alonso, Pensacola	7
2B	PCT	Jalen Miller, Mississippi	.975
	PO	Jalen Miller, Mississippi	91
	A	Jalen Miller, Mississippi	140
	DP	Carlos Sepulveda, Tennessee	41
	E	Brian Rey, Chattanooga	8
3B	PCT	CJ Alexander, Mississippi	.943
	PO	Robbie Tenerowicz, Chattanooga	59
	A	Robbie Tenerowicz, Chattanooga	124
	DP	Robbie Tenerowicz, Chattanooga	14
	E	2 players	13
SS	PCT	Braden Shewmake, Mississippi	.969
	PO	Braden Shewmake, Mississippi	98
	A	Braden Shewmake, Mississippi	187
	DP	Braden Shewmake, Mississippi	40
	E	2 players	13
OF	PCT	Cal Stevenson, Montgomery	1.000
	PO	Lorenzo Cedrola, Chattanooga	217
	A	JJ Bleday, Pensacola	11
	DP	4 players	3
	E	Izzy Wilson, Rocket City	9

PITCHING

G	Braden Webb, Biloxi	41
GS	Noah Zavolas, Biloxi	22
GF	Colton Hock, Pensacola	30
SV	Colton Hock, Pensacola	19
W	Ivan Pelaez, Montgomery	8
W	Randy Wynne, Chattanooga	8
L	Jesus Castillo, Biloxi	9
IP	Noah Zavolas, Biloxi	120.2
H	Blake Battenfield, Birmingham	128
R	Blake Battenfield, Birmingham	70
ER	Noah Zavolas, Biloxi	59
HB	Will Stewart, Pensacola	25
BB	Connor Curlis, Chattanooga	48
SO	Noah Zavolas, Biloxi	121
SO/9	Cam Sanders, Tennessee	10.74
SO/9 (RP)	Brooks Wilson, Mississippi	14.93
BB/9	Randy Wynne, Chattanooga	1.11
WP	2 players	12
BK	Javier Assad, Tennessee	4
HRA	Connor Curlis, Chattanooga	21
BAA	Max Meyer, Pensacola	.226

MINOR LEAGUES

BY EMILY WALDON

A lot changed in the minor leagues between the last pitch of 2019 and Opening Day 2021. The entire player development apparatus was overhauled, teams were cut and leagues took on new names and classifications.

The former Midwest League became High-A Central, it's classification changing from Low-A to High-A. The league dropped from 16 teams to 12.

One constant was the high talent level in the league, topped by West Michigan first baseman Spencer Torkelson, whom the Tigers drafted first overall in 2020. Torkelson started slowly but quickly lived up to his billing as an advanced hitter with huge power. He wasn't the only high-end prospect to spend time in High-A Central.

The Dodgers sent more prospects through the league than any organization. Great Lakes featured four league top 10 prospects: third baseman Miguel Vargas, righthander Bobby Miller, outfielder Andy Pages and middle infielder Eddys Leonard.

Vargas advanced to Double-A Central on June 17. He and league MVP Pages were recognized as first-team Minor League All-Stars after the season. Pages, a 20-year-old Cuban outfielder, led High-A Central with 31 home runs, 88 RBIs, 77 walk and a .933 OPS as he made his full-season debut.

Lake County placed three prospects in the top 10. The Indians affiliate began the season with shortstop Brayan Rocchio and outfielder George Valera. They were joined by righthander Daniel Espino on July 15. Rocchio and Valera moved to Double-A Akron in August. All three finished the season ranked as Top 100 Prospects.

While Quad Cities didn't have the type of prospect starpower as Great Lakes or Lake County, the Royals affiliate had one of the best teams in the minors. The River Bandits led the league in runs scored and placed second for fewest runs allowed.

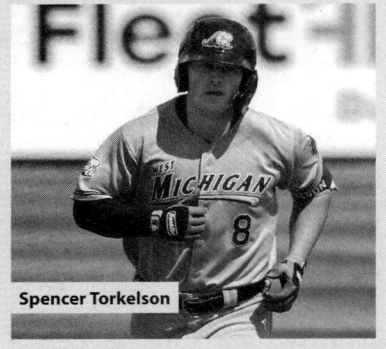

TOP 10 PROSPECTS

Spencer Torkelson

1. Spencer Torkelson, 3B/1B, West Michigan (Tigers)
2. Miguel Vargas, 3B, Great Lakes (Dodgers)
3. Jordan Walker, 3B, Peoria (Cardinals)
4. Bobby Miller, RHP, Great Lakes (Dodgers)
5. Andy Pages, OF, Great Lakes (Dodgers)
6. Daniel Espino, RHP, Lake County (Indians)
7. Brayan Rocchio, SS/2B, Lake County (Indians)
8. George Valera, OF, Lake County (Indians)
9. Eddys Leonard, 2B/SS, Great Lakes (Dodgers)
10. Joey Wiemer, OF, Wisconsin (Brewers)

Quad Cities' .653 winning percentage ranked fourth overall in the minors and was the best by a non-Rays affiliate. The River Bandits met Cedar Rapids in the High-A Central finals and took home a title with a dominant performance in a Game 5 that they forced after falling behind two games to one in the series.

Quad Cities won a thrilling Game 4 on a walk-off home run by Logan Porter, then won the clincher 5-0 on the strength of a two-hit pitching performance led by starter A.J. Block and finished by three relievers. Porter, John Rave and Nick Loftin delivered early RBI hits to stake the River Bandits to an early 3-0 lead the club would never relinquish. ∎

OVERALL STANDINGS

East Division	W	L	PCT	GB	Manager(s)	Attendance	Average	Last Penn.
Dayton Dragons (Reds)	65	55	.542	—	Jose Moreno	344,167	5,713	Never
Lake County Captains (Indians)	65	55	.542	—	Greg DiCenzo	126,191	2,081	*2010
Great Lakes Loons (Dodgers)	63	57	.525	2	John Shoemaker/Austin Chubb	124,896	2,070	*2017
Lansing Lugnuts (Athletics)	58	62	.483	7	Scott Steinmann	198,878	3,335	*2003
West Michigan Whitecaps (Tigers)	58	62	.483	7	Brayan Pena	228,071	3,778	*2015
Fort Wayne TinCaps (Padres)	54	66	.450	11	Anthony Contreras	219,044	3,718	*2009

West Division	W	L	PCT	GB	Manager(s)	Attendance	Average	Last Penn.
Quad Cities River Bandits (Royals)	77	41	.653	—	Chris Widger	163,263	2,763	2021
Cedar Rapids Kernels (Twins)	67	53	.558	11	Brian Dinkelman	100,161	1,688	*1994
Wisconsin Timber Rattlers (Brewers)	59	60	.496	18.5	Matt Erickson	156,646	2,598	*2012
Beloit Snappers (Marlins)	55	65	.458	23	Mike Jacobs	46,746	785	*1995
South Bend Cubs (Cubs)	52	67	.437	25.5	Michael Ryan	217,066	3,679	*2019
Peoria Chiefs (Cardinals)	45	75	.375	33	Jose Leon/Chris Swauger	69,725	1,165	*2002

Finals: Quad Cities defeated Cedar Rapids 3-2   * Refers to Low-A Midwest League prior to 2021

CLUB BATTING

	AVG	G	AB	R	H	2B	3B	HR	RBI	BB	SO	SB	OBP	SLG
Quad Cities	.261	118	4007	709	1045	222	35	144	657	516	1027	127	.352	.441
Great Lakes	.253	120	4102	698	1039	195	37	187	648	484	1305	120	.344	.456
Dayton	.246	120	3876	558	955	206	24	86	488	414	1089	145	.327	.378
Wisconsin	.244	119	3924	640	957	205	26	117	588	531	1250	186	.341	.399
Cedar Rapids	.239	120	3985	603	954	180	32	161	558	528	1284	95	.336	.422
Lake County	.236	120	3840	554	908	176	21	117	503	457	1160	151	.328	.385
West Michigan	.235	120	3854	571	907	209	36	95	516	441	1151	90	.320	.382
Fort Wayne	.234	120	3913	565	914	212	23	70	497	519	1244	118	.334	.353
Beloit	.232	120	4049	608	941	202	36	122	554	442	1327	127	.318	.390
Lansing	.232	120	3870	530	899	206	23	87	463	418	1109	157	.318	.365
Peoria	.231	120	3961	503	916	193	24	111	456	383	1260	90	.314	.376
South Bend	.230	119	3873	543	890	172	22	84	483	432	1114	159	.316	.351

CLUB PITCHING

	ERA	G	CG	SHO	SV	IP	H	R	ER	HR	BB	SO	AVG
Cedar Rapids	3.88	120	0	10	28	1052	873	527	453	82	429	1303	.221
West Michigan	4.09	120	1	8	28	1024	944	546	465	92	399	1086	.242
Lake County	4.12	120	2	10	37	1031	911	565	472	136	389	1234	.233
Quad Cities	4.15	118	0	6	33	1034	883	536	477	114	460	1220	.229
Great Lakes	4.24	120	0	6	19	1054	950	576	497	110	449	1153	.238
Dayton	4.45	120	3	6	36	1024	846	575	507	90	573	1240	.224
Lansing	4.46	120	1	7	29	1031	1006	608	511	114	407	1157	.253
Beloit	4.51	120	0	10	18	1063	1010	604	533	146	371	1173	.246
Fort Wayne	4.66	120	0	5	25	1035	957	599	536	101	460	1148	.245
South Bend	4.91	119	0	5	24	1028	931	639	561	115	574	1202	.239
Peoria	5.03	120	0	2	28	1031	1018	661	576	124	548	1173	.255
Wisconsin	5.18	119	2	5	27	1026	996	646	590	157	506	1231	.250

CLUB FIELDING

	PCT	PO	A	E	DP		PCT	PO	A	E	DP
Fort Wayne	.976	3106	995	102	76	Lake County	.972	3093	900	117	80
Great Lakes	.975	3163	1007	107	86	West Michigan	.971	3075	1033	121	81
Quad Cities	.975	3102	972	106	86	Lansing	.971	3093	969	121	71
Wisconsin	.974	3077	832	104	61	Cedar Rapids	.969	3156	985	132	54
Dayton	.973	3073	961	113	80	South Bend	.968	3083	964	135	71
Beloit	.972	3188	1020	121	65	Peoria	.968	3095	881	133	81

INDIVIDUAL BATING

Batter, Club	AVG	G	AB	R	H	2B	3B	HR	RBI	BB	SO	SB
Nick Loftin, Quad Cities	.289	90	356	67	103	22	5	10	57	42	60	11
Michael Massey, Quad Cities	.289	99	388	76	112	27	2	21	87	33	68	12
Troy Johnston, Beloit	.289	96	357	54	103	22	1	14	72	57	91	6
Jordan Diaz, Lansing	.288	90	333	46	96	24	1	13	56	25	58	2
Jacob Hurtubise, Dayton	.283	102	332	77	94	12	3	0	33	58	73	39
Jose Tena, Lake County	.281	107	413	58	116	25	2	16	58	27	117	10
Tucker Bradley, Quad Cities	.280	86	307	53	86	18	5	6	42	42	77	9
Yonathan Perlaza, South Bend	.280	99	357	54	100	24	1	15	64	38	95	6
Carson Taylor, Great Lakes	.278	79	291	52	81	16	1	9	54	45	63	1
Ryan Ward, Great Lakes	.278	109	439	91	122	21	3	27	84	47	118	8

INDIVIDUAL PITCHING

Pitcher, Club	W	L	ERA	G	GS	CG	SV	IP	H	R	ER	BB	SO
Wilfredo Pereira, Peoria	3	8	3.33	29	13	0	1	97	76	44	36	40	115
Eduardo Salazar, Dayton	4	5	3.49	19	19	1	0	98	81	43	38	32	107
Connor Lunn, Peoria	6	8	3.96	24	23	0	0	120	117	61	53	20	121
Hunter Gaddis, Lake County	4	11	4.16	20	19	1	0	97	83	65	45	28	127
Brendan White, West Michigan	3	9	4.17	26	18	0	0	101	103	55	47	27	107
Jesus Vargas, Great Lakes	8	4	4.40	24	14	0	0	102	102	58	50	14	88
Logan Gragg, Peoria	2	7	4.45	25	20	0	0	99	108	58	49	27	80
Reid Birlingmair, Lansing	4	10	4.54	21	21	0	0	103	88	56	52	52	84
Bryan Hoeing, Beloit	7	6	4.83	22	22	0	0	121	130	72	65	24	96
Mason Hickman, Lake County	8	8	4.88	20	20	0	0	98	89	59	53	37	110
Victor Castaneda, Wisconsin	5	7	5.20	20	20	1	0	97	90	58	56	37	114

ALL-STAR TEAM

C: Logan Porter, Quad Cities. **1B:** Vinnie Pasquantino, Quad Cities. **2B:** Michael Massey, Quad Cities.
3B: Jordan Diaz, Lansing. **SS:** Jose Tena, Lake County. **OF:** Griffin Conine, Beloit.
OF: Andy Pages, Great Lakes. **OF:** Ryan Ward, Great Lakes. **DH:** Troy Johnston, Beloit.
RHP: Ben Gross, Cedar Rapids. **LHP:** Anthony Veneziano, Quad Cities. **RP:** Charles Hall, Lansing.

MVP: Andy Pages, OF, Great Lakes. **Pitcher of the Year:** Anthony Veneziano, LHP, Quad Cities.
Top MLB Prospect: Andy Pages, OF, Great Lakes. **Manager of the Year:** Chris Widger, Quad Cities

DEPARTMENT LEADERS

BATTING

OBP	Jacob Hurtubise, Dayton	.413
SLG	Andy Pages, Great Lakes	.539
OPS	Andy Pages, Great Lakes	.933
R	Andy Pages, Great Lakes	96
H	Ryan Ward, Great Lakes	122
TB	Andy Pages, Great Lakes	236
XBH	Andy Pages, Great Lakes	57
2B	Tirso Ornelas, Fort Wayne	31
3B	Ricky Aracena, Beloit	11
HR	Andy Pages, Great Lakes	31
RBI	Andy Pages, Great Lakes	88
SAC	Eric Cole, Quad Cities	10
BB	Hayden Cantrelle, Wisconsin	77
BB	Andy Pages, Great Lakes	77
HBP	Andy Pages, Great Lakes	19
SO	Leonel Valera, Great Lakes	148
SB	Delvin Zinn, South Bend	42
CS	Ricky Aracena, Beloit	12
AB/SO	Nick Loftin, Quad Cities	5.93

FIELDING

C	PCT	Nick Kahle, Wisconsin	.996
	PO	Eric Yang, Dayton	764
	A	Eric Yang, Dayton	57
	DP	Carson Taylor, Great Lakes	8
	E	Zade Richardson, Peoria	13
	CS	Adam Kerner, Fort Wayne	26
	SB	Jake Washer, South Bend	76
	PB	Adam Kerner, Fort Wayne	12
1B	PCT	Tyler Durna, South Bend	.992
	PO	Troy Johnston, Beloit	681
	A	Troy Johnston, Beloit	48
	DP	Joe Naranjo, Lake County	54
	E	Troy Johnston, Beloit	9
2B	PCT	Michael Massey, Quad Cities	.989
	PO	Ricky Aracena, Beloit	155
	A	Ricky Aracena, Beloit	251
	DP	Ricky Aracena, Beloit	43
	E	Ricky Aracena, Beloit	19
3B	PCT	Seth Gray, Cedar Rapids	.933
	PO	Seth Gray, Cedar Rapids	52
	A	Seth Gray, Cedar Rapids	183
	DP	Seth Gray, Cedar Rapids	13
	E	Jake Slaughter, South Bend	19
SS	PCT	Jose Tena, Lake County	.988
	PO	Leonel Valera, Great Lakes	108
	A	Leonel Valera, Great Lakes	197
	DP	Leonel Valera, Great Lakes	37
	E	Leonel Valera, Great Lakes	21
OF	PCT	Matt Chamberlain, Peoria	1.000
	PO	Andy Pages, Great Lakes	180
	A	Michael Helman, Cedar Rapids	14
	DP	Andy Pages, Great Lakes	3
	E	Andy Pages, Great Lakes	10

PITCHING

G		Jared Tobey, West Michigan	45
GS		Logan Boyer, Great Lakes	24
GF		Zack Hess, West Michigan	31
SV		Zack Hess, West Michigan	13
W		Kevin Coulter, Lansing	9
L		Hunter Gaddis, Lake County	11
IP		Bryan Hoeing, Beloit	121
H		Bryan Hoeing, Beloit	130
R		Michael YaSenka, Peoria	75
ER		Bryan Hoeing, Beloit	65
ER		Michael YaSenka, Peoria	65
HB		Sam Keating, Fort Wayne	15
BB		Jacob Schlesener, Peoria	66
SO		Hunter Gaddis, Lake County	127
SO/9		Anthony Veneziano, Quad Cities	12.2
SO/9 (RP)		Will Klein, Quad Cities	15.48
BB/9		Jesus Vargas, Great Lakes	1.23
WP		Jacob Schlesener, Peoria	22
BK		Freisis Adames, Wisconsin	4
HRA		Hunter Gaddis, Lake County	20
BAA		Wilfredo Pereira, Peoria	.211

MINOR LEAGUES

MINOR LEAGUES

BY CHRIS HILBURN-TRENKLE

High-A East featured an embarrassment of prospect riches in 2021. A total of 10 Top 100 Prospects ranked among the league's top 10 talents. Two more just missed the list: Asheville catcher Korey Lee (Astros) and Greensboro righthander Quinn Priester (Pirates).

Wilmington righthander Cade Cavalli and Hudson Valley shortstop Anthony Volpe stood out the most to league managers, with Cavalli having the arsenal and poise of a frontline starter and Volpe showcasing the tools and instincts of a future above-average middle infielder.

Brooklyn led the way with three top 10 prospects: catcher Francisco Alvarez, shortstop Ronny Mauricio and third baseman Brett Baty.

Bowling Green righthander Taj Bradley, the overall minor league ERA leader, just missed the innings threshold to qualify for the list, as did Hudson Valley lefthander Ken Waldichuk and righty Luis Medina.

Bowling Green, the team with the best record in the league, had an impressive assortment of talent, with catcher Blake Hunt, shortstop Greg Jones and righthander Jayden Murray headlining the group of prospects who received praise from managers.

Bowling Green easily paced the league from start to finish, posting an 82-36 record and defeating a talented Greensboro squad that included Nick Gonzales, Liover Peguero and Priester in five games in the championship series.

It took a comeback for the Hot Rods to become champions, however.

After losing back-to-back games to fall into a 2-1 series hole, the Hot Rods battled back, scoring three runs in the sixth inning of Game 4 to break up a tie game, then taking the fifth game by a score of 6-3 to cement a remarkable season.

Bowling Green was one of four Rays affiliates to win a league championship, with the other three being Triple-A Durham, Low-A Charleston and the Florida Complex League affiliate.

Hudson Valley posted the best record in the North Division, thanks in part to the play of Volpe, but they faltered down the stretch, with an 8-10 record in September that included seven losses to Greensboro.

Greenville, meanwhile, bulldozed through the month of September, winning 10 of their final 12 games against the Hickory Crawdads and Aberdeen IronBirds. They were boosted by the play of 2020 first-rounder Nick Yorke, who joined the team in late August. The 19-year-old second baseman posted a .978 OPS in 21 games to help the Drive finish 14 games above .500. ■

TOP 10 PROSPECTS

Francisco Alvarez

1. Cade Cavalli, RHP, Wilmington (Nationals)
2. Anthony Volpe, SS, Hudson Valley (Yankees)
3. Francisco Alvarez, C, Brooklyn (Mets)
4. Michael Harris, OF, Rome (Braves)
5. Ronny Mauricio, SS, Brooklyn (Mets)
6. Oswald Peraza, SS, Hudson Valley (Yankees)
7. Brett Baty, 3B, Brooklyn (Mets)
8. Nick Gonzales, 2B, Greensboro (Pirates)
9. Gunnar Henderson, SS/3B, Aberdeen (Orioles)
10. Liover Peguero, SS, Greensboro (Pirates)

OVERALL STANDINGS

North Division	W	L	PCT	GB	Manager(s)	Attendance	Average	Last Penn.
Hudson Valley Renegades (Yankees)	71	49	.592	—	Dan Fiorito	125,599	2,082	***2017
Aberdeen IronBirds (Orioles)	58	61	.487	12.5	Kyle Moore	102,261	1,741	***1983
Jersey Shore BlueClaws (Phillies)	56	62	.475	14	Chris Adamson	150,873	2,533	*2010
Wilmington Blue Rocks (Nationals)	52	64	.448	17	Tommy Shields	78,690	1,290	**2019
Brooklyn Cyclones (Mets)	48	70	.407	22	Ed Blankmeyer	106,279	1,816	***2019

South Division	W	L	PCT	GB	Manager(s)	Attendance	Average	Last Penn.
Bowling Green Hot Rods (Rays)	82	36	.695	—	Jeff Smith	125,738	2,197	2021
Greensboro Grasshoppers (Pirates)	74	46	.617	9	Kieran Mattison	225,905	3,773	*2011
Greenville Drive (Red Sox)	67	53	.558	16	Iggy Suarez	243,362	4,084	*2017
Rome Braves (Braves)	56	60	.483	25	Kanekoa Texeira	78,538	1,357	*2016
Asheville Tourists (Astros)	54	62	.466	27	Nate Shaver	130,237	2,254	*2014
Hickory Crawdads (Rangers)	46	68	.404	34	Josh Johnson	88,453	1,505	*2015
Winston-Salem Dash (White Sox)	43	76	.361	39.5	Ryan Newman	206,333	3,372	*2003

Finals: Bowling Green defeated Greensboro 3-2   * Low-A South Atlantic League ** High-A Carolina League *** Short-season New York-Penn League

CLUB BATTING

	AVG	G	AB	R	H	2B	3B	HR	RBI	BB	SO	SB	OBP	SLG
Asheville	.262	116	3896	695	1020	223	15	186	637	400	1304	113	.337	.470
Bowling Green	.261	118	3945	723	1030	198	19	197	679	478	1252	127	.347	.471
Greensboro	.255	120	4112	723	1049	212	20	188	664	459	1244	173	.337	.454
Hudson Valley	.255	120	3933	628	1002	217	33	156	579	455	1154	149	.341	.446
Greenville	.253	120	4023	659	1018	218	28	153	614	465	1134	70	.337	.435
Hickory	.249	114	3783	615	943	165	13	137	561	382	1159	65	.330	.408
Aberdeen	.245	119	3950	577	966	212	37	103	533	469	1277	124	.337	.395
Wilmington	.240	116	3838	538	922	170	20	101	497	379	1035	109	.318	.374
Winston-Salem	.234	119	3885	531	909	183	16	131	497	380	1167	81	.310	.390
Rome	.234	116	3745	508	875	172	21	89	439	390	1103	129	.311	.362
Brooklyn	.227	118	3760	526	853	173	24	125	479	410	1166	70	.311	.385
Jersey Shore	.221	118	3763	495	830	138	26	105	447	415	1223	123	.306	.355

CLUB PITCHING

	ERA	G	CG	SHO	SV	IP	H	R	ER	HR	BB	SO	AVG
Bowling Green	3.95	118	0	8	33	1034	888	534	454	142	310	1187	.227
Rome	3.97	116	1	6	23	995	880	541	439	115	410	1143	.234
Hudson Valley	4.12	120	1	14	28	1034	844	546	473	115	439	1308	.219
Greenville	4.33	120	0	10	23	1047	983	569	504	145	375	1315	.245
Brooklyn	4.51	118	1	6	22	996	930	575	499	106	414	1071	.244
Jersey Shore	4.56	118	1	12	34	1015	957	586	514	118	479	1103	.248
Aberdeen	4.57	119	1	6	28	1031	949	586	523	151	374	1159	.243
Greensboro	4.67	120	0	8	36	1058	954	612	549	181	485	1197	.239
Wilmington	4.73	116	1	13	18	1004	991	610	528	127	410	1176	.256
Hickory	4.99	114	0	6	18	980	959	629	544	154	383	1218	.252
Asheville	5.68	116	0	4	23	992	1028	723	626	162	540	1198	.265
Winston-Salem	5.71	119	0	3	23	1012	1054	707	642	155	463	1143	.266

CLUB FIELDING

	PCT	PO	A	E	DP		PCT	PO	A	E	DP
Greenville	.976	3145	903	98	84	Winston-Salem	.974	3035	942	108	75
Greensboro	.976	3174	993	102	81	Brooklyn	.973	2987	995	110	88
Jersey Shore	.976	3046	948	98	97	Bowling Green	.972	3102	928	115	75
Aberdeen	.974	3093	1051	109	78	Wilmington	.970	3011	917	122	89
Hickory	.974	2942	906	104	60	Asheville	.970	2975	920	122	74
Hudson Valley	.974	3103	1001	111	66	Rome	.968	2986	958	132	83

INDIVIDUAL BATTING

Batter, Club	AVG	G	AB	R	H	2B	3B	HR	RBI	BB	SO	SB
Matt Fraizer, Greensboro	.314	75	303	64	95	14	3	20	50	43	74	14
Jared Triolo, Greensboro	.304	108	421	74	128	29	0	15	78	42	94	25
Nick Gonzales, Greensboro	.302	80	324	53	98	23	4	18	54	40	101	7
Cameron Cannon, Greenville	.302	74	311	46	94	24	0	8	39	17	34	9
Michael Harris, Rome	.294	101	374	55	110	26	3	7	64	35	76	27
Justin Connell, Wilmington	.293	98	372	52	109	11	5	6	38	33	72	21
Lenyn Sosa, Winston-Salem	.290	82	334	45	97	19	1	10	49	14	77	3
Christian Koss, Greenville	.271	104	428	65	116	18	7	15	55	31	100	10
Logan O'Hoppe, Jersey Shore	.270	85	318	43	86	17	2	13	48	30	63	6
Liover Peguero, Greensboro	.270	90	374	67	101	19	2	14	45	33	105	28

INDIVIDUAL PITCHING

Pitcher, Club	W	L	ERA	G	GS	CG	SV	IP	H	R	ER	BB	SO
Quinn Priester, Greensboro	7	4	3.04	20	20	0	0	98	82	40	33	39	98
Mitch Spence, Hudson Valley	7	6	3.94	23	20	0	0	105	99	52	46	37	118
Chase Shugart, Greenville	6	6	4.78	22	22	0	0	105	122	58	56	24	93

ALL-STAR TEAM

C: Francisco Alvarez, Brooklyn. **1B:** Blaine Crim, Hickory. **2B:** Nick Gonzales, Greensboro.
3B: Jared Triolo, Greensboro. **SS:** Ronny Mauricio, Brooklyn. **OF:** Tyler Dearden, Greenville.
OF: Matt Fraizer, Greensboro. **OF:** Jordan Qsar, Bowling Green. **DH:** Jhailyn Ortiz, Jersey Shore.
RHP: Quinn Priester, Greensboro. **LHP:** Jacob Lopez, Bowling Green. **RP:** Blake Brown, Jersey Shore.

MVP: Matt Fraizer, OF, Greensboro. **Pitcher of the Year:** Quinn Priester, RHP, Greensboro.
Top MLB Prospect: Ronny Mauricio, SS, Brooklyn. **Manager of the Year:** Jeff Smith, Bowling Green.

DEPARTMENT LEADERS

BATTING

OBP	Matt Fraizer, Greensboro	.401
SLG	Matt Fraizer, Greensboro	.578
OPS	Matt Fraizer, Greensboro	.979
R	Lolo Sanchez, Greensboro	79
H	Jared Triolo, Greensboro	128
TB	Ezequiel Duran, Hickory	202
TB	Jared Triolo, Greensboro	202
XBH	Luis Curbelo, Winston-Salem	51
2B	Jared Triolo, Greensboro	29
3B	Christian Koss, Greenville	7
HR	Tyler Dearden, Greenville	24
HR	Jesse Franklin V, Rome	24
RBI	Tyler Dearden, Greenville	80
SAC	5 players	6
BB	Evan Edwards, Bowling Green	56
HBP	Adam Hall, Aberdeen	16
SO	Luis Curbelo, Winston-Salem	152
SB	Lolo Sanchez, Greensboro	30
CS	Pedro Martinez, Bowling Green	18
AB/SO	Cameron Cannon, Greenville	9.15

FIELDING

C PCT	Logan Brown, Rome	.995
PO	David Garcia, Hickory	721
A	Israel Pineda, Wilmington	65
DP	Elih Marrero, Greenville	5
E	Elih Marrero, Greenville	13
CS	Maverick Handley, Aberdeen	28
SB	Logan Brown, Rome	85
PB	Francisco Alvarez, Brooklyn	13
1B PCT	Evan Edwards, Bowling Green	.986
PO	Evan Edwards, Bowling Green	609
A	Evan Edwards, Bowling Green	37
A	Eric Wagaman, Hudson Valley	37
DP	Drew Mendoza, Wilmington	49
E	Drew Mendoza, Wilmington	12
2B PCT	Cody Milligan, Rome	.956
PO	Cody Milligan, Rome	105
A	Cody Milligan, Rome	219
DP	Cody Milligan, Rome	45
E	Cody Milligan, Rome	15
3B PCT	Jared Triolo, Greensboro	.961
PO	Jared Triolo, Greensboro	81
A	Jared Triolo, Greensboro	163
DP	Jared Triolo, Greensboro	19
E	James Nelson, Hudson Valley	22
SS PCT	Christian Koss, Greenville	.961
PO	Christian Koss, Greenville	141
A	Ronny Mauricio, Brooklyn	237
DP	Christian Koss, Greenville	49
E	Yasel Antuna, Wilmington	36
OF PCT	Jordan Qsar, Bowling Green	.995
PO	Michael Harris II, Rome	203
A	Wilyer Abreu, Asheville	12
DP	Michael Harris II, Rome	3
E	Armond Upshaw, Wilmington	6

PITCHING

G	Austin Roberts, Greensboro	39
G	Jacob Wallace, Greenville	39
GS	Chase Shugart, Greenville	22
GF	Austin Roberts, Greensboro	26
SV	Derek Craft, Hudson Valley	10
W	Bear Bellomy, Greensboro	9
W	Josh Maciejewski, Hudson Valley	9
L	Alec Kisena, Brooklyn	9
L	Cam Opp, Brooklyn	9
L	Kaleb Roper, Winston-Salem	9
IP	Chase Shugart, Greenville	105.1
H	Chase Shugart, Greenville	122
R	Jaison Vilera, Brooklyn	77
ER	Jaison Vilera, Brooklyn	70
HB	Reid Anderson, Hudson Valley	10
BB	Mark Moclair, Asheville	50
SO	Avery Weems, Hickory	124
SO/9	Joey Estes, Augusta	11.55
SO/9 (RP)	Brendan Nail, Greenville	14.18
BB/9	Chase Shugart, Greenville	2.05
WP	Yeremi Ceballos, Asheville	15
WP	Michel Otanez, Brooklyn	15
BK	Tahnaj Thomas, Greensboro	6
HRA	Jaison Vilera, Brooklyn	22
BAA	Quinn Priester, Greensboro	.225

MINOR LEAGUES

BY JOSH NORRIS

As part of its realignment of the minor leagues, Major League Baseball got rid of all its short-season and Rookie-level affiliates outside of team complexes.

All except one.

The former short-season Northwest League survived the chopping block by dropping two teams—Salem-Keizer and Boise—and converting to a six-team full-season league.

The pandemic also threw the league an added wrinkle. Because the Canadian border remained closed deep into the season, Hillsboro acted as Vancouver's home park all year long, meaning that the Hops' stadium hosted a game nearly every day of the 120-game season.

Though six teams may not be an ideal setup in the long term, it meant that fans in the league's footprint got plenty of chances to see some of the circuit's top talent. That was especially true in the early going, when Everett boasted a roster that could easily make up part of the core of Seattle's next playoff team.

Outfielder Julio Rodriguez and righthander George Kirby, two of the game's very best prospects, were at the forefront, but they weren't the only attractions. The Aquasox roster also had a host of high-end pitchers, including righthanders Matt Brash, Levi Stoudt and Emerson Hancock and lefthander Brandon Williamson.

Everett also had league MVP Cade Marlowe, a 24-year-old outfielder who led the minors with 107 RBIs. Marlowe hit .259/.345/.566 with a league-leading 20 home runs for Everett after beginning the year with Low-A Modesto. Seattle drafted him in the 20th round in 2019 out of West Georgia.

By the second half of the season, the league was invaded by a host of high-upside shortstop prospects, including Giants top prospect Marco Luciano, who was part of the league-champion Eugene club, as well as the Blue Jays' Orelvis Martinez with Vancouver, the Rockies' Ezequiel Tovar with Spokane and, briefly, the Mariners' Noelvi Marte with Everett.

Hillsboro, too, opened with an extraordinarily talented rotation, with righthanders Luis Frias, Ryne Nelson, Drey Jameson and Brandon Pfaadt as well as lefthander Blake Walston helping the Hops finish first in the league with a 4.32 ERA and 1.34 WHIP. ■

TOP 10 PROSPECTS

George Kirby

1. Julio Rodriguez, OF, Everett (Mariners)
2. George Kirby, RHP, Everett (Mariners)
3. Matt Brash, RHP, Everett (Mariners)
4. Brandon Pfaadt, RHP, Hillsboro (D-backs)
5. Marco Luciano, SS, Eugene (Giants)
6. Orelvis Martinez, SS/3B, Vancouver (Blue Jays)
7. Ezequiel Tovar, SS, Spokane (Rockies)
8. Michael Toglia, 1B, Spokane (Rockies)
9. Levi Stoudt, RHP, Everett (Mariners)
10. Drey Jameson, RHP, Hillsboro (D-backs)

OVERALL STANDINGS

	W	L	PCT	GB	Manager(s)	Attendance	Average	Last Penn.
Eugene Emeralds (Giants)	69	50	.580	—	Dennis Pelfrey	91,315	1,520	2021
Spokane Indians (Rockies)	67	49	.578	0.5	Scott Little	140,623	2,448	*2008
Everett AquaSox (Mariners)	61	56	.521	7	Louis Boyd	102,423	1,787	*2010
Hillsboro Hops (D-backs)	52	60	.464	13.5	Vince Harrison	110,384	1,822	*2019
Vancouver Canadians (Blue Jays)	55	64	.462	14	Donnie Murphy	15,822	268	*2017
Tri-City Dust Devils (Angels)	43	68	.387	22	Jack Santora/Andy Schatzley	61,245	1,134	Never

Finals: Eugene defeated Spokane 3-1   * Refers to short-season Northwest League prior to 2021

CLUB BATTING

	AVG	G	AB	R	H	2B	3B	HR	RBI	BB	SO	SB	OBP	SLG
Everett	.260	117	3969	766	1031	274	38	158	694	572	1268	140	.361	.467
Spokane	.254	116	3864	638	982	169	28	113	570	484	1136	202	.346	.400
Vancouver	.254	119	4033	637	1023	240	22	108	583	487	1096	126	.344	.404
Eugene	.251	119	3941	648	988	216	25	145	590	455	1224	122	.338	.429
Hillsboro	.238	112	3606	510	858	154	31	93	462	386	1094	231	.319	.375
Tri-City	.222	111	3652	427	809	158	23	76	392	344	1244	102	.294	.340

CLUB PITCHING

	ERA	G	CG	SHO	SV	IP	H	R	ER	HR	BB	SO	AVG
Hillsboro	4.32	112	2	4	34	969	902	550	465	111	396	1074	.246
Spokane	4.58	116	1	5	31	1024	976	584	521	116	403	1129	.251
Eugene	4.61	119	2	7	33	1033	923	598	529	114	472	1311	.238
Tri-City	4.77	111	1	4	21	964	906	591	511	109	487	1140	.246
Everett	4.80	117	0	3	19	1023	986	626	546	142	401	1233	.250
Vancouver	5.02	119	0	2	25	1052	998	677	587	101	569	1175	.250

CLUB FIELDING

	PCT	PO	A	E	DP		PCT	PO	A	E	DP
Spokane	.978	3071	1044	94	96	Vancouver	.974	3155	1048	114	83
Eugene	.975	3100	938	102	73	Everett	.973	3069	946	112	71
Hillsboro	.974	2908	892	103	95	Tri-City	.965	2892	936	138	74

INDIVIDUAL BATTING

Batter, Club	AVG	G	AB	R	H	2B	3B	HR	RBI	BB	SO	SB
Ismael Munguia, Eugene	.336	81	333	57	112	22	3	9	53	13	27	15
Hunter Stovall, Spokane	.316	89	320	48	101	13	4	6	46	40	69	25
Isaac Collins, Spokane	.312	78	311	62	97	22	4	9	48	40	80	20
Spencer Horwitz, Vancouver	.290	105	389	65	113	28	1	10	62	70	66	4
Tanner Morris, Vancouver	.285	103	397	55	113	19	3	7	57	58	90	4
Jack Blomgren, Spokane	.284	86	278	61	79	13	4	3	32	45	74	30
Rafael Lantigua, Vancouver	.280	80	300	65	84	22	1	11	43	42	76	26
Brenton Doyle, Spokane	.279	97	390	70	109	16	2	16	47	30	134	21
Niko Decolati, Spokane	.264	100	371	67	98	14	2	11	56	40	98	26
Tyler Fitzgerald, Eugene	.262	103	382	71	100	28	2	19	65	38	139	12

INDIVIDUAL PITCHING

Pitcher, Club	W	L	ERA	G	GS	CG	SV	IP	H	R	ER	BB	SO
Chris McMahon, Spokane	10	3	4.17	22	20	0	0	114	119	57	53	32	119
Conner Nurse, Eugene	6	7	4.86	23	20	1	0	113	112	66	61	51	114
Paxton Schultz, Vancouver	5	7	5.28	22	21	0	0	102	108	69	60	45	114
Helcris Olivarez, Spokane	4	9	6.05	22	21	0	0	100	89	74	67	68	112
Adam Kloffenstein, Vancouver	7	7	6.22	23	23	0	0	101	96	76	70	61	107

ALL-STAR TEAM

C: Nick Dalesandro, Hillsboro. **1B:** Michael Toglia, Spokane. **2B:** Tanner Morris, Vancouver.
3B: Austin Shenton, Everett. **SS:** Tyler Fitzgerald, Eugene. **OF:** Isaac Collins, Spokane.
OF: Cade Marlowe, Everett. **OF:** Ismael Munguia, Eugene. **DH:** Spencer Horwitz, Vancouver.
RHP: Mitchell Kilkenny, Spokane. **LHP:** Nick Bush, Spokane. **RP:** Chris Wright, Eugene.

MVP: Cade Marlowe, OF, Everett. **Pitcher of the Year:** Mitchell Kilkenny, RHP, Spokane.
Top MLB Prospect: Spencer Horwitz, 1B, Vancouver. **Manager of the Year:** Dennis Pelfrey, Eugene.

DEPARTMENT LEADERS

BATTING

OBP	Jack Blomgren, Spokane	.406
SLG	Cade Marlowe, Everett	.566
OPS	Cade Marlowe, Everett	.911
R	Connor Hoover, Everett	77
H	Spencer Horwitz, Vancouver	113
H	Tanner Morris, Vancouver	113
TB	Tyler Fitzgerald, Eugene	189
XBH	Tyler Fitzgerald, Eugene	49
XBH	Connor Hoover, Everett	49
2B	Tyler Fitzgerald, Eugene	28
2B	Spencer Horwitz, Vancouver	28
3B	Livan Soto, Tri-City	8
HR	Cade Marlowe, Everett	20
RBI	Cade Marlowe, Everett	77
SAC	Tyler Keenan, Everett	8
BB	Spencer Horwitz, Vancouver	70
HBP	Jack Blomgren, Spokane	14
HBP	Philip Clarke, Vancouver	14
SO	Tyler Fitzgerald, Eugene	139
SB	Nick Dalesandro, Hillsboro	33
CS	Franklin Labour, Eugene	8
AB/SO	Ismael Munguia, Eugene	12.33

FIELDING

C	PCT	Nick Dalesandro, Hillsboro	.991
	PO	Philip Clarke, Vancouver	682
	A	Philip Clarke, Vancouver	59
	DP	Philip Clarke, Vancouver	7
	E	Axel Andueza, Hillsboro	8
	E	Franklin Torres, Tri-City	8
	CS	Philip Clarke, Vancouver	30
	SB	Philip Clarke, Vancouver	130
	PB	Nick Dalesandro, Hillsboro	13
	PB	Philip Clarke, Vancouver	13
1B	PCT	Spencer Horwitz, Vancouver	.994
	PO	Spencer Horwitz, Vancouver	603
	A	Michael Toglia, Spokane	69
	DP	Michael Toglia, Spokane	53
	E	Logan Wyatt, Eugene	7
2B	PCT	Cam Coursey, Hillsboro	.969
	PO	Cam Coursey, Hillsboro	93
	A	Cam Coursey, Hillsboro	129
	DP	Cam Coursey, Hillsboro	41
	E	Cam Coursey, Hillsboro	7
	E	Carlos Herrera, Tri-City	7
	E	Isaac Collins, Spokane	7
3B	PCT	Sean Roby, Eugene	.967
	PO	Brendon Davis, Tri-City	43
	A	Sean Roby, Eugene	85
	DP	Hunter Stovall, Spokane	10
	E	Ronny Brito, Vancouver	9
SS	PCT	Blaze Alexander, Hillsboro	.943
	PO	Blaze Alexander, Hillsboro	96
	A	Blaze Alexander, Hillsboro	202
	DP	Blaze Alexander, Hillsboro	46
	E	Blaze Alexander, Hillsboro	18
OF	PCT	Ismael Munguia, Eugene	.988
	PO	Ismael Munguia, Eugene	159
	A	Brenton Doyle, Spokane	13
	DP	Eric Rivera, Vancouver	3
	E	Jordyn Adams, Tri-City	8

PITCHING

G	Zac Kristofak, Tri-City	38
GS	Adam Kloffenstein, Vancouver	23
GF	Dugan Darnell, Spokane	29
SV	Chris Wright, Eugene	17
W	Chris McMahon, Spokane	10
W	Travis Perry, Eugene	10
L	Helcris Olivarez, Spokane	9
IP	Chris McMahon, Spokane	114.1
H	Chris McMahon, Spokane	119
R	Adam Kloffenstein, Vancouver	76
ER	Adam Kloffenstein, Vancouver	70
HB	Helcris Olivarez, Spokane	21
BB	Helcris Olivarez, Spokane	68
SO	Kai-Wei Teng, Eugene	142
SO/9	Kai-Wei Teng, Eugene	13.36
SO/9 (RP)	Taylor Rashi, Eugene	13.11
BB/9	Chris McMahon, Spokane	2.52
WP	Adam Kloffenstein, Vancouver	17
BK	Helcris Olivarez, Spokane	5
HRA	Conner Nurse, Eugene	21
BAA	Adam Kloffenstein, Vancouver	.243

MINOR LEAGUES

MINOR LEAGUES

BY CHRIS HILBURN-TRENKLE

Low-A East featured four Top 100 Prospects among its top 10—Gunnar Henderson, Nick Yorke, Taj Bradley and Daniel Espino—and an impressive group of players who took big steps forward and raised their stock during the 2021 season.

Augusta righthander Joey Estes, Down East third baseman Dustin Harris and Myrtle Beach lefthander DJ Herz were not highly touted coming out of the 2019 draft, yet all three turned in impressive seasons and earned praise from league managers for their play.

Charleston, the top team in the league with an 82-38 record, finished tied for the most prospects in the top 10 with two (Bradley, Curtis Mead), along with Delmarva (Henderson, Colton Cowser) and Down East (Harris, Luisangel Acuña).

Charleston carried its dominance into the postseason, disposing of Down East in a thrilling five-game series.

After losing the first two games of the series, the Wood Ducks rallied to tie it at 2-2 before heading into a decisive Game 5. But the RiverDogs' bats came alive, plating two runs in the third inning and five more in the fifth to take a commanding 7-0 lead. The Wood Ducks finished with just four hits on the day, falling 9-2.

Charleston boasted league MVP Diego Infante, an outfielder who led the league with 80 RBIs while hitting .296 with 16 home runs.

It looked like it would be the Salem Red Sox, not the Wood Ducks, who would challenge Charleston in the championship series, but the Red Sox faded down the stretch. Salem lost seven of its last 11 games, finishing with a 71-49 record, one game behind Down East.

Delmarva, who had the second best run dif-

ferential in the league at +147, and Carolina each battled for a postseason bid, but finished with identical 68-52 records, four games behind Down East for a spot in the championship series.

Due to the depth of talent in the league, there were notable omissions from the Top 10 Prospects list, such as Carolina outfielder Joe Gray Jr., whose power, speed and athleticism stood out; Lynchburg first baseman Jhonkensy Noel, who posted a 1.119 OPS in 38 Low-A games; and Down East outfielder Evan Carter, who missed significant time with injury but showed an impressive tool set. ■

TOP 10 PROSPECTS

Gunnar Henderson

1. Gunnar Henderson, SS/3B, Delmarva (Orioles)
2. Nick Yorke, 2B, Salem (Red Sox)
3. Taj Bradley, RHP, Charleston (Rays)
4. Daniel Espino, RHP, Lynchburg (Indians)
5. Joey Estes, RHP, Augusta (Braves)
6. Dustin Harris, 1B/3B, Down East (Rangers)
7. Curtis Mead, 3B/1B, Charleston (Rays)
8. Colton Cowser, OF, Delmarva (Orioles)
9. Luisangel Acuña, SS, Down East (Rangers)
10. DJ Herz, LHP, Myrtle Beach (Cubs)

OVERALL STANDINGS

Central Division	W	L	PCT	GB	Manager(s)	Attendance	Average	Last Penn.
Down East Wood Ducks (Rangers)	72	48	.600	—	Carlos Cardoza	85,586	1,426	**2017
Carolina Mudcats (Brewers)	68	52	.567	4	Joe Ayrault	98,976	1,655	**2006
Fayetteville Woodpeckers (Astros)	55	65	.458	17	Ray Hernandez	173,243	2,879	**2018
Kannapolis Cannon Ballers (White Sox)	40	79	.336	31.5	Guillermo Quiroz	162,031	2,701	*2005

North Division	W	L	PCT	GB	Manager(s)	Attendance	Average	Last Penn.
Salem Red Sox (Red Sox)	71	49	.592	—	Luke Montz	128,769	2,089	**2013
Delmarva Shorebirds (Orioles)	68	52	.567	3	Dave Anderson	110,281	1,838	**2001
Lynchburg Hillcats (Indians)	58	62	.483	13	Dennis Malave	68,032	1,139	**2017
Fredericksburg Nationals (Nationals)	44	76	.367	27	Mario Lisson	199,071	3,258	Never

South Division	W	L	PCT	GB	Manager(s)	Attendance	Average	Last Penn.
Charleston RiverDogs (Rays)	82	38	.683	—	Blake Butera	208,641	3,478	Never
Myrtle Beach Pelicans (Cubs)	59	61	.492	23	Buddy Bailey	199,704	3,319	**2016
Augusta GreenJackets (Braves)	54	66	.450	28	Michael Saunders	211,561	3,510	*2008
Columbia Fireflies (Royals)	48	71	.403	33.5	Brooks Conrad	153,547	2,541	*2013

Final: Charleston defeated Down East 3-2

* Low-A South Atlantic League ** High-A Carolina League

BRIAN WESTERHOLT/FOUR SEAM IMAGES

CLUB BATTING

	AVG	G	AB	R	H	2B	3B	HR	RBI	BB	SO	SB	OBP	SLG
Charleston	.267	120	3999	757	1067	212	36	129	671	557	1159	176	.364	.435
Salem	.264	120	4062	716	1073	225	38	103	619	477	1020	94	.347	.414
Carolina	.264	120	3973	770	1048	219	33	114	675	642	1176	186	.376	.422
Delmarva	.253	120	3964	720	1004	187	20	113	646	573	1097	152	.358	.396
Lynchburg	.253	120	4016	603	1015	205	43	92	519	390	1149	113	.325	.394
Fayetteville	.246	120	3950	651	971	194	27	111	591	527	1214	205	.347	.393
Down East	.244	120	3805	641	929	191	29	88	563	523	1122	290	.344	.379
Augusta	.234	120	3835	540	897	165	27	100	490	493	1256	145	.332	.369
Myrtle Beach	.229	120	3895	531	892	165	27	73	466	400	1154	71	.312	.341
Kannapolis	.228	119	3875	480	883	163	25	88	418	439	1321	92	.319	.351
Fredericksburg	.225	120	3899	499	879	181	21	55	439	439	1110	114	.313	.325
Columbia	.225	119	3821	583	859	171	29	86	493	538	1240	200	.332	.352

CLUB PITCHING

	ERA	G	CG	SHO	SV	IP	H	R	ER	HR	BB	SO	AVG
Charleston	3.45	120	1	15	32	1050	812	494	403	78	423	1269	.212
Salem	4.14	120	0	6	30	1042	1045	581	479	65	414	1066	.257
Delmarva	4.14	120	0	5	28	1028	929	573	473	95	432	1161	.236
Down East	4.27	120	2	5	32	1022	939	570	485	109	460	1203	.241
Myrtle Beach	4.39	120	0	7	25	1033	925	582	504	104	505	1215	.237
Columbia	4.42	119	0	6	21	1019	969	584	501	106	443	1141	.249
Lynchburg	4.43	120	0	3	23	1034	958	598	509	87	493	1176	.244
Fayetteville	5.00	120	0	3	23	1027	868	671	570	85	691	1224	.226
Augusta	5.11	120	2	6	24	1010	936	668	573	112	534	1257	.242
Carolina	5.21	120	3	3	32	1020	1010	677	591	104	541	1165	.258
Fredericksburg	5.22	120	0	5	17	1021	1034	738	592	109	492	1055	.258
Kannapolis	5.57	119	0	3	23	1012	1092	755	626	98	570	1086	.274

CLUB FIELDING

	PCT	PO	A	E	DP		PCT	PO	A	E	DP
Lynchburg	.974	3102	1011	110	91	Fayetteville	.967	3081	948	137	74
Columbia	.972	3057	1071	119	83	Charleston	.967	3150	1052	143	99
Down East	.972	3067	974	118	85	Delmarva	.965	3086	1020	148	78
Myrtle Beach	.971	3098	977	121	60	Augusta	.965	3030	826	140	57
Salem	.970	3127	1080	132	88	Kannapolis	.962	3036	1003	161	83
Carolina	.969	3061	910	128	82	Fredericksburg	.960	3064	1031	172	92

INDIVIDUAL BATTING

Batter, Club	AVG	G	AB	R	H	2B	3B	HR	RBI	BB	SO	SB
Nick Yorke, Salem	.323	76	294	59	95	14	4	10	47	41	47	11
Felix Valerio, Carolina	.314	85	309	71	97	24	3	6	63	54	49	27
Vaughn Grissom, Augusta	.311	75	280	52	87	15	4	5	33	34	49	13
Gilberto Jimenez, Salem	.306	94	373	64	114	16	6	3	56	19	86	13
Diego Infante, Charleston	.296	101	371	83	110	20	5	16	80	56	114	20
Cristian Inoa, Down East	.292	88	322	46	94	22	1	11	58	28	51	9
Jose Rodriguez, Kannapolis	.283	78	336	58	95	22	4	9	32	21	57	20
Gabe Holt, Carolina	.279	82	323	70	90	14	1	1	36	62	47	17
Willie Carter, Augusta	.278	101	349	46	97	12	3	8	68	45	109	18
Darell Hernaiz, Delmarva	.277	94	372	62	103	12	0	6	52	28	70	22

INDIVIDUAL PITCHING

Pitcher, Club	W	L	ERA	G	GS	CG	SV	IP	H	R	ER	BB	SO
Joey Estes, Augusta	3	6	2.91	20	20	1	0	99	66	39	32	29	127
Nick Krauth, Down East	5	9	4.30	20	20	1	0	103	103	56	49	28	79
Manuel Espinoza, Myrtle Beach	4	9	5.11	22	22	0	0	99	113	66	56	26	92
Adrian Alcantara, Columbia	5	9	5.33	24	20	0	0	96	102	67	57	30	98
Karlo Seijas, Fredericksburg	3	12	6.84	22	22	0	0	97	119	85	74	29	82

ALL-STAR TEAM

C: Yainer Diaz, Lynchburg/Fayetteville. **1B:** Dustin Harris, Down East. **2B:** Nick Yorke, Salem.
3B: Nicholas Northcut, Salem. **SS:** Luisangel Acuña, Down East. **OF:** Diego Infante, Charleston.
OF: Gilberto Jimenez, Salem. **OF:** Joey Wiemer, Carolina. **DH:** Felix Valerio, Carolina.
RHP: Joey Estes, Augusta. **LHP:** DJ Herz, Myrtle Beach. **RP:** Devon Roedahl, Salem.
MVP: Diego Infante, OF, Charleston. **Pitcher of the Year:** Joey Estes, RHP, Augusta.
Top MLB Prospect: Jhonkensy Noel, 1B, Lynchburg.
Manager of the Year: Blake Butera, Charleston.

DEPARTMENT LEADERS

BATTING

OBP	Felix Valerio, Carolina	.430
SLG	Nicholas Northcut, Salem	.513
OPS	Nick Yorke, Salem	.913
R	Diego Infante, Charleston	83
H	Gilberto Jimenez, Salem	114
TB	Diego Infante, Charleston	188
XBH	Nicholas Northcut, Salem	51
2B	Nicholas Northcut, Salem	32
3B	Ceddanne Rafaela, Salem	9
HR	Juan Carlos Negret, Columbia	23
RBI	Diego Infante, Charleston	80
SAC	Heriberto Hernandez, Charleston	8
SAC	Keyber Rodriguez, Down East	8
BB	Cade Bunnell, Augusta	91
HBP	Bryan Ramos, Kannapolis	18
SO	Cade Bunnell, Augusta	172
SB	Jayce Easley, Down East	70
CS	Braulio Vasquez, Augusta	13
AB/SO	Osleivis Basabe, Charleston	7.13

FIELDING

C	PCT	Onix Vega, Fredericksburg	.989
	PO	Andres Melendez, Lynchburg	521
	A	Victor Torres, Kannapolis	55
	DP	Andres Melendez, Lynchburg	6
	E	Alex Hall, Carolina	13
	CS	Ethan Hearn, Myrtle Beach	27
	SB	Darrien Miller, Carolina	116
	PB	Alex Erro, Carolina	16
1B	PCT	Bryson Horne, Augusta	.987
	PO	Harvin Mendoza, Kannapolis	513
	A	Harvin Mendoza, Kannapolis	38
	A	Matt Mervis, Myrtle Beach	38
	DP	Harvin Mendoza, Kannapolis	43
	E	Kevin Strohschein, Fredericksburg	12
2B	PCT	Nick Yorke, Salem	.971
	PO	Nick Yorke, Salem	128
	A	Nick Yorke, Salem	178
	DP	Nick Yorke, Salem	39
	E	Herard Gonzalez, Columbia	15
	E	Keithron Moss, Down East	15
3B	PCT	Junior Martina, Fredericksburg	.933
	PO	Junior Martina, Fredericksburg	48
	A	Junior Martina, Fredericksburg	133
	DP	Ashton McGee, Carolina	9
	E	Gage Hughes, Columbia	14
SS	PCT	Matthew Lugo, Salem	.911
	PO	Freddy Zamora, Carolina	102
	A	Matthew Lugo, Salem	239
	DP	Matthew Lugo, Salem	42
	E	Matthew Lugo, Salem	33
OF	PCT	Jayce Easley, Down East	.995
	PO	Stephen Paolini, Augusta	206
	A	Alexfri Planez, Lynchburg	12
	A	Joey Wiemer, Carolina	12
	DP	Ceddanne Rafaela, Salem	5
	E	Chase Krogman, Kannapolis	11

PITCHING

G	Devon Roedahl, Salem	37
GS	3 players	23
GF	Devon Roedahl, Salem	24
SV	Cam Robinson, Carolina	12
W	Taj Bradley, Charleston	9
W	Jordan DiValerio, Salem	9
L	Karlo Seijas, Fredericksburg	12
IP	Nick Krauth, Down East	102.2
H	Karlo Seijas, Fredericksburg	119
R	Karlo Seijas, Fredericksburg	85
ER	Karlo Seijas, Fredericksburg	74
HB	Michele Vassalotti, Carolina	25
BB	Jayson Schroeder, Fayetteville	65
SO	Joey Estes, Augusta	127
SO/9	Seth Johnson, Charleston	11.05
SO/9 (RP)	Matt Merrill, Fredericksburg	13.79
BB/9	Manuel Espinoza, Myrtle Beach	2.37
WP	Jayson Schroeder, Fayetteville	19
BK	2 players	6
HRA	2 players	18
BAA	Joey Estes, Augusta	.184

MINOR LEAGUES

MINOR LEAGUES

BY JOSH NORRIS

The last time the Low-A Southeast League took the field, it was called the Florida State League. And it was High-A. And it had 12 teams. And balls and strikes were called exclusively by humans.

All of that changed in 2021, after losing a year to the Covid-19 pandemic and the ensuing minor league realignment. The league is now the lowest full-season rung of the minors, lost two teams to contraction and served this season as a testing ground for the automated ball-strike system, which went through tweaks as the season went along.

The lost 2020 season created a bit of a logjam, and the league was full of a variety of players of varying experience levels. Collegians from high-pedigree schools were mixed in some cases with teenagers who hadn't played a day of pro ball.

Even so, there were players who stood head and shoulders above the rest. In the early going, that group included Tampa shortstop Anthony Volpe and Palm Beach third baseman Jordan Walker, first-round picks in 2019 and 2020, respectively. Dunedin shortstop Orelvis Martinez mashed in the middle months, and Daytona shortstop Elly De La Cruz took the league by storm as soon as he arrived.

Jupiter righthander Eury Perez, the youngest player in all the full-season minors, carved through the league with the poise of a much more experienced player before moving to High-A, where he continued to open eyes. His season as a whole helped vault him to the top of a heap of high-end pitching throughout Miami's system.

In all, the league looked a lot different in 2021 than it did in 2019, but there was still plenty of intriguing, high-upside talent.

The teams with New York-based affiliates each placed an 18-year-old prospect among the league's Top 10.

TOP 10 PROSPECTS

Anthony Volpe

1. Anthony Volpe, SS, Tampa (Yankees)
2. Jordan Walker, 3B, Palm Beach (Cardinals)
3. Orelvis Martinez, SS/3B, Dunedin (Blue Jays)
4. Mick Abel, RHP, Clearwater (Phillies)
5. Eury Perez, RHP, Jupiter (Marlins)
6. Elly de la Cruz, 3B/SS, Daytona (Reds)
7. Jasson Dominguez, OF, Tampa (Yankees)
8. Jared Jones, RHP, Bradenton (Pirates)
9. Endy Rodriguez, C/1B, Bradenton (Pirates)
10. Alex Ramirez, OF, St. Lucie (Mets)

For the Yankees, that was Jasson Dominguez, the celebrated outfielder whose highly anticipated debut was pushed back a year by the pandemic. While he didn't dominate the league, Dominguez showed improvement as the season went on and still stands as one of the Yankees' best prospects and made his debut on a national stage by making an appearance in the Futures Game after just a few official games in his pro career.

On the other coast, St. Lucie boasted its own teenage outfield phenom, Alexander Ramirez. The Dominican outfielder showed an excellent tool set during his time in the league, including speed, a strong arm and tremendous raw power. His .258 average also was good enough for fourth in the league among qualified hitters. ∎

OVERALL STANDINGS

East Division	W	L	PCT	GB	Manager(s)	Attendance	Average	Last Penn.
St. Lucie Mets (Mets)	60	55	.522	—	Reid Brignac	45,580	802	*2006
Jupiter Hammerheads (Marlins)	61	56	.521	—	Jorge Hernandez	20,197	674	*1991
Daytona Tortugas (Reds)	60	60	.500	2.5	Gookie Dawkins	79,361	1,313	*2011
Palm Beach Cardinals (Cardinals)	37	80	.316	24	Chris Swauger/Jose Leon	28,440	933	*2017

West Division	W	L	PCT	GB	Manager(s)	Attendance	Average	Last Penn.
Tampa Tarpons (Yankees)	73	43	.629	—	David Adams	34,842	556	*2010
Bradenton Marauders (Pirates)	71	48	.597	3.5	Jonathan Johnston	38,207	651	2021
Fort Myers Mighty Mussels (Twins)	60	54	.526	12	Brian Meyer	76,216	1,301	*2018
Dunedin Blue Jays (Blue Jays)	57	63	.475	18	Luis Hurtado	10,043	150	*2017
Lakeland Flying Tigers (Tigers)	55	63	.466	19	Andrew Graham	26,894	432	*2012
Clearwater Threshers (Phillies)	52	64	.448	21	Milver Reyes/Marty Malloy	108,111	1,884	*2007

Finals: Bradenton defeated Tampa 3-0

* Refers to High-A Florida State League prior to 2021

CLUB BATTING

	AVG	G	AB	R	H	2B	3B	HR	RBI	BB	SO	SB	OBP	SLG
Tampa	.260	116	3641	766	948	203	27	149	691	629	1144	163	.380	.454
Bradenton	.244	119	3856	675	940	191	29	109	596	607	1175	104	.357	.393
St. Lucie	.241	115	3648	594	879	167	28	68	495	544	1134	150	.352	.358
Palm Beach	.241	117	3749	515	903	204	23	73	459	498	1110	62	.340	.366
Daytona	.235	120	3831	567	899	211	33	108	492	475	1303	91	.327	.392
Dunedin	.233	120	3799	634	887	194	24	101	555	581	1307	227	.351	.377
Jupiter	.232	117	3762	527	871	154	37	51	446	442	1120	121	.322	.333
Lakeland	.224	118	3764	536	843	166	29	63	456	542	1129	146	.333	.334
Clearwater	.224	116	3648	517	817	154	21	91	461	511	1080	111	.330	.353
Fort Myers	.222	114	3568	543	792	156	24	73	474	586	1152	165	.343	.341

CLUB PITCHING

	ERA	G	CG	SHO	SV	IP	H	R	ER	HR	BB	SO	AVG
Fort Myers	3.96	114	0	8	30	968	871	533	426	60	457	1228	.234
Jupiter	4.01	117	2	6	27	996	888	531	444	79	447	1167	.236
Bradenton	4.17	119	2	10	30	1008	853	583	467	100	528	1288	.224
Daytona	4.22	120	0	3	36	1023	822	555	479	83	625	1183	.219
Tampa	4.48	116	0	4	24	944	770	546	470	75	551	1166	.220
Lakeland	4.50	118	1	5	23	1003	949	583	501	90	495	1131	.248
Clearwater	4.59	116	0	5	23	968	845	590	493	104	577	1182	.231
St. Lucie	4.65	115	7	10	32	959	868	570	495	97	513	1004	.242
Dunedin	4.94	120	2	8	30	1007	924	645	552	119	594	1131	.240
Palm Beach	5.66	117	0	3	14	975	989	738	613	79	628	1174	.261

CLUB FIELDING

	PCT	PO	A	E	DP		PCT	PO	A	E	DP
Lakeland	.973	3011	908	110	91	Clearwater	.968	2903	868	124	72
Tampa	.971	2833	899	111	71	Jupiter	.964	2988	927	147	82
Daytona	.970	3067	1043	126	98	Bradenton	.962	3024	906	156	88
Dunedin	.969	3020	900	126	83	Palm Beach	.962	2926	876	151	83
St. Lucie	.969	2877	963	124	99	Fort Myers	.960	2903	870	157	62

INDIVIDUAL BATTING

Batter, Club	AVG	G	AB	R	H	2B	3B	HR	RBI	BB	SO	SB
Endy Rodriguez, Bradenton	.294	98	377	73	111	25	6	15	73	50	77	2
Orelvis Martinez, Dunedin	.279	71	283	49	79	22	2	19	68	33	85	4
Victor Mesa Jr., Jupiter	.266	111	428	66	114	21	11	5	71	33	102	12
Alex Ramirez, St. Lucie	.258	76	302	41	78	15	4	5	35	23	104	16
Dariel Lopez, Bradenton	.258	98	361	52	93	17	1	10	64	41	103	1
PK Morris, Dunedin	.251	100	323	58	81	21	2	9	57	81	116	5
Warren Saunders, St. Lucie	.249	93	337	51	84	8	2	3	44	29	75	1
Addison Barger, Dunedin	.249	91	325	53	81	21	2	18	80	36	123	7
Miguel Hiraldo, Dunedin	.249	105	390	66	97	26	4	7	52	51	111	29
Brandon Leyton, Daytona	.248	80	303	47	75	22	2	6	36	17	60	4

INDIVIDUAL PITCHING

Pitcher, Club	W	L	ERA	G	GS	CG	SV	IP	H	R	ER	BB	SO
Naswell Paulino, Dunedin	7	4	3.82	23	23	0	0	97	75	50	41	57	109
Junior Santos, St. Lucie	6	6	4.59	21	16	2	0	96	108	60	49	38	79
Carlos Guzman, Lakeland	7	9	4.65	23	22	0	0	99	110	57	51	46	102

ALL-STAR TEAM

C: Endy Rodriguez, Bradenton. **1B:** PK Morris, Dunedin. **2B:** Trevor Hauver, Tampa.
3B: Jose Peroza, St. Lucie. **SS:** Orelvis Martinez, Dunedin. **OF:** Steward Berroa, Dunedin.
OF: Allan Cerda, Daytona. **OF:** Victor Mesa Jr., Jupiter. **DH:** Addison Barger, Dunedin.
RHP: Adrian Florencio, Bradenton. **LHP:** Naswell Paulino, Dunedin. **RP:** Enmanuel Mejia, Bradenton.

MVP: Endy Rodriguez, C, Bradenton. **Pitcher of the Year:** Adrian Florencio, RHP, Bradenton.
Top MLB Prospect: Eury Perez, RHP, Jupiter. **Manager of the Year:** Jonathan Johnston, Bradenton.

DEPARTMENT LEADERS

BATTING

OBP	Trevor Hauver, Tampa	.445
SLG	Orelvis Martinez, Dunedin	.572
OPS	Orelvis Martinez, Dunedin	.942
R	Endy Rodriguez, Bradenton	73
H	Victor Mesa Jr., Jupiter	114
TB	Endy Rodriguez, Bradenton	193
XBH	Endy Rodriguez, Bradenton	46
2B	Miguel Hiraldo, Dunedin	26
3B	Victor Mesa Jr., Jupiter	11
HR	Orelvis Martinez, Dunedin	19
RBI	Addison Barger, Dunedin	80
SAC	Victor Mesa Jr., Jupiter	10
SAC	Misael Urbina, Fort Myers	10
BB	PK Morris, Dunedin	81
HBP	Leo Jimenez, Dunedin	21
SO	Hudson Head, Bradenton	137
SB	Steward Berroa, Dunedin	55
CS	Nasim Nunez, Jupiter	10
AB/SO	Brandon Leyton, Daytona	5.05

FIELDING

C PCT	Daniel Vellojin, Daytona	.987
PO	Daniel Vellojin, Daytona	714
A	Daniel Vellojin, Daytona	73
DP	Carlos Narvaez, Tampa	6
E	Daniel Vellojin, Daytona	10
E	Carlos Narvaez, Tampa	10
CS	Carlos Soto, Palm Beach	29
SB	Charles Mack, Fort Myers	102
PB	Charles Mack, Fort Myers	17
1B PCT	PK Morris, Dunedin	.992
PO	PK Morris, Dunedin	601
A	Aaron Sabato, Fort Myers	51
DP	PK Morris, Dunedin	54
E	Ernny Ordonez, Bradenton	11
2B PCT	Brandon Leyton, Daytona	.973
PO	Brandon Leyton, Daytona	123
A	Brandon Leyton, Daytona	200
DP	Brandon Leyton, Daytona	47
E	Franklin Soto, Palm Beach	21
3B PCT	Nick Quintana, Lakeland	.941
PO	Andres Chaparro, Tampa	35
A	Nick Quintana, Lakeland	109
DP	Nick Quintana, Lakeland	15
E	Miguel Hiraldo, Dunedin	14
SS PCT	Maikol Escotto, Bradenton	.907
PO	Maikol Escotto, Bradenton	82
A	Maikol Escotto, Bradenton	153
DP	Maikol Escotto, Bradenton	37
E	Maikol Escotto, Bradenton	24
E	Keoni Cavaco, Fort Myers	24
OF PCT	Kingston Liniak, Lakeland	.983
PO	Kingston Liniak, Lakeland	222
A	Steward Berroa, Dunedin	9
A	Kingston Liniak, Lakeland	9
DP	Kingston Liniak, Lakeland	3
DP	L.J. Jones, Palm Beach	3
E	Willie Joe Garry Jr., Fort Myers	11

PITCHING

G	Matthew Swain, Fort Myers	35
GS	Naswell Paulino, Dunedin	23
GF	Gabriel Sequeira, Lakeland	24
SV	Gabriel Sequeira, Lakeland	10
W	Michael Giacone, Tampa	8
L	Carlos Guzman, Lakeland	9
L	Ludwin Jimenez, Palm Beach	9
L	Levi Prater, Palm Beach	9
IP	Carlos Guzman, Lakeland	98.2
H	Chris Mokma, Jupiter	122
R	Chris Mokma, Jupiter	75
ER	Chris Mokma, Jupiter	68
HB	Edwin Nunez, Palm Beach	17
BB	Levi Prater, Palm Beach	68
SO	Adrian Florencio, Bradenton	117
SO/9	Adrian Florencio, Bradenton	11.08
SO/9 (RP)	Steven Cruz, Fort Myers	14.66
BB/9	Chris Mokma, Jupiter	2.72
WP	Edwin Nunez, Palm Beach	35
BK	Luis Ortiz, Palm Beach	11
HRA	Chris Mokma, Jupiter	17
BAA	Naswell Paulino, Dunedin	.208

MINOR LEAGUES

BY KYLE GLASER

Everything changed in 2021 for the league formerly known as the California League.

The league's name changed to Low-A West. The level changed from High-A to Low-A. The composition of the league changed, with Fresno replacing Lancaster as the league's eighth team as part of MLB's minor league restructuring.

The rules of the league changed, too. Low-A West was used as a testing ground for experimental rule changes designed to increase the place of play, with 15-second pitch clocks instituted in June and pitchers limited to two pickoff attempts per plate appearance.

With the rule changes in place, the league's average time of game was 2 hours, 43 minutes, a reduction of 20 minutes compared to 2019.

Against that backdrop, the talent in the league was as strong as ever. First-round picks such as Stockton catcher Tyler Soderstrom, Lake Elsinore outfielder Robert Hassell and Fresno outfielder Zac Veen all starred in their professional debuts and a standout crop of international signees, led by San Jose shortstop Marco Luciano, Modesto shortstop Noelvi Marte and Rancho Cucamonga catcher Diego Cartaya shined in their first tastes of full-season ball.

While every team had talent, Fresno and San Jose stood above the rest.

Veen, catcher Drew Romo, shortstop Ezequiel Tovar and second baseman Eddy Diaz led a star-studded Fresno team of Rockies prospects that went 74-41, the best record in the league.

San Jose, a longtime Giants affiliate, boasted Luciano, outfielder Luis Matos, lefthander Kyle Harrison, outfielder Jairo Pomares, catcher Patrick Bailey and righthander Carson Ragsdale at various points in the season and went 76-44, the second-best record in the league.

Predictably, the two teams met in the championship series, with San Jose sweeping Fresno, three games to none, to win the league title.

TOP 10 PROSPECTS

Tyler Soderstrom

1. Tyler Soderstrom, C, Stockton (Athletics)
2. Marco Luciano, SS, San Jose (Giants)
3. Robert Hassell, OF, Lake Elsinore (Padres)
4. Zac Veen, OF, Fresno (Rockies)
5. Diego Cartaya, C, Rancho Cucamonga (Dodgers)
6. Luis Matos, OF, San Jose (Giants)
7. Noelvi Marte, SS, Modesto (Mariners)
8. Blake Walston, LHP, Visalia (D-backs)
9. Drew Romo, C, Fresno (Rockies)
10. Kyle Harrison, LHP, San Jose (Giants)

The Giants' pitchers combined to hold the Grizzlies to five runs in three games and a .182 batting average in a dominant staff-wide performance. Harrison (6.1 innings, one earned run) led the way in Game 1 and Ragsdale (six innings, two earned runs) picked up the win in Game 2 to set the table for a dominant group effort in Game 3, capped by five scoreless innings from the bullpen. Bailey went 4-for-10 with two home runs and four RBIs to lead the offense in the series.

Matos was named the league MVP after hitting .313 with 15 home runs, 86 RBIs, 21 stolen bases and an .853 OPS.

Harrison was named the pitcher of the year after going 4-3 with a league-best 3.19 ERA. Ragsdale led the league, and finished second in the minors, with 167 strikeouts. ■

OVERALL STANDINGS

North Division	W	L	PCT	GB	Manager(s)	Attendance	Average	Last Penn.
Fresno Grizzlies (Rockies)	74	41	.643	—	Robinson Cancel	176,395	2,940	Never
San Jose Giants (Giants)	76	44	.633	0.5	Lenn Sakata	62,569	1,043	2021
Modesto Nuts (Mariners)	64	51	.557	10	Eric Farris	42,200	771	*2017
Stockton Ports (Athletics)	42	75	.359	33	Rico Brogna	73,410	1,273	*2008

South Division	W	L	PCT	GB	Manager(s)	Attendance	Average	Last Penn.
Rancho Cucamonga Quakes (Dodgers)	67	53	.558	—	Austin Chubb/John Shoemaker	76,493	1,269	*2018
Inland Empire 66ers (Angels)	56	61	.479	9.5	Jack Howell	90,587	1,503	*2013
Lake Elsinore Storm (Padres)	55	65	.458	12	Mike McCoy	103,758	1,729	*2011
Visalia Rawhide (D-backs)	38	82	.317	29	Javier Colina	79,625	1,327	*2019

Finals: San Jose defeated Fresno 3-0

* Refers to High-A California League prior to 2021

BILL MITCHELL

MINOR LEAGUES

CLUB BATTING

	AVG	G	AB	R	H	2B	3B	HR	RBI	BB	SO	SB	OBP	SLG
Modesto	.277	115	4037	722	1117	253	35	87	642	545	1151	138	.371	.421
Fresno	.270	115	3917	635	1056	203	35	87	542	356	1004	221	.337	.406
Rancho Cucamonga	.268	120	4216	810	1130	257	51	165	735	498	1292	93	.357	.471
San Jose	.268	120	4176	706	1118	253	31	150	633	438	1119	91	.346	.451
Lake Elsinore	.264	120	4143	701	1094	227	42	78	606	475	1138	179	.348	.396
Inland Empire	.241	117	3953	617	954	196	52	91	541	483	1352	161	.331	.386
Stockton	.232	117	3931	573	912	195	29	98	511	455	1265	122	.322	.371
Visalia	.230	120	4029	599	928	201	27	114	532	468	1414	174	.323	.379

CLUB PITCHING

	ERA	G	CG	SHO	SV	IP	H	R	ER	HR	BB	SO	AVG
San Jose	3.59	120	0	11	30	1072	912	516	428	93	429	1439	.227
Fresno	3.79	115	0	8	39	1025	917	506	432	83	394	1119	.239
Inland Empire	4.66	117	0	6	31	1036	1031	654	537	101	431	1201	.256
Modesto	4.73	115	0	8	26	1018	993	666	535	79	512	1228	.250
Lake Elsinore	4.97	120	0	5	19	1054	1038	695	582	125	505	1218	.254
Rancho Cucamonga	5.03	120	0	3	28	1059	1104	701	592	125	415	1310	.262
Stockton	5.79	117	0	1	19	1023	1178	770	658	152	445	1064	.289
Visalia	5.96	120	0	0	18	1049	1136	846	695	112	587	1156	.273

CLUB FIELDING

	PCT	PO	A	E	DP		PCT	PO	A	E	DP
Fresno	.974	3076	1011	110	89	Inland Empire	.963	3109	1075	161	77
San Jose	.969	3216	953	135	74	Visalia	.961	3148	1108	171	91
Stockton	.968	3070	1006	133	100	Lake Elsinore	.961	3161	1082	171	92
R. Cucamonga	.964	3177	1035	158	68	Modesto	.958	3053	998	178	83

INDIVIDUAL BATTING

Batter, Club	AVG	G	AB	R	H	2B	3B	HR	RBI	BB	SO	SB
Euribiel Angeles, Lake Elsinore	.343	87	362	65	124	22	6	3	56	32	61	18
Braxton Martinez, Inland Empire	.333	79	282	50	94	27	3	12	59	56	52	1
Robert Hassell, Lake Elsinore	.323	92	365	77	118	31	3	7	65	57	74	31
Drew Romo, Fresno	.314	79	312	48	98	17	2	6	47	19	50	23
Luis Matos, San Jose	.313	109	451	84	141	35	1	15	86	28	61	21
Jorbit Vivas, Rancho Cucamonga	.311	83	328	73	102	20	4	13	73	27	42	5
Ezequiel Tovar, Fresno	.309	72	298	60	92	21	3	11	54	14	38	21
Brandon Valenzuela, Lake Elsinore	.307	82	329	50	101	21	3	6	62	44	80	3
Sam McWilliams, R. Cucamonga	.304	87	355	82	108	32	2	14	70	44	117	12
Zac Veen, Fresno	.301	106	399	83	120	27	4	15	75	64	126	36

INDIVIDUAL PITCHING

Pitcher, Club	W	L	ERA	G	GS	CG	SV	IP	H	R	ER	BB	SO
Kyle Harrison, San Jose	4	3	3.19	23	23	0	0	99	86	43	35	52	157
Prelander Berroa, San Jose	5	6	3.56	24	24	0	0	99	79	52	39	53	135
Wil Jensen, San Jose	7	3	3.59	23	19	0	0	103	96	46	41	25	109
John Swanda, Inland Empire	7	5	4.14	20	15	0	0	104	104	61	48	33	92
Carson Ragsdale, San Jose	8	6	4.43	24	24	0	0	114	107	61	56	45	167
Sam Carlson, Modesto	6	4	4.77	19	19	0	0	100	107	69	53	44	112
Jose Salvador, Inland Empire	6	6	5.91	20	17	0	0	96	100	66	63	47	115

ALL-STAR TEAM

C: Drew Romo, Fresno. **1B:** Braxton Martinez, Inland Empire. **2B:** Sam McWilliams, R. Cucamonga.
3B: Jorbit Vivas, Rancho Cucamonga. **SS:** Marco Luciano, San Jose. **OF:** Robert Hassell, Lake Elsinore.
OF: Luis Matos, San Jose. **OF:** Zac Veen, Fresno. **DH:** Noelvi Marte, Modesto.
RHP: Ryan Murphy, San Jose. **LHP:** Kyle Harrison, San Jose. **RP:** Randy Rodriguez, San Jose.

MVP: Luis Matos, OF, San Jose. **Pitcher of the Year:** Kyle Harrison, LHP, San Jose.
Top MLB Prospect: Zac Veen, OF, Fresno. **Manager of the Year:** Robinson Cancel, Fresno.

DEPARTMENT LEADERS

BATTING

OBP	Braxton Martinez, Inland Empire	.445
SLG	Braxton Martinez, Inland Empire	.578
OPS	Braxton Martinez, Inland Empire	1.023
R	Noelvi Marte, Modesto	87
H	Luis Matos, San Jose	141
TB	Luis Matos, San Jose	223
XBH	Luis Matos, San Jose	51
2B	Luis Matos, San Jose	35
3B	Ismael Alcantara, Rancho Cucamonga	7
HR	Neyfy Castillo, Visalia	21
RBI	Luis Matos, San Jose	86
SAC	Drew Romo, Fresno	8
BB	Alex De Jesus, Rancho Cucamonga	69
HBP	Robert Perez, Modesto	17
HBP	Jorbit Vivas, Rancho Cucamonga	17
SO	Neyfy Castillo, Visalia	170
SB	Eddy Diaz, Fresno	48
CS	Zac Veen, Fresno	17
AB/SO	Ezequiel Tovar, Fresno	7.84

FIELDING

C PCT	Drew Romo, Fresno	.992
PO	Drew Romo, Fresno	663
A	Patrick Bailey, San Jose	58
DP	Gilberto Vizcarra, Lake Elsinore	6
E	Brandon Valenzuela, Lake Elsinore	15
CS	Gilberto Vizcarra, Lake Elsinore	29
SB	Ty Duvall, Modesto	114
PB	Tyler Soderstrom, Stockton	15
1B PCT	Grant Lavigne, Fresno	.990
PO	Robert Puason, Stockton	120
A	Noelvi Marte, Modesto	225
DP	Robert Puason, Stockton	49
E	Noelvi Marte, Modesto	29
E	Robert Puason, Stockton	29
2B PCT	Jimmy Glowenke, San Jose	.976
PO	Jimmy Glowenke, San Jose	160
A	Jimmy Glowenke, San Jose	206
DP	Jimmy Glowenke, San Jose	46
E	Jimmy Glowenke, San Jose	9
E	Cesar Izturis Jr., Modesto	9
E	Ronny Simon, Visalia	9
3B PCT	T.J. Schofield-Sam, Stockton	.954
PO	Julio Carreras, Fresno	36
A	Julio Carreras, Fresno	97
DP	T.J. Schofield-Sam, Stockton	9
E	A.J. Vukovich, Visalia	17
E	Jeremy Arocho, Inland Empire	17
SS PCT	Noelvi Marte, Modesto	.920
PO	Robert Puason, Stockton	120
A	Noelvi Marte, Modesto	225
DP	Robert Puason, Stockton	49
E	Noelvi Marte, Modesto	29
E	Robert Puason, Stockton	29
OF PCT	Glenallen Hill Jr., Visalia	.986
PO	Junior Perez, Stockton	200
A	Alberto Rodriguez, Modesto	12
DP	3 players	3
E	Alberto Rodriguez, Modesto	8

PITCHING

G	Juan Mejia, Fresno	43
GS	Prelander Berroa, San Jose	24
GS	Carson Ragsdale, San Jose	24
GF	Clay Helvey, San Jose	35
SV	Robinson Hernandez, Fresno	14
W	Hyun-il Choi, Rancho Cucamonga	8
W	Carson Ragsdale, San Jose	8
L	Adrian Del Moral, Visalia	10
L	Austin Pope, Visalia	10
L	Nick Thwaits, Lake Elsinore	10
IP	Carson Ragsdale, San Jose	113.2
H	Sam Carlson, Modesto	107
H	Carson Ragsdale, San Jose	107
R	Junior Mieses, Visalia	81
ER	Austin Pope, Visalia	70
HB	Kyle Harrison, San Jose	15
BB	Junior Mieses, Visalia	72
SO	Carson Ragsdale, San Jose	167
SO/9	Kyle Harrison, San Jose	14.32
SO/9 (RP)	Randy Rodriguez, San Jose	14.66
BB/9	Kendall Williams, Rancho Cucamonga	2.12
WP	Junior Mieses, Visalia	21
WP	Pedro Santos, Stockton	21
BK	Carlos Duran, Rancho Cucamonga	5
HRA	Diego Granado, Stockton	15
BAA	Prelander Berroa, San Jose	.220

MINOR LEAGUES

BY BILL MITCHELL

The Arizona League was renamed the Arizona Complex League following Major League Baseball's restructuring of the minor leagues. The Rookie classification remained the same, but the number of teams shrunk from 21 in 2019 to 18 this season, with the Giants, Brewers and Royals each fielding two squads.

With the draft moving from June to July, the ACL was a tale of two seasons. Rosters in the first half consisted mostly of Latin American players, making the league feel more like an extension of the Dominican Summer League. As draft picks signed and joined the league in the second half, it more closely resembled a cross between Rookie ball and the old short-season level.

Challenges from the ongoing Covid pandemic wreaked further havoc with schedules and player transfers.

Eleven first-round picks from the 2021 draft made their professional debuts in the ACL. In order of selection, they were: D-backs shortstop Jordan Lawlar, Rockies outfielder Benny Montgomery, Mariners catcher Harry Ford, Giants righthander Will Bednar, Brewers outfielder Sal Frelick, Reds shortstop Matt McLain, White Sox shortstop Colson Montgomery, Athletics shortstop Max Muncy, Padres shortstop Jackson Merrill, Dodgers lefthander Maddux Bruns and Reds outfielder Jay Allen.

This year's ACL prospect crop was hitter-heavy and included several intriguing below-the-radar Latin players, such as top prospect Elly de la Cruz, a Reds third baseman, who was relatively unknown coming into the season.

It was one of De la Cruz's Reds teammate who won the league's MVP award: 18-year-old Dominican outfielder Yerlin Confidan. The lefthanded hitter topped the league with 11 home runs while hitting .315/.359/.573 in 50 games.

The ACL did not conduct a playoff series to determine a true league champion, but the Rockies led all teams with a 43-16 record. It was the Rockies' return to the complex league for the first time since 2000. For more than 20 years, the organization had eschewed the Arizona League in favor of affiliates in the Rookie-advanced Pioneer and short-season Northwest leagues. ∎

OVERALL STANDINGS

Central Division	W	L	PCT	GB	Manager
ACL Indians	34	23	.596	—	Jerry Owens
ACL Reds	33	26	.559	1	Bryan LaHair
ACL Dodgers	31	27	.534	3.5	Tony Cappucilli
ACL Angels	29	28	.509	5	Dave Stapleton
ACL White Sox	25	34	.424	10	Mike Gellinger
ACL Brewers Blue	21	33	.389	11.5	Rafael Neda

East Division	W	L	PCT	GB	Manager
ACL Rockies	41	15	.732	—	Jake Opitz
ACL Giants Orange	33	23	.589	8	Lance Burkhart
ACL Cubs	33	26	.559	9.5	Lance Rymel

	W	L	PCT	GB	Manager
ACL Giants Black	27	31	.466	15	Carlos Valderrama
ACL Diamondbacks	20	39	.339	22.5	Rolando Arnedo
ACL Athletics	15	37	.288	24	Adam Rosales

West Division	W	L	PCT	GB	Manager
ACL Mariners	39	18	.684	—	Austin Knight
ACL Brewers Gold	26	23	.531	9	None listed
ACL Rangers	31	28	.525	9	Jay Sullenger
ACL Padres	23	31	.426	14.5	Miguel Del Castillo
ACL Royals Blue	20	28	.417	14.5	Omar Ramirez
ACL Royals Gold	18	29	.383	16	Andre David

BILL MITCHELL

CLUB BATTING

	AVG	G	AB	R	H	2B	3B	HR	RBI	BB	SO	SB	OBP	SLG
ACL Rockies	.295	59	1680	376	495	96	16	46	316	248	399	115	.397	.453
ACL Cubs	.286	60	1871	384	536	100	29	57	334	252	564	67	.376	.462
ACL Indians	.280	58	1878	381	526	113	14	52	321	267	498	72	.379	.438
ACL Giants Orange	.271	59	1665	311	452	86	18	34	254	206	554	67	.369	.406
ACL Reds	.263	59	1839	331	483	101	24	69	276	241	590	86	.362	.456
ACL Brewers Gold	.256	51	1487	245	380	72	13	33	212	163	464	49	.344	.388
ACL Dodgers	.254	59	1888	328	480	98	18	41	276	242	577	31	.352	.390
ACL Rangers	.252	59	1848	328	465	97	32	43	290	245	621	92	.348	.409
ACL Giants Black	.250	59	1647	254	412	78	12	37	211	178	552	44	.334	.379
ACL Angels	.243	58	1811	321	440	91	23	32	259	264	616	80	.355	.372
ACL Mariners	.240	58	1608	315	386	84	18	49	274	276	554	78	.371	.406
ACL D-backs	.239	60	1712	273	410	73	16	29	230	213	543	76	.329	.352
ACL Brewers Blue	.237	54	1608	239	381	68	20	26	192	190	477	74	.325	.353
ACL Padres	.234	58	1573	252	368	85	14	28	209	243	497	59	.345	.359
ACL White Sox	.229	59	1824	267	417	91	9	43	226	210	670	33	.324	.359
ACL Athletics	.228	59	1459	202	333	56	11	18	164	210	519	32	.338	.319
ACL Royals Gold	.227	53	1331	230	302	66	16	28	186	200	473	66	.345	.364
ACL Royals Blue	.227	54	1346	210	305	69	8	30	177	188	532	66	.333	.357

CLUB PITCHING

	ERA	G	CG	SHO	SV	IP	H	R	ER	HR	BB	SO	AVG
ACL Giants Orange	3.90	59	0	6	15	425	370	221	184	34	174	530	.235
ACL Rockies	3.96	59	1	6	19	434	424	224	191	33	156	508	.255
ACL Mariners	3.98	58	1	4	20	436	355	238	193	29	245	573	.220
ACL Dodgers	4.06	59	0	4	10	488	428	269	220	38	221	617	.233
ACL Reds	4.31	59	0	3	16	486	438	310	233	40	239	670	.237
ACL Angels	4.48	58	0	4	13	476	440	306	237	34	223	562	.238
ACL Brewers Gold	4.90	51	0	3	12	379	341	251	206	26	248	455	.242
ACL Giants Black	4.93	59	0	4	9	422	439	279	231	34	198	561	.266
ACL Royals Gold	5.06	53	0	2	10	350	362	247	197	46	159	433	.261
ACL Padres	5.13	58	0	4	13	421	384	280	240	37	217	553	.241
ACL White Sox	5.34	59	1	3	14	473	495	324	281	48	270	599	.266
ACL Royals Blue	5.40	54	0	1	9	357	394	259	214	42	131	381	.278
ACL Cubs	5.43	60	0	4	7	470	426	359	284	37	274	564	.237
ACL Indians	5.47	58	0	3	8	477	479	341	290	68	247	564	.261
ACL Rangers	5.52	59	0	3	11	483	440	346	296	39	296	703	.240
ACL Brewers Blue	5.72	54	1	0	10	419	435	307	266	42	249	498	.266
ACL D-backs	5.99	60	0	2	7	448	494	370	298	41	291	505	.279
ACL Athletics	6.27	59	0	6	3	379	427	317	264	27	198	424	.283

CLUB FIELDING

	PCT	PO	A	E	DP		PCT	PO	A	E	DP
ACL Rockies	.969	1302	460	57	33	ACL Reds	.961	1459	426	77	32
ACL Giants Black	.966	1266	450	61	43	ACL Brewers Gold	.958	1135	353	65	42
ACL Indians	.965	1430	420	68	39	ACL Mariners	.957	1308	371	76	35
ACL Rangers	.964	1449	445	71	34	ACL Cubs	.953	1411	475	92	45
ACL Giants Orange	.964	1274	451	65	40	ACL Athletics	.951	1136	385	78	29
ACL White Sox	.964	1420	455	71	48	ACL D-backs	.950	1344	457	95	41
ACL Brewers Blue	.963	1256	405	63	31	ACL Angels	.950	1427	417	98	25
ACL Dodgers	.963	1464	489	75	40	ACL Royals Blue	.949	1070	367	77	31
ACL Padres	.962	1263	405	65	30	ACL Royals Gold	.947	1051	336	77	37

INDIVIDUAL BATTING

Batter, Club	AVG	G	AB	R	H	2B	3B	HR	RBI	BB	SO	SB
Adrian Sugastey, ACL Giants Orange	.358	43	148	23	53	6	0	2	25	12	26	1
Garrett Frechette, ACL Giants Orange	.331	50	169	20	56	13	1	4	28	13	52	2
Dayan Frias, ACL Indians	.322	42	152	32	49	12	3	4	24	27	38	3
Wilfred Veras, ACL White Sox	.322	46	152	25	49	16	2	4	26	21	42	3
Juan Guerrero, ACL Rockies	.318	47	148	32	47	13	1	4	26	16	29	9
Arol Vera, ACL Angels	.317	38	145	24	46	16	3	0	17	12	39	2
Yerlin Confidan, ACL Reds	.315	50	178	33	56	9	2	11	34	12	48	7
Alexander Suarez, ACL Giants Black	.311	55	193	43	60	15	2	6	25	10	72	16
Milkar Perez, ACL Mariners	.310	45	145	33	45	10	0	0	23	39	38	1
Luis Durango, ACL Indians	.308	46	156	37	48	6	0	3	20	18	31	28

INDIVIDUAL PITCHING

Pitcher, Club	W	L	ERA	G	GS	CG	SV	IP	H	R	ER	BB	SO
Esmerlin Vinicio, ACL Giants Black	3	3	2.64	14	11	0	0	58	49	22	17	29	70
Luis Devers, ACL Cubs	2	4	3.33	12	11	0	0	51	48	24	19	14	54
Dilmer Mejia, ACL White Sox	0	1	3.73	12	6	0	0	51	59	27	21	9	57
Trevor McDonald, ACL Giants Orange	2	3	3.86	15	13	0	0	68	67	35	29	31	69
Micah Kaczor, ACL Rockies	5	3	4.18	12	8	0	0	52	59	25	24	9	41
Manuel Mercedes, ACL Giants Orange	3	3	5.11	14	13	0	0	56	61	38	32	25	62
Sonny Vargas, ACL Giants Orange	5	5	5.33	16	10	0	2	54	45	36	32	18	62
Rafael Garcia, ACL Brewers Blue	2	4	6.16	12	10	0	0	50	49	39	34	29	52
Cristian Mena, ACL White Sox	1	4	7.82	13	12	0	0	48	69	44	42	21	62
Rafael Martinez, ACL Giants Black	2	6	7.88	13	9	0	0	48	64	47	42	28	55

DEPARTMENT LEADERS

BATTING

OBP	Milkar Perez, ACL Mariners	.463
SLG	Yerlin Confidan, ACL Reds	.573
OPS	Wilfred Veras, ACL White Sox	.949
R	Alexander Suarez, ACL Giants Black	43
H	Alexander Suarez, ACL Giants Black	60
TB	Yerlin Confidan, ACL Reds	102
XBH	Alexander Suarez, ACL Giants Black	23
2B	Miguel Fabrizio, ACL Cubs	16
2B	Arol Vera, ACL Angels	16
2B	Wilfred Veras, ACL White Sox	16
3B	Yosy Galan, ACL Rangers	7
HR	Yerlin Confidan, ACL Reds	11
RBI	Aeverson Arteaga, ACL Giants Orange	43
SAC	Jacob Gonzalez, ACL Giants Black	7
BB	Milkar Perez, ACL Mariners	39
HBP	Gunn Omosako, ACL Mariners	13
SO	Yosy Galan, ACL Rangers	80
SB	Luis Durango, ACL Indians	28
CS	Adael Amador, ACL Rockies	7
AB/SO	Diego Velasquez, ACL Giants Black	6.4

FIELDING

C PCT	Adrian Sugastey, ACL Giants Orange	.993
PO	Adrian Sugastey, ACL Giants Orange	356
A	Adrian Sugastey, ACL Giants Orange	41
DP	3 players	4
E	Enmanuel Pire, ACL Royals Blue, ACL Royals Gold	10
CS	Adrian Sugastey, ACL Giants Orange	19
SB	Malcom Quintero, ACL Cubs	50
PB	Andruw Salcedo, ACL Reds	11
1B PCT	Diego Maican, ACL Royals Blue	.977
PO	Garrett Frechette, ACL Giants Orange	267
A	Diego Maican, ACL Royals Blue	29
DP	Jesus Chirinos, ACL Brewers Blue, ACL Brewers Gold	29
E	4 players	7
2B PCT	Dilan Rosario, ACL Giants Black	.991
PO	Carlos Roa, ACL Brewers Gold, ACL Brewers Blue	46
PO	Dilan Rosario, ACL Giants Black	46
A	Hector Martinez, ACL Dodgers	64
DP	Carlos Roa, ACL Brewers Gold, ACL Brewers Blue	20
E	Donovan Antonia, ACL Reds	10
3B PCT	Anthony Rodriguez, ACL Giants Orange	.955
PO	Anthony Rodriguez, ACL Giants Orange	28
A	Anthony Rodriguez, ACL Giants Orange	77
DP	Anthony Rodriguez, ACL Giants Orange	7
E	Jose Bonilla, ACL Angeles	11
SS PCT	Carlos Santiago, ACL Dodgers	.952
PO	Carlos Santiago, ACL Dodgers	49
A	Aeverson Arteaga, ACL Giants Orange	127
DP	Aeverson Arteaga, ACL Giants Orange	21
E	Wilmin Candelario, ACL Royals Blue	12
OF PCT	Arbert Cipion, ACL Brewers Blue	1.000
PCT	Yorvis Torrealba, ACL Rockies	1.000
PCT	Rothaikeg Seijas, ACL Royals Blue	1.000
PCT	Logan Glass, ACL White Sox	1.000
PO	Luis Rodriguez, ACL Dodgers	88
A	Luis Rodriguez, ACL Dodgers	9
DP	Eduarqui Fernandez, ACL Brewers Gold	3
E	Alexander Suarez, ACL Giants Black	8
E	Deivid Alcantara, ACL Reds	8

PITCHING

G	Juan Mateo, ACL Indians	22
GS	Trevor McDonald, ACL Giants Orange	13
GS	Manuel Mercedes, ACL Giants Orange	13
GF	Cal Maduro, ACL Royals Blue	20
SV	Luis Amoroso, ACL Rockies	10
W	Raul Alcantara, ACL Mariners	8
L	Mauricio Bascunan, ACL D-backs	6
L	Rafael Martinez, ACL Giants Black	6
L	Luis Villar, ACL Royals Gold	6
IP	Trevor McDonald, ACL Giants Orange	67.2
H	Cristian Mena, ACL White Sox	69
R	Daury Cabrera, ACL Royals Blue	47
R	Rafael Martinez, ACL Giants Black	47
ER	Rafael Martinez, ACL Giants Black	42
ER	Cristian Mena, ACL White Sox	42
HB	Yovanny Cabrera, ACL Cubs	14
BB	Ronaldo Guzman, ACL White Sox	48
SO	Esmerlin Vinicio, ACL Giants Black	70
SO/9	Benony Robles, ACL Dodgers	12.02
SO/9 (RP)	Elvis Jerez, ACL Indians	18
BB/9	Micah Kaczor, ACL Rockies	1.57
WP	Luis Baez, ACL Mariners	19
BK	Jose Corniell, ACL Rangers	5
BK	Rynardo Cruz, ACL Reds	5
HRA	Micah Kaczor, ACL Rockies	10
BAA	Sonny Vargas, ACL Giants Orange	.226

MINOR LEAGUES

BY BEN BADLER

The Florida Complex League had a different feel in 2021.

The Rookie-level FCL, formerly known as the Gulf Coast League, felt the ramifications of the lost 2020 minor league season and of Major League Baseball eliminating all other short-season and Rookie-level leagues besides the Arizona Complex League.

As a result, the FCL has players from both the 2020 and 2021 draft classes in the league making their pro debuts. Multiple signing classes of international players filled the league as well in either their first official pro action or their United States debuts.

Several 2021 first-round picks played in the league, most notably the league's top prospect, Red Sox shortstop Marcelo Mayer. The No. 4 overall pick in the draft out of high school in SoCal, Mayer showed a calm, balanced swing from the left side with smooth, fluid actions at shortstop.

The No. 2 prospect in the league, Nationals shortstop Brady House, had an even louder pro debut. House hit .322/.394/.576 with four home runs in 66 plate appearances, showing off the power stroke that enticed the Nationals when they drafted him with the 11th overall pick.

Other first-rounders who impressed evaluators around the league included Phillies righthander Andrew Painter (13th overall), Marlins shortstop Khalil Watson (16th) and Rays shortstop Carson Williams (28th).

A pair of prominent third basemen from the 2020 draft—Blaze Jordan of the Red Sox and Coby Mayo of the Orioles—also stood out for their power during the league before getting promoted to Low-A later in the season.

The quality of the Marlins' 2019 international signing class, even with righthander Eury Perez on the fast track skipping the league, was evident with shortstop Jose Salas and second baseman Ian Lewis both standing out for their hitting ability

TOP 10 PROSPECTS

Marcelo Mayer

1. Marcelo Mayer, SS, Red Sox
2. Brady House, SS, Nationals
3. Jose Salas, SS, Marlins
4. Coby Mayo, 3B, Orioles
5. Blaze Jordan, 3B, Red Sox
6. Ian Lewis, 2B, Marlins
7. Joe Mack, C, Marlins
8. Izaac Pacheco, SS, Tigers
9. Manuel Sequera, SS, Tigers
10. Antonio Gomez, C, Yankees

and athleticism. That duo plus Watson all moves to Low-A Jupiter next season.

With no playoffs in the league in 2021, the Rays finished with the best record in the FCL, posting the best run differential (+162) with the most runs scored per game and the fewest runs allowed per game. Dominican shortstop/third baseman Willy Vazquez emerged as one of the Rays' better prospects at the lower levels, hitting .288/.382/.411 in 40 games.

The league's MVP award went to 18-year-old Tigers shortstop Manuel Sequera. Signed out of Venezuela in 2019 as more of a line-drive hitter, Sequera has tapped into more power as he has matured while also sharpening his batting eye. He led the FCL with 11 home runs and tied for the league lead with 40 RBIs. ∎

OVERALL STANDINGS

East Division	W	L	PCT	GB	Manager
FCL Mets	32	22	.593	—	Robbie Robinson
FCL Marlins	27	27	.500	5	Lou Dorante
FCL Astros	27	28	.491	5.5	Ricardo Rivera
FCL Nationals	26	30	.464	7	Jake Lowery
FCL Cardinals	24	29	.453	7.5	Roberto Espinoza

North Division	W	L	PCT	GB	Manager
FCL Yankees	36	16	.692	—	Julio Borbon
FCL Phillies	26	14	.650	4	Roly de Armas
FCL Blue Jays	25	29	.463	12	Brent Lavallee
FCL Tigers East	19	32	.373	16.5	Gary Cathcart
FCL Tigers West	18	33	.353	17.5	Ryan Minor

South Division	W	L	PCT	GB	Manager
FCL Rays	42	15	.737	—	Rafael Valenzuela
FCL Red Sox	37	20	.649	5	Jimmy Gonzalez
FCL Pirates Gold	30	14	.682	5.5	Gera Alvarez
FCL Pirates Black	19	23	.452	15.5	Steve Morales
FCL Braves	25	31	.446	16.5	Nestor Pérez
FCL Orioles Black	18	27	.400	18	Alan Mills
FCL Twins	19	38	.333	23	Takashi Miyoshi
FCL Orioles Orange	10	33	.233	25	Kevin Bradshaw

CLUB BATTING

	AVG	G	AB	R	H	2B	3B	HR	RBI	BB	SO	SB	OBP	SLG
FCL Blue Jays	.271	54	1697	361	460	100	14	35	309	292	449	100	.391	.408
FCL Red Sox	.267	57	1762	332	470	137	18	36	299	258	526	70	.368	.426
FCL Yankees	.261	52	1599	366	418	90	20	65	312	276	506	109	.378	.465
FCL Rays	.259	57	1785	363	462	96	20	34	294	275	498	127	.373	.392
FCL Pirates Gold	.256	45	1314	268	336	58	19	27	219	201	333	76	.367	.390
FCL Orioles Black	.252	47	1337	209	337	62	8	22	185	149	410	65	.338	.360
FCL Phillies	.252	40	1172	261	295	68	14	37	215	206	324	78	.383	.428
FCL Mets	.246	54	1645	258	404	108	12	42	219	182	529	55	.335	.402
FCL Tigers East	.243	51	1545	260	376	80	14	39	219	219	457	42	.350	.389
FCL Marlins	.236	55	1648	257	389	96	18	26	216	225	529	56	.341	.363
FCL Nationals	.234	56	1674	273	391	71	11	39	241	246	464	49	.349	.363
FCL Astros	.233	56	1634	249	381	70	11	34	206	209	544	78	.337	.352
FCL Tigers West	.231	51	1508	206	349	70	13	36	181	203	485	27	.338	.367
FCL Cardinals	.230	53	1595	235	367	70	12	19	191	225	491	48	.334	.325
FCL Twins	.227	59	1804	273	409	80	22	53	243	246	646	53	.333	.384
FCL Pirates Black	.226	43	1226	210	277	55	15	25	178	194	372	49	.345	.356
FCL Braves	.224	56	1659	221	372	67	17	19	178	190	522	101	.318	.319

CLUB PITCHING

	ERA	G	CG	SHO	SV	IP	H	R	ER	HR	BB	SO	AVG
FCL Rays	3.06	57	0	5	21	471	374	201	160	26	202	632	.214
FCL Astros	3.87	56	0	4	8	439	349	240	189	23	274	596	.214
FCL Pirates Gold	3.91	45	1	5	6	347	300	174	151	20	153	408	.232
FCL Mets	4.17	54	0	5	19	429	371	242	199	28	232	519	.231
FCL Red Sox	4.20	57	1	2	13	452	397	253	211	45	199	561	.230
FCL Marlins	4.32	55	0	1	9	435	399	251	209	35	197	498	.239
FCL Braves	4.50	56	0	7	11	440	364	282	220	39	294	503	.224
FCL Phillies	4.55	40	0	3	14	318	291	190	161	29	180	359	.238
FCL Nationals	4.56	56	0	5	12	440	417	273	223	31	194	478	.247
FCL Cardinals	4.62	53	1	5	11	419	396	266	215	43	190	466	.247
FCL Yankees	4.67	52	0	6	11	416	352	274	216	30	226	516	.226
FCL Pirates Black	4.82	43	0	3	7	325	302	238	174	21	184	353	.244
FCL Twins	5.05	59	1	2	8	476	477	327	267	33	227	544	.254
FCL Blue Jays	5.50	54	0	1	6	430	407	301	263	53	252	489	.249
FCL Orioles Black	5.80	47	0	0	7	337	354	262	217	32	174	375	.266
FCL Tigers West	6.43	51	0	0	9	396	393	333	283	52	297	435	.260
FCL Tigers East	6.78	51	0	2	7	401	455	356	302	48	241	422	.285
FCL Orioles Orange	7.11	46	0	1	4	337	402	332	266	21	237	341	.292

CLUB FIELDING

	PCT	PO	A	E	DP		PCT	PO	A	E	DP
FCL Pirates Gold	.972	1042	304	39	22	FCL Astros	.957	1317	381	76	34
FCL Mets	.971	1288	403	51	35	FCL Braves	.957	1319	444	79	43
FCL Nationals	.969	1320	480	58	39	FCL Tigers West	.957	1189	397	72	33
FCL Rays	.965	1412	448	67	41	FCL Yankees	.954	1249	425	81	29
FCL Blue Jays	.964	1291	401	63	40	FCL Orioles Black	.953	1011	356	67	19
FCL Red Sox	.962	1357	413	69	28	FCL Phillies	.953	955	338	64	28
FCL Marlins	.961	1306	475	73	34	FCL Pirates Black	.952	974	335	66	26
FCL Cardinals	.961	1258	448	70	34	FCL Tigers East	.952	1201	417	82	40
FCL Twins	.961	1428	470	78	26	FCL Orioles Orange	.939	1011	367	89	21

INDIVIDUAL BATTING

Batter, Club	AVG	G	AB	R	H	2B	3B	HR	RBI	BB	SO	SB
Brandol Mezquita, FCL Braves	.308	43	146	18	45	8	2	3	25	19	50	15
Juan Jerez, FCL Pirates Black	.296	43	152	26	45	9	2	6	28	24	46	10
Willy Vasquez, FCL Rays	.288	40	146	26	42	6	3	2	31	20	27	14
Rodolfo Nolasco, FCL Pirates Gold	.284	42	134	27	38	8	2	8	32	26	43	0
Danuerys de la Cruz, FCL Tigers East	.283	40	127	28	36	8	2	7	26	31	38	3
Kala'i Rosario, FCL Twins	.277	51	188	32	52	10	4	5	40	19	66	4
Isaac De Leon, FCL Orioles Black	.276	45	145	27	40	9	1	1	23	18	39	5
Alexander Vargas, FCL Yankees	.273	42	150	37	41	7	1	3	26	20	40	17
Jeremy Rivas, FCL Cardinals	.271	48	177	22	48	7	1	0	16	15	32	6
Jose de la Cruz, FCL Tigers East	.270	44	159	20	43	9	1	4	15	17	58	7

INDIVIDUAL PITCHING

Pitcher, Club	W	L	ERA	G	GS	CG	SV	IP	H	R	ER	BB	SO
Luis Vizcaino, FCL Marlins	4	2	2.92	12	8	0	0	49	35	23	16	24	51

ALL-STAR TEAM

C: Danuerys de la Cruz, Tigers East. **1B:** Adriel Sotolongo, Blue Jays. **2B:** Ian Lewis, Marlins.
3B: Juan Jerez, Pirates Black. **SS:** Manuel Sequera, Tigers East. **OF:** Carlos Dominguez, Mets.
OF: Kala'i Rosario, Twins. **OF:** Miguel Ugueto Red Sox. **DH:** Rodolfo Nolasco Pirates Gold
RHP: Juan Daniel Encarnacion, Red Sox. **LHP:** Yaifer Perdomo, Blue Jays.

MVP: Manuel Sequera, SS, Tigers East
Manager of the Year: Rafael Valenzuela, Rays

DEPARTMENT LEADERS

BATTING

OBP	Tsung-Che Cheng, FCL Pirates Gold	.449
SLG	Rodolfo Nolasco, FCL Pirates Gold	.552
OPS	Danuerys De La Cruz, FCL Tigers East	.975
R	Alexander Vargas, FCL Yankees	37
H	Kala'i Rosario, FCL Twins	52
TB	Manuel Sequera, FCL Tigers East	87
XBH	Manuel Sequera, FCL Tigers East	23
2B	Raul Beracierta, FCL Mets	16
2B	Eddinson Paulino, FCL Red Sox	16
3B	Ian Lewis, FCL Marlins	5
HR	Manuel Sequera, FCL Tigers East	11
RBI	Kala'i Rosario, FCL Twins	40
RBI	Manuel Sequera, FCL Tigers East	40
SAC	Ethan Workinger, FCL Braves	5
BB	Danuerys De La Cruz, FCL Tigers East	31
BB	Rayber Romero, FCL Pirates Black	31
HBP	Roilan Machandy, FCL Astros	12
SO	Adinso Reyes, FCL Tigers East	73
SB	Roilan Machandy, FCL Astros	30
CS	Alexander Vargas, FCL Yankees	8
CS	Luis Durango, ACL Indians	7
AB/SO	Tsung-Che Cheng, FCL Pirates Gold	8.71

FIELDING

C	PCT	Ricardo Olivar, FCL Twins	.993
	PO	Mario Fernandez, FCL Rays	274
	A	Brayan Hernandez, FCL Orioles Black	33
	DP	Mario Fernandez, FCL Rays	3
	E	3 players	7
	CS	Brayan Hernandez, FCL Orioles Black	20
	SB	Danuerys De La Cruz, FCL Tigers East	47
	SB	Brayan Hernandez, FCL Orioles Black	47
	PB	Agustin Ramirez, FCL Yankees	12
1B	PCT	Franrielis Bastardo, FCL Pirates Black	.995
	PO	Mahki Backstrom, FCL Braves	229
	A	Zach Zubia, FCL Marlins	14
	DP	Mahki Backstrom, FCL Braves	30
	E	Josue Cruz, FCL Orioles Black	9
2B	PCT	Rayber Romero, FCL Pirates Black	.964
	PO	Frank Veliz, FCL Tigers West	66
	A	Frank Veliz, FCL Tigers West	102
	DP	Frank Veliz, FCL Tigers West	25
	E	Yoneiry Acevedo, FCL Tigers East	11
3B	PCT	Marcos Cabrera, FCL Yankees	.887
	PO	Marcos Cabrera, FCL Yankees	30
	A	Marcos Cabrera, FCL Yankees	56
	DP	Emmanuel Sanchez, FCL Blue Jays	5
	DP	Brandon Hernandez, FCL Cardinals	5
	E	Adinso Reyes, FCL Tigers East	11
	E	Marcos Cabrera, FCL Yankees	11
SS	PCT	Alexander Vargas, FCL Yankees	.941
	PO	Jeremy Rivas, FCL Cardinals	47
	A	Jeremy Rivas, FCL Cardinals	111
	DP	Jeremy Rivas, FCL Cardinals	20
	DP	Manuel Sequera, FCL Tigers East	20
	E	Isaac De Leon, FCL Orioles Orange	15
OF	PCT	4 players	1.000
	PO	Jimmy Mojica, FCL Tigers East, FCL Tigers West	87
	A	Jimmy Mojica, FCL Tigers East, FCL Tigers West	9
	DP	5 players	2
	E	Luis Gonzalez, FCL Orioles Black, FCL Orioles Orange	5

PITCHING

G	Jesus Cruz FCL Tigers East	20
GS	Adolfo Bauza, FCL Tigers West	13
GF	Merfy Andrew, FCL Red Sox	15
SV	Maicor Leon, FCL Rays	7
SV	Omar Sanchez, FCL Cardinals	7
W	4 players	5
L	Daniele Di Monte, FCL Tigers West	8
IP	Luis Vizcaino, FCL Marlins	49.1
H	Jonatan Bernal, FCL Blue Jays	56
H	Ricardo Silva, FCL Tigers East	56
R	Hendry Nunez, FCL Tigers East	45
ER	Hendry Nunez, FCL Tigers East	40
HB	3 players	10
BB	Yefri Carrillo, FCL Astros	38
SO	Yaifer Perdomo, FCL Blue Jays	59
SO/9	Yaifer Perdomo, FCL Blue Jays	16.09
SO/9 (RP)	Ronaldo Alesandro, FCL Braves	15.14
BB/9	Samuel Perez, FCL Twins	1.21
WP	Wilmer A. Fenelon, FCL Tigers West	14
BK	Develson Aria, FCL Twins	9
HRA	3 players	8
BAA	Luis Vizcaino, FCL Marlins	.198

	TRIPLE-A EAST	TRIPLE-A WEST	DOUBLE-A CENTRAL	DOUBLE-A NORTHEAST	DOUBLE-A SOUTH
Best Batting Prospect	Wander Franco	Jake Meyers	Bobby Witt Jr	Adley Rutschman	Jose Barrero
Best Power Prospect	Jesus Sanchez	Jo Adell	MJ Melendez	Adley Rutschman	Shea Langeliers
Best Plate Discipline	Wander Franco	Yonny Hernandez	Nick Pratto	Austin Martin	Xavier Edwards
Best Baserunner	Kyle Isbel	Jake McCarthy	Bobby Witt Jr.	Samad Taylor	Justin Dean
Fastest Baserunner	Vidal Brujan	Jake McCarthy	Bobby Witt Jr.	Michael Beltre	Justin Dean
Best Pitching Prospect	Shane Baz	Josiah Gray	Cole Winn	Grayson Rodriguez	Nick Lodolo
Best Fastball	Hunter Greene	Julian Fernandez	Nick Snyder	Cade Cavalli	Hunter Greene
Best Breaking Pitch	Aaron Ashby	A.J. Puk	Matt Brash	Cade Cavalli	Nick Lodolo
Best Changeup	Jackson Kowar	Packy Naughton	Ryan Pepiot	Brayan Bello	Ethan Small
Best Control	Matt Liberatore	Darren McCaughan	Josh Winder	Caleb Kilian	Max Meyer
Best Reliever	Francisco Perez	Joe Barlow	Nick Snyder	R.J. Dabovich	Colton Hock
Best Defensive C	Payton Henry	Brian Serven	Matt Whatley	Adley Rutschman	Shea Langeliers
Best Defensive 1B	Lewin Diaz	Taylor Jones	Nick Pratto	Triston Casas	David MacKinnon
Best Defensive 2B	Andres Gimenez	Luis Rengifo	Jax Biggers	Jackson Cluff	Xavier Edwards
Best Defensive 3B	Emmanuel Rivera	Drew Ellis	Nolan Gorman	Oswaldo Cabrera	CJ Alexander
Best Defensive SS	Taylor Walls	Alan Trejo	Nick Allen	Ryan Kreidler	Braden Shewmake
Best Infield Arm	Gabriel Arias	Jake Gatewood	Bobby Witt Jr.	Oneil Cruz	Braden Shewmake
Best Defensive OF	Cristian Pache	Jake Meyers	Donovan Casey	Chavez Young	Justin Dean
Best OF Arm	Cristian Pache	Leody Taveras	Donovan Casey	Will Benson	Micker Adolfo
Most Exciting Player	Bobby Witt Jr.	Jo Adell	Bobby Witt Jr.	Oneil Cruz	Shea Langeliers
Best Manager Prospect	Brady Williams	Blake Lalli	Jared Goedert	Buck Britton	Justin Jirschele

	HIGH-A CENTRAL	HIGH-A EAST	HIGH-A WEST	LOW-A EAST	LOW-A SOUTHEAST	LOW-A WEST
Best Batting Prospect	Ryan Ward	Matt Fraizer	Austin Shenton	Joe Gray	Anthony Volpe	Luis Matos
Best Power Prospect	Andy Pages	Jesse Franklin	Michael Toglia	Joey Wiemer	Orelvis Martinez	Josh Mears
Best Plate Discipline	Justin Yurchak	Josh Smith	Tanner Morris	Gabe Holt	Edouard Julien	Robert Hassell
Best Baserunner	Max Schuemann	Greg Jones	Cameron Eden	Jayce Easley	Anthony Volpe	Eddy Diaz
Fastest Baserunner	David Hamilton	Greg Jones	Jordyn Adams	Jayce Easley	Steward Berroa	D'Shawn Knowles
Best Pitching Prospect	Bobby Miller	Cade Cavalli	George Kirby	Taj Bradley	Mick Abel	Ryan Murphy
Best Fastball	Bobby Miller	Cade Cavalli	George Kirby	Spencer Strider	Oliver Mateo	Kyle Harrison
Best Breaking Pitch	Daniel Espino	Luis Medina	Matt Brash	Jeremy Wu-Yelland	Oliver Mateo	Carlos Duran
Best Changeup	Landon Knack	Jared Shuster	Levi Stoudt	Ian Seymour	Adrian Hernandez	Blake Walston
Best Control	Zach McCambley	Jayden Murray	George Kirby	Emilio Marquez	J.T. Ginn	Ryan Murphy
Best Reliever	Will Klein	Felix Bautista	Chris Wright	Marc Church	Enmanuel Mejia	Chase Walter
Best Defensive C	Dillon Dingler	Blake Hunt	Nick D'Alesandro	Yainer Diaz	Cooper Johnson	Drew Romo
Best Defensive 1B	Joe Naranjo	Evan Edwards	Michael Toglia	Harvin Mendoza	PK Morris	Lawrence Butler
Best Defensive 2B	Michael Massey	Ezequiel Duran	Kaden Polcovich	Luisangel Acuña	Brandon Leyton	Eddy Diaz
Best Defensive 3B	Jake Slaughter	Jared Triolo	Aaron Schunk	Gunnar Henderson	Dariel Lopez	Casey Schmitt
Best Defensive SS	Jose Tena	Ronny Mauricio	Luis de los Santos	Freddy Zamora	Nasim Nuñez	Ezequiel Tovar
Best Infield Arm	Jose Tena	Ronny Mauricio	Blaze Alexander	Gunnar Henderson	Masyn Winn	Noelvi Marte
Best Defensive OF	Mike Siani	Michael Harris	Cameron Eden	Ceddanne Rafaela	Yhoswar Garcia	Robert Hassell
Best OF Arm	Andy Pages	Michael Harris	Eduardo Diaz	Joey Wiemer	Daniel Rivero	Jose Ramos
Most Exciting Player	Andy Pages	Ronny Mauricio	Julio Rodriguez	Joey Wiemer	Anthony Volpe	Zac Veen
Best Manager Prospect	Greg Discenzo	Jeff Smith	Louis Boyd	Joe Ayrault	David Adams	Mike McCoy

BY MATT EDDY

Many leagues received makeovers in 2021 after Major League Baseball took control of the minor leagues.

The Dominican Summer League carried on as usual. If anything, the league was stronger than ever as organizations continue to place more emphasis on developing Latin American players.

The DSL fielded 46 teams in 2021, one more than it had in 2019 and 13 more than in 2011. Even accounting for the defunct Venezuelan Summer League, MLB organizations fielded just 39 total Latin American complex teams a decade ago.

Among the players who gained valuable pro experience in the DSL after signing in January were 17-year-old shortstops Armando Cruz (Nationals), Carlos Colmenarez (Rays), Cristian Hernandez (Cubs), Cristian Santana (Tigers) and Wilman Diaz (Dodgers).

League MVP Adrian Pinto of the Rockies hit .360/.486/.543 with a DSL-leading 41 stolen bases. He is an 18-year-old Venezuelan second baseman.

ALL-STAR TEAM

C: Omar Martinez, Yankees2.
1B: Daniel Montesino, Padres.
2B: Adrian Pinto, Rockies.
SS: Leosdany Molina, Astros.
3B: Lyonell James, Red Sox.
OF: Yanquiel Fernandez, Rockies.
OF: Luis Paredes, Rockies.
OF: Samuel Zavala, Padres.
DH: Ismael Padua, Rangers1.
RHP: Jose Cedeño, Nationals.
LHP: Elvis Contreras, Rays2.
RP: Hugo Beltran, Orioles2.
MVP: Adrian Pinto, 2B, Rockies.
Manager of the Year: Eugenio Jose, Rockies.

NO PLAYOFFS: The DSL Blue Jays had the best record and were recognized as league champions.

NORTH

Team	W	L	PCT	GB
DSL Red Sox Blue	38	20	.655	—
DSL Rangers1	36	21	.632	1.5
DSL Pirates Black	34	22	.607	3
DSL Dodgers Shoemaker	29	28	.509	8.5
DSL Rays2	28	31	.475	10.5
DSL Cubs Blue	26	33	.441	12.5
DSL Royals White	20	32	.385	15
DSL Indians Red	21	38	.356	17.5

SOUTH

Team	W	L	PCT	GB
DSL Rockies	37	22	.627	—
DSL Phillies Red	33	24	.579	3
DSL Nationals	34	25	.576	3
DSL Angels	32	26	.552	4.5
DSL Yankees1	31	28	.525	6
DSL Mets1	25	33	.431	11.5
DSL Cardinals Blue	21	38	.356	16
DSL Twins	21	38	.356	16

NORTHWEST

Team	W	L	PCT	GB
DSL Royals Blue	32	20	.615	—
DSL Indians Blue	34	25	.576	1.5
DSL Dodgers Bautista	32	25	.561	2.5
DSL Red Sox Red	31	27	.534	4
DSL Rays1	29	30	.492	6.5
DSL Astros	24	34	.414	11
DSL Marlins	23	34	.404	11.5
DSL Athletics	20	36	.357	14

BASEBALL CITY

Team	W	L	PCT	GB
DSL Blue Jays	38	19	.667	—
DSL Padres	37	21	.638	1.5
DSL Reds	30	27	.526	8
DSL White Sox	26	33	.441	13
DSL D-backs1	23	36	.390	16
DSL Orioles1	13	39	.250	22.5

SAN PEDRO

Team	W	L	PCT	GB
DSL Phillies White	36	20	.643	—
DSL Rangers2	34	24	.586	3
DSL Brewers1	31	28	.525	6.5
DSL Cubs Red	28	30	.483	9
DSL Mets2	27	29	.482	9
DSL Cardinals Red	27	30	.474	9.5
DSL Giants Black	24	28	.462	10
DSL Tigers	23	36	.390	14.5

NORTHEAST

Team	W	L	PCT	GB
DSL Colorado	39	20	.661	—
DSL Mariners	35	24	.593	4
DSL Yankees2	30	29	.508	9
DSL Giants Orange	27	27	.500	9.5
DSL Brewers2	29	30	.492	10
DSL D-backs2	27	32	.458	12
DSL Orioles2	25	30	.455	12
DSL Pirates Gold	19	37	.339	18.5

INDIVIDUAL BATTING LEADERS

Player, Team	AVG	G	AB	R	H	2B	3B	HR	RBI	BB	SO	SB
Francisco Fajardo, DSL Blue Jays	.365	51	167	42	61	7	4	1	15	19	12	30
Adrian Pinto, DSL Rockies	.360	54	175	64	63	15	4	3	27	38	18	41
Pedro Ramirez, DSL Cubs Red	.359	50	195	37	70	11	7	1	30	13	20	9
Gabe Moncada, DSL Mariners	.358	54	159	29	57	16	2	4	30	37	46	2
Carlos Jorge, DSL Reds	.346	47	159	38	55	8	10	3	33	24	32	27
Jesus Bugarin, DSL Colorado	.339	51	165	37	56	6	0	4	31	18	25	14
Yanquiel Fernandez, DSL Rockies	.333	54	177	29	59	17	0	6	34	22	26	0
Maycol Justo, DSL Cardinals Blue	.331	47	166	38	55	5	2	1	14	21	25	6
Erick Brito, DSL Phillies White	.327	54	153	29	50	4	1	0	21	40	28	20
Luis Encarnacion, DSL Astros	.320	55	169	23	54	11	2	1	25	19	22	15

INDIVIDUAL PITCHING LEADERS

Player, Team	W	L	ERA	G	GS	CG	SV	IP	H	R	ER	BB	SO
Joel Diaz, DSL Mets2	0	2	0.54	15	15	0	0	50	29	9	3	9	63
Elvis Contreras, DSL Rays2	4	2	1.17	13	6	0	0	54	38	17	7	13	61
Kevin Ribon, DSL Mets1	3	1	1.20	17	8	0	0	53	39	15	7	13	40
Jose Cedeno, DSL Nationals	5	0	1.24	12	10	0	0	58	32	9	8	11	73
Stiven Cruz, DSL Brewers1	3	3	1.37	12	11	0	0	53	31	13	8	23	73
Jean Cabrera, DSL Phillies White	3	2	1.54	13	13	0	0	53	34	13	9	10	61
Jose Atencio, DSL Nationals	5	4	1.58	11	8	0	0	51	40	11	9	4	61
Joel Valdez, DSL Phillies Red	1	1	1.63	15	15	0	0	55	43	12	10	16	54
Diego Navarro, DSL Indians Blue	1	2	1.69	12	11	0	0	48	30	12	9	8	44
Manuel Urias, DSL Phillies Red	2	2	1.82	14	14	0	0	54	43	14	11	6	63

Excellence That Starts Off The Field

Triple-A

LAS VEGAS (TRIPLE-A WEST)

With the bright lights of the casinos on the famed Las Vegas strip illuminating and the attraction of the NHL's Vegas Golden Knights and the NFL's Las Vegas Raiders, there are certainly a lot of choices for the entertainment dollar in this desert city. But just 11 miles west of the strip and 7 to 10 degrees cooler, sits one of the finest ballparks in minor league baseball.

Las Vegas Ballpark, home to the Aviators, the Triple-A affiliate of the Athletics, is an 8,196-seat state-of-the-art ballpark located on eight acres in downtown Summerlin. The Aviators averaged 6,590 fans in 2021 despite a 50% seating capacity early in the season due to Covid-19 restrictions. There were six sellouts, including a season-high crowd of 10,190 on July 3 against Sacramento.

Baseball America has chosen Las Vegas as the recipient of the Triple-A Freitas Award. The Freitas Awards, named after longtime minor league baseball ambassador Bob Freitas, have been presented by BA annually since 1989 and recognize franchises for their community involvement, long-term business success and consistent operational excellence.

Double-A

HARTFORD (DOUBLE-A NORTHEAST)

By now, Hartford Yard Goats general manager Mike Abramson has a pretty good idea of what team owner Josh Solomon wants to know when he's on the other end of the phone during one of his frequent calls during the season.

Abramson explained it like this:

"He's not asking what the gate was or what we made at concessions, he wants to know if they completed the wave or, if we're having one of our Los Chivos nights or Copa nights. He wants to know if we had a good turnout from the population we

were honoring," Abramson said.

"He is super focused on the experience."

It's that commitment to customer service from the top down, and the successful execution of it, that made the Yard Goats this year's recipient of Baseball America's Bob Freitas Award at the Double-A level.

An affiliate of the Rockies that turned in the Double-A Northeast's worst record on the field at 39-79, Hartford once again excelled off of it, leading the circuit in attendance for a third straight season with a whopping 287,752 customers making their way through the gates at Dunkin Donuts Park this past year.

Tightly nestled in downtown Hartford, the 6,121-seat ballpark opened up in 2017, and has remained in pristine condition ever since, thanks in large part to an unmatched sense of pride from those who work for the organization.

Class A

GREENSBORO (HIGH-A EAST)

When the Greensboro Grasshoppers received the go-ahead that the 2021 season would happen, it came without the off-field equivalent of much of a spring training.

So president and general manager Donald Moore and vice president of baseball operations Katie Dannemiller relied on a foundation that had developed for more than a decade to pull it all together.

By summer, First National Bank Field was hopping again with excitement. As a bonus, the High-A East affiliate of the Pirates was stocked with prospects.

But the off-field successes might have been what allowed the Grasshoppers to stand out. Because of that, the club was named the Class A winner of the Bob Freitas Award, honoring excellence on the business side of operations.

LAST 10 WINNERS

	TRIPLE-A	DOUBLE-A	CLASS A	SHORT-SEASON
2010:	Louisville (International)	Corpus Christi (Texas)	Lynchburg (Carolina)	Idaho Falls (Pioneer)
2011:	Colo. Springs (Pacific Coast)	Harrisburg (Eastern)	Fort Wayne (Midwest)	Vancouver (Northwest)
2012:	Lehigh Valley (International)	N-West Arkansas (Texas)	Greenville (South Atlantic)	Billings (Pioneer)
2013:	Indianapolis (International)	Tulsa (Texas)	Clearwater (Florida State)	State College (NY-Penn)
2014:	Charlotte (International)	Montgomery (Southern)	West Michigan (Midwest)	Brooklyn (NY-Penn)
2015:	Salt Lake (Pacific Coast)	Richmond (Eastern)	Myrtle Beach (Carolina)	Grand Junction (Pioneer)
2016:	Round Rock (Pacific Coast)	Pensacola (Southern)	San Bernardino (California)	Pulaski (Appalachian)
2017:	Fresno (Pacific Coast)	Reading (Eastern)	Charleston (South Atlantic)	Hillsboro (Northwest)
2018:	Oklahoma City (Pacific Coast)	Tennessee (Southern)	Winston-Salem (Carolina)	Spokane (Northwest)
2019:	Nashville (Pacific Coast)	Tulsa (Texas)	Lexington (South Atlantic)	Hudson Valley (NY-Penn)

BY KYLE GLASER

Mesa defeated Surprise, 6-0, in the Arizona Fall League championship game at Salt River Fields on Nov. 20, concluding the 2021 AFL season.

Mesa was led by Cubs righthander Caleb Kilian, who turned in an outstanding outing when it mattered most.

Kilian pitched six perfect innings with eight strikeouts in a masterful performance and was named MVP of the championship game. The 24-year-old righthander effortlessly sliced through Surprise's lineup and completed his six innings in just 68 pitches.

Kilian reached 98.1 mph in the first inning, the hardest thrown pitch of the game, to set the tone immediately. His fastball ranged from 92-98 mph and sat 94-95 with alternating cut, sink and ride to keep Surprise's hitters waving through it fruitlessly. His sharp 86-90 mph cutter dove across the plate to get empty, off-balance swings and his twirling 75-77 mph curveball froze batters again and again. He didn't have command of his 83-86 mph changeup, but he hardly needed his fourth pitch.

"It was one of those days where kind of all of your stuff feels like it's on," said Kilian, who the Cubs acquired from the Giants in the Kris Bryant trade last summer. "I felt like all my pitches were working. I was throwing a lot of fastballs early on and I started mixing the other stuff and it started to come."

Kilian threw 48 of his 68 pitches for strikes and was ruthlessly efficient. He retired 16 of his 18 batters in five pitches or less.

The outing was a climactic finish to a breakthrough fall for the Texas Tech product. He surrendered five hits and seven runs without recording an out in his first AFL start. After that, he allowed only one earned run in his final 20 innings, including Saturday's masterpiece.

"I'm not making excuses, it was a terrible outing," Kilian said, "but it feels good to go from having one of my worst outings at the beginning of this league to one of the best at the end."

Here are the other top performers from the championship game, led by Mesa third baseman Logan Davidson.

Logan Davidson, 3B, Athletics (Mesa)

Davidson led Mesa's offense in support of Kilian, going 3-for-4 with a double, a walk, an RBI, a run scored and a stolen base. The switch-hitting infielder started Mesa's three-run first inning with a double down the right field line, smoked a single 110.5 mph off the bat in the second inning and dropped an RBI single into right field in the sixth to cap the scoring.

Davidson also showed smooth actions and an accurate arm while converting every play cleanly at third base and showed off his speed when he slid into second base just ahead of an on-target throw from Nationals catcher Drew Millas on his stolen base in the sixth.

Including the championship game, Davidson finished his time in the AFL batting .299 with five doubles, two home runs and 12 RBIs in 21 games.

JJ Bleday, OF, Marlins (Mesa)

Bleday had a sensational showing in the AFL and finished his time in Arizona strong. He reached base twice and drove in a pair of runs for Mesa and did most of his damage early to help the Solar Sox race out to a commanding lead.

Bleday showed a discerning eye in laying off close pitches from Reds lefthander Jacques Pucheau to draw a walk in the first inning and help set the table for Mesa's three-run frame. He lifted a sacrifice fly into center field to bring home a run in the second inning and extend the lead to 4-0, and he turned around a 96 mph fastball from Jackson Rutledge for a hard liner back up the middle in the fourth to single home another run that made it 5-0.

Bleday also stung a hard line drive the opposite way to left field in the eighth that was caught for a lineout.

Jackson Rutledge, RHP, Nationals (Surprise)

Rutledge had a difficult AFL on the heels of an injury-riddled season, but he flashed the ability that made him a first-round pick during a 3.1-inning relief appearance. Rutledge entered in the third inning and struck out the side to stop the early bleeding for Surprise. He continued to rack up swings and misses throughout his outing and finished with seven strikeouts.

Rutledge's 95-98 mph fastball was an effective pitch when he located it, but his 82-85 mph slider was his most dominant offering. Five of his seven strikeouts came on his slider, a promising development after his breaking ball was a focal point of his in the AFL. He also showed an effective 86-88 mph changeup with late dive that got both a called strike and a swing and miss.

Rutledge fell into ruts with his consistency and control—he threw only 38 of 73 pitches for strikes—and allowed three hits and two runs. Still, his flash of three swing-and-miss pitches represented a promising step forward.

MINOR LEAGUES

STANDINGS

East	W	L	PCT	GB
Mesa Solar Sox	15	13	.536	—
Scottsdale Scorpions	12	18	.400	4
Salt River Rafters	10	20	.333	6

West	W	L	PCT	GB
Surprise Saguaros	17	12	.586	—
Peoria Javelinas	17	12	.586	—
Glendale Desert Dogs	17	13	.567	0.5

INDIVIDUAL BATTING LEADERS
(Minimum 2 Plate Appearances/League Games)

Player, Team	AVG	G	AB	R	H	HR	RBI
Jose Tena, Scottsdale	.387	17	62	16	24	0	9
Nelson Velazquez, Mesa	.385	26	104	24	40	9	24
Nick Gonzales, Peoria	.380	19	71	18	27	2	13
Spencer Horwitz, Mesa	.375	16	64	14	24	1	12
Triston Casas, Scottsdale	.372	21	78	19	29	1	11
Elijah Dunham, Surprise	.357	23	84	15	30	2	14
Drew Lugbauer, Peoria	.346	16	52	14	18	6	18
Austin Wells, Surprise	.344	18	64	14	22	2	18
Jackson Cluff, Surprise	.342	22	79	18	27	1	14
Jacob Amaya, Glendale	.333	19	54	14	18	3	6

INDIVIDUAL PITCHING LEADERS
(Minimum .4 Innings Pitched/League Games)

Player, Team	W	L	ERA	IP	H	BB	SO
Joe Record, Glendale	0	0	0.00	14	5	4	14
Andre Pallante, Glendale	1	1	1.29	21	17	10	22
Zack Thompson, Glendale	3	0	1.56	17	14	15	22
Coleman Crow, Glendale	1	0	1.59	17	15	2	20
Owen White, Surprise	5	0	1.91	28	20	13	29
Jacques Pucheu, Surprise	1	0	1.93	14	10	4	13
Garrett Hill, Salt River	2	1	1.98	14	15	3	21
Zach Linginfelter, Glendale	2	1	2.19	12	11	8	10
Slade Cecconi, Salt River	1	0	2.40	15	15	7	14
Nick Vespi, Mesa	3	1	2.51	14	11	7	17

GLENDALE DESERT DOGS

Name	AVG	AB	R	H	2B	3B	HR	RBI	BB	SO	SB
Amaya, Jacob	.333	54	14	18	3	0	3	6	13	13	1
Cespedes, Yoelqui	.181	72	8	13	3	0	1	2	2	22	2
Donovan, Brendan	.308	52	10	16	5	0	2	8	10	8	2
Gorman, Nolan	.375	16	8	6	1	0	1	4	7	2	2
Hoese, Kody	.200	55	7	11	1	0	2	5	3	17	0
Jackson, Jeremiah	.161	56	10	9	1	0	3	10	2	23	0
Kessinger, Grae	.277	65	13	18	2	1	2	12	11	10	0
Lee, Korey	.258	62	8	16	2	0	1	6	9	19	1
Leon, Pedro	.257	70	9	18	3	0	1	9	13	20	4
Martinez, Orlando	.215	79	5	17	2	2	1	4	2	14	0
Mulrine, Anthony	.111	45	3	5	1	0	0	5	3	11	0
Nootbaar, Lars	.314	70	21	22	6	1	5	13	14	15	0
Outman, James	.284	67	17	19	7	1	3	11	15	23	2
Rodriguez, Jose	.226	62	5	14	1	1	1	13	4	10	2
Sanchez, Yolbert	.400	35	4	14	1	0	1	8	10	2	1
Taylor, Carson	.297	37	3	11	0	0	2	6	1	9	0
Yepez, Juan	.302	86	15	26	8	0	7	26	12	18	1

Name	W	L	ERA	G	GS	SV	IP	H	BB	SO	AVG
Belge, Jeff	0	1	19.96	9	0	0	8	9	15	12	.300
Burns, Nathan	2	0	0.96	9	0	2	9	3	5	10	.094
Crow, Coleman	1	0	1.59	6	3	0	17	15	2	20	.238
Dominguez, Johan	1	2	10.50	6	5	0	12	24	7	14	.429
Donato, Chad	1	1	6.30	4	0	0	20	26	6	17	.306
Freeman, Caleb	0	1	1.69	11	0	0	11	9	6	11	.231
Freure, R.J.	1	1	7.98	8	1	0	15	14	14	12	.250
Hicks, Jordan	0	0	9.64	2	2	0	5	4	4	5	.211
Hurt, Kyle	0	1	5.93	10	0	2	14	10	12	13	.222
Knack, Landon	1	0	3.68	5	2	0	15	13	5	16	.241
Linginfelter, Zach	2	1	2.19	10	0	0	12	11	8	10	.224
Macuare, Angel	1	0	4.50	3	2	0	6	1	4	4	.053
Miller, Bobby	0	1	9.90	5	3	0	10	10	7	10	.263
Moore, McKinley	0	0	4.22	10	0	0	11	11	5	9	.275
Olson, J.B.	1	1	6.23	10	0	0	13	15	2	12	.294
Pallante, Andre	1	1	1.29	7	4	0	21	17	10	22	.221

Pina, Robinson | 2 | 1 | 3.63 | 6 | 4 | 0 | 17 | 16 | 6 | 16 | .246

Pina, Robinson	2	1	3.63	6	4	0	17	16	6	16	.246
Record, Joe	0	0	0.00	9	0	2	14	5	4	14	.111
Thompson, Zack	3	0	1.56	9	0	1	17	14	15	22	.215
Walsh, Jake	0	1	8.10	11	0	4	10	15	6	10	.357

MESA SOLAR SOX

Name	AVG	AB	R	H	2B	3B	HR	RBI	BB	SO	SB
Banfield, Will	.231	39	8	9	2	0	1	8	5	7	0
Beck, Austin	.170	53	9	9	2	0	0	9	5	23	1
Bleday, JJ	.316	95	20	30	8	2	5	24	20	23	2
Bride, Jonah	.250	52	15	13	2	0	3	8	16	12	0
Cullen, Greg	.279	43	11	12	2	0	3	14	9	10	0
Davidson, Logan	.274	73	14	20	4	0	2	11	15	33	1
Diaz, Yusniel	.222	27	7	6	3	0	1	9	7	10	0
Eierman, Jeremy	.097	31	3	3	0	0	0	0	5	14	0
Horwitz, Spencer	.375	64	14	24	4	0	1	12	9	11	4
Jimenez, Leo	.237	38	6	9	4	0	0	4	8	8	1
Johnston, Troy	.296	71	15	21	3	0	0	11	9	21	2
Misner, Kameron	.205	78	21	16	3	0	7	14	20	34	4
Moreno, Gabriel	.312	93	16	29	11	0	1	19	14	14	0
Rodriguez, Ramon	.231	26	4	6	1	0	1	3	4	5	0
Stowers, Kyle	.200	10	2	2	1	0	0	1	2	6	0
Vazquez, Luis	.194	62	12	12	1	1	1	8	7	25	3
Velazquez, Nelson	.382	110	27	42	8	0	9	25	18	37	0
Weber, Andy	.273	88	19	24	3	4	2	20	17	24	0

Name	W	L	ERA	G	GS	SV	IP	H	BB	SO	AVG
Bishop, Cameron	1	0	8.03	5	2	0	12	10	15	11	.217
Conley, Bryce	0	0	5.23	10	0	2	10	12	9	7	.300
Correa, Danis	0	0	10.13	3	0	0	3	4	5	4	.333
Criswell, Jeff	2	1	6.75	6	3	0	23	26	12	32	.292
Dominguez, Michael	1	2	4.98	6	6	0	22	17	13	22	.207
Evans, Justin	0	1	10.29	6	0	0	7	13	4	6	.394
Finfrock, Cre	1	0	7.11	10	0	0	13	13	13	12	.265
Fitterer, Evan	1	1	3.86	2	2	0	7	8	4	9	.286
Gillaspie, Logan	0	1	9.00	5	2	0	14	18	7	18	.300
Harris, Hogan	0	1	7.20	6	2	0	10	7	14	14	.194
Jensen, Ryan	2	1	9.64	6	4	0	19	29	12	20	.363
Kilian, Caleb	1	0	5.14	5	2	0	14	12	5	18	.222
King, Zach	0	0	6.48	4	2	0	8	11	9	10	.306
Loeprich, Conner	2	1	8.38	6	4	0	19	32	18	15	.400
Rodning, Brody	0	1	7.71	11	0	0	12	14	5	16	.292
Santos, Pedro	0	1	16.20	5	0	0	5	8	7	3	.381
Simpson, Josh	0	0	6.08	9	0	1	13	9	10	18	.188
Spraker, Graham	0	0	0.00	11	0	3	11	4	2	17	.111
Vespi, Nick	3	1	2.51	10	1	0	14	11	7	17	.212
Whittlesey, Brock	1	1	9.00	11	0	0	13	22	3	8	.379
Yan, Jefry	0	0	8.31	9	0	0	9	8	9	18	.242

PEORIA JAVELINAS

Name	AVG	AB	R	H	2B	3B	HR	RBI	BB	SO	SB
Bae, Ji-hwan	.250	92	23	23	4	1	2	11	13	21	8
Batten, Matt	.270	63	11	17	2	0	0	7	12	14	4
Caballero, Jose	.224	58	4	13	1	0	1	11	5	19	4
DeLoach, Zach	.162	68	9	11	2	1	1	9	17	23	0
Franklin V, Jesse	.098	51	10	5	1	0	1	5	12	23	0
Gonzales, Nick	.380	71	18	27	4	1	2	13	13	14	4
Lugbauer, Drew	.346	52	14	18	0	0	6	18	10	20	0
Marlowe, Cade	.233	73	18	17	5	0	0	7	17	23	7
Muzziotti, Simon	.241	79	11	19	1	0	0	13	17	14	3
O'Hoppe, Logan	.299	77	19	23	8	0	3	17	21	15	3
Rosario, Eguy	.250	64	9	16	3	0	1	12	8	13	2
Seagle, Chandler	.233	30	6	7	2	0	1	7	1	8	0
Smith-Njigba, Canaan	.298	57	12	17	6	1	0	2	15	18	5
Stott, Bryson	.318	88	20	28	7	1	2	31	24	14	5
Waddell, Luke	.311	61	11	19	5	0	0	9	9	8	3

Name	W	L	ERA	G	GS	SV	IP	H	BB	SO	AVG
Arias, Dayeison	0	0	27.00	1	0	0	1	3	1	2	.600
Bellomy, Bear	1	0	3.86	8	0	0	12	10	4	9	.227
Burrows, Michael	1	0	3.52	5	1	0	15	13	5	16	.236
Contreras, Roansy	2	1	3.21	5	5	0	14	10	4	18	.196
Cosgrove, Tom	1	0	9.00	9	0	0	7	13	5	3	.419
Crouse, Hans	1	1	5.06	4	4	0	16	12	9	24	.211
Curvelo, Luis	0	0	7.11	6	0	0	13	14	4	15	.269
Diaz, Indigo	1	1	12.79	7	0	0	6	9	9	8	.333

Name	W	L	ERA	G	GS	SV	IP	H	BB	SO	AVG
Gore, MacKenzie	0	0	6.35	3	3	0	11	15	6	8	.319
Higginbotham, Jake	0	0	12.15	8	0	0	7	11	7	5	.367
Jones, Damon	1	0	0.87	8	0	1	10	7	7	14	.206
Kuhn, Travis	0	0	0.96	8	0	3	9	6	4	8	.182
McArthur, James	1	0	8.10	5	5	0	17	21	7	18	.292
Miller, Erik	0	0	1.80	6	0	0	10	6	7	12	.188
Mlodzinski, Carmen	1	0	4.91	7	0	1	11	9	5	9	.220
Quezada, Jose	1	2	4.66	8	0	1	10	12	2	8	.308
Scholtens, Jesse	0	1	2.38	8	0	0	11	10	6	10	.250
Sweet, Devin	1	0	4.32	8	0	0	8	6	4	11	.194
Then, Juan	1	3	12.46	4	3	0	13	20	9	16	.339
Vodnik, Victor	2	2	5.70	6	4	0	24	21	14	25	.239
Waldron, Matt	0	0	3.00	5	0	0	9	9	1	8	.257
Woods, William	1	1	4.29	6	5	0	21	19	10	20	.244

SALT RIVER RAFTERS

Name	AVG	AB	R	H	2B	3B	HR	RBI	BB	SO	SB
Baty, Brett	.292	89	16	26	5	1	1	15	11	31	1
Canzone, Dominic	.319	69	13	22	4	0	3	15	8	17	1
Cortes, Carlos	.236	55	7	13	2	1	0	5	10	18	0
De La Rosa, Eric	.220	59	8	13	1	0	2	7	5	19	4
Feliciano, Mario	.318	44	8	14	5	0	0	4	2	13	0
Gray Jr., Joe	.069	58	3	4	1	0	1	6	10	24	1
Hamilton, David	.293	41	5	12	3	2	0	5	12	6	4
Hummel, Cooper	.192	26	4	5	2	0	0	8	12	13	0
Kennedy, Buddy	.236	55	10	13	3	0	2	7	7	16	0
Kreidler, Ryan	.200	10	1	2	0	0	0	0	3	6	0
MacIver, Willie	.242	33	3	8	1	0	0	0	5	8	1
Reyes, Wilmer	.219	64	9	14	2	1	1	7	10	14	4
Senger, Hayden	.194	31	3	6	1	0	0	0	8	7	0
Toglia, Michael	.264	91	10	24	2	1	3	12	12	26	1
Torkelson, Spencer	.450	20	4	9	2	0	0	3	8	5	0
Tovar, Ezequiel	.161	87	10	14	2	0	3	10	5	20	2
Vilade, Ryan	.253	79	12	20	2	1	0	12	10	16	3
Wiemer, Joey	.467	30	6	14	3	0	1	4	4	5	2
Wilson, Weston	.214	14	3	3	1	0	0	0	3	7	0

Name	W	L	ERA	G	GS	SV	IP	H	BB	SO	AVG
Bird, Jake	0	1	2.84	12	0	1	13	14	8	12	.292
Bryant, Garrison	1	1	4.80	6	3	0	15	15	8	13	.259
Cecconi, Slade	1	0	2.40	5	3	0	15	15	7	14	.254
Curtis, Keegan	0	1	3.86	10	0	1	9	8	5	12	.235
Dennis, Matt	1	3	3.78	6	4	0	17	18	2	13	.273
Fernander, Chavez	0	0	3.38	8	0	1	8	4	6	7	.143
Flores, Wilmer	0	2	9.95	6	3	0	13	16	16	17	.308
Floyd, Taylor	0	0	7.27	9	0	0	9	11	6	10	.306
Grey, Connor	1	2	3.00	6	3	0	18	15	6	17	.214
Hess, Zack	0	1	9.00	10	0	0	10	14	7	12	.326
Hill, Garrett	2	1	1.98	5	3	0	14	15	3	21	.278
Hintzen, J.T.	0	1	5.02	11	0	0	14	9	5	16	.184
Holderman, Colin	0	1	8.71	11	0	2	10	10	7	10	.244
Jarvis, Justin	2	1	5.60	7	5	0	18	13	14	15	.206
Metoyer, Brian	0	1	10.45	10	0	0	10	10	10	17	.263
Sheffield, Jordan	0	0	0.00	1	0	0	1	0	1	0	.000
Stumpo, Mitchell	2	0	3.27	11	0	0	11	7	7	10	.189
Todd, Reagan	0	1	1.74	11	0	0	10	4	4	11	.114
Uribe, Abner	0	1	13.00	8	2	0	9	9	17	16	.257
Yoshikawa, Shumpei	0	2	5.00	7	4	0	18	17	12	15	.246
Zhao, Jolon	0	0	5.14	6	0	0	7	6	7	4	.222

SCOTTSDALE SCORPIONS

Name	AVG	AB	R	H	2B	3B	HR	RBI	BB	SO	SB
Amditis, Michael	.136	44	4	6	0	0	1	6	15	0	
Bailey, Patrick	.292	48	6	14	3	0	1	5	7	17	0
Bechtold, Andrew	.237	59	7	14	4	0	0	8	9	25	0
Bishop, Hunter	.262	42	4	11	5	0	0	6	8	20	1
Casas, Triston	.372	78	19	29	6	0	1	11	17	18	0
Cottam, Kole	.275	51	7	14	3	0	3	10	5	13	0
Downs, Jeter	.228	57	9	13	0	0	5	14	14	18	4
Dyer, Matthew	.173	52	8	9	1	0	1	6	6	19	4
Helman, Michael	.216	51	10	11	2	0	0	3	9	6	7
Hernandez, Heriberto	.133	15	2	2	0	0	0	2	3	5	1
Koss, Christian	.229	48	4	11	1	0	0	6	3	8	2
Luciano, Marco	.253	75	7	19	0	0	3	13	11	28	0
Mead, Curtis	.313	83	16	26	5	2	3	11	4	13	1
Palacios, Richie	.269	78	17	21	8	1	3	11	13	15	4
Qsar, Jordan	.200	25	3	5	0	0	2	5	3	8	1

Name	AVG	AB	R	H	2B	3B	HR	RBI	BB	SO	SB
Tena, Jose	.387	62	16	24	6	1	0	9	10	10	2
Wallner, Matt	.303	66	11	20	2	0	6	15	9	27	0
Wilson, Will	.164	67	9	11	3	0	2	8	6	19	0

Name	W	L	ERA	G	GS	SV	IP	H	BB	SO	AVG
Brigden, Trevor	1	0	4.73	11	0	0	13	15	8	8	.268
Casetta-Stubbs, Damon	0	1	5.59	9	0	0	10	10	10	10	.250
Cellucci, Brendan	0	1	6.94	10	0	0	12	15	7	11	.326
Corry, Seth	1	1	3.09	6	6	0	12	4	12	17	.105
Dabovich, R.J.	1	0	1.69	9	0	0	11	4	12	15	.114
Featherstone, Zach	0	1	8.10	11	0	0	10	13	9	12	.310
Funderburk, Kody	3	2	6.11	6	6	0	18	25	6	22	.325
Garcia, Carlos	2	0	3.60	9	0	0	15	14	5	15	.259
Laweryson, Cody	0	1	3.86	8	1	0	14	10	7	18	.189
Peguero, Matthew	1	0	3.60	8	0	0	10	7	12	.244	
Pinto, Aaron	0	2	6.75	9	0	0	12	18	6	13	.353
Politi, Andrew	0	0	5.84	11	0	2	12	15	8	10	.294
Sampen, Caleb	1	1	5.51	6	5	0	16	16	7	19	.250
Santos, Gregory	0	1	4.15	10	0	0	13	13	5	12	.271
Seabold, Connor	1	3	4.87	6	6	0	20	17	12	23	.224
Sisk, Evan	0	0	7.59	10	0	0	11	8	9	14	.200
Tully, Tanner	0	2	8.10	6	6	0	20	27	7	15	.325
Turner, Matt	0	2	12.27	8	0	0	11	20	6	8	.392
Waites, Cole	0	0	16.20	10	0	1	8	9	8	11	.273
Winckowski, Josh	1	0	6.55	6	0	0	11	15	4	3	.341

SURPRISE SAGUAROS

Name	AVG	AB	R	H	2B	3B	HR	RBI	BB	SO	SB
Casey, Donovan	.255	47	8	12	3	0	2	10	8	8	3
Chaparro, Andres	.268	82	18	22	9	0	4	17	13	20	0
Cluff, Jackson	.342	79	18	27	6	0	1	14	14	24	8
Dunham, Elijah	.357	84	15	30	6	3	2	14	14	10	11
Duran, Ezequiel	.278	72	16	20	7	4	3	12	5	9	0
Eaton, Nathan	.317	82	17	26	5	2	1	13	5	16	4
Foscue, Justin	.257	70	15	18	4	0	5	14	15	23	3
Huff, Sam	.167	24	2	4	0	0	0	1	4	8	0
Johnson, Ivan	.250	60	12	15	4	0	6	11	8	30	1
Matias, Seuly	.188	80	10	15	1	0	6	20	12	31	1
Means, Jake	.171	70	12	12	4	0	1	5	6	22	2
Millas, Drew	.196	51	8	10	1	0	1	5	13	4	3
Mount, Drew	.314	51	10	16	5	0	0	5	3	11	2
Pineda, Israel	.296	27	2	8	2	0	0	6	2	7	0
Siani, Michael	.300	40	11	12	3	0	1	6	10	9	10
Tresh, Luca	.125	24	1	3	1	0	0	1	0	8	1
Wells, Austin	.344	64	14	22	5	2	2	18	13	16	1

Name	W	L	ERA	G	GS	SV	IP	H	BB	SO	AVG
Abeyta, Blane	1	1	10.13	4	0	0	10	9	4	6	.238
Aguilar, Clay	1	1	10.24	6	1	1	10	18	2	2	.409
Brennan, Tim	1	1	5.59	7	0	0	10	15	7	3	.366
Byrne, Michael	0	0	0.00	3	0	0	4	4	0	4	.250
Cortijo, Harold	0	0	5.00	8	0	0	9	8	9	5	.242
Demurias, Eddy	0	0	8.31	9	0	0	9	11	11	7	.333
Ellis, Mitch	1	1	3.86	10	0	0	9	9	6	5	.300
Greene, Zach	0	1	4.91	8	0	0	7	8	3	9	.267
Haake, Chris	1	1	6.61	6	5	0	16	16	14	14	.258
Henry, Cole	1	0	3.32	6	3	0	19	12	9	30	.176
Lacy, Asa	2	0	2.35	4	4	0	8	5	6	15	.185
Lee, Evan	0	0	4.66	9	0	0	10	10	6	10	.270
Manon, Eudrys	1	1	7.45	9	0	2	10	11	9	8	.282
Marinan, James	0	1	7.00	6	5	0	18	18	9	18	.265
Marsh, Alec	0	1	27.00	1	1	0	1	3	1	3	.429
Mraz, Spencer	0	0	8.31	9	0	3	9	7	7	9	.226
Myatt, Tanner	0	0	13.50	8	0	1	6	8	13	9	.320
Peterson, Todd	1	0	2.61	8	0	1	10	8	4	8	.200
Pucheu, Jacques	1	0	1.93	8	0	0	14	10	4	13	.196
Rutledge, Jackson	1	3	6.98	6	4	0	19	28	10	17	.329
White, Owen	5	0	1.91	6	6	0	28	20	13	29	.202
Woods Jr., Stephen	0	0	4.67	10	1	0	17	20	11	17	.294

MINOR LEAGUES

INDEPENDENT LEAGUES

A New Branding For Independent Baseball

BY J.J. COOPER

In 2021, much of what has long been known as independent league baseball became partner league baseball.

Admittedly the new name doesn't roll off the tongue nearly as easily as "indy ball" and it doesn't have the same easy-to-explain description. In the past, indy ball was the renegade of professional baseball. Kept out of affiliated baseball, it revelled in its independence. Here were teams with no ties to the major leagues. They played to win and they went out and found (and paid for) their own players.

Nowadays, it's more complicated. The focus for these teams remains winning a championship rather than developing players to advance up a minor league ladder. And they still find and pay for their own players, but now the American Association, Atlantic League, Frontier League and Pioneer League are MLB partners, having signed agreements to have closer ties to Major League Baseball.

And in their first year as Partner Leagues, that partnership led to a whole lot of players being signed by MLB clubs. It's hard to say if this will be a one-year aberration or not, but in 2021 with the reduction of minor league rosters to a maximum of 180 players per org, seemingly everyone ran out of healthy players in April and May.

So they turned to partner leagues to fill out their rosters.

The rate of player transfer from partner leagues to MLB roughly doubled the normal flow. It was such a rapid increase in demand that the American Association doubled its in-season acquisition price from $5,000 to $10,000. The rate of player transfers didn't slow down at all.

The American Association's previous record for MLB signings in a season was 46. This year it ended up with 75. The Frontier League also sent 46 players to MLB (its record is 50).

That talent outflow also left partner league teams scrambling to find replacements. And it left everyone admitting that when it came to pitching, the talent level around the league dipped.

"To lose five guys in the first 16 days of the season, four of whom are pitchers, and three of them are big leaguers or Triple-A guys? That will put a dent in any pitching staff," said Josh Robertson, general manager of the American Association's

The Pioneer League completed its first season as a partner league in 2021.

Cleburne Railroaders.

Partner league managers and player personnel directors kept hitting up their contacts in MLB front offices, looking for an early word of pending releases. Almost always what they heard was that no one was going to be released, and by the way, do you have a shortstop or pitcher we could sign?

"We can't find replacements," Schaub said. "We can't find pro-level players to replace the players they sign."

To try to fill the spots, partner league teams scoured the college ranks to try to convince graduating seniors to sign with their teams. While MLB teams were prohibited from signing graduating seniors until they had passed through the MLB draft, partner leagues faced no such prohibitions.

The rush to sign partner league players quickly tailed off as the draft neared, however. In July and August, MLB teams were dealing more with roster crunches rather than empty spots. But in 2022, partner league teams will be looking to see if this was a one-year transitory blip or a newfound trend of increased player movement between them and their newfound partners.

Adam Brett Walker Revamps On The Fly

In 2020, Adam Brett Walker hit 22 home runs in just 57 games with the American Association's Milwaukee Milkmen. He averaged a home run once every 10 at-bats, a rate that seems relatively remarkable. He was the league's MVP for the coronavirus-shortened 2020 season as the Milkmen won the league title.

And when it was over, no affiliated team called. You see, everyone knows that Walker can hit home runs. He's done it virtually everywhere he's ever played.

After a 2013 breakout season when he hit 27 home runs for Low-A Cedar Rapids, Walker hit 25 or more home runs in each of the next four seasons. But even after hitting 27 home runs at Triple-A Rochester in 2016, Walker was designated for assignment by the Twins and bounced on and off of waivers throughout 2017. After the 2018 season, he found himself outside of affiliated ball for the first time since being drafted in the third round in 2012.

He returned home to Milwaukee to play for the newly formed Milkmen.

"I figured, if I don't perform well, at least I'll be in my hometown," Walker said. "At least if I finish up, I finish up in front of my family."

He wasn't finished. Walker hit 22 home runs in 2019 while playing through a sports hernia. He was the league MVP in 2020. But throughout that run, he'd been the same player who teams had seen for years—lots of home runs, few walks and usually a sub-.250 batting aver-

Adam Brett Walker

age. Walker has always posted exit velocities that demonstrate his plus-plus power, but the lack of affiliated team interest has made it clear that wasn't going to be enough to get him signed by an MLB club.

So for 2021, Walker decided to see if he could be something more.

"I had to use the whole field and if I get mistakes, the homers will come," Walker said. "I just tried to get my average up and be a more complete hitter, just for myself and to prove I could do it."

Consider it proven. Walker became a much more complete hitter in 2021. He hit .320/.369/.636 for Milwaukee. His 33 home runs led the league, but maybe more importantly he ranked among the league's best in batting average, hits (132) and stolen bases (24 in 26 attempts).

Pitchers rarely want to challenge him inside because of his power, but this year, when they stayed away from him, he was content to line the ball to the opposite field.

"He let the game come to him and he knows his value is more than hitting home runs," Milwaukee manager Anthony Barone said.

Walker is now 30, having played pro baseball for a decade. Where three years ago he thought he might be wrapping up by coming home and playing in front of friends and family, now there's a shot that he could get another chance at making it to the majors. After all, he's shown that he's more than just a slugger.

PREVIOUS WINNERS

1996: Darryl Motley, OF, Fargo-Moorhead (Northern)
1997: Mike Meggers, OF, Winnipeg/Duluth (Northern)
1998: Morgan Burkhart, 1B, Richmond (Frontier)
1999: Carmine Cappucio, OF, New Jersey (Northeast)
2000: Anthony Lewis, 1B, Duluth-Superior (Northern)
2001: Mike Warner, OF, Somerset (Atlantic)
2002: Bobby Madritsch, LHP, Winnipeg (Northern)
2003: Jason Shelley, RHP, Rockford (Frontier)
2004: Victor Rodriguez, SS, Somerset (Atlantic)
2005: Eddie Lantigua, 3B, Quebec (Can-Am)
2006: Ian Church, OF, Kalamazoo (Frontier)
2007: Darryl Brinkley, OF, Calgary (Northern)

2008: Patrick Breen, OF, Orange County (Golden)
2009: Greg Porter, OF, Wichita (American Association)
2010: Beau Torbert, OF, Sioux Falls (American Association)
2011: Chris Collabello, 1B, Worcester (Can-Am League)
2012: Blake Gailen, OF, Lancaster (Atlantic)
2013: C.J. Ziegler, 1B, Wichita (American Association)
2014: Balbino Fuenmayor, 1B, Quebec (Can-Am League)
2015: Joe Maloney, OF, Rocland (Can-Am League)
2016: Art Charles, 1B, New Jersey (Can-Am League)
2017: Alonzo Harris, OF, York (Atlantic League)
2018: Jordany Valdespin, INF, Long Island (Atlantic League)
2019: Keon Barnum, 1B, Chicago (American Association)

INDEPENDENT LEAGUES

AMERICAN ASSOCIATION

At the end of the 2019 season, the Kansas City T-Bones found themselves locked out of their stadium for failure to pay rent. Days later the team was sold to a group led by Mark Brandmeyer, who revitalized and rebranded the team for the 2021 season.

It was quite a successful takeover. The Kansas City Monarchs name paid tribute to one of the most famous and successful Negro League teams and made the team one of the most distinctive brands in the league, and led to a natural partnership with the Negro League's Baseball Musem. On the field, manager Joe Calfapietra's club could slug thanks to Gabby Guerrero, Ibandel Isabel and Casey Gillaspie and it could pitch thanks to Keyvius Sampson and Justin Shafer. The Monarchs swept Fargo-Moorhead to win the Miles Wolff Cup after posting a dominating .690 winning percentage during the regular season.

North Division	W	L	PCT	GB
Chicago Dogs	63	37	.630	--
Fargo-Moorhead Redhawks	61	38	.616	1.5
Milwaukee Milkmen	59	40	.596	3.5
Winnipeg Goldeyes	50	49	.505	12.5
Kane County Cougars	44	55	.444	18.5
Gary SouthShore RailCats	39	61	.390	24

South Division	W	L	PCT	GB
Kansas City Monarchs	69	31	.690	--
Cleburne Railroaders	54	45	.545	14.5
Sioux City Explorers	52	46	.531	16
Lincoln Saltdogs	53	47	.530	16
Sioux Falls Canaries	36	64	.360	33
Houston Apollos	17	83	.170	52

PLAYOFFS—First Round: Fargo-Moorhead defeated Milwaukee. Sioux City defeated Cleburne. **Semifinals:** Fargo-Moorhead defeated Chicago 3-2 and Kansas City defeated Sioux City 3-0 in best-of-five series. **Finals:** Kansas City defeated Fargo-Moorhead 3-0 in best-of-five series.

Attendance: Kane County Cougars 177,705; Chicago Dogs 155,582; Lincoln Saltdogs 149,204; Fargo-Moorhead RedHawks 145,553; Gary SouthShore RailCats 137,094; Kansas City Monarchs 102,257; Sioux Falls Canaries 82,932; Milwaukee Milkmen 79,741; Sioux City Explorers 59,802; Cleburne Railroaders 56,201; Winnipeg Goldeyes 52,014.

All-Star Team: C: Ryan Lidge, Chicago. **1B:** Kyle Martin, Winnipeg. **2B:** Ryan Grotjohn, Kansas City. **3B:** Jose Sermo, Sioux City. **SS:** Josh Altmann, Lincoln. **OF:** Adam Brett Walker, Milwaukee; Jordan George, Fargo-Moorhead; Gabby Guerrero, Kansas City. **DH:** Ramon Hernandez, Cleburne. **SP:** Myles Smith, Milwaukee. **RP:** James Pugliese, Lincoln.

Player of the Year: Adam Brett Walker, Milwaukee. **Manager of the Year:** Joe Calfapietra, Kansas City. **Defensive Player of the Year:** Chase Harris, Sioux City. **Rookie Position Player of the Year:** Wyatt Ulrich, Sioux Falls. **Rookie Pitcher of the Year:** Nate Hadley, Milwaukee.

BATTING LEADERS

Player	Team	AVG	AB	R	H	HR	RBI
Manuel Boscan#	F-M	.344	384	72	132	7	63
Kevin Krause	F-M	.341	305	66	104	13	55
Alay Lago	CLE	.337	419	68	141	5	50
Zach Nehrir	CLE	.334	347	55	116	6	41
Morgan McCullough*	KCM	.333	282	66	94	13	59
Jordan George#	F-M	.332	334	64	111	16	80
Ryan Grotjohn*	KCM	.329	331	76	109	10	60
Wyatt Ulrich*	SF	.327	364	69	119	1	37
Colin Willis*	KCM	.326	319	62	104	19	64
Kevin Lachance	WPG	.326	353	57	115	9	49

PITCHING LEADERS

Player	Team	W	L	ERA	IP	H	BB	SO
Kyle Kinman*	LS	8	3	2.9	96.1	80	48	109
Tyler Viza	KCC	6	2	3.05	91.1	92	21	96
Ryan Flores	F-M	9	2	3.33	94.2	73	30	129
Jheyson Manzueta	CLE	7	5	3.41	87	81	42	76
Myles Smith	MM	13	4	3.48	111.1	86	75	134
Greg Minier*	LS	9	4	3.87	86	87	33	90
David Holmberg*	MM	9	4	3.99	97	99	20	96
Jack Fox	KCC	3	5	4.26	80.1	81	32	51
Ryan Zimmerman	MM	10	6	4.26	114	95	59	120
Jordan Kipper	CHI	12	3	4.28	115.2	116	20	127

Josh Tols*	KCC	4	8	4.28	122	119	62	121

CHICAGO DOGS

Player	AVG	AB	R	H	HR	RBI	BB	SO	SB
Anfernee Grier	.308	347	51	107	10	40	33	73	35
Brennan Metzger	.270	319	70	86	7	34	81	76	7
Cosimo Cannella	.212	99	13	21	2	8	16	34	3
Danny Mars#	.299	378	67	113	6	68	51	91	20
Grant Kay	.272	294	37	80	6	45	34	88	7
Harrison Smith	.243	276	41	67	9	41	36	84	3
Johnny Adams	.234	351	47	82	10	39	33	92	5
K.C. Hobson*	.269	390	67	105	23	71	41	75	2
Mike Crouse	.277	303	59	84	13	64	44	86	33
Ryan Haug	.259	135	26	35	1	10	16	30	1
Ryan Lidge#	.312	282	41	88	6	45	49	54	0
T.J. Bennett*	.357	196	38	70	9	40	27	47	2

Player	W	L	ERA	G	SV	IP	H	BB	SO
A.J. Jones	4	3	5.77	9	0	48.1	55	8	28
Brendan Smith	1	0	5.48	18	0	23	22	17	20
Cam Booser*	1	2	1.93	21	2	23.1	20	10	39
Christian Friedrich*	3	1	4.21	6	0	36.1	42	2	30
Connor Grey	3	2	3.18	6	0	34	27	11	37
Garrett Christman	4	4	6.67	14	0	58	82	27	32
Jake Dahlberg*	6	2	3.05	15	0	62	50	11	76
Jase Dalton	2	1	4.00	20	0	27	22	13	26
Jeff Kinley*	5	1	1.46	40	18	55.1	27	12	64
John Baker	4	3	3.72	21	0	48.1	47	11	42
Jonathon Crawford	0	1	9.36	14	0	25	27	34	28
Jordan Kipper	12	3	4.28	20	0	115.2	116	20	127
Juan Echevarria	1	1	4.50	17	1	22	26	4	18
Justin Goossen-Brown	1	0	3.66	34	1	46.2	53	7	25
Kyle Murphy	4	2	2.64	8	0	44.1	36	18	27
Michael Bowden	7	1	2.92	12	0	52.1	37	10	52
Shane Barringer*	2	1	4.66	11	0	29	33	12	26

CLEBURNE RAILROADERS

Player	AVG	AB	R	H	HR	RBI	BB	SO	SB
Alay Lago	.337	419	68	141	5	50	33	60	13
Chase Simpson#	.250	360	53	90	11	61	50	99	10
Colton Pogue	.269	201	38	54	3	27	35	55	6
D.J. Peterson	.372	113	27	42	14	37	12	35	0
Grant Buck*	.187	134	15	25	3	13	23	45	1
Hunter Clanin	.264	345	58	91	11	45	37	88	29
John Nester	.212	255	27	54	5	35	24	75	2
Noah Vaughan*	.271	321	58	87	13	40	27	91	20
Osvaldo Martinez	.315	384	81	121	14	56	30	50	8
Ramon Hernandez	.324	386	74	125	21	100	32	77	13
Tyler Ryan	.179	140	15	25	5	20	7	75	0
Zach Nehrir	.334	347	55	116	6	41	17	70	22

Player	W	L	ERA	G	SV	IP	H	BB	SO
Austin Fairchild*	6	4	5.12	33	0	77.1	91	47	77
Brendan Bell	1	2	3.92	32	0	39	38	10	30
Edward Cruz	1	1	3.86	21	7	21	17	12	17
Garrett Alexander	8	7	6.70	26	0	95.1	109	75	103
Jalen Evans	2	3	4.89	8	0	38.2	35	22	41
Jesus Sanchez	3	0	4.40	5	0	28.2	39	3	20
Jheyson Manzueta	7	5	3.41	15	0	87	81	42	76
Kody Bullard	1	1	2.87	6	0	31.1	30	8	27
Kyle Chavez	3	0	1.78	25	5	25.1	25	6	14
Landon Holifield	0	1	3.60	21	0	20	11	12	27
Michael Gunn*	4	4	5.55	16	0	84.1	83	37	74
Michael Krauza	3	2	3.18	37	1	45.1	40	14	49
Taylor Wright	2	3	4.44	28	0	36.2	42	10	33

FARGO-MOORHEAD REDHAWKS

Player	AVG	AB	R	H	HR	RBI	BB	SO	SB
Alex Boxwell*	.296	274	47	81	5	33	16	58	14
Correlle Prime	.304	391	75	119	18	60	26	110	3
Dylan Kelly*	.313	291	40	91	6	56	23	37	0

Player	AVG	AB	R	H	HR	RBI	BB	SO	SB
John Silviano	.290	369	73	107	24	71	36	121	2
Jordan George#	.332	334	64	111	16	80	64	41	0
Kevin Krause	.341	305	66	104	13	55	29	41	1
Leobaldo Pina	.311	376	71	117	15	65	38	62	4
Manuel Boscan#	.344	384	72	132	7	63	41	56	10
Nick Novak*	.320	122	28	39	3	24	10	41	7
Nick Shumpert	.216	51	7	11	1	6	3	17	1
Sam Dexter	.268	336	51	90	8	55	14	38	3
Will Zimmerman	.243	136	29	33	3	21	22	42	3

Player	W	L	ERA	G	SV	IP	H	BB	SO
Alex DuBord	3	1	1.73	37	11	52	44	27	59
Andrew Tri	0	0	7.65	6	0	20	29	15	15
Austin Ver Steeg	3	3	5.46	30	0	62.2	59	34	43
Brent Jones	2	4	4.26	10	0	44.1	48	21	45
Bret Helton	7	9	4.79	21	0	118.1	116	47	107
Gage Hinsz	4	5	6.57	15	0	75.1	93	49	56
Jon Ludwig	2	2	4.71	7	0	28.2	40	6	23
Kevin McGovern*	4	0	1.41	4	0	32	14	3	37
Logan Nissen	6	5	4.56	19	0	71	80	32	54
Luke Lind	3	2	4.28	28	1	33.2	23	9	45
Mark Finkelnburg*	2	0	4.25	30	0	42.1	40	21	37
Matt Tomshaw*	4	0	2.33	5	0	27	23	7	30
Michael Hope	6	1	3.61	40	1	62.1	48	37	49
Ryan Flores	9	2	3.33	32	4	94.2	73	30	129

GARY SOUTHSHORE RAILCATS

Player	AVG	AB	R	H	HR	RBI	BB	SO	SB
Alec Olund	.280	214	41	60	5	37	30	43	5
Ben Andrews	.164	67	5	11	2	5	8	24	0
Billy Cooke	.301	166	18	50	1	15	4	36	18
Brandon Zaragoza	.245	53	3	13	0	3	5	13	0
Cam Comer*	.190	84	5	16	0	3	18	27	0
Daniel Lingua#	.281	313	37	88	3	42	45	86	13
Hayden Schilling*	.232	224	26	52	3	32	33	67	14
Jackson Smith*	.174	178	15	31	2	19	15	57	1
Jacob Talamante	.228	101	13	23	0	10	12	33	4
Jesus Marriaga	.284	292	35	83	2	31	22	77	19
Jose Mercado	.259	81	11	21	0	14	11	24	7
M.J. Rookard*	.259	224	35	58	2	24	20	57	9
Michael Woodworth	.367	120	22	44	2	17	8	16	8
Nikola Vasic	.218	78	12	17	0	6	11	20	6
Phil Caulfield*	.228	127	23	29	4	11	18	23	1
Ray Jones#	.241	237	28	57	4	30	29	71	4
Ryan Cash#	.254	138	21	35	0	14	12	21	0
Tom Walraven	.281	267	40	75	6	46	26	51	5
Tommy McCarthy	.221	113	15	25	0	9	15	33	3
Tyler Van Marter	.241	79	14	19	3	15	8	19	1
Zach Welz	.264	144	26	38	0	25	22	41	10

Player	W	L	ERA	G	SV	IP	H	BB	SO
Adam Heidenfelder	5	4	4.12	16	0	59	68	27	62
Cas Silber	3	1	5.88	13	2	41.1	52	19	44
Chris Erwin*	3	5	3.10	14	1	52.1	34	24	44
Cole Cook*	1	1	4.67	16	1	54	58	24	45
David Griffin	1	1	4.31	6	0	31.1	29	10	36
Jack Alkire	6	7	4.88	17	0	99.2	106	43	101
Jack Eisenbarger*	1	1	4.62	7	0	25.1	28	13	24
John Sheaks	1	6	5.40	9	0	40	50	9	38
Josh Vincent	2	4	6.20	9	0	45	59	31	27
Matt Vonderschmidt	1	0	4.29	16	0	21	28	2	15
Nick Garcia	1	5	5.40	25	5	50	63	14	40
Nolan Clenney	1	0	0.89	11	2	20.1	12	3	26
Tasker Strobel*	3	5	3.71	32	8	68	77	20	70
Trevor Lubking*	5	9	4.85	19	0	117	119	50	117
Yoel De Leon*	1	2	6.34	16	1	44	52	32	28

HOUSTON APOLLOS

Player	AVG	AB	R	H	HR	RBI	BB	SO	SB
Aaron Takacs*	.337	208	30	70	9	45	25	45	1
Alvaro Gonzalez	.260	169	17	44	5	17	16	50	2
Blake Berry*	.304	319	57	97	6	32	45	57	5
Breland Almadova	.242	91	10	22	0	8	16	20	3
Brian Dansereau	.226	230	33	52	7	26	19	59	7
Daniel Aldrich*	.213	155	19	33	4	20	13	54	0
Dom DeRenzo	.203	138	13	28	6	18	15	65	1
Hudson Bilodeau*	.280	318	39	89	3	34	18	45	0

Player	AVG	AB	R	H	HR	RBI	BB	SO	SB
Ian Yetsko	.210	352	33	74	10	39	34	143	1
Jared Fry#	.250	68	7	17	0	5	9	20	0
Jordan Pontious	.255	286	43	73	2	17	34	77	5
Mike Annone*	.186	86	9	16	0	5	10	13	0
Ramon Villa*	.216	102	14	22	1	7	28	31	0
Taylor Zeutenhorst*	.233	206	20	48	6	26	22	93	0
Yeiler Peguero#	.237	333	34	79	4	36	22	60	20

Player	W	L	ERA	G	SV	IP	H	BB	SO
Abdallah Aris*	0	9	6.75	13	0	58.2	73	34	64
Alex Merithew	3	7	7.66	34	1	74	107	37	73
Connor Berry	0	1	5.63	10	0	24	30	14	23
Derrick Sylve	0	5	7.71	30	2	49	59	29	42
Ian Codina	0	1	5.90	29	0	29	32	10	13
Jake Voss	0	2	7.92	11	0	30.2	41	24	10
Keisy Portorreal	1	4	4.23	22	3	27.2	23	9	31
Kenny Pierson*	0	3	13.29	23	0	21.2	38	18	17
Matt Bataska	0	0	7.34	17	0	30.2	40	13	15
Matt Cronin	4	11	6.60	19	0	90	126	52	59
Pierce Smith*	2	4	7.18	25	1	26.1	33	17	21
Tucker Smith	3	9	7.52	19	0	97	145	22	72
Yosmel Naranjo*	0	8	10.72	12	0	43.2	74	27	30

KANE COUNTY COUGARS

Player	AVG	AB	R	H	HR	RBI	BB	SO	SB
Anfernee Seymour#	.231	308	50	71	5	32	29	76	37
Anthony Ray*	.232	125	14	29	3	10	9	19	3
BJ Lopez	.219	114	16	25	3	12	15	22	0
Brandon Chinea	.267	131	17	35	3	13	7	17	1
Gavin LaValley	.270	289	47	78	12	45	39	56	0
Jack Surin	.186	59	6	11	0	4	4	22	0
Jeffrey Baez	.296	226	41	67	14	49	26	63	8
Josh Allen	.283	254	41	72	12	45	29	62	3
Josh Rolette*	.289	142	21	41	5	20	16	28	0
Kacy Clemens*	.278	288	43	80	12	43	44	72	1
Luis Roman*	.303	122	14	37	3	14	15	32	0
Mark Karaviotis	.327	205	34	67	9	31	21	51	1
Mitch Reeves	.280	322	43	90	4	41	31	67	2
Nick Anderson	.260	50	8	13	3	7	4	13	0
Nick Conti	.208	72	5	15	2	4	7	25	0
Nick Lovullo	.270	89	10	24	1	13	11	11	2
Nick Santoro	.210	124	16	26	1	13	9	25	0
Nick Zammarelli	.196	138	15	27	3	13	10	31	0
Tyler Friis#	.257	74	3	19	0	6	5	17	2

Player	W	L	ERA	G	SV	IP	H	BB	SO
Andrew Stout	1	1	5.54	26	0	50.1	49	33	39
Andy McGuire	1	0	3.06	26	2	32.1	25	16	22
Ben Allison	5	4	4.91	17	1	69.2	76	26	55
Christian DeLeon	6	3	5.73	34	1	48.2	61	21	39
Connor Berry	2	1	4.37	5	0	22.2	26	10	10
Eddie Medina	1	2	6.10	9	0	20.2	23	14	17
Jack Fox	3	5	4.26	17	0	80.1	81	32	51
Josh Tols*	4	8	4.28	21	0	122	119	62	121
Koby Bishop*	1	3	5.74	11	0	47	58	37	38
Kyle Huckaby*	4	2	4.09	31	0	33	27	15	34
Mark Seyler	2	6	4.00	26	3	36	30	17	35
Ryan Richardson	2	1	4.97	20	0	25.1	30	6	17
Ryley Widell*	0	2	8.27	13	0	20.2	24	26	20
Scott Harkin	0	3	3.41	5	0	29	33	11	26
Tom Curtin	3	3	7.56	16	0	25	23	26	19
Tyler Viza	6	2	3.05	14	0	91.1	92	21	96
Vance Worley	2	2	4.01	5	0	33.2	33	8	27

KANSAS CITY MONARCHS

Player	AVG	AB	R	H	HR	RBI	BB	SO	SB
Alexis Olmeda	.216	176	24	38	3	19	31	77	0
Casey Gillaspie#	.257	362	67	93	21	70	56	102	5
Charcer Burks	.286	213	43	61	4	28	28	41	7
Colin Willis*	.326	319	62	104	19	64	44	66	4
Daniel Wasinger#	.242	124	18	30	2	14	17	33	1
Darnell Sweeney#	.262	382	76	100	19	69	48	122	22
Gabriel Guerrero	.319	398	73	127	18	86	22	83	3
Ibandel Isabel	.320	103	25	33	11	24	7	27	0
Jan Hernandez	.318	211	45	67	19	66	24	73	5
Johnny Field	.198	111	21	22	3	11	10	38	3

Kevin Santa*	.337	95	18	32	1	14	4	5	4
Morgan McCullough*	.333	282	66	94	13	59	32	63	6
Ryan Grotjohn*	.329	331	76	109	10	60	55	69	12
Will Kengor*	.261	153	36	40	4	21	20	38	5

Player	W	L	ERA	G	SV	IP	H	BB	SO
Brian Ellington	3	4	4.33	27	0	27	21	17	41
Brock Gilliam	3	1	2.49	12	0	21.2	20	9	20
Carlos Diaz*	2	1	1.09	31	11	33	18	14	51
Cody Mincey	3	0	1.13	13	0	40	25	7	36
Dalbert Siri	2	1	3.98	19	3	20.1	20	10	21
Dylan Baker	2	0	2.57	4	0	21	17	7	22
Elroy Urbina*	2	1	5.56	30	1	45.1	51	26	31
Eric Stout*	2	1	1.96	4	0	23	17	5	30
Jacob Lindgren*	0	2	5.40	23	0	26.2	31	14	25
Jake Matthys	9	3	5.42	18	0	96.1	128	23	68
Jameson McGrane	6	1	3.71	34	9	70.1	56	33	90
Jose Taveras	1	1	5.20	8	0	27.2	31	13	19
Justin Donatella	5	1	3.35	16	1	45.2	34	14	47
Justin Shafer	7	3	4.63	18	0	70	68	30	79
Keyvius Sampson	5	1	3.93	8	0	36.2	28	21	45
Nick Travieso	8	8	5.92	18	0	86.2	106	38	64
Ryan Newell	1	0	6.75	14	0	25.1	26	18	28

LINCOLN SALTDOGS

Player	AVG	AB	R	H	HR	RBI	BB	SO	SB
Curt Smith	.280	332	44	93	10	51	37	59	4
David Vidal	.282	347	50	98	15	49	56	69	5
Edgar Corcino#	.268	306	47	82	12	49	21	77	8
Forrestt Allday*	.325	283	49	92	10	51	52	47	4
Garett Delano	.196	51	4	10	0	3	3	15	0
Gunnar Buhner	.158	95	9	15	0	8	12	35	0
Josh Altmann	.305	334	69	102	29	72	33	85	20
Justin Byrd*	.278	356	79	99	14	50	71	72	22
Pat Adams*	.213	122	19	26	0	7	16	47	8
Ryan Long*	.272	349	62	95	17	61	52	58	23
Skyler Weber*	.260	246	35	64	9	31	28	58	10
Yanio Pérez	.289	218	26	63	7	36	18	40	4
Zak Taylor	.239	180	17	43	1	13	12	40	0

Player	W	L	ERA	G	SV	IP	H	BB	SO
Ben Wereski*	3	3	4.54	9	0	41.2	44	18	34
Carson Lance	3	5	5.34	27	0	59	53	48	70
Carter Hope	3	0	4.12	35	0	39.1	39	16	34
David Zoz*	0	0	3.38	15	0	18.2	12	17	19
Garett Delano	1	1	3.55	9	0	38	30	8	51
Greg Minier*	9	4	3.87	25	0	86	87	33	90
Jake Hohensee	5	4	5.14	31	0	61.1	62	20	56
James Pugliese	3	3	2.47	42	25	43.2	47	15	46
John Richy	6	8	5.47	19	0	105.1	130	30	78
Josh Norwood*	2	0	4.32	25	1	33.1	25	23	27
Keenan Bartlett	2	5	5.60	15	0	62.2	80	26	51
Kyle Kinman*	8	3	2.90	19	0	96.1	80	48	109
Logan Lombana	1	2	7.84	23	2	20.2	27	10	17
Tyler Anderson*	4	1	5.59	41	0	38.2	55	13	29
Walter Borkovich	2	5	8.22	23	0	65.2	87	25	68

MILWAUKEE MILKMEN

Player	AVG	AB	R	H	HR	RBI	BB	SO	SB
Aaron Hill	.283	325	59	92	12	47	50	76	13
Adam Walker	.320	412	80	132	33	101	22	87	24
Aníbal Sierra	.188	234	19	44	6	20	13	67	3
Brett Vertigan*	.274	405	70	111	3	35	34	46	4
Christ Conley*	.213	183	20	39	7	20	38	54	0
Christian Correa	.282	298	42	84	13	51	31	41	2
Cole Sturgeon*	.256	121	13	31	2	15	1	4	4
David Washington*	.325	231	39	75	17	61	30	74	8
Jay Charleston	.121	66	12	8	1	6	8	26	4
Liam Scafariello	.067	60	6	4	1	4	12	43	3
Logan Trowbridge	.289	370	87	107	11	48	45	59	40
Mason Davis#	.321	53	8	17	0	4	5	6	3
Mikey Reynolds	.242	91	15	22	0	8	11	17	4
Tony Rosselli	.194	170	19	33	8	25	12	69	1
Trey Martin	.293	266	35	78	3	30	33	78	13

Player	W	L	ERA	G	SV	IP	H	BB	SO
David Holmberg*	9	4	3.99	15	0	97	99	20	96
Karch Kowalczyk	2	1	7.30	35	3	40.2	52	23	38

Kyle Mora	0	1	1.21	19	0	22.1	11	8	25
Matt Solter	3	8	4.74	16	0	93	96	33	94
Matthias Dietz	0	1	3.05	20	2	20.2	14	15	27
Misael Siverio*	2	2	5.79	7	0	32.2	52	11	30
Myles Smith	13	4	3.48	20	0	111.1	86	75	134
Nate Hadley	1	1	1.56	35	13	40.1	23	17	44
Nate Pawelczyk	1	2	6.00	26	0	42	35	31	43
Robbie Gordon	2	0	1.35	12	0	33.1	16	16	38
Ryan Boyer	6	3	2.72	30	1	46.1	38	14	64
Ryan Dunne	1	0	5.60	24	0	27.1	22	20	22
Ryan Kussmaul	2	2	4.25	7	0	42.1	42	10	37
Ryan Zimmerman	10	6	4.26	20	0	114	95	59	120
Zach Hartman	4	1	2.45	43	4	51.1	38	16	59

SIOUX CITY EXPLORERS

Player	AVG	AB	R	H	HR	RBI	BB	SO	SB
Blake Tiberi*	.272	195	28	53	7	32	35	50	7
Chase Harris	.251	295	51	74	5	27	36	78	33
Chris Clare	.339	186	38	63	1	26	28	32	8
DJ Poteet#	.231	65	7	15	3	12	9	25	2
Jared Walker*	.295	95	25	28	6	24	23	33	6
Jose Sermo#	.298	312	78	93	29	86	88	94	18
Joseph Monge	.262	286	33	75	2	34	36	88	14
L.T. Tolbert*	.295	349	51	103	6	43	33	38	1
Lane Milligan*	.245	257	45	63	12	37	57	62	5
Michael Lang	.220	173	30	38	1	8	25	49	6
Mitch Ghelfi#	.247	279	33	69	3	26	34	69	6
Nate Samson	.259	116	19	30	4	19	8	14	4
Seamus Curran*	.276	98	13	27	5	21	8	23	0
Sebastian Zawada	.259	320	54	83	16	62	25	83	0

Player	W	L	ERA	G	SV	IP	H	BB	SO
Brandon Brosher	4	2	2.51	39	6	46.2	40	22	69
Brett Adcock*	5	8	4.74	20	0	112	99	54	95
Danny Hrbek	1	5	5.44	36	2	51.1	50	31	61
Joe Riley	3	3	6.18	15	1	59.2	66	23	43
Jonah Smith	1	2	5.20	14	0	45	44	28	48
Jose Velez*	2	2	3.64	31	1	29.2	24	10	34
Matt Pobereyko	0	0	2.22	21	14	24.1	12	4	37
Max Kuhns	8	1	2.97	44	2	60.2	51	22	88
Nate Gercken	2	2	3.75	40	2	36	22	28	54
Patrick Ledet*	9	6	6.25	19	0	99.1	130	26	115
Tyler Beardsley	5	1	4.28	6	0	33.2	32	17	44
Tyler Koch*	1	2	2.95	21	0	36.2	27	24	49
Zach Hedges	8	5	4.58	21	0	120	133	37	71

SIOUX FALLS CANARIES

Player	AVG	AB	R	H	HR	RBI	BB	SO	SB
Angelo Altavilla#	.271	310	43	84	3	31	26	59	15
Cade Gotta	.327	257	44	84	6	36	49	53	24
Daryl Myers*	.259	58	9	15	0	7	8	27	1
Garrett Hope	.164	73	7	12	1	7	6	38	0
Jabari Henry	.292	312	67	91	21	77	85	78	0
Jordan Ebert	.263	160	28	42	2	21	15	23	2
Logan Landon	.390	118	23	46	7	32	8	25	2
Mike Hart*	.246	280	59	69	11	40	39	102	11
Mitch Glasser	.286	227	43	65	2	28	43	23	0
Nick Gotta*	.235	247	38	58	3	23	53	67	7
Shamoy Christopher#	.243	185	22	45	5	28	20	67	1
Trey Michalczewski#	.254	334	39	85	13	58	37	132	0
Troy Alexander*	.186	70	5	13	3	7	9	24	0
Wyatt Ulrich*	.327	364	69	119	1	37	42	49	20
Zane Gurwitz	.273	264	30	72	7	36	21	90	5

Player	W	L	ERA	G	SV	IP	H	BB	SO
Angel Ventura	7	7	5.14	22	0	119	142	34	89
Brady Stover*	0	3	9.27	11	0	22.1	35	16	17
Caleb Frare*	0	5	7.48	27	12	27.2	32	19	39
Carlos Pimentel	3	3	6.60	9	0	45	54	25	55
Charlie Hasty	2	4	6.40	28	0	70.1	94	29	65
Colby Wyatt	1	5	4.09	32	2	55	56	30	48
D.J. Sharabi	0	2	3.48	21	0	20.2	20	10	27
Eddie Medina	1	3	10.92	11	0	29.2	50	13	30
Grady Wood	3	6	6.20	29	3	40.2	55	8	40
Jack Maynard	0	1	6.28	20	2	28.2	40	13	32
Joey Wagman	3	3	4.50	5	0	30	36	7	20
Kevin Folman	0	1	6.75	3	0	5.1	7	0	7

INDEPENDENT LEAGUES

	W	L	ERA	G	SV	IP	H	BB	SO
Robbie Gordon	1	1	4.00	14	1	18	10	15	25
Trevor Simms	2	0	4.40	36	0	45	43	34	63
Ty Culbreth*	7	9	5.54	20	0	112	137	41	101
Tyler Garkow	6	9	4.97	21	0	116	115	33	114

WINNIPEG GOLDEYES

Player	AVG	AB	R	H	HR	RBI	BB	SO	SB
Austin Rei	.240	167	20	40	0	19	29	44	1
Dakota Conners	.235	179	24	42	1	15	21	46	6
Darren Seferina*	.231	117	28	27	3	14	19	30	2
Deon Stafford	.309	94	15	29	4	21	7	18	0
Jay Gonzalez*	.333	153	26	51	2	21	17	28	8
Kevin Lachance	.326	353	57	115	9	49	38	60	14
Kyle Martin*	.280	371	76	104	31	106	49	82	8
Logan Hill	.233	352	47	82	10	51	35	102	3
Max Murphy	.307	398	70	122	13	71	27	85	3
Raul Navarro	.310	313	48	97	2	45	42	60	20
Sonny Ulliana	.232	82	8	19	0	13	8	21	0
Tyler Hill	.294	350	67	103	4	45	74	52	20
Wes Darvill*	.307	264	48	81	5	30	25	45	21

Player	W	L	ERA	G	SV	IP	H	BB	SO
Austin Henrich	0	1	2.59	16	0	24.1	29	16	17
Christian James	3	3	6.65	29	1	44.2	52	26	37
Dan Kubiuk	1	0	6.63	17	0	19	21	11	20
Dylan Burns	1	2	5.59	7	0	29	43	12	19
Eduard Reyes	7	9	7.11	21	0	100	118	60	70
Greg Harris	3	5	7.00	9	0	36	36	29	29
Joey Gonzalez	3	5	5.08	14	0	78	84	30	70
Jorge Gonzalez	4	7	6.85	20	0	92	113	41	65
Jose Jose*	2	1	1.21	27	11	29.2	22	7	22
Jose Vasquez	0	3	5.97	8	1	28.2	40	7	27
Ken Frosch*	5	3	6.54	32	1	31.2	38	20	43
Kyle Thomas	1	3	6.96	12	0	32.1	52	13	24
Landen Bourassa	4	0	2.63	8	0	41	41	13	29
Mike Webb	0	0	7.33	6	0	23.1	36	12	16
Nate Antone	2	1	3.63	25	2	22.1	24	7	36
Pete Perez	4	1	5.29	12	0	51	67	14	40
Travis Seabrooke*	6	0	4.14	44	0	45.2	41	22	54

ATLANTIC LEAGUE

In the fall of 2020, the Lexington Legends officially learned that they would no longer be a part of affiliated baseball. A year later, they showed that there is life outside of affiliated ball.

Lexington won the Atlantic League title in its first season in the partner league by knocking off Long Island in the championship series. The Legends had gotten a sneak peek of their new situation in 2020, as Lexington fielded its own team as part of a two-team "Battle of the Bourbon Trail" with Florence, Ky. to play games during the coronavirus pandemic. That helped lay the groundwork for the 2021 Legends team, which included former big leaguers like Brandon Phillips, Ben Revere, Tony Cingrani and J.J. Hoover.

North Division	W	L	PCT	GB
Long Island Ducks	68	52	.567	--
Southern Maryland Blue Crabs	63	57	.525	5
Lancaster Barnstormers	56	63	.471	11.5
York Revolution	56	64	.467	12

South Division	W	L	PCT	GB
High Point Rockers	64	55	.538	--
Lexington Legends	60	60	.500	4.5
West Virginia Power/Charleston Dirty Birds	58	62	.483	6.5
Gastonia Honey Hunters	54	66	.450	10.5

Playoffs—Semifinals: Long Island defeated Southern Maryland 2-1 and Lexington defeated West Virginia 2-1 in best-of-three series. **Finals:** Lexington defeated Long Island 3-1 in best-of-five series.

Attendance: Long Island Ducks 224,120; Lancaster Barnstormers 182,132; Lexington Legends 163,798; Southern Maryland Blue Crabs 148,982; Gastonia Honey Hunters 114,416; York Revolution 111,628; High Point Rockers 108,200; Charleston Dirty Birds 85,398.

Player of the Year: Steve Lombardozzi Jr., Long Island. **Pitcher of the Year:** Daryl Thompson, Southern Maryland.

BATTING LEADERS

Player	Team	AVG	AB	R	H	HR	RBI
Michael Russell	HP	.360	283	58	102	7	48
Roberto Baldoquin	LEX	.355	403	90	143	14	75
Boog Powell*	GAS	.343	377	96	129	10	52
Teodoro Martinez	WVP/CDB	.339	384	66	130	5	53
Melky Mesa	YOR	.330	333	67	110	18	79
Steve Lombardozzi#	LI	.329	435	99	143	16	83
Kelly Dugan*	LAN	.326	316	77	103	15	88
Courtney Hawkins	LEX	.326	325	87	106	32	78
Alejandro De Aza*	LAN	.322	397	90	128	11	71
Tillman Pugh	LEX	.322	382	103	123	26	107

PITCHING LEADERS

Player	Team	W	L	ERA	IP	H	BB	SO
Daryl Thompson	SM	16	3	3.20	169	168	22	105
Austin Nicely*	YOR	9	9	3.74	142	151	50	75
Arik Sikula	WVP/CDB	11	7	4.35	136.2	127	35	103
Elih Villanueva	WVP/CDB	4	4	4.39	98.1	99	40	88
Darin Downs*	LI	6	5	4.50	98	104	35	93
Nile Ball	LAN	3	6	4.63	89.1	86	55	64
Joe Iorio	LI	13	2	4.65	127.2	145	48	73
Cooper Casad	HP	7	4	4.73	123.2	135	28	91
Tommy Lawrence	HP	11	4	4.82	117.2	122	23	80
Anderson DeLeon	LI	6	6	5.26	113	125	36	109

GASTONIA HONEY HUNTERS

Player	AVG	AB	R	H	HR	RBI	BB	SO	SB
Adrian Gomez	.286	70	12	20	1	12	14	6	1
Alexi Amarista*	.313	147	25	46	3	17	8	10	6
Boog Powell*	.342	377	96	129	10	52	64	54	35
Emmanuel Tapia*	.284	261	53	74	17	56	32	77	0
Ermindo Escobar	.286	175	28	50	5	32	19	29	0
Jake Romanski	.239	67	7	16	2	9	4	17	0
Jake Skole*	.270	366	84	99	23	85	76	122	30
Jason Rogers	.286	339	80	97	20	73	63	48	7
Jesus Sucre	.296	152	22	45	1	36	10	7	0
Jordan Howard#	.243	144	28	35	4	19	14	48	10
Josh Sale*	.284	415	94	118	34	104	76	96	13
Manuel Geraldo#	.264	231	43	61	7	35	18	50	10
Michael Osinski	.359	262	61	94	13	59	36	41	8
Mike Papi*	.243	292	57	71	14	60	38	57	8
Miles Williams	.194	67	9	13	2	6	10	19	2
Reece Hampton#	.350	143	39	50	10	27	19	34	10
Ryan Cordell	.231	104	21	24	7	23	20	28	7
Ryan Jackson	.305	82	20	25	3	13	12	18	2
Will Johnson	.226	124	16	28	2	14	23	29	6
William Salas	.194	103	12	20	0	9	15	16	4

Player	W	L	ERA	G	SV	IP	H	BB	SO
AJ Merkel	6	3	5.68	20	0	77.2	68	52	74
Alexis Candelario	0	4	9.74	9	0	32.1	50	19	21
Alsis Herrera*	1	5	6.59	6	0	27.1	36	12	17
Austin Glorius	5	2	6.67	17	0	79.2	102	55	62
Brock Knoten	0	1	8.44	13	0	21.1	40	10	7
Donnie Hart*	2	2	3.48	22	2	20.2	19	8	26
Euclides Leyer	4	1	7.97	21	0	40.2	46	30	47
Jacinto Garcia	0	2	10.59	16	0	26.1	42	21	19
Jailen Peguero	4	5	6.64	33	0	80	93	47	72
Jamie Callahan	2	0	7.04	26	0	23	33	17	25
Jay Gause	1	2	10.45	7	0	31	49	19	19
Jhonatan German	0	3	5.70	17	0	23.2	22	16	21
Joe Kuzia	0	2	14.91	20	0	22.1	32	28	23
John Anderson*	0	3	6.55	6	0	34.1	43	20	25
Jose Jose*	1	0	2.61	16	5	20.2	19	3	23
Kaleb Earls	6	2	5.93	36	4	44	52	24	52
Raibel Custodio	4	1	7.24	27	0	32.1	41	27	18
Reilly Hovis	1	2	2.96	6	0	24.1	16	9	21
Sam Burton	3	2	5.57	8	0	42	37	29	32
Spencer Bivens	4	8	7.26	14	0	74.1	106	31	62
Steven Farkas*	0	1	10.70	11	0	17.2	24	17	14
T.J. Goco*	0	2	8.77	24	0	25.2	41	26	17
William Kirwan	6	8	8.68	28	1	92.1	114	78	58

HIGH POINT ROCKERS

Player	AVG	AB	R	H	HR	RBI	BB	SO	SB
Adam Taylor*	.327	52	11	17	1	10	12	9	3
Cesar Trejo	.280	82	16	23	6	17	11	21	6
Edwin Arroyo#	.316	79	11	25	1	9	10	9	3
Giovanny Alfonzo	.273	352	51	96	2	49	37	52	10
James McOwen*	.267	333	55	89	7	61	47	59	8
Jared Mitchell*	.242	360	67	87	14	66	75	136	27
Jay Gonzalez*	.267	120	24	32	2	12	24	29	7
Jerry Downs*	.300	337	72	101	22	81	46	75	7
Johnny Field	.283	350	75	99	13	54	48	60	11
JR DiSarcina	.257	167	27	43	5	28	13	51	4
Logan Moore*	.209	91	15	19	3	12	21	31	0
Michael Martinez#	.286	192	22	55	4	30	21	27	5
Michael Russell	.360	283	58	102	7	48	34	26	21
Mike Gulino	.229	118	14	27	2	17	17	33	1
Quincy Latimore	.297	128	25	38	6	21	20	30	4
Randy Norris	.236	89	14	21	2	13	15	27	1
Stephen Cardullo	.289	325	73	94	20	76	55	46	16
Stuart Levy	.237	300	61	71	11	52	58	79	2

Player	W	L	ERA	G	SV	IP	H	BB	SO
Brian Clark*	0	4	9.50	22	1	18	23	14	19
Bryce Hensley*	6	9	6.07	24	0	109.2	146	34	55
Cooper Casad	7	4	4.73	24	0	123.2	135	28	91
Craig Stem	5	12	7.02	24	0	127	183	45	103
Joe Johnson	4	0	4.91	37	1	33	32	15	29
Joey Hennessey	1	2	4.18	19	0	23.2	14	26	30
John Hayes	2	4	5.34	31	0	32	40	17	25
Jonathon Crawford	4	0	2.70	21	0	23.1	14	13	33
Kyle Halbohn	1	1	3.35	45	13	43	34	11	42
Luke Westphal*	3	1	1.39	6	0	32.1	19	18	40
Mitch Atkins	2	1	4.37	8	0	35	36	5	30
Preston Gainey	1	1	3.72	20	7	19.1	15	15	31
Ricky Knapp	4	3	6.15	10	0	52.2	61	21	43
Ryan Chaffee	3	1	5.94	45	0	50	49	45	65
Tommy Lawrence	11	4	4.82	19	0	117.2	122	23	80
Tyler Garkow	1	0	5.40	5	0	20	18	9	29

LANCASTER BARNSTORMERS

Player	AVG	AB	R	H	HR	RBI	BB	SO	SB
Alejandro De Aza*	.322	397	90	128	11	71	57	63	11
Anderson De La Rosa	.257	253	38	65	4	49	35	52	1
Anthony Peroni	.268	198	19	53	1	30	31	44	1
Blake Allemand#	.251	386	95	97	21	59	57	73	6
Blake Gailen*	.279	287	59	80	18	72	68	60	4
Caleb Gindl*	.291	450	106	131	34	91	73	91	3
Cleuluis Rondon*	.247	376	67	93	6	49	52	93	5
Devon Torrence#	.258	186	24	48	0	26	17	63	16
Jake Hoover	.241	87	16	21	0	13	13	23	5
Kelly Dugan*	.326	316	77	103	15	88	55	67	5
LeDarious Clark	.265	268	56	71	18	65	23	99	28
Melvin Mercedes*	.301	249	50	75	2	34	44	32	14
Nick Shumpert	.204	206	25	42	1	22	21	70	13
Trayvon Robinson#	.235	294	57	69	8	46	52	97	12

Player	W	L	ERA	G	SV	IP	H	BB	SO
Andro Cutura	3	2	10.64	7	0	33	44	29	33
Augie Sylk*	5	7	9.09	24	0	97	116	108	85
Benny Wanger	0	1	5.67	15	0	27	29	17	31
Brent Teller	5	2	5.14	25	1	56	57	31	55
Cameron Gann	2	1	4.07	8	0	24.1	21	18	34
Cody Boydstun	2	5	5.68	8	0	38	50	16	20
Danny Taggart	0	2	10.87	12	0	27.1	42	21	16
Dom DiSabatino	11	9	7.36	25	0	118.2	149	63	97
Donald Goodson	2	3	5.09	51	0	53	49	42	55
Francisco Mendoza	0	2	12.77	9	0	31	59	16	24
Gabriel Moya*	3	1	2.36	44	2	45.2	30	13	51
Garrett Granitz	2	1	5.44	43	0	48	59	21	30
Jordan McCrum	1	2	4.22	18	0	21.1	23	4	25
Junior Rincon	0	2	7.67	21	0	27	33	18	30
Nile Ball	3	6	4.63	16	0	89.1	86	55	64
Scott Shuman	4	3	1.49	47	19	48.1	29	18	71
Tommy Shirley*	3	2	6.61	11	0	45	52	16	44
Yoel Espinal	3	6	10.89	30	0	41.1	36	68	26
Zach Smith	2	5	11.88	13	0	50	78	53	39

LEXINGTON LEGENDS

Player	AVG	AB	R	H	HR	RBI	BB	SO	SB
Ben Aklinski	.290	424	105	123	28	105	66	108	10
Ben Revere*	.300	50	10	15	0	14	3	5	1
Brandon Phillips	.276	221	37	61	14	52	17	31	5
Breland Almadova	.266	64	11	17	0	6	8	11	1
Chris Fornaci	.229	205	38	47	3	29	46	54	2
Cole Sturgeon*	.321	243	51	78	10	37	37	19	8
Courtney Hawkins	.326	325	87	106	32	78	49	68	8
D.J. Peterson	.311	164	43	51	15	44	25	42	0
Darian Sandford#	.291	103	25	30	1	11	22	27	23
Denis Phipps	.275	80	13	22	2	7	8	17	4
Derek Reddy	.180	61	13	11	0	6	17	14	5
Jake Romanski	.232	198	35	46	6	30	15	47	0
Jordan Pacheco	.370	138	23	51	4	29	14	11	4
Jose Briceno	.333	147	34	49	13	36	12	29	0
Juan Silverio	.229	70	10	16	2	10	6	10	3
Keon Barnum*	.291	275	55	80	24	74	32	69	1
Michael Choice	.328	137	25	45	6	24	23	28	1
Omar Artsen	.250	124	26	31	0	15	24	35	9
Pete Yorgen	.283	53	10	15	0	6	10	13	0
Roberto Baldoquín	.355	403	90	143	14	75	49	56	13
Sam Claycamp	.186	118	22	22	2	17	19	33	0
Tillman Pugh	.322	382	103	123	26	107	65	104	13

Player	W	L	ERA	G	SV	IP	H	BB	SO
Austin Adams	4	4	2.68	36	8	37	32	13	36
Braulio Torres-Perez*	1	3	6.58	5	0	26	32	7	22
Brett Schneider	0	0	4.60	19	0	29.1	27	11	24
Bryan Quillens	0	3	7.54	35	0	37	48	26	47
Daniel Gibson*	3	2	3.72	40	1	36.1	40	13	47
Davis Feldman	0	3	12.62	6	0	25.2	44	19	15
Derek Self	3	3	3.00	42	9	42	45	8	24
Dustin Beggs	1	0	4.15	5	0	26	25	10	20
Eli Garcia	5	5	7.70	16	0	78.1	117	49	63
Harold Myles	0	1	11.79	15	0	23.2	29	29	23
Henry Owens*	4	5	6.55	25	0	92	84	98	113
J.J. Hoover	7	1	6.06	20	0	108.1	141	39	95
Jeff Thompson	4	1	6.84	36	0	51.1	58	29	64
Jeremy Jeffress	1	1	6.45	23	2	22.1	20	18	27
Kevin McGowan	4	1	4.50	5	0	22	20	9	22
Liam O'Sullivan	4	1	5.44	10	0	44.2	58	6	36
Robert Carson*	2	4	8.00	39	0	45	64	25	33
Shawn Blackwell	6	9	6.93	30	1	88.1	111	50	59
Ty'Relle Harris	4	4	7.85	13	0	36.2	45	24	34
Zac Westcott	1	2	4.70	5	0	30.2	28	13	25

LONG ISLAND DUCKS

Player	AVG	AB	R	H	HR	RBI	BB	SO	SB
Breland Almadova	.226	93	17	21	1	17	20	19	6
Chris Shaw*	.219	155	29	34	5	18	25	42	0
Clint Freeman*	.276	58	10	16	2	9	9	7	2
Daniel Fields*	.299	184	36	55	12	48	31	52	5
Deibinson Romero	.252	258	53	65	10	47	51	44	1
Hector Sanchez#	.247	283	52	70	18	70	32	29	2
Jesse Berardi*	.241	216	37	52	8	32	28	40	4
Johnni Turbo	.301	316	68	95	7	29	25	44	31
L.J. Mazzilli	.303	373	77	113	11	69	45	25	19
Lew Ford	.311	151	23	47	3	31	9	17	1
Nick Bottari	.365	63	11	23	0	13	9	12	0
Ramon Flores*	.243	202	33	49	7	36	39	28	1
Rey Fuentes*	.222	63	15	14	2	11	10	18	6
Ryan Jackson	.287	188	30	54	6	40	24	19	3
Sal Giardina#	.317	230	45	73	6	38	25	47	6
Steve Lombardozzi#	.329	435	99	143	16	83	90	41	20
Ty Kelly#	.298	114	24	34	0	22	8	27	5
Vladimir Frias#	.286	357	72	102	10	60	38	48	19

Player	W	L	ERA	G	SV	IP	H	BB	SO
Anderson DeLeon	6	6	5.26	32	0	113	125	36	109
Brady Dragmire	5	5	4.31	43	0	48	45	15	28
Brendan Feldmann	8	4	5.49	26	0	118	128	59	91
Chris Reed*	1	2	7.98	23	0	29.1	45	21	41
Clint Freeman*	1	5	6.34	33	0	44	53	25	28
Danny Barnes	2	0	2.76	16	5	16.1	14	8	20
Darin Downs*	6	5	4.50	19	0	98	104	35	93

	W	L	ERA	G	SV	IP	H	BB	SO
Dylan Peiffer	3	2	1.69	21	1	26.2	23	20	30
Hunter Caudelle	1	0	2.55	8	0	17.2	15	12	20
Hunter Cervenka*	1	3	3.29	26	0	27.1	22	11	31
Joe Iorio	13	2	4.65	23	0	127.2	145	48	73
Michael Tonkin	2	1	0.53	16	9	17	9	5	21
Mike Bolsinger	1	4	5.31	15	0	39	42	24	37
Rob Griswold	4	0	3.34	32	8	35	31	8	30
Scott Harkin	5	0	3.42	10	0	55.1	52	14	33
Tanner Wilt	0	0	5.68	15	0	19	19	9	21
Vin Mazzaro	1	5	7.68	13	0	41	51	35	21

SOUTHERN MARYLAND BLUE CRABS

Player	AVG	AB	R	H	HR	RBI	BB	SO	SB
Alex Crosby*	.318	380	75	121	13	67	27	51	6
Cesar Trejo	.274	146	22	40	3	23	20	42	13
Dario Pizzano*	.324	142	21	46	5	24	30	16	1
David Harris	.272	382	67	104	15	79	35	74	3
Jake Luce*	.188	138	13	26	1	11	10	42	0
Jake Marshall	.261	69	6	18	0	8	7	24	0
Joe DeLuca#	.304	372	53	113	16	70	30	80	3
Jordan Howard#	.333	54	12	18	4	12	6	17	1
Josh McAdams	.272	401	66	109	22	90	51	108	5
Jovan Rosa	.252	127	22	32	4	18	9	23	0
Kent Blackstone*	.219	269	48	59	8	34	41	58	8
Matt Hibbert	.270	230	57	62	3	18	41	57	6
Michael Baca	.270	355	56	96	5	46	38	46	9
Rubi Silva*	.350	309	55	108	12	50	19	60	6
Will Decker*	.186	70	8	13	0	6	9	13	1
Zach Collier*	.324	293	76	95	14	58	54	75	8

Player	W	L	ERA	G	SV	IP	H	BB	SO
Austin Glorius	0	2	6.67	6	0	27	31	24	30
Blake Bivens	3	4	6.53	21	0	70.1	69	41	52
Brandon Barker	2	3	2.89	7	0	37.1	38	13	34
Carl Brice	5	5	6.10	12	0	59	61	44	49
Carlos Diaz*	2	0	7.36	30	0	25.2	30	19	32
Cody Strayer	0	2	5.26	19	0	25.2	26	13	14
Dalton Geekie	2	2	3.22	43	0	50.1	58	23	53
Daryl Thompson	16	3	3.20	24	0	169	168	22	105
Endrys Briceno	5	3	1.87	51	2	57.2	38	23	77
Greyfer Eregua	1	4	4.71	14	0	21	26	5	21
Kolton Mahoney	8	7	7.05	25	0	103.1	118	66	81
Mat Latos	2	5	2.76	43	24	42.1	32	11	46
Mike Devine	5	2	3.93	8	0	52.2	51	14	57
Misael Siverio*	1	4	6.30	9	0	40	49	13	38
Patrick Baker	3	3	5.47	35	0	52.2	57	36	59
Sam Burton	3	6	8.49	15	0	71	83	44	49
Ty Tracy	0	0	10.71	17	0	21	44	7	9

WEST VIRGINIA POWER/CHARLESTON DIRTY BIRDS

Player	AVG	AB	R	H	HR	RBI	BB	SO	SB
Al Reda	.182	55	11	10	1	4	16	17	0
Alberto Callaspo#	.335	334	62	112	6	57	85	30	0
Connor Kopach	.213	150	28	32	10	31	23	60	12
Connor Myers	.267	180	38	48	3	17	19	51	18
Dom Bethancourt	.245	110	15	27	5	17	14	40	1
Edwin Espinal	.307	358	46	110	10	66	27	52	0
Elmer Reyes	.252	309	33	78	5	34	16	50	2
Francisco Arcia*	.281	89	16	25	2	10	10	19	0
Jimmy Paredes#	.308	279	55	86	17	68	34	71	3
Jose Tabata	.354	82	15	29	4	18	11	10	0
Miles Williams	.262	145	23	38	14	37	8	55	1
Nate Easley	.235	166	35	39	5	20	21	51	16
Olmo Rosario	.323	155	26	50	7	26	18	15	2
Rubi Silva*	.263	137	15	36	6	21	6	31	4
Rymer Liriano	.297	290	53	86	9	42	57	76	5
Scott Kelly	.306	232	47	71	4	30	32	39	9
Teodoro Martinez	.339	384	66	130	5	53	47	30	9
Yovan Gonzalez	.269	223	33	60	3	34	23	35	0

Player	W	L	ERA	G	SV	IP	H	BB	SO
Alexis Candelario	3	5	6.11	14	0	56	72	37	53
Arik Sikula	11	7	4.35	24	0	136.2	127	35	103
Bret Clarke	0	2	8.14	11	0	24.1	31	25	21
Clinton Hollon	1	1	7.27	4	0	17.1	21	11	23

	W	L	ERA	G	SV	IP	H	BB	SO
Dakota Freese	0	3	5.96	11	0	22.2	21	16	17
Dave Kubiak	3	3	4.30	9	0	44	37	15	36
Edwin Quirarte	3	1	3.45	19	0	28.2	25	17	29
Eleardo Cabrera	3	4	4.57	34	1	43.1	35	34	46
Elih Villanueva	4	4	4.39	18	0	98.1	99	40	88
Emmanuel Rosario	0	3	9.31	15	0	29	42	31	21
Joe Harris*	0	2	6.00	8	0	24	27	12	12
Joe Testa*	5	4	5.76	17	0	50	56	18	51
Junior Figueroa	2	6	10.38	12	0	43.1	60	31	28
Junior Rincon	6	0	2.48	28	3	29	19	20	31
Luis Guzman*	3	0	3.86	33	0	35	29	16	46
Maddux Conger	0	0	6.28	12	0	14.1	12	13	20
Manny Corpas	1	2	13.00	4	0	18	35	12	11
Max Povse	1	2	5.82	22	0	51	49	21	42
Max Tannenbaum	2	0	7.71	25	0	37.1	43	18	26
Mike Broadway	3	2	2.30	39	14	43	32	11	46

YORK REVOLUTION

Player	AVG	AB	R	H	HR	RBI	BB	SO	SB
Andrew Dundon	.216	111	16	24	3	24	36	33	0
Carlos Castro	.352	261	47	92	17	59	15	50	0
Carlos Franco*	.311	167	38	52	13	56	48	54	0
Darian Sandford#	.228	289	58	66	1	14	45	51	55
Jack Kenley*	.288	319	66	92	12	57	68	80	4
James Harris	.280	350	74	98	14	56	66	90	18
JC Encarnación	.295	244	44	72	9	51	26	87	14
Josh Vitters	.157	51	6	8	0	5	6	22	0
Josue Herrera*	.256	242	42	62	9	40	22	71	0
Lenin Rodriguez	.205	156	21	32	1	13	23	32	0
Melky Mesa	.330	333	67	110	18	79	33	76	0
Mikey Reynolds	.319	72	18	23	3	11	3	12	2
Nellie Rodriguez	.316	310	65	98	25	81	69	94	0
Osmy Gregorio	.309	262	47	81	9	34	20	61	1
Rashad Crawford*	.283	60	16	17	2	10	10	17	3
Tyler Hill	.252	155	22	39	2	25	22	49	0
Walner Espinal	.186	70	7	13	3	8	3	29	0
Welington Dotel	.307	303	46	93	9	37	22	98	17
Yan Sanchez	.299	134	28	40	5	22	20	35	2

Player	W	L	ERA	G	SV	IP	H	BB	SO
Alberto Rodriguez	6	4	4.11	53	0	57	48	35	59
Alex Sanabia	3	0	2.43	6	0	33.1	27	11	24
Austin Nicely*	9	9	3.74	24	0	142	151	50	75
Austin Steinfort	1	4	8.88	11	0	48.2	49	61	29
Brandon Fry*	3	2	4.28	47	0	48.1	44	26	38
Bruce Bell	0	3	9.96	15	0	28	42	16	17
Bubby Rossman	4	3	5.40	36	0	33.1	26	25	48
Dalton Von Schamann	5	9	6.14	24	0	139.1	184	38	61
Eduardo Rivera	6	4	5.48	33	1	95.1	81	72	100
Edward Paredes*	1	1	3.38	35	1	32	22	17	32
Isaac Sanchez	4	0	5.04	44	0	44.2	52	25	53
Israel Cruz	1	2	4.24	26	1	23.1	17	11	25
Jake Welch	1	6	10.04	18	0	54.2	82	61	19
Jhoendri Herrera	2	4	8.80	10	0	44	53	31	19
Jim Fuller*	3	3	3.08	48	29	49.2	53	16	51
Joey Lara	2	3	8.70	9	0	40.1	57	26	14
Johan Lopez*	0	1	12.15	4	0	13.1	18	24	2
Luis Sanchez	2	1	5.34	20	0	28.2	29	17	20
Victor Capellan	3	3	6.32	37	2	37	44	9	32

FRONTIER LEAGUE

The Schaumburg Boomers joined the Frontier League in 2012. Within two years, they were starting to establish themselves as the league's most successful dynasty.

Schaumburg held off Washington, 10-4, in the deciding Game 5 of the championship series to win its fourth title in the past eight seasons. In just nine years, the Boomers have already become the winningest team in league history—no other team in the league has won more than two titles. Schaumburg manager Jamie Bennett became the second manager in league history to win four titles, joining Mal Fichman.

Kyle Arjona was named the championship series MVP as he won both the first and last game of the championship series.

After the season ended, the Southern Illinois Miners announced that they will not return for 2022 as owners Jayne and John Simmons said it is their intent to retire.

Atlantic Division	W	L	PCT	GB
Équipe Québec	50	41	.549	--
Tri-City Valley Cats	48	45	.516	3
New York Boulders	41	51	.446	9.5

Central Division	W	L	PCT	GB
Schaumburg Boomers	50	44	.532	--
Windy City ThunderBolts	43	49	.467	6
Lake Erie Crushers	40	51	.440	8.5
Joliet Slammers	35	54	.393	12.5

Northeast Division	W	L	PCT	GB
Washington Wild Things	56	39	.589	--
Sussex County Miners	48	44	.522	6.5
New Jersey Jackals	38	56	.404	17.5

West Division	W	L	PCT	GB
Florence Y'Alls	57	36	.613	--
Evansville Otters	53	38	.582	3
Southern Illinois Miners	50	39	.562	5
Gateway Grizzlies	33	55	.375	21.5

Playoffs—Semifinals: Schaumburg defeated Florence 3-1 and Washington defeated Quebec 3-2 in best-of-five series. **Finals:** Schaumburg defeated Washington 3-2 in best-of-five series.

Attendance: Schaumburg Boomers 157,112; Tri-City ValleyCats 100,519; New York Boulders 99,693; Joliet Slammers 86,067; Washington Wild Things 82,420; Sussex County Miners 79,762; Evansville Otters 76,482; Florence Yalls 73,099; Lake Erie Crushers 70,062; Southern Illinois Miners 66,099; Windy City ThunderBolts 65,022; Gateway Grizzlies 62,416; Equipe Quebec 43,819; New Jersey Jackals 43,722.

All-Star Team: CAN-AM—C: Jeffry Parra, Quebec. **1B:** Brad Zunica, Tri-City. **2B:** David Glaude, Quebec. **3B:** Juan Silverio, Tri-City. **SS:** Cito Culver, Sussex County. **OF:** Martin Figueroa, Sussex County; L.P. Pelletier, Quebec; Chuck Taylor, Sussex County. **DH:** Denis Phipps, Tri-City. **SP:** Ryan Hennen, Washington. **RP:** Trey Cochran-Gill, Tri-City.

MIDWEST—C: Trevor Craport, Florence. **1B:** Riley Krane, Evansville. **2B:** J.R. Davis, Evansville. **3B:** Brylie Ware, Joliet. **SS:** Luis Pintor, Florence. **OF:** Chad Sedio, Florence; Chase Dawson, Schaumburg; Nolan Earley, Southern Illinois. **DH:** Quincy Nieporte, Schaumburg. **SP:** Zac Westcott, Southern Illinois. **RP:** Logan Sawyer, Evansville.

Most Valuable Player: Quincy Nieporte, Schaumburg. **Pitcher of the Year:** Ryan Hennen, Washington. **Rookie of the Year:** Ryan Hennen, Washington. **Manager of the Year:** Andy McCauley, Evansville. **Coach of the Year:** Alex Boshers, Washington.

BATTING LEADERS

Player	Team	AVG	AB	R	H	HR	RBI
Martin Figueroa#	SCM	.352	236	54	83	5	53
Quincy Nieporte	SCH	.343	274	51	94	17	65
Chuck Taylor#	SCM	.340	359	74	122	11	63
L.P. Pelletier	EQ	.328	372	85	122	7	37
Ruben Castro*	EQ	.325	308	58	100	6	51
Bralin Jackson	WW	.323	347	48	112	7	68
Nolan Earley*	SIM	.321	346	59	111	13	66
Chad Sedio*	FLO	.319	357	68	114	15	69
Andres Regnault	GG	.317	265	32	84	13	46
Kaleo Johnson	SCM	.317	243	43	77	9	44

PITCHING LEADERS

Player	Team	W	L	ERA	IP	H	BB	SO
Ryan Hennen*	WW	11	3	2.12	106.1	84	18	93
Braden Scott*	EVAN	8	4	2.72	89.1	72	24	104
Ryan Feierabend*	LEC	8	5	2.79	100	98	12	108
Ryan O'Reilly	EVAN	5	4	2.89	84	67	29	72
Jared Cheek	FLO	8	1	2.94	79.2	80	10	74
Sam Curtis	LEC	4	1	3.03	77.1	58	24	80
Chase Cunningham	SIM	4	3	3.10	98.2	85	27	89
Ryan Middendorf	SCH	11	5	3.14	117.1	116	23	90
Logan Wiley	WC	6	4	3.20	98.1	90	22	54
Zac Westcott	SIM	14	3	3.29	123	103	27	103

ÉQUIPE QUÉBEC

Player	AVG	AB	R	H	HR	RBI	BB	SO	SB
Connor Panas*	.310	261	42	81	7	47	21	25	4
David Glaude*	.308	377	79	116	13	75	43	84	31
Elliott Curtis*	.244	90	12	22	2	13	12	24	3

Player	AVG	AB	R	H	HR	RBI	BB	SO	SB
Gift Ngoepe	.281	278	50	78	9	47	42	94	12
Jack Barrie	.203	79	9	16	1	10	5	25	1
Jeffry Parra	.287	348	52	100	15	73	34	68	2
Jesse Hodges	.238	277	43	66	7	50	35	73	4
Jonathan Lacroix*	.258	326	44	84	4	45	30	78	7
Kevin Whatley*	.189	53	12	10	0	4	8	12	2
L.P. Pelletier	.328	372	85	122	7	37	23	58	40
Nate Etheridge	.212	52	5	11	1	3	0	9	0
Raphael Gladu*	.375	176	34	66	3	38	11	22	1
Riley Pittman*	.189	122	13	23	2	12	11	20	0
Ruben Castro*	.325	308	58	100	6	51	49	48	29

Player	W	L	ERA	G	SV	IP	H	BB	SO
Andrew Case	2	0	2.61	20	10	20.2	18	2	18
Ben Hoffman	0	1	8.37	12	0	33.1	50	15	30
Codie Paiva	7	5	4.42	20	0	118	136	25	81
David Gauthier*	3	5	6.45	22	0	60	75	27	38
Evan Rutckyj*	3	1	0.86	27	6	31.1	17	13	34
Frankie Moscatiello	9	0	2.95	42	2	58	39	34	67
Henry Omana	2	0	4.50	6	0	30	23	20	30
Jared Mortensen	2	1	5.73	4	0	22	21	9	22
John Witkowski	2	1	3.95	14	0	27.1	20	17	29
Marshall Shill	3	2	1.91	39	2	42.1	26	16	54
Miguel Cienfuegos*	9	6	3.78	22	0	116.2	120	29	88
Nick Economos	1	2	8.89	7	0	26.1	34	21	28
Nick Horvath*	2	7	4.94	30	0	51	59	27	55
Pablo Arevalo	1	2	5.84	11	0	24.2	31	10	17
Stephen Knapp	1	1	2.37	26	1	38	33	9	26

EVANSVILLE OTTERS

Player	AVG	AB	R	H	HR	RBI	BB	SO	SB
Andretty Cordero	.195	123	11	24	2	16	9	18	1
Andrew Penner	.257	202	32	52	0	26	24	47	4
Andy DeJesus#	.295	336	51	99	4	34	23	77	16
Bryce Denton	.203	143	17	29	2	18	7	33	1
Cristopher Pujols	.194	98	14	19	1	14	10	28	6
Dakota Phillips*	.256	258	38	66	12	45	22	103	0
Elijah MacNamee	.292	325	62	95	7	45	45	74	10
Gary Mattis	.293	140	24	41	0	19	15	39	22
J.R. Davis	.316	342	54	108	8	56	35	49	4
Jeffrey Baez	.319	94	14	30	7	24	6	17	10
John Schultz*	.262	103	22	27	2	13	24	23	0
Josh Allen	.324	71	18	23	3	14	11	24	1
Justin Felix	.136	103	15	14	3	14	16	61	0
Miles Gordon*	.252	314	54	79	3	32	38	88	25
Riley Krane*	.271	384	64	104	17	73	19	93	5

Player	W	L	ERA	G	SV	IP	H	BB	SO
Austin Gossmann	2	7	4.22	16	0	89.2	88	28	101
Braden Scott*	8	4	2.72	14	0	89.1	72	24	104
Dalton Stambaugh*	2	0	3.57	4	0	22.2	22	7	24
Jacob Bowles	0	0	2.57	11	1	28	22	3	20
Logan Sawyer	3	5	2.97	38	25	36.1	36	6	48
Marty Anderson*	1	1	4.78	6	0	26.1	28	9	13
Polo Portela	10	3	3.69	19	0	109.2	112	36	93
Ryan O'Reilly	5	4	2.89	13	0	84	67	29	72
Samson Abernathy	1	0	3.86	29	0	35	28	23	33
Taylor Wright	0	6	2.91	29	1	34	25	13	29
Tim Holdgrafer	10	4	3.45	18	0	104.1	102	20	121
Tyler Spring	6	0	5.64	40	1	56.2	37	25	62
Tyler Vail	0	1	6.64	4	0	20.1	20	6	16

FLORENCE Y'ALLS

Player	AVG	AB	R	H	HR	RBI	BB	SO	SB
Andres Rios	.228	101	19	23	1	12	20	15	2
Axel Johnson*	.242	211	37	51	7	30	26	52	5
Chad Sedio*	.319	357	68	114	15	69	32	88	17
Connor Crane	.275	233	43	64	2	31	24	62	18
Harrison DiNicola*	.285	355	50	101	6	63	33	56	11
Jackson Pritchard	.210	100	12	21	1	9	15	46	3
Joe Lytle*	.260	177	26	46	4	25	19	28	5
Jordan Brower*	.272	265	37	72	9	42	14	42	13
Jose Brizuela*	.241	133	31	32	0	9	22	34	11
Luis Pintor	.316	285	61	90	7	45	29	48	19
Rodney Tennie*	.247	174	21	43	0	13	21	34	20
Taylor Bryant	.220	109	22	24	4	16	28	31	4
Trevor Craport	.308	344	68	106	19	85	34	59	18
Will Baker	.125	72	5	9	0	5	7	30	4

INDEPENDENT LEAGUES

Player	W	L	ERA	G	SV	IP	H	BB	SO
Alex Wagner	5	3	3.07	28	0	55.2	47	19	51
Andrew McDonald	1	2	4.19	22	5	34.1	34	13	35
Casey Grimm*	2	1	5.58	6	0	30.2	41	9	9
Christian Tripp	0	1	4.91	4	0	22	23	5	23
Edgar Martinez	7	3	4.58	19	2	90.1	85	42	94
Frank Valentino	3	4	6.91	12	0	57.1	70	23	52
Hayden Wheeler*	0	1	7.06	7	0	21.2	23	10	13
Jared Cheek	8	1	2.94	28	1	79.2	80	10	74
Joe Dougherty	2	0	2.06	35	15	35	19	14	32
Johnathon Tripp	9	1	4.15	24	5	84.2	95	15	85
Jonaiker Villalobos*	6	5	4.33	19	0	108	115	30	21
Karl Craigie*	2	3	2.56	30	1	31.2	28	12	43
Kevin Hahn	3	6	5.2	15	0	81.1	98	19	55

GATEWAY GRIZZLIES

Player	AVG	AB	R	H	HR	RBI	BB	SO	SB
Abdiel Diaz#	.269	308	37	83	1	17	36	57	18
Alonzo Jones#	.284	109	18	31	2	10	13	32	9
Andres Regnault	.317	265	32	84	13	46	22	67	4
Axel Johnson*	.209	86	6	18	2	12	15	26	1
Chase Vallot	.210	238	26	50	10	25	22	104	0
Connor Owings*	.190	221	30	42	10	38	33	82	4
Dustin Woodcock*	.249	301	63	75	14	49	29	82	7
Dylan Jones	.141	78	13	11	2	7	12	31	5
Jack Harris	.382	76	15	29	7	13	1	15	2
Jay Prather*	.272	302	35	82	4	35	23	40	4
Jose Rosario	.288	306	46	88	12	46	22	61	4
Justin Jones	.258	271	38	70	6	36	20	60	7
Nick Rotola	.250	176	25	44	7	20	14	63	9
Ty Moore*	.263	251	32	66	4	20	29	34	3

Player	W	L	ERA	G	SV	IP	H	BB	SO
Carlos Vega	3	4	5.32	25	0	71	70	34	84
Carter Hayes	3	2	3.98	33	0	40.2	27	23	36
Christian Camacho	1	1	3.33	6	0	24.1	10	10	21
Cody Thompson	1	4	4.57	33	0	43.1	43	23	43
Colton Easterwood	2	4	6.00	21	0	48	39	47	47
Drew Clavenna	2	2	9.28	5	0	21.1	35	20	6
Geoff Bramblett	1	0	1.66	18	8	38	22	9	39
Greg Duncan	0	2	5.46	9	1	28	33	15	18
Jack Jett	1	2	10.16	13	0	31	48	34	29
Jesse Remington*	0	1	11.85	3	0	13.2	22	7	12
John Murphy	0	0	4.66	14	0	19.1	16	12	28
Jordan Barrett*	4	8	7.19	18	0	82.2	85	75	84
Jorge Tavarez	6	5	6.01	16	0	76.1	94	26	67
Matt Mulhearn	2	5	5.60	8	0	45	46	17	26
Sam Gardner	5	3	4.24	12	0	70	74	23	72
Tanner Cable	1	2	2.03	28	6	26.2	13	25	45

JOLIET SLAMMERS

Player	AVG	AB	R	H	HR	RBI	BB	SO	SB
Alonzo Jones#	.291	141	15	41	0	5	17	35	11
Braxton Davidson*	.240	179	28	43	12	28	40	72	4
Brian Parreira*	.191	204	25	39	8	23	24	66	1
Brylie Ware	.299	278	36	83	5	37	44	39	1
Carson Maxwell	.257	113	22	29	7	20	15	42	1
Clayton Harp*	.196	51	6	10	0	8		17	2
Dave Matthews*	.207	87	10	18	1	12	5	33	2
Dylan Hardy	.235	293	37	69	2	23	29	76	11
Jackson Dvorak	.225	129	12	29	0	15	16	39	0
Jordan Rathbone	.215	79	12	17	2	11	4	18	0
Kyle Jacobsen	.194	217	27	42	5	33	14	66	10
Lane Baremore	.271	314	37	85	4	45	12	57	3
Luke Mangieri*	.323	65	10	21	2	12	6	18	0
Nick Lovullo	.257	70	8	18	1	8	4	17	1
Patrick Causa	.251	179	22	45	2	25	16	53	0
Scott Holzwasser	.266	169	26	45	5	20	10	43	6
Sean Green	.207	82	8	17	0	4	8	28	5
Tyler Depreta-Johnson	.178	253	27	45	0	22	25	49	9

Player	W	L	ERA	G	SV	IP	H	BB	SO
Adam Zuk	2	1	5.08	6	0	28.1	28	15	27
Austin Shea	1	5	5.58	11	0	40.1	38	34	38
Brad VanAsdlen	1	3	3.96	38	1	50	34	39	57
Brett Smith	5	3	3.67	15	0	34.1	29	16	29
Cameron Aufderheide	2	9	4.14	21	0	108.2	114	47	78

Chandler Brierley*	0	2	4.97	14	0	29	31	29	27
Chris Roycroft	4	4	5.81	26	0	69.2	77	30	62
Kaleb Honea	2	0	3.77	17	2	28.2	20	3	23
Keon Taylor	0	0	6	24	0	36	52	12	37
Logan Dubbe	3	3	4.44	8	0	46.2	47	10	47
Logan Lyle*	0	4	5.18	10	0	57.1	56	23	42
Mario Samuel*	2	4	4.24	23	1	40.1	43	20	42
Tom Walker	3	0	3.6	6	0	30	32	15	25
Trevor Charpie	4	5	3	43	16	54	33	20	62
Tyler Jandron*	1	5	4.81	17	0	73	75	32	64

LAKE ERIE CRUSHERS

Player	AVG	AB	R	H	HR	RBI	BB	SO	SB
Brody Wofford*	.212	274	24	58	7	29	24	82	1
Bryan De La Rosa	.184	212	26	39	2	20	25	53	4
Connor Oliver*	.272	228	28	62	7	34	28	66	5
Eric Callahan	.213	244	22	52	2	16	16	68	12
General McArthur	.173	75	8	13	1	5	5	29	2
Isaac Benard*	.309	191	32	59	5	25	21	30	6
Javier Betancourt	.237	245	26	58	5	22	12	31	2
Karl Ellison	.256	223	27	57	8	33	15	62	0
Shawon Dunston*	.247	267	41	66	0	12	33	64	37
Steve Passatempo	.214	257	32	55	9	31	27	98	0
Steven Kraft	.252	246	36	62	2	24	33	60	17
Trevor Achenbach	.275	338	54	93	15	57	28	73	7
Zach Racusin	.367	90	13	33	2	13	12	5	8
Zack Gray*	.162	130	13	21	2	15	21	44	0

Player	W	L	ERA	G	SV	IP	H	BB	SO
Aaron Glickstein	5	4	4.10	31	0	68	65	27	62
Daniel Kight	2	5	5.03	30	7	34	34	16	23
Dillon Larsen*	0	1	3.73	10	0	31.1	22	24	37
Ean Walda	3	0	3.09	25	0	58.1	43	33	51
J.T. Perez*	1	5	2.41	42	15	52.1	53	18	67
Jake Pilarski	3	4	5.32	15	0	66	72	37	66
Paul Hall*	3	10	4.81	19	0	103	117	41	97
Robby Rowland	2	1	3.27	4	0	22	25	11	18
Ryan Feierabend*	8	5	2.79	18	0	100	98	12	108
Sam Curtis	4	1	3.03	23	0	77.1	58	24	80
Sean Johnson	0	5	3.62	6	0	32.1	38	15	36
Taylor Sugg	4	4	3.98	35	3	61	68	23	54
Tyson Cronin	2	4	7.03	12	0	48.2	56	31	36

NEW JERSEY JACKALS

Player	AVG	AB	R	H	HR	RBI	BB	SO	SB
Alex Kachler	.250	64	8	16	2	15	5	15	1
Alfredo Marte	.279	147	24	41	7	29	12	27	4
Chris Carpio	.214	84	11	18	0	12	10	10	1
Dalton Combs*	.295	353	52	104	8	47	42	52	12
Demetrius Moorer	.256	281	51	72	2	31	47	70	34
Jason Agresti	.316	269	47	85	8	39	29	45	0
Josh Rehwaldt*	.300	170	29	51	11	35	9	52	0
Justin Wylie	.289	277	50	80	15	64	38	66	4
Nicco Toni	.300	140	17	42	3	17	4	29	1
Riley Mihalik*	.215	158	19	34	4	16	18	46	0
Russ Olive*	.296	169	29	50	8	39	31	29	2
Santiago Chirino	.305	275	44	84	0	35	25	25	1
Stanley Espinal	.269	323	54	87	5	36	40	41	1
TJ Ward	.257	101	16	26	2	11	15	24	0
Todd Isaacs	.304	207	44	63	11	32	13	56	9

Player	W	L	ERA	G	SV	IP	H	BB	SO
Angelo Baez	2	2	5.58	22	0	71	91	35	36
Chase Ingram	0	5	5.79	12	0	51.1	61	27	33
Chris Tessitore	2	6	6.45	17	1	51.2	70	34	36
Dakota Freese	1	2	4.74	9	0	24.2	23	20	24
Dylan Brammer	5	5	5.36	29	8	47	50	18	39
Jack Weinberger	6	2	4.81	30	0	58	50	35	44
Jared Milch*	4	4	4.74	17	0	76	76	21	64
Jason Zgardowski	4	4	6.68	31	0	62	83	28	56
Matt Vogel	2	4	4.20	35	1	40.2	31	23	62
Reece Karalus	4	2	3.77	34	4	43	30	20	60
Ricky Knapp	2	4	6.14	7	0	36.2	60	14	27
Ronald Herrera	2	2	4.68	6	0	32.2	31	13	23
Spencer Hereford	1	5	6.65	12	0	47.1	57	19	31
Thomas Spinelli*	0	1	4.70	17	0	23	24	14	31

NEW YORK BOULDERS

Player	AVG	AB	R	H	HR	RBI	BB	SO	SB
Gian Martellini	.290	169	29	49	8	33	9	44	1
Jack Sundberg*	.294	360	59	106	3	39	69	59	48
Kevonte Mitchell	.298	332	55	99	12	65	34	81	11
Marcus Mastrobuoni	.324	145	23	47	9	33	14	24	0
Milton Smith*	.275	284	52	78	4	33	37	58	35
Phil Capra#	.242	178	30	43	8	30	30	44	2
Phil Caulfield*	.242	194	27	47	2	17	24	34	14
Ray Hernandez	.261	348	65	91	23	58	20	92	11
Ryan Ramiz*	.267	217	38	58	5	35	29	50	4
Tucker Nathans*	.260	311	51	81	11	43	35	71	13
Zach Kirtley	.256	348	67	89	16	64	61	96	1
Zach Penprase	.254	118	16	30	1	15	16	31	14

Player	W	L	ERA	G	SV	IP	H	BB	SO
Alex Mack	0	2	6.31	10	0	25.2	32	11	19
Andrew Hammond	5	3	5.4	15	0	73.1	91	18	41
Ben Strahm	1	3	8.37	14	0	33.1	48	23	21
Brian Rapp	1	0	3.15	4	0	20	21	8	23
Danny Wirchansky*	4	5	4.08	20	0	106	97	58	105
Dylan Smith	1	0	4.91	22	0	25.2	22	14	41
James Mulry*	4	4	3.83	37	1	56.1	51	17	57
Luke Burton	2	1	5.77	29	1	39	40	19	45
Nate Roe	1	2	10.88	5	0	22.1	40	10	7
Nathan Alexander	3	4	5.65	29	2	43	36	25	46
Orsen Josephina	6	5	5.99	22	0	85.2	91	46	75
Robby Rowland	2	3	5.87	8	0	38.1	47	12	39
Ryan Munoz*	4	5	4.52	15	0	77.2	84	25	53
Tanner Kiest	3	9	6.53	32	6	40	30	30	66
Zach Schneider	3	1	3.18	24	5	34	39	8	25

SCHAUMBURG BOOMERS

Player	AVG	AB	R	H	HR	RBI	BB	SO	SB
Alberto Schmidt	.223	94	14	21	2	13	12	34	0
Alec Craig*	.247	295	55	73	5	28	76	80	43
Angelo Gumbs	.259	274	34	71	6	45	22	53	4
Braxton Davidson*	.363	102	23	37	10	30	24	39	0
Brett Milazzo*	.250	208	41	52	2	14	27	40	20
Chase Dawson*	.312	349	78	109	10	68	36	49	25
Clint Hardy	.253	281	48	71	6	45	27	63	9
Dusty Stroup	.210	62	9	13	5	10	7	21	0
Luke Becker#	.237	262	36	62	2	29	33	47	5
Matt Bottcher*	.268	231	22	62	3	27	14	55	2
Matt McGarry	.242	359	41	87	8	38	24	112	11
Nick Ames*	.223	157	16	35	5	18	11	49	0
Nick Oddo*	.204	211	27	43	4	23	18	72	0
Quincy Nieporte	.343	274	51	94	17	65	17	29	2

Player	W	L	ERA	G	SV	IP	H	BB	SO
Aaron Rozek	2	0	2.13	4	0	25.1	26	7	32
Andrew Cartier	2	1	4.56	28	0	25.2	25	12	33
Andrew Dean*	5	10	4.78	19	0	101.2	111	40	70
Bryan Ketchie*	0	5	6.57	7	0	37	53	7	28
Darrell Thompson*	2	0	3.86	21	5	21	26	7	31
Erik Martinez	3	2	5.60	5	0	27.1	35	14	32
Geoff Bramblett	2	0	2.16	3	0	25	18	12	18
Isaiah Rivera	2	3	5.02	26	0	57.1	54	35	62
Jack Snyder	2	1	2.14	14	0	21	14	9	30
Jake Joyce	2	2	4.19	37	5	38.2	29	27	55
Jesse Remington*	3	2	4.28	10	0	40	44	13	35
Kristian Scott	0	2	6.29	21	0	24.1	32	12	15
Kyle Arjona	8	6	3.38	19	0	119.2	113	30	91
Orlando Rodriguez	4	1	2.44	8	0	51.2	49	18	48
Ryan Middendorf	11	5	3.14	19	0	117.1	116	23	90
Ryder Yakel	0	1	5.54	15	1	26	29	6	20
Stephen Chamblee	0	2	6.75	12	0	22.2	32	3	13
Thomas Nicoll	2	0	2.19	34	7	37	24	8	55

SOUTHERN ILLINOIS MINERS

Player	AVG	AB	R	H	HR	RBI	BB	SO	SB
Anthony Brocato	.273	308	53	84	17	60	31	96	2
Ariel Sandoval	.287	167	23	48	3	26	5	23	14
Arturo Nieto	.226	146	16	33	1	16	14	35	0
Bryant Flete*	.315	124	24	39	4	11	14	13	0
Carson Bartels	.240	146	22	35	2	17	19	24	1

Player	AVG	AB	R	H	HR	RBI	BB	SO	SB
Gianfranco Wawoe	.153	98	17	15	1	8	13	17	0
Ian Walters*	.286	318	42	91	5	53	38	69	3
Jared Mang	.294	306	55	90	10	46	26	55	5
Jarrod Watkins*	.236	144	22	34	6	28	8	23	1
John Cable*	.197	71	9	14	1	8	7	20	0
Luke Mangieri*	.271	251	39	68	8	39	40	55	5
Marshall Rich	.200	70	10	14	0	6	13	22	2
Nolan Earley*	.321	346	59	111	13	66	47	57	5
Ryan Stacy*	.192	78	9	15	0	8	5	19	1
Yeltsin Gudino	.256	324	40	83	2	25	23	38	3

Player	W	L	ERA	G	SV	IP	H	BB	SO
Blake Stelzer	4	2	3.35	35	0	43	28	8	40
Chase Cunningham	5	4	3.10	17	0	98.2	85	27	89
Gunnar Kines*	3	3	4.79	15	0	67.2	60	23	70
Jake Fisher*	3	3	4.70	7	0	30.2	37	3	27
Joey Pulido	2	3	1.70	39	10	47.2	34	12	53
Kaleb Schmidt	4	1	3.88	15	0	51	45	25	48
Michael Austin	4	5	4.32	16	0	83.1	79	27	78
Mitchell Walters	0	5	3.58	25	0	27.2	17	23	38
Ryan Miller	1	1	2.89	25	6	28	19	14	38
Stevie Ledesma	5	1	2.83	26	4	54	50	16	48
Trent Johnson	0	4	3.18	11	0	45.1	38	11	40
Zac Westcott	14	3	3.29	21	0	123	103	27	103

SUSSEX COUNTY MINERS

Player	AVG	AB	R	H	HR	RBI	BB	SO	SB
Aaron Knapp*	.236	161	31	38	2	11	34	46	15
Audy Ciriaco	.303	343	58	104	10	61	28	51	13
Chuck Taylor#	.340	359	74	122	11	63	43	53	27
Cito Culver#	.275	309	47	85	7	45	51	65	5
Daniel Herrera#	.223	179	28	40	3	23	27	44	5
Eric Jenkins*	.137	51	9	7	0	1	4	21	7
Jackie Urbaez#	.261	184	32	48	1	14	25	42	5
Joey Rose	.198	91	13	18	4	12	8	32	2
John Jones#	.254	67	5	17	1	10	11	18	3
Juan Kelly#	.330	200	40	66	6	49	38	40	3
Kaleo Johnson	.317	243	43	77	9	44	18	65	1
LT Struble*	.273	77	15	21	0	4	13	20	10
Martin Figueroa#	.352	236	54	83	5	53	37	29	25
Nick Garland	.268	56	10	15	1	10	2	19	0
Nilo Rijo	.246	61	12	15	0	5	8	18	9
Trevin Esquerra#	.249	169	20	42	5	18	14	40	1
Trey Hair*	.260	50	17	13	0	3	8	8	8

Player	W	L	ERA	G	SV	IP	H	BB	SO
Alexander Vargas	4	7	5.77	20	0	92	121	24	44
Billy Layne	5	5	5.11	17	0	79.1	85	32	58
Dwayne Marshall	3	1	3.68	9	0	36.2	40	17	22
Gavin Sonnier	5	2	3.9	24	2	57.2	52	23	29
Jalen Miller	5	3	3.06	40	8	64.2	53	27	80
Max Herrmann*	5	5	4.33	16	0	79	81	25	57
Michael Mediavilla*	1	2	3.27	38	18	44	41	13	52
Mike Castellani*	5	6	6.26	21	0	83.1	126	23	44
Robert Klinchock*	4	1	6	40	0	51	63	20	38
Tyler Alexander*	2	3	2.23	5	0	36.1	34	2	42
Tyler Luneke	4	2	5.55	23	1	48.2	50	22	46

TRI-CITY VALLEY CATS

Player	AVG	AB	R	H	HR	RBI	BB	SO	SB
Brad Zunica*	.358	201	34	72	12	45	25	42	2
Carson Maxwell	.235	179	22	42	11	28	16	56	3
Carson McCusker	.324	102	24	33	6	23	15	23	1
Chris Kwitzer*	.261	142	23	37	5	17	6	38	0
Connor Lien	.224	85	12	19	5	21	6	39	2
Daniel Angulo*	.216	153	17	33	0	9	23	43	0
Denis Phipps	.277	336	54	93	21	62	36	79	7
Jhon Nunez#	.286	70	11	20	2	6	8	14	0
Juan Silverio	.310	345	59	107	16	53	29	49	6
Keaton Weisz	.261	111	9	29	2	12	2	34	4
Luis Roman*	.302	182	24	55	5	29	19	43	8
Nelson Molina*	.282	234	49	66	10	31	26	32	9
Oscar Campos	.305	233	38	71	3	27	6	17	5
Willy Garcia	.297	202	36	60	6	26	18	47	1
Zach Biermann*	.311	122	22	38	3	14	9	29	1

Player	W	L	ERA	G	SV	IP	H	BB	SO
Austin Cline	2	2	3.43	9	0	42	41	18	40

	W	L	ERA	G	SV	IP	H	BB	SO
Bruce Bell	0	2	6.08	5	0	23.2	36	10	16
Bryan Valdez*	1	0	5.24	7	0	22.1	26	9	12
Daniel Kreuzer	4	3	4.03	19	0	38	38	19	29
Erick Heredia	0	3	7.50	10	0	24	27	19	11
Francisco Jimenez	5	4	5.36	33	0	45.1	40	17	65
Jake Dexter	2	3	5.64	28	1	68.2	85	26	33
Jose Cruz	3	2	4.78	10	0	52.2	53	15	35
Josh Hiatt	5	4	5.01	17	0	79	86	31	54
Logan Dubbe	0	2	6.20	6	0	24.2	32	10	47
Parker Kelly	7	6	5.13	20	0	98.1	92	45	47
Patrick Murphy*	5	2	3.69	19	0	31.2	28	12	28
Ryan McKay	2	2	5.87	32	0	38.1	49	22	27
Trey Cochran-Gill	4	2	2.35	45	24	57.1	52	20	53
Turner Larkins	2	2	6.27	10	0	33	39	18	25

WASHINGTON WILD THINGS

Player	AVG	AB	R	H	HR	RBI	BB	SO	SB
Andrew Czech*	.271	262	37	71	15	38	43	58	0
Andrew Sohn	.257	230	41	59	2	26	21	58	11
Bralin Jackson	.323	347	48	112	7	68	22	58	12
Brian Sharp*	.167	90	15	15	2	11	20	36	3
Cam Phelps#	.164	61	13	10	0	4	12	22	7
Cody Erickson	.267	60	12	16	0	5	11	9	1
Cody Young	.290	69	14	20	4	10	6	19	0
Connor Perry	.250	56	8	14	0	10	6	16	3
Derek Reddy	.264	53	5	14	0	0	7	13	2
Gabe Howell	.190	63	6	12	1	4	5	15	7
Grant Heyman*	.240	342	48	82	11	52	13	91	6
Hector Roa	.296	338	51	100	12	59	17	79	15
Joe Campagna	.239	184	25	44	11	33	13	38	2
Nick Ward*	.269	279	50	75	5	37	67	37	21
Scotty Dubrule*	.374	187	35	70	1	21	31	21	3
Trevor Casanova*	.300	253	38	76	5	32	24	45	9
Tristan Peterson	.356	90	19	32	3	16	13	19	1

Player	W	L	ERA	G	SV	IP	H	BB	SO
Alex Boshers	4	3	5.11	15	1	44	54	12	31
B.J. Sabol*	2	0	3.48	41	0	33.2	29	23	60
Ben Vicini	9	0	2.03	24	0	48.2	35	10	52
Dan Kubiuk	2	0	1.29	22	1	21	12	3	32
Daren Osby	6	4	3.76	19	0	103	112	28	96
James Meeker	1	0	0.00	30	0	31.2	17	10	43
Jesús Balaguer	2	3	4.40	35	0	43	31	28	48
Keven Pimentel	7	7	5.80	19	0	94.2	104	37	72
Kevin McNorton	2	3	4.95	10	0	40	43	6	27
McKenzie Mills*	3	5	3.82	17	0	92	84	35	67
Ryan Hennen*	11	3	2.12	19	0	106.1	84	18	93
Steven Colon	2	0	2.70	10	0	36.2	33	22	39
Zach Strecker	2	7	4.97	51	22	50.2	62	5	33

WINDY CITY THUNDERBOLTS

Player	AVG	AB	R	H	HR	RBI	BB	SO	SB
Brynn Martinez#	.226	323	43	73	2	39	34	65	45
Dan Robinson*	.243	334	57	81	8	37	60	77	16
Donivan Williams	.273	88	13	24	1	10	3	18	5
Jace Mercer#	.244	86	20	21	5	18	21	20	12
Jack Strunc	.258	233	31	60	0	27	23	55	7
Jairus Richards*	.221	235	28	52	2	31	24	37	34
Jake Hirabayashi	.141	99	7	14	0	7	10	31	5
Jamey Smart*	.255	98	15	25	1	11	25	26	4
John Sechen	.175	114	22	20	3	9	21	47	5
Jose Layer	.239	67	9	16	0	4	2	20	4
Nikola Vasic	.224	85	15	19	0	8	15	28	6
Payton Robertson	.269	186	31	50	5	32	20	49	20
Peyton Isaacson*	.239	176	28	42	3	29	26	54	2
Rob Calabrese	.296	216	37	64	8	45	24	39	9
Rob Weissheier	.264	212	30	56	8	44	24	60	2
Zac Taylor	.245	273	38	67	6	29	27	83	9
Zach Racusin	.269	260	29	70	0	20	16	43	17

Player	W	L	ERA	G	SV	IP	H	BB	SO
Bryan Ketchie*	2	2	3.65	7	0	37	43	13	34
Danny Zardon	1	1	3.80	19	4	21.1	20	4	24
Garrett Christman	1	1	3.91	7	0	23	21	7	16
Jake Fisher*	2	6	6.11	12	0	56	80	11	47
Kenny Mathews*	8	9	4.82	19	0	104.2	133	14	81
Kyle Johnson	2	1	4.60	29	1	29.1	26	28	26

Layne Schnitz-Paxton	2	2	5.04	24	2	44.2	45	15	40
Logan Wiley	6	4	3.20	15	0	98.1	90	22	54
Miguel Ausua*	9	5	5.14	18	1	96.1	101	42	76
Neil Abbatiello*	3	4	3.49	29	2	56.2	44	31	69
Ryan Hare	1	1	2.83	18	3	28.2	23	14	29
Stetson Woods	0	1	1.74	21	1	20.2	13	10	29
Tyler Thornton	4	8	3.47	19	0	116.2	101	38	99

PIONEER LEAGUE

After many years as an affiliated league, the Pioneer League went through a massive transition in 2021. The league became a partner league. It also expanded to a lengthier 96-game season. And it adopted the "Knockout Round" where instead of extra innings, it had a home run derby to break ties.

With the longer season Missoula's Zac Almond broke the league home run record by hitting 26 home runs. His PaddleHeads won the league title, knocking off Boise.

Northern Division	W	L	PCT	GB
Missoula Paddleheads	62	28	.689	--
Idaho Falls Chukars	55	38	.591	8.5
Billings Mustangs	41	48	.461	20.5
Great Falls Voyagers	38	56	.404	26

Southern Division	W	L	PCT	GB
Ogden Raptors	52	39	.571	--
Grand Junction Rockies	51	41	.554	1.5
Boise Hawks	47	43	.522	4.5
Rocky Mountain Vibes	19	71	.211	32.5

Playoffs—Finals: Missoula defeated Boise 2-1 in best-of-three series. **Attendance:** Ogden Raptors 156,734; Boise Hawks 128,292; Rocky Mountain Vibes 124,762; Billings Mustangs 111,271; Idaho Falls Chukars 109,647; Grand Junction Rockies 73,518; Missoula Paddleheads 72,174; Great Falls Voyagers 62,976.

All-Star Team: C: Zac Almond, Missoula. **1B:** Webb Little, Idaho Falls. **2B:** Vinny Esposito, Grand Junction. **3B:** Cameron Thompson, Missoula. **SS:** Clay Fisher, Missoula. **OF:** Josh Broughton, Ogden; Matt Feinstein, Idaho Falls; Jakob Goldfarb, Ogden. **DH:** David Maberry, Ogden. **SP:** Matt Dallas, Boise. **RP:** Mark Simon, Missoula. **Closer:** Robbie Baker, Grand Junction. **MVP:** Zac Almond, Missoula. **Pitcher of the Year:** Mark Simon, Missoula. **Rookie of the Year:** Jalen Garcia, Billings. **International Player of the Year:** Jason Matthews, Great Falls. **Manager of the Year:** Michael Schlact, Missoula.

BATTING LEADERS

Player	Team	AVG	AB	R	H	HR	RBI
David Maberry	OR	.412	245	47	101	10	73
Clay Fisher	MP	.405	247	72	100	19	71
Josh Broughton	OR	.405	351	95	142	13	79
Kona Quiggle#	IFC	.381	273	77	104	14	84
Anthony Amicangelo	BIL	.378	296	57	112	5	85
Matt Feinstein	IFC	.366	358	110	131	22	116
Kyle Crowl	GF	.361	302	64	109	9	69
Zach Almond	MP	.354	333	83	118	26	91
Alejandro Rivero	BIL	.352	256	56	90	20	70
Alejandro Rivero	BH	.352	256	56	90	20	70
Cameron Thompson*	MP	.352	349	96	123	13	63
Nick Michaels	OR	.352	324	78	114	6	66

PITCHING LEADERS

Player	Team	W	L	ERA	IP	H	BB	SO
Matt Dallas	BH	9	4	4.35	97.1	94	53	119
Matt Mogollon	MP	2	3	4.40	73.2	70	25	77
Izzy Fuentes	GJ	7	4	4.56	81	105	17	81
Nick Floyd	IFC	8	2	4.60	86	97	34	64
Nico Tellache*	OR	6	4	4.96	78	86	17	60
Jake Binder	IFC	7	5	4.98	86.2	104	25	66
Daniel Silva	IFC	5	4	5.44	84.1	112	21	71
Mitch Lines	BH	7	3	5.44	87.2	101	33	69
Domingo Pena	MP	10	1	5.55	110.1	111	46	130
Brett Matthews	GJ	5	5	5.62	81.2	83	38	98

BILLINGS MUSTANGS

Player	AVG	AB	R	H	HR	RBI	BB	SO	SB
Alejandro Rivero	.352	256	56	90	20	70	14	37	1
Anthony Amicangelo	.378	296	57	112	5	85	31	42	2

	AVG	AB	R	H	HR	RBI	BB	SO	SB
Bo McClintock	.235	85	13	20	4	11	7	16	2
Brandon Pugh*	.246	130	24	32	2	16	22	24	1
Brandt Broussard	.212	170	34	36	2	16	36	44	4
Bryce Brown	.325	80	20	26	2	10	15	22	10
Byron Smith	.250	148	29	37	8	33	22	33	0
Caeden Harris	.227	110	17	25	1	8	9	33	7
Cam Comer*	.254	114	20	29	6	15	18	24	0
Chris Eusay#	.244	242	58	59	11	55	58	77	4
Chris Salvey	.284	81	7	23	5	14	8	31	0
Christian Funk*	.298	208	42	62	5	48	39	66	1
Christian Sepulveda	.317	161	47	51	7	42	17	27	16
Dalton Cobb	.250	84	26	21	3	9	37	32	15
Dalton Cornett*	.257	109	11	28	1	18	12	16	1
Daniel Cipriano	.212	99	14	21	1	13	8	20	0
Freddy Achecar*	.289	190	29	55	3	33	21	44	2
Greg White	.255	149	23	38	1	20	12	40	4
Hidekel Gonzalez	.308	195	30	60	5	33	15	36	3
Jalen Garcia	.349	372	97	130	16	75	33	89	29
Jason DiCochea	.334	305	67	102	10	66	27	28	2
Jerry Chavarria	.336	110	18	37	2	14	7	10	0
Jesus Azuaje	.284	250	35	71	2	29	36	27	1
Kolton Kendrick*	.260	100	17	26	2	17	17	35	0
Marcus Skundrich	.280	125	17	35	2	26	19	34	3
Myles Harris*	.228	197	34	45	6	27	34	74	1
Myles Miller*	.339	387	90	131	7	51	45	80	5
Nate Fisbeck	.360	100	27	36	10	28	10	19	0
Roby Enriquez*	.351	299	66	105	5	47	16	22	4
Tristen Carranza	.277	188	50	52	10	34	26	58	7
Tyler Jorgensen*	.306	307	57	94	5	49	20	42	8
Wladimir Galindo	.350	351	61	123	20	77	44	99	1

Player	W	L	ERA	G	SV	IP	H	BB	SO
Adolfo Espinoza	2	3	5.45	7	0	38	46	11	32
Alex Smith*	3	7	7.48	20	0	86.2	106	52	92
Chris Jefferson	3	1	7.91	6	0	33	44	9	34
Cody Hacker*	1	2	6.13	10	0	39.2	49	23	27
Colin Kelly	2	0	4.35	14	0	20.2	18	8	17
Gaylon Viney	2	7	8.31	15	0	56.1	78	31	55
Kelvan Pilot	3	2	5.32	11	0	44	45	29	49
Kollin Stone	2	0	8.41	19	1	20.1	29	21	23
Misael Castillo*	0	4	8.05	10	0	34.2	45	21	32
Neil Lang*	7	3	4.86	40	0	63	72	22	55
Taylor Bloye	2	2	4.15	6	0	34.2	32	14	28
Tyshaun Chapman	1	2	5.26	40	4	51.1	50	47	51
Yasnier Laureano	1	0	3.80	9	0	23.2	24	13	19

BOISE HAWKS

Player	AVG	AB	R	H	HR	RBI	BB	SO	SB
Alejandro Rivero	.352	256	56	90	20	70	14	37	1
Bo McClintock	.235	85	13	20	4	11	7	16	2
Bryce Brown	.325	80	20	26	2	10	15	22	10
Byron Smith	.250	148	29	37	8	33	22	33	0
Christian Funk*	.298	208	42	62	5	48	39	66	1
Greg White	.255	149	23	38	1	20	12	40	4
Hidekel Gonzalez	.308	195	30	60	5	33	15	36	3
Jason DiCochea	.334	305	67	102	10	66	27	28	2
Kolton Kendrick*	.260	100	17	26	2	17	17	35	0
Myles Harris*	.228	197	34	45	6	27	34	74	1
Myles Miller*	.339	387	90	131	7	51	45	80	5
Nate Fisbeck	.360	100	27	36	10	28	10	19	0
Roby Enriquez*	.351	299	66	105	5	47	16	22	4
Tyler Jorgensen*	.306	307	57	94	5	49	20	42	8
Wladimir Galindo	.350	351	61	123	20	77	44	99	1

Player	W	L	ERA	G	SV	IP	H	BB	SO
Cannon Chadwick	1	1	8.51	17	2	24.1	39	10	27
Conner Dand	3	2	3.69	25	5	31.2	29	15	40
Jake McDonald	1	2	6.23	11	0	30.1	41	19	23
Jared Price	4	2	7.28	31	4	59.1	82	27	64
Jay Baggs	2	3	13.06	12	0	31	37	47	24
Jayce Vancena	7	2	5.85	18	0	92.1	122	38	86
John Ellison*	1	1	6.75	7	0	21.1	32	11	11
Kenny Ogg	1	0	5.30	13	2	18.2	14	4	16
Liam Steigerwald	1	4	7.24	13	1	46	70	17	28
Luke Dawson	0	2	8.10	28	1	46.2	50	42	46
Matt Dallas	9	4	4.35	19	0	97.1	94	53	119
Matt Gabbert	3	6	5.55	14	0	61.2	84	13	44
Matt Terrones*	1	1	6.15	28	4	33.2	31	16	35

Mitch Lines	7	3	5.44	16	0	87.2	101	33	69
Tyler Tomaka	2	1	4.50	19	0	28	33	9	44
Zach Penrod*	3	4	5.66	14	0	68.1	65	42	85

GRAND JUNCTION ROCKIES

Player	AVG	AB	R	H	HR	RBI	BB	SO	SB
Alexis Monge	.328	119	23	39	0	18	13	28	11
Austin Elder*	.298	215	32	64	1	27	25	29	0
Conner Uselton	.198	86	14	17	1	10	6	19	1
Dondrei Hubbard	.338	311	75	105	20	81	35	48	15
Frankie Jezioro#	.381	147	41	56	5	30	13	42	8
Jake Anderson	.300	233	35	70	2	36	29	43	0
Jonathan Pino	.299	97	13	29	0	12	10	31	0
Jose Gutierrez#	.319	332	62	106	9	60	25	74	10
Josh Elvir*	.376	186	55	70	13	55	44	61	5
Kelvin Maldonado	.278	259	37	72	1	36	8	34	6
Luke Roskam*	.338	260	60	88	12	63	44	46	5
Nate Scantlin*	.330	339	91	112	6	54	56	85	24
Rolando Martinez*	.295	183	38	54	8	38	30	33	3
Tyler Sandoval	.267	75	12	20	2	10	7	29	0
Vinny Esposito	.299	374	86	112	23	85	53	103	3

Player	W	L	ERA	G	SV	IP	H	BB	SO
Brett Matthews	5	5	5.62	16	0	81.2	83	38	98
Cade Crader	3	3	6.75	11	0	56	67	14	34
Cody Clark	6	3	4.41	31	2	34.2	41	11	56
Isaiah Ramos*	1	2	10.33	14	0	49.2	87	23	45
Izzy Fuentes	7	4	4.56	15	0	81	105	17	81
James Varela	3	7	9.00	21	0	69	100	35	67
Jimmy Dobrash	3	1	8.62	12	0	47	72	21	41
Michael Flynn	2	4	9.26	12	0	45.2	59	34	51
Robbie Baker	4	1	0.77	29	12	35	20	5	50
Skyler Sylvester	2	3	6.12	5	0	25	37	6	31
Trevin Reynolds	1	2	3.56	10	0	43	46	11	47
Tyler Johnson	0	1	7.04	42	1	46	58	33	44
Winston Nicacio	2	3	11.73	21	0	33	47	18	33

GREAT FALLS VOYAGERS

Player	AVG	AB	R	H	HR	RBI	BB	SO	SB
Andy Atwood	.295	88	15	26	0	12	7	22	2
Ben Norman*	.356	163	36	58	13	59	18	30	6
Breydon Daniel#	.287	94	23	27	4	18	12	27	4
Chris Caffrey	.306	216	34	66	1	42	21	41	5
Cris Ruiz	.322	115	18	37	2	20	25	26	1
Dom Abbadessa	.353	221	65	78	5	42	23	48	15
Ernie Geraci	.275	69	20	19	0	12	12	15	1
Jackson Raper*	.316	133	33	42	10	34	15	40	2
Jacob Olson	.313	80	15	25	4	18	3	14	0
Jake Malec*	.217	69	18	15	0	2	15	31	6
Jason Matthews	.351	296	79	104	8	69	45	53	7
Kyle Crowl	.361	302	64	109	9	69	45	53	5
Kyle Hayes	.275	80	9	22	4	15	11	23	0
Michael Deeb*	.297	333	66	99	10	46	31	74	3
Nick Emanuel*	.284	109	20	31	0	21	21	24	0
Quintin Alexander	.278	237	37	66	1	29	23	54	7
Riley Jepson*	.355	76	14	27	3	16	17	16	3
Tavis Brunson	.277	119	25	33	2	20	11	34	4
Troy Dixon*	.264	193	37	51	5	30	32	56	4

Player	W	L	ERA	G	SV	IP	H	BB	SO
Aaron Kern	5	4	5.36	33	4	43.2	51	26	55
Anthony Becerra*	2	0	6.20	13	0	20.1	27	12	16
Ari Kaufman*	4	2	4.85	12	0	59.1	75	25	54
Austin Eggleston	0	3	7.62	19	0	26	38	12	29
Brad Demco*	2	0	9.25	20	0	24.1	19	30	37
CJ Grant-DeBose	1	2	5.59	19	0	48.1	44	28	43
Damon Ellis	5	1	6.32	11	0	57	79	30	45
Grant Larson*	2	5	3.18	35	8	45.1	46	9	46
Grey Lyttle	4	0	4.99	8	0	39.2	37	18	43
Lenny Gwizdala*	0	3	8.32	12	0	48.2	74	26	40
Malcolm Grady*	1	1	6.29	17	0	24.1	24	23	19
Matt Thomas	0	1	6.69	26	0	36.1	47	17	28
Nate Harmon	3	9	9.55	14	0	70.2	117	29	61
Quincy Jones*	4	7	6.68	18	0	95.2	139	27	53
Sean Hupp	0	10	7.94	20	2	45.1	65	15	26
Shane Gustafson	3	3	7.29	7	0	33.1	45	8	31

INDEPENDENT LEAGUES

IDAHO FALLS CHUKARS

Player	AVG	AB	R	H	HR	RBI	BB	SO	SB
Alexis Monge	.343	108	32	37	0	19	22	20	1
Andrew Don	.331	350	86	116	8	71	40	94	3
Brady West*	.301	153	41	46	8	39	19	52	0
Chuck Steele	.300	70	26	21	0	10	12	13	6
Daniel Martins-Molinari	.329	164	40	54	6	39	22	44	0
Hogan Brown*	.290	62	8	18	0	13	6	17	1
Hunter Hisky*	.347	219	59	76	4	55	32	40	1
Kona Quiggle#	.381	273	77	104	14	84	29	65	5
Matt Feinstein	.366	358	110	131	22	116	82	83	7
Sam Little*	.254	185	43	47	4	43	25	51	1
Steve Barmakian*	.348	325	95	113	3	51	50	46	3
Thomas DeBonville	.336	301	83	101	12	76	26	65	26
Tyler Kelly	.365	189	53	69	8	47	16	30	9
Tyler Van Marter	.327	208	35	68	2	43	20	31	0
Webb Little*	.341	381	100	130	15	102	54	66	4

Player	W	L	ERA	G	SV	IP	H	BB	SO
Alex Fishberg	0	1	3.52	13	0	23	14	13	28
Austin Dubsky	8	2	6.66	15	0	77	100	28	62
Damon Ellis	3	3	7.68	7	0	41	55	14	25
Daniel Silva	7	4	5.44	15	0	84.1	112	21	71
Eric Brodkowitz	3	1	5.40	7	0	36.2	43	5	32
Jake Binder	7	5	4.98	16	0	86.2	104	25	66
Jake Waters	3	1	5.29	26	1	47.2	40	39	39
Joe Slocum	4	5	7.10	15	0	58.1	102	20	27
Jon Nunnally	2	3	6.10	34	2	41.1	44	24	49
Keagan McGinnis	1	2	7.80	29	1	30	21	36	51
Matt Geoffrion	1	1	13.70	13	0	23	37	23	21
Nate Jenkins	1	2	6.80	37	3	45	60	19	36
Nick Floyd	8	2	4.60	22	0	86	97	34	64
Victor Rodriguez*	3	1	5.40	38	1	43.1	50	16	45
Yeison Medina	1	1	9.32	21	1	28	38	14	24

MISSOULA PADDLEHEADS

Player	AVG	AB	R	H	HR	RBI	BB	SO	SB
Aaron Bond*	.291	261	63	76	15	52	48	96	23
Brandon Riley*	.316	358	82	113	5	52	53	66	5
Cameron Thompson*	.352	349	96	123	13	63	48	86	15
Clay Fisher	.405	247	72	100	19	71	22	39	6
Dean Nevarez	.314	172	36	54	12	35	21	44	1
Jared Akins*	.293	280	62	82	13	56	41	72	5
Jayson Newman	.326	86	20	28	8	25	9	12	0
Jose Reyes*	.333	174	29	58	5	33	13	22	3
Luke Navigato	.340	153	49	52	6	39	26	20	2
McClain O'Connor	.315	241	51	76	15	43	18	51	6
Nick Gatewood*	.346	356	69	123	19	94	30	73	2
Sam Troyer	.256	82	19	21	1	16	17	27	7
Tristen Carranza	.307	88	20	27	3	16	12	22	7
Zach Almond	.354	333	83	118	26	91	53	49	0

Player	W	L	ERA	G	SV	IP	H	BB	SO
Andrew Bash	2	0	1.80	5	0	25	21	5	27
Andy Toelken	2	1	7.71	5	0	23.1	41	6	19
Chris Burica*	1	3	9.09	10	0	32.2	46	7	28
Dazon Cole	0	1	4.35	20	5	20.2	18	10	23
Domingo Pena	10	1	5.55	21	0	110.1	111	46	130
Felix Dieguez*	2	0	9.09	12	0	31.2	46	20	24
Garrett Westberg	2	1	4.43	24	1	20.1	10	17	28
Jason Seever*	2	1	6.20	8	0	20.1	25	8	12
Kevin Gould	4	2	7.29	21	0	33.1	42	16	30
Kevin Hilton	9	2	5.93	15	0	74.1	107	22	45
Kida De La Cruz	2	0	3.86	26	1	30.1	23	24	46
Mark Simon	9	2	3.00	36	7	60	55	14	87
Mason Schwellenbach	3	2	4.41	18	1	63.1	72	28	59
Matt Mogollon	2	3	4.40	32	1	73.2	70	25	77
Palmer Wenzel	4	0	4.71	18	0	42	52	24	28
Rabon Martin*	3	1	7.85	26	1	28.2	36	21	23
William Freeman	1	0	7.23	15	0	23.2	32	13	16

OGDEN RAPTORS

Player	AVG	AB	R	H	HR	RBI	BB	SO	SB
Andy Armstrong	.275	204	40	56	1	27	21	34	4
David Maberry	.412	245	47	101	10	73	31	52	1
Dom Abbadessa	.333	78	22	26	0	10	8	13	12
Frankie Jezioro#	.264	87	28	23	2	11	15	28	12
Jakob Goldfarb*	.342	351	116	120	24	90	50	78	45
Josh Broughton	.405	351	95	142	13	79	27	55	13
Kyle Kaufman	.316	114	18	36	4	27	7	10	0
Nick Michaels	.352	324	78	114	6	66	34	76	11
Niko Pacheco	.304	112	24	34	2	21	15	40	2
Owen Taylor#	.277	238	51	66	6	45	42	73	4
Pavin Parks*	.330	361	100	119	15	102	64	90	24
Raul Shah	.350	260	64	91	8	66	40	60	4
Reese Alexiades	.391	92	21	36	2	23	8	20	4

Player	W	L	ERA	G	SV	IP	H	BB	SO
Anthony Donatella*	5	1	6.35	26	0	73.2	102	17	62
Christopher Campbell	1	2	6.24	38	0	57.2	73	23	51
Colt Mink*	0	2	7.56	14	1	25	30	18	25
Dylan Pearce	6	0	4.26	24	1	38	36	20	52
Gavin Weyman	2	3	9.14	9	0	21.2	33	10	14
Jackson Cunningham	2	1	5.36	26	0	42	63	8	26
Jackson Sigman	3	0	2.30	17	0	27.1	21	13	36
Josh Broughton	1	2	9.28	10	1	21.1	27	8	16
Justin Watland	1	0	7.66	15	0	24.2	43	12	23
Mark Mixon	6	1	5.90	40	6	58	53	24	51
Mitchell Miller*	5	4	5.71	23	0	69.1	76	38	86
Nico Tellache	6	4	4.96	14	0	78	86	17	80
Reza Aleaziz	4	7	7.11	25	0	63.1	98	21	56
Tate Budnick	3	3	9.74	29	1	61	113	20	46

ROCKY MOUNTAIN VIBES

Player	AVG	AB	R	H	HR	RBI	BB	SO	SB
Aldo Buendia	.319	113	20	36	1	6	10	15	0
Aldo Nunez#	.259	259	48	67	1	20	15	60	15
Antonio Villaescusa	.295	105	5	31	0	8	5	23	0
Brandon Perez	.270	345	55	93	4	30	16	64	6
Carlos Gallardo	.243	107	18	26	1	9	18	35	0
Carlos Tirado*	.253	91	13	23	4	8	9	29	0
Edgar Salazar*	.300	190	35	57	5	26	18	36	2
Eduardo Ceballos#	.192	78	5	15	0	7	12	28	1
Ethan Lopez	.346	81	20	28	5	14	7	10	0
Griffin Barnes	.307	277	32	85	3	46	13	53	1
Jacob Barfield	.332	310	70	103	21	70	35	76	7
Joshua Esparza	.261	299	33	78	8	47	6	78	5
Juan Barboza	.211	90	12	19	0	7	20	18	3
Luis Matos	.200	70	6	14	0	8	5	24	3
Manny Olloque	.330	227	52	75	10	39	28	55	13
Mike Annone*	.308	117	13	36	3	22	13	17	0
Sergio Macias*	.323	127	22	41	8	30	15	30	1
Tyler Plantier	.177	62	2	11	0	4	2	26	0

Player	W	L	ERA	G	SV	IP	H	BB	SO
Agustin Herrera*	0	2	16.77	17	0	22	39	31	20
Angel Camacho*	1	3	9.00	6	0	23	30	18	21
Aron Solis*	2	9	8.17	20	0	82.2	127	40	76
Arturo Guajardo	1	1	6.94	11	0	23.1	25	15	26
Francisco Romero	1	0	15.78	15	0	21.2	48	17	19
Heriberto Sanchez*	1	6	9.00	16	0	46	81	26	32
Jassiel Ochoa*	2	10	8.09	24	0	79	101	51	61
Jean Correa	2	8	7.44	18	0	90.2	121	34	94
Jhonatan Lopez	2	9	8.95	36	3	62.1	100	34	54
Jose Gomez	0	0	12.76	20	0	30.1	59	33	32
Juan Pineda	0	3	8.34	30	1	41	67	19	33
Nattino Diplan	1	3	7.97	10	0	40.2	50	21	44
Onas Farfan*	1	1	5.00	30	4	45	52	21	58
Oscar Marcelino	1	1	4.57	17	4	21.2	25	12	26
Seth Davis*	2	3	5.88	17	0	26	30	15	26

PECOS LEAGUE

Because of coronavirus restrictions, the Pecos League crowned two champions in 2021. Tucson knocked off Roswell to win the Pecos League title while San Rafael knocked off Martinez in the Bay Series championship for the league's California teams. The title was Tucson's third Pecos League title and second in a row.

Mountain North Division	W	L	PCT	GB
Colorado Springs Snow Sox	29	14	.674	--
Garden City Wind	33	22	.600	4
Trinidad Triggers	19	31	.380	16
Salina Stockade	10	41	.196	25

Mountain South Division

Mountain South Division	W	L	PCT	GB
Tucson Saguaros	32	23	.581	--
Alpine Cowboys	30	25	.545	2
Roswell Invaders	30	26	.535	3
Santa Fe Fuego	27	28	.490	5

Pacific Division	W	L	PCT	GB
Bakersfield Train Robbers	33	5	.868	--
Martinez Sturgeon	23	17	.575	11
San Rafael Pacifics	21	18	.538	13
Santa Cruz Seaweed	16	24	.400	18
Monterey Amberjacks	14	24	.368	19
Wasco Reserve	10	29	.256	24

Playoffs—First Round: Roswell defeated Alpine 2-1 and Garden City defeated Colorado Springs 2-1 in best-of-three series. **Second Round:** Roswell defeated Garden City 2-1 and Tucson defeated Bakersfield 2-1 in best-of-three series. **Finals:** Tucson defeated Roswell 2-1 in best-of-three series.

BAY SERIES PLAYOFFS—Semifinals: San Rafael defeated Santa Cruz 2-0 and Martinez defeated Monterey 2-0 in best-of-three series. **Finals:** San Rafael defeated Martinez 2-1 in best-of-three series.

BATTING LEADERS

Player	Team	AVG	AB	R	H	HR	RBI
Dakota McFadden	BTR	.441	170	68	75	18	80
Bret Leiferman	ROS	.417	216	59	90	12	68
Gabe Wurtz	TUC	.414	220	70	91	22	86
Markus Bracey	CS	.413	155	51	64	5	54
Alex Jackson	CS	.412	177	80	73	9	53
Kokko Figueiredo	TUC	.407	209	69	85	5	50
Dakota Popham	CS	.404	178	46	72	14	92
Ozzie Millet	TT	.392	171	47	67	8	46
Vaughn Parker	TT	.384	164	38	63	1	41
AJ Pollack	MON	.384	125	47	48	6	31

PITCHING LEADERS

Player	Team	W	L	ERA	IP	H	BB	SO
Riley Cleary	MAR	4	1	1.92	32.2	22	7	37
Gabe Katich	SCS	0	4	3.13	46	45	12	56
Nathan Lu	MAR	1	2	3.37	34.2	32	14	43
Sam Wells	SRP	3	1	3.79	40.1	48	4	24
Rene Ramirez	MAR	4	0	3.89	39.1	41	15	31
Auggie Martinez	TUC	6	1	3.92	59.2	71	26	75
Jarrod Dumont	SRP	5	1	4.07	53	45	20	50
Zach Devon	BTR	7	1	4.15	52	47	27	58
Luke Kelley	BTR	2	1	4.40	32.2	41	20	34
Jonny Damon	BTR	2	2	4.55	51.1	61	14	42

UNITED SHORE LEAGUE

In a league with four teams sharing the same park, constructing a dynasty would seem to be difficult. But it hasn't been an issue for manager Jim Essian and the Utica Unicorns. Essian's Unicorns won their third consecutive USPBL title by edging the Eastside Diamond Hoppers, 6-5, in 10 innings in the league's 2021 championship game. Utica also dominated the regular season—it was the only one of the four teams to finish with a winning record. Jon Hodo was named the championship game MVP as he singled in the deciding run in the bottom of the 10th.

East Division	W	L	PCT	GB
Utica Unicorns	23	12	.657	-
Eastside Diamond Hoppers	19	16	.543	4

West Division	W	L	PCT	GB
Westside Woolly Mammoths	16	20	.444	-
Birmingham Bloomfield Beavers	13	23	.361	3

Playoffs—First Round: Birmingham defeated Westside. **Semifinal:** Eastside defeated Birmingham. **Finals:** Utica defeated Eastside.

BATTING LEADERS

Player	Team	AVG	AB	R	H	HR	RBI
Lamar Biggs	WEST	.359	117	26	42	6	24
Connor Bagnieski	BBB	.346	78	18	27	1	9
Trent Bauer	WEST	.324	108	18	35	1	11
Ben McConnell	EAST	.317	104	24	33	0	9

Player	Team	AVG	AB	R	H	HR	RBI
Jordyn Finney	WEST	.316	57	10	18	0	5
Joe Burke	EAST	.314	51	10	16	6	15
Juan Lopez-Rios	EAST	.303	66	7	20	0	6
Coleton Horner	WEST	.297	37	5	11	1	6
Adrian Guzman	WEST	.293	99	13	29	1	9

PITCHING LEADERS

Player	Team	W	L	ERA	IP	H	BB	SO
Adrian Cook	EAST	4	2	2.97	40	35	25	47
Charles Dunavan	BBB	3	5	2.97	40	38	16	54
Andrew Verbrugge	EAST	2	4	3.53	43.2	42	30	26
Miguel Cirino	UU	1	1	2.70	44	30	19	33
Donovan Thacker	WEST	0	4	4.26	44.1	54	17	25
Johnny Breidenthal	WEST	1	5	3.66	49.2	47	18	28
Zack Jones	UU	3	1	1.12	50	33	9	35
Greg Loukinen	WEST	5	2	1.39	55.1	30	27	77
A.J. Kullman	BBB	2	5	3.33	73.2	88	22	56

INTERNATIONAL

Japan Wins First Gold Medal In Baseball

Japan won its first baseball gold medal in the Olympics, and did so on its home soil.

BY J.J. COOPER

It took the Olympics coming to baseball-crazy Japan to get the sport re-entered into the Olympics after a 13-year hiatus.

Fittingly, baseball's return was celebrated by Japan winning its long-desired first baseball gold medal.

Masato Morishita and four relievers combined to shut out Team USA and give Japan a tense, 2-0 win in the gold medal game at the Tokyo Olympics.

The win is Japan's first gold medal in baseball since it became an official Olympic sport in 1992. Japan did win the 1984 tournament, but baseball was included in the Los Angeles Olympic games as a demonstration sport. Japan had won two bronze medals (1992 and 2004) and one silver (1996) since baseball became a medal sport. It also finished fourth in 2000 and 2008.

With the Olympics being played in Japan, the team pulled out all the stops to try to secure its first gold medal. As it has done before, Nippon Professional Baseball shut down its season to allow top players to play in the Olympics.

And it worked. Japan went through the six-team Olympics tournament undefeated. It beat fourth-place finisher South Korea. It beat the bronze medalist (Dominican Republic) and it beat the silver medalist (Team USA) twice.

In the gold medal game, Munetaka Murakami's home run in the third inning was all the scoring either side was able to get for most of the game. Murakami's blast gave Japan an early 1-0 lead, and Japan's pitching staff and defense held onto it.

The U.S. put runners on first and second in both the fifth and sixth innings, but failed to score in either situation. Nick Allen doubled with one out in the seventh to put the tying run in scoring position, but ground outs by Jack Lopez and Eddy Alvarez squelched the potential rally.

INTERNATIONAL

OLYMPICS STANDINGS

Team	W	L	Team	W	L
Japan	5	0	Korea	3	4
USA	4	2	Israel	1	4
Dominican Republic	3	3	Mexico	0	3

Gold Medal Game: Japan defeated United States, 2-0.
Bronze Medal Game: Dominican Republic defeated South Korea, 10-6.

BATTING LEADERS

PLAYER	TEAM	AVG	AB	R	H	HR	RBI	TB
Kim Hyeseong	KOR	.615	13	3	8	0	1	8
Joey Meneses	MEX	.500	12	2	6	1	4	10
Park Hae-Min	KOR	.440	25	7	11	0	5	13
Tyler Austin	USA	.417	24	5	10	2	7	19
Julio Rodríguez	DOM	.417	24	3	10	1	4	15
Mitch Glasser	ISR	.412	17	4	7	0	4	10
Kim Hyunsoo	KOR	.400	30	6	12	3	7	25
Kai Takuya	JPN	.385	13	3	5	0	3	5
Melky Cabrera	DOM	.381	21	0	8	0	2	9
Ryan Lavarnway	ISR	.350	20	3	7	2	3	14
Yamada Tetsuto	JPN	.350	20	7	7	1	7	12
Yoshida Masataka	JPN	.350	20	1	7	0	2	7
Kondoh Kensuke	JPN	.333	6	1	2	0	0	2
Murakami Munetaka	JPN	.333	15	6	5	1	3	8
Sakamoto Hayato	JPN	.333	21	3	7	1	4	13
Hur Kyoungmin	KOR	.320	25	2	8	0	1	11
Kang Baekho	KOR	.308	26	2	8	0	4	9
Asamura Hideto	JPN	.294	17	3	5	0	1	7
Nick Allen	USA	.286	21	3	6	1	2	11
Erick Mejía	DOM	.286	21	4	6	0	0	8

PITCHING LEADERS

PLAYER	TEAM	W	L	ERA	G	IP	H	BB	SO
Anthony Gose	USA	0	0	0.00	4	5.1	1	1	3
Itoh Hiromi	JPN	1	0	0.00	3	5	4	2	5
Scott Kazmir	USA	1	0	0.00	1	5	2	1	5
Ryder Ryan	USA	1	0	0.00	4	5	2	1	5
Ángel Sánchez	DOM	1	0	0.00	1	5	2	1	1
Cho Sangwoo	KOR	1	0	1.13	6	8	5	4	10
Yamamoto Yoshinobu	JPN	1	0	1.59	2	11.1	7	2	18
Nick Martinez	USA	1	1	1.64	2	11	9	1	16
Joe Ryan	USA	1	0	1.74	2	10.1	9	1	8
Morishita Masato	JPN	2	0	1.80	2	10	8	0	8
Kuribayashi Ryoji	JPN	2	0	1.80	5	5	3	2	6
Josh Zeid	ISR	0	0	3.12	3	8.2	6	2	5
Cristopher Mercedes	DOM	1	0	3.21	3	14	10	5	12
José Díaz	DOM	0	0	3.60	5	5	5	2	2
Lee Euilee	KOR	0	1	4.50	2	10	9	4	18
Ko Youngpyo	KOR	0	1	5.59	2	9.2	10	1	13
Raul Valdés	DOM	0	0	5.79	2	9.1	16	3	7

Tokyo 2020 All-Olympic Baseball Team
C: Takuya Kai, Japan. **1B:** Triston Casas, USA. **2B:** Eddy Alvarez, USA. **3B:** Erick Mejía, Dominican Republic. **SS:** Hayato Sakamoto, Japan. **LF:** Hyun-Soo Kim, Korea. **CF:** Hae Min Park, Korea. **RF:** Mitch Glasser, Israel. **DH:** Tyler Austin, USA. **RHP:** Yoshinobu Yamamoto, Japan. **LHP:** Anthony Gose, USA.
Best Defensive Player: Nick Allen, USA. **MVP:** Tetsuto Yamada, Japan.

Japan got an insurance run in the eighth. Tetsuto Yamada's single began the inning and a sacrifice bunt advanced him to second. On an 0-2 count, Masataka Yoshida golfed a ball into center field for a single. USA center fielder Jack Lopez, an infielder by trade filling in for the injured Bubba Starling, threw home while Yamada halted at third. But Lopez's throw was far up the third base line and got past USA catcher Mark Kolozsvary. Yamada sprinted home, barely beating the throw to give Japan a 2-0 lead.

That was enough for Japan's closer Ryoji Kuribayashi. He blew Jamie Westbrook away for a strikeout. Kolozsvary lined a ball to left field, but right at Masataka Yoshida for the second out.

Allen kept Team USA alive with a two-strike single to right field, but Lopez followed with a ground out to second, setting off Japan's celebration at the mound.

Team USA's silver medal finish marks only the second time the U.S. has played for the gold. Team USA now has one gold (2000), one silver (2020) and two bronze medals (1996 and 2008).

Meanwhile, Japan has a gold medal and two bronze medals in the Olympics. It continues what has become a healthy international rivalry as the two countries battle for international supremacy.

If Cuba was the dominant team of the 20th century when it came to international baseball, Japan and the United States have battled for that title this century.

Japan has two World Baseball Classic crowns. The U.S. has one. When it comes to lower-level international tournaments, the U.S. has won four of the last five U-18 World Cups. Japan won the most recent Premier12 tournament

The two teams are clearly the class of international baseball, and for now, Samurai Japan has bragging rights. The return of the World Baseball Classic in 2023 will give the two countries another chance to face off.

"The Japanese team, they were very, very tough. They were deep in pitching. They had a lot of situational hitters in their lineup and were able to do things when they needed to and they deserved to win," USA manager Mike Scioscia said. "They played the best. We tip our caps to them and we're a little disappointed we didn't get there, but we know we played as well as we could."

Juan Francisco hit the tiebreaking two-run double as the Dominican Republic scored five runs in the top of the eighth inning, and the D.R. rallied to beat South Korea, 10-6, in the bronze medal game of the Summer Olympics.

The U.S. once again put the tying run on base in the eighth on a Tyler Austin single. But Triston Casas couldn't check his swing on a slider off the plate, Todd Frazier popped up and Eric Filia grounded into a fielder's choice.

Tijuana Rallies Back To Win League Title

A year after the coronavirus pandemic wiped away the 2020 season, the Toros de Tijuana welcomed back the Mexican League by pulling off the remarkable.

In the first round of the playoffs, Tijuana rallied from a 3-1 deficit to win three straight games to edge Aguascaliente. After having an easier time in the second round of the playoffs and the North Division championship series, Tijuana then lost the first three games of the championship series—two of them at home—meaning that it was finished with one more loss.

But after a rainout delayed the series by a day, four relievers (Teddy Stankiewicz, Oliver Perez, Michael Tonkin and Fernando Rodney) held Yucatan scoreless for 6.1 innings as Tijuana rallied for a 6-2 win.

Rodney blew the save in Game 5, but he settled down to throw two scoreless innings after that and Xorge Carrillo singled to score Gabriel Gutierrez in a 4-3, 11-inning win. The Game 6 win was a much easier 10-3 Tijuana victory. The improbable comeback was finished off by Peter O'Brien and Stankiewicz. Stankiewicz threw the first six scoreless innings of a three-hit shutout and O'Brien homered in the third to kick-start the offense in a 3-0 Game 7 Serie del Rey clincher.

STANDINGS

NORTHERN DIVISION

	W	L	PCT	GB
Guadalajara	46	17	.730	-
Tijuana	40	25	.615	7
Saltillo	36	30	.545	11.5
Monclova	35	31	.530	12.5
Aguascalientes	30	31	.492	15
Laguna	31	33	.484	15.5
Monterrey	30	33	.476	16
Dos Laredos	30	36	.455	17.5
Durango	20	45	.308	27

SOUTHERN DIVISION

	W	L	PCT	GB
Mexico	41	23	.640	-
Tabasco	36	30	.545	6
Yucatan	34	30	.531	7
Veracruz	35	31	.530	7
Puebla	31	31	.500	9
Quintana Roo	32	33	.492	9.5
Leon	29	37	.439	13
Campeche	24	39	.381	16.5
Oaxaca	20	45	.308	21.5

Playoffs—First Round—Mexico defeated Quintana Roo 4-1, Guadalajara defeated Laguna 4-3, Yucatan defeated Veracruz 4-2, Tijuana defeated Aguascalientes 4-3, Monclova defeated Saltillo 4-1 and Tabasco defeated Puebla 4-1 in best-of-seven series.

Second Round: Tijuana defeated Monclova 4-1, Yucatan defeated Tabasco 4-1, Mexico defeated Veracruz 4-1 and Guadalajara defeated Aguascalientes 4-2 in best-of-seven series.

Division Finals: Yucatan defeated Mexico 4-1 and Tijuana defeated Guadalajara 4-2 in best-of-seven series.

Championship: Tijuana defeated Yucatan 4-3 in best-of-seven series.

BATTING LEADERS

Batter	Team	AVG	AB	R	H	HR	RBI	SB
Heras, Leo	GDL	.401	157	39	63	9	42	7
Vasquez, Niko	GDL	.387	212	51	82	11	51	1
Urrutia, Henry	SAL	.385	221	42	85	12	52	0
Rodriguez, Isaac	TIJ	.380	184	41	70	3	20	17
Murillo, Agustin	2 Teams	.379	169	33	64	4	28	2
Castro, Leandro	TIJ	.378	246	51	93	14	72	3
Polo, Tito	DUR	.375	168	41	63	5	16	11
Hernandez, Josuan	SAL	.372	247	53	92	7	31	7
Amarista, Alexi	VER	.369	244	56	90	14	42	2
Mendoza, Victor	MTY	.365	200	31	73	11	45	2
Drake, Yadir	YUC	.362	207	44	75	12	40	3
Garcia, Edwin	TAB	.362	213	28	77	1	35	1
Mayora, Daniel	DUR	.361	202	27	73	4	28	0
Castillo, Jesse	GDL	.357	221	51	79	11	49	3
Serrano, Maikel	TAB	.356	208	32	74	5	39	0
Rodriguez, Henry	2 Teams	.356	180	35	64	7	33	4
Olmedo-Barrera, David	PUE	.354	206	41	73	16	45	3
Tavárez, Aneury	DUR	.353	204	45	72	10	36	8
Guzman, Miguel	PUE	.346	217	46	75	6	31	4
Wing, Michael	AGS	.345	171	33	59	9	44	1

PITCHING LEADERS

Pitcher	Team	W-L	ERA	IP	H	BB	SO
Escobar, Luis	TAB	7-2	2.54	67	48	31	43
Thompson, Jake	YUC	4-3	3.02	60	48	16	35
Pineda, Rafael	LAG	4-4	3.16	77	74	19	47
Nakamura, Masaru	GDL	8-0	3.25	53	40	18	46
Torres, Edgar	MEX	7-0	3.38	53	56	17	35
Van Meter, Joe	TIJ	5-2	3.49	59	62	16	46
Marrujo, Ignacio	TAB	7-3	3.51	56	57	14	29
Oramas, Juan Pablo	TAB	4-5	3.62	60	53	22	35
Molina, Nestor	AGS	1-4	3.67	54	59	13	51
Negrin, Yoanner	YUC	4-4	3.79	62	65	13	29
Castillo, Cristian	LEO	4-1	3.88	70	76	12	35
Gutierrez, Demetrio	CAM	1-4	3.98	61	56	19	39
Araujo, Elvis	MTY	4-2	4.14	63	69	27	68
Cruz, Luis Leroy	LEO	4-2	4.23	55	61	25	33
Roeder, Josh	LAR	5-2	4.30	73	86	19	52
Vasquez, Anthony	GDL	5-1	4.39	53	59	13	24
Rios, Francisco	MVA	4-4	4.39	68	56	35	64
Colon, Bartolo	MVA	6-2	4.55	61	70	10	40
Martinez, Jorge	2 Teams	3-3	4.69	63	71	23	43
Rios, Wilmer	MVA	5-2	4.70	59	76	12	43

JAPAN

Yakult Clinches Japan Series Win

I t took 12 innings, but Shingo Kawabata's pinch-hit single drove in Yasutaka Shiomi with the winning run in the Yakult Swallow's 2-1 Game 6 victory that clinched the Japan Series.

The win was Yakult's first title since 2001 and its sixth overall. The Pacific League had won eight straight Japan Series before this year.

Unlike the World Series in the U.S., games in the Japan Series cannot go longer than 12 innings, so the game would have ended in a tie if Yakult didn't win in the bottom of the 12th.

The Japan Series was a remarkable pairing of two teams that had been downtrodden in recent years. The Swallows had finished in the basement of the Central League in 2019 and 2020 and five times since 2011. The Buffaloes had finished last in the Pacific League in 2019 and 2020 and four times since 2011.

The two teams bounced back because of some young stars. Corner infielder Munetaka Murakami hit 39 home runs for Yakult as a 21-year-old. For Orix, 22-year-old righthander Yoshinobu Yamato went 18-5, 1.39, while 19-year-old lefthander Hiroya Miyagi went 13-4, 2.51.

After the season Dennis Sarfate retired. The 40-year-old has spent the past 11 seasons pitching in Japan. He set an NPB record with 54 saves in 2017.

Masahiro Tanaka returned to play in the JPPL.

CENTRAL LEAGUE

Team	W	L	T	PCT	GB
Tokyo Yakult Swallows	73	52	18	.584	—
Hanshin Tigers	77	56	10	.579	0.5
Yomiuri Giants	61	62	20	.496	11
Hiroshima Toyo Carp	63	68	12	.481	13
Chunichi Dragons	55	71	17	.437	18.5
Yokohama DeNA Baystars	54	73	16	.425	20

Playoffs: First round: Yomiuri defeated Hanshin 2-0 in best-of-three series. **Climax Series:** Yakult defeated Yomiuri 2-0-1 in best-of-five series. **Japan Series:** Yakult defeated Orix 4-2 in best-of-seven series.

CENTRAL LEAGUE BATTING LEADERS

Player, Team	AVG	AB	R	H	HR	RBI	SB
Seiya Suzuki, Carp	.317	435	77	138	38	88	9
Shogo Sakakura, Carp	.315	422	58	133	12	68	4
Shugo Maki, BayStars	.314	487	73	153	22	71	2
Koji Chikamoto, Tigers	.313	569	91	178	10	50	24
Masayuki Kuwahara, BayStars	.310	519	84	161	14	43	12
Keita Sano, BayStars	.303	545	73	165	17	72	0
Toshiro Miyazaki, BayStars	.301	519	61	156	16	73	0
Kaito Kozono, Carp	.298	449	65	134	5	35	4
Yohei Ohshima, Dragons	.292	548	54	160	1	34	16
Ryoma Nishikawa, Carp	.286	504	57	144	12	60	3
Kento Itohara, Tigers	.286	441	34	126	2	30	6
Yuhei Nakamura, Swallows	.279	377	47	105	2	36	0
Yasutaka Shiomi, Swallows	.278	474	80	132	14	59	21
Munetaka Murakami, Swallows	.278	500	82	139	39	112	12

Ryosuke Kikuchi, Carp	.277	494	64	137	16	60	1
Dayan Vicciedo, Dragons	.275	480	44	132	17	70	1
Seiya Matsubara, Giants	.274	431	69	118	12	37	15
Takumu Nakano, Tigers	.273	466	45	127	1	36	30
Tetsuto Yamada, Swallows	.272	493	84	134	34	101	4
Hayato Sakamoto, Giants	.271	424	53	115	19	46	2
Yoshihiro Maru, Giants	.265	392	58	104	23	55	5
Kazuma Okamoto, Giants	.265	521	71	138	39	113	1
Yusuke Ohyama, Tigers	.260	466	55	121	21	71	2
Shuhei Takahashi, Dragons	.259	475	40	123	5	39	1
Jose Osuna, Swallows	.258	469	42	121	13	60	3
Jefry Marte, Tigers	.258	446	55	115	22	71	0
Norichika Aoki, Swallows	.258	446	57	115	9	56	0

OTHER NOTABLE HITTERS

Player, Team	AVG	AB	R	H	HR	RBI	SB
Tyler Austin, Baystars	.303	373	60	113	28	74	1
Zelous Wheeler, Giants	.289	384	44	111	15	56	3
Justin Smoak, Giants	.272	114	11	31	7	14	0
Jose Osuna, Swallows	.258	469	42	121	13	60	3
Ariel Martinez, Dragons	.244	82	7	20	2	7	0
Mel Rojas Jr., Giants	.217	189	18	41	8	21	1
Joe Gunkel, Tigers	.161	31	3	5	0	0	0
Mike Gerber, Dragons	.156	45	3	7	0	1	0
Yariel Rodriguez, Dragons	.133	15	0	2	0	0	0

CENTRAL LEAGUE PITCHING LEADERS

Pitcher, Team	W	L	ERA	IP	H	HR	BB	SO
Yuya Yanagi, Dragons	11	6	2.20	172	133	11	41	168
Koyo Aoyagi, Tigers	13	6	2.48	156	143	11	48	104
Yudai Ohno, Dragons	7	11	2.95	143	121	12	26	118
Masato Morishita, Carp	8	7	2.98	163	144	16	52	132
Daichi Ohsera, Carp	10	5	3.07	147	136	12	31	102
Shinnosuke Ogasawara, Dragons	8	10	3.64	143	141	16	51	115
Yuki Nishi, Tigers	6	9	3.76	144	143	12	40	95
Aren Kuri, Carp	13	9	3.81	149	150	18	51	102
Shosei Togo, Giants	9	8	4.27	152	130	19	58	138

OTHER NOTABLE PITCHERS

Pitcher, Team	W	L	ERA	IP	H	HR	BB	SO
Ryoji Kuribayashi, Carp	0	1	0.86	52	23	1	28	81
Robert Suarez, Tigers	1	1	1.16	62	40	0	8	58
Katsuki Matayoshi, Dragons	3	2	1.28	63	47	2	22	41
Raidel Martinez, Dragons	1	4	2.06	48	26	1	10	59
Noboru Shimizu, Swallows	3	6	2.39	68	55	12	18	74
Kota Nakagawa, Giants	4	3	2.47	55	47	2	10	49
Scott McGough, Swallows	3	2	2.52	64	43	7	23	76
Daisuke Sobue, Dragons	1	2	2.59	49	59	1	9	30
Suguru Iwazaki, Tigers	3	4	2.65	58	47	6	15	51

Player	W	L	ERA	IP	H	HR	BB	SO
Ryuta Konno, Swallows	7	1	2.76	62	55	1	25	63
Rubby De La Rosa, Giants	1	0	2.83	41	38	3	12	34
Thyago Vieira, Giants	0	3	2.93	55	38	3	26	64
Hiroto Fuku, Dragons	2	2	3.18	45	37	4	15	38
Yasuaki Yamasaki, BayStars	3	2	3.27	55	58	2	14	39
Edwin Escobar, BayStars	4	4	3.38	59	39	7	11	50
Taichi Ishiyama, Swallows	0	5	3.60	55	54	6	10	64
Yuhei Takanashi, Giants	2	2	3.69	39	34	2	21	47
Kazuki Mishima, BayStars	3	5	4.08	57	66	8	12	57
Atsuya Horie, Carp	5	4	4.25	42	48	4	25	29
Scott McGough, Swallows	3	2	2.52	64	43	7	23	76
Jon Edwards, Tigers	0	0	2.57	7	6	1	4	7
Joe Gunkel, Tigers	9	3	2.95	113	99	10	24	87
Randy Rosario, Dragons	0	0	3.00	9	8	1	6	3
Fernando Romero, BayStars	5	3	3.01	81	89	4	30	44
Cy Sneed, Swallows	6	2	3.41	68	60	9	23	69
Raul Alcantara, Tigers	3	3	3.49	59	55	6	14	48
Albert Suarez, Swallows	5	3	3.62	77	82	9	32	70
Cristopher Mercedes, Giants	7	5	3.77	86	96	5	22	74

PACIFIC LEAGUE

Team	W	L	T	PCT	GB
Orix Buffaloes	70	55	18	.560	--
Chiba Lotte Marines	67	57	19	.540	2.5
Tohoku Rakuten Golden Eagles	66	62	15	.516	5.5
Fukuoka SoftBank Hawks	60	62	21	.492	8.5
Hokkaido Nippon-Ham Fighters	55	68	20	.447	14
Saitama Seibu Lions	55	70	18	.440	15

Playoffs—First round: Lotte defeated Rakuten 2-0-1 in best-of-five series. **Climax Series:** Orix defeated Lotte 3-0-1 in best-of-seven series.

PACIFIC LEAGUE BATTING LEADERS

Player, Team	AVG	AB	R	H	HR	RBI	SB
Masataka Yoshida, Buffaloes	.339	389	61	132	21	72	0
Tomoya Mori, Lions	.309	431	70	133	11	41	5
Yutaro Sugimoto, Buffaloes	.301	478	73	144	32	83	3
Yuki Yanagita, Hawks	.300	516	95	155	28	80	6
Kensuke Kondoh, Fighters	.298	447	61	133	11	69	4
Takashi Ogino, Marines	.296	570	86	169	10	45	24
Takeya Nakamura, Lions	.284	430	50	122	18	74	0
Shogo Nakamura, Marines	.283	506	78	143	9	67	12
Takero Okajima, Hawks	.280	461	40	129	8	56	3
Daichi Suzuki, Eagles	.277	552	70	153	10	53	3
Ryoya Kurihara, Hawks	.275	531	71	146	21	77	7
Shuhei Fukuda, Buffaloes	.275	408	47	112	1	21	9
Yuma Mune, Buffaloes	.272	481	71	131	9	42	8
Sosuke Genda, Lions	.272	464	60	126	2	29	24
Hideto Asamura, Eagles	.269	483	70	130	18	67	1
Brandon Laird, Marines	.262	485	57	127	29	95	0
Eigoro Mogi, Eagles	.259	410	50	106	14	53	6
Hiroaki Shimauchi, Eagles	.257	486	64	125	21	96	2
Yudai Fujioka, Marines	.255	432	41	110	3	37	10
Takumi Kuriyama, Lions	.251	387	33	97	4	43	1
Daiki Asama, Fighters	.251	411	42	103	5	31	8

OTHER NOTABLE HITTERS

Player, Team	AVG	AB	R	H	HR	RBI	SB
Rangel Ravelo, Buffaloes	.429	7	1	3	0	0	0
Yurisbel Gracial, Hawks	.304	138	19	42	5	15	2
Alfredo Despaigne, Hawks	.264	261	27	69	10	41	0
Adam Jones, Buffaloes	.234	154	10	36	4	23	0
Cory Spangenberg, Lions	.232	181	30	42	7	27	3
Steven Moya, Buffaloes	.229	354	26	81	13	47	1
Rusney Castillo, Eagles	.225	71	4	16	1	3	0

PACIFIC LEAGUE PITCHING LEADERS

Pitcher, Team	W	L	ERA	IP	H	HR	BB	SO
Yoshinobu Yamamoto, Buffaloes	18	5	1.39	194	124	7	2	30
Hiroya Miyagi, Buffaloes	13	4	2.51	147	118	9	9	41
Naoyuki Uwasawa, Fighters	12	6	2.81	160	119	8	4	50
Hiromi Itoh, Fighters	10	9	2.90	146	125	8	6	47
Masahiro Tanaka, Eagles	4	9	3.01	156	131	17	5	52
Takahiro Norimoto, Eagles	11	5	3.17	145	123	18	3	51
Tatsuya Imai, Lions	8	8	3.30	158	123	15	11	58

Pitcher, Team	W	L	ERA	IP	H	HR	BB	SO
Shuta Ishikawa, Hawks	6	9	3.40	156	135	22	17	59
Takayuki Katoh, Fighters	6	7	3.42	150	136	13	3	57
Takayuki Kishi, Eagles	9	10	3.44	149	149	17	1	57
Daiki Tajima, Buffaloes	8	8	3.58	143	137	10	5	57
Kazuya Ojima, Marines	10	4	3.76	146	123	16	6	61
Kona Takahashi, Lions	11	9	3.78	174	157	23	6	73
Wataru Matsumoto, Lions	10	8	3.79	150	137	15	4	63

OTHER NOTABLE PITCHERS

Pitcher, Team	W	L	ERA	IP	H	HR	BB	SO
Yuki Matsui, Eagles	0	2	0.63	43	22	1	1	3
Kaima Taira, Lions	3	4	0.90	60	36	0	5	6
Livan Moinelo, Hawks	1	0	1.15	31	15	2	1	4
Chihaya Sasaki, Marines	8	1	1.26	57	36	4	2	8
Tomohiro Anraku, Eagles	3	3	2.08	56	45	4	2	13
Chia-Hao Sung, Eagles	3	3	2.23	61	46	2	2	15
Naoya Masuda, Marines	3	6	2.24	64	43	5	0	16
Tomohito Sakai, Eagles	4	3	2.28	51	33	3	0	13
Yoshihisa Hirano, Buffaloes	1	3	2.30	43	30	4	0	11
Mizuki Hori, Fighters	3	2	2.36	53	36	3	4	14
Tyler Higgins, Buffaloes	1	2	2.53	46	37	3	1	13
Yuki Karakawa, Marines	4	2	2.72	36	29	4	1	11
Bryan Rodriguez, Fighters	0	2	2.74	46	40	4	3	14
Toshihiro Sugiura, Fighters	3	3	2.96	55	34	9	1	18
Yuito Mori, Hawks	1	3	4.03	29	20	6	0	13
Sho Iwasaki, Hawks	2	5	4.17	45	37	7	0	21
Tatsushi Masuda, Lions	0	3	4.99	31	32	4	1	17
Frank Herrmann, Marines	1	1	5.19	43	47	7	1	25
Livan Moinelo, Hawks	1	0	1.15	31	15	2	19	42
Jose Flores, Marines	1	0	1.38	13	9	0	5	11
Enny Romero, Marines	1	0	1.54	23	19	2	9	20
Nick Martinez, Hawks	9	4	1.60	141	108	6	38	138
Colin Rea, Hawks	3	1	2.03	40	22	3	13	38
Tyler Higgins, Buffaloes	1	2	2.53	46	37	3	19	36
Robbie Erlin, Fighters	2	3	3.32	38	40	3	11	33
Reed Garrett, Lions	4	3	3.77	57	57	6	33	59
Drew VerHagen, Fighters	5	8	3.84	96	90	7	33	100
Alan Busenitz, Eagles	1	0	4.97	29	32	1	9	23
Matt Dermody, Lions	0	2	5.13	33	46	2	13	22
Zach Neal, Lions	1	6	5.85	60	76	3	15	26
Carter Stewart, Hawks	0	2	6.08	24	21	0	21	36
Glenn Sparkman, Buffaloes	0	1	6.88	17	15	4	8	14
Cesar Vargas, Buffaloes	1	1	11.00	9	13	4	4	7

KT Wiz Claim First Title

For the first time in KBO history, nobody beat the Wiz.

The KT Wiz swept the Doosan Bears in four games to claim their first-ever Korean Series title. The Wiz had joined the KBO in 2015. They didn't make the playoffs for the first time until last year. But this year, they were the class of the league, topping the league in the regular season and then rolling through the playoffs.

They knocked off Doosan, which was without Walker Lockett and Ariel Miranda, the team's best two starting pitchers, for most of the playoffs.

Miranda was the league's best pitcher during the regular season. He set the KBO record with 225 strikeouts and also led the league with a 2.33 ERA. The record had been held for 37 years by Choi Dong-won.

SSG third baseman Choi Jeong led the league with 35 home runs. He also became the second player in KBO history to top 400 career home runs—he now has 403. Lee Seung-Yeop is the KBO's all-time home run leader with 467.

Samsung lefthander Mike Montgomery was suspended 20 games after he threw a rosin bag at umpire Kim Sung-chul, effectively ending his time with the Lions. He had gone 1-2, 5.23 at the time of his suspension.

Kia manager Matt Williams was dismissed at the end of the season after the Tigers finished ninth in the 10-team league. Canadian slugger Jamie Romak announced his retirement at the end of the season. Romak hit 155 home runs in the KBO, which is third-most among foreign players.

STANDINGS & LEADERS

Team	W	L	T	PCT	GB
KT	76	59	9	.563	--
Samsung	76	59	9	.563	--
LG	72	58	14	.554	1.5
Doosan	71	65	8	.522	5.5
Kiwoom	70	67	7	.511	7
SSG	66	64	14	.508	7.5
NC	67	68	9	.496	9
Lotte	65	71	8	.478	11.5
Kia	58	76	10	.433	17.5
Hanwha	49	83	12	.371	25.5

Playoffs—First Round: Doosan defeated Kiwoom 2-1 in a best-of-three series. **Second Round:** Doosan defeated LG 2-1 in a best-of-three series. **Semifinals:** Doosan defeated Samsung 2-1 in a best-of-three series. **Korean Series:** KT Wiz defeated Doosan 4-0 in a best-of-seven series.

BATTING LEADERS

Player, Team	AVG	AB	R	H	HR	RBI	SB
Lee Jung Hoo, Kiwoom	.360	464	78	167	7	84	10
Jeon Jun Woo, Lotte	.348	552	88	192	7	92	6
Kang Baek Ho, KT	.347	516	76	179	16	102	10
Hong Chang Ki, LG	.328	524	103	172	4	52	23
Park Kun Woo, Doosan	.325	458	82	149	6	63	13
Yang Eui Ji, NC	.325	480	81	156	30	111	2
Son Ah Seop, Lotte	.319	542	88	173	3	58	11
Jose Fernandez, Doosan	.315	540	73	170	15	81	0
Kim Sun Bin, Kia	.307	501	55	154	5	67	0
An Chi Hong, Lotte	.306	421	58	129	10	82	3
Koo Ja Wook, Samsung	.306	543	107	166	22	88	27
Kim Hye Seong, Kiwoom	.304	559	99	170	3	66	46
Park Seong Han, SSG	.302	407	53	123	4	44	12
Lee Yong Kyu, Kiwoom	.296	459	88	136	1	43	17
Choi Won Jun, Kia	.295	589	82	174	4	44	40
Jung Hoon, Lotte	.292	486	70	142	14	79	8
Hwang Jae Gyun, KT	.291	453	74	132	10	56	11
Park Hae Min, Samsung	.291	454	78	132	5	54	36
Kang Min Ho, Samsung	.291	406	55	118	18	67	0
Lee Dae Ho, Lotte	.286	420	39	120	19	81	0

OTHER NOTABLE HITTERS

Player, Team	AVG	AB	R	H	HR	RBI	SB
Jose Pirela, Samsung	.286	553	102	158	29	97	9
Aaron Altherr, NC	.272	492	83	134	32	84	20
Zoilo Almonte, SSG	.271	225	18	61	7	36	1
Hernan Perez, Hanwha	.268	224	26	60	5	33	4
David Freitas, Kiwoom	.259	139	13	36	2	14	0
Ryon Healy, Hanwha	.257	249	27	64	7	37	2
Will Craig, Kiwoom	.248	222	25	55	6	30	0
Roberto Ramos, LG	.243	185	14	45	8	25	0
Preston Tucker, Kia	.237	468	42	111	9	59	0
Jamie Romak, SSG	.225	355	55	80	20	52	1
Justin Bour, LG	.170	100	7	17	3	17	0

PITCHING LEADERS

Player, Team	W	L	ERA	IP	H	HR	BB	SO
Ariel Miranda, Doosan	14	5	2.33	174	135	11	63	225
Baek Jung Hyun, Samsung	14	5	2.63	158	142	15	54	109
Ko Young Pyo, KT	11	6	2.92	167	147	9	27	130
Eric Jokisch, Kiwoom	16	9	2.93	181	171	12	46	131
Won Tae In, Samsung	14	7	3.06	159	147	11	51	129
David Buchanan, Samsung	16	5	3.10	177	173	13	59	162
Casey Kelly, LG	13	8	3.15	177	160	12	60	142
Drew Rucinski, NC	15	10	3.17	179	160	12	55	177
Nick Kingham, Hanwha	10	8	3.19	144	117	11	41	131
Choi Won Joon, Doosan	12	4	3.30	158	160	15	37	113
Odrisamer Despaigne, KT	13	10	3.39	189	175	10	78	165
Wilmer Font, SSG	8	5	3.46	146	114	12	45	157
Ryan Carpenter, Hanwha	5	12	3.97	170	150	16	72	179
Park Se Woong, Lotte	10	9	3.98	163	141	20	53	125
Kim Min Woo, Hanwha	14	10	4.00	155	131	15	76	125
Dan Straily, Lotte	10	12	4.07	166	162	12	67	164
Shin Min Hyeok, NC	9	6	4.41	145	155	17	44	107
Im Gi Yeong, Kia	8	8	4.88	153	155	15	45	129
Enderson Franco, Lotte	9	8	5.40	150	147	20	75	124

OTHER NOTABLE PITCHERS

Player, Team	W	L	ERA	IP	H	HR	BB	SO
Andrew Suarez, LG	10	2	2.18	115	91	4	41	126
Jake Brigham, Kiwoom	7	3	2.95	61	49	6	26	49
Walker Lockett, Doosan	9	9	2.98	124	132	5	42	112
Aaron Brooks, Kia	3	5	3.35	78	93	4	16	55
Wesley Parsons, NC	4	8	3.72	133	109	9	63	148
Arthur Lewicki, SSG	1	0	3.77	14	15	2	2	9
Bennett Lively, Samsung	0	1	4.05	33	23	4	13	38
William Cuevas, KT	9	5	4.12	133	131	11	51	137
Bo Takahashi, Kia	1	3	4.91	37	46	4	12	46

Lefthander Jose De Paula briefly pitched for the Yankees in 2015. Now he's the best pitcher in the Chinese Professional Baseball League and he won Game 1 of the Taiwan Series.

CTBC Brothers Win Title As De Paula Dominates

BY J.J. COOPER

Paced by the best pitcher in the league, the CTBC Brothers Elephants swept Uni 7-Eleven Lions to win the Taiwan Series title.

The win was Brothers' first title in 11 years.

Jose De Paula got the Brothers going with a dominating Game 1 win in the Taiwan Series. That wasn't surprising as De Paula had dominated all year. He was the league's ERA champ, striking out 187 in 178 innings. He was named the Brothers' most outstanding player in the Taiwan Series.

The Taiwan Series MVP was Chan Tzu-Hsien.

STANDINGS & LEADERS

Team	W	L	T	PCT	GB
&CTBC Brothers	66	49	5	.574	—
*Uni 7-Eleven	64	51	5	.557	2
Rakuten	56	61	3	.479	11
Fubon	54	62	4	.466	12.5
Wei Chuan	50	67	3	.427	17

& First half champion *Second half champion
Finals: CTBC defeated Uni 7-Eleven 4-0 in best-of-seven series.

BATTING LEADERS

Player, Team	AVG	AB	R	H	2B	3B	HR	SB
Chen Jun-Xiu, Rakuten	.352	338	67	119	15	2	7	8
Chen Jie-Xian, 7-Eleven	.325	394	69	128	11	7	3	22
Wang Wei-Chen, CTBC	.323	492	74	159	10	1	1	21
Zhu Yu-Xian, Rakuten	.311	366	54	114	12	1	22	2
Guo Tian-Xin, Wei Chuan	.308	406	46	125	10	3	5	22
Lin Jing-Kai, 7-Eleven	.303	445	70	135	33	3	3	23
Lin An-Ke, 7-Eleven	.302	387	70	117	14	2	16	17
Lin Hong-Yu, Rakuten	.295	386	60	114	34	1	14	1
Xu Ji-Hong, CTBC	.290	449	64	130	38	0	14	10
Lin Yi-Quan, Fubon	.286	388	39	111	29	0	11	1
Lin Li, Rakuten	.277	364	72	101	22	6	7	27
Chen Zi-Hao, CTBC	.276	388	56	107	15	5	14	3
Zhan Zi-Xian, CTBC	.275	364	36	100	21	0	10	3
Su Zhi-Jie, Wei Chuan	.275	375	69	103	22	3	8	15
Li Kai-Wei, Wei Chuan	.273	439	62	120	20	4	2	22
Jiang Kun-Yu, CTBC	.261	433	54	113	29	1	1	13
Wang Zheng-Tang, Fubon	.235	336	39	79	16	1	5	9

PITCHING LEADERS

Player, Team	W	L	ERA	G	IP	H	BB	SO
Jose De Paula, CTBC	16	4	1.77	26	178	151	25	187
Brock Dykxhorn, 7-Eleven	17	4	1.83	27	182	124	37	157
Bryan Woodall, Wei Chuan	12	5	2.90	34	152	151	26	83
Mike Loree, Fubon	7	9	3.03	25	157	154	26	125
Huang Zi-Peng, Rakuten	9	8	3.40	23	135	136	29	62
Tim Melville, 7-Eleven	8	7	3.74	26	123	120	47	84
Kevin Zheng, CTBC	12	7	4.08	22	130	151	18	90

ITALY

San Marino Wins Championship

BY J.J. COOPER

In 2021 to mark the return of baseball to full speed, Serie A grew from seven teams in 2019 to 33 teams. That led to teams playing group play in small pods, followed by a 12-game pool play format which led to San Marino and Fortitudo emerging to face off in the championship series. After the two teams split the first two games, San Marino won back-to-back games to claim the title. In the deciding Game 4, San Marino took a six-run lead into the bottom of the first. Fortitudo clawed back to trail 9-7 heading into the top of the ninth, but San Marino scored eight more runs in that half inning for a seemingly easy 17-7 clincher. It was San Marino's first title since 2013.

STANDINGS

Pool Play A	W	L	PCT	GB
Fortitudo	12	0	1.000	--
Parma	6	5	.542	5.5
Collechio	5	6	.458	6.5
Cagliari	0	12	.000	12

Pool Play B	W	L	PCT	GB
San Marino	11	1	.917	--
Nettuno	6	6	.500	5
Macerata	4	8	.333	7
Godo	3	9	.250	8

Championship: San Marino defeated Fortitudo 3-1 in a best-of-five series.

INDIVIDUAL BATTING LEADERS

Player, Team	AVG	AB	R	H	HR	RBI	SB
Exequiel Talevi, VER	.487	76	26	37	1	21	10
Ramon Bonilla, BOZ	.480	100	17	48	1	21	17
Noel Gonzalez, PAR	.436	101	25	44	1	24	6
Jesus Carrera, TOR	.432	111	30	48	5	33	14
Niccolò Maria Loardi, BOL	.430	79	28	34	5	34	0
Nathanael Batista, MAC	.429	105	19	45	4	27	4
Oscar Gamez, RSM	.424	92	27	39	5	33	1
Wilfredo Aroche, RES	.420	119	35	50	2	25	8
Jiandido Tromp, RSM	.415	94	34	39	5	26	4
Lorenzo Di Fabio, RSM	.406	64	22	26	0	13	0

INDIVIDUAL PITCHING LEADERS

Player, Team	W	L	ERA	IP	H	HR	BB	SO
Angel Calero, MOD	5	0	0.95	67	39	0	11	113
Yoel Suarez, SET	6	4	1.03	78	60	1	11	109
Eddy Garcia, RES	4	0	1.20	53	25	2	13	91
Frank Montieth, ATL	5	2	1.55	64	51	1	2	70
Aliangel F. Lopez, MAC	7	3	1.56	58	30	2	12	100
Nick Robles, CRO	7	2	1.59	96	60	2	25	117
Angel Guillen, TOR	6	3	1.70	79	51	0	36	106
Johan Belisario, SEN	4	6	1.77	87	47	3	22	108
Ruben Hernandez, RES	8	2	1.84	83	50	0	35	155
Jose Diaz, OLT	6	5	1.85	107	71	0	26	161

NETHERLANDS

Amsterdam Grabs Fifth Title

BY J.J. COOPER

Amsterdam right fielder Kalian Sams hit a three-run home run and Shairon Martis held Neptunus to two runs despite giving up nine hits as L&D Amsterdam knocked off Curaçao Neptunus, 4-2, in the deciding Game 7 of the Holland Series. This was the Pirates' fifth league title and their first since 2019.

Martis was once again the class of the league. A major leaguer with the Nationals and Twins, he had four complete games to go with his league-best 0.81 ERA.

STANDINGS

Team	W	L	PCT	GB
Curaçao Neptunus	34	8	.810	--
L&D Amsterdam	33	8	.798	0.5
HCAW	28	13	.679	5.5
Twins Oosterhout	22	19	.536	11.5
DSS/Kinheim	15	27	.357	19
Hoofddorp Pioniers	15	27	.357	19
Silicon Storks	12	29	.298	21.5
Quick Amersfoort	7	35	.167	27

Playoffs—Semifinals: Neptunus defeated Twins 3-0 and Amsterdam defeated HCAW 3-2 in best-of-five series. **Finals:** Amsterdam defeated Neptunus 4-3 in a best-of-seven series.

INDIVIDUAL BATTING LEADERS

Player, Team	AVG	AB	R	H	HR	RBI	SB
Denzel Brooks, AMS	.433	201	44	87	5	51	21
Ibrahin Redan, STO	.346	153	21	53	0	38	4
Roger Bernadina, NEP	.339	168	42	57	2	32	12
John Polonius, NEP	.332	196	54	65	3	43	23
Dudley Leonora, NEP	.330	194	27	64	0	41	12
Dwayne Kemp, NEP	.328	201	45	66	3	47	8
Stijn Van Der Meer, NEP	.327	196	52	64	1	32	10
Gilmer Lampe, AMS	.326	175	42	57	4	25	12
Jason Jakobus, DKI	.321	159	23	51	1	21	9
Arthur Bonevacia, HCA	.321	140	25	45	2	30	0

INDIVIDUAL PITCHING LEADERS

Player, Team	W	L	ERA	IP	H	HR	BB	SO
Shairon Martis, AMS	8	1	0.84	75	61	2	8	61
Kevin Kelly, NEP	4	1	1.07	59	25	1	25	63
Tom De Blok, AMS	3	2	1.59	34	17	0	11	46
Orlando Yntema, NEP	5	0	1.64	33	20	0	7	34
Naut Kragt, AMS	5	2	1.66	54	33	1	15	50
Diegomar Markwell, NEP	12	1	1.80	105	100	3	27	39
Lars Huijer, HCA	10	4	2.05	114	68	2	35	135
Scott Prins, PIO	4	1	2.06	48	43	1	15	44
J.C. Sulbaran, AMS	10	4	2.07	87	72	0	27	84
John-Michael Halley, PIO	3	2	3.23	39	36	0	15	32
Nick Boxelaar, DKI	5	1	3.27	52	51	3	26	39

Granma Takes Home The Title

During the regular season of the 60th Serie Nacional, Sancti Spiritus tied Granma for the best regular season record on the strength of its pitching staff. Sancti Spiritus ranked second in the league in runs allowed, trailing only Pinar del Rio in that category.

When it came time for the playoffs, though, Sancti Spiritus had a quick exit, as Pinar del Rio won three straight high-scoring games for a sweep in the quarterfinals.

Granma, meanwhile, fielded one of the most balanced teams in the league. It tied for third in the league in runs scored, ranked third in runs allowed and had a league-best +148 run differential. That balance carried over into the postseason as Granma won the championship.

Industriales first baseman Lisban Correa won the MVP after hitting .320/.457/.692 with 28 home runs, nine more homers than the No. 2 home run hitter in the league.

STANDINGS

Team	W	L	PCT	GB
Sancti Spiritus	48	27	.640	-
Granma	48	27	.640	-
Matanzas	44	31	.587	4
Santiago De Cuba	43	32	.573	5
Las Tunas	43	32	.573	5
Cienfuegos	42	33	.560	6
Industriales	42	33	.560	6
Pinar del Rio	42	33	.560	6
Camaguey	41	34	.547	7
Mayabeque	40	35	.533	8
Ciego de Avila	33	39	.458	13.5
Holguin	31	44	.413	17
Villa Clara	30	44	.405	17.5
Isla De La Juventud	27	44	.380	19
Artemisa	22	53	.293	26
Guantanamo	20	55	.267	28

Quarterfinals: Pinar del Rio defeated Sancti Spiritus 3-0, Las Tunas defeated Santiago de Cuba 3-1, Matanzas defeated Cienfuegos 3-0 and Granma defeated Industriales 3-2 in best-of-five series.

Semifinals: Granma defeated Pinar del Rio 4-2 and Matanzas defeated Las Tunas 4-2 in best-of-seven series.

Finals: Granma defeated Matanzas 4-2 in best-of-seven series.

BATTING LEADERS

Player, Team	AVG	AB	R	H	2B	3B	HR	RBI
Cesar Prieto, CFG	.403	318	78	128	21	7	7	51
Rafael Viñales, LTU	.387	261	59	101	14	0	19	66
Humberto Bravo, CMG	.380	255	67	97	10	4	0	41
Pavel Quesada, CFG	.376	242	47	91	10	0	12	63
Guillermo Aviles, GRA	.371	221	48	82	8	1	13	74
Frederich Cepeda, SSP	.369	214	49	79	21	0	10	48
Yordanis Samon, CMG	.369	268	48	99	20	0	11	66
Jeison Martinez, MAY	.365	271	68	99	15	4	7	49
Luis Sanchez, GTM	.364	242	30	88	15	0	5	24
Santiago Torres, SCU	.363	292	81	106	16	9	13	56
Yoelkis Guibert, SCU	.362	174	22	63	17	1	1	28
Luis Mateo, CFG	.361	277	63	100	13	4	3	54
Yariel Duque, MTZ	.358	176	33	63	7	0	8	48
Geyser Cepeda, SSP	.354	260	58	92	15	0	8	48
Jefferson Delgado, MTZ	.354	268	47	95	11	1	5	57
Daniel Perez, CFG	.352	270	42	95	7	4	4	47
Raico Santos, GRA	.350	246	69	86	14	0	4	50
Yordan Manduley, HOL	.350	214	47	75	9	0	9	43
Osvaldo Abreu, GRA	.348	264	54	92	13	3	0	37
Ariel Benavides, SCU	.348	198	34	69	12	3	1	29
Carlos Benitez, GRA	.347	219	40	76	19	0	6	59
Luig Baguet, SSP	.347	216	41	75	19	2	1	23
Andy Zamora, VCL	.341	173	35	59	8	3	0	21
Andres Quiala, LTU	.341	255	48	87	8	1	1	33
Laindel Leyva, HOL	.338	225	39	76	12	2	0	11
Yasniel Gonzalez, MAY	.338	207	40	70	17	0	10	57
Ivan Prieto, GRA	.337	166	28	56	11	0	2	34
Yuniesky Larduert, LTU	.334	287	58	96	7	2	3	34
Yunier Mendoza, SSP	.333	276	34	92	22	1	4	47
Abdel Civil, SSP	.332	211	28	70	16	1	5	30
Lazaro Cedeño, GRA	.331	236	38	78	19	0	11	50
Yosvani Alarcon, LTU	.328	296	57	97	8	0	15	72
Orlando Lavandera, MAY	.328	183	33	60	8	0	3	36
Estayle Hernandez, IND	.327	251	45	82	16	0	7	64
Juan Carlos Arencibia, PRI	.327	257	52	84	17	1	2	31
Luis Rivera, IJV	.325	212	28	69	11	0	3	29
Alexander Jimenez, CAV	.324	241	43	78	9	4	1	24
Alexander Ayala, CMG	.324	299	54	97	21	0	10	64
Osvaldo Vazquez, CAV	.323	217	46	70	9	0	14	61
Yoan Moreno, ART	.323	189	28	61	11	2	4	27

PITCHING LEADERS

Player, Team	W	L	ERA	G	IP	H	HR	BB	SO
Pablo Luis Guillén, VCL	4	3	2.52	14	78.2	75	0	44	47
Yoen Socarrás, SSP	11	4	2.63	18	99.1	75	3	29	92
Erlis Casanova, PRI	8	4	2.92	17	101.2	97	4	27	60
Yadián Martínez, MAY	8	6	3.01	20	143.1	152	8	50	73
Yander Guevara, CAV	8	3	3.04	15	94.2	89	4	21	31
Carlos Juan Viera, LTU	9	4	3.14	16	109	100	10	27	70
Frank Madan, CMG	13	5	3.30	22	141.2	122	13	40	109
Vladimir García, CAV	5	5	3.43	18	89.1	87	6	29	55
Yudier Rodríguez, LTU	12	5	3.43	19	123.1	127	12	32	67
Reinier Rivero, MTZ	10	5	3.47	20	109	104	6	53	51
César García, GRA	7	4	3.57	17	93.1	97	2	25	45
Noelvis Entenza, MTZ	7	3	3.64	12	76.2	72	5	42	41
Carlos Damián Ramírez, CFG	6	1	3.69	32	85.1	78	3	45	49
Frank Luis Medina, PRI	3	7	3.69	26	85.1	94	10	32	56
Luis Alberto Marrero, CAV	6	4	3.74	21	77	68	6	34	34
Alberto Bicet, SCU	10	5	3.83	19	105.2	138	7	20	39
Vladimir Baños, PRI	9	6	3.93	19	103	115	10	28	54
Leandro Martínez, GRA	6	7	3.98	17	81.1	109	5	17	32
Carlos Font, SCU	12	3	4.14	20	113	115	4	56	67
Wilson Paredes, HOL	7	5	4.16	25	93	101	8	35	38
José Eduardo Santos, SSP	7	4	4.17	16	77.2	77	7	44	40
Elier Carrillo, VCL	4	5	4.22	22	91.2	89	8	38	44
Miguel Angel Lastra, IJV	5	6	4.23	20	106.1	108	8	48	57
José Pablo Cuesta, IND	7	6	4.35	18	99.1	116	6	25	45
Marlon Vega, MAY	9	2	4.36	30	84.2	80	7	62	75
Joel Mojena, GRA	9	6	4.40	17	90	107	9	19	41
Jonathan Carbo, IJV	8	9	4.47	19	112.2	113	13	44	46
Yamichel Pérez, SSP	7	7	4.50	18	92	116	8	33	43
Carlos Alberto Santiesteban, HOL	4	4	4.64	15	73.2	86	8	23	23
Pavel Hernández, IND	6	6	4.72	16	80	92	5	42	76
Yunieski García, ART	3	6	4.95	32	72.2	72	3	56	64
Misael Villa, ART	5	9	4.95	19	96.1	133	4	33	49
Hermes González, CFG	5	5	5.42	26	79.2	93	6	53	27
Yasmany Insua, CFG	8	5	5.42	20	91.1	107	7	50	34
Yosimar Cousin De La, CMG	7	6	5.68	19	120.1	152	8	41	76
Mailon Cruz, MAY	6	4	5.73	22	77	103	6	35	36
Yunier Gamboa, IJV	5	9	5.87	17	79.2	87	8	55	26
Franklin Quintana, IJV	4	10	5.96	16	83	94	6	58	43

INTERNATIONAL

Aguilas gave the Dominican Republic its 21st Caribbean Series title.

Aguilas Cruise To A Caribbean Series Championship Win

BY J.J. COOPER

Simply pulling off the 2021 Caribbean Series was an accomplishment, as the tournament managed to be held despite the ongoing coronavirus pandemic.

And when the dust cleared, the Dominican Republic's Aguilas had once again won the D.R. the title. It was the Dominican Republic's 21st Caribbean Series title and its second in two years. The D.R. has won nine of the 20 titles in the 21st century. Aguilas swept through the round robin with a perfect 7-0 record and then beat Puerto Rico's Caguas club in the championship game, 4-1.

AUSTRALIAN BASEBALL LEAGUE

Team	W	L	PCT	GB
Melbourne	19	9	.679	-
Perth	12	9	.571	3.5
Adelaide	12	10	.545	4
Sydney	6	8	.429	6
Canberra	11	14	.440	6.5
Brisbane	8	18	.308	10

Playoffs—Wild Card: Canberra defeated Sydney. **Semifinals:** Melbourne defeated Canberra; Perth defeated Adelaide. **Championship:** Melbourne defeated Perth. **Third Place:** Canberra defeated Adelaide.

INTERNATIONAL

INDIVIDUAL BATTING LEADERS

Player, Team	AVG	AB	R	H	2B	3B	HR	RBI	BB	SO	SB
Young, Delmon, MEL	.400	100	17	40	7	0	5	24	6	18	0
Mead, Curtis, ADE	.347	72	11	25	7	0	3	12	3	13	2
Glendinning, Robbie, PER	.343	67	20	23	2	0	3	21	10	15	2
Witherspoon, Grant, PER	.333	72	17	24	9	1	4	20	9	21	7
George, Darryl, MEL	.331	124	21	41	9	2	4	27	4	19	2
Proctor, Ford, PER	.324	68	19	22	4	1	3	17	16	14	0
Perkins, Robbie, CAN	.319	69	12	22	8	0	3	12	8	18	1
Tomscha, Damek, MEL	.317	101	18	32	7	0	5	15	6	17	1
Willis, Colin, MEL	.304	56	14	17	4	1	1	5	12	14	2
Lutz, Donald, 2 teams	.300	80	12	24	4	0	5	20	11	22	1

INDIVIDUAL PITCHING LEADERS

Player, Team	W	L	ERA	G	SV	IP	H	BB	SO	AVG
Stoka, Dean, CAN	2	0	0.44	4	0	21	11	5	11	.155
Wiles, Nathan, PER	1	1	1.61	5	0	22	16	4	30	.190
Flynn, Brian, MEL	3	1	1.62	7	0	39	30	11	39	.210
Neunborn, Mitch, ADE	3	2	1.75	5	0	26	12	6	29	.135
Unsworth, Dylan, PER	0	1	1.93	6	1	28	20	1	23	.187
Morimando, Shawn, CAN	3	3	2.57	8	0	42	33	10	47	.219
Sulser, Beau, PER	2	0	2.63	5	0	24	20	2	23	.235
Gailey, Frank, CAN	3	2	4.03	7	0	38	43	20	30	.293
Beardsley, Tyler, MEL	2	2	4.19	7	0	34	29	12	30	.220
Guyer, Josh, SYD	2	1	4.22	4	0	21	18	12	23	.225

DOMINICAN LEAGUE

Team	W	L	PCT	GB
Aguilas	16	14	.533	-
Gigantes	16	14	.533	-
Toros	16	14	.533	-
Estrellas	15	15	.500	1
Escogido	14	16	.467	2
Licey	13	17	.433	3

Playoffs—First round: Estrellas defeated Escogido 2-0. **Semifinals:** Aguilas defeated Toros 4-3 and Gigantes defeated Estrellas 4-2 in best-of-seven series. **Finals:** Aguilas defeated Gigantes 4-3 in best-of-seven series.

INDIVIDUAL BATTING LEADERS

Player, Team	AVG	AB	R	H	2B	3B	HR	RBI	BB	SO	SB
Navarro, Yamaico, TOR	.361	83	10	30	4	0	2	13	14	9	1
Guzmán, Ronald, GIG	.360	111	25	40	3	0	5	13	17	23	2
Dunand, Joe, ESC	.319	72	5	23	7	0	3	12	9	25	1
Peña, Jeremy, EST	.306	121	18	37	2	2	3	9	7	23	7
Ravelo, Rangel, AGU	.303	109	13	33	5	0	1	6	12	18	0
Cabrera, Melky, AGU	.302	96	10	29	4	0	3	13	5	12	0
Lagares, Juan, AGU	.283	92	6	26	4	1	0	11	3	16	4
Siri, Jose, GIG	.282	110	21	31	7	0	3	14	12	34	7
Mercedes, Yermin, LIC	.276	87	9	24	2	0	2	16	7	9	0
Mejia, Erick, LIC	.273	77	12	21	2	1	1	7	9	21	4

INDIVIDUAL PITCHING LEADERS

Player, Team	W	L	ERA	G	SV	IP	H	BB	SO	AVG
Kubiak, David, ESC	1	0	1.73	7	0	36	20	10	32	.161
Maya, Yunesky, AGU	1	2	2.79	6	0	29	23	5	21	.213
Rosso, Ramon, AGU	1	1	3.12	7	0	26	15	6	31	.165
Valdes, Raul, TOR	2	2	3.20	5	0	25	24	8	15	.250
Negrin, Yoanner, AGU	3	3	3.27	7	0	33	36	9	30	.277
Espino, Paolo, TOR	2	3	3.72	6	0	29	22	6	21	.208
Harman, Casey, ESC	0	2	4.81	7	0	24	21	9	11	.226

MEXICAN PACIFIC LEAGUE

Team	W	L	PCT	GB
Obregon	37	22	.627	-
Hermosillo	33	23	.589	2.5
Guasave	31	26	.544	5
Monterrey	58	54	.518	5.5
Mexicali	30	28	.517	6.5
Jalisco	30	29	.508	7
Culiacan	29	29	.500	7.5
Mazatlan	28	30	.483	8.5
Navojoa	46	72	.390	20.5
Los Mochis	38	78	.328	27.5

Playoffs—Semifinals: Hermosillo defeated Monterrey 4-2 and Culiacan defeated Obregon 4-2 in best-of-seven series. **Finals:** Culiacan defeated Hermosillo 4-3 in a best-of-seven series.

INDIVIDUAL BATTING LEADERS

Player, Team	AVG	AB	R	H	2B	3B	HR	RBI	BB	SO	SB
Hernandez, Yadiel, HER	.339	177	32	60	10	1	4	24	34	47	5
Obeso, Norberto, HER	.329	207	30	68	10	2	1	26	25	27	10
Drake, Yadir, GSV	.321	218	37	70	15	1	8	40	17	21	3
Amador, Japhet, JAL	.319	207	34	66	11	0	15	52	18	38	0
Figueroa, Carlos, JAL	.316	228	43	72	10	2	0	19	28	35	10
Álvarez, Dariel, JAL	.309	230	28	71	10	0	8	39	17	19	3
Orlando, Paulo, 2 teams	.308	201	36	62	9	0	8	29	22	51	4
Renteria, Omar, NAV	.308	169	25	52	7	0	3	25	24	36	2
Sepulveda, Carlos, OBR	.305	203	40	62	13	4	2	32	34	32	12
Valenzuela, Roberto, MTY	.304	191	23	58	11	1	2	31	21	25	4

INDIVIDUAL PITCHING LEADERS

Player, Team	W	L	ERA	G	SV	IP	H	BB	SO	AVG
Pena, Miguel, MXC	4	0	2.08	10	0	56	41	15	31	.202
Solano, Javier, MXC	4	2	2.62	12	0	86	71	21	38	.229
Oramas, Juan Pablo, HER	8	2	2.80	12	0	71	77	18	57	.275
Reyes, David, MXC	4	5	3.12	12	0	78	65	19	39	.226
Lara, Orlando, JAL	6	2	3.21	12	0	62	53	22	51	.232
Barreda, Manny, CUL	5	5	3.95	11	0	66	66	20	64	.266
Torres, Edgar, MAZ	2	5	4.29	12	0	71	77	24	30	.287
Gutierrez, Santiago, MOC	2	6	4.63	11	0	56	60	30	36	.279
Acosta, Octavio, 2 teams	3	6	4.98	11	0	56	64	20	25	.283
Carrillo, Marco, NAV	6	2	5.04	12	0	61	66	26	30	.280

PUERTO RICAN LEAGUE

Team	W	L	PCT	GB
Caguas	14	4	.778	-
Mayaguez	13	5	.722	1
Manati	7	11	.389	7
RA12	2	16	.111	12

Playoffs—First round: Mayaguez defeated Manati 3-0 in a best-of-five series. **Finals:** Caguas defeated Mayaguez 4-0 in a best-of-seven series.

INDIVIDUAL BATTING LEADERS

Player, Team	AVG	AB	R	H	2B	3B	HR	RBI	BB	SO	SB
Morales, Jonathan, CAG	.394	33	8	13	2	0	3	9	12	6	0
Centeno, Juan, MAN	.356	59	6	21	4	0	4	15	3	7	0
Fargas, Johneshwy, CAG	.349	63	13	22	6	0	4	17	6	17	7
Machín, Vimael, CAG	.345	58	8	20	2	0	0	7	6	8	1
Ortiz, Danny, MAY	.339	59	10	20	4	0	2	8	8	6	0
Ramos, Henry, MAY	.322	59	9	19	5	0	1	6	13	8	0
Mars, Danny, MAN	.317	60	11	19	1	1	2	8	8	5	1
Miranda, Jose, CAG	.302	53	10	16	6	0	1	8	6	10	0
Rivera, T.J., MAN	.302	53	14	16	5	0	2	12	6	9	0
Rivera, Emmanuel, MAY	.292	65	12	19	6	0	3	9	6	13	3

INDIVIDUAL PITCHING LEADERS

Player, Team	W	L	ERA	G	SV	IP	H	BB	SO	AVG
Medina, Luis, MAY	1	0	0.54	4	0	17	7	6	32	.125
García, Jason, MAN	0	2	2.14	5	0	21	20	10	21	.260
Hernandez, Kenny, MAY	0	2	2.70	4	0	17	13	3	13	.220
De Leon, Jose, CAG	2	1	3.18	4	0	17	8	10	31	.145
Hogan, Miller, MAN	0	1	3.45	4	0	16	13	6	18	.224
Santiago, Hector, CAG	1	1	3.79	4	0	19	17	9	19	.243
Stout, Eric, MAY	1	1	4.08	4	0	18	22	4	25	.306
Herron, Tyler, MAN	1	2	4.34	7	0	19	15	3	15	.224

INTERNATIONAL

VENEZUELAN LEAGUE

Eastern Division	W	L	PCT	GB
Caribes	24	16	.600	-
Aragua	17	20	.459	5.5
LaGuaira	16	24	.400	8
Caracas	15	25	.375	9

Western Division	W	L	PCT	GB
Lara	25	15	.625	-
Magallanes	21	16	.568	2.5
Margarita	20	20	.500	5
Zulia	19	21	.475	6

Playoffs—Semifinals: Caribes defeated Magallanes 4-3 and Lara defeated Aragua 4-3 in best-of-seven series. **Finals:** Caribes defeates Lara 4-0 in a best-of-seven series.

INDIVIDUAL BATTING LEADERS

Player, Team	AVG	AB	R	H	2B	3B	HR	RBI	BB	SO	SB
Castillo, Ali, ZUL	.430	135	20	58	5	1	1	14	12	6	0
Vasquez, Danry, LAG	.414	87	25	36	8	0	5	28	24	18	4
Pérez, Hernan, ARA	.402	102	29	41	8	0	5	28	20	22	8
Rodriguez, David, MAR	.383	133	26	51	9	1	5	23	22	19	1
Astudillo, Willians, ORI	.379	145	27	55	7	0	7	25	10	4	1
Ortega, Dennis, MAR	.356	135	29	48	7	0	7	31	19	32	2
Sardinas, Luis, ORI	.355	124	17	44	12	0	2	21	14	10	1
Rodriguez, Reynaldo, MAG	.349	129	20	45	8	1	3	25	7	16	6
Reyes, Angel, ZUL	.349	109	19	38	12	1	4	25	19	25	0
Pereda, Jhonny, CAR	.338	133	16	45	8	0	1	16	19	23	0

INDIVIDUAL PITCHING LEADERS

Player, Team	W	L	ERA	G	SV	IP	H	BB	SO	AVG
Leal, Erick, MAG	5	1	1.31	7	0	34	29	9	24	.236
Centeno, Henry, MAR	2	0	2.04	8	0	40	39	10	24	.253
Diaz, Victor, LAG	2	1	2.89	9	0	37	35	18	16	.254
Rivero, Raul, LAR	2	0	3.38	8	0	35	36	9	23	.267
Duran, Logan, ARA	2	3	3.41	7	0	37	43	17	24	.299
Darnell, Logan, LAR	0	2	3.49	9	0	39	47	7	15	.297
Araujo, Elvis, ZUL	2	1	3.50	9	0	36	41	21	21	.287
Breto, Liarvis, ORI	1	2	3.94	9	0	32	40	10	30	.308
Herrera, Alsis, CAR	0	4	4.08	9	0	35	45	12	20	.317

COLLEGE

Righthander Will Bednar was named the College World Series Most Outstanding Player.

Mississippi State Wins First National Title

BY TEDDY CAHILL

Dudy Noble Field stands at the corner of the Mississippi State campus, a college baseball palace built on what used to be a cow pasture. The grandest stadium in the country built for perhaps the most audacious program in the country.

Because it took an audacious vision to turn Mississippi State into a powerhouse. The Bulldogs have had to work hard at it over the last 50 years in Starkville. Paul Gregory led them to their first College World Series appearance in 1971. Five years later, Ron Polk arrived in Starkville and took the program and the SEC to another level. He led the Bulldogs to the CWS three times in his first 10 years as head coach and nothing was ever the same for Mississippi State.

Fans came by the thousands to watch the Bulldogs, building makeshift personal boxes beyond the left field fence in truck beds. The Left Field Lounge, as it became known, was a unique experience and became part of the program's charm. Only Mississippi State has ever drawn a crowd of more than 14,000 fans to an on-campus college baseball game—and it has done so six times.

The program kept growing, getting bigger and bigger. Will Clark and Rafael Palmeiro brought the thunder and lightning to Starkville before being drafted in the first round in 1985. The stars kept coming—B.J. Wallace, Paul Maholm, Hunter Renfroe, Brent Rooker, Jake Mangum—and the Bulldogs won more and more. Mississippi State played for the national championship in 2013 but couldn't break through, losing that series to UCLA and falling short of the ultimate goal.

The Bulldogs would not be denied, however. Bigger and bigger the program grew. Dudy Noble Field was rebuilt, turning one of college baseball's iconic venues into a modern palace. The New Dude, a $68 million project opened in 2019, bridged history and tradition with modern amenities and a luxury condo building just beyond left field. The Lounge remains a unique experience but is no longer a makeshift series of contraptions and is instead built into the stadium.

Bigger and bigger, a behemoth growing in eastern Mississippi. All that remained undone was winning a national championship. Chris Lemonis, hired as head coach in 2019, knew his remit. Asked if the New Dude was missing anything, he could think of just one thing.

"A national championship sticker on the wall,"

COACHING CAROUSEL

School	In (Previous Job)	Out (Reason/New Job)
Alabama-Birmingham	Casey Dunn (Samford head coach)	Brian Shoop (retired)
Alcorn State	Reginald Williams (Reds minor league coach)	Bretton Richardson
Arizona	Chip Hale (Tigers third base coach)	Jay Johnson (Louisiana State head coach)
Arizona State	Willie Bloomquist (D-backs special assistant to the GM)	Tracy Smith
Cal State Fullerton	Jason Dietrich (East Carolina assistant)	Rick Vanderhook (retired)
Central Arkansas	Nick Harlan (Central Arkansas assistant)	Allen Gum (retired)
Grambling State	Davin Pierre (Grambling State assistant)	James Cooper (Yankees minor league coach)
Hartford	Steve Malinowski (Hartford assistant)	Justin Blood (Keene St. (N.H.) head coach)
Hawaii	Rich Hill (San Diego head coach)	Mike Trapasso
High Point	Joey Hammond (Wake Forest assistant)	Craig Cozart
Hofstra	Frank Catalanotto (New York Tech head coach)	John Russo (retired)
Houston Baptist	Lance Berkman (St. Thomas (Texas) assistant)	Jared Moon
Illinois-Chicago	Sean McDermott (UIC assistant)	Mike Dee (retired)
Iona	Conor Burke (Dartmouth assistant)	Paul Panik
Kennesaw State	Ryan Coe (Rangers scout)	Mike Sansing (retired)
Longwood	Chad Oxendine (Coastal Carolina staff)	Ryan Mau
Louisiana State	Jay Johnson (Arizona head coach)	Paul Mainieri (retired)
Merrimack	Brian Murphy (William & Mary head coach)	Nick Barese
Mississippi Valley State	Stanley Stubbs (Rust (Miss.) head coach)	Aaron Stevens
Mount St. Mary's	Frank Leoni (Marymount (Va.) head coach)	Scott Thomson
New Mexico	Tod Brown (North Dakota State head coach)	Ray Birmingham (retired)
Nicholls State	Mike Silva (Louisiana Tech assistant)	Seth Thibodeaux
Northern Kentucky	Dizzy Peyton (NKU assistant)	Todd Asalon (retired)
Northwestern	Josh Reynolds (Northwestern assistant)	Spencer Allen
Ohio	Craig Moore (Ohio assistant)	Rob Smith (retired)
Rice	Jose Cruz Jr. (Tigers assistant hitting coach)	Matt Bragga
St. Bonaventure	B.J. Salerno (St. Bonaventure assistant)	Larry Sudbrook (retired)
Samford	Tony David (Samford assistant)	Casey Dunn (UAB head coach)
San Diego	Brock Ungricht (USD assistant)	Rich Hill (Hawaii head coach)
Southern	Chris Crenshaw (Southern assistant)	Kerrick Jackson
Tennessee Tech	Matt Bragga (Auburn staff)	Steve Smith (Tigers minor league coach)
Texas A&M	Jim Schlossnagle (Texas Christian head coach)	Rob Childress
Texas Christian	Kirk Saarloos (TCU assistant)	Jim Schlossnagle (Texas A&M head coach)
Troy	Skylar Meade (South Carolina assistant)	Mark Smartt
UC Davis	TBD	Matt Vaughn
UC Riverside	Justin Johnson (UCR assistant)	Troy Percival
Utah	Gary Henderson (Utah assistant)	Bill Kinneberg (retired)
Utah Valley	Eddie Smith (LSU assistant)	Eric Madsen
Wagner	Craig Noto (Wagner assistant)	Jim Carone
William & Mary	Mike McRae (VCU assistant)	Brian Murphy (Merrimack head coach)

he said. "That's probably the only thing we've got left to put in. I think our fans are waiting on it."

In June in Omaha, the wait ended. Mississippi State defeated Vanderbilt, 9-0, in game 3 of the College World Series finals to win the national championship.

Mississippi State did it big, the only way befitting the program. Its fans flooded TD Ameritrade Park, which for game 3 packed in 24,052 fans and set a record for a CWS finals game. Among those fans were Polk, former Mississippi State righthander Jonathan Papelbon and Dallas Cowboys quarterback Dak Prescott, one of Mississippi State's most beloved alumni. They were there to see history as the championship was not just the first in program history but the first team sports championship in school history.

The Bulldogs routed the Commodores in a championship performance for the ages. Righthander Will Bednar, whom the Giants selected in the first round of the draft, threw six hitless innings on three days rest. Righthander Landon Sims, Mississippi State's All-American relief ace, nearly completed the no-hitter but had to settle for three scoreless innings and holding Vanderbilt to one hit.

Mississippi State's offense for the second straight game put together quality at-bat after quality at-bat. In the fifth inning, the Bulldogs knocked out All-American righthander Kumar Rocker, who had never before lost an NCAA Tournament elimination game, and ended the night with 12 hits, including two home runs.

The Bulldogs again didn't make an error, completing their seven games at the CWS with a perfect fielding percentage.

In short, it was an exemplary all-around effort.

"What an awesome night," Lemonis said. "Our kids played as free as you could be on the biggest stage, from the pitching to the defense, to the grind of having to be one of the best pitchers in college baseball history and the defending champions.

"So proud of them. And it's so awesome to bring

back the trophy to Starkville. It's our community and how much they love their baseball, it's pretty special."

Bednar was named CWS Most Outstanding Player after going 2-0, 1.47 in 18.1 innings over three appearances in Omaha. He struck out 26 batters and held opponents to three runs on five hits and six walks.

Bednar said it was "unreal" to be named MOP and was still trying to absorb the enormity of his performance in the aftermath of the game.

"I just kind of went out there treated it like every other outing, to be honest with you," he said. "So, I just kind of treated it like it was any other game, and just kind of rolled with it."

Bednar improved to 9-1, 3.13 on the season with 139 strikeouts and 26 walks in 92.1 innings. His powerful stuff and performance on college baseball's biggest stage helped him rise on draft boards. Two weeks after Mississippi State's triumph, he was drafted 14th overall by the Giants, becoming the program's highest drafted pitcher since Maholm went eighth overall in 2003.

Offensively, outfielders Tanner Allen and

Rowdey Jordan again led the Bulldogs offensively, as they have all season long. Jordan collected three hits and two runs and Allen added two hits and a run.

Jordan and Allen hit in the top two spots of the Mississippi State lineup all season long and were the Bulldogs' top two hitters. Allen, a first-team All-American and the SEC player of the year, this season hit .383/.456/.621 with 11 home runs and 11 stolen bases, while Jordan hit .323/.417/.546 with 10 home runs and nine stolen bases.

Allen, Bednar, Jordan and the rest of the 2021 roster will take their rightful place in Mississippi State history. In an unprecedented season that was played through the Covid-19 pandemic, requiring new restrictions and protocols throughout the year, Mississippi State found a way.

Lemonis continually told his team it wouldn't be easy, and it wasn't. The Bulldogs were swept at home by Arkansas early in the season and lost a series at Vanderbilt in April. They went 0-2 at the SEC Tournament and were blown out in both games. They overcame a tough Notre Dame team in the Starkville Super Regional and then had to

COLLEGE WORLD SERIES CHAMPIONS

Year	Champion	Coach	Record	Runner-Up	Most Outstanding Player
1948	Southern California	Sam Barry	40-12	Yale	None selected
1949	Texas*	Bibb Falk	23-7	Wake Forest	Charles Teague, 2B, Wake Forest
1950	Texas	Bibb Falk	27-6	Washington State	Ray VanCleef, OF, Rutgers
1951	Oklahoma*	Jack Baer	19-9	Tennessee	Sid Hatfield, 1B/P, Tennessee
1952	Holy Cross	Jack Barry	21-3	Missouri	Jim O'Neill, P, Holy Cross
1953	Michigan	Ray Fisher	21-9	Texas	J.L. Smith, P, Texas
1954	Missouri	Hi Simmons	22-4	Rollins	Tom Yewcic, C, Michigan State
1955	Wake Forest	Taylor Sanford	29-7	Western Michigan	Tom Borland, P, Oklahoma State
1956	Minnesota	Dick Siebert	33-9	Arizona	Jerry Thomas, P, Minnesota
1957	California*	George Wolfman	35-10	Penn State	Cal Emery, 1B/P, Penn State
1958	Southern California	Rod Dedeaux	35-7	Missouri	Bill Thom, P, Southern California
1959	Oklahoma State	Toby Greene	27-5	Arizona	Jim Dobson, 3B, Oklahoma State
1960	Minnesota	Dick Siebert	34-7	Southern California	John Erickson, 2B, Minnesota
1961	Southern California*	Rod Dedeaux	43-9	Oklahoma State	Littleton Fowler, P, Oklahoma State
1962	Michigan	Don Lund	31-13	Santa Clara	Bob Garibaldi, P, Santa Clara
1963	Southern California	Rod Dedeaux	37-16	Arizona	Bud Hollowell, C, Southern California
1964	Minnesota	Dick Siebert	31-12	Missouri	Joe Ferris, P, Maine
1965	Arizona State	Bobby Winkles	54-8	Ohio State	Sal Bando, 3B, Arizona State
1966	Ohio State	Marty Karow	27-6	Oklahoma State	Steve Arlin, P, Ohio State
1967	Arizona State	Bobby Winkles	53-12	Houston	Ron Davini, C, Arizona State
1968	Southern California*	Rod Dedeaux	45-14	Southern Illinois	Bill Seinsoth, 1B, Southern California
1969	Arizona State	Bobby Winkles	56-11	Tulsa	John Dolinsek, OF, Arizona State
1970	Southern California	Rod Dedeaux	51-13	Florida State	Gene Ammann, P, Florida State
1971	Southern California	Rod Dedeaux	53-13	Southern Illinois	Jerry Tabb, 1B, Tulsa
1972	Southern California	Rod Dedeaux	50-13	Arizona State	Russ McQueen, P, Southern California
1973	Southern California*	Rod Dedeaux	51-11	Arizona State	Dave Winfield, OF/P, Minnesota
1974	Southern California	Rod Dedeaux	50-20	Miami	George Milke, P, Southern California
1975	Texas	Cliff Gustafson	56-6	South Carolina	Mickey Reichenbach, 1B, Texas
1976	Arizona	Jerry Kindall	56-17	Eastern Michigan	Steve Powers, DH/P, Arizona
1977	Arizona State	Jim Brock	57-12	South Carolina	Bob Horner, 3B, Arizona State
1978	Southern California*	Rod Dedeaux	54-9	Arizona State	Rod Boxberger, P, Southern California
1979	Cal State Fullerton	Augie Garrido	60-14	Arkansas	Tony Hudson, P, Cal State Fullerton
1980	Arizona	Jerry Kindall	45-21	Hawaii	Terry Francona, OF, Arizona
1981	Arizona State	Jim Brock	55-13	Oklahoma State	Stan Holmes, OF, Arizona State
1982	Miami	Ron Fraser	57-18	Wichita State	Dan Smith, P, Miami
1983	Texas	Cliff Gustafson	66-14	Alabama	Calvin Schiraldi, P, Texas

fight past Texas, the top-seeded team to make it to Omaha. Their reward was a CWS finals against the Commodores, the reigning national champions. After losing Game 1 against righthander Jack Leiter, a first-team All-American and a projected top-five pick, Mississippi State faced two must-win games.

The Bulldogs won them both and, with them, the national championship. Mississippi State finished the season 50-18 and at last, dogpiled in Omaha.

To the end, the Bulldogs were gritty and resilient, the two ways Lemonis most often described his team. Now, that team has etched itself into the program's proud history.

"This team won't be together (again) on the field together," Lemonis said. "I'm just glad they'll finish as legends.

"When you go to Starkville, Miss., and you're around 20 years from now, they'll be remembered by everybody."

Mississippi State turned a cow pasture into a palace. It brought thunder and lightning to college baseball. Its most revered coach is known as the Godfather of SEC baseball for his role in turning the conference into a power.

But only now is the grand vision complete. The Bulldogs are finally national champions.

NC State Removed From CWS Due To Covid-19 Protocls

With North Carolina State one win away from reaching the CWS finals, a shocking turn of events led to the Wolfpack being removed from the tournament due to Covid-19 protocols.

NC State was scheduled to play Vanderbilt on June 26 in a winner-take-all game for a berth in the CWS finals. But the Wolfpack were missing an undisclosed number of players in their game June 25 against the Commodores due to Covid-19 protocols. They played the game with just 13 players—nine position players and four pitchers—and in the early hours of the morning of June 26 the NCAA's Division I Baseball Committee ruled the rematch a no-contest, eliminating NC State.

"This decision was made based on the recommendation of the championship medical team

Year	Champion	Coach	Record	Runner-Up	MOST OUTSTANDING PLAYER
1984	Cal State Fullerton	Augie Garrido	66-20	Texas	John Fishel, OF, Cal State Fullerton
1985	Miami*	Ron Fraser	64-16	Texas	Greg Ellena, DH, Miami
1986	Arizona	Jerry Kindall	49-19	Florida State	Mike Senne, OF, Arizona
1987	Stanford	Mark Marquess	53-17	Oklahoma State	Paul Carey, OF, Stanford
1988	Stanford	Mark Marquess	46-23	Arizona State	Lee Plemel, P, Stanford
1989	Wichita State	Gene Stephenson	68-16	Texas	Greg Brummett, P, Wichita State
1990	Georgia	Steve Webber	52-19	Oklahoma State	Mike Rebhan, P, Georgia
1991	Louisiana State*	Skip Bertman	55-18	Wichita State	Gary Hymel, C, Louisiana State
1992	Pepperdine*	Andy Lopez	48-11	Cal State Fullerton	Phil Nevin, 3B, Cal State Fullerton
1993	Louisiana State	Skip Bertman	53-17	Wichita State	Todd Walker, 2B, Louisiana State
1994	Oklahoma*	Larry Cochell	50-17	Georgia Tech	Chip Glass, OF, Oklahoma
1995	Cal State Fullerton*	Augie Garrido	57-9	Southern California	Mark Kotsay, OF/P, Cal State Fullerton
1996	Louisiana State*	Skip Bertman	52-15	Miami	Pat Burrell, 3B, Miami
1997	Louisiana State*	Skip Bertman	57-13	Alabama	Brandon Larson, SS, Louisiana State
1998	Southern California	Mike Gillespie	49-17	Arizona State	Wes Rachels, 2B, Southern California
1999	Miami*	Jim Morris	50-13	Florida State	Marshall McDougall, 2B, Florida State
2000	Louisiana State*	Skip Bertman	52-17	Stanford	Trey Hodges, P, Louisiana State
2001	Miami*	Jim Morris	53-12	Stanford	Charlton Jimerson, OF, Miami
2002	Texas*	Augie Garrido	57-15	South Carolina	Huston Street, P, Texas
2003	Rice	Wayne Graham	58-12	Stanford	John Hudgins, P, Stanford
2004	Cal State Fullerton	George Horton	47-22	Texas	Jason Windsor, P, Cal State Fullerton
2005	Texas*	Augie Garrido	56-16	Florida	David Maroul, 3B, Texas
2006	Oregon State	Pat Casey	50-16	North Carolina	Jonah Nickerson, P, Oregon State
2007	Oregon State*	Pat Casey	49-18	North Carolina	Jorge Reyes, P, Oregon State
2008	Fresno State	Mike Batesole	47-31	Georgia	Tommy Mendonca, 3B, Fresno State
2009	Louisiana State	Paul Mainieri	56-17	Texas	Jared Mitchell, OF, Louisiana State
2010	South Carolina	Ray Tanner	54-16	UCLA	Jackie Bradley Jr., OF, South Carolina
2011	South Carolina*	Ray Tanner	55-14	Florida	Scott Wingo, 2B, South Carolina
2012	Arizona*	Andy Lopez	48-17	South Carolina	Robert Refsnyder, OF, Arizona
2013	UCLA*	John Savage	49-17	Mississippi State	Adam Plutko, P, UCLA
2014	Vanderbilt	Tim Corbin	51-21	Virginia	Dansby Swanson, 2B, Vanderbilt
2015	Virginia	Brian O'Connor	44-24	Vanderbilt	Josh Sborz, P, Virginia
2016	Coastal Carolina	Gary Gilmore	55-18	Arizona	Andrew Beckwith, P, Coastal Carolina
2017	Florida	Kevin O'Sullivan	52-19	Louisiana State	Alex Faedo, P, Florida
2018	Oregon State	Pat Casey	55-12-1	Arkansas	Adley Rutschman, C, Oregon State
2019	Vanderbilt	Tim Corbin	59-12	Michigan	Kumar Rocker, RHP, Vanderbilt
2021	Mississippi State	Chris Lemonis	50-18	Vanderbilt	Will Bednar, RHP, Mississippi State

and the Douglas County Health Department," the committee said in a statement.

"The NCAA and the committee regret that NC State's student-athletes and coaching staff will not be able to continue in the championship in which they earned the right to participate. Because of privacy issues, we cannot provide further details."

The decision automatically advanced Vanderbilt to the CWS finals, where the Commodores ultimately lost in three games to Mississippi State. Had NC State won its first game with the Commodores to clinch a place in the finals, the winner of the other bracket final between Mississippi State and Texas would have been the national champion.

"What transpired over the last 36 hours, and especially since midnight last night, has been hard to comprehend and even much more difficult to accept," NC State athletic director Boo Corrigan said in a statement. "Every step of the way we fought exhaustively for our players, coaches and staff and program, and for the opportunity to play for the national championship this team has worked so hard to reach. But at the end of the day, several of our players tested positive for COVID and we were not allowed to continue playing. While we can't discuss publicly everything that transpired, please know every effort was made to fight for the best interests of our program."

NC State won its first two games of the CWS, meaning it needed to beat Vanderbilt just once over its next two games to advance to the finals. The Wolfpack fought hard Friday afternoon with limited substitutes, pushing Vanderbilt and ace Kumar Rocker, but ultimately fell short, losing 3-1.

NC State was without four regulars as well as most of its pitching staff. That forced some little-used players into action in a crucial game and the Wolfpack competed well.

Avent was asked in the aftermath of the first game whether or not he encouraged his players to get vaccinated.

"We talk about a lot of things, you know what I'm saying? But I've been coaching for a long time. And I think I'm the—you can call it caretaker, baby-sitter or the guy that the parents drop their young men off and leave them in my care," he said. "And they've raised them to be the quality people that we recruit. And my job is to teach them baseball, make sure they get an education and keep them on the right track forward. But I don't try to indoctrinate my kids with my values or my things that, my opinions. Obviously we talk about a lot of things. But these are young men that can make their own decisions and that's what they did."

In his statement, Corrigan clarified some of the discussion around vaccinations, noting that the

RPI RANKINGS

The Ratings Percentage Index is an important tool used by the NCAA in selecting at-large teams for the 64-team Division I tournament. These were the top 100 finishers for 2021. A team's rank in the final Baseball America Top 25 is indicated in parentheses, and College World Series teams are bolded.

Rank School	Record	Rank School	Record
1. Arkansas (5)	50-13	**51.** S.C.-Upstate	37-16
2. Mississippi St. (1)	50-18	**52.** Pittsburgh	23-20
3. Vanderbilt (2)	49-18	**53.** South Alabama	36-22
4. Texas (3)	50-17	**54.** Nevada-Las Vegas	20-13
5. Notre Dame (10)	34-13	**55.** Samford	35-24
6. Tennessee (8)	50-18	**56.** Maryland	30-18
7. Stanford (7)	39-17	**57.** Air Force	26-22
8. Arizona (9)	45-18	**58.** Florida Atlantic	32-25
9. Fairfield	39-5	**59.** San Diego	35-12
10. Texas Christian (17)	41-19	**60.** Wofford	36-21
11. Mississippi (12)	45-22	**61.** Clemson	25-27
12. N.C. State (4)	37-19	**62.** Oklahoma	27-28
13. Old Dominion (16)	44-16	**63.** Kansas	30-27
14. Texas Tech (11)	39-17	**64.** Mercer	35-22
15. East Carolina (13)	44-17	**65.** Virginia Tech	27-25
16. Oklahoma State	36-19-1	**66.** Kentucky	29-23
17. Oregon (15)	39-16	**67.** UNC Wilmington	32-22
18. Oregon State	37-24	**68.** San Diego State	30-16
19. Louisiana State (21)	38-25	**69.** Rider	23-18
20. South Carolina	34-23	**70.** Louisville	28-22
21. Duke	33-22	**71.** Kansas State	34-23
22. Southern Miss. (23)	40-21	**72.** Western Carolina	28-21
23. UCLA (24)	37-20	**73.** West Virginia	25-27
24. UC Irvine (18)	43-18	**74.** Georgia Southern	34-23
25. Connecticut	34-19	**75.** Rhode Island	28-26-1
26. Florida (19)	38-22	**76.** Iowa	26-18
27. Virginia (6)	36-27	**77.** South Florida (25)	31-30
28. Gonzaga	34-19	**78.** Cincinnati	29-26
29. Louisiana Tech (22)	42-20	**79.** Monmouth	24-13
30. Nebraska (20)	34-14	**80.** Florida Gulf Coast	28-20
31. Va. Commonwealth	38-16	**81.** Bryant	27-14-1
32. Miami	33-21	**82.** Southern Illinois	40-20
33. Wright State	32-13	**83.** Tulane	31-24
34. Charlotte	40-21	**84.** Central Florida	31-30
35. Liberty	41-16	**85.** Washington State	26-23
36. Alabama	32-26	**86.** Southeast Mo. State	30-22
37. Campbell	37-18	**87.** California	29-26
38. Indiana State	31-21	**88.** Wake Forest	20-27
39. Northeastern	36-12	**89.** Long Beach State	28-15
40. Arizona State	33-22	**90.** North Dakota State	38-19
41. Georgia Tech	31-25	**91.** Texas A&M	29-27
42. Dallas Baptist (14)	41-18	**92.** Texas-San Antonio	22-26
43. Nevada	25-20	**93.** Canisius	20-16
44. Georgia	31-25	**94.** Michigan	27-19
45. Florida State	31-24	**95.** Grand Canyon	39-21-1
46. North Carolina	28-27	**96.** Coastal Carolina	27-24
47. Baylor	31-20	**97.** Villanova	21-14
48. UC Santa Barbara	41-20	**98.** Stony Brook	31-18
49. Central Michigan	41-18	**99.** Wichita State	31-23
50. Ball State	38-18	**100.** Abilene Christian	36-21

university could not require the players to get vaccinated and that some players opted to put off getting vaccinated for fear of side effects from the shot, given that vaccination was not widely available for young people until the season was underway.

The move brings a bitter taste to what has been a highly competitive CWS, college baseball's pinnacle event. College baseball played through the pandemic this season without a significant number of games canceled. But the specter of Covid-19

FIRST TEAM

Pos. Name	Year	AVG	OBP	SLG	AB	R	H	HR	RBI	BB	SO	SB
C Henry Davis, Louisville	So.	.370	.482	.663	184	45	68	15	48	31	24	10
1B Niko Kavadas, Notre Dame	Jr.	.302	.473	.767	159	42	48	22	64	50	55	2
2B Connor Norby, East Carolina	So.	.415	.484	.659	246	64	102	15	51	33	34	18
3B Hunter Wells, Louisiana Tech	Sr.	.385	.456	.645	262	70	101	14	61	34	37	1
SS Trey Sweeney, Eastern Illinois	So.	.382	.522	.712	170	52	65	14	58	46	24	3
OF Tanner Allen, Mississippi State	Jr.	.383	.456	.621	261	72	100	11	66	23	35	11
OF Colton Cowser, Sam Houston State	So.	.374	.490	.680	203	61	76	16	52	42	32	17
OF Aaron Zavala, Oregon	So.	.392	.525	.628	199	64	78	9	38	50	31	11
DH Mat Nelson, Florida State	So.	.336	.436	.773	194	50	64	23	66	31	58	4
UTL Paul Skenes, Air Force	Fr.	.410	.486	.697	188	49	77	11	43	22	45	0

	Year	W	L	ERA	G	CG	SV	IP	H	BB	SO	AVG
SP Jack Leiter, Vanderbilt	Fr.	11	4	2.13	18	2	0	110	48	45	179	.129
SP Doug Nikhazy, Mississippi	So.	12	2	2.45	16	1	0	92	62	31	142	.186
SP Kumar Rocker, Vanderbilt	So.	14	4	2.73	20	1	0	122	75	39	179	.170
SP Gavin Williams, East Carolina	Jr.	10	1	1.88	15	1	1	81	57	21	130	.193
RP Kevin Kopps, Arkansas	Sr.	12	1	0.90	33	0	11	90	50	18	131	.162
RP Landon Sims, Mississippi State	Fr.	4	0	1.55	21	0	10	46	25	14	85	.154
UTL Paul Skenes, Air Force	Fr.	1	1	2.70	18	0	11	27	20	9	30	.208

SECOND TEAM

Pos. Name	Year	AVG	OBP	SLG	AB	R	H	HR	RBI	BB	SO	SB
C Daniel Susac, Arizona	Fr.	.335	.392	.591	242	48	81	12	65	19	47	0
1B Ethan Long, Arizona State	Fr.	.340	.417	.704	162	42	55	16	54	18	46	0
2B Jace Jung, Texas Tech	Fr.	.337	.462	.697	208	55	70	21	67	49	45	4
3B Tyler Locklear, Virginia Commonwealth	Fr.	.345	.515	.686	194	69	67	16	66	46	40	8
SS Brooks Lee, Cal Poly	Fr.	.342	.384	.626	222	48	76	10	57	18	34	3
OF Kyler Fedko, Connecticut	So.	.398	.483	.673	196	57	78	12	53	28	37	7
OF Quincy Hamilton, Wright State	Jr.	.374	.535	.771	179	78	67	15	65	56	32	20
OF Brock Jones, Stanford	Fr.	.311	.453	.646	206	56	64	18	62	49	59	14
DH Jacob Berry, Arizona	Fr.	.352	.439	.676	247	54	87	17	70	33	58	2
UTL Spencer Schwellenbach, Nebraska	So.	.284	.403	.459	183	43	52	6	40	30	44	9

	Year	W	L	ERA	G	CG	SV	IP	H	BB	SO	AVG
SP Rodney Boone, UC Santa Barbara	So.	11	4	2.31	16	1	0	97	55	39	128	
SP Geremy Guerrero, Indiana State	Sr.	10	1	2.08	14	2	0	99	65	14	98	.182
SP Ty Madden, Texas	So.	7	5	2.45	18	1	0	114	75	44	137	.188
SP Andrew Taylor, Central Michigan	Fr.	11	4	1.81	15	5	0	94	64	24	125	.189
RP Sean Hunley, Tennessee	Jr.	7	5	3.36	35	0	9	72	62	13	77	.229
RP Carson Palmquist, Miami	Fr.	1	1	2.22	25	0	14	45	22	8	75	.143
UTL Spencer Schwellenbach, Nebraska	So.	3	1	0.57	18	0	10	32	22	8	34	.198

THIRD TEAM

Pos. Name	Year	AVG	OBP	SLG	AB	R	H	HR	RBI	BB	SO	SB
C Hunter Goodman, Memphis	So.	.307	.401	.678	202	40	62	21	51	30	53	9
1B Liam McGill, Bryant	Sr.	.471	.541	.746	138	45	77	16	60	39	54	0
2B Jackson Glenn, Dallas Baptist	Sr.	.361	.429	.717	233	61	84	20	53	30	33	13
3B Jake Rucker, Tennessee	So.	.330	.399	.520	273	48	90	9	55	27	63	7
SS Benjamin Cowles, Maryland	So.	.287	.409	.632	174	42	50	18	51	20	57	9
OF Kyle Battle, Old Dominion	Sr.	.319	.464	.681	207	68	66	18	61	56	37	7
OF Jonny Butler, North Carolina State	Jr.	.376	.452	.663	202	54	76	14	53	26	45	16
OF Sal Frelick, Boston College	So.	.359	.443	.559	195	50	70	6	27	27	28	13
DH Wes Clarke, South Carolina	So.	.271	.428	.663	199	56	54	23	55	50	73	0
UTL Justin Campbell, Oklahoma State	Fr.	.269	.398	.388	67	10	18	1	10	14	20	0

	Year	W	L	ERA	G	CG	SV	IP	H	BB	SO	AVG
SP Andrew Abbott, Virginia	Jr.	9	6	2.87	19	0	0	107	89	32	162	.228
SP Brendan Beck, Stanford	Jr.	9	3	3.15	17	2	0	109	81	26	143	.200
SP Landon Marceaux, Louisiana State	So.	7	7	2.54	18	1	0	103	92	26	116	.238
SP Matt Mikulski, Fordham	Jr.	9	0	1.45	11	5	0	68	29	27	124	.127
RP Taylor Broadway, Mississippi	Sr.	4	3	3.44	30	0	16	50	46	9	66	.242
RP Nick Jones, Georgia Southern	Jr.	1	0	1.48	29	0	17	43	34	5	68	.213
UTL Justin Campbell, Oklahoma State	Fr.	7	2	2.57	14	1	0	84	66	27	102	.214

never went away and most weekends there were at least a few series that were altered by the virus. NC State itself previously had its season impacted by Covid-19, as its mid March series against Duke was canceled due to issues with the Wolfpack.

While other college sports experienced similar withdrawals from their championship events, none occurred at such a late stage of competition.

The men's hockey tournament was hit by three withdrawals, including the No. 2 seed Michigan, but all came before the Frozen Four. Virginia Commonwealth men's basketball was disqualified from the first round of the NCAA Tournament and Rice women's volleyball was also knocked out because of Covid-19 protocols.

NCAA Eases Transfer Rules

The NCAA Division I Council in April approved a rule change that allows all Division I athletes in all sports a one-time waiver to transfer and be immediately eligible.

The decision ends a long, protracted process to bring uniformity to the transfer rules and provide more freedom for athletes. Previously, baseball, men's and women's basketball, football and men's hockey required players to sit out a season when transferring. All other sports already operated with a one-time transfer exception.

The waiver change will have a significant effect on baseball. It long operated like other sports with the one-time transfer exemption but in 2008, in a series of moves designed to improve the sport's Academic Progress Rate and graduation rate, it was eliminated, and the sport was grouped with basketball, football and hockey. Within two years of the change, the percentage of players who had made a 4-4 transfer (a transfer from one four-year school to another) dropped from 8.4 to 3.5 and the percentage of players who had transferred at all (including those coming from junior college) fell from 26.2 to 22.4.

Now, the sport will return to the free transfer era. Every player will be able to transfer once without having to sit out a year (any subsequent 4-4 transfers would require a "year-in-residence"). The lone stipulation for baseball players (and all spring sports athletes) to receive the one-time waiver is that they must inform their current school of their intent to transfer by July 1. They don't need to have chosen a new school by then; they simply need to be in the portal by then to be eligible the following spring.

The transfer issue has long been contentious in college baseball. In 2005, Dave Keilitz, then the executive director of the American Baseball Coaches Association, told Baseball America, "I'm trying to think of the last time we had a Division I business meeting and it wasn't discussed."

Some coaches today believe it isn't right to restrict players in a partial scholarship sport from leaving to find a better situation, especially financially. Others remember the landscape before 2008 and aren't keen to return to it.

The transfer reform debate is now settled, not only for baseball, but for all sports. Conferences, schools and athletic directors could no longer find a justification for one set rules governing one set of players – who primarily play in revenue sports— and another set of rules for the rest.

Now, baseball goes back to the future with its transfer policy. The new rules will undoubtedly cause a significant amount of player movement this summer and require coaches to adapt their roster construction strategy. Transfer movement upticked in the first offseason of the new regulations and some programs dipped heavily into the transfer market.

COLLEGE WORLD SERIES

STANDINGS

Bracket One	W	L
Vanderbilt	3	1
North Carolina State	2	1
Stanford	1	2
Arizona	0	2

Bracket Two	W	L
Mississippi State	3	1
Texas	3	2
Virginia	1	2
Tennessee	0	2

CWS FINALS (BEST OF THREE)
June 28: Vanderbilt 8, Mississippi State 2
June 29: Mississippi State 13, Vanderbilt 2
June 30: Mississippi State 9, Vanderbilt 0

ALL-TOURNAMENT TEAM
C: Logan Tanner, Mississippi State. **1B:** Luke Hancock, Mississippi State. **2B:** Tim Tawa, Stanford. **3B:** Zack Gelof, Virginia. **SS:** Lane Forsythe, Mississippi State. **OF:** Tanner Allen, Mississippi State; Brock Jones, Stanford; Rowdey Jordan, Mississippi State. **DH:** Ivan Melendez, Texas. **P:** *Will Bednar, Mississippi State; Jack Leiter, Vanderbilt.

Named Most Outstanding Player.

BATTING
(Minimum 8 PA)

Player	AVG	R	H	2B	3B	HR	RBI
Chris Newell, Virginia	.600	4	6	1	0	2	5
Zack Gelof, Virginia	.583	3	7	2	0	0	2
Kyle Teel, Virginia	.583	0	7	1	0	0	1
Daniel Susac, Arizona	.500	1	4	3	0	0	4
Pete Derkay, Tennessee	.500	1	4	0	0	0	1
Drew Bowser, Stanford	.462	3	6	2	0	0	2
Brock Jones, Stanford	.429	3	6	2	0	2	8
Tim Tawa, Stanford	.400	3	6	1	0	1	1
Logan Michaels, Virginia	.400	4	4	0	0	1	2
Max Cotier, Virginia	.364	0	4	0	0	0	2

PITCHING
(Minimum 6 IP)

Pitcher	W-L	ERA	G	SV	IP	H	BB	SO
Luke Murphy, Vanderbilt	1-0	0.00	4	1	8	4	3	11
Sam Highfill, N.C. State	1-0	0.00	1	0	7	2	2	7
Andrew Abbott, Virginia	1-0	0.00	1	0	6	5	2	10
Landon Sims, Miss. St.	1-0	0.90	4	3	10	4	1	15
Mike Vasil, Virginia	0-0	1.29	1	0	7	4	1	8
Will Bednar, Miss. St.	2-0	1.47	3	0	18	5	6	26
Jack Leiter, Vanderbilt	1-1	1.93	2	0	14	7	4	23
Preston Johnson, Miss. St.	1-0	2.08	3	0	9	6	3	12
Nick Maldonado, Vanderbilt	0-0	2.08	3	1	9	8	1	11
Pete Hansen, Texas	0-0	2.35	2	0	8	6	2	8

REGIONALS

JUNE 4-7
64 teams, 16 four-team, double-elimination tournaments. Winners advance to super regionals.

FAYETTEVILLE
Host: Arkansas (No. 1 national seed).
Participants: No. 1 Arkansas (46-10), No. 2 Nebraska (31-12), No. 3 Northeastern (36-10), No. 4 New Jersey Tech (26-22).
Champion: Arkansas (3-1).
Runner-up: Nebraska (3-2).
Outstanding player: Kevin Kopps, RP, Arkansas.

AUSTIN
Host: Texas (No. 2 national seed).
Participants: No. 1 Texas (42-15), No. 2 Arizona State (32-20), No. 3 Fairfield (37-3), No. 4 Southern (20-28).
Champion: Texas (3-0).
Runner-up: Fairfield (2-2).
Outstanding player: Zach Zubia, 1B, Texas.

KNOXVILLE, TENN.
Host: Tennessee (No. 3 national seed).
Participants: No. 1 Tennessee (45-16), No. 2 Duke (32-20), No. 3 Liberty (39-14), No. 4 Wright State (35-11).
Champion: Tennessee (3-0).
Runner-up: Liberty (2-2).
Outstanding player: Drew Gilbert, OF, Tennessee.

NASHVILLE
Host: Vanderbilt (No. 4 national seed).
Participants: No. 1 Vanderbilt (40-15), No. 2 Georgia Tech (29-23), No. 3 Indiana State (30-19), No. 4 Presbyterian (22-21).
Champion: Vanderbilt (3-0).
Runner-up: Georgia Tech (2-2).
Outstanding player: Dominic Keegan, 1B, Vanderbilt.

TUCSON, ARIZ.
Host: Arizona (No. 5 national seed).
Participants: No. 1 Arizona (40-15), No. 2 Oklahoma State (35-17-1), No. 3 UC Santa Barbara (39-18), No. 4 Grand Canyon (39-19-1).
Champion: Arizona (3-0).
Runner-up: UC Santa Barbara (2-2).
Outstanding player: Garrett Irvin, SP, Arizona.

FORT WORTH, TEXAS
Host: Texas Christian (No. 6 national seed).
Participants: No. 1 Texas Christian (40-17), No. 2 Oregon State (34-22), No. 3 Dallas Baptist (37-15), No. 4 McNeese State (32-28).
Champion: Dallas Baptist (3-1).
Runner-up: Oregon State (3-2).
Outstanding player: Ryan Wrobleski, OF, Dallas Baptist.

STARKVILLE, MISS.
Host: Mississippi State (No. 7 national seed).
Participants: No. 1 Mississippi State (40-15), No. 2 Virginia Commonwealth (37-14), No. 3 Campbell (35-16), No. 4 Samford (35-22).
Champion: Mississippi State (3-0).
Runner-up: Campbell (2-2).
Outstanding player: Kamren James, 3B, Mississippi State.

LUBBOCK, TEXAS
Host: Texas Tech (No. 8 national seed).
Participants: No. 1 Texas Tech (36-15), No. 2 UCLA (35-18), No. 3 North Carolina (27-25), No. 4 Army (28-23).
Champion: Texas Tech (3-0).
Runner-up: UCLA (3-2).
Outstanding player: Kurt Wilson, OF, Texas Tech.

STANFORD, CALIF.
Host: Stanford (No. 9 national seed).
Participants: No. 1 Stanford (33-14), No. 2 UC Irvine (40-16), No. 3 Nevada (25-18), No. 4 North Dakota State (41-17).
Champion: Stanford (3-1).
Runner-up: UC Irvine (3-2).
Outstanding player: Tim Tawa, 2B, Stanford.

SOUTH BEND, IND.
Host: Notre Dame (No. 10 national seed).
Participants: No. 1 Notre Dame (30-11), No. 2 Connecticut (33-16), No. 3 Michigan (27-17), No. 4 Central Michigan (40-16).
Champion: Notre Dame (3-0).
Runner-up: Central Michigan (2-2).
Outstanding player: Niko Kavadas, 1B, Notre Dame.

COLUMBIA, S.C.
Host: South Carolina.
Participants: No. 1 Old Dominion (42-14, No. 11 national seed), No. 2 South Carolina (33-21), No. 3 Virginia (29-23), No. 4 Jacksonville (16-32).
Champion: Virginia (4-1).
Runner-up: Old Dominion (2-2).
Outstanding player: Devin Ortiz, DH, South Carolina.

OXFORD, MISS.
Host: Mississippi (No. 12 national seed).
Participants: No. 1 Mississippi (41-19), No. 2 Southern Mississippi (37-19), No. 3 Florida State (30-22), No. 4 Southeast Missouri State (30-20).
Champion: Mississippi (3-1).
Runner-up: Southern Mississippi (3-2).
Outstanding player: Tim Elko, DH, Mississippi.

GREENVILLE, N.C.
Host: East Carolina (No. 13 national seed).
Participants: No. 1 East Carolina (41-15), No. 2 Charlotte (39-19), No. 3 Maryland (28-16), No. 4 Norfolk State (25-26).
Champion: East Carolina (3-0).
Runner-up: Maryland (2-2).
Outstanding player: Matt Bridges, RP, East Carolina.

EUGENE, ORE.
Host: Oregon (No. 14 national seed).
Participants: No. 1 Oregon (37-14), No. 2 Gonzaga (33-17), No. 3 Louisiana (34-22), No. 4 Central Connecticut State (28-13).
Champion: Louisiana State (4-1).
Runner-up: Oregon (2-2).
Outstanding player: Gavin Dugas, OF, Louisiana State.

GAINESVILLE, FLA.
Host: Florida (No. 15 national seed).
Participants: No. 1 Florida (38-20), No. 2 Miami (32-19), No. 3 South Alabama (33-20), No. 4 South Florida (28-27).
Champion: South Florida (3-1).
Runner-up: South Alabama (3-2).
Outstanding player: Jake Sullivan, C, South Florida.

RUSTON, LA.
Host: Louisiana Tech (No. 16 national seed).
Participants: No. 1 Louisiana Tech (40-18), No. 2 North Carolina State (30-17), No. 3 Alabama (31-24), No. 4 Rider (23-16).
Champion: North Carolina State (3-0).
Runner-up: Louisiana Tech (2-2).
Outstanding player: N/A.

SUPER REGIONALS

JUNE 11-13
16 teams, best-of-three series. Winners advance to College World Series.

NORTH CAROLINA STATE AT ARKANSAS
Site: Fayetteville, Ark.
N.C. State wins 2-1, advances to CWS.

SOUTH FLORIDA AT TEXAS
Site: Austin
Texas wins 2-0, advances to CWS.

LOUISIANA STATE AT TENNESSEE
Site: Knoxville, Tenn.
Tennessee wins 2-0, advances to CWS.

EAST CAROLINA AT VANDERBILT
Site: Nashville
Vanderbilt wins 2-0, advances to CWS.

MISSISSIPPI AT ARIZONA
Site: Tucson, Ariz.
Arizona wins 2-1, advances to CWS.

DALLAS BAPTIST VS. VIRGINIA
Site: Columbia, S.C.
Virginia wins 2-1, advances to CWS.

NOTRE DAME AT MISSISSIPPI STATE
Site: Starkville, Miss.
Mississippi State wins 2-1, advances to CWS.

STANFORD AT TEXAS TECH
Site: Lubbock, Texas.
Stanford wins 2-0, advances to CWS.

Rocker exceeds the hype

PLAYER OF THE YEAR

BY TEDDY CAHILL

Kumar Rocker is listed at 6-foot-5, 245 pounds and cuts an imposing figure on the mound. Even bigger than his build on the mound, however, is the size of expectations he brought to college when he arrived in Nashville in the fall of 2018.

Rocker was one of the highest-rated recruits ever to reach college baseball. The righthander could have been a first-round pick that summer. Instead, he opted to become a Commodore, joining an impressive array of pitchers to matriculate at Vanderbilt.

Over the next three years, Rocker was an integral part of the Commodores' staff. He was named Most Outstanding Player in 2019 at the College World Series as a freshman after helping Vanderbilt win the national championship. While he fell just short of repeating that feat in 2021, losing the decisive third game of the College World Series finals against Mississippi State, his career—and season—were exemplary.

He this season went 14-4, 2.73 with 179 strikeouts in 122 innings. He led the nation in wins and tied with teammate Jack Leiter for the most strikeouts in the country. He finished his career at Vanderbilt 28-10, 2.89 with 321 strikeouts and 68 walks in 236.2 innings. In a stellar career, his 2021 season stands out as his best.

Kumar Rocker

No other player in college baseball this year combined the level of success, premium prospect status and impact as Rocker. For those reasons, he was Baseball America's College Player of the Year.

Rocker is the second Vanderbilt player to ever win the award, joining lefthander David Price (2007). He is the third player this century to win both the Freshman of the Year and Player of the Year awards during their careers, joining Rice third baseman Anthony Rendon (2009, 2010) and Louisville lefthander/first baseman Brendan McKay (2015, 2017).

Following the College World Series, Vanderbilt coach Tim Corbin was asked what he will most remember about coaching Rocker. He nearly broke down in tears while describing what it has meant.

"He's just a one-in-a-million kid," Corbin said. "His fibers are so real and so pure. He just loves team. He's connected to competition. He's connected to his teammates in such a way that (he's) just the ultimate college pitcher, ultimate college teammate. The ultimate college baseball player. He'll go down as one of the very best we've had at Vanderbilt.

"I don't like to categorize the kids because I don't want to slight anyone, but, my gosh, this kid—he's meant so much to our program. He's meant a lot to college baseball. He's meant a lot to the SEC.

"He's the best reflection of his parents. That's high praise. He's just done everything right. I love that young man."

PREVIOUS WINNERS

1982: Jeff Ledbetter, OF/LHP Florida St.
1983: Dave Magadan, 1B, Alabama
1984: Oddibe McDowell, OF, Arizona St.
1985: Pete Incaviglia, OF, Oklahoma State
1986: Casey Close, OF, Michigan
1987: Robin Ventura, 3B, Oklahoma State
1988: John Olerud, 1B/LHP, Washington St.
1989: Ben McDonald, RHP, Louisiana State
1990: Mike Kelly, OF, Arizona State
1991: David McCarthy, 1B, Stanford
1992: Phil Nevin, 3B, Cal State Fullerton
1993: Brooks Kieschnick, DH/RHP, Texas
1994: Jason Varitek, C, Georgia Tech

1995: Todd Helton, 1B/LHP, Tennessee
1996: Kris Benson, RHP, Clemson
1997: J.D. Drew, OF, Florida State
1998: Jeff Austin, RHP, Stanford
1999: Jason Jennings, RHP, Baylor
2000: Mark Teixeira, 3B, Georgia Tech
2001: Mark Prior, RHP, S. California
2002: Khalil Greene, SS, Clemson
2003: Rickie Weeks, 2B, Southern
2004: Jered Weaver, RHP, Long Beach St.
2005: Alex Gordon, 3B, Nebraska
2006: Andrew Miller, LHP, North Carolina
2007: David Price, LHP, Vanderbilt

2008: Buster Posey, C/RHP, Florida State
2009: Stephen Strasburg, RHP, San Diego St.
2010: Anthony Rendon, 3B, Rice
2011: Trevor Bauer, RHP, UCLA
2012: Mike Zunino, C, Florida
2013: Kris Bryant, 3B, San Diego
2014: A.J. Reed, 1B/LHP, Kentucky
2015: Andrew Benintendi, OF, Arkansas
2016: Kyle Lewis, OF, Mercer
2017: Brendan McKay, LHP/1B, Louisville
2018: Brady Singer, RHP, Florida
2019: Adley Rutschman, C, Oregon State

Lemonis leads Mississippi State to first title

COACH OF THE YEAR

BY TEDDY CAHILL

Mississippi State is one of the biggest programs in college baseball. It's the alma mater of Thunder and Lightning—Will Clark and Rafael Palmeiro—as well as Jake Mangum, the Southeastern Conference's hit king.

Longtime Mississippi State coach Ron Polk is known as the Godfather of the SEC for the way he brought the show of big-time baseball to the conference. Dudy Noble Field is an iconic venue and the home of the largest on-campus crowds in college baseball history.

The one thing Mississippi State was always missing, however, was a national championship.

From the time Chris Lemonis was hired as head coach following the 2018 season—when the Bulldogs made a Cinderella run to the final four of the College World Series under interim head coach Gary Henderson—he has never run from the program's championship expectations.

This year, in his third season at the helm, Lemonis and the Bulldogs made good on them. Mississippi State fended off Texas in the bracket final to reach the College World Series championship series against Vanderbilt. After losing Game 1 in the best-of-three series,

Chris Lemonis

the Bulldogs stormed back to twice rout the Commodores, 13-2 and 9-0, to win the national championship.

It was not only the baseball program's first national title, but also the first for a team sport in Mississippi State history.

The path to a national championship is never easy, and Mississippi State had plenty of challenges along the way, including a late-season series loss that cost it a shot at a conference title and then facing four elimination games in the NCAA Tournament.

Mississippi State's run to the national championship was a testament to the culture Lemonis fostered in Starkville and the team he built.

After a historic season, Lemonis is Baseball America's College Coach of the Year. Lemonis, 51, is the fourth man to win both Coach of the Year and Assistant Coach of the Year, joining Tim Corbin, Brian O'Connor and Dave Serrano.

Lemonis began his coaching career at The Citadel, his alma mater, as an assistant coach in 1995. He spent a decade there before joining Dan McDonnell, his college teammate, in Louisville in 2006. Lemonis helped build the Cardinals into a national power.

In 2013, Lemonis shared Assistant Coach of the Year honors with Louisville pitching coach Roger Williams. Two years later, Lemonis became a head coach for the first time when he was hired by Indiana. He led the Hoosiers to regionals in three of his four seasons before he was hired at Mississippi State.

PREVIOUS WINNERS

1982: Gene Stephenson, Wichita State
1983: Barry Shollenberger, Alabama
1984: Augie Garrido, Cal State Fullerton
1985: Ron Polk, Mississippi State
1986: Skip Bertman, LSU/Dave Snow, LMU
1987: Mark Marquess, Stanford
1988: Jim Brock, Arizona State
1989: Dave Snow, Long Beach State
1990: Steve Webber, Georgia
1991: Jim Hendry, Creighton
1992: Andy Lopez, Pepperdine
1993: Gene Stephenson, Wichita State
1994: Jim Morris, Miami

1995: Pat Murphy, Arizona State
1996: Skip Bertman, Louisiana State
1997: Jim Wells, Alabama
1998: Pat Murphy, Arizona State
1999: Wayne Graham, Rice
2000: Ray Tanner, South Carolina
2001: Dave Van Horn, Nebraska
2002: Augie Garrido, Texas
2003: George Horton, Cal State Fullerton
2004: David Perno, Georgia
2005: Rick Jones, Tulane
2006: Pat Casey, Oregon State
2007: Dave Serrano, UC Irvine

2008: Mike Fox, North Carolina
2009: Paul Mainieri, Louisiana State
2010: Ray Tanner, South Carolina
2011: Kevin O'Sullivan, Florida
2012: Mike Martin, Florida State
2013: John Savage, UCLA
2014: Tim Corbin, Vanderbilt
2015: Brian O'Connor, Virginia
2016: Jim Schlossnagle, Texas Christian
2017: Dan McDonnell, Louisville
2018: David Pierce, Texas
2019: Mike Martin, Florida State

Leiter sparkles in unique season

FRESHMAN OF THE YEAR

BY TEDDY CAHILL

Jack Leiter's first season in college was interrupted by the pandemic. He more than made up for lost time in 2021.

The righthander went 11-4, 2.13 in 110 innings. He tied teammate Kumar Rocker for the most strikeouts in the nation with 179.

He made waves March 20 when he no-hit South Carolina and then built a hitless inning streak that reached 20 and spanned three starts. He helped the Commodores to a runner-up finish at the College World Series and the Rangers made him the second overall pick in the 2021 draft.

No other freshman in college baseball this year combined the level of success, premium prospect status and impact as Leiter. For those reasons, Leiter is the Baseball America Freshman of the Year.

Jack Leiter

Leiter and all members of the 2020 freshman class were eligible for this year's Freshman of the Year award because they played only about a quarter of the 2020 season. If it had been an injury and not a pandemic that had ended their season at the same point, they would have been eligible for a redshirt and therefore still considered freshmen the following year. Baseball America applied the same standard for the 2021 season.

Leiter is the third Vanderbilt player to be named Freshman of the Year, joining third baseman Pedro Alvarez (2006) and Rocker (2019).

Vanderbilt coach Tim Corbin said the key for Leiter to reach his lofty level was the consistency he brings to everything he does.

"Consistency to what he's doing—he's the same every day," Corbin said. "Whether it's academically, socially or athletically, he's low-maintenance, mature, gets to the facility, and it's full-on go. He's wired to compete, too, every single day."

PREVIOUS WINNERS

1991: Brooks Kieschnick, RHP/DH, Texas
1992: Todd Walker, 2B, Louisiana State
1993: Brett Laxton, RHP, Louisiana State
1994: R.A. Dickey, RHP, Tennessee
1995: Kyle Peterson, RHP, Stanford
1996: Pat Burrell, 3B, Miami
1997: Brian Roberts, SS, North Carolina
1998: Xavier Nady, 2B, California
1999: James Jurries, 2B, Tulane
2000: Kevin Howard, 3B, Miami
2001: Michael Aubrey, OF/LHP, Texas
2002: Stephen Drew, SS, Florida State
2003: Ryan Braun, SS, Miami
2004: Wade LeBlanc, LHP, Alabama
2005: Joe Savery, LHP, Rice
2006: Pedro Alvarez, 3B, Vanderbilt
2007: Dustin Ackley, 1B, North Carolina
2008: Chris Hernandez, LHP, Miami
2009: Anthony Rendon, 3B, Rice
2010: Matt Purke, LHP, Texas Christian
2011: Colin Moran, 3B, North Carolina
2012: Carlos Rodon, LHP, N.C. State
2013: Alex Bregman, SS, Louisiana State
2014: Zack Collins, C, Miami
2015: Brendan McKay, LHP/1B, Louisville
2016: Seth Beer, OF, Clemson
2017: Matt Wallner, OF/RHP, Southern Miss
2018: Kevin Abel, RHP, Oregon State
2019: Kumar Rocker, RHP, Vanderbilt
Full list of winners can be found at BaseballAmerica.com/Stories/Baseball-America-Awards

FRESHMAN ALL-AMERICA TEAMS

All members of the 2020 freshman class were eligible for this year's Freshman of the Year award because they played only about a quarter of the 2020 season and were given an extra year of eligibility by the NCAA. To account for a larger than normal group of freshmen, a third team was added to the Freshman All-America teams.

FIRST TEAM

C: Daniel Susac, Arizona. **1B:** Ethan Long, Arizona State. **2B:** Jace Jung, Texas Tech. **3B:** Tyler Locklear, Virginia Commonwealth. **SS:** Brooks Lee, Cal Poly. **OF:** Enrique Bradfield, Vanderbilt; Dylan Crews, Louisiana State; Brock Jones, Stanford. **DH:** Jacob Berry, Arizona. **UT:** Paul Skenes, Air Force. **SP:** Will Bednar, Mississippi State; Jack Leiter, Vanderbilt; Parker Messick; Florida State; Andrew Taylor, Central Michigan. **RP:** Carson Palmquist, Miami; Landon Sims, Mississippi State.

SECOND TEAM

C: Kevin Parada, Georgia Tech. **1B:** Caden Grice, Clemson. **2B:** Carter Trice, Old Dominion. **3B:** Brayden Taylor, Texas Christian. **SS:** Jacob Gonzalez, Mississippi. **OF:** Dylan Beavers, California; Jared McKenzie, Baylor; Reed Trimble, Southern Mississippi. **DH:** Kyle Teel, Virginia. **UT:** Justin Campbell, Oklahoma State. **SP:** Pete Hansen, Texas; Jace Kaminska, Wichita State; Cam Schlittler, Northeastern; Drew Thorpe, Cal Poly. **RP:** Devereaux Harrison, Long Beach State; Max Rajcic, UCLA.

THIRD TEAM

C: Bennett Lee, Tulane. **1B:** Tre Morgan, Louisiana State. **2B:** Robert Moore, Arkansas. **3B:** Brock Wilken, Wake Forest. **SS:** Jordan Sprinkle, UC Santa Barbara. **OF:** Nathan Church, UC Irvine; Gavin Cross, Virginia Tech; Zach Rodriguez, UC Santa Barbara. **DH:** Josh Moylan, East Carolina. **UT:** Zach Neto, Campbell. **SP:** Ben Ethridge, Southern Mississippi; Thomas Harrington, Campbell; Nick Pinto, UC Irvine; Carter Young, Grand Canyon. **RP:** Tyler Cleveland, Central Arkansas; Jacob King, UC Irvine.

HITTING (MINIMUM 140 AT-BATS)

BATTING AVERAGE

Rk.	Player, Team	Pos.	AVG	OBP	SLG	G	AB	2B	3B	HR	RBI	BB	SO	SB
1.	Liam McGill, Bryant	1B	.471	.541	.746	37	138	9	1	9	50	22	23	2
2.	Dillan Shrum, Nevada	1B	.468	.527	.968	35	124	15	1	15	47	10	19	1
3.	Tristin Garcia, Alcorn State	2B	.445	.500	.582	27	110	10	1	1	27	7	8	7
4.	Kyler Castillo, New Mexico	LF	.439	.486	.665	38	164	16	0	7	40	12	11	5
5.	Ty Hill, Jackson State	3B	.432	.500	.662	37	139	13	5	3	43	15	13	9
6.	Jack-Thomas Wold, Nevada-Las Vegas	1B	.429	.491	.793	33	140	13	1	12	43	19	14	1
7.	Justin Starke, Virginia Millitary Institute	1B	.422	.525	.602	44	161	9	1	6	27	27	34	3
8.	Connor Norby, East Carolina	2B	.415	.484	.659	61	246	15	0	15	51	33	34	18
9.	Paul Skenes, Air Force	C	.410	.486	.697	48	188	21	0	11	43	22	45	0
10.	Dylan Hoy, Marist	SS	.410	.520	.538	29	78	3	2	1	10	15	12	2
11.	Matt Rudick, San Diego State	CF	.410	.484	.567	44	178	8	4	4	41	26	9	17
12.	Zach Neto, Campbell	SS	.405	.488	.746	44	173	17	3	12	58	17	30	12
13.	Bryan Rosario, Illinois-Chicago	LF	.399	.460	.500	46	168	8	3	1	21	18	34	12
14.	Kyler Fedko, Connecticut	RF	.398	.485	.673	52	196	14	2	12	53	28	37	7
15.	Tyler Hardman, Oklahoma	1B	.397	.481	.661	55	224	19	2	12	49	34	59	3
16.	JT Schwartz, UCLA	1B	.396	.514	.628	44	164	12	1	8	45	37	28	1
17.	Jared Gillen, Wagner	CF	.396	.437	.510	36	149	11	0	2	32	14	22	16
18.	Will Prater, Western Carolina	DH	.395	.457	.461	46	167	5	3	0	32	18	26	6
19.	Justice Bigbie, Western Carolina	LF	.395	.500	.621	49	195	15	1	9	50	36	37	11
20.	Myles Denson, Nevada-Las Vegas	RF	.395	.435	.605	30	114	6	0	6	22	8	20	1
21.	Bennett Hostetler, North Dakota State	SS	.394	.513	.606	61	213	13	1	10	58	36	38	19
22.	Matt Smith, Sacramento State	DH	.393	.452	.595	48	173	11	0	8	44	16	21	3
23.	Dario Gomez, Nevada	CF	.393	.415	.592	45	191	16	2	6	37	5	40	12
24.	Kai Moody, Cal State Northridge	2B	.393	.459	.486	36	140	10	0	1	25	22	14	10
25.	Aaron Zavala, Oregon	RF	.392	.525	.628	55	199	14	3	9	38	50	31	11
26.	Cole Tucker, Niagara	2B	.391	.482	.587	30	92	9	0	3	19	9	17	6
27.	Justin Janas, Illinois	DH	.391	.506	.449	42	138	6	1	0	28	20	19	0
28.	Jackson Feltner, Morehead State	1B	.390	.452	.652	44	164	10	0	11	42	17	40	0
29.	Trenton Jamison, Alabama State	3B	.390	.460	.634	39	164	12	2	8	43	16	27	3
30.	Reese Alexiades, Pepperdine	RF	.389	.481	.618	35	131	7	1	7	29	25	28	4
31.	Jaden Fein, San Diego State	RF	.389	.456	.553	46	190	19	0	4	53	16	35	8
32.	Chase DeLauter, James Madison	CF	.386	.508	.723	26	101	12	2	6	21	25	14	7
33.	Jake Gustin, Bryant	2B	.386	.463	.591	42	171	13	2	6	36	18	21	10
34.	Cole O'Connor, Niagara	RF	.385	.420	.471	30	104	9	0	0	16	7	14	0
35.	Hunter Wells, Louisiana Tech	3B	.385	.456	.645	62	262	20	3	14	61	34	37	1
36.	Tyler Black, Wright State	2B	.383	.496	.683	48	183	14	1	13	59	39	25	11
37.	Alec Sayre, Wright State	RF	.383	.479	.662	39	133	9	2	8	40	23	25	6
38.	Tanner Allen, Mississippi State	RF	.383	.456	.621	67	261	19	5	11	66	23	35	11
39.	Mitchell Dickson, Abilene Christian	C	.383	.465	.495	49	196	10	0	4	45	21	19	7
40.	Jared McKenzie, Baylor	CF	.383	.453	.626	51	214	14	4	10	44	15	35	3
41.	Michael Stygles, Oakland	DH	.382	.458	.549	46	144	12	0	4	38	17	32	3
42.	Trey Sweeney, Eastern Illinois	SS	.382	.522	.712	48	170	10	2	14	58	46	24	3
43.	Ruben Ibarra, San Jose State	1B	.381	.503	.850	35	113	9	1	14	32	28	24	0
44.	Thomas Smart, Illinois-Chicago	RF	.380	.505	.509	48	171	10	3	2	32	35	22	8
45.	Wyatt Hendrie, San Diego State	C	.379	.464	.633	45	169	12	2	9	57	22	25	8
46.	Alan Roden, Creighton	DH	.378	.476	.685	39	143	17	0	9	47	20	18	4
47.	Tyler Wilber, Southeast Missouri State	SS	.378	.446	.542	52	201	11	2	6	49	22	26	4
48.	Chris Meyers, Toledo	1B	.378	.509	.739	54	180	18	1	15	55	39	42	10
49.	Jonny Butler, North Carolina State	LF	.376	.452	.663	52	202	12	2	14	53	26	45	16
50.	Aaron Anderson, Liberty	LF	.375	.460	.567	57	224	25	3	4	42	33	38	0
51.	Brendan Hueth, Saint Joseph's	CF	.375	.444	.542	37	144	11	2	3	25	18	16	5
52.	Colton Cowser, Sam Houston	CF	.374	.490	.680	55	203	10	2	16	52	42	32	17
53.	Elijah Buries, Grand Canyon	1B	.374	.433	.553	51	179	10	2	6	38	18	29	13
54.	Quincy Hamilton, Wright State	CF	.374	.535	.771	48	179	18	4	15	65	56	32	20
55.	Joey Loperfido, Duke	CF	.374	.473	.612	53	206	19	3	8	29	24	50	12
56.	Zerek Saenz, New Mexico State	LF	.373	.471	.433	53	201	6	3	0	25	35	37	3
57.	Mason McWhorter, Georgia Southern	LF	.372	.445	.690	57	226	16	1	18	52	27	51	3
58.	Spencer Packard, Campbell	RF	.371	.488	.629	55	197	18	0	11	67	32	24	2
59.	Mack Chambers, New Mexico	SS	.371	.444	.624	41	170	16	3	7	31	16	12	5
60.	Henry Davis, Louisville	C	.370	.482	.663	50	184	9	0	15	48	31	24	10
61.	Kyle Baker, Delaware	RF	.370	.476	.496	34	135	9	1	2	19	26	25	5
62.	Nathan Church, UC Irvine	RF	.369	.424	.583	61	271	24	8	6	61	23	34	7
63.	Christian Del Castillo, Miami	CF	.369	.439	.495	54	198	11	1	4	40	22	26	7
64.	Branden Boissiere, Arizona	1B	.369	.451	.506	63	255	12	4	5	63	38	49	2
65.	John Thrasher, Hartford	CF	.369	.470	.680	36	122	11	3	7	23	15	21	37
66.	Alex Iadisernia, Elon	RF	.368	.448	.626	44	174	13	1	10	30	24	20	6
67.	Jack Rogers, Sam Houston State	LF	.367	.474	.696	55	207	18	1	16	55	31	58	12
68.	Jordan Schaffer, Indiana State	SS	.367	.432	.521	52	215	10	1	7	34	13	23	11

Rank	Player, Team	Pos												
69.	Jake McCaw, Illinois State	1B	.367	.424	.506	52	180	14	1	3	27	16	43	2
70.	Cristopher DeGuzman, Alabama State	SS	.367	.451	.506	41	158	8	4	2	31	21	25	8
71.	Mike Jarvis, San Diego State	SS	.367	.417	.544	46	215	17	3	5	32	12	20	16
72.	Trey Paige, Delaware State	3B	.366	.475	.592	43	142	13	2	5	32	29	21	7
73.	Connor OBrien, Bradley	1B	.366	.452	.549	39	142	12	1	4	26	17	36	1
74.	Chenar Brown, Jackson State	1B	.366	.432	.648	37	142	10	3	8	49	17	29	5
75.	Connor Kokx, Long Beach State	CF	.366	.481	.571	43	161	10	1	7	29	24	30	14
76.	Sky Duff, Pittsburgh	3B	.366	.461	.524	42	164	18	1	2	19	24	48	4
77.	Kyle Manzardo, Washington State	1B	.365	.437	.640	47	197	19	1	11	60	25	29	1
78.	Ryan Bliss, Auburn	SS	.365	.428	.654	50	211	14	1	15	45	23	30	6
79.	Alsander Womack, Norfolk State	2B	.364	.433	.472	52	195	12	0	3	37	25	20	17
80.	David Bryant, Radford	SS	.364	.480	.594	46	165	9	4	7	37	33	26	4
81.	Jahmoi Percival, Grambling State	LF	.364	.468	.600	44	165	10	7	5	43	32	27	31
82.	Conor Hartigan, James Madison	RF	.364	.414	.576	28	118	10	0	5	24	6	31	8
83.	Paul Komistek, Cincinnati	RF	.364	.459	.599	47	162	11	0	9	44	23	48	2
84.	Jackson Gray, Western Kentucky	RF	.363	.460	.592	52	179	13	2	8	32	29	45	7
85.	Nolen Hester, Wofford	RF	.363	.472	.463	52	201	11	3	1	39	34	20	13
86.	Cam Touchette, Kent State	RF	.363	.436	.500	52	190	12	1	4	30	17	41	7
87.	Zach Kokoska, Kansas State	RF	.363	.445	.675	57	212	19	1	15	46	27	45	9
88.	Tyler Jorgensen, Cal State Bakersfield	1B	.363	.390	.480	43	171	8	0	4	35	7	20	5
89.	Erik Stock, Connecticut	LF	.362	.436	.553	49	188	14	2	6	34	20	32	8
90.	Dylan Crews, Louisiana State	RF	.362	.453	.663	63	246	16	2	18	42	39	44	12
91.	Sammy Sass, Wright State	DH	.362	.456	.717	44	152	12	3	12	60	24	21	2
92.	Shawn Goosenberg, Northwestern	SS	.362	.426	.717	36	152	12	0	14	30	12	32	10
93.	Christian Encarnacion-Strand, Oklahoma State	3B	.361	.442	.661	56	227	17	3	15	66	20	50	4
94.	Coby Potvin, Central Arkansas	1B	.361	.474	.458	40	144	10	2	0	17	25	21	1
95.	Brian Ellis, Florida Gulf Coast	LF	.361	.489	.475	48	183	8	2	3	31	35	24	7
96.	Austin Kryszczuk, Nevada-Las Vegas	LF	.361	.457	.555	32	119	9	1	4	23	17	21	3
97.	Jackson Glenn, Dallas Baptist	2B	.361	.429	.717	58	233	19	2	20	53	30	33	13
98.	Chandler Dillard, Jackson State	RF	.360	.445	.435	42	161	4	1	2	39	25	28	17
99.	Matt Richardson, Utah	SS	.360	.451	.489	44	139	10	1	2	28	16	24	5
100.	Blaze Glenn, Youngstown State	3B	.360	.455	.513	54	197	14	2	4	35	29	36	10

ON-BASE PERCENTAGE

Rank	Player, Pos., Team	OBP
1.	Liam McGill, 1B, Bryant	.541
2.	Quincy Hamilton, OF, Wright St.	.535
3.	Mike Caruso, C, Fairfield	.532
4.	Dillon Shrum, 1B, Nevada	.527
5.	Aaron Zavala, OF, Oregon	.525
6.	Justin Starke, C, VMI	.525
7.	Mike Dorcean, C, Coppin St.	.524
8.	Trey Sweeney, SS, Eastern Illinois	.522
9.	Dylan Hoy, INF, Marist	.520
10.	Hunter May, C, Alabama St.	.519

SLUGGING PERCENTAGE

Rank	Player, Pos., Team	SLG
1.	Dillon Shrum, 1B, Nevada	.968
2.	Ruben Ibarra, INF, San Jose St.	.850
3.	Jack Wold, OF, Nevada-Las Vegas	.793
4.	Jared Dupere, OF, Northeastern	.781
5.	Mat Nelson, C, Florida St.	.773
6.	Griffin Doersching, 1B, Northern Ky.	.772
7.	Quincy Hamilton, OF, Wright St.	.771
8.	Niko Kavadas, 1B, Notre Dame	.767
9.	Liam McGill, 1B, Bryant	.746
10.	Zach Neto, SS/RHP, Campbell	.746

RUNS BATTED IN

Rank	Player, Pos., Team	RBI
1.	Andy Garriola, 1B, Old Dominion	72
1.	Reed Trimble, OF, Southern Miss.	72
3.	Jacob Berry, DH, Arizona	70
4.	Jace Jung, 2B, Texas Tech	67
4.	Spencer Packard, DH, Campbell	67
6.	Tanner Allen, OF, Mississippi St.	66
6.	Gavin Dugas, OF, Louisiana St.	66
6.	Christian Encarnacion-Strand, DH, Ok. St.	66
6.	Tyler Locklear, 1B, Va. Commonwealth	66
6.	Mat Nelson, C, Florida St.	66

HOME RUNS

Rank	Player, Pos., Team	HR
1.	Wes Clarke, DH, South Carolina	23
1.	Mat Nelson, C, Florida St.	23
3.	Niko Kavadas, 1B, Notre Dame	22
4.	Jared Dupere, OF, Northeastern	21
4.	Jackson Glenn, 2B, Dallas Baptist	21
4.	Hunter Goodman, C, Memphis	21
4.	Jace Jung, 2B, Texas Tech	21
4.	Bobby Seymour, 1B, Wake Forest	21
9.	Griffin Doersching, 1B, Northern Ky.	20
9.	Jud Fabian, OF, Florida	20

DOUBLES

Rank	Player, Pos., Team	2B
1.	Austin Knight, INF, Charlotte	29
2.	Brooks Lee, SS, Cal Poly	27
3.	Connor Denning, UTL, Campbell	26
4.	Aaron Anderson, OF, Liberty	25
5.	Nathan Church, OF, UC Irvine	24
5.	Gabriel Montenegro, OF, So. Miss.	24
5.	Tanner Smith, OF, Oregon	24
5.	Daniel Susac, C, Arizona	24
9.	Braydon Altorfer, C, Air Force	23
10.	Tyler Bosetti, INF, Nevada	22
10.	Rowdey Jordan, OF, Mississippi St.	22
10.	Alexander Marco, INF, Utah Valley	22
10.	Steven Moretto, INF, Sacramento St.	22

TRIPLES

Rank	Player, Pos., Team	3B
1.	Nathan Church, OF, UC Irvine	8
2.	Turner Grau, OF, Youngstown St.	7
2.	Ryan Guckin, 1B, La Salle	7
2.	Jahmoi Percival, INF, Grambling St.	7
5.	Joey Castellanos, INF, Mass.-Lowell	6
5.	Xavier Jefferson, OF, Prairie View A&M	6
5.	Will Vogelgesang, INF, Miami (Ohio)	6
5.	Jeff Wehler, INF, Youngstown St.	6
9.	19 players tied	5

STOLEN BASES

Rank	Player, Pos., Team	SB
1.	Enrique Bradfield Jr., OF, Vanderbilt	47
2.	Mike Antico, OF, Texas	41
3.	John Thrasher, OF, Hartford	37
4.	Braiden Ward, OF, Washington	34
5.	Connor Charping, C, Western Mich.	32
6.	Jahmoi Percival, INF, Grambling St.	31
7.	Jack Cucinotta, OF, La Salle	30
8.	Darren Baker, 2B, California	28
8.	Jack Renwick, INF, Wofford	28
10.	Elijah Brown, INF, Sacred Heart	27
10.	Albert Choi, OF, New Jersey Tech	27
10.	Gephry Pena, OF, Central Florida	27

RUNS

Rank	Player, Pos., Team	R
1.	Taylor Young, INF, Louisiana Tech	83
2.	Donta Williams, OF, Arizona	81
3.	Quincy Hamilton, OF, Wright St.	78
4.	Rowdey Jordan, OF, Mississippi St.	74
5.	Jacob Gonzalez, SS, Mississippi	73
5.	Tanner Allen, OF, Mississippi St.	72
7.	Hunter Wells, 3B, Louisiana Tech	70
8.	Mike Antico, OF, Texas	69
8.	Branden Boissiere, 1B, Arizona	69
8.	Tyler Locklear, 3B, Va. Commonwealth	69

HITS

Rank	Player, Pos., Team	H
1.	Connor Norby, 2B, East Carolina	102
2.	Hunter Wells, 3B, Louisiana Tech	101
3.	Tanner Allen, OF, Mississippi St.	100
3.	Nathan Church, OF, UC Irvine	100
5.	Branden Boissiere, 1B, Arizona	94
6.	Jacob Gonzalez, SS, Mississippi	93
7.	Jake Rucker, 3B, Tennessee	90
8.	Dylan Crews, OF, Louisiana St.	89
8.	Kevin Graham, INF, Mississippi	89
8.	Tyler Hardman, 1B, Oklahoma	89
8.	Tre' Morgan, 1B, Louisiana St.	89

TOTAL BASES

Rank	Player, Pos., Team	TB
1.	Jackson Glenn, 2B, Dallas Baptist	172
2.	Hunter Wells, 3B, Louisiana Tech	169

3. Jacob Berry, DH, Arizona 167
4. Dylan Crews, OF, Louisiana St. 163
5. Tanner Allen, OF, Mississippi St. 162
5. Connor Norby, 2B, East Carolina 162
7. Nathan Church, OF, UC Irvine 158
8. Mason McWhorter, OF, Ga. Southern 156
9. Clayton Rasbeary, OF, McNeese St. 153
10. Christian Encarnacion-Strand, DH, Ok. St. 150
10. Mat Nelson, C, Florida St. 150
10. Reed Trimble, OF, Southern Miss. 150

WALKS

Rank Player, Pos., Team	BB
1. Mike Antico, OF, Texas	63
2. Mario Camilletti, INF, Central Mich.	61
3. Kyle Battle, OF, Old Dominion	56
3. Quincy Hamilton, OF, Wright St.	56
5. Liam Spence, 1B, Tennessee	54
6. Wes Clarke, DH, South Carolina	50
6. Griffin Doersching, 1B, Northern Ky.	50
6. Niko Kavadas, 1B, Notre Dame	50
6. Donta Williams, OF, Arizona	50
6. Aaron Zavala, OF, Oregon	50

TOUGHEST TO STRIKE OUT

Rank Player, Pos., Team	AB/SO
1. Matt Ruddick, OF, San Diego St.	19.8
2. James Arakawa, INF, Pacific	16.4
3. Kevin Duburle, INF, Army	15.9
4. Kelby Weyler, SS, Lamar	15.2
5. Kyler Castillo, OF, New Mexico	14.9
6. Luke Waddell, SS, Georgia Tech	14.4
7. Danny Hosley, UTL, Norfolk St.	14.3
8. Mack Chambers, INF, New Mexico	14.2
9. Matt Toke, INF, Seton Hall	14.0
10. Luke Hancock, 1B, Mississippi St.	13.8

HIT BY PITCH

Rank Player, Pos., Team	HBP
1. Justin Bench, INF, Mississippi	29
2. Waldy Arias, INF, Campbell	27
3. Mike Peabody, OF, UC Irvine	27
4. Octavien Moyer,. INF, Florida A&M	26
5. Brett Harris, INF, Gonzaga	25
6. Troy Bellsmith, INF, Evansville	23
6. Billy Godrick, OF, Towson	23
8. Tyler Locklear, 3B, Va. Commonwealth	22
9. Gabe Matthews, 1B, Oregon	21
9. Jordan Rathbone, UTL, Central Florida	21

9. Hogan Windish, INF, UNC Greensboro 21

SACRIFICE BUNTS

Rank Player, Pos., Team	SAC
1. Kyle Cullen, OF, Stephen F. Austin	17
2. Ryder Giles, INF, East Carolina	15
3. Kaleb DeLaTorre, INF, South Alabama	13
4. Ryan Vogel, OF, Bradley	12
5. Nine players tied	11

SACRIFICE FLIES

Rank Player, Pos., Team	SF
1. Brian Leonhardt, UTL, San Diego St.	9
1. Jake Sullivan, C, South Florida	9
3. Connor Aube, OF, Texas-Arlington	8
3. Phillip Glasser, INF, Youngstown St.	8
3. Joshua Lamb, INF, Texas-San Antonio	8
3. Brooks Lee, SS, Cal Poly	8
3. Kai Moody, INF, Cal State Northridge	8
3. Robert Moore, 2B, Arkansas	8
3. Steele Netterville, OF, Louisiana Tech	8
10. 15 players tied	7

PITCHING (MINIMUM 40 INNINGS PITCHED)

Rk. Pitcher, Team	W	L	ERA	G	GS	SV	IP	H	R	ER	BB	SO
1. Kevin Kopps, Arkansas	12	1	0.90	33	1	11	90	50	9	9	18	131
2. Matt Mikulski, Fordham	9	0	1.45	11	11	0	68	29	11	11	27	124
3. Jake Noviello, Fairfield	9	0	1.47	10	10	0	67	50	14	11	9	59
4. Gordon Graceffo, Villanova	7	2	1.54	11	11	0	82	66	24	14	13	86
5. Sam Bachman, Miami (OH)	4	4	1.81	12	12	0	60	29	15	12	17	93
6. Andrew Taylor, Central Michigan	11	4	1.81	15	15	0	94	64	21	19	24	125
7. Cam Schlittler, Northeastern	8	1	1.88	13	13	0	77	58	18	16	20	85
8. Pete Hansen, Texas	9	1	1.88	19	14	0	91	66	22	19	23	80
9. Gavin Williams, East Carolina	10	1	1.88	15	12	1	81	57	18	17	21	130
10. Johnathan Lavallee, Long Beach State	8	1	1.89	11	9	0	62	35	15	13	16	73
11. Nick Mondak, St. John's	4	3	1.92	11	11	0	66	63	19	14	18	74
12. Jake Rice, Kennesaw State	9	2	1.93	13	13	0	75	48	21	16	24	79
13. David Festa, Seton Hall	6	4	2.00	15	11	0	72	44	27	16	33	67
14. Connor Cooke, Louisiana-Lafayette	7	3	2.03	18	12	1	80	44	25	18	37	90
15. Nicholas Sinacola, Maine	9	3	2.04	12	12	0	79	59	20	18	23	139
16. Geremy Guerrero, Indiana State	10	1	2.08	14	14	0	99	65	26	23	14	98
17. Patrick Wicklander, Arkansas	7	1	2.09	18	13	0	78	65	22	18	24	85
18. Jack Leiter, Vanderbilt	11	4	2.13	18	18	0	110	48	30	26	45	179
19. Trevor Delaite, Liberty	12	1	2.17	16	16	0	108	84	28	26	20	88
20. Miles Smith, South Alabama	7	1	2.18	19	7	2	83	66	25	20	21	79
21. Ryan Miller, North Carolina Central	10	0	2.21	13	12	0	73	55	26	18	22	74
22. John Gaddis, Texas A&M-Corpus Christi	5	3	2.25	13	10	0	64	42	19	16	18	72
23. Matt Svanson, Lehigh	4	4	2.30	13	12	0	70	60	30	18	24	65
24. Walker Powell, Southern Mississippi	10	2	2.31	15	14	0	90	76	28	23	18	86
25. Rodney Boone, UC Santa Barbara	11	4	2.31	16	16	0	97	55	33	25	39	128
26. Brennan Stuprich, Southeastern Louisiana	6	3	2.31	14	12	0	82	66	29	21	22	67
27. John Baker, Ball State	9	3	2.32	19	13	4	101	82	38	26	25	107
28. Jace Kaminska, Wichita State	8	1	2.32	12	10	0	62	51	18	16	19	51
29. Joe Rock, Ohio	8	3	2.34	14	14	0	89	67	29	23	27	117
30. Trenton Wallace, Iowa	7	1	2.34	36	13	0	73	54	20	19	37	106
31. Jose Fernandez, Alcorn State	1	7	2.35	10	9	1	61	50	30	16	21	55
32. Aaron Barkley, Arkansas-Little Rock	6	5	2.39	25	0	7	60	48	22	16	12	54
33. Tyler Cleveland, Central Arkansas	6	3	2.43	23	1	9	67	48	23	18	15	84
34. Doug Nikhazy, Mississippi	12	2	2.45	16	15	0	92	62	30	25	31	142
35. Ty Madden, Texas	7	5	2.46	18	18	0	114	75	37	31	44	137
36. Jordan Patty, Central Michigan	10	2	2.46	15	15	0	91	72	28	25	28	78
37. Tyler Mattison, Bryant	10	3	2.47	13	13	0	80	57	32	22	14	95
38. Christian Edwards, Jacksonville State	5	2	2.48	12	11	1	69	42	21	19	27	83
39. Tyler Thomas, Baylor	5	2	2.49	11	11	0	65	49	26	18	30	66
40. Adam Smith, UNC Wilmington	6	1	2.50	19	7	3	61	57	29	17	26	58
41. Robert Ahlstrom, Oregon	9	3	2.50	14	14	0	90	77	28	25	16	92
42. Alek Jacob, Gonzaga	8	1	2.52	17	11	3	86	60	25	24	18	112
43. Jake Miller, San Diego	6	2	2.52	12	12	0	61	50	24	17	17	77
44. Sam Turcotte, Stony Brook	6	3	2.53	12	11	0	68	59	32	19	26	66
45. Parker Scott, Oklahoma State	8	1	2.54	12	10	0	60	55	20	17	16	61

Rank	Pitcher, Team	W	L	ERA	G	GS	SV	IP	H	R	ER	BB	SO
46.	Jordan Marks, South Carolina-Upstate	10	2	2.54	15	15	0	96	85	32	27	20	101
47.	Landon Marceaux, Louisiana State	7	7	2.54	18	17	0	103	92	37	29	26	116
48.	Austin Vernon, North Carolina Central	5	4	2.55	12	12	0	71	41	30	20	31	109
49.	Kyle Smith, Prairie View A&M	4	3	2.55	9	9	0	71	63	26	20	15	57
50.	Hunter Stanley, Southern Mississippi	6	4	2.56	16	15	0	102	74	34	29	19	127
51.	Justin Campbell, Oklahoma State	7	2	2.57	14	13	0	84	66	28	24	27	102
52.	Will Warren, Southeastern Louisiana	7	2	2.57	14	14	0	91	71	33	26	25	95
53.	Collin Floyd, Youngstown State	9	4	2.58	15	15	0	101	75	33	29	23	108
54.	Austin Peterson, Connecticut	7	1	2.58	15	14	0	80	59	26	23	21	82
55.	Michael Sansone, Fairfield	9	2	2.58	12	9	1	66	52	20	19	15	73
56.	Landen Roupp, UNC Wilmington	8	5	2.58	16	15	0	101	69	40	29	42	118
57.	Dalton Rhadans, Wofford	6	0	2.59	24	0	7	59	50	19	17	20	62
58.	Pierson Ohl, Grand Canyon	10	2	2.60	16	15	0	100	79	30	29	12	103
59.	Nick Durgin, Stetson	6	2	2.61	11	10	0	62	46	19	18	17	67
60.	Robert Gasser, Houston	6	6	2.63	14	14	0	86	67	30	25	25	105
61.	Christian Peters, Portland	5	4	2.63	13	12	1	79	65	31	23	23	78
62.	Ryan Fischer, New Jersey Tech	5	3	2.65	14	14	0	82	72	30	24	15	53
63.	Gabe Bierman, Indiana	5	4	2.68	12	12	0	74	47	26	22	30	80
64.	Aidan Tyrell, Notre Dame	5	1	2.70	17	8	2	60	50	19	18	19	43
65.	Dylan Tebrake, Creighton	8	0	2.73	12	12	0	73	59	23	22	24	75
66.	Kumar Rocker, Vanderbilt	14	4	2.73	20	20	0	122	75	43	37	39	179
67.	Trey Dombroski, Monmouth	5	1	2.73	9	8	0	53	55	20	16	8	64
68.	Matt Amrhein, California Baptist	7	2	2.74	20	6	1	66	52	27	20	18	61
69.	Davis Feldman, Eastern Michigan	4	5	2.75	12	10	1	59	59	25	18	19	58
70.	Jon Snyder, Youngstown State	6	2	2.76	15	14	0	72	51	27	22	51	88
71.	Carter Young, Grand Canyon	7	1	2.77	15	13	0	68	69	24	21	27	59
72.	Rhett Kouba, Dallas Baptist	6	2	2.77	16	10	0	75	60	28	23	23	87
73.	RJ Petit, Charleston Southern	6	5	2.79	14	13	0	84	69	36	26	31	75
74.	Josh White, California	5	3	2.79	16	5	3	61	49	27	19	25	81
75.	Jack Noble, Long Beach State	3	2	2.79	12	10	0	48	38	17	15	24	62
76.	Cameron Weston, Michigan	7	4	2.81	14	14	0	83	68	32	26	29	69
77.	Ryan McLinskey, Seton Hall	4	1	2.81	12	12	0	58	51	22	18	28	66
78.	Isaac Coffey, Oral Roberts	9	2	2.82	14	14	0	86	73	32	27	13	92
79.	Jacob Key, Illinois-Chicago	7	3	2.82	13	13	0	89	69	29	28	26	58
80.	Wyatt Scotti, Northeastern	4	2	2.82	12	9	0	51	39	17	16	10	39
81.	Thomas Babalis, Binghamton	4	4	2.86	10	10	0	57	43	24	18	20	62
82.	Nick Dean, Maryland	3	1	2.87	9	9	0	53	47	22	17	11	39
83.	Andrew Abbott, Virginia	9	6	2.87	19	17	0	107	89	39	34	32	162
84.	Andrew Hoffmann, Illinois	3	0	2.87	11	11	0	63	49	23	20	15	64
85.	James Deloatch, Norfolk State	7	3	2.88	13	10	0	72	56	32	23	47	66
86.	Landen Bourassa, San Francisco	7	4	2.88	15	15	0	97	89	44	31	24	75
87.	Scott Randall, Sacramento State	7	2	2.89	15	14	0	87	87	32	28	9	103
88.	Edward Kutt IV, Ohio	8	4	2.92	22	5	5	74	55	32	24	13	84
89.	Michael McGreevy, UC Santa Barbara	9	2	2.92	16	16	0	102	109	41	33	11	115
90.	Jaret Edwards, George Washington	5	4	2.93	16	7	0	55	47	28	18	24	32
91.	Jack Jasiak, South Florida	6	7	2.93	16	16	0	98	76	39	32	23	93
92.	Hunter Gregory, Old Dominion	8	2	2.95	16	15	0	79	65	31	26	19	88
93.	Tyson Guerrero, Washington	3	3	2.96	11	11	0	55	50	25	18	18	50
94.	Trevor Olson, Xavier	5	3	2.97	14	10	0	64	53	23	21	18	50
95.	Ryan Twitchell, Rhode Island	5	1	2.97	14	14	0	76	81	37	25	24	58
96.	Noah Farmer, Southern Illinois	6	4	2.99	20	8	1	66	68	29	22	26	43
97.	Ky Bush, Saint Mary's	7	5	2.99	14	14	0	78	69	31	26	19	112
98.	Jonathan Ellison, McNeese	5	3	2.99	15	14	0	75	58	30	25	37	60
99.	Cullen Kafka, Oregon	5	3	3.00	15	15	0	78	73	38	26	35	84
100.	Joe Savino, Elon	0	3	3.02	12	9	0	60	55	30	20	10	70

WINS

Rank	Pitcher, Team	W
1.	Kumar Rocker, Vanderbilt	14
2.	Dominic Hamel, Dallas Baptist	13
3.	Trevor Delaite, Liberty	12
3.	Kevin Kopps, Arkansas	12
3.	Doug Nikhazy, Mississippi	12
6.	Rodney Boone, UC Santa Barbara	11
6.	Chad Dallas, Tennessee	11
6.	Jack Leiter, Vanderbilt	11
6.	Tristan Stevens, Texas	11
6.	Andrew Taylor, Central Michigan	11

SAVES

Rank	Pitcher, Team	SV
1.	Nick Jones, Georgia Southern	17
2.	Taylor Broadway, Mississippi	16

3.	Carson Palmquist, Miami	14
4.	Zach Grech, Stanford	13
4.	Evan Justice, North Carolina St.	13
4.	Jake Mulholland, Oregon St.	13
4.	Landon Sims, Mississippi St.	13
8.	Haylen Green, Texas Christian	12
8.	Parker Harm, North Dakota St.	12
8.	Frankie Scalzo, Grand Canyon	12
8.	Luke Sutko, Mercer	12

STRIKEOUTS

Rank	Pitcher, Team	SO
1.	Jack Leiter, Vanderbilt	179
2.	Kumar Rocker, Vanderbilt	179
3.	Andrew Abbott, Virginia	162
4.	Brendan Beck, Stanford	143
5.	Doug Nikhazy, Mississippi	142

6.	Will Bednar, Mississippi St.	139
6.	Nicholas Sinacola, Maine	139
8.	Ty Madden, Texas	137
9.	Dominic Hamel, Dallas Baptist	136
10.	Kevin Kopps, Arkansas	131

STRIKEOUTS PER NINE

Rank	Pitcher, Team	SO/9
1.	Matt Mikulski, Fordham	16.33
2.	Nicholas Sinacola, Maine	15.77
3.	Levi David, Northwestern St.	15.34
4.	Jack Leiter, Vanderbilt	14.65
5.	Gavin Williams, East Carolina	14.39
6.	McCade Brown, Indiana	14.31
7.	Sam Bachman, Miami (Ohio)	14.03
8.	Doug Nikhazy, Mississippi	13.89
9.	Ryan Cusick, Wake Forest	13.89

10. Austin Vernon, N.C. Central	13.88	

FEWEST HITS PER NINE

Rank Pitcher, Team	H/9
1. Matt Mikulski, Fordham	3.82
2. Jack Leiter, Vanderbilt	3.93
3. Sam Bachman, Miami (Ohio)	4.37
4. Connor Cooke, La.-Lafayette	4.97
5. Levi David, Northwestern St.	5.02

6. Kevin Kopps, Arkansas	5.02
7. Jonathan Lavallee, Long Beach St.	5.08
8. Rodney Boone, UC Santa Barbara	5.09
9. Kevin Abel, Oregon St.	5.16
10. McCade Brown, Indiana	5.16

FEWEST WALKS PER NINE

Rank Pitcher, Team	BB/9
1. Scott Randall, Sacramento St.	0.93

2. Michael McGreevy, UC Santa Barbara	0.97
3. Mario Lopez, Jackson St.	1.02
4. Zebby Matthews, Western Carolina	1.03
5. Pierson Ohl, Grand Canyon	1.08
6. Sean Bergeron, Western Kentucky	1.13
7. Gabe Levy, Davidson	1.15
8. Austin Parsley, UNC Greensboro	1.20
9. Jake Noviello, Fairfield	1.20
10. Braden Olthoff, Tulane	1.20

TEAM LEADERS

SCORING

Rank Team	G	R	R/G
1. Wright St.	48	502	10.5
2. Jackson St.	43	399	9.3
3. San Diego St.	46	420	9.1
4. Campbell	55	486	8.8
5. Va. Commonwealth	54	462	8.6
6. Arizona	63	537	8.5
7. Western Carolina	49	408	8.3
8. Alabama St.	42	346	8.2
9. Texas-San Antonio	48	378	7.9
10. Old Dominion	60	471	7.8
11. Texas Christian	60	468	7.8
12. Bryant	42	327	7.8
13. Arkansas	63	483	7.7
14. Nevada-Las Vegas	33	253	7.7
15. Dallas Baptist	59	451	7.6
16. Texas Tech	56	421	7.5
17. Mercer	57	428	7.5
18. Marist	29	217	7.5
19. Louisiana Tech	62	463	7.5
20. Illinois-Chicago	48	357	7.4
21. Southern Illinois	60	442	7.4
22. Oklahoma St.	56	412	7.4
23. San Diego	45	329	7.3
24. Samford	59	431	7.3
25. Abilene Christian	57	416	7.3
25. UCLA	57	416	7.3
27. UC Irvine	61	443	7.3
28. Connecticut	53	384	7.2
29. Washington St.	49	355	7.2
30. Northeastern	48	347	7.2
31. Nevada	45	323	7.2
32. Baylor	51	364	7.1
33. Mississippi	67	478	7.1
34. Wofford	57	404	7.1
35. Notre Dame	47	332	7.1
36. UC Santa Barbara	61	430	7.0
37. Mississippi St.	68	476	7.0
38. Tennessee	68	475	7.0
39. Auburn	52	363	7.0
40. Nebraska	48	335	7.0
41. Canisius	36	250	6.9
42. Oregon	55	379	6.9
43. North Carolina St.	56	385	6.9
44. Oklahoma	55	377	6.9
45. Charlotte	61	417	6.8
46. Central Michigan	60	408	6.8
47. Fairfield	44	299	6.8
48. Stanford	56	380	6.8
49. Dayton	51	346	6.8
50. Vanderbilt	67	454	6.8

BATTING AVERAGE

Rank Team	AVG
1. Wright St.	.339
2. San Diego St.	.335
3. Nevada-Las Vegas	.333
4. Arizona	.325
5. Jackson St.	.318
6. Nevada	.314
7. Marist	.313
8. Illinois-Chicago	.309
9. Alabama St.	.308
10. New Mexico	.307

HOME RUNS

Rank Team	HR
1. Arkansas	109
2. Old Dominion	105
3. Dallas Baptist	101
4. Tennessee	98
5. Louisiana State	93
6. Mercer	92
6. North Carolina St.	92
6. Vanderbilt	92
9. Wake Forest	91
10. Texas Tech	90

DOUBLES

Rank Team	2B
1. Arizona	145
2. Campbell	135
3. Tennessee	134
4. Charlotte	130
4. Louisiana Tech	130
4. Vanderbilt	130
4. Wright St.	130
8. Georgia Tech	127
9. Air Force	126
9. Tulane	126

TRIPLES

Rank Team	3B
1. Arizona	30
2. Youngstown St.	27
3. Texas Christian	25
3. UC Irvine	25
4. McNeese St.	23
6. Jackson St.	22
6. La Salle	22
6. Wichita St.	22
9. Vanderbilt	21
10. Old Dominion	20
10. Wright St.	10

SLUGGING PERCENTAGE

Rank Team	SLG
1. Wright St.	.579
2. Nevada-Las Vegas	.538
3. Old Dominion	.538
4. Nevada	.520
5. Campbell	.516
6. Dallas Baptist	.511
7. Arizona	.508
8. Mercer	.499
9. Illinois-Chicago	.497
10. Southern Illinois	.495

STOLEN BASES

Rank Team	SB
1. Jackson St.	139
2. Wofford	132
3. Texas Christian	121
4. Northeastern	118
5. Louisville	113
6. Norfolk St.	110
6. Southeastern Louisiana	110

8. Middle Tennessee St.	107
9. Campbell	101
10. Stony Brook	99

WALKS

Rank Team	BB
1. Texas	379
2. Arkansas	360
3. Texas Christian	346
4. Central Michigan	344
5. Tennessee	336
6. Texas Tech	322
7. Arizona	319
8. Wright St.	315
9. Mississippi St.	306
10. Dallas Baptist	305

PITCHING

EARNED RUN AVERAGE

Rank Team	ERA
1. Texas	2.93
2. Fairfield	3.14
3. Indiana	3.17
4. Monmouth	3.21
5. Northeastern	3.23
6. Louisiana-Lafayette	3.37
7. Florida St.	3.45
8. Vanderbilt	3.46
9. Oregon St.	3.48
10. Tennessee	3.51
11. Bryant	3.52
12. Liberty	3.57
13. Miami (Ohio)	3.61
14. Virginia	3.62
15. South Alabama	3.63
16. South Carolina-Upstate	3.68
17. Central Michigan	3.71
18. Oregon	3.71
19. Stony Brook	3.74
20. Southern Mississippi	3.74
21. Long Beach St.	3.75
22. Arkansas	3.77
23. South Carolina	3.80
24. UC Irvine	3.80
25. Nebraska	3.81
26. Lamar	3.83
27. Central Connecticut St.	3.85
28. UC Santa Barbara	3.86
29. Villanova	3.90
30. Georgia	3.91
31. UNC Wilmington	3.93
32. Georgia Southern	3.93
33. Creighton	3.93
34. UCLA	3.95
35. Notre Dame	3.95
36. Baylor	3.96
37. Grand Canyon.	3.98
38. Saint Mary's	3.99
39. East Carolina	4.01
40. Long Island	4.02
41. Mississippi St.	4.04
42. California	4.05
43. Marist	4.05
44. Michigan	4.09
45. Texas Christian	4.13
46. Ball St.	4.15
47. South Florida	4.16
48. San Diego	4.17
49. Middle Tennessee St.	4.19
50. Hawaii	4.20

STRIKEOUTS PER NINE

Rank Team	SO/9
1. Mississippi St.	12.2
2. Vanderbilt	11.9
3. Mississippi	11.7
4. Florida St.	11.4
5. Miami (Ohio)	11.2
6. South Carolina	11.1
7. Virginia Tech	11.1
8. Virginia	11.0
9. Ohio St.	11.0
10. Connecticut	10.9

FEWEST WALKS PER NINE

Rank Team	BB/9
1. Middle Tennessee St.	2.42
2. Southern Mississippi	2.44
3. Tennessee	2.49
4. Sacramento St.	2.55
5. Nevada-Las Vegas	2.62
6. Fairfield	2.62
7. Monmouth	2.65
8. Hawaii	2.65
9. Indiana St.	2.84
10. Northeastern	2.85

FIELDING

FIELDING PERCENTAGE

Rank Team	PCT
1. Liberty	.984
2. Creighton	.983
3. Sacramento St.	.982
4. Oregon St.	.982
5. Notre Dame	.982
6. North Carolina St.	.982
7. Gonzaga	.981
8. Oregon	.981
9. Northeastern	.981
10. Texas	.980
11. Arkansas	.980
12. Boston College	.980
13. Central Connecticut St.	.980
14. Mercer	.980
15. South Alabama	.980
16. Nebraska	.979
17. UCLA	.979
18. Cal Poly	.979
19. San Diego	.979
20. Stanford	.979
21. Nevada	.979
22. Pittsburgh	.979
23. Kentucky	.979
24. Florida Atlantic	.978
25. East Carolina	.978
26. Missouri St.	.978
27. Navy	.978
28. Cincinnati	.978
29. Stetson	.978
30. Wichita St.	.978
31. Monmouth	.978
32. Evansville	.977
33. Iowa	.977
34. Georgia	.977
35. Alabama	.977
36. Long Beach St.	.977
37. UC Santa Barbara	.977
38. Tennessee	.977
39. Auburn	.976
40. UC Irvine	.976
41. South Carolina	.976
42. Arizona St.	.976
43. Texas Christian	.976
44. Southern Illinois	.976
45. Lamar	.976
46. Fairfield	.976
47. Appalachian St.	.976
48. Kansas	.975
49. Virginia	.975
50. Wright St.	.975

DOUBLE PLAYS

Rank Team	DP
1. Arizona St.	60
2. Texas	57
3. Auburn	53
4. Fresno St.	52
5. Campbell	51
5. Oregon	51
7. Cincinnati	50
7. College of Charleston	50
7. New Mexico St.	50
7. Southern Illinois	50

1. MISSISSIPPI STATE

Coach: Chris Lemonis. **Record:** 50-18

Player, Pos., Year	AVG	OBP	SLG	AB	R	2B	3B	HR	RBI	SB
Allen, Tanner, RF, 4Y Jr.	.383	.456	.621	261	72	19	5	11	66	11
Clark, Kellum, INF, Fr.	.237	.355	.495	93	22	7	1	5	16	1
Cumbest, Brad, LF, 3Y So.	.306	.372	.537	121	23	9	2	5	21	2
Dubrule, Scotty, 2B, 5Y Fr.	.278	.384	.305	223	42	6	0	0	31	6
Forsythe, Lane, SS, Fr.	.231	.321	.274	186	30	5	0	1	21	1
Garner, Kace, C, 3Y Fr.	.154	.313	.231	13	4	1	0	0	3	0
Hancock, Luke, INF, 3Y So.	.262	.393	.408	233	40	4	0	10	63	3
Hatcher, Josh, 1B, 4Y Jr.	.189	.245	.284	148	17	8	0	2	12	6
James, Kamren, 3B, 2Y Fr.	.264	.354	.456	250	50	12	0	12	61	20
Jordan, Landon, 3B, 3Y So.	.281	.410	.344	32	2	2	0	0	5	2
Jordan, Rowdey, CF, 4Y Jr.	.323	.417	.546	269	74	22	4	10	45	9
Leggett, Tanner, 3B, 4Y Jr.	.235	.337	.321	81	18	4	0	1	10	5
McDonald, Kyte, OF, 2Y Fr.	.389	.421	.778	18	5	4	0	1	6	0
McGowan, Drew, LF, 2Y Fr.	.212	.364	.273	33	6	2	0	0	7	2
Meche, Davis, 3B, Fr.	.250	.400	.333	12	4	1	0	0	1	0
Pimentel, Brandon, INF/OF, 3Y So.	.286	.412	.500	14	3	0	0	1	6	0
Skinner, Brayland, LF, 4Y So.	.205	.333	.301	83	19	3	1	1	10	6
Tanner, Logan, C, 2Y Fr.	.287	.382	.525	244	45	13	0	15	53	0

Pitcher, Year	W	L	ERA	G	GS	SV	IP	H	BB	SO
Bednar, Will, 2Y Fr.	9	1	3.12	19	16	0	92.1	72	26	139
Carmouche, Dylan, Fr.	1	0	1.23	9	0	0	7.1	6	3	11
Cerantola, Eric, 3Y So.	0	1	5.71	10	4	0	17.1	13	11	24
Fristoe, Jackson, Fr.	3	3	5.69	16	13	0	49	41	37	68
Harding, Houston, 4Y Jr.	7	2	3.05	21	8	0	62	50	21	67
Hunt, KC, 2Y Fr.	0	0	4.80	14	0	0	15	15	8	14
Johnston, Preston, 3Y So.	4	0	3.82	22	0	0	33	25	14	50
Koestler, Carlisle, 6Y Sr.	3	0	4.12	11	2	0	19.2	20	7	23
Lovett, Xavier, Fr.	0	0	6.75	6	0	0	4	3	2	1
MacLeod, Christian, 3Y Fr.	6	6	5.23	19	19	0	82.2	79	33	113
Patrick, Chase, 4Y Jr.	0	0	2.57	19	0	0	14	14	6	10
Price, Spencer, 5Y Sr.	1	0	7.36	9	0	0	7.1	5	5	13
Rokose, Davis, 2Y Fr.	0	0	10.80	4	0	0	3.1	2	4	6
Self, Riley, 5Y Sr.	0	0	5.40	7	0	0	5	9	4	7
Simmons, Stone, 2Y Fr.	1	1	4.81	19	0	2	24.1	22	8	29
Sims, Landon, Fr.	5	0	1.44	25	0	13	56.1	29	15	100
Smith, Brandon, 3Y So.	4	4	4.12	21	2	1	39.1	36	12	43
Smith, Cade, Fr.	3	0	2.40	10	1	0	15	6	10	20
Stinnett, Parker, 3Y So.	1	0	2.41	17	1	1	18.2	8	16	31
Tepper, Mikey, Fr.	2	0	5.25	11	2	0	12	8	9	14
Tullar, Cameron, 3Y So.	0	0	6.86	23	0	1	19.2	23	11	25

2. VANDERBILT

Coach: Tim Corbin. **Record:** 49-18

Player, Pos., Year	AVG	OBP	SLG	AB	R	2B	3B	HR	RBI	SB
Bradfield, Jr., Enrique, CF, Fr.	.336	.451	.414	244	60	8	4	1	38	47
Bulger, Jack, LF, Fr.	.274	.369	.414	157	32	7	0	5	28	2
Casas, Gavin, INF, Fr.	.200	.273	.300	10	2	1	0	0	1	0
Davis, Cooper, LF, 4Y Jr.	.248	.339	.294	109	15	2	0	1	13	3
Duff, Will, UTL, 2Y Fr.	.143	.250	.143	7	2	0	0	0	0	0
Espinal, Alan, C, Fr.	.200	.200	.800	5	1	0	0	1	1	0
Gonzalez, Jayson, 3B, 4Y Jr.	.280	.391	.497	193	36	9	3	9	41	2
Hewett, Calvin, RF, Fr.	.571	.700	.857	7	3	2	0	0	3	0
Jones, Spencer, UTL, 2Y Fr.	.274	.346	.421	95	16	5	0	3	10	4
Keegan, Dominic, 1B, 3Y So.	.345	.427	.638	232	56	17	3	15	57	0
Kolwyck, Tate, 2B, 3Y So.	.290	.371	.507	138	28	10	1	6	25	2
LaNeve, Troy, LF, 2Y Fr.	.286	.326	.583	84	16	7	0	6	22	0
Noland, Parker, 2B, 2Y Fr.	.260	.336	.407	246	39	15	0	7	43	4
O'Dowd, Jack, INF, Fr.	.333	.400	.667	9	3	3	0	0	4	0
Rodriguez, C.J., C, 2Y Fr.	.249	.393	.378	185	28	9	0	5	36	1
Romero, Jr., Maxwell, C, 2Y Fr.	.300	.426	.620	50	14	4	0	4	14	1
Thomas, Isaiah, RF, 3Y So.	.305	.361	.583	223	45	13	5	13	40	12
Vaz, Jonathan, C, 4Y Jr.	.238	.396	.286	42	7	2	0	0	5	1
Young, Carter, SS, 2Y Fr.	.252	.341	.559	238	47	15	5	16	52	9

Pitcher, Year	W	L	ERA	G	GS	SV	IP	H	BB	SO
Berkwich, Nelson, Fr.	1	0	3.07	10	0	0	14.2	16	3	19
Bradley, Gage, Fr.	0	0	13.50	2	0	0	2	2	3	3

Player, Pos., Year										
Evans, Donye, Fr.	0	0	4.77	8	0	0	5.2	7	2	6
Fisher, Hugh, 4Y Jr.	0	0	2.46	16	0	0	11	5	11	13
Garrett, Miles, Fr.	1	0	2.79	9	0	0	9.2	8	2	8
Hliboki, Sam, 2Y Fr.	0	0	2.70	9	1	2	20	15	4	20
Leiter, Jack, 2Y Fr.	11	4	2.13	18	18	0	110	48	45	179
Little, Christian, Fr.	3	2	5.48	14	11	0	42.2	40	22	49
Maldonado, Nick, 2Y Fr.	1	2	2.31	28	0	9	50.2	32	7	59
McElvain, Chris, 2Y Fr.	5	1	4.34	22	1	2	45.2	39	27	58
Moore, Grayson, Fr.	0	0	9.00	5	0	0	6	8	4	6
Murphy, Luke, 3Y Fr.	4	1	2.40	27	0	9	41.1	24	15	61
Owen, Hunter, Fr.	0	0	10.26	14	0	0	16.2	22	15	19
Reilly, Patrick, Fr.	4	2	4.99	16	7	0	43.1	31	28	53
Rocker, Kumar, 3Y So.	14	4	2.73	20	20	0	122	75	39	179
Schultz, Thomas, 2Y Fr.	4	2	4.09	14	9	0	44	33	18	40
Smith, Ethan, Fr.	1	0	3.55	9	0	2	12.2	11	3	18

3. TEXAS

Coach: David Pierce. **Record:** 50-17

Player, Pos., Year	AVG	OBP	SLG	AB	R	2B	3B	HR	RBI	SB
Antico, Mike, CF, 5Y Sr.	.273	.436	.489	231	69	16	2	10	47	41
Ardoin, Silas, C, 2Y Fr.	.239	.389	.315	184	30	9	1	1	33	1
Campbell, Dylan, LF, Fr.	.189	.262	.302	53	10	3	0	1	7	2
Daly, Mitchell, 2B, Fr.	.316	.413	.416	209	35	15	0	2	31	8
Faltine, Trey, SS, Fr.	.249	.374	.401	217	51	18	0	5	37	7
Ford, Lance, 3B, 3Y So.	.100	.357	.100	10	6	0	0	0	0	0
Geib, Peter, INF, 3Y So.	1.000	1.000	4.000	1	2	0	0	1	3	0
Hodo, Douglas, RF, 2Y Fr.	.281	.384	.398	221	52	9	1	5	44	6
Kennedy, Eric, LF, 3Y So.	.253	.333	.352	233	42	7	2	4	27	18
Melendez, Ivan, INF, 3Y So.	.319	.438	.603	204	38	13	3	13	51	1
Peter, Caston, C, 3Y So.	.000	1.000	.000	0	0	0	0	0	0	0
Petrinsky, D.J., C, 5Y Sr.	.242	.363	.333	66	8	3	0	1	11	0
Porter, Dalton, OF, Fr.	.263	.391	.421	19	3	0	0	1	3	0
Powell, Peyton, C, 2Y Fr.	.273	.333	.545	11	4	0	0	1	2	0
Stehly, Murphy, 3B, 4Y Jr.	.294	.383	.373	51	8	2	1	0	7	2
Todd, Austin, RF, 5Y Sr.	.292	.346	.292	24	1	0	0	0	2	0
Williams, Cam, 3B, 4Y Jr.	.295	.415	.575	207	42	20	1	12	51	4
Witt, Tanner, INF, Fr.	.231	.286	.231	13	3	0	0	0	0	0
Zubia, Zach, 1B, 5Y Fr.	.286	.412	.502	231	45	11	3	11	61	2

Pitcher, Year	W	L	ERA	G	GS	SV	IP	H	BB	SO
Cobb, Coy, 3Y So.	0	0	7.50	6	0	0	6	7	3	5
Justin Eckhard, 2Y Fr.	0	0	6.75	6	4	0	13.1	10	10	5
Gordon, Lucas, Fr.	0	0	3.32	19	1	1	21.2	15	9	19
Hansen, Pete, 2Y Fr.	9	1	1.88	19	14	0	91	66	23	80
Kubichek, Kolby, 3Y So.	5	3	3.86	12	12	0	51.1	50	27	41
Madden, Ty, 3Y So.	7	5	2.46	18	18	0	113.2	75	44	137
Merryman, Dawson, 3Y So.	0	0	10.13	3	0	0	2.2	3	4	2
Nixon, Aaron, Fr.	4	3	2.12	27	0	9	34	26	10	35
Quintanilla, Cole, 3Y So.	5	1	1.35	26	0	4	40	22	11	42
Shifflet, Drew, 3Y So.	1	0	4.02	11	0	0	15.2	13	9	14
Southard, Jared, 2Y Fr.	0	0	0.00	12	0	0	10	4	7	16
Stevens, Tristan, 4Y Jr.	11	3	3.31	18	18	0	111.1	105	23	77
Walbridge, Sam, 2Y Fr.	0	0	9.00	3	0	0	2	3	0	4
Wenzel, Palmer, 5Y Sr.	3	0	3.32	17	0	1	21.2	22	9	13
Witt, Tanner, Fr.	5	0	3.16	28	0	5	57	40	25	73

4. NORTH CAROLINA STATE

Coach: Elliott Avent. **Record:** 37-19

Player, Pos., Year	AVG	OBP	SLG	AB	R	2B	3B	HR	RBI	SB
Highfill, Sam, UTL, 2Y Fr.	.750	.750	.750	4	0	0	0	0	0	0
Butler, Jonny, LF, 4Y Jr.	.376	.452	.663	202	54	12	2	14	53	16
McDonough, Tyler, CF, 3Y So.	.339	.423	.631	233	58	21	1	15	45	13
Murr, Austin, 1B, 3Y So.	.319	.376	.504	232	54	16	3	7	32	6
Tatum, Terrell, OF, 4Y Jr.	.317	.423	.543	186	37	2	2	12	36	16
Torres, Jose, SS, 2Y Fr.	.289	.343	.533	197	31	12	3	10	44	5
Brown, Devonte, RF, 4Y Jr.	.252	.363	.500	202	45	11	0	13	40	4
Jarrett, J.T., 2B, 4Y Jr.	.251	.341	.333	195	27	11	1	1	23	3
Mensik, Vojtech, 3B, 3Y So.	.239	.308	.358	201	29	7	1	5	24	11
Tresh, Luca, C, 3Y So.	.231	.310	.476	229	41	9	1	15	43	1
Soles, Noah, OF, 2Y Fr.	.207	.324	.241	29	4	1	0	0	2	0
Falsken, Carson, INF, Fr.	.200	.250	.200	15	1	0	0	0	0	0
Giles, DeAngelo, INF, 2Y Fr.	.083	.200	.083	12	0	0	0	0	1	0

Player	AVG	OBP	SLG	AB	R	2B	3B	HR	RBI	SB
Carnazzo, Danny, C, 3Y So.	.077	.143	.077	13	2	0	0	0	0	0
Eisert, Eddie, INF, Fr.	.000	.182	.000	9	2	0	0	0	0	0

Pitcher, Year	W	L	ERA	G	GS	SV	IP	H	BB	SO
Arnold, Cameron, Fr.	0	0	6.75	3	0	0	2.2	5	3	1
Bender, Logan, 4Y Jr.	0	0	27.00	2	0	0	1	1	2	1
Cotter, Cameron, 4Y So.	0	0	13.50	1	0	0	0.2	2	1	1
Feeney, Dalton, 5Y Jr.	1	1	8.83	17	0	0	17.1	24	17	17
Harrison, David, 4Y Jr.	0	0	3.72	4	2	0	9.2	10	3	8
Highfill, Sam, 2Y Fr.	9	2	3.66	16	16	0	93.1	77	26	84
Ingle, Coby, Fr.	0	0	2.57	11	0	0	14	10	6	13
Johnston, Reid, 4Y Jr.	9	3	4.47	16	12	1	96.2	84	23	96
Justice, Evan, 4Y Jr.	5	2	3.77	24	4	13	59.2	40	25	74
King, Cooper, Fr.	1	0	4.50	9	0	0	8	5	8	4
Klyman, Kent, 5Y Sr.	1	2	12.00	6	0	0	6	7	7	8
Miralia, John, Fr.	0	0	13.50	4	0	0	2.2	4	2	2
Nelson, Baker, 3Y So.	0	0	13.50	3	0	0	2.2	6	4	3
Payne, Garrett, Fr.	0	1	5.27	7	1	0	13.2	14	9	15
Silver, Canaan, 4Y Jr.	0	2	8.25	6	0	0	12	15	3	8
Sipple, Tristan, Fr.	0	0	4.77	6	0	0	5.2	3	2	7
Tillery, Andrew, 3Y So.	1	1	13.50	10	1	0	10.2	18	9	8
Villman, Chris, 2Y Fr.	5	2	4.35	18	7	2	60	45	16	71
Willadsen, Matt, 2Y Fr.	5	3	4.73	18	13	0	83.2	79	29	72

5. ARKANSAS

Coach: Dave Van Horn. **Record:** 50-13

Player, Pos., Year	AVG	OBP	SLG	AB	R	2B	3B	HR	RBI	SB
Bates, Ethan, RF, Fr.	.250	.333	.306	36	7	2	0	0	6	0
Battles, Jalen, SS, 3Y So.	.269	.371	.407	216	48	12	0	6	43	5
Franklin, Christian, CF, 3Y So.	.274	.420	.544	215	55	15	2	13	54	11
Goodheart, Matt, DH, 4Y Jr.	.264	.386	.481	208	43	6	0	13	38	3
Gregory, Zack, LF, 3Y Fr.	.245	.440	.412	102	21	6	1	3	19	2
Leach, Dylan, C, Fr.	.257	.469	.429	35	12	1	1	1	4	0
Moore, Robert, 2B, 2Y Fr.	.283	.384	.558	233	59	10	3	16	53	6
Nesbit, Jacob, 3B, 4Y So.	.205	.341	.288	73	12	0	2	2	14	0
Opitz, Casey, C, 4Y Jr.	.257	.367	.346	191	35	9	1	2	18	6
Slavens, Brady, 1B, 2Y So.	.284	.347	.560	218	49	12	3	14	63	2
Smith, Cullen, 3B, 5Y Sr.	.263	.395	.519	156	39	7	0	11	35	2
Wallace, Cayden, RF, Fr.	.279	.369	.500	240	52	11	0	14	44	0
Webb, Braydon, LF, 4Y Jr.	.174	.372	.413	92	25	4	0	6	16	6
Welch, Charlie, C, 3Y So.	.388	.494	.821	67	21	5	0	8	25	0
White, Zac, RF, Fr.	.250	.438	.250	12	4	0	0	0	1	1

Pitcher, Year	W	L	ERA	G	GS	SV	IP	H	BB	SO
Adams, Blake, 2Y Fr.	1	0	11.81	4	0	0	5.1	10	4	5
Bolden, Caleb, 4Y So.	2	0	4.50	17	10	1	44	38	24	44
Costeiu, Ryan, 3Y So.	8	3	5.10	26	0	0	30	21	15	40
Gray, Evan, 2Y Fr.	0	0	5.06	6	0	0	5.1	6	2	4
Kopps, Kevin, 6Y Sr.	12	1	0.90	33	1	11	89.2	50	18	131
Lockhart, Lael, 5Y Sr.	3	3	4.47	16	14	0	58.1	51	17	68
Magre, Matthews, Fr.	0	0	0.00	1	0	0	0.2	0	1	1
Monke, Caden, 3Y So.	5	1	3.71	27	0	0	34	19	21	42
Morris, Zach, 2Y Fr.	0	0	4.80	16	0	0	15	15	6	19
Noland, Connor, 3Y So.	1	0	6.91	9	0	1	14.1	15	4	15
Pallette, Peyton, 2Y Fr.	1	2	4.02	15	11	1	56	51	20	67
Pleimann, Miller, 3Y So.	0	0	3.00	2	1	0	3	1	3	5
Ramage, Kole, 4Y Jr.	2	1	6.75	13	3	1	24	33	8	29
Starks, Gabriel, Fr.	0	0	9.00	4	0	0	4	3	3	6
Taylor, Evan, 3Y So.	0	0	7.94	7	0	0	5.2	6	3	4
Tole, Heston, Fr.	1	0	2.25	10	0	0	12	8	2	20
Trest, Elijah, 3Y So.	1	0	3.14	10	0	0	14.1	12	8	15
Vermillion, Zebulon, 4Y Jr.	3	0	4.69	15	6	1	40.1	41	15	28
Wicklander, Patrick, 3Y So.	7	1	2.09	18	13	0	77.2	65	24	85
Wiggins, Jaxon, Fr.	3	1	5.09	17	4	4	23	20	14	28
Wohlgemuth, Nate, Fr.	0	0	6.75	3	0	0	1.1	2	6	1

6. VIRGINIA

Coach: Brian O'Connor. **Record:** 36-27

Player, Pos., Year	AVG	OBP	SLG	AB	R	2B	3B	HR	RBI	SB
Ballestero, Tate, 1B, 2Y Fr.	.219	.375	.219	32	3	0	0	0	2	0
Burrow, Addie, OF, Fr.	.125	.417	.125	8	1	0	0	0	1	0
Cotier, Max, 2B, 2Y Fr.	.262	.344	.306	229	30	8	1	0	30	3
Gelof, Jake, 1B, Fr.	.252	.336	.468	111	23	8	2	4	15	1
Gelof, Zack, 3B, 3Y Jr.	.312	.393	.485	260	50	18	0	9	41	12
Hamrock, Drew, INF/OF, 3Y So.	.167	.286	.167	6	1	0	0	0	0	1

Player, Pos., Year	AVG	OBP	SLG	AB	R	2B	3B	HR	RBI	SB
Hlinka, Christian, RF, 4Y Jr.	.233	.353	.326	43	4	4	0	0	5	0
Kent, Nic, SS, 3Y So.	.239	.338	.385	247	38	12	0	8	45	15
Lebreux, Marc, RF, 4Y Jr.	.232	.369	.246	69	12	1	0	0	6	5
Michaels, Logan, C, 5Y Sr.	.252	.346	.327	159	32	9	0	1	20	3
Newell, Chris, CF, 2Y Fr.	.258	.336	.397	194	29	6	3	5	34	13
Ortiz, Devin, 1B, 4Y Jr.	.270	.359	.432	222	41	10	1	8	34	3
Rivoli, Brendan, LF, 4Y Jr.	.272	.333	.349	195	26	10	1	1	24	4
Sullivan, Jimmy, INF, 4Y Jr.	.059	.111	.059	17	1	0	0	0	0	0
Tappen, Alex, RF, 4Y Jr.	.229	.311	.424	144	24	10	0	6	24	2
Teel, Kyle, C/OF, Fr.	.335	.416	.526	209	41	11	1	9	41	5

Pitcher, Year	W	L	ERA	G	GS	SV	IP	H	BB	SO
Abbott, Andrew, 4Y Jr.	9	6	2.87	19	17	0	106.2	89	32	162
Austin, Channing, Fr.	0	0	81.00	2	0	0	0.1	0	2	1
Bales, Blake, 4Y Jr.	3	0	0.71	25	0	0	38	17	15	54
Berry, Jake, Fr.	0	0	4.50	6	0	0	6	3	6	5
Kosanovich, Paul, 5Y Sr.	1	1	4.60	11	0	0	15.2	12	6	11
McGarry, Griff, 4Y Jr.	0	5	5.44	14	11	0	43	30	42	69
Messinger, Zach, 3Y So.	3	2	4.90	28	4	0	57	53	21	64
Neeck, Brandon, 3Y So.	2	0	1.93	22	0	0	23.1	20	11	40
Ortiz, Devin, 4Y Jr.	0	0	0.00	3	1	0	6	3	2	9
Price, Billy, 3Y So.	0	0	4.00	7	2	0	9	8	8	9
Richey, Rece, Fr.	0	0	0.00	1	0	0	0.1	1	1	1
Savino, Nate, 2Y Fr.	3	3	3.79	16	10	0	54.2	57	16	34
Schauer, Luke, Fr.	0	0	4.77	16	0	0	11.1	11	8	14
Schoch, Stephen, 6Y Sr.	4	2	3.00	22	0	8	36	30	16	52
Vasil, Mike, 3Y So.	7	5	4.52	17	16	0	81.2	101	18	73
Whitten, Kyle, 4Y Jr.	0	1	3.16	27	0	1	31.1	29	19	38
Wyatt, Matt, 2Y Fr.	4	2	3.86	21	2	1	39.2	36	23	51

7. STANFORD

Coach: David Esquer. **Record:** 39-17

Player, Pos., Year	AVG	OBP	SLG	AB	R	2B	3B	HR	RBI	SB
Barrera, Brett, 1B, 2Y Fr.	.215	.282	.415	65	10	1	0	4	7	0
Bowser, Drew, 3B, Fr.	.302	.361	.487	199	30	16	0	7	41	1
Brueser, Nick, 1B, 4Y Jr.	.304	.378	.536	194	30	10	1	11	34	3
Burton, Grant, CF, 3Y So.	.286	.500	.4571	7	4	0	1	0	1	0
Cobb, Owen, 2B, 2Y Fr.	.100	.217	.100	20	4	0	0	0	0	0
Crampton, Adam, SS, 2Y Fr.	.287	.348	.362	188	26	8	0	2	18	4
Gargus, Henry, RF, 2Y Fr.	.244	.375	.356	45	9	2	0	1	5	1
Graham, Carter, INF, Fr.	.091	.091	.091	11	0	0	0	0	0	0
Hinkelman, Cole, OF/INF, 2Y Fr.	.050	.136	.050	20	2	0	0	0	4	0
Huff, Kody, C, 2Y Fr.	.263	.336	.399	213	41	12	1	5	37	1
Jones, Brock, CF, 2Y Fr.	.311	.453	.646	206	56	13	1	18	62	14
Kretzschmar, Austin, 2B, 3Y So.	.320	.414	.320	25	2	0	0	0	4	0
Martinez, Vincent, C, 3Y So.	.312	.387	.500	154	36	8	0	7	22	0
Park, Eddie, LF, Fr.	.270	.377	.270	89	19	0	0	0	7	0
Rios, Alberto, C, Fr.	.000	.000	.000	1	0	0	0	0	0	0
Robinson, Christian, RF, 4Y Jr.	.318	.398	.500	198	36	12	0	8	48	8
Tawa, Tim, 2B, 4Y Jr.	.290	.357	.519	214	46	13	0	12	39	14
Troy, Tommy, 2B, Fr.	.247	.345	.487	150	29	6	0	10	28	4

Pitcher, Year	W	L	ERA	G	GS	SV	IP	H	BB	SO
Beck, Brendan, 4Y Jr.	9	3	3.15	17	15	0	108.2	81	26	143
Bruno, Ryan, Fr.	0	1	15.75	6	1	0	4	2	14	5
Dixon, Joey, Fr.	2	1	3.28	23	4	2	35.2	24	19	16
Dowd, Drew, Fr.	2	1	6.99	19	6	0	37.1	48	20	37
Fleischli, Nathan, 2Y Fr.	0	0	9.82	4	0	0	3.2	1	3	2
Grech, Zach, Fr.	5	5	3.62	31	1	13	49.2	42	12	34
Mathews, Quinn, 2Y Fr.	5	2	6.08	18	14	0	66.2	63	33	60
Meier, Max, 2Y Fr.	0	0	14.73	7	1	0	7.1	18	8	8
Moore, Justin, 3Y Fr.	0	0	8.31	4	0	0	4.1	4	4	3
O'Rourke, Tommy, Fr.	1	0	4.07	25	0	0	24.1	16	20	25
Palisch, Jacob, 4Y Jr.	2	0	3.97	21	0	2	34	38	11	29
Pancer, Brandt, Fr.	5	2	3.83	25	3	0	42.1	45	20	28
Weiermiller, Austin, 4Y Jr.	2	0	6.29	22	0	0	24.1	29	12	24
Williams, Alex, 3Y So.	5	2	3.42	12	11	0	55.1	38	17	54
Worley, Jonathan, 5Y Jr.	1	0	8.25	10	0	0	12	17	9	13

8. TENNESSEE

Coach: Tony Vitello. **Record:** 50-18

Player, Pos., Year	AVG	OBP	SLG	AB	R	2B	3B	HR	RBI	SB
Beck, Jordan, RF, 2Y Fr.	.271	.336	.523	258	42	16	2	15	64	8
Booker, Kyle, LF, Fr.	.310	.382	.448	58	16	5	0	1	10	1
Derkay, Pete, DH, 5Y Jr.	.291	.406	.423	182	35	10	1	4	21	5

	AVG	OBP	SLG	AB	R	2B	3B	HR	RBI	SB
Ensley, Hunter, OF, Fr.	.000	.000	.000	1	0	0	0	0	0	0
Ferguson, Max, 2B, 3Y So.	.253	.378	.461	245	46	11	2	12	46	15
Gilbert, Drew, CF, 2Y Fr.	.274	.341	.437	270	41	12	1	10	62	10
Greer, Jackson, C, 5Y Sr.	.271	.435	.471	70	13	5	0	3	9	1
Lawson, Cortland, INF, 2Y Fr.	.357	.438	.643	14	4	1	0	1	3	0
Lipcius, Luc, 1B, 5Y Jr.	.240	.357	.480	225	48	9	0	15	42	6
Lipscomb, Trey, 3B, 3Y So.	.310	.412	.517	29	7	3	0	1	9	1
Ortega, Jorel, INF, 2Y Fr.	.148	.333	.296	27	9	1	0	1	3	0
Pavolony, Connor, C, 3Y So.	.260	.365	.442	154	29	7	0	7	26	5
Payne, Ethan, 1B, 2Y Fr.	.182	.308	.182	11	5	0	0	0	0	0
Rucker, Jake, 3B, 3Y So.	.333	.399	.520	273	48	21	2	9	55	7
Russell, Evan, LF, 4Y Jr.	.238	.342	.500	206	41	10	1	14	43	3
Scott, Christian, CF, 3Y So.	.286	.415	.381	42	14	4	0	0	5	2
Spence, Liam, SS, 4Y Jr.	.336	.472	.459	244	63	11	2	5	36	5
Steenstra, Logan, SS, 3Y So.	.292	.462	.500	48	13	8	1	0	6	3

Pitcher, Year	W	L	ERA	G	GS	SV	IP	H	BB	SO
Brock, Luke, Fr.	0	0	0.00	1	0	0	0	3	1	0
Connell, Kirby, 2Y Fr.	1	1	3.00	26	0	2	42	44	3	39
Dallas, Chad, 3Y So.	11	2	4.19	17	17	0	103	95	20	122
Delashmit, Christian, 2Y Fr.	0	0	5.79	6	0	0	4.2	6	1	4
Fanning, Hollis, Fr.	0	0	6.75	4	0	0	2.2	5	0	2
Fitzgibbons, Jake, Fr.	1	0	8.31	7	3	0	8.2	13	6	6
Gilbert, Drew, 2Y Fr.	1	0	0.00	7	0	0	8.1	3	5	8
Heflin, Will, 4Y Jr.	3	3	4.07	18	16	0	79.2	82	17	77
Housley, Connor, 2Y Fr.	0	0	3.48	12	0	0	10.1	8	6	14
Hunley, Sean, 4Y Jr.	7	5	3.36	35	0	9	72.1	62	13	77
Leath, Jackson, 4Y Jr.	0	0	0.00	2	1	0	6.1	4	2	8
Mabrey, Will, 2Y Fr.	0	0	1.13	12	0	0	8	2	3	9
McLaughlin, Mark, 2Y Fr.	2	0	1.84	15	5	0	34.1	15	21	40
Pleasants, Elijah, 3Y So.	2	1	4.37	15	2	0	22.2	24	6	13
Rackers, Jason, 4Y Jr.	1	1	2.53	7	3	0	10.2	9	2	10
Scott, Shawn, Fr.	0	0	6.75	3	0	0	2.2	3	5	1
Sechrist, Zander, Fr.	2	0	2.89	8	0	0	9.1	8	1	11
Sewell, Camden, 3Y So.	4	1	2.82	23	3	2	51	33	15	46
Tidwell, Blade, Fr.	10	3	3.74	18	18	0	98.2	84	34	90
Walsh, Redmond, 5Y Jr.	5	1	2.52	28	0	5	39.1	36	10	40

9. ARIZONA
Coach: Jay Johnson. Record: 45-18

Player, Pos., Year	AVG	OBP	SLG	AB	R	2B	3B	HR	RBI	SB
Berry, Jacob, 3B/DH, Fr.	.352	.439	.676	247	54	19	5	17	70	2
Bingham, Mac, LF, 2Y Fr.	.305	.417	.390	141	34	7	1	1	33	1
Blas, Jacob, SS, 4Y So.	.257	.381	.340	144	31	1	1	3	23	3
Boissiere, Branden, 1B, 3Y So.	.369	.451	.506	255	69	12	4	5	63	2
Bullard, Tony, 3B, 3Y So.	.298	.369	.546	144	28	8	3	7	30	2
Casagrande, Tyler, LF, 3Y So.	.244	.347	.366	41	12	0	1	1	7	1
Davis, Chase, OF, Fr.	.233	.343	.400	30	5	3	1	0	4	0
Donahue, Kyson, 3B, 3Y Fr.	.250	.667	.500	4	3	1	0	0	1	0
Holgate, Ryan, RF, 3Y Sr.	.351	.421	.576	245	49	20	1	11	56	3
Hopson, Kaden, C, 2Y Fr.	.143	.333	.190	21	1	1	0	0	6	0
Kato, Kobe, 2B, 3Y So.	.350	.460	.469	226	58	16	4	1	34	6
LaLiberte, Cameron, C, Fr.	.333	.333	.333	3	0	0	0	0	0	0
McClaughry, Nik, SS, 3Y So.	.316	.412	.401	152	37	8	1	1	32	1
O'Tremba, Tanner, LF, 3Y So.	.269	.405	.448	67	14	2	2	2	14	1
Paugh, Blake, RF, 4Y Jr.	.258	.324	.468	62	13	6	2	1	9	0
Shaver, Jacob, UTL, 2Y Fr.	.286	.286	.286	7	0	0	0	0	1	0
Susac, Daniel, C, Fr.	.335	.392	.591	242	48	24	1	12	65	0
Williams, Donta, CF, 3Y So.	.342	.481	.538	240	81	17	3	8	49	9

Pitcher, Year	W	L	ERA	G	GS	SV	IP	H	BB	SO
Abshier, Randy, 3Y So.	4	0	2.91	20	0	1	21.2	22	11	26
Arias, Jr., George, 3Y So.	0	0	3.86	3	0	0	2.2	2	1	5
Churchill, Ian, 4Y Jr.	0	1	8.56	13	0	0	13.2	17	9	12
Cooper, Riley, Fr.	3	0	4.88	29	2	0	31.1	26	13	20
Fajardo, German, 2Y Fr.	0	0	27.00	1	0	0	0.1	2	1	0
Flanagan, Quinn, 4Y So.	0	4	3.99	19	4	0	38.1	37	23	45
Guardado, Jonathan, 4Y Jr.	0	0	0.00	1	0	0	1	2	0	1
Irvin, Garrett, 4Y Jr.	6	4	4.59	18	18	0	88.1	96	35	75
Long, Trevor, Fr.	2	0	10.66	6	0	0	12.2	23	4	8
Luna, Gil, 4Y Jr.	1	0	1.69	14	0	1	21.1	13	11	31
Murphy, Chandler, 2Y Fr.	7	0	4.29	20	8	0	63	71	26	56
Netz, Dawson, 2Y Fr.	0	0	4.50	28	2	0	34	26	10	36
Nichols, T.J., Fr.	6	3	4.77	17	9	0	60.1	50	31	66
Price, Preston, 5Y Sr.	1	1	3.38	16	0	3	21.1	14	12	35

	W	L	ERA	G	GS	SV	IP	H	BB	SO
Silseth, Chase, 3Y So.	8	1	5.55	18	18	0	97.1	112	29	105
Smith, Austin, 4Y Jr.	2	1	5.14	18	6	0	28	28	18	25
Vannelle, Vince, 5Y Sr.	5	3	2.78	26	0	8	32.1	34	12	38

10. NOTRE DAME
Coach: Link Jarrett. Record: 34-13

Player, Pos., Year	AVG	OBP	SLG	AB	R	2B	3B	HR	RBI	SB
Brait, Alex, LF, 5Y Sr.	.174	.174	.304	23	2	0	0	1	6	0
Brannigan, Jack, 3B, 2Y Fr.	.296	.388	.497	169	31	12	2	6	29	8
Coetzee, Brooks, RF, 3Y So.	.280	.344	.476	143	25	8	1	6	29	11
Cole, Ryan, LF, 4Y Jr.	.324	.445	.561	148	41	9	1	8	32	7
Hess, Kyle, 2B, 2Y Fr.	.250	.368	.344	32	4	3	0	0	6	1
Juaire, Nick, C/OF, 2Y Fr.	.308	.357	.308	13	1	0	0	0	0	0
Jung, Daniel, OF/1B, 5Y Sr.	.091	.091	.091	11	0	0	0	0	0	0
Kavadas, Niko, 1B, 4Y Jr.	.305	.479	.766	154	41	8	0	21	62	2
Kmet, Casey, INF, 2Y Fr.	.000	.000	.000	2	0	0	0	0	0	0
Lamanna, David, C, 4Y Jr.	.234	.335	.397	141	23	6	1	5	29	1
Miller, Jared, 2B, 4Y Jr.	.262	.333	.468	141	31	11	3	4	24	7
Murtha, Brock, INF, Fr.	.000	.000	.000	1	0	0	0	0	0	0
Myers, Spencer, CF, 4Y Jr.	.287	.364	.362	188	40	11	0	1	14	15
Neri, Danny, C, Fr.	.261	.346	.261	23	3	0	0	0	1	1
Prajzner, Zack, SS, 3Y So.	.288	.388	.458	153	32	8	0	6	23	2
Putz, Carter, INF, 3Y So.	.304	.367	.489	184	40	10	3	6	43	3
Williams, T.J., CF, Fr.	.333	.556	.333	6	7	0	0	0	3	0
Zyska, Jack, LF, 3Y So.	.189	.333	.216	37	4	1	0	0	0	5

Pitcher, Year	W	L	ERA	G	GS	SV	IP	H	BB	SO
Bertrand, John Michael, 5Y Sr.	8	2	3.25	14	14	0	88.2	80	21	65
Brannigan, Jack, 2Y Fr.	1	0	11.25	46	0	3	4	4	3	7
Brown, Cameron, Fr.	0	0	0.00	3	1	0	3	1	6	4
Cancellieri, Dominic, 2Y Fr.	0	0	6.60	10	3	0	15	20	13	18
Dennies, Jackson, Fr.	0	0	15.00	3	0	0	3	7	2	2
Hulbert, James, 5Y Jr.	0	0	0.00	1	0	0	0	0	1	0
Kohlhepp, Tanner, 3Y So.	7	2	3.08	23	1	2	61.1	42	22	65
Lynch, Ryan, Fr.	0	0	27.00	1	0	0	0.2	1	3	1
Megias, Mitch, 3Y So.	0	0	81.00	2	0	0	0.1	3	3	0
Mercer, Will, 3Y Fr.	4	2	4.53	17	10	2	55.2	60	17	44
Rao, Alex, 3Y So.	2	1	2.48	14	1	2	36.1	17	22	36
Scafidi, Christian, 5Y Sr.	1	0	1.50	2	2	0	6	4	6	5
Sheehan, Jack, 5Y Sr.	0	0	0.00	3	0	0	4.2	1	4	3
Sheehan, Tommy, 4Y Fr.	0	1	6.75	2	2	0	8	10	5	10
Sheridan, Joe, 5Y Jr.	1	2	5.27	16	3	3	41	52	17	30
Simon, Liam, 2Y Fr.	5	1	3.20	17	1	1	25.1	19	22	33
Tyrell, Aidan, 3Y So.	5	1	2.70	17	8	2	60	50	19	43

11. TEXAS TECH
Coach: Tim Tadlock. Record: 39-17

Player, Pos., Year	AVG	OBP	SLG	AB	R	2B	3B	HR	RBI	SB
Baker, Dru, LF, 3Y So.	.343	.406	.484	213	53	14	2	4	32	18
Jung, Jace, 2B, 2Y Fr.	.337	.462	.697	208	55	10	1	21	67	4
Conley, Cal, SS, 3Y Jr.	.329	.393	.587	225	46	13	0	15	55	7
Stilwell, Cole, 1B, 3Y So.	.288	.422	.548	146	29	12	1	8	33	0
Neuse, Dylan, CF, 4Y Jr.	.281	.440	.427	96	29	7	2	1	16	11
Wilson, Kurt, SS, 4Y Jr.	.274	.394	.453	106	23	6	2	3	16	3
Fulford, Braxton, C, 4Y Jr.	.264	.395	.590	178	38	12	2	14	45	0
Murrell, Easton, RF, 4Y Jr.	.250	.442	.417	144	37	8	2	4	20	2
Rombach, Nate, 3Y Fr.	.222	.359	.521	117	26	6	1	9	34	0
Carter, Dillon, CF, 2Y Fr.	.207	.318	.288	111	16	6	0	1	15	2
Runion, Braydon, INF/OF, 3Y So.	.195	.327	.341	41	10	3	0	1	4	0
Kelly, Parker, 3B, 4Y Jr.	.194	.333	.240	129	23	4	1	0	10	0
Masters, Cody, OF, 4Y Jr.	.192	.375	.551	78	22	3	2	7	23	1
Woodcox, Drew, 1B, Fr.	.167	.311	.333	36	6	0	0	2	7	0
Marusak, Max, LF, 3Y Jr.	.100	.129	.200	30	8	3	0	0	1	1

Pitcher, Year	W	L	ERA	G	GS	SV	IP	H	BB	SO
Beckel, Brandon, Fr.	0	0	16.20	5	0	0	3.1	6	5	6
Birdsell, Brandon, 3Y So.	4	1	3.06	8	7	0	35.1	27	9	36
Bridges, Derek, 2Y Fr.	0	0	3.97	19	0	1	11.1	12	0	11
Dallas, Micah, 3Y So.	4	3	3.51	17	10	2	66.2	61	20	79
Devine, Andrew, 2Y Fr.	1	1	12.00	17	0	0	15	17	21	23
Girton, Brendan, Fr.	2	0	4.74	18	2	1	24.2	21	19	23
Gorby, Nick, Fr.	0	0	0.00	3	0	0	3.1	4	3	1
Hamilton, Tyler, 2Y Fr.	0	0	6.75	2	0	0	1.1	0	4	1
Hampton, Chase, Fr.	4	1	3.86	18	7	1	44.1	36	17	34
Hitt, Jamie, Fr.	0	1	5.79	5	0	0	4.2	10	2	2

Pitcher, Year	W	L	ERA	G	GS	SV	IP	H	BB	SO
Key, Hayde, Fr.	2	0	5.52	10	1	0	14.2	15	6	17
LeJeune-DeAcutis, Brady, Fr.	0	0	4.91	4	0	0	3.2	5	2	4
Monteverde, Patrick, 5Y Sr.	7	4	3.75	16	16	0	86.1	79	21	101
Montgomery, Mason, 3Y So.	5	3	3.82	14	13	0	63.2	48	27	84
Petix, Brandon, 3Y Fr.	0	0	13.50	1	0	0	0.2	1	1	0
Queen, Connor, 4Y Jr.	1	0	4.15	18	0	6	21.2	21	9	19
Riechmann, Eli, 4Y So.	1	0	4.50	11	0	0	10	10	6	6
Sanders, Josh, Fr.	0	0	2.89	8	0	0	9.1	10	4	10
Sublette, Ryan, 4Y Jr.	6	3	2.34	19	3	0	42.1	28	17	62
Webster, Chase, 3Y So.	1	0	10.39	10	0	0	8.2	9	7	3
Wells, Levi, Fr.	1	0	7.64	17	0	0	17.2	15	23	21
Wilson, Kurt, 4Y Jr.	0	0	3.38	3	0	0	2.2	4	2	0

12. MISSISSIPPI

Coach: Mike Bianco. **Record:** 45-22

Player, Pos., Year	AVG	OBP	SLG	AB	R	2B	3B	HR	RBI	SB
Alderman, Kemp, UTL, Fr.	.125	.125	.313	16	2	0	0	1	1	0
Baker, Cael, 1B, 4Y Jr.	.208	.319	.331	154	25	4	0	5	28	0
Bench, Justin, 3B, 3Y So.	.307	.423	.440	241	56	7	2	7	39	14
Chatagnier, Peyton, 2B, 2Y Fr.	.271	.368	.412	221	41	13	0	6	43	0
Dunhurst, Hayden, C, 3Y Fr.	.280	.385	.435	232	40	11	2	7	43	3
Elko, Tim, 3B, 4Y Jr.	.325	.444	.675	160	41	8	0	16	55	0
Gonzalez, Jacob, SS, Fr.	.355	.443	.561	262	73	16	1	12	55	2
Graham, Kevin, LF, 3Y So.	.342	.422	.562	260	58	15	0	14	56	2
Harris, Calvin, C, Fr.	.208	.279	.347	72	10	4	0	2	18	1
LaFleur, Trey, 1B, 2Y Fr.	.133	.188	.367	30	2	1	0	2	2	1
Leatherwood, Hayden, RF, 4Y Jr.	.285	.348	.441	186	29	8	0	7	33	0
Loposer, Knox, C, 3Y So.	.235	.400	.353	34	8	2	1	0	5	0
McCants, T.J., CF, Fr.	.300	.369	.433	217	47	10	2	5	35	11
Plumlee, John Rhys, RF, 2Y Fr.	.267	.416	.383	60	21	4	0	1	7	7
Sammons, Cade, RF, 2Y Fr.	.111	.385	.111	18	7	0	0		1	3
Van Cleve, Ben, INF, 4Y Fr.	.255	.342	.333	102	14	6	1	0	15	0
Wood, Garrett, 2B, 3Y So.	.000	.300	.000	13	4	0	0		1	0

Pitcher, Year	W	L	ERA	G	GS	SV	IP	H	BB	SO
Adcock, Cody, Fr.	0	0	6.41	14	2	0	19.2	32	11	24
Baker, Cole, 2Y Fr.	0	0	8.10	4	0	0	3.1	4	6	5
Baker, Luke, Fr.	0	0	24.00	6	0	0	3	12	2	6
Broadway, Taylor, 5Y Sr.	4	3	3.44	30	1	16	49.2	46	9	66
Burton, Wes, 2Y Fr.	0	0	3.57	15	0	0	17.2	12	13	31
Cioffi, Max, 4Y Jr.	0	0	0.00	2	0	0	2.2	4	4	4
Diamond, Derek, 2Y Fr.	3	5	5.26	20	14	1	75.1	80	32	82
Dougherty, Jack, Fr.	2	2	5.40	12	2	0	25	23	7	36
Forsyth, Braden, 4Y Jr.	0	1	7.71	13	0	1	11.2	9	8	15
Hoglund, Gunnar, 3Y So.	4	2	2.87	11	11	0	62.2	40	17	96
Holston, Greer, 5Y Sr.	0	0	0.00	2	0	0	3.1	1	0	4
Johnson, Brandon, 3Y Fr.	1	0	4.70	18	0	1	23	24	10	28
Kimbrell, Jackson, 2Y Fr.	5	1	5.75	24	0	0	31.1	28	19	38
Mallitz, Josh, Fr.	4	1	7.33	17	6	0	27	41	10	35
McDaniel, Drew, 2Y Fr.	5	2	6.08	20	13	0	63.2	78	22	72
Miller, Austin, 4Y Jr.	1	1	5.00	21	0	1	27	26	11	30
Murrell, Mitch, 2Y Fr.	0	0	6.35	5	0	0	5.2	3	4	6
Myers, Tyler, 4Y Jr.	4	2	5.57	21	3	0	42	45	5	44
Nikhazy, Doug, 3Y So.	12	2	2.45	16	15	0	92	62	31	142
Savell, Logan, 3Y Fr.	0	0	40.50	2	0	0	0.2	6	0	1

13. EAST CAROLINA

Coach: Cliff Godwin. **Record:** 44-17

Player, Pos., Year	AVG	OBP	SLG	AB	R	2B	3B	HR	RBI	SB
Agnos, Zach, 3B, 2Y Fr.	.268	.397	.439	205	38	15	1	6	43	5
Berini, Joey, INF, Fr.	.250	.250	.250	16	0	0	0	0	1	0
Boyd, C.J., 1B/OF, Fr.	.182	.250	.455	11	3	0	0	1	2	0
Bridges, Matt, P, 6Y Sr.	1.000	1.000	1.000	1	1	0	0	0	1	0
Brooks, Skylar, 1B, 2Y Fr.	.200	.333	.800	5	1	0	0	1	3	0
Caddell, Seth, C, 4Y Jr.	.270	.373	.526	196	46	8	0	14	47	0
Chandler, Garrett, CF, Fr.	.500	.500	.500	12	1	0	0	0	1	0
Clonch, Cam, OF/1B, Fr.	.333	.333	.417	12	1	1	0	0	1	0
Francisco, Thomas, 1B, 3Y So.	.354	.416	.557	246	64	11	0	13	48	4
Giles, Ryder, SS, 3Y So.	.211	.329	.249	185	29	4	1	0	18	4
Hoover, Lane, RF, 3Y So.	.252	.376	.282	131	25	2	1	0	12	7
Johnson, Ryley, RF, Fr.	.257	.373	.443	70	16	4	0	3	13	8
Makarewicz, Alec, LF, 2Y Fr.	.295	.356	.464	183	30	9	2	6	33	2
Mayhue, C.J., P, 2Y Fr.	.000	.000	.000	1	0	0	0	0	0	0
Moylan, Josh, DH, Fr.	.310	.409	.460	187	35	8	1	6	38	0
Newton, Ben, C, 4Y Jr.	.325	.451	.438	80	13	6	0	1	17	0
Norby, Connor, 2B, 3Y So.	.415	.484	.659	246	64	15	0	15	51	18
Rezek, Joey, OF/C, Fr.	.000	.250	.000	3	0	0	0	0	0	1
Smallwood, Christian, OF, 5Y Jr.	.059	.238	.059	17	0	0	0	0	2	0
Starling, Jacob, INF/OF, Fr.	.150	.292	.200	20	6	1	0	0	1	0
Wilcoxen, Justin, C, 2Y Fr.	.000	.000	.000	3	0	0	0	0	0	0
Worrell, Bryson, CF, 4Y Jr.	.262	.356	.490	202	35	13	3	9	33	9

Pitcher, Year	W	L	ERA	G	GS	SV	IP	H	BB	SO
Agnos, Zach, 2Y Fr.	0	1	20.25	6	1	0	2.2	5	4	3
Beal, Danny, Fr.	1	0	2.25	15	0	0	12	6	8	8
Boyd, C.J., Fr.	0	0	0.00	9	0	0	1	2	0	0
Bridges, Matt, 6Y Sr.	5	0	2.25	30	1	5	36	30	12	45
Brooks, Skylar, 2Y Fr.	0	0	4.91	13	0	0	3.2	3	2	2
Colmore, Cam, 6Y Sr.	7	1	2.41	32	1	2	52.1	41	17	60
Giles, Ryder, 3Y So.	1	1	4.38	6	1	0	12.1	12	2	15
Ginn, Landon, Fr.	1	0	4.00	10	0	0	9	9	6	6
Grosz, Josh, Fr.	0	0	7.50	14	0	0	12	10	7	9
Kimmel, Trystan, 4Y Jr.	0	0	8.49	9	1	0	11.2	16	4	10
Kuchmaner, Jake, 4Y Jr.	2	4	5.97	19	14	0	57.1	74	10	45
Lawson, Dylan, 2Y Fr.	0	0	0.00	2	0	0	2	0	1	3
Logusch, Nick, 4Y Jr.	0	0	5.11	16	0	0	12.1	9	11	21
Mayhue, C.J., 2Y Fr.	3	1	3.06	34	0	8	50	44	21	76
Nahbolz, Nate, 2Y Fr.	0	1	6.00	4	1	0	3	3	3	3
Saylor, Garrett, 3Y So.	4	1	5.09	20	2	0	35.1	28	18	40
Smith, Tyler, 5Y Sr.	2	3	4.94	15	13	0	54.2	52	27	38
Spivey, Carter, 3Y So.	1	1	7.98	12	3	0	14.2	17	9	15
Whisenhunt, Carson, 2Y Fr.	6	2	3.77	13	13	0	62	50	22	79
Williams, Gavin, 4Y Jr.	10	1	1.88	15	12	1	81.1	57	21	130
Wilson, A.J., 2Y Fr.	1	0	4.22	21	0	0	10.2	12	5	18

14. DALLAS BAPTIST

Coach: Dan Heefner. **Record:** 41-18

Player, Pos., Year	AVG	OBP	SLG	AB	R	2B	3B	HR	RBI	SB
Bell, Austin, OF, 6Y Sr.	.277	.443	.555	155	40	13	0	10	39	4
Benfield, Andrew, 3B, 3Y Fr.	.280	.373	.487	189	39	12	0	9	41	8
Blessinger, Max, INF/OF, 2Y Fr.	.333	.333	.333	3	0	0	0	0	2	0
Boulware, Christian, C, 5Y Sr.	.264	.381	.442	129	34	8	0	5	24	8
Burgarello, Nico, SS, 4Y Jr.	.192	.317	.327	52	10	1	0	2	10	0
David, Jeffrey, CF, 2Y Fr.	.174	.333	.239	46	8	1	1	0	2	4
Glenn, Jackson, 2B, 5Y Sr.	.361	.429	.717	233	61	19	2	20	53	13
Grady, Jace, CF, 2Y Fr.	.341	.422	.540	176	46	17	3	4	40	15
Jones, Blayne, SS, 4Y Jr.	.229	.305	.477	153	28	5	0	11	34	1
Mach, Dylan, SS, Fr.	.250	.368	.250	16	6	0	0	0	2	0
Moore, Cole, 1B, 3Y So.	.329	.429	.606	170	39	14	0	11	46	4
Pruitt, Dan, DH, 4Y Jr.	.000	.556	.000	4	2	0	0	0	1	0
Sosa, Andres, 1B, 5Y Sr.	.241	.436	.481	133	42	5	0	9	32	2
Specht, George, LF, 3Y So.	.192	.316	.295	78	10	2	0	2	12	1
Town, River, RF, 3Y So.	.323	.433	.515	229	60	14	0	10	51	20
Wrobleski, Ryan, C, 3Y Fr.	.261	.343	.487	119	24	6	0	7	27	5

Pitcher, Year	W	L	ERA	G	GS	SV	IP	H	BB	SO
Arnold, Chandler, 3Y So.	3	0	3.94	15	0	1	29.2	31	23	33
Baker, Alec, 3Y Fr.	0	0	16.2	2	0	0	1.2	1	2	3
Carver, Ross, 4Y Jr.	1	1	6.35	9	0	0	11.1	11	4	12
Eldred, Luke, 5Y Jr.	4	0	2.23	10	9	0	32.1	20	10	32
Gaither, Ray, 5Y Jr.	3	2	5.32	15	7	1	45.2	50	29	45
Hamel, Dominic, 4Y Jr.	13	2	4.22	18	16	1	91.2	68	34	136
Heaton, Zach, 4Y So.	2	1	7.24	11	1	0	13.2	19	4	13
Kechely, Kragen, 5Y Jr.	3	4	2.61	20	1	2	31	22	15	34
Kouba, Rhett, 5Y So.	6	2	2.77	16	10	0	74.2	60	23	87
Martin, Joey, 3Y So.	0	1	13.5	8	0	0	4	4	9	6
Pettitte, Jared, 5Y Jr.	1	0	5.81	13	4	0	26.1	18	21	26
Reeves, Cole, 3Y So.	0	1	6.59	12	0	0	13.2	15	7	16
Rich, Kyle, 3Y Fr.	4	1	4.75	12	10	0	47.1	46	20	40
Russell, Zane, 2Y Fr.	1	0	2.25	14	0	2	20	14	10	16
Sagedahl, Chas, 4Y Jr.	0	1	19.29	2	0	0	2.1	6	3	0
Sherlin, Peyton, 4Y Fr.	0	1	2.56	23	0	4	38.2	22	24	46
Talbert, Tyler, Fr.	0	0	27.00	1	0	0	0.1	1	0	0
Trahan, Luke, 3Y So.	0	0	5.19	10	0	1	8.2	8	6	4
Young, Jacob, Fr.	0	0	13.5	3	0	0	3.1	7	0	2

15. OREGON

Coach: Mark Wasikowski. **Record:** 39-16

Player, Pos. Year	AVG	OBP	SLG	AB	R	2B	3B	HR	RBI	SB
Ashford, Robby, CF, 2Y Fr.	.200	.293	.286	35	6	1	1	0	2	3
Bellafronto, Nick, 3B, 6Y Sr.	.212	.372	.273	33	5	2	0	0	4	0
Boettcher, Bryce, CF, Fr.	.152	.310	.152	33	14	0	0	0	4	4
Cromwick, Josiah, C, Fr.	.280	.357	.320	25	3	1	0	0	1	1
Ganus, Tyler, OF/1B, Fr.	.286	.444	.286	7	1	0	0	0	3	0
Grant, Gavin, 2B, 3Y So.	.230	.348	.331	148	27	7	1	2	16	5
Haley, Jack, INF, Fr.	.500	.500	.500	2	3	0	0	0	1	0
Hall, Anthony, CF, 2Y Fr.	.286	.342	.470	168	25	11	1	6	36	3
Hanoian, Tristan, 2B, 4Y Jr.	.278	.372	.333	36	5	2	0	0	3	0
Kasevich, Josh, SS, 2Y Fr.	.324	.397	.444	216	32	10	2	4	50	7
Matthews, Gabe, 1B, 5Y Sr.	.322	.449	.559	202	48	20	2	8	35	0
Miller, A.J., OF, 3Y So.	.077	.133	.077	13	0	0	0	0	2	0
Novitske, Sam, 3B, 3Y So.	.246	.348	.311	167	24	8	0	1	24	10
Olsson, Sam, C, 4Y Jr.	.318	.420	.500	22	4	1	0	1	7	0
Scanlon, Jack, C, 2Y Fr.	.169	.275	.282	142	13	7	0	3	13	1
Shade, Colby, CF, Fr.	.250	.250	.250	12	2	0	0	0	2	1
Smith, Tanner, LF, 3Y So.	.324	.417	.533	225	49	24	4	5	36	4
Williams, Evan, CF, 4Y Jr.	.000	.000	.000	1	0	0	0	0	0	0
Yovan, Kenyon, DH, 5Y Jr.	.309	.407	.608	204	53	10	0	17	57	1
Zavala, Aaron, RF, 3Y So.	.392	.525	.628	199	64	14	3	9	38	11

Pitcher, Year	W	L	ERA	G	GS	SV	IP	H	BB	SO
Ahlstrom, Robert, 4Y Jr.	9	3	2.50	14	14	0	90	77	16	92
Ayon, Isaac, Fr.	2	1	5.21	22	2	0	38	40	15	44
Breault, Hunter, 4Y Jr.	1	1	4.70	15	0	0	15.1	19	6	17
Britton, Rio, Fr.	0	0	3.52	15	0	0	15.1	11	8	18
Ciuffetelli, Christian, 3Y So.	0	0	6.35	4	0	0	5.2	6	4	7
Ellis, Scott, Fr.	0	0	4.50	8	0	0	8	8	4	5
Fuller, Peyton, 4Y Jr.	1	0	2.38	3	3	0	11.1	12	6	4
Gordon, R.J., Fr.	3	0	4.19	14	3	0	19.1	24	9	20
Kafka, Cullen, 4Y Jr.	5	3	3.00	15	15	0	78	73	35	84
Mercado, Logan, Fr.	1	0	4.50	2	1	0	6	4	4	5
Mosiello, Andrew, 2Y Fr.	3	1	4.12	21	1	2	39.1	34	8	52
Sloan, Caleb, 4Y So.	1	2	4.30	12	0	0	14.2	19	3	18
Somers, Kolby, 4Y Jr.	2	2	3.08	20	0	11	26.1	14	14	37
Spears, Brayden, 2Y Fr.	0	0	9.00	1	0	0	1	1	1	1
Stedman, Decker, 2Y Fr.	2	0	4.82	8	0	0	9.1	7	9	12
Tellache, Nico, 5Y Sr.	3	0	5.35	20	1	0	33.2	35	14	37
Walker, Brett, 4Y Jr.	6	3	3.66	15	15	0	83.2	81	26	60

16. OLD DOMINION

Coach: Chris Finwood. **Record:** 44-16

Player, Pos., Year	AVG	OBP	SLG	AB	R	2B	3B	HR	RBI	SB
Barrientos, Robby, C, Fr.	.154	.389	.231	13	2	1	0	0	1	0
Battle, Kyle, LF, 5Y Sr.	.319	.464	.681	207	68	15	3	18	61	7
Bell, Tommy, SS, 4Y Fr.	.343	.421	.554	204	47	9	5	8	49	2
Claxton, Dominick, CF, 2Y Fr.	.077	.077	.077	13	5	0	0	0	0	2
Coldsnow, Zach, OF, 2Y Fr.	.000	.167	.000	5	2	0	0	0	0	0
Coutney, Matt, 1B, 4Y Fr.	.282	.418	.511	188	46	11	1	10	38	0
Dalatri, Andrea, 1B, 2Y Fr.	.182	.250	.318	22	5	0	0	1	4	0
Dengler, Chris, 2B, 2Y Fr.	.267	.421	.467	15	5	1	1	0	3	0
Gagliardi, Brock, C, 2Y Fr.	.316	.456	.561	155	39	11	0	9	35	0
Garriola, Andy, RF, 3Y So.	.318	.366	.564	236	53	16	0	14	72	0
Hancock, Jared, C, 3Y So.	.176	.259	.314	51	7	4	0	1	4	1
Levari, Kenny, 3B, Fr.	.298	.369	.441	238	49	10	0	8	36	2
Petracci, Robbie, OF, 2Y Fr.	.299	.381	.619	97	17	5	1	8	25	0
Ransom, Lincoln, OF, Fr.	.261	.333	.551	69	11	8	0	4	12	0
Teschko, Ryan, CF, 3Y So.	.275	.336	.508	120	24	5	1	7	23	2
Trice, Carter, 2B, Fr.	.355	.426	.632	234	57	17	3	14	54	8
Wheeler, Thomas, CF, Fr.	.271	.381	.450	140	34	6	5	3	26	15

Pitcher, Year	W	L	ERA	G	GS	SV	IP	H	BB	SO
Bashara, Vincent, Fr.	0	0	2.16	8	0	0	8.1	10	2	8
Busher, Matt, 3Y So.	0	0	3.00	3	0	0	3	3	3	1
Dean, Noah, 2Y Fr.	0	1	4.64	19	0	9	21.1	16	14	44
DeChiaro, Joey, 2Y Fr.	0	0	9.17	12	1	0	17.2	23	15	20
Dobzanski, Brad, 2Y Fr.	2	0	1.42	18	0	0	12.2	12	6	13
Fisher, Trey, 4Y Jr.	1	0	4.70	9	0	0	7.2	7	7	5
Gertner, Tommy, 4Y Jr.	2	2	4.95	15	15	0	56.1	51	23	54
Gomez, Jacob, Fr.	6	1	4.75	17	1	0	30.1	25	18	28
Gregory, Hunter, 4Y Jr.	8	2	2.95	16	15	0	79.1	65	19	88

17. TEXAS CHRISTIAN

Hartline, Jason, 4Y Jr.	5	0	1.88	27	0	3	48	42	10	60
Holiday, Aaron, 3Y So.	4	2	3.21	20	1	1	28	15	32	43
Moore, Ryne, 4Y Jr.	9	1	3.16	17	14	0	85.1	76	22	80
Pantos, Nick, 5Y Jr.	4	2	4.82	16	11	1	56	65	23	63
Rivera, Geo, 2Y Fr.	0	0	18.00	2	0	0	3	7	2	3
Rodriguez, Joey, 2Y Fr.	2	3	6.11	23	0	0	17.2	21	7	15
Scheffler, Tom, 5Y Jr.	0	1	4.50	15	0	0	16	12	10	13
Smith, Brett, 6Y Sr.	0	0	10.03	12	0	0	11.2	18	7	11
Vaks, Luke, Fr.	1	1	18.00	5	2	0	4	9	4	8

Coach: Jim Schlossnagle. **Record:** 41-19

Player, Pos., Year	AVG	OBP	SLG	AB	R	2B	3B	HR	RBI	SB
Berkley, Garrison, RF, Fr.	.000	.286	.000	5	2	0	0	0	1	0
Boyers, Luke, RF, Fr.	.307	.411	.353	150	35	4	0	1	22	10
Brown, Porter, LF, 3Y Fr.	.342	.444	.492	120	28	9	0	3	30	8
Byrne, Kurtis, C, 2Y Fr.	.333	.471	.556	27	8	3	0	1	9	1
Goodloe, Bobby, UTL, 3Y So.	.080	.207	.320	25	6	0	0	2	5	0
Henry, Austin, 1B, 5Y Sr.	.283	.368	.433	60	8	4	1	1	5	4
Humphreys, Zach, C, 5Y Sr.	.316	.425	.498	215	62	15	3	6	40	9
Maynard, Rhett, INF, 2Y Fr.	.000	.200	.000	10	0	0	0	0	4	1
Nunez, Elijah, CF, Fr.	.225	.375	.310	187	37	5	4	1	18	10
Rodgers, Gray, 2B, 4Y Jr.	.287	.383	.371	178	35	4	1	3	35	7
Sacco, Tommy, SS, 4Y Jr.	.231	.343	.313	208	27	12	1	1	27	10
Shepherd, Conner, 3B, 6Y Sr.	.261	.431	.489	88	25	4	2	4	19	3
Shope, Cruz, OF, 4Y Jr.	.500	.667	.500	4	3	0	0	0	2	0
Sikes, Phillip, RF, 4Y Jr.	.329	.427	.620	213	56	19	5	11	63	13
Speaker, Mason, C/INF, 2Y Fr.	.500	.667	.500	4	1	0	0	0	2	0
Taylor, Brayden, 3B, Fr.	.324	.445	.572	222	54	11	4	12	53	15
Thompson, Sam, OF, 2Y Fr.	.200	.333	.800	5	1	0	0	1	1	1
Wolfe, Hunter, OF, 3Y Fr.	.315	.397	.541	181	43	18	1	7	55	13
Wood, Gene, 1B, 6Y Sr.	.273	.392	.487	150	37	5	3	7	39	17

Pitcher, Year	W	L	ERA	G	GS	SV	IP	H	BB	SO
Beethe, Harrison, 4Y Jr.	0	0	5.06	8	0	0	5.1	3	11	7
Brown, Cam, Fr.	2	0	1.93	3	3	0	9.1	5	3	8
Brown, Dalton, 6Y Sr.	0	0	9.82	9	0	0	7.1	10	3	14
Cornelio, Riley, 2Y Fr.	1	1	4.91	5	2	0	7.1	6	3	7
Green, Haylen, 5Y Sr.	1	3	3.33	25	0	12	48.2	43	5	55
Hierholzer, Storm, Fr.	0	0	5.79	4	0	0	4.2	3	6	5
Hill, Drew, 4Y Jr.	3	1	3.90	16	0	0	32.1	35	8	40
King, Charles, 5Y Sr.	5	3	3.90	17	5	0	60	62	11	53
Kodros, John, 4Y So.	0	0	13.50	3	0	0	2	5	1	3
Krob, Austin, 3Y So.	8	1	3.81	16	16	0	85	80	37	96
Meador, Jacob, 2Y Fr.	1	1	5.68	10	4	0	19	18	11	24
Mihlbauer, Augie, 4Y Jr.	0	0	5.00	12	0	0	9	8	5	13
Pearson, Braxton, Fr.	0	0	9.82	4	0	0	3.2	10	3	3
Perez, Marcelo, 3Y So.	1	0	4.15	13	0	0	30.1	27	11	33
Ray, Johnny, 4Y So.	3	3	6.50	13	11	0	44.1	47	28	45
Ridings, River, Fr.	3	2	1.08	23	1	1	33.1	22	14	39
Savage, Luke, Fr.	3	0	3.32	7	3	0	19	18	4	20
Smith, Russell, 4Y So.	7	3	3.83	15	15	0	82.1	73	20	101
Speaker, Mason, 2Y Fr.	0	0	11.57	4	0	0	2.1	2	2	5
Wright, Garrett, Fr.	3	1	3.63	19	0	1	22.1	20	16	35

18. UC IRVINE

Coach: Ben Orloff. **Record:** 43-18

Player, Pos., Year	AVG	OBP	SLG	AB	R	2B	3B	HR	RBI	SB
Castro, Jacob, 1B, 4Y Jr.	.314	.411	.397	156	25	9	2	0	34	0
Church, Nathan, RF, 3Y Fr.	.369	.424	.583	271	62	24	8	6	61	7
Cosgrove, Jake, 2B, 3Y Fr.	.305	.468	.424	59	18	7	0	0	7	1
Damla, Adrian, 1B, 5Y Sr.	.236	.307	.297	148	23	5	2	0	17	1
Garcia-Pacheco, Abraham, C, Fr.	.214	.313	.357	14	0	0	1	0	3	0
Hadeen, Ryan, 2B, 4Y Fr.	.294	.446	.294	51	18	0	0	0	7	3
Ireland, Sam, 2B, 3Y So.	.143	.294	.357	14	4	0	0	1	1	0
Kasper, Riley, INF/OF, 4Y Jr.	.091	.167	.091	11	1	0	0	0	1	0
Kendle, Caden, LF, Fr.	.111	.172	.148	27	8	1	0	0	1	0
McCaffrey, Thomas, C, Fr.	.356	.449	.446	101	21	6	1	1	22	1
McGuire, Connor, 3B, 2Y Fr.	.297	.384	.423	182	38	13	2	2	44	0
Nakawake, Taishi, SS, 4Y Fr.	.261	.352	.312	199	35	10	0	0	32	3
Palmer, Jake, 4Y Jr.	.288	.430	.415	118	24	8	2	1	13	3
Peabody, Mike, CF, 4Y Fr.	.353	.481	.580	207	57	16	2	9	57	9
Sheck, Josh, INF, 3Y Fr.	.133	.235	.200	15	1	1	0	0	1	0
Spillane, Luke, LF, 2Y Fr.	.306	.385	.428	222	44	10	1	5	45	14

Player	AVG	OBP	SLG	AB	R	2B	3B	HR	RBI	SB
Tatum, Dillon, C, 3Y So.	.278	.401	.684	133	37	7	1	15	36	0
Torres, Justin, 2B, 3Y So.	.278	.395	.469	162	27	10	3	5	33	2

Pitcher, Year	W	L	ERA	G	GS	SV	IP	H	BB	SO
Antone, Andre, 4Y So.	1	0	4.32	13	0	0	16.2	14	9	20
Brooks, Tanner, 3Y So.	2	1	2.35	18	0	0	23	16	11	20
Denholm, Trenton, 4Y Jr.	6	2	4.61	16	16	0	82	94	28	70
Frias, Michael, 4Y So.	9	2	3.36	17	14	0	85.2	65	24	91
Ibarra, Josh, 4Y Jr.	2	2	4.03	20	0	2	29	25	9	26
Ingebritson, Gordon, 4Y Jr.	6	1	3.30	40	0	1	39.2	41	6	36
King, Jacob, 2Y Fr.	3	1	1.98	29	0	8	41	32	10	45
Pinto, Nick, 2Y Fr.	7	4	3.43	17	16	0	86.2	83	26	79
Riddle, Dylan, 6Y Sr.	0	1	4.32	17	0	2	16.2	16	3	15
Stanford, Michael, 3Y So.	1	0	4.26	10	0	0	12.2	14	13	10
Van Den Helder, Cole, 4Y Jr.	0	0	5.68	6	0	0	12.2	18	7	7
Van Loon, Peter, 4Y Jr.	5	3	4.42	15	14	0	73.1	77	20	87
Vergara, John, 5Y So.	1	0	5.06	4	0	0	5.1	4	1	7
Wentworth, Troy, 3Y So.	0	1	6.48	5	1	0	8.1	11	4	6
Wheeler, Cameron, 2Y Fr.	0	0	5.40	6	0	0	6.2	8	1	5

19. FLORIDA
Coach: Kevin O'Sullivan. **Record:** 38-22

Player, Pos., Year	AVG	OBP	SLG	AB	R	2B	3B	HR	RBI	SB
Acton, Cory, 2B, 3Y So.	.250	.438	.283	60	10	2	0	0	10	3
Armstrong, Kris, DH, 3Y So.	.289	.352	.535	142	23	9	1	8	30	0
Butler, Jordan, 1B, 4Y Jr.	.248	.321	.338	145	22	10	0	1	16	1
Calilao, Kendrick, 1B, 3Y So.	.274	.351	.434	113	22	1	1	5	19	0
Carrion, Joran, SS, Fr.	.244	.309	.279	86	15	0	0	1	8	4
Edge, Brock, OF, 4Y Jr.	.000	.000	.000	4	1	0	0	0	0	0
Fabian, Jud, CF, 3Y So.	.249	.364	.560	225	51	10	0	20	46	6
Greenfield, Cal, C, 4Y Jr.	.136	.240	.136	22	3	0	0	0	2	0
Guscette, Mac, C, Fr.	.298	.364	.351	57	10	3	0	0	9	0
Halter, Colby, 2B, Fr.	.302	.379	.453	159	31	11	2	3	32	1
Hickey, Nathan, C, 2Y Fr.	.317	.435	.522	224	40	15	2	9	50	1
Langford, Wyatt, C/1B, Fr.	.250	.250	.250	4	0	0	0	0	0	0
McMullen, Kirby, 3B, 4Y Sr.	.254	.347	.453	181	24	9	0	9	36	1
Rivera, Josh, SS, 2Y Fr.	.253	.324	.389	190	30	9	1	5	26	0
Thompson, Sterlin, RF, Fr.	.301	.396	.470	183	39	10	3	5	27	2
Young, Jacob, LF, 3Y So.	.315	.385	.461	254	56	16	3	5	41	13

Pitcher, Year	W	L	ERA	G	GS	SV	IP	H	BB	SO
Aleman, Franco, 3Y So.	2	4	5.74	23	9	4	69	75	21	65
Barco, Hunter, 2Y Fr.	10	3	4.01	16	16	0	83	77	26	94
Butler, Jordan, 4Y Jr.	1	1	7.71	7	0	0	7	6	4	9
Cabarcas, Ryan, 2Y Fr.	0	0	6.75	12	0	1	9.1	12	6	9
Carrion, Jordan, Fr.	0	0	0.00	7	0	1	6.2	4	3	8
Centala, Chase, Fr.	2	0	2.13	7	1	0	12.2	10	7	9
Leftwich, Jack, 4Y Jr.	7	4	3.36	24	6	5	69.2	54	22	78
Luethje, David, 3Y So.	0	0	1.50	11	0	0	12	6	7	7
Mace, Tommy, 4Y Jr.	6	2	4.38	16	15	1	90.1	91	21	113
Manning, Timmy, Fr.	0	0	6.60	8	4	0	15	13	13	16
Milchin, Garrett, 3Y Jr.	2	1	4.99	6	6	0	21.2	24	3	20
Mink, Hunter, 2Y Fr.	0	0	0.00	3	0	0	4	3	3	6
Scott, Christian, 3Y So.	4	2	3.00	26	1	2	54	46	9	51
Specht, Ben, 3Y So.	0	2	13.87	8	0	1	12.1	18	5	6
Sproat, Brandon, 2Y Fr.	2	1	6.65	16	2	0	21.2	29	15	18
Van Der Weide, Trey, 5Y Sr.	2	2	2.74	25	0	2	42.2	42	10	32

20. NEBRASKA
Coach: Will Bolt. **Record:** 34-14

Player, Pos., Year	AVG	OBP	SLG	AB	R	2B	3B	HR	RBI	SB
Acker, Joe, RF, 5Y Sr.	.283	.383	.466	191	49	15	1	6	26	7
Anderson, Max, 3B, Fr.	.332	.386	.500	184	35	8	1	7	32	3
Banjoff, Leighton, LF, 2Y Fr.	.255	.391	.345	55	12	2	0	1	7	0
Cervantes, Efrain, 3B, 3Y So.	.082	.250	.082	49	7	0	0	0	4	1
Chick, Cam, 2B, 3Y So.	.260	.387	.468	154	29	8	0	8	39	8
Everitt, Griffin, C, 3Y So.	.287	.370	.410	122	17	6	0	3	21	3
Foster, Logan, RF, 5Y Sr.	.213	.351	.295	61	7	2	0	1	10	3
Hagge, Mojo, LF, 5Y Sr.	.224	.289	.250	76	11	0	1	0	7	6
Hallmark, Jaxon, CF, 4Y Sr.	.342	.407	.546	196	48	4	3	10	23	16
Hellstrom, Gunner, C, 4Y Jr.	.158	.227	.211	19	2	1	0	0	3	0
Matthews, Brice, 2B, Fr.	.273	.381	.462	132	28	8	1	5	34	7
Roskam, Luke, 1B, 5Y Sr.	.307	.439	.527	150	36	6	0	9	38	0
Sartori, Luke, OF, 3Y So.	1.000	1.000	1.000	1	1	0	0	0	1	0
Schwellenbach, Spencer, SS, 3Y So.	.284	.403	.459	183	43	12	1	6	40	9

Player	AVG	OBP	SLG	AB	R	2B	3B	HR	RBI	SB
Steil, Jack, 1B, Fr.	.203	.282	.422	64	10	3	1	3	11	2

Pitcher, Year	W	L	ERA	G	GS	SV	IP	H	BB	SO
Bradford, Ethan, 2Y Fr.	0	0	0.00	3	0	0	3.1	1	6	3
Bragg, Braxton, 2Y Fr.	1	2	8.04	11	0	0	15.2	21	6	18
Bunz, Jake, 3Y Jr.	3	1	2.20	20	3	1	32.2	19	20	42
Diederich, Sayer, 2Y Fr.	0	0	9.00	3	0	0	2	1	2	2
Frank, Koty, 3Y So.	3	1	4.94	13	0	1	27.1	19	13	21
Freekin, Caleb, 3Y Fr.	0	0	3.18	11	0	0	11.1	10	6	13
Hallmark, Jaxon, 4Y Jr.	0	0	6.75	4	0	0	4	4	2	3
Hroch, Chance, 5Y Sr.	5	3	4.15	14	14	0	78	82	19	64
Kissack, Trey, 4Y So.	0	0	3.00	4	0	0	3	1	5	3
Martin, Tyler, 3Y So.	2	0	2.16	10	0	0	8.1	6	2	7
Mason, Quinn, 2Y Fr.	0	0	81.00	2	0	0	0.1	2	2	0
Olson, Emmett, Fr.	1	0	4.50	10	0	0	12	13	6	16
Perry, Kyle, 3Y So.	2	0	3.48	4	4	0	10.1	7	4	15
Povich, Cade, 3Y So.	6	1	3.11	15	15	0	81	74	22	88
Schanaman, Shay, 3Y So.	5	2	5.08	13	12	0	67.1	63	25	72
Schreiber, Max, 4Y Jr.	2	2	3.79	13	0	0	19	21	8	20
Schwellenbach, Spencer, 3Y So.	3	1	0.57	18	0	10	31.2	22	8	34
Wynne, Cam, 2Y Fr.	1	1	3.12	17	0	0	17.1	6	9	19

21. LOUISIANA STATE
Coach: Paul Mainieri. **Record:** 38-25

Player, Pos., Year	AVG	OBP	SLG	AB	R	2B	3B	HR	RBI	SB
Arnold, Zach, 2B, 2Y Fr.	.277	.325	.439	155	25	4	0	7	26	2
Beck, Matthew, P, 5Y Sr.	1.000	1.000	1.000	1	0	0	0	0	0	0
Beloso, Cade, 1B, 3Y So.	.226	.347	.354	164	21	10	1	3	29	0
Bianco, Drew, 2B, 3Y So.	.246	.378	.449	118	24	3	0	7	21	7
Cranford, Collier, 2B, 2Y Fr.	.106	.192	.128	47	7	1	0	0	4	0
Crews, Dylan, RF, Fr.	.362	.453	.663	246	64	16	2	18	42	12
DiGiacomo, Giovanni, CF, 3Y So.	.293	.330	.414	99	17	4	1	2	16	5
Doughty, Braden, C, 4Y Jr.	.211	.318	.316	19	3	0	1	0	4	0
Doughty, Cade, 3B, 2Y Fr.	.300	.368	.546	227	41	11	2	13	55	1
Drost, Brody, CF, Fr.	.226	.327	.440	84	14	3	0	5	14	1
Dugas, Gavin, LF, 3Y So.	.295	.407	.641	220	54	13	3	19	66	1
Hampton, Jr., Maurice, LF, 3Y So.	.500	.600	.750	4	3	1	0	0	1	0
Hellmers, Will, INF, Fr.	.000	.143	.000	6	0	0	0	0	0	0
Milazzo, Alex, C, 2Y Fr.	.135	.220	.183	126	13	4	1	0	7	0
Morgan, Tre, 1B, Fr.	.357	.441	.526	249	64	16	4	6	42	15
Safford, Will, CF, Fr.	.086	.273	.086	35	8	0	0	0	1	2
Sanford, Mitchell, CF, 2Y Fr.	.268	.325	.366	71	13	2	1	1	11	1
Thompson, Jordan, SS, Fr.	.250	.324	.392	212	32	4	1	8	26	5
Travinski, Hayden, C, 2Y Fr.	.271	.390	.542	48	10	1	0	4	13	0
Wyeth, Jake, C, 3Y So.	.118	.179	.176	34	1	2	0	0	6	0

Pitcher, Year	W	L	ERA	G	GS	SV	IP	H	BB	SO
Beck, Matthew, 5Y Sr.	0	0	0.00	3	0	0	3	1	4	3
Brady, Alex, 2Y Fr.	1	0	9.00	12	0	0	8	8	5	8
Coleman, Javen, Fr.	3	2	5.79	14	2	0	32.2	32	18	43
Edwards, Garrett, Fr.	2	2	3.41	24	2	4	37	36	13	34
Floyd, Ty, Fr.	0	2	4.44	20	0	0	24.1	17	14	39
Fontenot, Devin, 4Y Jr.	4	2	2.86	26	0	5	34.2	18	21	40
Fowler, Michael, Fr.	1	0	6.52	14	0	0	19.1	18	13	19
George, Aaron, 3Y So.	0	0	2.79	14	0	0	9.2	10	11	11
Hasty, Jacob, 2Y Fr.	0	1	4.24	19	0	0	17	21	9	15
Hellmers, Will, Fr.	6	2	4.08	18	9	0	39.2	35	17	36
Hill, Jaden, 3Y So.	2	3	6.67	7	7	0	29.2	29	12	25
Hilliard, MaKhail, 4Y Jr.	6	0	4.31	21	8	0	54.1	46	12	53
Kaminer, Brandon, 4Y Jr.	0	0	10.39	7	0	0	4.1	11	3	2
Labas, A.J., 4Y So.	4	2	5.55	16	15	0	86	104	17	74
Marceaux, Landon, 3Y So.	7	7	2.54	18	17	0	102.2	92	26	116
Millas, Theo, Fr.	1	0	3.00	11	0	0	15	13	4	6
Money, Blake, Fr.	1	2	8.68	15	2	0	28	39	10	28
Murray, Zachary, Fr.	0	0	0.00	2	0	0	1	1	2	0
Vietmeier, Trent, 4Y Jr.	0	0	3.93	21	1	0	18.1	15	5	16

22. LOUISIANA TECH
Coach: Lane Burroughs. **Record:** 42-20

PLAYER, POS., YEAR	AVG	OBP	SLG	AB	R	2B	3B	HR	RBI	SB
Bates, Parker, CF, 5Y Sr.	.346	.471	.583	228	64	13	4	11	62	1
Brantley, Ben, 1B, 2Y Fr.	.228	.330	.304	92	9	4	0	1	17	0
Corona, Jorge, C, 2Y Fr.	.269	.377	.401	167	26	7	0	5	29	0
Crigger, Kyle, 3B, 4Y Jr.	.000	.200	.000	4	1	0	0	0	0	0
Garcia, Manny, 1B, 5Y Sr.	.309	.376	.522	230	37	20	1	9	53	2

Player, Pos., Year	AVG	OBP	SLG	AB	R	2B	3B	HR	RBI	SB
Hasler, Kyle, C, 2Y Fr.	.230	.324	.393	61	12	1	0	3	12	0
Matulia, Philip, RF, 3Y So.	.311	.402	.521	167	35	7	2	8	37	3
McConnell, Cole, LF, 2Y Fr.	.347	.399	.503	167	38	12	1	4	30	4
McLeod, Logan, SS, 2Y Fr.	.176	.364	.294	17	5	2	0	0	1	0
Myers, Adarius, LF, 3Y Fr.	.244	.294	.422	45	8	2	0	2	11	1
Netterville, Steele, RF, 4Y Jr.	.283	.394	.572	180	45	14	1	12	57	0
Page, Shemar, INF, 4Y Fr.	.162	.200	.189	37	1	1	0	0	3	0
Ray, Alex, SS, 4Y Jr.	.255	.302	.293	188	26	7	0	0	19	1
Slaughter, Jackson, C, 2Y Fr.	.500	.500	.750	4	1	1	0	0	0	0
Wallace, Bryce, 1B, 3Y Fr.	.143	.250	.143	7	2	0	0	0	1	0
Wells, Hunter, 3B, 6Y Sr.	.385	.456	.645	262	70	20	3	14	61	1
Young, Taylor, 2B, 4Y Jr.	.331	.454	.504	242	83	19	1	7	36	10

Pitcher, Year	W	L	ERA	G	GS	SV	IP	H	BB	SO
Bales, Bryson, 2Y Fr.	0	0	13.5	3	0	0	1.1	1	3	1
Crigger, Kyle, 4Y Jr.	4	2	3.47	19	0	5	36.1	35	9	29
Ellis, Nick, 3Y So.	0	0	9.60	15	0	0	15	24	13	12
Fagan, Bryce, 5Y Sr.	0	0	0.00	2	0	0	1.1	1	0	3
Fincher, Jonathan, 4Y So.	8	3	3.05	17	16	0	100.1	80	23	85
Follis, Tyler, 5Y Sr.	1	1	6.75	17	0	2	9.1	11	10	6
Gibson, Cade, 5Y Jr.	4	3	6.41	23	11	0	71.2	95	19	66
Griffen, Kyle, 5Y Fr.	3	2	9.59	27	1	1	25.1	36	13	13
Hodges, Cade, 3Y So.	0	0	5.00	8	1	0	9	9	5	10
Jennings, Ryan, 4Y Fr.	5	4	4.48	17	16	0	84.1	88	26	73
Knight, Tanner, 3Y So.	0	0	2.53	11	0	0	10.2	11	7	12
Kreger, Wesley, Fr.	0	0	6.75	5	0	0	5.1	6	4	3
Martinez, Greg, 2Y Fr.	4	1	7.99	21	2	0	32.2	52	14	35
Ouellette, Casey, 2Y Fr.	1	0	5.19	11	0	2	8.2	7	7	11
Tomkins, Landon, 3Y Sr.	3	2	5.46	20	0	5	28	22	17	28
Whorff, Jarret, 4Y Jr.	9	2	4.00	16	15	0	83.1	89	30	67

23. SOUTHERN MISSISSIPPI
Coach: Scott Berry. **Record:** 40-21

Player, Pos., Year	AVG	OBP	SLG	AB	R	2B	3B	HR	RBI	SB
Crosby, Cade, 2B, 3Y Fr.	.100	.182	.100	10	0	0	0	0	1	0
Dickerson, Dustin, SS, 2Y Fr.	.279	.364	.376	197	39	11	1	2	20	2
Ewing, Reece, RF, 3Y So.	.250	.383	.403	176	32	7	1	6	25	0
Faust, Brady, INF, 2Y Fr.	.200	.167	.800	5	7	0	0	1	2	2
Fischer, Charlie, INF, 2Y Fr.	.304	.467	.491	171	29	11	0	7	37	0
Garrity, Billy, CF, 2Y Fr.	.053	.240	.211	19	5	0	0	1	3	0
Johnson, Blake, C, 3Y So.	.246	.340	.351	134	19	5	0	3	20	1
Lynch, D.J., 3B, 3Y So.	.320	.396	.571	203	41	11	2	12	36	2
McGillis, Will, 2B, 4Y So.	.236	.362	.503	191	40	12	3	11	35	4
Montenegro, Gabe, LF, 5Y Jr.	.345	.439	.504	238	50	24	1	4	29	6
Norris, Fisher, INF, 3Y Fr.	.333	.429	.333	6	0	0	0	0	0	0
Sargent, Christopher, 1B, 3Y So.	.227	.295	.483	238	41	11	1	16	57	2
Stanley, Andrew, C, 3Y Fr.	.203	.243	.297	64	11	3	0	1	8	1
Trimble, Reed, CF, 2Y Fr.	.345	.414	.638	235	59	14	2	17	72	12
Wein, Michael, 3B, 3Y So.	.152	.317	.212	33	6	2	0	0	2	0
Wilks, Slade, RF, Fr.	.158	.262	.351	57	6	3	1	2	8	0

Pitcher, Year	W	L	ERA	G	GS	SV	IP	H	BB	SO
Adams, Matthew, 2Y Fr.	0	1	5.06	12	0	0	10.2	12	5	14
Best, Chandler, 2Y Fr.	2	1	5.50	12	1	0	18	22	6	22
Boyd, Drew, 4Y So.	4	2	4.21	13	13	0	57.2	60	8	56
Carroll, Cody, 5Y Sr.	0	0	6.00	8	0	0	6	7	2	3
Dickerson, Dustin, 2Y Fr.	0	1	40.50	1	0	0	0.2	4	1	1
Ethridge, Ben, 5Y Jr.	6	2	3.25	16	14	0	74.2	65	13	82
Gillentine, Aubrey, 3Y So.	1	1	5.50	15	0	1	18	16	3	11
Hall, Tanner, Fr.	1	1	5.02	18	1	1	28.2	24	6	32
Lantz, Tyler, 4Y Jr.	0	0	3.86	4	0	0	2.1	5	3	1
Och, Ryan, 4Y So.	8	0	1.27	21	0	2	35.1	26	12	59
Powell, Walker, 6Y Sr.	10	2	2.31	15	14	0	89.2	76	18	86
Ramsey, Garrett, 3Y So.	0	1	4.50	17	0	9	14	12	13	20
Rhodes, Isaiah, 2Y Fr.	0	0	0.00	2	0	0	1	0	0	3
Shepard, Gabe, 3Y So.	0	1	81.00	3	1	0	0.2	4	6	2
Stanley, Hunter, 5Y Sr.	6	4	2.56	16	15	0	102	74	19	127
Storm, Justin, Fr.	0	0	4.66	12	0	0	9.2	8	5	10
Stuart, Tyler, 3Y Fr.	0	2	7.16	13	0	0	16.1	16	7	9
Waldrep, Hurston, Fr.	1	0	3.31	11	0	3	16.1	13	8	16
Wehunt, Blake, 2Y Fr.	1	2	15.12	11	2	0	8.1	14	3	10

24. UCLA
Coach: John Savage. **Record:** 37-20

Player, Pos., Year	AVG	OBP	SLG	AB	R	2B	3B	HR	RBI	SB
Beres, Tommy, C, 2Y Fr.	.143	.250	.143	7	1	0	0	0	0	0
Cardenas, Noah, C, 3Y So.	.268	.371	.404	213	42	12	1	5	32	2
Caulfield, Pat, LF, 4Y Jr.	.286	.402	.414	70	15	3	0	2	16	4
Cuellar, Kyle, LF, 5Y Sr.	.289	.409	.398	128	21	5	0	3	25	1
Curialle, Michael, RF, 2Y Fr.	.285	.366	.409	186	29	14	3	1	36	3
Dean, Emanuel, LF, 2Y Fr.	.292	.346	.375	24	1	0	1	0	6	0
Filby, Jack, 1B, 3Y So.	.188	.451	.271	48	10	1	0	1	12	1
Hahn, Josh, OF, 2Y Fr.	.250	.377	.430	100	17	4	1	4	26	1
Karros, Kyle, 3B, Fr.	.243	.292	.342	202	34	9	1	3	25	1
Kendall, Kevin, CF, 4Y Jr.	.356	.413	.498	247	58	17	3	4	37	10
McLain, Matt, SS, 3Y Jr.	.333	.434	.579	183	47	14	2	9	36	9
Moberg, Jake, 3B, 3Y So.	.297	.449	.432	37	7	2	0	1	10	0
Perez, Mikey, 2B, 3Y So.	.231	.347	.448	212	52	13	0	11	38	4
Perry, Darius, C, 2Y Fr.	.333	.600	.333	3	1	0	0	0	0	0
Reyes, Daylen, INF, Fr.	.200	.429	.200	10	3	0	0	0	1	0
Schwartz, J.T., 1B, 3Y So.	.396	.514	.628	164	44	12	1	8	45	1
Silva, Jarron, LF, 5Y Sr.	.288	.397	.318	66	12	2	0	0	12	2
Vaughns, Jon Jon, CF, Fr.	.239	.370	.537	67	19	5	0	5	14	1
Yates, Carson, LF, Fr.	.136	.208	.227	22	3	0	1	0	2	0

Pitcher, Year	W	L	ERA	G	GS	SV	IP	H	BB	SO
Bergin, Jesse, 3Y So.	6	4	4.18	16	16	0	79.2	85	23	65
Brooks, Jake, Fr.	2	0	5.31	16	3	0	20.1	22	6	18
Chaidez, Adrian, 4Y Fr.	3	0	2.20	30	0	0	32.2	14	17	48
Colwell, Daniel, 3Y So.	2	1	4.33	26	0	0	27	29	8	23
Filby, Jack, 3Y So.	0	0	9.00	7	0	0	7	10	4	4
Hahn, Josh, 2Y Fr.	0	0	6.75	2	0	0	1.1	2	0	2
Harrison, Charles, 2Y Fr.	0	0	3.55	16	0	0	12.2	13	3	12
Karros, Jared, 2Y Fr.	2	1	3.33	7	3	0	27	21	5	32
Mora, Kyle, 5Y Sr.	2	2	4.81	21	1	1	24.1	27	12	21
Mullen, Sean, 3Y So.	9	1	3.39	23	13	2	77	65	38	89
Nastrini, Nick, 3Y So.	2	2	6.89	12	7	0	31.1	19	38	48
Pettway, Zach, 4Y Jr.	3	5	4.56	15	14	0	79	76	16	74
Rajcic, Max, Fr.	2	1	1.65	24	0	7	32.2	23	8	36
Saum, Jake, 2Y Fr.	2	2	3.15	17	0	1	20	16	3	23
Townsend, Michael, 4Y Jr.	2	1	3.75	36	0	0	36	38	9	35

25. SOUTH FLORIDA
Coach: Billy Mohl. **Record:** 31-30

Player, Pos., Year	AVG	OBP	SLG	AB	R	2B	3B	HR	RBI	SB
Besnier, Dillon, RF, 2Y Fr.	.067	.067	.067	15	3	0	0	0	0	0
Brutcher, Drew, CF, Fr.	.294	.421	.546	119	25	6	0	8	17	6
Cantu, Daniel, RF, 2Y Fr.	.255	.379	.453	192	41	10	2	8	36	2
Collier, Cam, OF, Fr.	.200	.333	.200	5	2	0	0	0	0	0
Cortez, Julio, C, 3Y So.	.225	.257	.235	102	5	1	0	0	11	0
Eaton, Jarrett, LF, 3Y So.	.276	.366	.357	98	14	8	0	0	11	5
Gonzalez, Nick, SS, 3Y So.	.221	.286	.258	213	24	2	0	2	26	5
Hogan, Riley, 1B, 5Y Sr.	.292	.391	.504	236	41	12	1	12	40	1
Jacobs-Guishard, Keanu, INF, Fr.	.556	.556	.889	9	1	0	0	1	5	0
Lane, Carmine, 3B, 2Y Fr.	.306	.361	.496	248	44	14	0	11	43	1
Mitchell, Dontae, CF, 2Y Fr.	.158	.190	.158	19	3	0	0	0	3	0
Monque, Joaquin, LF, Fr.	.254	.377	.254	63	7	0	0	0	9	1
Pena, Roberto, 2B, 3Y So.	.236	.362	.476	225	39	12	3	12	40	7
Rivera, Nelson, C, Fr.	.263	.362	.313	99	15	5	0	0	12	2
Ruiz, Matt, 3B, Fr.	.265	.385	.386	223	39	15	3	2	22	8
Sullivan, Jake, C, 5Y Jr.	.256	.320	.307	176	18	6	0	1	22	0

Pitcher, Year	W	L	ERA	G	GS	SV	IP	H	BB	SO
Barr, Dawson, 4Y Jr.	0	0	1.50	5	2	0	6	7	7	8
Burns, Dylan, 6Y Sr.	5	5	4.33	18	10	0	77	72	34	84
Churchill, Connor, 4Y Jr.	1	0	7.36	12	0	0	11	12	7	10
Hemenway, Devin, Fr.	0	0	4.77	13	1	0	11.1	12	8	16
Jasiak, Jack, 2Y Fr.	6	7	2.93	16	16	0	98.1	76	23	93
Kerkering, Orion, 2Y Fr.	5	3	2.88	25	1	5	50	39	35	62
Lord, Brad, 3Y So.	3	5	4.77	17	11	1	62.1	68	18	63
Lozado, Alex, 2Y Fr.	0	0	3.18	5	0	0	5.2	5	1	2
Lyle, Logan, 5Y Sr.	5	1	1.99	26	0	4	45.1	31	17	46
Mink, Tanner, Fr.	0	1	7.71	17	0	1	11.2	13	15	13
Pundsack, Caleb, Fr.	0	0	7.27	10	0	0	8.2	10	9	7
Sanchez, Joseph, 5Y Sr.	0	2	4.77	19	1	1	34	29	3	23
Stuart, Baron, 4Y Jr.	3	2	6.62	17	3	1	35.1	32	23	34
Sullivan, Collin, 5Y Jr.	3	4	4.07	17	16	0	79.2	90	16	90
Wynja, Hayden, Fr.	0	0	27.00	2	0	0	2	4	3	2

CONFERENCE STANDINGS & LEADERS

NCAA regional teams in bold. Conference category leaders in bold.
*Team won conference's automatic regional bid. #Category leader who did not qualify for batting or pitching title.

AMERICA EAST CONFERENCE

	Conference		Overall	
	W	L	W	L
Division A				
Albany	20	18	22	25
Maine	16	17	22	22
Massachusetts-Lowell	18	20	19	28
Hartford	18	20	18	20
Division B				
Stony Brook	25	10	31	18
NJIT	23	17	27	24
Binghamton	16	20	16	20
Maryland-Baltimore County	12	26	17	26

ALL-CONFERENCE TEAM: C: Jon Tuccillo, Sr., Stony Brook. **1B:** Chris Hamilton, Gr., Stony Brook. **2B:** Johnny Marti, Jr., Albany. **3B:** Evan Giordano, Jr., Stony Brook. **SS:** Brad Malm, Jr., Albany. **OF:** John Thrasher, Sr., Hartford; Sean Lawlor, Sr., Maine; Albert Choi, So., NJIT. **DH:** Jimmy Sullivan, Fr., Massachusetts-Lowell. **UTL:** Julio Marcano, Sr., NJIT. **SP:** Nicholas Sinacola, Jr., Maine; Nick DeGennaro, Jr., Stony Brook; Thomas Babalis, So., Binghamton; Nicholas Dombkowski, Sr., Hartford. **RP:** Jake Rappaport, Sr., NJIT. **Player of the Year:** John Thrasher, Sr., Hartford. **Pitcher of the Year:** Nicholas Sinacola, Jr., Maine. **Coach of the Year:** Jon Mueller, Albany. **Rookie of the Year:** Albert Choi, So., NJIT.

INDIVIDUAL BATTING LEADERS
(Minimum 140 at-bats)

Player	AVG	OBP	SLG	AB	2B	3B	HR	RBI	SB
Sean Lawlor, Maine	.350	.428	.554	157	9	1	7	37	0
John Marti, Albany (NY)	.349	.422	.592	169	12	4	7	41	11
Brad Malm, Albany (NY)	.345	.415	.546	174	21	1	4	39	5
Vinnie Martin, UMass Lowell	.338	.451	.430	151	9	1	1	15	2
John LaRocca, Stony Brook	.329	.429	.487	158	10	3	3	23	18
Julio Marcano, NJIT	.322	.425	.567	180	12	1	10	42	7
Chris Hamilton, Stony Brook	.319	.381	.494	166	16	2	3	34	2
Daniel Franchi, Binghamton	.314	.370	.493	140	11	4	2	15	8
Evan Giordano, Stony Brook	.314	.412	.515	169	11	1	7	39	7
Albert Choi, NJIT	.311	.389	.515	196	12	5	6	36	27
Scout Knotts, Maine	.295	.403	.462	156	8	3	4	21	9
Joe Bramanti, Maine	.293	.374	.460	150	7	0	6	28	3
Daniel Helfgott, NJIT	.292	.416	.325	154	5	0	0	18	1
Connor Goodman, Maine	.287	.364	.333	174	8	0	0	18	3
Cam Climo, UMass Lowell	.285	.390	.583	151	13	1	10	39	1
Brett Paulsen, Stony Brook	.278	.335	.319	144	4	1	0	25	6
Quinn McDaniel, Maine	.268	.349	.458	153	9	1	6	20	2
Robert Gallagher, UMass Lowell	.266	.384	.427	143	5	3	4	21	19
John Tuccillo, Stony Brook	.261	.325	.411	180	9	0	6	34	10
Jason Bottari, Albany (NY)	.258	.340	.282	163	2	1	0	28	26
Dolan Ocasal, Albany (NY)	.252	.358	.314	159	8	1	0	13	9
John Daly, Albany (NY)	.248	.384	.383	141	4	3	3	22	14
Cedric Rose, UMass Lowell	.248	.315	.416	149	10	0	5	22	2
Nick Hussey, NJIT	.243	.328	.325	169	7	2	1	21	3
Paul Franzoni, NJIT	.236	.375	.424	144	7	1	6	18	3
Joey Castellanos, UMass Lowell	.221	.283	.355	172	5	6	2	23	0
Marc Wangenstein, Albany (NY)	.212	.320	.404	146	7	3	5	18	5

INDIVIDUAL PITCHING LEADERS
(Minimum 40 innings pitched)

Player	W	L	ERA	G	SV	IP	H	BB	SO
Nicholas Sinacola, Maine	9	3	2.04	12	0	79.1	59	23	139
Ryan Fischer, NJIT	5	3	2.64	14	0	81.2	72	15	53
Tommy Babalis, Binghamton	4	4	2.86	10	0	56.2	43	20	62
Sam Turcotte, Stony Brook	6	3	2.93	12	0	67.2	60	26	66
Jared Milch, Stony Brook	6	4	3.04	13	0	74	64	21	63
Nicholas Dombkowski, Hartford	4	3	3.13	10	0	60.1	42	27	72
Nick DeGennaro, Stony Brook	8	3	3.14	14	0	77.1	66	27	92
Joshua Becker, UMass Lowell	5	4	3.52	11	0	64	53	20	51
Brian Herrmann, Stony Brook	4	3	3.58	14	0	73	70	28	58
Jake Rappaport, NJIT	8	2	3.63	28	11	52	48	14	35

ECU righthander Gavin Williams solidified himself as a first-round pick in 2021.

Alex McKenney, Maine	4	6	3.67	17	0	56.1	43	23	43
Ray Weber, Albany (NY)	7	2	3.69	13	0	83	76	34	46
Cam Seguin, UMass Lowell	5	2	3.78	12	0	47.2	51	18	36
Anthony Germinerio, Albany (NY)	3	5	3.97	11	0	59	57	17	54
Jack Collins, Binghamton	3	3	3.98	10	0	52	42	30	46

AMERICAN ATHLETIC CONFERENCE

	Conference		Overall	
	W	L	W	L
East Carolina	20	8	44	17
Tulane	17	10	31	24
Wichita State	18	13	31	23
Cincinnati	18	14	29	26
Central Florida	18	14	31	30
South Florida	14	14	31	30
Houston	7	21	19	34
Memphis	7	25	18	39

ALL-CONFERENCE TEAM: C: Hunter Goodman, So., Memphis; Bennett Lee, Fr., Tulane. **1B:** Garrett Kocis, Jr., Wichita State. **2B:** Connor Norby, So., East Carolina. **3B:** Paxton Wallace, Jr., Wichita State. **SS:** Collin Burns, R-So., Tulane. **OF:** Jordan Rathbone, R-Sr., Central Florida; Corrigan Bartlett, Sr., Wichita State; Paul Komistek, Jr., Cincinnati. **DH:** Josh Moylan, Fr., East Carolina. **SP:** Gavin Williams, Jr., East Carolina; Garrett Schoenle, Sr., Cincinnati; Robert Gasser, Jr., Houston. **RP:** Aaron Haase, So., Wichita State. **Player of the Year:** Connor Norby, So., East Carolina. **Pitcher of the Year:** Gavin Williams, Jr., East Carolina. **Coach of the Year:** Cliff Godwin, East Carolina. **Newcomer Position Player of the Year:** Bennett Lee, Fr., Tulane. **Newcomer Pitcher of the Year:** Jace Kaminska, Fr., Wichita State.

INDIVIDUAL BATTING LEADERS
(Minimum 140 at-bats)

Player	AVG	OBP	SLG	AB	2B	3B	HR	RBI	SB
Connor Norby, East Carolina	.415	.484	.659	246	15	0	15	51	18
Paul Komistek, Cincinnati	.364	.459	.599	162	11	0	9	44	2
Thomas Francisco, East Carolina	.354	.416	.557	246	11	0	13	48	4
Collin Burns, Tulane	.353	.410	.571	238	20	4	8	50	20
Corrigan Bartlett, Wichita St.	.345	.403	.515	200	9	2	7	48	8
Jace Mercer, Cincinnati	.340	.440	.545	209	12	2	9	34	22

Paxton Wallace, Wichita St.	.322	.383	.553	208	11	2	11	49	5
Jack Sigrist, Wichita St.	.321	.390	.470	215	14	3	4	25	15
Josh Crouch, UCF	.311	.435	.574	209	10	0	15	36	0
Josh Moylan, East Carolina	.310	.409	.460	187	8	1	6	38	0
Hunter Goodman, Memphis	.307	.401	.678	202	10	1	21	51	9
Carmine Lane, South Fla.	.306	.361	.496	248	14	0	11	43	1
Joey Bellini, Cincinnati	.304	.361	.417	230	12	1	4	47	4
Tyler Bielamowicz, Houston	.301	.395	.458	166	6	1	6	24	6
Chase Engelhard, Tulane	.299	.361	.490	204	10	1	9	52	11
Jordan Rathbone, UCF	.298	.401	.555	238	9	2	16	54	8
Eric Santiago, Cincinnati	.298	.344	.465	228	17	0	7	26	9
Alec Makarewicz, East Carolina	.295	.356	.464	183	9	2	6	33	2
Riley Hogan, South Fla.	.292	.391	.504	236	12	1	12	40	1
Ryan Nicholson, Cincinnati	.291	.384	.412	165	3	1	5	32	5
Gephry Pena, UCF	.290	.405	.407	214	9	2	4	26	27
Hunter Gibson, Wichita St.	.289	.410	.487	152	7	1	7	33	2
Cole Harting, Cincinnati	.289	.373	.521	211	11	4	10	34	15
Alex Freeland, UCF	.288	.402	.429	219	10	0	7	37	3
Ryan Hernandez, Houston	.287	.345	.497	181	5	0	11	37	0
Couper Cornblum, Wichita St.	.285	.368	.380	158	5	5	0	24	12
Jacob LaPrairie, Tulane	.285	.415	.358	151	8	0	1	26	5
Jared Hart, Tulane	.277	.330	.340	188	7	1	1	23	11
John Montes, UCF	.275	.326	.389	167	10	0	3	29	3
Ross Cadena, Wichita St.	.274	.359	.403	186	14	2	2	26	1

INDIVIDUAL PITCHING LEADERS
(Minimum 40 innings pitched)

Player	W	L	ERA	G	SV	IP	H	BB	SO
Gavin Williams, East Carolina	10	1	1.88	15	1	81.1	57	21	130
Logan Lyle, South Fla.	5	1	1.99	26	4	45.1	31	17	46
Ben Vespi, UCF	1	1	2.08	24	1	47.2	38	20	46
Jace Kaminska, Wichita St.	8	1	2.32	12	0	62	51	19	51
Cam Colmore, East Carolina	7	1	2.41	32	2	52.1	41	17	60
Robert Gasser, Houston	6	6	2.63	14	0	85.2	67	25	105
Evan Shawver, Cincinnati	3	1	2.72	9	0	46.1	38	16	49
Colton Gordon, UCF	5	2	2.77	9	0	55.1	54	13	72
Derrick Cherry, Houston	2	3	2.85	26	5	41	36	21	44
Orion Kerkering, South Fla.	5	3	2.88	25	5	50	39	35	62
Jack Jasiak, South Fla.	6	7	2.93	17	0	98.1	76	23	93
C.J. Mayhue, East Carolina	3	1	3.06	34	8	50	44	21	76
Zack Hunsicker, UCF	2	3	3.38	22	1	45.1	36	22	36
Billy McKay, UCF	2	3	3.54	29	1	40.2	32	30	42
Jack Aldrich, Tulane	5	3	3.70	14	0	82.2	82	23	96

ATLANTIC COAST CONFERENCE

Atlantic Division	Conference		Overall	
	W	L	W	L
Notre Dame	25	10	34	13
North Carolina State	19	14	37	19
Florida State	20	16	31	24
Louisville	16	16	28	22
Clemson	16	20	25	27
Wake Forest	10	22	22	23
Boston College	10	23	21	28

Coastal Division	Conference		Overall	
	W	L	W	L
Georgia Tech	21	15	31	25
Miami	20	15	33	21
Virginia	18	18	36	27
North Carolina	18	18	28	27
Duke	16	17	33	22
Pittsburgh	16	17	23	20
Virginia Tech	16	20	27	25

ALL-CONFERENCE TEAM: C: Mat Nelson, R-So., Florida State; Henry Davis, So., Louisville. **1B:** NIko Kavadas, Sr., Notre Dame. **2B:** Cody Morissette, Jr., Boston College. **3B:** Luke Gold, So., Boston College. **SS:** Luke Waddell, Jr., Georgia Tech; Jose Torres, R-Fr., North Carolina State. **OF:** Sal Frelick, Jr., Boston College; Jonny Butler, So., North Carolina State; Gavin Cross, Fr., Virginia Tech. **DH:** Terrell Tatum, Jr., North Carolina State. **SP:** Parker Messick, R-Fr., Florida State; Austin Love, So., North Carolina; John Michael Bertrand, Gr., Notre Dame; Andrew Abbott, Sr., Virginia. **RP:** Carson Palmquist, Fr., Miami. **Player of the Year:** Mat Nelson, R-So., Florida State. **Pitcher of the Year:** Parker Messick, R-Fr., Florida State.

Defensive Player of the Year: Sal Frelick, Jr., Boston College. **Coach of the Year:** Link Jarrett, Notre Dame. **Rookie of the Year:** Parker Messick, Fr., Florida State.

INDIVIDUAL BATTING LEADERS
(Minimum 140 at-bats)

Player	AVG	OBP	SLG	AB	2B	3B	HR	RBI	SB
Jonny Butler, NC State	.376	.452	.663	202	12	2	14	53	16
Joey Loperfido, Duke	.374	.473	.612	206	19	3	8	29	12
Henry Davis, Louisville	.370	.482	.663	184	9	0	15	48	10
Christian Del Castillo, Miami (FL)	.369	.439	.495	198	11	1	4	40	7
Sky Duff, Pittsburgh	.366	.461	.524	164	18	1	2	19	4
Sal Frelick, Boston College	.359	.443	.559	195	17	2	6	27	13
Gavin Cross, Virginia Tech	.345	.415	.621	203	13	5	11	35	9
Tyler McDonough, NC State	.339	.423	.631	233	21	1	15	45	13
R.J. Schreck, Duke	.337	.435	.635	208	8	0	18	52	11
Ryan Cole, Notre Dame	.336	.455	.586	152	9	1	9	34	7
Kyle Teel, Virginia	.335	.416	.526	209	11	1	9	41	5
Matheu Nelson, Florida St.	.330	.436	.773	194	17	0	23	66	4
James Parker, Clemson	.324	.411	.500	210	13	0	8	38	1
Angel Zarate, North Carolina	.324	.424	.497	179	7	3	6	32	3
Cody Morissette, Boston College	.321	.398	.497	165	9	1	6	33	8
Luke Brown, Louisville	.320	.381	.422	206	13	4	0	20	17
Austin Murr, NC State	.319	.376	.504	232	16	3	7	32	6
Kevin Parada, Georgia Tech	.318	.379	.550	220	20	2	9	42	1
Caden Grice, Clemson	.317	.427	.618	186	9	1	15	53	2
Terrell Tatum, NC State	.317	.423	.543	186	2	2	12	36	16
Luke Gold, Boston College	.316	.364	.576	177	15	2	9	45	2
T.J. Rumfield, Virginia Tech	.315	.402	.478	203	12	0	7	37	2
Kevin Madden, Virginia Tech	.313	.361	.418	201	9	0	4	37	6
Nico Popa, Pittsburgh	.313	.381	.497	179	6	0	9	28	12
Zack Gelof, Virginia	.312	.393	.485	260	18	0	9	41	12
Trey Leonard, Virginia Tech	.312	.367	.458	144	7	1	4	25	7
Luke Waddell, Georgia Tech	.309	.402	.474	230	12	1	8	33	5
Dante Baldelli, Boston College	.308	.388	.453	159	9	1	4	27	5
Justyn-Henry Malloy, Georgia Tech	.308	.436	.558	208	17	1	11	43	4
Carter Putz, Notre Dame	.305	.369	.492	187	11	3	6	45	3

INDIVIDUAL PITCHING LEADERS
(Minimum 40 innings pitched)

Player	W	L	ERA	G	SV	IP	H	BB	SO
Carson Palmquist, Miami (FL)	1	1	2.22	15	14	44.2	22	8	75
Geoffrey Gilbert, Clemson	3	6	2.23	28	3	44.1	43	15	52
Gage Gillian, North Carolina	1	2	2.34	24	4	50	38	9	49
Jack Anderson, Florida St.	2	0	2.48	23	5	40	32	7	45
Luke Seed, Louisville	0	1	2.64	12	0	47.2	41	29	44
Aidan Tyrell, Notre Dame	5	1	2.70	17	2	60	50	19	43
Andrew Abbott, Virginia	9	6	2.87	19	0	106.2	89	32	162
Jimmy Loper, Duke	3	1	3.00	25	5	45	46	12	43
Chris Gerard, Virginia Tech	2	2	3.02	8	0	41.2	38	12	48
Luke Fox, Duke	2	2	3.05	20	0	56	59	15	76
Marcus Johnson, Duke	5	3	3.05	30	7	56	40	12	59
Tanner Kohlhepp, Notre Dame	7	2	3.08	23	2	61.1	42	22	65
Parker Messick, Florida St.	8	2	3.10	26	0	90	81	23	126
Mitch Meyers, Pittsburgh	5	5	3.21	13	0	81.1	78	23	83
John M. Bertrand, Notre Dame	8	2	3.21	15	0	92.2	82	22	68

ATLANTIC SUN CONFERENCE

	Conference		Overall	
	W	L	W	L
Liberty	19	2	41	16
Florida Gulf Coast	12	6	28	20
Kennesaw State	13	8	29	22
North Florida	11	7	22	23
Stetson	10	8	26	23
Lipscomb	8	13	18	29
Bellarmine	8	16	13	36
North Alabama	6	15	7	40
Jacksonville	3	15	16	34

ALL-CONFERENCE TEAM: C: Gray Betts, So., Liberty. **1B:** Alex Kachler, Gr., North Florida. **2B:** Will Wagner, Jr., Liberty. **3B:** Josh Finerty, Sr., Bellarmine. **SS:** Richie Garcia, Sr., Florida Gulf Coast. **OF:** Brian Ellis, So., Florida Gulf Coast; Aaron Anderson, Jr., Liberty; Hernen Sardinas, Gr., Stetson. **DH:** Garrett Hodges, Sr., Kennesaw State. **SP:** Trevor Delaite,

Sr., Liberty; Jake Rice, Gr., Kennesaw State; Nick Durgin, Fr., Stetson. **RP:** Fraser Ellard, Sr., Liberty. **Player of the Year:** Alex Kachler, Gr., North Florida. **Pitcher of the Year:** Trevor Delaite, Sr., Liberty. Defensive Player of the Year: Cam Locklear, Sr., Liberty. **Coach of the Year:** Scott Jackson, Liberty. **Rookie of the Year:** Trey Gibson, Liberty.

INDIVIDUAL BATTING LEADERS
(Minimum 140 at-bats)

Player	AVG	OBP	SLG	AB	2B	3B	HR	RBI	SB
Aaron Anderson, Liberty	.375	.460	.567	224	25	3	4	42	0
Brian Ellis, FGCU	.366	.494	.481	183	8	2	3	31	7
Alex Kachler, North Florida	.356	.450	.569	174	13	0	8	38	1
Hernen Sardinas, Stetson	.348	.427	.602	181	17	1	9	49	2
Alex Carballo, Kennesaw St.	.337	.452	.535	172	9	2	7	38	12
Will Wagner, Liberty	.333	.399	.538	210	16	3	7	52	6
Gray Betts, Liberty	.327	.434	.484	217	17	4	3	24	2
Jesse Sherrill, Kennesaw St.	.320	.411	.404	178	10	1	1	25	12
Malik Williams, Lipscomb	.320	.360	.431	153	9	1	2	23	1
Tyler Tolve, Kennesaw St.	.319	.393	.498	207	8	4	7	49	8
Jake Coro, Kennesaw St.	.310	.400	.445	155	10	1	3	25	1
Andrew MacNeil, Stetson	.310	.435	.551	187	16	4	7	33	8
Josh Finerty, Bellarmine	.304	.378	.492	191	14	2	6	26	0
Dakota Julylia, Jacksonville	.303	.342	.366	175	7	2	0	19	0
Jackson Grabsky, Jacksonville	.301	.343	.340	156	6	0	0	20	2
Clayton Mehlbauer, Bellarmine	.301	.400	.458	166	8	0	6	26	5
Garrett Hodges, Kennesaw St.	.298	.386	.482	191	11	0	8	38	1
Terence Norman, Kennesaw St.	.298	.413	.481	181	8	2	7	41	2
Blake Marabell, North Florida	.297	.351	.484	182	11	1	7	33	6
Ian Farrow, FGCU	.293	.402	.449	147	12	1	3	22	2
Ruben Someillan, Jacksonville	.293	.371	.351	208	6	0	2	19	4
Richie Garcia, FGCU	.292	.390	.443	192	9	1	6	42	6
Devne Daniel, North Ala.	.290	.362	.403	176	14	0	2	14	4
Brady Gulakowski, Liberty	.284	.349	.561	148	11	0	10	39	1
Jesus Pacheco, Jacksonville	.283	.344	.335	173	4	1	1	23	5
Drew Hudson, North Ala.	.282	.355	.401	177	13	1	2	10	13
Aidan Sweatt, North Florida	.282	.344	.384	177	14	2	0	22	3
Cam Locklear, Liberty	.278	.376	.454	216	16	2	6	31	9
Abraham Sequera, North Florida	.278	.340	.527	169	11	2	9	28	2
Tanner Clark, North Florida	.277	.367	.348	141	7	0	1	19	2

INDIVIDUAL PITCHING LEADERS
(Minimum 40 innings pitched)

Player	W	L	ERA	G	SV	IP	H	BB	SO
Jake Rice, Kennesaw St.	9	2	1.93	13	0	74.2	48	24	79
David Erickson, Liberty	8	1	2.08	25	1	47.2	25	31	52
Trevor Delaite, Liberty	12	1	2.17	16	0	107.2	84	20	88
Nick Durgin, Stetson	6	2	2.61	11	0	62	46	17	67
Jared Rine, Kennesaw St.	2	4	2.81	20	6	48	36	20	40
Mason Studstill, FGCU	7	3	3.02	13	0	83.1	70	32	73
Trey Gibson, Liberty	7	4	3.32	13	0	65	51	21	70
Austin Bogart, North Florida	4	2	3.58	44	0	70.1	79	16	39
Mason Meyer, Liberty	5	1	3.62	16	1	64.2	66	10	62
Fraser Ellard, Liberty	0	1	3.65	26	7	44.1	36	13	63
Tyler Tipton, FGCU	4	1	3.71	15	1	43.2	49	14	22
Tyler Shuck, FGCU	3	0	3.88	21	1	46.1	50	17	38
Ryan Kennedy, Kennesaw St.	8	2	4.16	14	0	71.1	77	16	56
Jovan Gill, Stetson	4	4	4.23	16	1	55.1	50	16	42
Tony Roca, North Florida	3	2	4.52	14	0	63.2	58	37	55

ATLANTIC 10 CONFERENCE

	Conference		Overall	
	W	L	W	L
North				
Rhode Island	13	6	27	26
Saint Joseph's	15	9	21	19
La Salle	15	9	32	21
Fordham	11	9	24	19
St. Bonaventure	6	14	7	24
Massachusetts	3	16	13	29
South				
Virginia Commonwealth	13	3	38	15
Dayton	13	4	25	27
George Washington	14	11	26	19
Davidson	11	13	27	24

Saint Louis	6	10	17	31
Richmond	5	11	19	17
George Mason	7	17	14	29

ALL-CONFERENCE TEAM: C: Andrew Cossetti, Jr., Saint Joseph's. **1B:** Ryan Guckin, Gr., La Salle. **2B:** Noah Levin, Jr., George Washington. **3B:** Tyler Locklear, Fr., Virginia Commonwealth. **SS:** Benjamin Blackwell, Jr., Dayton. **OF:** Domenic Boselli, Sr., George Washington; Trevor Candelaria, Jr., Davidson; Brendan Hueth, Sr., Saint Joseph's. **DH:** Marcos Pujols, Jr., Dayton. **SP:** Matt Mikulski, Sr., Fordham; Jared Lyons, Jr., George Mason. **RP:** Nolan Devos, So., Davidson. **Player of the Year:** Tyler Locklear, Fr., Virginia Commonwealth. **Pitcher of the Year:** Matt Mikulski, Sr., Fordham. **Coach of the Year:** David Miller, La Salle. **Rookie of the Year:** Tyler Locklear, Virginia Commonwealth.

INDIVIDUAL BATTING LEADERS
(Minimum 140 at-bats)

Player	AVG	OBP	SLG	AB	2B	3B	HR	RBI	SB
Brendan Hueth, Saint Joseph's	.375	.444	.542	144	11	2	3	25	5
Mariano Ricciardi, Dayton	.352	.469	.432	199	11	1	1	28	3
Benjamin Blackwell, Dayton	.349	.449	.508	189	12	0	6	31	10
Steve DiTomaso, G. Washington	.349	.438	.425	146	3	4	0	27	5
Marcos Pujols, Dayton	.346	.415	.585	188	9	0	12	53	6
Ryan Guckin, La Salle	.345	.403	.589	197	19	7	5	51	1
Tyler Locklear, VCU	.345	.515	.686	194	12	3	16	66	8
Riley Tirotta, Dayton	.337	.450	.696	181	13	2	16	58	14
Noah Levin, G. Washington	.333	.404	.519	162	8	2	6	47	4
Steven Barmakian, G. Washington	.331	.423	.446	157	14	2	0	24	9
Sonny Ulliana, Rhode Island	.331	.429	.538	169	18	1	5	35	2
Liam Hibbits, VCU	.326	.450	.456	193	13	0	4	60	3
Austin White, Rhode Island	.326	.434	.422	187	8	2	2	22	16
Cam Redding, Saint Louis	.322	.407	.537	177	14	3	6	47	1
Steven Carpenter, VCU	.320	.418	.442	181	12	2	2	38	1
Michael Haydak, VCU	.320	.443	.431	181	14	0	2	27	11
Tatem Levins, La Salle	.315	.416	.503	197	14	1	7	50	2
Hunter Vay, VCU	.314	.403	.564	156	10	1	9	39	3
Alex Fedje-Johnson, Davidson	.303	.450	.500	178	18	1	5	32	9
Colten Schild, Saint Louis	.301	.404	.368	163	7	2	0	10	3
Scott Morgan, George Mason	.300	.394	.536	140	9	3	6	27	0
Cade Fergus, G. Washington	.299	.437	.422	147	10	1	2	25	8
Nick Labella, VCU	.299	.415	.444	144	10	1	3	25	6
Connor Coolahan, La Salle	.297	.430	.348	155	8	0	0	21	4
Jason Coules, Fordham	.297	.404	.426	155	10	2	2	21	22
Domenic Boselli, G. Washington	.291	.378	.473	148	12	0	5	39	2
Josh Brodeur, Rhode Island	.289	.396	.335	173	8	0	0	19	8
Trevor Candelaria, Davidson	.285	.384	.576	172	17	0	11	32	13
Kyle Fitzgerald, Saint Louis	.285	.341	.441	179	13	0	5	37	1
Hogan Brown, VCU	.280	.409	.371	175	7	0	3	36	17

INDIVIDUAL PITCHING LEADERS
(Minimum 40 innings pitched)

Player	W	L	ERA	G	SV	IP	H	BB	SO
Matt Mikulski, Fordham	9	0	1.45	11	0	68.1	29	27	124
Jaret Edwards, G. Washington	5	4	2.93	16	0	55.1	47	24	32
Ryan Twitchell, Rhode Island	5	1	2.97	14	0	75.2	81	24	58
Colin Scanlon, La Salle	7	2	3.02	13	0	80.1	72	22	75
Bradford Webb, VCU	3	1	3.16	17	0	57	56	13	57
Mike Webb, Rhode Island	7	2	3.24	16	0	89	89	22	68
Frank Elissalt, La Salle	6	4	3.42	13	0	76.1	57	39	95
Jared Lyons, George Mason	6	2	3.73	12	0	72.1	50	38	76
Blake Hely, Davidson	4	2	3.78	11	0	64.1	52	27	61
Danny Watson, VCU	2	4	4.06	19	1	44.1	38	21	55
Evan Chenier, VCU	3	0	4.07	18	6	42	45	19	41
Trevor Harris, Saint Louis	4	4	4.32	12	0	56	61	20	46
Trystan Levesque, Rhode Island	5	2	4.37	18	1	45.1	49	10	41
Colby Wyatt, Richmond	4	2	4.38	10	0	51.1	37	21	47
Harrison Cohen, G. Washington	5	3	4.53	11	0	59.2	59	31	69

BIG EAST CONFERENCE

	Conference		Overall	
	W	L	W	L
Connecticut	13	4	34	19
Creighton	15	6	24	15
Seton Hall	16	11	23	25
Xavier	15	11	28	26

Villanova	9	12	21	14
St. John's	10	16	19	21
Butler	8	13	14	23
Georgetown	6	19	6	25

ALL-CONFERENCE TEAM: C: Jerry Huntzinger, Sr., Seton Hall; Natale Monastra, Sr., Xavier. **1B:** Matt Toke, Sr., Seton Hall. **2B:** Carson Bartels, Gr., St. John's. **3B:** Marty Higgins, RFr., St. John's. **SS:** Jack Housinger, Jr., Xavier. **OF:** Kyler Fedko, So., Connecticut; Chris Winkel, Sr., Connecticut; Erik Stock, Jr., Connecticut. **DH:** Alan Roden, Creighton. **SP:** Dylan Tebrake, So., Creighton; David Festa, Jr., Seton Hall; Nick Zwack, Sr., Xavier; Nick Mondak, RJr., St. John's. **RP:** Caleb Wurster, So., Connecticut. **Player of the Year:** Kyler Fedko, So., Connecticut. **Pitcher of the Year:** Dylan Tebrake, So., Creighton. **Coach of the Year:** Jim Penders, Connecticut. **Rookie of the Year:** Alan Roden, Creighton.

INDIVIDUAL BATTING LEADERS
(Minimum 140 at-bats)

Player	AVG	OBP	SLG	AB	2B	3B	HR	RBI	SB
Kyler Fedko, UConn	.398	.485	.673	196	14	2	12	53	7
Alan Roden, Creighton	.378	.476	.685	143	17	0	9	47	4
Erik Stock, UConn	.362	.436	.553	188	14	2	6	34	8
Andrew Walker, Xavier	.316	.407	.493	152	10	1	5	30	18
Matt Toke, Seton Hall	.310	.391	.405	168	14	1	0	31	0
Andrew Meggs, Creighton	.309	.380	.396	149	8	1	1	13	2
Casey Dana, Seton Hall	.306	.374	.512	160	12	0	7	36	3
Chris Winkel, UConn	.305	.384	.542	177	9	0	11	32	16
Jerome Huntzinger, Seton Hall	.301	.387	.366	183	10	1	0	24	24
Jack Housinger, Xavier	.297	.424	.480	175	17	0	5	28	13
Chris Brown, UConn	.296	.352	.475	162	10	2	5	38	2
Reggie Crawford, UConn	.295	.349	.543	210	11	1	13	62	2
Christian Fedko, UConn	.295	.386	.389	190	15	0	1	29	4
Nate Monastra, Xavier	.281	.386	.432	185	7	0	7	33	1
Pat Winkel, UConn	.279	.353	.515	204	13	1	11	42	2
James Gargano, Butler	.277	.360	.468	141	6	0	7	20	10
Zach Bushling, UConn	.245	.368	.380	192	8	3	4	25	9
Garrett Schultz, Xavier	.235	.349	.383	149	5	1	5	20	4
Alex Helmin, Xavier	.234	.335	.390	154	7	1	5	26	5
Ryan Hogan, St. John's (NY)	.233	.322	.327	150	11	0	1	20	8

INDIVIDUAL PITCHING LEADERS
(Minimum 40 innings pitched)

Player	W	L	ERA	G	SV	IP	H	BB	SO
Gordon Graceffo, Villanova	7	2	1.54	11	0	82	66	13	86
Nick Mondak, St. John's (NY)	4	3	1.92	11	0	65.2	63	18	74
David Festa, Seton Hall	6	4	2.00	15	0	72	44	33	67
Austin Peterson, UConn	7	1	2.58	15	0	80.1	59	21	82
Dylan Tebrake, Creighton	8	0	2.72	12	0	72.2	59	24	75
Ryan McLiniskey, Seton Hall	4	1	2.81	13	0	57.2	51	28	66
Caleb Wurster, UConn	4	1	2.85	25	9	41	31	14	52
Trevor Olson, Xavier	5	3	2.97	14	0	63.2	53	18	50
Nick Zwack, Xavier	6	5	3.15	15	1	80	69	33	75
Ian Murphy, St. John's (NY)	2	3	3.15	10	0	40	28	28	45
Ethan Bosacker, Xavier	4	3	3.34	12	0	62	52	24	54
Tyler Burnham, Seton Hall	3	5	3.42	12	0	50	38	25	45
Tyler Arella, Villanova	3	4	3.43	12	0	63	57	24	55
Nick Eaton, Butler	2	2	3.48	13	1	41.1	36	14	47
Joe Cinnella, Seton Hall	3	3	3.89	16	0	41.2	41	21	22

BIG SOUTH CONFERENCE

	Conference		Overall	
	W	L	W	L
Campbell	28	9	37	18
USC Upstate	28	12	37	16
Gardner-Webb	27	13	29	23
Presbyterian	18	16	22	23
Radford	17	19	23	23
Charleston Southern	18	22	18	26
Winthrop	16	21	19	27
UNC Asheville	14	26	15	33
High Point	12	25	14	31
Longwood	10	25	17	32

ALL-CONFERENCE TEAM: C: Straton Podaras, Gr., Radford. **INF:** Zach Neto, RFr., Campbell; Brandon Lankford, Sr., UNC Asheville; Matt Christian, RSr., Campbell; Jason Matthews, Sr., USC Upstate. **OF:** Spencer Packard, RSr., Campbell; Connor Denning, RJr., Campbell; Cam Pearcey, Sr., Gardner-Webb. **DH:** Patrick Ferguson, Sr., Gardner-Webb. **UTL:** Dominic Freeberger, Jr., UNC Asheville. **SP:** Jordan Marks, Jr., USC Upstate; Mason Miller, Gardner-Webb; R.J. Petit, So., Charleston Southern. **RP:** Logan Heintzman, RSr., Campbell; Kevin Davis, Jr., USC Upstate. **Player of the Year:** Zach Neto, RFr., Campbell. **Pitcher of the Year:** Jordan Marks, Jr., USC Upstate. **Co-Coach of the Year:** Justin Haire, Campbell. **Co-Coach of the Year:** Jim Chester, Gardner-Webb. **Freshman of the Year:** Thomas Harrington, Campbell.

INDIVIDUAL BATTING LEADERS
(Minimum 140 at-bats)

Player	AVG	OBP	SLG	AB	2B	3B	HR	RBI	SB
Zach Neto, Campbell	.405	.488	.746	173	17	3	12	58	12
Spencer Packard, Campbell	.371	.488	.629	197	18	0	11	67	2
David Bryant, Radford	.364	.480	.594	165	9	4	7	37	4
Matthew Christian, Campbell	.350	.400	.685	200	15	2	16	65	11
Eric Jones, Gardner-Webb	.345	.425	.515	171	11	0	6	30	4
Julian Rip, USC Upstate	.345	.457	.500	148	7	2	4	31	12
Jason Matthews, USC Upstate	.344	.427	.469	209	20	3	0	38	9
Brandon Lankford, UNC Asheville	.341	.433	.665	176	6	0	17	43	5
Connor Denning, Campbell	.340	.462	.686	194	26	4	11	42	6
Eliot Dix, Longwood	.340	.412	.488	162	6	0	6	39	2
Cole Singsank, High Point	.340	.429	.451	153	12	1	1	33	7
Devin Buckner, USC Upstate	.339	.482	.505	186	19	0	4	49	2
Cameron Pearcey, Gardner-Webb	.336	.386	.593	140	6	3	8	30	17
Dominic Freeberger, UNC Asheville	.333	.384	.512	201	12	3	6	30	2
Jack Hennessy, USC Upstate	.333	.438	.382	191	8	1	0	24	9
Hayden Harris, Longwood	.329	.411	.410	161	10	0	1	19	3
Jack Schnell, Longwood	.325	.423	.428	166	11	0	2	27	0
Bryce Arnold, Campbell	.324	.447	.511	182	12	2	6	39	9
Noah Rabon, USC Upstate	.321	.389	.459	209	14	3	3	45	7
Scout McFalls, Winthrop	.314	.379	.459	159	7	2	4	23	12
Joey Tepper, Winthrop	.314	.434	.443	140	9	0	3	21	4
Zacchaeus Rasberry, Presbyterian	.305	.357	.555	164	7	2	10	38	11
Peyton Carr, High Point	.304	.376	.494	168	11	0	7	33	1
Straton Podaras, Radford	.302	.434	.414	162	8	2	2	27	5
Cameron Macintosh, USC Upstate	.300	.381	.353	170	4	1	1	14	1
Patrick Ferguson, Gardner-Webb	.299	.415	.650	157	6	2	15	51	0
Joe Johnson, High Point	.296	.389	.484	186	15	1	6	19	4
Houston Parker, Charleston So.	.295	.403	.425	146	9	2	2	19	8
Mitch McLendon, Gardner-Webb	.293	.377	.423	215	14	1	4	31	6
Andrew Jenner, Winthrop	.292	.359	.386	171	11	1	1	21	5

INDIVIDUAL PITCHING LEADERS
(Minimum 40 innings pitched)

Player	W	L	ERA	G	SV	IP	H	BB	SO
Jordan Marks, USC Upstate	10	2	2.54	15	0	95.2	85	20	101
RJ Petit, Charleston So.	6	5	2.79	14	0	84	69	31	75
Andrew Potojecki, Longwood	2	2	3.24	13	0	41.2	43	13	33
Mason Miller, Gardner-Webb	8	1	3.30	15	0	92.2	73	30	121
Alex Garbrick, USC Upstate	7	3	3.39	14	0	66.1	61	29	74
Thomas Harrington, Campbell	6	3	3.45	16	0	75.2	65	28	75
Logan Heintzman, Campbell	7	1	3.46	18	0	41.2	38	15	26
Sean Hupp, USC Upstate	4	2	3.86	16	4	42	33	14	43
Ty Cummings, Campbell	2	2	3.88	21	1	46.1	47	15	39
Cade Kuehler, Campbell	5	2	3.89	16	1	44	51	22	41
Ben Ferrer, USC Upstate	4	2	4.09	8	0	44	47	9	38
Bruce Hudson, Radford	5	2	4.12	19	0	43.2	44	18	44
Kole Harris, UNC Asheville	2	2	4.33	25	0	60.1	68	26	49
Greg Duncan, Radford	6	3	4.38	13	0	78	95	26	64
Colton Rendon, Winthrop	4	2	4.46	15	3	42.1	44	9	32

BIG 12 CONFERENCE

	Conference		Overall	
	W	L	W	L
Texas	17	7	50	17
Texas Christian	17	7	41	19
Texas Tech	14	10	39	17
Oklahoma State	12	12	36	19
Oklahoma	11	13	27	28
Baylor	11	13	31	20
Kansas State	10	14	34	23

West Virginia	8	16	25	27
Kansas	8	16	30	27

ALL-CONFERENCE TEAM: C: Andy Thomas, Jr., Baylor. **INF:** Tyler Hardman, RJr., Oklahoma; Christian Encarnacion-Strand, So., Oklahoma State; Mitchell Daly, Fr., Texas; Cal Conley, Fr., Texas Tech; Jace Jung, Fr., Texas Tech. **OF:** Jared McKenzie, Fr., Baylor; Phillip Sikes, Jr., Texas Christian; Dru Baker, So., Texas Tech. **DH:** Ivan Melendez, RSo., Texas. **UTL:** Justin Campbell, Fr., Oklahoma State. **SP:** Jordan Wicks, So., Kansas State; Ty Madden, RSo., Texas; Tristan Stevens, RJr., Texas. **RP:** Luke Boyd, Sr., Baylor; Haylen Green, Sr., Texas Christian. **Player of the Year:** Jace Jung, Fr., Texas Tech. **Pitcher of the Year:** Ty Madden, RSo., Texas. **Coach of the Year:** David Pierce, Texas. **Newcomer of the Year:** Christian Encarnacion-Strand, Sr., Oklahoma State. **Freshman of the Year:** Brayden Taylor, Texas Christian

INDIVIDUAL BATTING LEADERS
(Minimum 2.5 at-bats per team game)

Player	AVG	OBP	SLG	AB	2B	3B	HR	RBI	SB
Tyler Hardman, Oklahoma	.397	.481	.661	224	19	2	12	49	3
Jared McKenzie, Baylor	.383	.453	.626	214	14	4	10	44	3
Zach Kokoska, Kansas St.	.363	.445	.675	212	19	1	15	46	9
Christian Encarnacion-Strand, Ok. St.	.361	.442	.661	227	17	3	15	66	4
Dru Baker, Texas Tech	.343	.406	.484	213	14	2	4	32	18
Jake Thompson, Oklahoma St.	.342	.502	.479	146	8	0	4	32	2
Jace Jung, Texas Tech	.337	.462	.697	208	10	1	21	67	4
Andy Thomas, Baylor	.337	.411	.575	193	11	1	11	60	1
Dylan Phillips, Kansas St.	.333	.422	.643	213	16	1	16	58	6
Cal Conley, Texas Tech	.329	.391	.587	225	13	0	15	55	7
Phillip Sikes, TCU	.329	.427	.620	213	19	5	11	63	12
Jack Pineda, Baylor	.327	.430	.493	205	16	3	4	33	5
Skyler Messinger, Kansas	.324	.398	.460	213	19	2	2	39	4
Brayden Taylor, TCU	.324	.445	.572	222	11	4	12	53	15
Austin Davis, West Virginia	.320	.390	.400	175	9	1	1	18	17
Ivan Melendez, Texas	.319	.438	.603	204	13	3	13	51	1
Mitchell Daly, Texas	.316	.413	.416	209	15	0	2	31	8
Zach Humphreys, TCU	.316	.425	.498	215	15	3	6	40	9
Tavian Josenberger, Kansas	.316	.392	.413	196	8	4	1	31	11
Hunter Wolfe, TCU	.315	.397	.541	181	18	1	7	55	13
Maui Ahuna, Kansas	.314	.413	.422	185	11	3	1	25	8
Conor McKenna, Oklahoma	.312	.402	.558	199	11	1	12	49	2
Tanner Treadaway, Oklahoma	.309	.391	.423	149	8	0	3	28	6
Tre Richardson, Baylor	.308	.389	.463	201	16	3	3	37	6
Luke Boyers, TCU	.307	.411	.353	150	4	0	1	22	10
Carson McCusker, Oklahoma St.	.305	.374	.519	154	10	1	7	35	1
Camryn Williams, Texas	.295	.415	.575	207	20	1	12	51	4
Peyton Graham, Oklahoma	.288	.400	.502	215	11	1	11	28	7
Cole Stilwell, Texas Tech	.288	.422	.548	146	12	1	8	33	0
Jimmy Crooks, Oklahoma	.287	.385	.502	223	18	0	10	39	3

INDIVIDUAL PITCHING LEADERS
(Minimum 40 innings pitched)

Player	W	L	ERA	G	SV	IP	H	BB	SO
Cole Quintanilla, Texas	5	1	1.35	26	0	40	22	11	42
Pete Hansen, Texas	9	1	1.88	19	0	91	66	23	80
Ryan Sublette, Texas Tech	6	3	2.34	19	3	42.1	28	17	62
Ty Madden, Texas	7	5	2.45	18	0	113.2	75	44	137
Tyler Thomas, Baylor	5	2	2.49	11	0	65	49	30	66
Parker Scott, Oklahoma St.	8	1	2.54	12	0	60.1	55	16	61
Justin Campbell, Oklahoma St.	7	2	2.57	42	0	84	66	27	102
Tyler Eckberg, Kansas St.	5	5	2.63	23	5	41	36	9	41
Jackson Wolf, West Virginia	6	5	3.03	14	0	89	66	37	104
Tanner Witt, Texas	5	0	3.16	34	5	57	40	25	73
Tristan Stevens, Texas	11	3	3.31	18	0	111.1	105	23	77
Haylen Green, TCU	1	3	3.33	25	12	48.2	43	5	55
Blake Helton, Baylor	4	3	3.44	13	0	52.1	62	21	40
Micah Dallas, Texas Tech	4	3	3.51	17	2	66.2	61	20	79
Jimmy Winston, Baylor	6	4	3.66	19	0	51.2	40	21	56

BIG TEN CONFERENCE

	Conference		Overall	
	W	L	W	L
Nebraska	31	12	31	12
Maryland	28	16	28	16
Michigan	27	17	27	17

Indiana	26	18	26	18
Iowa	26	18	26	18
Ohio State	22	20	22	20
Illinois	22	22	22	22
Rutgers	21	23	21	23
Penn State	18	23	18	23
Northwestern	15	21	15	21
Michigan State	17	27	17	27
Purdue	15	25	15	25
Minnesota	5	31	5	31

ALL-CONFERENCE TEAM: C: Luke Roskam, Sr., Nebraska. **1B:** Anthony Calarco, Jr., Northwestern. **2B:** Ted Burton, So., Michigan. **3B:** Jackson Raper, Sr., Illinois. **SS:** Benjamin Cowles, Jr., Maryland. **OF:** Grant Richardson, Indiana; Ben Norman, RSr., Iowa; Jaxon Hallmark, Sr., Nebraska. **DH:** Justin Janas, Fr., Illinois. **At-Large:** Shawn Goosenberg, Jr., Northwestern. **SP:** Trenton Wallace, RJr., Iowa; Steven Hajjar, RSo., Michigan; Cade Povich, Jr., Nebraska. **RP:** Spencer Schwellenbach, Jr., Nebraska. **Player of the Year:** Spencer Schwellenbach, Jr., Nebraska. **Pitcher of the Year:** Trenton Wallace, RJr., Iowa. **Coach of the Year:** Will Bolt, Nebraska. **Freshman of the Year:** Max Anderson, Nebraska.

INDIVIDUAL BATTING LEADERS
(Minimum 140 at-bats)

Player	AVG	OBP	SLG	AB	2B	3B	HR	RBI	SB
Shawn Goosenberg, Northwestern	.362	.426	.717	152	12	0	14	30	10
Jaxon Hallmark, Nebraska	.342	.407	.546	196	4	3	10	23	16
Max Anderson, Nebraska	.332	.386	.500	184	8	1	7	32	3
Matthew Shaw, Maryland	.332	.408	.543	184	16	1	7	30	7
Tito Flores, Michigan	.325	.429	.552	163	14	1	7	37	5
Kade Kern, Ohio St.	.325	.391	.438	160	10	1	2	30	9
Branden Comia, Illinois	.323	.457	.445	155	10	0	3	28	3
Miles Simington, Purdue	.322	.431	.493	152	14	0	4	27	4
Grant Richardson, Indiana	.320	.397	.517	172	9	2	7	33	11
Ben Nisle, Purdue	.318	.421	.580	157	11	3	8	26	6
Richie Schiekofer, Rutgers	.316	.403	.404	171	12	0	1	21	6
Benjamin Sems, Michigan	.314	.389	.479	169	8	1	6	30	4
Jackson Raper, Illinois	.311	.423	.634	161	11	1	13	44	4
Gavin Homer, Penn St.	.310	.429	.421	145	8	1	2	16	10
Zaid Walker, Michigan St.	.308	.367	.420	169	6	1	3	31	7
Luke Roskam, Nebraska	.307	.439	.527	150	6	0	9	38	0
Chris Alleyne, Maryland	.306	.409	.561	180	14	4	8	31	22
Ben Norman, Iowa	.306	.421	.612	170	14	4	10	53	12
Chris Brito, Rutgers	.302	.396	.527	169	8	0	10	43	1
Zach Dezenzo, Ohio St.	.302	.382	.550	169	11	2	9	31	0
Justin Williams, Penn St.	.302	.367	.472	159	12	0	5	23	1
Izaya Fullard, Iowa	.296	.395	.444	162	9	0	5	21	1
Anthony Calarco, Northwestern	.295	.379	.564	149	13	0	9	19	0
Cole Barr, Indiana	.292	.415	.526	154	8	2	8	35	4
Benjamin Cowles, Maryland	.287	.409	.632	174	6	0	18	51	9
Skyler Hunter, Purdue	.285	.385	.327	165	7	0	0	21	3
Johnny Piacentino, Penn St.	.284	.350	.525	162	15	0	8	32	0
Spencer Schwellenbach, Neb.	.284	.403	.459	183	12	1	6	40	9
Joe Acker, Nebraska	.283	.383	.466	191	15	1	6	26	7
Paul Toetz, Indiana	.281	.365	.407	167	18	0	1	24	1

INDIVIDUAL PITCHING LEADERS
(Minimum 40 innings pitched)

Player	W	L	ERA	G	SV	IP	H	BB	SO
Trenton Wallace, Iowa	7	1	2.34	36	0	73	54	37	106
Gabe Bierman, Indiana	5	4	2.68	12	0	74	47	30	80
Cameron Weston, Michigan	7	4	2.81	15	0	83.1	68	29	69
Andrew Hoffmann, Illinois	3	0	2.87	11	0	62.2	49	15	64
Nick Dean, Maryland	3	1	2.87	9	0	53.1	47	11	39
Steven Hajjar, Michigan	4	2	3.09	14	0	81.2	66	29	110
Cade Povich, Nebraska	6	1	3.11	15	0	81	74	22	88
Sean Burke, Maryland	6	3	3.27	14	0	74.1	48	42	107
McCade Brown, Indiana	5	4	3.39	12	0	61	35	43	97
Mason Erla, Michigan St.	5	6	3.50	13	0	79.2	76	30	80
Ben Wereski, Rutgers	6	2	3.67	13	0	76	64	11	56
Mike Doherty, Northwestern	1	4	3.69	11	0	63.1	64	15	32
Garrett Burhenn, Ohio St.	7	2	3.81	13	0	80.1	73	27	91
Nathan Lavender, Illinois	7	2	4.11	13	0	57	55	15	79
Chance Hroch, Nebraska	5	3	4.15	14	0	78	82	19	64

BIG WEST CONFERENCE

	Conference		Overall	
	W	L	W	L
UC Irvine	32	8	43	18
UC Santa Barbara	29	11	41	20
Long Beach State	26	14	28	15
Cal Poly	21	19	31	25
Cal State Northridge	21	19	21	19
UC San Diego	21	19	24	28
Cal State Bakersfield	17	19	20	23
Hawaii	16	24	24	26
Cal State Fullerton	13	23	20	35
UC Riverside	12	28	15	36
UC Davis	8	32	14	43

ALL-CONFERENCE TEAM: C: Myles Emmerson, Sr., Cal Poly. **1B:** Chase Luttrell, So., Long Beach State. **2B:** Kai Moody, Sr., Cal State Northridge. **3B:** Cole Cummings, So., UC Santa Barbara. **SS:** Brooks Lee, Fr., Cal Poly; Jordan Sprinkle, Fr., UC Santa Barbara. **OF:** Mike Peabody, Jr., UC Irvine; Nathan Church, Fr., UC Irvine; Connor Kokx, Fr., Long Beach State; Zach Rodriguez, Fr., UC Santa Barbara **DH:** Dustin Demeter, Jr., Hawaii. **UTL:** Tyler Jorgensen, Jr., Cal State Bakersfield. **SP:** Rodney Boone, So., UC Santa Barbara; Michael Frias, So., UC Irvine; Johnathan Lavallee, Jr., Long Beach State; Michael McGreevey, So., UC Santa Barbara. **RP:** Carter Benbrook, Fr., UC Santa Barbara; Gordon Ingebritson, Jr., UC Irvine. **CP:** Devereaux Harrison, Fr., Long Beach State; Jacob King, Fr., UC Irvine **Co-Player of the Year:** Mike Peabody, Jr., UC Irvine; Brooks Lee, Fr., Cal Poly. **Co-Pitcher of the Year:** Johnathan Lavallee, Jr., Long Beach State; Rodney Boone, So., UC Santa Barbara. **Coach of the Year:** Ben Orloff, UC Irvine. **Co-Freshman of the Year:** Brooks Lee, Cal Poly; Jordan Sprinkle, UC Santa Barbara. **Freshman Pitcher of the Year:** Devereaux Harrison, Long Beach State. **Tri-Defensive Player of the Year:** Myles Emmerson, Sr., Cal Poly; Denzel Clarke, Jr., Cal State Northridge; Taishi Nakawake, Jr., UC Irvine.

INDIVIDUAL BATTING LEADERS
(Minimum 140 at-bats)

Player	AVG	OBP	SLG	AB	2B	3B	HR	RBI	SB
Kai Moody, CSUN	.393	.459	.486	140	10	0	1	25	10
Nathan Church, UC Irvine	.369	.424	.583	271	24	8	6	61	7
Connor Kokx, Long Beach St.	.366	.481	.571	161	10	1	7	29	14
Tyler Jorgensen, CSU Bakersfield	.363	.390	.480	171	8	0	4	35	5
Mike Peabody, UC Irvine	.353	.481	.580	207	16	2	9	57	9
Jordan Sprinkle, UC Santa Barbara	.353	.402	.536	235	18	2	7	32	26
Michael Fuhrman, UC San Diego	.352	.457	.488	162	9	2	3	18	10
Zach Rodriguez, UC Santa Barbara	.348	.412	.511	221	11	2	7	55	9
Brooks Lee, Cal Poly	.342	.384	.626	222	27	3	10	57	3
Cole Cummings, UC Santa Barbara	.341	.469	.513	232	19	3	5	27	7
Caden Connor, Cal St. Fullerton	.325	.417	.387	191	12	0	0	22	2
Evan Berkey, CSU Bakersfield	.324	.427	.500	142	9	2	4	18	6
Denzel Clarke, CSUN	.324	.445	.570	142	11	0	8	25	15
Nathan Webb, UC Riverside	.324	.400	.524	185	10	0	9	43	1
Adam Fogel, Hawaii	.323	.382	.468	201	17	0	4	32	4
Chase Luttrell, Long Beach St.	.316	.347	.520	177	6	3	8	30	4
Jacob Castro, UC Irvine	.314	.411	.397	156	9	2	0	34	0
Kole Kaler, Hawaii	.314	.376	.435	207	13	3	2	22	15
Jalen Smith, UC Davis	.313	.388	.476	227	16	3	5	20	15
Myles Emmerson, Cal Poly	.312	.360	.380	234	14	1	0	23	0
Anthony Lucchetti, UC San Diego	.312	.399	.465	170	12	1	4	22	0
Travis Bohall, UC Riverside	.310	.369	.379	203	5	3	1	19	16
Dylan Orick, UC Riverside	.307	.357	.487	189	17	4	3	34	1
Luke Spillane, UC Irvine	.306	.385	.426	222	10	1	5	45	14
Joey Nicolai, UC Riverside	.302	.372	.396	159	9	0	2	28	1
Calvin Estrada, Long Beach St.	.298	.355	.548	168	8	2	10	36	2
Connor McGuire, UC Irvine	.297	.384	.423	182	13	2	2	44	0
Scotty Scott, Hawaii	.297	.435	.372	148	9	1	0	14	4
Jackson Kritsch, UC San Diego	.296	.398	.434	159	10	3	2	19	1
Broc Mortenson, UC Santa Barbara	.296	.409	.582	196	9	1	15	54	9

INDIVIDUAL PITCHING LEADERS
(Minimum 40 innings pitched)

Player	W	L	ERA	G	SV	IP	H	BB	SO
Jonathan Lavallee, Long Beach St.	8	1	1.89	11	0	62	35	16	73
Jacob King, UC Irvine	3	1	1.98	29	8	41	32	10	45
Rodney Boone, UC Santa Barbara	11	4	2.31	16	0	97.1	55	39	128

Jack Noble, Long Beach St.	3	2	2.79	12	0	48.1	38	24	62
Michael McGreevy, UC Santa Barbara	9	2	2.92	16	0	101.2	109	11	115
Michael Mitchell, UC San Diego	4	1	3.00	21	5	42	35	20	47
Carter Benbrook, UC Santa Barbara	7	1	3.02	25	5	53.2	52	19	62
Travis Weston, Cal Poly	5	6	3.28	14	0	82.1	82	17	74
Michael Frias, UC Irvine	9	2	3.36	17	0	85.2	65	24	91
Cory Lewis, UC Santa Barbara	7	4	3.38	15	0	80	55	31	86
Nick Pinto, UC Irvine	7	4	3.43	17	0	86.2	83	26	79
Buddie Pindel, Hawaii	3	2	3.43	13	3	42	47	5	26
Cade Halemanu, Hawaii	5	2	3.60	13	1	70	66	20	57
Tanner Bibee, Cal St. Fullerton	6	6	3.61	16	0	89.2	84	21	67
Aaron Davenport, Hawaii	3	6	3.74	13	0	86.2	82	21	97

COLONIAL ATHLETIC ASSOCIATION

	Conference		Overall	
North Division	W	L	W	L
Northeastern	20	3	36	12
Towson	11	12	21	36
Hofstra	8	16	17	22
Delaware	8	16	12	22
South Division	W	L	W	L
UNC-Wilmington	13	8	32	22
Elon	10	8	22	22
College of Charleston	12	12	27	25
William & Mary	10	14	14	29
James Madison	6	9	11	17

ALL-CONFERENCE TEAM: C: Matt Suggs, So., UNC-Wilmington. **INF:** Austin Gauthier, Sr., Hofstra; Scott Holzwasser, Sr. Northeastern; Cole Weiss, Sr., UNC-Wilmington; Ben Williamson, So., William & Mary. **OF:** Brooks Baldwin, So., UNC-Wilmington; Chase DeLauter, Fr., James Madison; Jared Dupere, So., Northeastern; Harrison Hawkins, Sr., College of Charleston; Alex Iadisernia, Fr., Elon. **DH:** Max Viera, Fr., Northeastern. **UTL:** Jack Cone, Jr., William & Mary. **SP:** Landon Roupp, Jr., UNC-Wilmington; Kyle Murphy, Sr., Northeastern; Cam Schlittler, Fr., Northeastern. **RP:** Hunter Hodges, Fr., UNC-Wilmington; Joe Sparke, So., Elon. **Player of the Year:** Jared Dupere, So., Northeastern. **Pitcher of the Year:** Landon Roupp, Jr., UNC-Wilmington. **Coach of the Year:** Mike Glavine, Northeastern. **Co-Rookie of the Year:** Alex Iadisernia, Fr., Elon; Cam Schlittler, Fr., Northeastern. **Defensive Player of the Year:** Matt McDermott, Sr., William & Mary.

INDIVIDUAL BATTING LEADERS
(Minimum 140 at-bats)

Player	AVG	OBP	SLG	AB	2B	3B	HR	RBI	SB
Alex Iadisernia, Elon	.368	.448	.626	174	13	1	10	30	6
Anthony Galason, Elon	.350	.428	.503	163	7	0	6	29	10
Max Viera, Northeastern	.348	.394	.589	141	12	2	6	26	3
Jared Dupere, Northeastern	.343	.457	.781	178	11	2	21	50	14
Harrison Hawkins, Col. of Charleston	.342	.409	.574	202	12	1	11	54	8
Danny Crossen, Northeastern	.336	.411	.473	146	13	2	1	31	6
Jeff Costello, Northeastern	.329	.405	.449	167	11	0	3	34	13
Brooks Baldwin, UNCW	.325	.353	.580	243	11	3	15	45	11
Joseph Mershon, Col. of Charleston	.314	.425	.467	169	10	2	4	20	11
Taber Mongero, UNCW	.307	.395	.367	166	5	1	1	29	1
Dillon Lifrieri, UNCW	.305	.355	.407	167	7	2	2	27	5
Ben Williamson, William & Mary	.303	.371	.429	175	11	1	3	19	6
Kip Brandenburg, UNCW	.299	.397	.448	194	15	1	4	26	5
Jared Kirven, Col. of Charleston	.299	.338	.422	147	6	0	4	18	1
Cole Reynolds, Elon	.292	.398	.444	144	7	0	5	25	1
Trotter Harlan, Col. of Charleston	.291	.338	.427	220	11	2	5	24	10
Matt McDermott, William & Mary	.289	.337	.494	180	15	2	6	25	9
Cole Weiss, UNCW	.289	.371	.433	201	9	1	6	40	8
Scott Holzwasser, Northeastern	.288	.438	.418	170	7	0	5	30	22
Matt Suggs, UNCW	.286	.403	.541	185	12	1	11	38	2
Ari Sechopoulos, Col. of Charleston	.285	.351	.468	186	11	1	7	40	6
Ben Malgeri, Northeastern	.280	.358	.458	168	7	1	7	28	23
Matt Thomas, William & Mary	.270	.354	.459	159	13	1	5	20	7
Billy Godrick, Towson	.259	.416	.378	185	11	1	3	24	8
Danny Becerra, Towson	.258	.381	.335	221	12	1	1	24	11
Javon Fields, Towson	.257	.384	.363	171	7	1	3	28	18
Nolan Young, Towson	.256	.388	.313	195	6	1	1	27	8
Anthony D'Onofrio, Hofstra	.253	.364	.333	150	8	2	0	20	15
Spenser Smith, Northeastern	.242	.335	.323	161	6	2	1	25	12

Player	AVG	OBP	SLG	AB	2B	3B	HR	RBI	SB
Noah Bridges, UNCW	.237	.305	.406	160	4	1	7	27	12

INDIVIDUAL PITCHING LEADERS
(Minimum 40 innings pitched)

Player	W	L	ERA	G	SV	IP	H	BB	SO
Cam Schlittler, Northeastern	8	1	1.88	13	0	76.2	58	20	85
Kody Reeser, Towson	4	6	2.02	25	1	49	41	11	53
Adam Smith, UNCW	6	1	2.49	20	3	61.1	57	26	58
Landon Roupp, UNCW	8	5	2.58	16	0	101	69	42	118
Wyatt Scotti, Northeastern	4	2	2.82	12	0	51	39	10	39
Joe Savino, Elon	0	3	3.02	12	0	59.2	55	10	70
William Privette, Col. of Charleston	1	3	3.60	14	0	45	39	12	36
Zach Tsakounis, William & Mary	3	2	3.63	11	0	62	57	18	45
Jimmy Joyce, Hofstra	3	4	3.70	11	0	73	67	21	89
Ty Good, Col. of Charleston	7	5	3.71	17	1	77.2	69	27	85
Kyle Murphy, Northeastern	6	1	3.86	13	0	65.1	48	15	87
Connor Campbell, Col. of Charleston	6	4	4.07	17	0	66.1	85	20	53
Brian Edgington, Elon	4	3	4.08	16	2	70.2	76	16	66
Sebastian Keane, Northeastern	6	1	4.09	12	0	70.1	64	20	73
Jordan Carr, Col. of Charleston	3	3	4.52	23	3	61.2	75	18	51

CONFERENCE USA

East Division	Conference		Overall	
	W	L	W	L
Charlotte	24	8	40	21
Old Dominion	22	10	44	16
Florida Atlantic	18	14	32	25
Western Kentucky	15	17	27	29
Florida International	11	19	20	31
Marshall	6	26	10	35
West Division	**W**	**L**	**W**	**L**
Louisiana Tech	22	8	42	20
Southern Mississippi	22	9	40	21
Texas-San Antonio	14	17	22	26
Middle Tennessee State	12	19	24	29
Rice	11	20	23	29
Alabama-Birmingham	11	21	18	36

ALL-CONFERENCE TEAM: C: Nick Thornquist, Sr., Texas-San Antonio. **INF:** Austin Knight, So., Charlotte; Taylor Young, Sr., Louisiana Tech; Hunter Wells, Sr., Louisiana Tech; Carter Trice, Fr., Old Dominion. **OF:** Parker Bates, Sr., Louisiana Tech; Kyle Battle, Sr., Old Dominion; Reed Trimble, Fr., Southern Mississippi. **DH:** Charlie Fischer, So., Southern Mississippi. **UTL:** Manny Garcia, Sr., Louisiana Tech. **SP:** Walker Powell, Sr., Southern Mississippi; Bryce McGowan, So., Charlotte; Jonathan Fincher, Jr., Louisiana Tech; Hunter Gregory, Jr., Old Dominion; Hunter Stanley, Sr., Southern Mississippi. **RP:** Christian Lothes, Fr., Charlotte; David Zoz, Sr., Middle Tennessee State. **Player of the Year:** Austin Knight, So., Charlotte. **Pitcher of the Year:** Walker Powell, Sr., Southern Mississippi. **Coach of the Year:** Robert Woodard, Charlotte. **Freshman of the Year:** Carter Trice, Old Dominion. **Newcomer of the Year:** Austin Knight, So., Charlotte. **Assistant Coach of the Year:** Christian Ostrander, Southern Mississippi.

INDIVIDUAL BATTING LEADERS
(Minimum 140 at-bats)

Player	AVG	OBP	SLG	AB	2B	3B	HR	RBI	SB
Hunter Wells, Louisiana Tech	.385	.456	.645	262	20	3	14	61	1
Jackson Gray, Western Ky.	.363	.460	.592	179	13	2	8	32	7
Carter Trice, Old Dominion	.355	.426	.632	234	17	3	14	54	8
LuJames Groover III, Charlotte	.351	.380	.489	188	14	0	4	38	0
Cole McConnell, Louisiana Tech	.347	.399	.503	167	12	1	4	30	4
Parker Bates, Louisiana Tech	.346	.471	.583	228	13	4	11	62	1
Braden Comeaux, Rice	.346	.419	.408	191	7	1	1	23	4
Gabriel Montenegro, Southern Miss.	.345	.439	.504	238	24	1	4	28	6
Reed Trimble, Southern Miss.	.345	.414	.638	235	14	2	17	72	12
Tommy Bell, Old Dominion	.343	.421	.554	204	9	5	8	49	2
Nolan Schanuel, Fla. Atlantic	.343	.444	.576	198	11	1	11	56	6
Austin Knight, Charlotte	.342	.398	.615	234	29	1	11	63	13
Griffin Paxton, UTSA	.335	.430	.543	188	16	1	7	43	0
Luke Edwards, Marshall	.331	.386	.556	142	16	2	4	21	7
Nick Thornquist, UTSA	.331	.442	.624	178	11	1	13	47	4
Taylor Young, Louisiana Tech	.331	.454	.504	242	19	1	7	36	10
Will Butcher, Charlotte	.328	.383	.506	180	8	0	8	40	4
Dylan Rock, UTSA	.326	.432	.516	190	12	0	8	38	11

Player	AVG	OBP	SLG	AB	2B	3B	HR	RBI	SB
Adrian Figueroa, FIU	.324	.397	.423	182	12	0	2	32	2
Joshua Lamb, UTSA	.324	.357	.481	185	14	0	5	39	4
Danny Lynch, Southern Miss.	.320	.396	.571	203	11	2	12	36	2
Kyle Battle, Old Dominion	.319	.464	.681	207	15	3	18	61	7
Andy Garriola, Old Dominion	.318	.366	.564	236	16	0	14	72	0
Mitchell Hartigan, Fla. Atlantic	.318	.394	.535	198	19	0	8	36	2
Brock Gagliardi, Old Dominion	.316	.456	.561	155	11	0	9	35	0
Philip Matulia, Louisiana Tech	.311	.402	.521	167	7	2	8	37	3
B.J. Murray, Fla. Atlantic	.311	.424	.584	209	11	2	14	52	0
Manny Garcia, Louisiana Tech	.309	.376	.522	230	20	1	9	53	2
Colton Schultz, UAB	.307	.384	.466	189	6	3	6	36	6
Charlie Fischer, Southern Miss.	.304	.467	.491	171	11	0	7	37	0

INDIVIDUAL PITCHING LEADERS
(Minimum 40 innings pitched)

Player	W	L	ERA	G	SV	IP	H	BB	SO
Jason Hartline, Old Dominion	5	0	1.88	27	3	48	42	10	60
Walker Powell, Southern Miss.	10	2	2.31	15	0	89.2	76	18	86
Hunter Stanley, Southern Miss.	6	4	2.56	16	0	102	74	19	127
Hunter Gregory, Old Dominion	8	2	2.95	16	0	79.1	65	19	88
Jonathan Fincher, Louisiana Tech	8	3	3.05	17	0	100.1	80	23	85
Christian Lothes, Charlotte	4	0	3.10	21	8	40.2	25	23	54
Ryne Moore, Old Dominion	9	1	3.16	17	0	85.1	76	22	80
Peyton Wigginton, Middle Tenn.	3	5	3.16	14	0	79.2	75	24	60
David Zoz, Middle Tenn.	6	3	3.21	24	6	42	35	5	40
Ben Ethridge, Southern Miss.	6	2	3.25	16	0	74.2	65	13	82
Riley Davis, UAB	4	5	3.74	13	0	79.1	83	24	60
Trent Siebert, Middle Tenn.	2	2	3.77	14	1	59.2	58	15	51
Zach Keenan, Middle Tenn.	2	5	3.86	14	1	65.1	61	13	62
Brandon Deskins, Rice	3	4	3.88	17	1	53.1	42	29	73
Aaron Brown, Middle Tenn.	7	5	3.99	14	0	85.2	67	15	113

HORIZON LEAGUE

	Conference		Overall	
	W	L	W	L
Wright State	28	4	35	13
Illinois-Chicago	28	11	30	18
Youngstown State	24	16	32	24
Milwaukee	17	23	22	33
Northern Kentucky	14	25	17	31
Oakland	11	24	17	29
Purdue-Fort Wayne	7	28	10	35

ALL-CONFERENCE TEAM: A.J. Blubaugh, Milwaukee; Griffin Doersching, Northern Kentucky; Matt Bottcher, Illinois-Chicago; Jacob Key, Illinois-Chicago; Bryan Rosario, Illinois-Chicago; Thomas Smart, Illinois-Chicago; Tyler Black, Wright State; Austin Cline, Wright State; Quincy Hamilton, Wright State; Sammy Sass, Wright State; Alec Sayre, Wright State; Collin Floyd, Youngstown State; Jeff Wehler, Youngstown State. **Player of the Year:** Quincy Hamilton, Wright State. **Pitcher of the Year:** Collin Floyd, Youngstown State. **Coach of the Year:** Alex Sogard, Wright State. **Freshman of the Year:** Cole Conn, Illinois-Chicago. **Relief Pitcher of the Year:** A.J. Blubaugh, Milwaukee.

INDIVIDUAL BATTING LEADERS
(Minimum 140 at-bats)

Player	AVG	OBP	SLG	AB	2B	3B	HR	RBI	SB
Bryan Rosario, UIC	.399	.460	.500	168	8	3	1	21	12
Tyler Black, Wright St.	.383	.496	.683	183	14	1	13	59	11
Michael Stygles, Oakland	.382	.458	.549	144	12	0	4	38	3
Thomas Smart, UIC	.380	.505	.509	171	10	3	2	32	8
Quincy Hamilton, Wright St.	.374	.535	.771	179	18	4	15	65	20
Sammy Sass, Wright St.	.362	.456	.717	152	12	3	12	60	2
Blaze Glenn, Youngstown St.	.360	.455	.513	197	14	2	4	35	10
Joshua Figueroa, UIC	.351	.402	.563	174	14	1	7	54	0
Matt Bottcher, UIC	.350	.437	.601	163	13	5	6	36	9
Zane Harris, Wright St.	.347	.460	.567	150	14	2	5	55	0
Dominick Bucko, Youngstown St.	.344	.446	.600	180	8	4	10	53	6
Cam Post, Oakland	.340	.402	.497	159	9	2	4	35	10
Damon Dues, Wright St.	.335	.438	.461	206	8	3	4	38	23
Jeff Wehler, Youngstown St.	.332	.390	.552	223	13	6	8	38	25
Phillip Glasser, Youngstown St.	.321	.423	.497	187	12	3	5	28	23
Thomas Norton, UIC	.318	.412	.494	154	10	1	5	29	3
Griffin Doersching, Northern Ky.	.316	.488	.772	158	12	0	20	48	2
Aaron Chapman, Purdue Fort Wayne	.312	.394	.468	154	5	2	5	24	8

Player	AVG	OBP	SLG	AB	2B	3B	HR	RBI	SB
Luke Seidel, Milwaukee	.312	.350	.438	192	9	3	3	21	16
Sam Hedges, Northern Ky.	.311	.410	.378	148	7	0	1	23	5

INDIVIDUAL PITCHING LEADERS
(Minimum 40 innings pitched)

Player	W	L	ERA	G	SV	IP	H	BB	SO
Collin Floyd, Youngstown St.	9	4	2.58	15	0	101.1	75	23	108
Jon Snyder, Youngstown St.	6	2	2.76	15	0	71.2	51	51	88
Jacob Key, UIC	7	3	2.82	13	0	89.1	69	26	58
Austin Cline, Wright St.	8	2	3.24	15	0	72.1	63	18	91
Riley Frey, Milwaukee	2	9	3.60	14	0	80	83	30	67
Chris Torres, UIC	7	2	3.94	14	0	48	46	17	19
Bradley Brehmer, Wright St.	8	4	4.11	14	0	76.2	65	25	85
Hayden Nierman, Oakland	4	6	4.60	17	3	43	45	13	47

IVY LEAGUE

	Conference		Overall	
	W	L	W	L
Pennsylvania	0	0	6	8
Brown	0	0	0	0
Columbia	0	0	0	0
Cornell	0	0	0	0
Dartmouth	0	0	0	0
Harvard	0	0	0	0
Princeton	0	0	0	0
Yale	0	0	0	0

-The Ivy League canceled its 2021 season due to the coronavirus pandemic.

ALL-CONFERENCE TEAM: N/A.

METRO ATLANTIC ATHLETIC CONFERENCE

	Conference		Overall	
	W	L	W	L
Fairfield	33	1	39	5
Monmouth	22	10	24	13
Rider	18	16	23	18
Marist	17	9	18	11
Canisius	17	13	20	16
Niagara	16	17	16	15
Siena	14	22	15	24
Manhattan	12	22	12	24
Quinnipiac	7	21	7	21
Saint Peter's	4	24	4	24
Iona	3	11	3	11

ALL-CONFERENCE TEAM: C: Mike Caruso, Fairfield. **1B:** Vinny Chiarenza, Canisius. **2B:** Dixon Black, Monmouth. **3B:** Jake Knop, Manhattan; Evan Vulgamore, Quinnipiac. **SS:** Justin Guerrera, Fairfield. **OF:** Jake Burlingame, Quinnipiac; Mike Handal, Fairfield; Sam Franco, Manhattan. **DH:** Tyler Kapuscinski, Marist. **UTL:** Alex Barker, Monmouth. **Pitcher:** Rob Hensey, Monmouth; Jake Noviello, Fairfield; Michael Sansone, Fairfield; Dan Klepchick, Monmouth. **Player of the Year:** Mike Caruso, Fairfield. **Pitcher of the Year:** Rob Hensey, Monmouth. **Relief Pitcher of the Year:** Bryson Cafaro, Fairfield. **Coach of the Year:** Bill Currier, Fairfield. **Rookie of the Year:** Dixon Black, Monmouth.

INDIVIDUAL BATTING LEADERS
(Minimum 140 at-bats)

Player	AVG	OBP	SLG	AB	2B	3B	HR	RBI	SB
Mike Handal, Fairfield	.357	.396	.560	168	7	3	7	34	9
Justin Guerrera, Fairfield	.340	.409	.685	162	13	2	13	45	8
Dan Ryan, Fairfield	.335	.422	.538	158	10	2	6	27	7
Sean Cullen, Fairfield	.318	.403	.424	151	3	2	3	37	9
Sean McGeehan, Rider	.229	.333	.421	140	10	1	5	32	12

INDIVIDUAL PITCHING LEADERS
(Minimum 40 innings pitched)

Player	W	L	ERA	G	SV	IP	H	BB	SO
Jake Noviello, Fairfield	9	0	1.47	10	0	67.1	50	9	59
Rob Hensey, Monmouth	5	0	1.54	7	0	41	30	6	41
Michael Sansone, Fairfield	9	2	2.58	12	1	66.1	52	15	73

Player	W	L	ERA	G	SV	IP	H	BB	SO
Trey Dombroski, Monmouth	5	1	2.73	9	0	52.2	55	8	64
Frank Doelling, Rider	5	3	3.30	10	0	57.1	46	29	56
Dan Klepchick, Monmouth	4	4	3.35	9	0	45.2	38	10	54
Pete Soporowski, Rider	6	3	3.86	11	0	60.2	59	16	59
Jacob Bruning, Niagara	3	3	4.30	8	0	44	40	24	39
John Signore, Fairfield	5	2	4.50	12	2	48	48	11	43
Logan Muratalla, Manhattan	3	5	5.01	10	0	46.2	51	24	51
Connor Bovair, Siena	4	5	5.34	10	0	55.2	48	20	75
Jack Mahoney, Manhattan	2	4	5.44	10	0	46.1	46	26	39
Mike McCully, Siena	3	7	6.89	10	0	48.1	62	22	29

MID-AMERICAN CONFERENCE

	Conference		Overall	
	W	L	W	L
Central Michigan	31	9	40	17
Ball State	29	11	38	18
Kent State	23	17	30	26
Western Michigan	23	17	24	26
Toledo	21	19	23	33
Ohio	19	21	28	25
Bowling Green	18	22	20	30
Miami	18	22	25	31
Eastern Michigan	15	25	21	30
Northern Illinois	15	25	16	38
Akron	8	32	15	36

ALL-CONFERENCE TEAM: C: Connor Charping, Western Michigan. **1B:** Chris Meyers, Toledo. **2B:** Mario Camilletti, Central Michigan. **3B:** Nathan Rose, Bowling Green. **SS:** Drew Devine, Western Michigan. **OF:** Zach Gilles, Central Michigan; Ben Carew, Kent State; Cam Touchette, Kent State. **DH:** Mike Monahan, Eastern Michigan. **At-Large:** Taylor Hopkins, Eastern Michigan. **SP:** John Baker, Ball State; Andrew Taylor, Central Michigan; Sam Bachman, Miami; Joe Rock, Ohio. **RP:** Eddie Kutt, Ohio. **Player of the Year:** Chris Meyers, Toledo. **Pitcher of the Year:** Andrew Taylor, Central Michigan. **Coach of the Year:** Jordan Bischel, Central Michigan. **Freshman of the Year:** Kyle Gurney, Bowling Green. **Freshman Pitcher of the Year:** Andrew Taylor, Central Michigan. **Defensive Player of the Year:** Chase Sebby, Ball State.

INDIVIDUAL BATTING LEADERS
(Minimum 140 at-bats)

Player	AVG	OBP	SLG	AB	2B	3B	HR	RBI	SB
Chris Meyers, Toledo	.378	.509	.739	180	18	1	15	55	10
Cam Touchette, Kent St.	.363	.436	.500	190	12	1	4	30	7
Zach Gilles, Central Mich.	.359	.484	.436	195	7	4	0	42	23
Connor Charping, Western Mich.	.355	.447	.464	183	9	1	3	35	32
Kam Smith, Northern Ill.	.355	.387	.560	200	8	3	9	33	8
Nick Powell, Ball St.	.351	.450	.530	185	13	4	4	37	5
Justin Miknis, Kent St.	.349	.432	.527	169	14	2	4	36	1
Jake Dunham, Northern Ill.	.333	.421	.530	183	16	1	6	36	3
Adam Furnas, Bowling Green	.331	.435	.444	160	9	0	3	28	1
Mario Camilletti, Central Mich.	.330	.502	.454	194	15	0	3	45	8
Collin Mathews, Kent St.	.330	.411	.505	194	14	1	6	49	17
Kyle Gurney, Bowling Green	.328	.385	.503	177	13	0	6	40	0
Nicky Winterstein, Toledo	.326	.388	.486	181	11	3	4	41	9
Justin Simpson, Central Mich.	.325	.473	.402	169	11	1	0	45	12
Will Vogelsang, Miami (OH)	.321	.386	.490	196	12	6	3	35	11
Ben Carew, Kent St.	.316	.395	.505	206	12	3	7	36	10
Trace Hatfield, Toledo	.316	.391	.444	187	12	0	4	35	0
Adam Tellier, Ball St.	.311	.408	.415	183	10	3	1	28	11
Sean O'Keefe, Western Mich.	.310	.349	.503	197	14	0	8	43	2
Zach Heeke, Central Mich.	.308	.419	.434	182	7	2	4	35	5
Taylor Hopkins, Eastern Mich.	.306	.394	.486	183	9	0	8	30	9
Noah Navarro, Ball St.	.306	.394	.489	186	11	4	5	31	12
Trenton Quartermaine, Ball St.	.306	.413	.425	193	9	1	4	40	0
Harry Witwer-Dukes, Ohio	.305	.413	.482	164	12	1	5	32	3
Drew Devine, Western Mich.	.303	.424	.479	165	14	0	5	29	2
Michael McNamara, Kent St.	.303	.410	.503	155	11	1	6	39	2
Justin Kirby, Kent St.	.301	.386	.473	146	8	1	5	25	10
Benji Brokemond, Miami (OH)	.295	.379	.382	173	6	3	1	19	8
Cameron Tilly, Akron	.294	.374	.425	153	8	0	4	21	2
Ross Messina, Ball St.	.288	.353	.429	205	12	1	5	41	3

INDIVIDUAL PITCHING LEADERS
(Minimum 40 innings pitched)

Player	W	L	ERA	G	SV	IP	H	BB	SO
Andrew Taylor, Central Mich.	11	4	1.81	15	0	94.1	64	24	125
Sam Bachman, Miami (OH)	4	4	1.81	12	0	59.2	29	17	93
John Baker, Ball St.	9	3	2.32	19	4	101	82	25	107
Joe Rock, Ohio	8	3	2.33	14	0	88.2	67	27	117
Jordan Patty, Central Mich.	10	2	2.46	15	0	91.7	72	28	78
Davis Feldman, Eastern Mich.	4	5	2.75	13	1	59	59	19	58
Eddie Kutt, Ohio	8	4	2.92	22	5	74	55	13	84
Chayce McDermott, Ball St.	8	2	3.05	15	0	82.2	59	36	125
Chace Harris, Ohio	3	3	3.25	13	1	44.1	39	16	43
Brandon McPherson, Northern Ill.	2	3	3.38	10	1	48	42	20	50
Luke Albright, Kent St.	6	4	3.40	15	0	82	65	40	102
Grant Hartwig, Miami (OH)	5	5	3.44	14	0	73.1	65	11	82
Lukas Jaksich, Ball St.	8	3	3.45	19	1	73	67	35	96
Cameron Wagoner, Eastern Mich.	2	3	3.49	18	2	49	53	22	56
Tyler Bosma, Miami (OH)	2	4	3.95	15	0	57	56	37	72

MID-EASTERN ATHLETIC CONFERENCE

Northern Division	Conference		Overall	
	W	L	W	L
Norfolk State	18	10	25	28
Delaware State	13	18	15	27
Coppin State	7	20	10	29
Southern Division	W	L	W	L
North Carolina Central	17	11	27	20
Florida A&M	15	13	22	33
North Carolina A&T	17	15	22	32

ALL-CONFERENCE TEAM: C: Mike Dorcean, RFr., Coppin State. **1B:** Mason Velasquez, Sr., Norfolk State. **2B:** Alsander Womack, Sr., Norfolk State. **SS:** Danny Hosley, Sr., Norfolk State. **3B:** Justin Williams, RJr., North Carolina A&T. **OF:** Trey Paige, So., Delaware State. **OF:** Dionte Brown, Jr., Norfolk State. **OF:** Justin Rodriguez, RJr., North Carolina A&T. **UTL:** Cole Garey, Sr., Delaware State. **SP:** Austin Vernon, RJr., North Carolina Central; Ryan Miller, RSo., North Carolina Central. **RP:** Scott Meylan, RJr., North Carolina Central. **Player of the Year:** Danny Hosley, Norfolk State. **Pitcher of the Year:** Ryan Miller, North Carolina Central. **Coach of the Year:** Jim Koerner, North Carolina Central. **Rookie of the Year:** Chet Sikes, North Carolina Central.

INDIVIDUAL BATTING LEADERS
(Minimum 140 at-bats)

Player	AVG	OBP	SLG	AB	2B	3B	HR	RBI	SB
Trey Paige, Delaware St.	.366	.475	.592	142	13	2	5	32	7
Alsander Womack, Norfolk St.	.364	.433	.472	195	12	0	3	37	17
John Weglarz, Delaware St.	.336	.410	.470	149	11	0	3	32	5
Kokko Figuerido, N.C. Central	.335	.424	.471	170	8	0	5	35	2
Luis DeLeon, N.C. Central	.315	.404	.488	168	15	4	2	31	8
Darren Hagan, Coppin St.	.312	.380	.454	141	7	2	3	25	6
Justin Rodriguez, N.C. A&T	.312	.386	.463	160	9	0	5	43	14
Dionte Brown, Norfolk St.	.307	.384	.398	176	7	3	1	17	19
Miguel Rivera, Delaware St.	.304	.421	.453	148	10	0	4	21	10
LJ Bryant, Florida A&M	.303	.423	.466	178	10	2	5	35	7
Dustin Baber, N.C. A&T	.301	.376	.393	183	4	2	3	32	8
Justin Williams, N.C. A&T	.298	.385	.489	178	10	0	8	38	6
Jared Weber, Florida A&M	.297	.378	.427	185	7	1	5	32	7
Cole Garey, Delaware St.	.295	.356	.425	146	7	0	4	30	0
Octavien Moyer, Florida A&M	.283	.435	.385	187	12	2	1	17	6
Cort Maynard, N.C. Central	.282	.426	.470	149	6	2	6	23	4
Cameron Norgren, N.C. Central	.280	.368	.476	164	5	0	9	36	6
Cameran Brantley, N.C. A&T	.277	.447	.434	166	9	1	5	24	7
Seyjuan Lawrence, Florida A&M	.277	.323	.387	173	7	0	4	28	9
Mason Velasquez, Norfolk St.	.276	.383	.425	174	9	1	5	24	8
Ty Hanchey, Norfolk St.	.271	.361	.434	166	8	2	5	30	13
Adam Haidermota, Florida A&M	.220	.312	.248	141	4	0	0	11	1
Tucker Rayburn, Florida A&M	.208	.306	.346	159	8	1	4	21	1

INDIVIDUAL PITCHING LEADERS
(Minimum 40 innings pitched)

Player	W	L	ERA	G	SV	IP	H	BB	SO
Ryan Miller, N.C. Central	10	0	2.21	13	0	73.1	55	22	74
Austin Vernon, N.C. Central	5	4	2.55	12	0	70.2	41	31	109
James Deloatch, Norfolk St.	7	3	2.88	13	0	72	56	47	66
Zach Morea, Florida A&M	4	1	3.81	32	1	54.1	52	17	31
Cole Parks, N.C. A&T	5	2	3.96	11	0	63.2	59	28	64
Danny Hosley, Norfolk St.	7	2	4.01	47	0	76.1	63	19	84
Kelyn Fox, Florida A&M	7	2	4.29	13	0	71.1	80	28	48
Evan Gates, N.C. A&T	4	4	4.37	22	5	47.1	48	15	79
Shawn Runey, N.C. Central	4	5	5.09	12	0	53	51	26	39
Michael Johnson, N.C. A&T	2	7	5.15	11	0	57.2	65	23	38
William Jackson, Coppin St.	1	4	5.44	11	0	46.1	57	19	32
Jordan Haddaway, Delaware St.	4	4	5.62	12	0	56	63	41	33
Derek Martinez, N.C. A&T	1	5	6.04	14	0	44.2	58	31	45
Cole Bates, Delaware St.	2	5	6.82	13	0	64.2	96	18	58
Ethan Chavis, N.C. A&T	2	4	6.97	11	0	40	48	19	31
Justin Walton, Norfolk St.	1	3	7.31	12	0	44.1	60	24	43
Kyle Coleman, Florida A&M	2	6	7.36	11	0	44	64	16	22
Josh Hancock, Florida A&M	4	8	7.60	13	0	58	77	32	37

MISSOURI VALLEY CONFERENCE

Team	Conference		Overall	
	W	L	W	L
Dallas Baptist	18	6	41	18
Indiana State	14	10	31	21
Bradley	12	10	20	22
Southern Illinois	15	13	40	20
Missouri State	11	13	21	23
Illinois State	12	15	23	34
Evansville	11	16	28	27
Valparaiso	9	19	16	35

ALL-CONFERENCE TEAM: C: Max Wright, RSr., Indiana State. **1B:** Connor O'Brien, So., Bradley; Jake McCaw, RSo., Illinois State. **2B:** Jackson Glenn, Sr., Dallas Baptist. **3B:** Brendan Dougherty, Sr., Bradley. **SS:** Jordan Schaffer, RJr., Indiana State. **OF:** Dan Bolt, Sr., Bradley; Ryan Cermak, Fr., Illinois State; Aaron Beck, RJr., Indiana State. **DH:** Austin Bell, RSr., Dallas Baptist. **SP:** Geremy Guerrero, RSr., Indiana State; Rhett Kouba, So., Dallas Baptist; Brad Harrison, Sr., Southern Illinois. **RP:** Peyton Sherlin, Jr., Dallas Baptist; Connor Fenlong, RSo., Indiana State; Trey Ziegenbein, Jr., Missouri State. **Player of the Year:** Jackson Glenn, Dallas Baptist. **Pitcher of the Year:** Geremy Guerrero, Indiana State. **Coach of the Year:** Dan Heefner, Dallas Baptist. **Freshman of the Year:** Kaleb Hannahs, Valparaiso. **Newcomer of the Year:** Aaron Beck, Indiana State. **Defensive Player of the Year:** Ryan Cermak, Illinois State.

INDIVIDUAL BATTING LEADERS
(Minimum 140 at-bats)

Player	AVG	OBP	SLG	AB	2B	3B	HR	RBI	SB
Jake McCaw, Illinois St.	.367	.424	.506	180	14	1	3	27	2
Jordan Schaffer, Indiana St.	.367	.432	.521	215	10	1	7	34	11
Jackson Glenn, DBU	.366	.438	.732	235	19	2	21	55	13
Connor O'Brien, Bradley	.366	.452	.549	142	12	1	4	26	1
Tristan Peters, Southern Ill.	.355	.463	.548	217	20	2	6	55	14
Jace Grady, DBU	.337	.417	.534	178	17	3	4	40	15
Troy Beilsmith, Evansville	.330	.457	.532	203	16	2	7	35	12
Cole Moore, DBU	.329	.429	.606	170	14	0	11	46	4
Dan Bolt, Bradley	.327	.462	.565	147	8	0	9	28	1
River Town, DBU	.326	.436	.519	233	15	0	10	51	20
Philip Archer, Southern Ill.	.322	.399	.552	230	20	0	11	60	2
Kenton Crews, Evansville	.322	.383	.489	174	12	4	3	34	6
J.T. Weber, Southern Ill.	.322	.375	.589	236	16	1	15	63	5
Brendan Dougherty, Bradley	.321	.423	.430	165	10	1	2	29	9
Tyson Hays, Illinois St.	.310	.412	.430	158	6	2	3	14	5
Jordan Libman, Illinois St.	.307	.403	.443	212	10	2	5	28	2
Max Wright, Indiana St.	.305	.453	.611	190	8	1	16	41	4
Tanner Craig, Evansville	.299	.384	.547	201	14	0	12	47	1
Nick Neville, Southern Ill.	.299	.373	.581	234	11	2	17	47	9
Kaleb Hannahs, Valparaiso	.296	.389	.387	186	6	1	3	22	4
Drake Baldwin, Missouri St.	.291	.411	.446	148	7	2	4	24	3
Simon Scherry, Evansville	.288	.333	.400	215	16	1	2	35	6
Ryan Cermak, Illinois St.	.284	.349	.553	190	10	4	11	40	3

Player	AVG	OBP	SLG	AB	2B	3B	HR	RBI	SB
Andrew Benefield, DBU	.280	.371	.482	193	12	0	9	41	8
Austin Bell, DBU	.278	.441	.551	158	13	0	10	39	4
Aidan Huggins, Illinois St.	.273	.361	.414	198	9	2	5	20	1
Parker Johnson, Valparaiso	.273	.330	.364	165	7	1	2	24	5
Josue Urdaneta, Indiana St.	.270	.335	.332	211	8	1	1	18	9
Ben Whetstone, Missouri St.	.267	.421	.420	150	6	1	5	21	2
Danny Borgstron, Evansville	.266	.387	.487	158	6	1	9	29	0

INDIVIDUAL PITCHING LEADERS
(Minimum 40 innings pitched)

Player	W	L	ERA	G	SV	IP	H	BB	SO
Geremy Guerrero, Indiana St.	10	1	2.08	14	0	99.1	65	14	98
Rhett Kouba, DBU	6	2	2.77	16	0	74.2	60	23	87
Peyton Sherlin, DBU	0	1	2.92	24	4	40	24	26	47
Noah Farmer, Southern Ill.	6	4	2.98	20	1	66.1	68	26	43
Trey McDaniel, Southern Ill.	6	4	3.07	30	9	44	43	20	51
Colton Johnson, Illinois St.	3	5	3.32	14	0	86.2	88	24	86
Shane Gray, Evansville	6	3	3.38	15	0	88	74	35	73
Logan Wiley, Missouri St.	5	4	3.47	15	0	72.2	60	22	58
Jared Viertel, Missouri St.	1	5	3.53	11	0	43.1	36	32	38
Brad Harrison, Southern Ill.	9	0	3.54	15	0	81.1	77	27	98
Trey Ziegenbein, Missouri St.	7	2	3.77	29	0	57.1	53	22	56
Jon Tieman, Valparaiso	2	3	3.92	17	3	41.1	36	26	48
Ben Chapman, Southern Ill.	7	5	3.97	17	0	81.2	87	18	78
Hayden Minton, Missouri St.	0	5	4.19	9	0	43	35	26	38
Dominic Hamel, DBU	13	2	4.22	18	1	91.2	68	34	136

MOUNTAIN WEST CONFERENCE

	Conference		Overall	
	W	L	W	L
Nevada	22	9	25	20
San Diego State	22	14	30	16
Nevada-Las Vegas	15	12	20	13
Air Force	18	16	26	22
Fresno State	16	18	20	25
New Mexico	10	17	16	19
San Jose State	2	19	6	30

ALL-CONFERENCE TEAM: C: Paul Skenes, Fr., Air Force; Wyatt Hendrie, So., San Diego State. **1B:** Jack-Thomas Wold, Jr., Nevada-Las Vegas; Dillan Shrum, Sr., Nevada. **SS:** Brendan Brooks, Jr., Nevada-Las Vegas. **3B:** Andrew Kachel, So., Fresno State; Tyler Bosetti, Jr., Nevada. **OF:** Dario Gomez, So., Nevada; Kyler Castillo, Jr., New Mexico; Matt Rudick, Jr., San Diego State. **Pitcher:** John Byrnes, Sr., Air Force; Cam Walty, Fr., Nevada; Shane Gustafson, Sr., Nevada; Justin Armbruester, Sr., New Mexico. **Player of the Year:** Dillan Shrum, Nevada. **Pitcher of the Year:** Justin Armbruester, New Mexico. **Coach of the Year:** T.J. Bruce, Nevada. **Freshman of the Year:** Paul Skenes, Air Force.

INDIVIDUAL BATTING LEADERS
(Minimum 140 at-bats)

Player	AVG	OBP	SLG	AB	2B	3B	HR	RBI	SB
Kyler Castillo, New Mexico	.439	.486	.665	164	16	0	7	40	5
Jack-Thomas Wold, UNLV	.429	.491	.793	140	13	1	12	43	1
Matt Rudick, San Diego St.	.410	.484	.567	178	8	4	4	41	17
Paul Skenes, Air Force	.410	.486	.697	188	21	0	11	43	0
Dario Gomez, Nevada	.393	.415	.592	191	16	2	6	37	12
Jaden Fein, San Diego St.	.389	.456	.553	190	19	0	4	53	8
Wyatt Hendrie, San Diego St.	.379	.464	.633	169	12	2	9	57	8
Mack Chambers, New Mexico	.371	.444	.624	170	16	3	7	31	5
Mike Jarvis, Nevada	.367	.417	.544	215	17	3	5	52	73
Ryan Higgins, Fresno St.	.352	.453	.667	165	13	3	11	41	4
Caden Miller, San Diego St.	.345	.464	.426	148	6	3	0	30	8
Braydon Altorfer, Nevada	.333	.437	.627	177	23	1	9	43	2
Cole Blatchford, Air Force	.330	.385	.471	191	12	0	5	32	6
Gabriel Garcia, Air Force	.330	.397	.534	191	14	5	5	37	7
Tyler Bosetti, Nevada	.328	.387	.641	195	22	3	11	47	3
Andrew Kachel, Fresno St.	.328	.422	.609	174	12	2	11	38	2
Willie Cano, New Mexico	.310	.363	.424	158	10	1	2	26	7
Jacob Cruce, San Diego St.	.308	.358	.476	185	11	1	6	46	0
Brian Leonhardt, San Diego St.	.305	.374	.404	151	7	1	2	47	0
Zach Morgan, Fresno St.	.295	.344	.389	149	5	0	3	19	1
Joshua Zamora, Nevada	.290	.399	.580	162	7	2	12	26	0
Cayden Zimmerman, Air Force	.288	.355	.432	146	11	2	2	25	9
Zach Presno, Fresno St.	.267	.379	.459	146	6	2	6	27	4

Player	AVG	OBP	SLG	AB	2B	3B	HR	RBI	SB
Tommy Gillman, Air Force	.262	.342	.355	172	7	3	1	29	4
Blake Covin, Air Force	.258	.345	.331	151	4	2	1	12	11
Alexander Pup, Air Force	.236	.324	.333	165	8	1	2	20	4

INDIVIDUAL PITCHING LEADERS
(Minimum 40 innings pitched)

Player	W	L	ERA	G	SV	IP	H	BB	SO
Shane Gustafson, Nevada	3	2	2.89	20	3	46.2	36	18	40
Justin Armbruester, New Mexico	5	2	3.58	13	0	78	66	21	101
John Byrnes, Air Force	5	4	3.86	14	0	67.2	61	27	59
Cam Walty, Nevada	5	3	4.02	12	0	56	52	30	48
Bradley Spooner, UNLV	6	3	4.24	11	0	57.1	67	17	57
Jamison Hill, Fresno St.	5	3	5.23	12	0	72.1	94	15	49
Jake Jackson, Nevada	5	4	5.45	15	0	74.1	112	15	44
Michael Paredes, San Diego St.	4	0	5.59	14	0	77.1	82	18	65
Josh Sharman, UNLV	1	4	5.69	11	0	55.1	64	13	26
Jake Dixon, Fresno St.	6	3	5.80	15	0	66.2	83	28	50
Troy Melton, San Diego St.	4	5	6.14	15	0	73.1	87	30	83
Alejandro Murillo, Nevada	2	2	6.25	15	0	59	73	22	49
Jonathan Clark, San Jose St.	1	7	6.55	8	0	44	43	30	47
Nathaniel Garley, New Mexico	1	4	6.58	13	0	53.1	80	12	30
Ricky Tibbett, San Diego St.	4	2	6.62	16	0	50.1	72	10	53

NORTHEAST CONFERENCE

	Conference		Overall	
	W	L	W	L
Bryant	21	4	27	14
Central Connecticut State	21	9	28	15
Sacred Heart	17	10	23	25
Long Island	18	11	20	15
Merrimack	13	14	19	22
Wagner	8	22	10	25
Fairleigh Dickinson	8	22	9	27
Mount St. Mary's	5	19	9	28

ALL-CONFERENCE TEAM: C: Sam Loda, Jr., Central Connecticut State. **1B:** Liam McGill, Gr., Bryant. **2B:** Jake Gustin, Jr., Bryant. **3B:** Jay DeVito, Jr., Central Connecticut State. **SS:** Anthony Warneke, Sr., Long Island. **OF:** James Cilento, Sr., Bryant; Jared Gillen, Gr., Wagner; Derek Smith, So., Bryant. **DH:** Robert Farruggio, Jr., Sacred Heart. **SP:** Tyler Mattison, Sr., Bryant; Andrew Braun, Sr., Central Connecticut State; Jordan Geber, Jr., Mount St. Mary's. **RP:** Rob Griswold, Sr., Long Island. **Player of the Year:** Liam McGill, Bryant. **Pitcher of the Year:** Tyler Mattison, Bryant. **Coach of the Year:** Ryan Klosterman, Bryant. **Rookie of the Year:** Jake Neuman, Central Connecticut State.

INDIVIDUAL BATTING LEADERS
(Minimum 140 at-bats)

Player	AVG	OBP	SLG	AB	2B	3B	HR	RBI	SB
Jared Gillen, Wagner	.396	.437	.510	149	11	0	2	32	16
Jake Gustin, Bryant	.386	.463	.591	171	13	2	6	36	10
Jay Devito, Central Conn. St.	.333	.498	.378	156	5	1	0	25	6
James Cilento, Bryant	.327	.417	.513	156	7	2	6	37	10
Derek Smith, Bryant	.321	.404	.479	165	12	1	4	39	6
Matt Woods, Bryant	.314	.407	.405	153	6	1	2	20	9
Joey Porricelli, Merrimack	.308	.461	.541	146	9	2	7	20	17
Danny Glendon, Sacred Heart	.306	.410	.415	147	11	1	1	16	3
Noah Martinez, Central Conn. St.	.305	.396	.503	167	8	2	7	37	0
Robert Farruggio, Sacred Heart	.298	.383	.447	141	9	0	4	26	2
Mike Veit, Fairleigh Dickinson	.298	.372	.371	151	8	0	1	24	8
Dave Matthews, Central Conn. St.	.293	.390	.503	167	14	0	7	33	13
Hunter D'Amato, Fairleigh Dickinson	.287	.323	.363	157	7	1	1	18	6
EJ Exposito, LIU	.286	.374	.442	147	5	0	6	29	6
Justin Jordan, Sacred Heart	.271	.418	.342	155	5	0	2	19	7
Myles Nicholson, Mount St. Mary's	.270	.309	.376	141	4	1	3	13	15
Isiah Daubon, Sacred Heart	.263	.361	.404	156	8	1	4	26	10
Nick Shumski, Merrimack	.262	.351	.445	164	11	2	5	31	3
Anthony Warneke, LIU	.260	.356	.360	150	7	1	2	29	17
Austin Markmann, Sacred Heart	.255	.324	.413	196	13	0	6	43	4
Elijah Brown, Sacred Heart	.250	.341	.361	180	11	0	3	22	27
Sam Loda, Central Conn. St.	.247	.371	.340	150	11	0	1	34	3
Joe Emerson, Sacred Heart	.241	.331	.333	141	10	0	1	25	10
Alex Haba, Merrimack	.236	.337	.403	144	8	2	4	19	6
Tommy DiTullio, Bryant	.212	.297	.258	151	5	1	0	14	2
Michael Jamele, Merrimack	.208	.252	.235	149	1	0	1	15	6

INDIVIDUAL PITCHING LEADERS
(Minimum 40 innings pitched)

Player	W	L	ERA	G	SV	IP	H	BB	SO
Tyler Mattison, Bryant	10	3	2.46	13	0	80.1	57	14	95
Tyler Schoff, Bryant	7	1	3.12	12	0	69.1	64	14	72
Vito Morgese, Bryant	4	2	3.49	12	0	59.1	70	19	57
Mike Lazos, LIU	7	1	3.56	11	0	43	45	9	26
Andrew Braun, Central Conn. St.	9	1	3.64	15	0	84	83	12	76
Jordan Geber, Mount St. Mary's	2	3	3.88	11	0	60.1	47	26	68
Alec Huertas, LIU	2	4	3.90	10	0	57.2	58	20	53
Riley Sorenson, Merrimack	5	3	4.06	11	0	71	57	31	50
Ryan Lauk, Wagner	2	6	4.40	12	0	73.2	63	26	86
Brandon Fox, Central Conn. St.	5	6	4.52	14	0	83.2	94	19	58
Jake Babuschak, Sacred Heart	5	2	4.65	14	1	60	55	28	45
Brendan Medoro, Fairleigh Dickinson	1	3	4.72	17	6	55.1	72	13	38
Chase Jeter, Sacred Heart	5	3	5.04	12	0	60.2	70	22	43
Anthony Mozzicato, Central Conn. St.	5	2	5.09	13	0	58.1	68	18	45
Joey Kosowsky, Fairleigh Dickinson	5	3	5.19	13	0	60.2	60	40	76

OHIO VALLEY CONFERENCE

	Conference		Overall	
	W	L	W	L
Southeast Missouri State	17	10	30	22
Murray State	18	12	33	25
Morehead State	13	11	24	23
Jacksonville State	16	14	26	27
Austin Peay	16	14	23	33
Tennessee Tech	15	15	22	25
Eastern Illinois	14	16	25	23
Belmont	14	16	22	30
Southern Illinois-Edwardsville	13	17	23	27
Eastern Kentucky	13	17	21	32
Tennessee-Martin	10	17	19	29

ALL-CONFERENCE TEAM: C: Alex Webb, Sr., Jacksonville State. **1B:** Jackson Feltner, Fr., Morehead State. **2B:** Jordan Cozart, RSr., Murray State. **3B:** Logan Jarvis, Jr., Belmont. **SS:** Trey Sweeney, RSo., Eastern Illinois. **OF:** Garrett Spain, Jr., Austin Peay; John Behrends, So., Belmont; Cody Littlejohn, Sr., Tennessee Tech. **DH:** Caleb Upshaw, Jr., Eastern Kentucky. **UTL:** Bobby Head, RJr., Austin Peay. **SP:** Dylan Dodd, Sr., Southeast Missouri State; Christian Edwards, Jr., Jacksonville State; Winston Cannon, Sr., Tennessee-Martin. **RP:** Corley Woods, Sr., Jacksonville State. **Player of the Year:** Trey Sweeney, Eastern Illinois. **Pitcher of the Year:** Dylan Dodd, Southeast Missouri State. **Coach of the Year:** Andy Sawyers, Southeast Missouri State. **Freshman of the Year:** Jackson Feltner, Morehead State.

INDIVIDUAL BATTING LEADERS
(Minimum 140 at-bats)

Player	AVG	OBP	SLG	AB	2B	3B	HR	RBI	SB
Jackson Feltner, Morehead St.	.390	.452	.652	164	10	0	11	42	0
Trey Sweeney, Eastern Ill.	.382	.522	.712	170	10	2	14	58	3
Tyler Wilber, Southeast Mo. St.	.378	.446	.542	201	11	2	6	49	4
Bryce Hensor, Morehead St.	.354	.439	.519	189	15	2	4	27	10
Jevon Mason, Southeast Mo. St.	.350	.447	.475	160	14	0	2	22	4
Logan Jarvis, Belmont	.346	.474	.570	179	9	5	7	53	10
Brett Roberts, Tennessee Tech	.343	.375	.490	204	13	1	5	39	17
Malcolm Tipler, Austin Peay	.335	.429	.443	176	10	0	3	20	2
John Behrends, Belmont	.332	.444	.554	193	15	2	8	42	13
Ed Johnson, Tennessee Tech	.331	.406	.483	172	9	1	5	28	4
Garrett Spain, Austin Peay	.330	.408	.515	206	7	2	9	43	14
Caleb Upshaw, Eastern Ky.	.325	.401	.560	200	12	1	11	48	2
Cody Littlejohn, Tennessee Tech	.324	.399	.635	170	5	3	14	37	6
Ryley Preece, Morehead St.	.324	.424	.490	145	7	1	5	22	4
Ole Arntson, SIUE	.321	.407	.591	159	8	1	11	38	1
Jordan Cozart, Murray St.	.317	.401	.648	227	18	0	19	59	1
Connor Kiffer, SIUE	.316	.386	.511	190	13	0	8	40	3
Brett Johnson, SIUE	.305	.444	.558	190	12	3	10	33	14
Alex Webb, Jacksonville St.	.304	.374	.521	217	14	3	9	54	1
Kendal Ewell, Eastern Ky.	.303	.390	.509	175	11	2	7	34	2
Bobby Head, Austin Peay	.303	.372	.481	208	11	1	8	39	10
Golston Gillespie, Tennessee Tech	.302	.439	.616	159	9	1	13	37	6
Nash Adams, Jacksonville St.	.300	.392	.418	170	14	0	2	22	4
Carson Crowe, Jacksonville St.	.299	.404	.548	157	16	1	7	21	1

Blake Daniels, UT Martin	.299	.382	.510	157	13	1	6	27	2
Brodey Heaton, Belmont	.298	.381	.417	168	9	1	3	44	1
Andrew Keck, Southeast Mo. St.	.298	.372	.424	205	9	1	5	25	17
Bryson Bloomer, Murray St.	.297	.364	.520	229	19	1	10	46	3
Raul Elguezabal, SIUE	.297	.356	.523	195	14	3	8	32	5
Jaylyn Williams, Jacksonville St.	.297	.422	.525	158	11	2	7	31	2

INDIVIDUAL PITCHING LEADERS
(Minimum 40 innings pitched)

Player	W	L	ERA	G	SV	IP	H	BB	SO
Christian Edwards, Jacksonville St.	5	2	2.48	12	1	69	42	27	83
David Hussey, UT Martin	3	1	2.59	23	6	41.2	27	12	52
Dylan Dodd, Southeast Mo. St.	9	2	3.17	15	0	96.2	85	17	120
Jacob Pennington, Murray St.	5	2	3.38	34	0	61.1	52	14	65
Cameron Doherty, Eastern Ill.	3	2	3.45	15	4	75.2	76	14	71
Colin Casey, Jacksonville St.	6	5	3.63	14	0	62	56	33	54
Kyle Brennan, Belmont	4	3	3.63	27	3	44.2	40	26	47
Winston Cannon, UT Martin	6	6	3.78	16	0	81	82	24	83
Kyle Miller, Southeast Mo. St.	4	2	3.86	20	5	51.1	54	15	52
Kyle Luigs, Jacksonville St.	3	1	3.95	18	1	41	36	24	30
John Bakke, Morehead St.	1	3	4.02	27	7	47	39	24	61
Drew McIllwain, Austin Peay	2	3	4.05	16	0	60	51	26	54
Darren Williams, Eastern Ky.	3	8	4.10	15	0	83.1	77	30	92
Andy Bean, Belmont	5	2	4.10	14	1	74.2	64	24	62
Cory Conway, Morehead St.	8	3	4.14	21	1	45.2	58	22	55

PACIFIC-12 CONFERENCE

	Conference		Overall	
	W	L	W	L
Arizona	21	9	45	18
Oregon	20	10	39	16
Stanford	17	10	39	17
UCLA	18	12	37	20
Oregon State	16	14	37	24
Arizona State	16	14	33	22
California	15	15	29	26
Washington State	13	17	26	23
Southern California	13	17	25	26
Utah	7	23	17	33
Washington	7	23	20	30

ALL-CONFERENCE TEAM: C: Daniel Susac, Fr., Arizona; Noah Cardenas, Jr., UCLA; Troy Claunch, Jr., Oregon State; Garrett Guillemette, Jr., Southern California. **1B:** Branden Boissiere, So., Arizona; Tristan Peterson, Gr., Washington State. **INF:** Darren Baker, Sr., California; Nick Brueser, Sr., Stanford; Ethan Long, Fr., Arizona State; Kyle Manzardo, Jr., Washington State; Gabe Matthews, Sr., Oregon; Matt McLain, Jr., UCLA; Ben Ramirez, RJr., Southern California; Quentin Selma, Sr., California; J.T. Schwartz, RSo., UCLA; Drew Swift, RJr., Arizona State; Kenyon Yovan, RJr., Oregon. **OF:** Dylan Beavers, So., California; Brock Jones, So., Stanford; Donta Williams, Jr., Arizona; Aaron Zavala, So., Oregon. **Pitcher:** Robert Ahlstrom, Jr., Oregon; Brendan Beck, Sr., Stanford; Adrian Chaidez, Sr., UCLA; Will Frisch, Fr., Oregon State; Zach Grech, Sr., Stanford; Jake Mulholland, Sr., Oregon State; Sean Mullen, Sr., UCLA; Max Rajcic, Fr., UCLA; Chase Silseth, So., Arizona; Kolby Somers, Jr., Oregon. **Player of the Year:** Aaron Zavala, Oregon. **Pitcher of the Year:** Brendan Beck, Stanford. **Coach of the Year:** Jay Johnson, Arizona. **Freshman of the Year:** Daniel Susac, Arizona. **Defensive Player of the Year:** Drew Swift, Arizona State.

INDIVIDUAL BATTING LEADERS
(Minimum 140 at-bats)

Player	AVG	OBP	SLG	AB	2B	3B	HR	RBI	SB
JT Schwartz, UCLA	.396	.514	.628	164	12	1	8	45	1
Aaron Zavala, Oregon	.392	.525	.628	199	14	2	9	38	11
Branden Boissiere, Arizona	.369	.451	.506	255	12	4	5	63	2
Kyle Manzardo, Washington St.	.365	.437	.640	197	19	1	11	60	1
Kevin Kendall, UCLA	.356	.413	.498	247	17	3	4	37	10
Jacob Berry, Arizona	.352	.439	.676	247	19	5	17	70	2
Ryan Holgate, Arizona	.351	.421	.576	245	20	1	11	56	3
Kobe Kato, Arizona	.350	.460	.469	226	16	4	1	34	6
Donta Williams, Arizona	.342	.481	.537	240	17	3	8	49	9
Ethan Long, Arizona St.	.340	.417	.704	162	11	0	16	54	0
Daniel Susac, Arizona	.335	.392	.591	242	24	1	12	65	0
Matt McLain, UCLA	.333	.434	.579	183	14	2	9	36	9

Player	AVG	OBP	SLG	AB	2B	3B	HR	RBI	SB
Darren Baker, California	.327	.402	.354	223	6	0	0	17	28
Jayden Kiernan, Utah	.325	.394	.364	154	6	0	0	17	0
Josh Kasevich, Oregon	.324	.397	.444	216	10	2	4	50	7
Tanner Smith, Oregon	.324	.417	.533	225	24	4	5	36	4
Gabe Matthews, Oregon	.322	.449	.559	202	20	2	8	35	0
Sean McLain, Arizona St.	.322	.386	.519	208	18	1	7	37	6
Kodie Kolden, Washington St.	.320	.382	.433	203	7	2	4	38	6
Christian Robinson, Stanford	.318	.398	.500	198	12	0	8	48	8
Nik McClaughry, Arizona	.316	.412	.401	152	8	1	1	32	1
Collin Montez, Washington St.	.316	.435	.500	190	10	2	7	36	0
Drew Swift, Arizona St.	.314	.380	.475	223	10	4	6	38	6
Vincent Martinez, Stanford	.312	.387	.500	154	8	0	7	22	0
Brock Jones, Stanford	.311	.453	.646	206	13	1	18	62	14
Jack Smith, Washington St.	.311	.389	.415	183	13	0	2	28	0
Will Simpson, Washington	.310	.381	.500	168	9	1	7	35	3
Kenyon Yovan, Oregon	.309	.407	.608	204	10	0	17	57	1
Mac Bingham, Arizona	.305	.417	.390	141	7	1	1	33	1
Troy Claunch, Oregon St.	.305	.379	.399	203	7	0	4	30	1

INDIVIDUAL PITCHING LEADERS
(Minimum 40 innings pitched)

Player	W	L	ERA	G	SV	IP	H	BB	SO
Will Frisch, Oregon St.	3	0	2.38	20	0	56.2	43	24	54
Robert Ahlstrom, Oregon	9	3	2.50	14	0	90	77	16	92
Josh White, California	5	3	2.79	16	3	61.1	49	25	81
Tyson Guerrero, Washington	3	3	2.96	11	0	54.2	50	18	50
Cullen Kafka, Oregon	5	3	3.00	15	0	78	73	35	84
Brendan Beck, Stanford	9	3	3.15	17	0	108.2	81	26	143
Jake Pfennigs, Oregon St.	5	0	3.24	13	0	58.1	54	19	50
Brayson Hurdsman, Utah	3	2	3.32	17	3	40.2	34	9	33
Sean Mullen, UCLA	9	1	3.39	23	2	77	65	38	89
Isaac Esqueda, Southern California	6	3	3.41	15	0	87	79	32	73
Alex Williams, Stanford	5	2	3.42	12	0	55.1	38	17	54
Kevin Abel, Oregon St.	3	5	3.62	16	0	82	47	61	109
Zach Grech, Stanford	5	5	3.62	31	13	49.2	42	12	34
Brett Walker, Oregon	6	3	3.66	15	0	83.2	81	26	60
Sean Sullivan, California	4	5	3.68	15	0	78.1	78	22	75

PATRIOT LEAGUE

North Division	Conference		Overall	
	W	L	W	L
Army	15	10	28	25
Lafayette	12	13	14	17
Holy Cross	9	15	10	20
South Division	**W**	**L**	**W**	**L**
Lehigh	17	10	24	19
Navy	11	12	17	15
Bucknell	11	15	11	22

ALL-CONFERENCE TEAM: C: Angelo D'Acunto, Jr., Holy Cross. **1B:** Casey Rother, Jr., Lehigh. **2B:** Nico Valdez, Jr., Navy. **SS:** Justin Johnson, Jr., Lafayette. **3B:** Anthony Giachin, Sr., Army. **OF:** Sam Ruta, Fr., Army; Chris Cannazzaro, Jr., Bucknell; Eric Cichocki, Sr., Lehigh. **At-Large:** Christian Policelli, Jr., Navy. **SP:** Mason Black, Jr., Lehigh; Chris DiFiore, So., Bucknell; Matt Svanson, Sr., Lehigh. **RP:** Sam Wurth, Sr., Lehigh. **Player of the Year:** Casey Rother, Lehigh. **Pitcher of the Year:** Mason Black, Lehigh. **Coach of the Year:** Sean Leary, Lehigh. **Rookie of the Year:** Sam Ruta, Army. **Defensive Player of the Year:** Tim Simoes, Army.

INDIVIDUAL BATTING LEADERS
(Minimum 140 at-bats)

Player	AVG	OBP	SLG	AB	2B	3B	HR	RBI	SB
Casey Rother, Lehigh	.329	.422	.494	158	6	1	6	34	3
Joe Gorla, Lehigh	.322	.420	.510	149	10	3	4	34	3
Jeremiah Adams, Army West Point	.316	.395	.471	155	12	3	2	22	11
Anthony Giachin, Army West Point	.304	.427	.478	184	13	5	3	32	8
Eric Cichocki, Lehigh	.297	.406	.424	158	12	1	2	10	9
Gerard Sweeney, Lehigh	.289	.403	.516	159	11	2	7	31	2
Tim Simoes, Army West Point	.287	.372	.369	160	6	2	1	24	8
Kevin Duburle, Army West Point	.283	.385	.365	159	9	2	0	29	4
Sam Ruta, Lehigh	.277	.376	.434	173	6	3	5	40	5
Nick Manesis, Army West Point	.267	.363	.430	165	8	2	5	22	2
Carter Macias, Army West Point	.264	.374	.344	163	5	1	2	29	12

Player	AVG	OBP	SLG	AB	2B	3B	HR	RBI	SB
Adam Retzbach, Lehigh	.237	.335	.421	152	9	2	5	26	1

INDIVIDUAL PITCHING LEADERS
(Minimum 40 innings pitched)

Player	W	L	ERA	G	SV	IP	H	BB	SO
Matt Svanson, Lehigh	4	4	2.30	13	0	70.1	60	24	65
Mason Black, Lehigh	7	3	3.11	13	0	72.1	64	31	95
Chris Difiore, Bucknell	5	3	3.51	10	0	51.1	57	18	46
Luke Rettig, Lehigh	3	4	3.59	13	1	62.2	55	26	62
Ray Bartoli, Army West Point	3	2	3.79	13	2	59.1	52	18	51
Matt Stamford, Lehigh	3	1	3.79	12	0	40.1	44	16	31
Tommy Goodridge, Navy	4	2	4.93	10	0	45.2	46	17	28
Anthony LoRicco, Army West Point	4	2	5.14	11	0	56	63	22	65
Will Greer, Bucknell	3	5	5.62	10	0	56	63	24	38
Robbie Buecker, Army West Point	3	4	6.95	13	0	57	58	28	37

SOUTHEASTERN CONFERENCE

East Division	Conference		Overall	
	W	L	W	L
Tennessee	20	10	50	18
Vanderbilt	19	10	49	18
Florida	17	13	38	22
South Carolina	16	14	34	23
Georgia	13	17	31	25
Kentucky	12	18	29	23
Missouri	8	22	15	36

West Division	Conference		Overall	
	W	L	W	L
Arkansas	22	8	50	13
Mississippi State	20	10	50	18
Mississippi	18	12	45	22
Louisiana State	13	17	38	25
Alabama	13	17	32	26
Auburn	10	20	25	27
Texas A&M	9	21	29	27

ALL-CONFERENCE TEAM: C: Sam Praytor, Alabama. **1B:** Will Frizzell, Texas A&M. **2B:** Robert Moore, Arkansas. **3B:** Jake Rucker, Tennessee. **SS:** Liam Spence, Tennessee. **OF:** Tanner Allen, Mississippi State; Enrique Bradfield, Jr., Vanderbilt; Jud Fabian, Florida. **DH:** Matt Goodheart, Arkansas. **SP:** Kumar Rocker, Vanderbilt; Doug Nikhazy, Mississippi; Jack Leiter, Vanderbilt. **RP:** Kevin Kopps, Arkansas. **Player of the Year:** Tanner Allen, Mississippi State. **Pitcher of the Year:** Kevin Kopps, Arkansas. **Coach of the Year:** Dave Van Horn, Arkansas. **Freshman of the Year:** Enrique Bradfield, Jr., Vanderbilt. **Newcomer of the Year:** Jack Leiter, Vanderbilt.

INDIVIDUAL BATTING LEADERS
(Minimum 140 at-bats)

Player	AVG	OBP	SLG	AB	2B	3B	HR	RBI	SB
Tanner Allen, Mississippi St.	.383	.456	.621	261	19	5	11	66	11
Ryan Bliss, Auburn	.365	.428	.654	211	14	1	15	45	6
Dylan Crews, LSU	.362	.453	.663	246	16	2	18	42	12
Tre' Morgan, LSU	.357	.441	.526	249	16	4	6	42	15
Jacob Gonzalez, Ole Miss	.355	.443	.561	262	16	1	12	55	2
Coltyn Kessler, Kentucky	.349	.439	.559	152	11	0	7	25	1
Dominic Keegan, Vanderbilt	.345	.427	.638	232	17	3	15	57	0
Connor Tate, Georgia	.344	.405	.545	189	6	1	10	33	1
Will Frizzell, Texas A&M	.343	.451	.686	204	13	0	19	50	3
Kevin Graham, Ole Miss	.342	.422	.562	260	15	0	14	56	2
Enrique Bradfield Jr. , Vanderbilt	.336	.451	.414	244	8	4	1	38	47
Liam Spence, Tennessee	.336	.472	.459	244	11	2	5	36	5
Joshua McAllister, Georgia	.333	.382	.562	153	6	1	9	29	4
Jake Rucker, Tennessee	.330	.399	.520	273	21	2	9	55	7
Austin Schultz, Kentucky	.329	.401	.481	216	11	2	6	26	22
Ray Alejo, Texas A&M	.325	.385	.430	200	10	1	3	23	18
Tim Elko, Ole Miss	.325	.444	.675	160	8	0	16	55	0
Rowdey Jordan, Mississippi St.	.323	.417	.546	269	22	4	10	45	9
Rankin Woley, Auburn	.320	.404	.533	197	12	0	10	31	1
Cole Tate, Georgia	.319	.379	.395	210	6	2	2	20	4
Nathan Hickey, Florida	.317	.435	.522	224	15	2	9	50	1
Jacob Young, Florida	.315	.385	.461	254	16	3	5	41	13
Tyler Miller, Auburn	.312	.354	.601	208	10	1	16	61	3
Zane Denton, Alabama	.308	.405	.489	221	10	0	10	40	2

	AVG	OBP	SLG	AB	2B	3B	HR	RBI	SB
Cade Doughty, LSU	.308	.368	.546	227	11	2	13	55	1
Justin Bench, Ole Miss	.307	.423	.440	241	7	2	7	39	14
Andrew Keefer, Missouri	.307	.384	.418	153	9	1	2	19	6
Isaiah Thomas, Vanderbilt	.305	.361	.583	223	13	5	13	40	12
Austin Bost, Texas A&M	.303	.343	.513	195	11	0	10	39	1
Colby Halter, Florida	.302	.379	.453	159	11	2	3	32	1
Trevor Austin, Mercer	.297	.393	.324	182	5	0	0	17	5
Bryce Hodge, ETSU	.295	.362	.575	146	11	0	10	40	0
Jack Renwick, Wofford	.295	.376	.390	200	16	1	1	29	28
Brandon Michie, Mercer	.291	.413	.539	206	15	0	12	46	5
Will Knight, VMI	.290	.397	.455	176	6	1	7	29	2
Ryan Crocket, Samford	.289	.376	.487	197	6	0	11	43	2

INDIVIDUAL PITCHING LEADERS
(Minimum 40 innings pitched)

Player	W	L	ERA	G	SV	IP	H	BB	SO
Kevin Kopps, Arkansas	12	1	0.90	33	11	89.2	50	18	131
Chase Lee, Alabama	7	0	1.33	22	7	40.2	29	14	51
Landon Sims, Mississippi St.	5	0	1.44	25	13	56.1	29	15	100
Patrick Wicklander, Arkansas	7	1	2.09	18	0	77.2	65	24	85
Jack Leiter, Vanderbilt	11	4	2.13	18	0	110	48	45	179
Brett Kerry, South Carolina	5	1	2.15	17	4	54.1	48	10	84
William Freeman, Alabama	2	1	2.22	24	1	56.2	43	11	39
Nick Maldonado, Vanderbilt	1	2	2.31	28	9	50.2	32	7	59
Luke Murphy, Vanderbilt	4	1	2.40	27	9	41.1	24	15	61
Doug Nikhazy, Ole Miss	12	2	2.45	16	0	92	62	31	142
Landon Marceaux, LSU	7	7	2.54	18	0	102.2	92	26	116
Kumar Rocker, Vanderbilt	14	4	2.73	20	0	122	75	39	179
Trey Van Der Weide, Florida	2	2	2.74	25	2	42.2	42	10	32
Camden Sewell, Tennessee	4	1	2.82	23	2	51	33	15	46
Julian Bosnic, South Carolina	4	2	2.84	22	4	50.2	22	25	78

INDIVIDUAL PITCHING LEADERS
(Minimum 40 innings pitched)

Player	W	L	ERA	G	SV	IP	H	BB	SO
Dalton Rhadans, Wofford	6	0	2.59	24	7	59	50	20	62
Elliot Carney, Wofford	6	3	3.07	15	0	88	62	22	107
Tyler Bradt, VMI	2	3	3.20	17	0	50.2	44	32	37
Colby Stuart, UNC Greensboro	6	1	3.22	14	0	86.2	74	23	73
Austin Parsley, UNC Greensboro	8	2	3.30	20	1	60	60	8	62
Zebby Matthews, Western Caro.	6	2	3.52	10	0	61.1	63	7	60
Jackson Kelley, Mercer	3	4	3.67	25	1	68.2	73	30	73
Jack Snyder, Western Caro.	2	1	3.88	21	1	46.1	42	11	37
Hunter Loyd, ETSU	4	5	4.11	14	0	72.1	57	32	83
Taylor Lobus, Mercer	9	3	4.25	24	0	72	66	30	73
Luke Sutko, Mercer	3	5	4.31	31	12	48	66	14	58
Garett Delano, Mercer	6	1	4.32	53	0	81.1	68	20	60
Hayes Heinecke, Wofford	2	4	4.40	8	0	43	41	11	43
Price King, UNC Greensboro	0	3	4.74	20	0	43.2	46	18	32
Zach Franklin, Western Caro.	7	4	4.96	18	3	45.1	46	21	48

SOUTHERN CONFERENCE

	Conference		Overall	
Blue Division	W	L	W	L
Samford	20	10	35	24
East Tennessee State	13	16	24	25
VMI	13	17	18	29
UNC Greensboro	12	18	27	25
Red Division	W	L	W	L
Wofford	21	9	36	21
Mercer	18	9	35	22
Western Carolina	14	11	28	21
The Citadel	4	25	12	39

ALL-CONFERENCE TEAM: C: Luke Robinson, Western Carolina. **1B:** Justin Starke, VMI. **2B:** Garett Delano, Mercer. **3B:** Jack Renwick, Wofford. **SS:** R.J. Yeager, Mercer. **OF:** Corey Rosier, UNC Greensboro; Justice Bigbie, Western Carolina; Colin Davis, Wofford. **DH:** Will Prater, Western Carolina. **SP:** Colby Stuart, East Tennessee State; Elliot Carney, Wofford. **RP:** Dalton Rhadans, Wofford. **Player of the Year:** Colin Davis, Wofford. **Pitcher of the Year:** Elliot Carney, Wofford. **Coach of the Year:** Todd Interdonato, Wofford. **Freshman of the Year:** Justin Starke, VMI.

INDIVIDUAL BATTING LEADERS
(Minimum 140 at-bats)

Player	AVG	OBP	SLG	AB	2B	3B	HR	RBI	SB
Justin Starke, VMI	.422	.525	.602	161	9	1	6	27	3
Justice Bigbie, Western Caro.	.395	.500	.621	195	15	1	9	50	11
Will Prater, Western Caro.	.395	.457	.461	167	5	3	0	32	6
Nolen Hester, Wofford	.363	.472	.463	201	11	3	1	39	13
Corey Rosier, UNC Greensboro	.354	.434	.604	212	9	4	12	51	17
Colin Davis, Wofford	.351	.434	.624	194	18	1	11	45	18
Tyler McManus, Samford	.346	.432	.612	188	13	2	11	53	0
Luke Robinson, Western Caro.	.345	.415	.597	206	13	0	13	52	0
Jeffery Brown, The Citadel	.341	.355	.413	208	8	2	1	19	13
Garett Delano, Mercer	.337	.433	.558	190	13	1	9	52	3
Pascanel Ferreras, Western Caro.	.329	.419	.624	213	11	2	16	56	5
Trey Morgan, VMI	.326	.411	.440	141	6	2	2	26	11
Bill Knight, Mercer	.325	.405	.544	228	16	2	10	50	4
Trey Yunger, Wofford	.321	.412	.400	215	11	3	0	45	20
Greg Hardison, UNC Greensboro	.312	.389	.465	170	15	1	3	36	0
Lawson Hill, Wofford	.309	.421	.409	220	17	1	1	43	10
RJ Yeager, Mercer	.308	.363	.564	234	17	2	13	50	10
Crosby Jones, The Citadel	.306	.347	.415	183	10	2	2	22	1
Daylan Nanny, Western Caro.	.306	.421	.440	193	14	0	4	44	8
Ethan Cady, ETSU	.305	.401	.641	167	12	1	14	44	5
Josh Madole, UNC Greensboro	.304	.413	.431	181	6	1	5	33	2
Daniel Walsh, Western Caro.	.304	.418	.429	168	8	2	3	37	9
Brooks Carlson, Samford	.301	.409	.478	186	13	1	6	37	2
Will David, Samford	.298	.396	.372	191	9	1	1	29	4

SOUTHLAND CONFERENCE

	Conference		Overall	
	W	L	W	L
Abilene Christian	25	13	36	21
Texas A&M-Corpus Christi	20	14	25	29
New Orleans	23	17	29	28
Sam Houston State	20	15	30	25
Southeastern Louisiana	22	17	32	24
Northwestern State	20	16	27	26
McNeese State	21	18	32	30
Lamar	17	19	25	23
Central Arkansas	18	22	23	28
Stephen F. Austin	17	22	20	31
Incarnate Word	17	23	21	28
Nicholls State	16	24	21	34
Houston Baptist	11	27	14	38

ALL-CONFERENCE TEAM: C: Mitchell Dickson, So., Abilene Christian. **1B:** Chase Kemp, Jr., Lamar. **2B:** Nate Fisbeck, RSr., McNeese State. **3B:** Itchy Burts, Sr., Texas A&M-Corpus Christi. **SS:** Bash Randle, Fr., Abilene Christian. **OF:** Colton Cowser, So., Sam Houston State; Colton Eager, Jr., Abilene Christian; Clayton Rasbeary, RSr., McNeese State. **DH:** Lee Thomas, Gr., Incarnate Word. **SP:** Will Dion, RSo., McNeese State; Brennan Stuprich, Fr., Southeastern Louisiana; Will Warren, Jr., Southeastern Louisiana. **RP:** Tyler Cleveland, RFr., Central Arkansas. **UTL:** Anthony Quirion, Sr., Lamar. **Player of the Year:** Colton Cowser, Sam Houston State. **Hitter of the Year:** Colton Eager, Abilene Christian. **Pitcher of the Year:** Will Dion, McNeese State. **Relief Pitcher of the Year:** Tyler Cleveland, Central Arkansas. **Coach of the Year:** Rick McCarty, Abilene Christian. **Freshman of the Year:** Brennan Stuprich, Southeastern Louisiana. **Newcomer of the Year:** Grayson Tatrow, Abilene Christian.

INDIVIDUAL BATTING LEADERS
(Minimum 140 at-bats)

Player	AVG	OBP	SLG	AB	2B	3B	HR	RBI	SB
Mitchell Dickson, Abilene Christian	.383	.465	.495	196	10	0	4	45	7
Colton Cowser, Sam Houston	.374	.490	.680	203	10	2	16	52	17
Jack Rogers, Sam Houston	.367	.474	.696	207	18	1	16	55	12
Coby Potvin, Central Ark.	.361	.474	.458	144	10	2	0	17	1
Brennen Bales, Houston Baptist	.356	.416	.469	160	8	2	2	22	6
Clayton Rasbeary, McNeese	.353	.417	.614	249	19	5	12	43	7
Colton Eager, Abilene Christian	.342	.421	.604	222	17	1	13	57	3
Ben MacNaughton, Lamar University	.336	.400	.452	146	9	4	0	19	18
Tommy Cruz, Abilene Christian	.335	.452	.421	164	11	0	1	29	0
Avery George, Lamar University	.333	.377	.385	195	8	1	0	19	13
Pearce Howard, New Orleans	.333	.398	.514	216	14	2	7	56	2
Grayson Tatrow, Abilene Christian	.325	.421	.560	209	15	2	10	39	4
Mike Williams, A&M-Corpus Christi	.324	.365	.465	185	6	1	6	37	6
Miller Ladusau, Abilene Christian	.322	.383	.494	174	6	0	8	35	1

Player	AVG	OBP	SLG	AB	2B	3B	HR	RBI	SB
Payton Harden, McNeese	.321	.392	.405	252	12	3	1	26	16
Tre Obregon III, McNeese	.321	.382	.442	165	10	2	2	34	1
Tyler Finke, Southeastern La.	.318	.412	.494	154	11	2	4	29	19
Kasten Furr, New Orleans	.318	.421	.388	201	11	0	1	12	10
Evan Keller, Southeastern La.	.313	.424	.427	211	15	0	3	27	19
Lee Thomas, UIW	.306	.420	.559	170	12	5	7	34	0
Kolby Johnson, Central Ark.	.305	.400	.378	164	6	0	2	27	5
Sebastian Randle, Abilene Christian	.305	.397	.417	187	13	1	2	39	3
Brendan Ryan, A&M-Corpus Christi	.305	.388	.461	141	5	4	3	19	6
Nate Fisbeck, McNeese	.302	.398	.509	232	17	2	9	63	2
Chase Kemp, Lamar University	.302	.395	.581	179	8	0	14	46	2
Luke Marbach, A&M-Corpus Christi	.301	.415	.510	153	9	1	7	28	11
Kelby Weyler, Lamar University	.301	.348	.399	183	12	0	2	27	8
Christian Garcia, Southeastern La.	.294	.422	.433	187	11	0	5	30	14
Luther Woullard, New Orleans	.294	.379	.512	201	17	3	7	48	3
Gaige Howard, New Orleans	.291	.419	.390	213	13	1	2	37	8

INDIVIDUAL PITCHING LEADERS
(Minimum 40 innings pitched)

Player	W	L	ERA	G	SV	IP	H	BB	SO
Drayton Brown, Northwestern St.	2	3	1.96	17	6	41.1	23	14	46
John Gaddis, A&M-Corpus Christi	5	3	2.25	13	0	64	42	18	72
Brennan Stuprich, Southeastern La.	6	3	2.31	16	0	81.2	66	22	67
Tyler Cleveland, Central Ark.	6	3	2.43	23	9	66.2	48	15	84
Will Warren, Southeastern La.	7	2	2.57	14	0	91	71	25	95
Coltin Atkinson, Sam Houston	6	1	2.72	13	2	46.1	43	12	52
Jonathan Ellison, McNeese	5	3	2.99	15	0	75.1	58	37	60
Will Dion, McNeese	9	4	3.07	17	1	99.2	79	19	121
Cal Carver, Northwestern St.	6	5	3.19	14	0	84.2	66	34	77
Bryson Hudgens, McNeese	2	3	3.19	13	0	48	43	22	26
Trevin Michael, Lamar University	6	3	3.29	12	0	68.1	56	29	77
Hayden Thomas, A&M-Corpus Christi	4	3	3.31	15	0	81.2	73	39	94
Dominic Robinson, Sam Houston	4	1	3.48	12	0	62	58	16	65
Kyle Backhus, Sam Houston	4	2	3.49	13	0	56.2	41	26	60
Zach Bravo, Lamar University	5	2	3.50	12	0	61.2	51	26	47

SOUTHWESTERN ATHLETIC CONFERENCE

East Division	Conference		Overall	
	W	L	W	L
Jackson State	24	0	31	8
Alabama State	14	7	23	17
Alabama A&M	11	13	11	18
Alcorn State	6	16	6	18
Mississippi Valley State	0	17	0	20

West Division	Conference		Overall	
	W	L	W	L
Prairie View A&M	12	7	12	16
Grambling	12	9	15	25
Southern	13	11	15	27
Texas Southern	10	14	11	33
Arkansas-Pine Bluff	8	14	8	30

ALL-CONFERENCE TEAM: C: Hunter May, Alabama State. **1B:** Chenar Brown, Jackson State. **2B:** Tristan Garcia, Alcorn State. **3B:** Ty Hill, Jackson State. **SS:** Christopher DeGuzman, Alabama State. **OF:** Chandler Dillard, Jackson State; Jahmoi Percival, Grambling; C.J. Newsome, Jackson State. **DH:** Santiago Garcia, Alabama State. **SP:** Anthony Becerra, Jackson State; Nikelle Galatas, Jackson State. **RP:** Steven Davila, Jackson State. **Player of the Year:** Ty Hill, Jackson State. **Hitter of the Year:** Ty Hill, Jackson State. **Pitcher of the Year:** Anthony Becerra, Jackson State. **Relief Pitcher of the Year:** Steven Davila, Jackson State. **Coach of the Year:** Omar Johnson, Jackson State. **Freshman of the Year:** Chenar Brown, Jackson State. **Newcomer of the Year:** Ty Hill, Jackson State.

INDIVIDUAL BATTING LEADERS
(Minimum 140 at-bats)

Player	AVG	OBP	SLG	AB	2B	3B	HR	RBI	SB
Trenton Jamison, Alabama St.	.390	.460	.634	164	12	2	8	43	4
Cristopher DeGuzman, Alabama St.	.367	.451	.506	158	8	4	2	31	8
Chenar Brown, Jackson St.	.366	.432	.648	142	10	3	8	49	5
Jahmoi Percival, Grambling	.364	.468	.600	165	10	7	5	43	31
Chandler Dillard, Jackson St.	.360	.445	.435	161	4	1	2	39	17

Player	AVG	OBP	SLG	AB	2B	3B	HR	RBI	SB
Oscar Ponce, Texas Southern	.342	.394	.543	184	16	0	7	40	2
C.J. Newsome, Jackson St.	.336	.426	.427	143	6	2	1	29	18
Cameron Bufford, Grambling	.319	.389	.573	185	7	2	12	40	7
Jabronski Williams, Alabama St.	.315	.449	.456	149	7	1	4	29	10
Tremaine Spears, Southern U.	.303	.421	.469	175	11	0	6	39	8
O'Neill Burgos, Southern U.	.298	.377	.482	168	8	4	5	32	10
Justin Cooper, Texas Southern	.295	.435	.397	146	7	1	2	21	18
Cameron Phelts, Grambling	.290	.391	.457	186	5	4	6	30	22
Zavier Moore, Southern U.	.288	.435	.459	146	13	0	4	31	6
Taj Porter, Southern U.	.280	.410	.453	150	8	0	6	24	4
Nic Garza, Texas Southern	.275	.438	.416	149	12	0	3	15	1
Wesley Reyes, Jackson St.	.273	.366	.407	150	8	3	2	32	13
Jeremy Almaguer, Grambling	.265	.354	.313	166	6	1	0	26	1
Tyrese Clayborne, Texas Southern	.238	.306	.320	172	10	2	0	19	18
Judah Wilbur, Southern U.	.324	.344	.314	188	10	1	1	18	8
Jordan Vidato, Texas Southern	.214	.354	.271	140	5	0	1	24	19

INDIVIDUAL PITCHING LEADERS
(Minimum 40 innings pitched)

Player	W	L	ERA	G	SV	IP	H	BB	SO
Payton Harris, Alabama St.	2	1	1.29	20	3	42	18	17	58
Jose Fernandez, Alcorn	1	7	2.35	10	1	61.1	50	21	55
Kyle Smith, Prairie View	4	3	2.55	9	0	70.2	63	15	57
Victor Mendoza, Prairie View	3	1	2.91	8	0	46.1	37	21	40
Anthony Becerra, Jackson St.	9	1	3.05	15	0	76.2	45	49	109
Nikelle Galatas, Jackson St.	8	2	3.12	15	1	86.2	65	34	89
Mario Lopez, Jackson St.	7	0	3.19	15	0	62	66	7	52
Breon Pooler, Alabama St.	5	3	3.36	13	0	64.1	41	32	84
Dimitri Frank, Southern U.	4	1	3.83	18	3	40	43	11	48
Osvaldo Mendez, Alabama St.	2	3	3.97	15	0	45.1	37	28	56
Kamron Fields, Texas Southern	4	6	5.03	13	1	68	69	37	79
Jason Alvarez, Grambling	4	4	5.19	13	1	60.2	58	26	77
Joseph Battaglia III, Southern U.	5	4	5.86	12	0	55.1	65	16	33
Marc Luna, Grambling	2	4	6.20	10	0	53.2	68	27	47
Tony Horn, Ark.-Pine Bluff	3	5	6.58	17	2	52	59	26	43

SUMMIT LEAGUE

	Conference		Overall	
	W	L	W	L
Oral Roberts	19	7	31	22
North Dakota State	20	11	42	19
Nebraska-Omaha	14	12	22	25
South Dakota State	9	19	15	32
Western Illinois	7	19	11	28

ALL-CONFERENCE TEAM: C: Alec Jones, Oral Roberts. **1B:** Jake McMurray, Oral Roberts. **2B:** Ryan Cash, Oral Roberts. **3B:** Mike Boeve, Nebraska-Omaha. **SS:** Bennett Hostetler, North Dakota State. **OF:** Jake Malec, North Dakota State; Caleb Denny, Oral Roberts; Joshua Cox, Oral Roberts. **DH:** Jordan Wiley, Oral Roberts. **UTL:** Hunter Swift, Oral Roberts. **SP:** Isaac Coffey, Oral Roberts; Matt Gaskins, Oral Roberts; Cade Feeney, North Dakota State. **RP:** Parker Harm, North Dakota State. **Player of the Year:** Bennett Hostetler, North Dakota State. **Pitcher of the Year:** Isaac Coffey, Oral Roberts. **Coach of the Year:** Ryan Folmar, Oral Roberts. **Newcomer of the Year:** Joshua Cox, Oral Roberts.

INDIVIDUAL BATTING LEADERS
(Minimum 140 at-bats)

Player	AVG	OBP	SLG	AB	2B	3B	HR	RBI	SB
Bennett Hostetler, North Dakota St.	.394	.513	.606	213	13	1	10	58	19
Jake McMurray, Oral Roberts	.343	.430	.444	216	9	2	3	30	2
Ryan Cash, Oral Roberts	.342	.406	.471	225	16	2	3	46	8
Jake Malec, North Dakota St.	.320	.415	.490	247	7	4	9	32	16
Mike Boeve, Omaha	.319	.401	.429	191	16	1	1	29	2
Derek Hackman, South Dakota St.	.319	.436	.542	144	8	0	8	26	0
Chris Esposito, Omaha	.301	.387	.515	163	5	3	8	37	13
Alex Dorethy, Western Ill.	.298	.344	.358	151	6	0	1	20	0
Joshua Cox, Oral Roberts	.293	.356	.455	222	17	2	5	33	12
Jack Simonsen, North Dakota St.	.293	.365	.415	188	8	0	5	35	7
Kevin Raisbeck, Western Ill.	.286	.361	.320	147	5	0	0	12	12
Caleb Denny, Oral Roberts	.284	.359	.456	204	14	0	7	39	3
Trenton Bauer, Western Ill.	.282	.321	.359	156	9	0	1	26	0
Anthony Martinez, Oral Roberts	.277	.361	.401	177	7	0	5	28	8
Masen Prososki, Omaha	.274	.379	.451	164	10	2	5	33	20
Blake Hall, Oral Roberts	.271	.356	.398	166	7	1	4	38	6

Player	AVG	OBP	SLG	AB	2B	3B	HR	RBI	SB
Luke Ira, South Dakota St.	.268	.337	.391	179	11	1	3	23	4
Zach Solano, North Dakota St.	.268	.335	.383	149	11	0	2	23	4
Jordan Wiley, Oral Roberts	.268	.368	.427	157	10	0	5	26	1
Peter Brookshaw, North Dakota St.	.263	.374	.388	224	9	2	5	38	12
Tucker Rohde, North Dakota St.	.261	.378	.300	207	8	0	0	36	6
Brett Bonar, Omaha	.254	.312	.355	169	8	0	3	25	1
Jess Bellows, South Dakota St.	.250	.355	.321	168	7	1	1	16	4
Calen Schwabe, North Dakota St.	.246	.319	.300	207	8	0	1	27	7
Adam Oviedo, Oral Roberts	.243	.344	.355	169	8	1	3	29	0
Charley Hesse, North Dakota St.	.229	.333	.301	166	6	0	2	27	1
Ryan McDonald, South Dakota St.	.218	.381	.361	147	3	3	4	17	1
Landon Badger, South Dakota St.	.201	.303	.403	159	10	2	6	31	4
Drew Beazley, South Dakota St.	.196	.293	.287	143	10	0	1	19	2

INDIVIDUAL PITCHING LEADERS
(Minimum 40 innings pitched)

Player	W	L	ERA	G	SV	IP	H	BB	SO
Matt Gaskins, Oral Roberts	3	1	2.41	9	1	41	31	6	36
Isaac Coffey, Oral Roberts	9	2	2.81	34	0	86.1	73	13	92
Cade Feeney, North Dakota St.	8	1	3.10	24	0	69.2	64	18	56
Evan Kowalski, Oral Roberts	7	2	3.18	14	0	56.2	49	20	53
Joey Machado, Omaha	5	4	3.84	14	0	63.1	67	35	59
Ryan Bourassa, South Dakota St.	0	4	4.04	14	2	42.1	36	24	65
Tanner Rogen, Oral Roberts	2	4	4.13	14	0	61	52	28	41
Cody Carlson, South Dakota St.	2	5	4.27	12	0	65.1	76	25	54
Jace Warkentien, Western Ill.	2	4	4.47	14	0	58.1	53	37	39
Richie Holetz, Omaha	3	5	4.52	14	0	79.2	72	33	68
Brian Raymond, Western Ill.	0	5	4.72	11	1	53.1	64	22	51
Evan Sankey, North Dakota St.	7	3	4.76	15	0	79.1	87	25	71
Max Loven, North Dakota St.	3	3	4.82	12	0	61.2	65	11	50
Tristen Roehrich, North Dakota St.	2	1	5.11	15	1	49.1	56	23	44
Mark Timmins, Omaha	5	2	5.12	11	0	45.2	45	17	37

SUN BELT CONFERENCE

East Division	Conference W	L	Overall W	L
South Alabama	15	9	36	22
Georgia Southern	14	10	34	23
Troy	13	11	27	26
Appalachian State	11	10	22	32
Georgia State	12	12	18	37
Coastal Carolina	9	12	27	24

West Division	Conference W	L	Overall W	L
Louisiana-Lafayette	13	11	32	23
Texas-Arlington	13	11	27	30
Louisiana-Monroe	11	13	26	26
Arkansas-Little Rock	11	13	21	30
Arkansas State	10	14	20	31
Texas State	9	15	21	36

ALL-CONFERENCE TEAM: C: Drake Osborn, Sr., Louisiana-Lafayette. **1B:** Robbie Young, Sr., Appalachian State. **2B:** Luke Drumheller, Jr., Appalachian State. **3B:** Ben Klutts, Jr., Arkansas State. **SS:** Drew Frederic, Sr., Troy. **OF:** Mason McWhorter, Gr., Georgia Southern; Logan Cerny, So., Troy; Ethan Wilson, Jr., South Alabama. **DH:** Ben Fitzgerald, Jr., Louisiana-Lafayette. **UTL:** Cameron Jones, Fr., Georgia State. **SP:** Connor Cooke, So., Louisiana-Lafayette; Hayden Arnold, Sr., Arkansas-Little Rock; Carlos Tavera, Jr., Texas-Arlington. **RP:** Nick Jones, Sr., Georgia Southern. **Player of the Year:** Mason McWhorter, Georgia Southern. **Pitcher of the Year:** Hayden Arnold, Arkansas-Little Rock. **Coach of the Year:** Mark Calvi, South Alabama. **Freshman of the Year:** Garrett Gainous, Troy. **Newcomer of the Year:** Drake Osborn, Louisiana-Lafayette.

INDIVIDUAL BATTING LEADERS
(Minimum 140 at-bats)

Player	AVG	OBP	SLG	AB	2B	3B	HR	RBI	SB
Mason McWhorter, Ga. Southern	.372	.445	.690	226	16	1	18	52	3
Christian Avant, Ga. Southern	.358	.428	.509	218	12	3	5	38	13
Liam Hicks, Arkansas St.	.344	.464	.548	157	11	0	7	30	0
Drake Osborn, Louisiana	.337	.415	.491	169	17	0	3	24	6
Logan Cerny, Troy	.332	.424	.694	193	17	4	15	47	12
Travis Washburn, ULM	.327	.393	.453	159	10	2	2	16	11
Josh Smith, Georgia St.	.324	.415	.544	182	8	1	10	35	10
Ben Klutts, Arkansas St.	.320	.400	.518	197	16	1	7	28	0
Parker Chavers, Coastal Carolina	.318	.407	.477	195	12	2	5	33	14
Drew Frederic, Troy	.318	.390	.545	220	15	1	11	31	13
Trace Henry, ULM	.318	.408	.430	179	16	2	0	13	17
Ethan Wilson, South Alabama	.318	.419	.528	214	13	4	8	34	10
Michael Sandle, South Alabama	.313	.389	.522	230	11	2	11	50	15
Brennan Breaux, Louisiana	.311	.376	.409	164	13	0	1	27	7
Andrew Miller, UT Arlington	.307	.367	.472	218	12	0	8	43	6
Tyler Duncan, Arkansas St.	.303	.382	.556	198	13	2	11	54	0
Santi Montiel, South Alabama	.295	.406	.480	200	16	0	7	34	1
Eric Brown, Coastal Carolina	.294	.413	.513	187	12	1	9	38	11
Ben Fitzgerald, Louisiana	.293	.391	.571	191	15	1	12	31	6
Ryan Humeniuk, ULM	.291	.367	.403	196	8	1	4	28	14
Will Mize, Georgia St.	.290	.339	.424	210	13	0	5	25	2
Luke Drumheller, App State	.289	.354	.423	201	10	1	5	39	4
John Michael Russ, Little Rock	.289	.376	.350	180	6	1	1	22	2
Boone Montgomery, UT Arlington	.288	.410	.439	205	13	0	6	17	3
Tyler Williams, Little Rock	.288	.316	.512	205	16	3	8	42	10
Robbie Young, App State	.287	.373	.387	181	7	1	3	28	6
Jason Swan, Ga. Southern	.284	.327	.381	194	14	1	1	22	10
Justin Thompson, Texas St.	.284	.352	.404	218	9	1	5	37	1
Connor Aube, UT Arlington	.283	.345	.509	230	12	2	12	43	8
Steven Curry, Ga. Southern	.282	.403	.410	188	10	1	4	24	3

INDIVIDUAL PITCHING LEADERS
(Minimum 40 innings pitched)

Player	W	L	ERA	G	SV	IP	H	BB	SO
Nick Jones, Ga. Southern	1	0	1.48	29	17	42.2	34	5	67
Connor Cooke, Louisiana	7	3	2.03	21	1	79.2	44	37	90
Miles Smith, South Alabama	7	1	2.18	19	2	82.2	66	21	79
Aaron Barkley, Little Rock	6	5	2.39	25	7	60.1	48	12	54
Kody Bullard, UT Arlington	7	4	3.02	15	0	89.1	70	34	83
Carlos Tavera, UT Arlington	3	4	3.04	15	0	83	51	33	117
Hayden Arnold, Little Rock	7	4	3.07	15	0	85	71	18	84
Spencer Arrighetti, Louisiana	7	6	3.12	16	2	83.2	69	29	91
Carter Robinson, Louisiana	1	1	3.17	12	0	48.1	46	12	39
Trey Lindsay, ULM	2	2	3.18	23	3	45.1	41	14	33
Tyler Tuthill, App State	4	6	3.32	14	0	89.1	52	43	76
Michael Wong, UT Arlington	3	2	3.38	22	5	40	34	5	31
Jeremy Lee, South Alabama	3	2	3.46	11	1	52	43	9	68
Ben Johnson, Ga. Southern	2	3	3.46	21	1	41.2	40	14	43
Eli Ellington, App State	3	0	3.50	26	5	46.1	30	17	52

WEST COAST CONFERENCE

	Conference W	L	Overall W	L
Gonzaga	20	7	34	19
San Diego	19	8	33	12
San Francisco	16	11	25	28
Brigham Young	15	12	23	27
Portland	14	13	24	26
Loyola Marymount	13	14	20	28
Pepperdine	12	15	20	25
Saint Mary's	11	16	25	26
Santa Clara	8	19	18	33
Pacific	7	20	16	33

ALL-CONFERENCE TEAM: INF: Billy Cook, Sr., Pepperdine; Thomas Gavello, So., Pacific; Brett Harris, Sr., Gonzaga; Luke Keaschall, Fr., San Francisco; Thomas Luevano, Sr., San Diego; Andrew Pintar, Fr., Brigham Young; Chad Stevens, Jr., Portland; Jack Winkler, Jr., San Francisco. **OF:** Reese Alexiades, Sr., Pepperdine; Holden Christian, Jr., Loyola Marymount; Jake Jacob, Sr., Gonzaga; Jake Miller, So., San Diego. **Player of the Year:** Thomas Luevano, San Diego. **Pitcher of the Year:** Alek Jacob, Gonzaga. **Coach of the Year:** Mark Machtolf, Gonzaga. **Freshman of the Year:** Luke Keaschall, San Francisco; Andrew Pintar, Brigham Young. **Defensive Player of the Year:** Brett Harris, Gonzaga.

INDIVIDUAL BATTING LEADERS
(Minimum 140 at-bats)

Player	AVG	OBP	SLG	AB	2B	3B	HR	RBI	SB
Brett Harris, Gonzaga	.350	.482	.535	200	17	1	6	43	7
Thomas Luevano, San Diego	.349	.421	.680	169	17	3	11	65	4

Player	AVG	OBP	SLG	AB	2B	3B	HR	RBI	SB
Cody Jefferis, San Diego	.341	.417	.434	173	11	1	1	32	6
James Arakawa, Pacific	.339	.403	.383	180	5	0	1	18	9
Alex LeForestier, Pacific	.339	.429	.385	174	4	2	0	22	4
Jack Costello, San Diego	.338	.402	.490	157	14	2	2	23	0
Julian Bury, LMU (CA)	.337	.403	.439	187	8	1	3	28	7
Thomas Gavello, Pacific	.335	.458	.601	173	12	2	10	28	0
Andrew Pintar, BYU	.333	.433	.556	189	9	3	9	32	4
Chad Stevens, Portland	.333	.402	.547	201	19	0	8	29	12
Ernie Yake, Gonzaga	.333	.423	.433	171	14	0	1	29	6
Wyatt Young, Pepperdine	.332	.405	.442	190	12	0	3	23	6
Kenny Oyama, LMU (CA)	.330	.412	.422	185	15	1	0	22	16
Luke Keaschall, San Francisco	.320	.406	.475	200	11	4	4	30	11
Mitch McIntyre, BYU	.318	.445	.484	192	14	3	4	29	3
Sam Brown, Portland	.315	.365	.495	184	16	1	5	21	0
Adam Lopez, San Diego	.314	.418	.471	140	10	0	4	37	2
Jack Winkler, San Francisco	.307	.382	.505	202	17	1	7	39	23
Jacob Talamante, Saint Mary's (CA)	.299	.414	.401	157	12	2	0	14	13
Jason DiCochea, Santa Clara	.297	.370	.396	202	11	0	3	33	3
Connor Bradshaw, Pepperdine	.291	.346	.426	148	11	3	1	12	8
Andrew Orzel, Gonzaga	.290	.389	.420	193	14	1	3	38	5
Grayson Sterling, Gonzaga	.288	.354	.425	146	9	1	3	23	2
Michael Bowes, Santa Clara	.287	.343	.464	181	8	0	8	30	8
Aharon Modlin, Pepperdine	.284	.354	.437	183	13	0	5	32	6
Tyler Rando, Gonzaga	.284	.406	.403	176	12	0	3	31	0
Jake Tsukada, Portland	.282	.323	.326	181	6	1	0	20	3
Caleb Ricketts, San Diego	.280	.366	.393	168	13	0	2	21	9
Shane McGuire, San Diego	.278	.389	.483	176	12	3	6	33	4
Guthrie Morrison, Gonzaga	.271	.356	.357	221	12	2	1	24	8

INDIVIDUAL PITCHING LEADERS
(Minimum 40 innings pitched)

Player	W	L	ERA	G	SV	IP	H	BB	SO
Brandon Buckley, Santa Clara	2	1	2.16	16	0	41.2	32	15	45
Alek Jacob, Gonzaga	8	1	2.52	17	3	85.2	60	18	112
Jake Miller, San Diego	6	2	2.52	12	0	60.2	50	17	77
Christian Peters, Portland	5	4	2.63	13	1	78.2	65	23	78
Jesse Barron, San Francisco	5	2	2.74	22	4	42.2	37	22	47
Landen Bourassa, San Francisco	7	4	2.88	15	0	97	89	24	75
Ky Bush, Saint Mary's (CA)	7	5	2.99	14	0	78.1	69	19	112
Josh Agnew, LMU (CA)	6	1	3.06	13	2	53	57	9	30
William Kempner, Gonzaga	3	3	3.10	11	1	40.2	31	29	34
Ivran Romero, San Diego	3	1	3.14	20	3	43	38	19	49
Freddie Erlandson, Santa Clara	1	7	3.22	16	0	58.2	51	22	46
Gabriel Hughes, Gonzaga	4	3	3.23	31	0	61.1	48	30	67
Peter Allegro, Portland	2	4	3.32	17	2	40.2	29	15	57
Brandon Ilewellyn, Pepperdine	5	1	3.38	14	0	50.2	44	23	43
Brad McVay, Portland	6	3	3.41	13	0	63.1	51	25	67

WESTERN ATHLETIC CONFERENCE

	Conference		Overall	
	W	L	W	L
Cal Baptist	29	7	40	16
Grand Canyon	29	7	39	21
Sacramento State	22	14	35	22
Dixie State	21	15	24	32
Texas-Rio Grande Valley	20	15	32	26
New Mexico State	16	20	20	34
Tarleton State	13	23	20	35
Seattle	10	22	18	33
Northern Colorado	7	24	11	36
Utah Valley	8	28	10	47

ALL-CONFERENCE TEAM: C: Kaden Hollow, Fr., Dixie State. **1B:** Ryan Walstad, Sr., Sacramento State. **2B:** Andy Atwood, Sr., Texas-Rio Grande Valley. **SS:** Channy Ortiz, Sr., Grand Canyon. **3B:** Jacob Wilson, Fr., Grand Canyon. **OF:** Damon Keith, Jr., Cal Baptist; Lane Pritchard, Sr., Dixie State; Zerek Saenz, So., New Mexico State. **DH:** Matt Smith, Sr., Sacramento State. **At-Large:** Elijah Buries, Fr., Grand Canyon. **SP:** Pierson Ohl, Jr., Grand Canyon; Scott Randall, Jr., Sacramento State. **RP:** C.J. Culpepper, Fr., Cal Baptist. **At-Large:** Kevin Stevens, Sr., Texas-Rio Grande Valley. **Player of the Year:** Damon Keith, Cal Baptist. **Pitcher of the Year:** Pierson Ohl, Grand Canyon. **Coach of the Year:** Andy Stankiewicz, Grand Canyon. **Freshman of the Year:** C.J. Culpepper, Cal Baptist.

INDIVIDUAL BATTING LEADERS
(Minimum 140 at-bats)

Player	AVG	OBP	SLG	AB	2B	3B	HR	RBI	SB
Matt Smith, Sacramento St.	.393	.452	.595	173	11	0	8	44	3
Elijah Buries, Grand Canyon	.374	.433	.553	179	10	2	6	38	13
Zerek Saenz, New Mexico St.	.373	.471	.433	201	6	3	0	25	3
Tommy Tabak, New Mexico St.	.342	.400	.483	149	5	2	4	26	5
Andy Atwood, UTRGV	.341	.450	.561	205	11	2	10	34	8
Ryan Walstad, Sacramento St.	.338	.422	.533	195	20	0	6	46	1
Damon Keith, California Baptist	.336	.434	.588	211	12	1	13	44	12
Chad Castillo, California Baptist	.333	.397	.428	201	10	0	3	30	9
Tayler Aguilar, Grand Canyon	.331	.411	.529	172	12	2	6	43	2
Jake Engel, Dixie St.	.328	.441	.574	183	13	1	10	39	6
Kevin Jimenez, New Mexico St.	.328	.451	.480	177	13	1	4	33	7
John Glenn, California Baptist	.326	.384	.474	215	9	1	7	46	7
Brock Burton, Grand Canyon	.324	.401	.468	216	13	0	6	39	6
Trevor Doyle, Sacramento St.	.324	.426	.417	204	11	1	2	25	1
Lane Pritchard, Dixie St.	.323	.388	.500	192	11	1	7	38	15
Kaden Hollow, Dixie St.	.322	.421	.559	177	15	0	9	41	1
Channy Ortiz, Grand Canyon	.313	.413	.454	227	8	0	8	33	9
Jacob Wilson, Grand Canyon	.313	.376	.440	182	11	0	4	29	1
London Green, Tarleton St.	.312	.396	.464	192	18	1	3	30	14
Blake Burns, Tarleton St.	.310	.399	.545	145	14	1	6	26	1
Coleman Grubbs, UTRGV	.308	.384	.469	211	14	4	4	37	7
Ethan Mann, New Mexico St.	.305	.392	.538	197	13	0	11	50	8
Cal Villareal, New Mexico St.	.304	.367	.391	161	8	0	2	38	4
Sam Leach, Northern Colo.	.301	.356	.399	163	8	1	2	17	2
Freddy Rojas Jr., UTRGV	.298	.407	.522	161	9	0	9	30	3
Josh Glenn, Northern Colo.	.297	.403	.462	145	10	1	4	42	3
Nick Plaia, California Baptist	.297	.371	.383	209	13	1	1	19	10
Harrison Spohn, California Baptist	.297	.339	.429	212	19	0	3	32	11
Tyler Fowler, Tarleton St.	.292	.383	.371	202	7	0	3	22	5
Gavin Rork, Seattle U	.292	.438	.348	178	6	2	0	15	22

INDIVIDUAL PITCHING LEADERS
(Minimum 40 innings pitched)

Player	W	L	ERA	G	SV	IP	H	BB	SO
Jack Zalasky, Sacramento St.	7	2	2.45	28	4	40.1	34	10	50
Pierson Ohl, Grand Canyon	10	2	2.60	16	0	100.1	79	12	103
Jacob McCarvel, California Baptist	5	1	2.68	26	4	53.2	43	7	50
Matt Amrhein, California Baptist	7	2	2.74	20	1	65.2	52	18	61
Carter Young, Grand Canyon	7	1	2.77	15	0	68.1	69	27	59
Scott Randall, Sacramento St.	7	2	2.89	15	0	87.1	87	9	103
Kevin Stevens, UTRGV	7	4	3.17	15	0	93.2	78	20	97
Chris Burica, California Baptist	8	5	3.36	15	0	104.1	94	18	72
Dawson McCarville, Grand Canyon	5	3	3.58	17	1	65.1	58	25	48
Andrew Necochea, California Baptist	4	0	3.62	15	1	49.2	39	18	34
JC Ariza, UTRGV	0	4	3.66	14	0	59	62	26	48
Brady Rodriguez, Sacramento St.	8	2	3.88	21	0	51	45	14	44
Max Balderrama Jr., UTRGV	3	1	3.97	13	0	47.2	47	21	40
Colten Davis, UTRGV	4	2	4.03	14	0	51.1	59	21	46
Riley Sinclair, Seattle U	0	5	4.03	13	0	51.1	49	28	30

NCAA DIVISION II

Wingate (N.C.) won the program's first national title in its first Division II College World Series appearance. After dropping its opening game against Angelo State, Wingate won five straight games to stave off elimination, defeating top-seeded Central Missouri 5-3 in the championship game.
After falling behind Central Missouri in the fourth inning, Wingate reliever Sam Broderson came on and threw five no-hit innings in relief to allow the Bulldogs to complete the comeback.
Wingate catcher Logan McNeely, who was named the most outstanding player of the event, drove in two runs. "It was heavy at the bottom of the dogpile," McNeely said "It's our third one this year, so we're kind of getting used to it. You learn where to be in the dogpile."

DIVISION II WORLD SERIES

Site: Cary, N.C.
Participants: 1. Central Missouri; 2. Seton Hill (Pa.); 3. Angelo State (Texas); 4. Trevecca Nazarene (Tenn.); 5. Tampa; 6. Wingate (N.C.); 7. Southern New Hampshire; 8. Northwest Nazarene (Idaho)
Champion: Wingate (N.C.)
Runner-up: Central Missouri

LEADERS: BATTING AVERAGE
(Minimum 140 at bats)

Rk. Player, Pos., Team	Class	AVG	OBP	SLG
1. Haydn McGeary, C, Colorado-Mesa	So.	.481	.541	.973
2. Matt Marlow, INF, Regis (Colo.)	So.	.441	.491	.664
3. Zion Pettigrew, INF, Illinois-Springfield	Jr.	.440	.514	.940
4. Joey Werner, OF, Minnesota State	Sr.	.439	.507	.769
5. John Michael Faile, C, North Greenville	So.	.438	.512	.901
6. Dayson Croes, INF, Quincy (Ill.)	Sr.	.436	.490	.716
7. Jake Anderson, INF, Colorado-Colo. Springs	Sr.	.427	.508	.860
8. Ben Ross, INF, Notre Dame (Ohio)	Fr.	.426	.494	.844
9. Cole Brooks, OF, Northwood (Mich.)	Sr.	.425	.509	.654
10. Carter Howell, OF, Augustana (S.D.)	So.	.423	.498	.679

EARNED RUN AVERAGE
(Minimum 40 innings pitched)

Rk. Pitcher, Team	Class	W	L	ERA
1. Zach Parish, Missouri Southern State	Sr.	11	1	1.21
2. Dylan Heid, Pittsburgh-Johnstown (Pa.)	Sr.	7	2	1.37
3. Nic Swanson, Northeastern State (Okla.)	Fr.	9	1	1.55
4. Alex Mack, St. Thomas Aquinas (N.Y.)	Sr.	7	1	1.61
5. Drew Moore, King (Tenn.)	Jr.	6	1	1.72
6. Charlie Cucciara, Molloy (N.Y.)	So.	5	2	1.80
7. Logan Workman, Lee (Tenn.)	Jr.	8	1	1.81
8. Bryan Ketchie, Catawba (N.C.)	Sr.	10	1	1.82
9. Nick Altermatt, Minnesota State	So.	5	2	1.90
10. Ethan Lauchart, West Virginia State	Sr.	6	1	1.94

CATEGORY LEADERS: BATTING
*Minimum 140 at bats

Dept.	Player, Pos., Team	Class	G	Total
OBP*	Haydn McGeary, C, Colorado-Mesa	So.	47	.541
SLG*	Haydn McGeary, C, Colorado-Mesa	So.	47	.973
R	Josh Elvir, OF, Angelo State (Texas)	Sr.	53	84
H	Haydn McGeary, C, Colorado-Mesa	So.	47	88
2B	Haydn McGeary, C, Colorado-Mesa	So.	47	26
3B	Alex Madera, INF, Central Missouri	Sr.	54	10
HR	John Michael Faile, C, North Greenville (S.C.)	So.	45	23
RBI	Haydn McGeary, C, Colorado-Mesa	So.	47	88
SB	Colby Johnson, OF, Charleston (W.Va.)	Sr.	38	26

CATEGORY LEADERS: PITCHING
*Minimum 40 innings

Dept.	Pitcher, Team	Class	Total
W	Mason Green, Central Missouri	Jr.	16
SV	Perry Bewley, Ashland (Ohio)	Sr.	11
	Kaleb Honea, Northwestern Oklahoma State	Sr.	11
G	Carson Childers, Angelo State (Texas)	Sr.	28
	Tiger Knox, Trevecca Nazarene (Tenn.)	Sr.	28
IP	Hunter Riggins, Delta State (Miss.)	Sr.	115

SO	Riley Martin, Quincy (Ill.)	Sr.	152
SO/9*	Riley Martin, Quincy (Ill.)	Sr.	17.39
BB/9*	Collin Denk, Minnesota State	So.	0.65
WHIP*	Dylan Heid, Pittsburgh-Johnstown (Pa.)	Sr.	0.67

NCAA Division III

At the end of an unbeaten run through the Division III College World Series, including a sweep of St. Thomas (Minn.) by 6-1 and 4-2 scores, Salisbury (Md.) won its first national title.
Salisbury starting pitcher Jackson Balzan won most outstanding player honors after giving up two runs in 14 innings across two starts in the CWS.
National runner-up St. Thomas, which won national titles in 2001 and 2009, is moving up to Division I in 2022.

DIVISION III WORLD SERIES

Site: Cedar Rapids, Iowa
Participants: Washington (Mo.); Johns Hopkins (Md.); St. Thomas (Minn.); Adrian (Mich.); Rowan (N.J.); Wheaton (Mass.); Salisbury (Md.); SUNY Cortland (N.Y.)
Champion: Salisbury (Md.)
Runner-up: St. Thomas (Minn.)

LEADERS: BATTING AVERAGE
(Minimum 120 at bats)

RK. Player, Pos., Team	Class	AVG	OBP	SLG
1. Adam Zebrowski, 1B, St. John Fisher (N.Y.)	Sr.	.500	.594	.993
2. Colby Martin, 2B, Shenandoah (Va.)	Fr.	.482	.544	.788
3. Bryce Novak, INF, Gustavus Adolphus (Minn.)	So.	.470	.500	.657
4. Tyler Chumita, INF, Wooster (Ohio)	Jr.	.465	.560	.638
5. Brett Williams, OF, Penn State-Harrisburg	Sr.	.450	.586	.915
6. Turner Hill, OF, Marietta (Ohio)	Sr.	.449	.515	.587
7. Sean Boylan, INF, Misericordia (Pa.)	Sr.	.444	.524	.699
8. Sam Beers, INF, Concordia Wisconsin	Jr.	.442	.500	.705
9. Jonathon Kelso, OF, Wisconsin-Platteville	Sr.	.442	.532	.782
10. Joe Battista, 1B, Utica (N.Y.)	Sr.	.442	.552	.600

EARNED RUN AVERAGE
(Minimum 30 innings pitched)

Rk. Pitcher, Team	Class	W	L	ERA
1. Jared Fong, Washington (Mo.)	Sr.	5	0	0.36
2. Jake Seymour, La Roche (Pa.)	Sr.	8	0	0.81
3. Matt Mulhearn, Webster (Mo.)	Sr.	12	0	1.90
4. Jordy Allard, Babson (Mass.)	Sr.	7	0	0.91
5. Daniel Johnson, Scranton (Pa.)	So.	5	0	1.99
6. Kyle Roche, Franklin & Marshall (Pa.)	Jr.	7	0	1.00
7. Westin Muir, Wisconsin-Whitewater	Sr.	9	1	1.93
8. Michael Simmerman, Alvernia (Pa.)	Sr.	5	0	1.27
9. Peyton Hood, Spalding (Ky.)	Sr.	7	2	1.27
10. Ryan Loutos, Washington (Mo.)	Sr.	11	1	1.33

CATEGORY LEADERS: BATTING
*Minimum 120 at bats

Dept.	Player, Pos., Team	Class	G	Total
OBP*	Adam Zebrowski, 1B, St. John Fisher (N.Y.)	Jr.	38	.594
SLG*	Adam Zebrowski, 1B, St. John Fisher (N.Y.)	Jr.	38	.993
R	Ryan Bixler, OF, Franklin	Sr.	39	67
H	Turner Hill, OF, Marietta (Ohio)	Sr.	44	88
2B	Brent Beals, INF, Millikin (Ill.)	Sr.	47	23
3B	Luke Lehnen, OF, North Central (Ill.)	Fr.	47	10
	Dom Listi, OF, North Central (Ill.)	So.	47	10
HR	Adam Zebrowski, 1B, St. John Fisher (N.Y.)	Jr.	38	20
RBI	Adam Zebrowski, 1B, St. John Fisher (N.Y.)	Jr.	38	70
SB	Nick Bastien, Marian (Wis.)	Sr.	41	36

CATEGORY LEADERS: PITCHING
*Minimum 30 innings

Dept.	Pitcher, Team	Class	Total
W	Matt Mulhearn, Webster (Mo.)	Sr.	12
SV	Carter Ballstadt, Piedmont (Ga.)	Jr.	10

	Jared Fong, Washington (Mo.)	Sr.	10
	Parker Primeaux, Centenary (La.)	So.	10
IP	Sam Carpenter, Piedmont (Ga.)	Sr.	100.1
SO	Matt Mulhearn, Webster (Mo.)	Sr.	137
SO/9*	Justin Garcia, Roger Williams (R.I.)	Sr.	15.27
BB/9*	Jordy Allard, Babson (Mass.)	Sr.	0.36
WHIP*	Kyle Roche, Franklin & Marshall (Pa.)	Jr.	0.60

NAIA

Georgia Gwinnett captured the program first national title with an 8-4 victory over Central Methodist (Mo.) in the championship game of the NAIA World Series. Georgia Gwinnett starting pitcher Hunter Dollander was named most outstanding player after he struck out nine batters in seven innings in the title-clinching win.

NAIA WORLD SERIES

Site: Lewiston, Idaho.
Participants: 1. Southeastern (Fla.); 2. Central Methodist (Mo.); 3. Lewis-Clark State (Idaho); 4. Oklahoma Wesleyan; 5. Georgia Gwinnett; 6. Faulkner (Ala.); 7. Indiana-Southeast; 8. Keiser (Fla.); 9. Louisiana State-Shreveport; 10. Concordia (Neb.)
Champion: Georgia Gwinnett
Runner-up: Central Methodist (Mo.)

LEADERS: BATTING AVERAGE
(Minimum 140 at bats)

RK.	Player, Pos., Team	Class	AVG	OBP	SLG
1.	Luis Vargas, OF, Wayland Baptist (Texas)	Sr.	.489	.531	1.098
2.	Griffin Keller, UTL, Georgia Gwinnett	Sr.	.469	.545	.855
3.	Cody Muncy, 1B, Oklahoma Wesleyan	Jr.	.465	.565	.945
4.	Jared Remspecher, INF, Hannibal-LaGrange (Mo.)	Sr.	.461	.526	.848
5.	Dylan Jacob, OF, Saint Katherine (Calif.)	Jr.	.451	.511	.969

EARNED RUN AVERAGE
(Minimum 40 innings pitched)

Rk.	Pitcher, Team	Class	W	L	ERA
1.	Ruben Ramirez, Point Park (Pa.)	Sr.	8	2	1.25
2.	Jake Fosgett, Concordia (Neb.)	Sr.	9	1	1.43
3.	Pablo Arevalo, Keiser (Fla.)	Sr.	10	3	1.50
4.	Cole Bellair, Tennessee Wesleyan	Sr.	13	2	1.67
5.	Tyler Morrison, Asbury (Ky.)	Sr.	8	1	1.77

CATEGORY LEADERS: BATTING
*Minimum 140 at bats

Dept.	Player, Pos., Team	Class	G	Total
OBP*	Cody Muncy, 1B, Oklahoma Wesleyan	Jr.	60	.565
SLG*	Luis Vargas, OF, Wayland Baptist (Texas)	Jr.	45	1.098
HR	Luis Vargas, OF, Wayland Baptist (Texas)	Jr.	45	29
	Bryan Leef, OF, Cumberlands (Ky.)	Sr.	54	29
	Isaac Wersland, OF, Oklahoma Wesleyan	Sr.	58	29
RBI	Cody Muncy, 1B, Oklahoma Wesleyan	Jr.	60	94
SB	Payton Robertson, UTL, Louisiana State-Shreveport	Sr.	57	45

CATEGORY LEADERS: PITCHING

Dept.	Pitcher, Team	Class	Total
W	Mason Schwellenbach, Central Methodist (Mo.)	Sr.	14
	Nick Merkel, Central Methodist (Mo.)	Jr.	14
SV	Kaden Sullivan, St. Francis (Ind.)	Jr.	11
	Cruz McFadden, Mount Vernon Nazarene (Ohio)	Fr.	11
IP	Pablo Arevalo, Keiser (Fla.)	Sr.	126
SO	Corey Jackson, Bellevue (Neb.)	Sr.	176

NJCAA Division I

McLennan (Texas) captured its first championship since 1983 with a 7-3 win over Central Arizona in the championship game of the NJCAA Division I World Series.
Freshman Logan Henderson gave up one run on two hits with 17 strikeouts in eight innings to help secure the crown for the Highlanders. Henderson won tournament most valuable player honors for his effort.

NJCAA DIVISION I WORLD SERIES
Site: Grand Junction, Colo.

Participants: 1. Crowder (Mo.); 2. Walters State (Tenn.); 3. San Jacinto (Texas); 4. McLennan (Texas); 5. Cowley (Kan.); 6. Central Arizona; 7. Florence-Darlington Tech (S.C.); 8. Miami Dade; 9. Shelton State (Ala.); 10. Indian Hills (Iowa)
Champion: McLennan (Texas)
Runner-up: Central Arizona

LEADERS: BATTING AVERAGE
(Minimum 140 at bats)

RK.	Player, Pos., Team	Class	AVG	OBP	SLG
1.	Savier Pinales, INF, Wabash Valley (Ill.)	So.	.498	.570	.744
2.	Nick Iannantone, OF, Johnson County (Kan.)	So.	.474	.540	.743
3.	Hunter Simmons, INF, Howard (Texas)	Fr.	.469	.580	.654
4.	Matt Goetzmann, OF, Southeast (Neb.)	Fr.	.468	.559	.891
5.	Alberto Osuna, INF, Walters State (Tenn.)	So.	.459	.530	.870

EARNED RUN AVERAGE
(Minimum 40 innings pitched)

Rk.	Pitcher, Team	Class	W	L	ERA
1.	Brandon Schaeffer, Potomac State (W.V.)	So.	7	1	0.94
2.	Jordan Armstrong, Chattahoochee Valley (Ala.)	So.	11	0	1.65
3.	Logan Henderson, McLennan (Texas)	Fr.	10	2	1.66
4.	Konner Copeland, Pensacola State (Fla.)	Fr.	7	1	1.74
5.	Jose Cabrera Jr., Wabash Valley (Ill.)	So.	10	0	1.83

CATEGORY LEADERS: BATTING
*Minimum 140 at bats

			Dept. Player,	
Pos., Team		Class	G	Total
OBP*	Payton Pennington, INF, Wabash Valley (Ill.)	So.	55	.582
SLG*	Josh Cameron, OF, Butler (Kan.)	So.	52	.938
HR	Damiano Palmegiani, INF, Southern Nevada	So.	63	26
RBI	Alberto Osuna, INF, Walters State (Tenn.)	So.	68	107
SB	Savier Pinales, INF, Wabash Valley (Ill.)	So.	57	64

CATEGORY LEADERS: PITCHING

Dept.	Pitcher, Team	Class	Total
W	Zane Morehouse, Dyersburg State (Tenn.)	So.	13
	Mat Olsen, Central Arizona	So.	13
	Hunter Omlid, Central Arizona	Fr.	13
SV	Antonio Knowles, Florida SouthWestern State	So.	13
IP	Logan Henderson, McLennan (Texas)	Fr.	97.2
SO	Logan Henderson, McLennan (Texas)	Fr.	169

NJCAA Division II

Junior college powerhouse Louisiana State-Eunice captured its seventh national championship with a 5-4 win over Western Oklahoma State in the NJCAA Division II World Series championship game. Righthander Jerry Couch of LSU-Eunice won pitcher of the tournament honors, while LSU-Eunice infielder Peyton LeJeune was named the player of the tournament.

NJCAA DIVISION II WORLD SERIES
Site: Enid, Okla.
Participants: 1. Louisiana State-Eunice; 2. Lincoln Land (Ill.); 3. Western Oklahoma State; 4. Kellogg (Mich.); 5. Madison (Wis.); 6. Kirkwood (Iowa); 7. Patrick & Henry (Va.); 8. Phoenix; 9. Frederick (Md.); 10. Lackawanna (Pa.)
Champion: Louisiana State-Eunice
Runner-up: Western Oklahoma State

LEADERS: BATTING AVERAGE
(Minimum 120 at bats)

RK.	Player, Pos., Team	Class	AVG	OBP	SLG
1.	Gage Little, OF, Mississippi Delta	So.	.496	.581	.777
2.	Dawson Perry, 1B, Miles (Mont.)	So.	.495	.586	1.000
3.	Jared Evans, C, Muskegon (Mich.)	Fr.	.490	.577	.621
4.	Brandon Ernst, C, Lackawanna (Pa.)	So.	.481	.547	.802
5.	AJ Henkle, OF, McHenry County (Ill.)	So.	.471	.536	.745

EARNED RUN AVERAGE
(Minimum 40 innings pitched)

Rk.	Pitcher, Team	Class	W	L	ERA
1.	Reagan Klawiter, Madison (Wis.)	So.	7	2	1.76
2.	Landon Gartman, Pearl River (Miss.)	So.	9	0	1.95

	Class	G	Total
3. Walker Johnson, East Central (Miss.)	So.	3	3 1.98
4. Payton Lawrence, Black Hawk-Moline (Ill.)	So.	10	2 2.03
Brad Wolfe, Bryant & Stratton (Ohio)	So.	6	1 2.03

CATEGORY LEADERS: BATTING
Minimum 120 at bats

Dept.	Player, Pos., Team	Class	G	Total
OBP*	Dawson Parry, 1B, Miles (Mont.)	So.	59	.586
SLG*	Dawson Parry, 1B, Miles (Mont.)	So.	59	1.000
HR	Dawson Parry, 1B, Miles (Mont.)	So.	59	26
RBI	Dawson Parry, 1B, Miles (Mont.)	So.	59	97
SB	Tristan McAlister, OF, Patrick & Henry (Va.)	So.	55	52

CATEGORY LEADERS: PITCHING

Dept.	Pitcher, Team	Class	Total
W	Jerry Couch, Lousiana-State Eunice	So.	12
SV	Kyle Stoddard, Black Hawk-Moline (Ill.)	So.	11
IP	Jerry Couch, Lousiana-State Eunice	So.	92
SO	Magnus Ellerts, Patrick & Henry (Va.)	Fr.	141

NJCAA Division III

Tyler (Texas) swept through the NJCAA Division III World Series to capture the program's sixth national championship. Previously, the Apaches won four straight national titles from 2014-2017. Tyler defeated Niagara County (N.Y.) 5-4 in the championship game, thanks in large part to a go-ahead two-run homer from Miguel Vega in the eighth inning.

NJCAA DIVISION III WORLD SERIES
Site: Greeneville, Tenn.
Participants: 1. Rowan Gloucester (N.Y.); 2. Tyler (Texas); 3. Oakton (Ill.); 4. Niagara County (N.Y.); 5. St. Cloud Tech (Minn.); 6. Coastal Bend (Texas); 7. Rockingham (N.C.); 8. Owens (Ohio)
Champion: Tyler (Texas)
Runner-up: Niagara County (N.Y.)

LEADERS: BATTING AVERAGE
(Minimum 120 at bats)

RK.	Player, Pos., Team	Class	AVG	OBP	SLG
1.	Scottie O'Bryan, OF, Niagara County (N.Y.)	So.	.475	.547	.777
2.	John M. Gonzalez, Jr., OF, Rainy River (Minn.)	Fr.	.450	.550	.806
3.	Cade Marquardt, C, Itasca (Minn.)	Fr.	.437	.520	.627
4.	Bradley Vondruska, INF, Milwaukee Area Tech	So.	.433	.493	.606
5.	Matt Wicker, INF, Westmoreland County (Pa.)	So.	.430	.483	.625

EARNED RUN AVERAGE
(Minimum 40 innings pitched)

Rk.	Pitcher, Team	Class	W	L	ERA
1.	Ryan Peterson, Niagara County (N.Y.)	So.	10	1	1.22
2.	Chris Widger, Rowan Gloucester	Fr.	8	0	1.26
3.	Terel Tillman, SUNY Adirondack (N.Y.)	Fr.	3	4	1.74
4.	Chad Gartland, Niagara County (N.Y.)	Fr.	6	2	1.88
5.	Jack Billings, Rowan Gloucester	So.	6	0	1.90

California Junior Colleges

No California CC Athletic Association state champion was crowned in 2021 due to some teams opting out of the season and others playing reduced schedules, but Orange Coast finished the shortened season ranked No. 1 in a ranking put together by the California Community College Sports Information Association after going 20-7-1 overall and 14-4 in the Orange Empire Conference. The Pirates are also still the reigning California state champs after winning the title the last time it was awarded in 2019. Butte, which won the Golden Valley Conference with a 23-3 record, ended the year ranked No. 2.

CALIFORNIA CC ATHLETIC ASSOCIATION
No champion crowned

LEADERS: BATTING AVERAGE
(Minimum 140 at bats)

RK.	Player, Pos., Team	Class	AVG	OBP	SLG
1.	BJ Vela, INF, Reedley	Fr.	.481	.560	.821
2.	Curran Ozawa-Burns, OF, West Valley	So.	.462	.550	.813
3.	Donte Valdez, OF, Sequoias	So.	.455	.547	.795
4.	Alex Vega, INF, Moorpark	So.	.435	.505	.620
5.	Michael Doerr, OF, Cerro Coso	So.	.433	.500	.656

EARNED RUN AVERAGE
(Minimum 40 innings pitched)

Rk.	Pitcher, Team	Class	W	L	ERA
1.	Ryu Umeda, Los Medanos	So.	4	0	1.09
2.	Matthew Lozovoy, Marin	So.	5	2	1.11
3.	Brody Eglite, Los Medanos	Fr.	4	0	1.13
4.	Connor Rudy, Contra Costa	So.	2	2	1.35
5.	Joe Murphy, Monterey Peninsula	So.	2	1	1.38

USA Baseball's Collegiate National Team played a summer unlike any before it. Due to travel restrictions and the continued fall-out from the Covid-19 pandemic, the team didn't compete in any international competition overseas or on home soil. Instead, the 48-man roster competed in a series of 11 intrasquad scrimmages mostly in the footprint of the Appalachian League and capped off the schedule with a three-game series in North Carolina against the USA Olympic team.

Because the CNT faced no foreign competition, the roster size had to be doubled and USA Baseball cast a wide net to for its player pool.

Among the standouts were already familiar top prospects like shortstop Brooks Lee (Cal Poly) and infielder Jacob Berry (Louisiana State) but also some other prospects who hadn't yet made their mark, like lefthander/first baseman Reggie Crawford (Connecticut), who hadn't pitched much for the Huskies before emerging as one of the top arms on Team USA.

No one will be eager to repeat the CNT's format for 2021, as international competition is a key part of every summer. But after a year without Team USA in any form, the CNT's return was a welcome sight.

COLLEGIATE NATIONAL TEAM STATS

Year indicates 2018-19 class standing

Player, Pos.	Year	School	AVG	OBP	SLG	G	AB	R	H	2B	3B	HR	RBI	BB	SO	SB
Gavin Cross, OF	So.	Virginia Tech	.455	.474	.879	11	33	7	15	2	0	4	13	3	4	3
Kevin Parada, C	So.	Georgia Tech	.400	.500	.520	10	25	5	10	3	0	0	3	4	9	1
Jacob Berry, INF	So.	Louisiana State	.387	.475	.871	11	31	9	12	3	0	4	12	6	6	1
Robert Moore, 2B	So.	Arkansas	.351	.415	.378	11	37	10	13	1	0	0	3	4	9	2
Dylan Crews, OF	So.	Louisiana State	.350	.435	.550	7	20	4	7	1	0	1	4	3	3	2
Ethan Long, 1B	So.	Arizona State	.333	.407	.458	8	24	2	8	3	0	0	3	3	8	0
Brooks Lee, SS	So.	Cal Poly	.306	.342	.444	11	36	3	11	2	0	1	4	1	6	2
Jordan Sprinkle, SS	So.	UC Santa Barbara	.300	.353	.467	11	30	3	9	3	1	0	5	3	11	3
Drew Gilbert, OF	So.	Tennessee	.294	.314	.382	11	34	4	10	1	1	0	3	0	7	2
Daniel Susac, C	So.	Arizona	.273	.273	.318	9	22	4	6	1	0	0	1	0	10	1
Jace Jung, INF	So.	Texas Tech	.267	.371	.400	11	30	4	8	1	0	1	1	5	10	1
Reggie Crawford, 1B/LHP	So.	Connecticut	.250	.286	.400	8	20	3	5	0	0	1	2	1	3	0
Brock Jones, OF	So.	Stanford	.242	.306	.576	11	33	5	8	0	1	3	8	3	10	1
Sean McLain, OF	So.	Arizona State	.242	.286	.273	11	33	3	8	1	0	0	2	2	8	4
Kyle Teel, OF	So.	Virginia	.233	.343	.333	11	30	7	7	3	0	0	1	4	7	0
Logan Tanner, C	So.	Mississippi State	.182	.217	.318	7	22	2	4	0	0	1	2	0	9	0
Jacob Gonzalez, SS	So.	Mississippi	.182	.308	.182	9	22	2	4	0	0	0	3	4	7	0
Hayden Dunhurst, C	So.	Mississippi	.160	.267	.160	10	25	3	4	0	0	0	1	3	10	1
Dylan Beavers, OF	So.	California	.143	.333	.286	9	21	4	3	0	0	1	4	5	9	3
Caden Grice, OF	So.	Clemson	.115	.207	.231	10	26	2	3	0	0	1	2	2	16	0
Carter Trice, INF	So.	Old Dominion	.056	.261	.222	9	18	5	1	0	0	1	2	5	9	1

Pitcher, Pos.	Year	School	W	L	ERA	G	SV	IP	H	R	ER	BB	SO	AVG
Reggie Crawford, 1B/LHP	So.	Connecticut	0	0	0.00	4	1	4	1	0	0	0	8	.077
Landon Sims, RHP	So.	Mississippi State	0	0	0.00	3	1	3	2	0	0	0	6	.167
Cole Kirschsieper, LHP	So.	Illinois	0	0	0.00	1	0	3	2	0	0	1	2	.182
Hunter Barco, LHP	So.	Florida	1	0	0.00	1	0	3	1	0	0	0	8	.100
Matthew Wyatt, RHP	So.	Virginia	0	0	0.00	1	0	3	3	2	0	2	2	.273
Tanner Witt, RHP	So.	Texas	1	0	1.50	2	0	6	4	1	1	4	3	.211
Carson Whisenhunt, LHP	So.	East Carolina	1	0	1.50	2	0	6	3	1	1	1	10	.150
Carson Palmquist, LHP	So.	Miami	0	0	1.80	5	1	5	3	1	1	0	7	.167
Devereaux Harrison, RHP	So.	Long Beach State	0	0	1.80	4	0	5	2	1	1	4	7	.118
Jaxon Wiggins, RHP	So.	Arkansas	0	0	3.00	5	0	6	6	2	2	0	9	.261
Brandon Sproat, RHP	So.	Florida	1	0	3.00	2	0	6	5	2	2	2	8	.227
Justin Campbell, RHP	So.	Oklahoma State	0	1	3.00	2	0	6	4	2	2	1	7	.200
Chris Villaman, LHP	So.	North Carolina State	1	0	3.18	3	1	6	7	2	2	4	11	.292
Josh White, RHP	So.	California	0	1	3.38	3	0	8	8	5	3	3	12	.235
Parker Messick, LHP	So.	Florida State	0	0	3.38	3	0	8	8	4	3	3	6	.242
Gabriel Hughes, RHP	So.	Gonzaga	1	0	5.14	3	0	7	8	4	4	1	2	.276
Adam Stone, RHP	So.	Harvard	1	1	5.62	3	0	8	12	5	5	5	8	.387
Will Sanders, RHP	So.	South Carolina	0	1	7.20	2	0	5	8	4	4	2	4	.364
Sam Highfill, RHP	So.	North Carolina State	0	0	7.20	2	0	5	9	5	4	2	7	.409
Nate Savino, LHP	So.	Virginia	1	0	7.50	3	0	6	7	8	5	3	7	.280
Blade Tidwell, RHP	So.	Tennessee	1	1	7.71	3	0	7	6	6	6	4	9	.222
Jack Washburn, RHP	So.	Mississippi	0	1	10.80	3	0	7	8	8	5	7	8	.308
Aaron Nixon, RHP	So.	Texas	0	2	11.37	5	0	6	12	10	8	3	4	.414
Drew Thorpe, RHP	So.	Cal Poly	1	1	12.38	3	0	8	19	11	11	2	11	.442
Jackson Fristoe, RHP	So.	Mississippi State	0	1	13.50	2	0	3	2	4	4	5	4	.222

Baseball Returns To Cape Cod

Baseball this summer returned to Cape Cod after the 2020 season was canceled due to the pandemic—the first time the Cape Cod League had missed a season since the end of World War II.

The league's return was a welcome sight for many around the game and especially for the people on the Cape. The league drew large crowds all season long and the play on the diamond was at a typically high level, despite some unusual circumstances.

Like everyone else in amateur baseball, the Cape had to deal with an abnormally late draft date, which led to a midseason disruption of many rosters. USA Baseball's Collegiate National Team was also twice the size as normal, which pulled more players away from the Cape. The flip side of that, however, was a shorter schedule for Team USA, which led to more of its players spending part of the summer on the Cape, including No. 1 prospect Brooks Lee.

The Cape's season culminated with Brewster sweeping Bourne in the best-of-three championship series. It was the second title in four seasons for the Whitecaps and manager Jamie Shevchik.

Brewster swept its way through the playoffs, beating Harwich in the first round before taking on Bourne, which was the top-seeded team in the playoffs, in the finals. Outfielder Chad Castillo (Cal Baptist) was named playoff MVP and the Whitecaps drew a record 5,217 fans to Stony Brook Field for the decisive second game of the finals.

New Appalachian, MLB Draft Leagues Debut

Major League Baseball's revamp of the minor leagues last year also led to the creation of two new college summer leagues: the Appalachian League and the MLB Draft League.

The two new leagues have similar overarching missions—the goal is to provide a high-level showcase for college players to be evaluated by scouts—but each occupies a slightly different space.

The startup MLB Draft League is exactly what it sounds like, a place for draft-eligible players to make a final impression on MLB organizations ahead of a draft that is now late enough in the calendar to allow for such a thing.

The revamped Appalachian League, a joint venture between MLB and USA Baseball that carries forward the historic name of the league that was until this season an affiliated minor league, is geared toward incoming freshmen and rising sophomores who will use their time in the Appy League as a developmental stop on the way to bigger things.

The Appalachian League wrapped its season in style in early August, with Greeneville winning the league championship over Pulaski in walk-off fashion. Along the way, it also had one of its best pitchers, lefthander Cole Kirschsieper of Kingsport, who plays his college baseball at Illinois, get a spot start with Team USA late in the summer.

The MLB Draft League did what it set out to do by having 39 of its players drafted in July, including eight players in the top 10 rounds. Eighteen more signed with MLB clubs as undrafted free agents and 24 others reached deals with independent league teams

But whether you judge each league's respective first season as successful or not, it's not really fair to draw conclusions about the long-term trajectory and viability of the leagues just yet. Consider that neither had anything approaching a normal lead-up to their inaugural seasons as college summer leagues.

Kerrick Jackson wasn't announced as president of the MLB Draft League until late November of last year and managers for the six clubs weren't announced until April. And the Appalachian League had to wait out MLB's decision with regards to minor league consolidation before it could conduct official business as a college summer league, so the announcement of its new function didn't come until late September 2020.

"We got such a late start, with the league not really announcing our formation until October 1, where you see a lot of summer college leagues already had signed their players in July and August of last year," Appalachian League president Dan Moushon said.

Becoming a successful college summer league can, on paper, be a tough nut to crack because of the inertia in the summer ball pecking order and changing attitudes around how college players should spend their summers.

Both of these new leagues are unique in that each is trying to fill a very specific niche and that can only help in their bid to stay relevant on the scene.

The MLB Draft League has a very clear mission to get its players into pro baseball right away, and previously, none of the higher-quality summer leagues were focusing on draft-eligible players. The Appalachian League, meanwhile, explicitly doesn't want to be seen as a competitor to the more prestigious summer leagues, as it looks to provide a place to play for younger college players who perhaps could be ready for a bigger stage later in their careers.

The focus for both of these new kids on the block is using the year ahead to apply lessons learned from challenging first seasons to serve the players in their leagues as best they can and to become established as permanent pieces of the colorful tapestry that is summer college baseball.

COLLEGE SUMMER LEAGUES

Shortstop Brooks Lee of Cal Poly was the No. 1 prospect in the Cape Cod League.

CAPE COD LEAGUE

East Division

	W	L	T	PTS
Orleans Firebirds	23	17	4	50
Brewster Whitecaps	22	11	3	47
Harwich Mariners	19	12	5	43
Yarmouth-Dennis Red Sox	16	14	7	39
Chatham Anglers	16	19	3	35
Orleans Firebirds	13	17	5	31

West Division

	W	L	T	PTS
Bourne Braves	24	9	3	51
Cotuit Kettleers	18	17	1	37
Wareham Gatemen	14	18	5	33
Falmouth Commodores	14	19	2	30
Hyannis Harbor Hawks	8	28	0	16

CHAMPIONSHIP: Brewster Whitecaps defeated Bourne Braves, 2-0, in best-of-three championship series.

TOP 50 PROSPECTS: 1. Brooks Lee, SS, Yarmouth-Dennis (So., Cal Poly). **2.** Brock Wilken, 3B, Harwich (So., Wake Forest). **3.** Chase DeLauter, OF, Orleans (So., James Madison). **4.** Jace Bohrofen, OF, Falmouth (So., Arkansas). **5.** Bryce Hubbart, LHP, Brewster (So., Florida State). **6.** Zach Neto, SS, Brewster (So., Campbell). **7.** Tommy Troy, 2B, Wareham (So., Stanford). **8.** Paul Skenes, C/RHP, Wareham (So., Air Force). **9.** Adam Maier, RHP, Yarmouth-Dennis (So., Oregon). **10.** Clark Elliott, OF, Hyannis (So., Michigan). **11.** Spencer Jones, OF, Brewster (So., Vanderbilt). **12.** Ryan Ritter, SS, Cotuit (So., Kentucky). **13.** Cayden Wallace, OF, Bourne (So., Arkansas). **14.** Teddy McGraw, RHP, Brewster (So., Wake Forest). **15.** Peyton Graham, 3B, Yarmouth-Dennis (So., Oklahoma). **16.** Jordan Beck, OF, Harwich (So., Tennessee). **17.** Victor Mederos, RHP, Chatham (So., Oklahoma State). **18.** Trey Dombroski, LHP, Harwich (So., Monmouth). **19.** Kody Huff, C, Yarmouth-Dennis (So., Stanford). **20.** Chris Newell, OF, Harwich (So., Virginia). **21.** Max Rajcic, RHP, Orleans (So., UCLA). **22.** Eric Reyzelman, RHP, Harwich (So., Louisiana State). **23.** Trey Faltine, SS, Brewster (So., Texas). **24.** Eric Brown, 2B/SS, Cotuit (So., Coastal Carolina). **25.** Christian Knapczyk, SS, Bourne (So., Louisville). **26.** Luke Keaschall, 2B/OF, Orleans (So., San Francisco). **27.** Luke Gold, INF, Cotuit (So., Boston College). **28.** Dalton Rushing, C/1B, Bourne (So., Louisville). **29.** Jace Grady, OF, Cotuit (So., Dallas Baptist). **30.** Eric Adler, RHP, Bourne (So., Wake Forest). **31.** Anthony Hall, OF, Falmouth (So., Oregon). **32.** Jack Jasiak, RHP, Falmouth (So., South Florida). **33.** Michael Curialle, SS, Falmouth (So., UCLA). **34.** Mason Barnett, RHP, Brewster (So., Auburn). **35.** Jack Brannigan, 3B/RHP, Wareham (So., Notre Dame). **36.** Bryce Osmond, RHP, Chatham (So., Oklahoma State). **37.** Luis Ramirez, RHP, Yarmouth-Dennis (So., Long Beach State). **38.** Andrew Mosiello, RHP, Harwich (So., Oregon). **39.** Jim Jarvis, SS, Wareham (So., Alabama). **40.** Adam Tulloch, LHP, Chatham (Jr., Arizona State). **41.** Orion Kerkering, RHP, Orleans (So., South Florida). **42.** Sebastian Keane, RHP, Chatham (So., Northeastern). **43.** Cy Nielson, LHP, Chatham (So., Brigham Young). **44.** Tyler Locklear, 3B, Orleans (So., Virginia Commonwealth). **45.** Maxwell Romero Jr., C, Chatham (So., Miami). **46.** Max Anderson, 3B, Bourne (So., Nebraska). **47.** Trevor Martin, RHP, Chatham (So., Oklahoma State). **48.** Dominic Johnson, OF, Hyannis (So., Kansas State). **49.** Pres Cavenaugh, OF, Harwich (So., UNC Greensboro). **50.** Owen Diodati, OF, Wareham (So., Alabama).

INDIVIDUAL BATTING LEADERS

	AVG	AB	R	H	2B	3B	HR	RBI	SB
Clark Elliott, OF, Harbor Hawks	.344	90	19	31	4	1	2	8	7
Pres Cavenaugh, OF, Mariners	.333	105	22	35	7	0	1	13	7
Tres Gonzalez, OF, Gatemen	.331	121	20	40	6	0	0	11	8
Ryan Ritter, SS, Kettleers	.330	91	17	30	4	1	1	8	2
Christian Knapczyk, SS, Braves	.321	109	27	35	8	1	0	11	6
Dalton Rushing, 1B, Braves	.314	118	23	37	9	0	6	24	1
Kris Armstrong, 1B, Commodores	.308	91	19	28	4	0	7	21	0
Tanner Schobel, SS, Braves	.302	86	11	26	5	0	3	17	0
Brock Wilken, 3B, Mariners	.302	129	26	39	10	0	6	26	3
Tommy Troy, 2B, Gatemen	.299	117	21	35	3	3	4	19	9

INDIVIDUAL PITCHING LEADERS

Player, Team	W	L	ERA	G	SV	IP	H	BB	SO
Trey Dombroski, Mariners	3	0	0.85	6	0	32	27	2	45
Bryce Hubbart, Whitecaps	3	1	0.87	6	0	31	14	8	45
Zack Morris, Firebirds	2	0	1.21	11	0	22	17	12	25
Adam Mazur, Gatemen	3	0	1.55	6	0	29	18	6	34
Andrew Mosiello, Red Sox	1	1	2.02	5	0	22	12	11	26
Austin Parsley, Braves	3	0	2.05	7	0	26	20	1	36
Michael Sansone, Braves	4	0	2.08	6	0	26	16	2	25
Cole Chudoba, Braves	3	0	2.08	7	0	22	18	2	17
Hayden Thomas, Firebirds	1	2	2.60	7	0	28	20	12	30
Eric Reyzelman, Mariners	2	0	2.66	5	0	24	18	6	36

BOURNE

Batting	AVG	AB	R	H	2B	3B	HR	RBI	SB
Zachary Agnos	.197	76	10	15	3	2	3	9	0
Max Anderson	.283	120	19	34	8	0	3	13	1
Colton Bender	.273	33	3	9	1	0	1	6	0
Peter Burns	.182	55	6	10	2	0	0	6	0
Lucas Costello	.056	18	1	1	0	0	0	0	0
Reggie Crawford	.296	27	4	8	2	0	1	2	0
Kyler Fedko	.220	50	1	11	0	0	0	5	0
John Garcia	.077	13	0	1	0	0	0	0	0
Nick Goodwin	.221	68	10	15	1	0	1	5	1
Benjamin Huber	.375	16	3	6	0	0	0	4	0
Hunter Jump	.056	18	2	1	0	0	0	0	0
Christian Knapczyk	.321	109	27	35	8	1	0	11	6
Joe Lampe	.269	108	18	29	1	1	0	11	6
Josh Moylan	.180	61	5	11	0	0	1	5	0
Dalton Rushing	.314	118	23	37	9	0	6	24	1
Tanner Schobel	.302	86	11	26	5	0	3	17	0
Colby Thomas	.228	92	14	21	5	2	4	15	4
John Thrasher	.167	6	1	1	1	0	0	1	0
Cayden Wallace	.290	62	12	18	5	0	2	14	1
Braylon Wimmer	.282	85	11	24	6	0	2	16	3
Pitching	W	L	ERA	G	SV	IP	H	BB	SO
Eric Adler	2	0	1.15	15	7	16	6	7	29
Jake Bennett	0	2	2.89	7	0	28	30	3	30
Dylan Bowers	2	0	1.64	6	0	11	10	4	15
Bryson Cafaro	0	0	10.80	3	1	5	9	1	4
Cole Chudoba	3	0	2.08	7	0	22	18	2	17
Reggie Crawford	0	0	0.00	2	0	2	0	0	4
Frank Doelling	0	1	1.69	3	0	5	3	4	4
Josh Ekness	0	0	3.95	8	0	14	8	13	12
Benjamin Ethridge	1	1	4.74	9	0	19	18	9	17
Gordon Graceffo	1	0	0.69	3	0	13	12	2	13
Matt Jachec	1	0	1.50	1	0	6	5	0	4
Xavier Lovett	0	0	7.50	11	2	12	13	9	12
Hunter Omlid	0	1	6.75	4	0	11	16	3	10
Austin Parsey	3	0	2.05	7	0	26	20	1	36
Jordan Patty	2	1	4.05	5	0	20	17	4	21
Michael Sansone	4	0	2.08	6	0	26	16	2	25
Cade Smith	1	0	7.11	5	0	6	7	4	7
Tyler Stuart	0	0	0.00	4	0	6	4	4	6
Andrew Taylor	0	0	1.29	2	0	7	3	3	11
Kenneth Turner	0	1	3.26	8	0	19	24	5	18
Peter Van Loon	0	0	1.35	2	0	7	6	2	7
Trystan Vrieling	2	0	1.04	7	0	17	7	7	21
Kelsey Ward	0	1	15.43	3	0	5	7	2	3
Nick Zwack	2	1	1.29	3	0	14	5	1	14

BREWSTER

Batting	AVG	AB	R	H	2B	3B	HR	RBI	SB
Nick Biddison	.147	75	7	11	2	1	0	10	6
Mac Bingham	.136	59	7	8	1	1	0	7	3
Porter Brown	.157	51	6	8	1	0	1	6	3
Tony Bullard	.242	33	3	8	1	0	0	4	1
Kurtis Byrne	.190	79	6	15	2	0	0	6	0
Dillon Carter	.138	29	7	4	2	0	0	3	2
Chad Castillo	.333	51	14	17	2	0	2	7	0
Gavin Cross	.105	19	3	2	0	0	2	2	0
Colin Davis	.420	50	11	21	0	0	2	10	13
Tyler Dellerman	.300	20	4	6	2	0	0	2	0
Trey Faltine	.154	65	13	10	1	0	2	8	4
Alex Freeland	.242	66	16	16	3	0	0	4	3
Shawn Goosenberg	.270	37	7	10	1	0	1	6	2
Spencer Jones	.312	77	14	24	4	0	3	18	6
Chris Lanzilli	.182	55	8	10	3	0	1	8	2
Zachary Neto	.304	46	7	14	4	0	3	10	4
Clayton Owens	.143	14	1	2	0	0	0	1	0
Christian Pregent	.000	11	1	0	0	0	0	0	0
Richie Schiekofer	.000	8	2	0	0	0	0	0	1
Dylan Simmons	.125	8	0	1	0	0	0	0	0
Will Simpson	.211	76	8	16	2	0	3	12	2
Jake Thompson	.278	108	16	30	9	2	3	18	3
Cooper Weiss	.118	51	11	6	0	0	3	8	3
Pitching	W	L	ERA	G	SV	IP	H	BB	SO
Thomas Babalis	0	1	8.31	3	0	4	6	4	3
Mason Barnett	1	1	4.95	5	0	20	19	6	23
Samuel Bello	0	0	6.75	5	1	11	18	1	8
Cooper Bowman	0	0	18.00	1	0	1	1	1	1
Donovan Burke	0	1	15.43	1	0	2	6	1	2
Ryan Cardona	2	0	1.35	3	0	7	6	4	6
Greg Farone	0	0	2.46	2	0	4	5	2	6
Brian Fitzpatrick	1	0	2.37	6	1	19	13	3	24
Brendan Girton	0	1	4.38	7	1	12	10	4	16
Griffin Green	0	1	2.60	8	1	17	12	6	19
Pete Hansen	1	1	6.32	4	0	16	14	7	15
Bryce Hubbart	3	1	0.87	6	0	31	14	8	45
Chris McElvain	2	0	4.85	4	0	13	12	4	13
Teddy McGraw	1	2	3.67	7	0	27	27	11	25
John Mikolaicyk	1	0	0.00	2	0	3	4	1	2
Hunter Owen	2	1	4.80	7	0	15	16	9	18
Brennen Oxford	1	0	2.70	3	0	7	6	4	8
Hunter Patteson	1	0	4.34	8	2	19	16	4	17
Michael Prosecky	2	0	2.35	9	1	15	10	10	21
Harrison Rutkowski	2	0	1.59	3	0	17	7	2	16
Dylan Simmons	0	0	4.91	7	1	11	12	7	12
Connor Staine	2	1	2.35	7	0	15	14	4	16
Dane Stanavich	0	0	2.25	12	6	16	10	8	30
Michael Walsh	0	0	0.00	1	0	2	0	3	3

CHATHAM

Batting	AVG	AB	R	H	2B	3B	HR	RBI	SB
Andrew Benefield	.167	36	3	6	2	0	2	7	1
Logan Britt	.174	46	5	8	2	0	1	3	1
Michael Brown	.308	13	2	4	0	0	0	2	0
Johnny Castagnozzi	.231	39	3	9	0	1	2	6	0
Cam Chick	.143	21	2	3	0	0	1	3	1
Jake DeLeo	.234	111	10	26	3	0	1	13	7
John Michael Faile	.227	22	1	5	1	0	1	2	0
Matthew Garcia	.150	60	8	9	3	0	0	3	1
Caden Grice	.250	28	7	7	0	0	2	3	0
Matthew Hogan	.227	88	14	20	6	0	4	10	5
Crosby Jones	.000	5	1	0	0	0	0	0	0
Kenny Levari	.162	37	2	6	2	0	0	2	0
Garrett Martin	.262	42	5	11	2	0	1	2	1
Nolan Mclean	.261	23	9	6	0	0	2	6	0
David Mendham	.161	31	4	5	1	0	0	1	0
Lyle Miller-Green	.248	125	17	31	3	0	8	28	0
Kevin Parada	.250	28	4	7	2	0	0	3	1
Josh Rivera	.248	117	15	29	6	0	1	7	4
Maxwell Romero Jr.	.264	91	14	24	6	0	5	20	0

Danny Serretti	.282	85	16	24	4	0	2	8	4
Seth Stephenson	.333	21	5	7	1	1	0	0	2
Dominic Tamez	.093	43	3	4	2	0	1	6	0
Caeden Trenkle	.186	97	17	18	5	1	1	10	3

Pitching	W	L	ERA	G	SV	IP	H	BB	SO
Kade Bragg	0	0	0.00	4	2	4	1	2	3
Dylan Carmouche	1	2	5.94	5	0	17	22	9	22
Logan Chapman	0	0	0.33	3	0	3	8	2	3
Garrett Crowley	2	2	5.13	8	0	26	23	10	39
Aaron Davenport	0	1	7.50	2	0	6	5	2	4
Dave Falco	0	1	6.40	9	0	13	16	8	18
Daniel Federman	0	0	0.93	3	0	10	8	0	15
Dawson Gause	1	0	7.20	2	0	5	7	4	6
Chase Hampton	0	1	4.91	4	0	11	11	4	14
Sebastian Keane	0	1	3.86	7	0	21	26	7	25
Kody Kubichek	0	0	2.25	1	0	4	2	0	3
Trevor Martin	3	0	2.79	8	1	19	19	9	27
Zach Maxwell	1	1	6.17	10	2	12	11	9	25
Alex McFarlane	2	2	4.03	7	0	22	17	14	28
Victor Mederos	1	1	4.64	7	1	21	17	12	19
Cy Nielson	2	2	5.70	8	1	24	28	11	26
Bryce Osmond	1	2	4.22	6	1	21	25	11	26
Adam Scoggins	0	0	0.00	6	0	6	0	3	16
Brandon Sproat	0	1	13.50	1	0	2	3	4	2
Adam Tulloch	0	0	4.03	8	0	29	26	8	43
Austin Vernon	0	0	6.52	3	0	10	5	8	15
Jacob Watters	1	0	6.00	3	0	6	5	8	11
Carson Winquest	1	0	2.79	8	1	19	15	11	22
Tanner Witt	0	2	3.00	3	0	12	11	5	17

COTUIT

Batting	AVG	AB	R	H	2B	3B	HR	RBI	SB
Brooks Baldwin	.239	67	13	16	3	1	1	7	7
Dylan Beavers	.233	30	4	7	2	0	0	5	0
Noah Bridges	.240	50	5	12	2	1	1	13	4
Eric Brown	.282	117	26	33	3	0	5	21	13
Drew Compton	.167	18	2	3	0	0	0	3	0
Cole Cummings	.288	52	10	15	3	1	1	4	4
Matthew Dolan	.254	67	7	17	3	0	0	6	0
Eldridge Figueroa	.083	12	2	1	0	0	0	0	0
William Gale	.000	2	0	0	0	0	0	1	0
Andy Garriola	.256	43	6	11	1	0	3	11	0
Luke Gold	.267	86	18	23	4	0	6	23	3
Jace Grady	.346	78	18	27	3	0	4	12	5
Cam Hill	.375	8	0	3	1	0	0	0	1
Trent Jeffcoat	.000	2	0	0	0	0	0	0	0
Blake Klassen	.200	20	2	4	1	0	1	1	0
Nathan Martorella	.264	72	12	19	4	0	1	9	1
Jack O'Dowd	.125	8	0	1	0	0	0	0	1
Raul Ortega	.100	10	1	1	1	0	0	0	0
Mikey Perez	.500	2	0	1	0	0	0	0	0
John Rhodes	.303	33	4	10	5	0	0	5	1
Ben Rice	.265	34	4	9	3	0	0	9	0
Ryan Ritter	.330	91	17	30	4	1	1	8	2
Brett Roberts	.305	82	14	25	4	0	2	17	3
Alec Sayre	.400	10	0	4	1	0	0	0	0
RJ Schreck	.231	39	9	9	1	0	1	6	1
Matthew Suggs	.171	41	6	7	0	0	1	4	2
Josiah Town	.200	25	5	5	0	0	1	2	0
Carter Trice	.213	47	12	10	3	0	1	8	2

Pitching	W	L	ERA	G	SV	IP	H	BB	SO
Alaska Abney	0	0	2.79	7	1	10	6	3	17
Logan Adams	0	0	14.73	3	0	4	8	3	3
TJ Brock	0	0	0.00	3	0	2	2	3	5
Jake Brooks	3	3	3.06	8	0	32	34	4	24
Zach Cable	0	1	9.00	3	1	2	3	3	3
Michael Ciminiello	0	0	0.00	1	0	2	3	3	3
Harrison Cohen	2	2	5.47	11	2	25	26	7	27
Ryan Deo	0	0	12.60	4	0	5	8	5	3
Ian Foggo	1	1	1.23	3	0	7	3	5	9
Zachary Fruit	3	0	4.15	12	1	13	16	10	16
Joseph Gieg	1	0	1.50	7	1	18	14	9	16

Andre Granillo	1	0	2.46	4	1	11	8	2	17
Trey Holland	0	1	8.31	3	0	4	8	1	4
Riley Huge	0	1	12.71	5	0	6	10	7	2
Will Jacobsen	1	1	10.69	8	1	16	22	9	12
Trevor Kuncl	0	0	2.89	6	0	9	6	5	10
Ryan Long	1	1	4.66	4	0	10	6	10	10
Logan Maitland	1	0	0.61	7	0	15	10	10	16
Joe Mancini	0	1	9.00	1	0	3	5	2	1
Quinn Matthews	0	0	1.56	4	0	17	10	11	22
Mike McCully	0	1	21.00	1	0	3	9	0	4
Justin Meis	1	1	2.08	4	0	17	11	3	17
Hambleton Oliver	0	1	8.10	10	0	17	23	8	15
Shaddon Peavyhouse	0	1	9.64	4	1	5	5	3	6
Shawn Rapp	0	1	4.50	3	1	8	8	2	13
Dalton Rhadans	0	0	2.70	7	0	7	12	3	10
Dalton Rogers	1	0	2.77	5	0	13	7	14	21
Jake Smith	2	0	0.00	2	0	10	8	2	12
Chris Troye	0	0	20.25	2	0	1	1	4	4
Joseph Walsh	0	0	12.00	6	0	6	9	3	7

FALMOUTH

Batting	AVG	AB	R	H	2B	3B	HR	RBI	SB
Walter Ahuna	.353	17	5	6	0	0	0	1	3
Kris Armstrong	.308	91	19	28	4	0	7	21	0
Michael Becchetti	.000	6	0	0	0	0	0	0	0
Jace Bohrofen	.279	129	25	36	8	3	5	19	8
Luke Boyers	.163	80	10	13	2	0	1	8	4
Cameron Bufford	.000	4	1	0	0	0	0	0	0
Michael Curialle	.243	115	17	28	6	1	3	20	3
Anthony DeFabbia	.400	5	0	2	1	0	0	0	0
Jake Dukart	.224	49	8	11	2	0	0	10	0
Jonathan French	.169	59	10	10	2	0	2	6	0
Anthony Hall	.283	106	18	30	7	1	4	13	3
Michael Handal	.364	22	3	8	1	0	0	5	1
Casey Harford	.236	55	6	13	1	1	0	5	0
Douglas Hodo	.194	31	2	6	1	0	0	2	1
Kodie Kolden	.171	111	13	19	3	0	2	12	3
Jake Meyer	.200	10	0	2	0	0	0	2	0
Brennan Milone	.167	36	5	6	1	0	0	3	1
Alec Sayre	.125	24	2	3	0	0	0	3	0
Taylor Smith	.187	75	15	14	4	0	5	9	0
Brayden Taylor	.269	104	18	28	6	0	2	14	3
JT Thompson	.250	4	1	1	0	0	0	0	0
Bryson Ware	.067	30	3	2	0	0	1	1	0

Pitching	W	L	ERA	G	SV	IP	H	BB	SO
Connor Bovair	0	1	5.63	2	0	8	10	4	9
Everett Catlett	0	0	0.00	1	0	1	1	0	1
Anthony DeFabbia	4	2	5.03	9	0	20	23	5	17
Jack Erbeck	0	0	0.00	1	0	1	0	0	0
Michael Esposito	0	0	3.00	3	1	3	0	5	4
Daniel Garcia	1	1	6.43	3	0	7	12	1	7
Lucas Gordon	1	0	3.86	7	1	14	11	5	22
Charles Harrison	1	0	5.06	9	0	16	20	9	16
KC Hunt	0	1	5.56	5	1	11	14	4	14
Jack Jasiak	2	0	2.89	4	0	19	15	4	16
Antoine Jean	0	1	4.19	5	0	19	17	9	15
Chase Jeter	0	1	3.60	8	1	20	18	5	19
Trey McLoughlin	1	0	0.00	2	0	11	6	2	7
Mason Pelio	1	3	7.13	6	0	18	24	12	17
Jackson Phipps	0	1	4.30	8	0	15	13	7	16
Alex Price	0	0	3.97	3	0	11	13	6	12
Paul Prue	0	0	10.80	1	0	2	1	2	1
Stephen Quigley	0	0	0.00	1	0	3	1	1	1
Jake Rons	0	0	0.00	1	0	1	3	0	1
Tommy Sommer	0	0	0.00	2	0	3	1	2	6
Adam Stone	0	1	12.96	4	0	8	12	11	5
Mitchell Stone	0	4	8.40	4	0	15	19	5	13
Welsey Sweatt	0	0	3.12	9	0	17	21	1	18
Mikey Tepper	1	0	0.00	3	0	9	3	4	5
Tyler Tuthill	1	2	6.33	8	0	27	28	9	29
Levi Wells	1	1	3.71	10	0	17	13	12	29
Andrew Yancik	0	0	1.23	4	1	7	6	2	7

HARWICH

Batting	AVG	AB	R	H	2B	3B	HR	RBI	SB
Cory Acton	.000	12	1	0	0	0	0	2	1
Jordan Beck	.267	90	11	24	4	1	2	10	7
Cade Beloso	.250	32	2	8	1	0	0	0	0
Pres Cavenaugh	.333	105	22	35	7	0	1	13	7
Max Cotier	.244	45	7	11	3	0	0	8	2
Josh Hood	.210	81	10	17	5	1	1	16	5
Hal Hughes	.180	50	7	9	2	0	1	3	1
Andrew Jenkins	.118	17	0	2	0	0	0	0	0
Jake Lazzaro	.194	31	6	6	0	0	0	1	4
Tatem Levins	.262	103	17	27	9	0	1	10	1
Nick Lucky	.138	29	3	4	0	0	1	2	0
Ben Malgeri	.262	42	9	11	0	0	2	6	4
Matt McDermott	.143	28	2	4	2	0	0	2	0
Aaron McKeithan	.143	21	5	3	0	0	1	3	0
Chris Newell	.250	76	13	19	2	1	5	14	4
Dylan Phillips	.293	58	11	17	4	0	4	15	1
Zack Prajnzer	.298	94	16	28	5	0	2	10	4
Carter Putz	.241	116	12	28	4	0	0	15	2
Brendan Tinsman	.250	28	4	7	2	0	0	3	1
Brock Wilken	.302	129	26	39	10	0	6	26	3
Pat Winkle	.154	13	1	2	0	0	1	1	0

Pitching	W	L	ERA	G	SV	IP	H	BB	SO
Owen Coady	0	0	3.29	12	5	14	6	3	22
Trey Dombroski	3	0	0.85	6	0	32	27	2	45
Kieran Garner	0	0	5.40	1	0	2	2	1	2
Spencer Giesting	1	1	4.79	6	0	21	19	16	22
Danny Heintz	0	0	0.00	1	0	3	1	1	2
Aaron Holiday	0	0	0.00	4	2	5	0	3	9
Beau Keathley	2	1	2.30	6	0	16	13	11	14
Timmy Manning	0	1	5.14	2	0	7	8	0	4
Andrew Mosiello	1	1	2.02	5	0	22	12	11	26
Matthew Pushard	1	0	0.00	4	0	9	7	4	11
Alex Rao	1	0	9.82	7	1	11	13	10	10
Eric Reyzelman	2	0	2.66	5	0	24	18	6	36
Cam Schlittler	0	3	5.40	6	0	25	25	11	21
Wyatt Scotti	0	1	5.56	4	0	11	12	4	14
Billy Seidl	0	0	2.87	4	0	16	14	9	17
Carson Seymour	3	0	1.23	4	0	7	4	3	14
Evan Shawver	0	1	0.00	2	0	12	8	0	22
Liam Simon	1	1	4.30	11	0	15	12	13	19
Nick Sinacola	0	1	8.00	2	0	9	5	5	13
Dalton Smith	2	0	6.05	9	2	22	24	15	34
Nick Stewart	0	0	9.00	3	0	4	6	5	6
Brandon Walker	0	0	11.46	6	0	11	15	13	7
Danny Wilkinson	2	1	4.96	8	2	16	14	7	29

HYANNIS

Batting	AVG	AB	R	H	2B	3B	HR	RBI	SB
Kyle Ball	.208	120	16	25	4	0	0	10	4
Jake Cunningham	.235	17	2	4	1	0	0	1	1
Clark Elliott	.344	90	19	31	4	1	2	8	7
Mason Greer	.146	82	4	12	1	0	0	2	0
Adam Hackenberg	.231	13	2	3	0	0	0	1	0
Zane Harris	.202	99	12	20	6	0	1	10	0
Mitchell Hartigan	.209	115	12	24	4	2	1	9	1
Dominic Johnson	.265	117	19	31	3	2	2	11	14
Luke Mann	.269	108	16	29	5	0	5	27	0
Caleb Pendleton	.222	45	10	10	4	0	2	8	0
Dylan Post	.190	21	3	4	1	0	0	1	0
Ryan Proto	.239	46	3	11	0	0	0	5	3
Marcos Pujols Martinez	.229	48	5	11	1	0	2	7	0
Joey Raffaele	.100	10	1	1	0	0	1	3	0
Mariano Ricciardi	.133	30	2	4	0	0	0	1	1
Nick Romano	.286	42	6	12	4	0	1	9	0
Ryan Romano	.188	74	10	14	3	2	1	11	7
Caden Rose	.191	89	10	17	2	0	1	6	7
Trent Taylor	.259	27	6	7	1	0	1	5	1

Pitching	W	L	ERA	G	SV	IP	H	BB	SO
Mark Adamiak	2	5	4.35	10	0	29	24	17	26
Andrew Baker	0	2	15	2	0	3	3	11	4
Sam Beck	0	0	0	3	0	6	3	4	8
Trey Braithwaite	0	1	3.68	5	1	7.1	8	3	11
Austin Brush	0	0	5.19	4	0	8.2	10	2	9
Anthony Casciola	0	0	0	2	0	2.2	0	1	2
Derrick Cherry	0	0	10.8	4	0	5	6	3	7
Nolan Crisp	0	0	3.68	8	1	14.2	15	8	16
Hunter Dula	0	1	5.19	3	0	8.2	7	4	11
David Furtado	0	4	7.76	8	0	26.2	37	8	21
Salvatore Fusco	0	0	8.79	5	0	14.1	19	13	13
Daniel Gill	1	2	8.49	3	0	11.2	17	6	9
Cade Halemanu	0	1	9	2	0	4	12	0	5
Noah Hall	0	1	20.25	2	0	1.1	3	2	2
Seth Halvorsen	0	2	12.27	3	0	7.1	10	10	6
Tristian Haught	0	0	4.5	4	0	4	3	3	5
Daniel Lloyd	0	0	0	4	1	4	2	2	7
Angus McCloskey	1	0	8.38	9	0	9.2	14	10	6
Tommy McCollum	0	0	10.57	5	0	7.2	10	9	11
Cooper McKeehan	2	1	5.14	9	0	21	25	12	36
Jaylen Nowlin	0	1	0	4	0	8	6	5	11
Trae Robertson	0	1	13.5	3	0	3.1	6	5	2
Jonah Scolaro	1	1	3.97	10	0	22.2	10	11	32
Adrian Siravo	1	3	4.39	7	0	26.2	28	9	22
Kyle Skidmore	0	0	0	3	0	2.1	1	1	2
Austin Wallace	0	0	6.23	10	0	21.2	20	15	15
Evan Webster	0	1	6.97	11	0	20.2	23	10	21

ORLEANS

Batting	AVG	AB	R	H	2B	3B	HR	RBI	SB
Cory Acton	.270	37	3	10	3	0	0	2	2
Benjamin Blackwell	.182	55	6	10	1	0	0	2	0
Jack Bulger	.000	10	0	0	0	0	0	0	0
Peyton Chatagnier	.232	99	19	23	3	0	4	14	6
Jeff Costello	.243	37	2	9	2	0	0	4	2
Chase DeLauter	.298	124	27	37	7	1	9	21	5
Matt Goodheart	.286	21	8	6	3	0	0	1	0
Garret Guillemette	.203	59	7	12	0	0	3	10	0
Trae Harmon	.357	56	3	20	6	0	1	10	0
Jace Jung	.219	32	2	7	1	1	1	9	0
Luke Keaschall	.321	84	10	27	4	1	2	15	2
Connor Kokx	.255	55	4	14	3	0	0	7	2
Tyler Locklear	.256	125	18	32	4	0	9	27	1
David Marcano	.171	35	7	6	0	0	1	2	4
Julio Marcano	.192	73	9	14	2	0	1	7	0
Jared McKenzie	.225	102	20	23	2	0	0	9	5
Justin Miknis	.231	52	12	12	1	0	1	6	0
Jack Moss	.071	14	1	1	0	0	0	0	0
Jordan Sprinkle	.250	28	8	7	0	0	0	1	3
Rhylan Thomas	.408	49	7	20	3	0	0	7	2

Pitching	W	L	ERA	G	SV	IP	H	BB	SO
Donovan Benoit	1	0	7.15	4	0	11	10	4	19
Jonathan Cannon	0	0	0.69	3	0	13	9	3	8
Chase DeLauter	0	1	6.75	3	0	4	4	2	2
Jack Filby	2	1	7.20	12	0	20	25	10	20
Nathan Florence	0	0	0.79	4	0	11	3	7	14
Marquis Grissom Jr.	0	0	3.00	1	0	3	1	2	2
Connor Housley	0	0	6.94	10	0	12	10	8	12
Nick Hull	0	0	1.59	4	1	6	5	2	6
Orion Kerkering	0	3	5.30	7	0	19	20	8	22
Nicolas Luc	0	0	2.08	2	0	4	4	0	4
Zack Morris	2	0	1.21	11	0	22	17	12	25
Dawson Netz	0	0	0.00	3	0	7	1	1	10
Michael Polk	1	1	8.47	11	0	17	23	11	20
Jeffrey Praml	1	0	11.30	8	0	14	25	3	11
Max Rajcic	0	3	4.32	7	0	25	25	8	28
Patrick Reilly	0	0	0.00	2	0	10	4	4	10
Jake Saum	1	2	6.41	12	1	20	22	8	27
Thomas Schultz	2	1	4.15	3	0	13	15	3	15
Carter Smith	0	0	7.20	4	0	5	4	8	6
Jared Southard	1	0	3.86	5	2	5	3	3	9
Hayden Thomas	1	2	2.60	7	0	28	20	12	30
Conner Thurman	1	1	6.75	4	0	8	3	4	9
Nick Wallerstedt	0	1	1.62	13	1	17	11	9	22
Brett Wichrowski	0	1	14.40	3	0	5	9	4	4

WAREHAM

Batting	AVG	AB	R	H	2B	3B	HR	RBI	SB
Jack Brannigan	.282	78	14	22	2	1	1	9	2
Ted Burton	.167	6	1	1	0	0	0	0	0
Nicholas Cimillo	.133	15	2	2	0	0	1	1	0
Kellum Clark	.190	63	10	12	3	0	0	3	3
Jimmy Crooks	.260	104	11	27	3	0	2	10	0
Angelo DiSpigna	.196	51	6	10	3	0	1	1	0
Owen Diodati	.246	138	14	34	5	0	7	23	2
Cade Fergus	.296	54	12	16	3	1	2	4	1
Anthony Frechette	.241	29	4	7	1	0	0	6	0
Tres Gonzalez	.331	121	20	40	6	0	0	11	8
Devereaux Harrison	.100	10	1	1	0	0	0	0	0
Kamren James	.159	63	4	10	0	0	2	8	4
Jim Jarvis	.289	128	16	37	7	1	4	21	8
Cody Jefferies	.174	23	3	4	0	0	0	0	1
Kade Kern	.215	93	15	20	3	0	2	16	4
Micheal Knell	.200	5	0	1	0	0	0	0	0
Sean McLain	.227	22	4	5	0	0	1	4	1
Yohandy Morales	.182	55	5	10	1	1	0	1	1
Paul Skenes	.143	14	1	2	0	0	0	0	0
Tommy Troy	.299	117	21	35	3	3	4	19	9
Justin Williams	.271	48	6	13	3	0	4	10	0

Pitching	W	L	ERA	G	SV	IP	H	BB	SO
Mack Anglin	0	0	0.00	3	0	13	7	3	16
Christopher Barraza	0	1	12.27	3	0	4	7	1	3
Jonathan Brand	0	0	2.57	2	0	7	1	1	8
Jack Brannigan	0	1	12.00	3	0	3	6	1	3
Bradley Brehmer	1	0	5.14	2	0	7	4	3	8
Erubiel Candelario	0	0	4.50	2	0	4	2	4	1
Ethan Chenault	0	0	6.40	8	0	13	15	5	9
Nick Clayton	1	2	3.44	5	0	18	18	5	15
Nicholas Conte	0	0	3.86	3	0	2	2	4	4
Kevin Eaise	1	2	6.23	7	0	9	11	5	10
Richard Fitts	0	1	7.94	2	0	6	6	3	7
Geoffrey Gilbert	0	1	6.48	3	0	8	5	4	10
Devereaux Harrison	0	0	4.91	4	1	4	4	1	2
Rob Hughes	0	0	0.00	3	0	5	3	0	8
Marques Johnson	0	0	0.00	2	0	1	1	4	1
Larson Kindreich	0	0	4.50	2	0	6	4	4	8
Cole Kirschsieper	1	0	0.75	3	0	12	3	5	19
Adam Mazur	3	0	1.55	6	0	29	18	6	34
Spencer Miles	0	2	2.55	6	0	18	10	9	24
Samuel Natera	0	0	0.00	1	0	4	0	0	7
Jack Noble	0	0	6.75	6	0	12	9	9	18
Alexander Pham	1	0	0.00	4	1	7	2	3	8
Christian Ruebeck	0	2	5.29	8	0	17	17	10	20
Carter Rustad	1	2	5.79	6	1	14	13	6	20
Eli Saul	0	2	10.32	7	0	11	12	10	10
Hunter Schilperoort	0	2	1.86	11	2	19	23	2	23
Garrett Schmeltz	2	0	1.90	7	0	19	9	7	27
Tyler Shingledecker	0	0	9.00	1	0	1	2	0	1
Kohl Simas	0	0	5.06	4	0	5	5	3	7
Paul Skenes	0	0	5.63	5	0	8	12	5	11
Blake Sodersten	1	0	0.00	4	0	17	7	3	20
Matt Svanson	1	0	0.00	2	0	9	6	1	10
Ian Villers	1	0	0.00	2	0	8	3	0	7
Andrew Walters	0	0	4.50	1	0	2	3	1	3

YARMOUTH-DENNIS

Batting	AVG	AB	R	H	2B	3B	HR	RBI	SB
Nathan Baez	.241	54	2	13	4	0	0	4	1
Drew Bowser	.194	72	5	14	2	0	1	4	0
Patrick Caufield	.100	10	2	1	0	0	0	0	1
Andrew Compton	.152	33	3	5	1	0	0	5	0
Pascanel Ferreras	.155	58	7	9	2	0	1	3	2
Fernando Gonzalez	.500	2	1	1	1	0	0	0	0
Peyton Graham	.247	81	20	20	4	0	2	7	3
Wyatt Hoffman	.270	126	14	34	8	0	1	12	2
Kody Huff	.241	108	12	26	3	0	4	18	1
Cade Hunter	.179	56	8	10	4	0	1	4	0
Dominic Keegan	.302	43	9	13	0	0	5	9	0
Briley Knight	.182	77	8	14	3	0	0	7	7
Brooks Lee	.405	84	16	34	4	0	6	13	0
Zach Lew	.150	80	12	12	2	0	0	7	1
Chase Luttrell	.239	134	14	32	4	1	0	15	7
Danniel Rivera	.625	8	4	5	2	0	0	1	1
Crew Robinson	.138	29	2	4	2	0	2	7	1
Tanner Smith	.278	115	19	32	6	0	4	23	2
Tyler Williams	.122	41	4	5	0	0	0	1	2

Pitching	W	L	ERA	G	SV	IP	H	BB	SO
Sam Beck	0	0	6.35	5	0	6	6	1	4
Bryce Collins	0	0	0.00	2	0	2	2	1	2
Christian Culpepper	1	0	1.72	10	4	16	10	2	23
Nicholas Dombkowski	3	0	2.20	3	0	16	13	2	16
Brandon Dufault	0	0	0.00	3	1	4	3	2	6
Ross Dunn	0	1	6.00	8	0	12	8	14	23
Zach Franklin	1	1	5.06	4	0	11	13	3	10
Patrick Gallagher	2	0	3.91	6	0	25	26	10	33
Jaret Godman	2	1	6.11	10	1	18	27	5	20
Zachary Jacobs	2	2	5.68	8	0	25	30	8	24
Briley Knight	0	0	9.00	1	0	1	2	0	0
Jared Lyons	1	1	2.40	3	0	15	11	6	16
Adam Maier	0	2	4.56	6	0	26	24	9	27
Andrew Marrero	0	1	5.40	6	0	7	4	8	13
Nolan McCarthy	0	2	31.50	2	0	2	6	4	3
Reid McLaughlin	0	0	0.56	9	3	16	8	7	17
Jacob Meador	2	0	3.62	10	0	27	20	8	34
Joe Moran	0	0	4.50	2	0	4	2	3	1
Eli Morse	1	0	1.23	6	0	7	6	3	5
Terry Murray	0	0	0.00	1	0	1	1	1	0
Ryan Patel	0	0	29.46	5	0	4	7	10	4
Zachary Patterson	0	0	5.40	3	0	8	7	3	4
Luis Ramirez	0	2	3.10	6	0	29	17	13	33
Owen Stevenson	0	0	0.00	2	1	4	3	0	3
Drew Thorpe	0	0	0.90	2	0	10	8	3	9
Ryan Wiltse	1	0	0.00	2	0	4	3	1	7
Eric Yost	0	1	5.79	8	0	14	19	8	14

ALASKA LEAGUE

	W	L	PCT	GB
Matsu Miners	30	13	.698	-
Chugiak Chinooks	22	20	.524	7.5
Anchorage Glacier Pilots	23	21	.523	7.5
Anchorage Bucs	18	27	.400	13
Peninsula Oilers	14	26	.350	14.5

CHAMPIONSHIP: Anchorage Bucs defeated Anchorage Glacier Pilots, 2-1, in best-of-three championship series.

INDIVIDUAL BATTING LEADERS

	AVG	AB	R	H	2B	3B	HR	RBI	SB
Ernie Yake, Bucs	.352	54	10	19	3	1	0	13	4
Ethan Mann, Glacier Pilots	.339	118	22	40	8	0	4	18	13
Garrett Pennington, Oilers	.336	107	22	36	10	1	6	22	2
Tom Tabak, Glacier Pilots	.331	142	22	47	9	4	2	18	13
John Marc Mullins, Chinooks	.297	148	17	44	6	1	0	17	13
Blake Wink, Glacier Pilots	.297	148	20	44	4	3	1	15	17
Josh Sheck, Chinooks	.295	88	13	26	5	0	2	14	3
Cole Moore, Bucs	.294	68	16	20	2	0	4	14	0
Jack Machtolf, Bucs	.292	144	23	42	3	2	1	21	3
Tyler Rando, Miners	.289	97	12	28	5	0	1	20	1

INDIVIDUAL PITCHING LEADERS

	W	L	ERA	G	SV	IP	H	BB	SO
Hayden Walker, Glacier Pilots	2	1	0.00	19	3	28	15	11	24
Easton Sikorski, Glacier Pilots	2	0	0.40	4	0	23	14	6	22
Ricky Tibbett, Glacier Pilots	1	1	0.98	7	1	37	27	8	26
Aaron Winkler, Miners	4	0	1.12	12	0	30	15	5	18
Honus Kindreich, Chinooks	2	1	1.36	17	0	40	28	16	26
Darwin Matos, Miners	1	1	1.40	4	1	19	9	8	17
Jimmy Galicia, Glacier Pilots	1	0	1.57	9	0	29	28	5	26
Joey Rodriguez, Glacier Pilots	1	1	1.65	14	3	16	10	8	13
Will Johnston, Miners	5	0	1.66	10	0	54	32	21	72
Nate Diamond, Glacier Pilots	3	2	1.74	7	0	41	26	13	41

APPALACHIAN LEAGUE

East Division	W	L	PCT	GB
Pulaski River Turtles	32	22	.593	-
Princeton WhistlePigs	30	22	.577	1
Danville Otterbots	29	24	.547	2.5
Blueville Ridge Runners	27	25	.519	4
Burlington Sock Puppets	18	34	.352	13

West Division	W	L	PCT	GB
Greeneville Flyboys	33	16	.670	-
Elizabethton River Riders	26	22	.542	6.5
Briston State Liners	24	22	.522	7.5
Kingsport Axmen	12	19	.387	12
Johnson City Doughboys	16	32	.337	15.5

CHAMPIONSHIP: Greeneville Flyboys defeated Pulaski River Turtles, 9-8, in championship game.

INDIVIDUAL BATTING LEADERS

	AVG	AB	R	H	2B	3B	HR	RBI	SB
Marcus Brown, River Riders	.407	118	35	48	13	2	2	30	12
Dylan Rogers, WhistlePigs	.335	185	48	62	4	5	10	41	3
Kendal Ewell, Ridge Runners	.333	141	43	47	15	3	6	42	22
Jonathan Hogart, Flyboys	.326	141	33	46	8	2	3	27	12
Homer Bush Jr., Flyboys	.316	171	34	54	6	1	0	17	21
Joe Vetrano, Doughboys	.316	133	31	42	14	3	5	30	5
Benji Gilbert, Sock Puppets	.315	149	32	47	11	4	1	23	15
Tre Morris, WhistlePigs	.314	140	35	44	10	1	2	24	3
Cameron Leary, River Turtles	.313	179	40	56	11	2	9	35	8
Nathan Holt, WhistlePigs	.309	178	44	55	14	3	0	11	22

INDIVIDUAL PITCHING LEADERS

	W	L	ERA	G	SV	IP	H	BB	SO
Cole Kirschsieper, Axmen	1	0	0.00	7	0	21	7	11	33
Nathan Ackenhausen, Ridge Runners	2	2	0.66	9	2	27	13	14	32
Grant Leader, Otterbots	1	1	0.98	15	3	28	14	15	50
Steven Casey, Doughboys	1	1	1.17	6	0	15	9	7	23
Zane Probst, WhistlePigs	1	1	1.37	15	6	20	14	5	33
Casey Keller, River Riders	3	0	1.42	13	0	19	16	4	23
Drew Gillespie, River Riders	1	1	1.47	8	0	31	26	6	42
Tyler Judge, Otterbots	2	2	1.69	10	0	32	28	7	48
Adam Parra, Axmen	3	1	1.89	9	0	19	12	6	19
Xander Rojahn, WhistlePigs	3	0	2.00	10	0	18	12	13	27

ATLANTIC COLLEGIATE LEAGUE

	W	L	PCT	GB
North Jersey Eagles	20	6	.769	-
Jersey Pilots	24	13	.649	1.5
Trenton Generals	25	15	.625	2
Quakertown Blazers	19	17	.528	6
Trenton Capitals	16	22	.421	10
New York Phenoms	12	20	.375	11
Ocean Ospreys	8	17	.320	11.5
New Brunswick MATRIX	8	22	.267	14

CHAMPIONSHIP: Trenton Generals defeated North Jersey Eagles, 2-0, in best-of-three championship series.

INDIVIDUAL BATTING LEADERS

	AVG	AB	R	H	2B	3B	HR	RBI	SB
Casey Caufield, Blazers	.397	116	28	46	9	0	0	16	13
Ben Watson, Blazers	.371	132	36	49	9	3	2	26	11
Mitchell Balint, Blazers	.368	87	19	32	4	1	1	20	3
Mark McNelly, Generals	.363	91	16	33	9	3	1	24	4
Jackson Tucker, Phenoms	.345	87	24	30	6	1	4	13	13
Vinny Dinicola, Pilots	.342	114	25	39	5	0	10	28	9
Jacob Kmiec, Capitals	.333	93	20	31	0	1	2	18	11
Robert Estrada, Eagles	.333	72	15	24	2	1	0	18	9
Andrea Dalatri, MATRIX	.319	91	15	29	6	1	5	21	2
Brian Nicolas, Blazers	.313	115	24	36	5	2	3	20	2

INDIVIDUAL PITCHING LEADERS

	W	L	ERA	G	SV	IP	H	BB	SO
Winston Allen, Pilots	3	0	0.29	7	1	31	13	9	23
Jake Reese, Blazers	2	1	0.78	4	0	23	16	10	26
Jack Carr, Eagles	2	0	0.98	6	1	18	11	6	21
Joe Skapinetz, Pilots	2	0	1.00	9	0	18	4	12	28
Christian Capuano, Pilots	5	1	1.66	7	0	38	32	11	43

	W	L	ERA	G	SV	IP	H	BB	SO
Hunter Curley, Generals	1	1	2.15	6	0	29	23	8	21
Joe Pucek, Pilots	4	3	2.42	8	0	41	38	6	42
Garrison LeGros, Capitals	3	2	2.92	13	1	25	19	10	23
Bryce Mangene, Generals	2	1	3.15	4	0	20	15	12	20
Joseph Sheets, Generals	2	1	3.19	8	0	31	19	17	44

CAL RIPKEN COLLEGIATE LEAGUE

	W	L	PCT	GB
Bethesda Big Train	27	8	.771	-
Alexandria Aces	20	15	.571	7
Gaithersburg Giants	19	17	.528	8.5
Silver Spring-Takoma T Bolts	16	20	.444	11.5
South County Braves	14	22	.389	13.5
D.C. Grays	11	25	.306	16.5

CHAMPIONSHIP: Bethesda Big Train defeated Alexandria Aces, 2-0, in championship series.

INDIVIDUAL BATTING LEADERS

	AVG	AB	R	H	2B	3B	HR	RBI	SB
Stephen Rice, Bolts	.377	106	32	40	2	2	1	25	13
Rocco Peppi, Big Train	.357	84	34	30	7	1	4	25	7
Scott Bandura, Grays	.351	97	28	34	3	0	4	26	31
Matt Thomas, Big Train	.350	100	34	35	4	0	7	32	7
Matt Kattula, Aces	.343	102	25	35	7	1	4	26	1
Trevor Doyle, Big Train	.338	74	15	25	2	0	0	13	4
Nolan Schanuel, Big Train	.333	75	17	25	5	0	3	24	4
Michael Marrale, Giants	.333	81	17	27	6	1	2	19	4
Garret Farquhar, Aces	.333	129	24	43	10	0	3	30	7
Darius Foster, Big Train	.327	101	37	33	3	1	0	11	25

INDIVIDUAL PITCHING LEADERS

	W	L	ERA	G	SV	IP	H	BB	SO
Cooper Vest, Grays	0	0	1.13	9	0	24	17	6	25
Blake Burkhalter, Aces	1	0	1.13	11	2	16	7	4	30
Matt Howat, Big Train	2	0	1.20	7	0	15	9	6	15
Matt Bedford, Big Train	2	0	1.50	8	0	24	11	6	27
Grayson Hitt, Big Train	4	0	1.64	6	0	22	9	9	39
Tucker Alch, Grays	3	0	1.82	6	0	30	22	4	29
JP Nolan, Bolts	1	2	1.86	11	0	19	16	12	19
Kieran Garner, Bolts	2	0	2.05	11	4	31	21	4	47
Cam Nolet, Giants	3	1	2.76	8	1	29	22	14	30
Zach Locke, Big Train	1	0	2.76	11	0	16	16	7	17

CALIFORNIA COLLEGIATE LEAGUE

Northern Division	W	L	PCT	GB
Healdsburg Prune Packers	29	5	.853	-
Lincoln Potters	16	16	.500	12
Walnut Creek Crawdads	12	18	.400	15
Solano Mudcats	6	24	.200	21

Southern Division	W	L	PCT	GB
Santa Barbara Foresters	23	7	.767	-
Arroyo Seco Saints	18	15	.545	6.5
San Luis Obispo Blues	18	16	.529	7
Conejo Oaks	15	18	.455	9.5
Orange County Riptide	13	17	.433	10
Academy Barons	8	22	.267	15

CHAMPIONSHIP: Healdsburg defeated San Luis Obispo, 8-7, in championship game.

TOP 10 PROSPECTS: 1. Daniel Susac, C, Lincoln (So., Arizona); **2.** Davis Diaz, SS, Orange County (Fr., Vanderbilt); **3.** Gabriel Starks, RHP, Santa Barbara (So., Arkansas); **4.** Ben Abram, RHP, Santa Barbara (Jr., Oklahoma); **5.** Andrew Kachel, 2B/3B, Santa Barbara (So., Fresno State); **6.** Steven Zobac, RHP/OF, Santa Barbara (So., California); **7.** Dylan Campbell, 3B, Santa Barbara (So., Texas); **8.** Kyle Booker, OF, Orange County (So., Tennessee); **9.** Josh Stinson, OF, Santa Barbara (So., Georgia); **10.** Matthew Sox, RHP, San Luis Obispo (Jr., Utah).

INDIVIDUAL BATTING LEADERS

	AVG	AB	R	H	2B	3B	HR	RBI	SB
Jesse Lopez, Prune Packers	.420	69	24	29	2	3	6	16	2
Chase Stanke, Potters	.418	55	8	23	5	0	1	7	1
Jeffrey David, Potters	.393	84	19	33	12	1	1	24	7
Ryan Targac, Prune Packers	.387	93	33	36	4	1	4	26	1

	AVG	AB	R	H	2B	3B	HR	RBI	SB
Anthony Pomilia, Crawdads	.383	47	10	18	5	0	0	9	0
Austin Bost, Prune Packers	.379	95	23	36	9	0	5	32	1
Braydon Runion, Prune Packers	.376	93	26	35	8	1	4	25	0
Garret Forrester, Potters	.371	62	15	23	9	0	1	15	1
Reagan Burford, Oaks	.367	49	14	18	4	2	2	22	3
Drew Cowley, Saints	.361	122	21	44	16	0	4	21	6

INDIVIDUAL PITCHING LEADERS

	W	L	ERA	G	SV	IP	H	BB	SO
Nick Proctor, Foresters	1	0	0.54	13	4	17	3	5	29
Nicholas Martinez, Barons	2	1	0.57	9	1	16	14	1	11
Marlin Brucato, Potters	2	0	0.84	9	0	21	12	2	21
Peyton Cole, Foresters	1	0	1.13	7	0	16	12	4	16
Justin Eckhardt, Foresters	3	0	1.23	4	0	22	14	7	23
Cooper Randall, Foresters	3	1	1.23	8	0	15	14	3	18
Tyler Stasiowski, Prune Packers	1	0	1.56	8	0	17	14	3	20
Marvcus Guarin, Prune Packers	5	0	1.57	7	0	23	18	6	30
Tommy Hannan, Saints	1	0	1.69	9	0	16	13	11	24
Ben Abram, Foresters	3	0	2.10	5	0	30	26	1	40

COASTAL PLAIN LEAGUE

East Division	W	L	PCT	GB
Peninsula Pilots	32	11	.744	-
Morehead City Marlins	29	14	.674	3
Wilmington Sharks	23	19	.548	8.5
Wilson Tobs	23	19	.548	8.5
Holly Springs Salamanders	24	20	.545	8.5
Florence Flamingos	11	30	.268	20
Tri-City Chili Peppers	7	34	.171	24

West Division	W	L	PCT	GB
Savannah Bananas	36	8	.818	-
High Point-Thomasville HiToms	25	19	.568	11
Lexington County Blowfish	24	19	.558	11.5
Asheboro Copperheads	23	21	.523	13
Forest City Owls	22	22	.500	14
Macon Bacon	15	26	.366	19.5
Martinsville Mustangs	15	28	.349	20.5
Spartanburgers	12	31	.279	23.5

CHAMPIONSHIP: Savannah Bananas defeated Morehead City Marlins, 2-1, in best-of-three championship series.

INDIVIDUAL BATTING LEADERS

	AVG	AB	R	H	2B	3B	HR	RBI	SB
Cam Fisher, Owls	.384	112	26	43	5	0	3	20	11
Drew DeVine, Tobs	.368	125	27	46	9	0	3	27	6
Benjamin Serrano, Mustangs	.368	106	18	39	9	1	0	19	9
Livan Reinoso, Bananas	.362	138	30	50	5	1	5	37	6
Riley Jepson, Tobs	.356	118	29	42	9	0	4	28	4
Matt Malone, Mustangs	.353	119	22	42	2	0	2	20	14
Dylan Brewer, Blowfish	.350	120	37	42	15	2	4	17	15
Will Butcher, Owls	.346	107	19	37	11	0	5	27	6
Connor VanCleave, Marlins	.343	108	21	37	6	0	7	29	0
Dylan Scaranda, Tobs	.340	147	35	50	9	3	9	28	4

INDIVIDUAL PITCHING LEADERS

	W	L	ERA	G	SV	IP	H	BB	SO
Ryan Kennedy, Bananas	5	1	0.73	8	0	37	24	14	53
Joseph Miller, Bananas	6	0	1.50	10	1	42	26	17	71
Dalton Mims, Blowfish	5	0	1.66	12	1	38	34	14	32
Joseph Kemlage, Sharks	3	1	2.00	9	1	45	34	15	51
Chris Ludman, Pilots	2	0	2.01	9	1	40	23	2	37
Will Lancaster, HiToms	5	0	2.18	11	0	41	31	14	54
Jared Mathewson, Copperheads	4	0	2.60	10	0	52	41	11	57
Kyle Lugis, Bananas	5	2	2.75	8	0	39	27	18	50
Justin Kleinsorge, Marlins	1	1	2.95	9	0	40	39	15	30
Gabe Golob, HiToms	5	1	3.23	9	0	39	36	19	43

FLORIDA COLLEGIATE SUMMER LEAGUE

	W	L	PCT	GB
Sanford River Rats	18	10	.643	-
Leesburg Lightning	18	11	.621	0.5
DeLand Suns	14	14	.500	4
Winter Garden Squeeze	14	15	.483	4.5
Winter Park Diamond Dawgs	14	16	.467	5
Seminole County Snappers	9	21	.300	10

CHAMPIONSHIP: Leesburg Lightning defeated Winter Park Diamond Dawgs, 2-1, in best-of-three championship series.

INDIVIDUAL BATTING LEADERS

	AVG	AB	R	H	2B	3B	HR	RBI	SB
Sterlin Thompson, Dawgs	.391	46	13	18	1	0	3	15	5
Jeslyn Whitehead, Snappers	.343	67	8	23	3	0	0	2	4
Brett Kelly, Lightning	.338	65	11	22	5	1	0	5	5
Bryce Jackson, Squeeze	.333	69	21	23	6	0	4	17	1
Joshua Pearson, River Rats	.333	93	30	31	10	0	4	14	23
Justin Farmer, River Rats	.324	37	12	12	2	0	3	11	7
Jeissy De La Cruz, Squeeze	.322	90	15	29	6	0	0	12	7
Edgar Alvarez, Squeeze	.315	89	15	28	5	0	2	9	0
Tyler McKenna, Squeeze	.313	48	11	15	1	0	1	4	2
Clay Stearns, Lightning	.312	77	13	24	7	1	1	15	5

INDIVIDUAL PITCHING LEADERS

	W	L	ERA	G	SV	IP	H	BB	SO
Gerry Kelly, Lightning	2	0	0.93	11	0	19	5	4	32
Demetrius Vizcarra, River Rats	1	3	1.19	7	0	23	18	14	16
Jacob Bradshaw, Lightning	2	0	1.23	7	0	22	18	5	10
John Sewell, Snappers	1	0	1.45	3	0	19	14	7	19
Walter Berry, Diamond Dawgs	2	0	1.57	6	0	23	14	11	25
Jarrod Cande, River Rats	3	0	1.80	4	0	20	12	10	24
Connor Udell, Suns	1	1	1.82	9	1	25	15	9	25
Colton Bruns, Lightning	1	0	2.37	8	0	19	18	5	12
Nathan Skinner, Suns	1	1	2.53	5	0	21	22	13	22
Myles Caba, Lightning	3	0	2.75	8	1	20	14	12	26

FUTURES COLLEGIATE LEAGUE

	W	L	PCT	GB
Vermont Lake Monsters	42	24	.636	-
Pittsfield Suns	38	25	.603	2.5
Brockton Rox	38	26	.594	3
Worcester Bravehearts	32	33	.492	9.5
Westfield Starfires	31	34	.477	10.5
Nashua Silver Knights	27	39	.409	15
Norwich Sea Unicorns	27	40	.403	15.5
New Britain Bees	25	39	.391	16

CHAMPIONSHIP: Vermont Lake Monsters defeated Pittsfield Suns, 2-1, in best-of-three championship series.

INDIVIDUAL BATTING LEADERS

	AVG	AB	R	H	2B	3B	HR	RBI	SB
Cole Bartels, Starfires	.389	167	43	65	15	0	6	35	1
Michael Golankiewicz, Rox	.359	145	38	52	11	3	5	34	9
Jaden Brown, Starfires	.336	149	30	50	8	1	2	33	6
Randy Flores, Bravehearts	.310	158	31	49	7	5	0	22	19
Ben Rounds, Rox	.306	147	41	45	17	1	4	41	9
Jake Blinstrub, Suns	.306	144	37	44	12	0	0	24	23
Hunter Pasqualini, Starfires	.299	167	39	50	10	0	0	21	6
Ryan Bagdasarian, Bees	.297	175	38	52	6	2	2	18	17
Jake Hyde, Bees	.296	179	34	53	7	0	1	32	2
Hunter Yaworski, Unicorns	.289	187	26	54	12	2	3	26	3

INDIVIDUAL PITCHING LEADERS

	W	L	ERA	G	SV	IP	H	BB	SO
David Vial Jr., Lake Monsters	0	0	0.00	12	5	16	5	7	18
Andrew Roman, Starfires	0	0	0.00	14	6	15	7	6	13
Griffin O'Connor, Bravehearts	1	1	0.81	17	2	22	22	9	20
Bryson Cafaro, Bees	4	0	1.00	8	2	17	5	3	27
Dennis Colleran, Bravehearts	2	0	1.11	12	2	24	16	7	37
Wyatt Scotti, Silver Knights	1	0	1.29	4	0	21	11	5	19
Dillon Ryan, Rox	5	0	1.36	9	0	40	21	16	66
Billy Oldham, Lake Monsters	3	0	1.40	10	0	45	36	11	39
David Hagaman, Suns	1	0	1.61	7	0	22	17	10	23
Tommy Benincaso, Bees	1	3	1.72	8	0	16	15	12	23

GREAT LAKES LEAGUE

North Division	W	L	PCT
Sandusky Ice Haulers	28	14	.667
Lima Locos	28	14	.667
Royal Oak Leprechauns	23	19	.548
Jet Box Baseball Club	20	20	.500
Muskegon Clippers	20	21	.488
Michigan Monarchs	18	24	.429

	W	L	PCT
Grand Lake Mariners	17	25	.405
Galion Graders	12	29	.293
South Division	**W**	**L**	**PCT**
Hamilton Joes	27	15	.643
Richmond Jazz	26	16	.619
Cincinnati Steam	24	18	.571
Xenia Scouts	21	21	.500
Licking County Settlers	18	24	.429
Ohio Marlins	10	32	.238

CHAMPIONSHIP: Hamilton Joes defeated Lima Locos, 2-1, in best-of-three championship series.

INDIVIDUAL BATTING LEADERS

	AVG	AB	R	H	2B	3B	HR	RBI	SB
Kerrington Cross, Steam	.419	124	31	52	7	2	4	23	14
Colton Ledbetter, Locos	.415	106	24	44	6	1	8	33	5
Zach MacDonald, Leprechauns	.394	94	31	37	7	3	3	25	20
Darryl Buggs, Locos	.388	103	32	40	9	4	1	19	6
Ben Huber, Jazz	.385	135	28	52	13	2	0	27	3
Noah Marcoux, Clippers	.384	151	30	58	13	1	9	47	0
Scott Mackiewicz, Ice Haulers	.375	152	46	57	10	2	9	51	11
Mark Connelly, Ice Haulers	.361	144	33	52	7	1	2	33	4
Cade Sullivan, Monarchs	.352	125	36	44	8	2	2	26	1
Trent Farquhar, Leprechauns	.345	113	30	39	9	3	1	34	18

INDIVIDUAL PITCHING LEADERS

	W	L	ERA	G	SV	IP	H	BB	SO
Lance Blaszak, Leprechauns	1	0	0.00	12	4	15	11	5	12
Garrett Navarra, Jet Box	1	1	0.72	6	1	25	10	13	41
Tanner Chafin, Jazz	2	1	0.83	17	7	33	25	11	28
Derek Clark, Leprechauns	2	1	0.95	4	0	19	23	4	21
Jonathan Machamer, Locos	2	1	0.96	9	2	28	16	15	34
Luke Leverton, Jazz	2	0	1.17	3	1	15	9	5	19
Zach Dugan, Joes	1	0	1.23	6	1	15	13	7	15
Isaac Danford, Settlers	1	0	1.29	17	2	21	11	12	44
Garrett O'Reilly, Locos	2	0	1.64	5	0	22	25	2	19
Dylan Freeman, Locos	5	0	1.69	11	0	37	26	11	40

MLB DRAFT LEAGUE

	W	L	T	PTS
Trenton Thunder	30	18	8	98
West Virginia Black Bears	30	19	6	96
State College Spikes	29	30	3	90
Mahoning Valley Scrappers	27	28	2	83
Williamsport Crosscutters	25	32	3	78
Frederick Keys	18	32	6	60

INDIVIDUAL BATTING LEADERS

	AVG	AB	R	H	2B	3B	HR	RBI
Nathaniel Butterworth, Thunder	.396	53	13	21	1	1	5	14
Bobby Sparling, Scrappers	.371	170	33	63	17	2	3	43
Haven Mangrum, Keys	.369	65	10	24	3	0	0	9
Kaeber Rog, Black Bears	.344	93	17	32	8	0	1	14
Carson Matthews, Thunder	.344	64	12	22	5	1	4	17
Breydon Daniel, Black Bears	.344	64	16	22	5	1	2	11
Nathan Church, Spikes	.343	70	10	24	6	0	4	17
Zach Dezenzo, Keys	.339	56	13	19	4	0	6	18
Lance Logsdon, Crosscutters	.338	136	22	46	7	0	1	13
Luke Seidel, Spikes	.333	93	23	31	3	1	0	9

INDIVIDUAL PITCHING LEADERS

	W	L	ERA	G	SV	IP	H	BB	SO
Kiernan Higgins, Spikes	1	1	0.36	16	2	25	18	9	39
Lane Flamm, Black Bears	1	0	0.52	5	0	17	9	4	25
Michael Hobbs, Black Bears	1	2	0.60	13	1	15	4	3	29
JP Williams, Thunder	2	0	0.87	8	0	31	22	8	30
Alec Whaley, Thunder	3	0	1.02	9	1	18	6	4	24
Jake Mulholland, Thunder	0	1	1.42	5	0	19	9	3	30
Ronan Kopp, Keys	1	1	1.46	8	0	25	12	30	45
Jacob DeLabio, Scrappers	1	0	1.46	17	0	25	15	5	43
TJ Czyz, Keys	2	1	1.50	4	0	18	12	7	22
Logan VanWey, Thunder	2	1	1.61	17	6	22	15	9	32

NEW ENGLAND COLLEGIATE LEAGUE

Northern Division	**W**	**L**	**T**	**GB**
Keene Swamp Bats	26	15	0	-

	W	L	T	GB
Upper Valley Nighthawks	23	18	0	3
North Adams SteepleCats	22	17	2	3
Vermont Mountaineers	21	20	0	5
North Shore Navigators	20	20	2	5.5
Sanford Mainers	16	26	0	10.5
Winnipesaukee Muskrats	14	26	0	11.5
Southern Division	**W**	**L**	**T**	**GB**
Martha's Vineyard Sharks	24	17	1	-
Valley Blue Sox	23	18	0	1
Mystic Schooners	23	18	1	1
Danbury Westerners	23	19	0	1.5
Newport Gulls	22	20	0	2.5
Ocean State Waves	18	24	0	6.5
Bristol Blues	12	29	0	12

CHAMPIONSHIP: Danbury Westerners defeated North Shore Navigators, 2-0, in best-of-three championship series.

INDIVIDUAL BATTING LEADERS

	AVG	AB	R	H	2B	3B	HR	RBI	SB
Travis Honeyman, Waves	.430	93	26	40	8	1	7	26	14
Brendan Cumming, Schooners	.398	133	36	53	10	2	1	20	12
David Bryant, Swamp Bats	.380	92	23	35	3	0	3	18	6
Alan Roden, Nighthawks	.357	140	32	50	9	1	5	25	28
Gehrig Anglin, Nighthawks	.351	97	24	34	7	3	6	27	14
Ryan Hernandez, Sharks	.337	104	19	35	8	0	8	32	0
Troy Schreffler, Swamp Bats	.336	137	26	46	11	3	6	29	6
Matthew Wood, Gulls	.336	116	26	39	8	0	5	18	3
Cole Johnson, Muskrats	.333	105	28	35	6	0	10	17	18
Parker Haskin, Nighthawks	.323	93	22	30	8	0	0	9	5

INDIVIDUAL PITCHING LEADERS

	W	L	ERA	G	SV	IP	H	BB	SO
Jackson Emus, Navigators	3	1	2.27	9	0	36	22	20	36
Noah Johnson, Sharks	3	1	2.57	9	0	35	24	22	50
Brian Zeldin, SteepleCats	3	1	2.75	8	0	39	33	12	28
Nicholas Payero, Waves	2	2	2.78	9	0	36	27	15	38
Austin Amaral, Navigators	2	3	2.97	8	0	36	25	17	31
Luke Marshall, Navigators	3	2	3.07	8	0	41	21	16	50
Mark Faello, Blues	1	2	3.27	7	0	33	35	17	35
Jordy Allard, Nighthawks	4	1	3.29	8	0	38	36	8	32
Zachary Davidson, Swamp Bats	1	5	3.47	9	0	36	25	25	52
Michael Bacica, Swamp Bats	2	0	3.52	9	0	38	25	18	42

NORTHWOODS LEAGUE

Great Lakes East Division	**W**	**L**	**PCT**	**GB**
Kokomo Jackrabbits	45	27	.625	-
Traverse City Pit Spitters	42	29	.592	2.5
Kenosa Kingfish	39	33	.542	6
Rockford Rivets	29	41	.414	15
Battle Creek Bombers	27	45	.375	18
Kalamazoo Growlers	26	46	.361	19
Great Lakes West Division	**W**	**L**	**PCT**	**GB**
Wisconsin Woodchucks	44	28	.611	-
Fond du Lac Dock Spiders	43	28	.606	0.5
Madison Mallards	39	32	.549	4.5
Wisconsin Rapids Rafters	38	34	.528	6
Lakeshore Chinooks	31	39	.443	12
Green Bay Rockers	25	47	.347	19
Great Plains East Division	**W**	**L**	**PCT**	**GB**
Waterloo Bucks	42	25	.627	-
Duluth Huskies	30	38	.441	12.5
La Crosse Loggers	28	40	.412	14.5
Eau Claire Express	27	41	.397	15.5
Minnesota Mud Puppies	10	26	.278	16.5
Great Plains West Division	**W**	**L**	**PCT**	**GB**
St. Cloud Rox	50	18	.735	-
Mankato MoonDogs	44	24	.647	6
Willmar Stingers	32	36	.471	18
Rochester Honkers	30	37	.448	19.5
Bismarck Larks	30	38	.441	20

CHAMPIONSHIP: Traverse City Pit Spitters defeated St. Cloud Rox, 9-3, in championship game.

TOP 10 PROSPECTS: 1. Kyle Teel, C/OF, Wisconsin (So., Virginia); 2. Chase Davis, OF, La Crosse (So., Arizona); 3. Tavian Josenberger, OF/SS,

Fond du Lac (So., Kansas); 4. Riley Cornelio, RHP, St. Cloud (So., Texas Christian); 5. Braden Forsyth, RHP, Kalamazoo (Jr., Mississippi); 6. Nate Wohlgemuth, RHP, Duluth (So., San Jacinto (Texas) JC); 7. Victor Scott, OF, Fond du Lac (So., West Virginia); 8. Justin Janas, 1B, Kenosha (So., Illinois); 9. Chandler Simpson, 2B, Fond du Lac (So., Georgia Tech); 10. Ethan Hammerberg, RHP, Duluth (So., Ohio State).

INDIVIDUAL BATTING LEADERS

	AVG	AB	R	H	2B	3B	HR	RBI	SB
Justin Janas, Kingfish	.402	174	29	70	12	2	2	43	3
Chandler Simpson, Dock Spiders	.377	204	52	77	3	1	0	23	55
Josh Kasevich, Bucks	.374	171	32	64	7	0	2	39	5
William Hamiter, Stingers	.353	184	28	65	13	0	1	37	6
Garrett McGowan, Bucks	.351	185	39	65	12	1	4	43	10
Alex Iadisernia, Mallards	.345	223	40	77	26	1	10	34	3
Chase Meidroth, Jackrabbits	.345	174	33	60	11	1	1	44	5
Max Jung-Goldberg, Bucks	.342	193	34	66	9	0	4	41	12
Mike Boeve, Huskies	.341	246	36	84	14	1	2	47	10
McKinley Erves, Rapids Rafters	.341	208	40	71	10	1	0	41	10

INDIVIDUAL PITCHING LEADERS

	W	L	ERA	G	SV	IP	H	BB	SO
Josh Gainer, Rox	4	0	0.00	14	0	23	16	4	36
Ben Livorsi, Jackrabbits	1	1	0.00	12	1	22	11	6	19
Seth Sweet-Chick, Dock Spiders	2	1	0.33	5	0	28	18	15	26
Vince Reilly, MoonDogs	3	0	0.41	16	8	22	13	10	26
Hunter Waldis, Rapids Rafters	1	1	0.41	12	0	22	12	5	32
Ivran Romero, MoonDogs	1	0	0.68	5	0	26	12	11	23
Cam Schuelke, Pit Spitters	4	0	0.68	15	0	53	32	17	48
Nick Herold, Express	3	2	0.75	17	7	24	9	12	37
Tucker Shalley, Rivets	4	1	0.78	19	4	23	15	9	26
John Beucklelaere, Pit Spitters	2	3	1.00	19	4	27	15	13	32

PERFECT GAME COLLEGIATE LEAGUE

East Division	W	L	PCT	GB
Amsterdam Mohawks	31	10	.750	-
Saugerties Stallions	27	12	.692	3
Albany Dutchmen	22	21	.512	10
Oneonta Outlaws	14	21	.403	14
Glens Falls Dragons	7	35	.167	24.5
Central Division	**W**	**L**	**PCT**	**GB**
Utica Blue Sox	24	17	.585	-
Auburn Doubledays	26	19	.578	-
Mohawk Valley DiamondDawgs	23	19	.548	1.5
Watertown Rapids	13	29	.310	11.5
West Division	**W**	**L**	**PCT**	**GB**
Jamestown Tarp Skunks	28	15	.651	-
Geneva Red Wings	23	18	.561	4
Batavia Muckdogs	22	19	.537	5
Elmira Pioneers	17	21	.447	8.5
Niagara Power	19	26	.422	10
Newark Pilots	12	26	.316	13.5

CHAMPIONSHIP: Saugerties Stallionss defeated Amsterdam Mohawks, 2-0, in best-of-three championship series.

INDIVIDUAL BATTING LEADERS

	AVG	AB	R	H	2B	3B	HR	RBI	SB
Griffin O'Ferrall, Doubledays	.404	151	43	61	12	1	0	27	29
Tony Santa Maria, Rapids	.388	103	28	40	4	2	0	14	13
Luke Mutz, Pilots	.387	93	17	36	4	4	0	18	11
Matt Shaw, Mohawks	.369	122	33	45	12	0	9	28	14
Haiden Hunt, Skunks	.351	94	29	33	7	0	0	13	22
Dylan Broderick, Rapids	.349	129	32	45	7	3	0	16	17
Evan Berta, DiamondDawgs	.349	109	30	38	6	0	1	22	12
Ryan Weiss, Outlaws	.347	95	14	33	5	1	1	19	0
Keaton Mark, Outlaws	.344	93	14	32	8	2	2	21	5
Nick Schwartz, Dutchman	.340	100	20	34	6	0	1	10	9

INDIVIDUAL PITCHING LEADERS

	W	L	ERA	G	SV	IP	H	BB	SO
Sam Stoutenborough, Power	2	0	0.00	5	0	26	7	5	36
Jacob Rosenkranz, Blue Sox	2	1	0.61	10	0	29	16	13	25
Nicholas Serce, Red Wings	2	0	0.68	7	0	26	18	9	46
Blair Frederick, Muckdogs	2	1	0.77	5	0	23	15	12	26
Alec Teska, Doubledays	2	0	1.00	3	0	18	11	5	13

Carlos Rodrigues, Muckdogs	2	1	1.04	10	1	17	4	13	36
Troy Butler, DiamondDawgs	1	0	1.20	7	0	15	7	9	19
Terry Murray, DiamondDawgs	3	1	1.50	13	2	30	30	6	33
Cam Hill, Pioneers	3	1	1.50	4	1	18	13	9	26
Nick Smith, Mohawks	4	1	1.51	10	0	36	24	9	46

PROSPECT LEAGUE

Ohio River Valley Division	W	L	PCT	GB
Chillicothe Paints	36	24	.600	-
Champion City Kings	28	30	.483	7
Johnston Mill Rats	24	34	.414	11
West Virginia Miners	23	36	.390	12.5
Wabash River Division	**W**	**L**	**PCT**	**GB**
Lafayette Aviators	41	18	.695	-
Danville Dans	36	22	.621	4.5
Illinois Valley Pistol Shrimp	24	36	.400	17.5
REX	20	40	.333	21.5
Great River Division	**W**	**L**	**PCT**	**GB**
Normal CornBelters	31	29	.517	-
Clinton LumberKings	29	31	.483	2
Burlington Bees	28	32	.467	3
Quincy Gems	27	32	.458	3.5
Prairie Land Division	**W**	**L**	**PCT**	**GB**
Cape Catfish	38	22	.633	-
O'Fallon Hoots	33	27	.550	5
Springfield Sliders	30	30	.500	8
Alton River Dragons	27	32	.458	10.5

CHAMPIONSHIP: Cape Catfish defeated Lafayette Aviators, 2-1, in best-of-three championship series.

INDIVIDUAL BATTING LEADERS

	AVG	AB	R	H	2B	3B	HR	RBI	SB
Ben Newbert, Mill Rats	.397	151	36	60	10	4	9	38	2
Denver Blinn, Miners	.379	140	42	53	16	1	4	42	5
Jake Skrine, Gems	.367	158	36	58	5	2	9	45	8
Trey Smith, Paints	.358	173	42	62	14	2	5	33	15
Nick Terrell, Sliders	.356	208	51	74	15	1	3	37	17
Ben Ross, Kings	.356	225	60	80	7	1	8	41	19
Alex Ludwick, Paints	.348	224	43	78	16	2	3	34	21
Cooper McMurray, Dans	.343	140	26	48	9	0	5	34	2
Ellison Hanna II, Catfish	.343	143	35	49	9	1	7	29	3
Kent Reeser, Paints	.336	137	38	46	8	2	5	47	14

INDIVIDUAL PITCHING LEADERS

	W	L	ERA	G	SV	IP	H	BB	SO
Kaleb Honea, Aviators	1	0	0.44	14	8	21	18	0	22
Braden Scott, REX	1	0	0.57	3	0	16	8	4	21
Anthony Klein, Hoots	5	1	0.81	19	5	33	14	15	39
Louis Lipthratt, Miners	4	1	1.36	8	0	33	23	15	39
Garrett Langrell, Bees	5	1	1.40	14	1	26	13	10	33
Peyton Havard, Dragons	4	1	1.72	6	0	31	31	7	29
Mac Hickman, Sliders	4	1	1.80	10	0	30	20	15	30
Sean Furlong, Mill Rats	0	0	1.84	5	0	15	14	6	9
Trey McDaniel, Catfish	2	1	1.93	13	5	23	11	4	35
Reece Wissinger, Bees	3	0	1.93	15	4	19	12	4	41

SOUTH FLORIDA COLLEGIATE LEAGUE

North Division	W	L	PCT	GB
Phipps Park Barracudas	21	17	.551	-
Boynton Beach Buccaneers	23	19	.548	-
Boca Raton Blazers	23	22	.511	1.5
Delray Beach Lightning	21	21	.500	2
Palm Beach Diamond Ducks	17	20	.461	3.5
South Division	**W**	**L**	**PCT**	**GB**
West Boca Snappers	25	11	.694	-
Palm Beach Xtreme	28	15	.648	0.5
Pompano Beach Clippers	14	17	.453	8.5
Fort Lauderdale Knights	14	24	.368	12
Florida Pokers	6	26	.206	17

CHAMPIONSHIP: Boca Raton Blazers defeated Palm Beach Xtreme, 2-1, in best-of-three championship series.

INDIVIDUAL BATTING LEADERS

	AVG	AB	R	H	2B	3B	HR	RBI	SB
Ross Maertz, Snappers	.427	75	24	32	4	0	2	19	12

	AVG	AB	R	H	2B	3B	HR	RBI	SB
Mason Maxwell, Buccaneers	.388	98	27	38	11	1	2	22	14
Justin Sierra, Barracudas	.372	78	23	29	2	1	0	7	14
AJ Orrico, Buccaneers	.370	92	30	34	2	0	0	8	25
Zach Benson, Snappers	.360	75	19	27	6	0	1	17	8
Edward Gonzalez, Knights	.353	51	14	18	2	0	1	11	10
Hunter Damato, Lightning	.344	96	15	33	5	0	1	12	9
Tarik Latchmansingh, Snappers	.338	71	14	24	5	0	2	16	6
Sam Faith, Blazers	.334	84	18	28	5	0	3	15	3
Christian Gemelli, Barracudas	.333	60	18	20	3	0	0	9	10

INDIVIDUAL PITCHING LEADERS

	W	L	ERA	G	SV	IP	H	BB	SO
Jordan Schulefand, Xtreme	2	0	0.00	8	2	16	7	5	19
Mason Adams, Barracudas	2	0	0.40	5	0	23	8	4	23
Ethan Rembish, Blazers	0	0	0.51	6	1	18	14	8	23
Zac Schultz, Blazers	1	0	0.83	9	1	22	14	11	26
Esteban Rodriguez, Clippers	2	0	1.06	5	1	17	7	8	27
Cole Stasio, Blazers	4	1	1.26	9	0	36	19	12	35
Coley Embry, Snappers	2	1	1.35	11	1	20	8	15	12
Jake Molloy, Snappers	5	2	1.39	10	0	26	26	6	27
Tyler Rapf, Diamond Ducks	4	1	1.47	7	0	18	13	7	23
Marc Degusipe, Barracudas	2	0	1.57	6	0	23	15	3	22

SUNBELT LEAGUE

	W	L	PCT	GB
Alpharetta Aviators	22	11	.667	-
Gainesville Braves	20	11	.645	1
Atlanta Crackers	18	11	.621	2
Gwinnett Astros	17	12	.586	3
Brookhaven Bucks	15	17	.469	6.5
Columbus Chatt-a-Hoots	15	19	.441	7.5
Waleska Wild Things	9	19	.321	10.5
Marietta Patriots	6	22	.214	13.5

CHAMPIONSHIP: Alpharetta Aviators defeated Columbus Chatt-a-Hoots, 2-0, in best-of-three championship series.

INDIVIDUAL BATTING LEADERS

	AVG	AB	R	H	2B	3B	HR	RBI	SB
Nathaniel Anderson, Crackers	.390	100	27	39	6	1	3	19	21
David Burke, Aviators	.362	94	20	34	10	0	0	22	4
Trenton Jamison, Bucks	.361	108	22	39	15	0	4	25	6
Graham Pauley, Aviators	.361	83	14	30	6	0	5	22	7
Joseph Hamilton IV, Aviators	.345	87	16	30	1	1	1	13	7
Antonio Brown, Astros	.338	74	22	25	1	0	0	9	20
Rob Gordon, Bucks	.333	72	28	24	10	0	2	19	15
Cameron Gray, Chatt-a-Hoots	.326	95	22	31	3	2	1	19	3
Carson Renz, Astros	.305	95	17	29	1	0	3	18	2
Jesse Donohoe, Chatt-a-Hoots	.297	101	15	30	7	0	1	18	1

INDIVIDUAL PITCHING LEADERS

	W	L	ERA	G	SV	IP	H	BB	SO
Charles Stephenson, Bucks	3	2	1.15	8	0	47	42	15	37
Leo Giannoni, Astros	2	1	1.35	17	1	27	20	7	38
Rob Hamby, Braves	5	1	1.47	8	0	37	26	8	42
Seth Clark, Astros	3	0	1.59	8	0	34	25	11	50
Daniel Holley, Chatt-a-Hoots	3	1	2.05	11	0	44	32	16	56
Davis Rokose, Crackers	2	0	2.08	6	1	26	14	9	40
Austin Wainer, Wild Things	2	1	2.26	8	0	32	26	10	34
Halton Hardy, Braves	3	2	2.33	9	0	39	25	8	33
Chase Allen, Wild Things	0	1	2.46	6	0	26	21	14	31
Blake Renner, Aviators	5	0	2.67	12	0	30	21	11	25

SUNFLOWER COLLEGIATE LEAGUE

	W	L	PCT	GB
Hutchinson Monarchs	26	8	.765	-
316 Sluggers	23	11	.676	3
Great Bend Bat Cats	21	13	.618	5
Cheney Diamond Dawgs	21	14	.600	5.5
Derby Twins	20	17	.541	7.5
Haysville Aviators	15	18	.455	10.5
Newton Rebels	8	26	.235	18
Sunflower Seeds	4	28	.125	21

INDIVIDUAL BATTING LEADERS

	AVG	AB	R	H	2B	3B	HR	RBI	SB
Conner Flagg, Sluggers	.410	117	40	48	8	0	0	17	8

	AVG	AB	R	H	2B	3B	HR	RBI	SB
Cole Cosman, Monarchs	.403	77	27	31	12	0	5	21	2
Nolan Riley, Rebels	.398	88	17	35	3	0	3	24	1
Cal Watkins, Monarchs	.397	63	12	25	1	0	0	11	2
Carter Young, Monarchs	.392	79	21	31	7	0	1	10	5
Enzo Bonventre, Dawgs	.388	80	14	31	6	1	5	24	0
Steven Saunders, Twins	.383	47	13	18	3	0	6	16	2
Lenny Ashby, Dawgs	.369	111	20	41	4	0	5	35	1
Justin Barnes, Rebels	.368	68	15	25	2	2	2	12	3
Zane Spinn, Bat Cats	.355	121	29	43	14	0	1	30	15

INDIVIDUAL PITCHING LEADERS

	W	L	ERA	G	SV	IP	H	BB	SO
Jarrett Seaton, Bat Cats	2	1	1.07	5	0	25	18	12	31
Zach Gillig, Rebels	1	0	1.07	18	0	25	24	16	48
Corey Wilson, Aviators	2	1	1.62	6	0	33	28	6	27
Mason Ashcraft, Diamond Dawgs	3	1	1.86	13	3	29	15	19	33
Matt Nedved, Bat Cats	3	1	2.16	8	0	17	10	7	20
Ethan Peterson, Sluggers	3	1	2.20	9	2	33	21	6	54
Zak Gould, Monarchs	1	1	2.25	6	0	28	22	12	33
Ryan Stuempfig, Monarchs	5	0	2.28	9	2	28	18	3	29
Megumi Fukuda, Twins	4	3	2.40	9	0	45	39	21	49
Conner Woods, Sluggers	0	0	2.40	9	0	15	18	3	15

TEXAS LEAGUE

	W	L	PCT	GB
San Antonio Flying Chanclas	29	7	.806	-
Acadiana Cane Cutters	21	17	.553	9
Brazos Valley Bombers	23	19	.548	9
Amarillo Sod Squad	17	23	.427	14
Victoria Generals	16	22	.423	14
Baton Rouge Rougarou	10	28	.263	20

CHAMPIONSHIP: San Antonio Flying Chanclas defeated Victoria Generals, 8-0, in championship game.

INDIVIDUAL BATTING LEADERS

	AVG	AB	R	H	2B	3B	HR	RBI	SB
Ethan Lege, Cane Cutters	.364	143	36	52	10	2	3	14	9
Ryon Knowles, Sod Squad	.343	108	19	37	8	1	2	16	0
Ryan Flores, Flying Chanclas	.311	151	29	47	4	0	2	34	0
Austin Trahan, Cane Cutters	.306	98	12	30	2	0	0	7	3
Grayson Tatrow, Bombers	.302	126	25	38	11	1	1	19	8
CJ Horn, Sod Squad	.292	89	17	26	5	0	0	16	0
Enrique Porchas, Sod Squad	.285	130	16	37	9	1	1	14	0
Ian Bailey, Flying Chanclas	.283	127	35	36	9	3	5	31	5
Adam Becker, Generals	.282	103	13	29	5	0	3	23	0
Nick Cupp-Allen, Rougarou	.274	95	15	26	6	2	1	9	8

INDIVIDUAL PITCHING LEADERS

	W	L	ERA	G	SV	IP	H	BB	SO
JT Moeller, Flying Chanclas	2	0	0.47	13	0	19	12	1	12
Matt Sessler, Flying Chanclas	1	0	0.67	11	1	27	17	5	25
AG Ayala, Flying Chanclas	1	0	1.08	11	0	17	10	5	19
Reed Vincent, Cane Cutters	1	0	1.15	10	1	16	8	8	13
Carson Atwood, Bombers	6	2	1.59	10	0	40	32	12	39
Alec Martinez, Flying Chanclas	6	0	1.71	9	0	47	33	15	51
Jaime Ramirez Jr., Flying Chanclas	1	0	1.72	4	0	16	12	4	19
Issac Crab, Bombers	2	0	1.88	9	1	24	12	14	22
Matthew Maloney, Sod Squad	3	0	1.93	12	0	23	13	14	22
Hoss Brewer, Sod Squad	2	2	2.12	7	0	30	17	17	27

VALLEY LEAGUE

North Division	W	L	PCT	GB
Strasburg Express	26	15	.634	-
Woodstock River Bandits	26	16	.619	0.5
Winchester Royals	22	19	.537	4
New Market Rebels	20	22	.476	6.5
Front Royal Cardinals	17	25	.405	9.5
Purcellville Cannons	12	29	.293	14
South Division	W	L	PCT	GB
Charlottesville TomSox	30	10	.750	-
Staunton Braves	19	20	.487	10.5
Harrisonburg Turks	19	21	.475	11
Waynesboro Generals	19	21	.475	11
Covington Lumberjacks	10	22	.313	16

CHAMPIONSHIP: Strasburg Express defeated Waynesboro Generals,

The Greeneville Flyboys had a dramatic win in the Appalachian League championship game.

2-0, in best-of-three championship series.

INDIVIDUAL BATTING LEADERS

	AVG	AB	R	H	2B	3B	HR	RBI	SB
Nate Furman, Royals	.400	100	38	40	7	1	3	22	25
Ryan Galanie, Express	.383	128	42	49	9	0	7	26	19
Austin Bulman, Royals	.379	124	31	47	14	0	7	40	7
Jackson Lancaster, Rebels	.371	97	22	36	5	4	6	23	7
Ryan McCarty, Braves	.356	104	29	37	9	3	4	16	17
Niko Amory, Cardinals	.349	86	19	30	11	0	3	15	4
Wyatt Langford, TomSox	.345	110	21	38	7	2	3	20	6
Will Long, Royals	.339	115	26	39	6	0	8	40	0
Aidan Nagle, River Bandits	.339	127	31	43	6	1	7	42	7
Chad Fairey, Express	.331	118	34	39	10	0	11	39	12
Tripp McKinlay, Express	.331	118	29	39	7	0	4	21	17

INDIVIDUAL PITCHING LEADERS

	W	L	ERA	G	SV	IP	H	BB	SO
Ryan Ammons, Express	3	0	0.96	12	4	19	8	7	32
Conor Miller, River Bandits	0	0	1.17	14	7	15	15	5	23
Seth Logue, Generals	1	1	1.40	6	1	19	11	3	23
Michael Darrell-Hicks, Royals	1	2	1.65	8	1	16	12	8	26
Christian Worley, TomSox	1	0	1.80	6	1	20	11	6	25
Jacob Cravey, Express	2	2	1.90	5	0	24	16	8	27
Gregory Martinez, Rebels	2	0	1.90	3	0	19	15	2	23
Brett Whiteman, Turks	2	1	2.04	7	0	18	16	13	15
Andres Rodriguez, Turks	3	2	2.25	7	1	28	21	11	36
Donovan Burke, Express	2	3	2.29	7	0	35	29	11	35

WEST COAST LEAGUE

North Division

	W	L	PCT	GB
Yakima Valley Pippins	29	19	.604	-
Bellingham Bells	24	24	.500	5
Wenatchee AppleSox	20	28	.417	9
Walla Walla Sweets	15	33	.313	14
Port Angeles Lefties	13	35	.271	16

South Division

	W	L	PCT	GB
Corvallis Knights	37	11	.771	-
Ridgefield Raptors	26	22	.542	11
Portland Pickles	26	22	.542	11
Bend Elks	26	22	.542	11
Cowlitz Black Bears	24	24	.500	13

CHAMPIONSHIP: Corvallis Knights defeated Yakima Valley Pippins, 2-1, in best-of-three championship series.

TOP 10 PROSPECTS: 1. Malakhi Knight, OF, Bellingham (Fr., UCLA); **2.** Jacob Kmatz, RHP, Bend (Fr., Oregon State); **3.** Travis Bazzana, INF, Corvallis (Fr., Oregon State); **4.** Nick McLain, OF, Bellingham (Fr., UCLA); **5.** Rikuu Nishida, INF, Cowlitz (So., Mt. Hood (Ore.) JC); **6.** Kelly Austin, RHP, Cowlitz (So., UCLA); **7.** Caden O'Connor, OF, Ridgefield (So., Cal State Fullerton); **8.** Ethan Ross, LHP, Corvallis (So., San Jose State); **9.** Tommy O'Rourke, RHP, Bellingham (So., Stanford); **10.** Leo Mosby, 3B, Portland (So., UC Santa Barbara).

INDIVIDUAL BATTING LEADERS

	AVG	AB	R	H	2B	3B	HR	RBI	SB
Travis Bazzana, Knights	.429	189	46	81	18	5	1	27	18
Rikuu Nishida, Black Bears	.370	119	29	44	6	1	0	14	28
Leo Mosby, Pickles	.369	141	23	52	7	1	6	40	7
Julian Kodama, Elks	.359	117	20	42	6	0	1	18	2
Nick Vogt, Knights	.351	134	25	47	5	2	2	24	23
Coby Morales, Raptors	.349	152	26	53	11	1	6	34	1
Reece Hernandez, Raptors	.325	117	27	38	8	0	0	21	0
John Peck, Raptors	.324	179	31	58	11	1	6	40	5
Matt Jew, Pickles	.320	122	27	39	9	0	3	18	2
Sam Linscott, Elks	.314	156	29	49	10	2	2	34	7

INDIVIDUAL PITCHING LEADERS

	W	L	ERA	G	SV	IP	H	BB	SO
Eric Chavarria, Bells	3	3	1.84	11	0	44	36	8	41
Alex Giroux, Pickles	4	1	1.93	11	0	42	35	12	38
Jaren Hunter, Raptors	4	0	1.93	8	0	42	42	12	35
Dillon Holliday, Elks	3	2	2.34	8	0	42	28	18	39
Kelly Austin, Black Bears	3	1	2.53	9	0	57	34	6	76
Ty Uber, Knights	4	0	2.80	11	1	45	25	24	55
Seth Kuykendall, Pippins	3	3	3.29	9	0	55	61	9	40
Caden Kaelber, Sweets	2	1	3.61	19	2	47	41	22	63
Travis Craven, Sweets	3	4	3.82	16	0	61	56	16	63
Dylan Bishop, Pippins	6	1	3.89	10	0	44	46	16	3

HIGH
SCHOOL

Madison Central High Takes The Prep Crown

Madison Central finished the season 34-2 and won the Mississippi 6A state championship.

BY ALEXIS BRUDNICKI

The stakes seemed higher to Patrick Robey this season.

As the head coach at Madison Central High in Mississippi, Robey believes coaching staffs around the country will understand and agree with him. But it wasn't the games that counted for more.

It was the time.

Before experiencing the loss of last season to the coronavirus pandemic, it had become easy to take the regular routine of spring and summer baseball for granted. Practices were a given. Motivational speeches from coaches were expected. The roller-coaster ride of a championship run was often the most significant emotional toll to be paid.

Heading into this year knowing his team would be reunited with a chance to return to some normalcy on the diamond, albeit missing several players who didn't get the sendoff their team felt they deserved, Robey's focus diverged from his usual preseason mindset. No longer was the game about the competition. It became about gratitude.

"I couldn't have cared less if we won or lost a game," Robey said. "I missed my guys. I missed the relationships, I missed the talks, I missed the bus rides, I missed my guys. That was the hardest thing for me. For the players, it was very tough. Every coach knows what I felt and what we felt."

While that sentiment was shared by many ahead of the beginning of this season, Robey and his players earned an entirely different set of emotions by the end of the year, winning Mississippi's highest classification (6A) championship after finishing 34-2 and being named the Baseball America High School Team of the Year.

"It's pretty remarkable," Robey said of the honor. "It's hard to explain. It's a credit to having years of success, and then to these young men who accomplished the goal this year. It's a credit to them and their families for a lot of sacrifice and hard work."

The state title was Robey's second with Madison Central in his fifth season and sixth year with the school. The Jaguars went undefeated in league play, and outscored opponents 422-64. The squad was led by draft prospects Braden Montgomery and Hunter Hines, but received contributions from across the roster.

"We were very talented, and you've got to be to finish No. 1 and win a state championship," Robey said. "But it goes a lot further than that. We had a group of very selfless kids who loved each other and didn't care who got the credit. They just wanted to win. You take a talented team with a team-first attitude and families who care about the team, that culminates into a very successful year.

"Offensively, we had some guys who could hit for power, some guys who could run, a lot of senior leaders who had a lot of at-bats under their belts and were all tough outs. There were three or four juniors in that group who were very key contributors. We had a group of guys who really enjoyed playing the game, they enjoyed being around each other, they didn't like to lose, whether it was checkers, ping pong, or baseball, so that was a pretty good combination."

Maybe it was the missed season. It might have been the result of an abundance of time apart. Perhaps it was the same feeling of gratitude felt by their head coach. But there's one word that primarily comes to mind for Robey when he thinks about the team he fielded this year.

"Lovable," he said. "They love each other, they truly did. I really believe God rewards faith, sacrifice and obedience, and those guys were not afraid to sacrifice for each other. They knew their roles and they accepted their roles. They knew they couldn't all be starting shortstop, they couldn't all hit third. But those guys have played baseball together for a long time and whether it was ping pong or baseball, they wanted to compete hard."

Though Robey can't expect the same level of camaraderie, he believes the same success that led him and his squad to become Team of the Year has a chance to be repeated because of the competitive spirit he's seen pass through his doors time and time again.

"We have a winning culture and a successful school," he said. "They want to win in the classroom, on the athletic field, on the basketball court, so the competitive nature is in our kids. Are we going to win a state championship every single year? Absolutely not. But our kids know they have to work hard to maintain the level of success we've had at Madison Central. We've got some really talented players coming back (and) we'll have a chance to make a good run next year too."

The 3D Sweets Expiriment Pays Off

For many players, the 2020 season and the coronavirus pandemic responsible for wiping it away represented nothing but lost opportunities.

For most high school seniors, it meant the last chance to play baseball with their childhood friends was taken away. For college and pro-caliber players, it meant lost development time. Or a missed chance to land a scholarship or impress big league scouts to improve their draft stock.

For everyone—regardless of ability or age—it was largely a season, and a year, of loss.

But for Southern California prep Thatcher Hurd it was also a year of discovery.

At the time, the junior was committed to UC Santa Barbara as a catcher. He pitched occasionally, but was mostly a reliever with a big arm who would throw a few innings here and there—and throw as hard as he could—for his team. When

HIGH SCHOOL RANKINGS

Rank	School	Record
1.	Madison (Miss) Central HS	34-2
2.	Barbe HS, Lake Charles, La.	38-2
3.	Stoneman Douglas HS, Parkland, Fla.	28-2
4.	Jackson (Miss.) Prep	35-3
5.	St. Mary Prep, Orchard Lake, Mich.	43-1
6.	Liberty HS, Peoria, Ariz.	21-3
7.	JSerra Catholic HS, San Juan Capistrano, Calif.	30-7
8.	Auburn (Ala.) HS	36-7
9.	Madison HS, Vienna, Va.	18-1
10.	Buchanan HS, Clovis, Calif.	29-3
11.	Bishop Gorman HS, Las Vegas	18-1
12.	Blue Valley HS, Stilwell, Kan.	19-3
13.	Parkview HS, Lilburn, Ga.	30-10
14.	Trinity HS, Louisville	41-2
15.	Harvard-Westlake HS, Los Angeles	27-4
16.	Houston County HS, Warner Robins, Ga.	31-7
17.	Thousand Oaks (Calif.) HS	29-1
18.	Keller (Texas)HS	31-5
19.	Mosley HS, Lynn Haven, Fla.	26-5
20.	Buford (Ga.) HS	35-2
21.	Barbers Hill HS, Mt. Belvieu, Texas	37-8
22.	Alhambra HS, Phoenix	23-2
23.	Ayala HS, Chino Hills, Calif.	26-4
24.	Fort Zumwalt West HS, O'Fallon, Mo.	29-4
25.	Orange (Calif.) Lutheran HS	30-6
26.	Danville (Ky.) HS	40-4
27.	Liberty (Mo.) HS	32-9
28.	Smithson Valley HS, Spring Branch, Texas	34-4
29.	Millard South HS, Omaha, Neb.	35-5
30.	St. Joseph HS, Montvale, N.J.	27-2
31.	East Catholic HS, Manchester, Conn.	25-0
32.	Roff (Okla.) HS	33-0
33.	Faith Academy, Mobile, Ala.	34-6
34.	Hamilton HS, Chandler, Ariz.	16-2
35.	Jasper (Ind.) HS	31-2
36.	Starr's Mill HS, Fayetteville, Ga.	31-11
37.	Bishop Eustace Prep, Pennsauken, N.J.	21-1
38.	Farmington (Minn.) HS	21-6
39.	Magnolia Heights HS, Sentobia, Miss.	30-3
40.	Sun Prairie (Wisc.) HS	27-2
41.	Tamalpais HS, Mill Valley, Calif.	19-1
42.	Jenks (Okla.) HS	27-6
43.	New Albany (Ohio) HS	29-5
44.	Rogers (Miss.) HS	19-7
45.	Puyallup (Wash.) HS	16-0
46.	Rio Rancho HS, Albuquerque, N.M.	21-1
47.	Bloomingdale HS, Valrico, Fla.	24-6
48.	Van Buren (Ariz.) HS	27-7
49.	Eastlake HS, Chula Vista, Calif.	25-10

the 2020 season was canceled, Hurd started to realize during bullpen sessions with his brother that his future just might be brighter on the opposite side of the battery.

"I just really started gravitating toward pitching," Hurd said. "I thought it was a perfect time to be in a controlled environment and just really hone the craft. And I fell in love with it."

Throughout the summer and fall, Hurd improved on the mound as he focused exclusively on pitching. He enjoyed the competitiveness that came with challenging one batter after another and felt comfortable within the rigors of a pitcher's routine.

Scouts took note, and Hurd entered the 2021

season as a top 100 prospect in the draft class.

"He is a guy to watch who could jump up," one scout said last winter. "He is not there yet, but if the velocity comes and he has a good season he could go pretty good. It wouldn't surprise me if he had a Quinn Priester ascent with a good offseason."

Comparing Hurd to the Pirates' 2019 first-round pick—the first high school pitcher off the board—is high praise. But as the year crept on and the pandemic continued to rage around the country, apprehension started to creep in.

What if 2020 happened all over again?

That fear was perhaps especially felt for players on the West Coast, where the safety guidelines were stricter than other areas of the country like the Southeast, where tournaments and showcases continued like normal.

"It was pretty hard," said Washington outfielder Malakhi Knight, thinking back to the lost 2020 season. "You know, everything shut down. The gym shut down, all of the batting cages shut down. I had to just focus on myself and self-motivate myself."

Knight, a prominent outfielder in the 2021 draft class, played travel ball with a number of other high-profile players from the Pacific Northwest, including 2021 righthander Max Debiec and 2022 righthander and infielder JR Ritchie. The players knew in November their 2021 season would at the very least be delayed.

Most places in the region were still closed or restricted because of Covid-19, and players began wondering if they were going to lose another season of development, exposure and the joy of playing the game they all love.

"A lot of the kids were getting depressed," said Ian Ritchie, JR's father and a partner in Alliance Baseball, which owns Baseball America. "Sitting around and stuck in Covid and to be honest, feeling like they were going to fall behind all of the guys (around the country) who were getting ready for college or their senior years and the draft and stuff. And there was a lot of, honestly, depression and anxiety and not knowing . . . For these kids it's not fair—they've been trying too long and chasing their dreams."

So Ian Ritchie, and Max Debiec's father Stan, wondered if they could figure out a solution. Perhaps Covid-19 created an environment with the kind of possibilities not found in a normal year. With students around the country already acclimated to online school, the new norm for high schoolers, what would stop them from getting a group of players together and heading down south for a month to play baseball every day?

Ian started asking around.

"Hey, you know, this might sound totally crazy," he said, "but what if we were able to rent a really, really big house, and take a really awesome group of kids to Arizona and play baseball and kind of control our own destiny?"

Hurd already had some experience turning a bad situation into something positive. Why not do it again?

"A total silver lining to Covid," Hurd said, chuckling. "Obviously this wouldn't even be possible in a normal year."

To pull off a plan like this, connections are required.

It just so happens there was a perfect man for the job: Dominic Robinson.

Robinson, who owns 3D Sports Performance and trains athletes, has been wanting to do something similar for four years. A former two-sport athlete at Florida State, Robinson previously coached college football before moving to the Phoenix area, where he has spent time as a trainer.

At times he would have athletes come train for a week here, a week there. Nothing much more extended than that. Robinson thought about holding a camp during Christmas break, but nothing materialized. The logistics always seemed to be just a bit too complicated.

So when Ian Ritchie called him, he was overjoyed.

"When he reached out to me, I couldn't even contain myself with excitement," Robinson said. "Because like I said, this was four years in the making for me. As (Ritchie) is talking through some of the thoughts, the way we were symbiotically connecting without ever having to have a conversation in terms of our thoughts on this—it was just so exciting to go, 'Wow, this is something we can really do.'

"The timing of this is right, for the first time."

With Robinson running 3D Sports and several of the players from the Northwest playing on the Sweets Baseball Club travel team, the players called themselves the 3D Sweets.

The two decided Ritchie would focus on getting a house for the players, while Robinson would focus his efforts almost exclusively on the baseball side. With Ritchie making sure players were getting their schoolwork done and not destroying the house, Robinson would be able to handle the logistics of setting up games, scheduling practices and keeping the players on a training program.

And that was certainly a challenge.

"We knew, one of the big conversations that we had early was, 'Hey, we are going to screw some of

AMATEUR/YOUTH CHAMPIONS 2019

ALL-AMERICAN AMATEUR BASEBALL ASSOCIATION (AAABA)

Event	Site	Champion	Runner-up
World Series (21U)	Johnstown, Pa.	New Orleans Boosters	New Brunswick Matrix

AMERICAN LEGION BASEBALL

Event	Site	Champion	Runner-up
World Series (19U)	Shelby, N.C.	Idaho Falls, Idaho	Honolulu, Ha.

BABE RUTH BASEBALL

Event	Site	Champion	Runner-up
Cal Ripken (10U)	Phenix City, Ala.	Cherry Hill	Williamsburg
Cal Ripken 12-year-old (60 feet)	Branson, Mo.	Owensboro	PBG Host - National
13-year-old	Demopolis, Ala.	—	—
13-15-year-olds	Bismarck, N.D.	Pacific Southwest	Middle Atlantic
16-18-year-olds	Mobile, Ala.	Onondaga	Mobile

LITTLE LEAGUE BASEBALL

Event	Site	Champion	Runner-up
Little League (11-12)	South Williamsport, Pa.	Michigan	Ohio
Junior League (12-14)	Taylor, Mich.	—	—
Senior League (13-16)	Easley, S.C.	—	—
Intermediate (50-70)	Livermore, Calif.	—	—

NATIONAL AMATEUR BASEBALL FEDERATION (NBAF)

Event	Site	Champion	Runner-up
Rookie (10U)	Tuxedo Park, N.Y.	Pelham Baseball	YBNR Raptors - New Rochelle N.Y.
Freshman (12U)	Tuxedo Park, N.Y.	—	—
Sophomore (14U)	Struthers, Ohio	Release Baseball	Astro Falcons
Junior (16U)	Struthers, Ohio	Ohio Longhorns	Astro Falcons
High School (17U)	Jackson, Miss.	Jackson 96ers 17U	Jackson 96ers 16U
Senior (18U)	Struthers, Ohio	Brooklyn Bonnie Jays	Troy American Legion Legends
College (22U)	Toledo, Ohio	Grand Rapids Brewers	Stark County Terriers

PERFECT GAME/BCS FINALS

Event	Site	Champion	Runner-up
12U	Fort Myers, Fla.	Velo Baseball 12U	5 Star Orlando 2027
13U	Fort Myers, Fla.	Burn Atlantic 13U Navy	TBT National White
14U	Fort Myers, Fla.	TBT Ballers National	5 Star National 14U RR
15U	Fort Myers, Fla.	US Elite 15U GA	eXposure 15U Prime - Church
16U	Fort Myers, Fla.	Eagles Baseball Scout Team	Ostingers Baseball Academy 2023
17U	Fort Myers, Fla.	Dallas Patriots 17U Stout	East Coast Lumberjacks 2022s
18U	Fort Myers, Fla.	Florida Legends	Marucci Elite Texas 18U Mayo

this up.' " Robinson said. "Nothing like this has ever been done. We are borrowing from a template that doesn't exist. We are going to forget some things. There are going to be some things that are going to fall short. We just have to be able to be flexible and handle it."

Robinson's connections around the Phoenix area allowed him to put together games against local high schools in Arizona and opened the doors to facilities where players could go to hit, throw or work out.

When scheduling problems arose because of Covid-19 issues with would-be opponents, Robinson would have to quickly figure out the next move.

In the middle of one game, Robinson heard from a coach who had to cancel a game the next day because of Covid-19. Before the final out, Robinson had reached out to another school, scheduled a game, locked down details for batting practice and alerted all of the scouts in the area to the change.

While Robinson was in charge of the logistics, the 3D Sweets also had an expert helping manage the pitching workload and schedules for many arms who were just ramping up for the season. That expert was Kevin Gunderson, who was familiar with almost every player on the team and previously helped train Phillies 2020 first-rounder Mick Abel.

"I was very, very cautious," Gunderson said, "because this last year has been so up and down, and the kids' throwing programs and game stuff has been so up and down that it was extremely critical we didn't get too far ahead of ourselves and fall into the excitement trap of wanting to go out and do more than what our bodies really wanted us to do."

That concern was warranted, especially when scouting crowds started growing from 30 to 40 and more, with front office officials as high as vice presidents showing up to games.

PERFECT GAME/WORLD WOOD BAT ASSOCIATION COASTAL SUMMER CHAMPIONSHIPS

Event	Site	Champion	Runner-up
14U	Mount Holly, N.C.	Mission Gold 14U	Virginia Venom 14U
15U	High Point, N.C.	5 Star Carolina 15U Johnson	Rawlings Tigers 15U Carver
16U	High Point, N.C.	TPA Nationals 16U Black	Stars Baseball 16U Freeman
17U	High Point, N.C.	Stars Baseball 17U Sisk	Wow Factor Patriots National
18U	Marietta, Ga.	—	

PONY BASEBALL

Event	Site	Champion	Runner-up
Pinto 8U	Mt. Vernon, Ill.	—	—
Mustang 9U	Mt. Vernon, Ill.	—	—
Mustang 10U	Youngsville, La.	—	—
Bronco 11U	Chesterfield, Va.	—	—
Bronco 12U	Laredo, Texas	—	—
Pony 13U	Whittier, Calif.	—	—
Pony 14U	Washington, Pa.	—	—
Colt 16U	Marion, Ill.	—	—
Palomino 18U	Laredo, Texas	—	—

REVIVING BASEBALL IN INNER CITIES (RBI)

Event	Site	Champion	Runner-up
Junior (13-15)	Vero Beach, Fla.	Atlanta Braves RBI	Roberto Clemente RBI
Senior (16-18)	Minnesota	Cincinnati RBI	RBI Austin

U.S. SPECIALTY SPORTS ASSOCIATION (USSSA)

Event	Site	Champion	Runner-up
10U/Majors Elite	Viera, Fla.	Prime Baseball 10U Lujan	SBA Nationals 10U
11U/Majors Elite	Viera, Fla.	Swamp Donkeys 11U Black	11U Scorpions Victus
12U/Majors Elite	Viera, Fla.	Dulin Dodgers Prime	Five Star Elite 12U
13U/Majors Elite	Viera, Fla.	T24 Gamecocks - Black	C35 Clark/Hill
14U/Majors Elite	Viera, Fla.	Puerto Rico by MSD	Lumberjacks

USA BASEBALL

Event	Site	Champion	Runner-up
14U West	Peoria, Ariz.	USA Prime National 14U	Saddleback Cowboys Black
14U East	Cary, N.C.	5 Star National	Canes National
15U West	Peoria, Ari.	MBA Navy	Trosky National
15U East	Cary, N.C.	Elite Squad	5 Star National
16U West	Peoria, Ariz.	TB SoCal Easton	MBA Navy
16U East	Cary, N.C.	Top Tier Roos American	East Coast Sox

"You put a bunch of people behind the backstop with a bunch of radar guns, you know it's tough for young kids to kind of say, 'OK, I am going to really stay within myself,' " Gunderson said. "But I commend the kids, they did a phenomenal job of sticking to their routines."

Thirty-six total players were involved, with some players staying for the entire process and others coming in for a week or just to pitch a game or two. In all, the 3D Sweets included 31 players committed to play for Division I programs. But talent alone was not enough.

"This could only work for this group of guys," Robinson said. "This is a lot more than just 'find good players and have them move here and play.' I have had very good players who this wouldn't have worked with. There is a maturity level, there is a level of engagement, there is a commitment level from the families, there is a commitment level from the kids. All of these things have to link up."

While there was plenty the kids could take away from the off-field experience, they were there to play baseball. In addition to competing in front of dozens of evaluators, players experienced a more beneficial playing environment—both in the quantity of games and the quality of the opposition.

"I think we have hopefully opened up some eyes and some minds to that outside-the-box thinking that this group has exhibited," Robinson said. "This will be a difference-maker in their lives. I have had many scouts tell us that this was a difference-maker for them, that this was huge for them in terms of being able to evaluate in a way they have never been able to evaluate and I think it's going to show come draft day.

"And I think that's the thing that talks louder than anything is, as these guys are flying off the board, why would you not do something like this if your kid is a 2022 or a 2023 for their draft?"

A year after Covid-19 threw everyone's world into chaos, it's strange to hear about anything being difficult in a world without it. But even if an experience like this doesn't come along ever again, it's something the 3D Sweets players will never forget.

Jobe excels as pitcher and hitter

BY ALEXIS BRUDNICKI

Wherever Jackson Jobe went this year, excitement followed.

As the centerpiece for Heritage Hall High, the 18-year-old helped lead his Oklahoma City team to the playoffs, then to regionals and finally onto a state championship victory. Jobe had an incredible regular season, and then somehow found another gear in the final stretch.

As the Chargers' starting shortstop, Jobe hit .469/.592/.927 in the heart of the lineup with seven home runs, five triples, 13 doubles, 21 walks, five strikeouts and 13 stolen bases in 32 games. On the mound, he went 9-0 with a 0.14 ERA and three complete games over 51.2 innings. Jobe walked five and struck out 122.

Those numbers led him not only to be named his team's MVP, and then to become the third overall pick in the 2021 draft, selected by the Tigers, but the performance was also enough to help him win the Baseball America High School Player of the Year award.

"He obviously brings a lot of eyes and attention to our program, and we love having those special players come through who help us succeed and put championship banners on the wall and trophies in the cases," Heritage Hall head coach Jordan Semore said. "That's something you don't find often, and Jackson was one of those guys who came in and completely turned things around for us.

"He was a guy we could really build around and put him in the middle of the lineup and let him do his thing, and with the (pitching) progression he had from junior to senior year, everything fell into place and was a special year for us because he had a guy like Jackson out there leading the way."

"I had a lot more to prove this spring," Jobe said. "So my first few starts were pretty nerve-wracking, but as it came down to it, I got more used to it. I wasn't really worried about the people in the stands, I was more worried about the game."

The number of postseason accolades Jobe has accumulated would suggest that talent and success like his is not often seen among high schoolers, and that his exemplary season stood out among the crowd this year.

"It means a lot being able to represent my

PLAYER OF THE YEAR

PREVIOUS WINNERS

1993: Trot Nixon, OF/LHP, New Hanover HS, Wilmington, N.C.
1994: Doug Million, LHP, Sarasota (Fla.) HS
1995: Ben Davis, C, Malvern (Pa.) Prep
1996: Matt White, RHP, Waynesboro Area (Pa.) HS
1997: Darnell McDonald, OF, Cherry Creek HS, Englewood, Colo.
1998: Drew Henson, 3B/RHP, Brighton (Mich.) HS
1999: Josh Hamilton, OF/LHP, Athens Drive HS, Raleigh, N.C.
2000: Matt Harrington, RHP, Palmdale (Calif.) HS
2001: Joe Mauer, C, Cretin-Derham Hall HS, St. Paul, Minn.
2002: Scott Kazmir, LHP, Cypress Falls HS, Houston
2003: Jeff Allison, RHP, Veterans Memorial HS, Peabody, Mass.
2004: Homer Bailey, RHP, LaGrange (Texas) HS
2005: Justin Upton, SS, Great Bridge HS, Chesapeake, Va.
2006: Adrian Cardenas, SS/2B, Mons. Pace HS, Opa Locka, Fla.
2007: Mike Moustakas, SS, Chatsworth (Calif.) HS
2008: Ethan Martin, RHP/3B, Stephens County HS, Toccoa, Ga.
2009: Bryce Harper, C, Las Vegas HS
2010: Kaleb Cowart, RHP/3B, Cook HS, Adel, Ga.
2011: Dylan Bundy, RHP, Owasso (Okla.) HS
2012: Byron Buxton, OF, Appling County HS, Baxley, Ga.
2013: Clint Frazier, OF, Loganville (Ga.) HS
2014: Alex Jackson, OF, Rancho Bernardo (Calif.) HS
2015: Kyle Tucker, OF, Plant HS, Tampa
2016: Mickey Moniak, OF, La Costa Canyon HS, Carlsbad, Calif.
2017: MacKenzie Gore, LHP, Whiteville (N.C.) HS
2018: Cole Winn, RHP, Orange (Calif.) Lutheran HS
2019: Bobby Witt Jr., SS, Colleyville (Texas) Heritage HS

family and my school and the program and all the people who support me," Jobe said. "It's been a really fun year and I'm really thankful . . . It was a long season. We didn't get to play last year and we thought we had a pretty good shot last year. We all came out and felt like we had something to prove, and we ended up proving it. There's not much more you can ask for."

As he continues to move forward beyond Heritage Hall, the High School Player of the Year understands that even foregoing his commitment to Mississippi would certainly not mean even the briefest of pauses in furthering his education.

"I'm excited to be able to learn more about the game and continue maturing as a person," Jobe said. "This year I've learned a lot about not only pitching, but myself, and being able to come home after each game and being able to learn something from it.

"Baseball's more fun than anything else I do, so I'm enjoying the ride and we'll see what happens."

ALL-AMERICA TEAM

Harry Ford

Jackson Jobe

FIRST TEAM

Pos.	Player, School	YR.	AVG	AB	R	H	2B	3B	HR	RBI	SB	Drafted
C	Harry Ford, North Cobb HS, Kennesaw, Ga.	Sr.	.341	88	25	30	11	2	5	23	16	Mariners (1)
INF	Brady House, Winder-Barrow HS, Winder, Ga.	Sr.	.549	91	52	50	14	0	8	20	21	Nationals (1)
INF	Wes Kath, Desert Mountain HS, Scottsdale, Ariz.	Sr.	.486	72	34	35	9	4	11	22	2	White Sox (2)
INF	Jordan Lawlar, Dallas Jesuit HS, Dallas, Texas	Sr.	.412	97	46	40	5	4	6	37	32	D-backs (1)
INF	Marcelo Mayer, Eastlake HS, Chula Vista, Calif.	Sr.	.378	90	42	34	5	0	13	40	17	Red Sox (1)
OF	Daylen Lile, Trinity HS, Louisville, Ky.	Sr.	.511	88	-	45	20	8	14	48	8	Nationals (2)
OF	Braden Montgomery, Madison (Miss.) Central. HS	Sr.	.479	96	-	46	7	5	7	50	17	Undrafted
OF	Will Taylor, Dutch Fork HS, Irmo, S.C.	Sr.	.441	59	29	26	6	1	6	25	-	Rangers (19)
DH	Peyton Stovall, Haughton (La.) HS	Sr.	.512	84	50	43	7	1	12	39	9	Undrafted

Pos.	Player, School	YR.	W	L	ERA	IP	H	R	ER	BB	SO	Drafted
P	Bubba Chandler, North Oconee HS, Bogart, Ga.	Sr.	8	1	1.61	45	22	15	8	21	96	Pirates (3)
P	Jackson Jobe, Heritage Hall HS, Oklahoma City, Okla.	Sr.	9	0	0.14	52	15	-	-	5	122	Tigers (1)
P	Frank Mozzicato, East Catholic HS, Manchester, Conn.	Sr.	9	0	0.13	56	9	2	1	22	135	Royals (1)
P	Andrew Painter, Calvary Christian HS, Fort Lauderdale	Sr.	6	1	0.31	45	18	5	2	14	91	Phillies (1)
P	Hagen Smith, Bullard (Texas) HS	Sr.	11	0	0.19	73	7	2	2	26	168	Undrafted

SECOND TEAM

Pos.	Player, School	YR.	AVG	AB	R	H	2B	3B	HR	RBI	SB	Drafted
C	Joe Mack, Williamsville East HS, East Amherst, N.Y.	Sr.	.500	56	41	28	8	1	8	22	-	Marlins (1s)
INF	Izaac Pacheco, Friendswood (Texas) HS	Sr.	.585	82	41	48	14	4	6	49	-	Tigers (2)
INF	Colson Montgomery, Southridge HS, Huntingburg, Ind.	Sr.	.407	59	38	24	9	1	6	21	23	White Sox (1)
INF	Kahlil Watson, Wake Forest (N.C.) HS	Sr.	.513	39	24	20	6	1	6	14	15	Marlins (1)
INF	Carson Williams, Torrey Pines HS, San Diego	Sr.	.500	72	31	36	8	2	8	27	-	Rays (1)
OF	Benny Montgomery, Red Land HS, Lewisberry, Pa.	Sr.	-	-	-	-	-	-	-	-	-	Rockies (1)
OF	Joshua Baez, Southfield HS, Brookline, Mass.	Sr.	.415	41	24	17	2	0	3	13	-	Cardinals (2)
OF	Jay Allen, Carroll Catholic, Fort Pierce, Fla.	Sr.	.422	83	35	35	9	1	3	17	-	Reds (1)
DH	Cam Butler, Big Valley Christian HS, Modesto, Calif.	Sr.	.736	72	52	53	18	4	12	50	27	White Sox (15)

Pos.	Player, School	YR.	W	L	ERA	IP	H	R	ER	BB	SO	Drafted
P	Anthony Solometo, Eustace Prep, Pennsauken, N.J.	Sr.	-	-	0.28	33	5	1	1	5	64	Pirates (1)
P	Chase Petty, Mainland Regional HS, Linwood, N.J.	Sr.	5	1	1.15	49	-	-	8	-	99	Twins (1)
P	Thatcher Hurd, Mira Costa HS, Manhattan Beach, Calif.	Sr.	5	1	1.15	39	14	9	5	21	57	Undrafted
P	Joshua Hartle, Reagan HS, Pfafftown, N.C.	Sr.	9	0	0.52	54	15	8	4	8	88	Undrafted
P	Ben Kudrna, Blue Valley Southwest HS, Overland Park	Sr.	2	0	1.59	45	23	10	8	10	84	Royals (2)

MIKE JANES/FOUR SEAM IMAGES

HIGH SCHOOL

DRAFT

Strong HS Shortstops Lead 20-Round Draft

BY CARLOS COLLAZO

Baseball largely put Covid-19 behind it this spring, but the 2021 draft class still felt the ripple effects of the pandemic. While it won't be remembered as the Covid draft in the same way the five-round draft in 2020 was, there's an argument to be made that the 2021 draft class is equally impacted by the virus—if not moreso.

Scouts wondered if that would be the case a year ago, as Covid largely blew up the summer evaluation period for scouts and players alike, especially among the college ranks. No Collegiate National Team. No Cape Cod League. No 18U National Team. While many high school events took place in the South, players from the West Coast were more limited in their options and scouts themselves had to miss events entirely due to personnel restrictions (and in some cases layoffs) and further step into the world of video scouting by writing reports remotely.

That dynamic has led to plenty of volatility during the season as players who previously didn't have a chance to establish a track record or baseline of performance stood out, and others with some history struggled. Teams were left to try to sort out the signal from the noise by more heavily relying on area scouts and their history and/

Jordan Lawlar was one of eight prep shortstops selected in the first round.

or adjusting their models to incorporate a much smaller sample of college stats.

Those factors—on top of the exceptional depth of the 2021 class thanks to the five-round draft last year that brought back many players who would have been drafted in a typical year—

FIRST-ROUND BONUS PROGRESSION

MLB's negotiated deal with the MLB Players Association to cut the draft from 40 rounds to just five for the 2020 draft also came with an agreement to use the same draft slots as 2019. Typically slot values are tied with increasing revenues around the league and the last few years that increase has hovered around 4%. This year that number was static, due to the Covid year that locked in draft bonus values for two years. While team spending in the first round is still over $4 million, the 2021 year is a slight decrease from the average bonuses value in 2020.

After the first draft in 1965, first-round bonuses rose by an average of just 0.6% annually for the rest of the 1960s and 5.2% per year in the 1970s. Bonus inflation picked up in the 1980s, averaging 10.2% annually, and soared to 26.9% per year in the 1990s.

Below are the annual averages for first-round bonuses since the draft started in 1965. The 1996 total does not include four players who became free agents through a loophole in the draft rules.

Year	Average	Change	Year	Average	Change	Year	Average	Change	Year	Average	Change
1965	$42,516	—	1979	$68,094	0.20%	1993	$613,037	27.20%	2007	$2,098,083	8.50%
1966	$44,430	4.50%	1980	$74,025	8.70%	1994	$790,357	28.90%	2008	$2,458,714	17.20%
1967	$42,898	-3.40%	1981	$78,573	6.10%	1995	$918,019	16.10%	2009	$2,434,800	-1.00%
1968	$43,850	2.20%	1982	$82,615	5.10%	1996*	$944,404	2.90%	2010	$2,220,966	-8.80%
1969	$43,504	-0.80%	1983	$87,236	5.60%	1997	$1,325,536	40.40%	2011	$2,653,375	19.50%
1970	$45,230	3.90%	1984	$105,391	20.80%	1998	$1,637,667	23.10%	2012	$2,475,167	-6.70%
1971	$45,197	-0.10%	1985	$118,115	12.10%	1999	$1,809,767	10.50%	2013	$2,641,538	6.70%
1972	$44,952	-0.50%	1986	$116,300	-1.60%	2000	$1,872,586	3.50%	2014	$2,612,109	-1.10%
1973	$48,832	8.60%	1987	$128,480	10.50%	2001	$2,154,280	15.00%	2015	$2,774,945	6.23%
1974	$53,333	9.20%	1988	$142,540	10.90%	2002	$2,106,793	-2.20%	2016	$2,897,557	4.42%
1975	$49.33	-7.50%	1989	$176,008	23.50%	2003	$1,765,667	-16.20%	2017	$3,880,723	25.4%
1976	$49,631	0.60%	1990	$252,577	43.50%	2004	$1,958,448	10.90%	2018	$3,754,123	-3.37%
1977	$48,813	-1.60%	1991	$365,396	44.70%	2005	$2,018,000	3.00%	2019	$3,791,729	1.01%
1978	$67,892	39.10%	1992	$481,893	31.90%	2006	$1,933,333	-4.20%	2020	$4,080,307	7.61%
									2021	$4,009,424	-1.74%

have led to less consensus on the class than ever.

"This year I have no expectations because it is so wide open," said one scouting director. "When I walk into that draft room the night of the draft I wouldn't be surprised if it was completely all over the place in terms of where guys go. Just not a lot of consensus."

There's not a consensus No. 1 player in the class and instead a group of five players are generally seen as the top tier of talent. That group includes toolsy prep shortstops Jordan Lawlar and Marcelo Mayer, renowned Vanderbilt righthanders Jack Leiter and Kumar Rocker and Louisville catcher Henry Davis, who was one of the best performers of the season.

After a full spring, the high school class looks more impressive than the college group. The 2021 class has a chance to be one of the best prep shortstop classes we've ever seen, with four potential top-10 picks at the position and a slew of intriguing depth options as well. Outside of the shortstops there is a bounty of up-the-middle position players with unusually impressive athleticism and tools.

The high school pitching group, led by righthanders Jackson Jobe and Andrew Painter, seems close to average, with several legitimate first-round talents and perhaps more lefthanded pitching depth than in an average class.

Scouting departments were worried about the college hitting class entering the year, but there was hope that throughout the spring players would step forward and make it at least average. That doesn't appear to have been the case. Most evaluators see the college hitters as the weakest demographic of the group—with a notable absence of shortstops and corner profiles with power—and it's a solidly below-average college hitting class overall.

The college pitching saw attrition during the season as potential top-10 players like Gunnar Hoglund and Jaden Hill suffered season-ending injuries, but the group seems solid or a tick above-average on talent—but significantly below-average in terms of innings and established track record.

Overall, the 2021 class seems weaker than teams would prefer at the very top, but with elite depth that might leave organizations more excited with their draftees on Days Two and Three than in a typical year.

Modern Record For HS Shortstops

We wrote back in March that this year's draft class had a chance to be historic for the prep shortstop demographic and that played out very

BONUS SPENDING BY TEAM

After breaking the bonus record in back-to-back years in 2018 and 2019, overall bonus spending for teams fell off a cliff during the 2020 and 2021 seasons. The 2020 draft was shortened to five rounds and resulted in a 25% drop in overall spending from the record 2019 year.

Going from five rounds to 20 meant the 2021 draft saw a 22% spending increase year over year, but the total spending in 2021 was still well short of the 2019 figure. The spending changes have largely impacted later draft picks, as top players continue to get large and record-breaking bonuses, while the shortened draft and shrunken minor league system caps the number of players entering professional baseball.

The Tigers spent more than any other club in 2021, thanks to owning a supplemental first round pick and also going to the 5% overage limit on their bonus pool, on top of handing out $100,000 or bigger bonuses to each of their 11-20 round draft picks. The Pirates had the first overall pick and had an extra pick in the second supplemental round and pooled their money at the top of the draft to hand out four signing bonuses over $1 million for C Henry Davis, LHP Anthony Solometo, OF Lonnie White and RHP Bubba Chandler.

The Astros spent the fewest of any team and didn't have a first or second round pick due to sign stealing penalties.

TEAM	2021	2020	2019
Tigers	$16,165,700	$13,978,600	$11,980,800
Pirates	$15,938,700	$11,067,400	$12,111,400
Reds	$13,638,300	$8,546,000	$11,273,400
Rangers	$13,362,000	$7,275,000	$12,858,300
Royals	$12,557,300	$12,520,000	$14,452,200
Orioles	$12,514,700	$13,672,300	$15,168,600
Diamondbacks	$11,946,900	$7,184,900	$17,045,500
Rockies	$11,372,200	$10,332,800	$8,073,300
Marlins	$11,257,290	$12,004,700	$14,832,700
Red Sox	$10,761,900	$5,250,000	$6,369,200
Angels	$10,722,500	$6,454,200	$9,751,300
Brewers	$10,623,400	$5,417,900	$6,908,200
Nationals	$10,106,600	$6,647,400	$7,683,580
Phillies	$9,530,600	$5,700,000	$8,779,800
Cardinals	$9,445,000	$8,290,000	$8,205,000
Mariners	$9,359,600	$9,961,100	$8,927,500
Giants	$9,213,200	$9,457,500	$10,384,500
Twins	$8,845,900	$4,330,000	$10,892,800
Rays	$8,694,800	$7,474,200	$11,685,800
Indians	$8,468,400	$7,390,000	$8,010,505
Yankees	$8,089,800	$3,687,400	$9,327,300
White Sox	$8,087,000	$7,757,500	$13,633,200
Padres	$7,763,300	$11,180,004	$13,010,900
Cubs	$7,748,300	$6,866,800	$6,987,900
Braves	$7,590,000	$3,991,800	$14,338,000
Athletics	$7,196,500	$5,447,400	$6,696,900
Blue Jays	$6,884,200	$10,202,325	$10,677,000
Dodgers	$5,754,000	$6,224,000	$10,539,300
Mets	$4,342,900	$7,499,000	$9,497,000
Astros	$3,427,500	$2,283,000	$6,462,099
Total	**$291,408,490**	**$238,092,829**	**$316,563,984**
Average	**$9,713,616**	**$7,936,428**	**$10,552,133**

obviously on Day One.

Eight high school shortstops were selected in the first round, matching the all-time record, set in 1971. This year's group is more impressive when you consider the context of the draft in the 70s and how little college players were valued collectively by the industry.

Perhaps it's also fair to consider the context of a down college bat year in 2021 that likely allowed some of the later-drafted first round prep shortstops to slip inside, but we've long thought the currency of this year's draft class was in the toolsy, athletic shortstops from the high school ranks.

Entering the draft we thought there was a good chance we would see the second year ever to have four prep shortstops taken among the top 10 picks, but Marcelo Mayer and Jordan Lawlar—the top two players on the BA 500—were the only two to fit in that range.

Brady House and Kahlil Watson slipped into the middle of the first round, but those four players alone still matched the previous all-time mark for prep shortstops in the Baseball America era (from 1981 onward).

At least four high school shortstops have been selected in the first round in the draft on just two previous occasions since the turn of the century—in 2016 and 2019.

The selections of Colson Montgomery (22), Max Muncy (25), Jackson Merrill (27) and Carson Williams (28) in the final third of the first round meant the 2021 class blew any other modern draft class out of the water when it comes to the demographic.

Vanderbilt righthander Jack Leiter was the first pitcher off the board at No. 2 overall.

HIGHEST BONUSES EVER

Five of the top six players drafted in 2021 joined the list of the highest bonuses ever: top four picks Henry Davis, Jack Leiter, Jackson Jobe and Marcelo Mayer, as well as No. 6 overall pick Jordan Lawlar. No player topped the all-time bonus record that Spencer Torkelson set in 2020, when the Tigers signed him for $8,416,300 as the No. 1 overall pick.

Player, Pos.	Team, Year (Pick)	Bonus
Spencer Torkelson, 1B	Tigers, 2020 (No. 1)	$8,416,300
Adley Rutschman, C	Orioles, 2019 (No. 1)	$8,100,000
Gerrit Cole, RHP	Pirates, 2011 (No. 1)	$8,000,000
Jack Leiter, RHP	Rangers, 2021 (No. 2)	$7,922,000
Bobby Witt Jr., SS	Royals, 2019 (No. 2)	$7,787,400
Stephen Strasburg, RHP	Nationals, 2009 (No. 1)	* $7,500,000
Bubba Starling, OF	Royals, 2011 (No. 5)	+ $7,500,000
Casey Mize, RHP	Tigers, 2018 (No. 1)	$7,500,000
Hunter Greene, RHP/SS	Reds, 2017 (No. 2)	$7,230,000
Andrew Vaughn, 1B	White Sox, 2019 (No. 3)	$7,221,200
Joey Bart, C	Giants, 2018 (No. 2)	$7,025,000
Brendan McKay, 1B/LHP	Rays, 2017 (No. 4)	$7,005,000
Austin Martin, SS	Blue Jays, 2020 (No. 5)	$7,000,825
Kyle Wright, RHP	Braves, 2017 (No. 5)	$7,000,000
Jackson Jobe, RHP	Tigers, 2021 (No. 3)	$6,900,000
Royce Lewis, SS	Twins, 2017 (No. 1)	$6,725,000
Jordan Lawlar, SS	D-backs, 2021 (No. 6)	$6,713,300
Kris Bryant, 3B	Cubs, 2013 (No. 2)	$6,708,400
MacKenzie Gore, LHP	Padres, 2017 (No. 3)	$6,700,000
Max Meyer, RHP	Marlins, 2020 (No. 3)	$6,700,000
JJ Bleday, OF	Marlins, 2019 (No. 4)	$6,670,000
Marcelo Mayer, SS	Red Sox, 2021 (No. 4)	$6,664,000
Asa Lacy, LHP	Royals, 2020 (No. 4)	$6,670,000
Carlos Rodon, LHP	White Sox, 2014 (No. 3)	$6,582,000
Jameson Taillon, RHP	Pirates, 2010 (No. 2)	$6,500,000
Dansby Swanson, SS	D-backs, 2015 (No. 1)	$6,500,000
Henry Davis, C	Pirates, 2021 (No. 1)	$6,500,000
Nick Madrigal, SS	White Sox, 2018 (No. 4)	$6,411,000
Danny Hultzen, LHP	Mariners, 2011 (No. 2)	* $6,350,000

*Part of major league contract. +Bonus spread over multiple years under MLB two-sport provisions

In several years, it's possible the 2021 class will be remembered for a player or players who have gone on to excel at the major league level, but for now 2021 seems like the year of the prep shortstop.

Kahlil Watson: Steal Of The Draft?

Speaking of prep shortstops, how about that Marlins pick?

Before the draft got started, it seemed like Kahlil Watson had a better chance to become the first overall pick than to slide all the way down the board to No. 16. That is to Miami's benefit, as it landed a top-six talent in the class and far and away the toolsiest player in that range of the first round.

Marlins scouting director DJ Svihlik summed up our own thoughts nicely when asked about whether or not he expected Watson to be available at No. 16.

"I would have said you're crazy, no way, not going to happen," Svihlik said. "Players move around the board for a number of different reasons. Like I said when we were on the call last time, the draft, very dynamic, this was a really, really challenging draft. Teams manage their drafts in different ways. You don't understand how everybody does it, how everybody has their own unique style.

"So I think when you add all those things together, players just tend to move around, and a player that's supposed to go No. 4, he goes No. 8, and a player who's supposed to go eighth might go 16th, and so on and so forth. For the most part, you look at the names that came off the board, all the right names came off the board, but it's very, very difficult to predict the exact order. And if you look at the top 14 or 15 picks, that's where you saw a lot of variety and changing of positions. So we just always take the best player that we have on the board at the time, and that's just how it fell."

It shouldn't be too surprising that the Marlins were able to land a talent that fit higher on the board, as they did have a pick in the competitive balance round and the 11th largest bonus pool, but still—it is surprising a player of the caliber of Watson made it that far.

He was solidly among the group of eight or so players who most teams expected to go among the top 10 picks, in some order or another.

"He was absolutely one of (the players we didn't expect to be available)," Svihlik said. "And I spent the last week down here with my staff and they probably got really tired of listening to me do it, but we constantly stress test our lists and our order, and we constantly ask the question of the whole fair catch. We did it again this morning. We went through our top of our board and said who are we going to fair catch? We know that a player is going to fall, who's it going to be? Is he too high? So we evaluate all the way to the very end, as more and more information comes in, and he was not a player that we anticipated was going to fall. I guess he would have been second maybe, or third, but he was not a player that we anticipated to fall."

While Watson falling to the Marlins was decided just as much by the teams in front of Miami, it's hard to not think the Marlins scouting department just walked away with the best pick of the draft after day one.

Surprise Pick At No. 7

There were plenty of surprises in the top 15 picks, but none came close to matching the jaw-dropping nature of Frank Mozzicato, ranked 42nd on Baseball America's Top 500 Draft Rankings.

Mozzicato had plenty of helium this spring thanks to his ability to consistently spin a plus curve. While his spring performance was sensational, it was expected to push him more into the mid to late first round consideration at best.

NO. 1 OVERALL PICKS

Year Team: Player, Pos., School	Bonus
1965 Athletics: Rick Monday, OF, Arizona State	$100,000
1966 Mets: Steve Chilcott, C, Antelope Valley HS, Lancaster, Calif.	$75,000
1967 Yankees: Ron Blomberg, 1B, Druid Hills HS, Atlanta	$65,000
1968 Mets: Tim Foli, SS, Notre Dame HS, Sherman Oaks, Calif.	$74,000
1969 Senators: Jeff Burroughs, OF, Centennial HS, Long Beach	$88,000
1970 Padres: Mike Ivie, C, Walker HS, Atlanta	$75,000
1971 White Sox: Danny Goodwin, C, Peoria (Ill.) HS	Did Not Sign
1972 Padres: Dave Roberts, 3B, Oregon	$70,000
1973 Rangers: David Clyde, LHP, Westchester HS, Texas	*$65,000
1974 Padres: Bill Almon, SS, Brown	*$90,000
1975 Angels: Danny Goodwin, C, Southern	*$125,000
1976 Astros: Floyd Bannister, LHP, Arizona State	$100,000
1977 White Sox: Harold Baines, OF, St. Michaels (Md.) HS	$32,000
1978 Braves: Bob Horner, 3B, Arizona State	*$162,000
1979 Mariners: Al Chambers, 1B, Harris HS, Harrisburg, Pa.	$60,000
1980 Mets: Darryl Strawberry, OF, Crenshaw HS, Los Angeles	$152,500
1981 Mariners: Mike Moore, RHP, Oral Roberts	$100,000
1982 Cubs: Shawon Dunston, SS, Jefferson HS, New York	$135,000
1983 Twins: Tim Belcher, RHP, Mount Vernon Nazarene (Ohio)	Did Not Sign
1984 Mets: Shawn Abner, OF, Mechanicsburg (Pa.) HS	$150,500
1985 Brewers: B.J. Surhoff, C, North Carolina	$150,000
1986 Pirates: Jeff King, 3B, Arkansas	$180,000
1987 Mariners: Ken Griffey Jr., OF, Moeller HS, Cincinnati	$160,000
1988 Padres: Andy Benes, RHP, Evansville	$235,000
1989 Orioles: Ben McDonald, RHP, Louisiana State	*$350,000
1990 Braves: Chipper Jones, SS, The Bolles School, Jacksonville	$275,000
1991 Yankees: Brien Taylor, LHP, East Carteret HS, Beaufort, N.C.	$1,550,000
1992 Astros: Phil Nevin, 3B, Cal State Fullerton	$700,000
1993 Mariners: Alex Rodriguez, SS, Westminster Christian HS, Miami	*$1,000,000
1994 Mets: Paul Wilson, RHP, Florida State	$1,550,000
1995 Angels: Darin Erstad, OF, Nebraska	$1,575,000
1996 Pirates: Kris Benson, RHP, Clemson	$2,000,000
1997 Tigers: Matt Anderson, RHP, Tigers	$2,505,000
1998 Phillies: Pat Burrell, 3B, Miami	*$3,150,000
1999 Devil Rays: Josh Hamilton, OF, Athens Drive HS, Raleigh	$3,960,000
2000 Marlins: Adrian Gonzalez, 1B, Eastlake HS, Chula Vista, Calif.	$3,000,000
2001 Twins: Joe Mauer, C, Cretin-Derham Hall, St. Paul	$5,150,000
2002 Pirates: Bryan Bullington, RHP, Ball State	$4,000,000
2003 Devil Rays: Delmon Young, OF, Camarillo (Calif.) HS	*$3,700,000
2004 Padres: Matt Bush, SS, Mission Bay HS, San Diego	$3,150,000
2005 D-backs: Justin Upton, SS, Great Bridge HS, Chesapeake, Va.	$6,100,000
2006 Royals: Luke Hochevar, RHP, Fort Worth (American Assoc.)	*$3,500,000
2007 Devil Rays: David Price, LHP, Vanderbilt	*$5,600,000
2008 Rays: Tim Beckham, SS, Griffin (Ga.) HS	$6,150,000
2009 Nationals: Stephen Strasburg, RHP, San Diego State	*$7,500,000
2010 Nationals: Bryce Harper, OF, JC of Southern Nevada	*$6,250,000
2011 Pirates: Gerrit Cole, RHP, UCLA	$8,000,000
2012 Astros: Carlos Correa, SS, Puerto Rico Baseball Acad., Gurabo, P.R.	$4,800,000
2013 Astros: Mark Appel, RHP, Stanford	$6,350,000
2014 Astros: Brady Aiken, LHP, Cathedral Catholic, San Diego	Did Not Sign
2015 D-backs: Dansby Swanson, SS, Vanderbilt	$6,500,000
2016 Phillies: Mickey Moniak, OF, La Costa Canyon HS, Carlsbad, Calif.	$6,100,000
2017 Twins: Royce Lewis, SS, JSerra Catholic HS, San Juan Capistrano, Calif.	$6,750,000
2018 Tigers: Casey Mize, RHP, Auburn	$7,500,000
2019 Orioles: Adley Rutschman, C, Oregon State	$8,100,000
2020 Tigers: Spencer Torkelson, 3B, Arizona State	$8,416,300
2021 Pirates: Henry Davis, C, Louisville	$6,500,000

Part of major league contract.

Instead he was the third pitcher off the board, ahead of all but one college pitcher.

"I'm speechless right now. I couldn't be more excited," Mozzicato said. "It was a little surprising. Six months ago I didn't think I'd be in this position."

The MLB draft does not allow teams to trade first-round picks, so if the Royals really liked Mozzicato, their only realistic shot to get him was with the seventh pick, as there was a chance he could be gone before Kansas City picked in the second round.

"Every draft is unique. They are all different," Royals GM Dayton Moore said. "We felt that going in, that if it fell the way it did up top it may be beneficial for us to factor in looking at all 20 rounds. The value that a lot of players put on themselves economically, it may be a wise strategy to not only take the best upside but also maximize what we can do later on with the other 19 selections."

So the answer to why the Royals took Mozzicato as high as they did very well will likely be answered on Monday. The Royals did something similar in 2013 when they took Hunter Dozier with the 13th pick. Dozier signed for $2.2 million, taking less money than the eight first-round picks who were picked after him. That year, the Royals selected Sean Manaea with their supplemental first-round pick and paid him $3.3 million.

There was no guarantee that the Royals would do something like that this time, but Moore made a point of noting that he didn't want to explain everything yet for strategic reasons with the draft still underway.

Fastball Metrics Playing A Role?

Texas RHP Ty Madden was supposed to be the player to break a surprising streak for Texas. No Longhorn player had been a first-round pick since RHP Taylor Jungmann in 2011.

The streak continues. Madden slid to the competitive balance round. The Tigers eventually ended his drop at pick 32.

Madden came into the draft with fastball metrics that don't fit what teams are looking for in 2021. He has plenty of velocity, but as we wrote last week, he struggles to beat hitters at the top of the zone.

Apparently that turned off enough teams that Madden fell out of the first round. It also means that the Tigers pulled off quite a first day of the draft. Detroit drafted Jackson Jobe, the consensus top high school arm in the draft class, with the No. 3 pick, and then added a college pitcher with

THE BONUS RECORD

Rick Monday, the No. 1 overall pick in baseball's first draft in 1965, signed with the Athletics for $100,000—a figure that no draftee bettered for a decade. The record has been broken many times since, including in 2019, when Adley Rutschman signed with the Orioles as the No. 1 overall pick for $8,100,000. Spencer Torkelson broke the record immediately, signing for $8,416,300 as the No. 1 pick in the 2020 draft with the Tigers..

The longest bonus record stretch dates back to Todd Demeter, whose $208,000 bonus in 1979 held the mark for nine years until 1988 when Andy Benes topped him with a $235,000 bonus.

The list below represents only cash bonuses and doesn't include guaranteed money from major league deals, college scholarship plans or incentives. It also considers only players who signed with the clubs that drafted them and doesn't include draft picks who signed after being granted free agency.

Year	Player, Pos. , Club (Round)	Bonus
1965	Rick Monday, OF, Athletics (1)	$100,000
1975	Danny Goodwin, C, Angels (1)	$125,000
1978	Kirk Gibson, OF, Tigers (1)	$150,000
	*Bob Horner, 3B, Braves (1)	$162,000
1979	Todd Demeter, 1B, Yankees (2)	$208,000
1988	Andy Benes, RHP, Padres (1)	$235,000
1989	Tyler Houston, C, Braves (1)	$241,500
	*Ben McDonald, RHP, Orioles (1)	$350,000
	*John Olerud, 1B, Blue Jays (3)	$575,000
1991	Mike Kelly, OF, Braves (1)	$575,000
	Brien Taylor, LHP, Yankees (1)	$1,550,000
1994	Paul Wilson, RHP, Mets (1)	$1,550,000
	Josh Booty, 3B, Marlins (1)	$1,600,000
1996	Kris Benson, RHP, Pirates (1)	$2,000,000
1997	Rick Ankiel, LHP, Cardinals (2)	$2,500,000
	Matt Anderson, RHP, Tigers (1)	$2,505,000
1998	*J.D. Drew, OF, Cardinals (1)	$3,000,000
	*Pat Burrell, 3B, Phillies (1)	$3,150,000
	Mark Mulder, LHP, Athletics (1)	$3,200,000
	Corey Patterson, OF, Cubs (1)	$3,700,000
1999	Josh Hamilton, OF, Devil Rays (1)	$3,960,000
2000	Joe Borchard, OF, White Sox (1)	$5,300,000
2005	Justin Upton, SS, D-backs (1)	$6,100,000
2008	Tim Beckham, SS, Rays (1)	$6,150,000
	Buster Posey, C, Giants (1)	$6,200,000
2009	Donavan Tate, OF, Padres (1)	$6,250,000
	*Stephen Strasburg, RHP, Nationals (1)	$7,500,000
2011	Gerrit Cole, RHP, Pirates (1)	$8,000,000
2019	Adley Rutschman, C, Orioles (1)	$8,100,000
2020	Spencer Torkelson, 3B, Tigers (1)	$8,416,300

Part of major league contract.

a very long track record of success in the competitive balance round.

Despite picking No. 3 and No. 32, Detroit landed two of the top four pitchers in the class and was the only team that managed to land not one, but multiple top-12 talents.

Notable Preps Opt Out Of Draft

While it's not unprecedented for high school players to opt out of the draft or ask teams not to select them, a large group of notable prep talents excused themselves from the goings on this year.

Delaware outfielder Lorenzo Carrier was one of the first high school players to opt out of the 2021 draft, but he was followed shortly thereafter by California prospects Nick McLain, Cody

BONUSES VS. PICK VALUES

The assigned slots for the 2021 draft have remained stagnant for the last two years and after Adley Rutschman and Spencer Torkelson topped the $8 million mark in 2019 and 2020, no player exceeded that signing bonus amount in 2021. Just five players exceeded the $6 million mark and four of those players came from the high school demographic.

The top-50 bonuses added up to $161,251,790 compared to a slot value of $158,573,300 for those picks. That overage came in spite of the deal-hunting that teams explored among the top picks, as seven of the nine first picks (not counting Kumar Rocker, who didn't agree to terms with the Mets at No. 10) signed to underslot or slot deals. By comparison, when MLB unilaterally determined slot recommendations in the last year of the previous Collective Bargaining Agreement (2011) but had no enforcement mechanism, the total of the first 50 bonuses ($120.5 million) dwarfed that of the top 50 slot values ($70 million).

Player, Pos., Team (Round/Overall Pick)	Bonus	Pick Value
1. Jack Leiter, RHP, Vanderbilt (1st round/No. 2)	$7,922,000	$7,789,900
2. Jackson Jobe, RHP, Heritage Hall HS, Oklahoma City (1st round/No. 3)	$6,900,000	$7,221,200
3. Jordan Lawlar, SS, Dallas Jesuit HS (1st round/No. 6)	$6,713,300	$5,742,900
4. Marcelo Mayer, SS, Eastlake HS, Chula Vista, Calif. (1st round/No. 4)	$6,664,000	$6,664,000
5. Henry Davis, C, Louisville (1st round/No. 1)	$6,500,000	$8,415,300
6. Benny Montgomery, OF, Red Land HS, Lewisberry, Pa. (1st round/No. 8)	$5,000,000	$5,176,900
7. Brady House, SS, Winder-Barrow HS, Winder, Ga. (1st round/No. 11)	$5,000,000	$4,547,500
8. Colton Cowser, OF, Sam Houston State (1st round/No. 5)	$4,900,000	$6,180,700
9. Matt McLain, SS, UCLA (1st round/No. 17)	$4,625,000	$3,609,700
10. Kahlil Watson, SS, Wake Forest (N.C.) HS (1st round/No. 16)	$4,540,790	$3,745,500
11. Harry Ford, C, North Cobb HS, Kennesaw, Ga. (1st round/No. 12)	$4,366,400	$4,366,400
12. Sal Frelick, OF, Boston College (1st round/No. 15)	$4,000,000	$3,885,800
13. Andrew Painter, RHP, Calvary Christian HS, Fort Lauderdale, Fla. (1st round/No. 13)	$3,900,000	$4,197,300
14. Sam Bachman, RHP, Miami (Ohio) (1st round/No. 9)	$3,847,500	$4,949,100
15. Will Bednar, RHP, Mississippi State (1st round/No. 14)	$3,647,500	$4,036,800
16. Frank Mozzicato, LHP, East Catholic HS, Manchester, Conn. (1st round/No. 7)	$3,547,500	$5,432,400
17. Gunnar Hoglund, RHP, Mississippi (1st round/No. 19)	$3,247,500	$3,359,000
18. Jordan Wicks, LHP, Kansas State (1st round/No. 21)	$3,132,300	$3,132,300
19. Colson Montgomery, SS, Southridge HS, Huntingburg, Ind. (1st round/No. 22)	$3,027,000	$3,027,000
20. Trey Sweeney, SS, Eastern Illinois (1st round/No. 20)	$3,000,000	$3,242,900
21. Bubba Chandler, RHP, North Oconee HS, Bogart, Ga. (3rd round/No. 72)	$3,000,000	$870,700
22. Ben Kudrna, RHP, Blue Valley Southwest HS, Overland Park, Kan. (2nd round/No. 43)	$2,997,500	$1,729,800
23. Max Muncy, SS, Thousand Oaks (Calif.) HS (1st round/No. 25)	$2,850,000	$2,740,300
24. Anthony Solometo, LHP, Bishop Eustace Prep HS, Pennsauken, N.J. (2nd round/No. 37)	$2,797,500	$1,999,300
25. Michael McGreevy, RHP, UC Santa Barbara (1st round/No. 18)	$2,750,000	$3,481,300
26. Izaac Pacheco, SS, Friendswood (Texas) HS (2nd round/No. 39)	$2,750,000	$1,906,800
27. Ryan Cusick, RHP, Wake Forest (1st round/No. 24)	$2,700,000	$2,831,300
28. James Wood, OF, IMG Academy, Bradenton, Fla. (2nd round/No. 62)	$2,600,000	$1,102,700
29. Chase Petty, RHP, Mainland Regional HS, Linwood, N.J. (1st round/No. 26)	$2,500,000	$2,653,400
30. Joe Mack, C, Williamsville East HS, East Amherst, N.Y. (supp. 1st round/No. 31)	$2,500,000	$2,312,000
31. Ty Madden, RHP, Texas (supp. 1st round/No. 32)	$2,500,000	$2,257,300
32. Jay Allen, OF, Carroll Catholic HS, Fort Pierce, Fla. (1st round/No. 30)	$2,397,500	$2,365,500
33. Carson Williams, SS, Torrey Pines HS, San Diego (1st round/No. 28)	$2,347,500	$2,493,900
34. Gavin Williams, RHP, East Carolina (1st round/No. 23)	$2,250,000	$2,926,800
35. Joshua Baez, OF, Dexter Southfield HS, Brookline, Mass. (2nd round/No. 54)	$2,250,000	$1,338,500
36. Tyler Black, 2B, Wright State (supp. 1st round/No. 33)	$2,200,000	$2,202,200
37. Maddux Bruns, LHP, UMS-Wright Prep, Mobile, Ala. (1st round/No. 29)	$2,197,500	$2,424,600
38. Cooper Kinney, 2B, Baylor HS, Chattanooga (supp. 1st round/No. 34)	$2,145,600	$2,148,100
39. James Triantos, 3B, Madison HS, Vienna, Va. (2nd round/No. 56)	$2,100,000	$1,276,400
40. Mat Nelson, C, Florida State (supp. 1st round/No. 35)	$2,093,300	$2,095,800
41. Jackson Merrill, SS, Severna Park (Md.) HS (1st round/No. 27)	$1,800,000	$2,570,100
42. Wes Kath, 3B, Desert Mountain HS, Scottsdale, Ariz. (2nd round/No. 57)	$1,800,000	$1,243,600
43. Daylen Lile, OF, Trinity HS, Louisville (2nd round/No. 47)	$1,750,000	$1,580,200
44. Ky Bush, LHP, St. Mary's (2nd round/No. 45)	$1,747,500	$1,650,200
45. Noah Miller, SS, Ozaukee HS, Fredonia, Wis. (supp. 1st round/No. 36)	$1,700,000	$2,045,400
46. Connor Norby, 2B, East Carolina (2nd round/No. 41)	$1,700,000	$1,813,500
47. Jaden Hill, RHP, Louisiana State (2nd round/No. 44)	$1,689,500	$1,689,500
48. Edwin Arroyo, SS, Central Pointe Academy, Kissimmee, Fla. (2nd round/No. 48)	$1,650,000	$1,543,600
49. Ethan Wilson, OF, South Alabama (2nd round/No. 49)	$1,507,600	$1,507,600
50. Lonnie White Jr., OF, Malvern (Pa.) Prep HS (supp. 2nd round/No. 64)	$1,500,000	$1,050,300
Total	$161,251,790	$158,573,300

Schrier, Alonzo Tredwell and Tyree Reed.

North Carolina lefthander Joshua Hartle also opted out of the draft to bring the total list of would-be BA 500 high school players to six.

There's a chance that multiple players in this group of opt outs could have gone on the first day of the draft and signed for $1 million or better bonuses, but instead their college programs will be happy with the tremendous talents they've added.

The group joins players like Louisiana State outfielder Dylan Crews and North Carolina righthander J.B. Bukauskas to opt out of the draft.

Team, Player, Pos., School	Bonus
1. PIT. Henry Davis, C, Louisville	$6,500,000
2. TEX. Jack Leiter, RHP, Vanderbilt	$7,922,000
3. DET. Jackson Jobe, RHP, Heritage Hall HS, Oklahoma City	$6,900,000
4. BOS. Marcelo Mayer, SS, Eastlake HS, Chula Vista, Calif	$6,664,000
5. BAL. Colton Cowser, OF, Sam Houston State	$4,900,000
6. ARI. Jordan Lawlar, SS, Dallas Jesuit HS	$6,713,300
7. KC. Frank Mozzicato, LHP, East Catholic HS, Manchester, Conn	$3,547,500
8. COL. Benny Montgomery, OF, Red Land HS, Lewisberry, Pa	$5,000,000
9. LAA. Sam Bachman, RHP, Miami (Ohio)	$3,847,500
10. NYM. Kumar Rocker, RHP, Vanderbilt	Did not sign
11. WAS. Brady House, SS, Winder-Barrow HS, Winder, Ga	$5,000,000
12. SEA. Harry Ford, C, North Cobb HS, Kennesaw, Ga	$4,366,400
13. PHI. Andrew Painter, RHP, Calvary Christian HS, Fla	$3,900,000
14. SF. Will Bednar, RHP, Mississippi State	$3,647,500
15. MIL. Sal Frelick, OF, Boston College	$4,000,000
16. MIA. Kahlil Watson, SS, Wake Forest (N.C.) HS	$4,540,790
17. CIN. Matt McLain, SS, UCLA	$4,625,000
18. STL. Michael McGreevy, RHP, UC Santa Barbara	$2,750,000
19. TOR. Gunnar Hoglund, RHP, Mississippi	$3,247,500
20. NYM. Trey Sweeney, SS, Eastern Illinois	$3,000,000
21. CHC. Jordan Wicks, LHP, Kansas State	$3,132,300
22. CWS. Colson Montgomery, SS, Southridge HS, Ind	$3,027,000
23. CLE. Gavin Williams, RHP, East Carolina	$2,250,000
24. ATL. Ryan Cusick, RHP, Wake Forest	$2,700,000
25. OAK. Max Muncy, SS, Thousand Oaks (Calif.) HS	$2,850,000
26. MIN. Chase Petty, RHP, Mainland Regional HS, Linwood, NJ	$2,500,000
27. SD. Jackson Merrill, SS, Severna Park (Md.) HS	$1,800,000
28. TB. Carson Williams, SS, Torrey Pines HS, San Diego	$2,347,500
29. LAD. Maddux Bruns, LHP, UMS-Wright Prep, Mobile, Ala	$2,197,500
30. CIN. Jay Allen, OF, Carroll Catholic HS, Fort Pierce, Fla	$2,397,500
31. MIA. Joe Mack, C, Williamsville East HS, East Amherst, N.Y	$2,500,000
32. DET. Ty Madden, RHP, Texas	$2,500,000
33. MIL. Tyler Black, 2B, Wright State	$2,200,000
34. TB. Cooper Kinney, 2B, Baylor HS, Chattanooga	$2,145,600
35. CIN. Mat Nelson, C, Florida State	$2,093,300
36. MIN. Noah Miller, SS, Ozaukee HS, Fredonia, Wis	$1,700,000
37. PIT. Anthony Solometo, LHP, Bishop Eustace Prep HS, N.J.	$2,797,500
38. TEX. Aaron Zavala, OF, Oregon	$830,000
39. DET. Izaac Pacheco, SS, Friendswood (Texas) HS	$2,750,000
40. BOS. Jud Fabian, OF, Florida	NOT SIGNED
41. BAL. Connor Norby, 2B, East Carolina	$1,700,000
42. ARI. Ryan Bliss, SS, Auburn	$1,250,000
43. KC. Ben Kudrna, RHP, Blue Valley Southwest HS, Kan	$2,997,500
44. COL. Jaden Hill, RHP, Louisiana State	$1,689,500
45. LAA. Ky Bush, LHP, St. Mary's	$1,747,500
46. NYM. Calvin Ziegler, RHP, TNXL Academy, Fla	$910,000
47. WAS. Daylen Lile, OF, Trinity HS, Louisville	$1,750,000
48. SEA. Edwin Arroyo, SS, Central Pointe Christian, Fla	$1,650,000
49. PHI. Ethan Wilson, OF, South Alabama	$1,507,600
50. SF. Matt Mikulski, LHP, Fordham	$1,197,500
51. MIL. Russell Smith, LHP, Texas Christian	$1,000,000
52. MIA. Cody Morissette, SS, Boston College	$1,403,200
53. CIN. Andrew Abbott, LHP, Virginia	$1,300,000
54. STL. Joshua Baez, OF, Dexter Southfield HS, Brookline, Mass	$2,250,000
55. NYM. Brendan Beck, RHP, Stanford	$1,050,000
56. CHC. James Triantos, 3B, Madison HS, Vienna, Va	$2,100,000
57. CWS. Wes Kath, 3B, Desert Mountain HS, Scottsdale, Ariz	$1,800,000
58. CLE. Doug Nikhazy, LHP, Mississippi	$1,200,000
59. ATL. Spencer Schwellenbach, RHP, Nebraska	$997,500
60. OAK. Zack Gelof, 3B, Virginia	$1,157,400
61. MIN. Steve Hajjar, LHP, Michigan	$1,129,700
62. SD. James Wood, OF, IMG Academy, Bradenton, Fla	$2,600,000
63. TB. Kyle Manzardo, 1B, Washington State	$747,500
64. PIT. Lonnie White Jr., OF, Malvern (Pa.) Prep HS	$1,500,000
65. BAL. Reed Trimble, OF, Southern Mississippi	$800,000
66. KC. Peyton Wilson, 2B, Alabama	$1,000,800

Prep lefthander Frank Mozzicato was a surprise selection at No. 7 overall.

Team, Player, Pos., School	Bonus
67. ARI. Adrian Del Castillo, C, Miami	$1,000,000
68. COL. Joe Rock, LHP, Ohio	$953,100
69. CLE. Tommy Mace, RHP, Florida	$1,100,000
70. STL. Ryan Holgate, OF, Arizona	$875,000
71. SD. Robert Gasser, LHP, Houston	$884,200
72. PIT. Bubba Chandler, RHP, North Oconee HS, Bogart, Ga	$3,000,000
73. TEX. Cameron Cauley, SS, Barbers Hill HS, Texas	$1,000,000
74. DET. Dylan Smith, RHP, Alabama	$1,115,000
75. BOS. Tyler McDonough, 2B, North Carolina State	$828,600
76. BAL. John Rhodes, OF, Kentucky	$1,375,000
77. ARI. Jacob Steinmetz, RHP, Hebrew Academy, N.Y	$500,000
78. KC. Carter Jensen, C, Park Hill HS, Kansas City, Mo	$1,097,500
79. COL. McCade Brown, RHP, Indiana	$780,400
80. LAA. Landon Marceaux, RHP, Louisiana State	$765,300
81. NYM. Dominic Hamel, RHP, Dallas Baptist	$755,300
82. WAS. Branden Boissiere, OF, Arizona	$600,000
83. SEA. Michael Morales, RHP, East Pennsboro Area HS, Pa	$1,500,000
84. PHI. Jordan Viars, OF, Reedy HS, Frisco, Texas	$747,500
85. SF. Mason Black, RHP, Lehigh	$708,200
86. MIL. Alex Binelas, 3B, Louisville	$700,000
87. HOU. Tyler Whitaker, OF, Bishop Gorman HS, Las Vegas	$1,500,000
88. MIA. Jordan McCants, SS, Pensacola (Fla.) Catholic HS	$800,000
89. CIN. Jose Torres, SS, North Carolina State	$622,500
90. STL. Austin Love, RHP, North Carolina	$600,000
91. TOR. Ricky Tiedemann, LHP, Golden West (Calif.) JC	$644,800
92. NYM. Brock Selvidge, LHP, Hamilton HS, Chandler, Ariz	$1,500,000
93. CHC. Drew Gray, LHP, IMG Academy, Bradenton, Fla	$900,000
94. CWS. Sean Burke, RHP, Maryland	$900,000
95. CLE. Jake Fox, SS, Lakeland (Fla.) Christian HS	$850,000
96. ATL. Dylan Dodd, LHP, Southeast Missouri	$122,500
97. OAK. Mason Miller, RHP, Gardner-Webb	$599,100
98. MIN. Cade Povich, LHP, Nebraska	$500,000
99. SD. Kevin Kopps, RHP, Arkansas	$300,000
100. TB. Ryan Spikes, SS, Parkview HS, Lilburn, Ga	$1,097,500

FREEK BOUW/FOUR SEAM IMAGES

Order Of Selection In Parentheses | Players Signed In Bold

ARIZONA DIAMONDBACKS (6)

1. Jordan Lawlar, SS, Dallas Jesuit HS
2. Ryan Bliss, SS, Auburn
2s. Adrian Del Castillo, C, Miami
3. Jacob Steinmetz, RHP, Hebrew Academy, N.Y.
4. Chad Patrick, RHP, Purdue-Northwest (Ind.)
5. Caleb Roberts, C, North Carolina
6. Luke Albright, RHP, Kent State
7. Scott Randall, RHP, Sacramento State
8. Gavin Conticello, 3B, Stoneman Douglas HS, Fla.
9. Jake Rice III, LHP, Kennesaw State
10. Hugh Fisher III, LHP, Vanderbilt
11. Tim Tawa, 2B, Stanford
12. Davis Diaz, SS, Acalanes HS, Lafayette, Calif.
13. Josh Swales, RHP, JC of Southern Nevada
14. Channy Ortiz, SS, Grand Canyon
15. Shane Muntz, C, Wake Forest
16. Jacen Roberson, OF, Cal State Bakersfield
17. Drake Varnado, SS, IMG Academy, Bradenton, Fla.
18. Joey Spence, C, West Bend (Wis.) East HS
19. Eric Hammond, RHP, Keller (Texas) HS
20. Ross Carver, RHP, Dallas Baptist

ATLANTA BRAVES (24)

1. Ryan Cusick, RHP, Wake Forest
2. Spencer Schwellenbach, RHP, Nebraska
3. Dylan Dodd, LHP, Southeast Missouri
4. Cal Conley, SS, Texas Tech
5. Luke Waddell, SS, Georgia Tech
6. Justyn-Henry Malloy, 3B, Georgia Tech
7. AJ Smith-Shawver, RHP, Colleyville (Texas) Heritage HS
8. Tyler Collins, OF, Boyd HS, McKinney, Texas
9. Liam McGill, C, Bryant
10. Dylan Spain, RHP, Honolulu (no school)
11. Adam Shoemaker, LHP, St. Benedict Catholic SS, Ont.
12. Andrew Hoffmann, RHP, Illinois
13. Adam Zebrowski, C, St. John Fisher (N.Y.)
14. Caleb Durbin, SS, Washington
15. Christian Robinson, OF, Stanford
16. Kris Anglin, LHP, Howard (Texas) JC
17. Tyler Tolve, C, Kennesaw State
18. Austin Smith, RHP, Arizona
19. Samuel Strickland, LHP, Samford
20. Ty Evans, OF, Lakeland (Fla.) Christian HS

BALTIMORE ORIOLES (5)

1. Colton Cowser, OF, Sam Houston State
2. Connor Norby, 2B, East Carolina
2s. Reed Trimble, OF, Southern Mississippi
3. John Rhodes, OF, Kentucky
4. Donta Williams, OF, Arizona
5. Carlos Tavera, RHP, Texas-Arlington
6. Collin Burns, SS, Tulane
7. Connor Pavolony, C, Tennessee
8. Creed Willems, C, Aledo (Texas) HS
9. Ryan Higgins, 3B, Fresno State
10. Billy Cook, OF, Pepperdine
11. Dylan Heid, RHP, Pittsburgh-Johnstown
12. Justin Armbruester, RHP, New Mexico
13. Jacob Teter, 1B, Florida Southern
14. Daniel Lloyd, RHP, South Carolina
15. Keagan Gillies, RHP, Tulane
16. Peter Van Loon, RHP, UC Irvine

17. Ryan Long, RHP, Pomona-Pitzer (Calif.)
18. Conor Grady, RHP, Florida State
19. Alex Pham, RHP, San Francisco
20. Trendon Craig, OF, Louisburg (N.C.) JC

BOSTON RED SOX (4)

1. Marcelo Mayer, SS, Eastlake HS, Chula Vista, Calif.
2. Jud Fabian, OF, Florida
3. Tyler McDonough, 2B, North Carolina State
4. Elmer Rodriguez-Cruz, LHP, Leadership Academy, P.R.
5. Nathan Hickey, C, Florida
6. Daniel McElveny, UTL, Bonita Vista HS, Chula Vista, Calif.
7. Wyatt Olds, RHP, Oklahoma
8. Hunter Dobbins, RHP, Texas Tech
9. Tyler Miller, 3B, Auburn
10. Matt Litwicki, RHP, Indiana
11. Niko Kavadas, 1B, Notre Dame
12. Christopher Troye, RHP, UC Santa Barbara
13. Zach Ehrhard, SS, Wharton HS, Tampa
14. Jacob Webb, RHP, Miami (Ohio)
15. Payton Green, SS, Crossroads Flex HS, Cary N.C.
16. BJ Vela, 2B, Reedley (Calif.) JC
17. Luis Guerrero, RHP, Chipola (Fla.) JC
18. Phillip Sikes, OF, Texas Christian
19. Tyler Uberstine, RHP, Northwestern
20. Josh Hood, SS, Pennsylvania

CHICAGO CUBS (22)

1. Jordan Wicks, LHP, Kansas State
2. James Triantos, 3B, Madison HS, Vienna, Va.
3. Drew Gray, LHP, IMG Academy, Bradenton, Fla.
4. Christian Franklin, OF, Arkansas
5. Liam Spence, SS, Tennessee
6. Riley Martin, LHP, Quincy (Ill.)
7. Parker Chavers, OF, Coastal Carolina
8. Casey Opitz, C, Arkansas
9. Chase Watkins, LHP, Oregon State
10. Peter Matt, OF, Duke
11. Gage Ziehl, RHP, Penfield (N.Y.) HS
12. Teo Banks, OF, Permian HS, Odessa, Texas
13. Erian Rodriguez, RHP, Georgia Premier Academy, Ga.
14. Frankie Scalzo, RHP, Grand Canyon
15. BJ Murray, 3B, Florida Atlantic
16. Zac Leigh, RHP, Texas State
17. Christian Olivo, SS, Leadership Academy, P.R.
18. Dominic Hambley, RHP, Belmont SS, Langford, B.C.
19. Daniel Avitia, RHP, Alhambra HS, Phoenix
20. Wilson Cunningham, LHP, JSerra Catholic HS, Calif.

CHICAGO WHITE SOX (23)

1. Colson Montgomery, SS, Southridge HS, Ind.
2. Wes Kath, 3B, Desert Mountain HS, Scottsdale, Ariz.
3. Sean Burke, RHP, Maryland
4. Brooks Gosswein, LHP, Bradley
5. Tanner McDougal, RHP, Silverado HS, Las Vegas
6. Taylor Broadway, RHP, Mississippi
7. Theo Denlinger, RHP, Bradley
8. Fraser Ellard, LHP, Liberty
9. Gil Luna Jr., LHP, Arizona
10. Tommy Sommer, LHP, Indiana
11. Christian Edwards, RHP, Jacksonville State
12. Johnny Ray, RHP, Texas Christian
13. Colby Smelley, C, Shelton State (Ala.) JC
14. Noah Owen, RHP, Golden West (Calif.) JC

15. Cam Butler, OF, Big Valley Christian HS, Modesto, Calif.
16. Terrell Tatum, OF, North Carolina State
17. Jayson Gonzalez, 3B, Vanderbilt
18. Adam Hackenberg, C, Clemson
19. Shawn Goosenberg, SS, Northwestern
20. Haylen Green, LHP, Texas Christian

CINCINNATI REDS (18)

1. Matt McLain, SS, UCLA
1. Jay Allen, OF, Carroll Catholic HS, Fort Pierce, Fla.
1s. Mat Nelson, C, Florida State
2. Andrew Abbott, LHP, Virginia
3. Jose Torres, SS, North Carolina State
4. Ruben Ibarra, 1B, San Jose State
5. Thomas Farr, RHP, South Carolina
6. JT Thompson, OF, North Carolina
7. Kevin Abel, RHP, Oregon State
8. Hunter Parks, RHP, Florence-Darlington Tech (S.C.) JC
9. Jack Rogers, OF, Sam Houston State
10. Donovan Benoit, RHP, Tulane
11. Shawn Guilliams, RHP, JC of Central Florida
12. Julian Aguilar, RHP, Cypress (Calif.) JC
13. Michael Trautwein, C, Northwestern
14. Carter Raffield, RHP, Clemson
15. Blake Dunn, LHP, Western Michigan
16. Owen Holt, RHP, Alvin (Texas) JC
17. Dennis Boatman, RHP, Sacramento JC
18. Austin Callahan, 3B, Hutchinson (Kan.) JC
19. Ryan Cardona, RHP, Marist
20. Javi Rivera, RHP, Florida Atlantic

CLEVELAND INDIANS (24)

1. Gavin Williams, RHP, East Carolina
2. Doug Nikhazy, LHP, Mississippi
2s. Tommy Mace, RHP, Florida
3. Jake Fox, SS, Lakeland (Fla.) Christian HS
4. Ryan Webb, LHP, Georgia
5. Tanner Bibee, RHP, Cal State Fullerton
6. Aaron Davenport, RHP, Hawaii
7. Jack Leftwich, RHP, Florida
8. Rodney Boone, LHP, UC Santa Barbara
9. Will Dion, LHP, McNeese State
10. Franco Aleman, RHP, Florida
11. Hunter Stanley, RHP, Southern Mississippi
12. Connor Kokx, OF, Long Beach State
13. Davis Sharpe, RHP, Clemson
14. Trenton Denholm, RHP, UC Irvine
15. Alaska Abney, RHP, Coastal Carolina
16. Zach Pettway, RHP, UCLA
17. Tyler Thornton, RHP, Arizona State
18. Tommy Ventimiglia, RHP, Longwood Prep Academy, N.Y.
19. Reid Johnston, RHP, North Carolina State
20. Jake Miller, RHP, San Diego

COLORADO ROCKIES (8)

1. Benny Montgomery, OF, Red Land HS, Lewisberry, Pa.
2. Jaden Hill, RHP, Louisiana State
2s. Joe Rock, LHP, Ohio
3. McCade Brown, RHP, Indiana
4. Hunter Goodman, C, Memphis
5. Evan Justice, LHP, North Carolina State
6. Braxton Fulford, C, Texas Tech
7. Evan Shawver, LHP, Cincinnati
8. Robby Martin, OF, Florida State
9. Cullen Kafka, RHP, Oregon
10. Zach Kokoska, OF, Kansas State
11. Nic Kent, SS, Virginia
12. Mason Green, LHP, Central Missouri

13. E.J. Andrews, OF, Fresno State
14. Tyler Ras, RHP, Alabama
15. Benjamin Sems, SS, Michigan
16. Braiden Ward, OF, Washington
17. Jarrod Cande, RHP, Florida Southern
18. Bryce McGowan, RHP, Charlotte
19. Elijah Trest, RHP, Arkansas
20. Tyler Ahearn, RHP, Florida State

DETROIT TIGERS (3)

1. Jackson Jobe, RHP, Heritage Hall HS, Oklahoma City
1s. Ty Madden, RHP, Texas
2. Izaac Pacheco, SS, Friendswood (Texas) HS
3. Dylan Smith, RHP, Alabama
4. Tyler Mattison, RHP, Bryant
5. Tanner Kohlhepp, RHP, Notre Dame
6. Austin Murr, OF, North Carolina State
7. Brant Hurter, LHP, Georgia Tech
8. Jordan Marks, RHP, South Carolina-Upstate
9. Garrett Burhenn, RHP, Ohio State
10. Austin Schultz, OF, Kentucky
11. Josh Crouch, C, Central Florida
12. Michael Rothenberg, C, Duke
13. Chris Meyers, 3B, Toledo
14. RJ Petit, RHP, Charleston Southern
15. Blake Holub, RHP, St. Edwards (Texas)
16. Jack Anderson, RHP, Florida State
17. Aaron Haase, RHP, Wichita State
18. Ben Malgeri, OF, Northeastern
19. Justice Bigbie, 1B, Western Carolina
20. J.D. McLaughlin, OF, Central Arizona JC

HOUSTON ASTROS (16)

3. Tyler Whitaker, OF, Bishop Gorman HS, Las Vegas
4. Alex Ulloa, SS, Calvary Christian HS, Fort Lauderdale
4. Chayce McDermott, RHP, Ball State
5. Quincy Hamilton, OF, Wright State
6. Spencer Arrighetti, RHP, Louisiana-Lafayette
7. Joey Loperfido, OF, Duke
8. Colton Gordon-Zimring, LHP, Central Florida
9. Aaron Brown, RHP, Middle Tennessee State
10. Michael Sandle, OF, South Alabama
11. Chad Stevens, SS, Portland
12. Rhett Kouba, RHP, Dallas Baptist
13. Kobe Kato, 2B, Arizona
14. Bryant Salgado, RHP, Oregon State
15. Adrian Chaidez, RHP, UCLA
16. Nic Swanson, RHP, Northeastern
17. Justin Williams, 3B, Penn State
18. Will Wagner, 2B, Liberty
19. Hector G. Nieves, SS, P.R. Baseball Academy, P.R.
20. Jackson Linn, OF, Cambridge (Mass.) Rindge & Latin HS

KANSAS CITY ROYALS (7)

1. Frank Mozzicato, LHP, East Catholic HS, Conn.
2. Ben Kudrna, RHP, Blue Valley Southwest HS, Kan.
2s. Peyton Wilson, 2B, Alabama
3. Carter Jensen, C, Park Hill HS, Kansas City, Mo.
4. Shane Panzini, RHP, Red Bank (N.J.) Catholic HS
5. Eric Cerantola, RHP, Mississippi State
6. Dayton Dooney, 2B, Central Arizona JC
7. Noah Cameron, LHP, Central Arkansas
8. Ryan Cepero, SS, Beltran Baseball Academy, Florida, P.R.
9. Parker Bates, OF, Louisiana Tech
10. Shane Connolly, LHP, Virginia Tech
11. Brennon McNair, SS, Magee (Miss.) HS
12. Tyson Guerrero, LHP, Washington
13. Patrick Halligan, RHP, Pensacola State (Fla.) JC

14. Caden Monke, LHP, Arkansas
15. River Town, OF, Dallas Baptist
16. Anthony Simonelli, RHP, Virginia Tech
17. Luca Tresh, C, North Carolina State
18. Harrison Beethe, RHP, Texas Christian
19. Cam Williams, 3B, Texas
20. Jack Aldrich, LHP, Tulane

LOS ANGELES ANGELS (9)

1. Sam Bachman, RHP, Miami (Ohio)
2. Ky Bush, LHP, St. Mary's
3. Landon Marceaux, RHP, Louisiana State
4. Luke Murphy, RHP, Vanderbilt
5. Brett Kerry, RHP, South Carolina
6. Jake Smith, RHP, Miami
7. Ryan Costeiu, RHP, Arkansas
8. Nick Jones, LHP, Georgia Southern
9. Braden Olthoff, RHP, Tulane
10. Andrew Peters, RHP, South Carolina
11. Chase Silseth, RHP, Arizona
12. Mason Albright, LHP, IMG Academy, Bradenton, Fla.
13. Mo Hanley, RHP, Adrian (Mich.)
14. Eric Torres, LHP, Kansas State
15. Glenn Albanese Jr., RHP, Louisville
16. Brandon Dufault, RHP, Northeastern
17. Mason Erla, RHP, Michigan State
18. Nick Mondak, LHP, St. John's
19. Nathan Burns, RHP, Oregon State
20. Marcelo Perez, RHP, Texas Christian

LOS ANGELES DODGERS (30)

1. Maddux Bruns, LHP, UMS-Wright Prep, Mobile, Ala.
3. Peter Heubeck, RHP, Gilman HS, Baltimore
4. Nick Nastrini, RHP, UCLA
5. Ben Casparius, RHP, Connecticut
6. Emmet Sheehan, RHP, Boston College
7. Ryan Sublette, RHP, Texas Tech
8. Ben Harris, LHP, Georgia
9. Lael Lockhart Jr., LHP, Arkansas
10. Michael Hobbs, RHP, St. Mary's
11. Justin Wrobleski, LHP, Oklahoma State
12. Ronan Kopp, LHP, South Mountain (Ariz.) JC
13. Antonio Knowles, RHP, Florida Southwestern State JC
14. Jordan Leasure, RHP, Tampa
15. Madison Jeffrey, RHP, West Virginia
16. Michael Sirota, SS, Gunn HS, Washington, Conn.
17. Adam Tulloch, LHP, West Virginia
18. Damon Keith, OF, California Baptist
19. Gabe Emmett, RHP, Folsom Lake (Calif.) JC
20. Charlie Connolly, RHP, Navy

MIAMI MARLINS (17)

1. Kahlil Watson, SS, Wake Forest (N.C.) HS
1s. Joe Mack, C, Williamsville East HS, East Amherst, N.Y.
2. Cody Morissette, SS, Boston College
3. Jordan McCants, SS, Pensacola (Fla.) Catholic HS
4. Tanner Allen, OF, Mississippi State
5. Brady Allen, OF, South Carolina
6. Sam Praytor, C, Alabama
7. Gabe Bierman, RHP, Indiana
8. Pat Monteverde, LHP, Texas Tech
9. Jake Schrand, RHP, Wright State
10. Hunter Perdue, RHP, Florida State
11. Jesse Bergin, RHP, UCLA
12. Brandon White, RHP, Washington State
13. Chandler Jozwiak, LHP, Texas A&M
14. Holt Jones Jr., RHP, Kentucky
15. Caleb Wurster, LHP, Connecticut

16. Ivan Melendez, 3B, Texas
17. Justin Fall, LHP, Arizona State
18. Bennett Hostetler, SS, North Dakota State
19. Noah Williamson, OF, Everett (Wash.) JC
20. Zach Zubia, 1B, Texas

MILWAUKEE BREWERS (15)

1. Sal Frelick, OF, Boston College
1s. Tyler Black, 2B, Wright State
2. Russell Smith, LHP, Texas Christian
3. Alex Binelas, 3B, Louisville
4. Logan Henderson, RHP, McLennan (Texas) JC
5. Ethan Murray, SS, Duke
6. Carlos Rodriguez, RHP, Florida Southwestern State JC
7. Tristan Peters, OF, Southern Illinois
8. Zack Raabe, 2B, Minnesota
9. Brannon Jordan, RHP, South Carolina
10. Wes Clarke, C, South Carolina
11. Roc Riggio, OF, Thousand Oaks (Calif.) HS
12. Caden Vire, LHP, Skyview HS, Vancouver, Wash.
13. Quinton Low, RHP, Chatfield HS, Littleton, Colo.
14. Jace Avina, OF, Spanish Springs HS, Sparks, Nev.
15. Hunter Hollan, LHP, San Jacinto (Texas) JC
16. Kaylan Nicasia, SS, Champagnat Catholic HS, Fla.
17. Will Rogers, C, Mounds View HS, Arden Hills, Minn.
18. Ryne Moore, RHP, Old Dominion
19. Carter Holton, LHP, Benedictine Military School, Savannah, Ga.
20. Samuel Mendeza, RHP, Cisco (Texas) JC

MINNESOTA TWINS (27)

1. Chase Petty, RHP, Mainland Regional HS, Linwood, N.J.
1s. Noah Miller, SS, Ozaukee HS, Fredonia, Wis.
2. Steve Hajjar, LHP, Michigan
3. Cade Povich, LHP, Nebraska
4. Christian Encarnacion-Strand, 3B, Oklahoma State
5. Christian Macleod, LHP, Mississippi State
6. Travis Adams, RHP, Sacramento State
7. Jake Rucker, 3B, Tennessee
8. Noah Cardenas, C, UCLA
9. Patrick Winkel, C, Connecticut
10. Ernie Yake, SS, Gonzaga
11. Brandon Birdsell, RHP, Texas Tech
12. Kyler Fedko, OF, Connecticut
13. David Festa, RHP, Seton Hall
14. Pierson Ohl, RHP, Grand Canyon
15. Mikey Perez, SS, UCLA
16. Johnathan Lavallee, RHP, Long Beach State
17. Dylan Neuse, 2B, Texas Tech
18. Mike Paredes, RHP, San Diego State
19. Jaylen Nowlin, LHP, Chipola (Fla.) JC
20. Dillon Tatum, C, UC Irvine

NEW YORK METS (10)

1. Kumar Rocker, RHP, Vanderbilt
2. Calvin Ziegler, RHP, TNXL Academy, Fla.
3. Dominic Hamel, RHP, Dallas Baptist
4. J.T. Schwartz, 1B, UCLA
5. Christian Scott, RHP, Florida
6. Carson Seymour, RHP, Kansas State
7. Kevin Kendall, SS, UCLA
8. Mike Vasil, RHP, Virginia
9. Levi David, RHP, Northwestern State
10. Keyshawn Askew, LHP, Clemson
11. Rowdey Jordan, OF, Mississippi State
12. Jack-Thomas Wold, OF, Nevada-Las Vegas
13. Matt Rudick, OF, San Diego State
14. Nathan Lavender, LHP, Illinois
15. Wyatt Young, SS, Pepperdine

DRAFT

16. Trey McLoughlin, RHP, Fairfield
17. Nick Zwack, LHP, Xavier
18. Kolby Kubichek, RHP, Texas
19. Drake Osborn, C, Louisiana-Lafayette
20. Justin Guerrera, SS, Fairfield

NEW YORK YANKEES (21)

1. Trey Sweeney, SS, Eastern Illinois
2. Brendan Beck, RHP, Stanford
3. Brock Selvidge, LHP, Hamilton HS, Chandler, Ariz.
4. Cooper Bowman, 2B, Louisville
5. Tyler Hardman, 1B, Oklahoma
6. Richard Fitts, RHP, Auburn
7. Robert Ahlstrom, LHP, Oregon
8. Will Warren, RHP, Southeastern Louisiana
9. Chandler Champlain, RHP, Southern California
10. Benjamin Cowles, SS, Maryland
11. Jack Neely, RHP, Ohio State
12. Ben Rice, C, Dartmouth
13. Zach Messinger, RHP, Virginia
14. Sean Hermann, RHP, Durant HS, Plant City, Fla.
15. Danny Watson, RHP, Virginia Commonwealth
16. Cole Ayers, RHP, State College of Florida JC
17. Grant Richardson, OF, Indiana
18. Bailey Dees, RHP, Penn State
19. Dominic Keegan, C, Vanderbilt | N
20. Sean Hard, RHP, St. Joseph Regional HS, Montvale, N.J. | N

OAKLAND ATHLETICS (26)

1. Max Muncy, SS, Thousand Oaks (Calif.) HS
2. Zack Gelof, 3B, Virginia
3. Mason Miller, RHP, Gardner-Webb
4. Denzel Clarke, OF, Cal State Northridge
5. CJ Rodriguez, C, Vanderbilt
6. Grant Holman, RHP, California
7. Brett Harris, 3B, Gonzaga
8. Drew Swift, SS, Arizona State
9. Shane McGuire, C, San Diego
10. Jack Winkler, SS, San Francisco
11. Eduardo Rivera, LHP, CADEST HS, Carolina, P.R.
12. Mitch Myers, RHP, Pittsburgh
13. Aaron Holiday, RHP, Old Dominion
14. Jonny Butler, OF, North Carolina State
15. Luke Anderson, RHP, Central Oklahoma
16. Colton Johnson, LHP, Illinois State
17. Kyle Virbitsky, RHP, Penn State
18. Mariano Ricciardi, 2B, Dayton
19. Blake Beers, RHP, Michigan
20. Hunter Breault, RHP, Oregon

PHILADELPHIA PHILLIES (13)

1. Andrew Painter, RHP, Calvary Christian HS, Fla.
2. Ethan Wilson, OF, South Alabama
3. Jordan Viars, OF, Reedy HS, Frisco, Texas
4. Micah Ottenbreit, RHP, Trenton (Mich.) HS
5. Griff McGarry, RHP, Virginia
6. Jose Pena, RHP, Tampa Prep HS
7. Christian McGowan, RHP, Eastern Oklahoma State JC
8. Jason Ruffcorn, RHP, Oklahoma
9. Gavin Tonkel, OF, Heritage HS, Brentwood, Calif.
10. Logan Cerny, OF, Troy
11. Andrew Baker, RHP, Chipola (Fla.) JC
12. T.J. Rumfield, 3B, Virginia Tech
13. Jared Carr, OF, Shepherd (W.Va.)
14. Jose Valadez-Acuna, OF, Veterans Memorial HS, Texas
15. Matthew Osterberg, LHP, St. Cloud State (Minn.)
16. Ty Collins, RHP, Glendale (Calif.) JC
17. Alex Garbrick, RHP, South Carolina-Upstate

18. Malik Binns, RHP, Benedictine Mesa (Ariz.)
19. Seth Halvorsen, RHP, Missouri
20. Cam Wynne, RHP, Nebraska

PITTSBURGH PIRATES (1)

1. Henry Davis, C, Louisville
2. Anthony Solometo, LHP, Bishop Eustace Prep HS, N.J.
2s. Lonnie White Jr., OF, Malvern (Pa.) Prep HS
3. Bubba Chandler, RHP, North Oconee HS, Bogart, Ga.
4. Owen Kellington, RHP, U-32 HS, Montpelier, Vt.
5. Jackson Glenn, 3B, Dallas Baptist
6. Mike Jarvis, SS, San Diego State
7. Wyatt Hendrie, C, San Diego State
8. Sean Sullivan, RHP, California
9. Luke Brown, OF, Louisville
10. Justin Meis, RHP, Eastern Michigan
11. Jack Carey, RHP, Duke
12. Chazz Martinez, LHP, Orange Coast (Calif.) JC
13. Owen Sharts, RHP, Nevada
14. Braylon Bishop, OF, Arkansas HS, Texarkana, Ark.
15. Tyler Samaniego, LHP, South Alabama
16. Daniel Corona, SS, Baylor HS, Chattanooga, Tenn.
17. Carlos Lomeli, RHP, St. Mary's
18. A.J. Graham, SS, Gaither HS, Tampa
19. Drew Irvine, RHP, Iowa
20. Brenden Dixon, SS, Weatherford (Texas) JC

SAN DIEGO PADRES (28)

1. Jackson Merrill, SS, Severna Park (Md.) HS
2. James Wood, OF, IMG Academy, Bradenton, Fla.
2s. Robert Gasser, LHP, Houston
3. Kevin Kopps, RHP, Arkansas
4. Jackson Wolf, LHP, West Virginia
5. Max Ferguson, 2B, Tennessee
6. Ryan Bergert, RHP, West Virginia
7. Ryan Och, LHP, Southern Mississippi
8. Lucas Dunn, 2B, Louisville
9. Garrett Hawkins, RHP, British Columbia
10. Colton Bender, C, Quinnipiac
11. River Ryan, RHP, UNC Pembroke
12. Marcos Castanon, SS, UC Santa Barbara
13. Kobe Robinson, RHP, Chattanooga State JC
14. Adam Smith, RHP, UNC Wilmington
15. Anthony Vilar, C, Miami
16. Alek Jacob, RHP, Gonzaga
17. Luke Boyd, RHP, Baylor
18. Gage Jump, LHP, JSerra Catholic HS, San Juan Capistrano, Calif.
19. Gabriel Rincones Jr., OF, St. Petersburg (Fla.) JC
20. Chase Burns, RHP, Beech HS, Hendersonville, Tenn.

SAN FRANCISCO GIANTS (14)

1. Will Bednar, RHP, Mississippi State
2. Matt Mikulski, LHP, Fordham
3. Mason Black, RHP, Lehigh
4. Eric Silva, RHP, JSerra Catholic HS, Calif.
5. Rohan Handa, LHP, Yale
6. Seth Lonsway, LHP, Ohio State
7. Nick Sinacola, RHP, Maine
8. Ian Villers, RHP, California
9. Mat Olsen, RHP, Central Arizona JC
10. Vaun Brown, OF, Florida Southern
11. Donovan McIntyre, OF, Marian Catholic HS, Ill.
12. Landen Roupp, RHP, UNC Wilmington
13. Jared Dupere, OF, Northeastern
14. Tyler Myrick, RHP, Florida International
15. Brooks Baldwin, SS, UNC Wilmington
16. Brett Standlee, RHP, Oklahoma State
17. Hunter Dula, RHP, Wingate (N.C.)

19. Irvin Murr III, 3B, Winter Springs (Fla.) HS
20. Vance Honeycutt, SS, Salisbury (N.C.) HS

SEATTLE MARINERS (12)

1. Harry Ford, C, North Cobb HS, Kennesaw, Ga.
2. Edwin Arroyo, SS, Central Pointe Christian Academy, Fla.
3. Michael Morales, RHP, East Pennsboro Area HS, Pa.
4. Bryce Miller, RHP, Texas A&M
5. Andy Thomas, C, Baylor
6. Bryan Woo, RHP, Cal Poly
7. Colin Davis, OF, Wofford
8. James Parker, SS, Clemson
9. Spencer Packard, OF, Campbell
10. Jordan Jackson, RHP, Georgia Southern
11. Will Fleming, RHP, Wake Forest
12. Corey Rosier, OF, UNC Greensboro
13. Ben Ramirez, SS, Southern California
14. Andrew Moore, RHP, Chipola (Fla.) JC
15. Cole Barr, 3B, Indiana
16. Jimmy Joyce, RHP, Hofstra
17. Jimmy Kingsbury, RHP, Villanova
18. Riley Davis, RHP, Alabama-Birmingham
19. Charlie Welch, C, Arkansas
20. Troy Taylor, RHP, Cypress (Calif.) JC

ST. LOUIS CARDINALS (19)

1. Michael McGreevy, RHP, UC Santa Barbara
2. Joshua Baez, OF, Dexter Southfield HS, Brookline, Mass.
2s. Ryan Holgate, OF, Arizona
3. Austin Love, RHP, North Carolina
4. Zane Mills, RHP, Washington State
5. Gordon Graceffo, RHP, Villanova
6. Alfredo Ruiz, LHP, Long Beach State
7. Alec Willis, RHP, Regis Jesuit HS, Aurora, Colo.
8. Mike Antico, OF, Texas
9. Trent Baker, RHP, Angelo State (Texas)
10. Osvaldo Tovalin, 3B, Azusa Pacific (Calif.)
11. Mack Chambers Jr., SS, New Mexico
12. Chris Gerard, LHP, Virginia Tech
13. Hayes Heinecke, LHP, Wofford
14. Andre Granillo, RHP, UC Riverside
15. Alex Cornwell, LHP, Southern California
16. Aaron McKeithan, C, Charlotte
17. Elijah Cabell, OF, Florida State
18. Andrew Marrero, RHP, Connecticut
19. Thomas Francisco, 1B, East Carolina
20. Xavier Casserilla, 3B, Eaton HS, Fort Worth

TAMPA BAY RAYS (29)

1. Carson Williams, SS, Torrey Pines HS, San Diego
1s. Cooper Kinney, 2B, Baylor HS, Chattanooga
2. Kyle Manzardo, 1B, Washington State
3. Ryan Spikes, SS, Parkview HS, Lilburn, Ga.
4. Dru Baker, 3B, Texas Tech
5. Mason Auer, OF, San Jacinto (Texas) JC
6. Mason Montgomery, LHP, Texas Tech
7. Logan Workman, RHP, Lee (Tenn.)
8. Patrick Wicklander, LHP, Arkansas
9. Alexander Ayala, LHP, Florida Southwestern State JC
10. Austin Vernon, RHP, North Carolina Central
11. Sean Mullen, RHP, UCLA
12. Johnny Cuevas, RHP, JC of Southern Nevada
13. Bobby Seymour, 1B, Wake Forest
14. Antonio Menendez, RHP, Wake Forest
15. Conor Angel, RHP, Louisiana-Lafayette
16. Ian Leatherman, RHP, Central Michigan
17. Conor Dryer, RHP, Central Missouri
18. Kenny Piper, C, Columbia (Mo.)

19. Sean Hunley, RHP, Tennessee
20. Kamron Fields, RHP, Texas Southern

TEXAS RANGERS (2)

1. Jack Leiter, RHP, Vanderbilt
2. Aaron Zavala, OF, Oregon
3. Cameron Cauley, SS, Barbers Hill HS, Mont Belvieu, Texas
4. Ian Moller, C, Wahlert Catholic HS, Dubuque, Iowa
5. Mitch Bratt, LHP, Georgia Premier Academy, Ga.
6. Chase Lee, RHP, Alabama
7. Bradford Webb, RHP, Virginia Commonwealth
8. Larson Kindreich, LHP, Biola (Calif.)
9. Liam Hicks, C, Arkansas State
10. CJ Widger, LHP, Rowan JC of South Jersey
11. JoJo Blackmon, OF, Escambia HS, Pensacola, Fla.
12. Jackson Leath, RHP, Tennessee
13. Thomas Ireland, LHP, Polk State (Fla.) JC
14. Tucker Mitchell, C, State College of Florida JC
15. Evan Elliott, RHP, Lethbridge (Alb.) JC
16. Ryan Ure, LHP, Eaton (Colo.) HS
17. Michael Alfonso, SS, Key West (Fla.) HS
18. Kyle Larsen, RHP, TNXL Academy, Ocoee, Fla.
19. Will Taylor, OF, Dutch Fork HS, Irmo, S.C.
20. Joseph Montalvo, RHP, Central Pointe Academy, Fla.

TORONTO BLUE JAYS (20)

1. Gunnar Hoglund, RHP, Mississippi
3. Ricky Tiedemann, LHP, Golden West (Calif.) JC
4. Chad Dallas, RHP, Tennessee
5. Irv Carter, RHP, Calvary Christian HS, Fort Lauderdale
6. Hayden Juenger, RHP, Missouri State
7. Jaden Rudd, OF, Mosley HS, Lynn Haven, Fla.
8. Hunter Gregory, RHP, Old Dominion
9. Conor Larkin, RHP, Penn State
10. Connor Cooke, RHP, Louisiana-Lafayette
11. Trenton Wallace, LHP, Iowa
12. Riley Tirotta, 3B, Dayton
13. Matt Svanson, RHP, Lehigh
14. Damiano Palmegiani, 3B, JC of Southern Nevada
15. Garrett Spain, OF, Austin Peay State
16. Micah Bucknam, RHP, Mennonite Educational Institute, B.C.
17. Cooper Benson, LHP, Arizona State
18. Jimmy Burnette, LHP, St. Leo (Fla.)
19. Juan Gonzalez, C, Miami Dade JC
20. Luke Holman, RHP, Wilson HS, West Lawn, Pa.

WASHINGTON NATIONALS (11)

1. Brady House, SS, Winder-Barrow HS, Winder, Ga.
2. Daylen Lile, OF, Trinity HS, Louisville
3. Branden Boissiere, OF, Arizona
4. Dustin Saenz, LHP, Texas A&M
5. T.J. White, OF, Dorman HS, Roebuck, S.C.
6. Michael Kirian, LHP, Louisville
7. Jacob Young, OF, Florida
8. Will Frizzell, 1B, Texas A&M
9. Cole Quintanilla, RHP, Texas
10. Darren Baker, 2B, California
11. Marc Davis, RHP, Florida Southwestern State JC
12. Andrew Alvarez, LHP, Cal Poly
13. Mack Anglin, RHP, Clemson
14. Erik Tolman, LHP, Arizona State
15. Jaden Fein, OF, San Diego State
16. Jack Sinclair, RHP, Central Florida
17. Brendan Collins, RHP, UNC Greensboro
18. Steven Williams, C, Auburn
19. Riggs Threadgill, RHP, McLennan (Texas) JC
20. Elie Kligman, C, Cimarron-Memorial HS, Las Vegas

DRAFT

APPENDIX

HANK AARON, the Hall of Fame outfielder and former home run king who hit 755 home runs and made 25 all-star teams in his 23-year career spent with the Braves and Brewers, died Jan. 22. He was 86.

Aaron captured three Gold Glove awards, two batting titles, and in 1957 won both the NL MVP and the World Series. He finished his historic career with a .305/.374/.555 slash line and is second all-time in home runs, first in RBIs (2,297), first in total bases (6,856) and third in hits (3,771). On April 8, 1974, he hit his 715th career homer, breaking Babe Ruth's all-time record.

TOM ACKER, a righthander who pitched in the major leagues from 1956-59 with the Reds, posting a 19-13, 4.12 mark with 256 strikeouts in 380.1 innings, died Jan. 4 in Narvon, Pa. He was 90.

DICK ALLEN, a third baseman and first baseman who played in the major leagues for 15 years from 1963-1977 with the Phillies, Cardinals, Dodgers, White Sox and Athletics and won the National League Rookie of the Year in 1964 and the American League MVP in 1972, died Dec. 7. He was 78.

Allen made seven all-star teams, posted a .292/.378/.534 slash line, hit 351 home runs and drove in 1,119 runs. In 1972, he led the AL in home runs (37), RBIs (113), walks (99), OBP (.420) and slugging percentage (.603).

JOE ALTOBELLI, a first baseman and outfielder who played in the major leagues for three seasons with the Indians in 1955 and '57 and Twins in '61 before managing the Orioles to a World Series title in 1983, died March 3 in Rochester, N.Y. He was 88.

Altobelli posted a .210/.277/.323 slash line in 257 major league at-bats. In addition to winning a World Series, Altobelli managed the Giants from 1977-79 and the Cubs in 1991. He posted a career 437-407 record in seven seasons.

VICTOR BARON, a catcher who played in the minor leagues from 1958-61 and in '66, died March 18. He was 82.

FRANK BAUMANN, a lefthander who pitched in the major leagues for 11 seasons with the Red Sox, White Sox and Cubs from 1955-65, won 45 games and took home the American League ERA title (2.67) in 1960, died Dec. 13. He was 87.

JOE BECKWITH, a righthander who pitched in the major leagues for seven seasons in 1979 and '80 and from 1982-86 with the Dodgers and Royals, died May 22 in Auburn, Ala. He was 66.

Beckwith was on the Royals squad that won the 1985 World Series, and he finished his career with an 18-19, 3.54 record. He appeared in 229 games, converted seven saves and struck out 319 over 422 innings.

MIKE BELL, a third baseman who had 27 at-bats with the Reds during the 2000 season before working for the D-backs in various roles for 13 seasons and most recently serving as bench coach for the Twins, died March 26. He was 46.

Bell was the younger brother of Reds manager David Bell and part of one of the great baseball family dynasties that includes the brothers' father Buddy, an all-star third baseman of the 1970s and '80s; and grandfather Gus, an all-star outfielder of the 1950s and '60s.

BING BENNETT, a righthander who pitched in the minor leagues in 1955 and '57, died Feb. 9. He was 88.

DICK BISIG, who pitched in the minor leagues in 1949 and '50, died Feb. 25 in Kittery Point, Maine. He was 90.

HOWARD BOLTON, a catcher who played in the minor leagues from 1952-54, died March 5. He was 91.

BILLY BOWMAN, a righthander who pitched in the minor leagues in 1953 and from 1955-59 before later serving as a coach for the Astros, died Aug. 21. He was 90.

DAVID BRASIER, who played in the minor leagues from 1965-66, died Feb. 11. He was 72.

TIM BRILL, a catcher who played in the minor leagues from 1977-79, died March 4 in West Reading, Pa. He was 65.

BOBBY BROWN, a third baseman and shortstop who played in the major leagues for eight years from 1946-52 and in '54 for the Yankees, winning four World Series titles, while also serving in World War II and the Korean War and later becoming the president of the American League for a decade starting in 1984, died March 26 in Fort Worth. He was 96.

ED BROWN, a third baseman/shortstop who played in the minor leagues in 1973 and '74, died March 12 in Chico, Calif. He was 67.

JAIRO CASTILLO, an international cross-checker for the Dodgers in the Dominican Republic who previously worked for the Brewers and Blue Jays as a scout after playing three seasons in the Dominican Summer League for the Mets from 2007-09, died Dec. 8. He was 31.

DOYLE CHADWICK, who played in the minor leagues from 1949-52, died Sept. 26 in Edmond, Okla. He was 90.

ROYCE CHANDLER, a righthander who pitched in the minor leagues from 1949-52, died Feb. 10. He was 92.

HY COHEN, a righthander who pitched in seven games for the Cubs in 1955, striking out four batters in 17 innings, died Feb. 4. He was 90.

BILLY CONIGLIARO, an outfielder who played in the major leagues for five seasons with the Red Sox, Athletics and Brewers, won a World Series in 1973 with the A's and was the younger brother of Red Sox star Tony Conigliaro, died Feb. 10. He was 73.

Conigliaro posted a .256/.311/.429 slash line with 40 home runs, 56 doubles and 10 triples in 347 career games.

RHEAL CORMIER, a lefthander who pitched in the major leagues for 16 seasons with the Cardinals, Expos, Red Sox, Phillies and Reds from 1991-97 and 1999-2007, died March 8. He was 53.

Cormier posted a career 71-64, 4.03 record with 760 strikeouts in 1221.2 innings pitched.

JOE CUNNINGHAM, a first baseman/outfielder who played in the major leagues for 12 seasons in 1954 and from 1956-66 for the Cardinals, Senators and White Sox, died March 25 in Chesterfield, Mo. He was 89.

Cunningham finished his career with an impressive .403 on-base percentage, good for 48th all time, and made one all-star team in 1959. That year he also led the National League with a .453 OBP. After his playing career ended, Cunningham managed in the Cardinals' farm system in the 1960s and '70s.

AUDREY HAINE DANIELS, who starred in the

All-American Girls Professional Baseball League, threw multiple no-hitters and was later inducted into the Canadian Baseball Hall of Fame, died Sept. 11 in North Ridgeville, Ohio. She was 94.

DALE DAVIDSON, who served as a replacement American League umpire in 1979, died Feb. 5. He was 89.

ART DITMAR, a righthander who pitched in the major leagues for nine seasons, posted a 72-77, 3.98 career mark and won a World Series with the Yankees in 1958, died June 11. He was 92.

HERBERT DUFF, a lefthander who pitched in the minor leagues in 1958 and '62, died Oct. 13 in Lynchburg, Va. He was 81.

AL EISELE, a righthander who pitched in the minor leagues from 1959-62, died June 29 in Falls Church, Va. He was 85.

Eisele went on to found "The Hill," a publication dedicated to covering politics in Washington, D.C.

NINO ESCALERA, an outfielder who became the first non-white player to play for the Reds during the 1954 season, died July 3 in Las Piedras, P.R. He was 91.

Escalera collected 11 hits in 69 at-bats during his lone season, but his impact on the sport went far beyond his play on the field.

JOHNNIE FENDERSON, an outfielder who played in the minor leagues from 1964-68 and in '70, died June 19 in Knoxville, Tenn. He was 76.

MARLIN FISCEL, a righthander who pitched in the minor leagues in 1953 and '54, died Sept. 30 in York, Pa. He was 86.

RAY FOSSE, a catcher who played in the major leagues for 12 seasons from 1967-77 and in '79 with the Indians, Athletics, Mariners and Brewers, died Oct. 13. He was 74.

Fosse, whom Cleveland drafted seventh overall in the first-ever draft in 1965, made two all-star teams and won two Gold Gloves during his big league career. He was also a two-time World Series champion with the Athletics in 1973 and '74.

After his playing career, Fosse served as a broadcaster for the A's, starting in 1986 and lasting for 35 years.

HELEN FOX, a righthander who pitched in the All-American Girls Professional Baseball League from 1943-52 and was considered one of the greatest players in league history, died July 25. She was 101.

Fox holds multiple AAGPBL records, including ranking first in career wins (163) and strikeouts (1,076). She appeared in 313 games, the most in history, pitching 2,382 innings.

BILL FREEHAN, a catcher who played in the major leagues in 1961 and from 1963-76, spending his entire career with the Tigers, died Aug. 19 in Petoskey, Mich. He was 79.

Freehan made 11 all-star teams during his career, won five Gold Gloves, finished top three in MVP voting twice and won a World Series in 1968. He posted a .262/.340/.412 slash line with 200 home runs and 1,591 hits.

ROBERT FRITZ, a righthander who pitched in the minor leagues from 1946-48, died June 15 in Alamogordo, N.M. He was 89.

TOM GANSAUER, a lefthander who pitched in the minor leagues from 1958-63, died Dec. 4 in Mount Vernon, Ill. He was 80.

DON GILE, a first baseman/catcher who played for the Red Sox for parts of four seasons from 1959-62, died March 5. He was 85.

Gile had 18 hits in 120 career at-bats to go with three home runs and nine RBIs.

GEORGE GLICK, who played in the minor leagues in 1948, died Aug. 18 in Spring City, Pa. He was 91.

PEDRO GOMEZ, who covered baseball for 35 years, including countless All-Star Games and World Series, for ESPN, Miami News, San Diego Union, San Jose Mercury News, Miami Herald, Sacramento Bee and Arizona Republic, died Feb. 7. He was 58.

JIM GOODWIN, a righthander who was selected by the Phillies in the second round of the 1970 draft and played one season in the minor leagues, died Sept. 13. He was 74.

CHARLIE GORIN, a lefthander who pitched in seven games over parts of two seasons with the

Braves, died Feb. 21 in Austin, Texas. He was 93.

JIM "MUDCAT" GRANT, a righthander who pitched in the major leagues for 14 seasons from 1958-1971 with the Indians, Twins, Pirates, Athletics, Cardinals, Dodgers and Expos, died June 11 in Los Angeles. He was 85.

Grant's historic career saw him become the first Black 20-game winner in American League history when he went 21-7 for the Twins in 1965 en route to the World Series.

Grant made two all-star appearances, that year and in 1963 for the Indians. He finished his career with a 145-119, 3.63 mark and later wrote a book titled "The Black Aces" in 2006, which documented the stories of the 13 Black pitchers who had won 20 games in a season.

JEFF HAINLINE, a first baseman who played in the minor leagues in 1988, died Aug. 12 in Spokane, Wash. He was 56.

JERRY HANKS, a Society for American Baseball Research member who authored "The Deacon's Daughter" with Carol McKechnie Montgomery, the daughter of Hall of Fame manager Bill McKechnie, died April 8. He was 89.

BILLY HARRIS, a second baseman and third baseman who played in the major leagues for parts of two seasons in 1968 and '69 with the Indians and Royals, died Dec. 20 in Hampstead, N.C.

CORY HARTBARGER, who played in the minor leagues in 1949, died Dec. 6 in Asheville, N.C. He was 93.

MYRON HOFFMAN, a righthander who pitched in the minor leagues from 1949-50 and from 1953-57, died Oct. 9 in Austin, Minn.

RON HOLMES, a catcher who played in the minor leagues in 1960, died Oct. 9. He was 83.

FREDDIE HOWARD, a first baseman who played in the minors from 1968-70, died Nov. 25. He was 71.

WILLARD HUNTER, a lefthander who pitched in the major leagues in 1962 and '64 for the Dodgers and Mets, died Feb. 3 in Omaha. He was 85.

Hunter posted a career 4-9, 5.68 record with 63

strikeouts in 114 innings.

RAY JARVIS, a righthander who pitched in the major leagues for the Red Sox in 1969 and '70 and posted a 5-7, 4.64 mark, died April 24 in Austin. He was 73.

RUSS JOHNSON, who played in the minor leagues in 1953, died Feb. 5 in Worcester, Mass. He was 90.

ART KELLY, who played in the minor leagues in 1944, '45, in '47 and in '49, died Dec. 5. He was 93.

JOAN MARIE KNEBL, an outfielder/middle infielder who played in the All-American Girls Professional Baseball League from 1950-54 with the Grand Rapids Chicks and Rockford Peaches, died Sept. 11. She was 87.

ELMER KOHORST, a catcher who played in the minor leagues from 1957-59, died Dec. 4 in Albany, Minn. He was 87.

GORDON LAMBERT, a lefthander who pitched in the minor leagues in 1957, died March 18 in Marion, Ill. He was 86.

LON JOYCE, who served as head baseball coach at Spartanburg (S.C.) Methodist JC from 1978-91 and posted a 473-170 record before later working as an amateur scout for the Dodgers starting in 1992, died Dec. 3 in Spartanburg, S.C. He was 72.

Joyce guided Spartanburg to seven conference championships and two appearances in the NJCAA World Series. He helped develop Reggie Sanders and other future big leaguers.

While with the Dodgers, Joyce signed future big leaguers such as Edwin Jackson and Corey Seager. Joyce was inducted into both the Professional Baseball Scouts Hall of Fame and the NJCAA Hall of Fame.

LEE LANDERS, a former minor league baseball executive and president emeritus of the Appalachian League, died May 17. He was 83.

Landers received numerous honors during his distinguished career, including being named executive of the year while with the Springfield Cardinals. He was named the "King of Baseball" in 2017 for his years of work promoting the sport.

TOMMY LASORDA, a Hall of Fame manager who posted a 1,599-1,439 record while managing the Dodgers for 21 years from 1976-96, died Jan. 7 in Fullerton, Calif. He was 93.

Lasorda guided the Dodgers to World Series titles in 1981 and '88, won four National League pennants and was twice selected as the NL manager of the year.

WILLIAM LENT, a righthander who pitched in the minor leagues from 1959-60, died Oct. 12 in Hudson, N.Y. He was 81.

DON LEPPERT, a second baseman who played in the major leagues in 1955 with the Orioles, posting 70 at-bats, died Jan. 5. He was 90.

CHUCK LINDSTROM, who played in one major league game in 1958 with the White Sox and later coached at Lincoln (Ill.) Junior College for over two decades, died Sept. 29. He was 85.

NICK LOBUE, who had served as a front office executive for the Triple-A Albuquerque Isotopes since 2003, died Nov. 27 in Albuquerque. He was 71.

PHIL LOMBARDI, a catcher and left fielder who played in the major leagues for three seasons in 1986, '87 and '89 for the Yankees and Mets, died May 20 in Stevenson Ranch, Calif. He was 58.

Lombardi collected 22 hits in 92 career at-bats with three home runs and nine RBIs.

ERNEST LOPEZ, a catcher who played in the minor leagues in 1962, died Feb. 9 in Klamath Falls, Ore.

MORRIS MACK, a third baseman who played in the minor leagues from 1951-53, died Nov. 6. He was 91.

MIKE MARSHALL, a righthander who pitched in the major leagues for 14 seasons in 1967 and from 1969-1981 for nine teams, including the Expos, Twins and Dodgers, and won the National League Cy Young Award in 1974, died May 31 in Zephyrhills, Fla.

Marshall appeared in 106 games in 1974, the most in a season in major league history, and pitched 208.1 innings for the Dodgers. He went 15-12, 2.42 with 143 strikeouts and 21 saves and finished third in NL MVP voting.

Marshall made two all-star appearances, finished in the top 10 in Cy Young voting five times and posted a 97-112, 3.14 career mark, appearing in 724 games and recording 188 saves.

JOHN MASON, a third baseman, second baseman and shortstop who played in the minor leagues from 1967-73 before serving as head coach for Louisville for six seasons from 1985-90, posting a 110-186-1 record, died Dec. 2. He was 75.

BILL MATTHEWS, a third baseman/catcher who played in the minor leagues in 1971 and '72, died March 16 in Smyrna, Tenn. He was 69.

BRENNAN MAY, an outfielder who played in the minor leagues from 2011-13, died Aug. 31. He was 30.

SKIP MCAFEE, a member of the Society for American Baseball Research and co-author of the third edition of the "Dickson Baseball Dictionary," died Nov. 22 in St. Petersburg, Fla.

DICK McCOY, a lefthander who pitched in the minor leagues from 1948-55, died recently. He was 92.

CHARLES MCGHEE, a righthander who pitched in the minor leagues from 1948-50, died March 26 in Chancellor, Va. He was 93.

DENIS MENKE, a middle infielder who played in the major leagues for 13 seasons from 1962-74 with the Braves, Astros and Reds and later managed in the minor leagues and coached in the major leagues for 20 years for four organizations, died Dec. 1 in Tarpon Springs, Fla. He was 80.

Menke made two all-star teams, in 1969 and '70, posted a career .250/.343/.370 slash line, hit 101 home runs and collected 40 triples.

TERRY MILANI, a first baseman and third baseman who played in the minor leagues from 1965-69, died Dec. 7 in Peters Township, Pa. He was 75.

BOB MILLER, a righthander who pitched for the Phillies from 1949-58 and later served as head coach at Detroit Mercy, where he posted a record of 896-780-2 from 1965-2001, died Nov. 27 in West Bloomfield, Mich. He was 94.

Miller posted a 42-42, 3.96 mark in the majors, converting 15 saves and pitching 23 complete games.

DON MILLER, who was the head coach at Chico State University from 1970-84, died Oct. 11. He was 86.

RAY MILLER, who managed the Twins in 1985 and '86 and the Orioles in 1998 and '99, posting a career 266-297 (.473) record, died May 5. He was 76.

Miller managed for four seasons but is best remembered as the pitching coach for the Orioles (1978-85, 1997 and 2004-05) and Pirates (1987-96). He worked with historic managers Earl Weaver and Davey Johnson in Baltimore and Jim Leyland in Pittsburgh.

Miller mentored six playoff pitching staffs, including the World Series-champion 1983 Orioles and three-time National League East-champion Pirates of 1990, '91 and '92. Miller's famous motto was "Work fast. Change speeds. Throw strikes."

ROWE MILLER, a catcher who played in the minor leagues from 1969-71, died Dec. 3 in Santo, Texas. He was 70.

KEVIN MILLICAN, a catcher and first baseman who played in the minor leagues for two seasons in 1994 and '95, died July 21. He was 49.

ROBERT MILLS, a third baseman, shortstop and first baseman who played in the minor leagues from 1983-87, died Sept. 12 in Hamilton, Ohio. He was 57.

LARRY MIMS, a second baseman and shortstop who was drafted five times and played in the minor leagues from 1986-89, died Aug. 17. He was 57.

GAYLE MOORE, a shortstop, third baseman and second baseman who played in the minor leagues from 1955-58, died Sept. 27 in Athens, Pa. He was 85.

WILCY MOORE, an outfielder who played in the minor leagues from 1948-59, died Sept. 25 in Muleshoe, Texas. He was 92.

ROGER MORET, a lefthander who pitched in the major leagues for nine seasons from 1970-78 with the Red Sox, Braves and Rangers, died Dec. 7 in Guayama, Puerto Rico. He was 71.

Moret posted a career 47-27, 3.66 mark with 408 strikeouts in 723.1 innings and converted 12 saves.

ED MORGENTHALER, who played in the minor leagues from 1945-50, died Sept. 29. He was 92.

MIKE OVERY, a righthander who made five appearances during the 1976 season for the Angels, died Sept. 22 in Sun City West, Ariz. He was 70.

JIM OWENS, a righthander who pitched in the major leagues from 1955-56 and from 1958-67 with the Phillies, Astros and Reds, died Sept. 8 in Houston. He was 86.

Owens posted a career 42-68, 4.31 mark with 516 strikeouts in 885.1 innings.

JAMES PACE, a second baseman who played in the minor leagues in 1960 and '61, died Sept. 24 in Newburgh, N.Y. He was 83.

STAN PALYS, a left fielder and pinch-hitter who played in the major leagues for parts of four seasons with the Phillies and Reds from 1953-56, died Feb. 8. He was 90.

Palys hit 10 home runs in 333 at-bats, posting a .237 average.

JOHNNY PAREDES, a second baseman who played in the major leagues in 1988, '90 and '91 with the Expos and Tigers and posted a .211/.292/.260 slash line, died Nov. 4 in Maracaibo, Venezuela.

HERKY PAYNE, who played in the minor leagues from 1952-53 and in '56 and also played tailback for the national title-winning Tennessee Volunteers in 1951, died March 30 in Knoxville. He was 92.

VINCE PICA, a shortstop who played in the minor leagues in 1949 and '50 before serving in the U.S. Army during the Korean War, died June 20 in Hartford, Conn. He was 90.

CLIFF POLITTE, a lefthander who pitched in the minor leagues from 1959-65, died June 21. He was 80.

JOHN PROKOPCHAK, a catcher who played in the minor leagues in 1952 and '55, died Sept. 27. He was 90.

CHARLEY PRIDE, a righthander who pitched in the minor leagues in 1955 and '60 before becoming a successful country music star, died Dec. 12 in Dallas. He was 86.

ROGER RADA, a first baseman who played in the minor leagues in 1950 and from 1952-54, died Dec. 6. He was 91.

KEN REITZ, a third baseman who played in the major leagues for 11 seasons from 1972-82 for the Cardinals, Giants, Cubs and Pirates, died March 31 in St. Charles, Mo. He was 69.

Reitz won a Gold Glove in 1975 and made one National League all-star team for the Cardinals in 1980. He finished his career with a .260/.290/.359 slash line, 68 home runs and 548 RBIs in 1,344 games.

VERNON RHODES, a catcher who played in the minor leagues from 1947-49, died Oct. 14. He was 96.

J.R. RICHARD, a righthander who was drafted No. 2 overall by the Astros in 1969 and pitched in the major leagues for 10 seasons from 1971-80, all with Houston, died Aug. 4 in Houston. He was 71.

Richard went 107-71, 3.15 and struck out 1,493 over 1,606 innings. He finished top five in Cy Young Award voting twice and led the National League in ERA (2.71) in 1979 and with 303 and 313 strikeouts in '78 and '79. Richard made one all-star team, in his final season.

EDDIE ROBINSON, a four-time all-star and a World Series champion who played in the major leagues for 13 seasons in 1942 and from 1946-57 primarily with the Indians, died Oct. 4 in Bastrop, Texas. He was 100 and the oldest living ballplayer.

Robinson's breakout season for the 1948 Indians coincided with the franchise's last World Series championship. He made his first all-star team the following year and hit 172 home runs in a 13-year career.

After he retired, he had a long career as a coach, front office executive—most famously as general manager of the Braves and Rangers—and later a scout.

OBITUARIES

KRIS ROUKEY, a team employee for the Indians for 20 years who most recently served as a coordinator for used goods and previously operated the department store at Thurman Munson Stadium in Canton, died May 2 in Akron, Ohio. He was 48.

Roukey, who was working as a Lyft driver, was shot and killed by his passenger after dropping the man off in Akron, according to police.

CHRISTIAN SALBERG, a shortstop and third baseman who played in the minor leagues in 1956 and '57 and in 1959 and '60, died Oct. 15 in Springfield, Neb.

RON SAMFORD, a shortstop and second baseman who played in the major leagues for parts of four seasons in 1954, '55, '57 and '59, died Jan. 14 in Dallas. He was 90.

DICK SANDERS, a third baseman and shortstop who played in the minor leagues in 1953 and from 1956-60, died March 20 in Wichita. He was 89.

STAN SANDERS, who pitched in the minor leagues in 1960 and served as head baseball coach at Toledo in two different stints from 1970-81 and from 1983-92, posting a 534-447 record, died July 23. He was 81.

DAVID SCHLEICH, a lefthander who pitched in the minor leagues in 1950 and '55, died Oct. 8. He was 91.

TOMMY SANDT, a longtime coach in the Pirates organization who served as first base coach for Pittsburgh teams that won three straight National League East titles from 1990-92, died Dec. 1. He was 69.

MIKE SHALIN, a longtime baseball writer for the Boston Herald who served as the official scorer for the Red Sox for the last 17 years, died Dec. 4. He was 66.

CHUCK SCHILLING, a second baseman who played in the major leagues for the Red Sox from 1961-65, died March 30 in West Chester, Pa. He was 83.

Schilling posted a career slash line of .239/.304/.317 with 23 home runs and 146 RBIs in 541 games. He led the American League in plate appearances (738) as a rookie in 1961.

WILLIAM SCHUDLICH, who worked in professional baseball as a scout for 54 years, primarily with the Tigers and Indians, died Sept. 19. He was 81.

ANDREW SEROKA, a catcher who played in the minor leagues in 1970 and '71, died March 18 in New Ringgold, Pa. He was 71.

DICK SHELDON, a righthander who pitched in the minor leagues from 1956-61, died April 6. He was 84.

JOHN SHIER, who played in the minor leagues in 1951, died Sept. 11 in McFarland, Wis. He was 91.

DWIGHT SIEBLER, a righthander who pitched for the Twins in parts of five seasons from 1963-67, died June 16 in Omaha. He was 83.

Siebler posted a 4-3, 3.45 career mark over 48 appearances.

LARRY SLUSSER, a territory scout for the Expos and Astros in the 1990s, died May 4 in Carlisle, Pa. He was 73.

DOUG SMITH, a first baseman who played in the minor leagues in 1953, from 1956-59 and in '62, died March 21 in Eau Claire, Wis. He was 86.

BILL SPANSWICK, a lefthander who pitched in the major leagues in 1964 for the Red Sox and posted a 2-3, 6.89 mark in seven appearances, died Dec. 2 in Enfield, Conn. He was 82.

RENNIE STENNETT, a second baseman, shortstop and left fielder who played in the major leagues for 11 seasons from 1971-1981 with the Pirates and Giants, died May 18 in Coconut Creek, Fla. He was 72.

Stennett, who won a World Series in 1979 with the Pirates, finished his career with a .274/.306/.359 slash line, 41 home runs, 432 RBIs and 75 stolen bases in 1,237 games.

PAUL SUSCE, who played in the minor leagues in 1957 before becoming a successful baseball coach for Wythe High School in Richmond, Va., died in May. He was 87.

Susce was the son of former big league player and coach George Susce and the brother of big leaguer George Susce Jr.

DON SUTTON, a Hall of Fame righthander who pitched in the major leagues for 23 years for the Dodgers, Angels, Brewers, Astros and Athletics from 1966-88, becoming one of 10 pitchers ever to amass more than 300 wins and 3,000 strikeouts, died Jan. 19 in Rancho Mirage, Calif. He was 75.

As a rookie in 1966, Sutton pitched alongside future Hall of Famers Sandy Koufax and Don Drysdale in the Dodgers' rotation. He finished his career 324-256, 3.26 and 3,574 strikeouts in 5,282.1 innings. He placed in the top five in National League Cy Young Award voting in five consecutive seasons from 1972-76 and won one ERA title in 1980 with a 2.20 mark. Sutton ranks 14th all time in wins, seventh in innings, seventh in strikeouts, third in games started (756) and 10th in shutouts (58).

TIM TALTON, a first baseman and catcher who played in the major leagues for two seasons with the Athletics in 1966 and '67, died July 22 in Goldsboro, N.C. He was 82.

Talton collected 112 at-bats during his career, mostly as a pinch-hitter. He hit .295 and homered twice.

DICK TIDROW, a righthander who pitched in the majors for 13 seasons with the Indians, Yankees, Cubs, Mets and White Sox from 1972-84 before serving as a scout for the Yankees and Giants and working in the Giants' front office, died July 10 in Lee's Summit, Mo. He was 74.

Tidrow posted a 100-94, 3.68 mark in his career over 620 appearances and 138 starts.

As the Giants' director of player personnel, Tidrow teamed with general manager Brian Sabean to shape the organization's pitching staff that included Madison Bumgarner, Matt Cain, Tim Lincecum and others who pushed San Francisco to World Series championships in 2010, 2012 and 2014.

LARRY TOMLINSON, a righthander who pitched in the minor leagues in 1957 and '58, died Sept. 25 in Fairhope, Ala. He was 86.

MIKE TRBOVICH, who scouted for the Giants and Dodgers, died Oct. 9 in Huron, Ohio. He was 92.

RALPH URBAN, who played in the minor leagues in 1949, died Dec. 7 in Newtown Square, Pa. He was 90.

VITO VALENTINETTI, a righthander who pitched in the major leagues for five seasons in 1954 and from 1956 to '59 with the Senators, White Sox, Cubs, Indians and Tigers, died Aug. 5 in New York. He was 92.

Valentinetti posted a career 13-14, 4.73 mark. He appeared in 108 games and made 15 starts, striking out 94 batters over 257 innings.

INMAN VEAL, a shortstop who played in the major leagues for parts of six seasons from 1958-63 with the Tigers, Senators and Pirates, died March 14 in Gray, Ga. He was 88.

Veal had 141 hits in 611 at-bats, a home run and 51 RBIs.

TED WIEAND, a righthander who pitched in six games for the Reds over two seasons in 1958 and 1960, died July 7 in Allentown, Pa. He was 88.

LEONARD WIESNER, a first baseman who played in the minor leagues from 1948-50 and from 1953-54, died Dec. 5. He was 91.

JOHNNY WILLIAMS, an outfielder who played in the minor leagues from 1969-71, died Nov. 25. He was 74.

STAN WILLIAMS, a righthander who pitched in the major leagues for 14 seasons from 1958-65 and from 1967-72, primarily with the Dodgers and Indians, died Feb. 20 in Laughlin, Nev. He was 84.

Williams posted a 109-94, 3.48 career mark, making one all-star team and winning a World Series in 1959 with the Dodgers.

RANDY WILSON, a first baseman who played in the minor leagues from 1971-76, died Nov. 23. He was 67.

DONALD YEATES, a righthander who pitched in the minor leagues in 1965, died June 3 in Sonoma, Calif. He was 78.

WAYNE YODER, a second baseman who played in the minors from 1949-51, died Dec. 9 in Springfield, Ohio. He was 91.

GARY YORK, a first baseman/third baseman who played in the minor leagues from 1965-69, died April 16 in Rome, Ga. He was 76. ∎

Austin Riley

Bowie	68
Erie	139
Harrisburg	348
Hartford	130
New Hampshire	338
Portland	79
Reading	254
Richmond	297
Somerset	234

DOUBLE-A SOUTH

Biloxi		201
Birmingham		100
Chattanooga		111
Mississippi		59
Montgomery		317
Pensacola		191
Rocket City	171	
Tennessee		89

DOUBLE-A CENTRAL

Amarillo		49
Arkansas		307
Corpus Christi		149
Frisco		327
Midland		244
NW Arkansas		160
San Antonio	286	
Springfield		276
Tulsa		181
Wichita	212	

HIGH CLASS A

HIGH-A WEST

Eugene	297
Everett	308
Hillsboro	50
Spokane	131
Tri-City	172
Vancouver	339

HIGH-A EAST

Aberdeen		69
Asheville		151
Bowling Green	318	
Brooklyn		224
Greensboro	267	
Greenville	80	
Hickory	329	
Hudson Valley	235	
Jersey Shore	255	
Rome	60	
Wilmington	349	
Winston-Salem		101

HIGH-A CENTRAL

Beloit	192	
Dayton		112
Cedar Rapids	213	
Fort Wayne	287	
Great Lakes	182	
Lake County	121	
Lansing	245	
Peoria	277	
Quad Cities	161	
South Bend	91	
West Michigan	140	
Wisconsin	202	

LOW CLASS A

LOW-A WEST

Fresno	132
Inland Empire	173
Lake Elsinore	289
Modesto	309
Rancho Cucamonga	183
San Jose	299
Stockton	246
Visalia	52

LOW-A EAST

Augusta	61
Carolina	203
Charleston	319
Columbia	162
Delmarva	71
Down East	330
Fayetteville	152
Fredericksburg	350
Kannapolis	103
Lynchburg	123
Myrtle Beach	92
Salem	81

LOW-A SOUTHEAST

Bradenton	268
Clearwater	257
Daytona	113
Dunedin	340
Fort Myers	214
Jupiter	193
Lakeland	142
Palm Beach	278
St. Lucie	225
Tampa	236

ROOKIE

ARIZONA COMPLEX LEAGUE

ACL Angels	174
ACL Athletics	247
ACL Brewers Blue	204
ACL Brewers Gold	204
ACL Cubs	94
ACL Diamondbacks	53
ACL Dodgers	184
ACL Giants Black	300
ACL Giants Orange	300
ACL Indians	124
ACL Mariners	310
ACL Padres	290
ACL Rangers	331
ACL Reds	114
ACL Rockies	133
ACL Royals Blue	163

APPENDIX

Trea Turner

ACL Royals Gold	163
ACL White Sox	104

FLORIDA COMPLEX LEAGUE

FCL Astros	154
FCL Blue Jays	341
FCL Braves	63
FCL Cardinals	280
FCL Marlins	194
FCL Mets	227
FCL Nationals	352
FCL Orioles Black	72
FCL Orioles Orange	72
FCL Phillies	258
FCL Pirates Black	269
FCL Pirates Gold	269
FCL Rays	320
FCL Red Sox	82
FCL Tigers East	143
FCL Tigers West	143
FCL Twins	215
FCL Yankees	238